PROCEEDINGS AND DEBATES OF THE VIRGINIA STATE CONVENTION

OF 1829-1830

Volume I

VIRGINIA. CONSTITUTIONAL CONVENTION, 1829-1830

PROCEEDINGS AND DEBATES OF THE VIRGINIA STATE CONVENTION OF 1829-1830

Volume I

DA CAPO PRESS • NEW YORK • 1971

A Da Capo Press Reprint Edition

This Da Capo Press edition of
Proceedings and Debates of the Virginia State Convention of 1829-1830
is an unabridged republication in two volumes of the one-volume first edition published in Richmond, Virginia, in 1830.

Library of Congress Catalog Number 71-139729

SBN 306-70077-8

Published by Da Capo Press
A Division of Plenum Publishing Corporation
227 West 17th Street, New York, N.Y. 10011

Manufactured in the United States of America

PROCEEDINGS AND DEBATES OF THE VIRGINIA STATE CONVENTION OF 1829-1830

Volume I

PROCEEDINGS

AND

DEBATES

OF THE

VIRGINIA STATE CONVENTION,

OF

1829-30.

TO WHICH ARE SUBJOINED,

THE NEW CONSTITUTION OF VIRGINIA,

AND THE

VOTES OF THE PEOPLE.

No free government, or the blessing of liberty, can be preserved to any people, but by a firm adherence to justice, moderation, temperance, frugality and virtue, and by *frequent recurrence to fundamental principles.*—Virginia Bill of Rights.

RICHMOND:
PRINTED BY SAMUEL SHEPHERD & CO.
FOR RITCHIE & COOK.

1830.

PREFACE

It is unnecessary to go into the history of the various attempts, which have been made in Virginia to revise her Constitution. It is enough to say, that after repeated failures in the Legislature, a bill was passed during the session of 1827-28, for taking the sense of the voters on the call of a Convention. In the course of the year 1828, the polls were opened, and the question was carried by 21,896 to 16,646 votes. Immediately a deep interest was spread through the Commonwealth. The people began to cast about for such men as were best qualified to serve them. There was no restriction in their right of selection, either as to the office which was held, or as to the place where the Delegate resided. Each of the twenty-four Senatorial Districts, into which the State had been previously divided, was entitled to four Delegates; and in some cases, the people of one District were induced to look into others for such men, as they thought best fitted to represent them. The consequence of this great excitement was, that an assembly of men was drawn together, which has scarcely ever been surpassed in the United States. Some have even held it to be equal to the celebrated Convention, which met in Virginia in the year 1788, to pass upon the Federal Constitution. Much of what was venerable for years and long service; many of those who were most respected for their wisdom and their eloquence; two of the Ex-Presidents* of the United States; the Chief Justice of the United States; several of those who had been most distinguished in Congress, or the State Legislature, on the Bench or at the Bar, were brought together for the momentous purpose of laying anew the fundamental law of the land.

The scene was truly an interesting one, not only to the State itself, but to the Union. Almost all eyes were fixed upon it. Several distinguished strangers, as well as many of the citizens of the State, were spectators. The great importance of the subject, as well as the high character of the members, diffused an interest over it, which has been very seldom equalled; and it may be truly said, that the reality did not disappoint the public expectation. The Debates were of the most animated sort. The fundamental principles of Government, the elements which should enter into the composition of all its various departments, were discussed at great length, and with much ingenuity. The struggles between the local interests of different parts of the State, were likewise maintained with great spirit and

* It is remarkable, that Mr. Madison was the only survivor of the Convention, which formed the first Constitution of the State, and one of the two surviving members of the Convention, which formed the Constitution of the United States.

perseverance. At length, after a session of three months and a half, and after a contest, which called into play most of the wisdom and eloquence of the House, a Constitution was formed, which was subsequently proposed to the people, and ratified by a vote of 26,055 to 15,563.

The present volume comprises the *Proceedings* and *Debates* of this important Convention. It is as complete a history of them, as can be obtained: Not a resolution, nor *projet*, nor vote, which has been designedly overlooked: Scarcely a Debate, which is not attempted to be sketched. The Publishers, fully aware of the deep interest which these proceedings would excite, not only at the moment of action, but for all future time, were anxious to rescue them, as far as possible, from oblivion; and they accordingly looked around for the best Reporter that could be obtained. The skill of MR. STANSBURY, of Washington, in reporting the proceedings of Congress, is well known to the citizens of the United States; and the Publishers deem themselves fortunate in having obtained his services, as a Reporter for the Convention. The public may be assured, that they have spared no pains in making their volume as perfect as possible. Many of the Speeches have since been revised by the members, and many of the Debates are now published for the first time. Yet the Publishers cannot be insensible to the imperfections of the work. No Stenographer can take down every thing accurately. No efforts of our own could supply what was defective. Some of the orators had neither the time nor the inclination, nor even the means, of enlarging the sketches of the Stenographer; and we feel it due to some of them, frankly to confess, that we are far from having done justice to some of their Speeches. It is not easy to report the Speeches of such orators as Randolph, and Leigh, and Giles; and if these, or any other gentleman, should think fit to complain, that their arguments have been omitted, or misrepresented, we can only assure them, and the public, that we have done the best within our power. If the volume we now lay before the public be not complete, we are sure at least that it is valuable; and we may be perhaps excused the harmless vanity of expressing our surprise, that instead of not doing *more*, we have done so *much*. Such as it is, it is calculated to assist in interpreting the provisions of the Instrument itself, by shewing the "*fundamental principles*," and the various views to which "*recurrence*" has been had in its formation.

We subjoin to the proceedings of the Convention, a copy of the Constitution which they framed, and the Votes of the people upon it.

All which is now respectfully submitted.

RITCHIE & COOK.

Richmond, August, 1830.

PROCEEDINGS AND DEBATES

OF THE

CONVENTION OF VIRGINIA.

MONDAY, October 5, 1829.

The Convention elected for the purpose of revising the Constitution of this State, assembled this day in the Capitol. The attendance was very general, the entire number of Delegates being present with the exception of six persons, detained by indisposition.

At a little after 12 o'clock Mr. Madison rose and addressed the Convention. He stated the propriety of organizing the body by the appointment of a President; and he therefore nominated James Monroe as qualified to fill the Chair; and one whose character and long public services rendered it unnecessary for him to say more than present him respectfully to the notice of the House.

No other candidate being put in nomination, the question was put on the nomination of Mr. Monroe; and he was elected *nem. con.*

Messrs. Madison and Marshall having conducted him to the Chair, he addressed the Convention nearly in the following terms:

Having served my country from very early life, in all its highest trusts and most difficult emergencies, from the most important of which trusts I have lately retired, I cannot otherwise than feel with great sensibility, this proof of the high confidence of this very enlightened and respectable Assembly. It was my earnest hope and desire, that a very distinguished citizen and friend, who has preceded me in several of these high trusts, and who had a just claim to that precedence, should have taken this station, and I deeply regret the considerations which have induced him to decline it. The proofs of his very important services, and the purity of his life, will go down to our latest posterity; and his example, aided by that of others, whom I need not mention, will give a strong prop to our free system of government.

I regret my appointment from another consideration: a fear, that I shall not be able to discharge the duties of the trust, with advantage to my country. I have never before held such a station, and am ignorant of the rules of the House. I have also been afflicted of late, with infirmity, which still exists to a degree, to form a serious obstacle. Being placed, however, here, I will exert my best faculties, physical and mental, such as they are, at every hazard, to discharge its duties to the satisfaction of this Assembly, and of my country.

This assembly is called for the most important object. It is to amend our Constitution, and thereby give a new support to our system of free republican government: our Constitution was the first that was formed in the Union, and it has been in operation since: We had at that period, the examples only of the ancient republics before us; we have now the experience of more than half a century of this, our own Constitution, and of those of all our sister States. If it has defects, as I think it has, experience will have pointed them out, and the ability and integrity of this enlightened body, will recommend such alterations as it deems proper to our constituents, in whom the power of adopting or rejecting them is exclusively vested.

All other republics have failed. Those of Rome and Greece exist only in History. In the territories which they ruled, we see the ruins of ancient buildings only; the

Governments have perished, and the inhabitants exhibit a state of decrepitude and wretchedness, which is frightful to those who visit them.

On the subject of order, and the method of proceeding, I need not say any thing to this Assembly. The importance of the call, and the manner of election, give ample assurance that no danger need be apprehended on that subject. Our fellow-citizens, in the elections they have made, have looked to the great cause at issue, and selected those whom they thought most competent to its duties. They have not devoted themselves to individuals, but have regarded principle, and sought to secure it. In this I see strong ground to confide in the stability and success of our system. It inspires me with equal confidence that the result of your labors will correspond with their most sanguine hopes.

Mr. Gordon then moved that the Convention proceed to the election of a Clerk, and nominated Mr. Spottswood Garland of Nelson, as a suitable candidate.

Mr. B. W. Leigh proposed the name of Mr. George W. Munford of this City, late Clerk of the House of Delegates.

Mr. Doddridge, that of Erasmus Stribbling of Augusta.

Mr. Morris, that of Edmund Pendleton of Caroline.

Mr. Green, that of David J. Briggs; and

Mr. Stanard, that of Thomas B. Barton.

These nominations were accompanied with recommendatory remarks, and in some cases with documentary testimony in favor of the respective candidates.

The Convention then proceeded to ballot; and a Committee, consisting of the gentlemen who had nominated the candidates, having been appointed to count the votes, Mr. Gordon of that Committee, reported them as follows:

For Mr. Munford,	38 votes.
" Stribbling,	18
" Garland,	6
" Briggs,	16
" Barton,	4
" Pendleton,	4

The entire number of ballots put into the box having been 86, and consequently 44 being requisite to a choice, it appeared that neither of the candidates had been elected.

Mr. Doddridge observed, that according to the rule of the House of Delegates, the lowest on the ballot is dropped on the next ballot.

The result of a second ballot was as follows:

For Mr. Munford,	45 votes.
" Stribbling,	19
" Garland,	18
" Briggs,	6
" Barton,	1
" Pendleton,	0

89 ballots were given in, and 45 being necessary to a choice, Mr. George W. Munford was declared to be duly elected, having received that number precisely.

Mr. Doddridge now stated that at a former Convention, the rules of the House of Delegates had been adopted, so far as they would apply, to regulate the proceedings: in conformity with that precedent, he then proposed the following resolution:

Resolved, That the Rules of the late House of Delegates be adopted by this Convention, as rules to govern its proceedings and deliberations, so far as they apply.

The resolution was adopted.

On motion of Mr. M'Coy, the Convention then proceeded to elect a Serjeant at Arms.

Mr. Powell nominated as a suitable person for that situation Mr. William Randolph of Frederick county.

Mr. Cabell nominated Col. James Sawyers of Pittsylvania.

Mr. Samuel Taylor proposed Mr. Wade Mosby of Powhatan.

Mr. Garnett nominated Mr. David Meade Randolph.

Mr. Morris nominated Mr. Samuel Jordan Winston; and

Mr. Campbell proposed the name of Peter Francisco.

The ballot being taken, the result was reported by Mr. Powell, from the Committee appointed to examine the ballots, as follows:

For William Randolph,	25 votes.
" James Sawyers,	14
" Wade Mosby,	12
" David M. Randolph,	4
" Samuel J. Winston,	14
" Peter Francisco,	17
Scattering,	3

The entire number of ballots having been 89, and 45 requisite for a choice, there was of course, no election by this ballot.

A second trial was equally unsuccessful, the votes standing as follows :

For	William Randolph,	39 votes.
"	James Sawyers,	12
"	Wade Mosby,	11
"	David M. Randolph,	0
"	Samuel J. Winston,	11
"	Peter Francisco,	16

A third ballot being taken, the issue was as follows :

For	William Randolph,	59 votes.
"	James Sawyers,	15
"	Wade Mosby,	0
"	Samuel J. Winston,	0
"	Peter Francisco,	13
	Scattering,	2

So William Randolph was duly elected Serjeant at Arms.

On motion of Mr. Clopton, the following resolution was then adopted :

Resolved, That the Reporters for the Newspapers in the town of Richmond, be admitted to seats for the purpose of taking notes of the proceedings of the Convention.

The Roll of the House was called, and the following was the result :

A LIST OF DELEGATES TO THE CONVENTION.

District of Amelia, Chesterfield, Cumberland, Nottoway, Powhatan, and Town of Petersburg,	John W. Jones, of Chesterfield, Benjamin W. Leigh, of Chesterfield, Samuel Taylor, of Chesterfield, William B. Giles, (Gov.) of Amelia.
District of Brunswick, Dinwiddie, Lunenburg, and Mecklenburg,	William H. Brodnax, of Dinwiddie, George C. Dromgoole, of Brunswick, Mark Alexander, of Mecklenburg, William O. Goode, of Mecklenburg.
District of the City of Williamsburg, Charles City, Elizabeth City, James City, City of Richmond, Henrico, New Kent, Warwick, and York,	J. Marshall, (C. J. U. S.) of Richmond City, John Tyler, of Charles City, Philip N. Nicholas, of Richmond City, John B. Clopton, of New Kent.
District of Shenandoah and Rockingham,	Peachy Harrison, of Rockingham, Jacob Williamson, of Rockingham, William Anderson, of Shenandoah, Samuel Coffman, of Shenandoah.
District of Augusta, Rockbridge and Pendleton,	Briscoe G. Baldwin, of Augusta, Chapman Johnson, of Augusta, William M'Coy, of Pendleton, Samuel M'D. Moore, of Rockbridge.
District of Monroe, Greenbrier, Bath, Botetourt, Alleghany, Pocahontas and Nicholas,	Andrew Beirne, of Monroe, William Smith, of Greenbrier, Fleming B. Miller, of Botetourt, John Baxter, of Pocahontas.
District of Sussex, Surry, Southampton, Isle of Wight, Prince George and Greensville,	John Y. Mason, of Southampton, James Trezvant, of Southampton, Augustine Claiborne, of Greensville, John Urquhart, of Southampton.
District of Charlotte, Halifax and Prince Edward,	John Randolph, of Charlotte, William Leigh, of Halifax, Richard Logan, of Halifax, Richard N. Venable, of Prince Edward.
District of Spottsylvania, Louisa, Orange and Madison,	James Madison, (Ex-P.) of Orange, Philip P. Barbour, of Orange, David Watson, of Louisa, Robert Stanard, of Spottsylvania.

District of Loudoun and Fairfax,	James Monroe, (Ex-P.) of Loudoun, Charles F. Mercer, of Loudoun, William H. Fitzhugh, of Fairfax, Richard H. Henderson, of Loudoun.
District of Frederick and Jefferson,	John R. Cooke, of Frederick, Alfred H. Powell, of Frederick, Hierome L. Opie, of Jefferson, Thomas Griggs, jun. of Jefferson.
District of Hampshire, Hardy, Berkeley and Morgan,	William Naylor, of Hampshire, William Donaldson, of Hampshire, Elisha Boyd, of Berkeley, Philip C. Pendleton, of Berkeley.
District of Washington, Lee, Scott, Russell and Tazewell,	John B. George, of Tazewell, Andrew M'Millan, of Lee, Edward Campbell, of Washington, William Byars, of Washington.
District of King William, King and Queen, Essex, Caroline and Hanover,	John Roane, of King William, William P. Taylor, of Caroline, Richard Morris, of Hanover, James M. Garnett, of Essex.
District of Wythe, Montgomery, Grayson and Giles,	Gordon Cloyd, of Montgomery, Henley Chapman, of Giles, John P. Mathews, of Wythe, William Oglesby, of Grayson.
District of Kanawha, Mason, Cabell, Randolph, Harrison, Lewis, Wood and Logan,	Edwin S. Duncan, of Harrison, John Laidley, of Cabell, Lewis Summers, of Kanawha, Adam See, of Randolph.
District of Ohio, Tyler, Brooke, Monongalia and Preston,	Philip Doddridge, of Brooke, Charles S. Morgan, of Monongalia, Alexander Campbell, of Brooke, Eugenius M. Wilson, of Monongalia.
District of Fauquier and Culpeper,	John S. Barbour, of Culpeper John Scott, of Fauquier, John Macrae, of Fauquier, John W. Green, of Culpeper,
District of Norfolk, Princess Anne, Nansemond and Borough of Norfolk,	Littleton W. Tazewell, of Norfolk Borough, Joseph Prentis, of Nansemond, Robert B. Taylor, of Norfolk Borough, George Loyall, of Norfolk Borough.
District of Campbell, Buckingham and Bedford,	William Campbell, of Bedford, Samuel Claytor, of Campbell, Callohill Mennis, of Bedford, James Saunders, of Campbell.
District of Franklin, Patrick, Henry and Pittsylvania,	George Townes, of Pittsylvania, Benj. W. S. Cabell, of Pittsylvania, Joseph Martin, of Henry, Archibald Stuart, jun. of Patrick.
District of Albemarle, Amherst, Nelson, Fluvanna and Goochland,	James Pleasants, of Goochland, William F. Gordon, of Albemarle, Lucas P. Thompson, of Amherst, Thomas Massie, jun. of Nelson.
District of King George, Westmoreland, Lancaster, Northumberland, Richmond, Stafford and Prince William,	William A. G. Dade, of Prince William, Ellyson Currie, of Lancaster, John Taliaferro, of King George, Fleming Bates, of Northumberland.

District of Matthews, Middlesex, Accomack, Northampton and Gloucester,	Thomas R. Joynes, of Accomack, Thomas M. Bayly, of Accomack, Calvin H. Read, of Northampton, Abel P. Upshur, of Northampton.

All the above members were present, and answered to their names, with the following exceptions:

Absentees—William B. Giles, from the First District; David Watson, from the Ninth District, who has notified the Executive of his inability to serve; Callohill Mennis, from the Twentieth District; William A. G. Dade, from the Twenty-third District, (and who, it is believed, will resign, in consequence of indisposition); Ellyson Currie, from the Twenty-third District, dead; and Calvin H. Read, from the Twenty-fourth District (sick.)

Mr. Doddridge then offered the following resolution:

Resolved, That the Secretary of this Convention, be authorised and required to provide the same with stationery, and that he do also contract for, and superintend all such public printing as shall be ordered by this Convention, on the most beneficial terms for the Commonwealth in his power.

In advocating the adoption of this resolution, Mr. Doddridge observed, that he had been induced to offer it to the Convention, by a desire to avoid the occurrence of any thing like strife or party collisions, so apt to be excited whenever the public printing of deliberative bodies was given by resolution or election to a particular individual. He understood that the public printing of Congress had, for many years, been confided to the management of the Clerk of the House of Representatives, and if he had been rightly informed, it was done as well, and as much to the satisfaction of the members, as it had been since the mode had been changed and a public printer appointed. He feared, if the Convention should proceed to the election of a printer, its members would be thrown into parties, and an unpleasant contest ensue. This he earnestly wished to avoid: he believed the resolution he had had the honour to propose was calculated to avoid it, and he thought it would be acknowledged to be practical, reasonable and fair in its character.

Mr. Nicholas was opposed to the resolution. He most fully agreed with the member, who had proposed it in deprecating the introduction of party spirit and party collisions into this body. But he did not see why such consequences must follow the election of a printer to the Convention, any more than the election of any other officer. He presumed that all the members would vote, in such an election, from the same regard to the public good and the same conviction of the fitness of the candidate proposed, as they would in any other, or as they had in the ballots just taken. He could perceive no necessity whatever of putting out the small amount of printing required by this body to be contracted for. The appointment of a public printer was the standing, permanent usage of this State. There had always been such a printer appointed by her Legislature, as well in the Senate as in the House of Delegates. He could see no motive for a change of that usage in the present case. The public work ought to be done by an officer responsible immediately to the House itself: where was the necessity for any intermediate agency? He was aware of the very respectable character of the Secretary, with whom the resolution proposed to place this trust, nor was it any objection to that officer which induced him to object to the measure; but he wished to avoid any subordinate agency as unnecessary and improper. Let the printer be appointed by the House itself: let him be responsible directly to the House which appointed him. As to the stationery, he took it for granted, that had already been furnished by the Clerk of the House of Delegates: if so, he saw no need of any farther provision on that subject. He was, however, uninformed on this point, being now for the first time a member of a deliberative body. Seeing no good end to be accomplished by the resolution which had been presented, he was opposed to its adoption: he hoped the House would reject it, and then proceed to appoint such person to execute its printing, as it should deem most fit and competent to that duty.

Mr. M'Coy said, that he also was opposed to the resolution which had been read. He had had some experience on this subject as a member of Congress, and he knew that so long as the public printing of that body had been put out on contract, it had been very badly executed. Constant complaints had arisen, and so greatly had the House of Representatives been dissatisfied, that it had been *driven* to resort to another mode, and had consequently employed a public printer appointed by law. As to the idea thrown out by his friend on the left (Mr. Doddridge) that the election of such an officer must necessarily excite party feeling, he could not for his part very well imagine why the election of a printer should produce this effect any more than the election of a door-keeper. Mr. M'Coy said, he did not exactly know what was the practice of the State Legislature on the subject of stationery, as it was now many years since he had held a seat there, but he believed it used formerly to be procured by the Clerk. His experience, however, was of long standing, and he did not know what might be the present practice in the matter; but he hoped what stationery they needed might be procured in the ordinary way.

Mr. Chapman Johnson said, that as there appeared to be some difference of opinion in relation to the resolution before the House, and its further discussion at this time might delay the full organization of the body, he would move that, for the present, it lie upon the table; and he made that motion accordingly.

Mr. Doddridge expressing his assent, the motion was agreed to *nem. con.*

Mr. Johnson then moved that the Convention proceed to elect two door-keepers; which being agreed to, the following persons were put in nomination: by Mr. Nicholas, Littleberry Allen; by Mr. Pleasants, Ellis Puryear; by Mr. Morris, Anselm Baily and Samuel Ford; by Mr. Tyler, John S. Stubblefield and Henry H. Southall; by Mr. Clopton, Pleasant Pomfrey, Ritchie Ayres, William W. Gray, Julius Martin, Christopher S. Roane, and Thomas Underwood.

The House having ballotted for the appointment of one of its two door-keepers, no choice was made: after a second ballot, Mr. Nicholas, from the Committee appointed to examine the votes, reported that they stood as follows:

For Littleberry Allen,	62
Ellis Puryear,	0
Anselm Baily,	2
Samuel Ford,	0
John S. Stubblefield,	7
Henry H. Southall,	0
Pleasant Pomfrey,	2
Ritchie Ayres,	0
William W. Gray,	12
Julius Martin,	0
Christopher S. Roane,	0
Thomas Underwood,	0
Thomas Davis,	1

So Littleberry Allen was declared duly elected.

Two ballots were also taken for a second door-keeper, on the ballot of which John S. Stubblefield had 20 votes, and William W. Gray, 55; 42 being the requisite majority, William W. Gray was declared to have been duly elected.

Mr. Wilson then offered the following resolution:

Resolved, That the Convention will proceed to-morrow, to the election of a Chaplain.

In introducing this resolution, Mr. Wilson said, that apart from all higher considerations which belong to the subject, he thought that a decent respect for themselves, as well as for the opinions and feelings of the community, requires of the members the adoption of a resolution of this kind.

Mr. Powell said, that he was by no means opposed to the object of the resolution just read: very far from it: it had, on the contrary, his most hearty approbation: he was, however, opposed to the mode in which the object was proposed to be attained. He thought a better course would be, to request the President of the Convention to present to the Clergy officiating statedly in Richmond, an invitation to serve in rotation as Chaplains to this House. This would obviate all imputation of invidious distinctions as implied in the election of a particular individual. Under this impression, Mr. Powell said he would move that the resolution lie for the present upon the table. He accordingly made the motion, and it was agreed to without opposition.

On motion of Mr. Johnson, the House then adjourned to meet to-morrow at 12 o'clock.

TUESDAY, October 6, 1829.

The President took the chair at a little after 12 o'clock.

Mr. William B. Giles, a Delegate from the First, and Mr. Mennis, a Delegate from the Twentieth Senatorial Districts, appeared and took their seats.

Mr. Doddridge of Brooke county, moved to take up the resolution he had yesterday offered on the subject of the public printing, with a view to its withdrawal. Mr. Doddridge said he was induced to take this course by a fear that his resolution, if pressed, might possibly lead to the very evil (the excitement of party spirit) which he had wished to avoid by its presentation.

The motion prevailing, the resolution was accordingly withdrawn.

Mr. Doddridge then submitted the following resolutions, not, he said, with any view to their being taken up at this time, but hoping that they might be permitted to lie on the table, as, probably, other gentlemen might have prepared resolutions on the same subject, more acceptable to the House.

1. *Resolved*, That a Committee be appointed to take into consideration the Bill or Declaration of Rights, and to report to this Convention whether, in their opinion, any, and if any, what amendments are necessary therein.

2. *Resolved*, That a Committee be appointed to take into consideration the Legislative Department of Government as established by the present Constitution, and to report to this Convention, either a substitute for the same, or such amendments thereto, as, in their opinion, are necessary.

3. *Resolved*, That a Committee be appointed to take into consideration the Executive Department of Government as established by the present Constitution, and to report to this Convention either a substitute for the same, or such amendments thereto, as, in their opinion, are necessary.

4. *Resolved*, That a Committee be appointed to take into consideration, the Judicial Department of Government established by the present Constitution, and to report to this Convention either a substitute for the same, or such amendments thereto, as, in their opinion, are necessary.

5. *Resolved*, That a Committee be appointed to take into consideration so much of the Constitution as relates to the Right of Suffrage and qualifications of persons to be elected, and to enquire whether any, and if any, what alterations or amendments are necessary therein, and report the same with their opinions thereon, to this Convention.

6. *Resolved*, That a Committee be appointed to take into consideration the proper basis of representation, and the proper mode of apportioning representation among the people, and to make report thereon to this Convention.

7. *Resolved*, That a Committee be appointed to take into consideration all such parts of the Constitution as are not referred by the foregoing resolutions, and to report to this Convention either substitutes for such parts or such amendments thereto, as, in their opinion, are necessary.

8. *Resolved*, That each Committee appointed under the foregoing resolutions, shall consist of ——— members.

On motion of Mr. Doddridge, these resolutions were accordingly laid upon the table.

Mr. Mercer moved that they be printed; but

Mr. M'Coy objected to this order being passed as premature, until a printer should be appointed; and, in order that the House might have such officer, he moved to lay the motion of Mr. Mercer, for the present upon the table, and that the Convention do now proceed to the election of a printer. The motion prevailed: whereupon

Mr. M'Coy nominated Mr. Thomas Ritchie as a suitable person, and accompanied the nomination by a few brief remarks in its support.

Mr. Clopton then nominated Mr. John H. Pleasants, in whose favour he said a few words.

Mr. Garnett added to these nominations the name of Mr. Thomas W. White, to whose competence he briefly bore witness.

The House then proceeded to ballot; when Mr. M'Coy from the Committee appointed to examine the ballots, reported that 89 votes had been given, and consequently 45 were necessary to a choice: that

Thomas Ritchie had received,	54 votes.
John H. Pleasants,	28
Thomas W. White,	7

Whereupon, Thomas Ritchie was declared to have been duly elected printer to the Convention.

Mr. Wilson now asked permission to withdraw the resolution he had yesterday offered on the subject of appointing a Chaplain; and having obtained it, he offered the following as a substitute, viz

Resolved, That the Secretary be directed to wait on the Clergy of this city, and request them by an arrangement between themselves, to open the session of the Convention each morning by prayer; and the question having been put on its adoption, Mr. Powell demanded that it be taken by yeas and nays; but having failed to make this demand in time, the question was taken in the usual mode, and the resolution adopted; 50 members rising in the affirmative.

Mr. M'Coy now moved that the series of resolutions previously offered by Mr. Doddridge and now lying on the table, be printed.

Mr. Johnson said he had not the least objection to the printing of the resolutions; but he had a proposition which he wished previously to offer to the House, and which, if adopted, might perhaps render that order unnecessary: He would state it for the consideration of gentlemen, and the mover of the order to print might determine whether it would not be best to withdraw that motion for the present. What he wished to ask, was, that a Committee might be appointed to report upon the best course to be pursued in relation to the subjects embraced in the resolutions which it was proposed to print. If such a Committee should be raised, the resolutions would, as of course, be referred to it for consideration, and this would supersede the necessity of printing for the consideration of the House.

Mr. J. said he should not at this time present the reasons which had induced him to suggest this course of proceeding, but would try the sense of the Convention upon his resolution, if the pending resolution to print should be withdrawn.

Mr. Doddridge expressed his hope that this would be done, as he approved of the object which seemed to be the aim of the gentleman's proposition.

Mr. M'Coy said, he would very cheerfully withdraw his motion, having made it under a sense of obligation, in courtesy to do so, as he had caused its postponement when made by another.

The motion to print was thereupon withdrawn, and

Mr. Johnson offered his resolution in the following form:

Resolved, That a Committee of seven be appointed to enquire and report what method will be most expedient in bringing before the House amendments to the Constitution which may be preferred.

Mr. J. said that he offered this resolution in conformity to a precedent set in the Convention held in the State of New York, where such a proposition had been presented and received with favour. He was well satisfied that the opinions of the members of this body as to many of the subjects embraced in the series of resolutions on the table, were very variant, and that there must be much difficulty in deciding on the proper course to be adopted. The resolution he had offered presented itself to him as being the best expedient which could be resorted to.

Mr. Powell suggested a modification of the resolution by changing the number of the Committee from seven (as originally proposed) to thirteen; to which modification the mover readily assented.

Mr. Mercer thereupon suggested that the resolution be farther modified by enlarging the number of the Committee, so as to embrace one member from each Senatorial District. This he thought would be a ready and the best mode of gathering the sense of the whole body. The trust committed to the Convention was an important one; the enlargement of the Committee would not be great, and each delegation would then be heard on the arrangement of the course of proceeding.

Mr. Johnson said he had no particular partiality to either of the numbers which had been proposed; his main anxiety had been that such a Committee should be raised; and if the enlargement last proposed met the sense of the House, he was content. He therefore adopted the modification suggested by Mr. Mercer, and the resolution was then agreed to, without opposition.

The President then rose and addressing the Convention, said that he had to express a wish that the appointment of this and of all subsequent Committees might be made, not by the presiding officer, but by the House itself. Such a course would be much more agreeable to him. He had now been long absent from deliberative assemblies: he had never presided in any. Many of the gentlemen present were, or had been members of the State Legislature, and were much better acquainted with the proper course of doing the business of such a body than he could be expected to be; his health, besides, was delicate, and it would be very gratifying to him if the Convention would consent to relieve him from the charge of making appointments of its Committees.

Mr. Johnson, though very desirous of lessening as far as practicable the burden imposed on the presiding officer, did not see how the wish just expressed would be complied with, unless by a resolution altering, so far, the rules by which the Convention had resolved to be governed. He would cheerfully offer such a resolution, did he not feel persuaded that the duty of appointing would be performed with more facility as well as greater propriety and more to the satisfaction of the Convention, in the mode at present prescribed. They were disused to such a course as was now suggested in any of the public assemblies in the State, and he could not but desire that the established mode should be adhered to.

Mr. Doddridge, taking it for granted that until the resolution now before the House should be disposed of, no farther business would be done, moved an adjournment to the afternoon, in order to give time for the selection of suitable persons to constitute the Committee proposed, but subsequently withdrew the motion.

Whereupon Mr. Macrae offered the following resolution:

Resolved, That a Committee of —— members be appointed to consider and report what rules of proceedings of the House of Delegates are applicable as rules of proceedings of this Convention, and what amendments thereof, if any, ought to be made.

In introducing the resolution, Mr. Macrae observed that from a defect of Parliamentary experience, he was unacquainted with the rules of the House of Delegates, which had in part been adopted for the government of the Convention; and unless those rules were to undergo some amendments, he should be obliged to move for their being printed in their present form. But he thought it best to afford the opportunity of their being modified, if necessary.

The resolution was adopted, and the blank, on motion of Mr. Scott, was filled with the word *seven*.

The following gentlemen were thereupon nominated by the President to constitute this Committee, viz:

Messrs. Macrae, Scott, Johnson, Mercer, Leigh of Chesterfield, Barbour of Orange, and Gordon.

On motion of Mr. Scott, a Committee of Privileges and Elections was appointed, and the following gentlemen were named by the President as its members, viz:

Messrs. Scott, Doddridge, Nicholas, Taylor of Norfolk, Taliaferro, Pleasants and Baldwin.

On motion of Mr. M'Coy, the House then adjourned till to-morrow, 12 o'clock.

WEDNESDAY, October 7, 1829.

The Convention met pursuant to adjournment, and its sitting was opened with prayer by the Right Rev. R. C. Moore, of the Episcopal Church.

The following Committee of twenty-four members, one from each Senatorial District, was announced as having been appointed by the President, viz:

William B. Giles from the	1st	District.
William H. Brodnax	2d	do.
John Marshall	3d	do.
Peachy Harrison	4th	do.
Chapman Johnson	5th	do.
Andrew Beirne	6th	do.
John Y. Mason	7th	do.
John Randolph	8th	do.
James Madison	9th	do.
Charles F. Mercer	10th	do.
Alfred H. Powell	11th	do.
William Naylor	12th	do.
John B. George	13th	do.
John Roane	14th	do.
Henley Chapman	15th	do.
Lewis Summers	16th	do.
Philip Doddridge	17th	do.
John W. Green	18th	do.
Littleton W. Tazewell	19th	do.
William Campbell	20th	do.
George Townes	21st	do.
James Pleasants	22d	do.
John Taliaferro	23d	do.
Thomas R. Joynes	24th	do.

On motion of Mr. Johnson, the resolutions introduced on the first day of the sitting of the Convention, by Mr. Doddridge, were referred to the above Committee; when the House adjourned to 12 o'clock to-morrow.

THURSDAY, October 8, 1829.

The Convention met at 12 o'clock, which it is understood will be the stated hour of meeting. After prayers by Bishop Moore,

Mr. Madison from the Select Committee, consisting of one member from each of the 24 Senatorial Districts, to whom the duty had been referred of devising the best mode of arranging the business of the Convention, made the following Report:

The Committee of one from each Senatorial District, appointed to enquire into the most convenient mode of proceeding in bringing to the consideration of the Convention, such amendments as may be proposed to the present Constitution, have had the same under consideration, and are of opinion that the most convenient method is to adopt the following resolutions, viz:

1. *Resolved*, That a Committee be appointed to take into consideration the Bill or Declaration of Rights, and to report to this Convention whether in their opinion any, and if any, what amendments are necessary therein.

2. *Resolved*, That a Committee be appointed to take into consideration the Legislative Department of Government, as established by the present Constitution, and to report to this Convention, either a substitute for the same, or such amendments

thereto, as in their opinion are necessary, or that no substitute or amendment is necessary.

3. *Resolved*, That the Executive Department of Government as established by the present Constitution, be referred to a Committee, to enquire and report whether any, and if any, what amendments are necessary.

4. *Resolved*, That the Judicial Department of Government as established by the present Constitution, be referred to a Committee, to enquire and report whether any, and if any, what amendments are necessary therein.

5. *Resolved*, That all such parts of the present Constitution as are not referred by the foregoing resolutions, be referred to a Committee, to enquire and report whether any, and if any, what amendments are necessary therein.

6. *Resolved*, That no original resolution offered to the Convention proposing any amendment to the Constitution or Declaration of Rights, be discussed on its merits in the House, till it shall have been referred.

On motion of Mr. Doddridge, the report was laid on the table, and ordered to be printed.

Mr. Tazewell then said, that as he took it for granted that the object in laying the foregoing report on the table and printing it, was that the other members of the Convention who had not been members of the Committee, might have an opportunity of informing themselves of the contents of the report, he presumed it would be agreeable to them also, to be made acquainted with some other propositions which had been moved in the Committee, but rejected; under this persuasion, he would move that the following resolution, which he had himself proposed to the Committee, but which had not received its approbation, should be printed and laid on the table together with the report, viz:

Resolved, That the most expedient method of bringing before the Convention any amendments to the Constitution which may be proposed, will be, to take up the existing Constitution or form of Government of Virginia, with the Declaration of Rights, and regarding them for the purposes of examination and discussion, merely, as a plan proposed and reported by a Select Committee, to refer the same to a Committee of the whole House, there to be examined section after section, and to be dealt with in all other respects as a bill so referred by the House to that Committee usually is.

The motion was agreed to.

Mr. Mercer said, that under impressions similar to those which had just been expressed by the gentleman from Norfolk, (Mr. Tazewell) he would move the printing of the two following resolutions, which he had had the honour to propose in the Committee, and which it was his purpose to make the subject hereafter of a motion in the Convention.

Resolved, That so much of the Constitution as relates to the right of suffrage, be referred to a Committee to consider and report whether any, and if any, what amendments are necessary therein.

Resolved, That so much of the Constitution as relates to the basis of representation, be referred to a Committee to consider and report whether any, and if any, what amendments are necessary therein.

Mr. Brodnax of Dinwiddie, observed that as in any conceivable disposition of the matter to be submitted to the Convention, the existing Constitution of the State, together with the Declaration of Rights, must be the substratum of the whole, it appeared proper that these also should be printed and should be in the hands of every member. The substance of them, it was true, was, he had no doubt, familiar to the minds of all the gentlemen, and the documents themselves might be consulted in the library, but as they would be a perpetual subject of reference in the approaching discussions, it was certainly convenient and proper that they should be printed, together with the report of the Select Committee. He therefore made a motion to that effect, which was agreed to.

Mr. Macrae, from the Committee appointed to revise the rules of the House of Delegates, made a report upon the subject.

After some conversation between Messrs. Green of Culpeper, Powell of Frederick, and Leigh of Chesterfield, it was agreed to take up this report and proceed to act upon it.

The rules reported were thereupon read successively at the Clerk's table, and after some verbal corrections in the 14th and 30th rules, and a modification of the 32d, which went to include members of both Houses of the State Legislature, among the persons privileged with admission to the floor of the Convention:

On motion of Mr. Leigh of Chesterfield, the 7th rule of the House of Delegates, which, as originally reported, forbids a member to vote on all questions in which he has a personal interest, was so amended as to confine this prohibition to questions "touching his own conduct in, and rights and privileges as, a member of this Convention."

Mr. L. considered this alteration as necessary, both as better expressing the true spirit of the rule, and because in the discussions of this Convention, very many questions must of necessity arise, in which every member would have a personal interest of the deepest kind.

Mr. Alexander of Mecklenburg, was desirous farther to amend this rule in that part of it, which forbids a member to vote on any question, unless he was present when the question was put. Mr. A. considered this prohibition as involving a question of grave importance, and as abridging improperly the exercise of a most important right. A difference of opinion might exist and had actually been expressed, as to the construction of the phrase "when the question was put." The understanding of its meaning in the House of Delegates was, that the question is put in the sense of this rule when it is stated from the Chair; but in the House of Representatives of the United States, a different construction prevailed: here the question was understood as being put to each member only, when that member was called upon to vote; then, the question was put *to him*. Mr. A. said, he would put a case to shew that the rule as it stood, might operate great injustice: he had indeed, himself, been subjected to its effects. When the yeas and nays were demanded, the roll is usually called from east to west. The question is put, and each member answers to his name. If a member residing in the west comes in while it is calling, he is precluded from voting, although his name has not yet been called, because the question has been put. So in the House of Representatives, when the yeas and nays are demanded, the names of the members are called in alphabetical order. If a gentleman enters the Hall, whose name happens to stand near the head of the list, he finds that the Clerk has already called it, and he is, of course, precluded from voting, while another gentleman entering at the same moment, but having the good fortune to stand lower on the list, is admitted to a privilege of which his colleague, though not more negligent than himself, and equally early in his attendance, is deprived. As almost every question likely to be presented to this Convention, would be of weighty consideration, Mr. A. considered it as highly important that every member should have a right to vote upon it, provided he should be present before the final decision was announced from the Chair.

Mr. M'Coy said that he did not see the hardships which his friend saw in this rule: the practice in the House of Representatives was, that members not in the House when the Speaker puts the question, are not admitted to vote; but when the yeas and nays are taken, the question is considered as put to each man when that man's name is called. When the members were called in alphabetical order, there was some hardship in the result: members whose names begin with A and B were sometimes taken by surprise, but that could not happen under the rule as interpreted in the House of Delegates; but even if some hardship did occur, Mr. M'Coy thought it best upon the whole to let the rule stand as tending to compel members to be present at their post. The more the rule was relaxed, the greater would be the negligence of the members.

Mr. Stanard of Spottsylvania, observed that the interpretation of the phrase in the rule had been so definitively fixed by the practice of the House of Delegates, that no sort of difficulty could occur in understanding its meaning. The construction referred to by the gentleman from Mecklenburg, was one which had never prevailed here. No additional chance of voting was enjoyed by any member of the House of Delegates from the fact of his name standing low upon the alphabet. The rules and the practice of that House, as was well known, had their origin in the Parliamentary law of England. By the established usage in the House of Delegates, no question was taken as definitively stated till the alternative had been propounded. If, therefore, a member entered the House after the affirmative votes had been collected, but before the members of the opposite opinion had been called upon to vote, his vote was received. When the yeas and nays were called for, so soon as one member had answered to his name, the question before the House was considered as definitively propounded, and if a gentleman entered the Hall after that time, his vote could not be received. Very great inconvenience must unavoidably ensue, should the Convention depart from this well established rule. He, therefore, earnestly hoped that the amendment would not prevail.

Mr. Alexander having so modified his amendment as to forbid voting only when a member had not been present before the final decision of the question:

The decision was taken on his amendment, and it was rejected by a large majority.

The question was then put on the whole report as amended, and carried *nem. con.*

The rules, as adopted, were as follows:

1. No member shall absent himself from the service of the House without leave, unless he be sick and unable to attend.

2. When any member is about to speak in debate, or deliver any matter to the House, he shall rise from his seat, and without advancing from thence, shall, with

due respect, address himself to the President, confining himself strictly to the point in debate, avoiding all indecent and disrespectful language.

3. No member shall speak more than twice in the same debate without leave.

4. A question being once determined, must stand as the judgment of the House, and cannot again be drawn into debate.

5. While the President is reporting, or putting any question, none shall entertain private discourse, read, stand up, walk into or out of the House.

6. No member shall vote on any question touching his own conduct in, or rights and privileges as, a member of this Convention, or in any other case, where he was not present when the question was put by the President or Chairman of any Committee.

7. Every member who shall be in the House when any question is put, shall, on a division, be counted on the one side or the other.

8. Each day, before the House proceeds to any other business, the Secretary shall read the Orders of the Day.

9. The Secretary shall not suffer any records or papers to be taken from the table, or out of his custody, by any member or other person.

10. A majority of the members of the Convention shall be necessary to proceed to business, and every question shall be determined according to the vote of a majority of the members present. Any smaller number shall be sufficient to adjourn, and fifteen to call a House, and send for the absent, and make any order for their censure or discharge.

11. When the House is to rise, every member shall keep his seat until the President passes him.

12. The Journals of the House shall be daily drawn up by the Secretary, and after being examined by the President, be printed, and one copy be delivered to the Secretary, and one to each member without delay.

13. A majority of any Committee shall be a sufficient number to proceed to business.

14. Any person shall be at liberty to sue out an original writ or subpœna in chancery, in order to prevent a bar by the statute of limitations, or to file any bill in equity, to examine witnesses thereupon, for the sole purpose of preserving their testimony against any member of this House, notwithstanding his privilege; provided that the clerk, after having made out and signed such original writ, shall not deliver the same to the party, or to any other, during the continuance of that privilege.

15. Any person summoned to attend this House, or any Committee thereof, as a witness in any matter depending before them, shall be privileged from arrest, during his coming to, attending on, or going from the House or Committee; and no such witness shall be obliged to attend, until the party, at whose request he shall be summoned, do pay, or secure to him, for his attendance and travelling, the same allowance which is made to witnesses attending the General Court.

16. If any person shall tamper with any witness, in respect to his evidence to be given in this House, or any Committee thereof, or directly, or indirectly, endeavor to deter or hinder any person from appearing, or giving evidence, the same is declared to be a high crime, or misdemeanor; and this House will proceed, with the utmost severity, against such offender.

17. No person shall be taken into custody by the Sergeant at Arms, on any complaint of a breach of privilege, until the matter of such complaint shall be examined by the Committee of Privileges and Elections, and reported to the House.

18. The Sergeant's fees shall be as follows, to wit: for taking any person into custody, two dollars; for every day he shall be detained in custody, two dollars; for sending a messenger to take any person into custody by warrant from the President, eight cents per mile for going, and the same for returning, besides ferriages.

19. On a call of the House, the doors shall not be shut against any member, until his name is once enrolled.

20. When any member shall keep his seat two days, after having obtained leave of absence, such leave shall be void.

21. No business shall be introduced, taken up, or considered, after 12 o'clock, until the Orders of the Day shall be disposed of.

22. Any member, on his motion made for that purpose, on being seconded, provided seven of the members present be in favor of the motion, shall have a right to have the ayes and noes taken upon the determination of any question, provided he shall give notice of his intention to call the ayes and noes, before the question be put, and in such case the House shall not divide, or be counted on the question, but the names of the members shall be called over by the Secretary, and the ayes and noes shall be respectively entered on the Journal, and the question shall be decided as a majority of votes shall thereupon appear: provided that after the ayes and noes shall be separately taken, and before they are counted, or entered on the Journal, the Secretary shall read over the names of those who voted in the affirmative, and of those who voted in

the negative; and any member shall have liberty at such reading to correct any mistake which may have been committed in listing his name, either in the affirmative or negative.

23. The petitioner who contests the election of a member returned to serve in this Convention is entitled to receive his wages only from the day on which such petitioner is declared duly elected.

24. Select Committees shall be composed of some number not less than five nor more than thirteen.

25. It shall be the rule of the House, in all cases of balloting, to fill one vacancy only at a time.

26. The Committee of Privileges and Elections shall report to the House in all cases of privilege or contested election, to them referred, the principles and reasons upon which their resolutions shall be founded.

27. In all cases of balloting for the election of any officer by this Convention, if on the first ballot no person shall have a majority of the whole number, on the second ballot the person who had the smallest number of votes shall not be balloted for; and so on each succeeding ballot till some person shall have a majority of the whole.

28. In all cases wherein a division of the House on any question propounded from the Chair, is rendered necessary, in the opinion of the President, by the equality of sound, or required by the motion of any member, the members voting on the question which occasions such division, shall be required to rise in their places; and if on a general view of the House, a doubt still remain in the President, or any member thereof, on what side the majority is, the members shall be counted standing in their places, either by the President, or by two members of opposite opinions on the question, to be deputed for that purpose by the President.

29. The Committee appointed to examine the ballot-boxes shall count no blanks therein.

30. The documents ordered to be printed by the House shall be printed on paper of the same size of the Journal of this Convention, and a copy shall be bound with each Journal, to be furnished to the members at the end of the session; and it shall be the duty of the printer of the House to print one hundred additional copies of each document ordered to be printed for the above purpose.

31. It shall be the duty of the Committee of Privileges and Elections to examine the certificates of election furnished by the sheriffs, in order to ascertain the members of this Convention duly elected, and to report thereupon.

32. Seats within this House, such as the President shall direct, shall be set apart for the use of the members of the General Assembly and of the Executive, of the Judges of the Superior Courts of this State, and of the United States, and of such other persons as the President may think proper to invite within the bar.

33. It shall be a standing rule of the House that the President be authorised to call any member of the House to occupy the Chair, and exercise the functions of President, until he may resume the Chair; with this proviso, that the power given by this rule shall not be construed to confer on the President a right to place any member in the Chair of the President for a longer period than one day.

On motion of Mr. Doddridge the Journal and other papers before referred to were ordered to be printed in the octavo form.

On motion of Mr. Mercer, it was ordered, that the act of the State Legislature which authorised the organization of this Convention, be added to the papers to be printed, and then the House adjourned.

FRIDAY, October 9, 1829.

The Convention met at 12 o'clock, and its sitting was opened with prayer by the Rev. Bishop Moore.

Mr. Scott from the Committee on Privileges and Elections, made the following report:

The Committee of Privileges and Elections have performed the duty assigned them by the rules of the House, and beg leave to report, that they have examined the returns of the sheriffs, and find that the following persons have been duly elected members of this Convention, to wit:

From the District composed of the counties of Amelia, Chesterfield, Cumberland, Nottoway, Powhatan, and the town of Petersburg—John W. Jones, Benjamin W. Leigh, Samuel Taylor and William B. Giles.

From the District composed of the counties of Brunswick, Dinwiddie, Lunenburg and Mecklenburg—William H. Brodnax, George C. Dromgoole, Mark Alexander and William O. Goode.

From the District composed of the counties of Charles City, Elizabeth City, James City, Henrico, New Kent, Warwick, York, and the Cities of Richmond and Williamsburg—John Marshall, John Tyler, Philip N. Nicholas and John B. Clopton.

From the District composed of the counties of Shenandoah and Rockingham—William Anderson, Samuel Coffman, Peachy Harrison and Jacob D. Williamson.

From the District composed of the counties of Augusta, Rockbridge and Pendleton—Briscoe G. Baldwin, Chapman Johnson, William M'Coy and Samuel M'D. Moore.

From the District composed of the counties of Monroe, Greenbrier, Bath, Botetourt, Alleghany, Pocahontas and Nicholas—Andrew Beirne, William Smith, Fleming B. Miller and John Baxter.

From the District composed of the counties of Sussex, Surry, Southampton, Isle of Wight, Prince George and Greensville—John Y. Mason, James Trezvant, Augustine Claiborne and John Urquhart.

From the District composed of the counties of Charlotte, Halifax and Prince Edward—John Randolph, William Leigh, Richard Logan and Richard N. Venable.

From the District composed of the counties of Spottsylvania, Louisa, Orange and Madison—James Madison, Philip P. Barbour, David Watson and Robert Stanard.

From the District composed of the counties of Loudoun and Fairfax—James Monroe, Charles F. Mercer, William H. Fitzhugh and Richard H. Henderson.

From the District composed of the counties of Frederick and Jefferson—John R. Cooke, Alfred H. Powell, Hierome L. Opie and Thomas Griggs, jr.

From the District composed of the counties of Hampshire, Hardy, Berkeley and Morgan—William Naylor, William Donaldson, Elisha Boyd and Philip C. Pendleton.

From the District composed of the counties of Washington, Lee, Scott, Russell and Tazewell—John B. George, Andrew M'Millan, Edward Campbell and William Byars.

From the District composed of the counties of King William, King & Queen, Essex, Caroline and Hanover—John Roane, William P. Taylor, Richard Morris and James M. Garnett.

From the District composed of the counties of Wythe, Montgomery, Grayson and Giles—Gordon Cloyd, Henley Chapman, John P. Mathews and William Oglesby.

From the District composed of the counties of Kanawha, Mason, Cabell, Randolph, Harrison, Lewis, Wood and Logan—Edward S. Duncan, John Laidley, Lewis Summers and Adam See.

From the District composed of the counties of Ohio, Tyler, Brooke, Monongalia and Preston—Charles S. Morgan, Philip Doddridge, Alexander Campbell and Eugenius M. Wilson.

From the District composed of the counties of Fauquier and Culpeper—John S. Barbour, John Scott, John Macrae and John W. Green.

From the District composed of the counties of Norfolk, Princess Anne, Nansemond and the Borough of Norfolk—Littleton W. Tazewell, Joseph Prentis, Robert B. Taylor and George Loyall.

From the District composed of the counties of Campbell, Buckingham and Bedford—William Campbell, Samuel Claytor, Callohill Mennis and James Saunders.

From the District composed of the counties of Franklin, Patrick, Henry and Pittsylvania—George Townes, Benjamin W. S. Cabell, Joseph Martin and Archibald Stuart.

From the District composed of the counties of Albemarle, Amherst, Nelson, Fluvanna and Goochland—James Pleasants, William F. Gordon, Lucas P. Thompson and Thomas Massie, jr.

From the District composed of the counties of King George, Westmoreland, Lansaster, Northumberland, Richmond, Stafford and Prince William—William A. G. Dade, Ellyson Currie, John Taliaferro and Fleming Bates.

From the District composed of the counties of Matthews, Middlesex, Accomack, Northampton and Gloucester—Thomas R. Joynes, Thomas M. Bayly, Calvin H. Read and Abel P. Upshur.

On motion of Mr. Mercer, the report was laid on the table.

On motion of Mr. Fitzhugh of Fairfax, a Committee was appointed to fix the compensation to be allowed to officers of the Convention; whereupon, the following gentlemen were appointed by the Chair, viz: Messrs. Fitzhugh, Loyall, Stanard, Barbour of Orange, and Bayly.

Mr. Doddridge moved that the report of the Committee of twenty-four, should now be taken up for discussion, but expressed his willingness to withdraw the motion, should any member express a wish for farther time to consider it.

No such wish being expressed, the motion was agreed to, and the report taken up accordingly. Previous to its discussion, however,

Mr. Mercer of Loudoun, explained to the House the reasons why he should not offer the resolutions which he had yesterday laid upon the table, and which had been printed together with the report of the Committee. He stated it to be his intention to offer at a suitable time, the resolution which he had yesterday read in his place, and which had subsequently been laid upon the table; the object and purport of which he now explained. It was to suspend that rule of proceeding which limits the number of members composing Select Committees to thirteen, with a view to move the reference of the first and fifth resolutions reported, to a Select Committee, consisting of one member from each Senatorial District, and then to refer the third, fourth and fifth resolutions to similar Committees. His design in this proposition was to avail himself of all the intelligence of the body in devising and maturing the best course to be pursued in arriving at the objects of its appointment. Should this plan be adopted, its effect would be to bring into employment the whole faculty of the House: the talent, knowledge and wisdom of all the members would thus be brought into requisition, and exerted at one and the same time. Mr. M. said, he had thought it his duty to give this explanation by way of apology for not now offering the resolutions, which at his request had been laid on the table and printed.

Mr. Tazewell, of Norfolk Borough, now rose and said that it would be more satisfactory to him, if the scheme to which he was desirous of offering his own resolution as a substitute, was made by its advocates as perfect as they desired it to be, before his substitute was considered: he had no wish to urge his own proposition as a substitute to another, while that other was confessedly in an imperfect form: he desired, on the contrary, that gentlemen would first make their proposition as perfect as they could, and when they had done this, that the House should judge between the scheme thus complete, and that which he presented to it. But, if the gentlemen who had reported the resolutions now before the Convention, were willing to wave this advantage, and leave their plan as it was, he should now proceed to redeem the pledge which he had given to the Convention yesterday, and move as a substitute for the resolutions, reported by the Committee of twenty-four, that which, at his request, had been printed and appended to them.

Mr. Tazewell then offered the following resolution:

Resolved, That the most expedient method of bringing before the Convention any amendments to the Constitution which may be proposed, will be, to take up the existing Constitution or form of Government of Virginia, with the Declaration of Rights, and regarding them for the purposes of examination and discussion, merely, as a plan proposed and reported by a Select Committee, to refer the same to a Committee of the whole House, there to be examined section after section, and to be dealt with in all other respects as a bill so referred by the House to that Committee usually is.

In making this motion, Mr. President, it is but fair, said Mr. T. to preface it by stating to the Convention that the same motion was made by me in the Committee, and rejected by a majority. But, Sir, notwithstanding this, I deem it due to the interest and importance of the subject, as well as to the solicitude of gentlemen who, not having been members of the Committee, have enjoyed no opportunity of recording their opinions in the case, to make this motion, in order that, at least, every member of this body may have the opportunity of expressing here his views and sentiments on the subject.

In examining the two schemes which are now before the Convention, it must at once be perceived by every gentleman, that in neither is there any principle involved. Each of them contemplates only the most convenient mode of conducting the business before us: it is a question merely of expediency and convenience. The simple question to be settled is, by which of two modes proposed, can the task imposed upon us by our constituents be best accomplished. The discussion is, therefore, narrowed down to a comparison of the different degrees of convenience presented by the two propositions. The difference between them lies in this only. By the scheme contained in my resolution, the existing form of Government is to be referred at once to the whole body, acting in Committee of the Whole, and to undergo a detailed examination there. The whole scheme will be before the whole body at the same time. Under such a state of things, every step that we take will be in reality a step in advance: whatever we do will diminish, so far, what remains to be done. But what will be the effect of adopting the scheme reported by the Committee? You dissect the subject submitted to you, and distribute its several parts to distinct and independent Committees. What then will be the condition of the body? If my plan be adopted, we shall, at once, on the spur of the occasion, begin to act. The Constitution will be printed immediately; we shall forthwith commence its revision; we shall make actual progress in our business, this very day, and so *de die* in *diem*, and the entire examination will very soon be completed. But if you pursue the other course, you cut up the whole subject into five, six or seven parts, and distribute these five, six or seven parts, among five, six or seven separate and distinct Committees; when this is done, what will remain to the body? Nothing, Sir. You have a Committee for what belongs to the Executive Department of the Government; another Committee for what pertains to the Legislative Department; another for what pertains to the Judiciary; and another Committee for what pertains to neither Executive,

Legislative nor Judicial, and then, Sir, what is this body itself to be doing? It must stand with arms folded, until the Committees, or some one Committee, give it something to do. Its faculties all suspended, it must meet only to adjourn; and how long such a state of things shall continue, must depend solely on the diligence of the Committees. But by my plan, the body can act at once; can act to-day, this very day it can begin and make actual progress in the great duties assigned to it by the people.

But, Sir, this is not all that will ensue upon the adoption of the report which has been presented by the Committee. The action of this body must be suspended, not only till some one of the Committees shall report, but till one certain particular Committee shall report. We are to have one Committee on the Bill of Rights; another Committee on the Executive; another on the Legislative; another on the Judiciary Department; another on some part of the plan of Government which is neither Executive, Legislative nor Judicial in its character, (though what that can be, I do not understand; for all writers that I have read, maintain that every function of Government is of necessity, either Executive, Legislative, or Judicial in its character:) thus, Sir, we are to have five Committees in operation all at one and the same time. On which of their reports must this body first act? On that relating to the Executive? No, Sir; on that relating to the Judiciary? No, Sir; on that which relates to neither of the Departments of Government? No, Sir. This body cannot act if all these reports were received, until the Committee on the Legislative Department have brought in its report; for this Department is universally and justly held to be the foundation of the system of all Government. How vain were it to proceed to any other part of the Constitution, till we had first settled that which is the supreme power in the State! How absurd to set about erecting an edifice, and to begin at the top! To attempt to proceed till the Legislative Committee shall have reported, must involve you in contradictions and difficulties at every step! For example; you come to take up the subject of the Judiciary; the very first question must be, how many judges are to be appointed? What shall be their duties? What their compensation? You take up the report of the Executive Committee, and your first enquiry is, what power shall your Governor have? Shall it be concurrent or exclusive? But all these things must depend on the report of the Legislative Committee; the details in the investigations of that Committee, are necessarily great; they must unavoidably consume a great deal of time; but be the delay ever so great, the Convention must wait till that Committee shall have completed its report; till then the whole body must remain on its oars, with nothing to do.

Nor is this all. He is little acquainted with the nature of Government, who does not at once perceive that in distributing its several functions into various Departments, it is utterly impossible to keep them completely distinct from each other; do what you will, like the colours of the rainbow, they will necessarily run into each other, and become more or less blended together. The ingenuity of man, never yet has devised a form of Government, in which the powers of the different Departments, were not more or less confounded. What, then, becomes of the Committees proposed by the report before you? We are to have one on the Executive Department; another on the Legislative; another on the Judiciary; and another on things anomalous. The first question to be settled, will necessarily be, what part of the Constitution is to be referred to this last Committee. If it is not to touch things Legislative, nor things Executive, nor things Judicial, it can, as I conceive, have nothing to do. If it does touch them, or either of them, what happens? You have two distinct independent bodies, acting at the same time upon the same subject; and in all human probability, rendering to this body different and conflicting reports. Sir, it must be so. It cannot be otherwise. Their duties are co-ordinate; their powers the same; and unless they exhibit more of unanimity than has ever yet been witnessed among mankind, they must and will differ from each other. Sir, it is asking too much, to expect that gentlemen so situated, should concur in their reports. What follows? Each of these conflicting reports will be referred to the Committee of the Whole, and then the Convention will have to begin just where I wish them to begin now. Your Executive Committee and your Legislative Committee both, for instance, report in relation to the veto of the Governor. One says he shall have an absolute veto; or a qualified veto. The other that he shall have no veto at all. Both these reports come into the Committee of the Whole; we take up one and decide upon it, and then comes a new report and a new discussion. We have passed on the report of the Legislative Committee, and then comes in the report of the Executive Committee. The first question which will present itself must be a question of order; and thus the Convention will soon find itself involved in the meshes which are of all others, the most unpleasant and perplexing. But suppose you get clear of the question of order; then comes each Committee, urging and defending its own views; and on the next report the same scene must be acted again; and so over and over again, so long as there remains any other Committee to report. Thus the scheme proposed by the Committee, must necessarily involve a waste of the time of the Convention: the stripping it of all power of action until the Committees shall please to give it something to do: the action of different independent Committees on the same subjects; the re-examination of discussions already gone through with, and the endless conflict of contradictory opinions, each urged by gentlemen already pledged by their votes in Committee; each and all of which present insuperable objections to the adoption of such a scheme, while to that which I have had the honour of proposing, none of them apply in whole or in part.

But there exists another objection; more perhaps in appearance than in fact, but one which I confess, weighs heavily with me. A bare majority of the people of Virginia, the majority was very small indeed, have given their decision in favour of the call of this Convention. A most respectable minority, (less by only a few votes than the majority which called us here,) though they admit the existence of some defects in the existing Constitution; yet think it "better to bear the ills we have, than fly to others that we know not of." This minority is every way respectable, as much so in character as numbers. And of what is the majority composed? Of a most mixed and heterogeneous mass, of which I will venture to affirm, that there are not ten men who agree in their objections to the Constitution. Each man has an objection of his own; all they agree in is, that they are objectors. Well, Sir, when one of the reports of these Committees shall come in, what will be the consequence? each man will be actuated by his own individual objection, and will of course, struggle for his own opinion. In the mean while, what becomes of the minority of the people? Is there no necessity of looking at all to their opinions? To their prejudices? Yes, Sir, to their false notions, if you please to call them so? Will a wise statesman ever disregard the opinion of his people? No, Sir, if he did, he would be no longer wise. Sir, we must have regard, and a respectful regard, to the opinions of the people of Virgina. What is proposed to you, Sir? Instead of taking up a Constitution to which a portion of that people have been long attached, and considering it section by section, and word by word, that we may cautiously discover and remedy its defects, by one fell swoop you seize at once upon the whole; tear it limbless, and scatter its various fragments to the winds of Heaven: then you set to work to gather these scattered and dissevered limbs, and you attempt to join and dove-tail them together, and piece them up into some other form. What will be the public impression from such a procedure? The public will very naturally conclude, that this Convention has determined to destroy at a blow, every vestige of their Old Constitution. This is the notion that must go abroad; the people will at once believe that you are resolved to explode every thing at a blast, and then to build upon the same, or on a different foundation, a Government, which but few can hope, *will* do as much for the public happiness and prosperity as that you destroy *has* done. Sir, it is due to this affectionate reverence, the people bear to their long-tried form of Government, to deal tenderly with it; it becomes us to take up this beloved offspring of theirs with every feeling of kind regard, to extol its virtues and to lay our correcting hand upon its vices alone. Thus, I have endeavored to show, that not only the convenience of the body, but the good opinion of the people, whose voice has brought us here, requires the adoption of the scheme I have proposed.

There are other considerations besides these which ought to lead you to the course I advocate; which ought to warn you to aim no fell and reckless blow at the existing Constitution. Will you dissect, will you dissever the body said to be gangrenous, before you know where the gangrene is? Will you at once cut into the vitals and separate it limb from limb, under pretence of searching for the unsound part? By whom was this Government formed? By a body which, I will say, united as much wisdom as can be found any where; with as much public virtue as will ever again be assembled. Is this an instrument to be torn to pieces and distributed fragment by fragment to Committees of thirteen men? Is it not due to such a document, that we shall contemplate the whole of it at once? That we shall take a view of its parts as sustaining their respective relations to each other and to the whole? Can we judge of it correctly if you judge of it only by parts? Is it wise thus to judge of any thing compounded and complex? Is it not the most ready course to err? A different course is surely due to the character and the virtues of those who formed the Constitution. And further, Sir, is nothing due to upwards of fifty years experience? This Constitution has been in operation for fifty-four years: it has borne us safely through peace and through war; through all the excitement of party contest, as well as the calmness of more tranquil times: And is there in this body a single member, or is there a single one of our constituents, who is able to name one practical evil it has brought upon us? Can more be said? A Government, born of wisdom and of virtue, which has been in operation for fifty-four years, and has done no harm. When was there a Government, of which this could be said? Certainly it is due to such a system, to consider it as *prima facie* good: it is due to it, to give it a close and deliberate examination: it must surely be rash, to cut it at once to pieces; scatter all its parts; and then see if we cannot make something out of them, that may peradventure do better. It is due to the feelings of a very large portion of the people of this State, who are attached to the Constitution in all its parts; to the whole and to every part; to refer such a document to all the wisdom which can be commanded for its contemplation; to the collective wisdom of all those whom they have deputed to the task of its revision. But, if the other course shall be pursued, what will be the result? We are to set thirteen men to examine the Legislative part of it; other thirteen to examine the Executive portion of it; other thirteen to examine the Judicial portion of it; and so on; piece by piece, through half a dozen different Committees. It is vain to reply, that all the reports of these various Committees, must come at last to this body; *how* are they to come? They will come with majorities of each respective Committee, enlisted in favor of their own report, and pledged for its support. It must be so. They stand openly pledged to their constituents and to the world. But, if my proposition shall be adopted, no man will be pledged to any thing, till he has the whole ground before him. Send it to Committees, and the majorities will be pledged; they must be: and they will enter this Hall in solid phalanx, each devoted to the maintenance of the work of his own hands. The consequence I need not predict.

Sir, the question before you, is one of mere form. I considered it as of importance to the time, and to the rightful deliberations of this body; and, therefore, thought something ought to be said upon it. I felt it a duty, to explain the nature of the course I wished to see pursued. I have done: and should consider it unwarrantable, to waste more of that time, which it is my aim and my desire to save.

Mr. Mercer rose in reply. He said, that when he at first rose, he had been well aware of the ingenuity and the ability of the gentleman who had just addressed the House, and was not ignorant of the generous feeling from which what he conceived to be the error of that gentleman proceeded. Yet he believed it only necessary to trace the course of the gentleman's own argument, to show him how widely he had departed from the principles with which he set out. That gentleman, said Mr. Mercer, early told us that the two propositions before the Convention involved no principle. Yet, in support of the substitute he has proposed to the resolutions reported by the Committee, he has gone back and traced the origin of the existing Government, and had delivered an eloquent eulogy upon the Constitution; to the greater part of which, my own heart very fully accords. Sir, was this no appeal to principle? The gentleman tells us, that if the course he advocates shall not be pursued, we shall bring into this House in solid phalanx, pledged and opposing majorities from the Committee rooms. Is there no principle in this? Sir, there *are* principles involved in any course we may pursue. How can we, who have thought that there are defects, and very serious ones in the Constitution, reconcile it to ourselves to be told that the course we have proposed, tears the Constitution to pieces? The honourable member from Norfolk, has treated the Constitution as if it were an organized sensitive being, and its reference to Committees, must necessarily tear it piece-meal and destroy it altogether.

I say, Sir, we purpose to treat the Committee with more respect. What is our proposition? It is first to see whether there be in this body a majority who do disapprove of its present form: and this before we submit it to the promiscuous and accidental motions (if the expression may be pardoned me) of every gentleman who chooses to attack it. We desire first to submit it to Committees of twenty-four members, who, coming from every Senatorial district, may be fairly presumed to represent the judgment of the whole State: and then, after we ascertain that a majority in such Committee of twenty-four concur in recommending an alteration in any of its features, to submit that proposed alteration to the deliberate action of the whole body. Sir, is this to treat the Constitution with levity? Is this tearing it asunder, and scattering its fragments to the winds of Heaven? Is this inconsistent with the tenderest and the deepest reverence for the work of our forefathers? No, Sir: Nothing like it: just the reverse. On the contrary, it is an expedient calculated to save the time of this assembly, and to promote the harmony as well as the speed of its decisions. Mr. President, even forms necesarily involve principles. If, however, our plan saved no time, the argument of the gentleman over the way would have more weight: but it does save time. How can it be otherwise? Surely it must be obvious that if every proposition before it be discussed, must be approved by a majority of a large Committee, we shall have the fewer propositions before us. It is most palpable that such an arrangement must save our time.

But the gentleman has said, that we cannot analyse the Constitution, so as properly to consider it by separate Committees. The honourable member very truly said, that all Governments are capable of being resolved into Executive, Legislative and Judicial Departments. Admit it. Yet, at another time, he says that these Departments melt like the colours of the rainbow into each other. The gentleman certainly reflects upon the authors of the report before you, when he says that the last Committee which they propose will have nothing to act upon. Sir, are there not many subjects, which standing in precisely the same relation to each one of the Departments, and having nothing in their nature to attach them to one more than the other, will very naturally be thrown out by each of the other Committees as not being appropriate to the subject of their examination? What is to be done with these? If the report be adopted, they will go to this last Committee, of which the gentleman speaks as if they must be idle. There are, for example, some principles laid down in the Bill of Rights, which pertain alike to all the Departments of Government; take as an instance that clause in the Bill of Rights which treats of rights not surrendered: the proposition there laid down belongs equally to all the divisions of Government; they are all alike bound to respect the residuary rights of the people.

But, Sir, let us leave theory for a moment, and look to the practical difficulties before us. What seems very imperfect in theory, is often found to be attended with no evil consequences, when reduced to practice, and submitted to the test of experience. The gentleman's theory is, that you cannot, in the nature of things, form a plan of Government, by the action of these independent Committees. But the simple remedy to this very formidable difficulty, is to let the Convention act upon the reports as they are received, or in the order in which they are taken up. This will prevent all collision of Committee majorities, and obviate the difficulty arising from contradictory reports, (if they shall prove contradictory.) For example: A report is received from the Committee on the Executive; the Convention takes it up and acts upon it, adopting or rejecting its provisions; that report recommends a certain course respecting the veto of the Executive. By and bye comes the report of the Legislative Committee, and recommends a different course respecting the veto; but this recommendation comes too late: the Convention has decided on the subject of the veto, and that subject is at rest; none can stir it anew. Here is an end to the gentleman's difficulty. The Convention loses no time; if any time is lost, it is that of the Committee which discussed a subject already anticipated. Why should the Convention decide upon it again? Has the Convention changed its judgment? It is to be presumed it has not. But granting that it has, all that is to be done, is to suspend the rule quod hoc, and open the subject for revision just as might be done in any other case. Nothing here is either gained or lost.

As to the period at which we must commence our discussions, the honorable gentleman from Norfolk says, that we must necessarily wait till we have the reports of all the Committees, and thus get the whole subject before us.

Sir, is this necessary? I say no: not at all. I heard a figure used the other day, (not here, but elsewhere,) in support of the gentleman's position, which strongly elicited this general remark: that figurative language has place in argument only for the purpose of illustration; and not as itself a source of argument. If we attempt to found arguments upon figures of speech, we shall ever be led astray. The figure used was this: it was said that a sculptor could not possibly know how to carve one limb of a statue, till he first knew the height and proportions of the whole figure he was to produce. This even, if true, would decide nothing in the case before us: for this body could decide, for example, on the question touching the unity of the Executive, without having any reference to the number of members of the House of Delegates, and so of many other branches of the general subject of Government. It is, indeed, true, that there are some points which have a bearing upon the whole system; but this is not true of all the points, nor is it true of many. Sir, were this not so, the House could not decide upon any question whatever; for, obviously, we can go but step by step; one subject only can be taken up at once, and we must and do presume the rest, and act accordingly. We must anticipate, and it will be fair and just to do so, that the coming reports will concur with what the Committees have already done. Give the gentleman all he asks: and suppose we go into Committee of the Whole, and take up the Constitution clause by clause. A member offers an amendment to the first clause; he does so, and can do so, only in anticipation of what is to be done, with the remaining clauses. So that it will come precisely to the same thing, and the difficulty, if it be one, applies as much to the one plan as to the other. I think we shall save much time, by adopting the plan of the Committee.

Besides, there will be this additional advantage. The several propositions will not only be each considered in Committee, but they will be considered in their bearing on all the other portions of that Department of Government to which they appertain, because all that Department will be in the hands of one Committee. Thus, for example, if, in the Legislative Committee, a proposition is reported to reduce the number of members in the House of Delegates, the same Committee will have it in their power to consider the propriety of also reducing the numbers of the Senate. Thus, there will be a harmony in the sub-divisions of each general Department of Government.

This puts an end to the gentleman's conjecture, that no ten men will agree as to what amendments should be made in the Constitution. But, if that were the fact, it only follows that there is the greater need for the Committees proposed; for there may, according to the gentleman, be no two in the Committee of the Whole, who will fully agree in all their views, and so the debates will be interminable. In Committee of the Whole, there is no restraint as to speaking; each member may speak as often as he pleases; and, for aught, I see, we shall be in session here till mid-winter, if his plan prevails. If the previous question to be taken is, whether the Constitution is to be amended at all, let it be taken. That, after all, is the argument of the gentleman from Norfolk, though it is not his plan. Such a resolution would be in order, and it proves that we have still a subject to act on here, even if the Committees shall be appointed. So we may also give instructions to the Committees. The whole subject is open to the body. I take it for granted, the delay produced by discussions in the Committees will not be great, and the gentleman can put an end to it whenever he will, the Convention concurring. But, Sir, to prevent the evil he suggests, I shall offer a proposition to enlarge all the Committees so as to make them each consist of twenty-four members. This will prevent the appearance of that solid phalanx which glares before the gentleman's imagination so formidably. If there shall be thirteen to eleven in each Committee, the majority will not be very large; and this is another advantage attending the scheme. The Committees, like the Convention itself, will in this way be prepared to act upon a knowledge of the whole subject before us.

Mr. M. concluded by an apology for having trespassed so long upon the time of the Convention, and then resumed his seat.

The question was then called for on Mr. Tazewell's amendment.

Mr. Randolph demanded that the question be taken by yeas and nays: it was so taken accordingly, and the yeas and nays were reported by the Secretary, as follows:

AYES.—Messrs. Jones, Leigh of Chesterfield, Taylor of Chesterfield, Giles, Brodnax, Dromgoole, Alexander, Goode, Marshall, Tyler, Nicholas, Clopton, Mason, Trezvant, Claiborne, Urquhart, Randolph, Leigh of Halifax, Logan, Venable, Madison, Barbour of Orange, Roane, Taylor of Caroline, Garnett, Barbour of Culpeper, Scott, Green, Tazewell, Loyall, Prentis, Townes, Taliaferro and Upshur—34.

NOES.—Messrs. Monroe, (President,) Anderson, Coffman, Williamson, Baldwin, Johnson, M'Coy, Moore, Beirne, Smith, Miller, Baxter, Stanard, Mercer, Fitzhugh, Henderson, Cooke, Powell, Opie, Griggs, Naylor, Donaldson, Boyd, Pendleton, George, M'Millan, Campbell of Washington, Byars, Cloyd, Chapman, Oglesby, Duncan, Laidley, Summers, See, Doddridge, Morgan, Campbell of Brooke, Wilson, Macrae, Taylor of Norfolk, Claytor, Mennis, Saunders, Cabell, Martin, Stuart, Pleasants, Gordon, Thompson, Massie, Bates, Joynes and Bayly—54.

So Mr. Tazewell's amendment was rejected by the Convention.

The report of the Committee was then read at the Secretary's table by sections:

And the question being on the first resolution by the Committee, as follows:

Resolved, That a Committee be appointed to take into consideration the Bill or Declaration of Rights, and to report to this Convention whether, in their opinion, any, and if any, what amendments are necessary therein.

A desultory conversation arose, in which Messrs. Johnson, Mercer and Doddridge took part, and which resulted in a motion by Mr. Mercer to lay the first resolution for the present upon the table: the motion was agreed to.

The second resolution having been read as follows:

Resolved, That a Committee be appointed to take into consideration the Legislative Department of Government as established by the present Constitution, and to report to this Convention, either a substitute for the same, or such amendments thereto, as in their opinion are necessary, or that no substitute or amendment is necessary,

Mr. Benjamin W. Leigh referring to the notice given by Mr. Mercer, that he should move to enlarge the Committees to twenty-four members each, protested against this being taken for granted as about to pass, and being thus made an argument with the House. He was opposed to such enlargement, and hoped it would not take place. Committees of twenty-four members would scarcely deserve the name; they would be so many debating bodies, with all the forms of debate observed elsewhere, instead of the colloquial discussion appropriate to Committees, and which constituted indeed their chief advantage. Mr. Mercer declined a formal reply till the resolutions should have been gone through with.

The third and fourth resolutions from the Committee were then read and adopted, as follows:

Resolved, That the Executive Department of Government as established by the present Constitution, be referred to a Committee, to enquire and report whether any, and if any, what amendments are necessary.

Resolved, That the Judicial Department of Government as established by the present Constitution, be referred to a Committee, to enquire and report whether any, and if any, what amendments are necessary therein.

The fifth resolution was then read as follows:

Resolved, That all such parts of the present Constitution as are not referred by the foregoing resolutions, be referred to a Committee, to enquire and report whether any, and if any, what amendments are necessary therein.

This resolution being amended, so as to add, "the Declaration of Rights," among the subjects transferred to the Committee, it was, thus amended, adopted by the House.

The sixth and last resolution of the Committee was then read as follows:

Resolved, That no original resolution offered to the Convention proposing any amendment to the Constitution or Declaration of Rights, be discussed on its merits in the House, till it shall have been referred.

Mr. Benjamin W. Leigh called for the reasons in its favor.

Mr. Johnson briefly stated them as consisting in a desire for the maturest discussion of every proposition before it was adopted, and for the prevention of the points referred to the Committees being mooted at the same time in the House.

Mr. Leigh objected to the words of the resolution as going to prevent any member who might propose an amendment in the House, from explaining the nature and intention of such amendments.

Mr. Johnson denied that such consequence would follow, and referred in support of his view of the case, to the usage in the House of Delegates, where it was a standing rule that no proposition could be discussed until it had been seconded, and still a gentleman offering a resolution was held in order to give a succinct explanation of its purport, provided the discussion stopped there.

The question being put on the adoption of the sixth resolution, a division was called for, and the votes being counted by Messrs. Leigh and Johnson, stood as follows: Ayes 48, Noes 32: so the resolution was adopted.

The first resolution was then taken from the table, and rejected; its contents having been superseded.

Mr. Mercer then moved the following resolution:

Resolved, That so much of the twenty-fourth rule of the Convention, as limits the number of a Select Committee to thirteen, be suspended, for the purpose of enlarging the three Committees required by the preceding resolutions, to such extent, as that each Committee shall comprehend one member from every Senatorial District, and composing the Committee required by the fourth resolution of such members as may not be placed on the preceding Committees.

Mr. M. now replied to the objections before stated by Mr. Leigh, and referred to precedents in the Journals of the House of Delegates, to shew that Committees of twenty, of thirty-three, and one of forty-three members, had been appointed on important subjects. No great evil, he thought, arose from the formal mode of discussion, pursued in large Committees, though he acknowledged, that he should prefer the colloquial mode of debate.

A desultory conversation ensued, in which Messrs. Leigh, Stanard, Mercer, Fitzhugh and Doddridge took part, and in which several modifications of the resolution were proposed. Mr. Marshall enquired of Mr. Mercer, if he intended to bring forward, at all, the two resolutions he had read yesterday?

Mr. Mercer replying in the negative,

Mr. Marshall said, that if he had brought them forward, he should have thought, that one Committee of twenty-four was sufficient; as the subject to be referred to it, was geographical in its nature, and had a bearing on members, according to the part of the State where they resided. In such a Committee, twenty-four members might be required, in order to collect the opinions of every part of the State; but this was not equally necessary on questions not geographical in their nature. When the measure proposed, was to affect all the citizens alike, there was not the same reason for a difference of opinion, in different districts. Still, if no objection arose from the proposed number of members in the Committees, Mr. Marshall said, he should have submitted to the arrangement; but there was an objection, and a serious one, which did arise from it: it was the wish, he presumed, of every member, that at least some portion of the business before the Convention, might be entered upon and completed as soon as practicable. But it must be obvious, that if each of the Committees were to consist of twenty-four members, more time would be consumed in preparing their reports, than if the number were smaller. If, for example, the Committees should consist of thirteen members, the reports, though he hoped not less considered, would be considered and reported upon in less time.

Mr. Scott moved to amend the resolution, by striking out the word "three," so as to read, "the first of the Committees," instead of "the first *three* of the Committees."

Mr. Mercer observed in reply to Judge Marshall, that there was not a part of the Constitution, in which all parts of the State were not deeply interested. How could the Convention know the opinions of the people, for instance, respecting the Executive Department of Government, but by consulting the people? and how could it consult them, but through their representatives? So respecting the Judiciary; he could assure the honorable and venerable gentleman that that was a question of a local character; there did exist on that subject, evils of very great magnitude; but those evils were not universal, but local in their extent. The gentleman was ready to admit that the principle involved in the first of the resolutions was such as required a Committee from all parts of the State; he believed the same principle would be found to apply to all the other resolutions. Mr. M. then stated the reasons why he should not offer his two resolutions, and concluded by a compliment to the judgment and standing of the gentleman from Richmond.

Mr. Marshall rejoined. If his friend had understood him to say that every part of the community was not interested in every part of the Constitution, he had greatly mistaken his meaning. But the interest they take in the other parts of the Constitution not geographical in their bearing, was not local or geographical in its kind. Gentlemen on one side of James River, for instance, had the same interest in the Executive Department of the Government, as those on the other side. That interest did not depend at all upon their residence; on that Department, therefore, he could see no reason for a Committee taken from all parts of the State; but the case was very different when the question of the basis of representation was involved. As that subject was not necessarily separated from the Legislative Department, he saw no need of reporting on it by a separate Committee. As there was nothing geographical in the Executive or Judicial Departments of Government, he could not see the need of having a Geographical Committee to consider them; and as a large Committee was likely to be slow in reporting, he preferred one of more limited numbers.

After some remarks of Mr. Johnson, going to shew the inconvenience of large Committees, he expressed his determination to vote for the amendment, leaving all other Committees but one to be appointed in the ordinary mode by the Chair.

The question was then taken on the amendment of Mr. Scott, and decided in the negative—Ayes 39, Noes 46. So the amendment was rejected.

The resolution was then carried, ayes 51.

A conversation now arose as to certain documents, the printing of which was desired with a view to ascertain as far as practicable, the present population of the State.

Mr. Joynes offered the following resolution:

Resolved, That the Secretary cause to be printed for the use of the members of this Convention 100 copies of the Census of this State, taken in the years 1790, 1800, 1810 and 1820; and also, in separate tables, 100 copies of the aggregate militia returns of each county in those years, and in the year 1829, and the three years preceding.

Messrs. Joynes, Claytor, Doddridge, Green, Mercer, Upshur, Scott, and B. W. Leigh, took part in this discussion; but before the gentlemen had agreed upon all the documents to be printed, Mr. Powell moved to lay the resolution of Mr. Joynes upon the table.

Whereupon, on motion of Mr. Stanard, the House adjourned.

SATURDAY, October 10, 1829.

The Convention met at 12 o'clock, and its sitting was opened with prayer by the Rev. Mr. Lee.

The following gentlemen were announced as having been appointed to constitute the several Committees ordered on Friday:

Committee to consider the Legislative Department of the Government.

Messrs. Leigh of Chesterfield,
Brodnax,
Tyler,
Anderson,
Johnson,
Beirne,
Mason,
Randolph,
Madison,
Mercer,
Cooke,
Pendleton,

Messrs. George,
Roane,
Chapman,
Summers,
Doddridge,
Green,
Tazewell,
Campbell of Bedford,
Townes,
Pleasants,
Taliaferro,
Joynes.

Committee on the Executive Department.

Messrs. Giles,
Dromgoole,
Nicholas,

Messrs. Campbell of Washington,
Garnett,
Cloyd,

Messrs. Coffman,	Messrs. Duncan,
M'Coy,	Morgan,
Smith,	Barbour of Culpeper,
Trezvant,	Loyall,
Leigh of Halifax,	Claytor,
Barbour of Orange,	Cabell,
Fitzhugh,	Gordon,
Powell,	Bates,
Naylor,	Upshur.

Committee on the Judicial Department.

Messrs. Jones,	Messrs. M'Millan,
Alexander,	Morris,
Marshall,	Mathews,
Harrison,	Laidley,
Baldwin,	Campbell of Ohio,
Miller,	Scott,
Claiborne,	Taylor,
Venable,	Mennis,
Stanard,	Martin,
Henderson,	Thompson,
Griggs,	Bayly.
Boyd,	

Committee to consider the Bill of Rights, and other matters not referred to the foregoing Committees.

Messrs. Taylor of Chesterfield,	Messrs. Taylor of Caroline,
Goode,	Oglesby,
Clopton,	See,
Williamson,	Wilson,
Moore,	Macrae,
Baxter,	Prentis,
Urquhart,	Saunders,
Logan,	Stuart,
Opie,	Massie,
Donaldson,	Read.
Byars,	

The President then laid before the Convention the following letter received by him from the honorable Judge Dade, a member elect to the Convention:

To the honorable the PRESIDENT *of the Convention, called to alter or amend the Constitution of the State of Virginia.*

SIR:—Being unable from ill health to attend my duties in the Convention, I take the earliest opportunity of enclosing to you my resignation of that high trust.

Occurring after the meeting of the Convention, it will, of course, devolve the filling of my vacancy on the remaining Delegates.

With the most earnest wishes for the success of your labours, and with the highest respect for yourself and the body in which you preside, I am your most obedient servant,

WM. A. G. DADE.

October 5th, 1829.

Mr. Taliaferro of King George, said, that he believed in expressing his unfeigned regret for the cause that had produced the communication just read, he should hazard nothing by saying, that in Judge Dade the Convention had lost one of its most valuable members. He was very sure he should hazard nothing in the view of all those to whom that gentleman was known. As he presumed that some authentic record of the fact of Judge Dade's resignation was requisite, it was his purpose to move that the letter announcing it, should be put on file by the Secretary, and entered upon the Journal of the Convention, but as a previous motion was required by order, he would first move that the letter be laid upon the table: which motion being agreed to, Mr. T. moved that the communication from Judge Dade be entered on the records of the Convention.

This motion was carried nem. con.

Mr. Joynes of Accomack, now moved again the resolution which he offered yesterday, and which was modified so as to read as follows:

Resolved, That the Auditor of Public Accounts, be requested to prepare and lay before this Convention, Tabular Statements, shewing the free white, free coloured, and slave population of each county of this Commonwealth, according to the Census taken in the years 1790, 1800, 1810, and 1820, respectively; the area in acres of each county; the quantity of land taxed in each county, in the year 1828; the amount of taxes assessed in each county, in the year 1828; the amount of tax paid into the Public Treasury, from each county, in that year; the amount of tax accruing on each subject of taxation; the white, free coloured, and slave tythables of each county, in the years 1800, 1810, 1820, and 1829; and also a statement of the free white, free coloured, and slave population of each county, in the year 1829, so far as he can deduce the same by a comparison of the tythables, and the entire population in the years 1800, 1810, and 1820.

Resolved, That the Auditor be also requested, in addition to such Tabular Statements, in reference to each county, to state the information above requested, in relation to the four following divisions of this Commonwealth, viz: 1st, from the sea-coast, to the head of tide-water; 2d, from the head of tide-water to the Blue Ridge; 3d, from the Blue Ridge to the Alleghany; and 4th, from the Alleghany to the wetward.

The above resolutions having been agreed to,

Mr. Green of Culpeper, moved the following:

Resolved, That the Auditor be also requested to furnish a statement, from the property books in his office, of the number of persons in each county and corporate town of this Commonwealth, assessed to the payment of any revenue tax, in the year 1828.

The resolution was adopted.

On motion of Mr. Doddridge, it was ordered, that the foregoing list of the members of Committees, be printed for the use of the House. And then the House adjourned till Monday 12 o'clock.

MONDAY, October 12, 1829.

The Convention met pursuant to adjournment, at 12 o'clock, and was opened with prayer by the Rev. Mr. Kerr (of the Baptist Church.)

Mr. Neal, from the District of King George, appeared and took his seat.

The President laid before the Convention the following letter, which was read at the Clerk's table:

Richmond, October 12, 1829.

Sir:—We discharge a melancholy duty in announcing to you the death of Calvin H. Read, Esq. a Delegate to the Convention of Virginia from the twenty-fourth District, who departed this life on the night of the 6th inst.

This event having occurred since the meeting of the Convention, we, the remaining members of that Delegation, have proceeded, according to the provisions of the act of Assembly, to fill the vacancy thereby occasioned. We have appointed William K. Perrin, Esq. of the county of Gloucester, as the successor of Mr. Read, as will appear by the document which we have the honor to enclose.

With high consideration we are, your ob't serv'ts,

THOS. R. JOYNES,
THOS. M. BAYLY,
A. P. UPSHUR.

The honorable James Monroe, *President of the Convention—Present.*

On motion of Mr. Joynes of Accomack, the letter was laid upon the table.

Mr. Joynes thereupon moved the following resolution:

Resolved, That the members of this Convention will wear crape for thirty days in testimony of their respect for the memory of Dr. Calvin H. Read of Northampton, who was elected a member of this Convention and who has died since the meeting of the Convention.

On offering the above resolution, Mr. J. said, that when he heard of the death of Dr. Read, he had at first been in doubt as to the propriety of moving such a resolution as he now had the honor to submit. He was not then apprised of the practice in the House of Delegates on such occasions; but he had since ascertained, that it was usual on the death of a member, to adopt such a mark of respect, as that he had just proposed. The gentleman, in remembrance of whom, he asked the Convention to wear crape for thirty days, was one of the most amiable and upright citizens of the State, and although this slight tribute of regard, was in itself, perhaps, but of little value, it might be some consolation to the weeping widow of the deceased, and to his family and friends, to know, that a testimonial of public respect, usual in other cases of a similar kind, had not been withheld from the memory of Dr. Read.

The resolution was unanimously adopted. Whereupon, Mr. Joynes moved the following additional resolution:

Resolved, That the Sergeant at Arms cause to be delivered, as soon as practicable, to Mr. William K. Perrin of Gloucester, a notification of his appointment as a member of this Convention, to supply the vacancy, occasioned by the death of Dr. Calvin H. Read, of Northampton.

Mr. Fitzhugh, from the Committee appointed to fix the compensation of officers, reported in part as follows:

"The Committee appointed to enquire into the compensation proper to be allowed the officers of the Convention, have agreed to the following resolution:

"*Resolved*, That the allowances to the officers of this Convention for their services, during its Session, shall be to the President, in addition to his mileage as a member of the Convention, eight dollars per day, to the Secretary one hundred and fifty dollars per week, to the Sergeant at Arms thirty dollars per week, to each of the door-keepers twenty-eight dollars per week, and to the person who cleans the Capitol, fourteen dollars per week."

Mr. F. observed in explanation, that the Committee had not found it possible to include in their report, a proper compensation for the public printer, inasmuch as no correct estimate could at present be formed of the amount of public printing he would have to execute. They had also included in their report, an allowance to a person not strictly an officer of the Convention, but performing a subordinate duty in its service, viz: the sweeping the Hall and passages. In taking this liberty, they conceived itself as acting in conformity with the spirit, though not the letter of their appointment, and in doing so they had followed a precedent set by the practice in the House of Delegates.

The resolution recommended by the Committee, was adopted.

Mr. Doddridge then offered the following resolutions:

"*Resolved*, That the several Committees consisting of a member from each Senatorial District, have power respectively to appoint a Clerk, and to cause such printing to be done as they may deem expedient in the performance of their respective duties.

"*Resolved*, That the Committee appointed to enquire into the compensation proper to be allowed the officers of the Convention, be instructed to provide and report a fit compensation for such Clerks as may be appointed under the preceding resolution."

The resolutions were agreed to.

Mr. Joynes then moved the following:

"*Resolved*, That the Auditor of Public Accounts be requested to prepare and lay before the Convention a statement of the number of persons in each county of this Commonwealth, who are charged on the land books of the years 1828 and 1829, with taxes on a quantity of land not less than twenty-five acres, or on a lot or part of a lot in a town established by law."

This resolution having been adopted,

On motion of Mr. Brodnax, the Convention adjourned to meet to-morrow at one o'clock.

[This alteration in the hour of meeting, being designed to allow further time to the several Committees now in session.]

TUESDAY, OCTOBER 13, 1829.

The Convention met at one o'clock, and was opened with prayer by the Rev. Mr. Kerr.

Mr. Marshall of Richmond said, that he was charged with a memorial from a numerous and respectable body of citizens, the non-freeholders of the city of Richmond. The object sought in the memorial, was an extension of the right of suffrage. The language of the memorial was respectful, and the petitioners accompanied their request with such arguments, as to them appeared convincing, in support of the object in view.

The memorial was thereupon received, and read as follows:

The Memorial of the Non-Freeholders of the City of Richmond, respectfully addressed to the Convention, now assembled to deliberate on amendments to the State Constitution:

Your memorialists, as their designation imports, belong to that class of citizens, who not having the good fortune to possess a certain portion of land, are, for that cause only, debarred from the enjoyment of the right of suffrage. Experience has but too clearly evinced, what, indeed, reason had always foretold, by how frail a tenure they hold every other right, who are denied this, the highest prerogative of freemen. The want of it has afforded both the pretext and the means of excluding the entire class, to which your memorialists belong, from all participation in the recent election of the body, they now respectfully address. Comprising a very large part, probably a majority of male citizens of mature age, they have been passed by, like aliens or slaves, as if destitute of interest, or unworthy of a voice, in measures involving their future political destiny: whilst the freeholders, sole possessors, under the existing Constitution, of the elective franchise, have, upon the strength of that possession alone, asserted and maintained in themselves, the exclusive power of new-modelling the fundamental laws of the State: in other words, have seized upon the sovereign authority.

It cannot be necessary, in addressing the Convention now assembled, to expatiate on the momentous importance of the right of suffrage, or to enumerate the evils consequent upon its unjust limitation. Were there no other than that your memorialists have brought to your attention, and which has made them feel with full force their degraded condition, well might it justify their best efforts to obtain the great privilege they now seek, as the only effectual method of preventing its recurrence To that privilege, they respectfully contend, they are entitled equally with its present possessors. Many are bold enough to deny their title. None can show a better. It rests upon no subtle or abstruse reasoning; but upon grounds simple in their character, intelligible to the plainest capacity, and such as appeal to the heart, as well as the understanding, of all who comprehend and duly appreciate the principles of free Government. Among the doctrines inculcated in the great charter handed down to us, as a declaration of the rights pertaining to the good people of Virginia and their posterity, "as the basis and foundation of Government," we are taught,

"That all men are by nature equally free and independent, and have certain inherent rights, of which, when they enter into a state of society, they cannot, by any compact, deprive or divest their posterity: namely, the enjoyment of life and liberty, with the means of acquiring and possessing property, and pursuing and obtaining happiness and safety.

"That all power is vested in, and consequently derived from, the people.

"That a majority of the community hath an indubitable, unalienable, and indefeasible right to reform, alter or abolish the Government.

"That no man, nor set of men, are entitled to exclusive or separate emoluments or privileges, but in consideration of public services.

"That all men, having sufficient evidence of permanent common interest with, and attachment to, the community, have a right of suffrage, and cannot be taxed, or deprived of their property, without their consent, or that of their representative, nor bound by any law, to which they have not, in like manner, assented, for the public good."

How do the principles thus proclaimed, accord with the existing regulation of suffrage? A regulation, which, instead of the equality nature ordains, creates an odious distinction between members of the same community; robs of all share, in the enactment of the laws, a large portion of the citizens, bound by them, and whose blood and treasure are pledged to maintain them, and vests in a favoured class, not in consideration of their public services, but of their private possessions, the highest of all privileges: one which, as is now in flagrant proof, if it does not constitute, at least is held practically to confer, absolute sovereignty. Let it not be urged, that the regulation complained of and the charter it violates, sprung from the same honored source. The conflict between them is not on that account the less apparent. Nor does it derogate from the fair fame of the Convention of '76, that they should not have framed a Constitution perfect in all its parts. Deliberating amid the din of arms, not merely on a plan of Government, but on the necessary means for conducting a most unequal struggle for national existence, it was not to be expected, that the relative rights of the citizens, could be maturely considered, or adjusted in detail. From any change of the regulation, in regard to suffrage, a subject prolific, always, of much dissention, they might have feared to generate feuds among those, upon whose harmony of feeling and concert of action, depended the salvation of their country. They left it, therefore, as they found it. The non-freeholders, moreover, unrepresented in the Convention, and for the most part, probably, engaged in resisting the common enemy, it is fair to infer, in the actual condition of the country, had neither the opportunity nor the inclination to press their claims. Nor should it be forgotten, that the Convention having been chosen by the freeholders, whose political power was derived from the abrogated Government, many of our wisest Statesmen regarded the Constitution itself, as wanting in authority, or at least as repealable by a succeeding Legislature: and, accordingly, it has, in point of fact, since undergone a material change, in the very provision now in question, touching the right of suffrage.

If the Bill of Rights may not challenge respect, the opinions of any individual, however eminent, will be still more lightly regarded. Yet your memorialists cannot but exult in the countenance their cause has received from him, who was ever foremost to assert the rights of his fellow men; the venerated author of the Declaration of Independence, and of the Act of Religious Freedom. When those rights are brought in question, they know of none whose sentiments are worthy of higher estimation. To none among the founders of our Republic, are we indebted for more in its institutions, that is admirable in theory, or valuable in practice. His name is identified with the independence of his country; with all that is liberal and enlightened in her policy. Never had liberty an advocate of more unaffected zeal; of more splendid abilities; of purer principles. Nor is there in ancient or modern times, an example to be found of one, who in his life and conduct, more strongly exemplified the sincerity of his faith, or more brightly illustrated the beauty of his tenets.

Your memorialists could not on this occasion, in justice to themselves, omit all allusion to the avowed sentiments of this illustrious Statesman, nor withhold from his memory, a passing tribute of admiration and gratitude.

Dreading the influence of the doctrines and opinions now adverted to, conscious of the futility of any attempt to reconcile with them their favorite policy, the enemies of extended suffrage have not hesitated to deride them as the crude conceptions of visionary politicians. The Bill of Rights, until it became necessary for their purposes to assail it, the theme of unqualified approbation, whilst they affect to admire the beauty of its theory, they paradoxically assert, tends in practice to mischievous results. Its principles, they cannot deny, are founded in truth and justice. But these practical politicians look to a higher sanction, and sacrifice without remorse both justice and truth on the altar of expediency. Would it not be well they should enlighten the world with a system of their own, which should conform to the practice they would approve, and substitute the exploded theories of the wisest Statesmen, the purest Patriots, and the soundest Republicans, who ever adorned any age or country.

But not to the authority of great names merely, does the existing restriction upon suffrage stand opposed; reason and justice equally condemn it. The object, it is presumed, meant to be attained, was, as far as practicable, to admit the meritorious, and reject the unworthy. And had this object really been attained, whatever opinions might prevail as to the mere right, not a murmur probably would have been heard. Surely it were much to be desired that every citizen should be qualified for the proper exercise of all his rights, and the due performance of all his duties. But the same qualifications that entitle him to assume the management of his private affairs, and to claim all other privileges of citizenship, equally entitle him, in the judgment of your memorialists, to be entrusted with this, the dearest of all his privileges, the most important of all his concerns. But if otherwise, still they cannot discern in the possession of land any evidence of peculiar merit, or superior title. To ascribe to a landed possession, moral or intellectual endowments, would truly be regarded as ludicrous, were it not for the gravity with which the proposition is maintained, and still more for the grave consequences flowing from it. Such possession no more proves him who has it, wiser or better, than it proves him taller or stronger, than him who has it not. That cannot be a fit criterion for the exercise of any right, the possession of which does not indicate the existence, nor the want of it the absence, of any essential qualification.

But this criterion, it is strenuously insisted, though not perfect, is yet the best human wisdom can devise. It affords the strongest, if not the only evidence of the requisite qualifications; more particularly of what are absolutely essential, "permanent common interest with, and attachment to, the community." Those who cannot furnish this evidence, are therefore deservedly excluded.

Your memorialists do not design to institute a comparison; they fear none that can be fairly made between the privileged and the proscribed classes. They may be permitted, however, without disrespect, to remark, that of the latter, not a few possess land: many, though not proprietors, are yet cultivators of the soil: others are engaged in avocations of a different nature, often as useful, pre-supposing no less integrity, requiring as much intelligence, and as fixed a residence, as agricultural pursuits. Virtue, intelligence, are not among the products of the soil. Attachment to property, often a sordid sentiment, is not to be confounded with the sacred flame of patriotism. The love of country, like that of parents and offspring, is engrafted in our nature. It exists in all climates, among all classes, under every possible form of Government. Riches oftener impair it than poverty. Who has it not is a monster.

Your memorialists feel the difficulty of undertaking calmly to repel charges and insinuations involving in infamy themselves, and so large a portion of their fellow-citizens. To be deprived of their rightful equality, and to hear as an apology that they are too ignorant and vicious to enjoy it, is no ordinary trial of patience. Yet they will suppress the indignant emotions these sweeping denunciations are well calculated to excite. The freeholders themselves know them to be unfounded: Why, else, are arms placed in the hands of a body of disaffected citizens, so ignorant, so depraved, and so numerous? In the hour of danger, they have drawn no invidious distinctions between the sons of Virginia. The muster rolls have undergone no scrutiny, no comparison with the land books, with a view to expunge those who have been struck from the ranks of freemen. If the landless citizens have been ignominiously driven from the polls, in time of peace, they have at least been generously summoned, in war, to the battle-field. Nor have they disobeyed the summons, or, less profusely than others, poured out their blood in the defence of that country which is asked to disown them. Will it be said they owe allegiance to the Government that gives them protection? Be it so: and if they acknowledge the obligation; if privileges are really extended to them in defence of which they may reasonably be required to shed their blood, have they not motives, irresistible motives, of attachment to the community? Have they not an interest, a deep interest, in perpetuating the blessings they enjoy, and a right, consequently, to guard those blessings, not from foreign aggression merely, but from domestic encroachment?

But, it is said, yield them this right, and they will abuse it: property, that is, landed property, will be rendered insecure, or at least overburthened, by those who possess it not. The freeholders, on the contrary, can pass no law to the injury of any other class, which will not more injuriously affect themselves. The alarm is sounded too, of danger from large manufacturing institutions, where one corrupt individual may sway the corrupt votes of thousands. It were a vain task to attempt to meet all the flimsy pretexts urged, to allay all the apprehensions felt or feigned by the enemies of a just and liberal policy. The danger of abuse is a dangerous plea. Like *necessity*, the detested plea of the tyrant, or the still more detestible plea of the Jesuit, *expediency;* it serves as an ever-ready apology for all oppression. If we are sincerely republican, we must give our confidence to the priciples we profess. We have been taught by our fathers, that all power is vested in, and derived from, the people; not the freeholders: that the majority of the community, in whom abides the physical force, have also the political right of creating and remoulding at will, their civil institutions. Nor can this right be any where more safely deposited. The generality of mankind, doubtless, desire to become owners of property: left free to reap the fruit of their labours, they will seek to acquire it honestly. It can never be their interest to overburthen, or render precarious, what they themselves desire to enjoy in peace. But should they ever prove as base as the argument supposes, force alone; arms, not votes, could effect their designs; and when that shall be attempted, what virtue is there in Constitutional restrictions, in mere wax and paper, to withstand it? To deny to the great body of the people all share in the Government; on suspicion that they may deprive others of their property, to rob them, in advance of their rights; to look to a privileged order as the fountain and depository of all power; is to depart from the fundamental maxims, to destroy the chief beauty, the characteristic feature, indeed, of Republican Government. Nor is the danger of abuse thereby diminished, but greatly augmented. No community can exist, no representative body be formed, in which some one division of persons or section of country, or some two or more combined, may not preponderate and oppress the rest. The east may be more powerful than the west, the lowlanders than the highlanders, the agricultural than the commercial or manufacturing classes. To give all power, or an undue share, to one, is obviously not to remedy but to ensure the evil. Its safest check, its best corrective, is found in a general admission of all upon a footing of equality. So intimately are the interests of each class in society blended and interwoven, so indispensible is justice to all, that oppression in that case becomes less probable from any one, however powerful. Nor is this mere speculation. In our ecclesiastical polity it has been reduced to practice; and the most opposed in doctrine, the most bitter in controversy, have forgotten their angry conflicts for power, and now mingle in harmony.

The example of almost every other State in the Union, in which the patrician pretensions of the landholder have, since their foundation, been unknown or despised, in many of which, too, manufacturing institutions exist on an extensive scale, ought alone to dispel these visionary fears of danger from the people. Indeed, all history demonstrates that the many have oftener been the victims than the oppressors. Cunning has proved an over-match for strength. The few have but too well succeeded in convincing them of their incapacity to manage their own affairs; and having persuaded them, for their own good, to submit to the curb, have generously taken the reins, and naturally enough converted them into beasts of burthen.

As to the danger from large manufacturing establishments in Virginia, when is their disastrous influence to be experienced? Is it not apparent that such establishments must, for an indefinite period, be at the mercy of those who affect to dread them, and may be shackled or suppressed, as fear or fancy may dictate? For how many centuries must the defranchised citizens be content to relinquish their rights, because, in some remote age of the world, a distant posterity, similarly circumstanced, may be powerful enough, and base enough withal, to trample upon the rights of others?

But if justice is not to be expected, if self-aggrandizement is to be assumed as the sole ruling principle of men in power, then, your memorialists conceive, the interests of the many deserve at least as much to be guarded as those of the few. Conceding the truth of the proposition assumed, what security, they would enquire, is there against the injustice of the freeholders? How is the assertion made good, that they can pass no law affecting the rights of others without more injuriously affecting their own? They cannot do this, it is said, because they possess, in common with other citizens, all personal rights, and, in addition, the rights pertaining to their peculiar property. And if this be a satisfactory reason, then one land-holder in each county or district would suffice to elect the representative body; or, the impossibility of injuring others being shewn, a single land-holder in the Commonwealth might still more conveniently exercise the sovereign power. But, is not the proposition obviously false? What is there to prevent their imposing upon others undue burthens, and conferring on themselves unjust exemptions? Supplying the public exigencies by a capitation or other tax exclusively or oppressively operating on the other portions of the community? Exacting from the latter, in common with slaves, menial services? Placing around their own persons and property more efficient guards? Providing for their own injuries speedier remedies? Denying to the children of all other classes admission to the public seminaries of learning? Interdicting to all but their own order, indeed, the power to elect, and the right to be elected, are most intimately if not inseparably united; all offices of honor or emolument, civil or military? Why can they not do all this, and more? Where is the impossibility? It would be unjust: admirable logic! Injustice can be predicated only of non-freeholders.

Still it is said, the non-freeholders have no just cause of complaint. A freehold is easily acquired. The right of suffrage, moreover, is not a natural right. Society may grant, modify, or withhold it, as expediency may require. Indeed all agree that certain regulations are proper: those, for example, relating to age, sex, and citizenship. At best, it is an idle contest for an abstract right whose loss is attended with no practical evil.

If a freehold be, as supposed, so easily acquired, it would seem highly impolitic, to say no more, to insist on retaining an odious regulation, calculated to produce no other effect than to excite discontent. But the fact is not so. The thousands expelled from the polls too well attest the severity of its operation. It is by no means easy or convenient for persons whom fortune or inclination have engaged in other than agricultural pursuits, to withdraw from those pursuits, or from the support of their families, the amount requisite for the purchase of a freehold. To compel them to do this, to vest that sum in unproductive property, is to subject them, over and above the original cost, the assessments upon it, and the probable loss by deterioration, to an annual tax, equivalent to the profits they might have derived from the capital thus unprofitably expended. What would be thought of a tax imposed, or penalty inflicted, upon all voters, for exercising what should be the unbought privilege of every citizen? How much more odious is the law that imposes this tax, or rather, it may be said, inflicts this penalty, on one portion of the community, probably the larger and least able to encounter it, and exempts the other?

The right of suffrage, however, it seems, is not a natural right. If by natural, is meant what is just and reasonable, then, nothing is more reasonable than that those whose purses contribute to maintain, whose lives are pledged to defend the country, should participate in all the privileges of citizenship. But say it is not a natural right. Whence did the freeholders derive it? How become its exclusive possessors? Will they arrogantly tell us they own the country, because they hold the land? The right by which they hold their land is not itself a natural right, and by consequence, nothing claimed as incidental to it. Whence then did they derive this privilege? From grant or conquest? Not from the latter. No war has ever been waged to assert it. If from the former, by whom was it conferred? They cannot, if they would, recur to the Royal instructions of that English monarch, of infamous memory, who enjoined it upon the Governor of the then Colony of Virginia, "to take care that the members of the Assembly be elected *only by the freeholders*, as being more agreeable to the custome of England:" he might have added more congenial also with monarchical institutions. If Colonial regulations might properly be looked to, then the right, not of freeholders merely, but of *freemen*, to vote, may be traced to a more distant antiquity, and a less polluted source. But, by our ever-glorious revolution, the Government whence these regulations emanated was annulled, and with it all the political privileges it had conferred, swept away. Will they rely on the Constitutional provision? That was the act of men delegated by themselves. They exercised the very right in question in appointing the body from whom they profess to derive it, and indeed gave to that body all the power it possessed. What is this but to say they generously conferred the privilege upon themselves? Perhaps they may rely on length of time to forestal enquiry. We acknowledge no act of limitations against the oppressed. Or will they disdain to shew any title; and, clinging to power, rest on force, the last argument of Kings, as its source and its defence? This were, doubtless, the more politic course.

Let us concede that the right of suffrage is a social right; that it must of necessity be regulated by society. Still the question recurs, is the existing limitation proper? For obvious reasons, by almost universal consent, women and children, aliens and slaves, are excluded. It were useless to discuss the propriety of a rule that scarcely admits of diversity of opinion. What is concurred in by those who constitute the society, the body politic, must be taken to be right. But the exclusion of these classes for reasons peculiarly applicable to them, is no argument for excluding others to whom no one of those reasons applies.

It is said to be *expedient*, however, to exclude non-freeholders also. Who shall judge of this expediency? The society: and does that embrace the proprietors of certain portions of land only? Expedient, for whom? for the freeholders. A harsh appellation would he deserve, who, on the plea of expediency, should take from another his property: what, then, should be said of him who, on that plea, takes from another his rights, upon which the security, not of his property only, but of his life and liberty depends?

But the non-freeholders are condemned for pursuing an abstract right, whose privation occasions no practical injury.

Your memorialists do not, perhaps, sufficiently comprehend the precise import of this language, so often used. The enjoyment of all other rights, whether of person or property, they will not deny, may be as perfect among those deprived of the privilege of voting, as among those possessing it. It may be as great under a despotism, as under any other form of Government. But they alone deserve to be called free, or have a guarantee for their rights, who participate in the formation of their political institutions, and in the control of those who make and administer the laws. To such as may be disposed to surrender this, or any other immunity, to the keeping of others, no practical mischief may ensue from its abandonment; or if any, none that will not be justly merited. Not so with him who feels as a freeman should; who would think for himself and speak what he thinks; who would not commit his conscience or his liberty to the uncontrolled direction of others. To him the privation of right, of that especially, which is the only safeguard of freedom, is practically wrong. So thought the fathers of the republic. It was not the oppressive weight of the taxes imposed by England on America: it was the assertion of a right to impose any burthens whatever upon those who were not represented; to bind by laws those who had no share, personal or delegated, in their enactment, that roused this continent to arms. Have the principles and feelings that then prevailed, perished with the conflict to which they gave birth? If not, are they not now grossly outraged? The question is submitted to your candor and justice.

Never can your memorialists agree that pecuniary burthens or personal violence are the sole injuries of which men may dare to complain. It may be that the freeholders have shewn no disposition greatly to abuse the power they have assumed. They may have borne themselves with exemplary moderation. But their unrepresented brethren cannot submit to a degrading regulation which takes from them, on the supposition of mental inferiority or moral depravity, all share in the Government under which they live. They cannot yield to pretensions of political superiority founded on the possession of a bit of land, of whatever dimensions. They cannot acquiesce in political bondage, because those who affect to sway over them the rod of empire, treat them leniently. The privilege which they claim, they respectfully insist, is theirs as of right; and they are under no obligation to assign any reason whatever for claiming it, but that it is their own.

Let the picture be for a moment reversed. Let it be imagined that the non-freeholders, possessing the physical superiority which alone can cause their political influence to be dreaded, should, at some future day, *after the manner of the freeholders*, take the Government into their own hands, and deal out to the latter the same measure of justice they have received at their hands. It is needless to enquire into the equity of such a proceeding; but would they not find for it in the example set them at least a plausible excuse, and to the freeholders' remonstrance retort the freeholders' argument? That argument your memorialists will not now recapitulate; they leave it to others to make the application.

Your memorialists have thought it due to the magnitude of the question, to examine at some length the grounds on which their political proscription is usually defended. If they have occasionally been betrayed into warmth of expression, the transcendant importance of the franchise they claim, and the nature of the objections they have been compelled to meet, will plead their apology. Deep would be their humiliation in now addressing you, delegated as you have been by those who hold them in political subjection, did they not but too well remember, it is their brethren to whom they impute their wrongs, and from whom they solicit reparation. Never, indeed, can they cease to protest against the measures which have made you, not the representatives of the people, but the organ of a privileged order. Still they approach you as the guardians of the public weal, however so constituted; as dispensers of the public justice; as an assemblage of distinguished citizens wielding the power, however irregularly conferred, of new-modelling the fundamental institutions of the State. They bow with respectful deference to the virtues and talents which have raised you to the eminent station you now occupy. They appeal, through you, to the justice of their country, and confidently trust, under your auspices, to assume that equal rank in the community, to which they conceive themselves justly entitled, and which, until they shall indeed be unworthy to enjoy it, they can never willingly renounce.

In behalf of the meeting,

WALTER D. BLAIR, *Chairman.*

Teste,

JOHN B. RICHARDSON, *Secretary.*

Mr. Marshall said that, however gentlemen might differ in opinion on the question discussed in the memorial, he was sure they must all feel that the subject was one of the deepest interest, and well entitled to the most serious attention of this body. He therefore moved its reference to the Committee on the Legislative Department of Government.

The motion was agreed to, and the memorial referred accordingly.

Mr. Mercer then presented a memorial, which, he said, came from a highly respectable body of citizens in Fairfax county. Its purport and tenor were very similar to that which had just been read; and he moved its reference to the same Committee.

The motion was agreed to, and the reading of the memorial having been dispensed with, it was referred to the Legislative Committee.

On motion of Mr. M'Coy, the House then adjourned, to meet to-morrow at one o'clock.

WEDNESDAY, OCTOBER 14, 1829.

The Convention met at one o'clock, and its sitting was opened with prayer by the Rev. Mr. Taylor, of the Baptist Church.

No business presenting itself,

Mr. M'Coy moved an adjournment, but withdrew his motion in favor of Mr. Doddridge, who moved a recess of the House till four o'clock, hoping that the First Auditor might have had time to prepare and lay before the House the documents which had been ordered by the Convention.

The President then laid before the House the following letter from the Auditor:

AUDITOR'S OFFICE,
October 13, 1829.

SIR:—In compliance with one of the resolutions adopted by the Convention on the 10th inst. I have the honor to transmit a statement of the number of persons in each county, and corporate town, within this Commonwealth, charged with State tax on moveable property, for the year 1828. The documents called for by the other resolutions will be furnished as soon as they can be prepared.

I have the honor to be, Sir,
With great respect and consideration,
Your obedient servant,

JAMES E. HEATH,
Auditor of Public Accounts.

JAMES MONROE, Esq.
President of the Convention.

Mr. Doddridge moved to lay the communication on the table and print it, and that the Auditor should deliver the residue when prepared to the public printer.

The motion was agreed to.

Mr. Johnson, with a view to give the Committees more time, moved that when the House adjourned, it adjourn to meet at two instead of one o'clock, which being agreed to, on motion of Mr. Doddridge, the Convention adjourned.

THURSDAY, October 15, 1829.

The Convention met at two o'clock, agreeably to adjournment, and was opened with prayer by the Rev. Mr. Kerr, of the Baptist Church.

Mr. Anderson presented a memorial from the non-freeholders of Shenandoah, praying the extension of the right of suffrage; which, on Mr. Anderson's motion, was referred to the Legislative Committee.

Mr. M'Coy rose to observe, that having no disposition to sit there, or see others sit there, without having something to do, he moved that the Convention rise; which was agreed to without opposition.

And then the Convention adjourned until to-morrow, two o'clock.

FRIDAY. October 16, 1829.

The Convention assembled at two o'clock, and was opened with prayer by the Rev. Mr. Taylor, of the Baptist Church:

And (having no business before them) on Mr. Naylor's motion, the Convention adjourned till to-morrow, two o'clock.

SATURDAY, October 17, 1829.

The Rev. Mr. Kerr offered up a prayer: after which, the Convention was called to order.

No business being yet ready to be laid before the Convention, Mr. Doddridge moved that the Convention adjourn; he stated that some additional documents had been prepared by the Auditor of Public Accounts, which would be placed in the hands of the public printer under a previous resolution of that body.

The motion to adjourn prevailed without opposition; and the Convention accordingly adjourned till Monday, two o'clock.

MONDAY, October 19, 1829.

The Convention met at two o'clock, and its sitting was opened with prayer by the Rev. Mr. Armstrong, of the Presbyterian Church.

Mr. Fitzhugh, from the Committee on Compensations, made the following farther report, in part:

The Committee appointed to enquire into the compensation proper to be allowed the officers of the Convention, have agreed to the following resolution:

Resolved, That the sum of sixteen dollars be allowed the Sergeant at Arms for notifying William K. Perrin of his election to the Convention.

The report was adopted.

Mr. Taylor of Chesterfield, from the Committee on the Bill of Rights, &c. made the following report:

The Committee to whom was referred the Bill or Declaration of Rights, and all such parts of the present Constitution as are not referred to the Committees on the Legislative, Executive and Judicial Departments of the Government, have had the subjects to them referred, under their consideration, and have in part performance of the duties devolved on them, agreed upon the following resolution:

"*Resolved*, That in the opinion of this Committee the Bill or Declaration of Rights, &c. requires no amendment."

The report was laid upon the table.

Mr. Harrison of Rockingham, presented a memorial from the non-freeholders of that county of a similar general import to those heretofore presented; and which was, on his motion, referred without reading to the Legislative Committee.

No farther business being before the Convention, on motion of Mr. Mercer, the House adjourned.

TUESDAY, October 20, 1829.

The Convention met at two o'clock, when its sitting was opened with prayer by the Rev. Mr. Hamner, of the Presbyterian Church.

Mr. Marshall, from the Committee on the Judiciary Department of Government, made the following report from the Committee:

1. *Resolved*, That the Judicial power shall be vested in a Court of Appeals, in such Inferior Courts, as the Legislature shall from time to time ordain and establish, and in the County Courts. The jurisdiction of these tribunals shall be regulated by law. The Judges of the Court of Appeals and of the Inferior Courts, shall hold their offices during good behaviour, or until removed in the manner prescribed in this Constitution; and shall, at the same time, hold no other office, appointment, or public trust: and the acceptance thereof, by either of them, shall vacate his judicial office. No modification or abolition of any Court, shall be construed to deprive any Judge thereof of his office; but such Judge shall perform any judicial duties which the Legislature shall assign him.

2. *Resolved*, That the present Judges of the Court of Appeals, Judges of the General Court, and Chancellors remain in office until the expiration of the first session of the Legislature, held under the new Constitution, and no longer. But the Legislature may cause to be paid to such of them, as shall not be re-appointed, such sum as, from their age, infirmities, and past services, shall be deemed reasonable.

3. *Resolved*, That Judges of the Court of Appeals and Inferior Courts, except Justices of the County Courts, and the Aldermen or other Magistrates of Corporation Courts, shall be elected by the concurrent vote of both Houses of the General Assembly, each House voting separately, and having a negative on the other; and the members thereof voting *viva voce*. The votes of the members shall be entered on the Journals of their respective Houses. Should the two Houses, in any case, fail to concur in the election of a Judge, during the session, the Governor shall decide the election, by appointing one of the two persons who first received a majority of votes in the Houses in which they were respectively voted for. But if any vacancy shall occur during the recess of the General Assembly, the Governor, or other person performing the duty of Governor, may appoint a person to fill such vacancy, who shall continue in office until the end of the next succeeding session of the General Assembly.

4. *Resolved*, That the Judges of the Court of Appeals, and of the Inferior Courts, shall receive fixed and adequate salaries, which shall not be diminished during their continuance in office.

5. *Resolved*, That on the creation of any new county, Justices of the Peace shall be appointed, in the first instance, as may be prescribed by law. When vacancies shall occur in any county, or it shall, for any cause be deemed necessary to increase their number, appointments shall be made by the Governor, by and with the advice and consent of the Senate, on the recommendation of their respective County Courts.

6. *Resolved*, That the Clerks of the several Courts shall be appointed by their respective Courts, and their tenure of office be prescribed by law.

7. *Resolved*, That the Judges of the Court of Appeals and of the Inferior Courts, offending against the State, either by mal-administration, corruption, or neglect of duty, or by any other high crime or misdemeanor, shall be impeachable by the House of Delegates, such impeachment to be prosecuted before the Senate. If found guilty by a majority of two-thirds of the whole Senate, such persons shall be removed from office. And any Judge so impeached shall be suspended from exercising the functions of his office until his acquittal, or until the impeachment shall be discontinued or withdrawn.

8. *Resolved*, That Judges may be removed from office by a vote of the General Assembly: but two-thirds of the whole number of each House must concur in such vote, and the cause of removal shall be entered on the Journals of each. The Judge against whom the Legislature is about to proceed shall receive notice thereof, accompanied with a copy of the causes alleged for his removal, at least twenty days before the day on which either House of the General Assembly shall act thereupon.

The report having been read, on motion of Mr. Marshall, it was laid upon the table.

Mr. Giles, from the Committee on the Executive Department of Government, made the following report, which was read, and on his motion, laid upon the table.

The Committee appointed on the Executive branch of the Constitution, have, according to order, had under consideration the subjects referred to them, and have come to the following resolutions thereupon:

1. *Resolved*, That the chief Executive Office of this Commonwealth, ought to be vested in a Governor.

2. *Resolved,* That there ought to be appointed a Lieutenant-Governor of this Commonwealth.

3. *Resolved,* That the Executive Council, as at present organized, ought to be abolished, and that it is inexpedient to provide any other Executive Council.

4. *Resolved,* That in case of the removal of the Governor from office, or of his death, resignation, or inability to discharge the duties and powers of his office, the said powers and duties shall devolve on the Lieutenant-Governor; and the Legislature may provide for the case of removal, death, or similar inability of the Lieutenant-Governor.

5. *Resolved,* That the sheriffs in the different counties in the Commonwealth, shall, hereafter, be elected by the voters qualified to vote for the most numerous branch of the Legislature.

6. *Resolved,* That the commissioned officers of militia companies be nominated to the Executive by a majority of their respective companies.

7. *Resolved,* That the field officers of regiments be nominated to the Executive by a majority of the commissioned officers of their respective regiments.

8. *Resolved,* That no pardon shall be granted in any case, until after conviction or judgment.

Both reports were subsequently ordered to be printed.

Mr. Giles farther stated, that he was instructed by the Committee, to ask that they be discharged from the farther consideration of the subjects referred to them, and he made that motion accordingly, which was agreed to, and the Committee was thereupon discharged.

Mr. Powell of Frederick, said, that having belonged to the Committee which had last reported, and having in that Committee been in a large minority of its members, who were in favour of a very different organization of the Executive Department of Government, from that which the Committee had adopted, and just reported to the House, he asked permission to read, and to lay upon the table, certain resolutions which he held in his hand. Leave having been granted, Mr. Powell then offered the following, which were read, laid upon the table, and ordered to be printed, viz:

Resolved, That the Executive Department of the existing form of Government ought to be amended as follows:

Sec. 1. The Executive power shall be vested in a Governor. He shall hold his office for years, and be ineligible for the term of years thereafter. And a Lieutenant-Governor shall be chosen at the same time, for the same term, and under the same restrictions.

Sec. 2. The Lieutenant-Governor shall act as President of the Senate, but he shall have no right to vote except the Senate be equally divided upon any question; in which case he shall have the casting vote.

Sec. 3. No person shall be eligible to the office of Governor or Lieutenant-Governor, except a citizen of the Commonwealth, nor any who shall not have attained the age of years, and who shall not have resided years next preceding his election, in the State.

Sec. 4. The Governor and Lieutenant-Governor shall be elected at the times and places of choosing members of the most numerous branch of the Legislature, by the voters qualified to vote for members of the General Assembly; provided that the election shall take place throughout the Commonwealth on the same day. The persons respectively having the highest number of votes for Governor and Lieutenant-Governor, shall be elected. In case two or more persons shall have an equal number of votes for Governor or for Lieutenant-Governor, the Legislature shall immediately by joint ballot of both Houses, choose of the persons having an equal number of votes for Governor or Lieutenant-Governor, the Governor or Lieutenant-Governor, as the case may be.

Sec. 5. The Governor shall be commander-in-chief of the militia. He shall have power to convene the Legislature on extraordinary occasions. He shall, from time to time, give information to the Legislature of the condition of the Commonwealth, and recommend to their consideration, such measures as he shall judge necessary and expedient. He shall expedite all such measures as may be resolved upon by the Legislature, and shall take care that the laws are faithfully executed.

Sec. 6. The Governor and Lieutenant-Governor, shall, at stated times, receive for their services, a compensation which shall neither be increased nor diminished during the term for which they shall have been elected.

Sec. 7. The Governor shall have power to grant reprieves and pardons after conviction, for all offences, except treasons and in cases of impeachment. Upon conviction for treason, he shall have power to suspend the execution of the sentence, until the case shall be reported to the Legislature at its next session, when the Legislature may pardon, or direct the execution of the criminal, or grant a farther reprieve.

Sec. 8. In case of the removal of the Governor from office, or of his death, resignation, or inability to discharge the duties of his office, his powers and duties shall devolve on the Lieutenant-Governor; and in case of the removal, death, or resignation, or like inability of the Lieutenant-Governor, the Legislature may provide by law upon whom the duties of Governor shall devolve, until such disabilities shall be removed, or a Governor shall be elected.

SEC. 9. The Governor shall have power to nominate, and by and with the advice and consent of the Senate, appoint Judges of the Supreme Court, or Court of Final Jurisdiction, and Judges of such Inferior Courts as may from time to time be established by law; all militia officers from the rank of Colonel inclusive; the Treasurer, Auditor of Public Accounts, Register of the Land-Office, and Attorney-General. The Legislature may by law vest the appointment of all other officers of the Commonwealth, whose appointments are not herein otherwise provided for, in the Governor, with the advice and consent of the Senate, or in the Courts of Law.

SEC. 10. The Governor shall have power to fill up all vacancies that may happen during the recess of the Senate, by granting commissions, which shall expire at the end of the next session of that body.

SEC. 11. The Governor shall have power to require in writing, the opinions of the Lieutenant-Governor, and of the Attorney-General, upon all matters appertaining to the duties of his office.

SEC. 12. No person, whose tenure of office depends on the pleasure of the Governor, shall be removed from office without the advice and consent of the Senate to such removal. But the Governor shall have power, at any time, to suspend such officer, and appoint another to discharge the duties of his office, until the next session of the Senate, and until their advice and consent to such removal shall be ascertained and expressed.

Mr. Gordon of Albemarle, presented a petition from citizens of that county, on the subject of freedom of religion.

The petition was received, and without reading, referred to the Committee on the Legislative Department.

Mr. Morgan said he was a member of the Committee which had been so unfortunate as not to agree upon all the propositions, properly referred to them, under the Executive Department of the Government, and like the gentleman from Frederick (Mr. Powell) he would ask leave to submit for the consideration of the Convention, several resolutions on the subject of that Department, which he wished read and laid on the table.

Permission having been granted, Mr. Morgan thereupon offered the following, which were read, laid upon the table, and ordered to be printed:

The Executive power shall be vested in a Governor and Lieutenant-Governor, to assist in the administration of the affairs of Government, when required by the Governor; and who shall act as Governor in case of the death, resignation, or removal of the Governor from office, until another be appointed; and in case of impeachment, temporary incapacity of any kind, or absence of the Governor from the seat of Government, until his restoration or return. And if at any time there should be no acting Governor, and the Lieutenant-Governor shall be impeached, or from any other cause not acting, the Executive authority shall devolve on, and be exercised by, some person appointed by law for that purpose.

The Governor and Lieutenant-Governor shall be annually appointed by joint ballot of the Senate and House of Delegates, and their terms of office shall end on the last day of December of every year; but no person shall be eligible to the office of Governor for more than three years at any one time, nor again, until after he shall have been out of that office four years; and in like manner after the end of every three years of service.

The Governor shall exercise the Executive power of the Government, according to the laws of the Commonwealth, and see that they shall be faithfully executed. He may, at his own discretion, and shall, on application of a majority of the Senate or House of Delegates, convene the General Assembly: And he shall have power to grant reprieves and pardons, except where the prosecution shall have been carried on by the House of Delegates, or the law shall otherwise particularly direct; in which cases, the House of Delegates shall alone have and exercise the power of granting them; but no pardon shall be granted in any case, until after judgment or conviction.

And then the Convention adjourned, till to-morrow, two o'clock.

WEDNESDAY, October 21, 1829.

The Convention met at two o'clock, and its sitting was opened with prayer by the Rev. Mr. Armstrong.

Mr. Marshall, from the Committee on the Judicial Department of Government, then rose and said, that although it was not probable the Convention would take up any one of the reports of the Select Committees which had been appointed, until the reports of all those Committees should have been received, yet, with a view to put the reports which had been rendered in a way to be acted upon by the Convention, if such should be its pleasure, he moved that the report made by the Committee on the Judicial Department, be referred to a Committee of the Whole Convention, and be made the Order of the Day for to-morrow.

Mr. Upshur of Accomack, said, that he had understood a wish to be entertained by some members of the House, that a smaller Committee than a Committee of the Whole, should be raised for the purpose of receiving and digesting the reports of the Select Committees, and laying the whole before the Convention to receive its action thereon. Should such a course be adopted after the report of the Judicial Committee had gone to a Committee of the Whole, it would have again to be withdrawn from their hands and put with the rest under the care of the Sub-Committee. He would, therefore, very respectfully suggest to the member from Richmond, whether it would not be expedient to withdraw for the present the motion which he had made. Mr. U. said that he was the rather induced to this course, by observing that the Chairman of the Committee on the Executive (Mr. Giles) was not in his place, and he knew that it was not the wish of that Committee, that their resolution should take the course now proposed.

Mr. Marshall said, that he was by no means solicitous that the motion he had made should be adopted: his only object had been to put business in such a train, that it might be taken up and acted upon whenever the House should wish to consider it. The reference of the report to a Committee of the Whole, implied no sort of necessity that the report should be immediately acted upon. As to the suggestion of the gentleman from Accomack, (Mr. Upshur) if the House should agree to refer all the reports to a Select Committee before the Committee of the Whole should have perfected its action on the particular report which was the subject of his motion; all that would have to be done, would be to discharge the Committee of the Whole from the further consideration of it: the motion he had made, would not be at all in the way of such a course. It seemed to him very possible, and extremely probable, that the House would not refer the respective reports to a Select Committee, until they should have received some report from the Committee of the Whole: nevertheless, he was entirely willing to withdraw his motion, if the gentleman insisted upon it.

Mr. Doddridge of Brooke, observed that if the suggestion of the gentleman from Accomack, (Mr. Upshur) had been occasioned by any thing that had fallen from him, (Mr. D.) the gentleman had certainly misunderstood him. The course he had desired to see pursued, was that each report should be referred to a separate Committee of this House, and after all the reports should then have been considered and fully discussed in Committee of the Whole, they be finally referred to one general Committee, which might properly be called a Copying Committee, who should transcribe and report the whole to the Convention.

Mr. Upshur, after a few words of explanation, withdrew the suggestion he had made, and the question having been taken on the motion of Mr. Marshall, it was decided in the affirmative, and the report of the Judicial Committee was accordingly referred to a Committee of the Whole Convention, and made the Order of the Day for to-morrow.

Mr. Leigh of Chesterfield, now moved the following resolution:

Resolved, That it be a standing order of the Convention, that the Convention shall every day resolve itself into a Committee of the Whole Convention, to consider the existing Constitution of the Commonwealth, and such propositions for amendment or alteration thereof, as shall be referred to or made in the said Committee.

Mr. Doddridge moved to lay the resolution upon the table, suggesting, as a reason, that its adoption would involve the Convention in difficulty. One of the rules they had adopted for their proceeding, required that the Order of the Day should be called at twelve o'clock. If the resolution of the gentleman from Chesterfield should take effect, the Convention would have to meet to-morrow at twelve o'clock, and take up the report of the Judiciary Committee at once: but he did not suppose it to be the wish of any gentleman to take up that, or any other of the reports, until the Legislative Committee should have reported. The course proposed would cut short the sittings of that Committee, which he was happy to say had now drawn so far toward a close, that some glimpses of the morning light could be perceived, and a hope was entertained that if they were allowed, as at present, to sit till two o'clock, they might, perhaps, finish their discussions to-morrow.

A debate on a question of order now arose, in which Messrs. Stanard, Doddridge, P. P. Barbour, Mercer, Leigh, M'Coy and Johnson took part.

It was affirmed on the one hand, that nothing would be gained by laying the resolution of Mr. Leigh on the table, because the report of the Judicial Committee, having been referred to a particular Committee of the Whole, and made the Order of the Day for to-morrow, the Convention would still have to meet, go into Committee of the Whole, and take up the report, unless the order were postponed; and a general order, if necessary, might as well be postponed as a specified one, though indeed, the general standing order would not involve any necessity of postponement. If the resolution should be adopted, the Committee of the Whole would be at liberty to take up, at its own election, either one of the reports referred to it; comparing each with the corresponding portion of the existing Constitution. It might pass, at will, from one of these reports to the other, without the ceremony of rising, reporting, and again sitting, for that purpose. It might sit on any day, without being confined, as must otherwise be the case, to a particular day specified: and its powers in this respect were illustrated by reference to the practice, as well of the House of Delegates, as of the House of Representatives of the United States.

It was insisted, on the other hand, that there was no rule which now bound the Convention, to make the consideration of a subject referred to a Committee of the Whole, the Order of the Day, for any particular day. That the Committee of the Whole existed already, and a subject had been referred to it: when that Committee met, it might take up any subject whatever, which might have been referred to a Committee of the Whole: in this Convention as in the House of Delegates, there existed but *one* Committee of the Whole; and all subjects referred in that form, belonged to it, as of course, and might be taken up in such order as the Committee itself should choose. There was no need of referring to it the existing Constitution, because a comparison of the proposed amendments with that which they proposed to amend, was necessarily involved in the discussion of such amendments; nor was it at all desirable, that the Constitution should go to such Committee, and there be taken up, and considered by sections, as though it were a reported bill. When an amendment to a law was referred, either in the House of Delegates, or in Congress, to a Committee of the Whole, it was never the usage to refer to that Committee the original law also.

The question being at length taken on the motion of Mr. Doddridge to lay Mr. Leigh's resolution on the table, it was decided in the affirmative—Ayes 40—Noes 37. So the resolution was laid upon the table accordingly.

Mr. Nicholas, who had been in a minority of the Committee on the Executive, in relation to some of the features of the report of that Committee, particularly that part of it which related to the abolition of the Executive Council, asked and obtained leave to lay the following resolutions on the table, and to have them printed, viz:

Resolved, That the ninth and tenth sections of the present Constitution be retained, and that the eleventh be substituted by the following resolution:

A Privy Council, or Council of State, consisting of four members, shall be chosen by joint ballot of both Houses of Assembly, either from their own members, or the people at large, to assist in the administration of Government. They shall annually choose out of their own members, a Lieutenant-Governor, who, in case of the death, inability, or necessary absence of the Governor from the Government, shall act as Governor. The Governor shall be the President of the Council, and shall in all cases of division, have the casting vote. Two members, with the Governor or Lieutenant-Governor, as the case may be, shall be sufficient to act, and their advice and proceedings shall be entered of record, and signed by the members present (to any part whereof, any member may enter his dissent) to be laid before the General Assembly, when called for by them. The members of the Council shall be elected by joint ballot of both Houses of the General Assembly, for four years. At the first election, the two Houses shall, by joint resolution, divide the persons elected into two classes: The seats of the Councillors of the first class, shall be vacated at the expiration of the second year; of the second class, at the expiration of the fourth year; so that one half may be chosen every second year; and if vacancies happen by resignation, or otherwise, they shall be filled by joint ballot of the two Houses of the General Assembly. An adequate but moderate salary, shall be settled on them, during their continuance in office, and they shall be incapable during that time, of sitting in either House of Assembly.

In consequence of the failure of Mr. Leigh's resolution, the order which directed the Committee of the Whole, to consider the report from the Judicial Committee *to-morrow*, was, on motion of Mr. P. P. Barbour, re-considered, and altered to *Monday* next; whereupon, on motion of Mr. Powell, the Convention adjourned to meet to-morrow, at two o'clock.

THURSDAY, October 22, 1829.

The Convention met at two o'clock, and its sitting was opened with prayer by the Rev. Mr. Armstrong, of the Presbyterian Church.

Mr. Giles moved, that the report from the Committee on the Executive, be now taken up; which motion being agreed to, he then moved that the report be referred to a Committee of the Whole.

Mr. Stanard suggested to him the propriety of forbearing his motion till the House should have come to some decision upon the resolution offered yesterday, by the gentleman from Chesterfield, (Mr. Leigh,) and now lying upon the table: the Convention had not yet determined whether it would have a Committee of the Whole, analogous in its duties and powers, to a Committee of the Whole, in the House of Delegates. If the motion should be pressed at this time, the effect would be, that the report would go to a distinct Committee of the Whole, from that to which had been referred the report from the Judicial Committee: for, as there has been separate orders, there would, of course, be distinct Committees. But if the Convention should agree to adopt the resolution upon its table, the order referring each report to a distinct Committee of the Whole, would have to be rescinded.

Mr. Giles observed, in reply, that not having been present yesterday, he was not apprised that any difficulty would arise from the motion he had made, but seeing that some embarrassment was apprehended, he would, with great pleasure, withdraw the motion; and he withdrew it accordingly.

Mr. Powell said, that although he did not regard it as at all important that the report should be referred at this time, he did not perceive the same difficulty as had presented itself to the member from Spottsylvania, (Mr. Stanard.) The report might, certainly, be referred to the same Committee of the Whole to which had been referred the report from the Judicial Committee; and in like manner, the reports from all the Select Committees, might be referred to one and the same Committee of the Whole; who would then have the whole before them at once. He saw, he said, the gentleman from Orange, before him (Mr. P. P. Barbour,) shake his head, and he was well aware that he had far less experience in Legislative proceedings than that gentleman; but unless he was greatly deceived, indeed, the course he had indicated was frequently pursued in the House of Representatives of the United States.

Mr. Barbour replied, that the gentleman from Frederick (Mr. Powell) was certainly correct, when he stated that several analogous subjects were often referred to the same Committee of the Whole; but then those subjects were not all held to be before the Committee at one and the same time; but were taken up consecutively, and each considered and discussed by itself, and as distinct from the others.

Mr. Taylor of Chesterfield, from the Committee on the Bill of Rights, made the following report in part, which, on his motion, was laid upon the table and ordered to be printed.

The Committee to whom was referred the Bill or Declaration of Rights, and all such parts of the present Constitution as are not referred to the Committees on the Legislative, Executive, and Judicial Departments of the Government, have, according to order, had the subjects to them referred, under their consideration, and have further, in part performance of the duties devolved on them, agreed upon the following resolutions:

1. *Resolved, as the opinion of this Committee,* That the Constitution of this State ought to be so amended, as to provide a mode in which future amendments shall be made therein.

2. *Resolved,* That the first and second sections of the present Constitution, ought to be stricken out, and that an introductory clause, adapted to the amended Constitution, be substituted in lieu thereof.

3. *Resolved,* That the twelfth, twenty-first, and twenty-second sections of the present Constitution, ought to be stricken out as no longer necessary.

4. *Resolved,* That the freedom of Speech and of the Press, ought to be held sacred and guaranteed by the Constitution.

5. *Resolved,* That no title of nobility shall be created or granted; and no person holding any office of profit or trust under the United States, or under any King, Prince, or foreign State, shall hold any office under this State.

6. *Resolved, as the opinion of this Committee,* That the Constitution ought to be so amended, as to provide, "that no man shall be compelled to frequent or support any religious worship, place or ministry, whatsoever, nor shall be enforced, restrained, molested, or burthened in his body, or goods, nor shall otherwise suffer on account of his religious opinions or belief; but that all men, shall be free to profess, and by argument to maintain, their opinions in matters of religion; and that the same shall in no wise, diminish, enlarge, or affect their civil capacities."

On motion of Mr. M'Coy, the House then adjourned.

FRIDAY, October 23, 1829.

The Convention met at two o'clock, and was opened with prayer by the Rev. Mr. Parks, of the Methodist Church.

Mr. Madison from the Committee on the Judicial Department, asked and obtained leave, that that Committee might sit for the discharge of its duties during the sittings of the Convention.

Mr. Taylor of Norfolk, a member of the Committee on the Bill of Rights, and other matters not referred to the previous Committees, asked and obtained leave to lay upon the table the following propositions, which were read and ordered to be printed:

Resolved 1st, That the elective franchise should be *uniform;* so that, throughout the State, similar qualifications should confer a similar right of suffrage.

Resolved 2d, That, among those entitled by the Constitution to exercise the elective franchise, there should be *entire equality of suffrage;* so that, in all elections, the suffrage of one qualified voter should avail as much as that of another qualified voter, whatever may be the disparity of their respective fortunes.

Resolved 3d, That equal numbers of qualified voters are entitled to equal representation throughout the State.

Resolved 4th, That as *individual suffrage* should be *equal*, without respect to the disparity of individual fortune, so an *equal number* of qualified voters are entitled to equal representation, without regard to the disparity of their *aggregate* fortunes.

Resolved 5th, That in all pecuniary contributions to the public service, regard should be had to the ability of individuals to contribute; and as this ability to pay, from disparity of fortune is *unequal*, it would be unjust and oppressive to require *each* citizen to pay an *equal* amount of public taxes.

On motion of Mr. Summers, the Convention then adjourned.

SATURDAY, October 24, 1829.

The Convention met at two o'clock, and its sitting having been opened with prayer by the Rev. Mr. Parks, of the Methodist Church,

Mr. Madison, from the Committee on the Legislative Department of the Government, made the following report:

The Committee appointed on the Legislative Department of the Government, have, according to order, had under consideration the subjects referred to them, and have agreed to the following

REPORT.

1. *Resolved*, That in the apportionment of representation in the House of Delegates, regard should be had to the white population exclusively.

2. *Resolved*, That a Census of the population of the State, for the purpose of apportioning the representation, should be taken in the year 1831, the year 1845, and thereafter at least once in every twenty years.

3. *Resolved*, That the right of suffrage shall continue to be exercised by all who now enjoy it under the existing Constitution: *Provided*, That no person shall vote by virtue of his freehold only, unless the same shall be assessed to the value of at least $ for the payment of taxes, if such assessment be required by law: And shall be extended; first, to every free white male citizen of the Commonwealth resident therein, above the age of twenty-one years, who owns, and has possessed for six months, or who has acquired by marriage, descent, or devise, a freehold estate, assessed to the value of not less than   dollars for the payment of taxes, if such assessment shall be required by law; second, or who shall own a vested estate in fee, in remainder, or reversion, in land, the assessed value of which shall be   dollars; third, or who shall own and have possessed a leasehold estate with the evidence of title recorded, of a term originally not less than five years, and one of which shall be unexpired, of the annual value, or rent of   dollars; fourth, or who for twelve months next preceding, has been a house-keeper and head of a family within the county, city, borough or election district, where he may offer to vote, and who shall have been assessed with a part of the revenue of the Commonwealth within the preceding year, and actually paid the same: Provided, nevertheless, that the right of suffrage shall not be exercised by any person of unsound mind, or who shall be a pauper, or a non-commissioned officer, soldier, sailor or marine, in the service of the United States, nor by any person convicted of any infamous offence; nor by citizens born without the Commonwealth, unless they shall have resided therein for five

years immediately preceding the election at which they shall offer to vote, and two years preceding the said election, in the county, city, borough or election district, where they shall offer to vote, (the mode of proving such previous residence, when disputed, to be prescribed by law,) and shall possess, moreover, some one or more of the qualifications above enumerated.

4. *Resolved*, That the number of members in the Senate of this State ought to be neither increased nor diminished, nor the classification of its members changed.

5. *Resolved*, That the number of members in the House of Delegates, ought to be reduced, so that the same be not less than one hundred and twenty, nor more than one hundred and fifty.

6. *Resolved*, That no person ought to be elected a member of the Senate of this State, who is not at least thirty years of age.

7. *Resolved*, That no person ought to be elected a member of the House of Delegates of this State, who is not at least twenty-five years of age.

8. *Resolved*, That it ought to be provided, that in all elections for members of either branch of the General Assembly, and in the election of all officers which may be required to be made by the two Houses of Assembly, jointly, or in either separately, with the exception of the appointment of their own officers, the votes should be given openly, or *viva voce*, and not by ballot.

9. *Resolved*, That no man shall be compelled to frequent or support any religious worship, place, or ministry whatsoever; nor shall be enforced, restrained, molested, or burthened in his body or goods, nor shall otherwise suffer on account of his religious opinions or belief; but that all men shall be free to profess, and by argument to maintain, their opinions in matters of religion, and that the same shall in no wise diminish, enlarge, or affect their civil capacities.

That the Legislature shall have no power to prescribe any religious test whatever, nor to establish by law any subordination or preference between different sects or denominations, nor confer any peculiar privileges or advantages on any one sect or denomination, over others; nor pass any law, requiring or authorising any religious society, or the people of any district within this Commonwealth, to levy on themselves or others, any tax for the erection or repair of any house for public worship, or the support of any church or ministry, but that it be left free to every person to select whom he pleases as his religious instructor, and to make for his support, such private contract as he pleases: Provided, however, that the foregoing clauses shall not be so construed, as to permit any minister of the gospel, or priest of any denomination, to be eligible to either House of the General Assembly.

10. *Resolved*, That no bill of attainder, or *ex-post facto* law, or law impairing the obligation of contracts, ought to be passed.

11. *Resolved*, That private property ought not to be taken for public uses without just compensation.

12. *Resolved*, That the members of the Legislature shall receive for their services, a compensation, to be ascertained by law, and paid out of the public Treasury; but no law increasing the compensation of members of the Legislature shall take effect until the end of the next annual session after the said law may have been enacted.

13. *Resolved*, That no Senator or Delegate shall, during the term for which he shall have been elected, be appointed to any civil office of profit under this State, which shall have been created, or the emoluments of which shall have been increased during such term, except such offices as may be filled by elections by the people.

Mr. Madison moved that the report be printed, and referred to the same Committee of the Whole, to which had been referred the report from the Committee on the Judicial Department.

Mr. Leigh of Chesterfield, requested the venerable mover to withdraw his motion for the present, until the Convention should have taken up, and decided upon, a resolution now lying on its table; and which, if adopted, would supersede the necessity of such a motion as had just been made.

Mr. Madison said, he would very readily consent to withdraw the motion, which he had made only in pursuance of the course taken with the other report; and the motion was thereupon withdrawn.

On motion of Mr. Leigh, the Convention then took up the following resolution, moved by him on Thursday last:

"*Resolved*, That it be a standing order of the Convention, that the Convention shall every day resolve itself into a Committee of the Whole Convention, to consider the existing Constitution of the Commonwealth, and such propositions for amendment or alteration thereof, as shall be referred to or made in said Committee."

Mr. Leigh said, that when this resolution had been offered, it had been encountered by objections from various quarters of the House, all of which, he hoped, further reflection had since removed. The whole purpose of the resolution was, to conform the practice of this Convention, in relation to its Committee of the Whole, to the course pursued in the House of Delegates; and did he believe that precisely the same object could be obtained in any other way, he should not have the least objection: but he did not think that that was the case. The original design, as proposed by some gentlemen, was, that the Convention should resolve itself into a Committee of the Whole, on the state of the Commonwealth, and there take up and discuss the various subjects reported upon by the Select Committees. But, said Mr. L. this Convention has not been charged with the state of the Commonwealth, but only with the revision of its fundamental law. The only duty assigned to us, is to consider the existing Constitution, and to propose therein such amendments as we may deem requisite and proper: for that reason, I suggest that instead of raising a Committee of the Whole, on the state of the Commonwealth, our's shall be a Committee of the Whole on the business before us. The course indicated by the resolution must be familiar to all who have served in the House of Delegates. I do not say that the practice there pursued, is the best that exists in the world; but it is the course best known to us.

Messrs. Mercer and Doddridge stated, that having had conversation with the gentleman from Chesterfield, in relation to the object and bearing of his resolution, the objections they had formerly entertained were removed, and they were now fully satisfied that it should be adopted.

The question being thereupon taken, the resolution was adopted *nem. con.*

Mr. Madison now moved the reference of the report from the Legislative Committee, to a Committee of the Whole; and it was so referred.

Mr. Giles made a similar motion, with respect to the report of the Committee from the Executive Department, which was also agreed to.

Mr. Marshall observed, that it was obviously convenient, that all the reports from the Select Committees, should be before the same Committee of the Whole; and as he believed, though he was not entirely sure, that the report of the Committee on the Judicial Department, had been referred to a particular Committee of the Whole, distinct from that recognized in the resolution this day adopted, he moved, if that were the case, that the particular Committee of the Whole, to which the report had gone, might be discharged from the farther consideration of it, and that the report might take the same direction, as had been given to those from the other Select Committees. The motion prevailed, and the report from the Judicial Committee was thereupon referred to the Committee of the Whole.

Mr. Powell moved, that certain resolutions, which at his request had been yesterday laid upon the table, and ordered to be printed, should now be referred to the Committee of the Whole.

The motion was agreed to, and then on motion of Mr. Leigh of Chesterfield, a general order was passed, directing that all reports made by any of the Select Committees, as well as all propositions, heretofore moved in the House, be referred to the Committee of the Whole.

On motion of Mr. Stanard, it was resolved, that when the House adjourned, it adjourn to meet on Monday next, at eleven o'clock, A. M.

Mr. Fitzhugh said, that he should have forborne to submit his personal views on the subjects referred to the Committee of the Whole, but for the course pursued by other gentlemen. As his views differed probably from both of what might be called the great parties in the House, he would ask the attention of the Convention to four resolutions, which he had drawn up, and which he asked leave to lay upon the table, and have printed, and referred to the Committee of the Whole.

Mr. F. then read in his place the following resolutions:

1. *Resolved*, That the Senate ought to be divided once in every   years into   election districts, containing as nearly as possible, equal portions of white population; and that each district should be entitled to one Senator, and   Delegates; the former to be elected by the whole district, and the latter to be distributed amongst, and elected by the counties composing the district, as nearly as possible, in proportion to their white population.

2. *Resolved*, That the power of the Legislature to impose taxes, ought to be so limited, as to prohibit the imposition on property, either real or personal, of any other than an "*ad valorem*" tax; and that in apportioning this tax, either for State or county purposes, the whole visible property (household furniture and wearing apparel excepted) of each individual in the community, ought to be valued, and taxed only in proportion to its value: Provided, however, that no individual, whose property (with the above exception) does not exceed in value   dollars, ought to be subject to any property tax whatever: And provided, moreover, that the Legislature may impose on all professions and occupations, usually resorted to as a means of support, such tax as may be deemed reasonable.

3. *Resolved*, That to prevent any unfair distribution of the revenue of the Commonwealth, the Legislature ought to be prohibited from making appropriations (ex-

cept by votes of two-thirds of the members of both its branches) to any road or canal, until three-fifths of the amount necessary to complete such road or canal, shall have been otherwise subscribed, and either paid or secured to be paid as the law may direct.

4. *Resolved*, That the right of suffrage ought to be extended to all free male white citizens of twenty-one years of age and upwards, who having been months preceding the election, freeholders or house-keepers in the county where they offer to vote, shall, within that time, have been assessed on property (exclusive of household furniture and wearing apparel) exceeding in value dollars, or in a tax other than a property tax, of the amount of dollars, and shall have actually paid all the taxes with which they may have been legally charged, during the current year.

The resolutions were referred accordingly.

On motion of Mr. Doddridge, it was ordered, that all the papers referred to the Committee of the Whole, should be printed consecutively, in one connected body.

Mr. Claytor of Campbell, offered the following resolutions, which, on his motion, were referred to the Committee of the Whole, and ordered to be printed.

1. *Resolved*, That the right of suffrage, belongs to, and ought to be exercised by, all free white male citizens within this Commonwealth, who have attained the age of twenty-one years, and are able to give sufficient evidence of "attachment to, and a permanent common interest with, the community."

2. *Resolved*, That nativity, or residence within the Commonwealth, for a sufficient time, and the payment of all taxes imposed, and performance of all public duties required by the laws of this Commonwealth, ought to be deemed sufficient evidence.

3. *Resolved, therefore*, That the right of suffrage ought to be exercised and enjoyed by all free white male citizens of this Commonwealth, who have attained the age of twenty-one years, except, first, paupers; second, persons convicted of infamous crimes; third, persons of unsound minds; fourth, persons who have refused or failed to pay all taxes assessed or imposed upon them by law, for the year next preceding any election at which they may offer to vote; fifth, persons in the military or naval service of the United States, or of this State; and sixth, persons not native born citizens of this Commonwealth, who have not resided at least three years within the same, and one year in the county, city, borough or election district in which they offer to vote, and been regularly assessed for taxation; and if liable to militia duty, enrolled in the militia of the same: Provided, however, that this last restriction shall not be so construed as to deprive any person of the right of suffrage, who had under this Constitution previously been qualified to exercise the same in any county, city, borough or election district, of this State: And provided, moreover, that wherever any question arises as to the right of an individual to vote, the *onus probandi* shall be upon the person claiming the right.

Mr. Campbell of Brooke, stating that he was in a considerable minority in the Judicial Committee on the propositions there adopted, would beg leave to submit his own views in the resolutions which had been rejected by that Committee. They were as follows:

Resolved, That the Judicial power shall be vested in a Court of Appeals, and in such Inferior Courts as the Legislature shall from time to time ordain and establish. The jurisdiction of these tribunals shall be regulated by law. The Judges of the Court of Appeals and of the Inferior Courts shall hold their offices during good behaviour, or until removed in the manner prescribed in this Constitution; and shall, at the same time, hold no other office, appointment or public trust; and the acceptance thereof by either of them, shall vacate his Judicial office.

Resolved, That the counties, cities and boroughs shall be divided into wards for the apportionment of Justices of the Peace among the people; and the persons authorized to vote for members of the General Assembly in each ward, shall elect the Justices of the Peace therein, who shall be commissioned to continue in office for the term of years, but removeable for any bribery, corruption, or other high crime or misdemeanor, by indictment or information, in any Court holding jurisdiction thereof.

Resolved, That the Constables shall in like manner be elected annually in said wards.

Resolved, That the appointment of the Clerks of the several courts, and their tenure of office, shall be regulated by law.

Mr. Campbell of Brooke, also offered the following, which were made the objects of a similar order.

1. *Resolved*, That all persons now by law possessed of the right of suffrage, have sufficient evidence of permanent common interest with, and attachment to, the community, and have the right of suffrage.

2. *Resolved*, That all free white males of twenty-three years of age, born within the Commonwealth, and resident therein, have sufficient evidence of permanent common interest with, and attachment to, the community, and have the right of suffrage.

3. *Resolved*, That every free white male of twenty-one years of age, not included in the two preceding resolutions, who is now a resident, or who may hereafter become a resident within this Commonwealth, who is desirous of having the right of suffrage in this Commonwealth, shall, in open court, as may be prescribed by law, make a declaration of his intention to become a permanent resident in this State, and if such person shall, six months after making such declaration, solemnly promise to submit to, and support the Government of this Commonwealth, and if he shall not have been convicted of any high crime or misdemeanor against the laws of this Commonwealth, such person shall be considered as having permanent common interest with, and attachment to, the community, and shall have the right of suffrage.

And then, on motion of Mr. Doddridge, the House adjourned until Monday, eleven o'clock.

MONDAY, October 26, 1829.

The Convention met at eleven o'clock, and was opened with prayer by the Rev. Mr. Sykes, of the Methodist Church.

Mr. Morgan of Monongalia, submitted the following resolutions, which, on his motion, were referred to the Committee of the Whole Convention:

" *Resolved*, That the Legislative power shall be vested in the General Assembly of Virginia, which shall consist of a Senate and House of Delegates. But no Minister of the Gospel of any denomination, or person holding any lucrative office, place, or appointment, shall be a Senator or Delegate.

" The Senate shall consist of thirty-two Senators, a majority of whom, and no less, shall form a quorum, to do business; for whose election the State shall be divided from time to time as equally as may be according to the number of free white citizens, into sixteen districts; and at the first election, there shall be two Senators chosen in each district; the Senator having the greatest number of votes, for the term of four years; the other, for the term of two years: And to keep up the succession, every second year thereafter, one Senator shall be chosen in each district, for the term of four years: But no person shall be a Senator, who shall not be a free white male citizen of the Commonwealth, of the age of twenty-five years, and an actual resident freeholder of his district, at the time of election.

" The House of Delegates shall consist of not less than sixty-four, nor more than one hundred and seventy-six Delegates, who shall be apportioned among the people, and chosen annually, in such manner that one equal sixteenth part of the whole number shall be elected in each Senatorial District: But no person shall be a Delegate, who shall not be a free white citizen of the age of twenty-one years, and an actual resident of his Senatorial District at the time of election.

" Each House shall have power to appoint its own officers; settle its own rules of proceeding; judge the qualifications, and determine the contested elections of its own members; issue writs of election to supply vacancies occurring during the sessions; originate bills, and adjourn without the consent of the other; but all laws shall be wholly approved and passed by both Houses.

" The General Assembly shall meet once or oftener in every year, and the members thereof, shall be exempt from arrest, and enlarged from imprisonment, in all cases except treason, felony, or perjury, during their sessions, and for the term of twenty days before and after: And no disqualification, prohibition or test, shall ever be declared, imposed or required by law, whereby to change or alter the eligibility of any person qualified under this Constitution to be a Senator or Delegate. But, all Senators and Delegates, before they shall enter upon the discharge of their duties, in presence of some person authorised to administer the same, shall make oath or solemn affirmation in this form, to wit: " I, ——, do declare myself to be a citizen of the Commonwealth of Virginia, owing no allegiance to any foreign power, Prince, or State; and I do swear (or affirm) that I shall be faithful and true to the said Commonwealth of Virginia, so long as I continue a citizen thereof, and that I will faithfully, impartially, and justly, according to the best of my skill and judgment, perform the duties of my office (Senator or Delegate.) *So help me God.*"

" That all free white men of this Commonwealth, are of right, and forever shall be, equally free and independent: And suffrage, without regard to birth or condition of estate, being the indefeasible right of every such effective man, proving permanent common interest with, and attachment to, the community, it is delared to belong to, and, in the election of Representatives in the General Assembly, shall be exercised by all free white male citizens of the Commonwealth, of the age of twenty-one years, who shall reside in the county, city, or borough, in which they respectively propose to vote, and shall have so resided for one whole year next before the time of election; other than those who shall have failed, in this Commonwealth, to pay any public tax or levy, or part thereof, within either of the two years next preceding the one in which they propose to vote; or paupers; or those under judgment of felony or other infamous crime; or soldiers, mariners, or marines in the service of the State, or of the United States: And that the right of suffrage may be exercised only by persons disposed for the prosperity and well-being of the Commonwealth, there shall be a tax of twenty-five cents per annum, levied on every free white man of the age of twenty-one years, to be collected and paid into the public treasury; and the Legislature shall annually set apart an amount of the property-tax equal to the whole amount of poll-tax so paid in; and these two sums shall be annually appropriated and constitute a principal fund, always to be preserved and vested in profitable stocks, or put to profitable uses, the interest and profit whereof, shall, in the best manner, be applied every year to the education of the youth of Virginia."

Mr. Leigh said, he perceived that it seemed to be the understanding of gentlemen, that under the rule reported by the Committee on rules of order, all propositions for amendments to the Constitution, must be made in the Convention itself, before they could be laid before the Committee of the Whole. Gentlemen, he saw, were acting on such an understanding. He had not so apprehended the meaning of the rule when it was adopted; on the contrary, he had supposed that members were at full liberty to move their proposed amendments in the Committee, without previously submitting them to the House. If this were not the just understaning of the rule, it ought to be known: and he now asked for information.

On motion of Mr. Mennis, the resolution containing the rule was read.

Mr. Doddridge said, that his understanding of the rule was, that when the Constitution in any of its parts, or the Bill of Rights, should be taken up in Committee of the Whole, it would then be in order for any gentleman to propose such amendments as related to the subject under consideration. If such a construction were not adopted, the Convention might have the whole political creed of every one of its members spread upon its minutes in the form of resolutions. The substance of the resolutions which had just been read, would have been properly presented in Committee of the Whole at the appropriate time. For instance: the great subject of the right of suffrage had been reported upon by the Legislative Committee, having been specified under three distinct resolutions. As each of these came before the Committee, every gentleman could propose to amend it in such way as to him seemed expedient, by striking out, for example, the property qualification, or that in relation to freehold, and so on. He trusted this course would be pursued, as it was obviously the most convenient.

Mr. Leigh said, that he had so understood the rule: All that it forbade, was the discussion and decision of any question of amendment, before it should have been submitted and considered in Committee of the Whole.

Mr. Stanard observed, that the resolution offered by the gentleman from Chesterfield, (Mr. Leigh,) would remove all difficulty on this subject. It includes in its provisions, a permission for new propositions being offered in Committee of the Whole. This was, indeed, the very end and purpose of that resolution: that the Committee of the Whole, in this Convention, might have the same liberty in this respect, as belonged to a Committee of the Whole, on the state of the Commonwealth, in the House of Delegates. He called for the reading of Mr. Leigh's resolution; and it was read accordingly.

On motion of Mr. Leigh, the Convention then proceeded to the Order of the Day, and went into Committee of the Whole, Mr. P. P. Barbour in the Chair.

The Chairman stated, that the subjects assigned to the Committee for its consideration, were the existing Constitution of Virginia, together with the several reports from the Select Committees, proposing amendments thereto, and such other amendments, as had been offered by individual members: the Committee were at liberty to take up any one of these subjects, in such order as might be determined on.

Mr. Doddridge observed, that the report from the Committee on the Legislative Department, would, he presumed, be generally considered at first in order of importance, among the reports before the Committee, from the nature of the subjects on which it treated. But, according to the form of the resolution under which the Committee had been appointed, *that* upon the Bill of Rights had precedence; and he therefore moved, that the report of the Select Committee on the Bill of Rights, be now taken up.

The motion was agreed to, and that report was thereupon read at the Clerk's table; and the question being on concurring with the Committee in their report, it was decided in the affirmative, *nem. con.*

So the report was concurred in by the Convention.

Mr. Powell now suggested, as a question of order, whether, as the report had declared, that the Bill of Rights needs no amendment, and the Convention had adopted that report, it was to be understood as precluding all *additions* to the Bill of Rights; and thereby shutting out the resolutions, which had, on Friday last, been submitted and laid upon the table, by his friend from Norfolk, (Mr. Taylor.)

The Chair replied, that, as the Convention had just decided, that the Bill of Rights needs no amendment, the propositions to amend it, whether by diminution, alteration, or addition, would be out of order.

Mr. Taylor said he was very unexpectedly called to address the Chair; he had had no expectation that the subject of the resolutions which he had had the honor to submit, would come up in any shape to-day; and so uninformed was he, as to the forms of parliamentary proceeding, as not to have apprehended that the rules of order would lead to such a decision as had just been pronounced by the Chair. It was not certainly for him to question that decision; but he should have apprehended, that when the Convention, by adopting the report of its Committee, had decided that the Bill of Rights needs no *amendment*, it had not in effect, said, that all *additions* were inadmissible. If, however, he was mistaken in the apprehension, he felt persuaded, that there existed in this body, a disposition that would lead it rather to consent to re-consider its vote, than, by insisting upon it, to exclude from consideration, resolutions, which, whatever might be their merit, referred to questions of the deepest importance. He asked, therefore, from the candour and generosity of the House, that they would consent to a re-consideration, with a view to let in the resolutions, he had had the honor to submit.

Mr. Johnson said, that perhaps he had misapprehended, either to what resolutions the gentleman referred, or else their true character. If they were those resolutions which he had seen printed in the papers, as offered by the gentleman from Norfolk, he could not conceive that they were at all excluded from the consideration of the Committee, by its having adopted the report in relation to the Bill of Rights. Those resolutions proposed an amendment, not to the Bill of Rights, but to the Constitution of Virginia. They pertained, as he understood them, to subjects reported upon by the Legislative Committee, and would be perfectly in order when the report of that Committee should be taken up for consideration.

The Chair observed, that it had expressed no opinion as to the *nature* or *tendency* of the resolutions, but had merely decided, that, if proposed as an *addition* to the Bill of Rights, they must be considered technically as an amendment to that instrument, and therefore out of order, inasmuch as the House had said the Bill of Rights should not be amended.

Mr. Doddridge now moved, that the report of the Legislative Committee be taken up and considered; and the motion was carried—Ayes 48—Noes 33.

Mr. Powell said, that he had thought there was a subject already before the Committee, viz: the question of re-consideration.

The Chair replied, that no express motion to that effect had been made, and the suggestion of the gentleman from Norfolk, had, as he understood, been waived in consequence of the remarks of the gentleman from Augusta.

Mr. Doddridge said, he had certainly so understood the matter, or he should not have made his motion: he trusted the vote would be re-considered.

Mr. Johnson said, that it was only necessary to lay the report of the Legislative Committee on the table; and he made that motion; which being agreed to, the report was laid upon the table accordingly. The vote, approving the report of the Committee on the Bill of Rights, was then re-considered, and the Bill of Rights itself was taken up, read at the Clerk's table, and afterwards read from the Chair by sections, for amendment.

No amendment being proposed by any other member of the Convention,

On motion of Mr. Campbell of Brooke, the resolutions offered on Saturday by Mr. Taylor were read, and the third resolution having been modified by the mover so as to read as follows; "Representation shall be uniform throughout the State," the whole were taken up for consideration in the following form:

1. *Resolved*, That the elective franchise should be *uniform;* so that, throughout the State, similar qualifications should confer a similar right of suffrage.

2. *Resolved*, That, among those entitled by the Constitution to exercise the elective franchise, there should be *entire equality of suffrage;* so that, in all elections, the suffrage of one qualified voter should avail as much as that of another qualified voter, whatever may be the disparity of their respective fortunes.

3. *Resolved*, That representation shall be *uniform* throughout the State.

4. *Resolved*, That as *individual suffrage* should be *equal*, without respect to the disparity of individual fortune, so an *equal number* of qualified voters are entitled to equal representation, without regard to the disparity of their *aggregate* fortunes.

5. *Resolved*, That in all pecuniary contributions to the public service, regard should be had to the ability of individuals to contribute; and as this ability to pay, from dis-

parity of fortune, is *unequal*, it would be unjust and oppressive to require *each* citizen to pay an *equal* amount of public taxes.

Mr. TAYLOR then rose and addressed the Committee in substance, as follows:

Mr. Chairman,—As the resolutions just read were offered by me, parliamentary usage requires that I should explain and defend them. I should enter on this duty, under the most auspicious circumstances, with great diffidence and embarrassment. The incidents, which have just occurred in the presence of the Convention, are by no means calculated to diminish these feelings. I do not affect not to have bestowed upon these resolutions the consideration which is due to their own intrinsic importance; due to the intelligence of the body which I now address; due to the deep influence which all that is done here is likely to have on the destinies of our country: nor can I forget that self-respect forbids me to lay before such an assembly a collection of crude, undigested thoughts. But I am taken by surprise, both as to the time and the manner in which this subject has been brought up, and have not, therefore, marshaled my ideas, humble as they are, in a manner to exhibit them as I could have wished them to appear. Nevertheless, I shall not shrink from the duty which I conceive to be enjoined upon me by every sentiment of manhood and patriotism; but shall perform it to the best of my poor ability, with all the sincerity which the deepest conviction of their truth can demand, with the zeal which its great importance ought to inspire; and, believe me, Sir, with all that deference, not of manner or of speech alone, but that deep deference of the heart which I ought to feel and to acknowledge, in the presence of such an assembly.

Sir, I will own frankly, that I have scarce any thing of reasoning or of argument to bring forward in support of these resolutions. This, I hope, however, will not throw any discredit upon them: for, I confess to you, it is the very circumstance which recommended them to my adoption. There are some truths, so simple and self-evident, that their most perfect demonstration is furnished by the terms of the proposition itself. Axioms, or self-evident truths, carry conviction to the human mind, the moment they are announced. And, it may be safely affirmed of all propositions which the wit of man can suggest, that the probability of their truth, is in an inverse ratio, to the reasoning and proof required to sustain them. Just in proportion as any affirmation approaches the axiomatic character, in that same degree is the range of argument in its support, limited and restrained. If the resolutions I have submitted have any merit, it lies in this solely: the principles they contain are so evident and obvious, that they neither require nor admit of argument to sustain them. What I have to say, therefore, is rather by way of explanation than of argument: believing, as I do, that this will constitute their sufficient defence and best apology.

I pray the Convention to recollect that the resolutions refer to two distinct objects; the *elective franchise* and the *principle of taxation;* and that their purpose is to give to these two great principles a constitutional consecration.

The principle of taxation, and the elective franchise, at all times most important, especially in a country of free institutions like ours, have now a peculiar interest, from their bearing on the great and paramount question, which occupies every head, and throbs in every heart in this Convention: I mean the question of *basis and apportionment of representation.* They are presented mainly with a view to their bearing on that object.

When I arrived here, my opinions on these subjects, were not formed: the only sentiment in my heart, was a most ardent and sincere desire to know what was truth, and when found, to pursue it. I sought light every where; conversed with gentlemen of various and opposite opinions; sought for facts in all directions, and listened to the reasoning which was founded on them, with the honest intention of giving due effect to both. But I confess to you, Sir, that as I proceeded, my own judgment became bewildered in this process. Nor is such a result at all surprising; for, the mental, like the bodily vision, we all know, may be destroyed as well by the excess, as by the absence of light. My intellect, I own, was insufficient to take in so many conflicting and various principles, at a single glance; still less was it able to pursue them, through all their multiplied and endless combinations; least of all, was it capable of blending them into one mass, giving to each fact, and to each argument, its proper force, and deriving a result, which should be satisfactory to my own mind. Under circumstances so perplexing, I resorted to what I conceived to be the only remedy: one which rarely had deceived me: it was, to simplify, to disentangle this skein of fact and argument, to analyse the materials of which it was composed; to search for principles; to learn the reasons of them; and finally, to draw a just conclusion, to the best of my humble capacity. The result is embodied in those resolutions: which, if they shall answer no other purpose, may at least furnish channels into which the thoughts and arguments of other gentlemen may be directed; by which means the talent and intelligence of the House may be drawn out and concentrated. I certainly should not have offered them, had I not believed them true. But, Sir, I value truth more than consistency: I will, therefore, endeavour to subdue in my breast, that pride of opinion, so natural to man; and am ready to abandon these resolutions the moment I shall be convinced of their fallacy. To have committed, and to have proclaimed, what shall afterwards prove to have been an error in judgment, is a venial offence; an offence, fully expiated by the mortification of confessing it (which I am ready to endure:) but to persist after the judgment is convinced of its error, is an unpardonable sin.

Four of the resolutions refer to the elective franchise: by the leave of the House, I will read them.

[Here Mr. T. read the first four resolutions.]

The Committee will perceive that all these several propositions grow out of one principle, and refer but to one object, the elective franchise, and the mode in which it is to be exercised. Permit me to preface what I have to say respecting them, by a very few general remarks.

All our institutions, whether State or Federal, in their character, are founded in the assumption of three political truths: 1. That a free Government is the best calculated to promote human happiness, if not universally in all countries and in all times, at least in the American States: 2. That the sovereignty resides, of right, and in fact, in the people: 3. That the best mode of administering Government is by agents, instead of the people personally. I shall not stay to enquire whether these assumptions be false or true: I do not indeed, for myself, hesitate to declare my unqualified belief that they are consonant with all the dictates of reason and of truth; and I believe that I express the sentiments of every individual in this Convention, when I make the declaration. But I allude not to these principles, either to justify or to condemn them; I only call the attention of the Committee to the fact, that all our institutions rest on these great principles of *Representative Republics:* Republican in this, that they repose the sovereignty solely in the people: *Representative* in this, that that sovereignty shall be exercised through the administration of agents, of representatives; and not personally, by the people. Nor is it my intention to enquire who are the people, in whom this sovereignty is supposed to reside? Some gentlemen think that they include every individual in the community, without regard to age or sex: others maintain that the people are, all who fight and pay; all who defend their country in the hour of peril, or contribute to supply its purse in "the piping times of peace:" while others, again, insist, that "people" means those only on whom the Constitution confers the right of exercising political power! (I used a wrong word; I will correct the language; I should have said not those *on* whom the Constitution *confers*, but *in* whom it *recognizes* the right of exercising political power.) Gentlemen may entertain as many different opinions on this point as they please; I meddle not with them now; the resolutions do not even approach these opinions. On the contrary, they pre-suppose that the Constitution has already determined by whom the elective franchise is to be exercised, and only attempt to regulate the mode of its action. The principle of the resolutions is as applicable to one *suffragan* (I know not if the term be strictly proper,) to one *voter*, as to another; and will be equally just, whether you shall adopt the plan of freehold suffrage, or any other, in its stead.

I have made these general remarks with a view of shewing that the elective franchise is an *essential* part of our system; that it furnishes the mode, and the only mode, whereby effect can be given to the principle of *representative administration.*

The elective franchise looks to two objects: first, the *persons* who are to exercise it; that is, *suffrage:* secondly, to the *effect of suffrage;* that is, *representation.*

Suffrage, then: shall it be *uniform throughout the* State? or shall it be *diverse in divers parts* of the State? so that, one man shall have a right in one part of the State, which, in circumstances exactly similar, shall not be enjoyed by another, in a different part of the State? This question, it is the purpose of the first resolution to settle. The Bill of Rights declares that all elections shall be free: I would farther add "and shall be uniform." Convenience recommends it. It will avoid the confusion of having different rules in different places; rules local and personal; instead of universal and uniform. Justice and equal rights require it. There can be no departure from the rules of uniformity, without conferring on some, immunities and privileges which are denied to others, in direct opposition to two other articles in this same Bill of Rights. The propriety of inserting such a resolution in your Constitution, arises from the fact, that the present Constitution has not so provided; but, on the contrary, establishes the very reverse. Its basis of representation, is the possession of freehold. In this, its rule may have been thought uniform; but there are portions of the State, in which the Constitution establishes a local rule, applying to that portion alone. In West Augusta, the existing Constitution recognized the right in "*landholders*" who were not freeholders. West Augusta, at the time the Constitution was adopted, comprehended a large extent of territory, from which many counties have since been formed. It then formed a barrier against Indian warfare; and their titles, founded on occupancy only, were held by the tenure of the rifle, and not by parchment. There were others, who were incapable of perfecting their title by the existing law. In 1752, it was the policy of the Colony, to erect a barrier against the Indians, on our western frontier. With a view to this object, we invited within our boundary "*foreign Protestants;*" aliens, who could neither hold nor transmit lands. So, in the Borough of Norfolk, and in the City of Williamsburg, the right of suffrage was extended to individuals, in a manner different from what it is in the other portions of Virginia. These rights I hope to see extended to others similarly situated. The object of my resolution is, to remove these anomalies, and to establish *one law*, and *one rule*, for all who enjoy the privilege of voting at all. To establish such *uniform rule*, is the only object of the first resolution.

Suffrage being established, whether uniform or diverse, another enquiry presents itself of great delicacy and importance. What shall be the effect of suffrage? I mean not as it regards representation, but as *between the voters themselves*. Are all to be units? *all of alike value?* or, will you graduate the votes given? Will you regulate their value by the *excess of the property the voter may own, over and above* the standard which you shall have erected?

The resolution proposes, when you have fixed the qualification to be possessed by all voters, to make all the votes *equal*, without regard *to any disparity of fortune among the voters:* and I pray the House to indulge me, while I attempt the development of the principle I advocate, by a particular application of it. But I premonish the House, that I offer an explanation on this subject, not because I suppose there exists among us any diversity of opinion, as to creating this uniformity *within* the same district. My object is, to ascertain *principles, with a view to their ulterior application.* Imagine a county containing three hundred qualified voters; of these, two hundred and fifty vote for A; the remaining fifty vote for B? Tell me which ought to be the representative of that county? The question may seem strange. Yet the House will perceive, that the decision of this question depends upon another, viz: whether you will graduate the votes given by *the wealth of the voters*, or whether you will make *all the voters count as units, all of equal value.* For explanation? Suppose of the two hundred and fifty voters for A, each owns a freehold worth one hundred dollars, and that the fifty who vote for B, besides possessing this qualification, own besides, each a large estate, say worth one thousand dollars. If *numbers* are to elect, A is elected, by five to one: but, *if wealth is to elect*, if property is to be taken into view, not merely for the safety, but for the effect of elections, then B is elected; fifty thousand dollars is on B's side; but twenty-five thousand dollars on A's. If numbers elect, A is chosen, five to one; if wealth, then B is chosen, two to one. But, suppose you adopt a *compound ratio*, produced by multiplying wealth into numbers; what will then be the result? While A gets but twenty-five thousand two hundred and fifty, B gets fifty thousand and fifty. So that the result is still precisely the same; the effect is just what it would have been, if reference had been had to *wealth alone.*

Perhaps I may be told, this is a subject about which it is impossible for gentlemen to differ. Excuse me: it is the subject on which *alone* there is any great difference of opinion in the House. For the contemplated ratio, the *compound of numbers and taxation*, so earnestly insisted on as the *true basis of representation*, is *neither more nor less, however it may be disguised, than this very thing.* Let me imagine an argument on this subject. Let me suppose the question between A's right and B's to come up here, and you to be the umpires between them; and then let me endeavour to imagine the argument in behalf of B, (having fifty votes.) The advocates of B would tell you that Government was formed chiefly, if not solely, for the protection of property: That there is a natural, inherent enmity between capital and labour: That the contest is interminable between *persons* and *wealth*, (for, strip the subject of the mystification, by which it is usually surrounded, and labour and capital mean no more!) That the two hundred and fifty voters who voted for A, though individually honest, are, through the ignorance and infirmity of human nature, not worthy of being intrusted with political power: Will they not appeal to experience, and insist that that touch-stone has tried what the nature of man is, and has decided that when the *many* possess the power of exercising rapine upon the *few*, it has ever followed that they exercise such power and commit the depredation: That, if the Government were so constituted as to give the power of representation by numbers only, and so admit the two hundred and fifty to elect their representative, the effect would be, that as he would be bound to obey his constituents, the rapine would still take place, with this only difference, that it would be accomplished by the forms of legislation, instead of force, without any form at all: That there can be no guarantee against the effect: That the guarantee afforded by the power of law, the sanctity of the Constitution, and the force of moral principle, however they may be found sufficient for the protection of life and of reputation, prove totally inadequate as a safeguard for *property:* That the only effectual, only sufficient guarantee, is to give to the fifty votes for B more effect than the two hundred and fifty votes for A: That, in a word, the only *means of guarding* property is to place the *power of Government in the hands of those who possess most property?* Would not these be the topics of argument by which the cause of B would be advocated on this floor?

It is not my purpose to fatigue the Committee or occupy its time by giving, in reply, the answers which might be adduced in A's behalf. This question is settled in the mind of every gentleman in the Convention: it is settled by the general sentiment of this nation: by the deep, the universal, and, I trust, the changeless feeling, which attaches us all to our free and happy institutions; a feeling which has its source in the conviction of *the equality they maintain among the citizens* of the Republic, and the *justice which flows from that equality*.

If I am right in this, can the House have any difficulty in adopting the resolution? What does it ask? Nothing but what, in the practical administration of the Government, already actually exists: But it proposes to give a *Constitutional sanction* to what does indeed *exist in fact*, but which the *Constitution does no where guarantee and secure*.

I pray you to refer to the existing Constitution. I say, that although *in fact* equality of suffrage does exist, it rests on *sufferance* merely. I wish it not only to exist, but to have a Constitutional consecration.

The only clause in the Constitution which bears upon the subject is this brief sentence: "The right of suffrage shall remain as it is exercised at present." I would not be hypercritical in examining this declaration; but to me it does appear to provide against *taking away* any rights already possessed and exercised, and not to regulate the equality of suffrage among the voters. All it prohibits is the stripping those of the right of suffrage, who now hold it: no more: it does not take from the Legislature the power of determining the relative effect of votes between the voters themselves. Yet, surely in a matter of such vital importance, nothing ought to be left to doubt and uncertainty. If the existing Constitution does what this resolution purports to do, all the effect of the resolution will be to confirm the declaration of the Constitution: but if it does not, then this resolution will supply the deficiency, and it is proper that the question should be settled now. Such are some of the considerations which unite to recommend the adoption of this resolution.

There are two others, the third and fourth, which have reference to *representation;* that is, to the *effect of the elective franchise, when exerted*.

The third resolution seems to be only a corollary from the first: it affirms, especially as now modified, nothing more than that the *uniformity* of individual suffrage shall be extended to its effect, that is, to *representation*.

The fourth resolution is nothing more than a corollary to the second. It is only the expansion and application of the same principle to representation, which is proposed to the voters themselves: i. e. that *representation* shall be *uniform*, that *like numbers shall confer like rights of representation, without regard to the disparity of fortune which may exist in the aggregate*.

One would think there could be no difficulty in admitting a conclusion like this. *Representation is but the effect of a number of suffrages*. If, then, the suffrages are all equal, it would seem perfectly plain that equal numbers of equal suffrages should produce an equal aggregate amount; and so equal representation. Would any gentleman here hesitate to adopt such a principle, except in a particular mode of its operation?

I stated a case supposed to exist in one county. Now imagine the same case to exist in every county. Is there any reason why fifty voters should outvote two hundred and fifty in one county rather than in another? Locality cannot alter right. If fifty voters are to do this in the county of Norfolk, then fifty voters should do the same in the county of Brooke; and in every other county in the State. There is no difference of opinion as to making the effect equal *within* any one county or district. On this, all are agreed. Where, then, does the difficulty arise in assenting to the principle? When you consider its operation not *within* any district, but between *different* districts, then only do gentlemen differ from me. But shall any one *district*, by any arrangement whatever, introduce a principle which *you all repudiate within a county?* Shall it give an effect to property when in extensive combinations, which is denied to property in a more limited field? Suppose you divide your district into three counties, containing each nine hundred voters. There is not one gentleman here who will hesitate to say, that a majority of qualified voters shall give the rule of election *within* each of these counties. But suppose, again, that in laying out your district boundary, you take the other rule, and say that property shall elect: what will the operation of such a principle be?

But the proposed compound ratio wholly disregards this principle of equality of right in the organization of districts. Let me illustrate this:

Three counties in Eastern Virginia, such as I have described before, are formed into a district, and the nine hundred qualified voters become entitled to one representative. In another part of the State, nine hundred other qualified voters claim similar representation. But it is found that in

the first district the nine hundred voters pay each say $1 tax, - - -	$ 900
And that there are one hundred and fifty persons among the nine hundred who pay beyond the others the sum of - - - - - - - - - -	600
Making an aggregate of taxes - - - -	$ 1,500
The other nine hundred persons who claim a representative, are also (like the seven hundred and fifty of the first district) all qualified voters, and pay $1 each, - - - - - - - - - - - - - - -	900
Leaving a difference of - - - - - - -	$ 600

This difference is wholly produced by the superior wealth of the one hundred and fifty persons in the first district. To equalize the district, the compound ratio proposes to throw a qualified voter into the scale to counterbalance this wealth.

Thus, then, said he, one county will contain nine hundred men, the other fifteen hundred; you add six hundred *men* to make up for the *difference* of property. And is the evil less, because it is disguised? Disguise it as you will, this is not *equal representation*; and if the principle of all our free Republican institutions cries out against *fifty* men electing a candidate *against two hundred and fifty in a single county*, why not in more extended portions of the State? You give to wealth in a *district* a power you refuse to it in a county, though the district is but a collection of counties. While there, it lies dormant; exerts no power at all: but the moment you go beyond the county line, it then receives vigour and effect; I fear, a pernicious vigour, and an effect fatal to freedom. Pray, let me be understood. I disclaim, in these remarks, the least possible disrespect toward gentlemen, who differ from me in sentiment: but in my judgment it is an oligarchical principle; it gives the *minority* power to *control the majority*, although admitted to be *equal participants* in political power. And, if you would consider this as an oligarchical principle, if introduced into counties, I conjure you to consider how you give to wealth, when in large masses, what you refuse it in the elements of which those very masses are all composed. If the principle be wrong in itself, it is only the more dangerous from being concealed. The danger which I know, courage may enable me to brave, or skill to elude; but if the danger approach unseen, if it assails me unwarned and unprepared, it only the more certainly destroys. Masses of men act with an effect not in exact proportion to their numbers. The effect increases more rapidly than the number. A single grain of gunpowder may explode in a lady's *boudoir*, without producing any effect sufficient to wave one of her lightest plumes; but when aggregated masses of those grains are exploded, castles topple to their foundations, and towers fall before its resistless power. Do not say the principle is harmless, because it operates on masses only: as you aggregate men into masses, instead of diminishing, you increase the mischief. I say that this principle, of giving the power to wealth, corrupts and vitiates the very persons it is intended to benefit. The safety of our free institutions, consists in the profound conviction of their justice and equality of operation. Destroy this conviction; weaken it; lead the people to doubt the salutary operation of those principles, and what will be the result? You have taken the first step in the downward road that has conducted all the free nations in the world, first to faction; then to convulsions; and finally to the sword, and a monarch, for protection. Oh, then, let no consideration induce us to weaken, in the slightest degree, that feeling of sacred regard towards free institutions, which is the best safeguard of their perpetuity. When you say, that nine hundred men in one district, and fifteen hundred men in another, shall have but the same representation in the Government, you bribe and tempt the honest simplicity of your fellow-citizens, to commit a fraud upon their brethren. You make them the instruments, willing instruments, if you please, by which the influence of property is brought to bear upon political power and civil liberty. Thus, you prepare them more readily to yield, whenever the influence of wealth, *within their own* county, shall advance its claims to the same power, it enjoys without the county line.

Men of property within all our counties, are deeply interested in this question. Let me remind such men, that the Chieftain in the border war who tempted their kinsmen and retainers, to pass the line and foray for spoil upon the land of their neighbours, destroyed their loyalty, corrupted their fidelity, lost their attachment; and at last have been actually compelled to pay *black-mail* to their own vassals for protection. We are all interested in preserving the great principles of Republican freedom: Men of property not less than others: It is to these principles that our most valuable institutions owe their being and preservation, and our people their national happiness.

Give me leave to ask of gentlemen one question. Representation; what is it? It is the effect of suffrage. Suffrage is the cause, representation the effect: Suffrage is the parent, representation only its offspring. What then ought to follow? What ought the relation to be between the cause and its result? What the similitude between parent and child? Should there be no family likeness? No correspondence between him who represents, and him who confers the power of representation? Is there to be in the Delegate no principle of resemblance to the individual who sends him? Surely the representative is but the mirror, which, if true, throws back the just image of *the voters* who gave him his place. Representation, to be perfect, must throw back such an image of the *people represented*, in all their proportions, features, and peculiarities. I hope gentlemen will excuse me for a remark, which may not correspond with their views and feelings; but to me it appears inconceivable, how there can be a *representative* without *constituents:* and how can there be constituents, without power to delegate? How can a *man* be a constituent, and him he creates not be *his delegate*. Property cannot vote; it cannot delegate power; and yet we are told that it is to have a representative. The *voter* surely, and the voter only is the representative, when we speak of representatives.

I hope, said Mr. T. that the Committee will perceive, that I have had no other object hitherto but merely to explain the nature and the effect of the resolutions I have proposed; that I am offering but little argument; relying as I do upon their own intrinsic truth. I have purposely avoided all answer to the objections, which may be urged against them: and I am led to adopt this course by two considerations: First, my object in only explaining, is that the undivided attention of the House might be drawn to the principles themselves: but I have another reason; I thought it decorous, fair and honorable, to allow to gentlemen who differ from me in sentiment, the advantage of presenting their own views in their own form; that those views may produce their entire effect upon the House. If in the progress of debate, it shall become necessary, I may pray the House to indulge me in reviewing the most important objections, when they shall have been made; and in fortifying my original resolutions, if I shall be able. To my course in this respect, there is but one exception; and *that* has reference to the fifth resolution:

[Here Mr. T. read the resolution.]

It refers to *taxation;* and I will own that I introduced it in connexion with the other subjects for the purpose of asserting what the *true principle of taxation is;* but I combined this principle of *taxation*, with the resolutions respecting *representation*, to show that one should have no influence in regulating the other. The one looks to *property only;* the other to *qualified voters only*. In the resolution, a proposition is affirmed in the first member of it; then, a fact is affirmed; and the last clause is an inference from the two, though not in strict syllogistic form. Some may think the premises are false; but none will deny that it is *unjust to require each citizen chargeable with taxes, to pay an equal amount*. What would be the effect of such a principle? Evidently this; that in time of foreign war or domestic need, be the exigencies of the State what they may, no greater sum can be raised by taxation, than the amount which the very poorest man in the community is required to pay, multiplied by the total number of the citizens of the State. You can lay nothing more on the richest man, than on the poorest; if each is to pay an equal sum; and thus the wealth of its citizens would be totally useless and unproductive to the Commonwealth, though the Republic be in danger.

Whence does the obligation to public contribution arise? Whence but from the consideration that each individual is bound to pay to the public for the protection of his property. The Government itself, I mean by its moral as well as physical force, is in fact the underwriter of all the property in the community: and each individual should pay for the general protection in proportion to the risk incurred; that is, according to the amount of property he has to be insured. The principle is founded in the eternal nature of justice; which requires that contribution should be in proportion to the good received. I think that even if my resolution should be convicted of false logic, and that neither the *major* nor the *minor* members of the syllogism were true, and that the conclusion did not follow; still, the proposition itself, contained in the conclusion, must be acknowledged by all to be true and evident. None doubts the *fact*, that property is unequally distributed; nor do I see how any can deny the principle, that each man ought to pay to the State in proportion to his *ability to pay*. I do not say in proportion to his capital, or to the profits upon his capital; but in proportion to his "*ability to pay*." I put the proposition in the broadest terms: and in such a form as will apply to any system of political economy, gentlemen may respectively think fit to adopt.

If the ground I have taken, be tenable, then we have arrived at the true sources of representation and taxation; they are not two twin streams, which have their common source in the same distant glen; which chance may have separated for a time, and which afterwards re-unite: they issue from different fountains; flow to different oceans, and never can be united but by some power which perverts the object for which nature destined them. When you look to *representation*, you look to *men:* when you look to *taxation*, you look to the ability to pay, and to the *property* from which this payment is to be made.

Mr. Taylor concluded by a short peroration; apologising for the time he had occupied, disclaiming all intention to offend, and deprecating such an imputation; and professing his readiness to renounce his views as soon as convinced they were untrue. He then moved that the resolutions be received and added as an amendment to the Bill of Rights.

The question being on the adoption of the first of Mr. Taylor's resolutions,

Mr. Green of Culpeper, said, that he should vote against all the resolutions, although he approved of some of the principles they contained; and he should do so because he thought their proper place was not in the Bill of Rights, but, if any where, in the Constitution of the State.

Mr. Nicholas of Richmond, said, that he did not rise to discuss the resolutions which had been submitted, although there were various considerations in respect to them, which forcibly struck his mind. Any man who had turned his attention much to politics must know, that in those matters, there was no such thing as abstract truth. Political maxims were valuable, only as applying to the actual circumstances of the country, and must always be considered as in connexion with them. It would not do to apply principles, suited to one state of society, to a state of things entirely different. He understood the gentleman from Norfolk, as having said that he had brought forward these propositions with a view to settle the great question which the Convention was called to decide. Mr. N. said, he was unwilling to decide that question *in this way*. That question grew out of various considerations in the state of the country, and must be considered as applying to them. He was willing to admit the abstract truth of some of the gentleman's propositions; there were others of them which he should be disposed to deny, and the two were so far blended that he could not assent to the resolutions. It seemed strange to him, that instead of waiting for the discussion of the report of the Legislative Committee, the Convention was, at this stage of its proceedings, called to decide upon doctrines in the abstract, without any attempt at applying their practical bearing. If they were adopted and added to the Bill of Rights, their effects would all have to be discussed again, when the other report came before the Convention. *Cui bono?* why go over the same matters twice? Besides, the Bill of Rights was drawn up by some of the wisest, most virtuous and most patriotic men this country had ever produced; it was truly a noble production, and it declared truth so well, that he felt unwilling to add to it, or substitute another in its room. But, surely the Convention should not attempt to decide on so great a question; a question, which would go to produce an entire revolution in the condition of the State without knowing something more of the effects of their decision. The gentleman had much better reserve his resolutions, till the Legislative report should come up. He would not be excluded, and that opportunity would be a more fit one. Mr. N. said he should have said nothing, but observing, that no other gentleman seemed disposed to rise, he had given briefly the reasons which would induce him to vote against the resolutions.

Mr. Johnson moved to lay the resolutions upon the table, but professed his willingness to withdraw the motion, if any member of the Convention was desirous of submitting his views. He was satisfied some gentlemen would vote against the resolutions now, who would vote for them when they should hear their practical application discussed. The proper time for that discussion would be when the report of the Legislative Committee should come up for discussion.

Mr. Taylor observed in reply, that he had not the least objection that the resolutions should be laid upon the table: but the gentleman had thought this was not the proper time to discuss these principles. He differed entirely on that point, and considered this as the "accepted time." If gentlemen thought the resolutions should be acted upon at all, it should certainly be in connexion with the Bill of Rights. What was the object of the Bill of Rights? It was to settle the very abstractions, to which the gentleman seemed so averse; to settle principles; to set up certain landmarks for the framing of a Constitution. It prescribed the general rules which it was the purpose of the Constitution to develope and expand. Its use was to familiarise the people to a consideration of these great principles of free Government, and thereby to control the action of the Legislature. If the principles he had brought forward were right in themselves, and worthy of adoption in any form, it should be in the Bill of Rights. Let them stand there as touch-stones, to try with what fidelity the Constitution should be drawn, and the legislation of the State carried on under it. Gentlemen object to abstractions: the Bill of Rights declares all men to be born by nature, free and equal. Does the gentleman call that an abstraction? Why is it any more so, when by another declaration, the equality of men is stated, not as in a state of nature, but as in a state of political society? It was but carrying out the object of that instrument. He could not agree with gentlemen, who thought the proper time for fixing such principles, would be when the report of the Legislative Committee came up for consideration.

On motion of Mr. Johnson, the resolutions were then laid on the table.

On motion of Mr. Doddridge, the Convention proceeded to consider the report of the Committee on the Legislative Department of Government. The report was read at the Clerk's table, and the first section having then been read by the Chairman for amendment, as follows:

"*Resolved*, That in the apportionment of representation in the House of Delegates, regard should be had to the white population exclusively."

Mr. Green moved to amend it by striking out the word "*exclusively*," and adding in lieu thereof the words "*and taxation combined*."

And the question being on this amendment:

Mr. Green stated, there were some documents expected momently from the Auditor, which had a bearing on the amendment; and he therefore wished the action of the House suspended till they should be received; and he, thereupon, moved that the Committee rise.

It arose accordingly, and the President having resumed his seat, Mr. Barbour reported, that the Committee had, according to order, had the subjects referred to them under consideration, and had made some progress therein; but had come to no conclusion thereon.

And then the Convention adjourned till to-morrow, eleven o'clock.

TUESDAY, October 27, 1829.

The Convention met at eleven o'clock, and was opened with prayer by the Rev. Mr. Parks, of the Methodist Church.

On motion of Mr. Scott, it then proceeded to the Order of the Day, and again went into Committee of the Whole, Mr. P. P. Barbour in the Chair.

And the question lying over from yesterday, being on the amendment proposed by Mr. Green of Culpeper, to the first resolution reported by the Committee on the Legislative Department of Government, viz: To strike out the word "*exclusively*," in the resolution, (which declares "that in the apportionment of representation in the House of Delegates, regard should be had to the white population *exclusively*,") and insert in lieu thereof, the words "*and taxation combined*."

Mr. Green observed, that he had proposed this amendment with a view to bring up the whole subject for discussion; so that both sides of the great question in relation to the basis of representation, might be before the Committee: and it was under the impression that the whole field being thus opened, some gentleman would enter upon the subject, by stating the grounds on which it was desired to introduce a new principle of representation into the Constitution. He now hoped that some gentleman, who was friendly to the change, would present to the Committee his views.

After a short pause,

Mr. Leigh of Chesterfield, said, that he did hope that the friends of the proposition reported by the Legislative Committee, would assign their reasons in support of a plan which proposes, in effect, to put the power of controlling the wealth of the State, into hands different from those which hold that wealth; a plan, which declares that representation shall be regulated by one ratio, and contribution by another: that representation shall be founded on the white population alone, and contribution on a ratio double, treble, and quadruple in proportion. He hoped the friends of these new propositions, new at least in our State, if not new throughout the world, would give to those who differed from themselves, some reasons in support of their scheme; some better reasons than that such principles were unknown to our English ancestors, from whom we have derived our institutions; better than the rights of man as held in the French school; better than that they were calculated in their nature to lead to rapine, anarchy and bloodshed, and in the end, to military despotism: a scheme, which has respect to numbers alone, and considers property as unworthy of regard. Give us, said Mr. L. some reasons; reasons which may excuse us in our own self-esteem, for a tame submission to this (in my opinion) cruel, palpable and crying injustice. Let us have at least some plausible reason; something which has at least the colour of reason, which may excuse us to ourselves: something which may gild the pill and disguise its bitterness: something to save us from the contempt of this present time, and the assured curse of posterity, if we shall betray their interest. Give us something which we may at least call reasons for it: not arithmetical and mathematical reasons; no mere abstractions; but referring to the actual state of things as they are; to the circumstances and condition of this Commonwealth; why we must submit to what I cannot help regarding as the most crying injustice ever attempted in any land. I call upon gentlemen for these reasons.

Mr. Cooke of Frederick, rose in reply.

Mr. Cooke said, that he could not but express his unfeigned astonishment, that the able gentleman from Chesterfield (Mr. Leigh) should have ventured to say to that assembly, that the principle of representation recommended by the Legislative Committee, was "new to him, and new in the history of the world." Can the gentleman have forgotten, (said Mr. Cooke,) that the principle which he treats as a novelty, and an innovation, is asserted in the "Declaration of the Rights of the people of Virginia?" And does he not know, that when the Convention of 1776 promulgated, in that instrument, the principles of Government on which their infant Republic was founded, they did but announce, in solemn form, to the people of Virginia, principles which had received, *a century before*, the deliberate sanction of the most enlightened friends of liberty, throughout the world?

Sir, the fathers of the Revolution did but *reiterate* those great and sacred truths which had been illustrated by the genius of Locke, and Sydney, and Milton: truths for which Hampden, and a host of his compatriots, had poured out their blood in vain.

Driven from Europe, by Kings, and Priests, and Nobles, those simple truths were received, with favour, by the sturdy yeomanry who dwelt on the western shores of the Atlantic. The love of liberty, aye, Sir, and of *equality* too, grew with the growth, and strengthened with the strength, of the Colonies. It declared war, at last, not only against the *power* of the *King*, but against the *privilege* of the *Noble*, and laid the deep foundations of our Republic on *the sovereignty of the people* and *the equality of men*.

The sacred instrument, for sacred I will dare to call it, notwithstanding the sneers which its very name excites in this assembly of *Republicans*, the sacred instrument in which those great principles were declared, was ushered into existence under circumstances the most impressive and solemn. The "Declaration of the Rights of the people of Virginia," was made by an assembly of sages and patriots, who had just involved their country in all the horrors of war, in all the dangers of an unequal contest with the most powerful nation on earth, for the sake of the noble and elevated principles which that instrument announces and declares. For the sake of those principles, they had imperilled their lives, their fortunes, their wives, their children, their country; and, in one word, all that is dear to man. For the sake of those principles, they had spread havoc and desolation over their native land, and consigned to ruin and poverty a whole generation of the people of Virginia.

And for what did they make these mighty sacrifices! For wild "abstractions, and metaphysical subtleties!" No, Sir. For principles of eternal truth; as practical, in character, as they are vital, in importance; for principles deep-seated in the nature of man, by whose development, alone, he can attain the happiness which is the great object of his being. Those principles are,

"That all power is vested in, and consequently derived from, *the people*."

"That all men are, by nature, *equally* free." And

"That *a majority of the community*" possesses, by the law of nature and necessity, a right to control its concerns.

These are the principles which the gentleman from Chesterfield regards as "wild and visionary;" as "abstractions and metaphysical subtleties;" and which are contemptuously styled by others, who think with him, "*mere* abstract principles." Passing by, without comment, the curious fact, that these "abstract principles" received but yesterday the sanction of an unanimous vote of this body (so far, at least, as a *nemine contradicente* vote can be called unanimous): passing by the fact, I say, that the resolution of a special Committee declaring that the Bill of Rights requires *no amendment*, was but yesterday adopted, without a dissenting voice, I will pause, for a moment, to enquire what these gentlemen mean by their favourite phrase, "mere abstract principles?" If I rightly apprehend the import of the term "abstract," when applied, in *a disparaging sense*, to any general principle, it means that the principle, though true, *as expressed*, is, nevertheless, expressed in terms so *general*, that when an attempt is made to apply it to any given subject, it is almost always found that the subject is included, not within the principle itself, but within one or other of those *exceptions*, which detract from the *universal* correctness of *all* general principles. That the principle is an unmeaning generality, and scarcely susceptible of application to the every-day business of men. In short, that it is wild, visionary and *unpractical*.

Let us see, then, whether the principles which are announced by the Declaration of Rights, as the "basis and foundation of Government," are of this wild and visionary character. Let us see whether they do not, on the contrary, come home to the "business and bosoms of men."

It declares, then, in the first place, "that all power is vested in, and consequently derived from, *the people*."

Look to the situation and circumstances of those who made this declaration, to the occasion on which it was made, and to its bearing and operation on the existing institutions of Virginia, and then say whether it was not a *practical* principle, and one too, of great pith and moment. The colonies had long been smarting under the tyrannical exercise of power, *not derived from the people:* Under the exercise of power assumed, by the King and Parliament of Great Britain, *without the consent of the people.* Here, then, is a bold denunciation of this usurped authority; an abolition of kingly power; a declaration that *the people* of Virginia are the only *sovereigns* of Virginia, and that they would tolerate, in all time to come, neither foreign Parliaments, nor Kings, nor Cæsars. A declaration that the only legitimate Government, is a Government of *magistrates*, deriving their power *from* the people, and responsible *to* the people.

With whatever colour of plausibility this might have been called an abstract principle, in Europe, in the time of Locke and Sydney, who first maintained and supported it, thanks to the indomitable spirit of our ancestors, it became *practical* in Virginia, in 1776; was gallantly sustained through all the vicissitudes of the war, and received the sanction of royalty itself, at the peace which ensued. It was then that the slavish doctrine of the *jus divinum* of Kings, openly supported, but a century before, in the country from whence we sprung, received its *practical* refutation; and it might have been hoped, in *Virginia* at least, *its final doom.* From the period of the revolution *till the meeting of this Convention*, the doctrine "that all power is vested in, and consequently derived from, the people," was considered *a great practical truth. Now*, it is an "*abstract principle*," a wild and visionary speculation!

But again, Sir. The Bill of Rights declares, "that all men are, by nature, *equally* free." And this is considered an abstraction *par excellence*; the very abstraction of abstractions. It is even pronounced to be "absurd on the face of it," because it amounts, as it is said, to a declaration, that "all men, all women, and all children, are entitled to an equal share of political power."

I shall briefly examine this principle, Sir, in connexion with that which stands by its side in the Declaration of Rights, which is, in effect, that the sovereign power, the supreme control of its affairs, is vested in the majority of every free community. And I hesitate not to say, that taken in connexion, and they *must* be taken in connexion, they are so far from being speculative and abstract truths, much less absurd speculations, that they constitute in fact, a compendium of the whole law of rational and practical liberty, and were peculiarly appropriate and practical in their application to the actual condition of Virginia. Taking first the insulated proposition, that "all men are, by nature, *equally* free;" I pronounce it to be a great practical truth; a self-evident proposition; the primary postulate of the science of Government. Sir, what does this proposition mean, but that no *one* man is born with a natural right to control any *other* man; that no one man comes into the world with a mark on him, to designate him as possessing superior rights to any other man; that neither God nor nature recognize, in anticipation, the distinctions of bond and free, of despot and slave; but that these distinctions are artificial; are the work of man; are the result of fraud or violence. And who is so bold as to deny this simple truth?

But is it a mere "*abstract*" truth? Was it not, when declared by the authors of the Declaration of Rights, replete with *practical* meaning? What was their actual situation? The Government of England, against which this principle was directed, was incumbered with privileged orders; there was the King with his *hereditary prerogative*, and the noble with his *hereditary privilege.* The colonists had found, to their cost, in the earlier stages of their struggle, that *prerogative* and *privilege*, derived from birth, were the sworn and mortal foes of liberty. In announcing and reinstating the original *equality of men*, they declared war against both, and from that time, neither privilege nor prerogative derived from birth, have been tolerated in the Commonwealth which they established. And is there nothing practical in this? Is this a mere abstract principle; a mere "metaphysical subtlety?"

But it is said, that if it be true that "all men are by nature equally free," then all men, all women, and all children, are entitled to equal shares of political power; in other words, that they are all entitled to the right of suffrage, which is, practically, political power.

Sir, no such absurdity can be inferred from the language of the Declaration of Rights. The framers of that instrument did not undertake to write down in it all the rules and all the exceptions which constitute political law. They did not *express* the self-evident truth that the Creator of the Universe, to render woman more fit for the sphere in which He intended her to act, had made her weak and timid, in comparison with man, and had thus placed her under his *control*, as well as under his protection. That children, also, from the immaturity of their bodies and their minds, were under a like control. They did not say, *in terms*, that the exercise of political power, that is to say, of the right of suffrage, necessarily implies *free-agency* and *intelligence;* free-agency, because it consists in *election* or *choice* between different men and different measures; and *intelligence*, because on a *judicious* choice depends the very safety and existence of the community. That nature herself had therefore pronounced, on women and children, a sentence of incapacity to exercise political power. They did not say all this; and why? Because to the universal sense of all mankind, these were self-evident truths. They meant, therefore, this, and no more: that all the members of a community, of mature reason, and free agents by situation, are originally and by nature, *equally* entitled to the exercise of political power, or a voice in the Government.

But at the same time that they recognized and expressed the general principle, the general right, they recognized and *expressed* a limitation of that general right imposed by *nature* and *necessity*. In affirming and declaring the *jus majoris* to be the law of all free communities, they did but declare the simple and obvious truth, that the essential character of a free Government, of a Government whose movements are regulated by numbers, involves the *necessity* of a submission by the *minority* to the *majority*. For the right of deliberation and *election* necessarily involves some *decision* between the men or the measures which are the subject of deliberation and election. All deliberation must come to a close, and every exercise of the right of election must terminate in a choice. To bring deliberation to *some* close, and election to *some* choice, it must of necessity be adopted as a rule, either that the majority or the minority must put an end to the deliberation, by pronouncing a decision: And the necessity of adopting the rule that the majority shall so pronounce, is founded on the necessity of a *sanction* to every law, on the fact that the majority possesses, in its superior physical force, *that sanction*, and on the certainty that it would not permanently submit to the opposite regulation. I say, *permanently:* Because, though the majority may be deluded for a time, by the artificial and vicious institutions of society, into a submission to the voice of the minority, they will arise, at last, and assert and enforce their natural superiority.

Neither did the framers of the Declaration of Rights carry out the *jus majoris* into certain other plain and obvious results: for they were not writing a treatise on political law, but merely announcing, in a brief and compendious form, its leading principles. They declared, for example, that the majority of every community has a right to adopt such a form of Government, and such a fundamental law, as to them seems best. They left unexpressed the plain and obvious propositions, that in forming that fundamental law, the majority have a right to act, and ought to act, on the principles, that the safety of the people is the supreme law; that the legitimate object of all Government, is to promote the greatest happiness of the greatest number; and that the perfect and entire protection of life, property, and personal liberty, constitutes the essential basis of the greatest happiness of the greatest number. That to effect these essential objects, the majority have a perfect right to prescribe, by a fundamental law, still further limitations to the universality of the right of suffrage. That they have a right to exclude, and ought to exclude, by their fundamental law, from the exercise of the right of suffrage, all those, who in the honest and deliberate opinion of the majority, cannot *safely* be entrusted with the exercise of it; or in other words, all those whose exercise of this right would be, in the honest and deliberate opinion of the majority, incompatible with the safety and well-being of the community, which is the supreme law. They did not set down, in express terms, all these distinct and consecutive propositions. But they *did* state the result to which they lead, when they said, in effect, that, in a well regulated community, those alone should be permitted to exercise the right of suffrage, who have "a permanent common interest with, and attachment to, the community."

I say, then, Sir, with a confidence inspired by a deep conviction of the truth of what I advance, that the principles of the *sovereignty of the people*, the *equality of men*, and the *right of the majority*, set forth in the "Declaration of the Rights of the people of Virginia," so far from being "wild and visionary," so far from being "abstractions and metaphysical subtleties," are the very principles which alone give a *distinctive* character to our institutions, are the principles which have had the *practical* effect in Virginia, of abolishing *kingly power*, and *aristocratic privilege*, substituting for them an elective magistracy, deriving their power *from* the people, and responsible *to* the people.

But it has been said that the authors of the Declaration of Rights themselves, admitted, in effect, the abstract and *unpractical* character of the principles which it contains, by establishing a Government whose practical regulations are wholly inconsistent with those theoretical principles. That while, in the Declaration of Rights, they asserted that all power is vested in *the people*, and should be exercised by *a majority* of the people, they established a Government in which *unequal counties*, expressing their sense by the representatives of a *selected few* in those counties, to wit, the *freeholders*, were the real political *units*, or essential *elements* of political power. That the right of the majority, in this frame of Government, was violated in two different modes: First, by vesting the power, within each county, in the freeholders, who are a minority of the people; and next by investing small masses of people in the small counties, and large masses in the large counties, with equal power in the Government.

Sir, the argument would be a good one if the premises which support it were correct. But it is *not true* that the authors of the Declaration of Rights *established* the anomalous Government under which we have lived these fifty years and more. There can be no grosser error than to suppose that the Constitution of Virginia was *formed* in 1776. Its two great distinctive features, the *sectional*, and the *aristocratic* had been given to it a century before. The *equal representation of the counties*, which was the remote cause of its sectional character, was established, in 1661, by a General Assembly representing a population residing exclusively in the tide-water country, and consequently, at that time, homogeneous in character and identical in interest. The *limitation of suffrage to freeholders* which gave to it an aristocratic character, was imposed on the Colony in 1677, without any act of Assembly, by a letter of instructions from the King of England to his Governor in Virginia, backed and enforced by two regiments of British soldiers, who had been sent to the Colony for the express purpose of suppressing a popular insurrection. At the æra of the revolution, then, these two provisions had been the constitutional law of the Colony for more than one hundred years. The freeholders had learned to pride themselves on their superior power and privileges, and the smaller counties on their equality with the larger. The body of the people were reconciled by habit to their actual condition.

What, then, was the situation in which the framers of the Constitution were placed?—While they framed that instrument they were almost within hearing of the thunder of hostile cannon. The invader was at the door. They were in continual danger of being driven from the very hall of legislation by the bayonets of the enemy. The whole undivided physical force of the country was barely sufficient to defend it against the superior force of a foreign enemy. It was utterly *impossible*, under such circumstances, to pull down, and erect anew, the whole fabric of Government. And it would have been to the last degree unwise and impolitic, at such a fearful crisis, to distract the minds of the people by attempting a new distribution and arrangement of political power. It would have been the very height of folly, at such a crisis, to create disaffection in the minds of the *freeholders*, by stripping them of their exclusive powers, and to exasperate the smaller *counties* by degrading them from the rank which they had held under the royal Government. In leaving the *freeholders* and the *counties* as they found them, the framers of the Constitution bowed to the supreme law of necessity, and acted like wise and *practical* statesmen. Weak and unstable, then, is the argument which infers the *unpractical* character of the principles contained in the Declaration of Rights from the inconsistency of the actual Government formed, with those principles. The very language resorted to in disposing of a subject of such vital importance as the regulation of the right of suffrage, the brief and summary way in which it is disposed of, would shew, in the absence of all other evidence, that it was a subject which the framers of the Constitution *scarcely dared to touch*.—"The right of suffrage shall remain as at present exercised."

No, Sir, it was not reserved for *us* to discover the inconsistency between their theoretical principles, and their practical regulations. They saw it themselves, and deplored it. In the very heat of the war which was waged for these "abstractions"—in the hurly-burly of the conflict, *one* statesman, at least, was found, to point out those inconsistencies, and to urge home on the people of Virginia the "new and unheard of" principle, that in the apportionment of representation, regard should be had to the white population only. As early as 1781, Mr. Jefferson exhorted the people of Virginia, in the most earnest and impressive language, to reduce the principle to practice, "so soon as leisure should be afforded them, for intrenching, within good forms, the rights for which they had bled."

From that time to this, the spirit of reform has never slept. From that time to this, the friends of liberty have continually lifted up their voices against the inequality and injustice of our system of Government. Incessantly baffled and defeated, they have not abandoned their purpose; and after a struggle of fifty years, that purpose seems at length on the eve of accomplishment. The Representatives of the people of Virginia have at length assembled in Convention, to revise the Constitution of the State. A special committee of this Convention has recommended, among other measures of reform, the adoption of a resolution,

"That in the apportionment of representation, in the House of Delegates, regard should be had to white population exclusively."

It is this resolution which has called forth the denunciations of the gentleman from Chesterfield. It is this proposition, "new in the history of our Government, if not throughout the world; new certainly to him," which he calls on us to support.

Sir, I have ventured to assert, in the commencement of the remarks which I have had the honour to address to the Committee, that this proposition, so far from being "*new and unheard of*," is but a reiteration, a practical enforcement, of those principles of political law which were solemnly announced by the fathers of the revolution, in that noble paper, the "Declaration of the Rights of the people of Virginia, which rights do pertain to them and their posterity, as the basis and foundation of Government." I proceed to redeem the pledge.

The Bill of Rights declares, that *the people* are the only legitimate source and fountain of political power.—The resolution of the Committee affirms this doctrine, by proposing, that in apportioning representation, or political power, regard shall be had to *the people* exclusively. Not to wealth, not to overgrown sectional interests, not to the supposed rights of the counties; but to the white population; to *the people* only.

The Bill of Rights asserts the political equality of the citizens.—The resolution proposes to give to that principle a practical existence in our Government, by abolishing the inveterate abuse of the *equal* representation of *unequal* counties, and equalizing, as nearly as may be, the electoral districts throughout the Commonwealth, on the basis of free white population alone.

The Bill of Rights pronounces the *jus majoris* to be the law of all free communities, by attributing to the majority of a community, the power to reform, alter or abolish, at its will and pleasure, the very Government itself, and consequently the lesser power of deciding, without appeal, in all matters of *ordinary legislation.*—The resolution proposes to give practical effect to the *jus majoris*, by making each Delegate the representative of an *equal number* of the people, so that the voice of a majority of the Delegates, will be the voice of a majority of the people. It proposes, in short, to establish that beautiful harmony between our theoretical principles and our practical regulations; the want of which, has been, for fifty years, the reproach of Virginia.

The resolution of the Committee, then, proposes no new and unheard of scheme; no innovation on the established principles of our Government. It calls on you to listen to the warning voice of the fathers of the revolution, who, in this despised "declaration," have told you, "that no free Government, or the blessings of liberty, can be preserved to any people, but by a frequent recurrence to fundamental principles."

But the accordance of the resolution with these great fundamental principles, has not obtained for it, the approbation of the gentleman from Culpeper, (Judge Green.) He proposes to amend it by striking out the word "exclusively," and adding the words "and taxation combined;" so that the resolution, as amended, would be,

"That in the apportionment of representation in the House of Delegates, regard should be had to white population *and taxation combined.*"

It will be perceived, at once, that the object of this amendment, is to substitute for the principle of representation contained in the resolution of the Committee, one of a totally new and different character. It proposes a mixed or compound basis of representation, the elements of which are *property* and *people*, in lieu of the simple basis of *people only*. For the total amount of *taxation* does, and must, bear a just proportion to the total amount of *property*, the possession of which constitutes the ability to pay. The direct tendency, then, of this amendment, is to give political power to the wealthy in proportion to their wealth, and to inflict political insignificance on the poor in proportion to their poverty. To confer on an electoral district, containing *few* electors but *great* wealth, equal power with another district containing *many* electors but *little* wealth. To give to the *few*, who are *rich*, a control over the *many* who are poor. So that if Stephen Girard, the great *millionaire* of the north, were to become a citizen of Virginia, and fiscal ingenuity could reach his abounding wealth, the direct or apparent operation of this amendment, would be to augment incalculably, the political power of the county he should select as his residence, while its real effect would probably, if not certainly, be, to confer all the accumulated mass of power, thus artificially produced, on Stephen Girard himself. If Richmond, in the vicissitudes of human affairs, should chance at a future day, to attain the opulence which is even now possessed by the commercial metropolis of the Union, the operation of the amendment would be, to give it uncontrolled power over the legislation of the Commonwealth.

But, Sir, without commenting further on the practical operation of the proposed amendment, let us apply to it the same test to which we have subjected the resolution of the Committee. Does it accord with the principles of the "Declaration of Rights;" with the principles to which the gentleman from Culpeper, in common with us all, has given, but yesterday, the sanction of his approving vote?

It will be perceived, on the slightest examination, that it violates, not one only of those principles, which I have mentioned, but *every one.*

1. It repudiates the doctrine that *the people* are the *only* legitimate source and fountain of political power, and that "all power is derived from the people," and makes property *one* of the sources of power, and declares it to be derived, in part, *from* property.

2. It denies the correctness of the principle, that all the electors in the Commonwealth are equal in political rights, by conferring on *a small number of wealthy electors*, congregated in one electoral district, the same power that it confers on *a large number of poor electors*, congregated in another electoral district.

3. It subverts the *jus majoris*, the third great principle alluded to, and which is, in fact, but a corollary from the first, that the sovereignty is vested in *the body of the people*, and substitutes for it the control of the wealthy few; or in other words, the most odious, pernicious and despicable of all aristocracies—an aristocracy of wealth.

And for what purpose, I pray you, are we thus to dilapidate the very foundations of our free institutions?—For what purpose are we to make this retrograde movement in the science of Government, and in the practical institutions of our country, which should rather keep pace with the improvements of that science, and the march of intellect?—While human liberty is making a progress, which, though slow, is yet certain, even in countries where the *jus divinum* of Kings is still the prevailing doctrine, why should we alone run counter to the spirit of the age, and disavow and repudiate the doctrines consecrated by the blood of our fathers?—While most of the old, and all the new Republics of this extensive confederacy, are carrying out the principle of the sovereignty of the people to its full extent, why should we alone, seek to narrow, and limit, and restrain its operation?—What mighty good is to be attained by this abandonment of the principles of the revolution?

The members of this Committee, in general, are left to imagine the objects and views of the learned and distinguished gentleman who has proposed the amendment in question. For though parliamentary usage, so far as I understand it, imposed upon *him* the task of developing the principles of his amendment, and though we were regularly notified yesterday, in the manner in which such notices are usually given, that he would proceed, to-day, to the performance of that duty, he has pursued a different course, and the friends of the resolution reported by the Select Committee, have been invited, or rather challenged, by the gentleman from Chesterfield, to commence the discussion.

Having been myself a member of that Committee, however, and having heard the arguments by which the same amendment was there sustained, I will endeavor to perform the duty of the mover by stating, and my own by answering them.

It is alleged, then, Sir, that the principles of Government contained in the Declaration of Rights, I mean those elevated and elevating principles which, in an assembly of *Virginia Statesmen*, I have this day been compelled to defend, are little better than mere abstractions. That whether they are correct or not, as "abstract principles," there is a great *practical* principle, wholly overlooked in the resolution of the Select Committee, of vital and *paramount* importance. The principle in question, and the argument by which it is sustained, when broadly and fairly developed, amount to this:

1. That the security of property is one of the most essential elements of the prosperity and happiness of a community, and should be sedulously provided for by its institutions.

2. That men naturally love property, and the comforts and advantages it will purchase.

3. That this love of wealth is so strong, that the *poor* are the natural enemies of the *rich*, and feel a strong and habitual inclination to strip them of their wealth, or, at least, to throw on them alone all the burthens of society.

4. That the *poor*, being more *numerous* in every community than all the classes above them, would have the *power*, as well as the *inclination*, thus to oppress the rich, if admitted to an equal participation with them in political power; and

5. That it is therefore necessary to restrain, limit and diminish the power of this natural majority; of this many-headed and hungry monster, *the many*, by some artificial regulation in *the Constitution, or fundamental law*, of every community. And if this be not done, either directly, by limitations on the right of suffrage, or indirectly, by some artificial distribution of political power, in the apportionment of representation, like that contained in the amendment, property will be invaded, all the multiplied evils of anarchy will ensue, till the society, groaning under the yoke of unbridled democracy, will be driven to prefer to its stormy sway, the despotic Government of a single master. And this is said to be the natural death of the Government of *numbers*.

Sir, if this statement of the argument be a little over-coloured by imputing to those who advance it epithets which they are too prudent to use, it is nevertheless, like all good caricatures, a striking likeness.

To this argument I answer that, like most unsound arguments, it is founded on a bold assumption of false premises. It is founded on the assumption that men are, by nature, *robbers*, and are restrained from incessant invasions of the rights of each other, only by fear or coercion. But, is this a just picture of that compound creature *man*? Sir, I conceive it to be a libel on the race, disproved by every page of its history. If you will look there you will find that man, though sometimes driven by stormy passions to the commission of atrocious crimes, is by nature and habit neither a wolf nor a tiger. That he is an *affectionate*, a *social*, a *patriotic*, a *conscientious* and a *religious* creature. In him, alone, of all animals, has nature implanted the feeling of *affection for his kindred*, after the attainment of maturity. This alone is a restraint on the excess of his natural desire for property as extensive as the ties of blood that bind him to his fellow man. Designing, moreover, that man shall live in *communities*, where alone he can exist, nature has given to him the *social feeling*; the feeling of attachment to those around him. Intending that for the more perfect development of his high faculties, and for the attainment of the greatest degree of comfort and happiness of which he is susceptible, man should associate in *nations*, she implanted in him a feeling, the glorious displays of which have shed lustre around so many pages of his history. I mean *the love of country or patriotism*. Designing that he should attain to happiness through the practice of virtue, and in that way only, she erected in each man's bosom the tribunal of *conscience*, which passes in review all the actions of the individual, and pronounces sentence of condemnation on every manifest deviation from moral rectitude. To add sanctions to the decisions of conscience, she also implanted in his bosom an intuitive belief in the existence of an intelligence governing the world, who would reward virtue and punish vice in a future state of being. Man is therefore, by nature a *religious* creature, whose conduct is more or less regulated by the love or fear of the unknown governor of the Universe. Above all, the light of revealed religion has shone for ages on the world, and that Divine system of morals which commands us "to do unto others as we would have them do unto us," has shed its benign influence on the hearts of countless thousands, of the high and the low, the wise and the foolish, the *rich* and the *poor*. But we are asked to believe that all these natural feelings, all these social affections, all these monitions of conscience, all these religious impressions, all these Christian charities, all these hopes of future rewards and fears of future punishments, are dead, and silent, and inoperative in the bosom of man. The love of property is the great engrossing passion which swallows up all other passions, and feelings, and principles; and this not in particular cases only, but in all men. The poor man is fatally and inevitably the enemy of the rich, and will wage a war of rapine against him, if once let loose from the restraints of the fundamental law. A doctrine monstrous, hateful and incredible!

But, Sir, if I were even to admit, for a moment, the truth of the revolting proposition that the desire for property swallows up all the other feelings of man, does it follow that the aspirants after the enjoyments that property confers, will seek to attain their object in the manner which the argument in question supposes? If it be contended that man is a greedy and avaricious, it will, still, not be denied, that he is a reasoning and calculating, animal. When he desires to *attain* property it is in order that he may *possess and enjoy it*. But if he join in establishing the rule that the right of the strongest is the best right, what security has he that he, in his turn, will not soon be deprived of his property by some one stronger than himself? Sir, the *very* desire for property implies the desire to possess it *securely*. And he who has a strong desire to possess it, and a high relish, in anticipation, of the pleasure of enjoying it securely, will be a firm supporter of the laws which secure that possession, and a decided enemy to every systematic invasion of the rule of *meum* and *tuum*. In other words, man is sagacious enough to know that as a general and public rule of action, the maxim that honesty is the best policy, is the safest and best maxim. And when he deviates from that rule he always hopes that the violation will go undiscovered, or otherwise escape punishment. So true is this, that I am persuaded that if a nation could be found consisting exclusively of rogues and swindlers, there would not be found in the legislative code of that nation a systematic invasion of the right of property, such as the argument for the proposed amendment apprehends and seeks to provide against.

Communities of men are sagacious enough to know and follow their *real* interest. And, Sir, I do not, and cannot believe that it is, or ever was the real interest of any class in the community, or of any community to commit gross and flagrant abuses of power, to disregard the monitions of conscience, to break down the barriers and obliterate the distinctions between right and wrong, and thus to involve society in all the horrors of anarchy. The principles of justice are the foundation of the social fabric, and rash and foolish is he and blind to his true interest, who undermines the foundation and tumbles the fabric in ruins.

Thus far I have reasoned *a priori*. But what are the lessons which history and experience teach us, in pursuing this enquiry?—We need not go far for examples. Let us look at the experience of our good old Commonwealth of Virginia. From the foundation of the Commonwealth the slave-holding population of Virginia has held the supreme power in the State. From the foundation of the Commonwealth there has existed and there still exists, a numerous population on our western frontier, who are comparatively destitute of slave-property, and whose wealth has ever consisted in cattle more than in any other description of property. Now if the argument of those who support the proposed amendment be a sound one, it would follow that as it is and always has been the interest (according to *their* views of interest) of the slave-holding population to shift from themselves, and to lay on others, the burthens of

Government, they would impose heavy taxes on the cattle, the property of the helpless minority, and oppress them by this and every other species of fiscal exaction. And yet the very reverse is the fact. For the slave-holders, invested with supreme power, and urged to its exercise by their "*interest*," have not only not overtaxed the cattle of their western brethren, but have, in fact, imposed on them, except at one period of danger and distress from foreign war, no tax at all, and when the pressure ceased the law imposing the tax was instantly repealed. And why?—Because they were governed by the principles of justice, and the feelings of honour. Because they thought, and justly, that the people of the frontier, burthened as they were with "the first expenses of society," and engaged in laying the very foundations of the social fabric, could ill endure the additional burthen of a tax on their flocks and herds. Because the non-slave-holders of the west were at their mercy, and every feeling of honour and magnanimity forbade them to oppress the weak. I say, then, Sir, that the slave-holders of Virginia have shewn by their conduct in this particular case, the incorrectness of the theory which supposes man to be habitually governed by a blind and reckless cupidity; by the sordid feelings alone of his nature, to the exclusion of the nobler.

I say, then, that arguing *a priori*, or taking for our guide the conduct of the slave-holders of Virginia, we are led to the conclusion, that the property of the wealthy would not be imperrilled, as gentlemen imagine, by entrusting the powers of Government to *numbers*, without regard to their wealth. That property would be abundantly secure, without investing its holders with a factitious power, derived from its possession. And that there is not the least necessity for the proposed innovation on the great principles of Government, asserted by our ancestors at the æra of the revolution.

But it is not in Virginia alone, that we see evidences of the futility of the apprehensions that are entertained for the safety of property. We have in the history of our Sister-Commonwealths, a rich fund of experience from whence we can draw arguments to illustrate the utter futility of these apprehensions. In *fifteen States of the Union*, representation is apportioned according to numbers alone, and wholly without reference to property, or the wealth of the electors. In eight of these States citizenship is the sole qualification of the elector, and in the remaining seven the payment of any tax, either local or general, is the only qualification superadded. The *numbers*, the needy *many*, have had the supreme control over the wealthy *few*, in some of those States for forty years, in some thirty, in some twenty, in some ten, and in some five. And what has been the practical result? Look at *their* situation, Sir, and look at *ours*. Do we not see among them the richest and most prosperous States of the Union? Has a single instance occurred of a Legislative invasion, by the poor, of the rights of the wealthy? Not one. The machine of Government has rolled smoothly on, and property has been found, as it ever will be found, able to protect itself, without *constitutional barriers* in the shape of *odious privilges*. So much for the *general question*, whether property is endangered by leaving the people in possession of their *natural and equal rights*.

But I know, Sir, incidentally, that the mover of this amendment entertains the opinion, that the case of Virginia is, from peculiar circumstances, a case *sui generis*. His opinion is that the comparatively non-slave-holding population of Virginia, must ere long constitute, if it does not now constitute, a decided majority of the people, and *that* majority inhabiting a particular section of the State, alienated from their slave-holding fellow-citizens, by distance, localities and dissimilar views on questions of general policy.—That it will be, or what amounts to the same thing, that they will suppose it to be, their interest to lay the burthens of Government almost exclusively on the slave property of their eastern brethren. And that it is, therefore, necessary to invest the slave-holding minority with *factitious power*, under the new Constitution, to enable it to protect itself against the injustice and oppression of the comparatively non-slave-holding majority.

Supposing the *facts* which I have just stated to be as he imagines them to be, I do not see any thing in the case stated, which takes it out of the operation of the principles of security which I have supposed to exist in regard to property in general. He *will not* contend that the people of the west are less operated on by the principle of honor, by sentiments of justice, and by a sense of their *real* interests, than the people of the east.—And if this be so, his fears are groundless. For the people of the east, under similar circumstances, have repelled the base suggestions of a sordid and short-sighted interest, and have been governed by nobler and more enlarged views of expediency and right. But, Sir, his premises fail him.—Look at the map of Virginia, and at the tables of population which have this day been reported by the Auditor. He estimates the white population east of the Blue Ridge of mountains, at 362,745, and the white population west of those mountains at 319,516. The people of the east have, therefore, a majority of 43,229 over those of the west. I need scarcely, Sir, tell this assembly, that the whole white population east of the Ridge is a slave-holding population. The black population is even more dense along the eastern base of the Ridge, than along the shore of the Atlantic. For while the two senatorial districts bordering on the ocean, contained, by the Census of 1820, one of them but 17,416, and the other but 18,363, three of the districts along the eastern base of the Ridge contained, one of them 27,417, another 27,514, and the third 30,621. Thus you perceive, Sir, that the slave population is crowded up to the very foot of the mountain. But this is not all. The slave-holding population extends *beyond* the Ridge. The district which I have the honor in part to represent, contains about 12,000 slaves. The four western counties of Berkeley, Jefferson, Frederick and Botetourt contain 17,070. They are therefore, fairly to be considered as slave-holding counties, to the practical intent of being interested in exempting slaves from undue taxation. These four counties are estimated to contain, at present, a white population of 47,013. Add this slave-holding population, west of the mountain, (to say nothing of other western counties which contain slaves to the amount of several thousands more,) to the slave-holding population east of the mountains, and you have an aggregate of 409,758. The comparatively non-slave-holding population in all the remaining counties of Virginia, is but 272,503. There is, therefore, a majority of slave-holding population, amounting to 137,255.

And yet, strange to tell, an apprehension is entertained, that if representation be *equally* apportioned among the white population, slave property will be burthened by unequal and oppressive taxes!—If the resolution of the Committee be adopted, the slave-holding population will possess, in the House of Delegates, a majority of representatives in the proportion of 409,758 to 272,503; and yet a fear is entertained, that the representatives of the 272,503 non-slave-holders will overtax the property of the 409,758 slave-holders! And to avert this imminent peril and flagrant injustice, you are asked to invest the 409,758 with *factitious Constitutional power*—to destroy the great landmarks of natural right, established at the æra of the revolution—to repudiate all the principles of Government which have been, until now, held sacred and inviolable. Such, Sir, is the argument by which the proposed amendment is supported.

Mr. Green said, it was with extreme diffidence that he rose to state his sentiments in support of the amendment. He was well convinced of his incapacity to do justice to the argument; but being urged by a sense of duty, he should make the effort, even though he might sink under it. The Committee were now apprised of what was to be urged as the foundation of the claim for a new basis of representation; they had been referred to the principles contained in the Bill of Rights. And according to the version of those declarations just given by the gentleman from Frederick, the declaration, that all men are by nature equally free, amounted to a declaration that every man in the community possesses, and ought to exercise, equal rights with every other man. And this was very true, if understood, as referring only to natural rights; but it was not true if applied, as the gentleman would wish to apply it, to rights of a political character. On the contrary, he hoped to shew that the Bill of Rights, so far from holding such a position, was explicitly opposed to it. The meaning of the declaration, as he understood, was this: that all men are by nature, so far equally free as that none might claim, in the social state, a natural right to govern others: this was the extent of the proposition: unless, indeed, they claimed to govern by the *jus majoris*, founded, as the gentleman contended, in the possession of physical force. To him, (Mr. G.) however, it seemed that there could arise no right from mere force. The gentleman from Frederick had determined, that because the majority possessed the physical force, they have, of course, the right to govern: but he thought that this did not follow.

Again, the gentleman had reminded the Committee, that the Bill of Rights declares that all power resides in the people. This was perfectly true; but it did not follow that the possession of the power of government by the people, gave to each member of the body politic equal weight in its government. Once more; the gentleman had contended, that according to the same Bill of Rights, a majority must govern in all things, and were of right entitled to supreme control. Such, no doubt, would have been the doctrine of the Bill of Rights, if the framers of that instrument had thought that its foundations were laid in the right of nature, or of conquest; and would have declared that to be the best Government which gives the most perfect effect to the will of the majority. Yet they do, in effect, instead of affirming this, deny it, by saying that Government being instituted for the security of the people, "that is best, which is capable of producing the greatest degree of happiness and safety, and is most effectually secured against the danger of mal-administration."

The affirmation is not that the majority shall rule by absolute power, but that they may establish such a Government, as shall produce the greatest amount of happiness, and as shall best be guarded against the dangers of mal-administration. I admit, said Mr. G. that in a community, where all the members are in circumstances of equality as to fortune, and so situated, that no one part of the society can injure the residue, without, at the same time, inflicting equal injury upon themselves, the rule that the numerical majority shall govern, is the best; and the foundation of all our institutions, is the assumption, that the people know, and will always pursue their own true interest; and, therefore, that a majority is likely to decide rightly. But, it is equally the principle of those institutions, that the majority have an *interest* in doing what is right. Unless this is taken for granted, the abstract proposition is of little value. Now, I ask of gentlemen, whether, in the peculiar situation of Virginia, circumstances will not present a strong inducement to the majority to oppress the minority for their own benefit?

My first proposition in support of the amendment is this: that it is perfectly certain that in a very short time, possibly within ten years, the majority of the free white inhabitants of this State will be found to the west of the Blue Ridge. A reference to the several enumerations of our population since 1790, will shew the grounds of this conclusion; a conclusion which is farther fortified by the report just received from the Auditor, and now in the hands of every member. In 1820, the difference of population between the eastern and western side of the Blue Ridge was near 100,000 in favor of the eastern side; now it is only 43,000. Thus, the western counties have experienced an increase in eight years, of more than 50,000 inhabitants: if such has been the ratio of gain in these eight years, it is not too much to believe that in ten years more, they will have a majority of the whole State.

The report of the Auditor makes the population of the Valley 10,000 more than I supposed: allowing for that difference (which is, as far as it goes, in favour of my argument.) The population west of the Allegheny mountains has increased in the same time 48,000; or about at the rate of thirty-six per cent. on its former population; while the Valley has increased 15,000; and putting both those divisions of the State together, their aggregate increase has been at the rate of twenty-five per cent. But what has been the rate of increase in the country *east* of the Blue Ridge? It has increased but by a ratio of four per cent!

Let us look, now, at the results of the system of taxation. The average amount of a capitation tax in the region west of the mountains was twenty-five cents per head: in the Valley, forty-eight cents: putting these two divisions of the State together, the average will be thirty-two cents. And what was it in the country *east* of the Blue Ridge? eighty-eight cents per head.

Look now at the *land* tax in these two grand divisions of Virginia; set slaves on one side. On the other side of the Ridge lands were taxed one dollar, while on this side they were taxed about two and a half: more than double.

From aggregate results go down to details: the same general result meets you still. During last war there was a tax on cattle in Virginia, (one of the articles which the gentleman has alluded to in his argument as more peculiarly pertaining to the western inhabitants) and even on cattle, more was paid on this side the mountain than on the other side. From all these facts, I am led to conclude that the existing inequality is likely to continue. If not, the amendment can do no harm. When there is no unequal taxation, it can do no harm to say that representation shall be regulated by taxation and population; for then it will result in the very thing the gentleman wants; he will have representation based upon the white population exclusively: or if it shall happen that the people of the west pay *more* taxes, then the effect will be to throw the weight of legislative power into that part of the State which now complains for the want of it.

The gentleman asks us, what *motives* the people of the west can have to misuse their power? I will state one inducement. They have one great object of desire, and the whole history of our State Legislature will prove it, and that is the construction of roads and canals. The desire of roads and canals has of late years grown into an enthusiastic passion among them. The whole of the country beyond the Ridge has passed those improvements by an unanimous vote, when they were proposed. The improvements on James River, in their extended form, were assented to solely for the benefit of the people of the west: a much more limited work would have answered all the ends and wishes of the people in the east of the State. A proposition was once before our House of Delegates to borrow three millions and about seven hundred thousand dollars for objects of this description, and every western man supported and voted for the scheme; nay, it was but last year that a loan of a million was brought forward, and, I believe, every western vote was given in the affirmative. Here, then, is an inducement, and here are actual efforts, to tax the lowlands for the benefit of western interests.

But it has been said that property has, and always will, protect itself. Sir, I admit that when property is unequally held by persons, all residing in one district together, and, therefore, having all one common interest, there may be truth in the position. But where it is dispersed in different and distant positions of the State, there is no such motive to restrain the attempts of those who have little common feeling with its possessors.

It has been farther said, that the restraints of conscience furnish an ample security; but, I believe, all political institutions, as well in this as in every other country, go on the assumption that all men, when acting, especially in large bodies, are governed by a feeling of interest, and do with little or no scruple, whatever they suppose their interest to dictate. I consider it as a self-evident proposition.

On the subject of slaves, it is true that one purpose of the amendment, is to secure them from undue taxation. The gentleman tells us that those living on this side the mountain, have a majority of the slaves; and a majority in the Legislature, and will continue to have both. But it will be found that if any question shall arise in the Valley on that subject, almost all the voters there are destitute of slaves. In those four counties the one class is to the other as nearly three to one.

Let us, in the next place, look at the relative effect upon the general state of our affairs from the adoption of the resolution as it stands, and with the amendment. If the *white basis* shall be adopted, the people in the lowlands will never feel secure; jealousies and an interminable hostility will be generated, and perpetuate feuds and heart-burnings between different sections of the State. But if you adopt the *compound basis*, although, possibly, the people of the west may, for a time, be very angry, as considering themselves deprived of political weight and privileges, they never can feel themselves insecure as to their *property*; for no law can be passed in the Legislature affecting property at all, that will not be felt to a much greater extent on this side the mountains.

I have heard in various forms, (though not as yet in this Committee,) of adequate *guarantees*. For myself, I believe that we can have no adequate guarantee but in representation. A majority in the Senate alone, I consider as wholly insufficient; the larger number of delegates in the other House will always, in the course of two or three years, prevail in carrying any object they have at heart: they always overwhelm the Senate in the end. I shall not advert to the other guarantees that have been proposed: for I am unwilling longer to detain the Committee. I feel regret at having already been compelled to trespass on their time. Important facts were what I wished principally to present to them, and those I have stated are in my judgment entitled to great weight in the mind of every reflecting man.

Mr. Campbell of Brooke, said, that he did not rise for the purpose of making a speech; nor of attempting a reply to the speech he had just heard: but to offer a remark or two in relation to the order of the Committee's proceedings. Order he considered as the first law of heaven: but if he were to judge of its importance by what he saw here, he should conclude that this body were departing from it entirely; and, by a constant law of nature, they were incurring the penalty of such a course, for confusion and darkness were likely to accompany their proceedings. Yesterday the Committee had been occupied in the development of the grand principles which lay at the bottom of the science of government, and it seemed to be the understanding, that this Convention would have for its object to settle those fundamental principles, the sub-basis, as they might be termed, of the fundamental law of the community. Some very interesting remarks had, in that connexion, been submitted to the Committee. But the positions taken were treated as mere abstractions, and it was held that the proper course was to lay these aside, until the Committee should first have gone down to the practical details of Government. Now, for himself, Mr. C. said, he knew of nothing that could rightly be called a *principle*, that was not an abstract idea. Justice, goodness, truth, might be so called, and they were all abstract ideas. All the principles in science were abstract ideas. But in reviewing the course adopted, he perceived that it had been taken on this ground, that it was said to be inexpedient to settle principles first, for they were mere abstractions, and gentlemen must try their practical effect first, before they could espouse them. They must go to the practical part of Government, irrespective of principles. This doctrine had thrown the Committee into complete confusion. It had been then proposed to take up the first resolution reported by the Committee on the Legislative Department, and thereupon came in the amendment now under consideration. The amendment certainly threw the *onus probandi* on the gentleman who proposed it; but as the mover yesterday asked delay, the amendment had been laid over, and was now pending. The expectation of the Committee had been that some proof should have been adduced in its support; but the gentleman from Culpeper (Mr. Green) had opened the debate by declining to offer any, and both he, and the gentleman from Chesterfield (Mr. Leigh) called on the advocates of the resolution for arguments in its support. Certainly the burden of proof lay upon the gentlemen themselves. *Onus probandi incumbit affirmanti.* The gentleman from Culpeper had offered an amendment, which he affirmed ought to be added to the resolution in place of a word which he proposed to strike out. To call on the friends of the resolution for arguments, when the obligation to argue lay on the opposite party, was as great an aberration from the correct principles of order as that which had taken place yesterday. Either adopt the principles in the Bill of Rights as canonical, and base all your subsequent proceedings upon them; or, if those principles are considered as unsound, let them be modified or amended; or else let gentlemen propose other principles as a substitute for them. Let them give us their principles distinctly and in numerical order, first, second, third, and so on: then, said Mr. C. we shall know where we are. In a word, I consider the order yesterday to have been "no principles;" that to-day seems to be "no proof."

The Chair having stated the question to be on the amendment of the gentleman from Culpeper, (Judge Green,) and the question being called for by several members,

Judge Upshur of Northampton, said, that it seemed to have been concluded by tacit agreement, that the debate was to be conducted by a member on each side alternately, and he considered that a convenient mode of proceeding. He felt disinclined to submit his own views at this time; and from the backwardness manifested by gentlemen on the opposite side of the question, (if, indeed, the Convention was to be considered as thus divided into *sides*,) he presumed they were taken somewhat by surprise, and were not now ready to submit their ideas. Instead, therefore, of carrying on the argument at present, with a view to give gentlemen time and opportunity for farther reflection, as well as that the order of discussion might be preserved, he thought it most fair and most expedient, that the Committee now rise; and he made that motion; but withdrew it at the request of

Mr. Mercer, who said, that he could not undertake to speak for other gentlemen; but he certainly could say, very confidently, as it respected himself, that the presumption just expressed by the gentleman from Northampton, was totally without foundation, viz: that the friends of the resolution reported by the Legislative Committee; in other words, the friends of the white basis, as it was technically and familiarly called, were not ready to reply: he hoped he might be permitted to say, that he was entirely prepared to reply, but was perfectly willing to rest the vote on the amendment upon the argument they had already heard.

Judge Upshur replied, that the gentleman from Loudoun mistook him if he supposed him to insinuate for a moment, that that gentleman, or his friends, were unprepared, in the sense he seemed to have supposed. He took it for granted, that gentlemen on that side of the question were all fully prepared to address the Convention, so far as familiarity with the facts and arguments pertaining to the subject was concerned: all he had meant to say was, that they did not seem desirous to proceed with the discussion on this day. He had rested his motion for the rising of the Committee, on the plan which seemed to have been agreed upon, of speaking alternately. He thought such a plan very fair, and on the whole the best course. If, therefore, it was not the intention of some of the gentlemen on that side to submit his views to the Committee, he hoped the Committee would rise: and he thereupon renewed his motion to that effect.

Mr. Mercer rejoined. If the gentleman from Northampton and his friends were not ready to speak farther in support of the amendment which they had brought forward, perhaps it would be better to pass it over for the present, and take up some other part of the report; but he hoped the House would not adjourn at so early an hour, and thus waste the residue of the day. For himself and those who acted with him, they were ready at any time to proceed.

The question being put on the motion for the rising of the Committee, it was negatived.

And the question then recurring on the amendment of Mr. Green, (viz. in adding the words "and taxation combined" to the first resolution of the Committee proposing the white basis of representation,)

Judge Upshur rose and addressed the Committee, nearly as follows:

I cannot say, Mr. Chairman, that I have been driven into this discussion without some degree of preparation. Yet I may be permitted to declare, that I did not anticipate that I should thus early be called on to submit my views to the Committee. It is true, Sir, that the few simple ideas which it is my purpose to submit, do not require a laboured preparation of any sort; but I should at least, have entered into the debate with more pleasant feelings, had not circumstances deprived me of the power of choosing my own time.

There seems to be some difference of opinion among us, as to the proper order of debate. A question has arisen whether the friends or the foes of the immediate measure before us, are bound to open the discussion. For my own part, I do not attach the slightest importance to that inquiry: to me it seems of no consequence whatever, whether the advocates of a compound basis of representation, or those of the popular basis, begin this discussion. I could have wished, so far as I feel any wish upon the matter, that the two parties should have addressed the Committee in alternate order; for this, it seems to me, would be at once, equitable and respectful, at the same time that it would best conduce to the elucidation of the subject. It was my wish that each party should be heard in turn; but it is still more my wish, that each should be heard with patience and candour, and answered in a spirit of kindness and respect.

For myself, Mr. Chairman, I trust that I have entered this body, without any feelings of local partiality or local prejudice. I entertain a deep conviction, that in the discharge of the solemn trust reposed in me, it is my duty to consider myself the representative of the whole State, and not of any peculiar part of it. I came here with an earnest, and an honest desire, to fix the foundations of Government with reference to the common welfare; and not upon the narrow basis of local interest. I brought with me also, another feeling; a feeling which is the result of long and mature reflection, and which I had hoped to make the guide of my conduct here. It appears to me impossible, that in a body like this, representing many differing, if not conflicting interests, any party can reasonably hope to carry all its measures. Nay, Sir, even if this were practicable, it admits of great doubt indeed, whether it would be in its results, either safe or wise. In a community like our own, no Government can gain the undivided affection, nor secure the undivided support of the people, unless it spring from a fair and equitable compromise of interests. It was therefore my earnest hope, that there would be no necessity for a formal array of parties upon this point. I have foreseen that we could not be much divided upon any other subject within the range of our duties; and it was therefore, peculiarly desirable, that on *this* subject, we should agree to meet on some middle ground. I was, and still am ready, to advance quite, nay, *more* than half way; for I feel entirely assured, that the great interests committed to our charge, require this temper in every one of us. Unfortunately, however, I have not found a single individual on the other side, who would agree with me in opinion.* I am therefore, driven to the necessity of relying on the strength of my own principles; and I shall attest the sincerity with which I entertain them, by the vote I am about to give.

It is contended by our opponents, that the proper basis of representation in the General Assembly, is white population alone, because this principle results necessarily from the right which the majority possess, to rule the minority. I have been forcibly struck with the fact, that in all the arguments upon this subject here and elsewhere, this right in a majority is assumed as a postulate. It has not yet been proved, nor have I even heard an attempt to prove it. It is for this proof that I was desirous to wait. Assuming this right as conceded, the whole scope of the argument has been to prove, that in the application of the right to the practical Government, we must of necessity, graduate political power according to white population alone. It may not perhaps, be more curious than profitable, to examine somewhat in detail, the grounds upon which this pretension rests.

There are two kinds of majority. There is a majority in *interest*, as well as a majority in number. If the first be within the contemplation of gentlemen, there is an end of all discussion. It is precisely the principle for which we contend, and we shall be happy to unite with them in so regulating this matter, that those who have the greatest stake in the Government, shall have the greatest share of power in the administration of it. But this is not what gentlemen mean. They mean, for they distinctly say so, that a majority in number only, without regard to property, shall give the rule. It is the propriety of this rule, which I now propose to examine.

If there be, as our opponents assume, an original, *a priori*, inherent and indestructible right in a majority to control a minority, from what source permit me to inquire, is that right derived? If it exist at all, it must I apprehend, be found either in some positive compact or agreement conferring it, or else in some order of our nature, independent of all compact, and consequently prior to all Government. If gentlemen claim the right here as springing from positive compact, from *what compact* does it spring? Not certainly from that Constitution of Government which we are now revising; for the chief purpose for which we have been brought together, is to correct a supposed defect in the Constitution, in this very particular. Not certainly from any other Constitution or form of Government, for to none other are we at liberty to look, for any grant of power, or any principle which can bind us. The right then, is not conventional. Its source must be found beyond all civil society, prior to all social compact, and independent of its sanctions. We must look for it in the law of nature; we have indeed been distinctly told, that it exists in "necessity and nature;" and upon that ground only, has it hitherto been claimed. I propose now to inquire whether the law of nature does indeed, confer this right or not.

Let me not be misunderstood, Sir. I am not now inquiring whether, according to the form and nature of our institutions, a majority ought or ought not to rule. That inquiry will be made hereafter. At present, I propose only to prove that there is *no original a priori* principle in the law of nature, which gives to a majority a right to control a minority; and of course, that we are not bound by any obligation *prior to society*, to adopt that principle in our civil institutions.

If there be any thing in the law of nature which confers the right now contended for, in what part of her code, I would ask, is it to be found? For my own part, I incline strongly to think, that, closely examined, the law of nature will be found to con-

* Judge Upshur takes great pleasure in acknowledging that he has learned, since the above remark was made, that there are some gentlemen on the other side, who have always been willing to meet any proposition of fair compromise. Their number however, is not large enough to authorise a hope that the measure could be carried, even with their assistance.

fer no other right than this: the right in every creature to use the powers derived from nature, in such mode as will best promote its own happiness. If this be not the law of nature, she is certainly but little obeyed in any of the living departments of her *empire*. Throughout her boundless domain, the law of force gives the only rule of right. The lion devours the ox; the ox drives the lamb from the green pasture; the lamb exerts the same law of power over the animal that is weaker and more timid than itself; and thus the rule runs, throughout all the gradations of life, until at last, the worm devours us all. But, if there be another law independent of force, which gives to a greater number a right to control a smaller number, to what consequence does it lead? Gentlemen must themselves admit, that all men are by nature *equal*, for this is the very foundation of their claim of right in a majority. If this be so, each individual has his rights, which are precisely equal to the rights of his fellow. But the right of a majority to rule, necessarily implies a right to impose restraints, in some form or other; either upon the freedom of opinion or the freedom of action. And what follows? Each one of three, enjoys the same rights with each one of four, and yet it is gravely said, that because four is a majority of the seven, *that* majority has a right to restrain, to abridge, and consequently, to destroy all the rights of the lesser number. That is to say, while all are by nature equal, and all derive from nature the same rights in every respect, there shall yet be a number, only one less than a majority of the whole, who may not by the law of nature possess any rights at all!

If, Sir, it be possible to carry our minds back to such a state of existence, let us suppose that the wild children of nature are for the first time, assembling together for the purpose of forming a social compact. Each one of them would bring with him all the rights which he derived from nature, and among these rights, would be found the right to say *whether a majority should rule him or not*. And, suppose a civil compact should be entered into by every member of the savage assembly, save one. Is that one bound by what the rest have determined? If he has originally a right to say whether he will agree to the compact or not, at what time does that right cease to exist, and by what authority is it taken away? *Until* the compact is formed, there is no majority in existence; and *after* it is formed, he is *no* party to it; and therefore not bound by its majority.

Again.—How is this majority to be ascertained? Who shall appoint the tellers, and who shall announce on which side the majority is? All these are necessary operations, without which the idea of a majority, is indeed, an "abstraction;" and yet these very operations presuppose a degree of order and arrangement inconsistent with a state of nature, and which cannot exist except in a state of society.

Again.—Within what limits is this majority to act? Is it a majority of the whole world, or only of a part of it? If of the whole world, then two millions of savages who range the forests of America, may prescribe the law to one million who inhabit the Asiatic Islands; two millions who live by hunting the elk and the buffaloe with a bow and arrow, have authority to say that one million, among whom these animals of the chase may not be found, shall not draw their subsistence from the ocean which surrounds them! Is this the law of nature? Has the Creator really ingrafted upon the nature of man, a principle which gives sanction to such monstrous cruelty and injustice?

But suppose, instead of looking to the whole world, you limit your majority to particular districts of it. It is impossible to do this, according to any fixed rule, except by supposing that the world is divided into separate and distinct communities, possessing separate and distinct interests. And this is precisely what we understand by a state of society, as contradistinguished from a state of nature; and of course, the majority which is to be found there, is not the majority which the proposition supposes.

But again. If nature really gives this right to a majority; if as the clear-minded gentleman from Frederick (Mr. Cooke) supposes, there be impressed upon us by nature, a principle of this sort, which is mandatory upon us, and which we are not at liberty to disregard, in what does the right consist? Is it in mere numbers? If so, every creature must be counted, men, women and children; the useless as well as the useful; the drone who lives upon the industry of others, as well as the most profitable member of the human family. The law of nature knows no distinction between these classes, and indeed, one of the very postulates on which gentlemen rely, is that "*all* are by nature equal." In point of rights, nature does not own any distinction of age or sex. Infancy has equal rights with mature age; and surely it does not consist with the gallantry of the present day, to say that the ladies are not at least the equals of ourselves. Nay, more Sir, nature as strongly disowns all invidious distinctions in complexion: in her eye, there is no difference between jet and vermilion. A distinction does indeed prevail here, Sir, and a wide one it is. But the same rule of taste would not answer in Africa; for the African paints the devil white. According to your rule of numbers, all these various classes and descriptions of persons must count. And if so, what estimate have gentlemen themselves put upon their own rule? If in the estimate of numbers, all are counted, why exclude any from the right of suffrage? Why are not women, and children, and paupers, admitted to the polls? The rule, even if it *exists* in nature, is worth nothing, unless its fair analogies will hold in a state of society. And how can gentlemen venture to limit themselves to *white* population alone, and yet found their claim on a law of nature which knows no distinction between white and black? By *their* rule, we are entitled to representation of every slave in our land; and if they will give us this, we shall dispute with them no longer. The majority will then be with us. God forbid, Sir, that I should propose this seriously. I am as ready as any gentleman here, to disclaim every idea of the sort. I use the argument only to shew to what consequences this demand, founded on a supposed law of nature, must inevitably conduct us. Gentlemen may not claim the benefit of a rule, which will not bear to be pushed to its legitimate results; a rule which they themselves are compelled to abandon, at the very first step which they take into practical Government.

If then, there be no inherent virtue in *numbers* which confers this right, in what else does it consist? I have heard elsewhere, of another ground on which gentlemen have been pleased to rest it, and it is now distinctly announced by the able gentleman from Frederick. It is *physical power*. I do not understand the gentleman from Frederick in the objectionable sense, of which his language was probably susceptible. He did not mean that this power in a majority would or ought to be applied, in the actual Government; it is impossible to attribute to the clear head and sound principles of that gentleman, any meaning so uncourteous as a threat. I understood him, as he meant to be understood, in this sense only:- Every law implies the necessity of some sanction; force is the only sanction in the case before us, and as this force is presumed to reside in the greatest degree, in a majority, it follows that a majority only can apply the sanction, and of course that a majority ought to give the law.

Here, Sir, we are under the necessity of looking back upon the preceding proposition. From what sources are we to derive this majority? I have endeavored to shew that by nature, all are equal and possess equal rights. Then women and children must be counted *here* also, as well as men. Now, we learn from good authority, that throughout the universe, the sexes rank to each other as thirteen and fourteen. Suppose then, the females to be all ranged on one side of the question, with a few children in their laps, and a few superannuated and decrepid men, at their sides. They may thus very well constitute a majority of the whole *number;* but will the *physical power* be with them? No Sir. That power has ever been found with personal strength, and intrepidity and skill. These qualities have at all times, and in all places, been an overmatch for mere undisciplined numbers. Here then is a case in which the majority do *not* possess the power of applying the sanction; and of course, the right to rule, which is supposed to follow the sanction, is in this case, with the *minority*. The case is quite as apt to occur, and quite as easy to be supposed, as that state of existence to which it refers, and from which gentlemen borrow their argument. And the necessary conclusion, upon the hypothesis assumed, is, that in one state of things a *majority* may have a right to rule, and in another state of things a *minority* may have that right; and this too, by the very same fixed and uniform law of nature!

To such absurdities are we inevitably driven when we attempt to apply principles deduced from a state of nature, to a state of society; a state which pre-supposes that nature with all her rights and all her laws, has been shaken off! Indeed, Sir, the whole reasoning is fallacious, because it is founded on a state of things which in all probability, never had existence at all. It goes back to a state prior to all history, and about which we know nothing beyond mere conjecture. The first accounts which we have of man, are of man in a social state. Wherever he has been found, and however rude his condition, he has been bound to his fellows by some form of association, in advance of a state of nature. If we may indulge any conjecture upon such a subject, the probability is that he was first urged into society, by a strong *feeling of property* implanted in his nature; by a feeling that he had, or at least, that he ought to have, a better title than another, to whatever his own labour had appropriated. The necessity of securing this right and protecting him in the enjoyment of it, in all probability, first suggested the idea of the social compact. Although property therefore, is strictly speaking the creature of society, yet a *feeling of property* was probably its creator. The result would be, that at the very moment that two human beings first came together, the social compact was formed. And gentlemen have fallen into another error also, of a kindred nature. They build their systems upon the notion of an abstract equality, for which there is no warrant in any thing we know of the history of man. Sir, I am about to use a borrowed idea; but it is valuable for its truth, and perfectly applicable to the subject. The first account that we have of man, is that contained in the Bible; and how will this notion of original equality stand, when tested by that orthodox book? Adam was the first of created beings;

Eve was created next; and the very fiat which brought her into existence, subjected her to the dominion of her husband. Here then was no equality. Cain was the first born of men, and at what period did he become the equal of his father? Was it at the moment of his birth, while he was yet scarcely conscious of his own existence, a helpless dependent upon the care of his parents? And if not *then*, at what age did this equality first attach? Was it at ten, or fifteen, or twenty-five, or thirty-five years of age? Where is the law, or the *doctrine* of nature, which enables us to say with certainty and precision, at what age the child becomes the equal of his father? Sir, the true meaning of the equality of men, as applicable to this subject, was happily expressed by the gentleman from Culpeper (Mr. Green) when he said that "all men are so far equal by the law of nature, that when they enter into a state of society, no one can claim a natural right to rule over another." And for the same reason, no ten men can claim a natural right to rule over any nine men.

The subject, Mr. Chairman, is scarcely worth the examination it has received. I will pursue it no farther, since I have no intention to give you a treatise on natural law, instead of an argument upon the practical subject of Government. I have thought it necessary to go thus far into an examination of the subject, because gentlemen have founded themselves upon what they are pleased to consider an axiom, that there is in a majority, an *a priori*, *inherent* and *indestructible* right to rule a minority, under all circumstances, and in every conceivable condition of things. And one of them at least has been understood by me, as referring this right to the law of nature; a law which he supposes, no society cannot repeal, and which therefore, is of original and universal authority. Surely this is a very great mistake. Nay Sir, there is proof enough before us that gentlemen themselves, who claim this right, and who seek to give it solemnity by referring it to the very law of our being, do not venture to carry it into the details of their own system. If there be a right in a majority of persons or of *white* persons, to rule a minority, upon what principle is it that the right of suffrage is restricted? *All* are counted, in making up the majority; and each one of the majority, ought of consequence, to possess a share in its rights. Why then do you not admit women to the polls? Nature has stamped no such inferiority upon that sex, as to disqualify it under all circumstances, for a safe and judicious exercise of the right of suffrage. And why exclude minors? Infants who have not acquired language, or whose intellects are not sufficiently unfolded to enable them to understand their own actions, may be excluded from the necessity of the case. But at what time, in the ordinary course of nature, do these disabilities cease? Gentlemen say, at the age of twenty-one years. And why so? Not certainly because nature declares it; for the faculties attain maturity at different periods, in different latitudes of the earth. In one latitude we are ripe at sixteen; in another, not until 30; and even among ourselves, we see many, under the age of twenty-one, who possess more wisdom and more power of general usefulness, than can be found in others of fifty; far more than in those who have approached their second childhood. What is there then, which indicates the precise period of twenty-one years, as the earliest at which these members of the ruling majority, may exercise the rights which belong to them? This, and this only: that the rule which is furnished by nature, is unfit for a state of society, and we are compelled, in our own defence, to adopt an arbitrary rule of our own, which is better suited to our actual condition. There is no one among us so wild and visionary, as to desire universal suffrage; and yet it is perfectly certain that, at the moment when you limit that right, in however small a degree, you depart from the *principle* that a majority shall rule. If you establish any disqualification whatever, there is no *natural necessity*, nor even a *moral certainty*, that a majority in any given community, will not come within the exception. And this state of things may by possibility, exist within every election district in the Commonwealth: and thus you establish a rule, with reference to the *entire body*, which is rejected in every *constituent member* of that body. Surely, gentlemen cannot claim the benefit of a principle, which will not bear to be pushed to its practical consequences; a principle which they themselves are obliged to desert as unwise, unsafe and impracticable, in the details of actual Government.

In truth, Mr. Chairman, *there are no original principles of Government at all.* Novel and strange as the idea may appear, it is nevertheless, strictly true, in the sense in which I announce it. There are no original principles, existing in the nature of things and independent of agreement, to which Government must of necessity conform, in order to be either legitimate or philosophical. The principles of Government, are those principles only, which the people who form the Government, choose to *adopt and apply to themselves.* Principles do not *precede*, but spring out of Government. If this should be considered a dangerous novelty in this age of improvement, when all old fashioned things are rejected as worthless; let us test the doctrine by reference to examples. In Turkey, the Government is centered in one man; in England, it resides in King, Lords, and Commons; and in the Republics of the United States, we profess to repose it in the people alone. The principles of all these Governments are essentially different; and yet will it be said that the Governments of Turkey and England are no Governments at all, or not legitimate Governments, because in them, the will of a majority does not give the rule? Or, will it be said, that our own Governments are not legitimate, because they do not conform to the despotic principles of Turkey, nor recognise the aristocracy of England? If there be these original principles at all, we must presume that they are uniform in themselves, and universal in their application. It will not do to say that there is one principle for one place, and another principle for another place. The conclusion resulting from the reasoning of gentlemen will be, that there is one Government in the world which is *really* a Government, rightful and legitimate; and all other forms of social compact, however long, or however firmly established, are no Governments at all. Every Government is legitimate which springs directly from the will of the people, or to which the people have consented to give allegiance. And I am not going too far, in asserting that Governments are free or otherwise, only in proportion as the people have been consulted in forming them, and as their rulers are directly responsible to them for the execution of their will. It matters not what form they assume, nor who are the immediate depositories of political power. It may suit the purposes of the people, as it once suited those of Rome, to invest all authority in a Dictator; and if the people choose this form of Government; if their interest and safety require that they shall submit to it, what original principle is there which renders it illegitimate? If the majority possess all power, they possess the power to *surrender* their power. And if it be just and wise that they should do so, it is still their own Government, and no one can impugn its legitimacy.

I have thus, Mr. Chairman, endeavored to prove, that there is not in nature, nor even in sound political science, any fundamental principle applicable to this subject, which is mandatory upon us. We are at perfect liberty to choose our own principle; to consult all the circumstances which attend our condition, and to mould our Government as our interests and necessities may require. We are now to ascertain what rule of representation, those interests and those necessities suggest, as wise, just and expedient.

I admit, as a general proposition, that in free Governments, power ought to be given to the majority; and why? The rule is founded in the idea that there is an identity, though not an *equality* of interests, in the several members of the body politic: in which case the presumption naturally arises, that the greater number possess the greater interest. But the rule no longer applies, when the reason of it fails. And here we should be careful to remember, that the question does not relate to the administration of an actual Government. It is not contended that the Legislature, when the Government shall go into operation, ought not to adopt the rule of a majority in acts of ordinary Legislation. The question before us, is prior to actual Government: it is not whether a majority shall rule in the Legislature, but *of what elements that majority shall be composed.* If the interests of the several parts of the Commonwealth were identical, it would be, we admit, safe and proper that a majority of *persons only* should give the rule of political power. But our interests are not identical, and the difference between us arises from property alone. We therefore contend that property ought to be considered, in fixing the basis of representation.

What, Sir, are the constituent elements of society? Persons *and property.* What are the subjects of Legislation? Persons *and property.* Was there ever a society seen on earth, which consisted only of men, women, and children? The very idea of society, carries with it the idea of property, as its necessary and inseparable attendant. History cannot show any form of the social compact, at any time, or in any place, into which property did not enter as a constituent element, nor one in which that element did not enjoy protection in a greater or less degree. Nor was there ever a society in which the protection once extended to property, was afterwards withdrawn, which did not fall an easy prey to violence and disorder. Society cannot exist without property; it constitutes the full half of its being. Take away all protection from property, and our next business is to cut each other's throats. All experience proves this. The safety of men depends on the safety of property; the rights of persons must mingle in the ruin of the rights of property. And shall it not then be protected? Sir, your Government cannot move an inch without property. Are you to have no political head? No Legislature to make laws? No Judiciary to interpret them? No Executive to enforce them? And if you are to have all these departments, will they render their services out of mere grace and favor, and for the honor and glory of the thing? Not in these money loving days, depend on it. If we would find patriotism thus disinterested, we must indeed, go back to a period prior to Bible history. And what are the subjects upon which the law-making power is called to act? Persons *and property.* To these two subjects, and not to one of them alone, is the business of legislation confined. And of these two, it may be fairly asserted that property is not only of *equal,* but even of *more* importance. The laws which relate to our personal actions, with reference to the body politic; which prescribe the duties which we owe to the public, or define and punish crime, are comparatively few in number, and simple in their provisions. And one half of these few find their best sanctions in public opinion. But the ramifications of the rights of property, are infinite. Volume upon volume, which few of us, I fear, are able to understand, are required to contain even the leading principles relating to them, and yet new relations are every day arising, which require continual interpositions of the Legislative power. If then, Sir, property is thus necessary to the very being of society; thus indispensable to every movement of Government; if it be that subject upon which Government chiefly acts; is it not, I would ask, entitled to such protection as shall be above all suspicion, and free from every hazard? It appears to me that I need only announce the proposition, to secure the assent of every gentleman present.

Sir, the obligations of man in his social state are two-fold; to bear arms, and to pay taxes for the support of Government. The obligation to bear arms, results from the duty which society owes him, to protect his rights of person. The society which protects me, I am bound to protect in return. The obligation to pay taxes, results from the protection extended to property. Not a protection against foreign enemies; not a protection by swords and bayonets merely; but a protection derived from a prompt and correct administration of justice; a protection against the violence, the fraud, or the injustice of my neighbor. In this protection, the owner of property is alone interested. Here, then, is the plain agreement between Government on the one hand, and the tax-paying citizen on the other. It is an agreement which results, of necessity, from the social compact; and when the consideration is fairly paid, how can you honestly withhold the equivalent? Indeed, gentlemen admit that property is entitled to protection; and that *our* property *is* entitled to it, when they offer us guarantees. I shall have occasion to speak of these by and by; at present I will only say, that although they are certainly offered in good faith, they would prove in practice, wholly unavailing.

Let us now inquire of *what kind*, this protection must be, if we would give it any value. I agree with the gentleman from Culpeper (Mr. Green) that it cannot be any thing short of a direct influence in the Government.

There is one consequence, supposed to result from our doctrine on this subject, which all the gentlemen opposed to us, seem to contemplate with a sort of horror: "What," say they, "will you balance money against the bone and sinew of the country? Will you say that fifty men on this side of the mountain, shall be counted against one hundred and fifty on the other?"

Sir, no man supposes that property should be represented *eo nomine;* it would be grossly absurd to place a bag of guineas upon your table, and call it a constituent entitled to representation. We do not propose to represent money, but the *rights and interests which spring from the possession of money*. This is not a metaphysical refinement, an unmeaning distinction. It is easily comprehended, and it ought to remove every shadow of odium from our proposition, considered in this view. If men enter into the social compact upon unequal terms; if one man brings into the partnership, his rights of person alone, and another brings into it, equal rights of person and all the rights of property beside, can they be said to have an equal interest in the common stock? Shall not he who has most at stake; who has, not only a *greater* interest, but a *peculiar* interest in society, possess an authority proportioned to that interest, and adequate to its protection? I certainly do not mean to say, that the right of suffrage in the *individual* ought to be in proportion to his property; that if a man owning one thousand dollars is entitled to one vote, a man owning two thousand is entitled to two votes. I do not expect to be so understood after the admission which I have already made, in announcing the precise limit to which my proposition extends. Where there is an identity of interest, no difference should be made in the rights of the voter, in consequence of a difference in the extent or degree of that interest. But where there is *not* this identity; where there are different and *distinct* interests, existing in masses sufficiently large to form important objects in the Government, (as I shall presently show is the precise case before us,) there the rule emphatically applies.

The view which we are now taking, presents a sufficient answer to an argument urged the other day by the eloquent gentleman from Norfolk, (Mr. Taylor.) He told us that representative and constituent were correlative terms: that there could be no notion of a constituent without a power of choice, and that it would be absurd to attribute this power to a mass of metal. Sir, money is in no sense, the constituent. Man is the constituent, and money has no other concern in the matter, than to regulate and graduate the rights and powers, which man, the constituent shall enjoy and exercise. Such a constituent has more interest in the community than another, and therefore he has, a *natural* right, if gentlemen please; certainly a *just* right to a greater weight in the management of its concerns.

Here Mr. Upshur gave way for a motion of Mr. Taylor of Norfolk, that the Committee rise. The gentleman, he said, must feel exhausted, and it was not probable that he could finish his very able argument during the present sitting of the Committee:

with a view, therefore, to the accommodation of the gentleman, as well as to allow the Committee time for further reflection, he moved that it now rise.

The motion prevailed, the Committee rose, and thereupon the Convention immediately adjourned.

WEDNESDAY, October 28, 1829.

The Convention met at eleven o'clock, and its sitting was opened with prayer by the Rev. Mr. Sykes, of the Methodist Church.

Mr. Fitzhugh, from the Committee on Compensation, reported, in part, as follows:

The Committee appointed to enquire into, and report on the compensation to be allowed the officers of the Convention, have agreed to the following resolution:

Resolved, That five dollars per day be allowed each of the Clerks of this Convention, for every day's actual attendance on said Committees. Which was agreed to by the Convention.

On motion of Mr. Doddridge, the Convention then proceeded to the Order of the Day, and again went into Committee of the Whole, Mr. P. P. Barbour in the Chair; and the question still being on the following amendment, proposed by Mr. Green of Culpeper, to the first resolution, reported by the Committee on the Legislative Department of Government, which resolution reads as follows, viz:

Resolved, That in the apportionment of representation, in the House of Delegates, regard should be had to the white population exclusively, viz: to strike out the word "*exclusively*," and to insert in lieu thereof "*and taxation combined*."

Judge Upshur continued his argument.

Mr. Chairman,—I have to express my acknowledgments to the Committee for the indulgence extended to me on yesterday; an indulgence which I should not have asked, had it not been necessary.

And now, it may perhaps, be proper, before entering further into the discussion, that I should recapitulate, and I will do it in as few words as possible, the leading propositions which it has been my object to prove. And I do this only that the continuity of the argument, may be preserved in the minds of such gentlemen as may have been pleased to attend to it. I commenced with the broad proposition that there is no original, abstract, *a priori* right, in the majority of any community, to control the minority. That if such a right did exist at all, it must be either by positive agreement, or by the law of nature. As it was not pretended that it existed by agreement, I then endeavored to demonstrate that it was not derived from another and a higher source. I admitted as a general proposition, (an *abstract* proposition, if gentlemen prefer the term,) that it might possibly be a safe *general* rule, that the majority should govern. But here permit me to remark on the doctrine I subsequently advanced, that the allowing a portion of political power to property, does by no means violate that rule. This may perhaps appear somewhat paradoxical, but it is susceptible of proof, without going very deeply into metaphysics. The question is as to what time the principle shall apply. If it applies only after the Government has been established, then those who established the Government, have already determined in what form the right of the majority shall be exerted; and, if they have said, that the majority which governs shall be constituted in part by wealth, and in part by the number of people, the rule, that the majority shall govern, is not violated. But prior to the existence of any Government, the question is, what rules it is *wisest* to adopt. I am willing to admit, that after the Government has been established, and put into operation, it is a safe and proper rule, that the will of a majority shall regulate the administration of its affairs; but this admission leaves the question still open, as to the materials of which that majority shall be composed.

I further endeavored to prove, that it was a fair and just principle that property is entitled to protection: first, because it is an important constituent element of society; without it, society could not exist for a moment, and if it did exist, could not move a single inch: Secondly, because, in the operations of Government, as they are concerned in legislation, the most numerous and most interesting class of subjects, on which the power is to be exerted, are all derived from property, and intimately connected with it. It must, therefore, necessarily receive protection, both in the form, and in the fundamental principles of Government, of which, property is always a part.

I will now proceed to the further development of this part of the subject. Sir, it is worthy of inquiry, in what the principles for which we contend differ from those, in defence of which, our ancestors of the American Colonies, felt themselves authorised to enter into that great and arduous struggle, by which they shook off the yoke of the mother country. What was, in the early days of the Revolution, the topic of complaint, which filled every mouth, and troubled every heart in these Colonies? It was the attempt to tax the people of the Colonies, without allowing them any voice in the matter. Here, then, is our doctrine already established: a doctrine testified, at the utmost hazard, by all the people of this country, that those who pay the taxes, ought alone to have the power of imposing them. They declared it to be oppression of the very worst kind, that they should be compelled to pay a tax, while they had no voice in imposing it. But why was this doctrine any more true, when applied to America and England, than in its bearing on matters now before us? If it be a dictate of eternal justice, that those who pay a tax ought to have a voice in the imposition of it, why is it not as just now, and here, as it was then, and there? This is that protection which property claims, and insists upon: and which it has always enjoyed, under every Government, which has proved either lasting or wise. And why does it require this particular form of protection? In reply, I ask, when you lay a tax, by what rule is it to be imposed? By the ability of the taxed party to pay; and that ability is regulated by the extent of his property. But, who can ascertain the extent of that ability, but the party himself? What right has another to judge of it? What right has the man who owns no land, to say to his neighbour, "you own a large and splendid farm, well stocked with slaves; you ought to pay a tax of a thousand dollars?" Would you not call it very presumptuous in him to undertake to measure the extent and value of your property, and to fix the price at which you ought to purchase the protection of it from Government? Would you not reply to him, "you cannot tell the labour, care and anxiety, attending the possession of this property, nor form any idea at what cost it is, that I derive the little income I receive from this soil. You do not know how small that income is; and would, no doubt, be surprised to learn, that splendid as it seems to you, it does not yield me one half the sum at which you say it ought to be taxed?" And would not this be a fair answer? It is an admitted principle, that property must pay for its own protection; but who can tell what that protection is worth, so well as he who receives it? Another man knows little, or nothing about the matter. He may impose upon it a tax which is greater than its annual income; and if it be an annual tax, the owner would of course rather surrender his property, than consent to pay it.

Again: I must remind the gentlemen, that they have admitted the principle, that property must be protected, and protected in the very form now proposed; they are obliged to admit it. It would be a wild and impracticable scheme of Government, which did not admit it. Among all the various and numerous propositions, lying upon your table, is there one which goes the length of proposing *universal suffrage*? There is none. Yet this subject is in direct connexion with that. Why do you not admit a pauper to vote? He is a person: he counts one in your numerical majority. In rights strictly personal, he has as much interest in the Government as any other citizen. He is liable to commit the same offences, and to become exposed to the same punishments as the rich man. Why, then, shall he not vote? Because, thereby, he would receive an influence over property; and all who own it, feel it to be unsafe, to put the power of controlling it, into the hands of those who are not the owners. If you go on population alone, as the basis of representation, you will be obliged to go the length of giving the elective franchise to every human being over twenty-one years; yes, and under twenty-one years, on whom your penal laws take effect; an experiment, which has met with nothing but utter and disastrous failure, wherever it has been tried. No, Mr. Chairman: Let us be consistent. Let us openly acknowledge the truth; let us boldly take the bull by the horns, and incorporate this influence of property as a leading principle in our Constitution. We cannot be otherwise consistent with ourselves.

I was surprised to hear the assertion made by gentlemen, on the other side, that property can protect itself. What is the meaning of such a proposition? Is there any thing in property, to exert this self-protecting influence, but the political power which always attends it? Is there any thing in mere property alone, in itself considered, to exert any such influence? Can a bag of golden guineas, if placed upon that table, protect itself? Can it protect its owner? I do not know what magic power the gentlemen allude to. If it is to have no influence in the Government, what and where is its power to protect itself? Perhaps the power to buy off violence; to buy off the barbarian who comes to lay it waste, by a reward which will but invite a double swarm of barbarians to return next year. Is this one of the modes alluded to? This, I am well assured, never entered into the clear mind of the very intelligent gentleman from Frederick (Mr. Cooke.) How else, then, may property be expected to protect itself? It may be answered, by the influence which it gives to its owner. But in what channels is that influence exerted? It is the influence which prevents the poor debtor from going against the will of his creditor; which forbids the dependent poor man from exerting any thing like *independence*, either in conduct or opinion; an influence which appeals to avarice on both sides, and depends for its effect on rousing the worst and basest of passions, and destroying all freedom of will, all independence of opinion. Is it desirable to establish such an influence as this? an influence which marches to power through the direct road to the worst, and most monstrous of aristocracies, the aristocracy of the purse? an influence which derives its effect from the corruption of all principle, the blinding of the judgment and the prostration of all moral feeling? and whose power is built on that form of aristocracy, most of all to be dreaded in a free Government? The gentleman appeals to fact, and says that property always *has* protected itself, under every form of Government. The fact is not admitted. Property never has protected itself long, except by the power which it possessed in the Government. There may, indeed, exist in some part of the world, a form of Government like that which the gentlemen wish to establish in the amended Constitution, where this influence is excluded; but if there does, it is utterly unknown to me.

Mr. Chairman, I will submit to the gentlemen; not tauntingly, but respectfully, and by way of illustration, this proposition. Will they agree to pay all the taxes and to take all the representation? Sir, they will not accept the offer; nor ought they to accept it: it is not seriously made. But still it may serve in some degree to show how necessary is the connexion between the duty of paying the tax, and the right of imposing it; at the same time that it will indicate the only point on which we feel alarm.

Every view, Mr. Chairman, which I am capable of taking of this subject, has led me to the conclusion that property is entitled to its influence in Government. But if this be not true as a *general proposition, it is true as to us.*

Gentlemen have fallen into a great error both in their reasoning and in their conclusion, by considering the subject before us, as if we were now for the first time, entering into a social compact. If we stood in the nakedness of nature, with no rights but such as are strictly personal, we should all come together upon precisely equal ground. But such is not the case. We cannot now enter into a new compact upon the basis of original equality; we bring more than our fair proportion, into the common stock. For fifty-four years we have been associated together, under the provisions of an actual Government. A great variety of rights and interests, and a great variety of feelings dear to the heart and connected with those rights and interests, have grown up among us. They have grown up and flourished under a Government which stood pledged to protect them; that Government itself, was but a system of pledges, interchangeably given among those who were parties to it, that all the rights and all the interests which it invited into existence, should be protected by the power of the whole. Under this system, our property has been acquired; and we felt safe in the acquisition, because under the provisions of that system, we possessed a power of self-protection. And by whom was that system ordained? Not indeed, by the same *men* who are now here assembled, but by the same *community*, which is now here represented. It was the *people of Virginia* who gave us these pledges; and it is the people of Virginia who now claim a right to withdraw them. Sir, can it be fair, or just, or honourable, to do this? The rights and interests which you are now seeking to prostrate, you yourselves invited into being. Under your own distributions of political power, you gave us an assurance that our property should be safe, for you put the protection of it into our own hands. With what justice or propriety then, can you now say to us, that the rights and interests which you have thus fostered until they have become the chief pillars of your strength, shall now be prostrated; melted into the general mass, and be re-distributed, according to your will and pleasure? Nay, Sir, you do not even leave us the option whether to come into your measures or not. With all these rights, and all these interests, and all these feelings, we are to be *forced*, whether willing or unwilling; we are to be *forced* by the unyielding power of a majority, into a compact which violates them all! Is there not, Sir, something of *violence* and *fraud* in this? Gentlemen are too courteous to suppose me capable of charging iniquity of this sort, upon them. They have too just an estimate, both of themselves and of me, to attribute to me so offensive a thought. If I really intended to express it, it might indeed expose me to just censure; but it would be worthless as an argument. I urge this view of the subject, because I feel entirely assured, that if gentlemen can discern either fraud or violence in their measures, they will themselves, be the first to abandon them.

I am sensible, Sir, that there is nothing in this view of the subject, unless the rights and interests to which I have alluded, are of a peculiar and distinctive character. What then are they? I purposely wave all subjects of minor importance, as too inconsiderable to give any rule. But a peculiar interest, and a great, and important, and leading interest, is presented in our slaves; an interest which predominates throughout the Eastern divisions of the State, whilst it is of secondary consequence West of the Blue Ridge. And what, let us now inquire, are its claims to consideration?

Will you not be surprised to hear, Sir, that the slave population of Virginia pays 30 per cent. of the whole revenue derived from taxation? Did there ever exist in any community, a separate and peculiar interest, of more commanding magnitude? But this is not all. It affords almost the whole productive labour of one half of the Commonwealth. What difference does it make whether a certain amount of labour is brought into the common stock, by four hundred thousand slaves, or four hundred thousand freemen? The gain is the same to the aggregate wealth; which is but another name for the aggregate power, of the State. And here permit me to remark, that of all the subjects of taxation which ever yet existed, this has been the most oppressively dealt with. You not only tax our slaves as property, but you also tax *their labour*. Let me illustrate the idea by an example. The farmer who derives his income from the labour of slaves, pays a tax for those slaves, considered as property. With that income so derived, he purchases a carriage, or a horse, and these again are taxed. You first tax the slave who makes the money, and then you tax the article which the money procures. Is not this a great injustice; a gross inequality? No such tax is laid upon the white labourer of the West, and yet the product of his labour is of no more importance to the general welfare, than the same product from the labour of slaves. Here then, is a striking peculiarity in our property; a peculiarity which sujects it to double impositions, and which therefore, demands a double security.

There is yet Sir, another view of this subject which is not only of importance with reference to the immediate topic under consideration, but which furnishes a strong argument against the change which gentlemen contemplate. One eleventh* of the power which we possess in the national councils, is derived from slaves. We obtain that power by counting three-fifths of the whole number, in apportioning representation among the several States. Sir, we live in times of great political changes. Some new doctrine or other is broached almost every day; and it is impossible to foresee what changes in our political condition, a single year may bring about. Suppose a proposition should be made to alter the Constitution of the United States in the particular now under consideration; what could Virginia say, after embracing such a basis as gentlemen propose? Would she not be told by those who abhor this species of property, and who are restive under the power which it confers, "you have abandoned this principle in your own institutions, and with what face can you claim it, in your connexions with us?" What reply could she make to such an appeal as this? Sir, the moral power of Virginia has always been felt, and deeply felt, in all the important concerns of this nation; and that power has been derived from the unchanging consistency of her principles, and her invincible firmness in maintaining them. Is she now prepared to surrender it, in pursuit of a speculative principle of doubtful propriety, at best, and certainly not demanded by any thing in her present condition? If you adopt the combined basis proposed by the amendment, this danger is avoided. You may then reply to the taunting question above supposed, "we have *not* abandoned our principle; on the contrary, we have extended it. Instead of three-fifths, *all* our slaves are considered in our representation. It is true, we do not count them as *men*, but their influence is still preserved, as *taxable subjects*. The principle is the same, although the modes of applying it may be different. We are *not* inconsistent with ourselves." To my mind, there is much force in this argument, and I think that the gentlemen opposed to us, to whom the influence of our common State is as dear as it is to us, cannot but feel and acknowledge it. The topic is fruitful of imposing reflections; but I will not pursue it farther.

I have thus endeavored to prove, Mr. Chairman, that whether it be right as a general principle or not, that property should possess an influence in Government, it is certainly right as to us. It is right, because *our* property, so far as slaves are concerned, is *peculiar;* because it is of imposing magnitude; because it affords almost a full half of the productive labour of the State; because it is exposed to peculiar impositions, and therefore to peculiar hazards; and because it is the interest of the whole Commonwealth, that its power should not be taken away. I admit that we have no danger to apprehend, except from oppressive and unequal taxation; no other injustice can reasonably be feared. It is impossible that any free Government, can establish an open and palpable inequality of rights. Resistance would be the necessary consequence; and thus the evil would soon cure itself. But the power of taxation often works insidiously. The very victim who feels its oppression, may be ignorant of the source from which it springs.

Gentlemen tell us that our alarms are unfounded; that even if we should give them power to tax us at their will and pleasure, there is no danger that they will ever abuse it. They urge many arguments to prove this; and among the rest, they tell us that there is no *disposition* among them, to practice injustice towards their eastern brethren. Sir, I do firmly believe it. It gives me pleasure to say, that in all my associations with the people of the west, I have never had reason to doubt either their justice or their generosity. And if they can give us a sure guarantee that the same just and kind feelings which they now entertain, shall be transmitted as an inheritance to their posterity forever, we will ask no other security? But who can answer

* Judge Upshur corrects a mistake in his calculation. The proportion is about one sixth.

for the generations that are to come. It is not for this day only, but I trust for distant ages, that we are now laboring; we are very unwisely employed, if we are not making provision for far distant times. And can gentlemen feel any assurance, that under no change which time may work in our political condition, there shall be found any clashing of interests, or any conflict of passions? Will they, who are just *now* be *always* just, under whatever temptations of interest, or whatever excitements of the feelings? Shall there be no jealousies in time to come? No resentments? Nothing to *mislead the judgment*, even if it does not corrupt the feelings? Even if no *disposition* to oppress us should exist, how can we be assured that the people of the west shall view their own acts in all time to come, in the same light in which they may appear to us? That which *they* may consider mere justice, may appear to us as the worst oppression. Surely it is not surprising that we should claim a right to say, whether we are oppressed or not.

Again.—We are told that slave-holders cannot be in danger, because in point of fact, they comprise a majority of our white population. If so, it would seem to follow that no good objection could be urged to the basis proposed by us; it is the basis required by the interests of the majority, and therefore right by our opponents' own rule. But while the fact as stated, is literally true, the conclusion deduced from it, is not so. How is this majority made up? By counting the slave-holders in all parts of the State; by taking a few, scattered here and there, through the western counties, where slaves are scarcely considered at all, and if considered, are absorbed in other and greater interests, and adding them to the numbers on this side the mountain, where slaves constitute the leading and most important interest. I need not press this view of the subject. It must be manifest to all, that the slave-holder of the east cannot calculate on the co-operation of the slave-holder of the west, in any measure calculated to protect that species of property, against demands made upon it by other interests, which to the western slave-holder, are of more importance and immediate concern.

We are told also, that slave population is rapidly increasing to the west, and that in a few years it will constitute a predominant interest there. If so, Sir, the same few years will, upon the principles of our own basis, transfer to the west, the very power which they are now seeking through another channel. They cannot lose more by waiting for this power, than we shall lose in the same time, by surrendering it. But, Sir, although it is admitted that slave population is increasing to the west, yet its increase is by a *continually decreasing ratio*. In the period between 1800 and 1810, the ratio of increase was sixty-five and a half; between 1810 and 1820, it was forty-six; and between 1820 and 1829, it was twenty-eight. Whence is this? It arises from causes which cannot for ages be removed. There exists in a great portion of the west, a rooted antipathy to this species of population; the habits of the people are strongly opposed to it. With them, personal industry, and a reliance on personal exertion, is the order of society. They know how little slave labour is worth; while their feelings as freemen, forbid them to work by the side of a slave. And besides, Sir, their vicinity to non-slave-holding States, must forever render this sort of property precarious and insecure. It will not do to tell me that Ohio no longer gives freedom, nor even shelter, to the runaway; that Pennsylvania is tired of blacks, and is ready to aid in restoring them to their owners. The moral sentiment of these States is against slavery; and that influence will assuredly be felt, notwithstanding the geographical line or narrow river, which may separate them from us. And again, Sir, the course of industry in the west, does not require slave labour; slaves will always be found in the grain-growing and tobacco country alone. This is not now the character of the western country, nor can it be, until a general system of roads and canals, shall facilitate their access to market. And when that time shall arrive, the worst evils which we apprehend will have been experienced; for it is to *make* these very roads and canals, that our taxes are required.

I think Sir, it must be manifest by this time, unless indeed, my labour has been wholly thrown away, that property is entitled to protection, and that *our* property imperiously demands *that kind of protection* which flows from the possession of power. Gentlemen admit that our property is peculiar, and that it requires protection, but they deny to it the power to protect itself. And what equivalent do they offer to us? The best, I own, which it is in their power to devise; and it cannot be doubted that they offer it in perfect sincerity and good faith. It is due to them to say this, but it is also due to us to say that they can give us *no* security, independent of political power. They offer us Constitutional guarantees; but of what value will they be to us in practice? No paper guarantee was ever yet worth any thing, unless the whole, or at least a majority of the community, were interested in maintaining it. And this is a sufficient reply to an idea of the gentleman from Norfolk, (Mr. Taylor.) "Will you," said he, "trust your lives and liberties to the guarantees of the Constitution, and will you not also trust your property?" Sir, every man in the community is interested in the preservation of life and liberty. But what is the case before us? A guarantee is offered us by that majority who claim to possess all power, and who have a direct and strong interest to violate their own pledges. In effect, it amounts to this. Gentlemen are indeed, ready to give us their bond, provided we will permit *them* to say whether they shall pay it or not. No guarantee can be worth a rush, if the very men who give it, have the power to take it away. Suppose your guarantee shall be violated, to whom are we to look for redress? Will the majority hold themselves responsible to the minority, for an abuse of their powers? To whom shall our complaints be addressed; on whom shall we call to relieve us from the unjust burthens which bear us down to the earth? On none, Sir, but the very men who have imposed them. We may appeal from Cæsar to Cæsar himself, and that is the only sanction which is given to this law for our security.

But let us examine the guarantees which are offered. The first is a Constitutional provision, that personal property shall never be taxed, except in a given ratio to land. The first objection to this is, that it is wholly unphilosophical; and must depend altogether upon accident for its fitness, so far as slaves are concerned. There is no fixed and uniform ratio between the value of slaves and of land. So far as labour is concerned, there may be indeed, something like a ratio: for the value of land itself, and of the labour which renders land productive, depend very much upon the same causes; and of course are subject to like fluctuations. But the value of slaves as an article of property; and it is in that view only, that they are legitimate subjects of taxation; depends much on the state of the market abroad. In this view, it is the value of land *abroad*, and not of land *here*, which furnishes the ratio. It is well known to us all, that nothing is more fluctuating than the value of slaves. A late law of Louisiana reduced their value 25 per cent. in two hours after its passage was known. If it should be our lot, as I trust it will be, to acquire the country of Texas, their price will rise again. Thus it appears, that their value depends on causes wholly extrinsic to us, and in no degree connected with the value of our soil.

But, even if this ratio were suitable, it may be useful to inquire in what manner we are to arrive at it, and what would be its operation upon society. You must either value the *whole* personal property of the country, or only *such parts* of it as you propose to tax. Let us view the subject in each of these aspects. I venture to affirm, that there cannot be a measure more directly hostile to the genius of free Governments, than that which proposes to value the whole property of every citizen who lives under it. Who is there that would submit to the exercise of such an inquisitorial power? Nay, can any measure be more *unwise* among a people essentially commercial in their character. Credit is necessary to the very existence of trade. It will not do to proclaim to the world, the uttermost farthing which a trading man is worth. It is not his interest that it should be known: this might, and in most cases, *would* frustrate the best planned speculations. But is it *practicable* to make this valuation? Will you permit the assessor to go into your chambers; to search among your wife's apparel for concealed treasure; to demand your purse, that he may count the dollars it contains? And, if you will not give him authority equal to all this, and more, what assurance can you have that his valuation is correct? You will compel the tax-payer to swear. And suppose he will *not* swear? Are you to excuse him from paying his tax because he will not tell you how much it ought to be; or will you punish him for not telling? Subject him to *peine forte et dure*, for resisting the impertinent exercise of an inquisitorial power? But suppose he *will* swear, and what then? The humble farmer who owes no man a shilling, and who is silently laying up his little gains from year to year, careless of the reputation of wealth, has a direct interest to put the smallest possible value, upon his taxable property. The less the assessor thinks him worth, the less will he have to pay. The merchant who lives by credit, and whose profits depend on the opinion which others may entertain of his wealth, has a direct interest to make the amount as large as possible. Here then is an invitation to perjury on both sides; a fiscal law whose direct tendency is, to corrupt the purity of the main channel of public justice! Nay, this is not all. Even if the citizen be *disposed* to swear to the truth, it is not always possible for him to do so. Suppose that A holds the bond of B for a thousand dollars, and that B holds the property for which the bond was given; to which of the two shall that sum be assessed? Not to B, because it is a debt which he owes; not to A, because the debt may never be paid. B may indeed, be taxed for the property which the bond has purchased, but A cannot be taxed for its equivalent, unless he will swear not only that the debt is due, but that the debtor is able to pay it. Who is there that would venture to do this? Not one.

Let us now take the other alternative. Instead of valueing *all* the property of the Commonwealth, let us suppose the valuation to be made of such articles only, as you propose to tax. Unless property is to have a fixed, permanent, and unalterable value: a value which is to experience no change among all the changes which are going on around us: you will be driven to the necessity of making your valuations so frequent, that the expenses of collection would add seriously to the burthen of taxation. And you could not do otherwise, than make them frequent, for property is continually changing hands; and he who, to-day, is liable to a heavy tax, may not, to-morrow, possess a single taxable subject. This Sir, must necessarily prove a fruitful source of discontent and murmuring. There is no man, whose justice is so unimpeachable, or whose skill is so great, as to satisfy every one, in the discharge of this delicate duty. Even in this view, the plan must be pronounced altogether unwise. But at what time is the valuation to be made? You must make it either at the moment of passing your tax law, or before, or after it. If at *the same time*, the Legislature themselves must be the assessors? Here then you have all the play in your own hands. It is the same to me, whether you value my property at two hundred dollars, and tax me five per cent. or value it at one hundred dollars, and tax me ten per cent. I pay the same sum in both cases. Of what value then, is your guarantee, if the same power which *taxes* my property, shall possess the right to *value* it? But, suppose your valuation to be made by a different power, and *before* the tax law is passed? What articles shall be valued? There is no law to guide the assessor; no law which declares what articles you mean to tax, and what you do not mean to tax. The consequence is, that every thing must be valued: the same impertinent scrutiny which I have already supposed, must be made in this case also; a scrutiny which would not fail to raise up more than one Wat Tyler in every county of the Commonwealth. But there is yet another horn of the dilemma. Suppose your valuation made, *after* the tax law is passed. It is the peculiar office of that law to fix upon the taxed subject, an ad valorem value: and this I presume, must always be regulated by the wants of the country. But how can you tell what rate per centum on property, is necessary to raise a given sum, unless the value of that property is previously ascertained? Either way, therefore, this scheme must be abandoned as wholly impracticable.

The next guarantee which gentlemen offer us, is a check on the power of appropriation. Much of the reasoning which has already been urged, would tend to prove that *this* also, would afford us no protection whatever. For myself, however, I desire no such guarantee; I should regret to see such a restraint imposed upon the power of the Legislature. My principle is this: As the payer of the tax, I have a right to be the judge of my ability to pay, and of the value of that protection *for which* I pay. But when my money has gone *rightfully* into the public fund, God forbid that it should not be applied wherever it may be most needed. It would rejoice me personally, to see every cent of it contributing to useful improvements beyond the mountain. I do not want any part of it back again; let it go wherever it will do the most good.

These, Sir, are the only Constitutional provisions which are offered us, in lieu of that power which we claim, as belonging of right to our greater stake in the Government, and as rendered necessary by the hazards to which our property is exposed. The conclusion to which I have arrived, (and I congratulate the Committee that I am fast drawing to a close,) is this: It is necessary to the well being, and even to the very existence of society, that property should be protected; it cannot in any case, and least of all, in *our own case*, hope for protection, except in the power of protecting itself; and no adequate substitute for that power, has been, or can be offered, in any other form of Constitutional provision. And now, permit me to ask, with whom can this power be most *safely* deposited? I grant, Sir, that gentlemen opposed to us, are equally patriotic in their feelings; equally just in their purposes, and equally sincere in their declarations, with ourselves. Still, I ask, even upon the very principle of this equality, where can the political power of this Commonwealth, be most *safely* deposited? So far as rights of person are concerned, we are all precisely equal, and the slave-holder can have no imaginable motive to do injustice in that respect. In the exercise of the tax-laying power, from which alone, injustice is to be apprehended, he has not the power to make any injurious discrimination. Among all the articles which have ever yet been made the subjects of taxation within this Commonwealth, which of them is not found on this side of the mountain, in just and fair proportion, at least? How, then, can we tax the west, without also taxing ourselves, in the same mode, and in just proportion? But reverse the case. There is not in the west, in any considerable degree, *one* species of property which constitutes the full half of our wealth, and which has always presented a ready subject for taxation. Give the power to the west, and will there be no temptation to abuse it? no temptation to shake off the public burthens from themselves, and throw an unjust proportion of them upon the slave-holder? Sir, there is much in this view of the subject. I am not indulging in mere speculation and conjecture. The experiment has been actually tried. For fifty-four years, the taxing power has been with with us, and who can say that it has ever been abused? The gentleman from Frederick (Mr. Cooke) himself, has admitted that we have never abused it. I heard the admission with great pleasure; it was honourable to his candour, and valuable to us, for the source from which it sprung. Why, then, change this deposit of power, which has been thus justly and safely exercised for more than half a century? Shall we, for the sake of mere theoretical principles, or speculative doctrines, throw our interests and our safety, upon new and hazardous experiments? Let us not forget, Sir, that after all, Government is a practical thing, and *that* Government is best which is best in its practical results. There is no end of speculative systems. The world has been full of them, from Plato, down through Harrington and Moore, and a host who succeeded them, even to the prolific bureaux of the French revolutionists. Of all their schemes, not one has ever been reduced to practice, in any part of the world. Experience is the best guide in Government. That guide we have; let us not shut our eyes to the lights which it affords us. For more than half a century, the political power of this Commonwealth, has been in the hands which now hold it. During all that time, it has not been abused. Is it then without cause, that I ask for a good reason why it should now be taken away?

Mr. DODDRIDGE now rose and addressed the Committee in answer to Judges Green and Upshur, as follows:

Mr. Chairman,—Although I had not the least expectation of embarking in this discussion, at the present time, yet seeing no one disposed to reply to the argument just concluded, (Judge Upshur's) I feel myself irresistibly invoked to submit a few remarks, in answer both to the gentleman from Northampton (Judge Upshur) and to the gentleman from Culpeper (Judge Green.) From want of proper time for arrangement, my remarks will be more desultory than I could wish, and I fear too diffuse for my own purpose, which is brevity in this debate. Having been the mover of the resolution under consideration in the Legislative Committee, I should not feel myself justified in permitting a vote to be taken until further discussion, which it is both my wish and my hope to elicit. In pursuing this subject, I feel myself both relieved and delighted, by the frank and friendly course of the gentlemen from Northampton and Culpeper, and particularly by that sincerity which the former displayed towards those opposed to him. Both gentlemen have furnished an example to us which I hope to imitate, while they have lessened our labours by such a candid statement of the principles relied on to support the amendment under consideration, as leaves us no room for doubt.

The gentleman from Northampton, yesterday, carried us back to the original state of man, in order, thence, to deduce the elements of the social state. His remarks were of such a general character, as not to require from me a close or critical examination. So far as the natural or supposed savage state of man has been referred to, the effort is entitled to the reproof of the late Judge Ashurst, in which the gentleman from Northampton more forcibly seems to concur. By both, this course is condemned as a vain effort to end our researches into the present rights and condition of society, in that rude chaos from which society is supposed to have originally sprung. I agree with the gentleman from Northampton, that if man ever existed in a savage state, in which he was under no control of Government, we must go back to a period anterior to Bible history, to find him. Although the barbarous tribes on our borders obey no written code, they have their unwritten laws, to which they yield obedience; which they not only permit to exist, but assist to execute. In our wilderness, we find not that supposed state of savage life, to which in disquisitions of this kind, reference is so often made. If this forced state of man ever existed, I will agree with the gentleman from Northampton, that, what he calls a "feeling of property," may have been one of the strongest inducements for leaving it, and for seeking in social life, and under a social compact, security for that property. This security consisted in the force of society, and it was for this, that man subjected himself to the restraints of the social compact; and as, in the nature of things, this force abides with the majority, man and his property became subject to their will. Of this position, I will say more hereafter, when I shall notice the gentleman's views of the rights of majorities, and contrast them with, what he supposes to be, those of minorities.

The gentleman from Northampton has said, that our Constitution is a compact made by all, for the benefit of all; that if there was in the majority a right to govern and control society, it must be derived, either from the law of nature, or from a Conventional source; and if from the latter, we must look for it in our written Constitution.

Here the gentleman first touched Virginia ground, and alluded to Virginia history; and here it is my purpose to meet him, and to follow him with frankness through each postulate maintained in his most able and eloquent argument.

Although not for the purpose of questioning its legal obligation, I deny the very first assumption of fact stated by the gentleman. The Constitution of Virginia is not a pact "made by all, for the benefit of all." It is well known, that the present Constitution was got up in a time of difficulty and danger. It was adopted as an expedient for existing circumstances, to serve the purposes of the time, and not looked upon as an instrument which would meet the wants and bear the test of experience for future ages. So far from all the members of society having had an agency in making this Constitution, none were, even, consulted except freeholders, and those only of a certain class, holding fifty acres of cultivated, or one hundred of uncultivated land; the property qualification then, being double what it is now. The Convention which made the election law under which that of 1776 was elected, was no other than the last House of Burgesses elected under the Colonial Constitution. When they were dissolved by an act of regal authority, they were reduced to the condition of so many private gentlemen freeholders. They possessed at least the confidence of the freeholding class of the community, of which their recent elections to the House of Burgesses was evidence. To the condition of private gentlemen they were constitutionally reduced; for the very act by which they were dissolved, was that by which the whole regal Government, of which they were but a part, was ended. Before their dissolution, they constituted only one of three legislative branches, yet when they met in March, and styled themselves a Convention, they assumed the exercise of all the powers of Government. In their March session, they passed many laws and resolutions, by the last of which, they declared that their powers were at an end. The country submitted to their authority, which it was wise to do, in the existing state of things. Seeing this, the members met again, and held another session, in the months of May and June, 1775; in the latter of which months, they passed an election law, which is the basis of that which now exists; and under this law, the Convention of 1776, who made our present Constitution, were elected.

When this election law was made, by whom was it made? to whom addressed? and by whom accepted and executed? The answers to these questions are plain, and are so many historical truths. The Convention of 1775, have certainly earned to themselves the thanks and gratitude of posterity; but this consideration by no means alters the facts. They were a body of freeholders, of a certain class, who, unauthorised by the whole, or any part of the people, assumed authority. They authorised that class of freeholders to which they belonged, to elect others of the same class, as their successors, and these latter made the present Constitution. The Constitution thus made is, therefore, not a compact, made by "all, for the benefit of all," as has been said, but by a part of society, for the benefit of that part, in a very great degree. Had there been but one class of men in Virginia at the time, holders of the necessary quantity of country or town property, the Constitution might have been considered as the agreement of all, for the common benefit; and for aught I know, might have been adapted to the wants and exigencies of future times. This, however, was not the case. The Convention of 1776, did little more than to continue the existing state of things. In the place of the old House of Burgesses, they erected the House of Delegates, while the Legislative Council gave place to the Senate; each new branch possessing precisely the powers, and privileges of its predecessor; and the members possessing the same qualifications respectively, and elected by the same electors. The Executive head was, alone, substantially changed.

Mr. Chairman: I have made the foregoing remarks, as I have already mentioned, not to disprove the legal authority of the present Government, but for another, and very different purpose. When we shall come at the discussion of the resolution concerning the right of suffrage, the foregoing remarks will serve to show who they were, who, not having been consulted in the formation of the present Constitution, will have a right to be consulted on the adoption of that which it is now proposed to make.

The greatest grievance proposed to be remedied, is the inequality in the representation, and this especially in the House of Delegates; the next, in point of magnitude and general concern, is the freehold restriction on the electoral franchise. The latter of these will claim more particular attention, when the third resolution of the Legislative Committee shall come under consideration. As to the first, the distribution of representation, as conferred by the Royal charter of Government, may have been tolerably fair and equal at the date of that charter. There were then but few counties or settlements, perhaps not more than six or seven, in the Colony. They were all contiguous; they had but one interest, and but one pursuit, which was agricultural. Each county had its frontier. When war existed on the border, it affected all; when peace reigned, all enjoyed it alike. In process of time, this state of things became materially changed. When the settlements extended far from the Capital, owing to the unprotected state of the country, and the sparseness of population, frontier counties were exposed to almost continual wars, while the interior enjoyed the blessings of profound peace. With few, and but short intervals, this state of things continued until Wayne's victory. Whatever may have been the justness, or equality of representation, at the beginning of the Royal Government, great changes were made before the Revolution. Around Williamsburg, the seat of Government, counties and settlements were sub-divided into small precincts, to each of which a representation of two members in the House of Burgesses was allowed, while no more was allowed to the large counties farther removed from the influence of Executive favor, and to those on the frontier. No more, indeed, was allowed to all West Augusta. Hence, if we look at the map, we will perceive representation distributed in double, treble, or even quadruple proportions round Williamsburg; and this representation grew up to be so unequal, and the consequent evils so intolerable, as no longer to be borne with.

In consequence, public opinion, in 1816, was brought to bear on the Senate, and in the session which commenced in that year, representation in that body, was distributed and apportioned on the basis of white population. I mention this fact now, in order to meet and refute a positive assertion, here and elsewhere, that the proposition to equalize representation on the basis of white population, is a new, cruel, and unheard-of innovation!

Since the year 1790, scarcely one session passed, in which petitions were not received in the General Assembly, praying for a reform of abuses in this particular, and in the law of suffrage. From the counties of Patrick and Henry, these petitions were as regularly looked for as the commencement of the session. In 1815, a bill was brought into the House of Delegates, for making a new arrangement of the counties in districts, for the choice of Senators, on this very abused white basis. At that time two-fifths of the free white population, were represented by *four* Senators, while the other three-fifths had *twenty*. This inequality was sensibly felt by those of our citizens who lived west of the Blue Ridge; and it is impossible for any gentleman to resist the conviction, that from that inequality, there must have resulted much misrule and practical evil. Every exertion was made, by western members, to pass that bill. Every effort, however, failed. The bill was nailed to the table after the second reading, and although motions were repeatedly made to take it up for consideration, they were scornfully rejected, by a silent vote.

At this time, 1815, there was not, in the House, one eastern constitutional lawyer, who did not maintain that no Legislative act could change the districts. They argued, that the same power that made the Constitution, had ordained the districts, and that they were as sacred as the Constitution itself, and could only be altered by a general Convention of the people.

One of the natural consequences of this doctrine was, that large assemblage of distinguished men, commonly called the Staunton Convention of 1816. That body addressed to the General Assembly, of 1816, an able memorial, praying for the passage of a law, to take the sense of the people on calling a Convention. Numerous petitions were, at the same time, received from various quarters of the State, on the same subject, and uniting in the same prayer. All who felt deeply aggrieved by the unjust rule of apportionment, looked forward to such a law, and to a Convention, as the only means of redress. All demanded that basis which we now demand. The bill which grew out of those memorials, and petitions, provided for taking the sense of the people, on the expediency of calling a Convention, with power to consider the propriety of adopting certain amendments. The friends of reform, did not then suppose the people prepared for one with full powers like the present. The amendments proposed, were, first, *to equalize representation among the free white people according to numbers*; second, to equalize the land-tax. To these was added a third, on the motion of a member from Fairfax, amended by his colleague, to extend the right of suffrage to all free white male citizens, twenty-one years of age, "who have evidence of permanent common interest with, and attachment to, the community."—The words of the Bill of Rights.

The bill passed in that limited form. It provided for taking the sense of the people on so amending the Constitution, as to extend the right of suffrage; to equalize representation on the basis of white population, and to equalize the land-tax. After ineffectual struggles to strike out the first and second clauses, it passed the House of Delegates, and was sent to the Senate. The majority in the House, on this vote, represented more than three-fifths of the whole white inhabitants. A gentleman, then from Norfolk borough, and now a member of this Convention, opposed that bill with all his zeal. In its progress, he moved an amendment to it, to introduce a representation of slaves. Whether he intended a representation of all, or three-fifths only, I cannot undertake to say, as no proposition was made to fill the blank in this amendment. This proposition was maintained, by the gentleman from Norfolk, with the most eloquent and cogent exertions of his matchless powers, I have ever yet heard. He was opposed by some of those who are opposed to him now; and notwithstanding his exertions, to the best of my recollection, there were but twenty-six votes on his side, in the whole House of Delegates. Of the precise number, I cannot be certain. The proposed amendment appears on the Journal, with the vote, but not the number on either side. Had that bill passed the Senate, the Convention, then to be called, would have represented the free white population according to numbers; and it is so far from being new and unheard of, that the demand for it in that session, and its establishment in the Senatorial bill of the same session, form parts of our record history.

When this bill was sent to the Senate, it was for a time laid on the table, and not acted on. The reason was as follows: The belief was suggested, and had gained ground, that some eastern Constitutional lawyers had changed their opinions touching the power to legislate over the districts, and hopes were entertained, that in order to tranquilize the public mind for a while, like throwing a tub to the whale, they would bring in a bill to equalize the Senatorial Districts, and to apportion representation in the Senate on the basis of free white population, which would relieve the Senate from the responsibility of accepting or rejecting the Convention bill. These hopes were not disappointed; for the opposers of a Convention brought in a bill to equalize the districts, and to apportion representation accordingly, and passed it. This bill is at present the law, and it establishes the Senate as the representative of the free white population, in equal numbers. Thus, in one and the same session, there were those politicians, who opposed and supported that very basis, which they now denounce as so new, unheard of, cruel and oppressive. That pure element was thus sustained, and is supported by the precedent then made, of so changing the districts from time to time, as to give to it its proper vigour. Nevertheless, there was, even then, some cause to complain. The only tabular statement of population in our power, was the Census of 1810, and from this the state of population had changed, so as to produce about the same injustice which the last General Assembly would have inflicted, if they had based our present representation here, on the Census of 1820, instead of the more gross injustice of establishing it on that of 1810. From these facts, Mr. Chairman, we perceive that our basis has been solemnly settled, and this not rashly, but after meeting opposition from the first talents in the land.

The change in the Senate was publicly known. It could not be concealed, as it not only appeared in the Statute Book, but affected the elections of the three following years, in giving to the new principle its full operation. This was not fully accomplished, until the election of 1820; and the Census of that year, shewed the people the extent of the inequality yet remaining, and which, according to the precedent of 1816, may be corrected after the next enumeration, by a new arrangement of districts. I admit that after power had thus, partially, changed hands in the Senate, the public mind rested from its excitement, and took a breathing spell, until the autumn of 1824, and spring and summer of 1825. During this period, the representation in the House of Delegates, and a proposition to equalize it on the white basis, became the subjects of newspaper controversy. Writers on one side endeavored, by exposing the misrule of the minority, and the evil tendency of that rule, to awaken public attention to the subject, and to bring about reform. On the other hand, attempts were made to alarm the people. They were taught to believe that those who proposed to reform, meant to destroy; that the judicial tenure of office, the right of suffrage, and even property of a certain description, nay, all that was valuable in society, would be hazarded by the call of a Convention. It was then maintained, as it is now maintained, that the majority suffered no practical evil from the government of the minority. Out of these discussions, arose the second meeting at Staunton, called the Staunton Convention of July 1825. That Convention was a body which would have suffered but little disparagement by a comparison with this. It contained upwards of one hundred delegates of the friends of reform. They came from the borders of the State; from the east to the west; from the sea to the Ohio. Their object was to increase the numbers, and strengthen the confidence of their friends; and to weaken and reduce the number of their opponents, by publishing to the whole Commonwealth the grievances of which they complained, and the redress they sought. In a word, they intended to act on public opinion, and in this they succeeded. Their coincidence in opinions and views was remarkable. It was matter of astonishment to themselves. They acted openly; they sat publicly, and kept and published a journal containing their proceedings and resolves. By their resolves, they claimed reformation of representation on the white basis; the reduction of numbers in the House of Delegates; the abolition of the Executive Council; a more responsible Executive, and an extension of the right of suffrage to all those, whether *freeholders or not*, who have evidence of common interest and permanent attachment. This journal was published in all the Gazettes. It was communicated to the General Assembly, and together with the memorial of that meeting, and the petitions of the people, became the subject of the most grave and animated discussions in the three following sessions, and until in that of 1827, their prayer was granted by the passage of the law for taking the public sense on calling a General Convention. All those principles were again discussed last winter, during the progress, and on the passage of the law under which we are now assembled. I will briefly notice the proceedings of last winter on this subject. The bill for organizing a Convention, was prepared and reported early in the session. It proposed representation by the Congressional Districts. This scheme was resorted to, to give representation in this body for three-fifths of the slaves, or what is called the Federal number. It was maintained on that ground most perseveringly, until towards the close of the session. The principle was then called the *black* basis, and it became so odious within these walls, and throughout the country, that its friends were compelled to abandon it. It was perceived, however, that if their arguments proved any thing to sustain a representation of *three-fifths*, they equally sustained a representation of *all* the slaves. From the moment that it was determined to abandon the black basis, the bill was sustained as one founded on the very combined ratio proposed by the gentleman from Culpeper, now under consideration. Some of those who had, by argument, maintained the black basis, denied that any thing but a basis of population and taxation, was ever contemplated, and they wound up their efforts by endeavoring to shew that the arrangement of Congressional Districts, reasonably effected their new pretensions, and had been resorted to for that purpose. After all this, it would be paying but a poor compliment to the intelligence of our constituents, to suppose them ignorant that the white basis would be here claimed, and that the battle between that and a compound one of some sort, would be the one most severely contested. In this brief review of the proceedings of last winter, I speak with confidence, and to the memories of many gentlemen now present, who must sustain me when I say, that the friends of the minority in this Convention, have commenced here, precisely where they ended last winter. It was then said, that if one slave ought to be represented, all ought, and in the form of taxation, the same thing is now claimed by the combined ratio of the gentleman from Culpeper. It is the same principle, in disguise. After the candid admissions of the gentlemen from Northampton and Culpeper, proof of this has become unnecessary. Whether you count him as a whole man, or as a fraction, it is still the same question, covered, indeed, by a few flowers and flounces, but it cannot be concealed, that a slave representation lies at the bottom of the combined ratio. Both gentlemen admit that, but for the purposes of security for that species of property, the principle would not be insisted on.

Mr. Chairman, I will now proceed to notice more particularly, and in their order of time, several postulates urged by the gentleman from Northampton.

Although that gentleman had agreed, that in order to settle our rights in the social, nothing could be deduced from the natural state of man, whether considered as a reality or as a fiction, I understood him to take up and espouse the position of the gentleman from Culpeper, "that the rights spoken of in the Declaration, are such as *were* natural, and do not pertain to the social state." To this position, the words in the first section of that Declaration are a conclusive answer, i. e. "All men are by nature equally free and independent, and have certain inherent rights, of which, when they enter into society, they cannot, by any compact, deprive or divest their *posterity;* namely, the enjoyment of life and liberty, with the means of acquiring and possessing property, and pursuing and obtaining happiness and safety." Now it is manifest, that what is here spoken of, are those *a priori rights*, which are supposed to exist in a state of nature, and are retained to man in society, so as to be social rights, secured by the social compact.

The gentleman from Northampton, however, qualified the position of his friend, by supposing him to have said that, "no man in a social state, has a natural right to control another." This may be true, and yet, in order to *pursue happiness and safety*, or even to *acquire and possess property*, a majority may well be supposed to possess the right, both natural and social, to prevent the minority from ruling them; from controling their actions, and from endangering their lives, liberty, properties or safety. I will say nothing as to the suppositious case of one savage tribe of hunters on this continent, dictating law to another of fishermen, on the isles of another. Nor will I follow the gentleman either to the first family of the human race, or into the enquiry, so often made and so often answered, why females, infants and lunatics are not counted as parts of society in settling the question of what majority should rule. The common sense and experience of mankind has determined that there is a state of infancy and a state of maturity, and the necessity, in all climes, of fixing on a certain period of human life at which, for legal purposes, the one shall terminate and the other commence. As to lunatics, the same common sense has excluded them for want of mind. All the excluded cases are founded on, either the imbecility of mind, or its subjection to the will of another, whereby it loses its freedom. The exclusion of the other sex, has been most eloquently accounted for by the gentleman himself. Of woman he says, that "the fiat of God which brought her into existence, subjected her to the will of her husband."

I dismiss all these speculations, as more calculated to amuse than instruct us, and proceed to the postulates of the gentleman from Northampton, which belong to the subject in dispute, and serve to explain it. The first ground insisted on is, that there are two majorities to be considered: one of persons, and the other of interests, both of which he contends ought to be counted, in order to arrive at and ascertain the majority which is entitled to rule. The gentleman has pushed his principles farther, and has contended that when men enter into society and form the social state, each brings with him his person and his property. Whether, indeed, on entering into society, man and his property become parts of that society, is a question which I will consider, briefly, as that is one of those in dispute. One Indian, we are told, enters society with two bows and arrows; another with one, and a third with none, while another brings nothing but his age, his infirmities and his wants. From these facts, it is attempted to draw the conclusion, that he who brings the most property to protect, is entitled to the most influence in Government, instead of the obvious one, that he should be subjected to the greatest share of the expenses of its protection. It has certainly been left to the men of Virginia of the present day, to make this discovery in the science of Government; for I may safely challenge them to produce any authority for it, ancient or modern. To get along with this argument, it was found necessary to denounce the principles laid down in the Declaration of Rights, which have already been sanctioned by an unanimous vote of this Convention. Their argument is, not that men alone constitute society, but that property enters into and forms a component element of it. The interests growing out of property, they say, must be represented. He who owns a tobacco field, must have representation for that interest, as well as his person. Not only do the gentlemen contend that the protection of property is one of the great ends of Government, but that, inasmuch as rights to property require more legislation to define and protect them than personal rights do, it is the principal and greatest end of Government. Property, then, it seems, is more entitled to consideration than persons. Simple laws, it is said, are sufficient for all personal rights, while those required for property are complex and voluminous. It seems that a large code of laws are requisite to define and protect our rights to a knife and fork, and to understand them the consumption of a thousand lamps; while those that concern our persons, may be studied in a week. By this course of reasoning, gentlemen have arrived at their conclusions as to the greatness of the interests of property, and the comparative littleness of all that concerns our persons. We are reminded, that he who enters into partnership with the greatest capital, is entitled to the greatest share of influence, and that the same principle must be carried into Governments. This, however, is not true, according to the laws of partnery. There, he who has the greatest capital, shares the greatest profit, and bears the greatest loss, which is precisely our doctrine. The greatest influence is not conferred on the largest capitalist by the laws of partnery. Wherever it does exist, it is by express stipulation in the articles of co-partnership. Will gentlemen push their principle to its legitimate results? Will they give to the largest capitalists, the largest suffrage in the State? I imagine they are not prepared for this. I will suppose the case of a man in any small county, who can bring two hundred able bodied slaves to the plough; will they confer on him votes according to the amount of his property? or, will not a man in the same county, with an house and lot in some decaying village, and who lives by catching the jumping mullet, be entitled to the same suffrage? This must be admitted, and yet the gentleman declares that he never will sustain a principle which will not bear to be pushed to its practical results. The argument must be carried to this extravagant length, or it must be abandoned altogether. The whole of this argument, is manifestly sustained, only by reference to some supposed original social pact made by men just emerging from a savage state; for surely gentlemen cannot say that the state of society here in 1775, furnished any thing to support these deductions, or that the social compact then formed, contained any such stipulations in favour of wealth.

I will here bestow some reflections upon the supposed analogy of the question of a combined ratio now, to the Colonial dispute with Great Britain. From this an attempt is made to prove the position that taxation should not only go hand and hand with representation, but that they should be measured by each other; that the amount of the former should determine the quantity of the latter. This was not the Colonial question. The Colonies claimed redress, not because taxation was not in proportion to representation, but because they were not represented at all. This was the point of all the appeals made by Statesmen of that day, whether addressed to King or People. The principle maintained was totally different. I refer here to a State paper written by Doctor Franklin in London. The Colonies were compared with the kingdoms of Ireland and Scotland before the union. Each of these was a separate kingdom or realm, to every intent and purpose, subject, only, to the same sovereign. Each had its Parliament, which could alone tax the subject or grant supplies; and it was maintained that the Colonies stood in the same situation. Each had its own Legislative Assembly, and each was subject, like Ireland and Scotland, to the same Crown; and the argument was, that as the Parliament of England had no right to grant supplies to be paid by the people of Ireland or Scotland, so neither could they vote supplies to be paid by the Colonies. The King, it was contended, could only draw a revenue from Ireland, or Scotland, before the union, in his political character of King of Ireland, or King of Scotland, granted by their respective Parliaments, and it was urged that each of these Colonies bore the same relation to the Crown and Parliament of Great Britain, that Ireland then bore. It had never been pretended that the discontents in the Colonies arose out of the question, whether taxation and representation were correllatives? They rested on the grounds I have just mentioned; for the correctness of which I might appeal to the personal recollections of several members of the present Convention, and to the historical reading of all. Representation is not the correllative of taxation. The question is by whom, or by what Government, were we to be taxed?

Whatever may have been the views with which the gentleman from Northampton endeavoured to enforce the position that man coming out of a state of nature into society, brought with him his property as an element of that society, I cannot pretend to say. Certain it is, however, that he yielded the whole of this argument, when he declared that when man enters into civilized life under a social compact, "nature and all her principles are swept away." Perhaps, in Virginia this doctrine might have been seriously and successfully urged, had it not been for the conservative words in the first article of the Bill of Rights, which I have before quoted. With the above declaration, the gentleman returned to the true point in dispute. He admitted that in arriving at the majority of society entitled to rule, if any be entitled, negroes, bond and free, were to be excluded, but that the *jus majoris*, could only apply to a majority of white persons and interests combined, calculating slaves as property.

The gentleman contends, that among the rights of individuals at the moment of forming a compact of Government, is the right to say whether a majority shall govern the minority or not? And he enquires what is to be done where one alone refuses his assent? The answer is an easy one: he must submit or leave the society, and thus preserve all his rights. It is again urged that the *jus majoris*, to rule the minority, does not exist in Virginia. Here the point of dispute at which we have arrived seems to be overlooked. We are now a majority, claiming to have our political powers according to our numbers. These powers are denied to us, and we have been met with a subtle distinction between civil and political rights. It is admitted that in relation to the former, each citizen, is equal to each other citizen; but it is contended, that the safety of the whole will not permit this equality in respect of the latter. If this equality of political power, and consequently the rights of a majority of numbers to govern does really exist, it is said that it must be found written in the Constitution. This shows how ingeniously gentlemen can vary their views of that document in which our rights are declared.—The *Declaration of Rights*. At one moment that document, and the makers of it, are extolled to the skies: at another, the principles it contains are termed metaphysical abstractions; as visionary theories, which appear very well on paper, but are wholly unfit for practical application. One of our opponents has seriously maintained that the Bill of Rights is, in fact, no part of the Constitution, although the contrary has been determined by the Court of Appeals. And it is absolutely necessary for gentlemen to get over the Bill of Rights, and to reverse their votes in its favour the other day, in order to get along with their argument at all; because the third article of that instrument is in their way. That article declares "that Government is, or ought to be instituted for the common (not unequal) benefit, protection and security of the people; and that whenever any Government shall be found inadequate to the purposes for which it was created, a majority of the *community* hath an indubitable, unalienable, and indefeasible right to reform, alter or abolish it," &c. Thus the very right in question; the *jus majoris*, is contained in the Declaration of Rights in express terms; and further, that whenever a Government shall degenerate into misrule and become unfit for the accomplishment of the great purposes for which it was instituted, the *majority of the community* have a right to amend it, or to pull it down and build up another. Here the right in question is given to the majority in express terms, and this is the *postulate* advanced and demanded. This right is always abiding with the majority, from whatever source derived, and with them, and with them alone, abides the sanction for its protection. This right is asserted by those whom we have been taught to look on as the greatest of men and the first of patriots. But the assertion of this right is only found in that part of the Constitution, called the Declaration of Rights, which as yet, although once re-enacted by ourselves, lies on our table and is open for discussion. Perhaps this state of the argument furnishes a clue to the desire we have manifested to write the book first, and last, the preface. However, in an evil hour for their argument, they had agreed to the preface first.

We have already decided by an unanimous vote, that the Declaration needed no amendment. It is true that vote has been rescinded, but this was only done to make room for the present debate. We have treated that document as one of the subjects committed to us by our constituents. As a part of the Constitution itself. We have treated it with the first respect among the Departments of Government by giving it the first reference, and by giving to the first report made on it the most prompt attention in the House. Our Committee has revised the Bill of Rights, and on their report we have concurred with them, that it needs no amendment. And shall we now be told that it abounds only in abstractions unfit for use? This report is, it is true, on the table, but is, professedly, to be disposed of, and every one knows what the disposition will be.

In our course we have not exactly followed in the footsteps of our predecessors who made the present Constitution. They acted as master builders: we have not. They laid the foundation first, and then proceeded to the superstructure. After they had declared the Government of the King of England at an end, the first thing they did was to appoint a Committee to prepare and report a *Declaration of Rights*. For what purpose? To *serve as a basis of* Government. They first determined the powers they would surrender, and the powers they would retain, and they acted upon and passed the Declaration of Rights first, and then, and not until then, they proceeded to erect upon their declared principles, the Constitution. If it must be so called, they made the preface first, and then the book.

In the course of his very eloquent argument, the gentleman from Northampton admitted, that it was the safest rule that a majority of the units of the community should govern, but only when property was equal. Unless property was equal he did not admit the principle at all.

[Mr. Upshur rose to explain. He said the gentleman from Brooke had mistaken his meaning. He had not said that the rule was only safe when the property of one individual was equal to that of another. He disclaimed, alike, the principle, and the effect that might be deduced from it. He applied the remark to large masses of population having not only unequal but discordant interests.]

Mr. Doddridge proceeded. I must have misunderstood the gentleman yesterday, but I did not misunderstand him to-day, and this, had he listened a little longer, he would have discovered. The gentleman from Northampton has laboured, and I am sure he thinks successfully, to maintain that, in Virginia the majority of free white persons have not the right (and he almost denies their power) to govern the State. This *jus majoris*, he says, is not derived to them, from the law of nature; ("that, with all its principles, is swept away,") nor from the exigencies of society; nor from the nature and necessities of Government; nor yet from any Conventional source, which can only be by an express provision in the present Constitution. *Argumenti gratia*, let the gentleman be right, and for this purpose let it be conceded that the majority could only derive this right, if at all, from some one of those repudiated sources. His conclusion then is, that a majority of freemen in this free land are not possessed of the right or power to govern. But Government there must be, or we instantly sink into anarchy Pray whence, then, will the gentleman derive the power in question to the minority?

Surely he will not go back to the natural state, where force prevailed. That state of things "with all its principles, was swept away," when the present Government was formed. He cannot deduce this right from the exigencies of society; nor from the nature or necessities of Government; nor if not from these sources, can he claim the right from any thing written in the Constitution or Bill of Rights. These look to, and declare the rights of the majority. Every source by which the right of governing could be derived to the majority, is repudiated by the gentleman's argument, and the same argument, conclusively denies the right claimed for the minority; and if the gentlemen are right, we are now in a perfect state of anarchy, which, we know, is not true.

Both gentlemen have, as I have before stated, admitted, that, but for the possession of slaves, in great masses, by the minority, residing mostly in a particular part of the State, the rule of the majority would be safe now. But this property they fear to subject to the Legislation of a majority, lest it might be oppressively taxed. Against this abuse the majority had labored to suggest a satisfactory guarantee; but nothing which their ingenuity could invent was satisfactory. Each plan was denounced as mere paper work, which the majority might disregard when invested with power, and that to complain of this, would be like appealing from Cæsar to Cæsar. To maintain the insufficiency of any Constitutional guarantee, it is insisted that neither the dictates of duty, the obligations of oaths, of conscience, and honor, are any thing when interest is concerned. That interest is the tyrant passion which can never be controled. Gentlemen have gone so far in their zeal, as to declare that there are no principles in Government at all. We are candidly told that the minority can accept no security at all except in representation; that the majority in this free land, cannot be trusted by the minority; and that unless the minority can be protected in the way they claim, they never can, nor will be satisfied; and it is to be feared, that their discontents may break out in something serious, because there can be, as they say, no security except in representation; that is, in the power to govern the State, and thus to rule the majority. This was the language of both gentlemen. Take away the gilding, what is it? The pill which could not be swallowed last winter; the black ratio again; not of three-fifths, but the whole. They say to us, "we have many slaves, and you have few, or none. The possession of this property by us, although it is not your crime, is the reason, however, that we claim to exercise over your persons, lives, and property, despotic power;" (for Government in the hands of the few is always despotic, whether it be called an aristocracy, or an oligarchy, it is still despotic;) "and though it be a despotism, yet we must claim, and you submit to it, as nothing else can secure us against your rapacity."

We are complimented, it is true, with many expressions of kindness; of confidence in our integrity; in our generous and liberal feelings. But then the most serious fears are entertained of our children. It is feared, that forsaking the example of their fathers, they will become freebooters; not that they will plunder their immediate neighbors, nor that they will have courage enough to attack the minority with open force. The fear is, that the rights of the minority may be invaded by a system of Legislative rapine, because "there are no principles in Government."

Were we disposed to act in that manner, or should our children be so disposed, it would only be necessary to look at the census of 1790, and the tabular statements since made, to enable you to discover how feeble would be the resistance you would shortly be able to make to such violence. You may there see, that a race is rising up with astonishing rapidity, sufficiently strong and powerful to burst asunder any chain by which you may attempt to bind them, with as much ease as the thread parts in a candle blaze. I refer gentlemen to the documents furnished us, to shew them how vain must be the attempt to impose a yoke, and how illusory the hope that it will be long worn.

In 1790, the whole white population east of the Blue Ridge, was 314,523, and the whole population west, 127,594; 1800, east of the Ridge, 336,389, and west, 177,476; 1810, east of the Ridge 338,837, and west 212,726; 1820, east of the Ridge 348,873, and west 254,308; 1829, by estimate, east 362,745, and west 319,516.

The balance of white population in 1790, in favor of the east was 185,932; in 1800, 159,903; in 1810, 126,114; in 1820, 94,965; and by estimate in 1829, 43,229.

In the first district, lying between the Alleghany and the Ohio, the increase of white population is truly surprising. In 1790, it amounted to 38,834 only, and in 1829, to 181,384, being nearly five times the number in 1790; and having increased by a ratio of 242¾ per cent. Within thirty years more, that district will contain a population more than equal to half the present white inhabitants of the whole State, if the same ratio of increase should continue. During the same period, the 4th district has only increased its white population 15,754, being at a ratio of eight per cent. only; and in the last year but little more than two per cent. This vast change is effected in thirty-nine years; a considerable period indeed, in human life, but a very short one in the life of a State. The whole population in 1790 was 442,117, and in 1829, 682,261. In 1790 the whole slave population was 292,627, and in 1829, 448,294. By which it appears that during a period of thirty-nine years, the white population has increased at a ratio of 36½ per cent. only, and slave population 44⅔, notwithstanding the drains made from the latter by sale and otherwise. The increase of free people of colour is yet more surprising. In 1790 this class amounted to only 12,866, and in 1829 to 44,212. This increase of coloured population, is a subject of regret and alarm. I looked over these statements of population last evening, and noted them down, with the different principles disclosed in this debate. This I did both for present and future use. A view of them will enable my constituents to appreciate the arguments and claims of the minority, and to discern, if we should be successful in reforming the Government as we hope, the depth of that gulph of political degradation, which was prepared for them, and from which they will have, happily, escaped! The arguments of the friends of the minority here, look to our perpetual slavery; for they maintain that the great mass of slave property, not only is, but always must be, in the east, because, they say, both the physical and moral constitutions of the western people, forbid the adaptation of that species of property to their uses. At the same time, it is admitted, that if a majority of white population is not now in the west, it will soon be there, and there increase forever. It will not vary their principles in the least, if at a future time, ten white men should be found west for one in the east. Their principle is, that the owners of slave property, must possess all the powers of Government, however small their own numbers may be, to secure that property from the rapacity of an overgrown majority of white men. This principle admits of no relaxation, because the weaker the minority becomes, the greater will their need for power be, according to their own doctrines. This, to be sure, is pushing their argument *in absurdum*, but the fault is in the argument, that it admits this criticism. It applies to a case far distant, in point of time, I own, when the tide-water population will be, to the whole, but as a drop in the bucket. East of the mountain, slaves are increasing more rapidly than whites. Between tide and the Ridge, this increase is truly alarming. In a short time, such will be the preponderance of numbers in the west, that the citizen will scarcely know where to find the power that rules him, and will be induced to ask with astonishment, to whom it is that he must submit? I say again, this western increase must proceed. It cannot be checked; it will go on while the east oppressed by the increasing weight of another race will be stationary; and if you have cause to fear us now, that cause will increase, and with it your fears and desires for power. I will not stop here to inquire into the causes of this western growth, but I can satisfactorily shew why it has not been much greater. In 1796, the United States' offices were opened for the sale of a tract of country separated from us only by the Ohio, at two dollars per acre. Ever since then, masses of public lands near us, have been brought into market in Ohio, Indiana and Michigan, first, at the price I have mentioned, and last, at one dollar and twenty-five cents. These land markets checked emigration to western Virginia from other States, and drew off some of its native population. Ohio is now filled up, and the lands nearest to us in Indiana and Michigan, are very generally sold out. The remainnig land markets are removed farther west, and to countries less inviting. It is owing to these circumstances that the ratio of increase during the last nine years, has been greater than during the nine or nineteen years preceding. The proximity of those land markets, have had an effect on all Virginia, but more especially beyond the Alleghany.

With the present state of population in view, and contemplating the prospects before us, with the full belief that upwards of 400,000 white people are with us, and that we are the majority at the present moment, should we be weak enough to agree to your terms, and submit ourselves to your Government, what would our indignant constituents say when a Constitution founded on your claims of superiority should be presented to them? They would scorn to accept it, and displace us from their confidence forever.

The Committee will be good enough to indulge me while I submit to their consideration a few reflections. We have often heard that wealth gives power, or that wealth itself, is power. By this axiom I suppose, is meant nothing more than the natural and moral influence which wealth gives to the possessor, by increasing his means of doing good or evil. Whenever power is directly conferred on wealth by Government, the additional power thus conferred, is a corrupt one. It is a *privilege* conferred contrary to the Bill of Rights, because not conferred *for merit or public services*. It is too, an *exclusive* privilege in its very nature. It is an immoral distinction that is conferred, because it makes no discrimination between the possessors of estates honestly acquired, and those of ill-gotten stores.

Perhaps no blessing of this life is so transitory as riches. To-day you are rich and powerful; to-morrow poor and despised. This thing property, while possessed, makes you a Sovereign, and the loss of it a slave.

We have long been in the habit of considering this Ancient Commonwealth, as the freest and happiest in the world; our Constitution as the best on earth, and ourselves the most fortunate of men. What would the citizen of another State think, or how would he feel, at the sight of an hundred wretches exposed to sale, singly or in families, with their master's lands, if in addition to the usual commendations of the auctioneer to encourage bidders, he should hear him tell them, that if they should purchase his goods, they would instantly become Sovereigns in this free land, and the present possessor would become their slave? Do I misrepresent or exaggerate when I say your doctrine makes me a slave? I may still live in the west; may pursue my own business and obey my own inclinations, but so long as you hold political dominion over me, I am a slave. We are a majority of individual units in the State, and your equals in intelligence and virtue, moral and political. Yet you say we must obey you. You declare that the rule of the minority has never oppressed us, nor visited us with practical evil; but of this, we are the best judges. We have felt your weight and have suffered under misrule. We never expected you to acknowledge this. You are not competent judges. It was not expected that you would make this acknowledgment, or part with power willingly. To do either, would be to furnish a precedent of the first impression.

We do not know to a certainty, what districts may vote with us, but if the results of the public polls furnish any sure indications, our strength in the community is to the minority as 402,000 to 280,000 souls. And if this be so, the heroic resistance made to our claims, proves a degree of moral firmness, equalled only by the moral worth of those who make it.

Among the propositions of the gentleman from Northampton, there was one which I wish to notice more particularly; that a majority in society, means not a majority of men, but of men and interests.

[Judge Upshur explained.—He did not intend to say, this was, of necessity, the case. He had said, that in fixing the apportionment of representation, there must be a majority of interests, and it did not necessarily follow, that it must be a majority of any particular character. It might be a majority of the units of society.]

Mr. Doddridge.—I did not misunderstand the gentleman. I understood him to say, that a *majority* combined of men and interests, did not *necessarily* mean a *minority* of men, but might possibly contain but a minority.

[Judge Upshur.—He had supposed the Government in operation, and he had never contended, that in the Senate and House of Delegates, a majority was not the proper rule. But we are engaged in the formation of a Government, and it is for us to say out of what elements that majority is to be formed. You may get one out of numbers alone, or out of numbers and property. In a state of Government a majority is the rule; but we are here assembled to fix the original law as to the materials out of which the majority shall spring, and we may determine whether it shall be composed of one element or of both.]

Mr. D. I am sure I understand the gentleman. The doubt is as to that majority which the Bill of Rights declares have the power to alter or amend the Constitution: whether the majority there spoken of, is composed of men, or of men and wealth. Surely the Declaration of Rights means numbers alone: that is the plain English of the text, which might be safely left to the decision of any man or woman, having a common knowledge of our mother tongue. Local interests, and slave property, existed in 1776, as well as now. These interests and localities bore the same relations and ratios to each other as now, yet they are neither alluded to nor provided for by the Bill of Rights or Constitution. Had it been intended to take property into the scale of representation, this silence could not have been observed. This brings me to the conclusion, that slaves were not regarded in 1776 as an element of society, but merely as property. The Convention of that day, left representation where they found it; based on the freehold qualification, just as it had been based in the Colony, when there was scarcely a slave in it. It results, that while gentlemen are demanding representation for this species of property, they are demanding a new thing, and are proceeding on a principle never before recognized in the Colony or State; while we are only endeavoring to assert those personal rights which spring up in every society, and can be absent from no Government or creature on earth. I therefore repeat, that when we demand equal political rights for ourselves, our constituents and posterity, we demand no new thing. It was never known before, that constituent powers were to be created out of a compound of this character. They certainly demand a new thing, who thus would exalt a minority into rule, and require a majority of free citizens to submit their persons and properties to their dictation.

I will now call the attention of the Committee to the state of our representation in this body. We have been elected here by a ratio marked by injustice. The Senatorial apportionment of 1816 was founded on the Census of 1810, which was unequal, to be sure; but that was then the last enumeration to which we could refer. In this body, we are apportioned by the same Census of 1816, although that of 1820 was in being, and could have been resorted to. For this injustice, no reason was, or ever will be assigned, except that those who practiced it, had the power to do so. This measure was a poor expedient for appeasing a discontented people. By it, the west were deprived of more than four members on this floor. By the Census of 1820, we were entitled to 40 293-603 members, instead of 36, and by the present population to 42 229-682. Yet, notwithstanding this injustice, I hope the cause of the people will triumph. The majority here may be small indeed, but I hope they will represent at least two-thirds of the inhabitants of the whole State.

One word more respecting the slave property, the increase of which is the subject of some uneasiness. To allay this uneasiness in some degree, I will state what I rather anticipate and fear than hope, because I have no desire to see the slave population of my country increased. This property will hereafter find a market, to some extent, in western Virginia. It has heretofore been of but little value near the Ohio river, because runaways received aid and protection from the people in the new territories and States. The State of Ohio, at an early day, passed a law requiring all people of colour migrating thither, to give bond and security to save them from becoming a public charge, and I believe to be of good behaviour. A general belief had prevailed, that this law was unconstitutional, and it went unexecuted, until lately. The Supreme Judges of that State have decided in favor of that law, and as their blacks cannot comply with it, they must remove. It is supposed their only retreat will be in Canada, as the people of Indiana and Illinois must follow the example of Ohio, in self-defence. In western Pennsylvania, public feeling is so far changed, that instead of the facilities heretofore afforded to fugitives, the master meets with no obstructions, but is even aided. Matters in Canada must soon take a turn. I have no doubt that there are many western citizens who will purchase slaves again, when the causes before mentioned, shall render the property secure. These considerations, with the acquisition of Texas, will greatly enhance the value of the property in question.

Mr. Chairman, I acknowledge my gratitude to the Chair and the Committee, for the attention with which they have listened to my remarks, desultory as they have been. Having been hurried into the discussion, without proper arrangement of materials, they require your indulgence.

Mr. Green rose, for the purpose of correcting a misapprehension into which the gentleman from Brooke (Mr. Doddridge) had fallen.

He had not, as that gentleman seemed to suppose, proposed, or supported, his amendment, merely as a security to slave property from excessive taxation: property of every other kind, was liable to the same sort of injustice: and he should have proposed the amendment, if there had not been such a thing as a slave in Virginia. The gentleman must remember, that two-thirds of all the taxable property in the State, was owned east of the Blue Ridge.

The question was now propounded from the Chair: when, after an extended pause, the Chairman rose to take the vote; whereupon, Mr. Leigh of Chesterfield, moved that the Committee now rise: the motion prevailing, the Committee rose accordingly, and thereupon, the Convention adjourned, to meet to-morrow, at eleven o'clock.

THURSDAY, October 29, 1829.

The Convention met at eleven o'clock, and was opened with prayer by the Rev. Mr. Parks, of the Methodist Church.

The standing order being read by the Clerk, Mr. Doddridge moved that the Convention proceed to execute the Order of the Day, which was accordingly agreed to, and the President called Mr. Stanard, of Spottsylvania, to the Chair.

The Chair having again stated the question before the Committee,

Mr. P. P. Barbour, of Orange, rose and said, that as the gentleman from Chesterfield (Mr. Leigh,) was entitled to the floor this morning, according to Parliamentary usage, I think it proper to state to the Committee, that I am about to occupy it with his consent. I am afraid, indeed, that I shall offer a very poor equivalent, for the rich repast which that gentleman would have spread before the Convention; but I have this consolation, that though it will be delayed, it will not be ultimately lost. But, Sir, I consider it a duty, which I owe to myself, to my constituents, and to the respect which I entertain for the opinions of my fellow-citizens of the Commonwealth at large, to state some of the views which I have taken of the subject under discussion, and to vindicate the course, which I feel it to be my duty to pursue. In doing this, I promise to be as brief as I can, consistently with rendering myself intelligible. I would do so, at all times and under all circumstances; but on the present occasion, I have the additional reason, that the able argument of the gentleman from Northampton, has relieved me from much of the labor, which would otherwise have devolved upon me; and I shall be much gratified, if it shall be in my power, to strengthen some of the strong points which were so ably occupied by him. I do not remember in my life, to have felt so deep a sense of responsibility, as on the present occasion; nor is this at all the language of affectation: I speak it in the sincerity of my heart. On former occasions, as a member of a deliberative assembly, I have been engaged in giving execution to the provisions of an existing Constitution; under such circumstances, if I should have chanced to fall into error, it would have been such, as would have found a speedy remedy in the ordinary process of legislation; but now, I stand on different ground. I am called upon, to aid, not in executing an existing Constitution, but in the creation of a new one; a situation, in which error, though not wholly irremediable, must continue for a considerable time; and if corrected at all, can only be corrected by the original power of the people, in their primary capacity, or in such other mode as may be adopted for the amendment of their organic law.

The task imposed upon us, is one of the grandest and most solemn import. We meet together as the representatives of a great community, to mingle our counsels for the common weal; to lay the foundation of a Constitution, which shall secure the permanent happiness and prosperity of a great Commonwealth. It has been the fate of most of the nations of the earth, to have a Government imposed upon them, without the least participation of their own will; it is our good fortune, on the contrary, both in our character of an individual State, and as constituting an unit in our great confederacy of States, to have a Government of our own choice. We meet, free as the air which we breathe, not only unawed, but uncontrolled by any earthly power, save only, the power of the people, who gave us our political existence; and before whom, as the ultimate arbiters of their own destiny, the work of our hands, must pass for their approval. I feel, Mr. Chairman, not only the importance and solemnity of the trust, but a more than usual deference towards the body which I am addressing. It is composed of individuals, all of whom have participated in the councils either of their native State, or of the United States; and some of whom, assisted, more than half a century ago, in laying the corner stone of the Constitution of this ancient Commonwealth, the first Representative Republic in the world, which we are now about to remove; and who as chiefs, either of the Executive or Judicial Departments of the Federal Government, have, for a series of years presided over the interests of our common country. If under these circumstances, I shall be somewhat embarrassed, in presenting my views to the Committee, they will perceive in my situation, an ample apology.

The most important of all our duties, is the organization of the Legislative Department of the Government; it is in that Department, that the public will is concentrated; since from it must issue in the form of laws, those rules of action, which control the lives, liberty and property of the people. Not only is this the most important Department of the Government, but the immediate question now under discussion, is the most important one, which the organization of that Department involves. It lies at the very foundation of our civil edifice; and it becomes us to examine, with the most guarded caution, how we lay it. The report of the Committee on this Department, has recommended, that in the apportionment of representation in the House of Delegates, regard should be had to the white population exclusively. An amendment has been offered by my friend from Culpeper (Mr. Green) which proposes the adoption of a compound ratio, consisting of the number of white population, *and taxation combined.* The precise question now to be decided, therefore, is between these two propositions. It will be my part, to endeavor to show, why the proposition of the gentleman from Culpeper, ought to be adopted.

With this view, let us first examine the arguments adduced in support of the other plan. At the threshold, we are met with a principle laid down in the Bill of Rights, *that all men are by nature, equally free.* And here, I cannot forbear to remark, whilst I am not controverting the position, that it appeared to me, to be singular, that the gentleman from Brooke, who relied so much upon this principle, denied the authority of the Constitution of the State, at the very moment when he was calling to his aid, that of the Bill of Rights, though confessedly, they both rested upon the same foundation, and consequently are of equal obligation. But let that pass. I shall not stop to enquire, whether this principle is, or is not abstract in its nature. But this I will say: That this, as well as every other principle in the Bill of Rights, is to be modified, by reference to the time when, and the circumstances under which, they were declared, and by reference also, to the people on whom they were intended to operate: otherwise, if you give to the language, all the force which the words literally import, (and they are, I believe, but an echo of those in the Declaration of independence,) what will they amount to, but a declaration of universal emancipation, to a class of our population, not far short of a moiety of our entire number, now in a state of slavery? And if you were to give to such a declaration, its full operation, without the modifications which I have stated, you might as a natural consequence, soon expect to see realized here, the frightful and appalling scenes of horror and desolation, which were produced in St. Domingo by a declaration of much the same tenor, issued by the famous National Assembly of France. I do not believe, Sir, that such is the intention of those gentlemen who rely upon this principle, in support of their proposition; I only meant to show, that if we would come to a right conclusion, in interpreting the meaning of this declaration, we must look at it, according to the condition and circumstances of the people, to whom it was intended to apply, and on whom it was expected to operate.

The principle taken from the Bill of Rights, is, *that all men are by nature, equally free;* and the conclusion which gentlemen draw from that principle, is, that therefore all men are entitled to an equal share of political power. With due submission, this conclusion is, in my estimation, wholly inconsequent. Suppose that all men are, by nature equally free: what sort of connexion has that proposition, with the civil and political rights growing out of the nature of Government?

Need I remind the Committee, that it is the very nature of the social compact, that all who enter into it, surrender a portion of their natural rights, in exchange for which, they acquire other rights derived from that compact, and dependent upon it, both in character and extent? Is it not a solecism, to say, that rights which have their very being only as a consequence of Government, are to be controlled by principles, applying exclusively to a state of things, when there was no Government? The question is, what are the political rights of the citizens? These political rights never existed, till Government was instituted. The same charter which created that institution, can alone create and define them; and yet in deciding this question, we are gravely asked, to refer, not to the charter itself, but to those original principles of Natural law, which not only existed, when the rights, whose extent is to be measured by them did not exist, but which in their very character, are in direct contradistinction, from those which govern the social state. Thus to exemplify: the present question is, what shall be the basis of representation? This term, by an irresistible association, conducts the mind to the idea of election; election necessarily involves the relation between the constituent and representative; and this relation derives its whole existence from Government: it did not, and could not exist before. Surely, then, it is only necessary to state the position, to show that it is utterly inapplicable to the case before us. No laws, no rights, can possibly bear on relations, which have subsequently come into being: relations, which belong to an entirely new state of things, and which state, has principles of its own, derived from the instrument which created it.

But, suppose it to be conceded, that the rights pertaining to a state of nature, and a system of rules deduced from the circumstances of that state, *had* relation to the subject; I ask, is the argument of gentlemen consistent with itself? They are themselves at the very outset, constrained to admit, that there are whole classes of persons, and numerous classes too, who are not entitled to political rights. Many of these have been already enumerated by the gentleman from Northampton: females, minors, paupers, convicts; and I will add, aliens. Now, Sir, females alone constitute a moiety of the human race; if to these be added all the minors who have reached years of discretion, and all the other classes under the acknowledged ban of exclusion, there is an overwhelming majority of the whole population. But how come they to be excluded? Is it by the provisions of the social compact? If that were the principle, it would be intelligible. Is it by the laws of nature? I should answer no. For those laws, of all invariable things, are the most invariable: they are the same yesterday, to-day, and forever, (so far as human affairs are concerned,) until modified by the ordinances of society. They operate upon all persons, of all countries, at all times, and under all circumstances. For example: the rights to life, liberty, and the products of labour, are natural rights. Are there any persons in the world, who by nature are not entitled to these? (I speak not now of the influences growing out of the domestic relations.) I answer without hesitation, none, no, not one. How then can it be said, that the laws of nature refer to the subject, since those laws are uniform and invariable; and it is conceded, that these political rights, are neither uniform, nor invariable, but subject to great diversity and exception? Sir, the concession that gentlemen are constrained to make, that all are not equally entitled to these rights, involves inevitably, the further consequence, that they are not regulated by the laws of nature; for *diversity* cannot be the effect, where *uniformity* is the cause.

But it is said, that two of the enumerated classes, to wit, females and minors, are excluded, by the laws of nature, for the want of *free agency* in both, and the want of intelligence in the latter class. The want of free agency is founded upon the idea, that these two classes, are subjected to the dominion of men. Let us first examine the condition of females in a state of nature: I call upon any gentleman to shew me a principle of natural law, which will sustain their exclusion, to the extent which is thus laid down. I will suggest one case, in which surely they could not apply their principle. We read of a nation which once existed, (I refer to the nation of the Amazons,) in which there were no men: the society consisted of females alone. Here, beyond all question, the principle could not be applied. But suppose a nation made up both of men and women. Can any gentleman shew me a reason drawn from *nature*, which subjects females, *as such*, and because of their sex only, to the dominion of men? Men might indeed govern them by a greater physical force; but so also, might they govern in the same way, all men as well as women, who were weaker than themselves. I repeat, that if gentlemen have found any such principle of natural law, they have had access to fountains of information, which are inaccessible to me. A female may change her relations by entering into the married state, and impair her original rights, to the extent of the obligations contracted by this change. But a female who is of mature age, and unmarried, is in possession of all her rights; those rights are by nature the same with those of the other sex; and men, merely as such, have no natural right to exercise any control over her whatsoever. And yet the reason assigned, for excluding females from the exercise of political rights is, that they are under the dominion of men. When a female is married, and the relation of husband and wife exists, then the power of the husband, is co-extensive with his duties; but co-extensive only. The utmost bound, therefore, of the dominion of men, even over married women, is limited to the circle of domestic relations. Gentlemen would find it difficult to prove, that if a woman were the wife of a man, blindly attached to despotic Government, she would be obliged to sacrifice the enjoyment of all the blessings of civil liberty, to his whim, by being constrained to abide there against her will. It will not be contended, that females are to be excluded for the want of *capacity*. I will not fatigue the Committee, by quoting many examples to prove the contrary. History presents us the records of multitudes, who have been illustrious in literature, in arms, and in council. Writers have selected the reign of Elizabeth, as one of the brightest periods of English history; and with respect to the II. Catharine of Russia, I need only remind the House of a single incident, which occurred in years long past by, but which proves the prophetic grasp of her mind, and which is illustrated by the almost literal fulfilment of the prophecy, in the events passing in Europe at this very hour; I allude to the fact, of her having inscribed over a splendid gate, which she erected, near the frontier of her empire, "*This is the road to Byzantium.*"

Let us look for a moment at the case of the minor: the father's power over him is precisely co-extensive too, and co-extensive only, with his duties, to wit, maintenance, education, &c.: from the moment that he is able to take care of, and provide for himself, he is by nature, utterly free from the control of his father; his subjection was only during his dependence; remove the one, and the other ceases.

Municipal laws have fixed arbitrary periods for the maturity of man, and his independence of paternal control: by some, it is fixed at twenty-one years; by others at twenty-three, and differently in others: nature has settled no period of months or of years: by her laws, whensoever he shall acquire strength of mind and body to provide for himself, from that moment, he is under no control on earth.

Is the argument consistent in another particular? Gentlemen say that taxation must in no degree, be permitted to form a constituent element of the basis of representation. Representation, say they, implies constituents; taxation does not. Well, Sir, does not the same reasoning apply, to exclude from the estimate of numbers, as a basis of representation, all who are excluded from representation itself? If you must exclude taxation, because it has no constituent for its correllative, does not the same reasoning apply to all, who do not possess the elective franchise? They, too, must be excluded from the basis; and so upon gentlemen's own grounds, that basis, instead of extending to all the white population of the Commonwealth, should be confined to voters alone.

The gentlemen have pressed upon us certain other positions from the Bill of Rights; the declaration that all power resides of right in the people, and that a majority, may alter, rescind, or new-model the Government at pleasure. I shall not call in question the truth of the doctrine, that all power resides in the people, nor is it necessary to enquire into the truth of the next proposition, that a majority of the people may alter their Government at pleasure. These two propositions, if I rightly understood the able argument of the gentleman from Brooke, were brought to shew that a majority must necessarily have the control in every free Government. I shall not retrace the ground so well occupied on this subject by the gentleman from Northampton, except so far as to confirm the truth of one of his remarks. As to any original and inherent right of the majority to rule, it could not exist, antecedently to Government. Majority is a relative term. It implies an interchange of opinion among persons convened for council, and whose decision is to control the action of the whole number so assembled, or of others conneoted with them. But this state of things could not exist in a state of nature. Nothing in the shape of Government belongs to that state. Each man stands upon his own intrinsic rights. Nay, so far does one writer carry this principle, as to maintain that, in order to form a social compact, which shall bind all those who enter into it, perfect unanimity is necessary among them all: and though the whole family of man were to enter into such a compact, if one single, solitary individual refuses his assent, the compact has no binding power as it respects him.

I do not say that to carry the doctrine to this length, meets my approbation. Permit me, while we are on this subject of majority, to make a few additional remarks. Some writers give us a very quaint and affected account of it. One of great celebrity, so defines the power of the majority, as to declare, that when a man is called upon to vote, he is not to vote according to his own opinion, but according to his notion of what is the public will: and if it shall turn out that the majority is against him, then it only appears, that he has mistaken the public will. I do not say that I adopt any such sentiment; but I mention this, as an example of one, among the infinite number of theories, which have been broached on the general subject. Sir, is there any rule, for the dominion of a majority, so invariable, as the gentleman seems to suppose? To test this, let us look at the history of our own country; both in the State and the Federal forms of its Government. Surely, if the gentleman is correct in supposing, that the right of a majority to rule, is derived from a natural law, it ought to have that character of uniformity, which distinguishes all such laws; and then it could not be subject to such multiplied exceptions, as we find to exist in fact, in its practical operation. Look first at the Federal Government, whether in its Executive, its Legislative, or its Judicial Department; and we shall find, that a majority is, in many instances, subject to the control of a minority, greater, but by a single unit, than *one-third* of the whole. If the President of the United States, shall refuse to sign a bill, passed by both Houses of Congress, and shall return that bill to them with his reasons for such refusal, the consent of two-thirds of the members of both Houses is requisite before such bill can become a law.

The Senate of the United States hold a double capacity, being a branch, as well of the Executive, as of the Legislative Department of Government; and when it acts in its Executive capacity, two-thirds of the members present must concur, before any treaty formed by the President, can receive its due ratification. Here, again, and in concerns too, of the utmost importance, a majority is subject to the will of the minority. So, in the Judicial Department, (the quasi Judicial, at any rate, for the Senate when it sits to try impeachments, is, in fact, a Judicative power, and acts entirely in a Judicial character;) when the Senate thus sits, two-thirds of the members present are necessary to convict the party impeached. Here, again, is found a minority, controlling the will of the majority.

Again, Sir:—Let us now look nearer home. What is our system of elections, as it exists in Virginia, and in most of the States of the Union, when brought down to its actual practical operation? Is it a majority only, which in each election district, has the power of sending a Delegate, to either House of the Legislature? No, Sir, a simple plurality enjoys that power. If, then, in a certain district, there be ten candidates set up, and neither one of the ten shall receive even *one-fifth*, (far less a majority) of all the votes given, yet, if he receive but a single vote *more* than either of the other candidates, he is returned to the Legislature as duly elected. And though so elected, he is to all practical purposes, the representative of *all* the people of that district; yet a majority of four to one was opposed to his election. Does the majority rule here, Sir? I need not refer to the well known case of our Juries, where the vote of *one* man balances the vote of *eleven* men; yet such an arrangement is thought wise, and has, for centuries past, challenged and received the admiration of all reflecting men. So far, then, from the rule's being a universal one, in all free Governments; in our own Government, the freest upon earth, a minority of one-third controls a majority of two-thirds: A minority of one-fifth may control a majority of four-fifths: Nay, Sir, a minority of one, does every day control a majority of eleven. It is not as gentlemen say, that a minority governs a majority; no, Sir, the minority under certain circumstances, not having the power of action themselves, are enabled to control the action of the majority: in the language of Tully, in relation to the Tribunes of the people at Rome, they have not the power to do mischief themselves; they have only the power, to prevent it from being done, by others. Let us pursue the chain one link further, and let us bring the principle into the Halls of Legislation. It is susceptible of mathematical demonstration, that you can have no certainty of hearing the voice of a majority of the people of any State, unless that State votes by a general ticket. Much as that practice has been objected to, as applied in another election, it may be demonstrated, that in many, if not in most cases, a will prevails, which is contrary to the will of a majority of the people. For example: If all the people of Virginia should assemble on one day, I do not say in one place, but at their several polls, and should all vote for the same individual, a majority of their votes would, no doubt, express the will of a majority of the people. But on any system of practical election, your State must be cut up into *districts*, and as the fractional minorities of these several districts, like the fractional minorities in different States, cannot be transferred from one district to another, it may happen, and does happen, that an individual may be elected contrary to the will of a very large majority of those who voted in the election; and then, of course, so far as representation is concerned, there is the will of a great majority against any measure which may be passed by Delegates so chosen.

What, then, is the conclusion to which I am brought by this train of reasoning? It is this: that there exists no such thing as a fixed, invariable rule, on this subject. The parties to the civil compact, in establishing a Government, and organizing its various Departments, impart to the system which is the creature of their will, such principles as they have found to be prudent and just. In politics, as in morals, the best test of propriety is practical utility. There can be no other. No other has ever been successfully acted upon. If you go to mere *a priori* principles, then a pure, unmixed, democracy would seem the best form of Government: but the experiment has been, long ago, abandoned; and why? upon grounds of practical utility.

The next step, in theory, is, that every one should vote: but this plan is abandoned even by the friends of the present resolution: and why so? for the same reason as before; it cannot bear the test of practical utility. The same principle applies to any other subject of enquiry. A majority of the people have a right to re-model the Government, in any way they may consider as most promotive of the public welfare. We, Sir, are now the representatives of that majority. What do we judge most for the public weal? Even if the doctrine of the power of the majority be conceded, it is only necessary to point gentlemen to what is daily the fact, to shew that the people, though they may not act nominally by a majority, yet do so substantially, and in effect. Suppose we shall determine that a mixed basis of representation is to be preferred to a basis of numbers only; then whether the voters be, as individual units, a majority or not, yet there would, in truth, be a majority of the people acting: all the members of the community would stipulate with each individual member, and each individual would stipulate with all the rest, that this shall be their form of Government. Because whatever should be afterwards done, no matter by whom, if according to the Constitution, would be done by the will of the majority, because the Constitution itself, would have been ordained by that will. A Judge sentences a prisoner: the Judge is a solitary individual; but he acts by the force of law, which law is created by a majority of the people acting through their representatives, whom they have appointed their agents to make the laws. The effect, therefore, is precisely the same as if the sentence of the Judge had been pronounced by a nominal majority.

If I am right, we must discard mere theory, adopt nothing on the ground of mere speculation, but proceed to men and things as they are. In the language of Solon, we must establish not the best *possible*, but the best *practicable* Government. We have our way open before us. There is no question as to our power to introduce what principles we please; the only question for us to ask is, whether the principle be fit; whether it be mete and expedient; whether it will bear the test of practical utility?

In that view, let us then investigate the principle which is now offered for our adoption.

If, when men unite to form a social compact, they surrendered only their personal rights, it might very plainly be concluded, that numbers, and numbers alone, constituted the proper basis for representation. Upon the ordinary principles of contracts made between man and man, (for the social compact is only a contract of all the members with each individual member, and of him with them,) if the contracting parties surrendered only their personal rights, all would give, and, in return, all would receive the same equivalent. But when they surrender, not only their personal rights, but their *property*, there the inequality commences. One man brings one amount of property, another man brings a different amount. I would put it on the principle of compensation; the principle of equivalents. Is it right, that he who has surrendered only his personal rights, should receive as much as he who surrenders much more? But, it is said, that the man who surrenders his property to society, receives, as an equivalent, the *protection* of that property, and that the two go on *pari passu* together. This argument is plausible; and it would be sound, if he could have an infallible security, that the society, or the Government, which is the same thing, should never demand from him a greater contribution from his property, than merely what is requisite for its due protection. But we know that Government claims the right (and exercises it too) of drawing on the purses of all the members of the community, and expends hundreds, yes, myriads, and millions of money, on schemes of internal improvement, and a thousand other objects connected with the internal police of the country. When we come to this consideration, does not the argument fail? It is conceded to be a good argument as far as mere equivalent for protection goes; but when you come to contribution far *beyond* such equivalent, the argument is good no longer, but ceases and is at a stand. The eloquent and ingenious gentleman from Norfolk (Mr. Taylor) compared the relation between the protection afforded to property on one hand, and the taxes levied by Government on the other, to the case of the underwriter and the insured. But, I need not to remind that gentleman of what has been so well and so justly said, that nothing is so apt to lead us into error as a simile. If we commence an analogy upon a subject where it will not hold throughout, and where there are other and strong points of discrimination, of all sources of error there is none so fruitful and so fatal as such mistaken analogy. Government, the gentleman tells us, is the underwriter: agreed. We, he proceeds, who pay taxes, are the insured. Sir, if in this case, as in ordinary cases of insurance, we were allowed to state the premium we are willing to give, and then hear on what terms the Government were willing to insure, there would be some such analogy as he supposes. But if the underwriter may first demand what *premium* he pleases, and after taking that, may confiscate what portion of the *capital* he pleases, besides, the case is altered. To a gentleman so well skilled in mercantile law, as I know that gentleman to be, it is unnecessary that I cite authorities. I admit that if we had the exact rate of premium fixed by compromise, as between buyer and seller, the analogy he gives might be tolerably accurate. But where the underwriter has the whole matter in his own hands, and the insured is neither consulted as to the rate of premium, nor can be sure of not forfeiting a large part of his capital into the bargain, the argument falls and comes to an end.

Mr. Chairman, the object to be attained by the amendment, has been spoken of in some parts of this debate, in terms which indicate that gentlemen consider us as aiming to perpetrate injustice. Sir, if I know my own heart, I would not contend for any object on this floor, which I did not conscientiously believe to rest upon the soundest principle. I may be wrong in my conclusions: I may mistake the causes from which the suggestions of my judgment have proceeded; but one thing I do know, that I shall never advocate here, (whatever be the supposed case elsewhere,) any principle or measure which I do not most sincerely believe to be right. Sir, is the principle for which the friends of the amendment are contending, a principle novel and unknown? One of the most ardent whigs that ever advocated the cause of free principles, a man who has done more to promote the cause of equal rights and of Parliamentary reform than almost any man of this day in England, a man who has pleaded for a more expanded right of suffrage in that country than any of his associates, sums up his doctrine, and his demand in this: that the most just and adequate representation would be, that *which is in proportion* to the contribution of the different portions of society to the public expenses. Yet this man was an enthusiast for liberty, burning with a holy ardour in her cause.

It is urged that numbers only are required, and a property qualification entirely disregarded in many of our sister States. So far as this argument goes, I answer that in North Carolina a property tax of some sort is required in the election of Senators; in South Carolina, the House of Representatives is founded upon just such a compound basis as this amendment proposes, and in Georgia, an allowance is made of three-fifths of all slave property, as in the Federal compact. And what is the fact in respect to our sister States to the East? In New Hampshire and Massachusetts, taxation, so far from being disregarded, is made the *sole* basis as respects elections to the Senatorial branch of the Legislature: and in reference to Massachusetts particularly, I say that the example is pregnant with useful instruction. The experiment there has borne the test of forty years experience; and when, a few years since, an attempt was made to alter this feature of their Constitution, after solemn argument, it was retained in her code. We are referred to the experience of our sister States: Sir, so far as *experience* goes, it is in our favor; so far as *experiment* is concerned, it is against us: and let it be remembered that there is a strong and marked line between the two. Experience is like the light of the sun, bright, constant, and uniform. Experiment is a meteor, transient in its splendor, and uncertain and irregular in all its movements. Talk to me of the *experience* of States which came into being but yesterday! Why, Sir, I have myself, assisted in the creation of some half dozen of them. States in their pupillage: or who have just escaped from it! tell the people of Virginia of an *ignis fatuus* like this for their guide! talk about the result of an experiment in Government which began but yesterday! Sir, I beg leave to decline to follow any such guide. If I must have guide and precedent, I had rather look toward the steady habits of Massachusetts, where the experiment has continued forty years and more: and where that experiment was in the full tide of successful progress, when those States, to whose experience we are so reverently referred, were naught but trackless wilds, roamed by savages in quest of game, and who have not had time even for an experiment. Admitting that there was some analogy between the condition of Virginia, and States, in circumstances so different, still I say, let me have experience, which, according to Lord Verulam, is "the Mistress of the world," and not experiment, which is the worst of all possible guides. And why, Sir? There is not a farmer in your State, who will try an experiment, that is suggested to him, till he finds out that somebody else has tried it before him. Shall we trust to an authority like this, in laying the foundation of our Commonwealth?

A strong case was put by the gentleman from Norfolk (Mr. Taylor) to shew the injustice that might flow from taking property into the account, in fixing our basis of representation. He supposed a country to contain a few individuals of great wealth, and others who were in comparatively humble circumstances, where fifty rich men might, through the weight of their property, out vote two hundred and fifty poor men. We are far from contending for such inequality among voters, nor do we desire to see it prevail. In the same district, we would make all the voters equal, no matter how unequal their property. But how did the gentleman get to his conclusion, from such premises? I believe he would find himself puzzled to make out the middle term of his syllogism. His argument, however, has been already answered by the gentleman from Northampton, and the gentleman from Chesterfield, (Messrs. Upshur and Leigh,) and the answer is this, that there can be no danger of the rich oppressing the poor by Legislation, where both reside within the same district of the State, and, therefore, have a community of local feeling and interest. I have another answer to it. It is of the nature of a representative Government, that it stands on the basis of responsibility. The representative is answerable to those who gave him his power. But if we are to be taxed, as a people, by individuals, not responsible to us for their public acts, the Government is done from that moment.

I make a distinction between civil liberty and political liberty. Under a Government of an oligarchical, or even a monarchical form, civil liberty may, nevertheless, be enjoyed, and to a very considerable extent. For Princes, born to even a despotic throne, may perchance, be of a gentle and benevolent temper, and in no wise disposed to exercise the oppressive power with which the Constitution has invested them. Augustus, as we all know, swayed the sceptre of the world, during, at least a part of his reign, with clemency and forbearance. But this is not political liberty. I may enjoy a large measure of personal freedom under such a Government, but I enjoy it by permission, by sufferance merely. To convert this freedom into political liberty, it must be made mine of right, and I must have the means of securing it. Now, to apply this doctrine to the argument of the gentleman from Norfolk. The delegate, who resides in the same district with his constituents, returns back to them, and is responsible to them for his political acts; the citizens hold him by a strong cord; and if he has not been a good steward, he may certainly calculate on meeting his reward. But, how does this principle apply, when he who lays the tax, and they who are to pay it, reside in different portions of the State? He may vote ruin to his fellow-citizens in a distant part of the State, and never be called to account for it! They did not elect him, and they cannot call him to any account for his stewardship.

[Mr. Taylor here rose to explain: He said he had waited until the gentleman from Orange had completed his argument on this point; he had not risen to answer it; but solely for the purpose of stating the position he had taken, and the principle on which he had relied, in the argument he formerly addressed to the Convention. What I say, observed Mr. Taylor, is, that our Government rests on the principle of equal rights, among all men who are worthy of political power; and I contend that on that principle rests the safety of our free institutions. If you fix the terms of qualification by a fundamental law, declaring who may vote, and who may not, then my position is, that there exists a perfect equality of rights, among all the voters thus qualified. If, in a district giving 300 votes, 250 votes shall not elect a representative, while the remaining 50 do elect him, I say that you destroy all free principle, and disguise it as you will, call it what you please, you do, in effect, establish an aristocracy, an odious aristocracy of wealth. You all oppose the admission of such a principle *within* your county lines; and repudiate it as aristocratical in its character. Why is it less aristocratical or less odious, when extended to districts, or to the State at large? These were my positions, and this was my argument.]

Mr. Barbour resumed. He had never knowingly misstated the argument of any gentleman opposed to him: and with due submission, he still contended, that he had neither misstated, nor misunderstood the argument of the gentleman from Norfolk. His argument, said Mr. B. was based on the equality of all the voters within a given district, and went to show that the same principle of equality ought to be extended to all other districts; and, in reply to this argument, I was going on to show the difference between the cases of a representative elected (by whatever rule) from the district where he resides, and returning again to that district, responsible for his public conduct, and that of a representative, chosen in *one* part of the State, and who has by his public acts, oppressively injured *another* and a distant part of it, to which he is not responsible, and by which he cannot be punished. And though rich and poor men, have an equal vote in the same district, yet there is safety to property, not only because there is a community of feeling and interest, but because of the responsibility which the representative thus elected, owes to all his constituents, both rich and poor, and who are interested in proportion to their respective property. And here permit me to make an earnest and most sincere disclaimer of all intention to impute to my fellow-citizens of Virginia, any thing like an improper purpose. I have no such belief whatever, but give to them all that credit for integrity of motive, which I claim for myself. But while *faith* is the surest of all foundations in matters of religion, the very reverse of faith, is the true foundation of all free Governments. They are founded in *jealousy*, and guarded by caution; nor can the spirit of liberty long survive among any people where this jealous vigilance is not kept in perpetual vigour. In Monarchies, its action is against the Monarch. Here, in the United States, so fully is it known and recognized, that the people have written it on all their gates, and exercise it not merely against their official agents, but even against themselves. To prevent the people of Virginia from being carried away, by their own partialities, into a premature confidence, they have themselves declared, that the people shall not elect any man to the House of Delegates, who is under 25 years of age, nor to the Senate, who is under 30. Sir, I speak of human nature as it is. I "nothing extenuate nor aught set down in malice." I draw no lines of partial discrimination: but I take my stand on the great principle which I have mentioned, that *not* faith, but the *reverse* of faith, is the foundation of all good Government, and that no nation is free, unless they possess *political* liberty, by which I understand the power to secure their own freedom.

We have heard much said against the principle of the amendment, as going in practice, to make an unjust discrimination in favour of the rich. But, gentlemen should recollect, that it proposes, within the electoral districts of this State, no distinction between the high and the low. But no man, Mr. Chairman, need to feel greatly alarmed, on the score of wealth among us. Those who have lived but for a few years, may see, from an inspection of the map of Virginia, how fleeting are all human possessions. The wheel of fortune never stands still, but is in a state of perpetual revolution. He who was on the summit yesterday, may be at the bottom to-day. It was well said that primogeniture, and the law of entails, are the two columns of Monarchy; and that the breaking down of entails, and passing the act of parcenary, secured a perpetual change in the possession of property. There exists not the slightest danger of a permanent concentration of wealth, in any one portion of our country, or among any particular class of our citizens.

With proper deference, I would take leave to suggest, that throughout a great part of this discussion, gentlemen have confounded *civil* rights with political power. An argument, which goes for the security of civil rights, involves considerations of one kind; while an argument for the distribution of political power, involves considerations of a very different description. All the individuals of the discarded classes, to which reference has already been made, are fully entitled to the enjoyment of civil rights. Minors, women, (for, in this respect, the ladies are as fully in possession of these rights, as any of the lordly sex,) and even aliens, except as to the tenure and transmission of real estate; and even that distinction has been gradually frittered away to a mere form. When the question has respect to civil rights, no distinction can take place from age, sex, or any of the other causes which operate in the other case, unless, indeed, under circumstances of an extraordinary kind; but, when the question has reference to political power, then we must have respect to age, to sex, to birth; and a variety of circumstances, which go, in practice, to exclude from the possession of it, a large majority of every community. Here we must of necessity look at the condition of the individual, and determine whether he has the requisites for the enjoyment and exercise of that power. Some items of qualification, all must admit, the payment of tax, and some residence within the State, are required by the gentlemen themselves: they call the possession of these qualifications, a fitness for the elective franchise; while some of them have so far extended the qualification, as to require permanent residence, and either nativity or naturalization.

Now, then, the question comes back upon us; if it be right, because Government operates on persons, that persons ought to be represented; is it not equally right, that because it operates on property, property ought to be represented? Take the converse of this position; and how will it work? What would the gentlemen say to a Government where property only was represented and persons excluded? None of them would accord to it; yet we have an example of such a state of things in the Roman Government.

It is the distribution of the State into *centuries*, where property alone was taken into view. Afterwards, indeed, according to their usual course, that people went into the opposite extreme; and then the State was divided into *tribes*, in which people alone were considered, and property was wholly disregarded. In the State of Massachusetts, as I have already stated, they go to the extent of making property the only criterion in voters for one branch of their Legislature. But I ask, neither for *Comitia* by *centuries*, nor *Comitia* by *tribes*. I ask for a compound ratio of both. Both are equally at the command of the Legislature, and both need security against an abuse of power. *A priori* indeed; as it is conceded by all, that because the Government acts upon persons, they should be represented, so in like manner, as Government acts upon property, the owners of that property ought to have some representation in reference to it, as between the different districts of the Commonwealth. If this be true as a general principle, it applies emphatically to the particular condition of Virginia; in the eastern part of which, there is almost half the population, which, *as such*, would be excluded upon the white basis, whilst at the same time, that population *as property*, pays an enormous disproportion of the tax; thus presenting the striking fact, that the very cause which would forever keep down the eastern representation, much below its standard, would forever aggravate their taxation, far beyond a just standard. The amendment under discussion, proposes some remedy for this great injustice.

It is the natural desire of us all, to lay the foundations of this Constitution in such a manner, that it shall stand and endure. If that be our purpose, we must rest it on these two great columns: Persons and property. Withdraw either, and you have a weak and tottering edifice, which never can endure the shocks of time. If I might venture upon a simile, I would compare our Constitution to an extensive and delicate piece of machinery. If the engineer who devised its structure, shall so arrange its internal wheels, that they act in opposite directions, and on antagonist principles, the result must, of necessity, be, that its works can easily be put out of order, and that the machine itself is not likely to last. But, if, on the contrary, he shall so arrange the various parts, that all its wheels shall move in one direction; that all the principles of its action shall be harmonious and uniform; that there shall be no clashing of wheel against wheel, but all shall move by one law, and to one end; then the machine, while it reflects credit upon the skill and ingenuity of its author, will accomplish the beneficial purposes for which it was designed, and will continue to work, without needing any material repairs, to an indefinite period of time. We have an instructive warning on this subject in the history and fate of the Ancient Republics. Whenever, in any of their Constitutions, persons and property, were set in opposition to each other, the result invariably was found to be, heart-burnings, conflicts, confusion, bloodshed, civil war, anarchy, and finally, the utter and disastrous downfall of liberty, and the establishment of Despotic Government. I would place these two principles side by side, in perfect harmony. I would encourage nothing like distrust, or conflict between them; but would blend their action into perfect concert, and thus produce lasting tranquillity. If persons remained safely protected, beneath the overshadowing power of the State, I would have property protected too. On the other hand, the safety of property was put under the guarantee of the Constitution; I would build upon the same organic basis, the perfect security of persons. It is the interest of this great community to keep the provisions of its Government, safe and inviolate: make those provisions just, and then they will abide long; and the edifice of State, subject only to that infirmity which is the inheritance and the characteristic of man, shall stand for posterity, secure from internal danger, and equally safe, as I trust and believe, from external violence.

Mr. Baldwin, of Augusta, after assigning his motives for addressing the Committee at that period of the debate, and his intention to present his views of the subject with as much brevity as practicable, proceeded to state the question under consideration. The resolution reported by the Legislative Committee, and the amendment proposed by the gentleman from Culpeper, present the question, whether representation ought to be apportioned equally amongst the citizens of this Commonwealth, who shall be admitted to the right of suffrage, according to numbers, or whether it shall be apportioned amongst them unequally, by adopting a basis compounded of numbers and taxation. It is a question, so far as relates to numbers, between equality on the one hand, and inequality on the other; and after the admissions made by gentlemen opposed to me in this debate, I may surely venture to assert, without much fear of contradiction, that according to the genius of our political institutions, whenever a question arises concerning the distribution of power, amongst the people themselves, the source of all power, the rule of equality ought to prevail, unless some good reason be shewn to the contrary. The gentleman from Culpeper (Mr. Green) and the gentleman from Northampton (Mr. Upshur) have both conceded, that under a Republican Government, it is correct, as a general rule, that the power of the State ought to be placed in the hands of the majority of its citizens; but they contend that peculiar circumstances may exist, which would render the application of that rule unjust and impolitic. On this occasion, they conceive that a sufficient reason to justify an exception, may be found in the contrariety of interests prevailing in different sections of this Commonwealth. If all the various portions of Virginia were entirely assimilated in territory, population, wealth and resources, neither of the gentlemen referred to, nor I presume any member of this Committee, would hesitate for a moment to approve the basis of representation proposed by the resolution we are now considering.

Notwithstanding the conflicting interests which some gentlemen suppose to exist between different sections of the State, none, I presume, are disposed to treat this controversy as a mere struggle for power. If it were so regarded, all discussion of the subject would be worse than useless. It would be mischievous. It would only serve to inflame our own minds, and scatter throughout the community, the fire-brands of discord. No, Sir, we all profess, and I trust sincerely, to be desirous of arriving at a correct conclusion, and to be engaged in this comparison of sentiments, for the purpose of obtaining light from the spirit of our institutions, the character and feelings of our people, the precepts of experience, and the dictates of sound policy. It has been said by several gentlemen in this debate, that all men are actuated by self-interest; and I have no objection to the proposition, when understood to embrace that noble and enlightened self-interest, which teaches us the love of truth and justice, and the sacrifice of all sordid and contracted prejudices, upon the altars of duty and patriotism.

In asserting the principles which in my opinion elucidate this subject, I shall not incur the imputation of indulging in abstract discussion; a mode of argument so much deprecated by some of the gentlemen who have preceded me, and which I acknowledge is less remarkable for its utility, than its intricate and almost interminable character. For my own part, Sir, having always regarded Government as practical in its very nature, I do not expect that we shall derive much useful information from the best constructed theories, though sustained with all the powers of intellect, and adorned with all the charms of eloquence. I was delighted, Sir, with the logical and beautiful abstract reasoning employed by the gentleman from Northampton (Mr. Upshur,) with the avowed object of proving that abstractions cannot be safely relied upon, in matters of Government. Let us leave, then, to school-men and sophists, all the theories concerning the origin and nature of Government in general, and save ourselves the trouble of enquiring whether it should be traced to patriarchal supremacy, physical force, or social compact. I would not dispute with any people, the propriety of any political system which they have thought proper to sanction by their approbation or acquiescence; even though they acknowledge the Divine right of Kings, and the duty of passive obedience, or boast the privileges and immunities extorted from the fears or conceded by the clemency of monarchs, or cherish the aristocratic notions of noble birth, subordination of ranks, and hereditary authority.

And yet, Mr. Chairman, I am far from admitting the broad proposition which has been asserted and reiterated in this debate, that there are no principles in politics. If, indeed, gentlemen mean only by this assertion, that there are no abstract principles of Government which must be regarded as true in all nations, in all ages, and under all circumstances, I should consider it a waste of time, to enter into any controversy with them upon the subject. But surely, Sir, there are principles of a practical nature, without which, no free Government can exist, and a frequent recurrence to which is indispensable, in order to justify and illustrate its institutions. A Government which rests upon public opinion, cannot be sustained without the aid of such principles; the result, if you please, of observation and experince, but sanctioned by the reason and cherished in the affections of the people, and which may be confidently appealed to, on all important questions, affecting their safety or happiness.

Ours, Mr. Chairman, is emphatically a Government of principles: principles established by the wisdom, and consecrated with the blood of our fathers. It is certainly not our purpose to tear up the foundations of our political system, and establish a new one out of the ruins; our object is to reform and amend, but not to revolutionize. Without, therefore, indulging in abstract theories, or referring to the systems of other nations, let us resort to those fundamental truths which constitute the basis of our own system. We shall find them all-sufficient for every useful purpose; they will serve as "a lamp to our feet, and a light to our path," upon this or any other subject of our duties.

In this country, highly favoured, as we believe, by Heaven, and distinguished for its civil and political liberties, we recognize the sovereignty of the people, the fiduciary character of all public agents. We consider the people not only as the objects and subjects of Government, but as the governors themselves in the last resort, and the only safe depositories of unlimited power. We regard the organs of legislative authority as representatives of the people, accountable to them, and constituted for the purpose of expressing their will. We acknowledge that this general or public will must prevail, whether in the ordinary legislative enactments, or in the construction and alteration of the fundamental laws. As unanimity in the operations of such a Government, is in the nature of things, impracticable, the general will is to be expressed by the voice of the majority. This, as the gentleman from Frederick (Mr. Cooke) has correctly stated, is a rule founded upon necessity; for otherwise, the public will would be nugatory, or would be expressed by the voice of the minority, the absurdity of which is manifest.

None of these principles have, as yet, been controverted in this debate. It has not even been denied, that the will of the majority ought to prevail; the only controversy is in regard to the application of the rule; some gentlemen contending that a majority does not mean, necessarily, a majority of numbers alone. On this point, it is only necessary that reference should be had to the language employed in our Bill of Rights, which asserts that a majority of the community hath an indubitable, unalienable, and indefeasible right, to reform, alter, or abolish the Government. It is impossible that any one can doubt the majority here spoken of, is a majority of numbers, and not a majority of interests, or of interests and numbers combined. It is true that this clause in the Bill of Rights was not intended as a declaration, that in all cases whatever, in which a conflict of opinions may occur, the question in controversy is to be decided by a majority of numbers; and the gentleman from Orange (Mr. Barbour) has stated various examples in which the rule is not applicable. The principle declared, is obviously in reference only to the sovereign right of the people, to establish or change the fundamental law; and it cannot be doubted, that the majority of the people may, if they so determine, give an ascendancy in the Government to the minority. But is it reasonable that they should do so? and would not such a transfer of power be a gross violation of the duty which they owe to themselves? The majority have the unquestioned right to change the very foundations of Government, and distribute political power according to their own discretion; and yet they are asked to subject themselves and their posterity, by their own voluntary act, to the control of the minority. Should they do so, they will shew themselves well worthy of becoming "hewers of wood and drawers of water." I would ask, Sir, if there is any one here who would venture to propose, that when the Constitution, which we are engaged in preparing, shall be submitted to the people for their approval or rejection, the question shall not be decided by the majority of qualified voters? And should there be reserved to the people, as undoubtedly their right, a veto upon the enactments of the Legislature, would they not, in the exercise of that direct power, decide according to numbers? The purpose of representation, is the delegation of power to agents, which the people cannot, with convenience, immediately exercise themselves, and no inequality ought to prevail, in regard to the delegated authority, which would not be admitted amongst those from whom it is derived, if retained by them in their own hands.

I have thus endeavored, by referring to well established principles, to shew that no inequality ought to exist in the exercise of the elective franchise. It is true that the right of suffrage itself, may, and ought to be limited. All those are to be excluded, who cannot be expected to exercise it discreetly; that is to say, in such manner as will promote the safety and happiness of themselves and the rest of the community. It is upon this principle, that various classes, embracing many individuals, are excluded; of which, obvious and familiar examples have been stated in the course of this debate. It is upon this principle alone, that any freehold or other property qualification can be required from the electors. The qualifications, of whatever nature, are the subjects of a sound and wholesome discretion, and ought to be fairly and impartially adjusted, with a view only to the public good, and not for the purpose of elevating or depressing any portions of society. But when once established, all those entitled to the right of suffrage ought to be admitted upon terms of perfect equality. We cannot with propriety, distinguish amongst individuals, or masses of individuals. There is no doubt a wide difference between the merits of individuals, intrinsic or adventitious. Moral integrity, talents, learning, reputable connections, the fruits of industry, acquired or inherited, always give the possessor an influence over the opinions and conduct of others; but those advantages are sufficient in themselves and require no artificial distinctions. Neither justice nor good policy requires that authority should keep pace with influence, and be in like manner unequally distributed. If the rule of equality for which I contend, be departed from, in order to distribute political power, in any degree, according to wealth, then I agree with the gentleman from Norfolk (Mr. Taylor) that the Government must, to that extent, be regarded as a monied aristocracy.

Having thus presented some of the considerations which, in my opinion, justify the resolution reported by the Legislative Committee, I shall now submit a few remarks upon the basis of representation proposed by the amendment. So far as taxation is a constituent, it is a scheme of property representation; and one of the arguments urged by its advocates is, that property ought to be represented, inasmuch as it is one of the great objects of Government. I beg, Sir, that the purposes of Government may not be confounded with the principles upon which it is to be organized. The protection of the people in the enjoyment of their property is doubtless an important duty of Government. But the same duty exists in relation to all the innocent and legitimate enjoyments of which they are capable. Those enjoyments are not, however, the proper subjects of representation. In a representative democracy, which is founded upon the supposed intelligence and virtue of the people, the purposes of Government are to be effected by a representation of the people themselves; and we have been taught to believe, that under such a system, none of the important interests of society will be prostrated or neglected. It can throw no light upon this subject to distinguish between personal rights and the rights to property; they are all equally entitled to the protection of Government; their relative importance cannot be graduated; nor is there any scale by which we can determine how much relative political power ought to be enjoyed by a citizen in order to ensure to him protection.

The advocates of the proposed amendment avow, that it is intended to operate upon the relative political power of different portions of the Commonwealth; and it is obvious that the only security which it can afford to property is by protecting it against the partial and unjust legislation, which may arise out of conflicting sectional interests. It can have no effect in securing proprietors throughout the State against the assaults of the indigent. Power would be unequally apportioned amongst the electoral districts, but in each district every elector would be entitled to an equal vote. If, therefore, a combination should be formed amongst the indigent against the affluent, property would find no protection in the basis of representation proposed by the amendment. If gentlemen are correct in the supposition that property ought to be represented in order to afford it protection, they ought not to stop short of their principle, and provide only a partial safe-guard; but should propose giving political power to each proprietor in proportion to the value of his property or the amount of his taxes. Now, I ask, Sir, what would be thought of a proposition that one elector should have twice, or thrice, or ten times as many votes as another, in consideration of his owning property to a greater extent; and yet the principle is the same, whether it be applied to individuals or masses of individuals.

Several gentlemen have urged upon us, that taxation ought to be regarded in the apportionment of representation, because it furnishes the means by which Government is supported; and we have been told, that those who pay the taxes ought to lay the taxes. If by this assertion is meant, that all who pay taxes ought to be admitted to the right of suffrage, it may be true as a general proposition, and will receive the consideration of this Committee when another resolution of the Legislative Committee shall occupy our attention. If the idea intended to be expressed is, that none but those who pay the taxes ought to have a voice in laying them, then the rule would amount to nothing more than an exclusive property qualification. But if we are called upon to believe that political power ought to be unequally distributed amongst the qualified voters, from a regard to the sums of money which they respectively contribute to the support of Government, it remains to be proved why contributions of that character confer a better claim to political power than those of any other description. There is no good reason why the aid which a citizen furnishes in the support of Government, in the form of taxes, should be placed on higher ground than that which he yields in personal services. He who devotes the energies of his body and mind to the welfare of his country, labours to promote her best interests, or defends her rights upon the battle field, may surely claim the merit of having contributed to the support of Government. He is not entitled to political power merely in consideration of such services, but his right is not inferior to that of him whose aid is furnished from his purse. There is not, as some advocates of the amendment seem to suppose, any peculiar relation between taxation on the one hand, and representation on the other, as is evident from the principles which govern their respective application. All are bound to contribute to the support of Government according to their means; all are entitled to the right of suffrage who have sufficient evidence of permanent common interest in, and attachment to, the community.

I am at a loss to perceive, Sir, how this subject can be elucidated, by the reference which gentlemen have made to the controversy with Great Britain, which resulted in our Independence. The British Parliament asserted the right of taxing us without our consent, although we were in no wise represented in that body; our representatives being here in our Colonial Legislatures. We resisted that despotic enterprize of a foreign Government, as we would have resisted any other invasion of our civil liberties, and engaged in the perilous and unequal conflict, not to obtain representation in Parliament, which we would not have been willing to accept, whether according to taxation or numbers, but because we would not submit to laws affecting our rights, to which we had not consented, either by ourselves or our representatives.

As this amendment is justified, in the opinion of its advocates, by the conflicting sectional interests supposed to exist in Virginia, in consequence of which the greater wealth of the minority might, without some such security, fall a sacrifice to the rapacity of the majority, I would ask gentlemen to reflect whether there is in point of fact, any permanent contrariety of interests of that alarming character. We are forming a Constitution which is to last for ages, and we should be careful not to mistake temporary and fluctuating varieties of interests, for those of a permanent and irreconcileable nature; and the changes in the relative wealth and population of different parts of the State, which have already occurred, and are still in progress, ought to be sufficient to remove all fears on this subject.

The only effect of the proposed amendment would be, to give permanency to any hostile sectional feelings which may now exist in this Commonwealth, and by exasperating those feelings, perhaps bring about that very insecurity of property which it is the object of its advocates to guard against. Representation in any degree, according to taxation, would not prevent schemes of internal improvement; by which, portions of the State may be made to aid in defraying the expenses of improvements in which they might not consider themselves immediately interested. If enlarged views of justice and sound policy should not satisfy the dominant party, however constituted, that the interests of the whole State will be promoted by useful internal improvements, wherever required, you may rest assured that the same result will be produced by combinations of various sectional interests. And we are not to expect that the east and the west will be always arrayed against each other upon such questions. The improvement of James River may, for example, be united with a project to connect it with the western waters; and in like manner a concert may be brought about between those interested in the navigation of the Potomac, and that of the Shenandoah.

All the arguments which have been urged to prove that Virginia is divided by hostile and irreconcileable sectional interests, only tend to establish that she ought not to continue united under the same Government, a conclusion abhorrent to the feelings of every patriot, and however ingenious and eloquent gentlemen may speculate upon the subject, not justified by any facts which have occurred in the whole course of our history. And after all that has been said to destroy our confidence in the justice of the majority, it is the only rational security which we can have for the peace, and happiness, and prosperity of the community. Our Republican Institutions rest for their support upon the virtue and intelligence of the people; and if they should not be sufficient to ensure a faithful and wise administration of the Government, the best hopes of human liberty and happiness which we have cherished must be disappointed, and we shall be compelled to abandon the scheme of self-government, and yield up the many to the protection of the few.

Mr. Baldwin concluded, by apologizing for the imperfect manner in which he feared he had discharged the duty he had undertaken, and for the omission of several views of the subject, which he had intended submitting to the consideration of the Committee.

Mr. Cooke of Frederick, availed himself of the pause which ensued, after the close of the above speech, to correct a misapprehension into which Mr. Upshur had fallen, in supposing him to have admitted, that in the whole period, during which the existing Constitution had been in operation, no instances of misrule had ever occurred in any department of the Government: he had gone no farther than to admit, that while the Gentlemen in the eastern part of the State, having the majority in the Legislature, had it thereby in their power to lay oppressive taxes on the cattle of the west, they had never exercised their power in that respect. As to instances of misrule, he had not said any thing, as he would gladly avow such a question. He went into a farther correction of the same gentleman, in relation to what Mr. Cooke had said, as to the balance between the population on the two sides of the Blue Ridge, and the relative number of slaves in the lower country, and in the Valley, and he made a statistical calculation to shew, that the fears entertained by the slave-holding part of the State were groundless.

Mr. Upshur replied, and regretted that the gentleman had thought it necessary to withdraw any part of a compliment, which, as coming from him, was highly appreciated by gentlemen from the east of the State. Still the argument remained the same; for, if when they had the power, they had not oppressed the west by taxation, he was at a loss to conceive, in what other way they were under any temptation to oppress them. Mr. Upshur still insisted on the ground he had before taken, as to the balance of slave population; and denied that any counties were to be reckoned to the slave-holding interest, but those in which that sort of population formed the preponderating interest.

Mr. Leigh of Chesterfield, asked whether it would be trespassing too far on the gentleman from Frederick (Mr. Cooke) if he asked him to state some of the prominent acts of misrule, which had taken place in the Legislature of Virginia, during the time the power of the majority in that body, had been in the hands of gentlemen residing in the eastern portion of the State? It had been a part of the fortune of his own very laborious life, to examine almost every act of that Legislature, since the Revolution. On the subject of misrule, he confessed himself a beggar for information, hungry and destitute. He did not ask the gentleman to go into particulars, but merely to state some of the prominent cases. Mr. Leigh would not say, that during that time no impolitic measures had been adopted, nor would he say the Government had always pursued the wisest and the best course; but, he wished to have pointed out to him any very impolitic measure, justly chargeable upon the structure of the existing Constitution, and to which the people of the west had not been as much parties as the people of the east; any wrong done either to individuals, or to classes of the community, springing out of the principles of the Constitution.

Mr. Cooke replied, that he had not asserted the existence of misrule, and, therefore, he was not called upon to prove what he had not asserted. Yet he would not admit, that he might not truly have made such an assertion. To make his meaning more distinct, he would now say that he did assert the existence of such misrule. Yet he should reserve to himself the right of taking what course he chose upon that floor; nor could he consent to have such course chalked out, and dictated to him by the member from Chesterfield. He said he might, perhaps, give at some other time the reasons on which his assertion rested; but at present there were many gentlemen who wished to speak to the question; and he did not choose to have the time of the Convention taken up by a discussion thus forced upon him by the gentleman from Chesterfield.

Mr. Leigh rejoined: he thought there had been nothing either unparliamentary or indecent in the request he had preferred to the gentleman from Frederick. The gentleman would certainly wait his own good time. But, in the mean while, he begged leave to join issue with him, and to pledge himself to meet the charge, come it on what ground it might: the history of the Legislature of the State would repel it.

On motion of Mr. Powell of Frederick, the Committee then rose, and thereupon the House adjourned.

FRIDAY, October 30, 1829.

The Convention met at 11 o'clock, and was opened with prayer by the Rev. Mr. Sykes, of the Methodist Church.

The Convention resolved itself into a Committee of the Whole, Mr. Stanard in the Chair.

Mr. Powell rose to address the Commmittee, in opposition to Mr. Green's amendment, and spoke in nearly the following terms:

Mr. Chairman: At no period, upon no occasion of my life, have I felt so much embarrassment as I do at this moment. I fear I have neither physical nor moral strength to sustain the weight. It is not wonderful that I should be embarrassed, when I look through this assembly, containing the assembled wisdom of the State; when I see before me, men grown grey in the pursuit of political service, and who have spent their lives in the application of their science, to promote the happiness and prosperity of their fellow men: men, who will hereafter be consecrated for their profound wisdom and tried patriotism. It would ill become so humble an individual to be otherwise than embarrassed. Mr. Chairman, I have nothing to offer to this Committee, but a plain, unvarnished statement of the grounds and arguments, which have brought me to my conclusions. I cannot invoke the rich stores of fancy or call the decorations of eloquence to my aid.

We have, Mr. Chairman, been deputed here, and clothed with ample powers by the people of Virginia, to form for them a compact of Government for the protection of their lives, their liberty, and for the security of their property. In the discharge of this duty, I know of but one moral or divine law which we are bound to respect and obey: this is, that we shall observe the immutable principles of justice in framing the instrument. There are certain political maxims, hallowed by time and sanctioned by the wisdom of the sages and patriots of former days, and embodied in our Bill of Rights, to which I shall have occasion to refer hereafter, that certainly have no binding or obligatory force upon us, either natural or divine, but which certainly are entitled to great respect and influence, where they are applicable. Our duty, as I have said, is to form a compact of Government; in doing this, certainly, every member has an unquestioned right to offer his propositions, and insist on their admission into the compact. In doing so, the member is the only proper judge of the justice and expediency of his proposition, and is not bound to yield his own opinion to the influence of any political maxim; except where such maxim has intrinsic worth to recommend it. We have, then, a moral rule to govern us, which, we are not at liberty to violate, and we have political maxims to guide us, so far as we regard these maxims as applicable to existing circumstances. There are also motives and rules of action, personal to ourselves, that ought tobe adverted to. We were not sent here, to gain in this compact, to seek to obtain advantages for those we represent, local or sectional advantages; for myself, I would have indignantly rejected the honorable trust conferred upon me, if it had been expected of me to struggle for local interests, at the sacrifices of the interests of the whole community. I regard myself here, as the representative, as much of the one as of the other sections of the Commonwealth. I regard it as my duty to look to the interests of the whole community, and to provide fundamental laws for the community at large.

With these preliminary views, I shall proceed to the consideration of the questions now before the Committee. It will be conceded, I presume, by every member of the Committee, that in the formation of a compact of Government, the great and leading object ought to be, to conform the Government to the character of the people over whom it is to operate. It will also be conceded, that a Representative Republic, founded upon elementary principles, essentially belonging to such a form of Government, is the best and happiest system for obtaining the end of all Government that can be devised, when the people have the essential qualities to suit them to such a form of Government. Those essential qualities are virtue and intelligence in the people. If they have those qualities, justice demands that they should receive this highest and best gift of Divine Providence, at the hands of those to whom is confided the power of framing their Government. If, on the contrary, they are deficient in those great essentials, such a Government would be to them a curse instead of a blessing. All history and experience prove the truth of this proposition. No wise politician would for a moment contend, that Turkey or Russia could live under such a form of Government. Visionary and dreaming politicians made the experiment in France: the result was a scene of carnage and horror, at which the mind revolts. But, in the same ratio as it would be unjust and impolitic in these countries, to attempt to establish a Republican Government, it would be unjust to refuse a Government of that description, to those who have those essential pillars, on which alone it can rest.

Our first duty, therefore, is to look to the character of the people of Virginia, for whom it is our duty to form a Constitution. If we find them virtuous and intelligent, it would be unpardonable in us, not to frame for them a Constitution, founded upon the pure and essential elements of Republicanism. It would be without excuse, if, in departing from those principles, we infused into the instrument, oligarchical, aristocratical, and monarchical principles, abridging, in any degree, their power of self-government. What, then, is the character of the people of Virginia? Have they virtue; have they intelligence, fitting them for such a system of Government? If they have not, it may be safely affirmed, that there is not, upon the face of the globe, a people of whom we have knowledge, that possesses these requisites; and we have only to deplore the verification of the predictions of all the enemies of civil liberty, who denounce the Republics in this country, as an idle and visionary experiment; and the friends of liberal principles, may sit down and lament over the prostration of their best and fairest hopes. But I confidently maintain, that the people of Virginia, is a community, who *love* virtue and intelligence. To sustain this proposition, I appeal to every member of this Convention, and ask him to look at the people with whom he lives in the district he himself represents, and to say whether they are not a virtuous, an honest, and an intelligent people? For myself, I could say, that the people of the district with whom I live, possess this character. No one will deny that the people of Virginia, were a virtuous and magnanimous people in 1776; that they gave the most striking and conclusive evidence of the most sterling virtue.

With a vindictive and ruthless enemy at their very doors; with every thing to appal and to alarm; in truth, with halters round their necks; the alternative was presented to them, of abandoning their virtue, their principles, and their country, and thereby securing their own safety, or nobly traversing the dangers that encompass them: are the people of Virginia the degenerate sons of such fathers? I think not. A similar occasion would produce similar evidences of virtue at the present day. The demoralizing principle, has not here had the inviting channels which have been opened to it in some other States of the Union. We have no large cities in Virginia, to present an inviting refuge for the vicious, the profligate, and the convicts of foreign countries, and in that way, to introduce them into the heart of the community, spreading their baneful influence in all directions.

But a conclusive evidence of the virtue of the people of Virginia is to be found in the body here assembled. I look around me, and of what materials do I find it composed? Does it not include men most distinguished for their wisdom and for their virtue, their patriotism, and public services? Were not these the qualifications which recommended them to the people of Virginia? Would the people, if themselves vicious, or demoralized, have selected them for such recommendations? What, I ask, is this? Does the report of the Legislative Committee, which we are now considering, recommend an essential, elementary principle, as the basis of a pure Republican Government, suited to a virtuous and enlightened people? If it does, and the principles which I have attempted to maintain, be correct; justice, wisdom, and policy demand that that report should receive our sanction. The principle there recommended, is, that representation in the Legislative Department of Government, should be based upon white population, exclusively. I have said, that there were great political maxims emanating from the wisest and most patriotic statesmen, and sanctioned by all the elementary writers upon the subject of Government; acted upon too, and approved by the people of this Commonwealth for fifty-four years, and embodied in our Bill of Rights; and that we ought to regard them, not as binding authority, but as lights to guide us to correct conclusions. One of these maxims is found in the second section of that instrument, which, among others, is declared, in the preamble of that section, to pertain to the people of this Commonwealth and their posterity, as the basis and foundation of Government. That maxim is, "that all power is vested in, and consequently derived from, the people; that magistrates are their trustees and servants, and at all times amenable to them." To see the application of this maxim, we must first ascertain in what sense the word "people" is there used. It is unquestionably intended to embrace all those within the pale of the community: in other words, all those who are participants in the enjoyment of political power. It follows, therefore, when the community is ascertained, that all political power is vested in that community. By the third article in the Bill of Rights it is provided that a majority hath an indubitable, unalienable, and indefeasible right, to reform, alter or abolish the fundamental laws as shall be judged, &c.

Thus it is perceived that, by the Bill of Rights, and without the Bill of Rights it would be equally true and undeniable, two great principles of Government are established.

1st. That all power is vested in the people.

2nd. That a majority of the people must control the minority, and regulate the exercise of that power.

Apply these two principles to the resolution of the Committee, and they sustain the proposition therein contained.

The truth of these two propositions must be denied, or the resolution must be sanctioned: does this require argument to prove it? The argument is brief. If all power is "vested in the people, and a majority is" to govern, in the exercise of that power, it follows of course, that such majority can only be ascertained by a general vote of the people, or by their agents representing equal portions of the people.

I have thus, according to my intention, endeavored to shew:

1. That Government must be conformed to the characters of the people.

2. That Republican Government is the happiest form of Government, that human wisdom can divine, for a virtuous and intelligent people.

3. That the people of Virginia, have the necessary virtue and intelligence.

4. That the resolution of the Legislative Committee, recommends a principle essentially and necessarily forming an element, of a pure Republican Government.

I will now, Mr. Chairman, proceed to the consideration of the amendment proposed by the gentleman from Culpeper. He proposes to strike out the basis of white population exclusively, as recommended by the Committee, and to insert a totally different basis; a basis to be composed of population and taxation combined:—As to the object of this proposition of amendment, there can be but one opinion; it is intended, distinctly, to give representation (to a certain extent) to wealth, and not to numbers. What is the avowed operation and effect of the amendment, as admitted by its friends and advocates? It will be to give representation to slaves, and political power to their masters in the Legislative Department of the Government; and this, not because they are rational beings, having free will, and the power of exercising such free will, but as *property* exclusively in the hands of their owners, by reason whereof, they are to have and exercise political power. To illustrate: If an individual has one hundred slaves, upon which he pays taxes, he is to have political power in proportion to his number of slaves. This doctrine is new in the political institutions of this State: it is moreover, not only a departure from what has hitherto been regarded as republican, but is in direct conflict with the political maxims, by which the statesmen and patriots of Virginia have heretofore been guided and governed. Let us look, for a moment, to some of the most leading and fundamental of these maxims: In the Bill of Rights it is asserted, that all power is derived from the people, and of right belongs to them. The proposed amendment affirms, that all power is not derived from the people, and vested in them, but that a portion of political power belongs to, and is vested in, *property*, and that not *property* in general, according to the argument, but in a particular species of property. There is another political maxim found in the same instrument, which asserts, that the majority of the people have an indubitable, unalienable, and indefeasible right, to reform, alter or abolish their fundamental laws. The amendment affirms, that this right does not belong to a majority, but that this great and absorbing right, belongs to a *minority* of the *people* and majority of *wealth:* both these propositions cannot be true. The one or the other must be false. Are gentlemen prepared to pronounce these maxims false? They certainly have high, and I would almost venture to say, controlling sanction, when applied to people capable of self-government: they emanated from the wisest and purest statesmen, in the best of times. They are hallowed by time and experience, and are interwoven with the habits and affections of the people of Virginia. Will the Committee at this stage of my argument, indulge me in a simple and practical illustration of the truth of these political maxims. I beg leave to use my illustration, not only to shew, to some extent, the reasons upon which these truths are founded; but also, as an answer to an argument of the gentleman from Orange, in which he insists upon the *quid pro quo*, in the compact we are engaged in making.

I will suppose that a community of fifty individuals have assembled together for the purpose of forming for themselves a system of Government. Of these individuals, forty are worth 100 dollars each: the residue ten, worth 2000 dollars each. They agree as to the object of the compact. It is to protect their lives, and their liberty, and to secure their property. The next object is the details of this compact. I will take the *joint-stock* principle of the gentleman from Northampton. Ten wealthy individuals bring into contribution, their lives, their liberties, and their two thousand dollars each. The poorer and most numerous class bring also their lives, their liberties, and their one hundred dollars each, which constitutes their all, into the joint-stock. The rich say, "we have two thousand dollars each: you have but one hundred dollars each. We have, consequently, twenty times as much property to protect by the provisions of this compact as you have. We, therefore, insist upon having, in all matters about which we are to legislate, ten votes for your one. This provision is necessary for the protection of our property, against your cupidity. Otherwise, having the majority of numbers, you might legislate our two thousand dollars out of our pockets into yours." What would be the obvious answer to such a demand? "It is true you have the most property; but our lives and our liberties are as dear to us, as your lives and your liberties can be to you. As to property, we bring into common-stock our all, you do no more. Our all is as dear to us, though not so great, as yours can possibly be to you. The compact can be only durable, as founded upon the mutual confidence of the contracting parties. Besides, if *you* shall have, by virtue of your property, the political power which you claim, you may exercise that power upon our lives and liberties, as well as upon our property. If, by virtue of our numbers, we are to be feared, as to matters of property, why may we not equally fear for our liberties, if we give to *you*, who are the *minority*, the power to govern us; especially as you have the wealth, which is power in itself?" At this moment, when the Convention is about to be broken up upon this matter, as to the distribution of power, a neighboring horde of marauders and plunderers are seen hovering round our supposed community, with the evident intent of conquering and plundering them. What would the wealthy minority think and say? "We have not strength to defend ourselves without your aid. Not only our property, but our lives and liberties will fall a prey to our enemies. It is our wealth especially which has allured them; we shall be the peculiar objects of their vengeance. We close with your terms: with your aid, our defence and protection is certain." The invading foe is repelled, at the risk, perhaps at the expense, of the blood of the majority. I would ask the gentleman from Orange, whether there would not be here a *quid pro quo*. Sir, I hope the day is far distant, when this Commonwealth will be exposed to war or invasion; but it is certainly wise to look forward and to make provision for such an event. When that day shall arrive, depend upon it, the wealthy few will find their remuneration for the loss of political power, which they now deprecate, in the dauntless bravery and ardent patriotism of the free white population of Virginia, in defending them from the only danger they have a right to apprehend to their property.

I have always thought, Mr. Chairman, that in a republican form of Government, so far from giving to wealth political power, the liberty of the citizen required that safe-guards should be provided, to prevent wealth from drawing to itself too great a portion of power. More than one successful conquerer has said, "give me money, and I will conquer the world."

But it is said, that Government is intended to protect property: this is certainly true. But where is this protection to be found? Is it to be found in parchment stipulations in the compact of Government? By giving to property, preponderating political power? By declaring that the minority of the people shall govern the majority, because of their wealth? By placing wealth in a hostile attitude to physical strength? Certainly not. This would truly be "a paper guarantee," which the eloquent gentleman described and rejected the other day, as visionary and delusive; and all his arguments, as to its inefficacy and futility, apply here with full force.

Sir, the only effectual guarantee, against the abuse of power in a republic, is to be found, and to be found only, in the *virtue* and *intelligence of the people*, in whom all power rests. While virtuous and intelligent, they will do no act of injustice or rapine. And when they become vicious, and fit for violence and spoil, it is in vain to attempt to restrain them by compact stipulations. When vice prevails, the republican form of Government cannot exist: it has, in itself, the elements of its dissolution. Some other form of Government must be resorted to: under which, indeed, the many may be restrained from plundering the few, but where the many will be plundered *by* the few.

Mr. Chairman, one leading objection to the amendment, which operates powerfully on my mind, is, that we have been deputed here, under a hope, entertained by the majority of the people of Virginia, that the very principle recommended by the Committee, may be incorporated in the Constitution. If this hope is disappointed, you will have a lasting cause of discontent. Sir, they will not be satisfied. The Constitution you offer them will be rejected. I do not, indeed, believe, nay, I am confident, that the people of Virginia would not, in such an event, so far as I know them, rise in their majesty, and demand the object of their wishes. I do not believe that there would be any disorderly or revolutionary manifestations of their displeasure. God forbid there should.

If I am mistaken, I pledge myself with my best powers, to prevent or delay any such feelings. But, I am satisfied, they would unceasingly, year after year, crowd the table of this Hall with their memorials and petitions, complaining of their wrongs and demanding redress, until the call of another Convention would be extorted, under a state of fearful excitement. Every gentleman would deprecate such a result.

Ought we, then, to infuse into the compact, any principle calculated to lead to such consequences, unless demanded by considerations in themselves irresistible.

Let us, then, attentively examine the grounds on which the principle is supported.

It is said, that the slave-holding portion of the community fear, that unless this amendment is adopted, their rights and interests in their slaves will be endangered, or abused; that the political power of the State, will, in the hands of the non-slave-holding portion of the community, be used to their oppression. These fears are either well, or ill founded. I think I have shewn, by the aid of the gentleman from Northampton, that if those fears are well founded, that no security is to be found in any paper stipulation on the subject, or by the adoption of the amendment; because these fears presuppose that the people are vicious, corrupt, and dishonest: and if such be the fact, no possible security can be formed, recognizing the right of self-government in the people. But, Sir, depend upon it, there is no ground of such fears, from any calculations I have been able to make. But, is there not a perfect security to the rights of the slave-holders, if it be a fact, that they will still retain the political power of the State, even upon the basis recommended by the Committee? My friend and colleague in his arguments to this Committee, proved, beyond question, by statistical calculations and facts, that the adoption of the resolution by the Committee, would *not* transfer the controlling political power to the non-slave-holding portion of the community; but that a majority in the Legislative Department of the Government, would still be left to the slave-holders. If this be true, surely, no gentleman would apprehend, for a moment, that those holding the power, would exercise it to the sacrifice of *their own* interests. I pray the Committee, to look for a moment, to their statistical tables, and they will find the most conclusive evidence, that the majority of the Legislative body, if the principle of the white basis be adopted, would still remain in the slave-holding portion of the community. Keeping out of view the slave-holding interest, which exists to some extent, in the country beyond the Alleghany, and assuming the eastern base of the Blue Ridge, as the western boundary of the slave-holding population, there it will be found the slave-holding interest predominates. If to this you add the slave-holding interest in the Valley, you give an overwhelming majority to the slave-holders. The fears of gentlemen must vanish before facts so conclusive. But, Mr. Chairman, we ask the high-minded honorable gentlemen of the east, to remember the charitable rule of judging others by ourselves. It is with unfeigned pleasure, that I bear testimony to the fact, that the slave-holding country of the east, have never done us injustice on the subject of taxation, though it has always been in their power to do so. They have most liberally contributed to the revenue of the State, by taxation on their slaves. Why, then, fear to trust the people of the west, if controlling political power, should devolve upon them? Have we less virtue and honesty? Are we made of different materials? We have not received injustice at *your* hands; why, then, should you apprehend it at *ours*?

It is said, that there is a diversity of interests in the different parts of the State, which must be harmonized by compromise. It is hardly possible to conceive a community in which there is *not* a diversity of interests.

Sir, diversity of interests is always to be protected by wise legislation; and there is no fear that every interest will not be fully and fairly represented in our Legislative body. If there be warring, and conflicting interests, the question would then be, could *any* Constitutional stipulations or provisions reconcile such interests? But it remains to be proved, that there *are* warring and conflicting interests within this Commonwealth. I do not admit the fact.

The gentleman from Northampton has asked us, whether we will consent to take all the political power, and bear all the pecuniary burdens? To this inquiry I indignantly answer no. The gentleman would reject such a proposal himself. We will neither *buy* nor *sell* political power; we regard it as the unalienable property of the people, which they have not a right to barter away or divest themselves of, either for themselves, or their posterity.

The gentleman from Orange, has reprobated the idea of giving political power to property alone. I concur with him in his reprobation. But has the gentleman reflected, how far the amendment he advocates, in effect, leads to the same result? He must admit, that the minority of the people ought not to, and cannot, govern the majority; but he contends, that property connected with that minority, ought to govern. What, then, is it that constitutes this right to govern, upon his hypothesis? It is certainly property.

Mr. Chairman, I have done. I have presented my plain views, in my plain way. I am thankful to the Committee for their polite attention, whether it proceeded from courtesy to myself, or from respect to any thing that I have said.

Mr. Morris of Hanover, then rose, and addressed the Committee substantially as follows:

After the able discussion this question has undergone, I cannot flatter myself with the hope of throwing upon it much additional light. But, as my constituents feel themselves very deeply interested in its decision, I hope to be indulged, while I assign the reasons which will govern my vote upon it. I promise, in so doing, not to detain the Committee long.

Mr. Chairman, it seems to me, that the question, which the gentleman from Frederick (Mr. Powell) has just been discussing, is not the question now before us for consideration. The question we have to decide, is, whether representation in the Legislative branch of our Government, shall be based upon numbers only, or on a combined ratio of population and taxation: from some of the remarks which have fallen from the gentleman from Frederick, he seems to have considered the question to be whether it should be based on *all who enjoy the elective franchise*, or on *all the fighting men in the community*. These are not the matters which we are now considering. When they shall be presented to us, if they ever shall be presented, the proper time will arrive to attempt an answer to what he has advanced. The question now before us is a very short one. Shall representation be based on numbers only? Or upon population and taxation combined? The question is short, but in its decision is involved much of the happiness or misery of this our ancient Commonwealth. Before I examine it more minutely, let me be allowed to make a remark or two, in reply to some of the observations of gentlemen on the other side of this question.

As the end of all good Government is the protection of property as well as of persons, it is not enough for those gentlemen to prove that their personal rights will be endangered unless representation shall be based upon numbers alone. If they had proved this, which I humbly conceive they have not, still, if we are not assured that our rights of property will be secure under such an arrangement, their observations fall short of the mark; they do not cover the whole ground. Even, if it be true, that they will not be protected in their personal rights, without the introduction of the new clause in the Constitution, yet, if that clause, in its practical effect, goes to lay prostrate our property at their feet, they have not proved to us that the article ought to be inserted.

Their argument might, indeed, shew us, that it will be right to propose to the people of Virginia *two* Constitutions instead of one; or else that some middle principle must be resorted to, which shall protect both persons and property; but if no mode can be found, of giving protection to both; if the incongruity between the two interests really be so great, that either one or the other must be sacrificed, I agree that the Convention should provide two different Constitutions. I earnestly hope, however, that no such necessity will be found to exist. I hope it will appear, that we may, at the same time, be able to secure to the west the enjoyment of their personal rights; and to the east, the safe possession of their property. I hope this, as a Virginian: for I feel my pride interested in keeping the lines of the State as they exist at present. Sorry should I be, to run a *new line* across the whole of our ancient territory; nor can I ever agree to such a measure, unless it shall be found necessary for the protection of the personal rights of one portion of the State, and the property of the other. I deprecate the existence of such a necessity. Whether gentlemen on the other side of the question, by the uncompromising perseverance with which they insist on carrying all the points they have in view, shall bring us to this necessity, I will not even allow myself to consider.

Let us see, Sir, whether there be any thing in representative Government, which so imperiously requires the insertion of this clause; whether it be indispensable for the preservation of a Republican Government, that representation in the Legislative Department shall be bottomed upon numbers only. If this principle be true, and our conflicting interests be, indeed, so irreconcileable, as some gentlemen seem to suppose, I know not, I confess, to what consequences it may lead. But whatever may be the basis, upon which representation is made to rest, I am satisfied that we must have a Republican Government. Our people are not only capable of enjoying that form of Government, and desire to have it, but we cannot make for them any other. Because there is another Government, of which we are also members, which has guaranteed to every State within its operation, a republican form.

But is it necessary that such a Government shall be based upon numbers only? When this debate commenced, it seemed that the principal source of argument was drawn from an inherent, independent, *a-priori* right by which a numerical majority were entitled to govern: such a right was urged upon us with great earnestness at first; but since the able and convincing address of the gentleman from Northampton (Mr. Upshur) it appears to have been nearly, if not quite abandoned: and now the position we are left to combat, is, that this right of the majority is a *Conventional* right; that it exists by the agreement of our ancestors, and, therefore, ought to prevail. They derive the proof in support of this position from the Bill of Rights, and the general principles there laid down; and without paying the least regard to the specifications in the Constitution itself, they insist that the general positions in the Bill of Rights ought to be received as giving the universal rule for all free Governments. And really, Sir, were we to look at the language of that instrument and to look no further, there might seem to be much force in their argument. But it is an established rule of interpretation, that in order to get at the true meaning of any instrument, you are not to look at one of its parts only, separately and apart from the residue, but you are to take the whole record, and compare one part with another, and thus judge of the connected meaning of the whole. If that rule is pursued here, we shall be obliged to concede that the venerable men who were the authors, both of the Bill of Rights, and of the Constitution of the State, were in the former stating general principles only: they were laying the foundation, not building the superstructure; and when they did afterwards build it, built on no such interpretation of the first instrument as is now contended for. The reason gentlemen give for this, is a very strange one. They tell us that those illustrious men were too much hurried; the roar of hostile cannon was too audible, and their place of meeting was too near a ruthless enemy, to make their work what it would otherwise have been. They, therefore, could not carry out the principles they had laid down in the Bill of Rights, in the subsequent structure of the Constitution. It does not seem to have occurred to gentlemen, that if the near neighborhood of the enemy, and the roar of hostile cannon, and the dangers and alarms of a state of war, operated with so much force upon their minds, when they were drawing up the articles of the Constitution, the same circumstances may reasonably be supposed to have operated with equal force when they were drawing up the articles of the Bill of Rights. If they were in too great a hurry to *carry out* general principles in the Constitution, we may as well suppose they were in too great a hurry to *limit* those principles, when they laid them down in the Bill of Rights. If we must conclude, that they would have made the one of these instruments very different from what it is, if they had had more time for deliberation, why is it not as fair, to draw the same conclusion with respect to the other? But, Sir, is the fact so? was the Constitution drawn up in all this haste? Were those wise men, after laying the foundation of the house on one plan, obliged to build the house itself on another? I am sure the gentlemen believe what they have stated to be strictly true, but nothing is more certain than that they are entirely mistaken. Sir, there are men now living, I was almost ready to say, there are men here present, who could inform this Committee, that every article in that Constitution was duly and diligently considered; aye, Sir, was debated, inch by inch. But I will not appeal to the living. I will appeal to the testimony of one of the most distinguished statesmen, whom this State or this country ever produced, but who is now no more. I could support by his testimony a multitude of facts on this subject, all going to verify the assertion I have made. I refer to Mr. Jefferson, who has left conclusive evidence to shew, that nothing like haste, nothing at all of the hurry supposed by gentlemen to have thrown the Constitution into its present form, had any existence. He says expressly, that that instrument was discussed, paragraph by paragraph, and disputed inch by inch: that the debate was protracted so as to produce weariness, and that in consequence of this weariness, a "projet" of his own, which he forwarded to a member of the Convention, was not submitted to its consideration, and, of course, not adopted, whilst its preamble was. I think, therefore, that those who are driven to contend, that while the Bill of Rights was drawn up with the utmost coolness and deliberation, the Constitution was hurried over amidst the roar of cannon, and from fear of the enemy, are mistaken in their facts: the evidence is all against them: and I am persuaded that they themselves, if they consult again the history of that time, will acknowledge that they have been in error. Let the consideration have its due weight, that both these instruments were drawn up by the same men, and at the same time; and that, in the exercise of the same wisdom, and with the same deliberation and care, they laid down, first, the principles, and then the form of a Government for Virginia. Apply, then, to these two valuable legacies of our forefathers, the principles of interpretation I have before mentioned. Do not take up one half the instrument, and say it means thus, and thus; but put both the parts together: They were both fashioned by the same hand: let all the strings sound, and then, if I mistake not, we shall be led to a different conclusion. If the framers of these two instruments understood themselves, and if on comparing the one with the other, it shall appear that the meaning of the Bill of Rights is not such as, taken alone, it might seem to bear; we must give effect to the provisions of the whole, so far as we can. For example, take the language of the Bill of Rights on the subject of the right of suffrage. Then take up the Constitution, and ask what it has enacted on the same subject? and see if there be any thing like contradiction between them. The Bill of Rights declares, that all persons "having sufficient evidence of permanent common interest with, and attachment to, the community," shall be entitled to vote. The question to be settled is, what is the true meaning of this declaration? Some gentlemen reply, that the fact of having been born within the State, furnishes all the evidence required; others tell us that a residence of two years is sufficient evidence; others require a residence of five years; and almost every gentleman has some qualification of his own. But do the framers of the Constitution and the Bill of Rights tell us any such thing? No, Sir; they say that the evidence they considered sufficient, is a FREEHOLD.

Do gentlemen tell me that here is a contradiction? Why, Sir, take the general principle in its abstract form; and you might argue from it till you bring us at length to universal suffrage. But take the naked principle, and view it in connection with the Constitution, and there you find, that freeholders, and freeholders only, were in the contemplation of those who laid down the principle. The one gives the interpretation of the other. The *general principle*, is in the Bill of Rights. The *limitation* is in the Constitution. The same remark is true, as applied to every other article. Let us apply the same mode of interpretation to the third article of the Bill of Rights.

The gentlemen say that all free white citizens in the State, are to be numbered, and that a majority of that number have the right to rescind, alter or new model the Constitution as they please; that they are to have the law-making power; in short, that they are to have all the power of the State: and we might have supposed that the framers of the Bill of Rights thought so too, had they not left on record a provision to the contrary. When they come to make the Constitution and ordain the law-making power, they *limit* the general principle laid down in the third article of the Bill of Rights, and confide that power, not to the *free white people*, but to the *freeholders in the several counties*.

Here, Sir, you find that they intended, not a majority of the free white male citizens merely, but a majority of citizens, capable of affording sufficient pledges that they would not abuse the authority entrusted to them. This is the majority to which they looked, and here is the limitation of the principle in the Bill of Rights. Let the gentlemen themselves say, if this comparison does not give the true interpretation.

It was said by the gentleman from Brooke, (Mr. Doddridge) that the Constitution has recognized no principle, by which slave-holders are to be protected.

[Here Mr. Doddridge explained. What he had said was, that the Constitution recognizes no such principle, as representation in virtue of property.]

Mr. Morris resumed. He had not misunderstood the gentleman; but would now undertake to shew that he was mistaken. It is true, said he, that the word "slave," is not mentioned either in the Bill of Rights or in the Constitution: neither do we ask that it should be inserted now. But when, in 1776, Virginia gave the control of her Government to *freeholders*, she granted it to *slave-holders*: nor could she have given to the latter a more effectual guarantee. The freeholder was himself a slave-holder. Was it necessary, expressly to say, that this was done for the protection of property? Sir, we infer it from the act. Virginia by her *act*, granted the power of the State, to men who held the very property, we desire to secure. And now let the gentleman from Brooke, give to the slave-holders the same power which was confided to them by the Constitution of '76, and so far as this subject is concerned, I am willing to adopt his proposition immediately.

It was said by my friend from Chesterfield, that this principle of basing representation upon numbers alone, is *new*: and I concur with him in that sentiment. The principle is not to be found in the existing Constitution: that instrument confides the power, not to a majority of free whites, but to a majority of freeholders. My friend did not say, that no such claims as are now advanced, had ever been made before. He was well aware of the abortive efforts, of which the gentleman from Brooke, has favored the Committee with an account: he knew perfectly well, that this doctrine had been asserted at Staunton twelve or fifteen years ago; but he thought, as I do also, that the memorial from Staunton, and the abortive efforts in the Legislature, had not affixed this new principle to the Constitution; a principle so different from those laid down by our forefathers in 1776, and which are calculated to protect, not only personal rights, but the rights of property also. The principle of a majority of mere numbers, was not only, not the basis of the existing Constitution, but it had been expressly and most solemnly declared, on various occasions, that it is unsafe to lay the basis of representation in any such principle. Such a declaration was the ground of the provision in relation to slaves, which is contained in the Federal Constitution; a provision, not which we *yielded*, but on which we ourselves *insisted*. Virginia, before she entered the confederacy, insisted that her representation in that confederacy should *not* be according to the numbers of her white population alone. And who, Sir, were the men that thus contended in the memorable Convention which framed the Federal Constitution? Some of those very men who framed our own State Constitution, and drew up the Bill of Rights. Yes, Sir, the very men, who laid down the abstract principles, from which gentlemen attempt to maintain the doctrine of a white basis exclusively, insisted that our Federal representation should be compounded of property as well as numbers. We did not acquiesce in the principle: We *demanded* the principle. We demanded it as a protection for all this great southern country, which was then filled with slaves. Protection against whom? against enemies? dishonest and rapacious? and who would be tempted by interest to depredation and rapine? No, Sir, against men, just as kind-hearted, just as upright, just as honorable, just as generous, as are our brethren now: Against men who had shed their blood in our common struggle for independence; men, who had lain with us side by side in the camp, and stood with us, side by side in the battle, not ten years before. And why, Sir? Why did we demand such a pledge? Because we held it *necessary* to our protection. Not that we suspected their motives; not that we imputed to them wickedness; but because we knew then, as all men know now, that unless property is protected, it will be invaded. Virginia stood in relation to the Union at that day, as we now stand towards our brethren of the west. And will our brethren deny, what our sister States of the Union granted? I do not deny, that other considerations entered into the Federal Compact, besides the mere distribution of power. *Union* was a most important object; so important, that almost any thing was to be sacrificed for the sake of attaining it: yet, notwithstanding the importance of union, and the earnest, anxious desire for it, which was felt by Virginia, she, nevertheless, insisted upon this point as a *sine qua non*: Unless that was inserted in the Federal Constitution, Virginia would not take that Constitution.

Sir, we are called upon now, when placed in like circumstances, to give up the great principle for which they thus contended; and can it be said that we have fewer motives to insist upon it than they had? If such is the fact, let it be shewn: but if not, as it is not, what apology can we make to posterity? Let Virginia give up this principle and what will be said? Will it not be said, that the great southern State, has given up the great southern doctrine for which she contended in 1789? And, when the decision of that question shall be agitated in the Federal Government, how shall we stand? "Virginia the great southern State, has given up the point. It is vain for the rest of the south, to attempt to maintain it." But, Sir, there is a necessity for our maintaining it. You have been told by the gentleman from Northampton, that one eleventh part of our power in the Federal Government, is derived from this principle, and rests upon it. Cut it down, by the act of this Convention, and how will the south sustain itself in our National Councils? Mr. Chairman, we have *more* motives than our fathers had on this subject. We have given up to the Federal Government, the entire power of laying duties upon imposts. We have surrendered all our most valuable sources of revenue into their hands, and now we have few resources left but direct taxation upon our lands and slaves. At the time of the adoption of the Federal Constitution, the wise men, who framed that instrument, knew that all the resources of foreign commerce were to be in the hands of the Federal Government, and that the necessity of resorting to direct taxation, would seldom arise. If, then, our ancestors thought it necessary, at that day, to insist on the principle; if they rejected a representation based on numbers, and insisted on a guarantee for the protection of property, can our motives be less for a similar policy? Surely not. They are magnified ten-fold. Those who framed the General Government, were well aware of the vast resources which must be derived to it, from foreign commerce: but, we know, by sad experience, that a State Government can have no resources for wealth, but what she derives from direct taxation. If our fathers insisted on a guarantee against the mere *contingency*, that the General Government might, sometimes be obliged to resort to direct taxation, how much more ought we to be on our guard, whose direct taxes are annually and daily recurring?

But, Sir, we have given other evidence, that, in our judgment, the interpretation which the gentlemen would put upon the Bill of Rights, is not the true one. Not only did the very men, who drew up our Bill of Rights, themselves insist upon a compound basis of numbers and property; but look, Sir, how we ourselves have disposed of power, in the structure of the Senate of the United States. I know the case is not, in all points, parallel; but I refer to it, as going to shew, that, in the judgment of Virginia, mere numbers never do constitute a fit basis for representation, (unless, indeed, where the peculiar nature of the case is such, that they are, in themselves, an all-sufficient guarantee;) but, wherever great interests, either political or pecuniary, are about to be placed in jeopardy, a different principle is instantly resorted to. I say, then, that in the construction of the less numerous branch of the Federal Legislature, so far from admitting the principle of a mere majority of numbers having the right to rule, we agreed, that that principle should be, in a still greater degree, disregarded, than is proposed now by the amendment before us. We stipulated expressly, that all the States should enjoy, in that body, a strictly equal representation. The little States of Delaware, Rhode Island, and New-Jersey, are precisely on a footing with Virginia, New-York, and Pennsylvania. Sir, is there any thing here like an equality of numbers? The inequality is vast; it is infinite: far, far beyond any thing that is asked or thought of between us and our transmontaine brethren.

Why was such an article as this, inserted in the Federal Constitution? It was for the purpose of preserving the political sovereignty of the small States; and it was necessary to that end. Numbers did not, and could not prevail. If they had, the small States would have been in jeopardy every hour. We deliberately agreed to the arrangement. We ourselves said, that in point of representation in the Senate, Rhode Island and Delaware should be on the same footing with Virginia or New-York.

I know it may be urged, that this was not a compromise among individuals, but among sovereign States. Granted. But, are we not making a compromise, similar in character and principle? A compromise to preserve the rights of individuals, as dear to them, and as important to them, as political sovereignty can be to a State. Is it not for the preservation of that on which their families are to subsist? For the preservation of their property?

It is a compromise, on the same principle and for the same end; with this only difference, that property is in the place of political power.

Numbers then, were not in '76 or in '87, the principle by which the people of Virginia, were regulated, in conferring power either on her own State authorities, or those of the Federal Government.

Is there no great interest concerned in this question? Shall we be told that it is not a great interest which is to be protected? Aye, but it is said that interest is not in jeopardy. Sir, what is the present actual condition of this State? In what position do we stand? In this position: The slave population on this side the Blue Ridge, amounts to 390,000; the slave population beyond the Blue Ridge, amounts to 50,000. On this side the Ridge is raised more than three-fourths of the entire amount of taxes paid in the State. Beyond that Ridge is raised less than one-fourth of those taxes. Beyond that Ridge, lie 40 counties. Some of these of rich and fertile land, and one of the most beautiful limestone valleys on which the sun shines. And yet, Sir, this whole region of country, from the Blue Ridge to the Ohio river, is drawing every year from the public chest, for the administration of justice, and the purposes of representative Government, a sum greater than it brings into the general fisc. And now, Sir, what are we asked to do? While we pay three-fourths of the taxes, and they one-fourth, and while they draw from the treasury, more than they pay into it, we are asked to adopt into our Constitution an article by which the whole political authority and tax-laying power of the State, shall be transferred beyond the Ridge ! Sir, I do not say, nor do I believe, that the people west of the Ridge, are any less moral, or in any respect, worse than those to the east of it: but I would ask them, with all frankness, whether *they* would feel safe in the like circumstances? Whether such a state of things could be called Republican? Or, whether it would not interfere with the very first principles of Republican Government? I ask, what is the money raised by taxation in a free Government? Is it a contribution *extorted* by the power of a despot? By the King or his Nobles? Has any power, existing in a Republic, a right to take away from me, 10, 20, 50 per cent. of my property, without any consultation with me or my representative? No, Sir. It is of the very essence of Republican Government, that all money raised for public purposes, shall be the voluntary donation of the people, by themselves or their agents. But what sort of a donation is that, where another lays the tax and makes the donation out of my property? Is that the donation of the holder? Sir, I was surprised when the gentleman from Norfolk said, the other day, that taxation and representation, sprang from different fountains, and flowed into different and distant oceans.

My little reading had led me to believe, that the representative principle in modern times, and as it now exists upon the American Continent, owed its birth to the British House of Commons; where representation, according to our notion of it, first existed. That was the *model* from which all the various forms of representative Government, in North and South America, have been taken. In some instances we have improved upon it: in others we have fallen below it; but varied as our forms are, the House of Commons was our original model. Now, that House had no authority in the beginning, but from the fact that its members were the tax-layers. They were called for the purpose of affording aids to the King, out of their property. Sir, it was this searching power of taxation, which gradually elevated the House of Commons, until they were enabled to say to the proudest of their Monarchs, we will not grant you the money for which you ask us, unless we know and approve the purpose to which it is to be applied. From this fountain have proceeded all the Republican Governments on the American Continent. The gentleman is much mistaken in supposing that these two powers are so little together. But let us now recur to the principle that the grantors have a right to be first consulted before their money is disposed of. We are told, Mr. Chairman, that we must rely on the morality, on the integrity and virtue of the majority as a sufficient guarantee. I know the people who live beyond the Ridge; I am acquainted with their character; and I most cheerfully admit that there are none on whose virtue and honor I would more readily rely. But the gentleman from Orange very truly said, that the principle on which all free Governments rest, is not confidence, but jealousy and watchfulness. Would not the good sense of gentlemen feel shocked, if any one here should propose that the Legislature of Ohio should be empowered to tax Virginia? Is there a man on this floor, who, on hearing such a thing mentioned, would not cry out that it was too monstrous a proposition to be tolerated? Now, Sir, I believe that the gentlemen who constitute the Legislature of Ohio, have a general feeling towards Virginia of kindness and good will; and that their integrity is as great as our own. But why revolt, then, at the very idea of their having power to tax us? Cannot we rely upon their morality, their integrity and virtue? Sir, it is not because we deny, or even suspect their morals, that we shrink from such a proposition; but because the Legislature of Ohio cannot know as accurately as we do, the situation of this part of the country, with which they have, comparatively, little connection, and no fellow-feeling; and because men vote taxes with much less caution and care when they do not expect themselves to pay any part of the tax, than when they are personally interested in its effects and responsible to those who must pay. It is one thing to give your assent to a requisition which falls upon those you never saw, and quite another to vote for it when you must go back and bear your own share in the contribution, and face those who are to bear the burden with you. If this principle, viz: that those alone should have power to lay a tax who will be required to pay it, be not a fundamental principle of a representative Government, why is it that the tax-laying power is, by the Federal Constitution, confided to the House of Representatives alone? Why, in a great majority of the States, is the same provision engrafted, that money-bills shall originate in the popular branch of their Legislatures? And if it be, on what ground does the principle rest? Obviously on the fact, that in that branch there will always be found more of the men who are to pay the tax, and who feel intimately with the people, the weight of their financial burdens. Sir, these principles are the very corner-stones of a free Government, and they constitute very striking features in all our State Constitutions. Grant now to the gentlemen, what they are asking by the resolution of the Legislative Committee; and will any one of these principles be brought to bear upon the property of the people who live in the south eastern portion of Virginia? People who hold about 400,000 slaves, and who furnish nearly all the revenue of the State? Taxation is the grant of a people holding property for the purpose of supporting the Government of their choice. But how is it to be a donation? If it is made by the Legislature of Ohio out of the funds of the people of Virginia, all men see at once that it can be no such thing. But if it be done by those who pay less than one-fourth, where we pay more than three-fourths, how is it more our donation than if it was given away by the Legislature of Ohio? Sir, all our property will be swept from us by the plan we are gravely asked to adopt as fair and equal. The people of the west, for example, want to make some Appian, or some Flaminian way, or some Roman aqueduct, or some other such splendid work of Internal Improvement: (It is not my purpose to ridicule works of Internal Improvement. There are some of those works, in support of which, under proper circumstances, I would go as far as they;) but they wish, perhaps, to unite the waters of the Ohio and Potomac, and so they must tunnel the Alleghany. Well, Sir; what will be done? Will they lay taxes to effect these great projects? No, Sir, not all: not at first: they will begin not with taxes, but with debt, and debt is always taxation at last: pay-day must come: and when it has come, then comes the tax; and how is the tax collected? Why, Sir, one-fourth part of it, and less than that, is collected to the west of the Blue Ridge, (i. e. where the great project is carried on) and the remaining three-fourths of it is collected; where, Sir? in the country south-east of that Ridge. When you come to the vote for laying the tax, every member from the south-eastern country is dissatisfied; every one of them is convinced the scheme is totally impracticable and a mere waste of the public money, and he speaks and votes against it. And what is the *effect* of their votes? just what it would have been had they all voted the other way. The donation is made; and it is made out of their property; but it is made by others: it is made by men who embrace entirely different views, and have entirely different interests; men who act most honestly in the matter, being sincerely and strongly of opinion that the project is of great importance; very practicable, and very desirable. Sir, is this a donation? I ask, are the three-fourths of this tax a donation of *ours?* No, Sir, the money is *taken:* it is taken from us: not by Legislative "rapine;" not by the perpetration of wickedness; not at all; but taken from us *against our consent*, because they are of a different opinion from us; and that with respect to matters on which there is confessed to be room for a wide, yet honest difference of opinion. Mr. Chairman, I fear to entrust my brethren with such a power: I fear it because they are not accountable to those whose money they take and have no common interest with them: that is the reason, the republican reason, on which I ground a refusal of their claims.

If I am right, then the highest degree of moral virtue, the most pure and unblemished integrity, and I had almost said, the most sublime intelligence, afford us no adequate protection: for men always have differed, and always will differ, in questions involving great and expensive objects of national enterprize. When the time comes at which the taxes must be levied (though they will not, as I said, begin by direct taxation; nay, it is probable there will be some diminution of taxes for a time, because they will resort to debt, which the people cannot feel, but come they must,) they will fall on those who were never consulted or who were voted down.

Sir, my friend did say that the great principle which lay at the foundation of our revolution, was involved in the amendment now before you; and I am, I confess, of the same opinion. Are not the cases parallel? do they not rest upon the same principle? viz: that the money of the people is not to be taken but by the consent of themselves or their authorised agents? Sir, what was the American Revolution? was it not the resistance of a claim set up by the British Parliament to tax the Colonies without their consent?

We have been told by the gentleman from Brooke (Mr. Doddridge) that America resisted the demand, because, though England and America were under the same Crown, they were different nations; just as Scotland and Ireland were before the union; and so the Legislature of the one could not tax the other. But, Sir, the Colonies came under the British Crown in a way very different from Scotland or Ireland. The question between America and the mother country could never have arisen if she had been situated toward the Crown as was either of those kingdoms. The Charter which fixed the boundaries of Virginia was granted by the King of England to English subjects; to subjects who resided in London; and for a long time, the whole Government of Virginia was conducted in London, subject, however, to the control of Parliament; and it was only after the Colony had become too populous to be thus managed any longer, that the grant was made to it of having a Provincial Assembly. Our situation was more analagous to that of British India, than it was to Ireland or Scotland. But, Mr. Chairman, it was not because Parliament undertook to tax us while we were not represented in that body, that America drew the sword: it was because our Colonial Charters had declared that the Colonists should enjoy all the rights of native-born British subjects; and one of these rights was, that you should not touch their property but by their own consent. That was the ground, and the true ground, of our revolutionary struggle. It was not that we had no representation in Parliament: for as to that, it was even pretended that as by our Charters, our lands were to be held as of the Manor of East Greenwich in the kingdom of England by the tenure of free and common soccage, we constituted a part of the diocese of one of the English Bishops, and were, therefore, virtually represented in the person of his lordship in the Upper House, and by the members from Kent in the other. But our ancestors well knew that representation in Parliament would be no security against oppression. Suppose, to quiet our discontents, Great Britain had offered to allow us to be represented, to how many delegates should we have been entitled? Let me see; there were the two Adamses, and Hancock, and Franklin, and Lee, and Henry, and the Rutledges. Why, Sir, upon the principle contended for by gentlemen, we could not have been authorised to have more than twenty or twenty-five of them; thirty perhaps. (Here a shrill and very peculiar voice was heard to say "less than the county of Wilts.") Less than the county of Wilts, I hear it suggested. Well, Sir; suppose them seated in the House of Commons. A tea tax is proposed. They get up and resist it: they tell the Parliament, in our own American phrase, that America "can't stand it." Suppose them to declare that she ought not to stand it, till at length, *waxing* warmer as they proceed, they tell the House, America *will* not stand it; she will resist the tax. Sir, would it answer any purpose to say this to the Minister in a body containing five hundred members? Some gentleman would immediately get up and say, "Why gentlemen, you are in a minority: you may vote against this tax, if you please; but we, who are more capable of judging what is best for America and for the whole empire, say the tax must be raised." What is the consequence? These old revolutionary men come back; they are asked in some town-meeting, or other assemblage of their fellow-citizens, "How came you to suffer this tax upon tea to be laid?" And they would say (according to gentlemen's doctrine) "we did not consent to the tax; we resisted it to the utmost of our power; we were fully heard; but, the majority was against us; we could not help it; and you must pay the tax; that's all. The money was wanted: It was necessary to aid Frederick to confirm his conquest of Silesia: it was indispensable to prevent a French Prince from mounting the throne of Poland: it must be had to enable the German troops to cross the Rhine." The citizens very likely would reply, "why, what are all these things to us? We care nothing about Frederick, or Silesia either: is our money to go for such projects?" The old men would shrug their shoulders, and reply, "you must e'en pay the tax." Would the men of the revolution, have suffered the powers of this great nation to be crushed in the cradle by miserable sophistications like these? Sir, I ask you, if they were not made of sterner stuff? Would they not have said to the people of the United States, (what they did say,) "unless you resist this, the resources of your country will never be unfolded: you can never reach the period of manhood: you must resist, or be ruined."

Sir, I bring no charge or accusation against gentlemen on the other side: I have no doubt whatever of the purity of their motives: but, for myself, I cannot imagine a more frightful despotism than to enable one great division of the country to set itself in opposition to another great division of it, and by a majority of one single vote, to take from them whatever they please.

We are told that when we have given them supreme power, they intend to exercise it with great mildness and moderation; that they will not avail themselves of it to do the least injustice, but will manage our affairs with great forbearance and liberality.

But might not the same language be held to the subjects of the most absolute despot on earth? Despotism does not consist in the actual *exercise* of arbitrary power. The greatest despot in the world may be constitutionally mild, and may rule his people with great clemency. But it is the *authority* to oppress, which constitutes despotism. And if we are to be so situated, as to be left absolutely dependent upon the will of others, and nothing we can do or say is to have the least effect in resisting it: if we are to rely for our security upon the mere *sic volo* of another man, what will they be but despots? and what shall we be but slaves? Sir, do we ask any thing which may enable *us* to be thus despotic over *them?* No, Sir, we are but asking what we have obtained already, in the Federal compact. We ask only that *that* shall be done in Virginia, which has been done in the Carolinas, and has produced nothing but perfect concord: and which has been done by our sister Georgia, and produced there the most entire domestic tranquillity. If you yield to our proposal, of a mixed basis of representation, it will not throw the people of the west at *our* feet, as the adoption of the other plan must infallibly throw *us* at *theirs*. Let us set off to lay what taxes we please, to operate beyond the mountain, and their operation must be precisely equal upon ourselves. With the exception of slaves only, the articles of taxation are the same on both sides of that boundary; so that we must either tax ourselves with them, or be guilty of the open barefaced villainy of saying in our law, that the tax shall operate on A, but it shall not in like circumstances, operate on B.

But, surely, Sir, there can exist no danger that either we or they will thus use the taxing power. Among honorable men, it is surely not necessary to say that taxes shall be made to operate equally on all in like circumstances. But, Sir, while we are thus restricted, so that we cannot tax our brethren unless we also tax ourselves, *we* have a species of property which *they* have not; and on which they may lay what tax they please, without themselves paying under that law, a single dollar. And this too, a sort of property, the most easy to be taxed of all others, and the most certain of raising the money. Payment is inevitable. But, suppose us to lay a tax upon cattle: when we go to look for the cattle of our brethren of the west, where are they to be found? Their's, Sir, are the cattle on a thousand hills: they raise enough for their own use, and ours: and have a large surplus besides, wherewith, to supply a foreign market; while we have so few, that we can hardly make our own butter; and yet, strange to tell, when we did once make the experiment, of laying such a tax, we had ourselves to pay the greater part of it. Sir, it depends, altogether, at what season the tax-gatherer happens to visit our brethren, whether *they* shall pay the tax or *we*. I don't believe, Sir, that the number of their cattle is known even to themselves; and I dare say, there are gentlemen here present, who would not know their own herds, if they should meet them on a mountain twenty miles from home. But, lay your tax upon slaves, Sir, and *they* are not fattened this week, and gone the next, before the tax-gatherer can come for his dues. They are here; I had almost said they are fixed here firmly; but I know there are some gentlemen, who tell us, that we shall, at some future day, get rid of them all. Sir, I give all credit to the integrity of the west; but, really, if this plan of their's shall succeed, the prophecy may possibly be fulfilled; for, then, I think, we shall be obliged to give them up. Not that I have any fear, that when these gentlemen get the power, they will pass a general emancipation law; but, if they raise the tax on slaves, much higher than it is, one of two things must happen: either the *master* must run away from the *slave*, or the *slave* from the *master*. The more fertile districts of the State; the rich low grounds of James River, for instance, may be able to bear a greater burthen; but upon the increase of the slave tax, much of it must be paid by that portion of the lower country which consists of sterile ridges. Slave-labour upon them cannot stand it, and if they go on to raise the taxes, our slaves must go somewhere else, because we cannot keep them.

Perhaps some gentlemen may consider it a very desirable thing, that we should be reduced to such a necessity; but, Sir, let it once be known, that this separation of the master and his slave is not a voluntary thing on either side, but a matter of compulsion, produced by the agency of the Government: I care not, whether this agency be manifested by the passage of a law of emancipation, or a tax-law depriving the master of the power of holding his slave: and soon a sword will be unsheathed, that will be red with the best blood of this country, before it finds the scabbard. This thing between master and slave, is one which *cannot* be left to be regulated by the Government. Compensation for 400,000 slaves, *can* not be made. The matter must be left to the silent operation of natural causes. Sir, I impute no evil purpose to our brethren of the west; but I never can, nor will consent that it shall be left for them to say what tax thall be paid on the slaves of Virginia, while their owners have no voice in the matter.

Sir, let us choose a middle ground: a ground which so many of the Republics of America have already taken: let us agree upon a compound basis of representation, and remain a united and harmonious people.

After Mr. Morris had closed, the Committee rose, and the Convention immediately adjourned.

SATURDAY, October 31, 1829.

The Convention assembled at eleven o'clock, and was opened with prayer by the Rev. Mr. Skidmore, of the Methodist Church.

On motion of Mr. John S. Barbour, the Convention resolved itself into a Committee of the Whole, Mr. Stanard in the Chair.

Mr. Campbell (of Brooke,) then addressed the Chair, in nearly the following terms:

Mr. Chairman—I have never been in the habit of making apologies; I never liked them. When I hear apologies from gentlemen, who, either have acquitted themselves well, or expect to acquit themselves well, I am reminded of the lady in the play;

> Who, in hopes of contradiction, oft would say,
> Methinks, I look so wretchedly to-day.

But really, Sir, I am compelled to make an apology on the present occasion. When I rise to address an assemblage composed of such illustrious patriarchs, sages and politicians; when I consider their superior age, experience and attainments, and that I am not only little experienced, but without experience in such addresses as I am now to make, I cannot but feel embarrassed and intimidated. But, Sir, this embarrassment arises most of all, from the fears which I entertain, that I may not be able to do justice to the cause which reason and conscience have compelled me to espouse. Nay, Sir, I know that I cannot do it justice; and I sincerely say, that I do not expect to meet the expectations of its friends. But I am compelled to contribute my mite; and well, I am assured, that it will be a very small contribution indeed.

I am a *man*, Sir, and as such I cannot but feel interested in every thing which concerns the prosperity and happiness of man.

I feel myself one of the race, and when I consider our origin and our destiny, I see so much to interest me, I cannot but feel a deep interest in every thing connected with the happiness of my species. I am not, Sir, believe me, under the influence of district or local feelings. In all matters to be discussed here, I am a Virginian. I feel myself inspired with that spirit, which regards the interest of every man, slave-holder or non-slave-holder in the State. If I lived in Northampton, I would advocate the same principles which I now do in coming from Brooke. It was *principles*, Mr. Chairman, which brought me here. *Principles*, Sir, which reason, observation and experience convinced me, are inseparably connected with the temporal prosperity of men; and of our State of Virginia: And principles, Sir, which are not to be sacrificed. I know, Sir, that local interests, and district feelings, can only yield to principles. Animosities and contentions must arise between rival interests, unless fellow-citizens are determined to be governed by principles. Too often it happens, from clashing interests, that—

> Lands intersected by a narrow frith,
> Abhor each other, mountains interposed
> Make enemies of nations, who had else
> Like kindred drops, been mingled into one.

But, Mr. Chairman, we are entirely out at sea in this debate. We set sail without compass, rudder, or pilot. So anxious were some gentlemen here to put to sea, that when we called for the compass and the pilot, they exclaimed: Never mind, we will get the compass and the pilot when we get to port. We are now a thousand miles from land. Gentlemen are making fine speeches upon the elements of the ocean, and now and then upon the art of sailing. It will be well if the *rari nantes in gurgite vasto*, apply not to us.

I wanted, Sir, to take the pilot, the compass, and the rudder aboard. But in the good old laconic style, the gentleman from Augusta, exclaimed, "*write the preface after you have written the book.*" Yes, Sir, we shall learn the language before we learn the grammar; we shall demonstrate all the propositions in Euclid, and then learn the *axiomata*, and the *postulata;* we must build the house and then lay the foundation; we must heal the constitution, and then feel the pulse.

I am sorry, Sir, that we did not first establish the principles, or at least, agree upon all the principles on which the frame of Government should be based, before we attempted to form the Constitution.

I see no reasonable bounds can be fixed to this discussion. Every gentleman here has to tell us his own principles, or to oppose those of others; and more than the half of every speech yet pronounced, has been in defence of mere abstractions, as some gentlemen would call them. For my part, I never could reason without some principles to reason from, and some point to reason to. The Bill of Rights of '76 has, it is true, been declared sound doctrine, but gentlemen seem to me, to be continually oppugning it.

Call me orthodox, or call me heterodox, I confess that I believe, that in the science of politics, there are as in all other sciences, certain fundamental principles, as true and unchangeable as any of the fundamental principles of physics or morals.

It is just as true, that Government ought to be instituted for the benefit of the governed, as that a whole is greater than a part; or that a straight line is the shortest possible distance between any two given points.

I had intended, Sir, to examine the arguments in detail, offered by gentlemen in favor of the amendment. Not as if these arguments had not been already refuted, if I may be allowed the expression, by other gentlemen who have preceded me, on the side of the question I espouse. But, Sir, I have found such a similarity of argument, used by the very eloquent pleaders for the basis of wealth and population, that I have this morning rather abandoned the idea of going into these dry details. It will still be necessary, that I pay some attention to some minor matters, which, in my judgment, involve important principles, and the more especially, as the public mind will consider every thing offered here, as of some importance. This community, Sir, will be much indebted to the gentlemen, who have been at so much pains to furnish all the deliberations of this Convention. They will furnish much information, necessary to prepare the public to judge of the merits of the Constitution, which we are to submit to them. Although I am not capable of throwing much, if any light, upon these subjects, I cannot but rejoice that so much will be elicited; and that the public, both our cotemporaries and posterity, will be able to decide upon the wisdom and utility of the various schemes advocated in this Assembly. Yes, Sir, posterity will be able to applaud or censure the views presented, and the course pursued by the advocates of the respective projects.

The remarks, which I am now to offer, will tend to establish four important items:

1. That the principles of the friends of this amendment, are based upon views of society, unphilosophic and anti-republican.

2. That the basis of representation, which they advocate, is the common basis of aristocratical and monarchical Governments.

3. That it cannot be made palatable to a majority of the present freeholders of Virginia: And,

4. That the white population basis, will operate to the advantage of the whole State.

1. I could wish, Sir, that my sole object now was, to fortify and illustrate these positions; but with a reference to the matters before me, I can only attempt this incidentally. My province is rather to follow those on the affirmative, or who plead the policy of the amendment, than to go into new details. Yet still, Sir, I expect, that some or all of these points will be illustrated in the review proposed.

The gentleman (Mr. Morris,) from Hanover, gave us yesterday, a splendid display of his rhetorical powers. I wish I could commend his *logic*, as sincerely as I do his rhetoric. His whole speech was founded upon two or three assumptions, as, indeed, have been those who preceded him on the same side. And, Sir, allow me two or three assumptions, and I don't know what I could not prove. He assumed, that the only legitimate meaning of the Bill of Rights, was to be learned from the Constitution: That the meaning of the phrase "permanent common interest with, and attachment to, the community," meant, a *freeholder*, with twenty-five acres of land, and a cabin on it. But again, he defined the term *freeholder*, as signifying in the year '76, a *slave-holder*. He assumed in the next place, that slave-property was protected, though not named in the Constitution, in confining the Right of Suffrage to freeholders alone. So I understood him. Now, Sir, let these matters be conceded, and the gentleman from Hanover, has the foundation for a fine oration. But another assumption was yet necessary to give wings to his imagination. He must, contrary to the very lucid and statistical expose of the gentleman from Frederick, whose speech he never noticed, he must, I say, assume, that if white population only, should be adopted as the basis of representation, then the non-slave-holders would have the exclusive control in all Governmental arrangements, and would, at once, interfere with the rights of masters to their slaves. Then, Sir, his feelings were roused to the height of true eloquence, and with an inspiration drawn from this view of the matter, he retires with a sword in his hand, stained to the hilt with the best blood in Virginia. I do not think it necessary, Mr. Chairman, to expose an argument, any farther, than to shew it is based upon *assumption* only. Thus shewn, and although it may please our fancy, it cannot inform our judgment.

He then took us with him to London, and shewed us the British Parliament, with some twenty or thirty Americans amongst them. The stamp and tea tax are in debate in the British Parliament, and the American Colonists are found of course debating and voting against it. But what are "twenty-five against five hundred!" Home they come, and tell the doleful tale. They inflame the people, and preach rebellion. They are a minority and must rebel, because they cannot submit. If this picture was pertinent, and designed to operate upon this Committee, then, Sir, it must have been designed either to discredit the popular doctrine of these Republics, viz: that the minority must submit to the majority, or that if the gentleman should find himself in the minority, he would not submit his property to the control of the representatives of white population alone: in fact, this doctrine would lead all minorities into rebellion. I forbear to follow him to Ohio, as this allusion had no reference to any sentiment expressed in this House.

I am sorry to observe so strong a dislike to the doctrine of a majority, appearing in many of the gentlemen's speeches on this floor. If this does not squint towards aristocracy, if it does not lead us towards the principles assumed by the monarchists of the old world, I am not a judge of such matters.

I go back to the honorable gentleman from Culpeper. His first axiom was, *that all men have equal* NATURAL RIGHTS, but not equal *political rights*. That they have the former, he has conceded; but why they ought not to possess the latter, he has not *shewn*. If they have equal *natural* rights, they ought to have equal *Conventional rights;* else, one part of them surrenders a larger share of their natural rights, when they enter into society, than another part. But logic is yet wanting to shew why A, in entering into society, should surrender more of his natural rights than B. Will some gentleman now, or at any future time, shew us the reason why A, in surrendering a part of his natural rights, should be obliged to surrender more than B?

I wish most sincerely, Sir, that that gentleman may yet be able to redeem a pledge which he has staked. He said, he hoped to be able to shew from *the Bill of Rights* itself, "that it was never contemplated to confer on *any man*, the right of governing another against his own consent." He and I most cordially concur in this sentiment, and I hope he may be inclined to go as far in this matter, as his honorable associate, the gentleman from Northampton, who has affirmed, "that he will hold no principle as true, which he will not carry out to its legitimate results." In this I concur with the latter gentleman: and if all the members of this Assembly, concurred with the gentleman from Northampton, Virginia would soon be generated from North to South, from East to West.

He next asserts that the *jus majoris* is not recognized as a *natural* right, but as a *Conventional* right. This may be true, but it will prove as much for us, as for him. In other remarks upon the Bill of Rights, this gentleman makes it a dead letter of very questionable import, and of as questionable authority. Yet, Sir, he decided it on one occasion, at least, to be a part of the Constitution of Virginia. In deciding the case of Crenshaw *versus* The Slate River Company, Randolph's Reports, vol. 6, p. 276, he says, "our Bill of Rights is a part of our Constitution, and the general principles thereby declared are *fundamental laws*, except so far as they are modified by the Constitution itself. They limit the powers of the Legislature, and prohibit the passing any laws violating these principles. The first article declares, 'that all men are by nature free and independent, and have certain inherent rights, of which, when they enter into a state of society, they cannot, by any compact, deprive or divest their posterity; namely, the enjoyment of life and liberty, with the means of acquiring and *possessing property*, and pursuing and *obtaining happiness* and safety;' to deprive a citizen of any property legally acquired, without a fair compensation, deprives him *quoad hoc* of the means of *possessing* property, and of the only means so far as the Government is concerned, besides the security of his person, of obtaining happiness." So decided the honorable gentleman from Culpeper, when the present question was not before him; but we have an excuse for him in this instance. He had been so much engaged in fortifying his amendment from deductions from Cocker's arithmetic the evening before to shew, that while the wise men all came from the East, the march of empire was to the West, that his mental lights were, for the time being, eclipsed.

But, Sir, it is not the increase of population in the west which this gentleman ought to fear. It is the energy which the mountain breeze and western habits impart to these emigrants. They are regenerated; politically, I mean, Sir. They soon become *working politicians;* and the difference, Sir, between a *talking* and a *working* politician, is immense. The Old Dominion has long been celebrated for producing great orators; the ablest metaphysicians in policy; men that can split hairs in all abstruse questions of political economy. But at home, or when they return from Congress, they have negroes to fan them asleep. But a Pennsylvania, a New-York, a Ohio, or a western Virginia Statesman, though far inferior in logic, metaphysics, and rhetoric, to an old Virginia Statesman, has this advantage, that when he returns home, he takes off his coat, and takes hold of the plough. This gives him bone and muscle, Sir, and preserves his Republican principles pure and uncontaminated.

Bidding adieu for the time being, to the gentleman from Culpeper, I proceed to make my devoirs to the honorable gentleman from Northampton.

This gentleman starts with the postulate, that there are two sorts of majorities; of numbers and interests; in plain English, of men and money. I do not well understand, why he ought not to have added, also, majorities of talent, physical strength, scientific skill, and general literature. These are all more valuable than money, and as useful to the State. A Robert Fulton, a General Jackson, a Joseph Lancaster, a Benjamin Franklin, are as useful to the State, as a whole district of mere slave-holders. Now, all the logic, metaphysics and rhetoric of this Assembly, must be put in requisition to shew, why a citizen, having a hundred negroes, should have ten times more political power than a Joseph Lancaster, or a Robert Fulton, with only a house and garden. And if scientific skill, physical strength, military prowess, or general literature, in some individuals, is entitled to so much respect, why ought not those majorities in a community to have as much weight as mere wealth?

We admit that fifty men in one district, may have as much money, as five hundred in another; but we can see no good reason, why the superabundant wealth of those fifty should be an equivalent, or rather a counterpoise, against four hundred and fifty citizens in another. Why should not fifty men, possessing as much talent, as much military, scientific, or general information, in one district, outweigh four hundred and fifty nabobs, who are mere consumers or political drones in the national hive, living in another? Amongst those who place mammon on the loftiest throne, I know nothing weighs like gold. But according to the logic of the honorable gentleman from

Northampton, if Stephen Girard, an old man, without wife or child, now worth 12,000,000 of dollars, were to buy up one or two districts in Virginia, and depopulate them, and cover them with sheep and cattle, he might, if he would, become a resident and elect himself, and become a member of both the Senate and House of Delegates at the same time. But the property basis of representation, never can become tolerably rational, until each vote is valued at a given sum, and every man have as many votes, as he has the stipulated price. Fix the votes at two hundred or five hundred dollars each, and let him who is worth one thousand dollars, have fifty or twenty votes. This will give some semblance of equity to the procedure; otherwise, a poor man in one district, may have the power of ten in another.

Yes, Sir, according to the doctrine of the gentleman from Northampton, one poor man, because he lives in the neighbourhood of a very rich man, would have more political power than the wealthiest citizen in the west, who lived in the neighbourhood of many poor men. This fact, alone, defeats the design of this gentleman's scheme, and shews its incompatibility with itself. This gentleman could find no law, or *right*, as he termed it, in nature, but the right of the strong to devour the weak. Brutal force governs every thing. He presented the lion devouring the ox; the ox driving the lamb, the lamb something weaker, but last of all, the worm eating the elephant.

This, Sir, is but a small part of the incongruity of this honorable gentleman's doctrine with Republican principles. But he concludes, there are *no principles* in Government; and his honorable associate (Judge Green) from Culpeper, declares, that men are governed by *interest* only. And, as for the poor, they have no affection, no love of country, no social feelings, no conscience, no religion; they are all governed by mere cupidity! No wonder the eloquent gentleman from Orange, affirmed that there is *no faith* in politics!

This gentleman, I mean the gentleman from Orange, in his clear and forcible oration the other day, began with the Bill of Rights, as usual, and with the first article too. I believe he admitted it to be true doctrine in theory, but dangerous in the application: *All men are born free and independent.* This is a position much older than these United States, and flowed from a gentleman, to whom, more than any other, these American States, are indebted for all their civil and religious liberties. Gentlemen may encomiaze whom they please; but there is no man more worthy of American admiration, than the statesman, the philosopher, and the christian who is the legitimate father of the first article of the Bill of Rights. I need not tell you, Mr. Chairman, that I allude to the Author of the Essay on Toleration, the Author of the Essay upon the Human Understanding. Now, Sir, I do not, because I cannot, concur with those gentlemen, who say that this article contains a truth, and yet maintain that it is dangerous in its application. Truth with me, Sir, is eternal, and what was true in morals, or in the science of man and Government five thousand years ago, is true still: truth is at least one day older than error. And, Sir, it is dangerous to depart from a truth so fundamental as that now before us. It will be found that the slightest departure from it in practice, will soon or late prove a curse to mankind. The departure may be gradual and imperceptible, like the gradual and almost imperceptible disinclination of two straight lines. Project them at one end, they meet in an acute angle; but extend them a great distance, and at the other end they will recede from each other to a great distance. So may our departure from correct principles issue in an ultimate abandonment of our form of Government. The acute and discriminating gentleman from Orange, seems also to find fault with the third article of the Bill of Rights, which declares that a majority of the citizens of any State, have a right to alter or amend the form of Government, when it becomes disagreeable to them. He gave us a long recital of our failures to obtain majorities. He instanced the pluralities which, in most instances, decide our County, State, and United States' elections; the usages in Congress; and finished his recitation of departures from the principle and practice in presenting one juror controlling eleven. The genius who could find in a jury of twelve men, called to decide a question of fact, or even a question in law, a proof for our departure from the principle of a majority, could easily infer that our republican institutions, might issue in a monarchy, and prove that we ought to establish a *minority* of men, with a majority of money! But, Sir, in all these examples, it is mere convenience, and the supposed majority of wishes, coinciding with the plurality obtained, which reconciles these communities to these usages. I except the allusion to the Senate, and Congress of the United States, and the reference to juries, as not applicable to the question at issue, and as explicable upon other principles.

But, since I am come to the subject of majorities, I wish to make a remark or two upon the origin of them. The gentlemen on the other side, have triumphantly called upon us, to find the origin of majorities in the state of nature. Nay, indeed, they almost ridicule the idea of men existing in a state of nature. We all know, that men roaming at large, over the forests, could have no idea of majorities: it is not applicable to them. But, so soon as men form a social compact, it is one of the first things, which, from nature itself, would present itself to them. The true origin of this idea, is found in the nature and circumstances of men. Man is a social animal, and in obedience to this law of his nature, he seeks society, and desires the countenance of man. But, as all men are not born on the same day, and do not all place their eyes upon the same object, at the same time, nor receive the same education, they cannot all be of the same opinion. Some arrangement, founded on the nature of man, for men's living together, must then be adopted. And the impossibility of gratifying their social desires, but in yielding to differences of opinion, presents itself among the very first reflections. In all matters, then, of common interest, when a difference occurs, one party must yield. They must either agree to yield, or to form a new community. But, which shall yield? All nature cries, the inferior to the superior; the weaker to the stronger; the less to the greater. It is, then, founded on the nature of things. And a moment's reflection will convince us, that, in case of a struggle, the minority must yield to the majority; for, they have the power, either to compel it, or to expel the disaffected. It is, then, as natural a conclusion and arrangement, as can be conceived.

But, Sir, there are some who deny the existence of a state of nature altogether. Were it imaginary, we can reason from it, as well as upon any other abstract subject whatever. But, Sir, it is not altogether imaginary. History affords some instances, of what is at least analagous to it, of dispersed individuals forming a social compact. We shall give an illustration of what history has recorded: History has informed us, that political communities have been broken up, and from their ruins, new ones have been formed. For example: Should some foreign enemy invade this country; and may Heaven long avert that day! I say, suppose that for our iniquities in Government, some foreign enemy should invade our country, and spread devastation, ruin and death through the land, a few might escape and flee to the most distant wilds, say beyond the Rocky Mountains. We shall select, for illustration of our principles, a few individuals, who will illustrate this state of nature, as well as many thousands. A community or a nation, is but a family on a larger scale. Suppose, then, A, B, C, D, and E, after having lived some two or three years, unknown to each other, in the wilds, should at some time meet. A, in making his escape, had snatched a bag of dollars; B had taken his wife; C, his rifle; D, his children; and E had nothing but himself. They are about to form a social compact. They have brought some of the old ideas with them, from their former society. A is an old Virginian, and begins the discussion. He says, "Gentlemen, Government is chiefly for *the protection of property*, and every man ought to have influence according to his property. I, therefore, contend for an influence, proportioned to my wealth. I know, that we have much need of wealth, in forming a comfortable settlement here, and many calls will be made upon me." B asks him, of what use was his bag of dollars to him since his arrival in the wilderness? Had he spent a dollar since he left the old society? Not one. "Society, Sir, continues he, is necessary to give use and importance to money; and you are as much indebted to us, for giving you an opportunity to spend your money, to obtain our aids, as we can be to you for such sums as we may call upon you for. Besides, Sir, without our society and assistance, you could not *protect* your money. We will afford you, not only the means of *enjoying*, but of *protecting* your wealth. I claim, Sir, twice as much influence in society as you; because, Sir, I have a wife. She has her interests and her wishes, as well as you or me." C rejoins: "I cannot, gentlemen, agree, that either of you shall have more power in our new Government, than myself. My *Rifle*, Sir, is of as much use, and my skill to use it, as either of your possessions. Nay, Sir, the day may be to-morrow, that the safety of our persons, and of our community, may depend upon me; and I think, that my claims, because founded upon the preservation of our very existence, are stronger than those of any other person, and entitle me, more than any other man, to greater political power. You recollect, Sir, that the great men of the Old World, were all Warriors and Military Chieftains. As for my neighbour B, claiming influence for his wife, it is absurd! Has she any separate interest from his? Has she not identified her interests with his? Can she have any will, affecting the community, but through him? Is not she his property, by the marriage compact?"

D rises. "My claims, gentlemen, are paramount to all others. I have many children. They are, Sir, the hope of every community. I claim an influence in Government, proportionate to my interest in it, and to the services which I may yet render it. I have no money, no rifle, it is true; but I have seven sons and daughters coming forward. They will be able yet, Sir, to create wealth, and to defend the community. I insist upon it, gentlemen, if any man in this community has a right to *any* more than his own voice, than his own personal weight; I have *seven* good reasons to offer, why I should have seven times more than he."

E says: "Gentlemen, I have neither wife, son, daughter, rifle, nor a single dollar. I am stripped of all extrinsic claims for superior weight in the Government. But,

Sir, I am not without other claims: I have learned to speak two or three of the Indian languages, since I became an inhabitant of these wilds. And, Sir, should any misunderstandings arise between us and them, I can be an *interpreter*, and may do more to prevent war, than any other member of our community. I claim, then, an influence, equal to this rarest and most useful endowment, which, Sir, requires so much labour and time to obtain, and which, when obtained, is so useful to society. But, I must protest against D's having seven votes for his seven children. They are minors, and under his control, and of immature reason. When they arrive at manhood, and are free agents, but not till then, shall they have a voice."

A rises: "Gentlemen, I see we all have claims for various portions of political power. I think we must abandon the idea of forming a social compact, upon these principles. I will claim only my single vote, and my single personal influence, and will yield my pretensions, if every other gentleman yields his. I will agree, that we all surrender ourselves, our property, our talents, and our skill, *pro bono publico;* that each man shall have his own personal influence, and in all contributions for the public service, each man shall contribute in his own way, according to his respective ability."

Mr. Chairman: Here we have in miniature something analagous to this state of nature, of which we have so often heard. And here we have the only true philosophy of the social compact. In this compact, Sir, as I understand it, every man surrenders himself to the whole community, and the whole community to him. We have no occasion to travel so far *South*, as the gentleman from Northampton, who penetrated those regions until he saw a *white devil.* Nor need we go so far *North* with the gentleman from Orange, who found a nation composed entirely of *women.* He seemed greatly concerned for the political rights of such a nation. But, Sir, he need not have troubled himself much on this account, for such a nation could not continue for more than five hundred years.

While, Sir, I am on the subject of such a state of nature, or viewing man as coming into society, may I not take occasion to observe, that man exhibits himself as possessing the right of suffrage, anterior to his coming into the social compact. It is not a right derived from, or conferred by, society; for it is a right which belongs to him as a man. Society may divest him of it, but they cannot confer it. But what is this right? It is that of thinking, willing and expressing his will. A vote is neither more nor less than the expression of a person's will. God has given to man the power of thinking, willing and speaking his will, and no man ever did as a free agent enter into any society without willing it. And, we may add, no men could form a social compact, without first exercising what we must call the Right of Suffrage. It is a right *natural* and *underived,* to the exercise of which, every man by nature has as good a reason as another. But this is only by the way.

Having now glanced at this state of nature, and the meaning of the social compact, which in my desultory and extemporaneous way I have done without much method, I would approach the great question, now pending before us: Remarking, however, that so soon as we depart from the doctrine, contained in the three first articles of the Bill of Rights, we abandon the radical principles of our Government, not only of the State of Virginia, but of every other State of the Union. [Here Mr. C. read and commented on the three first articles.] If the amendment should succeed, I shall consider these principles abandoned. A new principle will be sanctioned; the very principle on which the aristocracies and monarchies of the old world have been founded. Give men political power according to their wealth, and soon we shall have a legalized *oligarchy;* then come the thirty Tyrants; then follow the Quin decemviri; then the decemviri; then the triumvirate; and last of all, comes Julius Cæsar. Gentlemen talk of the docking of entails, and the laws of Parcenary; but a feeble resistance will these arrangements present to a reigning oligarchy. Men love power, and in proportion as they possess it, does that love increase.

This appears to me a controversy merely about power. One party speak as though they possessed it, and had it to bestow. Another contends for it as their right. It is not with me a struggle for power; it is for right, for principles, for justice. I do not think that in order to secure my comfort, happiness, or prosperity, it is necessary to invade the peace, comfort, or prosperity of any man. That I go for principles and not for power *per se,* I will now shew. And in shewing this, I will shew how unreasonable it is, for the opponents of reform to ask us for a *guarantee* against oppression. The power will be vested in the very hands of those who ought to hold it as umpires between the rival interests of the east and the west. We shall take the present number of Representatives for the data. That number is two hundred and fourteen: Of these, the forty-five counties and four towns on tide-water, have at present ninety-four representatives: on the white population basis, they would have only seventy-two and two-tenths representatives: That is, according to the Census of 1820; which will as correctly demonstrate the principle, as any document we could obtain. The country west of the Alleghany, containing thirty-three counties, has at present sixty-six representatives. On the white population basis, that district of country would have only sixty-one and four-tenths. We should then lose four and six-tenths representatives. Thus the nine Senatorial Districts on tide-water would lose twenty-two representatives, and we nearly five. In all, these two Districts would lose nearly twenty-seven representatives. Now, the question is, what sections of the State would gain this power. We lose, but who gains? I answer, the twenty counties making the six Senatorial Districts east of and along the base of the Blue Ridge, would gain nearly twelve representatives, and in this District, there are no less than 136,919 slaves. The remaining fifteen representatives would be gained by the seven counties, or three Senatorial Districts in the Valley beyond the Ridge, having 23,963 slaves. Thus, the power lost in the counties on tide-water and west of the Alleghany would be deposited in that part of the State, which, from its central position and from its dense slave population, would be the safest deposit which the fears of the slave-holders could devise, and which would afford to them the strongest and best guarantee against those encroachments of the non-slave-holders which the evil-boding imaginations of some gentlemen have conjured up. We are not, then, Mr. Chairman, contending for power for ourselves, but for principles, which, let them operate as they may, we believe, cannot fail to benefit the whole State, by distributing power where it ought to be, and by divesting our Government of those odious aristocratic features, which have caused and are daily causing the sceptre to depart from Virginia. So repugnant are many features in our Government to the Republican feelings which prevail in other States in this Union, that a majority of our own freeholders cannot approve them; and if they cannot approve them, how can we suppose that citizens from other States can be induced to locate themselves amongst us?

The statistical documents submitted, and the argument deduced therefrom, further prove the fallacy of the hypothesis upon which the gentleman from Hanover, based the greater part of his remarks. It shews these to have been as groundless as that other assumption of his: that we were going to lose, or in danger of losing, the 1-11th part of our power in the Federal Government, if the doctrine of making *three white men* out of *five* negroes, or of putting *five souls* into *three bodies*, should cease to be the popular practice in Virginia. He did not tell us, indeed, why Virginia gave up 2-5ths of her slave population to the Union; in this she erred, unless she intended to give up the other 3-5ths to her own white population.

But that I may not too far impose upon the time or patience of the Committee, I shall only now call your attention, Sir, to one or two other items.

I have been sorry, very sorry, Sir, to observe in sundry gentlemen on this floor, a disposition to treat us as aliens, or as persons, who have no *common interest* with the people of the east. We have given them no reason to suspect our want of fellow-feeling, or of common interest. Let gentlemen but reflect upon the circumstances of this State in the year 1814. When all the militia east of the Blue Ridge were employed, or chiefly employed in patrolling the counties on the seaboard, and generally east of the Ridge, in order to preserve that property for which a guarantee is now demanded: I say, when your militia, Mr. Chairman, were all needed to prevent insurrections amongst your own discontented population, who was it that fled to your succour and protection from an invading enemy, who were disposed to harrass your seaboard, and to augment the discontents of your slaves? The Valley and the west volunteered their aid. Yes, Sir, the single county of Shenandoah gave you twelve hundred men to fight your battles, or rather, the battles of their own State. They made a common cause with you. And, Sir, the bones of many a gallant and brave citizen of the west, lie in the sands of Norfolk. Men, too, who had no suffrage, no representation in your Government, sacrificed not their property only, but their lives also, in your defence. In one company, Sir, consisting of seventy-four persons, who marched from Culpeper Court-house, but two had the right of suffrage! Yet these men gave not sufficient evidence of common interest with, nor common attachment to, the community!!! Yes, Sir, from the very shores of the Ohio, from my own county of Brooke, they marched to your succour, and hazarded their all, their earthly all, in defence of that very country, and that very Government, which treated many of them as aliens in the land of their nativity.

We have been told that nearly 3-4ths of the tax has been paid by the counties east of the Blue Ridge. But these gentlemen tell us nothing about who fight the battles of the country. But, Sir, the disproportion between the east and the west, in the tax-paying department, will every day diminish. As the west increases in population and improvement, its ability to pay will increase, and its property will increase in value.

It were endless, Sir, to notice the many objections made against the surrender of power, or rather, the arguments offered, to retain a power already assumed and possessed. I will only remark, that it is said, that if the *white basis* should obtain, there will be endless discontentment among many of the citizens of this Commonwealth. But, Sir, if the *black basis*, or the *money basis*, as it should be called, should obtain, would it diminish, or terminate discontentment or complaint? No, Sir; in that case, a majority, a large majority of the freeholders, would be irreconcileably discontented. And, Sir, if discontents, murmurs and complaints must, on any hypothesis, exist, the question is, whether in policy and in justice, they had not better be confined to the minority, than spread through a majority of the citizens of this Commonwealth? And which party would have the best reason to be discontented, let the umpires throughout all Republics decide.

But, Sir, in the last place, I must say that the policy of those gentlemen who advocate the money basis, appears to me, not only an anti-republican, but a short-sighted policy. That policy which augments the power of wealth, which tends to make the rich man richer, and the poor man poorer, is the worst policy for such a community as this is, and must be, at least for some time to come. Little do the rich think, when charmed with the fascinations of wealth and power, when they are eager to secure and augment both, by Constitutional and Legislative provisions, that they are fighting against their own offspring, and proscribing their own posterity. And, Sir, is not posterity, is not our children's happiness dearer to us than our own? Do we not daily see that riches are ever making to themselves wings? Is not the great wheel of fortune, as some gentlemen call it, eternally revolving. Those at the summit must descend, and those in the mire must ascend. Where are the noble and wealthy families that flourished in this Commonwealth some sixty or seventy years ago? Some of their descendants may yet be found sustaining the name, the talents and respectability of their ancestry. But how many of them have, to use the words of Bonaparte, sunk down into the Canaille? There are few of the wealthy now living, who have not their poor relatives and connexions, and how long, or rather how short a time, will it be, till the decendants of most of us will have merged themselves amongst the humble poor and the obscure? My views of men, and of the revolutions in human affairs, make me a republican. My love for my own posterity would prevent me from voting for the amendment, if I had no other consideration to govern me. If I had the wealth of Stephen Girard, I could not, feeling as I do, viewing human affairs as I do, looking back into history, or forward into futurity, I could not consent to build up an aristocracy, because I should be erecting embankments and bulwarks against those dearer to me than myself. I do most sincerely wish that gentlemen would look a little before them, and remember the lot of man, lest they should, in attempting to secure themselves from imaginary evils, lay the foundation of real and lasting ones. To conclude, Sir, the policy of those gentlemen who are securing, or attempting to secure to themselves exclusive privileges, and to defend themselves from an imaginary evil, reminds me of a character which Dr. Johnson depicts in one of the papers in his Rambler. A young gentleman much afraid of thieves and robbers breaking into his room at night, became distrustful of all the locks and keys in common use, as *guarantees of his person and property*. He put his ingenuity to work, to invent a new lock and key, which could not be violated. He succeeded to his wishes. He had his room fortified to quiet all his fears. He one day called in a friend to exhibit to him his ingenuity. It required some two or three minutes to lock and unlock the door. The gentleman after admiring and commending his ingenuity, remarked, why, sir, said he, this is certainly a great defence against thieves and robbers, but it is so difficult to unlock, I should fear that if the house were to take fire, you might be consumed before you could open the door and escape. I declare, sir, said the young gentleman, I never thought of that. Hereafter I will sleep with my door, not only unlocked, but half open.

Mr. Scott of Fauquier, rose to ask for the reading of the question before the Convention; which being done, he proposed to amend the amendment by adding, "and in the Senate, on white population exclusively." (The effect of this proposition would be, to apportion the House of Delegates, by population and taxation combined, and the Senate by white population exclusively.)

Mr. Scott, rose and addressed the Committee as follows:

Mr. Chairman: Labouring under a disease which not only emaciates the frame, but clouds the intellect, were I to consult my own interest apart from that which I have in common with the inhabitants of that portion of the State which I have the honor in part to represent, I should abstain from troubling the Committee with any remarks on the question now before it. But, Sir, I have a duty to perform which compels me to make the effort, however unsuccessful it may prove. Mr. Chairman, the people whom I in part represent, have not been in the habit of singing hosannas to the present Constitution. They think it has defects, and that they have suffered evils under its operation. I have participated in these sentiments. To remedy these evils we have united with our brethren of the west to bring about this Convention. But I fear they will prove Roman allies, and we shall only have the privilege of changing our masters.

Mr. Chairman: After the frost-work of mere abstractions, constructed by the gentlemen on the other side, had melted before the rays of the genius of the gentleman from Northampton, the member from Ohio has endeavoured to build it up again, with what success I leave the Committee to judge. When I set about a task, Sir, my first enquiry is, what is the end to be accomplished? Having ascertained this, I then look about for the means which are at hand. The end which we all have in view, is to secure the blessings of liberty to the people of Virginia, and their posterity; the means by which we propose to accomplish it, is to recommend to them a frame of Government best calculated to attain that end. In constructing this Government, we are not necessarily driven back to the natural rights of man. If we are satisfied that the safety of the whole community requires, that the powers of Government should be placed in the hands of a minority, we are bound to recommend it to the people to place them there. And if they give it their sanction, the right of the minority is as legitimate as the *jus majoris* contended for by gentlemen on the other side. All the questions which can arise are mere questions of the fitness of means to an end. I would not be understood as discarding all principle. On the contrary it will be found that I agree with the gentlemen who are so very fond of theory in the principles which I shall take as my guide, although I shall apply them differently. The difference between these gentlemen, and myself, is this: they form a garment according to their ideas of exact symmetry without enquiring whether, or not, it will fit the person who is to wear it. I propose to take his measure before I apply the shears to the cloth. They profoundly skilled in the healing art, compound a medicine, containing the quintessence of the Materia Medica, and administer it in all cases. I propose to feel the pulse of the patient, and examine the symptoms, before I prescribe the remedy.

Mr. Chairman, I have already said, that the object of our labours, is to secure to the people of Virginia, and their posterity, liberty and safety of persons and property. To effect this, a certain quantity of power must be called into action. The first reflection which strikes us, is, that power entrusted to human agents, is liable to abuse. To guard against this abuse, constitutes the chief difficulty in framing a Government. The first expedient resorted to, is to call into action no more than is necessary to attain the end. Too much power is liable to run into abuse from its mere excess. The next expedient is not to confide all to the same hands: hence the separation of the Legislative, Executive, and Judicial Departments. But this separation has not in practice been found sufficient. It is not enough to check power by power. Some further security has been found necessary. The best reflection which I have been able to give to the subject, has brought me to adopt this maxim, "as far as practicable, to deposit power in the hands of those only whose interest it is not to abuse it." If we look around us into the ordinary affairs of men, we shall find that interest is the great spring of action. What is it that makes agriculture flourish? What is it that builds your cities, and makes commerce spread her wings? What inspires the poet and nerves the soldier's arm? It is love of wealth, fame, and distinction. In a word, it is self-love. I have not much experience in legislation, but I appeal to gentlemen here who are experienced both in Federal and State legislation, whether they are ever so sure of a vote as when they appeal to the interests of those whose vote they want. It would be out of order, Sir, to speak of the members of this House: One remark, however, I take leave to make: Although so much devotion is shewn to principles, the principles of gentlemen do quadrate most marvellously with the interests of their constituents. I do not mean to cast imputations on gentlemen. I do not mean to question the sincerity of their attachment to principle. But when I see honourable and intelligent men, with all their devotion to principle, unconsciously influenced by interest, I set an higher value on the security which interest gives against the abuse of power. The guarantee of interest constitutes the chief difference between Republican, and Aristocratic, or Monarchical Governments. The responsibility of public agents, resolves itself into this principle. By causing the law-maker to mingle with the people, and to be subject to the laws which he has enacted, you make it his interest to enact just laws. By subjecting him to re-election at short intervals, you make it his interest to consult the welfare of his constituents in order that he may be re-elected. Sir, I think I can boast of as many attached and disinterested friends as any gentleman here, but my experience teaches me, that I am never so sure of the good offices of another, as when I make it his interest to serve me. There are it is true, many bright exceptions to the influence of the selfish principle. The annals of mankind occasionally set before us examples of self-sacrifice on the altars of patriotism and virtue, but they are few when compared with the sacrifices of patriotism and virtue on the altars of ambition and avarice; and serve by their splendour, to render more visible, the dark shades of the human character. Here then we have a great principle founded in human nature, which will serve as a touchstone for every grant of power that we propose to make. Let us bring the question before the Committee, to this test. What will be the effect of the principle reported by the Legislative Committee? It will give to the people west of the Blue Ridge, if not immediately, in a very short time, a majority in the Legislature. No gentleman has questioned this, but my friend from Frederick. He seems to think that the majority of whites will remain, as it now is, east of the Ridge. If we look to the documents furnished by the Auditor, we shall find that the increase of whites west of the Ridge, greatly exceeds that on the east; and if it should continue in the same proportion, a majority will, in a very short time, be found west of the Ridge. If we look at the face of the country, we shall come to the same conclusion. A great proportion of the land below the head of tide-water, is worn and exhausted. That between tide-water and the Ridge, is in a similar condition, except a strip bordering on the mountain. This is capable of regeneration, and will sustain an increased population. It is of less extent than what is called, the Limestone Valley, which, from the fertility of its soil, is capable of sustaining a dense population. The country east of the Ridge, has no new lands to settle. There is no room for a great increase of population. A large portion of fertile land west of the Alleghany is yet unsettled; and when it is brought into cultivation by the influence of the Chesapeake and Ohio canal, it must give a vast accession to the population of that region. I will ask the gentleman, under whose patronage that work is progressing, whether he does not expect it will succeed? The population which this will add to the west, must be exclusively white. From the vicinity of the country through which it passes to Pennsylvania, slaves cannot be held there. But, Sir, it is unnecessary to pursue this argument farther. We have it on the authority of the gentleman from Brooke, (and no man is better acquainted with the situation and resources of that country,) that in thirty years a majority of the white population of the State will be found west of the Alleghany. I feel, therefore, warranted in assuming as the basis of my argument, that the country west of the Ridge, does now, or soon will contain a majority of the white population of the State.

Let us now enquire whether the people of that region can give the security we require against the abuse of the power which the Legislative Committee proposes to give to them. I agree with the gentlemen on the other side, that as a general rule, a majority ought to govern. A majority of persons will prima facie, comprise a majority of interests. But this rule is certainly liable to exceptions. The power of the majority must have limits. We all propose to limit it by denying to the Legislature the power of passing ex post facto laws, suspending the privilege of the writ of habeas corpus, &c. The only question is, what limitations shall we impose? I answer, all such as are necessary to protect the rights and interests of the governed. It is for me to shew that the limitation, which I propose, is necessary for our security. To that end, let us take a survey of the points of difference between the portions of the State, lying east and west of the Ridge. The first point of difference which strikes us, is the erroneous disproportion of the taxes paid by the two regions. I will not dwell on this part of the subject, after the luminous exposition given by the gentleman from Hanover. The next point of difference, is in the character of the population. Eight-ninths of the slaves are found east of the Ridge. In all laws relating to this species of property, the people west of the Ridge are interested to the extent of one-ninth only. But the gentleman from Frederick thinks that this property will not be in danger, because the slave-holders west of the Ridge, when added to those of the east, will give a majority. Suppose it is so. Why, I ask, should the people below the mountain, transfer all the power necessary for their protection, to the people above? This may be very agreeable to those who kindly offer to become our guardians. But the people whom I represent have a notion, (it may be a very unphilosophical one,) that their affairs will be never the worse managed, because they have a hand in the management of them. But, Sir, in that part of the Valley to which we are invited to look for protection, the slaves are to the whites as one to four. In the counties more particularly alluded to by the gentleman from Frederick, they are as one to three. The proportion which the slave-holders bear to the non-slave-holders, cannot be greater, and may be, and probably is less. It cannot be greater, because if the slaves be divided, so that no person shall hold more than one, there will be three who hold none, for one who holds one; and when the war between the non-slave-holders and the slave-holders shall be waged, the slave-holders will be out-voted at the polls. So far from protecting us, they will be unable to protect themselves. We cannot aid them, for they will have tied our hands. I ask the gentlemen representing that part of the State to which I belong, and which is deeply interested in this question, whether they are willing to accept of such a security as this? Would they not rather have the means of protection in their own hands? Will they not prefer the guarantee which I demand? With that security, we shall not want the lock of the gentleman from Ohio. I can trust my gold to a man whose interest it is to restore it to me.

There is another interest connected with this branch of the subject, which deserves our serious attention. Of the twenty-two members to which this State is entitled in the House of Representatives of the United States, seven represent the slave population. Now, if we establish it as a principle that the white basis is the true one for apportioning representation in the State Legislature, will it not follow that as between ourselves, it is also the true basis for apportioning members of Congress? And, if so, the seven members purchased, I may say, by the slave-holder, will be seized upon as common property, and divided between the east and the west. I ask gentlemen of the east, and more especially of the middle region, whether they are prepared for this?

And if not, what do they propose to do? Insert an article in the Constitution forbidding it? Gentlemen from the west may say we will promise you not to take from you the representation in Congress which your slaves give you. I know not whether they will be willing to do this. Some gentlemen may think that this is a common fund, and may have this very thing in view, as a consequence of the measures they are now pursuing. If such are their views, they will no doubt avow them. But suppose such an article to be inserted in the Constitution, I doubt very much its efficacy. I will not undertake to say that it will not be efficacious. But I will say that reasons may be found strong enough for those whose inclinations and interest lead them to disregard it. Less plausible reasons have in practice been found sufficient to justify violations of what we consider the spirit, if not the letter of the Constitution of the United States.

The power to prescribe the times, places and manner of electing members of the House of Representatives, is, by the Constitution of the United States, given to the State *Legislatures*, subject to the control of Congress. Not to the people of the States assembled in Convention. When we have constituted a State Legislature, this power, it may be contended, is not conferred by us, but is derived from a higher source, the Constitution of the United States. We have given it being, and a capacity to receive this grant of power, but the grant is not from us, but another, and the extent of the power cannot be regulated by us, but is regulated by the instrument which confers it. The argument may not be strong, but if we judge from experience, it will be found sufficient for those who seek power. I ask, are we willing to put this interest at hazard on no better security? I answer no. I will not be satisfied with the bond, I must have a surety.

There are other interests to protect, and other abuses of power to be guarded against, of greater importance than those to which I have called the attention of the Committee. The different divisions of the State are not more strongly marked by geographical features, than are the different interests of the people who inhabit them. The Committee must at once perceive, that I refer to the subject of internal improvement. Those different, and in some respects conflicting interests, cannot safely be confided to the people of any one division. The people below the head of tide-water do not stand in need of turnpike-roads and canals. The improvements which are suited to the country between the head of tide-water, and the Blue Ridge, will embrace the Potomac, James River, and Roanoke, as far as the Ridge, the branches of these streams which rise below that range of mountains, and the various branches of the Rappahannock. The scale of improvement of the larger streams, suited to the wants of the middle region, is much inferior to that demanded by the western people; they would therefore, be but partially benefitted by the improvements which the interests of the people of the middle region, would lead them to make. Those demanded by the people of the Valley, will afford for the most part, no benefit to the people of the middle region, and little to those west of the Alleghany. They require that the Chesapeake shall be united with the Ohio, the James River with the Kanawha. The scheme of the people of the Valley, as we learn from the sages assembled at Charlottesville, is, as soon as the Chesapeake and Ohio canal, shall reach the mouth of the Shenandoah, to improve that river for two or three hundred miles, and when it shall reach the mouth of the south branch of the Potomac, to improve that stream for some one or two hundred miles: and when all these improvements shall have been accomplished, some small attention is to be paid to the Roanoke. To shew that the scale of expenditure demanded by the western people, greatly transcends any thing that we of the middle region have any occasion for, I will beg leave to call the attention of the Committee to the project which was before the last Legislature. It proposed to subscribe for stock of the Chesapeake and Ohio Canal Company, to the amount of four hundred thousand dollars: a farther sum to make a lateral canal to the town of Alexandria in the District of Columbia, and to improve the navigation of James river the distance of twenty-four miles, in the county of Alleghany, at an expense of $260,000. This would have been a mere donation, for no man can pretend that the tolls would have been any equivalent for the expenditure. It was also proposed to subscribe the sum of $60,000 towards the improvement of the various branches of the Rappahannock. Unconditionally? No, Sir: whilst the appropriation of $260,000 to be expended in the county of Alleghany, was to be an unconditional gift, stock of the Rappahannock Company was to be subscribed for to the amount of $60,000, upon condition that individuals would subscribe for and secure, the payment of a like sum. Near half a million was to be allotted to the Potomac interest; $260,000 to be given to the county of Alleghany, paying a tax of $600; whilst $60,000 only, is conditionally allotted to the counties of Spottsylvania, Stafford, Fauquier, Culpeper, Orange, and Madison, which, united, pay a tax of more than $30,000. This is the measure proposed to be dealt out to the middle country, by our western friends, who ask us to place all power in their hands. I ask gentlemen representing this middle country, if they are willing to grant the demand. If we turn our eyes farther south, we find that at the instance of western men, a scale of improvement has been commenced on James river, which has resulted in the completion of twenty-nine miles of canal, near Richmond, and about six miles in the Blue Ridge, which, together, cost one million of dollars; and we have the authority of the Charlottesville Convention, for saying that this money has been thrown away, unless another million is expended, to connect these detached works. What benefit have the people, living immediately under the Ridge, derived from this expenditure? None. Worse than none. When the law passed, authorizing this large expenditure, a pledge was given them that no additional tolls should be demanded for the transportation of their produce, until, by the improvement of the navigation, the cost of transportation should be lessened. And how was that pledge redeemed? By a repeal of the law, and an increase of tolls upon their tobacco.

Whilst upon thirty-one miles of canal, to subserve western interests, one million of dollars have been almost thrown away, the improvement of the Rappahannock is estimated to cost about twelve hundred dollars a mile, including the great falls; and it is believed that it can be accomplished within the estimate. That of the Roanoke has actually cost about $1,500 a mile, including the purchase of a number of slaves now employed upon it.*

I do not make these statements to throw odium on the scheme for internal improvements, but to shew that the different sections of the State have separate interests, and that the interests of one, cannot safely be confided to the absolute control of another. I do not ask you to give to the region, which I in part represent, power to control any other; I ask you so to apportion representation in the two Houses, as to guard and protect the interests of all. I do not ask you to give us power to do *mischief*, but to avert *evil*.

Mr. NAYLOR then addressed the Chair to the following effect:

Mr. Chairman: If those gentlemen who have been long accustomed to legislative debates; gentlemen who were well able to sustain a distinguished station at all times when thus engaged heretofore, felt embarrassed in addressing that Chair before this Convention, how much more ought I to feel embarrassment in making the attempt, who, I may say, have never been accustomed to debate in an ordinary Legislature.

Yes, Sir, and I do most sensibly feel it; and nothing but the solicitude I experience, arising from the importance of the question now to be decided, which creates a still stronger sensation, could have overcome that repugnance which might have deterred me from arising to address this body.

But I cast myself with confidence on its benignity and indulgence, while I occupy a short space of time, while no other gentleman seems disposed to occupy the time of the Committee. I would premise the few observations I have to make, by stating, that though conflicting opinions on a matter in controversy may appear to coincide with the interests of those respectively, who maintain those opinions, yet they may be held on each side with all the honesty and sincerity which a conviction of their truth can produce. This I believe to be the case on the present occasion. With this persuasion, and with the highest respect for the opinions of those gentlemen from whom I am constrained to differ, I beg leave to state a few of those reasons which thus constrain me to differ from them.

In attempting to remedy that glaring defect in the existing Constitution of Virginia, whereby the citizens of one section of the State have so much weight on the floor of the Legislature, and the citizens of another section have so little, (which is in the extreme as twenty to one,) it is contended on the one side that representation in the Legislature ought to be based on white population and taxation combined; because, as it is urged by the advocates of this basis, that property or wealth is of so much importance in civil society, that it ought to be protected, by giving to it a voice through its owners in the Legislature; diminishing by so much the voice of the people. This, on the other side, is resisted, because it is inferior in its nature to persons, in the same ratio that persons are more valuable than property in a community, and that it would thus be substituting the inferior for the superior, and usurping the place of and taking from persons their natural rights; and farther because wealth is adventitious, incidental, and too fluctuating in its nature for the basis of a fundamental law, which ought to be founded on well ascertained and unchangeable principles. But it is denied by the gentlemen who contend for this mixed basis, that there are any fixed principles to govern us in this case.

* At this rate, the money thrown away on James River, would, if applied to the improvement of the streams which rise below the Ridge, have given us a navigation of near 1000 miles.

It is contended by them, that Government is just what you can make it, (and therefore a struggle in which the most powerful may succeed; a game at which the most skilful may win;) that it is altogether conventional, to be regulated entirely by expedience. Therefore, the whole effort of those gentlemen has been to disprove the existence of those principles which we contend for, and, indeed, of any principles whatever to regulate us in this case. It was necessary that they should do this, as they have denied the primary right of the majority to rule. This principle is a barrier in their way, and if they do not remove it they cannot get on. But this is not the only one to defend us, although we might rely upon it with safety. Nay, we have no cause to fear to meet them hand to hand in the open field of expediency. But if they had even carried this barrier, there is another just behind it which I think they never can pass; that is the public sentiment, and universally received opinion, not only of the people of Virginia, but of the whole United States. If there is any political sentiment common to them all, it is, that the majority ought to rule. You may travel any distance you please in Virginia, and ask the question of every man you meet, whether he thought the majority have a right to or ought to rule in a Republican Government; and if he did not laugh at what he thought so simple a question, he would unhesitatingly answer in the affirmative. Yes, Sir, and this would be universally the case, from the man of grey hairs down to the stripling of tender years. And it has been truly said by a wise and experienced statesman, that he was most unwise in framing a Government, who disregarded the fixed opinions, and even prejudices of the people. But by the proposed amendment it would be provided in the Constitution, that the minority might rule. Can it be supposed that a fundamental law like this, so much at war with all those political opinions which have grown with the people's growth and strengthened with their strength, and have become interwoven with all their thoughts, could prevail with them or be endured by them? Certainly not. A Republican Government can only be sustained by public opinion: erect it on any other foundation, and you build upon the sands: when the rain descends, and the storms beat upon it, it will fall. But the gentleman from Hanover (Mr. Morris) seems to think that we have given it up as a principle in a Republican Government, that a majority have an inherent right to rule. I, for one, have not given it up, and I do not know, nor am I persuaded that any other gentleman has. I do contend that there are fixed principles in the science of Government, as well as in other sciences, and that this is one of those principles, and a leading one. To stop now to prove that there are such principles, would be a work of supererogation, especially after what the gentleman from Frederick (Mr. Cooke) has said on that point. It would, indeed, be attempting to prove axioms or self-evident propositions.

I would as soon believe that there was no truth, no justice, no rule of right or wrong, as to believe this. If there is no undeniable truth here, such as are called first principles, we have nothing to reason from; we have no premises and can never come to any conclusion. If each is at liberty to choose their own premises, they must always come to different conclusions.

We would be thus at sea without star or compass to guide us, veering about to every purpose, on the great deep of expediency. But, that there are such first principles, the Bill of Rights declares, and in so many words recommends a frequent recurrence to them, and this has been the political creed of Virginia ever since she became a Republic, unless we have abandoned this creed and departed from the faith. And since the existence of these first principles is indisputable, the only enquiry now is, what are they? and how are they to be discovered? The answer is, that they are to be discovered in the same way as in all other sciences, that is, by tracing back those sciences to their primary elements. We must then, in this case, refer to man in his primitive condition. I know that the idea of man ever having been in what is called a state of nature, is ridiculed as being imaginary only, and as being a state that never had an existence in fact. It is not necessary to dispute about this, though more instances than one of this kind can be referred to in history. But in reasoning upon the subject, we have a right, for the sake of the analogy, to pre-suppose it, just as a mathematician pre-supposes a line and a point before he proceeds with the demonstrations which carry conviction with them, and cannot afterwards be disproved, by saying that the mathematical line and point were only imaginary, and that they never had a real existence. We cannot, indeed, divest ourselves of the idea of the state which man must have been in previous to the formation of the social compact. This was a treaty to which every member of the community became a party, by which they unanimously agreed to form one body, and so became incorporated as such.

This was formed not only by the consent of the majority, but by the consent of the whole. And when the compact was formed, it resulted from the very nature of the case, without any formal stipulation, that it could only act, move or be guided by the consent of the majority. True, they might afterwards by the consent of that majority, agree that a minority should rule, or they could agree to create a monarchy; but still the act that created the oligarchy or the monarchy, was the act of the majority.

This majority was still the fountain of the delegated power, which proves what I contend for, that there was an original, inherent right in the majority. For this, I have the authority of as great a political philosopher and constitutional jurist of the last or present age, viz: John Locke, Esq. A passage from his work on civil society, I beg leave to quote: "For when any number of men have, by the consent of every individual, made a community, they have thereby made that community one body, with a power to act as one body, which is only by the will and determination of the majority. For that which acts any community, being only the consent of the individuals of it, and it being necessary to that, which is one body, to move one way, it is necessary the body should move that way, whither the great force carries it, which is the consent of the majority; or else it is impossible it should act or continue, one body, one community, which the consent of every individual, that united into it, agreed that it should; and so every one is, bound by that consent, to be concluded by the majority. And therefore, we see, that in assemblies empowered to act by positive laws, where no number is set by that positive law, which empowers them, the act of the majority passes for the act of the whole, and of course determines, as having, by the law of nature and reason, the power of the whole. And, thus every man, by consenting with others to make one body politic, under one Government, puts himself under an obligation to every one of that society, to submit to the determination of the majority, and to be concluded by it." And, I think, it further goes to prove that man had an original, inherent right of suffrage, because it was by the exercise of this suffrage, that is consent, that he formed the social compact. He did not derive it from the social compact, for it existed previous to the existence of the compact, and by it he formed the compact; it was the cause of the compact, not the effect of it; it was, therefore, original and inherent. Property could not be regarded in this compact, for it was not recognized, and did not exist previous to it. There must, then, have been a second compact formed, before any one could claim representation for property. But if the majority of persons had and has an inherent right to govern, upon what principles can you give that right to a minority because they possess a majority of wealth? None certainly of justice, none according to the eternal fitness of things. This is what the gentleman from Northampton denominates a majority of interests; that is, the rich man and man of wealth: but this is the principle on which all aristocracies and oligarchies have been, and the Holy Alliance is founded, and therefore has tendencies to which that gentleman would be averse. But it is pressed upon us in answer to this, by the gentleman from Orange, why were not women and children, and all other persons taken into this majority, or counted as members having a right of suffrage? We answer that these are exceptions to the general rule, and that the Creator who gave the rule, formed the exceptions to it. He created women with all the tenderness, softness and delicacy of that sex, and when he placed them under the protection of man, he gave them an influence of another kind, more powerful than the right of suffrage; an influence which I have no doubt the gentleman from Orange will acknowledge. If suffrage at the polls had been added, they would have been entirely too powerful. They would have had all the Government in their own hands. And, therefore, I think it would have been difficult to form a society in the present day, like the Amazons the gentleman has mentioned; and I venture to say, that if ever such a society did exist, it did not exist long. It is not necessary to mention, why children are not taken in, or idiots, &c.; these exceptions do not impugn, but they prove the rule. Give a person one vote on his account, and another on account of his wealth, (which is ostensibly the amount of the demand embraced in the amendments under consideration,) and give another person one vote only, because he has not wealth, and it is the same thing as if you would give to the first person one vote only, and the latter none. For, by one of his votes, the rich man could annihilate the one vote of the poor man; and by the other, he could reign over him. It cannot be denied, that if a majority is to rule, a minority cannot; but if wealth is to be represented, a minority will rule, and if a majority of persons ought to rule, then wealth cannot be represented. [According to the standard proposed, the value of a vote will rise and fall from year to year, according to the taxes. If, in one year, the rich man pays twenty dollars tax, and the poorer man only ten, the rich man or his friends on his account, will have two votes, and the poor man only one; and if the taxes should be so lessened that the rich man the next year would have to pay only twenty cents, and the poor man only ten cents, still the rich man would have two votes to the poor man's one; so that the price of a vote would one year be ten dollars, and the next year only ten cents; a great variance in the price of that which ought to be above all price.] This would be throwing the elective franchise of men to the winds of uncertainty, to be driven about as something of no value.

In the scheme proposed, there appears to be no equivalents, no justice. It is the object of all good Governments, to produce the greatest possible good. In doing this, a choice of evils is often presented, that is of two evils, one of which is unavoidable, to choose the least. Now, it is said, to be an evil, that the poorer man should have an equal voice with the rich man, in laying the taxes of which the rich man has much the larger portion to pay; and this can only be avoided by another evil; and this is, by giving the rich man a decided control in making or passing all the laws, whereby the most valuable immunities of the poor man will be subjected to the will of the rich man. Now, from which of these two evils, is it possible, for the greatest degree of human misery to result? Certainly from that which might fall upon the poorer man in his personal safety and personal liberty, by so much as these are above all equivalents in money; and this proves the impolicy, injustice and total inadmissibility of the scheme proposed. But those who have the wealth, assure that those who have it not, are in no danger; that they will not abuse it. But why is not the virtue of those who have not the wealth, as much to be trusted? They have as much right to this confidence, as the wealthy; especially as the security required of them is so severe. But it is said, that the wealthy can pass no laws affecting the poor, which will not affect them: this is not so, for the cottager now, who is not wealthy enough to own two slaves, must work on the roads, while those who have two slaves, are exempt. They might also be taxed with double duty in the militia, poll taxes, &c. There is a further injustice in it than this. It is only in money bills, that the rich man can be endangered, and these are in proportion generally to other laws passed, as one in fifty; and so to have the control of the one money bill against the poor man, he must have the control of the other forty-nine against him.

In examining any thing which has been advanced by the gentleman from Culpeper, it is with diffidence in my opinion, in perfect unison with that high respect and esteem which is accorded to him by all his fellow-citizens, as well for his own personal worth, as for the manner in which he executes the duties of the office which he fills with his compeers on the highest seat of justice in the State. That gentleman admits, that all men are equal in their natural rights, but says, they are unequal in their political rights. It may then be enquired, at what point does the equality of natural rights end, and the inequality of political rights begin? And of what avail can the equality of natural rights be to a man, if the inequality of political rights may destroy them?

If personal liberty and personal safety, are natural rights, he must have a sufficient share of political power to preserve them; for political rights resolve themselves into the power which every man must have to preserve his natural rights; and it is a contradiction in terms to say, that he could hold his natural rights at the will of another, because that which is held at the will of others is no right at all. The gentleman from Northampton, (Judge Upshur,) denied that there was any inherent right in the majority, derived from nature, to bind the minority in any case. To illustrate this, that gentleman has said, that there was but one single right derived from nature, and that is, the right of all the creatures of God to use their powers in such mode, as may best promote their own happiness. That the lion devours the ox; the ox drives the lamb from the tender grass; and the lamb drives the creatures more timid than itself. This, then, is the right which superior strength gives, and according to this, they who have obtained illegitimate power, may keep it, if they can, and add to it if they are able.

But, perhaps, this was not exactly what the gentleman means; otherwise, we need not hope to adjust the matters in difference between us, as far as power could go. But I know he possesses more liberal sentiments; though we differ materially as to the points on which we should meet so as to agree. Indeed the fascinating strain of that gentleman's eloquence, was such, that I was sometimes astonished to find where it had carried me, by which I was imperceptibly led to substitute the truth of one proposition which could not be denied, as the proof of another which was still to be demonstrated. Most powerfully has the political doctrines which we contend for, been assailed, but I feel them to be a rock which torrents of eloquence cannot move, and we stand in no need of their adventitious aid. Thrice is he armed who hath his quarrel just. Truth is all powerful and must prevail. He has further said that property is one-half the compound in the social compact, and persons the other. Again, that it is not property, but the rights which grow out of it, which is to be represented. The conclusion, forcibly drawn from these propositions, is, that a certain proportion of the suffrage ought to be given to property, which would be so much taken from persons; for just in proportion as you give weight to property in the Government, you lessen that of persons. Now, wealth is defined to be the power, which he who possesses it has to command the labor of others. But the gentleman from Northampton would add to this power, by giving it Legislative power: that would be adding power to power, and according to the state of the case, it would be increasing one of the component parts of the social compact, so much as to destroy the whole equilibrium and proportion. Yes, Sir, wealth is power; and wherever wealth is, there power will exist independent of Legislation. Wealth is the object which keeps the world in motion; it is the supreme object of desire amongst men; they are dispersed every where to seek it with avidity, and to bow obsequiously before it; the pursuit of it was ardent enough, and the desire strong enough; it was not necessary to increase it; but it would seem by the gentleman's argument, to be exalted to a higher station than it ever possessed before; it is now to be brought even into the Legislative Hall, and set up as an idol to be worshipped. This would, indeed, be an idolatry which would corrupt the true republican faith, and such as we ought to hope and pray would never be introduced here.

But, if I am not much mistaken, this is the first attempt that ever was made in Virginia, formally to give representation to wealth, on the Legislative floor. Take the Bill of Rights and the Constitution together. The Bill of Rights states, that evidence of attachment to, and permanent common interest with the community, shall be sufficient to entitle a man to the right of suffrage; and if he possesses this evidence, he shall be entitled, whether he is rich or poor. And the Constitution only points out one circumstance which shall be evidence of this attachment, &c. That is, that he should be a freeholder. But, surely, it cannot be inferred from this, that there was any intention or design, in the framers of that Constitution, that wealth should be represented. For by that frame of Government, it could not, unless by mere contingency, because the poorest and least populous counties, were entitled to the same number of representatives with the most wealthy and most populous ones.

But I can shew now, that if the end was a good one, which the gentlemen seem to be all aiming at, the means proposed never will accomplish it. So far from it, it will operate directly the reverse. Instead of protecting the rich from the poor, if there is a danger of that kind to be apprehended, it would be increasing the power of the poor against the rich; which I can shew thus. It is proposed, as I understand, by this scheme of representation, according to white population and taxation, to divide the representation throughout the State, in such a manner that an equal number of white people shall send a representative. And then the taxes are to be divided into equal portions according to the number chosen in the mode above mentioned: and an additional representative is to be sent by every district or county, paying one-sixtieth part of the taxes. Now, suppose the State to be divided, by a line running, say from north to south, near the Blue Ridge, so that the white population in each division was exactly equal, and that there were thirty districts or counties in each, each of which would send a member on account of its population. But when we come down to distribute that part of the representation resulting from wealth or taxation it is found that there is so much more wealth in the eastern division, as to entitle it on the whole to double or one half the number of representatives more than the western division. But, suppose in that eastern division, ten of the counties or districts contain all the wealth which has given the whole number of districts or counties in it this increase of representation; and suppose the other twenty counties or districts in the eastern section are poor, possessing no more wealth on an average than the counties or districts in the west; then to protect the wealth of these ten counties in the Legislature, you give each of them one additional representative, but in doing that you give one additional representative to each of the poor counties. Thus while you advance them, or strengthen the rich by tens, you weaken them by twenties. But, suppose we take one of the rich counties whose wealth entitles it to double representation, and suppose in the rich counties, there are one thousand voters, but all the wealth in this rich county, which entitles it to this double representation, is possessed by one hundred of those voters, and the other nine hundred are poor men, of that class whose circumstances are below what might be considered mediocrity; all the men of this rich county may, then, in comparison with other poor counties, be considered as having two votes at the polls, to the voters in the other counties one. So then, to defend these rich men, you give them on the whole, one hundred votes, but in doing so, you give nine hundred to the poor voters, which, according to the gentleman's own hypothesis, must be directly against the rich. And thus, although the system contended for, may not come out in numbers exactly in this way, yet it will operate in a certain degree in that way, so as to increase the evil exactly in the same proportion that the poor do always out number the rich in all sections or districts.

There is no way of obtaining the end proposed, so as to give the man who pays the taxes, a voice in laying them exactly in proportion to the amount which he must pay, but by collating him with the tax-books at the polls, or by bringing him there with a certificate, or so marked and stamped, that it may be known for what amount he could be current at the polls: that is, to have it there ascertained, how many each ought to count according to his wealth, say one, two, three, or four. But this the gentlemen will not attempt: it would look too much like aristocracy to be endured in a free country. This, as far as can be learnt from the public journals, was introduced into the French Government. The deputies to the Legislative Assembly, are elected in this way. It was introduced by the ultra-royalists in that country, who seem to resemble those politicians in England, who are called Tories. It is called the double vote, and seems to have created great dissatisfaction among the people there. Those who are called Liberals, with La Fayette at their head, are violently opposed to it. But it is vain to disguise it, one way or the other. I do not say that the friends of the measure have made use of any disguise; but the project disguises itself, and when stripped of this disguise, its effects will only be, to marshal one part or section of the State, against another, producing sectional and hostile feelings continually. It will be productive of nothing but heart-burnings and jealousies. It would be producing a state of things, in some distant degree, between ourselves, like that which subsisted between this State and Great Britain, while Virginia was a Colony. Great Britain sought to rule the Colony for her own advantage; the Colony submitted with great forbearance, until provoked beyond endurance; Virginia, then, with other States, broke the connection with the mother country forever. I do not say that the State would be severed, but the section which thought itself oppressed, would have such alien feelings towards the other, that we can hardly anticipate what the consequences would be. We, in the unrepresented part of the State, have been seeking a redress of this our grievance, for more than twenty years, and now, when we have, with great difficulty, obtained an audience, the condition upon which it is offered, is worse than the penalty; the remedy is worse than the disease. Our situation is like that of those who asked for bread, and a stone was offered; for a fish, and a serpent was presented. Were the amendment of the gentleman from Culpeper to prevail, viz. that representation should be founded on the combined basis of wealth and population, the news would be answered from the west, with groans of deep disapprobation and discontent, if not with indignation. Those men of that large portion of Virginia, who are now earnestly seeking an amendment to the Constitution, never will accept of this. They would rather endure the ill they have suffered so long, than fly to others, the extent of which can hardly be foreseen. We would, indeed, rather wear the old yoke, which is almost worn out, and must of course fall of itself, before long, than to put our heads into a new one, to be riveted afresh, to last for generations to come. For, in the common course of human events, the present state of things in Virginia, cannot continue long. Public sentiment is on its march: it may have advanced slowly for some time; it never ceases. It is a phalanx, which becomes deeper and stronger as it advances, and will never stop short of its point. The people of Virginia, are not a volatile or fickle people: they are not easily aroused; but when they are, it belongs to such a character not to be stopped until they have obtained their object. They must and will accomplish it, not by physical force, but by moral force. To engraft that provision into the Constitution, would be to leave us where we are. Why should those gentlemen who advocate this amendment, be so tenacious of a state of things, under which Virginia has prospered so little? When a physician has pursued a certain mode of treatment of his patient, for a long time, during which, the patient has uniformly grown worse, he knows, or ought to know, that if he does not change his course, the patient will probably die. So Virginia has been long in a state of decline, during which time she has been strictly confined to a certain course of political regimen, but still she is sinking more and more. Is it not time to change it? Virginia was as fair a portion of the earth, as any under the sun; her soil in its virgin state, was as fertile as was by nature the most fertile, or best cultivated part of Europe: her coast is deeply indented with bays; and her territory intersected far within by the most numerous inlets for commerce, any where to be found in the same space: her multiplied rivers ready to roll down their tribute from the west: her climate congenial to all the most valuable agricultural productions; and Nature there, ready as it were to work for man with both hands, if he would extend but one of his; and yet, with all these natural advantages, she is retrograding from her rank, and other States without half her advantages, are going far ahead of her. Her population in the eastern section is stationary, her fields are deserted, and improvements abandoned. I could weep over her desolations; for I love Virginia. Now, though these things may proceed in part, but they do not proceed altogether from her slave population. For, go to the western part of the State where there are but few slaves, not enough to have any effect or influence on the people, and step over the line, in the adjoining States, in soil and climate of the same kind, and you will find the industry, the wealth, the population, the agriculture, and all the useful arts of life, two to one, in advance of Virginia. If, then, this difference between Virginia and other States, does not proceed from want of natural advantages, and but in part from her slave population, as I have shewn, what else can it proceed from, but a defect in her frame of Government? Let us remedy that, and see if Virginia is not regenerated, disenthralled, redeemed, and whether she will not again advance and regain the station she has lost.

Engraft the scion of genuine Republicanism upon the old stock of Virginian patriotism, and see whether it will not bud and blossom, grow and bear precious fruit, without becoming too luxuriant, as it is feared. But the gentleman from Hanover, and the gentleman from Fauquier, have objected to giving us our due weight in the Government, lest we should construct roads and canals. I need not take notice of the disparaging manner in which those gentlemen, (the gentleman from Hanover at least) have spoken of roads and canals. The gentleman from Hanover, having so little occasion for facilities of this kind, may not, indeed, set that value upon those improvements, which we do, who have many mountains and hills to pass, and rapid rivers to descend to get our produce to market; and therefore, we have been unfortunate enough to speak of those roads and canals to the Legislature, and to ask its aid to make them. Unfortunate I say, indeed, if that is to create an objection against us in obtaining our rights; which rights, whether roads and canals are made or not, must be at all times the same. But lest this should have an undue weight, or any weight at all, by inducing the belief that we are disposed to be unreasonable on the subject, I will first mention the true state of the case.

It was known, that we, as well as the rest of our fellow-citizens, had an interest in a large fund for internal improvement, which was thought, under its original constitution, to be sufficient to afford a benefit to each part of the State. When we sought a part of it in the first instance, we were told that the James river ought to have the benefit of it for the first two or three years, but then we should have it. At the end of that time, we applied again: the same answer was given us; and so from time to time, until we found that the whole fund was swallowed up in the James river, and the credit of the State mortgaged for further improvements. We thought then, that as we had been bound with our other fellow-citizens for the improvement of the James river, that it would not be presuming too much to ask for some assistance, not that we asked the State to become bound for us. And this is the head and front of our offending, which has given so much alarm to these gentlemen. For this we are to be held in political durance; and when we ask to be delivered from it, the answer is no, we are afraid if we give you your due weight, according to numbers, that you will make roads and canals with our money. And when we offer terms equal to giving security for our good behaviour, as to this, we still have the same denial, lest as it might be presumed, we might seek some indemnification for our portion of the fund for internal improvement, which has been taken from us. To give form and substance to the Constitution from such considerations as these, would be to shape that which is to last for many generations, (as we would hope) according to transient circumstances, whereby the distortions of the instrument would remain long after the incidents which produced them, were forgotten or were only remembered in the evil they had produced, and long after these roads or canals were made or abandoned. It would be a curious part of the history of this time, to be told, that the Constitution, then existing, would have been materially different, had it not been, that these internal improvements had been then or previously desired. Now, in conclusion, I would ask this highly respected and venerated body, one such, as with which I never again expect to be associated, not to permit this amendment to pass.

On the conclusion of Mr. Naylor's Speech, the Committee rose, on motion of Mr. Barbour of Culpeper.

On Mr. M'Coy's motion, the Convention determined (41 to 39 votes) to change their hour of meeting from 11 to 10 o'clock.

And then, on Mr. See's motion, the Convention adjourned till Monday morning, 10 o'clock.

MONDAY, November 2, 1829.

The Convention was opened with prayer by the Rt. Rev. R. C. Moore, of the Episcopal Church, and a few minutes after ten o'clock, the President took the Chair.

Mr. Stanard, after a few prefatory remarks on the inconvenience of meeting at this hour, moved that when the Convention shall adjourn, it adjourn to meet to-morrow, at eleven o'clock.

The motion was opposed by Mr. M'Coy, who asked for a further trial of the present course of proceeding. The question being taken, the votes stood, Ayes 37, Noes 37; the President voting in the negative, the motion was lost.

The Convention then passed to the Order of the Day, and went into Committee of the Whole, Mr. Stanard in the Chair.

And the question lying over from Saturday, being on an amendment proposed by Mr. Scott to the amendment offered by Mr. Green to the resolution of the Legislative Committee.

[The original resolution reads thus:

Resolved, That in the apportionment of representation in the House of Delegates, respect shall be had to the free white population *exclusively*.]

The amendment of Mr. Green proposes to strike out the word "exclusively," and insert in lieu thereof, the words "and taxation combined," so as to read, "free white population and taxation combined." And the amendment of Mr. Scott proposes to add, "and in the Senate to white population exclusively:" (the effect of which last amendment is, in substance, to adopt the mixed basis in the House of Delegates, and the white basis in the Senate.)

Mr. Green expressed his willingness to adopt the amendment of Mr. Scott as a modification of his own, (the effect of which would be to prevent the necessity of taking any distinct vote on Mr. Scott's amendment.)

The Chair decided this course to be contrary to the rules of order of the House of Delegates, (which the Convention have adopted as their own so far as they apply,) which require that after an amendment has been moved and debated, it cannot be modified by the mover, but must, if he wishes to alter it, be altogether withdrawn, and another substituted.

On this decision a debate arose; but as questions of mere order, though often disputed long and warmly, have usually more interest *in* the House than *out* of it, we are not in the habit of presenting more of them to our readers than the leading points. The leading point in this case was, that if the amendment of Mr. Scott was suffered to be united to that of Mr. Green, gentlemen who could not approve of both, might appear as if voting against the white basis in the Senate, while their vote was directed against the mixed basis in the House of Delegates. An appeal was even taken by Mr. Doddridge from the decision of the Chair, but subsequently withdrawn. Mr. Green also withdrew his motion to unite the two; and the question being as at first on the amendment of Mr. Scott only,

Mr. J. S. Barbour said, that he was gratified to find that by the amendment of his honorable colleague (Mr. Scott) the controversy could no longer be said to be one for power, but that it now resolved itself into a question of protection. In reaching his own conclusions on this subject, he had looked mainly to the preservation of certain great interests in the State, and he was anxious to take that course which would effectually defend them against encroachment. The end in view was one indissolubly bound up with the harmony and the liberties of the people, and the means should be adequate to the end. Power and protection seemed to him to be more closely allied than gentlemen had admitted. They are correlatives, necessary to the objects of civil society, and cannot be separated. Mr. B. said, it appeared to him that much of the vice which pervaded the arguments on the other side, might properly be traced to the misapprehension of the conservative principle of our political institutions.

Gentlemen had argued the question, as if the will of the majority should be the only rule of action. It was certainly entitled to great weight, and would always exert great influence. But it is not the only consideration which merits enquiry. The great safeguard in a Republican Government is, in my view, to be found in limitations of power; whether that power be vested in the many or the few. Responsibility cannot be disregarded in the public functionary without destruction to popular rights, and yet, in a society made up of numerous and diversified interests, this principle of responsibility would often fall short of compassing the objects of justice. For, if a majority of these interests be united in one common bond, the rights of a minority, having dissimilar interests, must be insecure. I have thought, said Mr. B. that there were two important securities necessary in our representative system. The first, to secure the fidelity of the representative to the constituent body; the second, to guard one part of the community against the injustice of the other. Without these, justice will be overthrown, and liberty cannot long survive the downfall of justice. The first of these securities we possess in the frequency of elections; to the other we have not given sufficient attention. No form of Government has ever subsisted, in which this principle of responsibility was not at times seen and felt. Even in the most frightful despotisms, it has often exerted a powerful dominion. The great struggles which have occurred between liberty and power, in the old as well as the new world, have almost invariably terminated by imposing further limitations upon power. If limitation upon power be unnecessary, and if the will of the majority is to be alone looked to, why is it that we have Constitutions at all? In all the contests in England, from 1628, when that act of Parliament passed, which is denominated the Petition of Right, to the Revolution of 1688, the first purpose seems to have been, to impose new checks, and additional restraints, upon those hands that wielded the sovereignty. If men were Angels; if justice and magnanimity were, at all times, to exert an uncontrolled sway; there would be no need of any Government upon earth. It is because we are not so constituted, that Governments are instituted; and political institution is unwisely constructed, if it be not so armed, and so restricted too, as to ensure its rightful, and restrain its injurious action. It is not a novel doctrine, that majorities, actuated by common interests, will unjustly encroach on the minority. We have at this moment a strong illustration of it, in the operation of those laws of the Federal Government, known by the name of Tariff Acts. Responsibility of the representative to the constituent body, is the direct cause of these oppressive encroachments, upon the suffering interests of the Southern States. The evil here, is not in the Government, but in the community; a community, united by interest, and acting under its influence, disregarding the obligations of justice, and preying upon the minor portion of that community. The principle is identical with that we are now discussing.

To shew that these unequal interests exist in the scale of contribution, gentlemen, agreeing with me in sentiment, have offered numerous calculations to our view, and it will be worse than idle for me to repeat them. That great disparity exists in the condition and the relations of this Commonwealth, must be apparent to all. Prudence, duty and safety, call upon us to lay along side this striking disparity, this exposed interest, a strong principle of protection. I look, said he, to the means of prevention, and these can only be obtained in representative power. We are, however, gravely told upon the other side, that we need no protection; that our fears, are the creatures of fancy; that justice, honour and magnanimity, will be the efficient guardians of our welfare. I make a just estimate of the virtues and integrity of gentlemen opposed to me, when I declare, in perfect sincerity, that I would confide to them as much as I could to any men whatever. But I confide to no man, that which it may become his interest to abuse; that which it is his interest to violate. When gentlemen tell me that my fears are idle figments of the imagination, I put in opposition to such suggestions, facts, experience, that which is known to me from personal knowledge. Let me ask the honorable member from Brooke (Mr. Doddridge) if he did not openly avow in 1823, the propriety of basing representation from this State to Congress, upon white population exclusively? And did he not refrain from moving it, only because he knew that it would be put down at that time, by force of numbers in the Legislature? With this fact staring me in the face, can gentlemen ask me to yield this protection for the eleventh part of our representative influence in the General Government? And to give up this representative power, as a mere gratuity to those who give nothing for it, and to which we are entitled only in consequence of our slave population. I do not blame gentlemen for entertaining or advocating such opinions, but they must pardon me for taking precaution against such schemes whenever they may be set on foot. Nor does this diversity of interest, with its correspondent influence, pervade one region of the State more than another. I have lived long enough, Mr. Chairman, to witness its operation in the General Assembly upon the East, as well as the West. Give me leave, Sir, to remind you of an instance occurring whilst we were both of us members of the House of Delegates. There was a time during the late war, in which the progress of events was well calculated to arouse and animate the patriotism of the whole land. It did arouse and excite it. The Capital of the country had fallen. The arrogant and insulting terms of the enemy had been promulgated at Ghent; and we had received an official communication from the Commander of the hostile fleets in our waters, that he would lay waste every assailable point. The indignation of the General Assembly was kindled into flame, and its feelings were expressed in the unanimous vote of the Legislative body. Yet, at that very moment, and under the influence of these exciting causes, both the East and the West, demonstrated the powerful and controlling sway of dissimilar interests and local apprehensions. I allude to the vote given on the passage of the bill, then denominated the "Defence Bill." With all the patriotism, chivalry and gallant devotion, which they possessed and had displayed in an eminent degree during the war, yet few, very few western members went along with us in support of that measure. The reason is obvious. They were remote from the theatre of danger, and could not have that community of feeling and sense of necessity, that pressed upon others not so situated. When the discussions occurred in the Senate, let me enquire of the honorable member from Augusta, (Mr. Johnson,) if he did not witness the influence of the same cause in its effects upon the debates of the Senate. The operation of the bill would have been to withdraw portions of the local militia from the tide-water country generally, and to concentrate military power, upon points more peculiarly exposed, and presenting stronger temptations to the incursions of the foe. Does he not remember the violent opposition that he encountered, in sustaining that measure, from the Senators from Lancaster and Mathews? I have mentioned these facts, for the single purpose of shewing that in times peculiarly calling for union of hearts and councils; for forbearance and oblivion of feuds; that local interests have exerted their influence upon men, high-minded, and elevated in honour, principle and patriotism. Sir, we are also told, that a sufficient and adequate guarantee will be given to us. No other guarantee, but representative power can be sufficient or adequate. The history of the world shews that in all contests between virtue and interest, the latter has finally prevailed. I wish to make them allies, not antagonists; for in the union of interest and virtue, have you the only safe pledge for happiness, for justice and liberty. But, what is this guarantee? Why, an article in the Constitution? And who is to tell us what that article means? How far it is to operate, and when it is to cease? Who is to construe it? Why, Sir, the majority; and it cannot be necessary for me to say, that wherever you deposit this power of construing, this right of interpreting its meaning, there do you also deposit a sovereign power over it. Then, the amount of this guarantee resolves itself at last into the will of the majority, who may make it mean what they please, or strike it out altogether at pleasure. And this brings me back to the enquiry, how far it is safe to trust even a majority with a power to oppress a minority, when united with temptations and inducements to abuse. It is said, that this defence of the interest of minorities is novel doctrine, incompatible with republican principles. Sir, there is no incompatibility between justice and republicanism; they can't exist apart. If I am to be oppressed, deprived of my rights or property by force, of what moment to me is it, whether that be the force and injustice of the many or the few? If an honorable member over the way, (Mr. Randolph,) will pardon me the use of a figure of his, I will say, that I go for the interest of the Stockholders against that of the President, Directors and Cashiers of this thing called Government. I am for guarding the Stock-holder's interest, even if the Presidents, Cashiers and Directors be multiplied into the more numerous body. I have high authority to answer the intimation that this is novel doctrine. I hope to be forgiven by a venerable gentleman on this floor for using it. In the Virginia Convention, Mr. Madison said:

"But on a candid examination of history, we shall find that turbulence, violence, and abuse of power, by the majority trampling on the rights of the minority, have produced factions and commotions, which, in republics, have more frequently than any other cause, produced despotism. If we go over the whole history of ancient and modern republics, we shall find their destruction to have generally resulted from those causes. If we consider the peculiar situation of the United States, and what are the sources of the diversity of sentiments which pervades its inhabitants, we shall find great danger to fear, that the same causes may terminate here, in the same fatal effects, which they produced in those republics."

The principle of numbers is strenuously urged upon us. Where do they get this principle? Not in Governments or societies situated like us. Where the wants, the necessities, and the contributions of the people were similar, if they acted alike upon every part, then the principle of numbers would be just, and representative responsibility a sufficient safe-guard against unjust encroachment. Numbers are looked to, because numbers indicate the ability of society, to pay its contributions. But what numbers? For taxation, you take the whole numbers of population, without regard to age, sex, condition or colour. The reason is apparent. Taxes are defined, by writers on political economy, to be contributions from the land and labor of the country, placed at the disposal of the Government. Contributions are made, and so levied upon the whole labor of the country; and if the principle of numbers is to be adhered to, the same reason that is assigned for the imposition of taxes, would justify representation. But to this, I should be unwilling. I discard the principle of numbers altogether, and recur to that of taxation.

In recurring to the question of taxation and representation as inseparable correlatives, we cannot avoid looking to the obligations of the Government, to protect property as well as persons. This principle is not only derived to us, from that country from which w have drawn most of our opinions of civil and religious liberty, but it is the foundation of that revolution, which made these States free and independent. From 1628 to 1688, it was the moving impulse to the great events then occurring in England, and which tended in a high degree, to secure the freedom of that country, and to inculcate here the genuine doctrines of civil and religious liberty. The Petition of Right, in Old England, did not only aim at enforcing the act against the exaction of arbitrary benevolencies, but to prevent the imposition of any other tax, loan, or such charge, without common consent in Parliament given. And to curtail the prerogative of the Crown, to cut up its *minora regalia*, there was an express prohibition against the power of imprisonment. The Petition of Right is known to be the product of Lord Coke's pen, who had a just right to say, that he had won all the honors of his distinguished life, "without prayers and without pence;" he courted nor flattered neither Church nor State. This important act of Parliament, conceded to the subjects of the Crown the right of taxing themselves, and a perfect security of person and property. There is nothing great and glorious in the history of England, that is not in some way associated with their indissoluble union of taxation and representation. The *Habeus Corpus* came from this contest, as the shield of the subject against the arbitrary power of the Crown. Nor do I hazard any thing of error in the assertion, that these conservative principles of liberty and law, were laid in the blood of that monarch, whose head the people brought to the block, as an appropriate sacrifice for the liberties of England. Principles, for which Hampden lost his life in Chalgrave-field, and in support of which, Russell and Sidney died upon the scaffold. I am unwilling, (said Mr. Barbour,) to surrender the principles of Locke, and of Milton, for the fancies of Rosseau, aye, as unwilling as I am to disregard the lights of our own revolution for the *ignis fatuus* of French politics and French irreligion, or rather for the delusions of anarchy and atheism. The American revolution is the fruit of the effort in the parent Legislature, to seize by taxation the property of the Colonies, without their free and common consent in making the gift and grant. The offer was made that representation be allowed the Colonies, but it was rejected, because such representation must be nominal only.

The sturdy Patriots and able Statesmen of that day, knew the inefficacy of such representation. They pointed to the instance of Scotland, and insisted that representation *in form, only*, was but an apology for greater plunder and more oppressive exaction. If we turn our attention to the Constitution of the United States, the same principle for which we contend, is therein engrafted. Direct taxes and representation in the popular branch of the Legislative Department, are locked together. If power is wanted, it is to be had upon condition, that it bear the expenses of the social and Federal system. Pay the taxes, and you have the representatives. With representation, power passes also, but the shadow must not and cannot quit its substance. My views are directed by practical utility, and not by speculative philosophy. In looking through the Debates of the State Conventions, that ratified the Federal Constitution, I perceive that the men of those days, recognized the principles for which I contend, and acted on them. In New-York and Massachusetts, Mr. Jones, Mr. Smith, Mr. Hamilton and Mr. R. King, and Mr. Samuel Adams, all contended, "that taxation and representation, should go hand in hand, and that it was the language of all America." Notwithstanding the lights of our own revolution, and those reflected by the lamp of history, we are now to disregard all, and to pursue a path as yet untrodden, either by prudence or success. And why, Mr. Chairman, let me ask? Because petitions, it is said, have poured in for reform. I venture to predict, that the people never dreamed of this sort of reform. Reform, which is to make one man's property the property of another, without the owner's consent, and in the end to enslave his person, by first stripping him of his property. When the gentleman from Brooke, spoke of the annual petitions from the counties of Henry and of Patrick, praying the call of a Convention, I was reminded of another sort of petition, that I have sometimes seen from those counties, and the county of Franklin. I knew well the character of the Delegates usually sent here by those people. Cautious, intelligent and patriotic; they sought reform for the protection of property, and the security of personal rights and equality. And the very men who held in one hand the petition for a Convention, brought in the other another petition to diminish disbursements of public treasure and to retrench expenses. They were plain men, but they had the sagacity to discern, as Mr. Dunning did, in maintaining his celebrated resolution, "that the power of the Crown had increased, was increasing, and ought to be diminished;" that reform was nothing without retrenchment and economy. I know well that those people looked to the diminution of expenditure and to lightening the burden of taxation. Had they imagined that all this thing of Convention and reform was to resolve itself into a grant of power to take their money *ad libitum* and *ad indefinitum*, they would have done as we did in Culpeper: they would have come to the "*right about.*" For, if I were to select sentinels to guard the purse of the State, I would as soon take them from that quarter of Virginia, as from any other; I should give full confidence to their vigilance, fidelity, intelligence and honesty. I well remember, some years since, that one of the gentlemen from that quarter, had even the name of the watch-dog of the Treasury. And I speak it with all due respect and with sincere commendation, that such representatives often make the best and most useful public servants. Gentlemen deceive themselves in supposing that the people are prepared to throw down the guards of prudence and self-love which usually defend their property from encroachment. They will be guided by experience, rather than follow the lights of the French Revolution. Lights that shone for a time upon the path of despotism, and were finally extinguished in blood, &c. &c. &c.

Mr. Gordon (of Albemarle) now rose and said:

That it would be presumptuous in him, to attempt to say any thing calculated to guide the Committee to correct decisions on the important subjects on which they were called to deliberate: That he had, however, some opinions and facts, which he felt it his duty to submit to the consideration of the Committee, that they might, at least, be enabled to judge, by comparing his views and theirs, how much he might be in error, or that he might derive light from the great ability which distinguished this Assembly.

The course of the debate had seemed to him, somewhat beside the question: most of the arguments in favour of the amendment, proposed by the gentleman from Culpeper, (Mr. Green,) had gone the full length in opposition to all reform whatever; and it would seem to a by-stander, that the gentlemen had not been called on to recommend amendments to the existing form of Government, but to determine whether there should be a Convention called or not. That question had been already decided. A majority of the freeholders of Virginia, after years of deliberation, had determined that a Convention should be called for the purpose of proposing amendments to the existing Constitution. Public opinion, said Mr. G., cannot be misunderstood on that subject; unless, indeed, the ingenuity of gentlemen, shall be able to make the people, (as has been said,) come to the right about; and persuade us, their representatives, to disregard the purposes for which we were sent here. Are there, in reality, any inequalities in the existing Constitution of Virginia, which need reform? To me, Sir, it seems evident that there are, and inequalities so great, that they cannot longer be borne with. They must be corrected, not, Sir, by force and violence, but by the mild operation of public opinion, acting through its appropriate representation on this floor. A reform is due to the character of Virginia before the American public.

But, Sir, an attempt is now made, in the modification of this Constitution, to infuse into it a new principle, unheard of till now, (so far, at least, as my knowledge extends,) in any free Government; a principle which is at war with every notion we, as Americans, have been taught to hold sacred, and which goes to make the elective power quadrate with *wealth*. The design is, in effect, either to make slaves constituents to the Legislature, or to make the tax paid on them an ingredient in Legislative power. To both these propositions, I have strong objections. Sir, the plan will be utterly unavailing to the object its advocates seek to accomplish by it. If the consequences which are to flow from granting us an equality of rights, are really such as they apprehend, this scheme will never operate to prevent the evil.

The gentlemen on the other side have discussed this question, as if the injury so much dreaded from equal rights of representation, and an extension of the right of suffrage, was to be confined, in its extent, to one peculiar part of Virginia alone. If the white basis is adopted, the most grievous oppression must, they think, ensue to that part of the Commonwealth, and nothing can save the interests of the majority of the wealth of the State from the danger of misrule, when the power shall go into the hands of a minority possessing little wealth or influence. But, Sir, what are the facts of the case? For it is not my purpose, even if I had the ability which some other gentlemen so conspicuously display, to indulge in beautiful speculation on mere abstract theories, or in the brilliancy of illustration by classical allusions to history. My view of this subject shall be altogether practical. I purpose to enquire how Virginia can be rendered most happy and prosperous? And what effect is likely to ensue, from the proposed alterations in our Constitution?

The State of Virginia contains one hundred and five counties and four boroughs, having representation. These counties are very various in their dimensions, in the comparative fertility of their soil, as well as in the character of their respective population. The variety in these respects, is very great indeed. Some of these counties, have more people than, by the present system, are fairly represented in the Legislature; and have this redundancy on any theory gentlemen may be pleased to adopt, whether we go on the white basis exclusively, or on the compound basis of population and taxation, or even on the plan of giving representation to all the blacks. Nor is it a fact that these diversities and discrepancies are scattered about the State, here and there only, at wide distances apart; but, on the contrary, large portions of the State, and numerous counties lying contiguous to each other, present a spectacle of these great and striking inequalities. The question is, whether we shall, soberly and calmly, set ourselves to remedy such a state of things; or whether we shall press a subject that is calculated to distress us all, and practically to divide us in feeling, by first teaching us that we are divided in interest: the result of which can only be to bring us to a conclusion, which all true friends of Virginia cannot but deprecate, and which I hope never to see.

Do gentlemen ask us for facts? Sir, I state this as a fact, for the truth of which I appeal to the documents furnished us from the Auditor's office. From the head of tide-water, (leaving out the counties of Spottsylvania, Caroline, Hanover, the county of my friend, Mr. Morris, and the one which gave the first impulse to the revolution; Henrico, Chesterfield and the City of Richmond,) what is the amount of population and taxation as far west as the Blue Ridge? This region contains a large proportion of the white population of the State: it wants but little of containing a majority of the whole number of slaves: it pays a share of the revenue greatly disproportionate to its present representation; and, if taken in connexion with the limestone valley, (which I consider as appertaining to the eastern portion of the State, in all essential interests,) the two together, by the Census of 1820, containing a *majority* of the *total white* population; a *majority* also of the *slaves;* and a majority of the *taxation* likewise, by a balance of $17,000. Well, Sir, what is the representation enjoyed by that portion of the State on this floor? The fourteen counties of the Valley have twenty-eight members. The region from the head of tide to the Blue Ridge, have twenty-nine counties and fifty-eight members, making in all eighty-six. Thus, Sir, we see that in a House containing two hundred and fourteen Delegates, a region of the State comprising a majority of whites, blacks, and taxation, is represented but by eighty-six members; leaving thus a majority of thirty-eight members in the Legislature, actually *against* a majority of the whole population and the whole taxation of the State. Gentlemen ask for facts; here they are. I do not discuss the sectional interests of these relative portions of the State: Would to God that I could consider the interest of them all as one and the same: but these views forced themselves on my mind in consequence of the course pursued on the other side.

Nor is this all: the grossest inequalities present themselves to our view in that part of the State, which extends from the head of tide to the ocean: inequalities glaring indeed, when the two parts of the State are compared together. The Senatorial District of which Richmond forms a part, and one other, have in the House of Delegates, exclusive of Richmond, twenty-nine, and inclusive of Richmond, thirty Delegates. Thus, while five counties, at the foot of the Ridge, paying a tax of $ 37,886, have ten Delegates, these two Senatorial Districts have twenty-nine Delegates, and pay a tax of $ 52,450 only; that being the actual amount of taxation paid by the counties; Richmond, which pays $ 18,073, being withdrawn.

Sir, I do not say, that the country below tide-water, (God bless the country below tide-water, and all Virginia!) does not pay its full proportion of taxes; but I ask whether the very able opposition on this floor, had not better unite with us, in devising and perfecting a feasible plan for the amendment of the Constitution, than obstinately to defeat every plan that can be proposed.

Sir, I have made other calculations, from which it will appear, that the representation in the extreme west of Virginia is redundant; that that in the extreme east, is also redundant; and that while both these parts of the State will, if the basis of white population shall be adopted, *lose* a portion of their representation, the middle region of the State, which lies between them, will *gain* as much as they lose. The strength will thus be carried to the centre, and if we suffer death, it will be from a disease of the heart, for which there is no remedy.

Agreeably to the Census of 1820, the whole white population of the State was 603,081 whites; 425,148 slaves, and the whole taxes in the year 1828, was $ 423,563. The people west of the Alleghany mountains were 133,112 whites, 13,306 slaves, and they pay $ 39,099 in taxes. They have at present twenty-six counties and fifty-two Delegates; but, on the basis of representation by white numbers, they would have forty-seven only, *five less than they have at present.*

The Valley between the Alleghany and the Blue Ridge, had a white population of 121,096, and 29,785 slaves; they pay $ 65,537 taxes; they have fourteen counties and twenty-eight Delegates. If equalized, they would have forty-two. There are in the region of the State above the head of tide-water to the Blue Ridge, 187,186 whites, and 205,500 slaves; and it pays $ 164,170 tax. They have twenty-nine counties and fifty-eight Delegates, and are entitled to sixty-six Delegates, *eight more than at present.* The country below the head of tide-water had 161,687 whites, 176,496 slaves, and pays $ 157,756 in taxes; they have thirty-six counties and four boroughs, and seventy-six Delegates. They are entitled to fifty-seven only, *making a difference of nineteen.*

I have made other calculations, which go to shew, that there is no material difference, in the result, between basing the representation on Federal numbers, and on a compound ratio of population and taxation. There will be not more than a difference of two Representatives in a House of Delegates containing one hundred and twenty members.

Now, Sir, I ask if it be wise to equalize the representation of the State on *any* principle? If it be, then I deny that there is any other principle on which it can be fairly done, but on a majority of the free white inhabitants.

Property, Sir, in any just scheme of representation, is not to be regarded but as claiming the protection of the society. It is in aristocracy, that the argument is urged which insists on giving it political power as possessed by *individuals.* When you admit *that,* you make *a House of Lords;* you give the rich man a power which he could not claim in the Government without the influence of his wealth. But, gentlemen propose to give this influence to property, not as property in the hands of individuals, but as lying in certain sections and sub-divisions of the State; and does this better the matter? Not in principle, for the principle remains the same; not in practice, for there its only effect can be (and is) to produce heart-burnings and jealousies of section against section, which is even worse than of man against man. Because one part of the State has fewer slaves than the residue, will you make your basis of representation rest upon that sort of property, of all others, the most objectionable? What must be the effect of such a policy? It must, it will produce discontent every where, save only among the slave-holders themselves.

Sir, I thought it unwise, and I feel that it is most unpleasant, to bring this subject into the discussion. I tried to prevent it last winter in the Legislature: but it is forced upon us, and we must meet it: the gentlemen will not let us avoid it.

I ask, what good would it do to Virginia, were we to admit representation on the basis of the whole black population? Gentlemen argue as if the whole of the eastern part of Virginia consisted solely of slave-holders; but so far from this being the case, I think it possible, and very probable, that there is, even in that portion of the State, a majority who are not slave-holders. If that be the fact, or any thing near the fact, do they not see that, adopt what numerical basis you please, the prevailing, moral influence of the State must be against this, class of persons and the sort of property they hold? And if power is given to the slave-holders with a view to protect their slave property, will not the non-slave-holding portion of the community feel it their interest to make the slaves pay for their own protection? Will not the non-slave-holders in east. Virginia immediately have a common feeling with those in western Virginia? Sir, whatever may be the natural passions of men, one thing is very certain, that there is no very peculiar sympathy between non-slave-holders and slaves. They will utterly oppose a principle which confers on this species of property any political power in the practical Government of Virginia.

Sir, my own portion of the country has a very deep interest in this matter; and I am as anxious as any one can be, to have their interest secured, and their apprehensions quieted; but I would effect this in a very different mode from that suggested by some of the very able and honourable men with whom, in time past, it has been my pride to act. Sir, do you not perceive, that if property be your basis, you *cannot* extend the right of suffrage? Do not gentlemen see, that an extended right of suffrage is the circle which includes all these powers? Do they not perceive, that in imparting power to make laws and to vote for representatives, if they extend that power beyond the freeholders, they instantly get up an interest in the State which is hostile to the very foundation of their scheme, and hostile to any Government that shall be founded upon it? Sir, this is not an interest to be laughed at and despised. Shall we not still be assailed year after year, with petitions from the north to ameliorate the condition of the slave population? That interference we may well despise: but if we get up this spirit at home, among our own people, and your State shall be sundered and severed in affection by those mountains, what I once looked to, as to the barriers of her strength and safety: Sir, I say, if they get up this spirit on the other side of those mountains, will it not come over? Aye, and spread too, among all that portion of the community who are not slave-holders? If you extend the right of suffrage, will not persons thus discontented and thus made inimical to the slave-holding interest, vote for the man who will lay the highest tax upon slaves? How do you now retain that description of property in perfect safety? I answer, by the power of the society itself. Yes, by that composed, silent, but tremendous power, which resides in the free white population of the State: that power which defends all, and without noise, or apparent effort, keeps all things still in Virginia: and if you adopt any other foundation of power, than the white people of the State, will not jealousies and excitement exist towards that species of property which you thus endeavour to protect, in all those who are not its owners?

If you do not extend the right of suffrage, most painful discontent will ensue, and if you do extend it, you put it into the power of those who exercise suffrage, and who are not slave-owners to oppress that property the more relentlessly because a peculiar power is claimed for it in the Government, and when, in truth, its guardianship springs in a degree from the very numbers whose political power is diminished, by making that property or taxes from it, an ingredient in the representative power of the State. One would think, that in a free State, each man would have protected along with his person, such property as his genius, talents, or industry might have obtained for him: but this slave property is like having the wolf "by the ear; you do not know whether to hold him fast or to let him go." It is a stumbling block in our way: it balks us in all our deliberations, and we seem almost at a stand, whether we shall adhere or not, to the principles of freedom and equal rights, for which our fathers bled.

I ask whether there is any thing in this doctrine of a compound basis of representation, like those doctrines of freedom for which Virginia has always contended? I will not go for examples to English history: my recollection of it, is too general to enable me to go into its particular detail. But I will go to the free Constitutions of our own happy country, and I ask whether there is any thing in this principle calculated to aid the reputation ever enjoyed by this ancient Commonwealth, for her zealous attachment to the true principles of Constitutional liberty?

Gentlemen have perplexed themselves with abstract disquisitions on the rights of majorities, and they point us to instances, where, in the Federal and other Constitutions, the majority is excluded from a controlling power: these instances we well knew and remembered; but they are only exceptions, and exceptions do but confirm the general rule to which they apply: yet gentlemen would make these cases of particular exception, to give the principle on which to lay the foundations of our Constitution: Sir, what would this be but, in the language of an eloquent man, "to make the medicine of the State, its daily food?"

The veto of the President; the provision requiring majorities of two-thirds of the Legislature, and others of the like kind are relied on, as proof that we are not to look to a majority of the people for an expression of the public will, but must get a will made up of slavery and freedom, of money and free will: and this is to be *our* protection.

I had hoped, gentlemen would have reserved this proposition for a mixed basis, till we came in regular course to consider the subject of representation in the Senate. The Senate, it seems, must be held as a check on the lower House: it is not to be itself a moving active body, but is to serve as a curb upon the enthusiasm of the other branch of the Legislature. But little did I expect that it was to be proposed to us, to make the first branch of our Legislature, unlike any other in the Union, unless it be where one of the slave-holding States have copied the Federal ratio of three-fifths of the black population. But there is no analogy between the case which gave birth to that ratio, and the case now before us. That was a treaty of one sovereignty with another. A Constitution was then being constructed, which was to combine different and totally distinct societies under one general Government, for their common benefit. It was a Government of limited powers, the residue of power being retained by those sovereignties as such. It is said, that able statesmen have doubted the wisdom of that provision in the Federal Constitution; and I myself shall regret it, if it be made a precedent, to infuse an aristocratic ingredient into our State Constitutions. The structure of the Senate of the United States, where States large and small have equal representation, is brought forward as furnishing a proof, that a majority of numbers does not, in fact, rule in this Republic. But the reason of the equality of representation, while numbers were so unequal, is manifest; the Delegates on that floor do not represent numbers at all; they have nothing to do with numbers; they represent sovereignties; and the sovereignty of a State, does not depend on its dimensions.

Gentlemen have denied the right of the majority to rule in part from the practical difficulties in applying the rule; and they have pointed us to the minorities in the Districts, as often being, if united, sufficient to contradict the vote obtained, by admitting a mere plurality to decide an election. Admitting this to be so, it does not reach the point: for I have not said either that the voice of the majority does always in practice prevail, nor that the majority always does what is right; but I ask gentlemen to point out a safer depository for the ruling power.

Allusions have been made to some of the Governments of antiquity, and to that of England, as supporting the opposite view. But, Sir, what is this Government of England, to which gentlemen so confidently appeal? Has it not at length become (notwithstanding the original freedom of its Constitution) little else than a military despotism? The people, it is true, submit; but take the arms out of the hands of the soldiery, and how long would that submission last? I suspect they would soon find out a very summary mode of paying their national debt. But the raw head and bloody bones of the French revolution is ever and anon made to pass before us, and we are reminded, as soon as we propose the least approach toward a greater equalization of rights, of the political and moral earthquake that shook that ancient empire to its foundations. Sir, I think there may be drawn from that very revolution a salutary lesson on our side of the question. The evils of that great convulsion did not grow out of the misrule of the *majority* alone, but out of the resistance of a minority. They refused to submit to the principle for which we contend, and rejected the concessions offered them by the mild spirit of their King; and it is not to be wondered at, that, in the issue, the will of the majority should prevail. It is very true that there succeeded a more settled state of things under Bonaparte; but though the country was to appearance quiet, it was not the calm of contentment, but of coerced submission; the spirit of liberty was still throbbing in French veins; and the issue has been, that after desolating all Europe, and laying waste in its course almost all the Kingdoms of the Old World, this very French revolution has terminated in advancing the rights of man. It has given to France a more limited monarchy; a free press, a representative chamber, and the trial by jury.

But, Sir, have we any proud and haughty nobility, for whose pleasure the yeomanry are to be taxed at will? A fat and indolent privileged order, who roll in luxury at the cost of the laboring classes of the community? No, Sir. There are none who propose such a thing. What then has the French revolution to do with a case no way analogous to that of France?

Various other topics have been introduced into the discussion, which, in my apprehension, have no legitimate connexion with it; (but I do not pretend to judge for others, or to cast the least censure on them.) And among others the subject of internal improvement has been conjured up; (I should not say *conjured* up, for it sprang up in our way.) And gentlemen oppose the white basis of representation on the ground that if it be adopted, the lower country will be heavily taxed for objects they do not approve, and the entire benefit of which will be enjoyed by the west. That this subject is known to be a favorite one among gentlemen who reside in that part of the State. But, I ask, was that attempt at internal improvement which has been made, a western project? Its advocates and the engineers, I own, deluded me when I first entered the Legislature; they told us we could unite the eastern and western parts of the

State at a small expense, and I reflected that we had a fund provided expressly for objects of that character, and the basis of which was wisely laid in the principle, that individual enterprize was first to be called out, and then aided by the hand of the Government. But, Sir, by whom was that wise restriction on the application of this fund ruptured? Was it by gentlemen from the west? Or was it not by what is familiarly denominated the James River interest? Was it not they who told us that the object was one of such vast importance, that it ought to be made an exception from the rule, and that a sum ought to be raised for that object expressly, without reference to the peculiar constitution of that fund? I am casting no injurious imputations upon the gentlemen: God forbid! I know they were all honorable and high-minded men, who were sincerely pursuing what they considered the best means of improving the State.

But what has this question of internal improvement to do with the question of a white or a compound basis for representation? Nothing at all, Sir: Yet, they themselves have introduced it, and I must be suffered to go a little into it, by way of reply. The gentlemen got little by their scheme: all the money, I believe, has been sunk in James River. They made large loans to effect it, and now those loans have to be re-paid, the country has come to a halt. The system of internal improvement cannot move a peg. I know that the distinguished Convention held at Charlottesville was got up with a view to revive the interest of the subject in the public mind; and what has been the result? I believe the gentlemen must own that it has been any thing else, rather than a revival of the public confidence in behalf of internal improvement. Unless these projects are carried on elsewhere in a very different manner from what they have been here, they will ever result in mere jobs, wherever the public or the Government have any concern in them. The meeting at Charlottesville has produced but very little effect in favor of the subject. very little indeed, Sir; insomuch that you cannot, at this day, get the people of Virginia to consent to be taxed for works of internal improvement any where, be it east or west, north or south. Freeholders or non-freeholders; all reject the proposition. The only way in which they can advance one step is by loans. and that mode I shall ever hereafter oppose.

My friend from Hanover (Mr. Morris), when the gigantic scheme was first presented to incorporate a Joint Stock Company, in which Virginia and other States were parties with individuals and the United States to make the Chesapeake and Ohio canal, supported it with great effect against my friend from Norfolk Borough (Mr. Loyall) and myself. Yet, notwithstanding this, such was the anxiety of the Virginia Legislature not to connect the improvement of the State with Federal authority, that the bill did not pass until a provision was made attempting to limit the Federal power, within the boundary of the District of Columbia, as to its subscription.

Reference had been made to an application to the Legislature, for certain improvements in the Shenandoah; but what argument could be drawn from a mere application, which was never granted, he could not perceive.

My friend from Orange (Mr. P. P. Barbour), for whose talents and character, I entertain the most exalted regard, has informed us, that he is against mere *experiments*, and in favor of experience alone; and so am I against experiments, when they are of a wild and visionary character. But we must not forget, that it is from experiment alone, that experience is obtained; and that the most valuable institutions of the country, that our whole free Government itself, is but the result of an experiment, which has happily succeeded, and has, as I fondly trust, converted this land into the abode of freemen, to endless ages. Yet, the very same arguments might have been urged against that experiment, as are urged now against this. It was a fearful conflict we engaged in, against the greatest nation in the world; the first in arts, and arms, and liberal science, and all that can ennoble or adorn the name of man. That was a fearful experiment; and the heart of the firmest man might well pause, if not tremble, at adopting it. But, Sir, is there any thing fearful in the little experiment we are now going to make? Almost all the States have re-modelled their Constitutions; and has any violence or public calamity ensued? I have heard of none. In the old world, indeed, you cannot take up at pleasure the foundations of your Government, and improve its form. Why? Because the principles of aristocracy and monarchy, are there infused throughout the whole system. A hundred ranks of dependent officers, are interested in upholding the existing abuses, and keeping down the people: and if the people obtain a mitigation of their evils, they must rise in their might, like the strong man, and tear down the temple which has become their prison. But, does an argument from that state of things, apply here, where we inhabit a free State, and are surrounded by twenty-three other States, equally free? Are arguments of this sort to appal us? Is there any demoniacal spirit gone abroad in the Commonwealth, so that there is nothing like justice or faith among men? Suspicion, it seems, is to be the order of the day; and jealousy the only safe foundation for a civil community. Sir, men do not associate in communities, because they *suspect*, but because they *love* each other: because society is necessary to the heart, and man is a savage without it. It is only when society has long been established, that the spirit of selfishness makes man a misanthrope, and persuades him to deny, that true "self-love and social, are the same." No, Sir. All the suspicion we ought to cherish, in laying the foundations of our new Constitution, is such as will teach us to be very jealous, lest so much as a grain of aristocracy or monarchy, should any where be found in it. Let us have no Nobles, no Kings; but give us, and our children, the equal rights of men.

Sir, if we shall fail in agreeing to any amendment to the Constitution, and shall return to those who sent us here, with nothing in our hands, what must be the consequence? Discontent, division, public confusion. Sir, it *must* happen. An excitement will take place, which cannot be allayed. The people expect that something shall be done. They expect, that the basis of representation of the State shall be equalized, and the right of suffrage extended: and they will be deeply dissatisfied, if it is not done. I said, that you could not extend the right of suffrage, and engraft this principle of a compound basis into your Constitution: and none are, or can be consistent, but those who oppose the whole. For, the very moment you extend the right of suffrage, you grant a power, which, if the white basis is rejected, will call another Convention. And, Sir, permit me to say, that the calmness with which we have met, and the mutual respect and decorum, which distinguish the present body, shew clearly, that we are in no danger of that bloody sword, which was so ominously brandished over us, by the gentleman from Hanover, (Mr. Morris); but, if we insist on what the people disapprove, we shall have east and west, lowlands and highlands, unite in the call of another Convention, who will put out the obnoxious principle, and then the just rights of the community will every where prevail.

And is there any thing to forbid this equalization of rights? If it shall prevail, the majority will still remain below the mountains: In a House of one hundred and twenty, there will be nineteen more Delegates from the eastern, than from the western side of the Blue Ridge. I do not go on the speculations of the gentleman from Brooke, (Mr. Doddridge.) I do not believe, that the majority will ever be found beyond the mountain, unless the policy of the Old Dominion shall be to encourage the growth of the black population, and discourage that of the white. I know, indeed, the immense tract of mountainous country which the State possesses; and I rejoice that she does possess it. It is her impregnable security; a stronger barrier than the Balkan. But it is a region, which never can possess a population so dense, as that below the mountains; nothing like it. Well, Sir, this negro property (it is very disagreeable to me to be obliged to touch the subject, but the fault is not mine; it lies in my way, and I cannot avoid it;) this negro property has increased, is increasing, and calls for the deepest consideration. I intend no idle appeal to the fears of Virginia; I know what the old Virginans are too well; a more gallant people is not on the earth: the only fear they know, is the dread of a dishonorable action. But what I state are facts. There exists below the head of tide-water, a mass of that population, which besides 23,000 free blacks, contains 150,000 slaves. There they are, Sir. The Colonization Society has failed to remove them. You cannot get them to go out of Virginia; and I think they would be blockheads if they did, living as comfortably as they do. This black population is fast increasing. The white population is nearly stationary. There lies a wide-spread region of country, as fair and fertile, and every way desirable, as any on which the sun shines: and when we contemplate its situation, to what conclusion are we naturally led? To this, Sir: that the whole tide of its population, both black and white, is moving with a steady but gradual current, to the west, and the time must, therefore, come when there will be in the residue of the State, a most decided majority *against* the tide-water country. Now, I ask, whether it is not better to have this majority as friends, animated by a devoted attachment to their brethren (notwithstanding a certain division on the details of the Defence Bill,) than to irritate them into a state of animosity, so that no reliance can be placed upon them in the time of war?

I claimed the Valley as an Eastern country; and I did so on the ground taken by the gentleman from Fauquier (Mr. Scott,) viz. because it was their interest to be so. The gentleman from Northampton, (Mr. Upshur) said that the Valley was not a grain-growing country; but if he lived as near it as I do, and saw as many of its huge wagons and fat horses, he could not have retained that opinion. Now, Sir, the trade of that region of the State must naturally follow the course of its rivers. Can any man believe that it will ascend the Alleghany Mountains, for the sake of going down the Ohio? And if not, what can be plainer than that that Valley has, and must have, the same interest as the lower part of Virginia? Why will gentlemen resolve to believe, that this our ancient Commonwealth, must be as distinctly divided by conflicting interests, as its several regions are divided on the maps?

No, Sir; it is the obvious interest of the Valley to be with us. Is it so on the Slave question? The tables we have received from the Auditor will shew, that there are only *two* white titheables to *one* black, through all the Valley. The slave population, though numerous, is, in that part of the State, much more diffused, than it is in East Virginia. The interest is divided among more owners in proportion to the number of slaves. Gentlemen to the west of the Alleghany, feel oppressed, as not being represented; but candour requires me to say, that the taxes in that part of the State are not paid in a manner proportionate to the population. Yet there are only five whites to one black, even there. In the mean while, the tide of the black population moves westward; and it increases more rapidly in the west, than in any part of the State. Now, Mr. Chairman, what is the conclusion from all these facts? Plainly this: That if any body is so wild as to be disposed that Virginia should get rid suddenly of her coloured people, the thing is impossible. They are fixed, fast rivetted upon us.

Here, then, the whole subject rises before us: and would to God, I had the power to do justice to it. But I feel that it is otherwise, and I must confine myself to a few of its most prominent points.

As it seems, that we *must* extend the right of suffrage, how vain will it be to introduce into our Constitution, a principle odious to the people, from its aristocratic character? Notwithstanding all that has been said on this floor, against the right of men to vote, you find few men who will deny that *they* themselves have that right, either by nature, or in some other way. I am for extending the right of suffrage, not merely because I think it proper in itself, that every free white citizen, should have some share in the Government, but because it is the only way to counteract the effects of the increase of the black population in Virginia. I am against offering a premium to induce our labouring white people to leave our soil. I would have that class of the community retained and encouraged among us, as the best means of preventing the disproportionate increase of the slaves. The labour of the country is the wealth of the country, be it performed by white men or black. The black labourer is represented through the person of his master, but the white labourer is not represented at all.

Here Mr. G. went into a series of illustrations on the relative importance of labour and money; contending that there was nothing valuable in the community apart from the soil itself, that was not the effect of labour; that the resources of the country had not been yet drawn out: and argued to shew that it was better entitled to representation than wealth could be: and from thence insisted on the necessity of an extension of the right of suffrage. He never thought that a freehold was the only qualification on which men ought to be allowed to vote. Society lives on its labour, not on its capital; if not, its capital would soon be exhausted. If, said he, you extend the right of suffrage in a fair and equitable manner, you will satisfy the country. There will be no excitement, and the whole effect of the alteration you produce, will be to remove the seat of power, not across the mountains, but only a little further up the country, than where it now resides. We, who live in the middle region of Virginia, have slaves as well as you. You profess to fear, that the Valley will go with the west, and that the two will unite their power to oppress and injure you. If that fear be well founded, the measure you propose offers no remedy. Let the Valley unite itself with the west, and let them be joined by all the non-slave-holders below the mountains, and any resistance of your's, on any scheme of representation, must prove utterly futile. You cannot withstand their will. Adopt what scheme you please, they must have a majority in the Legislature. It is the interest of my portion of the State to equalize representation on any basis; that effect cannot be avoided, and if it could be, there is nothing in that part of the State hostile to the interests of any other part.

The gentleman from Orange, when arguing for a minority, referred the Committee to the Senate of Massachusetts, where property is the sole basis. But there is a striking difference between the Senate of Massachusetts and the Senate of Virginia, as to the frequency of their election. In Massachusetts they are chosen annually; in Virginia, only once in four years. And as to taxation, the chief burden of the contributions in Massachusetts is imposed by the people themselves as divided into wards. The taxes laid, in the Legislative Hall are comparatively few; and for even these, the legislators are perpetually before the people in their annual elections.

Gentlemen talk about checks and responsibilities. Is the responsibility of which they speak, the responsibility of a Governor or of the Senate to the House of Delegates? We all know how such checks may be counteracted by combination. The only effectual responsibility in a free State, is responsibility to the people. They are never in favor of their own oppression; and although individually, may think them unjust to *their claims*, they are *rarely so to the general interests*. The gentleman from Fauquier (Mr. Scott) speaking about projects to tunnel the Alleghany, referred to the case of the James River canal, in which he supposed a pledge was given, or at least understood to be given, that if the Legislature would make the necessary grant to carry on the improvement, our produce should not be taxed. That a loan was obtained, and when difficulty was felt in paying the interest, a tax was imposed upon tobacco. I was here at the time, and was in favor of the project of improvement, and against the tax on tobacco. Now, I ask, who voted for that tax on tobacco? The whole lower Virginia interest. If there were any exceptions at all, they were (as we heard lately) *rari nantes*. They all voted by a simultaneous movement, to lay a tax of a dollar a hogshead on tobacco, notwithstanding the prohibition in the act of incorporation of the James River Company, by which they were bound not to raise their tolls, till the rate of transportation should be reduced. Yet the gentleman says, that the pledge then given, was immediately violated.

[Mr. Scott here rose to explain. He had not charged a breach of faith on any individuals. He had merely stated a fact, which he saw in the Statute Book.]

Mr. Gordon said, in reply, that it was much more agreeable to him to think, that all the gentlemen were equally just · and he had no doubt, that those who voted the tax, were upright and honorable men, and did what they supposed to be right. The case only proved, that a majority could sometimes do wrong : but, said Mr. G, come the imposition from where it may, one thing is certain, that we continue to pay it to this day : and when I hear the munificent power of lower Virginia lauded and magnified, by a strange association, this *tobacco* tax always comes into my mind. It was carried by a majority of one vote only : and well do I remember, with what ardour and ability the gentleman from Augusta (Mr. Johnson) resisted it to the last, in the Senate. Yet this case is brought up to have weight on the present question. Sir, I have no doubt that the gentlemen voted from the fairest motives. The motive avowed by some was to cure the country of middle Virginia, of its fondness for internal improvement, and, to speak the truth, I believe it has, thus far, operated very effectually to that end. Our country complained of the tax, and endeavored to get it repealed ; but in vain : all who voted to lay it on, voted to keep it on. But this case, so far from furnishing an argument for inequality of rights, has its whole bearing the other way. Do you give us our fair power in the Government, and then tax our tobacco, if you can? Sir, I am not against the tobacco country. As to the increase of the tolls, it was referred to a committee of two gentlemen, who reported in its favor. They were both enthusiastic advocates for internal improvement ; one of them was successfully prosecuting a work of great interest on the Roanoke, and the other had his own residence on the banks of James river, and was willing himself to be taxed.

And now, Sir, I ask, what have all these subjects of internal improvement to do with the question before us? What prevents us from going on to lay the foundations of a Republic, on those sacred principles of equal rights, for which the patriots of America have always contended? I, Sir, insist, that the people are capable of self-government, and that they ought to enjoy it ; that the power shall not reside in A or B, but in the whole community ; and that no free white male citizen should be excluded, but those who have excluded themselves, by the immorality of their character.

After an apology for occupying so long the time of the Committee, and a reference to the embarrassment under which he had spoken, Mr. G. then resumed his seat.

Mr. Morris here went into an explanation of the course he had pursued in relation to the incorporation of the Potomac Company, to which allusion had been made by Mr. Gordon. He had voted for the act incorporating the company, not conceiving it at all to involve the question, as to the right of the United States' Government to bring their spades upon the soil of Virginia. The application of this company to Congress, was totally distinct from their application to Virginia. They had applied to Congress merely as constituting the local Legislature of the District of Columbia, through a part of which District they wished to carry their canal. He could not perceive, what this had to do with the question before the Committee.

Mr. Mercer said, that he did not rise to enter into a discussion, which had already occupied the Committee for seven days : but simply to state the reason why he should vote against Mr. Scott's amendment. That amendment proposes a basis which is already acted upon in the election to the Senate ; and being attached to the amendment (of Mr. Green,) which proposes a compound basis for the lower House, the vote in favor of one must cover both. Such a vote he could not consent to give.

Mr. Johnson said, he had not risen to discuss the merits of the general question, but only to say a word on the last amendment ; for it was a little remarkable, that on this which, strictly speaking, was the only question before the House, not one word had yet been said, calculated to indicate, either how any one would vote upon it, or how any one ought to vote upon it. The latitude which had been unavoidably allowed in the course of the discussion, had resulted in this, that the whole debate hitherto had been occupied on the comparative merit of the resolution of the Legislative Committee, proposing the white basis exclusively in the House of Delegates ; and the amendment of the gentleman from Culpeper, (Mr. Green) proposing as a substitute the compound basis in that House. The last amendment offered by the gentleman from Fauquier, (Mr. Scott) sought to introduce the white basis in the Senate, going on the ground that the compound basis shall prevail in the lower House. Mr. Johnson said he should vote against this amendment; not because he thought white population an improper basis for representation in the Senate, but because he thought that question could be better considered, more fairly decided, as well as more fully understood, when the Committee should have disposed of the question of representation in the House of Delegates, and should come directly to consider the subject of the Senate. Besides, said he, this amendment takes it for granted, that we are to have representation on one principle in the one branch of the Legislature, and on another principle in the other. Those who are of this opinion, must have a preference in relation to which of the two shall be on the white, and which on the mixed basis. Those who prefer giving the white basis to the House of Delegates, will, of course, be against the amendment now last before us. I prefer it, as furnishing a check to the power of the Senate, and shall, therefore, vote against it also.

Mr. Scott said, that the very reason given by the gentleman from Augusta (Mr. Johnson) operated with him to vote the other way: But the gentleman from Loudoun (Mr. Mercer) had said that the present amendment gave them no more than they had already. He would ask of that gentleman to point out a single clause in the Constitution which establishes a white basis in the Senate: he, at least, had never seen such a clause.

Mr. Mercer replied that he had not asserted that the Constitution has such a passage, but the Constitution certainly does not forbid it, and it has been established by an act of the Legislature.

Mr. Scott said he was aware of that: but what he proposed by his amendment was, to give that arrangement a Constitutional sanction. Its whole authority, at present, is no more than that of any other ordinary bill passed by the Legislature. Gentlemen insisted on having a white basis of representation: he could not go with them the entire length they demanded, but was willing, as an *ultimatum*, to consent to that basis in the Senate.

Mr. Johnson would suggest one enquiry to the gentleman who advocated the amendment last proposed. Where was the precedent, or where could any just reason be found, to sanction such a course as it proposed? No man in the Convention, he presumed, was disposed to disturb that part of the Constitution which declares, that there shall be two branches of the Legislature; one, numerous, and frequently elected, and coming directly from the people, charged with their wishes and stored with a knowledge of all their wants, to present their petitions, advocate their rights, and claim the remedy of their wrongs:. The other, select in its character, few in its numbers, a longer term of service, and so graduated in the rotation of those terms as to render the body perpetual, charged with the duty of revising the proceedings of the representatives of the people, of detecting their errors, and correcting them: in whom confidence may be placed, that they will have the firmness to resist wrong, and the intelligence requisite to perceive, and to decide upon, what is right. These doctrines he understood to be acknowledged by all; and these rules, none that he knew of, wished to disturb. But the ground taken by those who wished to see the Constitution amended was, that in the popular branch of the Legislature, charged more especially with the wishes and wants of the people, the people do not now enjoy an equal representation; although in the other, and the controlling branch, they are justly represented. You wish, said Mr. Johnson, a censor (for you all contend for placing some limit upon the majority,) and for that end, you provide a Senate. But the effect of the present amendment, instead of making the Senate a censor upon the House, goes, in effect, to make the House of Delegates a censor upon the Senate. Now, I call upon all who have any regard to the just principles of Government, to its harmony and its consistency, to tell me why such a distinction should be established.

Mr. Scott observed in reply, that he would give the gentleman one or two reasons. Both the branches of the Legislature were popular in their character: both being chosen by the people, and responsible to them; and the question was, which of them should be placed as a guard upon the taxing power? We contend that we are entitled to place that guard in the stronger branch of the Legislature. We wish to have our rights protected, inasmuch as we bring a larger stake into the community: we bring our persons not only, but our property with us; and we ought, therefore to have the stronger security. Again, the interests of property are more easily infringed than those of persons. We expose our person in the streets, we place our less valuable property within the walls of our houses, but we lock up our gold in a strong box.

Mr. Nicholas said, that he wished to explain the vote he should give. He had listened with attention to the arguments urged on both sides, and his conviction was that the compound basis of representation was the only true and proper basis in *both* Houses. Why should the gentleman from Augusta, (Mr. Johnson) impute any improper motive to those who were in favor of the present amendment? For his own part, he thought that the arguments of the gentleman from Fauquier (Mr. Scott) went very conclusively to shew, not merely that the compound principle should be introduced into the larger branch of the Legislature, but that it ought to prevail in both branches. But, it was possible, that the vote on his amendment, might serve to try how far gentlemen of opposite views could come to some compromise, and yield a little of their respective convictions. Can it, asked Mr. Nicholas, be imputed to us as a fault, that we are willing, at least, to make the experiment? Or are the gentlemen resolutely determined to go to all extremities? The amendment appears to me wise in another aspect. What security have we who wish to take a middle ground, that gentlemen after having obtained that principle of representation which they desire in the lower House, will not, afterwards, when we come to fix the basis of the Senate, insist upon, and carry it there also? I am willing to take this amendment as an experiment, to try what are the views and feelings of other gentlemen; reserving to myself to pursue such a course in the issue, as I may then deem expedient. As to the propriety of establishing the white basis in the House of Delegates, rather than in the Senate, the argument of the gentleman from Augusta, goes on a *petitio principii.* It takes for granted the very question in dispute, viz. that the white basis of representation is the most proper in itself. We think otherwise. We prefer the mixed basis: and so thinking, we desire to have it first established in the most numerous House of the Legislature.

The question was now taken on the amendment of Mr. Scott, and decided in the negative. Ayes 43, Noes 49.

So Mr. Scott's amendment, (proposing the white basis in the Senate, and the compound basis in the House of Delegates,) was rejected.

The question then recurring on the amendment proposed by Mr. Green, viz: to strike out the word "exclusively" from the resolution reported by the Legislative Committee, and insert in lieu thereof, the words "and taxation combined," and the vote being apparently about to be taken,

Mr. Monroe, rose and spoke as follows:

It is with reluctance, Sir, that I now rise to address you, the reasons for which, I need not repeat, but being under the necessity of giving my vote, I owe it to my constituents who have generously placed me here, to the Commonwealth I have so long served, and to myself, to explain the grounds on which I act. I must do it with the utmost brevity, and I fear that I shall fail, in giving the explanation which I wish.

I have seen with the deepest concern, a concern I want language to express, the divisions which exist in this body, and in the Commonwealth; because I anticipate if they shall be persevered in, the most unhappy consequences. I consider it the interest of every section of the Commonwealth, to unite in some arrangement, which may be satisfactory to a great majority of this House and of the State; and even to sacrifice a portion of their respective claims, rather than to fail in the accomplishment of the great object, for which we have met. If we go home without having agreed upon a Constitution, or if we shall agree upon one, and it shall be passed by a small majority, what will be the effect? An appeal will immediately be made to the whole community, which will excite repellant feelings among the people, in one section against those of the other, which will endanger the dismemberment of the State. If it should be rejected by them, or passed by a small majority, the same result might follow. Sectional feelings already existing, will be nursed and cherished; they will increase and spread, till at length, one part of the community will be pitted against the other, and a deep and malignant acrimony ensue, and where will it end? In an actual dismemberment of the Commonwealth; which would be the worst evil that can befal us; a result which would be equally calamitous to all. Should it take place, the party which had pressed its claims with most earnestness, would suffer as much as the others. If the State should be severed, will the General Government agree, that the dismembered part shall be admitted as a separate State into the Union? I doubt it. But if it should agree to it, could we then get forward, with all our objects of internal improvement; objects which I have always advocated, and in the accomplishment of which I have taken a deep interest, with the same success, as in our present situation? I have considered these improvements, as very important to the strength and welfare of the Commonwealth, and stability of the Union. I have wished to see them prosecuted, but within the limited resources of the State, and with the aid of the United States. What else is there that can so effectually bind us together? If the Atlantic States should be separated from those of the west, the country would be ruined. The western States would then be arrayed against those on the Atlantic, and endless strife be the consequence. If Virginia should be dismembered, on the ground of the present controversy, will not the Carolinas and Georgia, experience the same fate? The same principles are involved, and causes exist there, though not to the same extent. Those causes do not exist in the new States, where the emigration was sudden, and the interests of all the emigrants, are nearly the same. There are causes of disunion among us, which do not apply to them, and if we can bind the States together, by opening communications between them, then our union will be perfected. nothing can ever break it

There are two great waters in Virginia, the James river and the Potomac, which I am very anxious to have connected, with the western waters to which they approach. The Roanoke is a third one, which may, in some degree, be connected with the western waters, and more intimately with those of the Chesapeake. These objects may be much better accomplished, if the State remains united, than if it should be dismembered.

What are the grounds of this division? On what does it rest? I regret that I am incompetent to go at large into a consideration of them. It is contended by those who reside in the western part of the State, that representation in the Legislature, shall be based on white population alone: It is contended on the other hand, by those who live in the east, that it shall be based on the principle of population and taxation combined. These are the two grounds of difference. I am satisfied, that the claim of those in the west, is rational under particular circumstances. It has often been suggested here, and I accord with that view, that putting the citizens in an equal condition, and the basis which they claim is just: It is founded on the natural rights of man, and in policy also, under certain circumstances. But look at the Atlantic country, and what is their claim? They are the oldest portion of the State; they have a species of property, in a much greater amount than the people of the west, and this they wish to protect. It consists of slaves. I am satisfied, if no such thing as slavery existed, that the people of our Atlantic border, would meet their brethren of the west, upon the basis of a majority of the free white population.

What has been the leading spirit of this State, ever since our independence was obtained? She has always declared herself in favour of the equal rights of man. The revolution was conducted on that principle. Yet there was at that time, a slavish population in Virginia. We hold it in the condition in which the revolution found it, and what can be done with this population? If they were extinct, or had not been here, white persons would occupy their place, and perform all the offices now performed by them, and consequently, be represented. If the white people were not taxed, they also would be free from taxation. If you set them free, look at the condition of the society. Emancipate them, and what would be their condition? Four hundred thousand, or a greater number of poor, without one cent of property, what would become of them? Disorganization would follow, and perfect confusion. They are separated from the rest of society, by a different colour; there can be no intercourse or equality between them; nor can you remove them. How is it practicable? The thing is impossible, and they must remain as poor, free from the controul of their masters, and must soon fall upon the rest of the society, and resort to plunder for subsistence. As to the practicability of emancipating them, it can never be done by the State itself, nor without the aid of the Union. And what would be their condition, supposing they were emancipated, and not removed beyond the limits of the Union? The experiment has in part been tried. They have emigrated to Pennsylvania in great numbers, and form a part of the population of Philadelphia, and likewise of New-York and Boston. But those who were the most ardent advocates of emancipation, in those portions of the Union, have become shocked at the charges of maintaining them, as well as at the effect of their example. Nay, Sir, look at Ohio, and what has she recently done? Ohio acknowledges the equal rights of all, yet she has driven them off from her territory. She has been obliged to do it. If emancipation be possible, I look to the Union to aid in effecting it.

Sir, what brought us together in the revolutionary war? It was the doctrine of equal rights. Each part of the country, encouraged and supported every other part of it. None took advantage of the other's distresses. And if we find that this evil has preyed upon the vitals of the Union, and has been prejudicial to all the States, where it has existed, and is likewise repugnant to their several State Constitutions, and Bills of Rights, why may we not expect, that they will unite with us, in accomplishing its removal? If we make the attempt and cannot accomplish it, the effect will at least, be to abate the great number of petitions and memorials, which are continually pouring in upon the Government. This matter is before the nation, and the principles, and consequences, involved in it, are of the highest importance. But in the meanwhile, self-preservation demands of us union in our councils.

What was the origin of our slave population? The evil commenced when we were in our Colonial state, but acts were passed by our Colonial Legislature, prohibiting the importation, of more slaves, into the Colony. These were rejected by the Crown. We declared our independence, and the prohibition of a further importation, was among the first acts, of State sovereignty. Virginia was the first State, which instructed her Delegates, to declare the Colonies independent. She braved all dangers. From Quebec to Boston, and from Boston to Savannah, Virginia shed the blood of her sons. No imputation, then, can be cast upon her, in this matter. She did all that was in her power to do, to prevent the extension of slavery, and to mitigate its evils.

As to our western brethren, I feel as deep an interest for them, as for those on the Atlantic border. I have so long represented the Commonwealth, that I have no sectional feeling. I look to the Commonwealth, and seek the welfare of the whole.

As to the question of boundary, what was the conduct of Virginia? Like the other Colonies, she claimed the boundaries, and the extent of territory, granted to her by her Charter. Virginia stood on the same footing with the other States. They all held, under their Charters. But as the revolution advanced, it began to be contended by those States, whose territory was covered with population, that those who held vacant lands, should throw them into a common stock, for the benefit of the whole, and the contest was pushed to such an extent that menaces of hostility begun to be uttered. To quiet this discontent, Virginia ceded to the United States, the territory which she held, to the north-west of the Ohio, out of which three States of the Union have been formed. Kentucky then, also a distant part of her territory, but separated by mountains from the rest of the State, claimed independence. Virginia consented to this also. And what did she then fix as the western boundary of the State? The Ohio River and the Cumberland Mountains. All the residue of her boundary, was left as it stood before, in confidence, that the extent was not too great, and that all the inhabitants within it, would be held together by a common interest. What has been her course, as to the settlement, quite up to the boundary line? It has been ever fair, open, manly, and generous. She has seldom refused the erection of a county, whenever it was sought. So at least I am assured, for I have been absent, in the performance of other duties, and cannot be expected, to recollect the details, of this subject. She has been guilty of no oppression, as has been acknowledged here, where, indeed, I have witnessed with delight, the mutual respect and confidence, with which gentlemen, on opposite sides, speak of each other; and I most earnestly hope, that they will remain, firmly bound together.

As to the best arrangement for the settlement of this question, I will frankly state my own views. I hold concession to be necessary on both sides. I think the claim of the West strong; but that that of those, who reside on the Atlantic side, is equally so. It is said, that by the principle, the latter contend for, the natural and political rights of men, would be violated. I do not so view the case. I think that it admits of a different view; that is, to a certain extent, and with the necessary modifications.

I am an advocate for the extension of the right of suffrage, and on that subject I am ready to go, as far as the most liberal can desire. I will here state an incident which occurred when I was in the Legislature of Virginia in 1810. Petitions were then presented, praying for a Convention, and one of the objects desired, or urged in the debate, was an extension of the right of suffrage. I had just seen the effects of this right in other countries: I had recently been in England and France, and witnessed popular movements in both countries, particularly in France. I was present during three of the great movements of the people, who seemed to act without any check or control. I saw one of these movements directed against their existing Government, and by which it was literally torn to pieces. It was at length repressed, with the bayonet, by Pichegru. In another the Convention was most violently assailed; the multitude, burst into the Legislative Hall; they were met and opposed, by the members; they killed one, and cutting off his head, marched with it on a pike to the President's Chair. I witnessed this scene. The third of these popular movements, was also an attack on the Convention. The Convention was about to pass over the Government to the Directory and the two Councils. The excitement among the people was great, (being fomented, as I believe, by the agents of foreign powers, for a political purpose,) and they had like to have overthrown the Government, but after much bloodshed, they were at length repulsed. I had seen also, popular movements in England, though not of so marked a tendency. I confess that this conduct of the people of France, under a Government which was exclusively their own, made me pause. I wished the tendency of the measures, asked for, to be carefully weighed. I hesitated, not from any thing I had ever seen in my own country, but from what I had seen of man, elsewhere. I reflected long, and at length, became willing, to extend the right of suffrage to all those, who have a common interest in the country, and may act, as free and independent citizens. We are differently situated from any other nation on the face of the earth. If self-government can exist any where, it is in these States, and in Virginia as well as in any other part of our Union.

I will carry the right of suffrage as far as any reasonable man can desire. Then the rights of all the citizens will stand upon the same ground: the poor man and the rich, will stand on the same level. As to the arrangement of districts, and the protection of property by some reasonable guarantee, I do not see how it can affect the question, of equal rights, among the citizens. It will not affect it, within any one district, where there are both poor and rich men. If the plan was to create an order of nobility, or to make the right of suffrage, depend on much property, it might enable the rich, to oppress the poor; but that is not the case; it leaves both on the same ground, and gives the one no advantage over the other. I only say, that representation should be based, on the white population, with some reasonable protection for property. But how is this to be done? It may be done in two modes. First it may be arranged, as it is in South Carolina, by taking both into consideration; base your representation on the white population of the State, and combine that, with the proportion of taxes throughout the whole; then each district will have its own share. The other mode is thus: Let one of the branches of the Legislature be placed upon the basis of white population alone, and the other branch, on the compound basis of population and taxation. If this plan be adopted, then the question arises, in which branch, shall the white basis prevail? and in which the compound? Will you give the basis of white population only, to the House of Delegates or to the Senate? I think it will be more safe, for both sections, for the western and Atlantic country, if you give it to the House of Delegates, and for the compound basis, to prevail in the Senate.

If you could agree on this arrangement, the country will, I think, be satisfied, and there will be an ample check upon the course of legislation, by the structure of the Senate. The popular branch, may then originate whatever it shall think most for the good of the country; and if, through the stimulus of heated feeling, they should propose any improper measures, the Senate will operate as an immediate check. It was on this principle, that I voted against the proposition to establish the white basis for the Senate.

Mr. Chairman, I thought it was my duty, to rise and state the grounds of my vote, so far as my ability, and the state of my health, would admit. I wish to see the basis of white population alone adopted for the House of Delegates, and the compound basis of representation, consisting of white population and taxation combined, for the Senate. This is my view.

Mr. Giles, in moving for the rising of the Committee, took occasion to express his gratification at the course and general tone of the debate, and his hope that some proposition for a compromise, would conduct it to a fortunate result. He intimated a doubt whether the state of his health would permit him to address the Committee to-morrow; and he did not wish to be considered as bespeaking the floor: but made a conditional promise, to present his views if able, and the attention of the Committee should not be otherwise occupied.

The Committee thereupon rose, and on motion of Mr. Johnson, the House changed its hour of meeting for to-morrow to eleven o'clock, and then adjourned.

TUESDAY, November 3, 1829.

The Convention met at eleven o'clock, and was opened with prayer by the Rev. Mr. Croes of the Protestant Episcopal Church.

The House having gone into Committee of the Whole, Mr. Stanard in the Chair, the question being on the amendment offered by Mr. Green to the first resolution reported by the Legislative Committee; which resolution is in these words: *Resolved*, That in the apportionment of representation in the House of Delegates, regard shall be had to the free white population *exclusively*: and which amendment proposes to strike out the word "exclusively," and insert in lieu thereof, "and taxation combined."

Mr. Leigh of Chesterfield, said he rose to address the Committee, on this vitally interesting question, under circumstances peculiarly disagreeable to him—having to follow the venerable member from Loudoun (Mr. Monroe) who favored the Committee with his views, yesterday—and who, from his advanced age and long experience, from the high place he had filled in the service and in the confidence of his country, and from the large space he occupied in the eyes of mankind, possessed great weight of character, to deepen the impression on the minds of others, of any opinions he might utter—weight of character, of which he himself (as he had often felt before and never more painfully than now) had none, literally none. Nevertheless, this was an occasion, on which he could take counsel only from his sense of duty. And, he believed, if George Washington were to rise from the dead, and to propose such a compromise as that offered by the venerable gentleman, so partial as in his conception it was, so ruinous, so destructive, so damnatory, to the dearest interests of the people who had sent him here, he should find the moral courage in his heart to reject and to oppose it, even coming from him. The *steterunt comæ*, he might experience—but not (he thought) the *vox faucibus hæsit*—on the contrary, he should be apt to utter a shriek of alarm and terror, that would strike the dullest ear and the dullest understanding, though not perhaps the hearts of such reformers, as were willing to make the experiment on the body politic, how large a dose of French rights of man it can bear, without fever, frenzy, madness and death.

He said, all the little knowledge he possessed, and all his habits of thinking, were merely professional; habits of thinking, confined to narrow questions of municipal law and justice, and little suited to the examination and discussion of great questions of State, which require the greatest reach and the widest range of thought. He felt himself under a sort of necessity to begin with a clear and fair state of the case and of the question.

He had then, in the first place, to inform the Committee, that there is *assessed*, of *land* tax, upon the twenty-nine counties lying below the Blue Ridge and above tide water, containing about 196,500 tax-paying inhabitants (average per head) 34 cents; upon the thirty-six counties and four towns, lying on tide water, containing about 184,500 tax-paying people, 31 cents; upon the fourteen counties between the Blue Ridge and the Alleghany, containing 124,000 tax-payers, 27 cents; and upon the twenty-six trans-Alleghany counties, containing 134,500 tax-payers, 12 cents. Of the tax on slaves, there is assessed on the people of the twenty-nine middle counties below the Blue Ridge and above tide-water, (average per head) 25 cents; on the people of the thirty-six counties and four towns on tide water, 24 cents; on the people of the fourteen Valley counties, 7 cents; and on the people of the twenty-six trans-Alleghany counties, 3 cents. The tax on horses and carriages, assessed on the tax-paying people of the twenty-nine middle counties (average per head) is 9 cents; on those of the tide water country, 8 cents; on those of the Valley country, 8 cents; and on those of the trans-Alleghany country, 7 cents. The total of these direct taxes, assessed on the people of the twenty-nine middle counties, is 72 cents; on those of the tide water country, 64 cents; on those of the Valley country, 42½ cents; and on those of the trans-Alleghany country, 22½ cents. The country east of the Blue Ridge contains about 381,500 tax-paying inhabitants, and the taxes assessed on them, averaged per head, stands thus—land tax, 32 cents 7 mills; slave tax, 26 cents 8 mills; horse and carriage tax, 8 cents 7 mills; total of direct taxes, 68 cents 2 mills—and the country west of the Blue Ridge contains about 258,500 tax-paying inhabitants, and the average per head of taxes assessed on them, is 19 cents 6 mills of land tax; 5 cents of slave tax; 7 cents 6 mills of the tax on horses and carriages; total 32 cents 2 mills.

The tax assessed on the people of the Congressional district composed of the counties of Sussex, Southampton, Surry, Isle of Wight, Prince George, and Greensville, (one of the least fertile tracts of country in the southern part of the State) is 62 cents, average per head; the tax assessed on the people of the district of Brunswick, Lunenburg, Mecklenburg and Dinwiddie, (an adjoining district of medium fertility) is 75 cents; that assessed on the people of the district of Halifax, Pittsylvania and Campbell, is 71 cents; and that assessed on the people of the district of Powhatan, Amelia, Nottoway, Chesterfield and Petersburg, is 97 cents; while the tax assessed on the people of the northern district of Loudoun, Fairfax and Prince William, amounts to an average of no more than 57 cents; and that assessed on the people of the rich and fertile Valley district of Frederick and Shenandoah, (the finest part of the State) averages only 43 cents per head.

The average per head of direct taxes assessed on the people of Frederick, is 56 cents; Loudoun, 56 cents; Jefferson, (the finest county in the State) 55 cents; Augusta, 54 cents; Berkeley, 38 cents; Shenandoah, 31 cents; Kanawha, 29 cents; Ohio, 21 cents; Brooke, 19 cents; Harrison, 17 cents; and Monongalia, 15 cents—while the average amount assessed on the people of Fluvanna, is 71 cents; Nelson, 79 cents; Amherst, 81 cents; Buckingham, 82 cents; Campbell, 84 cents; Orange, 88 cents; Albemarle, 90 cents; Goochland, 92 cents; Cumberland, 102 cents; Amelia, 106 cents; Nottoway, 119 cents; Powhatan, 122 cents; and that little despised county of Warwick, 75 cents; that is, 20 cents more than Jefferson.

In these estimates, it should be observed, free negroes were included as tax-paying citizens, because they were so in the eye of the law, though it is well known they in fact contribute little or nothing to the Treasury: the tax on merchants' and other licenses was excluded, though in truth they were borne by the consumers in the immediate neighborhood: the tax on tobacco inspected, imposed under the pretext of providing a fund for insurance of tobacco burned in the public warehouses, and borne wholly by the tobacco planters, was also excluded: and the gross taxes assessed were estimated instead of the amount paid into the Treasury. The estimate, too, was founded on the taxes of the year 1828, while the numbers of tax-paying citizens were ascertained by the Census of 1820, since which there has been a greater proportional increase of white population in the western than in the eastern part of the State.

Mr. L. said he had been furnished by his friend the honorable gentleman from Culpeper (Mr. Green) with an estimate, in which the free negroes were (as they ought to be) excluded from the number of tax-paying citizens, and the taxes on licenses and on tobacco inspected were excluded from the amount of taxation, and which was founded on the amount of direct taxes actually paid into the Treasury in 1828, and the estimate furnished by the Auditor of the white population in 1829. And it thence appeared, that the twenty-nine middle counties contained a white population of about 197,000, and pay (average per head) of land tax about 34 cents, of slave tax 28 cents, and of the horse and carriage tax 9 cents: the thirty-six counties and four towns on tide-water contain a white population of about 165,500, who pay an average of about 34 cents of land tax, 27 cents of slave tax, and 9 cents of horse and carriage tax: the fourteen valley counties* contain a white population of about 138,000, who pay an average of about 24 cents of land tax, 6 cents of slave tax, and 7 cents of horse and carriage tax: and the twenty trans-Alleghany counties contain a white population of about 181,300, who pay an average of about 9 cents of land tax, 2 cents of slave tax, and 5 cents of the tax on horses and carriages. The white population east of the Blue Ridge is about 362,500, and west of the Blue Ridge 319,300. The first pay of the land tax an average of 34 cents, the latter only 15 cents: the first pay of slave tax 28 cents, the latter only 4 cents: the first pay of the horse and carriage tax 9 cents, the latter only 6 cents.

Pursuing the comparison, Mr. L. stated, that for every dollar *levied* on the people west of the Blue Ridge, there was *levied* on the people east of the Blue Ridge $3 16 per head; and for every dollar *paid* by the Western people, the Eastern *pay* $3 24 per head. And these proportions of the burthens borne by the two great divisions of the State, have continued for a long series of years.

It had been supposed, Mr. L. understood, that a tax on neat cattle would prove comparatively light to the Eastern, and oppressively burdensome to the Western, people. He believed, it had been his fortune to be the first person to propose or rather to suggest that tax, when, in the session of 1812–13, he had the honor and the responsibility of being Chairman of the Committee of Finance. War was raging on our maritime frontier: the Federal Government told us, in plain terms, that the local authorities must look to the local defence, and depend on their own means: it was absolutely necessary to raise more revenue, a war revenue, by some means or other. Lands, slaves, horses and carriages, had been, time out of mind, the principal, he might almost say, the only productive, subjects of taxation; and thus the people of the eastern part of the State had always borne a great proportion of the burden. It was proposed to increase those standing taxes, and, casting about for means to reconcile the Eastern people to these additional burdens, by drawing a small increase of revenue from the West, the tax on neat cattle occurred as the best suited to the purpose. It was, therefore, suggested—but it was not then imposed. It was received with such a moaning low, as if the animal on which it was proposed to lay the tax, had smelt the blood of a slaughtered fellow-creature, and raised its plaintive voice for sympathy from man and brute. The war continuing, and the State Treasury as well as the Federal, uttering many a hollow groan, the tax on cattle was at length imposed in 1815, but never afterwards renewed, and ever since, the re-bellowing of that cow tax, and the spectres of our fellow-citizens whose deaths are imputed to the pestilential climate of Norfolk in the month of November (by the way, they were sent there by the Government of the United States, not of Virginia, and were not drafted from the tramontane militia alone, but from every part of the State) have been raised, again and again, on all occasions, to prove the enormity of the burdens borne, and the transcendant services rendered, for the defence of their Eastern brethren, by the people of the West. But what was the produce of that cow tax, and by whom was it paid? Excluding the counties of Jefferson, Accomac, Elizabeth City, Richmond, Norfolk, and Norfolk borough, (of which there are no returns,) the burden of that tax was borne, in almost exact equality, by the East and the West—the average being 3 cents 8 mills per head. Such is the fact, let it be accounted for how it may.

In 1815, in the extreme exigencies of the State, taxes were imposed on furniture, mills, tanneries, professions, trades, stamps, pictures, plate (for so they called silver spoons, the only article of the kind the people had)—in short, on almost every species of property, as well as additional taxes on lands, slaves, horses and carriages. Of these taxes, the country east of the Blue Ridge paid $495,589—and the Western country $141,360. For every dollar paid by the West, the East paid $3 50, average per head.

I will not affirm, said Mr. L. that these statements are absolutely free from all inaccuracy—but the inaccuracies, if any, are very trivial—the estimates have been examined by men more competent to the work than I pretend to be: I challenge investigation. And from these statements, some propositions, very material to be considered, flow by direct induction.

In the first place, there is one peculiar and most convenient subject of taxation, peculiar too and most delicate subject of legislation, of which the people of the West possess comparatively a mere modicum, and the farming country of the North a very moderate share, while the people of the East and of the more Southern planting counties hold a vast mass—I mean, *slaves*.

It is evident, in the next place, that it is hardly possible to find any subject of taxation, or to devise any tax, direct or indirect, of which the people of the East will not pay at least as much as those of the West; and as to the ordinary taxes, we pay a third more than the West, of the taxes on horses and carriages, more than twice as much land tax, and seven times as much of the slave tax.

And this may serve to account for another fact manifested by these statements, far more satisfactorily than that generous disregard of their own interests, which the gentleman from Frederick so courteously attributed to the people of the East—the acknowledged fact, that the existing Legislature has never abused its power as to taxation—of its acts of misrule in other respects, it seems, we are, in due time, to hear the charges and the proof. The East could not impose burdens on the West, without imposing far heavier burdens on itself. The West has had, all along, that very bond with surety from us, which my friend from Fauquier so justly demanded of the West for us—the pledge of our own interest and self-love—an interest in the depositories of power not to abuse it—no paper guarantee—but a hold upon the hearts of men, which beat true to self-interest, if to nothing else.

This also accounts for another fact, very observable in our history—that whenever any grand and munificent scheme of Internal Improvement has been offered to us, striking to the imagination and almost seducing the mind from the exercise of reason, it has found favour in the North and the West, while the South and the East have evinced a spirit, often described as niggardly—that the South and the East have shewed themselves loath to vote money for any such purposes, or for any purpose but to supply the pressing wants of the State. Taking the exactions of the Federal and of the State Governments together, I doubt whether there is a people on earth, more heavily taxed than the slave-holding planters of Virginia. We feel the weight of those State taxes, which our brethren of the West and North, paying no equal share, find so light and easy.

In the last place, seeing that the burdens of taxation are thus unequal now—if there be any man so strong of faith, as to entertain no fears that the inequality *may* be aggravated by transferring the balance of the power to the west—power over taxation and property—none can be so green, or so mellow, as to hope, that the inequality is likely to be *thereby* corrected. One of the main causes of discontent, which led to this Convention, that which had the strongest influence in overcoming our veneration for the work of our fathers, which taught us to contemn the sentiments of Henry and Mason and Pendleton, which weaned us from our reverence for the constituted authorities of the State, was an overweening passion for Internal Improvement. I say this with perfect knowledge; for it has been avowed to me by gentlemen from the west, over and over again. And let me tell the gentleman from Albemarle (Mr. Gordon) that it has been another principal object of those who set this ball of revolution in motion, to overturn the doctrine of State Rights, of which Virginia has been the very pillar, and to remove the barrier she has opposed to the interference of the Federal Government in that same work of Internal Improvement, by so re-organizing the Legislature, that Virginia too may be hitched to the Federal car. This also, in substance, has been often avowed to me, and that by gentlemen for whom personally I have the highest respect. The Federal Government points a road along the Valley, or along the foot of the Blue Ridge, or across the country at the head of tide-water; and State Rights fall or tremble at the very sight of this tremendous ordnance. It must be manifest to all men's minds, that without a vast increase of its revenue by the State, or the aid of the Federal Government, all those splendid schemes of Internal Improvement, so passionately supported by the North and West, must prove futile and abortive. If, therefore, the balance of power be transferred to the west, the taxes will in all likelihood be greatly augmented, and most certainly they will not be reduced.

And, then, Mr. Chairman, the question is, whether, when money is to be raised for any purpose—to defray the expenses of the civil list, or for the public defence, or for public education, or for Internal Improvement—the people of the west may justly claim power, forever hereafter, by one and the same vote, to give and grant three dollars of our money, for every dollar they give and grant of their own? And, then, to appropriate the revenue, according to their notions of justice and policy? Whether, while the people of Loudoun give and grant 56 cents of their money, those of Frederick 56, Jefferson 55, Augusta 54, Berkeley 38, and Shenandoah 31 cents—they may reasonably claim power, to give and grant, by the same vote, from the people of Fluvanna 71, of Nelson 79, of Amherst 81, of Buckingham 82, of Campbell 84, of Orange 88, of Albemarle 90, and of Goochland 92 cents? Whether, while the rich people of Berkeley give and grant 38 cents, and those of Shenandoah only 31 cents, of their money, they shall have power, by the same vote, to give and grant 75 cents from the poor people of Warwick? Whether, while the people of the thriving county of Kanawha, give and grant 29 cents, Ohio 21, Brooke 19, Harrison 17, and Monongalia 15 cents; they shall have power by the same vote, to give and grant 92 cents from the people of Cumberland, 106 cents from those of Amelia, 119 cents from those of Nottoway, and 122 cents from those of Powhatan? And that, for purposes, in which those who pay the most, can have little or no interest,—and those who pay the least, must have a great and direct interest? If the taxes be uniform, (as they must be,) the consequences are inevitable.

Sir, if the claim be yielded to, I know no happier illustration of the effects, than that furnished by the metaphor of the gentleman from Norfolk, the other day. He told us, that *representation* and *taxation* are not twin streams, rising in the same glen, separated by accident, uniting in the vale below, and rolling the joint tribute of their waters to the same ocean: they rose from different fountains, they flowed in different directions, and emptied into different oceans. Yes, indeed—if we adopt the principle reported by the Legislative Committee—*representation* will rise in the Mountains, and overflow and drown the Lowlands; while *taxation*, rising in the Lowlands, and reversing the course of nature, will flow to the Mountains, and there spend, if not waste its fertilizing steams, over every narrow valley and deep glen, and mountain side.

Gentlemen from the west, have exhorted us to discard all care for local interests—they tell us, that, if they know their own hearts, their opinions and course are not influenced by any such paltry considerations. Without doubting the sincerity of these professions, I doubt whether they do know their own hearts—without impiously setting up myself for a searcher of hearts, I doubt whether *they* have searched their hearts with sufficient scrutiny—nay, whether any scrutiny would have been successful. It is a divine truth, that the heart of man is treacherous to itself, and deceitful above all things. This we know with certainty, that the opinions of the western delegation, on this question, conform exactly with the interests of their constituents—they are perfectly unanimous—no division among them—none at all. And there is the great county of Loudoun—Why (as Louis XIV. said to his grand-son, when he departed to mount the Throne of Spain)—why are there no longer any Pyrenees?—Why is the Blue Ridge levelled from the Potomac to Ashby's Gap, though it swells again to Alpine heights, as it proceeds thence southward, to divide Fauquier from Frederick? This miracle has not been worked by turnpiking the roads. Look at the census, and observe that the white population of Loudoun, is three-fold that of the black; look at the Auditor's reports, and mark the fact, that Loudoun pays not half as much tax, as some of the poorer slave-holding planting counties; consider her common interest with all the upper Northern Neck in internal improvement, and their common opinions concerning State Rights: and then, if I mistake not, the question will be very easy of solution. The votes from the Orange, the Albemarle, the Campbell, the Pittsylvania, and the Norfolk districts, which (I know not why,) are all counted on as securely, as if they were already given; these are, indeed, disinterested, and can only be attributed to magnanimity. I presume not to enquire into the motives of gentlemen, much less to censure their conduct. I admire, but I cannot imitate their example. I have regard, especial regard, to the local interests of *my* constituents. They sent me here for the very purpose, that I might watch over them, guard, defend, and secure them, to the uttermost of my power. And, if I should disregard them, either through design or indolence—if I were even to profess to have no regard to them—it were better for me, that I had never been born—the contempt of some, and the hate of others, would pursue me through life; and if I should fly for refuge to the remotest corners of the earth, conscience—*Quis exul patria se quoque fugit*—conscience would still follow me with her whip of scorpions, and lash me to the grave.

Sir, I affirm with the gentleman from Hanover, (Mr. Morris,) that the contest we are now engaged in, though not the same in its circumstances, with that between our ancestors and Great Britain, is similar in principle. I have heard, and wondered to hear, many persons talk "of our having cast off the yoke of British slavery." The French minister, Genet, once dared to address General Washington in that same strain; and he began his answer with those memorable words,—"*Born in a land of freedom.*" Our fathers had no yoke of slavery to cast off—their merit and their glory consisted in resisting the very first attempt made to impose one. None but freemen would have perceived the danger; none but freemen would have spurned the yoke the moment they saw it prepared for them, and before they felt its weight. The humblest slave, the basest felon, the very beasts, will, when they can, cast off a yoke that galls them. At the peace of 1763, the Colonies were warmly attached to England; nor had George III. a more loyal subject in his dominions, that George Washington. The quarrel originated in the attempt of the British Parliament to tax us; and all the grievances we afterwards complained of, were but the effects of our determination not to submit to the taxes it sought to impose, and of the efforts of Great Britain to subdue our resistance. In the language of Lord Chatham, the Commons of Great Britain claimed a right to give and grant the money of the Commons of America, without allowing them any representation at all. Our western fellow-citizens only claim power to give and grant three dollars of our money for every dollar they give and grant of their own, allowing us representation indeed, but a representation not strong enough to refuse the grant. Suppose Great Britain had offered us a representation in Parliament, *proportioned to our free white population exclusively*—what would our fathers have said to it? What I, their descendant, now say to it—"It is mockery—you ask us to put ourselves in your power, bound hand and foot, and think because you gild our chains with a thin leaf that shews like golden freedom, we shall be so silly as to wear them." Great Britain might have offered us a representation in Parliament, proportioned to our population, and told us truly, that our country would soon be populous, that our vast forests would soon be felled, that our vast wildernesses would soon blossom like the rose, and that in the course of some forty years, we should have a population of ten or twelve millions, and then be entitled to an equal representation. Such language would hardly have prevailed with us. But our fellow-citizens of the west, reverse the proposition—they tell us, that in thirty years the majority will surely be found west of the Alleghany, and gravely ask us to assent to a principle, which will place us, and all we have, in their power and at their mercy—our slaves, our lands, our household goods, our—but I stop, Sir. The beauty of it is, they tell us all the while, to quiet our apprehensions, no doubt—"Remember the weight of a Back-Woods vote"—comply with all our desires, reasonable or unreasonable, or never hope more—"Remember the weight of a Back-Woods vote"—that force, which moves in solid phalanx, always advancing, never relenting, never breaking.

The Commons of Great Britain claimed power over our property, and we insisted that the control over it belonged, of right and exclusively, to us the owners: so our fellow-citizens of the west ask us to give them the absolute power of taxation over us, and we insist on retaining that power in our own hands. The Commons of Great Britain claimed to exact "a pepper-corn" from us, voting millions of their own: our brethren of the west only ask power to take three dollars of our money for every dollar they contribute of theirs. Let a fair comparison be made, and then determine which claim is the more reasonable, or the more abhorrent from justice, safety and liberty. Our fathers stood justified before the nations and before high Heaven too, in resisting the pretensions of Great Britain, by all the means that God and nature put into their hands.

And now, Sir, let me be distinctly understood. Attachment to this, my native State, to every foot of her soil, to every interest of all her citizens, has been my ruling passion from my youth—so strong, that it is now (what all attachments to be useful to its objects, must be) a prejudice—I hardly recollect the reasons on which it was founded. None that know me, will doubt this. I foresaw, I foretold, this fearful, distracting conflict. I looked to it with terror from the first, and I look to its consequences with horror now. I have trembled—I have burned. I raised my *Cassandra* voice, to warn and to deprecate—if I had the strength to make it heard, I wanted weight of character to make it heeded. Never till then had I felt the want of political influence, or lamented that I had disdained the ordinary methods of acquiring it in my earlier years, though probably no efforts would have been successful. My feelings, my reason, my prejudices, my principles, all assure me, that the dismemberment of the State must be fraught with cruel evils to us of the east, and still more cruel evils to our brethren of the west. Yet, Sir—and the blood curdles in my veins while I make the avowal—I shall avow, that the preservation of the Commonwealth in its integrity, is only the second wish of my heart: the first is, that it may be preserved entire under a fair, equal, regular, republican Government, founded in the great interests that are common to us all, and on a just balance of those interests that are conflicting.

Sir, the resolution reported by the Legislative Committee, in effect, proposes to divorce power from property—to base representation on numbers alone, though numbers do not quadrate with property—though mountains rise between them—to transfer, in the course of a very few years, the weight of power over taxation and property to the west, though it be admitted, on all hands, that the far greater mass of property is now, and must still be held in the east. Power and property may be separated for a time, by force or fraud—but divorced, never. For, so soon as the pang of separation is felt—if there be truth in history, if there be any certainty in the experience of ages, if all pretensions to knowledge of the human heart be not vanity and folly—property will purchase power, or power will take property. And either way, there must be an end of free Government. If property buy power, the very process is corruption. If power ravish property, the sword must be drawn—so essential is property to the very being of civilized society, and so certain that civilized man will never consent to return to a savage state. Corruption and violence alike terminate in military despotism. All the Republics in the world have died this death. In the pursuit of a wild impracticable liberty, the people have first become disgusted with all regular Government, then violated the security of property which regular Government alone can defend, and been glad at last to find a master. License, is not liberty, but the bane of liberty. There is a book—but the author was a tory, an English tory, and he wrote before the

American Revolution, so that I am almost afraid to refer to it—yet I will—there is an Essay of Swift on the dissentions of Athens and Rome, in which the downfall of those Republics, is clearly traced to the same fatal error of placing power over property in different hands from those that held the property. The manner of doing the mischief there, was the vesting of all the powers of judicature in the people; but no matter how the manner may be varied, the principle is the same. There has been no change in the natural feelings, passions and appetites of men, any more than in their outward form, from the days of Solon to those of George Washington. Like political or moral causes put in action, have ever produced, and must forever produce, every where, like effects—in Athens, in Rome, in France, in America.

The resolution of the Legislative Committee, proposes to give to those who have comparatively little property, power over those who have a great deal—to give to those who contribute the least, the power of taxation over those who contribute the most, to the public treasury—and (what seems most strange and incongruous) to give the power over property to numbers alone, in that branch of the Legislature which should be the especial guardian of property—in the revenue-giving branch. To my mind, Sir, the scheme is irreconcilable with the fundamental principle of representative Government, and militates against its peculiar mode of operation, in producing liberty at first, and then nurturing, fostering, defending and preserving it, for a thousand years. My friend from Hanover, (Mr. Morris) has already explained to the Committee, how the institution of the House of Commons in England, grew out of the necessities of the Crown to ask aids from the people. The free spirit of the Saxon laws, mingling with the sterner spirit of the feudal system, had decreed that property was sacred. The lawful prerogative of the Crown at no time extended to taxation; and if violence was sometimes resorted to, the supplies it collected were scant and temporary. Originally, the whole function of the House of Commons, was to give money; but the money being theirs, it belonged to them to say, when, how much, for what purpose, they would give it. From the first, and invariably to this day, the Commons have been the sole representative of property—the Lords never have been regarded in that light. And from this power of the Commons to give or withhold money, have sprung all the liberties of England—all that has distinguished that nation from the other nations of Europe. They used their power over the purse, to extort freedom from the necessities of the King—and then to secure and defend it—they made his ambition, his waste, his very vices, work in favor of liberty. Every spark of English liberty was kindled at that golden lamp. "I ask money"—said the Crown—"money to resist or to conquer your enemies and mine"—"give us privileges then" (was the constant answer,) "acknowledge and secure our rights; and in order to secure them, put them into our own keeping."—Sir, I know it is the fashion to decry every thing that is English, or supposed to be so; I know that in the opinion of many, it is enough to condemn any proposition, in morals, or in politics, to denounce it as English doctrine; but that is neither my opinion nor my feeling. I know well enough that the sentiment is unpopular—but I laid it down as a law to myself when I entered this Convention, to conceal no feeling and no thought I entertain, and never to vary in the least from an exact exhibition of my opinions, so far as it is in the power of words to paint the mind—and I have no hesitation in saying, in the face of the whole world, that the English Government, is a free Government, and the English people a free people. I pray gentlemen to cast their eyes over the habitable globe, survey every form of civil Government, examine the condition of every society—and point me out one, if they can, who has even so much as a conception, and much more the enjoyment, of civil liberty, in our sense of it, save only the British nation and their descendants. England was the inventor, the founder of that representative Government we so justly and so highly prize. I shall, therefore, still study her institutions; exercise my judgment in ascertaining what is vitious, or rotten, or unsuitable to our condition; and rejecting that, hold fast to all that is sound and wise and good, and proved by experience to be fit and capable to secure liberty and property; property, without which liberty can never exist, or if it could, would be valueless. Give me liberty in the English sense—liberty founded on law, and protected by law—no liberty held at the will of demagogue or tyrant (for I have no choice between them)—no liberty for me to prey on others—no liberty for others to prey on me. I want no French liberty—none; a liberty which first attacked property, then the lives of its foes, then those of its friends; which prostrated all religion and morals; set up nature and reason, as Goddesses to be worshipped; afterwards condescended to decree, that there is a God; and, at last, embraced iron despotism as its heaven-destined spouse. Sir, the true, the peculiar advantage of the principle of representative Government, is, that it holds Government absolutely dependent on individual property—that it gives the owner of property an interest to watch the Government—that it puts the purse-strings in the hands of its owners. Leave those who are to contribute money, to determine the measure and the object of contribution, and none will ever knowingly give their money to destroy their own liberty. Give to those who are not to contribute, the power to determine the measure and object of the contribution of others, and they *may* give it to destroy those from whom it is thus unjustly taken. From this false principle, the scheme of representation in question, is variant only in degree—it only proposes to give one portion of the people, power to take three dollars from another, for every dollar they contribute of their own. I say, therefore, that the plan is at war with the first principle of representative Government—and if it prevail, must destroy it—how soon, depends not on the wretched finite wisdom of man, but on the providence of God.

The resolution of the Legislative Committee, proposes to give the west power of taxation over the east, though it be apparent, that, in some respects, concerning as well the objects of taxes as the subjects of appropriation, the west has not only no common interest with the east, but a contrary or different interest. The interest of the west is contrary to ours, in regard to *slaves* considered as a subject of taxation, certainly and obviously. The unavoidable inequality of taxation upon all subjects, and the unavoidable equality of benefit from the revenue, give the west an interest to augment, and the east an interest to reduce, the amount of taxes. And, as to those internal improvements, those roads and canals, which seem, in the opinions of many, to be the only objects of Government, let any man survey the face of the country, and deny, if he can, that different, more extensive, and more expensive, works of the kind, are wanted, and even projected, in the west and in the north, than are wanted or have ever entered into the imagination of the east and the south. They would expend thousands where we would expend hundreds; that is, of our money; for if the expenditure was to be of their own, I cannot doubt they would grudge it as much as we do, or more. But this has been already fully explained by the gentleman from Fauquier. We are asked, gravely and importunately asked, and in a tone as if they thought the request the most reasonable in the world, to give them power to tax us three times as much as themselves, when their great object can only be, to apply the revenue (after providing for, perhaps stinting, the civil list) to those internal improvements they have so much at heart. Let it be always remembered, that as the east has never hitherto imposed any burdens, which have not borne more heavily on ourselves than on our western brethren, so neither will it ever be possible for the east, if the taxes be uniform, as uniform they must be, to levy any exactions on the west, which will not be more grievous to ourselves, so long as we hold a so much larger mass of taxable property: whereas the west may, by a uniform taxation, impose oppressive burdens on the east, which its own population will hardly feel the weight of. I should be sorry to say any thing offensive to gentlemen from any quarter—but I must follow the lights of my own mind, and declare it as my opinion, that the cunning of man, or of the devil, cannot devise a more vexatious and grinding tyranny for any people, than to subject them to taxation by those, who have not the same interest with them, much more who have interests contrary to or different from theirs.

The resolution of the Legislative Committee, proposes to give full representation to the labour of the west, with an exemption from taxation, while the labour of the east will be subjected to taxation deprived of representation.

The complaint seems to shock gentlemen—I shall repeat my words. (He repeated them)—In every civilized country under the sun, some there must be who labour for their daily bread, either by contract with, or subjection to others, or for themselves. Slaves, in the eastern part of this State, fill the place of the peasantry of Europe—of the peasantry or day-labourers in the non-slave-holding States of this Union. The denser the population, the more numerous will this class be. Even in the present state of the population beyond the Alleghany, there must be some peasantry, and as the country fills up, they will scarcely have more—that is, men who tend the herds and dig the soil, who have neither real nor personal capital of their own, and who earn their daily bread by the sweat of their brow. These, by this scheme, are all to be represented—but none of our slaves. And yet, *in political œconomy*, the latter fill exactly the same place. Slaves, indeed, are not and never will be comparable with the hardy peasantry of the mountains, in intellectual power, in moral worth, in all that determines man's degree in the moral scale, and raises him above the brute—I beg pardon, his Maker placed him above the brute—above the savage—above that wretched state, of which the only comfort is the natural rights of man. I have as sincere feelings of regard for that people, as any man who lives among them. But I ask gentlemen to say, whether they believe, that those who are obliged to depend on their daily labour for daily subsistence, can, or do ever enter into political affairs? They never do—never will—never can. Educated myself to a profession, which *in this country* has been supposed to fit the mind for the duties of the Statesman, I have yet never had occasion to turn my mind to any general question of politics, without feeling the effect of professional habits to narrow and contract the mind. If others are more fortunate, I congratulate them. Now, what real share, so far as mind is concerned, does any man suppose the peasantry of the west—that peasantry, which it must have when the country is as completely filled up with day-labourers as ours is of slaves—can or will take in affairs of State? Gentlemen may say, their labourers are the most intelligent on earth—which I hope is true—that they will rise to political intelligence. But, when any rise, others must supply the place they rise from. What then, is the practical effect of the scheme of representation in question? Simply, that the men of property of the west, shall be allowed a representation for all their day-labourers, without contributing an additional cent of revenue, and that the men of property of the east, shall contribute in proportion to all the slave-labour they employ, without any additional representation. Sir, I am against all this—I am for a representation of every interest in society—for poising and balancing all interests—for saving each and all, from the sin of oppressing, and from the curse of being oppressed.

Sir, the amendment offered by my honorable friend from Culpeper, is a scheme for balancing the various interests of the Commonwealth with exact and equal justice—not depriving *numbers* of their due weight, for it allows them full representation—yet allowing property also that fair, due and just share of representation, which is essential to its protection and security. It proposes to build up Government on the interests of society, with due regard to the rights both of persons and property; and to confide power to those whose self-love will forever prevent them from abusing it. If gentlemen prefer the federal number as the basis of representation, I shall be content. If they prefer a county representation, founded on any fair principle, respecting peculiar interests, and balancing the powers of Government accordingly—though I am sensible that this will be a more difficult operation—I shall be content. But I must forever contend, that a principle, which, in a Government professedly instituted for the protection and security of property as well as mere personal rights, disclaims all regard to the interests of property, and allows representation to numbers only, is dangerous and vitious, contrary to all the dictates of prudence and justice, and incompatible with the nature of representative Government, its wholesome operation and all its ends.

To reconcile us to a scheme so revolting, gentlemen tell us, in the first place, that the question has been settled by precedent—that it is *res adjudicata*. I said, that to found Government (meaning the *whole* Government,) on numbers alone, without regard whether the numbers quadrated with the interests of society or not, was a new principle in Virginia, and perhaps unknown in any other Government. I did not say, that no part or single branch of a Government had ever been laid on that foundation—I did not say, that no individual had ever maintained the principle—I learned at school, (from Tully, I think,) that there is nothing so absurd which some philosophers have not maintained for truth; and it might have been added, that there is nothing so unjust, which some politicians have not supported as right. The precedents which are supposed to have settled this question, are the vote of the Staunton Convention in 1815, forsooth, insisting that representation in the Legislature ought to be equalized on the basis of white population, and the act of 1816, equalizing and arranging the representation in the *Senate*, upon that principle, after full deliberation. But the principle was then applied to only one branch of the Legislature, and that not the tax-giving branch—and I, for one, shall be content with that principle of representation in the Senate now—I voted for it yesterday, and will abide by the vote, if gentlemen, on their part, will pay a just regard to the interests of property, in the tax-giving branch, the House of Delegates. Is not the difference wide as the poles asunder, between the two questions, whether there shall be a representation for the interests of property in the House of Delegates, the tax-giving House? and, whether property shall be represented in the Senate, which is not the tax-giving House? But I do not refer to the act of 1816, to repel its influence as a precedent, on the present question—I know to whom I am talking—there is not a man here who will pay the least regard to any such precedent. In another view, that transaction gave me a lesson, of which I hope I shall never cease to profit—I remember well every fact connected with its history, its origin, progress, and final consummation—and shall remember it all, to the last day of my life. They demanded the call of a Convention, of those, who, admitting that there were some defects in the Constitution which time had developed, (since no work of imperfect man can be perfect,) and especially the then inequality of representation in the Senate, yet thought that veneration for ancient and tried institutions, and loyalty founded in the heart rather than in the speculations of reason, were the best supports of Republican Government, and worthy to be preserved at any expense. The demand was addressed to such men as my friend from Norfolk (Mr. Tazewell) who had, like me, fallen into that fatuity of judgment, which deems virtuous prejudices virtuous principles. To avoid the call of a Convention, the bill for equalizing the representation in the Senate, on the basis of the white population, was, in an evil hour, passed—I had no share in it—I thank Heaven for all its mercies, none. They told us, they would be content—that that measure would satisfy all their wishes—that they too, loved the Government which the wisdom of our fathers gave, and with such a representation in the Senate, they would never seek to disturb it more. And the gentleman from Culpeper (Mr. Green) gave warning, that if the claim to representation in the Senate on the basis of white population was conceded, the concession would only be the motive to new demands. He has lived to be acknowledged for a prophet even in his own country. So, now, give them their favourite principle of representation in the House of Delegates—and guard property from taxation for any favourite purpose by any effectual guarantee, if such a thing be possible—or attempt to secure property, by giving it full representation in the Senate—the moment the new power of the State shall feel any check upon its action, and can no otherwise overcome it, it will raise another clamor for Convention, to cut the knot that cannot be untied. It is as true of the love of power as it is of the love of gold, *Quo plus habet, eo plus cupit.* Talk of power resting content while any power remains to be acquired—talk of it to any green, very green person—but for the love of mercy, mock us no more, by reminding us of the history of that Senatorial bill. As to the bill of the last session for organizing this body on the basis of the Congressional districts, it is not worth while to explain the way in which it was lost—the gentleman from Albemarle is best able to do it.

The next argument for the basis of white population exclusively, is deduced from the natural rights of man. I think the genius of the gentleman from Northampton (Mr. Upshur) has laid a spell on that doctrine, as one fit for any practical use. We are employed in forming a Government for civilized man, not for a horde of savages just emerging from an imaginary state of nature. If the latter was our purpose, I doubt whether we or they would think at all about their natural rights. Their political destiny would be determined by circumstances, which political philosophy would be little fitted to control. I cannot conceive any natural right of man contra-distinguished from social Conventional right—The very word *right* is a word of relation, and implies some society. While Robinson Crusoe was alone in his Island, what were his rights? To catch the goats and tame them—to kill their kids and eat them. When Friday came, how did they regulate their natural rights? He saved Friday's life—he gave him bread—and Friday became his servant. And that, I believe, was about as republican a Government as any men thus fortuitously brought together, would ever form—the stronger would be master. By the way, I think *Defoe's* a better book on the science of Government, than Cocker's Arithmetic or Pike's either. But gentlemen may have just what system of natural rights they like best—provided they will only grant me, that, either by natural law, or Conventional law, or municipal law, or the *jus gentium—aut quocunque alio nomine vocatur*—every man is entitled to the property he has earned by his own labor and to that which his parents earned and transmitted to him by inheritance—and that what is his property is his to give, and his to dispose of. These, I hope, are reasonable postulates: and I am much mistaken if they do not lead, by fair induction, to the utter overthrow of the resolution of the Legislative Committee, and to the establishment of the proposed amendment on irrefragable grounds.

Then gentlemen urge our own Bill of Rights upon us, as perfectly conclusive—and to the amazement of some and the amusement of others of this Committee, gentlemen, founding their whole argument on the Bill of Rights, deny the competency of the Convention of '76—and, by consequence, one would think, the authority of the Bill of Rights. Mr. Jefferson was the first person that brought this charge of usurpation against that Convention—and (so important are great men's errors) tho' with him it seemed rather matter of curious speculation only, yet ever since, when our old Constitution has been assailed for its supposed defects, this opinion of Mr. Jefferson has been referred to as conclusive authority. I had implicit faith in the opinion myself when I was at College—how long after I cannot say, not being able to fix the date when my mind came to maturity. At what period Mr. Jefferson discovered the incompetency of the Convention of '76, it were vain to conjecture—but I apprehend, it was not during the session of that body—for I know that Mr. J. himself prepared a Constitution for Virginia, and sent it to Williamsburg that it might be proposed to the Convention, during the session, from which the preamble and nothing more, was taken and prefixed to the present Constitution. Any one may see, at a glance, that that preamble was written by the author of the Declaration of Independence. I have seen the projet of the Constitution, which Mr. J. offered, in the council chamber, in his own hand writing, tho' it cannot now be found—and I have since cursed my folly that I neglected to take a copy of it, in order to compare Mr. J's democracy *of that day*, with George Mason's practical republicanism. But, Sir, the validity of the Constitution, as such, has been maintained by Pendleton, Wythe, Roane, by the whole Commonwealth for fifty-four years. If the Convention of '76 was incompetent to that act, it was incompetent also to abolish the Colonial Government, and that yet remains in force, in like manner as the Colonial form of Government of Connecticut was retained for years; and all the objections to the authority of our Convention of '76, might be urged with equal force, against all the Constitutions established in our sister States during the revolution. It is said the existing Constitution is not a lawful Government, because it was ordained by the representatives of the freeholders only, and never submitted to the great body of the people. To whom is it intended, that *our* amended or new Constitution shall be submitted? To those, I presume, to whom we shall allow the right of suffrage—that is, if gentlemen succeed according to their wishes in that particular, to lease-holders, house-keepers and tax-payers, as well as freeholders. It is a remarkable truth, in the natural history of man in this country, that the sons are invariably wiser than their fathers, such is the march of mind! Our sons may allege, hereafter, that our acts never had the sanction of the people—why did we exclude women and children? Why minors, tho' enrolled in the militia, and bound to bear arms? Why paupers, whose only sin is poverty? Nay, why the felons in the Penitentiary? All are part of the great body of the people. Sir, if we shall acknowledge, that we are at this moment in a state of nature; that men have resumed their natural rights, and are entitled to insist on them to the uttermost; we may live to see the day, when it will be claimed as matter of right, that the keeper of the Penitentiary shall bring his prisoners to the polls.

Now, as to the Bill of Rights—The first article declares, that "all men are by nature equally free and independent, and have certain inherent rights, of which, when they enter into a state of society, they cannot, by any compact, deprive or divest their posterity; namely, the enjoyment of life and liberty, with the means of acquiring and possessing property, and pursuing and obtaining happiness and safety."—The article enumerates *property* as equally dear and sacred with *life* and *liberty*, and as the principal means of happiness and safety—and with good reason—for, in order to live free and happy it is necessary that we live, and property is necessary to sustain life, and just as necessary to maintain liberty. Yet property is to be wholly disregarded in our fundamental institutions!—But, not to repeat what has been better said by others, I shall desire the committee to remember, that this article is expressed in the language of Locke's theory of government, then familiarly known; and that Locke, no more than the Convention of '76, understood the proposition in the broad sense now ascribed to it. Locke has had a singular fate. He was a zealous advocate of mixed monarchy—his Essay on Government was written to maintain the throne of William and Mary—his notions of practical Government, are exhibited in the Constitution he made for North Carolina, with its caciques and land-graves: yet, from *his* book, have been deduced the wildest democracy, and demented French jacobinism. He exploded the *right divine* of *Kings*—he showed that all Government is of human institution; yet he is supposed to have established the *divine right of democracy*. So, he was a pious Christian of the Church of England—of the low Church, however—yet, from his chapter on innate ideas, in his Essay on the Human Understanding, infidels have deduced the doctrines of materialism, infidelity and atheism. The truth is, that there is no proposition in ethics or politics, however true when duly measured and applied, which, if pushed to extremes, will not lead to absurdity or vice. It does not follow, that, because all men are born equal, and have equal rights to life, liberty, and the property they can acquire by honest industry, therefore, all men may rightly claim, in an established society, equal political powers—especially, equal power to dispose of the property of others.

It is very remarkable, Sir, that both the gentlemen from Frederick, (Mr. Cooke and Mr. Powell,) in founding the argument, they endeavoured to deduce from the third article of the Bill of Rights, read to the Committee, only the first and third sentences of it, which seem to suit their purposes, and omitted the intermediate sentence, so material to the just understanding of the doctrine the article inculcates, and so opposite to the conclusions at which they were aiming. I acquit them of all wilful unfairness—the respect I bear them, would not endure any suspicion of the kind—but the omission is a striking instance, how prone are the minds of men, studiously bent on maintaining a favorite point, to overlook, rather than to meet, difficulties, however obvious. The whole article reads,—"That Government is, or ought to be, instituted for the common benefit, protection and security of the people, nation or community.—Of all the various modes and forms of Government, that is best, which is capable of producing the greatest degree of happiness and safety, and is most effectually secured against the dangers of mal-administration—and when any Government shall be found inadequate or contrary to these purposes, a majority of the Commonwealth hath an indubitable, unalienable, and indefeasible right to reform, alter, or abolish it, in such manner as shall be judged most conducive to the public weal."—From the first sentence, the gentlemen deduced the perfect equality of men in a social state—not as to civil rights only, but political powers; and from the last, the absolute despotic right of a bare majority, to change the fundamental laws, and to assume to themselves under a new form of polity, the sovereign power to govern without limitation or check. Read the whole article, and it will be seen, that it means to declare, that when the existing Government fails to produce happiness and safety; fails to protect *property* as well as *liberty*, which in the first article are recognized, as the means of happiness and safety; and appears not to be effectually secured against the dangers of mal-administration: then, and not till then, the majority has the right to reform, alter or abolish it, and to substitute another, better calculated to produce happiness and safety; better suited to secure life, liberty, and *property* without which neither life nor liberty can be enjoyed or maintained; and more effectually secured against the dangers of mal-administration. But so long as the established Government answers those cardinal purposes of its institution, the majority may, indeed, have the *physical power*, but it can have no *moral right*, to overturn it. Now, we have the authority of the venerable gentleman from Loudoun, (Mr. Monroe) that under our present Government, in the course of fifty-four years, there has been no wrong, no oppression—Again: the sentence which the gentlemen overlooked, distinctly affirms the great principle for which we are so earnestly contending, that it behoves men engaged in framing a Government, to establish a just and wise Government—not a Government founded on theoretical principles, and squared according to the exact model of the natural rights of man, which, being necessarily the same in all societies of mankind, would, if followed, eventuate every where in the same form of civil polity—but a just and wise Government, adapted to the peculiar circumstances of the people for whom it is intended. No Government can be just, or wise, or safe, which, either wholly or in any material degree, gives one portion of the people the principal power of taxation, and imposes on the other, the principal duty of contribution—no Government can produce the greatest degree of happiness and safety, or fail to destroy them, which does not provide the most jealous security for property, which does not wed power to property, which disclaims, in the first principle of its organization, all regard to property. No Government can be just, or wise, or safe for Virginia, which shall place the property of the East in the power and at the disposal of the West. Whenever they shall take away the little earnings of my labour, or any part of them—whenever they shall seize the bread I earn for my children—for their own local purposes—against my consent, and the consent of all those who represent my interests—and I shall be bound to submit to such exaction, without means of redress; I shall be obliged to them, sincerely obliged to them, to take away my life too; I shall not desire to survive an hour. To return to the sentence in the Bill of Rights, which the gentlemen from Frederick overlooked; it was only by that omission, that they made George Mason's Bill of Rights pronounce sentence of condemnation upon George Mason's Constitution; condemned him out of his own mouth, of violating those sacred rights of man which he acknowledged and declared. So it happened to Zadig—I allude to Voltaire's tale—a fragment of paper was found, containing these verses in his hand-writing—

By crimes of deepest dye,
He's of the throne possess'd,
'Gainst Peace and Liberty,
An enemy professed.

And these lines were construed into a seditious and traitorous libel against the reigning Prince; and the unhappy author was doomed to death. But, as they were leading him to execution, a parrot flew to the place, with another fragment which saved his life; for it exactly fitted the former, and on it were written other words, which entirely changed the complexion of the supposed libel. The whole read thus—

By crimes of deepest dye, we've seen the earth made hell;
He's of the throne possessed, who all their power can quell—
'Gainst peace and liberty, love only wages war—
An enemy professed—and one we well may fear.*

The examples of our sister States, who are supposed to have framed their Governments upon the principle recommended by the Legislative Committee, has been as earnestly pressed upon us, as if it were true, that they have in fact set us any such examples, and certain, that what is suitable to their condition is also suitable to ours. Of the six New England States, it will be found, on an examination of their institutions, that not one of them has in fact adopted any such principle; which is remarkable enough, considering their dense and homogenious population, their comparatively small territory, and the consequent small diversity of their interests. The *new* Constitution of New York (whether it be an *amended* one or no, I shall not presume to say) *professes* to adopt the principle now recommended to us, and yet *departs* from it, in allowing each county, no matter how few its population, at least one vote; a very material modification: and, supposing the *city* of New York shall continue to grow for a few years longer, as it has done for a few years past, if the *State* of New York do not

* The English lines are doggrel, nor do we know where Mr. Leigh found the translation. The original French verses are quite pretty:

Par les plus grand forfaits j'ai vu troubler la terre;
Sur la trone affermi le roi sait tout dompter—
Dans la publique paix l'amour seul fait la guerre;
C'est le seul ennemi qui soit a redoubter.

rue the day it gave the *City* such excess of representation, out of mere respect to theoretical, and contempt of practical equality, I shall abandon all pretensions to political foresight. The Constitution of New Jersey gives each county an equal representation, so does that of Delaware. In Pennsylvania, the representation is apportioned according to the *taxable inhabitants:* and every county is allowed at least one. When the Constitutions of the North Western States were formed, their population was small, and all free, and there was no diversity of interests: and when those of the South Western States were formed, their population was small too, and they were all planters and slave-holders, so that they had no diversity of interests, which it was necessary to balance, in order to secure. North Carolina and Maryland are in a similar situation with us—and the Constitutions of both give to each county an equal representation. Suppose Maryland should be seduced, instead of being warned and deterred, by our example, and should be unwise enough to call a Convention to amend her Constitution, and to equalize her representation; does any man suppose her people will be weak enough, in deference to the rights of man, to give Baltimore a representation in proportion to its free white population, and thus, in effect, to constitute that city mistress of the State? Baltimore would have one-fifth of the whole representation; and, acting in mass, would almost invariably prevail over the rest, since the rest would be weakened by division. South Carolina, finding herself in circumstances similar to ours, though the diversity of interests is by no means so great there as here, has adopted that very compound basis of population and taxation, which the amendment of my friend from Culpeper proposes; and Georgia has adopted the federal number, in apportioning her representation, which comes very nearly to the same thing. It is wise to respect the institutions of our sister States—to obtain light, to borrow wisdom, to take warning, from any quarter—but, surely, to follow the examples of those, whose situation is different from ours, and who were under no necessity to exercise any jealousy of numbers for the safeguard of property; and to neglect the example of those, whose situation is similar to ours, and who yet had less occasion than we have, to provide such security for the interest of property—this would not be to profit by the examples of other States, but to despise them.

The gentleman from Norfolk (Mr. Taylor) and the gentleman from Augusta (Mr. Baldwin) have told us, that, disguise the principle of the compound basis of white population and taxation, as we may, or as we can, it is giving political power to the few over the many—to the wealthy few—to property over persons—and it is aristocracy. Now, I pray you, Sir, turn your attention to the Constitution of the United States, which apportions representation, and direct taxation too, to numbers, ascertained by adding to the free population, three-fifths of the slaves. And I ask those gentlemen to tell me, whether they are or are not zealous, devoted admirers, friends and supporters of the Federal Constitution? If they answer *no*, I have nothing more to say. If they answer *yes*—as I think they will and must—do they consider that principle in the Federal Constitution, *aristocracy in disguise?* Do they approve aristocracy in the Federal Constitution, and only abhor and abominate it in the State Government? Is it anti-republican in the one, to give property a representation for its security, and perfectly republican to give property the same kind of security in the other? What reason can ingenuity assign for the adoption of such a principle in either, which is not equally applicable to both? Sir, to charge the amendment of the gentleman from Culpeper with *aristocracy*, is out of the question—the amendment only proposes to provide effectual *protection* for the interest of property, by placing the care of them in the hands of those to whom they belong, nor are its friends to be deterred from demanding a just security for it, such as the Federal Constitution intended to provide, by any anathemas against the principle as aristocratical.

Mr. Taylor of Norfolk, rose to explain. He said he had never uttered any anathema against any gentleman. He never entertained the sentiment, and for that reason could not express it. He begged leave to state that he had offered his sentiments to the committee on every occasion, as the gentleman from Chesterfield said he would do. He would soften nothing—he would mitigate nothing, but would express the sincere conviction of his heart, and would conceal nothing he had said. He would not attribute improper motives to any gentleman, but he had to repeat, that the principles which the gentleman sought, honestly, no doubt, to introduce, were in his judgment inimical to all he was taught to respect—to all our free and equal institutions—and at any hazard ——

Mr. Leigh. Is it merely an explanation the gentleman is going to offer?

Mr. Taylor. Yes: he disclaimed any intention of imputing improper motives to gentlemen.

Mr. Leigh. I understood the gentleman correctly. He imputed aristocracy to the amendment we are insisting on, not to the friends of the amendment. I did not understand him to impeach *our motives;* and I assure him I do not question *his*, or those of any other gentleman. This is a vital question; and we must all be indulged with perfect freedom in debate.

Sir, we the people of the East demand of our fellow-citizens of the West, the same principle of representation for the security of our property, which the Southern States demanded of the Northern, and these conceded, in framing the Federal Government. Look to the experience of the Federal Government; and it will be found, that the representation apportioned to the Southern States has not been more than adequate to the security of their interests—no, not adequate. A gigantic system of protecting duties is proposed—the Southern States in vain exclaim against its partial and oppressive operation—in vain deprecate, remonstrate, struggle—a bare majority hesitates not to impose the tariff. Of the constitutionality of that system of measures—of its policy considered by itself, with a view to political economy—I shall give no opinion now: all I have to say, is, that in a Government constituted like ours, it never can be wise to persist in any system of measures, against which a large portion of the nation, though it be a minority, separated from the rest by geographical and political divisions, and by political interests too, so far as the proposed measures are concerned, raises its united voice. In my poor opinion, every commercial operation of the Federal Government, since I attained to manhood, has been detrimental to the Southern, Atlantic, slave-holding, planting States. In 1800, we had a great West India and a flourishing European trade—We imported for ourselves, and for a good part of North Carolina, perhaps of Tennessee—where is all that trade now? annihilated.—Where is the capital which carried it on? gone. Sir, we have not an adequate representation in the Federal Government. And as to that which we have, I have heard one gentleman doubt the wisdom and justice of the principle which gave it to us—the gentleman from Albemarle. [Mr. Gordon explained—he thought he had said, that wise statesmen might doubt the wisdom of that principle of representation.] If the gentleman does not doubt himself, I have only to ask his attention to another consideration. Suppose the Legislature of this State reformed and based upon white population; the time comes for making a new apportionment of our representation in Congress; the West insists, that that too shall be apportioned according to white population; the Loudoun district joins the West, as it does now; and Albemarle, in its zeal for the rights of man, forgets her old love and abandons State Rights—then shall we see Virginia, like Kentucky, hitched to the car of the Federal Government, for Internal Improvement and protecting duties.

Mr. Leigh, being fatigued, here gave the floor to Mr. Powell.

On the motion of Mr. Powell, who expressed a wish that the Committee would rise, in order to allow the gentleman from Chesterfield another day to conclude his remarks, the Committee rose and reported progress.

The Convention then adjourned till to-morrow at 11 o'clock.

WEDNESDAY, November 4, 1829.

The Convention met at eleven o'clock, and was opened with prayer by the Right Rev. Bishop Moore of the Protestant Episcopal Church.

The House having again resolved itself into a Committee of the Whole, Mr. Stanard in the Chair, and the question still being on the report of the Legislative Committee, as proposed to be amended by Mr. Green, by substituting for white population *exclusively*, white population *and taxation combined*,

Mr. Leigh of Chesterfield, resumed.—Mr. Chairman, I yesterday considered the examples of our sister States, and of the Constitution of the United States, so far as they have any bearing on the proposition of the Legislative Committee, and on the amendment of the gentleman from Culpeper, with a view to shew, that representation based on taxation and population combined,—and representation of persons and property, and of slaves as one or the other—were not, in the general sense of America, contrary to the principles of Republican Government, or at all obnoxious to the imputation of aristocracy. Gentlemen may think it strange, that I should take any pains to clear our proposition of that imputation. But, I have lived long enough to know, that words are things, and potent things too—and that if an odious epithet can be fixed on any proposition or measure, that will suffice to enlist thousands against it, and in the end, generally, to damn it forever. In truth, the question we are considering, is a question of State policy, unaffected by any theories, democratic, republican, or aristocratic—it is simply this: which scheme of representation ought we to adopt for the House of Delegates—that reported by the Legislative Committee, or that proposed by the gentleman from Culpeper? Which is the more politic, wise and just, having regard to all circumstances, and to the rights and interests of each and every part of the Commonwealth?

The Committee must pardon me, if I recur, for a brief space, to that provision of the Federal Constitution, commonly called the Federal number. Its history is somewhat curious. Originally, under the articles of confederation, each State was to contribute quotas in proportion to the assessed value of its landed property; but that principle being deemed inconvenient in practice, it was thought best to substitute a principle of contribution, apportioned to the population of the several States. In the discussion of this proposition—part of the debate has recently been published—the Northern States insisted; that slaves were *persons*, and that we ought to contribute in proportion to our whole population, bond and free; and the Southern States contended, that they were *property*, and ought not to be taken into the estimate of population, in settling the rate of contribution; each party maintaining that side of the question, on which, in that aspect of it, their interests lay. No wonder! all men do so—always have done,—and ever will do so. It was not till 1783, that Congress agreed to propose an amendment, by which the States were to contribute in proportion to their population, to be ascertained by adding to their free citizens three-fifths of their slaves. Whether or no this amendment was ratified by the States, I do not certainly know; but this was the origin of *the Federal number*. I have had recourse in vain, to every source of information accessible to me, to ascertain how that precise proportion of the slaves, *three-fifths*, came to be adopted—what mode or principle of estimate led to it. Some reason for it, there must have been—and it is remarkable, that if the Federal number be taken as the basis of representation, any where I believe, certainly in Virginia, it will give a result pretty nearly the same as the combined basis of white population and taxation—in Virginia, the difference, in a House of one hundred and twenty, would not be more than one delegate, to any *section* (speaking in modish phrase) or division of the State, divide it as you will, by lines East and West, or North and South. The Federal Convention of 1787 had, for the first time, to arrange a representation of the people in Congress. The Statesmen of the North and South now, doubtless, changed sides with their interests: in the view of the *former*, slaves were now *property*; in the view of the *latter*, they were persons. However, they made a compromise, and agreed on the same Federal number which had been proposed in 1783.

It is contended that there is no connexion between representation and taxation; that representation can only be of *persons*; that *property* has no claim to representation; that slaves are mere property, for which, therefore, we are entitled to no representation—and it has been gravely said, that the provision *of the Federal number* in the Constitution of the United States does not in fact, and was not intended by its founders to oppugn any of these propositions. On what ground, then, do gentlemen imagine, that the basis of the Federal number was adopted? They say, it was a compromise. And how far does that carry them in the argument? The question still recurs, what was the ground of compromise? and what were the interests compromised? The Constitution provides that representation and direct taxation shall both be apportioned to the same ratio, the Federal number; that is, that representation and taxation shall be proportioned each to the other. And, Sir, I shall affirm, and that without fear of contradiction after the proofs I shall adduce, that this provision was adopted and defended on the grounds, that there ought to be the same rule for representation as for contribution—that slaves are persons as well as property—and that whether persons or property, or of a mixed character partaking of both, the South was entitled to representation for them.

Sir, I refer the Committee to the 54th number of The Federalist (I know not who was the author of it*) in which this provision of the Constitution of the United States is discussed, and in which after maintaining that the Southern States rightly claimed a representation for their slaves as *persons*, the author proceeds—"It is agreed on all sides, 'that *numbers*,' (meaning gross numbers, bond and free) are the best scale of wealth, as they are the only proper scale of representation.—Would the Convention have been impartial or consistent, if they had rejected the slaves from the list of inhabitants when the shares of representation were to be calculated, and inserted them on the lists when the tariff of contributions was to be adjusted? Could it be reasonably expected, that the Southern States would concur in a system, which considered their slaves in some degree as men when burdens were to be imposed, but refused to consider them in the same light when advantages were to be conferred."—In the sequel of the same letter, it is said: "After all, may not another ground be taken, on which this article of the Constitution may admit of a still more ready defence? We have hitherto proceeded on the idea, that representation related to persons only, and not at all to property. But is this a just idea? Government is instituted, not less for the protection of the property, than of the persons, of individuals. The one, therefore, as well as the other, may be considered as represented by those who are charged with the Government. Upon this principle it is, that, in several of the States, and particularly in the State of New-York, one branch of the Government is intended more especially to be the guardian of property, and is accordingly elected by that part

* Mr. Madison afterwards avowed in his place, that he was.

of society, which is most interested in this object of Government. In the Federal Constitution, this policy does not prevail. The rights of property are committed to the same hands with the personal rights. Some attention therefore, ought to be paid to property in the choice of those hands."

Again, Sir—I presume it will be agreed, that no man better understood the reasons on which the various provisions of the Federal Constitution were grounded, than General Hamilton. Allow me, then, to refer the Committee to what *he* said, in the Convention of New-York which ratified the Constitution, on the subject of this *federal number*—"The first thing objected to (said he) is that clause which allows a representation for three-fifths of the negroes.—Much has been said of the impropriety of representing men who have no will of their own. Whether this be reasoning or declamation, I will not presume to say. It is the unfortunate situation of the Southern States, to have a great part of their population, as well as property, in blacks. The regulation complained of was one result of the spirit of accommodation which governed the Convention; and without this indulgence no union could possibly have been formed. But, Sir, considering some peculiar advantages we derive from them, it is entirely just that they should be gratified. The Southern States possess certain staples, tobacco, rice, indigo, &c. which must be capital objects in treaties of commerce with foreign nations, and the advantage which they necessarily procure in these treaties, will be felt throughout all the States. But the justice of this plan will appear in another view—*The best writers on Government have held, that representation should be compounded of persons and property.*—This rule has been adopted as far as it could be in New-York.—It will, however, by no means be admitted, that slaves are considered altogether as *property*. They are *men*, though degraded to the condition of slavery. They are *persons* known to the municipal laws of the States which they inhabit, as well as to the laws of nature. *But representation and taxation go together; and one uniform rule ought to apply to both.* Would it be just to compute slaves in the assessment of taxes, and discard them from the estimate in the apportionment of representatives? Would it be just to impose a singular burden, without conferring some adequate advantage?—Another circumstance ought to be considered. The rule we have been speaking of, is a general rule, and applies to all the States. Now, *you have a great number of people in your State, which are not represented at all,* and have no voice in your Government: these will be included in the enumeration—not two-fifths—nor three-fifths—but the whole. This proves, that the advantages of the plan are not confined to the Southern States, but extend to every part of the Union." —You see, Sir, that General Hamilton thought, that the Southern States had as just a claim to representation for their slave labour, as the Northern States for their free white labour—and he said this to the people of New-York, almost all of whose day-labourers were free white men.

Mr. Chairman, we have been told by several gentlemen, and particularly by the gentleman from Brooke, (Mr. Doddridge,) that if the amendment proposing the compound basis of white population and taxation prevail, which he regards as a simple claim for a representation of our slaves, the effect will be, to make the people of the West the slaves of the people of the East, to the end of time. If this was intended to excite the angry feelings of the West, it was surely well adapted to its purpose. But, if it was meant for argument, it exhibited a strange forgetfulness of the scheme reported by the Legislative Committee itself, and that in a particular, concerning which, there has been very little, if any diversity of opinion. The argument is founded, first, on the *fact*, that, at this time, the cis-montane country not only pays a far greater amount of revenue, but contains also the majority of white population, which, combined, must give us a majority of Delegates; and then, on the *supposition*, that the apportionment of the representation now to be made, is to be fixed and unchangeable. And yet, the same gentleman tells us, he has no doubt, that in thirty years, the majority of white population will be found on the West side of the Alleghany, let alone the Valley—and the Auditor's estimate informs us, that the cis-montane white population, which in 1820 was greater than that on the West of the Blue Ridge by 94,000, exceeds it now by only 43,000—and the gentleman must know, that it is a part of every scheme that has been suggested, and part of the report of the Legislative Committee, that there shall be new enumerations of the people, and new assessments of taxable property, and new apportionments of the representation, in 1835, and again in 1845, and afterwards once in every twenty years at least.—Now, as the *white population* increases in the West in a much greater ratio than in the East, the proportion of Western representation will increase in virtue of that element of the compound basis; and, as their population increases, their lands must be enhanced in value, all their taxable property must be augmented, and the revenue they pay into the Treasury must also increase, and they will gain a greater share of the representation in virtue of that element of the compound basis also—unless, indeed, it be supposed that, though their population increase and their wealth too, ever so much, they ought never to contribute a greater proportional amount than they now do, and that the taxation on them ought to be reduced, from time to time, so as to keep their contributions at the present reduced amount. The compound ratio, therefore, will work gradually, to augment their share of representation, both ways; and, in due time, to give them a greater share of it than us. I have not calculated the time which it will take, under the operation of the compound ratio, to transfer the balance of power to the West, nor am I very competent to the task; but if the gentleman from Brooke will ascertain the date when the majority of white population will be found on the West side of the Alleghany, I can venture to assure him that the tramontane country, upon our own plan, will, before that time comes, have the majority in the House of Delegates—and then, Sir, I am content that they shall have it. They will acquire it gradually, and as they *acquire*, learn to *use* it, with justice and moderation. They will not acquire it, till they learn to feel the weight of the crown they are destined to bear—and that feeling will chasten their love of power. They will not acquire it, till they shall contribute out of their pockets, under any scheme of uniform taxation, such a proportion of the revenue, as will give them a substantial community of interest with us in the imposition of taxes, if not in the appropriation of revenue. They can only acquire it, by giving us *that bond with surety*, which my friend from Fauquier (Mr. Scott) demanded—we shall have a security in their self-love, in their own interest, that they will not abuse their power. Sir, I have no unreasonable jealousy or distrust of them. Indeed, I have always known, that upon the principles of the existing Constitution, the balance of power would in time, and in no long time, be transferred to the West. Why, then, I shall be asked, have I been so strenuous a defender of our old institutions? Because, in preserving *them*, I should have preserved a great deal, apart from this, this question of the balance of power, which I dearly prize—because in preserving them, I should have avoided this very contest, which, terminate, as it may, is a sore evil in itself—because I should have preserved that sentiment of veneration for constituted authority, which is now forever lost, which gave sufficient moral force to execute the laws, and thus dispensed with the exertion of the strong arm of Government; for whenever physical force becomes necessary, the spirit of Republican Government must cease to direct the system, and even the empty form must soon perish. And now let me ask the gentlemen of the West, why are they so urgent for the immediate possession of power? for this sudden, abrupt transfer of it to their hands? when they surely ought to know, that it is impossible for us to make the transfer, without giving with it unlimited dominion over our property—without giving them power to take from the poor man of the East the fruits of his industry, and the bread from the mouths of his children. It is that rage for Internal Improvement—for wherever I see that passion, there I find the passion for reform, and thence I hear those scoffings at every sentiment of respect and veneration for the institutions our wise, prudent and virtuous ancestors bequeathed to us.

We have been told, Sir, that we have no dangers to apprehend from an immediate transfer of power to the West over the East—power to tax our property according to their ideas of justice, and to appropriate the revenue we are to pay, according to their views of policy; that we have ample security in the honesty of our western brethren; that we are mistaken in supposing, that *self-love* is the great spring of human actions; that the *moral sense* of mankind is sufficient to resist its promptings, and subdue its influence; that "self-love and social are the same." I know, that there are individual men—few, however—who, upon some occasions—very unfrequent—can disobey the dictates of self-love, and disregard their own interests, at the call of sympathy for other individuals, friendship, affection and gratitude. But, in the history of the human kind, of all nations and of all ages, from the earliest tradition to our own times and country, there has never been a single instance of any society of men, of men acting in masses great or small, who forgot self-interest, or what they supposed to be so, for a moment. It was not generosity, which prompted France to assist us in our revolutionary struggle—it was self-love—mistaken self-love, in my opinion—but still sheer self-love. It is not generosity, which has excited our so earnest wish for the independence of the South American States of Old Spain—it is our self-love—the desire to profit by her trade—mistaken self-love again, I fear; for we shall probably lose by their rivalry more than we shall gain by their custom. It is self-love alone that recommends the system of protecting duties—the American system—to our fellow-citizens of the Northern States; and it is self-love which incites the South to such strenuous opposition. It is self-love, which now divides this Convention, on this very question.

The moral sense and the honesty of the people of the West! I pray gentlemen to understand me—they are not to suspect me of the nonsense and folly of imputing to them any peculiar vice of disposition. I entertain no such opinion of the West or of the North—if I did, I would give my vote for separation this moment. I have marked the growth of native talent, of intellectual culture, of moral worth, in the West—I have watched young merit there, in its dawning, in its rise and its meridian—with hearty good will and sincere delight; and saying this, I think I may safely vouch any gentleman of the West, who knows me, for my witness. I admit, that the people of the West are as honest as those of the East; and I would refuse them no confidence which I would ask them to repose in us. And then I tell them, plainly, that, in my opinion, they, nor any body of men on earth, are honest enough to be entrusted with dominion over the property of others, uncontrolled by their own community of interest in that property, and in the disposition of it. This is the very dominion, which the gentlemen of the West are so importunately asking us to concede to them. Yes, Sir, they ask us to put our all into common stock with them, and then confide in the unerring dictates of their *moral sense*, that they will carve no unjust share for themselves—they ask us to put three dollars of our money into the treasury, for every dollar which they shall contribute of their own, and trust them to make a just, fair and impartial application of it for the common weal. This is the exact state of the case. The man, who, in private life, should accede to such a proposal, would be regarded as a simpleton—a natural fool—and the law would appoint a guardian to take care of his person and estate. Can the gentlemen of the West flatter themselves, that their *moral sense* is so strong, that it will always be proof against continual temptation? "Lead us not into temptation, but deliver us from evil."—So our Saviour taught us to pray—and, in my sense of the prayer, the *delivery from evil* depends on the *exemption from temptation*.

Sir, I fear we are in the habit of counting too much upon the purity and virtue of our society, as a permanent security against all political evils. I told the committee yesterday, that I intended to open my whole mind without reserve—This is the last scene of my political life; before I came here I weeded all the hopes of ambition from my heart; and I now declare my conscientious belief, unpopular as the avowal of it may be, that from the beginning of time, never any nation made a more rapid progress in corruption, than have these United States during the last quarter of a century. I beg leave to mention a few the most obvious of many symptoms. Even in this Good Old Dominion, for one place-hunter that was to be seen when I first grew up to manhood, there are ten now—Yes, the number is tenfold at the least. They swarm in the country and in the city—they infest our public places—they invade our privacy, and disturb the quiet of their industrious neighbours with their solicitations. They are themselves marketable commodities; they put up their principles, their opinions, their votes, at auction to the highest bidder, setting the highest value upon their services, but willing to take any price they can get. Men, hardly fit for a clerkship, aspire to embassies; and men, who aspire to embassies, will descend to a clerkship—Office!—office and emolument, high or low, State or Federal!—any sort of office, which will save them the pain of earning their living by honest industry. We hear a great deal about the corruption of all orders of men in Great Britain—What is it? Does any man suppose, that when Sir Robert Walpole said, that *every man has his price*, he was talking of a price to be told out in guineas? No—some are to be purchased with honors—some with the power to purchase others—some with the emoluments of place. The case is exactly the same here.—"Go to the ant, thou sluggard; study her ways, and be wise." There is a little white ant in the West Indies, the pest of the country—lay the smallest lump of sugar on a mahogany table, and in fifteen minutes, there will be hundreds around it—tread upon a lizard in the evening, and the next morning they will present you the cleanest and most perfect skeleton imaginable. So, Sir, the greedy expectants of office are continually on the look-out—let a poor Postmaster or Collector be *sick*, and they begin to collect their volume of recommendations—let him *die*, and before his remains are committed to his mother earth, the whole swarm is at Washington.—Then, Sir, look at the daily Press, which, in this country, is the true *exemplar vitæ morumque*. Why is it, that upon all political questions—presidential election, or what not—the whole argument turns on the single point, which side will get the majority? because that is the most effectual argument to carry the majority; for, the party that shall prevail, is to have the disposal of honors, and offices, and emoluments, and partizans are to be excited to exertion, or acquired, only by the hope of reward. There is another class of men, who (I think) have sprung up in Virginia, or rather began to be distinguished as a separate class, within the last fifteen years. They do not regard themselves as a part of the people—they profess themselves *the people's servants—the people's friends—the people's men;* meaning nothing more, in plain English, than that *they* are *the men for the people's money*.—They have no opinions and no will of their own—whatever the people think, they think—whatever the people desire, they desire—whatever the people *will*, they are content—and, therefore, whatever of honor or emolument the people have to bestow, they expect to receive it at their hands. Sir, *I am one of the people;* and I have noted the ways, and know perfectly how to appreciate the motives and the merits, of these our kind officious friends and servants. In Monarchies, the King is the fountain of honor and office: In Republics, the people. There are courtiers of the people as well as courtiers of Kings. The *motives* of both are exactly alike; their ends the same; their *conduct* is different only in mode; and it is equally true of the courtiers of the people, as of the courtiers of Kings, that, exactly in proportion to the contempt they entertain in their hearts, for the persons to whom their flatteries are addressed, is the extravagance of their adulation. Sir, the last hope of the Republic rests in that class—and, thank Heaven, it yet constitutes the great body of the people—who, possessing the means of subsistence, if improved by honest industry, placed above the temptation of poverty, and exempt from the temptations of prosperity, never so much as dream of the emoluments of office—the honest, hard-working yeomanry of this country, who hitherto have fed, cloathed, protected, and sustained society. But, how long will these pillars of the Republic remain stable and erect, under the mighty weight, with a Government, the first principle of which is, avowedly, to be an utter disregard of the interests and security of property.

Gentlemen who support the proposition of the Legislative Committee, aware that our apprehensions of danger from the practical operation of the principle are real, and seemingly aware too, that those apprehensions are not wholly destitute of foundation, have proposed to us a guaranty against any abuse of the power of taxation; a promise, so solemn, so clear, so strong, so binding on the conscience of the reformed Legislature, that its efficiency cannot be doubted. I have heard of such a guaranty, ever since this question was first started. It has been my misfortune, Sir, in all discussions concerning the necessity of reform, and the merits of the reforms proposed in our ancient institutions, not only never to convince the reformers on any one point, but hardly ever to succeed in making myself intelligible to them, though I take always the utmost pains to cloathe my thoughts in the plainest words of Anglo-Saxon root that I can find; and (upon this subject of guaranty, especially) I have ever found great difficulty in comprehending *their* meaning. What seems to them clear as the noon-day sun, has been to my eyes, mist and twilight, and sometimes utter darkness. Returning from Cumberland last spring, whither I went to present myself to the people as a candidate for a seat in this body—I found at night, in the lower end of Powhatan, a newspaper, in which was a letter, explaining the general views of the writer, on the questions most likely to engage the attention of this Convention; a gentleman, whose intelligence and virtue I have ever held in the highest respect and esteem, and with whom I have been always willing to confer, to put mind to mind fairly, and to abide the result. The letter suggested what *he* thought a sufficient guaranty. With a very painful exertion of the little eye-sight that remains to me—I wish the printer would look to the mending of his types, instead of mending the Constitution—I succeeded in making out the *words*; but then, to my surprise, I could not understand the *meaning* of them. Well, Sir, the first reformer I met with, after my return to this town, knowing my particular anxiety on this head, asked me, whether I would not be satisfied with such a guaranty as the letter I had read in Powhatan, proposed. I told him, I really did not understand it. He did not express in *words*, but he *looked*, a strong doubt of my sincerity. In the evening of the same day, I fell in company with the printer; who asked me, generally, what I thought of the letter; and, the guaranty being uppermost in my mind, I told him I could not understand the passage that related to that knotty subject; and that it reminded me of a piece of humour of Swift in his *Tale of a Tub*—He states some misty, unintelligible, metaphysical question, upon which, he says, he has bestowed much reflection, and having with infinite pains acquired a clear conception of it, he shall proceed to lay the matter open to his readers; and then follows half a page of asterisks, concluding—" And this I take to be a clear account of the whole matter." " Sir," (said my friend, the printer,) " I dare say you mean that for jest; but it is literally true, that there was an *out* of a line or two of that passage, in the manuscript copy of the letter, which was furnished for the press and printed." But, Sir, I do understand the meaning of the guaranty offered us by the gentleman from Fairfax (Mr. Fitzhugh.) Its meaning is very plain—There is, indeed, a fatal perspicacity in it, which leaves no doubt of the utter futility of the security it proposes to provide for us. These are the words—

" *Resolved*, That the power of the Legislature to impose taxes, ought to be so limited, as to prohibit the imposition on property, either real or personal, of any other than an " *ad valorem*" tax; and that in apportioning this tax, either for State or County purposes, the whole visible property (household furniture and wearing apparel excepted) of each individual in the community, ought to be valued, and taxed only in proportion to its value: Provided, however, that no individual, whose property (with the above exception) does not exceed in value   dollars, ought to be subject to any property tax whatever: And provided, moreover, that the Legislature may impose on all professions and occupations, usually resorted to as a means of support, such taxes as may be deemed reasonable."

" *Resolved*, That, to prevent an unfair distribution of the revenue of the Commonwealth, the Legislature ought to be prohibited from making appropriations (except by the votes of two-thirds of the members of both its branches) to any road or canal, until three-fifths of the amount necessary to complete such road or canal, shall have been otherwise subscribed, and either paid or secured to be paid as the law may direct."

Now, the first resolution only proposes to provide, that taxes instead of being imposed on specific articles of property, shall be *ad valorem* taxes. Of the inconvenience, and perhaps the impracticability, of the scheme, in a financial view, I have nothing to say. Suppose it be ordained, that, henceforth, all taxation shall be *ad valorem;* still the power of *laying* the taxes is to be confided to the West, and the duty of *paying* them to be imposed on the East; still, the duty of contribution will lie on us, and the right of appropriation belong to them; still, three dollars are to be exacted from the East for every dollar contributed by the West; and still, the West will have, and forever continue to have, purposes to answer in the expenditure of the public revenue, in which they have, and we have not, a direct interest, and far more expensive than any in which we *can* have any direct interest. And these are the very evils, against which the proposed guaranty is professedly intended to guard us. If my neighbour, having *ten* thousand and I *thirty* thousand dollars, should propose to me to throw the whole into common stock, and leave it to *me* to determine the distribution of it between us; I should accede to the proposal readily enough—I should be sure to take back all that I put in—and I *trust*—though I do not *know*—I should be loath to meet the temptation—but I *trust* I should restore the full amount of his contribution, to him or his family. But if he should propose such a community of property, and that *he* should have the power of distribution——

[Mr. Fitzhugh explained. His proposition only contained a simple statement. It did not go to making the taxes equal on all, but to give a security against the apprehension that the whole weight would be thrown on the slave property. It was intended to guard against that only.]

Mr. Leigh. It is, then, admitted, that the guaranty was intended to protect us against unequal and oppressive taxation on our *slave* property only. But, I shewed yesterday, that the far greater mass of taxable property *of every kind,* as well as of the *slave* property, lies on the East side of the mountain; and what odds can it possibly make to us, that the unequal exaction is to be made by a tax on one kind of property, rather than another? And how does the regulation against the abuse of the power of *taxation,* affect the correlative, and to us equally dangerous power of *appropriation?* But *this* is provided for by the second branch of the gentleman's guaranty.

He proposes in order to prevent an unfair distribution of the public revenue, to require a majority of *two-thirds* of both branches of the Legislature, to make appropriations of revenue, for any road or canal; meaning, generally, I presume, any work of public improvement. Does not the gentleman from Fairfax—I appeal to his good sense and candour—does he not himself perceive, that this proposal distinctly implies, that the scheme of representation, of which it is intended to provide a corrective, is in itself unfair? If it be fair, why should a bare majority be restrained from making appropriations to any conceivable object? Is not the requisition of this majority of two-thirds to appropriations of that kind, a plain admission, that the proposed scheme of representation does not give the East a representation adequate to the protection of our property? and are roads and canals the only objects, for which unequal distributions of public treasure can possibly be made? Is it a whit more fair or equitable, for example, that the East should contribute three dollars towards the education of the children of the people of the West, for every dollar they contribute towards the education of our children, than that we should contribute *three* dollars to their one, for the purposes of internal improvement? But, Sir, this same requisition of a majority of two-thirds of the Legislature, to appropriations of this kind, and to acts for several other purposes, has been ordained by the amended Constitution of New-York of 1820. And what is the efficacy of the provision, in its practical operation? I derive my information from an unquestionable source—from the gentleman from Loudoun, (Mr. Mercer.) I have learned from him, that the provision has been invariably defeated and rendered utterly nugatory, by combinations of the representatives of the different parts of the State, having different objects at heart, but uniting to carry the schemes of all, in order to gratify the particular wishes and to subserve the local projects of each. Now, can the gentleman from Fairfax devise any guaranty of force sufficient to prevent *Log-rolling?* (I borrow the metaphor from Kentucky, and a most apt and expressive one it is.) If he can, then I may safely promise—in the language addressed some years ago to the County Court of Giles, by the settlers of a remote corner of the county, whose only mode of punishing offenders was to refuse to *Log-roll* with them, in the literal sense of the phrase—then, I may safely promise him to come under *civilized Government*—for it seems to be imagined, that no Government is a *civilized* one, unless it be founded *on the natural rights of man, in a savage state.*

Sir, unless I be labouring under some strange delusion, it must now be apparent to the Committee, that the proposed guaranties are wholly nugatory.

But a compromise has been recommended to us, by the venerable gentleman from Loudoun (Mr. Monroe)—recommended to the hearts, rather than to the reason, of the Eastern delegation in this body—recommended in a tone of feeling, such as might be expected from a father seeking to heal discords among his children; and it is the feeling that dictated it, which alone, in my mind, gives any force to the recommendation. He proposes, that the representation in the *House of Delegates* shall be apportioned to the white population exclusively: and to guard the interest of property, to guard the property of the East against unjust and oppressive taxation, that the representation in the *Senate* shall be apportioned according to the combined ratio of white population and taxation. Let me ask the venerable gentleman—seeing, that his object is to provide a perfect security for the great mass of property held by the East, against abuses of the power of taxation by the reformed Legislature, that he acknowledges the right of the East to such security, and that his plan of giving us the security to which he admits our just claim, is, to found the representation in the two branches of the Legislature upon different bases—did he never reflect, that this kind of security for the interests of property, ought to be provided in the constitution of the *House of Delegates, the tax-giving branch*, rather than in the *Senate*, which is *not*, and no man intends should be, the tax-giving branch, of the Legislature? While the East is complaining of the injustice of being subjected to taxation by a power, which will not be restrained from abuse by any community of interest with them, and agitated with the most anxious apprehensions of the danger of such abuse of power, and these apprehensions are, in the opinion of the venerable gentleman, reasonable—the same gentleman, to appease our just complaints, and to allay our well-grounded apprehensions, would give us security against the abuse of the power of taxation in the frame of the *Senate* which is to have no original power of taxation, and deny it to us in the *House of Delegates*, in which the chief power of taxation is to be vested! The voice of truth and reason and justice must be silent.

But, Sir, let us suppose the proposed compromise, or a more efficient one framed on like principles, acceded to, and ordained in our reformed Constitution—let us suppose the representation in the House of Delegates based upon the white population exclusively, and the representation in the Senate based upon taxation alone, or upon the total population, bond and free, or upon the basis of white population and taxation combined—we shall then have a House of Delegates of from *an hundred and twenty* to *an hundred and fifty* members, and a Senate of *twenty-four* members. Let the relative powers of the two Houses, *as to money bills*, remain as at present—the power of originating *money bills* vested exclusively in the lower House, and the Senate restricted from amendment as to such bills, and bound wholly to reject them or take them without alteration. The lower House sends up a money bill—the Senate, thinking the taxation unjust or excessive, rejects it—the lower House returns the same bill, and the Senate again rejects it—a conflict ensues between the two Houses: is it not quite apparent, that the lower House has the power, either of compelling the Senate to take exactly such a revenue bill as they think equitable and politic, or of throwing upon the Senate the awful responsibility of stopping the wheels of Government? Follow the example of the Federal Constitution—leave the power of originating money bills in the lower House, give the Senate the power of amending them. The lower House sends up its revenue bill—the Senate, constituted (upon the supposed plan) the guardian of taxable property, finds the exactions unjust or enormous, and offers amendments to correct or reduce them—the lower House rejects the amendments: then, the same conflict must ensue, as in the other case, only it will now turn on the amendments of the Senate instead of the original bill of the other House; and the same consequences must follow. In any serious conflict between the two Houses, let us see which is likely to prevail. The members of both Houses are drawn from the same order of men, and the only difference between them consists in the duration of their service. The only operation of the Senate in all our State Governments (the Senate of the United States is organized on peculiar principles) is to suspend for a time, never to defeat entirely, the actions of the other House resolutely persisted in. The lower House is the more numerous body, more intimately connected with the people, and every way endued with greater moral and political energy. Accordingly, even under the present organization of the Legislature the Senate has never had the strength, for any long time, to resist any measure, in which the other House, session after session, strenuously perseveres; and when the proposed re-organization shall be made, making the lower House the representative of *numbers*, and the Senate the representative of *property*, the Senate will have still less relative strength. Let it attempt resistance to any favorite measure of the representatives of *persons, free white persons;* such a cry will be forthwith raised against the odious aristocracy on which its Constitution is founded, the aristocracy of wealth, as will make its members tremble in their seats, pause, waver, and at last yield, disheartened and impotent. The lower House may exercise another influence, if possible, of a more pernicious kind. As it is a numerous body, it has in fact the whole patronage in its hands, in respect of all appointments to be made by joint vote of both branches. A Senator of Virginia, nay, many Senators, may have an ambition to be a Senator of the United States, or a Judge, or Governor (we may change the mode of appointment as to the two last; but we cannot as to the first;) such a Senator, unless he be more than man, must wish to conciliate the lower House—and then *Remember the weight of a Back Woods vote!*

Sir, I insist, that the lower House is here, as it is in England, the proper representative of the interests of property; and it is for that very reason, and no other, that its responsibility to the people, is increased by the short duration of its term of service.

Let us, however, suppose, that the guaranties proposed by the gentleman from Fairfax, (Mr. Fitzhugh,) are efficient, or that some other efficient guaranties can be devised—and let us suppose too, that in addition to those guaranties, a check upon the power of taxation is provided, by so constituting the Senate as to make it a representative of property—and that these safeguards, if preserved, are completely adequate to the intended purpose: What security would they afford us? security only so long as they shall be continued. Is there, or can there be, any security that they will be continued? We may provide for future amendments, with the most jealous care to prevent reckless innovation; but we cannot destroy the inherent power of the people to call another Convention; and the moment the representative of *numbers* shall feel the check, *numbers may*, and *numbers will*, have another Convention to abolish the check.

But it is not a consideration of this vital power of taxation alone, which should impel us of the East, to resist, to the bitter end, this transfer of power to the West. There may be unjust legislation, as well as oppressive taxation. Our slave property is a subject, in the management of which, the owners cannot admit any interference, without the extremest danger. It seems to be supposed, in the United States and in Great Britain too, that those who possess the least portion of that kind of property, are better entitled, and more competent to manage it, than those who have the most; and by parity of reason, those who hold none, have the very best title, and the greatest degree of competency, to the management of it. Upon this principle it is, that Mr. Wilberforce, and the party of the Saints in England, insist on taking the regulation of the slave property in the West Indies into *their* hands, against the earnest remonstrances of the planters to whom it belongs. So, the statesmen of the Northern States, fancy themselves better acquainted with the subject, than those of the South; and our brethren of the Northern part of this State, claim greater fitness for the task, than their fellow-citizens of the Southern counties. The gentleman from Hampshire, (Mr. Naylor,) thinks, that slavery is one of the causes of the decline of Virginia; and I suppose he would be ready to promote her prosperity, by removing this cause of her decline——

[Mr. Naylor rose, and denied the inference which the gentleman had drawn, from any thing which he had said. He deprecated the idea which had been suggested, as to the emancipation of the slaves. And he took occasion further to state, that he considered it perfectly consistent with the principles of morality and justice, situated as we are, to hold them as we now do.]

Mr. Leigh—The gentleman from Hampshire is advanced in years, and may not change his sentiments—but, when Mr Wilberforce proposed to abolish the *slave trade*, he did not imagine, that he should ever find it wise to abolish *slavery* in the West Indies:—When men's minds once take this direction, they pursue it as steadily, as man pursues his course to the grave.

Sir, the venerable gentleman from Loudoun (Mr. Monroe) spoke of the impracticability of any scheme of emancipation, without the aid of the General Government. Is he, then, and if *he* is, are *we* reconciled to the idea of the interference of the General Government in this most delicate and peculiar interest of our own? What right can that Government have to interfere in it?

[Mr. Monroe here explained.

I consider the question of slavery as one of the most important that can come before this body: it is certainly one which must deeply affect the Commonwealth, whether the decision be to maintain it over those now in that state, or to attempt their emancipation. The idea I meant to suggest was, that the subject had assumed a new and very important character, by what had occurred in the other States, and particularly in those in which slavery does not exist. We had seen in the early stage a strong pressure for emancipation from the Eastern States, and equally so of late from the States in the West; but emancipation had thrown many of our liberated slaves upon them; in consequence of which, they have been driven back, and all interference on their part has ceased.

The subject is now brought home to them, as well as to ourselves, and the question to be decided by us is, whether their emancipation is practicable or not. Should the decision be that it was practicable, I did not mean to convey the idea that the United States should interfere, of right, as is advocated by many. I meant to suggest, that if the wisdom of Virginia should decide that it was practicable, and invite the aid of the General Government, that it should then be afforded at her instance, and not that of the United States, as having the least authority in the matter.]

Mr. Leigh—I thank the gentleman for his explanation. And now, will he give me leave to propound to him one question—Whether, with his knowledge and experience of the operations of the General Government, he does not know, that if once it be allowed, that that Government *may* constitutionally interfere at the instance of the State, it will not be inferred, that it *can* constitutionally interfere without any instance of the State Government? The moment such an attempt shall be, there will, there must be, an end of this Union.

I wish, indeed, that I had been born in a land where domestic and negro slavery is unknown—no Sir,—I misrepresent myself—I do not wish so—I shall never wish that I had been born out of Virginia—but I wish, that Providence had spared my country this moral and political evil. It is supposed, that our slave labour enables us to live in luxury and ease, without industry, without care. Sir, the evil of slavery is greater to the master, than to the slave: He is interested in all their wants, all their distresses; bound to provide for them, to care for them, to labour for them, while they labour for him, and his labour is by no means the least severe of the two. The relation between master and slave, imposes on the master a heavy and painful responsibility—but no more on this head.

Sir, the venerable gentleman from Loudoun has told us of the awful and horrid scenes he was an eye-witness of, in France, during the reign of democracy, or rather of anarchy, there. I wish he had told us, (as he told the House of Delegates in 1810, when he opposed the call of a Convention, and re-counted those same horrors) that "he had seen liberty expiring from excess"—these were his words. France was then arranged into equal departments, with equal representation, and general suffrage—in short, enjoying the unalloyed blessing of the natural rights of man! Have I lost my senses! Is the phantom that fills my breast with such horror—*the liberty of Virginia expiring with excess*—a creature of the imagination, that can never be realized! The venerable gentleman has described those horrors in France—has painted them to us in all the freshness of reality—and then told us, in the same breath, that he is prepared to vote for the same system here. The same causes uniformly produce the same effects.—I mean to speak with freedom, yet not without the respect due to the venerable gentleman, and which I should render as a willing tribute: I cannot forbear to express my astonishment, that he should be willing to adopt, for his own country, the principles that led to those horrors he has so feelingly described—

Mr. Monroe rose to explain:

Mr. Leigh—I request the gentleman to suspend his explanation, till I conclude what little more I have to say.

I am sensible, Mr. Chairman, that some of the opinions I have advanced, and some of the propositions I have maintained, are calculated to shock the principles, I might perhaps say, the prejudices, of many. I know, that the very propositions of the truth of which I am most firmly convinced, if pushed to extremes, would end in folly and vice; but it is an eternal truth, in all the moral sciences, that no principle, however just, will hold good to the utmost extreme; and there is no argument, which by that process is not capable of refutation. I pray the gentleman from Frederick (Mr. Cooke) to ponder well those lines, which, partly in sport, more in kindness, I handed him the other day—

Est modus in rebus—sunt certi denique fines,
Quos ultra citrave nequit consistere rectum.

It has pleased Heaven to ordain, that man shall enjoy no good without alloy. Its choicest bounties are not blessings, unless the enjoyment of them be tempered with moderation. *Liberty* is only a *mean*: the *end* is *happiness*. It is, indeed, the wine of life; but like other wines, it must be used with temperance, in order to be used with advantage: taken to excess, it first intoxicates, then maddens, and at last destroys.

Mr. Monroe now rose to explain. My worthy friend from Chesterfield, expresses his surprise at the view I now take after what I had seen in France. What I meant to convey, in the remarks to which he alludes, was, that the commotions I had witnessed inclined me in 1810, rather to oppose the petition from Accomac, in favour of a new Constitution and the extension of the Right of Suffrage, which was advocated in the debate, but that I had so far overcome that impression, as now to be in favour of extending that right. I will further explain, my opinion at that time, was not made up —I found cause to hesitate, but it was merely that the subject might be thoroughly analized and investigated to the bottom in a view of the conduct of men, in such circumstances through all ages. When we trace the popular movements in France to their causes, it will be seen that these causes do not exist here. The people of France had been ruled by despotism, and held in an abject and deplorable situation for ages. They were educated and reared under despotism. The idea of liberty was cherished among them. They were devoted to it—but rising out of slavery they were incompetent to govern themselves. The effect which despotic Government has on the intelligence and manners of the people under it, is supported by all history. The great mass are ignorant and trained to obedience. Those of France, had caught the spirit of liberty, and would no longer submit to the power of the crown and nobility. They rose in a body suddenly, and with violence, and overwhelming the existing Government, they took the whole power into their own hands, but were incompetent to a proper use of it. These remarks on the condition of France will apply to all Europe, but less to England than to other European nations. It was the effort of the people of England which repelled the despotism with which they were menaced, and laid the basis of that Constitution, from which, as it has been stated by my friend from Chesterfield, all our institutions have taken their origin. But there is no part of Europe, not England itself, I fear, that could support such a Government as we enjoy here. The power was vested essentially in the popular branch, during our Colonial State, in all the Colonies. There was little to oppose it, but the veto of the Crown. All America was arrayed against the Crown. We assembled in our revolution, and crushed it, and the power of the Crown then passed to the body of the people. The people of these Colonies never were slaves: they were an enlightened people who had fled from oppression in England, and came here in search of liberty. The love of it characterized us in our Colonial state, and continued to do so up to the period of our Independence. Look at Asia, at Africa, and even at Europe, and what is their condition? If there is a portion of the earth where self-government can be maintained, it is in these United States: and I say again, that Virginia is as competent to it, as any other part of the Union.

As to the slave population, it exists here, and whether we shall get rid of it or not is for those who own it to decide for themselves. The States where it does not exist, must never interfere unless authorized and invited to do it. But if the decision shall be, that they cannot be emancipated, (and I could never consent that they should be, unless you send them away,) it is equally the interest of the non-slave-holding as of the slave-holding States, to support the latter in their authority over their slaves. Where they are, they never can enjoy equal rights with the white population; and if emancipated, interminable war would ensue. If I say it shall be the sentiment of the Southern States, that slavery must continue forever, then what has passed will induce the other States to support us.

I would never, by any act of imprudence, raise up the non-slave-holding States into hostility against the others. If you marshal them against each other, what then must be the consequence? Dismemberment will be inevitable. The European powers all fight against each other, and we should go on the same way. The non-slave-holding States would incite insurrections among our slave population, as was done by the republics of ancient Greece, and desolate the country. I am for moving with great caution and circumspection in this matter.

Mr. Mercer then addressed the Committee:

In casting himself on the indulgence of the committee, in the present stage of the interesting debate by which its attention had been so long occupied, Mr. Mercer said, he laboured under the influence of feelings which he had not language to convey, and the expression of which he feared would disqualify him for the arduous task which he had undertaken to perform. The sentiment first at his heart was, that the depending question might terminate in a result, propitious to the union, and happiness to the whole Commonwealth. While desirous of extending to the people of the West a just participation in the political power of the Government; a power proportioned to their relative numbers, he entered upon the present discussion with no unfriendly feeling towards the East. Such a feeling would be equally at war with all his recollections and all his hopes. His cradle was rocked by the margin of the placid tide, though Providence had placed his dwelling by the side of the mountain torrent. He had not a drop of kindred blood flowing in the veins of any living being that did not warm the heart of some lowland man, or lowland woman. He came into this Convention not to assert the power of one portion of the State to control the other, but with a fixed determination to uphold the rights and interests of all, on the broad and solid basis of those great principles of political liberty which our forefathers had at all times struggled to maintain. Emphatically might he say this, and vouch this Assembly itself for his proof. Through what channel, he asked, did the resolution of the Legislative Committee, now in discussion, reach this Convention? By what hand was the report of that committee presented in this Hall? By that hand, which, more than any other now in being, had contributed to trace the outline and lay the foundation of the great structure of our free institutions. By whom had the principles of this report been just sustained? By his illustrious co-patriot, who, alone, of this Assembly, had enjoyed the high honor of consecrating those principles by his blood.

We are charged with asserting new and impracticable doctrines. Behold the proof of this allegation. Are they not founded on the principles, if the term may now be allowed him, of every Bill or Declaration of Rights of every State in this Union, which has framed a Constitution since our glorious revolution? Are they not sanctioned by the concurrent voice of the wisest statesmen, and the purest patriots, on both sides of the Atlantic? Are they not the principles of the father of English metaphysics, and champion of British liberty—the immortal Locke? Are they not the principles for which Milton successfully contended against the united power of political and ecclesiastical tyranny; and for which, in a still earlier age, the noble Sydney bled?

Could this question be tried, without prejudice, its issue would not long be doubtful. The very process, by which our assailants seek to over-power us, affords sufficient evidence of the strength of our cause. Principles must be true, which can be successfully controverted only by such arguments—arguments invented and most ably enforced, by gentlemen inured to the habits of a profession, which, above all others, teaches its professors how to discover, to touch, and to move all the secret springs of the human heart. What are the prejudices which seek to obstruct our better judgment on the present occasion? Some are too obvious to elude our perception, and must be dissipated when approached. The eloquent member from Chesterfield, proclaims with seeming regret, that, between the district, which I have the honor, in part, to represent, and the western counties of Virginia, there are no longer any Pyrennees. From Ashby's Gap to the Potomac, the Blue Ridge, he tells us, has disappeared. This illusion of his own imagination, the honorable member infers, from the sympathy subsisting in the present contest, between the people of Loudoun, and their fellow citizens of the West. To the other districts, on the Eastern face of the Blue Ridge, which espouse the same side of this cause with my constituents, and obviously for the same reason, he liberally awards the praise of magnanimity, which he denies to them.

Might he not have more impartially accounted for the zeal of Loudoun for a Convention, from the notorious fact that while she pays into the Public Treasury twenty times the amount of taxes paid by the county of Warwick, and has more than six-and-twenty times the free white population of Warwick—she has but the same political weight in the House of Delegates, under the Constitution of Government which this Convention has been deputed to amend. That twenty-six freemen of Loudoun have, in this branch of the Legislature, the weight of but one freeman of Warwick.

But the honorable member, disregarding this inequality, has found the origin of the present Convention in splendid schemes of internal improvement, to which the Constitutional scruples, manifested, by Virginia, in the councils of the Union, oppose a barrier, that the new distribution of political power sought to be effected by the resolution in debate, will enable the West to prostrate. In that ardent zeal, which had prompted so many other gentlemen, as well as the member from Chesterfield, to impute to the friends of a Convention, local, selfish and sordid motives for their present union of council, they have forgotten much, and in part, the history of our Legislation on this subject.

Internal Improvement—the cause of this Convention! Who, until the second day of March, 1817, had ever heard an objection started to the Constitutional power of the Federal Government to aid, by the resources of the Union, the efforts of the States, to construct roads, or canals of general interest. A few days only, prior to this period, a resolution, recommended by the unanimous report of the Board of Public Works, passed both branches of the General Assembly, with like unanimity, to request of the Government of the United States, pecuniary aid in promoting the then contemplated junction of the eastern and western waters of Virginia by the James and Kanawha rivers. A similar resolution had passed the House of Delegates without opposition at the preceding session of 1815. It was, however, near the close of that session, on the 8th February, 1816, that a bill, to take the sense of the people on the propriety of calling a Convention, first received the sanction of a majority of the House of Delegates, and that majority embraced both the delegates from Loudoun.

This bill was afterwards lost at its third reading: but a similar one finally passed the House of Delegates with the co-operation of the Loudoun delegation during the succeeding winter, and more than a month before the President's message, of the 2d March, 1817, had excited a doubt in the public mind, of the Constitutional authority of Congress to aid the several States in the construction of works of internal improvement. A State fund, for roads and canals, had been already created, and was in successful operation. How, then, can it be candidly maintained, that the efforts so steadily prosecuted, to amend the Constitution of Virginia, by a Convention, sprung from those impediments which this Commonwealth has since thrown in the path of internal improvement, whether by withholding from that object, her own resources, or restraining the application of those of the Union?

He would, said Mr. Mercer, proceed one step farther: and to refute this charge, very briefly state a few of the reasons which prompted the fruitless effort to obtain a Convention in 1815, and which have since been more successfully urged. Among the most prominent of those reasons, was that very inequality of representation, which has given rise to this debate, and which so shocks every feeling of political justice, that no argument has yet been heard in its vindication. Another grievance, then, also, pressing on the public consideration, was the overgrown and disproportionate numbers of the House of Delegates.

When our forefathers penned the present Constitution, there were about 140 members in that House; and they chose twenty-four, as a suitable proportion, for the number of the Senate; a body designed not only to revise the acts of the popular branch of the Legislature, but to constitute a check on the possible ambition of its leaders. But while the Senate, by the Constitutional limitation of its numbers, has been stationary, the House of Delegates has been extended, from time to time, by the multiplication of counties, to 214. More than seventy members have been thus added to the numbers of the Legislature, during a period in which the territory of the Commonwealth has been greatly reduced. For, from the county of Illinois, wrested from Great Britain in 1779, by the forces of the Commonwealth under the command of the gallant Clarke, and ceded in 1784, to the United States, no less than three States to the east, and one to the west of the Mississippi, have arisen. The county of Youghiogania, once represented on this floor, now supplies no less than eight counties to Western Pennsylvania: Kentucky has been erected into a separate State; and, along our southern border, North Carolina has a slip of our former territory, beginning at a point on the Atlantic, and gradually widening towards the Cumberland mountain.

While a reduction of the sphere of Legislation recommended a correspondent limitation of the numbers of the Legislative body, the progressive augmentation of its annual expenditure merited regard. In 1810, the entire cost of this Department of the Government did not exceed 50,000 dollars a year. It has, since, mounted up to more than twice that sum.

To restore the original proportion between the two branches of the General Assembly, and to prevent a still farther augmentation of the number of the House of Delegates, a measure required by no State necessity, and forbid by a due regard to economy, was always in the scope of that Constitutional reform contemplated by the friends of a Convention.

The abolition of the Council of State was another of their objects. Economy condemned this worse than useless appendage to the Executive, which, in destroying its unity, impaired both its vigor and responsibility. A feeble Chief Magistrate is but the tool of his Council, while to an able and unprincipled Governor, they serve as a cloak.

The friends of a Convention, with but few if any exceptions, had another and more aggravated cause of complaint. Is there a member of this body, who thinks that the right of suffrage now rests on a proper basis? Who would not, if disposed to restrict its exercise to a freehold qualification, substitute for quantity, a valuation of the land required to confer a vote. Should a freeholder be allowed to exercise the right of suffrage on fifty acres of land situated upon the summit of a barren mountain, where the crow would not build her nest, while this right is withheld from the proprietor of a farm of twenty-four acres in some fertile valley, which with its improvements may be worth as many thousand dollars? In one of the most flourishing townships of Connecticut, a territory of more than twenty square miles, there is not a farm exceeding twenty-five acres in dimensions, the minimum estate which the present Constitution annexes to the right of suffrage, without regard to its value.

Are we then, Mr. Chairman, with these apologies, to be regarded as coming here in the prosecution of schemes of narrow and sordid speculation? May I not pronounce such a charge to be the offspring of prejudice, and say that it is repelled by the history of the proceedings which have led to this Convention?

There is yet another of analogous birth which remains to be refuted before I proceed with my enquiry into the expediency of the proposed amendment of the gentleman from Culpeper.

It has been more than insinuated, that by the transfer of political power from the Eastern to the Western portion of the Commonwealth, the friends of a Convention design to shake the ascendancy of certain political doctrines, supposed to be essential to the rights of this Commonwealth, as a member of the Union.

If this transfer is required by political justice, how poor a compliment does this insinuation pay to the rights which it thus seeks to defend!

But of the members of the Virginia Delegation in Congress residing to the West of the Blue Ridge, how few are there who differ from a majority of the people of the State, in construing the Constitution of the United States, to say nothing of the gentlemen on this floor, from the counties below the mountain, who are alike advocates for the strictest construction of that instrument, and for a thorough amendment of our Constitution of State Government?

His venerable colleague, said Mr. M. had successfully repelled other prejudices which, if not utterly unfounded, might prove of fatal influence to the object of the Convention, and he now came to the consideration of the real proposition before the Committee.

The resolution of the Legislative Committee proposes to make the white population of the Commonwealth *exclusively* the basis of the apportionment of representation in the House of Delegates. It is moved by the member from Culpeper, to rest such apportionment on white population and taxation combined. After the most laborious attention to all the arguments as well of the mover of this amendment, as of the gentlemen who had sustained him, Mr. M. said he was at a loss to know how this combination was to be effected—in what proportions population and taxation were to be combined. If that of perfect equality, then what description of taxes were to be balanced against the rights of the freemen of Virginia? Shall one of the compounds be determined by taxing all the property of every citizen, visible and invisible? To this, almost insuperable objections might be urged; some of which had been forcibly pointed out, by the member from Northampton, (Mr. Upshur.) If visible property, only, shall be taxed, is all that a man possesses to be comprehended, moveable and immoveable? If one description only, or a portion only of each, which, or what part, and by what rule or ratio of numbers, quality or of value? Is it practicable to form this combined basis, and to impart to it, the simplicity, the stability, to say nothing of its intrinsic justice or propriety, which should, in a Constitution of Government, designed to be perpetual, form the ground-work of the representation of the people?

The author of the proposed amendment, since he designed to give to property, a certain practicable weight in the Government, would more readily accomplish his purpose by constituting as its measure, wealth for taxation; the thing taxed for the tax itself. This change of the basis of representation, in terms, would not alter the principles on which its justice and propriety rest, and both parties would by such conversion, be enabled better to comprehend the precise end, as well as the practicability of the proposed amendment.

For the sake of my own argument at least, I purpose making this substitution of wealth itself, for that which is its measure, in any equal system of taxation. Wealth! the basis of representation! It is proposed, indeed, to combine it with numbers, but the quality of the subject, must follow it through every possible combination, and what is true of it as a simple, may be affirmed of it as an ingredient, of any compound basis of representation, of which it may become an element.

Was wealth, then, ever before proposed in America, except in South Carolina, to be made the foundation of political power in the popular branch of a Government, professing to be free? An oligarchy this may be, open to all bidders for power; but if not an oligarchy, I have no conception of the import of the term.

And why prefer wealth, if equality of right be disregarded among the freemen of Virginia?

In savage life, mere personal qualities, as strength, courage, confer distinction, and not without reason. The term in our language, which denotes the perfection of moral worth, is borrowed from latin *virtus*, which originally signified strength, that quality of man, which barbarians esteem the first of virtues, because among them, the most useful. In the rudest as the wisest nations, age has its claims to veneration, of which my feelings, in this assembly, hourly remind me. To wisdom, all men yield respect: and as society grows older, birth asserts its more questionable claims to our homage, and learns at last, to back them by authority. Wealth, comes, last of all, to buy power and distinction, and if I must cease to be a freeman, 'tis the very last dominion, to which I will ever bow my neck. If I must choose between the aristocracy of birth or fortune, I do not hesitate a moment which to prefer. Had I not better trust my liberty, if I must have a master, to the descendant of honest parents, who may be presumed to have reared and educated their offspring with care and tenderness, than a man, I do not know, for his mere riches? If the latter be obtained, by sudden acquisition, or by secret or unknown means, I should think it incumbent on their possessor, if he claimed my confidence, and much more, if my obedience, to shew that he himself had honestly acquired his title.

To the argument of my friend from Frederick, (Mr. Cooke) that wealth would protect itself, the gentleman from Northampton, (Mr. Upshur) had replied, that it could do so, only by corruption, by the employment only, of the basest means. And shall representation be based on wealth? (Here Mr. Upshur explained.) Mr. M. said he had not misunderstood the eloquent member from Northampton, though he could not do justice to his former language, nor had the gentleman himself done so, in his explanation. If unexceptionable in all other respects, wealth (Mr. M. said) would be found in all countries, too fickle a basis of representation for a distribution of political power, designed to balance the interest of individuals, or of distinct portions even of the same community. Individual wealth! Who can fix it? He, who can stop the ever-revolving wheel of fortune. National wealth is subject, though not in the same degree, a like uncertainty. Of what does that of Virginia consist? Chiefly of lands and slaves. No estimate of the value of the 450,000 slaves of Virginia accompanies the Auditor's Report. The lands of the Commonwealth were valued in 1817, at 206,000,000 of dollars. What are they now worth? Half that sum? He had carefully sought, throughout the Convention, for information to correct the results of his own observation, within late years, as to the change of the value of lands in Virginia. After all his enquiries, he believed they had fallen to two-fifths, of their former estimated value; and could not, now, be computed, at more than 80, or at most, than 90 millions. Next, as to slaves.

A gentleman sitting near him, had, at the period to which he had just referred, of the passage of the equalizing land law, sold 85 slaves in families, at 300 dollars round: He had been assured by him, and by other gentlemen, equally well-informed, from other portions of the Commonwealth, that 150 dollars for each slave, taking them in families, would be a fair price at the present moment. This description of labour, then, has fallen one half, and lands more than a half, in very little more than ten years. In the estimate of the last, the tables supplied by the Auditor, comprehended $26,500,000 for city and town lots; chiefly, for the value of those at Richmond, Petersburg, Norfolk, and Fredericksburg: A value dependent on the fluctuations of domestic and foreign trade. What was once its extent in this city, the metropolis of the Commonwealth, we all remember. What it is now, I know not; since commerce, that inconstant handmaid of fortune, has turned her helm from our ports to the favoured harbor of New-York. Wealth attracts wealth. Fortune not only withdraws her gifts from those who abuse, but from those who fail to use them: taking from those who have little, that which they cannot spare, to pour it into the lap of abundance. While we have been quarrelling about Internal Improvement, New-York has swallowed up the commerce of America. Driven from us by our unkindness, it has gone where it was invited by wiser councils.

There are fluctuations of the value of property, however, which no wisdom can elude or avert. The value of our land and labor depends on the value of the staple commodities which they produce; this on the demand for them at home, and abroad, and that again on physical and moral causes which no Constitution of Government, which man himself, cannot controul; on the seasons, in other countries, as well as our own, on the policy of other nations, on peace, on the varying events of foreign war. The act of Congress reducing the minimum price of the national lands, struck down, at a blow, the value of every landed estate in Virginia. The tide of wealth which set in from Europe to America during the wars of the French revolution, rolled back at the general peace which succeeded our last contest with Great Britain.

If this uncertainty of wealth operated uniformly, on all the interests of our Commonwealth, their relative proportion would not be sensibly disturbed by it. Such, however, is not its effect. The cotton, the tobacco, the grain, and even the grazing interest, are affected, in different degrees, by the same agents: and, although the natural tendency of the profits of stock, the rent of land and the wages of labour, in the same country, is to one level, it requires time to still the successive agitations of their varying values. In the interim, new causes are continually arising to delay their subsidence to one common level; and this principle, the truth of which is unquestioned, though constantly operating, may never accomplish its end.

But had wealth the necessary stability to serve the purpose of the proposed amendment, is taxation in any known system, a just measure of that wealth?

Taxation is the instrument, by which legislation draws from the private revenue of each citizen, his fair proportion of the public expenditure. It should be proportioned to his ability to pay it. It should, therefore, be drawn from his income, and not from his capital, except with a view that his income shall supply the call. His income cannot be reached, if at all, by expedient means; and wisdom suggests the propriety of taxing his expenditure, which usually bears a certain proportion to his income.

The constitutional power of another Government restrains the application of these principles to taxation in Virginia, under the authority of the State; and, in other respects, diversifies the action of our local system of public revenue.

The gentleman from Culpeper, (Mr. Green) has not told us how he means to combine the taxes of the people, with their numbers, in his compound basis of representation. Will he add the annual sum of the present taxes, to the numbers of the people, and dividing the aggregate of men and dollars, settle the value, at which a legal voter in any district may be computed? A friend has informed me that such is to constitute a part of the details of the proposed compound basis, and that the value of each vote in the Commonwealth, will be rated at about fifty-eight cents! Or if this shall shock the ears of the Convention, or the sense of the people, who may set a higher estimate on their rights, will gentlemen adopt what in practice, will lead to a similar result, the plan of South Carolina; and distribute the territory of this Commonwealth into two descriptions of election districts, one in reference to free white population, the other, to taxation as it now exists?

[Mr. Green explained, but in so low a tone of voice, that the reporter could not catch his language.]

Mr. Mercer regretted that he had been unable to hear distinctly the explanation of the gentleman from Culpeper, but from the few words which had reached him, he inferred it to be his intention to adopt the system of South Carolina, and to divide the State into two sorts of election districts.

[Mr. Green having changed his seat in the Hall, again rose for explanation. He explained it to be his plan to take the white population of the State and the population of each county. Apply the rule. Population gives to representation, in proportion to numbers. See the number of representatives required. In like manner, take the whole taxes of the State, and those of each county, if the taxes give the like rule for the county, add them together, and that is the rule.]

Mr. M. thought this plan would only serve to increase the difficulty. To what portion of a representative will Warwick with her annual taxes at $500, and her white population of 620 persons, be entitled? The objection still applies, notwithstanding the explanation that a freeholder, or lawful voter of the Commonwealth, will be weighed in the same scales, with the taxes, he may chance to contribute to the wants or the caprice of the Legislature, and find himself balanced against the fraction of a single dollar.

Were a submission to such degradation, all that was required by this ingenious political composition of men and money, it would be possible, though it might be difficult to endure it patiently. But, is it possible to derive, from such materials, any equitable or stable proportion, or balance of political power, between the different sections, or interests, as they are called, of this Commonwealth, or, indeed, of any other, with which we are acquainted? I know its operation in South Carolina, said Mr. M. only so far as its details are disclosed in her Constitution. Let us turn to it. By this, it is provided, that sixty-two members of *the more numerous*, I will call it *popular* branch of her Legislature, shall be distributed among her pre-existing election districts, in number forty-four, from reference to their white inhabitants; and sixty-two among the same districts, from reference to "*the amount of all taxes raised by the Legislature, whether direct or indirect*, or of *whatever species*, paid in each, deducting therefrom, all taxes paid on account of property, held in any other district, and adding thereto, all taxes, elsewhere paid, on account of property held in such district." To give effect to this principle of representation, it is farther provided, that there shall be an enumeration of the people once in every ten years, and that, in every apportionment of representation, which shall take place, after the first, "the amount of taxes shall be estimated from the average of the ten preceding years:" "and the first apportionment shall be founded on the tax of the preceding year, excluding from the amount thereof, the whole produce of the tax on sales *at public auction*."

He had attended, Mr. M. said, the more closely, to these provisions, in order to ascertain, what portion to a House of one hundred and twenty-four members, would fall to the share of the city of Charleston. This city had, of the former House of Representatives of the State, including the parishes of St. Philips' and St. Michael's, fifteen members out of one hundred and twenty-four. The auction duties of South Carolina, there can be but little doubt, are paid chiefly, if not solely, in Charleston. They were not to be computed at all, in the first apportionment of representation, that of 1810; but the very exception, as well as the antecedent language of her Constitution, shews that they were to be reckoned, in every subsequent apportionment, founded on the taxes of the preceding ten years. They must have been computed, therefore, in 1820. The present representation of this city, in the House of Representatives of South Carolina, I have yet to learn; but if any part of it is founded on these auction duties, since her example is invoked to the aid of the amendment, in discussion, I ask if she is entitled to it on any principle which would not give to the citizens of Philadelphia, or New York, a like claim to representation, over and above their fair proportion to members in the Legislatures of their respective States? The extent of the auction duties annually collected in Charleston, is unknown to me: but the auction duties of Philadelphia, I believe, constitute a third of the entire revenue of Pennsylvania, whose State Government is sustained without any other tax whatever, except upon the dividends of her banks, and on collateral inheritances, devises and bequests. These taxes, together with her share of the annual dividends, accruing on her several road, bridge, canal, and bank stocks, make up the sum total of the public income, applied to the disbursements of a State Government, where neither a land nor a poll tax exists. More than a moiety of it arises in Philadelphia.

Similar views apply to New York. The auction duties levied in her great emporium, largely exceed a moiety of our State revenue, and are established and set apart for a special purpose, by an express provision of her Constitution.

The only tax we have in Virginia, analogous to this, is one on merchants' licenses; and both have a close affinity, in their principles and operation, to the impost duties of the United States. They are all levied at the marts of commerce,—all chargeable upon the commodities which enter into that commerce. They are, consequently, all paid, neither by the importer nor the vender,—neither by the auctioneer nor the merchant,—who are but the collectors of the tax, and charge a profit on their labour. They are all paid, in fine, by the consumer, who, for the opportunity of paying them, this amendment would require of him to surrender, not only the price in money of the articles which he purchased, but a most undue and enormous advance of political power, to his superiors, the tax-paying merchant and auctioneer. Apply this amendment to the condition of Pennsylvania and New York, and their chief cities would govern those States. These new heads of a monied aristocracy, the auctioneers, who pay, by far, the largest share of the taxes to the State, would, in the several State Governments, far out-rank the regular merchant, whose principal dues pass through the Collectors of the Customs, to the Treasury of the Federal Government; and, consequently, neither augment his own political power, nor that of his neighbours, however large they may be, and actually are.

If the payment of a tax, gives a right to a proportionate share of the power which levies it, my constituents have a fair claim to representation in the Legislatures of New York and Pennsylvania, since they pay no small share of these auction duties.

Sir, said Mr. M. the salt tax of New York, a State excise, is also set apart, by her Constitution, for a special purpose. Being twelve and a half cents on the bushel, and the quantity made, about 1,200,000 bushels, it does not fall short of $120,000 per annum, and being levied and collected on Lake Onondaga, near the town of Salina, it should entitle the inhabitants of that vicinity, to a very large portion of the political power of that great and flourishing State.

During the last war, we endeavoured to levy a similar tax in the counties of Washington and Kanawha; but with less success. Should the political weight of our several counties, be hereafter dependent on the amount of taxes they may severally pay, as the gentleman from Culpeper proposes, whatever the salt-makers may think of the renewal of that tax, the politicians and the people of those counties, might over-rule these objections, for the sake of governing the rest of the Commonwealth, by this newly-invented political power.

It must now be apparent, Mr. Chairman, that the district in which a particular tax is collected, may not be the district of the people by whom it is paid, and consequently that nothing would be more absurd than to rest the apportionment of political power on any such basis.

Indeed, the tax which is paid on a particular subject will have its locality, if I may be allowed the expression, determined, altogether, by the mode in which it is levied. The Supreme Court of the United States has defined a tax upon carriages, to be a tax on expenditure, and therefore an indirect tax, and to be the same in character, whether paid by the maker or the user of the carriage. Now, the maker and the user may live in the same Commonwealth many miles apart. If, however, the tax be paid by the maker, he would have credit for it; if by the user, it would inure to his benefit. To whom should the right of suffrage attach? If it attach to neither, it would seem to vest in the vehicle itself, and to suggest a similar difficulty to that propounded by Dr. Franklin, who, commenting on the case of a man, whose right to vote depended on the tax which he had paid on his ass, inquired after the death of the animal, and the consequent loss of the vote of his owner, whether the vote had been in the ass or the man.

It is impossible, Mr. Chairman, said Mr. M. to judge how far the rule of apportionment, adopted by South Carolina, would suit our condition, without knowing how it operates on her own. What is the character and operation of her system of taxation?

A similar rule is said to prevail in the apportionment of the Senators of Massachusetts and New Hampshire, under their respective State Constitutions. He had been informed, that no State tax had been levied in Massachusetts for seven years past, and he thought it highly probable that the same state of affairs, in the frugal Commonwealth of New Hampshire, would prevent a rule of apportionment, however offensive in theory, from exciting the public indignation. A rule, wholly inoperative, would be obnoxious to no one.

It can be readily perceived, that if applied to Pennsylvania, or New York, or even to Maryland, it would so far from restraining the political influence of the chief cities of these States, to a measure short of the just proportion of the number of their citizens in the scale of the population of their respective States, it would enable those cities by a combination of numbers and wealth to govern, without any control, beyond their corporation limits. And yet, this is one of the very evils against which the member from Chesterfield, the eloquent advocate of the amendment, is desirous to guard this Commonwealth: A Commonwealth, whose territory is so intersected by numerous rivers, that an overgrown market is not likely to spring up in its bosom.

Mr. M. said, he had considered these imperfections of the basis of representation, submitted by the amendment, arising from the nature of taxation, considered as an instrument for raising any given revenue required by the exigencies of the Commonwealth.

But if these exigencies shall vary between different periods of time, how unstable is this basis, and especially if the pressure of the public burthens shall grow more and more unequal, as they grow or decline in weight.

In Maryland there is no State tax: the expenses of her Government are defrayed out of the income of a public capital already acquired. The revenue of the two great canals of New York, the work of but a few years, reaches already near a million of dollars, and will shortly release that Commonwealth, which has now neither a land nor a poll tax, from the necessity of imposing any tax whatever on her citizens.

Such a principle of representation, as that, for which our opponents contend, would induce, under such circumstances, the imposition and distribution of taxes for the sake of power merely. On the plan of Carolina, half the political power of the State might be secured by the exercise of very little ingenuity, to a minority of the election districts, and with it the means of preserving it forever in the same hands.

We have sought as yet in vain to secure from misapplication, and to prescribe the use of the two great funds of the Commonwealth. If the new Constitution shall be silent on this subject, what will prevent a majority of a future Legislature from applying them to reduce the pressure of the taxes on one portion of the Commonwealth, with a view to its Government in all other respects, by a minority of the people, or those who lead such minority? Those funds are abundantly sufficient for any such purpose, and the amendment, if adopted, will furnish the opportunity so to abuse them.

Not only would every reduction of the taxes which affected their relative pressure affect the proposed apportionment of representation, but every augmentation of them.

In this view of the subject a new principle requires to be developed. A considerable augmentation of revenue cannot often be effected without increasing particular taxes on those subjects already taxed, which will bear augmentation, nor sometimes, without adding new subjects to the existing list of taxes.

War inevitably gives rise to both these necessities, by reducing or suspending some branches of private revenue, and supplying others, before unused or unknown.

The burthen of sustaining a foreign war, it is true, has been cast by the Federal Constitution upon another Government; but it cannot be forgotten, by any member of this Convention, that it had been found necessary to double the revenue of the Commonwealth during the late war, and to incur a considerable debt for its defence, part of which remains yet unpaid Can any man venture to predict, that a similar necessity will not again arise? Should he do so, would this Committee confide in the prediction: and found a provision in our Constitution upon it? No practical Statesman will believe that to be impossible which has actually happened, or reject the council which would provide for its recurrence.

Should an attempt be made to remedy the inequality of taxation, arising from war, or national distress, by averaging with a view to future representation, the taxes of a given period, according to the scheme of South Carolina: the effect of any war which varies the proportions of the public burthens, borne by the citizens of the same Commonwealth, will subsist in their representation, long after peace shall have been restored, and the inequality shall have ceased.

A review of our own system of taxation, both before and since the formation of our present Constitution, would supply all the facts necessary to sustain the positions I have assumed.

Prior to the war of 1756, called in Europe the Silesian war, from its object, and the seven years war, from its duration, and in America, the French war, from the foe whom it brought upon the western frontier of this Commonwealth, the only revenue of Virginia had been derived from a poll tax. The first land tax was laid in 1777, and was an ad valorem tax, the same in amount with that upon slaves—and these were then the only subjects of taxation. To these, before the last war, had been added taxes on horses, ordinaries, merchants' licenses, and law process.

The last war not only required a large augmentation of the taxes, on all these subjects, but the addition of a number which I will not fatigue the Committee by enumerating. Since the war the extraordinary subjects of taxation, have been released, but the pre-existing proportions of tax on the old subjects has not been restored. Allow me briefly to run over these changes with the date of their occurrence. In 1809 the land tax was 48 cents on the hundred dollars, or supposed value, according to the act of 1787. From 1816 to 1819 the land tax was 75 cents on the hundred dollars. In 1820 it was reduced by the new equalizing land law, the price paid by the West, for equalizing the representation of the Senate, to 12½ cents for every hundred dollars of actually assessed value. In 1821 it was brought down to 9 cents upon the same estimate; at which it remained till the last year, when it was again reduced to 8 cents, more than fifty per cent of the tax of 1820, having been struck off in eight years, and the land tax of 1829 made to bear to the land tax prior to the last equalizing land law an apparent ratio of one only, to more than 9.

In 1809, before the war, the tax on slaves above twelve years of age was 44 cents; in 1815 it was raised by the war to 80 cents, in 1819 reduced to 70 cents, in 1821 to 53 cents, in 1828 to 47 cents, and the last reduction brought it down to 40 cents, or 4 cents less than its amount prior to the war.

The tax on horses for several years prior to the last war was 8 cents. In 1815 it mounted up to 20 cents. In 1819 it was 18 cents; in 1821, 13½ cents; in 1823, 12 cents, and it is now 10 cents, or twenty-five per cent. more than it was prior to the war.

The war besides adding more than forty specific taxes to the three I have enumerated, raised essentially the proportions between those of ordinary use.

It greatly increased the ratio of the land and horse tax to the slave tax. The relative product of the taxes on lands, slaves and horses in 1809, was 141,000; 90,000, and 38,000 respectively. In 1816, 238,000; 161,000, and 40,000. In 1829, 175,000; 97,000, and 33,000 respectively. When the revenue from these three subjects stood highest, that is, after the equalizing law took effect in 1819, their proportions were 274,000; 163,000, and $ 52,000. Their proportions in the last year were 175,000; 97,000, and $ 33,000.

The land tax, it will be seen, has been gaining on the amount of the slave tax since 1809. Since when $ 34,000 has been added to the gross amount of the land tax, and $ 7,000 to the amount of the slave tax.

While these variations in the total amount of the taxes levied on the old subjects of taxation, have not been strongly marked, except during the continuance of war, the proportion paid by the several counties of the State have been more diversified.

The taxes of Loudoun paid into the State Treasury, in 1815, amounted to the sum of $ 12,885. Those of the county of Warwick to $ 1,285, or very near a tenth part of that amount. In each of the years of 1823 and 1824, Warwick paid only $ 500 and Loudoun $ 9,500. In the last year, Warwick paid $ 526, and Loudoun $ 10,507. Thus the proportion of taxes actually paid into the Treasury, by these counties which have, notwithstanding, an equal representation in the House of Delegates, was, in 1815, ten to one; and is, now, very near twenty to one. The proportion having varied in the ratio of very near two to one.

During the last war, nearly fifty specific taxes were added to three subjects of ordinary State revenue. Among the former were excises on salt, iron, lead and manufactured tobacco, objects all of limited production, and while consumed every where, taxed only where made.

They suggest one view of this subject which ought not to be omitted. It is that by resting the representation of the people of this Commonwealth on the basis of taxation and numbers, we place their relative political power over the operations of their own State Government, under the control of the Congress of the United States.

To develope this argument, it is necessary to refer to the Federal Constitution which gives to the National Legislature exclusively, the power of imposing duties on foreign imports, and a concurrent authority with the several States to tax every thing else within their limits.

Should Congress prohibit public auctions of foreign goods, as they have been earnestly entreated to do by the resident merchants of all our great cities, what would become of the revenue of New-York, Pennsylvania, and South Carolina, from this source? And should the revenue disappear, what of that portion of the representation of Charleston derived from the auction tax? May it not be said that those States who tax a particular mode of selling foreign commodities immediately after they are landed, while they are expressly debarred from taxing their importation, trench more directly on the powers of the Federal Government than that Government has done, upon the natural distribution of labour and capital within the several States by the imposition of a tariff for the encouragement of domestic manufactures?

Nor is it the *direct* action of the fiscal regulations of the United States, in particular branches of State revenue, to which I singly allude: the whole system of federal taxation exerts an indirect but constant control over all the subjects which a State can tax. Were the United States, for example, to repeal the 20 cent duty on salt, what would become of New-York excise on that commodity, an excise which enhances its price, not only to the people of that State, but of the Western counties of Pennsylvania and Virginia?

I trust, said Mr. M. that I need not adjure the Committee to exclude, if practicable, the action of the General Government, whether direct or indirect, on the representation of the people of Virginia in the Legislative Department of their State Government.

Had such a basis of representation obtained in the Federal Legislature, in lieu of federal numbers, what now would be the relative power of New-York, to the rest of the Union; and of the city of New-York to the rest of that great commercial State.

The duties there paid would overturn every just balance of political power, and overwhelm, in the vortex of a monied aristocracy, the liberty and happiness, not of that city only, but of the whole Union.

Before Mr. M. concluded his remarks, the Committee rose, and the House adjourned to meet to-morrow, at 11 o'clock.

THURSDAY, November 5, 1829.

The Convention met at eleven o'clock, and was opened with prayer by the Rev. Mr. Lee of the Episcopal Church.

Mr. Mercer resumed:

Having endeavoured, with what success it is for the Committee to determine, to shew that the basis of representation proposed by the gentleman from Culpeper, (Mr. Green,) if practicable, is unstable, unjust, and inexpedient, I beg leave to recur to the original resolution of the Legislative Committee, in order to demonstrate that it founds the representation of the people, on its only proper basis.

This course I deem the more necessary, since the friends of the amendment have sought to sustain it, rather by opposing the basis contained in the resolution, than by enforcing the justice, or expediency of the amendment itself. Their reasoning has shewn, if it has proved any thing, that the entire slave population of the State, or three-fifths of it at least, should be computed in any new apportionment of representation which shall be made.

The resolution asserts, that this apportionment should have reference exclusively to the numbers of the free white population of the Commonwealth.

Referring to free white population, alone, the Legislative Committee have designed to reject any computation whatever of slaves. Although no gentleman has so far offended the public sentiment in terms, as absolutely to confound slaves with freemen, yet in their arguments, in favour of a compound basis, they have laid great stress on the protection which a representation of slaves would afford to this species of property.

The gentleman from Chesterfield, (Mr. Leigh,) has gone so far as to urge the computation of the slave population, in whole or in part, on grounds of authority, of justice, and of expediency.

His leading authority is deduced from the articles of "Confederation and perpetual Union" among the States, which gave place to the present Constitution of the United States, wherein, three-fifths of the slave population are added to the white, to compose a standard of *direct taxation* and representation.

One of my purposes is to shew that these authorities are inconclusive in themselves, or inapplicable to the present question.

The honourable member insisted on a former occasion, that the articles of Confederation did actually authorise a computation of three-fifths of the slave population of the South. Had this been true, it would not have warranted the use of the fact as an authority in fixing the basis of representation in the Constitution of Virginia. The articles of Confederation formed a compact, not between individuals, but sovereign States, who regarded themselves as mutually independent of each other. This compact, like a treaty, could be ratified, only by the express assent of all the parties to it; which was not obtained, until the accession of Maryland, in March, 1781. In the Congress, which that compact provided, for the exercise of the authority of the United States, perfect equality of power subsisted among the States. The sense of a part indeed, was to govern the whole body, but this sense was taken by the votes, not of individuals, (any one, or several of whom, might represent a State) but of States, each State having one vote and one only. As the articles of Confederation could be ratified, so, they could be altered, or amended, only by the concurrent assent of all the States who were parties to them.

No rule of pecuniary contribution, in such a Government, for the power to tax did not exist, could therefore, have the remotest relation to any basis of representation whatever. The States were expected to contribute to the common expenditure according to their respective ability. Their representation was equal. The 8th of those articles, provided a common treasury, and required it to be supplied, by the several States, in proportion to the estimated value of all the lands granted in each State, with the buildings and improvements upon them. Until 1781, however, this like all the other articles of Confederation, had no validity whatever.

In the interim, the revolutionary Government sustained itself, by loans, and by the issue of paper money, till from the excessive issue of this paper, it lost all value, and ceased at length to circulate.

The authors of the Confederation discovered, that they had not the means of ascertaining the value of all the real property of the several States. Adam Smith, had informed them, that it took the Emperor of Germany, more than half a century, to complete a survey, of one only of the States of his dominions. The present day would add to this information the vast time consumed in the late triangular surveys of France and England. In Virginia, alone, it would then have taken several years, to have gone, with tolerable accuracy, through such an assessment as the 8th article of Confederation demanded. Amidst these embarrassments, and the alarm of national bankruptcy, it was proposed to substitute, as the standard of fiscal contribution by the States, a computation of the numbers of the people, for the actual valuation of all their estates. A new difficulty here arose, as to the proper subjects of such an enumeration. Whether it should be restricted to the free white population alone, of the several States, or comprehend the slaves also? The object being to measure the ability to pay, the South, naturally enough contended, and with truth, that their slaves were not regarded in their institutions of civil polity, as persons, but as property; and ought not to be enumerated. The North insisted on the other hand, that whether persons, or property, they subserved the end of other labour, and adding to the wealth of the community, should be counted in that estimate of the relative ability of the States, to contribute to the common treasury, of which it was proposed to make *numbers* the common measure. The discussion of this subject, in the Congress of the Confederacy, terminated in a vote to recommend it to the several States, to amend the articles of Confederation, by substituting, for the rule of apportionment, therein provided for revenue only, a triennial enumeration of the whole number of white, and other free citizens, with three-fifths of all other persons, except Indians, not taxed.

In the decision on this recommendation, in April, 1783, it was carried by ten votes out of twelve: Rhode Island being opposed to it; New York equally divided, Mr. Floyd voting for it, and Mr. Hamilton against it; and Georgia being absent. I am thus particular in relation to this vote, for reasons which I will, hereafter explain. The Legislature of Rhode Island persevered in the opposition begun by her delegates in Congress; and Virginia, after giving, retracted her assent; so that the recommendation totally failed. This state of things continued till the Convention assembled which framed the present Constitution of the United States, when the same topic of discussion and of disagreement was renewed. Nor was it easily adjusted in this body, as intimated by the member from Chesterfield, (Mr. Leigh.) No proposition which agitated the Convention, consumed so much of its time. As early in its deliberations as the 29th of May, 1787, it appears on the Journal of the proceedings of that Assembly, among the resolutions submitted by Governor Randolph of Virginia, in this form, "that the right of suffrage in the National Legislature, ought to be proportioned to the quotas of contribution, or to the number of free inhabitants, as the one or the other may seem best in different cases."

The following day Mr. Hamilton moved to alter this resolution, so as to cause it to read, "that the right of suffrage in the National Legislature, ought to be proportioned to the number of free inhabitants."

On the 11th day of June, it was moved by Mr. King of Massachusetts, and seconded by Mr. Rutledge of South Carolina, "That the right of suffrage in the first branch of the National Legislature, ought *not* to be according to the rule established in the articles of Confederation;" [the rule of equality among the States, as we have seen,] but according to some "equitable ratio of representation."

The same day, along with several other amendments of this resolution, it was moved by Mr. Wilson of Pennsylvania, and seconded by Mr. C. Pinckney of South Carolina, to add after the words "equitable ratio of representation," "in proportion to the whole number of inhabitants of every age, sex, and condition, including those bound to servitude for a term of years, and three-fifths of all other persons not comprehended in the foregoing description, except Indians, not paying taxes, in each State."

I will not weary the attention of the Committee, by reading all the references I have made to this volume, the Journal of the Federal Convention, with a view to the development of its course, in relation to these resolutions.

After passing and repassing through various Select Committees, and being frequently debated in Committee of the Whole, the proposition having assumed the shape in which it now stands in the Federal Constitution, was apparently settled on the 11th and 12th of July, by a vote of seven States to three, against striking out the "three-fifths" of the slave population. Had this motion prevailed, it would have caused *all* the slave population to be counted, as Delaware at first, and South Carolina and Georgia to the last, perseveringly insisted. By a motion on the second of those days, the attempt was renewed to produce this result, when Maryland, Virginia, and North Carolina, voted once more *against*, and South Carolina and Georgia, *for* computing the entire slave population.

What now becomes of so much of the authority relied upon by the gentleman from Chesterfield, as was derived from the suppos tion that the principle of computing three-fifths of the slave population, made part of the articles of Confederation; that, the slave-holding States were united in its support in the Federal Convention; and that it carried such conviction, to every mind, that it was interpolated in the new Constitution without resistance? The pages of this volume, [the Journals of the the Convention,] from the 75th to the 161st, manifest the contrary. The love of power did not, then, tempt Virginia to consider her slaves as parties to her social compact—as persons and not property. And is she, now, prepared to go to Washington, or to Boston, to learn the civil and political condition of the population, within her own limits? Whether it shall be regarded in her own councils, as property, or as a "peasantry," fitted to rank with "the free people of the West?" to use the language of the gentleman from Chesterfield (Mr. Leigh.)

Sir, said Mr. Mercer, is not the slave under our laws, as much an instrument in the hands of his master, as the wagon and team of the mountaineer? True, his life is protected from violence and his person from cruelty. So does the common law of England, which is ours, protect the horse and the ox from wanton injury. But the slave, like either, is by our law, mere property: and, as such, may be to-morrow shipped by his master to Cuba, or to Brazil. He may be smuggled into the United States from Africa, in violation of law, and exported again as an article of merchandize; having a known value in the market, and being the subject of frequent and profitable speculation. I speak not of the reason of the law, but of the legal fact.

Do not those who apprehend most danger to this species of property, from innovation, consider the slave as property, the *subject* of our social compact, not a *party* to it? What said New Jersey, to the Confederation, in the war of the revolution? "That slaves should be brought into the account," in the "requisition for land forces" to be supplied by the States, to the defence of the Union. She sustained this demand, by reasons, at least, as specious as those which we have just heard, for making this particular property the basis of representation. "Should it be improper, for special, local reasons, to admit them in arms for the defence of the nation, yet we conceive," says their memorial, "that the proportion of forces to be embodied ought to be fixed according to the whole number of inhabitants in the State, from whatever class they may be raised. If the whole number of inhabitants in a State, whose inhabitants are all *whites*, both those who are called into the field, and those who remain to till the ground and labor in mechanical arts, are estimated in striking the proportion of forces to be furnished by that State, ought even a part of the latter description to be left out in another? As it is of indispensable necessity in every war, that a part of the inhabitants be employed for the uses of husbandry and otherwise at home, while others are called into the field, there must be the same propriety that persons of a different colour, who are employed for this purpose in one State, while whites are employed for the same purpose in another, be reckoned in the account of the inhabitants." The prayer of this memorial received, in 1778, the sanction of three States, while one was divided, and six voted against it.

The argument of New Jersey in favor of a computation of slaves in distributing the personal burthens of a common war, bears a striking resemblance to that which the member from Chesterfield has so forcibly urged on the present occasion, and sustained by a comparison of the "peasantry" of the West, with the slaves of the East.

The answer to both arguments is the same. That, however regarded *elsewhere*, slaves, in Virginia, are considered as property, and property only. But if, as property, they are exempted, at the expense of the community, from obligations which would be onerous, not upon themselves, but their master; so as property merely, should they *not* add to the weight of a political power, of which they cannot and should not directly partake; and which is claimed for his benefit alone, to the public injury.

If, therefore, the Constitution of the United States has supplied a different rule, it should be remembered that it was founded in a compromise of principles, for the sake of uniting States, otherwise sovereign and independent, by a National Government of limited power. Its introduction, even there, as a principle of representation, was evidently founded on its prior assumption, by a majority of the Congress of the Confederation, as a principle of pecuniary contribution among the States. It is a price paid, by the small States, for their equality of power, in the Senate; and has long ceased, as was early anticipated, to be any security to the property it is supposed to have been originally designed to protect from unequal taxation. In the last House of Representatives, the proportion of the members from the slave-holding, to those from the non-slave-holding States, was 91 to 122. How that ratio will be augmented by the approaching Census, I need not intimate to the Committee.

At this point of my argument, it is proper, to allay the apprehension which has so often been expressed in this debate, that, to adopt the basis of representation recommended by the Legislative Committee for our State Government, would put to hazard that portion of representation, in the Federal Legislature, derived from a computation of three-fifths of the slaves of the Commonwealth.

This attempt upon our fears would seem to imply, that representation, under our present State Government, is founded, in part, on a computation of slaves. That of the Senate we know to have been apportioned in 1817, as nearly as practicable, to the free white population of the State; a concession, compatible with the existing Constitution, because made under it, and paid for, by doubling the land-tax of one portion of the State, and proportionably reducing that of another.

The origin of the House of Delegates was ably developed in an early stage of this debate, by my learned friend from Brooke, (Mr. Doddridge.) In the work of a venerable member of this Convention, "Marshall on the Colonies," it will be seen that the first representation of the people of this Commonwealth was of "settlements," then seven in number. The Assembly which their delegates formed was called the "House of Burgesses," from the names of those settlements, as Elizabeth City, James City, Charles City, which names, by a singular adherence to usage, they retained, as they now do, after those settlements were, for judicial purposes, erected into counties.

Representation in the House of Burgesses, therefore, preceded the existence of counties, as the counties did the existence of slavery; for that calamity was introduced among us by the Dutch, after the origin of county representation; that representation which has ever since existed in the House of Delegates.

In the Constitution of this branch of the General Assembly, therefore, slavery forms no original feature, and to change its foundation by an amendment, which shall derive its effect from periodical enumerations of the people, could expose the State to no loss of power in the councils of the Union.

If otherwise, what may be said of that very amendment for which these gentlemen have so zealously contended, and which proposes the mixed basis of *white* population and taxation? Would not this basis, unless explained by their arguments, be obnoxious to the very same fears which they labour to awaken? Unless indeed, if it prevail, their argument shall go abroad as a part of the Constitution itself.

But if our examples shall endanger a political influence, which some gentleman compute at 2-11ths of our present weight in Congress, and others, more correctly, at seven out of the twenty-two members, we have at present in the House of Representatives, what shall be said of that, which is supplied, by so many other States, interested like us, and some of them more deeply, in retaining this feature of our Federal Representation? Why has no slave-holding State, save Georgia alone, engrafted this principle on her Constitution of Government? Neither Louisiana, whose climate and productions approach so near the tropical sun, which has stained the complexion of Africa, nor Missouri, who formed her Constitution, amidst a moral and political excitement which might have excused such alarm, have felt its influence.

And if there is any truth in the origin of it, on the present occasion, why let me ask, did not the Hartford Convention, when it sought to exact a surrender of this power, from our fear of disunion, appeal to the example of every slave-holding State, except Georgia, to enforce their pretensions?

We have, Mr. Chairman, in truth, a substantial, and trusting as I do, to the obligation of solemn compacts, though recorded on mere parchment, a permanent safe-guard, for this portion of our political weight, which, though I deplore its origin, I neither deprecate, nor am prepared to yield, to any claims, whatever. This safe-guard is to be found, in that provision of the Constitution which, without naming expressly, confers this power, and in another clause of the same instrument, which provides that no alteration or amendment of it, shall take effect, unless with the sanction of three-fourths of the States.

To propose an amendment, which shall deprive Virginia of this power through the National Legislature, will require, by this clause, the concurrence of two-thirds of both branches of that body: and in one of them the slave-holding States have, now, inclusive of Delaware, twenty-four out of forty-eight members.

But it is, to the sanction, required of the States themselves, to any change of the Constitution, that I look, with absolute confidence for the preservation of this power.

At present any seven of the twelve slave-holding States could defeat any amendment which threatened its existence.

Looking forward to the admission of the territories of Florida, Arkansas and Michigan into the Union, I see this security confirmed by the addition of two slave-holding States, making the total number fourteen, exclusive of Delaware, which I do not count, because she is not likely long to continue of that number. Glancing to a futurity much more remote, and allowing for two additional States to the North of Illinois and Missouri, still the ratio between the number of the slave-holding and non-slave-holding States will be as fourteen to fifteen. If, in the madness of future conquest, for I never desired the annexation of Canada, to this Union, the whole North American provinces of the British Empire shall fall to our lot, and Upper and Lower Canada supply two States, in addition to Nova Scotia and New Brunswick, the proportion will be not less than fourteen to nineteen, and nine States of the fourteen, may prevent any change of the Constitution prejudicial to the rights and interests of the holders of this property. Let the Union, therefore, be extended, from Florida, to the northernmost limits of our continent—Let the States who compose it, be animated by what policy they may, a combination among them, to the prejudice of the political power of the South, so far as it rests on the principles of the present Constitution, can never be availing while that Constitution remains inviolate. The resources of the common Government may be applied to mitigate the evils of slavery by the aid of colonization, but its power can never be applied to endanger the peace of those who suffer from its existence. While the *number* of slaves, to the South, forbids their emancipation, without their consequent removal from the Commonwealth, no wise man can desire *its* augmentation. Whether it can be reduced in a mode consistent with the claims of justice and humanity, we are not now called upon to decide. I am on this subject no enthusiast; I look ever to the attainment of just ends by expedient means. These I am ready to discuss on any suitable occasion, in a temper to make every allowance for the rights of private judgment in others, and with a solicitude, which no consideration can sway, for the peace and happiness of the Commonwealth.

The eloquent member from Hanover, (Mr. Morris) in his fervid address to the Committee, acknowledged that he entertained no apprehension of sudden emancipation from any change of the present Constitution. Let my honorable friend then, and I apply this language to him, in the sincerity of a heart that never forgot a benefit, return to its scabbard the bloody sword which his fancy drew in the close of his animated and able speech. Having no terrors for him, it has none for me—The property of the master will be secured by the sad necessity from which it derives its existence. No gentleman has proposed that slaves shall be numerically represented. As property, is it better entitled to representation than any other estate in the Commonwealth? If so, on what is that title founded? Their value? Why not compute lands or horses? This argument I have already considered in relation to the amendment, by which it was proposed to combine taxation with population as a basis of representation. Were values to be regarded as a basis of representation, should we not compute the mineral treasures of the mountains of Virginia, which though latent, await but the hand of enterprise, to develope their extent, and to fit them for human use? As well might a British statesman propose to augment in the Parliament of that country, the representation of South Wales, whose naked mountains, barren in surface, as the Highlands of Scotland, have begun since the commencement of the present century to contribute to the wealth of Great Britain, as ample stores as the richest counties of England.

Before I leave the inquiry, whether slaves should be admitted to representation, regarded either as persons or property, an authority confidently urged by the gentleman from Chesterfield, remains to be considered—the fifty-fourth number of the Federalist, or the letters of Publius, addressed to the American people after the formation, and prior to the adoption of the Constitution.

While he should ever entertain not only the most profound, but the most grateful respect for the very eminent authors of that work, and regard the work itself, as a rich depository of political science, and an honor to American literature, it is proper to remark, that it was, in its character, controversial.

He who studies it with attention, will perceive that it is not only argumentative, but that it addresses different arguments to different classes of the American public, in the spirit of an able and skilful disputant before a mixed assembly. Thus, from different numbers of this work, and sometimes from the same number, may be derived authorities for opposite principles and opinions. For example, nothing is easier than to demonstrate by the numbers of Publius, that the Government, which it was written not to expound merely, but to recommend to the people, is, or is not a National Government; that the several State Legislatures may arraign at their respective bars, the conduct of the Federal Government, or that no State has any such power. I have in debate used this work for some one of these and other purposes, while my adversary has met me with passages from it alike genuine, which overturned my positions.

The authors undertook to defend every part of a Constitution, to which two of them at least, had in the Convention offered amendments that were rejected, and the whole of the numerous articles, of which, no man in America, of independent judgment, then approved. It was the offspring of mutual concessions, of compromise.

With these preliminary reflections on this very able work, which I trust will be regarded as compatible with the veneration and gratitude I cherish for its authors, I beg leave to turn the attention of the Committee to the particular number, quoted as authority by the member from Chesterfield, to prove not that three-fifths of the slaves of the several States are computed as a part of the basis of representation in the House of Representatives, but that, of right they should be so computed.

"The next view," says the author of this number, who appears in the volume I have, to have been Mr. Hamilton, "which I shall take of the House of Representatives, relates to the apportionment of its members among the several States, which is to be determined by the same rule with that of *direct* taxes." In the succeeding clause, the author, who had both in the Old Congress voted against this rule, and in the Convention submitted a different one, qualifies the approbation of the rule which his present purpose requires him to sustain, by a peculiar form of expression. "It is not contended," he says, "that the *number* of people in each State *ought not to be the standard* for regulating the proportion of those who are to *represent the people* of each State." He does not, therefore, impugn the identical principle for which we at present contend; and which, on another occasion, he had maintained. He proceeds as follows: "The establishment of the same rule," that of the Constitution, "for the apportionment of taxes," will be as little "contested; though the rule itself in this case," that is as to taxes, "is *by no means, founded on the same principles*. In the former case, the rule is understood to refer to the *personal rights* of the people, with which it has a *natural and universal* connexion. In the latter, it has reference to the proportion of wealth, of which it is, *in no case*, a precise *measure*, and in ordinary cases a *very unfit* one. But notwithstanding the *imperfection* of the rule, as applied to the relative wealth and contributions of the States, it is evidently *the least exceptionable among those that are practicable;*" and he adds, what the Journals of the Convention, now published, as well as the antecedent conduct of Rhode Island, New York, and Virginia, must be allowed at least to qualify to some extent, "that it had too recently obtained the general sanction of America, not to have found a ready preference with the Convention."

In another part of the same essay—"It is agreed," says the author, "*on all sides*, that *numbers* are the best scale of wealth and taxation, as they are the *only proper scale of representation*." The last is the doctrine for which the advocates of the resolution contend, against the doctrine of the amendment, which would found *representation* on *numbers* and *taxation* combined.

[Mr. Leigh rose and said, the gentleman would much oblige him by stating who was the author.]

Mr. Mercer said, the paper which he had read, had prefixed to it the name of Mr. Hamilton.

[Mr. Doddridge rose and said, that the paper from which the extract had been read, was attributed in some of the editions of the Federalist, to Mr. Jay.]

[Mr. Madison then rose and said, that although he was not desirous to take part in this discussion, yet under all the circumstances he was, perhaps, called on to state, that the paper in question was not written by Mr. Hamilton or Mr. Jay, but by the third person connected with that work.]

Mr. Mercer said, this volume, the third of an edition of "Hamilton's Works," the editor of which he supposed had derived his key to the names of the authors of Publius from a manuscript of Mr. Hamilton which he saw many years ago, in the possession of the late Richard Stockton, an eminent statesman of New-Jersey, would constitute, he hoped, an apology for the error into which, in common with many editors of this work, he had been betrayed; as he now perceived that the number of Publius, which he had quoted, was the work of a distinguished member of this Convention.

Although not able to avail himself of this paper, for the precise purpose which he had proposed, he was glad it came from such a source; from the venerable Chairman of the Legislative Committee, who had already yielded his support to the resolution in debate.

For the opinions expressed by Mr. Hamilton, the author of more than a moiety of these very able essays, in relation to the present topic of inquiry, Mr. M. said he would refer this Committee, not only to his votes in the Congress which preceded, as well as the Convention which made the Constitution, but to a prior number of those admirable essays written in favour of its adoption, and which bears his name.

"The right of equal suffrage among the States," Mr. Hamilton says in the 22d number, "is another exceptionable part of the Confederation. Every idea of proportion, and every rule of fair representation, conspire to condemn a principle, which gives to Rhode Island an equal weight in the scale of power with Massachusetts, or Connecticut, or New-York; and to Delaware an equal voice in the national deliberations, with Pennsylvania, or Virginia, or North Carolina. Its operation contradicts the *fundamental maxim of Republican Government*, which requires that the *sense of a majority should prevail*." The conformity of this language to that of the friends of equal representation in this Convention, is too apparent to need any other proof of it, than would arise from substituting the county of Warwick for "Delaware," and Frederick, or Loudoun, for "Pennsylvania," or "New-York." How far the answer to this reasoning, which Mr. Hamilton puts in the mouths of his adversaries, speaks the language of our opponents, I leave it to the Committee to judge.

"Sophistry," says Mr. Hamilton, "may reply that sovereigns are equal, and that a majority of the votes of the States, will be a majority of confederated America."

For the words "sovereigns," and "State," I have only to insert the word "counties," in behalf of those who desire no change of the present Constitution, and for "confederated America," the people of Virginia.

I close this quotation with Mr. Hamilton's rejoinder, which needs no commentary. "But this kind of logical legerdemain," he adds, "will never counteract the plain suggestions of justice and common sense. It may happen that a majority of States is a small minority of the people of America, and two-thirds of the people of America could not long be persuaded upon the credit of *artificial distinctions* and *syllogistic subtleties*, to submit their *interests* to the management and disposal of one-third. The larger States would, after a while, revolt from receiving the law, from the smaller. To acquiesce in such a privation of their due importance in the political scale, would be, not merely to be insensible to the love of power, but even *to sacrifice the desire of equality*. It is neither rational to expect the first, nor *just to require* the last. Considering how peculiarly the safety and welfare of the smaller States depend on union, they ought readily to renounce a pretension, which, if not relinquished, would prove fatal to its duration."

The Committee will readily excuse my substitution of the words of this able and eloquent writer, for any language that I could invent to express the same ideas. Such a course is the more expedient for my purpose, since it affirms all the truths which I labour to sustain, by the appeal of a statesman and patriot of the revolution to the people of America, in support of the principles, for which he had contended, as well in arms, as in council.

That he did not, any more than his equally patriotic associates, confound taxation with representation, as has been so often done in the course of this debate, a passage, which I beg leave to offer to the Committee from the preceding number of this able work, sufficiently manifests.

"The principle," says he, "of regulating the contributions of the States, to the common treasury, by quotas, is another fundamental error of the Confederacy." "I speak of it now, solely with a view to *equality* among the States." By *equality*, it will be seen, that he does not mean the payment of equal sums, by equal numbers, but in *equal*, or just proportion to the respective abilities of those who are required to pay them for the common benefit of all. "Those who have been accustomed to contemplate the circumstances, which produce and constitute national wealth, must be satisfied that there is no *common standard*, or barometer, by which, the degrees of it can be ascertained.—Neither the *value of the lands* nor the *numbers of the people*, which have been successively proposed, as the rule of State contributions, *has any pretension to being* a just representative." "Let Virginia be contrasted with North Carolina, or Maryland with New-Jersey, and we shall be convinced that the respective *abilities of those States*, in relation to revenue, bear little or no analogy to their comparative stock in lands, or to their comparative population. The position may be equally illustrated, by a similar process between the counties of the same State. No man acquainted with the State of New-York, will doubt, that the active wealth of King's county bears a much greater proportion to that of Montgomery, than it would appear to do, if we should take either the total value of the lands or the total numbers of the people as a criterion.

"The wealth of nations depends upon an infinite variety of causes. Situation, soil, climate; the nature of the productions; the nature of the Government; the genius of the citizens; the degree of information they possess; the state of commerce, of arts, of industry; these circumstances, and many more too complex, minute, or adventitious, to admit of a particular specification, occasion differences hardly conceivable in the relative opulence and riches of different counties. The consequence is, that there can be no common measure of national wealth; and, of course, no general or stationary rule by which the *ability* of a State to pay taxes can be determined. The attempt, therefore, to regulate the contributions of the members of a Confederacy, by any such rule, cannot fail to be productive of *glaring inequality and extreme oppression*.

"There is no method of steering clear of this inconvenience, but by authorising the National Government to raise its own revenues in its own way.

"It is a signal advantage of taxes on articles of consumption, that they contain in their own nature a security against excess. They prescribe their own limit; which cannot be exceeded without defeating the end proposed—that is, an extension of the revenue. When applied to this object, the saying is as just as it is witty, that 'in political arithmetic, two and two do not always make four.'"

May I not now affirm, without a presumptuous impeachment of the authority of the able authors of this vindication of the Federal Constitution, that whatever concessions it may contain of expediency or justice, to the Union of the States, they have not sanctioned the doctrines of our adversaries: that slaves are regarded as property by *our* laws, and as such have no other title to representation, than any other description of property in the Commonwealth.

The resolution, which I have undertaken to sustain, alike excludes a representation of counties. Such is the present representation in the House of Delegates, and its glaring inequality is one of the leading causes of this Convention. Although no voice has been heard in this Committee to vindicate this inequality, and the proposed amendment is as much at war with its continuance as the resolution itself, yet those who are opposed to any change of the present Constitution must be regarded as disposed to tolerate, and bound to defend it. It is equally incumbent on the advocates of the resolution to advert to its extent, and its operation on the principles for which the friends of a Convention have contended.

There are at present in this Commonwealth, 105 counties, entitled each to two Delegates, and four boroughs, having by law separate representation, entitled each to one Delegate. The House of Delegates consists, at present, therefore, of 214 members, of which 108 are a majority. Fifty-four of the counties of Virginia may, therefore, return such a majority. Omitting with all the boroughs, Williamsburg having a population of only 536 white inhabitants, and the small counties of Logan, Alleghany, and Pocahontas, which have been created since the last Census, this majority may be supplied by 180,000 of the 603,000 white inhabitants of the Commonwealth. It follows, therefore, that a minority of much less than a third of the people of Virginia, may govern the other two-thirds.

Of the thirty-nine counties below the Blue Ridge, selected to make this proportion, five have fewer than 2,000 white inhabitants, each; one has but 620, and another but 1,017.

Of the fifteen beyond that mountain, which I have added to the former, the smallest has a white population of very near 1,800, and that is the only one which has a white population below 2,000 in number.

In addition to the six counties having each less than 2,000 white inhabitants, there are eleven counties, whose population is known, which have between 2 and 3,000 only, and of these, there are but two West of the Blue Ridge.

On the other hand, there are thirteen counties, which have each more than 10,000 white inhabitants, of which, all but one, lie either West, or on the Eastern face of that mountain; and, of those, three, having each more than 16,000, lie connected together.

Similar inequalities, it has been urged by some of our opponents, exist without complaint, in the neighbouring States of Maryland and North Carolina, which have, like Virginia, equal county representation.

Neither position is true. Complaints of unequal representation, have been made in both these States, without effect, because the foundation of them, bears no proportion to the inequality for which we are assembled to provide.

Maryland has nineteen counties, the largest of which, Frederick, contains a few more than 40,000 inhabitants, of every description; and the smallest, Calvert, a few more than 8,000. The proportion being of five to one, on the whole population, and rather more than eight to one, if their white population alone, be computed.

North Carolina has sixty-two counties. Rowan, the largest, has 26,000 inhabitants, and Washington, the least, very near 4,000: The proportion being about six and a half to one, and if the white population be separately computed, 21,000 to 2,300, or about nine to one. While we have seen that the total population of the largest county of Virginia, was, to the least, as far back as 1820, in the ratio exceeding fifteen to one, and computing the white population alone, of twenty-six to one.

There is not a man within the sound of my voice, said Mr. M. nor would there be one who merited the appellation, could I be heard by the people of America, who would consent to be degraded by the application of such a scale of political power, to his own rights in comparison with those of his neighbour.

In one branch of the Legislature, a similar inequality was redressed in 1817, by a new arrangement of the Senatorial districts, on the basis of white population. At that time, four members, of a body consisting of twenty-four, represented two-fifths of the entire population of the State, and might have been outvoted by the representation of a twelfth. The evil called aloud for redress, and it was redressed in the manner, in which we now ask to have remedied a similar inequality in the other branch of the General Assembly. I was one of those who retired from this Hall in 1817, prepared to await the developement of the new distribution of the Senate, and acquiescing in the existing state of affairs. The arrival of a period of profound tranquillity among the parties which had divided, not Virginia, but the Union, (for a mere contest for the Presidency, could give rise to but transient excitement,)—a contest, in which for several years, he had felt scarcely interest enough to carry him to the polls, had prompted him to unite with his fellow-citizens, in endeavouring to amend the defects of their common Government.

Having disposed of the mixed basis of taxation and white population, of slave and free population, regarding, as he proceeded, the claim of the former to consideration, both as persons and as property; and exposed the inequality of county representation, he came now to an examination of the only remaining basis, or that which had been adopted and recommended to the Convention by the Legislative Committee—the numbers of the free white population exclusively, and that, with a view to give to equal numbers, equal portions of political power in the constitution of the popular branch of the Government.

A proposition had, indeed, been submitted to the Convention, by his eloquent friend from Norfolk, in the form of an amendment of the Bill of Rights, which asserted that equal numbers of legal voters throughout the Commonwealth, should have equal political power, without regard to the distinction of fortune. As such a proposition might be regarded as of a different character from that contained in the resolution of the Legislative Committee, Mr. M. said he would, as the incipient step towards the conclusion he was desirous to reach, undertake to shew their practical if not theoretical conformity. Whatever extent may be given to the right of suffrage, the only important distinction between these propositions will be found to consist in the superior facility of executing that which requires, simply, a periodical enumeration of the white population of the Commonwealth. To compute all the legal voters of the Commonwealth, supposing the extension of suffrage to be built upon the present freehold qualification, enlarged by the admission of other classes of citizens, not freeholders, to the same pivilege, would require the enumeration of all classes. If that labour be regarded in relation to the freeholders alone, it is not difficult to conceive its magnitude and the delays which must attend its execution.

In a computation of legal voters, instead of active agents, competent, at little cost, to take a Census of the people, learned Justices in Eyre must be provided in sufficient number to traverse every county, city, borough, or election district in the Commonwealth, in order to enquire who have freehold estates, and have been so seized for the period required by law. If to these, be added, the cases of constructive freeholds, and of tenants in common, whose names may not, and often do not, appear on the Commissioners' lists, and should claimants in reversion and remainder, of vested or contingent freeholds be empowered to vote, as some gentlemen propose, many years would elapse in making the necesssary enumeration and lists for the apportionment of Delegates. Nor would this painful and costly, if not impracticable labour, lead to a different result from that of the Census of the free white population, as we have good grounds to infer under any extension of suffrage. The more enlarged it may be, the more nearly will the numbers of those who are legal voters, approach the number of that population. But if restricted to landed qualification, or extended to all who pay taxes on moveable property, still the apportionment to white population will very nearly, if not exactly, conform to that which might be founded on a computation of the number of votes.

As evidence of this, Mr. M. referred to three of the tables lately supplied by the Auditor of Public Accounts.

To the first of these, that which professed to deduce white population of 1829, in the several counties, from the number of titheables voluntarily returned to that officer, at his request, Mr. M. could not yield implicit confidence. Indefatigable, faithful and intelligent as he knew that officer to be, he could not do more than use the materials supplied him. Mr. M. had seen that, in the district which he in part represented, one immediately below the Blue Ridge, intersected by three of the most extensive turnpikes in the Commonwealth, and having more of that description of improvement within it, constructed by individual enterprise, than is to be found in all the rest of the Commonwealth put together; this table manifested a reduction in nine years of the entire population of 1820, by 5,384 souls: a fact which he most confidently believed to be untrue. He would undertake to say that the county of Loudoun had, in that period, sustained no loss of white population, and Fairfax very little, if any. Another error, of almost equal extent, had occurred in the same statement, in adding to the population of Augusta a number equal to that which had been taken from Loudoun. Abandoning the conclusions to be drawn from a table, so inaccurate, Mr. Mercer said he would go back to the Census of 1820, in which he discovered that the white population West of the Blue Ridge bore very nearly the same ratio to the white population below that mountain, that the number of persons in the one territory charged on the land-books of 1826 with taxes on a quantity of land not less than twenty-five acres, or on a lot or part of a lot in a town established by law, bore to the same description of persons in the other? The first ratio being nearly that of 25 to 35, and the second that of 37 to 53: While the third table reported the number of persons, West of the same mountain, who are charged with a State tax on moveable property for the year 1828, to be 40,079: and the number of persons, East of it, charged in the same year, with the same tax, to be 55,514.

This ratio may be expressed with sufficient accuracy, by 40 to 55, and corresponds so nearly with that of 37 to 53, the ratio of the proprietors of lands and lots, in *these two districts*, and of 25 to 35, that of the white population of the same districts, that with little error, a common measure may be assumed for these three proportions. That measure would express both the relative proportion of the white population above and below this natural division of the Commonwealth, and of the legal voters of the same districts. Inferring from the identity of these three proportions, between the free inhabitants and the proprietors of real and moveable property in these extensive territories of the Commonwealth, the like identity throughout their minute sub-divisions, I shall consider myself, in the sequel of my argument, as sustaining, at the same time, the position of my friend from Norfolk, and that of the Legislative Committee.

In entering upon the last which I propose to consider, but by far, the most important enquiry, of the many, which have arisen in the progress of this debate, into "the right of the majority of any society to govern it," I find myself embarrassed, by the very simplicity of the truth, I have to maintain. What is obscure, may be explained; what is perplexed, disentangled: error may be detected, and falsehood exposed. But the mind is surprised, by the denial of a principle universally admitted, and at a loss to prove, what, for ages, no one has had the singularity, or the temerity, to question.

We are, however told, that there are no principles to be admitted any longer; that none in fact exist; and that whatever proposition we advance, as the basis of our reasoning, must be proved.

The natural equality of man is written on his heart and stamped upon his visage by the author of his being, after whose "express image" he was made.

While other animals look to the earth;

Os homini sublime dedit ad sidera tollere vultus,—

His rights spring from his affections and his wants, and these he derived from God, the author of his nature. He cannot exist out of society, because society is essential to his existence. His first relations are those of husband and father. That period, which in other animals is short, of dependence on a parent's care, is in man protracted for purposes the most beneficent. The infant gathers his first instruction in his mother's lap. His best virtues he imbibes from a father's care, a mother's tenderness. When age overcomes the parent, the son re-pays with kindness, the kindness he has received. If the crutch drops from the feeble grasp of his sire, he picks it up and restores it to his trembling hand. Patriotism is but filial love enlarged. When we think of our country, we dwell on the memory of our early years, on the forms of those who gave us our being and watched over its imbecility. When they are gone, we visit their remains, and from the unconscious dead imbibe anew the inspiration of their virtues. Does not the savage cherish these affections? The Tartar wanders over the interminable plains of Asia from climate to climate, accompanied by his flocks and herds; the Indian of America roams through forests, yet more wild. But they re-visit the tombs of their progenitors, and recount to their children the story of their deeds.

Are not these natural affections at the foundation of all the moral rights and duties of man?

Sympathy, is it not as natural to man as to the gregarious animals whom he gathers around him? Out of these feelings, spring the elements of society.

Is there no property known to savage life? Even the bird defends her nest, as the lion does his den, the former with less vigor, but with equal zeal. The hunter decorates his cave with the fur of the animals he has killed; and stores away, in time of plenty, the provisions which a season of want may require. He has his bow and arrows for the mountain deer, and when he approaches the water side, his canoe and spear for the finny tribe. In contempt of danger, he traverses the land and the water under the influence of the same feelings which prompt the civilized man to build permanent habitations, to till the land, and to lay up the fruits of autumn for the necessities of winter. How can labour and property be separated? Property is at once the fruit and the spring of labour. The author of the Essay on the Human Understanding, in his treatise on Civil Government, tells us emphatically, that he means, "*by property*," to denote "the life, liberty, and all the possessions of man."

I own that I was shocked, said Mr. M. when on opening the grammar of the law, I first met the phrase "Rights *of* things." Of Rights *to* things, I could readily conceive. Though things are external to man, and may be detached from him, yet the right to them is inseparably connected with his natural as well as social condition, and is, as personal, as his right to locomotion, the exercise of which, supposes a control over the objects around, and consequently without himself.

If it be contended that this early condition of man is not a state of nature, but of society, I am content, since it is one in which he is not bound to acknowledge a superior right, in another, to control his conduct.

The existence of the rights which he enjoys, supposes a correspondent obligation, on his part, to respect the similar rights of others; and hence the equality of right common to all.

The insecurity and inconvenience attendant on such a state of existence, would render it of transient duration; and nature who has given faculties to man which are susceptible of improvement, and made their exercise conducive to his happiness, cannot be supposed to have designed his continuance in a state unfitted for their cultivation.

It is a condition, however, in which, not Locke only, but all moral, and nearly all political writers, have supposed man to exist, for the sake of establishing, by the light of reason, his moral as well as his political rights and obligations. Upon the same basis rest the treatises that have been made upon the law of nature and of nations, which is but the just practical application, to sovereign States, of those rules which appertain to the relations of man in a state of nature. Vattel founds his code of international law, on the philosophy of Wolfius; and deduces the equality of States, from the same source from which Locke inferred the natural freedom and independence of man.

I trust I shall be pardoned for saying, that I have been alarmed, as well as shocked, at the levity with which the great apostle of English liberty and his doctrines have been treated by the greater part of our adversaries in this debate.

They reproach us with deriding the wisdom of past ages, in the pursuit of novel doctrines, while they claim, for themselves, to be wiser than their fathers who studied with veneration the political philosophy of Locke, and embodied its maxims in their Constitutions of Government.

He wrote, it seems, a Constitution for Carolina, and borrowed for his titular distinctions, terms of American and German origin—"Caciques and Landgraves." Names then are things; and the queen of flowers is less sweet, if not called, the rose. Locke cherished and sustained the great principles of liberty, by defending, as Milton, against the same foe, the infamous house of Stuart, the liberty of his countrymen, to frame what Government they pleased. That his enemies in England, as well as Scotland, were at that time neither few nor impotent, was manifested in the succeeding century by two rebellions. It is remarkable that his cotemporary and antagonist, Sir Robert Filmer, assailed the foundation of all his reasoning—the maxim, that all men are by nature and by birth *equally free*, with the same argument in behalf of the divine right of kings, that we have just heard used, not indeed for the same purpose, but in opposition to the same doctrine of natural liberty, which we infer from the Bill of Rights prefixed to our State Constitution. The ingenious member from Northampton (Mr. Upshur) used for this purpose one of Filmer's cases. Ascending to the creation of man, he historically proved, that our first parents formed the earliest human society of which there is any record, and he asked emphatically, if the doctrine of the natural equality of man be true, *when* Cain became equal to Adam, his father? "If it was at 10, at 15, or 30 years of age." I use the very words of the interrogation. In the language of Locke, I reply to it; *when Cain*, having arrived at maturity, no longer depended on his father for subsistence and protection; and the children, also, of Abel, when they sustained the wants and soothed the infirmity of their aged grandsire.

The gentleman from Chesterfield, following the example of the gentleman from Northampton, whose argument he applauded, has cast away Cocker, as well as Locke, and taken up with Robinson Crusoe and De Foe, as *his* authorities. "Robinson Crusoe," it seems, "saved Friday's life, and bound his heart to him:" "he gave Friday bread, and bound to him his body." I have heard of slavery, arising from the rights of conquest, and if my memory does not err, Grotius, I think, infers its legality from the power of the victor, to slay his enemy. But I never before heard this doctrine deduced from the rights of humanity and the obligation of gratitude.

"Robinson Crusoe gave Friday bread." They lived alone, but had commerce, introduced arts and money on their island, Friday might justly have claimed, for his labor, more than his bread: and if he preferred any other master, or to cease from labor, I know not the law, human or divine, which would have held him in subjection.

If, along with these two islanders, ninety-nine other men had settled and formed one society, Friday would have been as free as Robinson Crusoe himself.

Not one of these settlers would have been bound, by any will but his own, to form, or when formed by others, to remain in this society; but having made it, the majority of its members, until some other rule were provided, would of necessity govern it, as our majority does the proceedings of this body. So is governed every other body constituted like it, that is, without having a different rule prescribed for its government, by higher authority. We know none, except that of God, higher than the power of a Convention of the people, which is the power of the people themselves.

We have adopted the rules of the House of Delegates to regulate our proceedings; but we were not bound to choose these, any more than the rules of the House of Representatives of the United States, or of the Legislature of any of the individual States. We might have taken those of Massachusetts, or of Georgia. We might have required a majority of two-thirds to the decision of any question; for the election of a President, or of a Select Committee. But even the rule of two-thirds, absurd as it would be regarded, would derive its sanction from the will of a majority of this body. This doctrine is so interwoven in all our thoughts, habits of political action, and modes of judging, that to deny it, is to wound the common sense of every portion of the American people. Let us return, for a moment to the island of De Foe, and the newly formed society we left there. Suppose they desire to establish a political Government. To organize its Legislative, Judicial, and Executive Departments. Would they adopt any other rule of proceeding than by a majority? It has been contended that, in our Bill of Rights, the power of a majority to change the Constitution is limited to cases wherein the public good requires such change. But, who is to judge when the case occurs? The public good is made up of the good of all the individuals who compose the public. Each man judges for himself and the community, what is best, and the majority must consequently prevail, it being the majority of all the judgments so formed, and having the sanction of a majority for its execution. This sanction is, therefore, moral as well as physical. Suppose the settlers on the island of De Foe, to have brought their respective families with them, consisting of women and children. Count these or not, in the division by which the majority is ascertained, and the ratio is unchanged. For if, from any two numbers having a given proportion to each other, there be taken other numbers bearing to each other the same ratio, the former remains unaltered. And so will it be, if, in like proportion you augment those numbers. Women undoubtedly add to the physical force of society, and so do infants. I have voted in New Jersey, under a Constitution of Government, which does not exclude females from the right of suffrage. The Constitution has undergone no change in this State, but the society has. No woman votes, at present, because no lady will go to the polls.

Casuistry and sophistry may perplex the doctrine of the natural freedom and equality of man, and of the consequent right of the majority of society, already formed, to govern it, where no positive agreement has otherwise ordered; but the common sense of mankind will indicate their essential and natural rights.

The disorders of that Parisian mob, which overawed the deliberations of the constituted authorities of France, in the early stage of her late revolution, were the abuses of liberty, by mere brutal force, exerted against the principles by which its leaders professed to be guided.

The abuse of truth is no argument against its existence. What has not been abused? A cloud is now passing over the sun; but is that glorious luminary extinguished? The gospel of peace has been buried in superstition, after being shrouded in blood; but is our religion false? The most *precious things* are abused, and for the very reason that they are so. They interest the passions of man in the same degree that they are essential to his happiness.

Rejecting the authorities relied upon by the members from Northampton and from Chesterfield, I turn to others in favor of human liberty, which I deem more pertinent to my subject. Since the Bill of Rights prefixed to our own Constitution is deemed equivocal, in its language, by some of our opponents, and denied the validity of law, by others, I ask the indulgence of the Committee, while I look for authorities, less questionable, in the Constitutions of our sister States, to sustain the natural equality of man and the rights of a majority, or, in the language of my friend from Frederick, (Mr. Cooke,) who opened this debate, the *jus majoris.*

Before I consult the Constitutions of the New England States, I must be allowed to express to the gentleman from Orange, (Mr. P. P. Barbour) to whose lucid style of reasoning I always attend with pleasure, my surprise as well as regret, that he should have so highly complimented the political institutions of Massachusetts, and have, at the same time, denounced so unsparingly, those which have been planted "in the wilds of the west" by the emigrant decendants of this hardy race of freemen.

Ohio, Indiana and Illinois, are but swarms from the fruitful northern hive, as Kentucky, Tennessee, Alabama, and Mississippi, are descended from our own southern stock. As they have receded farther from our royal charters, and framed their institutions at greater leisure, with the advantages of the same experience and untrammelled by pre-existing disabilities, so they have carried out our principles with equal truth and greater simplicity.

But I will not offend the taste of any gentleman who may, however fastidiously, prefer the institutions of New England to those of the west.

Massachusetts formed her Constitution as our fathers did ours, in a period of war; but after expelling the enemy from her bosom: and the leisure with which she proceeded, is manifested by the time which she consumed in completing her labor, which was begun in September, 1779, and ended in March, 1780.

Her Declaration of Rights is expressly made a constituent part of her Constitution —and the first article of it affirms that

"All men are born free and equal, 'and have certain natural, essential, and unalienable rights,' among which, is that of seeking and obtaining their happiness."

The preamble sets forth " The end of the institution, maintenance and administration of Government to be—to secure the existence of the body politic, to protect it, and to furnish the individuals who compose it, with the power of enjoying in safety and tranquillity, their natural rights."

It asserts, that " The body is formed by a voluntary association of individuals. It is a social compact." And in the seventh article of the Declaration of Rights, these doctrines are repeated and fortified after a solemn assertion, that " Government is instituted for the protection, safety, prosperity and happiness of the people," by declaring that " the people alone have an incontestible, unalienable and indefeasible right to institute Government, and to reform, alter, or totally change the same"—and farther, that

" All elections ought to be free; and all the inhabitants of this Commonwealth, having such qualifications as they shall establish by their frame of Government, have an *equal right* to elect officers, and to be elected for public employments."

Article 10 asserts that, " Each individual of the society has a right to be protected by it, in the enjoyment of his life, liberty and property, according to the standing laws. He is obliged, consequently, to contribute his share to the expense of their protection, to give his personal service or an equivalent, when necessary." Here we see the origin of taxation. Its qualification comes next. " But no part of the property of an individual can with justice be taken from him, or applied to the public use, without his own consent, or that of the representative body of the people."

Again, we read—" The people have a right, in an orderly and peaceable manner, to assemble to consult upon the common good; give instructions to their representatives." How is such instruction to be given? By a representation of property? On the principles of a mixed basis, or by a majority of those authorised to give it? And if the majority of the voters may overrule the representative by instructions, what becomes of the supposed *majority of interests*, or of *property* in Legislation?

The Constitution of New Hampshire, as altered and amended by a Convention of Delegates in February, 1792, affirms in the first part of the first article, nearly in the language of Massachusetts, that " all men are born equally free and independent: *Therefore*, all government, of right, originates from the people, is founded *in consent* and instituted for the general good."

" Art. 2. All men have certain, natural, essential and inherent rights—among which are the enjoying and defending life and liberty: acquiring, possessing and protecting property: and in a word, of seeking and obtaining happiness.

" Art. 3. When men enter into a state of society, they surrender up some of their *natural rights*, to that society, in order to ensure the protection of others; and without such an equivalent, the surrender is void.

" Art 4. Among the natural rights, some are, in their very nature, unalienable, because no equivalent can be given or received for them. Of this kind are the rights of conscience.

" Art. 11. All elections ought to be free, and every inhabitant of the State, having the proper qualifications, has an equal right to elect and be elected into office."

The Constitution of Vermont was adopted July 4th, 1793.

The first chapter of the first article, declares:

" That all men are born equally free and independent, and have certain natural, inherent and unalienable rights, among which are the enjoying and defending life and liberty, acquiring, possessing and protecting property, and pursuing and obtaining happiness and safety."

The Charter of Rhode Island was granted by King Charles II. in the fourteenth year of his reign.

The inhabitants of this State are now, according to the argument of the gentleman from Chesterfield, in reply to that of my friend from Brooke, the subjects of George IV. since he contended, that if the Constitution of Virginia, be void, the people of Virginia are so; having, as he supposes, no other form of Government than that of their Royal Charter.

From this dilemma, however, if the Declaration of Independence did not relieve them, I presume the treaty of peace did, which ended the war of the revolution with the admission of that Independence, by the only nation that had an interest in denying it.

The Constitution of Connecticut also contains one of those silly instruments, called a Declaration of Rights. It begins, too, in a most exceptionable manner, for it uses in contradiction of all the arguments we have heard, to prove that there are no principles of Government, the following language as a preamble to its very first article:

" That the *great and essential principles* of liberty and free Government may be recognized and *established*—we (the people of Connecticut) declare—That all men, when they form a social compact, are equal in rights." What rights? Rights antecedent to the compact, I presume. " And that no man, or set of men, are entitled to exclusive public emoluments or privileges from the community." The following section of this article affirms, in the language of the Constitutions I have already noticed—"That all political power is inherent in the people, and all free Governments are founded on their authority, and instituted for their benefit: and that they have, *at all times*, an undeniable and indefeasible right to alter their form of Government, in such manner, as they may think expedient."

Both branches of the Legislature of this State, consist of members chosen annually, by the electors, who may be any white male citizen of the United States, above twenty-one years of age, having gained a settlement in the State, resided six months before the election at which he offers to vote in the town, in which such election is held, and shall have paid, if liable thereto, a State tax within the past year.

The Senate consists of twelve members, elected by the greatest number of votes of the whole people, or by a general ticket.

The Constitution of New York contains no Bill or Declaration of Rights; but it affords a practical exemplification of all the great maxims of natural liberty asserted by the States of New-England, from which the far greater part of her own population has been derived.

It establishes and appropriates certain taxes on salt, and certain auction duties, that then yielded the State more than half the annual revenue, but it allows no representation for either.

It establishes the right of suffrage on a very broad basis, requiring a freehold qualification only in persons of colour. The Senate which it creates, consists of thirty-two members, for the election of whom it divides the territory of the State into eight districts, with reference exclusively to the number of their inhabitants, to be ascertained by an enumeration to be made once in every ten years.

The Assembly consists of one hundred and twenty-eight members to be apportioned among the several counties of the State, according to the number of their respective inhabitants. It moreover provides, that every county heretofore established and separately organized, shall always be entitled to one member of the Assembly; but no new county shall hereafter be erected, unless its population shall entitle it to a member. This is rather an apparent than real, and at most but a transient qualification of equal representation as will be seen, by recurring to the actual population of the smallest county in this State, and comparing the extent of its fast peopling territory, with that of the oldest and most populous counties.

The Constitution of New Jersey was made while she recognized her Colonial dependence on Great Britain; and the only subsequent alteration of it has been effected by a law, substituting in its language, where the word "*Colony*" occurs, the word "State."

It is very nearly as ancient, as that of Virginia. But although ratified two days only, before the Declaration of Independence by Congress, it expressly provides that it shall be void in the event of a reconciliation with Great Britain. By her persevering struggle, through the calamities of the common war, waged in support of the principles, for which we now contend in debate—this gallant State, manifested the value, which she set on those principles, by her deeds, if not by the terms of her Constitution.

The Constitution of Pennsylvania made in 1790, is obnoxious both in its principles, and its details, to the criticism of all the gentlemen who have advocated the basis of taxation, and numbers, as the proper ground of representation. The 9th article, has the following remarkable preamble, "That the general, great and essential principles of liberty and free Government, may be *recognized and unalterably* established, we declare:

I. "That all men are *born equally* free and independent, and have certain *inherent and indefeasible* rights, among which, are those of enjoying and defending life and liberty; of acquiring and protecting property and reputation, and of pursuing their own happiness.

II. "That all power is inherent in the people, and all free Governments are founded on their authority, and instituted for their peace, safety and happiness. For the advancement of those ends, they have, at all times, an unalienable, and indefeasible right, to alter, reform, or abolish their Government, in such manner as they may think proper."

In giving effect to these principles, the Constitution of this State, provides that the number of representatives of the popular branch of her Legislature shall be apportioned according to the number of taxable inhabitants, without respect to the sum of tax paid by each, among the city of Philadelphia, and the several counties of the Commonwealth, in conformity with an examination to be made once in seven years.

The Senate consists of members to be chosen in districts, after a periodical apportionment to the number of taxable inhabitants in each district.

While the population of Philadelphia, is not denied its proportional weight in the Councils of Pennsylvania, no respect is paid to the superior wealth of that city, which yields a full moiety of the revenue of the State, in the shape of taxes.

To this State, belongs, moreover, the glory of having preceded Virginia, more than a century, in asserting the great principles of religious freedom.

The people of Delaware, the least State in the Union, fall not behind their more powerful fellow-citizens in asserting the natural rights of man, both civil, and religious.

In their Constitution made in 1792—"We," say the people of this Commonwealth, "hereby ordain and establish this Constitution of Government for the State of Delaware.

"Through divine goodness, all men have by nature the rights of worshipping and serving their Creator according to the dictates of their consciences, of enjoying and defending life and liberty, of acquiring and protecting reputation and property, and, in general, of attaining objects suitable to their condition, without injury by one to another; and as these rights are essential to their welfare, for the due exercise thereof, power is inherent in them; and, therefore, all just authority in the institutions of political society, is derived from the people, and established with their consent, to advance their happiness: and they may, for this end, as circumstances require, from time to time, alter their Constitution of Government."

The Constitution of Maryland dates its existence from 1776, the most memorable year of the war of the revolution, and maintains, the principles which gave rise to it, in the following declaration: "We, the Delegates of Maryland in free and full Convention assembled"—declare, "That all Government of right, originates from the people, *is founded in compact on y*, and instituted solely for *the good of the whole people*."

"That all persons invested with the Legislative or Executive powers of Government, are the trustees of the public, and as such, accountable for their conduct; wherefore, whenever the ends of government are perverted, and the public liberty manifestly endangered, and all other means of redress are ineffectual, the people may, and of right ought to, reform the old, or establish a new Government. The doctrine of non-resistance against arbitrary power and oppression, is absurd, slavish, and destructive of the good and happiness of mankind.

"That the right, in the people, to participate in the Legislature, is the best security of liberty, and the foundation of all free Government; for this purpose, elections ought to be free and frequent, and every man having property in, a common interest with, and attachment to, the community, ought to have a Right of Suffrage."

I fear, said Mr. M. that I have wearied the attention of the Committee, before I have reached the Bill of Rights of our own Constitution, if a Bill of Rights and Constitution we have, as I myself do not doubt, whatever may have been the defect of their origin. That Bill of Rights is so engraven on the memory of every member of this Committee, and has been so often referred to in this debate, that I will not read it. But I protest against that construction of the sacred truths which it contains, which seeks to impair their force, by combining them with the actual details of the Constitution.

The causes of the imperfections of the machine of Government, were truly and eloquently unfolded, by my friend from Frederick, (Mr. Cooke.) But the presence of danger, which may obstruct the labour of the most skilful artist in the fabrication of a complicated engine, need not impair his judgment of the plan by which he works. A re-organization of the counties of Virginia, or a Census of her population, at a time when no Census had ever been taken, of any people in modern Europe, or, for aught I know, in modern times; and at such a time—when a threatened invasion, by a foreign and most formidable enemy, was hourly expected to drive the people from their homes, and to waste their estates, was not within the compass of possible events. But, did it follow, that the great principles of freedom, for which the framers of the Constitution contended, in battle as well as in debate, should not be profoundly understood and ably elucidated? Was not the occasion calculated to quicken and invigorate all the operations of the human intellect; and although it might embarrass the movements of the principal actors, to enlighten, strengthen, and confirm their purpose?

Were the framers of our Constitution but half educated, as it is contended, all their descendants are? In such an age, truth flashes from mind to mind, with electric activity, and a force irresistible. Hence, we perceive not merely a conformity of opinion, but an identity of language, in all the State Constitutions of that period, from Massachusetts to Georgia, in relation to the foundation of my present argument, the natural equality in which men enter society, and the right of a majority of numbers to govern.

The direct tendency, the obvious as well as declared purpose of the basis of representation, adopted by the Legislative Committee, is to enable such a majority of the people of Virginia to govern this Commonwealth, as, of right, they should.

The member from Chesterfield, recurring to the same period with myself, and reasoning from a supposed inequality in the present taxes of this Commonwealth, invokes the principles of the Revolution to his aid. Our quarrel with the mother country, he, along with several of his predecessors, earnestly tells us, grew out of the violation of the principle, for which he and they are now contending, "of not being taxed without their consent," which they so define as to require a certain proportion between taxation and representation. On the other hand, it has been insisted by my friend from Brooke, that the Revolution sprung from a total denial, on the part of the Colonies, of the right of the British Parliament, to bind them to an obedience of any laws whatever, to which they had not given their assent, by their Colonial Legislatures.

No two gentlemen have precisely agreed on this topic; and yet, it seems to me, that none have erred in their statements so far as they have severally gone. Their disagreements have arisen from their severally referring to different periods of a contest of long duration. It began with the memorable Stamp Act, which imposed a tax to operate in the interior of each Colony, mingling with all the transactions of life. The tax was resisted, in argument, on both sides of the Atlantic, on the ground, that the Colonies were not represented in the Parliament of England; and, therefore, should not be taxed. The stamps were sent to America—a mob at Williamsburg threatened their destruction. The stamp-master resigned his station almost as soon as he landed; the city of Williamsburg was illuminated; the stamps re-shipped, and the act imposing them, shortly after rescinded.

The elder Pitt, and his eloquent co-adjutors, in opposition to the British ministry, of that day, contended, that the mother country had a right to bind the Colonies in all cases whatever of *legislation*, but that *taxation* was not *legislation*. That *taxes* were a *free grant* of money, by the Commons, to the Crown; and that, being so, the Commons of England could not grant away the money of the people of America.

Fortunately, as the event proved for us, but unluckily for Great Britain, Charles Townsend discovered a mode of obviating the objection to the Stamp Act, by the exercise of what, he considered, the unquestioned right of Parliament to regulate the trade between the Colonies and the mother country, which he deemed an office of ordinary legislation. Hence the imposition of a duty on tea, payable on being landed at the place of importation.

The Colonies found that they had nothing to gain by this distinction, since money could as well be drawn from their pockets, by commercial regulations, which were laws, as by taxation considered as, what few taxes ever are, the free grants of those by whom they are paid. They discovered, in fact, what their friends, for some time, appeared not to have contemplated, on the other side of the Atlantic, that to avoid taxation in some shape or other, they must maintain the doctrine that the British Parliament had a right to bind them, in no shape whatever, without their consent: That the Union of the Empire on both sides of the Atlantic, was, as that of Scotland with England, in the Crown, and, not in the Parliament. My friend from Brooke had, in his able argument, very truly described this stage of the controversy, at which, and not before, the tender of a representation in Parliament was made, to America, by England, and scornfully, as well as wisely rejected. Had a similar effort, at reconciliation, been made, at the period of the repeal of the Stamp Act, a different result might have happened, and the subsequent controversy delayed, if not prevented. To this early stage of the contest, between England and her Colonies, the gentlemen from Northampton, (Mr. Upshur,) from Hanover, (Mr. Morris,) and from Chesterfield, (Mr. Leigh,) had adverted in aid of their common opposition to the resolution in debate.

The last of these gentlemen has pushed the inference, which he deduced from the doctrine of the former opposition in England, relative to the nature of taxation, to a length as extravagant in some of its consequences, as inconsistent with the modern notion of taxation, on both sides of the Atlantic.

Are we to go back to the declension of the Feudal system, imported from Normandy, or yet farther, to the Saxon Wittenagemote, to learn from the antiquities of the English Government the nature of taxation in America? That taxes, are not the free grants of those who pay them, in a country where every thing is taxed from the cradle to the coffin? Where the exciseman seals up the key-hole of the door of the warehouse of the manufacturer, and carries away the key in his pocket!

That the House of Commons, gradually acquired the rank of a co-ordinate branch of the English Parliament, by firmly uniting to their grants of money to the Crown, the petitions of their constituents, for a redress of grievances, is an historical fact, which can reflect no light on the path of our present enquiry.

The legislative power of the Commons, is established in England, on the principles of the revolution of 1688. Taxation is a branch of legislative power, and was the instrument of its acquisition. In the last relation, it bears, however, no necessary affinity to the end which it accomplished. Who would trace to Syria or Spain, the origin of Magna Charta, because the sword blades of the Barons, who assembled at Runnimeads under the frowning turrets of Windsor, may have been forged at Damascus or Toledo? Shall we, at this day, repair to the British House of Commons to learn the true character of Legislative power in America? An instructive lesson it might teach us, against the inequality of representation of which we so justly complain. The corruption to which it has given rise, is no longer confined to the rotten boroughs in the gift of the nobility, but extends to the vitals of the people. Turn to the life of Sheridan, by More, and you may read this truth, in the reproaches which he makes to his friends, that they will not supply him with funds to purchase a seat in Parliament. There, indeed, a representative has to buy his constituents. Sometimes to travel through the kingdom to find them.

In attempting to assimilate the present controversy for political power between different parts of this Commonwealth, to that which subsisted between England and her Colonies in the war of the revolution, the member from Chesterfield relies on a supposed inequality in the distribution of the taxes of the Commonwealth. He would justify the lowland country, which is over-represented, in maintaining a political power disproportionate to the numbers of its white population, on the ground that it is at present over-taxed.

To sustain his position, he should show that the public taxes are not fairly proportioned to the ability of those by whom they are paid—and could he show this, the responsibility, for such injustice, would rest, not with those who claim a new apportionment of the legislative power of the Government, but with those who have so long ruled the Commonwealth.

It may not be amiss to examine the facts from which this supposed inequality of taxation is deduced. With this view, I beg leave to recall the attention of the Committee to some of those which I adduced, for another purpose, in an early stage of my argument. The revenue of this Commonwealth, except the income of the funds for Internal Improvement and Education, was before the last war, as it has been ever since the peace, principally drawn from three sources: taxes on land, slaves and horses.

If the actual value of the lands and lots assessed for taxation, be now assumed to be $ 90,000,000; of the slaves, amounting in number to 450,000, to be $ 67,500,000; and of 273,000 horses, at 50 dollars each, to be $ 13,650,000; then a comparison of the revenue derived from each of these sources in the last year, will by no means prove that the public burthens are unequally distributed, to the prejudice of the slaveholder.

The revenue charged upon this peculiar capital will be found to be less than that charged upon horses, and still less than that charged upon lands, estimating each subject of taxation at its fair value. For evidence of this, I refer to a table of the comparative revenue on each of these subjects since the equalizing land-tax and Senatorial district act of 1817, which went into complete operation in 1820.

For the first four years of the succeeding period, the average product of the land-tax, was $ 181,000, of the slave-tax $ 159,000, and of the horse-tax $ 38,000.

The revenue from these sources, for the current year, in round numbers, is, by the table supplied me, 175,000 dollars on lands, 97,000 on slaves, and 33,000 on horses. Notwithstanding all that has been said in the debate, these facts bear me out in the position, that in the current year, the capital in slaves is taxed less than that in land.

An error pervades all the reasoning of our adversaries on this subject, in considering the slave-tax as a tax on a certain territory rather than on a productive property; of the tax upon which, no complaint would be made, were it dispersed over the surface of the Commonwealth. For it is not easy to conceive an objection to a tax on this property that might not be made with equal propriety to any other tax whatever. It is founded as all taxes should be, on the ability of the persons taxed; and that ability is derived from the productiveness of this species of stock. The tables of the natural growth of this population demonstrate, when compared with the increase of its numbers in the Commonwealth, for twenty years past, that an annual revenue of not less than a million and a half of dollars is derived from the exportation of a part of that increase: While the proprietors of the lands of the Commonwealth, contributing a greater tax in proportion to the actual value of those lands, have derived no correspondent profit from the gradual augmentation of that value. The revenue of every country consists of the income of its land, its labour, and its stock. Taxation can draw from that income without oppression, only part of what remains, after sustaining the capital of every description which produces it, and the labour engaged in its production. If the numbers of the labourers were an exact measure of this income, taxation to be equal, should be proportioned to the aggregate number of all the slaves and free labourers of a country. But, the surplus which the former are able to supply after sustaining themselves, is, in fact, greater in proportion as their wants are less costly, and their natural increase conspires with the produce of their labour to swell the income of the proprietor who is chargeable with the tax they pay.

But while I do not admit, but on the contrary. am prepared to disprove that injustice has hitherto been practised towards the proprietors of this description of property, I am not only desirous, but deem it practicable to afford to them a protection from the oppression which they apprehend.

I am aware, Mr. Chairman, said Mr. M. of the extreme sensibility, with which the members of this body, who are opposed to the resolution on your table, receive every suggestion of a readiness on our part, to provide, by the Constitution itself, a security against the danger of unequal taxation. In whatever spirit it may be accepted, I am however prepared to submit a guarantee, which, to my poor judgment, will be both just in itself and adequate to its end. It will consist in a Constitutional provision, that no tax on slaves shall ever be imposed, without a general tax on lands and horses: and that every tax which may be levied on those subjects, shall be founded on a fair assessment of their value, and bear to that value an uniform proportion.

Compare the security which such a provision, would afford, with that supplied by the Constitution of the United States, to the same property, in the apportionment of all direct taxes; and will any question be made of the superiority of the former? How are direct taxes, which are to be apportioned among the States, according to their respective representation, distinguishable from indirect taxes, which are required to be uniform? In the judgment of the Supreme Court, in the case of the United States and Hilton, the boundaries of these two species of taxation, are designated mainly by reference to a single paragraph from the author of the Wealth of Nations. This was the case of the carriage tax, which the court regarded as a tax, not on capital, but expenditure, or income, which is commonly its measure. Some of the judges doubt their own ability to lay down characteristic distinctions which shall invariably serve to denote the appropriate subjects of these different taxes, required by the Constitution to be differently levied. The clause, on the other hand, which I propose as a security to the proprietor of slaves, against unequal taxation, if admitted into the Constitution, could receive but one construction, which there is not a magistrate in Virginia who would hesitate to pronounce, and by which, any law passed, in violation of it, would be promptly arrested. A similar security, I would leave it to those, who may deem it essential to dictate, for the protection of the tenure of this property. It will be repeated, "that these are but paper guarantees"—" mere parchment." And what else have we for our lives and our liberty? The trial by jury, the writ of habeas corpus, the freedom of speech, the liberty of the press, the rights of conscience, do they not all rest for their safety on the solemn compact of the people with each other, contained in the Constitution of the State, and of the United States?

When corruption and licentiousness shall have destroyed all the security which we derive from the Constitution, there will remain nothing else to preserve, or worthy of preservation. The proposed basis of free white population is represented, by our opponents, as an attempt to divorce property, from power. They speak, as if the whole property of the Commonwealth belonged exclusively to their constituents, and was about to be wrested from them by violence. The member from Chesterfield emphatically asserts, that what is *his*, *is* his. It is his, Sir, truly, but subject to the lawful claims of the Government, by which it is protected. Those claims are commensurate with the necessities of the Commonwealth, and the ability of its citizens to comply with them under a just and equal system of contribution.

Gentlemen imagine that a just and equal distribution of political power will expose all property to destruction. They have drawn lines across the Commonwealth, and exclaim, there, all is danger; here, all is security; as if they apprehended, from the West, an irruption of barbarians, as soon as a new basis of political power may be established.

Sir, no basis of representation can be formed, which will transfer the power of this Government from the hands of the slave-holding population, in less than twenty years from the first Census, which may be taken under a new Constitution.

I have pointed out some striking defects, in the table returned, upon conjecture, of the present white population of the various counties and corporations of the Commonwealth. It is safe to reason from our past, to our future growth. After adopting a course sanctioned by experience, and deriving its facts from the actual enumerations of the population of the Commonwealth—I have arrived at this result; and I appeal to the gentlemen who have expressed so much alarm, to disprove it if they can.

They conjure up imaginary dangers and reason from them, as if, instead of being the creatures of their own fancy, they were solemn realities.

All the foundations of property are to be uprooted! By whom? By men of frugal habits; who are laboring incessantly for its acquisition. Who can hope to acquire it, only, by the exertions of a hardy industry, from a stubborn soil, upon an uneven country, and who can hold and enjoy it, when acquired, but under the same protecting power of the laws? The tables I have already quoted, show, that property is diffused as widely to the West as to the East; and, consequently, the interest which guards its existence.

Do not our opponents perceive that the argument which they deduce against the augmentation of the power of the West, that it will be exerted to the prejudice of the East, may be retorted upon them, and with the greater force; since they desire to keep that, to which they have, in truth, no title; and which must consequently be maintained by that jealousy which ever accompanies injustice?

What, our opponents ask, has the *majority* to apprehend from the *minority;* the West, from the East? For if the proportions of the people be not thus, truly expressed, the East, has, itself, nothing to fear from the proposed apportionment of power. What, then, has the West to apprehend? I answer every thing, from the very alarm expressed by the gentlemen, who make the enquiry, in dread of the approaching ascendancy of the West? Laws, to discourage the improvement of a country, whose inhabitants are daily prompted to forsake it, by the temptations offered them, in cheaper lands abroad, and more liberal institutions, than they find at home.

Do you inquire what shall be the provisions of such laws? Some of them, I will borrow from our past; others from our existing code of Legislation.

I will not speak of the limitation of suffrage, in the Constitution itself, which degrades the non-freeholder to the level of the slave: but I will refer you to one of its consequences, the act of 1754, for Colonial defence. When threatened with a French and Indian war, the draft for compulsory enlistments, for military service, was extended by the General Assembly, to all persons, except such as were under twenty-one and above fifty years of age, and all *freeholders or voters*, and all *indented or bought servants*.

Need I go so far back? What is our present body of road laws, but one system of oppression upon the laboring poor, who are taxed in personal service as well as by a levy in money, equally with the rich, to keep that highway in repair, which they have not the power to injure, unless by their footsteps. Nay, to work on the roads is a duty from which any proprietor of *two slaves* is exempted, notwithstanding his use of the road is nearly in the direct proportion of his wealth?

What may I not say, of that system of poor laws, which extorts the resources of public charity, by an equal tax, from all men, without distinction of fortune, except what may arise from the application of a poll tax, to a country having slaves?

Such are some of the features of the old code. For the new, let us suppose every other branch of revenue lopped off from our present system, and a poll tax to be levied on the free white inhabitants of the Commonwealth, without reference to the distinction of wealth

If, instead of cherishing, it be desired to keep down the West, such are the present facilities for descending the river Ohio, and many of its tributaries, that, but a little ingenuity would make the trans-Alleghany country a wilderness again, fit only for the habitation of beasts of prey.

Gentlemen reason, as if the only power in Government was taxation; as they have represented the protection of property to be almost the sole end of Legislation. They forget the numerous laws, which protect the rights of persons, in peace, as well as the more important shield, which they cast around him in war.

It cannot have been forgotten, that during the last war, it was proposed, and not without apparent reason, to exempt a part of the militia on the sea board, from military service, beyond the limits of their respective counties; a regulation which might have been extended, so far, as greatly to augment the pressure of military duty on the West.

What are all the laws which limit, or extend the period of military service? That exempt apprentices and slaves from the obligation to perform it; but laws, the burthen of which, the wealthy can escape, by hiring substitutes; and, to which, the poor man must yield obedience, however reluctantly he may leave his home without a master; his wife, without a husband; or his children without a parent to protect them.

How many laws are there, with respect even to property, which operate, also, upon the very body, manners and character of society; disappointing labour of its fruits, and bringing discredit upon the country, which is obliged to acknowledge their sway? Such are those laws which withhold the payment, or suspend the legal remedies for the recovery of just debts: which in fine, drive commerce from a land, designed by nature to be her favoured abode, and turn her choicest blessings into absolute curses.

Society owes other obligations, to itself, or to its members. Protection from foreign violence and the administration of justice, are of indispensable necessity. But the intercourse and education of its citizens, have, also, claims upon its attention, that no wise Government has, hitherto disregarded.

These subjects are among those, however, that fill our opponents with the greatest alarm. They have denounced all attempts to improve the natural advantages of the State, at public cost, whether by roads or canals; and this, because of a single experiment which has, it seems, been badly conducted.

The people of James river, have been disappointed in the result of a favorite improvement—As the member from Albemarle demonstrated, they owe that disappointment to themselves alone. They bought a whistle, found it discoursed not such music as they expected; and like a spoilt child, they have broken it in two, and thrown it away. If I may presume to advise them, and I am at least sincere in what I say, I will tell them to finish their canal to Lynchburg; then quadruple, as they well may, the load of their boats: substitute a single horse, an old man, and a boy, for their impelling power, instead of a half a dozen able bodied hands, and they will no longer, find cause to complain of the money they have expended.

But what has this failure to do with the question before us? Did not the first vote in this Hall, in favor of a Convention, precede this James river scheme of improvement, and did that not spring up in this city?

As for the late Charlottesville Convention, it had any other than a western origin.

I will leave its vindication, to my venerable, learned and patriotic friend, (Chief Justice Marshall,) now sitting before me, who I fear, will not give his support, to our basis of representation, though certainly, from no prejudice against the improvement of the roads and rivers of the Commonwealth.

The education of the people is, also, an object of dread; and the bill of 1817, which passed the House of Delegates, by a very large majority, notwithstanding its present unequal basis of representation, has been the topic of special denunciation and complaint.

We are told that we wish to acquire the power of educating the poor man's child, at the expense of the rich. I confess, I am ashamed to hear such suggestions, at this day, and in the Capitol of Virginia. Although, I perceive no connexion between them, and the purpose of our present deliberations, yet they spring from a source so respectable, (Mr. Green,) that I must believe, being worthy of the gentleman from Culpeper, (Mr. Green,) they merit my notice. Such a cause ought not to suffer, for want of an advocate. The bill referred to, with all its imperfections, I am willing to let rest upon my head. But one word of defence.

Since 1819, we have applied $ 45,000 a year to the education of our poor, and 10,000 children are imperfectly taught for about six months in the year, by its application.

New York has, at present, in her free schools, open at all times, equally to the rich and the poor, more than 450,000 children; and to the State Treasury, the annual cost of their instruction is $ 100,000. By the judicious application of this sum, she has elicited individual zeal and wealth sufficient to do the rest of this beneficent labor.

Connecticut, whose school system is an improvement upon that of Massachusetts, and nearly as ancient, as its importation from Scotland in 1647, employs in its support a revenue of $ 80,000. She finds that sum sufficient to educate all her children, in number more than as many thousand. I once visited a gentleman in that State, the purest, if not the most perfect Commonwealth, in existence, who was worth several hundred thousand dollars, though with but four and twenty acres of land near his dwelling. He kept several carriages—and the son of his coachman went to the same school with his own grand-child. Both were well taught.

Except in the county of Brooke, where about five dollars a year suffices for the education of her poor children, the annual charge upon the Literary Fund, for every pupil whom it instructs, is no where less than eight dollars; while in Connecticut, this expense, as we see, is very little more than a fourth of that amount, corresponding, as it does, with the cost of instruction in the parochial schools of Scotland.

Will the rich any where complain of a system which, while the children of the poor are instructed enables them to educate their own, at a cost so reduced? And is the education of the people, who are every where in America, the acknowledged guardians of their own rights, the source of all political power, a subject of mere Eastern or Western interest, in Virginia?

Who are the people of the West? Are they not our fellow-citizens, our friends and brothers? Whence did they spring? From the East? Have they forgot their common origin? It was with extreme concern, that I heard the gentleman from Culpeper, (Mr. J. S. Barbour,) declare, a few days ago, that the West had not a proper sympathy with the East, and urge in proof of this charge, that during the invasion of the Commonwealth, in the last war, their representatives on this floor, voted against the Defence Bill of 1815. They did not hear, he emphatically said, the "sound of the cannon of the enemy, nor behold the distress of the East:" and, therefore, felt it not. He would not trust them with political power. Sir, said Mr. M. this very "Defence Bill," was the offspring of the joint labour of a delegate from Loudoun, and a gentleman from Augusta, now sitting in my view. I call upon my patriotic and liberal friend, to repel a charge, for which, there is not, in truth, the slightest foundation. If many Western delegates voted against this bill, so did many East of the mountains which divide us, as well they might. It became a law, as my honorable friend (Mr. Johnson,) can testify, who must well remember also the numerous imperfections which remained in it, and the complicated basis of taxation and enumeration, on which its most efficient provisions depended for their execution.

We trusted, in truth, to the moral feeling of the country, to supply those admitted defects. Nor, had the war continued, would that trust have been in vain—But while the war lasted, did it furnish no evidence of the common sympathy, which binds the West to the East? The gentleman from Chesterfield (Mr. Leigh,) himself, can attest the contrary. He had an official station, near the person of the commander of the army, which assembled for the defence of this Capitol; and if he was, as I then understood, the author of the proclamation which brought that army together, he must remember its effect. [Mr. Leigh shook his head.] There was not a mountain, a river, a valley of the West, that did not respond with animation, to this appeal to the patriotism of Virginia. At the cry of invasion and danger from the East, every man of the West, from the summit of the Blue Ridge, to the shores of the Ohio, capable of bearing arms, mounted his knapsack, and turned his face from home—there was no distinction of the rich from the poor. Gentlemen who had occupied conspicuous places in our halls of legislation—the ploughman from the fresh fallow field—officers, soldiers and citizens—all moved on with one accord. In a fortnight, 15,000 men were mustered in sight of the Capitol; among them the largest body of cavalry that ever was reviewed in our portion of this continent. In one morning, a thousand of them were discharged as supernumeraries. On their return home, they met the eagles of the West, still sweeping their flight to the East. Their course was turned to their mountains, only when danger had ceased.

Nor was this, the only proof, during that war, which the West afforded, of devotion to the East.

Shall I be told, by the gentleman from Chesterfield, while I labor to bind closer around my countrymen, the cords of union, that I haunt his imagination with the spectres of the men who died at Norfolk? I purposely omit the offensive association which accompanied the allusion. I will bear his reproaches.

It is full well known that, in the progress of that war, Virginia was thrown, in a great degree, upon her own resources, for defence. Her noble bay, was locked up by a British Admiral. Her State taxes doubled—Private income was nearly at an end. Her Banks had, by forced loans, been compelled to suspend the issue of specie. A currency of depreciated paper flooded the markets of the country, where there were any. The system of common defence by the forces of the Union, had so far failed, that the several States had begun to raise separate armies for their peculiar safety. It was a time to try men's hearts. And what did the West? March, without a murmur, from their health-inspiring mountains, to the marshes of Princess Anne. They descended from the remotest boundaries of the Commonwealth, traversing it for four hundred miles, from Washington and Brooke, to the sea-board. I witnessed their conduct, their sufferings, and the fortitude with which they bore them. No man of Princess Anne ever complained of the deportment of those men; that any soldier ever molested his person, disturbed his quiet, or wasted his property; that he had trodden down the grass of his fields, or traversed them, but by the paths, which he himself had made. The corn ripened around the tents of these soldiers untouched, in the midst of no ordinary privations, and a life of suffering, to which most of them were unused.

Disease made its way into their camps in various forms, and thousands ingloriously perished, of whose names no vestiges remain, but in the remembrance of their children. I have searched for their graves, but could find no trace of them except a few scattered stones, on the commons of Norfolk.

In the month of November next preceding the peace, which terminated this war, one hundred and sixty were buried, eight hundred discharged, because incapable of further service, and 2,300 returned on the sick list. These facts, Mr. Chairman, derived from an official source, were, you must well recollect, handed over to you, to serve as the basis of your argument in support of that very Defence Bill, of which, the member from Culpeper has reminded us. It was not till the close of this perilous season, or immediately before the return of peace, that any aid was ordered to our relief, from North Carolina, though Norfolk, is as much her sea-port, as ours: and her boundary crosses the canal in its vicinity.

Sir, the part which my friend from Norfolk (Gen. Taylor) who gave discipline, and character, and confidence to the militia army, I have described, has taken in this question, does equal credit to his heart and his head. It is worthy of the Bayard of Virginia, a man "*sans peur et sans reproche.*" And should he fall a martyr in the cause he has thus nobly espoused, I shall envy him his martyrdom. It will be the only unkind feeling I ever felt towards him.

And why, Sir, did we defend Norfolk, at so vast a sacrifice of life and money? We could have twice burnt it down and built it up again, with the sums spent in its defence; to say nothing of the mere labor of the men whose lives it cost us.

Was it not to protect the sea-board? Those very proprietors, who now deny our equal rights, with themselves, to political power in this Commonwealth, and that too, on the very ground, which then constituted their own insecurity and danger? Was it not, that the lowland gentleman might lie down in safety, or leave his dwelling, without fear, that, in his absence, the incendiary torch might fire it, and turn his wife and children out upon the world, if the mid-night dagger chanced to spare their lives? It was not the *value* of Norfolk, but its *position*, that we maintained, for the peace of the lowlands.

If the present were a mere question about taxation we should inquire into the ability of the taxed, to pay. As it is a question of representation, we inquire into the numbers of those, who are to be represented.

My friend from Norfolk, (Mr. Taylor,) had properly illustrated the difference of these two principles of taxation and representation, by comparing them to two fountains which rise in the same glen, but pursue their way to the ocean, by different channels.

The member from Chesterfield has told us, that the figure is inaptly applied, since they both spring from the same source: and with an infelicity, which rarely occurs in his figurative language, he has spoken of a torrent of representation rolling from, and another stream of taxation, ascending to, the West. If in the operations of peace, the balance be in favor of the West, it is evidently reversed, in war, for a heavier charge than a war on our sea-board, must ever bring upon the people who live remote from the actual theatre of its dangers, cannot well be conceived.

But why disfigure a Commonwealth so fitted for union by odious lines of discrimination founded on imaginary diversities of interests? If the "Pyrennees" have disappeared, at one end of their chain, why may they not do so, along its whole extent?

Were they, however, higher than the Alps, the new distribution of political power would not transfer the majority of the House of Delegates to the West of this natural division of the territory of the Commonwealth. In a House of 120 members, 70 would remain below the Blue Ridge: and, as I have said, a majority must continue there for years to come. The lenient agency of that very time, which the gentleman from Chesterfield would invoke, to mitigate all revolutions of power, is thus assured to those feelings which neither he nor I would revolt by sudden change.

If mere difference of local interests should sever States and people, 'tis not a division of Virginia by a single mountain which would suffice.

The member from Albemarle (Mr. Gordon) has illustrated this truth, in one of the histories which he gave us of the causes of discontent on James River. Even the slave-holding country has its tobacco and its cotton staples, below the line which divides us on the present question.

It is true with all local interests, that as you enlarge their sphere of action, you reduce their force. By circumscribing their limits, you only increase their vigor. To give each interest within this Commonwealth, power to regulate itself, not four divisions—but forty, must be made. Shall we, for such reasons, sunder the land of our birth?

Mr. Chairman, said Mr. M., as I decended the Chesapeake the other day, on my way to this city, impelled by a favoring west wind, which, co-operating with the new element applied by the genius of Fulton to navigation, made the vessel on which I stood literally fly through the wave before me, I thought of the early descriptions of Virginia, by the followers of Rawleigh, and the companions of Smith. I endeavored to scent the fragrance of the gale which reached me from the shore of the capacious bay along which we steered, and I should have thought the pictures of Virginia, which rose in my fancy, not too highly coloured, had I not often traversed our lowland country, the land not only of my nativity, but of my fathers—and I said to myself, how much has it lost of its primitive loveliness. Does the eye dwell with most pleasure on its wasted fields, or its stunted forests of secondary growth of pine and cedar? Can we dwell, but with mournful regret, on the temples of religion, sinking in ruin; and those spacious dwellings, whose doors once opened by the hand of liberal hospitality, are now fallen upon their portals or closed in tenantless silence? Except on the banks of its rivers, the march of desolation saddens this once beautiful country. The cheerful notes of population have ceased, and the wolf and wild deer, no longer scared from their ancient haunts, have decended from the mountains to the plains. They look on the graves of our ancestors, and traverse their former paths. And shall we do nothing to restore this once lovely land? There was a time when the sun in his course shone on none so fair.

Let us elevate the condition of that population in Virginia, which constitutes the bone and sinew and strength of every nation. Let us lift it up to a condition above our slaves, diffuse throughout it, knowledge, which is power; and, instead of driving it, by political proscription, from our bosom, invite it from abroad.

The gentleman from Chesterfield, bound by ties that do not connect me with the world, tells us that the integrity of the Commonwealth is but the second wish of his heart—Sir, unlike him, the affections of mine centre on my country. My last wish will be like my first, for her liberty, her peace, her happiness, and as the firmest bond of all these blessings, her Union. In life, and in death as in life, such will be my prayer. Oh America! patria op ima; Virginia, mater amatissima, esto perpetua!

Mr. J. S. Barbour here rose to explain:

The gentleman from Loudoun has referred, I presume, to myself, in some of the remarks which had fallen from him, in relation to the people of the West. His fervid defence of their conduct during the last war, was wholly unnecessary. Believe me, Sir, I know too well what is due to their patriotism and bravery, ever to have entertained or expressed the slightest distrust of either. All I was endeavouring to shew, was, that there exists a diversity of interests between different parts of the State, which could not but exert its influence on their views and course of action. The West had one set of interests, the East another. The gentleman from Loudoun knows that I went with him in support of the Defence Bill. I never felt or thought that there was any deficiency manifested by the people of the West, in this season of public danger.

Mr. Mercer said he was happy to hear the gentleman express the opinion he had jvst uttered; but the gentleman from Culpeper must forget the tenor of his own remarks, which certainly went to convey the idea, that the people beyond the mountain not having heard the sound of hostile cannon, nor witnessed the scenes of distress occasioned by the presence of an invading enemy, did not sympathize with their brethren in the lower part of the State. He was very happy to find that the gentleman now harboured no suspicion in his breast toward his brethren in the Western part of the State.

Mr. Doddridge said he had been repeatedly alluded to in the course of this debate, as if he had contended that the Constitution was not legal and obligatory. He had made no argument nor expressed any opinion to that effect. When alluding to the circumstances under which the Constitution had been formed, he was replying to the argument of the gentleman from Northampton, who had contended that the existing Constitution, had been made "by all and for the benefit of all:" and his object was to shew, that so far from having been made by all, for the benefit of all, it had been made by a particular description of freeholders only, and for the benefit of freeholdors of the same description with themselves, perpetuating the power which they themselves possessed. Mr. D. had made the statement more particularly with reference to the right of suffrage, (should the Convention ever reach that subject, of which he began to entertain some fear:) he had done it to shew that there was a numerous class of citizens who had never been consulted at all in the formation of the Constitution, and his inference from that fact was, that they had a right to be consulted now.

Mr. Joynes next addressed the Committee.

Mr. Chairman: The subject now under the consideration of the Committee, is one of great importance to the future happiness and prosperity of Virginia; and I have to ask the attention of the Committee, for a short time, while I present to the Committee the views I have taken of this subject. In doing this, I shall not indulge the expectation that any thing that I can say will change the vote of any member of this Committee. Every gentleman in this Convention has, no doubt, maturely considered the subject, and honestly made up his opinion;—and, if the able and eloquent arguments which have already been addressed to the Committee, have been insufficient to change the opinions of gentlemen, I have not the vanity to suppose that any thing which I may say, would have that effect. This subject is interesting to the whole State, and particularly to that portion of it in which I live; and if I were to permit this question to be decided without expressing the opinions I entertain, and the reasons on which these opinions are founded, I should be wanting in duty to myself and to those who sent me here.

When I was elected a member of this Convention, Mr. Chairman, I endeavoured to persuade myself, that while it was my duty, in concert with my colleagues to watch over and protect, so far as I could, the particular interests of my constituents, yet that I was a representative, in some degree, of the whole people of Virginia, and bound to consult the interests of the whole community. I came here, Sir, actuated by a spirit of compromise toward other members of this Convention. I came here, prepared to reconcile, as far as was practicable, by mutual concessions, all sectional and conflicting interests, and to agree in the adoption of such a Constitution as we might reasonably hope would permanently promote the interest and happiness of Virginia. It was idle for any man to calculate that every measure was to be adopted precisely according to his wishes. It is by mutual concessions alone, that any beneficial results can be expected to arise from our labours. There was no subject which it was probable could come before the Convention, on which I felt more strongly actuated by a wish for mutual concession than on that now under the consideration of the Committee;—and I was gratified the other day, when my friend from Fauquier (Mr. Scott), proposed an amendment to the amendment proposed by the gentleman from Culpeper (Mr. Green), which would afford me an opportunity of manifesting, by my vote, that I was really disposed to compromise this interesting subject; and I regret that a majority of the Committee entertained different views from me relative to that amendment.

We have been told in the course of this debate by the gentleman from Albemarle (Mr. Gordon), that the amendment proposed by the gentleman from Culpeper (Mr.

Green), was incompatible with the extension of the right of suffrage. The right of suffrage, Mr. Chairman, is not by any means involved in this question, nor have they any necessary connexion. The question here is not, to whom the right of suffrage shall be granted, but in what proportions shall the political power of the Commonwealth be distributed amongst the different sections of the State: whether it shall be distributed, having reference to white population alone, by which those portions of the State which pay less than one-fourth of the whole revenue of the Commonwealth, shall have the entire control of the legislative power; or shall it be so distributed, that those who are compelled to pay more than three-fourths of the revenue, shall have it in their power to protect themselves from improper taxation. I am in favour of the extension of the right of suffrage as far, perhaps, as any man in this Convention; and much farther, I dare say, than I shall be sustained by the votes of a majority of the Convention. I am willing to extend it to all free white male citizens of this State upwards of twenty-one years of age who have committed no crimes against the State, and who actually *pay* taxes to the State or county—whether they be freeholders or not. And, I would allow to the poorest man who went to the polls, precisely the same vote, that I would allow to his wealthy neighbour who might be the master of five hundred slaves.

I shall not pretend to question the correctness of the general rule, that the majority should govern; and a majority of persons in general furnishes the best evidence of a majority of interests. Since the eloquent argument of my colleague from Northampton (Judge Upshur), most of the gentlemen who have engaged in this debate on the other side, have placed this question on the ground of expediency alone. One of the greatest errors which can be committed in the science of Government, it appears to me is, to lay down certain general fundamental principles, and, like the bed of Procrustes, compel every community to conform to them, without regard to circumstances. A Constitution, to be of any value, must be adapted to the particular circumstances and situation of the country for which it is intended. That Government which would be best for one country might be worst for another. Every man in this Convention; nay, every man, I am sure, in America, would unite in saying, that a Republican form of Government was best adapted to the situation of the people of the United States and to the individual States: but *he* would be an unwise politician indeed, who would attempt at this day to establish a Republic in Russia or Turkey; and humanity has had to mourn over the unsuccessful efforts to establish a Republic in France; and, from recent indications, we have too much reason to apprehend that Republican Government is not suited to the late Spanish possessions on this Continent. The only question that a wise Statesman should ask is, whether the measure proposed, is *best* calculated to promote the liberty, interests and happiness of the people on whom it is intended to operate as they really *are;* and not, whether the measure conforms to certain rules of *theoretical perfection*, and would be best adapted to a people such as he would have them *to be.* If this were a question between the protection of personal rights on the one hand, and property on the other, and it was impossible to reconcile the two, I should not hesitate in giving the preference to the protection of personal rights; but I humbly conceive, that there is no incompatibility in the protection of the two. Property asks not for a sword to enable it to do injury to others: it only asks for a shield to protect it from injury.

This question has been discussed, Mr Chairman, by most of the gentlemen on one side, and by all on the other, as if the only object was the protection of the slave property of Eastern Virginia from oppressive taxation. And the gentleman from Albemarle (Mr. Gordon), has said, that no gentleman on the other side has advocated the amendment to the report of the Legislative Committee on any other ground. For myself, Sir, I have no hesitation in saying, that if there were not a slave in Virginia, or if, by the unanimous consent of the Convention, a clause were inserted in the Constitution exempting them forever from taxation, I should still think the amendment ought to prevail. The power of imposing taxes upon a community, whereby the Government can at pleasure withdraw from every individual any portion of his hard earned property, is one of the most important powers which can be conferred by the people, in their sovereign character, upon their Government. And, it is of the utmost importance, that that responsibility of public functionaries to the people for the faithful discharge of their duties, which is the life and security of representative Government, should be preserved in the fullest and most perfect degree, with respect to the power of laying taxes,—and this responsibility never can exist in a proper degree, unless those who have the power of laying the taxes are directly responsible to those who are compelled to pay them. If the report of the Legislative Committee be adopted by the Convention, then those who pay less than one-fourth of the taxes of the State would have the power of imposing taxes on the residue of the State; and the majority, who imposed the taxes, would be subject to no kind of responsibility to those who were compelled to pay the greater part of the taxes.

The wealth of a country, Mr. Chairman, depends upon the productive industry of that country; and whether these productions arise from the labour of freemen, or of slaves, they add equally to the wealth of the community at large. The tobacco of Virginia, the cotton and rice of the Carolinas and Georgia, and the sugar of Louisiana, add as much to the wealth of the nation as if they were the produce of the labour of free white men. Yet, I am still unwilling to place the slave labourer, on an equality with the white man: There are prejudices on this subject, arising from a difference in colour, and various other considerations, which are insuperable: These prejudices I feel as strongly as any man in the West; and, if the question now under consideration was, whether, in an apportionment of representation having reference to numbers, and *to no other consideration*, slaves should be included, I should feel no hesitation in saying that I would not include slaves in the enumeration.

Although the protection of slave property from the danger of unjust and oppressive taxation, be not the only object of the proposed amendment to the report of the Legislative Committee, yet the large portion of slaves held in Eastern Virginia, and the comparatively small number held in the Western part of the State, deserves serious consideration in deciding upon the subject. The slave tax is about 30 per cent. of the whole revenue of the State: they constitute one-third of the whole property of the State, and more than one-half of the property of that part of Virginia lying to the East of the Blue Ridge of mountains. We have been told by the two gentlemen from Frederick (Mr. Cooke and Mr. Powell); by the gentleman from Brooke (Mr. Campbell); by the gentleman from Albemarle (Mr. Gordon); and by the gentleman from Loudoun (Mr. Mercer), that if the white basis of representation be adopted, still the slave-holding interest would be protected—because, they say, there are a great many slaves in the Valley, where they are generally distributed amongst the people: and several of these gentlemen referred particularly to four counties in the Valley, which they say contain *great numbers* of slaves, and that the white population of these four counties added to the white population of the country East of the Blue Ridge, would make a white population of 400,000, who have peculiarly a slave interest; and the balance of the white population being only 280,000, the slave-holding interest would have a large majority, and would always have a majority. The respectability of these gentlemen repudiates the idea that they intended to deceive the Convention; and their splendid talents added to their weight of character, gives an imposing authority to every statement they make; but I think, Sir, it can be very easily shown, that these gentlemen are intirely mistaken in their calculations. The slaves constitute 38 per cent. of the whole population of the State;—and no county having less than 38 per cent. of slave population, can have such a controlling slave interest, as would induce it to unite with the slave-holding interest in other parts of the State, in resisting attempts to burthen that species of property with excessive taxes, for the relief of other property from taxation. To illustrate my idea, I will suppose that the taxes of the State are so arranged that, one half arises from land, and the other half from slaves: If these slaves be distributed in equal proportions, according to white population, amongst the several counties of the State, and it should become necessary to increase the taxes of the State, it would be immaterial, so far as intire counties were concerned, whether the increased taxation be imposed on land or slaves: But if the slaves, instead of being distributed equally amongst all the counties, should be so distributed, that one half of the counties contained three fourths of the slaves, and the remaining half contained only one fourth; and it should become necessary to increase the taxes, is it not perfectly manifest, that those counties containing only one fourth of the slaves would be interested to impose all the taxes on slaves, to the exclusion of land? There cannot be a doubt on the subject. The slaves West of the Alleghany are 8 2-3 per cent. of the whole population West of those mountains; in the Valley the slaves are 17 per cent. of the whole population; and in the country East of the Blue Ridge, the slaves exceed the whites.

But, Mr. Chairman, we have been told that four counties of the Valley, particularly, have a slave interest, which will induce them to unite with the slave-holders of the East in the protection of that kind of property. Let us examine whether these four Valley counties to which the people of the East have been asked to commit the guardianship of their slave property, *have* such a common interest in the subject as will render it prudent for the slave-holders of the East to choose them as guardians of that kind of property. If they *have not* such interest, Mr. Speaker, prudence would forbid their being selected as guardians. Let us say what we will of the virtue and integrity of man, the best security that can be had for another man's honesty is, to place him in a situation where it is his own interest to be honest. "Lead us not into temptation," are the words of the Saviour himself.

The four Valley counties to which gentlemen allude, are, no doubt, Frederick, Augusta, Botetourt and Jefferson. These counties contain together 20,534 slaves, and 50,241 free whites; the slaves being 27 per cent. of the whole population. These counties pay $16,630 55 cts. of the land tax, which is equal to 9 47-100 per cent.

of the whole land tax, and they pay $4,935 of the slave tax, which is equal to 4 3-10 ⋈ per cent. of the whole slave tax. Suppose there was a proposition before the Legislature, to raise for the exigencies of the State, an additional sum of $100,000 by taxation, and a member from the West should propose to raise this additional sum by a tax exclusively upon slaves: and a member from the East proposed to raise it intirely by a tax on land, how would these four guardian counties vote? If the additional tax be raised on land, these four counties would pay $9,474: and if it be raised on slaves, they would pay only $4,305. If they were actuated by that great spring of human action—self-interest, they are interested more than two to one, to impose the additional tax intirely upon slaves. If they were governed by interest alone, they would make bad guardians, and I fear the East would share the fate of too many wards.

The gentleman from Brooke (Mr. Campbell), and the gentleman from Albemarle (Mr. Gordon), have told us, no doubt to allay the apprehensions of the East, that if representation be apportioned according to white population alone, the West would lose representation in comparison with the present apportionment, and the gain would be in the slave districts. In order to prove this, they disregard the calculations of the Auditor as to the supposed population of 1829, and rely upon the Census of 1820. And the gentleman from Loudoun, (Mr. Mercer), has also told us, that the Auditor has committed a great mistake in the supposed population of 1829, as to that county; and he, therefore, has no confidence in the Auditor's calculations, but prefers to rely on the Census of 1820. The gentlemen who advocate the white basis, do not agree in the value they are disposed to place upon the Auditor's estimate of the population of 1829. A gentleman from beyond the Alleghany, whose opinions are intitled to great weight upon this and all other subjects, (Mr. Doddridge) told us, that the Auditor's calculations did not give to the country beyond the Alleghany, a greater increase of white population than it was really intitled to; and I know that other gentlemen entertained the same opinion. In fact, the gentleman from Brooke (Mr. Doddridge), in his speech the other day, rather vauntingly, said, that in thirty years the majority of the white population of the whole State would be *West of the Alleghany Mountains:* And he referred to the Auditor's estimate of the population of 1829, in support of that assertion. And he told us, too, that the white population beyond the Blue Ridge, would continue to increase until (to use his own language) "the white population East of the Blue Ridge would be but a drop in the bucket, to that of the West." The Auditor's estimate of the population of 1829, although called for on my motion, was called for on the suggestion of another gentleman from the West of the Alleghany, who was a good *Judge* of the subject, and after the Auditor had satisfied that gentleman and myself that, from the documents in his office, he could be enabled with tolerable accuracy, to estimate the population of 1829. I cannot consent to allow gentlemen the advantage in argument of relying on the correctness of the Auditor's statement one day, and then, when it suits their argument on another day, to tell us that no confidence should be placed in that estimate, and *that* the Census of 1820 should alone be relied on. If we were now about fixing the representation according to the white population, and which was to remain unchanged for ten years to come, would gentlemen then be content to rely on the Census of 1820? I presume we should then be told again that the Auditor's estimate was correct and ought to be relied on. I have but little doubt that the Auditor's estimate of the population of 1829, is very nearly correct, and I shall not hesitate to assume it as the basis of my calculations,—and let us see upon that estimate how the representation would stand in comparison with the present apportionment of representation. According to the Auditor's estimate, the whole white population of the State in 1829, is 682,261. If this number be divided by 120 (which is the number of delegates recommended by the Legislative Committee), we shall find that 5,685 are the number of free whites necessary to furnish one delegate. On this estimate, the country West of the Alleghany (containing twenty-six counties) would be entitled to thirty-two delegates,—the Valley (containing fourteen counties) to 24 1-3,—the country from the Blue Ridge to the head of Tide (containing twenty-nine counties) to 34 2-3: and from the head of Tide to the Sea Coast (containing thirty-six counties and four towns intitled to representation) to 29 delegates. If the number of delegates were reduced to 120, and distributed in proportion to the present distribution, the result would be that the first District would be intitled to 29 delegates,—the second District to 16,—the third District to 32 1-2,—and the fourth to 42 1-2 delegates. So that, on the basis of white population, in comparison with the present apportionment, the different Districts would stand thus:

The 1st District would gain	3 members.
The 2d District would gain	8 1-3 members.
The 3d District would gain	2 members.
The 4th District would lose	13 1-3 members.

So that the 3d and 4th Districts, which are slave-holding Districts, would lose 11 1-3 members; and the two Western Districts would gain 11 1-3 members.

The gentleman from Albemarle (Mr. Gordon) has told us, that the Valley and the middle country, which he calls the "heart of the State," have a majority of white population and pay a majority of taxes, and ought to have a majority of Delegates; whereas, at present they have only 86 Delegates out of 214. I agree that these two Districts ought to have a majority; and let us see how they will stand on the white basis and on the compound basis of representation. That gentleman, to insure the majority of Delegates to the "heart of the State," again refers to the Census of 1820; whereas, by the Census of 1829, which I have endeavoured to show ought to be relied upon, on the basis of white population, they would have only 59, out of 120 Delegates; and these two Districts, on the white basis, never can have a majority, because the white population West of the Alleghany, increases much faster than in the Valley; and in the other two Districts there is very little increase. The present white population of the second and third Districts together is 335,354, and the first and fourth Districts together have a white population of 346,907. It is only on the combined basis of population and taxation, that the second and third Districts can have that majority which the gentleman from Albemarle, so ardently desires they should have. On the combined basis, the first District would have 21 Delegates: the second District 21: the third District 41: and the fourth District 37; and the second and third Districts, "the heart of the State," would have, together, 62 Delegates; instead of 59 on the white basis.

The gentleman from Albemarle (Mr. Gordon), and the gentleman from Loudoun (Mr. Mercer) have also told the Committee, that if representation be apportioned according to white population alone, there would still be a considerable majority of Delegates East of the Blue Ridge. The first gentleman says the majority would be 19, and the other says it would be 20. Here again the gentlemen are compelled to resort to the Census of 1820, to sustain their positions. If, in argument, you will grant gentlemen their premises, it is very easy to prove any thing they wish; but I must again insist on holding gentlemen to the Auditor's estimate of the population of 1829. I cannot consent that they should adopt it when it suits them, and abandon it when it makes against them. Why, Mr. Chairman, should we talk about the Census of 1820, when it is manifest that no apportionment of representation under the new Constitution which may be recommended by this Convention to the people, ever can be made under that Census? The Delegates in 1830 are to be elected under the old Constitution, and in 1830 a new Census will be taken under the authority of the General Government, and the first apportionment of Delegates that can ever take place under the new Constitution, will be conformable to the Census of 1830.

The gentleman from Loudoun (Mr. Mercer) has told the Committee, that there would not be a majority of white population West of the Blue Ridge before 1850; and that the transfer of political power to the West would be gradual. This information is no doubt kindly intended by that gentleman, to allay the apprehensions of the East. While I may be disposed to admire the philanthropy which prompts the information, I cannot admit the premises necessary to enable the gentleman to prove his position. Here again, he refers to the Census of 1820. According to the Auditor's "*Census*," the white population West of the Blue Ridge, is now 319,516; and on the East of the Ridge 362,745. If the white population continue to increase in the same ratio as it has increased since 1820, then in 1835, the white population West of the Blue Ridge will be 375,310; and East of the Blue Ridge 372,293, being a majority of 3,017 West of the Blue Ridge. I acknowledge, Mr. Chairman, that on this subject I have heretofore been mistaken, and, possibly, I may have induced some others to adopt my errors. I did not suppose, until I saw the Auditor's estimate, that the majority of white population would be West of the Blue Ridge so early as 1835.

I have said, Mr. Chairman, that if there were no slaves in the State, or if by unanimous consent they were to be forever exempted from taxation, I should still vote for the amendment under consideration. Those who have the power of laying the taxes, ought to be directly responsible to those who are compelled to pay them—not merely in name, but in fact. If the report of the Legislative Committee be adopted, then taxes to any amount may be imposed, contrary to the unanimous wishes of those who pay three-fourths of the taxes, and imposed by agents who owe no responsibility, express or implied, to those who are compelled to pay the greater portion of these taxes. Like the gentleman from Hanover (Mr. Morris), I can imagine no despotism more oppressive than that which gives to one man the power of laying taxes, and imposes the duty of paying the taxes on those who have no control over laying them. Why is it, Sir, that the Constitution of the United States, and of all the several States, give the power of originating laws imposing taxes, to the most numerous branch of the respective Legislatures? It is because the most numerous branches of the Legislature are more immediately the representatives of the people; they are elected for shorter periods, and are compelled more speedily to return to the people and give an account of their stewardship. Those who pay the taxes ought to have complete control over those who have the power of laying the taxes; otherwise the taxes, which in a free Government should be considered as the voluntary contributions of the citizen for the services of the State, would be, in fact, arbitrary exactions made by irresponsible agents. If the amendment to the report of the Legislative Committee be adopted, this salutary and necessary control will be preserved; but if the amendment be rejected, then taxes may be laid by those who are not responsible to those who are compelled to pay them.

Let us see, Mr. Chairman, what has been done by other States in this Union, in fixing the basis of representation in their respective Legislatures. We have been told in the progress of this debate, that fifteen States of this Union have adopted the white basis, without regard to any other consideration; and we have been urged to follow their example. Here again, I am sure that the honourable gentlemen who have made this assertion had no intention to deceive the Committee; but I am equally certain that they have reckoned without their hosts. Instead of fifteen States having adopted the white basis, *unqualified*, there are but six who have adopted that basis without modification. And of these six, neither of them are of the Old Thirteen States of this Union—and four of them are States created within the last few years. The only States which have adopted this basis, *unqualified*, are Kentucky, Ohio, Indiana, Illinois, Mississippi and Alabama. I must beg the indulgence of the Committee while I refer to the Constitutions of the other States, particularly on this subject.

In Massachusetts, where they have no slaves, the representation in the Senate is based intirely on taxation; and in the House of Representatives every town having 150 rateable polls is intitled to one representative; and every town having 375, is intitled to two representatives.

In Maine, every town containing 1,500 inhabitants, is intitled to one representative; and so on, increasing until a town has 26,250 inhabitants, when it shall be intitled to seven representatives; *and no town shall ever have more than seven representatives.*

In New-Hampshire, the representation in the Senate is based on taxation alone. In the House of Representatives, a town having 150 rateable polls is intitled to one representative, and a town having 450 is intitled to two.

In Vermont, towns containing 80 taxable inhabitants are intitled to two representatives; and all others, without regard to population, are intitled to one.

In Connecticut, (that land of steady habits, to which the gentleman from Loudoun wished he could transport all the members of this Convention, to witness the beneficial results of her wise institutions) each new town, *without regard to population*, is intitled to one representative.

In New York and Pennsylvania (so often referred to in a commendatory manner in this debate,) each county, however small the population, is intitled to one representative, and the larger counties to more than one—according to population in the one and taxable inhabitants in the other State. When the gentleman from Loudoun to-day was reading parts of the Constitutions of different States, he read that part of the Constitution of Pennsylvania which directed that representation should be apportioned according to taxable inhabitants; and the very next sentence after that read by the gentleman, commenced with these words, "Every county shall have at least one representative," &c. I am sure the omission of the gentleman to read that clause was intirely accidental: I know him to be too honorable to wish to impose upon the Committee. In New Jersey, Delaware, Maryland, and North Carolina, the representation in both Houses is apportioned by counties, without regard to numbers; and in Virginia, the House of Delegates is apportioned by counties, and the Senate according to white population. In South Carolina, the representation in both Houses is apportioned according to population and taxation combined; but every district shall have one, whatever may be the population and taxation. In Georgia, the Senate is equally apportioned amongst the counties, without regard to population; and the House of Representatives is apportioned according to federal numbers, but subject to this modification, that each county shall have at least one and not more than four members; and counties having 3,000, to have two delegates; 7,000 three; and 12,000 and upwards, four delegates. In Tennessee, both Houses are apportioned according to taxable inhabitants, including slaves. In Louisiana, the Senatorial districts are to remain forever unchanged, without regard to the increase of population. And in Missouri, each county is to have one representative at least, and the larger counties more than one, according to population. If, Sir, we are to be influenced by the example of other States, by which ought we to be influenced; by the example of seventeen States, twelve of which are old States, some of whose Constitutions have have been tested by the experience of near half a century? Or, shall we follow the example of our younger sisters, some of whom are so young that they have not yet had a sufficient opportunity of testing the wisdom of their measures? The gentleman from Loudoun (Mr. Mercer) read to the Committee extracts from the Bills of Rights, prefixed to the Constitutions of a number of the States, to prove the equality of all men, and to convince the House that the white basis, without regard to any other consideration, ought to be adopted. It is true, that seven of the States have Bills of Rights declaring the equality of all men; and that the majority have a right to alter and modify the Government as they please. Notwithstanding all these Bills of Rights we find the wise men who made these Constitutions, like George Mason and his compatriots of 1776 who made the Constitution of Virginia, wisely modifying general principles, so as to adapt them to the particular situation and circumstances of their several States; they made the coat to fit the man who was to wear it, rather than to make the coat without regard to the dimensions of the man, and compel him to wear it whether it fits him or not. Thus, Mr. Chairman, will all wise lawgivers act. A Constitution, although it may be made according to the most approved ideas of theoretical perfection, is of but little value, unless it be adapted to the circumstances of the country for which it is intended. And, cotemporary expositions of the meaning of an instrument made by the authors of the instrument themselves, are intitled to more respect than the most elaborate and ingenious essays of subsequent commentators.

We were told yesterday by the gentleman from Loudoun, that for the last seven years, there had been no State tax in Massachusetts and New Hampshire; and therefore, although they had a provision in their Constitutions for basing representation in the Senate according to taxation, it had ceased to operate in practice, and white population was now alone regarded. I am willing to follow precisely in the footsteps of New Hampshire and Massachusetts on this subject. Let us have the power of protecting ourselves from unjust taxes as long as it is necessary, and the moment those, into whose hands the political power of Virginia seems destined shortly to pass, can so wisely manage our concerns as to exempt us from taxation, I for one, am ready to adopt the basis of white population alone. Yes, Sir, I am prepared this day to agree to it on these conditions; and on our own principles, if the amendment prevails, as soon as we have no taxes to pay, white population alone will be regarded.

In order to show the inequality of taxation, and the necessity that should induce those sections of the State paying the greater part of the taxes, to adopt the proposed amendment, I beg leave to refer to some statements and calculations I have made on this subject, founded on the Auditor's report. The whole revenue of the State *paid into the public treasury* in the year 1828, and arising from taxes on land, slaves, horses, carriages and licenses, amounted to $385,429 50. If this sum be divided by 682,261, which is the whole number of white inhabitants, according to the Auditor's calculation, it will give 56 cents 5 mills as the average taxes paid by each white person in the State. In making this calculation, I have excluded free negroes from the estimate of persons paying taxes to the *State*, because I have no doubt of the fact, that throughout the State, free negroes contribute very little indeed to the public revenue; so little as not to affect the accuracy of my calculations. The county in which I reside, contains, unfortunately for us, the one-twentieth part of the whole free negroes of the State, and the free negroes of that county do not pay $30 of revenue to the Commonwealth; and, from the information of other gentlemen, I believe it will be found that free negroes are equally worthless throughout the State. If any portions of the State have a more respectable class of free negroes than we have, I congratulate them. With us, instead of contributing to the wealth or revenue of the State, they are perfect nuisances.

While the average taxation for each white person in the State is 56 cents 5 mills, the average paid in the different districts is as follows:

In the first district, (West of the Alleghany) 18 cents 6 mills; in the second district, (the Valley) 41 cents 2 mills. The whole country West of the Blue Ridge, averages 28 cents 4 mills.

In the third district, (from the Blue Ridge to tide) 76 cents 2 mills; in the fourth district, (from the head of tide to the sea) 87 cents 2 mills. The average of the whole country East of the Blue Ridge is 81 cents 2 mills.

There is no subject of taxation on which the West pays as much tax per head, according to white population as the East. To show this, I must beg the indulgence of the Committee, while I refer to another calculation I have made:

The whole land tax *assessed* in the State *(but not all paid in)* amounts, for each white person, to 25 cents 7 mills.

In the first district, for each white person, it amounts to 9 cents 2 mills; in the second district, for each white person, it amounts to 24 cents 6 mills. West of the Blue Ridge, the average is 15 cents 8 mills.

In the third district, for each white person, it amounts to 33 cents 8 mills; in the fourth district, for each white person, it amounts to 34 cents 7 mills. East of the Blue Ridge, the average is 34 cents 4 mills.

So that for every dollar of the land tax for each white person paid by the people West of the Blue Ridge, those on the East side pay $2 18 cents for each white person.

The slave tax assessed amounts, for each white person in the State, to 16 cents 8 mills.

In the first district, it amounts to 2 cents 3 mills; in the second district, it amounts to 6 cents 2 mills. West of the Blue Ridge, it averages 4 cents.

In the third district, it amounts to 28 cents 5 mills; in the fourth district it amounts to 27 cents 6 mills. East of the Ridge, it averages 28 cents 1 mill.

So that the whole country East of the Blue Ridge pays, on an average, for each white person, a slave tax amounting to more than seven times as much as is paid by the whole country West of the Blue Ridge—and more than twelve times as much as the country West of the Alleghany.

The taxes assessed on horses and carriages amount, for each white person in the State, to 7 cents 7 mills.

In the first district, it amounts to 5 cents 1 mill; in the second district, it amounts to 7 cents 4 mills. West of the Ridge it averages 6 cents 2 mills.

In the third district, it amounts to 9 cents 2 mills; in the fourth district, it amounts to 9 cents. East of the Ridge, it averages 9 cents 1 mill. Which is fifty per cent. more than the average to the West of the Ridge.

Taxes on licenses average throughout the State, for each white person 11 cents 8 mills.

In the first district, the average is 4 cents 7 mills; in the second district, the average is 7 cents. West of the Blue Ridge, the average is 5 cents 7 mills.

In the third district, the average is 11 cents 2 mills; in the fourth district, the average is 24 cents. East of the Ridge, the average is 17 cents. Which is more than three times as much as the average to the West.

It thus appears, that on every subject of taxation, the country East of the Ridge pays a great deal more for each white person, than is paid to the West. Even of the land tax, the poor and worn out country from the head of tide to the sea coast—a country which has been settled for two hundred years, and has been suffering under a most injudicious and ruinous system of agriculture, for each white man, the land pays near fifty per cent. more than is paid in that Valley, which we have been told, and no doubt correctly, is the finest Valley on the face of the globe.

But if the slave tax be rejected intirely from the estimate, it will be found that of the other taxes *assessed*, the different districts will stand for each white person thus: The first district, 19 cents; the second district, 39 cents; the third district, 54 cents 2 mills; the fourth district, 67 cents 7 mills. The average West of the Ridge, 27 cents 7 mills; and the average East of the Ridge, 60 cents 5 mills. It thus appears, that for every dollar of taxes (exclusive of slave tax) assessed for each white person West of the Alleghany, there are about $ 3 50 cents assessed on each white person in the tide water district—and for every dollar for each white person (exclusive of slave tax) assessed on the whole country West of the Blue Ridge, there are $ 2 18 cents assessed on each white person East of the Ridge. And if the slave tax be included, it will be found that the disparity is much greater. If we examine the amount of taxes paid into the Treasury, from some separate counties, we shall find the inequality to be still more glaring. In the large counties of Monongalia and Harrison, lying to the West of the Alleghany Mountains, the average taxation for each white person is 13 cents 5 mills. In Powhatan and Nottoway, lying East of the Ridge, the average of the counties is $ 1 33 cents 2 mills.*

I will now proceed to examine, Mr. Chairman, how the representation on the white basis will stand in comparison with the taxes paid in different Districts of country. The whole amount of taxes *paid into* the Public Treasury, per Auditor's statement, amounts to $ 385,429 59 cents. If this sum be divided by 120 (the number of Delegates recommended by the Legislative Committee) it will give $ 3,211 91 cents as the average taxation paid by the constituents of each Delegate in the State. Instead of the constituents of each Delegate paying this sum, they will pay as follows, viz:

In the first District, for each Delegate will be paid	$ 1,055 32
In the second District, for each Delegate will be paid	2,340 90
In the third District, for each Delegate will be paid	3,954 34
In the fourth District, for each Delegate will be paid	4,980 06

From this statement it will appear that the constituents of each Delegate in the Tide Water District, pay nearly five times as much taxes, as will be paid by the constituents of each Delegate West of the Alleghany mountains. I will now show how it will stand in regard to some individual counties. In Monongalia and Harrison together, the white population amounts to 26.243, and they together pay taxes to the amount of $ 3,553 02. For a Delegate from these counties, therefore, their constitu-

* In Grayson county, the average taxes paid for each white person, is 10 cents. In Giles, 13 cents; in Lewis, 12¾ cents; in Preston, 12 cents; in Logan, 9¼ cents; and in Nicholas, 8¼ cents.

ents would pay a tax of only $ 768 71.* In Powhatan and Nottoway together, the white population is 5,434, and the taxes amount to $ 7,238 51. For a Delegate from these counties, the constituents would pay a tax at the rate of $ 7,572 85. The constituents of a Delegate from Powhatan and Nottoway, would therefore be compelled to pay nearly ten times as much as the constituents of each Delegate from Monongalia and Harrison: and the average paid by the constituents of each Delegate in the Tide Water District, would be near seven times as much as would be paid by the constituents of each Delegate from Monongalia and Harrison.

In order to render the representative really and effectually responsible to the constituents, in the exercise of the important power of taxation, there should not be a great disparity in the burthens imposed by any proposed system of taxation on the aggregate constituents of each delegate: the disparity should never be greater than is produced by a combination of persons and taxation. But on the white basis, as applied to the situation of Virginia, while a member West of the Alleghany on the principles of taxation heretofore adopted (and the East cannot have any reason to calculate on any change of that system being made beneficial to them) votes to impose a tax of one dollar on his own constituents, he at the same time votes to impose a tax of near five dollars on each of the constituents of every delegate from the tide water country; and when a delegate from Monongalia or Harrison votes to impose a tax of one dollar on his own constituents, he at the same time votes to impose a tax of near seven dollars on the people of the tide water country, and near ten dollars on the people of Powhatan and Nottoway. Under such an inequality of taxation and representation, the responsibility of the representative to his constituents, is merely nominal. The gentleman from Albemarle (Mr. Gordon,) told us the other day, Mr. Chairman, that there was a district of country in the neighborhood of Richmond, having twenty-nine delegates, which did not pay as much taxes, and had not as many inhabitants as another district of country at the foot of the Blue Ridge, having only ten delegates. This, I admit, as the gentleman tells us, is a disease of the body politic, and *this* the gentleman from Albemarle proposes to cure by the application of the white basis, as a panacea. But, I think, from the analysis which I have given of the remedy, it will be found that, like many quack medicines applied to the human body, it only serves to make the patient worse.

Mr. Chairman, although we may talk a great deal about our disinterestedness, yet if we will examine ourselves, and the suggestions of our own hearts, we shall be very apt to find, that self-interest in some degree actuates us even when we appear to be the most disinterested and patriotic—and we are very apt to calculate how particular measures would operate at home. I confess, Mr. Chairman, I have examined, what would be the effect of the white basis upon the district in which I live: and I dare say, other gentlemen have made similar calculations as to their respective districts. I think it not improbable that my friends from the West, who I have no doubt are as honest and disinterested as any men upon earth, have calculated the relative operation of the white basis and compound basis in their section of country—and if they have not, there is a marvellous coincidence of opinion amongst them and acting intuitively in the direction their own interests would point out.

If the white basis be adopted, as gentlemen contend it should be, in both branches of the State Legislature, and the report of the Legislative Committee, recommending that the number of Senators should remain at twenty-four, be adopted, then according to the supposed population of 1829, 28,425 white inhabitants will be necessary to intitle a district to a Senator. The Accomack Senatorial district would require a considerable addition to give it a sufficiency of white population to intitle it to a Senator. Having regard to contiguous territory, I propose to add the counties of York, Elizabeth City, Warwick and Essex, and the whole district would then contain only 247 white inhabitants more than the number required. This district, thus enlarged, pays a revenue of $ 19,491 08, while the average which would be paid in each Senatorial district West of the Alleghany, would be only $ 5,276 60, and in the district of Harrison and Monongalia only $ 3,843 55.

Although the Accomack district shows a striking inequality in taxation and representation compared with some other districts, yet there is another district in which the inequality is much greater. There is a district of country, Sir, not fifty miles from Richmond, in which a Senatorial district composed of contiguous counties (on the basis of white population, and the number of Senators being retained at 24,) would pay at the same rate of taxation paid in 1828, within less than $ 600 of as much revenue on lands, slaves, horses, carriages and licenses, as the whole country West of the Alleghany mountains, paid in 1828, on the same articles; that is the Chesterfield district. This district is now composed of the counties of Chesterfield, Amelia, Powhatan, Nottoway, Cumberland and the town of Petersburg. This district now

* In Nicholas county, the taxes are at the rate of $ 466 for a delegate; in Logan, $ 540; and in Grayson $ 568 50.

contains 24,572 white inhabitants; and in order to bring it up to the number, which will be required on the white basis, I propose to add the adjoining county of Lunenburg. The district would then have within nine of the number of white inhabitants required for a Senator; and the revenue paid from that district in 1828, amounted to $ 33,194 80, on the articles enumerated above, while the whole country West of the Alleghany only paid $ 33,770 14 on the same articles, being an exces of only $ 575 34.

By an examination, I have made in the Auditor's office, I have ascertained some facts at the result of which I confess I was myself astonished. From the examination and calculations I have made in the Auditor's office, I think I can make it satisfactorily appear to the Convention that the whole country West of the Blue Ridge, from the Auditor's report of the taxes on lands, slaves, horses, carriages, and licenses, does not contribute one cent to the general revenue of the State for general purposes, but on the contrary is largely in arrear; that is to say, they do not pay as much revenue as their own citizens receive back as members of the Assembly and for claims and services which may be considered of a local character. The Valley, taken by itself, I admit, pays a large surplus; but the country beyond the Alleghany does not pay much more than half enough for its own purposes; and by adding the two districts together, there appears to be a considerable deficiency.

The expenses of the General Assembly—Commissioners of the Revenue and Cleks for examining Commissioners' books—Criminal charges and Guards—Contingent expenses of Courts—Militia, for Adjutants, Brigade Inspectors, &c.—Comparing Polls—Salaries of General Court Judges and Chancellors, amount, rejecting cents to about $ 259,573. If this sum be divided amongst the different sections of the State, according to counties equally, it will be found that the country West of the Blue Ridge receives $ 97,035, and the revenue paid West of the Ridge, (according to the Auditor's report to the Convention, above referred to,) amounts to $ 90,732—being $ 6,303 less than it receives. In making the calculation of the sum received by each section of the State by counties, the result is favorable to the West; because their members of the Assembly, Judges, and Guards attending convicts, receive a great deal more mileage than is received by the Eastern half of the State. In making this calculation, I have omitted the salaries of the Governor and Council—Judges of the Court of Appeals—Attorney General—Auditor and Treasurer, and their Clerks—Public Guard at Richmond and *Lexington too*—Contingent fund—and in fact all expenses which can be regarded of a general character. To this deficiency of $ 6,303, add for Lunatic Hospital at Staunton $ 7,500, and also add $ 8,374 for the Literary Fund, (being the difference between $ 18,968 of the annual appropriation of $ 45,000 for Primary Schools received by the West, according to the ratio of white population by which it is distributed, and $ 10,594 for the amount paid by the West, on the supposition that that fund was raised from the different parts of the State in the same proportion that the revenue is now paid) and we have the sum of $22,177, received every year by the country West of the Blue Ridge from the Treasury more than they contribute, according to the Auditor's report, without charging them with any part of the expenses of a general character.*

If the basis of white population be adopted, the country West of the Blue Ridge, which is now a charge of $ 22,000 annually, for their individual purposes on the rest of the State, will have immediately nearly one half of the delegates in the State Legislature; and, after 1835, will have a majority of delegates; and will have the power of imposing taxes at pleasure on the rest of the State. With these facts before us, can it be expected that Eastern Virginia, if there was not a slave in the State, could consent to give to their fellow citizens of the West the absolute and irresponsible control of their property. I think not. For myself, I confess that I am not willing to do it.

We are told, Mr. Chairman, by our Western friends, that the people of the East should rely on the integrity and honesty of their brethren of the West, and that the restraints of conscience will be sufficient to prevent any oppression of their Eastern brethren. I have no doubt the people of the West are as honest as any people on earth, and a gentleman from that country told us a few days ago that they were *peculiarly honest*. I know them them to be honest, brave and patriotic; but I know they are also *men*, and subject to the infirmities of poor fallen man—*I* would not trust Aristides himself to tax me, unless he were responsible to me for the faithful execution of the trust. It was said, by one of the wisest statesmen America ever produced, that *faith* was necessary to salvation hereafter, but in this world *jealousy* was the best

* The tax on law process was not included in the Auditor's report to the Convention, and is not included in this calculation. It has since been ascertained that the whole amount of the tax on law process paid into the public Treasury from the country West of the Blue Ridge in the year 1828, was $ 7,638 61. If this sum be deducted from $ 22,177, there will still be a deficiency of $ 14,538 39, without taking into the estimate any appropriation for Internal Improvements West of the Blue Ridge—The precise amount of deficiency was not deemed important; the principle object was to show, what is believed to be a fact, that the whole country West of the Blue Ridge did not pay as much into the Treasury as it received back.

security for the preservation of man. I have no fears of private property being endangered from individual rapine. No, Sir, not the slightest; but I am unwilling to subject property to taxation by agents who are not responsible to those who are compelled to pay the taxes.

This Hall, seems to me, Sir, to be the last place in America in which this doctrine of political faith ought to be held out. This Hall has been repeatedly made the theatre on which the ablest men Virginia ever produced, have eloquently appealed to their fellow citizens to resist the usurpations of the General Government in violation of the Constitution of the United States. For thirty years, the violations of that Constitution have been the theme of complaint by Virginians. We are told that the Constitution has been twice violated by the establishment of the Banks of the United States—has been violated by the Alien and Sedition laws—and by the whole system of Tariff laws for the protection of domestic manufactures. These violations, too, are said to have been committed by those who were bound by the solemn obligation of an oath, to support the Constitution. Prudence forbids my inquiring, here, whether these complaints be well founded or not; it is enough to know that they exist to prevent Virginians from trusting to a sense of honour and the restraints of conscience alone, to prevent men from pursuing their own interests when there are no Constitutional provisions in the way, and when their own discretion is the sole measure of their power. What is it that induces one part of the country to support and another to oppose the Tariff laws? Is it not probable that interest has something to do with it? There is no doubt of it.

It has been frequently said in the progress of this debate, that the object of Western gentlemen in wishing the white basis to be established, was to enable them to obtain the passage of laws for the promotion of a system for the internal improvement of their country. I thought the magnanimity and candor of gentlemen would prevent them from denying that that was one of their primary objects. What else can be their object? Does any gentleman pretend that the security of personal rights requires the adoption of this principle? Is it mere theoretical perfection they aim at? Or is it not rather some *practical* advantage, which they expect to result from it? I had like to have said, is it not self interest, that in *some degree* prompts them?

I know, Sir, that some of the leading politicians of the West have the promotion of internal improvement greatly at heart. I mention this in no reproachful spirit—it is honorable to them—and if they did not wish to improve their country, and facilitate the means of intercourse by roads and canals—they would be unworthy of those salubrious hills and fertile vallies with which their delightful region abounds. I am myself a friend to internal improvement. I consider that every road and every canal, connecting the East and the West, is a strong bond of union—a union which I hope may be perpetual. If you make it the interest of men to be united, they will be very apt to remain united; and if you make it their interest to be separated, nothing but the strong arm of power can hold them long together. If I were a member of the Legislature, I would grant pecuniary assistance to my Western fellow citizens, in no grudging spirit, for the improvement of their country. But while I declare, with perfect sincerity, my willingness to aid my fellow citizens of the West in this great work of internal improvement, I want those who are to pay the expense to have the power of judging and deciding *when, for what purpose*—and to *what extent* they will contribute to that object. No one is so competent to decide upon the ability of a man to pay, as that man who is compelled to pay. And no person should have the power of deciding how much shall be paid, and for what purposes, except the tax-payer himself, or his immediate and responsible representative—and least of all, should the power of imposing the taxes be given to those who are directly interested to make large impositions.

The gentleman from Brooke (Mr. Doddridge) told us, that the masters of slaves in the East, wished their fellow citizens of the West to bow their necks and become political slaves—and that if the amendment proposed by the gentleman from Culpeper prevails, the West will forever be subject to the political power of the East. With due respect to that gentleman, I must beg leave to differ from him. If the white population of the West continues to increase as rapidly hereafter, as it has done since 1820, and the taxes for each white person in the different sections of the State shall be the same they now are, then, on the combined basis, in 1856 one half of the delegates will be West of the Ridge, and one half East; and in 1857, the majority would be West of the Ridge. When the population of the West shall so increase that the majority of political power shall be West of the Blue Ridge, that country will not be near so populous as the Eastern country now is. The trans-Alleghany district would then have about 17 inhabitants to the square mile, and the Valley about 26: and at present the middle country has 28, and the old and *impoverished* tide water country 33 to the square mile. If other gentlemen are disposed to object to this estimate of the future population of the Western sections of this State, my friend from Brooke cannot object to it, because it was in that same speech he told us that in thirty years the majority would be West of the Alleghany, and the population of the East would be to the West but as a "*drop in the bucket*."

Although, Mr. Chairman, I decidedly prefer the combined basis to the white basis of representation, yet I should be willing to abandon it in favor of a *graduated* county plan of representation, if such an one can be adopted as will protect those who pay the taxes from oppressive burthens. Many of the counties of Virginia have been in existence for 200 years, and the people have been so long in the habit of forming county associations and having separate representation, that no plan could be acceptable to the people which broke up these ancient county boundaries. I would adopt a *graduated* county representation, for the same reason that induced George Mason and the other wise men who formed the Constitution of 1776, to depart in the Constitution from the *literal* meaning of the Bill of Rights: I would do it, because it is best adapted to the situation of Virginia. By this plan, the political power of the country will gradually pass to the West, as the wealth and taxes of that country increase; and as the increasing population of that country shall render the formation of new counties necessary in that section of the State; while no new counties would be formed to the East.

I am sorry, Mr. Chairman, that I have detained the Committee so long at this late hour of the day; I thank the Committee for their attention, and will conclude with expressing the ardent wish that this important question may be so settled as will be satisfactory to the whole people of Virginia, and will permanently promote their prosperity and happiness.

Mr. Joynes having resumed his seat, the Committee rose, and thereupon the House adjourned.

FRIDAY, November 6, 1829.

The Convention met at 11 o'clock, and its sitting was opened with prayer by the Rev. Mr. Lee of the Episcopal Church.

Mr. Townes of Pittsylvania, submitted a resolution, which, if the Convention thought worthy of its attention, he hoped would be referred to the Committee of the Whole.

This resolution, read by the Clerk, is as follows:

"*Resolved*, That all propositions for laying the taxes, or appropriating the public money, or for the loan of money upon the credit of the State, the votes of the members of both branches of the General Assembly, representing the divisions of the State hereafter mentioned, shall avail, in proportion to the amount of public revenue collected in each division of the preceding year. A majority of the members from each division, shall give the vote of the division; to which end, that part of the State which is composed of the counties of ———, shall be one division; that part which is composed of the counties of ———, shall be another division; that part which is composed of the counties of ———, shall be another division; and that part which is composed of the counties of ———, shall be another division."

Mr. Townes moved, that the resolution be referred to the Committee of the Whole, which was agreed to.

The President then submitted a letter from the Presbyterian Synod of Virginia, (which had just had its meeting in this city,) expressing their cordial concurrence in the principles of toleration, which had marked the proceedings of the Convention. This letter was read as follows:

"At the Sessions of the Synod of Virginia, held in the First Presbyterian Church in the city of Richmond, on the 31st of October, A. D. 1829, the following resolution was *unanimously* adopted:

"*Resolved unanimously*, That the Synod of Virginia have observed with great satisfaction, that the Convention now assembled to form a new Constitution for the People of this Commonwealth, are proposing and doubtless intending to preserve and perpetuate the sacred principle—*Liberty of Conscience*—declared in the Bill of Rights and developed in the Act establishing Religious Freedom, as a part of the fundamental law of the land; and they do hereby solemnly proclaim, that they continue to esteem and cherish that principle for which the Presbyterian Church in this State, and throughout the United States, have ever zealously and heartily contended, as the clearest right and the most precious privilege that freemen can exert.

"*Resolved*, That John H. Rice, D. D. Conrad Speece, D. D. and William Maxwell, be a committee to communicate a copy of the foregoing resolution to the President of the Convention, to be very respectfully submitted to that body at such time as he shall deem most proper and convenient.

"WM HILL. *Moderator.*

"FRANCIS M'FARLAND, *Clerk of Synod.*"

On Mr. Naylor's motion, this paper was laid on the table—Mr. N. moved also to have it printed, and on taking the question, the voices seemed to be against it: on Mr. Naylor's saying, that he would be content with the spreading of it on the Journals of the Convention, no count was taken.

The Convention having gone into Committee of the Whole, Mr. Powell in the Chair:

Mr. FITZHUGH addressed the Committee:

I had determined, Mr. Chairman, to take no part in this discussion, but to give a silent vote on the question before you, and to rest my justification for doing so, on the character of this body. Circumstances, however, have recently occurred, which have changed my determination. My sentiments, at all times fully, fairly, and freely expressed, and on no subject more fairly or more fully expressed than on this, have, it seems, become a matter of speculation amongst those whom I have the honor to represent. By what agency this has been effected, I have not yet been able to learn. Nor is it material. I know very well, however, the means by which an honorable and high-minded people may be disabused, in relation to a faithful representative; and, if in seeking to employ them on the present occasion, I should seem to be offering instruction to the venerable men around me, who are so much better fitted by their age, their wisdom, and their experience, to give, than to receive instruction, I trust I shall find a sufficient apology with them at least, in the peculiarity of my situation.

I am an advocate, Sir, for the resolution of the Legislative Committee. I am so, because I believe its design to be, what I am sure its effect must be, so to organize the Government of the State, that its future laws shall emanate from a majority of its recognized voters. In declaring my preference for this principle, I hope to relieve myself from the imputations so profusely cast upon its advocates, by disclaiming all authority for it, as derived from the laws of nature, and all support for it, founded on metaphysical abstractions. I view it, on the contrary, as one of those plain and practical principles, which the common sense and experience of mankind have almost constituted into a political axiom.

Let me not be understood as wishing to impair, in the smallest degree, the character of the Bill of Rights. No, Sir. I recognize almost all its principles, when practically construed, as sacred. All men, for instance, are by nature "equally free and independent." But, God forbid that I should so far disregard the lights of reason and of common sense, as to infer from hence, a political equality that must accompany man through all the various modes and changes of political society. Political right, Sir, or more properly, political power, is the creature of Convention, and the very same instrument that ascribes to all men a perfect equality in the formation of this Convention, recognizes in the community of its creation, a perfect right not only to establish that Government, which it deems "capable of producing the greatest degree of happiness and safety," but to change it "whenever found inadequate or contrary to the purposes for which it was intended."

When, then, we speak of the natural equality of man, we mean only that no one, in the original organization of Government, can claim a natural superiority to another; that all may enter, or refuse to enter, into the compact proposed, as to them may seem best; and that they may, in the language of the Bill of Rights, select that Government, which they deem "capable of producing the greatest degree of happiness and safety." The relative power of each, is of course to be determined by the compact itself; and all that can be asked on this subject, is, that it should be regulated by reason and justice.

With the gentleman from Orange, (Mr. Barbour,) I agree in regarding as the wisest political maxim ever uttered, the declaration of Solon "that he had given to the Athenians, not the best Government *he* could have framed, but the best *they* were capable of receiving." This, in truth, is the foundation of all good Government. In opposition to the gentleman from Northampton, (Mr. Upshur,) it admits the existence of principles in politics. It recognizes a standard in Government, as well as in morals and in taste; and it recognizes also, the propriety of varying from that standard, as circumstances may require.

With these admissions on my part, Sir, I only claim from gentlemen opposed to me, the acknowledgment, that of all forms of Government, the Republican form is best; that in the exercise of its power, all other things being equal, the supreme authority should be vested in the majority, rather than in the minority; and that as all departures from this principle are evils, they should go no farther than may be required by the actual necessity of the case; and this enables me to proceed at once to the practical consideration of the question before us.

The resolution of the gentleman from Culpeper, (Mr. Green) proposes so to amend the report of the Legislative Committee, as to base representation on population and taxation combined. For the present, it is true, it embraces but one branch of the Legislature; but I feel myself justified in inferring from the arguments urged in its support, both here and elsewhere, that the real design is to organize the whole Legislative Department on this principle; and of course to transfer to a minority of the recognized voters of the State, the exclusive power of enacting all the laws of the State.

When a proposition of this extraordinary character, totally at war with the principles I have heretofore sustained, is made, I must be pardoned for examining both its extent and the reasons by which it is supported, before I yield it my assent. I lament that in doing so, I shall be compelled to resort to any thing in the shape of statistical exhibits.

I know very well, that in debate, statistics are always disgusting, and seldom efficient; but I feel, that on the present occasion, I cannot more clearly illustrate the propositions I mean to sustain, than by a few short and simple details, extracted from the reports of the Auditor.

If a line be drawn from the waters of the Chappawamsic, (a stream insignificant in itself, but rendered classic by the eloquent allusions so often made to it elsewhere,) to the southwestern corner of the county of Patrick, the State will be thrown into two divisions; each embracing eleven Congressional Districts. And if, as I understand from those who have made the calculation, a representation based on Federal numbers be but little different from a representation based on population and taxation combined, each of these divisions will be entitled, on the principle of the amendment, to an equal number of representatives in the future Legislature. But the documents supplied us by the Auditor shew, that while the western division, embracing among others the District I have the honor to represent, contains 349,720 white inhabitants, the lower or Eastern division, contains only 253,361; leaving a balance in favour of the former, of 96,369.

I think it proper to remark, in relation to this statement, that it is derived from the Census of 1820, as presenting the only authentic source of information on this subject. And I have felt the less difficulty in resorting to it, rather than to the uncertain calculations of the Auditor, as to the probable population of the State in 1829, because, although the use of the latter might have occasioned a little difference of result in figures, it would not have affected, in the smallest degree, the principle for which I am contending.

But the subject may be presented in a still stronger point of view, by a reference to the relative vote of the two divisions. I find that on the Convention question, the Western division gave 23,096 votes; while the Eastern gave only 15,437; leaving a majority in favour of the former, of 7,559. An idea, I know, at one time prevailed, that a large number of bad votes had been given in the Western country, and that the expression of public opinion on that occasion, furnished of course no fair test of the relative strength of the different parts of the State. But it so happens, that the vote of the two divisions was very nearly in proportion to their population in 1820. Whereas, if the relative increase of population has been as much greater in the West, as has been supposed, and a full vote had been taken, the majority ought to have been very far beyond what was actually obtained.

But taking the case as it is, it presents this obvious result: that 23,096 voters in that division of the State from which I come, are, on the plan of the gentleman from Culpeper, to elect no more representatives in the legislative body than 15,436 in the lower division. In other words, that sixteen votes *below* tide-water, are hereafter to outweigh in the political scale, twenty-three votes *above* tide-water; and that solely on account of their superior wealth.

I will not stop for the present, to inquire whether this be reasonable and just; but I do ask, in the same spirit in which the question was propounded by the gentleman from Norfolk, (Mr. Taylor,) whether such an arrangement of political power would be consistent with the republican principles of our Government? If it were proposed to introduce it into our county elections, to graduate the influence of votes by the wealth that accompanied them, to give to sixteen affluent men the power to select their favorite representatives in opposition to the united voices of three and twenty of their poorer neighbours, can there be a doubt of the spirit in which it would be met? Would it not encounter a tone of indignant remonstrance, in every corner and section of the State, mingling itself, as well with the lowland wave, as with the mountain torrent?

And is the principle varied? Is its enormity lessened? Are its evils avoided by the sectional character with which it is proposed to invest it? To my mind, Sir, this is its most objectionable shape. When inequalities are created amongst those who are living in constant communion with each other, and whose general interests are one and the same, the spirit of oppression is controlled by the influence of social intercourse; and the lust of power, if it yield not to the suggestions of patriotism, is lost amid the calculations of extended and uniform interests.

But when these inequalities are sectional; when the few in one quarter are empowered to control the many in another; where, to what benignant influence are the latter to look for protection to their feelings and their interests? Not to the justice and magnanimity of those in power; for we have been emphatically told by gentlemen, that interest is the ruling, if not the only spring of action to man; and surely they will not ask from the majority, a confidence, on which, from the beginning, they have refused to rely. Nor can that majority depend for security, on the prevalence of a general interest throughout the country; for the very concession demanded of them rests for its justification on the existence of separate and distinct interests.

But, again, Sir, if sixteen voters are, by the instrumentality of wealth alone, to be made superior to twenty-three, where are you to stop? Where are you to draw the precise line of demarcation to Republican Government? Must not the same principle, under a change of circumstances, concentrate power in yet fewer hands? If, as the gentleman from Northampton (Mr. Upshur) supposes, a majority of interests must always prevail, may not that majority, which is now confined to sixteen in thirty-nine, attach itself, in the progress of individual accumulation, to nine, to three, or even to one? And when, under the influence of their favorite principle, power shall be thus concentrated, shall I be told that we are yet a Republican people? I will not say, that in the progress of events, such a change in our Government may not become necessary. I will not say, that a state of things might not be imagined, in which I myself should be constrained to vote for it. But the same page that would contain the record of my vote, would present in connection with it, the declaration that Virginia was no longer fitted for a Republican Government. But suppose that in all this I am mistaken, and that our Republican principles are not endangered by the proposition of the gentleman from Culpeper. We are certainly about to depart, and in no measured degree, from that plain and simple rule of Government, sustained by expediency, no less than by reason and justice, which confides the power of legislation to a majority rather than a minority. Is there any reason for this departure? And if there be, is it not now proposed to go far beyond what the necessity of the case requires? The lower division, to which I have referred, it is acknowledged, contains a larger amount of property and pays a greater proportion of taxes than the upper, (the excess about $54,000,) and hence it is inferred, that unless the power contended for, be obtained, property will be without an adequate protection. If this can be made manifest, I pledge myself to abandon the principles I have brought with me to this discussion, and to go along with, and under the guidance of, the gentlemen from below.

Security to property, Sir! who does not feel its necessity? Who of the numbers that are present, does not concur with the gentleman from Northampton, in thinking that security to property is the most efficient, if not the only security to personal rights? Is it of any consequence to me to be able to keep my body beyond the limits of a jail, to roam where I please, to do what I please, or even to contribute by my vote to organize the Government under which I am to live, if that very Government is to be empowered, whenever it shall think proper, to wrest from me the means of my subsistence, and to throw me poor and pennyless on a heartless world!

No, Sir, the property of the country ought to be, and must be protected, at all hazards; but let gentlemen beware, lest in providing for its security, they expose it to dangers that do not naturally surround it; lest in attempting to throw around it the robes of protection, they incautiously invest it with the shirt of Nessus. To a certain extent, property carries within itself the means of its own protection. Not in its corrupting influence, as referred to by the gentleman from Northampton; but in the facilities it affords for acquiring knowledge and diffusing benefits. It ought to be the aim, as it is within the scope of political institutions, to fortify and strengthen this power of self-protection. Let them guard it by just regulations against improper invasions. Let them increase its facilities for action, in all cases where its aim is to procure legitimate advantages to its owner, or gratuitous benefits to the community in which it exists. And let it be limited in its power of corrupting and oppressing, not by giving to it political power, but by rendering it amenable to the majesty of the laws it would violate, and to the indignant justice of the people, whose honesty it would corrupt.

But this is not all. I would not stop here, even though in proceeding farther, I may stray from the ranks in which I have hitherto been fighting. I would provide for the protection of property in the very foundations of Government. I would furnish to it, that very security, modified in form only, to which the gentleman from Hanover appealed, as an evidence of the sentiments of our forefathers. With them, I would commit the right of suffrage to such only as "could give evidence of permanent common interest in the community." I would allow no man to participate in laying the taxes, who did not also participate in paying them. This I hold to be the best security for property; a security which gives to it the only political power to which it is entitled, or with which it can be safely entrusted. Here then, let gentlemen plant their standard; here unfurl their banner; and they will draw around them, if not all, a very large proportion of the intelligence as well as the property of the State.

But this general security to property, I am told, is not the object aimed at; and that nothing is accomplished while the many are authorized to levy on the few, a heavier tax than they themselves are required or have it in their power to pay. The gentleman from Hanover, indeed, has gone so far as to declare, that this is the very principle, against which, our ancestors so gallantly and so successfully contended; and that it constitutes in fact the very consummation of tyranny. And does the gentleman really think, that if the Government be organized as we propose, the people of the lower country will stand to their Western brethren, in the same relation that our forefathers occupied towards Great Britain—or to use his own words, that we now occupy towards the Government of Ohio? Will he consider himself taxed without his consent, because his representative may be ranked among the minority in the legislative vote—or because some particular tax may possibly bear harder on himself or his county, than on other parts of his State? If so, we have hitherto lived under the rankest despotism; for it will be found by reference to the tabular statements of the Auditor, that the middle country lying on either side of the Blue Ridge, while it possesses a large majority of the property of the State and is annually paying nearly $30,000 more than the rest of the State, has in the House of Delegates forty-two representatives less than the Western and Eastern divisions united.

Gentlemen must pardon me for saying, that on this subject, their arguments have gone beyond the proposition they have intended to support; and that in pourtraying what they deemed the incompatible interests of the East and of the West, they have gone far to establish another proposition, that the Ancient Dominion is no longer fitted for a single Government. I confess, indeed, Sir, that I was shocked and alarmed, when I heard the solemnity with which the gentleman from Chesterfield, in particular, declared the integrity of the State to be now only the second wish of his heart; and that unless the whole powers of legislation were thrown into the hands of a minority, he for one, was prepared for a division of the State.

[Mr. Leigh here rose to explain. He said the gentleman from Fairfax had strangely misconceived the character of his remarks. What he had said, was, that the preservation of the State entire, was the second consideration with him. The first was, that the entire State should have a free and regular Republican Government, founded upon the mutual interests of all, with a just balance of those interests, where they are conflicting.]

Mr. Fitzhugh resumed. I did not misunderstand the gentleman. I sincerely wish I had done so. He did not, it is true, desire the division of the State, if the Government should be organized on what he deemed fair principles; but when he came to explain himself in relation to these principles, they consisted in throwing the whole power of legislation into the hands of a minority of the people. Against the doctrine of disunion, I have uniformly protested, let it come from what quarter it might. I would preserve the integrity of the State at all hazards. (Mr. Upshur here nodded assent.) The gentleman from Northampton agrees with me. I rejoice at it. He is one of the earliest of my friends, whom I have had the pleasure to meet on the present occasion; and I thought, from my recollection of his character in former days, as well as from what I have seen of him here, I might rely on his zealous co-operation in whatever would have a tendency to promote the harmony of our deliberations, and to preserve the unity of the State.

But, Sir, to return to the subject from which I was called off by the gentleman from Chesterfield. If it be really so tyrannical to vest in a majority, a power to levy taxes to which they themselves are to contribute in proportion to their property, what shall we say to the converse of the proposition, where the minority are to be entrusted not only with the purse strings, but with the lives and liberties of those, in whom they are unwilling to recognize any general community of interest with themselves? If there be tyranny in the case, it is here, where the interests and wishes of a few are to be substituted for the interests and wishes of the whole.

To that argument which has been deduced from the peculiar character of the property most prevalent in the Eastern section of the State, I am willing to allow its full weight. Participating very largely in that description of property myself, I cannot be otherwise than alive to any dangers that may seem to threaten it. And be assured, Sir, that my own interest independently of a sense of justice, will at all times secure my zealous co-operation, in whatever may be necessary to protect it against dangers, either present or in prospective.

What then are the dangers to which it is really exposed? None, I apprehend, and none, in truth, to which reference has been made, but that of excessive taxation.

And even this is acknowledged to be very much diminished by the diffusion of the property in question over every portion of the State. Yes, Sir, slavery unfortunately exists even in the remotest regions of the West, and if its subjects be less numerous there, than along the shores of the Atlantic, their general distribution, in smaller numbers, especially in the Valley, ensures an interest in relation to them, that will not fail to unite with the more powerful interest in the East, in opposing any attempted injustice, in relation to them.

But I for one, am not disposed to rest on this as my only dependence. The very fact, that this description of property has hitherto borne so disproportionate a part of the public burdens, renders it a fit subject for constitutional protection. And it is with this view, that I have already proposed so to limit the power of taxation, as to distribute the impositions of Government among the different descriptions of property, exactly in proportion to their relative value. The effect of this must of course be, what all will acknowledge to be just, to reduce the tax on slaves to precisely the same level with all the other taxes of the State.

But I am told by the gentleman from Chesterfield, that this is a mere paper guarantee, to be executed or not, as the whim and caprice of the majority may hereafter determine.

A paper guarantee! And what, Sir, are all the limitations on the powers of the Government, provided by the present Constitution? What, that very organization of the Legislative Department you are so pertinaciously seeking to establish? What, in fine, is the Constitution itself? All, all mere paper guarantees! And when these shall have become, in truth, as valueless as they are represented to be, the fact itself will furnish conclusive evidence of the progress of corruption, and of the unfitness of the State for the continuance of Republican Government. Until then, however, I must be permitted to hope, that the provision in question, if adopted, will furnish us ample security against the apprehended danger of excessive taxation.

Nor, Sir, does it seem to me more difficult to provide against another apprehended evil. I mean the unjust distribution of the public revenue with a view to internal improvement. The gentleman from Fauquier (Mr. Scott) has exhibited this danger in all its details. He has presented to us every variety of interest, Eastern and Western, Northern and Southern, upland and lowland, and has called on us of the middle country especially to look to our own immediate interests on this subject. Mr. Chairman, I cannot act in this spirit. I should deeply lament its introduction into this body. I am an advocate for the improvement of every portion of the State, and I am willing, for myself as well as my constituents, to contribute fairly and freely to its accomplishment. All that I require, is, that the public funds shall be judiciously distributed, and with a national and not a sectional spirit.

With this view, and especially to quiet any well founded fears of the East, I would consecrate in the Constitution, that wise provision on which our Fund for Internal Improvement so long reposed, and from which I, amongst others, was tempted, in "evil hour," to depart. Yes, Sir, the best security for a just and judicious application of the public treasure, is to dispose of it only in connection with individual contribution. Had this principle been sustained until now, we should have been gratified by the general diffusion of our system over every part of the State; and instead of contemplating a Bankrupt Fund, buried in the waters of a single stream, we might have prepared ourselves to enter upon a new career of internal improvement, with unimpaired resources and unbroken spirit.

I beg leave to return, for a single moment, to the idea of the gentleman from Northampton, that the Legislative power of the Government should rest with a majority of interests rather than of persons. Does he really think that this ever was or ever can be accomplished in a Republican Government? Does he believe that the interests of the majority, by which the Legislature is elected are ever predominant? or that in any county the selection of representatives can be made by those who are to contribute most largely to the revenue of the State. I hold in my hand, Sir, a letter from the Commissioner of the revenue in my own county, giving this important information; that of 1281 male titheables, paying upwards of $3,500 taxes, 535 contribute only $35. His examination has gone no farther; but I have very little doubt that if prosecuted, it would have shewn that three-fourths of the taxes of the county are paid by less than 100 of its citizens. And does the gentleman think that to these 100 individuals, the entire control of the county could be given consistently with the general character of our Republican institutions? To attempt it, in reference to the State, would be not less impolitic, and infinitely more unjust.

To any proposition, then, Mr. Chairman, going to confide to a minority of the legitimate voters of the State, the entire control of *both* branches of the Legislature, I cannot, under any circumstances, give my assent. Hardly less objectionable, is the proposition of the gentleman from Culpeper, now under consideration, to give such control, over the most popular branch. Even this goes very far beyond what gentlemen profess to ask, the protection of property, and in all cases of the joint action of the two Houses, whether referring to persons or property, elevates the minority above the majority. The former and not the latter are to elect your Senators, your Governors and your Judges; and to proclaim, from time to time, the relation in which you stand to the General Government. Sir, I cannot assent to this. To the will of the community, fairly and legitimately expressed, I shall at all times bow with perfect submission. But I cannot recognize as the deliberate sentiment of the whole, the will of a minority, congregated in a particular section of the State, and expressing the peculiar feelings and wishes of those, whom they more immediately represent.

Gentlemen are mistaken in the precedents on which they rely. There is not one of them that goes to sustain the proposition contended for here, that the whole power of legislation ought to be confided to a minority. The case of the United States is hardly applicable at all. That Government was a compact amongst independent sovereignties, and regulated in almost all its Departments, on a principle of compromise. If Virginia obtained in one branch of the National Legislature, a representation beyond her white population, she fully paid for it in the other, by admitting the little States of Rhode Island, Delaware, &c. to an equal participation of power with herself. Nor does any State that I know of, furnish an example of organization in *both Houses*, with a view to the representation of property. In the States of New Hampshire, Massachusetts, South Carolina, Georgia, and perhaps one or two others, property, it is true, is avowedly provided with a check in *one House;* but in a large majority of the States, both old and new, so far as Legislative representation has been controlled by any thing beyond mere convenience, it has been fixed solely in reference to white population.

Whether we ought to depart at all, from this latter principle, must depend on contingencies that cannot yet be calculated. If the legitimate claims of property to protection be not sufficiently regarded in the other provisions of the Constitution, it becomes a question of expediency, how far they ought to be secured by a check on the power of the majority, in the less numerous branch of the Legislature; and this, like all other questions of expediency, must be decided, in some degree, by its probable effect on the object we ought all to have in view, the adoption of a Constitution that will be acceptable to a majority of the people.

I lamented, Sir, that I could not follow the gentleman from Accomack, (Mr. Joynes) through the statistical details with which he yesterday favoured the Committee. The late period at which he rose, rendered me utterly incapable of giving to his statements, the attention they no doubt deserved. I heard enough, however, to satisfy me, that while he had done less than justice to that portion of the Western country denominated the Valley, in charging it with paying into the public Treasury, less than it received from it, he had measured out rather more than justice to his own section of the State, by exhibiting it in connection with the fertile and heavily taxed country immediately under the mountain. I learn, indeed, from the gentleman from Albemarle, that if the cities of Norfolk and Richmond be excluded from the Eastern division of the State, it is very doubtful, whether it may not be found in the very predicament prescribed by the gentleman from Accomack, to the whole Western country.

I cannot concur with these gentlemen, Sir, who would resolve all our actions into base and sordid interest; though it were useless to complain of the remarks of the gentleman from Chesterfield, in relation to the district I represent; as in denying to us, any other motive of action, than our own peculiar interest, he has only placed us by the side of himself. But I do trust, Sir, that in spite of the growing corruption of the times, he has so eloquently and so justly described, there is yet in this body at least, enough of public spirit, to induce us to look to the great interest of the Commonwealth, uninfluenced by either personal or sectional considerations. If there be not, the sooner we adjourn the better. Let us go back to our constituents, and tell them honestly and candidly, that we are not the men they had supposed us, and that we are in truth, as unfit to give, as they to receive a Republican Government.

I have submitted these remarks for no other purpose, Mr. Chairman, than to explain both here and elsewhere, the course I am about to pursue. It would be folly in me to hope, that the Government about to be formed, will be based exclusively on the principle I have advocated; and I should hold myself unfit for the station with which I have been honoured, if I did not feel myself at all times prepared to make every reasonable concession, to insure either harmony here or tranquillity abroad.

The Chair having twice enquired, whether the Committee were ready for the question, it was about to be put, when,

Mr. Taylor of Norfolk, rose, and said that he had not had the slightest suspicion that the question would be taken at this time; but as it seemed that no gentleman intended to address the Committee, he would move that the Committee do now rise, and he owed it to himself to explain why he made such a motion.

I received, said Mr. T. the honor of a seat here, with a distinct knowledge, on the part of my constituents, of the sentiments I held in regard to the reforms contemplated in the Government of the State. I had given to them no *pledges*, express or implied. I had made a distinct avowal of my opinions in respect to most of the matters in controversy, and an open promulgation of them, on the last day of the election. On the immediate subject now before us, I had formed no definite opinion : nor had any such opinion been formed, or expressed, by the people of my district. If there had, I was ignorant of it.

The opinions I hold with regard to this resolution, have already been indicated to this body, by the resolutions I had the honor to submit to it, some days since : which resolutions were considered in part, and now sleep on your table. When I offered them, I did believe, and I do still believe, that the amendment is inconsistent with our free institutions, that it is hostile in its principle, to equal rights among qualified voters, and tends directly, in its practical effect to introduce an oligarchy, fatal to the continuance of free Government. If the present amendment had been rejected, it was my purpose to have moved another, the object of which would have been to strike out the words "*white population*," and to insert in lieu thereof "qualified voters, without regard to disparity of fortune ;" and I meant to do this, not only because I considered it more philosophical to commence with presenting principles, rather than facts ; but also, because I considered it important not only to myself, but to the friends who agree with me in opinion, and to the interests of the whole State, that the public should understand the subjects which are in discussion here, that they should understand, that this Convention is debating whether a majority of the qualified voters of the State, shall have the control of the State, or whether a minority shall possess that control on account of their superior wealth. I am willing to stand or fall on this question, when it shall be rightly understood by the people.

I do not now intend to enter into the debate. Peculiar circumstances render it improper for me to do so at present, and it is in reference to these circumstances that I am induced to ask the Committee to rise.

I have learned, recently, that although no opinion had existed among my constituents when I came here, on the subject of the amendment, there *does* now exist among them a very decided opinion on that subject, insomuch that I have received direct instructions as to the course they wish me to pursue. I have some reason to believe that a vast majority of my people (I call them so, as they have honored me with an appointment to this body,) concur in the sentiment expressed in these instructions. It has been the sentiment of my life, that representation is only the means by which the opinions of the constituent body are to be expressed and effectuated. No act of mine shall ever impair that principle. But, Sir, there are limits to obedience. Had my constituents instructed me in some matter of expediency, or asked me to do what was possible to me, I should have taken pleasure in showing with what cheerful submission I would give effect to their opinions rather than my own. But they ask what is impossible. To obey them I must violate my conscience, and the sacred obligation I owe to my country. I must do that which would dishonor me as a man and cover me with shame as a patriot. I cannot do it without being guilty of moral treason to the free institutions of my country. If I fall, I will meet the blow with dignity and firmness, and I shall only regret that the victim is not more worthy of the God. But, Sir, a man of integrity knows how to reconcile all his duties : and I am constrained to ask a postponement of this question, because it is my fixed purpose not to give a vote upon it, but *to resign my seat in this body*. I have had a communication with the member first chosen in the delegation from Norfolk, and I have asked him to consult with his colleagues as to the selection of some other person who may be more fortunate than I am, and agree in sentiment with my constituents, and to do so with as much expedition as propriety will allow, in order that they may not remain unrepresented on this question. He informed me that there was no need of acting yesterday, as there was no probability whatever that the question would be taken for some days to come. Under these circumstances, I throw myself on the generosity of this body, that I may not be compelled to act against either my own conscience or the will of my constituents, and that time may be given for the selection of another delegate in my room. I shall, therefore, move that the Committee rise, hoping that before it is again called to deliberate, some gentleman may occupy my seat, who shall be more fortunate than myself, in harmony of opinion, though none can be more devoted to what I conceive to be the best interests of my constituents.

Before I take my seat, I hope it will not be deemed criminal in me, to profess that I brought to this House the sentiments so well expressed by the gentleman from Northampton, (Mr. Upshur.) I came here, Sir, as a Virginian ; prepared to promote the interest of Virginia : fully believing that the petty and temporary interests of my district are as nothing, in comparison to the interest it has, in the general prosperity of the State.

Permit me, Sir, to state the comparative effect which will be produced in my District, by the adoption of the resolution and of the amendment ; in other words, by the white, and by the compound basis of representation. My District consists of the counties of Norfolk, Princess Anne, Nansemond, and the Borough of Norfolk. In the county of Norfolk, (I state from memory,) the white population is about 9,000: In Princess Anne, 5,400; in Nansemond, more than 5,000; and in Norfolk Borough, 4,600. Now, if the resolution reported by the Committee shall prevail, and the *white* basis be adopted, what will be the result? Go by numbers, and the county of Norfolk having twice the population of the Borough, will be entitled to twice the number of representatives. Princess Anne will have its representation in proportion to that of Norfolk 1 and 16—100 to 1. Nansemond also will have a larger representation than Norfolk Borough. I speak now of qualified voters; and I refer to the Census, only as a mean of ascertaining them. But, should the amendment prevail, and the *mixed* basis of population and taxation be adopted, see what will be the result: $ 10,280 are paid in taxes by Norfolk Borough. Add its population, and the compound ratio for that Borough, will be within a fraction of 15,000. In the county of Norfolk, the taxes amount to $ 5,528: Add the 9,000 people, and the sum is less than 15,000. So that the whole county, with a double population, will have a less representation than the Borough. The county of Princess Anne, which pays $ 2,716 in taxes, will, on the same plan, be surpassed by the Borough of Norfolk, in the proportion of 1 and 17—100 to 1. And, in like manner, the county of Nansemond will be surpassed, in the proportion of 1 and 94—100 to 1. Thus, with greater population, each of these counties will have less representation than the Norfolk Borough.

Mr. Taylor concluded, by renewing his request, that the question might be postponed, and that the Committee would rise. He did not feel at liberty to enter upon its discussion; but he afterwards consented to withdraw the motion at the request of

Mr. Moore of Rockbridge, who then took the floor in support of the resolution, and spoke as follows:

Mr. Chairman: It was my intention, until very recently, not to have troubled the Committee with any remarks upon the proposition now under consideration. I had supposed, that long before we assembled in this Hall, the opinion of every member of this Convention, would have been unchangeably fixed, upon this question at least, if upon no other; and that consequently, every argument which might be adduced on either side, would be entirely thrown away. I find, however, from the great zeal which has been manifested by gentlemen who have advocated the opposite side of the question from that which I intend to espouse, that they do not altogether despair of making converts to their cause.

Confident, as I am, that in asking that the representation in the House of Delegates, shall be based upon white population exclusively, I am asking nothing more than that which is right in itself; and unwilling that it should be supposed for a moment, that I, or those whom I represent in this Convention, are demanding any thing more than justice at your hands, I beg leave now to present to the Committee, my views upon this highly important subject. I claim, Sir, for myself, and for my constituents, to be actuated by higher considerations, and more honorable motives, than those of mere sordid interest, in the course we are pursuing in relation to this matter. And I call upon those gentlemen who pay so poor a compliment to themselves and to their fellow-men, as to assert that interest is the great, if not the sole motive of human action, to turn their attention to the Senatorial District from which I come, and to inquire, what is the relative proportion of white and black population there, to what it is in other parts of the State; and what has been the relative increase of the whites and the blacks; to ascertain what is the nature of our soil and products; what is the extent of our property of every description; and if they please, what taxes we pay, in proportion to other portions of this Commonwealth; and then to say, whether or not, we can reasonably expect, to gain any permanent advantage from the adoption of the basis for which I contend, in preference to that which they propose. The gentleman from Accomack, it is true, has endeavoured to shew, that the people of the Valley have very little interest in common with the people on this side of the Blue Ridge of mountains; and has made a calculation, by which he endeavours to prove, that the former will always find it to their interest, to impose taxes upon slaves, in preference to lands. He assumes, that in all the counties in which the slaves do not bear a proportion of 38 per cent. to the whole population, the people will find it to their interest, to throw as much as possible of the burthens of taxation, on that species of property. Perhaps, if the gentleman could have shewn, that the proportion of voters in the Valley counties who hold slaves, to those who hold none, was less than 38 per cent. there might have been some force in the argument which he advanced. But the proportion of persons in those counties entitled to vote, who hold slaves, to those who hold none, being something like two to one, it is apparent from his own reasoning, and upon his own principles, that they cannot be interested in taxing slaves, in preference to other property. And that a majority of those at least, who have the power in their hands, have a common interest with the Eastern people, in protecting slave property from unjust taxation.

It is said, Sir, that all comparisons are odious; and I confess, that none are more so to me, than those which have been made in this Committee, upon the subject of taxation. Not because the result of these comparisons will be to the disadvantage of my own particular District, (for I think I can demonstrate to the satisfaction of the Committee, that we pay a full proportion of all the taxes paid in the State :) but because they are calculated to engender the most unkind feelings, between the good people of this Commonwealth. I did not like the manner in which the gentleman from Accomack was pleased to divide the State, by the Blue Ridge, and then endeavoured to prove, by shewing that we (the Western people) drew more money out, than we paid into the Treasury, that we were all a set of paupers, dependent on the charity of the East. I do not choose, that we, who pay our full proportion of the taxes, shall be classed with those who pay less than their proportion, in order to make us all out paupers. According to this mode of proceeding, I can prove *his own constituents* to be nothing but a set of paupers; for if he will add *his* District, to the whole country West of the Blue Ridge, he will find, that all taken together, we do not pay as much into the Treasury as we draw out of it. And after all, there is nothing so very discreditable in a county or district of country, paying less money into the Treasury than it draws out of it; for if you divide the State into two parts, containing equal numbers of people, by any line you please to run, unless they draw out of the Treasury in exact proportion to what they pay into it, one division or the other, will draw out more money than it puts into it; and according to the gentleman's mode of reasoning, all the people of that division must be considered as dependent upon the charity of those of the other division. I had always supposed that the people of every portion of this Commonwealth, contributed to the support of Government, both in personal services, and in money, in proportion to their ability to contribute, and that this was all that could reasonably be demanded of them. I am not willing to give to those who pay more money than we do, a greater representation than we have; nor will I ask of those who pay less, to be satisfied with a smaller one. I have ever believed, that when a man, however poor he may be, has paid as much money into the Treasury as he is able to pay, that nothing more can be required at his hands; and that his having done so, ought, like the widow's mite, to entitle him, to equal privileges, with those, who are enabled, out of the abundance of their wealth, to pay a much larger sum.

Permit me now, Sir, to call the attention of the Committee once more, to the declarations contained in our Bill of Rights, about which there appears to be so great a diversity of opinions. It is not my intention to follow those who have preceded me in this debate, over all the ground which they have occupied in discussing the principles asserted by these declarations; my only purpose will be, to explain to the Committee, what has been my understanding of these declarations, so solemnly made by our ancestors. I have been in the constant habit, from my earliest infancy to the present moment, of regarding the whole Bill of Rights as a sacred instrument, in which the only true principles upon which Republican Governments can be founded, had been proclaimed to the world. And I trust, Sir, I shall be pardoned, (for I assure you I mean no offence to any man,) when I say, that although I did believe that individuals might be found in foreign countries, who (misled by the prejudices of education, or blinded by interest,) might be disposed to question their authenticity; yet I did not believe, that in this boasted land of liberal principles, one man could be found, who would refuse to acknowledge them as the foundation, upon which the whole superstructure of Government should rest. Entertaining such sentiments as these, it has been, as you may well imagine, Mr. Chairman, with extreme pain, that I have listened to the very able and ingenious arguments of gentlemen, which to my apprehension, are but too well calculated to sap the very foundations of this, and every other Republican Government.

The first section of the Bill of Rights asserts, "that all men are by nature equally free and independent," &c. Now, Sir, is there any man here who doubts that all men are "by nature equally free and independent?" I presume there is not one individual in all this Assembly, who is prepared to express a doubt upon the subject. But, say gentlemen, our ancestors did not mean to assert that all men are in the actual enjoyment of equal rights and privileges; they only meant that by nature, they are entitled to equal rights and privileges; and in this opinion I entirely concur with them. But when gentlemen undertake to pronounce this to be a mere abstract principle, which can never be applied to the actual condition of men, I differ with them *toto cælo*. And I hesitate not to affirm, that it is a principle which not only *can be*, but which *must* be acted upon by all men, whatever their condition in life may have been; whether they have been in the enjoyment of their natural rights, or held in the most degraded state of slavery, whenever they are about to form a Constitution; otherwise, the Government which they establish, must in the very nature of things, be nothing more or less than a despotism. We have been asked, if this be really a correct principle, and susceptible of universal application, why was it that the slaves were excluded by our ancestors, and why do we not now propose to admit them as parties to the social compact? The answer to this question is so easily given, and is so obvious, that I am surprised it should ever have been asked. The answer is, that we do not *choose* to form or enter into any such compact with them. And is not this a sufficient answer?

We exclude *them*, for precisely the same reasons that we would exclude foreigners of every description; for the same reasons that we would refuse to extend the right of citizenship to the inhabitants of Texas, or of Canada, or to any race of Indians who might wish to be acknowledged as a part of the community to which we belong: namely, that we do not *choose* to grant their request. And we would not choose to grant such a request, because we believe that they would not make good citizens. We do not propose to admit our slaves as parties to the social compact, because we believe that they would not make good citizens, or because we are prejudiced against their colour; or if you please, because we think proper to disregard their natural rights, and to hold them in slavery, that we may reap the benefit of their labour. And it is perfectly immaterial what the reason for excluding them may be, if it be sufficient to induce us to do so. By excluding foreigners, however, or Indians, we do not interfere with their natural rights; but leave them at liberty to form any sort of Government they please for themselves. The mistake is in supposing that the principle, if true, is one which must, in its application, be extended, to all, to whom, it can be extended: whereas, it is one, which may, or may not, be extended, so as to embrace any particular race or class of people, as may seem best to those who are about to establish a Government: but which must be extended to all whom it is intended, shall become parties to the compact, or members of the community. It is evident, that such was the understanding which our ancestors had of this principle, and of its application, at the time when our Bill of Rights and Constitution were established by them. They, excluded foreigners from the enjoyment of all the rights and privileges of citizenship in this State, except upon certain conditions: they excluded the Indians altogether, and they excluded the negroes altogether, and the reasons for excluding the latter, were stronger than those for excluding the former. All those, however, who were admitted as members of the community, were admitted upon terms of perfect equality. Let us suppose the agents of the British Government, with a view to induce them to return to their allegiance to the British Crown, to have addressed them in language like this: "You have declared, that all men are by nature equally free and independent, and that the majority of the people have an indubitable and unalienable right, to alter, reform, or abolish Government at their pleasure; and we have a strong party amongst the white people in this State, who are in favour of abolishing the Government which you have established, which added to the whole number of Indians and negroes in the State, (who are also in our favour,) will make a majority; which, according to your own principles, has a right to change the Government at its pleasure. We therefore demand that you submit to the will of this majority, and give up the power which you are no longer entitled to hold." What are we to suppose would have been their reply to such a demand? Would they not have said, "these Indians and negroes constitute no part of the community for whose advantage this Government was formed, and consequently have no right to express any opinion upon the subject; and although we admit that their natural rights are equal to our own, yet they not having been permitted to become parties to the compact from which we derive our authority, they can have no voice in changing or destroying it." And they might well have added, "these negroes whom you see so totally unfitted by their habits, and want of all the moral virtues, to enjoy the blessings of liberty and of a free Government, have no just cause of complaint against any one for placing them in their present degraded condition, except it is against your own King, who sent them amongst us, and compelled us to receive them, contrary to our own inclinations, which is one of the grievances complained of in the preamble to our Constitution."

Having expressed my belief that our slaves are by nature equally as free and independent as ourselves, or in other words, that they are by nature, entitled to equal rights and privileges, it may not be improper, that I should make one or two remarks, which though they have no immediate bearing upon the question before us, may serve to prevent any misapprehension of my sentiments upon a subject of such vital importance to this State as that of slavery. I give it then, as my deliberate opinion, that although our slaves are by nature, entitled to equal rights with the rest of the human race, and although it would be both our interest and our duty to send them out from amongst us, if any practicable scheme could be suggested for effecting that object; that yet, all questions as to their rights, are questions between them and our selves exclusively. It is moreover my opinion, that if the necessity of the case does not furnish a sufficient excuse for our retaining them in servitude, (as I hope it does,) that we are answerable for our injustice towards them, only to our own consciences, and to the Great God of all: and that no foreign people or power, have a right in any manner, under any circumstances, or under any pretence, to interfere between them and us. And so far do I carry my ideas of exclusive right, upon this subject, that if the majority of the people of Virginia, or of their representatives, were to determine to reduce all the free negroes amongst us to a state of slavery, although the proposition in itself would be most abhorrent to my feelings; yet I should regard myself as a traitor to my country, if I did not resist by all the means in my power, any attempt which might be made, on the part of any other people, to interfere.

We have been asked, why it is we exclude the women from all participation in the formation of Government, if it be true that all the human race possess equal natural rights? I answer, that it is not because we deny to these an equality of natural rights, or because they are inferior in intelligence, morality, or virtue, to ourselves: for I will be as ready to admit as any gentleman on the opposite side of the question, that in all these particulars they are our equals at least, and in most of them, our superiors. And I was not a little surprised the other day that the gentleman from Orange, should have thought it necessary to go into a historical argument, to prove what no one here was disposed to dispute in relation to their capacity for conducting the affairs of Government.

It will be a sufficient answer to this question, to say, that the women have never claimed the right to participate in the formation of the Government, and that until they do, there can be no necessity for our discussing or deciding upon it: more especially as no one believes that any such claim will ever be insisted upon by them. There surely can be no reason why we should attempt to impose upon them, burthens which they are unwilling to bear. If I were to attempt to assign the reason why they do not make any such demand, I would say that it is because their interests are so completely identified with our own, that it is impossible that we can make any regulation injuriously affecting their rights, which will not equally injure ourselves. And because they have such unlimited confidence in our sex, that they cannot suspect us of any disposition to act unjustly towards them. A confidence which I hope is by no means misplaced, unless gentlemen on the other side of this question, are disposed to impose some unjust restrictions upon them, of which I am sure I am very far from suspecting any member of this body.

We have been called upon to assign a reason why infants under the age of twenty-one years, should be excluded from a share in the formation of the Government, if the principles for which I have been contending are correct? I answer, that it will be time enough to assign the reasons for it, when they claim the right; and as it is very certain they do not intend to make the demand at present, we need not waste our time in making unprofitable enquiries, into the extent or nature of their rights. The question asked by the gentleman from Orange, (Mr. Barbour) as to our right to exclude the free negroes from the rights of citizenship, is sufficiently answered by saying, that we choose to exclude them for reasons which must be obvious to him, and therefore need not be assigned.

There has been one other question asked, which deserves our most serious consideration. It is this: What right have we, if the principles asserted by the Bill of Rights are correct, to exclude paupers from taking any part in the formation or amendment of the Constitution? It is important in the consideration of this question, to know precisely what is meant by the term paupers. If this term is intended to embrace all the non-freeholders, as I presume it is, (for it is on account of their poverty, and the want of common interest with and attachment to the community, which is supposed to be consequent upon their state of poverty, that they are excluded,) there can be no difficulty in making a suitable reply to the question. The reply which I am disposed to make, is this: These paupers or non-freeholders, being admitted to belong to the community, and acknowledged as parties to the compact of Government, and they having demanded permission to exercise their rights, as they have done, in language not to be misunderstood, or disregarded; we have no right to exclude them from a share in the alteration of the old or the formation of a new Constitution. And, Sir, if I am not deceived by the language of their memorials now upon your table, they are determined not to be prevented from exercising their rights. When we come to consider the question, of who shall be permitted to vote in favor of the adoption or rejection of the new or amended Constitution, I may perhaps endeavor to satisfy the Committee, that every free white man above the age of twenty-one years, will be entitled to vote upon that question, inasmuch, as the people will then be engaged, in the actual exercise of those equal rights, secured to them by our Bill of Rights: And to draw the distinction between these natural rights, and the right of suffrage, which is a mere conventional right, and can only be claimed or exercised, by those on whom it has been conferred by the majority which created the Constitution. For the present, it is enough for me to deny our right to exclude them from voting, for or against the new Constitution.

The second section of the Bill of Rights asserts: That all power is vested in, and consequently derived from, the people, &c. To this proposition I understand no objection has been made. I shall therefore pass on to the third section, which asserts: That Government is, or ought to be, &c. (here the third section of the Bill of Rights was read.) And it has been in discussing this proposition, that most of the questions I have endeavored to answer, have been propounded: but which I have thought had more immediate relation to the first principle asserted by the Bill of Rights.

A question has been raised, whether the right of the majority to govern which is here asserted, is a natural or conventional right; and we have been called upon to prove that it is a natural right. For my own part, I conceive it to be wholly immaterial, as to the effect it is to have upon the decision of the question now before us, whether it is considered as a natural, or as a conventional right. If it be not a natural right, its existence must at least be acknowledged, before the social compact can be formed. For unquestionably, it is essential for any body of men, who may be about to form a Constitution, to determine in the first place how the questions which may arise shall be determined. It would perhaps be impossible for me to furnish a better illustration of my views upon this subject, than that which is afforded by a reference to the course which has been pursued by the Convention itself. When we assembled in this Hall as the representatives of the people, we met upon terms of perfect equality, notwithstanding the great inequality which must exist among so many individuals, both as to intellectual qualifications, and to physical power. A motion was made to appoint a President, and the venerable gentleman from Loudoun was put in nomination by the venerable gentleman from Orange. It being understood that a majority of the members were in favor of the election of the gentleman from Loudoun, he took his seat as President. And if another person had been put in nomination, and had received less than the majority, and the member from Loudoun had obtained but a majority of one vote, still he would have been entitled to take his seat as President: and any man who would have questioned his right to do so, would have been regarded as little better than a madman.

We proceeded in the next place to elect a Clerk, a Sergeant at Arms, and two Door Keepers, and in every case we continued to ballot, over and over again, until it was ascertained who had the majority. Thus was the right of the majority to rule, acknowledged time after time by this Convention, without a single dissenting voice: and all this took place before we had become organized as a Convention.

So soon as we were organized, we again acknowledged the right of the majority to rule, by every vote which we gave upon the adoption of the rules by which our deliberations are regulated. And the only binding authority which those rules have over us at this moment, is derived from the sanction given to them by the vote of the majority. Is it then for us to question the right of the majority to rule, after having so often acknowledged it, in a case exactly in point? Surely it is not. It would be idle after this, to go into the enquiry, as to the origin of the right of the majority to rule. Nor need I go into the enquiries suggested by the gentleman from Northampton, as to the mode in which the majority is to be ascertained, how the votes are to be given, or who would appoint the tellers. If the majority be ascertained, it is immaterial how it is ascertained; and I presume it would be impossible to form any Government in a country where parties were so equally balanced as to require a count in order to ascertain the majority. I do not imagine that our ancestors, when they dissolved the old Government, and established the existing Constitution, waited to take the votes, or appointed tellers for that purpose, before they began to exercise the powers incident to Government. It was sufficient for them to know that they were the majority.

It is not correct to suppose, as has been done by some of those who have preceded me in this debate, that the acknowledgment of an unqualified right in the majority to govern, is incompatible with the existence of any rights in the minority. The minority still retain their natural rights unimpaired by the establishment of Government; but it being impossible that two separate social compacts can be formed, or rather, that two independent communities, can exist in the same country at the same time, the minority being the weakest party, must either submit to the will of the majority, or leave the country. Thus we see the Cherokee and Creek tribes of Indians compelled to leave the Southern States, and the Royalists flying from Mexico at this very time, and seeking an abode in countries where they may enjoy all their rights unimpaired.

The gentleman from Northampton, speaking of the right of the majority to govern, says: "The very advocates of this doctrine abandon it, because they cannot but perceive, that it is impossible in practical Government, to push it to its fair results;" and asks "if free whites alone are to give the measure of political power, upon what principle is it, that any one individual is deprived of his share in that power?" The gentleman will pardon me for saying that he has done the advocates of this principle, great injustice, and that he and all the other gentlemen who have followed him upon the same side of the question, have fallen into a very great error, by attempting to apply the principle or rule improperly. The rule is applicable when a Government is to be formed, but can with no propriety be thought to be applied to mere conventional regulations, which owe their existence to the will of the majority as expressed in the Constitution.

If it is provided by the Constitution, that none but persons possessing the freehold qualification, shall be entitled to the right of suffrage, or that a plurality of votes only shall be required to elect members to the General Assembly; or if the Legislature, in pursuance of authority derived from the Constitution, declare that there must be unanimity in jury trials, &c: all these things are right and proper, because the majority have willed that it shall be so. And if the majority think proper at any time, they have full power to vary these regulations and to adopt others in their stead: there can be nothing discovered then, inconsistent with the unlimited right of the majority to rule, in any of these mere conventional regulations which have been so often, and so triumphantly referred to during this debate.

The gentleman from Northampton attempts to avoid the force and effect of this principle, as applicable to the question before us, by asserting that "there are in fact no original fundamental principles of Government; that the principles of Government do not apply to another; and that the same principles will not apply in the same country at different times and under different circumstances." He also asserted, that "this principle (that the majority shall govern) does not prevail in England or in Turkey, and that yet there are Governments in both these countries." I beg leave to differ with the gentleman in every one of the positions he has taken. I affirm, that there *are* original fundamental principles of Government, which must and do prevail in all countries, at all times, and under all circumstances. And that this very principle of the right of the majority to govern has prevailed at all times, both in England and in Turkey. Every change which has been effected in the British Government, from the days of King Alfred to the present moment, has been made with the consent of the majority, without which it could not have been effected at all. In France, this principle has been applied in the last half century, to change the Government from an absolute Monarchy to a limited Monarchy; from a limited Monarchy to a Republic; from a Republic to a Despotism; and from a Despotism back again to a limited Monarchy. And all the dreadful convulsions of that country, grew out of an attempt of the minority to resist the will of the majority. The power of the majority over the Government is unlimited, and they may, at any time, convert the Government from a Monarchy into a Republic, or from a Republic into a Monarchy, at their pleasure. In fine, the majority have "an indubitable, unalienable, and indefeasible right to reform, alter, or abolish" the existing form of Government at their pleasure.

We have been informed by the gentleman last alluded to, that there are two sorts of majorities, viz: a majority of numbers and a majority of interests. I confess, Sir, I do not exactly understand what is meant by a majority of interests, any more than I should have been able to comprehend his meaning, if he had talked to me about a majority of air, or of religion, or any thing else, in speaking of which he could not, with any propriety, use the term majority. I understand by the word majority, as used in the Bill of Rights, precisely what nine hundred and ninety-nine men out of a thousand throughout the United States understand by it, that is, a majority of numbers. And if the gentleman had consulted his own constituents upon the subject, he would have found that the whole of them understand it as I do.

In order to sustain this doctrine of a majority of interests, the gentleman advanced a proposition, which I shall endeavor to shew is utterly incorrect, that is, that property is one of the elements of society. For the purpose of ascertaining the truth of this proposition, we must look back to the original rights of men in a state of nature. Each man had a right to that which was in his immediate possession, and to nothing more, and the moment he abandoned that possession, any other individual could acquire a perfect title to it, by seizing and appropriating it to his own use. And the title which man acquires in a state of society to property, owes its existence and its validity, entirely to the consent, expressed or implied, of the other members of the society to which he belongs. For example, when the Legislature, acting under authority derived from the majority, have said that the possession of a deed executed with certain formalities, shall entitle a man to hold real estate, or that the possession of a bond, shall give the holder a right to claim property in the hands of another: the validity of these claims depends entirely upon Legislative enactment, and have no foundation whatever in nature. And I hesitate not to affirm, that whenever individuals possessing property have entered into, or become members of any social compact, that they must have derived their title to that property from the consent of some other society in which they had lived. Property then is not an element of society, it is only one of the strongest *inducements* which men have, for entering into the social compact. It was said by the learned gentleman from Northampton that we have no knowledge of any people since the period when Bible history commenced, who went into a state of society without any property. I do not pretend to be so accurately acquainted with Bible history as that gentleman, but I am inclined to think, the Israelites themselves, must have had very little property to begin with, after passing through the wilderness;

and I could name several other nations, who, in the commencement, must have been as destitute of property as we can conceive of men being.

Not being entirely satisfied with this new doctrine of a majority of interests, the gentleman from Northampton, in the next place endeavored to shew that there was a large majority of numbers on this side of the Blue Ridge, if we take the slaves into the estimate. I have already endeavored to prove that the slaves, not being a part of the community, or belonging to the body politic, cannot be counted at all. But if they are to be counted on either side, (which God forbid) what title has he, to count them on his side? Is it because their interests and his are the same? Surely not; for every interest they have on earth is adverse to his, and if counted at all, they must be counted against him.

But, Sir, there is another very numerous and respectable class of men in this country, whose claims have as yet been but little noticed in this body, but who have a right to be taken into the estimate; who, as I have already stated are determined boldly to assert their rights; and who must be counted upon one side or the other. I allude, Sir, to the non-freeholders. And if it be true, as has been so often and so forcibly remarked, by gentlemen on the other side of this question, that interest is the main spring of human action, I would ask what interest *they* have, in common with the slave-holders?

Does the gentleman expect them to unite with him, because they find the advocates of their rights among those who are in favor of the mixed basis? If this were the fact, such an expectation, would not be altogether unreasonable. But unless these non-freeholders, be both blind and deaf, they cannot be ignorant of the fact, that in all the struggles which have taken place in the Legislature, upon the Convention question, it has been by the advocates of the white basis of representation alone, that their claims have been attended to, and supported against the most violent opposition on the part of those who are now in favor of the mixed basis. Nor can they forget by whom they have been excluded from being represented in this very Convention. The whole body of non-freeholders on this side of the mountain then, together with all other non-slave-holders, must be added to the whole population on the west, and a large proportion of the freeholders immediately on this side of the Blue Ridge and counted against him: and then let us see, what sort of a minority we have, attempting to dictate terms to the majority.

I have thus, Mr. Chairman, endeavored to express to the Committee what has been my understanding of some of the declarations contained in the Bill of Rights: to prove that the assertion contained in the third section, that is, "that the majority have an indubitable, unalienable, and indefeasible right, to reform, alter, or abolish it" (the Government) is true; and that there is a large majority of the community, who must be fairly presumed to be in favor of making the white population the basis of representation, in the General Assembly.

I shall proceed in the next place, to consider the amendment which has been proposed by the gentleman from Culpeper, (Mr. Green) to the resolution reported by the Legislative Committee. His proposition is, that representation in the House of Delegates, shall be based upon a combined ratio of white population, and of taxation. The first remark which I shall make upon this proposition, is, that I cannot perceive how it will be possible, if the amendment shall prevail, ever to apply the rule which it is intended to establish. Do gentlemen mean to make the taxes now paid the permanent basis of representation? If they do, they will find, that in a very short time, owing to the constant fluctuation in property, and the consequent change in the relative proportion of taxes paid, in different sections of the State, that the representation will soon cease to be just, even upon their own principles. I cannot suppose that gentlemen intend to make the law now in force, imposing taxes for the support of Government, a part of the Constitution; for, if they do, they might as well dispense with the Legislative body altogether; the most important part of its duty being to regulate the taxes according to the ability of the people to pay, and the necessities of the Government. If the amendment prevails, I do not see how the Legislature are to be prevented from imposing the taxes in such a way, as to give to one portion of the community, the whole amount of power or representation, which it is proposed to derive from the payment of taxes. For example, if the slave-holders, having the majority in the Legislature, choose to take to themselves the whole representation arising from taxation; all they have to do, will be to collect the whole revenue of the Commonwealth from a tax upon slaves. But granting that the rule, if adopted, can be applied, which I think more than doubtful, let us examine the principle which it establishes, and the justice of applying it.

The principle is, that every portion of the community shall be represented in proportion to the taxes it pays into the treasury. And those who avow this principle, attempt to sustain it by saying, that taxation and representation must always go together; and by comparing the social compact to a partnership between merchants, or a Bank association, in which every member is entitled to power, in proportion to the capital or stock he furnishes. In order to test the correctness of this principle, let us see how it will work, when applied to individuals; and this is the only way in which principles of this sort can be properly tested; for it is always true, that a principle, which cannot be justly enforced between individuals belonging to the same community, can never be justly enforced against the inhabitants of a particular district, who constitute a part of that community. If this be a correct principle, then the man who owns, or pays taxes on two slaves, is entitled to twice as much power as he who owns, or pays taxes on but one; and he who owns or pays taxes on a thousand slaves, will be entitled to five hundred times as much power, as he who owns but two, and one thousand times as much as he who owns but one; and he who owns no slave, or pays no taxes, will be entitled to no power at all. Suppose a proposition was made at this time to act upon this principle, and give to every man power at the elections (that is to say, a number of votes,) corresponding to the amount of taxes which he pays, is there any man here who would have the hardihood to vote for it? Surely there is not one. And if such a provision were engrafted in the Constitution, do you believe that the people would submit to it? Do you believe that the non-slave-holders would agree to be deprived of all share in the elections; or that those who own but from one to twenty, would agree to see the elections entirely controuled by a few, who own from one hundred to a thousand? It is impossible any man can believe such a system could be enforced. And yet, Sir, we are gravely called upon to enforce this principle against the people west of the Alleghany, which we *dare* not even propose to establish amongst ourselves. I say amongst *ourselves*, Sir, because I affirm it as my belief, that the people of my district have as much, or nearly as much interest in this question, as the great body of the people on the eastern side of the Blue Ridge. And I shall endeavor, before I take my seat, to prove that we are much more strongly connected with the people of this part of the State, by motives of interest, than the people of either the Accomack or the Culpeper districts, from whose representatives we have heard so much on the subject of imaginary separate interests.

The true rule as to taxation, (and it is one which prevails every where,) is, that every man shall pay in proportion to his ability to pay, without any sort of regard being had to the political rights which he enjoys. This is the rule which has constantly been acted upon by the Legislature of Virginia, in all times past. I have been astonished, not to say amazed, to hear gentlemen complaining of the great inequality betwixt the taxes paid by the people of the East, and those paid by the people of the West; and especially of the taxes paid upon slaves over and above what is paid upon any other species of property, as if these taxes were unjust, and had been imposed upon them against their own consent. And who was it imposed these taxes? Was it the people west of the Alleghany mountains? No, Sir, they have never had the power to impose them. Was it not the Eastern people themselves? Nay, more, was it not the slave-holders themselves who imposed them? Unquestionably it was; for, as you were very correctly told by the gentleman from Hanover, the slave-holders are the freeholders in this country. Was it to please the people west of the Alleghany, that these taxes were imposed in the manner, and on the particular species of property on which they were imposed? No, Sir, it was to please the people here that it was done. The true reason why these taxes have been imposed in the manner so unjustly complained of, is, that the principle, that men shall pay taxes in proportion to the property they own, prevails in practice every where, and is universally considered among the people, to be the only correct principle. If any gentleman doubts the correctness of this position, let him propose to the Legislature to take off the taxes from the shoulders of the wealthy, and impose them upon the poor, and see how the proposition will be received by the people; or let him propose to take the tax off the negroes, and impose it on other kinds of property, and see how that proposal will be received by the non-slave-holders and the holders of few slaves in Eastern Virginia. Sir, I hesitate not to say, that if the Legislature was, at its next session to make either of the changes in the laws, which I have suggested, that the people of Eastern Virginia would not submit to it, and that it would be impossible to enforce the law; for no man, who is either poor, or in moderate circumstances, will ever consent to pay as much tax as his neighbour, who is worth an hundred times as much as himself. What is the rule which prevails in this and all other cities, in regard to taxation? Is it not, that every man shall pay according to his ability? Does he, who is the humble tenant of a hut in the suburbs of the town, pay as much towards the support of the corporate authorities, and keeping up the police, as the owner of those splendid buildings which adorn and beautify the city? No, Sir, and yet they all meet at the polls upon terms of perfect equality. And no man could be found fool-hardy enough to propose, either that all should pay alike, without regard to property, or that each man should have votes in proportion to the amount which he pays into the town treasury. Let us not then, I again beseech you, attempt to act upon, and enforce a principle, against the people west of the Alleghany, which we cannot, and I repeat it, which we *dare* not attempt to enforce among ourselves? Let us give them representation according to their numbers, and tax them according to their ability to pay.

Upon the subject of guarantees, of which we have heard so much during this discussion, I concur entirely with gentlemen on the other side of the question, in the opinion, that none can be given. For my own part, I will neither offer nor accept of any guarantee, in relation to the taxes which are to be imposed for the support of Government. The only guarantee which ought either to be tendered, or received, betwixt the parties to the social compact, is the mutual confidence which ought always to subsist between them, and without which, the compact ought never to be formed. This was the only guarantee, given by our ancestors to each other, when they formed the old compact, which was sealed with their blood, and it is the only one I will give, or take, now. And, Sir, all the arguments we have heard, founded upon the diversity of interests supposed to exist, between the Eastern and Western people of this State, are arguments in favor of a division of the State, and not in favor of a guarantee, or in favor of putting the Government into the hands of the minority. And if gentlemen can convince me, that our interests are so distinct, or so conflicting as they have represented them to be, I for one, am in favor of an immediate division of the State. And no happier illustration of what I am endeavoring to impress upon the Committee, could be desired, than that afforded by the eloquent gentleman from Hanover, when he called upon us to imagine, what would have been the course which the Adams's, Franklin, Washington, Lee, and the Rutledge's, would have recommended their countrymen to pursue, had this country been equally represented in Parliament according to numbers, at the time the tax was imposed upon the tea consumed in this country. And had the taxes been imposed by the majority in Parliament, against all their united votes, and remonstrances, for purposes which could in no way benefit or interest the people of this country, according to the principles now contended for by that gentleman, and all those who have spoken on the same side, they should have recommended to the people to ask for more power, that being the only guarantee which, in their opinion, can be received, as sufficient for the protection of property. And they should, upon this principle, now so strenuously contended for, (that is, that representation should be in proportion to population and taxation combined,) have asked, that an estimate should be made of the value of all the property in the two countries, or of all the taxes paid in each, that the representation might be equalized according to this combined ratio. But according to my ideas of what would have been proper, they should have done, what they certainly would have done, under such circumstances, that is, they should have recommended, as they did recommend to their countrymen, to refuse to submit to those laws, and declare themselves an independent people. That, Sir, was the only course which was left to the people of this country to pursue then; and if the interests of the people in the Eastern and Western divisions of this State, are so incompatible with each other, that we cannot trust one another, without overturning the fundamental principles of our Government, and putting the power into the hands of the minority, there is no other course left to us now, but to divide the State. But, Sir, I do not believe there is any such diversity or clashing of interests amongst us; if there be, the gentlemen asserting it, have entirely failed in the proof; and until it be shewn, we are bound to presume it does not exist.

I promised to prove, before I took my seat, that the people of the district in which I live, are more united by the ties of common interest with the people in this part of the State, than the people of the Culpeper or Accomack districts can be. And I now proceed to redeem that promise.

It is known that this City and the town of Lynchburg, and the intermediate country, afford our only market for our surplus produce, upon the disposal of which, we depend, for all the luxuries and many of the comforts and even necessaries of life. Of course we feel a deep interest in their prosperity. The people of the Culpeper district, trade altogether to Fredericksburg and Alexandria; and the people of Accomack, to Baltimore; they of course, feel a deep interest in the prosperity of those towns, but certainly none in that of Lynchburg or Richmond. We would be disposed to defend this City from an enemy, if it were only to secure to ourselves a market hereafter: they, on the contrary, might find it to their interest that this City should be burned to ashes, inasmuch as it might be the means of driving some of its capitalists to live in the towns which they are in the habit of looking to for a market. We have no other channel, by which we can carry on a commercial intercourse with the world, except the James River; it is therefore our interest to keep up a good understanding with those who live on its banks, and to endeavor to get it improved: they, on the contrary, might be benefited by the navigation being entirely destroyed, as it would keep a great many competitors out of the market In truth, our interests are so intimately connected with those of the people along the whole course of the James River, that we might as well attempt to make our streams flow in an opposite direction, as to attempt to sever them. Their interests, on the contrary, all tend to attach them, to people living either out of this Commonwealth, or in some other part of it than this.

A great deal has been said upon the subject of roads and canals, but without much bearing upon the question under discussion, as far as I am capable of judging. The gentleman from the Culpeper district, (Mr. Scott,) for instance, undertook to prove, that all improvements cost more as you advance westward, by comparing the cost of the Potomac canal with some little improvement on the Rapidan. He also made some remarks upon the subject of the James River Canal, which it will not be improper for me to notice. The gentleman seems to be of opinion, that this improvement was undertaken at the instance of some Western man. I think in this he is mistaken, for I have always been under the impression, that this improvement was first suggested by some person living East of the Blue Ridge. I thought it a little curious, that the gentleman should have changed his original ground, which was, that improvements cost more as you go Westward, than they do in the East, when speaking of the James River Canal, and seem disposed to attribute the immense cost of this work, not to its situation in the West, but to the fact of its having been a Western scheme, for the benefit of the Western people. But, Sir, I deny that this improvement was undertaken exclusively for the benefit of the West. It was expected greatly to benefit the coal trade; and as soon as it had reached a certain point, and all the advantages which the East expected to gain from it, had been secured, it was stopped short; and we are now taxed with double tolls, to pay the expense of a work, which has never been of the least benefit to us. And the great cost of this, and other works of the kind, is now to be made the pretext for depriving us of our just share of power in the Legislature, it being apprehended, that we will impose unjust taxes upon our Eastern brethren, to make improvements in the West. I conscientiously believe, that the suspicion is not well founded, and that the whole argument, which has been attempted to be deduced from the supposed disposition of the Western people, to improve their country, at the expense of the East, is unsound, and only calculated to deceive and mislead the members of this Convention.

It has been very often repeated in this debate, that each man in the Eastern part of the State, pays more than three dollars for every dollar that is paid by each Western man into the Treasury. I cannot perceive any good reason why this circumstance should have been so often brought to our view, for I can hardly believe that the Eastern people would be so unreasonable as to expect that they should derive the principal part of the benefits from the existence of the Government, and that the Western people should pay all the expense attending its administration. I have already endeavored to prove, that each individual ought to pay taxes in proportion to his ability to pay, upon the ground, that he who owns most property, derives the greatest benefit from the existence of the Government and of the laws; and upon the same principle, the Eastern people, owning three times as much property as the Western people, and consequently deriving three times as much benefit from the Government, ought to pay three times as much of the expenses. I am also inclined to think, that if there is three times as much money paid into the Treasury by the Eastern people as is paid by the West, there is a still greater proportion of the money expended in the East. Nearly all the money which has ever been expended in the West, has been, what has been expended in improving the Kanawha river, and in making the Kanawha road; and for that, the State derives a tolerable equivalent in the tolls collected. Whilst hundreds of thousands of dollars have been expended in Eastern Virginia, in building and inclosing this very Capitol; in erecting the other public buildings in this city; in making the James River Canal, and in establishing the University, to say nothing of the immense expenditure of public money in building fortifications on the sea coast, which money, although not drawn out of the State Treasury, is expended among the Eastern people for their peculiar benefit, and is collected from the whole people of the United States.

The Western men having been charged with voting away the public money, for Western purposes, it is proper for me to say, that in the course of several years during which I have been in the Legislature, I have always voted very cheerfully for all appropriations which have been asked for, for improving the country, uninfluenced by any local considerations whatever; and that I have always voted as willingly for the expenditure of the public money in the East, as in the West.

There was one idea advanced by most of the gentlemen who have advocated the opposite side of this question, which appeared to be very much relied upon, as proving the propriety of our granting to the minority, the power they ask for, and which I should have noticed before, if the gentleman from Fairfax, (Mr. Fitzhugh) had not sufficiently refuted it already. I allude to the expression so often used, that those who lay the taxes, ought to be responsible to those who pay the taxes. I will barely remind the gentleman from Accomack, who advanced this idea last, that it is not now the case, and never can be the case, to the extent which he seems to contend for, that those who lay the taxes, shall be responsible to those who pay them. For that whilst his county has more than a thousand voters in it, the principal part of the taxes are paid by about two hundred; and yet the members of the House of Delegates will always find themselves compelled to obey the wishes of the eight hundred who constitute the majority, rather than the minority, who pay the greater part of the taxes. And any member obeying the instructions of the minority, in opposition to those of the majority, would be sure to lose his seat at the next election.

I have only, in conclusion, to notice the proposition for a compromise, made by the venerable gentlemen from Loudoun, for the purpose of remarking, that I am opposed to it; for I fear, if it prevails, there will be constant jealousies and dissentions betwixt the two Houses; and I cannot willingly give my vote for a proposition, subversive of the great fundamental principles of Republican Government, viz: that the majority shall always govern.

Mr. Moore having concluded his remarks, he moved for the rising of the Committee; when

Mr. Doddridge enquired of Mr. Taylor, whether it was probable the difficulty to which he adverted, would be removed in time for the meeting of the Convention to-morrow?

Mr. Taylor answered, that he presumed it would. He had intimated his purpose to the senior member of the delegation; and he should to-morrow send in to the President, his letter of resignation. He hoped his colleagues would be able, by to-morrow, to have the vacancy supplied.

The Committee then rose, and the House adjourned.

SATURDAY, November 7, 1829.

The Convention was opened with prayers by the Rev. Mr. Lee of the Episcopal Church, and the President took the Chair.

The President laid before the Convention a letter from Robert B. Taylor, Esq. (a Delegate from the Norfolk District,) which was read as follows:

Sir,—Many of my constituents have instructed me to support the proposed plan of apportioning representation, with regard to white population and taxation combined; and I have reason to believe that a large majority of the people of my District concur in the desire, expressed in those instructions.

It is due to myself to prevent all misrepresentation of my official conduct. I was elected to this body, with the full knowledge of my constituents, that I favored reforms in the existing Constitution. I came here untrammelled by instructions; and restrained by no pledges. I am unfortunate, indeed, in this, that my opinions do not harmonize with those of my constituents; but I have disappointed no expectation; violated no engagement; betrayed no trust.

Having always believed, and maintained, that the value of representative Government mainly depends on the principle, that representation is only a mean, whereby the deliberate will of the constituent body is to be expressed and effectuated, no act of mine shall ever impair the principle. Had my constituents instructed me on some matter of mere expediency; or required me to perform any thing, which was possible; it would have afforded me pleasure to testify with how cheerful a submission, I would give effect to their opinions, rather than my own. But they ask what is impossible. They require me to violate my conscience and the sentiment of filial devotion, which I owe to my country.

Believing, as I conscientiously do, that the measure I am instructed to support, is hostile to free institutions; destructive to equality of right among our citizens, and introductive of a principle, that a minority, on account of superior wealth, shall rule the majority of the qualified voters of the State, I should be guilty of moral treason against the liberty of my native land, if I allowed myself to be the instrument by which this mischief is effected. In this state of mind, by executing the wishes of my constituents, I should justly subject myself to their reproaches, for my baseness, and to the more insufferable reproaches of my own conscience.

One mode only remains to reconcile my duties to my constituents, to the higher and more sacred duties I owe to myself, and my country. It is to resign the office, which they conferred upon me; and thereby to enable my colleagues to select a successor, who more fortunate than I am, may give effect to their wishes, without violating any sentiment of private and public duty.

Allow me to ask that this letter may have a place on your Journal. Forgive the feeling, which prompts this request. If any eye shall hereafter read my humble name, I wish that the same page, which records my retirement from your service, may also record the motives (mistaken perhaps, but not unworthy,) which occasioned it.

I leave the Convention, Sir, with sentiments of profound respect, and veneration for the virtue and talent, which ennoble and adorn it. My heart will still attend your counsels; and I shall not cease to supplicate the Almighty, that he may so inspire and direct them, that Virginia may be regenerated, united, free and happy.

I have the honor to be, your obedient servant,

ROBERT B. TAYLOR.

James Monroe, Esq.
President of the Convention.

On Mr. Mercer's motion, the letter of Gen. Taylor was laid on the table.

Mr. Grigsby, of the Borough of Norfolk, has been elected by the rest of the Delegates as a Delegate to serve in the place of Robert B. Taylor, Esq. resigned.

The standing order having been read, the Convention resolved itself into a Committee of the Whole on the Constitution, Mr. Powell in the Chair.

Messrs. Scott and Green made some explanations in relation to the remarks presented by Mr. Moore of Rockbridge on Friday, on the improvement of the James River.

Mr. Scott referred to the Journals of the House of Delegates, to shew that on various occasions members from the region of country below the Ridge and in the Valley had voted with the West for objects of internal improvement, even when their own country was not specially interested.

Mr. Green detailed the circumstances of the compromise, by which the members from the lower country were induced to consent to a larger appropriation for the James River improvement, than they would otherwise have done, in consequence of a stipulation in the act for that object, that the tolls should not be raised until the rate of transportation was lowered.

Mr. Moore explained on the same subject; shewing that he had voted for internal improvements which were on the West or East of the mountains. He disclaimed all sectional feelings, however other gentlemen might entertain them.

Mr. Leigh hoped that the Committee would rise, to give a gentleman on this floor (Mr. Giles) an opportunity of addressing them to greater advantage hereafter; his indisposition this morning was aggravated by the state of the weather. He said besides, that there were at least five gentlemen absent. He said he was perfectly willing to withdraw his motion, if any other gentleman was prepared and willing to take the floor.

Mr. Doddridge repeated the same sentiment, and hoped that some gentleman would rise, if ready to address the Committee.

But no one rising for that purpose, Mr. Doddridge made a motion for the Committee to rise, which was carried without opposition; and then Mr. Powell reported that the Committee had, according to order, taken into consideration the subject referred to them, but had adopted no resolution thereon.

And then, on Mr. M'Coy's motion, the Convention adjourned until Monday, eleven o'clock.

MONDAY, November 9, 1829.

Convention met at 11 o'clock, and was opened with prayer by the Rev. Mr. Horner of the Catholic Church.

According to the standing order, the House went into Committee of the Whole, Mr. Powell in the Chair.

The following is the substance of Mr. Giles' remarks, taken down by a stenographer, in his own language, and corrected by Mr. Giles himself.

Mr. Giles said: After all the subjects of this debate have been so fully elaborated, and thoroughly exhausted, it may be deemed presumption in him to attempt a further elucidation of them; repetitions too, might be deemed intrusive on the time, and even wanting in respect to the intelligence of the Committee. Notwithstanding these discouragements, he felt impelled by an irresistable sense of duty, to extend the debate still further, not with a vain hope of throwing new interesting lights on the subject; nor with a hope of obtaining a lean majority. A lean majority on either side would be a poor triumph of friends over friends; and still more so, on the affirmative than negative side of the proposed amendments to the Constitution, and would be better calculated to attract the distrust than the confidence of our constituents. But his principal inducement for continuing the debate, was a faint glimmering hope of approaching nearer to unanimity in whatever measures may be adopted, than we seem to be at present, from any indications now before us. Unanimity would, indeed, be an effect worthy of this great occasion, and worthy the sacrifice when he considered every individual member called upon to make, to obtain the objects of the Convention. Without some approach to unanimity, he feared all our labours here, might be worse than unavailing. Why should we not approach this unanimity? All see that there are sufficient inducements to make the best effort, and fortunately, not without the authority of great example on this occasion. The existing Constitution which we are called upon to examine, modify, or abolish, was produced by unanimity. Our forefathers were magnanimous enough, after a laborious investigation, conducted with the most ardent zeal, to agree to it by an unanimous vote. And why should not we follow their noble example? It was said that this unanimity, and this very Constitution were produced by a sense of danger; and were the effects of haste and alarm. He was sorry to hear this suggestion repeated, because it was unfounded. It is true that our forefathers did act in imminent peril, and under full sense of that peril, but it is not true, that the instrument they produced, was the effect of haste or alarm. Though they were highly sensible of the danger; it never disturbed the equanimity of their minds, during their whole proceedings. They went on coolly and dispassionately, notwithstanding the dangers that surrounded them, and the final result, was the production of this Constitution. This danger, far from being appalling, was viewed by them with sport, contempt, and even derision. He had been frequently told, that nothing was more common, than that the members should sportively jeer each other, with saying, we *must* hang all together, or *be* hung one by one. Is it possible, that any state of mind could have produced a stronger incentive to exert their best efforts, for arriving at the best results? Did not this state of mind afford the strongest incentives for calling into action every feeling of the heart, and every dictate of the head, to the perfection of their great work, with one united voice? They accordingly presented to us, the best Constitution that was ever presented to any people under the sun; accompanied too, with perfect unanimity. The history of their proceedings, will show that although, in the commencement of their discussion, there was as much difference of opinion amongst them, as amongst ourselves, and those opinions maintained with as much ardour and zeal; yet they nobly compromised all their differences, and came to an unanimous result. We are in a different situation. We are in a state of perfect security. No danger threatens us. We are perfectly free. Yes, Sir, perfectly free to indulge the wildest speculative visions of our imaginations in search of philosophical abstractions, to introduce into our fundamental laws for practical purposes. Whence arises this state of security? Surely from the patriotic and heroic labours which our venerable ancestors performed under different circumstances: We are so secure from the moral tendency of those fundamental laws, with which we were blessed 54 years ago, that there is no fear that we shall *hang one by one*, even if we should refuse *to hang all together*. Although we are perfectly free from the apprehensions of personal injuries, we are not without the strongest inducements, to make us combine to use our best efforts in producing unanimity in our proceedings. Should we fail in the objects for which we are called together, we would lose the confidence of our constituents, and whatever political fame and standing we have acquired; and should disappoint the expectations of our fellow-citizens, and of the world.

He mentioned these circumstances, to show us the necessity of banishing all prejudices, passions, and prepossessions; and, if possible, to be unanimous in our results, whatever they may be. He begged to be permitted to remark, that he had been delighted with all the arguments presented to the Committee, not only on account of their elaborate researches, and their splendid display of talents, eloquence, and instruction; but on account of their honorable frankness and candour. This remark was intended to apply equally to both sides of the question. The whole debate appeared to him to have afforded a new and conspicuous example of the just celebrity which Virginia has obtained for morals and for principles. The arguments on both sides, were presented front to front, and with so little disguise, equivocation or evasion, that to form a just comparison of their respective merits, it was only necessary to re-view them in their state of confrontation. But, while he felt this pleasure at the progress of the argument, he could not avoid expressing the deepest regret, that a difference of local interests, should have interposed to interrupt this happy spirit, in conducting this discussion. Such local interests, however, do exist, and they are too important either to be overlooked or disregarded. To obliterate them, would seem to be impossible. This difference of interests consists in the unequal position of the slave property in this State, and this interest is so important, that the production of the labour of the slaves, forms the foundation of one third of the whole taxes of the State. Although confronted at the threshold by this unfortunate stumbling block, it was the duty of all to meet and subdue the difficulty, or to apply such remedy as would be acceptable to all.

The venerable gentleman from Loudoun, (Mr. Monroe,) thinks emancipation impossible, without the aid of the Federal Government; and, perhaps, it would not be possible even with that aid—an aid which, could it be had, surely would not be desirable to any. He hoped the venerable gentleman would excuse him for saying, that he did not see the precise applicability of his remarks to the precise subject under consideration, and he could not avoid saying, that his feelings were much excited at the mere suggestion of calling upon the Federal Government for aid in so delicate a question. What would be the effect of calling on the Federal Government, to aid us in the common, ordinary, municipal regulations of the State. Some gentlemen call for the aid of the General Government in the prosecution of Internal Improvements. The venerable gentleman from Loudoun, thinks it may be required for the emancipation of our slaves, and says, "he even doubts if we were disposed to divide the State, whether we should be permitted to do so by the General Government." What will be the effects of all these dependencies on that Government? The effects must be the annihilation of all State rights—the destruction of the State Governments—and more, the amalgamation of a great mass of power in the Federal Government. Have gentlemen reflected on the tendencies of a vast momentum of power, collected in any hands, which are beyond their control? Is it not inevitable, that it must beat down the barriers of all political powers, which may be interposed to palsy its influence by division? The best we could hope under such an amalgamation, would be a consolidated despotism. This consummation could be desirable to none. He had merely made these general remarks with a view of protesting against the interference of the General Government, and of preventing their intrusion in the discussion before us, by disposing of them at this early period. Were it not for this important difference of sectional interests, he would indulge the most flattering hope that the Convention should be enabled to improve the condition of man, by adding to the great political lights heretofore shed on this State, and the whole world, by our venerated forefathers. He considered the science of politics yet in a state of infancy. While he observed the march of the human intellect, in bringing to perfection all the other arts and sciences, viewing with wonder the improvements which have been made in the last century, or perhaps still more in the last half century, he could not but observe, that the science of politics, had not kept pace in improvements with any of the other arts and sciences. The only effort at improvement, was the one originally adopted by the framers of our Constitution. This was only fifty-four years ago; a mere speck in the progress of time; and had introduced a new and just principle in the science of politics—one in direct hostility to the pre-existing basis on which all other Governments were founded. It opened a new æra in the science of politics, and, he hoped, sincerely hoped, that our American statesmen would abandon that system which had so long prevailed, and had proved so destructive to the rights and liberties of the human race; and found a new science upon the great discoveries of our forefathers. We have not done so. We have rather retrograded to those principles which our forefathers had abandoned. We have gone back to imitate the British system, as far as regards practical, political economy, after having established the most happy and beautiful fundamental system of our own. And this is one cause why we have not added a new science to the existing political economy, suited to our great developements in fundamental principles. There is another cause. All other Governments were, as he conceived, founded on fraud and backed by force. The few who had by combinations usurped the rights of the many, and possessed themselves of all the proceeds of their productive labour, have employed all their means to prevent further improvements in the science of politics, to avoid the detection and exposure of the fraud, which was the foundation of their systems. We know it was their great object to prevent an examination of these subjects, and to such an extent did they carry their rigorous vigilance, that the first patriots, Hampden and Sydney, fell victims to their patriotic enquiries into the science of politics. These causes contributed to throw the science of politics back, and to prevent it from making its way under the influence of that march of intellect which pressed forward all the other sciences.

He should suppose it was the duty of this Convention, to turn their researches into political science. A great discovery had been made in opposition to former systems: that all the rights of Government are founded in the consent of man, and that consent is ascertained through the social compact, or, in other words, the written Constitution. There is a difference of opinion, however, in regard to the true characteristics of the social compact, and particularly in relation to the parties to it. In the origin and progress of the social compact, every member is a party to it; each representing his own individual interests, as his own sovereign, uninfluenced by the majority. At its completion, the parties become changed by the consent of all its members. The compact is then made to consist of only two parties, the governors and the governed; and whether the majority shall exercise the Government or not, or to what extent, must depend solely on the written compact. Gentlemen had imputed to the honorable gentleman from Orange, to whom he listened with great pleasure, the assertion, that a minority ought to govern, as well as a majority. This imputation had been extended too far, if he had rightly understood the gentleman from Orange. He did not understand that gentleman, as declaring, that a minority ought, in any case, to exercise active, affirmative legislation, but that a minority was sometimes invested with authority to legislate, in a negative capacity. A minority cannot rightfully *govern*, in any case, but it is often used, as a fit instrument to prevent a majority from doing what it ought not to do. The rights of the majority depend solely upon the compact. It will be seen, there, how far a majority may govern, and how far it ought to be checked. Here we have a local interest, which is admitted by all to be applicable to peculiar sections of the State, but not to the whole of it. This local interest must be secured by provisions in the fundamental laws; if not, upon general principles, the majority would govern it. If it be improper that the majority should govern, where there is a *particular*, local interest, the minority should have a power of controlling the majority, so far as to afford protection to such particular, local interest. Such was the case in the Federal Government, as was illustrated by the gentleman from Orange; from whose lucid remarks he derived both pleasure and instruction. He took it for granted, that the majority had no rights but those that were vested in them by the compact.

Under our written Constitution, or social compact, the science of politicts was divided into two parts. One great branch of the science, is that which relates to the organization of the fundamental laws. And the other branch is, that which relates to the policy to be observed by the practical government, as established by these laws. No effort has been yet made to enquire into these subjects, as distinct branches of political science. The American mind has been drawn from the contemplation of these subjects by imitation. The love of imitation is one of the strongest passions of the human mind; and instead of elaborating a new system, suited to our own discoveries, we have been led into the imitation of British systems of practical, political economy. Here, then, is a new field opened before us, for the extension of political science.

An example of this spirit of imitation, may be seen in the organization of the Executive of the United States. There we have exhibited the anomaly of an Executive, attached to a republican Legislature, having more monarchical than republican tendencies. We have thrown so much power and patronage into the hands of the Federal Executive, that we must see the danger which threatens us from its organization. Yet that Executive is now held up to us for our imitation. How this happened he could not perceive, if gentlemen had the same views of the organization of the Executive of the Federal Government, that he had, and the same views of the peculiar fitness of the Executive Government of Virginia, as it is now established to a republican form of Government. So far from abandoning the old system, and falling into the gulph of imitation, an error, the strongest of the natural propensities of man; we should call on those who may hereafter aid in amending the Federal Constitution, to follow the example of Virginia. If the Virginia system were transferred to the United States, it would be the best improvement that could be adopted. The events of the last four years must be sufficient to satisfy every gentleman, that instead of calling on us to imitate the Executive of the Federal Government, if that Government could be brought to imitate our system, it would be the most important amendment that could be devised in the formation of its organic laws.

The gentleman from Loudoun (Mr. Mercer) whose eloquence he had listened to with great pleasure, had pointed to the Executive Department, as one of the great defects in the present Constitution of Virginia. He was not so much surprised at the reference, as he was at the grounds upon which the gentleman had rested his objections. They were founded on a supposed want of responsibility. That want of responsibility should be alleged against it, Mr. G. said, attracted his wonder. If there was any responsibility in any Executive under the sun, it is in ours, as at present organized. The gentleman, therefore, has taken up his notions, without a sufficiently minute examination; for, in fact, the responsibility of the Virginia Executive, was the strictest that human wisdom could devise. What is the responsibility of the Executive? The Executive Council are required to keep a journal of their proceedings, which is signed by every member present.

The agent thus renders an account to his principal, under his own hand, which can always be referred to, as evidence of the manner in which his duties are fulfilled. What are the duties of the Governor? His accountability is as strict, though not as severe as that of the Council. He is at liberty to follow or refuse to follow the advice of the Council. He acts on his own responsibility; he is not bound by the Council. The journal shows his own acts also, and consequently his responsibility. How, then, is he screened from his own responsibility? This Executive, then, is wisely ordained. It is the wisest effort of the great genius of the writer of our Constitution, in making the whole Executive responsible to their electors, as connected with a republican Legislature. He had been struck with the remarks of the gentleman from Loudoun, (Mr. Mercer) and had wondered how a gentleman of such intelligence should have fallen into such an error, as it appeared to him to be. He had felt it to be his duty to do away the imputation, not only from a sense of justice to the Council, but to this and to all nations. This Council had been in operation fifty-four years. If there had been any misrule, the gentleman could point it out. He invited gentlemen to attend to the condition of the Executive, not only at the present moment, but from the commencement of its organization, and would thank them for any criticisms on any of its pr ceedings, and particularly those of the present day. There was no merit in the administration, but a merit of principle arising from responsibility. If we have had an Executive in Virginia, which has gone on so smoothly, so easily, so little known, and scarcely felt for fifty-four years, discharing all its duties, why should it now be changed? If it should have done all that was expected, he would ask if there was not some hazard, some boldness, in changing it for something untried and unknown? As to want of power in the Executive, so far as his experience had gone, although he had been often accused of an inordinate love of power, he then had as much power as he wished to have, or ought to have, or as any other human being should ever have. Executive patronage and power were the sure causes of all political mischiefs. The demoralizing influence which we have seen throughout the whole United States, arose mainly from giving too much patronage to the Federal Executive. But, gentlemen had gone further, and made some more general charges against the Constitution. The gentleman from Brooke (Mr. Doddridge) to whom he always listened with pleasure, had said, that the Constitution was made amidst peril and alarm—that it was constructed hastily—adopted under the exigencies of the times, and was never considered as a permanent, organic law. He begged to be permitted to repeat the words of the gentleman, as taken down in the newspapers, not with a view of throwing them back upon him by way of retort; he was incapable of such rudeness; but from his extreme reluctance at mis-stating the words of any gentleman. The words are the following:—"The history of the State would show that the present Constitution was adopted in a period of danger and alarm; that it had been hastily enacted, was never considered as an organic instrument, deliberately agreed upon with a view to its being permanent, but adopted under the exigencies of the times, merely as a temporary expedient." Suppose, for a moment, the Constitution was a chance-medley—a God-send. If it were a God-send, it was the most blessed God-send with which man was ever favoured. So happy have we been under it, we have lived so harmoniously, and enjoyed ourselves so much at our ease, as almost to forget that there was any government. Government may be said to approach perfection, when man does not know that he is governed at all. Would gentlemen discard the Constitution merely because they conceived it to be a lucky hit, and not a dictate of wisdom; because they deemed it a special interposition of Providence rather than the production of the wisdom of man? We ought to cherish it and make the best possible use of it, for such is the manner in which Christians ought to treat every God-send. So directly contrary was the argument of the gentleman, to the views he entertained as to the manner in which the Government was formed. To show the mistake into which the gentleman from Brooke had fallen, with respect to the Constitution, he would read an account given by the President of the Convention, the celebrated Edmund Pendleton, whose name, in itself, should give to every thing he said, the most unquestionable sanction. He would not fatigue the Convention with much reading, but the mistake was so serious, and called so loudly for correction, that he must beg its attention to a single paragraph, because these mistaken opinions prevailed on this subject throughout the whole State. The paragraph he should read, is found in a letter from the late Mr. Jefferson to the late Judge Woodward, giving an account of the proceedings of the Convention. He would read but a few sentences.

"He (Mr. Pendleton) informed me (Mr. Jefferson) afterwards, by letter, that he received it on the day on which the Committee of the Whole had reported to the House, the plan they had agreed to; that that had been so long in hand, so disputed inch by inch, and the subject of so much altercation and debate, that they were worried with the contentions it had produced, and could not, from mere lassitude, have been induced to open the instrument again: but that being pleased with *the preamble* to mine, they adopted it in the House by way of amendment to the report of the Committee; and thus my preamble became tacked to the work of George Mason."

He begged the gentleman's best attention to this historical account of the proceedings of the Convention, and they could not avoid seeing the direct contrast between it and the account given by others. So far as he was enabled to do so, it would now be his pleasing task to defend the Constitution from other imputations. He regretted his inability to do justice to the subject. In the first place, the wisdom of our forefathers fixed the basis of the Constitution, on land—on earth—mother earth. We are taught, when we pray, to say to our Creator, "in thee we live, and move, and have our being." He would extend the reflection so far, as to show that the instrument in the hands of God, was land—earth—emphatically our mother earth, through which we do "live, and move, and have our being." We look to it for our existence, and we look to it for our subsistence. It gives us the coarsest food, which indigence requires, and supplies us with all the highest luxuries which refinement can desire. It yields our ordinary covering, and affords all the ornaments which decorate the fair of the land. From the lowest necessity to the highest luxury, we are indebted for all to our mother earth. Are there not, then, an affinity and an association between our mother earth, and the beings who exist on it? Would it not be unreasonable and unphilosophical to establish a Government for the inhabitants of the land, without reference to the land itself? He thought it certainly would be—he might be too much enchanted with the idea, that there existed an intimate connexion and relationship between the land, and its inhabitants—but it had grown out of the best reflection he had been able to give to the subject. Yes, he considered land as too important an instrument in the affairs of mankind, to be entirely disregarded, in the formation of the organic laws for the government of its inhabitants. He would say land is the best and only solid, indestructible foundation for Government, unless we re-assert the divine right of Kings, which is nothing more than a mere human invention, founded in fraud and falsehood. The wisest provision that ever was made in any Constitution, is that which declares, that the right of suffrage should remain as it then was. It was then based on the freehold right of suffrage. But he did not mean to examine that question now. He mentioned it merely to attract the reflections of other gentlemen. If any other occasion should occur, and his health would permit, he would then go into a further examination of the subject, but he was fearful that he should not be able at this time to go through all the observations he had intended to make. Our forefathers then fixed on land as the basis of our Constitution, and adopted the Republican form of Government. The means for carrying the Republican system into effect, are made to consist of individual and intermediate elections combined. He conceived this to be the wisest combination of the elective franchise, that ever was devised. It is indispensable in these United States. The necessity arises from the extent both of territory and population. He knew that the popular current was running strongly against the principle of intermediate elections, and that an attempt was making in this country, to throw all governmental duties, in relation to elections, upon the people, in their individual capacity. This is visionary and impracticable: A mere *ignis fatuus*, and calculated to be onerous on the people, whom it is intended to benefit. He was satisfied, that the people could not beneficially exercise this right, to its full extent, in a great, extended, populous community; and, therefore, he thought it was proper for them, in certain cases, to delegate it to their legislative representatives. Intermediate elections are a refinement in the representative system, known only in the United States; and instead of extending its utility, we are throwing ourselves back upon the original principle of representation, by man, solely in his individual character. After this compound system of election, the Government is based, as far as practicable, upon a separation of departments, as checks on each other—the Legislative, Executive, and Judicial. These checks are introduced for the purpose of controlling the unlimited will of the majority. Unlimited will, wherever it be found, whether in the hands of a majority or a minority, is despotism. He had bestowed much reflection on this subject, and it had produced the most perfect conviction, that despotism is the inevitable effect of unlimited will. The utility of these checks, then, is seen in controlling this unlimited will, wherever it may exist. These are the fixed and stable pillars, upon which rests the useful and beautiful superstructure of our Constitution. These pillars, he feared, were now about to be torn down, and their fragments scattered to the winds, although he could not help hoping for better things. The merits of this Constitution were demonstrated by its beneficial results for 54 years; conspicuously seen by the present moral condition of our society, over any other known to him. If any other equalled it, in morals and in principles, he should be glad to be informed of it. The merits of the Constitution are still further seen, in the harmonious co-operation of all its parts, to produce an unity of object—one great, common good. Its merits are still further seen, in the peculiar favor and protection afforded to non-freeholders.

In all complicated controversies, between the poor and the rich, it is known that there exists a very strong bias in favour of the poor. That during the short time he was engaged in the practice of the law, he recollects, that he deemed it a compliment to any County Court, in which justice might be had by the rich, in any complicated controversy with the poor; not from any disposition in the Court to do injustice to any, but from the difficulty of counteracting the popular bias in favour of the poor; and he believed this was a general impression. He hazarded nothing in saying, that the poor are better protected against the influence of the rich, under our Constitution, than any other in the United States. Whilst, therefore, he disclaimed all popular views, he considered himself the real friend of the poor, in endeavouring to sustain our system. Under its peculiar organization, justice is administered to the poor freely, without reward; and the whole of his contributions, of every description, do not exceed 2*s*. 3*d*., whereas, the costs of a single warrant, under the perquisite system, which is proposed to be substituted for the existing one, would cost him, perhaps, ten times as much as all his present contributions put together. He begged to call the attention of the Convention to another point. Much had been said about the order and decorum of our elections, and nothing more was said than was merited. What do we hear from other

States, to which we have been referred for precedents; but which the gentleman from Orange had truly regarded as experiments, in opposition to experience? Look at every State where Suffrage has been extended to Universal Suffrage, and you will see universal disorder, intoxication, and demoralization of all sorts. He had been amused for a day or two past, in noticing what was doing in the State of New-York. The Convention of that State, had, a few years ago, conferred a blessing on themselves, by extending the Right of Suffrage to people of all colors—red, black, white and yellow. It was *philosophically* asserted, that mere difference of colour ought not to have any influence whatever, on any question of rights. He had read with amusement, one production headed, "confusion worse confounded." In the elections just had in New York, he found that there were two parties, Jackson and Anti-Jackson, each nominating a regular ticket for their elections. Another nomination, however, unexpectedly appeared, supported by what was designated Miss Fanny Wright's party. Yes, she started on the principle of the Agrarian Law; dividing property, morals, and all the gifts of God equally, in common, and indiscriminately amongst the whole of "We the people." For the two first days, Miss Fanny Wright's ticket was far ahead, and great was the alarm, lest it should succeed. By great exertions of all parties in New-York, and by Providential interposition, Miss Fanny Wright's ticket did not succeed. (Since the delivery of this speech, it appears that one of the persons on Miss Fanny Wright's ticket did actually succeed.) Thus that State has escaped from an Agrarian Law, and an utter subversion of morals and principles for the present, but for how long, God only knows. Gentlemen will probably reply, that the population of New-York is heterogeneous, and not like ours, homogeneous. This, however, all must admit, is a slender distinction, on which to place all the dearest rights and liberties of man: A mere presumed difference between heterogeneous and homogeneous. Suppose this presumption to exist in degree. All must admit that it must be a very limited degree. May not gentlemen be mistaken in the conclusions they have drawn from it? Under similar circumstances, men are the same every where; and similar causes will always produce similar effects. Its merits may still further be inferred, from the honorable compliments awarded it in this debate, even by its adversaries, in the frank and candid admission of the honorable liberality of the slave-holders to the non-slave-holders west of the Ridge, and yet more from their total failure to show any misrule whatever under it, although emphatically called upon to do so by his most worthy and honorable colleague, (Mr. Leigh of Chesterfield.)

Under its benign influence, we have enjoyed all these great, civil and political blessings, in the midst of many others, for 54 years. In no one instance has the wisdom of our forefathers been more conspicuously displayed, than in the means chosen to effect these great ends. These have consisted in the peculiar organization of the County Courts, and in throwing a great preponderancy of power into the hands of the middling class of society. He would rather have a Government dependant on the middle classes, relying upon their uniform moral tendencies, without any check or balance whatever, than a Government entrusted to either of the extremes of society, with all the checks which wisdom could devise. The organization of the County Courts is marked with peculiar wisdom. The County Court magistrates, with their judicial functions, are also entrusted with a portion of the Executive powers. These magistrates are scattered in neighborhoods, nearly equally, throughout the whole State: Each of them possessing a degree of moral influence in his own neighborhood, which, with his official influence, when combined together, forms the strongest Executive in the world.

Hence, the celebrity of Virginia, for obedience to law. Hence, it has been so frequently and emphatically said, that *law* is the only *despot* here. Here is seen an exception of the common maxim of an unity of the Executive, and is exhibited at the same time the most numerous and most efficient Executive in the world; substituting for physical force, in a single hand, its moral and official influence combined; acting more upon the affections, than upon the fears of the people. Another peculiarity of this organization, is, that the magistrates are totally destitute of compensation or reward, while acting in their Judicial and Executive capacities. Their only perquisite is their monopoly of the Sheriffalty, and it is now proposed to deprive them of even that inadequate chance of compensation. Even that compensation is never received in their Judicial capacity: and this is one of the peculiar merits of the system. Justice being thus administered freely, without reward, tends to keep its current pure and unpolluted. We received our County Court system directly from our Anglo-Saxon ancestors, but it may be traced back more than 1500 years from the present time, and beyond the period when the Saxon became converted into the Anglo-Saxon. During that long period of time, and amidst all the fluctuations of human affairs, it has been attended with the happiest effects.

He had thought proper thus to present to the Committee, this mere outline view of the subject, but it was far from being exhausted, and he greatly feared that he had fallen far short of its merits. He hoped, however, that he had in some degree rescued the

Virginia Constitution, from the unmerited imputations thrown against it; and that he had proved it to be founded on the true principles of political science.

He would now accept the invitations of several gentlemen, to enquire into the condition of man, "previous to a state of society," about which he found some differences of opinion. He observed he was placed in a singular dilemma. He felt himself compelled to agree with gentlemen in their premises on one side of the question, and to differ with them in their conclusions; whilst he agreed with gentlemen on the other side in their conclusions, and differed with them in their premises. Although he was charmed with the eloquence of his worthy colleague (Mr. Leigh of Chesterfield,) and of the hon. gentleman from Northampton (Mr. Upshur,) he was reluctantly compelled to differ with them, in the opinion, that there never existed a state of nature; whilst he concurred with them in the conclusion, that majorities had no right to govern, but that derived from the social compact. At the same time, notwithstanding he concurred with the hon. gentleman from Loudoun (Mr. Mercer,) who had displayed all his powers of reasoning, calling to his aid all the brilliancy of oriental imagery on this occasion, in the opinion that man had existed in a state of nature, he nevertheless felt himself constrained to dissent from the conclusion, that majorities had necessarily a right to govern in such a state. Mr. G. said, he would tell a plain tale, and his only effort would be to be understood. He believed there was a state of nature, and that it was susceptible of proof, both from history and from the reason and nature of things. A single fact and remark only, he conceived, ought to be sufficient to satisfy every reflecting mind, that there must have been some condition of man previous to his social condition. All admit that the social compact was made by men —by numbers of men. Man, therefore, must have preceded the social compact. If so, in what state was he? Surely in that state which has generally been designated a state of nature. He believed there was an intermediate state between the two. It might be called the domestic or family state of man. If so, both the natural and family state of man must have preceded the social. Although the hon. gentleman from Northampton, had partially denied the existence of a state of nature, and had referred to Bible history on that point, he had, however, admitted that the social compact was grounded on a feeling of property. This is admitted as one ground, but it is denied that it is the principal or the strongest ground. Whence was this feeling of property derived? It could only be from a right of property and a sense of that right. He insisted that the social compact was founded more in a feeling of weakness and of want. This feeling was so strong, as to amount to an absolute necessity for entering into the social compact. In his reference to the Bible history, the hon. gentleman had given some account of the subjection of Eve to Adam, and of the condition of that family, at the early period of their creation. The hon. gentleman should have extended his historical researches somewhat further, and he would have found that they abundantly proved, not only the right and possession of property in a state of nature, but also the existence of a domestic or family condition of man. He would have found, that Cain and Abel both made offerings to the Lord. The one, the first fruits of his land and labour—the other the firstlings of the flocks he tended. Abel's offering was most acceptable to the Lord, but the right of property was not denied by any one—the right being derived from occupancy and labour, and sanctioned by the innate or moral sense of man, ascertained by common consent. Mr. G. said, we were apt to fall into errors for want of due reflections upon the longevity of the anti-deluvians, compared with the little span of life permitted to the present race of man. To avoid such errors, he had made enquiries as to the age of Cain, at the time he committed the bloody murder upon his brother—and he had found that Cain was at that time, a mere lad approaching to puberty, but had not yet once thought of matrimony, although he had reached the age of one hundred and twenty-eight years, and his brother Abel one hundred and twenty-seven. Here, then, is complete evidence of a state of nature—at least one hundred and twenty-eight years after the creation. The right of property being unquestioned in each of them, and there being no one to punish Cain for his bloody crime—Adam having relinquished all parental authority over him. God, however, took Cain into hand, put a mark upon him, and sent him into the land of Nod, where, it is said, he married a wife and built a city. Should there be any sceptics bold enough to doubt the account given by the sacred historian, from a suspicion that there were other families existing at the time of Adam, of which the sacred historian was unapprised, Mr. G. would reply, that presuming that to be the case, the account given of the family of Adam, would form the Natural History of any other family which might be in existence, previous to the social compact. (For Cain's age at the time of the death of Abel, see Rees' Cyclopedia, corresponding upon this point with Lemprier's Chronological table prefixed to his Classical Dictionary.)

Mr. G. said, he was of opinion, that there had been such a state, as a state of nature; and that man had been driven from that state by the wants of nature. Indeed, that all creation was founded upon a principle of relative dependance; and man rendered more dependant than any other animal—clearly manifesting thereby, a Providential intention to drive him from a solitary, to a social state. The same principle of relative dependance, is observable amongst nations, as well as individuals, and is the true foundation of commerce. The mischiefs arising from the mistaken, barbarous notion of the positive independence of nations, introduced into the practical Government, by our late miserable and incompetent rulers, have been incalculable. Yes, Sir, greater than could be compensated for, in all time, by the same deluded, unfortunate political economists, if their lives were prolonged to the age of Methusaleh, and spent in the performance of good instead of evil deeds. Their miserable cabalistical false misnomers or nick-names—"National Industry;" "Domestic Industry;" "Home Market;" "Protection of Manufactures;" and above all, the "American System," he verily believed, had each of them cost the State of Virginia above 1,000,000 of dollars, since the year 1816; and he was confident that every gentleman would come to the same result, who would take the trouble to make the calculation from correct premises.

Whilst he admitted a state of nature, he denied that majorities had any influence in such state. Whence the derivation of the term "*Sovereign* People?" Surely from man in a state of nature, where he was his own sovereign. If he were not sovereign there, he was sovereign no where. If he were sovereign there, then we have the basis of his subsequent sovereignty. This seems to him to be a self-evident proposition. This enquiry leads to another more important one—to ascertain what are the duties of Government; and what is the object of the social compact? He would correct the expression. What is the object of the social compact, and what the objects in the formation of every free, legitimate Government? Exclusive of the public safety, one object is the protection of persons, the other the protection of property. Government was instituted for the protection of all human rights: adequate powers ought, therefore, to be given to the Government, to ensure the protection both of persons, and of property. A question, then, arises, how much power ought to be given? Is it to be unlimited power over all the rights of man? If so, all his natural rights must be taken from him. If only a portion of his rights are to be taken, what portion? How can the Government be so organized as to make a distribution of rights between the individual in his native character, and the Government in its corporate character? Here a question arises; ought a Government to be an active, or a passive machine? If Government be an active machine, you must give all the requisite powers and properties which belong to an unlimited Government. If it be a passive machine, less power is necessary, and the only difficulties will be found in the proper distribution of rights between the governors and governed. Upon this important point, differences of opinion exist. There are some gentlemen who claim for the General Government, the whole proceeds of the labour of the nation, as the great desideratum of its political economy. If so, in vain do we sit here; in vain are we here, if the proceeds of all labour must be given up to the General Government, not leaving even a modicum for ourselves, as the basis of our Constitution. Presuming, then, that Government is to be formed by a distribution of the natural rights of individuals between themselves, and the Government, what portion ought to be given to the Government? Surely the smallest portion which will suffice for governmental purposes. If all be given, none of course can be left to the management of the individual. He had bestowed much reflection upon the inquiry, as to that portion of rights, which should be surrendered to the Government, and that which should be retained to the individual. Perhaps the most effectual mode of ascertaining this point, would be to enquire what rights of nature, man, in his individual capacity, can manage better than the Government, and what portion Government can manage better than the individual. From all his reflections upon the subject, he had concluded that there were but two descriptions of rights, which the Government can manage better than the individual. One is, the right of every individual to do himself justice in his natural state; the other, the smallest portion of property that will suffice for governmental purposes. It will be perceived, that an exact distribution of rights, according to the preceding rule, must necessarily approach nearly to the production of a perfect Commonwealth. Here is opened a still wider field for extending the researches of all lovers of political science. He had himself concluded, that all rights, of every description, which individual man could manage at all, he could manage, and would manage better than the Government; and the degree of liberty enjoyed by him, would depend upon the greatest portion of these rights, left to his own management. The only reason why any rights should be given to Government, arises from the incapacity of man to execute them by his own means. He has not power to do justice to himself in a state of nature, because he will necessarily be brought in conflict with others, and he will be compelled to abandon that power merely from his incapacity to execute it. Hence, a portion of power must be given to Government to enable it to do, what the individual cannot do. Hence, the necessity for any concession of power, and he thought that no concession ought to extend beyond the right of doing justice, and the surrender of that portion of property, which is found indispensable for defraying the expenses of Government. In that case, Government would be a passive machine, ensuring liberty and safety to the people—rendering justice to all. Mr. Giles could not help expressing his surprise, that several gentlemen, and amongst the rest, the gentleman from Brooke, who seemed to be most desirous of great changes in the Constitution, after throwing the most serious imputations against it, had resorted to the Bill of Rights as the consummation of human wisdom, and insisted upon the observance of the rules there laid down by the present Convention, particularly the first three articles; and some of them have also called to their aid the 15th article, with the practical commentary upon them in the Constitution itself; and the gentleman from Brooke, had gone so far as to assert that in demanding a free white basis of representation, he demanded nothing new under the sun. It was the slave-holding minority, who were demanding a new thing under the sun. The following are the gentleman's own words: "He, (Mr. Doddridge) therefore, concluded that, in demanding a free white basis of representation, he and those who acted with him, were asking no new thing under the sun; but were forwarding a principle already existing and recognized; principles deeply founded in the nature and necessities of society. It was the slave-holding minority who were demanding a new thing." Here the gentleman admits that he is demanding something, and that thing, a change; he yet denies that this change is a new thing under the sun, and proceeds to charge the slave-holders with demanding a new thing under the sun, whilst they demand nothing at all, under the sun, neither new nor old, but are perfectly content with the Constitution in that respect as it now stands. Mr. G. said, he was willing to be governed by the Bill of Rights according to his interpretation of it. The Bill of Rights detracted nothing from the Constitution by preceding it, and he deemed it an essential part of the Constitution. Permit me, said Mr. Giles, to turn to the sections to which gentlemen invited our attention. The first article is:

"That all men are by nature equally free and independent, and have certain inherent rights, of which, when they enter into a state of society, they cannot, by any compact, deprive or divest their posterity; namely, the enjoyment of life and liberty, with the means of acquiring and possessing property, and pursuing and obtaining happiness and safety."

The eloquent and learned gentleman from Loudoun, read to us a number of Constitutions, and particularly that of Massachusetts, in the formation of which he told us, the Convention sat in deliberation for months.

He (Mr. G.) had already read the first article of the Virginia Bill of Rights. Let us look at the comparative merits of the Bill of Rights of Virginia and Massachusetts. The first article of the Massachusetts Bill of Rights says, that "all men are *born* free and equal." He denied this to be true, either in law or in fact; while he agreed that "all men are by *nature* equally free and independent." The condition of man, from free to bond, or from bond to free, is changed by municipal or conventional, and recognized by international law. Slaves are born slaves before us every day, which directly disproves the assertion, that "all men are *born* free and equal." Yet the Constitution of Massachusetts unequivocally asserts, that all men are born equally free. Are slaves born free? No. And if an enquiry be made as to the means, by which their condition is changed, the answer is, by municipal law—by conventional law—by force—or by conquest. Upon what authority do we hold Africans in bondage? Surely, by the municipal laws of that country, recognized by international law. Slavery was not only recognized by international law, but it was acknowledged by the law of God, if the scriptures may be deemed sufficient evidence of that law. As to matter of fact and of law, directly the reverse of the declaration in the Massachusetts Bill of Rights, is the universal legal maxim, "*partus sequitur ventrem*"—the offspring follows the condition of the mother.

This Constitution is presented to us as a model of excellence for our imitation, which declares that the bond are not born bond, which is not true—in preference to our own, which asserts the truth, that "all men are by nature free." And this strange preference has been strangely attributed to a greater degree of deliberation in the one case than in the other. He observed that this clause in the Bill of Rights contained another important declaration, that man possesses the means of "acquiring and possessing property" in a state of nature, thereby clearly sanctioning the existence of such a state. The second section is in the following words:

"That all power is vested in, and consequently derived from, the people; that Magistrates are their trustees and servants, and at all times amenable to them."

This section contains the great declaratory principle in direct hostility to the basis upon which all pre-existing Governments were founded; that "all power is derived from the people"—and that Magistrates are the servants of the people—and affords the first great example of reducing that principle to use in the affairs of mankind. It meets my most hearty approbation, and exalted admiration. The third section is:

"That Government is, or ought to be, instituted for the common benefit, protection and security, of the people, nation, or community: of all the various modes and forms of Government, that is best, which is capable of producing the greatest degree of happiness and safety, and is most effectually secured against the danger of mal-administration; *and that, when any Government shall be found inadequate or contrary to these purposes, a majority of the community hath an indubitable, unalienable, and indefeasible right, to reform, alter, or abolish it, in such manner as shall be judged most conducive to the public weal.*"

His worthy colleage, (Mr. Leigh) had so fully explained his views on one branch of this subject, and particularly on the clause, omitted by the gentleman who had introduced this section, that he considered all repetition superfluous. This section clearly proves that conditions are imposed upon majorities. His colleague had pointed out one, he would point out another. Whilst the majority have a right to alter, reform, or abolish the Government, there is no right conferred on them to do so, according to their own unlimited, capricious will. An obligation is imposed upon them, to act "in such manner as shall be judged most conducive to the public weal." This is the very business we are now engaged in performing—" to alter, amend, or abolish the Constitution, in such manner, as we shall judge most conducive to the public weal." Surely we should feel ourselves restrained by this clause from injuring, or even putting at hazard, any local or particular interest, even should it be the interest of the minority. Mr. G. called the attention of the Committee to that clause in the Bill of Rights, which required a permanent attachment to the community, as a qualification for voting, and asserted that the word 'permanent' was introduced with reference exclusively to land, nothing being deemed permanent but land; and the provision in the Constitution, which requires, that the Right of Suffrage should remain as it then was—being the freehold Right of Suffrage, was the practical commentary of the framers of our Constitution, upon the word '*permanent*' in the Bill of Rights. This demonstrably proves that there is no discrepancy whatever between the two instruments.

Some gentlemen plumed themselves upon a notion that our forefathers had earnestly invited us to a frequent recurrence to fundamental principles, with a view, as they suppose, to change those principles. This notion they had derived from the 15th section, in the following words:

"That no free Government, or the blessing of liberty, can be preserved to any people, but by a firm adherence to justice, moderation, temperance, frugality, and virtue, and by frequent recurrence to fundamental principles."

Why recur to fundamental principles? If these principles were true at that time, they are true now. Fundamental principles are eternal and unchangeable. Could our forefathers invite us to recur to fundamental principles, for the purpose of changing unchangeable things? But, if this were not the object, what could the object be for inviting a frequent recurrence to fundamental principles? Evidently for the purpose of watching the proceedings of the practical Government, and to draw them back from their aberrations, if any they had committed, to these great fundamental principles. It was not his intention to have referred to the General Government, if it had been possible to avoid it, notwithstanding its intimate connection with the State Governments, and its even constituting a part of them. But he found it impossible to avoid it. It would be all important, if we could prevail on that Government to recur to fundamental principles. Such had been its monstrous aberrations from the fundamental principles of the Federal Constitution, that they were violated every day. Scarce a semblance of its most important, original features remained. After he had been absent from the Government for some time, when he returned to it, he was astonished at the new-fangled nomenclature, which was introduced in substitution of the old Governmental phraseology; one effect of which was a splendid Government which the people are made to feel. How important then, would it be, could we prevail on this Government to have recurrence to original, fundamental principles. Instead of a splendid Government, which the people are now made to feel, we should then have a happy Government which they could not feel. He feared he had detained the Committee very unprofitably in presenting to their view mere general propositions without any attempt at minute, logical demonstrations. Those he left to the intelligence of the Committee. He would now examine some points of difference between himself and other gentlemen more especially, and as far as possible, would avoid repetitions. He would come to consider the actual difference of local interests as regards the slave population. The point is, whether there shall be any special provision for this local interest.

Mr. Giles was proceeding to remark on the argument of the gentleman from Loudoun, (Mr. Mercer) with respect to the salt-works of New York, and to deduce from it a confirmation of the views of the gentleman from Orange, (Mr. P. P. Barbour) with respect to those cases where a minority governs a majority; when

Mr. Taylor (of Chesterfield) rose, and moved that the Committee rise, in order to give his colleague another opportunity of presenting his views to the Committee, which, as he was then considerably fatigued, he could do more to his satisfaction and ease.

Mr. Giles expressed his willingness to proceed, although he was much exhausted, rather than protract the business of the Committee. He was willing to strain every power, physical and mental, he possessed, to continue his remarks.

The motion that the Committee rise was then put and carried, and the Convention adjourned.

TUESDAY, November 10, 1829.

The Convention met at eleven o'clock, and was opened with prayer by the Rev. Mr. Sykes of the Methodist Church.

According to the standing order, the House went into Committee of the Whole, Mr. Powell in the Chair.

Mr. Giles then rose in continuation of his remarks. He said, that he had never, at any period of his life, been in the habit of complaining, and as little now as ever, but it was only common justice to himself to state that he had risen yesterday, under a sense of debility so paralyzing, that he feared he would not be able to controul the operations of his own mind, nor to command that portion of physical strength which was requisite to sustain him through the task he had before him. This naturally produced some delay and confusion both in his manner, and in the course which he had prescribed for his own government. When he first rose, he had intended to read several extracts, but soon found himself compelled to change that determination, and to avoid reading as much as possible; being aware that reading tends much more to debilitate, than even the effort of speaking. He had intended to have read some of those extracts in relation to the first point which he had yesterday brought into discussion: he alluded to the remarks which had fallen from the venerable gentleman from Loudoun (Mr. Monroe) respecting the emancipation of slaves. This was a subject of such peculiar delicacy, that it was proper to present to the Committee the character of the existing relations, in respect to jurisdiction over slaves between the General and State Governments. He thought it proper now to complete what he had yesterday intended.

The General Government, at all times, from the first Congress, had disclaimed all sort of jurisdiction over the emancipation or the management of slaves; and thus jurisdiction, in both cases, was peremptorily denied to the General Government. He intended to have introduced the Journal of the twenty-first session first Congress, but as it was not before him, he would state from his recollection, what the resolution contained in the Journal upon that point was. The resolution went to disclaim on the part of the General Government, all jurisdiction over the emancipation or treatment of slaves. This resolution was entered on the Journal, as declaratory at that time, of the true interpretation of the Constitution; and at that day such an excitement existed among the Southern members against having the subject even mentioned, that they voted against this declaratory resolution. The honorable and venerable gentleman who is a member of this Convention, and who was then a member of Congress, he meant the gentleman from Orange, voted decidedly in favor of it. This was the mere declaratory act of one House; but in consequence of it two bills were passed, either at that or at some subsequent session, prohibiting the citizens of the United States from interfering with the slave trade, for the purpose of supplying foreign nations with slaves.

Mr. G. then referred to a memorial, which was presented to Congress by the representatives of several societies of Quakers. He happened to be a member of the Committee, to whom the subject was referred. He had relied on the declaratory resolution, in the negotiation which he had to carry on with the Quakers. All the Committee were, in principle, in favor of the measure; but it was his duty to satisfy these persons, that Congress had no right to interfere with the subject of slavery at all. He was fortunate enough to satisfy the Quakers, and they agreed, that if Congress would pass a law, to prohibit the citizens of the United States from supplying foreign nations with slaves, they would pledge themselves and the respective societies they represented, never again to trouble Congress on the subject. The law did pass, and the Quakers adhered to their agreement. He did not know whether or not the documents, on the subject of this negotiation, were still in existence; but he believed they had been filed away with other papers.

Subsequently, an Act was passed, prohibiting the introduction of slaves into the United States, in which this principle was again touched, in a more specific, but a different form. It was again his fortune to be on the Committee to whom that subject was referred, and he drew up two provisos to a bill then pending before Congress, for prohibiting the introduction of slaves into the United States after the year 1807; the object of which, was to draw a distinct line of demarcation, between the powers of Congress, for prohibiting the introduction of slaves in the United States, and those of the individual States and territories. It was then decided, by an unanimous vote, that when slaves were brought within the limits of any State, the power of Congress over them ceased, and the power of the State began, the moment they became within those limits. He would beg leave to refer to these provisos. He would read as little as possible; but recent events made it important to revive the recollection of these facts, which appear strangely to have been forgotten. He had drawn up these provisos with all imaginable care.

The first proviso, after the powers of Congress to a certain extent had been declared, and the words therein were critically examined—and, indeed, he might say, not only every word, but every syllable, and even every stop, by the best talents which Congress could afford, be found—proceeded thus: "And neither the importer, nor any person, or persons, claiming from, or under him, shall hold any right or title whatever, to any negro, mulatto, or person of colour, nor to the service or labour thereof, who may be imported, or brought into the United States, or territories, in violation of this law; but the same shall remain subject to any regulations, not contravening the provisions of this Act, which the Legislatures of the several States or territories, at any time hereafter, may make, for disposing of any such negro, mulatto, or person of colour."

This was then considered as a legislative interpretation of the Constitution, as may be seen by its phraseology. It disclaimed all power over slavery, in all time to come. But it did not stop there. The power was not only relinquished to the States, but also to the territories, to wit: the unlimited jurisdiction over all the slaves brought within their limits respectively.

The second proviso is in the following terms: "Provided, that the aforesaid forfeiture, shall not extend to the seller, or purchaser, of any negro, mulatto, or person of colour, who may be sold, or disposed of, in virtue of any regulation which may hereafter be made, by any of the Legislatures of the several States, in that respect, in pursuance of this Act, and the Constitution of the United States."

Here, then, in these declaratory provisions of the Act, there is an explicit demarcation of the boundary line between the power of Congress, and of the Legislatures of the several States and territories. The Committee would observe that the word "territories" was omitted in the last proviso. An abstract right is admitted to the territories in the first proviso, but the word territories was not used in the second proviso, Congress having had a revisory power over the laws of the territories, and were unwilling to yield that power. The word was therefore omitted, but the right in the territories was recognized to exercise exclusive power over slaves, within their limits. He had understood that the Legislature of South Carolina, passed a law on the subject, and the State of Georgia assumed similar jurisdiction, in consequence of this law of Congress. This had led to two results—first, the admission on the part of Congress, that the State Governments are vested with the authority to declare persons within their limits, slaves; and second, the exercise of that authority, by the State Governments.

This brought him to the consideration of the proceedings which have lately taken place in the State of Ohio, and which had been very properly referred to by several gentlemen in this debate. It appears that Ohio, acting under a mistaken zeal, amounting to a fanatic desire, to meliorate the evils of slavery, invited a number of those unfortunate persons to take refuge in that State. Some remarks appeared in the newspapers, some years since, in regard to the State of Ohio, in which was suggested the possibility that in some future capricious mood, she might convert the coloured persons, who had been induced to enter her limits, into slaves, and that this she might do, because Congress had no right to prevent it. The remarks to which he referred, were as follow:

"Again, suppose Congress even could constitutionally exercise such power, would it be wise, or desirable that it should do so? when the effect would be, to place the different States in the Union upon different footings, as to rights? Nay, as to the most important right, with which the original States are invested? That is, the right of jurisdiction over persons within its own limits. This inquiry may be extended further. Suppose any of the free States, self-called, Ohio for instance, in some capricious mood, should determine that all the coloured people, who have been invited to take refuge in that State, against the slavery of other States, should be slaves within that State; would the Federal Government have the right to exercise any control over such determination? Certainly not—the jurisdiction over persons within the limits of Ohio, being exclusively with the State authorities. Here, then, Ohio would be invested with the power of jurisdiction over persons within its limits, which would be denied to another State admitted to the Union, subject to the bargained condition. Such are always the consequences of substituting bargains for principles in legislation."

What has Ohio now done? Becoming perfectly sensible of the mischiefs which have resulted from her former fanaticism, she has passed a law, which, if carried into execution, must entail upon those unfortunate and deluded people, who came into her State, in the belief that they should find protection there, a greater evil than slavery itself. The mischief has arrived at such a pitch, that the State has passed a law, requiring that all coloured persons in the State, should give security for their good behaviour, to an amount beyond their means to obtain. And not being able to do this, they must either be incarcerated, or quit the State. No asylum is provided for them, but if the law should be carried into effect, they must be driven forth—find refuge where they can—perhaps in Virginia; and surely Virginia ought to be upon the alert to counteract this most probable effect of the law. The next step which Ohio may take, may be to declare those people slaves, and it is more likely now that she should do so, than it was when the preceding remarks were made, that she should now take this step, which is more onerous and disastrous to her invited guests than slavery itself. It is, indeed, strange, that these coloured people should have been invited into that State, and should now be driven abroad as vagabonds, not on the face of the earth, but to find their way to the clouds, if they can, or wherever else they could find a refuge. He mentioned this subject to show how scrupulous the States ought to be, in touching the subject of slavery, and particularly of emancipation.

There was another point, which he was compelled yesterday to omit, having then been nearly exhausted. It was the difference between the rights of the majority, claimed from the various misconceived sources, to which gentlemen had referred, and such as were given by the Constitution or Social Compact. The specific question before us, is, not what relates to the powers of the majority, nor who shall be the majority; but who shall be the constituents to make that majority. The question now is, who are to be the constituents? By whose votes a majority of the members forming the practical Government, is to be created? And, then, what degree of jurisdiction should this majority have? This must depend on the Social Compact, or written Constitution we are now engaged in forming; and that brought him to the real point of inquiry, as contained in the Bill of Rights. In determining who shall be the constituents, the rule he had agreed to observe, which he still agreed to observe, and which he hoped all gentlemen would observe, is, that these constituents are to be made, "in such manner as shall be judged most conducive to the public weal." The rule imposed on us, is to perfect the great work now before us, in such manner as may be most conducive to the public weal. He had now arrived at the point at which he left off yesterday.

He would now consider the actual, local differences, arising from the unequal, sectional divisions of our slave property. The question which has arisen, is, whether slaves ought to be counted, in forming the basis of representation, either as persons or property? It is a plain question, if we agree as to the objects of the formation of Government. Why should they not be counted? They are persons and property both. Because they are property, shall we divest them of their existence—of their personal character? They are both persons and property in law and in fact. He did not state this with such positiveness, because he pretended to claim any superiority for his own opinions. Far from it. He would present to the Committee the few grounds on which his opinion rests, and leave them to decide. He would point out some of the supposed aberrations of the gentlemen on the other side. The fact, that they are property, is authorised by the federal law, the laws of the State, international law, and the sanctions of all laws. Great Britain may be referred to on this subject, on account of the peculiarity of her policy in that respect. She is so fastidious in her ideas of the relation of master and slave, that the moment they touch British ground, in that relation, such relation between them is entirely cut asunder. Where then shall we look for the British sanction of slavery? We found it first here—we found the curse upon us, for a curse he must consider it. It is admitted that we cannot avoid it. That very nation which is so fastidious on the subject of slavery in British land, fixed it on us against our consent. She has lately, in a treaty with this country, admitted slaves to be property, and has paid for them as such, and thus she has again admitted the principle of slavery. Look first at her West India possessions. Slavery is there, in its essence. The condition of the slave there is miserable in comparison with what it is here. There is abundant evidence around us to prove that we are making the best use of our power, to meliorate the condition of slaves.

He here begged to correct an aberration of the gentleman from Loudoun (Mr. Mercer,) as he conceived it to be. That gentleman had laid it down positively, that a slave in Virginia had no civil rights—that he was property—mere property. He compared him even to cattle. He presumed, however, that that gentleman would admit the existence of laws which treat slaves as persons: protecting them as far as wrongs are committed on persons in the character of persons, and consequently that slaves have civil rights. All persons, whether they be bond or free, not even excepting the *master himself*, who commit the higher order of wrongs, such as murder, &c.

on slaves, are subject to the punishment of death. The distinction on which this law is founded, is, that the offence is committed on them in the character of persons, and on the cattle in the character of property. The law in minor cases, for wrongs done to slaves, punishes through the master. As to the civil personal rights of the slave, they are more strictly enforced here than those of the white population. The protection which they receive under the law is most efficacious. The gentleman from Loudoun then, was in error. If rich or poor, white or black, murder a slave, death is the punishment. Did gentlemen ever hear of punishment of death for killing a cow? No, not even if the murderer eat her afterwards; yet these are the analogies of the gentleman from Loudoun.

He would say, that the laws in relation to slaves are wise and just. The law requires that the record of every offence charged against a slave, for which a white man would be punished in the Penitentiary, shall be laid before the Executive, for its decision: thus submitting by mere act of law, the case of every slave, found guilty of a criminal act, to the pardoning power. According to the humane provision of the law, the slave enjoys privileges which are not allowed to any one else. The best counsel is provided for him by his master, or by the Court, if the master should fail, and his rights are protected with the utmost vigilance and care. If we look at the police records of London, we shall see that thousands are hung in that city with almost as little ceremony as if they were brutes. Under this view, then, as the laws recognize the civil rights of bond as well as free, why are slaves not to be counted? The fact is, that whether persons or property, their labour produces a third of the taxes of the State. He cared not in what character the slaves produced them. The practical result, whether counted as persons or property, is nearly the same. But here is a case in point, of the unequal taxation of an important interest which requires some provision in the Constitution. Gentlemen admit there should be some provision, and offer a guarantee against the principle which they desire to insert in the Constitution. What is the object in establishing the fundamental laws? It is to draw from nature, certain great general principles, for the government of society, producing good moral tendencies, through their own intrinsic operations. According to the wise or unwise selection of these principles, would moral or immoral tendencies be produced in society. If we selected principles conducive to the public weal, the effect is visible, in the moral organization which the community gradually assumes. If the contrary, the effect is disclosed in their corrupt tendencies. It is then manifestly our duty, to select principles, which would intrinsically produce good and not evil tendencies upon society. He would here remark, that the condition of the population of Virginia, is now believed to be as sound as that of any other country in the world, because the great principles which our forefathers selected, had continued to produce good moral tendencies from that time to the present—a period of more than 54 years. Is there any wonder then, in our present moral condition? What are the consequences of the want of good principles in other communities, but the existence of immoral tendencies in their fundamental laws. It is a conclusive proof that gentlemen on the other side, are selecting principles, which have bad tendencies, that they are providing remedies against those very tendencies. This reminded him of a silly fellow who insisted upon making himself sick, merely for the purpose of ascertaining, whether physic would kill or cure him, when it was more likely to kill than cure him.

He had paid every attention to the pathetic complaints, which had been made by gentlemen on the other side, but more particularly to those of the gentleman from Hampshire, (Mr. Naylor) to whom he had listened with peculiar delight, not only on account of the eloquence, but the philanthropy which pervaded the whole of his remarks. That gentleman had called upon us for justice to the people of the West. Mr. G. said, could he see the injustice complained of, he would obey the call with pleasure. But he could not see any analogy in the cases, which it was said called for the exercise of this act of justice. The complaint is, that the people East of the Ridge demand protection for their property, and, at the same time, refuse protection to the persons of those West of the Ridge. This, in the first place, is not the case; for the exclusion of persons, which is demanded for the protection of property, applies equally to the East and to the West. There is no analogy, however, in the two cases. The Eastern people have persons as well as property to protect. The Western, persons only, so far as the exclusion is intended to go—and the exclusion of persons is the same both on the West and the East side of the Ridge. The Eastern people have as much interest to protect person as property. The Penal laws are the same and must always be the same on both sides of the Ridge. The Western people, who had no property to protect, and into whose hands it was now proposed to place the power of protection, were not only not interested in affording, but were interested in depriving property of that protection. They would be aided too, in doing this without injury to themselves, by the difference in the kinds of property on this and the other side of the Ridge—and particularly the great disproportion in the slaves,

He asserted, that on the formation of the social compact there were two parties—the governors and the governed, and that the conditions of the compact, were formed upon the principle of the *quid pro quo*. The governed give up a portion of their rights to be compensated for, by the protection of other rights to be afforded by the Government. There was then a stipulated obligation on the part of the Government to protect property, and there was a greater difficulty in complying with this obligation than in the protection of persons. The gentlemen admit both these obligations. No one would deny them. Is not the Government bound therefore, on this principle of *quid pro quo*, in return for property given up to protect the residue? This admission seemed to him to settle the question absolutely. What are we now doing? We are about to constitute an agent to protect both person and property. Here are two interests. The great object is to protect both. Would it be wise to choose an agent who had an interest in protecting both or one only? Surely all the world would agree, that he ought to have an interest in protecting both, and not one only. Here another question is presented. A great deal has been said about the protection of wealth, a term which seems to have been substituted for property. Property *in se*, is not wealth. It is property, in large masses, which constitutes wealth. Property in small portions is not wealth; and no one has ever insinuated or thought of affording more protection to large than to small portions of property. Hence, the poor man's property is to be as much protected as the rich man's. It is property which is to be protected then—whether in large or small portions, and not wealth—the property of the poor as well as of the rich; and the property of the poor in this country is vastly more extensive than that of the rich. And the protection of property indiscriminately, would strip the argument of the protection of wealth, by higher sanctions never thought of, of all its terrors.

Several gentlemen, and particularly the gentleman from Frederick (Mr. Cooke) most earnestly invites us to place the protection of our property, on the morals of the people West of the Ridge, and not on their interests. Will the gentlemen return the compliment to their brethren East of the Ridge, and place their protection on our morals? If so, we are then to act upon the principle, that we are all moral—"all honorable men"—disregarding altogether the selfish notions of interest. If this be really the case, he would respectfully ask these gentlemen what would be the use of Government at all? Government is not intended for moral, honorable men; but as a protection against the vices and imperfections of man; and if man were totally exempt from all vices and imperfections, there would be no necessity for Government at all. It was strange to him that gentlemen did not see, that this was a new emanation of the French philosophy of the perfectibility of man; and that if adopted here, would be attended with the same results which attended it in France. It failed in France, and will fail in every other country in which it may be tried, simply, because it is founded in a false, though flattering hypothesis. The notion of the perfectibility of man affords the most flattering unction to his vanity, but unfortunately for him it has no real existence, and is nothing more than a mischievous, delusive vision of the mind. The gentlemen, in support of this fallacious doctrine, refer us to the liberality of the slaveholders on the East side of the Ridge towards the non-slaveholders on the West, as an example in point, in favor of his proposition. It is true Virginia was thus liberal in that particular case, and is always liberal. She gave up her western lands, sufficient to form an extended empire in themselves. She was liberal to Kentucky; and she has ever been liberal, in her intercourse with her sister States. Whence the causes of this celebrity of Virginia liberality? Surely, from the moral tendencies of her fundamental laws for fifty-four years. They teach her that it is to her interest to be liberal, and that honesty is the best policy for nations. Could there be higher compliments to the wisdom of the fundamental laws of Virginia than are contained in these demonstrations? He begged to call the attention of the Convention to an example, forming an awful contrast to the one presented by the gentleman. It was furnished by the Federal Government. An excessive tax has been imposed by that Government, as he conceived, in direct violation of morals, principles, and the plainest provisions of our written Constitution. It originated in combinations of particular sections of country to tax other sections. These combinations were effected by invitations given by certain political fanatics to other fanatics, to meet in Convention, at Harrisburg, during the recess of Congress; excluding all the sections of country intended to be made tributary from these invitations. Virginia was not honored with an invitation, nor any State South or South-West of Virginia. This Convention, thus composed, unblushingly met at Harrisburg in open day; organized themselves into a Convention, with all the assumed honors and formalities awarded to this Convention; and there laid the foundation of the Tariff Act which was subsequently sanctioned by an Act of Congress. This Act was passed in direct violation of every principle of taxation heretofore held sacred, and was addressed to the worst passions of the human heart. It was dictated by a spirit of electioneering and of avarice, which reckless of all principle, invited the manufacturer to rely upon the labor of others, instead of his own labor, not only for support, but even for the accumulation of wealth; and actually furnished him with means, of taking the proceeds of the labor of another, which, if done without the sanction of this iniquitous Act, would amount to a criminal offence. The effect of this Act has been to demoralize the whole country, and to impoverish the whole of the tributary parts of it. It has taken from his own pocket every current dollar he possessed; and would go on to prevent him from ever re-possessing another. Nor is there any hope for any relief against this unprincipled imposition, so long as this baneful, electioneering spirit shall continue to direct our councils. It is the most unrelenting spirit, and, instead of our hoping for relaxation, it is constantly in search of some little modicum of property remaining untaxed for the tax of the next year. *(See note at the end.)* Such are the effects of the unprincipled measures recommended by this fanatical Convention at Harrisburg; which, after usurping all the powers of an authorised Convention, kept a regular journal of their proceedings, and after their adjournment, officially forwarded him a copy thereof. Now, he would ask all men, above and below the mountains—all christians—all lovers of right and haters of evil, to determine whether such proceedings can, or ought to be tolerated? If so, how deplorable is our condition below the mountains! The General Government first plunders us under a pretext of protecting manufactures, of every dollar within their reach; and then our trans-mountain brethren gravely ask us to trust the residue, if there be any, to their morals. The gentlemen then charge Virginia with impoverishment and degradation, and seem to intimate that both have arisen from the imperfections of our organic laws. It is true that Virginia is impoverished, but not degraded. Is that impoverishment confined to Virginia, or does it not extend to South Carolina, and the whole of the tributary scene of country? If so, then the extravagant impositions under the Tariff Act, must be the true cause of that impoverishment: Not the supposed imperfections of the organic laws of Virginia. They have moral tendencies which never could produce impoverishment. The bankruptcy of Virginia, is in *cash*—not in morals, nor in principles. Amidst all her misfortunes and impoverishment, she stands now as erect and distinguished in morals and in principles, as she has ever done at any former time. The true cause, then, of the bankruptcy of Virginia *in cash*, is the Tariff Act. This plunders all our *cash*, and that being taken away, impoverishment is the necessary consequence. Here, then, is a direct and immediate cause for this deplorable effect, without resorting to imputations against our fundamental laws as the cause of it: The attributable cause having no affinity nor relationship to the effect suggested to be produced by it.

We here have to encounter another pathetic appeal to our feelings. Several gentlemen, and particularly the learned gentleman from Loudoun, (Mr. Mercer) whose absence he regretted, had urged with great earnestness, claims for military services, rendered during the last war, by our brethren of the West. The absent gentleman drew in the most vivid colours these patriotic services—exhibited so much sensibility and exhausted so much time on the occasion, as to satisfy every hearer, that he must himself have been an honorable partaker in the scene. But Mr. G. hardly expected that he would have exhausted so much declamation in eulogiums upon the patriotism and heroism of these defenders of their country, because this tribunal was the last in the world to whose *fee ings* appeals of any kind should be made. No, Sir; ours is the severe duty to search for principles, and not to indulge our feelings. There was no member of the Committee, more ready than himself, to do ample justice to the heroism and patriotism of the soldiers of the West on that occasion. But he could see no affinity, whatever, between those feelings, and the claims so pathetically urged by the gentleman, for extending to them the right of suffrage, or any other civil right whatever. To ascertain this point, it would be necessary to resort to first principles. It would be observed, that from the origin of society to the present time, some of its members possessed physical powers, and others possessed money. It is the duty of those who possess the physical power, to defend the society by arms. It is the duty of those who have money, to pay their defenders full compensation for their services. The militia laws are the arbiters between those who fight and those who pay. In the present case, our brave and patriotic defenders were fully paid, and when that was done, there was an end of all obligation between the parties. If they have not yet received compensation enough—in the name of God, give them more. It must be presumed that they have received enough, because there is no grumbling upon that score. But the great objection to this principle is, the intermixture of civil and military rights. What would be the effect of placing military claims for services at the fountain of all power? It would be to subvert the order of the civil and military authorities—making the civil subordinate to the military, instead of the military subordinate to the civil authority; and thus, with a mere scrape of a pen, convert a free, republican Government, into a military, despotic one. Pay, then, the military in land, in money, in military honors, in gratitude, in love, if you please; but for God's sake, never pay them in your civil nor religious rights. But keep forever military and civil rights separate and distinct from each other. Some gentlemen have most gravely and seriously complained that we withhold their rights from them. He should be glad to know what rights they mean. He would be happy to hear what rights they are. He knows of none—nor has he heard any described. The only right, which he conceived the gentleman could allude to, is the *right* to do *wrong*. They call upon us to surrender to them the power of taxing a species of our property without taxing their own. To do so would be a *wrong*, not a *right*—certainly not a *right* included in his system of ethics. They complain of our refusing them their natural right of suffrage. They say it is cruel to deprive the poor of their natural right of voting. Yet, in the next breath, they, themselves, exclude more than half the nation from the exercise of the same right. They must necessarily carry the right to its whole extent, or abandon it altogether; otherwise they would be guilty of the most evident inconsistency in their own doctrines. Let a case be put including a youth of twenty-one years of age, according to their rule, and excluding one of twenty. Let the youth of twenty take up the memorial recently presented to us—written with great ability and eloquence—and read it to the youth of twenty-one included within the rule, which arbitrarily excludes himself; and then address him as follows: "I am a much smarter fellow then you are. I can out-read you—out-write you, and out-cipher you. I can out-run you—out-jump you—throw you down, and whip you after you get up. In the point of the fashionable consummation of the qualifications for a voter, such is the thickness of my pericranium, that I can drink a quart of whiskey to your pint, and give a better vote than you can afterwards. Is it not cruel, then, that one so highly gifted for a voter as myself, should be excluded by a rule of right, which includes such a booby as you are?" What reply could be made to so just and pathetic complaint? Certainly none, if the rule be right. This would prove incontestably, that all claims grounded on natural rights must be abandoned, and that we must act upon expediency alone. That we must observe the injunction of the Bill of Rights to extend the right of suffrage in such manner only, as we shall judge most conducive to the public weal, and to those only, who shall possess sufficient evidence of a common, *permanent* attachment to the community.

Mr. G. said, he was now approaching a point in the debate, which filled him with pain and regret; because he could not avoid seeing in it some departure from that spirit of decorum, as well as of confidence and affection, which had heretofore characterised the debate. He alluded to certain observations made by the gentleman from Brooke, (Mr. Doddridge) which he could not help construing into polite threats, from the influence of the physical power West of the Ridge. The language used by the gentleman, was not presented to us in the insulting terms of "war, pestilence and famine;" but it was equally intelligible, and to him not less repulsive. He had no intention of reciprocating either the spirit or language of these threats. God forbid that he should infuse one drop of bitterness into this debate! The first object of his heart was, to improve the spirit of conciliation and concession. Such language as "war, pestilence and famine," had been heretofore banished from this Convention; and he thanked God for it. But can any other interpretation be put upon the following observations of the gentleman from Brooke, but polite threats of the physical force of the West against the East:

"How fatal, then, will be the effects, should you be guilty of misrule! You say, to be sure, that we are a minority: of the freeholders, perhaps we may be: but look at the votes given at the polls, where the true voice of the people of Virginia was heard; and it will appear, that while *you* represent 280,000 of that people, *we* represent 402,000 of them. I acknowledge that so vast an odds proves one thing, at least; it proves that heroic, moral boldness which inspires the gentlemen who are opposed to a new Constitution. It proves that they are as daring and firm, as I well know them to be upright and honorable."

What is the meaning of this language? What is the meaning of presenting the odds between 402,000 whites on the West side of the Ridge, and 280,000 on the East? Why call upon us to exert heroic, moral boldness, in giving a vote upon the present question, agreeably to the dictates of our own conscience? He meant not to press this argument upon the minds of others, similarly circumstanced with himself. But he could not abandon the duty of stating its impressions upon his own mind. It would not be possible for him to surrender the power demanded under the influence of these threats, especially when the uses intended to be made of the physical power were openly avowed. Other gentlemen, similarly circumstanced, might do so; but in such case, their only reliance, so far as he could see, must be in the morals of our Western brethren, for the protection of their own interests and the interests of their constituents. If so, amiable may be the thought—philanthropic the intent—and generous the act, but deadly the mistake in his judgment to their own interests, and to the interests of their constituents—vain, indeed, he feared, would be this reliance.

If threats thus bold are to be presented to us, while the physical force of the West is restrained by the Constitution and the laws, with how much more force will they assail us, when we shall yield up the Constitution at their bidding, and they shall have made the laws, under their own interpretation of it. In that case, instead of being restrained by a sacred respect for the Constitution and the laws, they will have both co-operating with the threatened physical force on their side. He should think, that these circumstances would present a most awful question, for the consideration of every member as well as of every individual inhabitant East of the Ridge. Whilst, however, he left other gentlemen to their own reflections, he would state with frankness, their effect on his own mind. He could never, for a moment, think of voting against his own conscientious convictions, under the influence of any threats whatever. So far from it, they would serve to fortify him in acting fully up to those convictions. He should vote, therefore, with more firmness, than if he had not been told, that there were 402,000 whites on the West side of the Ridge, who could be arrayed against 280,000 on the East side, at least as early as the year 1850; and even if he had doubted before, these threats, with the avowals they contained, would serve to dissipate those doubts, and fix more decidedly his impressions. The arguments of the gentleman, may have their full force upon those, who expect to reap a beneficial effect from that influence; but they could only be repulsive to him, who was threatened, as well as his own constituents, to be the victims of that influence. He could not avoid also, suggesting to the gentleman, although he did so with great reluctance, but in a spirit of good feelings, that these threats may serve to teach him two most important lessons. The first; that the people below the Ridge, will always be found to have as much of that "heroic, moral boldness," and to be as "daring and firm," as any occasion shall require. Second; that they will necessarily be driven, with however great reluctance, to the ascertainment, to the full extent of all their energies and capacities, fiscal and physical.

Mr. G. said, these reflections had naturally drawn his attention to some remarks made by the venerable gentleman from Loudoun, (Mr. Monroe) in relation to a probable separation of this State. That gentleman had earnestly admonished us of the danger of such separation, which was much enhanced by our divisions and collisions of opinion here. Surely, such danger must be visible to all, when they see this array of force presented against force; and surely all will admit that it is the first duty of the Convention to guard against an impending evil of so much magnitude. The mere comparisons of force against force, must be fraught with danger; particularly when a geographical line of demarcation is drawn between the parties placed in opposition to each other. He feared the danger was greater than was generally apprehended, and that the best mode of subduing it, would be to command our own passions, and to bring our own deliberations to harmonious results. The moment the suggestion of the separation of Virginia was made by the gentleman from Loudoun, it entered deeply into his own mind, and extended itself into a thousand ramifications, which he felt it impossible to trace in all their various bearings. He verily believed that more extensive consequences would result from that deplorable event, than could at once enter into the contemplation of any gentleman. Can any gentleman believe that the separation of Virginia would stop there? If there be really any one who thought so, he could not have devoted much reflection to the subject. The forcible separation of Virginia, must and will lead to a separation of the United States, come when it will. This would be the probable effect of the forcible separation of any State in the Union, but particularly so of Virginia, in consequence of her relations—and especially her geographical relations to the United States. Have we not awful indications of the probable separation of Virginia, not only from what is passing in this Hall, but also out of doors? What is going on in the country at this moment, from excitements produced by our debates here? An anxious and ardent spirit is seen to exist in the country generally; and the excitement in one district has displayed itself, in actually sending instructions to a distinguished member of this body.

Mr. G. said, that he saw from the newspapers, that the people of other districts were actually taking the business of this Convention into their own hands. He saw that a single vote given by two of the most venerable and distinguished members of this body (Messrs. Madison and Monroe) was calling for instructions from their respective districts. Could not every gentleman see in these extraordinary excitements and actual movements of the people, great danger of a separation, particularly where a geographical line of demarcation was already designated, for separating the combatants. No human being can foresee the extent of these excitements, nor the excesses to which they may be carried. We have already seen one honorable member of this body called upon under their influence to abandon his conscience or his seat, and who had actually abandoned his seat rather than his conscience. Mr. G. said, he was far from making these remarks, with a view of depriving the people of their unquestionable right of instructing their members on this floor. He thought it not only their unquestionable right, but their indispensable duty to do so, if they thought the magnitude of the occasion called for their interference; and he begged leave here to repeat an opinion which he had already expressed, that a division of this State necessarily involved a division of the United States. In regard to the force held up *in terrorem*, he could only say, that whenever the awful occasion should arise for calling in force to settle collisions and divisions amongst ourselves, the destinies of this country will not be settled by the physical force on the West side of the Ridge, nor of the whole United States alone. No gentleman could have thought much upon this alarming subject, who would not perceive, that the physical force of the commercial nations of Europe, would settle the destinies of this country in that deprecated event. The mind, in contemplating consequences, could not avoid discerning, in a crisis so awful, that the great and splendid city of New York would have much more to dread than the city of Richmond; for the very existence of that great city depends upon contingencies beyond her own control; and, in the event of divisions and collisions amongst ourselves, would have more to dread than any other spot in the United States. Have gentlemen, employing these threats, ever contemplated the absolute certainty, that, in the event of divisions amongst ourselves, the future destinies of the United States must be determined by the physical force of foreign nations? And then extended their thoughts to the *douceurs* which they have to offer, for the purpose of obtaining such physical force? If they have not done so heretofore, they surely have omitted to perform a most essential and indispensable duty; and he begged now to be indulged in calling their best reflections to that important subject. If the people of Virginia could be so wild and so foolish, as to rush forward to a separation of the State, let the enquiry now be made, what *douceurs* have our transmontane brethren to offer for the physical force of the commercial nations of Europe? Nothing—literally *nothing;* whilst the people on the East side of the mountains, have the most attractive and influential douceur that could possibly be offered—commerce—the most valuable and seductive in the world. Commerce—consisting of the most suitable staples, which any part of the world can produce, for the commercial nations of Europe; and which may be given in exchange for their productions equally suited to our own wants. Hence our douceurs might consist of advantages, not sacrifices. Notwithstanding these convictions, and although he never had been in the habit of making professions of patriotism, or of the motives which govern his conduct, he would take this occasion to say, that he would deprecate a division of this State, or of the United States, as much as any gentleman in them. But he felt it his duty to speak of things as they are—things so irresistibly fixed, in the relation of nations, that neither himself, feeble as he was, however he might wish it, nor the whole power of this Convention—nor of the United States, could alter or avoid. The venerable gentleman from Loudoun, had expressed his doubts whether the Government of the United States would permit a division of this State, even were she to require it. He would respectfully ask, how could the Government of the United States prevent it? He knew that there was a clause in the Constitution which required the consent of Congress to the separation of any State in the Union. But when force is once brought into action, it puts at defiance all civil regulations whatever. *(Inter arma silent leges.)* Whenever this is the case, all our civil relations become changed, and we must look to force alone to give the law. In that case, he would respectfully ask gentlemen, how the General Government could prevent such a deprecated calamity, if it would? What means have they, which they could employ for such a purpose? Could it be prevented by degrading us still further by more Tariffs, or by physical force? These means would be feeble, aggravating and incompetent. He would again recur to the remark which he had before made, that the destinies of this country would not be settled by the physical force of this country alone; and whilst he looked at that circumstance with as much awe and regret as any gentleman on this floor, he could not shut his eyes to what was passing before them. Independently of the separation of this State, the General Government has already produced excitements enough in the country to hazard the Union, by the unprincipled and oppressive measures, which he had already mentioned. He saw in the newspapers that enquiries had already commenced, into the probable effects of the Tariff, Internal Improvements, and other usurpations of the General Government upon the Union of these States. Mr. G. said that he had seen some most able and eloquent dissertations, said to be written by one of the ablest statesmen and patriots in the United States, (he alluded to the Rev. Mr. Channing of Boston,) containing inquiries, into the probable separation of the Union, resulting from the various usurpations of the General Government, but particularly from the Tariff and Internal Improvement Acts. These causes he seemed to think were at least sufficient to hazard the integrity of the Union.

Mr. G. said, that he had gone into this course of reflection in the hope of attracting the reflections of others, and bringing about conciliation and harmony amongst ourselves, but he greatly feared that they would be utterly unavailing. He would now most respectfully ask gentlemen, seriously to reflect upon the best mode of avoiding our own embarrassments, and of relieving the country from existing alarms and difficulties. The best that had occurred to him, was, to banish as far as possible our own dissentions, and to approach to unanimity in something—that we should banish our own passions and prepossessions, and calmly, coolly, and confidentially consult with each other, as to what could be done with a nearer approach to unanimity. He would warn gentlemen against the effects of carrying any question—especially one of great magnitude—by a lean majority. He thought nothing good could be gained by such a proceeding. The country never could be tranquillized so long as the people see that we have no confidence in our own measures—measures of so high a character as imperiously to demand both our own confidence and theirs. This redeeming spirit of harmony, of confidence, of conciliation and concession, should commence in this Hall. It is our imperious duty to be the first in making manifestations of this saving spirit here. Let us then, with a magnanimous disinterestedness and self-denial, set a noble example to our constituents, and thus tranquillize their passions and relieve their alarms. He would ask no more from other gentlemen, than he was disposed to yield himself. He sincerely wished to ascertain the propositions for amendment, which would command the confidence of the greatest majorities. He would himself agree to amendments, which he could not fully approve, provided gentlemen on the other side would make similar relaxations on their part. For the purposes of union and harmony, he was disposed to go to the utmost points which his conscience would permit; but he should deeply deprecate the adoption of any measure whatever, which would not command the confidence of a great majority. Less than that, he was perfectly convinced, would never relieve our present deplorable embarrassments.

There was one impression upon his mind, which he wished to impress upon the minds of others with peculiar emphasis. It was, that small changes could never produce a division of a State, whether produced by unanimity or not; whilst great changes would at least hazard such a result, unless unanimously adopted; or at least by a majority approaching to unanimity. Great changes made by an almost equal balance of opinion, are the best calculated to produce great hazards, and will necessarily do so, unless checked by an interposing Providence. In this stage of our business he had no specific propositions to offer. All he could do, was to throw out these ideas, and solemnly to pledge himself to indulge to the utmost, a spirit of conciliation and concession. He earnestly invited other gentlemen to turn their minds towards making propositions of conciliation, and in that case, pledged himself to do so, in the further progress of the business before the Convention. But, above all things, he begged to guard the Convention against the adoption of great changes by lean majorities; because, as he said at the beginning, it would only be a poor triumph of friends over friends, and could not possibly eventuate in any good result.

Mr. G. expressed his regret at having detained the Committee so long, and promised to close his remarks, with only two or three further reflections. It must occur to all, that the task of mere pulling down, is an easy one. Every booby, possessed of sufficient physical power, with a trowel in his hand, can take down every brick of the most solid, useful and magnificent building, erected upon the true principles of architectural science. But it requires thought, care, study and science, to build up one, which shall be durable, useful and ornamental, upon the same principles. Such a structure is now before us, wisely and fearlessly reared up for us, by our God-like forefathers, in the midst of imminent peril; and he feared, greatly feared, that every member of this Convention, with the best intentions, had brought here a trowel in his hand to take down his brick. He sincerely hoped better things; and should continue to do so, although hope, he feared, would be unavailing. He said, Mr. Chairman, is it possible that we can be content to become mere dilapidators, to tear down the most stupendous fabrick, which has proved the greatest blessing which God, in his infinite mercy, has bestowed upon us; and set up nothing better in its stead? And, Sir, ought we not to be scrupulously careful how we set up any thing, which would bear but a poor comparison with that which we have torn down? On the other hand, how honorable would it be to contribute our mite to sustain the noble institutions we have received from our forefathers:—to give them support, instead of dooming them to destruction. Suppose we do but little. We shall have done all that could be required of us—all that we conscientiously could do. We may, then, honorably return home with satisfaction to ourselves and to our constituents. Gentlemen have asked, and particularly the venerable gentleman from Loudoun, (Mr. Monroe) emphatically asked—what is to be the effect of doing nothing? What is to be the effect of going home, without doing something? Aye, Sir, permit me to reiterate the question, what would be the effect of doing nothing? It surely would be a great deal better than doing mischief. But no one calculates on doing nothing. All are disposed to do something—to do a great deal. Let us then unite, Sir, and do all we can do with unanimity or some near approach to it. If we find nothing to do, we shall do a great deal by refusing to tear down this noble edifice. We can then go home with approving consciences, and tell our constituents, that after its having passed through the severest ordeal, we found our present Constitution better than we expected: that we had discovered some unthrifty scions: that we had applied the pruning knife—cut them off—and put into their places grafts which would produce good fruits. He was satisfied that we could not discharge the great duties entrusted to us—nor satisfy our own consciences so well in any other way.

He hoped to be indulged in making another remark. Our wise, heroic, patriotic forefathers gave us this blessed Constitution. They framed it under the same feelings of zeal, and amidst the same honest differences of opinion which now exist amongst us. But *they* succeeded by compromising, and by sacrificing all their variegated opinions and feelings upon the altar of patriotism and virtue. We are now called upon to examine and improve their great work. In performing this high and honourable task, let us recollect and imitate their exalted example.

Mr. G. said—Mr. Chairman, with pain and sorrow of heart, I speak it—these our God-like forefathers are now mouldering in a state of oblivion and forgetfulness. Their names are blotted out from our remembrance. Ought this, Sir, to be longer permitted? If so, would it not be to our shame, and ingratitude? But, Sir, it is neither. It is merely the effect of thoughtless inattention. Virginia was never ungrateful. Virginia never can be ungrateful so long as she is composed of Virginians. A stain may be cast upon her for forgetfulness—for inattention—but she is incapable of ingratitude. Why, then, should we suffer our venerated ancestors to sleep longer in oblivion? We have even permitted the greatest day in the political calendar, when under their influence, the great light of liberty first burst forth upon a benighted world, to be also lost in oblivion. Yes, Sir, that day, the 29th of June, has become merged in the 4th of July, which has been permitted to usurp all its own appropriate honours. Let it not, then, be longer said, that our noble forefathers rest in oblivion. Instead of tearing down the splendid structure they have raised, instead of letting them longer sleep in silence, let us call them from their tombs, and award them the highest posthumous honours. And here he begged to be permitted to renew a proposition he had once before made, to testify our sacred veneration for their memories; let us fill with their busts the vacant niches in this Hall. Let us fill with them all the niches in the whole Capitol; for there are worthies amongst them sufficiently numerous to fill the whole. Let us relieve ourselves from the sin of ingratitude, by taking them from their silent incarceration, and placing them where they will be seen and venerated by every true-hearted Virginian—by our posterity and by the whole world, to the end of time.

NOTE.—*(Accompanying Mr. Giles's Speech.)*

Extract from page 247, vol. 2, Raymond's Elements of Political Economy—"There is no part of the Statute Book, that requires such frequent revision as the Tariff Act, although we sometimes hear it said, that a tariff, should be permanent, and seldom if ever changed, but this is a great error. A year does not pass, in which the tariff upon some particular articles may not be raised with advantage. The most general rule on this subject is, that a tariff ought not to be reduced, although it may frequently require to be raised."

Again, page 248—"The reduction of a tariff is one of the harshest and most violent measures that a Government can possibly adopt."

Comment.

What an unblushing spirit of avarice is here displayed? The manufacturers, whose insatiable cupidity seems not satisfied with the extreme injustice of the present tariff, are still to be upon the watch, and every year some new addition is to be made to it. Every imported article is to be strictly watched, and if not already burdened to its highest pitch, is to be strained up annually a little higher, whilst "the reduction of a tariff is one of the harshest and most violent measures that a Government can possibly adopt." What elementary logic! What political morals! Every occasion is to be greedily seized upon, to add to the plunder of the proceeds of the labour of one man, and give them to another, who did not labour for them—but to cease from further plundering, is "one of the harshest and most violent measures that a Government can possibly adopt." Is this also the doctrine of the new political school? Is this doctrine to be honoured by the sanction of its future enactments? On the other hand, the writer contends—that the practical Government is now called upon by every motive that moral honesty, and by every principle, that the general welfare "can suggest to suspend this plunder, and to leave to every individual labourer, the proceeds of his own honest labours."

The rule laid down in the foregoing extracts of Raymond's Political Economy, has been scrupulously observed since the year 1824. New subjects for higher duties—or new duties have been hunted up and brought forth from that time to the present. What an encouragement of furtive propensities is this encouragement of manufactures? What a general corruption of morals? The manufacturer is authorized and empowered by law to pick the pockets of his neighbour, and encouraged to sharpen his wits to increase his plunder, and to stop his plunder would be the essence of cruelty.*

Mr. Giles having resumed his seat, the Committee rose.

Mr. Venable observed, that it must be evident from the progress which had as yet been made in the business of the Convention, that there was no probability that it would get through its labors before the meeting of the Legislature. The present Hall did not present very convenient accommodation to those who were desirous of listening to the debates. They attended in numbers, not as he believed, from a vain curiosity, but from the deep interest very naturally felt in what was doing here; he, therefore, thought it was time that measures should be taken to provide some other place of meeting—with which view he offered the following resolution:

Resolved, That a Committee be appointed to enquire whether a convenient room can be obtained for the sitting of the Convention, should they judge it expedient to retire from the Legislative Hall, and report.

The question being taken, the resolution was rejected without a count; and thereupon, the House adjourned.

WEDNESDAY, November 11, 1829.

The Convention met at eleven o'clock, and its sitting was opened with prayer by the Rev. Mr. Horner of the Catholic Church.

On motion of Mr. P. P. Barbour, the House again went into Committee of the whole, Mr. Powell in the Chair, when,

Mr. Johnson rose and addressed the Committee as follows:

Mr. Chairman—The question under consideration, has occupied much time, in the discussion, and no doubt much more, in the deep deliberations of the Committee. Its great importance and exceeding delicacy, entitle it surely, to all the aid, which temper, forbearance, conciliation, free, frank and full interchange of opinion, laborious investigation and candid argument, can afford. It has on the one hand encouraged the most animated hopes, and, on the other, alarmed the most anxious fears. The whole country looks to it with intense interest—convinced that on its issue depends much of weal or woe.

We are engaged, Mr. Chairman, in a contest for power—disguise it as you will—call it a discussion of the rights of man, natural or social—call it an enquiry into political expediency—imagine yourself, if you please, presiding over a school of philosophers, discoursing on the doctrines of political law, for the instruction of mankind, and the improvement of all human institutions—bring the question to the test of principle, or of practical utility—still, Sir, all our metaphysical reasoning and our practical rules, all our scholastic learning and political wisdom, are but the arms employed in a contest, which involves the great and agitating question, whether the sceptre shall pass away from Judah, or a lawgiver from between her feet.

In this contest, I feel a peculiar interest—because I stand towards the parties in a relation of some delicacy. With the one, are my present residence, the land of my nativity, almost all the friends of my youth, and most of those to whom my affections are bound, by the ties of affinity and blood—With the other, are my property and my constituents—those who are endeared to me, by a residence among them of more than twenty years, by many a proof of recollected kindness and friendship, by gratitude for early patronage, and for political confidence, bestowed before it had been earned, and continued after every claim, I could have pretended to it, had been lost by my removal from them. In this state of divided allegiance I ought perhaps to have taken counsel from prudence, and have chosen the part of neutrality. But I had been long in the habit of considering both parties to this controversy as children of the same family, constituent and inseparable parts of the same community—somewhat diversified, it is true, in their possessions, their pursuits, their manners and their character, having some interests, perhaps not altogether in accordance—nevertheless identified in the leading characteristics of a plain agricultural, republican people, having the same great interests, and one common object, the integrity, freedom, happiness, and glory of a common country. I had long, too, cherished the fond, perhaps the delusive hope, that it was possible to reconcile all differences, to appease all angry feelings, to remove all causes of jealousy, and to unite all parts of the community in harmonious action, in common labor for the common weal; and to realize this hope, I had often exerted to the uttermost my humble power. I could not, therefore, at this most interesting crisis in public affairs, when heated, if not angry controversy

*See Appendix, for Mr. Giles' address to the Executive Committee, as prefatory to the foregoing speech.

was expected by all; when serious, if not fatal dissension was feared by many; when all might be lost by inattention or imprudence, or all might be saved by care and pains—I could not decline the honorable call to duty, from my old constituents. I could not refuse the trust, when, well knowing my opinion, they confided their great interests here in part to me, and left me at full liberty, without pledge and without instruction, to profit by the experience and wisdom of those around me, and following the dictates of my own judgment, to shape my course, with a single view to the public good.

After listening attentively to every thing that has been said—and much has been ably and eloquently said—I am satisfied, that by advocating the resolut on of the Select Committee, and resisting the proposed amendment, I shall best discharge my duty to my constituents and my country.

Mr. Chairman: I am no friend to change—I have been no advocate for the call of this Convention. True, I have thought the old Constitution, in some respects, imperfect in theory, and defective in practice. I have thought its principal defect that very inequality in representation, which the resolution of the Select Committee proposes in part to remedy.

I thought it also a defect in the Constitution, that it contained no provision for a just apportionment of taxes, or just distribution of the burthens of the Government, among the people of the Commonwealth. I had been, for some years, a member of that branch of the Legislature, in which the inequality of representation was most glaring. I represented in the Senate, a district composed of six counties, in the Valley, containing then, perhaps, about one-eighth of the white population of the State, and I with only three others, represented the whole country West of the Blue Ridge, containing about one-third of the white population. I thought I perceived the injurious operation of this inequality. On questions of local concern, I had often seen the interests of the East arrayed against those of the West, and controversies thence arising, attended with much excitement, and sometimes with great asperity, and angry feeling. It had occasionally been my good fortune to interpose between the contending parties, and reconcile their differences. But I was satisfied that a settled discontent was arising, that jealousies were daily increasing, which threatened to foment discord, to alienate brother from brother, and to countenance the opinion, that there were important differences of interest in the different parts of the State, which the same Government would not equally protect. When the Western people complained, that they had not a just participation in the power of the Government, they were often reproached with their poverty, and almost always reminded, that they did not contribute their just proportion of its revenue. The Act of 1782, made for equalizing the land tax, had thrown the State into four great districts, the counties into four classes, and had fixed a standard, in each class, of the average value of the land per acre. The first class comprised all the tide-water counties, with several of the large midland counties, and the standard value of its lands per acre, was ten shillings;—the second class comprised the other midland counties, except Pittsylvania and Henry, and embraced the two Valley counties of Frederick and Berkeley, and its standard per acre was 7*s.* 6*d.*—the third contained Pittsylvania and Henry, with the Valley counties, not included in the second, and the standard value of its lands was 5*s.* 6*d.*—to the fourth belonged the trans-Alleghany counties, rated at the standard value of 3*s.* per acre. This standard, probably just and fair at the time when it was adopted, had in process of time become unjust, and operated injuriously. The relative value of land in the several districts had essentially changed; those of the Western districts having risen, and approached much more nearly to equality with those of the Eastern. But the taxes continued to be imposed according to the same standard; in consequence whereof, the tide-water district was unduly burthened, and the other districts, especially the third and fourth, paid less than they ought. These inequalities, in the imposition of taxes, and in the representation in the Senate, had been the subject of frequent discussion, and I was informed that several ineffectual attempts had been made to correct them, by an ordinary act of Legislation. These fruitless efforts served only to increase the general discontent, to inflame animosities, and by giving to the discontented a solid reason for objecting to the organization of the Government, enabled them with more success to seize on all occasions of public distress or popular excitement, and turn them to the purpose of rousing a spirit of heedless reform. Thus it happened, that in 1816, the people of the large districts being disappointed in some favorite measure, and much dissatisfied with the proceedings of the Legislature, were persuaded that they had been grossly injured; that the cause of their wrongs was to be found in the unequal distribution of the power of the Government; and that their remedy was to be sought in a general Convention to reform this, and many other fancied or real defects of the Constitution. Under the excitement of this occasion, that meeting in Staunton was held, which has been denominated the Staunton Convention. The county of Augusta did not participate in the feverish excitement which then prevailed, and while it was willing to seek by temperate and prudent measures, substantial relief from acknowledged evils, it was unwilling to encounter the hazard of general reform. It therefore deputed to the meeting two members, of whom I was one, and charged them with the duty of endeavouring to infuse into the proceedings as much of temper and prudence as possible, and to restrain them to a respectful memorial, asking of the Legislature that proper measures might be adopted for organizing a Convention to amend the Constitution of the State, but with powers limited to the objects of equalizing the representation and taxes, and of providing under proper cautions, for future amendments. The deliberations of this meeting resulted in a memorial to the Legislature, asking a general Convention; and in a protest by a small minority, to which the Augusta deputies belonged, the object whereof was to limit the powers of the Convention to the three subjects which I have mentioned. The memorial and protest were laid before the Legislature at their session of 1815, and a bill passed the House of Delegates, providing that the sense of the people should be taken on the question, whether a Convention should be called, with powers limited to these three objects and one other only, the extension of the Right of Suffrage. This bill was amended in the Senate, so as to limit the powers of the Convention to taxes and representation only, and was laid on the table to await the coming of a bill then in progress, for reforming the Senatorial Districts, and for a re-assessment of the lands. This bill came to the Senate, and passed by a majority, I think, of one: the bill for the Convention having been rejected by a majority of two. Both were very obnoxious to the Eastern members, and were opposed by them: both were acceptable to me, and advocated by me. I preferred the Convention bill, because I thought it would give more adequate and more permanent relief; but when it was lost, I espoused the other, though its operation was inconvenient and harsh, and its relief temporary. The Convention bill was in truth, preferred to its rival, by a large majority of the Senate, and would have passed, but for one of those amusing incidents in legislation, by which false calculations of majorities sometimes cheat us of our votes. [Here Mr. J. related an anecdote, shewing that one of the Senators, being deceived in his calculations, had been induced to give a vote, which secured the passage of the bill, which he most desired to defeat.]

This bill reforming the districts upon the basis of white population as ascertained by the Census of 1810, gave to the country beyond the Blue Ridge, nine Senators. That country had then about its due share in the representation of the House of Delegates, upon the same basis; and an adequate provision was made, for a just apportionment of the taxes.

Believing that the Legislature would follow this precedent—would preserve something like a practical equality of representation, in both Houses, by occasional reforms of the Districts, and by the division of counties, I was content to submit to the remaining imperfections in the Constitution, rather than to put to hazard every thing valuable that it contained. I did think there was much in it, worth preserving. I thought it suited to our genius and character, calculated to protect our rights and promote our interests—taking it "all in all," comparing it with every Constitution of which I had any knowledge, and especially with those which our extensive confederacy affords, I preferred it to any of them;—and I venerated it, because it was the work of our wise and virtuous ancestors; a child of the Revolution, born with the State, and consecrated by all the associations, which make us proud of our country. I have, therefore, ever since the session of 1816, opposed the call of a Convention, whether limited or general, and have laboured much to prevent it. Step by step have I followed the march of my noble friend from Chesterfield, in the campaigns he has made in defence of the Constitution, and though I have not emulated the gallantry or prowess of my leader, he will bear me witness that I have been a faithful soldier, and that I never laid down my arms, till the victory was fairly won from us. It was not till a majority of the freeholders had desired the call of a Convention, that my opposition to it ceased. From that time, my friend from Chesterfield, and all our other wise men, I believe, united in opinion, that the will of the people should be obeyed, that the Convention should be organized without delay, and that all the subjects of complaint should be considered, and as far as possible adjusted.

I have detained you, Mr. Chairman, with these explanations, because I thought them due to myself, if they were not strictly due to the Committee. I neither expect nor desire, that they should recommend to your favourable attention, the poor remarks I have to offer, on the great question in debate. These remarks I shall submit, with a consciousness, that they are but little worth; though with an humble trust, that if they have any value, it will not be lost on the candour and intelligence of the Committee.

The first duty, perhaps, which I owe to the Committee, is to acknowledge an error, into which it seems I had fallen, at an early stage of your proceedings, in not approving the order of debate, which was proposed by the gentleman from Norfolk, (Mr. Taylor,) who no longer holds a seat among us. I had been weak enough to suppose, that we had already learned the rudiments of political science—that we had not come here to be taught the horn-book of politics—to be schooled and lectured on the elements of Government; that a great proportion of this Convention, at least, had been selected for their presumed knowledge of its doctrines, and their long experience in public affairs. But, my friends tell me I was wrong, and I am compelled to acknowledge it, by the course of argument, which some of our adversaries have pursued. It was the misfortune of my friend from Frederick, (Mr. Cooke,) of falling into a similar error,—to suppose that there were settled principles in *our* Government; at least, that they were clearly and fully enunciated, in our Declaration of Rights, and that he had succeeded in proving all that was necessary, when he had shewn, that the proposition which he advocated, was sustained by these principles, and that they condemned that which he opposed. This opinion, and the argument founded upon it, have furnished the apology for a discursive enquiry into the natural rights of man. The very eloquent gentleman from Northampton, (Mr. Upshur,) condemning abstract doctrines and metaphysical reasoning, as misapplied here, has indulged himself, in a very elaborate course of metaphysical reasoning, and refined abstraction: has cast his eye through all time; appealed to all history; vainly endeavored to imagine unimaginable things; conjectured a state of nature, which he supposes never to have existed; endeavored to ascertain its laws, and finding not even light enough respecting them, to guide him in a simple enumeration of whole numbers, or in counting a majority, has at last arrived at the bold conclusion—bold, he himself seemed to consider it—that there were no principles in Government. We cannot, Mr. Chairman, understand the gentleman from Northampton, according to the literal import of his phrase. His own principles are too well settled—his character and talents are too well known, and too highly esteemed, to allow us for a moment to believe, that he would deny to the science of Government, those elementary truths, which constitute its principles—without which, all reasoning concerning it, is destitute of foundation, and incapable of conducting us to any conclusions. He was betrayed into the language he has used, by an over-anxiety to withdraw from his adversaries, the aid of those settled doctrines, on which they have rested their argument, to persuade us, that these doctrines are mere abstractions; and to bring the question in discussion, to the test of expediency. Indeed, he has told us, that every question of Government, is a question of expediency; and that every Government should be constructed, not with reference to original principles, but with a sole view to the character and circumstances of the people, for whom it is ordained. Admit this doctrine of expediency—admit the propriety of conforming the Government to the character and circumstances of the people—and no one admits it more readily than I do—yet it does not follow, that there are no principles, by which to decide the question of expediency, none to aid in constructing the Government, so as to make it suitable to the people. The plan of every building, for the use of man, presents a question of expediency, on which the purposes for which it is destined, and the circumstances of the tenant, are to be duly considered; but no wise man would disregard, in its structure, those principles of architecture, which belong to the humblest cottage, as well as to the loftiest temple. Is it more wise, by representing the principles of our Government, as metaphysical abstractions, furnishing no aid to the deliberations of the Statesman, no safe guide to his conduct, to disparage those principles in our estimation, endanger disloyalty to the Government which rests upon them, and confound all our political reasoning? This has not been the wisdom of ancient or of modern times. From the days of Plato, down to the period of the last Southern Review, wise men have labored to establish the principles of Government, to inculcate political truths, to recommend them to the respect of mankind, and to place them in the hands of Statesmen, as guides to direct their measures, and as weapons to defend them. The author of Publius, who had profoundly studied these principles, and understood these truths, commences his thirty-first number with the postulate, that "In disquisitions of every kind, there are certain primary truths, or first principles, on which all subsequent reasonings must depend."

For the primary truths, which belong to this discussion, we can look no where, with so much propriety, as to that solemn act, which announces the doctrines of our revolution—that "Declaration of Rights," which proclaims the principles pertaining to the Government of a free people, and is made the "basis and foundation" of our own. This Declaration, Mr. Chairman, faithfully embodies the doctrines, which gave to Algernon Sydney his crown of martyrdom, and to John Locke imperishable fame. These distinguished men, inspired by the spirit of freedom, which the history of the English Government had infused into the people, and emboldened by the accessions which the rights of the people had gradually gained from the power of the Crown, openly assailed the slavish doctrines by which the parasites of power had endeavored to defend the tyranny of the Stuarts, denounced and confuted the dogmas of Sir Robert Filmer, which asserted the divine right of Kings, and traced the origin of Government to its legitimate foundation, the will of the people. Guided by the experience of their own Government, enlightened by the history of all others, and above all, examining, with the sagacity of wise men, the natural and unvarying relations, between the governors and the governed, they maintained those doctrines, which the Whigs in England partially recognized in their Constitution at the revolution of 1688, and which the American Statesmen made the basis of their Governments at the revolution of 1776. Ought these doctrines to be treated as vain abstractions, metaphysical subtleties, visionary theories? Ought they not to be acknowledged as solemn truths, confessed as the articles of our political faith, made the standard of our political conduct? Ought we not, as we regard the permanency of our institutions, to recommend them to the respect and deference of the present generation, to the love and veneration of posterity? "To recall men to original maxims is generally recalling them to virtue;"—this is the language of a distinguished political writer; and is the language of truth, which does not require the support of authority. The advocates for liberty, the friends of good government in all time, have endeavored to inculcate respect and reverence for principles, and have thought it wise to hold up high standards of excellence for the emulation of the people. Plato's Republic was not written with the vain hope that its perfection would be realized; but with a view to inspire a love of excellence, and create emulation. Cicero's work *De Republica* was written for the purpose of recalling the Roman people to the fundamental principles of their Government, and of recommending them to their affections and their reverence. But it came too late to reform the degeneracy of the age, or to preserve the freedom or the glory of Rome. The celebrated Edmund Burke, who dreaded the contagion of French principles, and the levelling hand of French equality quite as much as any good republican here can do, when with so much eloquence and ability and prophetic talent, he traced the causes of the French revolution, deplored its sanguinary excesses, pointed out its errors, and indicated its dangerous tendencies, when he endeavored to allay the evil spirit of reform which was rising in England, and to warn his countrymen against the ruinous example which they seemed disposed to imitate. What did he appeal to, as most dear to Englishmen? He appealed "to the word and spirit of that immortal law," the English Declaration of Right. It is to the word and spirit of our Declaration of Rights, to that law, which we should desire to make immortal, that in my humble judgment we should at all times appeal, not only to guard us against the danger of heedless reform, but to guide us in making wholesome amendments.

We have been taught, Mr. Chairman, that the education of a people should always be conducted with reference to the principles of their Government, in order that sentiments of loyalty may be sown in their early affections. The same wisdom instructs us to mould the subordinate laws, in conformity to the fundamental law of the country. It is in the spirit of these lessons, that, having adopted the Republican form of Government, we have constantly inculcated the love of liberty, of virtue, of simple, unostentatious manners, and that, to prevent an injurious inequality in the fortunes and conditions of men, the laws have been passed which abolish entails, and the rights of primogeniture. The act abolishing entails, which is coeval with our Government, and that prescribing the law of descents, which very quickly succeeded the war of the revolution, were not founded on any supposed injustice or intrinsic impropriety, in limiting the estate of the parent to his remotest descendants, or making the first-born son, the exclusive heir, but were founded on reasons purely political; reasons, which induced our ancestors to believe, that however wise, however necessary in England, for the preservation of their Government it might be, to preserve family distinctions and perpetuate family wealth, such distinctions and such wealth were unsuited to a Republican Government, and that the laws for promoting them, would be, here, not less impracticable than unwise.

It is submitted to this Committee, whether all these considerations do not recommend to their most respectful attention, the principles which lie at the foundation of our Government. If they think so, it is hoped they will not deem the time misspent, which shall be employed in further consideration of the Bill of Rights, where these principles are declared. In performing this duty, I shall not follow the example of the judge who condemned Zadig to death, upon the evidence of the torn fragments of his manuscript:—I shall not sunder the different parts of the same instrument, the text from the contemporaneous commentary, the Declaration of Rights, from the Constitution, based upon it at the same time, and by the same hands.

The first article declares, "that all men are by nature free and independent; and have certain inherent rights, of which, when they enter into a state of society, they cannot, by any compact, deprive or divest their posterity: namely, the enjoyment of life and liberty, with the means of acquiring and possessing property, and pursuing and obtaining happiness and safety." The first line of this article, is taken almost literally from Locke, who declares, that "all men are by nature free, equal and independent"—and it has given rise to the discussion here, concerning the natural rights of man. Gentlemen have endeavored to investigate those rights, in a condition of man which is supposed to have preceded society; a condition, which they have termed the state of nature. Not being able to satisfy themselves, that such a condition of man ever existed, they reasonably conclude, that the rights pertaining to it, cannot be ascertained, and that whatever they may be, they cannot influence his rights, in a state of civil society. I readily concur in the opinion, Mr. Chairman, that such unsocial condition of man has never existed, unless under such accidental circumstances as attended the fabled case of Robinson Crusoe, quoted by the gentleman from Chesterfield, except the single instance with which the Bible history commences. That we know was of short duration, continuing only, while "man the hermit sighed"—and terminating, when "woman smiled" and dispelled forever the gloom of his solitude. Man was created for society; and social intercourse is as much a law of his nature, as that he should support his existence by food, promote his comfort by raiment, procure supplies by labor, protect himself from aggression by force. In every state of society—whether savage or civilized—whether patriarchal or political—laws arising from the nature of man, from his weakness, his dependance, his wants, his desires, his appetites, his passions, and his intelligence, must necessarily govern his social relations—regulate his rights and duties. These are deduced by reason, from the known character and condition of man, and these are the laws of his nature. They accompany him in all conditions of life, and it is to them, that the Bill of Rights, in this first article refers. This article means not to declare those political rights, which may be varied by compact, but those natural rights only, which spring from the invariable relations of man to society. It affirms to all equal freedom and equal independence, as the gift of nature—not equal political power—because that arises from compact between those, who, having equal freedom and independence, have associated together, and regulated by agreement, the political power of the society. It is reserved for the fifth article to declare the political power of the respective members of society, by indicating the basis of the Right of Suffrage—and by referring us for guidance in this behalf—not to natural, but to conventional law.

The first article of the Bill of Rights has another function, not less important than the declaration of equal freedom and independence, and certainly more practical in its character—the declaration of those inherent rights, of which men do not and cannot divest their posterity by any compact of society. As Government is instituted for the protection of life, liberty, property, to secure happiness and safety, so no Government can be legitimate to which these are sacrificed. It is happy for us that this part of the Bill of Rights has been solemnly adjudged to be constitutional law; for, to it the citizen owes the protection of his property from the power of the Government.

The second article of the Bill of Rights is a further affirmance of the doctrines of Locke and Sydney, in opposition to Sir Robert Filmer; recognizes the people, not the Prince, as the fountain of political power, and declares magistrates to be their trustees, answerable to them, not their irresponsible masters. No one here has denied these to be the genuine doctrines of our Government.

The third article affirms, that Government is instituted for the common benefit—that "*that* is the best which is capable of producing the greatest degree of happiness and safety, and is most effectually secured against the danger of mal-administration; and that when any Government shall be found inadequate or contrary to these purposes, a majority of the people hath an indubitable, unalienable and indefeasible right to reform, alter or abolish it, in such manner as shall be adjudged most conducive to the public weal." Here we have plainly declared the object of Government, the standard of its excellence, and the rule for its reform—its object, the common benefit; the test of its excellence, its capacity to attain that object, by producing the greatest degree of happiness and safety, and being secured against mal-administration; and the rule for its reform, the judgment of the majority pronouncing it inadequate to its purposes, and altering it, with a sole view to the public weal. We are saved then the necessity of looking to natural law for the right of the majority to reform; we have positive conventional law; the most solemn declaration on the face of our social compact, that the majority have a right, an indubitable, unalienable and indefeasible right, to reform, alter or abolish. It is true, that this power is to be employed when the Government is found inadequate to its object, the common benefit, and must be employed with a single view to the public good.

But, who is to judge whether the Government has been adequate to the object of its institution; who to judge of the manner of its reform? Surely the people, who ordained it, the people for whose happiness and safety it was instituted; the people, to a majority of whom the right of reform is declared unquestionably to belong—the people are the sole, the exclusive judges. It is their duty, I admit, to listen with all deference and respect to the counsels of their wise men, who may tell them—"We have been long and attentive observers of the operations of your Government; we have compared it with all the Governments of the world, ancient and modern; we are satisfied it is the best that ever existed; we can demonstrate that it has fulfilled all the great ends of its institution; that it has secured you all the happiness and safety, which it is the province of Government to secure, and that an attempt to change it essentially, is a wanton experiment to make that better which is already good beyond the common lot of human institutions; it is to sport with the blessings of Providence, and encounter the imminent hazard of losing all that is valuable in practice, in the vain pursuit of all that is perfect in theory." After attentively and impartially considering all the arguments adduced to sustain these counsels, and carefully weighing every fact on which they rest, if convinced by them, it is a solemn duty to themselves, to posterity, and to all mankind, to reject all propositions to reform, to preserve a model of so much excellence as an example to the world, and as a rich inheritance to the generations that are to come. But, if they are not convinced; if, on the contrary, their judgments are satisfied, that they have not enjoyed the degree of happiness and safety, which good Government ought to assure; that their Government is not only imperfect in theory, but defective in practice; that its defects may be safely remedied, and its practical good much enhanced—then there is but one answer which they can give to these counsels:—"We acknowledge your experience, your wisdom, your virtue—the great superiority of your attainments, and the entire sincerity of your opinions—we admire the plain, candid and manly language, in which you have spoken disagreeable truths—we thank you, sincerely thank you, for the parental solicitude with which you have raised your warning voice; but you must allow, that we too have some experience in the operations of our own Government—that we have enjoyed its blessings, suffered its evils, and have some opportunity of judging, whether the one may be abated, or the other increased—You must remember that you are endeavoring to prove to us, by rhetoric and logic, that we are prosperous and happy, when our own senses, and the reflections of our own minds, have conducted us to a different conclusion—ours is the stake in this Government—ours the loss, if ill should result—ours the gain, if happiness should attend our reform—ours, therefore, is the province to judge, and you must excuse us, if dissenting from your opinions, we feel bound to follow the dictates of our own judgments."

The people, then, Mr. Chairman, must judge for themselves, when the *casus fœderis* has occurred, when the defects of the Government require reform;—and judging that time to have arrived, the unquestionable right to reform belongs to the majority. But to the majority of whom? A majority of the community is the answer which the Bill of Rights gives; and that answer is perfectly intelligible, when we consider in connexion, the several clauses of the Bill of Rights and the Constitution. The *community* referred to in the third article, cannot mean the whole people, because they never are, and never can be consulted, either in the formation of the organic law, or in the administration of the Government. It can mean none other than those to whom, in the sixth article the Right of Suffrage is declared to belong—those to whom the Constitution itself was submitted to be carried into effect—the qualified voters. To those, then, enjoying the Right of Suffrage, it was submitted, whether they would accept or reject the Constitution, by electing or refusing to elect the members of the General Assembly. To them, the Convention held in effect this language:—"We have formed a Constitution for your Government, and have declared the rights which pertain to you and your posterity as the basis on which that Constitution rests:—we have declared that it is instituted for the common benefit, and that when it shall be found inadequate to this purpose, a majority of you have an indubitable, unalienable, and indefeasible right to reform, alter or abolish it, in such manner, as shall be adjudged most conducive to the public weal. We believe it well suited to your condition—well calculated to attain its object;—but, if experience shall teach you that we are mistaken, the corrective is in the power of a majority of you, who may alter, reform or abolish, as you may judge most conducive to the public weal;—it is referred to your wisdom to accept or reject." Thus submitted, it was accepted by the freeholders, the qualified voters, without opposition; and their act, by which they elected the members of the first General Assembly, was as effectual, if not as solemn an adoption of the Constitution and Declaration of Rights, as if an unanimous vote of approbation had been given on a formal call of the Ayes and Noes. I never entertained any doubt of the validity of our Constitution, for the want of a formal ratification;—or, if any doubts on that subject were ever impressed on my youthful mind, such as my friend from Chesterfield once felt, both he and I must have been disabused of them, I think, by the lectures of the distinguished master under whom we studied our professions, and whose memory we both revere. The Constitution being thus accepted by the qualified voters, they became the parties to the social compact; they shared the sovereignty, they constituted the *community*, to the majority of whom the right of reform belongs.

It does not necessarily follow, from the right of the majority to reform the Constitution, that the powers of ordinary legislation should be vested in the majority. This, I agree, is a question of expediency, which it belongs to the majority to decide—and in deciding it, they are bound to look to the great object of Government, the *common benefit*, and to enquire, by what organization, it will be *capable of producing the great-*

est degree of happiness and safety, and be most effectually secured against the danger of mal-administration. Upon the result of this interesting enquiry, it depends whether the majority should hold in their own hands the power of legislation, or confide it to the minority. But this doctrine of expediency, Mr. Chairman, not well understood, is of dangerous tendency, and calculated grossly to mislead us. In adopting it as the guide of our deliberations here, it may become us to bestow a moment's attention on its character. Enlightened and liberal expediency, which looks to consequences immediate and remote, calculates effects, temporary and enduring, and regards all interests, partial and general, which in short has the lasting public good for its object, and truth and justice for its guides, lies at the foundation of moral and political law, and is the true test of moral and political propriety :—while that blind and narrow expediency which regards only immediate consequences, temporary effects, and partial interests, which has for its object the present good, disregards the precepts of justice, and delivers itself up to the guidance of sophistry, is the parent of all that is false and mischievous, in morals and politics, teaches in the schools of modern philosophy, upholds the pernicious theories of Condorcet, Rousseau, and Godwin, justifies usurpation and tyranny, and recommends the most visionary and heedless scheme of reform.

The wise man, when he enjoins a rigid observance of faith, strict performance of promises, when he enforces filial duty and parental love, and commands you to do no murder, is not unmindful, that partial evil might often be avoided, and temporary good obtained, by violating your faith, disregarding your promise, failing in duty to your parent, forgetting your affection for your son, and even by imbruing your hand in human blood :—But looking beyond the narrow circle which bounds the vision of modern philosophy, he tells you that all these partial considerations must be foregone, and that the lasting peace and happiness of society imperiously require that the moral duties, he has taught, should be held in constant reverence. So the wise Statesman, looking beyond the partial evils and temporary benefits which guide the expedients of political quackery, walking in the light of experience, and governing himself by principle, will take all his measures with reference to the great and enduring interests of the community. If such light and such guidance shall conduct us to the conclusion, that the great and permanent interests of this community require that the power of the Government should be entrusted to the minority, it becomes the solemn duty of the majority to withdraw their claim, to yield the power, and with it their confidence to the minority, whether that minority consists of thousands, or hundreds, or tens, or even a single unit,—whether the Government shall continue a republic, or become an oligarchy, an aristocracy, or a monarchy. All that I require is, that the evidence of this duty should be clear and conclusive :—that in a Government instituted for the benefit of the people, and acknowledging their will to be sovereign ; in a country where, under the most favorable auspices in the world, the interesting experiment is yet in progress, which is to solve the problem of man's capacity for self-government,—we should be very careful to consult our judgment rather than our fears—we should be quite sure, that in protecting an obvious, though subordinate interest, we are not leaving the paramount interests of society unguarded ; that in surrendering the power to the minority, we are not abandoning the principle, that the will of the people is sovereign, and acknowledging that the question of self-government must be decided against the liberties of mankind.

With these views of the rights of the majority, and of the test of expediency to which every measure of reform must be subjected, let us proceed to the question before the Committee. The people who adopted the present Constitution, with a declaration on its face of their right to reform it, having lived under it for more than fifty years, have thought it required alteration, and have deputed us to enquire and report to them, what amendments, if any, ought to be made. The Select Committee have reported a resolution, declaring "that in the apportionment of representation in the House of Delegates, regard should be had to the white population exclusively." The gentleman from Culpeper has proposed so to amend this resolution, as to place the representation on the basis, not of the white population simply, but of the white population and taxation combined :—and the question is upon the adoption of the proposed amendment. In considering this question, we must not be deceived by the literal import of the two propositions, and I beg permission to explain my understanding of each.

When the resolution of the Select Committee refers us to the white population "*exclusively*," I do not understand that in the practical application of this rule, there is to be a rigid adherence to its terms :—I do not understand that the Commonwealth is to be laid off into election districts, containing a precise equality of white inhabitants, and entitled to an equal number of Delegates. I understand this word "*exclusively*," in that sense, which would refer us to the white population, in exclusion of the black population ; in exclusion of property and taxes—not in exclusion of all regard to county limits—of all regard to the interests, the convenience, the ancient habits and customs of the people. My object in applying the rule, would be to lay off the State into a given number of districts, composed of contiguous counties, having interests as nearly identical as possible—to give to each of these districts a number of Delegates, in proportion to its white population, and to distribute the Delegates, in each district, among the several counties therein, so as to give to each county in the district, at least one member, if the number of members were equal to the number of the counties. To illustrate :—Suppose the State divided into four districts, by the lines of the Alleghany, the Blue Ridge, and the head of tide water—and suppose the House of Delegates to be composed of one hundred and twenty members. Then upon the basis of the white population, according to the Auditor's estimate of its present numbers, the trans-Alleghany district, would be entitled to about thirty-two members—the Valley district, to twenty-four—the Middle district to thirty-five—and the Eastern to twenty-nine. The thirty-two trans-Alleghany members, would be distributed among its twenty-six counties, so as to give one to each; and assign the surplus six to the six larger counties. In like manner the twenty-four Valley members would be distributed among its fourteen counties, and the thirty-five members for the midland district among its twenty-nine counties. The twenty-nine members for the Eastern district would not supply one to each of its thirty-six counties and four boroughs, and therefore in that district no county or borough would have more than one, and some of the smaller counties, must form together, election districts for single members. By such an arrangement as this, though each county would not have its exact proportion in the representation, each large district would; and in order to give to each local interest in the Commonwealth, its just weight in the Legislature, you have only to take care, that in laying out your large districts, you embrace in them respectively only those counties whose interests are essentially the same. This being done, the spirit of a just equality would be observed, whilst the regard had to county limits would soften the asperities of the reform, and be attended with many advantages, which it would be out of place here to recount.

Again, the resolution of the Committee, in referring to the white population exclusively, literally imports, that the whole number of white persons in the several districts, shall give the ratio of representation—and this was intended to be the practical operation of the rule. But this is not in the spirit of the doctrine for which we contend. We do not insist, that each white person, male and female, infant and adult, whether entitled to the Right of Suffrage or no, is entitled to equal representation. No!—Our doctrine is, that each person entitled to the Right of Suffrage, each who shares in the sovereignty, is entitled to equal political power, and therefore to equal representation. We espouse the principle of the resolution offered by the gentleman from Norfolk (Mr. Taylor,) though we do not adopt its mathematical precision. We have advocated the basis of white population, instead of qualified voters, because the former gives a more certain and convenient rule, and because it was believed, that it was substantially equivalent in effect. But examination and reflection lead me to believe that there may be, and possibly is, a material difference, in the effect of the two rules; that the number of white persons in the different districts would not be a fair index of the number of qualified voters; and that the basis of qualified voters would be more favourable to the Eastern part of the State, than the basis of white population. If there be any gentleman on this, or the other side of the House, who prefers as the basis of representation, the qualified voters, rather than the white population, who thinks that the superior justice of the former, countervails the greater convenience and certainty of the latter, I am prepared to go with him, and give it my support. I will not press the principle for which I contend beyond its reason and justice. In advocating then, the basis of white population, I must be understood as maintaining the right of the qualified voters to share equally the power of the Government; and as pressing their claims, not to a precise mathematical equality, but to a rational practical equality, assuring to every local interest, as far as can be, its due weight and just protection.

The proposition to amend, which offers the basis of population and taxation combined, is not very definite in its terms, but as explained by its mover is very intelligible. It does not propose to compound the number of dollars paid for taxes in each district, with the number of white persons therein, and thence derive the rule for apportionment, but it proposes to compound the ratios of taxation and numbers, thus—to give one-half the Delegates, according to the ratio of taxes paid, and the other half according to the ratio of white persons—or thus take for each district the mean proportional between the number it would be entitled to according to the ratio of white persons, and the number it would be entitled to according to the ratio of taxes paid. To illustrate: The trans-Alleghany district, would be entitled—on the basis of white population to thirty-two—on the basis of taxes to eleven—on the compound basis to twenty-one and a half. The Valley, on white population twenty-four—taxes ten—compound basis twenty-one and a half. Middle district, on white population thirty-five—taxes forty-nine—compound forty-two Eastern district, on white population twenty-nine—taxes forty-one—compound thirty-five.

The proposition to amend is liable to other objections for want of precision; but candour requires us to suppose, that they will be obviated, when the proposition is carried out into its details, and therefore they need not be now pointed out.

With these explanations, the question before the Committee may be thus stated:—Shall the power of the Government be apportioned among its districts, according to the simple ratio of those who partake of the sovereignty, the qualified voters, in each;—or shall it be apportioned according to the combined ratio of white persons and taxes?

Those who advocate the simple ratio, endeavour to maintain it upon principle; to deduce it from the fundamental doctrines of our Government, and to vindicate it upon considerations of sound political expediency.

The advocates of the compound ratio, not seeming directly to controvert the general rule, that the majority should govern, and some of them admitting it, insist nevertheless that it is liable to exceptions; that it is subject to the control of these considerations of expediency which may prove it unfit for the good government of the people to whom it is to be applied, and that the circumstances of the people of Virginia render it unfit for them. They contend that a primary object of Government is the protection of property; that when its title is unsafe, no other rights can be secure, and that the peculiar condition of property in Virginia is such that no adequate protection can be given it, if the power of the Government is put into the hands of the majority. They endeavour to prove, that power in the minority is essential to the protection of their property, and that such is the singular constitution of our society, that while the property of the minority is exposed to certain injury, by giving power to the majority, the property and all the personal rights of the majority, are effectually secured by giving the power to the minority. The evidences of this peculiarity they find, in the unequal distribution of the slave property, among the different districts of the State; the unequal contributions of revenue from those districts; the variety and supposed conflict of their local interests. They show that the great body of the slaves is held by the Eastern districts of the Commonwealth; they endeavour to show, that the taxable inhabitants in those districts pay a much greater average tax *per capita*, than is paid by the taxable inhabitants of the Western districts; that there is no subject of taxation in the West which is not also found in the East, and on which a tax would not be quite as burthensome to the Eastern as to the Western people, and no subject of legislation, on which the interest of the East could be promoted at the expense of the West:—that on the interesting subject of internal improvements, particularly, while the interests of the Eastern and Western districts are variant, if not hostile, and plans might be adopted to enrich the latter, which would impoverish the former, yet the East would have no adequate motive to do injustice to the West;—and they thence infer the propriety of giving to the East a power in the Government, somewhat proportioned to their contributions of revenue, a power adequate to the protection of their property;—they thence also infer, the perfect security of the West, against the power of the East,—and the alarming danger,—that, if the power of the Government, were in the hands of the Western people;—whither they think the rule of the majority would probably soon carry it,—the property of the Eastern people would be unjustly taxed, unwise laws affecting the value of their slaves and dangerous to the peace of the community, would be enacted, and schemes adopted, which might apply the revenue contributed by the East, to the improvement of the estates of the West.

This is believed to be a fair outline of the principal grounds on which the friends of the compound ratio rest its defence. Some subordinate considerations have been called to their aid, and many ingenious, able and eloquent arguments have left it wanting in nothing, but intrinsic merit, to recommend it to our affections and our judgment.

I readily subscribe, Mr. Chairman, to the proposition, that an indispensible object of every good Government, is the security of property, and that no Government which does not afford that security, can be a safe depository of the liberty and life of the citizen;—but I utterly deny that there is any thing in the peculiar situation of Virginia, which should induce us to look for that security, in the power of the minority, or which threatens the serious dangers which gentlemen apprehend, from the power of the majority. On the contrary, I insist, that the majority have more to fear from the power of the minority, than the minority has to fear from theirs:—that under the rule of the majority, property will be more secure, legislation more just and wise, the people more happy, and the country more prosperous.

Before we proceed to a more particular consideration of this question, it may be well to review the statements which have been submitted to us, deduced from the tables furnished by the Auditor, and to make such corrections as they may be found to require.

The tables of population show us that there are probably in the Commonwealth at this time, about 682,000 white persons, and about 448,000 slaves, thus distributed amongst the different districts:—In the first or Western district, about 181,000 whites, and 17,000 slaves; more than ten whites for each slave:—in the second or Valley district, about 138,000 whites, and 33 500 slaves, little more than four whites to a slave:—in the third or middle district, about 197,000 whites, and 221,000 slaves—the slaves exceeding the whites by about 24,000, nearly one-eighth of the white population; and in the fourth or Eastern district, about 165,000 whites, and 176,000 slaves—the slaves there, also exceeding the whites, about 10,500, about one-sixteenth of the white population. Thus, it appears that the aggregate of slaves on the East of the Blue Ridge is about 397,000, while the aggregate on the West is about 50,500, nearly eight to one—while the aggregate of white population on the East of the mountain is about 362,500, and that on the West 319,000—the difference only about 43,500. It is, therefore, true as is stated on the other side, that the slave population is very unequally distributed at this time, and is at present essentially an Eastern interest.

From the tables of taxation, the gentleman from Chesterfield deduced, that the people of the first district paid of the whole taxes on land and personal property, an average *per capita*, of 23 cents 8 mills; and the people of the second district 42 cents 6 mills, while the people of the third district paid 72 cents 2 mills, and those of the fourth 63 cents 9 mills—making an average for the people on the West of the Blue Ridge of 32 cents 2 mills; and for the people on the East of 68 cents 2 mills. He selected individual counties in the different districts, between which there was a still more striking inequality, and showed that the average contribution of the slave tax *per capita*, in the several districts, was the most unequal of all.

That there are inequalities in the contributions of revenues from the different districts of the State, owing to the unequal distribution of wealth, no one doubts. It is certainly so, in our country, as it is in all countries, and as it must be, so long as taxes are laid upon property and not on polls; so long as the ability to pay shall be regarded as furnishing any criterion of the amount of contribution. But the statements which have been exhibited to you are calculated to deceive. They make the impression that the several sums stated, show the average *per capita*, actually assessed on the tax-paying inhabitants of the several districts—this, however, is not the case: the calculations are made by distributing the whole amount of taxes assessed, in each district, on the whole number of free persons in the district, on whom by law a tax could be assessed, whether black or white, male or female, infant or adult. I have made an estimate of the average *per capita*, actually assessed, on the tax-paying inhabitants of the several districts, and the result is materially different; showing inequalities, it is true, as must have been anticipated, but inequalities less glaring, and less calculated to excite alarm, or, to countenance the extravagant claim for power which has been founded upon them.

The Committee will remark, that I have made this estimate from the Auditor's tables of the taxes assessed for the year 1828, and his lists of persons charged with taxes on lands or other property, in the several counties and corporations in the Commonwealth. There will be a slight inaccuracy in the estimate of the land tax, resulting from the circumstance, that this list excludes all those charged with a tax, on parcels of land in the country, less than twenty-five acres. But this inaccuracy cannot materially vary the result.

Calculating from these data, I find the average tax *per capita* as follows:—in the first district, land tax 80 cents, tax on other property 59 cents, total $1 39; in the second district, land tax $2 30, tax on other property $1 12, total $3 42; in the third district, land tax $2 31, tax on other property $2 43, total $4 74; and in the fourth district, land tax $2 07, tax on other property $2 43, total $4 50. We thus see that the average land tax of the Valley district is equal to the average land tax of the middle district within one cent, and is superior to the average land tax of the Eastern district, 23 cents—that its average total tax is less than the average total of the middle district, $1 32—that is about 28 per cent. and less than the average total of the Eastern district, by $1 08—that is about 22 per cent. But, the taxes on slaves have been reduced 8 cents for the present year, and this reduction would cause the average of the several districts to stand thus—first district $1 36—second district $3 34—third district $4 43—fourth district, $4 19, bringing the Valley district within $1 11 of the middle district, and within 85 cents of the Eastern. It must be farther remarked, that in these estimates, the towns of Richmond, Petersburg and Fredericksburg have been included within the tide-water district. Now, although these towns are situated at the head of tide-water, they do not, for any of the purposes of this argument, belong to the tide-water district. Their sympathies, their interests are with the country that lies above them, which founded them, supplies their trade and furnishes their wealth. Withdraw them from that district, and you diminish very materially its average tax. We have not the means of estimating the taxes paid in Fredericksburg, our tables containing no separate return for that town. Subtracting Richmond and Petersburg only, for which we have separate returns, and then the average of the Eastern district will be, of land $1 84, of tax on other property, $2 12, total $3 96; thus reducing its average land tax 46 cents below that of the Valley, and leaving its total average only 53 cents above it.

In all these estimates it will be observed that the contributions of the trans-Alleghany district are very much below par. It is easy to understand why the average tax on personal property, is much lower there than in the other districts, because of the small number of its slaves—but why the average land tax should be so, is an enquiry, the answer to which does not lie on the surface. It is probably to be found in two considerations: First, very large quantities of land, in different parts of that district, on which large arrears of taxes are due, have been vested in the Literary Fund, by the operation of the tax law of 1814, and are now stricken from the tax books, because the lands belonging to that fund pay no taxes—secondly, and chiefly, in the year 1817, when all the lands of the Commonwealth were assessed, it is well known that the public mind was acting under a delusion, which misled its estimates of the value of every thing, and perhaps of nothing more than of the value of land. The combined influence of protracted war in Europe, which for many years had given an extensive market, and high prices, to the products of our soil—our own war, which throwing a large amount of mercantile capital out of its regular employment, left it to seek investment in land; and the great multiplication of banks, which creating a large fictitious capital, increased to an extravagant degree the speculations in real property—had inflated the market price of that property beyond any reasonable relation to its intrinsic value. These causes, in Virginia, had exerted their principal force in the agricultural country, of the Valley, and the Eastern side of the Mountain, and especially the banking towns, and their immediate vicinities. They were but little felt in the trans-Alleghany country, remote from the influence of the banks—remote from market, and from the scenes of speculation. Its lands were the less sought either by the emigrant or the speculator, because of the difficulty in their titles. The land law of 1779, drawn, it is said, by the same George Mason, the author of our Constitution—men are not equally wise in all things!—the land law of '79 had operated to produce infinite confusion in the land titles of the West; and this cause, as well by retarding settlements as by discouraging purchasers, had depressed the market value of their lands. Thus, while extraneous causes of one kind contributed to enhance the market value of lands East of the Alleghany, extraneous causes of another kind conspired to depreciate the market value of the lands West of that mountain. I should have inferred, therefore, that the assessment of 1817, which the law required to be made according to the market value, would have overrated the lands on the Eastern waters, and underrated those on the Western. We all know that the lands on the Eastern waters were assessed too high, and I am informed that those on the Western waters were, in truth, assessed too low. Looking at a statement made from the assessors' tables, we find that while the average value of the lands on the Western waters was but 92 cents per acre, those of the Valley were $7 33, those of the Midland district $8 20, and those of the Eastern district $8 43 per acre. These causes, added to the great increase of population in the Western district since the assessment, leave no reasonable doubt that a new assessment would reduce the average of all the lands of the three districts upon the Eastern waters, especially of the tide-water district—would raise the average of the lands in the Western district, and would place the land-tax of that district nearly upon a ground of equality with the land-tax of the other districts of the State.

It does not follow, Mr. Chairman, from the inequalities of contribution in the different districts, that there is any injustice in the measure of taxes imposed, or that those who pay least can best bear the burthen imposed on them. If taxes are imposed on the property of the country, in the proportion of the ability of its owners to pay, those who have more property, and therefore pay more taxes, have, surely, no cause to complain. With equal prudence, economy, and good management, the rich will be always able to pay their contributions to the Government with more ease than the poor. The contributions of the rich man are paid from his abundance, and if they restrain his enjoyments at all, they curtail only his luxuries—while the poor man withdraws his modicum from a bare competency, leaving scarcely enough behind for the necessaries and the ordinary comforts of life. It has been the object of our laws to distribute the taxes among the people in proportion to the value of their property, assuming that as the best criterion of their ability to pay, and adopting such general rules to effect their object as were found by experience to be most convenient in practice. If they have failed in this object, as no doubt in some degree they have, the failure has not been greater than was to have been anticipated from the intrinsic difficulty of the subject. If you will measure the ability of the several districts by the amount of their labor, and allow the whole number of their inhabitants, respectively, to be a fair standard of their comparative labor—you have a test by which to try this question. I do not vouch for the accuracy of this test, though a better one does not now occur to me—and if you will apply it, by dividing the whole amount of taxes in each district, by the whole number of its inhabitants, you will find the average *per capita* not very unequal in the several districts East of the Alleghany—and unequal in the Western district, no doubt, because of the accidental under value of its lands as already explained. The taxes of the several districts for the year 1829, distributed among all the inhabitants of each, gives an average, *per capita*, nearly as follows: In the first district, 15 cents; in the second, 29 cents; in the third, 31 cents; and in the fourth, 30 cents.

Mr. Johnson being much exhausted, asked the indulgence that the Committee should rise.

It was accorded to him on the motion of Mr. Giles, and the Committee rose accordingly—and on the motion of Mr. Mason of Southampton, the Convention immediately adjourned.

THURSDAY, November 12, 1829.

The Convention met at eleven o'clock, and its sitting was opened with prayer by the Rev. Mr. Horner, of the Catholic Church.

Mr. Johnson resumed his speech of yesterday, and continued to occupy the floor till the hour of adjournment.

I have been thus particular in examining the manner in which the taxes are distributed among the different districts of the Commonwealth, not because it was essential to the merits of the question now before the Committee, but because I thought it would remove from our minds the alarming spectacle of poverty making war upon wealth, and would satisfy impartial men that each district pays, as nearly as the operation of laws always imperfect could be expected to produce, a just contribution to the Government—that no district is in a state of pauperism—none in a situation to be tempted to seize unlawfully on its neighbor's property—and that in all human probability, when, hereafter, a Western man shall vote from the pocket of his Eastern brother, one dollar, in the form of taxes, he will vote from his own pocket, at the same time, nearly an equivalent sum, one at least, which he can as ill spare, and will be as little able to pay. I regretted very much to hear that part of the remarks of the gentleman from Accomack, (Mr. Joynes) in which he endeavored to show that the whole country West of the Blue Ridge did not pay into the treasury a sum sufficient to defray the expenses of its delegation to the General Assembly, and of the administration of justice within its own limits. Remarks tending to institute odious comparisons, and to excite unpleasant sensations, coming from a gentleman who has manifested so much liberality, so much kind and good feeling, are exceedingly to be regretted—and I felt them the more because they came from that part of the State, the extreme East, from which on former occasions, I have so often heard remarks leading to collision and controversy, between the extreme West and extreme East, which required the interposition of moderate men to compose. I have not examined the gentleman's calculation to ascertain whether his conclusion is right or wrong. After having ascertained the precise amount of taxes paid by each district; after ascertaining the average amount *per capita*, paid in each—what possible influence on the question before us can it have—to know that the contributions of any district are not adequate to that part of the expenses of the Government, which the calculations of gentlemen may choose to assign to it? Surely the expenses of legislation, and of the administration of justice are not local in their character, pertain to no district, and can be charged to none. They are, if any can be, the expenses of the whole Commonwealth, incurred for the common weal and justly payable from the common purse. Such imputations as these, if it were proper to repel them, would lead to the unpleasant and unprofitable enquiry, into the objects to which the public revenue was applied; the districts in which it was expended; the local causes which increased the expense of Government, and would impose on us the invidious duty, which I certainly shall not perform, of indicating the various counties, in the Eastern district, which do not contribute their share of the expenses of Government. But we must forbear from such topics, they do not become the occasion.

It will be proper, Mr. Chairman, to disarm this question of some of its terrors to one party; disrobe it of some of its charms for the other, by examining with care its effects on the distribution of power, among the different districts of the Commonwealth. The calculations on this subject, have been made with reference to the House of Delegates, and upon the supposition that *that* House should consist of an hundred and twenty members. They are made upon the Auditor's estimates of the population of the present year. These are supposed by some gentlemen to be inaccurate, and the Auditor does not himself rely with confidence upon them;—but I assume them as approximating the truth sufficiently for the purposes of the present argument.

Let us, then, compare the power of the four great districts of the State, in such a House of Delegates, as it would be on the present basis, the equal representation of counties, as it would be on the compound basis proposed by the gentleman from Culpeper, and as it would be on the basis of white population. The Committee will understand my references to the districts, if they will remember, that I number them from West to East, denominating the Western, the first district.

In such a House of Delegates, the relative power of the several districts would stand thus:

On the basis of equal county representation.

First district, 27—2d, 16—3d, 32—4th, 43.

Compound basis.

First district, 21½—2d, 21½—3d, 42—4th, 35.

Simple basis of white population.

First, 32—2d, 34—3d, 35—4th, 29.

Divided by the Blue Ridge, the East and West, would stand thus:

By equal county representation,	W. 45	—E. 75
By the combined ratio,	43	" 77
White population,	56	" 64

In making these calculations, we disregard small fractions, and convert large ones into integers, that we may give the results in whole numbers.

By this method of calculating the effect of the two propositions, it would appear, that, adopting the compound basis, the West would lose, and the East gain two members out of one hundred and twenty, and that, adopting the simple basis, the West would gain, and the East lose eleven. But if instead of taking the whole number of white persons, as the basis, you take such only as are qualified to vote, there is reason to believe that the result would be materially varied. We have no means of ascertaining the number of qualified voters; there is no record of them any where, and we have certainly no *data* from which we would estimate them accurately. But we may approximate them perhaps sufficiently near, to answer the purpose of illustration, by estimates from such *data* as we have.

Until I came into this Convention, Mr. Chairman, I had habitually considered a representation apportioned according to the whole number of white people in the different districts, and one apportioned according to the qualified voters in each, as substantially equivalents. I had supposed, that the ratio of the one, would be a fair index of the ratio of the other. I had never carefully examined the subject, 'till my duties in the Legislative Committee, called my attention to it, and induced me to doubt the correctness of my former impressions. The able argument of the gentleman from Chesterfield, rivetted my attention to it, and induced me to think, that those impressions were probably wrong. There is much weight due to the consideration, that those who perform menial services—the day-labourers, the cultivators of land which they do not own, are in the Eastern districts, principally slaves—while those who perform similar functions, in the Western districts, are chiefly white persons; and this consideration tends to the conclusion, that the ratio of qualified voters, to the whole white population, would be greater in the East than in the West. I have appealed to the only documents in my power, to test this conclusion—the lists of persons charged with taxes, furnished us by the Auditor. He has furnished two lists—the one, of the number of persons in each county and corporate town, charged with any tax, on a town lot, or part of a town lot, or any parcel of land, not less than twenty-five acres—the other, of the number charged with any tax on property. Now, although each of these lists, contains male and female, young and old, black and white, without discrimination; and, therefore, cannot inform us correctly of the actual number of adult white males, upon either, yet I have thought, that, probably, they would not very far mislead us, if we regard them as an index of the relative number of free adult white males, in the several districts, and as an index of the relative number of qualified voters in each. If we take the list of those charged with taxes on land, as giving the ratio of freehold voters, and the other list as giving the ratio of voters, when the Right of Suffrage shall be extended to house-keepers, who pay a revenue tax, then, upon the basis of the qualified voters, the relative power of the districts would stand thus:

According to the land list—1st, 27—2d, 20—3d, 37—4th, 36.

According to the property list—1st, 29—2d, 21—3d, 39—4th, 34.

Dividing by the Blue Ridge, the power would be,

According to the first—West, 47—East, 73.

According to the second—West, 50—East, 70.

Thus, according to the most favourable of these estimates, the West would gain, and the East lose five members, in a House of an hundred and twenty, and the majority on the Eastern side of the Blue Ridge, would remain twenty.

These statements may serve to show, that although upon any basis of representation which has been yet suggested, a large portion of power will pass from the tide-water district, to those above it—yet upon no basis, can the power pass now, from the Eastern to the Western side of the Blue Ridge, and that upon the principle for which we contend, if it pass at all, it must pass at a distant day, slowly, gradually, safely—unaccompanied by the dangers which have been apprehended—they may serve to show to calm reflection, that the stake depending on the present contest, is not so great, the prize to be won not so valuable, the loss to be sustained not so dreadful, as has been pictured to our imaginations. I may have occasion again to refer to them in illustration of my views.

In taking leave, for the present, of those calculations which I have introduced as correctives of the estimates made on the other side, I cannot forbear remarking on the seeming inconsistency of gentlemen, who losing no occasion to throw ridicule on numbers, and political arithmetic, have arrayed them against us, in a most formidable phalanx, and have drawn from them their strongest and most impressive arguments. I have no doubt, that the tables of population and taxes, which have gone out to the public, with the arithmetical calculations of gentlemen, on the other side, which have accompanied them, and their inferences of change of power, and danger of oppressive taxation, have been the principle cause of the great excitement in the public mind, and of the alarm which is felt in the Eastern districts of the Commonwealth; an excitement and alarm which have already done mischief, and threaten to do more; which have already, through the instrumentality of instructions, deprived an honorable member of his seat on this floor, and may soon confound the councils of this Convention. I mean not at all to interpose between the district and its delegate:—it is not for me to enquire into the causes which led to the instruction and the consequent resignation—but as a member of this Convention, anxious for the harmony and profitable issue of its labours—as a citizen of the Commonwealth, deeply interested in its welfare, I cannot but lament the example, which, if followed generally, must deprive this Assembly of its deliberative character, and deprive it of all power to effect the purposes for which it was appointed. While we are sitting here deliberating on the great interests of the State, candidly comparing our opinions, endeavouring to reconcile discordant views, adjust conflicting claims, secure every right, and protect every interest, ambiguous words are to be scattered among the people, scraps from newspapers and shreds of arguments to be circulated among them—in a moment of tumultuous agitation, they are to be collected, at the hustings and muster grounds, at the taverns and cross roads, to form specific instructions, for their delegates on the most delicate and difficult of all the subjects of their deliberation—thus, depriving them of the power of making or receiving concessions, and putting an end to all further consultation. Can any considerate man be blind to the confusion and mischief to which such measures must tend? Do not understand me, Sir, as questioning the right of the constituent to instruct his representative—this I regard as one of the settled doctrines of our Government, to which I most cheerfully subscribe. But surely I cannot be mistaken in supposing that there never was a more unfit occasion for exercising it, than that on which the people have endeavoured to put in requisition, the experience, the wisdom, and prudence of the State, not to enact laws, but to propose for the consideration of the people themselves, amendments to their fundamental law. If this example is to be followed, had we not better return home, restore to the people the trust they have confided to us—tell them that all hope of amending their Constitution is perfectly illusory—that the solemn declaration of the right of the majority to reform, is indeed a visionary theory, since it is utterly impracticable for the people to exercise this right without the aid of representatives, and since those representatives cannot be trusted even to confer together, and propose amendments? I beg pardon for this digression, and will return to the question before the Committee, whether the compound or simple basis shall be preferred.

It has been urged as an objection to the report of the Select Committee, that it proposes to introduce something new into the Constitution. It certainly is not new to the American Republics, to apportion representation according to the ratio of white population; and whether it is new to our own Constitution, it cannot be material, to enquire, since the objection must equally lie against the proposed amendment. Both propose a change in the Constitution, and the question is, which is preferrable.

We are cautioned, however, against all change, unless called for, by strong reasons;—we are referred to the nearly equal division of parties, which probably exists here, on this question—and are emphatically warned against the impropriety of an important change, by a lean majority of one or two, forcing upon a large minority, a Constitution that would be abhorrent to them. I readily admit, that no important changes should be made, that are not called for by clear and strong reasons, and no one can be more sensible than I am, of the imprudence of forcing upon a large minority, a Government that is odious to them. But the existing inequalities in the representation are so glaring, and the discontents produced by it are so strong, that every one seems to concede the propriety of some reform, and both the propositions under consideration will effect that reform to a considerable extent. If the reform proposed by the Select Committee, be objectionable, because it is unacceptable to a large minority, would the reform proposed by the gentleman from Culpeper, be the less objectionable, it being at least as disagreeable to a small majority? Or, shall we be told that the gentleman from Culpeper, and his friends, are not insisting on any reform, but are content with the present Constitution? Still, however, the objection recurs:—it is with the present Constitution, that we suppose the majority is discontented, and the question again arises, shall they be compelled to submit to it? In whatever light we view it, therefore, a nearly equal division of opinion would present matter for serious consideration, and not less serious regret. In this view of the case, it may be worthy of some attention, that if the majority here should be found in favour of the report of the Committee, and we faithfully represent the will of our constituents, it is probable that the majority of the people who approve it, will be larger. This House being composed of an equal number of members from each Senatorial district, these districts having been arranged according to the Census of 1810, so as to contain as nearly as convenient, equal numbers of white population—and the population of the Western districts, having since increased by a much greater ratio than that of the Eastern districts, it is fair to conclude, that a proposition sustained here, by a majority consisting chiefly of Western members, would be sustained by a larger majority of the people. We have no warrant, however, for counting majorities, at present, on either side, and it is our duty to proceed with candour, and liberality to examine the merits of both propositions, and to recommend that which shall be found best, to as much favour as possible.

When we have established that the people are the fountain of political power, and their happiness its object—that a majority of those entitled to suffrage have a right to reform their Constitution, and thereby regulate the political power—it must necessarily follow, that the majority may rightfully retain the power of ordinary legislation, unless it can be shown that the object of good Government will not thereby be obtained. Gentlemen have, therefore, with great propriety, assumed upon themselves the burthen of proving, that in Virginia, this power in the hands of the majority, would be inconsistent with the public welfare. They insist, that as a leading object of all Government, is the protection of property, so, there is no mode of affording that protection so effectual and so proper, as giving it a direct influence in the Government, by entitling it to representation. It is by thus claiming representation for property, that they insist on placing power in the hands of the minority. Let us examine the arguments by which this claim is sustained.

Gentlemen tell us, that by our own concessions, we surrender the power of numbers, the right of the majority, and admit the propriety of giving property an influence in Government, when we agree to exclude many from the polls, and require a qualification in property, to give the Right of Suffrage. This argument is founded in mistake; we have never advocated the power of numbers without distinction of persons; all that we have endeavoured to maintain, is the equal power of those who share the sovereignty and the consequent right of their majority. The qualification of property which we require, to give admission into this number is, with no view to give power to property, but is, like the qualification of age, and sex, an evidence only of fitness for the exercise of political power. If it were intended to give power to property, the richest and the poorest voter could not enjoy equal portions of power. So far then, as this illustration is entitled to respect, the argument founded upon it turns in favour of the equal right of every voter, without reference to property, in favour of the simple basis of representation.

Experience and precedent have been appealed to, and the learned gentleman from Orange, (Mr. P. P. Barbour,) has warned us of the very just distinction between experience and experiment; and giving us wise caution against the dangers of the one, has prudently commended us to the guidance of the other. It was hardly to have been expected, after this salutary lesson, that the gentleman, to sustain his argument, and to enlighten the path of our duty, would have looked for examples in the twilight of Roman history. When we substitute for our own, the experience of other nations, and other ages, we should at least require that it should come to us well attested by authentic history. But I am willing to allow to the argument all the aid it can derive, and avail myself of all the light that can flow from the example referred to. The centuries and tribes of Rome are the examples to which our attention has been called —the former as furnishing a precedent of the representation of property in a republic. The centuries, it is true, in which the richest class of society was represented, furnish to my mind, so far as the dim light of my information enables me to judge, a fair illustration of the representation of property; and I ask whether this example in the Roman Government is seriously recommended to our imitation?

[Here Mr. Barbour, in explanation, said, that he had referred to the Roman republic as furnishing an example at one time of the representation of property alone, by centuries, and at another time, of the representation of numbers alone, by tribes.

He had said that he did not approve either of these extremes—he would prefer to combine them, as in the proposition of the gentleman from Culpeper.]

This explanation, Mr. Chairman, does not vary the view I have taken of the subject, nor can it add force to the example which has been quoted. The centuries and tribes of Rome, were not extremes of aristocracy and democracy of which the Roman people made experiment at different times and separately. They existed together, and for ages. They were at the foundation of the patrician and plebeian orders—originated during the monarchy, and were continued in the time of the republic. They were the inspiring cause of the angry dissentions between the different orders of the people—of the grinding oppressions of the poor, and the lawless inroads upon the property of the rich. The power of the monarch was necessary to balance the contending factions, and restrain the dangerous excesses of each—and in a few short years, less than twenty, after the expulsion of the Tarquins, and the destruction of the monarchy, these excesses led to the appointment of the first Dictator, the recession of the people to the sacred mount, and the first serious petition for an agrarian law. In the tribes the people were not represented, but appeared in proper person to act their part in public affairs. The scheme of centuries and tribes was designed to balance numbers and wealth against each other; but, the history of the republic affords more of warning against its mischiefs than commendation of its success. I will not, however, claim the benefit of this example and urge it as a caution against the danger of giving representation to property in our republic. I know that our condition and that of the Roman people is so essentially unlike—our representative republic so radically different from their mixture of aristocracy and democracy, that it is not safe to reason from one to the other. The Roman Government, indeed, in the op nion of Cicero, its greatest admirer, and ablest vindicator, owed its chief excellence to its strong aristocratic character—a merit to which our Government surely has no claim.

It is utterly in vain, Mr. Chairman, that we appeal to any of the ancient republics for information to guide us. We know them all most imperfectly, and the little we do know teaches us only that they contain no instruction for us.

The modern European republics will supply as little aid to our deliberations. We should look in vain to Venice or St. Marino, to Holland or Switzerland, for the experience of a system like ours, operating upon a people like ours—or for information to guide us to the best means of protecting the peculiar interests which arise out of the peculiar population of Virginia. How would it avail us, for example, to know what causes preserved so long the little Italian republic, with a few thousand inhabitants only on a mountain top, contented and happy, though poor, safe amidst surrounding nations, though without military force, and perfectly tranquil in the operations of its Government, though without the ordinary checks and balances! Or what would it profit us to inquire, how it has happened that in the small democratic cantons the liberty of the people, with all the rights of person and property, were preserved for centuries, though every male citizen, above fifteen years of age, was admitted, in proper person, to share in the legislation of the country?

Just as little useful information or salutary warning is furnished us on this question by the experience of the French republic—a Government that was thrown up by a convulsion from the abyss of despotism, floated for a few years on the waves of a bloody revolution, and sank again, as they subsided, into the bottomless deep. Such experience might teach us the utter unfitness of any people for a Government to which they have been wholly unused—and the great dangers which attend violent and sudden transitions from one extreme to another—but, none of the examples of the European republics can assist us in deciding, whether it is wisest in Virginia to base the representation upon numbers, or property, or a combination of both.

The British House of Commons has been referred to, for the purpose of showing the intimate connexion between taxation and representation, and of proving that in England, where our system of representation had its birth, its foundations were laid in the power of imposing taxes.

To the experience of England, Mr. Chairman, the American Statesman may in general safely refer. We are better acquainted with her history, more familiar with her institutions, than with those of any other foreign country. From her common law, her jury trial, *habeas corpus* and *magna charta*, we learn the most valuable lessons of jurisprudence, and from these our ancestors imbibed their love of civil liberty, their respect for the rights of persons and the rights of property. In her Government we see a well-adjusted balance of power; and with all its imperfections on its head, it is probably better suited than any other to her own peculiar condition. I can readily understand how its king, lords and commons, with all the inequalities of its representation, may be well adapted to the Government of England, and yet neither of them be a fit model for our imitation. A mixed monarchy, for the Government of an insular people, surrounded by powerful nations, and under the necessity of maintaining expensive naval and military establishments, may find its strength and its efficacy in those very provisions, which, in a country like ours, would be justly regarded as intolerable defects. We could not here tolerate either its monarchy, its aristocracy, or the corruptions of its House of Commons.

But, the example of the House of Commons is quoted to prove that representation is founded on taxation. True, Sir, that at an early period of the English history, the independent spirit of that people contested with their monarch, the right of taxing them without their consent, and at last succeeded in maintaining that no contributions should be levied upon them, but such as were freely given in Parliament through their representatives. It is true, also, that the Knights and Burgesses, originally summoned by the monarch to vote supplies only, availed themselves of this power to extort from the throne, a participation, with the King and his nobles, in the legislation of the kingdom. But, what Monarch or noble Barons have we here, from whom to purchase, with our treasure, the right of legislation? And what peculiar connection can there be, between taxation and representation, in a country, where it is as much the settled doctrine that the people shall be bound by no laws made without their consent, as it is that they shall not be taxed without their consent? When you have established that the people cannot be taxed without the consent of themselves or their representatives, you have advanced no farther in ascertaining how representation is to be apportioned among the people, than when the broad principle is acknowledged that no law, affecting life, liberty, or property, is binding on the people without their consent. Surely, the example of the House of Commons can give no support to the proposition, that representation should be apportioned in any degree to taxation. The people of England never insisted, that each man should vote his own contribution, that the votes of their representatives should be valued according to the amount of their respective contributions, or that the several interests on which contributions were levied, should be represented, in the proportion of their wealth. The poorest borough, and the richest city, the largest and the smallest shire, has its representation, without any reference to wealth, amount of taxes or population. The forty counties in England, send each two members to Parliament, notwithstanding their great disparity in wealth and population, and the residue of the 513 members, furnished by England, are supplied by the large cities and the small boroughs without the least regard to their wealth, or their contributions to the Government: the large majority of them, are comparatively poor and insignificant, while some of them would scarcely be able to defray the expenses of their members during a single session, perhaps not able to pay for the wine drank by them at a single dinner. The great county of Middlesex, and its towns of London and Westminster send eight members to Parliament. If they were represented in proportion to their taxation, they would probably furnish a majority of the House of Commons. A statement made by Burgh, the great advocate of English reform, referred to, probably by the gentleman from Culpeper, (Mr. J. S. Barbour) shews that in the latter part of the seventeenth century, Middlesex and its towns paid 265 parts out of 513, of the whole land tax of the kingdom, permanent and annual; so that a proportionate representation would have given them a decided majority of the whole number of English members.

I cannot here forbear to remark, that gentlemen have seriously objected to the representation of numbers, because of its tendency to throw the power of Government into the hands of small populous districts, whose representatives, acting in concert, would exert an injurious influence over the legislation of the country. They tell us that Boston, or New York, or even Baltimore, represented in proportion to its numbers, would soon controul the councils of its State. And what is the remedy proposed for that evil? Instead of a salutary check, by limiting the representation in such overgrown districts; by anticipating the probable growth of the tide-water towns in wealth and population, and limiting their representation to a prescribed number, it is proposed to give them additional power in the Government, by adding their wealth to their numbers. The city of Richmond, which, upon the ratio of the white population, would be entitled, at this time, to one member only, would be entitled on the ratio of its taxes to more than four, and on the combined ratio to nearly three.

The principles of our revolution have been appealed to; and it has been supposed that the spirit of our fathers, which refused submission to taxes imposed by a Government, in which they were not represented, should inspire a just opposition to every scheme of representation, which was not apportioned, in some degree, to the amount of taxes imposed. If this, indeed, were the true principle of the revolution, is it not wonderful, how little regard was paid to it by the fathers of the revolution? That it did not find some conspicuous place in their Declarations of Rights, or have a controlling influence in the provisions of the Constitutions which they themselves formed? But do gentlemen seriously believe, that the war of the revolution originated in a desire to obtain a representation in the British Parliament, proportioned to our population, or, indeed, any representation at all? They certainly do not; for they ask us, almost in derision, what would have been the fate of a proposition from the British Parliament, to grant her colonies a representation in the House of Commons, proportionate to their population, on condition that they would submit to be taxed? I unite with the gentlemen in supposing, that our fathers had too much good sense, too much prudence and foresight, to have consented to surrender their own House of Burgesses, their own power of legislating for themselves, and taxing themselves, subject only to the royal negative, to have bound themselves indissolubly to a Government, acting at the distance of 3000 miles from them; to have sunk their consequence and their power, by becoming an integer of the British nation; and have abandoned forever, all hope of independence. I unite with them in believing that the proposition would have been rejected; and not less certainly would it have been rejected, if they had been offered a representation, proportioned to their population and taxes combined. The principles of the revolution teach us, that no people should be taxed by a Government, in which they are not represented; but they do not instruct us, that representation and taxation should bear any given ratio to each other. They would rather lead to the conclusion, that as representation is the organ, through which the public will acts upon the public interest, it should be proportioned with the sole view of fairly embodying that will.

Gentlemen, endeavoring to fortify themselves with authority, and seeming desirous to supply force by numbers, have invoked the Constitution of the United States, and of several States of the Union.

They suppose the Constitution of the United States, to furnish an example worthy of great respect; because, in apportioning representation among the several States, it has abandoned the guide of white population; has adopted the Federal number, which, in effect, gives representation to property, and has provided, that representatives and direct taxes, shall be apportioned, according to the same standard. Need I remark on the inconsistencies of gentlemen, who, while they quote the example of the Federal Constitution, lose no opportunity to reproach the Federal Government, with corruption and mal-administration?—who, while they hold up the provisions of that Constitution, as fit models for our imitation, take great pains to inform us, how utterly it has failed to attain the great ends of its adoption; how it has been wrested from its original purpose, and made the engine of injustice and oppression? No, Sir, I entertain too much respect for the Constitution of the United States, to allow myself to repel the argument drawn from it, by relying on the imputations which have been made on its practical operation. I regard it as one of the happiest efforts of human wisdom, prudence and foresight. Considering the intrinsic difficulty of the subject—the delicacy and importance of the interests to be adjusted—the jealousies to be soothed—the diversity of opinions to be consulted and harmonized—the opposing powers to be balanced—it is really wonderful how admirably the work has been performed, with how much fitness the means have been adapted to the end, and how much practical good has been attained. The errors and abuses in the Government, which certainly have not been few or trivial, and which deserve not to be excused or palliated, are incident to the imperfection of human institutions, and the incurable frailty of human nature, and ought not, perhaps, to be ascribed to any particular fault in the Constitution. To the example of this Constitution, then, I am willing to pay great deference and respect; but we must be careful not to misapply the example. We must recollect, that we are not the deputies of thirteen independent sovereignties, endeavouring to form a confederacy, and establish a Government, charged with its foreign relations, commercial and diplomatic, with the conduct of its wars, with the common defence, and with the preservation of peace and harmony among its several members—that we are not charged with the duty of surrendering a part, and retaining a part of the sovereignty of independent States—that we are the delegates of a single people, members of the same political society, owing an undivided allegiance to the same Government—living under a Constitution which acknowledges the right of the majority to reform—and now charged with the duty of making such reforms as will best assure a fair, just, and wise expression of the public will, on those measures of internal domestic legislation, which are intended to secure the property, liberty, and life of every citizen, and promote the prosperity and happiness of all.

It is obvious, then, that as the districts which we represent, have no separate independent sovereignty, none of them can impose a veto on our measures, none prescribe indispensible conditions of our action—while, in the Federal Convention, each State, even the smallest, could dictate the terms, on which alone it would be bound by the measures agreed upon. Whatever, therefore, we can fairly trace to that spirit of compromise and concession, which was indispensible to the success of the Federal Convention, will lose its authority here, in a discussion of what is right in principle—what will be just and wholesome in practice—what the majority ought in prudence to adopt. A little attention to the history of the Constitution of the United States, will show, I think, that the apportionment of representation among the several States, was the result of that spirit of compromise and concession.

When the articles of confederation were reported to the old Congress in July, 1776, they proposed that contributions to the General Government should be apportioned among the several States, in proportion to the whole number of inhabitants in each, and that each State should have an equal vote in the councils of the nation. Both these propositions were strenuously debated. It was agreed by all, that contributions should be in proportion to the wealth of the respective States—in proportion to their ability to pay—but there was great difference of opinion as to the measure of that wealth. The Southern members seriously contended, that the most accurate measure was the number of freemen; that slaves were property only, and no more a standard of wealth than cattle or other property; while the Northern members contended, that the whole number of inhabitants was the better measure; because, although slaves were property, they were productive labourers, and the labour of a country was the surest measure of its wealth. A member from Virginia suggested, that the labour of two slaves was not more than equivalent to the labour of one white man, and proposed that two slaves should be counted as one, in the apportionment of taxes:—And a member from Pennsylvania, Dr. Witherspoon, was of opinion, that the best measure of the wealth of a nation, was the value of its lands and houses. On the question of Suffrage, the smaller States insisted, it was due to their independence, and essential to their preservation, that they should each have an equal vote with the larger States, while the larger contended, that the vote of each State should be proportioned to the numbers represented in each, or if not, to the amount of their contributions. Mr. Wilson of Pennsylvania thought "that taxation should be in proportion to wealth, but that representation should accord with the number of freemen." These articles of confederation having been debated from time to time for two years, were adopted in July, 1778, making the value of lands and houses, the standard of contribution from the several States, and giving to each State an equal vote in Congress; the larger States thus surrendering their claim to power, as the price of that union which was indispensible to success to the common cause, in which the interests of all were embarked.

Experience soon demonstrated, that however just the standard of contribution which had been adopted, it was too expensive and inconvenient for political purposes. Remonstrances were presented against it, which resulted in a resolution of Congress to propose as a substitute for it, the apportionment of contributions, according to the federal number, in which the labour of five slaves is regarded as equal to the labour of three free men. This resolution was adopted in April 1783, and a committee consisting of Mr. Madison, Mr. Ellsworth, and Mr. Hamilton, was appointed to address a communication to the several States recommending it with other amendments to their adoption. In their address to the States, the Committee thus speaks of it: "This rule, although not free from objections, is liable to fewer than any other that could be devised. The only material difficulty which attended it, in the deliberations of Congress, *was to fix the proper difference, between the labour and industry of free inhabitants and of all other inhabitants.* The ratio ultimately agreed on, was the effect of mutual concession."

The substitute had been approved by eleven out of the thirteen States, but the concurrence of the other two not having been signified, and unanimity being necessary, it does not appear to have been adopted as an article of the confederation.

When the Federal Convention assembled in 1787, and had agreed to transfer to Congress the exclusive power over imposts and duties, almost the whole power of indirect taxation—there seems to have been no difficulty at all in regulating the proportions in which direct taxes should be levied in the several States. The Federal number, as recommended by Congress, and approved by eleven States, gave the obvious rule of apportionment, and I believe it was adopted without opposition. It was, however, an arduous task to regulate the power of the several States, in the new Government. Here arose the delicate and difficult questions, between sovereigns having equal rights, claiming equal power, but possessing unequal numbers, and unequal wealth:—The smaller States preferred again their claim to equal power—the larger, their's to a just apportionment; and among themselves, they differed as to the rule of apportionment, whether according to the whole number of inhabitants, the number of free inhabitants, or the amount of contributions. These conflicting claims, after protracted debate, presenting difficulties which threatened entire abortion to all the labours of the Convention, resulted in compromise. Mr. Wilson of Pennsylvania, who, in 1776, had expressed the opinion, that, while taxation should be in proportion to wealth, representation should accord with the number of freemen, proposed as the basis of representation in the House of Representatives, the Federal number, and recommended it, as having been approved, by eleven of the thirteen States, as the proper measure of contributions. It was acceded to by a majority, and submitted to by all, when the small States had been conciliated, by a provision, that each should have equal power in the Senate.

It is manifest, from this review, that the ratio of representation in Congress, was adjusted less upon considerations of what was just and right, in relation to the persons represented, or of what was wise and proper, for the protection of property, than upon principles of concession and compromise—and it follows, that the example cannot be proper for our imitation, till that day shall arrive; which, may God, in his mercy, forever avert!—when the large districts of our State, having separated from each other, and formed independent Governments, shall have sent deputies to form for them, a Federal Constitution.

That the apportionment of representation according to Federal numbers was not intended to afford protection to the slaves of the Southern States, is plainly to be inferred from the utter inadequacy of the means to the end. It could afford no such protection, because it left the five Southern States, the principal slave-holders, in a decided minority, in the House of Representatives, while they were in a still smaller minority in the Senate. The protection to that property, from the power of Congress, is to be found, in the absence of all authority to legislate concerning it, except by the imposition of taxes, and in the restraint upon the power to lay any capitation or other direct tax, unless in the proportion of the Federal numbers.

The provisions of the Constitution of the United States do not warrant the conclusion, that it was intended to apportion representation, in the popular branch of the Legislature, to the contributions of the respective States. The contributions of the States are drawn essentially from imposts and duties, and there is no attempt to apportion representation to them. It was manifest that the revenue from this source would furnish the ordinary income of the Government, and that direct taxes would be the subject only of occasional resort. Yet the representation is the same whether direct taxes are levied or not. In truth, direct taxes and representation are not apportioned to each other; they are only referred to a common standard, the Federal number, which is to govern the one always, whether the other exist or no, and govern that other casually when called into existence.

But suppose it conceded, that it was the object of the Federal Constitution to apportion representation and contributions, to each other; and conceded, moreover, that such apportionment was right upon principle; is there nothing due to the consideration, that while to the General Government is committed the conduct of our external relations alone, the State Governments have charge of all our internal affairs—while the Federal Government acts in the general upon great and common interests, and upon large masses, the State Governments act upon the minor sub-divided interests and upon each individual, in every relation which he bears to society? Is there no fair inference from this consideration, that while a representation apportioned to taxes, might fairly embody the public will, in the Federal Councils, and give sufficient protection to the various interests on which they act; a representation in proportion to the number of free men, might be required in Virginia, to express fairly the will of her people, to represent and protect all the various interests on which her Government continually acts?

The Constitutions of Massachusetts, New-Hampshire, South Carolina and Georgia, are referred to, as furnishing examples of a representation of property in Republican Governments; and the gentleman from Orange, (Mr. P. P. Barbour,) particularly commends to our attention the experience of Massachusetts, who, after thirty or forty years' trial of her Government, has approved this representation, by refusing to alter it, at a late revision of her Constitution. In Massachusetts, the representation in the Senate is based upon the ratio of taxes, with a provision that no district shall send more than six members; and in the House of Representatives, it is based on the number of taxable polls, each election district being entitled to one for the first one hundred and fifty polls, and one in addition for every two hundred and twenty-five above that number. The election districts are large, and have become populous, so that each is now entitled to many representatives—Boston, for example, to about seventy. But the districts are not required to elect the whole number; each sends such proportion of its whole delegation as it thinks proper—and generally they send but a small proportion of them. It is this Constitution which the experience of Massachusetts has not induced her to alter. Would any gentleman recommend the constitution of both branches of her Legislature, as a model for our imitation? Would he give to our election districts the power of electing from one to seventy members, as they thought fit? If he would not be governed by the experience of Massachusetts, as to one branch of her Legislature, why should he desire us to be governed by it, with respect to the other? But if we are to be governed by it, what does it teach us? Surely, not that a check upon the power of the people, should be introduced into the popular branch of the Legislature, by giving representation to property there; but that such check should be introduced into the Senate: it teaches us to reject the amendment of the gentleman from Culpeper, which it has been invoked to support.

The Constitution of New-Hampshire is similar to that of Massachusetts, and requires no particular commentary. That of South Carolina has been most relied on, as furnishing a more appropriate example. South Carolina, a slave-holding State, by her Constitution adopted in the year 1790, had a prescribed number of Representatives and Senators from each election district, not varying with the changes of population, and not apportioned thereto. In 1803, the constitution of her House of Representatives was changed, by introducing into it the precise compound basis, now proposed to us by the gentleman from Culpeper—the Senate was left as formerly, composed of a prescribed number of members from each election district. The precedent, as it regards the popular branch of the Legislature, seems to be in point, and how far we shall respect its authority, it is for the good sense of this Committee to decide. The slave population, I learn, abounded in the lower districts of South Carolina, as it does in the lower districts of Virginia; there, as here, the slave population was small in the Western districts, the white population rapidly increasing—its representation very unequal—the people of those districts insisting on a more equal representation—and the people of the Eastern districts fearing, that if the power passed into the hands of the Western people, their property would be endangered. The Eastern districts anticipating the time when they would not be able to resist the demands of the growing population of the West, and availing themselves of their great ascendancy in both branches of the Legislature, adopted the amendment which fixed the basis of representation in the popular branch upon the compound basis of taxes and white population. Their Constitution authorised amendments, by majorities of two-thirds of both Houses of the Legislature, at two successive sessions. It was by such a concurrent vote that this amendment was adopted, and there can be no stronger evidence of the ascendancy which at that time the Eastern districts had in the Legislature. That an overwhelming majority then, should have imposed such terms upon the minority, can, in my humble judgment, furnish no good reason, why the minority here should impose like terms upon a majority. But the subsequent history of South Carolina furnishes the strongest refutation of the argument which upheld the policy of this measure there, and now recommends it to us; for, notwithstanding this expedient of the compound basis, the political power, in the popular branch of the Legislature, has passed from the Eastern slave-holders to the Western freemen, and yet the Government proceeds in perfect harmony, and I am well informed, that danger to the property of the East, is in no wise threatened, and is no longer feared. Why then should danger be feared, from permitting the Western freemen of Virginia, to acquire political power in the popular branch of the Virginia Legislature?

By the Constitution of Georgia, adopted in 1798, their Senate is composed of one member from each county, and their House of Representatives has a graduated representation based upon the Federal number. How this operates in the practical distribution of power, or upon the interests of society, we are not informed. We cannot therefore appreciate the example.

But, if this question were tried by the example of our sister States, surely the weight of authority would greatly preponderate against the limitation which is proposed, upon the power of the free inhabitants. Among the slave-holding States, while Maryland and North Carolina have a county representation without regard to numbers, Louisiana has its House of Representatives apportioned according to the qualified voters, and a Senate with fixed numbers from prescribed districts—Kentucky, its representatives apportioned to the qualified electors, and Senate to the free male inhabitants above twenty-one years—Mississippi has representatives apportioned to free white inhabitants, her Senators to the free white taxable inhabitants—Alabama has both Houses based upon free white inhabitants—Missouri, both based upon free white male inhabitants—and Tennessee upon the *taxable* inhabitants—that is, as I am well informed, free inhabitants, on whom taxes may be imposed. Here are six slave-holding States, in most, if not all of which, the slave population is very unequally distributed. In none of them has it been deemed necessary to protect their slaves by restraints on the power of the free inhabitants, and in none of them do we learn that there has been the least cause to apprehend any danger to this property from the exercise of that power. Of these States, Kentucky and Tennessee has each had between thirty and forty years' experience.

In States where there are no slaves, and where political power is distributed among the different districts essentially in proportion to the number of inhabitants, we have the examples of Pennsylvania, New-York, Ohio, Indiana and Illinois, in which there has been no attempt to guard property by giving it representation. In the old Constitution of New-York, there was a distinction made between the qualification of voters for members of the two Houses; a higher property qualification being required for the voter in elections to the Senate; but this has been abandoned in the recent change of their Constitution.

I profess, however, Mr. Chairman, to pay but little respect to any of the examples from the Constitutions of our sister States, quoted on the one side or the other. None of them can be very well understood by us; all of them have been subjected to the test of but a span of time, compared with the life of nations; and all of them are taken from the infancy of our institutions, where our sparse population, the facility of acquiring property, and our agricultural pursuits, secure to us more virtue, and more freedom from temptation, than, in future times, we can reasonably hope to enjoy.

Having disposed of the precedents which are supposed to bear on the question in debate, let us consider the two propositions with reference to their practical operation—and in approaching this subject, I must express my deep regret at the appeal which has been made to the spirit of party politics. We are told by the gentleman from Chesterfield, that one of the objects of this Convention is to change the policy of this State in reference to the measures of the General Government; and he has endeavored to alarm the party politician, with the apprehension that his favorite doctrine of State Rights would be endangered, by a transfer of power from the East to the West. Mr. Chairman, has not the subject under consideration intrinsic difficulties enough? Are there not prejudices, naturally, perhaps inseparably belonging to it, which present almost insuperable obstacles to candid discussion, to just and wise conclusions respecting it? Shall we, by invoking the demon of party spirit, multiply these difficulties, inflame these prejudices, bring discord into our ranks, and confusion to our councils? Has it come to this—that public opinion is to be controlled, by retaining political power in the hands of the minority? Do our brethren of the East mean to deny us freedom of opinion respecting the affairs of the General Government? Do they insist upon the privilege of thinking for us, as well as legislating for us? The generous feelings of my friend from Chesterfield, when the excitement of ardent debate has subsided, will disclaim, I am sure, all aid from blind party zeal; and I trust that this Committee will not for a moment submit to its influence.

It has been objected to the resolution of the Select Committee, that by transferring the power to the West, it will endanger the basis of representation in the House of Representatives of the United States; that is to say, that if the basis of white population should be established for the House of Delegates, the people of the West, following the precedent, will insist on arranging the Congressional districts in this State upon the same basis, instead of the basis of Federal numbers, upon which they have heretofore been arranged. I do not believe, Sir, that any such danger exists; the propriety of arranging the Congressional districts upon the Federal basis is so obvious, and has been so long practised, that I do not believe the change would ever be attempted. But if you fear it, provide against it in the Constitution, by an express declaration that the Federal number shall forever govern in arranging these districts. But the gentleman from Fauquier tells us, he does not know that such a provision would be regarded as obligatory; he does not know but that the Constitution of the United States would be appealed to as paramount to the authority of the State Constitution on this subject. Does the gentleman from Fauquier entertain the least doubt that such a provision in our Constitution would be obligatory? Can he doubt that the State Legislature is imperiously bound by the State Constitution, in all things not contrary to the Federal Constitution? And can he find any thing in the Constitution of the United States upon which to rest a doubt, that it is lawful to prescribe that the districts for electing members to Congress, shall be formed upon the basis which the Constitution of the United States itself has established for the whole representation of the State. If we are to be driven from the path of duty by such scepticism, our labours are at an end; for, why prescribe a qualification of suffrage? The gentleman from Fauquier does not know that in this age of metaphysical abstraction, it will be held obligatory upon the people. Why prescribe any basis of representation at all? The gentleman from Fauquier does not know that the Legislature will hold it obligatory upon them. Let us not, Sir, deliver ourselves up to the blind guidance of what we do not know; but rather let us be governed by what we do know or might know, if we would consult our reason. We ought to know, that it is our duty to settle this question of representation without influence from imaginary dangers. We ought to know that the Legislature of Virginia would never incur the risk of losing its whole representation in Congress, by electing all its members in direct violation of the State Constitution; that they would never incur the reproach of mankind by so palpable a violation of duty.

We are threatened with another danger, in relation to the Federal Government, from adopting the basis of white population. We are told that if Virginia, the largest Southern State, disregards her slave population, in apportioning representation in the State Legislature, it will weaken the argument, by which the Southern States support their right to representation for that property, in the Government of the United States, and may endanger the loss of power, which that representation gives us.

It should be recollected, that the power which this population gives us, in the General Government, does not rest upon argument, but upon compact—was not allowed us upon principle, but upon compromise—and cannot be taken away from us, but by a total departure from the spirit of the compromise and an amendment of the compact agreed to by three-fourths of the States, in the Union—and the gentleman from Loudoun (Mr. Mercer) has shown how utterly impracticable any such amendment would be. But, Sir, this argument, that the slave population was not regarded in the representation of those States where slavery existed, was in full force when the Constitution of the United States was adopted—it was then urged and repelled. The argument is noticed, in the fifty-fourth number of Publius. The fact on which it rests is admitted, and the argument ably repelled by a clear exposition of "the compromising expedient of the Constitution"—"which regards the slave as divested of two-fifths of the man." By adopting the basis of white population, then, we furnish to our adversaries no new and fearful argument—but we leave the old refuted argument in the quiet grave which has covered it for forty years.

We come now to consider this question, with reference to the protection of property. By adopting the basis of white population, shall we expose to danger that peculiar property, in which the Eastern districts have so deep an interest? I am perfectly satisfied, Mr. Chairman, that you would more effectually protect this property by granting us the simple basis, than by imposing on us the compound basis, proposed by the gentleman from Culpeper. Let us attentively and impartially examine this question.

The whole danger apprehended, rests upon the supposition, that the basis of white population will carry the power of the Government into the hands of those, who will be, comparatively, but little interested in this property: And if it can be shown, that this supposition is not correct, then it must be admitted, that the danger is unreal. I do not believe that it is correct—and will submit to your candid consideration, the reason of that opinion.

I have already shown you, that taking the Auditor's estimates of the present population, and apportioning the representation according to the whole white population, there would be a majority of eight members in the House of Delegates, on the East of the Blue Ridge; and apportioning it according to the qualified voters, there would probably be a majority of twenty. If the basis of qualified voters should be adopted, there is no definite period of time, within the present century or the next, at which any person could say, with confidence, that this majority of twenty would be overcome, by the increasing population of the West. Indeed, it is very doubtful whether the majority of qualified voters will ever be West of the Blue Ridge. Any one, who will carefully examine this subject, in his closet, with reference to the tables of population; the number of square miles in each district; the quantity of mountain and arable land in each; their capacity to sustain population; their distance from market; the probable growth of their towns; the pursuits of their people, whether commercial, manufacturing, or agricultural; planting, farming, or grazing; will, I think, be satisfied, that if that time should ever come, it is too distant to have the least influence on our deliberations.

The period is not so distant when the majority of the white population, will probably be West of the Blue Ridge; but when that period will arrive, is exceedingly uncertain. The tables of population show us, that the relative increase of the different districts, heretofore, has been very irregular; and we shall find our calculations of their future increase, in a great measure conjectural. The ratio of increase of the white population, from the year 1790 to the present time, appears by these tables, to be as follows:

In the first district, from	1790 to 1800	83 3-4 per cent.
	1800 to 1810	47 per cent.
	1810 to 1820	27 1-2 per cent.
	1820 to 1829	36 1-5 per cent.
In the second district, from	1790 to 1800	20 per cent.
	1800 to 1810	3-4 per cent.
	1810 to 1820	11 3-4 per cent.
	1820 to 1829	14 3-4 per cent.
In the third district, from	1790 to 1800	11 1-2 per cent.
	1800 to 1810	1 per cent.
	1810 to 1820	3-4 per cent.
	1820 to 1829	5 3-10 per cent.
In the fourth district, from	1790 to 1800	2 per cent.
	1800 to 1810	1-4 per cent.
	1810 to 1820	5 1-2 per cent.
	1820 to 1829	2 2-5 per cent.

Thus you see, that in the Western district, the ratio having decreased between the years 1790, and 1820, from 83¾ per cent. to 27½—appears by the Auditor's estimate to have risen in the last nine years, to 36 1-5 per cent. which is equivalent to 40 per cent. for ten years—this may be owing to some error in the Auditor's estimate, or it may perhaps be accounted for, upon the supposition that emigration from that district diminished, within the last nine years, and migration to it increased. It is certainly, however, not according to the usual course of things, that the ratio of increase in a newly settled country should rise, as the population becomes more dense.

You will observe, that the Valley district having remained nearly stationary for ten years from 1800 to 1810, increased 11¾ per cent. for the next ten years, and 14 2-5 per cent. for the last nine: that the middle district remaining nearly stationary for twenty years, from 1800 to 1820, appears to have increased upwards of 5 per cent. for the last nine; and that the tide-water district being nearly stationary for twenty years from 1790 to 1810, increased in the next ten years 5½ per cent., and in the last nine, about 2½ per cent.

There can be no doubt, that these irregularities proceed in a great degree from the difference of emigration from all the districts in the State, fast diminishing, as the Western States and territories are becoming populous, and Western lands rising in price. The time, therefore, is probably not distant when the increase of our population will be left chiefly to its natural causes, and when the ratio in each district will be nearly the same.

I have made a calculation of the probable white population of the several districts, in the year 1850, upon the supposition, that the Auditor's estimates are correct, that the Western district will increase 20 per cent. for the next ten years, and 10 per cent. for the succeeding ten; that the Valley district will increase 10 per cent. for each period of ten years; and that the two Eastern districts will increase 5 per cent. for each period of ten years. The result of this calculation is, that in the year 1850, the white population of the Western district, would be about 234,000—that of the Valley 167,000—of the middle district 217,000—and the tide-water district 178,000—giving to the West of the Blue Ridge, about 406,000, and to the East, about 395,000. This I am persuaded is a calculation more liberal to the West than they are entitled to, and it results in giving them a small majority of white population in 1850. From thenceforward they can have no reason to expect that their population would increase more rapidly than that of the East. Look for a moment at the comparative extent of the two districts, and at some of the causes which would affect the increase of their population.

The two districts West of the Blue Ridge, contain 38,896 square miles:—the two East of the Ridge, contain 26,774 square miles. Considering the vast extent of mountains beyond the Blue Ridge, it would be giving to the West a most liberal estimate of its arable lands, to suppose them equal in quality to the arable lands East of the mountains. Reflect, then, on the circumstance, that the whole lands of the East must be always employed in planting and farming, while a very large proportion of those of the West, the whole extensive district from the North Mountain to the Western boundary, with the exception only of those narrow valleys which lie convenient to the navigable waters, must for ages to come, be in the hands of the grazier:—recollect too, that if we should ever have large towns and extensive manufactories, they will seek the marts of foreign commerce, and probably be found about the falls of the Eastern rivers—and I think you will find strong reason to believe, that the Eastern side of the mountain will always maintain a greater population than the West, and can never be much inferior to it in white population.

I have heard it said, that the Eastern districts contain already, nearly as much population as they could sustain. Nothing can be more erroneous. The middle district, counting all its inhabitants, has a population of about twenty-eight, and the tide-water district, a population of about thirty-two, to the square mile. Compare this with the population of older countries. In 1811, Scotland had a population of about sixty-four—Wales, seventy-nine—England, one hundred and ninety-six, to the square mile—France, about the beginning of this century, had a population of one hundred and seventy-nine, to the square mile. Can any one doubt, that the country between the Blue Ridge and the ocean, is capable of sustaining more population than Scotland or Wales:—and can any good reason be assigned, why it may not be as populous as England or France?

If I am right in my estimate of the future progress of white population, and we can be satisfied, that in the course of twenty years, there will be a few populous counties beyond the mountains, essentially slave-holding counties, having a kindred interest with the East, in the good government of that property, and its exemption from unjust burthens, then you have assurance that the basis of white population will not carry the power of the Government, into unfriendly hands.

Referring again to our tables, we find that the tide of slave population has been setting strongly to the West, and that it is now swelled to its greatest height, at the very base of the Blue Ridge: That in due time, it will find its level through the passes of that mountain, there can be little reason to doubt. We have seen by how much the slave population exceeds the white population, in the two Eastern districts, and by how much it falls short, in the two Western. Let us now see what has been the ratio of increase, from 1790, to the present time. It stands thus:

In the first district, from	1790 to 1800—138 per cent.
	1800 to 1810—65 1-2 per cent.
	1810 to 1820—46 per cent.
	1820 to 1829—28 1-2 per cent.
In the second district, from	1790 to 1800—40 1-2 per cent.
	1800 to 1810—31 1-4 per cent.
	1810 to 1820—25 1-2 per cent.
	1820 to 1829—12 1-5 per cent.
In the third district, from	1790 to 1800—28 1-2 per cent.
	1800 to 1810—20 3-4 per cent.
	1810 to 1820—10 3-4 per cent.
	1820 to 1829—7 7-10 per cent.
In the fourth district, from	1790 to 1800—6 1-4 per cent.
	1800 to 1810—4 per cent.
	1810 to 1820—1 1-4 per cent.
	1820 to 1829—loss of 13-100 of one per cent.

You find then, that, while in the tide-water district the slave population is rather decreasing, it is increasing in the middle district by a much smaller ratio than in the Valley and the Western districts. You perceive too, until within the last nine years, the increase in the Valley and Western district has been very rapid. A strong reason why, within that time, the increase has not been so great in those districts, may be found in the depressed prices of agricultural products. For the last ten or twelve years, the products of the farming districts have scarcely been of value sufficient to justify their transportation to distant markets. In consequence of this, farmers of the Valley, and no doubt of other Western districts, have become graziers, and the labour of slaves has been less in demand. The price of tobacco has been better sustained than the price of other agricultural products—it better bears the expense of transportation to market; and this has kept up the demand for the labour of slaves, in the planting districts of the middle country. This too, is fostering the culture of tobacco in some of the Valley counties, where it is grown of fine quality, and to much advantage; and will, no doubt, extend its culture very considerably in the Western districts. As the demand for slaves in the Southern States of the Union diminishes, and their laws restraining the importation of them, become more rigid—as the tobacco lands of the middle district decrease, and the tobacco culture in the Western districts is extended; and as the products of the farming districts shall become more valuable; the demand for the labour of slaves will diminish in the middle districts, and increase in the Western; the price of them will become lower, the Western man will be more able to purchase them, and the Western country will be sure to possess them, in large numbers. In Rockbridge, where the culture of tobacco has been lately introduced, the slave population has increased about 33 1-3 *per cent.* in the last nine years, and in Botetourt, where the plant has been longer and more extensively cultivated, the slave population has increased more than an hundred *per cent.* in the same time. These two counties together, have a white population of 20,927, and slave population of 7,592. It cannot be doubted, that in twenty years, they will be essentially slave-holding counties; and their white population, added to that of the East, in the year 1850, will cast the balance of power decidedly in its favour. But many other counties of the West, and among them, the rich and populous counties of Frederick and Jefferson, under the influence of the causes I have referred to, must, in the course of twenty years, have so strong an interest in the slave population, as to insure their co-operation in its protection. Nearly one-third of the population of these two counties is, at this time, slaves. Their aggregate white population is upwards of 27,000; their aggregate slaves, upwards of 11,000.

These are some of the reasons which have satisfied my mind, that the power of the Government, under the influence of the basis of white population, will abide with the slave-holders.

But, suppose I should be mistaken; suppose the ratio of white and slave population to continue as it is, and that the basis of white population would transfer the power of the Government to the West, would you secure protection to the interests in the slave property, by rejecting this basis, and imposing on us the compound basis? I think not.

If by conceding to the Western people, a right which has been so long, and, as they think, so injuriously withheld from them, by this manifestation of generous confidence in them, by thus acknowledging them really as brethren, equal with you in right, you could not inspire a feeling of affection and sentiment of justice, on which some reliance might be placed; if you could not trust to their general though deep interest, in maintaining the rights of property, and the peace and good order of society; if you could not accept the justice of your own Government, your own forbearance to invade their property for more than fifty years, as evidence, that they too will govern justly, and will respect your property; if you must act upon the distrust, which the known frailty of human nature prompts, upon the apprehension, that large masses of men, acting together, cannot resist the temptation of large masses of property, exposed to their power, then, there are other considerations which deserve your most serious attention.

Let it be once openly avowed and adopted as a principle of your Constitution, that the price which the Western people must pay for the protection of your slaves, is the surrender of their power in the Government, and you render that property hateful to them in the extreme, and hold out to them the strongest of all possible temptations to make constant war upon it, to render it of no value to you, and to induce you to part with it. A large district of your country, marked out by a geographical line, containing a large minority of the freemen of the country, and expected soon to contain the majority; having a large representation in both branches of your Legislature, where its voice can be constantly heard, and its complaints will be perpetually poured forth; this district is to be placed under the ban of the Empire, and its people to be told, that your slaves exclude them from the pale of authority. I will not say, you will madden them into acts of violence or disloyalty, by such a measure—I believe it not—the people of the West, though zealous and persevering in pursuit of their rights, are in general an industrious and contented people, as obedient to the law, as prudent and as loyal as any people under the sun. But will you not make them zealots on that subject, on which your right of property depends, and which is so intimately connected with your domestic peace? Will you not drive them to seek allies among your own people, associates in the measures, which are necessary to remove the obstacle that stands in their road to power?

Unless I am deceived, very grossly deceived, Mr. Chairman, they would find many and ardent auxiliaries, in the bosom of your own society. How many are there, who owning none of this property, and doomed to the laborious offices of life, feel a sort of degradation in being compelled to perform them in common with the slave, and a sentiment of envy towards their owners? How many who professing conscientious scruples, are even now continually propagating doctrines, which tend to insubordination? Remember too, Sir, that the Right of Suffrage will be extended. How many of this class of auxiliaries, will be brought to the polls by this extension, remains yet to be known. But I put it to the sober judgment of the Eastern Statesman to say, whether he can feel security against the combined action of the whole Western country, and all the discontented of the East, when you shall have established the compound basis, and materially extended the Right of Suffrage? Sir, nothing in my estimation can be more unwise, or threaten more serious mischief, than the united operation of these two causes. You cannot with safety extend the Right of Suffrage materially, and force upon us the compound basis.

But, if the evil I have hinted at should not follow, what then? Will the people of the West sit down tamely under the privation of even a portion of the power which they now enjoy? Will the majority of the freemen of the country, who share the political power, acquiesce in the rule of the minority, under the persuasion that while the minority would have virtue and wisdom enough to protect the property and secure all the rights of the majority, that majority could not be trusted with power over the property of the minority? This is impossible. A Constitution founded upon such a principle would not last ten years. There would be no rebellion, no civil war, no blood-shed. The peaceful remedy is in the hands of the people, and they will employ it. You do not mean to disavow the doctrine, that the majority may reform the Constitution. You have already, by an unanimous vote, sanctioned this doctrine in agreeing to the resolution, that the Bill of Rights required no alteration. Your new Constitution then is to be sent forth, with a proscription against the majority, and with an invitation to the majority to alter, reform or abolish. Will not this invitation be most certainly accepted? The qualified voters, with the increased power which the extension of the Right of Suffrage will give them, will make themselves heard at the polls, and heard in your halls of legislation. Do not flatter yourself, Sir, that your majorities in the Legislature can resist the petitions of a dreaded majority, earnestly pressed, and long persevered in. Your new voters will sympathise with them and not with you—they will owe their power principally to the people of the West, and they will not regard your power as necessary to their protection. If your own constituents do not take part against you, nevertheless, you will be compelled to yield, as the Legislature has heretofore yielded to the force of public opinion—and another Convention will be called to do that which you now refuse to do. The surrender of your power may then come too late, to allay the animosities which the protracted controversy will have inflamed, heal dissention, soothe wounded feeling, inspire confidence, and cement the bond of union among the people of the Commonwealth.

Why then will you persist in contending for that which it is so hazardous to possess, so impossible to retain? Better, far better is it, in my humble opinion, to turn your attention to that which is practicable, safe, enduring and effectual—to the prudent limitation of the Right of Suffrage. This is a ground on which we could meet and confer together, I should hope, with some prospect of settling at once the basis of political power, and the mode of apportioning it. Let the qualifications of suffrage be judiciously defined, and the basis of representation be the ratio of qualified voters. I have shown you how such a provision accords with the principles of our Government, how mildly it would operate in the distribution of power, how perfectly secure it would leave our rights of property.

It is to the qualifications of suffrage, Mr. Chairman, that we must look for the essential character of our Government, for the security of all our rights, and especially for the protection of our property. Hold in steady view the word and the spirit of the Bill of Rights—admit to the enjoyment of political power, those, and if possible those only, who "have sufficient evidence of permanent common interest with, and attachment to, the community"—and you have the best security that we can devise for the protection of our property and our rights—you have the bond which gentlemen have demanded, founded in self-interest and self-love. I am not so visionary as to suppose, that human wisdom can devise a rule of suffrage, which would include all, who have, and exclude all, who have not, the requisite interest in the community and attachment to it. But there can be no doubt, by a careful attention to the circumstances, which indicate *permanency* of interest, *community* of interest, *attachment* to the country, much might be done, to exclude the unworthy, and to commit the political power, to the great body of the people, who must look to the good government and prosperity of the country, for the prosperity and happiness of themselves individually, their families and their posterity. Let your qualification of property be fixed with no view to aristocratic pride and distinction; let it be fixed so low, that the industrious of all classes, professions and callings, may acquire it in a few years of persevering labour; and so high as to be out of the reach of the habitually idle, who in all stations of life, are habitually worthless. Whether it be of real or personal property—real I should prefer—let it be certain, simple, easy to understand, and convenient in practice. Such a safeguard for property, as this, would be permanent; it would not array the great districts of your State against each other; and could not produce any serious discontent. What excluded class would oppose it? Not our slaves—their masters will keep them better employed; nor our children—the discipline of the rod, will secure their allegiance; not our daughters—Heaven bless their maidenly modesty!—they would not for the world be suspected of desiring power; nor our wives, who would be perfectly contented, that their husbands should give their votes for them; nor yet those, who are no longer wives; for they will have been taught, in Heaven's best school, the vanity of human power, and the necessity of seeking happiness in devotion. No other classes, but the aliens and free coloured, are excluded, and from them, nobody has any apprehension. All besides who are excluded, are individuals belonging to all classes, who are for the time without the requisite qualification. The industrious young man, whether a cultivator of the soil, a merchant or mechanic, whether lawyer, doctor or divine, who is engaged in laying the foundations of his fortune, and who looks with confidence, as every industrious man in this community may, to the time when he shall have acquired a comfortable subsistence for himself and his family, and with it the qualification of suffrage—can he now complain that he must for a few years submit to that exclusion which has been deemed necessary to secure him the profits of his own labour, the protection of the property he is endeavoring to acquire? The sons of freeholders, who have not yet come to the possession of the estates which their fathers have in keeping for them, and have earned none of their own—they surely cannot complain, that while they depend upon their fathers for property, they should depend on them also for its government. Can the imprudent or the unfortunate, who have lost their property, and with it their right of suffrage, complain that they are not permitted to participate in the management of public affairs, when they have been so unsuccessful in the conduct of their private estates, as to be left without the qualification of a voter? With still less reason, could the idle man, whether young or old, who had acquired no property, and was pursuing no means to acquire any, complain that he was not permitted to share in the government of that society, to which he contributed nothing better than the evil example of his bad habits. It is very manifest, that among all these various descriptions of excluded persons, there could be no bond of sympathy, no union of action—and that from their discontents, if they had no rallying point of real grievance, no organized corps of dissatisfied voters to conduct their opposition, society would have nothing to apprehend.

There is but a single point of view in which the connexion of the basis of representation with the Right of Suffrage, as I have suggested, would seem to threaten mischief. If the qualified voters in the several districts were made the standard of their power, the extension of the Right of Suffrage, as it would probably vary the ratio of qualified voters, might become a question of power between the different districts. I have been fully aware of this consequence, and it induced me to hesitate in proposing the connexion. But I have been encouraged to hope that this very expedient may be made the means of settling the question of suffrage here more satisfactorily than it could otherwise be settled. And if adjusted here to the satisfaction of both parties, I should have no fears of future consequences. No general discontent could possibly be excited among the people upon this subject—at least not for years to come. The influence of the extension of the Right of Suffrage, upon the relative power of the several districts, will diminish hereafter, in the exact proportion, that the slave population shall become more equally distributed through the State—and if I am right in my calculations upon this subject, the extension of the Right of Suffrage, as a question of relative power, will be every day losing its interest. I should hope then, Sir, that this question would engage the serious attention of gentlemen on both sides.

Mr. J. proceeded to discuss the subject of internal improvements, but being much fatigued, he gave way to a motion of Mr. Stanard for the Committee to rise, (Mr. J. stating that he should scarcely expect to detain the Committee more than fifteen minutes on the following day.)

The Committee rose, and immediately on Mr. Leigh's motion, the Convention adjourned.

FRIDAY, November 13, 1829.

The Convention met at 11 o'clock, and was opened with prayer by the Rev. Mr. Hoorner of the Catholic Church.

Having again resolved itself into a Committee of the Whole, Mr. Powell in the Chair,

Mr. Johnson resumed and concluded his speech in favor of the resolution reported by the Legislative Committee, and in opposition to the amendment of Mr. Green, proposing a mixed basis of representation. He said, that

Another subject, on which gentlemen express great apprehensions of danger, from transferring the power of the Government to the majority, is that of internal improvements. They fear that expensive schemes of improvement will be adopted, in which the Eastern districts have little, if any interest; and which, if successful, will be principally beneficial to the West, while the expense will be chiefly defrayed from taxes levied in the East.

In considering this question, Mr. Chairman, I do not feel myself at all called upon to vindicate the Western people from any imputation upon their motives or character. If any such had been made, it would have been so entirely gratuitous, that it could not have required an answer. But none such has been made. Gentlemen have explicitly disclaimed all personal distrust of the Western people—all imputation upon them. They have reasoned from the known character of man, from the ordinary motives and influences of human action. The correctness of their reasoning alone I controvert; its candor and liberality I cheerfully admit. I do not believe that the danger apprehended exists, nor do I think that if it did, it would be avoided by the means proposed.

I do not hesitate, in the outset, to avow myself a decided friend of the policy of internal improvement; not, Sir, a system of internal improvement forced upon us by the Government of the United States, without our consent, and without our authority—a system less suited perhaps for making roads and canals, than for making Presidents and Secretaries—less used for the purpose of facilitating transportation from one part of the country to another, than for the purpose of transferring popularity from one set of politicians to another. I advocate the policy of internal improvement conducted by our own internal Government, for the *bona fide* purpose of lessening the expense of transportation, facilitating the intercourse between distant places, increasing the value of our property, and with it the wealth and resources of the State. I am no friend of any system conducted, no matter by what authority, which robs one man's purse to improve another man's land. I think that no improvement ought ever to be undertaken, unless the local districts immediately benefitted by it will bear a tax, in the form of tolls or otherwise, adequate at least to pay a reasonable interest upon the money expended in its execution; and that Government ought never to advance its money or credit for the purpose of such improvement, without the best assurances that such return can be made, and exacting an adequate toll on transportation, or tax upon the district. With these limitations, which, cautiously observed, would guard every part of the State from unjust burthens, I think that the best interests of the country require the patronage of the Government, in the improvement of its roads and rivers.

The policy of internal improvement, Mr. Chairman, is not an invention of the West for enriching themselves, and impoverishing their neighbours. It is the policy of the Statesman and the Patriot. It was recommended to us in Virginia, by the father of his country; and has found its most zealous and distinguished advocates, in the Eastern districts. When adverse circumstances had thrown it into some discredit, darkened its prospects, and damped the spirits of its friends—who, I ask, were foremost in their efforts, to vindicate its character and re-animate its hopes? Let the meeting at Charlottesville during the past year answer this question—a meeting invited by a voice from the lowlands, attended by a few members from the West, and many from the East of the Blue Ridge, whose presiding officer was the distinguished member of this Convention from the county of Orange, once the President of the United States, and among whose most active members were the President of this Convention, the Chief Justice of the United States, the gentleman from Chesterfield, and other very distinguished Eastern men, now members of this Convention.

Let us look on the map of the State and see what part of the country is directly interested in the policy of internal improvement. Its narrowest limits will be found prescribed, by the Potomac on the North, the Ohio on the West, the line of North Carolina on the South, and the head of tide-water on the East. Add to this extensive district the towns of Norfolk, Petersburg, Richmond, Fredericksburg and Alexandria, with the counties adjoining them, in which the direct interest is quite as manifest as in any other part of the State, and you leave but a very small district, not directly interested in this subject. But in truth, Sir, the interest of internal improvement pervades the whole Commonwealth. The tide-water country, which requires no improvement in its roads and rivers, has an important interest in the improvement of its markets. Whatever will increase the population, the wealth, the mercantile capital of their market towns, must enhance the value of every acre of their lands. And permit me to suggest, that under a prudent system of internal improvement, patronised by the Government, the benefits to the tide-water country, though they might not be so great, would be more certain, and the risk of loss less, than to the immediate district in which the improvement might be made. Suppose, for example, the Government to borrow the money necessary for completing the James river improvement, and to provide by law for a tax on the land, or a toll on the products of the James river district to meet the interest on the loan—in this case, the whole risk incurred by the tide-water country is, that the means employed to pay the interest on the loan may not be effectual—and this risk they encounter, in common with the James river district and every other part of the State. If the improvement should succeed, that would secure the means of paying the interest on the loan, and lay a sure foundation for the prosperity of their principal market town; and thus, without paying one dollar for it, the tide-water country connected with Richmond would enjoy the benefit of an improved market.

And what would the James River district enjoy? The benefit of an improved market, it is true, and of improved transportation—but subject to the tax necessary to pay the interest on the loan. It would depend entirely upon the comparative value of this tax, and of these benefits, whether the James River interest would be promoted or injured, by the successful improvement. If the tax were equivalent to the diminution of freight resulting from the improvement, then the James River interest would have gained nothing; if more than equivalent, it would be injured; and it would be benefitted only in the event, that the saving of freight would be more than equivalent to the tax imposed. This interest then would incur the double risk of loss—first, by the failure of the improvement; secondly, by having to pay for it more than it was worth. Apply this illustration to all our navigable streams which require improvement, to the towns connected with them, and the country interested in their markets, and you will perceive how essentially the interest in a well-conducted system of internal improvement, is an interest of the Commonwealth, and how unwise it would be to regard it as a partial interest, and to excite local jealousies concerning it. Considering it in this light too, you will acknowledge the injustice of regarding it as the means of taxing one part of the Commonwealth for the benefit of the other. Indeed, the very moment you adopt the principle of making the local districts pay the interest upon the expenditure, and hold their lands mortgaged for the payment, you secure from those districts the utmost practicable caution in all their plans of improvement; you make them as careful in accepting loans, as the State should be in granting them, and you give to the agency of the Government its true paternal character, employed in assisting the prudent and solvent members of its family in laying the foundations of their fortune.

But it is not to such a system that the objections of gentlemen on the other side apply. Most of them, I doubt not, would be its patrons. They fear the operations of a different system, one which, whatever might be its object, would result in throwing the expenses of every great improvement upon the State at large, while its profits would be partially enjoyed. Let us then examine whether this would be the probable consequence of adopting the basis of white population, and whether it would be avoided by the compound basis.

When danger is apprehended from the prevalence of local interests against the interests of the State, the most obvious inquiry is, whether any one local interest, or any combination of them, can probably command the power of the Government. Looking to the divisions of our State, with reference to the various interests in the subject of internal improvement, you will find the general interest guarded against the local power, by more natural ramparts, than were ever created upon the face of any country on earth, capable of half the improvement to which ours so strongly invites. It is this very capacity for improvement, the numerous objects which so strongly solicit it, that constitute the real difficulty in our system—and present almost an insuperable barrier to any improvement at all.

The country East of the Alleghany, and above tide-water, is divided into three great interests, the Potomac, the James River, and the Roanoke, and two subordinate; those of the Rappahannock and Appomattox, not to mention the yet smaller interest of the Pamunkey. The trans-Alleghany interest might be associated in part with the three greater interests in plans of very extensive improvement, but as to all minor objects would be sub-divided, with reference to its own navigable streams. An inspection of the map and the tables of population will show you, that the whole local interest, Eastern and Western, attached either to the Potomac, the James, or the Roanoke, upon any plan of improvement, however magnificent, will embrace less than one-third of the white population of the State—and so it must be forever. Neither, therefore, alone, could command the power of the Government—each would guard the Commonwealth against any improvident scheme which the other should espouse. It must then be from a combination of different interests, that any danger would be apprehended. Is such a combination probable?

That which would be most natural, perhaps, would be between the James and the Roanoke, because their principal market towns, Norfolk and Richmond, have commercial connexions, which might be advantageously extended. But such a combination is feared by nobody; it is in no wise probable, and if formed, its local interests would not embrace a majority. That which seems to be apprehended, and which is least improbable, is a combination between the James and Potomac. Is not this apprehension unfounded?

It ought to be remembered, that one of the most interesting objects of an enlarged plan of improvement connecting the Eastern with the Western waters, is the Western trade; that, in this object, the Potomac and the James would be rivals—and therefore, that combination between them would be less probable.

The vast expense of the two improvements, which should connect the James and Potomac, with the Western waters, would present another serious obstacle to the combination--an obstacle, which the known reluctance of the people of Virginia, to raise the taxes, or incur debt, would render almost insuperable. But suppose these obstacles removed, suppose the local interests of James River and Potomac prepared to lay down their rivalry and at every expense to seek the attainment of a favorite object, how then will stand the question of power?

Upon the basis of white population, the Western vote is estimated at fifty-eight. But of the Western country, the counties of Grayson, Montgomery, Wythe, Washington, Scott, Lee, Russell, Tazewell, Logan, and Cabell, belong neither to the James River nor the Potomac interests. Their population entitles them to twelve votes, which must be deducted from the fifty-six, leaving forty-four. To this add the vote of those counties on this side of the mountain which have heretofore espoused either the James River or the Potomac interest—Loudoun, Fairfax, Albemarle, Amherst, Nelson, Fluvanna, Goochland, Bedford, and Campbell; also the vote of the city of Richmond, in all thirteen, and you give to the combination the power of fifty-seven against sixty-three. It must then seek other alliances to be successful. Where will it find them? Will the South-Western counties that I have enumerated unite with them?

That bond of sympathy originating in a common feeling of common injury, which has heretofore given so much power to the Western vote, may unite them, unless you dissolve it, by adopting the basis of white population and causing every local interest to sympathise only with the interests of the Commonwealth. Do this, and there will be no better reason, why the South-Western counties should unite themselves with the James and Potomac, than there would be for such a union of the Roanoke counties, below the mountain.

Will the Appomattox or Rappahannock interests unite? This could only be on terms which would promise them the achievement of their objects of improvement; terms, which would swell the whole expenses still higher, and multiply the difficulties of success. And if this object is to be obtained, only by combination of this sort, it will be easy to show that the compound basis would be no security against them.

The compound basis, if any thing could, would carry the whole Western vote, in unbroken phalanx, upon this subject. I have elsewhere, Mr. Chairman, referred to the well known influence of this vote in the Legislature of Virginia; and this reference has been treated here as a threat used to influence the proceedings of this Convention. Never was the meaning of any one more entirely misconceived, if it has been thought for a moment, that I referred to the influence of the back-woods vote, with any the remotest intention of holding it *in terrorem* over the members of this Convention. Sir, I mentioned it, with far different motives—and it is wonderful that they should not have been understood. I mentioned it as an evil, which it was desirable to remedy—as the natural effect of that sense of injustice, which the Western people had so long felt, as a reason for believing, that an attempt to deprive them of power, by denying them their just share in the representation, would on many occasions defeat its own object, as it might give more power to their concert than you had taken from their numbers. If I had believed that there was a single member of the Convention, capable of being influenced by such an appeal to his fears, I would have disdained to address myself to him. But, I repeat, Sir, that if there is any thing, which could unite the whole Western vote, in favor of the combined scheme of improvement, which we are now considering, it would be your compound basis.

Suppose them thus united—the Western vote upon the compound basis, is forty-three—the vote of the nine Potomac and James River counties, on this side of the mountain, would be sixteen—that of the city of Richmond, nearly three—making in the whole sixty-two votes, a small majority. If the ten South-Western counties, or any of them should not unite, the combination must only look for an equivalent, in an alliance with the Rappahannock or Appomattox. The whole force of the ten South-Western counties upon the compound basis is but eight votes—which subtracted, would leave the strength of the James River, and Potomac interest fifty-four votes—and leave them to seek seven allies from the other districts.

These views of the subject serve to show you, that upon either basis, the State is perfectly safe from the domination of any one great local interest—that upon neither is it safe from combinations of them, if such combinations be practicable at all—that in this respect, if there be any difference between the two, it can only be, that on the compound basis the combination required may be a little more extensive, and, therefore, a little more mischievous in its consequences. But, Sir, when we ascertain that the great body of the State above and below the mountain is directly interested in its internal improvement, of what great consequence is it to calculate the probability of combinations? The policy must and will be cherished, and whenever plans are presented, which recommend themselves to public approbation, by their apparent practicability and usefulness, they will be adopted. Gentlemen have supposed, that, as the more expensive improvements were best suited to the Western interests—as the estates of the Western people were to be most improved by them, and as they contributed the smallest proportion of the taxes, which might be necessary to defray the expense—they would be less careful in counting the evils and more disposed to encourage extravagant and ruinous projects.

Without stopping to enquire whether the Western people have most interest, in the more expensive improvements, I am content to have shown you that the Valley people at least contribute man for man, nearly as much tax as the Eastern people—that the whole West, when the inequalities of the last assessment shall have been corrected, will contribute fully in proportion to their ability to pay—that a man of small property, parts with a tythe of his profits, with as much caution and reluctance as the man of large property, and that the local tax, in the form of tolls or otherwise, which the local district must pay for every improvement will at once secure a rigid attention to its economy and usefulness, and guard the public interest. My purpose in adverting to the argument, now, is to show the consequence to which it leads. Observe, the argument is, that the Western people will advocate improvident expenditures of public money, in the improvement of their estates, because they contribute unequally to the public treasury—to control which, power should be given to the Eastern people, by giving them representation in proportion to their taxes and numbers combined. Now, it is obvious, that if the money is to be expended, in the improvement of Western estates, the inequality of contributions cannot be the only or the governing motive with Western men, looking to their interest, for advocating the expenditure. Suppose the contributions equal, suppose the Western man to pay dollar for dollar with the Eastern man, and their joint contributions to be applied to the improvement of western estates—would not the expenditure still be an object of desire to Western cupidity? How much difference would it make in the conduct of an interested man whether, for the improvement of his own property, he was voting half a dollar of his own money with a dollar of yours, or one dollar of each? You would have as little confidence in him, in the one case as in the other. If it be true then that the Western people are interested in improvements that do not interest the East—and that they would be tempted by selfish considerations to expend the public money in those improvements, without adequate indemnity, then it is manifest, that no safe-guard would be found for the interests of the East, in the circumstance that the West paid an equal proportion of the public taxes. In such a state of things some other argument must be found, and doubtless would be found, to justify the refusal of power to the West. We should be told then as we are told now, that to secure the property of the East from the power of the West, the Government must remain in the hands of the Eastern people; and some new basis of representation would be devised to effect it. Would not this lead to the conclusion, that the tide-water country, as least of all interested in internal improvements, as the most impartial arbiter between the various local interests, is the only proper depository of the power of this Government?

Before I take leave of the subject of internal improvements, allow me a brief explanation relative to one, which seems to have been much misunderstood here. I allude to the James River improvement—which has been treated in a manner calculated to cast imputation on its friends, and throw discredit on the system.

In the year 1784 a private company was incorporated, for the improvement of the navigation of this river, and fixed tolls on transportation allowed them. They made the contemplated improvement, and had been for many years in the enjoyment of very large profits upon their stock. Much complaint, however, was made against them, for imputed neglect of duty and violation of their charter. These complaints were most earnestly and perseveringly urged from the South side of the river, and the Legislature was repeatedly pressed to charter another company with privileges incompatible with those of the James River company—and to declare its charter forfeited and void. These measures resulted in a resolution of the General Assembly, directing a prosecution in the General Court, to ascertain whether the charter was forfeited. Pending this prosecution, the Legislature, by a compact with the company, assumed the whole interest, and entire control of the subject, and passed a law for effecting an improvement deemed of great importance to the Commonwealth, by a continued Canal from Richmond to the mouth of Dunlap's Creek; a turnpike road from thence to the Great Falls of Kanawha, and removing the obstructions to the navigation of that river, from thence to the Ohio.

This law provided for the assessment of tolls upon the transportation for the purpose of indemnifying the Government for the expenses of the improvement; and in order to give assurance to the local interest that it would not be prematurely or unjustly burthened, a pledge was given in the law itself, that the additional tolls imposed should not exceed one-third of the saving in the price of transportation, effected by the improvement. Great pains had been taken by repeated surveys and reports of commissioners and engineers, to ascertain the probable expense and value of the improvement; and some confidence was entertained in the opinion that it was practicable, at an expense not burthensome to the State; that its consequences would be very beneficial; and the reduction of freight so great as to justify a toll which would re-pay the interest of the money expended, and not exceed one-third of the saving in the price of transportation. Nevertheless, the Legislature, with wise precaution, so laid out the whole into convenient sections, as to give themselves the benefit of actual experience in the progress of the work, and to enable them, if they thought fit, to arrest it at such points, as falling far short of the whole plan, would have achieved objects valuable in themselves, and promising a reasonable profit upon the expenditure. The first section was the canal from Richmond to a convenient point on the river, beyond the limit of the rich mines of coal which lie in the vicinity; the second, the turnpike road; and the third, the improvement of the navigation of the Kanawha. The tolls upon coal were expected to indemnify the expenses of the first; the tolls upon the road, the second; the tolls on the valuable salt trade then growing up on the Kanawha, were relied on to indemnify the expenses of the third; and it was believed, that if experience should forbid the further prosecution of the improvement, these three sections would be permanently useful. They were therefore immediately provided for, and in the course of a few years completed. The mountain section—the canal through the Blue Ridge, was the result of subsequent legislation. When the three first sections had been finished, the expenses of the canal had so far exceeded the estimates, that the most zealous friends of the improvement, doubted the propriety of prosecuting the whole plan to its completion. It was in this state of things that the additional toll on tobacco was recommended to the Legislature by the Board of Public Works, and was advocated on two grounds;—first, that the interest of the tobacco-planters would well justify this offering, which, by increasing the revenue of the company, would restore confidence, and might ultimately secure success to the improvement in which they were deeply interested; and secondly, that justice required it, inasmuch as the toll on tobacco had been originally too low, in comparison with the toll on flour and other products. A bill passed the House of Delegates, imposing this additional tax; and in the Senate, of which I was then a member, representing a farming and not a planting district, I united with the most decided friends of the James River improvement, in the tobacco districts and elsewhere, in a zealous opposition to the law, insisting that it would be a breach of faith; that it was wrong in itself, and would alienate from the improvement the affections of some of its most constant friends. The bill, however, was carried, by the vote of the East, combined with the enemies of the improvement every where, and with a few Western members, who were, or had been friendly to it. It is not just, therefore, to charge this law to the bad faith of the West. I charge it not to bad faith or improper motives any where. Gentlemen, no doubt, acted as they thought was right:—but the law is unquestionably to be charged to the vote of those in general, who were unfriendly to the James River improvement. I have but one word more to say in relation to this improvement—and that is, that notwithstanding the bad economy with which the work has been done, it having cost at least one hundred per cent. more than we now think it ought to have cost, yet the income from the tolls furnishes a reasonable profit upon the whole amount expended:—and that the freight upon transportation, from the district at the head of the first section, which can avail itself of the full benefit of that improvement, has been reduced one half.

I thought this explanation called for, by the remarks of the gentleman from Fauquier, (Mr. Scott) and others, and hope that it may remove some prejudices and quiet some fears.

I learn, Mr. Chairman, that other fears are indulged by the gentlemen of the East, from the transfer of power to the West: They fear not only that the estates of the West are to be improved, but that the poor of the West are to be educated, at the expense of the East. It is most deeply to be regretted, that there is any thing in the local situation of a particular property in Virginia, which gives rise to so many and such apprehensions. Interests the most general and most important; those most intimately connected with the prosperity and happiness of the whole people; the general protection of property, the improvement of all our roads and rivers, the education of our people, and the organization of our Government; all, by the malign influence of this unhappy cause, are made the subject of local jealousies, and party contests. What is the foundation, Sir, of this new alarm? For nearly fifty years, we have had, from time to time, various plans of public education, submitted to us, and discussed in the Legislature and before the people. Some of them, no doubt, have been wild and visionary; but, I believe, not one of them has ever been so extravagant, as to propose a general tax for the education of the poor. The farthest that any one of them has gone, has been to propose, that the school districts should be taxed, in aid of the contributions from the Literary Fund, for the education of the poor of those districts respectively. But, what warrant is there for supposing, that the education of the poor from the public purse, is a Western interest; that their poor are more numerous or less educated than yours? There is none; and it ought to be remembered, that the most extensive schemes of public education, if not all, that ever have been submitted for the adoption of this State, have proceeded from Eastern politicians.

But, suppose that the danger which has been apprehended to the security of property, the danger of an unjust levy and application of the public taxes, will really attend the unqualified transfer of power; is the appropriate remedy to be found in retaining that power in the hands of the minority? I think not.

Appeal, if you please, to that cautionary doctrine of the gentleman from Fauquier, which teaches that the greatest merit of a Constitution, is in giving to Government those powers only which are essential to the general welfare, and apply the remedies which it suggests.

If you think that your slaves will be unjustly taxed, prescribe in the Constitution a proper limit upon the legislative power: fix the ratio between the tax on slaves and real estate, according to some just standard; declare that the tax shall be *ad valorem*, and equal on both, and that the one shall never be taxed without the other. In this, I will cheerfully co-operate with you, satisfied that such a provision would be just and effectual. Any law imposing a tax in violation of it, being forbidden, by the Constitution, would be void; every one interested, might resist the payment of the tax, and he would be sustained by an independent judiciary.

If you think there is real danger, that the public revenue will be unjustly applied to partial objects of internal improvement; if you really think that the spirit of internal improvement requires rather to be checked than encouraged, limit the powers of Government upon this subject also; provide, that no law appropriating the public revenue to such objects, or borrowing money for them, upon the public credit, shall be enacted without the concurrence of specified majorities in both Houses; majorities of four-sevenths, three-fifths, or whatever else might be equivalent to the whole restraining power, which your favourite basis would give you. However reluctant I should be to add to the very strong shackles, which nature has imposed upon the power of legislation on this subject, I could not hesitate to adopt such limitations upon the power of the majority, rather than yield it to the minority.

If you think that guards are necessary to restrain the improvident application of public money, to the purpose of educating the poor, prescribe them at your pleasure; for myself, I give you a *carte blanche* on this subject.

If none of these expedients will impose an effectual restraint; if the power of the majority is so great, that you fear its irresistible strength will burst all the bonds imposed upon it, do not claim this uncontroulable power for the minority: there is an expedient, by which it may be denied to both. Apply your basis to the Senate, and let ours be applied to the House of Delegates. You have told us you do not ask power; you only ask for protection; and you say that power only can resist power. There is certainly no method by which you can use the power of the minority as a check to the power of the majority, but by giving to each the power in one branch of the Legislature. Do not understand me, as advocating such a distribution of power, upon principle, or as conceding that it is required by the peculiar condition of Virginia. All I say is, that it is the utmost extent to which your own principles would carry you. You object that such a Senate would be no sufficient safe-guard, because being the smaller body, and representing in some degree the property of the country, it would be stigmatized as the aristocratic branch of the Government, and would not be able to resist the measures of the popular branch of the Legislature. We are told, that though it may resist for a short time, it must yield to the popular voice in the course of a few years, as all experience proves.

These objections, I think, are wholly unfounded. My experience in the Senate of Virginia, induces me to think that it is admirably suited to guard the legislation of the country against injustice, and the influence of popular clamour. It has nevertheless been reproached as the aristocratic branch of the Legislature, wherever it opposed itself firmly to the popular branch, as it often did, to the almost unanimous vote of the House of Delegates. The four years term of service, the classification, which carries out one fourth of its members each year, and leaves the other three fourths to render their account to their constituents, only when they have had one, two or three years' experience of their measures and reflection upon their conduct, gives a confidence to their opposition of injustice, and of the mischievous measures which popular excitement dictates, that is very rarely subdued. It is true, Sir, that a Senate constituted as ours is, cannot for a series of years, resist the settled wishes of the people: Nor should they. Like all other representative bodies, they ought to yield, and must yield, to the deliberate will of their constituents. And so ought, and so must your Senate formed upon the compound basis, yield to the settled will of their constituents. Nor can you desire that it should be otherwise. Their constituents will be that very minority, that very people to whom you desire to give the power: But, they will not yield to the will of the House of Delegates, nor to the will of the constituents of the House of Delegates. The two constituent bodies will be different, and as the members of each House will look to their own constituents for a renewal of the trust confided to them, and for approbation of their conduct, so they will look to the same source for instructions, and for that settled popular will, which must habitually guide the representative. I cannot doubt that such a Senate would afford ample protection against all the dangers to property, which have been apprehended from the power of the majority.

I have endeavored to show that no such protection is necessary, that no such danger exists. I have said in another place, and I will repeat here, that your peculiar property does not require representation in order to give it influence and power in the Government. You having more wealth—your lands being cultivated by slaves—all the menial duties in your families being performed by slaves—your white people have more leisure to devote to the cultivation of their minds, better opportunity to prepare themselves for those stations in society, which give distinction and power to talent, than can possibly be enjoyed by your Western brethren. In answer to this, it is said to be a ridiculous mockery to speak of the wealth of the lower country, and I have been asked whether I know a single man in the Commonwealth, who has been more than half educated since the revolution. I know not by what standard gentlemen would estimate wealth or education; and I have said nothing of great riches or finished educations. But the whole argument of the Eastern gentlemen, and the scheme of representation they propose, are founded upon the superior wealth of the East, and I can appeal to numberless witnesses, among the living and the dead, who will bear ample testimony to the fact, that in the East have been born and educated, almost all our distinguished orators, jurists and Statesmen. Where do you find the eminent men, who in former or latter times, have ornamented your bar and your bench, have enlightened and guided your Legislative Councils, State and Federal? Whence your long list of Governors, and your race of Presidents? It is the natural, the necessary effect of your slave population to give these advantages; and they must give political power. But I am asked, whether if superior wealth gives superior intelligence, that intelligence does not give superior virtue—and whether I would withdraw the power of the Government from its intelligence and virtue.

This is ingenious catechism, Mr. Chairman, but not sound reasoning. It does not follow, that when superior numbers are on one side, and superior talent on the other, the power of the Government will be with the superior numbers—This conclusion would deny the influence that talent exerts over numbers. And much less does it follow, that superior intelligence gives superior virtue in that condition of life to which this argument applies. I might very safely concede, and I do concede, that in the retired walks of private life, intelligence cherishes, if it does not create virtue; rebukes and restrains, if it does not repel or subdue vice. But I cannot admit, that the school of politics, is the school of virtue. I should not look for the most virtuous men among that class, however enlightened, who have been long disciplined in the arts of electioneering and intrigue; who have been accustomed to the simulation, and dissimulation practised in the management of men; who have been drilled in the tactics of party warfare, and have become veterans in the conduct of political campaigns. I should, with more confidence, look for them among the independent and intelligent in the middle class of society; who obey a call into the public service as a matter of duty; whose ambition is satisfied, if that duty is faithfully performed; who find their chief happiness in this life, in the bosom of their own families, and limit their principal desires to the boundary of their own farms. I cannot allow, then, to your superior intelligence any necessary superiority of virtue; and though we are willing that you should enlighten the path of our duty and persuade us to follow it, we cannot consent that you should prescribe it.

While I would most cheerfully submit to the natural influence of your talents; while I would most cordially co-operate with you, in any reasonable measure to guard your property against all injustice from the power of the majority, I never can consent to surrender the power into the hands of the minority—to give them the complete dominion over the persons and property of the majority. You ask, what security we can give you for the protection of your property? We ask, what security you can give us for the protection of our persons and property? You tell us you have not abused your power, you have been guilty of no injustice, no oppression for fifty years. We tell you, that you admit us to be the same people with yourselves, entitled to equal confidence, and that if your good conduct, for fifty years, is evidence that the minority will rule justly, it is equal evidence that the majority of the same people will rule justly. But you place your principal reliance on the position, that the legislation which you would adopt for the promotion of your own interests and protection of your own rights, would necessarily promote our interests and protect our rights. Let us examine this.

Upon the subject of internal improvements, have you not told us, that the interests of the West required one system, and the interests of the middle country another; and is it not a very general opinion, in the Eastern district, that their interests require none? Consult, then, the supposed interest of the East and abandon all improvements, or consult the views of the middle country, and adopt the system best suited to them, adopt a narrow, selfish policy, and stop all your improvements at the base of the Blue Ridge, take our money to make them, and what becomes of the necessary connexion between your interest and ours, of the protection you were compelled to give us, in protecting yourselves?

Again; you have already told us that your slaves were too highly taxed—a position which we controvert. Suppose you reduce the tax one-half, and throw the burthen on lands?—or suppose that you persuade yourselves, that retributive justice requires that as your slaves have been taxed too high for the last fifty years, they should not be taxed at all for the next, and act accordingly; would this measure adopted to promote your interests, necessarily promote ours also?

Is it, as you have supposed, that there are no subjects of taxation in the West, that do not equally abound in the East—none on which a tax could be levied, that would not bear as heavily on the East as on the West? The gentleman from Chesterfield supposed that the tax on horned cattle would bear as heavily on the planting districts of the East, as it would on the grazing districts of the West, and quotes the experiment of a single year, during the late war, to sustain his conclusion. He tells us that this experiment produced as much revenue from the East, as from the West. He supposes that he himself, a few years before, had made the first proposition that ever was submitted to the Legislature, for imposing a tax on cattle—and that this single experiment, resulting so differently from what was anticipated, is good assurance that the tax can never be resorted to, as the means of imposing undue burthens on the

West. Without examining the result of the tax laid during the late war, or enquiring into its cause, I should be very sceptical in the opinion that a cattle tax could operate equally, in the East and the West—equally upon a corn, a cotton, or tobacco plantation, and upon a grain-growing or grazing farm; and I, with all other Western men, would be very unwilling to see the question brought to the test of *experience*. Time may come, when it will be. My friend from Chesterfield is mistaken in supposing that he first proposed this tax. It was habitually levied during the revolutionary war, and for some years afterwards; and no doubt, there had been paid the assessed three pence upon the head of that very bullock which was impressed by an officer of the revolution from John Hook, and whose " moaning low" figured so conspicuously in the eloquence of Patrick Henry.

But, Sir, it would not be difficult to find many subjects of taxation in the West, in which the Eastern people have comparatively no interest. Even their extensive coal mines may, at a future day, be the subject of a burthensome tax, in which they would find no sympathy East of the mountains, except in the counties of Chesterfield and Henrico. But look at the boundless stores of metallic ore which the Western mountains every where contain, and their extensive salt works, to the growth of which there is scarcely an assignable limit; and you cannot doubt that a disposition to impose unjust burthens on the West, could readily find the means. Does any one doubt how unequally an excise on distilled spirits would operate? I must not be understood as imputing to the people of the East any disposition to impose unjust taxes, or injurious legislation of any kind on those of the West. I do not believe they have any such disposition—but it is my duty to show that if they had, it might be indulged; and that, therefore, we have the same reason for withholding extraordinary confidence from them, which they think they have for withholding from us the ordinary confidence which is extended to the majority of equals.

To the proposed compound basis, Mr. Chairman, I have insuperable objections. As its direct object and effect will be to give the power to the minority, so its natural, if not necessary consequence will be to propitiate that power, even although the reasons for bestowing it should pass away. In process of time, the works of internal improvement may cease to be a subject of jealousy, and the slave population may become so generally diffused, as to quiet all fears on that score—and yet the power of the Government being in the hands of the minority, they might so regulate the taxes, as to retain that power at pleasure. They would be the sole judges, whether they would pay the purchase money. Was it to this event, Mr. Chairman, that the gentleman from Northampton sagaciously looked forward, when he asked the emphatic and significant question, whether we were willing to pay the whole expenses of Government, and take its whole power? No, Sir, I do not believe that *that* gentleman had in contemplation any such abuse of the power, which he desired to bestow on the minority—I believe that his was a mere rhetorical question—and yet it could not fail to remind us of the value which ambition sets upon power, and led us to enquire what price the minority might be willing to pay for that which the majority would not, or could not purchase. Looking back but a few years into the history of our own Government, we are taught, by the extreme reluctance with which that minority parted with their power in the Senate, for which they paid the price of a double or a triple land tax—how highly it was valued by them. Considering the very small amount of the taxes of the State, it can scarcely be deemed unreasonable to suppose, that the people East of the mountain would always be willing to pay a double portion of them, as the price of the power of the Government. Whether they would or no, *they* ought not to be exposed to the temptation—we ought not to be exposed to the danger.

Another, and perhaps more serious objection to the compound ratio, is the tendency of the principle on which it is founded. Although, in the actual condition of Virginia, it would establish no aristocracy or oligarchy, would leave us still a popular Government, yet it is wise to examine its bearing, and consider how far it is proper to admit it into our republic. The principle is, that as property must be protected, it must have a representation, which would give its owners the power of the Government as the only effectual means of protection. Now it is manifest, that the argument in favor of such protection strengthens, as you increase the value of the property and diminish the district in which it is situated—So that if the whole slave population of Virginia were confined to the tide-water district, that district might *a fortiori* claim the power of the Government as essential to its protection. But, would such a claim be tolerated for a moment? Could it be allowed, and leave any longer a popular Government? No, sir! But, yet there is in the nature of our Government an appropriate protection for property thus situated, thus exposed to danger—and a wise majority would not fail to furnish it. They would not surrender the power to this small minority or to any other; but they would erect constitutional barriers to the exercise of their own power—and if they believed every other inefficient, they would give to the minority a veto upon those laws which might invade their rights. It is in this veto, that the checks and balances of well adjusted Governments must be found, where the object is to protect warring interests from the power of each other. The various instances of the restraint upon the power of the majority, referred to by the gentleman from Orange, (Mr. Barbour,) are all either restraints upon the power of the majority, for the protection of the rights of the minority, or expedients to secure deliberation, and protect the majority itself from the effects of inconsiderate action. None of them are intended to give power to the majority. Let us not then admit into our Constitution the principle that the property of the country, as essential to its protection, must possess the power of the Government.

In conclusion, Mr. Chairman, I beg the Committee carefully and impartially to compare the two propositions which are submitted to their choice—to reflect on the simplicity, the uniform character and operation of the one, its entire conformity with the great principles of our Government, and on the complex and varying character of the other, its proneness to abuse, and its strong tendency to discredit, if not to condemn the doctrines which we have been taught most to respect and reverence—to enquire, whether the one, with a proper limitation of the Right of Suffrage, does not afford the best possible assurance of protection to all interests, and security to all rights, while the other endangers the very objects it seeks to secure—and, above all, to remember, that the one leads to the restoration of confidence and good feeling, the establishment of lasting peace and harmony, the preservation of the power, the character, the integrity of the State—while the other sows the seeds of never-dying jealousy and contention, and threatens mischief which no human wisdom can calculate, and no patriot can look upon without horror.

I beg the Committee's forgiveness, for having detained them so long, in a very laborious and unprofitable effort to discharge my duty, and I have now only to ask, that if any thing has escaped me, importing any manner of disrespect, or in the smallest degree wounding the feelings of any one—gentlemen will recollect that I have not that happiness of phrase, which always faithfully translates my thoughts into language, and be assured that I have too much real respect and kind feeling towards every member of this Committee, to allow me for a moment, to entertain towards one of them an offensive sentiment.

Mr. Stanard now rose and addressed the Committee in nearly the following words:

My sincerity, I am sure, will not be doubted when I avow the reluctance I feel in addressing the Committee at this stage of the debate. Conscious that I have but little title to claim attention, at any time, I cannot hope that at this any will be acknowledged, or that I shall be able to requite the attention which courtesy may accord, by any thing that I can extract from a theme already so elaborately discussed. A jaded audience, and an exhausted subject, are certainly very strong discouragements; and the force of these discouragements is augmented by the circumstance, that I follow the able gentleman who has just closed his argument.

Powerful considerations alone could overrule these dissuasives, and by such I am impelled. They arise out of the situation, (not entirely peculiar, but not common to many,) which I hold in this Assembly. Though for many years separated by residence from those whose interests I here represent, they, disregarding this almost insuperable objection, have selected me as one of the depositories of the important trust with which this Assembly is charged. By so touching a proof of kindness and confidence, they have entitled themselves to my most grateful and devoted service. The question in debate involves some of their dearest interests, and the vote that I shall give on it, will, as I believe, sustain those interests, while it will accord with the opinions of a great majority of my constituents. These interests have been assailed, and these opinions have been stigmatised, and I feel that the generous confidence which has placed me here, requires of me the requital of an attempt to uphold those interests and vindicate those opinions, though I should sink under the effort.

The amendment proposed by the gentleman from Culpeper, and which it is my purpose to sustain, has been characterised as anti-republican, aristocratical, oligarchical; and these epithets, I have cause to apprehend, may be fastened by popular delusion, to the opinions of which I am the organ, to their disparagement, and to the injury of the interests connected with them. It is due to my constituents, that I should endeavor to redeem their opinions from these stigmas.

I yield my ready concurrence to the sentiment of gratulation, which has been repeatedly expressed on the temper of this debate. It has my entire approbation. Here passion should have no voice, because here it ought not, and, as I trust, it cannot find a proselyte. While I shall conform myself to the spirit which has thus far governed the discussion, I have no hope to imitate those who have preceded me in the impressiveness and strength of their argument. Their eloquence I shall not attempt to emulate. Did I feel myself competent to do so, I should find in the recent experience of this Committee a lesson of dissuasion, too impressive to be unheeded. For who, Sir, has forgotten how instantaneously the spell attempted to be thrown over this body by the impassioned peroration of the gentleman from Loudoun was dissolved, and the memory of it obliterated by the sober realities, the ponderous facts, the luminous statements, and the cogent arguments by which they were connected, of the gentleman from Accomac (Mr. Joynes.) The instruction I draw from this lesson is, that this is not a proper theatre for such displays. And here permit me to say, that I would not stint to the West the eulogy they merit. I would not deny the meed of praise for the services and sacrifices so eloquently commemorated by the gentleman from Loudoun. It would not suit my feelings or sense of justice to do so. But, this claim is no novelty. It has been urged on this floor, by lips as eloquent as those of the gentleman from Loudoun. It has been repeated, and reiterated again and again, within these walls. The claim has been acknowledged, whenever it has been asserted. It was heard here in 1816, when an extensive scheme of banking was brought before the Assembly, and though in that instance it failed to produce the intended effect on that measure; yet if evil averted, may be permitted to stand, as good conferred, the West was certainly more than indemnified, for all its sacrifices, by having averted from its borders a moral pestilence, which would have contaminated its morality, and overwhelmed its property. It was heard again on this floor, when the expenses of the very epoch at which the serv.ces were rendered, were returned to us by the United States, and Virginia was indemnified for her advances, and when a destination was to be given to the large amount then received by the State. That sum, which, in the proportion of three or four to o e, had been advanced by the East, was, with a commendable generosity, partition d, not in the proportion of three to one, nor of two to one, but of one to one, or at least three to two, with the people of the West. How often it has been heard since, all those cannot fail to recollect, who have had any share in our public councils. I say not this by way of disparagement, nor from any want of gratitude: but may I not be permitted to ask, is this service of the West always to stand without any counterpoise? Is it to endure for all time and for all purposes, as an undiminished charge against the East on which to demand forever new sacrifices and new concessions? Must it be considered like our obligations to our Creator, "a debt immense of endless gratitude, still paying—still to owe?"

Is the service such that nothing can requite it, but the surrender of the power over the whole property of the East? Nor do I mean to question the virtue or intelligence of the people on which you, Mr. Chairman, so earnestly insisted, when you recently addressed the Committee. I yield on this subject all that was claimed by you. But may I not ask, are the means resorted to, to preserve it, judicious? Is it wise, when we would guard our virtue, to separate interest from duty; to expose that virtue to the strongest temptation? Ought we to do this at a time, when we propose to break up the existing order of society, and to change its organic law; at a time, when the minds of men are cut loose from their moorings, and all things and all principles are set afloat?

Nor do I mean, gentlemen of the West, one and all, (I speak with the utmost sincerity, and that my language is not the profession of the day or for the occasion, I appeal to my public course when I was a public man,) I mean not to question your honor, nor to say, nor to insinuate, that you have a desire to revel in the spoil of the East: I do not ground my course of action on the belief, that any spirit of rapine will govern you or your sons. No, gentlemen, I have full faith in your sincerity. I have confidence in your honor personally and politically—I question not the sincerity of the gentleman from Loudoun, (in truth I do not.) Even when shedding tears of anguish over the desolate fields and mouldering mansions of the tide-water country, and bewailing them with a pathos that almost extorted tears from others, and looking with rapt vision to the consummation of his hopes of future improvement, he surrendered himself to the illusion, that verdure and fertility could be restored to these wastes, by taking from their owners a portion of their scanty products to improve the highlands and torrents of the West. No, Sir. I have not attained the years which I now number, without instruction from experience, which assures me how possible it is for the strongest mind, and the purest heart, to be exposed to delusions of this kind.

It is important, that before advancing in the discussion, we should have a correct conception of what is the real question before us; that we should clearly understand what is the matter in issue. It is not the issue which the gentleman from Augusta made up, (Mr. Johnson.) That gentleman essentially changed the issue presented by the resolution of the Committee, and the amendment proposed to it. And here let me say in passing, that if he was right in all he said, then we are disputing about a mere form of words, and nothing more. Both the resolution and the amendment are only means to an end; that end once attained, it is a matter of little consequence whether the means be preserved or not: they are from that moment of little value. What do we learn from the statistics of the gentleman from Augusta, as applied to his interpretation of what he makes the riddle of the Committee? The first thing that we learn, is, that the ratios furnished by the entire number of the white population, are different from the ratio arising from that portion of the community which are Catholic, which belong to the body politic, and exercise the Right of Suffrage. He, in apportioning representation, is for excluding all but those who have the Catholic qualification; and applying this rule to the data furnished by the Auditor's statements, it is shown that the masses of power in the four grand divisions of the State, scarce differ by units from those which will be quoted to them by the adoption of the amendment, and the application of the rule it would furnish.

After this digression, (to which I have been led by the strong impression his statement made on my mind,) let me turn back to the line of argument I intended to pursue.

The first thing it becomes us to look at, is the erroneous representation of the question before the Committee, and the gratuitous assumption of the principles which are to resolve it. The question has been treated, as if it were one now before the sovereign power of the State, in its primary assemblies, and the people were called to give their final vote upon it. It has been treated, as if the integers of this assembly were to be reckoned for more or less, according to the mass of population in their several districts, as if, telling over the members of the Convention, name by name, and putting a value on each, the question was to be decided, not by the numbers present in this body, but by the numbers of the population they represent:—and the majority of these latter numbers having been ascertained, those representing this majority, should prescribe the terms of the Constitution, and the minority have no further voice. Sir, is this correct? Or, is not such an assumption at war with the very ends of our appointment, the very nature of our trust, and derogatory to that intelligence we are so lavish in ascribing to this Assembly? If this be the true question, instead of prudence, knowledge and virtue, the sum total of the qualities required in us, is the capacity to add, subtract, and strike a balance, and the entire argument consists in the force of that balance, when struck. If this be the true question, and these the means of solving it, then is this Convention a mere bed of justice, and its entire function is to record the pretended edict of the people. The terms of that edict are to be dictated by a self-selected portion of this body, and its obligation is to be found by summing up the quantity of the people, young and old, children and men, male and female, and thus fixing the value of the votes of those (the self-selected part of this assembly) who represent them. What is the use of deliberation? Why did we resolve ourselves into special Committees; into miniature Conventions? Why do we sit here discussing questions from day to day, and from week to week? Why did the people look round to collect the patriarchs of the land, that they might bring their prudence, and wisdom, and experience here? Why all this, if all we have to do is only to add and to subtract? No, Sir; this representation of the question, which, I believe, has had more effect both here and elsewhere, than all other arguments, is utterly fallacious. Considerations of majority or minority do not belong to the initiatory inquiry. If they did, they would annul the functions of counsel and deliberation. And what is the character of this Assembly? We were sent here to counsel and deliberate; to take a broad survey of this widely-spread nation; to take the measure of its interests and its capacities; to weigh facts, to draw cautious and sagacious inductions; and then to submit to the people, not what they have prescribed, but that which we think a majority of the people ought to ratify. We are not to be forestalled by calculations: we are to present the result of a wide view of the true interests of the State, taken by the congregated wisdom of this body. We are to carry into effect the principle of our selection. We are to have the influence of the patriarchs of the land, to recommend the result of our investigations. We are to have the inestimable value of the weight of their authority. They are to stand before the people as instructors, not as the passive instruments of a foregone decree.

The true question is, what in the opinion of this Committee, with all its experience, and all its political prudence, after all its inductions from an extended observation of the interests, circumstances, habits, and physical aptitudes of the State, a majority of the people ought to accept as their organic law.

Here we are on a foundation where we can exercise our minds; not fettered by the results of calculations, which, by pre-supposition, has the authority of a mandate, takes away from us all free will and counsel, and leaves us mere instruments to ascertain numbers, and to record a pretended decree.

I have remarked, that the argument, which if it be not most frequently used, is yet really the most prevalent and irresistible, is the argument of epithets.

I shall address myself to that first.

Let us then enquire, whether the amendment and the principles on which it proceeds, merit the disparaging epithets which have been applied to them. I shall be vindicated by the judgment of the Committee, in addressing myself first to this part of the argument, because I am satisfied that there is not one who has looked upon recent and passing scenes, and has anticipated others, still not developed, who will not concede that the argument of epithet is a most potent one, if not the most potent one, on all political themes. I beg pardon. I have been too hasty. I agree with my friend from Chesterfield, that there is one yet more potent, and it is this: We are, or shall be, the majority. Yet even this is of little value, unaccompanied and unaided by the other. It shall be my humble effort to disarm my opponents of this argument, by showing that it has been gratuitously assumed, and most wantonly applied. I shall endeavor to do this, from the reason of the case, from the concessions of our adversaries themselves, (adversaries I hope only, as they are our opponents in argument,) and from the examples furnished by the political institutions of our sister States, and of the United States.

As the means of fixing a stigma on an opinion held by so many, gentlemen have assumed that that opinion commences with the postulate, that there are no principles in Government. I am under no need of vindicating the gentleman from Northampton from this imputation. He is able much more effectually to vindicate himself. Whether such a sentiment is justly ascribed to him, whether in fact it was ever uttered by him, and if it was, whether it must not, in common charity, be received as only a strong expression of the opinion, that a single principle is not a safe guide in adapting political institutions to a mature people, (the opinion which I shall maintain,) I leave for gentlemen to determine.

[Here Mr. Upshur rose and declared, that he never uttered the opinion.]

Mr. Stanard resumed.

I did not hear the gentleman utter the sentiment, and his disavowal of it conforms to my recollection of his argument. Such a position is no part of my political creed. My creed instructs me in opposition to this dogma, that the principles of Government are numerous and multiform; as much so as are the interests, habitudes, moral condition and physical situation of the people to be governed. No principles in Government! Every one of these considerations is the fruitful parent of numerous principles, and it is the business of the Statesman, by wide and extended observations, and searching investigations, to extract the principles which ought to regulate their organic or municipal law. Principles multiply with the diversities in situation, habits and interests, of the people to be governed. They are few and simple among a new people, whose population is homogeneous, whose interests are united, and among whom, no great disparities or contrarieties are to be found: they become numerous, and they multiply in geometrical ratio, as such a people advance to maturity, as they diversify their interests, and by long continuance under one system of organic law, they become gradually moulded by it in all their habits and interests. These principles often take their origin from different parts of the social circle—they traverse and intersect each other—one principle often encounters an antagonist principle—and then it is the province of wisdom to discern, and of prudence to allow the due proportion of force to each. Under the government of reason, all of them are entitled to their own prerogatives—though not equal, (like a fancied republic of men where all are equal,) all have a voice—and the ear which will not hear all, is deaf from the influence of prejudice, and averse from the policy which alone can conduct to peace and happiness. No one principle is to have a despotic sway, and to hush to silence all the rest. All are to be heard—and here is our point of difference.

Gentlemen have imputed to the supporters of the amendment of my friend from Culpeper, the avowal or the maintenance of the sentiment, that there are no principles in Government—and they, on the opposite hand, have given to one solitary principle, despotic sway, silencing all the rest. Gentlemen have applied themselves to what they were pleased to call an analysis of the principles of Government—and the result has been the evolution from the concrete mass of one single principle—and that they administer in its essence, utterly disregarding all those which modify and give to it all its sanative efficacy. They treat the subject of Government as a chymist would the food which sustains us, and in which, in its native, healthful state, is found in combination with many others—one ingredient which gives it all its flavour and much of its nourishing quality—but which, when extracted from the mass, and administered in a state separated from that which assuages and dulcifies it, maddens the brain, while it ministers no nutriment to the body.

Let me tell the Reverend gentleman from Brooke, (for, among the fallacies of the day, is his attempted application of analogies drawn from the exact sciences to that of Government,) to whom we are indebted for the reference of the forty-seventh proposition of Euclid's first book, that geometry, whether superficial or solid, furnishes but a poor guide, when we would measure the force, ascertain the value, and fix the relations of moral and political quantities.

Under the guidance of a fallacious analogy, the gentleman thinks it would be wise to set out with certain *a priori* principles, certain postulata and axiomata, and then to keep ourselves within the exact parallel lines which these guides shall prescribe to us. Let me tell that gentleman, that for the construction of political and moral theorems, there are no postulata, which give him a straight line, that may be indefinitely extended; no definition of a point, without length or breadth; no axiom which allows that a given number of integers combined, is of the same value as the like number, indicated by summing up separate and detached integers. All these guides will fail him, and he will find himself betrayed into the most desperate and fatal errors, by submitting himself to their absolute sway. Proceeding on his straight line, he will go on, linking consequence to consequence, and induction to induction, to an almost interminable extent; like Jacob's ladder, which led from earth to Heaven—only, that this, I fear, takes the opposite direction.

I said, that in constructing moral and political theorems, especially when providing an organic law for society, already mature, whose interests have been growing up for two centuries, numerous principles are necessarily required, in order to give form to a Government, which will secure to each the enjoyment of life, liberty, property, and the pursuit of happiness, and to produce the greatest sum of public good.

Let me now attempt to furnish some illustrations, and to correct some paralogisms, by which gentlemen attempt to fix on us, that which we condemn in them, viz: the following out of one principle to extremes, disregarding all others.

Look to England—grown as she is to a magnitude of opulence and aggrandizement, with interests distinct in their nature, enormous in their amount, and diverse as to the parties possessing them. Is there a fanatic in the land, who would take up *a priori* principles, if he were called to make a Constitution for that people, and be governed by them alone? Is there one who has so entirely surrendered his mind to certain simple abstractions, as that he would undertake, at one blow, to level all these interests, and give a free and equal representative Government to that people? Yet the general principle of Republican Government is no less true, and without it, no free Government does or can exist. It is found in the British Constitution—modified, indeed, and maimed—and far below what it is in this country—but, still enough to make that a free Government, so far as mere civil rights are concerned.

But, supposing him to get rid of the most obvious impediments to the practical application of this famous political theorem, (viz: the equal rights of man, and the equal enjoyment of political power;) suppose, I say, that he gets rid of the Nobility—the Clergy—the Corporations—and the Monarch—and then has only the People themselves to provide for, and he is called to apply his principles; is there one here, who respects the rights of man, as a means to the end of public happiness, that would extend the principle, so as to give, in the language of the propositions of the gentleman from Norfolk, to every man an equal portion of political power, and make the sole measure of that equality, equal numbers, however they may be situated or combined? Sir, equal numbers are, in this matter, not always of equal value. Their value depends on their localities, their circumstances, and the interests which bind them together. Would any give, for example, to the county of Middlesex and city of London, power in proportion to the number of polls within the bills of mortality? Far less according to the property within those limits. The man who would do this, would prove himself to be a mere driveller—a poor closet speculator, who knew nothing of man, his interests, or his passions. I have selected this example, in order to show the limits I set to my own principle. So far would I be from giving to London and Middlesex, an average of power according to their numbers, that I would look to the lessons of experience taught us, and as the wisdom brought into practical operation in our sister States of Massachusetts and New-Hampshire. The former gives a term to the number of representatives of the town of Boston, whatever may be the number of inhabitants or their wealth; and both require, as the numbers of population multiply in a township, a larger and still larger number, in order to obtain another integer of political representation. They could not, in consistency with the preservation of the darling principle of political equality, (darling it is to me as to any,) mete out to large masses of population combined in one interest and directed by one will, a representation equal to that enjoyed by population of equal numbers dispersed in numerous smaller townships. Let us take lessons not from theory, but from practice—and that of these descendants of the pilgrims reads us a lesson which we may profitably consider.

What, then, becomes of the reproach attempted to be fastened on the friends of the amendment? that their object is to give superiority to wealth? So far from giving wealth the prevailing influence, I would, in the case to which I have resorted for illustration, strike it out altogether; and to counterpoise the consolidated force of numbers in the city, I would look to the wealth and numbers combined in the country—or apply the principle that has been adopted in Massachusetts and New-Hampshire, of requiring larger and larger numbers to entitle the growing masses of the population combined by one interest, to an additional representative in the Legislature.

For further illustration, let us take our position, not on foreign ground, not in a country where the Government and the community are the growth of so many centuries, but in our own land. Let us look at the State of New-York. Were I called upon to frame a system of organic law which should protect all the interests of society, and preserve them in their proper orbits, I certainly would not give to their great commercial emporium a representation according to its numbers; far less would I add its two hundred millions of property, still farther to enhance its overgrown power. Gentlemen may not, perhaps, in our day, witness any very evil effects from such a feature in the Constitution of that State—but when that great city shall have extended itself over the whole island on which it is seated, and shall have engulfed all the neighbouring villages, then those who shall have been misled by the pragmatical idea of measuring moral qualities by rules which apply to physical quantities only, may rue the day, when they adopted a principle which will have given the city of New-York practical dominion over the whole State.

Mr. Chairman, I am sensible that I have occupied too much time in these illustrations: but I was anxious, at the threshold of the discussion, to withdraw from gentlemen on the other side, the authority to turn upon us the reasoning we condemn in them. I know it would be easy to show, that if the principle contained in the amendment, were to be applied at all times and in all circumstances, such an application of it would sacrifice the main principles to an antagonist and subordinate one.

We renounce such a course. When we are called, not to sum up figures, but to ascertain the existing state of society; to take the measure of its various interests; to collate its diversities; to look at its physical aptitudes as a source of other diversities in future; I never will consent that I am bound to carry out one single principle beyond the necessity which is imposed by considerations of practical utility.

It is always useful to recur to fundamental principles, and I call back the debate to the point I started from, when I undertook to show, that the argument of epithet is assumed gratuitously, and most wantonly applied to our opinions.

I said I should endeavor to prove, from the concessions of gentlemen directly, or by clear implication, that the epithets employed by some of them were gratuitously assumed. In order to do so, let us fix the expression of this paramount, and all-in-all principle of theirs, and see how it works in the hands of those who attempt to fetter us with it. Let us give it, if not the precision, at least the terseness of a mathematical proposition, and throw it into a syllogistic form. All men are by nature equal: ergo, all men, when in society, should enjoy equal portions of political power. This is not strictly in the syllogistic form. It wants the minor proposition, and is what the logicians call an enthymeme. If, as gentlemen contend, this be the sole and all-sufficient principle in the construction of all just Government, then my first remark is, that the world, from the time of Solon till now, has been under a great mistake. It has been the idle prejudice of civilized man, every where, to suppose, that a Statesman is constituted, not by the conception of a theme, which is within the comprehension of a school-boy in his first form, but that it required the exercise of the higher faculties of the human mind. It has been thought till now, that an able Statesman was the product of labour; of sagacious and widely extended observation; of deep research; of clear induction from the treasures of experience; of power to bring within its grasp the whole horizon of human affairs, and laborious exercise of that power. But this, it seems, has been a mere prejudice; it must have been so, if the gentlemen are correct in maintaining, that the whole business of a Statesman is to understand and apply their propositions; and that, if he deviates in the slightest degree from it, he sacrifices that, without which, he must lose all his force—I mean the name of a republican: a cabalistic word brandished by the demagogue at the hustings, and made to work with magic force in the columns of the public prints. Without this, whatever his wisdom or his virtue, he is ostracised from public trust. The channels of public service are closed against him. Sir, this is a new patent mode of making a Statesman; a sort of labour-saving machinery, in which they are made with a celerity that nails are struck in a factory, and requiring intellect of no higher order to construct Governments, than that which computes the weight of the iron or the number of nails into which it is fabricated. This is the first consequence which follows from attempting to give simplicity to political science, and this alone is enough to ensure its condemnation. To attempt to provide for all the diversified interests of a mature people by such a proposition, is the height of political madness.

There is another value in this political theorem, by which all Republican Governments are made, and without which was not made any that was made. A theorem adapted to all purposes, it requires only the form of rules of arithmetic to put into complete operation; addition and subtraction, according to the pretensions of some gentlemen, as we have seen suffice to fix the principles that should govern this body. The other two rules, multiplication and division, suffice to reduce them to practise it.

It has another value. It is the grand catholicon, the political specific to make new, and repair infirm Constitutions. It also serves as an amulet for the physician to keep off all harms from former political transgressions, and those who profess full faith in it, shall have no reckoning to make, for acts and opinions of passed times. In these remarks I must be permitted to say, that I have no individual in view. I aim them not. They are the suggestions of the moment, without particular reference to any one.

Well, Sir, with this mathematico-political theorem, your Statesman goes to work; and the moment he tries to put it in practice, the case categorical becomes a case hypothetical. All men are possessed by nature of equal rights, ergo, all men in a state of society, should have equal portions of political power; *if* they are not women; *if* they are not under twenty-one years of age; *if* they are not paupers; *if* they are not insane; *if* they are not convicted of crime; limitations which I believe are conceded by the most thorough-going supporter of this new patent for Republicanism on the simple specification, before stated, though he may have no other title to that designation.

As he advances, his case categorical becomes more hypothetical. Yes, Sir, much more so. Look at the report of the Legislative Committee, and look at the other hypothesis by which it limits this grand theorem, for making a Republican Government. You find they have *if's* in abundance; *if* he owns land; *if* it is so many acres; *if* it is of such value; *if* he is a house-keeper; *if* he has paid taxes; *if* he resides in the State; *if* he has resided in the county so many years; *if* he owns an estate in reversion; and so before he gets to work, he will have stricken from the numbers of the people, a mass equal to two-thirds of the whole—and then these gentlemen bring their doctrines to this; all men in a particular predicament have equal political rights, and what that predicament is, we (the patentees) are to prescribe—all beyond the line we lay down, is damnable Heresy; all within the line is Catholic and orthodox. But, why exclude any? Reason, say they, instructs us, that children, who have minds not matured, cannot vote understandingly; and the law declares that all under twenty-one, are to be viewed as children; and our feelings tell us, that the sex ought not to contaminate its purity, by the pollutions of a political canvass. Very well, this is all fair. But, why make your opinions the standard? Why is Republicanism to be emblazoned on your escutcheon, notwithstanding your admission of these modifications, and denied to others, who, on equally sound considerations, would make or admit other modifications?

The gentleman from Brooke, (the Rev'd. gentleman from Brooke,) tells us, that those who do not choose to pass all the way on his straight line, (though they may think it leads to the hell of anarchy, not to the heaven of peace,) are wholly unphilosophical, and are acting in direct opposition to all the established principles of political gravity. I fear this analogy from the doctrine of gravity, is more close than that from his mathematics. I fear that the downward tendency of his scheme is so strong, as to put in requisition all the wisdom, prudence, and firmness here assembled to arrest its career, and even that, that may be unavailing.

The other gentleman from Brooke, sets his pipe to a different key, and his tune is, that the Government is oligarchical—a plain aristocracy—anti-republican, and, he says, to us of the East, you are insisting on your right to make us your political slaves, in order that you may keep your black slaves in subjection.

I would not take advantage of a warm expression uttered in the heat of debate, and hold the gentleman down to the literal meaning of the terms he employed, but I will refer it to himself, whether he has not sacrificed justness of sentiment to mere antithesis of expression; whether his statement is not an exorbitant exaggeration, and his charge unwarranted: Whether he is not confronted by his own doctrine, and if so, whether candor and self-respect, do not demand that he shall retract his words? Does that gentleman mean to say to paupers and minors, and the other persons he proposes to exclude from suffrage, (for he, I believe, is not one of the patentees,) you are slaves? You are bondsmen? And if not, will he predicate slavery of all those who are not precisely equal in power, numerically divided, when he does not predicate it of those who have none at all?

Let us, then, have the argument disarmed of this reproach, that our present Government is anti-republican and oligarchical.

Let us come to the issue made up by those on the other side, who have forborne to press this argument of epithet; for, most of those of the other side, have themselves renounced it. The question then is, not what is the principle which every true Republican requires in constituting a Republican Government, but first, are there no principles which limit it? On this point all agree—most of the gentlemen on the other side admit, that with perfect consistency with Republican principles, the very limitation proposed by the amendment may be made, and that whether it should be made in this particular case, is a question of expediency to be decided by justly weighing all the considerations, which such a question involves. If so, then secondly, it is a mere question of degree. It is not the enquiry, what are the primary principles of Republicanism, but it is the enquiry, to what degree other and antagonist principles ought to arrest the march of this primary one.

[Here, upon an intimation of a wish that the Committee should now rise, Mr. S. stated, that he had arrived at a part of his argument where it could be interrupted without affecting its conclusion, and gave way for a motion. The motion was made, and the Committee rose and reported progress, and the House thereupon adjourned.]

SATURDAY, November 14, 1829.

The Convention met at 11 o'clock, and was opened with prayer by the Rev. Mr. Hoerner of the Catholic Church.

Mr. Stanard, resumed his speech in support of the amendment of Mr. Green, proposing the mixed basis of representation in the House of Delegates :

I endeavoured yesterday to show from the reason of the case and the concessions of my opponents, either directly or by fair implication, that their argument of epithets was unfounded, and that the epithets they have attempted to fasten to the doctrines maintained by me and my coadjutors, have been gratuitously assumed, and wantonly applied by them.

I thought that I satisfactorily showed from both sources, that the question, how far the general principle, insisted on as the sole and exclusive rule in the construction of Republican Government, ought to be carried, was a question of degree and not of principle ; and that what we have to determine is, at what point that principle is to be intersected, traversed, and modified by other and controlling principles, which all must admit ought to be consulted in adapting a Government to the actual state of society.

Permit me now to attempt a farther illustration, by showing what must be done, if they shall prevail in establishing their proposition, either in the form in which it has been reported by the Legislative Committee, or according to the gloss which has been put upon it by the gentleman from Augusta. Their elementary proposition is this, that as all men are by nature equal, all men have a right to enjoy equal portions of political power ; and they insist that this must be carried out, or there is no such thing as a Republic. Now, I will give them this principle, and let them apply it to a mature condition of society, and then see how far they will be compelled to renounce some portion of it. In the nature of things, to the obtention of the desired equality, you must have given, first, the mass on which the principle is to operate, as a dividend ; then the given number of representatives as a divisor ; and applying this divisor to this dividend, the quotient will be the number of individuals to be represented by each Delegate. Then you come to the existing society—and you find dividing lines all over the State, which have existed, some of them, for two hundred years, and the population scattered in unequal masses within these lines. The number which your quotient indicates for one representative is, of course, an unvarying quantity—while the numbers to which it is to be applied, are all variable. One county contains three thousand free whites—another county eight thousand—and your quotient is five thousand—what are you to do ? Must you break up the county lines ? Must you add one county to another and sub-divide for the average ? Is this to be your process ? Is such a process practicable ? The gentleman from Augusta, I am sure, does not look to such a process ; none of the gentlemen avow themselves in favour of it. It would be cutting up not one, nor two, nor three of your counties ; but every existing partition of the State—every one—without exception. All the present lines, all of them, must be obliterated. And even when you shall have been reconciled to this, by any practical process to cut off and to define the several portions to be taken from one and added to another, so as to produce perfect equality between the counties or districts, is beyond the power of man.

If the principle cannot be thus applied, what is to be done ? What must be its effect in practice ? Here you have one county containing three thousand inhabitants, and another containing eight thousand ; while your invariable divisor is five thousand. Will you give the former of these counties a representative ? Suppose you do : and what will you allow to the second ? Not any more : but say, you give it two—yet I apprehend you would not give two to a county containing six or seven thousand. And what then ? Why then, a county containing eight thousand, will have two representatives, while a county containing six or seven thousand, will have one representative : and this is their exact mathematical proportion ! It turns out in practice so variant and unequal, that eight gives two, and seven one, and three as many as seven.

I shall not pursue this view of the subject farther : there can be no necessity of pushing it to other obvious consequences before this Assembly.

My next voucher for clearing away the incumbrances to our title to Republicanism, is the Constitution of this State—which shows the principle embodied and in a concrete form, and in that form consecrated by an authority which gentlemen invoke to their aid and then disparage. They all eulogize in the most exalted strains, the wisdom, the virtue, the patriotism of our ancestors, and yet they endeavour to make their principles condemn their own work. Their patriotism, their virtue, their wisdom, their intelligence, are all set forth in order the more to consecrate the principles they laid down; but all these cannot mitigate the sentence of condemnation which is pronounced upon their labours, and on the structure which they themselves reared on these very principles.

But, the gentlemen have a salvo for discrediting at one time an authority which they cry up as irrefragable and infallible in every respect in which they want to make use of it; and that is, that while the principles they laid down are the result of mature reflection, the happy inductions of sagacious minds, from an extended view of past times, all these qualities were dissolved and dissipated by the hurry and alarm in which they constructed their work. That assumption has been shown to be inconsistent with historical facts.

They go in pursuit of some pretext, on which to discredit their own authority. It is catholic, as far as they choose to use it, and heretical, just as far as they wish to reject it. They indulged themselves in an elaborate examination of analogous provisions in the Constitutions of our sister States.

The gentleman from Loudoun, in particular, presented us with a most elaborate and extensive analysis, on this subject—all with a view to maintain the authority of the Bill of Rights, and to repudiate that of the Constitution.

To give the more emphasis to these precedents, it pleased that gentleman not only to bring before us, in detail, various Bills of Rights, adopted in different parts of the Union, but to apprize the Committee, with more than usual solemnity, that these were not the work of men, intimidated by the presence of an enemy at their doors, and by the roar of hostile cannon, but the mature results of profound and tranquil investigation, when peace was in all our borders, and their authors enjoyed the advantage of the experience of the revolution, and the councils of many of the master spirits of that epoch. All these things were brought in solemn array, and for what purpose? To cast discredit on the work of our progenitors. But, surely, the evil genius of the gentleman from Loudoun must have been presiding, when he was allured to adopt this course.

Most unfortunately, the very circumstances, he so confidently relies on, when collated together, and not presented in detached fragments, torn from their context, but compared with the work of the same men, in framing the Constitutions of the States, furnish an irrefragable argument against his pretensions.

In every one of the States, noticed by the gentleman from Loudoun, aye, in every one of them, without a single exception, (unless it be that modern scheme of representative Government, with which the State of New York has favored the world,) the work and structure of those very sages, with all their advantages of mature experience, and tranquil times, and deliberate investigation, show, most convincingly, the utter fallacy of the pretensions he upholds.

The Constitution of Massachusetts, of New Hampshire, of Maine, of Connecticut, of Vermont—all show, that this political dogma, in its adaption to a mature society, with interests far advanced, and long established—this idea of carving and cutting out the mass of society, so as to assign to each man an equal portion of political power, has not been attempted by them: and notwithstanding all the facilities, which the condition of some of these States, in respect to their localities, municipal arrangements, and state of society, afforded for the application of this principle of equality, having regard to naked principles only, it has been disregarded in one branch of their Legislature, and traversed by greater and stronger checks in the other branch, than any we propose to adopt. Let me tell him too, that though the feature does not now appear in the Constitution of Pennsylvania, yet if he will look into the proceedings of the Convention which formed it, he will find, that even in that State, homogeneous as it is in population, and uniform as it is in almost all its interests—in that Convention, containing some of the master-spirits of the revolution, and the standard republicans of the day, it was proposed to introduce the same limitation in the Senate of that State, which we propose, by basing representation, not upon the number of the taxable inhabitants only, but upon a ratio deduced from a combination of taxation and numbers of taxable inhabitants.

But is it not a little remarkable, that the gentleman from Loudoun, after going into such an elaborate investigation of the Constitution and Bill of Rights, of other States in this Union, should all at once have stopped, at that precise point, when he would have come in contact with States, whose interest and situation, in respect to population, are analogous to ours? North Carolina, South Carolina, Georgia, and Tennessee, are all kept carefully out of view. They probably do not deserve enquiry, precisely for the very reason which, of all others, ought to recommend their example to us, viz: a conformity of their interests to ours, and the claim of those interests, to the modifications in their political institutions, which we propose in ours.

My next voucher is the Constitution of the United States. Yes, Sir, the Constitution of the United States. And here, it pleased the gentleman from Loudoun, (I speak, of course, of the *tendency* of his remarks,) to disparage that instrument, and the eminent men who recommended it to the adoption of the American people, by holding up that series of papers, which I have so often heard gentlemen on this floor refer to as containing the articles of their political creed, (I speak of the Federalist,) as obnoxious to the criticism, that the arguments in one part of it directly traverse and contradict those used in another part. It gave me some surprise, I confess, from the known sagacity of that gentleman, that he had not found a solution for the apparent contradiction to which he alluded; that he had not discovered the means by which he at once would solve it completely; that he did not, as the authors of that work had done, discard from his mind the influence of one dominant principle, and allow the antagonist principles their proper place and effect in controlling it.

That would have explained all the seeming contrariety. It is worthy of remark, that in his zeal to sustain his proposition, not merely as a means, but with a steady gaze towards the end, he added to the principles of the Bill of Rights, the doctrine in one of those papers which regards numbers as one of the elements of power, and exultingly referred to it—and yet the very work furnishes direct condemnation of the use he proposes to make of it, that is, to show that numbers form the sole element of power.

What is the character of the Government of the United States? It is not a full and plenary Government for all purposes; but it is a complete political entity, for the purposes of conducting the foreign relations of the United States, and as between the States of the same confederacy to settle their differences as members of that confederacy. It is shorn of all power to interfere with the municipal regulations of the States; but its limitation to our foreign relations, does not change its classification. It does not cease to be republican, because it refers to external concerns only; yet it is, in effect, contended that the same Government, if applied to our internal concerns, is aristocratic and oligarchical. Surely, the limitation of the uses of its power does not qualify or change the designation of the Government itself; and if a Government is republican, when charged with a part of our concerns, it does not cease to be republican, if charged with the whole of our concerns as one people.

Now, look at the principles which enter into the Constitution of that Government. The Federal Government is a Government formed by an association of sovereigns; the Governments of the several States by associations of individuals. Now, it happens in respect to States, that the principle of their equality is not admitted by us only, but by all Christendom: all civilized people admit equality of States. Whether their Governments be republican or monarchical—whether political power be exercised by the people in person, or by their representatives, or by the autocrat upon his throne, none are denied equality among themselves. But the equality of individuals has not the same force of authority: that is denied by all the rest of Christendom. States are artificial entities—they are political corporations, and with us they are associated to form a Government, just as individual men would associate for the same purpose. Their primitive equality is confessed; none dispute it; yet how are these equals dealt with in the details of the Federal Government? Looking, indeed, to one of the departments of that Government, we find their equality preserved strictly; but if we look to other departments of it, we shall find, that other considerations have supervened; which political considerations required to be weighed, and due allowance to be made for, in order to effect the great end of Government, viz: the protection of all. In other departments, these entities are treated not as integral, but as representing different masses of population; and power is allowed them according to the proportion of those masses to each other; while, in a third branch of the Government, we find a compound principle made up of both combined. The Executive branch is the progeny of an union of these principles. There is an equality of the parties in one sense, and there is a difference of power in another; yet is not this a Republican Government? Will the gentleman from Loudoun, (Mr. Mercer,) or the gentleman from Brooke, (Mr. Doddridge) pronounce their anathema against it as an aristocracy, or an oligarchy? Look at the modification of the principle. In order to fix the relative dimensions of entities which are equal in one sense, one part of the population is allowed a value according to its numbers, and the other according to a certain proportion of its numbers.

Well, Sir, has this changed it into any other than a Republican Government? It is said, that this arrangement was the result of a compromise. Admitting this, I demand to know, whether all compromises are not the fruit of a modification of antagonist principles? Are they made by mere guess, in a manner perfectly arbitrary? Have they no principles to guide them? Or is not the compromise to fix the precise point where antagonist principles intersect each other, so as to give to both their due operation?

I refer to the Constitution of the United States, not merely to vindicate our scheme from the stigma which is attempted to be fixed upon it, but for another, and a more important purpose. That Government has been referred to, not only as an example to show the consideration of all population, bond and free, in the apportionment of political power, but because of its influence on this State, as a member of the confederacy, and subject to that Government; a Government, charged with the external relations of this, and the other States. In that Government, all the inhabitants of the Union are taken into account: from which arrangement, a large portion of the weight of this State in it, is derived. Expel that principle from the Constitution, and you at once contract the State of Virginia. You bereave it of one-third of its political dimensions, in its connexion with a Government, which in various forms exercises a more powerful sway over all the States, than is equal in amount to all the residuary power left in their possession. When the other States were called upon by the South to make the compromise, the same arguments, now so strenuously urged, were at hand to resist the claim. The arguments were heard: they were profoundly considered. They were weighed with all the temper, deliberation and sagacity which that eminent body could bestow. That body did not find the allowance of this claim an insuperable obstacle; nor did they consider it as fixing upon the Government the stigma of anti-republicanism. It is found in the Constitution. The principle has been questioned since. Its influence on the pending question, direct and incidental, has been urged on this House, by my friend from Chesterfield, with a force and eloquence which I cannot pretend to emulate. His argument had been anticipated by one gentleman, and it has been attempted to be answered by two others. In one of its members, it has been evaded and it has been entirely unnoticed in the other. The argument is this: If this assembly pronounce, that the infusion of this principle converts any Government from a republic to an aristocracy, can you consistently, when that declaration shall be invoked against you, refuse to abide by your own decree? You must consent either to exhibit an open, undisguised, and glaring inconsistency, or you must surrender your rights so soon as you are confronted by your own declaration. The argument goes still further. If you countenance and sustain this pretension, may you not expect that that will be attempted, which has already many political converts, though it has not yet been attempted in the Legislature? It has, I say, many warm advocates, viz: that this power is a State acquisition, and like its Literary Fund, ought to be made common property, and distributed to all parts of the State, according to the ratio of white population. Sir, is this a mere gratuitous suggestion, thrown out for the purpose of alarming this Assembly, and having no foundation in fact? Will the gentleman from Loudoun, and the gentleman from Brooke reply? Will they stand up in the face of this Assembly, and say that such a doctrine has not been gravely insisted on heretofore? I mean, urged as a matter of political speculation among others, to show that the interests of the West have been sacrificed? I bear testimony to the fact, that it has been so urged.

[Mr. Mercer here rose and said, that he had never heard such an idea broached either in or out of the House of Delegates.]

Sir, I did myself hear it urged on this floor at the time when the distribution of the Literary Fund was discussed in the Legislature.

[Mr. Doddridge here enquired to what distribution of the Literary Fund, does the gentleman allude?]

I allude to the distribution of it, among the counties of the State, according to the numbers of white population in them respectively.

[Mr. Doddridge then said, on that occasion, the member from Brooke was not present.]

If the gentleman from Brooke was not, another gentleman, who is a conspicuous member of this House, was present. It was said, on that occasion, that the people of the West had been injured by the unequal distribution of this power acquired in the General Government, and claimed as the common property of all the white inhabitants of the State; and one injury ought not to be made the foundation of another. But, Sir, the suggestion will have at least this value. I propound the question now. I desire to have the disavowal of the claim to an apportionment of the Congressional representation according to the numbers of free white population, now under bond, sealed and delivered: Is this claim now disavowed? Am I to understand that it is disavowed by the gentlemen? If so, I have their own authority against that doctrine in future. If not, the argument is left in its full force.

I said, that the other part of the argument had been evaded. Its spirit has not been met. How has it been eluded? The gentleman from Albemarle made an argument, which implied that he did not approve of, or justify the provision of the Constitution of the United States. I do not say, that he expressly condemned that provision, or renounced the claim, to apportion our representation in Congress, on what is called the Federal numbers, or that he explicitly declared what his sentiments were; but he certainly did renounce it by implication. An explanation was drawn from him, which amounted to this, that wise men had doubted the propriety of this provision of the Constitution of the United States. Surely the gentleman did not wish me to suppose that he did *not* think so, because wise men did think so. I, therefore, say, as the case now stands before the Committee——

[Here Mr. Gordon asked leave to explain. He said he was sorry to have opinions imputed to him which he had not expressed. He had said that the propriety of the provision had been doubted by wise men, and that he should be of the same opinion, if it was to be made the basis of an aristocratic system of Government for Virginia. That was still his opinion.]

Sir, the gentleman is perfectly correct; and I represented him to have said what in explanation he avows he said. He did say that wise men had so doubted, but he did not express his own opinion further, than he should be opposed to the principle when made to exceed its function in the Government of the United States. We are left still in uncertainty as to what the gentleman thinks of the direct operation of the Federal Constitution in this part of it. How was the argument pressed by my friend from Chesterfield? He said to us, will you treat the principle on which rests a large portion of our power in the Federal Government, as if it would, being introduced into our own Government, contaminate it with aristocracy? and will you deny that it has the same influence in the other case? If you think so, then you are prepared, whenever the claim shall be made by the Northern States, to have that principle in the Federal Constitution abolished, or to own that we retain in it, this taint of aristocracy, because it serves our interests. This was his argument. And what answer was vouchsafed by the gentleman from Loudoun, (Mr. Mercer?) This: You have the power in your hands, and can keep it—it can never be surrendered but by your own consent—your *sic volo*. And is that an answer to the argument? Is that an answer to the enquiry, are you prepared to follow out your own principles, when the like appeal shall be made to you from another quarter? They say not one word to that. Respect for the gentlemen compels me to say, that when the claim shall be urged, they will surrender.

What, then, is the result on this branch of the argument? I wish I could express it with more force and precision. It is this: We maintain in its full spirit and extent, and say that it ought to be so maintained—the whole principle in the Bill of Rights—as an essential ingredient in all Republican Government; nay, as being so sacred that a Government, where it is not paramount, ceases to merit the epithet of Republican: but that that principle, (dear as it is—and it is dear to me—as giving to the whole mass, its flavor, relish, and nutritive quality,) is not to be taken separately and uncombined with other principles: That it is liable in its application, to be checked, controlled and modified by other principles, which make it sanative and salutary: and that the idea of giving to each and every man in the community equal portions of political power, is so far from being effected by counting numbers only, (disregarding their combinations,) that that will be the very means by which it must certainly be frustrated—and that the gentlemen, who are contending so strenuously, for the simple, naked, unmodified principle, will find, when it is reduced to practice, that it produces the very results which it is their avowed purpose to avoid.

And now, let me ask my highly esteemed friend from Augusta, whether, in these sentiments, he can find any warrant for saying that the friends of the amendment cast ridicule upon the Bill of Rights? and overthrow the very foundations of Government in their eager grasp for power? and whether a more dispassionate consideration ought not to exact from him the avowal that these imputations were hasty, and are not merited? Let us not be misunderstood. It may occur to some, that I have been anxious to make this vindication of the amendment, not only for the sake of my constituents, but that regard to self has had much sway in prompting the effort. Not so. Not so. Differing as I do, from the gentleman from Loudoun, in his opinions, I must also dissent from some of his sentiments. And though I can truly avow that self-vindication, apart from the important interests implicated in the question under discussion, has had but little or no influence, I can assure that gentleman, that *I* am no candidate for the Martyr's Crown. He, it seems, envies the distinction, and pants for the glory of martyrdom. I have no such aspiration. I do not wish to expose myself to trials, which well require heroic virtue to endure. I do not so certainly know, whether mine would avail me in the hour of need; I am sure I should not better bear by rashly courting the trial. I wish not, therefore, to tempt myself by making the experiment; nor can I consider the loss of popular favour, or the offices to which it may lead, as meriting the distinction of martyrdom. No, Sir. Yet I do not pretend to that stoical insensibility which is unconscious of the glow which public approbation imparts to the bosom. I am not insensible to popular applause, nor would I depreciate the value of popular favour. But that favour only which is spontaneous, and which is the best test of public approbation, is the object of my ambition. I value not that which is gained as a charitable dole, reluctantly bestowed on importunate solicitation—not that which is retained by the pliancy, which looking with steady eye at the signs of the political Zodiac, conforms to the horoscope it there finds? I thank God I have so regulated my desires, that a very small portion of my happiness depends on such popular favour, or on the acquisition of office; and if for the opinions I on this occasion avow and maintain, I shall be stricken from the ranks of those on whom the rays of popular favour may or is to beam, I shall more deplore the infatuation which directs the blow, than suffer pain from its infliction.

I think I have shown that the question before us is now reduced to this: whether, on a full and fair survey of the actual condition of the Commonwealth; its past history; its existing and multiform interests; its connexion with the Federal Government; and primarily, and above all, the peculiar location of one peculiar and important species of its property—any thing is due to those inductions, which can be fairly made from this survey, that ought to control or limit the sway of the (confessedly) primary principle of Republican Government?

The right in some form to the power we claim, has not been seriously questioned. The objection is, not that this power may not properly be conceded; but that, in the concession of this, we get a power beyond the necessity of the case on which we found our claim: not merely enough to protect this interest, but over persons and rights of a different kind. I mean not to enter at large on this argument. I could not do so, without bringing again before the Committee, many of those very able views which have already been much better presented by others.

Let me again call the attention of the Committee to the examples of other States, as being persuasive, if not irresistible, in this matter. I also call gentlemen's attention to the nature of the interest, and will endeavor to show what has not been distinctly unfolded by my coadjutors—that there is some object ulterior to that of protection against unjust taxation, which justifies the claim we advance. If in States, homogeneous in their population, and uniform in their condition, it has been found necessary to interpose a check either in the Senate, or by an apportionment of power to masses, so arranged as to control the power of mere numbers, is not the necessity enhanced incalculably, when we refer to the influence of this consideration in our own State? Do we claim protection for property only as such? The property we seek to protect, not merely serves the uses of man, but itself supplies the place of men. Its value does not consist in consumption—it is not mere brute matter, contributing to the comfort and ornament of life, but it consists of intelligent, sentient, responsible beings, that have passions to be inflamed, hearts to feel, understandings to be enlightened, and who are capable of catching the flame of enthusiasm, from the eloquent effusions of agitators, if not here, at least in other parts of the State: and who may not only be lost to their masters as property, but may change conditions, and become masters themselves; so far, at least, as the ravages of a servile war shall have any subject to be ruled over. These are the dangers which necessarily belong to the existence of this species of property within our borders. Are these considerations to have no weight? Will gentlemen still consider our slaves as mere brute matter? Will they shut their eyes to the fact, that there are and will continue to be political missionaries, who, with malignant purposes, or under the stimulation of a misguided philanthropy, industriously spread a contagion which no power may be able to arrest? Shall we shut our eyes and ears to all experience? Nothing is so easily propagated as such enthusiasm, when it comes with all the force of an apparent respect for human right, and a spirit of general philanthropy. Sir, is this the day when such principles will not be propagated? Are the people of the South so steady, as to be impregnably shielded against the sway of such a spirit? Can any gentleman look to the recent history of this country, and say that there are not some feelings, which, under the impulse of enthusiasm, may pass with the rapidity of lightning across the whole extent of this Union?

Looking to this subject, let me be permitted to state, in the presence of this audience, what I have often professed before, with a most perfect sincerity. I have told you that I entertain no distrust of the honour and sincerity of the people of the West; and further, that I did not distrust their sons, as the gentleman from Brooke considered the gentleman from Northampton to have done: and feeling this, I think it due to the candour which belongs to this debate, to declare my full and entire conviction, that if the power to the very uttermost of their claim, shall be transferred to the people of the West, their sense of justice will restrain them from wilfully doing the open and apparent wrong of levying unequal taxes on this species of property to the exoneration of property of a different kind. I do not believe they will do any such thing. There is not to be found in this land, any body of men prepared to commit gross, apparent and wanton wrong. Much less would I impute such a purpose to gentlemen from the West, some of whom, I am glad to regard as personal friends, and all of whom, I hope, will long continue to be brethren of the same political family. But, will this honesty be any guard against such influence as I have described? Sir, I dread not the vices of my brethren, but opinions that to them have the show of virtue. I fear not their meditated wrong, but their misguided philanthropy.

I extend the remark to the exercise of the taxing power, for objects in which we have little interest. Do I apprehend this from the wantonness of power and the recklessness of rapacity? I disclaim such a thought. No, Sir. I have no fears of their wilful injustice. But, is there any safe-guard against delusion on this subject? Can I shut my eyes against the light that beams from all experience, and shows the facility of persuading men that they are in the line of duty and patriotism, though interest alone stimulates the effort and sways the judgment? And on such occasions the virtues of the representative stand not as our security, but as the very source of our danger, when he shall think, that he is conforming to the wishes of his constituents, and cherishing the interests of all. I may say, therefore, without much violence to gentlemen's feelings, that if there are any dangers arising from the power of taxation, they are to be resolved into no distrust of their integrity, but that all the danger proceeds from the different views and different interests of parts and the whole Commonwealth, and the representative virtue of cherishing those of his constituents.

There is another view of the subject. They allow that we are entitled to some security, but insist that the form in which we ask it extends too far, and enables us to inflict the very injustice on them in other respects which we profess to fear from them on this. I call the attention of gentlemen to the different functions of the taxing power as in one, and in the other hand. With us it is conservative and defensive merely. We do not seek for its exercise by ourselves, but to prevent its exercise by others. In them, the danger is from action—not from the power's being fettered, but from its being left free.

I admit that the power, if given us for our protection, exists for other objects, and may be used for personal oppression. But, I beg leave to call the attention of gentlemen to the position on which I rest the argument—I have no distrust in the honour and virtue of the West—and I claim the same confidence as due to the East.—I anticipate in no quarter the exercise of mere arbitrary power; and I found the argument on that very principle: Their security is that which is furnished by considerations which they urge in vindication of the West. How can we oppress them in their personal rights without affecting all parts of the State equally? unless we be guilty of an open, confessed, naked act of arbitrary power? How can any Constitution be so framed as to guard against violence and arbitrary power? I turn gentlemen's argument against themselves—If any part of the Commonwealth shall have made up their minds to face the opprobrium of such conduct, your Constitution and all its guards cease to be of any value. No matter where power is by constitutional regulation, it cannot be retained. Resort must be had to an arbiter, and that arbiter sweeps your Constitution and your Republican Government together, from the face of the land.

And here let me notice one of the arguments of the gentleman from Augusta, (Mr. Johnson.) He made an ominous remark which I have not forgotten. He said, that "if we of the East had no slaves, their places would be supplied by white men." In what signification did he make this remark? Suppose their places were filled by white men? Then we are asking much less than we are entitled to.

But, their places are not supplied by white men. What then? Are you to form a Constitution as if they were not here? As if they did not belong to the Commonwealth, and formed no part of its interests? The observation shows, either that we ask less than is our due, or it gives cause for the foreboding that the new Constitution is to be fashioned as if slaves were mere intruders here, to whose existence no regard is to be given.

Permit me to make another observation. I told you that in looking at this important and delicate interest, it was to be regarded not merely as a subject of taxation, but that we ought to look steadily on all the dangers which surround it. Is it necessary for me to tell this Assembly, that in regard to these interests, respect is to be had to legislation which affects it even as property? That a wise regard to interests and feelings of the Eastern part of the State, present an irresistible claim on our brethren of the West, not to push their theories so as to take away from us the power to govern our slaves, and make laws of police for them? By the transit of power to hands not acquainted with our situation and dangers, and shielded by a barrier of mountains, who have no fears to sharpen their intellect to the approach of evil, and who know not how to adapt laws to the wants, the condition, the feelings, and the passions of the slaves in regard to those who retain them in bondage, interests, not of property merely, but of life itself, are implicated; these, and all their dearest connexions.

I pass with much pleasure from such a subject, to a view more congenial to the spirit in which I entered this Convention. Sir, I came here not to exasperate, but to soothe the asperities of other minds: not to arrest the march of reform, (as far as reform ought to be allowed to go,) but to enter on the task of repairing the Constitution, in perfect good faith: with professions not upon my lips merely, but springing from my heart: not made on this floor to suit the occasion, but resolved on and promulgated before I came here. I reject as an unworthy suggestion, the idea, that the course of any member here is intended as a mere deception to beguile this Assembly, and to cheat the people out of their rightful claim to reform. It must be obvious to you, Sir, and to this Committee, that it is my earnest wish to avoid every topic calculated to disturb the tranquil, judicious, and candid consideration by this body, of every subject which comes before it. In the process of the debate, it has pleased many gentlemen who are in favour of adopting the report of the Legislative Committee, to represent the West as having suffered for years under the most cruel neglect of its rights.

They have been represented to us, as year after year, bringing their complaints to the Legislature, and as being either rudely repelled, or treated with the most callous indifference. Sir, I feel that it is in my power to show, that the principal ground of this complaint, is a gross mistake of the nature and state of things. Even the last and latest complaint; that which gentlemen urge upon us, as a most aggravated grievance; that is, the manner in which this Convention is constituted, is utterly without foundation. I regretted to hear the gentleman from Augusta urge this topic with a view to influence this body. After enumerating other causes of complaint, he reminded us of our responsibility resulting from the gross injustice committed in the apportionment by which the representation in this body was prescribed, and that a majority of this Assembly represented a minority of the people of the State.

I did not understand him to complain on this subject, that the question, whether there should be a Convention or not, was first propounded to the freeholders of the State? I am sure he could not complain of this. If any such complaint is heard in any quarter of this House, let it at once be silenced; for, this limitation was prescribed by the advocates of Convention themselves. It was those who sought to have this Convention assembled, who volunteered in proposing such a restriction. The qualified voters of Virginia, to whom her sovereign power is confided, were those to whom they made their appeal to decide the question, whether the Convention should be called or no, and on the same principle they were made the electors of this body. Instead of claiming the utmost extent of the principle here insisted on, and giving uncontrolled sway to numbers of all classes, reference was had to the voters only. Now, I find from the result of the calculation of a friend in whom I have all confidence, that the following is the amount of representation in this body of the different sections of the State, having regard only to the number of voters. The whole number of persons charged, in 1829, with a land tax, was 92,000 in round numbers. This sum is to be taken as a dividend; 36,000, out of this 92,000, are on the land books of the counties beyond the Blue Ridge, and 56,000 on those East of that Ridge. According to the apportionment of that number, among the twenty-four Senatorial Districts, that dividend divided by twenty-four will give the quotient of 3,800 freeholders to each district. Take the 36,000 which includes every name on the land books for the counties beyond the mountains, divide that by 3,800, and the quotient is nine; nine districts, therefore, beyond the Ridge is the utmost claim that can be asserted by the West, and have they not nine? But, let us look further. That number of 36,000 includes all the names on the Commissioners' books in all the counties West of the Ridge. Now, I appeal to the candor of gentlemen of the West, and to the Sheriffs' returns, when I say that a large number of these names—one tenth at least—are the names of non-residents. Am I not correct? Is not much of that land ideal? And is not much of it owned by residents of the Eastern part of the State, for non-residents of the State? I earnestly desire, and it would give me inexpressible pleasure, to disabuse the minds of our Western brethren on this subject. I ask those conversant with the Western counties, to take up the land book and to say if one-tenth is not less than the due allowance. The consequence is, that they have nine districts, when, if the principle of the gentlemen from Norfolk and Augusta, (Mr. Taylor and Mr. Johnson,) were to be strictly applied, they would not have more than eight. They have then a larger representation than they are entitled to, and this, though we totally disregard the slave population of Eastern Virginia.

This view is profitable in its bearing on another object. These returns are for 1829, and therefore adapted to the augmented strength of the West at the present time. Now, permit me to use their own claim of rapid increase—and thus to show how far short these estimates must have been of the number of voters in the year 1817, when, by a new arrangement of the Senatorial Districts, the West was then allowed a larger representation in the Senate than they are now entitled to. I ask, therefore, whether in the change of the Senatorial Districts, instead of being depressed and defrauded, they have not been assigned even a larger share of political power than on their own principles they were entitled to. Yet, it is said, and said again, and great stress has been laid on the assertion, that they are languishing under the oppressive legislation of a hard-hearted minority. Look at their representation in the House of Delegates. They have eighty members out of two hundred and fourteen, that is, more than nine to fifteen. Reduce it to the proportion of eight to sixteen, and their title on the same basis is only one-third of the entire number, viz: to seventy-one. During this whole time, therefore, while all these doleful complaints have been uttered, they have been in the practical enjoyment of representation ten per cent. greater than they can justly claim. Now, Sir, I do not bring this as a matter of reproach, or an item of debit or credit, but my sole object is to disabuse their minds and free them from the influence of imaginary grievances, and then bring them to the real questions before this body with all that spirit of conciliation, harmony and good will which a frank correction of errors, is calculated to produce; cherishing, as I do, the earnest hope that the result of the labors of the Convention may conduce to the future good feeling, confidence and affection of different parts of the State. I do this that I may expel that festering sore, that they may be convinced that they have misconceived their own situation, that no wrong has been done them on their own principles, and that power has been meted to them by their own scales and by their own weights.

In the same spirit, and swayed by similar influences, I will now advert to the statement of the gentleman from Augusta, to show that on the very foundation he laid, if we disregard means and look only to results, the question is, in fact, reduced to a mere form of words.

But before I go to that, let me bring to the notice of the gentleman from Augusta the influence of the principle when reduced to practice, according to the terms of the resolution of the Legislative Committee, as explained by his coadjutor from Loudoun (Mr. Mercer,) viz: the principle of representation on the basis of white population. The gentleman from Loudoun took this process. He did not controvert the proposition contained in the resolutions of the gentleman from Norfolk, but maintained the report of the Legislative Committee, on the ground that the two were equivalents. He claimed that equal amounts of population would produce equal numbers of qualified electors. On this postulate, he assumed, that the total numbers of white persons in any region of the State was a fair exponent of the number of voters it would furnish, and the numbers of population and of voters, having the same ratio, however different their sum, the result would be the same, whichever should be resorted to, in making the apportionment of representation. If one hundred of gross population, wherever situated, gave ten voters and in that proportion, it would be just as accurate to take a gross population for your computation of the amount of representation, as to take the voters.

The gentleman from Augusta, does not deal with these equivalents, or go on these postulates. He has tried the effect, and has not conjectured that if a given number of whites, in one part of the State, furnish a certain number of voters, the same number of whites in any other part would furnish a like number of voters. He has found the postulate of the gentleman from Loudoun to be fallacious, and the result shows one of the most striking and irresistible proofs of the sagacity with which my friend from Chesterfield seized the true criterion of the question in debate. Though in its form his proposition was supposed to be revolting to the feelings of the West, the result of these calculations furnishes demonstrable proof of its correctness.

I need not go into an examination of the classifications of the gentleman from Augusta, made of the quantum of power to each portion of the State, deduced by his different processes. The necessity of this is removed by the fact that we have the amount in gross, and that the question is between the two sections of the State, divided by the Blue Ridge.

On the basis of qualified voters, on the Commissioners' books, the Western district has nine more members than its due in the lower House, and one more in the upper. The gentleman shakes his head when I designate the Blue Ridge as separating the rival interests of the State. Be it so. But let me tell him, that it is a matter of some little value to us, to look to any line. We can advance one step with the aid of the elements of apportionment we have obtained from his estimate, by first taking this primary division of the State. We can say these are to be the estimated amount of representatives beyond the Blue Ridge, and leave the sub-division to them. Leave that estimated for the East to us, and we will easily sub-divide. There will be no difficulty on this score. But, look to the estimated amounts for the sub-divisions of the State. What are they? I could not take down the results of the gentleman's calculations, and so cannot speak with precision, as to the particular sums; but, I received this impression from the whole, that taking the whole number of those who pay land tax in the East and West, divided by the Ridge, and giving them representation in proportion, and then making a re-partition between the two sections of the East, and the two sub-divisions of the West, I think the difference between the results of this, and an apportionment on the ratio, that the amendment under consideration supplies, will not amount to an unit. The gentleman may say, whether or not I am right. That the numbers do very nearly approximate, is certain. How much the difference may be, is unworthy serious deliberation. Here, then, the gentleman from Augusta, and the gentleman from Loudoun, stand on a ground of apportionment, which leaves the four grand divisions of the State, almost as they will stand on the mixed basis.

If you take the Federal number and work by that rule, it will bring you to nearly the same result. Now, it deserves to be mentioned as a memorable fact, that this concurrence of three different processes, all leading to the same result, shows the justice and sagacity of the scheme of the gentleman from Culpeper (Mr. Green.)

He resorted to the plan of a mixed basis of taxation and representation, not arbitrary—nor with a view to claim and to conquer power, but on mature deliberation, weighing various interests as they exist—and not from mere speculation—and it does happen, such is the influence of the slave property, (which is not property merely, but men) on the other classes of persons and property, in the community, as to render it indispensable that they should be considered in the ratio. And it is another and most striking evidence of the sagacity and wisdom of those who originated the Federal number. It acts on the just principles of political economy. The slave population acts, not only as the laboring power of society, but it takes the place of men. Wherever slavery exists, and you look to the freemen of society for its government, and there is any property qualification, you arrive at the same object, or very nearly so, by adding three-fifths of the slave population, as by ascertaining all the voters, and apportioning your representation according to numbers.

This view of the subject is consoling. It presents us a point where all the processes meet and coincide: and then the only question is (seeing this is the result by either calculation,) not which ratio shall be employed just this moment, but what shall be fixed upon as the rule of future apportionments. On that subject, every consideration of wisdom and of convenience, requires that we discard at once, other modes of calculation, and take the easy, simple, practical plan of the Federal number, and make our apportionment by that.

Why are we to take this? Not arbitrarily, but because it agrees with the other processes, and because, if any other is resorted to, for the future rule, you force an artificial state of things, by holding out to politicians and individuals, inducements to produce it, with a view to an unequal distribution of political power. If you take taxation as your rule, legislation may be moulded, not by right principles, but sinister views to it; influence on political power and taxation may be managed, so as merely to affect the balance of that power.

If you take the rule of qualified voters only, then you encounter the difficulty of accurately determining their number. The very element of calculation is wanting. If you go to the Commissioners' books, you encounter the toil and expense of registering all the lawful voters throughout this land: and you encounter, besides, the active principle alluded to by the gentleman from Augusta, leading men to make a false and fraudulent representation of the number of those votes, and give an artificial exaggeration of it; and thus you will have on your books, a host of men of straw, who disappear at the polls. You do more. And I wonder that the strong and masculine mind of the gentleman from Augusta, did not see this danger, and repudiate the rule. If I understood him aright, there is no one who regards, with a stronger feeling of foreboding and solicitude, that part of our duty which consists in prescribing the qualification of voters, than the gentleman. I have the authority of his whole political life, (and the life of no man can be more confidently appealed to, to determine the future from the past,) for this assertion. And what must be the consequences, if he adopts this principle as a future test of political power?

The very first effect of it, will be to turn the thoughts of this Convention, not to the consideration of the reasons which legitimately belong to the subject, but to its influence on the grand question of power.

The effect will be, that you interpose a barrier to a fair, candid, and judicious decision of the questions affecting the limits of the Right of Suffrage. I am not sure that I am exempt myself from the operation of such an influence. I fear that my mind may be turned away, from considerations justly belonging to those questions, by the important and decisive influence of whatever principles we adopt, to regulate the Right of Suffrage, on the all-absorbing question now under consideration.

This is the inevitable effect of fixing upon the ratio of voters, as a principle of future action. But, what will be the effect in future? Fraud and simulation in fixing the number of voters. Insuperable difficulty will arise in getting at the real number of voters. And allowing you to get at it first, what will be the result hereafter? We propose, by the resolution in the report of the Legislative Committee, to extend the Right of Suffrage, so as to include many new classes of voters. We embrace all who are house-keepers, and have been assessed for, and have paid revenue taxes. I know not if it will be carried to that extent—but that has been proposed. But, assuming that that rule shall obtain, what is the number of qualified voters when we look to the numbers, not now, but in after time? When we fix the time the Census shall be taken, we cannot look to a former Census, but to that taken in the same year the apportionment shall be made; and that is to be the foundation of the allotment.

Well. And what is the expense at which the ascendancy of political power may be purchased? Aye, purchased?—put up to auction—and you the offerers. The delinquents in the payment of a county levy shilling tax will probably average one hundred and fifty or two hundred for each county, and they, it may be presumed, have not taxable property. The number of voters at this time, taking as the criterion of suffrage, the payment of a revenue tax, are probably about 35,000 West of the Ridge; and by the calculation of gentlemen on the other side, there are 15,000 or 20,000 more above the age of twenty-one, who either have no property at all, or no taxable property. You, Sir, well know, as every member of this Convention knows, that from the manner in which the assessments are made, every individual, by his own mere ipse dixit, may qualify himself to vote, so far as that qualification depends on having his name on the commissioner's book, and an assessment of a tax on property. Suppose the case of a contractor or manufacturer who has in his employ five hundred day-labourers, every one of them subject to his beck and call—though not one of them may own a dollar's worth of taxable or other property, yet every one of them may at pleasure, when called on by the commissioner, affect to own a horse or some property not subject to a higher tax than four cents, and give in that as property owned by him and liable to a revenue tax; and this tax being paid, he ranks as a voter, and more than that, he will enter into the computation when representation is to be apportioned. By this process, 20,000 may be added to the number of voters, at an expense of $800, and the addition of this 20,000 may, nay, will change the entire balance of political power. You would thus put up that balance at a wretched auction, and sell it for a miserable pittance. Will gentlemen close their eyes to this view of the subject? If we are to proceed in this downward course, let us go the whole length at once, and not require these petty frauds to bring upon us all the practical consequences of the utmost extreme to which we may go in extending the Right of Suffrage. Let us at once adopt the plan of Universal Suffrage—admit paupers and all to the polls. Let us give full efficacy to the so much loved principle of numbers to its whole extent. Let us no longer struggle with each other under vain disguises, but consent like men in the face of day, that we will take Universal Suffrage as one of the principles of the Constitution.

I appeal to the gentleman from Fairfax, (Mr. Fitzhugh,) the gentleman from Augusta, (Mr. Johnson,) the gentleman from Brooke, (Mr. Doddridge,) and to all the gentlemen on that side the House, if they do not render this almost inevitable; if they resort to such a principle as is now proposed, not for the present only, but for all future times, as the rule for the apportionment of representation: and then I solemnly ask them, are they prepared with their opinions on the subject of Suffrage, to incur this consequence?

Sir, I renounce it. I call on others, and especially the gentlemen to whom I have appealed, to join me in renouncing it, and to unite to furnish some ground on which all can meet, and this vexed question be terminated, at least, so far as results are concerned. Let us renounce all our processes. This I hold out to our antagonists as an olive branch—I tender it as a peace-offering—let us renounce all our processes, and take results and fix *them* in the Constitution, and wrangle no longer about a form of words. Let us endeavor to fix on some principle to guide us in all our future changes. But if we cannot do this, then let the Constitution be silent, as to the rule to govern in future, and leave to future times to provide for future exigencies. Not that I prefer or approve the omission in the Constitution of some rule applicable in such exigencies. I would acquiesce in it, however, rather than continue the tedious and pernicious struggle in which we are engaged. If our brethren in the West will discharge from their minds imaginary injuries, and unseasonable fastidiousness, there is a principle in which we all might meet, simple, practicable, already established, and sustaining a most important interest of the State: a principle which adapts itself to all changes—and which, if the prospects held out in the West, be not the creations of fancy, but the prophetic augury of wise observation, will carry there, along with its increasing prosperity and population, the power which is its due.

I have already adverted to the principles on which I became a member of this Convention. They were known to the public before I became a depository of the trust I hold here, and permit me to say to the gentlemen of the West—brethren of the same community, if my wishes shall prevail, brethren of the same community, we will remain in all time to come; for I will not permit my mind to indulge even in the hypothetical anticipation of a state of things that would reconcile me to a separation of the State, or to a disunion of the United States. In that term DISUNION, are included all the master ills that can affect a people or a State. Though we may, and certainly will, suffer less by the separation than the West, how heart-sickening is this estimate, not of blessings, but of woes! Come disunion when it may, it is due to the candour of this debate, to say, that strong as we are, it will bring to us a measure of evil, at least equal to that which our Northern neighbours will suffer. Nay, I fear, that if the extremity of suffering to which the several parts of the Union would be exposed by so disastrous an event, could be accurately guaged, the painful pre-eminence of superior suffering would be found to belong to the Southern States.

I have not myself, been indifferent to the interests of the West. I am a friend to internal improvement. I have manifested it not by professions merely, but by acts in discharge of my solemn duties as a member of the Legislature. To the gentleman from Loudoun, (Mr. Mercer,) I allow the meed of praise, of being the author of the law which established the Board of Public Works, and munificently endowed it. To his zeal and influence, its success is mainly to be ascribed—If praise it be, I may claim for myself, that which belongs to an humble but earnest ally in the same cause. It had my support—and therein, I think I gave no indication of hostility to Western interests. I still continue the friend of internal improvement within those limits which its true friends are disposed to assign to it. I am hostile to gorgeous and visionary schemes, calculated only to delude the public mind, to play before the imagination the image of a great but unattainable good, or if not unattainable, to be accomplished only at a cost more than all the benefit it can yield will counterbalance. The true test of the expediency of attempting improvements of every kind, is that which was laid down by my friend from Augusta, (Mr. Johnson.) Let that be always applied, and with caution and care. When I see presented to me a scheme for any work for improving the state of the country, and I find it to be such, that those who receive the aid will be able themselves to return the sum expended, or a reasonable interest on it, I shall always be willing to advance for their aid the treasure and credit of the State. And let me add, that this is not a singular sentiment by any means in the Eastern portion of the State: and nothing can exterminate that feeling and turn all the kindly and wholesome affections of the people of the East, to gall and bitterness, but a callous indifference to the mighty interests they hold, and the tremendous dangers to which those interests are exposed, and expose those who hold them. If the East shall find or have just cause to suspect that callous indifference, not to their property merely, but to their happiness and their safety; not to a matter of pence and farthings, but to their existence itself; the effect will be a state of constant inquietude, of uninterrupted apprehension—a total destruction of quiet and happiness. If to this indifference shall be added a grasping and intractable spirit—a resort to themes of angry declamation to overbear by passion and prejudice, and delusion, instead of weighing with candour their claims, and estimating them with the kindness of fraternal feeling—then, that will be done in the East, which some gentlemen think has been done in the West. There will be concert and combination. Stimulated by the feelings produced by that most intolerable evil, and ever-present sense of insecurity, they will regard the inexorable authors of it, with fierce and angry hostility, and every collision will heat the blood, and tend to melt into one common mass, all their interests and passions, and then the two divisions of the State will stand confronted with each other; with passions aroused; fraternal feelings exasperated into bitterness; and then the minority in the East, impelled by one feeling, and directed by common will, will, (as the gentleman says that of the West has done,) practically control the power of the majority. The tendency of the claims so inexorably urged in total disregard of the rights and security of the East, is to break the cement which has heretofore so consolidated Western feelings and interests, and to fuse all the people of the East, as it were, into one body having but one soul.

I invoke gentlemen to take this view—I ask them, whether they can think of acting so as to produce this violent wrenching of all the feelings which ought to bind us as members of one political family, and plant a thorn in the wound made by the violent divulsion which will rankle for all time to come, and as an eloquent advocate of American rights said, in the British Parliament, in an analogous case, produce that *immedicabile vulnus*, for which time has no lenitive, and no physician a cure.

Mr. Stanard having resumed his seat, the question was propounded from the Chair, and after a pause, seemed likely to be taken, when

Mr. Randolph rose, and addressed the Committee as follows:

Mr. Chairman: It has been with great disappointment, and yet deeper regret, that I have perceived an invincible repugnance on the part of gentlemen representing here, a large portion of the Commonwealth, extending from Cape Henry to the Mountains, along the whole length of the North Carolina line, that portion of it in which my own district is situated, to take a share in this debate—a repugnance not resulting—I say so from my personal knowledge of many of them—not resulting from any want of ability, nor from the want of a just, modest, and manly confidence in the abilities they possess. I have looked to Norfolk; I have looked to Southampton; I have looked to Dinwiddie; I have looked to Brunswick, for the display of talent which I knew to exist: but, Sir, I have looked in vain.

And it is this circumstance only—I speak it with a sincerity, I have too much self-respect to vouch for, which has induced me to overcome the insuperable aversion; insuperable until now; that I have felt, to attract towards myself the attention of the Committee.

As long as I have had any fixed opinions, I have been in the habit of considering the Constitution of Virginia, under which I have lived for more than half a century, with all its faults and failings, and with all the objections which practical men—not theorists and visionary speculators, have urged or can urge against it, as the very best Constitution; not for Japan; not for China; not for New England; or for Old England; but for this, our ancient Commonwealth of Virginia.

But, I am not such a bigot as to be unwilling, under any circumstances, however imperious, to change the Constitution under which I was born; I may say, certainly under which I was brought up, and under which, I had hoped to be carried to my grave. My principles on that subject are these: the grievance must first be clearly specified, and fully proved; it must be vital, or rather, deadly in its effect; its magnitude must be such as will justify prudent and reasonable men in taking the always delicate, often dangerous step, of making innovations in their fundamental law; and the remedy proposed must be reasonable and adequate to the end in view. When the grievance shall have been thus made out, I hold him to be not a loyal subject, but a political bigot, who would refuse to apply the suitable remedy.

But, I will not submit my case to a political physician; come his diploma from whence it may; who would at once prescribe all the medicines in the Pharmacopœia, not only for the disease I now have, but for all the diseases of every possible kind I ever might have in future. These are my principles, and I am willing to carry them out; for, I will not hold any principles which I may not fairly carry out in practice.

Judge, then, with what surprise and pain, I found that not one department of this Government—no, not one—Legislative, Executive or Judicial—nor one branch of either, was left untouched by the spirit of *innovation;* (for I cannot call it reform.) When even the Senate, yes, Sir, the Senate, which had so lately been swept by the besom of innovation—even the Senate had not gone untouched or unscathed. Many innovations are proposed to be made, without any one practical grievance having been even suggested, much less shown.

Take that branch of the Government which was so thoroughly reformed in 1816, and even that is not untouched. Sir, who ever heard a whisper, *ab urbe condita* to this day, that the Senators of Virginia were too *youthful?* I never heard such a sentiment in my life. And in the House of Delegates, what man ever heard that the members—I speak of them, of course, in the aggregate—that the members were too young? Yet, even there—it is to be declared, that all men who might be elected to that body between the ages of twenty-one and twenty-four, are to be disfranchised; and as regards the Senate, all between the ages of twenty-one and thirty. Yes, Sir, not only the spring and seed-time, but the summer and harvest of life; that delightful season which neither you, Sir, nor I can ever recal; the dearest and the best portion of our lives; during this period of nine years, the very prime of human life, men are to be disfranchised. And for what? For a political megrim, a freak—no evil is suggested. The case is certainly very rare, that a man under thirty is elected a member of the Senate. It will then be said, there is no privation, and, therefore, no injury. But, Sir, there is a wide difference between a man's being not elected, and a fundamental law stamping a stigma upon him by which he is excluded from the noblest privilege to which no merit or exertion on his part can restore him. But, all this, I suppose, is in obedience to the all-prevailing principle, that *vox populi vox dei;* aye, Sir, the all-prevailing principle, that Numbers and Numbers alone, are to regulate all things in political society, in the very teeth of those abstract natural rights of man, which constitute the only shadow of claim to exercise this monstrous tyranny.

With these general remarks, permit me to attempt—(I am afraid it will prove an abortive attempt) to say something on the observations of other gentlemen, to which I have given the most profound attention I am capable of. Sir, I have no other preparation for this task, than a most patient attention to what has been said here, and in the Committee, of which I was a member, and deep, intense, and almost annihilating thought on the subjects before us. This is all the preparation that I have made. I cannot follow the example which has been set me. I cannot go into the history of my past life, or defend my political consistency here or elsewhere. I will not do this for this reason: I have always held it unwise to plead 'till I am arraigned, and arraigned before a tribunal having competent and ample jurisdiction. My political consistency requires no such defence. My claim to Republicanism rests on no patent taken out yesterday, or to be taken out to-morrow. My life itself is my only voucher, a life spent for thirty years in the service of the most grateful of constituents.

The gentleman from Augusta, who occupies so large a space, both in the time and in the eye of the House, has told us that he fought gallantly by the side of his noble friend from Chesterfield, so long as victory was possible, and that it was not until he was conquered, that he grounded his arms. The gentleman farther told us that, finding his native country and his early friends on this side the mountain, on whose behalf he had waged that gallant war—he found he hesitated what part to take *now*, until his constituents, aye, Sir—and more than that, his property, on the other side—and he has taken his course accordingly. Well, Sir, and will he not allow, on our part, that some consideration is due to our constituents, although they happen to be our neighbours; or *to our property*, although we reside upon it? Are either or both less dear on that account?

But, Sir, I put it to the Committee, whether the gentleman is not mistaken in point of fact? Whether the victory *is* indeed won? Every one, to be sure, is the best judge whether he is beaten or not. But, I put it to the gentleman himself, whether, if he were now fighting along side of his noble friend from Chesterfield, the scale might not possibly turn the other way? No man, however, is compelled to fight after he feels himself vanquished.

Sir, I mean no ill-timed pleasantry, either as it regards the place where it is uttered, the person to whom it refers, and least of all, as it respects him by whom the remark is made, when I say, that in this prudent resolution of the gentleman from Augusta, he could not have been exceeded in caution and forecast by a certain renowned Captain Dugate Dalgetty himself. Sir, the war being ended, he takes service on the other side:—the sceptre having passed from Judah, the gentleman stretches out his arm from Richmond, to Rockfish Gap, to intercept and clutch it in its passage.

Among various other observations with which he favoured the Committee, he protested with great earnestness against opinions relating to the Federal Government or its administration being introduced here. Sir, the gentleman is too great a lawyer not to know, that the Federal Government is *our* Government:—it is the Government of Virginia:—and if a man were disposed to shut his eyes to the Constitution, and the administration of the Federal Government, he could not do it: they would be forced open, Sir, by the interests, and feelings, aye, and by the passions too, which have existed, do exist, and will continue to exist, as long as Virginia herself shall have existence.

It is not the least of my regrets that one of the most inevitable consequences of these changes, if they shall take effect, will be totally to change all the politics of Virginia in reference to the Federal Government; (without considering the hands in which it may happen to be placed.) and I do confidently believe, that the very greatest cause of them is to be found in the hope of producing that all-desired change. In many cases I know it to exist, of my own personal knowledge.

Sir, we can't shut our eyes to the Federal Government.

When in 1788, the Convention of Virginia adopted the Federal Government as a part of her Constitution, they effected a greater change in our Constitution than the wildest reformer now suggests to us: to estimate the amount of that change we must have reference to her interests and power at that day: if not, we may call *ourselves* Statesmen, but the world will apply to us a very different epithet. Among innumerable causes why I now oppose a change, is my full recollection of the change which was then brought about. I have by experience learned that changes, even in the ordinary law of the land, do not always operate as the drawer of the bill, or the Legislative body, may have anticipated: and of all things in the world, a Government, whether ready made, to suit casual customers, or made per order, is the very last that operates as its framers intended. Governments are like revolutions: you may put them in motion, but I defy you to control them after they are *in* motion.

Sir, if there is any one thing clearer than another, it is that the Federal Constitution intended that the State Governments should issue no paper money; and by giving the Federal Government power "*to coin money*," it was intended to insure the result that this should be a hard money Government:—and what is it? It is a paper-money Government. If this be the result, in spite of all precautions to the contrary—(Sir, this is no time, as the late illustrious President of the Court of Appeals was wont to say, to mince words,) and these Governments have turned out to be two most corrupt paper-money Governments, and you could not prevent it; how can we expect, now, to define and limit the operation of new and untried principles? For new and untried they are; and if God lends me strength, I will prove it.

I have very high authority—the authority of the gentleman from Augusta—to say that the Federal Government was intended to be charged only with the external relations of the country: but, by a strange transformation, it has become the regulator, (abandoning the Colonial trade by negligence, or incapacity, or both, and crippling all our other trade,) it has become the regulator of the interior of the country; its roads; its canals; and, more than all, of its productive, or rather its *unproductive* labour, (for they have made it so.)

Yet, with these facts staring us in the face, we are gravely told not to look at the Federal Government at all. And this in the Government of Virginia, where, to use a very homely phrase, but one that exactly suits the case, we can't take a step without breaking our shins over some Federal obstacle.

Sir, I can readily see a very strong motive for wishing to do away all past distinctions in politics, to obliterate the memory of old as well as of recent events, and once more to come with something like equal chances into the political lottery.

Let me return to my illustration. What provision is there, Mr. Chairman, either in the Constitution of Virginia or the Constitution of the United States, which establishes it as a principle, that the Commonwealth of Virginia should be the sole restraining and regulating power on the mad and unconstitutional usurpations of the Federal Government? There is no such provision in either:—yet, in practice, and in fact, the Commonwealth of Virginia has been, to my certain knowledge, for more than thirty years, the sole counterpoise and check on the usurpations of the Federal Government—so far as they have been checked at all: I wish they had been checked more effectually.

For a long time, our brethren of the South, because we were the frontier State of the great Southern division of the Union, were dead to considerations to which they have, I fear, awaked too late. Virginia was left alone and unsupported, unless by the feeble aid of her distant offspring, Kentucky. It is because I am unwilling to give up this check, or to diminish its force, that I am unwilling to pull down the edifice of our State Government from the garret to the cellar; aye, down to the foundation stone. I will not put in hazard this single good, for all the benefits the warmest advocate of reform can hope to derive from the results of this body.

The gentleman from Augusta told us, yesterday, I believe, or the day before, or the day before that, (I really do not remember which,) that slaves have always been a subject of taxation in Virginia, and that a long while ago neat cattle had also been taxed. In regard to these horned cattle, I think they have occupied full as much attention as they are entitled to in this debate. But, let it be remembered, that we were then, not taxing the cattle *of the West*, for there was no West, but a few scattered settlements beyond the mountain; and what we have been discussing was the proportion of taxes paid by the East and the West. No sooner was an interest in this subject established beyond the mountains, than the tax was laid aside. At that time, Sir, the Commonwealth of Virginia was throughout, a slave-holding Commonwealth: (would to God she were so now.) And is it then so wonderful that slaves should have been a subject of taxation? Yes, Sir: Virginia was then not only throughout, a slave-holding, but a tobacco-planting Commonwealth. You can't open the Statute Book—I mean one of the Old Statute Books, not those that have been defaced by the finger of reform—and not see that tobacco was, in fact, the currency, as well as staple of the State. We paid our clerks' fees in tobacco: verdicts were given in tobacco: and bonds were executed payable in tobacco. That accounts for it all. While a large portion of the State has ceased to be a slave-holding, and a still larger portion has ceased to be a tobacco-planting community, the burden has rested on the necks of a comparatively small, unhappy, and I will say it, a proscribed caste in the community. Not that any such effect was intended, when all were tobacco-planters, taxes on slaves and tobacco were fair and equal. But, time, the greatest of innovators, has silently operated to produce this great and grinding oppression. My nativity cast my lot there. I am one of them. I participate in all their interests and feelings. And if I had been told, until I had the evidence of fact to prove it—that one of the great slave-holding and tobacco-planting districts, would lend itself to the support of the report of the Legislative Committee, unmitigated, or, to use a term for which I am indebted to the gentleman from Spottsylvania, *unmollified*, or *undulcified* by any thing to give it a wholesome operation, I would not have believed it. Nothing but ocular and auricular demonstration, would have made me believe it possible. For my part, I had not only, as the gentleman from Chesterfield has said, never have been born, but, being born and grown up as I am, it were better for me that a mill-stone were hanged about my neck, and I cast into the uttermost depths of the sea, than to return to my constituents after having given a naked vote for the report of the Committee.

Sir, when I speak of danger, from what quarter does it come; from whom? From the corn and oat growers on the Eastern Shore, the Rappahannock and the Pamunkey? From the fishermen on the Chesapeake? The pilots of Elizabeth City? No, Sir—from ourselves—from the great slave-holding and tobacco-planting districts of the State. I could not have brought myself to believe it—nothing could have persuaded me to believe, that the real danger which threatens this great interest, should spring from those districts themselves. And, arrogant and presumptuous as it may appear in me, (these epithets have been applied to us by the gentleman from Augusta,) I will risk any thing short of my eternal salvation on the fact, that when the people of that region come to understand the real question, you will as soon force ratsbane down their throats, as a Constitution with such a principle in it.

The gentleman from Augusta told us, yesterday, or the day before, I cannot be certain as to the precise day, with some appearance as if it were a grievance, that the people had interfered; and he asked if we are to be instructed out of our seats? I answer, yes. Such as cannot be instructed *in* their seats, must be instructed *out* of their seats. He says the voices of the people from county meetings and cross roads and taverns, will come here and interrupt the harmony of our deliberations.

I trust they will. Though the people have hitherto been supine, on this side the mountains, I trust they will take the matter into their own hands. I hope they are beginning to rouse from their torpor: and I know it. I will state one fact, to show that the current of public sentiment, is fast setting in on our side. I do not say whether it was for or against us before. I have heard, not one, not ten, not fifty, (and when I say not fifty, I mean not less, but more than that number,) of intelligent men declare, that if by any possibility, they could have foreseen, (poor innocents,) that such were to be the results, they never would have voted for this Convention. In the mean while, not a single convert has been made from our cause; if there has, name the man; I could name ten, twenty, aye, fifty; and if I were to resort to documentary evidence, I could name more. So far am I from being one of those, who wish to precipitate the question, I am glad, I rejoice in the prospect, that our Session will run into that of the Virginia Assembly. In politics, I am always for getting the last advices. You can never get at the true temper of the public mind, till the occasion presents itself for decisive action.

I have made, and shall make, no disclaimer of having intended offence to any person or party in this body—and this for the same reason I before stated. I never will plead, till I am arraigned by a competent tribunal—and the disclaimer would be misplaced. Gentlemen on all sides, have spoken of the *intention* with which they are demanding power, (for the gentleman from Augusta lifted the veil, and owned to us, that power, and power alone, is the object he is in pursuit of.) Sir, I mean no disrespect, when I say, that however important it may be to themselves, to me it is a matter of perfect indifference—I speak in reference to the operation of their measures—whether their intents be wicked or charitable. I say, the demand which they make, is such as ought to alarm every considerate and fore-thoughted man; and that there is nothing to mitigate that alarm, in the stern, unrelenting, inexorable, remorseless cry, which they raise for power, and their determination to listen to no compromise. One gentleman, indeed, has abated somewhat, of his tone of triumph. Perhaps, the prospect of speedy enjoyment, has calmed his exultation, and sobered him down.

Mr. Chairman, since I have been here, the scene has recalled many old recollections. At one time, I thought myself in the House of Representatives, listening to the debate on the Tariff; at another time, I imagined myself listening to the debate on the Missouri Question; and sometimes I fancied myself listening to both questions debated at once. Are we men? met to consult about the affairs of men? Or are we, in truth, a Robinhood Society? discussing rights in the abstract? Have we no house over our heads? Do we forget, that we are living under a Constitution, which has shielded us for more than half a century—that we are not a parcel of naked and forlorn savages, on the shores of New Holland; and that the worst that can come is, that we shall live under the same Constitution that we have lived under, freely and happily, for half a century? To their monstrous claims of power, we plead this prescription; but then we are told, that *nullum tempus occurrit Regi*—King whom? King Numbers. And they will not listen to a prescription of fifty-your years—a period greater, by four years, than would secure a title to the best estate in the Commonwealth, unsupported by any other shadow of right. Nay, Sir, in this case, prescription operates *against* possession. They tell us, it is only a case of long-continued, and, therefore, of aggravated injustice. They say to us, in words the most courteous and soft, (but I am not so soft as to swallow them,) "we shall be—we will be—we must be your masters, and you shall submit." To whom do they hold this language? To dependents? weak, unprotected, and incapable of defence? Or is it to the great tobacco-growing and slave-holding interest, and to every other interest on this side the Ridge? "We are numbers, you have property." I am not so obtuse, as to require any further explanation on this head. "We are numbers, you have property." Sir, I understand it perfectly. Mr. Chairman, since the days of the French Revolution, when the Duke of Orleans, who was the richest subject, not only in France, but in all Europe, lent himself to the *mountain* party in the Convention, in the vain and weak hope of grasping political power, perhaps of mounting the throne, still slippery with the blood of the last incumbent—from that day to this, so great a degree of infatuation, has not been shown by any individual, as by the tobacco-grower, and slave-holder of Virginia, who shall lend his aid to rivet this yoke on the necks of his brethren, and on his own. Woe betide that man! Even the Duke of Orleans himself, profligate and reprobate as he was, would have halted in his course, had he foreseen in the end, his property confiscated to the winds, and his head in the sack of the executioner.

I enter into no calculations of my own, for I have made none, nor shall I follow the example which has been set me. I leave that branch of the argument, if argument it can be called, of the gentleman from Augusta, to be answered by himself.

The gentleman told us, the day before yesterday, that in fifteen minutes of the succeeding day, he would conclude all he had to say; and he then kept us two hours, not by the Shrewsbury clock, but by as good a watch as can be made in the city of

London. (*Drawing out and opening his watch.*) As fifteen minutes are to two hours—in the proportion of one to eight—such is the approximation to truth, in the gentleman's calculations. If all the calculations and promises of the gentleman from Augusta, which he held out to gull us—I speak not of his intentions, but only of the effect that would have ensued—shall be no nearer the truth than these, where then should we be who trust them?

In the course of what I fear will be thought my very wearisome observations, I spoke of the Tariff Law. When the people of the United States threw off their allegiance to Great Britain, and established Republican Governments here, whether State or Federal, one discovery since made in politics, had not yet entered into the head of any man in the Union, and which, if not arrested by the good sense and patriotism of the country, will destroy all Republican Government, as certainly and inevitably as time will one day destroy us. That discovery is this: that a bare majority—(the majority on the Tariff was, I believe, but two—my friend, behind me, (Mr. P. P. Barbour,) tells me that I am right—and on one important branch of that law, that I mean, which relates to cotton bagging, the majority was but one, and that consisted of the casting vote of the Speaker,) that a bare majority may oppress, harass, and plunder the minority at pleasure, but that it is their interest to keep up the minority to the highest possible point consistent with their subjugation, because, the larger that minority shall be, in proportion to the majority, by that same proportion are the profits of the majority enhanced, which they have extracted and extorted from the minority. And after all our exclamations against this crying oppression; after all our memorials and remonstrances; after all our irrefragable arguments against it, (I refer not to the share I had in them, I speak of the arguments of other gentlemen, and not of my own,) shall we in Virginia, introduce this deadly principle into our own Government? and give power to a bare majority to tax us *ad libitum*, and that when the strongest temptation is at the same time held out to them, to do it? It is now a great while since I learned from the philosopher of Malmesbury, that a state of nature is a state of war; but if we sanction this principle, we shall prove that a state, not of nature, but of society, and of Constitutional Government, is a state of interminable war. And it will not stop here. Instructed by this most baneful, yes, and most baleful example, we shall next have one part of a county conspiring to throw their share of the burden of the levy upon the other part. Sir, if there is a destructive principle in politics, it is that which is maintained by the gentleman from Augusta.

But we are told that we are to have a stay of execution. "We will give you time, say the gentlemen: only give us a bond binding all your estate, secured by a deed of trust on all your slaves." Why, Sir, there is not a hard-hearted Shylock in the Commonwealth, who will not, on such conditions, give you time. Are we so weak, that, like the spend-thrift who runs to the usurer, we are willing to encounter this calamity, because it is not to come upon us till the year 1856? A period not as long as some of us have been in public life? Sir, I would not consent to it, if it were not to come till the year 2056. I am at war with the principle. Let me not be told, that then I am at war with the Bill of Rights. I subscribe to every word in the Bill of Rights. I need not show how this can be. It has been better done already by the gentleman from Spottsylvania, (Mr. Stanard,) to whom I feel personally indebted as a tobacco-planter and a slave-holder, for the speech he has made. The Bill of Rights contains unmodified principles. The declarations it contains are our lights and guides, but when we come to apply these great principles, we must modify them for use; we must set limitations to their operation, and the enquiry then is, *quousque?* How far? It is a question not of principle, but of degree. The very moment this immaculate principle of their's is touched, it becomes what all principles are, materials in the hands of men of sense, to be applied to the welfare of the Commonwealth. It is not an incantation. It is no Talisman. It is not witchcraft. It is not a torpedo to benumb us. If the naked principle of numbers only is to be followed, the requisites for the Statesman fall far below what the gentleman from Spottsylvania rated them at. He needs not the four rules of arithmetic. No, Sir, a negro boy with a knife and a tally-stick, is a Statesman complete in this school. Sir, I do not scoff, jeer or flout, (I use, I think, the very words of the gentleman from Augusta; two of them certainly were employed by him,) at the principles of the Bill of Rights, and so help me Heaven, I have not heard of any who did. But I hold with one of the greatest masters of political philosophy, that "no rational man ever did govern himself by abstractions and universals." I do not put abstract ideas wholly out of any question, because I know well that under that name I should dismiss principles; and that without the guide and light of sound, well understood principles, all reasonings in politics, as every thing else, would be only a confused jumble of particular facts and details, without the means of drawing out any sort of theoretical or practical conclusion.

"A Statesman differs from a Professor in an University. The latter has only the general view of society; the former, the Statesman, has a number of circumstances to combine with those general ideas, and to take into his consideration. Circumstances are infinite, are infinitely combined, are variable and transient: he who does not take them into consideration, is not erroneous, but stark mad—*dat operam ut cum ratione insanat*—he is metaphysically mad. A Statesman, never losing sight of principles, is to be guided by circumstances, and judging contrary to the exigencies of the moment, he may ruin his country forever."

Yes, Sir—and after that ruin has been effected, what a poor consolation is derived from being told, "I had not thought it." *Stulti est dixisse non putaram.* "Who would have thought it? Lord bless me! I never thought of such a thing, or I never would have voted for a Convention."

If there is any country on earth where circumstances have a more important bearing than in another, it is here, in Virginia. Nearly half the population are in bondage—yes, Sir, more than half in the country below the Ridge. And is this no circumstance? Yet, let me say with the gentleman from Accomac, (Mr. Joynes,) whose irresistible array of figures set all figures of speech at defiance, that if there were not a negro in Virginia, I would still contend for the principle in the amendment. And why? Because I will put it in the power of no man or set of men who ever lived, or who ever shall live, to tax me without my consent. It is wholly immaterial whether this is done without my having any representation at all, or, as it was done in the case of the Tariff Law, by a phalanx stern and inexorable, who being the majority, and having the power, prescribe to me the law that I shall obey. Sir, what was it to all the Southern interest, that we came within two votes of defeating that iniquitous measure? Do not our adversaries, (for adversaries they are,) know that they have the power? and that we must submit? Yes, Sir. This whole slave-holding country, the whole of it, from the Potomac to Mexico, was placed under the ban and anathema of a majority of two. And will you introduce such a principle into your own State Government? Sir, at some times during this debate, I doubted if I were in my right mind. From the beginning of time till now, there is no case to be found of a rational and moral people subverting a Constitution under which they had lived for half a century—aye, for two centuries, by a majority of *one*. When revolutions have happened in other countries, it was the effect of a political storm, a Levanter, a tornado, to which all opposition was fruitless. But did any body ever hear of a revolution affecting the entire condition of one half of a great State, being effected by a majority of one? Did it ever enter the head of the wildest visionary, from the days of Peter the Hermit, to—a day I will not name—to accomplish a revolution by a majority of *one?* Sir, to change your Constitution by such a majority, is nothing more than to sound the tocsin for a civil war. It may be at first, a war of words, a weaponless war, but it is one of those cases in which, as the lawyers tell us, fury supplies arms. Sir, this thing cannot be: it must not be. I was about to say, it *shall* not be. I tell gentlemen now, with the most perfect deliberation and calmness, that we cannot submit to this outrage on our rights. It surpasses that measure of submission and forbearance, which is due from every member of an organized Government, to that Government. And why do I so tell them? Sir, we are not a company of naked savages on the coast of New Holland, or Van Diemans Land—we have a Government; we have rights; and do you think that we shall tamely submit, and let you deprive us of our vested rights, and reduce us to bondage? Yes, vested rights! that we shall let you impose on us a yoke hardly lighter than that of the villeins regardant of the manor? We are now little better than the trustees of slave-labour for the nabobs of the East, and of the North, (if there be any such persons in our country,) and to the speculators of the West. They regulate our labour. Are we to have *two* masters? When every vein has been sluiced—when our whole system presents nothing but one pitiful enchymosis—are we to be patted and tapped to find yet another vein to breathe, not for the Federal Government, but for our own? Why, Sir, the richest man in Virginia, be that man who he may, would make a good bargain to make you a present of his estate, provided you give him bond upon that estate, allowing him to tax it as he pleases, and to spend the money as he pleases. It is of the very essence of property, that none shall tax it but the owner himself, or one who has a common feeling and interest with him. It does not require a plain planter to tell an Assembly like this, more than half of whose members are gentlemen of the law, that no man may set his foot on your land, without your permission, but as a trespasser, and that he renders himself liable to an action for damages. This is of the very essence of property. But he says, "thank you, for nothing—with all my heart, I don't mean to set my foot on your land; but, not owning one foot of land myself, I will stand here, in the highway, which is as free to me as it is to you, and I will tax your land, not to your heart's content, but to *mine*, and spend the proceeds as I please. I cannot enter upon it myself, but I will send the Sheriff of the county, and he shall enter upon it, and do what I cannot do in my own person." Sir, is this to be endured? It is not to be endured. And unless I am ignorant of the character and the feelings, and of what is dearer to me than all, of the prejudices of the people of the lower country, it will not be endured. You may as well adjourn *sine die*. We are too old birds to be taken with chaff, or else we are not old enough, I don't know which. We will not give up this question for the certainty, and far less for the hope, that the evil will be rectified in the other branch of the Legislature. We know, every body knows, that it is impossible. Why, Sir, the British House of Peers, which contains four hundred members, holding a vast property, much more now, it is true, than when Chatham said, they were but as a drop in the ocean, compared with the wealth of the Commons: If they, holding their seats for life, and receiving and transmitting them by hereditary descent, have never been able to resist the House of Commons, in any measure on which that House chose to insist, do you believe that twenty-four gentlemen up-stairs, can resist one hundred and twenty below? especially when the one hundred and twenty represent their own districts, and are to go home with them to their common constituents? Sir, the case has never yet happened, I believe, when a Senator has been able to resist the united delegation from his district in the lower House.

Mr. Chairman, I am a practical man. I go for solid security, and I never will, knowingly, take any other. But, if the security on which I have relied, is insufficient, and my property is in danger, it is better that I should know it in time, and I may prepare to meet the consequences, while it is yet called to-day, than to rest on a security that is fallacious and deceptive. Sir, I would not give a button for your mixed basis in the Senate. Give up this question, and I have nothing more to lose. This is the entering wedge, and every thing else must follow. We are told, indeed, that we must rely on a restriction of the Right of Suffrage; but, gentlemen, know, that after you shall have adopted the report of the Select Committee, you can place no restriction upon it. When this principle is in operation, the waters are out. It is as if you would ask an industrious and sagacious Hollander,* that you may cut his dykes, provided you make your cut only of a certain width. A rat hole will let in the ocean. Sir, there is an end to the security of all property in the Commonwealth, and he will be unwise, who shall not abandon the ship to the underwriters. It is the first time in my life, that I ever heard of a Government, which was to divorce property from power. Yet, this is seriously and soberly proposed to us. Sir, I know it is practicable, but it can be done only by a violent divulsion, as in France—but the moment you have separated the two, that very moment property will go in search of power, and power in search of property. "Male and female created he them;" and the two sexes do not more certainly, nor by a more unerring law, gravitate to each other, than power and property. You can only cause them to change hands. I could almost wish, indeed, for the accommodation of the gentleman from Augusta, that God had ordained it otherwise; but so it is, and so it is obliged to be. It is of the nature of man. Man always has been in society—we always find him in possession of property, and with a certain appetite for it, which leads him to seek it, if not *per fas*, sometimes *per nefas*; and hence the need of laws to protect it, and to punish its invaders.

But, I am subjecting myself, I know, to a most serious reproach. It will be said that I am not a friend to the poor. Sir, the gentleman from Chesterfield and the gentleman from Spottsylvania, have dealt with the "friends of the people" to my entire satisfaction. I wish to say a word as to the "friends of the poor." Whenever I see a man, especially a rich man, endeavoring to rise and to acquire consequence in society, by standing out as the especial champion of the poor, I am always reminded of an old acquaintance of mine, one Signor Manuel Ordonez, who made a comfortable living, and amassed an opulent fortune by administering the funds of the poor. Among the strange notions which have been broached since I have been on the political theatre, there is one which has lately seized the minds of men, that all things must be done for them by the Government, and that they are to do nothing for themselves: The Government is not only to attend to the great concerns which are its province, but it must step in and ease individuals of their natural and moral obligations. A more pernicious notion cannot prevail. Look at that ragged fellow staggering from the whiskey shop, and see that slattern who has gone there to reclaim him; where are their children? Running about, ragged, idle, ignorant, fit candidates for the penitentiary. Why is all this so? Ask the man and he will tell you, "Oh, the Government has undertaken to educate our children for us. It has given us a premium for idleness, and I now spend in liquor, what I should otherwise be obliged to save to pay for their schooling. My neighbor there, that is so hard at work in his field yonder with his son, can't spare that boy to attend, except in the winter months, the school which he is taxed to support for mine. He has to scuffle hard to make both ends meet at the end of the year, and keep the wolf from the door. His children

*Looking to the Chevalier Huygens, the Dutch Minister, who was in the Hall.

can't go to this school, yet he has to pay a part of the tax to maintain it." Sir, is it like friends of the poor to absolve them from what Nature, what God himself has made their first and most sacred duty? For the education of their children is the first and most obvious duty of every parent, and one which the worthless alone are ever known wholly to neglect.

Mr. Chairman, these will be deemed, I fear, unconnected thoughts; but they have been the aliment of my mind for years. Rumination and digestion can do no more; they are thoroughly concocted.

In the course of not a short or uneventful life, I have had correspondence with various persons in all parts of the Union, and I have seen gentlemen on their return from the North and the East, as well as from the new States of the West; and I never heard from any of them, but one expression of opinion as it related to us in Virginia. It was in the sentiment, if not in the language of Virgil; Oh, fortunate, if we knew our own blessedness. They advise us with one voice, "Stick to what you have got; stick to your Constitution; stick to your Right of Suffrage. Don't give up your freehold representation. We have seen enough of the opposite system, and too much." I have received and seen letters breathing this spirit from men who dare not promulgate such a sentiment at home, because it would only destroy their hopes of usefulness—from North Carolina, from South Carolina, from Georgia, from Alabama, from Pennsylvania and from New York.

Sir, the day, come when it may, which sees this old and venerable fabric of ours scattered in ruins, and the mattock and the spade digging the foundation for a new political edifice, will be a day of jubilee to all those who have been, and who must be in conflict with those principles which have given to Virginia her weight and consequence, both at home and abroad. If I understand aright the plans which are in agitation, I had sooner the day should arrive, that must close my eyes forever, than witness their accomplishment. Yes, Sir, to this Constitution we owe all that we have preserved, (much I know is lost and of great value,) but all that we have preserved from the wreck of our political fortunes. This is the mother which has reared all our great men. Well may she be called *magna mater virum*. She has, indeed, produced men, and mighty men.

But, I am told, that so far is this from being true, we have been living for fifty-four years under a Government which has no manner of authority, and is a mere usurpation at best. Yet, Sir, during that time, we have changed our Government; and I call the attention of this body to the manner in which that change was made. The Constitution of '88 was submitted to the people, and a Convention was called to ratify it, and what was that Convention? It was the old House of Burgesses with a nickname—the old House of Delegates, Sir, with a nickname—in which the same municipal divisions of the State were regarded—the same qualifications required—the same qualified freeholders were returned from the same districts and by the same sheriffs—and yet, by the waving of a magic wand, they were converted into a Convention—in which Warwick was made equal with Culpeper, then by far the largest county in the State. Do not gentlemen see where the point of their own argument leads to? If it is a sine qua non of a legitimate Government, that it must have the assent of a majority of the people told by the head, then is the Federal Government an usurpation—to which the people *per capita*—King Numbers—has never given his assent.

It is now thought necessary to have another Convention, and what is it? It is nothing but the Senate of Virginia, elected from the same districts, by the same voters, and returned by the same sheriffs; many of them the self-same men; yet when multiplied by four, by talismanic touch, they become a Convention. Yes, Sir. You can't trust the House of Delegates and Senate with your affairs, but you can trust a smaller body. You can't trust the whole, but you can trust a part. You can't trust the Senate, but you can trust the same men, from the same districts, if multiplied by four. Sir, are we men? Or, are we children? For my share, this is the first Convention in which I ever had a seat; and I trust in God, it will be the last. I never had any taste for Conventions; or for new Constitutions, made per order, or kept ready made, to suit casual customers. I need not tell *you*, Sir, that I was not a member of the Staunton Convention. No, Sir, nor was I a member of the Harrisburg Convention—nor the Charlottesville Convention. No, Sir, nor the Anti-Jackson Convention—though I had the honor, in very good company, of being put to the ban and anathema of that august Assembly—and when, to their very great surprise and alarm, we returned their fire—they scattered like a flock of wild geese.

Mr. Chairman, the wisest thing this body could do, would be to return to the people from whom they came, *re infecta*. I am very willing to lend my aid to any very small and moderate reforms, which I can be made to believe that this our ancient Government requires. But, far better would it be that they were never made, and that our Constitution remained unchangeable like that of Lycurgus, than that we should break in upon the main pillars of the edifice.

Sir, I have exhausted myself, and tired you. I am physically unable to recall or to express the few thoughts I brought with me to this Assembly. Sir, that great master of the human heart, who seemed to know it, as well as if he had made it, I mean Shakespeare—when he brings before our eyes an old and feeble monarch, not only deserted, but oppressed by his own pampered and ungrateful offspring, describes him as finding solace and succour, only in his discarded and disinherited child. If this, our venerable parent, must perish, deal the blow who will, it shall never be given by my hand. I will avert it if I can, and if I cannot, in the sincerity of my heart, I declare, I am ready to perish with it. Yet, as the gentleman from Spottsylvania says, I am no candidate for martyrdom. I am too old a man to remove; my associations, my habits, and my property, nail me to the Commonwealth. But, were I a young man, I would, in case this monstrous tyranny shall be imposed upon us, do what a few years ago I should have thought parricidal. I would withdraw from your jurisdiction. I would not live under King Numbers. I would not be his steward—nor make him my task-master. I would obey the principle of self-preservation—a principle we find even in the brute creation, in flying from this mischief.

Gentlemen seem to press the question—let it, for me, be taken. It was only because I felt unwilling to delay the Committee to another week, that I have been induced now to address them under every disadvantage.

It being now past four o'clock,

The question was called for on all sides; it was accordingly taken, after having been distinctly announced from the Chair; and the votes, (as counted by Mr. Fitzhugh and Mr. Loyall,) stood as follows: Ayes 47, Noes 47.

Whereupon, the Chairman giving his casting vote in the negative, the amendment of Mr. Green, proposing that, "in the apportionment of representation in the House of Delegates, regard shall be had to white population *and taxation combined*," was *rejected* in Committee of the Whole.

[N. B. There must have been an error in the count, as the whole Convention, consisting of *ninety-six* members, was present. The true vote, as since ascertained, was 47 Ayes, and 49 Noes.]

Mr. Scott of Fauquier, moved an amendment to the first resolution reported by the Legislative Committee, to insert after the word "exclusively," the words "and in the Senate to taxation exclusively;" to make the whole resolution read:

"*Resolved*, That in the apportionment of representation in the House of Delegates, regard shall be had to white population exclusively; and in the Senate to taxation exclusively."

Mr. Leigh now moved that the Committee rise.

It rose accordingly, and thereupon the House adjourned.

MONDAY, November 16, 1829.

The Convention met at 11 o'clock, and was opened with prayer by the Rev. Mr. Armstrong of the Presbyterian Church.

The President laid before the Convention a letter from Elisha Bates, a preacher belonging to the Friends' Society, in the following words:

Richmond, 11th Mo. 10th, 1829.

Respected Friend,
James Monroe, President of the Convention:

Elisha Bates, a minister in the Religious Society of Friends, respectfully requests the opportunity of a religious meeting, with the members of the Convention, this evening, at five o'clock.

ELISHA BATES.

On motion of Mr. Dromgoole, the letter was laid upon the table.

Mr. Henderson of Loudoun, presented a memorial from the non-freeholders of that county, on the subject of the extension of the Right of Suffrage, which, on his motion, was referred to the Committee of the Whole.

On motion of Mr. Scott, the House then resolved itself into a Committee of the Whole, Mr. Powell in the Chair; and the question being on the amendment offered yesterday by Mr. Scott, which proposed to add to the first resolution reported by the Legislative Committee, the words "and in the Senate to taxation exclusively"—so as to make it read:

"*Resolved*, That in the apportionment of representation in the House of Delegates, regard shall be had to *white population exclusively*, and in the Senate to *taxation exclusively*."

Mr. Scott asked and obtained leave to withdraw his amendment.

And the question recurring on the original resolution,

Mr. Leigh of Chesterfield moved to amend it, by striking out all after the words "Resolved that," and inserting in lieu thereof, as follows:

——— "representation (in the House of Delegates) be apportioned among the several counties, cities and towns of the Commonwealth, according to their respective numbers, which shall be determined by adding to the whole number of free persons, including those bound to service for a term of years, and excluding Indians not taxed, three-fifths of all other persons."

In supporting the amendment, Mr. Leigh observed, that it had already been explained to the Committee, that the general result of the scheme he proposed, when applied to the present circumstances of the Commonwealth, would be, substantially, the same as that derived from the adoption of the plan of the compound basis, which had been rejected by the Committee. My motive, said Mr. L. in presenting this amendment, is to try the sense of the Committee in reference to the adoption of the *Federal number*, as the basis of representation. The proposition varies in one particular from that of my friend from Culpeper, (Mr. Green.) In the debate on his amendment, it was suggested, by way of objection, that the plan of a mixed basis put it in the power of the delegation from the Eastern part of the State, by avoiding to tax the Western districts, to keep the weight of power constantly in the East; and that such was the desire of the inhabitants of that part of the State to retain the power in their own hands, (manifested, as was said, by their general opposition to the call of this Convention,) that we might expect, in future, a majority of the Legislature to be anxious to lay the heavier burdens on the East, and the lighter on the West. This was urged as an objection, not so much against the principle of the scheme, as one likely to operate in its practical details. And I am not sure but that some, perhaps several, voted not against the *principle* of the mixed basis, but against the inconvenience and abuse of power that might grow out of the *application* of the principle. Without entering into that argument, I shall be content to substitute for the mixed basis, against which this objection is thought to be, a basis on the Federal number. I am satisfied it is a wise provision in the Federal Constitution, and that here, its results will be as beneficial as those of any other scheme: and it is recommended to my mind by the facility and certainty with which it can be applied in practice. The plan has long been in operation amongst us; we are acquainted with its effect; and I earnestly hope that it may be adopted by the Committee.

Mr. Nicholas rose in support of the amendment.

Ever since I have taken my seat, said he, in this Convention, I have felt a very awful sense of my personal responsibility. I have felt it, not only as one representing a portion of the Commonwealth, and therefore, in reference to the whole State, but in a peculiar manner, with regard to the particular district I have the honor in part to represent. The change now contemplated in our institutions, is radical in its nature. We are called upon to change the *whole* system of our civil polity: and give me leave to say, that, superadded to my responsibility as a citizen of the Commonwealth, at present, I am called to decide a question which must affect the peace and happiness of our remotest posterity. Besides, Sir, I am the representative of one of those districts which must suffer most, should the change be adopted. On the issue of our present proceeding, will, in a great measure, depend the future peace and tranquillity of the State: and though I have not the vanity to believe that I can bring to the Committee any thing worthy of them, and should greatly have preferred to listen to the wisdom of others, than to present my own crude remarks, still, had it not been for the feeble state of my health, for many days past, I should have held it to be my duty to make at least a feeble effort in behalf of those, who have honored me with a seat on this floor.

Sir, we have arrived at an awful period in our deliberations. It was predicted by my honorable friend from Charlotte, (Mr. Randolph,) whose solemn appeal, so recently addressed to us, left a deep impression on my mind, that the rejection of the amendment would be effected by a majority of one, or at most, of two votes. The fact has justified that prediction; and, Mr. Chairman, I cannot conceive a more awful state of any country, than that it should be about to change its fundamental law, by such a majority: to change its entire Constitution, when *one half* of the country vote against the change. So meagre a majority, made up, not of Delegates coming from beyond the Blue Ridge, but, in part, by the addition of members from this side the mountain, members on whom we fondly counted, as being our natural allies, (I cast no censure on their conduct, I know that they act conscientiously, and I presume that they speak the wishes of their constituents;) I say, so meagre a majority plainly shows what is the sense of the country, as to a change in its Constitution. And can it be wise to effect so radical a change, when half the country pronounces it to be unwise? When they loudly declare that the change will subvert the rights, prostrate the interests, and destroy the happiness of one half the State? What must be our situation, if we adopt such a measure? Can we ever be a happy and tranquil community, while one-half its members conscientiously believe, that the change we shall have made, has not only injured their interests, but destroyed all prospect of quiet and happiness? Surely we all must know, that no country ever can prosper under such circumstances. The best, the only effectual support of any Government, is in the confidence of the people; but when the people believe themselves oppressed by the Government, what prospect can there be of their yielding it a cordial and enduring support? What can we look forward to, but eternal jealousies and animosities? Can any wise man, however wedded he may be to his own theories, can any good man, wish to see the Commonwealth in such a situation?

Mr. Chairman, I am one of those who believed it unwise to call this Convention. I do not say, and never did say, that our Government is perfect theoretically; that it is absolutely free from all defects. But every wise Statesman, in judging of a system of Government, will look to *the whole* of that system. He will form his estimate of all the good it contains, and then he will determine whether that amount of practical good does not overbalance any merely theoretical objections. It was on this ground, that I was opposed to the call of a Convention. This business of theoretical perfection, may have an inviting appearance; but all experience proves, that absolute perfection is unattainable—a mere *ignis fatuus*—that must lead to disappointment, and, ultimately, to misery, and public convulsions. Lycurgus and Solon, were supposed to be among the wisest men of their day, and they established Governments on what they thought a system of absolute perfection; but what has become of them? Where are all the ancient Republics? They are gone, and in their room has come the most frightful despotism. Wisdom surely dictates, that when we have enjoyed a practical good more than half a century, we should not give it up for what theorists may recommend to us. The Government of Solon did not last even during his life; the liberties of his people were usurped by Pisistratus during his own life-time.

It has been said, that the object of some gentlemen, who have attended this body, is merely to prevent any thing from being done. That is not my case. I did oppose the calling of the Convention; but when the people said that it should be assembled, I came here with the honest intention to stick to what was good in the Constitution, and this I mean to do as long as possible. The gentleman from Charlotte, (Mr. Randolph) laid down a rule which, I think, was full of practical wisdom. He asked, whether we will reform our Government, on mere theory? And he said, (and so I say,) " no: but let us first see some practical evil; and when it is clearly proved, then let us reform our Government in that particular respect and in that only." I have once been an officer under the Government for twenty years—I was Attorney General of the State at an early period of my life, (and if I ever did, I certainly did not then deserve the trust;) but the situation afforded me a good opportunity to judge, from observation, of the practical effect of this Government. And I declare to God, that in the whole period of those twenty years, I knew of no instance of oppression, or injury to any man's rights caused by the operation of the Government. It is not then wonderful that I should part from it with reluctance.

Permit me now to make a few observations, on the amendment offered by the gentleman from Chesterfield.

I was always of opinion, that the true ground of representation was that of the Federal number. I voted in favour of the mixed basis, because it appeared to me that it might have the effect of securing the rights of the Eastern portion of the Commonwealth: and not because I preferred it. The other mode had my decided preference. The Federal number was adopted from considerations which operate in what is now before this body. It was not adopted on grounds of compromise. Look at the speeches of that day: look at the number of the Federalist on that subject: it was fixed upon not as a compromise, but as being in itself the correct basis of representation. Here we have both property and persons protected: and here, we find, the happy medium between the two extremes of universal suffrage and aristocratic Government.

It was the ground taken by gentlemen from the North (all of them strongly prejudiced against slavery,) as a ground which afforded a just protection to property. The principle was viewed not only as vital to the Southern States, but as a fair principle for all. Any gentleman who will look at the debates of the Federal Convention, will find full evidence that it was not a compromise. The United States' Government, though in many features of it, it is Federal, is, in others a *National* Government. Representation is one of those features. In its representation, it is National, and not Federal. Its representation is not founded upon concessions of one State to another State, but is laid as a correct basis for the whole. The mixed basis, as proposed by the gentleman from Culpeper, must necessarily be fluctuating and very hard to reduce to practice. The taxes will often differ in the same district. The whole basis must be eternally fluctuating, and will require to be re-adjusted from time to time. But the ratio of three-fifths of the slaves furnishes a certain criterion, that is easily measured, and cannot change. Gentlemen represent this proposition as unjust, and fit for one portion of the Commonwealth only; but this is not true. We do not say that the Eastern part of the State only shall have the three-fifths added, but that all the Commonwealth shall; wherever there are slaves, there the principle will take effect; and if, as has been very ingeniously represented, it be, indeed, probable, that the slaves will go beyond the mountain the moment they do so, the West gets the power. Indeed, this argument of theirs, appeared to me at the time, to be *felo de se*, or else, to be in opposition to the other arguments adduced by them in favour of a white basis. If the slaves shall emigrate, every five slaves that pass over the mountain, give them additional representation. The rule is general, and operates alike on all.

I said, we had arrived at an awful period in our deliberations. Yes, Sir, we have reached the brink of a precipice. Gentlemen must here decide for themselves; and I put it to gentlemen of the West, whether they will consent to form an entirely new Constitution for the State by a majority of one, or of two, or of five, or ten? It is an awful responsibility for them; and all the ills which may grow out of it, be on their heads! I say this, not in anger, but in sorrow. Some of my dearest friends and nearest relatives, reside beyond the Blue Ridge. I deprecate the calamity which I behold impending, for their sakes, as much as my own.

Much has been said as to the moral influence of Virginia. I believe, she has frequently saved the Union; and though gentlemen are pleased to say, that she is retrograding in wealth and influence, we have this proud consolation, that if we *have* refused the lures and boons of the General Government, we are at least poor on principle. Virginia may be a victim to her honour, but I, for one, hope she may be poor forever, if she can only become rich at the sacrifice of her principles.

Gentlemen are under a great mistake, if they impute to me any wish for confusion, or any desire that we may make a change that shall prove unpalatable to the people. But, we, whose districts are to be sacrificed, have an important duty which we owe to our constituents. I am disposed to conciliate. I wish the State to remain united. I had rather be the citizen of a great Commonwealth than a petty State. But, there is something yet better than union. Oppression is worse than division. I am ready to go as far for conciliation as any, but I am not ready to offer up my country as the sacrifice. I think it vastly better, that freedom should be preserved, even if disunion must be the price. I speak, God knows, with affliction at my heart. But, how is this evil to be averted? Here we are arrayed against each other. The West advances its demands, and they say, "there are provisions which we must have." The East remonstrates, and says, "you will destroy us." To every compromise there must be two parties; but do we hear one whisper, aye, so much as one low voice, that talks of compromise? No. Gentlemen stand on their rights: they stand perfectly stationary: they call to us to come up to them: but that we never can. I am willing to adjust the difference. Do gentlemen ask how? By a plan which shall give security to the East, for the preservation of all that is dear to them and their posterity. While we shape our course towards conciliation, we must have effectual security. All security from equality of taxation, is purely imaginary. What boots it to us, that the taxes are made equal, if they are all to be paid by one part of the State? It would be the interest of the West, to pay even a heavy taxation, if they are to have the sole distribution of the money raised. The only possible security, is to give us such a share in the administration of affairs, as shall ensure a good and just Government; as will secure to us the rights which we believe to be in jeopardy.

Let me say, in conclusion, that whatever vote I may give in the final issue, I reserve to myself the right, first to see *the whole* extent of the security gentlemen propose to give: and, then, when they have modified their proposition into its last form, then comes the awful question, is this security adequate? If I shall judge that it is not, I never will give my assent to any system which will jeopardize the rights of my constituents.

Mr. Monroe, now rose and addressed the Committee, in substance, as follows:

Mr. Chairman: The House, I hope, will indulge me in a few remarks. I will promise to be very concise. My faculties of debate, always humble, have been impaired by long disuse while I occupied another station in the public service, and have, of late years, been yet farther weakened by bodily infirmity; yet duty impels me to make some remarks on this occasion. They shall be but few, and more a sentiment than an oration. My situation is one of peculiar delicacy as it relates to my constituents, and my country. When I retired from the office I last held, it was with the expectation that that retirement would be permanent. My age admonished me that it was welcome and becoming. When I received an invitation to come here, (for the seat I hold was not sought by me,) I consented with regret, for causes which must be obvious to all. Yet I would not shrink from the call of my fellow-citizens, and at their call I came. But it was with the disposition to look to the whole Commonwealth: from the Potomac to the Roanoke, from the mountains to the ocean, from Kanawha, to Monongalia, from the Blue Ridge to the Ohio; all was one to me.

I could have been content to reside in any part of the Commonwealth. I left one part of it, where I had spent the greater part of my life, for another, where I was almost unknown. Its citizens kindly manifested their confidence, and I came with a disposition to look to the interests of the whole. I consider myself as their servant, and I consider them, as having a right to instruct me. If they should think fit to do so, I shall either obey them or withdraw from this Assembly. When I find myself in that dilemma, I shall do so without a word. But I do not know that it will arrive. In the course I shall pursue here, I shall make it my principle to look to the State at large. I shall look also, to the divisions and to the state of acrimonious feeling which existed, long before the calling of this Convention, and which I consider this body as having a tendency to tranquilize.

My idea has been, that it will be wise to base representation on the white population in the House of Delegates, and to place an adequate check on the result of their deliberations in the Senate. This is my opinion. By basing the representation on the white population, we are resting on principle; on a principle corresponding with the Bill of Rights and with the Constitution; for, our Government is in the hands of the white people. We shall by this means rest on fundamental principles, and gratify the feelings of the people, in every part of the community. Our Constitution rests on that basis.

And by whom was it framed? By the most enlightened of our citizens; by men who have given proof of their patriotism, wisdom, and knowledge of mankind. I wish to preserve its important features and to alter it as little as may be, considering that it was the first of our Constitutions ever made here, and will be an example through all ages. Where do we find a free Government in history, except in Greece, to a certain degree in Carthage, and in Rome? Every where else we find only barbarism, and all mankind kept in a state of degradation. With this example before them, these men framed a Constitution better than had ever existed before.

By resting representation on the white population, in the House of Delegates, we leave that body free from any check: but to control its hasty decision, you resort to the Senate, and therefore I thought that the plan of the mixed basis, ought to be confined to the Senate. For my part, I am ready to vote for it. But I think the Federal number liable to fewer objections. It makes our system correspond to that of the Federal Government. It is more easy of execution, and it is not against principle.

By adopting the white basis in the House of Delegates, we shall tranquilize the people, and if we adopt the mixed basis in the Senate, I hope that the other gentlemen will meet us there.

I hope, Sir, that this will be done. Why do men enter into society? What are their objects, whether rude or civilized? Is it not for the protection of life, liberty and property? Is not this the declaration of our Constitution and of all the Constitutions since adopted throughout the United States? Is there any other motive for society, whether rude or civilized? In a rude state, the protection of life is the principal motive, but even there, property also is a motive. What kind of Government do we find prevailing among our native Indians? They are not governed by written compacts, but the principal chief or elder as he is called by them, rules over the tribe, and they submit; he following the will of the tribe.

Look at civilized society: is the obligation to submission not stronger? Can you separate property from either state? There is a difference, however. In the rude state of society there is the game—all is open and free to all—and property exists only round their cabins. But, what is the case with civilized man? There man presses on man—society presses on society: each individual must have something of his own or he starves. There the people are the guardians, and they must protect property, as well as life and liberty, or society perishes.

This protection is in no degree incompatible with the adoption of the white basis of representation in the House of Delegates; and I hope that this body will unite in some plan that may correspond to the general views of the community, and may correspond with our relations to the General Government, for which I have a very high respect. But, I know the duty of a representative to his constituents, and, I hope, we shall all draw to that end—we shall gain a grand object—and it may lead to what we cannot tell. I would, myself, rather have a representation that may correspond to the Federal number.

It has been suggested, that it will be best to keep the qualification of voters as it exists at present, or to reduce it but in a small degree. I differ from that opinion. I think we must modify and reduce it. Who are they who are pressing for a new Constitution? Those, who suppose themselves deprived of their just Right of Suffrage. Reduce the requisites for this, and you carry tranquillity into the body of the community. Our situation in reference to this subject, is different from that of any people who ever existed before us. What was the condition of the ancient republics? In

Greece, Carthage, and Rome? The question there was, whether power should be held by the people *en masse?* Whether it should be exercised by the people in a body? Their Governments originated with a prince or with the nobles. They had always great weight; and the contest was between the rich and the poor. The people originated no measure—they heard what was proposed by the prince, but they proposed nothing. In Athens they had what has been called a free Senate—and as to Lacedæmon it was the same—the same thing applies to Rome, and in a degree to Carthage; but they only adopted or rejected what was submitted to them. The people had no stake in the property of the State, it was all in the hands of the prince or the ancient nobility.

But our Government is in the hands of the people. We have no privileged orders. We have no overgrown wealthy to oppress the poor—and they cannot do it if we fix the grade of representation on a moderate scale. The President of the United States, the Governor of the State, the Senators, all are servants of the people. The property of the country rests on the people alone. Therefore, I say, our situation is different from that of all who ever existed before us.

I would adopt a plan that may harmonize the feelings of the community on the subject of Suffrage, and of representation in the popular branch. I would place a check in the other branch.

I thought it my duty, though in a feeble manner, to explain these views to the House—and I wish, also, that my sentiments should go to my constituents.

Mr. Tazewell said, that when he came to the House this morning, he had but little expectation, and certainly not the slightest inclination, to take any part in this debate. He had not felt any wish to participate in the discussion of a question so general and undefined in its terms, as that which the Committee would soon be called upon to decide. All which he had ever seen of man, and all the information which he had ever been able to acquire in the science of politics, combined to teach him, that no good ever had, and that no possible good ever could, result from the discussion of any mere general propositions, in order to elicit by such discussion an agreed basis, which, by mutual consent, might be adopted, as a foundation for some *unknown* practical, political scheme. All such schemes, when fully developed (and developed they must be at some time or other,) must at last be brought to the test of experience and utility; and as it ought not to be considered as constituting any just objection to any useful political plan, that it was not constructed according to the most nice and precise rules of any art, so nor will it be any recommendation of any other plan, that it is a clear syllogistic deduction from any supposed general truth. If the details of any intended scheme, when fairly exhibited, should be seen to be mischievous, they would surely be rejected, although in strict accordance with the agreed basis; and if believed to be good, they would infallibly be adopted, although at war with, and contrary to, all the admitted general truths announced by such basis. Discuss whatever general proposition you please, settle whatever general basis you choose, and you will at last discover, when you come to fix the details of the plan, that each of these must be adjusted by a regard to its own particular merits, and by no special reference to any general rules. Entertaining these opinions, it was with much regret he had seen at first, the course and direction intended to be given to the deliberations of the Convention; and he had then almost resolved, to say not one word in relation to the matter now under consideration, until it should assume a more certain and defined form than it yet presents. But the discussion had now proceeded so far, that it would perhaps be an economy of time, to extend it a little farther; and by endeavoring to show, not the truth or falsehood, but the tendency and effect of the general proposition, so as to bring our future, if not our present labors, to a more speedy termination, than they seem at present likely to reach. It was with this view he would ask the attention of the Committee to a few remarks which he proposed to address to them, in the course of which, he would notice some of those they had just heard from the venerable gentleman from Loudoun, who had but just now taken his seat.

Whatever may be the form of the question now presented to us, the general proposition included in it is; what is the proper basis whereon to erect representation in the Legislative Department of a Government designed for such a State as is Virginia? In examining this question, a most apt enquiry at once presents itself to our consideration. Upon what basis is such representation founded now? When the venerable member from Loudoun, and other much respected gentlemen on every side of this body, unite in telling us, that the existing Constitution of Virginia is the best the world has ever seen—when the experience of many here assure us, that this Government has endured for more than half a century, producing as much of good as could be expected to result from any Government—and when not a solitary witness has appeared to testify to the existence of a single mischief as its effect—we surely ought to examine carefully the foundation of such a Government, before we should wish to change it. For his part, he was free to declare, that he would not compare the knowledge derived from such experience, with that obtained by an examination of the visions of Plato or Aristotle, the theories of Locke or Sidney, or of any other mere speculative scheme whatever.

The basis of representation here, was established more than two centuries since. It rests not upon a prescription of fifty odd years only, as his friend from Charlotte had supposed, but it traces back its origin to a period much beyond the independence of the Commonwealth, and is coeval with the very first Legislative Assembly that ever convened in Virginia. During the long interval that has since elapsed, representation itself has undergone many changes, but the foundation wherein it rests, has ever remained the same. He prayed the Committee, therefore, to accompany him in the enquiry he was about to institute, as to the basis whereon this ancient scheme of representation was erected.

In the year 1619 or 1620, the first House of Burgesses assembled at Jamestown. The members of that body were elected by the different plantations as they were then called, or as we should now denominate them, the different settlements, then existing in the Colony. The early settlers had established themselves in different societies, along the margin of James River, from its mouth to near this spot.

These societies, separated either by wide water courses, difficult to be passed, or by thick forests dangerous to penetrate, differed widely from each other, in the numbers of their population, in their wealth, and in the extent of the territory occupied by them: but each was entitled to representation, and each sent its Burgess to the Grand Assembly. Variously circumstanced, while each had a common interest in the prosperity of all, each had also a particular interest peculiar to itself. With a view of enabling each to promote the good of all, in that mode which would be most suitable to its own convenience; and with a view of enabling all to advance the prosperity of each, by any means not inconsistent with the common good, representation was allowed to every society then existing; and this, without having regard to the population, or the wealth of any, or even to these things combined, but merely to the peculiar interests existing in the different societies, occupying the undefined space, then termed a plantation or settlement. The basis of representation, then, was the interests of the different plantations; and as these interests were various and peculiar, each interest had its proper representative, whether that interest concerned many or few persons, or involved much or little wealth. If the peculiar interest of the part, was of sufficient importance to claim the regard of the whole, that interest was entitled to, and was allowed a representative, whether the population of the plantation amounted to fifty or to five hundred persons, or whether their wealth was £100 or £1,000.

In process of time, the different settlements became extended in every direction, and were so brought in contact with each other. The various interests then existing in the Colony, became more assimilated and consolidated than they had been before; but still a diversity of particular interests existed. The wants and wishes of the settlers in Accomack, must have been very different from those of the persons dwelling near the Falls of James River, and the pursuits and situation of the inhabitants at Point Comfort, must have been very unlike those of persons abiding far from them, on the other side of the great water. This union of the settlements, had superceded the necessity of allowing representation to each of what had been the different plantations; but the reason for allowing representation to the various interests existing in the Colony, still remained as before. The abode of these different interests, had, indeed, been much enlarged and extended; but the interests themselves, remained still various. In this state of things, public convenience required a new division of the settled parts of the Colony; and accordingly, in 1634, it was divided, for the first time, into eight shires or counties, as they were afterwards called. These shires, our history and laws inform us, were very different in extent of territory, in the numbers of their respective inhabitants, and in the taxable property possessed by these inhabitants: but still the same basis of representation was preserved. Within each of these shires, a particular interest, peculiar to itself, was supposed to exist; and to that peculiar interest, representation was allowed, whatever might be its comparative numbers, or wealth, or extent of territory.

Pursuing the examination further, you will find, that as the frontier counties extended into the wilderness, new interests sprung up in each. The pioneers and advanced guards of the society, must have had very many wants, and wishes, and necessities, different from their former associates in the same county. The advance of the one, in exposing them to new perils and difficulties, gave peace and security to those they left behind; and the peculiar interests of the frontier inhabitants of Northampton, and York, and Isle of Wight, and Henrico, must have been very different from those of their brethren in the other parts of these counties, resting, as the latter did, upon the interior shires. Thus, it came to pass, that within the same county, where at first, a single interest only existed, two different interests arose. If both these interests were to be represented by those chosen by a majority of the two, it was very certain, that one of these two would be neglected; and hence arose the necessity for dividing the frontier counties, by such lines, as might allow to each interest, its proper representation. In this manner, we went on regularly dividing the frontier counties, as new interests sprung up in each, until the whole territory of Virginia was thus distributed.

Nor did this process of allowing representation to every peculiar interest in the community stop here. Whenever an interior county became so populous, or its territory was found so wide spread, as to justify a belief, either that different interests had or might arise within it, such county was always divided, whensoever a division of it was asked for—nay, in many cases where neither the extent of territory, nor the number of inhabitants was so great, as to render it probable that different interests would arise, yet if the county was found intersected by wide water-courses, or rapid torrents, or rugged mountains, or if any other cause existed, calculated to interpose permanent obstacles in the way of free and frequent intercourse between the inhabitants of different parts of the same county, it was always divided upon the application of either part, where particular convenience, (which must always be considered as its peculiar interest,) required such a division.

Nor is this all. Our history will further inform us, that after the first division of the State into shires or counties, peculiar interests arose within the bodies of some of these counties, which interests were not of a character to justify or to require the dismemberment of the county, in order to provide special representation of them. When such interests appeared, they were, therefore, incorporated, and by their several charters of incorporation, were allowed a representation different from that which had always been given to the peculiar interests existing in the counties themselves—such, most probably, was the origin of the representation allowed to Jamestown, and afterwards to that which was certainly allowed to the city of Williamsburg, to the borough of Norfolk, and to the College of William and Mary. Neither the comparative population nor wealth, or extent of either of these corporations, at the time their several charters were obtained, could possibly have entitled it to representation, if representation had then been erected upon either of these bases. But the interests of navigation, of trade, and of science, which were believed to exist in these corporations, were each important to the community, and being then peculiar to these interests, were respectively allowed a representative, as all other interests had been before.

Such was the basis of representation established in the Colony of Virginia at the moment when a representative Legislature was first introduced here; and upon this basis was every thing of that sort afterwards founded, up to the period of the revolution of 1776. It rested upon the peculiar interests existing in particular districts, the limits of which districts were at first accidental, but were afterwards delineated and marked out by the convenience of the inhabitants within them.

When the Convention who formed the existing Constitution of Virginia assembled, they found representation established on the basis just stated; and being desirous of preserving all of our ancient institutions which they could preserve, consistently with the principles of the new Government they were about to create, they continued to each county and corporation then existing, the same right of representation it then enjoyed. No departure from this rule occurred, except in two cases, and these exceptions prove strongly the existence of the rule itself. Jamestown, the ancient metropolis of the Colony, had become so much reduced in its population, that it was inconceivable that any peculiar interest could abide there; and the College of William and Mary was no longer the peculiar residence of most of the science in Virginia, and, therefore, no longer entitled to representation on that account. Jamestown and the College, were, therefore, deprived of their particula representation, while every thing else was preserved as it had before stood; and the same power was given to the new Legislatures, which had always been exercised by the former, of dividing the existing counties, and of establishing new corporations, whenever, in its opinion, the general interest of the whole community, and the peculiar interest of any part of it, required the exercise of such power.

Such is the basis of representation in Virginia now. This basis was probably just and perfect when first established, and would yet be regarded in the same light, but for a single circumstance, to which none here probably are indisposed to apply the proper corrective. That circumstance is this: In the original distribution of the counties, lines of demarcation were necessarily drawn, within which limits peculiar interests did then abide, although these limits circumscribed in some instances very narrow spaces. The Convention of 1776, acting upon the opinion, that it would be unwise to change any thing then existing, except when such change was necessary to prevent practical mischief, had regard to the existing electoral precincts; and intending to preserve to each precinct, the rights of representation it then had, inserted a provision in their Constitution, that each county should continue to have two representatives. The object was wise and just at the time. But, while they prudently provided for the probable case of new interests thereafter to spring up in the existing counties, and, therefore, gave to the Assembly the power of dividing counties and of creating corporations at their will, they did not probably foresee, and therefore did not provide for the event, of any county or corporation ceasing to be the abode of some interest peculiar to itself, the existence of which peculiar interest, was the sole cause of giving to such county or corporation, any particular representation at first. In providing for the birth of future peculiar interests, they omitted to provide for the extinction of such as then existed; and while the Legislature, by this Constitution, was authorised to give representation to any new interest, by dividing the counties or creating new corporations within which it might appear, the mandate of the Constitution, that each of the existing counties should have two representatives, deprived the Legislature of the power of taking from such counties, any portion of their rights of representation, even after the cause which originally gave to them such rights, had ceased to exist.

In consequence of this provision in the Constitution, it has occurred, that after some of the smaller counties, (Warwick for example) have ceased to be the abode of any interest peculiar to its inhabitants, it still retains a right of representation equal to that enjoyed by Shenandoah, the largest county in the State; nor is it competent to the Legislature to remedy this inequality, without producing much greater mischiefs than any which ever have or ever can result from that cause. Because, if the larger counties should be so divided and cut up, as give to their respective parts equal to Warwick in any thing, a right of representation equal to that which Warwick now enjoys, the Legislative body must become much too numerous, unwieldy, and expensive, to be any longer useful; and the people of many of the sub-divisions would be most grievously oppressed, by the necessary burthens of their own mere municipal police. Thus it happens, that while the causes for allowing equal representation to all the different counties in the State, have ceased to apply in many instances, and while the effect of this is remedyless under the provisions of the existing Constitution, the incapacity of the Legislature to provide the proper cure for this confessed evil, has become the source of all the murmuring and complaint we have heard, and is the true cause of the assembling of this Convention. It is not, that the East or the West, the cis-montane or ultra-montane regions of the State, have too much or too little political weight in the Assembly—it is, that the largest counties are put upon a par with the smallest; that Warwick and Loudoun, Halifax and Alleghany, are equalized in representation. This is the inequality complained of, and this is the inequality which we are sent hither by the people to reduce and reconcile, so far as we may find it practicable to do so.

If we confine ourselves to this task, the work to be performed is by no means difficult of execution. The addition of a single line to the provisions existing in the present Constitution will accomplish it; and to such an addition, but little objection will probably be urged. Give to the Legislature the discretionary power of uniting any of the present electoral districts, within which no peculiar interest is believed to exist, to other contiguous districts having similar interests, and the desired object will be attained. Then, under the power they now have, of dividing the larger counties; and under this new power so conferred upon them, of consolidating the smaller, every desirable and practical equality will be at once accomplished. The whole scheme of representation will then remain upon its ancient, unaltered basis, and can be accommodated from time to time to every future condition of things, without changing any principle, or seeking to establish any new foundation.

Instead of adopting a course so simple, so easy, and which, in all probability, would be so satisfactory, as this, it seems to be proposed, to apply a sponge to all the division lines within the State, and to make a perfect *tabula rasa* of the whole Commonwealth. When this is done, new lines must be drawn, and new associations created, in the establishment of which, no regard is to be had (according to the report of the Select Committee) to any thing else but to the number of the free white population, existing within such limits. Such an idea, he believed, never entered into the mind of a single man, before this Convention met, and will not now be regarded without amazement and almost consternation, by any other than a member of this body.

For my part, said Mr. T. I will cordially unite with any, in consolidating the smaller counties every where, until the very least shall assume a proper size. I will unite then in dividing the larger counties, wherever it is desired, until the largest shall cease to be considered as over-grown. In the progress of this work of equalization, however, I can never consent to regard numbers of any sort, *exclusively*, or taxation or property of any kind *exclusively*, or any thing else *exclusively*. I must consider what the interests and convenience of the people to be represented require; and in deciding this question, I must do, what every wise Statesman ought to do: I think, I must regard and pass in review before me, every single circumstance which exists, to influence any part of the State materially.

Let me illustrate my views of this subject, by an example. If you will cast your eye over the map of Virginia, you will see on its extreme Eastern border, a little peninsula, containing within its limits not a fiftieth part of the territory or population, or probably of the wealth of the State. Suppose this territory, and population, and wealth, reduced to any thing less you please, but still remains respectable, the situation of that peninsula would yet be what it now is. It would still be contiguous to a neighbouring State, washed by the great Atlantic on the one side, and separated from the rest of the State on the other by a great bay, wider than the English Channel at Dover, or than the Mediterranean at the Straits of Gibraltar. This situation, you must perceive, exposes its inhabitants to much greater perils than those of any other part of the Commonwealth; and, at the same time, deprives it of all hope of aid from any other quarter, even in the hour of its greatest need. In the Revolution, and during the late war, these people defended themselves by their own means alone, receiving no particle of assistance from any other portion of the State. Whatever may be thought of the ingratitude of another part, in not erecting monuments to mark the spots where rest the bones of the brave men who fell victims to the diseases of either camp or climate, no tear ought to bedew the cheek of the gentleman from Loudoun (Mr. Mercer) at similar ingratitude here—no Western hero is there interred, for the foot of no Western hero ever pressed that soil. The people of this little peninsula unaided, have maintained and defended themselves from the beginning, will continue to do so to the end, and I thank God that they are able so to do. But this is not all. Our history will inform us, that the people of this peninsula, are the descendants of the earliest settlers in Virginia. Their insular situation must inform us, that the ancient manners and customs of the country, are there preserved more perfectly, probably, than in any other part of the State, where the frequent attrition of various associations, has long since blunted and smoothed down the asperities and sharp points of the habits of antiquity—a different climate, soil, and situation, has necessarily yielded various productions, and invited to the pursuit of occupations there, very different from those existing elsewhere. In short, all these diversities have created an interest peculiar in that section of the country, the like of which is to be found no where else. Now, with a full knowledge of all these facts, would any wise Statesman, in adjusting a scheme of representation for the whole Commonwealth, ever conceive the idea of allowing no representative to such a society as I have described, merely because their numbers, or their wealth, did not rise to the exact height of that arbitrary standard of number or property which he had fixed? Would common prudence justify him in saying to such a people, "It is true an ocean rolls between us; it is true, your situation, manners, habits, pursuits, and interests, are different from ours; it is true you are contiguous to another State, where juxta-position to you may better qualify it to learn the true nature of your wants, and to extend to your peculiar interests, more protection than we can; but nevertheless I cannot regard any of these things. My rule is, that in allotting representation, respect should be had to the number of free white inhabitants *exclusively;* and as your natural limits contain not a sufficient number of these, no representation can be allowed to you, and you can, therefore, have no share in the administration of the Government designed for the benefit of all." I need not state what must be the inevitable result of such a course. Every man who hears me, must at once perceive it.

Mr. T. then adverted to the little county of Warwick, containing, as he said, not more than about forty thousand acres of land, and but little more than six hundred white inhabitants. He said, that regarding the situation of that county, or the convenience of its inhabitants, it was scarcely possible to conceive, that any interest could there exist at this day, which was not common to the circumjacent contiguous counties, upon the principles of the basis of representation as now established; therefore, this county could not be considered as longer entitled to a separate representation. But, suppose, Sir, said he, that the river which runs through this little county, precipitated itself in its course over such a cataract as that of Niagara? Does not every one discern in such a circumstance, a cause sufficient to convert the inhabitants of that county into a body of manufacturers? And then is it not obvious, that such an interest would require a separate representation, notwithstanding the limits of the county, its population and property might each remain not greater than they are at present? Justice and policy would surely require this. If so, it is perfectly clear, that the existing basis is the true basis of representation; and, that in the allotment of representation, regard should be had, rather to the interests and convenience of the people, than to their actual numbers, or wealth, or territory.

But, my venerable friend from Loudoun, (I beg pardon of the gentleman for the familiarity of the phrase, but he has ever been my friend) has said, that the principles of all Republican Government required, that representation should be apportioned according to numbers alone, and should be founded on the white population only. Yet, Sir, that gentleman himself tells us, that our existing Government is the best the world has ever known. Is not this Government a Republican Government? Were not the patriots who formed it, wise Republicans? And is it not founded on the purest Republican principles? If gentlemen contend that it is not a Republican

Government, what are we to infer from that eulogy which represents it to be the best Government in the world? Here Mr. T. shewed the inconsistency of the argument urged on the other side, which, while it conceded that the present was not only a Republican Government, but the best of such Governments, yet denied to such a Government any one of the ingredients necessary to the construction of a Republic.

He next referred to the arguments on the subject of the natural right of a majority to govern; contending that a radical objection to all such arguments, would be found in the arguments themselves. Gentlemen contend, that a majority of the people have an indefeasible right to rule the minority; and having established this proposition, to their own satisfaction, at least, they immediately undertake to define who are the people; and by their own definition exclude not less than seven-eighths of the whole population, from the enumeration of that society, the majority of which, derives from eternal and immutable justice, a supposed right to rule the minority. Gentlemen assert, that according to an eternal rule of right, the majority must govern, and then instantly exclude from the enumeration, all except free *white* persons; so making the eternal rules of justice and reason, to depend, not upon the condition of the population as bond or free, but upon the accidental circumstance of the colour of their skins: and pray, Sir, said Mr. T. to what standard are we to refer in order to decide the question of colour, which is considered as so important in deducing a natural right? The native inhabitants of Japan, of China, of Hindostan, of all Southern Asia, of Egypt, the Moors of Africa, the Natives of the Greek Islands generally, together with all the unmixed descendants of the original inhabitants of America, will now be embraced within this supposed rule, that deduces the right of a majority of whites to govern any society from the supposed source of natural law.

If gentlemen had said, that sound policy required, that in Virginia, negroes and mulattoes, whether bond or free, should not participate in the active exercise of any political power, most willingly would he have assented to such a proposition. But when the question is not, who shall possess and exercise political power, but upon what basis ought such power to be erected, he could not comprehend the force of the argument, which, while seeking to fix population merely as that basis, would nevertheless disregard all other than the free white population. Domestic slaves of every sort, whether black or white, may be excluded, under the idea that they ought not to be considered as persons, but as property merely: but why none but a free white person should be enumerated, in establishing the number of the people as the basis of representation, he could not conceive. Women, minors, even aliens, and many others whom none propose to admit to the enjoyment of the Right of Suffrage, are all, nevertheless, to be counted, (provided they be white,) in forming the basis of representation: but none others are to be computed, although they be free, virtuous, intelligent, and rich, as any white man, in the whole State. Suppose, said Mr. T. a Hong merchant was to come hither from Macao, bringing with him numerous connexions and much wealth; or suppose some convulsion in the neighbouring Republics of the South, Mexico for example, should force hither many of the inhabitants of that country, free, virtuous, intelligent, and wealthy; can any possible reason be assigned, why the unmixed descendants of such emigrants, natives of Virginia, should be excluded from the computation of numbers, while every emigrant from any part of Europe, even before he becomes a citizen, must be estimated? Such a rule cannot be traced to any principle of right, or to any maxim of sound policy. The true rule is, that in a representative Government, every important interest in the society should have its particular representative; and that in the election of such a representative, the majority of persons duly qualified according to law, whose peculiar interest he is to represent, should have the privilege of electing him—and as, in defining the society so to be represented, it must be measured by territorial limits, so by apportioning representation to the different electoral precincts of the State, you attain the great desideratum of all representative Government.

Mr. Chairman, said Mr. T. capital and labour are the two great elements of the prosperity of every State; each of these is necessary to the existence of the other, for without labour, capital would be worthless, and without capital, labour would be useless. But although thus essential to each other, between the two there has existed a struggle from the beginning, which, in the very nature of things, must continue to the end of time. To reconcile these jarring elements, and to confine each within its proper sphere, is the business of good Government. But in the adjustment of the powers of Government, if too much influence be given to either of these elements, mischiefs must result to society. If too much weight be allowed to capital, labour will surely be oppressed, and if too much influence be given to labour, capital is at once endangered. Oppressed labour seizes power to redress its wrongs; capital endangered, must purchase power to protect its rights. Although in perpetual conflict, it passes human wisdom to separate these conflicting forces. You might as well expect to separate the soul from the body of man, and to preserve his existence, as to separate capital from labour, and to preserve society. You may subject either you please to the dominion of the other, but the experiment can only be made by that sort of revolution, which of necessity must end in anarchy and despotism. All which the friend of free Government can desire; all that the wisest Statesman can accomplish, is so to resolve these opposing forces into a third, as to give a new direction to each, which may be sufficient to check, restrain and balance both. This resulting force is Government, which, when deriving its power from both capital and labour, will receive the support of both.

But how is such a Government to be constructed? Certainly not in the mode suggested by the venerable member from Loudoun, as that which he prefers. His plan is, to divide the Legislative Department into two branches, both to be chosen by the same electors; to allow to numbers, that is to labour exclusively, representation in the more numerous branch, which is to be elected annually, and to capital and numbers combined, representation in the other branch, which is to be elected quadrennially; and so to check and balance these opposing forces. Now, Sir, is it not obvious at once, that two bodies, each deriving their authority from the same common source, can never check each other; but that both must obey the direction given to either by the power from which they both proceed? Does not our own experience too, inform us, that a Senate consisting of twenty-four members, sitting up-stairs, can never restrain the power of a House of Delegates consisting of one hundred and twenty members, sitting here? The Senate may sometimes prevent the hasty and incorrect legislation of the House of Delegates; they may dot the i's or cross the t's, or correct the orthography in bills which have passed the House, (if it be allowable to suppose that any member of that body may not know how to spell,) but it never has and never can arrest any deliberate measure which the House is disposed to persist in. The reason of this is very obvious. The Senate is elected for four years in the large divisions of our territory, while the Delegates are elected annually, by the smaller sub-divisions of these large districts. The Delegates, therefore, understand and represent more truly the opinions of their common constituents than the Senators; and whensoever a division of opinion exists between them, the Delegates must therefore prevail. I do not know the fact, but I think I hazard nothing in saying, that the case has never occurred, in which a Senator, voting differently from the Delegates representing the different counties of his district, upon any matter of much importance, has ever been re-elected. What security, then, can property find in such a body as a Senate, against the attack of numbers, represented exclusively in the other House!

But suppose, to avoid a result so obvious as I have stated, the plan should be somewhat changed, and a higher property qualification should be required of the electors of the Senate, than of the electors of the Delegates, the case would not be changed materially. The gentleman from Brooke would immediately proclaim this little body to be a band of oligarchs—others would style it a body of aristocrats, and many would be found to denounce it as the rotten part of the Government, which ought to be put down. With this cry of mad-dog uttered against it, the Senate would be sent forth to the people as an object of their scorn and hatred, and could furnish little protection to rights, for the security of which such an anomalous institution was at first designed.

In every society, there will always be found individuals, who, from the mere fondness of notoriety, and popularity, will oftentimes neglect their own interests, and who may, therefore, be expected to disregard the interests of their constituents. Such was the Duke of Orleans formerly in France: and in the conflicts between persons and property, which must take place in every election of Senators, upon this basis of numbers and property combined, the result must be, that numbers will certainly select the first Mons'r Egalite who presents himself as the professed guardian of the rights of property. In such a society as that which now exists, and I hope ever will exist in Virginia, if ever a separate representation is allowed to persons and to property, if ever they are so arrayed against each other by Government or in Government, we may talk as we please about checks and balances, but it is a delusion to believe, that the smaller can ever stop the progress of the greater power. An Almighty hand may part Dives and Lazarus by an impassable gulph, but the Statesman, who expects to keep them asunder, deceives himself; the struggle for power will and must bring them together again, and although Dives may remain in the place assigned to him, Lazarus cannot. If you wish to secure both persons and property, you must not add fuel to the flame which their natural collisions will always kindle. Instead of dividing them in action any where, you must resolve and combine their forces every where. Your effort should be by mingling them to render it impossible to distinguish the voice of the one from that of the other, and not to arrange them so as that each should be separately heard and understood. You can only accomplish this object by pursuing the example of our ancestors, by arranging representation neither upon the basis of one or the other, but upon the basis of interests, comprehending both within the limits of some certain territory, delineated by convenience.

Let me illustrate this in another way. The capital and labor of every country must be employed in the pursuits of either agriculture, commerce, or manufactures. Here, then, are three great interests existing in every community, all of which are so useful and important to its prosperity, that each ought to be represented, to the end that each may be preserved and promoted. Now, from what cause do these various and distinct interests proceed? It is from local circumstances merely; from the peculiar situation of the spot where they exist. By allowing representation to territory, therefore, you will in effect give representation to the particular interest which inhabits it. Do the trans-Alleghany people ever expect to become commercial? The thing is impossible. They may cut canals wherever they live, and call their boatmen sailors if they please, but God and nature have decreed that commerce shall never find a home there. It must abide upon navigable waters, made so, not by man, but by Him who made man. The interests of commerce, therefore, can never be represented by those who represent that section of the country. Do the people of the alluvial plain, watered by the tide-water, destitute as it is of every mineral production, and without a water-fall of a single foot, expect to become manufacturers? Such an expectation would be equally idle on their part: and the middle region of the State, must ever contain what it now does, the great agricultural interest of the Commonwealth. Each of these great interests ought to be represented; and the proportions of their representation will always be found well measured, by the capital and labor employed in each, and these again by the total population contained within the respective territories wherein they exist.

Again, if you will examine the territories of Virginia, wherein the great agricultural interests are found, I mean on this side of the mountain, (for my topographical knowledge of the tra-montane region does not enable me to speak of that,) you will discover, that taking the line of North Carolina as a base, the Blue Ridge as one of its sides, and some point near the county of Culpeper as its apex, a line drawn from thence to the termination of the tide-water region, will form a great triangle, within which, a slave-holding, tobacco-planting interest predominates. From the termination of the base of the first triangle, the North Carolina line so very near the Atlantic, furnishes the base of a second great triangle, whose apex is on the Potomac, and within which is to be found a slave-holding cotton-planting interest. The residue of this lower country will comprehend the grain-growing interest. Now all these three great interests, although agricultural, are, nevertheless, as distinct from each other as are those of agriculture, commerce, and manufactures; and like the latter, each of the former interests proceeds from local circumstances, easily to be ascertained, and circumscribed by well-defined geographical lines. But this is not all. The territory occupied by each of these three great agricultural interests, will be found intersected in all directions by wide water-courses, cutting off and preventing all intercourse and association between those who may chance to dwell on their opposite sides. Convenience will, therefore, require, that in allowing representation to each of these great agricultural interests, regard should be had to these local circumstances, to the end that the responsibility of the representative may be secured. Having fixed representation upon such a basis as this, in graduating and apportioning it to the different precincts delineated by a due regard to the convenience of their inhabitants, you may then, but not until then, resort to numbers, as furnishing the scale and measure by which the different interests abiding within these precincts may be ascertained and compared. But in resorting to numbers, you should not confine yourself to white numbers exclusively, but should consider every other circumstance in any way connected with this subject. Such was the course pursued in re-arranging the Senatorial Districts in 1816; and if a similar course was pursued upon this occasion, it would lead to a conclusion satisfactory and agreeable to all.

Mr. T. said, that having referred to this Act of 1816, which had been several times mentioned in the course of debate, and which, as he believed, was not understood generally, it might be well for him, who had a great share in the passage of that law, to give some account of its history, and of the principles upon which it was established.

During the course of the debate on the proposition to call a Convention in the year 1816, it was frequently said that the Western country was most unequally represented in the Senate; and that this inequality being created by the existing Constitution itself, could not be remedied by any act of the ordinary Legislature. This idea was new to him. He had never heard it suggested before, nor had he any confidence in the suggestion then. These opinions were stated by him in the debate, coupled by the declaration, that he had entertained little doubt it was competent to the Legislature, to arrange the Senatorial districts, whenever, in their discretion, they saw fit to do so; and, that this had been done several times already. In consequence of this declaration, after the Convention Bill passed, he was applied to by one of the members from the Western part of the State, to assist in an effort to re-arrange the Senatorial districts, in a manner more equal than they were then arranged. To this application, he yielded a ready assent; and supported, with all his ability, the motion for leave to bring in such a bill. This motion was opposed by the gentleman from Brooke, (Mr. Doddridge,) and others, upon the ground, that it was a measure, not warranted by the Constitution. But, after a warm debate, the motion was carried, and a Committee was appointed, (of which he was one,) to bring in such a bill.

He said, that according to the basis of taxation, the West was found entitled to seven members, and a small fraction over—according to the basis of Federal numbers, they were entitled to seven members, and a large fraction over—and according to the basis of white population, they were entitled to nine members, and a small fraction over—computing according to the Census of 1810. Then, by adding all these results together, and dividing by three, it was found, that the West would be entitled to eight members, and a fraction over. Believing that the East, which would be entitled to fifteen members and a fraction, could better spare the fraction than the West; and being entirely averse to differing with his Western brethren concerning a fraction of a representative merely, for his part he willingly assented to give up this fraction to the West, who thereupon would have nine Senators, while the East retained fifteen—and upon a perfect understanding of these proportions, were all the arrangements of the original bill made.

The gentleman from Brooke is mistaken when he says, that I offered an amendment to this bill, the object of which was to compute slaves in the apportionment of the Senators. I never made any such proposition, or wished to amend the bill in any other way whatever.

[Mr. Doddridge said, that he had not meant to refer to this bill. His reference was to the bill for calling a Convention.]

Mr. Tazewell said, he was satisfied, that the gentleman from Brooke did not intend to make a mis-statement, but it was certain that he had referred to the Senatorial bill, not only in his speech here lately, but upon several other occasions both here and elsewhere. When the Senatorial bill was to be adjusted in the Committee, it was distinctly understood by every member, that the proportions between the West and the East were to be nine and fifteen; and although from what he had since heard, he thought it highly probable, that afterwards, while adjusting these proportions to the different parts of the State, gentlemen might have had regard to white numbers only, yet if they did so, no such idea was ever suggested to him, either in or out of the House. He was content with the proportions mentioned and agreed upon, and for his own part, was perfectly indifferent as to the further details of this bill.

In conversation with the friends of the measure, it was agreed, that as the West was then entitled to representation in the Senate, fully proportioned to their quota of the land-tax paid by them, if they wished to augment this representation, they ought to have a re-assessment of the lands, and so to enlarge their quota of this tax. This suggestion was readily accepted by the gentlemen from the West, favourable to the bill, which, therefore, assumed the shape it now wears, of a bill to re-apportion the land-tax, and to re-arrange the Senatorial districts.

Such was the history of this law; and he had hoped, that a perfect knowledge of the benefits derived from it, and the general satisfaction with which it had been adopted, would have induced the pursuit of a similar course now. The people of the West were then satisfied. They confessed, that they had no cause to complain of unequal representation in the lower House; and when the inequality of representation in the Senate was so redressed, they expressed their entire content with the arrangement made. Let but a similar course be again adopted, and it will terminate in a similar result. Add but a single line to George Mason's Constitution, authorising the Legislature, from time to time, in their discretion, to deprive counties and corporations which may have declined too much in population or in wealth, of the representation to which they are now entitled, and every evil of unequal representation which is now complained of, will be at once removed.

But the gentleman from Augusta, (Mr. Johnson,) has told us, that this is a contest for power merely; that disguise it as we might, it must still present itself as a question of power. If this be so, we cannot surrender the smallest fraction, without an abasing degradation. The power we now possess, we are well content to share with our brethren of the West, provided they can satisfy us, that it is right we should do so. But if the power is demanded by them merely because it is wanted; and if it is expected, that the East must yield until the West is satisfied, he for one would yield nothing to such a demand. He would at once place his foot on the spot from whence he would never recede, be the consequence what it might. To a spirit of just compromise he was prepared to yield much, but to a strong demand nothing.

Mr. Chairman, said Mr. T. I came here anxious to preserve so much of our long-tried Constitution, as in practice had been found good, and no more. I came here prepared to reform at once every part of it, from the operation of which any practical mischief had been found to result. Nay, I am willing to go still further, and am ready to provide a seasonable remedy for any probable mischief, which may be reasonably supposed likely to result hereafter. But I cannot consent to pull down the whole venerated fabric to its foundation, merely to build up another; to change every thing, to reform every thing, and to alter all. Those whom I represent have no such wish as this, nor did they depute me to co-operate in any such undertaking. They had heard complaints and murmurs at different times, proceeding from different quarters, that the existing Government had produced mischievous effects. Such mischiefs they have never felt themselves, but believing it probable that they might exist, although unknown to them, they sent me hither to enquire into the fact; and when it should be seen to exist, to apply to the evil the proper corrective. To the attainment of this object, I will honestly and sincerely co-operate with any. But when I am told, that the question to be discussed and decided is nothing else than a mere question of power; that the West want that which the East have, I can only say that such a question can never be decided here. Jurists may discuss and decide questions of right; Statesmen may settle and adjust matters of political expediency; but there is but one earthly forum to which an appeal can ever be made for the determination of a mere question of power; and before that forum, there is but one argument which ever can produce the slightest effect. We are told, that in former times, a strong demand was made upon the Government of ancient Sparta, accompanied by a declaration, that if the demand was not granted, the demandant would come and take it. The laconic answer to this demand was, 'Come and take it.' The demandant came, but did not obtain that which he meant to take.

Mr. Doddridge said, he wished to make some observations in reply to the statements of the gentleman from Norfolk. That gentleman had said, that by the law of February, 1817, reforming the Senatorial representation, reference was had, not only to white population, but to interests and other circumstances, from an examination of which it resulted that the West were entitled to eight Senators and a fraction, and that the East yielded that fraction to the West, which gave them nine members. Mr. D. said, he would not rely on his memory and oppose it to that of the gentleman from Norfolk, but he would appeal to facts which could not err, whether they were tested by Pike, Gough, or Dilworth.

The Senatorial bill of February, 1815, was based on the Census of 1810. In 1810 the whole white population was 551,000, disregarding the fractions of a thousand—of this population, 212,000 were found West of the Blue Ridge. Out of twenty-four members of the Senate, this population entitled the West to nine members, and a large fraction which they *lost;* so that the Senatorial arrangement of that year was regulated by white population, and by nothing else. By the law of 1817, it required several annual elections to give the West their nine members. These members did not come into the body until 1820. The Census of that year showed that at that period the West had upwards of 48,000 unrepresented. Since 1810, the increase of Western population has been nearly 107,000 and of the Eastern 23,000, leaving West of the Ridge upwards of 82,000 souls now unrepresented in the Senate.

The gentleman had said that in 1817, the West had their full share in the House of Delegates. How correct that statement may be, will appear from the following facts: In 1817, there were ninety-nine counties and four towns represented. This produced a House of two hundred and two members. There were then thirty-four counties West of the Ridge, having sixty-eight members. The population being 551,000 inhabitants, and the number of members two hundred and two—the Western population being 212,000, entitled them to seventy-eight and a half members instead of sixty-eight, being a deficiency of ten and a half members, which being added to the East gave that quarter of the State an advantage on a divided vote of twenty-one.

There was as little accuracy in the other assertion, that the West were satisfied with the Senatorial arrangement, declaring it to be one that justice and equity required. So far from this, most of the members from the West voted against the Senatorial bill in all its stages, and never agreed to accept it until the Convention bill which went to the Senate was lost.

The inequality of Western representation in the House of Delegates has increased since 1817. The whole white population is now 682,000 of which 319,000 are West of the Ridge. Since 1817, the following counties have been erected in the West, viz: Morgan, Preston, Alleghany, Pocahontas, Nicholas and Logan, making the Western counties forty, and giving to the West eighty votes in our House of Delegates of two hundred and fourteen members. By the above numbers, the West are entitled to something more than one hundred members instead of eighty, and the deficiency of twenty being added to the East, gives to that quarter an advantage of forty votes.

Mr. Chapman Johnson said, he was sorry there was some misrepresentation of his remarks, by the gentleman from Norfolk, (Mr. Tazewell.) He regretted that this should have been the case, as he believed that gentleman was disposed to consider what he had said in a spirit of fairness and candor. He did say, that the question we were considering was a contest for power. He had said, disguise it as we would, view it in any aspect we could, if we come back to a candid consideration of it, it was a question of power and nothing else. He did not mean to be understood as intimating that this was a lawless controversy for power, in which each was trying to get what he could, *per fas aut nefas.* This was far from his opinion, and his reason for addressing the Committee, was to show that in the principles of either party this question was not so intensely important as either imagined. He did not mean that either party contended for power on any principles but those which they could justify to their own consciences as right, but this question of representation was a question of power, although certainly all the business of the Convention was not of that character. Is it not the question whether you will give the *power* of representation to interest, numbers or wealth? To any or all of them? Is it not the question whether you will distribute the power of the Government among the elements of the Commonwealth? No matter what is the basis, it is the same. He did think that his language would have been viewed in this way, as it ought to have been. It would be found that no one was more disposed to settle the question of power, so as to meet all the wishes and interests of the State, than he was. He knew it was impossible to meet those wishes, but he would come as near as possible, for it was his sincere desire that all things should go on harmoniously. He should vote against the proposition to make the Federal numbers the basis, for reasons which it would not now be necessary to repeat. If what he had said was remembered, his reasons would be known. He would vote against it, as much on account of its effect on the people he represented, as on account of its effect on the whole population. He should consider as satisfactory, qualified voters for both branches. If he could not choose—if Federal numbers should be preferred, as the limitation to be given to the Senate to operate as a check on the House of Delegates, he should have very little to regret on account of the power given over his constituents by that basis, over that which would have been given by the basis he recommended. A single remark as to the power of the Senate to check the power of the House of Delegates. He did not mean to refer to his experience there, nor to resist the argument, that the Senate for one, two, three, or four years might withstand the House, but that it must at last yield, because both branches are from the same people. He would say nothing farther on that argument, except, that if the Federal numbers were adopted in the Senate, and the House of Delegates established on the basis of white population, we ought to suppose that each should concur in two or three years in any great question. It ought to be so. He thought the responsibility of the representatives was a sufficient security for their continued regard to the public interests. The members of the Senate are elected for a longer period of time, and that circumstance might render that body less efficient as a check—but the member of the House goes back to his own constituent body annually; so that when you give the white basis to this body, you establish the best of all checks. He had thought it right to state this much; he should not attempt further argument. The Committee ought not to indulge him any more, as he had already consumed so much of their time. He would not sit down without saying, that to the bitter sarcasms, gratuitous imputations and learned jests of the gentleman from Charlotte, (Mr. Randolph,) he had no plea to enter, no answer to give. However low he might stand in the opinions of others, and they could not estimate him lower than he estimated himself, yet he had self-respect enough not to answer that gentleman, and if he had not, respect for this Committee would impose silence upon him.

Mr. Mercer, rose to corroborate what had fallen from the gentleman from Brooke, on the subject of the Senate Bill in 1816. The basis of that Bill was rested on the white population, and ought there to stand. He was second on the Committee, and owing to the indisposition of the Chairman, who could not attend, the duties of Chairman devolved upon him. A gentleman from Berkeley, not a member of this Convention, was the one who collated the counties to form the basis. He had heard no complaints. Another word and he had done. The gentleman from Norfolk, had said, that in the original formation of this Government, regard was had to the representation of interests, and that the old House of Burgesses was composed with reference to that distribution of interests. He saw no evidence in the topographical or other character of the country, to sustain the view of the gentleman from Norfolk. The gentleman from Norfolk, had gone so far as to divide the Commonwealth into a number of triangles, to shew the different interests into which the State was divided. He considered these interests as forming a basis as fluctuating as any other that could be determined.

Cotton was of recent cultivation. In Loudoun, where there were formerly tobacco fields and wheat-patches, there are now wheat-fields and tobacco-patches. The plan, therefore, of the gentleman from Norfolk, might be applicable one day, and altogether inapplicable a few years hence. Mr. M. made some other observations in reply, but we did not correctly catch their import. He concluded with stating, that the counties had been created for judicial, not for legislative purposes; and all applications to divide counties were founded in the difficulty of going to the courts to serve either as jurors or witnesses. He had never heard any other causes assigned, although he had been in this Hall on many occasions, when applications of this kind were made. He hoped that the new basis would not supersede that of the free whites.

Mr. Cooke said, that if he was correctly informed in the Constitutional History of Virginia, the gentleman from Norfolk, (Mr. Tazewell) had been singularly infelicitous in attempting to support, by a reference to that history, his theory of the true principles of representation. For I find, said Mr. Cooke, that he, too, has his *theories* of Government, as well as the wild democrats of Middle and Western Virginia.

His theory is, that there should be a representation of *interests*, in the legislative bodies, as contradistinguished from the representation of numbers; and, to support this theory, he has attempted to shew that it has been uniformly acted on in Virginia, even from the first establishment of legislative bodies in the Colony. For this purpose, he has drawn a picture of the Colony at that period of its infancy when the population was dispersed in detached settlements, or plantations, separated from each other by "mighty waters" and impenetrable forests. He next *assumes* it as a fact, without even *attempting* to prove it, that each of these settlements had some peculiar interest of its own—I mean an interest variant from that of its neighbour settlements. He alleges that a separate representation was given to each of these settlements, *because of the existence* of these separate and variant interests: That, in process of time, when the settlements were enlarged so as to come in contact with each other, it became necessary to designate, by artificial boundaries, the limits of these separate and distinct interests: That, to effect this purpose, the Colonial Legislature, in 1634, erected them into counties, giving to each county an equal representation in the House of Burgesses. And thus he shows that his favorite theory of the representation of interests, *as interests*, and contradistinguished from the representation of numbers, was the theory of the earliest law-givers of the Colony; and he asserts that it has remained, to the present day, the theory of representation practically adhered to in the Constitution of Virginia, and so is entitled to prescriptive respect.

Now, Sir, I apprehend that in taking this view of the subject, the gentleman has fallen into a mistake not uncommon with theorists. Instead of conforming his theory to the facts, he has made his facts conform to his theory.

I apprehend that a more accurate version of our early Constitutional History will shew, that if any principle of representation has been adopted in Virginia, it is substantially, the principle which is recommended in the Report of the Select Committee—the principle, that in apportioning representation, regard should be had to the free white population exclusively.

The first chapter in the Constitutional History of Virginia is, the ordinance of the 24th of July, 1621. On that day, "the Treasurer and company of adventurers of the city of London, for the first Colony in Virginia," passed an ordinance establishing the Constitution of the Colony. (1) By this ordinance, they constituted a General Assembly, to consist in part, of Burgesses, or Representatives, to be chosen by the "*inhabitants*" of the different plantations, or settlements. And, as there were, at that time, no slaves in the Colony, the free inhabitants of the country were of course the *basis of representation*. And though the ordinance did not direct, that the free inhabitants should be *equally* represented, yet, as *equal* representation, where there is a representation of the *people*, is the most obvious, and natural idea, it is to be presumed, that the company contemplated a representation substantially equal. I see no trace, in this first organic law of Virginia, of the representation of *interests*, and no evidence, any where, that there were any peculiar, separate and distinct interests, appertaining to the different plantations or settlements. Their contiguity, would seem to contradict the idea; and, in fact, their interests were homogeneous, if not identical.

Proceeding to the next era in the Constitutional History of the Colony, we find the gentleman from Norfolk, asserting, that in 1634, when the forests, which had constituted, for a time, the natural barriers between, and limits of, these supposed distinct interests, had disappeared, and they were in danger of being blended together, artificial limits were substituted, counties erected, and *two Burgesses, or in other words, equal representation, given to each county*. And this measure, he says, was adopted, with a view to preserve the separate representation of these distinct and separate *interests*. Here is, indeed, a singular adaptation of the *facts* to the *theory*. But, Sir, it happens, unfortunately for the *theory*, that the *facts* are not historically true. It is true, that the Colony was first divided into counties in 1634; but it is not true, that the counties were created with any, the most remote, reference to *representation*, at all. The counties were created for *two avowed purposes, and for no other*. I mean the organization of the military force of the Colony, for defence against the Indians, and the administration of justice. (2) Not a word is said about the *representation* of

(1) See Hening's Statutes at Large, vol. 1, p. 110.
(2) See Hening's Statutes at Large, vol. 1, p. 224.

these counties, or about the representation of *interests, or any* representation at all. And, in fact, the counties were not represented *as* counties, till the year 1661; nor does any, the smallest *connexion* between *counties* and *representation* appear in the Legislative History of the Colony, till 1645. It is true, that in the last mentioned year, an Act was passed, declaring that not more than *four* representatives should be sent from each county, except James City county, which was allowed six—besides one for the town. (3) But, it is equally true, that at the time of, and after the passage of that Act, the parishes also were allowed to send representatives to the Legislature, whenever they thought proper. (4)

It was not until 1661, as I have said, that the counties, *as* counties, were represented in the General Assembly. In that year an Act was passed, declaring in effect, that the House of Burgesses should consist of two representatives, and no more, from each *county*, together with one from James City, "the metropolis of the country." And, by the same Act, it was declared, "that every county which should lay out one hundred acres of land, and people it with one hundred tithable persons," should have the privilege of sending an additional Burgess. (5)

By adverting to the recital of that Act, you will find that the cause assigned for the reduction and *equalization* of the representation of the counties, was the *expense* of maintaining the great number of Burgesses sent from the counties and *parishes*. "Whereas, the charge of assemblies is much increased by the great number of Burgesses," &c.

Thus you perceive, Sir, that the principle of representation in Virginia, if it deserves the name of a principle, received its final consummation, its last finish, from a Colonial Legislature of unlettered tobacco-planters in 1661. The Constitution of Virginia, which is gravely declared, even on this floor, to have been the work of the sages and patriots of 1776, *was actually formed and finished in 1661, and has never since been modified, in this great and leading feature of the representation of the people.* This *admirable* regulation—the equal representation of the counties, which is recommended to our love and veneration, as the work of our glorious ancestors in 1776, was, in fact, a paltry Colonial regulation—a device to save money—a matter of pounds, shillings and pence!

It is true, that the men of '76 did not alter it. And *why* did they not alter it? Simply because *they could not*. The infant Commonwealth was engaged, as I had occasion to remark in a former debate, in a war, in which its very existence was at stake—in a war which required the united direction of all interests, and of its whole strength, against a foreign enemy. The sages and patriots who composed the Convention of 1776, were wise and *practical* men. What extreme folly, what absolute insanity, would it have been, when hostile squadrons were riding at anchor in Hampton Roads, to say to the smaller counties, exposed by their position to the full operation of all the seductions and all the threats of the enemy, "*you must surrender a part of the power you have enjoyed under the Kingly Government for one hundred and seventy years.*" Sir, the members of the Convention of '76, had too much good sense; too much practical wisdom—to *attempt* so mad and ill-timed a reform. They said, what they were obliged to say, that the representation of the counties should remain as it was.

Thus, Sir, it appears, that the idea of the gentleman from Norfolk, that the representation of interests, *as* interests, contradistinguished from the representation of numbers, has been from the first settlement of the Colony, the theory of our Government, has no foundation in history; and that the statement of facts which he has made to support his theory, is altogether erroneous. That the Act of 1661, which established the equal representation of the counties, considered at this day as the highest stretch of political sagacity, so far from having been intended to establish the principle that *interests* and not numbers should be thereafter represented, or *any* principle, was a mere fiscal regulation, of which penuriousness, and not political wisdom, was the author and source.

In fact, Sir, since the ordinance of 1621, no *principle* of representation, deserving the name of a principle, has ever been acted on. We are assembled here to declare what the principle of representation *ought to be*, and shall be, in all time to come.

The question what *is* the true principle, is one which I have heretofore discussed, and shall not now touch. The gentleman from Norfolk says, that the true principle by which to regulate the apportionment of political power, is the representation of all the different *interests* of society—*as* interests. The Bill of Rights declares, that the true principle is the equal representation of *the people*. I am content to rest the question on the relative weight of the two authorities.

(3) See Hening's Statutes at Large, vol. 1, p. 299.
(4) See Hening's Statutes at Large, vol. 1, pages 411, 421, and passim.
(5) See Hening's Statutes at Large, vol. 2, p. 20.

Mr. Leigh said, that reference having been made to the Colonial Government, to disprove the statement of the gentleman from Norfolk, he would read an extract from the history of that Government, for the accuracy of which he would vouch, as he took great pains to ascertain facts. Mr. Leigh then read a note which is appended to the Revised Code, first volume, page 38.* It appeared, he said, that Bacon, a rebel, was the first who adopted the notion of Universal Suffrage in the country, and that he had it from the soldiers of Cromwell's army.

He stated, that the substance of the note which he had read, was confirmed in its accuracy by the late Judge Roane, and said a few words as to the manner of dividing the State into plantations, districts and hundreds, all founded on that principle of interest which the gentleman from Norfolk had alluded to. If that principle was not avowed, there could be no doubt that it was the principle.

Again, he stated that the College of William and Mary was allowed a representative until the commencement of the revolution. It was represented in the Convention of 1775. Why was this, but that the principle of the interests of different branches was acted on in the apportionment of representation? Here was a representation of the learning of this College, which had been until lately a most useful institution, and he hoped might become so again. He considered that the gentleman from Norfolk had been fully sustained in his statements and views.

Mr. Cooke said, that he had not learned the constitutional history of Virginia from the *notes to the Revised Code*, but from the documentary and legislative records set

* As to the form of the Colonial Government, for which this Constitution was substituted, see 1 *Chart.* § 7. 8. 15. 1 *Hen. st. at lar. p.* 60, 1, 4. *Royal instructions for the government of the Colony, Ibid. p.* 67. 75. 2 *Chart.* § 8. 9. 10. 11. 12. 13. 14. 15. 23. *Ibid. p.* 89, 90, 1, 2, 5. 3 *Chart.* § 6. 7. 8. *Ibid. p.* 102, 3.—By the 14th section of the second charter and the 8th of the third, the power of establishing a form of government and magistracy for the Colony, was vested in the council and general court of the Virginia company in England; which, on the 24th July, 1621, ordained a form of government accordingly; whereby the powers of the Colonial government were vested in a governor and council of state, appointed by the company in England and holding during its pleasure, and a house of burgesses, *two* from every town, hundred and particular plantation, to be respectively chosen by the *inhabitants*; and this council of state and house of burgesses formed the Colonial legislature, called the General Assembly. The Colonial government was directed to conform, in legislation and jurisprudence, to the English government and laws; and it was provided, that no law or ordinance made by the General Assembly, should be valid, unless ratified by the general court of the company in England, and returned so ratified under its seal. *See this Constitution, and the commission and instructions to the first governor under it,* 1 *Hen. st. at lar. p.* 110. 113. 114. In 1624, the crown suppressed the Virginia company by proclamation, and resumed the powers granted to the company; but the form of government it had given the Colony, remained in substance unchanged. It appears, that the constitution of the Colonial government was amended by George I. and instructions were given by George II. to the governor Lord Albemarle, for the regulation of the government according to the amended constitution: but these papers are not to be found. The King always retained the control over the Colonial laws, and even exercised the power of suspending and repealing them; powers, often exercised capriciously, always complained of as a grievance, sometimes disputed, and at length assigned as one of the causes of the revolution; see 5 *Hen. st. at lar.* 432. This royal prerogative had a most important influence on the legislation of the Colonial government. Counties or shires were first established in 1634. 1 *Hen. st. at lar. p.* 224. It seems from our ancient records, that at first, in practice, neither the towns, hundreds and plantations, while they were represented, nor the counties, after the burgesses were elected from them, were restricted to *two* or *any fixed number* of burgesses. In 1645, the number was limited to four for each county, except James City, which was allowed five, besides one for Jamestown, the seat of government; 1 *Hen. stat. at lar. p.* 299. Afterwards, *particular* parishes, and then *all* parishes, were allowed to send *one* or *two* burgesses; *Ibid.* 250. 277. 421. In 1660, the number of burgesses was limited to two for each county and one for Jamestown in James City county, with like privilege to every county, that would lay out 100 acres of land, and people it with 100 titheable persons; 2 *Ibid. p.* 20. 106.—The 7th article of the present constitution, provides that the *right of suffrage for members of both houses of Assembly, shall remain as exercised at present.* By the constitution of July 1621, above cited, the *right of suffrage* was given to the *inhabitants*; afterwards, it seems, only *freemen* were allowed to vote; 1 *Ibid. p.* 333, 4. then *only housekeepers; Ibid. p.* 412. then *all freemen* again, *Ibid. p.* 403. 475. then "*freeholders and housekeepers, who only are answerable for levies;*" 2 *Ibid.* 280. then, by Bacon's laws, *all freemen* again; *Ibid.* 356. But in 1677, the King instructed the Governor, that the members of Assembly should be elected by *freeholders only; Ibid. p.* 425. In 1684, it was resolved, that *all tenants for life* had an undoubted *right of suffrage*; 3 *Ibid.* 26. In 1699, the right of suffrage was confined to *freeholders* (excluding women, infants and recusants convict) resident in the respective counties and towns; *Ibid. p.* 238. In 1736, the right of suffrage was confined to *freeholders* of an hundred acres of unsettled land or twenty-five acres of improved land, and all freeholders in towns, but with a right to vote, only in the county where the land or the greater part of it lay; 4 *Ibid.* 475, 6. The city of Williamsburg and the borough of Norfolk were allowed a representative, by their charters, by which the *right of suffrage* of the citizens and burghers was regulated, but afterwards somewhat narrowed by law; *Edi.* 1769, *p.* 122. 287. It seems, that till 1723, *free negroes, indians and mulattoes,* might vote at elections; but by the acts of that year, c. 4. § 23. *Edi.* 1733. *p.* 344, they were disqualified; and that particular section of the act was not repealed, though the rest of it was by royal proclamation in 1724. *Edi.* 1769. *p.* 15. *note* (a.) *Edi.* 1762. *p.* 103. By the act of 1769. c. 1, the quantity of unimproved land, necessary to qualify a freeholder to vote, was reduced to fifty acres; but this act was suspended until the royal approbation should be signified, and such approbation was never signified. The ordinance of the convention of 1775, providing for the election of delegates to the convention of 1776, extended the *right of suffrage* to free white men, inhabitants of Fincastle and West Augusta, in possession of the requisite quantity of land, and claiming freeholds therein, though they should have obtained no patents or legal titles to their lands.—Thus stood the *right of suffrage* when the constitution was adopted. By the act of 1785, c. 55. § 2. the qualification of the freeholder in respect to the quantity of unimproved land was reduced from 100 to 50 acres; the legislature either regarding the act of 1769, as effectual, notwithstanding the want of the royal assent; or, perhaps, considering that while the principle of freehold qualification was preserved, a change as to the quantity of land was consistent with the constitution.

forth at length in "Hening's Statutes at Large." I am, nevertheless, thankful, said he, to the gentleman from Chesterfield, (Mr. Leigh,) for reading the long and elaborate note from the Revised Code, which has refreshed my recollection of sundry particulars which I pretermitted in the sketch that I gave of the history of representation in Virginia, because I did not consider them precisely "germane to the matter" under consideration. I am yet to learn, however, in what point or particular I have misstated the historical facts which I undertook to state. I said, and I repeat, that the ordinance of 1621 recognized the free "*inhabitants*" of the Colony as the basis of representation, and I have heard nothing inconsistent with that statement in the history that has been read by the gentleman from Chesterfield.

I *thank* him, however, for calling the attention of the Committee to the history of Suffrage in Virginia, as I think *that* history replete with valuable and interesting facts. The learned gentleman, Sir, has ventured to say to this Committee, that the idea of Universal Suffrage was never heard in Virginia, till it was started in England by those crazy enthusiasts, the "*agitators*," in the time of Cromwell; and that it was through them introduced into the Colony. I confess that I heard this statement made with no small surprise.

What is the meaning, Sir, of the phrase "Universal Suffrage," as commonly used and understood by intelligent men? Does it mean a Right of Suffrage belonging to, and exercised by, all the men, all the women, and all the children of the community? Such an absurdity never entered into the head, even of "*a reformer*," however "*hardened his heart might have become by experimenting on the rights of man, to ascertain how large a dose of French principles might be administered without causing their destruction.*" It means a Right of Suffrage exercised by all the free *men* of a community. And precisely to this extent was the right exercised in the Colony of Virginia from the year 1621 till the year 1655. The ordinance of 1621 secured the Right of Suffrage to all the free "inhabitants" of the Colony. And I defy the gentleman from Chesterfield, with all his constitutional lore, to show, by a reference to the legislative history of the Colony, that it was taken away, or even assailed, before the passage of the act of 1655. In that year an act was passed declaring, "that all house-keepers, whether freeholders, leaseholders, or otherwise tenants, should only be capable to elect Burgesses: Provided, that this word house-keepers, repeated in this act, extended no further than to one person in a family." (1)

And here, Sir, we have presented to us, the curious discrepancy between the statement made by the gentleman from Chesterfield and the real facts of the case: and not discrepancy only, but absolute contrariety. His statement is, that Universal Suffrage originated in England, with the military "agitators" in the time of Cromwell, and was thence, and *at that period*, transplanted into Virginia, where it was before unknown. The *fact* is, that it had existed in the Colony from the earliest period of its legislative history, and was *first assailed* in the time of the "agitators" of Cromwell, who, in 1655, was at the height of his power and the sovereign of Virginia. Thus, Sir, these crazy "agitators," these English republican enthusiasts, *destroyed*, instead of introducing Universal Suffrage. They were the first to introduce rationality into the theretofore irrational regulation of the Right of Suffrage. I say *rationality*, Sir, because I am no advocate for Universal Suffrage. God forbid that I ever should be.

The act of 1655 was repealed, however, in the following year. The repealing act declares, in the quaint language of the age, that it is conceived to "be something hard and unagreeable to reason, that any persons shall pay equal taxes, and yet have no votes in elections; and that so much of the act for choosing Burgesses be repealed, as excludes *freemen* from votes." (2)

With the exception of this interval of a year, Universal Suffrage prevailed in Virginia, from 1621 till 1670. In the year last mentioned, an act was passed declaring that "none but freeholders and house-keepers, who only are answerable to the public for their levies, should thereafter have any voice in the election of any Burgesses."(3) This limitation of the Right of Suffrage was unpalatable to the colonists, and was set forth as *one* of the grievances by which the popular insurrection of 1676 was justified. I call it a popular *insurrection*, because the phrase is more agreeable to my republican notions than the word "*rebellion*," used by the gentleman from Chesterfield. *Rebellion*, Sir! then what were the men of 1776, but rebels against the royal authority! Nathaniel Bacon was a *rebel*, who, perhaps, wanted only a wider theatre of action and a more protracted span of existence, to be the Washington of his age. He rose in arms against oppression, and a democratic Legislature, or one under his control, while it redressed many *real* grievances, repealed the limitation of Suffrage,

(1) See Hening's Statutes at Large, vol. 1, page 412

(2) See Hening's Statutes at Large, vol. 1, page 403. The repealing act *precedes* the act repealed in the *paging* of "Hening's Statutes at Large," in consequence of a mistake in the *MS.* "not discovered in time."

(3) See Hening's Statutes at Large, vol. 2, page 280.

imposed in 1670. His democratic code was repealed in its turn, in 1677, and two regiments of British soldiers were sent by his most gracious Majesty, King Charles II. whose Government the gentleman from Chesterfield calls, by way of distinction, "the lawful Government," to disseminate in the Colony more *correct notions* concerning civil and political liberty. This worthless tyrant—the *most* worthless that ever filled the throne of England—did not condescend to ask of the trembling Burgesses, whom he assembled at the very mouths of his cannon, and at the very point of his bayonets, *a legislative act* establishing *the freehold limitation of the Right of Suffrage in Virginia.* He *ordered* his Governor, in his private letter of instructions, under his royal hand, "to take care that the members of the Assembly should thereafter be elected by *freeholders only*." (4) And *thus*, Sir, the freehold limitation of the Right of Suffrage became the *law of Virginia;* and so it has remained to the present day: Modified, to be sure, from time to time, by subservient Colonial Assemblies, in regard to the quantity of land necessary to confer the right, but still the *freehold limitation.* And with these slight modifications, it remains the law and the Constitution of Virginia to the present day. It was, in 1677, then, and not in 1776, that this boasted regulation, the acme of political wisdom, became a part of the Constitution of Virginia. It was dictated by a tyrant, and thrust down the throats of the people of Virginia at the point of the bayonet. And *this* is the principle of our Constitution which we are called on to venerate—to bow down and worship, as the wisest and best of all the institutions *formed in* 1776 *by the sages and patriots of the revolution. This* is the institution which is the great safeguard of property, and the palladium of our liberties.

Sir, I have said that the Constitution of Virginia, as it regards this great and vital provision, was matured and completed in 1677. The Convention of 1776 *found it* established and matured, and they left it *untouched.* And WHY did they leave it untouched? Were they in love with the memory of its author? Or were they true republicans, as they unquestionably were partial to aristocratic distinctions and priviledged orders? No, Sir; they left it untouched, because they dared not touch it. It had taken deep root, and could not be torn up with safety, while so many elements of discord were already at work, and threatened to add the horrors of a *civil* to the dangers of a *foreign* war.

Moreover, the poisonous plant, *aristocracy*, had grown up and flourished under the shadow of the tree of *royalty.* A privileged class had been created, not only by the establishment of exclusive political privileges, but by extensive grants of land to the favorites of the Crown. There was, therefore, a *landed*, as well as a *political* aristocracy. It was, like all privileged classes, tenacious of its exclusive privileges, and like all wealthy aristocracies, proud of its wealth. To a class like this, the authors of the Bill of Rights, genuine and bold republicans as they were, did not *dare* to say, in the heat of a war which put in requisition all the wealth and all the resources of the country, "Your reign shall cease—your power and influence are at an end."

They said, with a mournful and sententious brevity, "The Right of Suffrage shall *remain* as at present exercised."

This, Sir, is a true history of the rise and progress, and unhappily, of the present state of the Right of Suffrage in Virginia.

Mr. Leigh said, that the gentleman from Frederick needed not to inform him that he had not learned the history of Virginia from the note to the Revised Code. His object had been merely to put the Committee in possession of the facts which were there stated. The gentleman had not only studied out of a different system of law, but also out of a different system of general history, or he would not have said that Bacon's insurrection, which grew out of a private feud, was a stand in defence of the rights of man.

The question was then taken on the motion of Mr. Leigh, to amend the resolution, which motion was decided in the *negative*—Ayes 47, Noes 49.

Some difficulty occurring in the count, the names of members were called over; but as the vote was taken in Committee of the Whole, the rule of order does not permit the yeas and nays to be recorded on the Journal. We have obtained, however, the following list, which we submit to satisfy the curiosity of readers.

Ayes—Messrs. Jones, Leigh of Chesterfield, Taylor of Chesterfield, Giles, Brodnax, Dromgoole, Alexander, Goode, Marshall, Tyler, Nicholas, Clopton, Mason, Trezvant, Claiborne, Urquhart, Randolph, Leigh of Halifax, Logan, Venable, Madison, Barbour of Orange, Stanard, Holliday, Roane, Taylor of Caroline, Morris, Garnett, Barbour of Culpeper, Scott, Macrae, Green, Tazewell, Loyall, Prentis, Grigsby, Mennis, Taliaferro, Bates, Neale, Rose, Joynes, Bayly, Upshur, and Perrin.—47.

Noes—Messrs. Anderson, Coffman, Harrison, Williamson, Baldwin, Johnson, M'Coy, Moore, Beirne, Smith, Miller, Baxter, Monroe, Mercer, Fitzhugh, Henderson, Cooke, Powell, Opie, Griggs, Naylor, Donalson, Boyd, Pendleton, George, M'Millan, Campbell of Washington, Byars, Cloyd, Chapman, Mathews, Oglesby, Duncan,

(4) See Hening's Statutes at Large, vol. 2, page 425.

Laidley, Summers, See, Doddridge, Morgan, Campbell of Brooke, Wilson, Campbell of Bedford, Claytor, Saunders, Cabell, Stuart, Pleasants, Gordon, Thompson, and Massie.—49.

So the Committee of the Whole rejected the proposition to base the representation in the House of Delegates, on what is called *the Federal number*, consisting of the free whites, together with three-fifths of the slaves.

The Committee then rose, and the House adjourned.

TUESDAY, November 17, 1829.

The Convention met at eleven o'clock, and was opened with prayer by the Rev. Mr. Taylor of the Baptist Church.

Mr. Mercer moved that when the Convention adjourn, it adjourn to meet to-morrow at ten o'clock, (instead of eleven.) The motion was opposed by Mr. Stanard, and advocated by the mover and Mr. Doddridge: and the question being taken, the House appeared equally divided—Ayes 40, Noes 40. The President giving his casting vote in the affirmative, the motion was carried.

The House then went into Committee of the Whole, Mr. Powell in the Chair.

Mr. Scott, professing his earnest desire to see the Convention come to some compromise of the opposing parties, and believing that object would be promoted by passing over this subject until something should have been determined on the limits of the Right of Suffrage, made a motion to take up the next resolution reported by the Legislative Committee.

Mr. Mercer opposed the motion, and desired that the amendment to the first resolution should first be finally disposed of in the Committee. He referred to other important questions which had been decided by small majorities, and disclaimed on the part of the majority any thing like an uncompromising spirit.

Mr. Doddridge rose to notice a remark of Mr. Scott, on what had fallen from Mr. Johnson. He understood Mr. J. to have stated it as his understanding of the first proposition, in the report of the Legislative Committee, that representation was to be apportioned on the basis of qualified voters; and he had added that he supposed this to have been the intention of the mover of that resolution in the Legislative Committee. Now Mr. D. said, that he had himself been the mover of it, and such an interpretation was certainly very far from his purpose. He had never intended any such thing; nor, so far as he knew, had such an interpretation entered into the mind of the Legislative Committee. His doctrine, and his desire was, that representation should be apportioned according to the entire white population. If this was settled, the next question would be, to whom should the elective franchise be extended? and then a third would present itself, viz: to whom should the Constitution be finally submitted for adoption or rejection? The gentleman had added a word of caution, to so small a majority as to their undertaking to control a minority so numerous. He admitted that the majority here was numerically but little larger than the minority; but if the population which the two portions of the House represented was to be taken into view, it would be found that the difference was far greater. The gentleman had said, that a majority so small ought not to expect to carry all the points it might have in view; but surely, if this was a good argument to a majority, the argument applied with still greater force to those who represented a comparatively small minority of the free citizens of this Commonwealth.

Mr. Scott said, that the gentleman from Loudoun seemed averse to any thing like compromise. The gentleman said, that he did not possess the spirit of divination, and therefore could not tell that the measure which they were pressing would finally succeed.

Mr. Mercer explained. The gentleman from Fauquier had inferred, from his unwillingness to postpone the subject of the basis of representation, that the majority were actuated by an uncompromising spirit.

Mr. Scott said, that he had brought no such charge against the majority. Mr. Mercer then said, that he must have misunderstood him.

Mr. Scott resumed. The gentleman says, that he has not the spirit of divination, and that therefore he cannot know that his measure will succeed; but on that principle, no compromise can ever be effected, because no one can tell whether it will succeed until it is first proposed; and so unless its friends have the spirit of divination, they are not to make the experiment.

The gentleman from Brooke says, that though their majority in this House is small, it represents a large majority of the people of the State. However this may be, I am very sure of one thing: and that is, that the minority in this House represents a large majority of the freeholders of Virginia. There are at least four freeholders East of the Blue Ridge, to three on the West of it. The proportion of tax-payers, even of the smallest tax, down to a single cent, is nearly the same. There are four thousand two hundred tax-payers East of the Ridge, to three thousand six hundred West of it. So that the minority represented a large majority of those who owned the soil, and bore all the burdens of the Commonwealth.

Mr. Mercer replied. He had certainly understood the gentleman to say, that the experience of the Committee manifested the fact, that the majority was actuated by an uncompromising spirit: and to such a remark, it was certainly pertinent to reply, that he did not know, when he voted for his own proposition, whether it would be accepted or not. The gentleman from Fauquier possessed very different facts, or else proceeded on a very different system of arithmetic from himself; and he averred that the gentleman was totally mistaken in the statement he had made. If the gentleman confined the majority to those beyond the Ridge, he might perhaps be right; but if he added those in the large counties immediately below the Ridge, it would be found, that a large majority of the tax-payers of the State, were represented by a majority on this floor. In support of this statement, Mr. M. referred to two tables exhibiting the number of tax-payers in the counties, and insisted that from those tables, it would appear that the white population West of the Blue Ridge, bore to the white population East of the Ridge, the same proportion, as the tax-payers West, did to the tax-payers East; and that the freeholders of twenty-five acres West of the Ridge, were to those East of the Ridge, in the like propo[illegible]on. The persons charged with land-tax in the whole State, were 93,000; of the[illegible], 39,000 were West of the Ridge, and 53 East. The persons who paid tax on moveable property in the whole State, were 95,000; of whom, 40,000 resided West of the Ridge, and 55,000 East of it. Of the white population, the total number was 600,000; of whom, 250,000 were West of the Ridge, and 350,000 East of it. Here, then, there was little difference between the three ratios. The gentleman from Fauquier had argued on the illusory idea, that the distribution of property was different on the two sides of the Ridge. Such a notion was entirely unfounded, and inconsistent with the actual state of the fact. If the gentleman would add those in favour of a new Constitution, who live below the Ridge, to those who live beyond it, he would find that there was a large majority.

Mr. Stanard said, that if it was regular to receive the statements of the gentlemen on the other side of the House, as going to support one view of a subject, it must be regular to receive statements from the same side, when bearing in an opposite direction. Now, the statements just given by the gentleman from Loudoun, were in hostility with those of his coadjutor from Augusta. The gentleman insisted, that the ratio of freeholders and of tax-payers on the two sides of the Ridge, did not differ from that of the white population. He should confront this assertion, by the statements made by the gentleman from Augusta. According to the gentleman from Augusta, the freeholders from the West, were to those in the East, as thirty-six to fifty-six. According to the gentleman from Loudoun, they were as forty to fifty-three. The gentleman asserted this, in total disregard to a consideration which all knew ought to have great influence on the calculation: that a large proportion of persons charged with land-tax in the West, are non-residents there, and live either in Eastern Virginia, or without the bounds of the State. If due allowance were made for this circumstance, the proportion would not be thirty-six to fifty-six, but thirty-three to fifty-six; or rather thirty-three to fifty-nine, if the three taken from the West were to be added to the East. In Richmond alone, there were more than one hundred persons who owned freeholds to the West of the Ridge. He would now proceed to confront the statement of the gentleman from Loudoun, with that of the gentleman from Augusta.

Mr. Doddridge enquired whether this discussion was in order.

Mr. Stanard contended that it was, as he should not go one word beyond correcting the mistake, the great and extravagant mistake, of the gentleman from Loudoun: and in doing so, he should employ the statements of the gentleman from Augusta, only as a means of giving more force and effect to the correction. The gentleman from Loudoun had affirmed, that the ratio of the white population on the two sides of the Ridge, was nearly the same with that of the tax-payers and land-holders. But what said the tables of the gentleman from Augusta?

Mr. S. after quoting them at large, stated the result to be as follows:

The ratio of white population was fifty-six on the West, to sixty-three on the East: of land-holders, forty-six West to seventy-three East: and of tax-payers, fifty on the West to seventy on the East.

With these statements staring him in the face, the gentleman had told the Committee, without reserve, and without qualification, that the ratios were nearly the same. He had felt it due to the Committee, and to the public, that the assertion should not go unconfronted with the document.

Mr. Mercer said, in reply, that he owed many obligations to the gentleman from Spottsylvania; but the correction of his facts, was not one of the number. He protested against this mode of collating his remarks with the calculations made by another gentleman. He was responsible for his own statements and his own calculations, and for them alone. The gentleman from Augusta would be the last to require his support. The tables to which the gentleman had referred, went upon the estimated population of 1829. He had already said, that he repudiated those tables, and rejected them as utterly incorrect: he had shown how grossly erroneous they were, in reference to his own district, and he certainly was not bound to abide by tables which he did not admit.

Mr. Stanard replied, that the statements of the gentleman from Augusta, which he had quoted, did not rest on the computations of the Auditor, to which the gentleman from Loudoun now referred. The computation of the Auditor, whether accurate or inaccurate, had nothing to do with the question.

Mr. Mercer replied, that the gentleman's explanation was wholly unanswerable. The tables referred to, were based on some calculation of the white population, as existing in 1829. He rejected these calculations, as uncertain, and adhered to the Census of 1820. According to that Census, the white population West of the Ridge, amounted to 250,000, and that East of the Ridge, to 353,000; that is, they were in the proportion of twenty-five to thirty-five.

Mr. Mercer then referred to the list of county taxes, which went to show, that taxation on the two sides of the Ridge, was in the proportion of forty to fifty-five. Of those who were taxed for freeholds of twenty-five acres and over, 39,110 resided West of the Ridge, and 53,055 resided East of it. He would lay the paper containing these calculations on the Clerk's table, that any gentleman, wishing to examine it, might have an opportunity of doing so. He did not pretend to know where all the persons resided, who were charged with taxes on real estate; nor did he know how many persons residing East of the Ridge, owned land to the West of it; but he had travelled over the State ten times as much as the gentleman from Spottsylvania had ever done, and he claimed to know as much of the condition of its people.

Mr. Fitzhugh recalled the Convention to the motion of Mr. Scott, which he opposed as likely still farther to procrastinate the decision of the Convention on the questions before it: he then proposed, as a measure calculated to bring the House to some result in part, and hasten the disposal of the other questions, that the Committee should rise, and report the first resolution of the Legislative Committee to the House; announcing it to be his intention subsequently to move, that the whole of the residue of the business be turned over to a small Select Committee, to be chosen by the Convention from its most moderate and influential members, who should be charged with the duty of reporting the draft of a Constitution. With this understanding, he moved that the Committee rise.

Mr. Leigh, opposed the object of Mr. Fitzhugh, as likely to lead to a repetition of all the difficulties already felt, and in the end to produce greater delay than the present course.

Mr. Doddridge, concurred in these views, but was in favour of the Committee's rising and reporting the first resolution, that its fate might be decided in Convention. And the subject of representation being thus disposed of, it might serve as a guide to the Convention in the rest of their discussions. He could not fix upon his course as to the Right of Suffrage, till he knew what was to be done as to the basis of representation.

Mr. Leigh, opposed the motion to rise, and wished the Committee to proceed to the question of Suffrage, laying the resolution now under consideration, aside for the present.

Mr. Stanard, took, in substance, the same view, and earnestly opposed the motion for reporting on one resolution in a series of resolutions, all intimately connected: this he contended, to be wholly without precedent in Parliamentary usage. Besides, the sense of the resolution to be reported was not fixed: The gentleman from Augusta, understanding it to apply *only* to *qualified voters*—the gentleman from Brooke understanding it as referring to *all* the *white population* whether voters or not.

After some explanation as to the point of order,

Mr. Johnson opposed the rising of the Committee: he thought the two great and leading subjects of Representation and the Right of Suffrage, ought to be considered in connexion with each other. He was therefore in favour of Mr. Scott's proposal, to pass over the first for the present, and to go on till the other should be arrived at in order.

The question was now taken on Mr. Fitzhugh's motion, for the rising of the Committee, and decided in the negative—Ayes 40—Noes 48.

On motion of Mr. Leigh, the Committee then passed by the first resolution reported by the Legislative Committee, (viz. that which refers to the basis of representation,) and took up the second resolution, which is in the following words:

"*Resolved*, That a Census of the population of the State, for the purpose of apportioning the representation, should be taken in the year 1831, the year 1845, and thereafter, at least once in every twenty years."

Mr. Doddridge, moved to amend this resolution, by striking out in the third line, all after the word "year," and inserting a clause to make the whole resolution read—

"*Resolved*, That a Census of the population of the State, for the purpose of apportioning the representation, should be taken in the year 1835, and at least every ten years thereafter, if the Assembly shall deem the same expedient; and that a new apportionment of representation shall be made after each Census, if the state of the population shall have been so changed as to require it."

Mr. Doddridge explained his reasons for offering the amendment. The State Census, if taken at the periods he proposed, would fall into the intervals of the General Census of the United States, and would correct the inaccuracies of that enumeration; which had, in some cases, been made in a very loose manner.

Mr. Leigh suggested, that though the amendment made it imperative that a Census should be taken, as the basis of representation, it did not require any *assessment* to accompany it. It secured to the West all the benefits of increased representation, but did not require a corresponding increase of taxation.

Mr. Doddridge, requested Mr. Leigh to add a clause to supply this defect: which he declining,

Mr. Mercer, moved to add the clause, "and an assessment thereof made." He insisted that the duty of taking the Census ought not to be left discretionary, but should be made imperative on the Legislature. He dwelt upon the advantage of having the Census taken frequently, and so made as to include a variety of statistical information: the expense would be but small.

After some further conversation between Messrs. Leigh, Doddridge and Mercer, the resolution was amended by striking out the clause which leaves it discretionary with the Legislature; and, after some further opposition, on the part of Mr. Stanard, the resolution was, at the suggestion of Mr. Cooke, passed over for the present, to give the gentleman from Brooke a better opportunity of digesting his proposition.

The Committee then proceeded to the consideration of the third resolution reported by the Legislative Committee, in the words following:

"*Resolved*, That the Right of Suffrage shall continue to be exercised by all who now enjoy it under the existing Constitution: Provided, that no person shall vote by virtue of his freehold only, unless the same shall be assessed to the value of at least   dollars, for the payment of taxes, if such assessment be required by law: and shall be extended, first, to every free white male citizen of the Commonwealth resident therein, above the age of twenty-one years, who owns, and has possessed for six months, or who has acquired by marriage, descent, or devise, a freehold estate, assessed to the value of not less than   dollars for the payment of taxes, if such assessment shall be required by law: second, or who shall own a vested estate in fee, in remainder, or reversion, in land, the assessed value of which shall be   dollars: third, or who shall own and have possessed a leasehold estate with the evidence of title recorded, of a term originally not less than five years, and one of which shall be unexpired, of the annual value, or rent of   dollars: fourth, or who for twelve months next preceding, has been a house-keeper and head of a family within the county, city, borough, or election district, where he may offer to vote, and who shall have been assessed with a part of the revenue of the Commonwealth within the preceding year, and actually paid the same: Provided, nevertheless, that the Right of Suffrage shall not be exercised by any person of unsound mind, or who shall be a pauper, or a non-commissioned officer, soldier, sailor or marine, in the service of the United States, nor by any person convicted of any infamous offence; nor by citizens born without the Commonwealth, unless they shall have resided therein for five years immediately preceding the election at which they shall offer to vote, and two years preceding the said election, in the county, city, borough, or election district, where they shall offer to vote, (the mode of proving such previous residence, when disputed, to be prescribed by law,) and shall possess, moreover, some one or more of the qualifications above enumerated."

Mr. Leigh, pointed out an effect which he presumed was not seriously intended, but which would arise from the resolution, as it now stood. According to the proviso, no freeholder was allowed to vote unless his freehold was of a certain value (not yet fixed upon;) but, according to a subsequent clause, any house-keeper who has paid "any part of the revenue of the Commonwealth," is allowed to vote. Suppose the value of the freehold be fixed at any given sum, say twenty dollars; and suppose a freeholder owns a house worth nineteen dollars; and suppose, further, that in that house, there resides a tenant who owns a single horse; the result will be, that the landlord, who owns the house, is forbidden to vote, while the tenant who pays a tax of four cents on his horse, is admitted to the polls. Could it be seriously intended not merely to abolish the freehold qualification, but to make it a *less* qualification than the payment of the very smallest tax? Taking it for granted, that this could not be the purpose of the resolution,

Mr. Leigh, moved to amend it, so as to make the fourth qualification read, "or who, for twelve months next preceding, has been a house-keeper and head of a family, within the county, city, borough, or election district, where he may offer to vote, and who shall have been assessed with a part of the revenue of the Commonwealth, *to the amount* of within the preceding year, and actually paid the same."

Mr. Randolph said, that he rose simply to make a suggestion to the gentleman from Chesterfield, and one to the Committee. I believe, said he, that I shall hardly be contradicted, when I state that the great moving cause, which led to this Convention, has been the regulation of the Right of Suffrage. After all the out-cry that has been raised on this subject, judge my surprise, when I found that a proposition coming from the Legislative Committee, and which extends the Right of Suffrage almost *ad indefinitum*, to many entire classes of persons within the Commonwealth, contained a blow at the elective franchise of the freeholder, the present sovereign of this land. We are met to extend the Right of Suffrage; nobody can tell how far under the out-cry that it is *too much* restricted, and the very first step we take, is to restrict it *still farther, quoad* the freeholder. Do gentlemen suppose the freeholders will be blind to this? What becomes of all the considerations of philanthropy of which we have heard so much? What becomes of all the gentlemen's abstractions? Sir, the only good I ever knew these abstractions to do, is to abstract money out of the pockets of one great division of the country, to put it into the pockets of another, a species of abstraction the least of all others to my taste.

Sir, I demand, as a freeholder, in behalf of the freeholders, on what plea you are to put them, and them only, to the ban of this Convention? Other and large classes of persons are selected to be drawn within the range of the elective privilege, while the poorer classes of the freeholders are to be disfranchised. So, after all, this great and illustrious Assembly are met to make war on the poorer classes of the freeholders of the Commonwealth. You are not only to extend rights, but you are to take away the rights, the vested rights, of a large and respectable, however they may be a poor, class of your fellow-citizens. Sir, I will never consent to deprive the freeholder of his rights, however trivial in the view of assessors or patricians, his humble shed may appear. I saw this measure in the Legislative Committee, and I thought I saw, what I think I now see, (here Mr. R. pointed with his finger,) a snake in the grass. I will never consent to be the agent in taking away from any man the Right of Suffrage he now enjoys.

Mr. Mercer observed, that the proviso was not chargeable upon the advocates of the Convention, having been moved in the Legislative Committee by a gentleman, (Mr. Green,) who had always opposed it. Mr. M. explained the object of the mover to have been the prevention of frauds, but thought it unnecessary, as by a subsequent clause, paupers were excluded from the polls; and fraudulent evasions of the Constitution must be left to be remedied by the Legislature.

Mr. Leigh, consented to withdraw the amendment he had offered; but announced his intention to be, after the resolution should have been made as perfect as was in the power of its friends, to move to strike out the whole, and substitute another, which he read in his place, (and which went, in his view, to extend the Right of Suffrage to such tenants, as were in circumstances to vote independently of their landlords.)

Mr. Mercer, moved to strike out the whole proviso, fixing a value to the freehold.

Mr. Green said, the proviso had been introduced at his suggestion. It was a notorious fact, that in the Western part of the State there were bodies of land not worth a cent an acre, which had been taken up by speculators with a prospect of imposing on foreigners, and that in some cases, several different patents had been issued for the same land. If the freehold should be regulated by quantity alone, and no prescribed value be required, it was manifest, that one of these large land-holders would be able to create at will, as many freeholders as he pleased. Practices of that sort had, in some instances, already prevailed, and would, doubtless, again be resorted to. The sole purpose of the proviso, had been to exclude such as were merely nominal freeholders, who paid no taxes, and were entitled to no voice in the Commmonwealth. His object had been to lay down such a plain and practical rule as it would be hard to evade by fraud. Gentlemen from that part of the country confirmed the existence of such practices.

Mr. Stanard said he should vote against expunging the proviso. Not because he thought with the gentleman from Charlotte, that it would deprive the poor freeholder of the Right of Suffrage, but for the purpose of guaranteeing and giving security to his right, and with a view to make the general provision operate with some degree of equality. It would make that which was not a real limitation in the Eastern part of the State, to be a real limitation in the Western part of it. No one could cast his eye over the Western part of Virginia, without being satisfied, that the physical condition of the country was such, as put it in the power of any person, at an expense not exceeding the price of the paper on which a deed could be executed, to qualify himself as a voter; and there were individuals there who could qualify voters by the hundred. The quantity of land on the Assessors' books, bore, in some cases, scarce any relation to the land actually in the county, yet deeds could be given for these imaginary freeholds, which existed no where but on paper, to almost any amount.

The average valuation of all the lands, in some of the counties, was less than five cents an acre, good and bad. Much of it was fit only for lairs for wild beasts. It was not worth one mill per acre. In this situation of things, how would the rule operate on the rights of persons in different parts of the State? The rule gives the Right of Suffrage, not to value, but to quantity. In the West, a certain quantity of land, not worth five cents in all, was sufficient to make a man a voter, while in the East, the smallest quantity of land, communicating the same privilege, was worth from fifty to one hundred dollars. This, surely, was great inequality, and the limitation in the proviso, was all that prevented it. He understood that the mountain land, West of the Ridge, consisted, for the most part of rocks and shrubbery of no conceivable value. No person who visited it, could so much as conjecture, that it ever could become of any value, unless this State should become as full of people as China is, or unless the mountains contained minerals which gave them a value that was concealed from the eye. But, to provide for this possibility, when deeds were made, the title was conveyed with a reservation for any minerals that the soil might contain. He enquired of gentlemen, whether such a state of things was not worthy of consideration, and whether it did not imperiously require, that some amount should be fixed as the value of the freehold. The limitation he would give, would be such as should not only embrace all the poor freeholders now entitled to vote, but should confer that right on many who were now deprived of it. Freeholds of the present size, if situated near a town, were worth more than he would require. The proviso went to extend the basis of representation, yet it confined the Right of Suffrage to a landed qualification, while it excluded freeholders who were merely nominal.

Mr. M'Coy said, that the gentleman last up, appeared to labor under some strange mistake, in relation to the lands and the soil of the West. He underrated, in a surprising manner that portion of the handy works of the great Creator. Between the Blue Ridge and the Ohio, there lay a beautiful and fertile valley, of which the gentleman seemed to have but little knowledge, nor did he seem to be any better acquainted with the mountains than with the vallies of that country. The gentleman had represented the land, as belonging, in great part, to individuals who lived East of the Ridge, and had said that one-tenth part of the whole soil was the property of owners living elsewhere. The gentleman was much mistaken. That country was surveyed in 1795, in large tracts of from fifty to one hundred thousand acres. The number of owners were then not very great. Where the land turned out not to be valuable, the taxes upon it were not paid, and the lands had become forfeited to the Literary Fund of the Commonwealth: The owners, therefore, had it not in their power to make such batches of freeholders as some gentlemen seemed to suppose. Mr. M. said, he happened to live where there was much of this sort of land, and as to what had been represented by the gentleman from Culpeper, (Mr. Green,) as so very common a practice, he had known of but four freeholders having been created in fourteen years, and their votes had been pronounced good for nothing, because the law required six months possession. It was very true that a young man might purchase the right to vote for forty or fifty dollars; but not for five cents, as was supposed, because all the lands not fit for cultivation had been forfeited to the Commonwealth. The gentleman in one breath, had represented the country as being the finest in the world, and had said in the next, that it was not worth one mill an acre. He was astonished at the language of the resolution; he had not come to the Convention to take away the Right of Suffrage from any who possessed it, but to extend it, though in a very limited degree. He should vote to strike out the proviso, so far as taxes went as a rule for extending the Right of Suffrage: a small amount of tax was not the best evidence of an interest in the community, or of attachment to it. A mechanic, born and raised in Virginia, would scorn to go to the mountains to buy the Right of Suffrage. A father having four or five sons, while he gave each of them a plantation, would keep the title in his own hands. Many of the most respectable farmers in Virginia, resided on land that was not yet theirs, but which they expected to get a title for. He would limit the Right of Suffrage to all who now possessed it, and to such heads of families and house-keepers as had had a sufficient residence, from which to infer their attachment to the State. He considered residence, as much better proof of such attachment than the possession of property.

Here he would stop. He would cover all who lived on rented land, all mechanics and mercantile men who lived in rented houses, and there he would stop. He should vote to strike out the proviso.

Mr. Leigh rose, simply to state the reason why he should not vote to strike out the proviso. It was meant, only to get rid of the objection he had stated, and to render the first provision of the resolution consistent with the last. To the last he was ready to accede. He had never yet seen a freeholder who was a pauper, nor had he ever heard that such a freeholder existed in Virginia, until he heard it from the gentleman from Loudoun. But he had seen many house-keepers, and heads of families, who owned nothing but a single horse, with which they were hauling wood that belonged to other people. They resided by courtesy on land they did not own, and who received parish aid. He remembered about thirty or forty such, who lived on both sides of the river. For his part, he did not know what a house-keeper and head of a family was, unless it was a man who lived in a house with a family. He was sorry to see gentlemen so ready to place all persons of this description on a footing with the freeholders.

Mr. Mercer said, that the purpose which the gentleman from Spottsylvania wished to accomplish, could not be attained. Suppose the proviso should be suffered to stand, and the blank it contained should be filled with one dollar. There were thousands of such freeholds near the Kanawha river—or supposing the blank to be filled with fifty cents for fifty acres. The Commissioner would enter fifty acres in his book, of the average value of four cents. There would be no security against fraud in such a provision; but, if fraud was so strongly to be apprehended, the Legislature had ample power to guard against it in any manner that might be necessary.

Mr. Stanard was surprised, that the gentleman from Loudoun should suppose, that a sworn Commissioner would put down land in his book at any rate the owner might desire. Such a means of evading the law did not apply to the case. The persons who appear as the owners of freeholds, were often but the transient population of the day, who are provided with a freehold for the occasion, and who would be succeeded by a new swarm, whenever the sinister purposes of a canvasser should require it. He desired to enquire of the gentleman from Kanawha (Mr. Summers) whether such practices did not exist, and whether the known facility, with which votes might thus be obtained, had not in practice, throughout a large extent of the Western country, broken down all limitations to the Right of Suffrage? And such being the case, whether all enquiry into the right of a voter to vote, must not be made at the hazard of losing the election. He hoped the proviso would remain, and that the blank be filled with twenty-five dollars. He would take the minimum of the gentleman from Loudoun. He should prefer fifty dollars but would be content with twenty-five.

Mr. Mercer said, that it was painful to him to be obliged again to trouble the Committee, but when a gentleman questioned the facts he stated, it was necessary for him to protect himself. None could change the value at which land was assessed, but this was only law, it was not the Constitution. Every owner had a right to have his land assessed. If he had a tract worth $20,000 and should sell part of the land, he could not be made to pay on the residue, an average of the whole. Mr. M. insisted, that a man who bought land should be charged with a tax only on its value. If he bought a freehold of twenty-five acres, and should pay tax at the rate of two cents, that would cover the sum in the blank.

Mr. Stanard reminded the gentleman that the assessment was made by a sworn officer.

Mr. Wilson of Monongalia enquired of the Chair, whether it would be in order to offer a substitute for the proviso.

The Chair replied, that he must know first what the amendment was, and then he should be able to decide whether it could be admitted as an amendment to the amendment now pending.

Mr. Wilson thereupon read his resolution.

"*Resolved*, That every free white male citizen of this Commonwealth, of the age of twenty-one years, and upwards, who shall have resided in the State two years, and in the county where he proposes to vote, one year, next preceding the time of offering such vote; who shall have been enrolled in the militia, if subject to military duty; and who shall have paid all levies and taxes assessed upon him, or his property, for the year preceding that in which he offers to vote, shall have a right to vote for members of the General Assembly: *Provided*, That no person shall be permitted to exercise the Right of Suffrage, who is a pauper; who is of unsound mind; who has been convicted of any infamous crime; or who is engaged in the land or naval service of the United States; and the Legislature shall prescribe the mode of trying and determining disputes, concerning the said qualifications of voters, whenever the right of a person to vote shall be questioned."

The Chair pronounced the resolution to be in order.

After some discussion on the point of order,

Mr. Wilson concluded to withdraw his amendment for the present.

Mr. Summers said, the reference of the gentleman from Spottsylvania, (Mr. Stanard) required from him some explanation, and in giving it, he begged to be permitted to remark, that he was not disposed to make war either upon the *small* or the *large* freeholder. He not only wished to preserve the Right of Suffrage to all who now enjoy it, but to extend it to large classes who are now deprived of this important right.

The imputation of frauds upon the election laws, general and notorious in the Western district, is, he imagined, the result of misrepresentation or misapprehension. Called upon by this charge for its verification or denial, he had subjected his memory to a rigid scrutiny, without being able to recollect a single instance of a fraud of this character, within his own observation. He then appealed to the rumors of the country, which furnished but a single instance, and that in a period of great party excitement, of an attempt to increase the number of electors by deeds made expressly with that view; the extraordinary number of the grantees gave notoriety to the attempt, and may have induced the gentleman from Spottsylvania to suppose that such occurrences were common. Not so, Sir. He owed it to that quarter of the State, to assure the Committee, from information entitled to his full confidence, that many, very many of those intended to be made voters by this deed, refused to exercise the right on a ground so objectionable; and that the commisioners appointed to hold a very important election in which their political character had been consulted in their appointment, resisting all party consideration, decided with great firmness, and unanimity against this fraudulent attempt to increase the freehold list, and to the entire satisfaction of the country.

He did not mean to be understood as affirming that no other abuses of our election laws have taken place. He thought it probable that occurrences of this sort happen occasionally, both in the East and in the West, but not more frequently in the latter than in the former.

To him, the limitation of the freehold right by the value of the land, was very objectionable. It adds to the misfortunes which are inseparable from the cultivation of poor land, the serious evil of political disfranchisement; and aggravates the misfortune in no slight degree. The *minimum* value proposed by the gentleman from Spottsylvania, lessens, but does not remove the objection—the average value of the land of the Western district, by the assessment of 1817, is ninety-two cents per acre, and to require a freehold of twenty-five dollars value, will be to require more than twenty-five acres of the average land of the country, to constitute a voter. His views of political equality and justice will extend the same rights to the humblest cottage of the mountain side, which are enjoyed by the most splendid mansions of the wealthy. Permanent common interest, however small, ought, in his humble judgment, to be invested with the rights of protection, and placed on a level in the political institutions of the country, with the most elevated ranks of society.

Mr. M'Coy said, that most of these masses of unproductive lands, which had not paid the taxes, were forfeited to the Literary Fund, and thus could not be cut up. He went into his own views of the Right of Suffrage, stating that in his country there were a great many lease-holders, who had not deeds from their fathers, perhaps, and who ought to have the Right of Suffrage. There were also many mechanics who were heads of families, and deserved to have the right. He said, he was perfectly willing to give the Right of Suffrage to all those who had it at present, and to heads of families, and house-keepers. This was his idea of the limitation of Suffrage.

The question was then put on striking out the proviso, and decided in the affirmative.—Ayes 62.

So the provision which went to restrict the right of freehold election to freeholds of a certain value, to be fixed in the Constitution, was stricken out of the resolution reported by the Legislative Committee.

The Committee then rose, and on motion of Mr. Leigh of Chesterfield, the Convention adjourned.

WEDNESDAY, November 18, 1829.

The Convention met at 10 o'clock, and was opened with prayer by the Rev. Mr. Taylor of the Baptist Church.

Mr. Massie of Nelson, presented the following memorial from the citizens of that county, which, on his motion, was referred to the Committee of the Whole on the Constitution:

To the Convention of Virginia:

Your memorialists beg leave to represent to your honorable body, that it was with deep concern they received the intelligence, that a proposition to make a change in the mode of appointing Magistrates, was rejected by the Judicial Committee. Your memorialists do consider the present mode of those appointments to be aristocratic in its features, and tending to the establishment of a privileged order in this Commonwealth: that a body should be established in this Commonwealth, with self-creating powers, appears to them an anomaly of most alarming tendency, and in practice, well calculated to dethrone the supremacy of the people's will. It must be known to your honorable body, as it is known to your memorialists, that the present mode of appointing those officers, is well calculated to place the Judicial powers of the country, as well as the destinies and well-being of the counties, into the hands of a few families. It is known, that the County Courts have been invested, in this State, with the extraordinary powers of appointing militia officers—of supplying vacancies in their own body—of the appointment of overseers of the poor—of establishing and changing roads—of levying county taxes at their own discretion—and of managing the whole county police, according to their own will and pleasure, without consulting the supreme will of the people; their powers are great, and often improperly exercised, because the Courts are in no way responsible to the people; in fact, they are a power without responsibility. Your memorialists have thought proper to make this very brief statement, in order to call the attention of your honorable body, particularly to this subject. They, therefore, pray that some mode may be adopted by you, which will take away a self-creating power from the County Courts—and they will ever pray, &c.

(*Here follow the signatures.*)

The House then went into Committee of the Whole, Mr. Powell in the Chair:

And the question still being on the third resolution of the Legislative Committee, (which relates to the Right of Suffrage—see proceedings of yesterday,)

Mr. Wilson of Monongalia, offered the following amendment, by way of substitute for that of the Legislative Committee:

"*Resolved*, That every free white male citizen of this Commonwealth, of the age of twenty-one years, and upwards, who shall have resided in this State two years, and in the county where he proposes to vote, one year, next preceding the time of offering such vote; who shall have been enrolled in the militia, if subject to military duty; and who shall have paid all levies and taxes assessed upon him, or his property, for the year preceding that in which he offers to vote, shall have a right to vote for members of the General Assembly: *Provided*, That no person shall be permitted to exercise the Right of Suffrage, who is a pauper; who is of unsound mind; who has been convicted of any infamous crime; or who is engaged in the land or naval service of the United States; and the Legislature shall prescribe the mode of trying and determining disputes, concerning the said qualifications of voters, whenever the right of a person to vote shall be questioned."

Mr. Wilson addressed the Committee as follows:

Mr. Chairman,—As there can be no difference of opinion about the propriety of my presenting at this time, the resolution which I offered yesterday, but subsequently withdrew, I now submit to the consideration of the Committee the following substitute for the third resolution of the Legislative Committee. (Here Mr. W. read his proposed resolution on the subject of the Right of Suffrage, which being reported by the Chair, he resumed, in substance, as follows:)

It must be evident, Sir, from the various objections which on yesterday came from every quarter, to the resolution of the Legislative Committee, that it meets the views of a very small portion of the members of this Convention. I have, therefore, thought it proper to rid the Committee at once, of the labour and trouble of innumerable amendments and modifications of that resolution, by placing before it the subject of the Right of Suffrage on its broadest ground. I wish to march boldly up to the question and meet it at once, and present it in such a shape that there will be no room for the imputation of ambiguity or insincerity. The substitute I propose is short, plain, simple, and easy to be understood. This proposition, at least, is not liable to the imputation uttered yesterday by the gentleman from Charlotte, (Mr. Randolph,) of being "a snake in the grass."

The scheme here proposed for the regulation of the Right of Suffrage, is not open to the objection raised yesterday, by the gentleman from Chesterfield, (Mr. Leigh,) to the resolution of the Legislative Committee. It does not exclude from the polls the owners of small freeholds, whilst it admits the payer of a four cent horse-tax, who, although he might even be a lease-holder under one of those small freeholds, yet would be entitled to a vote, whilst his landlord is excluded. The substitute includes both these classes. Nor is it open to the objection of the gentleman from Charlotte, (Mr. Randolph.) It aims no fatal blow at the rights of the freeholders, for it includes them all. Nor is it liable to the objections raised by the gentleman from Spottsylvania, (Mr. Stanard,) yesterday, against the resolution for which it is intended to be a substitute. He dwelt strongly and truly on the difficulties attending any attempt to estimate the value of a man's property per annum, for the purpose of measuring his right to vote. The plan now proposed, looks not to property as the test of a man's attachment to the community, and, therefore, avoids the difficulties which must ever attend any scheme of property qualification. It seems to be admitted, that the arbitrary limitation of the Right of Suffrage to the ownership of any fixed number of acres of land, is absurd and unjust, because of the inequality of the value of land. It is, therefore, proposed, that the property of the citizen, either real or personal, or both, shall be valued, and his right to vote be tested by that value. This scheme would indeed be liable to great objection, arising out of the difficulty of carrying it into execution, and the fraud or negligence of the valuers.

Two qualifications seemed to be required by the sixth section of the Bill of Rights, in every person, before he shall be entitled to the Right of Suffrage. And, notwithstanding the lacerations which this venerable instrument has undergone, in the course of our past debates, I still feel disposed to take my text from it, whenever I am about to discourse upon political subjects, and matters of Government.

The first qualification required by that instrument is, that the man shall furnish sufficient evidence of permanent, common interest with the community—and secondly, that he shall furnish sufficient evidence of attachment to the community. In other words, we should be convinced that his interests and his affections, bind him to us, before we admit him to any share in the government of our State. The question then arises, by what means can we ascertain where his interests and attachments are centred? What test shall we apply? What requisites shall we demand, without which, the man shall be excluded from the exercise of this, the most honorable and precious of his natural rights? And, here, Sir, permit me to observe, that, notwithstanding all the ridicule which has been cast upon the natural rights of man, by certain gentlemen; notwithstanding the repeated denial of their existence, except in the brains of moon-struck reformers, I still believe, that Nature, or Nature's God rather, has conferred certain original rights upon man; and among these, none appears to me more clear and undeniable, than the right of appointing our own agents. And this right may exist apart from, and anterior to, any regular, social compact. The fact of my having authorised a certain individual to transact a piece of business for me, does not necessarily imply any social compact with him, or any other individual of my race. But, although this right of appointing our agents exists in man by nature, yet, when he enters into society, that right becomes limited, and ought to be controuled, by a due regard to the interests of that society, or if the gentlemen please—by expediency. Private and individual conveniency must yield to the good of the whole. We must give up a portion of our natural liberty, in order to enjoy the advantages of social union, and be secured in the undisturbed enjoyment of those rights which are not surrendered, and which the necessity of the case does not require us to surrender.

But, Sir, this surrender should not be required to an extent greater than is necessary and expedient for the good of the whole community. If you require the citizen to yield up to the Government a larger portion of his natural independence and free agency, than is necessary for the security of the community at large, and its members, in particular, then, Sir, you take from him that, for which you render him no equivalent. The moment you say to the citizen, yield to the Government *more* of your natural liberty than is requisite for the security of the community, you pass out of the field of freedom, and enter upon the domains of tyranny. This, I conceive, to be the true rule. And the application of it will produce very different results, according to the virtue, intelligence, and patriotism of the people, to whom it is applied. When applied to the corrupt and ignorant Italian, the result will be absolute monarchy. When applied to the more virtuous and enlightened inhabitants of England, the result will be, a limited monarchy. When applied to the intelligent, virtuous and patriotic people of Virginia, the result will be a free representative Republic, wherein the administrators of public affairs are the agents of the people, and chosen by those of the people, who have, or are supposed to have, a free will, a matured intellect, and an interest in, and attachment to, the community. With regard to freedom of will, and maturity of intellect, I have only to observe, that if gentlemen do not already perceive the propriety of excluding women, children, paupers, idiots, and slaves, from the polls, vain will be any attempt, on my part, to convince them of it. The beams of the noon-day sun will be useless to him, who wilfully shuts his eyes against the light.

But, I recur to the question, what is the proper test of a man's interest in, and attachment to, the community? It is answered, that property, and especially landed property, is the only true and safe test. To this I cannot assent. It assumes, that a man cannot love a country, or take an interest in its good government, unless he owns a portion of its soil. It is not my intention here, to enter into a detailed history of the rise and progress of the freehold Right of Suffrage. That duty has been ably and eloquently performed by my friend from Frederick, (Mr. Cooke.) He has shown, that it originated in despotism. It is my business to show, that it is absurd and unjust in its nature.

It is said, that the possession of property is the only test. Now, Sir, if the security of property were the only object of Government, there might be some truth in this assertion. But, when we know, that the object of all good Government, is to protect the citizen in the enjoyment, not only of his property, but also of his life, his personal liberty, his limbs, his character, the freedom of speech and action, and the pursuit of happiness; and that these are all objects of equal, and some of them, of higher importance than property, we see, at once, the fallacy of the test. In all these, the rich and the poor, stand on a level—they are all equally valuable to both—or, rather, the poor are *more* interested in the security of these rights, because the enjoyment of them furnishes to the poor man his only defence, against the overweening influence and power, which wealth confers upon the rich, and which we know, are too often tyrannically exercised. Besides this, however poor a man may be, unless he be an absolute pauper, (and paupers are excluded,) he yet possesses *some* property; and, Sir, the poor man's pittance is just as dear to him, as the rich man's treasure, because it is his all; aye, and more dear to him, because it is but a pittance, and, therefore, more liable to be exhausted. Supposing, therefore, that the rich and the poor have equal virtue, (and this I imagine will not be denied,) the poor man must, and does take as great an interest in the good government of the country, as the rich man.

The truth is, that permanent residence is the best evidence of attachment to the community, and an interest in its welfare. The value of land is too fluctuating, and its tenure too uncertain, to furnish this evidence. It may be said, that if a man loses his land, and it passes into other hands, that other persons will possess this evidence, and will be entitled to the vote, and so on through every mutation of property; but from this it would seem, that the Right of Suffrage is in the land, and not in the people! Suppose a virtuous and intelligent man to-day possessed of a farm upon which he resides with his wife and children, surrounded by a large circle of beloved friends and relatives. Every body will say, he is entitled to the Right of Suffrage. Well, suppose that by one of those sudden reverses of fortune, which in the uncertainty of human affairs, are continually occurring, he should be deprived of his farm the next day; is he to be deprived of the Right of Suffrage? He is yet virtuous, intelligent, patriotic—he has yet in this State his residence, his family, his friends, his all that is left him. Do you suppose that his attachment to his native State, and his interest in its welfare, is less now than before? Certainly not. Being now deprived of the all-commanding influence of wealth, he is still more concerned in the procurement of equal and just laws, by which he, and all that is near and dear to him, shall be protected from oppression.

Do you measure a man's right to vote by the *value* of his landed property? How uncertain and unjust a test will this also be, of a man's attachment and interest! Will you say that he shall own real estate of the value of twenty-five dollars, as was suggested by one gentleman? Surely, we all know that a piece of land which this year may be worth twenty-five dollars, may, by some of those causes which are producing continual changes in the value of land and its produce, be next year reduced far below that value. And yet you will next year deprive the owner of his vote, although he owns precisely the same land, which this year conferred upon him the Right of Suffrage. If you don't do this, you abandon your principle of regulating the elective franchise according to the value of a man's landed property. And if you do this, a man may always hold the same tract of land; the same portion of the soil, and yet have, or not have the right to vote according to the variations of the price of his land and its produce!

Upon your own principles, Sir, this standard is unjust. You propose to measure a man's right to vote, by the value of his land, and in the same breath you give to a man owning twenty-five dollars worth of land, one vote, and to the man owning twenty-five thousand dollars worth of land, *no more* than one vote! Is this just on your own plan? But, it may be replied, that though the disparity of fortune is great, yet the interest is the same; that though there is not an equality of interest, yet each has *an interest* in the welfare of the State. If this be so, then you do not measure a man's right to vote by the quantum of his interest; the existence of *an interest* is sufficient. Agreed then—he who has no property in the State, but resides here, has his family here, and is here pursuing some business to procure a livelihood, is interested in the good government of the community. A man may own twenty-five dollars worth of property in this State, and yet care little or nothing about its general interests. Yet, a man who has not property valued at twenty-five dollars, but who has all his relatives, friends, and *associates* in the country—all his affections concentrated in its welfare, would be deprived of his vote, and it would be given to the other, who happens to own as much property as amounts to twenty-five dollars in value. Such is the result of your real property qualification.

If we advert to moveable property as the basis of the Right of Suffrage, it will be evident at first sight, that the same objections apply to it with accumulated force; for we all know, that personal property is, if possible, more uncertain in its tenure, and subject to greater and more frequent mutations in its value, than landed estate. In fact, whenever you attempt to prescribe such a standard, you will always find it imperfect. I admit that no *perfect* rule can be prescribed on the subject: but I confess, I think *that* general rule too imperfect for practical application, the exceptions to which, are more numerous than the cases which it includes. There can be no *perfect* standard: but I think at the same time, that there can be none found more worthy of adoption, than residence, bearing arms, and paying taxes. The possession of property furnishes not an exclusive, but a probable evidence of attachment to the community; and my proposition includes all the possessors of property who reside here, and I presume, gentlemen do not intend, to permit non-residents to vote, because they may own a tract of land here. But, some period of residence must be fixed. It will not do to let every bird of passage that flits through our State, enjoy the Right of Suffrage. What shall that term of residence be? Gentlemen may differ in opinion on this subject; but it appears to me, that a residence in the State, of two years duration, does furnish sufficient evidence of a man's present intention to continue a resident of the State, so far as outward acts can furnish such evidence. If gentlemen think this too short a period, let them amend the resolution by inserting three, or four or five years residence, or any other term, provided they do not consume too much of the man's life in ascertaining his intention to spend his life amongst us; and thus deprive him of the right of voting, during a considerable portion of his earthly existence, in order to ascertain that he will exercise that right wisely, during the remnant of his mortal career. All I think necessary in this case, is, that we should be satisfied of his present intention to reside with us, that he has cast in his lot with us; and for this, I deem two years residence in the State, and one in the county, sufficient. When you have a man's person here, you will, in general, have his property also; and this, together with every thing dear to him, will bind him to the country, and deeply interest him in its welfare. Let me put a case, Mr. Chairman, by way of illustration. Suppose two men embarked on board a ship, the one, carrying with him merchandize to the value of ten thousand dollars, and the other goes aboard with nothing but his wearing apparel. They launch into the ocean. Storms soon succeed to fair weather. The billows threaten to swallow up the ship with its cargoes and crew. I ask you, Sir, whether the poor man in this hour of peril, will not feel himself as much interested in the preservation of the ship, as the rich merchant. It is true, he has not the same pecuniary interest at stake, but his life, and his present all, is at stake; and he will enter into every scheme and make every exertion for the salvation of the ship and its contents, with as much ardour, energy, and passion, as the owner of thousands. How is it possible, that the interest of the poor sailor in such case, can be less than that of the wealthy trader? The one has his all embarked—the other has no more.

It seems to be generally admitted, Sir, that men are as much influenced by hope and expectation, as by actual fruition. Anticipation is said, and perhaps truly, to be superior to enjoyment. If so, the man who comes into this State poor, but with the hope and expectation, that by the pursuit of some profession or avocation, learned or unlearned, he shall support his family, and acquire a fortune; while engaged in this pursuit, he has, in my opinion, an attachment to, and an interest in this community, which should entitle him to the Right of Suffrage. Although he has no property, yet he expects to gain it. He would, therefore, have a strong motive to promote the good government of the State; and this arising from an interest, and an attachment, as strong as that of the owner of property. He would be anxious to have a protection for whatever property he might acquire; and this he would know, he could only have, under a good government and equal laws.

But, Mr. Chairman, not only does the present limitation of the Right of Suffrage prevent the increase of population by migration from other States, but it drives from the bosom of the Ancient Dominion, many of her most valuable sons. It may not be known to the gentlemen of the East, but it is a fact well known to those from the Western part of this State, that many valuable citizens have left their native State, and availing themselves of the facility of emigration, presented by that great river which washes the greater part of our Western border, have departed to those splendid regions of the West, where, in addition to the exuberant fertility of the soil, and other physical advantages, they can enjoy the rights of freemen. Yes, Sir, your Government banishes vast numbers of our young men to the Western States, where this odious restriction does not exist. Those States, in general, require little more than residence, as evidence of attachment and interest, so as to entitle persons to the Right of Suffrage. The consequence is, that many of our citizens, virtuous, intelligent, industrious men, forego all their attachments to their native soil, their house, and the scenes of their youthful sports, and pass away into some of those Western

States, where they can enjoy the privileges appertaining to freemen, by right of nature, not by purchase. Although a freehold may be cheaply bought, they disdain to purchase that which is of right their own.

Sir, there is a continual, and an exterminating warfare, carried on throughout this wide extended Commonwealth. She bleeds at every pore. And who are the parties to this desolating war? It is the Government against the people. A most unnatural war! Every member of the community driven out from us, by the operation of an unjust Constitution, is as much lost to us, as if the bayonet or cannon ball, had done its work upon him. Yes, Sir, it is a cruel and exterminating war. I speak of Western Virginia, when I say, that if the State were called upon to furnish annually her quota of troops to aid the General Government in resisting the attack of all Europe combined, it would not consume our strength, nor retard our population more, than do the restrictions imposed by her laws upon the Right of Suffrage. Many a soldier goes to the battle-field and returns again to his home with its comforts and endearments: but the voluntary exile; he, who is compelled for conscience sake, to rend asunder all the ties which bind him to his native country, and like the pilgrim fathers of New-England, seek liberty in a distant land, never returns. Sir, I have known respectable, intelligent, virtuous men; men who had been honoured with seats on the benches of our County Courts; to whom their fellow-citizens cheerfully confided the protection of their rights of property, and their personal rights, who were regarded as the efficient guardians of the public peace and welfare; I have known such, Sir, prohibited by your laws from exercising the Right of Suffrage. Is there not something wrong in all this? I have seen the respectable young men of the country—the mechanic, the merchant, the farmer, of mature age, of intelligence superior to that of one half the freeholders, and glowing with a patriotism which would make them laugh at death in defence of their country: I have seen such commanded to stand back from the polls, to give way to the owner of a petty freehold, who presses forward, saying to him in effect, "Away! I am holier than thou—this is sacred ground, upon which you have no right to tread." Ought such things to be? Is it for the good of our country that such things should be? Surely not.

Mr. Chairman, I shall not extend my remarks any farther. It was not my intention to enter into a detailed enumeration of all the evils of the present system of Suffrage, or of the advantages of that which I have now the honour to submit to the Committee. My present remarks were only intended to call the attention of the Committee to the plan I have proposed. It is a broad one I admit. I submit this project to gentlemen, as a base upon which they may build their schemes of Suffrage. It is open to amendment, and I have no doubt, requires amendment. Such as it is, I submit my substitute to your consideration.

Mr. Henderson of Loudoun, moved to amend the amendment of Mr. Wilson, by striking out the words "who is engaged in the land or naval service of the United States," and inserting in lieu thereof the following: "Who shall be a non-commissioned officer or private soldier, seaman or marine in the regular service of the United States, or of this Commonwealth." And stated his reason for it to be, that he did not wish to exclude gallant officers, such as Thomas ap Catesby Jones in the naval, or Roger Jones in the land service, (both from his own district,) from the Right of Suffrage; nor would he exclude the subalterns, and soldiers, &c. could he believe them capable of an independent exercise of the Right of Suffrage.

In reply to an enquiry of Mr. Claytor, Mr. Henderson said it was his intention to include the militia as well when in as out of actual service.

Mr. Wilson having accepted this amendment as a modification of his own,

Mr. Henderson addressed the Committee in support of the substitute of Mr. Wilson as amended. He expressed the gratification he had felt on account of the manner in which the interesting question, recently under the consideration of the Committee, had been debated by the gentleman from Northampton, (Mr. Upshur,) and the gentleman from Hanover, (Mr. Morris.) He remarked, that he felt pride in making the tribute of his acknowledgments to these gentlemen, distinguished alike for their ability and eloquence, and for their courteous treatment of those who, with himself, differed from them in opinion. He intimated an earnest wish, that the same temper might mark the debate about to obtain upon the great subject now before the body.

Mr. H. said, before I proceed, Mr. Chairman, to trouble the Committee upon the merits of the question under consideration, I will briefly advert to the origin and history of the freehold Suffrage in Virginia. It is now, Sir, two hundred and ten years since the assemblage of the first House of Burgesses. From 1619, when it met, till 1677, a period of fifty-eight years, the Suffrage, with the exception of a single year, was exercised by all the *freemen* of the Colony. During the excepted year, it was limited to *house-keepers*. In the year 1677, after the death of the gallant Bacon, the *freehold* Suffrage was first introduced, not by any Act of the Legislature, of the English Parliament, or of the people of either country. It was the offspring of regal interposition entirely, as has been most aptly and forcibly shown by my friend from Frederick, (Mr. Cooke.) Yes, Sir, said Mr. H. it was the precious fruit of despotism. Charles II. one of the most odious and profligate tyrants who ever wielded the British sceptre, transmitted to Sir William Berkeley, then Governor of the Colony, an instruction, signed by his own royal hand, commanding him to permit none except *freeholders*, to exercise this inestimable privilege. It is curious to observe the refined spirit of tyranny which reigns throughout this document. It commands Sir William not to permit the House of Burgesses to meet more than *once in two years;* to limit its sessions to *fourteen days*, and to *reduce* the moderate recompence for their services, which the freemen of the Colony had cheerfully accorded to their representatives. It is obvious, Sir, that the policy and aim of this disgusting edict was to dishearten the people; to degrade their agents; to make a mockery of their legislation. A fortnight for the whole business of a new and rising Colony, by agents who were to be humbled by subsisting upon "*low and coarse diet!*" I ask, Mr. Chairman, if, in the face of these striking and graphic facts, gentlemen can cover with the hoary mantle of antiquity, the monopoly which I assail? If an abuse founded in a flagitious and scornful disregard of all decency and right, and fastened, at the point of the bayonet, upon an indignant people, can challenge to itself the favourable notice of the freemen of Virginia, in the nineteeth century? Having thus, continued Mr. H. stripped the argument of our opponents of the interest which it claims from the pretended *revolutionary* origin of this usurpation, I respectfully invite the Committee to follow me in the imperfect effort which I shall make to discuss it on its merits. I lay down these principles as applicable to the subject. I deem them clear as day; postulates in the science of politics: First, that *all the men of a society are entitled to a voice in framing its organic law;* secondly, that a *majority* of these men has an undoubted right to decide what that law shall be; thirdly, that as a corollary from the second proposition, this majority has a legitimate authority to prescribe *who shall exercise the Right of Suffrage in the ordinary legislation of the society;* and, fourthly, that to withhold the exercise of this right from any man in the society, *except where it is necessary for the common good*, is unjust and tyrannical. I do not think, said Mr. H. that the truth of these principles, or either of them, will be denied in the United States, *save only in Virginia*. Let us proceed to apply them to the subject of the present debate. I assume, that there are in the State of Virginia 100,000 men having attained the age of twenty-one years, either natives of the State, or having resided therein for a reasonable time, and who are willing to pay, rateably with their fellow-citizens, its taxes in peace, and to fight, by their sides, in war. The real number is no doubt greater. I assume it for convenience. I farther assume, that, of the 100,000, 40,000 are freeholders, and 60,000 non-freeholders. This exposition of the subject shows at once its importance. Yes, Sir, on the one hand, you have the political power; the political life and death of three-fifths of the freemen of the Commonwealth; on the other, the order and stability of the Commonwealth itself. I am deeply sensible of my inability to do justice to such a theme. But, impelled by a sense of duty to my constituents, whose memorial I have had the honor to present, and by a sacred regard to the great principles involved in the issues of our deliberations, I will endeavor to prove that neither the lights of history, the results of comparison, nor the inductions of reason, demand, at our hands, the tremendous sacrifices which gentlemen desire us to make.

The history of ancient times, Sir, continued Mr. H. will give us very little aid in the development of this subject, as has been justly observed by my venerable colleague, (Mr. Monroe.) No gentleman will point us to any nation of antiquity except the Grecian and Roman Republics. There man attained to greater excellence in arts, in literature, and in arms, than under institutions less free. Greece, the mention of whose name awakens so many classic associations, and the memory of whose recent woes makes the heart bleed with sympathy, can afford us no material aid. The subtile, but versatile Athenian, eagerly catching the strains of that eloquence, the charm of succeeding ages, and deciding by acclamation, *in proper person*, great questions of public concern, is no example for us. Rome laid the foundations of her power in violence, and completed it by incessant war. Her victorious Generals, laden with the spoils of conquered nations, and dragging at their chariot-wheels the Kings of the earth, afford a poor illustration of the principles of representative Government. And the American turns with disgust, from a half-civilized people, who sported in the groans of the gladiator weltering in his blood, while he bent his sinking eye towards his native hills.

The able and eloquent gentleman from Chesterfield, (Mr. Leigh,) referred us the other day, in the discussion of a kindred topic, to France and England. We were counselled by that gentleman, to take warning from the French Revolution; and the Government of England was extolled as resting on liberty and law. Law, Sir, is to be found every where. No country in Europe exhibits the disgraceful picture of property insecure. The spirit of the age forbids it. The revolutionary horrors of France were set before us in bold relief; and we are earnestly premonished not to act them over again. Let us follow out this parallel. The Kings, Nobles and Priests of France, for a succession of ages, governed the people by an oppression so intolerable, that they rose at length, in their strength, and shook off their detested tyrants as the lion does the dew-drops from his mane. Grief and rage, drove them to excesses revolting to humanity. Now, Sir, what is this but social confusion and misery, produced by the injustice and cruelty of the aristocrats of France? Had they been just and moderate, these horrors would never have occurred. We seek to confer upon the body of the people their rights; and we are gravely, and most pathetically urged not to do it, because the tyranny of the *few* in France, and the suffering of the *many* led to social convulsion. That is, as I take it, opposite causes, produce like effects; or do not relieve the people of Virginia, because the oppression of those of France led to blood-shed. To this logic, I cannot subscribe. And, after all, what is now the situation of that beautiful country? A representation of the people; the establishment of the trial by jury; a free press, and a vastly more equal division of property, proclaim that with great temporary evil, much lasting good has flowed from the revolution. The Jesuit no longer tramples on the man. Happy change for this gallant people! Let not the brilliant and ravishing description which Burke gives us of the unfortunate Marie Antoinette, beguile us into the belief that any argument against our principles can be founded on the story of her sorrows, or of those of her country. For England, said Mr. H. I have great respect. She is crowned with too much glory not to awaken our admiration; and has too much in common with us, not to attract our sympathies. But is England, in truth, a land of liberty? Are the people happy? Is her Government a fit model for our imitation? Do not those who wield the power of the country, the *privileged few*, lavish its resources with wanton prodigality, while about two millions of the people are on the poor lists, and as many more, on the confines of pauperism, eke out a bare subsistence by a degree of toil which makes life itself a burden? A single ecclesiastical character in Ireland receives annually, and chiefly, too, from those who differ with him in religious belief, more than five times as much as the salary of the President of the United States, while hundreds of thousands of the people are huddled, like beasts, into mud-huts, half naked, and subsisting on potatoes, often, too often, scantily supplied! A man dares not in England, unless he is worth £100 a year, shoot a hare on his own land. Yet England, renowned and dreaded, has power beyond any nation over which the sun holds his course; a glory which Princes and Potentates may envy. But this power belongs to the few; this glory is the property of her leaders; and she owes a debt of four thousand five hundred millions of dollars. From such a union of wretchedness and splendour, of injustice and oppression, Heaven preserve the land of my nativity!

Let us, said Mr. H. turn our eyes towards our own country. Of the twenty-four States that form our Federal Family, Virginia alone has the freehold Suffrage throughout. In North Carolina, *freeholders* alone vote for Senators; but, as if to atone for this political sin, she permits *free negroes* to vote for members of the "House of Commons." In New-York, also, there is a singular anomaly; for the *free negro* there, is the only man of whom the freehold qualification is required. Every other citizen, without pecuniary qualification, is allowed to exercise this privilege, so dear to freemen. The effect is, that, of twenty-four States spread over the wide bosom of our happy country, Virginia, and *Virginia alone, proscribes and brands, with utter political opprobrium, the far greater part of her sons.* In Massachusetts, New-Jersey and Connecticut, a moderate pecuniary qualification is demanded; and in South Carolina, a tax of three shillings is required. In the other nineteen States, no pecuniary qualification is established, although some two-thirds of them impose as a prerequisite to the exercise of Suffrage, the payment of such taxes as may be assessed. I appeal to the members of this Committee; to the American world, if property is not as safe, and social order as effectually sustained, in the other States in this Union, as in Virginia? Look to South Carolina, to Louisiana, every where around you. Ask Ohio, the daughter of yesterday, now an empire in herself, if property is safe within her confines? If social order be not inviolate? Her population, I mean, Mr. Chairman, her white population, is now greater than that of the renowned and *once powerful* Commonwealth of Virginia.

After all, Sir, what is required of the voter? Simply the capacity and the will to choose good public agents. The gentleman from Chesterfield, before alluded to, in treating by anticipation, the question now under debate, denied that men who labored were able to perform this duty; and intimated, that even he, acute and accomplished as he is, was so engrossed with professional pursuits, as not to leave him leisure for the study of political science. Surely the same remark would apply to the other classes of society; for, by the fiat of an overruling Providence, we are doomed to earn our bread by toiling in our several vocations. Shall we cast the Government, then, into the hands of the idle and worthless? Heaven forbid! But, it does not require, in order to the proper exercise of the Right of Suffrage, that the citizen be a master of political science. Were it otherwise, how many voters would you have? Sir, the "*peasantry*" are competent to the performance of this duty. All who know men, and are versed in their concerns, in the various walks of life, are aware that individuals of limited education, observe character, with eyes at once steady and clear; unengrossed by books, wide awake to the world around them, they acquire and digest that every-day knowledge, that prevailing and discriminating common sense, which enable them to select their public functionaries with judgment. Sir, we have a very pretty antithetical line written by a sweet poet who was a very lazy fellow, "Those who think, must govern those who toil:" Nothing is so apt to delude a man and expose him to error in politics as poetry and metaphor. They lead him to make sense yield to sound, principles to flourishes of rhetoric. There lived in the last age another poet, and he will live for countless ages to come. He invigorated his understanding, and sharpened his perceptions by labor. You will recognize, in this description, the low-born but high-souled and enchanting Burns. He was a flax-breaker. His contemporary and acquaintance, Alexander Wilson, to whom the republic of science owes so much for his inimitable work on ornithology, was a *peasant* too. Yes, Sir, I myself have seen Horn, a weaver by day, a poet at night. Benjamin Franklin too, was of the peasant class. He labored hard for his daily bread. Gentlemen abhor abstractions. Let them learn, then, from those illustrious peasants this *practical truth, that moderate labor inspires sound sense.* I ask the Committee to test the correctness of my position, by inquiring how the non-freeholders in our sister States have chosen their representatives in the Federal Congress, as compared with the wiser freeholders of our native State? Lowndes of South Carolina, James Lloyd of Massachusetts, Rufus King of New York, William Pinckney of Maryland, *cum multis aliis*, were, or are the peers of the first talents that Virginia has sent forth. And now, Sir, are not Webster and M'Duffie, and Berrien, without naming others, additional living examples of the truth of my proposition? Such facts speak volumes. It were a most ungracious consumption of the valuable time of this enlightened and honorable body, to attempt, by any enlarged scope of argument, to prove that a man loves his birth-place as he does his mother, with an ardor that no time can efface, no circumstance extinguish. Sacred love of country, ineffable attachment to the natal spot, art thou the offspring of a churlish interest; or can gold purchase thee? Sir, the landless peasant clings to the rocky cliffs on whose summit he sported in the halcyon days of his boyhood, as the ligaments of his own heart bind it to his bosom. Away, then, with the idea of the gentleman from Spottsylvania, (Mr. Stanard) that a twenty-five dollar freeholder, a whole Commonwealth of whom Stephen Girard could create without impairing materially his resources, has a stronger, a more elevated, or more enduring attachment to his country, than the man I have faintly attempted to describe.

But, continued Mr. H. gentlemen have denied the propriety of permitting a man without property to vote equally with the rich man, because the latter brings into the common stock his fortune, as well as all that class of rights strictly denominated personal. In the first place, how is this position to be reconciled with the concession, that a man who has $25 in land shall vote? If one man have $100,000 and another $25, the ratio is so very inconsiderable as to withdraw from the argument of my opponents the greater part of its force. Examine this branch of the subject in its true lights. A man without property stakes his liberty, his life, his reputation, his happiness, and *his right to acquire property.* While we surround property with so many fences, and guard it with so much solicitude, shall we not duly appreciate the right to acquire it? Shall we not, in the emphatic language of Napoleon, preserve for it "the open theatre?" Again, if the rich man brings in his property, does he not create the necessity of an expensive Government? It is mainly for his property that law is piled upon law in your Statute book, and that the onerous labors of your judiciary are demanded. He, too, engrosses the honors and emoluments incident to the operations of Government. It is rarely that you incur expense in making or administering law for the citizen without property, and still more rarely does he share in those distinguished and interesting functions. How stands the account in war? Are wars waged for the interest of the poor? Do their passions prompt or their possessions invite them? No, Sir. The ambition of the great men of Rome raised her armies to invade Britain; after over-running the fairest portion of the Island, they returned to enjoy their spoil, leaving the highlands unconquered. The poor and hardy Caledonians boasted that their gallantry had rolled back the tide of battle; but Gibbon says more truly, that the proud Eagle of Rome scorned to perch on the naked hills of "the land of the mountain and the flood:" Sir, the cottager is always the instrument and often the victim of war, but he is never its author, and seldom shares its glory. Let not wealth, then, complain that it is taxed for its own interest, and its own protection and honor. But, Sir, property, as has been well said, has influence. It confers knowledge, and gives facility for improving the virtues of the heart and the graces of the manner. This is power, concentrated, legitimate, resistless power, ever has been, and will continue to be, till time shall be no more.

Gentlemen intimate, that the enlarged and liberal Suffrage will engender tumult at elections, and impart to the populace, habits of dissipation. Have you not now mirth and irregularity and riot at your elections? What real evil springs from this source? The gentry drink wine and the lower classes alcohol. This is a subject of regret, but not an adequate cause for disfranchising the one or the other. A celebrated man in England, remarked that it was better the Nobleman's coaches should be bespattered by the mob than that the people should be made slaves. And it is better that cultivated taste be offended here, than that three-fifths of the body politic be powerless. For these transient inconveniences, a perfect remedy may be found in the creation of moderate election districts.

Mr. Chairman, we have one small, but conspicuous example of the correctness of the doctrine which I have the honor to maintain, in Virginia itself; and gentlemen, justly tenacious of the character of our ancient Commonwealth, ought to weigh it. The borough of Norfolk is entitled, as we all know, to a delegate in the lower House of our Legislature. In that borough, *pot-boilers and mechanics, who have served an apprenticeship*, are invested with the Right of Suffrage. How, Sir, have they exercised it? Look at their representation on this floor. One of those who exemplified their political fitness, in war the defence, in peace the ornament of the State, is here no longer. It is, Sir, an indisputable fact, that the *borough* of *Norfolk* has been represented in the Legislature, with an ability and patriotism which do honor to the city itself, while it is a *living and constant proof* of the capacity of the non-freeholders of Norfolk. And are not the non-freeholders of the county of Frederick as competent as they are? Is there any thing in the air of a city which gives light and purity to its populace, when citizens of corresponding grade throughout your wide confines are involved in darkness or steeped in impurity? We have been taught to believe that the multitude in cities was more depraved and more liable to political delusion than that dispersed over the surface of the country. Allowing them to be no worse than their fellow-citizens of Norfolk, time, the best instructor, establishes their claim. It is vain to contend that we are happy, and, therefore, that no amendment would be proper. Suppose the State were governed by an absolute monarchy, whose character was as benign as that of a Trajan or Antonine, and who made them happy for the time, would not the citizens assert their *political rights* as the sole security for the continuance of their *civil immunities?* Would they be content to hold their comfort, and peace, and all that is dear to man, upon courtesy? If not, ought the vast mass of citizens, the subject of our present debate, to remain content, because not actually *oppressed?* Ought they not to be placed in a predicament which would enable them to guard themselves from *possible oppression?* But, Sir, I respectfully insist that the non-freeholders of Virginia have been politically wronged, and that they are so now. Permit me, since we are boldly called upon to point out a solitary instance of misrule, to name a few, simply by way of example. Some of them will demonstrate the injustice done to those who do not vote; all of them manifest the unsound policy of the representatives of those who do.

This is an invidious task. I enter upon it with no feelings other than those of regret and pain. Professions are of little use. I will proceed with the argument. In Hening's Statutes at Large, vol. 6, page 439, and in the same book, page 532, may be found two Acts of Legislation, which will serve to exemplify, in a lively manner, the idea which I advance. I will notice, briefly, the last. It provides, that all the people of the country shall perform the arduous and perilous military duties incident to their circumstances, except certain official dignitaries, and owners of *four slaves*. The official characters were compelled to furnish arms and equipments as a substitute for their personal services; but the overseer of the opulent man was neither compelled to fight nor to pay. By the Act of 1754, to be found, page 438, two justices might cause to be seized any man not having a calling or support, except *voters or servants indented or bought*, have him dragged before them, and finally decide to consign him or not to all the hazards and sufferings of war. If this was right in the general, why except voters, or, in other words, *freeholders?* Why except servants, *the property of these freeholders?* Can any man believe so gross a discrimination would have been made, if these freeholders had not held all the power, and the remainder of society been a proscribed caste? This example is not the less apt or illustrative, because it occurred under the Colonial Government.

Is not every gentleman somewhat struck with the fact, that the long denial of justice to thousands of citizens, is itself evidence of misrule?

The manner of working the roads of Virginia is little short of the odious *corve* of France. If a man has two slaves, he is exempt from the imposition, while his poor neighbor, with all his sons, is liable to it. Imagine a wealthy man, often the case in the county where I reside, to have a large crop to carry to market, and a family for whose accommodation good roads are essential; this individual has six negro men;

his poor neighbor has six sons, who, together with their father, earn their daily bread by their daily labor. This man, with his six sons, is obliged to work upon the roads along side of the six slaves of his wealthy neighbor. The poor man, in the interim, never uses the road.

The entire county and parish levies are raised by a poll or capitation tax. In the county where I reside, this charge, for the four years next succeeding the last Census, was $12,000, more than our whole contribution to the revenue of the State itself.

If a poor man owes 15 or $20, his creditor may, in one month, sell under scire facias, at auction, the bed on which his sick wife languishes, and the cow that affords aliment to his children. Nothing is spared. Until within a few years, a man might own large landed estates, or valuable stocks, and unless he had personal property, his creditor might seize his person, and the law interposed, and, under the kindly facilities of the prison rules, he might live like a nabob. Even now, if he chooses to convert his prison into a drawing-room, he may employ his income in riot and luxury. I submit it to this Committee, to that part of it, at least, who do not conclusively assume that to be wise which has existed long, if these examples do not indicate too forcibly the exceptionable spirit of our legislation? I am aware, Sir, that I am now addressing gentlemen elected by freeholders. I appeal to their candor and good sense, and through them, to the liberal and dispassionate citizens of Virginia.

Sir, I ask if the state of the Judiciary of the country is not a reproach to the Legislature? Truly, we add the "law's delay" to the "proud man's contumely." I will not enlarge on this topic.

What is the general condition of the Commonwealth? A commerce inferior to that of the little State of Rhode Island, an agriculture languishing, the mechanic arts in a state of depression and thriftlessness, and provision made for the education of about one-eighth of the children annually educated by the small State of Connecticut. Yes, Sir, and they are not half so well educated.

As for the development of the natural resources of the State, through the medium of a system of improvement, the very mention of the subject is calculated to inspire melancholy. What, Sir, is your great James River Canal? Between one and two millions of dollars have been lavished on it, in the course of forty years—some thirty miles are completed! and the people of the State, provoked with this gross absurdity and waste, look on the whole enterprize with disgust.

But, if there be a Commonwealth on earth, where the Right of Suffrage is fairly and rationally susceptible of a most liberal enlargement, it is that of Virginia. Her people are habitually steady in their conduct; the mass of them are reflecting; and, libel them who may, every man who really knows the state of society, and is willing to be just to it, will attest the truth of the declaration, that morality and virtue are growing amongst us. Who is not struck with the temperance and sobriety of the rising generation, compared with that which is passing away? Vice and crime, I boldly affirm, have, within ten years, rapidly diminished; individual industry and energy, are increasing. Schools are multiplying, and religion is diffusing its genial influence over the land. Over this picture, rudely but faithfully sketched, I rejoice with filial joy; and while I cheerfully admit the virtue and stability of the freeholders, the middle classes, as they are termed, I cannot yield my judgment to the dictum, which confines virtue to any description of men. The gentleman and the cottager too, are pure. Yes, Sir, with individual exceptions, all deserve to share in the government of the community, that rules the land of their birth, the theatre of their joys and sorrows, that embosoms the ashes of their fathers, and unites the hopes of the children of their affections. The composition and circumstances of the society themselves, invite to the infranchisement of the people. No large or populous cities agitate or corrupt us; few foreigners are intermixed with us; our pursuits, for the most part, agricultural; an extensive territory sparsely peopled; and a respect for order, for the character of the Commonwealth itself, animating all classes of citizens. Such is Virginia; such, the material for her Statesmen and law-givers. Are we to apprehend rapine, disorder, disorganization, from a paternal and generous course? Besides, more than three-fifths of the inhabitants, comprehending far the greater part of those termed in European countries the rabble, are slaves. This single circumstance, is enough to quiet all the apprehensions of gentlemen. It cannot be successfully contended, that a community, thus characterised and composed, is not to be trusted to govern itself; that its powers must be confided to the chosen few. From the days of Homer, to this day, it has been conceded, that to enslave a man, was to impair his worth; and, that to clothe him with the privileges appropriate to his nature, elevated his sentiments.

If it were questionable, whether the reasoning I employ were just originally, still half the force of the conflicting argument is taken away by the fact, that no other State in the Union retains the odious distinction which I combat. If the freehold Suffrage existed in the other States, the problem would exist in all its force and interest; but, when it is abandoned by twenty-three States, to retain it here, were insufferable. The humble citizen of Virginia cannot pass the confines of Maryland, Pennsylvania, Ohio, Kentucky, or Tennessee, without being taunted by his neighbours with his vassal condition. The borderer on North Carolina beholds, amidst the most perfect social order and security, the very free negro exercising that privilege which is withheld from him. This is galling and most humiliating.

Let those who feel solicitude, and who does not, for the future destiny of the State, inspect, with a Statesman's eye, its diversified population. There are four distinct classes—the freeholder, the non-freeholder, the free negro, and the slave. Pause, Mr. Chairman, and examine this interesting subject. May not occasions arise when the common weal will loudly call for the united exertions of your white population? A large part of them have already poured their murmurs into your ear. Will you deafen it? I adjure you, Sir, I adjure this Committee to bind in the chords of common affection, the whole people, and to treat them as one family.

I cannot but think, that the condition of the world is greatly improved and rapidly improving. All virtuous men venerate their progenitors. But, how was it possible, in ancient times, to diffuse through society the knowledge which now prevails? The art of printing, itself, was sufficient to change the face of the world, and it is certainly changing it. The mariner's compass, post-offices, the application of steam in facilitating intercourse amongst men, and in the mutual transmission of information, are, with a steady pace, pressing us on in the career of mind. These, with many ancillary causes, are exalting and meliorating the species. Why shall we alone, lag and faulter in the generous race? Adopt a well-devised, wise, and economical system of education for all classes, and all will be capable of performing the cardinal duties of the citizen, will be worthy to become depositories of political power, and all will love with filial regard, the land of their birth.

After all, we are merely commissioned to sketch, for the adoption or rejection of the people, the plan of a Constitution. If they approve, they will establish it; if, on the contrary, they disapprove, they will reject it—and then our work will terminate. Why, then, do gentlemen attempt to alarm us? Why this cry of separation, intestine war, and all the horrors that eloquence can paint, or ingenuity conjure up? Rather, Sir, let us be calm, and endeavour to do our duty in a spirit of conciliation and harmony. One gentleman, for whom I entertain great esteem, distinguished by his talents and virtues, (Mr. Nicholas,) announced to us, the other day, that we were in a most awful situation, that clouds and darkness hovered over us, and terrible calamities beset our path. Permit me to congratulate that amiable gentleman upon the tranquil and serene aspect, which he exhibited to us in the midst of the storm he raised or fancied. I had the pleasure to sit near him, and marvelled at the placidity of his brow in a scene so appalling. Is there, Mr. Chairman, no rhetoric in those horrors? The same gentleman informed us that he had held an official station under the Government for some twenty years, and that things had flowed on with wonderful smoothness during the whole time. That may be, Sir, so far as the gentleman is concerned. A good official station has a charming effect in smoothing the asperities of life, and imparting brighter tints to the scenes around one. But, it does not follow, from all this, that the people are content with their disfranchisement. I wish the worthy gentleman a long continuance of the advantages he has so richly merited; but my first wish is for my country.

Another honourable gentleman, in speaking of the determination of the minority to retain its power, was pleased to hold to us of the West, for it seems I too am a Western man, the language which Sparta held to the Persian Monarch, when he demanded the surrender of their arms, "come and take them." Sir, here are no Spartans, no Persians. We are all Virginians. During the war of 1812, the citizens of Norfolk talked to us in a different language. They then said, "come and help us." And we went; and ranging ourselves under the banner of his gallant townsman, we bade the enemy "come and take the city." Aye, and we are ready to repair again to his succour. In fighting, there is no sectional line, no exclusion. Whenever the standard of freedom of Virginia, the "Star-Spangled Banner" is unfurled, in the East or the West, the North or the South, then will every true-hearted American be found to face, not his brothers, but the foes of his beloved and common country. Permit me, Mr. Chairman, humble as I am, to make a passing effort to relieve this learned gentleman from a distressing state of perplexity into which he has fallen. He seems to apprehend, that we shall not be able to discern and define the white man, with any sort of distinctness, and that the people of China and of the South American Republics, when they come hither, will puzzle our modicum of physical and political science to arrange them. This is a most embarrassing question, it must be admitted; but if the learned gentleman will concede our principle, we will endeavour to relieve him in the labour of its application; and should we not be competent to the solution of this matter ourselves, we have yet a resource which may save the Republic. We will call Dr. Mitchell into consultation, and from the acumen and erudition which he displayed upon the occurrence of a similar difficulty in the celebrated case of the Almshouse *vs.* Alexander Whisteloe, he will doubtless prescribe with effect.

Mr. Chairman, it is not a question who is white; but how shall the wrongs of the people be redressed. *Sixty thousand men*, in a land of liberty, ask their fellow-men to admit them to an equal participation in their political rights: they ask in the spirit of brotherhood, but, in the unquailing voice of conscious rectitude and firmness. Every where around them they see those who have the same claims with themselves, and none other, standing up and giving assurance that they are men. Shall they, they alone, bear the stamp of political villinage?

The Committee assenting, the resolution respecting the Right of Suffrage was, for the present, laid aside, and

Mr. H. having resumed his seat, Mr. Pleasants asked as a favour of the Committee, that the resolution now under consideration might be laid aside long enough to afford him an opportunity of presenting to this body a proposition of his own, which he offered as the basis of a compromise.

Mr. Pleasants then offered the following amendment to the fourth resolution of the Committee:

The original resolution reads,

"*Resolved*, That the number of members in the Senate of this State ought to be neither increased nor diminished, nor the classification of its members changed."

The amendment proposes to strike out all after the words "Resolved, That" and to insert as follows:

——— "representation in the Senate shall be based on the whole number of free persons, including those bound to service for a term of years, and excluding indians not taxed, and adding to the aforesaid number of free persons, three-fifths of all other persons; and the Senate shall consist of a number not exceeding   , and its term of service and classification remain as at present."

In supporting the amendment, Mr. Pleasants spoke, in substance, as follows:

I have risen to make the motion just now intimated to the Committee—which motion, I had hoped some other member would have made. I had hoped some gentleman of standing in this body, some gentleman of standing in the community, and of weight of character, would have risen to make some such motion; but I have been so far disappointed. I will then present the proposition, under the hope that it may tend to bring about a reconciliation, and lead to those concessions, which are so desirable, and which many gentlemen think absolutely necessary to the further progress of our proceedings.

The district I represent, has received the notice of several gentlemen, in the course of this debate. It is what I fully expected, and what I am very glad to see. The respectable and intelligent people whom I represent, (I hope I shall be permitted to term them so, for it is no more than the truth,) have put themselves in that point of view in which they are entitled to stand before this body. I have heard it frequently insinuated here, that the people are in the dark, and are therefore not competent to decide on that branch of the subject which has occupied our attention so long: that they want more light, more information, and that they ought to receive it. Sir, this is all well: the people will receive with thankfulness, all the information which may be given them. But, I have never been disappointed in the expectation that they will always come to correct conclusions if left to themselves, and not misled in their judgment by some who have more influence than is wholesome for this Commonwealth. In saying this, I have no particular reference to the present juncture, nor do I point the remark at any individuals. I have given the most profound attention to the discussions which have taken place. The various subjects which have come before us have been most ably handled. The best talents of the State, talents which I have often witnessed and long admired, have been employed upon them. The country has been illuminated, and I have myself been greatly profited. An intense interest has been excited every where, but my district has not changed its position as far as I am informed. The majority of the little county in which I live, has, it is true, been against the opinions of the majority of the district, but they have honoured me with a seat here. It is an honour which I duly appreciate, and a proof of their respect and confidence which I can never forget. I should be a villain, if I could wipe the remembrance of it from my heart. No, Sir—it will be there when I die. I am more singularly situated, not only as it regards the geographical position of my district, but in some other respects, than many other gentlemen. I did not go through my district, nor did I know the sense of the people, till the day of the election. I heard that my name had been mentioned as a candidate, and I hastened to promulgate my sentiments, in the fullest and most explicit manner. Give me leave to say, that the subject was fully canvassed. A gentleman who is particularly conversant with the finances of the Government, and who is very thoroughly acquainted with all matters relating to it, laboured with his utmost energy to produce an impression contrary to that which the people entertained, but without success. He exerted his utmost ability, but his efforts did not succeed.

Gentlemen have made their appeal to the Albemarle district, and to its position in relation to this question. I felt the full force of their appeal, and had I thought they were wrong, and could I consent to violate the known will of a majority of my district, I would have yielded to that appeal. But my attachment to numbers, and to the principle that the majority who are bound to fight and to pay, ought to have the power to vote, was not for one second shaken. I concluded the appeal to be in part directed to myself, from what an honorable member from Chesterfield said, in relation to a certain letter which he had seen. My disposition was to do all I could for the security of the slave property in consistency with my view on the great principles of Republican Government. The district I represent, is deeply interested in whatever touches that property, as it probably contains as many slaves in proportion to its extent, as any other portion of the State. And I should be the very worst of men, if I could voluntarily jeopardize such an interest. It had been my opinion, that some standard for taxation might be taken from the relative value of land; and that the one property should not be taxed save in a given ratio to the other; but on this point, I have found myself in a very small minority. I did believe that the thing might be made practicable, and that there would be no difficulty in stopping the violation of the Constitution, *instanter*. But, as the project was disapproved in the Legislative Committee, I do not know that I shall offer it here. In the proposition I now advance, I am convinced, that I go beyond the opinions of my constituents, as it was at the time of the election. But what is to be done? The Convention is almost equally divided. Gentlemen ask us whether we will press measures with so small a majority? But, Mr. Chairman, what must we do? Can they expect us to desert our own principles, and to fly in the face of a majority of our constituents? Must we be willing to yield to a minority? Sir, such an expectation cannot, and ought not to prevail. The venerable gentleman from Loudoun, (Mr. Monroe,) gave us most parental and conciliatory counsel, and expressed his own predilections in favour of the plan embodied in my amendment; but he did not follow it up with any specific motion. I have felt it my duty to bring the plan before the Committee. I have done so in the very best spirit, and with a strong hope of effecting the compromise. I have proposed the Federal number, because it is most simple, best known, and the most easily reduced to practice. But if gentlemen prefer introducing in the Senate, the principle of a mixed basis of representation, I am perfectly ready to modify it in that way.

Mr. Nicholas observed, that as he was one of those who voted for affording his highly esteemed friend from Goochland an opportunity to offer his resolution, he thought it proper to state, that he was influenced in giving that vote by a spirit of courtesy, and by a wish to gratify that gentleman. But, as his proposition goes ahead of the discussion, and refers to a resolution which will come on hereafter, it would be improper to take it up at this time. There were considerations connected with the proposition, which he wished to weigh in his own mind; he, therefore, moved that the resolution offered by the gentleman from Goochland, be for the present passed over.

Mr. Pleasants seconded the motion, and stated that, as his resolution was closely connected with the subject of the basis of representation before the Convention, he deemed it proper to submit it, whilst that subject was undisposed of. He hoped, therefore, that his resolution might lie on the table, and be printed. The Chairman took the question: Shall the resolution be passed over for the present? which was carried.

Mr. Pleasants then moved that the subject, the consideration of which had been suspended, should be resumed; which was carried.

Mr. Nicholas, after requesting the Chairman to report the amendment, spoke, in substance, as follows:

My sentiments, Mr. Chairman, are so different from those just expressed by the gentleman from Loudoun, (Mr. Henderson,) upon this interesting subject, and my district is so much opposed to the measure now under consideration, that I feel it an imperious duty to submit to the Convention my views on it. The amendment has certainly the merit of advancing boldly to the question, and proposes, what I conceive, amounts essentially to Universal Suffrage. There cannot be a more fit occasion to enquire, what ought to be the basis of Suffrage, than when it is proposed to extend that right to almost every man in the country. I find myself, Mr. Chairman, placed in a new attitude. If we are to take the sentiments of myself, and those with whom I act, from the representations of the gentleman from Loudoun, we should be induced to suppose, that we are not only inimical to the whole class of the poor in this country, but to Republican institutions in general. I do not mean to make professions of my principles. But I may be permitted to say, that though in the different political scenes and vicissitudes which have taken place in this country, my situation may have been humble and obscure: though I have not filled high stations, I have not stood by with apathy as to passing events. I have always taken a deep interest in them, and have not been inactive. It is true that I have served as a private, but have felt as much zeal, as others who were more elevated. I had supposed that from my boyhood, I was engaged in defending free principles, by fighting under the banners of the most distinguished patriots of the land; but now the gentlemen on the other side, endeavor to take our weapons out of our hands, to defeat us with them. This policy of attempting to alienate the people from their friends, is as old as the days of Æsop. We are told in one of his fables, that certain shepherds had their flocks protected by their watch-dogs, who proved faithful sentinels, and resisted every effort of the wolves to break into the fold. Baffled in their attempts, the wolves persuaded the shepherds that it was an useless expense and trouble to maintain these faithful sentinels, and made solemn promises, that if they would dismiss them, they should sustain no injury. Deluded by these assurances, the shepherds complied with the request, but the consequence was, that the wolves broke into the fold and destroyed all the flock. But such policy will not be effectual in this country; the people are intelligent; they know who are their friends, and they will never abandon them.

The gentleman from Loudoun has been pleased to say, that when on a former occasion I depicted the evils which would result from an attempt to force a Constitution upon a large portion of the people, which they believed to be oppressive and ruinous to them, and that by a meagre majority, and stated that the consequences might be awful, that I could not be in earnest, because my countenance, at the time, expressed no strong emotion, but was placid and unmoved. But that gentleman is yet to learn that a placid countenance is not incompatible with firmness of purpose; and I trust that in the discharge of the duties which I owe my constituents, I shall not flinch from the assertion of their rights, but be as firm and immoveable, as any gentleman, with whatever fervor of manner, he may support his opinions.

I cannot, Mr. Chairman, promise the Committee to gratify them with the great variety of topics and illustrations, which the talents of the gentleman from Loudoun has enabled him to lay before them. It shall be my humble endeavour to discuss the question before the Committee. I shall not doubt the sincerity of the gentleman's opinions, though he would appear to question mine. [Mr. Henderson here stated, that he did not doubt the sincerity of the gentleman, but only whether under momentary excitement, he might not have expressed, what in calmer moments he would have repudiated.]

Mr. Nicholas observed, that he did not know how he could be understood to have spoken under excitement, when a placidity of countenance at the moment was attributed to him, incompatible with the feelings he expressed. He continued—I received with pleasure the assurances of good will, and good feelings expressed by the gentleman from Loudoun, and cordially reciprocate them. He said he should disdain himself, if he suffered difference of sentiment on public subjects to inspire him with ill will to any gentleman. It was not his habit. Every thing which had occurred in his intercourse with the gentleman from Loudoun, during their short acquaintance, had impressed him with far different feelings.

Mr. N. said, he should proceed to discuss what was the real question before the Committee, stripped of those extraneous considerations, which do not bear upon it, and which are rather calculated to mislead, than to enlighten. This subject has received from me, Mr. Chairman, my anxious consideration; not only since it has been agitated in this Convention, but whilst during the canvass, which preceded the elections, it was discussed in the public prints, in speeches to the people, and in the addresses of various gentlemen who were called on to declare their sentiments. Amongst the arguments relied upon by the advocates of a very extended Suffrage, one of the most fallacious, is, that which attempts to found the right upon principles of natural equality. This pre-supposes that Suffrage is derived from nature. Now, nothing can be clearer, than that Suffrage is a conventional, and not a natural right. In a state of nature, (if such state ever existed except in the imagination of the poets,) every man acts for himself, and is the sole judge of what will contribute to his happiness. When he enters into the social state, which he is compelled to do, to guard himself against violence, and to protect him in the enjoyment of the fruits of his industry, he gives up to the society the powers of Government, and surrenders to it, so much of his natural rights as are essential to secure to him such portion of those rights which he retains, or such other rights as grow out of the new relations in which he is placed.

In the rudiments of society, and whilst the people are few, the making laws and the decision on the most important concerns, such, for instance, as war and peace, were exercised by the body of the people in their collective capacity. Such was the ancient republic of Athens, and some of the other Grecian States, and such is said to be the little republic of St. Marino. When the community became large, it was found impracticable to exercise their sovereignty in their primary Assemblies. These were too numerous for deliberation, and were too much under the control of violent passions, and too liable to be influenced by the seductions of artful men, who flattered the people only to destroy them. It was found absolutely necessary, to entrust the making of laws and the management of the public affairs to agents, or deputies, and this gave rise to representation. The power of voting for these agents or deputies constitutes the Right of Suffrage. This plain exposition of the origin and formation of society, incontestibly shows that both Representation and Suffrage are social institutions. It proves that it is a solecism to insist, that it is proper to refer back to a state of nature, for principles to regulate rights which never existed in it—which could only exist after mankind abandoned it, rather than by a correct estimate of those relations, which are to be found in a state of society, of which, both Representation and Suffrage are the offspring. It has been attempted to sustain almost unlimited suffrage, (I know not whether in the Committee, as I did not come in until after the gentleman from Loudoun had been speaking some time, but certainly elsewhere,) by reference to those general phrases in the Bill of Rights, which declare, "that all men are by nature equally free and independent." But the same section of the Bill of Rights plainly discriminates between the state of nature, and the social state, and admits the modification which natural rights may receive by entering into society. It is true it speaks of inherent rights, of which men, when they enter into society "cannot by any compact deprive or divest their posterity;" "namely, the enjoyment of life and liberty, with the means of acquiring and possessing property, and pursuing and obtaining happiness and safety." But it is most obvious that this last clause does not comprehend suffrage, or representation, or any fancied rights growing out of them; first, because these are not natural rights; and next, if they were, as the clause last referred to enumerates the rights which a man in a social state cannot alienate, and that enumeration has nothing to do with suffrage or representation, it must in candour be admitted, that these subjects are surrendered (so far as the Bill of Rights is concerned) to the regulation of society. These considerations, Mr. Chairman, appear to me clearly to prove, that in deciding upon suffrage, we are deciding a question of expediency and policy, and that we ought so to regulate it, as will best promote the happiness and prosperity of society. Our opponents have themselves afforded unequivocal evidence of the truth of what we contend for, by advocating schemes of suffrage which profess to impose restrictions on the exercise of the right, though those restrictions (in my humble judgment) are totally inadequate and illusory.

I have reflected much on this subject, because every one must have anticipated, that it would be, save one, the most important which could employ the deliberations of this assembly, and that with the one alluded to, it had the most intimate connexion. In forming my opinion, I am perfectly satisfied, that the rule laid down in our Bill of Rights, is the true one on this subject. And here, Mr. Chairman, permit me to join most heartily in the eulogiums which have been so repeatedly pronounced by the gentlemen on the other side, on the profound wisdom, exalted patriotism, and unbounded devotion to free Governments, of the framers of our Bill of Rights. I subscribe entirely to every part of it, and adopt it as containing the articles of my political faith. It is much, however, to be deplored, that whilst these gentlemen pay such adoration to the Bill of Rights, and its authors, they should in the same breath deny that they understood their own principles, and assert, that in the formation of every essential part of the Constitution, they were guilty of a flagrant violation of them! What then, is the rule laid down by the authors of our Constitution on this subject? It is, "that all men having sufficient evidence of permanent, common interest with, and attachment to, the community, have the Right of Suffrage." Every part of this definition, Mr. Chairman, is highly important. First, there must be "sufficient evidence," and next, it must be the evidence "of permanent, common interest with, and attachment to, the community." Now, I contend that this sufficient evidence of common, permanent interest, is only to be found in a lasting ownership of the soil of the country.

This kind of property is durable, it is indestructible; and the man who acquires, or is the proprietor of it, connects his fate by the strongest of all ties, with the destiny of the country. No other species of property has the same qualities, or affords the same evidence. Personal property is fluctuating—it is frequently invisible, as well as intangible—it can be removed, and can be enjoyed as well in one society as another. What evidence of permanent interest and attachment, is afforded by the ownership of horses, cattle, or slaves? Can it retard or impede the removal from the State, in times of difficulty or danger impending over it? What security is the ownership of Bank or other stocks, or in the funded debt? None. A man may transfer this kind of property in a few moments, take his seat in the stage, or embark in the steamboat, and be out of the State in one day, carrying with him all he possesses.

The same objection applies to admitting persons who have only a temporary interest in the soil: besides, that these temporary interests give a control to others, over the votes of the holder, just as certainly, as that "a control over a man's subsistence, is always a control over his will." In vain do gentlemen refer to the example of other States. Here we have a safe rule laid down, by the wisdom of our ancestors, whom gentlemen unite in canonizing, and tested and approved by the experience of more than half a century. Sir, I always thought I was a republican, but gentlemen would argue me out of my belief. I have always supposed, that our Right of Suffrage was so constructed, as to protect both persons and property. God forbid that I should wish to exclude any, who I can be convinced ought to be admitted, or that I would oppress any portion of my fellow-citizens. My principles would lead me to admit all I could, consistently with what I believe the welfare of society requires. I am no enemy to the non-freeholder; but I must vote for that rule, which by securing the tranquillity and happiness of society, secures those inestimable blessings to every member of it. I do not deny to the advocates of greatly extended suffrage, either in this House or out of it, perfect rectitude and sincerity of motive. Enthusiasm is always sincere—but that truth does not at all mitigate the evils and desolations, which it has often inflicted on mankind.

Sir, I know it has become fashionable to represent those who are opposed to many of the innovations which are contemplated, as the enemies of the people. Whether I am their friend, I shall endeavor to manifest by my acts, and not by my professions. No denunciations have any terror for me. They will pass by me "like the idle wind which I regard not." There is what I consider a very strong and decisive argument in favor of the rule I lay down, for suffrage to be drawn from the act of the framers of our Bill of Rights, which is contemporaneous with it. It is that part of the Constitution, which declares "that the Right of Suffrage in the election of members of both Houses, shall remain as exercised at present." Now, the freehold suffrage was then the established mode. The framers of your Constitution declare to you in the most emphatic manner, that the rule which they laid down in the Bill of Rights as to suffrage, could only be complied with, by requiring a permanent interest in the soil. Here then, is contemporaneous exposition always deemed the best. Nay, more, here is a declaration of these wise men who framed the Bill of Rights, as to what they intended in it. Will gentlemen contend, after their splendid eulogiums on them, that they did not understand their own words and intentions, but that the men of the present day, are better expositors of both? But the intelligent gentleman from Frederick, endeavours to obviate the force of this argument, by insisting that this part of the Constitution is not to have the same authority as other parts, because the framers of the Government did not, for the first time, establish the rule of suffrage, but merely left it as they found it. This may be specious, but in my poor judgment, is not solid. The framers of our Government were employed in establishing a system adapted to the changes produced by the revolution. It was not incumbent on them to change every thing. It was only wise and proper to abolish such parts of our former system, as were irreconcileable with the republican form we were about to carry into effect. Thus, we find in several parts of the Constitution, portions of the old institutions were retained. But they were retained upon due consideration, and by adoption became just as much the act of the framers of the Government, as the parts which were created by them. If the framers of the Government had said the suffrage should be conferred on the freeholder, it would be admitted, I presume, that in every sense, it was a rule established by them. Now, can it make any difference, except in mere form, that a phraseology is used, which retains the rule of suffrage which had previously existed. But the same gentleman contends, that the retention of the Right of Suffrage, as theretofore exercised, resulted probably either from the Constitution being made in haste and amid the noise of hostile cannon, or that it was a sacrifice made to propitiate, or rather to avoid the alienation of the freeholders. Both these hypotheses appear to me to be incorrect. As to the Constitution being the result of hasty or timid councils, the gentleman from Chesterfield, (Mr. Giles,) in a former debate, has clearly shown, on the best evidence, it was not the case. And as to this provision being an oblation to the freeholders, I find no trace in the Constitution itself, in the history of the times, or even in any tradition which has come down to us, to justify the idea. I believe that at the period spoken of, there was such a devotion to country, such a love of liberty, and such disinterestedness, that the Convention might, with perfect safety, have made any arrangement which they believed would contribute to sustain free principles. But they were wise and practical statesmen, and they knew and felt, that they had established a rule which was perfectly compatible with republican institutions. The force of the argument derived from their authority, as well as from the experience under it, remains complete and unimpaired. Gentlemen argue this question as if it was one between the Satraps, (the existence of whom they choose to suppose) and the poor of the land. Instead of making war upon the middling or even the poorer classes, we believe we are defending their best interests. We go not for the interests of wealth, when we say, that we are of opinion that an interest in the soil is the best evidence of permanent attachment. This idea of an aristocracy of freeholders, is not only incorrect but ludicrous. Are we contending for giving wealth in the distribution of suffrage, a weight in proportion to its extent? The answer is, that a freeholder, whose farm is worth fifty dollars, has as available a suffrage as one who has land worth two hundred thousand dollars. Are we for fixing a high property qualification? We reply, that it appears from this debate, that a man can get a freehold in almost any county in the State for fifty dollars, and in some (indeed many) for twenty-five dollars, or for a smaller sum. And yet we are gravely told, that these freeholds, accessible as they are to the industry and exertions of all, constitute an odious aristocracy. Sir, we do not even require that these freeholds should be productive, (as many of them are not) of one cent of revenue. Sir, the beauty of this system, its republican feature, is, that the humblest freeholder is put on a footing with the richest man in the State. It was a little remarkable that the report of the Legislative Committee proposed what I conceived to be a violation of our Constitutional principles on this subject, by requiring that in addition to the quantity of acres required by law, there should be a tax to a certain amount paid. I voted against this restriction, and I am glad it was stricken out by a large majority. I am for depriving no man of a vote, now entitled to it. I care not whether a man's freehold be productive or otherwise. It is his all, and is as dear to him, as the freehold of the owner of thousands of acres is to its proprietor. But it is said, that every man who pays a tax ought to vote—now, what evidence of interest in the community, is furnished by the payment of four cents upon a horse, or paying a poor rate and county levy? Is it even the semblance of testimony, that the person paying it, intends to remain in the Commonwealth? It is also contended that service in the militia, is a proper and valid claim to a vote. It is said the non-freeholder fights your battles—but does not the freeholder do so too? And does he not do another thing, pay for the support of the non-freeholder? War cannot be carried on by men alone: you require munitions of war, provisions and every thing necessary to equip and sustain an army. Without these, numbers are of no avail, indeed injurious. Your army would soon be disorganized without them. In time of peace, the militia service which is common to freeholder and non-freeholder, is light, if not nominal. In time of war, you draw heavily on the property of the country, and then the freeholder is not only bound to fight, but to pay. We have a strong example of this during the last war. During that war, Virginia was thrown very much upon her own resources, and having found that the keeping very large bodies of militia in the field, was very harassing to the people, very expensive, and not very efficient, the Assembly determined on raising ten thousand men for the defence of the State. The law provided, that the expenses of these troops should be assessed on the property of the country, and it would have fallen with great and oppressive weight on the land and slave-owners. Happily, the intervention of peace saved the country from the severe burthens, to which the property-holders would have been subjected. But it serves to show, what ever will be the case, when we are exposed to the calamities incident to war.

The gentleman from Loudoun has stated, that he knows of no particular virtue attached to the soil, that we should select the owners as the sole depositories of political power. All professions are on a par in his estimation. I do not pretend that great virtues may not be found in all the professions and walks of life. But I do believe, if there are any chosen people of God, they are the cultivators of the soil. If there be virtue to be found any where, it would be amongst the middling farmers, who constitute the yeomanry, the bone and sinew of our country. Sir, they are men of moderate desires, they have to labor for their subsistence, and the support of their families; their wishes are bounded by the limits of their small possessions; they are not harassed by envy, by the love of show and splendor, nor agitated by the restless and insatiable passion of ambition. When they lay their heads at night upon their pillows under the consciousness of having spent the day in the discharge of their duties to their families, they enjoy a sweeter sleep under their humble roofs, than frequently do those who repose in gilded palaces. Amid the same description of persons, I should look for independence of character. It is a fact, that our voters are less exposed to influence and intrigue, than any, I believe, in the United States. A man may be popular enough to be elected himself, but he cannot dictate to the voters to elect any other. A man who would attempt this would be apt to be insulted, and I have known illustrious examples of some of the most popular men; aye, Sir, in the zenith of their popularity, who could not control an election in favour of another. Do you ever hear in this State of a man being called, as in some of the States, the partizan of some great name? A Livingston man, or a Clinton man for example? Ask one of our freeholders whose man he is, he will tell you he is his own man. These men know that their land is their own, that they are the lords of the soil; that according to the principles of the common law, their house is their castle, and that no man dare invade either, with impunity. Do you believe, Mr. Chairman, that there is any property which attaches a man so much to the country as the land? There is none. His attachment to his home, is connected with the best sympathies of the human heart. It is the place of his boyish sports, the birth place of his children; and contains the bones of his ancestors. He will love his country which contains a home so dear to him, and defend that country at the hazard of his life.

There is one consideration which shows the propriety of making land the basis of political power. It is, that the land, has always been, and will ever continue to be, the principal source from which all your taxes are derived. The freeholders, if they are an aristocracy, are the most lenient aristocrats who ever existed. From the foundation of our Republic, and long before, land-holders, who are the largest slave-holders too, have paid your principal taxes. We have parted with the customs to the General Government, and the only other sources of revenue of any great extent, are your lands and negroes. The freeholders too, pay a large share of the other taxes, such as taxes on licenses, horses and carriages. You can never expect to see a capitation tax, nor an income tax. They both are odious in their character; the first is very unjust, and the second must be attended with such inquisitorial powers to your officers, and be so easily eluded by fraud, that it will not be attempted. They tried it in England, and it was the cause of overturning the ministry which introduced it. But the great advantage of the freehold system is, that it keeps the Government in the hands of the middling classes. So far from being aristocratic, it is the best safeguard against aristocracy. It places the power in the hands of those who are interested to guard both property and persons against oppression. The idea of aristocracy is absurd. Did you ever hear of an aristocracy of fifty dollar, or twenty-five dollar freeholders? In the hands of these freeholders, personal rights are just as secure as the rights of property. Many of the non-freeholders are the sons of freeholders. Would they support measures which would oppress their own sons? Besides, have not the great body of the freeholders such perfect identity of condition with the non-freeholders, that they could pass no law for the regulation of personal rights which would not equally affect them as well as the non-freeholders. To those who take a superficial view of things, it might appear that placing the power in the hands of men, without regard to their condition, would advance the cause of liberty. Many will tell you, Sir, that they would do this to counteract the influence of wealth in society.

But these men, many of whom are ardent friends of liberty, are unconsciously laboring to undermine the cause of which they mean to be the strenuous advocates. As long as political power is placed as it now is in Virginia, in the hands of the middling classes, who, though not rich, are yet sufficiently so, to secure their independence, you have nothing to fear from wealth. But place power in the hands of those who have none, or a very trivial stake in the community, and you expose the poor and dependent to the influence and seductions of wealth. The extreme rich, and the extreme poor, if not natural allies, will become so in fact. The rich will relieve the necessities of the poor, and the latter will become subservient to the ambition of the rich. You hear nothing of the bribery and corruption of freeholders. No man is hardy enough to attempt it. But extend the Right of Suffrage to every man dependent, as well as independent, and you immediately open the flood-gates of corruption. You will undermine the public and private virtue of your people, and this your boasted Republic, established by the wisdom of your ancestors, and defended at the hazard of their lives, will share the fate of all those which have preceded it, whose gradual decline, and final extinction, it has been the melancholy task of history to record.

Mr. Chairman, the revolution of France has been frequently invoked into this debate, by the gentlemen on the other side; but I cannot see to what useful purpose of argument they have applied it. I do not see that there is any thing very inviting in the progress or termination of that revolution, from which we can infer the propriety of a hasty, inconsiderate and radical change of our institutions. The French, I believe, had cause to be greatly dissatisfied with their ancient Government. During that revolution, though young, I was an enthusiastic admirer of what I believed to be the cause of the people resisting oppression. But the excesses of that revolution, have done more injury to the cause of freedom, than any thing which has happened in modern times. Those excesses have served to rivet the chains of despotism in all the monarchies of Europe. Those who set the revolution in motion, were many of them, I have no doubt, virtuous and enlightened men. But they were more of philosophers and theorists, than practical statesmen. They enlightened the minds of the people. They pointed out the oppressions and tyranny under which they suffered. They raised a storm, which they had not the power to direct, and of which they became the victims. They devised schemes of Government, which were either not adapted to the state of the times, or which the people were incapable of living under. They did not know how free Governments would work: meanwhile, there arose factions, to which revolutions not unfrequently give birth, consisting of men who had nothing to lose and every thing to gain—men dissolute and depraved—who, under the mask of patriotism, were bent on the acquisition of wealth and power. Those persons collecting round them all the men of desperate fortunes, aided by the mobs of

Paris, began by pushing revolutionary principles to an extreme, which those who commenced the work of reformation never contemplated; and because they would not sanction the crimes which were perpetrated by the mountain and other factions, they were brought to the guillotine. Every man must recollect with horror, the bloody scenes, which took place in France, when no age, no sex, no virtues were safe from the infuriated monsters who perpetrated crimes under the profaned name of liberty. I mention not these things in derogation of the cause of freedom. I should rejoice to see free institutions established in every country which willed to be free. But what was the result? After spilling oceans of blood, France flew to the arms of despotism as a refuge from crimes and miseries inflicted under the abused name of liberty—and where is she now? Restored to the dominion of the same odious dynasty, to escape which, she suffered so long and so cruelly. The misfortunes she has undergone, have strengthened what is called the cause of legitimacy, by uniting all the despots of the world, in a crusade against liberty, and rendering desperate the friends of liberal principles in every part of Europe. I have dwelt too long on this subject, and should not have said thus much, but that the example of France has been so often quoted on us. Our lot in this Commonwealth is a happy one, if we would but be content with it. Our institutions are free, no man is oppressed, and every man is secure in the enjoyment of the fruits of honest industry. Our Government has no taint of monarchy, or aristocracy, and power is in the hands of the great body of the yeomanry of the country. What can a people want more!

It was not my purpose to answer the gentleman from Loudoun in detail. I wished to give a general view of the principles, on which I vindicate the freehold Right of Suffrage, though it may be capable of some modifications. I will make a few remarks, however, on the charges of oppression and misrule, which the gentleman has brought against the existing Government. The gentleman must have been hard pressed for facts to illustrate his opinion, when he has resorted to a period of remote antiquity, the year 1656, to quote an insulated provision in the Statute Book, to shew oppression in the freeholders. I allude to the exemption of voters and overseers from militia services. This law remained in force only a few years—we hear of no instance of complaint against it—and we do not know but it originated in sound policy, which might have required, that in the then state of infancy of the Colony, surrounded as they were by hostile tribes of Indians, and trembling for their existence, it might have been necessary to keep a certain portion of the population employed in raising the means of subsistence, whilst others were engaged in guarding the frontiers, or repelling incursions.

The other specifications of supposed abuses, appear to me unimportant in their character, and susceptible of easy answers. But I have already trespassed too long on the indulgence of the Committee, and will conclude with observing, that when the talented gentleman from Loudoun, after the other side have been so long called on, to point out any abuses which have existed under this Government, has only been able to find such as he has enumerated, it amounts to the highest eulogium, which can be pronounced on our institutions.

Mr. Leigh now moved that when the Convention adjourned, it adjourn to meet at eleven o'clock; which motion gave rise to a desultory debate, in which Messrs. Leigh, Mercer, Stanard, Doddridge and Nicholas took part, and which resulted in the adoption of Mr. Leigh's motion, by a large majority; and then, on Mr. Doddridge's motion, the House adjourned.

THURSDAY, November 19, 1829.

The Convention met at 11 o'clock, and was opened with prayer by the Rev. Mr Taylor of the Baptist Church.

The House went again into Committee of the Whole, Mr. Powell in the Chair:

And the question being on the following amendment of Mr. Wilson, as modified at the request of Mr. Henderson:

"*Resolved*, That every free white male citizen of this Commonwealth, of the age of twenty-one years, and upwards, who shall have resided in the State two years, and in the county where he proposes to vote, one year next preceding the time of offering such vote; who shall have been enrolled in the militia, if subject to military duty; and who shall have paid all levies and taxes assessed upon him, or his property, for the year preceding that in which he offers to vote, shall have a right to vote for members of the General Assembly: *Provided*, That no person shall be permitted to exercise the Right of Suffrage, who is a pauper; who is of unsound mind; who has been convicted of any infamous crime; or who shall be a non-commissioned officer or private soldier, seaman or marine in the regular service of the United States, or of this

Commonwealth; and the Legislature shall prescribe the mode of trying and determining disputes concerning the said qualifications of voters, whenever the right of a person to vote shall be questioned."

The Chairman rose to put the question, when

Mr. Trezvant of Southampton took the floor in opposition to its passage.

Mr. T. said, that he had not intended to have said any thing upon the subject under the consideration of the Committee, nor had he expected to have said any thing upon any other subject which might be discussed in the Convention; but as the proposed amendment, the question under debate, notwithstanding its importance, was about to be submitted without any other discussion than that which it received yesterday, he felt himself impelled to submit a few remarks—remarks of course, which could not be the result of any previous preparation, and which necessarily must be desultory in their character. What was the question under consideration? The object of the amendment was to abolish the present modification of the Right of Suffrage, and to substitute in its place, one entirely new to us. When a people undertake to make a change in their political institutions, affecting the foundation of Government, it behoves them to proceed with the utmost caution and circumspection. We should recollect that we are about to introduce an experiment which is to operate upon the affections, prejudices, and long-established habits of the community, and the consequences cannot be distinctly foreseen or foretold. A numerous population, falling not much short of a million, cannot at once throw off their old usages and customs, and accommodate themselves to an entirely new order of things, radically different from that under which they had lived in peace and tranquillity, without incurring the risk of many and great evils. This Government had existed for more than fifty years, and under it, the people had enjoyed happiness and contentment. There were, it is true, occasional clamors arising from local causes and prejudices, and not from any real defects in the form of Government; and he hoped this amendment would not be adopted to allay such complaints. In that part of the State in which he resided, he had not heard of any serious complaint touching the Right of Suffrage. The people there, in this respect, at least, were satisfied; why then adopt this new qualification of the Right of Suffrage, which in his poor opinion, would put to hazard the best interests of the country, and even endanger the liberties of the people? We are called upon to substitute for the Freehold Suffrage, that which, if it be not Universal Suffrage, falls but little short of it. It is proposed that those who are twenty-one years of age, who bear arms, and have resided twelve months in the county in which they propose to vote, should have this right, and the adoption of the principle amounted in effect, to what he called Universal Suffrage. He was told by one gentleman, (to the correctness of whose statistics he did not, however, feel himself bound to subscribe,) that the adoption of this measure would add to the number of voters in the State more than 60,000, the present number being somewhat more than 40,000. Thus, the power of the Government is to be transferred from the hands of the 40,000, who have the deepest interest at stake, to the 60,000, who have comparatively but little interest. It is no idle chimera of the brain, that the possession of land furnishes the strongest evidence of permanent, common interest with, and attachment to, the community. Much had been already said by gentlemen on both sides, demonstrating the powerful influence of local attachment upon the conduct of man, and he could not be made to comprehend how that passion could be more effectually brought into action, than by a consciousness of the fact, that he was the owner of the spot which he could emphatically call his home. It was upon this foundation he wished to place the Right of Suffrage. This was the best general standard which could be resorted to, for the purpose of determining whether the persons to be invested with the Right of Suffrage, were such persons as could be, consistently with the safety and well-being of the community, entrusted with the exercise of that right. Much had been said in the discussion yesterday, of the oppression and impolicy resulting from an adherence to the present restricted Suffrage, which he presumed was intended to produce some effect upon public opinion, for he could not suppose it was intended as a serious argument addressed to this Committee.

Among other things, we had been seriously told by one gentleman, that many of the citizens of this Commonwealth, non-freeholders, labouring under a sense of the great injustice done them in withholding this Right of Suffrage, were known to abandon their native State, and to emigrate to other States in the Union where Suffrage was Universal, that thereby they might enjoy that most invaluable right. This was a mere figment of the fancy. It is admitted on all sides, that to obtain the qualification of a voter, the expenditure of a trifle in amount, would be all that was necessary. Yet, we are told that the persecuted citizens of this Commonwealth are migrating to other parts of the Union, to avoid this odious principle, and doing this at an expense too, much beyond what would be required to make them freeholders. Gentlemen deal in fanciful suggestions. He would venture to hazard the opinion, that no man that ever lived in that portion of the State from which he came, was ever known to fly to other countries to avoid that or any other kind of political oppression. The idea was a new one, and he hoped it had sprung from the fruitful imagination of the gentleman. Let those who indulge in these fancies, enquire of such Virginians as may have emigrated to other States, what their opinions are upon this subject. Will they be found to revile Virginia with curses, because, while citizens here, they enjoyed not the Right of Suffrage? No. They would hold a very different language, and instead of complaints of tyranny and oppression, they would speak in terms of the profoundest veneration of her political institutions. Virginia had not so completely fallen from her high estate, as some gentlemen had been pleased to represent; and if she had suffered any deterioration, it did not result so much from her own councils as from those of another Government, which in many respects exercises a controul over her destinies. Is it because she, in common with the other Southern States, is labouring under a deplorable commercial depression, that we are called upon to abandon the old and established order of things, and look for an improvement of our condition from the future councils of the State Government? We may pull down this Government under this vain expectation, but he entertained serious apprehensions that we could not build up another which could long endure. No, Sir; the condition in which we find ourselves, has not arisen from, nor can it be improved by, the policy of the State Government, in the regulation of her internal and domestic concerns. It could not be effected by the introduction of Universal Suffrage, as intended by the proposition of the gentleman from Monongalia; for since, so few would be excluded, he felt himself justified in calling it Universal. He indulged a sanguine hope that the Committee was not prepared to adopt this bold innovation—he would say this dangerous experiment, fraught in his opinion, with mischief inconceivable. He said that he had listened with much attention to the gentleman from Loudoun, (Mr. Henderson,) who addressed the Committee yesterday. He had expected that that gentleman would have furnished some strong and conclusive arguments in support of that side of this question which he had espoused—he had been much disappointed, not because the gentleman did not possess the requisite talents and ingenuity to sustain himself with ability in the maintenance of any opinions he might advance, but he was disposed to ascribe his disappointment to the fact, that the subject did not admit of more conclusive arguments. This Committee no doubt would look at the facts according to that gentleman's own statement, uninfluenced by his eloquent effusions. And what are those facts? To substitute for the freeholder, a class of sixty thousand people, who are to controul the operations of a Government, in the correct and judicious administration of which the forty thousand freeholders, with the whole land of the Commonwealth in their hands, and of course possessed of all other species of property, in an amount greatly exceeding that held by the non-freeholders. In other words, the great landed interest is to be placed in the keeping of a majority of twenty thousand, who have no direct and immediate connection with it, and who even as it regards all other property, have an interest infinitely short of that which the freeholders possess. If this principle were introduced in a Government administered without the intervention of public agents, it would be neither more nor less than a pure democracy; and we have yet to learn whether, if introduced in our Government, it will not end in ruinous consequences. Gentlemen who advocate this extraordinary extension of the Right of Suffrage, are compelled to admit the necessity of fixing upon some limitation. Upon their own principles, they exclude three-fourths of the white population from the possession of any political power. According to their own favourite theory, we do not violate any existing rights by depositing this power where it can be safely lodged, in the hands of the freeholders—he said he was willing to accede to a proposition extending the Right of Suffrage, but it should rest upon, or be closely and intimately connected with, the ownership of land—that interest must be considered in any extension of the Right of Suffrage which would meet with his support.

The gentleman from Loudoun rests the claim of non-freeholders to the Right of Suffrage, upon the military services which they are called upon to render to the country. An apt reply has been already given to this pretension. Freeholders are called upon to render like military services, and in addition thereto, are required to furnish the "sinews of war." They fight by the side of non-freeholders in their country's battles, and almost exclusively furnish the pecuniary means of sustaining the Government in peace, as well as war. It would be a waste of time to detain the Committee longer, in discussing this subject, with a view to expose the extravagance of the scheme presented by the proposition under consideration. He would not refer to passing events of the day, in support of what he was about to say, but he would remind gentlemen that history did not furnish an example of a Government founded upon Universal Suffrage, that had not degenerated to a despotism.

A comparison had been made between the other States of this Union and this State, much to the disparagement of Virginia. It was not his intention to have passed any encomiums upon his native State. It did not become him to deal in empty or substantial compliments on her institutions or her people. It should be left to others less interested, to pass judgment upon these matters—but he trusted he should be excused in expressing the opinion, that in most respects she could bear a comparison with any of her sister States. In what is she deficient? In what respect is she behind them? Are her people deficient in patriotism? Are they wanting in those virtues which ennoble man? Is she inferior to any of the States in moral character? In all these respects, he would say she stood pre-eminently high. With all the supposed defects in her character, he would be unwilling to exchange it for that of any other country—not even for that of the land of steady habits. Passing in review the whole Union, from Maine to its most Southern border, no cause of mortification would result from the comparison. Has she not produced a long line of Statesmen, and given birth to a galaxy of warriors, whose names she can proudly point to in refutation of this charge? Sir, in point of character, she yields nothing to her sister States, and for this character she is mainly indebted to those political institutions which it seems we are resolved shall give place to a new order of things; so far at least, as that can be effected by the adoption of the proposition offered by the gentleman from Monongalia.

We have been referred to France, by the gentleman from Loudoun, and have been told that the oppression on the part of the nobles and priesthood, had brought on the revolution in that country. We have no nobles here, neither have we any priesthood practising oppression upon the people. He was sure that no oppressions of that kind were practised in the Eastern part of the State. He had no personal knowledge of the actual state of things beyond the Blue Ridge, but he had always believed the people of that region of the State to be an honest, virtuous, and intelligent race of men, and as little disposed as any people upon earth, to submit to the sort of oppression spoken of by that gentleman. It is true that these oppressions did exist in that country, and did give rise to that revolution which was attended with such horrors and waste of human life. But, Sir, this very principle—this Universal Suffrage, had its full share in bringing upon that devoted country, the calamities to which it was exposed.

He was sensible that his observations were of an extremely desultory character. He had appeared before the Committee as he had before stated, unexpectedly to himself, and his principal object was to occupy a small portion of its time, that others who he knew could do greater justice to the subject, might have an opportunity of submitting their views. He was sorry that he had detained the Committee so long. He hoped the Committee would reject the proposition under consideration. If, however, the proposition could be modified or amended, so as to accord with his views, he would vote for it: otherwise, he could not. He was not disposed to trust to speculative theories. He begged leave, however, before he resumed his seat, to ask the Committee to advert to the manner in which our popular elections were conducted, and he would appeal to them if we were not placed in an enviable situation in that respect, compared to the condition of those States in the Union where Suffrage was more extended than in this. We hear nothing of those commotions in this State which frequently occur at the elections in other parts of the United States, where Universal Suffrage, or something approaching nearly to it, prevails. He had been for many years familiar with the manner in which the elections in this State had been conducted, as he supposed every other member of this body had been, and had no doubt he should be sustained by all, when he said that Virginia in this respect would bear an honorable comparison with any other part of the world. No popular elections were conducted with more respect for the laws, or could be conducted with more regard to decorum. If we add sixty thousand to the number of voters, we must necessarily change the mode of voting. He was attached to the viva voce manner of voting, because it was the most honest and manly mode. Extend the Right of Suffrage, and you must resort to the ballot-box: otherwise, these voters cannot act independently—they must have the means of concealing their votes. That change, as simple as it might appear to some, in his estimation, would let in a flood of fraud and corruption which would end in the destruction of every thing like honesty and independence in our elections.

Mr. Doddridge proposed that in taking the vote, the names of the Committee should be called over.

The Chair in reply, remarked, that it was not strictly in order, in Committee of the Whole, to call over names. He begged to make the suggestion, that the divisions on questions in Committee were to be regarded only in the light of comparisons of views; and when the names are announced, such is the pride of opinion, that members might be inclined afterwards to adhere to opinions, which they might have been disposed to change, but for their premature committal before the public eye. He merely made the suggestion. The Committee might take it for what it was worth.

The Chairman rose to put the question, when Mr. Bayly addressed the Chair:

Mr. Chairman,—Before you put the question on the amendment, I wish to express my opinion in favor of extending the Right of Suffrage, which is now under consideration. I am not in the habit of apologizing, when I consider it to be my duty to address this Committee, and I shall not do it now. I will say, that although I did intend to speak on the proposition now under discussion, at some other time, and expected that other gentlemen would have occupied your attention on this day; yet, as the question is about to be taken, and as my constituents are among the foremost in the call for this Convention, for the express wish of having the Right of Suffrage extended, I owe it to myself and to them, to give the reasons why I shall vote for the amendment of the gentleman from Monongalia.

In the year 1807, the people of Accomack petitioned the General Assembly to call a Convention, to extend the Right of Suffrage to other persons than freeholders, and to redress grievances existing under the Constitution. At that time, very few freeholders, in the other four counties, which I represent in part, wished for such a measure. But at this time, with the great change of public opinion that has taken place in these counties, and the almost unanimous wish of the freeholders of the county of Accomack, there can be no doubt, but a very large majority of the freeholders of the district, are in favor of extending the Right of Suffrage to others than land-holders.

When I was elected to this Convention, I considered it to be my duty to inform myself of the alterations and amendments to the existing Constitution, which the people in every part of the State demanded, and to correct these evils in the new Constitution. And when I shall frankly state to this Committee some of the great amendments in the Constitution, which my constituents wish us to make, and as I most cordially unite with them, in the hope, that those improvements will be made, I am not to be considered a leveller, a revolutionist, or a radical reformer: such a character does not belong to me, it is far from me. A sense of duty points to me, to pursue that course, which will lead to the correction of the evils complained of in every part of the State; which I hope and expect, will be so amended by the Constitution we shall submit to the people, that they will cheerfully ratify it.

If I thought that the adoption of this amendment would endanger the safety of property, or would put power in the hands of those, who would in any manner abuse it, I would not vote for the amendment, but would give it my most decided disapprobation. It may be dangerous, perhaps, where the non-freeholders are destitute of property and principle. Such is not the character nor condition of the people among whom I live, who were among the first to favor the extension of the Right of Suffrage, and are now so unanimous for it. It may be, that the peculiar situation of that people; the difficulty for all to acquire a freehold, and the denial of that right, to those who have a freehold less than twenty-five acres of land, may be a great cause in creating that unanimity, which at this time exists among them upon this question. They have not the facilities of acquiring freeholds, that exist in other parts of the State, to qualify themselves to be voters, where there is so much waste and useless land. If a man could by law vote in the county where he resides, upon the requisite freehold, situated in any other county in the State, he might purchase a freehold in the West, where the rocks and mountains cover half their counties, for one or two dollars.

Penned up in a peninsula, every one who wishes to obtain a vote, cannot realize that blessing under the present system, however much he may prize the privilege, whatever may be his standing or even his means. The territory is small, and the tracts of twenty-five acres, which are necessary to make the qualification, are not easily to be obtained at any price; but, although the qualification of electors are thus confined to the soil, the respectability of the inhabitants is not exclusively derived from that source. I have never believed, that the qualification ought to depend on the right in the soil. No such principle is believed to be correct among the people with whom I live. They do not draw their subsistence solely from the land. A great proportion of them are worthy mechanics, and many earn their bread by ploughing the ocean. It is not easy for such men, on their first entering into life, to lay up 2 or $ 300, to purchase the requisite freehold, to qualify them to vote. However easily that might be obtained in other parts of the State, having vast mountains of worthless land, where fifty acres may be acquired by a week's labour, enterprize and industry cannot always be so soon rewarded in a dense population, where land is in great demand, and is of high value. I have never considered the possession of a freehold, as the best evidence and test of permanent and common interest with, and attachment to, the community. I believe, that many situations and circumstances in life furnish tests as certain.

The Bill of Rights declares, "that election of members to the General Assembly ought to be free, and that all men having sufficient evidence of permanent common interest with, and attachment to, the community, have the Right of Suffrage." And yet so much has been said on the necessity of disfranchising the soldier! No such necessity applies to the Eastern Shore. There it is considered the sacred duty of all to protect their country against any invading enemy. During the two wars in which this country has been engaged, there were no exempts, nor was there one example of any man shrinking from his duty; all rushed to the post of danger the moment the alarm was given, poor and rich. The most aged was found quite as ready as the young. No man was then disqualified from the protection of the property of the freeholder; for, all showed that they had a common interest with, and attachment to, the community.

It is said, that the soldier cannot be trusted—the militia-man cannot be trusted, without he has a freehold. This is a doctrine which ought not to be entertained. Compare these objections—a more patriotic band of men never entered the army of Washington, than the 9th Virginia Continental Regiment—they fought by his side at Brandywine, Germantown, Trenton, Princeton and Monmouth, and their valor is well known to the venerable President of this Convention; and I rejoice that he has not forsaken the soldiers of the revolution, for they never have forsaken him. But, Sir, the independence of the country being obtained, they disband themselves and return home in beggary: and these men who have saved the Constitution of their country, by that very Constitution, are *expelled* from the polls to make way for some old tory: they have no *right* to be there, because *they* have *shewn* no *permanent interest* in, and *attachment* to, the community. Sir, this scene has occurred in every old county in the State, and in many is yearly witnessed. Such things roused the people to complain, and induced them to vote for a Convention—I mean the freeholders. They cannot, they will not believe, that such aged and virtuous men ought not to participate in the elective franchise, under the very Government that their valor established.

Is the proposition of the gentleman from Monongalia, a project of the non-freeholders? No, Sir; it is the wish of the freeholders themselves, to restore to the non-freeholders those rights which they ought always to have had. If 21,896 to 16,637, gives any expression of their will, they have said that they are desirous to abandon the distinction they now hold.

If this Government belongs to the freeholders, it is *they* who say we are willing to part with this exclusive power, and share it with our brethren. The freeholders possessing the Government, and the sovereignty being in the people, and the freeholders desire that the rest of their fellow-citizens shall be admitted to participate in political power—what good reason can, or has been assigned for this Convention to oppose that desire? It is not the non-freeholders merely: it is the freeholders themselves, who complain of the existing state of things. I have never heard the non-freeholders half so loud to call for this Convention, as the freeholders themselves.

It was from the most thickly settled part of the county of Accomack, and from those who reside near the Maryland line, that the demand to extend the Right of Suffrage was most earnest. Many of the freeholders have cut up their farms already into small tenements, to give to their sons the right of voting; so that they can lop off no more, without depriving themselves of that privilege. And those who reside in the north of the county, having a constant intercourse with the people of the State of Maryland, trading to their town, they become acquainted with their institutions, and they see how the extended Right of Suffrage operates there, and finding no evil resulting from it, consequently they are anxious for the change in their own State.

Farms are divided and sub-divided so often, that even that cannot be further done to any advantage, so as to leave a support to a family practising the greatest industry and frugality. The farm being now so small that it can only be given to one son, and generally the first born, he remains at home with his father—cultivates the land—supports him in his old age—and at his death inherits the freehold. The other sons are sent from home, generally to the towns in Maryland and Pennsylvania, to learn useful mechanical trades; they return, they will not leave the view of the smoke of their father's dwelling; the old man, perhaps, can cut off an acre of land from his little farm, or purchase one in the neighbourhood, on which is erected a ship yard or a blacksmith shop—these young men enter with great skill and industry on their trades, and very soon marry: these useful mechanics, having returned to your State, full of patriotic love for this Commonwealth, and as much attached to her interests as the freeholder. Yet, you are going to say to them, in the Constitution you are now making, "Young man, you have returned to your country, with a perfect knowledge of your useful profession, you are raising up a family of great promise to the welfare of Virginia, but you get your living by throwing the broad-axe, the sledge-hammer, or the saw, you cannot be trusted, you have not that attachment to your country as your oldest brother, who has remained at home, and followed the plough-handles; he must be trusted to vote for himself and you."

Gentlemen say the non-freeholders do not wish this privilege to be extended to them. I know of no such description of men; and if there be many of that opinion in this ancient Commonwealth, they are fit subjects for a King. A free man who is willing to be governed by laws, and voluntarily prefers to relinquish to other men the authority to elect the Lawgiver, is a slave already, and he is not a fit member of a Republic.

Much has been said about confusion at elections. I do not believe, if we extend the Right of Suffrage as far as any of us wish, that there is danger on this score. Our people are not of that riotous character. I have never seen any confusion in that part of the country where I live, at elections. I have never seen nor heard of any confusion in any part of Virginia at elections. But reject this proposition, and let the old restrictions and disqualifications continue, and you will not be long without confusion, and great confusion, at the polls, and from the polls. You *must* show a disposition to *redress* the evils of which the people complain, or you must expect that their complaints will assume a louder tone. But suppose the people shall ever become corrupt, and their own worst enemies at elections, (I entertain no fear that they ever will,) and that riot and bloodshed should be the consequence. There is a remedy for this, and a simple one: it is to lay off the counties into small electoral districts, and you prevent all danger of riot; (and as a gentleman near me suggests,) let the elections be held on the same day in all the districts, and that will prevent large collections of people at one place, and consequently prevent confusion. No, Sir, there is no such danger. Have your people ever shown a disposition for insurrection? Have you ever seen or heard of a disposition among them to riot and insurrection? Have you ever seen or heard of a disposition among them to rise in arms against the General Government? although at times they have been so much excited against the administration of that Government. They can be trusted; they may with the utmost safety, even if you extend to them the utmost limits of the elective power, *be trusted*.

My worthy friend from Richmond, (Mr. Nicholas,) (and I use that expression only in reference to old and tried friends,) tells us about revolutionary France, and the evils which grew out of it, in that country. Much good has resulted to the people from that revolution. Why, Sir, it may have happened, that the heads of one or two contemptible nobles may have fallen into the sack of the executioner, brought on by their own vices and treason, but nobody lamented their fate. The people were bound down in chains, which the Government refused, not only to knock off, but to slacken: they were broken and torn asunder; and like the bursting of a volcano, desolated all around. But, is that the state of things here? Is there any monarch, or rich nobleman, to throw his gold among the people at our elections, to promote the utmost confusion and riot? Let us not take for our guide facts recorded by pensioned authors during the French revolution, and pretend that what has happened to that country and its institutions, will happen to our institutions, but rather take for authority the Whigs of *this* country. Jefferson saw the scenes at the commencement of the revolution; he was Minister of the United States to France. Was he the enemy of Universal Suffrage? No, Sir; on the contrary, the longer he lived, the more he was attached to it, even unto death.

Did the sight of the scenes of that revolution, even under Robespierre, cure the venerable gentleman from Loudoun, (Mr. Monroe,) he also was Minister to France, from his attachment to the rights of man? He has told you that there is nothing to fear from extending Suffrage in this country. Ours are a different kind of people, and on them I place all my confidence. They will not break out in mobs of sanguinary violence: they only ask their rights as freemen, and for this purpose the amendment is offered. I am desirous to know why it is that certain parts of the Commonwealth adjacent to other States where Suffrage is enjoyed to the fullest extent, are all in favor of this great change? I mean the freeholders in those districts. You see the South-West part of the State which joins Tennessee and Kentucky; the North-West which joins Ohio and Pennsylvania; and the North-East which joins Maryland, all anxious for this change. Can it be, that all the wisdom lies in the centre of the State? The people of those parts of the State to which I have referred, have witnessed and know how this thing operates upon their neighbours; and are, with very few exceptions, in favor of extending this right to freemen. The result of the trial is conclusive. We are not making an experiment, we are following those already made. Yes, the experiment is not to be made; the plan has been tried by other States; and the result is, that their population and prosperity has most rapidly increased, and they prove that man can govern himself.

The question of Internal Improvement in this State, has somehow got into this debate—how, I do not comprehend exactly. I am in favor of Internal Improvement to a limited extent, with the aid only of the fund set apart for that purpose; and my main reason for having gone with the West on the subject of their roads and division of counties, has been my pride—yes, Sir, my pride as a Virginian. I believe it is our interest and duty to hold out and to give every inducement to emigrants from the Northern States and from Europe, to settle that part of the country, and to retain our own population at home. We have seen Virginia fall from being the first State of the Union, to that of the third; and without great exertions on our part, she will fall still lower. I look to the West as my hope, to see her maintain her present station in these States. Extend the elective franchise, make your system of Government liberal and republican, and you will fill Western Virginia with inhabitants, and all parts of your State with a more dense population. The Right of Suffrage has hitherto been confined to freeholders exclusively. Will any one give me a reason why it should be required of a voter for members of the General Assembly, when the same requisite is not demanded of those who fill the high departments of the State? Your Generals, your Governors, your Judges, your Treasurer, your Auditor, are not required to be freeholders. *They* are not required to possess this emblem of "permanent, common interest with, and attachment to, the community." That *evidence* is exacted alone from the native born citizen, the honest planter, when he goes to the polls. So also in the Federal Government. The President, the Senators, the Representatives, the Judges, and all others from them downward are placed in office, without enquiring whether they are freeholders or not. Can any man give a plausible reason, why a man is fit to fill all those high offices, and not fit to come to the polls? If you can trust men in all high offices without an interest in the soil, why cannot you trust a voter also, without that interest in the land? I will not reply to epithets that gentlemen have used on both sides—such as aristocrat, republican, &c. I may be called either: those who know me best, are republicans by acts and deeds, and *not* by words. They have confided their interest to me, and, I trust, it will not be abused. Make a Constitution that the people will gladly approve—redress all the evils complained of by the old Constitution, and you may call it aristocracy, oligarchy and every thing but a Republic; yet the people will ratify it.

In Virginia, epithets have lost their power: I will vote for such a Constitution as my constituents wish; nor will I concede to my friend from Richmond (Mr. Nicholas,) that he and those who are with him on this question, are the exclusive friends of the people; I know of no act they have done, which entitles them to use the phraseology, "*We the friends of the people.*" If his friend meant, that they were the friends of the freeholders, he will find that a majority of the freeholders are in favor of this change; and if he meant that they were the friends of the non-freeholders, I suspect that the friendship will not be accepted.

The gentleman has told you, that he was Attorney General for twenty years. Was this said to give his opinions greater weight with the community? I know the gentleman was Attorney General, and Virginia never had a better; and I know also, that I aided to put him there. At the age of twenty-two, I voted for the gentleman, (who was then about the same age,) and I have never repented for so doing, because I have never had cause for such repentance. At that time, I knew him only from report, which was strong in his favor; a young man of great expectations to them who knew him; but I had a stronger reason; he was the son of that old revolutionary and genuine Whig, Robert Carter Nicholas, Treasurer of Virginia; and a scion from that pure stock, might safely be trusted in any station he desired, for he would honor it. I cannot admit that he and those who act with him on this question, are the only friends of the people; if so, why did he cease to be the agent, the officer, the representative of the people, I will not say servant, I dislike the word? I trust my friend will excuse me, if I recommend to him to strike out all that part of his speech relating to Bank stock, lest his friends, the people, enquire what *office* he now holds.*

Another idea the gentleman suggested—perhaps I mistake him—I hope I do—I take no notes. He told the Committee, I think, that no reliance was to be placed on men, who hold Bank stock; that the man who holds Bank stock, is not to be trusted like a man who stands upon the soil. Sir, in that opinion I agree. Yes, Sir, I agree with the gentleman—the Bank stock-man may sell out to-day and be gone to-morrow; and a man who stands on his *own* land, is more entitled to confidence, than he whose estate is in Bank stock; a Bank stock-man is not a Virginia man. The Bank stock-man now, is not like the Bank stock-man when the old Constitution was made. The people, at that time, when they went to the Treasury, of which Robert Carter Nicholas held the key, received *hard* money and gold, and would be content even with cut money, bits and half bits. There was then in the Treasury the old English guinea, and the Spanish doubloon, half joes and pistoles. But now they are all gone, and with them, the golden American Eagle, with all its brood, has taken flight to a distant land. Go now to the Treasury, and what do you get? To be sure the paper currency is good now, but few there are who know how long it will be good.

Virginia before has had a paper currency; the old continental paper money was good, when first issued; and although it fell to nothing, the people even now keep it, venerate, and revere it, and think it a great blessing that it was made, and so it was: for it carried this Commonwealth triumphantly through the revolution, and thus rendered a blessing on the country. Not so with all the Bank paper—*the paper money* of the present day; for, some Bank paper has become so worthless, as to be of no other use than to be given to the children.

* Mr. Nicholas is President of the Farmers' Bank of Virginia. The money of the Treasury is kept in that Bank and in the Bank of Virginia.

I know the time has been when the people of the United States might be caught by names, and, if my friend from Richmond will take it in good humour, I would request him and his associates, if ever they should happen to be put upon a Central Committee, and should send printed tickets to some remote parts of the State upon the supposition that the people could not write, not to head the tickets the "People's Ticket," the "American System," "Internal Improvements," "Rail Roads;" for it will give their friends trouble to cut such trash off. For, I can assure him, that in some parts of the State, this will be absolutely necessary. Such titles are mere chaff. The people are not now to be deceived by names any longer, nor prevailed on to agree to a restriction of the Right of Suffrage to the freehold. You may christen the new Constitution by whatever name you will; if you do not liberally extend the Right of Suffrage, and reform other great abuses which has got into the Government under the old Constitution, they will not vote for the new Constitution, but will have another Convention, which will do what this Convention *ought* to do.

Another cause of dissatisfaction, is the personal labour exacted of the non-freeholders, in making and repairing the roads of the Commonwealth. My constituents do not of themselves complain of the labour, for it is scarcely felt in the county: the roads there are kept in repair by one day's labour in the year, and are the best roads in the State; but their complaint is of the principle. You exclude them from the polls, and you compel them to labour on the road, against the wish of 21,896 freeholders, who voted for a call of this Convention, to 16,637, who voted to continue this oppressive system; and if you send a Constitution to the people with such oppression not redressed, how long do you expect the people will suffer them to remain so? You have to insert a clause in the Constitution you are now making, providing for the mode and power of future amendments. After that, is it expected that this odious restriction of the Right of Suffrage will remain in the Constitution three years? And if you do not engraft such a provision as to amendments, you will have another Convention in less than three years. Sir, is it not wise—is it not politic—to give up something to the feelings and wishes of the people—and if you please so to call it, even to their prejudices and ignorance? And he is an unwise statesman who does not consult even the prejudices of the people of this country. We are here for that very purpose to consult their wishes and opinions, and make a Constitution accordingly. It is not expected that we can make the best Constitution that can be made, but it *is* expected that we shall make such a one as our constituents wish, and is suited to the times and to them, to the end that they shall be prosperous and happy under it. We have only to make the changes which are asked for by our sovereigns, the people, and they will be grateful, and we shall be honoured with their approbation. Mr. Chairman, I have a very great desire that the amendment of the gentleman from Monongalia should prevail. It will be like oil thrown on the troubled ocean. It will calm the agitation of the public mind, which is now so alarming. I hope this debate will be extended. I wish to hear what the people of every part of the State think and wish upon this subject. There are gentlemen in this Committee, who are not accustomed to speak, but have the strongest intellect. I think it is their duty to cast light upon this question, and state particularly the wishes of the people with whom they live. I have endeavoured to discharge this duty, although not to my satisfaction. I have heard eloquence, and great eloquence in this House. But there is in this Assembly, another class of members, besides the eloquent speakers. I refer to the silent members, who, I believe, know more what the people wish upon this occasion, and feel more for what the people complain of, than the eloquent gentlemen who have so often occupied the floor. To them I look with hope, and I trust I shall not look in vain. I repeat my desire that the debate should be continued.

Mr. M'Coy said, that under the present state of things he would not vote for this amendment. He would not say he would not vote for it under another state of things. It would depend upon what basis of Representation would be adopted. If the white population should be taken, he would be willing to restrict the Right of Suffrage; but if the basis of property be taken, then he would be willing to extend the right of voting to more persons, for the purpose of balancing that influence of wealth which might be infused into our system. He made this remark to obviate any charge of inconsistency which might be hereafter brought against him.

Mr. Scott asked, what would be the condition of any who have the qualification, if they have not paid their tax. If he who has the property, and is assessed, should be returned on the pay books as delinquent, will he not be entitled to vote? If the man who is not assessed in any property may vote, will not the man who is assessed, but who has not paid his tax, be entitled to his vote?

Mr. Wilson said, it was his intention to include those who were not assessed for any tax, provided they were not subject to any of the disqualifications which were specified. But as to the man who has property, and is fairly assessed, yet refuses to pay, he evinces such a disregard for the community, that he ought to be excluded from the privilege of giving his vote.

Mr. Morgan of Monongalia, then rose and addressed the Committee as follows:

Mr. Chairman: Before the question be put to the Committee, I wish to submit a few remarks in favor of the adoption of the amendment now under consideration.

The subject is very properly deemed by every member of this body, one of great importance. It involves the sovereign rights of the people—rights too, which when restrained, ought to be restrained with great care. We are told by able writers on the subject, that the right of voting in the appointment of Legislators, is a sovereign right, and one of the first importance in free Governments. It is a sovereign right, and must be so considered here. I presume then, Sir, that it can only be abridged so far as shall be necessary for the public safety and the public good. And our inquiry is, how far can this right be safely extended? or what is a proper restraint upon it? We all agree that good Government depends very much upon the determination of this question.

I believe, Sir, that the very best form of Government for the promotion of human happiness and safety, is dictated by the natural love of liberty and equality, implanted in every human heart; and in every act of mine upon this floor, I shall be guided by this notion. I shall pursue that course which I think best calculated to secure the enjoyment of the greatest possible portion of the rights of man to the people of this Commonwealth. Government is, or ought to be instituted, not for the restraint of those rights, but for their security and enlargement. We are not to look for man by himself in the forest, but in society, where he can only be found. He is a social being by nature—he was made to live in society, and cannot live without it. In my humble judgment, (which, however, I do not presume to put in competition with the judgment of this body,) society may be so ordered as to enable man to enjoy all his natural rights, in a much more perfect and ample manner, than he can possibly do alone, in the unbroken forest.

In the few remarks which I propose submitting for the consideration of the Committee, I shall endeavor to argue from facts to conclusions, and not by mere declamation, as I think was the course of the gentleman who preceded me in opposition to the amendment of my colleague, (Mr. Wilson.) It is from facts we are to look for correct conclusions, and I know of no better course of reasoning on the affairs of Government, than to look into facts and circumstances connected with other Governments, similar to those in our own, and the effects, and to conclude that similar facts and circumstances here, would produce similar effects.

The gentleman of the city of Richmond, (Mr. Nicholas,) on yesterday, from his course of declamation, came to the conclusion, that non-freeholders could not love Virginia. His principal argument consisted in the fact, that the holder of Bank stock in this city might go to the office, transfer his stock, and in a few hours have himself conveyed to the State of Maryland. I pray you, Sir, cannot the land-holder do the same, by going to another office, (the clerk's office,) and there transfer his land? This sovereign right never can, or ought to depend upon the ease or facility of the mere alienation of property. No, Sir, it must depend upon higher considerations.

The gentleman across the way, (Mr. Trezvant,) seems alarmed at the amendment, because it contains what he calls *Universal Suffrage*. I would call it General Suffrage. It is possible, however, that his objections have been induced by an intimate acquaintance with the improper exercise of the Right of Suffrage by free negroes in the elections in North Carolina. I believe the gentleman resides near that State. Or, perhaps his argument is drawn from the fact, which he has given the Committee, that some gentleman of his acquaintance, raised in Virginia, who removed to some of the Western States, where the Suffrage may be said to be general, resided there several years, again saw the gentleman, and told him that he still loved Virginia: *ergo*, the Right of Suffrage as fixed by the Constitution of Virginia, is the very best in the world! This may be a conclusive argument with that gentleman; it is not with me. Before I enter upon the argument, it will be proper to observe to the Committee, that I had the honor a few days ago of laying upon the table a scheme for the regulation of the Right of Suffrage, differing somewhat from the one now under consideration. It requires the citizenship of every free white man, and one year's residence in his county, city, or borough, and the payment of all taxes or levies, levied upon him the two years next preceding the one in which he proposes to vote; and also, that a tax of twenty-five cents shall be levied on every free white man, to be collected and paid into the public treasury. All such citizens, having so paid their taxes, would be entitled to vote. It also requires that a portion of the property-taxes equal to the whole amount of the taxes so required to be collected and paid in, shall be set apart, and these two sums annually appropriated and vested in the permanent Literary Fund, for purposes of education. The amendment now under consideration requires two years' residence in the State, and one in the county, city, or borough, and the payment of all taxes and levies, levied on all such free white men within the year next preceding the time of election, as a qualification. It requires no specific tax to be levied, but the payment of those which shall be levied. This amendment meets my approbation as fully as my own, except as to the subject of education. It is, perhaps, as great an extension as we may now expect to get.

It is possible, Mr. Chairman, that I shall not call up for consideration that part of my scheme which relates to education. I have seen too much opposition already expressed by several gentlemen (in the discussion of another question) to the establishment of any system of general instruction, and I presume it would be useless to urge my views on the consideration of the Committee. We have heard expressed the fears and objections of the gentleman from Chesterfield, (Mr. Leigh,) the gentleman from Spottsylvania, (Mr. Stanard,) and other gentlemen too, Sir; which fears and objections seem to be, that some system may be adopted to tax the people of the East, for the education of the children of the West. I believe, Sir, I am not mistaken in saying that at least two of these gentlemen were educated at William and Mary, an institution which had authority, and did tax the buck-skins, and the pelts of the beavers and otters taken by the Western hunters, through the medium of the surveyors' fees. Yet they fear that the East will be taxed for the benefit of the West.

I will, however, state to the Committee, that it can be demonstrated by documents to be relied on, that the plan which I had the honor of proposing, (if adopted,) would at the end of twenty years, furnish the means of giving five years education to every free white child, born in the Commonwealth of Virginia: and as well, Sir, to those of the Eastern part of the Old Dominion, as to those of the West. Yes, Sir, to all! And whatever other gentlemen may think upon this subject, I think even that would render more substantial benefit to the people, than all we have done; (indeed, we have done nothing,) I may say, more than all we can now possibly expect to do. But it must be abandoned for the present.

This brings me, Mr. Chairman, to the question before us, and as I have before said, I will endeavour to argue from facts to conclusions.

The proposition now under consideration, justifies an enquiry into the state of the Government; and I believe, it will be found to be aristocratical in its principles. If you agree that an aristocracy is properly defined to be a Government of the few over the many, and that those few hold their authority by virtue of their estates, I can prove that our Government is an aristocracy, or at least aristocratical in its nature and principles. If it shall be found, that the powers of the Government are in the hands of the few, to the exclusion of the many, and these few are to be ascertained and known by the estates they hold, surely it must be aristocratical in its nature. And I venture to say, that such is the situation of the Government of Virginia, at this time.

In 1828, when the election was before the people, to determine whether they would call this Convention or not, thirty-eight thousand five hundred and thirty-three votes were given, and returned from the whole State, (20,275 East of the Blue Ridge, and 18,258 West.) And here, Sir, I must beg leave to correct some of the very erroneous calculations of the gentleman from Spottsylvania, made a few days ago, in the discussion of the question upon the basis of Representation. The gentleman's calculations were taken from the argument of the gentleman from Augusta, whose argument was founded upon documents furnished by the Auditor, known by every person here to be inaccurate, fallacious, and not to be depended upon. These documents purport to exhibit the number of freehold-estates in the Commonwealth, which will authorise voters. It must be recollected, that they included all such estates, whether held by men, women, children, foreigners, or even free negroes, if any such persons have freeholds. But not only so, each person's freehold in every county is counted; so that the same man is counted once for his freehold, or freeholds, in each county. Many men are counted three, four, and five times, and some, perhaps, oftener. It is very common, particularly in the Eastern part of the State, for gentlemen to have freeholds in many counties, but not so frequent in the West. But this is not all. In several of the Western counties, a few years ago, large quantities of lands were returned delinquent for the non-payment of taxes, and sold. Most of these lands now belong to the Literary Fund. They do not appear on the commissioners' books; and, consequently, were not reported by the Auditor. These documents are not to be relied on, I can assure you.

I give you better proof: I offer you the freeholders themselves when called to the polls, and not at one time, but several times, when all felt an interest, and when nearly all attended. I offer you the list of votes from all the counties, cities, and boroughs, both from the East and from the West. It is known that every voter did not attend, but more, I presume, were prevented from attending in the West, than in the East. There were circumstances in that country to prevent their attendance, which did not operate here. In some of the large counties, where there were no district elections, some were prevented from attending the polls by intervening mountains and water-courses; and even where there were districts, all who failed to attend on the first day, were compelled afterwards to go to the court-houses; for the law only required the polls to be kept open after the first day, at the court-houses during court days. Those difficulties were not much felt in this part of the State.

I can assure you, that the votes were taken, and the polls examined with great care, and I doubt whether the vote of any non-freeholder, ever reached the Executive Chamber. The judges qualified to take votes and purge the polls were vigilant, and performed their duty with the utmost strictness, so far as I have been informed. Indeed, they were, of all men in the Commonwealth, the last to permit improper votes to be counted; for it must be recollected that these gentlemen, (the county court clerks, sheriffs and commissioners of the revenue,) had but little feeling or desire for the formation of a Convention. They did their duty fully and amply.

The number of freehold-voters in the State, may be estimated at 45,000, and not more. I shall consider them as of that number. From the free white population of 1820, and the hypothetical increase since that time, there are now in the State more than 140,000 free white male citizens over 21 years of age. Deduct from this number the voters, and you find 95,000 free white men excluded from the polls. But, Sir, deduct from this last number, 5, 10, or if you please, 15,000 for paupers and others who ought to be excluded, and you still have 80,000; leaving the Government in the hands of little more than one third of the people. I am then justified in saying that the Government is in the hands of the few; that it is held and exercised by that few, who hold it by virtue of their freehold estates. I ask you, now Sir, if our Government be not to some extent aristocratical in its form? It is so considered by some men of great wisdom, and I believe generally by the people of the other States of this Union. Are we to close our eyes to these facts? or are we to consider them as having some influence on our deliberations? Sir, we ought to consider them.

When I use this argument to prove the aristocratical principles of our Government, I do it with due respect to the opinions of all the members of this body, and also, with due respect to the freeholders who sent me here; whose opinions and interests I wish to represent. But, Sir, from these facts, I must contend that the Right of Suffrage ought greatly to be extended. The freehold Suffrage is contrary to the genius of our people; and I may well say, contrary to the genius of the people of all these United States. Is it not unwise to contend for a principle so much opposed to the will of the great body of the people?

I shall now attempt to shew that the freehold Right of Suffrage is contrary to the genius of the American people. In doing this, I will introduce, for the consideration of the Committee, a general analysis of the regulations on the Right of Suffrage in each of the States of this Union, which will develop some curious facts, and correct some improper impressions made on the public mind on this subject. And although it may be tedious and uninteresting to the Committee, yet some valuable lessons and correct conclusions may be drawn from a careful examination of all the provisions in the several States on this subject. I know that the Constitutions of other States will not be received as conclusive evidence to convince the Committee of the propriety of adopting the principle for which I contend, nor, indeed, do I presume they will have much weight here. But, Sir, these Constitutions are looked to by the people, and are respected by them. They will have some weight, in shewing that the principle of General Suffrage is neither new nor dangerous.

I proceed, Mr. Chairman, with the twelve slave-holding States, as they are called:

Missouri.—Every free white male citizen of the United States, 21 years of age, who shall have resided one year in the State, and three months in the county or district, shall be deemed a qualified voter, except soldiers, seamen or marines.

Alabama.—Every male person of the age of 21 years, being a citizen of the United States, and who shall have resided in the State one year, and in the county, city or town, three months, shall be deemed a qualified elector, except soldiers, seamen or marines.

Mississippi.—Every free white male person of the age of 21 years, being a citizen of the United States, and having resided in the State one year, and the last six months in the county, city, or town, where he offers to vote, being enrolled in the militia, (if not exempted,) or having paid a State or county tax, shall be deemed a qualified voter.

Louisiana.—Every free white male citizen of the United States, who at the time being, hath attained the age of 21 years, and resided in the county in which he offers to vote, one year next preceding the election, and who, in the last six months, has paid a State tax, shall enjoy the right of an elector; and every such citizen who shall have purchased lands from the United States, shall have the right of voting, when he shall have the other qualifications of age and residence.

Kentucky.—Every free male citizen, (negroes, mulattoes, and indians, excepted,) who at the time being, hath attained to the age of 21 years, and resided in the State two years, and the county or town he offers to vote, one year next preceding the election, shall enjoy the right of an elector.

Tennessee.—Every free man of the age of 21 years and upwards, possessing a freehold in the county wherein he may vote, and being an inhabitant of the State; and every free man being an inhabitant of any one county in the State six months, immediately preceding the day of election, shall be entitled to vote.

Georgia.—The electors of members of the General Assembly shall be citizens and inhabitants of the State, and shall have attained the age of 21 years, and have paid all taxes which may have been required of them, and which they may have had an opportunity of paying agreeable to law for the year preceding the election, and who shall have resided six months within the county.

South Carolina.—By the old Constitution, the Right of Suffrage was confined to free white males 21 years of age, possessed of freeholds in 50 acres of land, or town lots, and such of them as paid two shillings sterling of taxes the year before the election. But by the amended Constitution:

Every free white man of the age of twenty-one years, (paupers and soldiers of the United States excepted,) being a citizen of the State, and having resided therein two years previous to the election, and who hath a freehold of fifty acres of land, or a town lot, of which he hath been seised or possessed six months before the election; *or not having such freehold or town lot*, hath been a resident in the election district in which he offers to vote, six months before the election, shall have a right to vote.

North Carolina.—All free men of twenty-one years of age, having been possessed of a freehold estate in fifty acres of land for six months, and having resided twelve months in the county, may vote for Senators—and all free men of the age of twenty-one, who have been inhabitants of any one county twelve months, and shall have paid public taxes, shall be entitled to vote for Commons. It is nearly the same in towns having separate representation.

Maryland.—By her old Constitution, *all free men* above twenty-one years of age, having freeholds of fifty acres of land, or thirty pounds value of any property, and having resided one year in any one county, were authorised to vote. But by the amendment of 1802, every free white male citizen of the State (and no others) above the age of twenty-one years, having resided one year in any county, or the city of Baltimore, or Annapolis before the election, shall have the Right of Suffrage.

Delaware.—Every white free man of the age of twenty-one years, having resided in the State two years next before the election, and within that time paid a State or county tax which shall have been assessed at least six months before the election, shall enjoy the right of an elector; and the sons of those so qualified, between the ages of twenty-one and twenty-two, may vote without having paid a tax.

Virginia we know is freehold.

From the Constitutions of these twelve slave-holding States, the various facts will be discovered, that six of them require fixed times of age and residence of their male citizens, as the only qualifications of electors; four require the payment of some kind of taxes in addition to age and residence; and only two require a freehold qualification: these two are Virginia, and North Carolina in the Senate.

I will not detain the Committee in giving a full analysis of the Constitutions of the non-slave-holding States, but will merely submit this statement, shewing that six of them require age and residence as qualifications, and that the other six require the payment of some kind of taxes.

States which require particular terms of age and residence as qualifications of electors:

Slave-holding.	*Non-slave-holding.*
Missouri,	Illinois,
Alabama,	Indiana,
Kentucky,	Maine,
Tennessee,	New Hampshire,
South Carolina,	Vermont,
Maryland—6.	Rhode Island—6.

States which require the payment of taxes in addition to age and residence:

Mississippi,	Ohio,
Louisiana,	Pennsylvania,
Georgia,	Massachusetts,
Delaware—4.	Connecticut,
	New Jersey,
	New York—6.

States which require freehold estates in addition to age and residence:

Virginia,	
North Carolina—2	
12	12

Now, Sir, I have presented for your consideration twelve States of this Union, in which the Right of Suffrage is extended generally, to all the free white male citizens of twenty-one years of age. Some of them, but not all, have excluded paupers, soldiers and seamen; and some have not even excluded free negroes. Six of them, like Virginia, hold slaves, and six do not. I have also presented you with ten States, which require the payment of taxes in addition to the qualifications of age and residence—

four of them slave-holding, and six not. South Carolina, Maryland, Massachusetts and New York, have changed their former Constitutions in this particular, and have abandoned the freehold qualification, except as to free negroes, in New York. The Constitution of that State authorises free negroes, being male citizens of that State, of full age, who hold estates of freehold, of the value of $250, clear of debts and incumbrances, and who shall have paid taxes on their estates, to vote. But, I have heard that the Legislature refused to tax these freeholds, and thereby deprived the owners of voting. There is an express provision in the Constitution, that no free negro's real estate under the value of $250, shall be taxed; so that no man is taxed in that State without representation. I believe, Mr. Chairman, from these facts, I may conclude that the freehold Right of Suffrage is contrary to the genius of the people of the present age, and the Republican institutions of the United States.

If any confidence can be placed in the people of the United States, (and I presume there can be some) so far as example and precedent taken from them can have any influence on our deliberations, that influence is in favour of an extension, even beyond the amendment of my colleague. The example of these States has a very powerful influence on the people of Virginia, I am well assured. My residence is near Pennsylvania and Ohio; and I see and know the influence of those States, and their institutions, over the people of the Western part of this State. They see and know the benefits of General Suffrage on society—they approve, they desired a change. And, Sir, look around you; and you find members on this floor from the Tennessee line, round to that of Maryland, who advocate the same principles for which I contend. But to the South, on the North Carolina line, we meet with opposition.

The gentleman over the way, (Mr. Trezvant,) has told us that every Republican Government in the world, where *Universal Suffrage* was instituted, has gone to ruin and perdition. Now, Sir, I would like the gentleman to name the Government to which he refers us, that we may know the force of his precedents. I shew him twelve Republican Governments where suffrage, although not *Universal*, is very general, which have not yet gone to ruin.

[Here Mr. Trezvant remarked that his reference was to the ancient Republics of Greece and Rome, where Suffrage became Universal.]

Then, Mr. Chairman, the gentleman's cases are not in point, and cannot, therefore, be considered as having any influence on the question. It is not necessary to discuss them. They were either democratic or very imperfect Republics, and their history shews that they are not examples for us. Sir, we must look to our sister States, whose history we know, and whose example we feel. They sustain us: and we are sustained in our principles by the opinions of some of the best and wisest men of our own country—men whose names will go down to posterity when many of us will be forgotten. We are not contending for a wild and untried scheme. No! It is one founded on the eternal principles of liberty and equality, which must characterize every good Republican Government which now is, or which ever can be.

But there is another objection. Those who pay no taxes are unworthy of the privilege of voting. It must be observed that taxes may be imposed in various ways, and services may be required instead of the payment of money, for the support of Government. Every thing contributed for the support of any branch of the affairs or concerns of Government, may be legitimately considered as part of the taxes; and it is a curious fact, that the taxes and services imposed on the people of Virginia, have been so arranged, that the greatest burthens have been put upon those who do not vote. Yes, Sir, I say that those who do not vote, are burthened greatly beyond what is right, and even more than is generally imagined. On a former occasion I attempted to shew, and did shew, that such is the fact.

This scheme of taxation is effected by authorising those one hundred and nine little Governments spread over the whole territory of the State, (the county, city and borough court,) to levy taxes to any amount. It is true they levy on voters, as well as those who are not; but it is a capitation tax, and very frequently far exceeds the whole revenue levied upon all the property of the counties. Look to all the items of county taxes and county services—military duty—labour on the public roads—county levies for various purposes—poor levies, (the poor supporting the poor,) and patrols in the counties. Add all these little items together, and it will be found that they make large sums—that they are very important contributions to the Government, and highly necessary for its good being. The voters pay in general the same; but the number of those who do not vote, so far exceeds them, that the whole contribution of the non-voters, is even greater than that of the voters.

A few days ago we were told that wealth and political power could not be divorced; that capital and labour could not be separated; and that labour must be represented. Yet, Sir, on the present occasion, we find that labour is only to be represented by the votes of *freehold-labourers;* and the whole power of the Government is to be placed at the control of the capital of the country, if possible. It is not for me, however, to reconcile these inconsistencies in gentlemen's arguments. I hesitate not to say, that those sixty or eighty thousand persons, to whom it is proposed to extend the Right of Suffrage, constitute the great mass of actual productive labourers of the State. Mr. Chairman, I believe it cannot be otherwise.

We have been told that we shall have a war of the poor against the rich, and that the right of property will be destroyed, if the amendment be adopted. It is not so, and no man can or ought to believe it. If the people of the East, West or South, have given us examples worthy of our imitation, we can fear no such thing. There has been no instance of war upon property in any of our sister States. It is just as secure in them as in Virginia. There is more of it in the North—greater estates, and perhaps more of them than here. There is a greater distance between the rich and the poor, and yet the poor is in a better condition than they are with us. Sir, we can find nothing like physical rapine in any of the States where General Suffrage has been adopted. All live in peace, happiness, prosperity and tranquillity, and every man is secure in his own person and property, under his own roof.

It has been argued, that General Suffrage has a tendency to bring together the rich and the poor, and that the one will have means, and be able to buy up the other, to the prejudice of the liberty of the people. This argument always comes from those who advocate the power of the few over the many. Yes, Sir, from the real aristocracy of the country. It is an argument to be found in nearly all the treatises of theoretical writers, who support aristocracies. The object is to alarm the people with fear that the poor will be bought, and made engines of their own ruin. It is only for purposes of alarm, and is not true. If the Constitution shall require of electors, the payment of a small tax just before elections, there will be a possibility of an improper influence, if there can be candidates corrupt enough to buy, having the means to buy, and voters base enough to sell their votes. But I know of no case of corruption, in any of the States, having such a qualification. Cases of mere suspicion, perhaps, have occurred. If the payment of taxes be made a qualification, they ought not to be required immediately before the election, but some one or two years preceding, at a time when they cannot be paid with a view to any particular election. But, Sir, I would not tax a man merely to qualify him to vote, although it may be proper, in this way, to require a man justly and honestly to pay the public demands. All free men ought to vote, because they are free men. Then they will act independently. Such men can never be purchased by the cash of candidates, or the power of demagogues. No, the poor will be as independent in their opinions, as the greatest land-holders of the State.

There is one other argument which ought to have some influence on this question. It is one of delicacy, and I will say but little upon the subject of this argument; however, I will say something. We find that all the slave-holding States South of us, deemed it of the utmost importance to make all the free white men as free and independent, as Government could make them: and why? Sir, it is known that all the slave-holding States are fast approaching a crisis truly alarming: a time when freemen will be needed—when every man must be at his post. Do we not see the peculiar condition of society? Yes, all see, all feel, and all lament the approach of the crisis before us. It must be in the contemplation of gentlemen, who presume to look upon the progress of events, that the time is not far distant, when not only Virginia, but all the Southern States, must be essentially military; and will have military Governments! It will be so! We are going to such a state of things as fast as time can move. The youth will not only be taught in the arts and sciences, but they will be trained to arms—they must be found at every moment in arms—they must be ready to serve their country in the hour of peril and of danger. Is it not wise now, to call together at least every free white human being, and unite them in the same common interest and Government? Surely it is. Let us give no reason for any to stand back, or refuse their service in the common cause of their country. These considerations had their influence on the Southern States, when forming their Constitutions, I doubt not; and ought to have great influence with us.

I would ask, Mr. Chairman, where are the evils to be apprehended from General Suffrage? I have been unable to find them. It is true, we have been told that it produces mobs, confusion, and turmoil at the polls. Turn your eyes upon all the States of this Union, and let me ask for the evidence of these mobs and turmoils? Look to the South, and have you heard of them? No! Look to the West, and do you find them there? No! Look to the North, and do you see them even there? No! They are no where to be found except in large towns and cities, where it is perfectly well known, that restraint on the Right of Suffrage, has no influence over them whatever.

Where many thousands of persons are brought together upon election days, there will be disputes, and sometimes turmoils. But no danger to the public safety need be apprehended in mere disputes in the choice of public officers. These disputes only serve to show that the body politic is in a good and healthy condition; that it has energy and power. It is not like the cold calm of perfect aristocracy or despotism, where few men dare express opinions on the public affairs. No, Sir; all are at liberty, and all are free to discuss the affairs of Government. I fear not mobs or turmoils in

Virginia; and none who are at all conversant with elections in Pennsylvania and other States, where Suffrage is general, can fear them. Those States are generally divided in small election districts, so that few persons are brought together. Why not do as they have? Our counties may be districted; and even a less number of persons brought to the polls at a single place, than now is, under the existing Constitution. This is the best remedy against mobs or turmoils.

I must conclude my remarks, Mr. Chairman, by telling you, that from the facts which I have laid before the Committee, we may safely argue that there is no danger of rapine or robbery by the poor upon the rich; nor of mobs, turmoils, ruin or despotism; nor indeed, of the Government getting in the hands of demagogues. I have a sanguine hope that the Convention will extend the Right of Suffrage generally; that the people will accept it, and that if it shall at any time be found inconvenient or improper, that they will change it. Several States, as I have said, have abandoned the freehold Suffrage, and all are doing well; all are happy and prosperous. Virginia can do the same, and the effects will be similar.

I beg the Committee not to consider that we advocate a mere wild and untried scheme. But on the contrary be assured, that we in good faith, advocate what we deem to be the sacred rights of the people. We do it to promote the happiness and welfare of our country.

Mr. Wilson now modified his amendment, so as to require that the taxes should have been demanded of the voter before he was rejected for not having paid them.

The question was then taken and decided in the negative: Ayes 37, Noes 53.

(Messrs. Madison, Monroe and Marshall, voting in the negative.)

So the amendment of Mr. Wilson was rejected.

Mr. Campbell of Brooke, then offered the following amendment as a substitute for the 3d resolution reported by the Committee:

1. *Resolved*, That all persons now by law possessed of the Right of Suffrage, have sufficient evidence of permanent common interest with, and attachment to, the community, and have the Right of Suffrage.

2. *Resolved*, That all free white males of twenty-two years of age, born within this Commonwealth, and resident therein, have sufficient evidence of permanent common interest with, and attachment to the community, and have the Right of Suffrage.

3. *Resolved*, That every free white male of twenty-one years of age, a citizen of the United States, not included in the two preceding resolutions, who is now a resident, or who may hereafter become a resident within this Commonwealth, who is desirous of having the rights of a citizen, in this Commonwealth, shall, in open court, in the county in which he resides, as may be prescribed by law, make a declaration of his intentions to become a permanent resident in this State: and if such person shall, twelve months after making such declaration, solemnly promise to submit to, and support the Government of this Commonwealth, such person, shall be considered as having permanent common interest with, and attachment to, the community, and shall have the Right of Suffrage.

4. *Resolved*, That all persons, except such as shall have rendered important services to their country; all persons of unsound mind, and all persons convicted of any high crime or misdemeanor against this Commonwealth, possessing whatever qualification they may, shall not be permitted to exercise the Right of Suffrage in this Commonwealth.

Mr. Campbell then addressed the Committee as follows:

Mr. Chairman,—If I had been asked what in the reason and nature of things, would have first demanded and occupied the attention of this Convention, I would have answered in accordance with *reason*, as I think that the first question to be discussed is, *who shall be a citizen of this Commonwealth?* The next question, embracing the very basis of Government, would have been; *what shall be the privileges and duties of a citizen of this Commonwealth?* On these two questions, as I think, Sir, depends the whole system of Government. These questions correctly decided, and the frame of our Government would have been reared. I would call the attention of this Committee, Sir, to the propriety of the *term* citizen; I need not inform you, Sir, nor any gentleman present, that the term inhabitant, is not equivalent to the term *citizen*. Every citizen is an inhabitant, but every inhabitant is not a citizen of Virginia. They are not convertible terms. In Great Britain, every person is a subject of the King. Every person from the Duke of York, down to the most obscure native of the British Isles, is a subject of his Majesty the King of Great Britain. It is so in all Monarchical Governments. We have repudiated that term in these United States, and we have consecrated the term citizen. But, Sir, though we admire the term, and in a sort of complimentary way, address all men as citizen, we do not in fact, recognize all men as citizen. In Virginia, we have comparatively few citizens. What, let me ask, Sir, does the term fairly import? A citizen is a freeman, who has a voice in the Government under which he lives, who has the privilege of being heard in the councils of his country, by his agent, or representative. No disfranchised man is a citizen. He may be an inhabitant, alien, or what you please, but without a vote he cannot be a citizen.

But, Sir, I have long thought, and I am more fully convinced from the debates which I have heard in this House, that the science of politics, and the science of Government, are yet in progress. We have not yet attained to perfection. Very far from it, Sir. Man in society, is capable of much greater enjoyment than any Government on earth has as yet afforded him. I allude, Sir, to the social enjoyments, which directly, or indirectly, flow from Government, and which every good and wise Government ought to aim at producing. The Constitution of Virginia, is the result of all the discoveries and improvements of nearly six thousand years. Yes, Sir, the present Constitution was the result of all the improvements in the science of Government in the history of the world; *perfect or imperfect*, it was the best the world ever saw, till the year 1776. But how much more light have we attained in the science of politics since? So much at least, as to authorise us to say, that that instrument is by no means perfect.

But, Sir, the great error of mankind, and the common error of all ages, has been, to suppose that all reformations are perfect, or so nearly, as to admit of little or no amendment. It is equally true in religion and politics. We have had both sorts of reforms. After many ages of darkness and superstition, two men arose called Reformers; and they achieved what has been called a great reformation. But while Luther and Calvin effected much, and laid the foundation of a real reformation, their successors and admirers considered their work perfect, and pushed their enquiries no farther. Since then, Sir, during an interval of three hundred years, their adherents have not advanced an inch. So in politics. Some fifty or sixty years ago, many distinguished men, deservedly called reformists, arose in the political world. They carried their views of reform to a very considerable extent, and not only laid the foundation, but actually accomplished a very great reformation in Government. Those illustrious fathers of the American Revolution, and founders of these Republics, are entitled to the admiration and gratitude of all the friends of the rights of man. But it was not to be expected that these sages, great and wise, and good, as they were, could have perfectly emerged out of the political darkness and errors, consecrated by the prescriptions of the monarchies of the old world for thousands of years.

We are wont to admire antiquity, and to venerate long established usages. We think our ancestors were the wisest and best of men. Many of the ancient sages attained reputation, merely because they advanced a little beyond the ordinary stature of their times. Plato, Aristotle, and Socrates, *cum multis aliis*, were men of only ordinary stature, but they lived amongst *pigmies*. Yet these men, famous as they were, and still are, were but pigmies compared with myriads in after times. But, Sir,

> Pigmies though perched on Alps, are pigmies still;
> And pyramids, are pyramids, though placed in vales.

I do not say that amongst the ancients there were not great men, but I do say, that light and science are progressing, and that many of those reputed great, are not worthy of the admiration bestowed upon them. They owe their fame to the age in which they lived. The greatest of these sages, statesmen, and orators, have been far surpassed by the moderns. It was well for the reputation of Demosthenes and Cicero, that they lived so long before the days of Sheridan and Burke.

The science of politics and Government is as well understood in this age as in any former age of the world. I would say better understood. Yes, Sir, and I would say more, better understood in these United States, than in any other country upon the face of the earth. But though our present Constitution was the best production of nearly six thousand years, experience and the progress of political light have discovered some defects in it.

I did expect, and did promise myself, that Virginia would at this time present to the world a model, the best model of Government the world ever saw. When I heard of the talent which was to be assembled here, and which I now see convened around me, I thought myself warranted in expecting that such would be the result of our deliberations. All eyes have been turned to Virginia: all these United States are looking with intense interest to Virginia. She owes it to herself, to the whole United States, to the world, not to disappoint the general expectation. Will the Ancient Dominion respect herself, and realize the hopes of her friends? I am, Sir, beginning to despair, and to fear that we are again to prove that *retrogression* rather than *progression* is the common characteristic of man.

Some call every attempt at reformation, and every new suggestion, a *new theory*. With them, the reformist is a theorist, and his amendments are mere theories. I am no friend to mere theories, but all reformations and all improvements are first theories. I cannot call every effort to ameliorate the political condition of man a mere theory, a visionary theory. And yet, Sir, I am no friend to new theories; but remembering as I do, that we owe all our improvements which have raised the present above all past ages, to mere theories, as some gentlemen please to call them, I cannot disparage theories in the gross. Yes, Sir, printing itself, this art which has revolutionized, and is revolutionizing the world, as well as all the American systems of Government, were once but *mere theories*.

I have no new theory now to offer; I only wish to see the principles already defined, understood, and canonized, carried out to their proper extent. I think we are prepared for nothing more; we can reasonably ask for no more at present. But I am very far from thinking that the social compact has yet been perfected, or that society is yet prepared for the best possible political institutions. That Government is best for any people that is best adapted to their views, wants, wishes, and even prejudices: Not that which is best administered, but that which best suits itself to the great mass of society. This seems not to have been overlooked by the framers of the Bill of Rights, and the founders of this Government. They declared the principles, the just and righteous principles of the social compact; and progressed so far in the application as they supposed the then existing state of society required and permitted. But foreseeing that changes would take place, and that the human mind was progressing and would progress, they revised, and most prudently advised, a frequent recurrence to fundamental principles: Not to change those principles as one gentleman, (Mr. Giles,) asked, but to purge and reform our institutions by bringing them up near to the unchangeable principles; by a continual approximation to the cardinal principles which they propounded. Amongst all the great political truths which these sages declared, not one is more just or evident than this; "That no free Government, or the blessing of liberty, can be preserved to any people, but by a firm adherence to justice, moderation, temperance, frugality and virtue, and by frequent recurrence to fundamental principles."

Mr. Chairman, I have based the resolutions which I have had the honor to submit, upon the doctrine contained in the 6th article of the Bill of Rights. And, Sir, permit me to say, that I am more attached to the Bill of Rights, than I was before the late discussion commenced. I have seen that this instrument has been our palladium, and the only bulwark against the demolition of our republican citadel, and the destruction of the Republican character of our Government. Nothing has now saved us from the establishment, the canonization of the most prominent features of an aristocracy, but this same Bill of Rights. Have not the efforts of all the gentlemen anti-reformists been directed in some way or other against the letter of this instrument? Some have oppugned it one way, and some another. But all who have plead the mixed basis and the freehold qualification, have found it in their way, and have made it in whole, or in part, a dead letter. Whether they intended it or not, such has been the effect of all their criticisms upon it. And, Sir, give me leave to add, if those gentlemen had succeeded in their efforts, and at this time carried the *taxation basis*, upon their constructions of the Bill of Rights, would it not be possible some fifty years hence upon a more liberal construction, and with the precedent of these proceedings before another Convention, to originate a legalized aristocracy in the fullest sense of the term? Yes, Sir, if in the short period of *fifty-four* years, so great a departure from the principles developed and prescribed by the framers of the existing Constitution, should have been completed as the basing of this Government on wealth, on wealth, Sir, I repeat, disguise it as gentlemen may, fifty-four years more, and another Convention following such examples, and such interpretations, and we would have an oligarchy *in propria forma*, a by-law established nobility. Seeing the warfare which has been waged against this now more than ever dear to me instrument, and seeing the barrier which it has thrown in the way of all encroachments upon our free institutions, I shall vote for its being perpetually a part of the fundamental law of our country.

I was glad on yesterday morning, to hear the gentleman from Henrico, (Mr. Nicholas,) begin his speech with the doctrine of this section of that instrument; not, Sir, with the application which he made of that doctrine. According to his interpretation, no man has any attachment to the community or country, but a freeholder. You will observe, Sir, that I have, in the resolutions before you, only developed the meaning of the 6th section of the Bill of Rights; the plain English interpretation of the words. If a single idea, not founded on the fairest and most just interpretation of these words, is found in any one of those resolutions, I hope it may not be retained. Some gentlemen allege, that in the year 1776, the words *common interest with*, and *attachment to*, the community, meant neither less nor more than a freeholder. According to what dictionary or mode of interpretation, this meaning is made out, I have not as yet learned. Words may be used in an appropriated sense, I own; but some proof of this appropriated sense must be produced; as yet, I have not heard any authority other than assertion. Please observe that the words "*common interest*" do not mean *equal* interest. That they do not, the single fact of the *inequality* of the freeholds from twenty-five to one thousand acres in extent, and from twenty-five to one hundred thousand dollars in value, unquestionably indicates. *Common* interest admits of the greatest variety in the extent and value of that interest. One gentleman had spoken of the interest which one man might have in a ship which had a valuable cargo aboard, and another who had only his person. They both had a common interest, it was true; but he might have given to the figure a greater extent, and supposed that many individuals might have had different stakes embarked on the same bottom. Besides their own persons, they might have a great diversity of interests, and though disproportioned in value, equally interesting them all in the safety of the ship. No two interests are precisely equal, yet all have a *common interest*. But it is said that this common interest must also be a *permanent* interest. This further defines the nature of this common interest. This restrictive term denotes that it is not to be a transient interest. But still this word *permanent* is only comparative and necessarily limited. The various interests which we found embarked in the same ship, are as permanent as the voyage from port to port. It may be a long voyage or a short voyage. So it may be, and so often is the journey of human life. Our interests in the State are as transient and as uncertain as our lives. We all have a common interest in the State, but how permanent or how transient that interest may be, cannot be defined. Besides, it may in any given instance, be more transient than our lives. He who has a freehold of any given extent, may either sell or spend it in a very short time, and if we make his tenure of that estate the test of his permanent interest in the State, we have fixed upon as great an uncertainty as can be well conceived. It is a very precarious permanency, as uncertain as the tenure of life, and not necessarily of longer duration than any other man's interest in society. The landlord and the tenant may have, as far as law or reason can determine, the same permanency of interest.

But there is another consideration mentioned in this article, to which I presume this permanent, common interest is subordinate, and to which it stands rather in the relation of means to end. This is comprehended in the word *attachment*. This is the desideratum. Attachment to the community is the best guarantee, and indeed the only guarantee. A person may possess the property of a freehold without the attachment, and the attachment without the property. No man can intentionally, by his vote, injure that community to which he is attached. And as property in the earth was supposed, and justly supposed, in most instances, to attach persons to the community, it has been selected as one proof, (and it is but one,) and not the strongest proof of such attachment. Nativity is a stronger, a much stronger, and a more invariable evidence of attachment to a community, than wealth or any other consideration. It is upon this incontrovertible fact, which I presume no person will impugn, that I base my second resolution. My first embraces all the present voters in Virginia. And, taking for granted that the Bill of Rights makes *attachment* to the community, the great consideration which qualifies an elector, I contend that it is the letter and spirit of this article to extend the Right of Suffrage to every free white male of the age of twenty-two years, born within this Commonwealth. The reason why I fix upon the age of *twenty-two* years rather than *twenty-one*, is to meet a fastidious objection, which I had anticipated as possible to be presented upon a very literal interpretation of the text. It might be said, and with some plausibility too, that a young man of the age of twenty-one, has, by no act of his life, afforded any evidence of permanent, common interest with, or attachment to, the community, who has just arrived at the age of twenty-one, inasmuch as he has, till that moment, been under the guardian and compulsory authority of his parent or guardian. His living one year after he has become a free agent, destroys that objection, and, in addition to his nativity, affords all necessary evidence of his attachment to the community. This is the *rationale* of the second resolution.

To fortify or illustrate this position, or, in other words, to prove that nativity is the best guarantee for attachment to any community, I deem, at this time, a work of supererogation. I feel no disposition to repeat arguments already offered on this and other topics connected with it. After the very able argument of the gentleman from Loudoun, (Mr. Henderson,) which, like a tornado, left nothing behind it, I think such an effort on my part altogether superfluous. True, Sir, one gentleman from Southampton, (Mr. Trezvant,) called it "*empty declamation*," but I would like to see him or any other gentleman attempt by a fair analysis to *prove* it declamatory, and not argumentative. I do think that no gentleman can refute the arguments of the gentleman from Loudoun. They carried irresistible conviction to my mind; and I think it unnecessary to repeat or defend them, until they have at least been formally assailed. The memorials laid upon that table, sufficiently argue this question.

My third resolution, Mr. Chairman, has respect to another class of inhabitants in this Commonwealth. And the only difficulty, as indeed, the only question of much consideration, which occurs in settling who shall be citizens of this Commonwealth, is, what shall be required of those not natives of Virginia, nor embraced in the present laws conferring the Right of Suffrage? You see, I prefer residence and a *moral qualification*, to a pecuniary or property qualification. The payment of any given tax imposed on the purchasing of a piece of land, does not present to my understanding, according to my views of human nature, such evidence of common interest with, and attachment to, the community, as that submitted, and it certainly does not present such temptations to corruption, or to that buying of votes of which some gentlemen speak, as the fixing of a certain amount of tax as the qualifying consideration. Where there is no price proposed, there is no temptation offered, and therefore, corruption is rendered as impossible as the freehold can be supposed to make it. If we desire to see men act a dignified part, we must treat them according to the dignity of human nature. If you put the tax at one dollar, you make the price of a thousand votes only a thousand dollars. But, according to the principle of this resolution, every improper incentive is removed out of the way. A person who becomes an inhabitant of this State, and who desires to become a citizen, a permanent resident, not upon the excitement of an election immediately approaching, calmly and dispassionately goes to the court in the county in which he resides, and declares his intention of becoming a permanent resident. Twelve months afterwards, he returns to the same court, and promises to submit to, and support the Government of, this Commonwealth. Now, I ask, is not this the strongest evidence which the native of any other State can give of his attachment to, and of his feeling a common interest with, the community? I think it must appear so to all, except them who think that virtue, intelligence and patriotism, spring up out of the soil, and grow like mushrooms upon its surface, after a person has paid a stipulated price for it. But in these United States, the principle embraced in this resolution is regarded as a higher proof of attachment to the community, than the purchase of any amount of real estate. When a foreigner from any other country expatriates himself, and desires to become a citizen of these United States, the purchasing of no amount of real or personal estate, will prove his attachment to the country. He must, if he will become a citizen, go into court and make a solemn renunciation of every foreign Prince and Potentate, of all allegiance to any foreign Government, and promise to submit to and support the Constitution of these United States. This, in the estimation of the good and wise framers of our State and Federal Governments, is the highest proof of attachment to, and of feeling a common interest with, the community, which can be afforded. Now, although I would not require all the same formalities, I contend that the principle of the third resolution warrants us to entertain more confidence in the person who thus becomes a citizen, than the mere possession of any freehold. For, unless gentlemen will argue that moral qualities are in the soil, and spring up in a man's mind from the ownership of it, they cannot, I presume, prefer it to the plan proposed upon any principle implied in, or derivable from, the Bill of Rights. The second and third resolutions, I conclude from these and other considerations, are equitably based upon the sixth section of the Bill of Rights.

One word upon the fourth resolution, and I dismiss this part of the subject. I cannot consent to disfranchise all paupers. Ingratitude is one of the greatest crimes against Heaven and man. If then, Sir, any pauper shall have rendered any important service to his country; if he shall have fought her battles, and his virtues have made him a pauper, it would be as cruel, as ungrateful, as it would be *impolitic*, to disfranchise him. It would be a bad precedent; it would evince a destitution of the noblest principle which can dignify a man, or exalt a nation.

This, Mr. Chairman, is the whole *rationale* of the scheme proposed. I was not so studious of the terms, as of a clear development of the principle. But, I will be told by Dr. Expedient, that however reasonable, or however just, and however accordant with the spirit of the age, and the meaning of our fundamental principles of the social compact, it is not expedient. I never liked this doctrine of expediency. Its grand-father was a *Jesuit*. It was the popular doctrine in the Catholic Dominions of the Roman Hierarchy. It kindled all the fires, heated the furnace, and prepared the red-hot pincers of the Holy Inquisition. His *Majesty* the King of Great Britain, and his Court, on the doctrine of expediency, established Episcopacy in England, Presbyterianism in Scotland, Popery in Canada, and Paganism in the East Indies. Yes, Sir, it was expedient to lay a capitation tax upon the worshippers of Juggernaut, just as the Turks levied a capitation tax upon the pilgrims who went to visit the Holy Sepulchre. This, Sir, I believe, furnished the first model, and is the true origin of the Virginia "*poll-tax*." This doctrine of expediency is an off-set against all reason, argument, and principle too. It was not expedient for England to let France govern itself. It was not expedient to permit any other sort of Government to be erected so near the British Throne, than that which accorded with the genius of the English Monarchy. Thus, the flame of war spreads over Europe, and England, from her regard to the doctrine of expediency, made Buonaparte the wonder of the world. Had she permitted France to manage her own affairs, the ambition of Napoleon would not, in all human probability, have transcended the ancient limits of France. But, she made him acquainted with his own military prowess, and forced him to extend his sceptre in the year 1813, over 64,000,000 of human beings. But, Sir, it would be endless to detail the enormities which have been perpetrated, the blood that has been shed, the havoc of human life which has been made, in obedience to the suggestions of this popular doctrine of expediency. It has invaded and destroyed every right of man. Pardon me, Sir, for mentioning *the rights of man*. For it would seem, that man has no rights but what the different Governments in the world please to bestow upon him. His rights in Russia, Turkey, France and England, are just what the Governments please to bestow upon him. Believe this who may, I cannot. He has, in my judgment, certain inherent and inalienable rights, of which he cannot be divested with impunity. Amongst those is the right of a voice in the Government, to which he is to submit.

But I am told that Universal Suffrage, (I am no advocate for Universal Suffrage,) or more correctly *General* Suffrage, was the invention of the age of the Lord Protector Cromwell—that it sprung up for the first time, during the Commonwealth of England. It is called *novel* doctrine. Were it so, that would not prove it false. Steamboats are a novel invention, and many other useful arts are comparative novelties. The new race of men which modern science has created and made, is a new invention. I mean the wooden, brazen and iron men, which neither eat, drink, sleep, nor get tired; which are adults without being infants, full grown men as soon as born. These new men, these novelties, are likely to be a very useful race; for when inspired by steam, they are as rational as our black population. England has two hundred millions of them, and these United States have more than ten millions of them. They are all revolutionists and will as certainly revolutionize the world as ever did the art of printing, or any conquering invader. They are all novel too. No prophetic eye, nor prophetic pen, can describe their progress, or foretell their destiny. All novelties are not fictions. But, Sir, notwithstanding the general historic accuracy of gentlemen on the other side, they have mistaken the date of the origin of General Suffrage. It is more ancient than the British, the Roman, the Grecian, or the Persian Governments. It is now three thousand three hundred and twenty-nine years old. I have heard gentlemen quote the Mosaic history on this floor. It will be no sin, I hope, for me to quote the same authority. Now, Sir, if gentlemen will look into the Exodus of Israel, they will find that the Virginia Constitution was not the first *written* Constitution, nor the General Suffrage the invention of Oliver Cromwell. Cromwell, Sir, was a prodigious genius, but this he did not invent. When Israel became a Commonwealth, and, Sir, they were a Commonwealth, and were so denominated two thousand years ago by a very high authority, I say when Israel became a *Commonwealth*, they received a Constitution from him who led them through the Red Sea. Israel in the wilderness amounted to six hundred thousand fighting men. The God of Israel first proposed a social compact. It was called in Hebrew *Berith*, in Greek *Diatheke*, in Latin *Constitutio*, in Scotch *Covenant*, after the manner of the "Solemn League and Covenant." It is precisely equivalent to our English word *Constitution*. This was *written*, and it is the oldest written document upon earth. After it was written, it was submitted to every man upon the *muster roll* of Israel. Their vote was required and they voted for its adoption as their national compact. So old, Sir, and so venerable is the origin of General Suffrage.

It is no novel doctrine in this country. My colleague and friend from Monongalia, (Mr. Morgan,) this morning, presented us with the history of General Suffrage in these United States. He has anticipated my remarks on this topic. It is enough for me to observe, that no less than half the States in this Union, have totally discarded the property qualification of electors. And half of these, Sir, are slave States. And it has appeared too, Sir, that so far from impairing the safety of property or the progress of improvement, or the peace and happiness of these States, it has contributed to the prosperity of all of them.

The gentleman from Southampton, (Mr. Trezvant,) informed us, that all history shewed, that in all Governments where General Suffrage prevailed, a military despotism ensued, and ultimately the liberties of the people were destroyed. I know not, Sir, whence this gentleman has derived his historic information, but one thing I will venture to affirm, that he can shew no one instance of the practice of General Suffrage issuing in a despotism, civil or military, where the Government was *representative*. Such an instance will be necessary, if not to sustain his position, at least to give it any application to the question now before the Committee.

But, Sir, what was the overthrow of every Government that hitherto fallen into ruins? And many Governments have been subverted; many great empires have gone to perdition. When the real, the true cause is ascertained, the cause which all history developes, it will appear that a disregard of the rights of man was the sole cause of their subversion. Yes, Sir, one party, and always the governing party of the community, invaded the rights of the other. An infraction of these inherent rights, these natural rights of man, has proved the overthrow, the ruin of every Government now extinct in the world. Search the annals of all time, and not an instance can be found contrary to this fact. No Government which has paid a due regard to the rights of man has ever been subverted. Where are all the ancient empires of the world? The Egyptian, Assyrian, Persian, Grecian, Roman? All, all, Sir, dilapidated, all gone to ruin. And what was the cause? Either they were not founded on a just regard of social rights, or ceased justly to regard man according to his nature. Their perdition is, and ought to be, a beacon, a caveat to us. I said upon another occasion, that every departure from the principles of the true philosophy of man was dangerous. The illustration which I used has been perverted by the gentleman from Spottsylvania. I did not say that the laws and rules of mathematical science were to be applied to civil Government, but that there was as much certainty, as much truth in morals, in politics too, as in mathematics. It is not always so perceptible, but it is nevertheless just as certain, and as unchangeable. And, Sir, however slow, however gradual, the departure from correct and fundamental principles, if persisted in, if continued, it must result in very great and fatal enormities.

I was sorry to hear, the other day, the eloquent gentleman from Charlotte, (Mr. Randolph,) protest against his majesty *King Numbers*, and declared his readiness to revolt from his government, and to migrate from his dominions. King Numbers, Mr. Chairman, is the legitimate sovereign of all this country. General Jackson, the President of these United States, is only the representative, the *lawful representative* of King Numbers. And, whither, Sir, can that gentleman fly from the government of this King? In the North, in the South, in the East and in the West, he can find no other monarch. Except he cross the ocean, he can put himself under no other King. And whenever he may please to expatriate himself, he will find beyond the dominions of King Numbers, there is no other monarch, save King Cypher, King Blood, King Sword, or King Purse. And, Sir, permit me to add, there is none of those so august as our King. I love King Numbers; I wish to live, and I hope to die, under the government of this majestic personage. He is, Sir, a wise, benevolent, patriotic and powerful prince—the most dignified personage under the canopy of Heaven.

I heard that same gentleman, Mr. Chairman, with pleasure too, refer to a saying of the immortal Bacon. Twice he alluded to it; twice he spoke of the great *innovator*, time. I did wish to hear him quote the whole sentence, and apply it. Lord Bacon said, (I think I give it in his own words)—"*Maximus innovator tempus; Quidni igitur tempus imitemur?*" Why then, says he, can we not imitate time, the greatest of all innovators? The Romans long ago learned this lesson. Their moralists taught it to their children—"*Tempora mutantur, et nos mutamur in illis.*" Why, then, Sir, cannot we learn to imitate time?

I am glad, Sir, to find myself associated with many gentlemen on this floor, who are inspired with the spirit of this age, who have not only grown up *under* this age, but grown up *with* it. They are willing to learn what time, the great teacher, and the greatest revolutionist, teacheth. And, Sir, she is an eloquent preceptor. These gentlemen, Sir, who feel the current of time, who are in heart, in unison, with this age, have no idea of making Chinese shoes for American feet; or of constructing a new bedstead after the manner of Procrustes, for men of American stature.

But, Sir, there is one most august tribunal to which we must all bow. Time will make us all do homage before it. This, I need not inform you, is the tribunal of *public opinion*. This is the supreme tribunal in all this extensive country. No sentiment is canonical in this country, which this tribunal reprobates. All our acts must be judged by it, and I rejoice to live in a country in which this is the supreme law—and in which no political maxim can prevail which does not quadrate at all angles with the *dicta* of this tribunal.

I am assured, Mr. Chairman, that it is in the power of this body to make this land one day, the happiest land on the earth—to infuse into our institutions, such principles as would elevate, enlighten, and happify this community, greatly beyond any thing yet experienced on this continent. I mean to say, Sir, that from the lights which concentrate their influences upon us—from the wisdom and talent assembled here, we have every facility for carrying to a much greater extent improvements into the social compact. Were this assembly far inferior to what it is, such a result might reasonably be expected. Standing as we do, upon the shoulders of all former Conventions, and being furnished with all the experiments which have been made in ancient and modern times, much is reasonably expected from us. But I fear these monosyllables *mine* and *thine*, are about to frustrate all attempts at a thorough amelioration of our condition.

I did hope that we would feel a little more in accordance with the progress of improvement and the spirit of the age, than to put forth all our energies in a contest about mere local interests, which a few years will change in defiance of all our efforts. Yes, Sir; a few years will settle all these questions about *miney* and *thiney*. But should the improvement of the condition of society have been taken into consideration—should the adaptation of our political institutions to the actual condition and circumstances of the great mass of the community have engrossed our attention or entered into our hearts, I doubt not but we could have endeared our memory to the latest posterity. To mention only one instance; we have been told that it is quite practical now to give birth to a system of education, which in *twenty* years from this day would render it impossible for a child to be born in this Commonwealth and to live to manhood, without receiving a good education, and that too, Sir, without the laying any tax after that day for the support of such a system. I have understood, Sir, and from good authority too, that in some parts of Massachusetts, particularly in the environs of Boston, any child, without the contribution of a single cent, may receive not only a good English, but a classical education. Such is the extent to which the common school system has been carried in that enlightened community.

Yes, Mr. Chairman, we might now bless Virginia with a social compact which would, in the gradual progress of time, develop and improve the intellectual and moral powers of every member of the community, and contribute to the political good of the whole Commonwealth. Is not such an object worthy of such a Convention? And would not the origination of such a splendid scheme carry down, for a thousand generations, the grateful admiration of our services? But, if we exhaust our energies on these little localities, time, the great innovator, will break our arrangements to pieces: For it is decreed, that every system of Government not based upon the true philosophy of man—not adapted to public opinion, to the genius of the age, shall fall into ruins.

But, Sir, one gentleman, (Mr. Randolph,) referred us to the *great men*, which the present system in Virginia had produced. We doubt it not, Sir. I have lived in a country in which there were many great men: very learned and very powerful men. But how were they created, Sir? For one noble Lord, there were ten thousand ignoble paupers, and for one great scholar, there were ten thousand ignoramuses. That is the secret, Sir. I never wish to see this mode of making great men introduced into this Commonwealth. I trust, Sir, we will rather strive to make many middling men, than a few great or *noble* men. When we adopt the English way of making great men, we will soon adopt the English way of speaking to them. I have heard of but one "*noble* friend" in this Committee, as yet; but, Sir, it is a contagious spirit. There are many sorts of great men. It is not necessary to create them in advance of the demands of society. Peculiar crises call them into being. This sort of great men, has always been the creature of circumstances. One of them was once found on Mount Horeb, another on the way to Damascus—one at Mount Vernon, and another was found in the county of Hanover, with a fishing rod in his hand. The Island of Corsica produced one, when he was wanted. There is no occasion to devise any plan for creating this sort of great men. But, Sir, under a proper system of Government, we should be able to multiply other sorts of great men a hundred fold, and we should not fail to derive benefits of every sort, intellectual, moral, and political, incomparably surpassing any sacrifice we should be obliged to make in commencing such a system.

One word more, Sir, and I will not further trespass upon the patience of the Committee. The scheme which is contemplated in these resolutions, is not only, I think, adapted to the general good of the whole State, but especially to the Eastern part of it. I was much pleased with the suggestion of the gentleman from Albemarle, (Mr. Gordon,) it was founded on a correct knowledge of man. When we disfranchise one class of men, or deprive them of their political and natural rights, to secure any property or privilege we possess, we endanger that very property and those very privileges, more by such disfranchisements, than we protect them. We give an invidious character to those interests and privileges, and we create antipathies against ourselves. It is in the nature of man to hate, and to attempt to impair and destroy, that which is held at his expense, and which degrades him in his own estimation. For the safety, then, and preservation of those very interests, I would conceive this extension of the Right of Suffrage indispensable. If the extension sought for in these resolutions, can be obtained, I am not tenacious of the words or of the form in which it is sought. I chose thus to develop the principle. I aimed at no more, than to shew, that it is in accordance with the Bill of Rights. I did not expect to have addressed the Committee at this time; but on the failure of the scheme submitted by the gentleman from Monongalia, (Mr. Wilson,) I thought it expedient to make another experiment. Had it been my object to do more than to expose the principle, I should have, in a more syllogistic form, fortified and defended the grounds on which it is based. But, even in this, I have been, in a great measure, anticipated by the gentlemen who have preceded me.

The question being then taken, it passed in the negative by a very large majority, eleven only rising in the affirmative.

Mr. Scott then gave notice that in case the resolution offered by Mr. Pleasants yesterday shall be rejected, he will move the following:

Resolved, That in the apportionment of representation in the House of Delegates, regard should be had to the white population exclusively, and in the Senate to taxation exclusively: That the House of Delegates shall consist of one hundred members; and the Senate of forty-eight: That the Senate shall have the same Legislative powers in all respects as the House of Delegates—and all appointments to office, which by the Constitution shall be referred to the two Houses of the Legislature, shall be made by a concurrent vote.

The Committee then rose and the House adjourned.

FRIDAY, November 20, 1829.

The Convention met at 11 o'clock, and was opened with prayer by the Rev. Mr. Taylor, of the Baptist Church.

Mr. Thompson of Amherst, offered the following resolution:

Resolved, That during the remainder of the session of this Convention, the 22d rule thereof shall be observed in the Committee of the Whole, and that "it shall be the duty of the Clerk hereafter to keep a Journal of the proceedings of said Committee, and to insert in such Journal, if they can be ascertained, all the proceedings heretofore had therein."

Mr. Wilson called for the reading of the 22d rule.

The 22d rule is as follows:

"Any member on his motion made for that purpose, on being seconded, provided seven of the members present be in favor of the motion, shall have a right to have the Ayes and Noes taken upon the determination of any question, provided he shall give notice of his intention to call the Ayes and Noes, before the question be put, and in such case the House shall not divide, or be counted on the question, but the names of the members shall be called over by the Secretary, and the Ayes and Noes shall be respectively entered on the Journal, and the question shall be decided as a majority of votes shall thereupon appear: provided that after the Ayes and Noes shall be separately taken, and before they are counted, or entered on the Journal, the Secretary shall read over the names of those who voted in the affirmative, and of those who voted in the negative; and any member shall have liberty at such reading to correct any mistake which may have been committed in listing his name, either in the affirmative or negative."

In supporting the resolution, Mr. T. observed, that it might have been foreseen, and must now be obvious to all, that the whole of the important business of this Convention would be done in a Committee of the Whole; the Convention, as such, having little left for it to do but to give its sanction to the acts of the Committee of the Whole, and embody them in a regular form. If then the privilege of recording his vote was important to a Delegate any where, it was eminently so here; for, the Committee was nothing else but the Convention in another form. The adoption of the resolution, would be productive of an economy of time. All the members came charged with some grievance his constituents desired to have redressed. If they were allowed the opportunity of satisfying their constituents, that they had made an attempt to discharge the duty entrusted to them in the Committee of the Whole, there would be no need of repeating their motions to that effect, in the Convention: the District having seen the course pursued by their Delegate, would be satisfied, and much time would be saved. Such a measure was not unsupported by precedents. A similar regulation had been adopted in the Federal Convention, when the Constitution of the United States was framed: the Yeas and Nays were recorded, and a regular Journal kept in the Committee of the Whole. Another precedent was to be found in the records of the New York Convention, in 1820. He hoped that gentlemen, who professed to hope every thing from a re-action in the public mind, would offer no opposition to a proposal of this description.

Mr. Leigh was opposed to the resolution. He had supposed that if there was any body of law in the world approved by the experience of mankind, and altogether unexceptionable, it was the body of Parliamentary Law. The Committee of the Whole was one of the most valuable institutions ever devised for facilitating the business of a deliberative body. It gave opportunity for full, fair and free discussion, untrammelled by the forms necessarily attendant upon the definitive action of a Legislative Assembly. Yet here, said Mr. Leigh, we have a proposition to abolish all distinction between the Committee of the Whole, and the House in its Conventional capacity. Its effect will be to make the Committee of the Whole, the Convention—the only remaining difference will be that the presiding officer of the one is called a Chairman, and the other a President. I differ entirely from the gentleman's view of the matter. I hold that there is a great and essential difference between the two, and in that difference it is that the excellence and advantage of the Committee of the Whole entirely consists. But there is precedent for it. The gentleman has quoted two, but the first of them is no precedent at all; for the Convention of '87 voted not by members, but by States, and it was necessary to declare, which States were for, and which were against any proposition, in order to determine the question. It is true that such a rule was adopted by the Convention of New York, which sat at Albany in 1820. Why, I do not know; but this I do know, that there was in that Convention such bidding in the auction of popularity, as never was known on earth before. It seems to have been adopted there in order to record the bids, but here there is no bidding that I know of, and if there shall be any, there can be no need of recording it; for the opinions we deliver here, are as well known by the public, as if they were recorded on our Journal.

Mr. Thompson thought the gentleman from Chesterfield, had not been very happy in his appeal to experience; he had said that no such example could be furnished. There have been many deliberative bodies, they are of ancient origin; but there have been only a few Conventions, and they belong to modern times. We have adduced the experience of two of these Conventions; whether the same expedient be resorted to in the others which have been holden, I cannot tell: but it is very probable. But, how has the gentleman succeeded in shewing, that the case of the Federal Convention was so entirely dissimilar, as to furnish no precedent for this body? The gentleman says, it is because the votes there taken, were given, not by individuals, but by *States*. But, surely there was no more need to record the votes on that account, than if they had been given by individuals. I can see no distinction whatever, in principle; we may just as well record our votes, as they recorded theirs. The experience we have already had in this Convention, proves the utility of the plan; for we have already been compelled to resort to it. We have been greatly crowded by company, who have almost mingled themselves with the members. This may be the case again, and we may be again compelled to take the same course. It occupies little more time to record the names than it does to call them, and surely we have not shewn ourselves penurious of time. As to the auction of popularity, of which the gentleman spoke, I have nothing to say, because he has disclaimed any personal allusion. Whether he is right in his opinion of the New York Convention in this respect, I cannot tell. I have read the Journal of their Debates, and I did not perceive the evidence of any thing of the kind. I thought their proceedings were such as did honour to the State, and I consider them well worthy of our imitation.

Mr. Stanard said, that judging from appearances as to what the gentleman's object was, he thought he had taken a very round-about way to get at it: his more direct and obvious course would have been to move at once to abrogate the Committee of the Whole. His resolution did that in effect; for, why have any Committee of the Whole, if its proceedings are to be attended with the same formality, and to have the same effect as those of the original body? The gentleman had better march up at once, fairly, to his object. He has quoted precedents, said Mr. S., and what are they? He ventures to *suppose* that the precedents in the Conventions of all the States are in his favour: it is a bold supposition. Yet it is a little extraordinary, that that gentleman has contented himself with supposing, and has forborne to examine. This will appear strange to any one who knows with what accuracy that gentleman furnishes information, and what pains he takes to be exact in all his facts. If, indeed, the gentleman has examined, he cannot be ignorant that there have been thirty Conventions in this country, which have had the same service to perform as this; and yet out of that whole number, there have been but two which have so much as thought of recording their proceedings in Committee of the Whole. One law seems to have governed bodies of that kind, ever since they existed, and I am not in favour of any innovation. It is a measure likely to end in no good, and there is not the least shadow of necessity for it.

The question being now about to be put,

Mr. Gordon demanded that it should be taken by Yeas and Nays. It was accordingly so taken, when the Yeas and Nays stood as follows:

Ayes—Messrs. Goode, Anderson, Coffman, Williamson, M'Coy, Moore, Beirne, Smith, Baxter, Mercer, Henderson, Cooke, Opie, Naylor, Donaldson, Boyd, George, M'Millan, Campbell of Washington, Byars, Cloyd, Chapman, Mathews, Oglesby, Duncan, Laidley, Summers, See, Doddridge, Morgan, Campbell of Brooke, Wilson, Claytor, Saunders, Cabell, Martin, Gordon, Thompson and Joynes—39.

Noes—Messrs. Monroe, (*Pres't.*) Jones, Leigh of Chesterfield, Taylor of Chesterfield, Brodnax, Dromgoole, Alexander, Marshall, Tyler, Nicholas, Clopton, Harrison, Baldwin, Johnson, Miller, Mason, Trezvant, Claiborne, Urquhart, Randolph, Leigh of Halifax, Logan, Venable, Madison, Barbour of Orange, Stanard, Holliday, Powell, Griggs, Pendleton, Roane, Taylor of Caroline, Morris, Garnett, Barbour of Culpeper, Scott, Macrae, Green, Tazewell, Loyall, Grigsby, Townes, Pleasants, Massie, Taliaferro, Bates, Neale, Rose, Bayly, Upshur and Perrin—51.

So the House refused to rescind the rule as proposed, and to record their proceedings in Committee of the Whole.

The Convention then proceeded to the Order of the Day, and went into Committee of the Whole, Mr. Powell in the Chair; and the question still being on the third resolution reported by the Legislative Committee, and amended by the Convention, in the following words:

"*Resolved*, That the Right of Suffrage shall continue to be exercised by all who now enjoy it under the existing Constitution; and shall be extended, 1st, to every free white male citizen of the Commonwealth, resident therein, above the age of twenty-one years, who owns, and has possessed for six months, or who has acquired by marriage, descent or devise, a freehold estate, assessed to the value of not less than dollars, for the payment of taxes, if such assessment shall be required by law; 2d, or who shall own a vested estate in fee, in remainder, or reversion, in land, the assessed value of which shall be dollars; 3d, or who shall own, and have possessed a leasehold estate, with the evidence of title recorded, of a term originally not less than five years, and one of which shall be unexpired, of the annual value or rent of dollars; 4th, or who for twelve months next preceding, has been a house-keeper and head of a family within the county, city, borough or election district, where he may offer to vote, and who shall have been assessed with a part of the revenue of the Commonwealth within the preceding year, and actually paid the same: *Provided, nevertheless*, That the Right of Suffrage shall not be exercised by any person of unsound mind, or who shall be a pauper, or a non-commissioned officer, soldier, sailor or marine, in the service of the United States, nor by any person convicted of any infamous offence; nor by citizens born without the Commonwealth, unless they shall have resided therein for five years immediately preceding the election at which they shall offer to vote, and two years preceding the said election, in the county, city, borough or election district, where they shall offer to vote, (the mode of proving such previous residence, when disputed, to be prescribed by law), and shall possess, moreover, some one or more of the qualifications above enumerated."

Mr. Leigh of Chesterfield moved to amend the resolution by striking out all after the words "Resolved, that," and inserting the following as a substitute:

"Every male citizen of the Commonwealth, resident therein (other than free negroes and mulattoes,) aged 21 years and upwards, qualified to exercise the Right of Suffrage by the existing Constitution and laws,—

And every such citizen being possessed, or whose tenant for years, at will and at sufferance, is possessed, of land of the assessed value of dollars, and having an estate of freehold therein,—

And every such citizen being possessed, as tenant in common, joint-tenant or coparcener, of an interest in or share of land, and having an estate of freehold therein, such interest or share being of the value of dollars,—

And every such citizen, being entitled to a reversion, or vested remainder in fee, expectant on any estate for life, or lives in land of the assessed value of dollars,—

And every such citizen, being possessed of a leasehold estate in land, claiming under a lease, renewable at the option of the lessee, absolutely, or upon payment of a fine, or performance of other condition, the yearly value of such land being dollars,—

Each and every such citizen, unless his title shall have come to him by descent, devise, marriage or marriage settlement, having been so possessed or entitled for six months,—

And no other persons,

Shall be qualified to vote for members of the General Assembly, in the county, city, or borough, respectively, wherein the land lieth:—

Provided, That no person shall be entitled to vote more than once, or at more places than one, in any election;—

And, provided, That non-commissioned officers, soldiers, sailors, and marines, in the land or naval service of the United States, shall not be qualified to vote;—

And, provided, That the Legislature may, by law, deprive any persons of the Right of Suffrage, for crimes, whereof they shall or may be convicted."

The amendment having been read, and the question upon it propounded from the Chair, Mr. Leigh rose, and spoke to the following effect—

Mr. Chairman,—It may be, perhaps, that in submitting this proposition, and in the earnest endeavour I am going to make to explain the principle it is founded on, to maintain it as the wisest and surest foundation of a Representative Republic, and particularly suited to the circumstances of this Commonwealth, and thus to recommend it to the favourable consideration of the Committee, I am taking a task upon myself, utterly nugatory, as well as laborious and ungracious. For, it seems, plainly enough, to be the general opinion, that any effort to preserve a landed qualification of the Right of Suffrage must fail. Yet, if it shall fail, the principal reason of its failure, I am persuaded, will be found in the prevalence of the opinion that it certainly will fail, rather than that it ought to fail. It happens in most political questions and controversies in our day and nation, that the first exertion of men's minds is to ascertain which way the majority is, and if that point can be ascertained, it generally in fact (and in the opinion of many, rightly too) sways and determines the majority. For my own part, however, the landed qualification of the Right of Suffrage stands approved in my judgment, by principle and experience, and the more I have reflected and the more I have observed upon the subject, the more strongly approved; and a departure from it is condemned, in my view of things, by the experience of the other States of this Union. In almost every instance, in which our sister States have broken up old foundations, and departed from the landed qualification of Suffrage, they have proceeded eventually and instantaneously, to Universal Suffrage—I say, instantaneously—for speaking in regard to the life of a nation, the transition is instantaneous. States never go upward, in affairs of this kind—their course is always downward—the downward course is easy, the downward tendency constant; and down, down they go, to those extremes of democracy, which have always ended, and will always end, in licence and anarchy, and thence, by inevitable consequence, in despotism. The first wish of my heart is for a practical, regular, stable, Republican Government; to which, in my apprehension, violent extremes of all kinds are equally dangerous and hostile. And perceiving (as I do but too clearly for my own peace of mind) that if we too depart from the landed qualification of Suffrage, we shall not stop short of Universal Suffrage, in the end—believing, indeed, that it is Universal Suffrage, in effect, to which the views of many gentlemen obviously tend—and feeling the most anxious forebodings of danger to all regular Government, from the admission of the principle into our institutions—I am, therefore, desirous to extend the Right of Suffrage only to those who are within the equity of the original principle of the freehold qualification, on which the founders of our Government placed it.

When my friend from Augusta (Mr. Johnson) gave the Committee his interpretation of the first resolution of the Legislative Committee, and endeavoured to shew us, that the proposal to apportion the representation according to the white population only, was tantamount to, and really meant, an apportionment of representation according to the qualified voters; and then endeavoured to reconcile us to that scheme of apportioning the representation, thus expounded and understood, before it was yet determined who should be the qualified voters, I saw at once, and wondered he did not see, that that argument went beyond and beside the purpose for which he used it—that it would chiefly affect the question concerning the qualification of the Right of Suffrage—that, with the exception of himself, and a very few others, all those who are for apportioning representation according to white population only, if that should be understood to mean according to the qualified voters, would be intent on making every white man a qualified voter. That this was the effect of the argument, soon appeared from the sentiments avowed by one of his own colleagues (Mr. M'Coy). The gentleman from Augusta has thus lent the most efficient aid to the principle of Universal Suffrage; which, I am sure, he deprecates as earnestly as I do. He has borne a main part in bringing us into this fearful strait between *Scylla* and *Charybdis;* and, confidently trusting that the Siren's voice cannot lure him to the fatal shore, I implore him to lend *me* his aid, now—or rather, to put his own strong and skilful hand to the helm, and, if possible, save us from being dashed against the impending rock of destruction. Our hopes of avoiding the whirlpool which threatens to ingulph all, must rest on others.

There is, Sir, one feature in the resolution of the Legislative Committee on this subject, so strikingly unjust, I may say, so glaringly absurd, that I can hardly think it was intended; but I mentioned it here, some days ago, and no friend of the principle of the resolution, has proposed any amendment of its details in this particular. Observe, Sir—the resolution provides, that the owners of the smaller freehold estates in land, shall not be allowed to vote, unless their land be of a certain assessed value, though the owners must pay some land tax, no matter how trivial the value of their land may be; but, if a house-keeper and head of a family shall reside on one of these small freeholds, as tenant of the owner or by his permission, paying any revenue tax, of what kind or how trivial soever, such house-keeper and head of a family shall be allowed to vote, though his landlord shall not. Can this be right? Can it possibly be intended? I must still think, that it is to be imputed to inaccuracy in the details of the resolution, which will be, as it easily may be, corrected: and I mention it now again, as I did before, chiefly for the purpose of shewing how cautious we ought to be against indulging in an intemperate zeal for innovation, miscalled reform, lest we run into gross inconsistencies, and produce new and greater inconveniences or wrongs than those we propose to remedy.

Permit me now, Sir, to explain succinctly my own proposition.

In the first place, I propose, that all who now enjoy the Right of Suffrage, shall continue to exercise it. According to the existing provisions of the Constitution and laws on this subject, it is land, a freehold estate in land, of a certain quantity, without regard to its quality or value, which ascertains the right of the owner to vote.* We are told,

* For the existing freehold qualification of Suffrage in Virginia, see Rev. Code, vol. I. c. 51. § 3—"Every male citizen of this Commonwealth, aged twenty-one years, (other than free negroes or mu-

that these regulations operate very unequally; for that, in some parts of the State, land is worth ten, twenty, fifty dollars per acre, while in other parts, and often in the same county, it is worth less than a dollar per acre. And this is very true. Again we are told, that, in many parts of the State, there are large tracts of barren land, and in the Western country, particularly, vast bodies of mountainous land unfit for cultivation; that these lands afford the holders of them the means of creating freeholders and voters, *pro re nata*, to answer occasional electioneering purposes; and that this is a shameful and intolerable abuse. And, since the meeting of this Convention, I have heard the existence of this abuse, in some parts of the Western country, to a very enormous extent, asserted by a delegate from that quarter of the State; but to my great satisfaction (though, considering from whom the first information came, much to my surprise) I have since heard the fact of such abuses being either frequent, or carried to any great extent, strenuously denied, on this floor, by another gentleman from the same quarter. Some abuses of the kind, I doubt not, there have been, in the West and in the East too; but, upon reflection, I cannot but think, that they must have been very rare. For, the provision of the election law, which requires that the title in the land, unless derived by marriage, descent or devise, shall have been acquired six months before the owner of it presents himself at the polls to vote, which was intended to prevent such abuses, must, in practice, have proved generally effectual to prevent them; since it cannot often happen, that the person who desires to make a voter by making a freeholder, does or can foresee the want of the vote so long before the election at which it is to be given. Such abuses too, are in their nature, very open to detection, and easy to be exposed. Although, therefore, I am sensible, that the existing regulation of the Right of Suffrage, does operate unequally, by reason of the inequalities in the value of lands—and although it may be liable (for what regulation is not liable?) to some abuse—yet I am very sure, that it brings to the polls, the great body of the settled residents of the Commonwealth, the free, allodial cultivators of the soil for their own use; and admits but few, very few others. Imperfections there may be in the present regulation—but imperfections which ought not to condemn it—such imperfections as are incident to all general regulations, and indeed to all human institutions; such as perhaps, it would be hardly possible to avoid. Besides, Sir, I hold that there is a wide difference between the refusal in the first instance, to confer a right, which ought not to be conferred, and the taking away a right, which has been already conferred and long enjoyed, because in justice and good policy it ought originally to have been withheld. If I had found the Right of Suffrage extended ever so far beyond what I consider the proper point, however I might have lamented it, I should have hesitated long before I touched it. Imperious necessity only should have induced me to assent to new restrictions. There is no such necessity here. Though a freehold of twenty-five acres of land in Jefferson, may be worth five hundred dollars, while the like quantity of land on the sandy ridges of the East or in the broken mountainous districts of the West, may not exceed in value fifty or even twenty dollars, still the owner of the one, cultivating it for his maintenance, has a common interest in the soil, as well as the other, and is affected by whatever affects the general interests of the State or the local interests of his own county. I have explained my views on this point the more fully, because I know there are some gentlemen who differ with me in opinion concerning it, while they concur with me as to the general principle of a landed qualification.

In the next place, I propose to extend the Right of Suffrage to all freeholders of land, which though not equal in quantity to that now required as a qualification, is yet equal in value to the average of the smaller freeholds which now constitute the qualification. A man may be the owner of one or two acres of land, with a mill,

lattoes, or such as have refused to give assurance of fidelity to the Commonwealth,) being possessed, or whose tenant for years, at will, or at sufferance, is possessed, of twenty-five acres of land, with a house, the superficial content of the foundation whereof is twelve feet square, or equal to that quantity, and a plantation thereon, or fifty acres of unimproved land, or a lot or part of lot of land in a city or town established by act of General Assembly, with a house thereon of the like superficial content or quantity, having, in such land, an estate of freehold at the least, and unless the title shall have come to him by descent, devise, marriage, or marriage settlement, having been so possessed six months, and no other person, shall be qualified to vote for delegates to serve in General Assembly, for the county, city, or borough respectively, in which the land lieth. If the fifty acres of land, being one entire parcel, lie in several counties, the holder shall vote in that county wherein the greater part of the land lieth, only; and, if the twenty-five acres of land, being one entire parcel, be in several counties, the holder shall vote in that county wherein the house standeth, only. In right of land holden by parceners, joint tenants or tenants in common, but one vote shall be given by all the holders capable of voting, who may be present, and agree to vote for the same candidate, or candidates, unless the quantity of land, in case partition had been made thereof, be sufficient to entitle every holder present to vote separately, or unless some one or more of the holders may lawfully vote in right of another estate or estates in the same county; in which case, the others may vote, if holding solely they might have voted: *Provided, nevertheless*, That no person inhabiting within the District of Columbia, or elsewhere, not within the jurisdiction of this Commonwealth, shall be entitled to exercise the Right of Suffrage therein, except citizens thereof employed abroad in the service of the United States, or of this Commonwealth, and whose foreign residence is occasioned by such service."

tannery, or other fixtures upon it, equal or far exceeding in value, many tracts of fifty acres of unimproved land, or of twenty-five acres with a small dwelling house upon them. I would extend the Right of Suffrage to freeholders of this class; to all freeholders of land of a certain assessed value; say, fifty dollars, or if you please, twenty-five dollars—I am not particular about the sum with which the blank shall be filled. Then, Sir, I propose to extend the right, to all parceners, joint tenants and tenants in common, of lands of such an assessed value, that the share of each shall be equal in value, no matter how small in quantity, to the value of the small freeholds held in severalty, which I have just now described. I propose to extend the right, further, to all remainder-men and reversioners in fee, expectant on estates for life or lives, so that the assessed value of the land be such that the estate in remainder or reversion may be fairly estimated at an equal value with that of the small freeholds held in possession. I know that the value of such interests depends on the complement or duration of life of the tenant in possession; but there is no occasion here for the accuracy which would be proper in making a bargain; and a general rule may be easily laid down, which will answer the present purpose; as if we should estimate the life estate equal to one-third, and the remainder in fee equal to two-thirds, of the whole fee-simple value of the land, and regulate the extent of this particular qualification accordingly. Lastly, I propose to give the Right of Suffrage to all tenants for years, holding under leases renewable at their own option, upon the payment of a fine or performance of other condition. These are estates for years, only in name; they are, in truth, fixed, permanent and independent interests. Such leases are generally purchased for a consideration presently paid; and only a ground-rent, very small and very far short of the annual value of the property, is reserved. Such lessees are little, if at all, dependent on the favour of their landlords. But I would require, that the property should be of a given value; if estimated with respect to the value of the fee-simple, it should be somewhat greater than the assessed value of the small freeholds; if estimated with respect to the amount of rent reserved, that should be very small. I am at present regardless of details, being only desirous to explain the principle on which I propose to regulate the Right of Suffrage, which is, to require some certain, fixed, permanent, independent interest in land, as the qualification of the voter. And to any extent to which this principle can in reason be carried, to that extent I am willing to go: but, to go farther—to depart, in any degree, from the principle of a substantial and permanent landed qualification—this is what, in my opinion, the true theory of pure Republican Government, and all experience of the practical operation of political institutions, at home and in our sister States, far from dictating to be done, warn us not to do.

The Legislative Committee proposes to extend the Right of Suffrage, to every leaseholder of a term originally not less than five years, yielding an annual rent of a certain amount, though but a month or a week of the term shall be left unexpired when the lessee shall present himself at the polls; and to every person, who for twelve months next preceding, has been a housekeeper and head of a family, within the county or town where he may offer to vote, and who shall have been assessed with, and shall have paid, a revenue tax, of any kind, on any subject, or to any amount. As to these housekeepers and heads of families, which the proposition distinguishes from termors of five years, as well as from freehold owners of land, they must be persons resident on the lands of others—they must be either tenants from year to year, paying rent—or tenants at the will of others, on whose bounty they are dependent for a home and a shelter—or squatters, who have trespassed and seated themselves on the lands of others. These last, to be sure, may be independent of the owners of the land, and ready enough, quite too ready, to set them at defiance; and they, I hope, are not within the intent, though they are within the words, of the new regulation of the Right of Suffrage, which the Legislative Committee has proposed to us. But what will be the condition of the tenant at will, who is indebted to the mere bounty of his landlord, for the shelter that covers his head? or of the tenant from year to year, or of the termor of a five years lease, rendering a rent quarterly, half-yearly or yearly, equal to the full annual value of the land? Is it expected, is it really believed, that men in this situation, will or can vote without any regard to the wishes of their landlords? that the tenant, when he goes to give his vote, will have no care to conciliate the favor, or to avoid the resentment, of the man, who may issue his distress warrant whenever the rent is in arrear, and take the bed on which his sick wife is lying, or the cradle from his new-born child? Sir, the landlord holds such a tenant by the very strings of his heart. He has the power, with the slightest twitch, to drag him to the polls, and to dictate his vote. Not the pusillanimity only, but the very virtues of the man, may serve to ensure his dependence, and implicit obedience to the master-power which constrains his will. If the landlord be indulgent and kind—if with power to exact his due by summary process of distress, he yet forbears to do so, out of a kind regard to the interests of the tenant, or a generous sympathy with any misfortunes which have befallen him, he binds the tenant to him by favor: if there be gratitude in the human heart, such a tenant will respect the wishes of such a landlord; and the case will be rare indeed, in which he will hesitate to give his vote at the polls, according to the landlord's desire or suggestion, or his slightest hint. On the other hand, the hard and rigorous landlord may address his dictation to the distresses or fears of his tenant; and may, in general, command his vote, by the terror of a constable at his door, with a distress warrant in his hand. The poor man, who loves his wife and children, will look to their welfare and comfort as the first object of his care, and will find in the pride of political independence, no consolation for the misery in which it may involve them. Thus it is, Sir, that all extremes approach. This extension of the Right of Suffrage, professedly (and, I will not doubt, sincerely) designed to raise the poor to a level with the rich in political power, will only increase the power of the rich: for, it may safely be affirmed, as a general consequence of the principle, that, to give the Right of Suffrage to tenants at will, the mere dependents on the bounty of the rich, or to tenants from year to year, or to your termors of five years, rendering a full rent, is, in effect, to give the landlord as many votes, in addition to his own, as he has tenants. We have all heard of the interest of landlords of England in their counties—an interest transferrible at their pleasure, which is continually influencing, and often determining, the fate of elections. What is it? how acquired? and how exerted? The explanation is very simple. The great landholder lets to his tenant a petty forty shilling freehold, which qualifies him to vote in elections; and with this, he leases to him a farm for a term of years, at a full rent of £50, £100, or £500, with a clause of re-entry, and the legal power to distrain, for rent in arrear. Such a tenant is expected to give his vote, whenever he shall be called upon, according to his landlord's will and pleasure, just as much as he is expected to pay his rent when due; and the vote, is given, as certainly, I doubt not far more certainly, than the rent is paid; it being the only part of the consideration, which the tenant finds no trouble in paying. I shall be told, no doubt, as I have been often told, that *we* may rely on the political virtue of this people, as a complete safeguard against the exertion, or even the existence, of any such influence of the landlord over his tenant. The virtue of the people is resorted to to solve all difficulties. To me it seems passing strange, that an argument should be drawn from the present existence of political virtue, against the system, under which that virtue has grown up and attained its utmost strength, and in favor of a new principle, the obvious tendency of which is, to expose that virtue to temptation and corruption. And, with regard to that political influence, which a landlord may acquire over his tenant, by kindness, indulgence and favor, it is quite obvious, that the virtues both of the one and of the other, far from tending to counteract such an influence, have a tendency to beget, to foster and confirm it. I own, that, at this time, and perhaps for some ten or fifteen years to come, it is not probable, that any landlord will dare to exercise a political influence over his tenant, by a rigorous exertion of the powers which such a creditor has over such a debtor; but the time may come, the time sooner or later will surely come, when, in the agitation of those violent political contests, which certainly no man hopes or believes to be impossible or improbable in this Commonwealth, and which are so peculiarly calculated to excite the passions of men, and to make them regardless of the political morality of the means by which party purposes can be accomplished, we may expect to see landlords exerting their influence over their tenants, in whatever way such an influence may be most effectually exerted. Let there be one successful example of the kind, and there will soon be imitation enough; and the exertion of this corrupt and corrupting influence, which viewed at a distance and in the abstract, is an object of just abomination, will soon come to be regarded, as natural, fair and legitimate. What expedient will then be resorted to to preserve the tenant's independence, and exempt him, as a voter at the polls, from the influence of his landlord? Sir, I have heard it hinted already—not yet indeed openly upon this floor—but it has been hinted, that the remedy is quite obvious and easy—only abolish the right of the landlord to distrain for rent in arrear. Suppose it shall be adopted—as in my conscience I believe it will be, and that at no distant day—what then? Would the genius of reform also deny the landlord his action of debt to recover his rent, and his execution to enforce the judgment? Shall all clauses of re-entry for non-payment of rent, inserted in any lease, be declared null and void by statute? The very suggestion of the possibility of such expedients to counteract the tendency of the proposed extension of the Right of Suffrage, is the strongest sentence of condemnation of the principle itself, since it serves to shew, that the adoption of it is only a prelude to a direct attack upon the rights of landed property.

It may be thought extraordinary, that I, who maintain, that property is justly entitled to representation—that, being inert in itself, to take from it all influence in the Government, would be to make it, not an object of the most jealous care (as it ought to be), but an object of plunder—that I should, nevertheless, reject the proposed extension of the Right of Suffrage, on the ground that it tends to increase the political influence of the fee-simple owners of land. And, to my knowledge, there are some to whom the proposed extension of the Right of Suffrage is recommended, precisely by the consideration which I have been urging as a vital objection to it—namely, that it will increase the political influence of the landholder. Sir, I am for giving property a fair, just, direct influence in the Government—an influence little (if at all) liable to abuse—an influence, which promotes, instead of undermining, public virtue; an influence, which obviates the possibility of corruption—that kind of influence, which it has hitherto had in this Commonwealth, and which has contributed, above all things, to the preservation of political purity in the community at large, and in the administration of public affairs. But, regarding public virtue as essential to the very being of a Republic, as the vital spirit which animates healthful liberty, and makes her the parent of every blessing and the dearest object of our affections, I shall be the last man to give property that kind of influence which can work only by corruption; an influence, which will corrupt alike the citizen by whom it shall be exercised, and the citizen on whom it shall be exerted.

Sir, these house-keepers and termors of five years, stand in a relation towards their landlords, to which the influence of the one, and the dependence of the other, are, in my opinion, almost inseparably incident; and, therefore, they are the last class of men (except paupers) who ought to be admitted to the polls.

I am, Sir, for retaining, unchanged and unimpaired, the *principle* of the freehold qualification of the Right of Suffrage, as established by the existing Constitution and laws, only extending the right to such as come within the reason on which the principle itself was established by our forefathers. Shall I be again told, that the Convention of 1776 found this principle in the Constitution of the Colonial Government, and preserved it unaltered—that it was copied from the institutions of England—that it was in truth dictated to us, originally, by King Charles II. in 1667—and that its origin and its history stamp upon it, indelibly, the odious character of aristocracy? Whence did we derive the institution of jury-trial? Whence the principle of representative Government itself? Did we copy them from the Republic of Rome, or the democracy of Athens? Were they suggested by the wisdom of Aristotle, or of Plato, or of Tully? Are gentlemen prepared to abolish the institution of jury-trial, and the principle of representative Government itself, merely because they are (as undoubtedly they are) of English origin? Are they prepared to draw the very blood from our veins, because that too is derived from British ancestors? Are they prepared to abrogate the whole body of the Common Law, because it is the Common Law of England?—that Common Law, which our ancestors brought with them to this land, and claimed and enjoyed as their birthright—that Common Law, the genius of which is found standing by the side of liberty, wherever liberty is found upon the globe, her companion and her handmaid. As to the freehold qualification having been dictated to the Colonial Government of Virginia, by a royal mandate in the reign of Charles II., I do not question the fact; nor have I the least doubt, that it was a high-handed arbitrary measure, transcending the lawful authority of the crown, and essaying to usurp powers, which the Constitution of the Colonial Government (such as it was) vested in the whole Legislature: but it is not true, that the freehold qualification of Suffrage was established in the Colony, by force of the royal mandate; it was established and regulated by the only competent authority—by an act of the whole Legislature. He who attributes this measure to the personal interference of Charles, has given very little attention to the character or history of that scoundrel King (as he has been justly called.) It was only a measure of that reign—a measure of the minister, whoever he was, that was charged with the care of Colonial affairs—and it was intended, as it certainly was calculated, to give stability and dignity to the Colonial Government. The King himself, intent only on sensual gratifications, pleasure and ease, hardly bestowed a serious thought on the condition of his subjects at home, much less on the political institutions of his distant Colonies. But this freehold qualification of Suffrage in Virginia, was a measure of Charles's reign! So was the act, which is now the great safeguard of personal freedom, in England and America—the act which secured the privilege of the writ of *Habeas Corpus!* I hope, Sir, we shall hear no more declamation on this subject—no more addresses to our prejudices: I hope we shall discuss the merits of the freehold qualification of Suffrage, as a question of political expediency, or (if gentlemen please) of political justice, or natural right, without the least consideration of the Colonial or English or regal source, from which it was originally derived.

In the various discussions I have heard on the subject of the qualification of the Right of Suffrage, as well before as since the meeting of this Convention, I have understood those who are opposed to the freehold qualification, to contend, that the Right of Suffrage belongs, *of natural right*, to all men who are subject to the Government, and bound to contribute to its support, and to bear arms in defence of the State. Now, Sir, for my own part, I am incapable of conceiving any *natural right*—(a right, distinct from, antecedent to, independent of, social conventional law—a right inherent in man, derived from the law of nature, and with which he is indued by the God of nature)—which is not common to every human being. Take the definition of the first article of the Bill of Rights: "All men are by nature equally free and independent, and have certain inherent rights, of which, when they enter into a state of society, they cannot by any compact deprive or divest their posterity; namely, the enjoyment of life and liberty, with the means of acquiring and possessing property, and pursuing and obtaining happiness and safety." It is manifest, these rights belong not only to every man who pays public taxes and bears arms, but also to every woman and child in the community. Again; natural rights are rights inherent in man, vested in him before he enters into society, distinct from and independent of social institutions. Can there be a greater contradiction in terms, than to say that the Right of Suffrage is one of these natural rights, pertaining to man in a state of nature?—the Right of Suffrage, which supposes a state of society—which can never be exercised, which can have no value, no effect, and no imaginable ideal existence, till society is formed and regulated by laws, nor indeed till it has attained to a very high degree of civilization and refinement. The friends of Universal or (as it is now the fashion to call it) General Suffrage, are themselves obliged to admit, that it is not a natural right—that it is a merely conventional right: for, at the first stroke of the pen, they exclude from the polls all women without exception, that is, about half of the community; and then, all minors, that is about half of the male sex; and then, all paupers and convicts—so that this right, which gentlemen claim as one of the natural rights of man (and if so common, to all mankind), they themselves propose to confine to less than a fourth of the people. We all agree, then, that the Right of Suffrage is a subject of conventional regulation—we all agree, that some limitation of it, and a very extensive limitation too, is just and necessary. The question is, what qualification is the most just, the most politic, the best suited to the nature and ends of a Representative Republic, and, in particular, to the peculiar circumstances of this Commonwealth? The question between us, is only a question of degree. And believing, as I do most conscientiously believe, that the landed freehold qualification is preferable, far preferable, to any other that can be devised, I am bound to maintain it with the utmost exertion of my poor ability.

Gentlemen say, it is imperfect—that there are lazy, idle, drunken, vitious men, who hold freeholds which may entitle them to vote, while their next neighbour, though ever so industrious, honest and intelligent, may be excluded from the polls, because he owns no freehold—that the man who owns a freehold to-day, and sells it to-morrow, is in all likelihood equally worthy to be entrusted with the exercise of political power after he has made the sale as before, and that the purchaser can hardly be deemed more worthy, the day after than he was the day before he made the acquisition—that, surely, intelligence, or independence, or any of the social virtues, cannot, with truth, be ascribed to all the freeholders, or denied to all the non-freeholders; and I admit all this. It has been said too, that there are freeholders who are paupers; but that I cannot conceive the possibility of. But I admit, that the freehold qualification is imperfect. What then? I still say—and I appeal to every man who hears me, whether or no I say the truth—that, in Virginia, the great mass of intelligence and virtue resides in that stout and generous yeomanry, the freeholders of this land; that to them belongs not only all the real property of the Commonwealth, but almost all of the personal property also; that they are the class, who feed, who clothe, who educate all classes; who hold the greatest stake in society; who are the only persons who have any stake that may not be withdrawn at pleasure, in the twinkling of an eye; who, therefore, have, and actually take, the deepest interest in the public welfare. They alone support Government, constantly in peace, as well as occasionally in war—they fight as well as pay—and they feed and clothe and pay all who do fight. It has been my lot to mix, a great deal, in the society of these freeholders—aye, Sir, with the very poorest of them. I think I know the character of our poor freeholder perfectly. Look at him—modest, unobtrusive, and unassuming, in his manners and deportment, almost to humility, the idea has never entered into his head, that he is a nobleman—the limb of a great aristocracy: on the contrary, the first impression of a stranger would be, that he is not sensible of his dignity as a freeman. But try him—go to his house, and you will find him, and especially his wife, hospitable to the utmost of their means—trust him, and you will find him proudly faithful to his trust—appeal to him in any distress that may befall you; you will find his heart warm with generous sympathy, and his hand ready to aid you—Do him a service or a kindness, he will remember it to the latest hour of his life; and if ever opportunity occurs, he will pay it back to you, or after your death, to your children, with interest—let any one wrong him; he knows as well as the wisest, how to seek and obtain redress—insult him, and he will fight you. I copy the portrait, Sir, from the picture of the original painted on my own heart. I can hardly imagine a higher degree of virtue, public or private, than that of the great body of the freeholders of Virginia. Has one man of them all ever been bribed for his vote? has any gentleman ever heard of a single instance? The wealth of this Commonwealth cannot bribe the freeholders of that little despised county of Warwick, so often referred to, on account of its size, as the opprobrium of the existing Constitution. I say, therefore, that the freehold landed qualification—though it is not absolutely perfect, as I willingly own it is not—though, like all other general regulations, it may admit some to the polls, who, if regard could be had to their individual character, ought to be excluded, and excludes some, whom, regarding individual merit, all would be willing to admit—is still, in Virginia at least, if not in all Republican States, the preferable qualification of Suffrage—the best criterion for ascertaining the class most worthy to be entrusted with the political powers of the State.

No general regulation on the subject, can be exempt from imperfection. We all (I believe—I am not quite sure of it) concur as to the qualifications of sex and age—that all women and all minors, without exception, ought to be excluded from the polls. Yet, I presume, no man entertains the opinion, that there is not a single woman, that there are not many, very many women, fully equal to the most meritorious of the other sex, in intelligence, in public spirit, and every other quality that constitutes a good citizen. I have known women, Sir, who possessed, not only the gentler virtues of their sex, and passive fortitude (in which, I think, they generally surpass men), but such active courage, as might shame many of the stronger sex. Is that a perfect rule, which excludes all women, the firm and wise, as well as the silly and the vain? As to the qualification of age, we all concur in admitting to the polls, the most imbecile of mankind—men in the last extremity of dotage—men of any degree of mental weakness short of legal incapacity to manage their own affairs—while we exclude all youths under twenty-one years of age, whatever be their attainments or their merits. Considered, then, in reference to individuals, gentlemen must perceive, that even these qualifications of sex and age, which as yet no statesman surely has ever doubted the propriety of, are imperfect.

Let us not waste our labour in a vain search after unattainable perfection in our political institutions. If, in regulating the Right of Suffrage, we can find a rule which will exclude the fewest of those who ought to be admitted, and admit the fewest of those who on any account ought to be excluded, with that rule we ought to be content. And I shall forever maintain, that (in this Commonwealth particularly) the freehold qualification is that rule.

It is, I suppose without question, the object of us all, to establish a wise, just, patriotic, Republican Government. And, looking to the accomplishment of that end, I insist, that to ensure wisdom in the Government, and a strict observance of justice, and a spirit of patriotism in the administration of public affairs, we ought to vest the Right of Suffrage (the fountain, in our system, of all political power) in that class of men, in whom we find, generally, the greatest degree of moral and intellectual cultivation; in that class of men, who, holding the property of the State, are the most interested in the administration of justice; in that class of men, whose own interests are the most completely identified with the interests of the Commonwealth. And this is the class of freeholders.

Now, Sir, is the freehold qualification contrary to any sound principle of Republican Government? Gentlemen insist that it is—and they appeal to the Bill of Rights, in which it is declared, that "all men, having sufficient evidence of permanent common interest with, and attachment to, the community, have the Right of Suffrage." We acknowledge the principle, in its utmost extent—but we tell them, that it is only the general abstract principle, and that the question is as to its application in practice—what is the sufficient evidence of common interest with, and attachment to, the community, which ought to be required as the qualification of Suffrage? We tell them, that the very men, who laid down the abstract principle, did, at the very same time, in their practical application of it, require a freehold in land, as the qualification. The only answer they give us, is, simply, to repeat the principle: relying on the authority of the Bill of Rights for the principle, which nobody disputes, and rejecting the authority of the Constitution, framed by the same men, as to the practical application of it, which is the point in debate, they eternally repeat the principle. Now, I affirm, as the Convention of 1776 affirmed in the Constitution, that a freehold, or other certain, permanent, independent interest, in land, is the best and the only sufficient evidence of permanent common interest with, and attachment to, the community.

For, I think it may safely be assumed, that not only all the land of the country is owned by the freeholders, but at least nineteen twentieths (I believe the proportion is much greater) of the visible, taxable, personal property also is owned by them. Suppose one of these men purposes to sell his land, and migrate to the West; still he is interested in whatever affects the general weal of Virginia, to the last moment he holds the land, since he cannot divest himself of his interest in its value. But mere personal property has no locality. Slaves without land to work them on, are more valuable in the South Western States than here. Money, Bank stock, stock in the public funds, are of equal value every where: the owners of such property (it is with us, a very small part of the national wealth) have not, by reason of such ownership, any common interest with or attachment to our community, in any sense of the words.

I shall forever contend, that those who must bear the burden of paying taxes, ought to have the power of laying them. Is it right, that the land-holders of Virginia, who must pay almost the whole revenue of the State, as well that raised on land, as that raised on personal property, should be taxed by those who pay little or nothing, and who by no contrivance can be made to contribute more?

There is another view of this subject, which is very obvious, and yet seems to have altogether escaped the attention of those who deny the propriety of the freehold qualification. The Commonwealth of Virginia has three several classes of political interests. One is the interest she has, in common with all the States of the Federal Union, in relation to foreign nations; this is confided to the Federal Government. Another is, the interest of Virginia, in relation to the Union, and to the several States which compose it; this is confided, partly to the Federal, and partly to the State, Government. In regard to both these classes of interests, every citizen of Virginia has, or ought to have, the same common interest. But, as to the other class, the local interests of the several parts of the State in relation to each other—which are confided exclusively to the State Government—which are continually brought home to every man—I defy the wit of man to discover any evidence, or devise any cause, of community of interest with or attachment to any particular county, other than the ownership of land in it. What is the bond, which attaches the resident of the county of Chesterfield, who has only a slave, or a horse, or a gainful trade, to the peculiar interests of that county, more than those of Henrico? What is his community of interest with the people of Chesterfield, for whose representative he is to vote? I pray gentlemen to tell me; to tax their ingenuity, to exercise their invention, or their imagination, and point it out to me, if they can. There is none; none conceivable.

There are those who affect to think, that the mere fact of the citizen being born in the State, is enough to attach him forever to the interests of the Commonwealth, and even of the particular county in which he is born; and that birth, therefore, with actual residence and mature age, is a sufficient qualification of the Right of Suffrage. I wish I could think this reasoning well founded in fact. For my own part—though I have never avowed the sentiment without exciting a smile—I yield all pretensions to philosophy, and I am proud to own, that I cherish a narrow attachment for the spot of earth where I was born, and where sleep in peace the ashes of my parents, and of all the dead whom I have loved and honoured in my youth; and a grateful affection for the people among whom I was bred, and from whom, from my childhood to this hour, I have been experiencing continual kindness. Would to God, this sentiment was general! But we see men, every day, leaving this their native land, and migrating to the most distant regions of the West, without a single pang at the separation from the home and the friends of their youth, and with no concern but that which springs from the thought of their being obliged to pay for the land they have bought of the United States.

While the freehold owners of the land, being owners also of the great mass of visible taxable personalty, have a community of interest, of which they never can divest themselves, with every other class of the community, the other classes have no necessary community of interest with them. Retain the powers of Government in the hands of the freeholders; and they can never adopt any course of measures, or impose any public burdens, which will not affect themselves equally or more than the non-freeholders. Place the Government in other hands than theirs; and they may be ground to dust and ashes by those who have no fellow-feeling for them. All men, we are told, are by nature equally free; and thence it is inferred, that every man is equally entitled, in a political way, to dispose of the property of others. The direct contrary is the true inference—that every man is best entitled to dispose of his own. This principle intended to operate as a protection of the rights of individuals from the power of others, and expressly so applied by those who declared it, is converted into a principle of power over others. Sir, these manifold perversions of the plain words and simple elementary truths of the Bill of Rights, which I daily hear, are, to my apprehension, the most alarming symptom of the times: they jeopard the very principle of property; they portend serious danger to all regular Government.

But it is contended, that the freehold qualification is an odious system of exclusion; and every word we have heard on the subject here—and all the reasoning of that famous memorial, which was presented to us at the commencement of our session, and which has been so much lauded—proceed on the assumption that this is the true character of the principle. A stranger unacquainted with our institutions, and relying for information concerning them on the language of our reformers, would conclude, that the freeholders constitute a separate and higher rank in our society, and the non-freeholders an inferiour degraded caste, from which the one can never rise, nor the other descend; that the freeholder can never part with his qualification and cease to enjoy the Right of Suffrage, nor the non-freeholder acquire it. Yet, in truth, there is not the least restraint on the alienation of freehold lands in Virginia; and every farthing's worth of real estate is open to the fair and honest acquisition of all. No law secures the possession of the soil to luxury and idleness, or denies it to honest labour and persevering industry. An odious system of exclusion! where every man may acquire freehold estate in land enough to confer the Right of Suffrage for fifty dollars. There is not a county in the State (unless, perhaps, the county of Jefferson) where a sufficient freehold may not be bought for fifty dollars; in many counties, it may be bought for twenty, in many for five dollars. No honest industrious citizen is excluded, who chooses to gain admission; no, none but the veriest paupers and drones in the community, whom all agree upon excluding. An interest in the soil is only required, because it affords the best and only certain general test of community of interest with the great body of the State. It was, then, with surprise, ineffable surprise, that I heard the information which the gentleman from Monongalia (Mr. Wilson) gave the Committee the other day—that in his part of the country, men of the highest merit, "of civic virtue and literary talent," debarred by the requisition of the freehold qualification from exercising the invaluable Right of Suffrage, and disgusted with this "odious exclusion," this degradation from the rank of citizens, were seen to abandon their native land, and seek "in the free States," that equality with others which our institutions sternly deny them. I should be glad to know of the gentleman, what a sufficient freehold to give the Right of Suffrage, would cost in the county of Monongalia? I suppose it might be bought for ten dollars; twenty dollars would be a large estimate. And if these gentlemen of "civic virtue and literary talent" felt, so very acutely, the evil and degradation of their exclusion from the polls—if an attachment to this State formed any ingredient in their "civic virtue"—if their taste for literature had not spurned the vulgar processes of calculation—they would have considered, that the expense of the first hundred miles of travel, in their emigration to "the free States," would have sufficed to purchase a freehold at home, and this invaluable Right of Suffrage into the bargain. The very facility, with which, for the slightest or for no reason, these non-freeholders abandon the State, of which we have now, from one of their advocates, the most authentic information, is conclusive proof to my mind, that it is wise to exclude them from the polls—precisely, because it evinces, that they have no permanent common interest with or attachment to the community.

The war of epithets too, which I hoped had spent its rage in the debate upon the question of the basis of Representation, has been renewed upon this question of the qualification of Suffrage. The freehold qualification is a remnant, a shred, a taint of aristocracy, which we ought carefully to expurgate from our political institutions! Any person is at full liberty to think me an aristocrat—aye, and to call me so, if he pleases—provided it is not done with design to insult me: I have no office to gain; no office, no emolument, no political fame or consequence to lose—naught is never in danger—political proscription cannot harm me. I shall still enjoy the personal confidence of the generous people, whom it is my pride to represent here—I shall still enjoy the affections of all those whose regard is at all necessary to my happiness in life—these I can only forfeit by departing from the course (I wish I were sure I could persist in it) of virtue and honour: and as loyalty of personal attachment is with me a ruling motive and principle of action, so I look to it as my principal solace and support. I, therefore, trust, that I shall have the fortitude to bear any political odium that can be heaped upon my head; and the courage to face any clamour that can be raised, however fierce and loud. To constitute the *justum et tenacem propositi virum*, it is not more necessary that he should be capable of withstanding the *vultus instantis tyranni*, than that he should be capable of beholding, unmoved, the *civium ardor prava jubentium*. The freehold qualification is aristocratical! Was Patrick Henry an aristocrat? was George Mason? was Edmund Pendleton? was Spencer Roane? Were all the great and good men in Virginia, since the revolution, who have, so steadily, so anxiously adhered to this principle, aristocrats? Has Virginia herself been aristocratical for these fifty-four years past? Is this blasphemy of our glorious forefathers to be endured? I understand the term "aristocracy," to describe political power vested in a particular order of men, either designated by birth, or by election for life, which, by the Constitution of the State, is unalienably vested in them, and in which no other order of men in the community, can, by any act of their own, participate. Generally, in Governments where orders of nobility are admitted, the rank and the political power incident to it, are descendible. But what is the condition of this nobility of ours—this aristocratic body of freeholders? The freeholder sells his land to the plebeian non-freeholder: the plebeian is exalted to the patrician order, and, *eodem flatu*, the patrician descends into the plebeian; and these ups and downs are continually going on. Even gentlemen's termors for years, and house-keepers, are nobility too, if enjoying the Right of Suffrage gives the patent of nobility; but, in their case, the landlord has only to say "quit," and not only their patent of nobility is revoked, but they are turned out of house and home. To call the freehold qualification aristocratical, if not a wilful abuse of words, implies a confusion of ideas.

But if this institution is not an aristocracy, it is an oligarchy—the Government of a few (for that, I believe is the meaning of the word)—the number of freeholders does not amount to a moiety of the free white citizens of the Commonwealth, of full age, who contribute to the public revenue! I know who it was that first said it—and I know how little logic can avail to refute faith—but if undeniable facts have any virtue in argument, our opponents have been at the pains to collect such facts as common reason, not sustained by faith, will hardly be able to resist. They have called on the Auditor, for "a statement of the number of persons in each county and town charged with a State tax for the year 1828"—and, for "a statement of the number of persons, charged on the land books of 1828, with taxes on a quantity of land not less than twenty-five acres, or on a lot or part of a lot in town." These statements have been laid before us.* The first ascertains the number of tax-payers, to whom it is proposed by some to extend the Right of Suffrage; the other ascertains with sufficient accuracy, the number of freehold estates of the extent which gives the Right of Suffrage. And it appears, that the number of freeholds is ninety-two thousand eight hundred and fifty-six—and the number of tax-payers only ninety-five thousand five hundred and ninety-three. There ought to be a deduction from the number of freeholds, on account of the double, or rather the manifold charges of the same land on the commissioners' books of the Western counties, in consequence of the number of patents that have been issued for the same tracts: my friend from Spottsylvania (Mr. Stanard) thinks this deduction ought to be ten thousand—which will leave the number of freeholders about eighty-two thousand. The deductions of femes covert and minors are to be made equally from both lists. It is apparent the number of freeholders is to that of the tax-payers (which, of course, includes all the freeholders) more than eight to ten. And, then, we have an oligarchy—*a Government of a few*—vested in more than eight-tenths of the people!

I have no doubt myself, that a great many of the tax-payers, who are not also freeholders, are the adult sons of freeholders, not yet married and settled in life; because whoever owns a horse, pays a revenue tax; and, among that class of people in Virginia, who, in my part of the State, are called good-livers, the first present, which a father makes to his son, when he puts on the *toga virilis*, is a horse; which horse makes that son chargeable with a State tax. And, gentlemen ask, why are the sons of freeholders—those sons, who are to inherit the lands of their fathers—those sons, who have a common interest in the soil with their fathers—why are they excluded from the polls? I believe, there would be little or no practical difference, in the mere result of elections, between the admission and the exclusion of them. But suppose them admitted: the sons would either vote with their father, or against him. If they should vote with him (as it is to be expected they generally would) the result would only be, to give the father as many votes, in addition to his own, as he has sons of full age. If they should vote against him (and a puppy scoundrel son may take a pride in voting against his father) then they would only countervail their father's vote, and stifle his voice in the Government—which can only be justified by that very peculiar trait in the natural history of man, which is found in this country, (such is the march of mind), though never imagined to exist in any other age or nation under heaven; namely, that the son is, of course, wiser than his father. Has it come to this pass? Are the sons of this land to be taught, that they cannot safely trust the political powers of the State, to their own fathers? Not only are all sentiments of generous chivalry to be decried, renounced, banished from our society—not only is the order of private gentleman to be abolished, as aristocratic and odious—but even filial piety is to be discouraged as incompatible with civil liberty. What manner of democracy is this which teaches these doctrines of impiety and abomination? Not that democracy which our fathers loved and cherished—no, Sir; but a siren democracy—gifted with the voice of the charmer, indeed, and with face and breast of maiden beauty, but declining into a foul and scaly serpent armed with mortal sting. *Procul! O Procul!* Sooner would I embrace monarchy at once, in any form, than democracy of that family, which is sure after years of crime and blood and horror, to engender military despotism.

We are urged to abolish the freehold qualification of Suffrage, in order (as we are gravely told) to subvert the lowland oligarchy—the lowland aristocracy—the aristocracy of wealth! And of the existence of this aristocracy of wealth, there stands Col. William Allen of Surry, the living example and proof! Truly, Sir, but for him, I apprehend gentlemen would have been somewhat at a loss to find an instance to their purpose. That gentleman inherited a large estate from his ancestors, and instead of squandering it away, he has kept it together, and improved his fortune; which, in my opinion, is proof of good sense and virtue too. He owns some thousands of acres of land, and certainly a large number of slaves—eight hundred, I think we were told at the commencement of our session, but now (wonderful increase) twelve

* See these statements appended to the Journal of the Convention, Nos. 6, 7.

hundred—and he has a park stocked with deer—and he undoubtedly drinks, or rather gives his guests to drink, the oldest and best wine in Virginia. Long may he live, say I, to enjoy it all! Because there are a few, a very few, wealthy individuals among us, it seems to be supposed, that the great body of our freeholders are opulent. Gentlemen take no note of Col. Allen's poor neighbors. The wealthy freeholders! Would to heaven, they were wealthy! I am sorry to know, with perfect certainty, that the reverse is the true state of their condition; it is mockery to taunt them with their overgrown wealth. The statute of descents is alone sufficient to prevent the possible growth of aristocracy. This talk of the lowland aristocracy—the landed aristocracy—the aristocracy of wealth—is downright slang.

Gentlemen have advanced one argument against the freehold qualification, which, from the frequency with which they have recurred to it, and the earnestness with which they have pressed it upon us, I suppose they think irrefragable—a sort of *argumentum ad hominem*, or *reductio ad absurdum*, which they seem to think it impossible to escape from or resist—an argument, therefore, which it is my business to state and meet fairly and directly. Indeed, to some it might seem uncourteous, and to others sheer recreancy, if I were to decline it. The argument is this—Gentlemen say to us, if you contend, that, in framing a Republican Constitution of Government for the State, a freehold landed qualification of Suffrage is wise and proper, in order to preserve a due regard to the interests of property in the ordinary administration of public affairs, why do you not carry the principle out to all its consequences and to its utmost extent, and allowing one vote to the man that owns ten acres of land (for instance,) allow ten votes to the owner of a hundred, and fifty to the owner of five hundred acres, and so on? Will you pretend, that this would be right? or that it would be compatible with the true principles of a Representative Republic? I answer, without hesitation, no. But, in the first place, the argument, if of force to condemn the freehold qualification, concludes against a property qualification of Suffrage of any kind; and is inconsistent with the views of every man, who is not for Universal Suffrage in the utmost latitude ever heard of. In the next place, I by no means allow, with respect to any moral or political principle whatever, that because it would end in vice or folly if pushed to extremes, it is therefore vitious and unwise, when applied with moderation and caution; for I doubt, whether there is a single moral or political truth, however generally admitted and acted upon by men, that might not be condemned by the same process of reasoning. Then, Sir, we have never contended, that an *undue* influence in the Government should be allowed to property, but that *due* regard and consideration should be had to the interests of property, and only so much weight allowed to it in the Constitution of the Government, as will suffice for its preservation and security; and the fair state of the question is, whether, in insisting on the freehold qualification, we ask more than political prudence dictates? Now, Sir, the owner of a thousand, or ten thousand acres of land, may safely trust the owner of a hundred acres, or of ten, with an equal share of power over property, and especially over taxation; in other words, with an equal vote at the polls, because the owner of the smaller property, has a common interest with the owner of the larger; he must feel precisely the same kind of interest in every public measure, which affects the owners of real estate, either beneficially or injuriously; and as the modicum of the poorer freeholder, and the broader lands of his more opulent neighbour, are equally dear to the respective proprietors, each will unite with the other to promote or defend the interest of all. If the poor freeholder contributes less, his means of contribution are less; the burden is proportioned to the ability; and the more opulent freeholder finds ample security in the self-love of the poorer, and the poorer in that of the more opulent. All we desire is, to place the political power of the State, in the hands of those who have a community of interest in whatever befals the State, whether of weal or woe.

Comparisons have been made between the condition of Virginia, who has so long and so pertinaciously adhered to her freehold qualification of Suffrage, and that of our sister States, who have adopted more liberal principles, in this particular; and, in painting the portrait of Virginia, gentlemen seem to have thought that nothing but shade is necessary to a likeness, and in the portraits of our sister States, nothing but light. Where, they ask, are our arts, our literature, our manufactures, our commerce? What is the state of our agriculture? What has become of our political rank and eminence in the Union? Whither, in the language of Henry, whither has the Genius of Virginia fled? As to arts (if gentlemen mean the fine arts) and literature, I grant we have a very moderate share indeed of the one, and none of the other—but, whether owing to my ignorance, or to my national vanity, or national prejudices, I have never been sensible of any great superiority of our fellow-citizens of other States in these respects, while I am very sensible of the very great inferiority of us all to the nations of Europe, though none of them enjoy, and not one (I believe) is capable of enjoying, the blessing of Republican Government in any form. Gentlemen will hardly, upon reflection, impute our defects in arts and in letters, to the freehold qualification of

Suffrage. And how any man can impute the low state of our manufactures, and the decay of our trade, to any measures or to any neglect of the State Government, I am wholly at a loss to imagine; since the interests of commerce belong exclusively to the Federal Government; and it has assumed the care of manufactures also—but I do not mean to discuss the justice or the policy of that system of measures. But that which seems to me, the oddest of all the oddities and novelties which I have heard advanced on this floor, is the opinion, that the languishing condition of our agriculture, is owing to the neglect of that great interest by the State Government, and that neglect imputable to the circumstance of all political power being vested in the allodial cultivators of the soil. For my own part, I only wish the Federal Government would unite with the State Government, in leaving manufactures and commerce and agriculture to their natural course—but this no wise concerns our present question; and, I say again, I shall not enter into that field. But, say gentlemen, Virginia has declined, and is declining—she was once the first State in the Union—now she has sunk to be the third, and will soon sink lower in the scale—New York has taken the lead of her. I envy not the pre-eminence of New York, or of any other State, in population or in wealth. Do gentlemen really believe, that it is owing to any diversity in the principles of the State Governments of the two States, that New York has advanced to be the first State in the Union, and that Virginia, from being the first, is now the third, in wealth and population? Virginia ceded away her Kentucky, to form a new State; and New York has retained her Genessee—there lies the whole secret. The conduct of both States was determined by a just regard to the geographical situation of their original territory; and I am well content, that Virginia did make the cession, and that New York retained her territory. The truth is, that so long as new and fertile lands remain to be settled in the Western States, the old States never can advance in population, as rapidly as they otherwise would; and of all the old States, none has contributed more to the peopling of the new States, than Virginia—I dare to say, not one so much. This is the reason of what gentlemen call the decline of Virginia. Her Government could not by any conceivable means have prevented it; nor if it could, ought it to have done so. Virginia, in common with most of the old States, must of necessity forego, for a long time to come, the advantages of a full population; and may, meanwhile, content herself with an exemption from the evils incident to a State of a crowded population. Is Virginia inferiour to any of her sister States, in social peace and happiness, in intelligence, in the virtues of private life, in political purity, in national character? No, Sir—I say, proudly and confidently, no. I shall not vaunt of her superiority—but I acknowledge no inferiority. I have been happy to observe, that if she has, at times, been an object of some jealousy in other States, she has still always enjoyed the respect of them all. And I shall add (what is peculiarly pertinent to the present debate) that she has been chiefly respected for the even tenor of her system, and the steadiness and probity of her character and her course; which the most sagacious Statesmen of other States—I say it with the most perfect conviction, or rather the most certain knowledge—have attributed, mainly, to this very principle of the freehold qualification of Suffrage, which it is now proposed to abolish.

And, Sir, the only point of comparison between the condition of Virginia and that of any of our sister States, which is at all pertinent to the present question, is the comparison of the practical effects of Universal or General Suffrage in those States in which it has been adopted, with those of the freehold qualification of Suffrage in Virginia: a point on which it would not become me to speak my thoughts with perfect freedom. I take a deep interest in whatever concerns the happiness of our sister States—not so deep, indeed, as that I feel for my own State, to which I owe and cherish the most perfect allegiance of mind and heart—but yet a deep and sincere interest. I am the last man to take pleasure in finding fault with their institutions, much less with the political character or conduct of their citizens; to think hardly concerning them, or to speak unkindly. I hope it will not be thought inconsistent with these sentiments, if I say, as I must say to this Committee, that I have never conversed with any observant reflecting man, who has migrated from Virginia to a land where Universal or General Suffrage prevails, who has not earnestly deprecated the abandonment of the freehold qualification in this his native State; and that I have never known any Virginian, that had witnessed an election campaign, or even a single scene of contested election, in New York, Pennsylvania, Maryland or Kentucky, however he may have been smitten with a passion for reform in this particular before he left home, who did not return completely cured of it. Neither does the passion ever recur. [Here a member said aloud—"It is like the small pox."] Yes, Sir—it is like the small pox in that respect—but there is this difference, that distance seems necessary to the communication of the Universal Suffrage fever—a near exposure to it, in its utmost intensity, generally proves a cure and an antidote. A close observation of the practical workings of the principle of Universal Suffrage, has rarely if ever failed to produce disgust, reprobation, deprecation. Shall we learn wisdom from the great State of New York, and profit by her experience and example? Her example, Sir, is a beacon to warn, not a guide to direct. I will not say—for I do not think—that the scenes which but yesterday were exhibited in the elections held in the city of New York—the open attack on the very principle of property, and on the principles of all regular Government, which excited serious alarm there—that these scenes afford any fair criterion of the sentiments of the body of the people of the State of New York. But, Sir, they afford abundant evidence, to my mind, that the poison has begun to work; and they afford us a lesson and a warning, by which we shall profit if we are wise, never to administer a drop of that same poison to our own body politic. As to our sister Maryland, the practical operation of her Universal Suffrage, is more open to our observation, from her nearer neighbourhood; and I shall say, that it was the actual view of it there, that first cured me of that plausible and tempting but deluding philosophy (so called) which most men imbibe in their youth, and which teaches that civil liberty is so good, that there is no necessity for moderation in the enjoyment of it—that no intemperance can disturb its healthful action. I received, very recently, by the mail, a newspaper printed at Cumberland in that State, with a note on the margin, calling my attention to an advertisement of nine hundred and forty acres of land, for sale by a constable, to satisfy a judgment rendered by a single justice of the peace; and with this remark—"See the effect of Universal Suffrage." Neither do I doubt, in the least, that the principle tends, in its practical operation, to indifference and unconcern for the rights of property, and especially of real property. How can it be otherwise, when those who hold no property, have a full share of the Government on which the security of property depends? In many, perhaps, in most of the States, where the principle of Universal, or General, or Extended, or Free Suffrage (call it by which name you please) prevails, I observe, the ballot has been substituted for the old method of voting *viva voce*, on the avowed principle, that it is necessary to enable the voter to give his vote with independence, that he should be allowed to vote secretly. Now, the introduction of the ballot, as part of the system and proper accompaniment of Universal Suffrage, is a plain distinct acknowledgement, that the Right of Suffrage is extended too far—extended to men who cannot be expected to give an independent vote, openly, in the face of day—to men liable to the influence of others, and desirous to conciliate their favour, or to avoid their resentment. And this method of preserving the spirit of political independence, by substituting the ballot for the public poll and *viva voce* vote, I fully expected to hear proposed to us, as part of our plan of reform. It is a very odd expedient for cherishing the political independence of the citizen, to take away all occasion for the exercise of it; as if political independence were not a virtue of the mind, and, like all other virtues and faculties, sure to be invigorated by exercise, and to wane and be extinguished by inaction. One remark more, before I leave this topic—I pray gentlemen to observe, how generally the introduction of Universal Suffrage has been followed by the caucus system of nomination—I know the name of caucus has recently been discarded, and that caucuses, now a days, are conventions, but the only difference is the name—caucuses or conventions to make a regular nomination of candidates, to discipline parties, to whip in all who hope a share of the loaves and fishes in their turn, and to whip out all who show a disposition to rebel against "regular nomination." They cheat the people with the shew of popular election; the elective body, in fact, is the caucus. Where there is a people capable of being drilled, there will not be wanting leaders to drill them. The freeholders of Virginia require no caucus or convention, to direct them how they are to vote—they require no drilling, and would submit to none—they want no ballot-box to hide their votes from their neighbours, and to screen them from the indignation of others—they feel their independence, and it costs them no effort to exercise it on all occasions.

Gentlemen tell me, however, that men who have once enjoyed the blessing of Universal Suffrage, can never be induced to forego it—that the farmers of Pennsylvania and Maryland, are not to be tempted by the offer of the most beneficial leases, to migrate hither; and our landholders can get no tenants, because the requisition of the freehold qualification debars such tenants from the invaluable privilege of Suffrage. If this is meant as an argumentative deduction from the supposed operation of political causes, I have nothing to say to it: but if intended as the assertion of a matter of fact, I must say, that I am incredulous. Let gentlemen name a single instance, in which any man has been prevented from migrating to Virginia, by any consideration of the laws regulating Suffrage. I should be curious to see such a man—for sure I am that I should see the most thorough bred philosopher of modern times, or at least a sample of the utmost extreme of political fanaticism. The true reason, I apprehend, why the farmers of Pennsylvania and Maryland, do not turn their attention to the beneficial leases which court them in Virginia, is, that if they find it prudent to migrate at all, they know very well whither to go, to procure land, and the best land, upon the easiest terms, in absolute property, which they may enjoy during life, and leave to their children. If the good people who dwell on our northern border, hope advantage of this kind from the proposed reform, I fear that hope will be disappointed.

It is remarkable—I mention it for the curiosity of the fact—that, if any evil, physical or moral, arise in any of the States south of us, it never takes a northerly direction, or taints the southern breeze; whereas if any plague originate in the North, it is sure to spread to the South and to invade us sooner or later: the influenza—the small-pox—the varioloid—the Hessian fly—the Circuit Court system—Universal Suffrage—all come from the North—and they always cross above the falls of the great rivers: below, it seems, the broad expanse of waters interposing, effectually arrests their progress.

I thought before the Convention met, that I was already familiar with the utmost extravagance of theoretical politics; but I have heard one proposition advanced on this floor, which is absolutely new to me—namely, that none but those who are allowed the exercise of the Right of Suffrage, are citizens—that all who are denied that right, are, in every just political view, slaves. Whence I learn, that our mothers, wives and daughters are not and never can be citizens; and that our sons never become citizens till they attain the age of twenty-one years, and acquire the legal qualification of Suffrage, whatever it may be. For my own part, I fondly imagine, that the mother who bore me was a free woman and a Virginian citizen—that my wife, and my children—male and female, are free born citizens of Virginia—and that I myself enjoyed exactly the same civil liberty before I attained to full age as I have ever done since—in short, that civil liberty, much more citizenship, depends not at all on the right to exercise political powers. Neither shall I render any thanks, (for I feel no gratitude) to those who have taken the pains to correct my errors in these points. It is, indeed, a great blessing—it is the first and the highest of social blessings—to live under a regular, free, Representative Republican Government; to belong to a society, fitted to enjoy, capable of enjoying, such a Government; but neither the blessing itself, nor any happiness which it can confer upon any individual, depends on the right of that individual to exercise, in his own person, the Right of Suffrage. The blessing of free Government, and all the happiness that can flow from it, is best secured to each individual, by the wisest general regulation of that right, whether such regulation admits him or excludes him. And in this view of the subject, gentlemen will see, upon a little reflection, the general opinions and feelings of men concur with perfect unanimity: for no one ever heard of any vendor of land demanding any consideration for the surrender of his Right of Suffrage in making the alienation, or of any purchasers advancing a cent more in the price for the acquisition of the right; and though I have known many to buy freeholds, in order to entitle themselves to receive the votes of others, I have never known any man to buy land, merely for the sake of acquiring a right to vote, however trivial the cost would be.

It has been said, that the people, that the great body of the freeholders themselves, are not only willing but desirous to abolish the freehold qualification—that the desire to reform the Constitution in this respect, was the ruling motive which led to the calling of this Convention. Willing the freeholders may be, and I believe are, to extend the Right of Suffrage, as I propose to extend it, to all who come within the reason of the principle of freehold qualification—but, that they are willing to abolish the principle itself, I never can believe. The vote in favour of calling a Convention, given by the freeholders in this cismontane part of the State, I am sure was dictated by no such motive. I do know that many, very many of them, were cheated into a belief that the freehold qualification was in no danger; and I heard a member of the Legislature, and as sagacious a man as any in Virginia, declare, that he gave his vote for a Convention, in the firm belief that it would put an end to all disputes about the Right of Suffrage, and confirm and establish the freehold qualification forever. He was sincere, but he was deluded.

I little expected, Sir, after what passed in this Committee, in the debate upon the question of the basis of Representation, to see the attempt renewed, in this place, to discredit the Convention of 1776, and the Constitution it framed for the State, by reference to the untoward circumstances in which it was placed—but we have been again told, that that illustrious body was in a state of too much hurry and alarm to execute with due deliberation a work so important; that the enemy was at their door; and the roar of hostile cannon resounding in their ears; that other and more pressing affairs occupied their attention; and that, therefore, (as gentlemen would have us infer) they were content to leave the qualification of the Right of Suffrage as they found it in the Colonial Government, rather than devote the necessary time to improve it. It has been already shewn, that no part of this representation is justified, in point of fact, by the truth of history; and I shall not repeat what has been better said by other gentlemen. I have always thought, and shall forever think, that the circumstances in which the Convention of 1776 were placed, were the most propitious imaginable to the work that body had to perform; precisely the circumstances best calculated to repress the spirit of faction, and to kindle every spark of patriotism; to stimulate political wisdom to its utmost exertion, to force men to look only to practical good, to stifle all propensity to the vain speculations of theory, and to enforce on them the observance of the lessons of experience. But I find my sentiments on this subject expressed so exactly, so clearly, and so forcibly, by another and a far wiser man than ever I hope to be, that I shall borrow his language—and I do so the rather, because, very probably, it was the source from which my own sentiments were originally derived. The writer of the 69th number of the Federalist—I know not which of the three it was—speaking of a celebrated scheme of Constitution-mending, by which it was proposed, "that whenever any two of the three branches of the Government, shall concur in opinion, each by the voices of two-thirds of their whole number, that a Convention is necessary for altering the Constitution or correcting the breaches of it, a Convention shall be called for the purpose"—says: "It may be considered as an objection inherent in the principle, that as every appeal to the people would carry an implication of some defect in the Government, frequent appeals would in great measure deprive the Government of that veneration which time bestows on every thing, and without which perhaps the wisest and freest Governments would not possess the requisite stability. If it be true, that all Governments rest on opinion, it is no less true that the strength of opinion in each individual, and its practical influence on his conduct, depend much on the number which he supposes to have entertained the same opinion. The reason of man, like man himself, is timid and cautious, when left alone; and acquires firmness and confidence, in proportion to the number with which it is associated. When the examples, which fortify opinion, are *ancient* as well as *numerous*, they are known to have a double effect. In a nation of philosophers, this consideration ought to be disregarded. A reverence for the laws, would be sufficiently inculcated by the voice of an enlightened reason. But a nation of philosophers is as little to be expected, as the philosophical race of Kings wished for by Plato. And in every other nation, the most rational Government will not find it a superfluous advantage to have the prejudices of the community on its side. The danger of disturbing the public tranquillity by interesting too strongly the public passions, is a still more serious objection against a frequent reference of Constitutional questions, to the decision of the whole society. Notwithstanding the success which has attended the revisions of our established forms of Government, and which does so much honour to the virtue and intelligence of the people of America, it must be confessed, that the experiments are of too ticklish a nature to be unnecessarily multiplied. We are to recollect, that all the existing Constitutions were formed in the midst of a danger which repressed the passions most unfriendly to order and concord; of an enthusiastic confidence of the people in their patriotic leaders, which stifled the ordinary diversity of opinions on great national questions; of a universal ardor for new and opposite forms, produced by a universal resentment and indignation against the ancient Government; and whilst no spirit of party, connected with the changes to be made, or the abuses to be reformed, could mingle its leaven in the operation. The future situations in which we must expect to be usually placed, do not present any equivalent security against the danger which is apprehended." Now, I pray gentlemen to hearken to these words of wisdom, and to weigh them well. As to that veneration for ancient institutions, which has hitherto constituted the great moral force of our Government, and sufficed alone to execute the laws; all that is gone—forever gone—extinguished by the agitation which produced this Convention. Our children will hardly comprehend the sentiment. Then, let gentlemen, if they can bear to do so, institute a comparison between the Convention of 1776 and this body. That Convention, after full and free debate, adopted the Constitution it framed, by an unanimous vote. This Convention is torn by dissensions, and divided by parties marked by geographical lines—incited by mutual opposition to the extremes of political animosity—engaged (in the opinion of one party at least) in a mere contest for power; such a contest, as in any other country on earth, and, but for a sense of the controlling influence of the General Government, in this country too, would and could only be decided by the sword. No good that we can now accomplish, can ever compensate for the mischief which this contest has already engendered, and entailed upon the State.

I am not casting censure on others—I take to myself my full share of blame for the heats, which the collision of interests and opinions have produced in this assembly—my heart rises above all petty personal resentments and party views, and feels only for the woes of my country. Though I shall continue to resist to the uttermost of my power, all unreasonable demands from the West, I do not feel—whatever others may think of me—I do not, I cannot feel (heaven forbid that I should!) any hostility to my fellow-citizens of that part of the country, any disregard of their just rights, any indifference for their happiness. Gentlemen who have any knowledge of me, must know, that these sentiments are not uttered for the occasion, to serve a purpose here. In the paper I addressed to my countrymen in 1824 (commonly called *The Substitute*) after having exhibited the state of the existing representation in the Legislature, and shewed that the representation of the Western counties, compared even with that of the Eastern counties, was excessive, I said: "The *Western* counties have at present about *one-fourth* of the representation in the House of Delegates. Comparing the population of these counties (about one hundred and forty-five thousand five hundred) with that of the Commonwealth (about one million and fifty thousand) it is plain, that no plan can be devised for equalizing the Representation, which will not reduce their proportion to something less than a *seventh*. He who thinks, that the people of those counties ought to consent to such a diminution of their weight in the Legislature, has no fellow-feeling for them: he who thinks that they ever *will*, counts the heart of man for nothing, in his political speculations. The schemes of equalization, which would work such consequences, could only be imposed on them by force. There is, indeed, one principle, on which the *Western* people might consent to such equalization; one, on which they would lose none of their relative strength in the Legislature. If, in apportioning the Representation, the *slave* population, so inconsiderable in the *Western* counties, so large in the *Middle* and *Eastern*, shall be wholly disregarded, the *Western* counties will perhaps as eagerly embrace, as the *Middle* and *Eastern* will strenuously resist, this blessing of equality. And let the attempt be made when it will, this question, (which seems to be the very dæmon of discord,) will be sure to rise up to confound our peace. In the apprehension of this meeting, the very agitation of this subject is calculated to do great mischief. It is a searching blast, which will find every weak part of the body politic. And we implore those, who are prosecuting this design, to beware, lest, while they mean only an equitable arrangement of the Representation, they be not striking a fatal blow at the integrity of the Commonwealth. For, we feel the most painful conviction, that the actual attempt to execute the design, will array in direct opposition, all the conflicting interests of the State, growing out of natural diversities in the face of the country, and out of the moral diversities of our population; and wake into action, all the latent causes of civil contention, which good men should wish, and wise men should labour, by all means, to allay." The same sentiments I entertained then, I entertain still. Did my fears magnify the danger? The evil has now come upon us in a form more aggravated—the storm is raging with greater violence—than even my anxious mind foreboded.

But, upon this question of the qualification of Suffrage, I do not discern any reason for difference of opinion among us, growing out of diversity of local interests. And I implore gentlemen to pause in their adventurous career of experimental reform; to preserve every part of our ancient institutions, which they cannot alter with any certain assurance of amendment; and, especially, to leave us unimpaired the essential principle of the freehold qualification. If the State shall make a false step here—particularly, here—that step she can never hope to retrace, any more than we can recal the hour which has passed away and brought us so much nearer to the grave.

After Mr. Leigh had concluded his speech, a short explanation took place between himself and Mr. Doddridge, on a point of law involved in the amendment; when Mr. D. moved that the Committee rise.

It rose accordingly, and thereupon the House adjourned.

SATURDAY, November 21, 1829.

The Convention met at 11 o'clock, and was opened with prayer by the Rev. Mr. Courtney of the Methodist Church.

The Convention having again resolved itself into a Committee of the Whole, Mr. Powell in the Chair, and the question being on the amendment offered by Mr. Leigh of Chesterfield to the third resolution reported by the Legislative Committee:

Mr. Doddridge, (who, having moved for the rising of the Committee yesterday, was, by Parliamentary usage, entitled to the floor,) signified his intention of yielding that privilege to the member from Amherst, (Mr. Thompson,) but previously gave notice, that should the amendment now before the Committee (Mr. Leigh's) be rejected, he should offer the following amendment to the third resolution—viz:

Third resolution, second and third lines—from the word "resolution," strike out to the word "provided," in the twenty-third line, and insert:

"And shall be extended to every free white male citizen, aged twenty-one years or upwards, who shall have resided at least one whole year in the county, city, borough or district, in which he shall offer to vote, immediately preceding the time of voting; and who, during that period, shall have actually paid a revenue tax legally assessed—And to every free white male citizen, aged twenty-one years or upwards, who shall have actually resided at least one whole year in the county, city, borough or district, where he offers to vote; and who, for the period of six months at least, shall have been an house-keeper therein."

Mr. Thompson of Amherst, addressed the Committee as follows:

Mr. Chairman: The gentleman from Brooke, who by Parliamentary usage, was entitled to the floor this morning, having for the present waved his right, I rise to solicit for a short time the attention of the Committee, whilst I endeavour, in my poor manner, to discharge an obligation of duty, which I owe to the constituents in part represented by me in this Convention. It is, as you well know from personal experience, Mr. Chairman, a painful and embarrassing duty. I would to God it had been committed to other and abler hands. When I consider the time, place, and circumstances that surround me, the momentous interests involved in our deliberations, and the weighty responsibility that rests on each and every one of us, in connection with the humility of my own pretensions, I almost shrink from the task that lies before me: but on the other hand, when I call to mind that I am the representative in part of many thousand free-men, who spontaneously, and without any solicitation of mine, have clothed me with this high, delicate and responsible trust, all personal considerations vanish, and I resolve fearlessly to speak their sentiments on this floor, regardless of all the sarcasm, wit, ridicule and even derision, with which principles they hold dear and sacred, have been assailed in the progress of the debates of this Convention. Had not imperious duty, in my humble estimation, forbidden silence, my lips had been sealed, hermetically sealed, during the session of this august Assembly. But I should forever despise myself, if whilst I am the representative of freemen, I could sit by in silence and hear the sacred and unalienable rights of man derided, and should tamely shrink from their defence, under the influence of any unmanly fear of criticism, or of any personal consequences whatever.

I feel that I shall need much of the polite attention and kind indulgence of this Committee to sustain me in the task I have imposed on myself; and the wonted magnanimity and courtesy of a Virginia Assembly, I am sure, will always accord it to a member of its body, so long as that member shall merit it, by courtesy and decorum on his part. Like an honorable gentleman, who addressed you on a former day, of this Convention, I too may disclaim any intention of entering the lists to break a lance, with the redoubtable knights who have contended for victory on this arena. I have neither the prowess to impel, the strength to sustain, nor the panoply to protect me in so unequal a conflict. In common with this Committee, I have participated in the delight of listening to the luminous and eloquent arguments of gentlemen who have addressed you on this and other questions. And after so long rioting on the rich banquet they have spread before us, I but the more regret that I have nothing but the homeliest fare to offer in return. I lament my inability to reciprocate light for light—I have the consolation, however, to know that the same spirit which prompted to the offering of the widow's mite, has dictated this poor attempt of mine; and I therefore trust, that my offering, however humble, will meet a similar fate, from the benignity of this Committee. Mr. Chairman, I somewhat regret that in the order of debate, it is my lot to follow the talented and eloquent gentleman from Chesterfield. I have not the vanity to suppose, under the most auspicious circumstances, that I could interest this enlightened Committee by any view I could present of a subject, much less when preceded in the debate by that gentleman. Believe me, Sir, I have not the vanity to contest with him the palm of victory in the fields of rhetoric, of erudition, or of wit. No, Sir. As to them, so far as I am concerned, I leave him the undisputed victor of the field. I do mean, however, in the course of my remarks, to question many of his facts, or rather assumptions, and the conclusions he has adduced from the facts assumed.

Mr. Chairman, I scruple not *in limine* to avow that I am one of those *visionary* politicians who advocate General Suffrage, what gentlemen are pleased to term *Universal* Suffrage. And, in this avowal, I believe I speak the sentiments of a large majority of my constituents. What I mean by General Suffrage, is the extension of that inestimable right of voting in the election of all public functionaries, made eligible by the people to all white freemen of the age of twenty-one years and upwards, who are citizens by birth or residence for a certain time, and who have discharged all the burthens personal, including militia duties, and pecuniary, such as taxes, imposed upon them by the laws of the land, and excluding such as are rendered infamous by the commission of crime. In other words, I wish to establish a qualification that is personal, and respects age and residence, and to abolish forever the freehold qualification, which to me has always appeared an invidious and anti-republican test. Like the gentleman from Charlotte, (Mr. Randolph,) I did not come here to vote for the disfranchisement of one human being qualified to vote under the old Constitution, but to aid in the enfranchisement of all who come within the foregoing description. I came here to contribute my feeble aid in the great cause of *non-freehold* emancipation, but not to imitate an example set us elsewhere, of disfranchising the forty shilling freeholders. I am, therefore, diametrically opposed to the amendment proposed by the gentleman from Chesterfield, as I am to all amendments that go to restrict the Right of Suffrage; and upon this question, I will meet and take issue with the friends of freehold qualification, amongst the most strenuous of whom, the gentleman from Chesterfield, has proved himself, by the argument which he yesterday addressed to this Committee. I am willing to rest this argument upon the authority of reason and common sense, the Bill of Rights, upon the doctrine of expediency, or upon experience, which, *visionary* as *I am*, I consider more valuable than volumes of speculation and theory. It is with me perfectly indifferent, whether this right be regarded as a natural, a social, a civil, or a political one; the conclusion at which I arrive, satisfactorily at least to myself, is the same.

Before I proceed with my argument, I must trouble the Committee with a few general observations suggested by the course of this debate. I cannot forbear to express my surprise and regret at some of the principles avowed by gentlemen on this floor, and the change which public sentiment seems to have undergone in this ancient Commonwealth. In the opinion of some gentlemen, Government has no principles. The idea of patriotism and virtue even are exploded, and self-love and self-interest are the only springs of human action. The rights of men are a mere chimera of distempered imaginations, and in this debate have been made the theme of ridicule and derision, rather than eulogy. Against this, I solemnly protest. There was a time when this would not have been endured, when such language would have been offensive to republican ears. In the whole progress of this debate, the name of Thomas Jefferson, the great Apostle of liberty, has never once been invoked, nor has one appeal been made to the author of the Rights of Man, whose immortal work, in the darkest days of our revolution, served as a political decalogue and operated as a talisman to lead our armies to victory. There was a time when it was honorable to profess the faith of these great fathers of the church, when it was perilous to be a sceptic, when the name of Fox was venerated, and the principles of Burke abhorred—but the sentiment of the Latin poet quoted in this debate are but too true, "*tempora mutantur*," &c. rendered into English,

> "Men change with manners, manners change with climes,
> "Tenets with books and principles with times."

Then, the authority of the sage of Monticello would have stood against the world; now, there are "none so poor as to do him reverence." Then, was Burke regarded as the enemy of human rights and the firmest defender of aristocracy and monarchy—but now, Burke, Filmer, and Hobbes, judging from their arguments, have become the text books of our statesmen.

Mr. Chairman, I have spoken of political faith and political church—it recalls to my mind an observation I have often made, and no doubt has often occurred to the mind of every member of this Committee—and that is the great similarity in the conduct of the votaries of religion and politics. In these days, you find no atheist and few professed deists, but how many practical ones? men who, whilst they yield a sort of historical belief or assent to divine truths, live in the open and daily disregard of them, and utterly refuse all practical obedience. They cannot impose upon themselves that forbearance, self-denial, and humility enjoined by the author of that religion—their pride and their manhood revolt at that text, which informs them that they must emulate the simplicity of infant innocence ere they can enter the kingdom of Heaven. So, Mr. Chairman, with a large class of our politicians, who, whilst they have not the bold daring to deny the great principles of our political faith, whilst they profess to keep that faith, they refuse all practical obedience. They say the theory is very good—but the pride of intellect and of wealth, that inherent love of distinction in man, that overwhelming self-love, and that pharasaical spirit which induces frail man to plume himself on his own supposed perfections, and to congratulate himself on the infirmities of his fellow-man—revolt at that political equality taught us by the precepts and practice of our forefathers. I like not their theoretical republicanism. I care not for professions unless the precept and the practice correspond—as I will judge the tree by its fruit, as I will judge the christian by his works, so I will judge the professor of republicanism by his practice.

Let us now, Mr. Chairman, return to the subject immediately under consideration—the Right of Suffrage—I shall bestow but little time upon the consideration of the question, whether it is a natural, social, civil, or political right—for the inquiry is rather curious than useful. What boots it, if it be a valuable right, whether it be the one or the other? Nor shall I, like other gentlemen have done, resort to any laborious inquiry into the question, whether a state of nature ever in fact existed? I leave this task where those gentlemen have left it, who have endeavoured by most metaphysical arguments to prove it a creature of abstraction. This, however, I will say, that whether it ever did or could exist or not, it is as fair and necessary to suppose its existence, and to assume it as a postulate on which to bottom a political deduction, as for the mathematician to suppose the existence of a straight line on a point, as a postulate on which to found his demonstrations; nor are maxims in politics less useful in practical results to the statesman, than are the axiomata and postulata to the practical geometrician.

What, then, is the Right of Suffrage? Not what gentlemen seem to understand it, in its technical and confined sense, the right to vote for public functionaries only, in a regular organized Government: in its enlarged sense, it is the right by which man first signifies his will to become a member of Government of the social compact—the means by which that same man gives expression to his will in the formation of that compact, his consent to, or his veto upon, measures of the Government in legislation in a pure democracy, as at Athens, and in others of the ancient republics, and some of the modern, or the right of voting for public functionaries as above mentioned, in a Representative Democracy such as ours, where the people do by their agents what they could not conveniently or even possibly do in person. This being its definition then, is it a natural right? I understand natural rights to mean such as appertain to man in a state of nature; this appertained to him in a state of nature, for it was by its exercise in that state that he agreed to relinquish the natural state and enter into society—But, say the gentlemen, such a state never existed—the consequence is that man has no natural rights, if my definition of natural rights be correct—but the gentlemen admit he has natural rights, life, liberty, the pursuit of happiness, and the means of acquiring and enjoying property. Suffrage is the substratum, the paramount right upon which all these rest for protection, preservation, and safety. This right, as has been very properly said, has its origin in every human being, when he arrives at the age of discretion: it is inherent, and appertains to him in right of his existence; his person is the title deed, unless it be those on whom the same natural law has pronounced judgment of disability, or those who have forfeited it by crime or profligacy; and one other class in this country who must be the victims of necessity, that can never be urged as an example for disfranchising the white man. It is said not to be a natural right, because we curtail, restrict, and confine it, as before said; that it is forfeitable, and that our exceptions include more than our rule. Life, liberty, &c. are curtailed, restricted, and forfeitable, and subjected to exceptions, yet they are admitted to be natural rights. Natural rights may be transplanted into the social, civil, and political state, yet they are still natural rights. A distinguished statesman has informed us that most of our civil rights have natural rights to rest upon—nor do I think I should be far wrong, were I to assert that all our important rights, whether civil, social, or political, are, properly speaking, natural rights. The exceptions, we all admit to the universality of the right, by which the gentlemen endeavour to overthrow the rule itself, I shall notice a little farther on. But suppose it be not a natural right, it must be one of the other three, and I care not which—why should a majority of freeholders have it in exclusion of a minority of non-freeholders? If the non-freeholders were consulted, and upon the score of expediency voluntarily made the surrender, there would be no cause of complaint on their part—but it is claimed of them as a right. Have they ever been consulted? No. Do you purpose to consult them? No. Then it comes to this, that a minority of one class have taken possession to the exclusion of a majority, not by the consent of that majority, but by consent among themselves, or by accident, or by *jure divino* I suppose, and now claim to hold the possession against the right. Have not the majority as much right to exclude the minority as the minority the majority? Yea, more. But we claim for the poor no right to exclude the rich, for the many no right to exclude the few; we claim only equality (which is equity,) for all, and deny the right of any arbitrarily to exclude the rest. These claims and these denials, I stated in the beginning, to be founded upon reason and common sense, upon our declaration of rights, which is a plain and simple deduction of principles from that paramount source, *right reason*, upon experience, and expediency, the gentlemen's own grounds.

By the way, I would ask if it be a question of expediency, why is the non-freeholder not permitted to pass upon the question by his vote? Why will you deny to him an opportunity of making a merit of necessity, if he must be disfranchised? Why is it, that Virginia has presented the first instance of a Convention called to form a Constitution without consulting the non-freeholder, any more than your free negroes, and without allowing him any voice in the election of delegates that compose that Convention? And why is it, that you purpose to carry the injustice still farther by submitting this Constitution to the ratification of freeholders only? If expediency be the plea, and it be true, and has been true for more than half a century, why should gentlemen now labor so hard to prove it? Are these arguments to convince the freeholders they ought to hold on, or to reconcile the proscribed to their fate? The object, Sir, is to induce the freeholder to hold on, not to convince or to reconcile the non-freeholder; for believe me, Sir, that were impossible; you cannot convince a freeman in this country that his neighbour has more political rights than himself, and that it is expedient for him to be guilty of committing the suicidal folly of surrendering up all or any of his rights into the hands and keeping of others—You will find many men willing to admit, that their neighbours are incapable of exercising the rights of sovereignty, but none that will ascribe that incapacity to themselves—and I congratulate the country upon the march of liberal principles, that the freeholders themselves are prepared to surrender these pretensions. This is a freehold Convention, and I believe that a large majority of the constituent body have decided upon the abolition of the freehold test—unless the worthy gentlemen who have undertaken to rejudge their justice—should succeed in their attempt to induce them to retrace their steps, which God forbid! Mr. Chairman, I said the proposition affirming the right of General Suffrage could be sustained upon the principles of reason and common sense. Is it not so? Does it not command the assent of every unprejudiced and unsophisticated mind as almost a self-evident truth? Is it not the affirmation of a principle written by the pen of nature upon the heart of every human being, whose spirit is not bowed down by oppression and political degradation? Who doubts the proposition when it is announced? Not the great body of the people, in whom of right the sovereignty resides, whose polar star is right, and not expediency. None but those statesmen who make human rights any thing or nothing to suit their varying ideas of expediency, which has been, in all ages, the pretext for every atrocity, the tyrant's plea, and the Jesuit's watchword. But why need I detain the Committee in discussing principles derived from reason and common sense, which, more than half a century ago, were deduced by our forefathers, and so happily expressed in our Bill of Rights? Here is a text that no commentary can illustrate, written in characters so legible, that he who runs may read, and in terms so simple, so intelligible, and so consonant to the love of equal liberty implanted in our hearts, that it "comes home to the business and bosoms of men." To this text let us appeal for the evidence of that Right of Suffrage for which I contend; a "right inestimable to freemen, and formidable to tyrants only." The first article of the Bill of Rights reads thus: "That all men are by nature equally free and independent, and have certain inherent rights, of which, when they enter into a state of society, they cannot by any compact, deprive or divest their posterity, namely, the enjoyment of life and liberty with the means of acquiring, and possessing property, and pursuing and obtaining happiness and safety." The second declares, "that all *power* is vested in, and consequently derived from, the people: that magistrates are their trustees, and servants, and at all times amenable to them." The third declares the end and object of Government to be, "the common benefit, protection and security, of the people, nation, or community," and affirms the right of a majority, "to reform, alter, or abolish it, in such manner, as shall be deemed most conducive to the public weal." The sixth affirms, that "elections ought to be free, and that all men, having sufficient evidence of permanent, common interest with, and attachment to, the community, have the Right of Suffrage."

Now, Mr. Chairman, if I were to ask a plain man, who were entitled to vote under these provisions, would he answer land-owners only, or such persons as I have heretofore described, including the great body of the people, a majority at least? He certainly would not answer freeholders; there would be no doubt in his mind, unless indeed, he should chance to take the advice of counsel, who like Doctor Doubty, finds doubts in every thing; then perhaps a doubt would be suggested; but to understand the Bill of Rights, requires not the aid of counsel, or statesman, nor of wise, nor learned men: it is intelligible to the most unintelligent above the grade of *non compos mentis;* and well it is, Mr. Chairman, that it is so. If only the wise and the learned were capable of comprehending the fundamental rights of a free Government, such a Government could never have existed, and if it had, would necessarily have been of short duration. But when we quote the Bill of Rights upon our opponents, they do not flatly deny its force and authority, but explain it away by the Constitution. They say their authors are the same men, and that they have given a contemporaneous and practical exposition in the one, of what they meant by the other, in establishing Freehold Suffrage in the Constitution. A conclusive answer to this has been furnished by the arguments of more than one gentleman, that has preceded me in the debate.

The circumstances in which our forefathers were placed, and under which they acted, would have rendered it very unwise and impolitic to carry out at that time to their full results all the principles established by the Bill of Rights. They had not the time, had it been wise to do so. They acted in haste, and it was then more than problematical what would be the issue of the struggle they had just embarked in. Why should they then create division at home, by disturbing the settled order of things, when harmony was so essential to the success of their great enterprise? They thought it wise to leave the perfection of their work for more auspicious times; this we are told by the immortal Jefferson, and as every one must infer from the instrument itself. Is this not proved by the ordinance of the Convention, passed only three days after the Constitution, by which we adopted for a system of distributive justice the common law of England and the statutes made in aid thereof, up to the fourth year of James the 1st? By this, we had engrafted upon our code the law of primogeniture, of entails and the institutions of the hierarchy. Might not the same reasons now assigned for adhering to the freehold test, have been urged against our statute of distributions, the statute for docking entails, and the act of religious toleration, the work of the immortal Jefferson? To the same causes, that we assign for the adoption of the freehold Suffrage in part, want of time for reflection and deliberation, must be ascribed another imperfection or inconsistency in the Constitution; a failure to prescribe any qualification whatever for your Governor, your Judges, your Magistrates, your Militia officers, &c. Now, is it not absurd to say, that before a man can vote for his neighbor, to represent him in the Assembly, he must furnish as a test of his independence or patriotism, the possession of his fifty acres? yet no test either of property, residence, or citizenship, is required of your Governor; for aught the Constitution contains, your highest Executive, your highest Judicial, and your highest Military officers may be aliens. This surely proves the imperfect character of the instrument, and the cause of that imperfection, as before assigned; but it proves also another thing; it proves the absurdity and inutility of the freehold test. If you can trust your Governor to execute your laws, and to temper them by the high prerogative of mercy, in the exercise of the pardoning power; if you can trust your lives, liberty, and property to your Judges; the defence of your homes and your fire-sides to Military commanders and militia-men, though they possess not one acre of land, and though they be as poor as Lazarus; in the name of common sense, why is it that you cannot trust a citizen without fifty acres of land to go to the polls, and vote in the election of public functionaries?

Mr. Chairman, it has been said by the gentleman from Chesterfield, and by other gentlemen, that we derive a rule from the law of nature and the Bill of Rights, in relation to Suffrage, that is in its terms universal, and that we ourselves abandon it, and thereby prove its fallacy: the females, including one half of the population, are disfranchised at one fell swoop; minors, convicts, paupers, slaves, &c., which together, compose a large majority of every community: and hence they argue, that as our rule, if carried out to its extreme results, will not work well, it must be erroneous. For this argument, I have a short answer; it will not do to test any rule by extreme cases. I presume it cannot be necessary for me to assign a reason for the exceptions. In this the gentleman and myself would doubtless agree. He has himself very happily assigned the reason for excluding females; and could assign reasons as satisfactory for the other exceptions. In the foregoing exceptions we are all agreed. I do not understand any of those excepted classes, as now complaining, nor that any member of the Committee wishes to include them. Why then lug their claims into this debate? For what purpose do the gentlemen so generously step forward to their relief, who seek no relief, and for whom none is intended by either party? I can tell you, Sir; the gentlemen seek by argument to elevate their rights, in order to disparage ours. I object to this change of issue; the question is now between freeholder and non-freeholder; to which contest these others are no parties. I insist upon a comparison of our titles in this our writ of right, if I may be allowed to borrow a figure from that profession of which I am an humble member. In this form of action, and not as an ejectment, neither party can rely upon the weakness of his adversary's title, provided it be better than his own; it is simply as before stated, a comparison of titles; this I insist to be the law of this case. If the freeholder and non-freeholder have usurped the rights of other classes, it is no reason in the mouth of the freeholder, against an equal division of the spoil. I have always heard that honour was observed among thieves and robbers. I have thought it necessary to say this much, to shew that the exclusion of females, &c. had not legitimately the least connexion with this question. If it be a good argument, carried out to its results, it would justify any man to make a slave of his neighbour, provided that neighbour happened to be the owner of a slave. The argument of the kidnapper would be this, to his enslaved captive; "you, Sir, held a fellow-creature in bondage, because you thought it expedient to do so. I have the same right to enslave you, and I think it expedient to do so. I justify myself by your own example. I try you by your own rule." So with the freeholders, when they are challenged to shew a better title than the non-freeholder, they resort to the plea of expediency; that it is expedient they should have the power, and that as females, &c., are excluded by mutual consent, *ergo*, we the freeholders will exclude the non-freeholders, because they concurred in the exclusion of females, minors, &c. In what does the case just supposed, differ from this? So we find that *their* arguments will not abide the test of being carried to their extreme results. And this is not the only argument of the gentlemen, obnoxious to the same criticism. In the discussion of the question of Representation, they contended for the mixed basis: we replied, that it was inadmissible, that it was anti-republican, to give out political power, in proportion to the wealth of the voter; and that if it was just, to give one district weight in proportion to its wealth, it was equally so to divide power among citizens of the same county in the same ratio, and so it is: but of this argument they complained as being unfair, and founded on extremes, which they said was an unfair mode of treating their proposition. And this reminds me of a discrepancy between the first and last argument of the gentleman from Chesterfield. In the argument of the question of Representation, we contended that the fears of the East were unfounded; for, that all the country between the Alleghany and the sea-shore, was slave-holding; that it therefore had a common interest, and would always have the power, as it now had; that although the Valley had not as many slaves as the East, yet taking the ratio between the tythables and slave-owners; it appeared that the slave property was more generally diffused there, than in the East; there were more small slave-holders; and that the owner of one slave was as safe a depository of power, as the owner of one thousand; inasmuch as the tax on that one would be as onerous to him, as the tax on the one thousand would be to their owner; and would make him as vigilant to guard and protect that right. This argument, then, from our side of the question was wholly repudiated, and if I remember rightly, by the gentleman from Chesterfield; yet on yesterday he used that very identical argument to prove that Col. Allen's poor neighbour owning but one slave was as safe a political partner for the Colonel, as though he owned one thousand slaves, and assigned the very identical reasons heretofore assigned by the friends of the white basis. But, other discrepancies exist in the arguments which could not have escaped the attention of this Committee. They complain, that by extending Suffrage, you augment the power of the rich; a singular complaint coming from the friends of restricted Suffrage, and most generally, if not always, used by the rich themselves. They say that tenants are not to be trusted, because they will vote for their landlords, or as they direct; the poor will vote for the rich, or as they direct; yet these very same gentlemen claim power in Representation, for the protection of the property of the rich. They disguise the effect of the claim by telling us, they claim it not for individuals, nor counties, but for sections of country; and that the effect of it is, to ascribe power to the poor, in right of their vicinity to wealth, for its protection; in other words, to give them all equal portions of this surplus power reserved on the score of wealth, in trust for the benefit of their rich neighbours. If this be so, why should the gentleman from Chesterfield and his associates, fear the subserviency of the tenant to the landlord, or of the poor to the rich? If they hold power for the benefit of the landlord and the rich, they must either yield to the views of those persons, or set up for themselves; if they set up for themselves and disregard the wishes of the property-holders, they would prove unfaithful trustees, and the object of property Representation would be defeated; if, on the contrary, they should prove subservient, then only could the object of protection be accomplished by the means of property Representation; and the gentleman should, therefore, not complain, of this effect of universal or extended Suffrage. But again: the gentleman, on yesterday, objected to tenants being voters, because, said he, the landlord held them by their very heart-strings; could distrain upon them, sell their last cow, and even the cradle on which their infants reposed. If the gentleman's argument be a good one, I think it will prove too much. I think it will prove that his favourite freehold test, is not quite so good a one as he seems to think, unless there be something in the ownership of land, that by enchantment or magic converts frail erring man, into an infallible and impeccable being. I think all the tests, except those of age and residence, will be found too imperfect to act upon. A moral test no man would advocate, neither a religious; an independence test founded on the possession of property is equally Utopian, equally unjust, and equally fallacious; no man contends that the land is a test of patriotism; and even if it were, should it, therefore, be established as the test of Suffrage? I presume there are as many degrees in patriotism as there are men; and as there are degrees in any other virtue. Every man is more or less a patriot, if patriotism means love of country. A man that loves not his country, is a monster; such a one as I have never yet seen, though such have lived, and live to infamy on the page of history, as Benedict Arnold, and a very few such. The love of country is formed in the heart of man in childhood, in youth, and does not, as seems to be supposed, grow out of the self-love and self-interest of mature years; it springs from the affections and the associations of childhood and youth, before the sordid and selfish cares of manhood have taken possession of the heart. Did the patriotism of Aristides, of Marcellus, and of other great names that might be mentioned, rest upon the freehold; were they less patriots in exile, than the ungrateful men that banished them? I humbly answer no.

Mr. Chairman, will not the reasons assigned by the gentleman from Chesterfield, for the exclusion of tenants, operate in equal degree to exclude his own favorite freeholders? will it not furnish a good reason for excluding every man that is indebted, and for putting the Government in the hands of the creditor class of the community? And if this be the rule of exclusion, how many of the freeholders, think you, will be excluded? I venture to affirm at least one half or three-fourths: is there not that proportion indebted to their neighbours, their merchants, to the Banks, &c., by account, by bond, and by trust deed, or otherwise; and will not a debt have the same influence upon a freeholder, as upon a tenant or other non-freeholders? Indebtedness is, in substance, the reason assigned for excluding the tenant; and can it be a matter of any importance what sort of debt it be, whether it be for rent or any other consideration; whether it be collectable by distress-warrant, or by fieri facias, whether the cow or the cradle be sold by the constable, the sheriff, or a trustee or marshal, or whether the person indebted be turned out of possession by notice, to quit if a tenant, or by a *habere facias possessionem*, or *sesinam* if a mortgaged freeholder? I, therefore, conclude, the gentleman's own rule, tried by his own arguments, would include as much too many voters as it would exclude, improperly, tried by our arguments. The gentleman's argument has evidently on several occasions varied with itself. This has not been the fault of the gentleman's ingenuity or ability, but the fault of the principles he advocates; his premises are wrong; "he has laboured under a cause too light to carry him, and too heavy to be borne by him."

The gentleman from Chesterfield, has said Universal Suffrage originated in Cromwell's army. He has been well answered by the gentleman from Frederick, (Mr. Cooke.) Did the gentleman, when he made this assertion, forget the *pure* democracies of antiquity, where all voted and legislated in *propria persona;* did he forget those of more modern date, but still more ancient than the age of Cromwell? I mean the Swiss Cantons. Their Suffrage was more universal than it ever was before or since: every male of the age of fifteen years was allowed to vote, and I take it upon me to say, that no evil there resulted from this extended Suffrage.

The gentleman from Chesterfield, in his argument in favor of property Representation, warned us against the white basis, equal Representation. He said it would inevitably lead to the subversion of our free Government and to despotism. He cited as examples, Greece, Rome, and all the ancient Republics, and held up to us the English Government as an example in many respects worthy of our imitation. He yesterday predicted that the same effect must necessarily result from Universal Suffrage, but instead of again vouching the ancient republics to sustain him in this prophecy, I think he said these Republics furnished no light for our guidance, but that England was the country we must look to for our analogies and for lessons of instruction and experience, it being the only Representative Government bearing a real similitude to ours, in the world, or that ever existed. Then all free Governments have perished by these formidable foes of liberty: equal Representation, and Universal Suffrage. How do the gentlemen account for the fall of despotisms? they too, have perished, and free Governments established on their ruins. Did Universal Suffrage, and equal Representation, produce these effects too? if so, they have done as much good as evil, and deserve not such utter reprobation. But the truth is, gentlemen have been misled; they knew only the historic fact, that Governments free and despotic have perished, have shared the fate of every thing mortal, have obeyed that great law, which sooner, or later, consigns to the tomb, man, and all the works of man; but the remote and hidden causes, that produced these effects, ever have been, and ever will be, mere matter of speculation. The ancient or the modern Republics, are surely incapable of teaching us any lessons of instruction, or of furnishing any beacons for our warning; they are not cases in point; there is no resemblance between the pure democracies of antiquity, and the Representative democracies of the United States. Here was made the first experiment of that form of Government, and ours are the only Representative democracies that ever existed. Had the Republics of Rome and Greece, been based as ours, upon the Representative principle, their liberties might have been immortal; for, if that attribute can, without impiety, be ascribed to any Government, it must be to a Government like ours. I fondly trust ours will be immortal. For this Representative principle we are indebted to England, and she borrowed it from the woods of Germany; but in borrowing this part of her Government, we discarded her monarchy, and her aristocracy, infusing instead, the pure democratic spirit into our institutions. Greece and Rome have furnished us models of architecture, statuary, poetry, and painting, but not of Government. It would be as just to compare their beautiful temples to our steam-boats, cotton-gins, and printing-presses, as to compare our institutions of Government with theirs; they are as dissimilar. They, therefore, can shed no light on our deliberations, much less, Mr. Chairman, than the Cherokee nation of Indians, who have recently established a free Constitution of Government, and laws. Mr. Chairman, we have heard many professions of patriotism, and love of country. I doubt not their sincerity, but I shall make none myself, after telling you that the man who loves not his country, is a monster in human shape.

Nor shall I, Mr. Chairman, join in the war of epithets, so much complained of by the gentleman from Chesterfield, and the gentleman from Spottsylvania. I submit it to the candour of this Committee to decide, who cast the first stone, and whether if aristocrat and monarchist, be obnoxious epithets; whether visionaries, abstract theorists, demagogues, bidders at the shrine of popularity, slang, &c., be not entitled to the same appellation. I submit it to the candour of the gentleman from Chesterfield, whether in his zeal, he has not been betrayed into the same fault, which he has imputed to our side. For one example among others, that might be enumerated, of intemperate zeal and harsh epithet, we had asserted the claims of the sons of freeholders to the Right of Suffrage, he replies, that if they are permitted to vote, the consequence will be, that the son will vote with, or differently from his father—if with his father, the man with four sons will have five votes—if they vote differently from the father, these four sons, will be four scoundrels and puppies. Surely the gentleman's reflections cannot sanction now such opinions; if they do, I would ask him at what age may a son, a freeholder, ever vote independently, without meriting the epithet of scoundrel and puppy; and this, Mr. Chairman, is a sentiment expressed by one, who has so strenuously contended for the independence of voters!

I agree with the gentleman from Chesterfield, in the eulogy he has paid to the freeholders of the State: there is not in the world a more respectable body of men. I have cause to respect, and love them—it was their partiality, undeserved I am sure on my part, that sent me here—I am sure they will not consider me as disparaging their claims, when I say, that the non-freeholders are a respectable body of men. There are virtuous and vicious amongst both classes. Indeed, Mr. Chairman, we have been told by a very philosophic poet, and I think truly,

> "Virtuous and vicious every man must be,
> "Few in the extreme, but all in the degree."

But I cannot agree with the member from Chesterfield in the *compliment* he has paid to the intelligence of the so much lauded freeholders, by supposing them to have been cheated out of their votes in calling this Convention, or in the elections to this body, or cheated into sentiments so hostile to their true interests. After attributing to them the suicidal folly of calling this Convention, not in terms, but by the tenor of all his arguments, it was indeed the most charitable supposition, as to them, to suppose them to have been misguided. The people in my district, I venture to say, were not cheated; I cannot say how it was in others.

Mr. Chairman, I cannot see what the ballot boxes (or Pandora's, if it better please the gentleman), and the constable's advertisement sent by some anonymous correspondent from Maryland, have to do with the subject of this debate. The gentleman very confidently expresses his preference for the *viva voce* election, reprobates the mode of voting by ballot, then gratuitously assumes this latter mode to be the necessary consequence of extended Suffrage, and by this assumption he readily justifies his reprobation of the cause of this consequence. I agree with him in preferring the *viva voce* mode of voting, but I am not prepared so confidently, as he seems to be, to pronounce an anathema upon the other. We should, at least, pause and reflect well before we condemn a practice adopted by many of our sister republics, and, so far as I am informed to the contrary, with good effect; a practice, the adoption of which is now advocated by some of the Whigs of England, as the very best guaranty of independence in voters—but I do not mean to argue this question at this time; it would be travelling out of the record—all I intended to say was, that there was no affinity between the question of the extension of Suffrage and the mode of voting.

And as little, as it seems to me, is there between the Maryland advertisement and this question: the gentleman did not even attempt to shew how the supposed cause produced the supposed effect. If Universal Suffrage produced the passage of the law, that subjected land, however large the tract, to the payment of its owner's debts, however small, it is my humble opinion, an eulogy on Universal Suffrage. It proves that the voters, instead of being lawless free-booters, are lovers of justice. Mr. Chairman, may it not be that this correspondent is the debtor and the owner of the land, and that it is because he is made to feel the operation of a wholesome law, that he feels no very good opinion of it? According to Hudibras,

> "A thief ne'er felt the halter draw,
> "With good opinion of the law."

But we are told, if the Right of Suffrage be extended, the rights of property will be invaded: we shall have an agrarian law, tumults, confusion, civil discord, and finally despotism. The only answer I have to make to arguments so derogatory to the dignity of human nature in these United States, is, that twenty-two out of twenty-four sister Republics, many of them situated precisely as we are in relation to slave population, have this Free Suffrage, called by the gentleman Universal, and none of these results have happened, or are likely to happen there, so far as we are informed. Virginia and North Carolina are the only States that adhere to the freehold test, and the latter only in one branch of the Legislature. What length of time the gentleman requires for the fulfilment of his lugubrious prophecies, he has not informed us. Believe me, Sir, it is all speculation and theory, against the rights of man, and we have this advantage, if we are theorists and speculators, we speculate and theorise in favour of equal rights, and our theories and vagaries have been reduced to successful operation. They have been called on, and cannot shew one case in point: on the contrary, we can triumphantly point to the example of twenty-two Republics, our sisters in this great confederacy of States. I have now a gentleman in my eye, who has informed me, that he owns a large real estate in Ohio, and that no where are the rights of property more secure. His language was, "that a twig could not be cut from his premises, without exposing the transgressor to reparation in damages." During the session of this Convention, I have conversed with a distinguished functionary from the State of Mississippi, a native of Virginia, and he informs me, that in that State, the Legislature is in the hands of the non-property holder; and that so far from their having any oppressive taxation of property, their civil list is actually defrayed by a capitation or poll-tax. During the past summer, I was informed by a citizen of Alabama, that a part of that State, which owned least property and fewest slaves, wielded the power of Legislation—situated as to slave property, as the East of this State is to the West, and yet that no abuse had intervened, and that none was apprehended. Let us turn our eyes to the States North, West, East and South of us, and we look in vain for any of the evils pourtrayed in such glowing colours by the gentlemen on the other side of this question. Liberty and law, equality and justice, peace, prosperity and good order, reign throughout their borders; with those few exceptions of popular excitement, incident to, and inseparable from, all free Governments under the sun. Mr. Chairman, the little temporary excesses of a free people must be borne: it is the evil inseparable from the good; there is no human good without its alloy of evil. I prefer even the hurricanes and the tempests of liberty, to the calm of despotism.

And is Virginia less fit for free Government than her sister States? Would the same causes produce different effects here? In my poor judgment, we are better situated to adopt the principle of extended Suffrage than the free States, according to the gentlemen's own theories. The presence of upwards of four hundred thousand slaves entitled to no political power, and excluding perhaps as many of that class denominated by the gentleman from Chesterfield as peasantry, at once diminishes the number of dangerous voters by that amount, dangerous in the estimation of others, not in mine. In addition to this, we have no overgrown cities—no overgrown manufactory establishments. With a population proverbial for their attachment to law, order, and public tranquillity, I boldly say, if any State in this Union can adopt Free Suffrage with safety, Virginia is that State. The extension of the right does not endanger the tranquillity of election—as the experience of the Eastern States has conclusively proven—and if we adopt it, and pursue the policy now in progress, of establishing precinct or separate elections, we disarm these primary assemblies of any dangerous tendencies to excess, which they may be supposed to have.

Have not the non-freeholders of the United States, shewn their capacity for self-government in the election of members of Congress? and your Presidents, from Washington down to the present incumbent? I say the present incumbent, because whatever be my opinions of him, he was the choice of Virginia. Are the delegations in Congress from other States less talented and respected than our own? I mean no disparagement, when I say no. And can a non-freeholder vote discreetly for a Federal and not for a State officer? Look to the New York Convention of 1821, the first fruits of this General Suffrage, which numbered among its members, *Kent*, *Spencer*, *Lansing*, *Rufus King*, *Sanford*, and many others, though less known to fame, not the less entitled to distinction. Here we have seen a body of men elected by General Suffrage; a comparison with which, in my humble opinion, whatever be the opinions of others to the contrary, would not disparage this freehold Convention of ours, talented as I am willing to admit it to be. Look too, to the Bench, the Bar, the Legislative Halls of New York: you behold a blaze of talents, a constellation of great men, unsurpassed by those of any other State.

Mr. Chairman, the non-freeholders are told they are contending for a shadow—a right, if extended to them, would be of no great importance—that under the old state of things, every thing has gone on well—we have lived happily, and that their complaints are unfounded, and their grievances imaginary. We are told, the owners of the country should govern the country: that the freeholders are the safest depositories of power; that they hold it in their trust for the whole community, and that through them all are virtually represented. My reply to this is, that a man who has no voice in the Government, holds his rights by the sufferance of him who has; and he that thus holds his liberty at the will of another, is already half a slave. Because the non-freeholders have not been hung up without a Judge or Jury—because they have been allowed their civil rights, the gentlemen say they have not been injured. Free negroes are allowed all their civil rights; the non-freeholders no more: and here I would recall to mind a very proper distinction heretofore taken by the gentleman from Orange, (Mr. Barbour,) between civil and political rights. Civil rights may be, often are, and have been, respected and secure under the veriest despotism: and he very properly illustrated his remark by a reference to the reign of Augustus, and many of his successors. I consider the denial to any man of any portion of his political rights, or giving to his neighbour more than his own, an injury of the gravest character. If the right be ideal, existing only in the fancy of men, equally so are many of the possessions men hold dearest—liberty itself, reputation, fair fame, all dearer than life, and the invasion of which inflicts the deepest wound on the peace and happiness of their possessors. But I have shewn sufficient injury done to the non-freeholders, by simply announcing, that a Convention has been called and members delegated to it, without consulting them any more than if they were slaves or free negroes—an example, so far as I am informed, never before set in these United States.

Mr. Chairman, in answering the arguments of gentlemen, I have, in some measure, anticipated the grounds of expediency and experience, to which I promised to appeal in the commencement of my remarks: I intended, however, to have carried out my remarks on these two branches of the subject, for the purpose of supplying such views as I had not presented in answering the arguments of gentlemen, who had appealed to expediency and experience. I had intended to endeavor to shew the beneficent effects of extending Suffrage, by allaying discord and discontent, restoring harmony and good feeling among all classes and conditions. I intended to shew its moral and political tendencies, and amongst these its direct influence and operation—to elevate the character of the enfranchised; but finding my strength exhausted, and my voice failing, I will detain the Committee with but a few more remarks in conclusion.

We are told there is a great crisis in our affairs, big with danger to the peace, safety and integrity of the State. I doubt not the sincerity nor the moral courage of those gentlemen, who have admonished us of these dangers; but, Mr. Chairman, I have no faith in these predictions—I am not perturbed by the alarms that have been sounded: the dangers so much dreaded by gentlemen, are the creatures of their own imaginations: that bloody sword which has been brandished over our heads by the gentleman from Hanover, reeking with the best blood of the land, has inspired no terror, in my mind; because I trust that his sword, and that of every true Virginian, like the noble Roman's sword, "for their friends have only leaden points," and that they will never be formidable except to the enemies of the Commonwealth. I trust that ere the time shall arrive to unsheathe a sword to shed each other's blood, "consideration will, like an angel, come to save us from the obloquy." Is it possible that Virginia, of all the States in this Union, the birth-place of sons whose sires were foremost in the revolutionary struggle, has not the wisdom and the patriotism to reform her fundamental law without violent revolution and blood-shed—to perform quietly, and without tumult, an act of sovereignty, which even the Cherokee Indians can perform without violence; for, they lately established for themselves a Constitution for their government? For one moment to suppose separation, disunion, or dismemberment possible, is to pronounce a libel upon the wisdom and the patriotism of our constituents. Believe me, Sir, it would be beyond our power to produce such a result, were each of us to return to our constituents, and exert our utmost powers to bring about so calamitous a consummation. In vain would be all our puny efforts to agitate into a tempest the great body of the people. They would remain, in despite of all our efforts, as tranquil as the great ocean, when it is unruffled by the storm—that ocean, whose awful sublimity, the people in their sovereign power and grandeur, so much resemble.

Let us, then, banish from our minds, and from our deliberations, all intemperate feelings. Let us practice towards each other the republican virtues of temperance, moderation and forbearance, maintaining our opinions always with firmness, but with deference for the opinions of others—feeling the *fortiter in re*, but practising the *suaviter in modo*—eschewing violence, and cultivating harmony and good feeling—for, depend upon it, that as much wisdom and worth as I admit to be concentered in this body, there is yet more in the community we represent. The eyes and the thoughts of that community are now directed towards this ancient metropolis, the seat of our deliberations—a community, in whom dwells an abiding sense of justice, and a deep-rooted loyalty to social order and law: and that community will not hold *him* guiltless who throws the first firebrand into the fair temple of our political liberty, and saps the deep foundations of our ancient and beloved Commonwealth.

Mr. Thompson having resumed his seat,

Mr. Doddridge took the floor, and addressed the Committee as follows:

Mr. Chairman,—I am forced to meet the question of Suffrage at a period of our discussions when I did not expect it. With a very few exceptions, the friends of reform had determined to adjust the basis of Representation in both branches of the General Assembly first. In this they have met with difficulties which they have been unable to overcome. My own opinion was, that this basis in both Houses ought to be established by the same resolution, and such was my first proposition. That proposition was divided at the suggestion of those who thought otherwise, to enable them to sustain the white basis in the House of Delegates, and some other in the Senate. A different basis in the Senate was claimed on two grounds: first, to protect the owners of slaves from oppressive taxation on that species of property, and secondly, to preserve the title from being affected by any species of Legislation. The present views of a majority are sufficiently known, but it is uncertain whether the Senate will not be placed on a worse ground than this Convention found the House of Delegates. Should that be the case, the greatest end for which the people called us together will have failed, and in this state of things the question of Suffrage is pressed, and we are impelled, while considering it, to act, in some degree, as if the very worst that can happen to the people in adjusting representation, had actually happened. Thus situated, Universal Suffrage would be rendered acceptable to thousands, who never dreamed of its introduction. The proposition of my colleague, from Monongalia, has not yet been fully tested, because of the existing uncertainty of the real ground on which we stand. Should a slave, with a white, Representation be introduced into the Senate; or an exclusive Representation of taxation, or of property, there will be a necessity to array all that the denounced King Numbers, can command. The amendment of my colleague fell but little short of Universal Suffrage. It required the payment of taxes if assessed, but did not require their assessment. It excluded paupers, soldiers, persons adjudged infamous, and all such as had not resided a sufficient time to furnish evidence of permanent attachment to the community. The uncertainty of the ratio, both acquired and lost friends to Suffrage, on the rejection of my colleague's amendment. The rejection of the resolutions of my colleague from Brooke, followed as a matter of course. They did not, subtantially, differ from my other colleague's amendment, except in the facilities proposed for a foreigner to acquire Suffrage without an oath, and the exclusion of a native until twenty-two years of age. In these particulars, I would have proposed a small alteration to remove, perhaps, but a seeming objection; but that the fate of these resolutions had already been decided, and that decision, according to known rules, governing a Committee of the Whole, as well as the House, stands as their judgment, until reversed in the House. So far as the propositions of my other colleague from Monongalia, have relation to Suffrage, they are in like manner disposed of. That in relation to education is, indeed, untouched. That most important subject may find another place in our deliberations, or if not, it will remain a subject of legislation, and may form an important adjunct to the Literary Fund.

The question of extending Suffrage in the manner proposed by all my colleagues, although at rest in this Committee, will remain open for decision in the House, where I hope it will be renewed by them, or some of them, when every vote may be spread before our constituents, and the world.

I will, in my turn, offer an amendment, presenting Suffrage in another form—not quite so extended, yet falling but little short of the plans already discussed. My plan is to leave the present right untouched, and to extend it to all those, whether freeholders or not, to whom Government looks for support, whether by revenue taxes or county levies; by impositions payable in money or to be discharged by labour. To go farther than this, would be to trench on the decisions of the Committee; and to stop short of it, would be disobedience to the well known wishes of my constituents.

Mr. Chairman: In support of the principles asserted by the amendment now under consideration, I need not detain the Committee long. My constituents have been so fully heard, and their rights and interests so ably defended by each of my colleagues, that I have, indeed, little more to do, than to implore the Committee, to bear in their recollections, the able, and as I think, unanswerable, arguments of each of them, while I endeavour, briefly to arrange and pass in review the principal topics touched in this debate, as well by them as others. The decisions of the Committee on the resolutions of my colleagues, have settled the principle, so far as the Committee are concerned, that Suffrage shall not be extended to those not taxed, and they have settled nothing further. My effort now, is to extend it to all such as are taxed. This I know, at least, to be conformable to the wish of the whole body of my constituents. My colleagues are equally certain that the public wish is to go farther. Having been very generally from home the last five years, my information is less exact than theirs, but I have no doubt they are correct, and therefore voted with them for the extension they desired.

I admit, the proposition of the gentleman from Chesterfield offers one valuable extension of Suffrage: I mean that which embraces freeholders now excluded. These are the holders of less than twenty-five acres of land, and of lots in towns without dwelling houses, where the value shall come up to the amount required. These freeholders are numerous, and the estates of many of them worth more than sufficient to purchase an hundred freeholds at the prices at which Suffrage has been estimated in this debate. The other class embraced by his proposition, are termors, in a legal sense only. They are virtually freeholders, and are so considered by the gentleman himself. Leases of the description proposed to be provided for, are unknown in the West, and perhaps, are only to be found in or near Norfolk, so that the effects of the provision in their favor will be both limited and local. If Suffrage is not to be extended farther than the gentleman from Chesterfield proposes, this Convention might as well not have been called, if its principal object was, what the gentleman from

Charlotte (Mr. Randolph) affirms it to have been—the *extension of the Right of Suffrage.* The extension of Suffrage, proposed by the gentleman from Chesterfield, is not that which has been called for by public opinion. It is not such an extension of that privilege as was claimed from 1806 to the present time, nor is it that for which a majority of freeholders voted in 1828, when they spoke this body into existence. A brief review of the Legislative proceedings which led to the present Convention, will not only prove the objects for which we have been convened, but that their publicity has been such as to render it almost incredible that in calling this Convention any portion of freeholders who voted for it could have been cheated out of their votes, as has been alleged, or could have been ignorant of the extent to which it would be attempted to extend the Right of Suffrage.

Before entering into this review, I wish to get rid of a difficulty which has been constantly thrown in the way of the present debate. That difficulty arises from the sensitiveness of gentlemen at the use of the terms *aristocracy* and *oligarchy.* By the use of these terms, I have never meant an application of them to the hearts, feelings, or characters of those opposed to me ; but to the tendency and effects of the principles they maintain. I have never meant them as personal, or as offensive or abusive epithets. The term aristocrat has been applied to me nearly all my life, and I never took personal offence, because, I knew none was intended by those who used it. They supposed my political principles to be aristocratical, in which I knew they were honestly mistaken. The gentleman from Chesterfield says, he has so far forgotten his Greek as not to remember the meaning of these terms in that language, and he only knows their meaning in good old English, and not the modern dialect of that tongue. I will, in that dialect, explain my meaning of both terms. They are in fact synonymous. Each of these terms is descriptive of a Government whose powers are vested in a minority. A Government thus described, is contradistinguished from a monarchy, or Government in the hands of one man, and from a pure democracy, or Government in the hands of every man. By Government in the hands of a few, we do not mean a small select few. Few and many, as the gentleman from Chesterfield says, are relative terms. In their just sense they are equivalent with the terms majority and minority. In this sense I use them. A Government to be an aristocracy or oligarchy, is not necessarily one in which power is acquired by descent or by patent. This is the sense in which I use the terms, and if I am correct, to constitute a statesman an aristocrat or an oligarch, it is only necessary that he should be one of those holding and exercising the powers of the few over the many—of the minority over the majority. And I maintain, and before I sit down will attempt to prove, that our opponents are not only sustaining in this Convention the powers, wishes and principles of a minority over those of a majority, but the power of the *minority of a minority* over the majority. I will now proceed to the proposed review of Legislative proceedings leading to the call of this body.

In the session of 1806, after many preceding efforts, a resolution, requiring the sheriffs to take the votes of the freeholders at their next election, on calling a Convention, passed the House of Delegates. In the Senate it was postponed indefinitely. At that period we were so divided into political parties, and such was the heat and animosity prevailing, that prudent men on every side feared the call of a Convention. We were not qualified for cool and dispassionate discussion. The causes of our divisions were of a temporary character, and we all hoped to survive them with their effects. We hoped to see the tranquillity of the present hour. But we would not reject the resolution, lest it might be inferred that we acknowledged no defects to exist, or, at least, none of sufficient magnitude to authorise its adoption. The subject, moreover, had not been sufficiently canvassed to elicit public opinion, and in that state of things, the measure was calculated to excite, rather than quiet the public mind. A preamble assigning those reasons as the grounds of it was drawn up, concluding with a resolution of postponement. I now see before me two Judges of the General Court, not members of this body, and another gentleman who is a member, all of whom were partakers of these councils, and, if the curiosity of any one should be excited, he can satisfy it by inspecting the Journal of the Senate of that day. In the year 1814, a bill in the House of Delegates was rejected by a small majority of votes. On that occasion those in the affirmative represented a considerable majority of the people. As that bill was reported, it had the following preamble, viz: " Whereas, it is represented to the present General Assembly of Virginia, that many good citizens desire various amendments to the Constitution of this State; *among the most important is the extension of the Right of Suffrage, and equalization of Representation, and a diminution of the numbers of members elected in pursuance of the present laws and Constitution of this Commonwealth,*" *&c.* The words describing the causes of discontent were stricken from the preamble before the question on the passage was taken. This was done to avoid any legislative commitment of members, as to the causes of complaint or necessity of redress. Although that bill did not pass, and is not to be found on the Journals, a printed copy is to be found in the clerk's office. By this measure, it is made manifest, as well as by the resolution of 1806, and all the intervening efforts, that the people had settled upon freehold Suffrage as one of the evils demanding redress. The rejection of the bill of 1815, by those representing a minority of the people, increased the public discontent, and led first to a meeting of a political character at Winchester, and after that to the assemblage at Staunton, called the Staunton Convention, of 1816. The memorial of that body, together with numerous petitions, were referred to a committee in the House of Delegates of 1816. Their report underwent a tedious discussion. The bill ordered to be brought in contained a provision looking to the same object with that of 1815, but the objects were more particularly described in the bill of 1816, viz: "To call a Convention to equalize the representation of the free white people of this State, in both Houses of the General Assembly—to equalize taxation—to extend the Right of Suffrage to all persons having sufficient evidence of a permanent common interest with, and attachment to, the community, and provide for such future amendments in the Constitution of State as experience shall suggest to be necessary."*

Here the complaints are specified, and the redress suggested—"to equalize the representation," of whom? "the free white people;" and not of white people and negroes, nor of white people and taxes. Again, where is their representation to be equalized? and the answer is "in both Houses of the General Assembly," and not in the House of Delegates alone. The Convention of 1825, at Staunton, need not be mentioned. Their memorial was the subject of the most laboured debates in the House of Delegates of that year, and in both Houses in the two years following, in the latter of which the prayer of it was granted. Thus it appears, that the question of Suffrage is one among others which has agitated the public mind incessantly since the year 1806; and after it has undergone so many discussions in the General Assembly—in the newspapers and at the Hustings, where it was made a test, is it not paying a miserable compliment to the judgments or recollections of our freeholding-constituents to suppose them ignorant in the spring of 1828, when they voted for this Convention, that the contemplated extension of Suffrage would be among the most prominent of its measures? I will not say how this may have been elsewhere, but I will fearlessly affirm, that my constituents were not imposed on, and that no man was capable of practising such an imposition in my district. Mr. Chairman, permit me to ask, whether after this review, it is fair to deny, *that the freeholders of this State have, in fact, decided the question under consideration, and that we, ourselves, are called here by their authority to execute their judgment.*

While on the question of Suffrage, permit me to follow the example of others, by bringing to view, as connected with it, the principal questions in dispute, and to cast from the consideration of it all such matters as we agree about. The remarks I intend to offer on this head will serve to shew, and I think to demonstrate what I promised to prove, that our opponents here are but the representatives of a minority of a minority.

In determining, then, who are, according to all our principles, the only safe depositories of political power, whether we commence with the fall of Adam—whether we draw our maxims from the savage, the natural or the social state of man—by whatever path we have travelled in our researches or reasonings, we have all arrived at the following results—We all agree to exclude the other sex—We all concur in excluding infants, those under military bondage in actual service—those rendered infamous by their crimes, and those of unsound mind. Who then are they whom we all agree to be fit and capable depositories of power? They are males of twenty-one years of age and upwards—of sound mind, not infamous, nor subject to another man's will—that is, freemen. So far we are all agreed, from whatever reasoning we may have arrived at this agreement. Questions of policy, however, present themselves for our decision, and as a matter of policy we require citizenship and residence for a certain time, but those opposed to us require in addition to age, citizenship and residence, an ownership of part of the soil of the State, believing that nothing less than this furnishes sufficient evidence of interest and attachment to it. In this we differ, and this presents the great question of policy on which we are so seriously divided. The gentleman from Chesterfield said, very significantly, the other day, that he knew who he was who had asserted that the non-freeholders were a majority over the freeholding class of the community. I do not know to whom he alluded, but I will say that the non-freeholders in the Western country are to the freeholders a majority of about three to two. I have understood that a census of population was lately taken in the county of Frederick, from which it appeared that there were about two thousand five hundred non-freeholders in that single county, excluded from Suffrage, and who would be otherwise safe depositories of power under all our principles, and I cannot doubt that they are a majority throughout the State. We perfectly agree as to those who are the depositories of every scintilla of power, but differ only in the

* See Journal of House of Delegates of 1816, page 180.

evidence of attachment to the community that such ought to possess before we admit him to participate in its exercise. On our part we agree that this evidence ought to be afforded, but we insist that residence, birth, business, choice and other circumstances, furnish this evidence, with satisfactory certainty. If I am right in believing the non-freeholders to be a majority of the qualified depositories of power, then I must be right in charging those opposed to us with supporting the pretensions of a minority to govern a majority. But the proof does not stop here.

I have understood that the freehold vote on the question of calling a Convention, was a very full one. From all the information I have been able to collect, from conversations with members of this Convention, and of the last House of Delegates, I have come to the conclusion that about one-seventh part of those qualified to vote did not exercise that right on that occasion. If I am right in this estimate, the numbers of qualified voters under the present laws will be ascertained thus:

They who voted for a Convention were,	21,893
And they who voted against it,	16,887
Making,	38,780
To this number add one-seventh, not voting,	5,540
Making the number of voters,	44,320

If this be true, and if none but freeholders ought to vote, then gentlemen are here sustaining the pretensions of a minority of those, who alone ought to be entitled. Add to the number who voted against a Convention sixteen thousand eight hundred and eighty-seven, one seventh part of that number, and we have nineteen thousand three hundred and twenty-nine freeholders, who are opposed to reform, and if all the freeholders are but a minority of qualified persons, then it is manifest that the gentleman from Chesterfield and those who act with him, are exerting themselves here to carry into effect the principles of a minority of a minority—*a minority* of the freeholders who are *a minority of the whole*; and the intentions of nineteen thousand three hundred and twenty-nine men alone, if carried out into the form of a Constitution will result in establishing the will of that handful as the Government of this whole people. This will be an oligarchy. Nor less will their will be effectual to rule and control the community, if it should *prevail to* prevent those amendments of the Constitution, which are required by the majority. This latter consequence, I fear, is but too probable, and should this be the result of our labours, the effects will be deplorable.

The gentleman from Southampton, (Mr. Trezvant,) joining in self-commendation of our public morals, attributes their purity to our Constitution and laws; urging, that Governments have a tendency to form and correct public opinion. That legislation has this effect, is a political truth—it is not the whole truth, however, but only half.

The law-giver, to be wise, must regard public opinion. Wise laws, in a great degree, spring out of that opinion and conform to it. While public opinion acts on the legislator, his laws act back on that opinion and assist to enlighten and control it. Thus, legislation and public opinion mutually act on each other as moral cause and effect. This consideration suggests the duty of Government to consult the will and feelings of the people under every aspect and every change—a duty so well defined, and so ably enforced by my worthy colleague from Brooke, (Mr. Campbell,) that I have only to beg the Committee to bear his argument on this topic in mind. I will not attempt to add to it.

Having shewn how many persons are entitled to Suffrage at present, I will proceed to enquire what number will be added to them by extending the privilege to all persons paying a revenue tax, and how many more, if those subject to levies and not taxes were embraced. Those charged with land tax are ninety-two thousand—From this whole number are deducted, first, all females; second, all male minors, and persons of unsound mind; third, all foreigners; and fourth, all freeholders holding real estates less than that which at present confers the right. These deductions leave, as I suppose, the number I have already stated as that of the qualified voters, viz: forty-four thousand three hundred and twenty—The number of persons paying taxes on personal property are ninety-five thousand; of these, I may say, each person paying a land tax is one, and therefore, deducting the qualified voters from those paying a property tax, there will remain about fifty-one thousand; but to ascertain what portion of these will be admitted to Suffrage by my present proposition, I have had examinations made to ascertain what proportion of the ninety-five thousand are females, and find them to be one-ninth of the whole, and supposing that male minors and persons labouring under disabilities, may amount to as large a proportion as all females of every description, (which is allowing too much,) I arrive at the result in the following manner:

Number of persons paying taxes on personal property as stated in the Commissioners' books,		96,856
Deduct for females of all descriptions one-ninth,	10,650	
Ditto for infant males and others,	10,650	
Ditto all those now entitled to vote, as freeholders, and also on the property list,	44,320	
		65,620
		30,236

This would leave thirty thousand two hundred and thirty-six persons to whom, by my present proposition, I would, extend the Right of Suffrage. By this addition the number of voters will be augmented to seventy-four thousand five hundred and fifty-six. Should this proposition prevail, it will encourage me to propose its further enlargement to all persons subject to levies, or other county impositions payable in money or labour. It is difficult to arrive at any correct estimate of the number of males twenty-one years of age, who are subject to road laws and levies. From militia returns, and from imperfect lists of titheables in our power, it is reasonable to estimate them at about twenty-two thousand. These added to the thirty thousand two hundred and thirty-six, who pay a property tax, make a total of fifty-two thousand two hundred and thirty-six men, twenty-one years of age, of sound mind, and therefore safe depositories of political power, who are wholly disfranchised in Virginia; others make this number greater, but I am sure my calculation is within bounds. The class, thus excluded, have been claiming their rights ever since 1806. They have not been noisy and troublesome, because they depended on their freeholding brethren, whose honorable exertions in their favour have been incessant. The excluded classes were told from every quarter to be patient, and the freeholders, their neighbours, would deal liberally with them. When the vote was taken on the law of 1827, whether a Convention should be called or not, they were excluded, as they had been on the passage of that law. They were again excluded from the polls when the members of this body were elected, because those who made the law of last session were, like ourselves, the agents of freeholders. Last June these people were assured that this Convention would make full provision for them: this they believed and rested in quiet. A majority of freeholders are here ready by their delegates to redeem every pledge: they are manacled, however, by the law which scaled their power by the census of 1810. Instead of relieving the majority of qualified persons, members of this body, representing nineteen thousand three hundred and twenty-nine freeholders, are tendering to us with an unrelenting hand, their ratios of representation in three forms—first, white persons and taxation; second, the Federal number, and third, taxation alone in the Senate, as if determined on an aristocracy of wealth in one house at least. I have shewn, that the freeholding class qualified to vote by the present laws are to the number of qualified persons as forty-four thousand three hundred and twenty, to fifty-two thousand two hundred and thirty-six; of the former number, twenty-one thousand eight hundred and ninety-three voted for relief: to these are to be added one-seventh of their number, who omitted to vote, and three thousand one hundred and twenty-seven, making twenty-five thousand and twenty freeholders on the side of the non-freeholders, and of course, against every basis except the free white population. To come at a satisfactory estimate of popular strength, I think it fair to add to the excluded classes, the freeholders who voted for this Convention and their proportion of qualified voters who did not vote: this will present us with an astonishing state of things; nineteen thousand three hundred and twenty-nine freeholders, opposing the will of twenty-five thousand and twenty of their own class, and of fifty-two thousand two hundred and thirty-six qualified persons, not of their class; that is, nineteen thousand three hundred and twenty-nine men, against seventy-seven thousand two hundred and fifty, and (owing to the injustice of the law under which we are acting) with a fair prospect of success. Here we behold that oligarchy we deprecate! After the rise of this Convention, if nothing be done for their relief, this large proscribed class will not again be lulled to sleep—their eyes are on us at this moment—not a paragraph in the Gazettes escapes them—they will discover in these, that they have no attachment to their country in common with a freeholder. They will read in the speeches of members, that *their* allegiance is that of the heart, that there is another allegiance which is the creature of reason. After all this, should this country be again involved in war, how can these oppressed, excluded, disgraced men, be entrusted to bear arms in its defence? When the gentleman assures us, that the allegiance he bears the Commonwealth is that of the heart, I believe him—not because he declarés it, I know it by comparing him with myself, and such as I am, I suppose every other member to be. Rely upon it, all those to whom Government looks for support, either of general or county administration, in peace or in war, owe it the allegiance of the heart, or they ought not to be trusted with its defence; and thus allegiance ought not to be worn down by that oppression which breaks the heart.

I have always considered our system of making and repairing public roads as peculiarly oppressive. Farmers and others in the West, who employ white labour, feel it in the wages they are compelled to give. In some places a poor man walks ten or fifteen miles with his spade, axe, or mattock, to work on roads. In many places, ten and twenty days in the year are required, and this from journeymen, who have not yet acquired stock enough to commence for themselves—from labourers and others who have no property in the world. I had hopes, that after reforming Representation, one of the first measures of legislation would be, to abolish our present road laws, and with them every species of poll-tax; until then, I have no hope to see this great evil cured. I have witnessed so many abortive efforts to put down these oppressive regulations, that until Representation is reformed, I never hope for a successful one.

Mr. Chairman, I do not concur in the expressions of alarm for our divisions. There is not the least danger without. When I before spoke of numbers, I meant any thing else than a threat of forty-two thousand bayonets. I said that if our hopes were to appease the anxiety of so many men, these hopes would be fatally blasted by a rejection of their just claims, and to urge, that soon, very soon, these claims must prevail. I am happy to find that but one gentlemen, (Gov. Giles,) considered me as uttering a threat, and that but one other gentlemen, (Mr. Stanard,) looked on my language as uncourteous. Many expressions escape us in the heat of debate which our own reflections would chasten. Of this description, was the figure of the bloody sword used by the gentleman from Hanover, (Mr. Morris,) and the declaration of the gentleman from Chesterfield, (Mr. Leigh,) that a Government in the hands of a majority of numbers, would be such an oppressive and insupportable tyranny, *as no man ever did or would submit to*. There is no danger of a dismemberment of this State, I hope, and yet it *will soon* be ruled by numbers. To those who are in the habit of looking to such an event, I will communicate an advice once given to myself, by Major Jackson of Philadelphia, who I was told, was the last surviving member of General Washington's military family. Speaking of the purchase of Louisiana as an acquisition likely to produce a division of the Union of these States in time, the gentleman I have mentioned, cautioned me in a low voice thus: "when any man speaks of a division of these States, as a thing desirable or possible, he does more than commit an error." And I can assure gentlemen here, that when they speak of a division of this State, as a thing to be desired, they do "more than commit an error."

We are told from several quarters, that if Suffrage be extended, the purity of our elections will be destroyed, and tumult and riot take place of peace and order. The gentleman from Chesterfield, almost questions the words of my colleagues, when speaking of matters within their own knowledge. They had said that their constituents were well acquainted with the effects of General Suffrage, in the States on our border, and that they nevertheless desired that privilege extended here as far as we propose. That gentleman declares, he never heard of one Virginian, who had ever seen an election in Pennsylvania, Ohio, or Kentucky, who was not cured, forever cured, of a desire to see Suffrage extended, or the ballot introduced. I, in my place, am bound to confirm what my colleagues have declared. My experience is not great; indeed, I never saw many elections in Pennsylvania, and none in Ohio; those I saw in Pennsylvania were on the border of Virginia, where many of the inhabitants were of Virginia origin, having been inhabitants of our county of Yohioghany, so gallantly given away by the wisdom of the men of 1776. I never saw there, a more riotous election, than that of 1799, in this city, when one of the candidates for Congress, was a gentleman now a member of this House, and the other, the father of another member; he was personated on that occasion, by a third member of this Convention, who, since then, held for twenty years, the office of Attorney General, during all which time, he says, the whole Government went on very well.

Mr. Chairman,—The effort we are making is one, the object of which, is to reform our Constitution, on our own principles, and to give practical effect to those declared in the Bill of Rights. What we contemplate is not a revolution. The Government is an elective Republic, and we mean to leave it so. Yet we are warned of the dangers and horrors of revolution. Revolutions, it is said, never stop at the objects first had in view, but the ball once set in motion, goes downward on the road to anarchy or despotism, and never stops. One false step can never be recalled; the descent to ruin is easy, but to return, difficult, if not impossible: *hoc opus, hic labor est*. Could we forget where we are, and listen to the speeches of gentlemen in opposition, we should forget the business we are engaged in; we should imagine we were listening to Burke on the French Revolution. All the horrors of that volcano are set before us, as if in our madness, we were ready to plunge into it. We are likened to the impious priests of France in the last age; we are called fanatics, dreamers, and even drivellers, by a gentleman of this city: the history of the ancient Republics is invoked to alarm us: at one time it is said, that each of these perished when Suffrage was made general, and Governments established on the rights of numbers. With much more truth we are again told, that these Republics with all their temporary Governments, have fallen, without leaving in their histories any thing for our instruction: the truth is, that neither in antiquity, nor in the ages succeeding the fall of Rome, were there any Governments formed on our model; not one. Before ours, there never existed one Government in the world in which the whole power was vested in the people, and exercised by them through their Representatives; in which, powers were divided between separate and distinct bodies of magistracy, and in which no nobility or privileged order existed. It is in vain, therefore, that we are incessantly lectured like school-boys about the Republics of Greece, Sparta, Lacedæmon, Rome, and Carthage. In our sense of the term, in the Virginia sense of it, neither of these was a Republic; they have perished indeed, as all others of the same age have done; some by war and conquest, some by one cause, and some by another. Perhaps, among the inscrutable decrees of Providence, there is one by which all Governments like the men composing them, are to have a beginning, a maturity, and an end.

Gentlemen who oppose us, continually turn our attention to England, as the country whose history is replete with instruction, and from whose Constitution and laws, we have borrowed the trial by jury, *habeas corpus*, and the scheme of Representation itself. I concur with the gentlemen in their appeals to this source of information. I believe with the gentlemen opposed to us, that the Government of England is the best that could exist for that people; it would not do for us. We have dispensed with king, nobility, and hierarchy; we have no use for these establishments. I do not believe the English people could be governed by our Constitution and laws, and I am the more proud of them and my country, in proportion as I am satisfied that no people on earth, ourselves excepted, could sustain our free institutions. It cannot be denied, that in the elective system of England, in her common law, in her charters, and customs, we are to look for the sources from which we and our ancestors have extracted our best principles. Thus far I do most heartily concur with the gentlemen from Chesterfield, from Richmond, and from Orange.

But the ball of revolution, once set in motion, rolls down to anarchy first, and then to despotism! It never returns! And is it really so? Permit me to call the attention of the Committee to some of the civil revolutions of England, (for there have been several,) in which the ball of revolution *ascended*, and stopped at the point desired; and the fruits of which, are now the boast, both of that country and of this. On what does the Englishman pride himself, when contrasting his condition, with that of the subject of any other country? The answer readily occurs; the great and lesser charters of English liberties; jury trial, the habeas corpus, the common law, the Right of Suffrage; in short, the Englishman rejoices in his civil and religious liberties; in a Government of laws. Among all his blessings, he is in the habit of naming *magna charta* as the first: when and how was that charter obtained? It was obtained by *revolution* at Runny Meade. A majority of the Barons demanded of King John a charter of privileges and liberties, as English subjects: the King refused, and this majority of Barons armed themselves, (*for numbers* ruled there.) The King wrote to them, to know, what were these liberties and privileges about which they were so anxious. The Barons answered, that the privileges they demanded were granted by the King's father. From this answer it is supposed, that the great charter had first been granted by King Henry the third. This fact is not certain however, nor is it important: the King signed certain articles of agreement, promising a charter of the rights demanded, which the Barons had drawn up in writing, as we propose to do: he engaged to meet them on a certain day, in July, 1215, to give full effect to this agreement. Instead of performing what he had promissd to do in good faith, the King interposed a difficulty; that difficulty was not a ratio of freemen and villains, of men and taxes, or of federal numbers. He wrote to the Pope, and placed his kingdom under his protection, offering himself for a crusade to the Holy Land, and when the day arrived, instead of performing his engagement, he informed the Barons of his intentions, and that his kingdom being now the patrimony of St. Peter, they could not touch it without impious, (if I recollect we have heard this word here,) hands. The Barons, on receipt of this evasive answer, attacked and carried several of the King's castles; and, as the Pope could give no assistance, and St. Peter came not to claim his heritage, the King and his *minority* had to yield to a *majority* of Barons. The charter was signed and sealed, and with the agreement which preceded it, is preserved in the tower of London to this day. This charter is a body of what we would now call common law, of family law. The ladies of that day were as effectually represented by those Barons, as they of the present, are by us. Their rights of dower; of quarantine; of protection during minority against disparaging marriages, are enforced; not granted, for they had existed from time immemorial.

This glorious civil revolution, was effected in two or three short months, in the year 1215. Between that year, and the year, 1688, several revolutions occurred and were attended with the same happy results, the consequences of which, were frequent renewals of the great, and the additions of the lesser charter, and the *articuli super cartas*. In each of these revolutions the ball was rolled up, and, at the end of each, the rights of the people who rolled it, acquired additional strength.

I pass on to the well-known revolution of 1688. Until this time, England had never known the blessings of an independent Judiciary. The tenure *quamdiu bene se gesserit*, had never been inserted in but one commission. Great as was the value placed by our Whig ancestors in 1688, on their charters, their laws, their jury trial, and their writ of *habeas corpus*, they looked upon these rights and privileges, as in some degree of danger, so long as the Judges were dependent on the King or his ministry. The gentleman from Chesterfield said the other day, that when the King is weak and profligate, the rights of the people gain ground. William was weak at least: his ruling desire was to insert in the act of settlement, a provision limiting the succession to the heirs of his kins-woman, the Princess Sophia of Hanover: he was too weak to perceive that his Parliament were determined to do this at all events; that no other course could consist with their policy. The Parliament practised on the King's weakness, and as a consideration for the settlement of the Crown, extorted his concession, that the Judges of England should hold their commissions *during good behaviour*. Unfortunately for Scotland and Ireland, this provision was omitted in each of their acts of union with England, and the effects of Judicial dependence and independence, have been manifested in the three kingdoms in our own days. A great effort, common to the Whigs of England, Ireland, and Scotland, was made at the same time. The object was Parliamentary reform. The necessity of reform was manifest. The means proposed were orderly and constitutional. Government endeavored to suppress the United Irish in Ireland, the friends of reform in Scotland, and corresponding societies in London. In conflicts between Government and people, considerable excesses happened in each kingdom. The laws of Ireland differ from those of Scotland, and the laws of each from those of England; I mean those relating to crimes and punishments: the greatest difference was in the Forums, before which the subjects of each kingdom were brought for trial. The Englishman, was brought before independent Judges; those of Ireland and Scotland, before Judges amenable to the King and his ministers. The Irishman suffered death; the Scotchman banishment; while the Englishman was acquitted and greeted as a patriot. Englishmen were not yet satisfied with the concession of William; the Judges were not secure from a demise of the Crown, and this defect, at length, was remedied by statute, in the reign of one of the George's. Here is a brief outline of the history of four or five civil revolutions, if our present effort may be called one. All these happened in our mother country. Before the first, the Government of that country was a feudal monarchy, a despotism; since the last, it is a free limited monarchy. These civil revolutions have made that Government such, that it is receiving every day the warm and reiterated plaudits of our opponents on this floor. From the last of these revolutions, we have copied our independent Judiciary; and, although, I will aid to create more responsibility there, I pray, that we, and our posterity to remotest time, may never be weak enough to part with this surest, greatest, sheet-anchor of every free State.

Mr. Chairman, what do we hear on this occasion, more than the alarming predictions, melancholy forebodings, and evil auguries usual on every question of reform? When were men in power ready for reform? When did they yield power except to force or fear? We have lived to see Catholic emancipation in Ireland, after the failure of many attempts to accomplish that measure. On each of these occasions, ministers answered according to custom; sometimes, that the country was at war with France, or the whole Continent; sometimes, the Christian religion was in danger; and at others, that reform would jeopardize both Church and State. Their predictions were never more fearful and gloomy, than on the eve of Catholic emancipation. They were precisely of the same nature, and of the same justice, with those of our opponents here. The Catholics are emancipated, and England has gained strength by that act of justice. By a similar act of political emancipation, Virginia will increase her strength and happiness, notwithstanding the forebodings of men about to part with power.

Permit me to ask, if all civil revolutions go downward, and necessarily tend to anarchy and despotism, what do gentlemen make of that of 1776? Perhaps, there are those who think us anarchists at the present moment.

History does not present us with the arguments of King John and his minority, in 1215; these are lost in the mists of time. The same may be said of all revolutionary transactions before that of 1688. With the Tory arguments of that time, we are well acquainted. The exclusive friends of the old Constitution of England, treated all innovation as dangerous, and as tending to destroy the royal prerogative. There was a respectable party opposed to that revolution, when it took place, and many an honest Englishman is of that opinion at the present day. There always was, and there always will be, a strong party in every country opposed to reform, however necessary, and however apparent that necessity, and their intentions are generally honest, and their views patriotic. Between the contending parties on such occasions time is the judge, and experience the arbiter.

Mr. Chairman,—I acknowledge the kindness of the Chair and Committee, manifested in their attention to my remarks on this trying occasion.

Mr. Stanard offered, by way of conciliation and compromise, the following amendment to the amendment of Mr. Leigh:

"And every such citizen who shall be a lessee of a tenement of the yearly value of dollars, for a term of or more years, by deed duly recorded three months before the time he may offer to vote, and of which lease at least years shall be unexpired at the time he offers to vote.

"And every such citizen who shall within one year before he may offer to vote, have a tax or taxes to the amount of assessed on property, whether real or personal owned by him, and shall have actually paid such tax or taxes at least three months before he shall so offer to vote."

Mr. P. P. Barbour called for a division of the question, and it was divided accordingly.

Mr. Johnson suggested, that if the present amendment should be adopted, it would supercede that part of Mr. Leigh's amendment which admits termors with leases renewable at pleasure. He pointed out as an objection to that part of Mr. Leigh's amendment, that leases of the description he has mentioned, instead of being as now confined to Norfolk, would be multiplied every where, and so drawn as to confer the Right of Suffrage, and yet not to extend beyond a single year or other limited term: this could easily be effected by making the fine to be paid for the renewal of the lease so large that no tenant could pay it.

Mr. Nicholas felt embarrassed in voting for Mr. Stanard's amendment before the blanks were filled. He thought Mr. Leigh's more safe.

After some desultory conversation on the details of Mr. Stanard's amendment:

Mr. Mercer expressed his regret at the present course, and his preference to have the resolutions of the Legislative Committee taken up and decided on in their order. The present amendments applied to the first three resolutions—he wished to see the fourth taken up, which related to house-keepers.

The question was now put on the first member of Mr. Stanard's amendment, viz:

"And every such citizen who shall be a lessee of a tenement of the yearly value of dollars, for a term of or more years, by deed duly recorded three months before the time he may offer to vote, and of which lease at least years shall be unexpired at the time he offers to vote;" and decided in the negative: Ayes 37, Noes 52. So the first clause of the amendment was rejected.

The question now recurring on the second part of Mr. Stanard's amendment, Mr. Johnson expressed his decided predilection for the amendment of Mr. Leigh (slightly modified)—but expressed his willingness to vote for Mr. Stanard's proposition, if it should prove the best that can be got. He declared himself the advocate of a landed basis for the Right of Suffrage—which he pressed as a ground on which both parties might meet.

Mr. Monroe then said: It is with great regret that I rise to address the Committee at this late hour; but, as I presume the House will take a vote on the question to-day, I deem it my duty to do it. Having stated, in an early stage of this debate, that I thought that the Right of Suffrage might be extended beyond the limit prescribed by the present Constitution, and with advantage to every class in the community, it is my desire to show to what extent, I think it may be carried, and within what limit it should be confined. I feel bound to do this in explanation of my own conduct, and that my principles may be understood by my fellow-citizens. I will be very brief.

By the resolution as reported from the Legislative Committee, as well as by the amendments to it, which have been proposed, the Right of Suffrage is secured to all who now enjoy it. This is perfectly right, and if any individual holds a freehold interest which has come to him by descent, devise, marriage, or marriage settlement, or by reversion of a voter, which it is proposed to make very moderate, the Right of Suffrage is to be extended to him also: and by another amendment which is now before the Committee, it is proposed to extend this right to lessees. I confess, that under certain modifications, I shall readily agree to this. But my object is to confine the elective franchise to an interest in land: to some interest of moderate value in the territory of the Commonwealth. What is our country? is it any thing more than our territory? and why are we attached to it? is it not the effect of our residence in it, either as the land of our nativity or the country of our choice? Our adopted country? And of our attachment to its institutions? And what excites and is the best evidence of such attachment? Some hold in the territory itself; some interest in the soil: something that we own, not as passengers or voyagers, who have no property in the State, and nothing to bind them to it. The object is to give firmness and permanency to our attachment. And these are the best means by which it may be accomplished. Mere transient passengers may be foreigners. As to the citizens of other States of the Union, I consider them as citizens of Virginia, and so identified with us, that they may be relied on in that character. But our country is an asylum for the oppressed of all countries; they fly to us from all regions of the globe, particularly from Great Britain; and more especially from Ireland—they fly to us from poverty and oppression. I am willing to receive them; but I consider those people as very different from ours; and as they are not fit to be at once admitted to equal political rights among us, they should not be permitted to participate in the sovereignty, nor get hold upon the Government till they have been rendered fit for it by the acquirement of different feelings and principles.

Ours is a Government of the people: it may properly be called self-government. I wish it may be preserved forever in the hands of the people. Our revolution was prosecuted on those principles, and all the Constitutions which have been adopted in this country are founded on the same basis. But the whole system is as yet an experiment; it remains to be seen whether such a Government can be maintained; and that it may, in our Union, I have no doubt. But wise provisions, as to the exercise of the Right of Suffrage, and the powers of Government, are indispensable for its preservation. We ought to profit by the examples of every other nation; we ought to look at the history of other Republics, and see the causes which led to their overthrow. When we find that the most important and democratical among them have been soon overthrown, we ought to guard against the causes which led to their downfall. We have come here that we may prepare a form of Government for our native State. The experience of all the other States and our own experience are before us. But the experiment is still in operation, and nothing can be considered as conclusive, especially in the new States, which are of such recent establishment. Of the effect produced by the original organization, in the other States, and by the changes they have severally made in it, different reports are given in this House, on the representation of different parties in each State, which proves, that the experiment is still depending and its result unknown. I have the utmost confidence in the integrity of gentlemen on both sides of the question in this House. I can see great cause for a difference of opinion between them. It is very natural that those on the one side should feel a strong inclination to give the greatest possible extent to the rights of every citizen, whatever may be his circumstances. It is equally natural that doubts should be felt on the other side, when the experience of other Governments has admonished them of danger.

There are three great epochs in the history of the human race in regard to Government! The first commenced with the origin of the ancient Republics and terminated with them. The second commenced at the overthrow of the Roman Empire; with the Governments that were established on its ruins, and comprises their career to the present time. The third and last, commenced with the discovery of this hemisphere, the emigration of our ancestors, to this section, with their colonial state, the revolution which followed, and the Governments founded on its principles. Each of these epochs, is marked by characters, peculiar to itself. The Governments of the two first, warn us of dangers which we should always have in view. Athens and Lacedæmon are the best specimens among the Greeks—Carthage and Rome are the only others worth considering. And first let us look at the state of Athens. There we find the people *en masse* in one great assembly, possessed of the power of the Government under certain modifications. The Government and sovereignty were united in them; but the people could originate nothing. A Senate must propose all that was done—and that Senate consisted of the wealthy. The Government had commenced with nobility and a Prince, and so it continued till Solon formed the Government and instituted a Senate. This State consisted, therefore, of two classes, the rich and the poor. And as was truly observed by the gentleman from Richmond (Mr. Nicholas,) it lasted but ten years, when it was overthrown by Pisistratus, who deceived the people.

Lacedæmon was under two Kings and a Senate who held their places for life. This Government lasted longer. And why? The lands were divided equally; the people fed together, Kings, Senators and people at the same tables. This had a tendency to connect them together; at the same time all intercourse with foreign nations was prohibited. The bonds were close; and the Government was never overthrown until these bonds were first broken. Commerce introduced war and acquired plunder, whereby the manners of the people were changed. But would any body think of introducing such a Government here?

The same remarks apply, in substance, to Carthage and to Rome. My idea is, that the causes which overthrew all these Governments are so many warnings for us to profit by. Of the peculiar characteristics of the second epoch, and of the differences between ours and both, by which we were placed on more advantageous ground than either, I cannot now enter into.

I think if the Right of Suffrage should be so extended as I have suggested, I can see in that event no remaining cause of variance. All who wish to enjoy it can procure it by a few months' labour, and if public virtue and the general abhorrence of corruption shall prevail, as I hope and believe they will, we shall have those who enjoy the right, so nearly on a level with those who do not, that their influence will operate to tranquillize the whole mass of society, and induce the poor man to use exertions which will soon obtain for him the right of voting.

I thought it my duty to shew to the Committee how far I wished the right should be extended, and where we ought to stop: I think we are not in a situation to go farther.

Mr. Randolph said, he believed he was not singular in the opinion he was about to express, (though he might be the only member of the Convention, by whom it was uttered,) of sincere gratification, on finding that the gentleman who had just taken his seat, was in favour of what he (Mr. R.) conceived to be the only safe ground, in this Commonwealth, for the Right of Suffrage—he meant *terra firma:* literally *firma:* The land. The moment, said he, you quit the land, (I mean no pun,) that moment you will find yourselves at sea: and without compass—without land-mark or polar star. I said that I considered it the only safe foundation IN THIS COMMONWEALTH. For whom are we to make a Constitution? For Holland? For Venice, (where there is no land?) For a country, where the land is monopolized by a few? where it is locked up not only by entails, (I do not mean such as the English law would laugh at,) but by marriage settlements, so that a large part of the people, are necessarily excluded from the possession of it: but for a people emphatically agricultural; where land is in plenty, and where it is accessible to every exertion of honest industry. I will venture to say, that if one-half the time had been spent in honest labour, which has been spent in murmuring and getting up petitions, that the signers might be invested with that right, all-important at muster-rolls, at cross-roads, and in this Convention, yet not worth three months' labour, the right would have been possessed and exercised long ago.

I will not go into the discussion; I rose merely to express my extreme satisfaction, that the gentleman who has just taken his seat, is of opinion, that we ought to abide in the land.

The amendment of the gentleman from Chesterfield, as proposed to be modified by the gentleman from Spottsylvania, is one which I do not exactly understand. So far as it depends on a landed qualification, (which is the great principle of our present Government,) the proposition of the gentleman from Chesterfield, appears to be only an equitable modification of it, and to retain the great stable, solid qualification of land, which I view as the only sufficient evidence of permanent, common interest in, and attachment to, the Commonwealth.

I had thought, that the experience of this Commonwealth, and of the United States, had read us such lessons on the subject of personal security, that we never should think of leaving real. As I am not sufficiently acquainted with the measure proposed by the gentleman from Spottsylvania, I respectfully move that the Committee do now rise.

The Committee rose accordingly, and the House adjourned.

MONDAY, November 23, 1829.

The Convention met at 11 o'clock, and was opened with prayer by the Rev. Mr. Armstrong of the Presbyterian Church.

The President laid before the Convention the following letter from Mr. Taliaferro:

RICHMOND, 23d November, 1829.

SIR,—A domestic occurrence, which threatens the most serious family affliction, demands my immediate presence at home. In obeying this call, my first object is to provide, in the most effectual manner, for the future execution of the important trust with which I am now charged; and as I do not, under existing circumstances, consider it safe and proper, that the District, in whose delegation I am associated, should be left by me without its entire representation, my design is to resign. I therefore, beg leave, through you, to announce to the Convention, that my right to a seat in that Assembly is hereby vacated: My colleagues will proceed at once to execute the function which the Act of Assembly, in such a case, devolves on them. May I be allowed to say, that very many considerations combine to excite in me feelings of deep regret at the necessity I am under to withdraw myself from the Convention—and to add, that no considerations, certainly none personal to myself, could prevail on me to do so, unless the power existed to supply my place without possible embarrassment to my constituents, from my resignation. I cannot, in justice to my feelings, close this communication, and not express the cordial hope, that the result of the work in which you are engaged, may unite, in harmonious accord, the affections and interests of all the citizens of this Commonwealth; and that, with sentiments, Sir, of the most profound respect for you, and for the body in which you preside, I am your friend and fellow-citizen,

JOHN TALIAFERRO.

The honorable JAMES MONROE,
President of the Convention.

The letter was laid upon the table.

Mr. Neale then rose and signified to the Convention that the remaining Delegates from the District to which Mr. Taliaferro belonged, had selected as a suitable person to fill his place, John Coalter, Esq. of Stafford county, (one of the Judges of the Court of Appeals.)

The Convention then went into Committee of the Whole, on the Constitution, Mr. Powell in the Chair, and the question being on the amendment proposed by Mr. Stanard to Mr. Leigh's amendment of the third resolution of the Legislative Committee. [See Saturday's proceedings.]

MR. MONROE then addressed the Committee in nearly the following terms:

Mr. Chairman,—On Saturday, I engaged the attention of the Committee for a few moments in explaining my views with regard to the extension of the Right of Suffrage, but as it was near the hour of adjournment, I was unwilling to prolong my remarks. There are some ideas which I did not then state, and which I beg leave now to explain. I stated it to be my view, that the Right of Suffrage should be confined so as in some form to be connected with the soil—it was my idea that those who enjoyed it ought to possess some interest in society, and to have a home: at the same time I wished to see the interest limited as much as possible, and made as moderate as prudence would allow. My reasons for desiring that the elective franchise should be connected with the soil, were then stated, and need not now be repeated. My reasons for wishing to make that interest as moderate as practicable, I wish now more fully to explain.

I observed, that in fixing a Constitution for the State, either by the amendment of the old one or the adoption of a new, we ought to profit by the examples of other Governments, and particularly of the ancient Republics, as furnishing us with a warning of the dangers to which free Governments are exposed, but that none of them could present to us such an example as we ought to follow: but as a warning, it may be very profitable that we should keep them in view. Here the sovereignty resides in the people: ours may truly be called a system of self-government: and my object is, to preserve it in their hands forever. It is with that view, I would look at the dangers to which it is exposed.

I remarked that there were three great epochs in history, as it respected Government. The first of them commenced with the ancient Republics, and ended with their overthrow. The second, with the overthrow of the Roman Empire, and the establishment of those Governments which were erected on its ruins. The third and last commenced with the discovery of this hemisphere: the emigration to it by our ancestors, the Governments which were formed in our colonial state, and after our revolutionary struggle, with the Governments which were formed on the principles of the revolution. I gave an illustration of this remark, so far as relates to the first period, viz: during the continuance of the ancient Republics.

What are the characteristic features of those Governments, and what the warning they hold out to us? The people who settled on the ruins of the Roman Empire were rude in their condition and character: their Governments were monarchical, accompanied with an order of nobility. In all the great powers, with the exception of England, the Government was despotic; and in England herself, liberty had, through a long space, no solid basis on which to rest. The effort there was to avoid despotism; and the most that the friends of liberty aspired to, and contended for, was to rescue the people from slavery, and acquire for them some hold in the system. A representation in one branch of the Legislature was all that they sought, and all that they obtained. I will not go into further details. From such a Government, what example is afforded, which we ought to imitate? It was during this struggle that our ancestors fled from persecution—and settled on this Continent, under charters from the Crown, which charters formed the connecting link between the Colonies and the parent country. In all these Colonial Governments, the power was in the people: the Governor was the agent of the King. His powers were limited. Every proposition originated with the people—there was a negative in the Crown. This was the only check upon their authority. There was no nobility or prince. The revolution transferred the whole power to the people. There were no privileged orders; nor was the Government hereditary. It consisted of a House of Burgesses, a Council, and a Governor. Every proposition originated with the people, under our Colonial Government; and, therefore, liberal and free principles were inculcated, which were made perfect by our revolution. The whole Government, in all its branches, is now that of the people: every proposition may be said to originate from them; for, when checks on the most popular branch are provided, as by the Senate, for example, on the House of Delegates, they are formed by representatives of the people, and intended to give greater stability and permanence to their Government. Such a condition, therefore, as the rich and poor, and such a struggle between them, as overthrew the Government of Athens, and prostrated the power of the people, did not and does not exist here in the slightest degree. In the ancient Republics, and especially in that of Athens, the people possessed the whole power: the sovereignty and the Government were united in them: with us it is different. The sovereignty is in the people, but the exercise of Government is in their representatives. Every voter partakes a share of the sovereignty; and thus the Right of Suffrage is the basis of our system of Government. And hence the necessity for caution how we extend the right to such as have no permanent interest in the community. When we see that the representatives are so numerous, and that the voters constitute so great a mass, we have the certainty that they never can pass laws in favor of one class of society to the injury of another class.

Many reasons urge us in looking to self-government, to cause this Right of Suffrage to draw as near as possible every class in society together. But it should be connected with an interest in the soil. I wish to see no distinction, order, nor any thing like rank introduced amongst us. Let all be in the hands of the people. Let a majority rule. The laws of primogeniture and of entail are gone, and what is the tendency of such a state of things? The father brings up his sons, in his own principles and habits, and when he dies he divides his estate among them; or if he dies intestate, the law of descents comes in and divides it for him. His sons live without labour, and thus in two or three generations the largest estates become subdivided until the owners become reduced into one mass; and the whole aspect of society becomes nearly the same. Does not this present a reason why the Right of Suffrage should be connected in some degree with the soil? But let the test be made as moderate as it can be. Here we see none of those causes which overthrew the ancient Republics. The bases of our society are different from theirs. Our interests are more combined. The mass of the people are more connected with each other. Here are no great divisions of rich and poor existing distinct from each other, and engaged in perpetual conflicts. For these reasons, I should like to see the Right of Suffrage connected with the soil, but to an extent as moderate as circumstances will admit.

The question was then taken on Mr. Stanard's amendment, and decided in the negative—Ayes 41, Noes 44.

(Messrs. Madison, Monroe, and Marshall, voted in the affirmative.)

The question was then taken on Mr. Leigh's amendment, and decided in the negative—Ayes 37, Noes 51.

Aye—Mr. Monroe. *Noes*—Messrs. Madison and Marshall.

Mr. Cooke then offered the following amendment:

Strike out from the resolution of the Legislative Committee, all after the words "Resolved, that" and insert: "the election of all Executive, Legislative, or other functionaries, in this Commonwealth, whose election shall be submitted directly to the people, by the provisions of any new Constitution, or amendment of the old, to be framed by the Convention now assembled, shall be:

"All white male citizens of the United States, of the age of twenty-one years, or upwards, and resident in the county, city, borough or other electoral district, where they shall respectively offer to vote, at the time of any election; except

"That citizens of the United States, born in the United States, but without the limits of the Commonwealth, shall not enjoy the Right of Suffrage, unless they shall have resided therein for   years immediately preceding the election at which they shall respectively offer to vote; and   immediately preceding such election in the county, city, borough or other electoral district, where they shall respectively offer to vote: the mode of proving such residence to be prescribed by law:

"That naturalized citizens of the United States, shall not enjoy the right until, in addition to the qualification of residence required by the next preceding clause, they shall have respectively acquired by marriage, by descent or purchase, a freehold estate in land of the assessed value of   dollars, situated within the Commonwealth, (the title to which shall have been evidenced by a recorded deed, or will, and shall have been in possession of the same for the space of   before any election at which they shall respectively offer to vote; the mode of proving the previous residence required by this clause to be prescribed by law.)

"That no person shall exercise the Right of Suffrage at any election unless he shall have paid a State, county, or corporation tax, imposed on him by law, and legally demanded of him, during the two years immediately preceding such election: the mode of proving or disproving such payment, if disputed, to be prescribed by law.

"That no person convicted of any infamous offence, shall, at any election thereafter, enjoy or exercise the Right of Suffrage; the enumeration of such offences to be made by law.

"That the Right of Suffrage shall not be enjoyed or exercised, by any pauper—(the definition of the term pauper to be made by law:)

"By any person who shall have been declared, by a lawful tribunal, to be of unsound mind, during the continuance of such disability; or,

"By any non-commissioned officer, or private soldier, seaman or marine, in the regular service of the United States, or of this Commonwealth."

(The preceding is the shape which Mr. Cooke's proposition assumed, after being modified by subsequent amendments.)

Mr. Cooke said, that the Convention was now in the eighth week of its session, and had decided almost nothing. He added, that notwithstanding the ability with which the various subjects had been discussed, it was quite apparent that the Committee was absolutely surfeited with discussion and debate. It would ill become him, under such circumstances, to trespass on the time and patience of the Committee, by what was commonly called a "set speech." Nothing was farther from his purpose. Indeed, if the views comprehended in the amendment he had just offered on the subject of Suffrage, had been presented by any other member, he should have contented himself, after a discussion so protracted, with giving a silent vote in their support.

Under existing circumstances, he deemed it his duty to explain and support those views, but would endeavor to do it with as much brevity as possible. He hoped it would not be considered a departure from this plan of brevity, to make a few remarks on the two amendments yesterday proposed by the gentleman from Spottsylvania, (Mr. Stanard,) as he should in explaining the reasons which induced him to vote against both of the amendments alluded to, present at the same time the grounds of his preference for those which he had had the honour himself to submit.

The gentleman from Spottsylvania had proposed to extend the Right of Suffrage to

1st. "Every such citizen as shall be a lessee of a tenement of the yearly value of dollars, for a term of or more years, by a deed duly recorded three months before the time he may offer to vote, *and of which lease at least years shall be unexpired at the time he offers to vote.*" And

2d. "Every such citizen as shall, within one year before he may offer to vote, have *a tax or taxes to the amount of* assessed on property, whether real or personal, owned by him, and shall have actually paid such tax or taxes at least three months before he shall so offer to vote."

Now, Sir, said Mr. C., I am opposed to both of these modifications of the Right of Suffrage, because of the fluctuating and mutable character of the qualification they prescribe. I am opposed to the first, because it confers the right on a lessee in 1829, and deprives him of it in 1830. In 1829, his lease has two years to run, and he is a voter: he enjoys a share in the *sovereignty of the country:* in 1830, it has but one year to run, and he is disfranchised, and yet he is the same man—possesses the same moral and intellectual qualities—the same love of country—the same stake in the community—the same "evidence of permanent common interest with, and attachment to, the community"—in short, the same fitness to exercise the Right of Suffrage as in the preceding year. He has done no act to change his relation to the community in any respect, and yet he finds himself degraded from the rank of one of the sovereigns of the country, and a member of a disfranchised class. Sir, it ought to be borne in mind, that in forming a Constitution for the people of Virginia, we are not dealing with mere machines—with those "men of wood and brass and iron," to which the gentleman from Brooke (Mr. Campbell) the other day so forcibly alluded; but with sentient beings, whose feelings must be consulted and respected. And in this view I would ask, whether the free and high-spirited people of Virginia would submit, with patience, to a regulation so arbitrary and capricious in its character! Would not its enforcement produce disaffection, if not turmoil and confusion, in the class of persons subjected to its operation? I apprehend that such consequences would inevitably flow from the enforcement of a rule not only fluctuating, but in itself unjust and arbitrary.

The same principle of mutability pervades and vitiates the other qualification proposed by the gentleman from Spottsylvania. He proposes that the qualification shall consist in the payment of *a certain sum of money* to the Government, in the shape of an assessed tax on property, real or personal, owned by the voter, and that the right to vote shall *cease* when the tax shall be either abolished or reduced in amount below *that certain and specified sum.* There are, incident to this qualification, two principles of mutability or destruction, one *extrinsic*, the other *essential and inherent.* Although recommended as a part of the *fundamental law of the country*, which of course should not be changeable by ordinary legislation, it is liable to be destroyed, at any moment, by the whim, or caprice, or settled policy, if you please, of the Legislative bodies. And this too, on the colourable and popular pretext of diminishing the burthens of the Government, by the abolition or reduction of the taxes. You put the tax, for example, the payment of which is to confer the right of voting, at twelve and one-half cents, and at the time of the adoption of the Constitution of which this provision forms a part, there happens to be a tax on horses of twelve and one half cents a head. A Legislature is chosen, in which there is found a majority of members, who honestly and deliberately think, that the poorer classes of the people cannot safely be entrusted with a participation in political power—that the good order, and well-being of the community, require them to be disfranchised. A Legislature composed of such materials, has only to abolish the tax on horses, and it disfranchises at once all those poorer citizens, who have beasts of the plough, but neither land nor slaves. And this, too, as I said before, on the popular pretext of diminishing the burthens of Government. Nay, Sir, the tax on horses, may become, in the course of events, wholly unnecessary; for, one of the great objects of our assembling here, is to reduce the expenses of Government, and dispense with as many taxes as possible. But by adopting the resolution in question, you would put it out of the power of the Government to perform one of the most beneficent functions of a Government, the diminution of the burthens of the people, without, by the same act, disfranchising a considerable part of them. Can a Constitutional provision, which involves such consequences, recommend itself to the good sense of the people of Virginia?

But I have said that there is, in the qualification which I am now considering, a principle of mutability *essential* and *inherent*. I alluded to the provision which makes the payment of *a certain fixed and unchangeable sum of money*, in the shape of taxes, the qualification of the voter. Now, Sir, it appears to me, that few things are more unsteady in their value than money, and that a worse standard could scarcely be found, by which to measure and apportion political power.

If we look back into the history of other ages, and nations, we shall find that, in England, the value of silver decreased between 1570 and 1640, seventy-five per centum. So that *forty shillings*, in 1640, would command no more labour, would purchase no more of the necessaries of life, than *ten* shillings in 1570.

We shall find that the perpetual rents, reserved *in money* some centuries ago, have become, by reason of its diminished value, a mere nominal incumbrance on the land in the hands of the tenant, while those retained in *corn*, have preserved their proper proportion to the fee simple value of the land: That in the same manner the *medus*, or commutation of tythes *in kind* for a fixed sum of *money*, payable annually, established by contracts, made some centuries ago, by the church, and the proprietors of particular tracts of land in England, has become a mere nominal incumbrance on land so situated.

But we need not resort, for instruction, to the history of remote ages or distant nations. We have seen, in our own times, and in our own country, a still more forcible illustration of the unsteadiness and mutability of that standard by which it is now proposed to measure political power, and distribute it among the people. Between the year 1812 and the year 1817 the dollar depreciated, in Virginia, sixty-six per cent. so that a dollar would command in 1817 no more labour and no more of the necessaries of life than thirty-three cents would command in 1812. But a still more striking illustration is seen in the fact, that since 1817 the dollar has risen in value *two hundred per cent.*—so that thirty-three cents, at present, will command as much labour, and as great a quantity of the necessaries of life, as one hundred would have commanded or purchased in 1817.

The scheme of qualifications which I have had the honour to submit, possesses at least, the negative merit of being free from these objectionable features. It will be perceived that the proposed amendment of, or substitute for, the resolution of the Select Committee, is founded on the assumption or postulate that all the free white male citizens in the Commonwealth of mature age, have, *prima facie*, a right to a voice in the Government. I shall not repeat the arguments by which this proposition has been sustained, in the discussions which have taken place on an analagous subject. I hope I may be allowed to express the opinion that those arguments have not been answered, and the belief that they are unanswerable.

But those who believe in the original universality of this right, insist, at the same time, for reasons which have been given again and again, that the majority of the male adults, or members of the community, have a right to adopt and enforce a fundamental law, by which certain classes or descriptions of persons shall be excluded from the exercise of the right. That the majority have a right to say that the good order, well-being and safety of the community, require such exclusion. In conformity with this view of the subject, I have submitted to the Committee, a series of disqualifications, to which I now beg leave, with the utmost brevity, to call its attention.

The first disqualification includes all citizens born in the United States, but without the limits of the Commonwealth, until they shall have manifested, by a residence of some duration, an intention to reside permanently among us; until they shall have afforded by residence at least, evidence of "permanent common interest with, and attachment to, the community." This disqualification attaches great, and I think deserved importance, to the feeling of love for the natal soil. I shall not attempt, Sir, to *prove* to this Assembly, *that men love their country*.

The second disqualification is but another exemplification of the same principle. It supposes that foreigners, though naturalized, want the *attachment of the heart* which is felt by the natives of the country, and should be required to bind themselves to the community by the acquisition of *land*—by the factitious tie of *interest*, before they shall be admitted to a share of the sovereign power.

Passing by the disqualification of persons convicted of infamous offences, because they have shewn by their conduct, that they are not merely indifferent, but hostile to the community in which they live—of persons of unsound mind, because of their incapacity to exercise the right—of paupers, because of their dependent condition, and consequent want of free agency, and of their want of interest in the well-being of a community in which they have no stake, I ask the attention of the Committee to the only one which remains.

It is that which denies the Right of Suffrage to those who neglect or refuse to pay to the Government or the local authorities, the taxes and levies imposed on them by law. I confess, Sir, that I attach to this disqualification, great practical importance. I need not tell those whom I address, that there are many citizens in this Commonwealth, and I fear, not a few freeholders, who are regularly returned delinquent by the collecting officers, and whose delinquency arises not so much from their want of ability to pay, as from their utter worthlessness. Where the public contributions are so light and trifling in amount as those demanded by our Government, it may be safely assumed as *a general principle*, that those who do not pay them, are idle and worthless. And, *in fact*, the class of delinquents *includes* a great proportion of the habitual drunkards and idle vagabonds who are a dead weight, and worse than a dead weight, on the country which supports them. The practical effect of this disqualification, then, is to deny political power to those who constitute, in fact, "the rabble" of this and every country.

In this exposition of my views, Mr. Chairman, I have been studiously brief; and I regret that a sense of duty has compelled me to trespass, even as long as I have, on the valuable time of the Committee.

Mr. P. P. Barbour then addressed the Committee in nearly the following terms:

I shall certainly emulate the example set me by the gentleman from Frederick (Mr. Cooke) in brevity at least. I have no idea of going into any set speech; I am satisfied the temper of the Committee is not now such as to endure it, if it has been at any time. As I am most decidedly opposed to the whole scheme, I shall vote under an utterly different view of it from that which has been taken by the gentleman; and since he has seen proper to impute very grave charges to those who insist that the Right of Suffrage shall be connected with the soil, I shall present to the Committee, and to the public, two or three of the reasons which influence the vote I shall give.

I throw out, in the mean while, as a mere suggestion to the gentleman from Frederick, the enquiry, whether his resolutions will not conflict with some of the provisions in the Constitution of the United States? I do not say that I have formed any clear opinion as to this bearing of the subject, but I throw out the enquiry, as one that may be worthy of consideration. One of the articles of the Constitution declares, "that the citizens of each State shall be entitled to all privileges and immunities of citizens in the several States."

How far the distinction which the gentleman proposes to make between the rights of citizens of Virginia and those of the citizens of sister States, consists with the observance of this Constitutional principle, presents a subject for enquiry: but to the question before us.

We have been engaged in discussing the enquiry, in what proportion power shall be divided, among the body politic? and the question now before us is, of whom does this body politic consist? who constitute the body politic of the State of Virginia? It is hardly necessary to enter on the enquiry now as to the power of this body to declare, who shall, and who shall not, exercise the Right of Suffrage. All agree that we possess such power, in its utmost latitude; the only limitation upon its exercise is the consideration, what is just? what is proper?

My purpose is to put, if possible, the vessel of State at a sure anchorage; such as shall enable her to outride the political storms, which all history combines to prove, will ever continue to agitate the great ocean of human affairs. My purpose is to lay the foundations of the Government on a permanent basis, such as shall endure the shocks of time. I wish to sanction no unjust exclusion of any portion of the community. I seek to divide the State into no *castes* or classes. God forbid! Such a design was utterly incompatible with the spirit of the Constitution: but I want to establish sound and equitable criteria to determine who shall, and who shall not, enjoy the elective franchise, and thereby exercise a control in the Government.

Is not some landed qualification the best surety for such a permanent interest in the community as justly entitles any citizen to the exercise of this right? In answer to this inquiry, I might derive an argument from the gentleman from Frederick himself: for, when he comes to provide for the exercise of the right by aliens, he himself proposes to exact a landed qualification, as the only adequate security. He then thinks the soil presents the only solid foundation: that a right in the soil presents the best and surest evidence of a permanent common interest with, and attachment to, the community, none will dispute. Other things may indicate an interest in the community, but whether they indicate that degree of permanency in that interest which is required by the Bill of Rights, may well admit of dispute. The distinction between any and every other qualification, and that derived from an interest in the soil, is as broad as the Ecliptic. As to all other property, it is transient and perishable in its nature: it has no local habitation, and scarce a name. It is with us to-day, it is with another to-morrow. It pertains not to one person, or to one State, but may be said to belong to the Universe at large. Does the immense personal wealth of Stephen Girard belong to the State of Pennsylvania? No, Sir. It may be at New York to-day, and at Charleston to-morrow. Permanence is an attribute which has nothing to do with personal property. It belongs to landed property alone. Landed estate has another advantage: it is visible, tangible, immovable; the man who owns personal property *may* be benefitted or injured by the operations of your Government, but the man who owns the soil, *must* be benefitted or injured by them. If called to regulate the affairs of your household (and the principles of right reason which apply to a household, apply in their degree to the body politic,) would you invite those who sojourn upon your estate for a week or a month, or would you ask such as were members of your household, and were personally connected with the interests of your farm? While I am disposed, like the gentleman from Loudoun, (Mr. Monroe,) to adhere to the soil, I am willing to go to every reasonable length in extending the Right of Suffrage under that sole modification. I would not confine it to freeholders alone: I would go to the reversioner, and to the lessee: all I ask is for some indication from an interest in the soil, that the voter has some sort of permanent interest in the well-being and the fortunes of the Commonwealth.

The gentleman from Frederick objects to admit the lessee on the ground that his lease is to be valued, and that that value is mutable.

[Here Mr. Cooke rose to explain. He said the gentleman from Orange had slightly misapprehended his meaning. He had objected to the clause respecting the lessee, because it gave the Right of Suffrage to such lessee so long as his lease had yet a certain time to run, and then took it away from him, when the period for which he held it approached within a certain distance of its termination. If it was just to confer the Right of Suffrage on the ground of the lease, it certainly was unjust to take it away from the lessee until the lease was expired.]

Mr. Barbour replied, that he had understood that to be one ground of the gentleman's objection, and he would now proceed to answer it. Did not the gentleman perceive that his argument turned in a circle? that it immediately recoiled upon him? Did he not see that the argument in its utmost extent might be turned against himself? Did not the gentleman himself lay down requirements which extended retrospectively from the period of voting? and according to which a man who voted last year, would be deprived of the right of voting this? and so the Right of Suffrage would be as unsettled as a pendulum? Let him look at his own resolutions; certain classes of persons must have dwelt for two years within the county before they were admitted to vote: so, that one year before the election they would lose that privilege. In other parts of the resolutions, voters were required to have paid taxes for a certain time previous to voting: the same objection applied in that case. Take the case of the freeholder: while he continued to own the land, he was permitted to vote, but the moment it passed out of his possession, the privilege went with it. The same objection applied to the case of the minor, who could vote this year, though he could not last. The gentleman must certainly abandon this argument.

But, I am told that to insist upon connecting the Right of Suffrage, with an interest in the soil, is aristocracy; rank aristocracy. Sir, this is a grave charge, and I shall certainly be the last to advocate any measure, against which such a charge will justly lie. The gentleman from Chesterfield, presented to the Convention, some happy illustrations on this term aristocracy. According to the idea he so forcibly illustrated, if you are about to make an aristocracy, you must create a certain class in the community, distinguished from the rest by privileges and immunities, which are not only peculiar to them, but which continue to be theirs, under all changes of circumstances: which adhere to their persons and cannot be separated from them. Thus, the House of Lords in Great Britain, are a class of persons separate and distinct from all other subjects, with privileges, which they possess by hereditary descent, except a few, who, from time to time are added to the class by patent from the Crown. The aristocracy of a country all belong to a distinct class, and must remain distinct and separate, *ad indefinitum*. How can a term, which designates such a class as this, be applied in this country to freeholders, who derive the power to vote, from owning a portion in the soil? Must a man who owns a freehold to-day, own it forever? Does not this interest in the soil pass from hand to hand? is it not actually changing every day and hour? Besides all the mutations which it suffers from buying and selling, it is exposed to another and a more serious cause of change; that which arises from its partition among the descendants of those who possess it. This operation is continually widening the foundation on which freehold Suffrage rests. Thus the dreaded aristocracy is a matter of bargain and sale, and the moment any man purchases the land of his neighbour, behold! a new aristocrat! What propriety can there be in applying the term aristocracy to a body of individuals, whose claim to power is based on a foundation as fluctuating as the waves of the ocean? a body of men, into which, a man may enter to-day, and out of which he may pass again to-morrow? To make the two cases alike, it should first be shewn, that the aristocracy in England can sell at pleasure their patents of nobility, and that any commoner may become a noble, who is rich enough to pay the market price. But every body knows, that no man in England can enter this privileged order, but by the sovereign pleasure of the King, and that a man who has once been admitted, cannot lose his privileges, but by a process of law. Has the Committee, asked Mr. B., turned its attention to our law-parcenary? Here is an individual who owns ten thousand acres of land; he has a family of six children; the first descent divides this tract into six parts. Suppose each of his children should have as many children as his father had, then the second descent divides the tract into thirty-six parts; and on the same principle, a third descent would break it down into two hundred and sixteen portions. Where then is the danger of a landed aristocracy? when but the third link in the chain of descent breaks up by a mere operation of law, the largest estate, into portions, too small to support a family? Unless with every new apportionment, there is bequeathed such an energy of character, as enables each descendant to add largely to his patrimony, the posterity of the most formidable aristocrat must inevitably come to poverty. Of the truth of which assertion, the past history and present condition of Virginia will furnish abundant proof to every man. The territory of the State contains about sixty-five thousand square miles, each mile containing six hundred and forty acres of land. A process of arithmetic will speedily show, that there is soil enough in Virginia, to give a fifty acre freehold to one hundred and thirty thousand persons, after first supplying every man, woman, and child in the State. Yet, gentlemen are alarmed at the prospect of a landed aristocracy. So far is the community from such a danger, that to base the Right of Suffrage on a landed qualification, (considering the area of the State, the ease of transmutation, and the inevitable effect of partition,) is to place that privilege on a basis perpetually extending, and to make it the property of no man or set of men. Such a provision does not confine the right of voting to merchants, to farmers, or to professional men; it gives it to whoever may hold the land; to whoever may purchase the land; and, who is disposed to gratify his ambition to be an aristocrat, at the small expense required to possess himself of a freehold. It places the elective franchise within the reach of every man in the community, who possesses ordinary industry and economy. From such an arrangement, no danger can arise to the liberties of the people.

This danger being removed, I ask, whether the possession of land will not be confessed, to furnish the best evidence of a man's permanent interest in the well being of the community. Every man who has remained for any length of time in the Commonwealth, without possessing himself of some interest in its soil, gives reason to doubt whether he intends to stay among us, and whether he is disposed to identify his interest with ours. It is so very easy to acquire sufficient land to entitle a man to vote, and the privilege of voting is in its nature so far beyond all price, that the presumption is a fair one, that he, who acquires no freehold, either underrates that privilege, or does not mean to become permanently a citizen among us. But, we are told that under the present Constitution, many valuable citizens of great talents and virtue, are excluded from the polls. It may be so; but what line can possibly be drawn, which will not leave excluded some angles of the State? No regulation can be adopted, under which some cases of hardship will not possibly occur. Is it not a hard case, that a young man, who lacks twenty-four hours of being of age, should be deprived of the privilege of voting, for the want of those twenty-four hours, especially if he be something of a precose and forward youth? Such an argument will not do, unless gentlemen can shew it to be possible for imperfect and fallible men, to make rules which shall be beyond all imperfection: to shew, that the rule we propose, will be attended with some inconvenience, is only to shew, that our rule is human, and is like all other rules, that have men for their authors. As to the case of those citizens, who own such vast amounts of personal property, as have been represented by gentlemen, and whose exclusion from the polls has drawn forth so much commiseration, if, with all their wealth, they are unwilling to purchase one poor fifty acre tract of land, their case certainly receives little commiseration of mine: their exclusion is their own fault, their thousands remain intangible to our taxation, and if they will not subject the price of one poor freehold, to the reach of the Government, they deserve to have neither part nor lot in its control.

MR. LEIGH next addressed the Committee. According to my understanding of the resolutions now moved by the gentleman from Frederick, a man who has never been assessed with a tax of any sort, is to be allowed to vote; but the man who has been assessed with a tax, and has not paid it, is to be excluded from the polls! It comes then to this, that those "drunken vagabonds," against whom the gentleman manifests so earnest a zeal, are only to be excluded, if they chance to have property enough on which to be assessed; but such vagabonds as have no property, and whom no man would ever think of taxing, are the peculiar objects of his favour. They must have a right to vote. If I had used such a phrase, it would doubtless, have been attributed to my aristocratical prejudices; it would immediately have been imputed to my political creed. But I submit to the Committee, whether a man who has some property and some means of subsistence, or a man who has none at all, is more likely to be a "vagabond," and to belong to "the rabble;" yes, Sir, to "the rabble." It is a proper phrase, and it is a phrase too, used by a gentleman on the other side. Mr. Chairman, I do not contend that the possession of property is a security against vice. I know better, and sorry I am that I do; but this I say, if you look at the state of mankind with a view to determine who is the most likely to become base and undeserving; to become drunken vagabonds, and a part of the rabble, you will be constrained to confess, that those who have some property, are at least more apt to be virtuous, than those who have none. You will be almost sure to find, among those without property, no industry and no economy; and if you then look to those who exhibit the greatest degree of vice, you will find them to consist of persons precisely of this description. I throw out these objections to the details of the gentleman's plan, that it may the better be compared with the amendment I proposed. It is hardly to be imagined, that the gentleman seriously intends such consequences to result from his measure. I shall not attempt to enter on the question of a landed qualification as the basis for the elective franchise. On that subject hope is winged, and ready to take its departure. I feel it dying in my heart. This very morning, I heard the venerable gentleman from Loudoun, (Mr. Monroe,) insist on connecting that privilege with the soil, and I then saw him vote in favour of a proposition of the gentleman from Spottsylvania, the object of which was to dispense with all landed qualification whatever. After this I can hope for nothing more; far less, can I expect that my shoulders will be broad enough to sustain the weight of such a cause. I consider that question as at an end. Whether I shall ever revive, depends upon circumstances; but I never shall abandon it, while one scintilla of hope is left me.

There is one consideration, which I consider of much more importance, than the question of freehold qualification: whether the voter is to possess a freehold or not, is comparatively of little consequence. But gentlemen insist, that every form of a landed qualification, amounts to an exclusion of all who do not possess it, and they argue on a similar assumption as to all other qualifications. Sir, this is no exclusion whatever, of any man, who, according to the gentlemen themselves, would be entitled to vote; (for, they themselves advocate a permanent exclusion of all females and coloured persons.) When gentlemen talk of the EXCLUSION of any free white man, from the privilege of voting, I am at a loss to understand their meaning. Is there a free white man in all Virginia, who may not obtain the right to vote? If he has his health, and is industrious, he may compass enough to purchase ten or twenty, or even fifty acres of land, which is the most that any one thinks of requiring as a freehold. Who then is excluded? Those only, who are too lazy to earn, or who do not think proper to acquire it. There is not a man who may not acquire even the qualification demanded by the existing Constitution. He may possess it at pleasure, if he is an industrious man. Far less is he prevented from acquiring the reduced qualification, which is proposed to be acquired by the new Constitution.

Mr. Chairman,—I do not agree in the position, that no man who is not qualified to vote for members of the General Assembly, is not a member of the body politic. I insist, that the wife and the daughters of such voter, are members of the body politic. They are not the slaves of their husbands or their fathers; they are free-born citizens of this Commonwealth. God forbid they should be otherwise! It is not a necessary qualification of a citizen that he should be entitled to vote; it would be most absurd to exclude from the privilege of citizenship, every female, and every minor in the community.

We hear gentlemen on the other side constantly speaking of the Right of Suffrage, as being of inestimable value; the dearest right of freemen; dear as life itself, &c. I have heard this language all my life, and I once thought, (it was when I was fresh from school,) that I understood it; but latterly I have ceased to understand it, and I cannot recall the ideas I once had on this subject. It is certainly a most invaluable privilege to live under a Government freely elected by the most virtuous portion of the community; to live under rulers, who can pass no act injurious to me, that will not be equally injurious to themselves, and more so. But, is the privilege that I individually should vote for them an invaluable privilege, when I can purchase it for fifty dollars? I ask gentlemen to reflect upon this view of the subject. When a young man is twenty years old and six months, is this privilege a whit less inestimable, than after he is of age? But I go farther, and I ask, is the blessing of Republican Government confined to the *men* who live under it? does it not belong to the women also? do they not enjoy the free benefit of it? The enjoyment of the inestimable blessing does not then depend on our exercising the Right of Suffrage, but it consists in this, that those govern, who themselves hold property, and that they cannot injure others, without in the same degree injuring themselves; that those govern the community who feed, clothe, and educate the whole community, and pay all its burdens. This is the privilege, and it is a privilege indeed. Does any man believe, I consider it an invaluable privilege to vote for a member of the General Assembly? Without the least disrespect for that body, I may say, that I consider this, as a matter of no moment. I do not regard him alone as my Representative. I put my confidence in the great body of the Legislature as a whole; as the body which in its collective capacity protects my rights and gives me my share of the general liberty and safety. The only benefit they are to me, consists in this; that they protect all the happiness which I succeed in carving out for myself. But according to the doctrine of the invaluable privilege, unless I vote, I enjoy no share in the political sovereignty of the community. Now, if I vote against a candidate who succeeds in his election, I am worse off than if I had not voted, because I see others share in the Government, in direct contradiction to my wishes and efforts. I wish in conclusion, distinctly to say, that the advantage I derive from a free Government consists in this, that the Government is administered by those who have a common interest with me, and that I cannot be injured unless others are, and among those, the rulers themselves. If I am protected, that is all I desire. Mr. L. concluded by expressing his conviction, that to insist upon a landed qualification for the Right of Suffrage, involved no exclusion of any man; established no order of nobility, but was simply a provision, that those who were in general the most fit to rule should exercise the powers of Government.

Mr. Stanard said that he should reply to Mr Cooke's criticism on his amendment, if this was the proper time to do it; but the amendment having been rejected, could not now be discussed.

Mr. Monroe now explained,—I feel it incumbent on me to give an explanation of the ground on which I gave the vote that has been remarked upon by my very worthy friend from Chesterfield, for whom I feel great respect and regard. I am for adhering to an interest in the territory. I am for providing some tie which shall connect the voter with the soil. Perhaps I did not distinctly understand the proposition of my friend from Spottsylvania, but I viewed it in this light: that the person who had been assessed to a certain amount which was left blank, and who had paid his assessment, should be admitted to vote. My idea was, that if he was taxed, he must of course be a resident: and if taxed to the extent which I expected, (and it was my view that the tax should be made to exceed the value of a freehold or a lease,) it would enjoin upon him an obligation to purchase or lease real property. I had no idea of abandoning a hold upon the land, not in the least. The proposition is still before the House, and after all the amendments should have been proposed and passed upon, the result of the whole proposition would still be in our power. It was my purpose to take a deliberate view of the proposition as it should appear in its last stage, and then to vote for or against it as my best judgment should dictate. I never meant to abandon some hold upon the land, but to give security by it to our system of Government. I am for giving permanence, if possible, to a system of self-government. But you go afloat, the moment you put the Right of Suffrage in the hands of a transient population. You can have no security. Go to Great Britain, I name that country because its history and condition are most acceptable and best known by us. Put the Government there in the hands of the people; and they would immediately behead the King and cut off the heads of the Nobility, and throw every thing into confusion: the reason is, they are incompetent to self-government. But we are competent. We are altogether in a different situation. The general diffusion of knowledge among our people inspires me with the strongest confidence in the success of our system. Still, let us be on our guard as to the exercise of the Right of Suffrage, on which the sovereignty rests, which is in the people.

All the officers of the Government, though many of them are not elected immediately by the people, are their Representatives, since they derive their appointments from the people, by the agency of those whom the people do elect. My object is to connect the Right of Suffrage with the territory.

The Chair now said that the remarks of Mr. Cooke on the amendment of Mr. Stanard had been permitted, not as a discussion of that amendment after it had been rejected, but as a part of his argument intended to bear on his own amendment.

Mr. Leigh gave an assurance of his personal regard and respect for Mr. Monroe, and expressed his satisfaction at learning that he still adhered to a landed qualification for voters.

He then urged this farther objection to Mr. Cooke's amendment; that its effect would be to give the elective franchise to persons like some in Richmond and Petersburg, who were the mere factors for the manufacturing houses of the North, and who had not only no common interest with the people of Virginia, but an interest directly hostile to theirs. It would admit every man who owns a horse: and there were numbers in his own county who owned nothing else, living by charity on the lands of others and wholly devoted to their will in every thing that was not directly dishonest. All these would give the votes not of themselves, but of their benefactors.

Mr. Campbell in reply to Mr. Monroe, referred to the fact that in twelve States of the Union, nothing more is required of a voter than residence and the payment of taxes. No condition of the ancient Governments had been analogous to this, and therefore their downfall was no warning against it. As to the case of procuring a freehold, no man with due respect to himself and his rights, would stoop to purchase what he had a right to demand.

Mr. Cooke replied to Mr. Leigh, whose criticism he thought more witty than candid. He wished to sweep off all, who from moral degradation, were incapable of an upright and proper exercise of the elective franchise. His amendment would not admit vagabonds without any property, while it admitted vagabonds who nominally had some; because it excluded all who did not comply with county levies; now the rabble of whom Mr. Leigh had spoken, were all included in the poll-tax; and if returned delinquent, all these would be excluded.

In reply to Mr. Barbour, he thought there was a distinction between the word "rights" and the terms "privileges and immunities." The elective franchise was included in the former term, but not in the latter; and, therefore, the amendment would not contradict the Constitution of the United States.

Mr. Leigh observed that Mr. Cooke had said, and repeated three times that which *he* had said was more witty than *candid*. He desired that Mr. Cooke would have the goodness to recall that word *uncandid*.

Mr. Cooke was about to reply, when the Chairman interposed, and remarked that he had not understood Mr. Cooke as imputing any intentional misrepresentation to Mr. Leigh, otherwise he should have stopped him.

Mr. Leigh repeated his call on Mr. Cooke, to recall the word.

Mr. Cooke said, that he had not the slightest objection to saying, with the utmost frankness, what was precisely the fact, that he had not imputed, or intended to impute, to Mr. Leigh, any intentional misrepresentation. He added, that he wondered greatly at the excitability manifested by Mr. Leigh, since nothing that he had said could be fairly construed into an intention on his part, to wound Mr. Leigh's feelings; which, in fact, he had not the remotest idea of doing. That he meant nothing more than that Mr. Leigh's remarks, made in the ardour of debate, had, in their effect, presented an unfair view of his (Mr. Cooke's) proposition. Deliberate or intentional unfairness, he had not imputed to him.

Mr. Leigh said, that, personally, he was satisfied. But he had appealed to Mr. Cooke in the course of his remarks to say, whether the interpretation put by him (Mr. Leigh) on his (Mr. Cooke's) proposition was not correct; to which Mr. Cooke had nodded assent. After that he thought it was rather singular, that Mr. Cooke should impute to his argument any want of candour.

Mr. Cooke replied, that the proposition which his assent to, or dissent from, was asked by Mr. Leigh, was simply this—that Mr. Cooke's scheme of qualification, admitted persons to vote who had no taxable property, and excluded from Suffrage those who had taxable property, and failed to pay the taxes assessed on it. To the correctness of that construction of his proposition, Mr. C. had nodded assent.

Mr. Doddridge now objected to that part of Mr. Cooke's amendment, which had relation to aliens; he moved to strike out that clause. He briefly explained his objections to it, as going farther than the laws relating to aliens go, respecting real estate.

Mr. Cooke modified his amendment, by inserting the words, "if acquired by purchase"—(requiring the deed to be recorded, when the freehold was acquired by purchase.)

Mr. Joynes expressed an objection to Mr. Cooke's amendment, as going to admit the poorest man in the county, while the richest might be excluded, if the poll-tax should ever be repeated.

The question being put on striking out, it passed in the negative, without a count.

Mr. Coalter, after an apology, referring to his recent occupation of a seat, expressed his opposition to cutting down the venerable tree planted by our forefathers and planting another in its stead; he would endeavour to strike one blow for Virginia, and bear down on the enemy; by whom he meant the passions and prejudices of members, his own included. To pluck up the tree, would be the sin of *man* only; for Eve, looked on with deep anxiety clutching her child to her bosom. He expressed his decided approbation of the present form of Government, as the best in the world, under which the people had lived contented and happy. He reflected on the injustice of the friends of Internal Improvement laying the burden on those who had no personal interest in the object, and imposing a lasting mortgage on the lands of the State.

Mr. Campbell thought the gentleman's alarm about the axe imaginary; it was only a pruning knife to lop off a few aristocratical branches.

Mr. Cooke farther modified his amendment at the suggestion of Mr. Joynes, so as to include any State, county, or corporation tax.

In this form the question was taken upon its adoption and negatived.—Ayes 43, Noes 49.

Mr. Doddridge now moved the amendment he had referred to on Saturday, and which is in these words:

"And shall be extended to every free white male citizen, aged twenty-one years or upwards; who shall have resided at least two years in the county, city, borough, or district, in which he shall offer to vote, immediately preceding the time of voting, and who, during that period, shall have actually paid a revenue tax legally assessed; and to every free white male citizen, aged twenty-one years or upwards, who shall have actually resided, at least two years in the county, city, borough or district, where he offers to vote, and who, for the period of six months at least, shall have been an house-keeper therein, and shall actually have paid a State, county, or corporation tax."

Mr. Mercer wished to know why Mr. D. desired to strike out the first and second class of persons included in the resolution of the Legislative Committee?

Mr. Doddridge replied, because the generality of his proposition covered them all, provided they paid taxes.

Mr. Mercer stated that he could not vote for the proposition. The gentleman from Brooke himself had agreed that all who now have the Right of Suffrage should retain it. Was it his object to make the right to vote to depend on the payment of a tax? In eight States of the Union there is no tax whatever imposed. Even within sight of this Capitol, there is a gentleman who has an estate worth twenty-five thousand dollars, but who has no right to vote because there is no tax imposed on his property. Why were such persons to be excluded? He was in favor of comprehending all those whom that gentleman intended to include; but he would not vote to exclude those who held by exactly the same tenure, but who were denied the right to vote because they were not taxed. The gentleman from Brooke himself, insisted that there should be a sufficient evidence of permanent common interest. He moved to amend the proposition to amend, by inserting the amendment in the fourteenth line, after the word "dollars"—the effect would be to leave the first and second classes untouched.

The Chair decided that the amendment was not in order; but

Mr. Doddridge having accepted the proposition, modified his amendment accordingly.

Mr. Joynes moved to amend the amendment by adding the words "and who shall have actually paid a State, corporation, or county tax."

Mr. Doddridge accepted the amendment as a modification of his amendment.

Mr. Mason asked for a division of the question; and,

The question was then taken on striking out, which, after an unsuccessful motion by Mr. Henderson, that for the sake of accuracy the names of members should be called over, was decided in the affirmative.

The question was then taken on inserting the words moved by Mr. Doddridge, and decided in the negative.—Ayes 44, Noes 48.

Mr. Mercer then moved to fill the blank occasioned by striking out, with the fourth class of persons included in the report of the Legislative Committee, in the following words:

"Or who for twelve months next preceding has been a house-keeper, and head of a family within the county, borough, or election district, where he may offer to vote, and who shall have been assessed with a part of the revenue of the Commonwealth within the preceding year, and actually paid the same."

Mr. Mercer said, he would not presume to violate the rule which had been laid down by others, of abstaining from going into the merits of the general question. There was one view which he wished to take: while gentlemen on one side represent the acquisition of the Right of Suffrage as to be gained with the greatest facility, they seemed to attach the greatest importance to the exclusion of others from its exercise. If it were so easy to acquire a qualification, and it was of such importance, why could not faction purchase the freehold? According to the gentleman from Orange, (Mr. P. P. Barbour,) the multiplication of the square miles in the State by the acres, gave sufficient quantity of land to every individual in the State, and left a considerable surplus. He computed that putting the value of the freehold, as estimated by gentlemen, it would take a capital of three millions of dollars to supply the sixty thousand now excluded with the qualification. He then reviewed the proposition by gentlemen on the other side, denying that the land qualification was necessary. The people who lived in a shepherd state, had other property besides land, and that was considered quite as permanent and essential as land. Was it necessary for him to direct the attention of gentlemen to England? Is not the fixed capital in that country as important as land? Is it not here in the low-land country, where labor is capital and is an essential ingredient in the wealth of the country? Implements of trade are essential, and every one will thus perceive, that other property is as essential as land. If this principle be true, what becomes of the foundation of the argument, which rests on the durability of land? The right is not founded on the land, but the relation in which the proprietor stands to it. And so it is with other capital. It is the relation of the proprietor to it; as it is between the freeholder and the soil. Personal property is an essential ingredient in the wealth of the country, and the title to it is as good, as that of the land-owner to the land. By shutting out the sixty thousand free whites who lack the qualification of land, we shut out not only the majority now, but the increase of that majority. He referred to the time, when tenants for life were every where to be found; when all that part which was now called the back-woods and the part where he lived, were cultivated by tenants for life. The practice had been discontinued, because of its effect on the independence of the tenants, and so completely had this class disappeared, that in twenty years, he had known but two instances of tenants for life. Suppose, men of fortune found it to their interest to divert part of their capital from manufactures to land, would it not be better to introduce the tenantry-system again, and to supercede slave-labor? In his part of the country, tenantry for years had superceded slavery. Gentlemen imagined that sixty thousand non-freeholders, might be easily converted into freeholders. He requested them to look at the consequences of this. Suppose sixty thousand persons purchased freeholds of fifty dollars each; three millions would thus be expended merely for the Right of Suffrage.

He took a view of the different value of land in different sections of the country, and resisted the idea, that a qualification could at any time be purchased at a moderate price. In the district he represented, the non-freeholders greatly outnumber the freeholders, and he supposed, that all the non-freeholders there, desired to purchase a freehold each, and taking this for his basis, he asserted, that it would take ten millions to purchase freeholds for the non-freeholders, in order to give them the qualification to vote. You would make all these men farmers. He repeated, that the basis of the qualification, was not the land, but the relation in which the owner stood to his land.

He adverted to the assertion of gentlemen, that this question which we are now settling, was of limited importance, only embracing the Commonwealth. It was forgotten that the United States had a representation from this State, which would be affected by our measures, and which taxes our productions, to the amount of six times our whole State revenue. He did not believe, that his venerable friend and colleague, (Mr. Monroe,) intended to exclude house-keepers, who have an interest in the soil.

Mr. Johnson moved to amend the amendment, by inserting after the words "and who shall have been assessed with a part of the revenue of the Commonwealth, within the preceding year," the words "not less than cents."

But his motion was negatived.—Ayes 42, Noes 51.

Mr. Leigh again pointed out the inconsistency of letting a tenant vote who paid a ten cent tax, and excluding his landlord, because his freehold did not come up to the value fixed by the Constitution.

Mr. Mercer acknowledged this, but reserved that for another time, when the whole should be referred to a Select Committee to revise. He pressed the question; and it was then taken and decided in the *affirmative*.—Ayes 53, Noes not counted.

That whole resolution, as amended, will now read:

"*Resolved*, That the Right of Suffrage shall continue to be exercised by all who now enjoy it under the existing Constitution: and shall be extended, 1st, to every free white male citizen of the Commonwealth resident therein, above the age of twenty-one years, who owns, and has possessed for six months, or who has acquired by marriage, descent, or devise, a freehold estate, assessed to the value of not less than dollars for the payment of taxes, if such assessment shall be required by law: 2d, or who shall own a vested estate in fee, in remainder, or reversion, in land, the assessed value of which shall be dollars: 3d, or who for twelve months next preceding, has been a house-keeper and head of a family within the county, city, borough, or election district, where he may offer to vote, and who shall have been assessed with a part of the revenue of the Commonwealth within the preceding year, and actually paid the same: *Provided, nevertheless*, That the Right of Suffrage shall not be exercised by any person of unsound mind, or who shall be a pauper, or a non-commissioned officer, soldier, sailor, or marine, in the service of the United States, nor by any person convicted of any infamous offence; nor by citizens born without the Commonwealth, unless they shall have resided therein for five years immediately preceding the election at which they shall offer to vote, and two years preceding the said election, in the county, city, borough, or election district, where they shall offer to vote, (the mode of proving such previous residence, when disputed, to be prescribed by law,) and shall possess, mereover, some one or more of the qualifications above enumerated."

The Committee then rose and the House adjourned.

TUESDAY, November 24, 1829.

The Convention met at 11 o'clock, and was opened with prayer by the Rev. Mr. Douglass, of the Presbyterian Church.

The House then resolved itself into a Committee of the Whole, Mr. Powell in the Chair, and the question being on the third resolution reported to the Convention by the Legislative Committee, viz:

"*Resolved*, That the Right of Suffrage shall continue to be exercised by all who now enjoy it under the existing Constitution: and shall be extended, 1st, to every free white male citizen of the Commonwealth resident therein, above the age of twenty-one years, who owns, and has possessed for six months, or who has acquired by marriage, descent, or devise, a freehold estate, assessed to the value of not less than dollars for the payment of taxes, if such assessment shall be required by law: 2d, or who shall own a vested estate in fee, in remainder, or reversion, in land, the assessed value of which shall be dollars: 3d, or who for twelve months next preceding, has been a house-keeper and head of a family within the county, city, borough or election district, where he may offer to vote, and who shall have been assessed with a part of the revenue of the Commonwealth within the preceding year, and actually paid the same: *Provided, nevertheless*, That the Right of Suffrage shall not be exercised by any person of unsound mind, or who shall be a pauper, or a non-commissioned officer, soldier, sailor or marine, in the service of the United States, nor by any person convicted of any infamous offence; nor by citizens born without the Commonwealth, unless they shall have resided therein for five years immediately preceding the election at which they shall offer to vote, and two years preceding the said election, in the county, city, borough or election district, where they shall offer to vote, (the mode of proving such previous residence, when disputed, to be prescribed by law,) and shall possess, moreover, some one or more of the qualifications above enumerated."

Mr. Summers of Kanawha, offered the following amendment, (applying to the third class of voters added) being the same he had offered in the Legislative Committee, with a slight modification, substituting occupancy for possession:

"Or who shall own and be himself in actual occupation of a lease-hold estate, with the evidence of title recorded, of a term originally not less than five years, *and one of which shall be unexpired*, of the annual value or rent of dollars."

The amendment was very briefly explained by the mover, and supported by Mr. Claytor.

At the suggestion of Mr. Leigh,

Mr. Summers farther modified his amendment, so as to confine the occupancy to the *termor* himself, and not extend it to his tenant.

Mr. Henderson of Loudoun, moved to amend the amendment, by striking out after the words "of a term originally not less than five years," the words which immediately follow, viz: "*and one of which shall be unexpired*."

The motion prevailed, Ayes 48—(Mr. Marshall was observed to vote for it, Mr. Madison and Mr. Monroe against it.) So the words requiring one year of the lease to remain unexpired, were stricken out.

Mr. Leigh moved to strike out the word "five" (in the original length of the lease) with a view to insert a longer period.

This motion was supported by Mr. Doddridge, as tending to benefit the tenure of lease-hold property, by encouraging long leases.

Mr. Johnson wished first to know how the blank was to be filled.

Mr. Leigh said, he meant to insert ten, instead of five years.

Mr. Claytor said, he should then move to fill the blank with three instead of five.

Mr. Leigh then varied his motion, so as to strike out, and insert *ten*. The motion was negatived.

Mr. Claytor moved to strike out five and insert three.

Mr. Scott called for a division of the question; and then the question being put on striking out five, it was negatived.

So the term of *five years* as the original length of the lease, was left unaltered.

Mr. Tyler asked, and obtained a re-consideration of the motion to strike out the unexpired term of one year; but the vote being again taken, the striking out was again carried—Ayes 45, Noes 44.

Mr. Wilson moved to amend the amendment of Mr. Summers, by striking out the words (in respect to the lease) "*of the annual value or rent of dollars.*"

But the motion was negatived.

The question was then put on Mr. Summers's amendment as amended, and carried by a large majority.

Mr. Leigh now moved to amend, by inserting after the word "year," (in reference to the payment of a part of the revenue within the preceding year) the words "*to the amount of* ." But the motion was negatived—Ayes 43, Noes 44.

Mr. Stanard then moved to insert, (in the same place, and in reference to the same subject, namely, the tax paid,) the words "*by a tax on property owned by him.*"

Mr. Mercer explained the effect of this amendment to be, to exclude the tenant who pays a tax on his house, the merchant who pays a tax on his licence, or a slave-employer on the slaves he hires.

Mr. Stanard thought differently: when the tenant paid the tax, it formed a part of the rent. The amendment would exclude mountebanks, pedlars, &c. Those who had not some little modicum of property hung loosely on society.

Mr. Moore opposed the amendment, as leading to disputes at elections, and afterward as to the votes to be admitted.

Mr. Green said, the resolution as it stood, would give the Right of Suffrage to every man who sues out a writ, with or without cause of action, for there is a tax on all writs.

The amendment of Mr. Stanard was negatived—Ayes 41, Noes 48.

(Messrs. Madison, Monroe and Marshall, against it.)

Mr. Stanard, (to avoid disputes about votes,) varied his amendment, so as to read, "by a tax on property charged to him on the Commissioners' books."

Mr. S. explained his object to be, to exclude all who paid tax on their profession or trade merely. It was unfair that the mechanic, who sells the work of his own hands, should be excluded, and the merchant, who sells foreign goods, admitted to vote.

Mr. Mercer said, of all books, printed or in MS., the Commissioners' books were the most inaccurate. Besides, this would be fixing the Right of Suffrage on a variable mode of taxation, liable to continual change.

Mr. Leigh had never heard the Commissioners' books charged with inaccuracy before. As to the tax on merchants' licenses, it was not the merchant who paid them, but the consumers.

Mr. Mercer replied, that he had known the same tract of land to be charged *three times* over, on the Commissioner's book, and *never* to its right owner in either case. Many merchants would be glad if the fact was as stated by Mr. S., and lawyers too.

The question was taken on Mr. Stanard's amendment, and the votes stood—Ayes 47, Noes 46.

(Messrs. Madison and Marshall for it, Mr. Monroe against it.)

The Chair voting in the negative, produced a tie; and of course the motion was lost.

Mr. Summers, after expressing his satisfaction that there was now, as he hoped, a *final end to the freehold Right of Suffrage in Virginia*, moved the following amendment:

"Or who having resided two years in the county, city, town or election district, should have been assessed with, and paid to the Commonwealth any part of the revenue of the preceding year."

The amendment was to be inserted immediately before the proviso.

Mr. Stanard enquired whether this was not, in substance, the same provision, which had been three times rejected already?

The Chair thereupon compared the present amendment with all those which had been rejected; and then announced, that though this proposition had been rejected, it had always, heretofore, been *in connexion* with some other proposition, and had never, until now, been presented specifically, and alone; it was therefore in order.

Mr. Johnson strongly objected to this amendment, as going in effect to put the extent of the Right of Suffrage, within the control, and at the discretion of the Legislature: who, by increasing or diminishing the taxes, could enlarge or lessen the number of voters at pleasure. A tax of one cent a head would at any time introduce *Universal Suffrage*.

Mr. Randolph then rose and addressed the Committee, nearly as follows:

As one of not the least zealous of those who wish (in company with the gentleman who stands at the head of the delegation from Loudoun, and presides over this Convention, the benefit of whose vote I trust we shall have when we come into the House,) to restrain the Right of Suffrage to the possession of *land*, I feel almost indifferent whether this amendment shall prevail or not. I will go farther, and say, that if the proposition, written in sport, by my old friend and fellow-labourer, who sits behind me (Mr. Garnett,) and which gives the Right of Suffrage to every free white man who has been twenty-four hours within the bounds of an election district, should be offered by him, I do not know, if I should have any great objection to that proposition.

But I will say, with the most perfect sincerity, that I had rather this Committee should rise, after having adopted a resolution committing the whole powers of the State, Legislative, Executive, and Judicial, to the Legislature of Virginia, than that any of the propositions inserted in the third resolution of the Legislative Committee, should become a part of the Constitution. I believe it would be safer to trust solely to the discretion of the Legislature, than to adopt these propositions; for, we should then at least rest upon the good sense of the people. Sir, I put it to every gentleman who hears me, whether it would not be safer to give the Legislature *a carte blanche*, and make them as omnipotent as the Parliament of Great Britain, rather than to give them these propositions as the fundamental law by which they are to be bound. I have said, and I will now repeat it, that if the first resolution in the report of the Legislative Committee shall be adopted, in the naked form in which it now stands, it will be a matter of indifference to me, personally, what shall be done by this body hereafter, on any subject. And it is only because this first resolution lies as yet, in abeyance on your table, that I am disposed to struggle in relation to what I consider next in importance. Sir, if the freeholders of this Commonwealth, in whom is the power, shall be weak and mad enough to surrender this question, they will have effaced, (were it not in Holy Writ,) all record of the stupidity of Esau. If we, the proprietors of the soil, the land-owners, who can give *notice to quit*, aye, and compel to quit too, all those persons who insist on taxing our land, submit to this, our "ineffable stupidity" ('I thank thee, Jew, for teaching me that word,') I say our "ineffable stupidity" will have effaced, (were it not inscribed by the pen of inspiration on the pages of Holy Writ,) all record of the stupidity of Esau. I do not know whether I shall take the trouble to rise, or keep my seat, when the question shall be called on the amendment of the gentleman from Kanawha.

I had no expectation of entering into this debate, but the appearance of apathy, which I witness (with a *solitary* exception,) is to me most afflicting and painful. There is one class of non-freeholders toward whom my heart yearns, if it were not restrained by my judgment: I mean the sons of freeholders; whose fathers cannot yet afford to lay them off their little modicum of land, and who, therefore, have to wait. To that class, I would now address myself, and I would say to them, cannot you trust your fathers? cannot you have a little patience? must you not, necessarily, succeed to this power? if not by inheritance, or bequest, at least by a few years industry? Will you go into joint stock with those "*vagabonds*" and that "*rabble*," so well designated by the gentleman from Frederick, who never mean to have a freehold? the profligate, the homeless; who, as was well said by the gentleman from Spottsylvania, "hang very loosely on society," but stick very closely to her skirts, and who are determined to pick up their vile and infamous bread, by every despicable means? I call on the young non-freeholders, the sons of freeholders, (and if I had a son, he should be my *own* son) I call on them to wait, and not to unite themselves with those who, in the nature of things, can have no permanent interest in the Commonwealth. I am very sure, that when they shall have understood this question, they will rally round their fathers and their brothers. I have no belief, that a Constitution with such principles in it, will ever be received by the sober sense of this good old Commonwealth. I would rather wish that all powers, Executive, Legislative and Judicial, should be at once entrusted to the General Assembly, and then trust the good sense of the people of Virginia, than inflict on them the curse of such provisions as those which the Committee have adopted.

Mr. Summers, in reply to Mr. Johnson, expressed regret at not being able to attach as much weight to his opinion in this case, as he was accustomed to do. He thought the expansive power attending this amendment, was its most valuable feature. He was willing to commit it to the wisdom of the Legislature, believing it to be a just principle, that all who contribute to the burdens of society, should have some voice in its affairs.

Mr. Stanard thought the amendment of the gentleman from Kanawha, went, at least, a bow-shot further, toward Universal Suffrage, than any proposition yet submitted to the Committee. He did not know how the gentleman would manage the matter with his friend from Loudoun, who, in his speech on a former occasion, had insisted that all taxes on consumption were paid by the consumer. If this were true, and an excise should be laid on spirits, every man who bought a gill of rum, would thereby pay a tax and get the Right of Suffrage; and thus the "vagabonds" and "rabble" of the gentleman from Frederick, (very properly so called,) would be entitled *par excellence* to that privilege. He insisted on the objection urged by Mr. Johnson, and then shewed that the lightest cattle-tax, would give a vote to every man west of the mountains; inferred the ease of introducing Universal Suffrage, and concluded with a strong appeal to the Committee, against so sweeping an amendment.

The question being taken, the amendment was *rejected* without a count.

Mr. Henderson now moved to amend that clause of the resolution which requires a residence of five years, of citizens of other States moving into Virginia, before they can be permitted to vote. He thought two years residence in the State, and one in the county, a sufficient test of permanent interest in the Commonwealth.

Mr. Nicholas said he should vote for the amendment. He was willing to give these citizens the right of voting after a residence of two years, but he would superadd to the qualification of persons of this class, the attainment of a freehold. He did not think that his part of the country would be injured by this proposition; and he thought it impolitic to throw impediments in the way of emigration to the State. He did not go with the gentleman from Orange, (Mr. P. P. Barbour,) in his doubts, that by prescribing one Right of Suffrage, we should interfere with the Constitution of the United States. He thought that this construction of the Constitution, went to impair the sovereignty of the States. He thought that we ought to extend courtesy towards the sister States, and endeavour to promote harmony with the States, by adopting a system of indulgent courtesy, and not restrict the rights of citizens of other States to such as have resided five years. He would, however, require a freehold, as the citizens of the other States cannot claim to be put on a footing with the citizens of Virginia.

Mr. M'Coy concurred in the sentiment, that the period of probation was too long, and that citizens of other States ought to be put on the same footing with our own: but he conceived this case provided for by that clause in the first part of the resolution, which declares that "the Right of Suffrage shall continue to be exercised by all who now enjoy it under the existing Constitution:" a residence of six months only is now required.

Mr. Leigh thought this clause superceded by the effect of the subsequent proviso. He, however, disapproved of the whole of that part of the resolution relating to citizens of other States, as unjust, and hard in its bearing.

On motion of Mr. Henderson, the whole of that clause was stricken out, from the word "nor," to the end of the proviso. [See above.]

The Committee now proceeded to the fourth resolution of the Legislative Committee; which is in the following words:

"*Resolved*, That the number of members in the Senate of this State ought to be neither increased nor diminished, nor the classification of its members changed."

Mr. Pleasants moved to amend the resolution by striking out all after the words "Resolved that" and substituting the following:

"Representation in the Senate shall be based on the whole number of free persons, including those bound to service for a term of years, and excluding Indians not taxed, and adding to the aforesaid number of free persons, three-fifths of all other persons, and the Senate shall consist of a number not exceeding , and its term of service and classification remain as at present."

Mr. Pleasants said, that he was not very sanguine in the hope that the resolution which he had the honour to submit, would be carried by a large majority, but he hoped that something would be done; that a meeting of the two parties into which the question had divided the Committee, would take place. It was a subject of serious consideration what must be done. He observed at the time, that this mode of basing representation in the Senate was not acceded to by some of his friends. Provided that any gentleman thought the compound basis preferable, he was at liberty to modify his proposition. Such mode was suggested by the gentleman from Fauquier, but it did not meet his approbation.

He would take the liberty of making a few remarks in support of his proposition. The first idea which suggested itself to him was, to base the Senate on Federal numbers, or three-fifths of the slaves. His proposition, he thought, was more simple, less complex, and less fluctuating than the other mode. Besides, it produced nearly the same results as taxation and numbers combined. Under these circumstances, it was preferable to the mixed basis. He would add another reason which was mentioned out of doors, and which suggested itself to him. There was a strong objection to reject the Federal numbers, as it would give a plausible pretext to the other States to disturb the Federal basis in the United States, and to take away the influence of the Southern States. This idea would reconcile even those who were fanatical (if he might be permitted to use that term,) in their attachment to the other basis. In any amendment hereafter proposed by the States to the Constitution, such a pretext could not be assumed. These were the reasons why he gave the basis of Federal numbers a preference.

He was sanguine in the hope that this proposition would be adopted, as it would afford every security against the unequal taxation which was apprehended from basing the House of Delegates on numbers alone. A Senate so constituted, particularly when its numbers are extended, (as he hoped it would be extended to thirty-six, and he intended to fill the blank with that number,) it would give every degree of security which could be wished for. He was satisfied in the belief, that security would be obtained—he used the word security, as gentlemen objected to a guarantee—if the Senate was so constituted. He may be mistaken, though he had not much confidence in his opinion, but it would have the effect he mentioned, if the basis were so modified. He adverted to the resolution offered by the gentleman from Fauquier, which was in the following words:

"*Resolved,* That in the apportionment of representation in the Senate, regard shall be had to taxation exclusively; that the Senate shall consist of thirty-six members, and shall have the same legislative powers, in all respects, as the House of Delegates, and all appointments referred by the Constitution to both branches of the Legislature, shall be made by a concurrent vote of both Houses."

This appeared to him to give to the Senate a power of originating tax bills—to give them a concurrent power. Even the United States' Senate has not this power—it was prohibited by the Constitution. But if this proposition of the gentleman from Fauquier prevail, it will give to the Senate a power of originating money bills which is not enjoyed by any other Senate. He had a strong predilection for his proposition. He had no hesitation to allow the Senate to exercise the power of a veto on the measures of the House of Delegates. He had experience in this matter, and he preferred the practice of the Virginia Senate to that of the United States. The last year he had the honour to serve in the Senate of the United States, it reported almost as many bills as the House of Representatives. It was customary to present memorials to the Senate, and to originate bills thereon, after they had been rejected by the House of Representatives. He recollected this perfectly. He had no doubt, that this subject being so long under the consideration of the Committee, gentlemen had made up their minds upon it. He would therefore leave it to the consideration of the Committee. He was prepared to listen to the arguments of gentlemen, and he would adopt that proposition which to him appeared best.

Mr. Doddridge moved to amend the amendment by striking out all after the word "based," and inserting the following:

"On the whole number of free white persons, including those bound to service for a term of years, and taxation combined."

Mr. Tazewell submitted to the Chair whether the motion was in order. The gentleman from Goochland, (Mr. Pleasants,) had moved an amendment to the original proposition—the gentleman from Fauquier, (Mr. Scott,) had moved an amendment to that amendment, and now the gentleman from Brooke offers an amendment to an amendment.

The Chair decided that the motion was in order. The gentleman from Fauquier having merely given notice of his intention to offer an amendment at a proper time, but not having offered it.

Mr. C. Johnson said, no difficulty on the point of order could arise in regard to this proposition, nor would any difficulty be thrown in the way of the gentleman from Fauquier. The question now before the Committee, related to the comparative merits of the two propositions relative to the Federal and the compound basis. Whether he should afterwards prefer the simple proposition of the gentleman from Fauquier to both, he could not now say; but he did not hesitate to say that of the propositions now presented to him for his choice, the Federal and compound basis, he should prefer the Federal numbers. He knew that on the minds of the people there was an unpleasant impression respecting the introduction of the Federal numbers in any way into the State Constitution, but he was not to be deluded by names. He looked to the character of the thing, and examined the consequences, whether if the mixed basis or the Federal numbers were adopted, the apportionment of power would be nearly the same. He was induced to favour the principles of the Federal numbers, because it was simple in its character, easy to be ascertained, known to the laws, had been habitually applied in practice—was not variable at the will of the Legislature, nor leaving with them the discretion to change it as they might think fit. The compound basis was liable to these objections, and this led him to vote for the Federal numbers, and against this amendment.

Mr. Doddridge said he would make but a very few remarks. If any thing was due to the feelings of those, who, if not the majority, are a large minority, it should impress itself now. If the East should obtain the mixed basis in either House, the Western people will believe it to be an improper decision of the Convention. As to numbers, if there be any change, he would prefer to that, the combined basis of persons and taxation. The effect would not be the same. The people of colour in the East were increasing in a ratio greater than the whites. From 1790, the ratio of increase of blacks had been forty-four and a fraction, while that of the whites had been but thirty-six and a fraction. The increase of the blacks will be still greater hereafter. By the increase of population, and the improvement of the lands in the West, the amount of taxes made to the revenue has increased, and its burdensome relation to the General Government has diminished. As to the propositions before the Committee, he was disposed to go far for the purpose of conciliation. If harmony could be produced, it would be almost sufficient to reconcile him to any sacrifice. Still if we must submit, it was but fair to allow us a choice.

One word more: propositions have been made to increase the number of the Senate. He from reflection was particularly opposed to such an increase. If we retain the number twenty-four in the Senate, we have a divisor of the House of Delegates.

Concurring in the views of gentlemen on the other side so far, as to be unwilling to disturb the existing Constitution where there is no absolute occasion for it, he was desirous to have it undisturbed in this particular. To twenty-four as the number of the Senate, we have been long accustomed. For all the purposes of a check it is sufficient. The Senate has heretofore been what it was intended to be—a body of calm, reflecting men, not disturbed by any agitation originating with themselves, but having time to regulate and check those of the other branch—having in fact a much more elevated and useful duty to perform than merely to dot the i's and cross the t's of the other body. The proportion of bills from the House of Delegates which had been rejected in the Senate had been large—it was less than usual at the last session—he believed about ten. Some of these were bills which in their passage in the House of Delegates excited considerable sensation. There was one bill which was *five* times rejected during a single session, and its discussion lengthened the session about a week. A great excitement prevailed in the Capitol on that occasion, but he believed that it did not extend beyond the Capitol. He mentioned this for the purpose of shewing, that the Senate was a serious check on the other House, particularly in relation to revenue bills, and he had never heard any complaints of that body. He was willing to increase the number, if that would give the Senate a larger scope of action, but this would depend on the collateral increase of public confidence. He who had greater confidence in large bodies than in small ones, would wish to increase the number, in order to increase the influence of the Senate. But he who thinks that in small bodies there exists a greater proportion of wisdom and stability, will not wish to increase the number. Thinking a small body better calculated to proceed with caution and wisdom, his confidence was in the opposite ratio to numbers. He therefore had more confidence in a Senate of twenty-four members, than he should have in one of twice that number. If an increase is not called for by the people, why should the Senate be increased? The people are taught to believe that one of the motives for the diminution of the number of the House of Delegates, is to diminish the ordinary expenses of the Legislature. Instead of a diminution, an increase of expenditure must be the result of an increase of the number of the Senate. He hoped there would be no diversity of opinions on this subject. It had been already said, that the Senate was deprived of the power to originate bills, or schemes of finance, and this leaves them sufficient time for deliberation and digestion. Here then we have something by which to demonstrate that the Senate deliberates more than the House of Delegates, and we have found it to be so. An augmentation of the number would be productive of an increased expenditure, both on account of the addition to the present number, and of the lengthening of the session. He hoped that his amendment would be favourably received by the Committee.

Mr. Leigh in rising to address the Chair, said that he would not enter into any comparison between the two propositions. Both of them were abhorrent to his ideas. He desired a different basis. He merely intended to remark on the argument which had been used by the gentleman from Brooke, in comparing it with the argument which the gentleman had used in the discussion of the white basis. The gentleman now tells us that as the population of the West increases, taxation will also increase; that the slaves are increasing in the West in a greater ratio than in the East, but that the increase of power in the West would not be in proportion. Now, he had understood the other day, that considering the course taken by the States of Ohio and Pennsylvania as the cause, slave property had not increased in the West. If there is to be this increase of slaves in the West, cannot the West obtain the power which they wish by taxation, in the Senate, as they would surely have it in the House of Delegates? He might have misunderstood the gentleman from Brooke, but he could not avoid considering his two arguments in opposition to each other.

Mr. Doddridge said, he could not suppose his argument on the basis of Representation in the House, was at all forgotten. The question in the discussion was this, whether if the power was in the West, there would not be danger of oppression to the slave-holder in the East? To prove that there was no danger, he shewed the probability of the increase of slaves on the Western waters. With the slaves already there, and their natural increase, there would be an increasing confidence in the East that they had nothing of injury to themselves to apprehend. But now he was proceeding to shew, however it may be, that we should be less oppressed—for, oppression it would still be—we should have less to fear from the principle of taxation and numbers, than from the Federal numbers. He begged to bring the view of the gentleman to the present state of the country. The lands from the head of tide-water to the ocean, are nearly worn out; so are they in a great degree, worn out between tide-water and the Blue Ridge. There is not much to be gained, therefore, in those parts of the State, from any system of reclaiming culture. There might be something gained by increased persons and population. He believed there was no inconsistency in the arguments he had advanced. He had alluded to the vast number of slaves or this side the Blue Ridge, and the ratio of increase as compared with the ratio of in crease to the West. How was it possible for him to bring any thing which could occur in the West, to counterpoise this increase in the East?

Mr. Leigh rejoined: He said, this was a singular kind of explanation—under pretence of explanation the gentleman had taken the floor from him, and interposed in the midst of remarks he was making, a new argument on the point in debate. He did not admit the explanation as satisfactory, and urged and enforced the charge of inconsistency. He was indifferent which plan should prevail: he objected to arsenic as much in a preserved *cherry*, as in a preserved *strawberry*. It had been lately necessary to administer calomel to a little son of his, and sweetmeats were employed to cover it; but the child could not be deceived by it; neither could his father by a similar process. The mixed basis in the House of Delegates had been opposed on principle as "aristocracy." The principle here was the same, though not the degree; and were the gentlemen on the other side in favour of an "aristocracy" to a degree? The only way he could conceive to account for their apparent inconsistency, was in their conviction (in which he agreed) that the mixed basis in the Senate would be *valueless*, and no effectual security whatever against the power of the House of Delegates. He said that he had a peculiarity of temper, which rendered him perfectly indifferent to the charge of aristocracy imputed to him *personally*, but at the same time very sensitive to the imputation of aristocracy to any measures or principles, which he thought calculated to advance the general weal.

Mr. Doddridge rose to suggest a single remark. The proposition assumed, had been treated as if it had originated with them. If a physician present me with two pills—one more nauseous than the other, I am surely at liberty to select which I will take. I regard either the mixed basis, or the Federal basis, as an evil; but I suppose one or the other must be taken, and I must take that which is the least nauseous.

Mr. Mercer suggested, that as they had a Constitution, and were called to amend it, if they could not get what they esteemed the *best* amendment, they must then try and get the *second best*. If he must swallow either arsenic or calomel, he should prefer the calomel. If his child was very sick, and in great pain, it might possibly be induced to swallow arsenic itself, (which, administered in a certain measure, may be taken without injury,) to continuing under the pain it endured. They had never advocated the propriety of basing representation on property, and, therefore, the charge of inconsistency did not hold. The existing Constitution bases Representation, neither on property nor numbers, but on an arbitrary arrangement of districts, by which one hundred and eighty thousand men were made to out-vote four hundred and twenty thousand: and by which, one man on the sea-board, was made equal to twenty-seven men in the interior. He remarked to Mr. Pleasants, that if the Senate remained of its present number, he should vote for allowing it concurrent power with the House of Delegates, in the joint election of officers; but *not*, if its numbers were enlarged.

The question was then taken on Mr. Doddridge's amendment, and decided in the negative: Ayes 34, Noes 59.

(Messrs. Madison, Monroe and Marshall, all voting against it.)

So the Committee refused to sanction the mixed basis in the Senate.

Mr. Scott now moved the amendment he had formerly read, and which is in the following words:

"*Resolved*, That in the apportionment of representation in the Senate, regard shall be had to taxation exclusively; that the Senate shall consist of thirty-six members, and shall have the same legislative powers, in all respects, as the House of Delegates; and all appointments referred by the Constitution to both branches of the Legislature, shall be made by a concurrent vote of both Houses."

The question being taken, the amendment was negatived: Ayes 39, Noes 54.

(Messrs. Madison, Marshall and Giles voting *for* it.)

The question then recurring on the amendment of Mr. Pleasants,

Mr. Joynes moved to fill the blank for the number of Senators, and to strike out the words "a number not exceeding."

The motion was negatived: Ayes 42, Noes 51.

(Messrs. Madison and Marshall in the affirmative, Monroe and Giles in the negative.)

Mr. Summers now moved to fill the blank with the number thirty-two; Mr. Brodnax with forty-eight, and Mr. Doddridge with twenty-four.

Mr. Upshur expressed his desire to see some Constitution formed which should be acceptable to the people; and if there should be such a distribution of power between the two Houses as he could approve, he should vote in favour of the plan. But this he would never do, unless there was a *large increase* in the number of the Senate. Without this, it was vain to tell him of any security. Give us, said he, such a number as will at least afford us, in our own view, something like security. Every feeling of my heart would urge me to the most amicable course. I have none but the most friendly feeling toward those whose views differ from mine. Yet, I must be permitted to say, that it is, in effect, (though not in their intention,) a mere mockery to tell us of security, while they adopt such a basis for the Right of Suffrage, and are pursuing a course to render the Senate as little of a check upon the other House as possible. Even there my best feelings lead me to meet them (a compromise is out of the question,) on such ground as will permit us to believe that we have some security. I believe that I could be contented with some modification of the Senate. Nothing would delight me more, than to be able to go home and advise my constituents to adopt the Constitution. But if gentlemen will base the House of Delegates on the white population, and then refuse to give us more than twenty-four members in the Senate, they afford us no security, and their very best friends on our side of the House will be driven from them. I could wish a Senate of forty-eight members, but I will be content with thirty-six. Lower than this, I cannot go.

Mr. Doddridge said, he had no doubt the gentleman would be gratified to see the Constitution adopted; but if he wished to send a Constitution to the people, which they *could* not accept, he was taking the very course to do it. The people already are represented on the white basis in the Senate: they stood as they wished in that branch of the Government. You then proposed to afford us a correction of the evils of which we complained, by a new basis in the House of Delegates; but now you are for *taking away* from us all the relief we got in 1816, and you propose to turn the Senate, in effect, into a new House of Delegates, adding to the basis three-fifths of your slaves, and giving such a Senate the power to originate all bills. If this is to prevail, our evils will only have *changed sides*, and we shall be worse off than we were before.

Mr. Baldwin, after some remarks upon the difficulty of their situation, proposed to lay the present resolution on the table, until that fixing the basis of representation should be settled. Let there be a full, fair, and manly compromise on that subject, and then give gentlemen as large a Senate as they desire. He declared himself in a clear and emphatic manner, as opposed to all higgling. He concluded with submitting a motion to lay the resolution upon the table.

Mr. Mercer suggested, that a better course would be, to append the resolution with respect to the basis of representation to the present resolution, in the form of an amendment, but

Mr. Baldwin, not accepting this suggestion, persisted in his motion to lay on the table.

Mr. Naylor was opposed to it, wishing first to know what price he was to get, if he consented to a compromise. Before, however, any vote was taken,

On motion of Mr. Baldwin, the Committee rose, and thereupon the House adjourned.

WEDNESDAY, November 25, 1829.

The Convention met at 11 o'clock, and was opened with prayer by the Rev. Mr. Armstrong of the Presbyterian Church.

The House then went into Committee of the Whole, Mr. Powell in the Chair; and the question being on the several numbers proposed wherewith to fill the blank in the resolution, fixing the number of members in the *Senate*,

Mr. Bayly rose and said, that he would take this opportunity of proposing that the blank should be filled with the word *forty*.

He did not believe that the number forty-eight, which had been proposed by the gentleman from Brunswick, (Mr. Brodnax,) would be agreed to, and the number thirty-six had been rejected. He had offered forty, and would explain his reasons.

When I first saw (said Mr. B.) the report of the Legislative Committee, declaring that the present number of the Senate (twenty-four,) should neither be increased nor diminished, I had determined to vote against the resolution; for I had believed, before I came to this Convention, that forty members would not make the Senate too large. The proposition is, therefore, not made in reference to the basis of representation in the House of Delegates, nor did it originate with me to affect any principle of compromising that great question, which agitates this Assembly. On most occasions, I do not like compromising rights, but some concessions must be made; and if the Senate can be so constituted, as to effect that most desirable object, it must be by increasing their number, and giving them concurrent power to originate laws. I shall, however, advocate the motion entirely upon its own merits, because I am convinced, that constitute the House of Delegates as you please, and make the number of members one hundred and twenty, or more, your Senate ought to be one-third the whole number of Delegates, and with equal powers of legislation.

Sir, I have had some experience on this subject. By the old Constitution, "all laws must originate in the House of Delegates, to be *approved* of *or* rejected by the

Senate, *or* to be *amended* with the consent of the House of Delegates, except money bills, which, in no instance shall be altered by the Senate, but wholly approved or rejected;" and under this power of amendment, many of the most important laws now in your Code, have been introduced original bills in the Senate and concurred in by the House of Delegates, as amendments to bills sent to the Senate; for example, the House of Delegates pass an act, making a trivial alteration in the law respecting the Courts, and the Senate amend, by striking out the whole after the enacting clause, and re-model the Judiciary system, not as it relates to one Court only, but to every Court; for, the title of the bill has given the power, and the Constitution jurisdiction, by the term *amendment*.

The Senate do not consider their power, by this word *amendment*, restricted merely to verbal or critical alterations. You had better expressly give equal power of originating laws to both Houses of the General Assembly, and thereby prevent collisions between them, than to permit it to be used by implication, which has heretofore protracted the sessions many days. On one occasion the Senate amended the appropriation bill, and were unanimous, that they had the right; the House of Delegates rejected the bill and amendment, with unanimity, denying the right to the Senate, and insisted, that an appropriation is a money bill. In that instance only, did the Senate succeed against the House of Delegates, and maintained the doctrine, that laws *laying* the taxes were the money bills contemplated by the Constitution, and that when the money was in the Treasury, the Senate had equal power over it. Sir, the Senators are equally the representatives of the people, and have no interest separate and distinct from them; this jealousy of the two Houses of Assembly towards each other, ought to be guarded against by the Constitution we are endeavoring to make, by conferring upon the Senate the authority to originate any bills, even *money* bills. This restriction upon the Senate respecting money bills, is borrowed from the Constitution of England into our own. It is refused to the Upper House of Parliament to lay the taxes, because the Lords do not derive their power from the people, are created by the Crown, and have a separate and distinct interest from the Commons. No such reason exists in this country.

Should this power be given to the Senate, they will freely confer with the Delegates, and each knowing what acts of Legislation it is necessary to pass for the good of the State, both Houses will be employed at the same time perfecting the public business upon different subjects. But now, the Senate after eight or ten days session, adjourn for two or three weeks, because the House of Delegates before that time, will not probably pass any important bills, and the Senators having nothing to act upon, some go home, others remain without any public duties to perform. Give the Senate power to originate bills, and all will be right.

The Senate of the United States may be compared to an Assembly of Ambassadors, representing Sovereign States, and their duties are complicated and various: they participate in and greatly control the Government in the policy towards foreign nations: this, with their Executive duties, which is often very perplexing, occupies as much of their time as is bestowed on Legislative business; and yet, they possess equal power in originating laws as the House of Representatives. I may appeal with confidence to gentlemen in this Convention, who now are or have been members of the Senate of Virginia, to say whether the power to originate bills would not greatly contribute to shorten the sessions of the General Assembly.

The long and expensive sessions was one great cause for calling the Convention, though it certainly was not the leading cause. The House of Delegates now consists of two hundred and fourteen members; the Senate of twenty-four. If we organize the House of Delegates with one hundred and twenty members and the Senate with forty, the General Assembly will be reduced seventy-eight members, which will shorten the sessions perhaps one-fifth of their usual length of late years, which, together with the reduction of the members, we may calculate on a saving of public money of 40 or 50,000 dollars annually, and have the business of the State better done.

The last General Assembly was in session ninety days, and cost the State 108,773 dollars 85 cents, which was more than 1200 dollars a day. The memorable General Assembly of 1798, was in session fifty-three days. The Delegates were one hundred and seventy-nine: the pay of the members being two dollars a day, the whole expenses of the session were $29,332 60. The General Assembly the next year, 1799, continued in session fifty-seven days; the daily pay of the members was raised to three dollars, and the expenses of that session were $40,631 19. And I believe it is universally admitted, these two General Assemblies possessed more eloquence, talents and wisdom, than any that has ever since assembled in Virginia.

The present number of the Senate, twenty-four, is too small: the House is considered very full with twenty members, and many of the most important laws now in the Code, were passed into laws by not more than eight or nine votes, and with a majority of one or two. This is too small a number of men to give law to this Commonwealth, or to controul the immediate representatives of the people, if they fall into error. Increase their number, give them employment by originating laws, and the State will have the benefit of their wisdom, experience and industry; the business of legislation will progress equally in the two Houses, with harmony and expedition, and will have the confidence of the people.

In 1776, when the Constitution was made, the Convention then wisely fixed the number of the Senate to twenty-four. At that time the population was not one-half what it now is, and was condensed on the East of the mountain; it was then absolutely necessary to have a most economical Government: a revolution was commencing, and the State had little money or credit. There were twenty districts below the Blue Ridge, and they were small: the local interest well known and respected; and should the number be increased to forty, each district will contain more population, than under the present Government, when first put into operation, and for many years afterwards. The Senate must represent the people, and the Representative should be known personally to a large portion of his constituents, to obtain their confidence and respect: this will not be the case in large districts.

Examine the Map of Virginia and the position of the water courses, and more especially the district I have the honor in part to represent. Two counties on the Eastern Shore, Accomack and Northampton, and three on the Western Shore, Gloucester, Matthews and Middlesex, separated by the Mediterranean of the United States, the Chesapeake. On the East of that water, the trade is to New York, the London of America, or to Philadelphia, while the produce of the Western Shore of that Bay finds a market within the Capes of Virginia. The people of the district, thus separated, and their trade going to different places, and having no intercourse, they are as unknown to each other, as if they resided in different States. The Senators who represented that district the two last terms of four years each, resided on the Western Shore, and were unknown to the people on the Eastern Shore when the election commenced, and I do believe, never trod on that land before they commenced their canvass. Do you believe that these Senators being unknown to that people, would command their respect and confidence equal to a Delegate that was known to them, should a difference of opinion exist, respecting a great and important political measure. On such an occasion, the people would espouse the opinions of that man who resided among them. Before the great change of the Senatorial Districts took place throughout the State in 1816, the Eastern Shore from the adoption of the Constitution to that time, formed a separate Senatorial District; and although one county had more than three votes to the other's one, the people having great intercourse and confidence in each other, their interests being the same, it was not considered by them material in which county the Senator resided, and immediately after the first election under the Constitution, it was considered wise, that each county should alternately have one of its citizens sent to the Senate, which arrangement continued forty-one years, in harmony and good feeling between the people of these counties, as a strong illustration of the advantage of small districts, to the peace and happiness of the country. The situation of other parts of the State, also requires the election districts to be small. The counties of Brooke and Ohio, formed from a long strip of land, bounded by the States of Pennsylvania and Ohio, and united to Virginia by a line of fifteen or twenty miles, and having more intercourse with these States than with Virginia, the people of these counties cannot be presumed to have great intercourse with the people of Kanawha, so as to judge of the qualifications of the Senator residing so remote from them. The same argument will apply to other parts of the State, divided by great rivers and mountains: for example, take the country situated between the wide rivers of James and York, and extending from Hampton towards Richmond, and before you get the requisite population to form a district for a Senate of twenty-four members for the whole State, you will pass this city, and your district will be one hundred and fifty miles long; and is it probable that the home-staying and industrious farmer, will be sufficiently acquainted with the character and talents of gentlemen who reside at the extremity of the district, to give him his vote?

The Northern Neck is similarly situated: commencing at Smith's Point, and proceeding up between the Potomac and Rappahannock, before you form a district of sufficient population, you will be in full view of the mountains. The same difficulty is to be met with in some of the sections of the Alleghany country. The Senator from such large districts, will not know the grievances of the people, or their local interest, but must depend for information upon others, when called to act; and he will not long possess the affections of the people. Sir, should the Senator put himself in opposition to the five or six Delegates of the district, (and his duty will often compel him so to do,) and they go before the people supporting their own views and opinions; the Delegates thus united, will defeat the re-election of the wisest and most patriotic Senator that ever sat in the Senate-house; nor will his virtue, integrity and talents shield him against the attack of those who are so much better known to the people.

I have examined the Constitutions of several of the States, to see what proportion of the number of members the two Houses of the Legislature are to each other; and I find,

Delaware has nine Senators and twenty-one Representatives:

North Carolina, sixty Senators and one hundred and twenty members of the House of Commons:

Ohio, Indiana, Illinois and Tennessee, the Senate shall never be less than one-third, nor more than one-half of the number of Representatives:

Mississippi and Alabama, the Senate never less than one-fourth, nor more than one-third of the number of the Representatives:

Louisiana, the Senate always fourteen, the Representatives never less than twenty-five, nor more than fifty.

Should the motion prevail to fill the blank as I have proposed, it will give the Senate a controling power, which it ought to have, and make it such a representative body, as to secure the respect and confidence of the people.

Mr. Baldwin explained what would be his proposition for compromise, viz: to propose the white basis in the House of Delegates, and the Federal number in the Senate, and make the number of the latter thirty-six: but as it was not in order to move it now, he moved first, that the Committee pass over the propositions for filling the blank, in the resolution prescribing the numbers of the Senate.

Mr. Doddridge said, if that motion should prevail and the proposition of the gentleman be presented to the Committee, he should immediately call for a division of the question upon it, and take its parts separately.

Mr. Mercer gave notice that after the Committee should have passed on the proposition of the gentleman from Augusta, (Mr. Baldwin,) he should move the consideration of the report of the Executive Committee, with a view to settling the power of the Senate before determining its number. He would consent to give them concurrence in the appointing power, if on the white, or on the mixed basis, but not if its number was to be so enlarged as to open a door for faction. The power of the Senate would be more strengthened by the power of appointment than by an augmentation of its numbers.

Mr. Leigh was in favour of passing by for the present, the propositions for fixing the number of the Senate, and then taking up the report, not of the Executive, but of the Judicial Committee. He had in his mind, a proposal, different from any that had yet been submitted and which he hoped would unite the assent of all, (provided gentlemen, as they said, were willing to give and take,) but before he could announce it, he wished to consult the delegations from one or two of the districts which would be most affected by the plan. If they should refuse their assent, he would not propose it.

Mr. Coalter then rose to address the Committee, as follows:

I threw myself, most *improperly*, and I now find *unnecessarily*, on the Committee the other day. I had been elsewhere engaged, and knew not the stage of the proceeding.

My friend from Chesterfield, seemed to say that the *crisis* was at hand, and I knew not that I could again be regularly heard.

I am peculiarly situated. I belong, by *birth*, *growth* and every kind of obligation to the transmontane country.

The good opinion and good feeling of that country towards me, and of every member of it on this floor, is a cordial which I will not have dashed from my lips or from my heart, if I can help it. I give you my heart's blood, Sir, *freely*, if that will cure all the evils that now afflict Virginia; but leave me that cordial.

I may be *mistaken* in my opinions, and I may err in my course here; but I will yield to no *native of the West* in my love for the land of my birth; nor in the anxious desire I feel to see it every thing which I know it is capable of being.

But, I now have *new interests* and *new connexions* on this side of that line, and these may lead me astray. This is very true, and I am very willing that it should be thrown into the scale, to weigh against *my judgment*. *I* ought to weigh it *myself* against *myself*. The words of truth say that the heart of man is deceitful, &c. I may have *vanity* enough to suppose I am above this. But that most wise and excellent of all Governors, *Sancho Panza*, has said, that there is nothing *more vain* than *vanity*.

I *know* I may be wrong—I *fear* I may be wrong in all I may say or do.

I have seen the day when I would have had no such fears—when I would with as little fear of error, have drawn a new Constitution for this State—yes, on my knee in a Court yard, as I would have drawn a declaration on a *plain bond*. I was perfectly persuaded that the great mass of the people were capable of every thing; that Universal Suffrage was the true palladium and safeguard of our rights, founded in nature, and that all mankind must finally yield to it—that it was a millenium fast approaching—that France was *regenerated*, and that all mankind would follow in the train—America, glorious America at the head!!—that our Senate was an aristocratic body, thwarting the good sense of the people in their Hall of Representatives—that the Council was a *fungus*—that the people ought to elect their own Governor, and their Executive and Ministerial Officers, civil and military, for which they were *created for* them, and *by* them, and they alone were the proper judges of their fitness and capacity. But, suppose I was now a Western man, and joined with Western men in all their views, could I be more certain that there was no *alloy* of interest, no feeling that has been produced by excited passions in myself or those around me—no real, or supposed sense of past injustice, which may have warped my judgment, which may have led me back to the visions of my youth, and courted me to go back to opinions once solemnly abandoned? Surely this would be a fit cause for serious *self-examination*.

I have lived, Sir, either to have much weaker nerves; or, having witnessed what has passed here and elsewhere, during the last thirty years, to have acquired a sounder judgment, and a more correct view of things—perhaps, I have become *too fearful*—*Discretion*, it is said, is the better part of valor; and perhaps a little *fear* is not a bad ingredient in a politician, who is about to put forth his hand to tear up—plant a-new, or even *to prune* away and replace portions of a Government, under which such a people as these of Virginia have lived, until within a few short weeks, safely and happily. I confess *I am afraid*—perhaps I have caught the epidemic which prevails in the country. Who is there then who is not afraid? Not one! I must nerve myself though, as well as I can, at least against *idle fears*.

I must try and make such amendments to the Constitution, that I will neither be afraid nor ashamed to recommend to the confidence and affections of this people.

But, I must have a very large majority of this body to back me in it; or my strength will depart from me.

There is one thing which I now wish distinctly to make known to this body, and to my constituents.

It is of little consequence to me, in this, or any future stage of the business, whether I fall into the minority or majority, provided that minority is large, or that majority is small. This is not ordinary legislation; to be re-examined at the next session, and the evils, if any growing out of it, corrected with as much ease as they are inflicted. When we adjourn, we adjourn *sine die*.

There is no *locus penitentiæ* left to us. We can only go home, and as *individuals*, oppose or approve the work of this body.

I consider a large minority as an *equal division* of this body—as a state of things which does not admit of final action; and if in the course of human events I am in a small majority, I will not impose on a large minority a Constitution against which their feelings or judgments rebel. I will vote down *finally*, so far as my voice goes, all innovations of that kind; as believing it most safe and wise to leave the present Constitution as to such matter, where we found it.

If my constituents disapprove of this, the sooner they recall me, the better; I will most willingly obey that call.

I feel a responsibility that is almost deadening to me, and would willingly shift it to abler hands.

I believe—*I can't think otherwise*—that I will be in a majority, finally, on this point.

Surely—*surely*, we are not prepared to enter the great arena of the human passions, with the anathemas of *Aristocrat*—*Monarchist*—*Oppressor* of the Poor—*Enemy of the People*, and of human rights, on the one side, in order to carry through our work,—and with the denunciations of *Demagogue*—*Agitator*—*Radical*, &c. on the other!! No, Sir; the few hairs I have remaining, rise on my head at the bare supposition.

No, Sir; we were sent here by the people, as their *sure and true friends;* to see whether we could confer on them any *additional blessing: To be sure*, that we could confer this on them, before we deprived them of what they had: Not to inflict on them the countless miseries which must arise from such a state of things.

No, Sir; we must either return to them the *gold* which they have entrusted to us, without farther alloy; or we must purify it yet more, and put the *Tower Stamp* on it. This can only be done by a large majority of this body.

We can't return it to them mixed up with the *dregs* of contending passions and interests, and put it on them to purify and refine it.

They can only *reject* such a mass, and, if indeed man is capable of self-government, *they will reject it*. *They* will say, as I say, we will not impose on a large minority of our fellow-citizens a Constitution which *they* think a *bad one*, for one which they and we know is a *good* one. *We* may be mistaken; some of our wisest men, and most tried patriots think we are mistaken, and we will not risk it.

Surely all would say, that this would be *wisdom*—*patriotism*—*magnanimity* of the highest order. But can we say that the great body of the people will take this course, if we set them a contrary example? We are now to say whether such would be the correct course. If we say no; you must bandy words and epithets; call in the passions; avail yourselves of every prejudice. *This* is the way to establish your liberties and the happiness of the State; then indeed the foundation of the great deep will be opened, and *woe* be to those who do not seek safety in that *Ark of the Covenant*, the *old Constitution*, which has borne us triumphantly through so many dangers and difficulties!

Impressed with these views, I hailed with pleasure unspeakable, the proposition of my friend from Augusta; seconded by my trusty friend and coadjutor on another interesting occasion, from Hampshire, to see if a *fair*, *open*, *manly*, and *honourable* compromise of conflicting interests and opinions could not be made.

They very wisely want to see the *quid pro quo;* this is precisely what I want to see, also.

But, it seems to me we cannot see this at present. There are other great interests to discuss, besides those which have been before the Committee. How are we to agree on *them?* It is of no consequence to me when the evil is to creep in, which shall put it out of my power to vote for the amendments which may be offered. I might yield much on some points, for a *safe Constitution* on others; and which I would not yield but for that *quid.* All would avail nothing, if *Mordecai* still sits at the door; I want to see the whole ground; the whole instrument, before I can sign and seal any part. I must tear off my seal, if I don't agree to the whole instrument.

I plead *non est factum*—in fact, it seems to me impossible to come to any available compromise, until we have the whole ground before us. There are things to come that may be equally, or even more objectionable to me, *if possible,* than extending the Right of Suffrage, substantially beyond what it now is.

I allude particularly to the mode to be agreed on for electing the Governor. As to the Judiciary, I never have entertained any fears about it. I fear unwise legislation in regard to it, it is true; having much experience on that point; but I have no fears as to the *fundamental laws* in regard to that department; I mean as to the Superior Courts. As to the county magistracy, there may be danger; but of what character I am not apprized. These, Sir, are my views at present; I am not prepared to propose any thing; I thought it due to myself to state candidly what were my general views.

Mr. C. concluded by saying that he had not seen any of the documents printed for the Committee; that he had no specific propositions to make; but that he would prefer with the gentleman from Loudoun (Mr. Mercer,) to pass on to the Report of the Executive Committee.

Mr. Baldwin withdrew his motion to pass by filling the blank with numbers for the Senate; but

Mr. Mercer renewed it, with a view to taking up the Report of the Executive Committee.

Mr. Gordon, after some remarks on his peculiar situation, and his earnest desire to effect a compromise, read in his place the following amendment to Mr. Pleasants's proposition, as a plan to effect that object:

" *Resolved,* That the Representation in the Senate and House of Delegates of Virginia, shall be apportioned as follows: that is to say,

" There shall be ten Senators West of the Blue Ridge of mountains, and fourteen East of those mountains.

" There shall be in the House of Delegates one hundred and twenty members; of whom twenty-six shall be elected from that part of Virginia lying West of the Alleghany mountains; twenty-four from the Valley between the Alleghany and Blue Ridge; thirty-seven from the Blue Ridge to the head of tide-water; and thirty-three thence below."

He commented at some length on this proposal, shewing what would be its practical effect. It would leave in the whole House of Delegates a majority of twenty to the East of the mountain.

The twenty-six counties West of the Alleghany, would have twenty-six Delegates: the fourteen counties in the Valley, twenty-four Delegates; the twenty-nine counties of middle Virginia, would have thirty-seven Delegates; and the thirty-six counties and four boroughs of the tide-water country, would have thirty-three Delegates.

He preferred the county basis for representation; and thought it might with some little accommodation be arranged in the tide-water country as in the rest of the State; a few of the smallest counties giving up their claim to individual representation.

He placed this copy of the resolution on the table for the inspection of the members.

The question being taken, it was determined to pass by filling the blank for the present: Ayes 51.

Mr. Mercer now moved to take up the report of the Executive Committee: the motion was opposed by Messrs. Brodnax and Nicholas, and *negatived.*

The Committee then proceeded with the report of the Legislative Committee, and took up the eighth resolution, which reads as follows:

" *Resolved,* That it ought to be provided, that in all elections for members of either branch of the General Assembly; and in the election of all officers which may be required to be made by the two Houses of Assembly, jointly, or in either separately, with the exception of the appointment of their own officers, the vote should be given openly, or *viva voce,* and not by ballot."

Mr. Brodnax now moved as a substitute for the above, the following:

"*Resolved*, That it ought to be provided in the Constitution, that in all elections in this State, to any office or place of trust, honor or profit, with the exception of the appointment of the officers of the General Assembly, the votes should be given *viva voce*, and not by ballot."

On the suggestion of Mr. Randolph, he asked leave to withdraw the clause which permits the officers of the House of Assembly to vote by ballot for their own officers.

Mr. Claytor, approving the general principle of *viva voce* elections, objected to carry it into all Legislative Assemblies, so as to open a poll for the choice of their officers. He was about to reinstate the clause; when

The Chair suggested that to vote against leave to withdraw it, would have the same effect.

Mr. Brodnax defended the principle, and contended that there should be no exception on its application. In some elections in Congress, resort had been had to ballots of different colours that members might have the opportunity of letting their votes be known to all.

Mr. Claytor thought there was no need of enjoining it by Constitutional provision: the Legislature might use their discretion in the case.

Mr. Johnson concurred in this view. There was no danger of intrigue and corruption in the election of the officers of the Assembly; and it was not desirable, that officers who were continually to come in contact with the members, should know who had voted for and who against them.

Mr. Randolph said, that he hoped in common courtesy the Committee would not refuse the leave asked by the gentleman from Dinwiddie. In the whole course of his Parliamentary life, he had never known the leave denied. If the gentleman from Campbell, (Mr. Claytor,) felt strenuous on the subject, he would move to re-insert the clause. As I am on my feet, said Mr. R., permit me to say that there are many who remember the important election of Speaker to the House of Burgesses in 1799—1800; an election, in which the Commonwealth of Virginia felt as much interest as she has done in any one election from that day to this. It was during that session that the venerable gentleman who is at the head of the Orange delegation, and, I may say—speaking of his experience and weight of character—at the head of this Assembly, brought in his celebrated report on the Alien and Sedition Laws, which put a curb in the mouth and a hook in the nose of the great Federal Leviathan, and which some gentlemen seem so anxious to remove. As to the saving of time, the Clerk can call over the names of the members in far less time than it takes to collect the ballots, count them and ascertain and report the result. All gentlemen know the difference in time between merely calling the yeas and nays, and conducting an election by ballot. The Clerkship of the House of Delegates is an office of great profit, and of yet greater trust and honour. I can see no ground of discrimination between an election in the House of Delegates, and an election elsewhere. But it was not with this view that I rose, but merely to vindicate what I consider as in common courtesy, the right of the gentleman from Dinwiddie: I could not justify it to myself to offer such an act of rudeness and indignity to that gentleman, as to refuse the leave he has requested.

Mr. Claytor disclaimed all intention of offering any rudeness or indignity to the gentleman from Dinwiddie: on the contrary, the course he had originally chosen, was the very one pointed out by the gentleman from Charlotte, (Mr. Randolph.) He did not rise to prolong the debate, but only to vindicate his own conduct.

The Chair said, he had not understood the gentleman from Charlotte as having any personal allusion in his remarks.

Mr. R. disclaimed it entirely.

Mr. Johnson explained himself as intending to refuse no courtesy to the gentleman; but as having understood this as the mode of trying the question, whether the clause should remain or be stricken out.

After some farther explanation, the question was taken on granting leave, and carried: Ayes 50.

Mr. Claytor now moved to re-instate the clause—(so as to leave it discretionary with the Legislature, to vote for their own officers, by ballot or *viva voce*.)

And the question being taken, the votes as counted by the Chair stood, Ayes 44, Noes 43: but the Chair fearing some inaccuracy in the count, appointed tellers; and then the vote appeared: Ayes 43, Noes 46. So the Committee refused to re-instate the clause—thereby requiring all elections to be held *viva voce*.

The Committee then proceeded to the ninth resolution, which reads as follows:

"*Resolved*, That no man shall be compelled to frequent or support any religious worship, place, or ministry whatsoever; nor shall be enforced, restrained, molested, or burthened in his body or goods, nor shall otherwise suffer on account of his religious opinions or belief; but that all men shall be free to profess, and by argument to maintain their opinions in matters of religion, and that the same shall in no wise diminish, enlarge, or affect their civil capacities."

Mr. Brodnax explained this to be a literal transcript from the celebrated act drawn by Mr. Jefferson, and passed in 1785, for the freedom of religion.

He moved to amend the resolution by adding to the first member of it, a clause, declaring all persons who disbelieved in a God or a future state of rewards and punishments, as incapable of being received as witnesses in any Court of law in the Commonwealth. He did not himself consider such a clause absolutely necessary, as the same thing was virtually included in the resolution, or not contradicted by it: but it was best to add the clause by way of caution.

On the suggestion of Mr. Randolph, Mr. Brodnax withdrew his amendment.

Mr. Cooke moved to amend the second member of the resolution, by striking out the proviso (which disqualified ministers from being elected to the Legislature.)

Mr. Doddridge was in favour of the motion. He disapproved the election of ministers to a legislative body as much as most men; but he would not vote to prevent the people from making whom they would their Delegate to their own Hall of Legislation. He considered the exclusion as at war with the principle of the whole resolution: which allowed men to promulgate their religious opinions free from all political consequences; but the language of this proviso was—*unless they uttered them in the pulpit*, then they must be disfranchised.

Mr. Brodnax said, the gentleman from Brooke had forgotten the Hall of Legislation. Ministers might vent their opinions every where, and any where, but in that Hall. The gentleman from Brooke was commonly very felicitous in appealing to the example of other States, and sometimes carried that appeal farther than he was disposed to follow him. He believed, all the States in the Union went to the extent of this resolution, and many of them much farther. In the new Constitution of New York, which had been *lugged* in—(He begged pardon—which had been brought in most gracefully) into this debate, ministers were disabled from holding any civil office whatever. Mr. B. disclaimed all want of respect for the clergy, either personally, or in their clerical capacity; but there was a proper place for them; and that place was not in the Legislative Hall. He entertained, indeed, no fear as to a union of Church and State in this country. The fears of our forefathers, he believed, were well founded: but the progress of time, and the division of the Church into four, five, or six, he might almost say into four, five, or six thousand, different fragments, rendered that danger nugatory. This was the best and strongest of all guards on that subject. But there were numerous reasons which forbade the appearance of ministers of the Gospel in the political arena. It was totally inconsistent with their sacerdotal habits and sentiments; every power of their mind ought to be, and he believed, was, turned in different and opposite directions from temporal legislation. He adverted to the influence (not consciously indulged) of sectarian attachments, and its operation on all questions where the interests of a sect were directly or indirectly involved; and the influence of a minister over the numerous individuals attached to him—both of which were foreign to impartial legislation on his part or impartial judgment on theirs.

Mr. Doddridge assured the gentleman from Dinwiddie, that he did know the difference between the pulpit and the Hall of Legislation—having seen both more than once. But he still insisted on his former ground. The resolution declared, that a man's religious opinions shall not affect his civil capacities: but the proviso declares, that if those opinions are uttered in the pulpit, the utterance of them shall affect his civil capacities, even to disfranchisement. At the *polls* he should probably act with the gentleman; but why tie up the hands of the people?

Mr. Cooke considered it as at war with the whole spirit of our institutions, to disfranchise an entire class of our citizens, without any good reason assigned; a class too, which he considered far the most virtuous and efficient in the community. He insisted on the objection urged by Mr. Doddridge.

Mr. Coalter said, that it was precisely because he wished the clergy to remain what he now believed them to be, that he was against striking out the proviso. Their master had said that his kingdom was not of this world; he had commanded his servants to render unto Cæsar the things which are Cæsar's, and unto God the things which are God's. He had been himself willing to have nothing to do with politics, and his servants ought to have no more to do with them than He.

Mr. Brodnax, in reply to Mr. Doddridge and Mr. Cooke, observed, that a proviso, is, of course, something which involves a discrepancy and exception. It might be deemed very sinful in him to wish to exclude ministers, but he found himself, at any rate, in very good company. The exclusion was carried yet further than this by the old Constitution of Virginia. He called it the old Constitution: he knew it was spoken of very commonly now with great contempt; and perhaps he ought to beg pardon for mentioning it at all; but this old Constitution had been formed by men, not half so wise, to be sure, as they, (because, as the Committee had been informed by the gentleman from Chesterfield, sons were younger, and of course wiser than their fathers,) but by men who had some little reputation in their day; and those men had said that ministers should not be eligible as members of the Governor's Council. He knew that the act on Religious Freedom was no part of the Constitution, but it had received universal sanction from the people of Virginia.

But Kentucky, Tennessee, and New York, while they had the same general provision on the subject of Religious Freedom, added besides this exclusion of the clergy from the Legislature: and in New York they are excluded from "any civil or military place or office whatsoever."

Mr. Cooke said, that on the ground of authority, he was not prepared; but he was informed that in eighteen States out of the twenty-four in this Union, ministers are admitted to a full participation in all civil and political rights with other men. He admitted, that the Constitution of Virginia did treat the clergy with not very high respect: but probably this arose from old habitudes derived from England, where the clergy were excluded from the House of Commons, because they had a House of their own.

Mr. Morgan said, there seemed to be but a single question to be settled; which was, whether the Constitution shall be so formed that the clergy shall be dispossessed of all modes of amassing power over the people. Now, there were two modes of effecting this object, either to exclude them from the Legislature; or to divest the Legislature of all jurisdiction whatever over the subject of religion.

If the Committee adopted the latter mode, there could be no necessity of resorting to the former.

Under the existing Constitution, their exclusion is *personal* only: the Legislature may give them any degree of patronage, and any amount of support, but not a seat in the Legislative Hall. But they now proposed to forbid the Legislature's granting them any aid or patronage, and, therefore he was for admitting them to a seat, if the people chose to elect them. He was in favor of striking out the proviso.

Mr. Moore was opposed to it. He thought any clergyman who offered himself as a candidate for a seat in the Legislature, shewed himself unworthy to be trusted any where. He considered their habits and studies as totally unfitting them for politics; and, in the last place, he owned that he was *afraid* of them. Keep them in their proper place, and there is no danger; but allow them to be connected with the State in any way, and you have the dreaded union of Church and State at once.

Mr. Randolph then said:

To me this is a most unlooked-for proposition. There is not one single article of my political creed, about which I have not a greater disposition to doubt, than of the propriety of excluding a class of men, dedicated to the office of religion, from the possession of political power. A gentleman told us, that but for the insertion of that proviso in the Constitution, he should be for excluding them from the Legislature. I would much rather vote to strike out the whole, and to leave the Constitution as it now stands; and for this plain reason: I am, and have been, and ever shall be, a practical man; and when I meet with legislative provisions of this kind, I rather smile at the fears which dictated them, than applaud the caution they exhibit. The Constitution is just as safe without, as with them. The Legislature of Virginia cannot, and if it could, it dare not, attempt such legislation as is forbidden in the body of this resolution. I feel myself perfectly safe. I find, somewhere else, a provision that we shall have no orders of nobility in this country. Who dreams that we ever can? Sir, when the time shall come that the people of this country are ripe for a union of Church and State, or for orders of nobility either, they will have them in spite of all the moth-eaten parchment in your archives. I fearlessly pronounce, that the admission of gentlemen of the cloth into your Legislative Halls is *ipso facto* the union of Church and State. Sir, are there no other considerations which weigh with us in altering? or in keeping the Constitution as it is? They are now excluded. Are there no other considerations? None that every well regulated mind belonging to the clerical profession ought of itself to suggest? I have had the pleasure (I was about to say I have had the honor, but the term would be misplaced) to be acquainted with many of them: with men of the most unaffected piety, of high attainments and great talents; and who, moreover, were clothed with that *humility* which is the Alpha and Omega of the christian character—Yes, Sir, its all in all: and I never knew one of them who dared to trust himself in such a situation. Not one, who if such an offer had been made him, might not justly have said, "lead us not into temptation." Sir, what are the offices of the clerical body? Do they not mingle with all classes of society? and above all, in the domestic circle? Is not their influence there paramount to that of all others? Is it not their duty to serve a master whose kingdom is not of this world? As well to reprove as to console?

Figure to yourself, Sir, a minister of the gospel of peace, about to reprove for his sins, a man of wealth and influence in his county; having, at the same time, a desire himself to represent that county. Sir, this is no exclusion on account of the profession of any opinions. It is an exclusion of an occupation; of an occupation incompatible with the discharge of the duties of a member of either branch of the Legislature. The task of legislation is at war with the duties of the pastor. The two are utterly incompatible. Sir, no man can busy himself in electioneering, (and in these times who can be elected without it?) No man can mingle in Legislative cabals; I say no man can touch that pitch, without being defiled. No man can so employ himself, without being disqualified for those sacred duties which every minister of the gospel takes upon himself; and for which he is accountable, not to his constituents at home, but to the God who made him; and who will call him to a much more rigorous account than that he renders to his parishioners.

Sir, there is an indecency in this thing. We have heard much about exclusion of the ladies; but there is not greater indecency and incompatibility in a woman's thrusting herself into a political assembly and all its cabals, than in a clergyman's undertaking the same thing. One of the greatest masters of the human heart, and of political philosophy too, declares, that while the French are in their manners more deferential to woman than any other people, they have less real esteem for woman than any other nation on earth.

Let me illustrate this. The Turk shews that he values his wife, by locking her up; it is, to be sure, a mistaken mode: but he shews that he estimates the value of the treasure, by putting it under lock and key. The Frenchman permits his wife to mingle in political affairs; and if Madame Roland had not been engaged in such affairs, Madame Roland would never have ascended the scaffold. If women will unsex themselves; and if priests—(what shall I say?) will degrade themselves by mingling in scenes and in affairs for which their function renders them improper and unfit, they must take the consequences. If ladies will plunge into the affairs of men, they will lose the deference they now enjoy; they will be treated roughly—like men. Just so it is with priests. They lose all the deference which belongs, and which is paid to their office, (whether they merit it or no.)

Sir, rely upon it, if you permit priests to be made members of the Legislature, they will soon constitute a large portion of all your assemblies. And it has been truly said, that no countries are so ill-governed as those which were ruled by the counsels of women, except such as have been governed by the counsels of priests.

The question was now put on striking out the proviso, and decided in the negative; only twelve members rising in its support. (Mr. Madison being one.)

Mr. Brodnax now moved a further amendment, to be added at the close of the resolution, viz:

"Nor shall be so construed, as to deprive the Legislature of the power of incorporating by law, the trustees or directors of any Theological Seminary, or other Religious Society, or body of men created for charitable purposes, or the advancement of piety and learning, so as to protect them in the enjoyment of their property and immunities, in such case, and under such regulations, as the Legislature may deem expedient and proper. But the Legislature of this State, during all future time, shall possess the power to alter, re-model, or entirely repeal such charter, or act of incorporation, whenever they shall deem it expedient."

Mr. Giles rose in opposition to the amendment, which he hoped would not be passed upon without due consideration. He then went into a series of observations on the injurious effect of the incorporating power, when the corporations were of a civil character, and much more when they were of a religious description. He considered their multiplication a serious evil which had already accomplished much mischief, and which threatened much more. They were bodies very irresponsible, and were gradually absorbing to themselves all the powers of the Legislature. He dwelt especially upon the injurious effects of Banks; and he hoped no sanction would be introduced into the Constitution, tending to encourage the Legislature in granting incorporations of any kind.

Mr. Brodnax spoke in reply. He agreed in the sentiments expressed by that gentleman, but contended that the amendment he had offered went to modify, and restrain, not to increase the evil. The Legislature had now Constitutional liberty to incorporate Theological Seminaries, and if once incorporated, their charters could not be altered or revoked, unless legally forfeited: But this amendment conferred on the Legislature, power to alter or amend their charters at pleasure. He spoke of the degradation of being obliged to send young men who were seeking, and who would get, and ought to get, a clerical education, *out* of the State to be educated. Two Theological Seminaries raised by Virginia capital, and supplied with Virginia students, had, through sheer necessity, been built and incorporated, *beyond* the limits of the State, because they could not be incorporated within it. He denied that the amendment gave any preference to one sect over another; and, as there would be a ministry in society, and that ministry must possess great influence, was it not better to provide the means of giving them a becoming education? As to the danger of Church and State, it was a chimera. Not *one-eleventh* part of the inhabitants of the United States, were members of a church of any denomination whatever: and when it was remembered into how many various and incompatible sects, this small fraction was itself divided, all fears of any thing like a religious establishment in this country, must be acknowledged to be visionary in the extreme. He did not believe, that any one sect would wish, or accept such a distinction if it were offered to them: and sure he was, that if they should, all the other sects would be in hostility to them immediately. The experience of England on this subject, had taught a lesson which could never be forgotten. Union with the State was deadly in its effect on any religious denomination, and none in this country were so weak as to desire it.

Mr. Campbell of Brooke said, that every argument he had heard from Mr. B. went to prove the necessity of a religious establishment. For himself, he had no partiality for religious incorporations of any sort. He had, on the contrary, a great abhorrence to them in every form. He had many objections against them; but having heard no good reasons brought forward to prove that any advantage would attend them, (those hitherto used only professed to shew that they would be attended with no danger,) he should urge but one objection, and that was, that one feature of such institutions must be, to put it in their power to compel persons to the support of religion. If not, they were of no use; and all such compulsion was incompatible with the spirit of christianity. He, as a republican, should vote against compelling any person to support any ministry whatever.

Mr. Brodnax rejoined. The Reverend, or the *Right* Reverend gentleman from Brooke, has discovered an objection to his amendment, which, he confessed had never entered into his brain. He must certainly have been very unhappy either in the selection or the expression of his argument, if he had conveyed no better idea of his meaning. The Rev. gentleman said, he had pointed out no good consequence whatever, as likely to attend Theological Seminaries. He hoped they would, at least, have this good effect, to teach ministers of the gospel good morals and good manners. The gentleman had said, that such incorporations could be of no use, unless they compelled contributions to the support of their ministry: but could the gentleman forget that in the body of the resolution, such a power is expressly prohibited, not to a mere corporation, but to the Legislature of the State? a clause which had been introduced with the precise view to prevent that compulsion which some other States had sanctioned.

The question being now taken on the amendment, it was promptly negatived, twelve only rising in its favour.

The tenth and eleventh resolutions were passed over without amendment. They read as follows:

10. "*Resolved*, That no bill of attainder, or *expost facto* law, or law impairing the obligation of contracts, ought to be passed."

11. "*Resolved*, That private property ought not to be taken for public uses without just compensation."

The Committee then proceeded to consider the twelfth resolution, which is in the following words:

12. "*Resolved*, That the members of the Legislature shall receive for their services, a compensation, to be ascertained by law, and paid out of the public treasury, but no law increasing the compensation of members of the Legislature shall take effect, until the end of the next annual session after the said law may have been enacted."

Mr. Naylor moved to strike out the word "end" and insert in lieu thereof, the word "commencement."

Mr. Chapman of Giles, (who had introduced this resolution in the Legislative Committee,) explained the reason why he did not wish the amendment to prevail. Supposing a Legislature, sitting this year, to pass a resolution increasing the amount of the wages of a Representative: and supposing the people to be dissatisfied with what was done: when the Legislature meets the next year, they must meet under that law, and receive the extra compensation, until time should elapse to pass a bill to repeal the law. This he was desirous to avoid; and in order to avoid it, he would not have the law take effect, till the end of the session. Then there would be ample leisure to consider the subject, and to introduce, mature, and pass a bill for the repeal, if it should be deemed advisable.

Mr. Naylor thought this was an excess of caution; it was looking too far ahead to legislate at the distance of two sessions off. If the people shall be dissatisfied, according to the case put by the gentleman, the remedy is easy. Let there be an understanding that the extra wages shall not be received.

The question being put, the amendment was negatived. Ayes 37, Noes 50.

The thirteenth resolution, which is the last reported by the Legislative Committee, was then passed by without amendment. It is in the words following:

"*Resolved*, That no Senator or Delegate shall, during the term for which he shall have been elected, be appointed to any civil office of profit under this State, which shall have been created, or the emoluments of which shall have been increased during such term, except such offices as may be filled by elections by the people."

Mr. Doddridge now moved to take up the second resolution, (on the subject of the census,) but after some conversation as to the next subject to be considered,

Mr. Nicholas moved that the Committee rise: the motion prevailed. Ayes 44, Noes 42.

The Committee rose accordingly.

Mr. Mercer moved a resolution, which was referred to the Committee of the Whole, viz:

"*Resolved*, That all taxes on lands, slaves, and horses, shall be founded on a fair assessment of their value, that no one of these subjects shall be taxed separately from the other two, and that when taxed, the same rate shall be charged and levied upon all."

Mr. Doddridge moved to take up the second resolution *about the census;* and then proposed the following substitute to his former proposition:

Second resolution, second line, after "taken," strike out to the end of the resolution, and insert "in the year 1835, and in every tenth year thereafter, and upon every such census being taken, and also upon the next census taken under the authority of the United States, a new apportionment of Representation shall be made, according to the principles declared in the foregoing resolution, (if the state of the population shall have so changed, as to render the same necessary,) and upon every apportionment hereafter to be made, there shall be a new assessment of lands for the purposes of taxation."

Mr. Massie then moved that the resolution proposed by Mr. Gordon be printed for the use of the members; and Mr. Goode made a similar motion respecting Mr. Doddridge's amendment in relation to the census; and the printing was ordered accordingly.

And thereupon the House adjourned.

THURSDAY, November 26, 1829.

The Convention met at 11 o'clock, and was opened with prayer by the Rev. Mr. Douglass of the Presbyterian Church.

On motion of Mr. Mason, the Convention passed an order, authorising the Committee of the Whole to have such printing executed, as they might judge conducive to the dispatch of the public business; and then,

On motion of Mr. Macrae, certain documents were ordered to be printed.

The House went into Committee of the Whole, Mr. Powell at first, in the Chair; but, his voice being impaired by a severe cold, he soon after requested Mr. P. P. Barbour to take his place as Chairman.

And the question being on the following amendment offered by Mr. Doddridge, to the second resolution of the Legislative Committee:

Second resolution, second line, after "taken," strike out to the end of the resolution, and insert "in the year 1835, and in every tenth year thereafter, and upon every such Census being taken, and also upon the next Census taken under the authority of the United States, a new apportionment of representation shall be made, according to the principles declared in the foregoing resolution, (if the state of the population shall have so changed, as to render the same necessary,) and upon every apportionment hereafter to be made, there shall be a new assessment of lands for the purposes of taxation."

Mr. Johnson objected to the amendment, and stated the expense which would have to be incurred, if an assessment was made every five years, (reckoning the State and Federal Census:) he referred to a statement from the Auditor's Office, for the expense of the last assessment of lands, to shew that it cost $51,399 94. This would occur every ten years, in addition to the cost of the Census. He concluded with a motion, that this resolution be, for the present, passed over, which was carried.

The fifth resolution, which is in these words, was also passed by:

"*Resolved*, That the number of members in the House of Delegates, ought to be reduced, so that the same be not less than one hundred and twenty, nor more than one hundred and fifty."

The Committee then proceeded to take up the sixth resolution, which reads as follows:

"*Resolved*, That no person ought to be elected a member of the Senate of this State, who is not at least thirty years of age."

Mr. Bayly moved to amend the resolution, by striking out the word "thirty" and inserting "twenty-five."

In support of this amendment, he addressed the Committee as follows:

Mr. Chairman,—I cannot agree to the resolution which requires the age to be longer in the Constitution we are endeavouring to make, than in the old Constitution, without very strong reasons to justify the change. For, although we have heard very many and great complaints from various parts of the State against the Constitution, in most parts of its organization, yet I have never heard a whisper of disapprobation from any portion of the Commonwealth, or from any man, that the Senators were not of sufficient age at twenty-five. It seems to me, that this part of the Constitution, heretofore, has been considered by all, free from exception, until we have met in Convention, and an imaginary evil is now supposed to exist. And yet gentlemen, who are very unwilling to make, and resist with all their force and power of argument, any and every change in those very great defects in the Constitution which have compelled the people to convene this Convention to remove, seem determined to change some of those parts of the Constitution which now place no restraint upon the people. But, such parts of the Constitution as the people have demanded shall be so altered or amended, whereby they shall have greater power in the Government than they have heretofore possessed, are to remain unaltered and unalterable, and a strong limitation put upon their right of electing the man of their choice, who they desire to be their representative, and upon the supposition that they cannot distinguish between the merits of old and young men; the young man without experience, and the old man who has not profited by experience.

Has a single or solitary instance been quoted, where the Commonwealth has received any injury from the very numerous number of young men of great merit and promise, which the people, the freeholders, have introduced into their two Houses of General Assembly, that thereby in early life, they may acquire those useful and necessary accomplishments, which will in due time fit them for the Councils of the Union? The people are to be restricted from selecting a man under thirty years of age, to deliberate with grave Senators, who will be quick to correct any error which will lead him from his duty; but should his aged companions in the Senate, not restrain the youthful Senators of twenty-five years from doing wrong, his constituents will, at the next election, apply the corrective. You add restriction upon the people when they elect or appoint to office, but when the General Assembly or your Executive elect or appoint to office, no restriction will then be met with in your Constitution. Your Judges, your Generals, your Auditor, Treasurer, and all the host of civil and military officers, will be created without the requisite of any qualification of age: I might add your Councillors of State; but they are dead, and nothing but a miracle can bring to life. The only cases where age will be required as a qualification to office, is, when the people choose; then they are to be restrained in their election, to members of the General Assembly, and in the election of the Governor, who is to be thirty years of age and elected by the people, as *seems* to be at *this time* the determination of the Convention, which I hope and trust will be adhered to.

When we consider the reduction we are making of the number of Legislators, and that half the counties which heretofore have been privileged with two Law-givers, will hereafter only have one, it may readily be supposed that they will be more solicitous upon whom their choice will fall, and will select their brightest man, be he young or old. A majority of the States finding no evil resulting, from permitting their young men early in life to enter into their service in deliberative assemblies, have required the age of twenty-one for a Representative, and twenty-five for a Senator; and some of these modern Constitutions may have been copied from the Virginia Constitution, which is not only the oldest written Constitution of any of the States of this Confederation, but it is believed it is the oldest written Constitution of Government in the world. Why then shall we change this feature which has been approved? Sir, the people *may*, *can*, and *ought* to be trusted, to select without restriction as to age after twenty-five, whosoever they wish to be their rulers. It will not do so often to say, that the citizens of Virginia are so virtuous, wise and independent in voting *viva voce* for their agents, and yet restrain them from promoting their interest by selecting a rising genius of great expectations to advocate their rights. By this resolution, you compel them to turn away from a man who has every qualification except age, to another who has no other qualification. But, Sir, so far from this provision producing mischief, and I think it has produced none, for none has been stated or complained of, it has produced much good. Soon after the age of twenty-one, the three venerable gentlemen who stand at the head of this Convention, (Ex-Presidents Madison and Monroe, and Chief Justice Marshall,) entered into the service of Virginia: to these I may add the gentleman from Norfolk, (Mr. Tazewell.) Another gentleman from Norfolk, (Mr. Grigsby,) in this Convention, is not now twenty-three years old, and yet he has been twice elected by the citizens of that Borough, to represent them in General Assembly. I may mention the names of many more illustrious citizens of Virginia to justify my motion; one more I will refer to, the gentleman from Charlotte, (Mr. Randolph,) when elected to Congress, it was supposed he had not acquired the age of twenty-five years, (which I believe was the fact,) and when called upon to take the usual oaths in the Hall of the Representatives of the Nation, the Speaker demanded as by authority, "*Sir, are you twenty-five years old?*" The reply of the young Statesman struck him dumb: "Go and ask my Constituents;" and that was the proper reply. His constituents were the rightful judges of his qualifications, and if that gentleman had studied from that to this time, for an answer more proper to have been given, he would not have succeeded.

A newspaper I have received this morning, gives the ages of the fifty-six illustrious men at the time they signed the Declaration of Independence of the United States.

Edward Rutledge was twenty-six years old, Thomas Lynch, jr. twenty-seven; Thomas Heyward, jr. thirty. These three, the youngest of the fifty-six, were from South Carolina. Benjamin Rush thirty; Elbridge Gerry thirty-one; William Hooper thirty-one; Thomas Stone thirty-two; Thomas Jefferson thirty-three; James Wilson thirty-three.

It is not probable, that the first entrance into public life of these men, was in that glorious Congress, and I may safely presume, that they had often been chosen by their countrymen, to fill public stations, before they were selected for that great and trying occasion.

William Pitt the younger, who is considered by Englishmen, the wisest Minister England ever had, took upon himself the government of that wonderful people, at the age of twenty-two or twenty-three, and sustained himself against every opposition, for twenty-three years, and until his death.

Taking the example of our own and other States and countries, it does appear to me, that the restriction upon the people which we are about to impose in choosing their Representatives, is not necessary, and therefore I have made the motion.

Mr. Joynes addressed the Committee, in substance, as follows:

Mr. Chairman,—The resolutions relative to the ages of Senators and Delegates, having been adopted in the Legislative Committee on my motion, it may, perhaps, be expected of me to state the reasons which induced me to propose to change the provisions of the present Constitution on these subjects. I confess I do not regard it as a matter of *very great importance*, that Senators should be thirty, rather than twenty-five years of age; but there are several considerations which induce me to prefer thirty as the age of Senators. There is no general rule without exceptions; and I admit, that one of the greatest Statesmen England ever produced, was Prime Minister of that Kingdom at much less than thirty years of age. And our own country has produced some splendid examples of very early developments of great powers of mind. Some of the greatest orators the world has ever known, have attained very high distinction before the age of thirty; but these exceptions do not disprove the propriety of the proposed change.

It is not enough to fit a man for the duties of a Senator, that he should be a man of brilliant genius, or great powers of eloquence; but it is necessary that he should possess a maturity of judgment, and a knowledge of the Constitution and laws of the State, which very few young men possess. It is proposed that the Senate should be retained at its present number of twenty-four members; and a bare majority being necessary to form a quorum, the votes of seven members (which is a majority of a majority,) will be sufficient to enact or repeal the most important laws. The territory of Virginia, from its extent and fertility, is able to sustain more than twice the number of its present population; and with this increased population, and from other causes, it may reasonably be expected that new interests will spring up, and whatever may be the increased population, and however diversified may be the interests of society, it is proposed forever to limit the number of Senators to twenty-four.

In addition to the ordinary powers of legislation, it is proposed in the Convention to confer new and important powers on the Senate. It is proposed, to give to the Senate the power of trying all impeachments—to give it a *concurrent* vote with the House of Delegates in the appointment of all important officers of the Government, or to constitute it as a Council, by whose advice and consent, the Governor is to make such appointments; and it is also proposed to give to the Senate and House of Delegates, by *concurrent vote*, the power of removing Judges from office. All these important powers to be exercised by twenty-four men, it seems to me, require that these twenty-four men, should be men who possess great wisdom and experience, and that maturity of judgment and discretion, which age alone can give.

But, Mr. Chairman, there is another consideration which it appears to me, is entitled to some weight upon this subject. Although I ardently hope that the Union of these States may be perpetual, yet in modern times, a *dissolution of the Union* is so frequently spoken of, that there is some reason to apprehend that *that* is not merely a possible event. If such a catastrophe should ever happen to this confederacy, the Legislature of Virginia, will not then, as at present, be confined to legislation for the internal concerns of the State, but other new and important duties will devolve upon them in reference to the connexion of Virginia, with the great family of nations. Such important duties as would then devolve upon the Legislature, ought not to be performed, except by the wisest and most experienced of the sons of Virginia.

It is said, that the people may be safely trusted on this subject, and that they are the best judges of the fitness of candidates for office, and that there is no danger of their electing a man to the Senate who is not well qualified for the station. I should be the last man to question the competency of the people to decide upon the qualifications of candidates for office; or to impose any improper restrictions upon the exercise of their discretion; but the arguments of gentlemen upon this subject prove too much. The restraints imposed by a people upon themselves in their fundamental laws, are restraints imposed by them for their own benefit. If *no restraint* should be imposed upon the right of selection by the people, why do gentlemen propose that Senators should be *twenty-five* years of age? Why not trust the people to elect Senators at twenty-one years of age? Nay, Sir, even less than twenty-one; for, I dare say that *some young men might be found* even under twenty-one, who would, *possibly*, make good Senators.

The same argument would apply with equal force to the Constitution of the United States. The wise men who made that Constitution, required the President to be thirty-five, Senators thirty, and Representatives twenty-five years of age; and the Constitution having been adopted by the people, shews that they approved of those limitations on their own discretion. The united voice of the people of the United States would not be sufficient to elect to the Presidential Chair the most distinguished man in the nation, unless he were thirty-five years of age. Why not remove all these Constitutional restraints, and confide to the discretion of the people and to the State Legislatures, the power of electing a President, Senators and Representatives, of whatever ages they choose? The people of other States have thought it wise to impose limitations upon themselves in their Constitutions upon this subject. In four of the States, Senators are required to be thirty years of age, in one twenty-eight, in four twenty-seven, in one twenty-six, and in all the rest of the States, twenty-five years of age are required. In two of the States, Representatives are required to be twenty-five years of age, in three twenty-four, and in one twenty-two.

But, Mr. Chairman, I consider it much more important to require Delegates to be twenty-five, than Senators thirty years of age. Between the ages of twenty-one and twenty-five, young men ought to be engaged in study, and in preparing themselves to become members of the Legislature; and the observation of every man who has been a member of the House of Delegates, I am sure, has furnished him with opportunities of seeing young men under twenty-five years of age in that House, who had not sufficient experience and judgment to fit them to be Legislators.

I know that some gentlemen are opposed to changing the existing state of things, unless great practical evils have resulted from them. Innovations upon established regulations on important subjects, I admit, ought to be cautiously made; but in the proposed changes, no possible danger can arise. If the proposed changes would exclude some young men well qualified, they would also, probably, exclude more who had not sufficient experience for the important duties of legislation; and those who were qualified, would be still better qualified, after a few more years devoted to the acquisition of knowledge and experience.

The question being taken, the motion of Mr. Bayly was negatived—Ayes 37, Noes 45. (Mr. Marshall *Aye*, Messrs. Madison and Monroe, *No*.)

The seventh resolution was then read as follows:

"*Resolved*, That no person ought to be elected a member of the House of Delegates of this State, who is not at least twenty-five years of age."

Mr. Henderson moved to amend it, so as to make the age of a Delegate twenty-one instead of twenty-five.

Mr. Doddridge opposed the motion, and it was lost—Ayes 37. (Mr. Madison among the Ayes.)

On motion of Mr. Mercer, the Committee then proceeded to the consideration of the report of the Executive Committee.

The first resolution having been read as follows:

"*Resolved*, That the Chief Executive Office of this Commonwealth, ought to be vested in a Governor."

Mr. Doddridge moved the following amendment:

"To be elected once in every three years, at the time of the general annual elections, by the persons qualified to vote for the most numerous branch of the General Assembly."

Mr. Henderson moved to amend Mr. Doddridge's amendment, by inserting the words "most numerous branch of," which was accepted by Mr. D. as a modification.

Mr. Leigh moved to amend the amendment by striking out the words after "elected," and inserting "to be elected by the two Houses of the General Assembly."

Mr. Leigh said here was a proposition of the Legislative Committee to elect a Governor. The second resolution is to abolish the Council. The proposition of the gentleman from Brooke, is to give the election to the qualified voters. If this amendment were rejected, the Constitution would stand as it now stands. He wished to know if such be the fact.

At the suggestion of the Chair, who said that if no proposition to amend were carried, the Constitution would remain as it was, Mr. Leigh withdrew his motion to amend.

Mr. Leigh then called upon gentlemen for some reasons, founded on practical views, for the change they required. Upon them was the *onus probandi.*

Mr. Powell regretted that the state of his voice prevented him from taking the course which he otherwise would, by presenting the amendment which he had himself moved to this whole report. Mr. P. then moved to pass by the resolution, and to take up the other reports.

Mr. Doddridge said he did not know that the gentleman from Chesterfield had any right to call upon him to answer interrogatories. It was a practice growing upon the Convention. He had been a few days ago charged with being cognizant of a motion in the House of Delegates, when he was not a member of that branch, but he was not permitted to explain, and to deny that he was a member; and the gentleman then proceeded to ask him questions as to what he would do in certain cases. He denied this right, and declared that he was at liberty to address the Committee on the subject of his proposition, or to submit it to a silent vote. He suggested to the gentleman from Frederick, to permit the question now to be taken on the report, and reserve his argument for a future stage of the proceedings.

Mr. Powell persisted in his motion, and gave the reasons which induced him to view the election of the Governor, as the most important question which was likely to arise in the consideration of this report.

Mr. Mercer said that as it was at his instance, the report of the Executive Committee was taken up, he felt it necessary to make a few observations, with respect to the motion made by the gentleman from Frederick, (Mr. Powell). If he thought that the gentleman from Frederick, from his present indisposition, would do any injustice to the advocacy of the substitute which he submitted, for the Executive report, *he* certainly would not press the decision at the present time. But if that gentleman would reflect and perceive the converse of his argument, he would find that we were involved in the same difficulty from which he wished to extricate himself. On this principle we cannot proceed one step; we cannot move at all. It was objected the other day when it was proposed to take this report under consideration, that it would be improper, until we had settled the whole basis of Representation. There is no report, which does not, in part, involve in its consideration, that of another report. The Executive depends on the Legislative, and the Judicial on both the Legislative and Executive Departments. We cannot decide any proposition separately: every question is argued hypothetically in the Committee, and inferences are drawn in this manner. Suppose the Executive power is to be enlarged, then we are to consider the expediency of vesting the power of appointment in the people; if the Executive powers remain as they are, then we must consider whether he is to be appointed according to the present Constitution. At last when we have settled the question in the Committee, we then go into the House, with a full knowledge of the whole principles of the proposition, and we can vote and decide, not hypothetically. If then it was decided, that the Executive is to be elected by the people, he would vote to give him powers to act independently of the Legislature. If the Executive was made the creature of the Legislature, he would regulate his vote accordingly. He said the gentleman from Frederick, would have an opportunity to offer his substitute hereafter. The Executive report will be open to amendment: he hoped, therefore, he would withdraw his motion, so that the report might be considered.

Mr. Leigh asked, if it was or was not parliamentary, to ask of the friends of a proposition to give their reasons for it.

The Chair said there was no parliamentary rule on the subject. The only rule is to avoid personality, and imputation of motive.

Mr. Leigh said, he was sure he had attributed no personal motive. He asked the gentleman from Brooke, if he supposed, he had any authority for carrying a proposition through the House, without assigning any reasons, or, if he had a right to take offence against any one for requiring reasons? He wished to know, if it was to be expected that a system which has all the sanctions of time in its favour, was to be at once changed at the suggestion of the gentleman, without any reasons being assigned. He had thought our object was to compare our reasons, and he was willing to meet the consequences of any change of reasons. When he submitted a proposition, he considered himself required to state any reasons without any specific call.

Mr. Doddridge wished to say one word. The gentleman from Chesterfield had made an amendment to his proposition, and before he sat down, seemed to call on him in a somewhat peremptory manner. He stated that he was as little disposed as any man to look at the conduct of any one in an unfavourable view; and was as ready to make this explanation to the gentleman from Chesterfield, as to any gentleman. He said, that as this proposition was to be submitted to the people, and the subject had been sufficiently discussed, he had a right to leave the question to be taken, without giving any reasons.

After an explanation from Mr. Leigh and Mr. Doddridge, Mr. Powell withdrew his motion to pass by the proposition.

Mr. Doddridge said, he would now assign his reasons for the proposed change in the Executive, and he would do so, without adverting to any of the existing abuses in its constitution. In the first place, he objected in theory to its power of appointment, as sufficient to show that the Executive Department should undergo a new organization. If we are agreed on any one principle which has been discussed amongst us, it is that the Executive, Legislative, and Judicial Departments of the Government, should be separated, and that the duties of neither should be exercised by another department. This, with some exceptions, would be admitted as a general rule.

What is the Executive of Virginia? It is nothing more nor less, than an emanation of the Legislative power. He is appointed every year, and is responsible, only to those to whom he is looking for a re-appointment. And the Executive Magistrate by an interpretation of the Constitution, has been deprived of all Executive power. By a construction which was given to it, in the time of General Wood, it was decided, that when the Executive Council was divided, the Governor had no power to give a casting vote. This was the prevailing doctrine to the present time. The Governor requires no other qualification, than to be a gentleman, to be enabled to fill his office. All he has to do, is to write his name when commanded; and not till he is commanded by the Executive Council, can he do so. He is the creature of the Legislature and not of the people, and he is responsible to the Legislature alone, except when the process of impeachment is resorted to; and from the tenure of office, it would be useless. He understood from the Notes of Mr. Jefferson, that the Executive was nothing but an emanation of the Legislative power. He had not the Notes here now, but he had read them so often, and they made such an impression on him, that he could readily give their substance. Mr. Jefferson proved, that the Executive was not a co-ordinate branch of the Government; that it was not responsible to the people. The conclusion was, that the Executive power resulted in the Legislative body. It was asked had the Judicial body a sufficiency of independence. Their tenure is, *quam diu sese bene gesserint*. This did not make a Judge independent, because after providing an adequate salary, the words, "which shall not be denied during the continuance of office," are omitted.

The Legislature could thus starve a Judge out of office. The Judiciary is in fine dependent on the Legislature. What are the words of Mr. Jefferson? "When all the powers of Government, Legislative, Executive and Judicial, result to the Legislative body, and the concentration of them is in the same hands, it is a precise definition of despotic power." Independent of this authority, is it not so in fact? What can prevent the Executive Council from doing an unpopular act, since they are not farther accountable to the General Assembly, and have no motive to induce them to act properly, except that the General Assembly may not re-elect them?

Another defect is, that effectually and efficiently they are in no manner responsible. In the Council, which consists of eight members, unless there is a majority on every question, the Governor has no responsibility. The Executive Council is periodically removed, not appointed, and this was a most odious and disgusting office. Two of the eight must go out, and this circumstance creates amongst them a disposition to electioneer in the General Assembly against each other. The result is, the dishonour of him who is removed from office.

Among the complaints which brought this Convention together, and which were published in the Gazettes of the country, was one against the Executive. After the extension of the Right of Suffrage, what the people next desired, was the establishment of an independent, responsible Executive. If the Executive Council be abolished, the Governor will be responsible for whatever abuse may be committed, and there will be no necessity to refer for the Ayes and Noes to the Executive Council book. The objections against the Executive, would come with greater force, especially if he be invested with the power of making appointments.

The objection, therefore, to the constitution of the present Executive, is, being an emanation of the Legislative body; as lacking independence, and, as not possessing the power necessary for the Executive of any country. He would not go further in his argument. It was said that no abuses existed; that none had taken place under the present system. He was not prepared to go into this subject; yet all had not given satisfaction. Many of the appointments have given dissatisfaction; there have been many made independent of, and against the nomination of the county courts. There was another subject which he had omitted to mention. An increase of power has devolved upon the Executive by an enactment of the Legislature. He referred to the administration of the Literary Fund, and of the fund for Internal Improvement; the distribution of which the Executive possesses, not in virtue of any constitutional power it enjoys in this respect, but by an enactment of the Legislature. The consideration surely shews the necessity of there being a greater responsibility on the part of the Executive. He had briefly and imperfectly assigned his objections to the present system. As to the power of impeaching the Executive, it was futile. We were not an impeaching people. There was but one impeachment which ever took place here, and that was made at the request of the gentleman himself. But as to the impeachment of a Governor, whose tenure of office is but one year, it was useless, as his time would expire before the impeachment could be effected.

Mr. Morgan said, he would suggest an amendment to his colleague, to strike out the word "three," and leave a blank. He had intended to vote for the appointment of the Executive by the Legislature, if the election was made annually. His reason for making this motion was, to have the most responsible Executive in the United States, which he thought would be thus attained. The blank may be again filled with "two," or with "three," if the Committee prefer the latter number. For himself, he preferred that the appointment should be made every two years, if the Executive is to be elected directly by the people; but if by the General Assembly, he preferred an annual election, as the Executive was thus held as a tenancy from year to year, and therefore more responsible. An annual election by the people would be inconvenient; an annual election by the Legislature, constituted as that body now is, he would never consent to. He would move that the word "three" be stricken out.

Mr. Doddridge accepted the modification proposed by his colleague.

Mr. Morgan said, he would further remark, that he was opposed to the augmentation of power in the Executive branch of the Government. It was dangerous. He thought the weakest Executive in the world to be the best. It was the safest. No original good whatever can result to the people from the power of this branch. It is the business of the Executive to see that the laws shall be faithfully executed. All good resulting from Government to the people, must originate and come from the Legislature. It can originate no where else. But so far as the Executive is concerned in the execution of the laws, there ought to be a high responsibility. He would vote for the amendment, but against every thing calculated to augment Executive power or influence. He wished to keep that branch feeble.

Mr. Doddridge accepted the motion as a modification of his amendment, so as to leave the term of service blank for the present.

Mr. Nicholas addressed the Committee as follows:

It appears to me, Mr. Chairman, that we are passing over vital interests, rapidly, and without due consideration. This is one of the most important branches of the Government, and a sense of duty impels me, to state the result of my reflections on the subject. There is also, a relation, in which I stand to this question, which renders it proper that I should address the Committee. I had the honour to submit to the Executive Committee, of which I was a member, a proposition relative to the Executive Department; which since, with the consent of the Convention, was laid on the table, and referred to this Committee. I have announced my intention, to submit it as a substitute for a part of the report of the Executive Committee. The resolution now before the Committee, is limited to the declaration, that the Governor ought to be elected by the people, instead of the Legislature. But there are other matters connected with the organization of the Executive Department, which have been already adverted to in debate, and which, in truth, will have an important bearing on the question now before the Committee. The proposition I submitted, was, that the ninth and tenth sections of the Constitution should be retained, and that the eleventh should be substituted by a new section, which provides for retaining four members of the Council, one of them to be chosen and act as Lieutenant Governor; half the Council to go out at the end of two years, the other two at the end of four, so that though the members are to be re-eligible, it shall be in the power of the Assembly, if necessary, to renovate half the body once in two years. It is also proposed to abolish the present mode of ejecting members from the Council, and to allow them salaries, moderate but adequate.

It is stated by the gentleman from Brooke, (Mr. Doddridge) that one object of calling the Convention, was to abolish the Executive Council. I do not know what other gentlemen's constituents may think on the subject, but I believe mine have expressed no opinion on the matter, and I feel myself free to consult my own views of what is right and proper.

I admit, that I have my fears, that any attempt that I may make to defend the Council, will prove fruitless, because many seem to entertain strong prepossessions against it. But this will not deter me from doing my duty, in endeavouring to demonstrate, that the public interests will be promoted, by preserving this branch of the Executive, under certain modifications. Whether the Council ought to be abolished, depends upon our ideas, of what are the proper characteristics of the Executive Department. I take it for granted, that every gentleman would think it proper, to construct the Executive Department on principles suited to republican institutions. The Government from which we were separated by the Revolution, was one which concentrated inordinate authority in the hands of a single Executive Magistrate. The monarch had the powers of war and peace, was the fountain of honour and office, and could increase the House of Peers, who are a body of hereditary nobles, to an unlimited extent. Look at the preamble to your Constitution, which enumerates the causes which induced our ancestors to separate from Great Britain, and you will see, that our revolution was to a great extent, founded on the tyrannical and oppressive exercise of the vast powers and prerogatives of the British King. Smarting as our ancestors did, under what they declared to be "a detestable and insupportable tyranny," it was natural as well as proper, that in the Government they were about to establish, they should endeavour to conform the structure of the Executive Department to the genius of a Republic. But, now, we are about, it would seem, to depart from these principles. We are to have a splendid Executive. It is contemplated to vest this authority in a single magistrate; and the appointment to all offices in the gift of this Department, is to be given to him, as some contend, without controul, and as others maintain, with no other check, save the power of rejecting his nominations by the Senate. I am not prepared for this. The gentleman from Monongalia, (Mr. Morgan,) says he is for a feeble Executive. This is not precisely the phrase I would adopt. I wish the Executive to have power enough to execute the laws and no more. I would not invest it with splendor, or extensive patronage, or make it the mark, or instrument of inordinate ambition. Our Executive as at present constituted, is simple and unostentatious. Your Governor is nothing more than a citizen called upon, temporarily, to execute the laws; this done, he returns to the level of the great body of the people. Whilst in office, he has with the advice of the Council all the power which is necessary to give efficacy to your Government. What more can be desired? If you invest all power and extensive patronage in a single magistrate, you create a petty monarchy. The gentlemen who are on the other side of this question, admit the propriety of interposing checks to prevent the abuse of power in the other Departments of Government; but the framers of our Constitution felt that these checks were equally, indeed, more necessary in the Executive. The check they interposed, was the Executive Council. This is a constitutional body, not dependent on the Governor.

The President of the United States has enormous powers and patronage, and he has no constitutional Council. The Constitution authorises him to call for the opinion of the principal officer, in each of the Executive Departments, upon any subject relating to the duties of his office; and usage has erected these officers into what is called the Cabinet. But there is all the difference in the world between such a body, and a Council organized as ours. These Executive officers hold at the will of the President, and he can act without, or contrary to their advice. The Governor can do no important act, without the advice of Council. They not only know his acts, but they understand the motives and secret springs which set these acts in motion. If you entrust power to one man to act in the dark, and without the possibility of determining his motives, you give facilities and temptations to do wrong, you enable him to indulge a spirit of favouritism, and to confer offices, in promotion of objects of personal ambition.

By a constitutional Council, you superadd to the responsibility of the Governor, the means, if not of preventing the formation of improper schemes, yet of their being carried into effect.

But, it is proposed to give the election of Governor to the people. It seems to me, that the power is essentially exercised by the people, when carried into effect by their immediate representatives. Both the Governor and the members of the Legislature are elected for short periods, which constitutes a sufficient security for the proper exercise of this power of appointment, by those to whom the present Constitution has entrusted it. This is one of those selections for office, which can be best exercised by intermediate agents. It is impossible that the candidates for Governor, can be known but in a very few counties of the State. But, to the members of the Legislature, who are on the scene of action, all the public men of the State, who would be fit for the station, would be known, and they could make the best choice. If the Governor is to be elected by the people at large, they must depend upon the representations made to them of the characters of the candidates. The persons who may make these representations, will, in effect, control the election. In the one case, then, the elections would be made by the representatives of the people, acting under a sense of duty and official responsibility; in the other, by the influence of heated and interested partizans.

But it is said, that the creation of a single Executive magistrate, and vesting his choice in the people, will increase responsibility. Strange, that a large increase of power, and the investiture in a single hand, should have that effect. It is further said, that the existence of the Council destroys all responsibility in the Governor. This is not so. The Governor cannot act without the advice of Council, and that advice is to be spread on their journal, signed by each member, and laid before the Legislature when required; besides, any member may enter his protest. The Governor and Council then, are both responsible; the former for following, or not following their advice, and the latter for that which they give. I beg gentlemen before they adopt a system which gives all power and patronage to one man, and the election of him to the people, to turn their eyes to the operation of this system in our sister States. Look at New York, Pennsylvania and Kentucky. It appears from the debates of the Convention in New York, that before the recent change in her Constitution, about eight thousand offices, were in the gift of the Executive, including militia appointments, prothonotaries and a multitude of smaller offices. Whenever the election comes round, in some of these States, the community is convulsed to the centre. Every man is made an office-hunter and dabbler in elections. As soon as a new Governor is elected, all the incumbents in office go by the board. And then begins a new struggle, so that the State is kept in continual ferment and agitation. The inevitable effect of these systems is, not only to destroy the peace and happiness of the people, but to undermine their political morality. Under our plan, the machine of Government works so smoothly, that whilst our Executive possesses power all-sufficient to execute the laws, no sensation is felt on the change of the Chief Magistrate, and it is not unlikely that many citizens of the State are frequently ignorant who the Governor is, unless he happens to be a man who has acquired distinction in other political stations.

But it is objected by the gentleman from Brooke, (Mr. Doddridge,) that in giving the election of the Governor to the Legislature, you violate that valuable political maxim, which requires the different departments to be kept separate and distinct. If the gentleman will advert to the forty-seventh Number of the Federalist, in which this subject is discussed, he will find that the true meaning of the maxim laid down by Montesquieu, is "that where *the whole power* of one department is exercised by the same hands which possess *the whole power* of another department, the fundamental principles of a free Constitution are subverted." And that he did not mean, "that these departments ought to have no *partial agency in*, or *no controul over*, the acts of each other." And this Number also demonstrates by reference to the British Government, and the Governments of the different States (to which may be now added, that of the United States,) that it is extremely difficult, if not impossible, to prevent the powers of one department from running into those of another. Besides, how does the power of appointment of Governor, confer on the Legislature, Executive power in the sense in which the maxim before quoted, can alone apply? As well might it be contended, that the appointment of the Judges, confers on the Legislature, Judicial powers.

But the gentleman from Brooke, says the Governor has no power; he is a mere cypher. I do not think so. He is not bound to obey the advice of the Council. It is true he cannot act without their advice, but he can, after they give it, execute it or not, on his responsibility. This is the uniform construction which has been put on the Constitution. Besides, my plan proposes, that when the Council is divided, the Governor shall have the casting vote. How does it appear, that the Governor and Council have not adequate power? Have they not the power to execute the laws? And have not the laws been always executed? Why give them more power? It can only be necessary to confer splendor and patronage. The powers of the Executive are very considerable. It must be so in every Government in a State as large as this. The power of executing the laws must always be commensurate with the legislation of a country. They have the power of appointing magistrates, sheriffs, all the militia officers, and many others, and the power of filling vacancies in various offices during the recess of the Legislature. They have also a general superintendence of all the departments, subordinate to them, the Treasurer's office, those of the Auditors, the Penitentiary, to which may be added, the Boards of Internal Improvement and the Literary Fund. Can any one man discharge these various important duties? In the exercise of the power of appointment, can the Governor possess the local information, or the knowledge of men dispersed over this great State which would enable him to make proper selections? With a Council of four, elected with any reference to this object, he would have always at hand, the means of making a judicious choice.

There is one power vested in the Executive, which I should be unwilling to confer on any individual. I mean the power of pardon. Is there any gentleman here, who is willing so to invest this power, which may involve the liberty, and even the life of any citizen of the land? There is no man, however elevated, however prosperous, however virtuous or circumspect, such is the frailty of our nature, and such are the accidents and vicissitudes of life, who may not either in his own person, or that of his connexions, have a deep interest in the exercise of this power.

The idea advanced by some, that the Council may be dispensed with, by taking the advice of the Treasurer, Auditors, and some other officers of Government, is not, in my mind, one which can be sustained. The objects for which these officers are selected, are entirely distinct, and they may require different qualifications. But what seems conclusive, is, that these officers are under the supervision, and to a certain extent, the controul of the Executive, and have already laborious duties to perform, which occupy all their time. It is the opinion of others, that we should conform our Executive to the model of that of the United States. I should be more disposed, had I the power, to reverse this proposition. The powers of the Federal Executive are enormous, and its patronage most extensive. For this cause, we see the nation frequently convulsed in the choice of this magistrate. The office of President overshadows every other part of the Government. His election absorbs the wishes and thoughts of a large portion of the nation. Other elections, and political measures of vital importance, are too often made subservient to the advancement of the interests of favorite candidates for the Presidency. It is much to be feared, that the conflicts which take place for this glittering object of ambition, may more endanger the permanency of our General Government than any thing else which can happen to it. The remedy would be found in diminishing the power, or, at least the patronage of the Executive of the United States.

It may be well supposed, however, that there are some of the powers which are conferred on the Executive of the Union which may be necessary to it, but would be entirely otherwise, as applied to the State Government. In the United States, are invested, the powers of war and peace, the regulation of commerce, and the management of our external relations. The cares of the State Government are principally confined to the regulation of our internal affairs. And for the management of these, the powers we have given the Executive have been found amply sufficient, and to have been judiciously arranged, under the existing Government.

The gentleman from Brooke says, that the impeachment to which the Governor is liable, is a mere nominal thing; it contains no terror, because he can only be impeached after his office ceases. But will the gentleman recollect, that if convicted on impeachment, he may be disabled to hold any office in future, and subjected to such pains and penalties as may be prescribed by law?

The gentlemen who are against the Council, under any modification, have not agreed upon what they will substitute for it. Now, I am persuaded, that whenever they bring forward a plan, it will be found that it will not be as efficient, or economical, as the small Council I propose to be retained.

The Executive Committee have decided there shall be a Lieutenant Governor, but have as yet, assigned him no duties.

He must, if the Council be abolished, be a salaried officer. There must be also, some other subordinate and auxiliary officers, to transact the public business. By my plan, the Lieutenant Governor is to be one of the Council, as at present, and to receive no additional salary.

The Committee will, however, be better enabled to decide, on the intrinsic, or comparative merits, of what is intended to be substituted, for a Council under any modification, when gentlemen shall see fit, more fully to develop their views on the subject.

Mr. Henderson remarked, that it was his misfortune, again to differ with the estimable gentleman who had just favored the Committee with his views. I will not, said Mr. H., detain the Committee long, because I am aware, that what I may say, will come recommended neither by weight of reputation, nor by any grace of manner. I agree, Mr. Chairman, that the friends of the proposition under consideration, are bound to give reasons to this Convention, and to the people themselves, for the contemplated change, and sound and strong reasons too. Unless this can be done, let the existing mode of election continue. Such, I admit, is the course of prudence and common sense. It really does appear to me, Sir, that it were not difficult to place this matter in a point of light, clearly shewing the propriety of electing the Chief Magistrate of the State by the citizens in their primary capacity. The gentleman from this city, who has just taken his seat, has amused us with something like a declamation upon the topic of a splendid Executive. In this, the gentleman has leaped before he reached the stile. He has invested the Governor with an imaginary splendor; and, having done this, he has very gravely proceeded to prove that this gorgeous pageant ought not to be elected by the people. Now, Sir, this is varying the question in a manner singular enough. We contend that the Governor should be elected by the people; and to prove this political position untrue, we are told that he ought not to be so elected, because he is to be armed with great powers, and arrayed in great magnificence. The presumption is, that this body, in its wisdom, will give to this department of the Government, such powers as are consistent with the interest and honor of the Commonwealth. Thus presuming, we are called upon to decide on the mode of his election. My opinion is, that he ought to be elected by the people, and for the space of three years. I voted for striking out the term of years, conceiving it more regular to test the principle first, and fill the blank afterwards.

Let us then, Mr. Chairman, without heeding nicknames, by which principles are too often prejudiced, proceed with the enquiry. And here, Sir, I venture to assume a ground, the soundness of which may defy criticism, that, *as an individual ought, in no important concern, to do by another what he can as well do by himself, so a people ought not to execute by agency that to which it is competent in its proper original character*. If this be true, then, we have to ascertain whether the citizens at large can perform this duty, as well as their Legislature, or not. I maintain the affirmative, not only of this proposition, but of the other one; that they can perform it better; and that strong, very strong objections to the action of the Legislature upon the subject, exist.

What is the nature of the duty? What the qualifications necessary to its discharge? Sound understanding and honesty. Are there any recondite principles of science in the matter? Is it complete in its parts? Do any peculiar difficulties attend, or obscurities hang over it? No man ought to be a Governor of Virginia, who has not attained considerable age, performed eminent public services, and required a diffusive reputation, a high standing. All men of that description are, in the very nature of the thing, generally known to the people. Have the people, then, not judgment enough to discern who is fit, and rectitude enough to have a sufficient regard, indeed, for their own interests and dignity, to choose him when discerned? I cannot, and will not, impute to the sovereign people of this ancient Commonwealth, so much folly, or obliquity as to doubt it.

It may not be amiss, Sir, to advert to our sister States for a moment: eighteen elect their Chief Magistrates by the people; six, including Virginia, by their Legislatures. This is not referred to, in the expectation, that we shall blindly follow their example; but, in the hope that gentlemen will be persuaded to pause, and ponder on the fact, that three-fourths of the States in our Union, have adopted the system which we advocate.

He who will study the European Governments, and especially that of England, will be struck with the idea, that they are built upon the ground of making the principles of *monarchy*, *aristocracy*, and *democracy*, conflict with each other in such proportions, as to preserve the energy of the whole. Such is the theory of the British Government. I will not examine it now, in the abstract, or in its supposed aptitude or inaptitude, to the circumstances or character of that or any other people. Suffice it to say, that no American politician ought to resist the declaration, that the theory of our Governments is the *sovereignty of the people*, and the *responsibility of their agents*. And, to maintain this responsibility in its full vigor, the wise men who framed our institutions, have so ordered, that the Legislative and Executive Departments, should emanate *directly from the people themselves*. Thus, each looking to its source, will feel that jealousy of the other, which inspires mutual vigilance, perpetuates liberty, and establishes public security. This is the broad, the vital, the beautiful principle, which stands substitute for the European plan of checks and balances. This it is, that gives to the Governments composing our happy political fraternity, the spirit which assures us, they will not prove disloyal to the societies over which they preside. Remove this responsibility, destroy this laudable and manly jealousy; and, although circumstances may prostrate the existence of free institutions, they are the sport of casualty. It is no answer to this argument, to say, that all the powers of the Government are vested, not in *one man*, but in *many*. *Many tyrants are not more tolerable than one*. It is against the *principle* of tyranny, that I struggle with, in its *details*. Sir, said Mr. H., I am advancing no novelties. I am the humble echo of the voice of the fathers of the Revolution; the Statesmen whom Virginia has delighted to honor. Few of those to whom I allude, are gathered to their fathers; another graces, by his venerable presence, the deliberations of this body.

Here Mr. H. read from Jefferson's Notes on Virginia, as follows: "All the powers, Legislative, Executive, and Judiciary, result to the Legislative body. *The concentration of these, in the same hands, is precisely the definition of despotic Government*. It will be no alleviation, that these powers will be exercised by a plurality of hands, and not by a single one. *One hundred and seventy-three Despots, would surely be as oppressive as one*."

Again: Mr. H. read, "They, (meaning the Legislature,) have, accordingly, in many instances, decided rights, which should have been left to Judiciary controversy; and *the direction of the Executive, during the whole time of their session, is becoming habitual and familiar*."

He then referred to the 47th No. of the Federalist, written by Mr. Madison, and read as follows: "No political truth is of greater intrinsic value, or is stamped with the authority of more enlightened patrons of liberty, than that on which the objection is founded. The accumulation of all powers, Legislative, Executive and Judiciary, in the same hands, whether of one, a few, or many, and whether hereditary, self-appointed, or *elective*, may justly be pronounced the very definition of tyranny." Mr.

H. here called the attention of the Committee to the 40th No. of the same work, written by the same gentleman, and read as follows: "It is agreed on all sides, that the powers properly belonging to one of the Departments ought not to be directly and completely administered by either of the other Departments. It is equally evident, that in reference to each other, neither of them ought to possess, directly or indirectly, *an overruling influence* in the administration of their respective powers." Mr. H. then referred to the 51st No. of the Federalist, written by General Hamilton, and read as follows: "In order to lay a due foundation for that separate and distinct exercise of the different powers of Government, which, to a certain extent, is admitted to be essential to the preservation of liberty, it is evident that each Department should have *a will of its own;* and, consequently, should be so constituted, that the members of each should have *as little agency as possible in the appointment of the members of the others.*"

Again: "But the great security against a gradual concentration of the several powers in the same Department, consists in giving those who administer each Department, the necessary constitutional means, and personal motives, to resist the encroachments of the others. The provision for defence must, in this, as in all other cases, be made commensurate to the danger of attack. Ambition must be made to encounter ambition. The interests of the man must be connected with the constitutional rights of the place. It may be a reflection on human nature that such devices should be necessary to control the abuses of Government. But what is Government itself, but the greatest of all reflections on human nature? If men were angels, no Government would be necessary. If angels were to govern men, neither external nor internal controls on Government would be necessary." I may, continued Mr. H., have fatigued the attention, or offended the taste of the Committee. My excuse, Sir, is this: We are boldly called on to give reasons for the alteration we project. I am without consequence, true; unknown to fame, and without those powers which enable some men to spread a charm over every topic which they touch. I am also one of a class of men denounced as innovators, visionaries. All that I can hope is, that my arguments, when sustained by the names of Jefferson, Hamilton, and of the honored fellow-labourer of Hamilton, shall be particularly and soberly considered. I ask, Sir, if my doctrine is not fully borne out by the writings of those great men, who, however they may have differed on other subjects, all unite in proclaiming the principles of the *sovereignty of the people*, the separation of the different Departments of Government, and their *independence of each other*, the folly and danger *of permitting the one Department to appoint the other*, and that to allow one an undue influence *indirectly*, is equivalent to a *direct* control. These, Sir, are the springs of republican Government, its vital elements, the pledges of its durability, the rock of its safety.

Mr. Chairman: Gentlemen in the face of one of the greatest men in America, the political patriarch of Virginia, over the ashes of his illustrious compatriots, persist in denying these great political truths. They pronounce our Governors wise and good, and challenge us to specify acts of official abuse or turpitude. Surrounded as we are by gentlemen who have acted in the affairs of the Executive; mingling as many of these respectable gentlemen do in our deliberations, shall we perform the invidious and painful office to which we are invited? And for what? We are not scanning the official conduct of any body. We came here on no such errand. Their acts are embodied in the history of the Commonwealth: the citizens know them well. In the year 1781, Thomas Jefferson prepared his Notes. He had recently filled the Chair of Governor, and knew better than any man in the State, the action of the Legislature on the Executive. What does he say? That the direction of the Executive by the Legislature was *habitual* and *familiar*. He had felt it. This is history, not speculation. It proves that your *Governor has no will of his own;* that he is the creature of the Legislature; a very man of straw.

The gentleman to whose remarks I have heretofore alluded, gave us a fine picture of Executive excellence; and finished it by informing us, that so harmless an Executive had we, that *a great portion of the people actually did not know who the Governor was.* Is this desirable? A free people, professing to be intelligent, and to take an interest in their *own affairs*, not to know who their Governor is! and to be felicitated upon it in this assemblage. Truly, the gentleman has placed the sovereign people in a most dreamy and beatified state! Sir, I wish to arouse them from their unmanly torpor. I wish, Sir, that the people *may* know their Governor, and that the Governor may *know the people.* Mr. Jefferson in his Notes, states, "in December, 1776, our circumstances being much distressed, it was proposed in the House of Delegates to create a *Dictator*, invested with every power, Legislative, Executive, and Judiciary, civil and military, of life and death, over our own persons and over our own properties; and in June, 1781, again under calamity, the same proposition was repeated, *and wanted a few votes only of being passed.*" Is there a living man who will doubt the wisdom and patriotism of the Legislatures of 1776, and 1781? Surely the gentleman from Chesterfield, who seems so confident that we can give no good reasons for the course we recommend, is not that man. The cause, then, of this most extraordinary and appalling project of clothing one man with absolute despotism, *in order that the Republic might receive no harm*, is to be found in the utter imbecility of the Executive Department of the Government. Any other supposition, imputes treason against the freedom of the people, to the fathers of the Revolution. Are we, in the teeth of reason, against the advice of the wise, the warnings of history, to continue an Executive utterly incompetent? An Executive for the "piping times of peace," that will tremble to its centre when war blows its blast? A fair-weather Government, that may be wrecked on the first billow of the tempest? I trust not, Sir. No, let us embark our fortunes in a vessel that will ride proudly amidst the roarings of the storm, and bear unshaken, that broad pendant of freedom under the lightning's flash.

Mr. Chairman,—I am not a gloomy politician; on the contrary, I hope the best of men and things; but I cannot shut my ears to what passes around me. An able gentleman told us, we ought to prepare for a state of affairs within the scope of possibility, and to which all good men look with mournful apprehension. The day may come, when Virginia may be compelled to take her rank amongst the nations of the earth. Suppose a scene of turmoil, of peril, is there a man of sense in the Commonwealth, who would rest securely, at such a crisis, on an Executive constructed like ours? Let us, for Heaven's sake, frame such a Government as will bring out and wield the energies of the whole people, when the fortune of war imperiously demands it. Again, Sir; the very term *Legislature* indicates the appropriate functions of the body. It is no part of that duty to elect the Executive. How many, how various, how difficult the subjects of legislation! What labour, reflection, devotion, and sober-minded men are necessary to do justice to them? Surely, our law-givers have ample employment, if confined within their legitimate sphere. We all know how the passions, intrigues, combinations, incident to these elections, agitate any body of men, and unfit them for that cool thought, accurate analysis, and profound research, so indispensable to public usefulness in this great department. I appeal to the people of Virginia, if the past is not a lucid commentary upon this doctrine. Some gentlemen are so very tender of the public repose, that they would not expose the people to the agitations arising from the election of their Governor. Sir, I maintain that a moderate exercise of the public mind, has a most salutary effect in instructing the people, in habituating them to think of their rights and interests, and in preserving that vigilance and self-respect, which are the strength and glory of a Republic. The people will not thank gentlemen for consulting their *ease* by curtailing their *rights*. I am not one of those zealous and minute politicians, who would continually teaze the citizens of the country with the election of constables and all the little machinery of place. I despise it; I will not

> "Ocean into tempest work,
> To waft a feather, or to drown a fly."

But the great Legislative and Executive Departments of Government ought to be elected, not by each other, but by the people themselves.

The gentleman from this city told us, that the citizens elected the Legislature, and the Legislature the Governor; and that, therefore, the citizens elected the Governor. Sir, this is very good doctrine at that forum where the gentleman plays an eminent part; but he will not be able to satisfy the common sense of his fellow-citizens by this political special pleading. And he will permit me to express my surprise, that he should so far play upon their credulity, as to present them a law-adage in lieu of their political privileges. We are informed, that our Councillors are endued with great wisdom and efficiency. It may be so. But I remain to learn that they are the superiors, or the peers of the Attorney General and Auditor of Public Accounts. At any rate, we certainly can provide an inexpensive and dignified advisory Council. It is objected, that we are about to confide the interesting prerogative of mercy to a single man. Why so? May we not provide, that advice shall be taken under our plan as well as under that the abolition of which we seek?

I have trespassed too long on the patience of the Committee, in making these desultory remarks. And I close by asking, if their spirit be not approved by the best theories of Government, supported by the highest authorities in America, and vindicated by the history of the Commonwealth itself?

Mr. Leigh followed Mr. Henderson, and expressed the desire he had long felt, to know more about a fact stated in Jefferson's Notes, and adverted to by Mr. H. concerning a proposal twice made, in 1776 and 1781, by the Legislature of Virginia, to appoint a Dictator. He wanted to know, whether this was Mr. J's. account of his own view of the effect of the proposition, or whether the proposal was actually made in terms. It was not to be found on the Journals of the Assembly, but might have been offered in Committee of the Whole. As to another passage, also quoted from the same work, expressing Mr. J's. views as to the practical subserviency of the Governor to the Assembly, he could not understand its meaning. The Governor was merely an Executive officer, and had no independent power to exercise, unless it was the prerogative of pardon. He adverted to the investigation into Mr. J's. conduct, and his honorable acquittal, as part of his general position, that *no one abuse* had occurred in the Executive Department from the foundation of the present Government to the present day. To this statement he challenged contradiction. He himself then stated one instance, viz: the granting a few barrels of damaged powder to be fired on the public square. [Here a well known voice was heard to remark, that the grant had made far more noise than ever the powder did, for that would not burn.] Mr. L. denied that the Governor was dependent on the Legislature in any other sense than every other Governor was; and asked if gentlemen wished a Governor with a prerogative like that of the Crown, and power to call out the militia against the will of the Legislature? He remarked, with some severity, on the proposition to abolish the Council, and concluded, it had answered precisely the end of its appointment; which was to reduce, by dividing the Executive power, and so render it incapable of evil.

He retorted the charge of aristocracy, by charging the plan to give power to the Executive, with a spice of monarchy. He contended the Executive of the United States was an elective monarch; and went into a long digression on the effect of patronage in the General Government, and concluded with insisting, that if the Executive of Virginia was to have similar powers, the election of a Governor would immediately grow into as great importance in Virginia, as the election of a President was to the United States.

Mr. Doddridge promising to answer the gentleman's call for information to-morrow, moved that the Committee rise.

It rose accordingly.

The President laid before the Convention the following letter from Calohill Mennis:

RICHMOND, November 26th.

SIR—My health having become so feeble as to prevent my discharging the duties of a member of the Convention, I resign my seat. With high respect,

CALOHILL MENNIS.

JAMES MONROE, *President of the Convention.*

Mr. Claytor then announced, that the Delegation from Mr. Mennis's District, had agreed upon Samuel Branch, Esq. of Buckingham, as a suitable person to fill the vacancy caused by his resignation; and moved that the Sergeant at Arms, cause Mr. Branch to be notified of his election: Which was ordered accordingly.

The House then adjourned.

FRIDAY, NOVEMBER 27, 1829.

The Convention met at 11 o'clock, and was opened with prayer by the Rev. Mr. Armstrong of the Presbyterian Church.

The House resolved itself into a Committee of the Whole, Mr. P. P. Barbour in the Chair; the question being on the amendment of Mr. Doddridge to the first resolution of the Executive Committee.

(The resolution reads,

"*Resolved*, That the Chief Executive office of this Commonwealth ought to be vested in a Governor."

Mr. Doddridge's amendment is in these words:

"To be elected once in every three years, at the time of the general annual elections, by the persons qualified to vote for the most numerous branch of the General Assembly.")

MR. DODDRIDGE took the floor in explanation of his amendment:

I observed yesterday evening, said he, that the discussion was becoming too latitudinous, and I will now endeavour to confine myself to the question raised by my amendment, and to that alone. This question is, not, whether we shall build up a splendid Executive, or whether any spice of monarchy shall be infused into it. The question is, should the first resolution prevail, whether the Governor of this Commonwealth shall be elected by the people, or by the General Assembly as heretofore. The amendment involves nothing more. The decision of this question will greatly influence our votes on others. If the people shall elect their Governor, to the people he will be responsible, and not to the Legislature. It is hereafter to be determined whether the Executive shall be entrusted with additional powers, and if so, whether these shall be exercised by him alone, or with the advice and under the direction of a controlling Council. The decisions of these latter questions will greatly depend on the fate of the present amendment. I do not mean at this time, to give an opinion whether additional powers of any description ought to be conferred, but simply to enquire whether the election of our Governors ought not to be given to the people. My remarks, will, of course, lie within a narrow compass. In my remarks of yesterday, I referred to the opinion of Mr. Jefferson on the very question propounded by the amendment under consideration. This opinion is contained in the Notes on Virginia. The words of the author were yesterday quoted from memory only. Since then the book has been furnished me by a friend and I will use it for greater accuracy. I am the more induced to do this, as the authority of that gentleman, contained in a private letter, has been used against me in this body by one of his friends.

I acknowledge, that I did not generally approve the conduct of Mr. Jefferson as a practical politician. Many of his opinions, formed at a time when he had attained to a maturity of age and judgment, ripened by much experience—when the Constitution of the United States with its honours and emoluments was not thought of—when these States were bound together by the feeble cords of the Confederation alone—I have approved of since my youth. Such are his opinions on the great principles of our present Constitution, and particularly the organization of the Executive and Judicial Departments. After urging as an objection to the latter, the omission to provide that their salaries shall not be reduced during their continuance in office, and to the former, the entire dependence of the Executive on the Legislature, and the uselessness of the Council, Mr. Jefferson proceeds thus: (See Notes on Virginia, pp. 126, 7.) "All the powers of Government result to the Legislative body. The concentration of these in the same hands is precisely the definition of despotic Government. It will be no alleviation, that these powers will be exercised by a plurality of persons, and not by a single one. One hundred and seventy-three despots would surely be as oppressive as one. Let those who doubt it, turn their eyes on the Republic of Venice. As little will it avail us that they are chosen by ourselves. An elective despotism was not the Government we fought for; but one which should not only be founded on free principles, but in which the power of Government should be so divided and balanced, among several bodies of magistracy, as that no one could transcend the legal limits without being effectually checked and restrained by the others. For these reasons that Convention which passed the ordinance of Government, laid its foundation on this basis; that the Legislative, Executive, and Judiciary Departments should be separate and distinct, so that no person should exercise the powers of more than one of them at the same time. But no barrier was placed between these separate powers. The Judiciary and Executive members were left dependent on the Legislative for their subsistence in office, and some of them for their continuance in it."

Thus we see, that shortly after the adoption of the present Constitution, it was objected that the Executive, instead of being elected by the people and responsible to them, was appointed by the General Assembly and only responsible to them. The theory maintained in the Notes on Virginia is our theory. I will now show, that after Mr. Jefferson's retirement from the Presidency of the United States, he maintained the same opinions, and expressed them with such force as to assure us, that his intellect not only remained unimpaired, but that his convictions were strengthened by a longer experience of the defects in our present system, which he had so early pointed out.

In a letter to his friend, dated July 12, 1816, Mr. Jefferson says: "The question you propose on equal representation, has become a party one, in which I wish to take no public share. Yet if it be asked for your own satisfaction only, and not to be quoted before the public, I have no motive to withhold it, and the less from you, as it coincides with your own. At the birth of our Republic I committed that opinion to the world, in the draught of a Constitution annexed to the Notes on Virginia, in which a provision was made for a representation permanently equal. The infancy of the subject at that moment, and our inexperience of self-government, occasioned gross departures in that draught from genuine republican canons. In truth, the abuses of monarchy had so much filled all the space of political contemplation, that we imagined every thing republican that was not monarchy. We had not yet penetrated into the mother principle, that 'Governments are republican only as they embody the will of their people and execute it.' Hence our first Constitutions had, really no principle in them. But experience and reflection have more and more confirmed me in the particular importance of the representation then proposed. On that point then, I am entirely in sentiment with your letters, &c.

"But inequality of representation in both Houses of our Legislature is not the only republican heresy in this first essay of our revolutionary patriots, at forming a Constitution. For, let it be agreed that Government is republican in proportion as every member composing it has his equal voice in the direction of its concerns (not indeed in person, which would be impracticable beyond the limits of a city or small township, but,) by representatives chosen by himself and responsible to him at short periods; and let us bring to the test of this canon every branch of our Constitution.

"In the Legislature, the House of Representatives is chosen by less than half the people, and not at all in proportion to those who do choose. The Senate are still more disproportionate, and for long terms of responsibility. In the Executive, *the Governor is entirely independent of the choice of the people and of their control; his Council equally so, and at best but a fifth wheel to a waggon.*"

Again. "But it will be said, that it is easier to find faults than to amend. I do not think their amendment so difficult as is pretended. Only lay down true principles and adhere to them inflexibly. Do not be frightened into their surrender by the alarms of the timid, or the croakings of wealth against the ascendancy of the people. If experience be called for, appeal to that of our fifteen or twenty Governments for forty years, and shew me where the people have done half the mischief in these forty years, that a single despot would have done in a single year, or half the riots and rebellions, the crimes and the punishments, which have taken place in any single nation under Kingly Government during the same period. The true foundation of republican Government is, the equal rights of every citizen in his person and property, and in their management. Try by this, as a tally, every provision in our Constitution, and see if it hangs directly on the will of the people. Reduce your Legislature to a convenient number, for full, but orderly discussion. *Let every man who fights or pays, exercise his just and equal right in their election.* Let the Executive be chosen in the same way, and for the same term, by those whose agent he is to be, and have *no screen of a Council*, behind which to skulk from responsibility."

Mr. Chairman: I will make a further quotation from the same author, to shew the advantage of a single Executive head, uncontrolled by any species of Council. The words are these: "Nomination to office is an Executive function. To give it to the Legislature as we do, is a violation of the principle of the separation of powers. It swerves the members from correctness, by temptations to intrigue for office themselves, and to a corrupt barter of votes; and destroys responsibility, by dividing it among a multitude. By leaving nomination in its proper place, among Executive functions, the principle of the distribution of powers is preserved, and responsibility weighs with its heaviest force, on a single head."

They who have sought the present Convention, generally agree in the following principles, as comprehending the amendments desired; first, an equal apportionment of Representation among white population: second, an extension of the Right of Suffrage to all who pay taxes: third, a total abolition of the Executive Council: fourth, a single Executive Head, or Governor, to be elected by the people and responsible to them: fifth, future apportionments to keep representation equal among the people: sixth, a provision for future amendments. Our theory requires that every man to whom Government looks for support is a member of the community, and entitled to an equal share of power, and that to separate the Executive from the Legislative Department, it is necessary that the Governor should be immediately responsible to the people as the members of the Legislature are, and as completely independent of them as they are of him; and to secure Executive responsibility to the people, we are disposed to give him "*no screen of a Council, behind which to skulk from that responsibility.*" Every principle for which we contend, is supported by the deliberate opinions of Mr. Jefferson, who has been quoted against us to disprove an historical fact. He is even an authority for us as to that fact. We have asserted that our present Constitution was got up in haste, and not intended by those who made it as a durable instrument. We are so far from being contradicted by Mr. Jefferson in this, that he goes beyond us, and says that the Convention of 1776, were not even elected with a view to independence and a final separation from Great Britain.

His opinions are thus expressed in the Notes, page 128: Speaking of the Conventions of 1775, and 1776, he says, "These were first chosen, anew, for every particular session. But in March, 1775, they recommended to the people to choose a Convention, which should continue in office a year. This was done accordingly in April, 1775; and in July following, that Convention passed an ordinance for the election of Delegates in the month of April annually. It is well known that in July, 1775, a separation from Great Britain, and establishment of republican Government, had never yet entered into any person's mind. A Convention, therefore, chosen under that ordinance, cannot be said to have been *chosen for purposes which certainly did not exist in the minds of those who passed it.* Under this ordinance, at the annual election in April, 1776, a Convention for the year was chosen. *Independence, and the establishment of a new form of Government were not even yet the objects of the people at large.*" In Mr. Jefferson's views of the historical fact we are more than supported by his assertion, that they who made our Constitution were not elected for such a purpose. It is not to be wondered at, therefore, that in page 124 of the Notes, he should speak thus of the Constitution made by them, viz: "The Constitution was formed when we were new and inexperienced in the science of Government. It was the first, too, which was formed in the whole United States. No wonder, then, that time and trial have discovered very capital defects in it."

So much, then, for the authority of Mr. Jefferson, who has been dragged into this debate by his friends, to serve purposes directly contrary to his own principles, which are proved to be in strict accordance with ours throughout.

I have already said, that the Governor is not a responsible officer, even to the General Assembly, who appoint him. This position I now repeat, for the purpose of meeting more directly the arguments of gentlemen opposed to me. In sustaining this position, I beg leave to notice the actual organization of the Executive Council. This body is composed of eight members appointed by joint ballot of the Senate and House of Delegates. The appointing power can only remove two of them at the expiration of every three years. Each third year has on this account acquired the title of scratch year. Should every member of this body become at once obnoxious to the General Assembly; should all become rotten at the same time in this little *State of Denmark*, what can the Assembly do? At the end of three years they can remove two, and three years afterwards two more, and so on. Thus an operation of twelve years is required to displace eight Councillors, although every one of them has lost public confidence. In the mean time, those appointed to succeed the members removed may have become just as obnoxious as they. Practically, therefore, there may always be an Executive Council, possessing neither the confidence of the Assembly nor the country. Universal experience has proved, that when responsibility is divided among many agents, it ceases to be responsibility. This I consider a political truth of universal acceptation. If Councillors are not thus responsible to the Assembly, the gentleman from Richmond, (Mr. Nicholas,) triumphantly says, that this circumstance proves the *Executive* Department to be as independent as we claim it should be. But the gentleman forgets that our argument is, that the *Governor* is not an independent Executive officer, and therefore, not responsible for the manner in which the Executive functions are performed. The Council is, at least, too imperfectly responsible to the General Assembly, while to the people the members are not accountable at all. Yet these Councillors are a shield to the Governor, behind which he may skulk with the most perfect security. Not only is this evident from the Constitution itself, but the very explanation of the gentleman from Amelia, (Gov. Giles,) makes it more plain, if possible. According to the Constitution, and the practice thus explained, the Governor, except when acting as Commander-in-Chief, can do no Executive act, without the advice of Council. Without that advice he cannot even award a Commission on recommendation of the County Court. Is it not idle then, to hold him accountable for the omission to act, when the Council shall have omitted or refused to advise him to do his duty? But it is said, that he is not bound to act on the advice when given, and is therefore, independent of the Council. This may be true; yet when he is advised to violate the most important and sacred of his duties, and he follows that advice, all experience has taught us, that the advice he receives is his perfect and sure defence, and I have heard that defence made within these walls against a motion for an impeachment; and there are now sitting by me two members of this Convention who have given their votes against an impeachment on that very ground. If, therefore, the Governor is advised to commit a malfeasance in office, and he does it, he is not responsible, because the advice is his protection; and if he and the Council concur in the omission to discharge an important duty, he is not responsible for non-feasance, because he could not act without advice. From this view, it is manifest that the Governor of this Commonwealth is a mere creature of the General Assembly; a political irresponsible cypher, and the Council of State a perfect nuisance.

There is another view of the situation of the Executive Council which I feel it necessary to take, and in doing this I will beg to be understood as having no reference to any member of that body, past, present, or to come. In this view I will only have reference to the weakness of our nature; that weakness, of which I acknowledge myself a large partaker. Whoever feels himself exempt from frailties has not studied himself. Since the fall of our first parents we are indeed all exposed to be led astray, by the suggestions of interest, and even to be deluded through our virtues and the amiabilities of our natures. The situation of an Executive Councillor peculiarly exposes him to temptation. When he takes his seat at the board, he does not expect to be the victim of the first, or of any future scratch, as it is called. He hopes to hold his office for life or until he can obtain some higher preferment. His salary will not maintain him as a private gentleman in this city; much less will it sustain or enable him to provide for a family. He must follow the law, physic or some other laudable occupation, with the profits of which and the aid of his small salary he can get along. A Councillor, in fact, becomes to every intent and purpose, a citizen of Richmond, in which, surrounded by his friends, associates and dearest connexions, he intends to live and expects to die. The Councillor elected from the country, ceases to be its representative, and being blinded by the interests of the city, becomes, without his own knowledge, its advocate at the Council board. Should the Governor with advice of Council expend the public money too profusely on the Penitentiary, Armory,

Warehouse or James river, or other city interests, this profusion, although a practical evil, is not felt in the city. Nay, it is unknown there—those living within the circle and influence of these expenditures feel a benefit, without knowing or dreaming of any wrong. They have full confidence in their neighbours and friends, the Governor and members of the Council of State. It is not their business, nor their immediate interest to suspect or enquire after abuses, and believing that none exist, they are ready to join in the declaration, so often repeated here, that "all has gone on smoothly—all has worked well!" &c. If such be the tendency of things—if the residence of Councillors in the city, and of the habits formed there, withdraws their allegiance from the country and attaches them to city interests, it is not to be expected that where there is any competition between these and country interests, the latter will be fairly represented. Considering the large sums expended here by Government, and the incessant opportunities afforded for gain by improper disbursements, it cannot be doubted that by one means or another many have been drawn into temptation. The means of temptation are of no importance. The abuse is the evil, and it is our desire to prevent it.

[I wish to know, Mr. Chairman, whether, following the example of others, I am at liberty to refer to the remarks of the gentleman from Chesterfield in the Committee.

Here the Chair stated, that it could only be tolerated now, because such violations of Parliamentary practice had been permitted before.

Mr. Leigh said, that he was willing that any thing he had said any where should be the subject of remark.

The Chair, in its decision, disclaimed any reference to any individual.]

Mr. Doddridge resumed: I only desired to make a reference to certain remarks on our general tendency to corruption with our growth in years. The gentleman stated, that from his early manhood to the present day, he had marked its growth, and had especially traced its effects in the increasing love of office, and in the character of the means to which men resort to obtain it. There is much truth in the observation. I am not disposed to look altogether on the dark side of things. There is a German or Dutch writer of aphorisms, (I do not remember which,) who says, that a man who has known a great many villains is an old man, and that he who has not known them is still young, though in years he may be as old as Methusaleh. Our growing old in the knowledge of man, exposes more, his weakness to our view. Along the toilsome path of life we make so many discoveries of error and abuse, that we too easily give ourselves up to the distressing belief that all is growing in corruption around us—a belief, which may serve to increase our distrust, but should not be allowed to lessen our enjoyments or diminish our confidence in our friends and countrymen generally. Whether men of the present age are more corrupt than those of ages gone by, or not, is a question about which men may form different opinions. That human nature is the same every where and in all times, is a practical truth. Human nature both formerly and now, has been such that to insure order, discipline and integrity in the administration of public affairs, real, substantial, and not formal, responsibility, in public functionaries, is indispensable.

While discussing this subject, I understood the gentleman from Chesterfield as saying that he was acting for the Commonwealth. I have turned myself round to reflect what that Commonwealth can be, for which the gentleman had taken a stand so distinct from others. Who is this Commonwealth? Against whose assaults is it to be defended? According to some, it consists of certain freeholders alone; according to others, of all tax-paying citizens; while others again, compose it of the whole white population. This latter is the Commonwealth I am supporting. What then is that which the gentleman from Chesterfield defends? Is it the sixteen thousand freeholders who voted against a Convention?

[Mr. Leigh expressed some surprise at the manner in which the gentleman from Brooke was treating a somewhat idle remark which fell from him. He had considered the member from Frederick as preferring a bill of indictment against the Legislature, and he had set himself up for the defence, thus considering himself for the Commonwealth, in as much as he stood to defend the Commonwealth against charges of abuse of power by the Legislature.]

Mr. Doddridge: It is unnecessary for me to express the respect I feel for the public and private virtues of the gentleman from Chesterfield; that I believe is known to him, and he may rest assured that I would not willingly misunderstand him. In his remarks yesterday, that gentleman had enquired what act of abuse by the Executive could be pointed out and sustained, and I understood him to say he would yield the present question if one could be sustained, and moreover be thankful to any gentleman who would thus add to the knowledge he at present possessed of the manner of discharging Executive functions.

[Mr. Leigh said, he spoke of *usurpations* of power. He was not about to defend the Executive against *errors of judgment*.]

Mr. Doddridge: I understood the gentleman to say, an *abuse of power*, and I had then in my recollection a case, the production of which would entitle me to the gentleman's thanks. I will request the Secretary to read from the Journal of the House of Delegates in the session of 1808-9, the report of the Armory Committee from page 108 to 114, inclusive. (That report being read, Mr. D. resumed.)

Mr. Chairman,—Before that year, strong grounds existed for suspecting abuses, although the Executive reports of each successive year were of the most flattering character. It was supposed by some, that many of the arms were deficient in quality, and by others that their cost was greatly beyond that at which good arms of the same description could be purchased. These doubts increased every year; and every year, the Governor's message with the Armory report was calculated to dispel them. I refer to this report as furnishing record evidence of abuses which occupied a period of eight years of unexampled expenditure. I do not refer to it as censuring the Governors under whose administrations those abuses happened; nor any one else. My sole purpose is to shew, that while thousands and hundreds of thousands were in a course of expenditure on the Armory and its fixtures, and in the manufactory of arms, there was no system of care, accountability or supervisorship observed by the Executive Council. The Governors, (for, these proceedings occupied the whole administrations of several Executives,) were as unqualifiedly honest as any of their predecessors or successors. The fault was that of the Council, without whose advice the Governors could not act—Nay, could not act in one single instance otherwise than in conformity with that advice.

The officers of the Armory were of Executive appointment. The Executive was invested with full power to make all contracts, supervise their performance, and certify their execution with the sums due, to the Auditor. For payment of claims, the Auditor had no voucher except the Governor's warrant, drawn in pursuance of the advice of Council. In fine, the Executive power over these extraordinary expenditures was ample, and if our constitutional theory had been right, the Executive responsibility would have been commensurate with their power; instead of which, none was found to exist, except in the humble power of removing two members from the Council every three years.

From the report of the Committee it appears, that the Executive contracted with the Superintendent for finishing the buildings and fixtures within a limited time, and to pay the contractor for this labour in certain instalments as the work progressed. This contract was in writing, but being filed with the Council, it was in their power, and they permitted the contractor, who was Superintendent, to vary this contract from time to time to suit his own convenience, or as changes were suggested by his judgment; these changes resulted in immense additions to the contract under the head of "extra work." These alterations were never reduced to writing, because of the unlimited confidence reposed in the Superintendent.

Thus, public moneys were paid away in immense sums on contracts between the Executive Council and the contractor, of which contracts neither the Auditor, General Assembly, nor people, had any evidence; nor was there any record, book, voucher, or paper of any description kept, at the Armory, in the Council chamber or Auditor's office, by which the accounting committees of the Senate and House of Delegates could detect an excess in payment, if any existed. The Superintendent, in this "extra work," employed the labour of his own slaves, and certified the number of days and the amount of pay; and this certificate was the only evidence on which the advice of Council was founded. An illiterate man was examined before that committee, whose investigation was the most laborious I ever witnessed. This man testified that he kept the number of days' work on small slips of paper which he returned to the Superintendent, who made up (what he supposed to be) the results on sheets of paper, which he certified or deposed to. These sheets constituted the only evidence on which the Council advised payment of something like fourteen thousand days' work. When the committee of investigation called for evidences of this labour, neither the sheets containing the general results, nor the slips of paper, nor book, nor voucher of any kind could be found; nor does there exist to this hour one letter, or vestige of a letter, whereby this account can be either refuted or supported. The Journal of that session contains (I think in page 124 or 125,) a proposition to pass a resolution of censure with a view to an impeachment. That resolution was neither adopted nor rejected. It was postponed; and it was on that occasion I heard the advice of Council urged as a defence of the Governors as to all these transactions; and it was this defence, that induced at least two members of this Convention to vote for the postponement of that resolution.

A bill providing against future abuses of this kind grew out of the Armory report, and passed both Houses, which is now the law. This law may be found in the first volume of the Revised Code of 1819, page 130.

That law divested the Executive of the power of appointing Armory officers. It provided that *in future* no money should be drawn from the Treasury, except in pursuance of *written contracts*, and that all contracts whereby money should be so drawn, should be filed with the Auditor of Public Accounts, instead of the Executive Council. To the best of my recollection the bill as it passed the lower House had a clause to this effect, "that the officers of the Armory be removed." This clause contained a direct censure, which was unnecessary, and I believe it was stricken out on my motion. Here, then, is record evidence of the irresponsibility of the Governor to the General Assembly, and of the entire independence of the Executive Council, of all the world. They are convicted of negligence, carelessness and gross improvidence in the money transactions of Government committed to their controul, through a long series of years. For this, what did the Assembly do? Why, took from them the power of appointment—they disabled them from making or varying a contract otherwise than by *writing, and they deprived them of the custody of their own contracts when made.* They imposed many other restraints, as may be seen by the law referred to. Here the confidence of the General Assembly was completely withdrawn, yet they had *to content themselves with the slow operation of the scratch.* Such is the Executive responsibility of which the gentleman, who is now at its head, has boasted so much, and of which, he and others have so often declared, that, "it works so well that all has gone on smoothly."

At the time of the investigation to which I have alluded, a new Governor was appointed, of whom I would more particularly speak, but that his son is present, a member of this body. The Armory report shewed that the Superintendent claimed yet, a small balance, the payment of which had been suspended during the investigation. It was at the time, a current report in this city, that the Council, indignant at what they heard within these walls, retired to their chamber and advised the payment of that balance, and that the new Governor refused to act on that advice. This part I cannot assert to be true, as I did not enquire into it. But this I can assert, that the citizens of Richmond appeared to be as much excited against the investigation of the Armory Committee *then*, as they are against some of the efforts made in this Convention *now*. I will mention another fact. Governor Tyler, after having heard what passed in the Hall of Delegates, appointed a committee of men, commonly called here, back-woods-men, to examine the rifles. They tried them, and found them as they said, more dangerous to those who would use them than those against whom they were employed. Many pistols were reported to be unfit for use, on account of largeness of calibre, being made out of the barrels of muskets, bursted in the proof.

These remarks, Mr. Chairman, I thought it my reasonable duty to make; they are crude I know. It has been but a short time since the report of the Executive Committee was taken up, and I found it necessary to examine the Legislative Journal of 1808, rather than trust my frail memory.

Mr. Leigh rose in reply, and went into a history of the causes which led to the appointment of the Committee of Investigation. He referred to the determination of a party to put down the Armory; the means resorted to to libel the Superintendent; the unfair and oppressive course which was pursued in denying him an opportunity of defence: he then went on to give a farther history of the suit at law instituted against that officer; the elaborate trial of the cause before the General Court of the Commonwealth; the ample admission of the testimony from all quarters, and the result in his honorable and triumphant acquittal. His innocence was farther confirmed by his poverty. This one fact, he considered as an answer to Mr. D's. whole argument: for, if the Superintendent (Major John Clarke) had been guilty of no injury to the public, the Council had not permitted an injury to be done, and so were free from the charge which had been brought against them. Mr. L. defended Mr. Clarke (who resides in his District) with ardent zeal, and challenged the world to disprove his statement.

Mr. Doddridge rejoined. Major Clarke's acquittal did not touch his argument, or weaken it in the least. He had not charged him with malfeasance, but the Council with the grossest negligence; and though Major Clarke's honesty saved the State from injury at his hands, no thanks were due to those who had left power in his hands by which he might have depredated to a vast extent upon the public money. He knew Clarke well, and was his personal friend.

Mr. Cooke, after adverting to what had fallen sportively (and once more seriously) from Mr. Leigh, as to defending the Commonwealth in an indictment to be brought by him against the past course of legislation, said, that if he had not before been convinced of the imprudence of the pledge extorted from him to bring such an indictment, what he had now witnessed would be sufficient to admonish him, that to prefer any further charges would be imprudent indeed. He, therefore gave notice, that the day for the trying of that indictment would never come. He was far from blaming his friend from Brooke for what he had done, and as far from blaming his friend from Chesterfield, for his eloquent defence of an injured man; but he plainly saw, that if such charges, with their specifications, were to be tried here, the Convention would sit, not only till Christmas, but till Christmas of next year.

(Here Mr. Randolph's *voice* was heard to sav. "Enter then a *nolle prosequi*.")

The British Isles

Modern London

An air view looking northeastwards down the river Thames. In the centre foreground is Westminster Abbey with the Houses of Parliament to the right. Left foreground the dome of the Methodist Central Hall and numerous government buildings on each side of Whitehall. The bridges are Westminster, Charing Cross (railway), Waterloo and Blackfriars. Across the river are the County Hall (headquarters of the Greater London Council), Waterloo Station and the 1962 skyscraper of Shell Centre. In the centre distance St Paul's Cathedral can just be seen.

The British Isles

A Geographic and Economic Survey

L. Dudley Stamp
C.B.E., D.Lit., D.Sc., LL.D., Ekon.D.

and

Stanley H. Beaver
M.A., F.R.G.S., Professor of Geography, University of Keele

SIXTH EDITION

St. Martin's Press, New York

For information, write: St. Martin's Press, Inc., 175 Fifth Avenue, New York, N.Y. 10010
Printed in Great Britain
Library of Congress Catalog Card Number: 70–174725
New edition first published in the United States of America in 1971

Affiliated publishers: Macmillan & Company, Limited, London—also at Bombay, Calcutta, Madras and Melbourne—The Macmillan Company of Canada, Limited, Toronto

Contents

Preface to the sixth edition		vii
1	The position of Britain	1
2	The physiographic evolution of the British Isles	9
3	The physiography of the British Isles	26
4	British weather and climate	59
5	The inland waters of the British Isles	88
6	The soils of Britain	103
7	The natural vegetation of Britain	118
8	Forestry and afforestation	134
9	Land use in the British Isles	148
10	Agriculture	160
11	Agricultural regions of Scotland	229
12	Agricultural regions of England and Wales	236
13	The British fisheries	254
14	Fuel and power	277
15	Mining industries other than coal and iron	356
16	Iron and steel	369
17	Iron and steel: the secondary industries	418
18	The non-ferrous metal industries	459
19	The textile industries: woollen and worsted	488
20	The textile industries: cotton	525
21	The textile industries: other textiles	554
22	The chemical industries	578
23	Miscellaneous industries	599
24	The peopling of the British Isles	625
25	The evolution of the form and functions of British villages and towns	642

26 London 663
27 The growth of communications 689
28 The seaports of Great Britain 717
29 The Irish Republic 762
30 Northern Ireland 791
31 The foreign trade of the United Kingdom 801
References and further reading 815
Index 835

Preface to the sixth edition

The death of Sir Dudley Stamp in 1966 deprived this book of its senior author and certainly delayed the production of this sixth edition. The writing of economic geography becomes increasingly difficult in this age of rapidly changing technology and fluctuating economic progress, and when in addition nearly two years may elapse between the completion of a revision and its publication the task of keeping a book up-to-date is almost impossible. So much has happened in Britain since the fifth edition was prepared in 1962, that certain sections of the book have had to be completely re-written; and some re-arrangement of the material has been undertaken as well. A new chapter on Fuel and Power includes the former chapter on Coal plus sections on gas, coke, thermal and hydroelectricity that were formerly scattered through other chapters. The chapter on Chemical Industries has been completely re-cast.

I am grateful to various friends and colleagues for substantial contributions to the new text. Professor J. T. Coppock has completely revised the chapters on Agriculture, Mr Trevor Thomas re-wrote the section on Coal, and Dr T. D. Kennea re-drafted the Fisheries chapter. Mr T. W. Freeman gave much good advice on the chapters relating to Ireland. Mr S. W. Rogers assisted in the revision of the Forestry chapter. Professor I. T. Millar helped me to sort out the problems of the chemical industries.

Other chapters to which substantial alterations, necessitated by changing technological and economic circumstances, have been made, are Iron and Steel and Miscellaneous Industries. The Textile chapters presented a special problem in that, especially in Lancashire, these industries have altered almost beyond recognition through contraction and the substitution of man-made fibres. So the chapters on Cotton and Wool have been left as studies in historical geography, with additions explaining some of the modern developments.

Over sixty new maps and diagrams have been included, and for the drawing of these I am indebted to my technical staff, Mr G. Barber and Miss E. Smith. The resources of the Statistics Library at the London School of Economics were tapped for me by Mr L. Baker, whose help is gratefully acknowledged.

This edition appears at a time when the process of metrication is in full swing. At the risk of cluttering up the text with figures, it has been felt advisable to give English equivalents in brackets after the metric measurements. Perhaps when the seventh edition is called for, students and the public at large will be sufficiently familiar with the metric scales to allow the English equivalents to be dropped.

Keele S. H. BEAVER
August 1970

Acknowledgements

We are grateful to the following for permission to reproduce photographs:—

Aerofilms Library Ltd: Frontispiece and Plates 20, 21, 23–25, 29–31; Peter Baker: Plates 6, 8, 27; Barnaby's Picture Library: Plates 16, 28; V. Blankenburgs: Plate 2; British Petroleum Co. Ltd: Plate 32; British Railways: Plates 26, 33; British Steel Corporation: Plates 17, 19; Central Electricity Generating Board: Plates 11, 12; The Forestry Commission: Plates 1, 3; National Coal Board: Plate 9; North of Scotland Hydro-electric Board: Plate 13; John Topham Ltd: Plates 4, 5. Plates 14, 15, 18 and 22 are by S. H. Beaver.

1
The position of Britain

No philosophy of British history can be entirely true which does not take account of the facts of the position of Britain. So wrote Sir Halford Mackinder over half a century ago in that book *Britain and the British Seas*, which must for ever remain a landmark in the progress of thought in this country, for it marks an important stage in the resurrection from the dead of the forgotten or discredited science of geography—the study of the earth as the home of man and of the interrelationship between man and his environment. It will be the purpose of this book to examine the natural environment afforded by the British Isles for their human inhabitants; to examine the advantages and the disadvantages of that environment; to analyse the natural resources of value to man which are proper to these islands; to see the use which the inhabitants have made of those resources, and so to lead up to a study of the present position—the capital which has been accumulated in consequence of past exploitation, and the outlook for the future in the utilisation of the resources which remain.

The philosophers of ancient Greece knew well that the earth was a sphere, and 'every schoolboy knows' of the experiments of Eratosthenes by which the actual size of the sphere was measured. But the known world of the ancients occupied but a small portion of the surface of the sphere. It centred round the Mediterranean Sea. To the south it was bounded by the Sahara, beyond which there were but legendary lands. On the southeast it extended to the Indian Ocean, to the east so far as Central Asia, beyond which again lay the mysterious land of Cathay known only because of the silks and porcelain brought by traders to Mediterranean Europe. On the north-western margin of the known world lay the islands of Britain. The name 'Albion', which is still sometimes applied to the larger of the two islands, perpetuates the point of view of the ancients. The British Isles were approached and explored from the Continent, and it was the white chalk cliffs of Dover, facing as they do the land of Gaul, which suggested a name for the whole country. The Celtic lands of Ireland, Wales and Scotland lay on the outermost fringe, so little known that in many of the ancient maps Scotland is represented as an island. Throughout early Christian or medieval times the marginal or terminal position of the British Isles became accentuated as the scientific concepts of the ancients became lost during the Dark Ages. The fantastic maps of the medieval monks show

Jerusalem as the centre of a flat earth separated by the blue curtain of the sky from the celestial Jerusalem above, but again with the British Isles on the margin and doubtless near the dangerous 'edge' of the world.

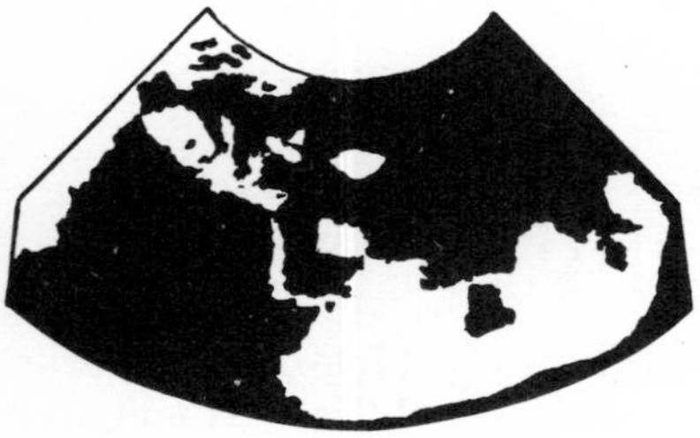

FIG. 1. Map showing the terminal or marginal position occupied by Britain in the world as known to the ancient Greeks and medieval geographers. (*After Ptolemy*)

The year 1492 not only marks the discovery of the Americas by Columbus, but it marks the end of the dominance of the countries of the Mediterranean basin. It released the British Isles from the disadvantage of being on the fringe of world politics and placed London in the centre of the land of the globe, and the British Isles in a dominating position relative to all the world. This reorientation was not the result of an accidental discovery. Columbus's voyage was based on a firm belief that the earth was a sphere and that it was consequently possible to sail round it. Anyone holding such a view at that time did so not only in opposition to public opinion but also in constant danger of being branded 'heretical'. One may wonder why the land on the far side of the Atlantic remained so long unknown to Europeans.

FIG. 2. The world position of Britain today—the centre of the 'land hemisphere'

True the coasts of Greenland, of Labrador, and of Newfoundland were doubtless known at a much earlier date to Icelandic and Norwegian fishermen; but however attractive the fisheries might be, the character of the lands was not such as to cause enthusiastic wonder. Flowing southwards, parallel to the coast of Greenland, is a cold current bearing a constant stream of icebergs from the Arctic, and whilst a vessel may sight land, the crossing of this belt of cold water and actual landing on the shores is a matter of extreme difficulty, and climatic conditions are obviously not those to attract such attempts. The navigators of the Mediterranean, a sea which, with its great extent and its treacherous sudden storms, was no mean school for navigators, knew that when they passed through the Pillars of Hercules, or the Strait of Gibraltar, and turned southwards they were in the belt of the constant northeast trade winds, that would always blow them *from* known lands and would allow the venturous mariner no hope of return. Over the north of France and the south of Britain, the winds, though variable, were on the whole from the southwest; but to venture with a sailing vessel of a few tons, which could be victualled only for a limited period, merely to test the theory that one could go outwards by the northeast wind, and at some far distant point find it possible to get in the current of wind which was on the whole southwesterly, required the efforts of a dominating and fearless leader, and Columbus's own sailors nearly lost faith in their leader before land was sighted. Once the discovery had been made no one can fail to be impressed by the rapidity of events which followed—the exploration and settlement of the American continent—and by the consequent opportunity afforded to those countries of Europe which faced the Atlantic and of which the British Isles formed one. The Mediterranean became a backwater, its commerce and its cultures decayed, and it was not until 1869–70 that the opening of the Suez Canal afforded a resuscitation of its ancient trading glory. By that time the world position of Britain was too firmly established to be shaken by the revived importance of the Mediterranean. Instead, Britain profited by yet another route to the Far East.

It may be thought that in this modern world, with all the improvements in transport and communications which have characterised the last hundred years, position would be of little importance to these islands. Such, however, is far from being the truth. An attempt has been made in Fig. 3 to show facts which can much more readily be appreciated by a glance at a globe. From the thickly populated industrialised countries of northern Europe to the corresponding area of urban development on the far side of the Atlantic, characterised by the northeastern United States and by the St Lawrence Basin of Canada, the shortest route (the Great Circle route) lies across the British Isles. Presuming that the proverbial crow really does take the shortest route, that sagacious bird bound either from New York or from Montreal for any one of some fifteen or sixteen capital cities in Europe would, of necessity, have to pass over the British Isles. Actually, all ocean traffic from the ports of the northern seaboard of continental Europe bound for North America has to make a detour to escape the British Isles and passes down the English Channel. The vessels are not taken out of their way by dropping anchor for a short time at one of the ports on the south coast of England, for example Southampton.

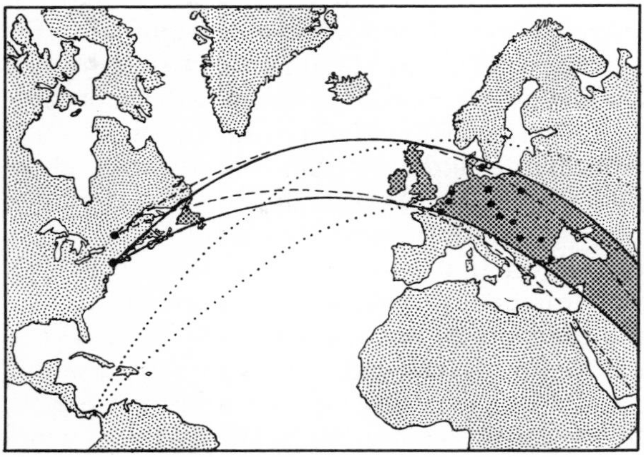

FIG. 3. Great circle routes from Europe to North America

Within the two dark lines are the shortest routes between New York and the capitals of European states marked by dots; in each case the shortest route passes through the British Isles. The pecked line shows the same relationship for Montreal; the dotted line for the Panama Canal.

The importance of constructing a Channel tunnel is once again before the public eye. The scheme is interesting geographically because if the tunnel were completed a British port, such as Liverpool, would almost automatically become the railhead of the whole European system—providing a new route for passengers and mails from Europe to America. However, where speed is important airways have replaced both seaways and railways. It is an interesting experiment to take a globe and a piece of string and to notice the shortest distance between Europe and various other parts of the world, and also to calculate the saving of distance—not to say the saving of time—which results by the utilisation of new routes. In any case they all serve to stress the importance of the position of Britain at present and the importance which its position is likely to maintain in the future. The modern development of trans-Atlantic air transport has already demonstrated this. Eastward bound it is not difficult to make Montreal or New York to London in one hop and from New York London may be bypassed en route to a continental airport. The westward flight, however, was often a battle against headwinds and convenient stops are afforded by Prestwick (Ayrshire) or Shannon (near Limerick), Goose Bay (Labrador) or Gander (Newfoundland). Not infrequently surprised passengers found themselves touching down in Iceland. In recent years however the increasing range and speed of aircraft have to some extent altered the position. In 1956 Scandinavian Air Services (SAS) established a regular passenger service from Copenhagen to Tokyo via the North Pole as shown in Fig. 4. Canadian Pacific Airlines make the journey Vancouver to Amsterdam with only one stop. British Overseas Airways Corporation (BOAC) pioneered with jet-liners in 1952 doubling previous speeds of 320–480 kilometres (200–300 miles) per hour. The jumbo-jet, in service in the nineteen-seventies, ferries 500 passengers at over 960 kilometres (600 miles) per hour. One strategic result is that Europe and North America now have polar frontiers to guard. In 1958 for the first time more passengers crossed the Atlantic by air than by sea: each year since the air lead has increased.

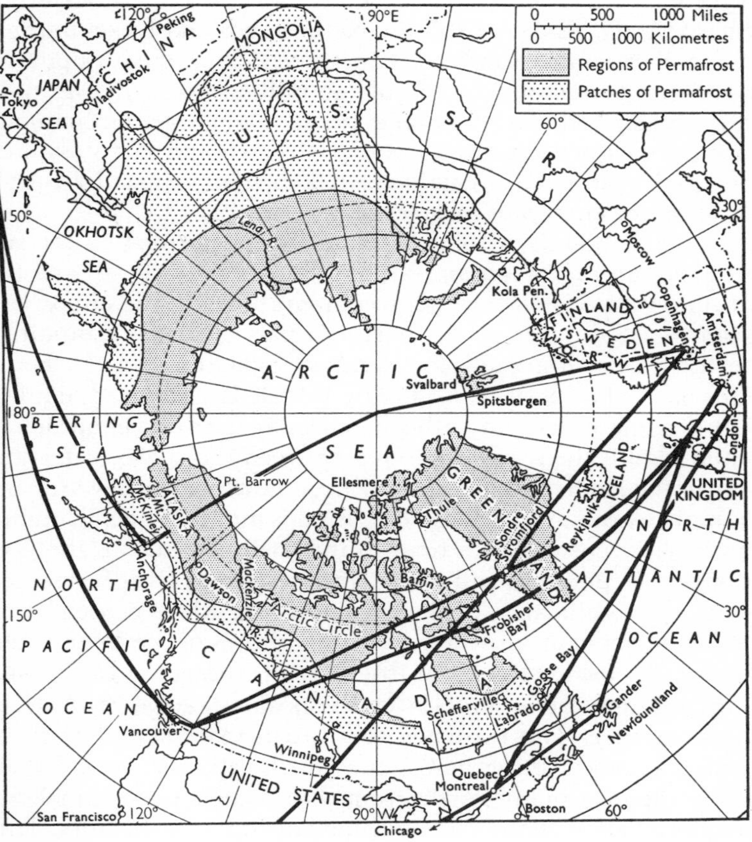

FIG. 4. Trans-Atlantic and trans-Polar air routes

The world relations of Britain reflect in many ways her world position. If, by virtue of situation, the British Isles belong to the Continent of Europe, it is still not too much to say that the British Isles do not really belong to

Europe. Viewed from the other side of the Atlantic, it seems obvious that Britain would form an essential unit in a United States of Europe or Western European Union. But the countries of continental Europe are more 'foreign' to the people of Britain than are countries overseas more distant but more closely related, such as the United States of America and, still more, the countries of the British Commonwealth. Some years ago Professor C. B. Fawcett carried out an interesting calculation in studying the direction of foreign mails from the British Isles. Eliminating business correspondence, the mail to America and our overseas dominions was overwhelmingly more important than that to the countries of continental Europe. Blood ties, linguistic ties, social ties and economic ties are with the new lands of the world. However, after six countries of the heart of Europe —West Germany, Italy, France, Belgium, Netherlands and Luxemburg— had linked themselves as the European Economic Community, popularly called the European Common Market, of 300 million people it was difficult for Britain to ignore certain advantages which might accrue from membership. Negotiations, opened in 1961, were protracted and many conflicting views emerged before the breakdown in February, 1963. In 1967 a further application for entry was unsuccessful.

The British Isles lie mainly within the quadrilateral formed by the two lines of longitude 0° and 10° West and the two lines of latitude 50° and 60° North. In latitude the position is roughly comparable with the almost uninhabitable lands of Labrador, to the northern part of British Columbia, and again to the almost uninhabitable lands of Sakhalin and the Kamschatka Peninsula of the coasts of Asia. The British Isles, indeed, enjoy a more favourable climate than any other land so far from the equator. To the north of the islands the sea way is open between the coasts of Iceland and of Norway to the Arctic Ocean, and a constant drift of warm water and of correspondingly warm air passes by these islands into that open channel. We have long been accustomed to refer to this drift of water as the Gulf Stream, and if purists prefer to call it the North Atlantic Drift it does not alter the fact of the significance of the phenomenon. More especially, of course, is the fact significant in winter, since the shores of the British Isles lie in the winter gulf of warmth. Apart from the advantages of world position, there are numerous advantages from the position of the British Isles more local in character. The existence of a broad Continental Shelf on which the warm waters drifting across the North Atlantic are piled up ensures not only the maximum benefit from these waters in the amelioration of climate, but it accentuates the movement of water by the tides. Thus our ports, always free from ice, are kept free from silt by the strong tidal scour, while the shallow seas on the Continental Shelf afford the richest fishing grounds in the world, where variety, caused by the constant movement and mixing of the waters, is the spice of life in the fish world. The English Channel, narrowing eastwards to the Strait of Dover, which is only twenty-one miles (under 34 kilometres) wide at the narrowest part, separates the south of England from France. The North Sea lies between Britain and Holland, Germany, Denmark and Norway.[1] Whatever may be the opinion of travellers crossing the 'silver streak', these separating seas are a great advantage to the islands rather than the reverse. The part they played in saving Britain from invasion during the Second World War is too well known to need emphasis. But Britain is double-faced. The ports on her southern and eastern shores face the most important and most developed parts of northern Europe. The embouchure of the Thames is opposite that of Europe's most important river, the Rhine. On the other hand, Britain's west coast ports face the most developed parts of America. This is again symbolic of the intermediate position which Britain occupies, political, financial, and commercial, between America on the one hand and the countries of Europe on the other.

Note

In citing statistics and statements relative to the British Isles the greatest care must be taken to note the area to which reference is made in each specific case. The island of Great Britain consists of three countries—Scotland in the north, Wales in a part of the west, and England occupying the remainder. England, Scotland and Wales have been joined under one monarch since 1603; but whilst England and Wales are usually considered together for many purposes, Scotland is distinct. Thus the Ministry of Agriculture, Fisheries and Food refers to England and Wales but not to Scotland. Statistics and details which are published by this and other Ministries refer, therefore, to England and Wales only. Since 1920 Ireland has been divided into Northern Ireland and the Irish Free State (now known as the Irish Republic or Eire). Northern Ireland has a parliament of its own, but is otherwise closely united to Great Britain. But the Republic of Ireland is an independent republic. Thus 'United Kingdom' used to mean the United Kingdom of Great Britain and Ireland, now it means the United Kingdom of Great Britain and Northern Ireland. The distinction is important when comparing pre-1914 with later statistics. For many purposes the Isle of Man, with a parliament (or House of Keys) of its own, is not part of the United Kingdom. Again, the laws of Great Britain do not apply to the Channel Islands unless such application is specifically laid down and approved by the islands. The table on p. 8 is given for reference purposes.

The table shows that the total area of the British Isles, including the Isle of Man and the Channel Isles, is 313 076 square kilometres (120 879 square miles) excluding inland water. This area is equivalent to about one twenty-fifth of continental United States. Out of this total the larger island of Great Britain is roughly 230 500 square kilometres (89 000 square miles)

1. Notice the shape of the North Sea. It is relatively narrow at its northern end, and the Shetland Islands lie almost halfway between the north of Scotland and the coast of Norway.

	AREA (SQ. KM)	AREA (SQ. MILES)	POPULATION 1921	POPULATION 1931	POPULATION 1951	POPULATION 1961	POPULATION 1968[3]
England	131 763	50 874	35 681 019	37 789 738	41 147 938	43 430 972	45 873 000
Wales	19 337	7 466	2 205 680	2 158 193	2 596 986	2 640 632	2 720 000
Scotland	78 748	30 405	4 882 497	4 842 554	5 095 969	5 178 490	5 187 000
Isle of Man	572	221	60 284	49 338	55 213	48 151	50 423[5]
Channel Islands	194	75	90 230	93 061	157 983	104 378	104 378[6]
Northern Ireland	13 564	5 237[1]	1 256 000[3]	1 243 000[3]	1 369 579	1 423 127	1 502 000
Republic of Ireland	67 897	26 601[1]	2 971 992[2]	2 965 854[4]	2 958 878	2 834 000[3]	2 884 002[7]

[1] Excluding water areas. [2] 1926. [3] Estimated. [4] 1936.
[5] 1965 census. [6] 1961 census. [7] 1966 census.

with over 53 million people, the smaller island 82 900 square kilometres (32 000 square miles) with about 4.4 million people. The population of the United Kingdom of Great Britain and Northern Ireland with the Isle of Man and the Channel Islands passed the 50 million mark about 1950—on its total area of 244 179 square kilometres (94 278 square miles). The census population of the whole United Kingdom in 1966 was 53 788 000. The figures of area given on p. 151 are smaller because inland water is excluded.

The Registrar-General's mid-year estimates for 1968 gave the population of the United Kingdom as 55 282 500.

2
The physiographic evolution of the British Isles

The present surface features of the British Isles, as well as their relationship to the features of the neighbouring parts of the Continent of Europe, are the reflection of the long and complicated geological history of the area. Geology has been described as geographical evolution, but, conversely, the existing physical geography of a country is the result of its geological evolution from the dawn of geological time to the present day.

The geologist has divided geological time into at least five great eras and each of those eras into a number of periods. On broad lines the rocks which were laid down in each of those periods can be made to tell the story of the earth's history. Each period was characterised by its own sets of animals and plants, the remains of which have been entombed in the rocks and can be found today as fossils. Nor are these episodes in the past history of the earth merely of academic interest. Whether it be in the search for minerals of economic importance or the study of the disposition of these deposits when found in its relation to economic costs of mining; whether it be the study of the rocks of the earth's crust in relationship to the soils which they afford or in relationship to construction on the earth's surface, the studies of the geologist are of fundamental importance. No excuse, therefore, need be made for considering in this chapter the physiographic evolution of the British Isles, by attempting to trace the history of these islands from the earliest times to the present.

The five eras—the Pre-Cambrian (in the rocks of which earliest era no remains of life are commonly found), Primary or Paleozoic, Secondary or Mesozoic, Tertiary or Kainozoic (Cenozoic), and, finally, the Quaternary or Modern Period—are the great divisions which the geologist has made in the geological time scale. Subdivisions of these are shown in the diagram overleaf. Further subdivisions are of course made, but those listed are of fundamental importance in that they are in common use for numerous purposes.

Little is known of the geography of Pre-Cambrian times. The rocks of this great era found in the British Isles fall into three main groups:

(*a*) Crystalline or metamorphic rocks, the descriptive name 'metamorphic' indicating that they have changed their form: as the result of heat and pressure they have become recrystallised. They are hard, resistant to

ERA	PERIODS OR systems		EARTH MOVEMENTS	IGNEOUS ACTIVITY	CHARACTERS OF ROCKS AND SOILS
QUATERNARY	RECENT PLEISTOCENE AND ICE AGE				Drift, alluvium and gravel deposits.
TERTIARY OR CENOZOIC	PLIOCENE			W. Scotland & Antrim Volcanics Mourne Mts Granite	Crags of East Anglia and some gravels.
	MIOCENE		Alpine Earth Movements		Almost absent in Britain.
	OLIGOCENE				Sands and clays, where mixed giving good loams; clays give heavy soils, sands very light (London and Hampshire Basins).
	EOCENE				
SECONDARY OR MESOZOIC	CRETACEOUS				Great mass of chalk forms the upper part; sands, sandstones and clays in lower part.
	JURASSIC	OOLITES			Alternations of sandstone or limestone (giving cuestas) and clays (giving vales).
		LIAS			
	RHAETIC				
	TRIASSIC				Upper Keuper rocks give wet red soil of Midlands. Lower Bunter sandstone, poorer sandy soil.
PRIMARY OR PALEOZOIC	PERMIAN		Armorican Earth Movements	Cornish Leinster Granites &c.	Magnesian limestone and red marl giving fair to good red soil.
	CARBONIFEROUS	COAL MEASURES			Sandstones and shales often very fair soil.
		MILLSTONE GRIT			Grit or sandstone; uplands, poor soil.
		CARBONIFEROUS LIMESTONE			Limestone and sandstone forming uplands except in Ireland.
	DEVONIAN		Caledonian Earth Movements	Many Volcanic Rocks, Newer Scottish Granites	Upper part of Old Red Marl often fertile red soil. Lower part of Old Red Sandstones, flaggy, poor soil.
	SILURIAN				Hard old sedimentary rocks, slates, grit, sandstones, etc. Poor siliceous soils. Igneous rocks stand out as hill masses.
	ORDOVICIAN			Lavas &c. Wales & Lake District	
	CAMBRIAN				
PRE-CAMBRIAN			Charnian & Other Movements	Older Scottish Granites	Hard metamorphic and crystalline rocks. Poor siliceous soil. Upper part with sandstones.

Table of geological time periods

weathering, and, except where the continuous action of the agents of denudation through untold ages has slowly but surely worn them down almost to sea-level, they tend to form hill masses. It used to be thought that these hard crystalline rocks represented the original crust of the earth. But in one area after another the Pre-Cambrian crystalline rocks have been shown to represent sediments deposited on a solid crust of an already existing world and which were later much altered.

(*b*) Ancient volcanic, and other igneous rocks, of the same period.

(*c*) Sedimentary rocks, such as sandstones and shales, which have suffered less alteration but which are nevertheless older than the most ancient of the rocks which have yielded fossils.

It seems clear that in Pre-Cambrian times there were at least several great periods of folding or earth movement and volcanic activity, and that the earliest rocks were highly folded and ridged up into great mountain chains, before the deposition of those sandstones and other sediments mentioned under (*c*). Thus it is possible, for example in the northwest Highlands of Scotland, to see the way in which the coarse red sandstones known as the Torridonian and which are themselves Pre-Cambrian, rest in hollows amongst the still older mountains of Pre-Cambrian times. One system of folding developed in some of the small ancient blocks of the Midlands of England, notably in Charnwood Forest, has produced northwest to southeast or 'Charnian' folds.

During the first three periods of the Paleozoic era, that is during the Cambrian, the Ordovician, and the Silurian, the earth was inhabited almost exclusively by lowly creatures which had not yet attained the dignity of possessing a backbone. It is possible that during most of these periods a great land mass lay to the northwest of Scotland, and that a broad sea trough ran across the British Isles. At certain times islands occupied part of Britain and, particularly during the Ordovician, volcanic activity was rife. Some of the volcanoes were submarine and poured out their lavas on the sea floor; others were volcanoes of an explosive type which threw out huge quantities of ashes. Thus we find that the deposits of the Cambrian, the Ordovician, and the Silurian periods are, for the most part, marine sediments, originally clays, silts, sands and coarser deposits; but interbedded with these are found the lavas of contemporary volcanoes and beds of ashes. Intruded amongst the sediments are other masses which came up in a molten condition from the lower layers of the earth's crust and which solidified before reaching the surface. Most of the old sediments have become hardened. The clays have become hard shales and slates, the silts and sands have become sandstones, quartzites and other hard rocks, so that again the sediments of these three periods tend to form hill and mountain masses, and to occur in what will later be described as the Highland Zone of the British Isles. The various igneous rocks are even more resistant to the agents of weathering than are the sediments, and many of the highest mountains of the British Isles are formed of the ancient lavas which were extruded at this time, familiar examples being Snowdon and Cader Idris in North Wales.

Towards the close of Silurian times occurred one of the great periods of mountain building which from time to time have played an enormous part in the determination of the present surface features of the earth. It was during this great period of earth movements that the Highlands of Scotland

Fig. 5. The geography of the British Isles in Devonian times

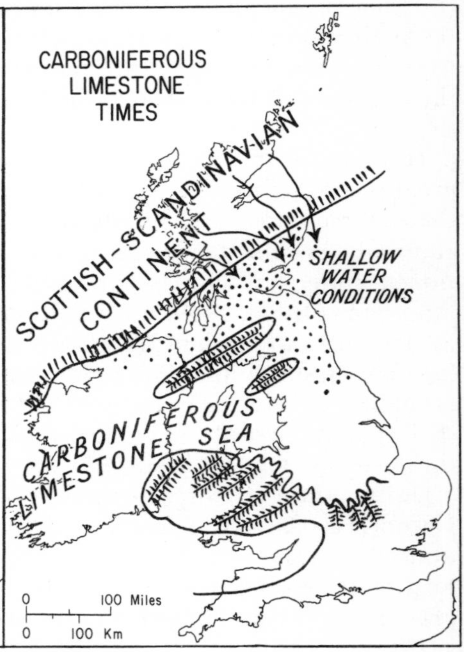

Fig. 6. The geography of Carboniferous Limestone times

and the Southern Uplands were formed, and because of its great importance in Scotland the period of folding and the folds produced are known as Caledonian. The Caledonian system of earth movements in these islands resulted, for the most part, in the formation of a series of mountain chains which ran from southwest to northeast. So characteristic is this direction for the mountains that it is known commonly as the Caledonian trend. This dominant trend is very clear in the mountains of the Highlands of Scotland, in the Southern Uplands and their continuation into Ireland, in the mountains of north Wales, and to a less extent is apparent, but nevertheless important, in the Lake District. The Caledonian earth movements commenced towards the end of the Silurian and they were prolonged into the succeeding Devonian period, and the sea-trough of Silurian times disappeared. Most of the British Isles became a land mass, but between the great ridges of mountains were deep mountain-girt valleys or basins. In these torrential streams from the recently formed mountains deposited great thicknesses of coarse conglomerates and sandstones. These are the deposits which we know under the famous name of Old Red Sandstone, and it is remarkable that the Old Red Sandstone deposits often occupy hollows even at the present day, particularly in Scotland. It was only over the south of England that there existed contemporaneously a sea, and in this sea were deposited the Devonian rocks—muds, sands and silts with local limestones—which form the Devonian Series in Devon, Cornwall and the adjoining parts of Somerset and are found also over areas in South Wales. In South Wales and the Welsh border they mingle with deposits of Old Red Sandstone type. It may be that the characteristically red colour of the Old Red Sandstone reflects desert conditions in the neighbouring mountains. Not unnaturally the few fossils which are found in the Old Red Sandstone are of fish, the first backboned creatures (which lived in the transient lakes of the great mountain valleys) and primitive land plants. The enormous thickness of many of the Old Red Sandstone deposits testifies to the rapidity with which the Caledonian mountains were worn down by the agents of atmospheric weathering. Towards the close of the Devonian period the mountains were already mere remnants of their former selves and they yielded only fine sand and red mud or marl. The beginning of the succeeding period—the Carboniferous—was marked by a great invasion by the sea of practically the whole area. The sea flowed into the pre-existing mountain basins, except in the north where there still existed the great continental mass, the remnants of which now form the Highlands of Scotland. Over England and Wales and much of Ireland the mountains had been worn down to such an extent that they yielded but little sediment. In the waters of the Carboniferous sea there flourished a wealth of corals and other organisms which are favoured by clear water; and so the deposits laid down were limestone (Carboniferous Limestone). The name once used for Carboniferous Limestone was Mountain Limestone indicating the association of this limestone with mountain or upland areas, particularly of the Pennines. But the great continent which extended from Scotland to Scandinavia yielded sediments which prevented the extensive growth of clearwater organisms in what is now the north of England and the Midland Valley of Scotland. So here one does not see the great thicknesses of Carboniferous Limestone found farther south; instead there are thin beds of limestone in a mass of sandstones and shales. These sandstones and shales represent material brought down by rivers draining from the northern continent. In the middle of the Carboniferous period a huge river gradually began to overwhelm the British area and to spread its great deposits of sand on top of the limestone which had been just formed. We have really in Britain the formation of an enormous delta, and because of the former use of the sandstone of these deltaic deposits as millstones the deposits are known as the Millstone Grit. The Millstone Grit delta extended from Scotland right across the Midlands of England as far as an island, or perhaps a peninsula from an European mass, known as St George's Land, which extended from central Wales through the heart of England.

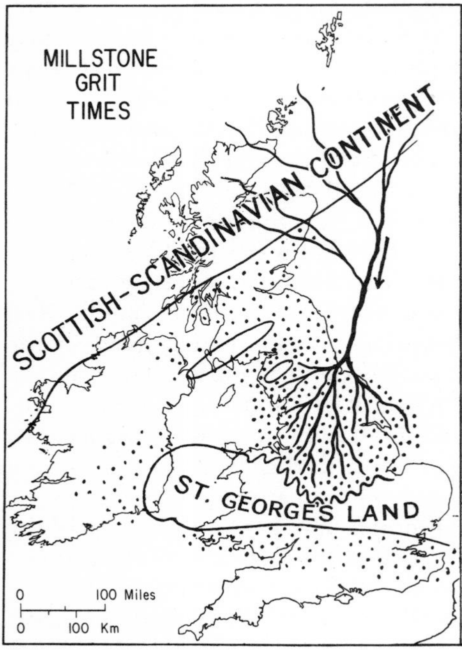

Fig. 7. The great river delta of Millstone Grit times

Fig. 8. The geography of Coal Measure times. The shaded portion shows the area where the coal forests flourished

The great delta which was formed during Millstone Grit times prepared the way for the very widespread growth of swamp forests in the succeeding period of the Coal Measures. The forests of tree ferns and allied plants, the remains of which form the coal seams of the present day, flourished in swampy tracts which have been compared by some to the mangrove swamps of the tropics of today, and by others to freshwater swamp forests such as the Everglades of the United States in Florida. Conditions suitable for the growth of such forests were to be found along the margins of the Scottish land mass as early as Carboniferous Limestone or Millstone Grit times, but it was not until the deposition of the great Millstone Grit delta that conditions became suitable over the huge area between the Scottish land mass, where now one finds the Scottish Highlands, and that land that existed across the middle of Britain and to which the name of St George's Land has been given. There is little doubt that the Coal Measure forests grew over continuous areas from what is now the Scottish border to the

Midlands of England, and right across the area where now the Pennine Upland is found. To the south of St George's Land, in what is now South Wales, the Forest of Dean, the Bristol area, and right across southern England through east Kent into northern France and Belgium there were similar conditions equally suitable for the growth of forests. It is clear that at intervals the forests were overwhelmed, and indeed entombed, by masses of sand and mud which were brought down by rivers similar in character to those which deposited the Millstone Grit. At other times the slight changes in surface level caused an inrush of the sea, and so in parts of the British Coal Measures there are found thin marine bands. Under most of the British coal seams there are found beds of clay, often with traces of roots, and it would seem that these Coal Measure swamp forests grew in a dark muddy slime, not very different from that in which mangrove swamps grow at the present day. Sometimes this layer of clay underneath the coal seams is of value in that it furnishes fireclay. Occasionally it has become silicified and is important as 'ganister'. There is little doubt that the land masses of Coal Measure times had been worn down greatly, in fact almost to sea-level, and towards the close of the period there is evidence that desert conditions prevailed on the neighbouring land masses.

The close of Coal Measure times is marked in many parts of the world by a great series of mountain-building movements, frequently known as the Carbo-Permian earth movements, since the succeeding period is that of the Permian. In the British Isles these movements resulted in four sets of folds:

1. In the north and northwest of the islands the Carbo-Permian movements resulted in the accentuation of pre-existing folds which had been formed by the Caledonian earth movements.
2. In such areas as central Wales new folds were formed, broadly speaking parallel to the pre-existing Caledonian folds, that is with a trend from southwest to northeast. The great anticline of the Vale of Towy in central Wales is a good example.
3. The most characteristic folds, however, of the Carbo-Permian earth movements are those which have an east and west trend and which are best exemplified in the folding of South Wales and the formation of the South Wales coal basin. The highly complex folds with their axes roughly from east to west which are found in Devon and Cornwall are also of this period, and there they were accompanied by the intrusion of vast masses of granite. On the other side of the Channel the east–west folds of Brittany are of the same age. Brittany, or 'Armorica', shows the folds of the Carbo-Permian earth movements so well that they are known as the Armorican earth movements or, alternately, as the Hercynian, from the Harz mountains of Germany.
4. In other parts of England north–south folds characterise this period, and there is little doubt that the general uplift of the Pennines which resulted

in the separation of the Coal Measures into an eastern and a western series of basins originated at this time. Another north–south structure of Carbo-Permian age is the line of the Malvern Hills, which now forms the eastern limit of the massif of ancient rocks making up Wales.

As a result of these great Armorican earth movements, at the beginning of Permian times Britain was occupied by an important series of mountains, between which there were deep mountain-girt desert basins—and naturally the earliest Permian deposits are usually coarse breccias which are of the nature of screes from the newly formed mountains. Beds of coarse conglomerate and boulders, laid down by torrential streams, are also found. There is one very well known Permian basin containing rocks of this character, and that is the one which occurs in the southwest, over the eastern parts of what is now the county of Devon and the neighbouring parts of Somerset. A great sea, or possibly salt water lake, comparable to the Caspian at the present day, covered much of Germany. It may, or may not, have been continuous with the main ocean which lay to the south of Europe. This German sea stretched across the North Sea and its western shores were to be found in northern England. After the early sandy deposits the well known Magnesian Limestone was laid down in the north of England and is found in its best development in Durham and Yorkshire. The waters of the Magnesian Sea seem to have found their way round the southern edge and perhaps across the north of the newly formed Pennines, and attenuated remnants of the Magnesian Limestone are therefore found on the western side of the Pennines. There is little doubt that the land surrounding these areas was under desertlike conditions; most of the sandstones and marls of Permian age are red; many of them contain grains of sand worn smooth by wind action. The Permian deposits thus form the lower part of what the older geologists described as the New Red Sandstone. This name was not ill-chosen, since the conditions of deposition of the beds must have closely resembled those of the Old Red Sandstone.

Although the Permian is the youngest of the Primary or Paleozoic systems, there is little break in England between the Permian deposits and those of the succeeding Trias, the oldest of the Secondary or Mesozoic. The Trias takes its name from the threefold division which is possible in the rocks of this series in most parts of northern Europe into Bunter, Muschelkalk and Keuper. The coarse red sandstones and pebble beds of the Bunter period were laid down in roughly the same areas as the Permian deposits. Like the Magnesian Limestone, the Muschelkalk of Germany and much of Europe was laid down in an inland sea, doubtless a saltwater sea, which, like the Magnesian Limestone sea, stretched from Germany across towards England. The Muschelkalk itself as a limestone is, however, absent from England. Here the Bunter Sandstones are succeeded by a considerable thickness of red sandstones and marls (Keuper) which were clearly laid down in a shallow basin surrounded by desert country. At intervals this basin was dry, for one finds deposits of salt (of considerable economic importance) and gypsum, representing salts that were deposited when the shallow basins dried up. Many of the deposits are ripple-marked; others show pittings due to rain storms on the scarcely dry mud. This was an age when giant reptiles first began to be important and the remains of some of them are entombed in the Triassic deposits. Some of the masses of older rocks—the remnants of the Carbo-Permian Mountains—stood up as islands in the Triassic salt lake or sea of the Midlands of England. Examples are preserved to us today in the Wrekin, the Lickey Hills, the Mendips and the hills of Charnwood Forest, so that one finds the red Keuper deposits wrapping round the margins of the ancient rocks. It is the red Keuper Sandstones and Marls together with glacial drifts largely derived there-

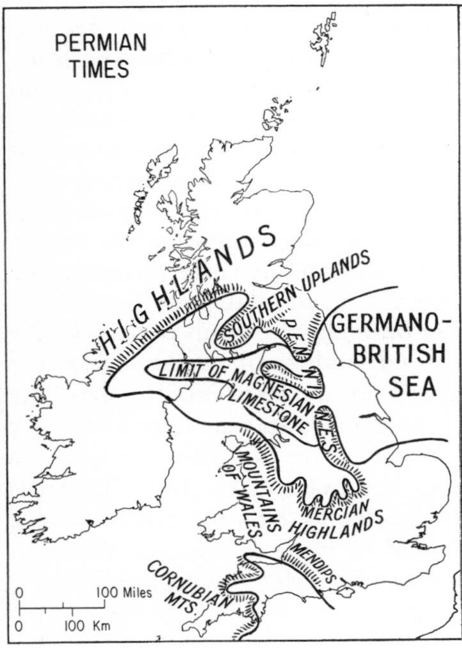

FIG. 9. The seas and salt lakes of Permian times after the Carbo-Permian earth-building movements

FIG. 10. The geography of Keuper times

from which are in the main responsible for the red soils so common in the Midlands of England. The Marls give rise to a soil which is rich, though tending to be waterlogged, but fertile for agricultural purposes if well drained.

The next phase in the physiographic evolution of the British Isles began with the irruption of a sea into the old Triassic basins. Many of the creatures living in the Triassic Sea, such as fishes, were killed off by this sudden incursion of marine waters, whilst organisms which were brought in by the marine waters found themselves unable to survive under the new conditions. Hence it is not surprising to find the earliest deposits of the Rhaetic, as the succeeding period is called, consist frequently of 'bone beds', built up entirely of the remains of fishes and reptiles. But in time the sea covered the whole area of the Triassic basins and even overstepped them on to the neighbouring land masses. By this time the land masses were worn down so that the material they yielded was more often of the nature of fine sands and muds, rather than coarse deposits. Conditions favoured the development of certain types of limestone. Deposits attributed to the Rhaetic on the Continent of Europe often attain a great thickness but in Britain the whole period is represented by only a thin series of deposits. The important Jurassic period which succeeds it is represented by a great series of beds which can be divided into three great groups. The Lower Jurassic deposits were the Liassic deposits and are mainly of clay or mud, argillaceous limestones, and occasional sands. In the water of the Jurassic seas enormous numbers of ammonites flourished, and these are really the dominant fossils of the period. Although there were no great earth-building movements during the Jurassic period, there were doubtless small folding movements; and the deposits of the Middle Jurassic comprise limestones, sandstones, and clays laid down in the tranquil waters of basins more or less cut off from one another.[1] Where the waters were clear and free from sediment the conditions were particularly suitable for the accumulation of the Oolitic Limestones, and the famous freestones of Bath belong to this period. In the Upper Jurassic, on the other hand, clays and sands again predominate over the calcareous deposits though the famous Portland stone is of this age. The difference between the soft and easily eroded clays and the harder beds by which they are separated has been a factor of the utmost importance in determining the relief of the present day southeast of England. Towards the close of the Jurassic period the sea retreated to the northeast, while the extreme southeast of England was covered by a great lake, the Wealden Lake, which stretched across what is now the English Channel into France. In this Wealden Lake were laid down deposits of sand and clay, such as the Hastings Sand and the succeeding Weald Clay found at the present day in the heart of the Weald of Kent, Surrey and Sussex. Around this Wealden Lake lived enormous numbers of giant reptiles such as iguanodons, whose remains are found in the lake deposits. In the seas which still covered the northeast of England were deposited various beds, including the Speeton Clay of Yorkshire.

Just as the Triassic Lake basins were later invaded by Rhaetic seas, so the Wealden Lake basin and the northern marine area were afterwards invaded by the sea of the earlier Cretaceous period. Naturally the earlier deposits were sands and muds, but there had been no extensive earth-

1. This accounts for the discontinuous character of the scarps formed by the harder beds (see pp. 47–8).

building movements affecting Britain since Carbo-Permian times, so that the lands surrounding the invading Cretaceous seas were low and yielded but little sediment. There is evidence that on these lands a desert type of climate prevailed. After the formation of the Greensand and Gault Clay deposits the waters of the Cretaceous seas became deeper and were extremely clear. The conditions thus favoured the deposition of one of the most famous of all the deposits found in the British Isles, that remarkably pure white limestone which we know as Chalk. It used to be thought that the Chalk was laid down in deep water under conditions comparable to those prevailing in the open Atlantic Ocean where white 'oozes' are being formed at the present day, but it is now believed that the Chalk sea was

FIG. 11. Map showing the area *probably* covered by the Chalk Sea

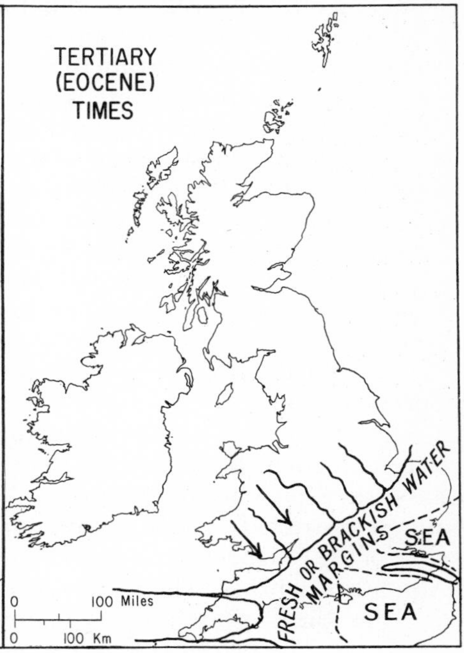

FIG. 12. The geography of Eocene times

not necessarily a deep sea, but merely one in which the water was clear owing to the absence of sediment brought from the land. The Chalk itself consists partly of the remains of multitudes of tiny organisms, particularly of foraminifera. It is partly a precipitate of lime. The exact limits of the Chalk sea in Britain are not easy to determine. It is believed by many that the peneplanation or the smoothing of the mountains of Wales, and possibly even of parts of the Highlands of Scotland, is due to the action of the waves of the Chalk sea.

The Cretaceous is the youngest of the periods of the great Mesozoic or

Secondary era. Although in Britain there is comparatively little discordance between the bedding-planes of the Chalk and of the succeeding deposits there is a great change of character between the two. There was actually a considerable lapse of geological time between the deposition of the highest Chalk and the succeeding beds. The earliest of the Tertiary deposits in Britain are the Eocene, and with this period Britain began to assume some of the relief features which are so familiar at the present day. Most of Britain seems to have risen so as to form a great land mass and only the southeast of the country was covered by a sea. Into this sea there emptied one or more great rivers coming from the west from a continental mass which is now beneath the waves of the Atlantic Ocean. The rivers laid down sands and other deposits of predominantly continental origin in the western parts of what we call the Hampshire and London Basins, while towards the east of these same basins there were being deposited clays or muds containing marine fossils. There is on the whole an alternating succession of deposits of marine and continental origin which marks the various backward and forward movements of the marine waters of the Eocene sea.[1] The same sea covered the Paris Basin in the northern part of France as well as considerable tracts in Belgium and Holland. It was during the Eocene period that there occurred some of the earlier earth tremors which were gradually to increase in strength and to culminate in those earth-building movements which were the most important of all in determining the present physiography of Europe—the Alpine earth movements. It seems likely that the Wealden dome in southeastern England began to rise during the Eocene period.

The Oligocene period, which succeeds the Eocene, has left but little trace in Britain. If there were Oligocene deposits laid down in the London Basin they have been removed by denudation and Oligocene deposits are almost restricted in this country to the Hampshire Basin. Towards the close of the Oligocene and during the succeeding Miocene period the great Alpine storm broke. This great period of earth-building movements formed the Alps, the Carpathians and many of the other great mountain chains of the world. The British Isles were comparatively little affected, since earlier folding movements had exerted their full influence in the north and the northwest of the country and resulted in the formation there of great stable blocks too rigid to be further folded by the earth-building movements so paramount in central Europe; they were at the same time too distant from the main seat of the Alpine storms. It is to be expected that the southern parts of England would be the areas most affected by the Alpine movements; that is actually the case. The folds, for example, which run across the Isle of Purbeck and the Isle of Wight are of this age. The main folding of the Weald is also of the same date. Although the ancient rocks of the north

1. Economically this is of the utmost importance because of the variety of soils and consequent land utilisation which result.

of the British Isles were not folded they were rent and torn, and through some of the fractures burst enormous flows of molten rock giving rise to the lava plateaus of Antrim in Northern Ireland and of many parts of western Scotland, whilst some of the great granitic intrusions, such as the Mourne Mountains in Northern Ireland, some in Scotland, and Lundy Island belong to the same period. The succeeding Pliocene period saw Britain taking on very much the form that it has at the present day. The Pliocene sea lingered in what is now the London Basin and later retreated farther north to occupy the position of what is now the North Sea, so that Pliocene deposits in this country are restricted, broadly speaking, to the London Basin and to East Anglia. More important than the deposits left behind was the work of Pliocene seas, in cutting those flattened surfaces, bevelling many of our hills especially in southern England. It is only in recent years that the geological history of the times has been worked out from this fragmentary evidence.

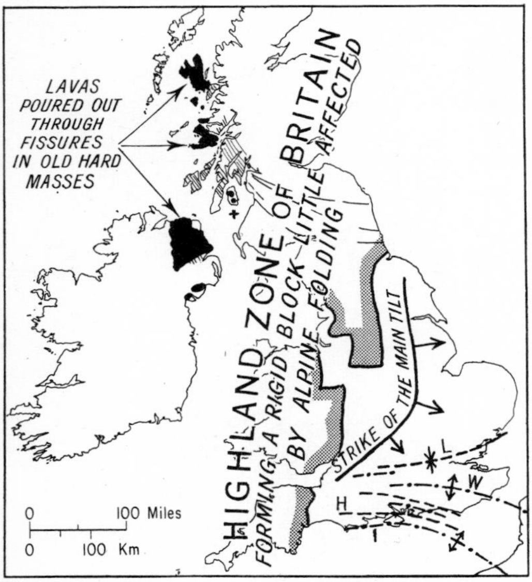

FIG. 13. Map of the British Isles showing the effects of the Alpine earth movements. The arrows show the dips of the rocks. The fine black lines in the north of England and in Scotland are dykes of igneous rock of the same age filling cracks

There was still to come, however, an episode in the geological history of these islands which has left its mark in nearly all places: and that was the Pleistocene Ice Age. At least three times during the Glacial Period the greater part of the British Isles was covered with ice sheets. Some of these were of local origin and had their centres in such upland areas as the Highlands of Scotland, the Southern Uplands or the mountains of Ireland, whilst other parts of the British Isles, particularly the east, were affected by the enormous ice sheet which crossed the North Sea from the main centre of the Scandinavian mountains. The southern limit of the ice sheets in Britain ran roughly along the present day line of the Thames, so that Britain south of the Thames and of the Bristol Channel was not actually covered by the ice sheets, though it must have been subjected, like the presentday Arctic regions, to tundra conditions, with the ground permanently frozen to a considerable depth.

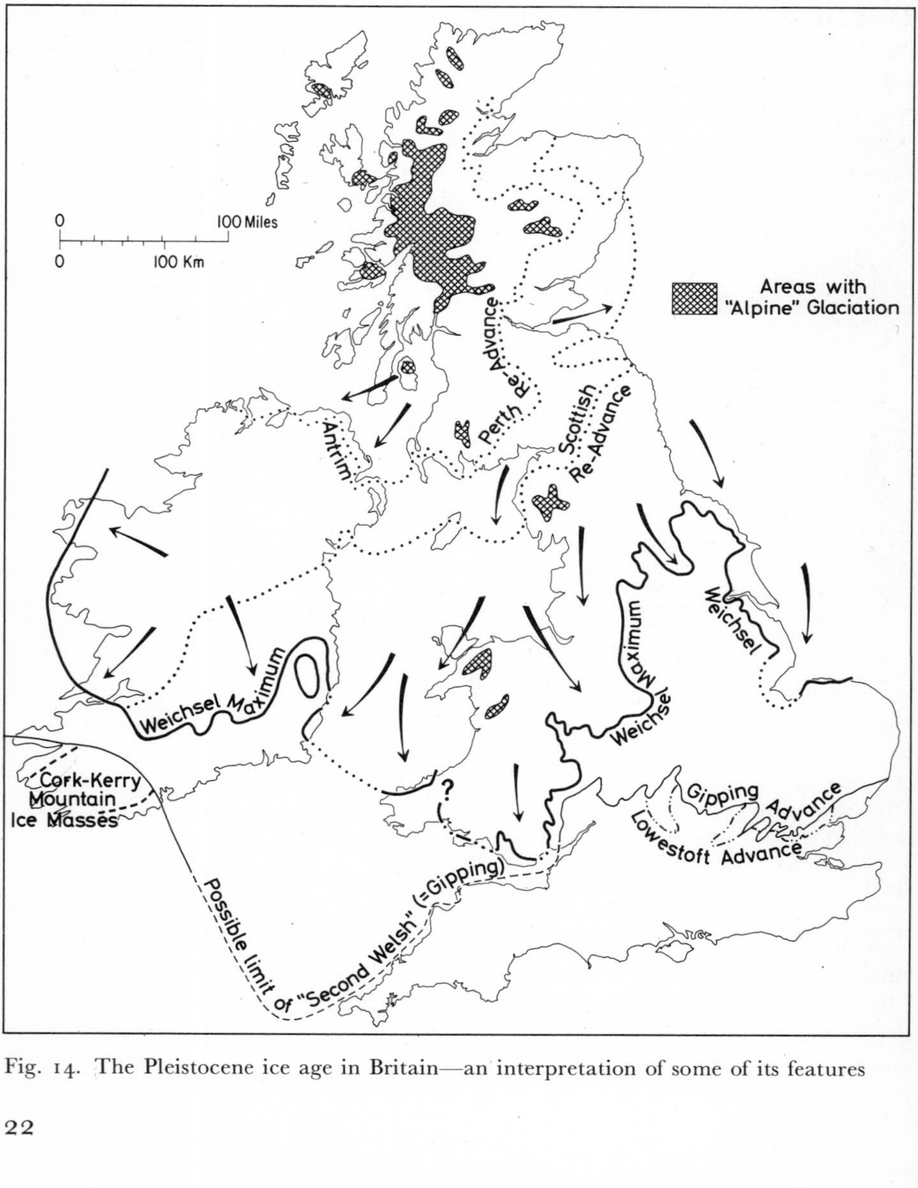

Fig. 14. The Pleistocene ice age in Britain—an interpretation of some of its features

Of the four or perhaps five ice advances that are recognisable in the Alpine regions of Europe, only the last three are known to have affected the British Isles. During the first of these cold periods, known in the Alps as the Mindel, in northern Europe as the Elster, and in England generally as the Lowestoft, the ice front penetrated as far south as Oxfordshire and the lower Thames valley. During the succeeding warmer or interglacial period (called in England the Hoxne interglacial, from a locality in East Anglia where its deposits have been recognised) the ice may well have left the country entirely. But it advanced again during the period known in the Alps as Riss, in northern Europe as Saale, and in England as Gipping (another East Anglian locality), reaching roughly the same southerly limits as before, except for a probable southerly excursion across the Bristol Channel to North Devon, the Cornish coast and the Scilly Isles. After a further warm interglacial period (known in Europe as the Eemian and in England as Ipswichian) the last re-advance is known as the Würm (in the Alps) or Weichsel (in northern Europe and in England, though other more local names such as Smestow—a valley near Wolverhampton—have also been given to it). The Weichsel ice covered most of Wales, and the Irish Sea ice-sheet sent a broad tongue across the Cheshire–Shropshire plain into the West Midlands; but in northern England the middle and southern Pennines were ice-free, though another broad ice tongue stretched down the Vale of York, and a further tongue impinged on the east coast as far south as north Norfolk. Another Irish Sea ice stream just touched the Pembrokeshire and Wexford coasts, whilst over Ireland itself the southern limit extended roughly from Dublin via Tipperary to the mouth of the Shannon, with an ice cap on the mountains of Cork and Kerry.

Naturally enough, except in Midland and eastern England which were not overrun by the Weichsel ice sheets, far more is known about the Weichsel advance and retreat than about the earlier ones, the evidence of which has been largely obliterated; and various stages in the retreat of the Weichsel glaciers are recognisable on the ground (see Fig. 14). During these later stages, too, the higher mountains must have risen above the general ice level, so that they were subjected to frost-shattering, with the formation of corries and small valley glaciers of alpine type that have given character to the landscape, as in Snowdonia, the Lake District and many parts of the Scottish Highlands.

The Ice Age is of enormous importance in the physiography of the British Isles, because the ice sheets and glaciers moulded the surface of the country and left behind them various superficial deposits which are frequently of much greater importance in determining the character of surface utilisation than are the underlying solid deposits to which the geologist pays greater attention. Thus the ordinary geological map of the British Isles is really of comparatively little use to the geographer in his attempt to interpret the effect of soil on human activities and as a factor in the human environment. It is of utmost importance that he should consider what the geologist calls

2

Chronology of the Great Ice Age

	STAGES	NOMENCLATURE	HUMAN REMAINS AND CULTURES (mainly EUROPE)	IMPORTANT EVENTS AND DEPOSITS IN BRITAIN
UPPER PLEISTOCENE	Last glaciation	WEICHSEL (Würm) (Smestow)	Cresswell Cave man *Homo Sapiens*	Corrie glaciers in Highland Britain York moraine Lower terraces of Avon, Severn, Thames, Trent Hessle and Hunstanton till
	Last interglacial	EEM (Ipswich)	Neanderthal man First Mousterian implements Levallois techniques	Kidderminster terrace (Severn)
	Penultimate glaciation	SAALE (Riss) (Gipping)		Taplow Terrace (Thames) Coombe Rock (glacial sludge) in south Chalky Boulder Clay in Eastern England 'Early Scottish' glaciation and 'Second Welsh' drift
MIDDLE PLEISTOCENE	Penultimate interglacial	HOLSTEIN (Hoxne)	Swanscombe man	Boyn Hill terrace (Thames) Hoxne deposits (E. Anglia)
	Ante-pen-ultimate glaciation	ELSTER (Mindel) (Lowestoft)	First Acheulian implements Heidelberg (Mauer) man Vértesszöllös man First Clactonian tools Abbevillian implements	Plateau gravel (Thames and Chilterns) 'Pennine' and 'First Welsh' drift Lowestoft till Cromer till
	First interglacial	(Cromer)		Cromer Forest Bed
LOWER PLEISTOCENE (upper part of)	Early glaciation	Günz Danubian (Europe only) / Preglacial in Britain	First tools in Europe	120 m (400 ft) Pebble gravel (Thames)

the 'drift' map, the map which shows not only the solid rocks underneath but the superficial deposits, many of which are directly or indirectly connected with the great Ice Age. In general it may be said that the great Ice Age had at least the following effects:

1. The ice removed much of the soil which must previously have been formed in the mountainous areas and has rendered huge tracts of the Highlands of Scotland, for example, almost devoid of soil and therefore comparatively useless for agricultural purposes. The older rocks are exposed at the surface and have been smoothed by ice action, and one sees in the rounded outlines of the relief of the Highlands some of the results of the work of ice. Tongues of ice scooped out pre-existing valleys and smoothed the sides and gave the characteristic U-shaped valleys, with sides almost devoid of soils, which one finds throughout the Highlands and, indeed, in many parts of northern England and Wales and of Ireland.

2. Over the low-lying areas glacial deposits were laid down. Some of these consist of coarse sands and even of boulders of morainic character. Elsewhere there are boulder clays—stiff clays full of boulders of various rocks. Or again, there are outwash fans of gravel and sand which were laid down by torrential waters caused by the melting of the glaciers. In the fourth

place, some of the finer glacial deposits were redistributed by wind, and while the climate of England seems to have been too humid for the formation of vast quantities of loess, which are found in regions where conditions south of the ice masses were drier, the brick-earth of England has many of the characters of loess, and is really loess deposited under more humid conditions or under water. These brick-earths are essentially characteristic of the south of the country.

3. Then the glaciers profoundly altered the drainage of the British Isles and there are innumerable examples of pre-existing drainage which has been affected by the Ice Age. Many ice-dammed lakes were left during and after the retreat of the ice and today the fine sediments deposited in these glacial lakes afford some of our most fertile lands.

Since the retreat of the ice sheets from the British Isles there have been several fluctuations in level. Evidences of these fluctuations in level are found in the raised beaches which occur in many places along the coasts, whilst movements of the opposite character are evidenced by submerged forests. Then, again, one must always remember that there has been a progressive change from the extreme cold of the great Ice Age to the climatic conditions which are found at the present day, though the change may have been interrupted by cyclic fluctuations. The spread of the present vegetation into these islands must have been governed by the changing climatic conditions; doubtless, very considerable portions of the preglacial flora managed to persist in the south of the country and formed the nucleus for the reclothing of the British Isles.

The evolution of the rivers and drainage system of Britain will be separately considered; but it should be borne in mind here that there was a drainage system in existence prior to the formation of the ice sheets of the great Ice Age, that this earlier drainage system was profoundly affected by ice action, and that the present river system of these islands reflects in most cases the result of glacial interference.

3
The physiography of the British Isles

In the last chapter, by considering the changes in the distribution of land and water over successive geological periods, we traced in bare outline the evolution of the physiography of these islands. In the present chapter we must analyse the physiography as it is at the present day. Leaving on one side for the moment the island of Ireland, the island of Great Britain is broadly divisible into two parts: a Highland Zone on the north and west, a Lowland Zone on the south and east. It is possible to suggest more than one line which may be used to separate these two divisions, but the most satisfactory seems to be that used in Fig. 15 and elsewhere in this book (see Chapter 24) and which cuts across the country, following a somewhat irregular course, from the mouth of the River Exe in the southwest to near the mouth of the River Tees in the northeast. It is roughly the line separating the outcrop of the old Paleozoic rocks on the one hand and the younger Mesozoic and Tertiary rocks on the other. To the north and west of the line lie the remnants of the great mountain chains which were built up by successive earth-building movements of Pre-Cambrian, Siluro-Devonian and

FIG. 15. The Highland and Lowland Zones of Britain

Carbo-Permian times. The mountains are but remnants of their former mighty selves, but they still comprise the major mountain and hill masses of Great Britain. Generally the most ancient masses are those which occur, as in the case of the Highlands of Scotland, farthest to the northwest. Naturally the margins of the ancient rocks are not infrequently covered by strata of later ages.

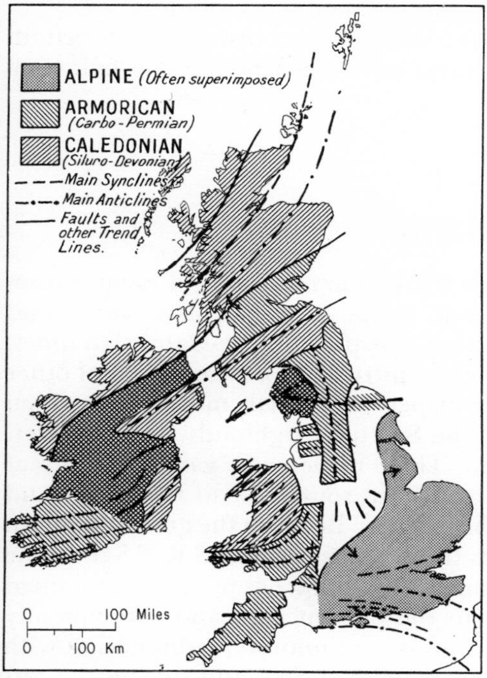

FIG. 16. Morphological map of the British Isles, showing the spheres of influence of the main folding movements

To the south and east of the line one finds first the broad plains or low-lying plateaus, built up mainly of Triassic rocks, which constitute the Midlands of England. Not infrequently small remnants of the ancient mountains stand up as islands in the midst of these plains of younger rocks. Farther southwards and eastwards the Midland plains give place to what may be called, in the broadest possible sense, the scarplands of England. Indeed, it is possible to draw another line across England, again somewhat irregularly, from the Dorset coast to the north Yorkshire coast. To the south and east of this line lie low ridges, separated by shallow valleys, which mark respectively the outcrop of the harder or more resistant and softer or less resistant beds of the geological sequence from the early Jurassic onwards. Like the Triassic rocks of the Midlands, these rocks rest upon an ancient platform which lies buried beneath them at a greater or less depth.

Sometimes, as for example under London, the ancient platform is within 300 metres (1000 feet) of the surface. At other times the Paleozoic platform lies at such a depth that the full thickness of the overlying beds has never been penetrated by the boring tools of the well-engineer. The Jurassic and later rocks have themselves been gently tilted, usually towards the southeast, by the Alpine system of earth movements; but it is only in the extreme south that there are signs of what might be called severe folding.

For the purposes of a preliminary account we may distinguish in Britain the broad physiographic and structural units described in the following pages.

THE HIGHLAND ZONE

The Highlands of Scotland

The Highlands of Scotland are built up for the most part of great masses of ancient metamorphic or crystalline rocks—gneiss, schists, slates, and quartzites. Some of the folding doubtless took place in Pre-Cambrian times, and it would seem that some of the great intrusions of granite and of other rocks are of the same date. The great period of earth movements which determined the major structures of the Scottish Highlands was, however, the Caledonian, or Siluro-Devonian. These movements gave rise to great mountain chains with a general trend from southwest to northeast, and this is still the dominant 'grain' of the country. Between the great mountain chains were the deep basins in which the deposits of the Old Red Sandstone were laid down. Much of the Highlands of Scotland has probably remained land from those very remote ages to the present day, and consequently subaerial denudation has gone on almost continuously, culminating with the work of the great ice sheets which covered Scotland during the last glacial epoch. As a result, the Highlands of Scotland of today no longer present the highly accidented scenery of the younger mountain belts of the world, but rather the rounded outlines which betoken the results of aeons of subaerial denudation and the work of ice. On the whole, then, the Highlands form an irregularly surfaced plateau with its greatest elevation along the western margin, sloping on the whole towards the east. The plateau surface has in general an average elevation of between 2000 and 3000 feet (600 and 900 metres); some of the higher points often marking the outcrops of granite, of both Pre-Cambrian and Siluro-Devonian ages. The highest points may reach over 4000 feet (1200 metres), and included amongst them is Ben Nevis, the highest mountain in the British Isles, of 4400 feet (1341 metres). The Scottish Highlands are divided into the Northwest Highlands and the Central Highlands or Grampians by the great cleft of Glen More. The Northwest Highlands are by far the more rugged and the grander, and meet the Atlantic Ocean in the intricate fiorded and island-bounded coast of western Scotland. It seems possible that the Alpine earth movements, being unable to fold the old stable block, tended to fracture it instead, and the belts of crushed rock which were formed along the fractures have been more easily excavated by rivers and by ice, and by the waves of the ocean, thus giving rise to the fiords with their remarkable rectangular bends.[1] Through some of the major cracks, too, igneous rocks of Tertiary age have welled up and give rise to the marked lava plateaus of Skye and some parts of the western coast of Scotland, comparable in character to those found in Iceland. The Old Red Sandstone, originally deposited in valleys, still tends to occur in valley or lowland

FIG. 17. Physical regions of the British Isles

1. The system of major cracks developed along the western coasts of Scotland may be due to pressure exerted from below by masses of molten rock attempting to find an outlet. Just as when one presses with the point of a stick on a sheet of ice covering a pond, or when a stone is thrown through a window, both concentric and radial cracks would be developed, and it would seem that this explains the varied directions followed by the fiords and valleys of the area. See J. W. Gregory, 'The origin and nature of fiords'; and J. W. Gregory, 'The Scottish lochs and their origin', *Proc. Roy. Phil. Soc. Glasgow,* **45**, 1914, 183–96.

situations, but the more resistant rocks of the period may cover considerable stretches, as they do over Caithness.

The ancient rocks of the Highlands on the whole give rise to a poor type of soil, while much of the soil which must previously have been formed has been swept away from most of the higher areas by the ice sheets of the glacial epoch. The tracts occurring on the Old Red Sandstone are, on the whole, more fertile. The same is true of the lower eastern margins of the ancient rocks themselves, as for example in the area known as the Buchan

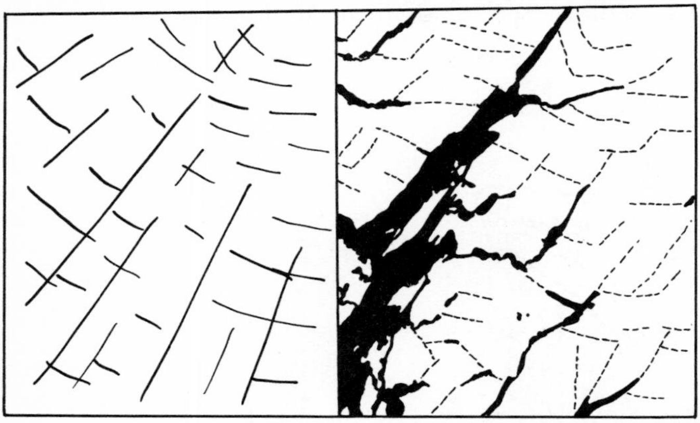

FIG. 18. The diagram on the left shows cracks which would be developed in a rigid block by pressure from below at a point near the northeast corner. On the right is shown a part of the fiord coast of western Scotland—water in black, main valleys dotted

Plateau. Geographically, the eastern margins, whether they are on the ancient rocks or on Old Red Sandstone, are somewhat distinct from the main mass of the Highlands and are frequently considered as a separate region under the title of Northeastern Scotland. It should be noted that the Orkney Islands form a detached portion of this area, whilst the Shetland Islands, farther north, resemble more closely the central part of the Highlands themselves. The southern limit of the Highlands of Scotland is remarkably well defined by the great Highland boundary fault, actually a succession of faults, which runs across the country with a Caledonian trend, from the mouth of the Clyde to the east coast in the neighbourhood of Stonehaven. The faults seem to have been initiated at the same time as the Caledonian earth movements, but intermittent movements along them have undoubtedly occurred from that time until the present.

The Southern Uplands

The Southern Uplands consist of the denuded remains of a great mountain chain of Siluro-Devonian age, which runs across the south of Scotland from the southwest to the northeast, that is with a characteristically Caledonian trend. There is, however, a marked difference between the Southern Uplands and the Highlands, in that the rocks of which the Southern Uplands consist are sediments, mainly of Ordovician and Silurian age, very highly folded. In the southwest, particularly in Galloway, there are large

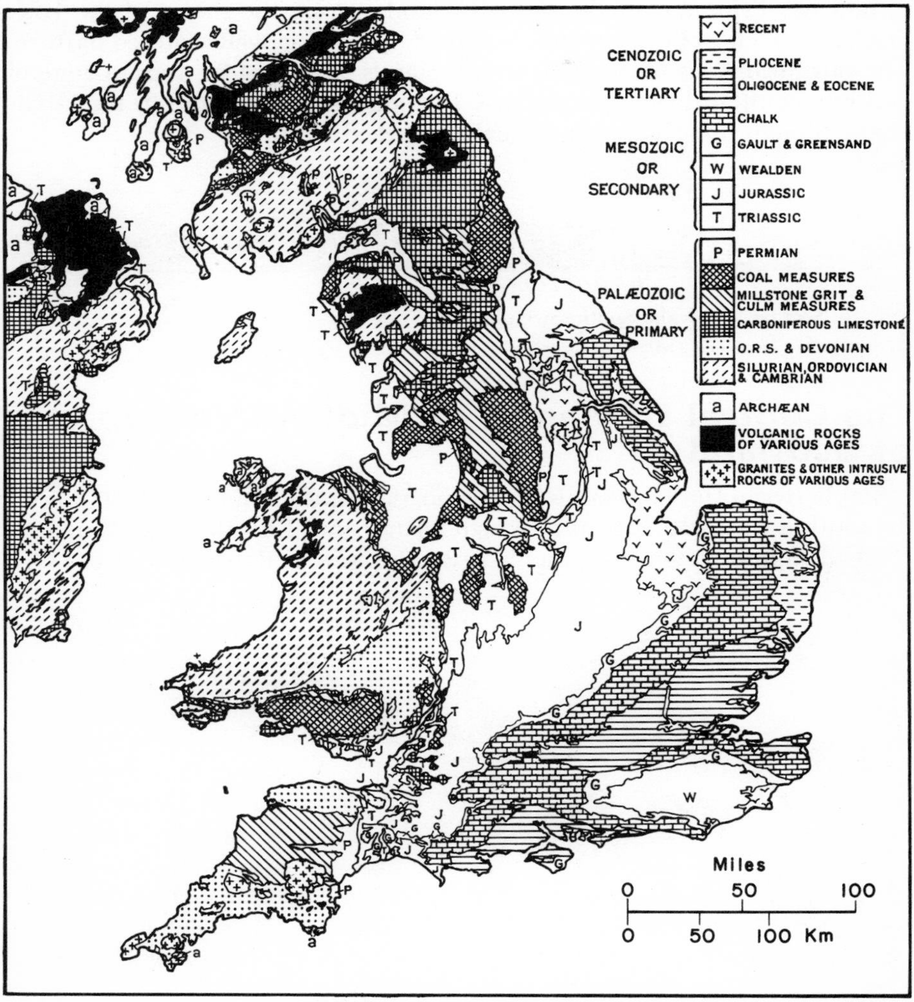

FIG. 19. A simplified geological map of England and Wales

For reference purposes use should be made of the Geological Map of Great Britain on the scale of 1:625,000 (approximately 10 miles to one inch) published in two sheets by the Geological Survey (HMSO).

granitic intrusions, but ancient metamorphic rocks, such as those constituting the greater part of the Highlands, are absent. Consequently all the higher parts of the Southern Uplands are formed of moorland country with rounded outlines, passing on lower ground in the east, particularly in the Tweed basin, to quiet rolling pastoral, and often well-wooded country. In the southwest, cutting across the main mass of the Southern Uplands, are the well-known dales. These dales are comparatively straight clefts running from north-northwest to south-southeast and afford important routeways. Fringing the Southern Uplands, along the shores of the Irish Sea, are stretches of low ground, occupied by smiling, well-watered pasture. The northern limit of the Southern Uplands is formed by a great zone of faulting, comparable in character to the faultline which bounds the Highlands, though not giving rise to such a marked feature.

FIG. 20. Section across the Southern Uplands
ORS = Old Red Sandstone; Carb. = Carboniferous

The Central Lowlands, or Midland Valley, of Scotland

Lying between the Highlands on the north and the Southern Uplands on the south is the great rift valley which forms central Scotland. Initiated by the Caledonian earth movements it was a basin of deposition of the Old

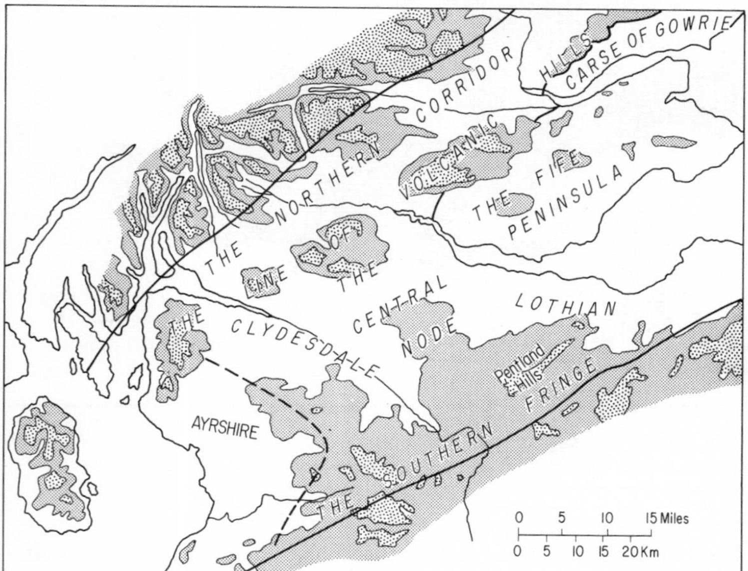

FIG. 21. Subregions of the Midland Valley

Red Sandstone, and was later occupied by a shallow arm of the Carboniferous sea, so shallow that at an early stage it was suitable for the growth of the swamp forests which have left their traces at the present day in seams of coal. At the same period volcanic activity was rife, and as a general result at the present day neither the relief nor the geology of the Midland Valley of Scotland can be described as simple. It is only in the broadest possible sense a valley. It is possible to distinguish a northern fringing corridor or broad valley, then a line of volcanic hills, then the central lowlands wherein lie the great Lanarkshire or Central Coalfield and the Midlothian-Fifeshire Coalfield, then a line of hills along the south and an ill-defined valley separating them in turn from the Southern Uplands. These subdivisions of the valley and their correlation with the geology may be seen in Figs 21 and 22.

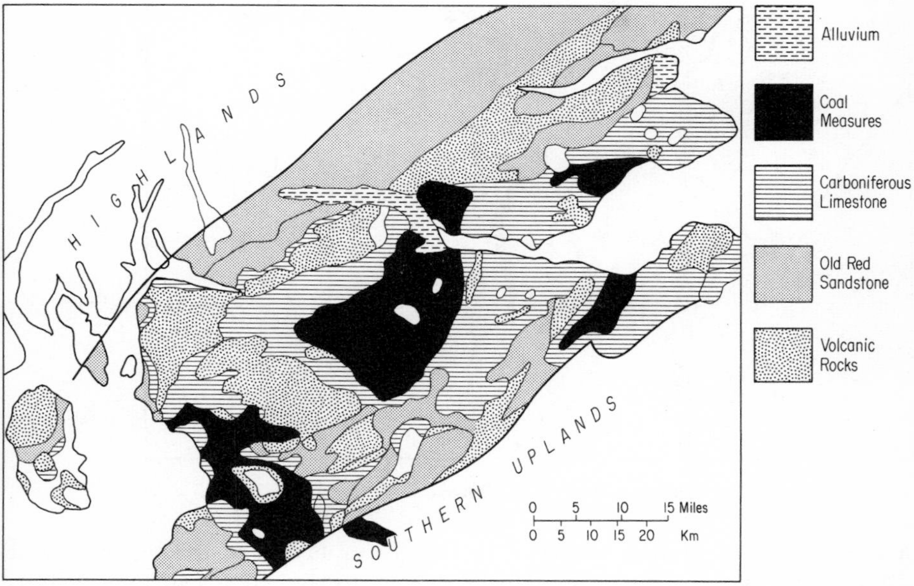

FIG. 22. The geology of the Midland Valley

Note the separation of the Ayrshire and Central coal basins by the Cunningham axis of uplift (NW–SE) and the separation of the Central and Midlothian by the Pentland axis (SW–NE).

The Lake District or Cumbria

The folding of the mountains which now make up the Lake District probably commenced even as early as Ordovician times, but the main earth movements responsible for the formation of the group were, like those of the Southern Uplands and of the Highlands, the great Caledonian movements. Consequently the geological structures in the main part of the Lake District have a trend from southwest to northeast and there is no doubt that originally the Isle of Man and the Lake District were joined and formed a single great chain of mountains. But the mountains suffered great denudation, and at a later stage the waters of the Carboniferous sea washed round them and may even have submerged the whole, so that Carboniferous Limestone was deposited on the flanks of the old central core. At a later stage—probably during the Alpine earth movements—a local uplift occurred in the heart of the Lake District. The uplift may have been due to

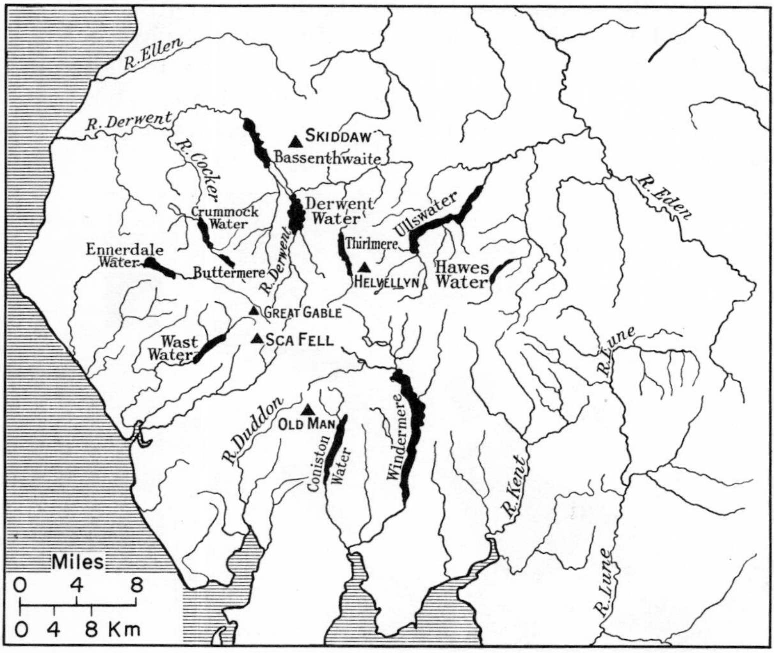

FIG. 23. The radial drainage of the Lake District

a great mass of molten material in the lower layers of the earth's crust attempting, without success, to force its way to the earth's surface. Whatever its cause, the uplift has undoubtedly resulted in the two great characteristic features of the area of the present day. These two features are the occurrence of the main mass of ancient rocks in the heart of the area, surrounded by younger rocks which in general dip away from the centre core. In the second place the uplift seems to have been responsible for the initiation of one of the most remarkable examples of radial drainage which is known. The well-known lakes of the Lake District radiate like the spokes of a wheel from a central hub, and it is because this uplift took place at a comparatively late stage that the forces of denudation are still active. Thus the Lake District has some of the finest rock scenery and, despite their relatively low altitude, rugged mountains in the British Isles. Geographically there is a remarkable contrast between the area of ancient rocks in the heart of the Lake District and the surrounding ring of younger strata. Only on the southeast do the Shap Fells connect the Lake District proper with the hill masses of the Pennines.

Wales or the Welsh massif

For the purposes of a general account the whole of the Welsh massif may be considered together. For this purpose the massif may be described as embracing all the hill masses which lie to the west of the English Midlands, excluding only the southern part of the county of Glamorgan, which ought to be considered as part of the English plain or scarplands. The eastern margins of the area so defined can be quite clearly traced from any physical map. In the north the Welsh hills abut quite abruptly on the Cheshire and north Shropshire plain; along the margin lies the North Wales Coalfield. The hills of central and southern Shropshire belong structurally to the Welsh massif, and from central Shropshire southwards to the mouth of the Severn the eastern limit is defined by the line of hills running southwards from the Wrekin in Shropshire to the Abberley Hills and the Malvern Hills. The oldest part of the Welsh massif is in the northwest, where the ancient crystalline rocks of the isle of Anglesey underwent folding in Pre-Cambrian times. The folding was continued during the Caledonian earth movements and post-Carboniferous foldings followed along the same lines, so that one finds narrow bands of Carboniferous Limestone pinched in amongst the ancient rocks. The whole of Anglesey, as the result of later denudation, has been worn down to a low plateau, almost to a sea-level plain, and its complicated geological history is scarcely suggested by the somewhat uninteresting surface features of the island. The mainland of north Wales is still, on the other hand, a land of rugged mountains. On the whole the grain of the country is from southwest to northeast, indicating that the mountains owe their origin in the main to the Caledonian earth movements. The rocks involved in the folding are, for the most part, Cambrian, Ordovician and Silurian, but the mountains owe their rugged character of today to the large masses of contemporaneous lava which were extruded as well as to other igneous masses which were intruded into the rocks before and during the folding. The igneous rocks have proved themselves more resistant to weathering, and most of the higher points, such for example as Snowdon and Cader Idris, mark the outcrop of one or more masses of igneous rock. As one passes from north into central Wales, the igneous masses become less numerous, and this is one reason for the less rugged relief of central Wales. The age of the folding of the rocks, too, becomes successively younger as one goes towards the south. Whilst north and central Wales, which at that time were probably continuous with southeastern Ireland, formed the land mass which we have already called St George's Land in Carboniferous times, South Wales was occupied first by the Carboniferous Limestone sea, then by the fringing swampy lands on which grew the Coal Measure forests.

Coal Measures were laid down over a huge area in south Wales, and at the end of the Carboniferous period were folded by the Carbo-Permian or Armorican earth movements. These earth movements resulted there in folds with an east–west trend, thus causing the great coal basin of the South Wales Coalfield. It would seem that the Armorican earth movements were unable to fold the already highly complicated and hardened masses of north Wales, and that the earth-building waves broke against this resistant mass both along its southern and eastern sides. Thus there are east–west folds in the south, but north–south folds in the east. Some of the latter are remarkably sharp, and one forms that curious line of hills, the Malvern Hills. The Malvern Hills folds are typical of the group with a north–south trend which is sometimes referred to as the Malvernian group. Where the north–south and east–west folds cross, small nodes and basins were formed of which the Forest of Dean coalfield is an excellent example.[1]

It will be seen that a triangular space remains between the east–west Carboniferous folds of south Wales, the north–south Malvernian folds of the eastern margin, and the south–west to north–east Caledonian folds of central Wales. This triangular space is occupied mainly by rocks of Old Red Sandstone age. Where the rocks consist mainly of hard red sandstones and conglomerates, they give rise to high moorland country such as that of the Brecon Beacons, including indeed some of the wildest moorland country in the whole of the British Isles. Where the Old Red Sandstone consists, on the other hand, of comparatively soft red marls lower ground has resulted, in particular the famous fertile lands of central Hereford which is thus a basin lying within the bounds of the Welsh massif. Even here thin irregular limestone bands (cornstones) have resulted in a diversified relief. An attempt has been made in Fig. 25 to divide the Welsh massif into its smaller constituent regions.

The peninsula of Devon and Cornwall

The southwestern peninsula is the third of the masses of ancient rocks which occur on the western side of England and Wales. It is very different in character from the Lake District massif, and also from the Welsh massif. The folding of the rocks is very complicated and took place, for the most part, during the Carbo-Permian or Armorican earth movements, and the strike of the folds is east to west. During the folding there was an intrusion of large granite masses. Thus from early Permian times onwards, as already pointed out, there must have been great east and west mountain chains separated by deep rock-girt basins in which the Permian and Triassic rocks were laid down. But through the long ages since, denudation has been active, and the ancient mountain chains have been worn down until now there are certainly no rugged mountains in Devon or Cornwall. Instead

1. Still better shown in the complicated Bristol district, and the Mendips.

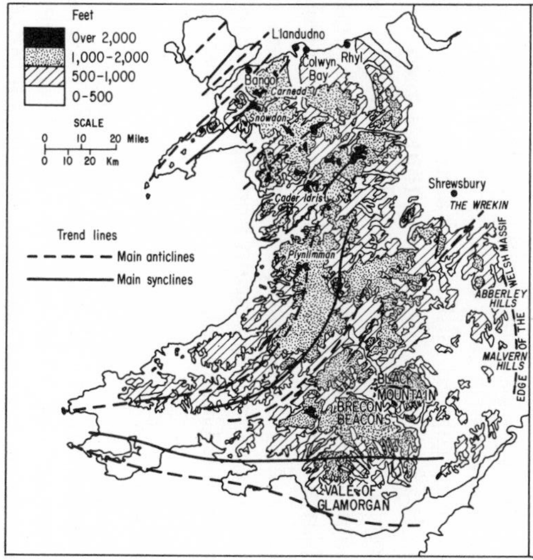

Fig. 24. Physical map of Wales showing trendlines

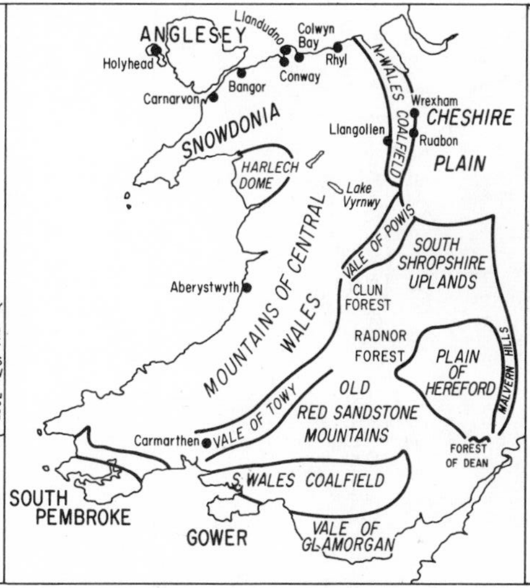

Fig. 25. Wales, showing a division into physiographic regions

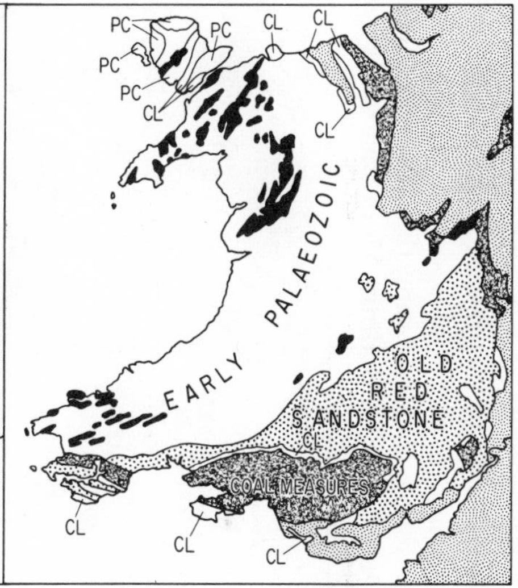

Fig. 26. Geological map of Wales

Black = igneous rocks; PC = Pre-Cambrian; CL = Carboniferous Limestone

there is an elevated plateau rising to its greatest heights either where the old rocks are very hard or tough, as in Exmoor, or where the granite masses have offered a greater resistance to denudation than the surrounding sediments, as they have in Dartmoor and Bodmin Moor and other areas. The

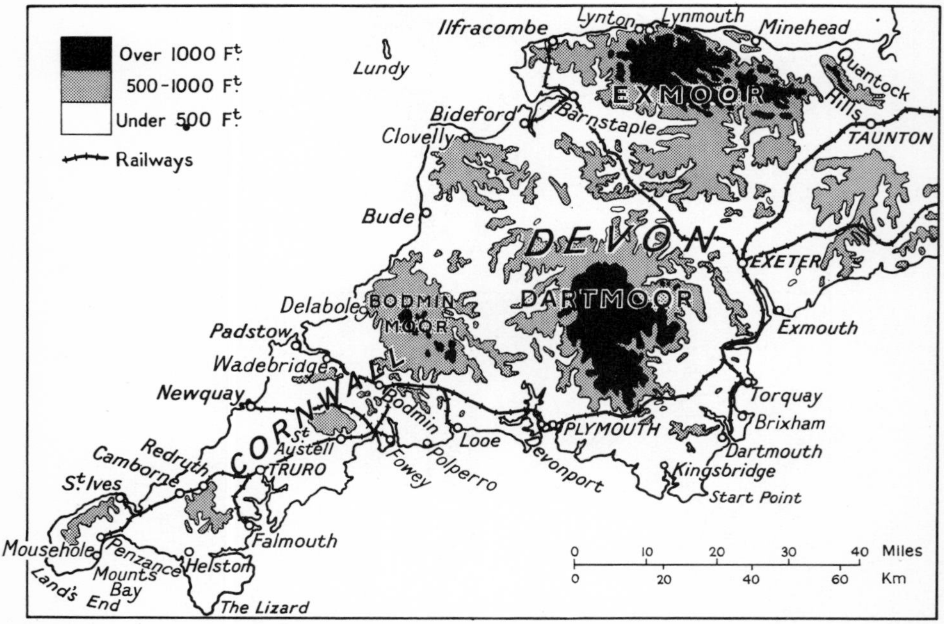

FIG. 27. Physical and general map of the southwestern peninsula

southwestern peninsula also seems to have undergone, at least since mid-Tertiary times, a general though intermittent uplift, so that at the present day we may best describe the area as a succession of plateaus or platforms generally believed to be of marine origin—plateaus which meet the present ocean in the long succession of rugged cliffs, so characteristic of the coasts of Devon and Cornwall. It should be mentioned that a part of western Somerset (the Quantocks) is also included within this region. The higher levels are occupied by moorlands, but much of the remainder is cultivated, since the Devonian and Carboniferous rocks break down into a moderately rich soil. The comparatively mild climate, especially of the more sheltered valleys, is responsible for the special vegetation and utilisation features of these valleys both in Devon and Cornwall.

The Pennines

The Pennines, or the 'Backbone' of England, are sometimes wrongly referred to as a chain of mountains. This term is entirely incorrect, and it is not wise to apply even the term 'range' to them. It is much more suitable that they should be referred to as the Pennine Upland. It is probable that Coal Measures were deposited, as we have already seen, right across the north of England, and that the Pennine Uplift dates from post-Carboniferous times, that is from the the Carbo-Permian earth movements. The

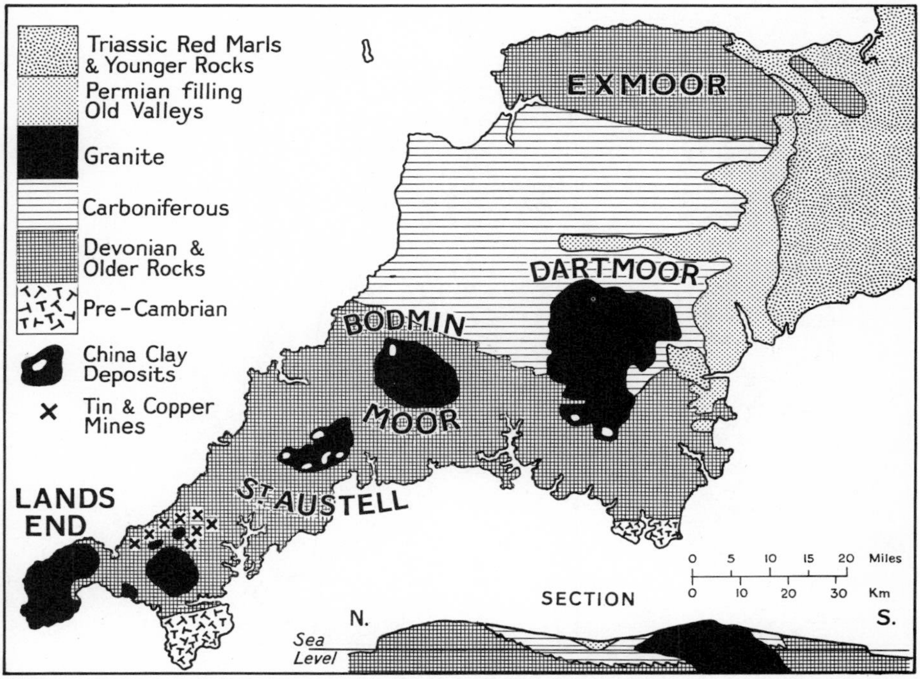

FIG. 28. Geological sketch map of the southwestern peninsula

A comparison with Fig 27 will suggest the correlation between the granite masses and higher areas of the plateau surface—with Exmoor as an exception. The section is from Exmoor through the Dartmoor granite.

Pennines are often represented in diagrammatic sections as if they were a simple anticline. Broadly speaking, however, the fold, if such it may be called, is defined by a series of great faults on the west, and consequently the highest portion of the Pennines is usually the western margin overlooking the lowlands to the other side of the boundary faults. The Carboniferous Limestone and Millstone Grit rocks which make up the bulk of the moor-covered Pennine Uplands are themselves but slightly folded, often almost horizontal, but towards the east they take on a general dip towards the North Sea, so that on the eastern side the Pennines fade gradually into the lower ground bordering the North Sea itself. Important transverse valleys divide the Pennines into four blocks; these are shown on Fig. 29 in relationship with the main outcrops of Carboniferous Limestone and Millstone Grit. In the north the Cheviot Hills, largely built up of volcanic material, form a connecting link between the Pennines and the Southern Uplands of Scotland.

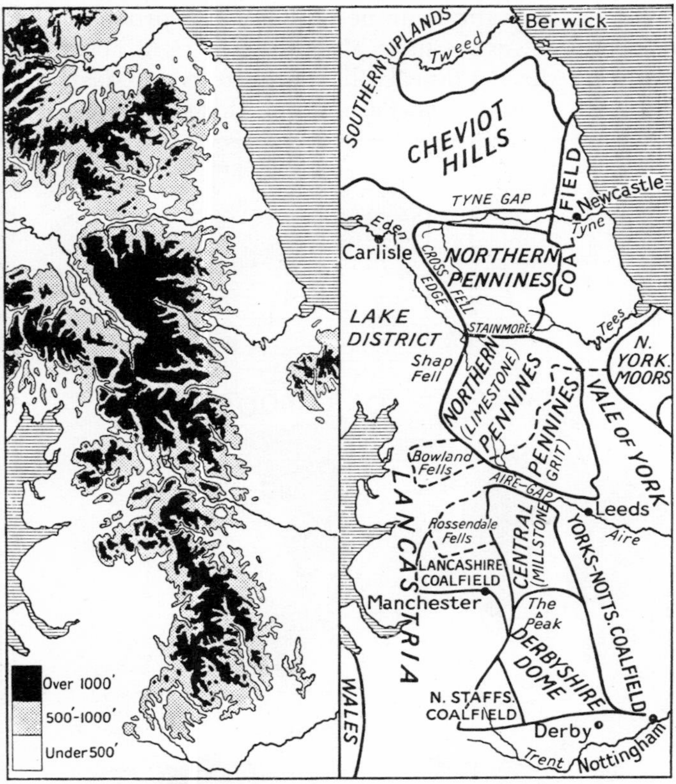

FIG. 29. The Pennines

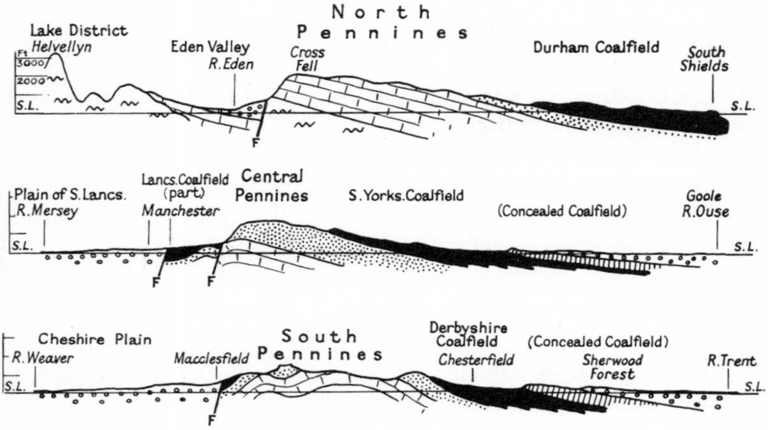

FIG. 30. Sections across the Pennines

The geological formations shown are: Lower Paleozoic Slates (wavy lines), Carboniferous Limestone (brickwork), Millstone Grit (dots), Coal Measures (black), Magnesian Limestone (vertical lines), Trias (circles). Note the asymmetrical character of the uplift and the variation in structure from north to south.

THE LOWLAND ZONE

The remainder of England is occupied for the most part by lowlands, and is built up mainly of rocks younger than those which form the Highland Zone. For purposes of description, the following broad regions may be distinguished.

The Triassic plain of the Midlands

The Midlands of England, in a somewhat restricted sense, consist for the most part of lowland, and occupy a V-shaped area. The southern end of the Pennines fits into the centre of the V, the left arm of which joins the lowlands of Cheshire and Lancashire, through the Midland Gap, while the right arm joins the lowlands of the Vale of York by way of the broad lower Trent Valley. Geographically the Midlands so defined may be regarded as bounded on the southeast by the first of the scarps which make up the scarplands of southeastern England. On the west the Midlands

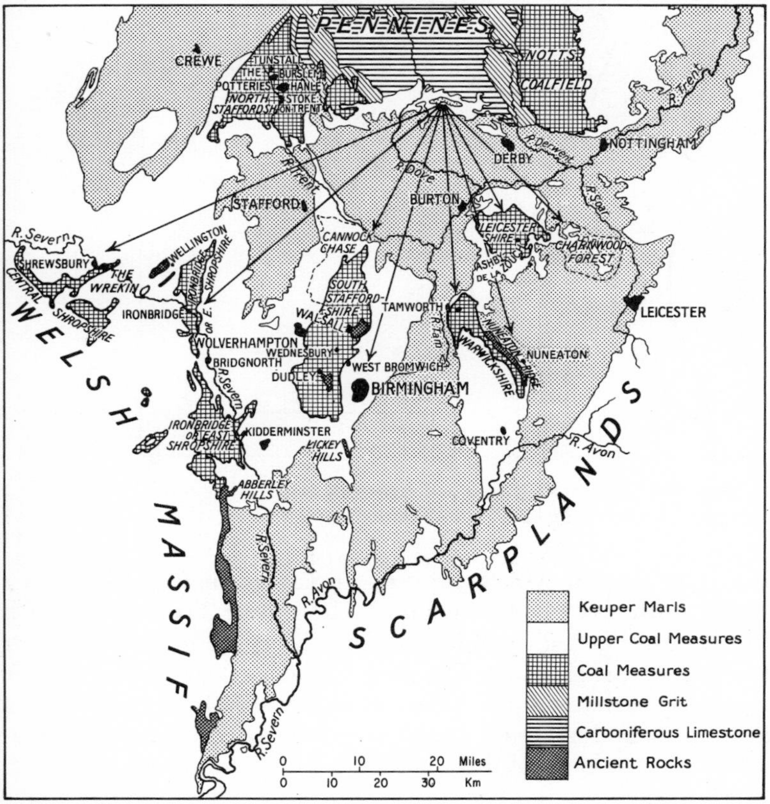

FIG. 31. The ancient islands of the Midlands

stretch as far as the edge of the Welsh massif, which has already been described. The point of the V stretches to the Severn estuary and extends through the interesting, if complex, Bristol–Mendip region into the Plain of Somerset. The most important of the geological formations in the Midlands is the Upper Trias or Keuper Marls with the fine-grained Keuper Sandstones, which weather to a rich red soil excellent for cattle pastures and

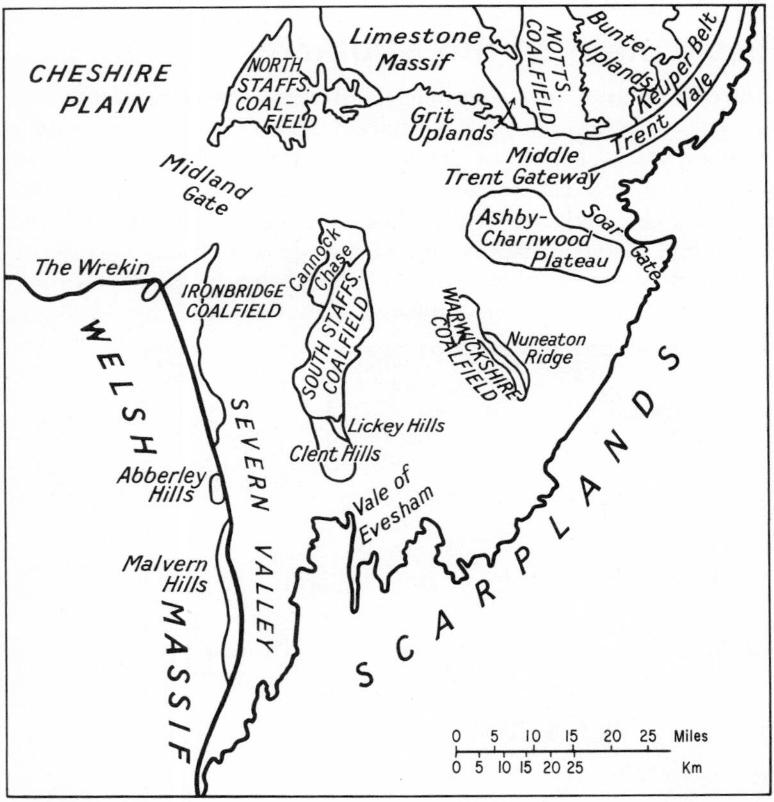

FIG. 32. Sketch map showing physiographic subdivisions of the Midlands. The northeastern part is after Professor H. H. Swinnerton

for cultivation. The Triassic Marls are very similar to the Old Red Marls of Herefordshire. Both give rise to lowlands. The Lower Trias or Bunter is a formation of sandstones and pebble beds which results in rather higher and less fertile country, such as the Cannock Chase plateau. The whole of the Trias, as already explained in Chapter 2, was originally laid down in a shallow inland basin under almost desert conditions (compare the Great Salt Lake of Utah at the present day), and the Triassic deposits are found wrapping round masses of older rock which formed islands in the old lake basin. The 'islands' include the small coalfields of the Midlands, and since they give rise to industrial areas in the midst of country otherwise agricultural they should be considered separately, together with the 'islands' of still older rocks.

The 'islands' of old rocks in the Midlands. These islands of old rock are best considered in relation to the southern end of the Pennines. Taking a point at the southern end of the central limestone core of the Pennines, just west of Derby, it is possible to draw radiating lines each passing through one of the old islands. This has been done in Fig. 31.

Charnwood Forest lies to the southeast of the southern Pennines. It consists of very ancient (Pre-Cambrian) rocks, though all but the highest hills of the ancient island have been covered with Triassic deposits. But the geology makes Charnwood Forest quite different from the surrounding country. There are pretty wooded hills and winding leafy lanes, and the whole area is one of the playgrounds of the Midlands. Some of the old rocks are quarried for road metal, which is used all over southern England.

The Leicestershire coalfield lies next to Charnwood Forest on the west. It is one of the few coalfields of England which has not given rise to an extensive industrial area. The coalfield and Charnwood Forest form an upland area which has been called (as on Fig. 32) the Ashby-Charnwood Plateau.

The Nuneaton Ridge, a narrow ridge of ancient rock including the Cambrian Hartshill Quartzite, lies almost due south of Derby.

The Warwickshire coalfield, sometimes called the Nuneaton Coalfield, lies to the west of the Nuneaton Ridge, just as the Leicestershire field lies to the west of Charnwood Forest.

The Lickey Hills. Slightly west of south from the centre of the Pennines a line passing through Birmingham reaches a very small island of ancient rocks comparable with the Nuneaton Ridge—these are the Lickey Hills.

South Staffordshire coalfield. This large and important coalfield lies immediately to the northwest. The northern part is a broad plateau, continued northwards by Bunter Sandstones and known as 'Cannock Chase.' Associated with the southern part of this coalfield is the famous 'Black Country.' A hard breccia at the top of the Coal Measure sequence gives rise to the ridge of the Clent Hills.

The Ironbridge and Forest of Wyre coalfield (East Shropshire Coalfield) is a long, narrow coalfield stretching southwards from Wellington and lying along the edge of the Welsh massif. It is cut through by the gorge of the Severn.

The Wrekin, a hill of ancient rocks near Wellington, has already been mentioned as part of the outer rampart of the Welsh massif. It is part of the area of old rocks which occupies central Shropshire.

Having now dealt with the islands of old rocks which give rise to most of the industrial areas of the Midlands, it remains to note a few points about the surrounding regions of Triassic rocks.

The Bunter Sandstones and Keuper Sandstones, as already noted, coincide with low uplands, the Keuper Marls with low ground, gently undulating but otherwise rather featureless. It must be remembered that over very many areas the underlying solid rocks are masked by the glacial drifts.

To the southeast the Keuper Marls are succeeded by the Rhaetic and Liassic rocks. Unless the Rhaetic or lower Lias contains hard or resistant beds sufficiently important to give rise to a scarp there is little to mark the junction. Thus the Vale of Evesham is partly on Keuper, partly on Lias; so also is the Vale of Berkeley.

The plain of Lancastria

The plain of Lancastria forms a continuation of the Midland Plain through the Midland Gap or Midland Gate. It occupies the northern half of Shropshire, nearly the whole of Cheshire and that part of Lancashire which lies between the Pennines and the Irish Sea. There are two broad tongues of moorland, called respectively Bowland 'Forest' and Rossendale 'Forest', which extend westwards from the Pennines into Lancashire and which coincide with outcrops of Carboniferous Rocks (Millstone Grit and Lower Coal Measures). Again, where Bunter or Keuper sandstones outcrop there may be low hills, as in Delamere Forest. Elsewhere, the Lancashire–Cheshire plain is an undulating lowland underlain by Keuper Marl; the actual character of the surface, however, depends largely on the thickness and type of the mantle of glacial deposits. Physically the plain of Lancastria lies between the Welsh massif and the Pennines: on the west the undulating country of the North Wales Coalfield forms a transition belt; in the east the coal measure country of the North Staffordshire Coalfield forms another transitional belt.

The northeastern lowlands

These lie in Nottinghamshire, Yorkshire, Durham and Northumberland. On the eastern side of the Pennines, and thus corresponding to the Plain of Lancastria on the west, is a broad belt, mainly of lowland. The Carboniferous Limestone and Millstone Grit formations which make up the bulk of the Pennines dip eastwards, and are succeeded in turn by the Lower Coal Measures, the Middle and Upper Coal Measures, the Magnesian Limestone and higher Permian beds, the Bunter Sandstone and the Keuper Marls. In general terms each succeeding formation gives rise to its own characteristic type of country. Thus there is a succession of physiographic zones roughly parallel to the Pennines. The Lower Coal Measures give rise to rather barren land with patches of moorland separated from one another by river valleys. The more fertile country of the Middle and Upper Coal Measures has a gentler relief, but resistant beds may form westward facing scarps (see Fig. 188). Tongues of lowland extend into the heart of the Pennines along the famous 'Yorkshire Dales'—particularly those formed, from north to south, by the Swale, Ure, Nidd, Wharfe, Aire,

Calder and Don. The Magnesian Limestone usually forms a distinct westward facing scarp, often with attractive cliff scenery, especially at those places where the scarp is cut through by rivers. The Bunter Sandstone, as in the Midlands, coincides with sandy, rather elevated tracts, infertile and hence often well wooded as in the Sherwood Forest. Occasionally marked bluffs are found, such as that on which Nottingham Castle is situated. The final belt is that of the Keuper Marls and is the lowland belt which stretches from the mouth of the Tees to the Trent Vale of Nottinghamshire, but the Keuper Marls are masked by superficial deposits over large areas, particularly over that huge tract known as the Vale of York, and the interesting area of the Isle of Axholme.

The Bristol-Mendip region

To the southwest the Midland Plain narrows and passes first into the Vale of Gloucester and then into the Vale of Berkeley between the Forest of Dean or the Severn on the west, and the fine scarp of the Cotswolds on the east. But farther southwards, in what may be called the Bristol–Mendip Region, the plain disappears. Its place is taken by country of varied relief

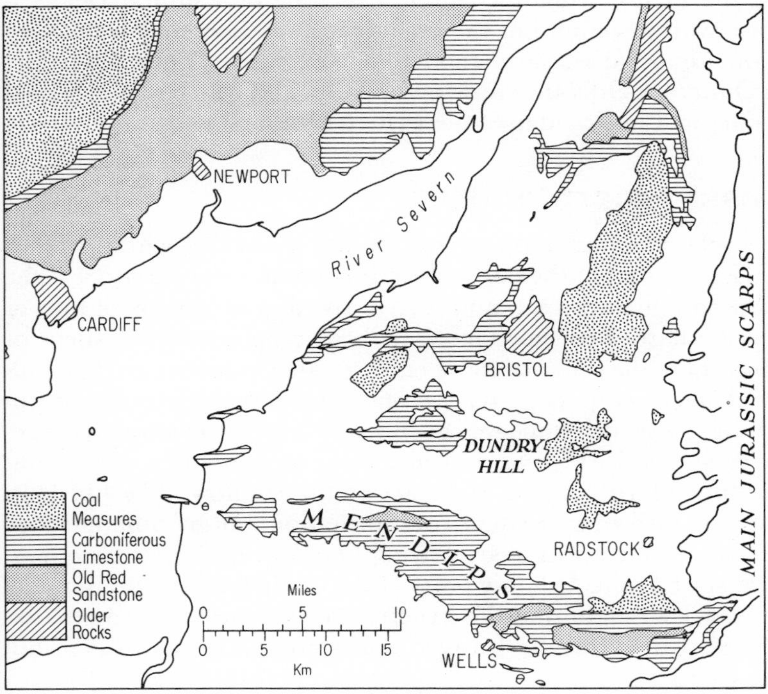

FIG. 33. The Bristol-Mendip region, showing the islands of old rocks. The unstippled land areas are Triassic and lower Jurassic rocks and recent deposits

lying between the Severn and the westernmost of the Jurassic scarps. This region repeats, on a smaller scale, the features of parts of the Midlands. It really consists of 'islands' of old rocks wrapped round by the softer Triassic and Liassic deposits. But there are several points of difference: the islands are relatively larger and more numerous, the amount of low ground correspondingly small. The islands, too, are of rocks of varied age; there are the large Carboniferous Limestone masses of the Mendip Hills, and the important coal basins, as well as quite tiny patches of Silurian, Old Red Sandstone and Carboniferous Limestone. The 'islands' are remnants of Armorican folds, and it is in this region that the north–south Malvernian folds cross the more normal east–west folds. Thus some of the old blocks are elongated in a north–south direction, such as the Tortworth Ridge north of Bristol and the Carboniferous Limestone edges of the Kingswood coal basin. In the Mendip Hills a succession of east–west folds *en echelon* has resulted in a broad upland trending from westnorthwest to eastsoutheast.

The plain of Somerset

In some ways this plain resembles that of the Midlands from which it is separated by the Bristol–Mendip region. The Vale of Taunton Deane is thus a Keuper Marl lowland, but the great feature of Somerset is the very extensive plain, almost at sea-level and liable to extensive floods, which lies between the Quantock Hills and the Mendip Hills, and which is interrupted only by the narrow Liassic ridge of the Polden Hills.

The Jurassic scarplands

The Jurassic rocks of Britain crop out over a belt of varying width extending from the Dorset coast to the north Yorkshire coast. Over large areas the beds dip to the southeast or east, and so give rise to a succession of hills or ridges where the harder or more resistant beds crop out, and valleys or negative relief where the softer or more easily eroded rocks occur. The hills usually have a steep scarp slope on the one side, generally to the northwest, and a long gentle dip slope on the other. While the general arrangement is that suggested in Fig. 34, it is a mistake to imagine a continuous Jurassic limestone scarp running right across the country. The hill belts and scarps are not formed by a single rock formation, but by different rock groups in different areas. The scarps swing about in different directions, die away, and start again. In some parts of the Midlands, the dip slope of the resistant beds is so slight that the structure of the country becomes that of a dissected plateau. Thus the Jurassic scarps are not nearly as constant as that of the Chalk.

In the first place the Jurassic rocks were laid down in shallow water, and consist of a varied series of clays, fine and coarse sands, sandstones and limestones. Some of the latter are oolitic, but the importance of the oolitic limestones has been overemphasised as a result of their economic value as building stones or for lime. The variability of the Jurassic succession was enhanced by the presence within the sea of three axes of uplift which, by separating the sea into four different basins, allowed a different succession of clays, sands and limestones to accumulate in each basin. Along the axes, which lay respectively east–west across south Yorkshire, northwest to southeast across Oxfordshire and westnorthwest to eastsoutheast along the line of the Mendip Hills in Somerset, the whole Jurassic sequence is naturally thin.

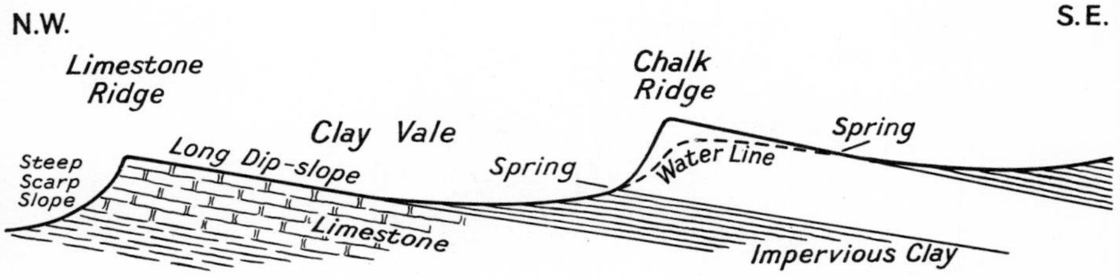

FIG. 34. Diagrammatic section illustrating the succession of clay vales and limestone or sandstone ridges found in the southeast of England

An attempt has been made in Fig. 35 to show the actual position of the true scarps.[1] Those shown have a minimum slope of 1 in 10. The scarplands may be divided as follows:

1. *The northern basin of deposition.* The Cleveland and Hambleton Hills of North Yorkshire. Here the wavy dissected scarp, 200 metres (600 ft) high, with its deep valleys and its plateau-like surface, is formed by thick sandstones of Inferior and Great Oolite age, accentuated by the resistant nature of the underlying Upper and Middle Lias beds which form the lower portion of the cliff. There are also tabular hills of Corallian rocks.
2. *The Market Weighton uplift* of South Yorkshire. The thin Jurassic rocks are overlapped by the Chalk and there is no Jurassic scarp.
3. *The central basin of deposition*—in Lincolnshire and Northamptonshire.
   (*a*) In Lincolnshire the remarkable Lincoln Cliff, from 30 to 60 metres (100 to 200 ft) high, runs north and south in an almost straight line, broken only by the Witham Gap on which Lincoln is situated. It is formed by the Lincolnshire Limestone (Inferior Oolite); to the west is the low ground on soft Liassic Clays; to the east low ground again.
   (*b*) In south Lincolnshire and Leicestershire there are three distinct scarps. The Rhaetic and Lower Lias limestones form a small ridge, of no great extent, some 16 kilometres west of Grantham. Eastwards are wide lowlands on Lower Lias Clays; then, beginning near Caythorpe, and increasing in height as it swings south-westwards to form the Melton

1. For full details see S. H. Beaver, 'The Jurassic scarplands', *Geography*, **16**, 1931, 298–307.

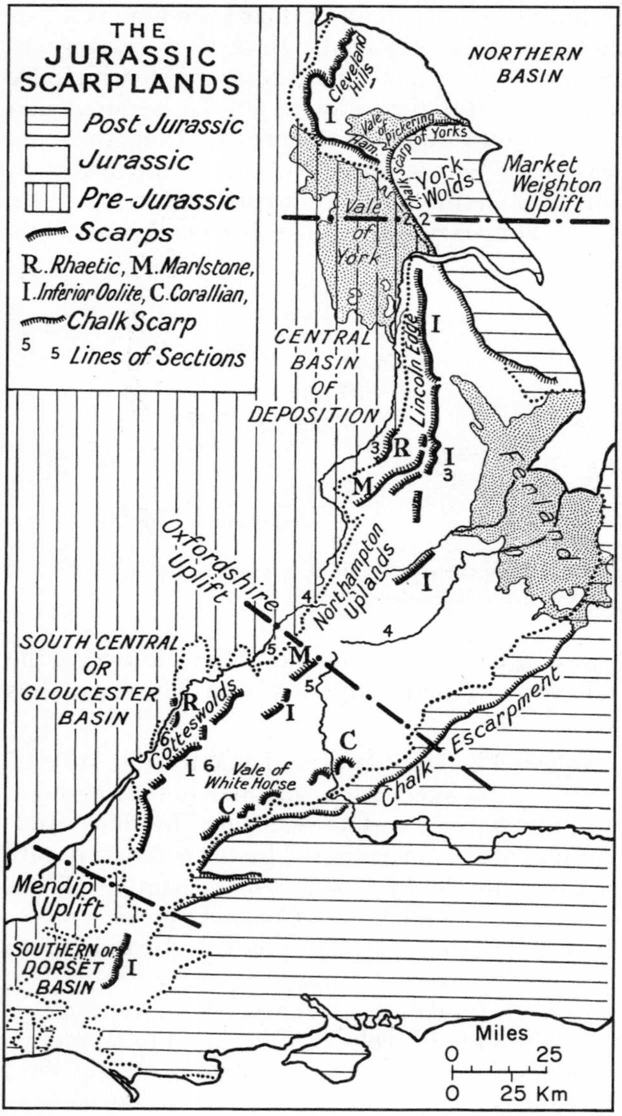

FIG. 35. The Scarplands of England

Mowbray ironstone ridge, is the scarp, about 45 metres (150 ft) high, formed by the Middle Lias marlstone. Farther east is the Upper Lias clay vale, then a scarp 60 metres (200 ft) high which marks the edge of a Lincolnshire limestone plateau. The last scarp continues, rather more broken, south of Grantham and overlooks the Vale of Catmoss in Rutland and the Welland Valley in Northamptonshire.

(*c*) In eastern Warwickshire and Northamptonshire there are really no scarps (partly owing to Boulder Clay cover), but instead an undulating area and a watershed where a number of important streams rise. Many of the rocks present are resistant, so the area is in the main an upland.

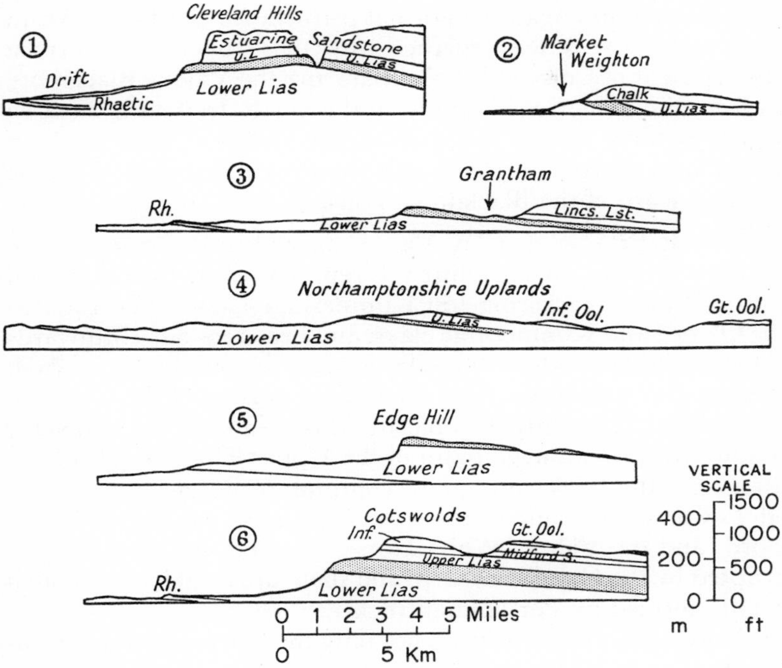

FIG. 36. Some typical sections across the scarplands

The numbers refer to the lines of section shown on Fig. 35. Stippled band = Middle Lias (mainly sandstone and marlstone).

4. *The Oxfordshire Uplift* in southeastern Warwickshire and north Oxfordshire. Here the Lower Lias limestones continue to form an upland and the Marlstone makes the marked feature of Edge Hill, but the Inferior and Great Oolites are poorly developed and give rise to undulating ground.

5. *The South-Central or Gloucestershire Basin of Deposition.* Here the great scarp of the Cotswolds, 200 metres (600 ft) high, dominates the whole country. The scarp is formed in the main by the Midford Sands and the limestones and grits of the Inferior Oolite, but the extensive dip slope is usually capped by the Great Oolite limestone and Forest Marble. Frequently the main scarp is 'stepped', a lower step or shelf being formed by the Middle Lias Marlstone. To the west there is locally a small Rhaetic scarp; to the east the Cotswolds slope gradually towards the great Clay Vale (including the Vale of the White Horse) and only in some places is the eastern side of the Vale interrupted by a small scarp formed by the Corallian.

6. *The Mendip uplift.* The Oolitic escarpment ceases to be clearly recognisable south of Bath. All the Jurassic divisions tend to become thin and to lose their normal lithological character towards the Mendips where there was an axis of uplift during the time of their deposition.
7. *The southern or Dorset basin of deposition.* Southwards from the Mendips the Jurassic succession resumes again its normal features (in the Dorset basin of deposition), and the Oolites, together with the Upper Lias, form a prominent escarpment of Cotswold type separating the Vale of Blackmore on the south from the Somerset lowlands on the north. In detail, the area is very complex as there are no less than eleven different resistant beds which in places form scarps. Farther south the area is dominated by the Upper Greensand scarp of the Blackdown Hills.

It will be clear that the great Clay Vale is formed in the main by the clays of the Upper Jurassic. In Yorkshire it is represented by the old glacial lake basin of the Vale of Pickering (on Kimmeridge Clay). The Lincoln Vale is on the Oxford and Kimmeridge clays, and broadens out southwards to the great flat of the Fens where the solid geology is completely masked. Beyond this is the clay vale drained by the middle portion of the Ouse, on which stands Bedford. A low divide separates this area from the wide clay Vale of Aylesbury in the drainage basin of the Upper Thames. This Vale owes its existence to the thick and almost continuous succession of Upper Jurassic and Lower Cretaceous Clays. It is continued westwards in the Vale of Oxford, and the Vale of White Horse, but here the clay vale becomes interrupted by the Corallian scarp, and there are local features, such as Shotover Hill, formed by Portlandian rocks.

The accompanying sections illustrate not only the scarp-forming formations, but also the general Jurassic sequence.

The chalklands

The fine white limestone known as chalk, although soft, is more resistant to weathering than the clays or sands which underlie it and the more recent sediments by which it is sometimes succeeded. As a formation it is thick—about 200 to 300 metres (600 to 1000 ft) generally—and varies but little from Yorkshire to the Isle of Wight. Consequently it gives rise to a scarp, in general westward facing, which is both more conspicuous and more continuous than the scarps formed by the Jurassic rocks. Only rarely—as in the East Anglian Heights—is this feature inconspicuous, even more rarely almost absent. The dip slope of the chalk is characteristically 'rolling' country and innumerable dry valleys are a constant feature. Where the chalk is almost horizontal large stretches of rolling downland (typified by Salisbury Plain) result; where the dip of the beds is steep there is little difference between the dip slope and the scarp slope and 'hog's back' lines of hills result, like the Hog's Back between Guildford and Farnham. The belt of chalklands commences in the north in Yorkshire (where it forms the Yorkshire Wolds). It is interrupted by the Humber and forms the ridge through which that river passes just before reaching Hull. Southwards are the Lincolnshire Wolds, as far as the second interruption caused by the Wash. In both the Yorkshire and the Lincolnshire Wolds the character of the chalklands is modified by a thick mantle of glacial deposits. From the chalk cliffs of Hunstanton in Norfolk the scarp is represented merely by low hills overlooking the Fens. In the neighbourhood of Newmarket, the chalk hills become more distinct (East Anglian Heights) and gradually the great

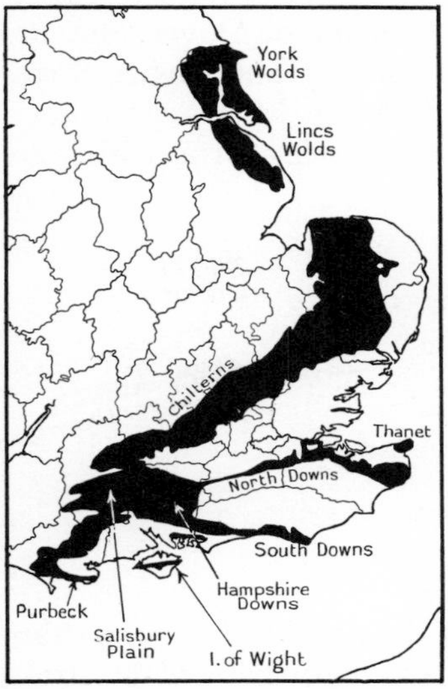

FIG. 37. The Chalklands of England

stepped scarp of the Chiltern Hills becomes increasingly marked. The River Thames cuts through the chalk ridge by the Goring Gap. In Berkshire and northern Wiltshire the chalk outcrop broadens to form the Lambourn and Marlborough Downs. In this part of England certain beds below the chalk, especially the Upper Greensand (here a close-grained loamy clay), assume a special significance. The important Vale of Pewsey is floored by the Upper Greensand and the morphological features of this Vale are particularly interesting. To the south is the great stretch of Salisbury Plain. The chalk downs extend into Dorset. From there westwards an important feature is formed by the Greensand deposits—here with more resistant beds—which give rise to the Blackdown Hills.

Along the south coast tracts, Britain was considerably affected by the Alpine earth movements, and the highly folded chalk—almost vertical in places— gives rise to a ridge through the Isle of Purbeck and then the Isle of Wight.

To the north and south of the Weald are the North Downs and South Downs respectively (see Fig. 38).

The Weald

Originally the whole of southeastern England was covered with a thick mantle of chalk, and the uplift of the Wealden dome took place during the Alpine earth movements. The crest of the dome, which is elongated from east to west, trends on the whole in that same direction, but the axis curves towards the southeast when followed over the Strait of Dover into the northern part of France. The Weald of Kent, Surrey and Sussex forms classic ground in many respects, for it was here that W. M. Davis[1] studied the evolution of the river system and applied the following terms which are

FIG. 38. Diagrammatic section across the Weald from north to south

now commonly used. From the central ridge of the upfold, the rivers drain off to north and to south. Their direction was a consequence of the structure of the ground, and hence such streams are called 'consequent'. As the rivers and other agents of denudation continued their work so the chalk was entirely removed over the central area and the underlying rocks were exposed. The softer beds, such as the clays, were worn away by streams running into the consequent rivers at right angles. These streams developed subsequently to the earlier ones and so are called 'subsequent'. Still smaller streams, which joined these at right angles in such a way that their direction of flow was often opposite to that of the consequent streams, are known as 'obsequent'. The rocks underlying the chalk in the Weald belong to the Lower Cretaceous Series, and there are alternating soft, or easily eroded, beds, mainly clays, and harder, or more resistant beds, mainly sands and sandstones. One thus has a repetition in miniature in the Weald of the features of the scarplands of England, with each successive ridge showing a scarp facing towards the centre, as suggested in Fig. 38. At a late stage in the history of the area, the Strait of Dover was cut and occupied by the sea across the eastern end, so that the extreme east of the Weald is actually in

1. 'The development of certain English rivers', *Geogrl J.*, 5, 1895, 127.

France. In the heart of the Weald as it is today is a group of sandy beds forming hills once covered with thick forest, and so often known as the Forest Ridges. Surrounding these hilly central tracts is a belt of lowland where the Weald Clay and certain other clayey beds are found, then a belt of hills formed by the harder beds of the Lower Greensand, then again a valley, called Holmesdale in Surrey and Kent, which marks in the main the position of the soft Gault clay. Then comes the main ridge of all, formed by the chalk, well known as the North Downs in the north and the South Downs in the south. The Downs present a steep scarp slope inwards towards the heart of the Weald, and then a long gentle dip slope in the reverse direction. Sometimes the dip of the chalk is steep, as in the famous Hog's Back west of Guildford, and the apparently simple structure shown in the diagram may be complicated locally, especially where the escarpments are 'stepped' and certain horizons, e.g. the Lower Chalk, give rise to platforms. Although the Weald is thus a well-marked region, it will be seen that it comprises a number of different parts, which may now be separately considered.

The Forest Ridges or the High Weald, usually built up of various groups of sand, particularly the Ashdown Sands, the Tunbridge Wells Sands, and the Hastings Sands, once densely forested and important for the supply of timber for charcoal for the now defunct iron industry.

The Weald Clay Vale, a region of negative relief, still very wet, mainly occupied by pasture lands with scattered remnants of the once continuous cover of damp oak woodland. It is a tract in which older settlements and villages are relatively few.

The Greensand Ridge or the tract of well drained land with numerous springs on the flanks. Sometimes the land is highly cultivated, but where the sand is coarse the soil may be poor and there are wide stretches of heathland. The Greensand Ridge passes towards the western edge of the Weald into a broad tract of undulating, dry, heathy country which has been called the Western Heights. It should be noted that the Lower Greensand does not give rise to a distinctive region on the southern side of the Weald.

Holmesdale is another tract of damp clay lands, but at the foot of the downs there is usually a strip where the Upper Greensand and Lower Chalk outcrop and where there are good, rich mixed soils, largely cultivated.

Romney Marsh is a separate area within the Weald, now drained and occupied by pastures, whilst *Pevensey Marsh* is a similar area though its utilisation is different (see p. 253).

Strictly speaking the Weald may be regarded as limited by the main crest of the chalk scarp, but it is often convenient to consider as belonging to it the chalk downs as well. When one remembers that the chalk ridge maintains an average elevation of about 150 to 220 metres (500 to 700 ft), and that there is a drop of 120 metres (400 ft) or more to the Gault Clay Vale, the importance of the gaps through the ridge is at once apparent. Along the

North Downs the chief gaps and gap towns from west to east are (the letters refer to Fig. 39):

(*a*) The Wey Gap—Guildford.
(*b*) The Mole Gap—Leatherhead and Dorking.
(*c*) The Merstham Dry Gap—Redhill and Reigate.
(*d*) The Darent Gap—Otford and Farningham.
(*e*) The Medway Gap—Rochester.
(*f*) The Stour Gap—Canterbury.

Along the South Downs are:

(*a*) The Arun Gap—Arundel.
(*b*) The Adur Gap—Steyning.
(*c*) The Ouse Gap—Lewes.
(*d*) The Cuckmere Gap.

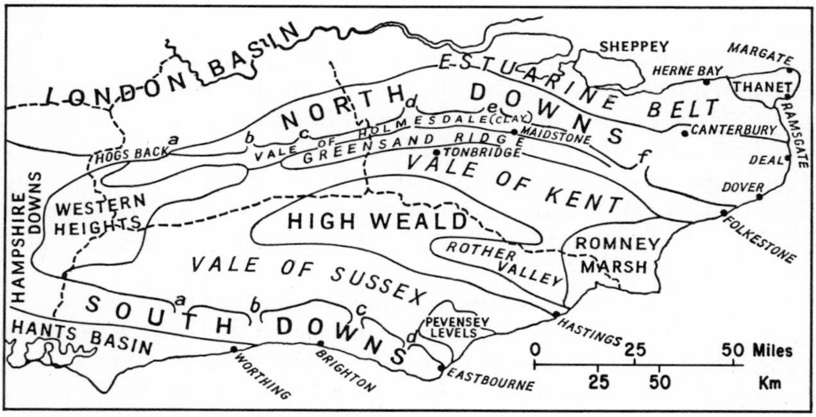

FIG. 39. The minor regions of the Weald

Apart from the features associated with the normal scarplands there are morphological characters of great interest in the Weald in the presence of platforms, probably cut by the Pliocene sea—the last sea to occupy this part of Britain.

The London Basin

The London Basin is both a geographical and a geological unit. Geologically, it is a broad synclinal basin with a clearly defined chalk rim and a central portion occupied by sands and clays of the Tertiary sequence, by gravels of varied origin, and by alluvium. The chalk which underlies the London Basin in turn rests directly, or with but a small intervening thickness of older deposits, on the ancient Paleozoic platform which, like its

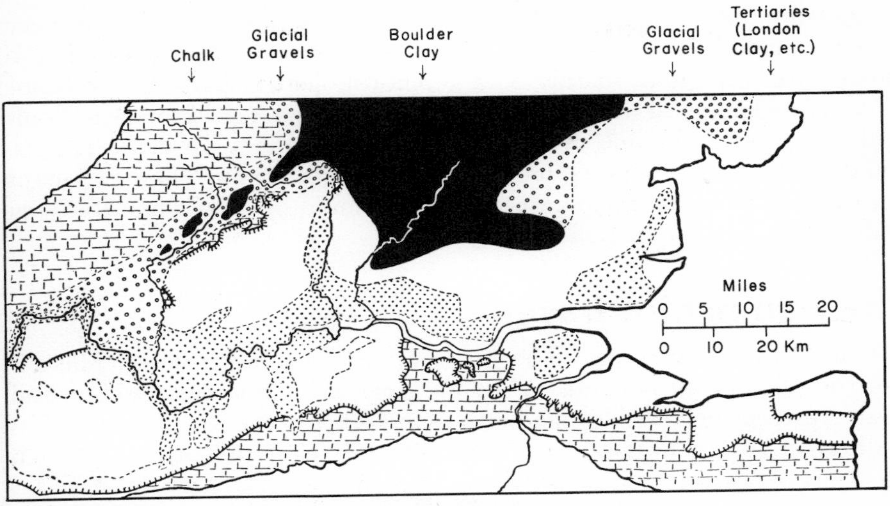

Fig. 40. The geology of the London Basin (simplified)
Lightly dotted area = river gravels; for alluvium, see dotted area on Fig. 41. (*After S. W. Wooldridge*)

analogues in South Wales or northern France, is highly folded and fractured. It is probable that renewed movements along the folds and fractures of the Paleozoic platform have been responsible for the existence in the London Basin of minor structures. The London Basin, a syncline as a whole, is not symmetrical. Its axis is towards the southern edge, and it is to be noted that it is along this line that the lower River Thames flows. Then there is quite an important fold in the centre with an east–west trend, sometimes known as the Thames Basin or the London Basin Anticline. These minor structures, combined with the very varied character of the

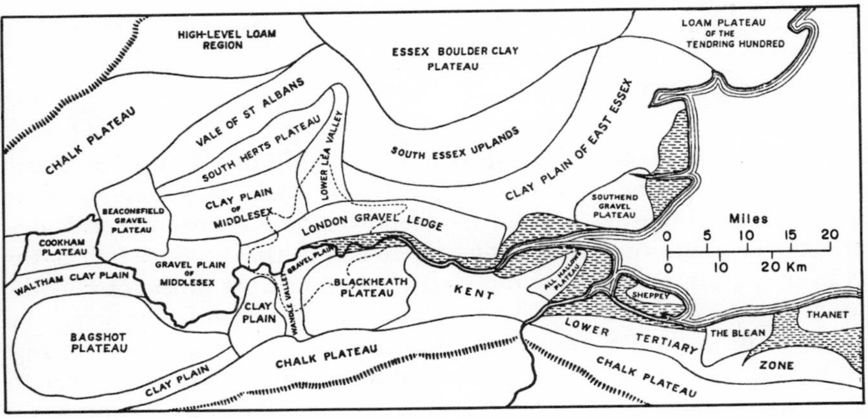

Fig. 41. The minor physiographic regions of the London Basin, according to the late Professor S. W. Wooldridge

3

young sedimentary rocks which fill in the basin, are responsible for its very varied morphological character. It has, accordingly, been divided into minor natural regions, mainly on a geomorphological basis, by Professor S. W. Wooldridge.[1] Two maps are here reproduced from Professor Wooldridge's account, the one showing the position of the main drift deposits, and the other a suggested regional subdivision of the basin. These two maps must be left to speak for themselves. They should be used when studying in detail the position of London itself.

The Hampshire Basin

In many ways the Hampshire Basin resembles the London Basin. There is a surrounding girdle of chalk downs and a central region of later clays and sands. Instead, however, of the basin being open to the sea to the east, its southern chalk rim has been cut through by the sea in two places—at each

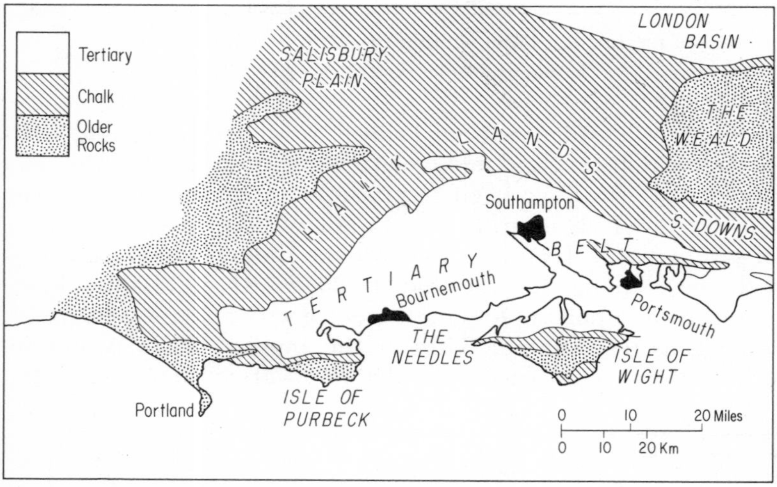

FIG. 42. The Hampshire Basin

end of the Isle of Wight. Although strictly speaking the Hampshire Basin might be limited to the central area of Tertiary rocks, it is convenient to consider the surrounding area of chalk downs also in any general geographical consideration of the Basin. There is thus the Tertiary belt of the heart of the basin, and the surrounding chalk lands. As in the case of the London Basin, subsidiary folds occur, and one important one brings up the chalk to form the Portsdown Hill to the north of Portsmouth (see Fig. 42). The Tertiary belt differs from that of the London Basin in the rather larger proportion of coarse or mixed sands. These are especially important

1. 'The physiographic evolution of the London Basin', *Geography*, **17**, 1932, 99–116.

in the southwest, where the New Forest is found on sandy areas of this character. The more varied of the Tertiary rocks give rise to sandy and loamy soils suitable for mixed farming, and have a low but varied relief. The southern rim of the Hampshire Basin is formed by a sharp fold of chalk which cuts across the Isle of Wight, following its longer axis. To the south of this central ridge in the Isle of Wight there are early Cretaceous rocks, giving rise to varied country repeating on a small scale some of the features of the Weald. In the so-called Isle of Purbeck still older rocks appear, and one sees part of the Jurassic sequence of the Jurassic scarplands.

East Anglia

East Anglia corresponds roughly with the counties of Norfolk and Suffolk. Chalk underlies most of the western two-thirds of this tract and later Tertiary rocks the remainder, but the whole tends to be so thickly covered with glacial and other deposits that East Anglia is very far from resembling the well-known chalk downland. At the present day it is difficult to realise the former isolation of East Anglia. It is bounded on the north and east by the sea. To the south it stretched as far as the once thickly forested damp lowlands of Essex; on the west lay the impassable marshes of the Fenlands, and it was only to the southwest that East Anglia could be approached along the comparatively dry route afforded by the chalk country of the East Anglian Heights. Though the former isolation has disappeared, East Anglia remains a remarkable geographical entity. The character of East Anglia varies mainly according to the nature of its surface deposits. The whole is a low plateau with an undulating surface, often indeed almost flat, and in which those towns and villages situated along the river courses tend to be hidden, as, for example, in the case of Norwich. A special feature of interest is that area known as the Broads—wide stretches of shallow water, probably resulting from the excavation of peat—where the rivers have been ponded back by the formation of bars preventing the free flow of their waters to the North Sea. As East Anglia is mainly agricultural, its division into subregions will be considered relative to agriculture.

IRELAND

The geography and natural regions of Ireland have been reserved for special treatment in connection with agriculture (see Chapter 29), but it may be noted here that its physiographic units connect very closely with those of England and Scotland. In the northwest there are masses of ancient metamorphic rocks which form a continuation of the Highlands of Scotland. In the northeast there is the natural continuation of the Southern Uplands of Scotland. Between the two there should be a western extension of the Midland Valley of Scotland, but this is obscured by the huge spread of lava which makes up the so-called Antrim Plateau, a saucer-shaped basalt plateau with the large but shallow Lough Neagh in the centre. The Mourne Mountains are formed by a mass of granite intruded into rocks which are a continuation of the Southern Uplands of Scotland. The south-east of Ireland is occupied by the Wexford Uplands and the Wicklow Mountains. Doubtless the Wexford Upland area was formerly continuous with the main mass of Wales with which it is geologically and structurally allied, whereas the Wicklow Mountains represent an enormous mass of granite, the largest in the British Isles. Southwestern Ireland is characterised by a succession of sandstone ridges and limestone valleys. The sandstone is mainly of Old Red Sandstone age, the limestone is the Carboniferous Limestone. The folding is Armorican; the folds are not quite east and west, the general trend being from westsouthwest to eastnortheast. The heart of Ireland is occupied by a great plain—the Central Plain—represented on geological maps as consisting of an enormous mass of Carboniferous Limestone. Through this there appear isolated mountain masses consisting either of older rocks, which appear in the form of anticlinal masses from beneath the limestone, or which represent the remnants of younger rocks of Coal Measure age. Actually the Carboniferous Limestone in the heart of Ireland is very rarely seen. It has been covered to a great depth, either by a mask of bog and peat or by sands, clays, and other deposits which were left behind during the retreat of the great ice sheet.

4
British weather and climate

The variability of British weather has long been a byword and, as every holiday-maker knows, the most reliable of British weather experts are apt to be misled, at least at times, in their attempts to forecast the coming weather. Until recently atmospheric conditions at or near the surface of the earth were those which most concerned its human inhabitants. With the coming of the airplane the conditions in the higher layers of the earth's atmosphere suddenly became of considerable importance. It was during the First World War that innumerable investigations had almost perforce to be carried out in the higher layers of the atmosphere in studying the behaviour of air currents and the occurrence of air pockets. It was largely as a result of these investigations, previously of interest mainly to the scientific meteorologist, that ideas concerning the causation of weather conditions were fundamentally changed. The dogmatic statements of the earlier text-books can no longer be accepted, but at the same time it is not yet possible to state fully in simple terms, or with general assurance, the results of modern studies.

The old concept of the planetary wind systems placed the British Isles in the belt of the 'Southwest anti-trades', later described more accurately as the Westerlies or Variables. The development of the Polar Front hypothesis associated especially with the name of Bjerknes and his colleagues of the Norwegian school of meteorologists led to the current concepts of air masses of differing origin and the phenomena associated with the fronts along which these air masses meet. The development of radar led to entirely new knowledge of the character of the upper atmosphere, and this has been greatly extended by the use of space-craft.

Nevertheless, we can still state simply that a number of factors have a determining influence on the character of British weather and climate. The factors may be grouped as follows:

(*a*) The shores of the British Isles, more especially the western shores, are bathed by a warm drift of water, the North Atlantic Drift, which is a continuation of the Gulf Stream. The existence of this warm drift of water has undoubtedly an important effect in ameliorating winter conditions. To the north and northeast of the British Isles no land barrier exists to prevent the flow of water. It therefore makes its influence felt right along the coast of

Norway to well within the Arctic Circle, with the result that even the Murmansk coast of northern Russia remains free from ice throughout the winter. The British Isles thus lie within the winter gulf of warmth and possess a milder climate than any other region in corresponding latitudes. They afford a remarkable contrast in this respect to lands such as northern Japan or Labrador, which are situated on the eastern side of continental masses, and which are under the influence of cold ocean currents. It must be remembered that the direct effect of the warm waters themselves is much less important than the warmth which is communicated from the water to the prevalent southwesterly winds. The existence of the Continental Shelf round Britain enhances the influence of the waters in that they are spread out over a wide area and thus exert a maximum influence in warming the overlying air.

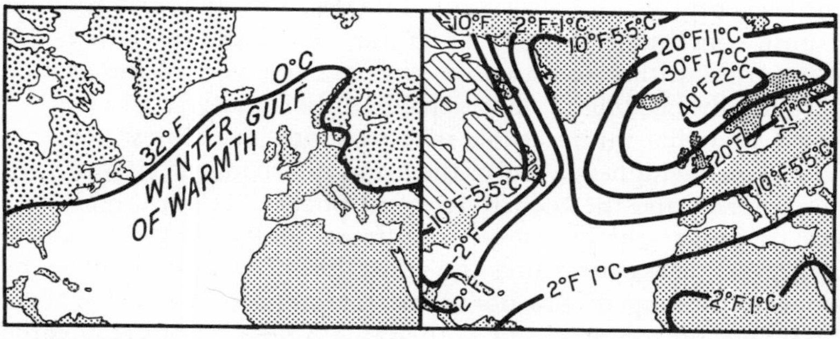

FIG. 43. The figure on the left shows the 'winter gulf of warmth' in which the British Isles lie. The isotherm shown is that of freezing point for January. The figure on the right expresses the same facts in terms of isanomalous lines. All parts heavily stippled are more than 20 Fahrenheit degrees or eleven Centigrade degrees above the average for their latitude. Note the negative anomalies over eastern Canada

(*b*) Except perhaps for certain periods in winter the British Isles lie wholly within what has long been called the westerly wind belt. There is not, of course, at any season of the year a constant westerly or southwesterly wind, although the southwesterly is the *dominant* wind in these islands. What is perhaps more important is the fact that the greater part of our weather comes from the west, that is from across the Atlantic, and that these islands are greatly affected by what are now described as maritime tropical (mT) air masses. The sequence of British weather depends very largely on a series of whirls and eddies in the atmosphere (to which we give the name depressions, or 'lows') and intervening wedges of high pressure which move across these islands in a direction which is generally from between southwest and northwest. By comparing the daily weather maps published by the Meteorological Office for successive days, it is often possible to trace the movements of the individual depressions across the Atlantic Ocean. On the other hand, any long range forecasting based on the weather experienced on the other side of the Atlantic is obviously liable to go wrong, since the depressions may become filled up and disappear in the course of their passage across the Atlantic or their path may lie to the north or to the south of the British Isles. The sequence of weather during the passage of a depression is well known, but changes in the rate of progression and in the intensity of depressions present considerable difficulties to the forecaster. Further reference will be made later to the character and causation of these depressions.

(*c*) The configuration of the British Isles, particularly the existence of numerous inlets, so that no part of the country is far from the sea, makes the penetration inland of oceanic influences more than would otherwise be the case. The existence of the principal hill masses of Britain on the western side of the islands, combined with the fact that the main rain-bearing winds blow from the southwest, results in a very marked difference in the amount of rainfall on the west and on the east. If it were not for this surface relief the whole of the British Isles would experience a moist climate, more like that of Ireland.

It will now be clear that the passage of depressions, or cyclones,[1] over these islands has a dominating influence in determining the character of our daily weather. Thus the causation of these whirls in the air is a matter of some importance. According to the Polar Front hypothesis first developed by the Norwegian school a very important difference is found between cold polar air and warm air moving from the southwest, that is from tropical and subtropical regions. The position and the amount of the cold polar air varies with the seasons, and this mass of cold heavy air may be regarded as having a front, or southern limit, known as the Polar Front, lying normally somewhere to the north of the British Isles, not infrequently at least in the neighbourhood of Iceland. It has been suggested that in winter the Polar Front may be regarded *very roughly* as following the 0°C (32°F) isotherm. It is the meeting of the current of tropical warm air and the cold polar air that is believed to give rise to the succession of depressions which we associate with the Polar Front. The formation of depressions on this hypothesis is best understood by reference to the diagram. It will be seen that a whirling motion of the air is set up in which the winds blow round a centre, actually a low-pressure centre, in a counterclockwise direction. Where the warm moisture-laden air meets the cold polar air condensation takes place, especially as the warm air rises naturally over the cold air. The indraught of cold air from the north which marks the passing of the depression is accompanied by a drop in temperature, but, after an initial cloudiness explained in Fig. 49, by a clearing of the sky. If one accepts this explanation of the formation of depressions, the fact that the Polar Front is approximately over Iceland would result in a continuous succession of depressions passing

1. It has now become more usual to restrict the term 'cyclone' to tropical storms.

across Iceland in a northeasterly direction. If one takes an average of such conditions one gets the conception of a semipermanent low-pressure system situated approximately off Iceland.

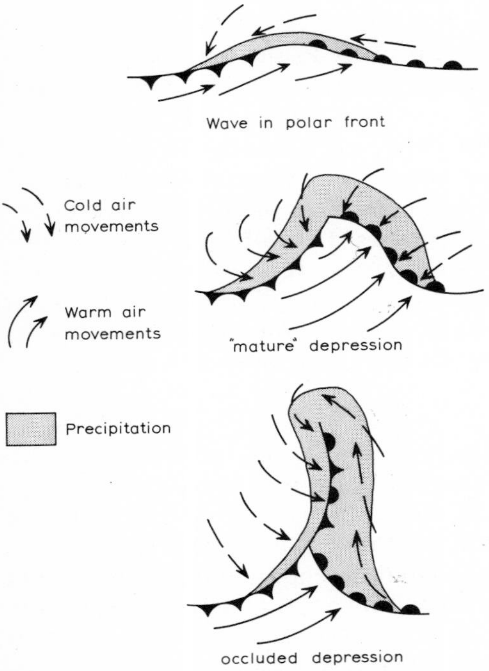

Fig. 44. Diagram illustrating the Polar Front hypothesis of the formation of depressions

Weather and climate of northwest Europe

Before considering the weather conditions in the British Isles in particular, it will be necessary to look at the weather conditions affecting the whole of Europe, and it is simplest to do this by contrasting the winter and the summer conditions.

Winter conditions

In the winter months the Continent of Europe lies in the belt of westerly winds, warm moisture-laden winds from the Atlantic Ocean. The extra-tropical belt of high pressure at this season lies well to the south of the Continent—over the Sahara and its continuation into the Atlantic Ocean to the south of the Azores. Thus there is a high pressure area over the Azores and, as we have already seen, a semipermanent low pressure system roughly over Iceland. But the eastern part of the Continent is very near the great land mass of central Asia, of which it is indeed a continuation, and so at this season gets extremely cold. One may picture a great mass of cold heavy air over Asia and eastern Europe, giving rise to a permanent high pressure system in the winter. The warm moisture-laden air from the Atlantic blows up against this, as against a wall, and either finds a way of escape to the northeast along the coast of Norway, or a way of escape to the south along the Mediterranean. At times this great high pressure system of eastern Europe, with its cold outblowing winds, may exert its influence even as far as the British Isles and may therefore give rise to cold and frosty, though often sunny, weather. Indeed it may be said that the winter weather of the British Isles is determined by the relative strength or importance of

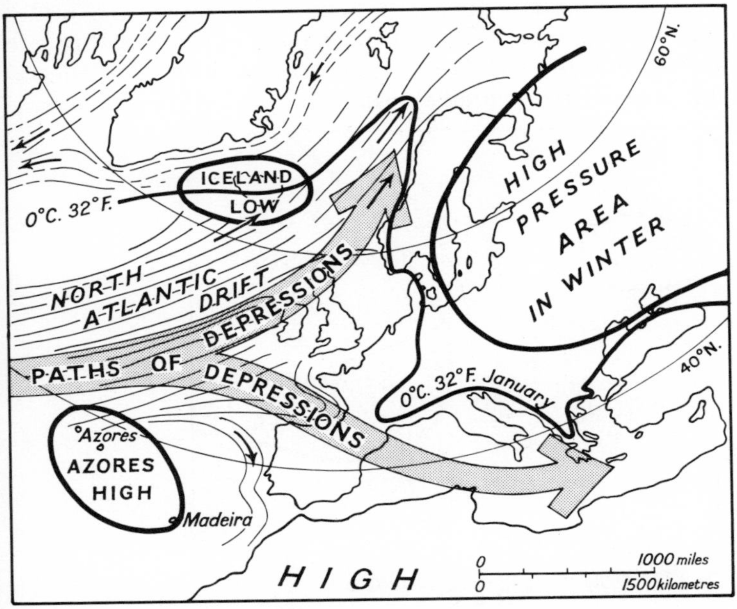

FIG. 45. Generalised winter conditions

Many of the depressions moving along the southern path do not, in fact, penetrate farther than Italy.

these three great pressure systems—the semipermanent low pressure system over Iceland, the permanent high pressure system over eastern Europe, and the high pressure system south of the Azores. Bearing these facts in mind it is not difficult to understand why in the winter months it becomes steadily colder as one travels eastwards across the British Isles and, indeed, as one travels eastwards in Europe. In Europe the isotherm of 0°C (32°F), or freezing point, divides the Continent roughly into two halves and, as we have already noted above, we may look upon this isotherm as marking approximately the position at this season of the Polar Front. Thus the cold mass of air over Russia and eastern Europe may be regarded as lying within the Polar Front. At this season the moisture-laden winds from the west deposit their moisture on the western sides of the land masses; they are unable to penetrate very far towards the east and so there is comparatively little precipitation in the east. This is apparent even in the British Isles, where in the western half of the islands more than half of the total rainfall comes in the winter months, whereas in the eastern half of the islands the greater rainfall is during the summer months (see Fig. 59).

Summer conditions

At this season the wind systems of the world have moved to the north of their average position, so that only the northern part of Europe comes under the influence of the westerly winds. The southern parts of Europe, that is to say the countries surrounding the Mediterranean Sea, lie within the influence of the high pressure belt which almost girdles the globe just outside

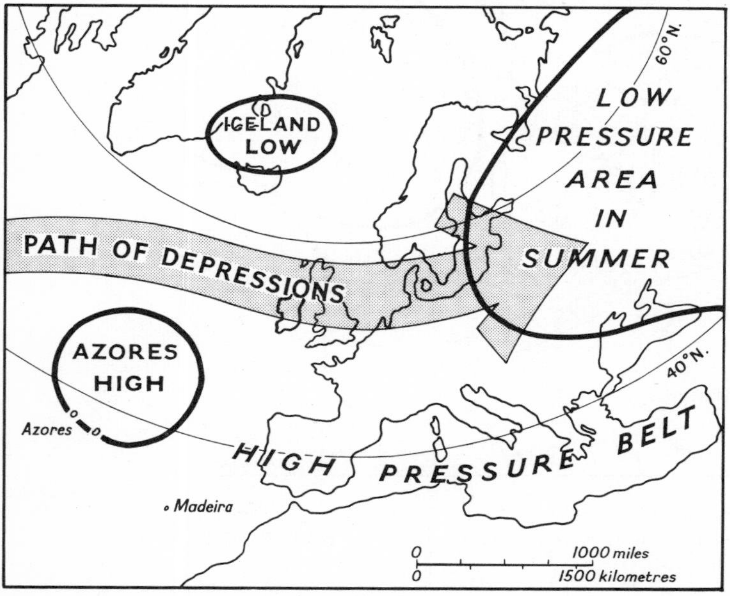

FIG. 46. Generalised summer conditions
The main depression path might more justifiably be shown north of the British Isles.

the Tropics. The high pressure reigning in the summer months over the Mediterranean prevents the penetration of the cooling, or rain-bearing, winds from the Atlantic Ocean. Consequently the Mediterranean lands suffer from considerable heat and comparative, or even complete, rainlessness. In the Atlantic the high pressure centre of the Azores, which forms part of this belt of high pressure, is north of its winter position and frequently extends its influence as far as the British Isles. On the other hand the Polar Front is farther to the north and the belt of depressions which is associated with it tends to be rather north of the island of Iceland and to affect the British Isles far less than in the winter. In eastern Europe the conditions of winter are reversed. The great continental land mass is greatly heated and a large low-pressure area is the result. There is a tendency for the low pressure to be particularly marked over southern Russia; towards this area the rain-bearing winds from the Atlantic blow, and result in the light spring rains of the steppelands of southeastern Europe. Thus central and eastern Europe have the greater part of their rain, that is to say more than half the annual total, in the summer half of the year rather than in the winter.

It needs but a glance at a map of Europe to realise that the British Isles tend to be centrally situated between the three main pressure systems, and actually our weather, both in winter and summer, is largely determined by their relative strength. In winter there is a distinct tendency for the low pressure system over Iceland to be the most potent in determining the weather of these islands, except in those years when the high pressure system over eastern Europe is exceptionally strong and extends its influence as far as the east coasts of Scotland and England. For example, in the winter of 1928–29, and again in 1939–40, 1946–47 and 1962–63, when settled cold weather prevailed for long periods at a time, with cold easterly or north-easterly winds, it was found that the pressure system of eastern Europe was extending its influence as far as these islands. It should be noticed that when one of the high-pressure systems extends its influence in this way there is a distinct tendency for the weather to remain settled for considerable periods of time. Thus in summer, when the high pressure system of the Azores stretches rather north of its normal position, there is a possibility that at least the south of England will enjoy long spells of fine weather. This happened in the summer of 1921,[1] again in 1929, in 1931, 1947 and 1959. These summers were marked, during the months of August and September, by fine and hot weather over the whole of the southern three-quarters of the islands; but in 1929 in particular the summer was marked in northern Scotland by an extended period of bad weather: in other words, the path of the depressions from the Atlantic lay along the northern fringe of the high pressure system which remained comparatively stable over southern Britain. On the other hand, there are years like 1968, in which the depression tracks in August lay across southern England, giving that area an extremely cool and wet holiday season, while northwest Scotland basked in the unaccustomed sunshine of its finest summer for several decades.

So far we have considered only the three great pressure systems which are dominant factors in determining European weather, but actually the weather in these islands is determined to an even greater extent by the passage of a succession of secondary depressions with intervening ridges of high pressure. Since the British Isles are intermediately placed between the

1. *Q. Jour. Roy. Met. Soc.*, **48**, 1922, 139–68 (dealing with droughts in general).

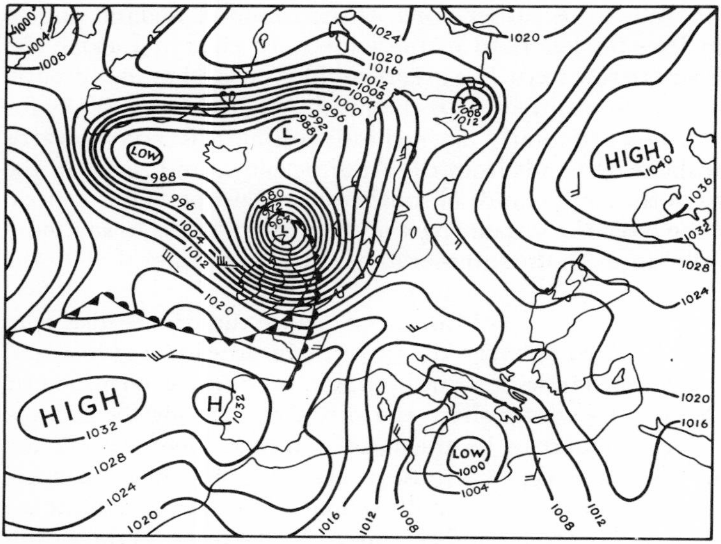

FIG. 47. Weather conditions on Sunday, 30 December 1951

This weather chart shows typical winter conditions with a high pressure system over eastern Europe; a 'high' over or near the Azores; and a low pressure area, with several centres, between Scotland, Iceland and Greenland. Such a situation, with warm and cold or occluded fronts, passing across the British Isles, gives the characteristically variable weather of the British winter. A characteristic small depression is passing over the Mediterranean. Isobars are shown with values expressed in millibars.

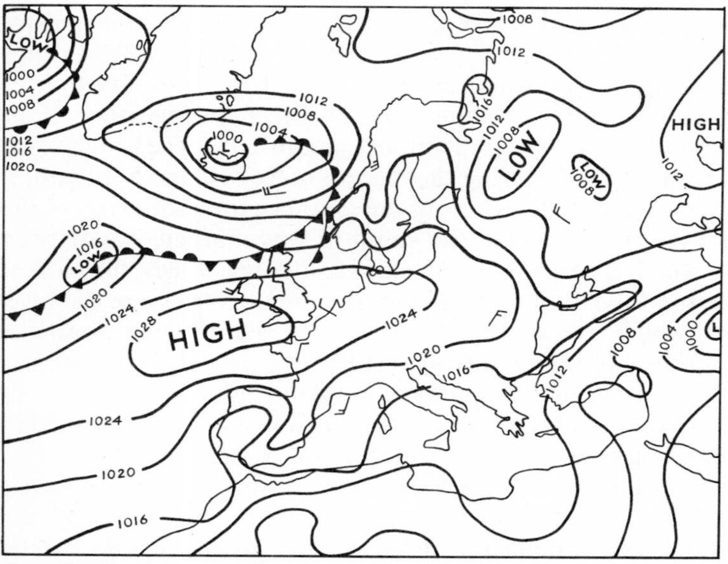

FIG. 48. Weather conditions on Sunday, 1 July 1951

This weather chart shows typical summer conditions, with low pressure systems over Iceland and eastern England and a 'high' extending from the Azores to Britain. The 'polar front' lies for the most part to the north of the British Isles, which are bathed in mT air. But in many summers the fronts frequently pass farther south so that rain and incursions of mP air are common.

three great pressure systems of Europe both in summer and in winter, it follows that the line of passage of these secondary depressions must lie across these islands in both seasons of the year. Since this is the case it is desirable to examine in a little more detail the succession of weather which results. One must remember that a depression in the northern hemisphere is marked by a low-pressure centre with upward currents of air. Winds tend to blow round this centre, for reasons which have already been explained, in an anticlockwise direction, and at the same time towards the centre, where they rise. When a depression is approaching these islands from the Atlantic the barometer will fall and winds will be southerly to southwesterly,

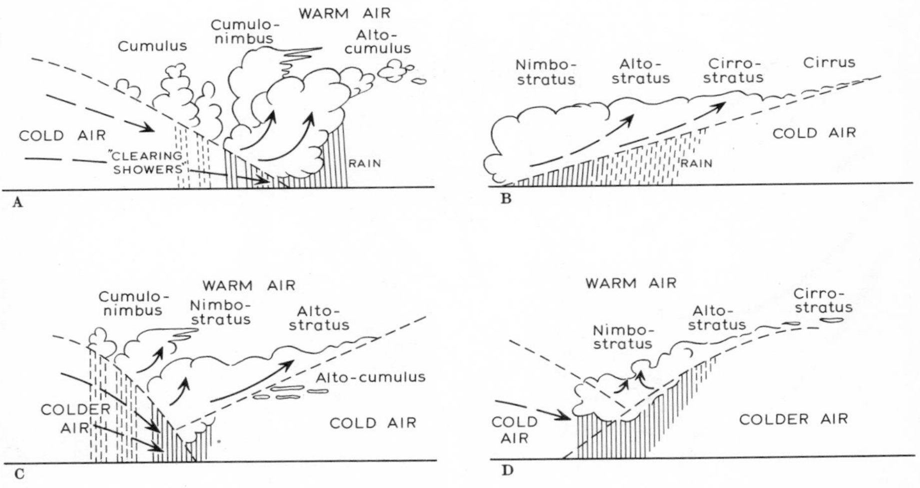

FIG. 49. Sections through typical depressions. A and B: the cold front and warm front as usually developed south of the centre of low pressure; C: a 'cold' occlusion; D: a 'warm' occlusion

veering westerly later. Coming from the Atlantic, they will be warm and moisture-laden, blowing northwards towards cooler regions and also towards the central depression where they will rise, so that rain begins to fall. Where the oncoming warm southwesterly winds meet the colder air, the 'warm front', as it is called, is formed, and along this warm front, where the air is cooled by rising over the cold air, rain is likely to occur, and prolonged steady rain may result. Subsequently there is usually a break in the weather. After the centre of the depression has passed across the islands, usually in an easterly, or northeasterly, direction, the barometer will again rise and the normal air currents will now be the colder winds from the north or northwest. These winds are comparatively dry, but where they impinge on the flanks of the southwesterly current intense rain with squalls may result. This is shown in the diagram as the 'cold front'. Of course the exact sequence of weather at any locality depends on its position in relation to the centre of the depression. If the centre passes to the north of the locality, both warm and cold fronts, with the intervening warm sector, may be experienced; but if it passes to the south, no fronts will cross and there may simply be a prolonged rainy period with the wind gradually backing from east to northwest. The passage of such a depression is often, one might say usually, followed by the passage of a ridge of high pressure, ushered in by the continuation of the cold northerly winds and a steadily rising barometer. Fine sunny weather may result in the summer, but as the winds decrease and calm conditions prevail the passage of such a ridge of high pressure is often marred in winter by the occurrence of fogs.

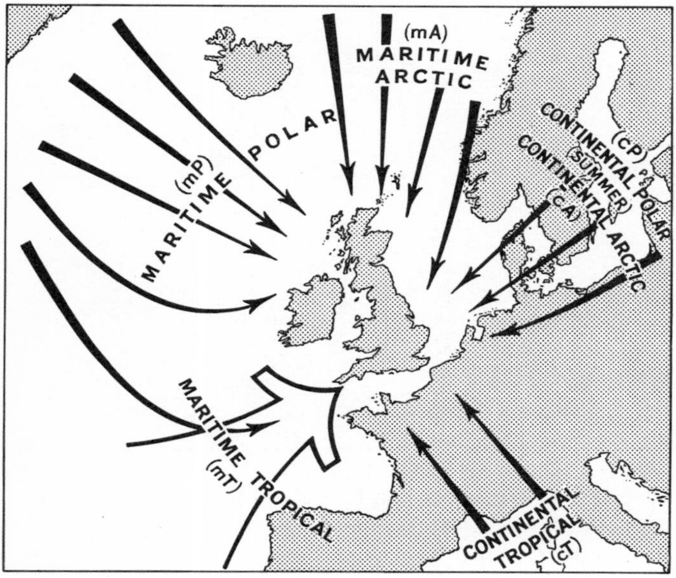

FIG. 50. Diagram showing origin of air masses reaching Britain

Compare with Figs 45 and 46.
The large generalised arrow for mT air is not intended to indicate that this is more important than mP air.

Air masses reaching the British Isles

It is now possible to restate what has been said in the last few pages in modern terms by stating that the British Isles are affected by six principal types of air or air masses. Most of the air reaching Britain can be traced to one of four main source regions—regions where the air has had sufficient time, such as a number of days, to acquire a degree of homogeneity of temperature, humidity and vertical structure throughout its mass. These four source regions are the northern (and especially the northwestern) Atlantic, the Arctic, eastern or continental Europe, and the middle Atlantic

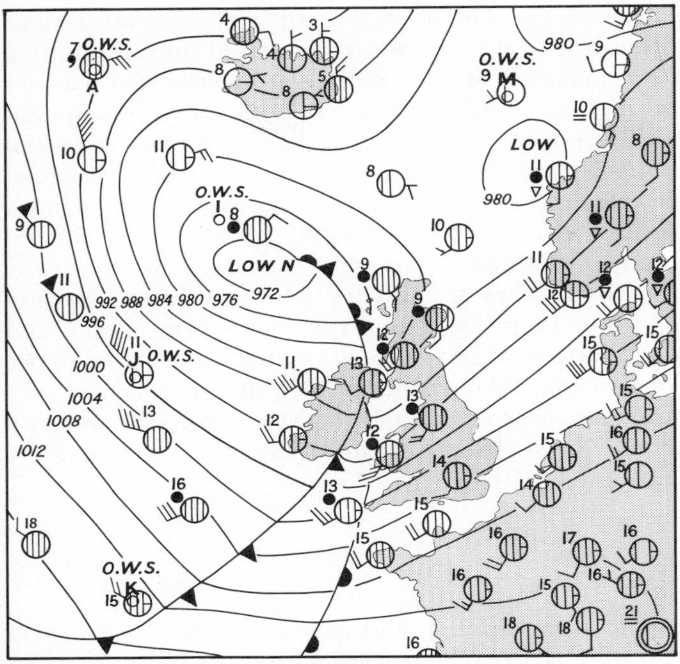

FIG. 51*a*. A typical depression; for key to symbols see Fig. 51*b*

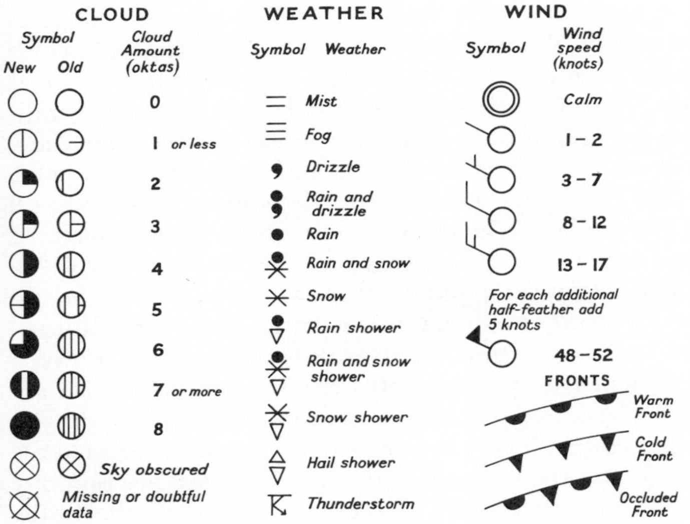

FIG. 51*b*. Symbols used on the Daily Weather Reports. The *cloud* symbols were changed on 1 January 1969 and are shown in the left hand column

high-pressure area of the Azores. The north Atlantic yields the air streams that are called Polar maritime (mP); these are damp and unstable, with a high lapse rate that is increased as they move southwards into warmer latitudes. The Arctic (mA) air masses originate over the polar ice cap and move southwards from the region of Spitzbergen; they seldom occur except in winter, and are bitterly cold, and also somewhat damp and unstable. Polar continental (cP) air masses originate over eastern Europe; in winter, especially if they are drawn from northern Russia, they are very cold and dry; they are less common in summer, but when they do occur, generally under anticyclonic conditions, they are also dry. The mid-Atlantic area of the Azores yields maritime Tropical (mT) air masses, warm, damp, and relatively stable, though capable of giving much rainfall when forced to rise over relief obstacles or over cold polar air masses. Continental Tropical (cT) air masses, derived from northern Africa and the Mediterranean area, are dry and very warm; they occur but rarely in summer, and are virtually unknown in winter.

The equinoxes

In the analysis of the general conditions in Europe we referred to the formation of a great high pressure centre over eastern Europe in winter and the formation of a low pressure centre over the same area in summer. Naturally there must be two seasons of the year when the change from one to the other takes place, and it is very largely the resulting disturbance of atmospheric conditions which is responsible for the well known equinoctial gales experienced in this country. Whilst in the early part of the year high winds are associated with the month of March and the fame of March winds is perpetuated in many a nursery rhyme and popular ballad, the change indicated by these winds does not always take place at exactly the same time. In some years March may 'come in like the lion and go out like the lamb', in others it may come in like the lamb when the winter conditions still prevail, but go out like the lion. The corresponding high winds associated with the disturbances at the autumnal equinox are the equinoctial gales of September and October. After the equinoctial gales of March come the still unsettled conditions of April, when numerous small secondary disturbances in the unstable polar maritime air streams result in April showers. The small rainfall of the early spring months can be correlated with the small evaporation. Indeed, evaporation is almost confined to the six months of April to September. There is a definite lag between the increase of evaporation in April and the increase in the mean rainfall per rain day which does not exceed the average for the year until July. Similarly the mean rainfall per rain day continues above the average for the year for some three months after the evaporation has practically ceased at the end of September.

Temperatures

So far we have been dealing with the weather conditions of the British Isles, and owing to the irregular succession of weather it is sometimes said that the British Isles have no climate, since climate is described as the average state of the weather. This may at least serve as a useful reminder that we should use averages with care owing to the variability from year to year. Taking, first, temperature conditions in the winter, it may be said that in

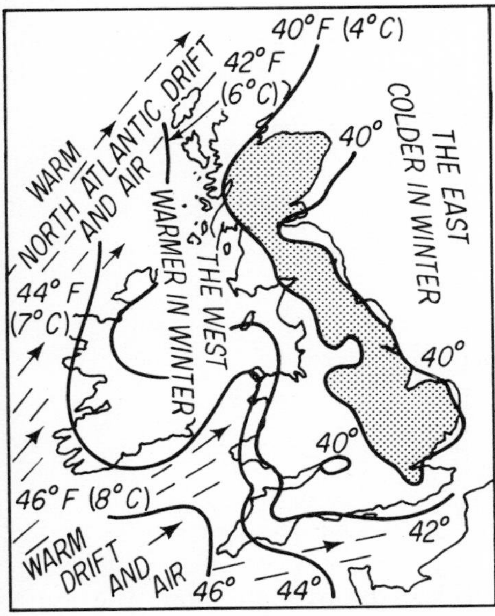

Fig. 52. Temperature conditions in January (1906–35)

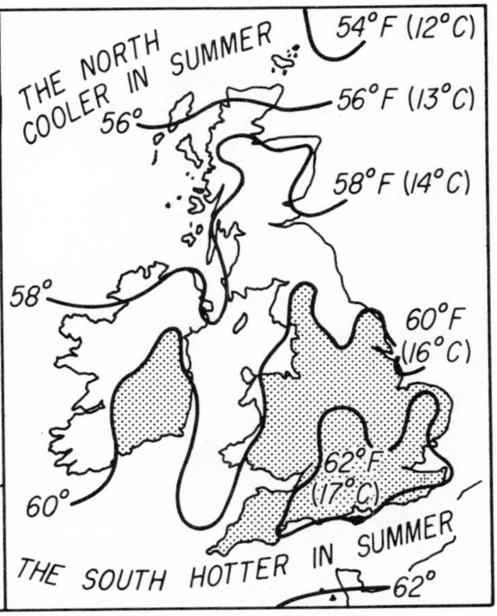

Fig. 53. Temperature conditions in July (1906–35)

Mean temperatures reduced to sea-level (after E. G. Bilham).

general conditions in the British Isles reflect in detail those prevailing in Europe as a whole. In winter the west is warmer than the east and the isotherm of 14°C (40°F) in January roughly divides the islands into two. Its curve should be carefully noted. As one would expect at this season, the extreme southwest of Britain and southwestern Ireland are, taking the average conditions in January, the warmest parts of the islands. The Scilly Isles have an average temperature in January of no less than 7°C (45°F), whilst snow and frost are both rare. The important effects which this has on the products which are possible in these areas, and on the use of warmer parts of Britain in winter as winter resorts, may be mentioned. Taking the evidence afforded by the isotherms alone the coldest parts in the British Isles in winter are certain tracts down the east coast, and it would seem that the east coast of Scotland in the neighbourhood of Aberdeen is not as cold as some parts of the coast of East Anglia farther south, but the ordinary dry-bulb thermometer is scarcely an adequate measure of temperature in so far as it affects human beings and there is perhaps a rawer quality in the air in northern tracts. In summer, by way of contrast, the south of the British Isles is warmer than the north. The isotherm of 15.5°C (60°F) in July runs roughly from east to west. The southeast quarter is the warmest of all in

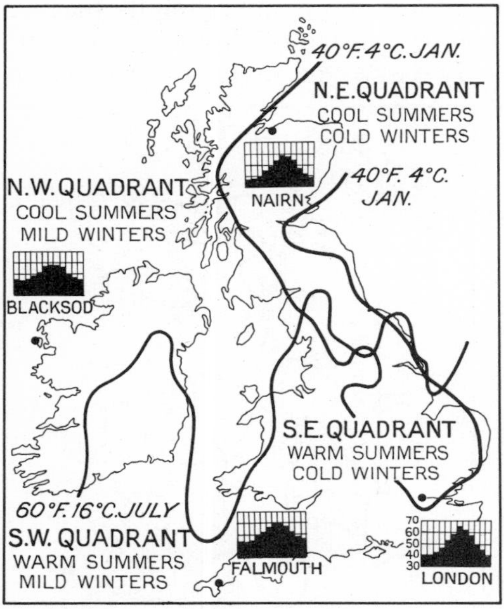

FIG. 54. The four quadrants of the British Isles

July in the neighbourhood of London, but the average along the south coast is high. The coolest parts of the islands at this season of the year are the extreme south of Scotland, the Orkneys and the Shetlands. Though geographers have long been accustomed—perhaps too slavishly—to take January and July as the typical winter and summer months, they are not in the British Isles the coldest and warmest months respectively. It frequently happens in oceanic or insular climates that there is a considerable lag between the period when the sun's rays strike least obliquely or most obliquely on the surface of the ground and the time when the highest and lowest average temperatures are reached, so that for many parts of the British Isles February is the coldest month and usually August the hottest month. Even, however, taking January and July and noticing the course of the isotherms across the islands, it will be seen that the 4°C (40°F) isotherm for January and the 16°C (60°F) isotherm for July divide the islands roughly into four quarters. The northwest quadrant is the most 'oceanic', and it is possible to find stations in the Outer Hebrides which have a range of only 13°–6° (= 7 degrees) C or 56–43 (= 13 degrees) F between the winter months and the summer months. The southeast quadrant is the most nearly 'continental', if that adjective can be applied at all to any part of the British

Isles. Nevertheless, the temperature range of London is from 18°–3°C (64°–38°F)—no less than 15 degrees C (26 degrees F)—quite a remarkable contrast to the stations just mentioned.

So far we have been considering temperature as it affects lowlands, and the isotherms which have been discussed are sea level isotherms. If one considers the actual surface temperatures as recorded the theoretical difference between actual temperature and temperature reduced to sea-level is 0.6°C for every 100 metres (1°F for 300 ft). Since the greater part of Lowland Britain is less than 200 metres (600 ft) above sea level the theoretical difference does not exceed 1.2°C (2°F). Elevation begins to exert an important effect on the higher ground of Highland Britain and on the top of the highest point in the British Isles, Ben Nevis (1341 m: 4400 ft), the temperature if reduced to sea level equivalent would be nearly 8°C (15°F) higher.

The effect of elevation justifies us in regarding the Highlands of Scotland in January as the coldest part of the country. The factor of elevation is readily apparent when snowfall is considered (see Fig. 60). Whilst in the southwest of the country, in Devon and Cornwall, snow does not normally fall on low ground on more than five days in each year, and is not found to be lying for more than five days, such lofty tracts as Dartmoor are frequently seen to have a powdering of snow. Indeed, on the higher parts of Dartmoor snow normally lies for more than twenty days in every year.

The effect of elevation on temperature is however far from simple. Cold air behaves much like cold water. It flows downhill and will collect in a valley or basin where there is no outlet and gives rise to a 'frost pocket' or 'frost hollows'. Some extremely low temperatures have been recorded in such obstructed valley situations amongst the Chiltern Hills. On the other hand, where cold air can drain freely as it does down river valleys and out over the sea, such frost pockets are absent.

Studies which have been undertaken in connection with the growing of fruit and the siting of fruit orchards have shown how very important it is to secure free drainage of air. Even a high hedge can hold up air movement and increase the hazards of frost (see Fig. 58). In addition aspect plays a much greater part in the determination of local climates than was suspected in the past. If one attempts to determine the upper limit of cultivation in such areas as the Pennines, one finds that cultivation is almost invariably to a higher level on the northern sides of valleys, that is to say on those slopes facing southwards towards the sun, than it is on the southern sides of the valleys.

Hills running from east to west afford a remarkable protection from cold northerly or northeasterly winds. The attraction of Ventnor, on the southern side of the Isle of Wight, is very largely due to the protection of the town from northerly winds by the high chalk downs which lie immediately behind. The early cultivation of tomatoes along a strip of the Sussex coast in the neighbourhood of Worthing is in large measure due to the protection

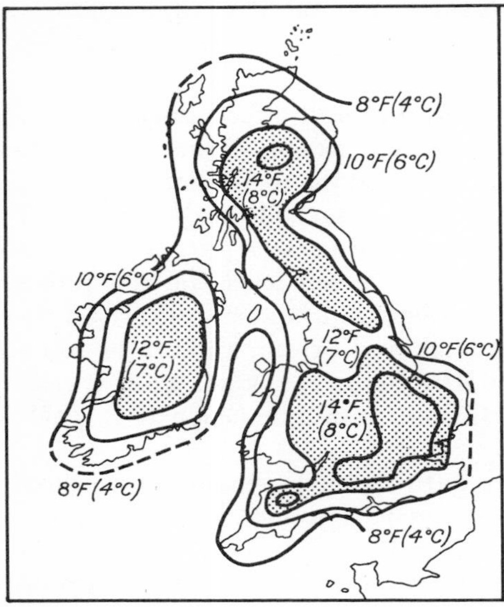

Fig. 55. Mean daily range of temperature (whole year), 1906–35

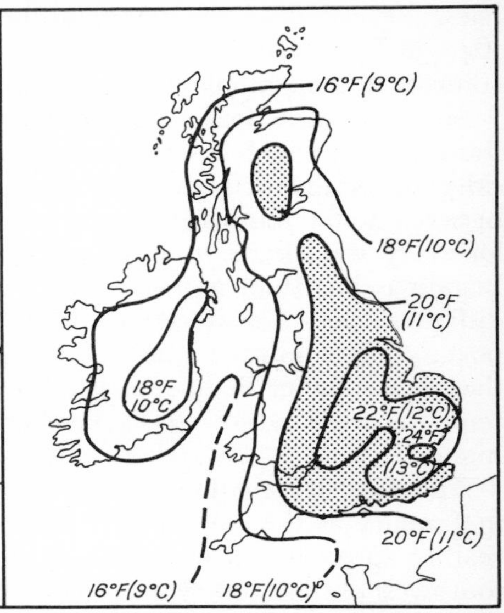

Fig. 56. Mean annual range of temperature 1921–35

Both these maps are after E. G. Bilham and clearly illustrate the moderating influence of the sea in lowering the range of temperature both diurnal and annual, whilst Fig. 56 illustrates the relative continentality of south-eastern England.

afforded by the South Downs in the immediate hinterland. The delightful mildness of Aberystwyth, which is important to the town as a resort, is again partly due to the protection by the Welsh hills behind. By way of contrast some of these sheltered resorts are described as enervating by those who prefer the more bracing conditions from the vigorous winds of the east coast in the winter. This brings us to a consideration of the very important question of frost. The following table shows the normal number of days when ground frost occurs at some widely scattered stations in Britain:

Normal number of days with ground frost

STATION	METRES	HEIGHT FEET	J	F	M	A	M	J	J	A	S	O	N	D	TOTAL FOR YEAR	DAYS WITH SNOW
Balmoral	283	930	23	21	21	17	9	3	2	1	5	10	18	21	151	50
Glasgow	55	180	12	10	11	8	3	1	0	0	4	8	10	12	79	16
Birmingham	163	535	17	15	15	11	5	1	0	1	3	7	14	13	102	11
London	3	18	15	15	15	13	4	1	0	0	2	8	14	14	101	13
Clacton	15	54	12	13	11	7	1	0	0	0	0	1	7	9	61	16
Liverpool	57	188	14	14	18	9	1	0	0	0	0	1	10	13	80	11
Falmouth	51	167	8	8	10	5	0	0	0	0	0	1	6	9	47	5
Guernsey	90	295	6	6	5	3	0	0	0	0	0	0	3	4	27	—

A distinction is made between days on which snow is seen to fall (given in this table) and days with snow lying (Fig. 60).

Late frosts in spring are particularly dangerous in such enterprises as fruit farming. They may occur after blossoming and affect the young fruit before it has had time to grow large enough to resist damage. There are many plants which are killed by the first frost of the autumn, e.g. soft-stemmed plants like the vegetable marrow, or flowers such as nasturtium. It is the shortness of the growing season between the last killing frost of spring and the first of autumn, as well as the absence of really high summer temperatures which prohibit the cultivation in the British Isles on a farm scale of such a crop as maize.

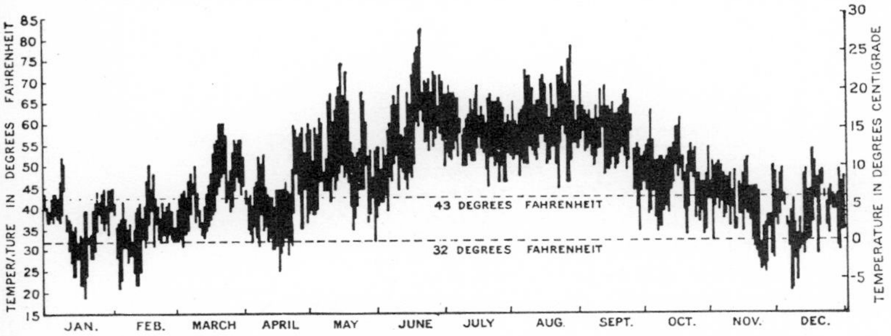

FIG. 57. Diagram showing the temperature range for each day in a typical year (1936) at Macclesfield, Cheshire, 152 metres (500 feet) above sea-level

Notice the number of days when the temperature exceeded 6°C (43°F), the crucial temperature for plant growth. By adding together the number of degrees shown in this diagram above 43°F one gets the concept of accumulated temperature expressed in day degrees.

Another crucial temperature is 6°C (42° or 43°F). At temperatures below this figure most plants are dormant and vegetative growth takes place only when temperatures rise above this figure. This factor is important where fodder grasses are concerned. Since the average temperatures for the coldest month are above this crucial figure in the southwest of England some vegetative growth is going on even in the coldest month, and stock left out in the open can find at least some sustenance in new growth which may be rare or completely absent in colder eastern regions.

Most of the preceding references have been to average temperatures. Considerable importance must be attached to temperature ranges both daily and annual. The two figures (Fig. 55 and Fig. 56) show how the mean daily range throughout the year increases steadily inland from the coasts. This is in some contrast to the mean annual range of temperature which is actually greatest near the southeast coast, and least over the windy islands of northwest Scotland.

Considerable importance must also be attached to absolute maxima and absolute minima, especially the latter. A maximum temperature during the day exceeding 32°C (90°F) in the shade is not infrequently recorded at many stations. Records of 38°C (100°F) and over are extremely rare but have been recorded. For long it was doubted whether a temperature as low as −17°C (0°F) had ever been recorded. Any doubt, however, regarding the possible occurrence of such low temperatures in the British Isles was removed once and for all during the long cold spells of the winters of 1939–1940, 1946–47 and 1962–63 when temperatures down to −20°C (−4°F) were officially recorded. Though very rare such very low temperatures were found to have an unexpected importance. Many plants normally hardy failed to survive and a good example was the widespread destruction of the Californian *Cupressus macrocarpa*. Trees of this species which had flourished for ten to fifteen years were killed by the very low temperatures, probably because the low temperatures were maintained for several days.

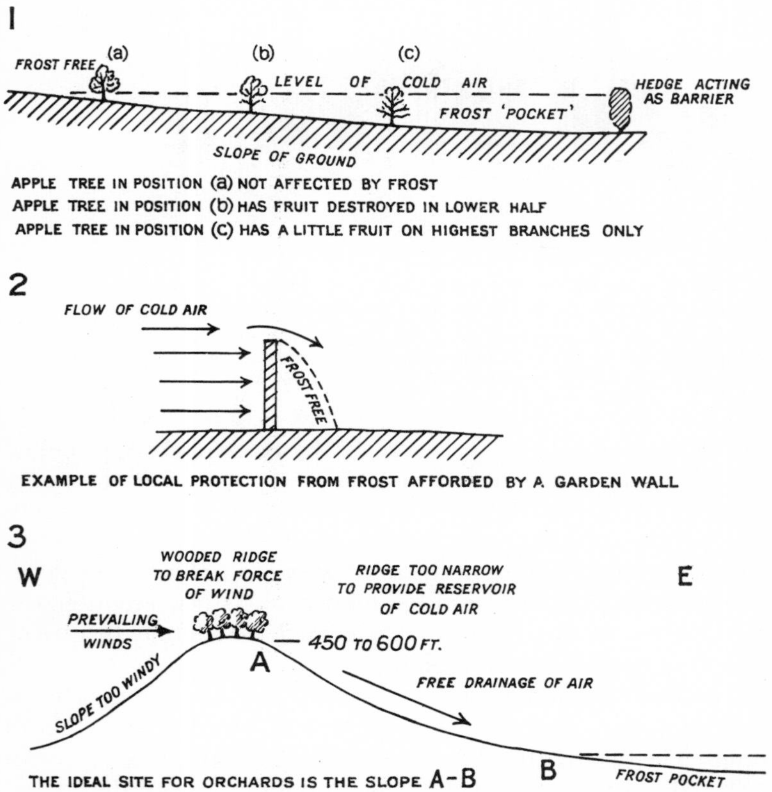

FIG. 58. Diagrams showing the relationship of air drainage to frost pockets and frost-free slopes

Precipitation

In the British Isles precipitation includes drizzle, rain, sleet or hail, and snow, which fall on to the surface of the ground, whilst moisture may also be precipitated from the air as dew and hoar frost or rime, which are directly deposited on exposed surfaces. The distinction between drizzle and rain is now commonly made on the basis that a drizzle drop, from 0.3 millimetres to 0.25 millimetres (one-eightieth to one-hundredth of an inch) in diameter, is only one-quarter to one-twentieth of the size of a raindrop. Whereas raindrops usually fall, drizzle is drifted by the wind.

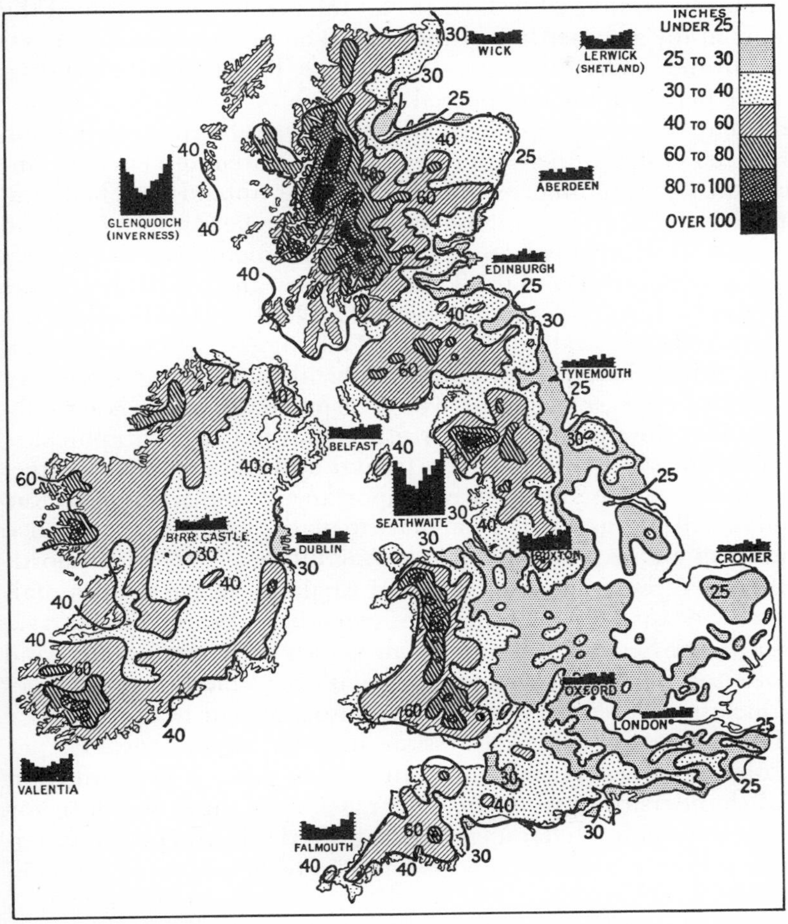

FIG. 59. An annual rainfall map of the British Isles

With the steady accumulation of data, refinements and changes in such a map are possible. For a detailed modern map of Great Britain that in the National Planning Series on the scale of 1:625 000 (in two sheets, Ordnance Survey; second edition, 1968) should be used.

The measurement of moisture deposited as dew or hoar frost is difficult and its influence on vegetation is imperfectly understood. The other forms of precipitation are usually reduced to rainfall equivalent and the remarks which follow regarding rainfall distribution must be taken as including also these other forms of precipitation. A map has been prepared showing the average annual rainfall of the British Isles, together with rainfall graphs showing the distribution of rainfall in the different months of the year. These indicate certain important points: the first is the well distributed rainfall throughout the year, characteristic of the British Isles; the second is the general tendency for stations on the west to receive the greater part of their precipitation in the winter, while farther east the greater proportion of the rainfall occurs in the summer half of the year. The third is that in general there is an autumn maximum, usually reached in October, extending roughly for the period of the equinoctial gales.

Then the map illustrates quite clearly the general broad distinction between the drier east and the wetter west, with the areas of heaviest rainfall—more than 1500 millimetres (60 in)—on the upland and highland areas, particularly of Scotland, the Lake District, the Pennines, Wales and western Ireland. The average annual rainfall is about 500 millimetres (20 in) in the neighbourhood of the Thames estuary and probably reaches 5000 millimetres (200 in) over small areas in the Western Highlands, at the head of the River Garry and on Snowdon. This suggests at once that the rainfall of the British Isles is mainly orographical, but if it were entirely orographical, then the east, of course, would be much drier than is actually the case. In reality the rainfall of the British Isles is partly orographical—due to the relief of the islands—partly frontal and, in a smaller degree, brought by thunderstorms. The relative importance of the different factors causing rainfall will of course vary from place to place, largely in accordance with relief, aspect and exposure. The following figures, for Keele in north Staffordshire, are representative of Midland England: of the total rainfall in the fifteen years 1952–66, 22.6 per cent came from Warm Fronts, 12.4 per cent from Warm Sectors (the tropical air masses between the warm and cold fronts of a normal depression), 14.9 per cent from Cold Fronts, 17.6 per cent from Occlusions, 18.9 per cent from unstable mP air masses, 8.7 per cent from Polar Lows (frontless depressions in polar air streams), 1.7 per cent from Polar Continental and Arctic air masses, and 3.1 per cent from convectional thunderstorms in tropical air masses. Of these, warm-sector rain is largely orographic in character, whilst frontal rain and precipitation from unstable mP air masses are always liable to be accentuated by relief and elevation.[1]

It may be said at once that the rainfall in all parts of the British islands is adequate for agricultural purposes and, in many of the more hilly regions, the rainfall must actually be classed from this point of view as excessive. The coasts of Ireland, western Scotland, and many parts of western England and Wales receive too much moisture to make farming possible or at least profitable. A severe limitation is applied by excessive moisture on crops which can be grown by the arable farmer, and it is not too much to say that farming of all types may be prevented in certain areas. Further considera-

1. See papers by E. M. Shaw referred to on p. 817.

FIG. 60. Snowfall in the British Isles, showing the number of mornings with snow lying, annual average 1912–38 (after Gordon Manley)
(Simplified from the *Meteorological Magazine*, **76**, 1947, by permission of the Controller of H.M. Stationery Office)

tion will be given to this question later, but it may be said that cereal farming, with the exception of the cultivation of that hardy crop, oats, is largely restricted to the regions having less than 760 millimetres (30 in) of rain per year. It has, indeed, been suggested that England can be divided into four agricultural provinces by using the 15.5°C (60°F) July isotherm and the

760 millimetres (30 in) rainfall line, since the 15.5°C (60°F) isotherm marks the approximate northern *economic* limit of the cultivation of certain crops (e.g. wheat).

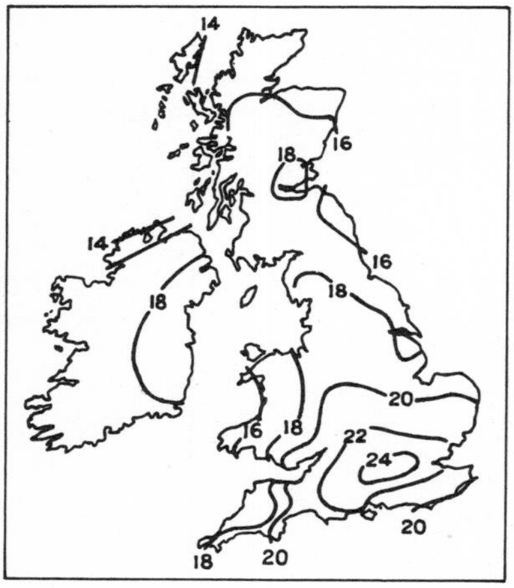

FIG. 61. Evaporation from open water in the British Isles. Average annual amount in inches (after J. Wadsworth)

Rainfall by itself is not, of course, an adequate measure of the relative wetness or dryness of a country from the agricultural point of view, but with cloudy skies and comparatively low temperatures throughout the year evaporation is relatively small;[1] long periods of drought are unknown. Further, the variability of British rainfall from one year to another is comparatively slight; it is rare for any part to experience more than 160 per cent, or less than 50 per cent of the average. There are occasions when the British farmer, robbed of showers of rain at just the seasons when he considers his crops require moisture, complains of drought;[2] but the British Isles may be said never to suffer from drought in the way in which that scourge may affect such an area as Australia. The difference in moisture conditions between the western and eastern sides of Britain is perhaps greater than would appear from an examination of rainfall figures. Since the largest proportion of the rain on the eastern side is cyclonic in character, periods of heavy rain tend to be separated by days when rainfall is practically nil. On the other hand, in the west, particularly in Ireland, there is a much greater

1. Evaporation from exposed water surfaces has recently been shown by J. Wadsworth to vary more than was previously believed—from under 355 millimetres (14 in) per annum in northwest Ireland and northwest Scotland to over 610 millimetres (24 in) in the heart of the London Basin (Fig. 61).

2. He is right; evapotranspiration studies have shown moisture deficiencies in at least some months of the year in the drier parts of Britain in most years and the use of supplemental irrigation for valuable crops such as vegetables is spreading.

tendency for a succession of days of light drizzle. It is a common greeting in Ireland for one farmer to say to another, 'Fine soft day today', meaning a day characterised by warm gentle drizzle. The average number of days with rain increases very steadily from the southeast to the northwest of the British Isles. This is due to the greater frequency of depressions to the north of these islands. Unlike the actual quantity of rainfall, geographical position is of more importance than altitude in determining the number of days with rain.

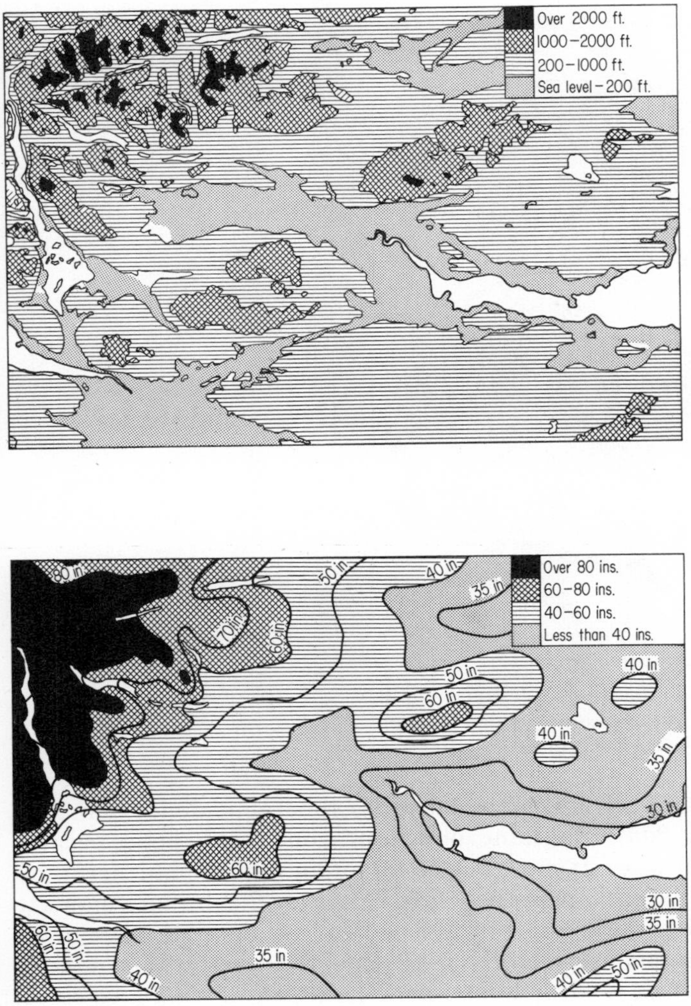

FIG. 62. The correlation between relief and rainfall in the Midland Valley of Scotland (after H. R. Mill)

Sunshine and cloud

Some measure of this difference is afforded by the accompanying sunshine maps of the British Isles. Fig. 63 illustrates the advantages of situation along the south coast and along the east coast, and in lowland areas some distance

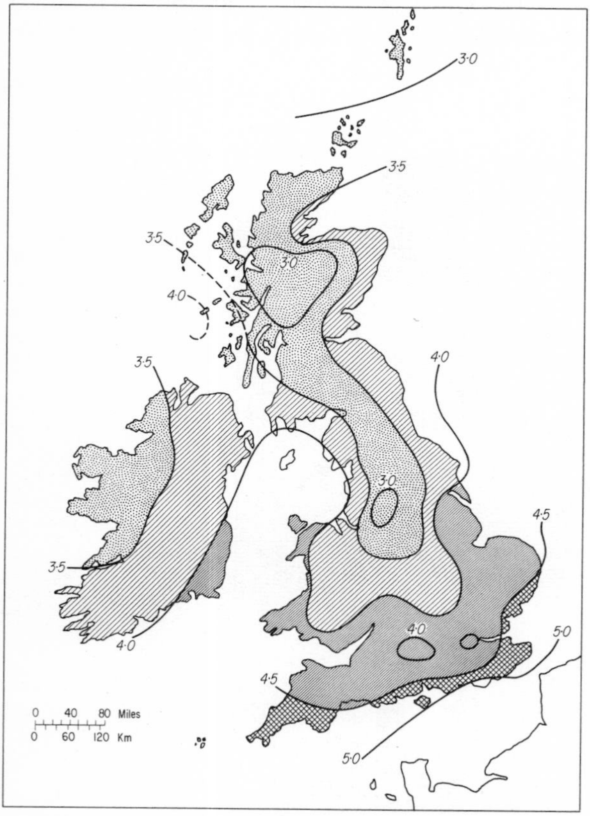

Fig. 63. Sunshine map of the British Isles, showing the average number of hours of sunshine per day throughout the year, 1906–35 (after E. G. Bilham)

from mountains which attract cloud. There is a general tendency, too, for a larger proportion of winter sunshine in the south, one reason being because of the longer winter days. It must not be forgotten that the northernmost part of Britain is sufficiently near the Arctic Circle for the summer nights to pass without complete darkness being reached, at least that is the case in the Shetland Islands in the latter part of June and July, when it is possible to read by the twilight. It is of some interest to note the way in which resort towns have seized upon salient facts of British climate for advertisement purposes. Common slogans include, 'South for Sunshine', while Skegness on the 'drier side' of Britain is 'so bracing'. It may, however, be mentioned that the west coast scores in that slightly more rain falls at night than during the day, while along the east coast slightly more rain falls during the day than at night, the east coast districts experiencing thunderstorms during the late afternoon rather more frequently. The fame of the mild winters of the

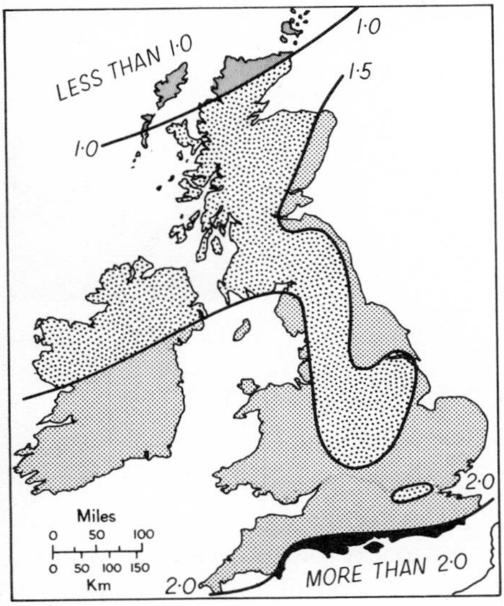

Fig. 64. January sunshine, expressed in number of hours per day

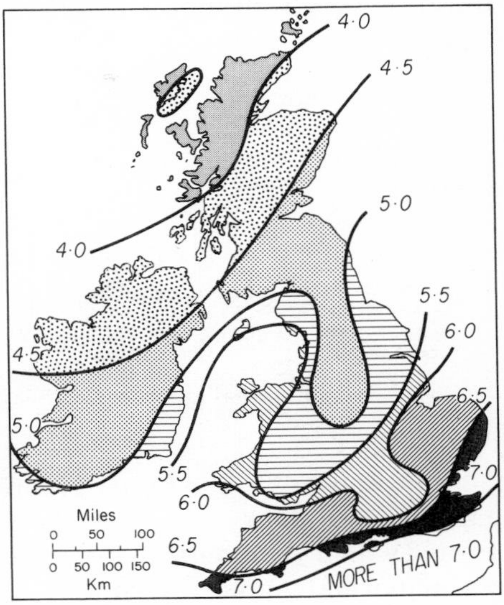

Fig. 65. August sunshine—the number of hours per day in the chief 'holiday month'

Mediterranean coast of France, or the French Riviera, was doubtless responsible for the application of the name 'Cornish Riviera' to the coast of Cornwall. Many years ago a poster on the Cornish Riviera express of the old Great Western Railway showed the Cornish peninsula on one side pointing to the southwest and the Italian peninsula on the other side pointing to the southeast, intending to suggest, of course, the similarity between the two. It is interesting to note that if one takes just the temperature records of coastal towns there is little difference between those of Cornwall and those of the French Riviera. For example, the mean January temperature of Penzance is 7°C (44°F), the January temperature of Nice is 8°C (46°F). The main difference comes in the sunshine records of 25 per cent of the possible for the months of December, January and February for Penzance and over 50 per cent for the same months for Nice. Even so the figures are sufficient to explain the reason why one should find such warmth-loving plants as the palm and the *Yucca* growing outdoors in the sheltered Cornish resorts and why they should justify their existence as winter resorts. Torquay, more accessible and developed with the amenities of a winter resort, has a January temperature of 6.8°C (42.3°F) and a sunshine record for that month of two hours per day.

Wind, fog and atmospheric pollution

The dominant direction of the wind in the British Isles is from the south-west, though wind roses for differing situations show that the degree of dominance varies widely. Exposed situations on the western coastlines illustrate very well by the deformed growth of trees how important wind can be.

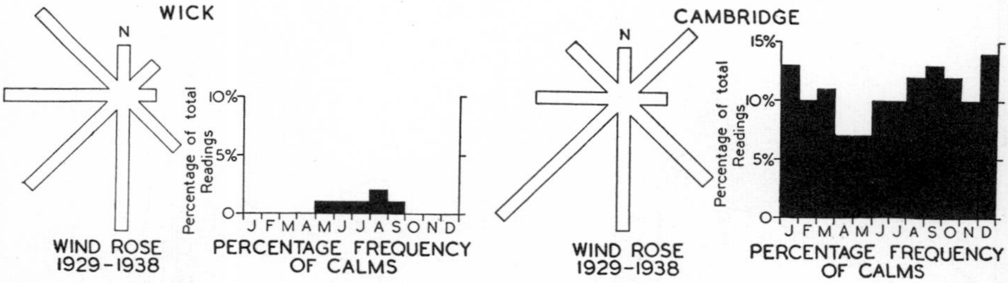

FIG. 66. Wind conditions in Wick, Caithness and Cambridge, 1929–38

At Stornoway in the Outer Hebrides the average number of 'days with gale' reaches 48 in every year; the Scilly Isles record 25. This may be contrasted with Tynemouth on the east coast with only four, and Kew, London, where normally none is recorded. A gale is defined officially as 'wind with a mean velocity exceeding 34 knots (63 kilometres per hour)'.

At least abroad, the British Isles have a reputation for fog, in very large measure undeserved. An attempt has been made, in the table adjoining, to show the number of foggy days in parts of the British Isles. Settled anti-cyclonic conditions in the winter are the most dangerous period. Sea mists, driving up the Channel, are most important, these being caused, of course, by the slight movements of damp, moist air reaching the colder air over Britain itself. Fog or sea mist of this sort is not infrequently responsible for delaying ocean vessels and was directly responsible for the discontinuance of a very useful way of crossing from Britain to the Continent—from Tilbury to Dunkirk (Dunkerque).

Fogs in and around urban areas are frequently accentuated by atmospheric pollution. The old 'pea-soup' fogs of London, Manchester and other great cities were connected with the excessive use of imperfectly combusted coal and the humidity of the atmosphere. It was the disastrous London 'smog' of December 1952 that finally moved the Government to take action that ultimately resulted in the Clean Air Act of 1956. This disaster was caused by an excess of atmospheric pollution by soot and by sulphur dioxide derived from coal burning and the exhaust from internal combustion engines, under meteorological conditions that involved an absence of wind and a temperature inversion. Atmospheric pollution in some form, however, is always with us, particularly in and around large urban and industrialised areas; its local effects vary enormously with wind direction and the nature of the air masses: polar maritime air with its high lapse rate and instability wafting the polluting elements aloft whilst stable air masses, often accompanied under anticyclonic conditions by temperature inversions, confine the pollution to lower atmospheric levels. Much has been done in recent years, through the introduction of smokeless zones in towns and the increasing efficiency of the combustion processes in, for example, thermal power stations, to reduce the incidence of pollution—but no attempt has yet been made to tackle the increasing menace in congested urban streets of motor vehicle exhaust fumes.

Number of days per year on which fog is normally recorded (data from official pilot's manuals)

Falmouth	10	Yarmouth	43	Malin Head	16
Plymouth	30	Hull	30	Valentia	5
Portsmouth	11	Scarborough	46	Cork Harbour	18
Dungeness	38	Tynemouth	39	Donaghadee	6
Dover	17	Leith	14	Glasgow	9
Margate	11	Aberdeen	18	Liverpool	18
Shoeburyness	42	Wick	21	Pembroke	45
Greenwich	46	Stornoway	5		

London, Greenwich: Jan. 7; Feb. 4; Mar. 3; Apr. 1.5; May 0.5; June 0.8; July 0.1; Aug. 0.7; Sept. 4; Oct. 7; Nov. 10; Dec. 7.

Calculating the average duration of the fog at four hours on each day recorded, nowhere at the stations shown would fog occur during more than 2 per cent of the year, i.e. 98 per cent of the year is fog-free at the worst stations and 99.7 per cent at the best. Including sea mist, some stations, it should be noted, may be only 85 per cent mist-free.

The term 'fog' is used by international agreement whenever the visibility is less than one kilometre (about 1 100 yards).

Climate and health : urban climates

In recent years attempts have been made to measure more exactly the effects of different elements of climate on the health of human beings and on the prevalence of disease. Very little is really known of the direct effects of climate and what causes 'bracing' or 'enervating' and similar conditions. Prof. Melvyn Howe's work for the Royal Geographical Society and the British Medical Association on the *National Atlas of Disease Mortality* (1963) leaves no doubt as to the localisation of certain diseases but the factors are obscure. *Sudden* changes of weather act as dangerous irritants (e.g. in bronchitis) and, contrary to popular belief, cold dry snaps may be particularly serious. There are certain definitely 'urban' diseases, notably bronchitis, lung cancer, and pneumonia, and intensive studies are being made of urban climates. As T. J. Chandler has shown for London (*Geogrl. J.*, **128**, 1962, 279–302) most cities form in winter a definite 'heat-island' with a much smaller temperature range than in the surrounding green belt or countryside. Both vertical and horizontal air currents are set up—some comparable to those shown in Fig. 58.

Variations in British climate

There is a widespread belief that the climate of the British Isles is changing, and people are fond of saying that we do not get as severe winters now as occurred in the days of our forefathers; and they point out that it is now no longer possible to roast an ox on the ice of the Thames frozen over. In this particular example, as in so many others, the full facts of the case are not taken into consideration. If the Thames of the present day were allowed to flow almost unrestricted through banks very wide apart, it would doubtless freeze over just as easily now as it did of old. Some authors have been at great pains to collect accurate information, and it would seem that the weather of the British Isles does tend to occur in cycles, and a correlation may perhaps be possible between these cycles of weather and the occurrence of sun-spots. Gordon Manley in his *Climate and the British Scene* reviews the evidence and the present state of knowledge at some length; it would seem that there may be both major and minor cycles of weather. At the same time it is, of course, important to remember that in the early days of man's habitation of Britain, the country was under the influence of the great Ice Age, and there has, *on the whole*, been a steady change from that time to the present, with an increase in temperature and a decrease in humidity, though there is evidence for relatively wet or 'pluvial' periods in Neolithic and Roman times inter-

		CLIMATE		VEGETATION
Post Glacial	800 B.C.–present	Sub-Atlantic	Cool and wet	Zone VIII Alder–birch–oak (beech)
	3000–800 B.C.	Sub-boreal	Drier	VIIb } Alder–mixed oak–elm–lime
	5000–3000 B.C.	Atlantic	Warm and wet	VIIa }
	6800–5000 B.C.	Boreal	Warm and dry	{ VI Hazel–pine; V Hazel–birch–pine
	8000–6800 B.C.	Preboreal	Rapid amelioration	IV Birch
Late Glacial	8800–8000 B.C.	Upper Dryas	Cold	III Park tundra (birch copses)
	10,000–8800 B.C.	Allerød	Milder	II Birch woods
	12,000–10,000 B.C.	Lower Dryas	Cold	I Park tundra (local birch)

The Upper paleolithic corresponds with the Late Glacial, the Mesolithic lasted till about 2500 B.C., the Neolithic and Bronze Ages to 800 B.C., followed by the Iron Age and Romano-British.

rupting the general change in an interglacial period, and evidence is lacking as to whether the climate as a whole is still getting milder or not. Climatic fluctuations since the disappearance of ice from Britain have played a major part in the development of the present flora and fauna.

The table on p. 86 is based on the tentative one in H. Godwin's *The History of the British Flora* (1956), p. 62, and takes account of radio carbon dating.

It is probable that these climatic fluctuations are intimately connected with the final separation of Britain from the continent, and the establishment of the present oceanic circulation. The climatic periods in Britain are not necessarily contemporary with those established on the continent.

5
The inland waters of the British Isles[1]

Of the rain that falls on the surface of the British Isles, part evaporates, part soaks into the ground, and part, usually a large part, runs off to form streams and rivulets, and eventually finds its way into the rivers of the country. That which percolates into the soil and into the rocks of the earth's crust is in part utilised by plants growing therein, and may eventually pass back into the atmosphere; but some of this water joins the underground water table and becomes part of an underground supply, being gradually returned to the open where the water table comes to the surface, and the water thereupon reissues in the form of springs. Although work discussed in the last chapter has shown considerable variation in evaporation from one part of the country to another, over a large part of lowland Britain from exposed surfaces of water (e.g. lakes and reservoirs) it is equivalent to about 400–600 millimetres (16–24 in) of rainfall (Fig. 61). Thus in areas with a rainfall of 600–1500 millimetres (25–60 in) from 30 to 60 per cent (over large areas between 40 to 50 per cent) of the rainfall is lost by evaporation. This takes into consideration the greatly varying evaporation from land surfaces. It is not the purpose of this chapter to study the behaviour of underground water, or even of surface streams; but to regard the sum total of rain falling upon the surface of the British Isles as one of the natural resources of this country, and to study its utilisation.

The evolution of British rivers

The evolution of the existing British river system falls into three phases:

(*a*) The preglacial phase;
(*b*) the period of glacial interference;
(*c*) the period of man's interference.

It is certain that the main lines of the present relief of the British Isles were outlined before the coming of the great Ice Age. On the whole, many of the rivers must have followed substantially their present courses. In England and Wales, it is probable that the Highland Zone on the north and west of the country exercised a greater influence than it does at the present day, and that there were many rivers draining from the higher lands of Wales, or the

1. We are indebted to Professor W. G. V. Balchin for valued help in the revision of this chapter.

north of England, following the general slope of the land towards the southeast (see Fig. 13). The tectonic depression of the Thames Basin considerably antedates the glacial period, and it is likely that these southeasterly flowing rivers made their way into what may be called the proto-Thames.[1] The extreme southeast of England—the Wealden area—is the classic area in the study of river development, mentioned above. The coming of the great Ice Age and the formation of huge ice sheets over the north of the country

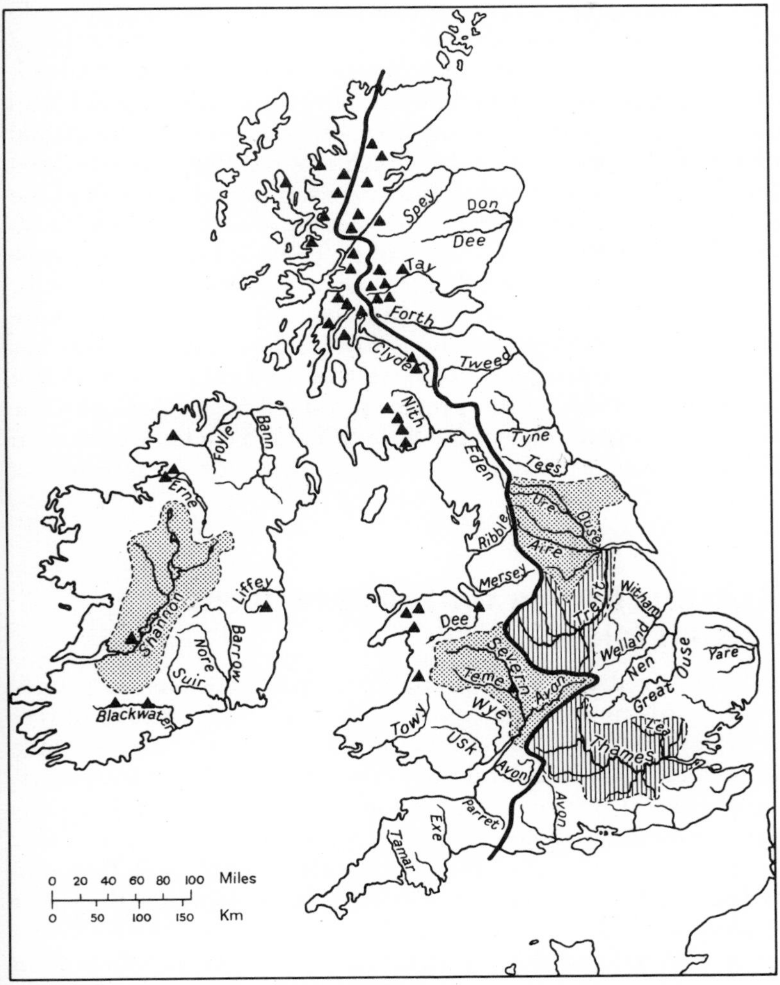

FIG. 67. The chief rivers of the British Isles

The heavy line shows the main water parting; five of the larger basins are separately indicated. The black triangles are some chief points where water power has been developed.

1. For correction of this oversimplified statement see S. W. Wooldridge and D. L. Linton, *Structure, Surface and Drainage in South-east England*, Publication no. 10, *Inst. Br. Geogr.*, 1939, reissued, 1955.

must have obliterated there the free surface drainage. As the ice spread southwards so natural drainage channels were in many cases blocked and pent-up waters were compelled to find their way into new channels; in many cases they have never gone back to the old ones. The tongues from the ice sheets were responsible for the deepening of many of our valleys, especially in the Highland Zone. Thus many of the lochs of Scotland are of glacial origin, so also are the lakes of the Lake District; whilst amongst the higher parts of the mountains of Wales the circular 'cwm' or corrie lakes do much to add to the beauty of the scenery of that country. With the gradual departure of the ice sheet many pre-existing valleys were thickly covered, perhaps even obliterated, with glacial debris, effectively blocking old lines of drainage. In the lower parts of the country, especially where the glacial debris was clayey or impervious in character, there resulted the ill-defined drainage which to this day is characteristic, for example, of so much of the Central Plain of Ireland. Amongst the other marshy lands left behind were the Vale of York and the Fenlands of England.[1] The third stage in the evolution of the river system of the British Isles has been marked by the small, but cumulatively important, efforts of man to control drainage and more especially to drain some of the lower lying areas. How successful this has been can be judged by the complete conversion of the Fenland into what it is today—one of the best agricultural regions in the British Isles—and the almost equally complete drainage of the Vale of York. To a less extent man has controlled the drainage of the country for his own ends, for purposes of water supply.

The utilisation of the water resources of the British Isles

It is remarkable, indeed well-nigh incredible, that there has been until comparatively recently no comprehensive study of the freshwater resources of Britain. Whilst almost from time immemorial such rivers as the Nile have been studied day in and day out, and their exact flow measured by gauges, few such records exist for British rivers. The seasonal rise and fall of rivers is a study of the utmost importance in many countries of the world. Their characteristic regime, as this rise and fall is called, may be a factor of national significance. The Thames, because of its importance for the water supply of London, was the only river whose resources were comparatively accurately known. What was the reason for this neglect of the study of an important national resource? It is in the main a reflection of the climatic conditions of these islands. Broadly speaking, in the past we have always had a superabundance of water for our requirements. The trouble has

1. For an account of some outstanding examples of glacial interference with drainage, see L. J. Wills, *The Physiographic Evolution of Britain*, pp. 211–28. Many of the papers listed under References for this chapter deal with the evolution of drainage (see p. 815).

usually been too much water, and the difficulty of getting rid of the surplus. Thus the necessity of organising a survey of our national water resources has not, until comparatively recent times, become apparent.

The Meteorological Office, as mentioned in the last chapter, is responsible for the collection of statistics of rainfall. The Geological Survey has concerned itself with underground water and since 1899 has published a series of water-supply memoirs on the counties. In these details of underground supplies from water-bearing deposits or aquifers and existing wells are given. The importance of water in the war effort of the Second World War led to a systematic recording of information in which the Water Unit of the Geological Survey played an active part, and notification of the results of well boring is now compulsory. What remained neglected was the surface water—the behaviour of rivers and the supply which is available from them for all purposes. In 1932 the British Association for the Advancement of Science appointed an Inland Water Survey Committee to study the means whereby such a survey could be undertaken. An Inland Water Survey Committee was set up by the Government in 1935 and a *Surface Water Year Book* published for 1935–36 and 1936–37. Both the Committee and the Year Book faded out during the War, to be resuscitated later. The Committee sponsored the publication of the *Surface Water Year Book of Great Britain*, 1937–1945 before the Committee was again suspended as an economy measure. It is clear that engineers of all important water supply and power undertakings must have an accurate knowledge of their resources and so carry out river gauging and flow measurements. The information available is collected in the *Year Book*. Some river basins (such as the Ness in Scotland, the Nene and Wye in England and Wales) are reasonably well covered: for much of the country there is still little information despite the anticipation by the Government in 1944 of a national water policy.[1]

As the standard of living rises and all houses have running water and baths, 205 litres (45 gallons) or more per day must be allotted to every individual. Indeed, this figure is constantly being increased. In some parts of the United States it has exceeded 680 litres (150 gallons). Some modern industries, e.g. paper making and rayon manufacture, make enormous demands on water. The great urban centres seek their supplies in distant mountainous areas and the water is brought by aqueducts across rural land which may be very short of water. A modern dairy farm requires at least 136 litres (30 gallons) per cow per day, but few reach this standard unless they can have mains supply. In the country as a whole, domestic consumption is now running at the rate of some 2.7 million million litres (600 000 gallons) a year, and industrial consumption at about 1.36 million million litres (300 000 million gallons) a year.

In the utilisation of our water resources it may be said that there are at

1. *A National Water Policy*, Cmd 6515, HMSO, 1944.

least five frequently conflicting interests which regard the water resources of the islands from five different points of view:

land drainage,
water supply for domestic, agricultural and industrial purposes,
transport (i.e. navigation),
water power,
fisheries and recreation.

Land drainage

In 1927 a Royal Commission, under the chairmanship of Lord Bledisloe, was appointed to inquire into the whole question of land drainage in England and Wales. In the evidence presented to that Royal Commission it was stated that there were 710 750 hectares ($1\frac{3}{4}$ million acres) of land in England and Wales alone in urgent need of drainage, and that 1 766 610 hectares (4 362 000 acres), about one-seventh of the land in agricultural use, depended absolutely on artificial drainage.

Land drainage is a complex matter. With the heavy rainfall over much of Highland Britain there is commonly an excess of water for agricultural purposes. Unless this is drained away soils become more and more acid and incapable of yielding good crops, grassland becomes waterlogged and the place of nutritious grasses is taken by reeds, rushes and mosses such as *Sphagnum* till the land becomes a useless bog. Two types of drainage are needed, one to drain off surface water, hence open ditches, the other to drain the soil, hence pipes a foot or so below the surface or channels cut underground by an implement which works like a mole (mole-drainage). It has been estimated that in 1939, 3.6 million hectares (9 million acres) or 40 per cent of the farmland, excluding rough grazings, or a quarter of the total surface of England and Wales was in need of drainage of these types. Much work was carried out during the Second World War especially by prisoner of war labour but in 1952 the Drainage Division of the Ministry of Agriculture estimated that 1.4 million hectares (3.5 million acres) were still in urgent need of drainage.[1] It will be seen that these greatly exceed the figures previously given to the Royal Commission.

The more effective the drainage of agricultural land, the greater the run off and the greater the danger of flooding from rivers overflowing their banks. There are still many parts of the British Isles which are subject to disastrous floods. To quote one example, in the valley of the lower Don, no less than 79 per cent of the total area of 86 062 hectares (212 500 acres) of the Doncaster area is below the 8 metre (25 ft) contour, and in urgent need of provision of adequate drainage.

The position is that the natural river channels are only sufficient to take off the surface water in times of normal flow and prove quite inadequate in

1. See also *Land Drainage in England and Wales*, Cmd 916, HMSO, 1959.

times of excessive rainfall, which therefore results in widespread flooding. In the past, land drainage engineers have had to take a purely arbitrary figure in calculating the run-off from the catchment basin with which their works would have to deal. It has been considered as reasonable to take as a normal maximum run-off one-hundredth part of the average annual rainfall over the catchment area for twenty-four hours. Thus, if the average rainfall of the catchment area is 635 millimetres (25 in) per year, it has been considered necessary to construct the drainage works to take off the equivalent of 6 millimetres (0.25 in) per twenty-four hours. This is admittedly insufficient to deal with exceptional floods, but the cost of providing for a flood which might occur once in fifty years is entirely prohibitive. Taking the case of the River Thames, for which some accurate figures do exist, the largest flood recorded was due to very exceptional rainfall in the year 1894 when the discharge at Teddington Weir reached 92 million litres (20 236 million gallons) per day or 37 600 cusecs on 18 November. This is equivalent to 15.25 cusecs[1] per thousand acres over the whole catchment area, or equivalent to 9 millimetres (0.36 in) of rain on the whole area of the Thames Basin. In the 26 days from 23 October to 17 November 1814 over 203 millimetres (8 in) of rain fell in the Thames Valley, or an average of 7 millimetres (0.31 in) per day. The Thames when it is running bank high was able to discharge 20 457 million litres (4 500 million gallons) per day—a quantity which has been exceeded on about twelve days per year since 1883. Improvement works later undertaken between Weybridge and Teddington enabled the river to discharge roughly double this quantity. It is not considered practical to provide for floods of greater magnitude which are of very rare occurrence. Thus it must be accepted that some 60 750 hectares (150 000 acres) in the catchment area of the River Thames are subject to inundation in times of high floods and that they must remain so subject. By way of contrast, the minimum flow recorded for the Thames at Teddington is 75.9 million litres (16.7 million gallons) per day or 31.0 cusecs on 29 October 1934.

Broadly speaking, it is only in the smaller catchment basins that a single day's heavy rainfall will be reflected in a serious flood. Thus in east Norfolk, one of the most disastrous floods on record of the river Wensum (on 6 August 1912) was due to a fall of rain of 505 millimetres (7.3 in) in one day, though the river provided itself automatically with water storage by overflowing the lowland on each side to the extent of 4047 hectares (10 000 acres). Similarly the disastrous flood in August 1952, which destroyed much of the Devon village of Lynmouth with a serious loss of life, was due to a cloudburst higher up the tiny valley: 228 millimetres (9 in) of rain fell in one day, most of it in three hours.[2] In 1959, as a result of a dry summer, a

1. Cubic feet per second. One cusec = 538 000 gallons a day and 1 000 000 gallons a day = 1.86 cusecs.
2. C. Kidson and J. Gifford, 'The Exmoor Storm of 15th August 1952', *Geography*, **38**, 1953, 1–17.

quarter of the people in England and Wales were restricted in their use of water, whereas in 1960 and 1968 the wet summer led to serious flooding in many areas.

FIG. 68. Water areas under the Water Resources Act 1963

Summarising, much land in the British Isles still requires drainage to render it of greater agricultural value, though much has been done in recent years. The channels of main rivers in particular require improvement so that they are able to take off up to about twice the water which they can take off at present. Payment for such work may be obtained by rates on the owners of land situated below the flood level, taken normally as 2.4 metres (8 ft) above the mean level of the river, but it is often contended that upland owners should pay for the privilege of discharging their surplus water with danger to lowland owners and that rates should be levied over the whole of a basin.

The Land Drainage Act 1930 provided for the division of England and Wales into forty-seven catchment areas for which Catchment Boards were constituted. This was an important step, but it was the Water Act 1945 which laid the foundations of a national water policy. At the time of the 1930 Act there were over a thousand statutory water authorities—borough, urban and rural councils—and about a thousand water supply companies in England and Wales alone. The decisive legislation was however the Water Resources Act 1963, setting up a new central authority, the Water Resources Board, charged with the duty of conserving, distributing or otherwise augmenting water resources, including supplies from watercourses, lakes, and underground water. The Act set up twenty-six River Authorities for England and Wales and to them were transferred the powers and duties of the former River Boards. The Ministry of Agriculture remains responsible for land drainage and fisheries. A 'river basin' in English usage is called 'watershed' in America and the function of the new British River Authorities is what would be called watershed management in America.

Water supply[1]

The object of the land drainage engineer is to drain the land effectively and conduct the water as easily and as quickly as possible to the sea; the object of the water supply engineer is to conserve a supply of pure, good quality water so that it may be available in quantity to the populace at large at all seasons of the year, independent of periods of drought. The supply is derived from three main sources:

(*a*) Shallow wells which go down as far as the permanent water table, and from which the water can be pumped up.
(*b*) Deep wells tapping deep-seated, including artesian, water.
(*c*) River supplies, or gathering grounds whose water has been conserved in natural lakes or artificial reservoirs.

In country districts the normal water supply is still obtained to a certain extent from wells, supplemented in many cases by supplies from natural springs. In 1914 out of 12 869 parishes in rural districts in England and Wales, only 4874 had a piped water supply even to some of the houses. In 1939, according to the Scott Report, 3432 parishes and at least a million of the rural population were still without piped water. In the same areas the method of disposal of sewage is by cesspools or pits in the ground, and the relative siting of well and cesspool is a matter of the first importance. There is in the underground water table a definite movement of water, usually, but by no means always, down hill by relationship to the surface of the ground, and obviously the cesspool should be on the downflow side from the well. Even with the utmost precaution pollution is likely to occur and with an increase in population the provision of a piped water supply is a

1. For matters relating to water supply the standard work is R. C. S. Walters, *The Nation's Water Supply*, 1936, which is a mine of information. For later statistics see successive editions of *British Waterworks Year Book and Directory* and the official publications already quoted.

first essential. The drilling of deep wells is perhaps most frequently undertaken by firms and individuals who wish to have an assured supply apart from that provided by water supply companies.[1] Where there are numerous wells drawing upon a deep-seated underground supply, particularly an artesian supply, as under London, it has become quite clear that the water is by no means inexhaustible, and the level of the artesian water under London has been lowered appreciably within the last fifty years.

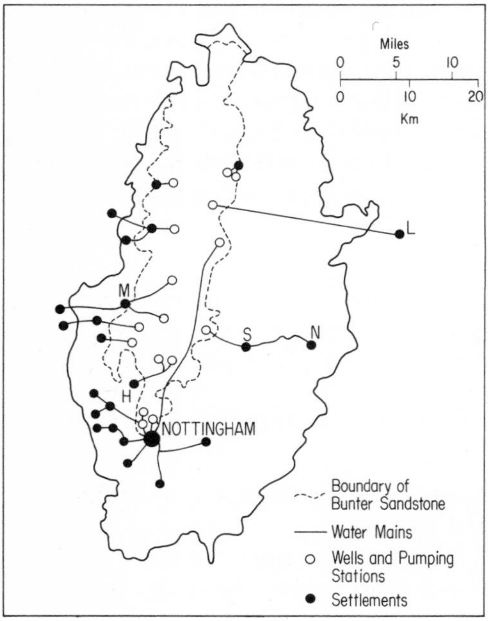

FIG. 69. Sketch map illustrating the importance of certain geological horizons (in this case the Bunter Sandstone) as water-bearing beds (after Professor H. H. Swinnerton). The most valuable water-bearing formation in south-eastern England is the chalk, but many permeable or partly permeable beds such as sandstones and fissured limestones are locally important. Surface gravels are liable to pollution

The problem of water supply is obviously most acute in the large conurbations. In many cases, as for example, London, provided the quantity of water removed does not affect the use for transport, navigation, and other

1. In England and Wales every landowner has the right to use, but not to sell, water naturally flowing through, past, or under his land provided there is no interference with the rights of neighbouring landowners. There is now however a certain restriction on new borings. Private rights to impound rivers and draw water are drastically restricted by the Water Resources Act 1963.

interest of the riverine owners, it is possible to draw a water supply from all the larger rivers. In some cases the water is drawn directly from the river and simply passed through filtration plant before being distributed but in other cases it is drawn off first into storage reservoirs. Amongst the rivers whose water is used may be noted the Yorkshire Ouse and the Trent, the Wye, Severn and Bristol Avon, the East Anglian rivers and those draining to the Wash, the Tees and Derwent and many smaller rivers. The outstanding example, however, of the use of river water is that of the Thames for London. The bulk of London's water supply is taken from the Thames above Teddington, supplemented by a considerable supply from the River Lea or the New River Waterworks, and from wells. The springs and wells used to supply London from early times proved inadequate as early as the sixteenth century and the 'New River Scheme' to bring water from Chadwell and from Amwell near Ware in Hertfordshire was sanctioned by Parliament in 1606 and completed in 1613. The Thames water, more than two-thirds of the whole London supply, is taken off and stored in great reservoirs.[1] Fears of a shortage have led to various proposals for distant supplies, notably from south-central Wales.

In some of the other conurbations the problem is not quite so simple. Obviously the most suitable collecting grounds for water supply for a large city are the open moorlands or hilly areas which have a heavy rainfall, but where there is not a large animal or human population living on the hills which would naturally pollute the supply of water. Thus it is not too much to say that there has been a scramble amongst the more powerful city corporations to secure rights for this purpose over the more thinly inhabited parts of Wales, the Pennines, the Lake District and elsewhere. There is great competition amongst the towns on the two flanks of the Pennines to secure the rights for areas of drainage and water supply from the Pennines themselves.

Water from the Pennines supplies the needs of over 20 million people, and reservoirs, as shown in Fig. 70, are closely spaced. But the supplies were obviously becoming inadequate. The Corporation of Liverpool cut the Gordian knot by damming the Vyrnwy valley in Wales, thereby creating Lake Vyrnwy, with a surface about 250 metres (825 ft) above sea-level. It formed the largest single inland sheet of water in Wales and at that time the largest artificial reservoir in Europe—8 kilometres (five miles) long and on an average nearly 1.5 kilometres (a mile) wide. It was constructed between the years 1881 and 1892, and has a surface area of 454 hectares (1121 acres), its storage capacity being 55 147 million litres (12 131 million gallons), and the catchment area nearly 94 square kilometres (36 square miles). The aqueduct is 105 kilometres (65 miles) long. The Vyrnwy, it should be

1. It is thus true to say that the bulk of London's water supply is in fact purified sewage—for the Thames has received the effluent from all the towns on its banks upstream of the Metropolis.

added, is the chief Welsh tributary of the river Severn, and was formerly a small stream meandering across a marshy flat. The suitability of the site depended to a considerable extent on the hard old rocks of the neighbourhood forming a suitable foundation for the masonry of the reservoir dam.

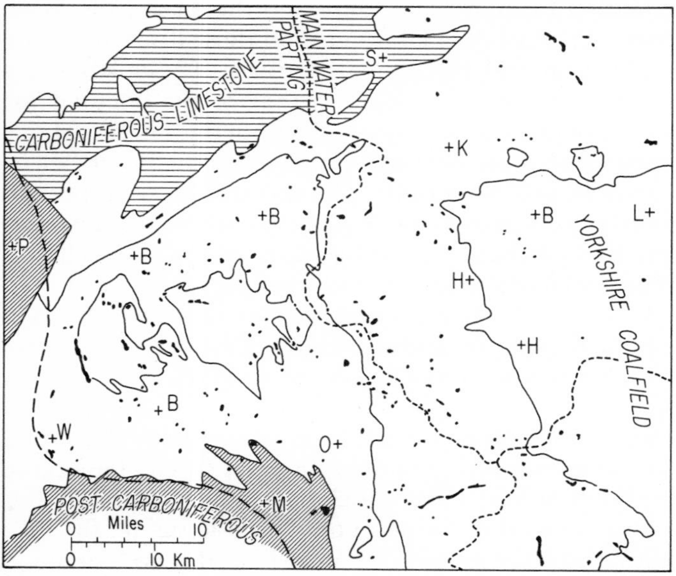

FIG. 70. The Pennines as 'gathering grounds' for water supply
All the black areas are reservoirs and no less than 220 are shown on this map. The blank areas are Millstone Grit and Coal Measures, on which nearly all the reservoirs are situated. The broken line in the west is the western limit of 'soft' water (see Chapter 20).

The Corporation of Birmingham followed suit by constructing a series of four reservoirs in the beautiful valley of the Elan about four miles west of Rhayader. These were completed in the years 1893–1904 at a cost of no less than £5,750,000. They cover 364 hectares (900 acres) and yield a daily supply of 341 million litres (75 million gallons) from a gathering ground of about 181 square kilometres (70 square miles), the storage capacity exceeding 45 461 million litres (10 000 million gallons). Provision was made for later extensions of the supplies. From the reservoirs there are, of course, gigantic aqueducts, for the most part near the surface, though hidden, running for more than 117 kilometres (73 miles). Parts of the aqueduct, totalling 59.5 kilometres (37 miles), are actually siphons where the water is under pressure from the heart of Wales to Birmingham. In 1952 a further supply was obtained from the new Claerwen reservoir. Manchester has utilised the natural lake Thirlmere in the Lake District under the shadow of Helvellyn. A fear that the supply from Thirlmere would be insufficient for the growing city led to the development of another scheme in the Lake District for using Haweswater. Manchester had secured the rights to Haweswater against much opposition from those interested in local supplies and there were indignant protests when the scheme was postponed in 1932 as not immediately necessary. In due course, however, Manchester not only developed Haweswater but again fearing a shortage negotiated in 1962 for the right to use Ullswater. Countrywide opposition, mainly on amenity grounds, caused the project to be shelved, at least for the time. The necessity for sharing available supplies had been accepted as early as 1899 when an Act of Parliament apportioned the waters of the Derwent valley between the cities of Leicester, Sheffield, Derby, and Nottingham and the counties of Derby and Nottingham. Great works have been constructed on this basis of which the most noteworthy is the Ladybower Reservoir.

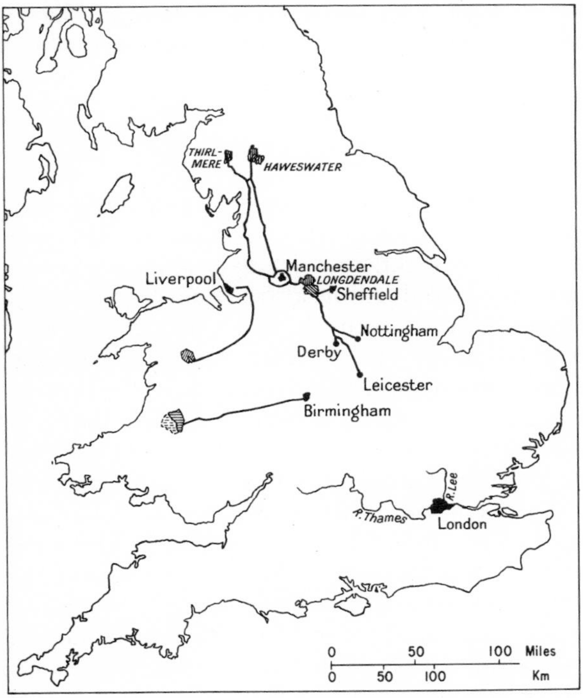

Fig. 71. Map of England and Wales showing some of the long-distance urban water supplies

During the Second World War, the needs of agriculture for water became apparent and were stressed in the Scott Report, but the Water Resources Act was not passed until 1963.

For certain industrial purposes, the quality or type of water is of importance. Thus it is well known that the supplies of soft water were in part responsible for the location of the textile industries of Lancashire and Yorkshire, since soft water is so essential for washing and dyeing the raw materials and fabrics (see Chapters 19 and 20). But with the modern development of water softeners, it is relatively easy, though expensive, for firms concerned to install the necessary apparatus, just as the railways did, in the days of steam locomotion, for softening their water. Similarly, although the local well water from the gypseous Keuper Marls with its considerable permanent hardness was largely responsible for the development of the brewing industry at Burton, 'burtonisation' or artificial hardening of water for brewing is now commonplace. For other purposes, too, soft water may be a disadvantage. If passed through lead pipes it is apt to dissolve so much lead as to become poisonous.

Although for domestic supplies, emphasis is on the 'purity' of water it is now recognised that for maintenance of health certain salts should be present. In particular fluorine is needed for the development of children's teeth and many water authorities now undertake a fluoridation of drinking supplies.

Transport

The utilisation of British inland waterways for transport and navigation purposes and their linking by canals is considered elsewhere (see Chapter 26). It may be noted here, however, that the land drainage engineer in embanking the rivers to prevent excessive flooding also benefits the users of waterways in that the firmness of banks is secured, and a deeper and narrower channel tends to be formed. Many of our rivers have been changed out of all recognition in this way. Thus it is difficult to imagine at the present time a ford across the Thames, as undoubtedly there was in early times, in the neighbourhood of London Bridge. The river has been so enclosed by embankments on either side that the current has become swift, and the actual watercourse deep. It may be appropriate to mention at this point, too, the enormous importance of the mouths of British rivers. The river mouths are often more important than the rest of the river because of the situation thereon of many of our great ports. Here the climate of these islands, with its well-distributed rainfall, is responsible for the steady flow of most of our rivers throughout the year. This, combined with the marked tidal scour consequent on the large tidal range characteristic of the continental shelf round the British Isles, has been in a large measure responsible for the development of so many of our ports.

Water power

The water power resources of the British Isles are not large. In the days before the extensive use of coal, small swift streams such as those running down from the Pennines were extensively used for driving machinery. The sites of the early forges and grinding works—for example in the Sheffield district—were determined by the water power available from the streams.

In the Sheffield area it is still possible to see the 'hammer ponds' in which water was impounded and so used for turning water wheels which operated mechanical hammers for working the iron. Similarly the water was used for working the bellows in the forges. Some of the cotton mills in South Lancashire were likewise located, as were woollen mills in Yorkshire, where water power was available from the streams. In many parts of the country water power was used in small flour mills, but most of these primitive establishments have fallen into disuse. A water wheel where such exists for grinding grain or for sawing wood has now become a tourist attraction, and more money is likely to be earned by the proprietor in providing teas for visitors than in any benefit he derives directly from his mill.

About fifty years ago the Board of Trade appointed a Water Power Resources Committee to enquire into the hydroelectric power resources of the British Isles. They calculated that if all the schemes up before them were developed 250 000 kW could be generated out of which 210 000 were regarded as developable on an economic basis. This was the total for Great Britain, made up of 195 000 kW in Scotland, 36 000 in Wales, and 26 500 in England. It was estimated that the output would reach 1840 million units or kilowatt-hours per annum, and would represent a saving of some 3 million tons of coal a year. This theoretical possibility was actually equal to 40 per cent of the total units generated in 1917–18. Since then the enormous increase in the demand for electricity has altered the picture completely, and the modern development of hydroelectric power is considered in Chapter 14.

Fisheries and recreation

Most of the British rivers were once celebrated for their trout, their salmon, and for other fish. Many have become so polluted that the fish have disappeared, but in others fishing is carefully preserved and the sporting rights guarded by angling societies and private owners. Fishing rights on the best trout streams in the south of England let at £5000 per mile of stream. It is difficult to calculate the value of freshwater fish in British rivers. Possibly the value of salmon and other fish obtained in Ireland approaches £1 million annually; the annual value of salmon from Scottish rivers is officially estimated at the same figure. In recent years increased attention has been paid to the restoration of inland fisheries by preventing further pollution. In the new hydroelectric power schemes it is now standard practice to provide fish ladders. In some, such as that near Pitlochry, the salmon are automatically counted as they ascend.

Apart from sport fishing the inland waters of Britain have assumed in recent years a new or renewed significance in the recreational life of the country. Nearly every lake has, if the controlling authorities permit, its quota of pleasure boats—canoes, rowing boats, outboard motors, yachts, and motor boats of all types. The advent of the speed boat, disturbing by its noise and wave-creating habits fishermen, nature-lovers, and the users of other craft, has created difficulties and dissension. Many stretches of inland water now have their 'marinas'; both rivers and canals are valued more for boating than for any other purpose and active steps have been taken in many areas for the preservation of canals as rural amenities.

6
The soils of Britain

Pedology, or the study of soils, is a study which as a modern science is still young, but much progress has been made since this book was first published. The soil is, broadly speaking, the surface layer of the earth in which plants grow. The mineral matter is in the main derived from the underlying rocks which have weathered and it might be thought therefore that this part of the soil would vary directly according to the character of the underlying rocks, and that therefore a geological map would form the necessary basis for the construction of a soil map. More and more of recent years however it has been recognised that climate plays a leading, even a dominant, part in determining the character of the surface soil. So much is this the case that it is possible to distinguish, as American writers have done, two great soil groups in middle latitudes. The *pedalfers* are those commonly formed where rainfall is in excess of evaporation, and where there is normally therefore a tendency for the more soluble mineral salts, including lime, to be dissolved out of the surface layers and washed downwards, leaving a soil rich in the elements aluminium (al) and iron (fe), hence the name pedalfers. Where on the other hand evaporation exceeds rainfall there is an upward movement of moisture in the soil, and when the moisture is evaporated the previously dissolved salts are left behind in the surface layers, which thus become rich in such salts as calcium carbonate, hence the name *pedocal*. Where there is an approximate balance between rainfall and evaporation conditions are often particularly suitable for the accumulation of organic matter, and the development of a *chernozem*, or black earth. These great soil groups are termed 'zonal' in the sense that we may speak of major world climatic zones.

It has already been noted in the preceding chapter on climate that in all parts of the British Isles rainfall normally exceeds evaporation, and hence the soils of the British Isles are normally pedalfers. Further, the whole of the British Isles lie in one climatic region, and that is not one of extreme conditions. Hence the soils of the British Isles do not show the great differentiation due to climate which is characteristic of such large tracts as the plains of European Russia, or of the heart of North America. Most of the soils of the British Isles belong to two of the great world soil groups, the podzols and the brown forest soils, together with a limited development locally of special types. Actually in the British Isles the soils vary enormously but according to parent material or human influence, and Britain has thus, despite the uniformity of climate, a remarkable range of soils which are sometimes for obvious reasons described as 'aclimatic' or 'intrazonal'.

The pioneer studies of soil in Britain were mainly the work of agriculturalists concerned in the use of soil. In 1793 a state-aided independent organisation known as the Board of Agriculture and Internal Improvement was set up, and it prepared a series of county studies each of which bore the general title *General View of the Agriculture of the County of X with Observations on the Means of Improvement*. These were published first in a preliminary form, inviting comments, and later in a permanent form from 1794 onwards. In each the first chapter has a section devoted to soils, and most of the volumes include a soil map, sometimes a hand-coloured folding plate. In many of the counties of Britain this remains, more than 150 years later, the only soil map of the county. The descriptions of the soils were based primarily on texture, e.g. loams, clayey loams, black peat earths, and so on, with special types in certain counties such as the brashy soils on the Oolites, or descriptions which would be appreciated by farmers, such as 'a turnip soil'. These primitive soil maps are of such interest that they have been reproduced in black and white, sometimes simplified, in the County Reports of the Land Utilisation Survey of Britain, published under the title of *The Land of Britain*.

When the Geological Survey was set up in 1835 it was laid down as one of the objectives that maps of surface deposits and soils should be prepared to serve the needs of agriculture. For the most part this objective remained in abeyance, and although the Survey has now mapped the solid geology over the whole country, there is still no complete drift map.[1] In a few areas the Geological Survey found time from its work of mapping geology to produce a soil map, the basis of which was the texture of the soil. Two coloured maps, covering a large part of Ayrshire, were published, and a soil survey was carried out of a considerable part of the Eden Valley in Cumberland. The maps distinguish such groups as light sand, coarse sand, light, medium, and heavy loams, and so on, but a different scheme is adopted for each sheet. These maps are interesting because they represent a breakaway from a geological basis of classification and a return to the basis of texture.

An important landmark was the publication in 1911 of *The Agriculture and Soils of Kent, Surrey, and Sussex*, by A. Daniel Hall and E. J. Russell (afterwards Sir Daniel Hall and Sir John Russell). They were concerned with the soil as a medium for farming and their mechanical analyses were based on a well mixed sample of the surface layers, a procedure entirely different from the modern methods which study the separate layers in the soil, or the soil profile. The foundations for the modern concepts of pedology, or soil science, were laid particularly by the Russians under the leadership of V. V. Dokuchaiev, and by the Americans under the leadership of C. F. Marbut.

1. A small scale map was prepared in 1958–59 by Prof. K. M. Clayton for publication as Plate 18 of the Oxford *Atlas of Britain*, 1963.

The move in Britain to establish a separate soil survey and to carry out detailed studies and mapping on the 6-inch scale developed slowly, but in due course, shortly before the outbreak of the Second World War, a Soil Survey of England and Wales was established, with the late Professor G. W. Robinson as its first Director.

Under the Agricultural Research Council, through the Soil Survey Research Board, the Soil Survey of Great Britain is now engaged in detailed mapping in England, Wales and Scotland. The initial surveys were published on the one-inch scale, and by the end of 1970, eighteen sheets had been issued in the English series, with five more in progress, and ten Welsh sheets were available. Since there are 360 sheets to cover England and Wales it is clear that there is a long way to go. But present policy is to survey and publish on the scale of 1 : 25 000, and in 1970 sixteen sheets in this series had been published. In Scotland, 28 one-inch sheets had been completed out of 131, with work in progress on 21 others. It is also interesting to record that the basis of classification of soils being used for the Scottish sheets differs from that for England and Wales, an indication that modern soil scientists are as yet by no means agreed.

The soil profile

There is, however, general agreement on the importance of studying the soil profile. The parent material of the soil may be the underlying rock, using the word 'rock' in the geological sense, and independent of hardness. In some cases the soil is simply the surface layer of the rock and the two merge imperceptibly into one another, as for example the soils which overlie river alluvium or clay. But in many cases mechanical weathering has broken up the underlying hard rock into smaller fragments, and chemical weathering due to the solvent action of rainwater has played its part. On almost all slopes there is soil creep, the soil sliding or being washed downhill, so that especially towards the lower slopes of valleys there is a layer of transported material from a few centimetres to several metres in thickness between the soil and the underlying rock, and it is this hillwash which forms the true parent material in the soils.

The normal climatic conditions in Britain result in the differentiation of three layers, or horizons. The upper, or A, horizon is subject to downward washing or leaching; the finer material is washed down mechanically and soluble constituents are gradually removed in solution by the percolating waters. The result is to leave a greyish or whitish layer of insoluble quartz sand or rock fragments. Between this whitish layer and the surface there may actually be two thin levels, that at the surface (A_0 horizon) being dark or almost black and owing its colour to remains of vegetation, humus and sometimes to sooty material from forest or heath fires. Below this the A_1 horizon, though suffering from leaching, remains dark because it receives from above the addition of organic matter. Then follows the main leached

A_2 horizon. Below the A horizon is the B horizon often stained brown from oxides of iron, redeposited by the percolating waters from above. The iron oxides may actually form concretions or even cause the consolidation of the level to form a hardpan. The fine mineral particles washed down from above may cause this B horizon to be quite different mineralogically from that above. The C horizon is that of the weathered parent material.

This division of the soil profile into A, B, and C horizons is characteristic of the great world soil group known as the podzols. It may be regarded as normal in Britain in all but the wettest parts where there is impeded drainage and perhaps the drier parts of the east. Actually the podzol profile is broken up wherever the land is ploughed and is therefore seen developed naturally only in sandy heathland or under coniferous woodland. In wet regions such as the level floors of valleys the permanent water table is near the surface and the horizons are somewhat different. Again the surface, or A, horizon may be leached but the intermediate, or B, horizon is saturated for part of the year and relatively dry for the other. As a result oxidation and reduction alternate, producing a characteristic mottling of grey or yellow or brown which is a sure sign of impeded drainage. Below it in the C horizon air cannot penetrate and the conditions are permanently reducing so that greys and blue greys predominate. This is the characteristic profile of the gley or glei soils, though some writers restrict the term gley to the mottled horizon.

In the drier parts of southern and eastern Britain there is less difference between rainfall and evaporation and leaching is less intense. In certain summer months evaporation may even exceed rainfall. It is here that deciduous woodland normally predominates and the annual leaf fall provides a surface layer of brownish humus in contrast to the acid black humus of the podzol. The bleached A_2 horizon of the typical podzol is absent, its A horizon differing little in colour from the B horizon, which is rich in flocculated iron, commonly yielding a good crumb structure. Such soils are commonly known as brown earths or brown forest soils and the effect of ploughing and cultivation is normally to promote the development of a soil of brownish colour and to prevent the development of a podzol.

It may thus be said that there are three major soil groups present in Britain—the podzols, the brown earths and the gley soils. Under special local conditions other groups such as peat soils or fenland soils may be present whilst in the hills and mountains the weathering of the old rocks has not proceeded long enough to provide the necessary basis for a proper soil profile. In such areas the so-called skeletal, immature or *azonal* soils (including lithosols) are found. In other cases the surface layers may be washed away with the result that some soils are described as having a truncated profile. Some very interesting soils occur on limestones, particularly chalk. Although there is always an excess of lime in the subsoil, B and C horizons, the surface layer may be so leached as to be even acid in reaction.

Soil series

Within the great world soil groups one of the most commonly used units of classification, comparable perhaps with the genus amongst plants or animals, is the 'soil series'. This is defined as 'a group of soils derived from the same or similar parent materials under similar conditions, and showing similar profile characteristics'. It is the soil series which is now commonly mapped in detailed soil survey, and the series are named very often from localities where they were first studied—and the series names are unfortunately not, therefore, descriptive. Soil series commonly contain several soil types which are differentiated mainly on the basis of texture. For example, we may speak of the 'Ashley sandy clay loam'. It should be noted that a soil series may include a considerable range of texture and may also include shallow or deep phases so that from the point of view of cultivation a single soil series may embrace land of very different quality agriculturally.

The description of each soil series is based on the character of the profile. Since ploughing and cultivation generally prevent the formation of a profile it is somewhat difficult to fit agricultural soils into this classification. Consequently there is much still to be said in favour of the older approach to the study of soils which was concerned particularly with the texture, the structure, and the chemistry. The Scottish surveyors still recognise the overriding importance of the geological background and are grouping their soil series into associations which have a close relationship to the underlying geology. In England and Wales on the other hand the surveyors are mapping soil series and do not recognise the same type of grouping into associations.

As no detailed soil survey has been carried out over the greater part of the British Isles to date, efforts to show British soils on small scale maps leave much to be desired. An attempt was made by H. Stemme in his *Soil Map of Europe* (1927). This map is useful as a first approximation, but has been severely criticised. It was revised with international collaboration in 1958–62 under the auspices of FAO (scale 1 : 1 m)—see p. 116.

We may now proceed to look at British soils from what may be called the older point of view.

Broadly speaking, it may be said that four factors have determined the distribution of the different types of soil in the British Isles.

1. *Parent material, including solid rocks and drift.* We have seen that five-sixths or more of the British Isles were at one time or another covered by great ice sheets, that the ice sheets removed soil from huge areas, mixed fragments of rock of very varying character, and eventually distributed over the surface of the land a mantle of deposits of very varying thickness which are collectively known as drift. Quite a large proportion of these drift deposits were further resorted by water action—in some cases by waters derived from the melting of the ice, in other cases by more recent streams.

It may even be that some of the finer particles were partly resorted by wind or by wind and rain. What is of fundamental importance is that these surface deposits are very widespread. The geologist who is concerned mainly with the structure of the earth's crust tends rather to regard these mixed drift deposits as of little importance, very often as a distinct nuisance in that they obscure the character of the underlying solid rocks. It is perhaps significant that there is not in existence at the present day a complete one-inch map of Great Britain showing the distribution of drift deposits, and for Ireland the only complete map is an old one by Sir A. Giekie, made many years ago on a scale of 10 miles to 1 inch. Because of the absence of a general drift map of Great Britain the geographer is too often thrown back on the solid geological map, and it is a fundamental, but very common, error to suppose that this is a satisfactory basis for studying the soils of England, Wales and Scotland. In the southern counties, which were little affected by glaciation, this may sometimes be the case, but north of the Thames it certainly is not.

FIG. 72. The drift-covered areas of England and Wales

The stippled areas are almost wholly drift covered: the black areas would be submerged if the drift and later deposits were removed (after L. J. Wills and G. W. Lamplugh). For greater detail the reader is referred to Plate 18 of the Oxford Atlas of Britain 1963.

Where drift deposits are absent, or where the drift is very thin, then the character of the underlying rocks is of the greatest importance in determining the type of soil. Thus the stiff Weald Clays give rise to the stiff clay soils of the Wealden area, the sands of the Lower Greensand to sandy soils, and so on; but it is a mistake to pay too much slavish attention to the geological map, for the poorer siliceous soils of the Highland belt, as for example of

Wales, vary but little in character whether they are derived from Cambrian, Ordovician, or Silurian rocks, although there may be considerable variation *within* any one of these groups or in rocks of the *same* age in different parts of the country.

FIG. 73. The principal boulder clays of eastern England (after F. W. Harmer, *Geology in the Field*)

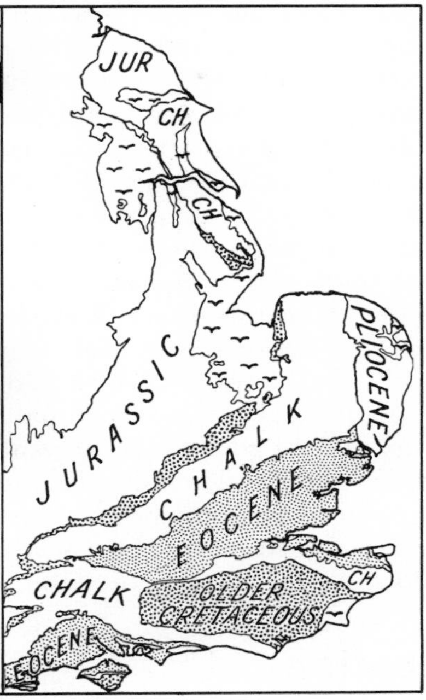

FIG. 74. The solid geology of eastern England

2. *Climate*, including soil climate. On the whole, of course, there is a general increase in the amount of rainfall as one goes from east to west in the British Isles. On the whole there is a general tendency for peat formation to increase as one goes in the same direction. An important point, not always realised, is that one must regard the rainfall of a considerable part of the British Isles as excessive; even if drainage operations were undertaken it is likely that the climatic conditions are such that the soils would not even then be suitable for arable farming. This applies, for example, to many parts of the Highlands of Scotland.
3. *Vegetation*, including former vegetation. The former vegetation cover of numerous areas plays an important part in the character of the soil which is found at the present day.
4. *Relief*. The degree and direction of the slope of the land is important in its relation to drainage.

It has been found that a distinction must be drawn between the texture of a soil and the structure of a soil. When organic matter has been eliminated it is possible, as indicated above, to separate the mineral particles of the soil according to size, that is to determine differences in texture.

If however we take an ordinary worked agricultural or growing soil, dry it thoroughly and, say, place some in a closed jar, it is found that the particles remain grouped together and give the soil what is commonly called a 'crumb structure'. The soil does not immediately break down into a powdery mixture of large and small particles. This crumb structure is recognised as being of enormous importance where growing plants are concerned, and the maintenance of a good crumb structure is what the farmer understands by 'keeping the soil in good heart'.

Certain modern methods of soil treatment, notably the patented substance known under the trade name of Krilium, aim at creating a suitable crumb structure in heavy soils which are otherwise almost amorphous clay.

A great deal of nonsense has been written about the relative value of artificial or chemical fertilisers which add to a soil the chemical nutrients required by plants, and natural or animal manure. There are those who go so far as to say that for good health vegetables and fruits must be grown on land enriched with natural manure. Whilst it is difficult to substantiate such an extreme point of view it is probably true that animal manure helps to maintain the crumb structure of a soil whereas that crumb structure may be broken down by the addition of chemical fertilisers alone.

Classification

We may now attempt a classification of British soils, especially in relationship to their effect on agriculture and the natural vegetation cover. Two broad groups are to be distinguished:

(*a*) Mineral soils. Those which owe their principal characteristics to the size and character of the mineral particles present.
(*b*) Organic soils. Those whose dominant characteristics are determined by the character and relative quantities of organic compounds present.

Mineral soils

Apart from the presence or absence of calcareous material, the properties of mineral soils are determined largely by the proportion of particles of different sizes. For purposes of study particles have been grouped arbitrarily under the following types:

Diameter above 2 millimetres—stones.
Diameter between 0.2 and 2 millimetres—coarse sand.
Diameter between 0.02 and 0.2 millimetres—fine sand.
Diameter between 0.002 and 0.02 millimetres—silt.
Diameter below 0.002 millimetres—clay.

Sandy soils usually contain more than 60 per cent of coarse and fine sand and less than 10 per cent of clay. Owing to the large size of the particles they present but a small surface for retention of water; they are easily permeable by air and also by water, and hence plant roots can not only penetrate such soils easily but can also 'breathe' easily. Water may drain rapidly away from the roots so that plants may suffer from drought. Not infrequently they are deficient in plant foods because the freely moving water dissolves the nutrients and removes them. For that reason they are called 'hungry' by the farmer, but they are easily cultivated.

Loamy soils contain a smaller percentage of coarse and fine sand, but a larger proportion of silt and clay. They are less easily permeable, but sufficiently so to allow the ample aeration of roots and to prevent waterlogging. Thus loamy soils are suitable for all types of crops and are the most valuable of the mineral soils.

Clayey soils, or clays, containing a high proportion of clay, are much less permeable, liable to become waterlogged, very sticky when wet, but hard and difficult to cultivate when dry. It is usually difficult for plant roots to penetrate clay soils, and in the summer months when the clay soil is dry and cracked the roots may be torn asunder. They are thus not naturally very suitable for arable cultivation (though they can be much improved by liming and addition of organic matter) and in Britain are very largely given over to permanent grassland. Many of the 'marginal lands' of Britain, once cultivated, but where now cultivation is uneconomic, have clay soils.

Calcareous soils. Calcium carbonate and calcium phosphate are both of vital importance to a plant, and in small quantities they usually tend to improve the character of any soil, especially a clayey soil. The term marl is variously applied in Britain, but is sometimes, and rightly, given to a loamy soil or a clayey soil which has a considerable proportion of calcareous material. In soils derived directly from limestone such as chalk, the proportion of calcium carbonate may naturally be very high. On such soils occur plants which are definitely calcicolous, or lovers of lime, whilst on other types of soil calcifugous plants, or haters of lime, occur—especially on acid soil types. It may be noted here that in some cases the soils found in limestone areas are curiously deficient in calcium carbonate, the whole of it having been leached out by the solvent action of percolating rainwater.

Other types. Mention should also be made of those soils which have special characteristics due to the presence of quantities of salts—for example, the salt marshes—and a separate category must be preserved for rocky soils or hard rock, not covered by loose earth or by soil in the generally accepted sense.

Organic soils

Fenland, or black earth, soils. The organic matter in soils is, of course, derived mainly from plants. When plants die the very varied organic compounds of which they consist are very rapidly attacked by the various micro-organisms in the soil which tend to break them down again into simple compounds, such as carbon dioxide, water and ammonia, the ammonia rapidly becoming oxidised to form nitrates. But there are other organisms in the soil which build up their own substance and also reconstruct complex organic compounds. In a well aerated soil a great variety of micro-organisms is present, giving rise to innumerable substances of organic origin, varying

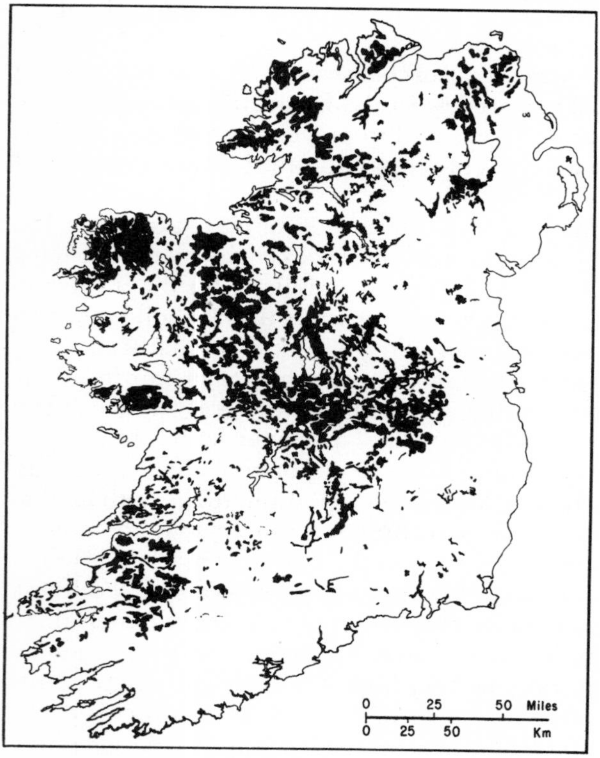

FIG. 75. The peat-bogs of Ireland

All areas in solid black are covered with peat and bogland. The predominance in the Central Lowland and in the West should be noted. For the utilisation of peat see p. 328.

from the complex organic compounds formed by the decaying plants themselves to the simpler compounds and elemental substances which result from their final alteration. Among the most characteristic of the intermediate products present are those compounds, usually black and sticky, collectively known as humus. They are colloidal like clay, but, unlike clay, they do not make the soil sticky; on the contrary they render it more friable. A loamy soil with a good proportion of humus may be described as the most fertile of all soils, and where the Fenlands of England have been drained are some of the most fertile agricultural lands anywhere to be found; it will be noticed that the characteristic colour of the soil is almost black, due to the large proportion of humus present.[1] Where, however, the aeration of the soil is deficient, usually due to the excess amount of moisture, then there tends to be an accumulation, not of humus but of humic acid. *Peaty and moorland soils.* In peaty and moorland soils the great defects are acidity due to the excess of humic acid and poor aeration, in turn due to excessive moisture and low temperatures. In some cases by draining, or by the admixture of a proportion of calcareous material, a peaty soil may be converted into a very rich humic soil; but there are other areas where the acidity is so great that the expense of treatment is prohibitive even by these simple means. This, of course, is particularly the case in moorland areas where the drainage is bad.

Perhaps a better classification of organic soils would be:

Mild humic soil or mull, such as is normally found on the floors of deciduous woods, in meadows, gardens, etc., and has a neutral reaction or is only slightly acid or alkaline, being well aerated by earthworms, etc. (brown earth).

Fen or mild peat, formed where there is an excess of water but a deficiency of oxygen, as on the margins of lakes; but the water gives an alkaline reaction because of the presence of lime or other bases in quantity. When drained this is the rich humic or the black soil of the Fenland area.

Raw or acid humus is formed on soils deficient in lime and is characteristic of podzolised soils under coniferous woodland and on dry heaths. Oxidation is not necessarily deficient, but the soil must be so acid that the humus is unsaturated and earthworms are absent.

Acid peat. Under conditions of excessive moisture, low temperature and oxygen deficiency acid peat accumulates and a pure peat soil is produced. If the conditions are maintained this acid peat soil may reach a great depth giving the characteristic moor ('mor') soil with moorland vegetation.

The distribution of soil types in the British Isles

Mineral soils derived from drift deposits

The deposits left behind after the retreat of the ice sheets of the great Ice Age vary enormously in character. The following broad types of soil derived from these and other superficial deposits may be distinguished:

Boulder clay. This is usually a stiff clay with numerous boulders of rock of very varied size transported from a distance. As a rule the soils derived from boulder clay are stiff heavy clay soils and hence little cultivated but rather left as grassland. In the wetter parts of Scotland and Ireland particularly

1. Though humus is dark in colour some of its constituents are not.

they tend to be waterlogged and to give rise to acid humus soils or acid peaty soils. The same happens with compact soils even if not true clays.

Chalky boulder clay. A special place must be made for the boulder clay, common in parts of eastern England, where there is a considerable admixture of chalk. This ameliorates the normal character of the clay soil

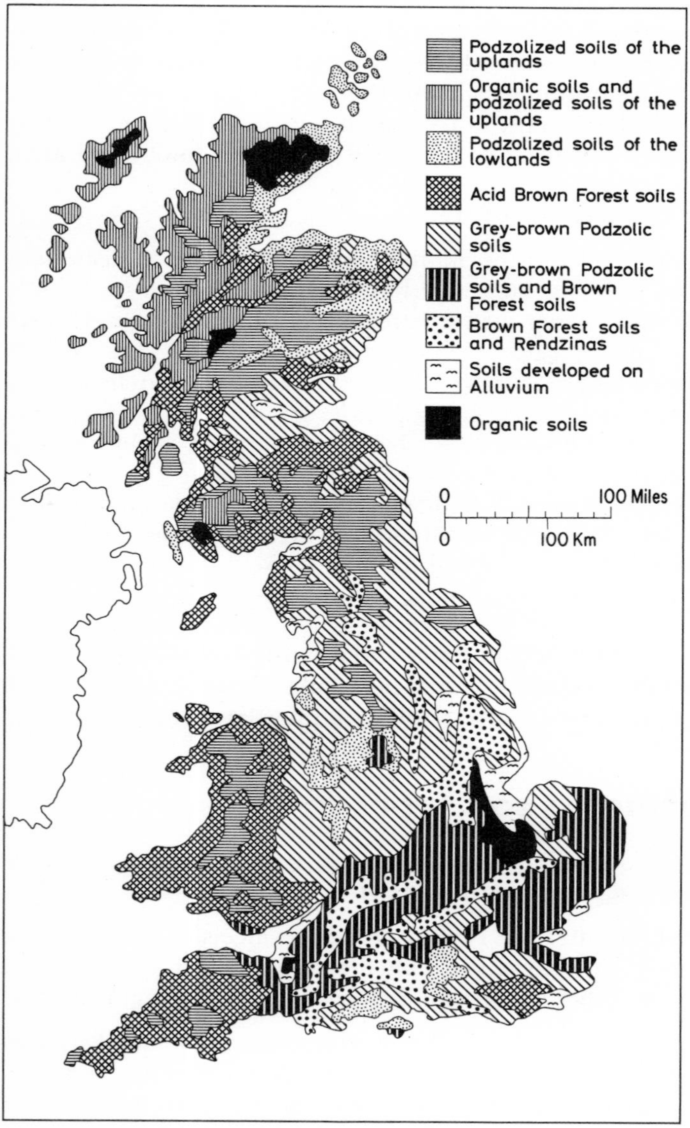

FIG. 76. The main soil groups in Great Britain

From information supplied by the Director of the Soil Survey, from the British contribution to the soil map of Europe (see p. 116).

derived, and the chalky boulder clay is frequently very fertile (see p. 256).
Loamy glacial drifts, such as those derived from the Old Red Sandstone in Scotland and in parts of England. Because the soils are well mixed they may be very fertile and hence the land is largely cultivated. This is the case in the Lothians of Scotland around Edinburgh.
Glacial sands. Particularly conspicuous in Ireland are the dry grass-covered gravel ridges, known as eskers, and the sandy, loamy or stony, sometimes clayey, knolls of glacial drift called drumlins. Where the sands are coarse and the water drains away quickly the soils are light and sandy, but the drumlins are often selected in Ireland for agricultural purposes because of the better drainage when compared with the low-lying levels by which they are surrounded.
Brick-earth. In the south of England there are some fine loamy or silty soils which are derived from what is commonly called brick-earth. Brick-earth (cf. French *limon*) seems to be in the main composed of the finest particles which result from glaciation, probably distributed partly by wind and thus corresponding to loess, but resorted under conditions of heavier rainfall in England, and so differing in character from typical loess. Soils derived from brick-earth are very fertile.
Gravelly soils. There are numerous sheets of gravel both at high levels and at low levels, particularly in England, some of which may be derived from outwash fans when the ice had melted, others of which are the normal deposits of rivers and some perhaps coastal deposits laid down under marine conditions. The high level gravels often give rise to infertile soils whereas the low level gravels, especially if covered by a thin layer of brick-earth, may be particularly fertile. Special reference will be made later to cultivation on such areas as the Thames terraces.
Clay with flints. A special type of deposit is widely distributed on the surface of the Chalk Downs, especially the North Downs of Kent. It consists of a stiff clay, brownish in colour, with sharp angular flints—a residual deposit from weathering of chalk. All the lime has been leached out so that it is a stiff clay soil deficient in lime, commonly, therefore, left to grassland or to damp oak woodland contrasting with the surrounding chalk country itself.
Alluvium. The fine grained deposits of the alluvium of flood belts and riverine tracts need no further description, except to point out their wide distribution in this country. To them may be added the marine silts such as are important round the Wash.

Mineral soils derived from the underlying solid rocks themselves

Two broad divisions may at once be distinguished:

(*a*) The siliceous soils derived from the older rocks, mainly Paleozoic rocks, of the 'Highland Zone' (see p. 26) of the north and west of England and Wales, Scotland and Ireland. Although technically they may be classified into sands, loams and clays, according to the size of the particles, they tend to differ from the better known soils derived from later rocks in the southern and southeastern parts of England. They are comparatively well drained, but usually lack the fertility of soils derived from later rocks because the weathering processes have failed to form soils of great depth. Where drainage is bad and moisture excessive peat and moorland soils predominate, as, for example, in many parts of the Highlands of Scotland. Indeed the soils of Scotland derived *directly* from underlying solid rocks seem to be limited. Among the soils derived from the Paleozoic rocks are extensive stretches of limestone soil, as in parts of the Pennines.

(*b*) Soils derived from the younger Mesozoic and Tertiary rocks of the 'Lowland Zone' (see p. 26) of the south and east of England. Of the Secondary rocks the marls of the Trias and the clays of such belts as the Lias and the later Jurassic rocks, the Cretaceous of the Weald and the Tertiaries (e.g. London Clay) give rise to tracts of heavy clay soil. Between these there are the ridges formed by the outcrops of sandstone and limestone. On these will be found sandy soils, as on the Lower Greensand, and the calcareous soils characteristic of the Oolitic Limestone and of the Chalk. Again, it must be remembered that on these limestones, including the Chalk, leaching is often important and lime may be practically absent. What is often important is the rapid and very marked local variation in many parts of the Lowland Zone, e.g. the London Basin.

Organic soils

The distribution of organic soils in the British Isles will have been made clear from the descriptions given above.

International Soil Map of Europe

The British contribution to the United Nations (Food and Agriculture Organisation) Soil Map of Europe, 1961–63

As indicated in the preceding pages there is far from being general agreement on soil classification. What has been said of British soils is factual and non-committal. For purposes of the International Soil Map of Europe, the British Soil Survey drew a small-scale map (1 : $2\frac{1}{2}$ m) which showed, apart from soils developed on alluvium and the organic soils of upland peats and lowland fens, six categories (Fig. 76):

1. Podzolised soils of the uplands—the highlands of Scotland, Pennines, Lakes, Wales, and the southwest—with patches of peat.
2. Podzolised soils of the lowlands, mainly in the northeast of Scotland but including the coarse sandy lands of England in the Hampshire basin, Bagshot country, etc.

3. Acid Brown Forest soils, dominant in Wales, the southwest peninsula, and the wet southwest of Scotland.
4. Grey-Brown Podzolic soils, found over much of the Midlands of England and the Central Lowlands of Scotland.
5. Grey-Brown Podzolic soils and Brown Forest soils mixed, over much of southeastern England.
6. Brown Forest soils with Rendzinas (chalk and humus-rich soils lacking a B horizon), on the main limestone areas of the Cotswolds and chalklands.

7
The natural vegetation of Britain

It is frequently stated that except for areas of fenland and marsh the natural vegetation of the whole of the British Isles was forest or woodland, and the small extent of woodland at present remaining—only about 6 per cent of the surface of the whole country—is frequently quoted as evidence of the extent to which man has cleared the natural vegetation of the country and artificially altered the appearance of the surface. While it is perfectly true to say that natural woodland has been cleared over vast areas—as, for example, over the Weald of Kent, Surrey, and Sussex—it may be that there is a tendency to exaggerate the former extent of forest land in the British Isles as a whole, and to ignore other types of natural vegetation. Further, when one is discussing the former extent of natural vegetation it is necessary to say exactly to what period one is referring. Before dealing with the different types of vegetation which may be found in the country at present, it will be useful to outline the changes which one may postulate as having taken place since the close of the great Ice Age.

It has already been pointed out (p. 22) that during the great Ice Age ice sheets covered Great Britain as far south approximately as a line joining the Thames and Severn, and also the whole of Ireland, with the exception possibly of certain tracts in the south. Whatever may have been the pre-glacial vegetation of the British Isles, it is clear that the conditions prevailing in the south of both Britain and Ireland at the time of the maximum extension of the ice sheet (the Lowestoft or Elster Glacial, cf. p. 24) must have been the conditions of the tundra lands. With the final retreat of the ice after the last or Weichsel Glacial and the amelioration of climatic conditions Britain was gradually recolonised by plant species from the continent, that is from the south and east. Indeed, there are numerous species still restricted to the south and east, and on the whole the flora of the British Isles becomes poorer in species as one goes northwards and westwards. Just as in northern Russia and Finland at the present day, to the south of the tundra belt the dominant trees of the great forests are birch and pine, so we have good evidence that as the ice finally receded in Great Britain these were the first trees to invade the country. The analysis of pollen in the successive layers in peat deposits—work associated especially with the name of Dr H. Godwin—has enabled an exact sequence to be worked out and this is summarised in the table on p. 86.

After the early postglacial birch–pine forests (Zone IV of Godwin) pine became dominant (Zone V), then pine with hazel (Zone VI). This was throughout a period with dry cold winters (the Boreal Period) when Britain was probably still joined to the continent and was inhabited by Neolithic man—using polished stone implements. The submerged forests round the coasts of Britain are largely of this age. There seems then to have been quite a sudden change to wet, mild conditions (the Atlantic Period) which may be due to the final severance of Britain from the continent and the establishment of the present system of oceanic circulation. The change was marked, probably about 5000 B.C., by a great development of oak but in association with alder, elm and lime (Zone VII), and later with alder, elm, birch and beech (Zone VIII). During these periods Neolithic culture gave place to Bronze Age and then Iron Age man.

It is still uncertain how far north some of the invading trees and other vegetation extended, but in Iron Age times, shortly before the Roman invasion and the Christian era, we can picture the British Isles as for the most part forest-covered, the types of forest present being determined by climate and by soil, and ranging from forest in the north, in which the Scots pine and birch were dominant, to the great stretches of oak woodlands on damp soil in the Midlands and south, and to the beech and hornbeam forests of the drier areas in the south.

The forest cover may have been interrupted over wide tracts by other types of natural vegetation. Fenland and freshwater marshland probably covered very large areas, such as in the region still known as the Fens, of which a description will be given later. Proofs exist that much of the heathland and moorland of the present day was formerly forested, but this may not apply to the whole of the great areas that are now moorland. Scrubland, which can be defined as the transition phase between grassland or heathland and forest, may also have covered very considerable areas. It is much more difficult to assess how far grassland may be regarded as a natural type of vegetation in Britain. At present there are three or four kinds of grassland which correspond broadly with the main types of forest. Thus the chalk or fescue grassland which is characteristic of the shallow soils derived from the chalk corresponds with the beech forests found on the same soils. These chalk grasslands may have been typical sheep pastures from very early times, whilst more recently the ravages of rabbits and other small grass-eating animals have contributed to prevent the growth of forest on these upland tracts.

It may have been the more open character of the vegetation on the higher limestone tracts made them attractive to the Neolithic settlers. There is no doubt that the Neolithic settlements occurred in such areas, and early Neolithic roads are found for the most part on such elevated tracts, despite difficulties of an adequate water supply (see Chap. 24). Another type of grassland, often called grass heath, occurs on sandy soils and shows many transitions to and from heath proper. A third and very common type of grassland is that which is called neutral grassland, and which corresponds to the oak forests of the heavy clay lands. This on alluvial soils, or where the water level is high, passes naturally into waterside meadow, corresponding broadly with the willow and alder woodlands.

There can, however, be little doubt that most of the grassland of the present day owes its character to human influence.

An attempt will now be made to describe very briefly some of the more important types of the natural and seminatural vegetation which are found at the present day in the British Isles. Before doing so it will be well to understand the principle involved in plant succession. Each type of physical environment, that is each combination of climate, soil, etc., may be regarded as having an association of plants peculiar to itself, and this plant association would form the natural vegetation cover, provided interfering factors are absent. This natural vegetation association is known as the climax association, but it must not be supposed that a tract of country such as Britain must have been when the ice sheet left it, or a tract of land which has been cultivated by man and then deserted, will immediately become covered with the climax vegetation. It is instead invaded and colonised by plants whose dominance is limited in that they will in time become ousted by others until the climax community eventually establishes itself. Thus the natural vegetation cover passes through a succession of stages; owing to the depredations of animals such as rabbits, the interference of man and his domestic animals, certain of the stages in the plant succession may become quasipermanent, and the climatic climax may not have an opportunity of establishing itself at all.[1] Thus in attempting to describe the natural vegetation cover of the British Isles we shall be dealing with various stages in the plant succession as well as climax communities.

Referring to the table given on p. 149, showing the utilisation of the surface of the British Isles, we may regard natural and seminatural vegetation as embracing the first two categories—namely, the woods and the rough grazing land, which broadly speaking is moorland and heathland, and at least to some extent the permanent pasture—whilst under the heading of other lands are included certain areas of marsh, etc., which are definitely natural vegetation.

TYPES OF NATURAL VEGETATION

The following brief account of the chief types of natural vegetation found in the British Isles has been based in part upon the standard work on the subject, *The British Islands and their Vegetation*, by A. G. Tansley. The types have been arranged in the following summary under the three broad headings of forest and woodland, heathland and moorland, and grassland, and

1. Reference should be made to the important studies by Dr E. Wyllie Fenton, *The Influence of Man and Animals on the Vegetation of Certain Hill Grazings in South-East Scotland*, Edinburgh School of Agriculture, I and II, 1951–52.

thus correspond with three main categories which were distinguished in the maps of the First Land Utilisation Survey of Britain. Thus the types described under the forest and woodland will include the principal types of natural vegetation to be found in those areas coloured dark green on the Land Utilisation maps. Similarly the type described as heathland and moorland will be the types which make up the areas of yellow colour on the map, whilst the types described under grassland will be those which correspond to the light green areas on the Utilisation maps.

Forest and woodland

Damp oakwood or pedunculate oakwood

In more ways than one the oak is the characteristic British tree, and there can be little doubt that the whole of the lowlands of Britain with clayey or loamy soils were at one time covered with oak forests. Most of the woods still existing on these soils, with the exception of those, of course, planted with exotic species, are also oakwoods or derived from oakwoods. The dominant tree of the heavier soils and those well supplied with mineral salts is *Quercus robur* (*Quercus pedunculata*), or the pedunculate oak. Most of the British oakwoods have been heavily exploited for timber in the past.[1] Oak was in special demand for shipbuilding before the extensive use of iron and steel. The rise of the English Navy and Mercantile Marine coincided with a rapid using up of extensive oak forests, particularly in the southeast of England, where the oak forests were within easy reach of navigable waters and harbours. During the Middle Ages, too, when most of the iron was smelted by means of charcoal, there was an enormous destruction of oak forests. It is of course well known, as explained elsewhere in this book, that the disappearance of the Wealden iron industry was not due to the exhaustion of the ore, but to the virtual exhaustion of the supply of wood for charcoal. Most of the oakwoods which remain have been sadly neglected from the forestry standpoint and really good standard trees, suitable for the production of timber, are few. In the south and midlands of England the majority of oakwoods are now in the form of coppice with standards. That is to say there are some eight to a dozen 'standards' or large trees per acre, while the intervening area is occupied by 'coppice', trees of other species. By far the most common of coppice trees is hazel. The tree is cut near the ground and the stump sends up a number of shoots. After a period of ten or fifteen years the main branches thus formed are cut for the provision of fencing posts, etc., the smaller ends having a small market as bean sticks and pea sticks. Ash and birch are also common in coppice woods, and oak itself may be coppiced, in addition to the oaks which grow as the stan-

1. Primitive woodland can frequently be distinguished even from very old plantations by a greater richness in plant species of the ground vegetation.

dard tree. Another important coppice tree is the Spanish chestnut, much favoured for fencing because it splits evenly into two half-round sections. It is urged by some that these woodlands of coppice with standards are legacies from the Middle Ages when the oak woods were thinned in such a way that the remaining trees branched freely and thus gave a supply of curved timber and 'knee' pieces which were particularly useful in shipbuilding; obviously quite contrary to the usual requirements of modern industry of good straight timber. The copse or coppice with standards will clearly present a very different appearance shortly after it has been cut, and a recently cut woodland is usually characterised by a rich growth of ground plants, including the favourite primrose and bluebell. These almost disappear as the coppice trees once more grow up and cast a greater shade over the ground. The wood anemone and dog mercury are other characteristic ground plants. 'On the edges of burnt oakwoods which have been carelessly exploited a scattered scrub is commonly found with spaces of turf between the clumps of bushes and an occasional isolated oak tree. This vegetation represents degenerate oakwood from which the trees have nearly all quite disappeared.' Many of the species present in this scrub are spiny species, and this is doubtless due to the fact that they are protected by their spines from browsing animals. This kind of land is occasionally used for pasturing, but has economically no value as woodland (recorded by the Land Utilisation Survey as Fc).

Dry oakwood

Oakwoods also occur on dry sandy soils. The oak may either be *Quercus robur* or *Quercus sessiliflora*, or the two may be mixed. Birch is usually found in the dry oakwoods in varying proportions, but the hazel and the ash are commonly absent. The ground vegetation is often poor, but a common feature is the presence of large quantities of bracken. The beech may occur, particularly in societies or clumps, and as usual in beechwoods the undergrowth is here almost absent. Scrub may occur on the margins of these dry oakwoods, and the woods, especially oak with birch, often grade insensibly into heathland. As Tansley points out in his later writings there is no fundamental difference between damp and dry oakwoods. Reference will be made later to the oak–birch heath.

Sessile oakwoods (Durmast oakwoods)

On the older rocks of the British Isles, which, as already described, furnish poor siliceous soils, oakwoods again occur, but here the dominant tree is the Durmast oak, *Quercus sessiliflora*. The soils are shallow and are usually deficient in soluble salts, especially calcium, and often show a marked tendency to allow the accumulation of acid humus. Durmast oakwoods occur, however, on a great variety of soils, but always with soils poor in mineral salts. The trees are therefore on the whole of small dimensions;

where larger, the trees are of a more upright habit[1] than *Q. robur*. The birch (*Betula tomentosa*) commonly occurs, the beech is sometimes found in larger woods. Conifers are not indigenous, but both the larch and the Scots pine are commonly planted. The holly (*Ilex aquifolium*) is usually found in the oakwoods on the Pennines. On the hills such as the Pennines and in Wales, it would seem that these oakwoods formerly extended to higher levels than at the present day. They tend to degenerate now into scrubland and there is every passage from scrub to grassland and moorland. In the intermediate stages, especially on the drier soils, bilberry and bracken are very common. In the Pennines and drier regions the ash is usually confined to wetter situations and the sides of streams, but in the regions of the British Isles which have a heavy rainfall, for example in the Lake District, most of the oakwoods contain a very large proportion of ash, and one really has an oak-ash woodland. The same is true, for example, of some of the Devonshire woods.

Birchwoods

Anyone who knows the great northern forests of Russia and Lapland will know the extent to which the birch is there intermingled with hardy coniferous trees. It is not, therefore, surprising to find a fringe of birchwood occurring above oakwoods in the British Isles, and forming in the Highlands of Scotland characteristic woods at the sides of the valleys, sometimes even occurring up to 600 metres (2000 ft). The birch is a light demander, but can stand great exposure. Because Scots pine thrives under much the same conditions, birchwoods and pinewoods are largely interchangeable. Oakwoods from which the oak has been removed are often replaced by the less valuable birches and become birchwoods, whilst wood clearings often seem to pass into birchwoods rather than back to the original oakwoods. Thus the birchwoods may replace the oakwoods or may occur definitely as a vegetation layer above them.[2]

Pinewoods

Although the Scots pine (*Pinus sylvestris*) was formerly native in many parts of England and Ireland, it is generally agreed that it disappeared from the south of England, and has only recently been reintroduced (in the eighteenth century or perhaps earlier). In Scotland pinewoods at one time covered large areas in the broad valleys or straths of the Highlands and the

1. These oakwoods may be coppiced on a twenty-year rotation.
2. It has been pointed out by Sir E. J. Salisbury that primitive man, working with stone tools, would find the birch easier to cut down than oak, and it may be that he was attracted to higher ground in many parts of Britain not because the ground was already clear but because the birch forest was more easily cleared.

glens, extending for considerable distances up the mountain slopes. Owing to heavy exploitation the area occupied by these pine woodlands is now rather seriously restricted. On its introduction into the south of England the Scots pine spread very rapidly over tracts of sandy soil, and it now forms extensive subspontaneous woodland, as on the Bagshot Sands of the London Basin and on the Lower Greensand of the Weald. But whether in Scotland or in the south of England, there is a very close association between pinewoods and heathlands, and it is often difficult to decide whether an area should be classified as a pinewood, or as heathland with many scattered pines. It will be seen that on the dry soils of the south these pinewoods are competitors with dry oakwoods and with beechwoods. The close pinewoods are very poor in other species, partly on account of the deep shade and partly because of the thick layer of pine needles which carpets the floor of the woods. Where more open, bracken is common, whilst over large areas the bilberry (*Vaccinium myrtillus*), as in the great coniferous forests of the north of Europe, is very characteristic, associated of course with the heath (*Calluna vulgaris*).

Beechwoods

By pollen analysis Godwin has now proved that the beech (*Fagus sylvatica*) invaded Britain in Atlantic times, but afterwards it retreated from the southwest and elsewhere. Because it behaves as a native only in the southeast it was long thought to be a recent introduction. Beechwoods occur characteristically on the chalk, occupying the steep valley sides or the scarp faces on the North and South Downs as well as large areas in the Chiltern Hills and in parts of the Cotswolds. They are absent from the northern chalk areas of Yorkshire and Lincolnshire as well as of Norfolk. On the Continent the beech tends to occur rather on the marly or damper limestone soils. In England the beech is natural to the drier limestone soils, possibly as a result of the generally damper character of the English climate. The way in which the beechwoods occur on the steep sides of the chalk valleys has given rise to the commonly applied name of 'hanger' to this type of wood. The beech is not only the dominant tree in the beechwoods, it is very frequently the only tree, and indeed typically forms pure high forest in close canopy. Shrubs and ground vegetation are scarce, in fact the latter is often quite absent, and the ground covered with nothing but the delightfully brown fallen leaves. Thus, walking through a beechwood, there are many characteristic points of difference to be noticed from other types of English woodland. Occasionally the yew occurs as a shrub in the beechwood forest, and locally the yew has become dominant and forms yewwoods. Beechwoods are not restricted to the chalk; the beech has migrated to lighter sandy soils, much more rarely is it found on heavier clay soils. It is essential that there should be free drainage round the roots. The beech cannot grow with its 'feet in water'.

Ashwoods

Ashwoods are characteristic of limestone soils in the north and west of England, where, as already pointed out, beechwoods are absent. They are thus well-known features of the limestone dales of the Carboniferous Limestone of Derbyshire and of the Mendips. Wych elms are commonly found in these ashwoods whilst shrubs are characteristically abundant (including a number of species), partly owing to the high light intensity, even in summer, resulting from the translucent canopy of the trees. On marly soils the oak becomes important and one may really distinguish an ash–oak woodland association as characteristic of marls and calcareous sandstones. Again, hazel is common, and where the oaks have been left as standards one may have an ash–oak–hazel coppice, very common indeed in the south of England, especially towards the rather damper west, taking the place of the oak–hazel coppice, which occurs on clay soils that are poor in lime.

Alder–willow associations

The alder (*Alnus rotundifolia*) and the willows (*Salix*) are the characteristic trees of very damp situations. By the sides of streams in oakwoods the alder usually appears, whilst the alder–willow association is the woodland association which corresponds to marshland.[1] The osier (*Salix viminalis*) is of course usually planted—on tracts of alluvium by the sides of rivers where the surface of the ground is only a few inches above the permanent water level. The ground vegetation in such situations is that of a typical marsh. In the wet areas of East Anglia the woodland formation, occurring associated with fens, is known as swamp carr and marsh carr.

Heathland and moorland

Under the title of Rough Grazing, Mountain Heath, Moor or Downland, the published statistics of the Ministry of Agriculture, Fisheries and Food include a considerable variety of types of natural vegetation. This category is identical with the Heathland, Moorland, Commons, and Rough Hill Pasture distinguished by the First Land Utilisation Survey of Britain and shown on their maps in yellow.

In 1940 Sir George Stapledon and Mr William Davies extended to England a reconnaissance survey they had previously carried out in Wales and later a map on the scale of 1 : 625 000 was published and is usually referred to as the Grassland Map. It shows, highly generalised and ignoring both woodland and ploughland, lowland grassland divided into eight

1. Sir E. J. Salisbury believes that alder woodland was formerly very widespread in low, damp ground, but, because of the relative ease with which the alder could be cleared by primitive man with stone tools, was largely destroyed at an early date. Compare the early settlements on valley gravels (see p. 642) where the lowland water-side meadows were an added attraction.

categories according to agricultural quality. The heathland, moorland and rough pasture are shown divided into eleven types:—heather moor, heather fell (i.e. with many boulders), lowland heaths; cotton grass and deer-grass moors, molinia moor and nardus moor; mountain or hill pastures and grassland invaded by bracken, gorse, etc; basic pastures of mountains, downland and lowland grass heaths.

This scheme was extended and enlarged for use in Scotland and a map prepared using existing data which was published as one of the National Planning Series (1:625 000 in full colour) with an explanatory text by Arthur Geddes.

It will be found that these schemes agree generally with that given below, based on Tansley.

Heathland or heath associations

In heathland by far the most widespread and abundant species is ling or heather (*Calluna vulgaris*). With it are usually associated other members of the Ericaceae of which *Erica tetralix* is one of the commonest; whilst towards the north of Britain the bilberry (*Vaccinium myrtillus*) becomes dominant over considerable tracts. Under the dense shade of *Calluna* very few other species can exist. Heathland is usually found on gravelly or relatively coarse sandy soil, or on similar soils derived from the older rocks in the north. The coarse, gravelly or sandy soil usually has a dark surface layer coloured by much humus, below which there is a layer of leached sand, often pale grey, or even whitish in colour. Between this and the unaltered sands below there is frequently a compact stratum of hard moorpan. The moorpan may be only a few inches but perhaps several feet below the surface, but it is this which prevents the invasion of heathland by trees, and heathland in which the hard pan is present cannot be afforested unless the pan is broken up or holes made in it for the roots of young trees to penetrate. Thus the heath association is usually a stable association, either resulting from the final degeneration of the oak–birch–heath association or a stage in the succession on poorer sandy soils.

Where the hard pan is absent there may be every gradation from the pure heathland to the oak–birch association, or to pinewood. It is frequently difficult in studying a tract of country to decide what should be called pinewood with a ground vegetation of heather and heathland with scattered pine trees. Indeed any distinction must be a very artificial one. Gorse is often found on the margins of heathland where conditions are less acid, though it is not essentially a typical member of the heathland itself. Local bogs are common in heathland. Some of the better known regions of English heathland include the stretches of flat sandy country in northwest Norfolk, and southeast Suffolk on the crags or on the more sandy members of the overlying drift deposits. Heaths are well developed on the Bagshot Beds of the London Basin, and on the sandy Tertiary beds of the Hampshire

Basin. They are common, too, on the sandy beds which occur in the Wealden area. Both the sandy soils of the New Forest region and the sandy soils of the Weald afford excellent examples of the way in which heathland dovetails into the oak–birch woodland and pinewood. In the west heathland occurs both on Devonian Sandstones, as on Exmoor, or on the granite masses, such as Dartmoor. Here, being in the wetter part of the country, there is frequently a gradation into true moorland with heather growing on peat. In Yorkshire the name 'moor' is often applied to true heathland, and here varieties have been distinguished according to the dampness of the areas. Heathland in Scotland does not usually occur at greater elevations than 600 metres (2000 ft), and is found in those parts of the Highlands where the mean annual rainfall is comparatively low—less than 1500 millimetres (60 in). The heathlands of the Highlands are usually called moors, and are indeed the typical grouse moors. As such they are systematically burned in rotation every ten to fifteen years. In various regions, the association of bracken with typical heathland should be noticed. Bracken usually indicates a relatively good soil.

Limestone heathland

In the ordinary way heather is a plant that dislikes lime, and it is therefore not found on calcareous soils. But some plateau areas of limestone, owing to leaching action, tend to lose their lime; in such areas heather may occur, but it is associated with plants which have long roots, and which therefore reach the limestone below and are thus lime lovers. This accounts for some heathlike vegetation occurring in limestone areas. Of rather a different order are the limestone pavements which occur as striking features on some of the summits of the Carboniferous Limestones, as in the north Pennines and in the great limestone plain of County Clare in western Ireland. The exposed surface of the rock is very bare, and although rather rich in mosses it is extremely poor as regards larger plants which are more or less restricted to crevices. Heather (*Calluna*), though a calcifuge, may be present partly because of the existence of little pockets of soil from which the lime has been leached.

Moorland

Moorland is a comprehensive term, and includes many different types of natural vegetation. Moorland is essentially the vegetation of peaty soils. Frequently the soil is deep, practically pure peat; in other cases there is only a shallow layer of surface peat much mixed with mineral substances from the underlying rocks, in which case there is naturally a transition stage between the moorland and heathland, as one finds in the 'moors' of the North Riding of Yorkshire. There are also peat soils, especially those relatively rich in lime (hence called mild peat) and developed particularly, as far as Britain is concerned, in East Anglia, to which the name black fen is frequently applied. Separating moor and fen, moor has a relatively wet peat soil of considerable depth, fed by water poor in mineral salts, suffering from lack of aeration so that the humic acids produced give rise to a soil water which is acid in reaction. Fen, on the other hand, has a peat or peaty soil fed by water which is relatively rich in mineral salts, with the result that the ground water is alkaline in reaction. When drained, the peaty soil of the fens gives rise to a very dark coloured but extremely rich soil; whereas even when drained it is difficult to carry out cultivation on many tracts of moorland because of the essentially acid nature of the soil.

In moorland a broad distinction is possible between lowland moors, such as those areas known as 'mosses' in Lancashire, and upland moors. *Sphagnum* is a very common constituent of lowland moors and in the valley moors which occur in the south of England in the wetter parts of heathland. Amongst the different types of upland moor which have been distinguished in the wettest areas there is the *Sphagnum*, or bog moss moor, of comparatively limited extent. The cotton grass moors are characterised by the cotton grass (*Eriophorum vaginatum*) and are much more extensive in their occurrence. Cotton grass moors are widely distributed on the summit plateau of the Pennines, and sections through the peat of these areas show that considerable areas of these moorlands were once forested. *Scirpus* or reed moors occur in the wetter regions of the northwest Highlands of Scotland, as well as in some parts of Ireland, such as the Wicklow Mountains. The dominant plant is *Scirpus caespitosus* with often a considerable quantity of heather. There is evidence that some of these moors, too, were formerly forested, the remains of Scots pine and birch having been found in the peat.

Bilberry moors

The dominant plant here is *Vaccinium myrtillus* (the bilberry) and this type is common in the Pennines and in the central part of the Highlands of Scotland, but not in the northwest nor the Hebrides.

Heather moors

These differ from the heathland mainly in the occurrence of a greater thickness of peat, and the frequent association of heather and cotton grass or heath and bilberry.

Grass moorland

Grass moorlands cover large areas of Boulder Clay, such as in the southern part of the Southern Uplands, and also in the western Highlands of Scotland. The grass moorland tends to be intermediate in character between the *Scirpus* moor, already described, and siliceous grassland. The vegetation is mainly composed of a variety of grasses, rushes and sedges, but as in other moors, the soil is peaty, acid, and generally wet during most of the year.

Grassland

Five or six main types of grassland may be distinguished and may be regarded as seminatural formations in that they correspond with different types of woodland, and are found where the woodland has been cleared.

Neutral grassland

The adjective 'neutral' indicates that the soil of these grasslands is neither very acid on the one hand nor particularly calcareous on the other. The neutral grassland is the ultimate phase of degeneration of damp oakwood and so occurs associated with damp oakwood on the same types of soil. It consists of a close turf of grasses with associated herbaceous plants. The plants characteristic of calcareous pasture on the one hand are absent, and so are those which are characteristic of heath pastures. Neutral grassland affords excellent permanent pasture and is usually heavily grazed, but where less heavily grazed, as on the borders of some of the village greens of central and southern England, has many of the plants common to the ground flora of the damp oakwoods, including the anemone and the primrose. Where clay soils are low-lying, and ground water approaches the surface, the appearance of various species of rush (*Juncus*) may be noticed in neutral grasslands and marks a gradual passage towards rough marsh pasture. The line is often very difficult to draw, and this was found to be the case in surveying for the First Land Utilisation Survey. The best neutral grasslands are the permanent pastures dominated by rye grass (*Lolium perenne*) and wild white clover (*Trifolium repens*).

Acidic grasslands

Grassland dominated by bents (*Agrostis* spp.) together with sheep's and red fescue (*Festuca ovina* and *F. rubra*) probably covers a greater area than any other type of grassland in Britain. It is the typical community of the 'grassheath' and 'siliceous grassland' of earlier writers. Grass heath is associated with dry oakwood. Although transitions to ordinary heath are found, in the grass heath true heath plants, such as *Calluna*, *Erica*, etc., may be, and usually are, entirely lacking; but the grasses are those which prefer a sandy soil and usually form a close short turf. These grasslands are less valuable as grazing lands than the neutral grasslands, and so one often finds patches of gorse coming in on the margins of such areas. The East Anglian heaths sometimes include quite considerable stretches of dry grassland of this character, and it is believed by some writers that they represent a survival of steppe, or semi-steppeland, conditions in Britain. The better 'siliceous grasslands' correspond with the sessile oakwoods which grow on the thin soils of the older rocks. In such areas as the Pennines they tend to occur, not only associated with the oakwoods, but at higher levels.

Nardus and Molinia moors

On land with poorer soils or more acid conditions, grassland gives place to what is better described as moorland although dominated by grasses. On poorer drier areas the characteristic grass is the mat grass (*Nardus stricta*); whilst on the wetter soils the purple moor grass (*Molinia caerulea*) is the characteristic grass. In the southwest, the characteristic grass is *Agrostis setacea*. The dominance of grass is sometimes interrupted by stretches of bracken, whilst the small gorse comes in abundantly in such areas as the Malvern Hills, Devon and some of the hilly areas of Ireland. In wet areas rushes appear.

Limestone or basic grasslands

The springy turf that is characteristic of the chalk downs is almost proverbial. It is commonly referred to as downland. Similar grassland is found on other limestones in this country notably on the Jurassic limestones of the Cotswolds and a somewhat similar plant association reappears on some basic igneous rocks. The grasses of the siliceous grasslands are absent, and the bracken, the gorse and the rushes are on the whole uncommon. The heaths, too, are practically unknown. No one who is familiar with the delightful chalk downlands in the south of England will need to be reminded of the characteristic herbaceous flora, with numerous flowering herbs peculiar to itself, including many of our orchids. Generally the dominant grass is the red fescue (*Festuca rubra*) or sheep's fescue (*F. ovina*). Although a great proportion of the chalk pastures in England are old, it is going too far to say that the area has never been occupied by woodland. The chalk and limestone grasslands have, of course, long been famous as sheep pastures. Rabbits also were very abundant, and where they did occur in numbers the turf was even more closely nibbled than by the sheep. The fescue, with its wiry herbage, is very largely responsible for the springy nature of the turf, which is thus so delightful for walking. Myxomatosis almost wiped out the rabbit population in 1954.

Arctic-Alpine grasslands and mountain vegetation

Arctic-Alpine grassland is practically restricted to the higher levels in the Highlands of Scotland. The grasses and other plants tend to have a rosette habit, and naturally the species occurring are of particular interest in view of what has been said above as to the possible origin of this vegetation. This, with certain very wet types of grassland, may be the only type of truly *natural* grassland in Britain.

Fenland and freshwater marshland

The vegetation of fens, freshwater marshes, mosses and bogs is ecologically very interesting but economically unimportant. Some very reedy pastures are intermediate in character and can be used for rough grazing, but the true fen and freshwater marsh are of little use except for the yield of rushes for such purposes as thatching.

Salt marsh

The vegetation of regions which are characterised by the presence of salt in the soil or which are periodically flooded by salt water, whether regularly by the tide or only occasionally, consists of plants specially adapted to withstand these curious conditions, and known as halophytes. They are commonly fleshy plants of which the glassworts (*Salicornia*) are particularly characteristic. Some of the drier types of salt marsh can be used for occasional pasture. The numerous types of salt marsh are of particular interest to the ecologist, but are rather outside the scope of the present work. Those plants which bind and hold marine muds and enable land to be reclaimed are clearly of economic importance. Of these *Spartina townsendii* has colonised large areas in the south of England.

Sea coast and sand-dune vegetation

Hard, wiry grasses are characteristic of the vegetation of young sand-dunes. Some of them are particularly valuable because of their ability to bind sand-dunes and prevent their movement over valuable land. The sea couch grass (*Agropyrum junceum*) and the marram or star grass (*Ammophila arundinacea*) are specially interesting in this connection. Occasionally a few goats find pasturage on sand-dune grasses, and there is quite a considerable use of older dunes as golf courses. The study of grasses suitable for planting as greens for the golf courses is thus a matter of some general interest.

It might be thought that the study of the natural and seminatural vegetation of the British Isles has comparatively little practical importance. This is very far from being the case. The natural vegetation of an area forms a perfect index of the sum total of conditions, particularly of soil and climate, which affect the growth of any plants which may be introduced by man. For example, in introducing foreign species of trees for afforestation experiments in Britain it may be essential that they should be introduced in regions where the environment corresponds with the environment where they are found to flourish in their own home localities. The character of such environment in this country can be gauged by the natural vegetation ordinarily existing though some exotic species when introduced are found to require conditions here different from those of their homeland. Further, a detailed study of the natural vegetation existing, for example, in our moorland tracts, is an indication as to what is wrong with the soil from the point of view of its further utilisation in other directions, e.g. in agriculture. The presence of rushes in ordinary meadows is definitely indicative of wet conditions. The occurrence of heath is clearly indicative of an entirely different set of conditions. It is to be feared that some of the expensive early experiments in afforestation were carried out without a sufficient study of the local natural vegetation.

Fig. 77. National parks, forest parks, long distance paths and new towns, 1969

National Parks and nature conservation

The increasing pressure of population on land resources has led in Britain to a comprehensive system of town and country planning, based mainly on an Act passed in 1947. An attempt is made to balance the needs of land for industry, housing, recreation, communication, service use and other 'urban' needs against agriculture and forestry. Arising out of the need to provide large areas of natural beauty primarily for recreation has come the demarcation of National Parks in England and Wales—the Lake District, Northumberland, Peak District, Yorkshire Dales, North York Moors, Snowdonia, Dartmoor, Exmoor, Brecon Beacons and the Pembrokeshire Coast. These are under the general supervision of the National Parks Commission. Other areas are protected by being named 'Areas of Outstanding Natural Beauty' (AONB). There has also arisen a particular need to conserve areas where our native flora and fauna can continue to exist and be scientifically studied. The Nature Conservancy was established in 1949 and has general charge of this task, including the establishment and maintenance of nature reserves. The Reserves are usually small—the 72 demarcated in the first ten years totalled 57 000 hectares (140 000 acres)—and in contrast to National Parks it is often necessary to *limit* public access. The Conservancy has also notified a large number of Sites of Special Scientific Interest (SSSI) and as far as possible these are protected from building and other forms of development.

8
Forestry and afforestation

Enough has been said in the chapter on Natural Vegetation to indicate that the climate of the whole of the British Isles is one favourable to the growth of forests, and that one must regard forests as the natural vegetation cover of the major part of the islands at least below 300 metres (1000 ft). As we travel about much of Britain, particularly the lowland counties of England, the southern part of Scotland, the valleys amongst the Highlands, as well as the valleys of Wales, we are, perhaps, impressed by the well-wooded nature of the country. But the impression is in reality an illusion, for under eight per cent of the surface of the United Kingdom is at the present day covered with forest and woodland (see p. 149). The lowlands of Britain are, of course, preeminently characterised by numerous small fields, usually separated by hedges, and almost inevitably one sees along these hedges isolated trees which have been allowed to grow up or perhaps were planted at the time of the Enclosures. Viewed from a distance, the isolated trees of the hedgerows and the scattered trees of our numerous parks give an impression of a well-timbered country which is in reality entirely false.[1] Yet in the past forests have played an important part in the economic life of Britain. In the early days the clearing of heavily forested land, particularly the damp oakwoods of the lowlands, presented a task beyond the capability of the early inhabitants of these islands. In the Middle Ages the products of our forests and woodlands played an essential part in the economic development of the country. To quote from an article written some years ago:[2] 'The three great uses of wood in the preindustrial period may be broadly said to be for construction, for domestic fuel and for industrial fuel. In the days when timber occupied a place in domestic architecture even more fundamentally important than it does today, when timber was the only material for the construction of ships and when timber rubbed against timber in the moving parts of the coach or the mill wheel, it was strength and durability which counted rather than ease of working. Consequently the old oak beams

1. It should be noted, however, that in many parts of Britain, particularly the arable areas, hedges are being grubbed up in the interests of mechanised farming, whilst the regeneration of hedgerow trees is prevented by the use of mechanical hedge-cutters in place of the skilled hedge-layer of the past.

2. L. D. Stamp, 'The forests of Europe, present and future', *Empire Forestry Journal*, **7**, 1928, 85–102.

of the manor house, the massive timbers of the *Victory*, or the elaborately carved panels of a Jacobean press are symbolical standards of value which were the essential standards of the Middle Ages. The emphasis is obviously on the hard woods rather than on the softwoods. The association of the latter is rather with the blazing pine logs of the baronial hearth—the second great use of wood in the Middle Ages. Characteristic of the third great use is the now defunct iron industry of the Weald. The presence of large quantities of wood suitable for the manufacture of charcoal was the first consideration in determining the location of numerous industries, of which the smelting of iron was one.'

The Industrial Revolution was followed by the development of coal (including gas and electricity derived therefrom), and later of oil, as the principal domestic and industrial fuels and the rise to first rank of iron and steel as constructional materials. It would almost seem as if timber had become a superfluous commodity. Entirely supplanted by iron and steel in the construction of ships and machinery, very largely replaced in countries such as England as a domestic fuel and entirely as an industrial fuel, timber seemed to have been relegated to a position of minor importance in the economic life of the world.

The history of forestry in the nineteenth century reflects the unconscious reaction of these changes on the public mind. By that time British forests had almost gone: in the new lands of the world people of British stock were failing to appreciate forest wealth. The reckless depletion of forests by unregulated felling; the 'clearing' of enormous areas for agriculture by the incredibly barbarous method of burning off virgin forest; the lack of precautions against fire, and a dozen other things too familiar to necessitate enumeration, all indicate the low ebb of public appreciation of forest wealth.

But the present era is by no means an era which can do without forest products. There are innumerable uses now absorbing huge quantities of timber, such as the manufacture of wood pulp, chipboard and paper, as well as the constant demand for the time-honoured purposes of domestic architecture and the construction of furniture, and the now decreasing requirements of the railways for sleepers and the coal mines for pitprops.

The peculiar and serious position of Britain may be judged in several ways. In the first place there is the remarkable contrast with the remainder of Europe. Europe as a whole has roughly 30 per cent of its surface covered with forest, an average of about 0.32 hectares (0.8 acres) of forest for every inhabitant. Compared with the other countries of Europe, the United Kingdom is in the anomalous position of having the smallest proportion of forest area, as well as the smallest area per capita, of any major country. The useful forest and woodland covering the surface is only about 8 per cent of the whole and is equivalent to only about one-tenth of an acre per inhabitant. Europe, excluding the British Isles, is roughly self-supporting in the matter of timber, but there is certainly not sufficient surplus to supply the huge requirements of this country. Forest resources have been so depleted in most of the European countries that it is with the utmost difficulty that an export of timber is maintained from such countries as Finland, Sweden, Poland, Norway, Czechoslovakia, Austria and Romania. There remains, of course, the greatest potential exporter, Russia. All the time there exists in the background the fact that Britain herself could supply, and should supply, a much greater proportion of her requirements than the 10 per cent which was characteristic of the 1960s. Despite recent progress, there are still vast areas of heathland and moorland and mountain side of little value which are capable of growing excellent timber or at least wood of economic value.

The attention of the Government was focused on the timber resources of the British Isles during the First World War. Shipping which was urgently required for the transport of food and troops had to be utilised for the importation of that very bulky commodity—timber. There was ammunition to be made, for which factories were required; they needed fuel and that fuel was provided by the coal mines. Coal could not be mined without the extensive use of pitprops. As early as 1916 the Reconstruction Committee set up a Forestry Sub-committee to consider ways and means whereby, in the event of another national emergency, an adequate supply of home-grown timber could be assured. The Sub-committee set before it the ideal that the British Isles should be self-supporting as regards timber throughout a period of at least three years. Among the recommendations of the Committee was that a Forestry Commission should be set up, and this Commission was actually appointed in 1919. The Forestry Commissioners calculated that it would be necessary to afforest 719 000 hectares (1 777 000 acres) in order to cover a national emergency lasting three years. Their scheme provided for the planting of this large area in the course of eighty years, two-thirds of the programme to be completed within the first forty years. In addition, the existing woodlands were to be rescued from the state of neglect into which they had long since drifted.

One of the first tasks undertaken by the Forestry Commissioners was a census of woodlands of Great Britain and a census of production of home-grown timber. Most of the information gathered related to the year 1924. The results showed that there were approximately 0.8 million hectares (1.9 million acres) of woodland of all types, including scrub and devastated forest, in England and Wales and 0.4 million hectares (1 million acres) in Scotland. The exact total for the whole of Great Britain was 1 198 212 hectares (2 958 673 acres) or 5.3 per cent of the land surface.

A similar census of woodlands was carried out in 1947–49 and the results published in 1952. By that time the total had reached 1 472 321 hectares (3 635 362 acres) (including an estimated 75 735 hectares (187 000 acres) for areas under 5 acres not actually measured) or 6.5 per cent of the land surface. The effects of the work of the Forestry Commission are at once apparent.

A further census was taken in 1965–67 and the results published in 1970. This revealed that the area of woodlands had still further expanded, as a result of a revived interest in commercial forestry as well as through the activities of the Commission, to 1.7 million hectares (4.3 million acres) or 7.6 per cent of the land surface. The two following tables summarise the data of these last two censuses.

Distribution of woodlands by types and sub-types, 1947

TYPE	ENGLAND ACRES	%	WALES ACRES	%	SCOTLAND ACRES	%	GREAT BRITAIN ACRES	%
High forest:								
Conifers	331 275	18	97 438	31	439 084	34	867 797	25
Mixed	117 996	6	10 835	3	37 235	3	166 066	5
Hardwoods	580 286	31	77 633	25	97 017	8	754 936	22
Total high forest	*1 029 557*	*55*	*185 906*	*59*	*573 336*	*45*	*1 788 799*	*52*
Coppice with standards	227 423	12	2 276	1	89	—	229 788	7
Coppice	102 637	6	17 082	5	487	—	120 206	3
Scrub	200 040	10	40 228	13	256 683	20	496 951	15
Devastated	105 415	6	12 013	4	33 636	3	151 064	4
Felled:								
before Sept. 1939	33 492	2	21 578	7	233 433	18	288 503	8
since Sept. 1939	166 482	9	37 395	11	169 174	14	373 051	11
Total felled	*199 874*	*11*	*58 973*	*18*	*402 607*	*32*	*661 554*	*19*
Total	1 865 046	100	316 478	100	1 266 838	100	3 448 362	100

Distribution of woodlands by types and sub-types, 1965

FOREST TYPE	ENGLAND TH. HA	ENGLAND TH. ACRES	%	WALES TH. HA	WALES TH. ACRES	%	SCOTLAND TH. HA	SCOTLAND TH. ACRES	%	GREAT BRITAIN TH. HA	GREAT BRITAIN TH. ACRES	%
High forest:												
Coniferous	332	822	38	131	323	65	453	1121	69	917	2267	53
Broadleaved	285	705	32	25	63	13	39	97	6	350	864	20
Total high forest	*617*	*1527*	*70*	*156*	*386*	*78*	*492*	*1218*	*75*	*1267*	*3131*	*73*
Coppice	29	73	3	—	—	—	—	—	—	29	73	2
Scrub and felled	238	590	27	44	110	22	163	402	25	446	1101	25
Total	884	2189	100	200	496	100	655	1620	100	1742	4305	100

Figure 78 shows the approximate distribution of woodlands in Great Britain in 1947, and it will be noticed that the most heavily wooded portion of England was that immediately south of London, including the counties of Sussex (with as much as 15.5 per cent), Surrey (15.0), Kent (10.5) and Hampshire (14.9). In Scotland the most densely wooded part was the Buchan plateau between the Moray Firth and the Firth of Tay, including the counties of Nairn (with 19.1 per cent), Moray (21.6), Banff (10.0) and

Aberdeen (11.6). Farther south, Kincardine had 13.4 per cent. In the north and west the proportion dropped in Scotland to 0.4 in Caithness. All other Scottish counties had more than 2 per cent, but the western isles, considered separately, only 0.8 per cent.

Details were collected at both the 1924 and 1947 censuses as to the age of the trees in the forests, and a summary of these, together with somewhat similar data for 1965, is given in the following table.

Age of woodlands (high forest)

AGE (YEARS)	PERCENTAGE OF TOTAL AREA		1965			
	1924	1947	TOTAL	CONIFEROUS	BROAD-LEAVED	AGE (YEARS)
1–10	8.5	14	42	58	10	1–15
11–20	9	16	10	13	5	15–25
21–40	18	15	18	21	8	25–45
41–80	39.5	15	7	4	13	45–65
Over 80	25	14	21	4	64	Over 65

These figures show very clearly three things; first, that stands of useful timber (over 20 years and especially over 40 years) were much depleted during the Second World War; secondly, the enormous amount of planting, and particularly of coniferous species, that has been done since the war, and thirdly, the fact that almost all the really mature forest is of broad-leaved species. It must be understood that forest grown for timber has a definite rotation over a number of years. Thus a coniferous forest in Britain was reckoned to be fit for cutting over for timber about every 80 years, that is to say it has an 80-year rotation. Hardwoods, on the other hand, based especially on the oak, have a longer rotation, and forests can only be cut over for large timber every 150 years. Mixed forests are calculated on a 120-year rotation.[1]

Coppice, and coppice with standards, represented nearly 18 per cent of the total area of woodlands in 1924, but only 10 per cent in 1947. Most of this area was to be found in southern England; indeed almost half the woods of this description were in the four counties of the southeast—Kent, Surrey, Sussex and Hampshire—where the coppice with standards was very largely the remnant of the former covering of damp oakwoods on the heavier soils in this part of England. The produce from these woods—mainly chestnut and hazel—was largely hop poles—which are no longer in demand owing

1. These are approximate figures used in the earlier census reports. Actually, various rotations are employed when woodland is regularly managed, and Forestry Commission calculations of yield are now based on a rotation of between 55 and 70 years for all conifers except Scots pine; the reduction results from improved techniques of planting, thinning and general forest management.

to the substitution of semipermanent wiring—and fence poles—now replaced by concrete or metal posts. It is thus not surprising that in 1965 the areas worked as coppice represented only 3 per cent of the total English woodlands, with almost none in Wales and none at all in Scotland. Those coppiced woodlands no longer worked as coppice were reclassified in the 1965 census as high forest or as scrub, according to their condition.

The large area of scrub and felled woodland—446 000 hectares (over a million acres) in 1965, or 25 per cent of the total woodland area—represents

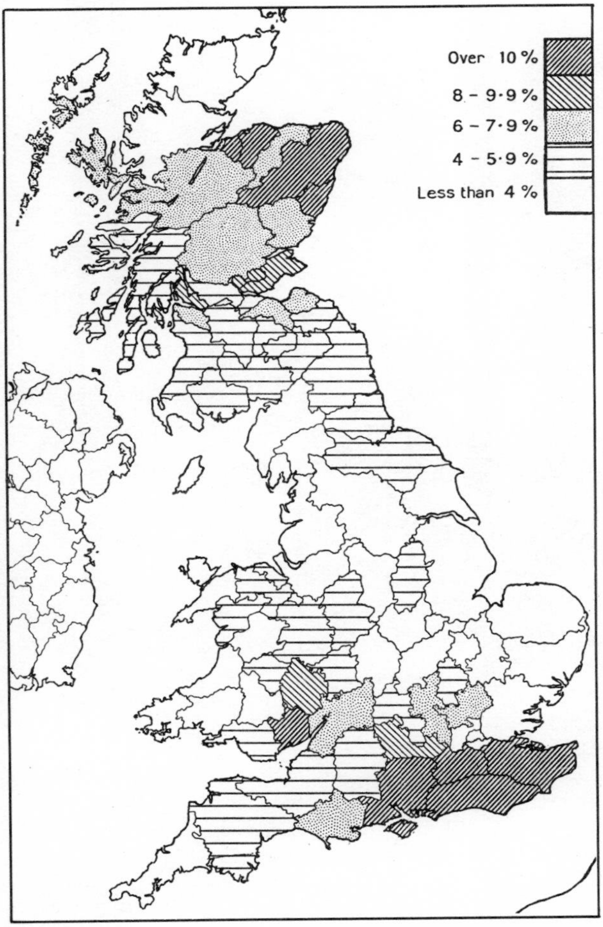

FIG. 78. The wooded areas of Great Britain, according to the census of woodlands of 1947, showing the proportion of the surface of each county occupied by forest and woodland. In 1965 the following counties were also included in the 'over 10%' class: Northumberland, Perth, Glamorgan, Brecon and Montgomery (the last two shown as 'under 4%' in 1947)

PLATE 1. Beechwood at Slindon, Sussex. Very sparse ground flora

a possible reserve of afforestable land. About 15 per cent of it could be called low-grade high forest, capable of yielding some timber, but the remaining 85 per cent, mostly in private ownership, is unutilisable, though much of it could undoubtedly be replanted with high forest crops. There are considerable areas in the Scottish Highlands, particularly in Argyll and Inverness, consisting of sparse stands of birch. In the west of Wales a poor cover of dwarf oak is common and similar tracts in parts of Dartmoor are believed to be true primeval forest remnants. In addition there are overgrown coppices, and woods devastated during the Second World War and not replanted.

Since the Second World War afforestation has become more and more a matter for the State. With the heavy incidence of death duties and the consequent breaking up of large landed estates, there has been little if any incentive for private owners to plant trees which cannot mature in the lifetime of the planter. In 1924, 96 per cent, and in 1947, 82 per cent of the woodland area in Great Britain was in private ownership but by 1965 this had been reduced to 62 per cent—74 per cent in England, 54 per cent in Scotland and 42 per cent in Wales. There is a very important contrast between these private woodlands and those of the Forestry Commission, for of the 1 087 500 hectares (2 687 000 acres) of private woodlands, 298 700 hectares (738 000 acres) or 27 per cent consisted of broadleaved high forest, and this represented 85 per cent of all the broadleaved high forest in Great Britain. On the other hand, only 37 per cent of the coniferous high forest is in private hands, the remaining 63 per cent being owned by the Forestry Commission.

The Forestry Commission's policy of planting mainly coniferous species (in response to the known economic demand) proved unpopular with the general public in the early years. Britain is a land of deciduous trees and has only three native conifers—the Scots pine (*Pinus sylvestris*) which is the only timber tree, the juniper and the yew—and a considerable section of the public, having grown accustomed to the open, windswept moorlands and mountains, disliked the regimented plantations of introduced conifers, arranged in straight-sided blocks and all of one age. The amenity objections are still sometimes raised—but at least the forests do not normally take up agricultural land (apart from moorland sheep-runs) and with the increasing maturity of the forests and a policy of limited public access the Commission's work is now more generally appreciated, particularly in the areas where it has provided employment and homes. In addition to its own forests the Commission now supervises private woodlands 'dedicated' for the purpose.

At the census of 1965, 28 per cent of the high forest was of broadleaved species and 72 per cent coniferous. Within the broadleaved category, oak forests represented 13 per cent of all the high forest area (but 23 per cent of that in England). The chief stands were to be found in southeast England and the Forest of Dean, and the only major areas outside the southern half

PLATE 2. Sprucewoods in Kielder Forest, Northumberland

of England and Wales were in the valleys on the southern fringe of the Lake District. Beech (*Fagus sylvatica*) occupied 5 per cent of the high forest area—mostly on the chalk and limestone of the Chilterns and Cotswolds, and in the New Forest of Hampshire. Other important broadleaved species included ash (*Fraxinus excelsior*), birch (*Betula verrucosa*), sycamore (*Acer pseudoplatanus*) and elm (*Ulmus* spp).

Conifers in 1965 were headed by Scots pine with 20 per cent of the high forest area. Pines—natural and planted—are to be found in the sandy-soiled lowland areas of England such as the New Forest, Thetford Chase, the Bagshot area, Cannock Chase and Sherwood Forest, and in northern Scotland on the lowlands around the Moray Firth. The pine produces excellent pitprops as well as timber for other purposes. In recent years however, largely in response to the increasing demand for wood pulp and chipwood for paper and board manufacture, the spruce, especially Sitka spruce (*Picea sitchensis*) and Norway spruce (*P. abies*) has been very widely planted, especially in the Border forests, in western Scotland and in Wales. In 1965 Sitka spruce represented 20 per cent of all the high forest area (but 28 per cent in Scotland and 37 per cent in Wales), and in 1967 out of 86 million new trees planted by the Forestry Commission, no less than 41 million were Sitka spruce, mostly in Scotland and north Wales. In these high rainfall regions the spruce is capable of producing up to three times as much timber per acre as the pines. Other conifers include the lodgepole pine (*Pinus contorta*) of which 17 million were planted in 1967, the Corsican pine (*P. laricio*), the Japanese and European larches (*Larix kaempferi* and *L. europaea*) and the Douglas fir (*Pseudotsuga menziesii*).

The State Forests of the Forestry Commission are widely distributed (Fig. 79). The largest is Kielder in Northumberland, with nearly 20 000 hectares (48 000 acres) planted; others in the Border country—including Wark and Redesdale—bring the total for this area up to 48 500 hectares (120 000 acres). Thetford Chase, on the former Breckland of Norfolk and Suffolk, has 19 000 hectares (47 000 acres), whilst the former Crown Woodlands of the New Forest and Forest of Dean have 11 700 hectares (29 000 acres) and 8 500 hectares (21 000 acres) respectively. Allerston forest in northeast Yorkshire has 11 300 hectares (28 000 acres) planted, and Hambleton forest, also in Yorkshire, has 5 600 hectares (14 000 acres); whilst Sherwood forest in Nottinghamshire covers nearly 5 600 hectares (14 000 acres). In Wales the largest forests are Coed Morgannwg in Glamorgan with 13 700 hectares (34 000 acres) and three forests in Merioneth and neighbouring counties which together cover 20 000 hectares (48 000 acres). The largest in Scotland are Glen Trool 9 700 hectares (24 000 acres) and the Forest of Ae 5 200 hectares (13 000 acres) in the southwest, Clashindarrock 5 200 hectares (13 000 acres) and Speymouth 4 800 hectares

PLATE 3. Pitprops from thinnings in Monaughty forest, Morayshire

(12 000 acres) in the northeast, Black Isle in Ross-shire 5 600 hectares (14 000 acres) in the north, and Loch Ard 6 500 hectares (16 000 acres) in the central Highlands. Only a few others cover more than 4 000 hectares (10 000 acres), but the total area was 817 300 hectares (2 019 500 acres) at 31 March 1969. At this date the Forestry Commission employed about

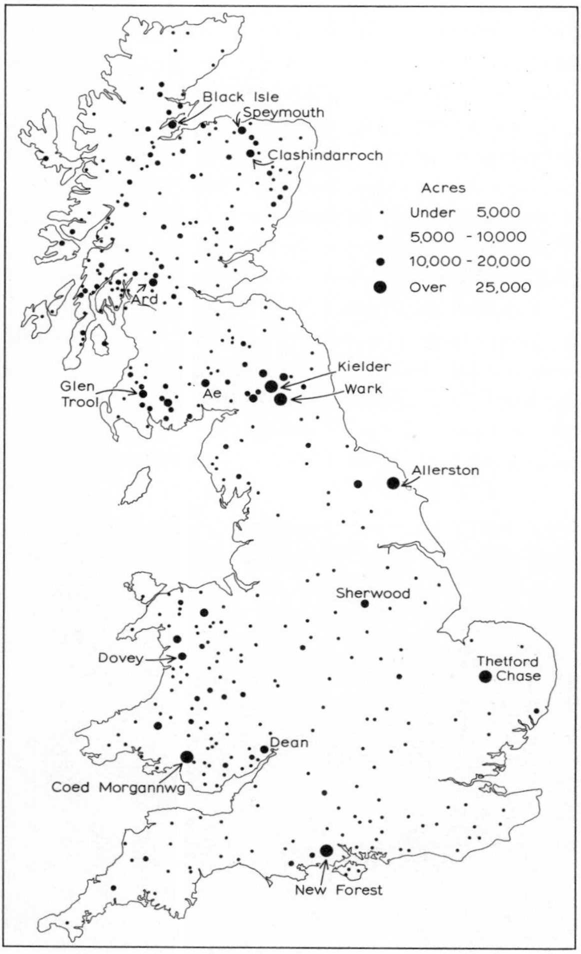

FIG. 79. Forestry Commission plantations

10 000 people out of a United Kingdom total in forestry of about 22 000.

Afforestation can undoubtedly bring about an amelioration of conditions for human life in many parts of the country. A good example is afforded by the western Highlands of Scotland.[1] Over most of this area

1. See J. Claxton, 'Afforestation in the Western Highlands and its effect on repopulation', *Geography*, **17**, 1932, 193–203.

there has long been a steady rural depopulation, commencing with the disruption of the Clan system after the 1745 rebellion and carried on through later years when the crofting population of the valleys was replaced by a small number of shepherds; and then later an equally small, or smaller, number of gamekeepers and stalkers replaced the shepherds. The large acreage of deer forest has already been noted. In 1883 it was less than 0.8 million hectares (2 million acres), but by 1930 it had increased to approximately 1.4 million hectares (3.5 million acres); and it must be admitted that this does not represent the highest utilisation of the land. Many of these rough grazings and deer forests have since 1930 been or are being acquired by the Forestry Commissioners. The permanent forest employees have a cottage and some cultivable land, giving them a definite interest in the countryside quite apart from their work in the forests; and each worker's holding means the establishment not of one person only but of a family of four or five. The work in forest areas does not, of course, end with the planting operations, more especially when one remembers that it is not the intention to plant the units purchased for afforestation all at one time, but rather to spread the work over ten to thirty years. In this case by the time the forest unit has been fully planted it is time to begin thinning —the cutting down of certain trees to provide increased room for selected ones. On this basis it is estimated that every 40 hectares (about 100 acres) of forest will supply permanent employment for one man and his family until the first clear fellings are made when the trees are sixty or eighty years old. Actually, because of the large amount of afforestation work undertaken, the northwest Highlands of Scotland have shown that it requires about one man for every 20 hectares (50 acres). Nor does this represent the full total for there is obviously a demand for schools, for shops, for professional men, for transport workers supplying motor bus services, and so on, and a permanent rural population of some twenty per square kilometre (fifty per square mile) in afforested areas of the Highlands of Scotland is probably not a bad estimate.

Uses of homegrown wood

Three major types of wood are produced. First, softwood small roundwood; this is mainly spruce, Scots pine, lodgepole pine, larch and other conifers, of a diameter between about 7.5 and 20 centimetres (3 and 8 in). In 1965, some 41 per cent of the output went into coal mines, 23 per cent for pulp manufacture and 19 per cent for fibreboard and wood chipboard; but the market is changing rapidly, and by 1980 the mines may well consume under 10 per cent whilst the pulp-mills take over 60 per cent.[1] At present the country supplies only 3 per cent of its pulpwood requirements (cf.

1. B. W. Holtam, 'Homegrown roundwood', *Forest Record*, **52**, H.M.S.O. 1966.

p. 616), but 70 per cent of its pitwood (compared with under 10 per cent before the Second World War).

Secondly, softwood logs for the production of sawn planks, mainly for use in building: at present only 2.5 per cent of the country's requirements is home-produced, for our conifer forests are not yet mature enough and large imports from Canada, the Scandinavian countries and Russia are necessary. Thirdly, hardwood logs, of which the country produces 25 per cent of its requirements (the remainder comprising 25 per cent temperate hardwoods, mainly from European sources and 50 per cent tropical hardwoods). Most of the oak, beech and other broadleaved forests and woodlands old enough to produce merchantable timber are in private ownership, and mainly in the southern half of England and Wales.

Figure 80 shows the location of the principal wood-processing industries that are based wholly or in part upon homegrown wood. Most of these produce chipboard or fibre building boards; a few produce mechanical

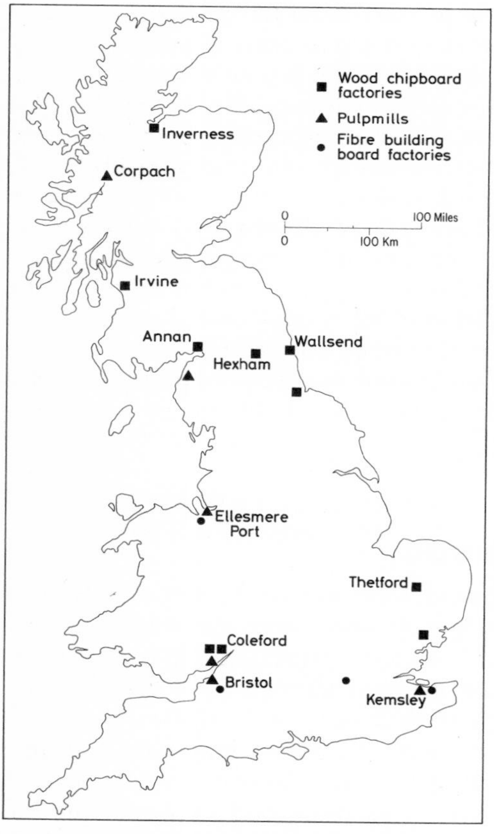

FIG. 80. Wood-processing industries based on home-grown timber

pulp from ground-up wood, for use in paper or cardboard manufacture, but the most interesting and novel is the chemical pulp mill, integrated with a paper mill and a sawmill, at Corpach, near Fort William, established in 1966. The logs for this mill are brought by lorry, by rail or by water from coniferous forests within a radius of some eighty kilometres (fifty miles), and cargoes of wood chips arrive from Canada. Some 700 people are employed in the mill—an obvious advantage to a Highland area that is suffering from a severe lack of employment opportunities; but the economic margin is a delicate one, for the mill must compete with north American and Scandinavian plants that depend on wood that is derived from forests that are natural and not created by the expenditure of heavy capital resources as in Scotland.

Northern Ireland[1]

The position in Northern Ireland is somewhat different from that in Great Britain. In early historical times Ireland was a land of bogs and forests inhabited by small clans who lived by herding, hunting and raiding rather than agriculture. Over the whole the clearing of the woodland came later than in Britain, but was eventually far more complete. That small area around Dublin known as the English Pale where direct English rule was established by the Normans was cleared of forest for military reasons and the clearance was extended to the Central Main so that by Elizabeth's reign it was reported nearly destitute of trees. It was not however till 1608 that the power of the last native chieftain in the northern province was broken and in 1609 began the systematic settlement of Ulster with English and Scottish colonists—the so-called Plantation of Ulster. The settlers cleared the woods to make room for agriculture and the process was continued by the Stuarts and the Cromwellian settlement of 1652; there was also a reckless exploitation for fuel, for the ironworks and for export, so that by 1698 the first of several abortive Acts was passed requiring the planting of trees.

Although the Royal Dublin Society from its foundation in 1831 did much to encourage planting, as did landowners individually, Northern Ireland remained a comparatively treeless country. When the Government of Northern Ireland was established in 1921, it became the forest authority. At that time less than 1.5 per cent of the land area was classed as forest and woodland. By following a policy comparable with that of the Forestry Commission the area has crept up gradually. An average of 400 hectares (a thousand acres) a year were planted from 1928 to 1948 and lately five times that rate. In 1962 the total forest area of Northern Ireland was recorded as about 283 000 hectares (700 000 acres) or roughly 3 per cent of the land area.

1. J. Pimlott, 'The history of afforestation in Northern Ireland', *Advmt Sci.*, **9**, 1952, 297–303.

9
Land use in the British Isles

In England and Wales the Ministry of Agriculture, Fisheries and Food is responsible for collecting and publishing in outline statistics showing the principal uses of the land of the country. In Scotland the same function is performed by the Department of Agriculture for Scotland; in Northern Ireland by the Ministry of Agriculture; and in the Irish Republic by the Department of Agriculture. In England and Wales every year 'the Minister of Agriculture, Fisheries and Food requires a return in writing to be made' by each owner or occupier of agricultural land exceeding 0.4 hectare (1 acre), specifying the acreage of the several crops and of land in fallow or used for grazing, the number of livestock on the land and the number of persons employed thereon on 4 June. Similar returns are made in Scotland, Northern Ireland and in the Irish Republic. The returns so made are strictly confidential, but the acreages given are added together for each parish, and parish figures may be obtained on payment from the Ministry concerned. The published statistics refer to administrative counties. In addition the Forestry Commission collects statistics of forest, woodland and plantations in England, Wales and Scotland, so that the acreages of these are available from time to time.

Combining the statistics available and expressing the figures in percentages of the whole areas the following tables show in comparative form the use which was made of the land of the British Isles in the depression year 1933 and for the year 1950 when the country was still faced with the need of maintaining food production from agricultural land, together with the position in 1960.

The tables demonstrate certain salient points. In the first place there is the extremely small area actually covered by woods, forests and plantations in all parts of the British Isles. Forest and woodland actually occupy a smaller proportion of the surface in the British Isles than in any other important European country. This is notwithstanding the fact that the natural vegetation of the greater part of the British Isles is forest, and two thousand years ago forest must have covered the greater part of the country at least below 300 metres (1000 ft). Further, it is curious because, to the casual observer, the British Isles still appear to be well wooded. This, of course, is very largely due to the numerous small woods, shaws, and hedgerows with isolated trees, as well as the large proportion of parkland which is so characteristic of the country, especially in the southeast. It must be admitted that the position until recently was little short of a scandal when one has a country which is essentially one which could be forest-covered and which has incredibly large tracts of moorland or heathland which might well be productive of good timber.

Land use, 1933 and 1950 (in brackets)

	WOODS AND PLANTATIONS PER CENT		ROUGH GRAZING LAND PER CENT		PERMANENT PASTURE PER CENT		ARABLE PER CENT		OTHER LAND PER CENT	
England	5.1	(5.8)	11.3	(8.0)	42.8	(28.2)	26.5	(40.0)	14.3	(18.0)
Wales	5.0	(6.2)	33.8	(27.4)	41.8	(29.1)	11.9	(21.1)	7.5	(16.2)
Scotland	5.6	(6.6)	66.8	(57.3)	8.3	(6.2)	15.9	(16.8)	3.4	(13.1)
Great Britain	*5.6*	*(6.6)*	*28.2*	*(29.0)*	*31.4*	*(20.8)*	*21.8*	*(30.6)*	*13.0*	*(12.8)*
Northern Ireland	1.3	(1.7)	15.7	(21.2)	45.6	(32.6)	27.9	(36.0)	9.5	(8.5)
United Kingdom	*5.4*	*(6.4)*	*26.5*	*(28.7)*	*33.0*	*(21.4)*	*22.4*	*(30.8)*	*12.7*	*(11.7)*
Irish Republic	1.4	(1.7)	12.0	(10.0)	47.3	(44.7)	21.4	(23.3)	17.9	(20.3)

Land use, 1960

	WOODS AND PLANTATIONS	ROUGH GRAZING LAND	PERMANENT PASTURE	ARABLE	OTHER LAND
England	6.5	10.3	28.1	39.9	15.2
Wales	8.9	32.8	34.2	16.1	8.0
Scotland	8.4	65.7	6.7	16.0	3.2
Great Britain	*7.4*	*31.2*	*21.2*	*30.4*	*9.8*
Northern Ireland	1.8	34.2	25.0	30.0	9.0
United Kingdom	*7.0*	*31.3*	*21.5*	*30.4*	*9.8*
Irish Republic	1.8	—[1]	43.3	22.6	32.3

[1] Included in 'other land'.

The rough grazing land referred to in the second column is for the most part heathland and moorland occupying upland tracts. In England a considerable percentage represents land on the Pennines, the upland areas of the southwestern peninsula and the heaths of southeastern and central England. In Wales the much higher proportion reflects the large extent of moorland in the mountainous areas. It is scarcely surprising to find two-thirds of the surface of Scotland listed as rough grazing land in view of the large extent of the Highlands and of the Southern Uplands (Fig. 81). Lowland Ireland, with its improved pastures, has on the other hand comparatively little rough grazing. By adding together the figures for permanent pasture and arable land one gets the proportion of the country which may be regarded as improved farming land—nearly two-thirds of the whole in the case of England, only a little over half in the case of Wales, only a quarter in Scotland, but approximately three-quarters in both the Irish Republic and Northern Ireland. Perhaps the most interesting column in this table is the last one, headed 'Other land', for which official details are not available. It is curious that until recently we had no statistics as to what exactly is the use made of a seventh of the surface of England.

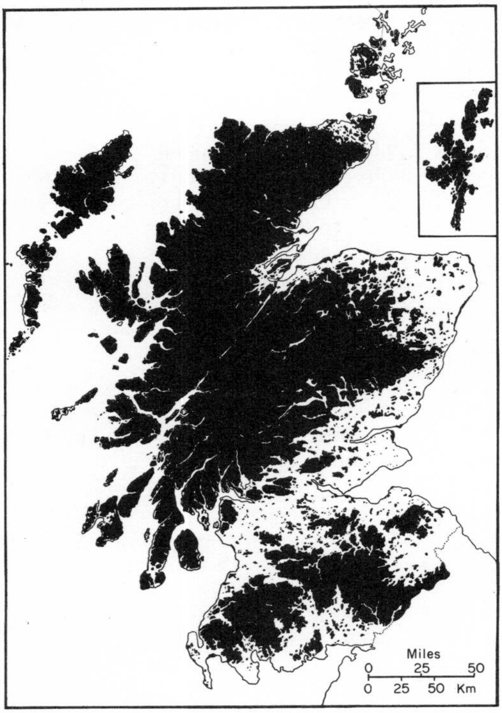

FIG. 81. The moorland (or rough grazing land, including deer 'forests') of Scotland

A comparison of the two tables opposite shows that in 1925 72.3 per cent of the surface of England and Wales and 74.2 per cent of Scotland was agricultural land of which particulars were furnished annually by owners or occupiers, whereas in 1960 the totals had been swollen by the inclusion of open grazing in common ownership. If one takes improved farm land only (crops and grass) the total in Great Britain (England, Wales and Scotland) had dropped from a total of 12 332 250 hectares (30 450 000 acres) in 1925 to 11 665 400 hectares (28 803 500 acres) in 1960. This is a loss of 666 800 hectares (1 646 500 acres) in thirty-five years or 19 000 hectares (47 000 acres) a year, despite some reclamation and is a measure of the spread of industry, housing, mineral working, etc. Actually the loss is greater, as returns of agricultural land are more complete than formerly.

Agricultural statistics of the British Isles, 1925

		ENGLAND AND WALES	SCOTLAND	NORTHERN IRELAND	IRISH REPUBLIC
Area exclusive of inland water and tidal land	acres	37 136 000	19 070 000	3 351 500	17 024 500
	hectares	15 040 000	7 723 300	1 357 300	6 894 900
Arable	acres	10 682 000	3 229 000	573 800	1 552 000
	hectares	4 326 200	1 307 700	232 300	628 600
Permanent grass	acres	15 073 000	1 476 000	1 217 200	10 704 000
	hectares	6 104 600	597 800	493 000	4 335 200
Rough grazing (private)	acres	1 104 000	9 250 000	514 500	not recorded
	hectares	447 100	3 746 200	208 400	not recorded
Not accounted for in the annual agricultural returns	acres	10 277 000	5 115 000	1 046 000	4 768 000
	hectares	4 162 100	2 071 600	423 600	1 931 100
		(27.7% of whole)	(26.8% of whole)	(31.2% of whole)	(28.0% of whole)

Figures exclude the Isle of Man and Channel Isles.

Agricultural statistics of the British Isles, 1960

		ENGLAND AND WALES	SCOTLAND	NORTHERN IRELAND	IRISH REPUBLIC
Area (as above)	acres	37 134 100	19 068 700	3 351 500	17 024 000
	hectares	15 039 300	7 722 800	1 357 300	6 894 700
Arable	acres	13 681 500	3 142 000	1 005 500	3 847 400
	hectares	5 541 000	1 272 500	407 200	1 558 200
Permanent grass	acres	10 792 400	1 187 600	838 000	7 385 600
	hectares	4 370 700	481 000	339 400	2 991 200
Rough grazing	acres	4 999 300	12 524 800	1 146 000	not recorded
	hectares	2 024 700	5 072 500	464 100	not recorded
Not accounted for	acres	7 660 900	2 214 300	362 000	5 791 000
	hectares	3 102 600	896 800	146 600	2 345 300
		(20.7%)	(11.6%)	(10.8%)	(34.1%)

The total land area of the United Kingdom (England, Wales, Scotland and Northern Ireland) is 24 110 865 hectares (59 533 000 acres) or 240 925 square kilometres (93 021 square miles). On this area live 52 673 221 people according to the 1961 census. This means that the share per head of popu-

6

lation of land of *all types* is a little over 0.45 hectares (1⅛ acres) per head. The acreage per capita of improved farm land (crops and grass) at 12.3 million hectares (30.5 million acres) is under 0.24 hectares (0.6 acre). If England and Wales are considered apart from Scotland and Northern Ireland, it is only 0.32 hectare (0.8 acre) of land of all types or 0.21 hectare (0.53 acre) of improved farm land per head. Taking the world as a whole the land area represents about 4.8 hectares (12 acres) of land of all sorts per head of population of which about 0.5 hectare (rather over 1 acre) is productive farm land. The experience in the intensively cultivated countries of northwestern Europe suggests that, with present systems of farming it takes about 0.5 hectare (one acre) to produce the food for one person on an adequate northwest European standard. On this basis, Britain can or should produce 55 per cent of the food consumed or alternately can feed from home resources some 55 per cent of the population. Actually the 'target' of the postwar government in 1950–53 was about 55 per cent of the food consumed, leaving 45 per cent to be imported.

These figures illustrate the extreme pressure on land in Britain and the need for land use planning.

The Land Utilisation Survey of Britain

Official statistics record acreage under certain types of land use, but do not permit the areas to be precisely located. Moreover, as the table on p. 151 shows, more than a quarter of the whole country was left unexplained.

It was in order to map the distribution of different types of land use and to supplement the statistics collected by the Ministry of Agriculture that the Land Utilisation Survey of Britain was formed in 1930, and carried out a survey of the country in the years 1931 to 1939. The aim of the Survey, an organisation whose work was carried out by volunteers all over the country, was to show what use was being made of every single field in the whole of Great Britain.[1] The field work was done on the maps published by the Ordnance Survey on the scale of 6 inches to the mile, since these show the individual fields. The classification adopted by the Survey was drawn up so as to correspond as closely as possible with that used in the official statistics.

1. *Forest and Woodland.* Woodland is marked on the one-inch maps and the six-inch maps published by the Ordnance Survey, and the character of the woodland is broadly indicated by symbols showing whether the trees are coniferous, deciduous or mixed, whilst other symbols indicate woodland of a scrubby nature. A classification of British woodland was drawn up by the Forestry Commissioners for the purpose of the Census of Woodlands taken in 1924, and this classification was adopted by the Land Utilisation Survey.

1. At a slightly later stage a similar survey was carried out in Northern Ireland under the direction of Mr D. A. Hill and the results published.

Description	*Letter marking*	*Colour marking*
1. Forest and woodland	F	Dark green
2. Meadowland and permanent grass	M	Light green
3. Arable or tilled land, fallow, rotation grass, and market gardens	A	Brown
4. Heathland, moorland, commons, and rough hill pasture	H	Yellow
5. Gardens, allotments, etc.	G	Purple
6. Orchards	O	Purple ruling
7. Nurseries	N	Purple hatching
8. Land agriculturally unproductive, e.g. buildings, yards, mines, cemeteries, etc.	W	Red
9. Ponds, lakes, reservoirs, ditches, dykes, streams, and anything containing water	P	Blue

(*a*) *High forest* (Fa) of trees which are being grown primarily for timber or which can be used for that purpose. When fully grown the trees in the high forest are sufficiently close for their crowns to touch. High forest can be divided into forests of conifers (Fa^c) and hardwoods (Fa^d) and of mixed conifers and hardwoods (Fa^m). The hardwoods are, of course, the ordinary deciduous trees, but the deciduous larch is included as one of the conifers.
(*b*) *Coppice* (Fb), or coppice with standards, woodland that is cut over every ten or fifteen years for fencing, posts, etc. The number of large trees or standards left varies, but they are not sufficiently close for the woodland to be called high forest.
(*c*) *Scrub* (Fc) consisting of small bushes or trees unfit for the production of timber.
(*d*) *Derelict forest* (Fd) which has been cut or devastated.
2. *Meadowland or pasture and permanent grassland.* In the annual returns made by farmers or other occupiers of agricultural land a distinction is drawn between permanent grassland for mowing and permanent grassland used as pasture. Owing to changes in practice from year to year the distinction was not made by the Land Utilisation Survey, but the category of course excludes rotation grass—grass grown in rotation with crops.
3. *Arable, or tilled, land.* In any one year land normally ploughed may fall into one of three divisions: that used for clover or rotation grasses, that occupied by crops, and that lying fallow. The three are included together in the maps of the Land Utilisation Survey.
4. *Heathland, moorland and rough hill pasture.* This type of land is usually distinguished on the six-inch maps and in some cases on the one-inch maps. Swampy or reedy pastures and marshland which can be used as rough pasture have been included here by the Land Utilisation Survey. In the agricultural returns farmers make a return of this type of land, over which they have exclusive grazing rights, but only estimates are available of the

areas where grazing rights are communal and of areas of similar character which are not actually used for grazing purposes (see below, p. 156).

5. *Gardens, allotments, etc.* In the scheme drawn up by the Land Utilisation Survey houses with gardens sufficiently large to grow a few vegetables, or even flowers, are included in this category; but where there are only back yards or small areas which must be agriculturally unproductive, land used for housing falls into another category. Broadly the line is drawn where houses are fewer or more than 12 per acre. Allotments are to be regarded as gardens at a distance from the cultivator's house. Large private parks have been split up by the Land Utilisation Survey according to the actual use which is made of the land, much of it naturally being permanent pasture.

6–7. *Orchards* and *nurseries* have been separately shown on most of the published maps.

8. *Land agriculturally unproductive.* This category includes buildings, yards, railways, mines, cemeteries, as well as waste land, i.e. all ground of which the soil is not productively used. On the maps of the Land Utilisation Survey, the difference between land in this category covered with buildings and land which is purely waste is readily apparent—except in the case of recent developments—because of the presence or absence of symbols for buildings.

It will thus be seen that the work of the Land Utilisation Survey was to show for the years 1931–39 the exact use being made of every portion of the surface. The bulk of the work referred to the years 1931–33, only some of the remoter areas being covered at a later date and the whole was complete before the outbreak of war in September 1939. The Survey thus recorded the utilisation of land at a time which may well represent the *nadir* of British agriculture.

The material collected by the Survey was published in several ways. The coloured 1-inch maps (with usually the same sheet lines and the same base maps, including water and contours, as the Popular Series of the Ordnance Survey though sometimes combining two sheets) which were published totalled 168 sheets covering the more populous parts of Britain—the whole of England and the whole of Wales, and the South and Midland Valley of Scotland—as well as sample areas elsewhere. For the remainder of Scotland, the MSS coloured 1-inch maps can be consulted at the Royal Geographical Society in London. Finally, a generalised map on the scale of 1 : 625 000 or roughly 10 miles to 1 inch, in two sheets, covered the whole of Great Britain.

The details shown on the maps were analysed and the factors influencing present land use and its evolution were studied in detail in the series of county memoirs. This Report, under the title of *The Land of Britain*, was issued in 92 parts, one for each county, the whole forming nine quarto volumes (1937–46) to which a separate part covering the Channel Islands was added later. The main results have been summarised in Stamp, *The Land of Britain: its use and misuse*, which should be consulted on matters relative to the use of Britain's land. In common with all the county reports, details are given of historical and economic aspects of land use and special attention is given to factors of permanent importance affecting town and country planning. When the present utilisation is compared with that in the past it is found that on the best and also on the poorest land there is considerable stability of land use (except where housing or industrial development has taken place) but on land of intermediate quality economic factors have completely altered the type of utilisation in the last hundred years.

Summary table of the findings of the Land Utilisation Survey

	ENGLAND		WALES		ISLE OF MAN		SCOTLAND		GREAT BRITAIN	
	ACRES	%	ACRES	%	ACRES	%	ACRES	%	ACRES	%
Arable	8 339 400	26.0	535 900	10.5	65 500	46.5	3 128 600	16.4	12 069 400	21.4
Permanent grass	15 239 400	47.7	2 167 800	42.5	19 900	14.2	1 470 400	7.7	18 897 500	33.5
Orchards	257 100	0.8	3 400	0.1	—	—	800	—	261 300	0.5
Forest and wood	1 827 900	5.7	294 200	5.8	2 800	2.0	1 094 300	5.8	3 219 200	5.7
Rough grazing	3 812 700	11.9	1 906 400	37.4	44 800	31.6	13 011 300	68.2	18 775 200	33.3
Houses with gardens	1 487 500	4.6	73 300	1.4	3 800	2.7	155 300	0.8	1 719 900	3.1
Agriculturally unproductive	1 069 600	3.3	117 700	2.3	4 200	3.0	207 700	1.1	1 399 200	2.5
Total	32 033 600		5 098 700		141 000		19 068 400		56 341 700	

This table refers to conditions as they were before the plough-up campaign of the Second World War. (1000 acres = 404.7 hectares)

It is also clear, when viewed over the past century and a half, that the natural or geographical factors are of increasing importance. Whereas in the past a country village, cut off by poor communications, had of necessity to grow most of its requirements, and did so independently of the suitability or otherwise of local soils and other factors, at the present day conditions of soil and climate determine much more what is economically possible.

It is interesting though by no means easy to break down the large figure for houses with gardens including allotments and for land agriculturally unproductive. In 1936–39 acreage of allotments was officially given as 49 653 hectares (122 600 acres) in England and Wales, 1659 hectares (4100 acres) in Scotland. In 1942 during the Grow More Food campaign of the war the total increased to 72 439 hectares (179 000 acres). A rough estimate gave 185 182 hectares (457 240 acres) occupied by roads (public highways with a total length of 289 024 kilometres (179 630 miles) in 1937–38) and 101 000 hectares (250 000 acres) for railway and railway yards. R. H. Best and J. T. Coppock (*The Changing Use of Land in Britain*, 1962) attempted a more positive approach and found the total 'urban area' of Great Britain, including railways and roads, 1 648 595 hectares (4 070 607 acres) in 1950.

Stamp calculated a round total of 1 861 500 hectares (4 600 000 acres) in 1960–61.

Best calculated that from 1900 to 1950 7 per cent of all agricultural land passed to urban uses.

The classification of land

When the British Government declared its policy of conserving good agricultural land wherever possible for food production, the classification of land assumed a major practical importance which has since been accentuated by the development of town and country planning. Under the Act of 1947 it is compulsory on every county and county borough to prepare development plans. Inherent land quality must not be confused with productivity, which may vary greatly under different forms of management but in a long settled country such as Britain present and past use usually affords a useful pointer to potential use.

A simple tenfold classification into types of land was developed as a result of the work of the Land Utilisation Survey. It is described in detail in *The Land of Britain* and was reached after extensive discussion with the soil scientists. A map on the scale of 1 : 625 000 (Land Classification) was published in two sheets in the National Planning Series.

Classification of types of land

I Good	1 (A)	First Class General Purpose Farm Land, capable of intensive cultivation, especially of vegetables and fruit for direct human use.
	2 (AG)	Good General Purpose Land, suitable for cash crop production.
	3 (G)	First Quality Land, but with a high water table or liable to flooding.
	4 (G)	Good Land, but heavy.
II Medium	5 (AG)	Medium Quality Light Land, including Downland, Basic Grassland with certain areas suitable for arable cultivation (usually light land).
	6 (AG)	Medium Quality, General Purpose Farmland, which is or can be productive whether under crops or grass.
III Poor	7 (G)	Poor Quality Heavy Land.
	8 (H)	Mountain Land, Mountain or Rough Hill Pastures.
	9 (H)	Poor Quality Light Land (Lowland Heaths and Moors).
	10	Saltings, Rough Marsh Pasture, Wastelands, etc.

A, G, H, indicate suitability for arable, grassland, or heathland.

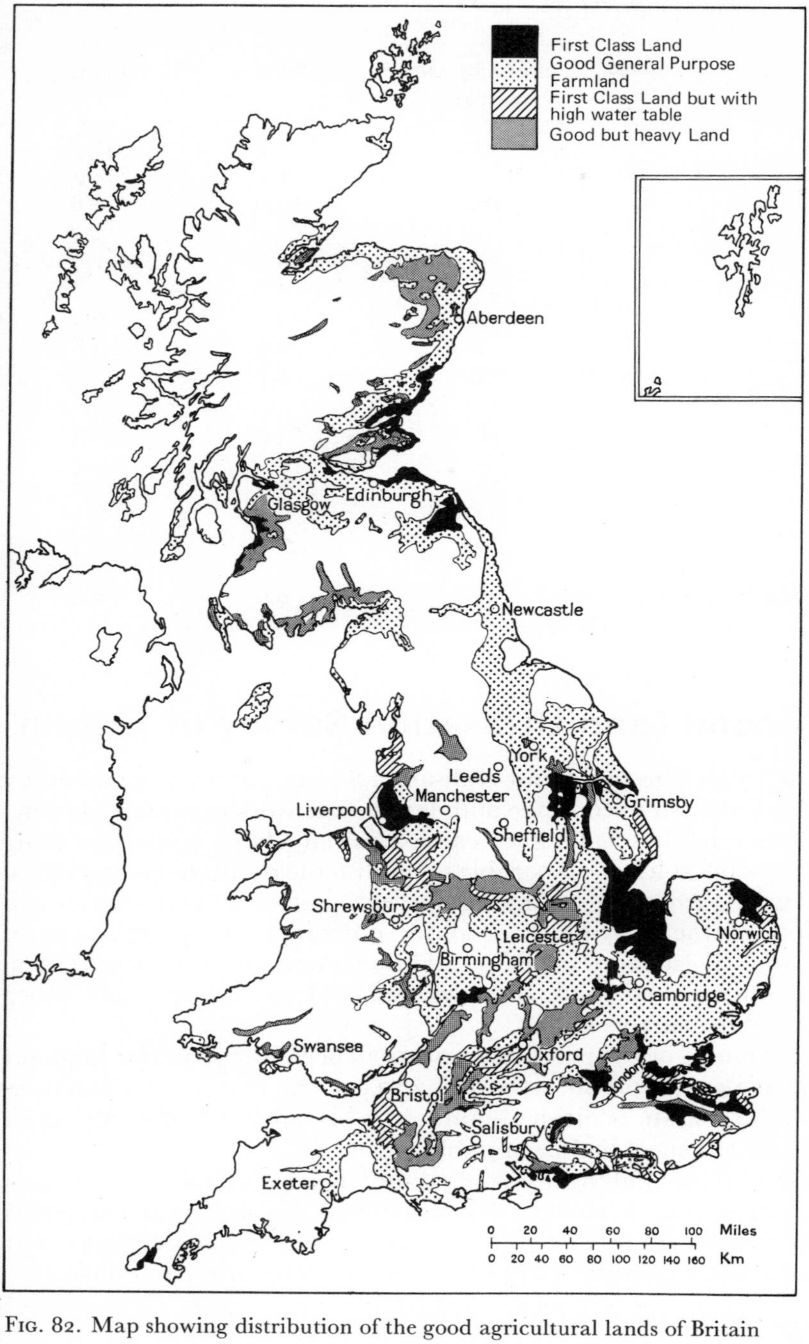

FIG. 82. Map showing distribution of the good agricultural lands of Britain

Proportions of land of different types in Britain

	ENGLAND AND WALES	SCOTLAND	BRITAIN
I *Good*	*47.9*	*20.8*	*38.7*
1	5.3	2.1	4.2
2	26.0	10.1	20.6
3	3.3	—	2.2
4	13.3	8.6	11.7
II *Medium*	*32.0*	*15.1*	*26.3*
5	7.0	0.4	4.8
6	25.0	14.7	21.5
III *Poor*	*17.0*	*63.5*	*32.8*
7	2.2	0.3	1.6
8	12.1	62.9	29.3
9	2.2	0.3	1.5
10	0.5	0.0	0.4
Residue—Built over, etc.	3.1	0.6	2.2

The Second Land Utilisation Survey of Britain

During the 1960s a Second Land Utilisation Survey has been organised by Miss A. M. Coleman to continue and develop the work of Stamp's survey. The field mapping has again been carried out largely by volunteers using six-inch maps but it has been possible to publish the results in greater detail than previously, using the Ordnance Survey's postwar 1 : 25 000 series as a base. Most of the sixty-four categories portrayed are subdivisions of Stamp's original categories, but in addition there are four new classes: transport, unvegetated land, derelict land and recreational and other tended but unproductive land.

By the beginning of 1969 the field survey had been completed for England and half of Wales and 110 sheets covering 13 per cent of their area had been published. A separate Scottish committee is organising field mapping in Scotland and one sheet had been published.

The task of data analysis, using a computer, is being taken up. A preliminary interpretative analysis has organised the sixty-four categories within the framework of a general land use model, which recognises that the land of Britain consists of five basic land use territories, as follows:

Townscape—fully urbanised areas;
Farmscape—areas of viable agriculture, including villages;

Wildscape—areas of indeterminate use (i.e. intermittent uses, multiple uses or uses lacking visible boundaries) where use-mapping has to give place to the mapping of cover types;

Rurban fringe—the zone of confrontation and conflict between townscape and farmscape or less commonly between townscape and wildscape; the rurban fringe is usually relatively inflationary and in need of planning control;

Marginal fringe—areas of marginal farming, which typically occupy the zone between the farmscape and wildscape; the marginal fringe is usually relatively depressed and in need of planning assistance.

10 Agriculture[1]

While in some ways the British Isles form an agricultural unit they cannot easily be treated as such in any geographical analysis, for much of the available information relates only to parts of the United Kingdom, and somewhat different policies have been pursued in the Irish Republic from those adopted in the United Kingdom. The emphasis in this chapter will be mainly on the latter country, and especially on Great Britain; more detailed discussion on Ireland will be deferred to Chapters 29 and 30.

It is important at the outset to appreciate the place which farming has come to occupy in the British economy. In the course of the great industrial expansion of the Industrial Revolution, British exports of manufactured goods and investment in overseas territories increased greatly; in return, imports of foods and raw materials grew in volume. Up to the period of high farming in the 1850s and 1860s, British agriculture had been able to feed the industrial population in the rapidly growing towns, but, with the repeal of the Corn Laws in 1846, barriers to exclude foodstuffs grown in other countries were reduced and finally eliminated. Although the effects of these measures were delayed, the rapid expansion in food imports which followed, especially with the agricultural colonisation of the temperate grasslands of the New World and Australasia, brought profound changes in British agriculture and reduced it to a severely depressed condition by the 1930s, producing only one-third of the food supply of an admittedly much larger population. This policy of cheap food certainly benefited those living in towns, who represented the majority of the population from the middle of the nineteenth century onwards; but owners of rural land, farmers and farm workers undoubtedly suffered. Largely because of the expansion of other sectors of the economy, agriculture's contribution to the gross national product declined in relative importance from about one-fifth in 1850 to about 3 per cent in the 1960s; at the same time there was a steady movement of labour out of agriculture, which now employs less than 4 per cent of the occupied population. The proportion is still considerably higher in Ireland, which was much less affected by industrial development. In the Irish Republic, 35 per cent of the employed population was engaged in

1. This chapter has been completely rewritten by Professor J. T. Coppock, to whom I am deeply indebted (S.H.B.).

agriculture in 1961, and farming accounted for 24 per cent of the gross national product (though it must be remembered that over a third of those born in Ireland are working in the United Kingdom, mainly in non-agricultural occupations); even in Northern Ireland, agricultural employment still accounts for 13 per cent of all employment.

Nevertheless, despite these changes in the relative position of agriculture, it would be quite wrong to consider British farming as unimportant, even in the depression years of the 1930s. The value of produce sold off farms at that time was ten times that produced by the fishing industry, and was greater than the output of the mining industry; and, despite the movement out of farming, agriculture still occupied more people in the United Kingdom than in any of the great agricultural exporting countries of the Commonwealth, such as Australia and Canada. Furthermore, as agriculture's share of employment decreased, its dependence on those employed in non-agricultural occupations, like the manufacture of machinery and fertilisers and the processing of agricultural produce, increased; so that while agriculture in the 1930s employed only 6 per cent of the occupied population, it was estimated that one in ten of the population was dependent on the land directly or indirectly for a livelihood. Agriculture also remains the largest user of land; if rough grazings are included as farmland, the proportions in England, Wales, Scotland and Northern Ireland are respectively 78, 84, 80 and 81 per cent, and that in the Irish Republic 84 per cent, an average of about 80 per cent for the whole of the British Isles.

Although agriculture's share of employment and production has continued to decline since the 1930s, the position of agriculture has greatly improved in recent decades. The government of the United Kingdom has come to accept a large measure of responsibility for the state of British agriculture through a complex system of production grants and guaranteed prices, minimum wage rates, and an increasing degree of control over food imports. Free trade was abandoned in the early 1930s, and in recent years governments have been increasingly concerned, chiefly through voluntary agreements with overseas suppliers, to restrain the value of food imports. At the same time, what has been called the second agricultural revolution has led to greatly increased productivity, despite a reduction of some 3 per cent in the area of agricultural land and of 35 per cent in the number of farm workers, so that British agriculture now supplies half the country's food requirements (or two-thirds of those products which could be grown in temperate latitudes) for a population more than twice as large as in the 1850s and a seventh larger than in the 1930s. The Irish government has similarly intervened in Irish agriculture, although here the situation is rather different, for the population of Ireland is less than two-thirds of that in the mid-nineteenth century and Ireland is a net exporter of foodstuffs; consequently there have also been measures to expand agricultural exports, which accounted for 59 per cent of all exports in 1961, dropping to 55 per cent in 1967.

The development of agriculture in the British Isles before the First World War

The agricultural colonisation of the British Isles is the counterpart of the destruction of the natural vegetation which was discussed in Chapter 7, although, as has been shown, interpretation of the processes whereby the present agricultural landscape came into being is complicated by both physiographic and climatic changes, so that evidence of former limits of cultivation must be viewed with caution. The sequence of events is highly complex and only the broadest outlines can be sketched here; furthermore, changes in highland Britain, where conditions have generally been less suited to the growth of crops on account of the heavier rainfall, lower summer temperatures and often shorter growing season, have been rather different from those in lowland Britain, although recent research has shown that some of the differences between the mainly pastoral west and the arable east are less clearcut than was thought formerly.

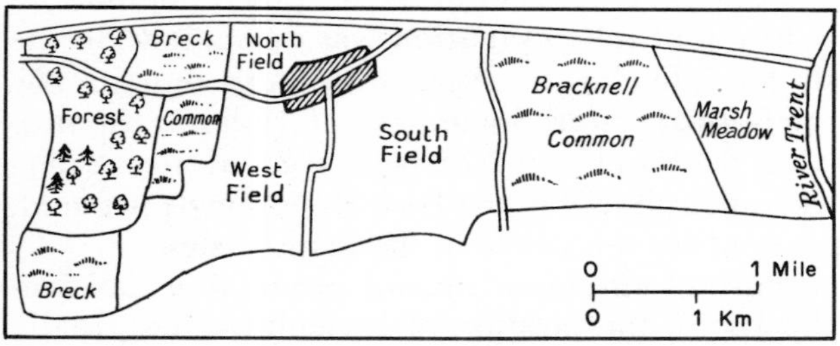

Fig. 83. A Nottinghamshire parish before enclosure, showing the nucleated village, the three fields, the waterside meadows, the common or waste lands and the woodland

In lowland England attention was first directed to the areas of light soil, perhaps because they were more easily cleared and because the heavier soils could not readily be cultivated with the equipment then available; but, especially from the fifth century with the coming of the Anglo-Saxons, the heavier soils were increasingly cleared for cultivation. Throughout much of lowland England the basis of colonisation was the nucleated village and its associated farmlands, which fell broadly into three categories: the common arable fields, the meadows and the waste. The large open arable fields were divided into strips, each of which represented part of the holding of an individual farmer, and were cropped on a common rotation. Where there were three fields a triennial rotation was practised, with one field under a winter corn crop (wheat or rye), one under a spring corn crop (barley, oats, peas or beans) and one under bare fallow; where there were two fields, crops and fallow alternated. Fields were cultivated in common and after harvest were thrown open for the farmers' livestock to graze the weeds and stubble. The meadowland was often sited on low-lying land near a stream and was used for the production of hay; it too was thrown open for common pasturage after the hay harvest. Grazing was also provided in the waste, the land which had not yet been cleared for agriculture, although grazing animals, by preventing the regeneration of trees, must have contributed materially to the clearance of the natural woodland and to its replacement by heath and moor and ultimately by farmland. Those who held land were generally entitled to a share of such grazing and often possessed other common rights, such as the cutting of turf and brushwood for fuel, the cutting of bracken for litter, the quarrying of stones for house-building and the like. Figure 83 shows the layout of the farmlands of a Nottinghamshire village before enclosure and some idea of the appearance of such a village can be obtained by visiting Laxton in Nottinghamshire, where the open fields (though not the scattered strips) still survive.

Such an economy was primarily a subsistence one, wheat and rye being the bread grains, barley the basis of beer, and cattle, pigs and poultry providing meat; sheep were especially important for their wool, while oxen were the main work animals. There was thus a variety of products, a characteristic of much British farming which has persisted to the present day; but yields were very low, with perhaps 6.5 quintals of wheat per hectare (ten bushels per acre), a fivefold increase, rather more for barley and less for oats. Livestock production was also low, for the quality of grazing was poor and there was little fodder for winter; as a result, large numbers of animals were killed in the autumn and salted down to provide a supply of meat. Moreover, since the livestock were herded together and tended by the village cowherd, shepherd or swineherd as the case might be, improvement of livestock was difficult, as was that of crops grown in the common fields.

Land was held under the feudal system by which all land rights devolved in theory from the Crown and were granted by the Crown to tenants-in-chief, who in turn sublet to various classes of lesser tenants in exchange for services. Originally feudal superiors had held strips in the common fields and grazed their livestock in common with those of lesser tenants, but gradually they came to consolidate scattered strips and to enclose them and also to enclose land direct from the waste. Lesser tenants, too, consolidated holdings, perhaps also commuting their obligations to their feudal superiors for money rents which came in time to replace feudal obligations. From quite early on the system which has been briefly described began to break down, in part because fields were enlarged in size and increased in number as new land was cleared for agriculture, but also because of the tendency to enclose land for individual use. This process was facilitated by depopulation during the Black Death in the fourteenth century, while during the Tudor period the high price of wool made it advantageous for landlords to enclose land and lay it down to grass; as M. W. Beresford has shown, whole villages were depopulated and replaced by large fields for grazing. Nevertheless, half the arable land in England and Wales was still in open fields by the middle of the eighteenth century. In the next hundred years all but a handful of these disappeared under a succession of Acts of Parliament, to be replaced for the most part by regularly-shaped fields, bounded by hedges, and compact holdings in individual occupation which were normally held on lease from a large landowner. On the larger holdings, too, new farmhouses and steadings were often built in the farm territory away from the village. Large areas of heath and down were also brought into cultivation at this time and laid out in farms, generally with steadings dispersed among the fields.

The situation which has been described was most characteristic of the country between the estuary of the Tees and that of the Exe, but in many other parts of the lowlands, open fields, if they ever existed, disappeared early and the agricultural landscape has long been enclosed. Both customs of land holding and physical conditions contributed to these contrasts; in the Chilterns, for example, where there is little level land, open fields were small and complex and soon disappeared, so that Leland in the seventeenth century contrasts the 'champion' (open) Vale of Aylesbury and the Chilterns 'full of enclosures'. In Scotland, Ireland and some areas of poor land in England, the arable land was farmed on the infield/outfield system which resembles shifting cultivation or bush fallow in that some land, the outfield, was cropped intermittently and allowed to revert to rough vegetation until its fertility was restored, while other land, the infield, was continuously cultivated and manured. Such land was unenclosed and farmed in scattered strips. In Scotland much of it remained in this condition until the end of the eighteenth century, when, in a period of less than fifty years, it was rapidly transformed into a landscape of enclosed fields and individual holdings. Most infield/outfield farming in Ireland had also disappeared by the nineteenth century. Throughout these areas of highland Britain, there is increasing evidence to show that the present pattern of dispersed farms was preceded by one of small nucleations, surrounded by small arable fields divided into strips, on which subsistence crops would be grown.

The extensive rough grazings of the uplands of highland Britain were also grazed in common and were generally managed on a system of transhumance, whereby temporary summer dwellings were occupied while mixed flocks of sheep and cattle grazed the pastures, to be abandoned in winter for a permanent settlement at lower altitudes. From the sixteenth century onwards large scale sheep farming, begun by the Cistercian monasteries in the Pennines, gradually extended to these upland areas, reaching north Scotland in the early nineteenth century. As a result, the summer grazing by mixed flocks was replaced by a monoculture of sheep and by the nineteenth century nearly all the uplands were being grazed throughout the year by sheep. The common grazings have disappeared in a variety of ways and in England and Wales large areas were enclosed by Act of Parliament between 1750 and 1900, although approximately 0.6 million hectares (one and a half million acres) of common land still survive. In

Scotland and Ireland common grazings mainly disappeared without legislation, although they survive in the crofting areas of Scotland and in parts of the Irish uplands.

Towards the end of the sixteenth century there was increasing trade with other parts of Europe, especially Flanders, and largely as a result, new crops and livestock and new methods of farming came to be introduced into lowland England. Turnips, clover and fodder grasses were the most important of these; because of the capacity of the bacteria in the root nodules of clover to fix atmospheric nitrogen, clover improves the fertility of the soil, while clover, grasses and turnips provided a supply of winter feed for livestock. There evolved the Norfolk four-course rotation (and variants of it) especially on light land; under this rotation, wheat is succeeded by a root crop, mainly turnips, then by barley and finally by a leguminous crop. As a result yields increased greatly, and by the middle of the eighteenth century, that of wheat had doubled to some 13 quintals per hectare (20 bushels per acre). Enclosure and associated improvements in crop husbandry enabled both tenants and owners to carry out controlled experiments in animal breeding; from these emerged the breeds of sheep, like the Leicester and the South Down, and of cattle, like the Hereford and Shorthorn, which are now important in the major wool- and meat-producing regions of the world. Much of this work was done by tenant farmers, but it was often the enthusiasm and enterprise of the great landlords that created the necessary conditions. These improvements were slow to be adopted in Scotland, where farming remained backward until the late eighteenth century; they then spread rapidly, and Scottish farming, especially in the eastern Lowlands, came to be known for its high standards of husbandry.

The early Victorian period was one of great scientific progress in British farming. The requirements of the different crops came to be scientifically studied and the use of artificial fertilisers began to spread. The first consignments of nitrate of soda arrived in 1830 and of Peruvian guano about 1840, while in 1843 Lawes, who founded Rothamsted Experimental Station in Hertfordshire, began the manufacture of superphosphate at Deptford and quickly proved the value of ammonia salts (which could be made easily from byproducts of the already important gas industry) as fertilisers for crops. Land drainage received scientific study; tile drains, available from the 1830s, were extensively used for underdraining, and this led to considerable improvement in the productivity of heavy land. Imported feeding stuffs for livestock, such as linseed and cottoncake, also came to be widely used, improving livestock nutrition and, in effect, importing the fertility of other lands. As a result crop yields increased and that of wheat had risen to 20 quintals per hectare (30 bushels per acre) by 1870. The demands of the expanding industrial towns were also a stimulus to improvement and the rapid development of the railway network between 1840 and 1870 brought many areas within easy access of urban markets. These years are sometimes spoken of as the period of high farming, when the area of improved land probably reached its greatest extent ever and land was farmed intensively for high profits.

This remarkable period of agricultural prosperity and development came to an end about 1874. High prices had been occasioned by the Franco-Prussian War of 1870–71, but this was followed by a trade depression and a series of bad seasons. A new factor came into operation, the growth of railway networks overseas and the development of steamship traffic, which greatly facilitated international trade in agricultural produce. Rapid settlement of the new lands in Canada, the United States, Argentina and Australia soon followed, and supplies of foodstuffs from these regions began to appear in quantity. As a result, the prices received for domestic produce fell sharply and continued to do so until the end of the century. Wheat was the first to suffer, but meat prices followed as refrigeration enabled distant countries like New Zealand, Australia and Argentina to compete in British markets. However, the decline in meat prices not only began later, it was also less severe. Increasing imports of dairy produce, especially cheese, also had an adverse effect on the prices received by British farmers.

Unlike their counterparts in other European countries, many of whose governments erected tariff barriers to keep out the flood of cheap food, British farmers were left to fend as best they could. Those most severely affected were farmers who depended on wheat, which was the chief cash crop in most of the principal areas of arable farming. Even these parts of the British Isles were not as well suited to wheat growing as the temperate grasslands, nor could British farmers grow the hard wheats which were desirable for breadmaking; consequently, they were unable to compete with the produce of these more favoured lands. Low prices led farmers to economise by laying land down to grass and by neglecting necessary cultivations; rents were reduced because farmers could not pay them and landowners were consequently deprived of the resources to make necessary changes in order to accommodate new systems of farming, and large areas could not be let and were extensively farmed by landowners. It was particularly in areas of heavy or poor land in central and eastern England that the greatest changes took place.

As far as possible, farmers tried to adopt systems of farming which were economical and were less severely affected by competition from imported produce. Livestock farming increased in importance because it was less expensive of labour and because meat prices had fallen less than those of cereals, and the rapidly growing towns and the general rise in living standards provided new demands for milk and vegetables. Milk consumed fresh enjoyed a natural protection against competition, although that manufactured into cheese and butter competed with imported produce. Up to the middle of the nineteenth century, milk had been produced either in town dairies, with stalled cattle fed on purchased feed, or on the immediate outskirts of towns; but improved transport and developments in the technology of milk treatment extended the distance over which milk could be carried, and dairying was adopted by farmers whose systems of farming had become unprofitable, while those in traditional dairying areas, who had formerly concentrated on the production of butter and cheese, turned increasingly to milk production. So great was the increase in dairying along the Great Western Railway line to Wiltshire that it was said to be known as the 'Milky Way'. Market gardening also developed, both around the towns and, with the aid of railways, in more distant localities, like west Cornwall, the Fenland and mid-Bedfordshire; in the latter area, there was a two-way traffic of vegetables to London and manure from London work-horses which helped to improve these light soils. Increasingly, too, arable farmers grew vegetables to provide an additional cash crop, so that the once clearcut distinction between farming and market gardening began to break down.

These changes affected primarily eastern and midland England; elsewhere the emphasis was already mainly on pastoral farming, although even in these areas there was a tendency for marginal land to revert to rough grazing and for the general level of farming to deteriorate. Rural depopulation became widespread and was especially severe in Ireland, where the acreage under crops was more than halved.

The interwar years

In the early years of this century the position of British agriculture improved somewhat, for many of the necessary adjustments had been made and the downward trend of prices had slackened and was reversed during the blockade of the First World War, when the government adopted measures to increase the home supply of food. Mechanisation, though still on a small scale, was encouraged and administrative machinery established to stimulate production and to increase the acreage under crops, both by guaranteeing minimum prices for the main products and by means of county agricultural committees, whose tasks included indicating what land should be ploughed. As a result, the area under tillage in the United Kingdom rose by 1.25 million hectares (3.1 million acres). This achievement was shortlived and the downward trends were resumed after the war. Although some attempts were made in the 1925 British Sugar (Subsidy) Act, which provided a subsidy for homegrown sugar, to improve the position of arable farmers by providing them with an alternative cash crop, this was an isolated incident and government still stood aloof from farming, apart from the promotion of research and the enforcement of health regulations.

This situation was greatly changed by the worldwide depression of the early 1930s. The policy of laissez-faire was abandoned and a variety of measures adopted to protect the British farmer and to improve his bargaining position. Agricultural products, with the exception of those from Empire sources, had to face import duties and, in the case of horticultural crops, these varied seasonally depending on the marketing of the home crop; attempts were even made to regulate the volume of imports. Guaranteed minimum prices were also introduced for wheat and fat cattle and, from the late 1930s, the first of a number of production grants was introduced, to subsidise the liming of land; with war imminent in 1939, a grant was also made available for the ploughing of grasslands. Although the wheat subsidy did result in a sharp, but shortlived, increase in the wheat acreage, it cannot be said that any of these measures had a marked effect on trends in British agriculture. The area under tillage continued to decline, although this was in part due to the loss of land to non-agricultural uses, which was running at the rate of 20–25 000 hectares a year in England and Wales alone in the 1930s. Perhaps the most significant change was that introduced by the Marketing Acts which allowed agricultural producers to form statutory marketing boards in order to promote the orderly selling of produce. Boards were established for hops, milk, pigs and potatoes, but their fates and their powers were very varied. The most important were the Milk Marketing Boards, especially that established for England and Wales. By acting as a sole buyer and seller of milk, the Board was able to prevent the price of milk manufactured into butter, cheese and other products from undercutting the price of milk sold liquid. Furthermore, by a system of interregional levies, the more remote producers were subsidised by those nearer the markets, so that some of the advantages of proximity were reduced. This fact, together with the certainty of a market for milk at a known price and the attraction, particularly for the small farmer, of a regular monthly income, encouraged an increasing number of people to take up dairying; between 1933, when the Board was established, and 1938 the volume of milk sold by the marketing boards increased by 30 per cent.

From the 1870s until the 1930s certain broad trends can be discerned. Over most of the country it had become uneconomic to grow crops when there were regularly available supplies from overseas countries where physical conditions and farm structure were often more favourable. As a result, the area under pasture steadily increased, except where most of the land was already down to permanent grass or where conditions were most suitable for crop growth and were least favourable to livestock farming, as in eastern parts of lowland Britain. At the same time, numbers of cattle increased steadily throughout the country, while those of sheep remained fairly stable, and sheep became increasingly concentrated in upland and grassland areas because of the high labour costs of keeping them under arable systems.

The Second World War and after

Although the measures adopted by the government in the 1930s represented an important change in attitude, the Second World War is the watershed between the agriculture of the depression years and that of today. When war began, plans which had been prepared for the expansion of home food supply were rapidly implemented, largely through the agency of County War Agricultural Executive Committees which provided assistance and advice to farmers, for example through the loan of machinery, had powers to prescribe cropping and to take over and work land where this was being neglected. Considerable attention was paid to the upgrading of agricultural land through clearing, ditching and draining, and between 1940 and 1950 grants were paid to improve 2.8 million hectares (seven million acres) in England and Wales. Fields which had been infested with scrub were cleared and considerable tracts of moorland and heathland reclaimed.

The key element in wartime policy was an increase in the acreage of ploughed land, for this was more productive than permanent grassland and more flexible in its use, in that many crops could be used either for direct human consumption or for feeding to livestock. With considerations of nutrition and import-saving in mind, emphasis was placed upon greater production of grain, potatoes, sugar beet and milk. Meat production, which is expensive of land, was reduced and the numbers of sheep, pigs and poultry declined. The use of machinery was greatly accelerated; for example, there were less than 50 000 tractors in Great Britain in 1939, most of them in eastern England, but by 1946 there were over 200 000 and these were much more widely distributed throughout the country. Consumption of fertilisers, too, rose dramatically and, by recruiting members of the Women's Land Army and employing prisoners of war, the total labour force was actually increased. As a result of all these measures, the supply of homegrown wheat increased by approximately a third, the acreage under potatoes doubled and production of fodder crops rose by a third; on the other hand, supplies of meat fell by a third and those of eggs by a half. Net farm output as a whole increased by 20 per cent between 1939 and 1944, but the gross increase was rather smaller (5 per cent), partly because much of the output was required to replace imported feedingstuffs and store stock.

The effects of war time measures were widely felt. As Figs 84 and 85 show, the greatest proportional increase in the extent of arable land was in the midland and western counties of Great Britain, where the arable acreage was formerly small; in most Welsh counties, for example, there was more ploughed land in 1944 even than in the 1870s, although the total acreage in the United Kingdom was 2 per cent lower than that in 1871. In eastern counties of Great Britain, where most of the farmland had remained under the plough, the scope for increase was more limited, but even here there was a large expansion in the acreage of ploughed land, especially on heavy land like the clays of Essex and west Cambridgeshire, where poor arable land had tumbled down to grass in the period of agricultural depression.

The campaign to increase agricultural production in wartime also saw a considerable extension of state aid to agriculture. Prices for agricultural produce were fixed at levels which would encourage production, grants were made towards the cost of improvement and recognition was given to the needs of particular types of farming for special help in the provision of subsidies on hill sheep. In the postwar period these measures were extended and consolidated into a comprehensive policy of state support for agri-

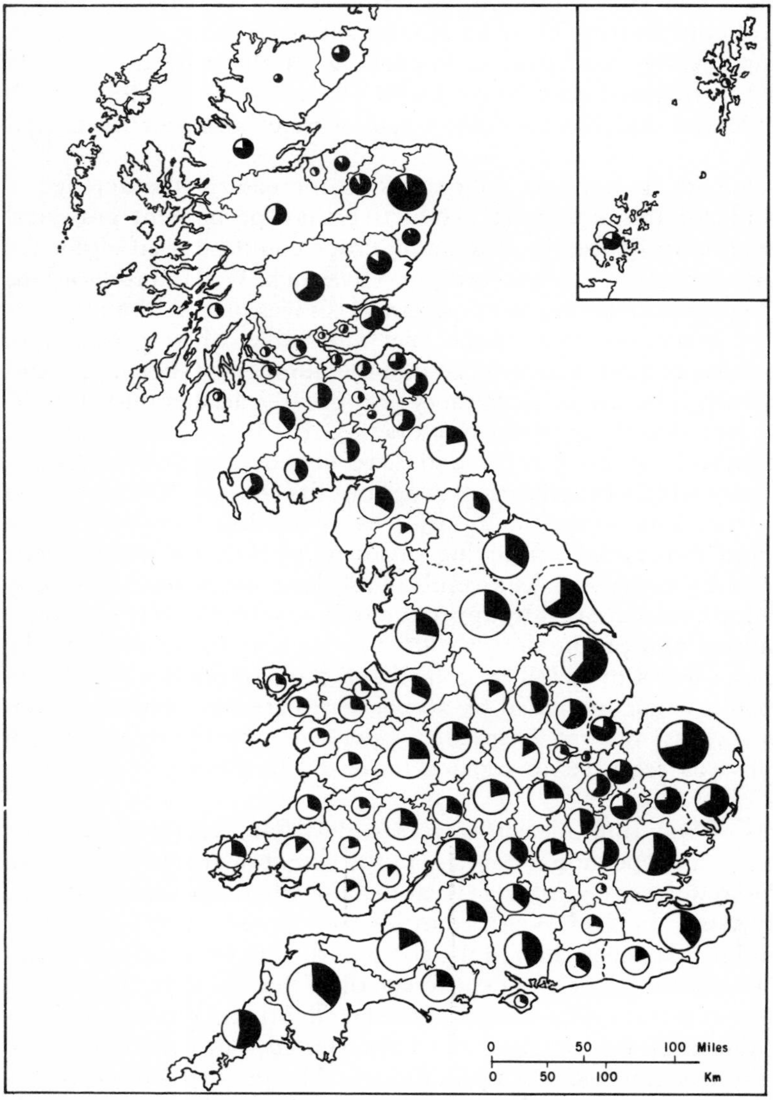

FIG. 84. The use of farm land in Great Britain, 1937

This map shows that arable land was mainly important in the drier counties of eastern England and in Scotland. Each circle shows area of arable land in black, permanent grass white.

culture. It was accepted in the 1947 Agriculture Act that the government of the United Kingdom had a duty, not only to promote a stable and efficient agriculture which would provide an appropriate part of the nation's food supply at competitive prices, but also to ensure that the levels of living of those engaged in agriculture were comparable to those enjoyed by the rest of the community and that landowners received an adequate return

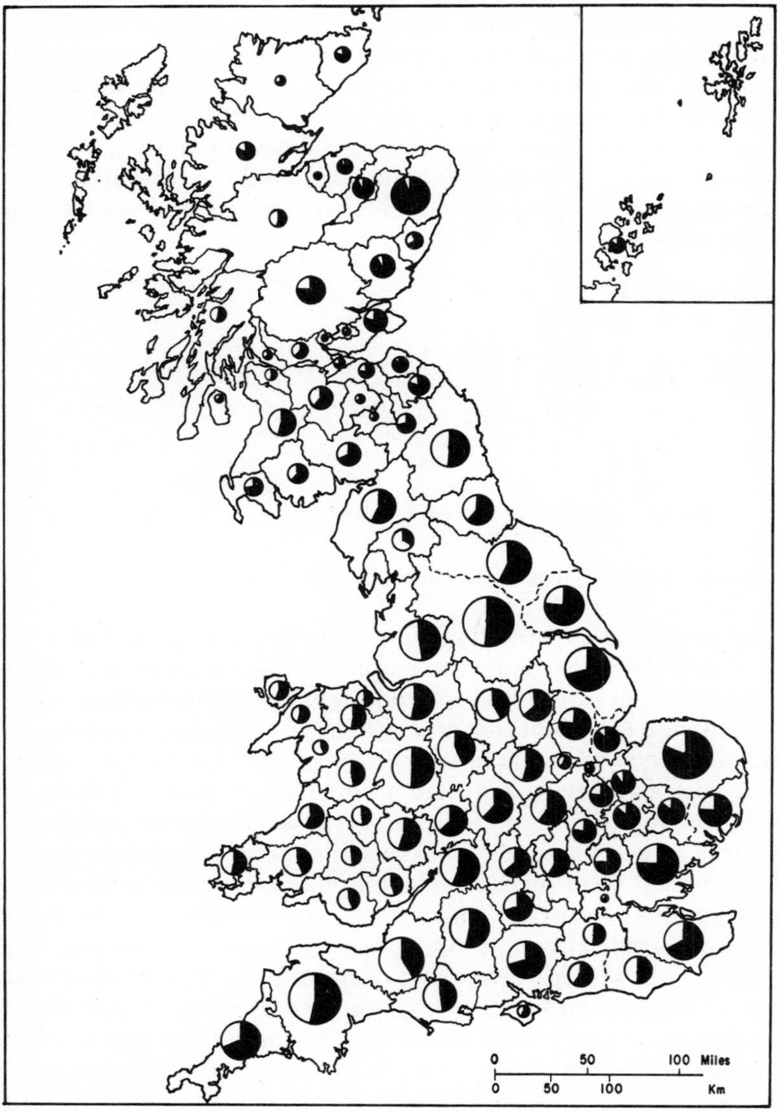

FIG. 85. The use of farm land in Great Britain, 1944
This map shows the effect of the wartime ploughing campaign.

on the capital they invested in the industry. The main method of achieving these aims was by means of an annual review of prices, at which the ministers responsible for agriculture considered changes in agricultural costs and supplies and determined a level of guaranteed prices for the main agricultural products in the succeeding year. For the most part these guarantees were implemented by deficiency payments, i.e. the difference between the actual price achieved on the free market and the guaranteed price, although the production of oats and barley was supported by acreage payments. In addition there was a variety of production grants to encourage desirable practices, like the grassland ploughing, lime and fertiliser subsidies; grants were also payable towards the cost of land improvement and drainage, to promote the production of particular commodities, like the calf subsidy, and to assist the farmers in areas which did not benefit directly from guaranteed prices, like those producing store cattle and store sheep on the upland margins.

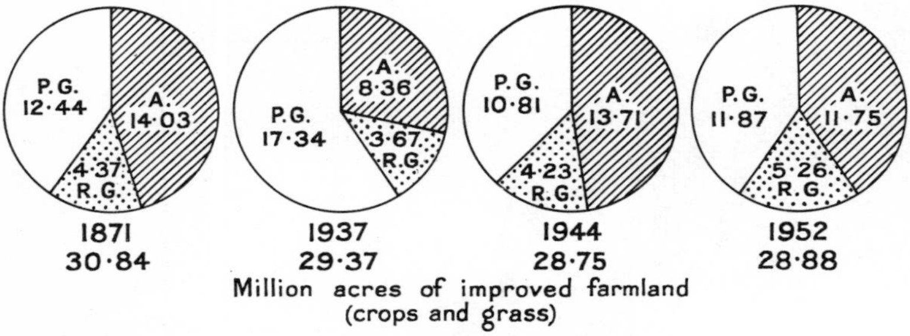

FIG. 86. The changing use of farmland in Great Britain, 1871–1952

The postwar period can be broadly divided into two in respect of government policy. Until the mid-1950s, the emphasis was on increasing agricultural production and in the later period on efficient production. After the war, a worldwide food shortage and problems of foreign exchange to pay for imports led governments to encourage production by favourable prices with the aim of achieving a level of production 50–60 per cent above that of prewar. During the 1950s, however, surpluses of certain commodities began to appear and the total cost of subsidies grew till it was approximately as large as net farm income. The emphasis therefore switched to production at competitive prices and guarantees for some commodities have even been reduced, although, under the 1957 Agricultural Act, the Government sought to provide a measure of stability by undertaking that both the total subsidy bill and the level of guaranteed prices for individual commodities should vary only within quite narrow limits from year to year. Attempts have been made to shift an increasing proportion of the subsidy bill to production grants, and the Government have also sought to limit their commitment to pay subsidies on some commodities by nominating standard quantities to which the guaranteed prices apply and to limit the volume of imports of competing products by voluntary agreement with the overseas producers. Increasing involvement by Government in the determination of agricultural production in the United Kingdom is thus one of the most distinctive features of the postwar period. The increased emphasis on efficient production has led farmers to simplify farming systems, and has contributed to the pressures to enlarge farms in order to achieve a satisfactory standard of living and to make the most efficient use of resources, especially machinery and labour. Governments have directly assisted this process through the Small Farmers' Scheme, introduced in 1958, which has provided grants towards the cost of reorganising those small holdings which are thought capable of providing an adequate income and through recent legislation which has encouraged the amalgamation of farms which are not viable and provided compensation for elderly farmers who are willing to retire.

The other major feature of British farming in the postwar period has been the rapid rate of technological change, summed up in the phrase 'second agricultural revolution'. The trend towards greatly increased mechanisation begun during the Second World War has continued and, although the number of tractors has changed little since the late 1950s, there has been a sharp increase in other kinds of mechanical equipment; the stability in numbers of tractors also conceals a steady replacement by larger and more powerful machines. Tractors are now widely found

PLATE 4. Combine harvesting of barley on Salisbury Plain, Wiltshire

throughout the United Kingdom and serve not only to draw tillage implements, but also as a means of farm transport and even of personal transport in hill areas. As a result, the horse as a work animal has virtually disappeared from British farms and has ceased to be enumerated in the agricultural censuses in Great Britain; an interesting byproduct of this change has been the release of land, estimated at between 1.2 and 1.6 million hectares (three to four million acres), which was formerly needed to support these work animals. The use of lime and fertilisers, encouraged by government subsidies, has become much more widespread and applications of lime have increased sixfold since 1939 and those of nitrogenous fertilisers almost eightfold. Plant breeders have produced new varieties with high yields, greater resistance to disease and often adapted to particular environments; the great expansion in barley growing since the Second World War owes much to the development of new varieties. The use of pesticides and herbicides to combat plant pests and diseases has also increased greatly and once common weeds of cereal fields like the cornflower and the poppy are now almost extinct. Similar developments have occurred in animal husbandry from better understanding of management and nutrition, from the use of chemicals both to promote growth and to control disease, and through the development of artificial insemination, which enables the influence of high quality stock to be felt much more widely; less than half the cattle born in the United Kingdom are now the product of natural mating. As a result of these changes agricultural production has continued to rise steadily and in the United Kingdom is now almost double the level of prewar years, despite a continued reduction in the area of agricultural land through losses to housing and industry, mineral working, forestry and other uses, which are running at a rate of some 40 500 hectares (100 000 acres) a year, and a continued fall in the labour force which declined by 38 per cent between 1939 and 1967.

Changes are also taking place in marketing. A rise in the proportion of food which is processed and the growing share of food purchases made by chain stores, supermarkets and other large buyers has increased the importance of grading and packing; the encouragement to improve marketing and grading given by governments in exporting countries also provides an incentive to British farmers to improve the presentation of their products and to organise themselves in order to strengthen their bargaining position. Government support has been provided to help the reorganisation of horticultural marketing, and a Home Grown Cereal Authority and a Livestock and Meat Commission have been established to promote better and more orderly marketing of these products.

British agriculture today is in process of rapid change. Economic pressures and the needs of mechanisation are encouraging a move to larger farms and fields, especially in eastern arable districts. Farming systems are tending to become simpler, both from economic necessity and because the chemicalisation of agriculture appears to have removed the need for rotations in the interests of crop hygiene, at least in the short run. With these trends are associated greater areal specialisation as agricultural enterprises show an increasing tendency to be localised in particular parts of the country. These trends can be expected to continue.

The distribution of crops and livestock

The main features of agricultural land use have already been discussed in Chapter 9, but these now need to be placed in an agricultural context. When the first Land Utilisation Survey was undertaken in the 1930s there was a fairly clearcut division of agricultural land, in eastern England at least, into arable land and permanent grassland. In Scotland the distinction was more difficult to make because most rotations included a grass

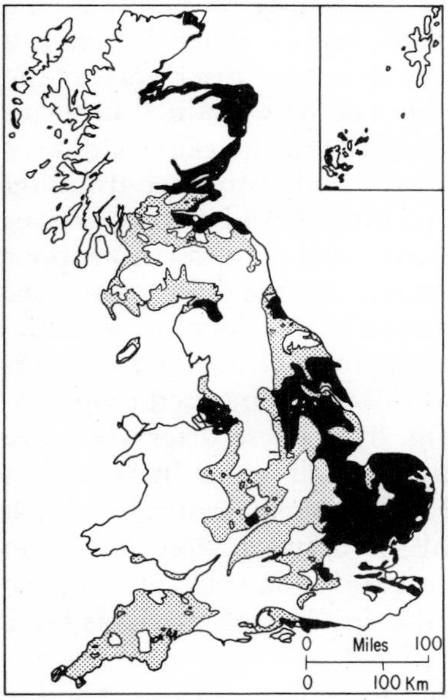

FIG. 87. The chief arable areas of Great Britain

Main areas in black; mixed arable and grassland dotted. In England it is easy to see that the chief factor concerned is climate. In southern Scotland the same factor operates, but in the Highlands of Scotland it may be said that if the land is worth 'improving' from the main mass of moorland it is ploughed rather than put down to permanent grass.

crop which was left down for several years; in northeast Scotland, for example, a common rotation included three years of cereals and roots and three years of grass. In many western parts of Great Britain also much of the improved land was periodically ploughed and returned to grass after one or more other crops had been taken. Since the Second World War, the acreage of temporary grass has greatly increased and such ley farming or alternate husbandry has become much more widely practised in England and Wales, assisted by the ploughing grants which were available between 1939 and 1967. Many of the grassy shires of midland England now show a wide scatter of ploughed fields which will soon be put down to grass and other grass fields ploughed in their place. As a result, it is now more useful to distinguish between the land under tillage crops, i.e. crops other than grass, and grassland, rather than between arable and permanent grassland, and this practice has been adopted in the Second Land Use Survey. (see above, p. 158).

Land under tillage crops is mainly concentrated in eastern parts of Great Britain, and this tendency has become even more marked in the 1960s than it was in the 1930s. The highest proportions, exceeding 80 per cent, are found in the Fenland, where there is little grass, and in general there is a gradient of a decreasing proportion of tillage from the drier east to the wetter west. Most of the exceptions to this rule can be explained in terms of soil and climate. Thus, the Welsh borderland lies in the rain shadow of the uplands, while southwest Lancashire has a low rainfall and free-draining soil; conversely, most of the areas in eastern counties with low proportions of agricultural land in tillage crops have heavy soils or suffer from poor drainage. The principal controls are thus climatic, for the drier conditions which tend to prevail in the east are better suited to the ripening and harvesting of crops; but, by a fortunate coincidence, most of the land which is well-suited by virtue of its altitude, relief and soil to mechanised crop production is also found in eastern counties (Fig. 87). These drier areas are also less suitable for grass, especially on the lighter soils where little growth is possible in dry seasons. The best grassland areas are generally those with the fairly heavy soils and moderate rainfall of between 900 and 1300 millimetres (35 and 50 in), as in Cheshire and Somerset. In wetter areas, high soil acidity is likely to affect the quality of the grassland adversely.

The distribution of grassland and tilled land in Ireland is rather similar in that most of tilled land is found in the east of the country; but, because of the higher rainfall, Ireland as a whole is less suitable for crop production and only in a small part of the southeast is more than 30 per cent of the agricultural land in tillage crops.

Cropping in the British Isles is dominated by cereals which together account for 76 per cent of the area under tillage crops; the remainder is made up of cash crops such as potatoes, sugar beet and vegetables, and by a variety of fodder crops, including turnips, kale and rape, which are consumed mainly on the farm of origin. The following table shows the acreage, yield and production of the main crops in the United Kingdom in 1938 and 1966.

Area, yield and total product of the principal crops in the United Kingdom, 1938 and 1966

CROP	AREA		YIELD		TOTAL PRODUCE 1938	
	(*thousand*)				(*thousand*)	
Wheat	acres	1 928	cwt per acre	20.4	long tons	1 965
	hectares	780	kg per ha	2 561	metric tons	1 996
Barley	acres	988	cwt per acre	18.3	long tons	904
	hectares	400	kg per ha	2 497	metric tons	918
Oats	acres	2 395	cwt per acre	16.6	long tons	1 992
	hectares	969	kg per ha	2 084	metric tons	2 024
Potatoes	acres	733	long tons per acre	7.0	long tons	5 115
	hectares	297	metric tons per ha	17.5	metric tons	5 197
Turnips and swedes	acres	753	long tons per acre	14.3	long tons	10 710
	hectares	305	metric tons per ha	35.7	metric tons	10 881
Mangolds	acres	219	long tons per acre	17.0	long tons	3 705
	hectares	88	metric tons per ha	42.5	metric tons	3 764
Hay	acres	6 406	cwt per acre	21.0	long tons	6 127
	hectares	2 592	kg per ha	2 636	metric tons	6 225

CROP	AREA		YIELD		TOTAL PRODUCE		
	(*thousand*)				(*thousand*)	1966	1968 (estimate)
Wheat	acres	2 238	cwt per acre	31.2	long tons	3 496	3 515
	hectares	905	kg per ha	3 917	metric tons	3 552	3 571
Barley	acres	6 130	cwt per acre	28.7	long tons	8 809	8 274
	hectares	2 481	kg per ha	3 603	metric tons	8 950	8 407
Oats	acres	907	cwt per acre	24.4	long tons	1 102	1 212
	hectares	367	kg per ha	3 063	metric tons	1 120	1 231
Potatoes	acres	669	long tons per acre	9.7	long tons	6 476	6 738
	hectares	271	metric tons per ha	24.2	metric tons	6 580	6 846
Turnips and swedes	acres	300	long tons per acre	19.2	long tons	5 770	5 429
	hectares	121	metric tons per ha	48.0	metric tons	5 862	5 516
Mangolds	acres	42	long tons per acre	24.8	long tons	1 041	803
	hectares	17	metric tons per ha	62.0	metric tons	1 057	816
Hay[1]	acres	5 302	cwt per acre	31.9	long tons	8 468	8 395
	hectares	2 145	kg per ha	4 005	metric tons	8 604	8 742

[1] 1965.

Wheat

The acreage under wheat in the whole of the British Isles in the year 1931 was 514 755 hectares (1 271 000 acres), the lowest ever recorded. Of this area, only 20 234 hectares (50 000 acres) were in Scotland and 9713 hectares (24 000 acres) in Ireland. The total production was about 1 046 000 metric tons (1 034 000 long tons), compared with roughly 6 063 000 metric tons (5 968 000 long tons) which were imported in the same year. Following the abandonment of Free Trade in 1932 and the introduction of a guaranteed price for a specified quantity of wheat, the acreage in the United Kingdom rose to 780 840 hectares (1 928 000 acres) in 1938. Similar measures in Ireland led the acreage there to rise sharply to 103 275 hectares (255 000 acres). During the Second World War the area under wheat increased rapidly to a maximum of 1 402 925 hectares (3 464 000 acres) in the United Kingdom in 1943 and 268 110 hectares (662 000 acres) in Eire; the acreage under wheat has since declined to 906 390 hectares (2 238 000 acres) and 53 055 hectares (131 000 acres) respectively in 1966.

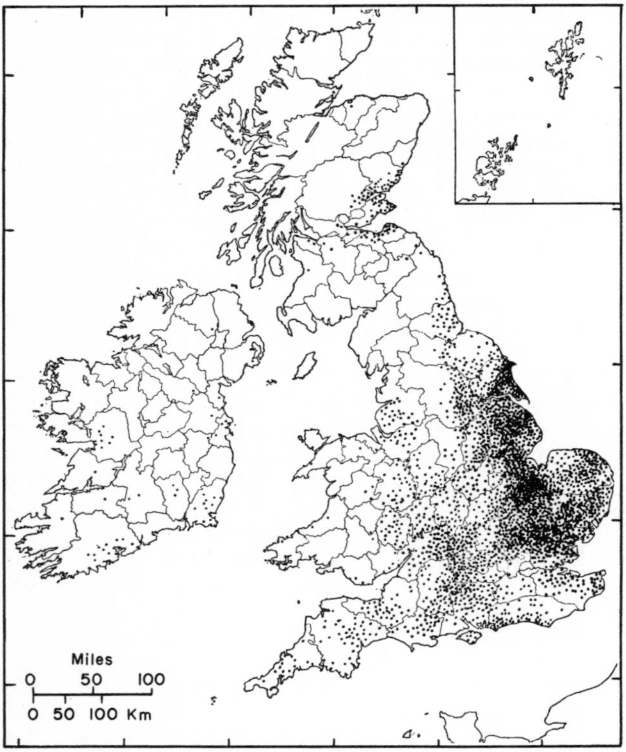

FIG. 88. Map showing the distribution of wheat cultivation in the British Isles

Each dot represents 500 acres in 1931, the year when acreage reached its lowest recorded and when wheat was being grown only where physical conditions were especially favourable.

Figure 88 shows the distribution of wheat in the depression year of 1931. It illustrates the remarkable concentration of wheat cultivation in East Anglia, which has the combined advantages of low rainfall, comparatively high summer temperatures and sunshine, large tracts of gently undulating or level land suitable for ploughing, and fertile mixed soils. In Scotland the small acreage of wheat was restricted mainly to the south of the country and to its eastern margin, which also has a comparatively low rainfall of less than 760 millimetres (30 in). The northernmost extension of wheat cultivation was found on soils developed from the Old Red Sandstone around the Moray Firth. It is, however, broadly true that the 15.5°C (60°F) isotherm for the month of July roughly (see Fig. 54) marks the northern limit of significant wheat cultivation. The distribution of wheat growing in the British Isles thus suggests two quite different types of limit. Broadly speaking, it may be said that the possible limits of cultivation of any crop are determined by physical, primarily climatic conditions. So far as wheat is concerned, this ultimate limit is almost reached in the north of Scotland, and Caithness, Orkney and Shetland lie outside the limit; but the whole of Ireland, Wales and England, and the southern two-thirds of Scotland fall within it. However, as the ultimate limits for the cultivation of any crop are approached, there is usually a belt where harvests are uncertain and may fail completely in some years, although in others bumper crops of good quality may encourage farmers to gamble. There is thus a second limit of cultivation which may be described as the economic limit. Within this, natural conditions are such that an annual crop is generally assured and failures are rare. Here, too, a given crop can be grown in competition with others. In broad terms, the economic limit for wheat in the British Isles may be said to correspond with roughly the 760-millimetre (30-in) isohyet on the west and with the 15.5°C (60°F) July isotherm on the north, although there are specially favoured outliers. The whole of Ireland and Wales, much of western England, and the greater part of Scotland lay beyond these limits in the 1930s. It is true that in the nineteenth century and earlier when competition from foreign wheat was unimportant, this crop was grown in large quantities over the fringing tracts outside the economic limits of the 1930s, but conditions in that outer fringe were never near the optimum for wheat. It is frequently urged that the decline in wheat cultivation in such areas as Ireland is due primarily to economic and historical causes, but the truth would seem to be that Ireland, like many other countries, was producing a crop for which it was not climatically suited. Detailed agricultural statistics have been collected in Ireland since 1847 and in Great Britain since 1866 and the maximum acreages recorded under wheat are as follows:

England and Wales	1 378 620 hectares	(3 404 000 acres)	in 1871–75
Scotland	54 960 hectares	(135 700 acres)	in 1872
Northern Ireland	36 200 hectares	(89 400 acres)	in 1858
Eire	371 750 hectares	(671 000 acres)	in 1847

In Ireland, wheat has never been a crop of primary importance; in what is now Northern Ireland, it occupied only 8 per cent of the ploughed area even at the time of its maximum extension in 1858 and in the Irish Republic, the proportion was even less. By contrast, even as late as 1925, wheat occupied 28 per cent of the total arable area in the English counties of Huntingdon and the Isle of Ely, where conditions approach as near as possible in this country to the optimum. Elsewhere, natural conditions were less favourable and, with a temporary halt in 1917–18, the acreage dwindled until positive action by governments in the 1930s halted the decline. During the Second World War the acreage in 1943 almost equalled that in 1871 and wheat was grown in every county.

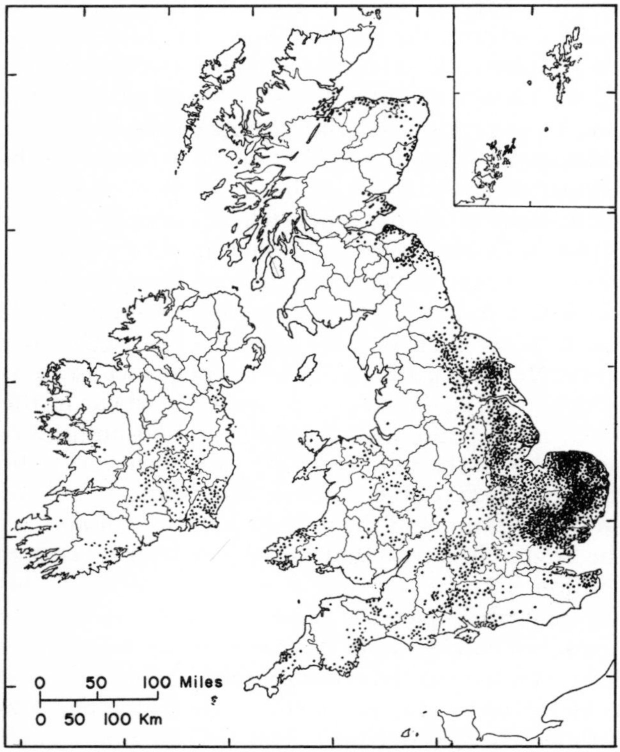

FIG. 89. Map showing the distribution of barley cultivation in the British Isles

Each dot represents 200 hectares (500 acres) in 1931 (Ireland, 1930). The reason for the choice of this year is the same as for wheat. The considerable cultivation now in Northern Ireland is a recent phenomenon.

This wartime expansion was in part made possible by selection of varieties suitable for local conditions. The majority of wheats grown in the British Isles were soft wheats which are not very suitable for breadmaking though they are of good quality. British strains of harder wheats, such as Yeoman and Holdfast, were developed and their cultivation extended. In the cooler northern counties, such as Durham and Northumberland, it was Swedish wheats which did well, in the dry east, Dutch varieties such as

Wilhelmina and Little Joss, and in parts of the south, wheats of French origin. The influence of climatic considerations on the choice of variety is unmistakable.

The bulk of British wheat is winter-sown and yields are higher than those for other cereals. For the ten years 1934–43, the yield in the United Kingdom averaged 2347.6 kilograms per hectare (18.7 cwt per acre) and by 1955–64, the yield in the United Kingdom was averaging 2603 kilograms per hectare (28.7 cwt per acre).[1] It is interesting to note that near the limits of wheat cultivation the yields are often high, probably because the area is small and more care is taken in choosing fields.

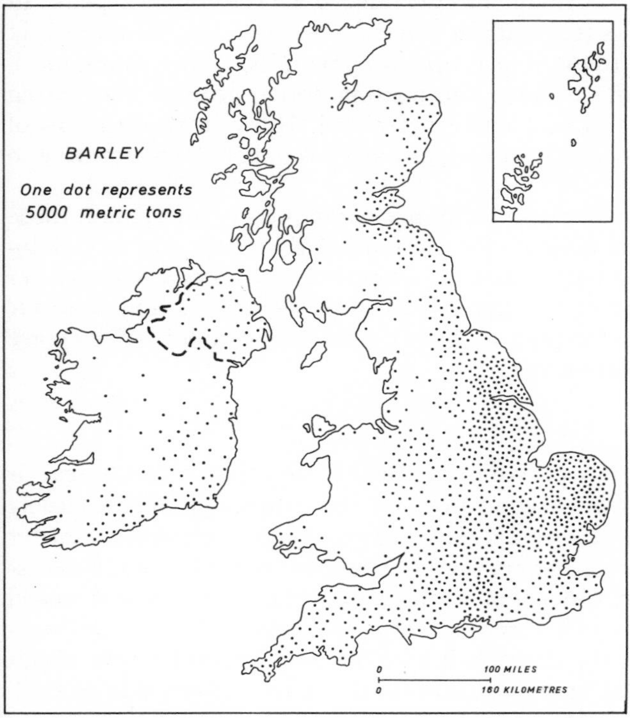

FIG. 90. Barley cultivation in the British Isles, 1966

Barley

In the 1930s barley was the least important of the cereals occupying only about 400 000 hectares (a million acres), and was confined largely to eastern parts of Great Britain and to southeast Ireland (Fig. 89); the principal areas were in East Anglia and the main aim of farmers was to grow a crop of malting quality. Barley was, however, grown in more northern latitudes

1. Yields of all grain crops have risen appreciably since 1964, and in 1967 the UK figure was 4180 kilograms per hectare.

than wheat, possibly because it can take advantage of the longer summer days; in Scandinavia, barley will even ripen within the Arctic Circle. At the wartime peak there were 485 900 hectares (1.2 million acres) grown and, since the 1940s, there has been a dramatic increase in the importance of barley production. New short-strawed varieties out-yield oats and are well suited to mechanised corn growing and to heavy dressings of artificial fertilisers. Barley has thus become a profitable crop to grow and its lower susceptibility to the diseases which beset wheat and oats has enabled farmers to grow several crops in succession; it has also come to be accepted as a suitable feed for cattle. As a result, the area under barley has risen steadily, even though the amount of tillage has declined since the wartime peak; in 1966, 2.6 million hectares (6.5 million acres) were grown, or more than six times as much as in the 1930s. The crop has come to be grown much more widely and has gradually become the leading cereal crop in every area except northwest Scotland and western Ireland. Heavier applications of lime have probably helped this spread, as barley is particularly sensitive to soil acidity.

Most barley is spring sown and yields are consequently lower than those of wheat; in 1955–64 the average for the United Kingdom was 2251 kilograms per hectare (25.9 cwt per acre),[1] compared with 2134 kilograms per hectare (17.0 cwt per acre) in 1934–43. Most of the crop is now used for livestock feed, especially for pigs, and the demands for malting barley are much less important than formerly.

Oats

Oats are much more widely grown in the British Isles than either wheat or barley, although the optimum conditions for the cultivation of oats closely resemble those for wheat. However, oats will grow and ripen under moister conditions and are more tolerant of high soil acidity; they can also, if necessary, be harvested green. Hence, of all the grain crops, oats are best suited to the climatic conditions of Ireland, the west of England, Wales and Scotland. Figure 91 records the distribution of the acreage under oats about 1931 and shows a similar concentration on the drier eastern side of both Ireland and Great Britain; but oats here compete with wheat and barley, and a comparison of the proportion of arable under oats would show that it occupied the lowest proportions in these eastern areas and the highest in western counties.

Since the Second World War, oats have been losing ground steadily to barley, partly because of the decline in the number of horses, to which oats were an important source of feed, and also because barley now out-yields oats; oats are also said to be less suitable for combining and much of the crop in western districts is still cut by reaper-binder. The total acreage in the United Kingdom has fallen from 1.5 million hectares (3.7 million acres)

1. In 1967 the UK yield had risen to 3780 kilograms per hectare.

in 1944 to 367 300 hectares (907 000 acres) in 1966 and that in the Irish Republic from 382 725 hectares (945 000 acres) to 98 400 hectares (243 000 acres). The decline has been widespread and barley has gradually replaced oats as the leading cereal in western counties, although oats still remain a relatively important crop in these areas of high rainfall. Oats are primarily grown for fodder and are consumed mainly on the farm on which they are grown; oat straw is also important for animal feed and is more highly regarded than either wheat or barley straw, much of which is now burnt after harvest.

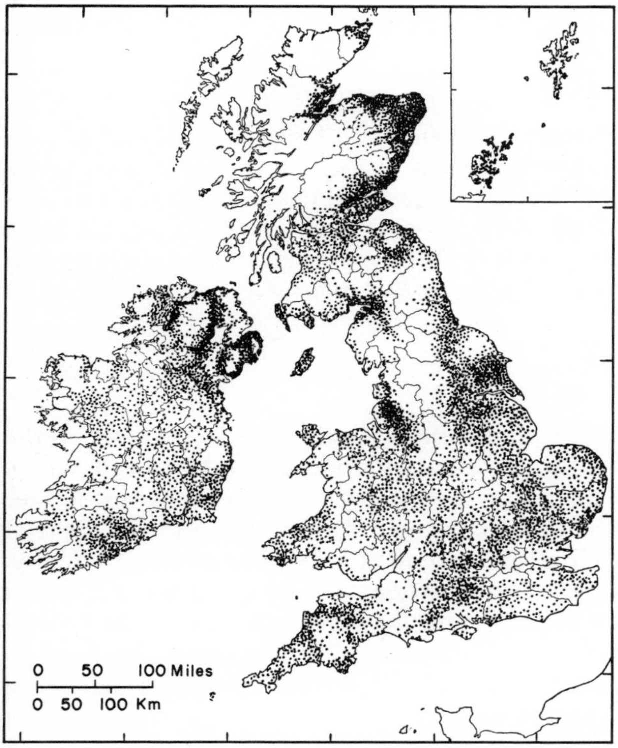

FIG. 91. Oats cultivation in the British Isles, 1931

Each dot represents 500 acres; the accompanying text explains the changes that have taken place.

Rye

Rye is often described as the poor relation of wheat and flourishes under similar conditions. However, it will tolerate far poorer soils and is thus widely grown on those derived from the glacial deposits of the north European Plain, which are the counterparts of those found in central Ireland and much of Scotland. Except as seed to produce green crops for sheep feed, there is little demand for rye in the British Isles and the acreage grown was very small until the Second World War, when rye was mixed with wheat in the 'National Loaf'. In medieval Britain, rye was quite an important grain, but the British people lost, if they ever had, the taste for the rather sour though nutritious rye or black bread, which is familiar to all visitors to Germany and eastern Europe. The area in the United Kingdom jumped from 6800 hectares (17 000 acres) in 1938 to 52 200 hectares (129 000 acres) in 1943, in addition to that grown as green fodder, but by 1966 it was almost back to the 1939 area. Rye is grown mainly on areas of very light soil and some of the homegrown Irish rye is used in the distillation of rye whiskey.

Beans and peas

Beans and peas, when allowed to ripen, were formerly included as corn crops, but it is now necessary to make a distinction between those grown for fodder and the vegetable crops. Beans are a heavy land crop and peas are better suited to light land. Both have declined greatly in popularity as fodder crops since the nineteenth century, although there has been some revival of interest in beans in recent years as farmers searched for alternative break crops.

Mixed corn

The growing of mixed corn was of comparatively little importance in the British Isles in the 1930s except in a few counties such as Cornwall, where barley and oats (dredge) have long been grown together to provide fodder for livestock. Mixed corn can be cut green if necessary and the yield as grain is usually higher than that of either of the two grains grown separately. The prohibition on feeding wheat to livestock during the Second World War led to a considerable expansion in the acreage grown in the United Kingdom, which rose from 38 400 hectares (95 000 acres) in 1938 to 339 000 hectares (838 000 acres) in 1950. However, by 1966 it had fallen again to 29 500 hectares (73 000 acres).

Potatoes

The distribution of potato cultivation in the British Isles provides one of the most interesting examples of the interaction of physical and economic factors. In the first place, potatoes are grown mainly for human consumption and there is not the important production for distillation of industrial alcohol that is found in continental Europe, especially Germany. Secondly, because of the character of the crop itself and its relatively low value per ton, potatoes enter little into international trade. Whereas in the British Isles as a whole most of the wheat which is required for human consumption is imported, nearly all the potatoes consumed are homegrown. Imports consist mainly of early potatoes sold at high prices before the home crop is ready. Thirdly, potatoes have played rather different roles in the agricultural economy of Ireland and the crofting centres of northwest Scotland, and in the remainder of the British Isles. The peculiar suitability of potatoes to the humid soil and atmospheric conditions of Ireland were not appreciated until 150 years ago, prior to which, wheat and barley were the staple crops. It is not too much to say that the increased cultivation of potatoes

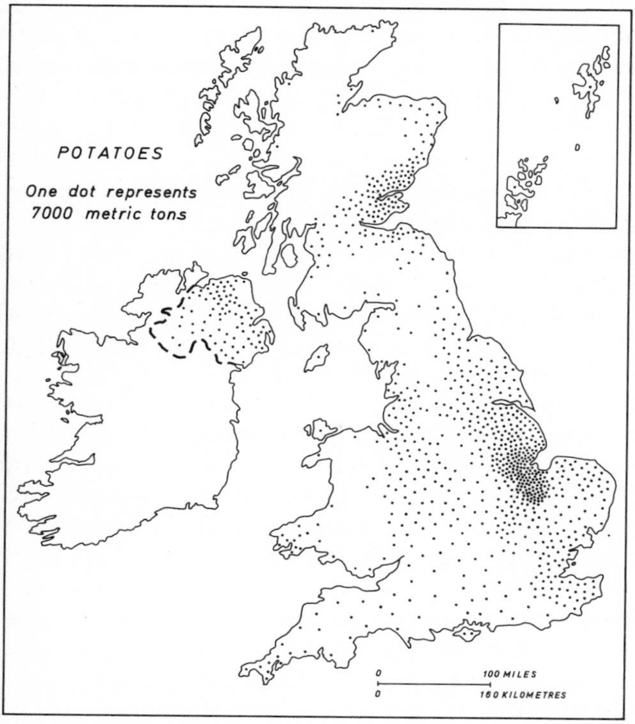

FIG. 92. Potato cultivation in the United Kingdom, 1966.
See also Fig. 270.

made possible the large increase in population and perhaps actually occasioned the overpopulation of rural districts prior to the terrible famines of the 1840s. The area reached a maximum in 1859 when there were 373 400 hectares (923 000 acres) under potatoes in what is now the Irish Republic and in the decade 1847–56 potatoes occupied 19 per cent of the area devoted to crops. The potato is still widely grown as a food crop to supply local needs, irrespective of favourable soil or climatic conditions. The potato also plays a rather similar role in the Highlands and Islands of Scotland.

Elsewhere in Great Britain potatoes are grown mainly as a cash crop for urban markets, although surplus small potatoes are fed to stock and there is an important trade in seed potatoes, which are grown in western and northern districts, notably in Scotland and western Ireland, where the risk of attack by aphids is low. In the Scottish Lowlands, potatoes are grown as a main crop, as an early crop or as seed; the deep loams of the eastern parts of the central Lowlands are particularly favourable for main-crop potatoes. The principal areas for the production of early potatoes in Scotland are situated in the southwest, especially along the coasts of Ayrshire. Close proximity to the sea permits sowing as early as February and the crop is lifted towards the end of June or early in July. Here the soil is light and sandy and has to be enriched by heavy manuring. Markets for these early potatoes of Ayrshire and for the later main crop are near at hand in the densely populated parts of the central Lowlands, but there is still a surplus available for sending southwards to England. In England and Wales also potatoes are widely grown for local consumption, but there is a remarkable concentration of cultivation in several areas.

Two factors are paramount. The first is the suitability of soil, deep, rich loams being the best, especially if free of stones which interfere with the free growth of tubers and handicap mechanical harvesting. Secondly, there must be ready accessibility to the main centres of consumption. The leading area of cultivation is to be found on the fine rich soils surrounding the Wash. In the Holland division of Lincolnshire and the Isle of Ely potatoes occupied nearly one-fifth of the total arable area. The development of potato growing here is a romance of the last hundred years. The silt lands were formerly cattle pastures, but perseverance with disease- and rot-resisting varieties of potatoes rewarded the effort of a local potato buyer and a local farmer. In neighbouring counties, especially on the Fen peats, the area under potatoes is also large. Potatoes from this area are destined very largely for the London market. The second great area is the Lancastrian Plain in Lancashire and Cheshire, where potatoes occupied respectively 12 and 10 per cent of the tillage acreage in 1966. Here potatoes are grown in the lowlands on the loamy soils derived from glacial material and supply the great industrial towns of Lancashire. On the fertile drift soils of the southern part of Durham there is an important production for the industrial northeast. Production in the West Riding and in Staffordshire again reflects the requirements of local industrial centres, while the London market encourages the growing of potatoes in Surrey and Kent. Special mention must be made of the movement of early potatoes from Cornwall, which are the first to be marketed in Great Britain; this is a matter of some importance because the earlier supplies are available the more valuable they are. Pembrokeshire has also become an important area for early potatoes in recent years, and still earlier supplies are available from the Channel Islands, where much of the arable land on the island of Jersey is devoted to potato cultivation.

The acreage under potatoes in the United Kingdom is now less than before the Second World War and is well below the wartime peak; however, owing to the steady improvement in yields, the volume of potato production is larger than prewar. In 1938 296 600 hectares (733 000 acres) were grown, giving a yield of 5 197 000 metric tons (5 115 000 long tons); by 1966 the figure had fallen to 267 000 hectares (660 000 acres), but the yield was 7 577 000 metric tons (7 458 000 long tons), compared with a wartime peak of respectively 574 900 hectares (1.42 million acres) and 9 980 000 metric tons (9 822 000 long tons). In Ireland the area under potatoes rose from 128 300 hectares (317 000 acres) in 1938 to 1939, to 173 200 hectares (428 000 acres) in 1941, but with only 68 000 hectares (168 000 acres) in 1966. In England especially, it should be noticed that, in addition to these quantities from farms, potatoes are widely grown in gardens and allotments.

Turnips and swedes

The principal root crops grown for animal fodder in this country are turnips, swedes and mangolds; but a small proportion of the turnip crop is now grown for human consumption. In general, these root crops demand conditions similar to those required by potatoes, viz. deep stonefree soils, although this is less important with turnips that develop largely above ground and are fed to stock *in situ*. These root crops are largely grown as winter feed for sheep, and to a lesser extent for cattle, and it is often possible to correlate a reduction in the area, especially under turnips and swedes, with the reduced sheep population of the same areas. The introduction of turnips as winter feed for stock marked the turning point of British agriculture during the agricultural revolution, for stock previously slaughtered in the autumn could be kept throughout the winter on turnips stored in clamps. They do best under cool moist conditions, but yield is irregular and growth may be checked by early autumn frosts, especially in the northeast. In England and Wales there has been a steady decline in the area under turnips and swedes associated with the decline of sheep keeping on arable farms; in 1880 the crop occupied 11 per cent of the arable area in the country, by 1925 this proportion had fallen to 7½ per cent and it now stands at less than 1½ per cent. In Scotland and Ireland the crop remains more popular, but here, too, there has been a considerable decline.

Mangolds

It is interesting to compare the distribution of mangolds, the other major root crop used for fodder, with that of turnips and swedes. The land under mangolds in Scotland is negligible; the summer is too short and the crop too susceptible to frost for there to be any extensive cultivation. On the other hand, in England, especially in the drier and warmer south, mangolds grow well and are definitely superior to turnips and swedes, for the yield is considerably higher. The average for the whole of England and Wales reached over 61 250 kilograms per hectare (24.5 tons per acre) in 1961–65, and exceeded 75 000 kilograms per hectare (30 tons per acre) in the rich soil surrounding the Wash. Mangolds are also grown in southeast Ireland. Although the area under mangolds in England and Wales changed little between 1880 and 1930, with the general decrease in the area of arable land, this represented an increased proportion of the arable and illustrated the superiority of mangolds for cattle feed over other root crops. In recent years, however, high labour costs have led to the replacement of mangolds by other fodder crops and the acreage under mangolds has fallen by more than half.

Sugar beet

Until after the First World War only a small acreage of sugar beet was grown, but in the 1920s the United Kingdom Government provided encouragement for its production in order to help arable farmers to grow an alternative cash crop. The acreage grown, some 180 500 hectares (446 000 acres) in 1966, is limited by agreement with other Commonwealth sugar producers and there is little doubt that more would be grown if this was permitted. Within this limitation, the distribution of sugar beet growing is governed by physical conditions and by the location of sugar beet factories, which have been erected in the main arable areas (see below, p. 220 and Fig. 99). Sugar beet is mainly confined to areas of deep, well-drained and stonefree soils in the drier and warmer parts of Great Britain, notably the Fenland and East Anglia; a small acreage is grown in Fife near the sugar beet factory at Cupar. In the Irish Republic beet is produced for a protected home market, and the 21 800 hectares (54 000 acres) grown in 1966 is sufficient for home needs. The crop is confined mainly to the eastern and southern counties, although a factory at Tuam has led to some planting in Galway; this factory is under-used and could support a larger acreage if markets were available, but there is little prospect of this.

Kale

In recent years kale, especially marrow-stem kale used as winter feed for dairy cattle, has had an effect comparable with the spread of turnips during the Agricultural Revolution. Cattle are fed on the standing crop so that the cost of lifting and storage is avoided; the crop is nutritious and palatable. It is mainly grown in southern England.

Miscellaneous fodder crops

The chief of these crops are rape, cabbage and other brassicas, vetches or tares, fodder mustard and lucerne. Rape is widely grown in western and northern districts as a fodder crop for sheep and as a pioneer crop. Vetches were formerly important as sheep feed, but only a small acreage is now grown. Lucerne is largely confined to neutral or alkaline soils in eastern and southern England; its deep roots make it particularly suitable for areas where the water table lies some distance below the surface, as in the Breckland.

Clover and rotation grasses

One of the major changes following the ploughing campaign of the Second World War was the reduction in the acreage under permanent grass. To a considerable extent this was counterbalanced by an increased acreage under clovers and sown grasses, which now occupy about one-third of the total area of arable land, although the proportion in the eastern counties, notably in the Fenland, is lower and that in the midland counties rather higher. In western counties of England and Wales the proportion is considerably greater; in Cornwall it exceeds 50 per cent, suggesting that land which is sown to grass in that county is left unploughed for at least three or four years. In Scotland, too, there is a marked difference in practice between the east and west. In the west, in Ayrshire for example, it is quite common practice to leave land under grass for ten to fifteen years and then to plough it for two; in the east sown grass for three years out of six was long the rule. The Scottish farmer improving rough hill grazing prefers to convert it to arable rather than to lay it down to permanent pasture. Clover and rotation grass may, of course, be grazed by livestock, but some is cut as green fodder and a considerable proportion is cut for hay. In Scotland rather over a quarter is so used, and in England and Wales normally a half, although the proportion is considerably higher in eastern counties. Hay made from sown grass is usually distinguished as seeds hay in contrast to meadow hay made from permanent grass. Special mention should be made of the timothy meadows which occupy considerable areas in central Scotland, particularly in northern Ayrshire and the adjoining parts of Lanarkshire and the Carse of Stirling; timothy grass is suited to heavy clay soil where the yield of other crops is uncertain. Much of the nutriment in grass is lost when it is made into hay and climatic conditions often make haymaking difficult; yet, despite these considerations, silage has not yet become very popular with farmers, although a subsidy on silos has encouraged the construction of large numbers. Dried grass, too, is handicapped by high drying costs.

Flax

Flax can be grown either for fibre or for seed. In the United Kingdom, the growing of flax for fibre was once important in England, but it became almost entirely restricted to Northern Ireland until wartime needs brought back cultivation in many parts of England during the Second World War; it has now ceased to be of any importance anywhere in the United Kingdom, although Fig. 93 is retained as a reminder of its former importance. There has been a similar decline in the Irish Republic.

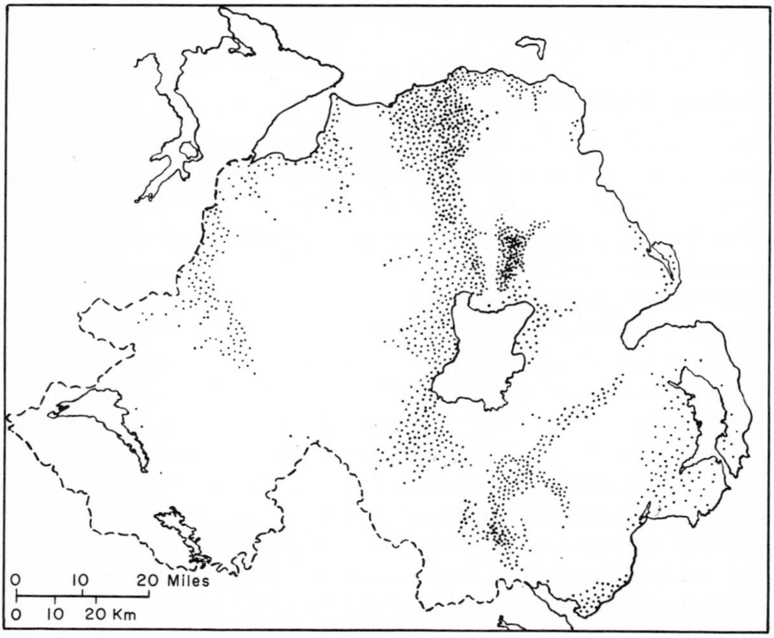

FIG. 93. Map showing the former distribution of flax in Northern Ireland
Each dot represents 25 acres in 1928. By 1959 the acreage had dropped to under 500—broadly flax production was dead except for a few acres for experimental purposes.

Hops

In recent years about 8000 hectares (20 000 acres) of hops have been grown, mainly in southern England. Considerably more than half is grown in Kent on the northern slopes of the Downs and in the Weald. The other centre of cultivation is the county of Hereford and the neighbouring parts of Worcestershire and Shropshire. Hops require deep, well-drained soils; they are demanding crops and require heavy manuring. In the past proximity to towns was thus advantageous. Formerly they were also noted for their heavy labour requirements and the harvest in Kent was undertaken by casual labour from east London. The harvesting of this crop is now largely mechanised and the former temporary hop-poles have now been replaced by semipermanent wiring, so that labour needs have been greatly reduced. The area of land planted is now controlled by the Hop Marketing Board, with which all producers must register. The marketing and processing of hops has now been largely centralised, but the oast-houses in which hops were dried and stored are still familiar features in southeastern England.

Vegetables for human consumption

In 1939 the land under vegetables in the United Kingdom was nearly 118 000 hectares (291 000 acres); it rose to 204 000 hectares (504 000 acres) during the Second World War, largely owing to an expansion in the production of dried peas, but has since declined to 149 000 hectares (368 000 acres). It is difficult to analyse earlier trends because of changes in the

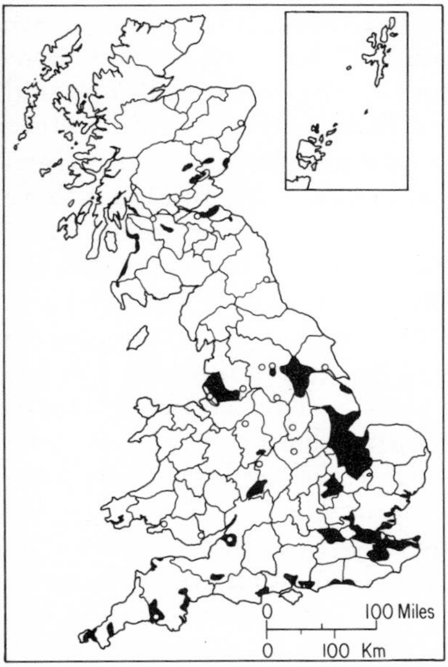

FIG. 94. The main market gardening and fruit farming districts of Great Britain

nature of statistics. These were originally confined to the acreage of market gardens, but it became so difficult to decide what to include in this category that the practice was abandoned and although land under the main vegetables continued to be recorded, there was no estimate of the total area. Nevertheless, it is clear that there has been a major change over the past century as vegetables have ceased to be the monopoly of market gardeners, and a large amount, admittedly of a relatively few common vegetables which lend themselves to field production, has come to be grown as a cash crop on arable farms. Vegetable growing is thus more widely dispersed than formerly; but it is still fairly localised and there are several highly distinctive areas which specialise in vegetable growing. Some of them also produce small and top fruit. The main areas for the intensive growing of fruit and vegetables are shown in Fig. 94.

Over thirty different kinds of vegetables are grown, each with a different distribution and its own requirements of soil and climate. A broad distinction can be made between the choice vegetables, which tend to be grown in small acreages, often by specialist vegetable growers, and the coarse vegetables, which are grown on a field scale by arable farmers. The former tend to be more demanding in their requirements and more localised, although the distribution of any particular category may owe a great deal to chance, to purely local circumstances, or to individual initiative; the latter are often more tolerant in respect of soil and climate. Such field crops as cabbages, which have low value in relation to weight and bulk, are grown widely throughout the arable areas and are favoured by those conditions which favour crop production in general; they also tend to be sold in nearby towns. For the areas of more specialised production, the nature of the soil is often important; deep, well-drained and stonefree soils which can be worked for long periods are well suited to most vegetables, but there is some tendency for soils of lighter texture, which warm up quickly and can be easily worked, to be preferred over heavy soils. Deficiencies of such light soils can more readily be made good by application of fertilisers and increasingly by irrigation, although a number of areas which depended on supplies of town manure have been handicapped in maintaining soil fertility by the great decline in the number of horses. Soil derived from the silts of the Fenlands or the brick-earths of the lower Thames Valley are particularly suitable, but in some areas, like the parts of the West Riding devoted to rhubarb growing, soils are largely manmade.

The climatic conditions suitable for tillage crops in general are also relevant to the growing of vegetables, but earliness is of much greater importance because of the high premiums which early crops of vegetables can command. Coastal areas are favoured, especially in southwest England, where winters are mild and crop growth begins early in the year. Most of the vegetables are grown in southern England, but it must not be too readily assumed that northern and western areas are unsuitable. In Scotland, it seems likely that dietary preferences play some part in explaining the relatively small acreage under vegetables.

Markets are thus also a major consideration in the distribution of vegetable growing. The development of road and rail transport has made proximity to urban markets less important than formerly, although there are still advantages in locations near towns, partly because produce may be fresher but also because supplies can more easily be provided at short notice. However, the complex nature of horticultural marketing and the role of central markets like Covent Garden make it dangerous to draw conclusions from the location of vegetable production in relation to towns and cities; and important areas, like the Fenland and mid-Bedfordshire, lie some distance from urban markets. A new kind of relationship to markets has also developed with the establishment of canneries and, more recently, of quick-freezing plant in the principal arable areas. Large acreages of peas, French beans and other crops are now grown near such plant, often on contract; for quick-freezing in particular, only a short time must elapse between harvesting and processing, so that proximity is of great importance. As a result of the growing popularity of quick-frozen vegetables, the area devoted to such crops has risen sharply in recent years; there were 18 200 hectares (45 000 acres) of peas for quick-freezing in England in 1965, compared with 12 000 hectares (30 000 acres) in 1962, and although the land under vegetables in Ireland is small, there has been a similar expansion of vegetable growing for freezing and canning.

Small fruit

Most of the small fruit produced in the United Kingdom is grown in three areas. The first of these includes Kent, especially the mixed soils of the fertile northern belt of the county, although small fruits are also grown in the neighbouring counties of Essex, Middlesex, Surrey and Sussex. This whole area accounts for a quarter of the total acreage. The second area, one-third of the total, lies around the Wash, includes parts of Norfolk, Cambridge, the Isle of Ely and the Holland division of Lincoln, and has an important centre at Wisbech. The third tract is the county of Worcester, together with the neighbouring parts of Gloucestershire and Herefordshire. In addition, Hampshire has important areas devoted mainly to strawberries, as have Devon, Cornwall and Somerset. Some 45 per cent of the area devoted to small fruit in England is under strawberries, and 33 per cent under blackcurrants. In Scotland the emphasis is on raspberries and strawberries and there is a similar concentration of small fruit growing, notably in the Carse of Gowrie, which has suitable soils, comparatively low rainfall and a generally southern aspect; this area specialises in raspberries and 75 per cent of the British crop is grown in the counties of Kincardine and Perth.

The great difficulty faced by growers of small fruit in the British Isles is the short ripening period in the summer; the markets are suddenly glutted for about a fortnight with each type of fruit and supplies are considerably in excess of demand. Jam-making, canning and deep-freezing play an important role in using this surplus.

Orchards

Orchards are of negligible importance in Ireland, Scotland and Wales, although there are local concentrations south of Lough Neagh, in the Clyde Valley and in Monmouthshire; apart from the considerable number of orchard trees in gardens, there were 75 300 hectares (186 000 acres) of orchards in England in the 1966 agricultural census, of which 60 000 hectares (148 000 acres) were commercial orchards. Apples are the most important fruit, followed by plums, pears and cherries. Most of the fruit is grown in southern England and four groups of counties contain four-fifths of the orchards: Kent, where orchards occur on the high Weald, around Maidstone and in the fertile northern belt, leads with 25 500 hectares

(63 000 acres), mainly of apples and cherries (1966). Worcester, Hereford and Gloucester, with large acreages of plums and apples, come next with about 11 000 hectares (27 000 acres), followed by Devon and Somerset with 3600 hectares (9000 acres). These are old-established areas and a later development has occurred in Essex, Norfolk and Suffolk, which have 9300 hectares (23 000 acres); this is now the most rapidly developing area, with a high proportion of productive orchards under apples. The average yield of orchard fruit is far more variable than that of small fruit as the following table for two contrasting years shows; in any given orchard there is often an alternation of high and low yields per tree.

Average yield per tree of orchard fruit in 1941 and 1947

DESCRIPTION	1941		1947	
	kg	lb	kg	lb
Apples				
Dessert and cooking	8.8	19.5	38.7	85.4
Cider	15.5	34.2	48.8	107.8
Pears				
Dessert and cooking	6.9	15.3	18.9	41.8
Perry	26.8	59.1	60.1	132.5
Plums	18.0	19.8	25.7	56.6
Cherries	6.7	15.7	32.3	71.3

It is difficult in a short space to summarise the essential climatic differences between these two years, but the following brief notes give some indication of the characteristics of the various months; the months March–May affect the blossoming and fruit setting, the months of July–September the ripening.

Months	*1941*	*1947*
March	Cool; excess of E. winds	Very cold; snow
April	Dry and cold, excess of E. winds	Wet
May	Cold; severe frosts	Very warm
June	Dry	Warm
July	Warm	Warm with thunder
August	Cool and wet	Hot, dry and sunny
September	Dry and dull	Unusually warm

Both climate and soils are important in the distribution of orchards, although, as with vegetables, the needs of the different crops vary considerably. Top fruit of good quality is likely only in the drier sunnier parts of the country. Frost is a particular hazard for the fruit grower and late spring frosts provide an additional disincentive to commercial fruit growing in northern areas; but frost is a widespread risk, which can be minimised only by careful siting, and it is a major cause of the variability of yield. Deep, well-drained soils are generally advantageous, though there are differences; cherries are particularly susceptible to poor drainage, while plums do well on fairly heavy soils, provided they are not poorly drained. However, orchards are a long-term investment and, once planted, tend to persist even where they are not well sited.

Kent and Worcestershire are long-established areas which remain important, but orchards in western England are decreasing as old unproductive orchards are grubbed up. Since new planting is taking place mainly in eastern counties, there is a marked eastward shift of emphasis. Even the composition of the remaining orchards in the West Country is changing, for in addition to the grubbing up of entire orchards, it has been a practice for many years to plant dessert apples in gaps in orchards. The marketing of orchard fruit, especially dessert apples, is also undergoing change. Cooperatives and business groups are becoming more important and an increasing proportion of apples is stored in low-temperature gas stores, so that marketing of the home crop can be spread over a longer period.

Flowers

Flowers and hardy nursery stock occupied some 13 750 hectares (34 000 acres) in the United Kingdom in 1966. The growing of bulbs for sale is largely confined to the Holland division of Lincolnshire and the bulb fields on the friable fertile soils derived from the Fen silts are now a considerable tourist attraction; the only other major area for bulbs is southern Cornwall, although there are interesting projects for developing bulb growing in northwest Scotland. Flowers for cutting are widely grown, but are found in two characteristic locations, around large towns and cities, especially London, which is the largest and wealthiest centre in the country; and in Cornwall and the Scilly Isles, where early crops can be produced, mainly between January and April. The growing of hardy nursery stock is also widespread and associated with large urban markets. It is especially prominent on the sandy soils of Surrey.

Crops under glass

There were about 1620 hectares (4000 acres) of glasshouses in the United Kingdom in 1966. Like the distribution of flower-growing, that of glasshouses is both widely dispersed, with small amount of land in many localities, and highly localised in a few areas. The most important of these is the lower Lea valley, although it is less prominent than formerly; the growing of crops under glass developed here partly because of its proximity to the London market, but atmospheric pollution and urban expansion are now both considerable hazards. Other prominent areas are the south coast of England around Worthing, where average hours of sunshine are among the highest in the country; west Lancashire, especially near Blackpool, and around Hull; the Channel Isles, especially Jersey, also have a large area under glass. More than one crop a year can be grown in glasshouses and the crops differ throughout the year; tomatoes are the principal crop in summer, accounting for nearly two-thirds of the land under glasshouse crops, but lettuces and flowers are the chief crops in winter. Apart from general considerations of proximity to markets, expressed more in premiums of freshness and for the reputation of 'local grown' produce than in lower costs and prices, the reasons for the location of glasshouse production are complex and often idiosyncratic. Physical factors play a minor part and, despite lower sunshine and higher heating costs, tomatoes from glasshouses in the Clyde valley are able to compete successfully with those grown by producers in other areas.

Distribution of livestock in the British Isles

Livestock are the most important feature of British farming and most of the agricultural land is used for their support, whether as grazing on leys, permanent pasture or rough grazing, or for the production of fodder crops. Moreover, they have become gradually more important and, although the acreage of agricultural land in Great Britain has been declining steadily, numbers of most of the different classes of livestock, with the exception of horses and of older beef cattle and sheep, are higher than in the 1870s. The composition of the livestock population has changed considerably over the last hundred years, as numbers of cattle have risen steadily; the most marked changes have occurred in the last two decades, as the horse has ceased to be a major source of power on British farms and as intensive, large-scale production of pigs and poultry has increased in importance. The various branches of livestock farming have also tended to become more localised in different parts of the British Isles.

Horses

It is difficult to get a correct view of the distribution and importance of the horse in the British Isles. There has been a steady decrease in the number of agricultural horses, especially in the post-Second World War period; numbers reached a peak just before the First World War, when there were just over 1.1 million in Great Britain and 394 000 in Ireland, but had fallen to 649 000 and 400 000 by 1939, and to 21 000 and 105 000 by 1965. The number of work-horses other than those on farms has also declined, though it is difficult to get actual statistics. On the other hand, horses and ponies for riding have probably increased in numbers in recent years. The breeding of horses as hunters, racehorses and others for pleasure purposes, including the production of bloodstock for export, is also important. In the British Isles as a whole, the location of breeding establishments is determined by the proximity to well-known race courses; thus, there are such centres of breeding as Epsom, Newmarket and Lambourn, where the existence of downland suitable for exercising horses has had an important influence. The United Kingdom is supplied to a considerable extent from the well-known racehorse breeding industry in the Irish Republic, located mainly in the hinterland of Dublin. The decrease in number of agricultural horses is closely connected with the growth of mechanisation and detailed statistics are now published of agricultural machinery. In 1939 there were an estimated 56 000 tractors in Great Britain and only a small number in Ireland; by 1966 and 1965 respectively there were 496000 and 60 000. In general terms, every full-time farmer in the United Kingdom now uses at least one, and usually two, tractors and a full range of other machines.

Cattle

In 1931 there were nearly 12 million cattle in the British Isles, 7 million in Great Britain and the remainder in Ireland. In 1966 there were 17.8 million, of which 11 million were in Great Britain. Yet, despite this growth, numbers in England and Wales did not at first keep pace with the rise in population, as the following table shows:

YEARS	NOS. OF CATTLE PER 405 HA (1000 ACRES) OF LAND UNDER CULTIVATION			NOS. OF CATTLE PER 1000 OF POPULATION		
	COWS AND HEIFERS IN MILK OR IN CALF	OTHER CATTLE	TOTAL	COWS AND HEIFERS IN MILK OR IN CALF	OTHER CATTLE	TOTAL
1867–76	68	104	172	78	119	197
1877–86	70	109	179	74	115	188
1887–96	76	115	191	72	110	181
1897–1906	80	122	201	67	102	169
1907–14 (8 yrs)	86	127	213	66	96	162
1915–24	95	129	224	69	94	163
1925	105	134	239	70	89	158
1939	90	170	280	—	—	—
1945	94	216	310	56	122	178
1950	104	237	300	63	149	212
1960	149	230	349	94	132	226
1966	157	211	347	79	106	186

There is a broad distinction between dairy cattle and beef cattle, although, as will be seen later, many of the animals slaughtered for beef are derived from dairy herds. About a third of the total cattle are cows and heifers and, in the United Kingdom, where it is possible to distinguish those being kept mainly for dairy herd from those rearing calves for beef, dairy cows outnumber those rearing calves for beef by four to one. Beef animals are more important in Ireland and Scotland.

Dairy cattle

The number of dairy cattle in the British Isles has been rising steadily since statistics were first collected and dairying is now the most important single enterprise on farms in the United Kingdom; in 1866–70 there were 2.1 million cows and heifers in Great Britain and 1.5 million in Ireland, compared with 4.6 million and 2.1 million respectively in 1966, although these numbers also include animals in beef-rearing herds. Dairy cattle are widely distributed throughout the British Isles, but they are most common in the western lowlands of Great Britain, notably in Cheshire, Somerset, Carmarthen and southwest Scotland, and in southwest Ireland. The most important among the many reasons for this distribution are the physical requirements of dairy cattle, characteristics of the markets for milk, and the structure of farming in the British Isles.

Fig. 95. Map showing the main dairy-farming areas in Great Britain

Although the different breeds vary in their requirements, dairy cattle are more sensitive to exposure and low temperature than other grazing livestock. The optimum temperature for milk production is said to be about 10°C (50°F) and, while adverse weather can be evaded by housing dairy cattle in winter months (and there is a south–north gradient of increasing length of housing), the greatest densities are found in the southern half of the British Isles, especially in the milder climates of the west. Feed requirements also contribute to this distribution, for dairy cattle must be well fed if they are to produce high yields of milk and, while they can be and are fed on arable crops and purchased concentrates, grazing provides the cheapest feed and dairy cattle are most prominent in those areas where there is an abundant pasture of good quality and a long growing season.

The better grasslands of the west and southwest thus provide the optimum physical conditions for dairy cattle, but the distribution of such animals is also affected by the outlets for milk. Milk has two quite different markets, for it may either be made into butter, cheese or other milk products, or sold for consumption as liquid milk. Since milk is perishable and loses both weight and bulk in the manufacture of products which can be more easily transported and stored than liquid milk, location theory indicates that dairy cattle supplying milk for liquid consumption will be kept near towns and that cattle producing milk for manufacture, which fetches a lower price, will be found in remoter areas where physical conditions are suitable for dairying. Such a relationship was true of Great Britain a hundred years ago, for most milk for liquid consumption came from stall-fed cattle in town dairies or from farms on the outskirts of towns, while dairy cattle kept in areas like Cheshire and Somerset supplied milk for making butter and cheese; but this situation has been transformed by the growth of the urban milk market, by improvements in the transport of milk and by the creation of producer-controlled marketing boards, so that more than two-thirds of the milk produced in Great Britain is now sold for liquid consumption and only that which is surplus to the requirements of the liquid milk market is manufactured; for a safety margin is necessary to ensure that supplies are always available.

Improvements first in rail transport and then in road transport have gradually extended the distance over which milk can be transported without deteriorating until virtually all lowland areas of Great Britain are now capable of supplying urban markets with milk; an increasing proportion of milk is now being collected by bulk tankers direct from farms. At the same time, the demand for liquid milk was expanding with the rapid growth of the urban population and a general rise in the standard of living. The keeping of dairy cattle to supply milk was becoming increasingly attractive to farmers in many parts of Great Britain who had been hard hit by competition from imported produce; for, unlike milk products, liquid milk enjoyed virtually complete natural protection against imports. These trends towards a wider distribution of milk production were accentuated by the creation of milk marketing boards in 1933. These, by pooling the returns from sales of liquid and manufacturing milk, and by the pricing policies they adopted, minimised (for the individual farmer at least) the importance of location. The farmer received the same price for his milk irrespective of its destination and did not pay the full cost of its transport to markets.

The assured market and a regular monthly income which the marketing boards provided for milk producers made the keeping of dairy cattle particularly attractive to those with small farms. Dairying is also an intensive system of farming, requiring large inputs of labour, and hence is suitable for occupiers of small holdings who can increase the effective land of their farms by purchasing feed. Such farms are found in many parts of Great Britain, but they are particularly numerous in western counties and, where physical conditions made milk production possible, dairying was often adopted in such areas in place of more extensive systems like stock rearing.

In the last decade, this tendency towards a wider distribution of dairy cattle has been reversed. Rising yields have led to surpluses of liquid milk and dairying has become less profitable. Many farmers, especially in eastern counties where other enterprises are possible, have therefore ceased to keep dairy cattle and, as a result, the proportion of the national dairy herd in western counties is rising.

PLATE 5. A Friesian dairy herd in Kent: strip grazing controlled by electric fences

Despite these developments some differences between areas of Great Britain producing milk for liquid consumption and those producing milk for manufacture survive, and in Ireland, where the urban milk market is much smaller, a clearcut distinction remains. Thus, much of the milk surplus to urban requirements in Great Britain is produced cheaply on grass in summer in areas like southwest England, Wales and Scotland and a higher proportion of milk is manufactured in these areas. In Ireland the keeping of dairy cattle to supply milk to urban markets is largely confined to the area around Dublin and other large towns, while milk produced in the main dairying areas is sent to creameries for manufacture.

While the Friesian is the most important single breed of dairy cattle in the British Isles, there are considerable regional differences in breed structure of dairy herds. The Friesian predominates throughout England and Wales, but the Ayrshire and Dairy Shorthorn account for most of the remainder. The Shorthorn is overwhelmingly the most important breed in Ireland and the Ayrshire, a relatively hardy animal, occupies a similar position of dominance in Scotland. Among the minor breeds, Channel Island cattle (Guernsey and Jersey) are important only in southern England. The Friesian has been increasing in popularity because of its high yields and because surplus calves are suitable for rearing and fattening ing as beef animals.

Dairy cattle differ from other grazing livestock in that there is relatively little seasonal movement of animals between different parts of the country, apart from the sales of surplus calves and cows to be fattened for beef; most dairy herds are self-contained and breed their own replacements. However, there are regional differences in the seasonal pattern of calving and of milk production, reflecting differences in outlets for milk and in the availability of feed. In western counties of Great Britain, where milk can be produced cheaply on grass, there is a higher percentage of spring calving and more milk is produced in summer, while in eastern counties, where fodder from arable crops is abundant and there are advantages in concentrating on more profitable winter milk production, the balance is more even.

Beef cattle

Beef cattle have also increased in importance, especially in the post-Second World War period when the British Government has been encouraging the production of beef. However, it has never been easy to draw a sharp line between dairy cattle and beef cattle, and it has become more difficult with the increasing use of artificial insemination and with the expansion of dairy farming; thus, some two-thirds of the young animals reared for beef are the offspring of dairy cows and about a quarter of the cattle slaughtered for beef are old cows and bulls, many of which have come from dairy herds. In Ireland, too, most beef cattle originate on dairy farms. However, changes in numbers of cattle other than cows and heifers do give some indication of the expansion of beef production, although this category includes dairy herd replacements as well as cattle intended for slaughter. In 1866–70 such other cattle numbered 3.1 million in Great Britain and 2.2 million in Ireland, compared with 6.4 million and 4.7 million respectively in 1966. These figures conceal quite important differences in the composition of the national herd, for whereas cattle of two years and over have been declining in numbers in recent years, those between one and two years old have been increasing rapidly, reflecting a fall in the average age of slaughter.

Beef cattle are relatively more important in Ireland and Scotland, but it is necessary to consider the British Isles as a whole in examining their distribution because of the large movements of dairy cattle from Ireland to

Great Britain. Figure 96 shows that beef cattle are most numerous in the Irish lowlands, southwest England, the Midlands and northeast Scotland; there are fewest beef cattle in the uplands. However, this map is somewhat misleading in that it includes all stages from breeding to fattening, each of which exhibits a somewhat different regional pattern. Cattle intended for slaughter as beef may be born of dairy cows on farms in many parts of the country; they may also be born to cows of beef breeds, like Herefords and Aberdeen Angus, either on lowland farms or on farms on the margins of the uplands. Surplus calves on dairy farms are likely to be sold shortly after birth, but others will probably spend some time on the farm on which they are born.

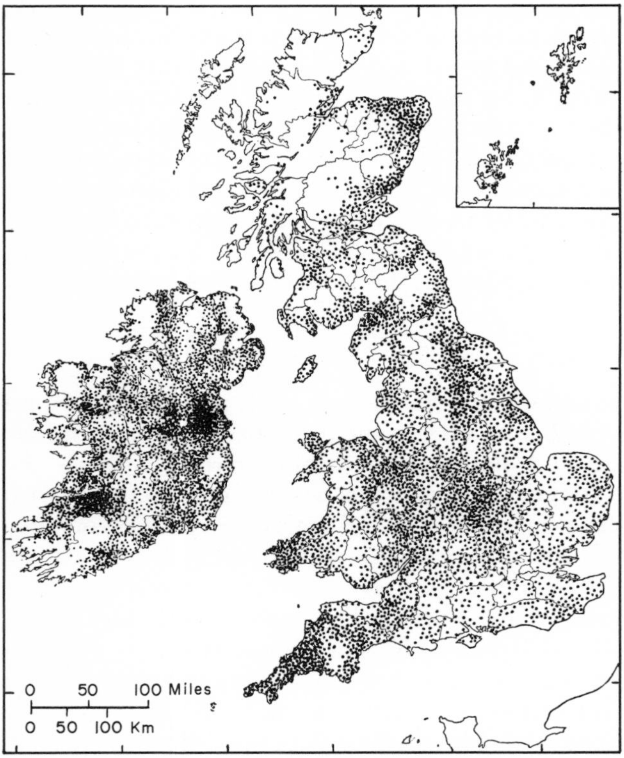

FIG. 96. Map showing the distribution of beef-cattle in the British Isles

Each dot represents 1000 animals.

The breeding and rearing of young beef cattle is especially characteristic of family farms on the upland margins in areas like the Welsh borderlands and northeast Scotland, for beef cattle are less demanding than dairy cattle in the early stages of their lives and can use the rough grazings and poor pastures; about half the cows in beef herds in the United Kingdom are found in such areas and qualify for the hill cow subsidy. Older animals may be found on farms in most parts of the British Isles, either being kept as store animals for a limited period to use surplus grazing or fodder, or being reared and fattened. In general, beef cattle tend to move eastwards to other farms in the lowlands as they get older, although the detailed pattern of movement is highly complex. Furthermore, over half a million animals are exported from Ireland to Great Britain, either for slaughter or to be fattened on farms in eastern counties. Beef cattle may be fattened on farms in many parts of the lowlands, either on grass in the summer months or on arable crop residues during the winter. However, certain areas have tended to specialise in the summer feeding of cattle, notably the plains of Meath in Ireland and the east Midlands in England, where there are pastures of high quality. Fattening in yards in winter has long been characteristic of arable districts in eastern counties in England and Scotland, and such cattle are often kept as much for the manure they provide as for the contribution they make to farm income. In recent years there has been increasing interest in the intensive rearing and fattening of beef cattle on arable farms, with animals being slaughtered at under fifteen months; in 1964 between 5 and 10 per cent of beef supplies in the United Kingdom were thought to have been produced in this way.

Sheep

The British Isles have long been famous for their sheep. Not only was wool a staple product and export in the Middle Ages, but at a later stage British sheep became well known for their meat. Most of the British breeds are heavy animals, producing good, well-flavoured meat, and at the same time having a heavy fleece of excellent quality wool. The large sheep populations of the great grassland countries of the southern hemisphere, such as Argentina, Uruguay, South Africa and New Zealand, are very largely of British origin. The only rival of the British breeds is the Merino, a wool-producing sheep suitable for arid conditions. There are normally as many sheep in the British Isles as in the whole of New Zealand and between a quarter and a third of the total in the Australian continent. Numbers of sheep, though large, have fluctuated more markedly than those of cattle and their distribution has also changed more markedly. In 1866–70 there were 27.9 million in Great Britain and 4.6 in Ireland, compared with 28.9 and 5.7 million respectively in 1966; there has been a rapid increase since the Second World War when numbers were deliberately run down and there were only 19.4 million in Great Britain in 1944. As Fig. 97 shows, sheep are to be found mainly on and around the uplands of the north and west, especially the Southern Uplands in Scotland, the northern Pennines and the Lake District, and Wales; the principal lowland areas where sheep are prominent are the east Midlands, where both sheep and cattle are fattened, and Romney Marsh, which has the highest density of sheep anywhere in the British Isles. Although numbers in Ireland are much smaller, sheep are also found mainly on and around the uplands. A century ago sheep were more widely distributed and there were many more in the lowlands, especially in the arable areas of eastern England, where sheep were

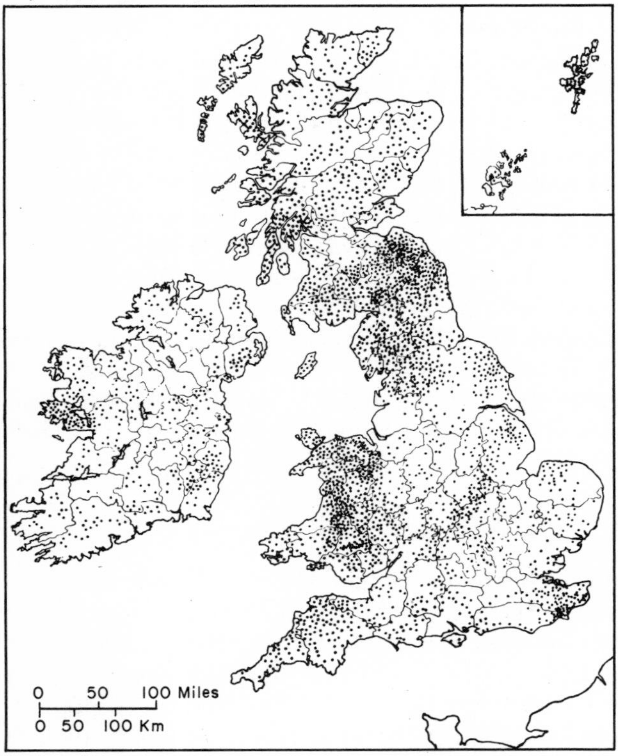

FIG. 97. Map showing the distribution of sheep in the British Isles

Each dot represents 10 000 animals. Total in the United Kingdom 29 million in 1961.

folded on arable land; increasing labour costs have tended to exclude sheep from arable farms, except as scavengers of crop residues, and sheep compete with dairy cattle for available grazing on lowland pastures. This trend towards the concentration of sheep in the uplands has become more marked since the Second World War as numbers have increased in western counties of Great Britain and declined in the east, although in parts of the uplands afforestation has reduced the acreage of hill pasture and numbers have either fallen or increased at a much lower rate than elsewhere. But there have also been changes in the composition of the sheep flocks; the decline in the demand for mutton has led to the virtual disappearance of wether sheep and most flocks now consist mainly of breeding ewes, ewe replacements and lambs.

Sheep are a source of both wool and meat, mostly lamb, but only in the uplands is wool an important source of farm income; such wool is not of the best quality and is mainly used for carpet-making. The reasons for the

PLATE 6. Dorset horn lambs folded on swedes and kale

present distribution are in part economic and in part the physical requirements of sheep. It is clearly fallacious to claim that sheep cannot thrive under damp conditions, for they are most numerous in the wetter areas of the British Isles; the actual rainfall is not so important, provided that drainage is good. The hardier breeds of sheep are better able to withstand exposure and cold than other livestock; they are also less demanding in their requirements of feed, water, housing and attention than cattle and are able to graze the poorest upland pastures which would otherwise go unused. Their distribution in the uplands is in part an index of the quality of grazing, with the lowest densities in the Scottish Highlands where the environmental conditions are most extreme and the carrying capacity is very low. The extent of common land, which tends to be overstocked, and the size of the predominant breeds are also factors which need to be taken into account in explaining differences in density of sheep. Conditions in the uplands are far from ideal for sheep and numbers tend to fluctuate greatly in response to weather conditions; the sheep population of Great Britain was reduced by over 3.5 million (about one-sixth) between 1946 and 1947 because of the severe weather of the intervening winter. Sheep are thus numerous in the uplands because no other enterprise is possible on much of the land grazed by them; by contrast, sheep tend to be excluded from lowland areas because the keeping of sheep is less profitable than other enterprises.

Like beef cattle, sheep tend to be reared and fattened in farms in different parts of the country and there is also a marked stratification of sheep farming with altitude, in which the degree of dependence on sheep declines with height above sea-level and farms at higher altitude supply those lower down with stock for fattening. On the poorest uplands, where sheep are often the only enterprise, ewes of hardy breeds graze for several seasons, bearing a crop of lambs each spring. The ram lambs are generally sold to occupiers of lowland farms where they are fattened, although there is an increasing tendency for upland farms to fatten lambs where this is possible; many of the female lambs are required for flock replacements and these are often sent away during their first winter to the kindlier conditions of lowland farms. Mortality rates are much higher than on lowland farms and those ewes which survive the severe conditions for several seasons are usually sold as cast ewes to lowland farmers, who may cross them with a ram of lowland breed to produce a flock of half-bred lambs for fattening. Offspring of these crosses may similarly be crossed with rams of arable breeds. Pure breeds of hill sheep may also be kept on upland farms which specialise in cattle rearing and lowland farms may also support purebred flocks whose role is in part to provide rams for crossing with ewes of upland breeds. Thus, in general, this stratification of sheep farming results in a progressive mixing of breeds at lower altitudes, a decreasing importance of sheep in the farm economy and a shift of emphasis from breeding to fattening. It is claimed that such an arrangement represents a more efficient use of resources, in that the poorer quality land is used for less profitable breeding and the better for fattening, and that the role of the uplands as a reservoir of breeding stock produces animals which combine the hardiness of the upland breeds with the rapid growth and larger size of the lowland breeds.

This account shows that crossbreeding plays an important part in sheep farming and that no simple picture of the distribution of sheep breeds is possible. There are more than thirty different breeds, many of them adapted to local environments. In Scotland two breeds predominate, the Blackface and the Cheviot, the former mainly on the heather-covered hills, the latter especially on the grass moors of southern Scotland, although a special strain, the North Country Cheviot, is found in Caithness. In northern England, the distinctive Herdwick is characteristic of the Lake District, and the Teesdale, Swaledale and Wensleydale in the northern Pennines; while in Wales the small Welsh mountain breed is common. Characteristic breeds of the lowlands include both grass sheep like the Leicester, arable sheep like the Suffolk, and the Down breeds. In Romney Marsh and the rest of Kent, most sheep are of the Romney Marsh breed. There are, of course, many permutations of upland and lowland breeds, resulting in a great variety of first and second crosses. In Ireland the Cheviot is by far the most important breed, followed by Down breeds.

This progressive concentration of the sheep population in upland counties has led to considerable investigations of the possibility of improving upland pastures, which provide sufficient food for growth only in the short summer period. Pioneer work in this respect was done by the late Sir George Stapledon at the Welsh Plant Breeding Station at Aberystwyth. He pointed out that, after the Napoleonic Wars, isolated but well chosen areas were ploughed for oats on the Welsh hills up to 450 or even 500 metres (1500 or 1700 feet), and that these areas can still be distinguished by the better pasture they provide. It is clear from these patches, with their comparative abundance of *Agrostis* rather than moorland grasses, and the occurrence of white clover and such weeds of cultivation as hawksweed, that the surrounding areas of pasture might in any case be much better than they are. When he made his survey of the hill lands of Wales in the 1930s Stapledon found something like 800 000 hectares (2 million acres) of rough hill pastures, about half mainly of grass, of which he considered half favourable from the point of view of aspect and other considerations for improvement. The very wet areas of cotton grass, sphagnum and other types of bog would be expensive to drain, but there remained three types of grass pasture suitable for consideration: (*a*) *Molinia* or flying-bent pasture; (*b*) *Nardus* or mat grass pasture; (*c*) bent-fescue (*Agrostis-Festuca*) pasture. The natural defects of these pastures are that *Molinia* is deciduous and is used by sheep for about one month; *Nardus* is unpalatable to sheep and, whilst the bent and fescue are palatable, they are of low feeding value, particularly in that they lack lime. Further disadvantages are the lack of leguminous plants such as white clover, and of herbs, such as daisies, which have an excellent feeding value.

The need is to introduce wild white clover, and more palatable grasses with a longer growing season. Even by the simple process of cutting, grazing hard and then manuring, the bent and fescue, i.e. the better grasses, are increased in numbers; large areas can also be improved by surface cultivation and reseeding. Stapledon claimed that 10–15 per cent of the land of the sheep walks might be improved and, by the proper alignment of fences, this improved land could be used in such a way that each of the major sheep walks had a proportion of it. He further suggested that much also might be done by the planting of trees as shelter belts, so that it would be possible for sheep to be kept on the fells or hill pastures throughout the year. Heather moorlands can be improved in the same way, by the simple process of burning, since young heather itself has an important nutritive value for sheep feeding. Stapledon considered it would pay also to keep limited numbers of cattle on the hill pastures, not because the cattle themselves could be expected to pay, but they would gradually benefit the ground by their manure. In the event not much of the uplands has been improved, despite the availability of grants towards the cost; hill sheep farmers have generally lacked the resources necessary, even with grant aid.

Pigs

Pigs have also increased greatly in importance over the past hundred years. There were 2.5 million in Great Britain in 1866 and 1.2 million in Ireland, compared with 6.3 million and 2.1 million respectively in 1966. Numbers fluctuate considerably in accordance with the pig cycle (which has a periodicity of some four years) and partly in response to government policy, as during the Second World War, when numbers fell by more than half. Pigs, which are sensitive to cold and exposure, are confined to the lowlands, but their distribution is very patchy and there is none of the regionalisation of breeding and fattening that characterises the keeping of beef cattle and sheep, although there is some specialisation of function between those who rear and those who fatten pigs. Pigs are often associated with small holdings and a tenth of those in the United Kingdom may escape enumeration because they are on holdings of 0.4 hectare (1 acre) or less (the minimum size recorded in the annual agricultural census).

Pigs can be fed on waste human food and there are often considerable numbers around large towns and cities, as in Greater London. There is also an association between pig keeping and arable farming, especially the growing of barley and potatoes, but pig keeping was sometimes established for reasons which now have little validity, as with the association between pigs and farmhouse cheesemaking in Cheshire. In the main, size of holding seems a more important consideration and most pigs are found on small holdings; in Ireland more than two-thirds are on holdings of under 40 hectares (about 100 acres). Large Whites predominate in both countries, with Landrace as the second breed.

Poultry

It is not easy to obtain accurate estimates of the number of poultry or to make comparisons over time. In the United Kingdom numbers of poultry have been regularly recorded in the agricultural census only since 1926, but many farmers do not know accurately how many they have and possibly a quarter of all poultry escape enumeration because they are not on agricultural holdings of over 0.4 hectare (one acre). Whatever the truth about earlier changes, numbers in the United Kingdom have been rising rapidly since the Second World War, when they were drastically reduced as part of the Government's programme for home food production. There were 119 million in 1966, compared with 55 million in 1944 and 72 million in 1938. Poultry keeping in the Irish Republic has been adversely affected by these developments in the United Kingdom, particularly by the low price of eggs, and there were only 11 million in 1966, compared with 21 million in 1950. Like pigs, poultry are largely confined to the lowlands and require little land. The largest concentration is in Lancashire, which had 8 per cent of the poultry in Great Britain in 1966, although the dominance is less marked than formerly; other important areas are in the east Midlands, East Anglia, and the counties around London. In Ireland poultry are most numerous in Connacht and Ulster. The great majority of poultry in both countries are fowls; small numbers of other kinds of poultry are found in many lowland areas but there are important concentrations of ducks and turkeys in East Anglia.

In the past poultry have shown an even more marked association with small holdings than have pigs, and on many larger farms the poultry flock was the perquisite of the farmer's wife. In recent years, however, there have been major changes as a result of industrialised methods of poultry farming which is increasingly being undertaken by specialists on a large scale. This change has been very rapid; for example, in England and Wales in the 1950s the numbers of fowl kept free range fell from over nine-tenths to under a third. A rising proportion of egg-laying fowl are kept in large units under intensive systems requiring little land, but much capital for buildings, while there has been a rapid increase in the number of broilers (intensively reared table birds), which numbered 31 million in June 1966. Similar developments, although on a much smaller scale, have been taking place in Ireland and Scotland. Intensive rearing of ducks and turkeys on a large scale is also being practised, notably in East Anglia. Location is not a major consideration and little land is required; the distribution of such holdings is thus very patchy.

Number and size of agricultural holdings

This discussion of the distribution of the different kinds of crops and livestock has shown that farm size is an important factor. Unfortunately there is little information on farms as such, although the number of farmers is enumerated in the population censuses. The data for the agricultural censuses are collected by holdings, many of which are not farms in the ordinary sense. In the United Kingdom a holding is a unit of more than 0.4 hectare (one acre) of agricultural land and many smaller holdings are accommodation fields, grounds of large establishments and the like which serve some agricultural purpose. Any concept of an average farm obtained by dividing the acreage of farmland by the number of holdings must clearly be treated with considerable reserve. In 1966 there were 374 000 holdings in Great Britain, of which 73 000 were under 2 hectares (five acres) and occupied less than 0.5 per cent of the agricultural land, and nearly 12 000 were of 200 hectares (500 acres) and over and occupied 41 per cent. In Northern Ireland there were 66 000 holdings in 1963, but only sixteen were of 200 hectares (500 acres) and over (as measured, not by total area but by the land under crops and grass), occupying 0.5 per cent of the area in crops and grass. In the Irish Republic there were 283 000 holdings in 1965, 2605 of them exceeding 120 hectares (300 acres) in size.

Although the evidence is ambiguous, there is little doubt that farms are tending to increase in size; and the great expansion in mechanised farming has provided an incentive to enlarge holdings, especially in the eastern counties of England where the proportion of land in holdings of 120 hectares (300 acres) and over rose by more than 15 per cent between 1939 and 1965.

In interpreting the regional distribution of holdings, it should be noted that much of the information about holdings relates only to improved land, i.e. rough grazings are excluded. This does not matter in most lowland areas, but it can give quite misleading impressions in the uplands; for example, a hill sheep farm of 400 hectares (a thousand acres) or more will include little improved land. Even where rough grazing is taken into account, it must be remembered that there are about 607 000 hectares (1.5 million acres) of common rough grazings in England and Wales, about 490 000 hectares (1.25 million acres) of common pasture in the crofting counties of northwest Scotland, and an unknown quantity in Ireland; such land in effect enlarges the size of holding of those who have rights to use such common grazings.

Although a wide range of holdings of different sizes occurs in most areas, there are quite important regional tendencies. Large holdings are associated particularly with areas of mechanised arable farming, especially cereal-growing on the chalk lands of southern and eastern England. Large holdings of a very different kind are found on the rough grazings of the uplands, with the largest holdings on the poorest land, as in north Scotland. Small holdings are similarly characteristic of two quite different situations: the areas of intensive horticulture, like the Fenland and Worcestershire; and poor grazing land on the margins of the uplands and on the west coast of Ireland and northwest Scotland and the islands. Many of these holdings on poor land are too small to provide an acceptable standard of living and their occupiers often have other employment. Both the crofting districts of northwest Scotland and the congested district of western Ireland present problems in this respect.

Size of holding provides some indication of regional difference in size of farm, but, as has been shown, size alone is clearly unsatisfactory; for a small holding associated with an intensive kind of farming may provide full-time employment, while a larger holding devoted to extensive grazing cannot. Various attempts have been made to improve the kind of information available. Before the First World War occupiers of holdings in England and Wales were asked to say whether they farmed mainly for business or not; only 5 per cent said they did not, although this proportion reached 19 per cent in Surrey. During the Second World War, a National Farm Survey of England and Wales, confined to holdings of 2 hectares (5 acres) and over, showed that 74 per cent were full-time farmers, 11 per cent part-time farmers, and 15 per cent spare-time and hobby farmers. This last category was particularly common around large cities and in areas like Cardiganshire where there had formerly been an association between mining and farming. Spare-time and hobby farming appears to have increased in importance since this survey, especially in the area around the London conurbation.

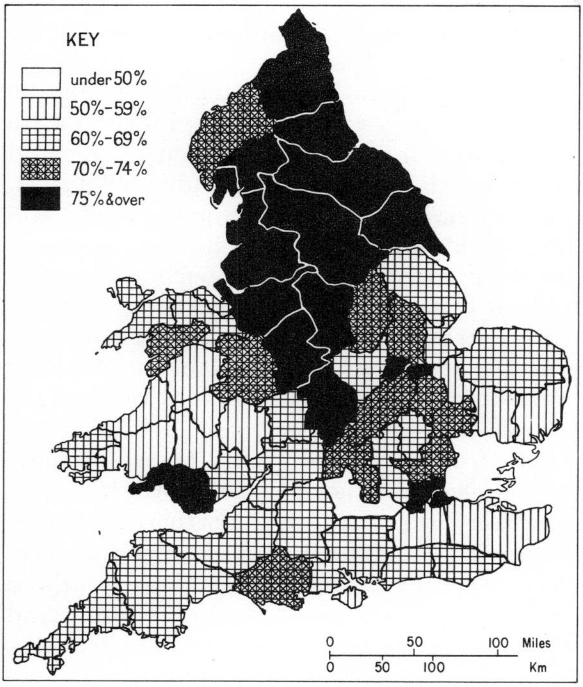

FIG. 98. Proportion of tenant farmers in England and Wales

Although tenant farmers are most numerous where there are large estates in the north and fewest in the home counties with their numerous smallholdings this map reflects local custom more than geography. (From *National Farm Survey of England and Wales 1941–43*, by permission of the Controller of H.M. Stationery Office.)

More recently, agricultural economists in the United Kingdom have extended this approach by analysing holdings by size of business rather than by area, using standard labour requirements as a basis for comparison. Those holdings which require fewer than the standard labour requirements for one man (275 standard man days, except in Northern Ireland, where 200 has been adopted) are regarded as part-time holdings; on this basis half the holdings were part-time, though an analysis in 1955 showed that a third of the occupiers of such part-time holdings in England and Wales had another full-time occupation. Part-time holdings were also shown to be most numerous around the large cities and in Wales and southwest England. In Scotland only 43 per cent of the holdings were full-time; as might be expected, part-time holdings were most numerous in the crofting counties of the northwest. In Northern Ireland nearly two-thirds of the holdings were part-time, although these included some 20 000 holdings which are let seasonally and generally run with other farms. There are no comparable data for the Irish Republic, but fewer than half of those occupying holdings of less than 30 acres gave their principal occupation as farmer in the 1961 census.

There are also great contrasts in agricultural land tenure throughout the British Isles. In Ireland nearly all farmers own the land they farm (or are paying annuities to acquire it), although there is both common grazing and some moorland held jointly by a number of owners in undivided shares. There is also a form of short-term tenancy known as conacre, where land is let for eleven months or less, mainly for grazing; such land represents about 10 per cent of the land used for agriculture. The proportion of owner-occupiers is much smaller in Great Britain, although it has risen considerably since the beginning of this century, when most farms were tenanted. Most holdings are either owned or tenanted, but some consist of mixed tenures. In England and Wales about 57 per cent of holdings and half the agricultural land were owned or mainly owned by occupiers, while in Scotland the proportions were 38 and 59 per cent respectively. There are, however, considerable regional differences and, as Fig. 98 shows for 1941, tenancy was then the characteristic form of tenure in northern England, while owner-occupation was more important further south. A special form of tenancy is found in the seven crofting counties in northern Scotland (Argyll, Caithness, Inverness, Orkney, Ross and Cromarty, Sutherland and Zetland) where occupiers of certain small holdings enjoy a high degree of security of tenure under the supervision of a Crofters Commission. There are about 20 000 such crofts, occupying some 72 800 hectares (180 000 acres) of improved land and 166 000 hectares (410 000 acres) of rough grazings, and crofters also have grazing rights over some 49 000 hectares (1.25 million acres) of common pastures. However, the legal position of tenants in general has improved steadily since the 1870s and they now enjoy a high degree of security of tenure and freedom of action, provided land is properly farmed. Statutory smallholdings have also been created, originally to foster a peasant economy, and then to help ex-servicemen to settle on the land after the First World War and to alleviate unemployment in the 1930s. In England and Wales there are some 15 000 owned by county councils and 1300 owned by the Ministry of Agriculture, while in Scotland the Department of Agriculture owns 4000 holdings, mainly in the crofting counties.

Many of the changes in the number of holdings in the United Kingdom since the middle of the nineteenth century have concerned small holdings which are not farms, and the number of farmers has remained remarkably stable until recent years when it has begun to decline; numbers of farm workers, on the other hand, have fallen steadily.

Types of farming

There are marked contrasts between one part of the British Isles and another in type of farming; and, while in many localities a variety of types can be found, individual types often show a tendency to be localised in particular regions. The reasons for these differences are to be found primarily in the physical condition of the land, in relief, soil and climate; but accessibility, especially to roads and hence to markets, farm size and type of tenure also play a large part. Furthermore, although hill sheep farms would seem to have little connection with intensive market gardening, in reality British farming forms a closely integrated whole. As has been shown, hill farms provide lowland farms with young stock for fattening, as well as some breeding animals, the surplus calves from dairy farms are sent elsewhere for fattening, and crop farms in eastern counties may provide those further west with fodder. Farms throughout the United Kingdom are thus linked by complex transfers of stock and crops and there are similar movements of stock in Ireland, as well as between the Irish Republic and the United Kingdom. Formerly this integration was achieved almost wholly through farmers buying in the cheapest market and selling in the dearest, although traditional links between one area and another may have played a part. There is, however, a growing tendency (if still on a small scale) for widely separated farms of different kinds to be permanently linked in this way under the same ownership or management; for example, a mixed farm in the English Midlands may be worked in conjunction with an upland farm in Wales owned by the same farmer. These links between different areas must always be remembered when the various types of farming are under discussion.

Types of farm can be recognised by reference to the relative importance of the enterprises, such as crop production, dairying and pig-keeping, which make up the farming system; many of these have already been discussed in the preceding sections on crop and livestock distributions. In the past, farm types were recognised on the basis of both land use and a subjective assessment of enterprises; thus, on the *Types of Farming* map prepared in 1937 by the Ministry of Agriculture and Fisheries, a threefold division was made in respect of the proportion of arable and grassland and these areas were then subdivided according to what were thought to be the leading enterprises. It is now widely held that all land which can be ploughed benefits from being so treated, and the spread of ley farming has blurred the distinction between arable and grassland and made this criterion less useful. More recently attempts have been made to make more objective estimates of the contribution which different enterprises make to the farm business. For this to be done some common measure has to be found by which the relative importance of the various crops and livestock can be compared. Sales of farm produce would seem an obvious choice, but there is little information about these, and most studies have used estimates of labour requirements, calculated from crop acreages and livestock numbers by means of standard factors. Farms are classified according to the enterprise which accounts for half or more of the labour requirements, although some note is also taken of other enterprises. Those farms where no enterprise accounts for 50 per cent are classified as mixed, but it must be appreciated that many other farms have a number of enterprises. Unfortunately, classification in the various parts of the United Kingdom is not identical. In England and Wales in 1965 farms of the following type were recognised:

Type	*Number*
Dairy	60 800
Livestock	24 700
Pigs and poultry	9 600
Cropping	26 600
Horticulture	15 000
Mixed	19 500

Only full-time farms have been classified. Livestock farms are those which concentrate on the rearing and/or fattening of sheep and cattle; 4400 of these are mainly sheep farms in hill areas and correspond broadly with the hill sheep farms recognised in Scotland. A further 8400 are also in hill areas, but rely on both sheep and cattle and resemble to some extent the upland farms in Scotland.

In Scotland in 1965 the following types of farm were recognised:

Type	*Number*
Hill sheep	1300
Upland	2900
Rearing with arable	4800
Rearing with intensive livestock	1100
Arable rearing and feeding	2000
Cropping	3500
Dairy	7000
Intensive	1200

Of the three types of mixed rearing and arable farms, the emphasis in the first is on the rearing of sheep and cattle, in the second on cattle, pigs and poultry, and in the third on the rearing and fattening of cattle. About half the intensive farms are specialist pig and poultry farms and the remainder horticultural holdings.

In Northern Ireland in 1964 the following types were recognised:

Type	*Number*
Mainly dairying	9900
Beef and sheep	5700
Mixed	6200
Pigs and poultry	1400
Cropping	900

These figures alone give some indication of the regional differences in farm type, but the reality is far more complex. The distribution of different types of farm in Scotland in 1952 has been shown in a publication by the Department of Agriculture and Fisheries, *Types of Farming in Scotland*, but the predominance of moorland helps to make the pattern of farming in Scotland somewhat simpler than that in England and Wales, where farm types have not yet been mapped in detail. Some idea of their complexity can be gained by examining a map, based on a sample of holdings, which appears in a publication by the Farm Economics Branch of the University of Cambridge, *Farming in the Eastern Counties*. The following account summarises the main features of the principal types and should be read in conjunction with the generalised *Types of Farming* map of Great Britain, published by the Association of Agriculture. Reference should also be made to a new mapping technique based upon computerised farm data, published in *Outlook on Agriculture*, 5, 1968.

Hill sheep farming

Most of the moorlands which cover one-third of Great Britain and also those in Ireland are grazed by sheep of hardy breeds. The flocks are mainly on hill sheep farms, which are unusual among farming types in that the breeding of sheep is often the only enterprise, chiefly because the land is too poor or the climate too harsh for any other kind of farming to be practised. On a hill sheep farm most of the land is rough grazing and, in general, the poorer the land the larger the size of the farm. There are usually several enclosed fields where fodder may be grown or where ewes may lamb, but winter feed is a major problem. In the uplands of England and Wales, the occupiers of such farms may have rights to pasture their sheep on common grazings, which often tend to be overstocked. Although large in area, hill sheep farms are often small as businesses and may employ only a single shepherd; both the carrying capacity and the income per acre are low. The main products from such farms are wool, store lambs sold in the autumn for fattening, and ewes sold for breeding on lowland farms. Only wool has a guaranteed price in the United Kingdom and prices of stock may fluctuate widely; the hill sheep subsidy, under which a payment may be made for each breeding ewe, was introduced to meet this problem.

Livestock rearing

The only other enterprise likely to be found on hill sheep farms is the breeding and rearing of hardy cattle, but at lower elevations, where the proportion of improved land is higher, cattle form a main enterprise, often with a subsidiary sheep flock. Such farms occupy a smaller area, but grow more fodder crops; their output per acre, however, is still low by comparison with lowland farms. Cattle may run on the rough grazings in summer, but are kept on the improved land in winter. Cows normally calve in spring and calves are often sold in the autumn, although they may be kept longer if adequate feed is available. Except where stock can be fattened, wool is again likely to be the only product which has a guaranteed price, and the hill cow subsidy was introduced to help such farmers on marginal land.

Dairy farming

Dairying is the most important enterprise on many farms in the lowlands, especially in western England and Wales, and in the southwest of both Ireland and Scotland. Such dairy farms are generally small in area, but dairying is a much more intensive enterprise than livestock rearing and output per acre is high. In Ireland there are few large urban markets and milk is mainly manufactured, but in Great Britain most milk goes to the towns for consumption as liquid milk and only the surplus is manufactured. Nevertheless, except in the case of cities like Aberdeen, which are remote from the main centres of population, proximity to markets is not a major determinant of the location of dairy farms, most of which are to be found in areas of moderate rainfall and mild climate where good grass can be grown and there is a long grazing season. Dairying may also be found combined with crop production and other enterprises in drier eastern areas, where there is an emphasis on more profitable winter milk production. In the 1930s and 1940s dairying became important on large farms on the chalk downs in counties such as Hampshire and Wiltshire. Since the mid-1950s, there has been a tendency for occupiers of dairy farms in eastern districts to give up dairying, since other enterprises have proved more profitable; dairy farms are thus becoming more localised in western counties of Great Britain.

Beef fattening

Beef cattle are rarely the main enterprise on farms in the British Isles and many of the farms on which beef cattle are reared and fattened in England and Wales are included in either the livestock category or, if livestock are not sufficiently important, in the class of mixed farms; however, there are farms in areas of good grazing, like the east Midlands, where beef cattle are the major enterprise. Such farms are much more important in Scotland, especially the northeast where there are many arable and feeding farms. In Ireland, where many beef fattening farms are found in the plains of Meath, the emphasis is on fattening on grass.

Mixed farming

In one sense, nearly all farming in the British Isles is mixed farming, in that there is more than one enterprise on most farms; but mixed farms in which no single enterprise predominates are to be found mainly in western England. The occupier of such a farm may keep both beef and dairy cattle, grow and sell some crops, and keep pigs and poultry; but such diversity is becoming increasingly uncommon as economic pressures encourage farmers to simplify their farming systems.

Crop farming

Farms on which crops account for at least half the labour requirements are found mainly in eastern England and Scotland, where much of the land suited to arable farming lies and the climate is more favourable to crops and less favourable to grass than in any other part of the British lowlands. Such farms are generally well above average size and there are strong economic forces encouraging further enlargement. Barley, wheat, potatoes and sugar beet are the principal crops sold, although field crops of vegetables, like peas for canning and quick freezing, are of increasing importance. Most crop farms have other enterprises, such as pig and poultry keeping and the fattening of cattle in winter, but there is a growing (though small) number of crop farms on which there are no livestock at all.

Horticulture

Horticultural crops were once grown very largely in market gardens on the margins of towns, but though specialist horticultural holdings are still found in such localities they are most numerous in areas like north and mid-Kent, the Vale of Evesham, mid-Bedfordshire and the Fenland. Most horticultural holdings produce both fruit and vegetables, and less than a third have more than half their business in either fruit or vegetables. Such holdings are generally small when measured by acreage, but represent a very intensive type of agricultural production. They are often highly specialised with subsidiary enterprises playing a minor part.

Pigs and poultry

Farms specialising in pigs and poultry are also small when measured by the land they occupy, but they, too, are very intensive and the degree of specialisation is often marked. This is particularly true of holdings specialising in poultry, for the last decade has seen the rise of large broiler units and poultry flocks; in lowland England, where most pig and poultry farms are found, nearly two-fifths of laying birds and more than two-thirds of broilers are on specialist poultry holdings. Pig and poultry holdings are widely scattered throughout the lowlands, but are most numerous in eastern and southeast England, reflecting the dependence of this type of farm on cereal feeding stuffs, and in Lancashire.

More detailed accounts of the distribution of different types of farming will be found in the chapters which follow on the agricultural regions of Scotland, England and Wales, and on Northern Ireland and the Irish Republic.

The agricultural output of the United Kingdom and the Irish Republic

We are now in a position to examine the relative values of the principal types of produce which are sold off British farms. These figures take no direct account of produce retained on the farm, most of which is used to feed livestock, nor of the large purchases of feeding stuffs.

The figures for the United Kingdom, which show the position in both 1925 and 1965, illustrate the importance of livestock and livestock products at both periods, despite the very considerable changes in agriculture which have taken place in the interval.

Agricultural output of the United Kingdom (value)

	1925 PER CENT		1965 PER CENT	
Cereals	10.5		12.6	
Potatoes	5.2		4.0	
Sugar beet	0.5		2.1	
Others	4.0		0.6	
Total farm crops		20.2		19.3
Livestock	36.2		34.8	
Milk and milk products	26.4		19.6	
Other livestock products	9.3		15.3	
Total livestock and livestock products		70.8		69.7
Fruit	3.5			
Vegetables	3.1			
Other horticultural products	2.4			
Total horticultural products		9.0		10.9

Among livestock products, the most important change has been the sharp increase in egg production. Cattle now account for 36 per cent of the livestock output, pigs for 35 per cent, poultry for 17 per cent and sheep for 13 per cent.

The contribution of livestock and livestock products is even more marked in the Irish Republic. The corresponding proportions for 1965 are:

Cereals	7.7	
Potatoes	3.0	
Sugar beet	3.0	
Other crops	3.8	
Total crops (including fruit and vegetables)		17.5
Livestock	52.3	
Milk and milk products	23.9	
Eggs	4.9	
Other livestock products	1.4	
Total livestock and livestock products		82.5

The high proportion contributed by livestock is in part a reflection of the suitability of the British Isles for grass and grazing livestock and, equally, of its unsuitability for crops. It is also related to the high standard of living of most of the inhabitants and to the advantages of proximity to markets enjoyed by those who produce perishable products like fresh milk. In interpreting these figures, account must also be taken of the fact that half the food consumed in the United Kingdom is imported, whereas the Irish Republic is a net exporter; a third of the coarse grain used to feed livestock is also imported into the United Kingdom, representing a quantity more than ten times as large as the imports of coarse grain into the Irish Republic.

Some agricultural industries

Sugar beet

One of the most remarkable features in the history of sugar is the fact that the British Isles remained for so long without a homegrown sugar industry, despite the existence of a large sugar beet industry in continental Europe, where the first sugar beet factory had been established as early as 1801. Efforts to establish factories in this country were made from 1909 onwards, factories were planned, and promises were extracted from farmers to grow the necessary beet. But the competition of bounty-fed cheap continental sugar in the open British market rendered all these schemes abortive. It is interesting to note, however, that the Cantley factory was built in 1912 before the First World War, very largely with Dutch capital, and thus the beginning of the modern industry in this country was mainly due to Dutch initiative. It was, of course, during the First World War that the United Kingdom felt the severe effects of not having a home sugar industry, for the shipping necessary to bring supplies of sugar to the British Isles could ill be spared. The normal imports of sugar had approached 2 million long tons, so that supplies had to be carefully rationed in wartime. In March 1917 the Treasury sanctioned an advance of £125 000 to the British Sugar Beet

Society as a loan for the development of the Kelham estate in Nottinghamshire, but for various reasons the factory was not ready to operate until March 1921. In the meantime, the Cantley factory, which had been disused during the war, was reopened in 1920, and took beet which had been grown for the then uncompleted Kelham factory. At that time there was an import duty on sugar and great assistance was given to the home industry in March 1922 by the remission of the excise duty; but it was recognised that high import duties could not be maintained indefinitely. The passing of the British Sugar Subsidy Act, in March 1925, marked the beginning of a long and complicated story of direct state aid to the home sugar industry.

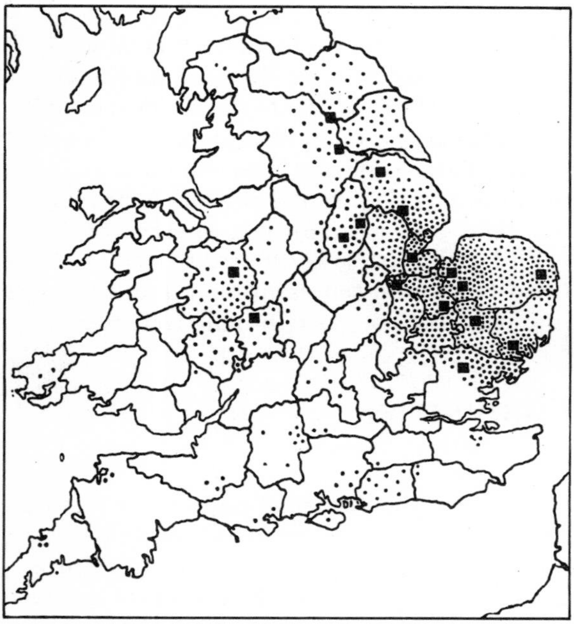

FIG. 99. Sugar beet in England and Wales

Each dot represents 500 acres of sugar beet in 1951–52. Each square represents a beet sugar factory.

By 1927–28 seventeen factories in England had been established and by 1930–31 the industry had taken on almost the pattern it still has nearly forty years later. Since 1942 the area under sugar beet has changed little and now stands at some 182 000 hectares (450 000 acres). There is one factory in Scotland at Cupar in Fife; two factories are located in the west Midlands, at Kidderminster and Allscott (Shropshire). The remaining fifteen, at Bardney, Brigg, Bury St Edmunds, Cantley, Colwick, Ely, Felstead, Ipswich, Kelham, King's Lynn, Peterborough, Poppleton, Spalding and Wissington, are all in eastern England in an area stretching from Yorkshire to Essex (Fig. 99).

By 1931 the average yield of sugar beet was 17 800 kilograms per hectare (7.1 tons per acre) and the sugar content 17.3 per cent. The yield of beet has climbed steadily from 23 800 kilograms per hectare (9.4 tons per acre) in 1938–48 to 38 350 kilograms per hectare (14.4 tons per acre) in 1959–62 and the sugar content has also increased. The production of sugar thus averaged over 3765 kilograms per hectare (1.5 tons per acre) and has been maintained at 600–700 000 long tons (1951–60) or more than a quarter of British consumption.

The conditions necessary for the cultivation of sugar beet agree in general with those required for other root crops. It requires a well-drained fertile loamy soil, whilst a certain proportion of lime in the soil is essential. It is an annual plant raised from seed and sown in the spring. The whitish parsnip-like roots are ready for digging towards the autumn; they are washed and topped and are then ready for delivery to the factory, where the sugar is extracted. The pulp or residue from the beet makes excellent manure applied either direct or as dung from the cattle fed on it, and there is a steadily increasing demand in this country for wet pulp mixed with molasses, for it is both a palatable and a valuable cattle food. Two difficulties in the establishment or maintenance of the sugar beet industry must be mentioned. One is the need for close cooperation between the factories and the farmers, for the supply of sugar beet must be assured from year to year. The second difficulty is that sugar beet is a heavy, bulky commodity and transport costs are heavy, so that little beet is grown more than forty miles from a factory. At the same time, beet must be grown in rotation with other crops, and the amount of land which can be sown to beet immediately around the factory, however large it may be, is therefore strictly limited. These factors tend to restrict the size of the factories which are possible in the British Isles.

A similarly protected sugar beet industry has grown up in the Irish Republic, where there are factories at Carlow, Mallow, Thurles and Tuam.

The canning industry

One of the spectacular developments in British agricultural industries in the years between the wars was the rise of the canning industry. There is no official return of output, but the following table gives an estimate of the output of canned fruit and vegetables in the 1930s when the great rise occurred. In seven years the output increased tenfold, from under 10 million cans in 1925 to over 100 million cans in 1932. Towards the close of 1932 there were nearly sixty factories (ten of which had come into production during that year) employing mass production automatic machinery.

The early rise of output of British canned fruit and vegetables (*cans*)

1913	negligible	1929	16 340 000
1924 } 1925 }	very small	1930	34 200 000
		1931	83 000 000
1926	7 000 000	1932	100 000 000
1927	7 840 000	1934	120 000 000 from 76 factories
1928	7 930 000		

In the past one of the great difficulties faced by the British farmer growing fruit and vegetables for market has been the shortness of the season. Too often a good season means a good season for everybody, a glut of fruit and vegetables and very low prices. Canning provides a way of dealing with such a glut; provided the area of production is near the cannery, the fruit can be picked when the weather is suitable and the operation of canning completed within twenty-four hours. A danger is that sufficient care will not be taken in the grading of the fruit for maintenance of quality is essential for the prosperity of the industry. Similarly, it is undesirable for fruit to be brought from a distance and to suffer the disadvantages of carriage before being canned. Consequently the major canning factories in Great Britain are near the main areas of production, especially East Anglia. The shortness of the season also affects the economic working of the canning industry. Broadly speaking, fruit and vegetables are available for canning in this climate only for about four months, from June to September. To run a factory and to secure an adequate labour supply for four months out of the twelve is difficult. If a canning factory can be built near the seaboard, for example, at Ipswich, it may be possible to combine the canning of fish with fruit and vegetable canning, so as to occupy the machinery for the greater part of the year.

The canning industry suffered a severe setback during the Second World War, partly because of the scarcity of tinplate. Thus, 32 000 metric tons of fruit were canned in 1938, but an average of only 4000 metric tons in 1939–1943. Production recovered quickly after the war and reached 94 000 metric tons in 1955.

The quick freezing of vegetables (especially peas), fruit and fish began in earnest about 1947. The quantity of frozen vegetables increased rapidly from 2882 metric tons in that year to 68 000 in 1961, as did the tonnage of fish, which reached 56 000 metric tons in 1961. There was only a small increase in frozen fruit which rose from 1000 to 1500 metric tons. There are now over twenty major establishments in the growing areas.

There are also canneries in the Irish Republic, especially in Cork and Dublin; quick freezing plants have been erected by the Irish Sugar Company.

The brewing industry

Since a large quantity of homegrown barley and homegrown hops are used in beer making, brewing may be classed as an agricultural industry. In the manufacture of beer, the barley is first malted, then ground into coarse meal and mixed with warm water. After this liquid, or wort, is strained off, the remains of the barley are dried and sold to farmers as a valuable cattle food. From about 560 kilograms (11 cwt) of barley about 150 kilograms (3 cwt) are thus returned to the farmer for use in feeding his cattle, and in many ways this cattle cake is a better feed than the original barley itself. The wort is then boiled with hops and fermented.

The brewing of beer used to be carried out mainly in small farmhouses, but it has become more and more concentrated into large breweries; even the smaller breweries are disappearing. One reason is the precision needed at each stage in the complex operation. For example, the quality of the water used in the malting process is very important. The best results are obtained from water which possesses a considerable permanent hardness due to the presence in solution of calcium sulphate. The well water from the Keuper Marls at Burton-on-Trent is of this character and is therefore particularly suitable; the brewing industry of that town is no doubt largely a result of this supply. Manchester, Warrington, Chester, Liverpool and Tadcaster are other brewing centres situated on the Trias, but in some cases the salt is added artificially to the water (the process commonly known as 'burtonising').

The annual consumption of beer in the United Kingdom (1951–62) is between 24 and 30 million barrels, a barrel containing 145.5 litres (32 gallons or 256 pints); this is about 68 to 85 litres (120 to 150 pints) per head of population per year. Consumption reached its highest level in 1945 (33 million barrels), but later dropped steadily, only to rise again to 27.9 million in 1962.

Distilling

There are three stages in the manufacture of whisky: malting and mashing the barley, or the preparation of the wort, as in the manufacture of beer; the fermentation of the wort to produce the wash, and the separation of the spirit from the wash by means of distillation. For Scotch whisky, barley is practically the only material used. In Irish whiskey, barley, oats, wheat, and rye are generally mixed.

Despite the decrease in consumption which is due to high excise duties, changes in popular taste and the demands of the export trade, especially to America, whisky may still be regarded as the native drink of Scotland and Ireland, as beer is of England. In 1913–14 nearly 123 million litres (27 million proof gallons) were consumed in the British Isles (81.3 million litres (17.9 million gallons) in England and Wales, 28.1 million litres (6.2 million gallons) in Scotland and 10.4 million litres (2.3 million gallons) in

Ireland) representing 2.27 litres (0.5 proof gallon) per head of population. By 1926–27 the total had fallen to less than 54.5 million litres (12 million gallons) (38 million litres (8.4 million gallons) in England and Wales; 14 million litres (3.1 million gallons) in Scotland), representing only about one litre (0.24 proof gallon) per head of population. In the decade 1941–50 total consumption of all spirits (i.e. whisky, gin, rum and brandy) in the United Kingdom dropped to between 36 and 46 million litres (about 8 and 10 million gallons). As home consumption has fallen, so exports have increased, both to North America and to continental Europe; indeed, markets are worldwide.

The food supply of the United Kingdom

The introduction of subsidies and the changing value of money render invalid comparisons between present and past expenditure on food, whether by the individual or the nation, but a comparison of quantities per head of population is both interesting and instructive.

The following table shows some striking changes since the early part of the present century. There is no doubt that the British people are now better fed than ever before, although supplies of meat, bacon, butter, eggs and fruit were greatly curtailed during the Second World War. The war left a surprising legacy in the continued high consumption of potatoes, although this in part represents a change of habit in a rising consumption of manufactured potatoes, such as potato crisps. Compared with sixty years ago, there is less reliance on bread and the amount of butcher's meat is lower, although this figure conceals considerable changes in the pattern of meat consumption; for whereas 16 per cent of home-killed meat was pork before the Second World War, the proportion is now 29 per cent. One of the most striking changes is the increase in consumption of poultry meat which is now more than three times as large as in the 1930s, a consequence of the spread of broiler production and the relative cheapness of poultry compared with other kinds of meat.

As has already been noted, despite an increase in population, the United Kingdom is now less dependent on imported food than before the Second World War. Forty-seven per cent of wheat is now home grown, compared with 23 per cent; 70 per cent of carcase meat is home produced, compared with 51 per cent; 98 per cent of shell eggs compared with 71 per cent, and 43 per cent of cheese compared with 24 per cent. But the dependence on imports of oils and fats (89 per cent imported) and butter (92 per cent imported) is greater and most of the bacon consumed is still imported.

The figures for 1907 are calculated from the *Agricultural Output and the Food Supplies of Great Britain, HMSO*; those for liquid milk and eggs are estimates from numbers of gallons and eggs respectively. The remaining figures are taken from the *Annual Abstract of Statistics* and are not strictly comparable; the figures given for bacon and ham include all pig-meat and lard.

Estimated food supplies in the United Kingdom in pounds and kilograms per head per annum

COMMODITY		1907	1934–38 AVERAGE	1946	1965
Flour	lb	208.0	194.5	221.2	155.2
	kg	94.3	88.3	100.3	70.4
Sugar	lb	79.9	100.6	79.5	110.4
	kg	36.2	45.5	36.1	50.0
Fresh and frozen meat	lb	102.0	92.4	70.8	92.6
	kg	46.2	41.9	32.0	42.0
Bacon and ham	lb	42.8	26.4	15.1	25.7
	kg	19.4	12.0	6.8	11.6
Poultry	lb	—	5.1	4.0	16.5
	kg	—	2.3	1.8	7.5
Fish	lb	43.5	21.8	26.3	17.8
	kg	19.7	9.8	11.9	8.1
Liquid milk	lb	195.0	217.1	309.4	325.2
	kg	88.5	98.4	140.3	147.5
Cheese	lb	8.8	8.8	10.0	10.1
	kg	4.0	4.0	4.5	4.5
Eggs—shell	lb	14.2	25.9	18.0	32.0
	kg	6.4	11.7	8.1	14.5
Butter	lb	15.9	24.7	11.0	19.5
	kg	7.2	14.0	4.9	8.8
Margarine	lb	4.9	8.7	15.1	12.0
	kg	2.2	3.9	6.8	5.4
Dried and fresh fruit	lb	74.1	86.5	60.0	79.1
	kg	33.6	39.2	27.2	35.9
Canned and bottled fruit	lb	—	10.3	2.4	18.7
	kg	—	4.6	1.1	8.4
Potatoes	lb	188.8	190.0	281.2	223.2
	kg	85.6	86.1	127.5	101.2
Fresh vegetables	lb	—	115.3	130.7	115.2
	kg	—	52.3	59.3	52.2

Before the sources from which the United Kingdom derives her food are considered, it is necessary to have at least a generalised picture of the changing pattern of world trade.

Before the First World War many of the 'newer' countries were producing a surplus of food (including animal feeding stuffs) and raw materials which they were anxious to exchange for British manufactured foods and were sometimes even willing to 'dump' or sell below cost. The United

Kingdom had many investments overseas and payment of interest came largely in the form of foodstuffs, as did payment for services rendered, such as banking, insurance, shipping and technical services. Tariff barriers were comparatively few and the flow of world trade was unhindered. British supplies of food could have come from many areas: they tended to come from those countries with which the United Kingdom had the closest ties.

The submarine menace of the First World War, shortage of shipping and the spectre of starvation turned attention, if only temporarily, to increasing home supplies of food, but when that war was over, home production became an even smaller proportion of total consumption than before. There was, however, a deliberate attempt to stimulate trade within the British Commonwealth. Empire Free Trade became a slogan, the Empire Marketing Board was set up and various trade agreements involving imperial preference were negotiated. The increase of food imports from Commonwealth countries was only a little greater than the increase from foreign countries.

The advent of the Second World War brought many changes. There was the tremendous drive to increase food production at home while the Ministry of Food undertook the planning of the nation's diet. The Government purchased in bulk both the home production and overseas supplies and then rationed the total amongst the civilian and service populations. Private wholesale trading in food practically disappeared. When the war was over, relaxation of controls and the return to private trading took place very slowly. The international situation was completely changed as far as the United Kingdom was concerned. There was no longer any automatic flow of food into the country as interest on overseas investments, for the investments had for the most part been sold or otherwise liquidated to pay for the war. The world was divided into blocs: the Soviet bloc behind the Iron Curtain which played little part in foreign trade; the dollar countries; and the sterling area (the Commonwealth and certain other countries linked with the £ sterling—see Fig. 279). There was comparatively free trading between members of the sterling area, but shortage of dollars resulted in stringent restrictions on food imports from the United States and, despite membership of the Commonweath, from Canada. Whereas, therefore, comparisons between the sources of supply of food for the United Kingdom before and after the First World War indicate changes in the world's supply position, such comparisons of before and after the Second World War reflect the influence of manmade barriers.

The change in origin of wheat and wheat flour supplies is particularly noteworthy. Before the First World War huge quantities came from the United States, but later Canada became easily the chief source, followed by the United States, Argentina and Australia, these four countries providing on average over 90 per cent of the total. The pre-1914 supplies from Russia have, of course, almost disappeared. Of other grains imported, maize was very important in the interwar years as food for livestock, and

1.77 million metric tons (1.75 million long tons) were imported annually, five-sevenths coming from Argentina, one-seventh from South Africa, and the remainder from Romania and the United States; 60 per cent now comes from the United States. The United Kingdom imported annually 1.52 million metric tons (about 1.5 million long tons) of meat, of which over 1.2 million was chilled beef from Argentina; it is noteworthy that imports exceeded the home supply, only about 43 per cent of the beef consumed being produced in the United Kingdom in the interwar years. Imports now account for a quarter of supplies and Argentina is still the chief supplier. 250 million kilograms (5 million cwt), mainly of mutton and lamb, came from New Zealand and Australia, while the 250 million kilograms (5 million cwt) of meat from Denmark was mainly bacon; these countries remain the chief suppliers. Other supplies in smaller quantity came from the United States, Uruguay, the Netherlands and Canada, while a notable feature was the import of bacon from Poland. The increased home consumption of meat in the exporting countries is at least one reason for the shortage of world supplies of meat.

Nearly all eggs used in this country are now home produced, but imports reached 3000 million in the interwar years, half this huge quantity coming from Denmark and the Netherlands, rather less than a fifth from the Irish Republic and a tenth each from Poland and Belgium. Changes in world communications have been responsible for quantities of poultry coming from Australia and South Africa, whereas formerly the only country sending poultry to Britain was the Irish Republic; imports are now only a small proportion of consumption and come mainly from Denmark. In dairy produce there is practically no import of fresh milk, but considerable quantities of condensed milk are imported. Forty per cent of the butter imports came in the interwar years from the Empire, from New Zealand, Australia and Ireland, Denmark sent a third, and Argentina was another important source; New Zealand, Denmark and Australia are now the principal suppliers. New Zealand, easily first, and Canada provided 60 per cent of imports of cheese, the other countries being the Netherlands and Italy. The details for vegetables and fresh fruit deserve a chapter to themselves, because they illustrate in a remarkable way what can be done with improved methods of transport, as with the specially constructed ships with refrigerating machinery, to extend the markets for a commodity. Nevertheless, homegrown vegetables can compete satisfactorily in terms of quality with anything imported which is grown under similar climatic conditions.

British agriculture is now more efficient and productive than before the Second World War, but about a quarter of the temperate products which could be homegrown are still imported. There is considerable controversy about the proportion that should be produced in the United Kingdom, but there is little doubt that more could be, provided there were adequate incentives to farmers; but the British would lose the cheap food supplies they have enjoyed for over a century.

Strictly comparable figures are not available for the Irish Republic, but the pattern of food consumption is rather different. Ireland is, of course, a net exporter of food, importing only those products like hard wheat and tropical produce which cannot be homegrown. In 1965, only 28.8 kilograms (63.6 lb) of sugar were consumed per head, compared with 50 kilograms (110.4 lb) in the United Kingdom; consumption of meat was about the same, but that of fresh milk nearly 50 per cent higher, at 211 litres (46.4 gallons) per head, and of butter over 70 per cent higher. Less than half as much cheese (1.8 kilograms (3.9 lb)) was eaten in the Republic of Ireland, but consumption of potatoes (at 148 kilograms (326 lb)) was nearly 50 per cent larger. These differences reflect both the nature of Irish domestic production and the differences in the standard of living.

11
The agricultural regions of Scotland

In his *Agricultural Atlas of Scotland*, H. J. Wood divided Scotland into a number of simple agricultural regions. Although the work of the Land Utilisation Survey enabled the regions to be defined more exactly, and although the production campaign of the years 1939 to 1945 wrought certain changes which have persisted, his regions were based on environmental factors which remain. It does not, therefore, seem necessary to change the regional division which has been used in the earlier editions of this book, though the map (Fig. 100) should be compared carefully with the

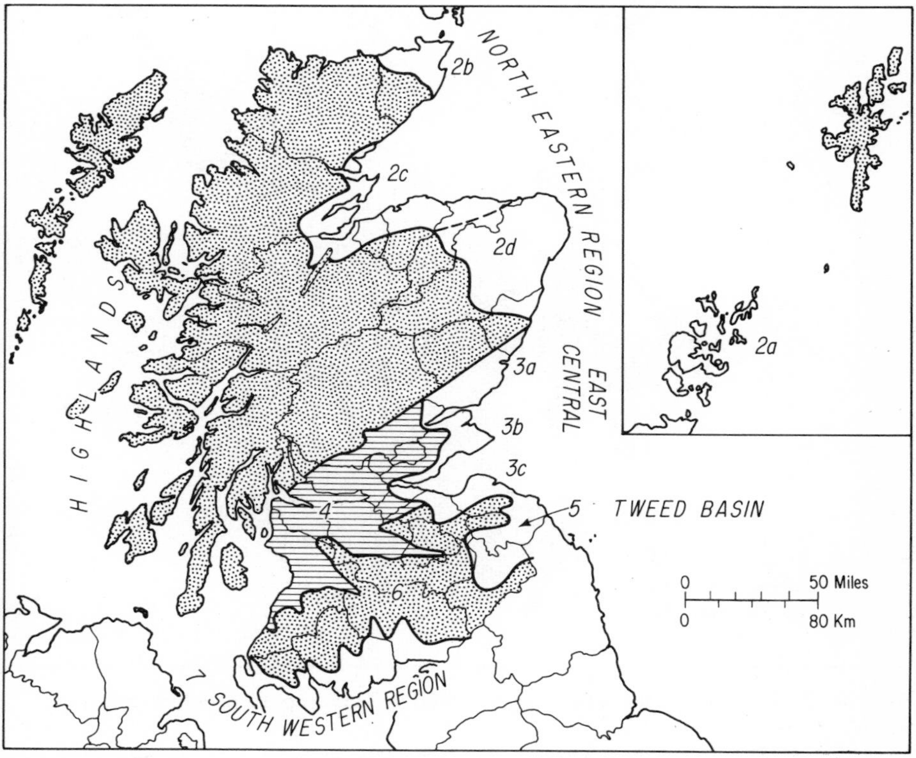

FIG. 100. The Agricultural Regions of Scotland (after H. J. Wood).

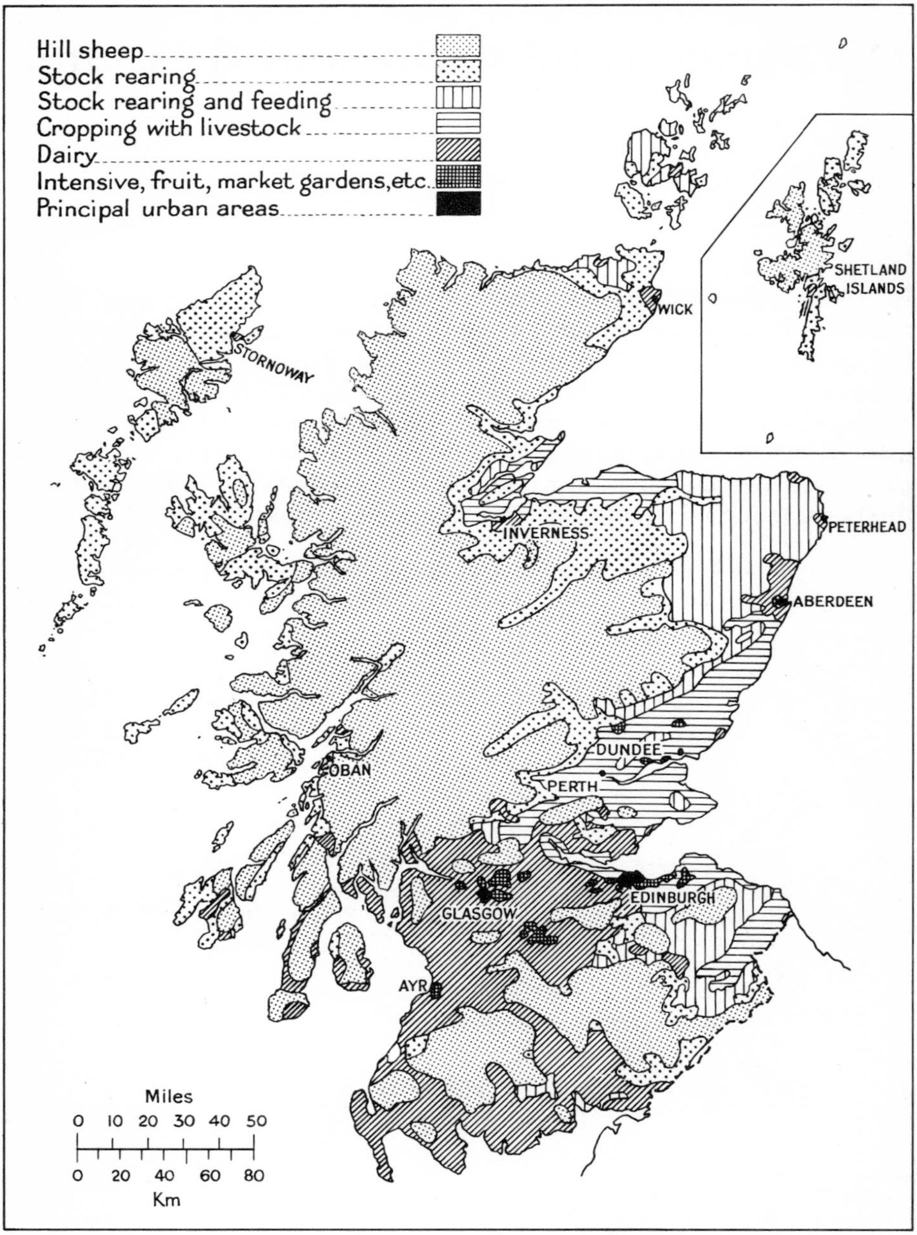

FIG. 101. Predominant types of farming in Scotland. This map refers only to full-time farms

(Modified from *Types of Farming in Scotland*, 1952, by permission of the Controller of H.M. Stationery Office.)

map of predominant types of farming prepared by the Department of Agriculture for Scotland (Fig. 101), which is itself a post-Second World War revision of the map based on statistics for 1938, and published at a scale of 1 : 625 000 in the National Planning Series.

For Scotland as a whole, it is remarkable that in the interwar years, 98.7 per cent of the total area occupied by crops and grass was represented by permanent grass, rotation grass, oats, barley, wheat, turnips and potatoes; the postwar position is very much the same. The specialist crops, which are sometimes of great importance in England, play a smaller part in Scotland and the relative distribution of these major crops thus gives a key to the farming economy of the various regions.

The Highlands and Western Isles

The Highlands of Scotland form a well-marked region from both the physical and the agricultural points of view. It is the most extensive region in Scotland and includes all the islands, with the exception of the Orkneys. The southeastern boundary approximately follows the line of the Highland boundary fault; only here and there are valleys which belong rather to the fringing corridor of lowland. To the east the boundary with the north-eastern agricultural region is not a sharp one, Highland conditions disappearing gradually as one passes eastwards. Although there are variations within this huge area, it is generally true to say that there are central cores of highland virtually uninhabited by man and his domestic animals. These are the deer forests, though almost devoid of trees, which in 1938 occupied about 1.3 million hectares (3.3 million acres), nearly all in the Highlands, or 17 per cent of all Scotland. In that year only 3 per cent of the hill sheep were inside the deer forests, the bulk being found in hill sheep farms which occupied much of the remainder of the Highlands. These farms are large and generally have over 95 per cent of their area in rough grazings; but most have a small acreage under such feed crops as rape. Sheep are mainly Scottish Blackface and the ewes are eligible for Hill Sheep Subsidy. On the lower and rather better margins, the proportion of rough grazing declines and hill sheep-farming gives place to cattle-rearing. On the west coast and in the islands, crofting prevails. Crofters enjoy a special status as tenants, but most have other occupations as well; for crofts are generally too small to provide a living, even with access to common grazings. Formerly, many crofters combined fishing and farming, but few do so now; providing 'bed-and-breakfast' for summer tourists is less arduous and much more lucrative.

The hard, resistant old rocks, from which the great ice sheets swept much of the previously accumulated soil, have combined with climate to create conditions where only a few small areas are suitable for agricultural settlement. High rainfall, humid conditions, cool moist summers and a lack of sunshine result in an abundance of surface water and wide areas of moor and bog. Drainage is difficult and even where it has been carried out, the wide extent of acid peat soils militates against cultivation. Limestone is rarely available locally to ameliorate the acidity. Towards the east conditions become slightly more favourable as the rainfall diminishes. But population densities are low and rural depopulation has long been the rule, as people gravitate towards more favoured agricultural lowlands or to urban centres, and to foreign countries where better opportunities await them. The drier or wider glens, especially those of the Tay system towards the east, and tracts along the western coastal fringe are the most suitable for settlement; permanent grass and small acreages of oats, turnips, potatoes and barley are found here. The Highlands remain a problem area. Recent developments include afforestation (see above, p. 144) and hydroelectric power (see below, p. 346). No longer are there wealthy tenants able to pay large sums for the rent of deer forests and hunting lodges, though shooting, especially on the drier grouse moors, is still popular and an important source of revenue. Hill sheep farms and cattle-rearing supply healthy stock to lowland farms, for fattening and breeding, and the future may in part depend on the improvement of hill grazings by the use of Stapledon's methods and the development of large-scale ranching.

The northeastern region

This is a coastal region of varying width which can be divided into four parts:

The Orkney Islands;
The northeastern part of Caithness;
The Moray Firth lowlands;
The Buchan Plateau or the 'shoulder' of Aberdeenshire and Banffshire.

Most of the three northern tracts are underlain by Old Red Sandstone, and most of Aberdeenshire by granitic and metamorphic rocks, but there is generally a covering of drift which gives rise to moderately acid soils. The dominant crops are rotation grass, oats, turnips and, increasingly, barley. The summers are too cool for the ripening of wheat, but in the favoured areas, particularly around the Moray Firth and along the coastal strip from the Moray Firth to the shoulder of Aberdeenshire, barley is of considerable importance. There is extensive grazing for sheep and cattle on the fringes of the moors, but little permanent grass; where the land is improved it is ploughed and was once worked on a six-year rotation of oats, turnips, oats, grass, grass, grass. In this area, as in other parts of Great Britain, barley is now replacing oats as the leading cereal, at least on the lower lands. The economic development of this region owes much to the introduction of turnips, valuable both for fodder and as a cleaning crop. As shown on Fig. 101, each of the main towns (Thurso, Wick, Inverness, Peterhead and Aberdeen) has given rise to a small dairying area to supply local needs, but the larger coastal towns, with their interest in fishing, are rather apart from the main agricultural belt as a whole. Over most of the remainder, stock rearing and feeding predominate, especially of beef animals of the Aberdeen-Angus breed, and farms are small. On the richer Moray Firth Lowlands the feeding is based on arable cropping. The areas as a whole are too remote for dairying to have developed on any scale and in recognition of this two separate Milk Marketing Boards were created, the North of Scotland and the Aberdeen and District. The Buchan plateau, with much of inland Banff and Aberdeen, is very extensively forested.

The east-central region

This is the drier part of the Central Lowlands of Scotland. It is favoured by varied and often fertile soils, many of them derived from material of glacial origin, and by good climatic conditions, with drier sunnier summers than are usual farther north and an annual rainfall which is generally less than 760 millimetres (30 in) and sometimes less than 635 millimetres (25 in). Arable farming is the rule and farms are large. Commonly a six-year rotation is practised, of oats, potatoes, wheat, turnips, barley, grass; but in recent years barley has become a much more important crop. Sugar beet, vegetables and small fruit provide other cash crops. However, much of the produce of the arable land is devoted to the fattening of sheep and cattle.

The region is divided into three parts by the Firths of Tay and Forth:

(*a*) The Angus Region lies mainly in the county of that name, southern Kincardine and eastern Perth. It includes part of Strathmore and the coastal belt, and the Carse of Gowrie is noted for its small fruit, especially raspberries.

(*b*) The eastern half of Fife is an undulating lowland, where sugar beet, processed in the factory at Cupar, is a distinctive crop.

(*c*) The northern strip of West Lothian and Midlothian and the greater part of East Lothian, limited roughly to the south by the 150 metre (500 ft) contour, has long been famed as one of the most favoured agricultural regions of Scotland. Edinburgh and the other towns of the area have long exercised an influence, and this has resulted in the increased importance of market gardening and other forms of intensive cultivation.

The west-central region

This region occupies the larger part of the Central Lowlands and has a higher rainfall, which may exceed 1500 millimetres (60 in) per annum in the west. The volcanic hills, with their rough sheep pastures, may be regarded as outliers of the Highlands from the agricultural point of view. The summers are cooler and wetter and have less sunshine than the eastern region, and thus the proportion of grass is high. Cereals other than oats are uncommon, but barley is increasing in importance; turnips play a smaller part in farming economy here than they do in the east of Scotland, whilst potato production on a large scale is limited to certain localities. This is pre-eminently a dairying area, the home of the famous Ayrshire cattle, but the Carse of Stirling is noted for hay production, and the raised beaches along the coast of Ayrshire, with their sandy soils and mild spring weather, have given rise to a specialised early potato industry centred on the town of Girvan. The demand from the towns, especially greater Glasgow, obviously exercised an influence here, as it does noticeably on the main centres of the dairy industry. The old-established orchard area of Lanark is the only area in Scotland where top fruit is grown on any scale; it lies in the Clyde Valley and is protected from the winds which sweep over the uplands. The Clyde Valley also includes the largest concentration of glasshouses in Scotland.

The Tweed Basin

The Tweed Basin is a mainly arable region of large farms; it is enclosed on three sides by moorland and extends into Northumberland. Permanent grass and rotation grass are of almost equal importance, barley is the leading cereal, and turnips (winter food for sheep) are still an important crop in a region where upland and lowland are integrally linked in a pastoral farming regime. Towards the mouth of the Tweed, the Merse of Berwick is distinctive in that it has a considerable acreage under wheat. Potatoes and other cash crops are unimportant. Cattle are numerous in the lower-lying districts of mixed farming, but the Tweed valley is unique in the whole of Scotland for the number of sheep it carries. In the upper basin, in Tweeddale, Ettrickdale, Teviotdale and Lauderdale, the density of sheep population is very high and large sheep farms are characteristic. The poorer sheep pastures support the Scottish Blackface, the better pastures at lower levels the Cheviots, whilst an improvement of breeds on lowland farms has been carried out by crossing ewes of these breeds with Border Leicester rams to produce the Greyface and the Scottish Halfbred respectively. An account of the woollen industry is given in Chapter 19.

The Southern Upland region

The greater part of this region is occupied by moorland, but the Southern Uplands differ from the Highlands in their lower elevation, the gentler relief of the hills and the better grazing which they afford, and hence in the greater density of the sheep population. In the postwar period there has been extensive afforestation which has reduced the area under rough grazing, especially in the west. Settlements are mainly located in the valleys, and on the river terraces of these valleys there are fields, usually of permanent grass, sometimes of sown grass and less frequently of oats and turnips. Most of the larger valleys afford important routeways and the improved access which results led to the extension of dairying from the lowlands on either side; in the west, rearing hill sheep may also be combined with the keeping of young dairy stock.

The southwestern region

This lowland region borders the Southern Uplands from the head of Solway Firth in the east to Wigtownshire in the west. In the east are the dales which dissect the southern Uplands and in the centre is the coastal tract or the Rhinns of Galloway. In common with other parts of western Scotland the limit of cultivation is quite low, reaching 60 metres (200 feet) in Wigtownshire, but rising eastwards. The region has a relatively heavy rainfall of up to 1270 millimetres (50 in) and cloudiness is a characteristic feature. Wheat is little grown under such climatic conditions; oats were the principal crop, but have been giving way to barley in recent years. The greater part of the land is under permanent or sown grass. The whole region has large numbers of cattle, especially dairy cattle, usually Ayrshires; the native Black Galloway cattle are also characteristic. The mild climate allows a longer period of grass growth than elsewhere in Scotland. The manufacture of butter and cheese is far less important than formerly and quantities of milk are now sent to the towns of central Scotland; before the creation of the Scottish Milk Marketing Board, this area also supplied milk to Newcastle and other areas in England. There is a tendency, not so marked as in Ayrshire, to lay down under grass for as much as ten or even more years land which has been ploughed, and then to plough it for two or three years before laying it down again to grass. It is thus difficult to decide whether this is strictly rotation or permanent grass. Indeed, this is true of Scotland as a whole and in 1959 the distinction between permanent and rotation grass was abandoned in official statistics.

12
The agricultural regions of England and Wales

It would be hard to find elsewhere in the world an area of comparable size to the British Isles with such a variety of agricultural conditions. Wide variation in types of soil consequent upon complicated geological structure

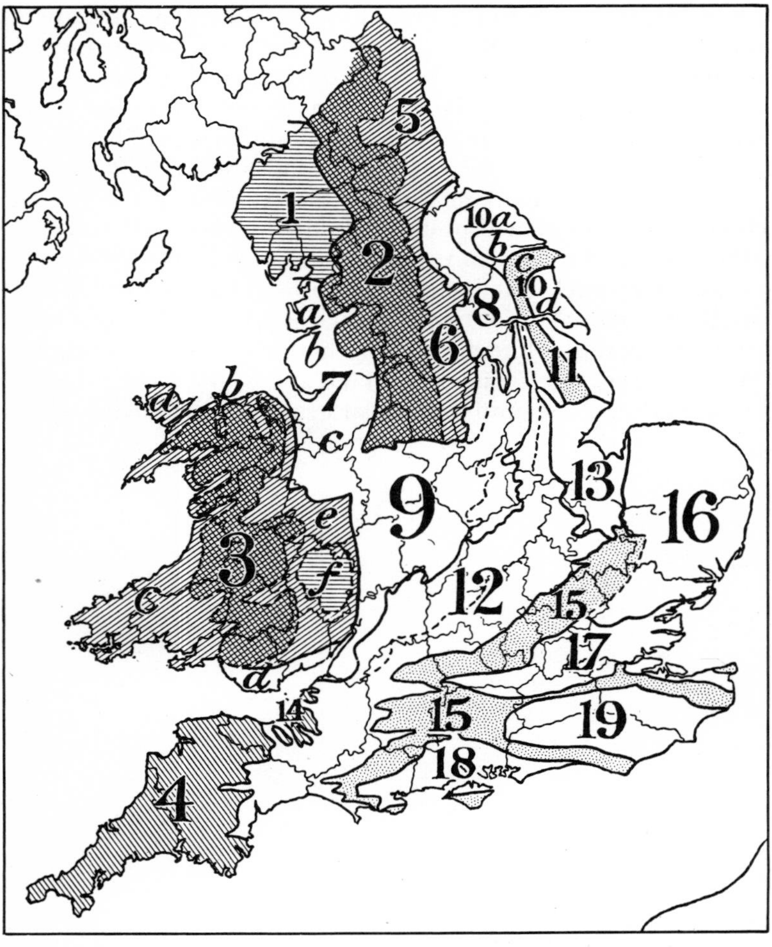

FIG. 102. The agricultural regions of England and Wales

and physiographic history, considerable variation in relief, and by no means unimportant differences in climate between west and east and south and north, all contribute. It may even be foolish to talk of the economic condition of British farming or of the British farmer, or to put forward sweeping proposals for the amelioration of present conditions without due regard for local, even parochial, conditions. Because of the immense importance of this aspect of British agriculture, an attempt is made in this

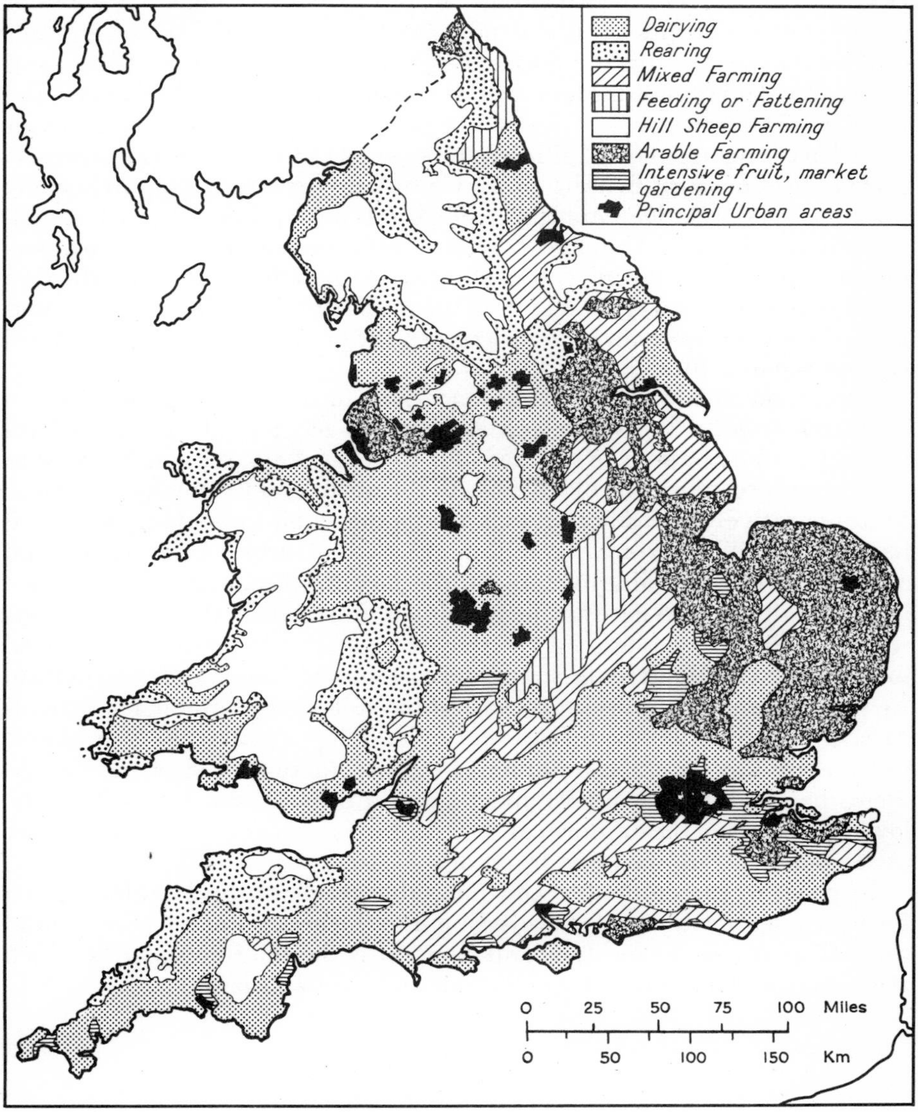

Fig. 103. Predominant types of farming in England and Wales

chapter to divide England and Wales into broad agricultural regions, and in some areas to suggest a tentative division into subregions. These agricultural regions show little or no relationship to administrative divisions, and statistics arranged on a county basis can be very misleading in forming comparisons. Even the unpublished parish statistics are frequently insufficient in detail, for a large proportion of English parishes owe their peculiar form, as in the long narrow parishes stretching from the North Downs to the heart of the Weald, to the necessity of sharing fairly between neighbouring parishes good and poor land, upland and lowland pasture suitable for sheep and cattle respectively, friable loamy land for tillage and heavy clay land unsuitable for crops. It was one of the main objectives of the Land Utilisation Survey of Britain to provide for the first time an exact record of the distribution of different types of use, by recording the use made of every field in Great Britain. In the County Reports an attempt was made to evaluate the relative importance of various physical factors, such as soil, elevation, aspect and drainage, as well as certain economic factors, in determining the type of farming in each area. Although the food production campaign of the 1939–45 war altered the proportion of arable and grass and pushed back the moorland fringe in places, the broad pattern of agricultural regions remains little changed.

The broad division into a Highland Zone in the north and west and a Lowland Zone in the south and east, which has already been used repeatedly, affords also a broad basis for dividing England and Wales into agricultural regions. The older rocks to the north and west, which give rise to comparatively poor siliceous soils, are on the whole upland regions which have a rainfall exceeding 760 millimetres (30 in) nearly everywhere. Soil and climate thus combine to render arable farming of secondary importance in nearly all areas. Where arable farming is undertaken, the range of crops which can be grown is limited and they serve mainly to provide winter feed for livestock. The land to the south and east, on the other hand, is underlain by younger and less resistant rocks and has soils more suitable for agriculture. Over the Midlands and eastern England the rainfall tends to be almost everywhere less than 760 millimetres (30 in), though most of the escarpments have a higher rainfall; and there is a broad distinction within the lowlands between the damper cattle-farming tracts of the west and the drier predominantly crop-farming tracts of the east.

In general, the cultivable and habitable tracts of the Highland Zone form tongues of varying size projecting into the great expanse of moorland and hill pastures: in the Lowland Zone, it is the infertile uplands which tend to form islands in a sea of cultivable and habitable land.

REGIONS OF THE HIGHLAND ZONE

The Lake District or Cumbria

This region, consisting of a central knot of mountainous country with a very heavy rainfall and a surrounding fringe of lowlands (broken only in the southeast), exhibits considerable differences from an agricultural point of view; but because of the movement of animals (particularly sheep) from one part to another according to season, there is a certain essential unity in the whole region. Broadly it consists of four parts:

The Central Mass comprises rough hill pastures supporting fell sheep and valleys where dairy cattle graze. The uplands are the home of the Herdwick sheep and large tracts are common land. This area forms most of the Lake District National Park and is increasingly under heavy pressure for outdoor recreation.

The Eden Valley, on the lee side of the mountains, has a well-drained red soil and a lower rainfall which is as low as 760 millimetres (30 in) in places. As a result, there is a considerable proportion of arable land, but, owing to the northern situation, no wheat is grown, the leading crops being rotation grasses, turnips and swedes (grown for the fattening of sheep and cattle), oats and barley.

The Solway Plain has rather similar conditions and large numbers of fell sheep are fed in the winter months when the fell pastures are snow covered.

The southwestern and southern fringes consist of undulating land more exposed to rain-bearing winds, and hence with a heavier rainfall and less arable farming. There is much woodland and permanent grass, and cattle rearing takes a leading place.

The Pennines

The easterly slope of the Pennine uplands is occupied by moorland or rough hill pasture. Considerable tracts, especially of the Millstone Grit areas of the central Pennines, are 'reserved' as water gathering grounds for the large towns on the flanks of the uplands (see Fig. 70), and here both animals and human inhabitants are few. Air pollution and recreational pressures from the surrounding towns provide additional handicaps to agriculture. North of the Aire Gap the Pennines are largely under hill sheep farms, and there are extensive tracts of common land; on the lower slopes sheep tend to share the pastures with beef cattle, which are sold to lowland farmers for fattening.

South of the tabular masses of sandstone which form the High Peak, the Pennines take on a very different aspect. This area is largely underlain by Carboniferous Limestone and soils are more fertile than elsewhere in the uplands; most of the land is under permanent grass and, despite its elevation, is devoted to dairy farming. The limestone scenery is attractive and the area lies within the Peak District National Park and is under heavy recreational pressure.

Wales and the Welsh Borderland

Agriculturally the Welsh massif consists of a core of moorland or rough hill pasture and a surrounding fringe of better agricultural land. The central core of rough hill pasture covers some 800 000 hectares (two million acres), about 200 000 hectares (half a million acres) of which are common grazings, out of a total for Wales of over two million hectares (five million acres). Much of the uplands is used for water gathering, large areas have been afforested since 1919, and recreational pressures are increasing, especially in Snowdonia. Almost the only tenants of the hill pastures are the sheep of the Welsh Mountain Breed.

The surrounding fringe may be divided as follows:

Anglesey, with its low surface and its rainfall averaging about 1000 millimetres (40 in), has remarkably little rough pasture, but a high proportion of permanent grass. This island was once the granary of Wales, but it is now largely devoted to grass or to barley and oats, all other crops being relatively unimportant. Until 1939 cattle farming for beef production rather than for milk was the leading occupation, though sheep were also numerous; but subsequently there has been a considerable expansion of dairy farming.

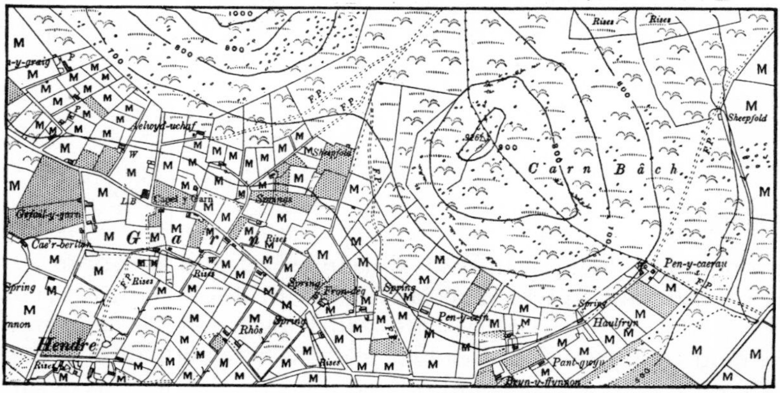

FIG. 104. A section of marginal hill land in North Wales
Typical of farming areas in the highland masses of the western part of Britain—innumerable tiny fields of which about 15 to 20 per cent are ploughed (shown by dotted areas), the remainder under grass (M), but which may be ploughed at intervals. All have been wrested with difficulty from the main mass of moorland, which will be seen to have re-invaded many of the enclosed areas. This is a section of one of the original field sheets of the Land Utilisation Survey (1932). The result of the war was to show much reclamation in land of this sort. Scale, 4 inches to 1 mile. (By permission of the Ordnance Survey and of the Land Utilisation Survey of Britain.)

The valleys of North Wales and the Lleyn are largely under grass, as might be expected from the heavy rainfall. On the arable land the leading cereals are oats and barley, and, as everywhere in the west, wheat is unimportant, as are fodder root crops such as turnips, swedes and mangolds. These areas are, of course, cattle and sheep lands, and there is an important movement of sheep between the hill pastures in summer and the lowland pastures in winter.

Southwestern Wales includes the western two-thirds of Cardiganshire, the whole of Pembrokeshire and Carmarthenshire, and the small western portion of Glamorgan, and lies to the west of the great belt of upland rough grazings. Until 1939 these counties were for the most part under permanent grass and there was comparatively little ploughed land. In contrast with similar areas in Ireland, potatoes are of little importance, although south Pembrokeshire has risen to prominence in the post-Second World War period as an area for early potatoes. This is preeminently cattle country, with a large proportion of dairy cows, while sheep are now relatively unimportant. Farms accessible by good roads were quick to turn to dairy farming; those not accessible to the daily milk lorry are compelled to carry on mixed farming. During the Second World War, there was a great increase in ploughland, but this has now reverted to permanent pasture.

The Vale of Glamorgan and Plain of Gwent lie to the south of the moorlands of the South Wales coalfield. Although this tract lies within the boundaries of Wales, it is physically a detached portion of the Midlands and scarplands of England. The Vale of Glamorgan is an area of mixed farming, with dairying as the principal enterprise, but with large numbers of lambs also being fattened. To the east of the coalfield is the red land of Gwent in Monmouthshire.

The Welsh Borderland lies to the east of the main central mass of the Welsh mountain moorland or hill pastures. It stretches eastwards as far as the limit of the Welsh massif (which may be described as running north and south along the Malvern Hills) and is a varied area with broad valleys penetrating amongst the mountains. It includes, for example, the Vale of Powis, in which Welshpool and Montgomery are situated, but comprises also uplands such as those which occupy the southern half of Shropshire, Radnor Forest, and Clun Forest, as well as the rolling country which merges into the Plain of Gwent in the county of Monmouth. Two areas may be separately distinguished. One is the Forest of Dean (still largely forested) and the other is the Plain of Hereford. For the remainder, the hill areas are largely devoted to sheep, especially of breeds such as the Kerry Hill and Clun Forest, and to the rearing of beef cattle, while dairying is an important enterprise in the lowlands.

The Plain of Hereford is a varied lowland with rich red soils derived from the marls and cornstones of the Old Red Sandstone and the overlying drifts. It lies in the lee of the Welsh Uplands and most places have a rainfall of under 760 millimetres (30 in) a year. There is little mountain pasture, and although permanent grass is an important feature, the distinctive character of this tract is the considerable acreage under the plough. Barley, oats and appreciable quantities of wheat are grown, as well as root crops, including sugar beet. The eastern part, like the neighbouring areas of Worcestershire, is well known for its hop gardens, the only other centre of importance outside the Weald. Fruit orchards, particularly of apples, occupy a large though diminishing area and Herefordshire is an important cider-producing county. Cattle, especially of the Hereford breed, and sheep are reared and fattened, although sheep are not as important as in most parts of the Welsh massif. The Plain of Hereford is a 'basin' amongst the hills and may sometimes form in winter a 'frost pocket' where cold, heavy and stagnant air tends to remain; in summer, fair warm conditions may prevail for longer periods than elsewhere.

The southwestern peninsula

Although this is another area where old rocks tend to yield an indifferent soil, two features distinguish it agriculturally from other regions in the west of England. One is the plateau character of much of the surface which makes the land easily ploughed, though some areas are ill-drained; the other is the remarkable mildness of the winter which encourages certain crops to mature early. The higher lands of Exmoor and its outlier, the Quantock Hills, in the the north, and the granite masses of the south, particularly Dartmoor and Bodmin Moor, as well as Land's End and the Lizard area, are given over to rough hill pasture, much of it common land, on which sheep and some cattle are reared. On the improved land, permanent grass came to occupy a larger share than tilled land in the 1930s, but the southwest, and Cornwall especially, was remarkable for the large amount of land remaining under the plough. The plough-up campaign of 1939–44 produced a great change in Cornwall and to a less extent in Devon, and the practice of taking the plough round the farm led to nearly all land being ploughed in some areas; since 1945 much of this land has been laid down again to grass. Certain of the drier tracts with more favourable soil conditions favour the production of limited quantities of wheat, and barley has become the dominant grain crop; formerly, the southwest was distinguished by the prominent place occupied by mixed corn, a mixture of barley and wheat. Most of the ploughed land is occupied by fodder crops which tend to emphasise the great importance of cattle-rearing and dairy-farming. Formerly the emphasis was on butter, cheese and cream rather than on milk, since the southwestern peninsula long remained too inaccessible from the great centres of milk consumption for fresh milk to be a first consideration. But for direct supply of milk to factories the position is different, and Nestlé's and other firms established collecting stations in the area. Since the creation of the Milk Marketing Board, an increasing volume of milk for liquid consumption has been produced in the southwest. The western half of Cornwall is remarkable for the high density of the pig population, a legacy of the once-abundant supply of skim milk on farms; large numbers of store pigs are sent eastward for fattening. The mildness of the sheltered valleys, especially around Penzance and north of Plymouth, is reflected in the large output of early flowers, potatoes and vegetables, for example, winter cauliflower or broccoli.

TRANSITIONAL REGIONS

Northumbria

This region, which may alternatively be described as northeastern England, occupies the eastern halves of the counties of Northumberland and Durham and a portion of the North Riding of Yorkshire. Broadly, there are two parts: (*a*) the gentle eastern slope of the Pennines and the undulating country between the Pennines and the sea in Northumberland and the northern part of county Durham, and (*b*) the lower Tees basin. The first is a region of indifferent, rather heavy soils, and the proportion of arable land to permanent grass steadily increases as one gets on to lower ground towards the coast. Durham is world famous for its Shorthorn cattle or 'Durhams', but the crops which can be grown are those which do not have exacting requirements. There is very little wheat, for example, and root crops are comparatively unimportant. Near the Scottish border, however, the richer land supports a considerable production of barley, turnips and swedes. Elsewhere the emphasis is on fodder crops, reflecting the importance of cattle-rearing and sheep-breeding. Lowland Northumberland is also an important area for fattening cattle. On the lighter drift soils of the lower Tees basin and in the Magnesian Limestone belt of east Durham conditions are much more favourable for arable farming. Wheat, barley, oats, potatoes, turnips and swedes are grown, and there are large tracts under fodder grasses.

The eastern slopes of the Pennines in Yorkshire and Derbyshire and the Nottinghamshire border

This region is terminated eastwards by the fertile Vale of York. Its agricultural conditions generally resemble those in Northumbria. Spurs of moorland separate the fertile and attractive Yorkshire dales of the Swale, Ure, Nidd, and Wharfe, but farther south in the drainage basins of the Aire and Don, agricultural utilisation is overshadowed by industrial development.

In the western parts of the coalfield there is a long tradition of small holdings, many of them occupied by retired industrial workers. Small dairy farms, dependent largely on purchased feedingstuffs, are still characteristic of this area. Pigs and poultry are also present in large numbers. The unique rhubarb-growing area south of Leeds is on largely manmade soil; the underlying Coal Measures otherwise give rise to heavy acid soils.

REGIONS OF THE LOWLAND ZONES

The Plain of Lancastria

Geographically and agriculturally the Plain of Lancastria comprises the western half of Lancashire, that is west of the moorland, practically the whole of Cheshire, the detached portion of Flintshire, and the northern half of Shropshire, including the area round Shrewsbury, although the industrial development of south Lancashire has tended to obscure the very great importance of that county from the agricultural standpoint. Practically the whole area is lowland, with a rainfall varying between 635 and 760 millimetres (25 and 30 in), and is underlain by the red rocks of the Triassic period. The soils derived from the Upper Series, the Keuper Marls, are comparatively heavy, and thus differ from the light soils derived from the Lower Series, the Bunter Sands. However, the greater part of the plain has been covered with glacial drift, and it is the character of these drift deposits which largely determines local agriculture. In some areas, especially near the hills, heavy boulder clay is found; such land is unsuitable for cultivation and hence is devoted in the main to permanent pasture. Where the soils are lighter and more loamy, arable farming becomes important, and there are intensively farmed areas of reclaimed peatland.

Three main areas may be distinguished in the Plain of Lancastria:

Lowland Lancashire north of the Ribble basin, including the Fylde district, is an area where heavy soils prevail and are mainly under permanent grass. This is an important dairying region with a very large number of dairy cattle, pigs, and remarkably high densities of poultry. A large proportion of its products is destined for the industrial towns of the southern half of Lancashire. In addition large numbers of sheep from the neighbouring moorlands are pastured, especially in winter.

Southwestern Lancashire and the Mersey valley are almost entirely under arable crops. It is almost the only area in the west of England where wheat is an important crop, but the distinctive crops are potatoes and vegetables, while pigs and poultry are relatively important.

Cheshire and North Shropshire, where the heavy soils are mainly under grass, although large acreages were ploughed during the Second World War. It is preeminently a dairy-farming region, with the highest density of dairy cattle in Great Britain. The farms are small, often run by the farmer and his family, who, under pre-1939 conditions, often sold milk in the winter when prices were good, and made cheese in summer. Little farmhouse cheese is now made and most milk goes for liquid consumption. Pigs and poultry are both numerous.

The Vale of York

This is in the main a tract of glacial drift, lake silts, and alluvium. It was formerly marshy, but is now well-drained and mainly fertile land. There is much land under pasture, but this may be described as one of the northernmost arable areas of any importance in England. It is certainly the northernmost area where wheat is a crop of significance and large quantities of barley and oats are also grown. The deep fertile soils favour root crops, notably potatoes, turnips, swedes, mangolds and sugar beet, with carrots on very light land. Around the head of the Humber large acreages of vegetables are grown. Cattle-fattening is also important.

The Midlands of England

It is by no means simple to give a general account of the agriculture of the large triangle in the heart of England to which this name of the Midlands has been applied. It lies east of the Welsh massif, south of the Pennines, and is bounded on the southeast by the first of the major scarps of the Jurassic rocks which cross England. The southeastern boundary thus defined does not coincide with any one geological horizon, but with a physical feature which, though discontinuous, can be well seen on the ground. The large

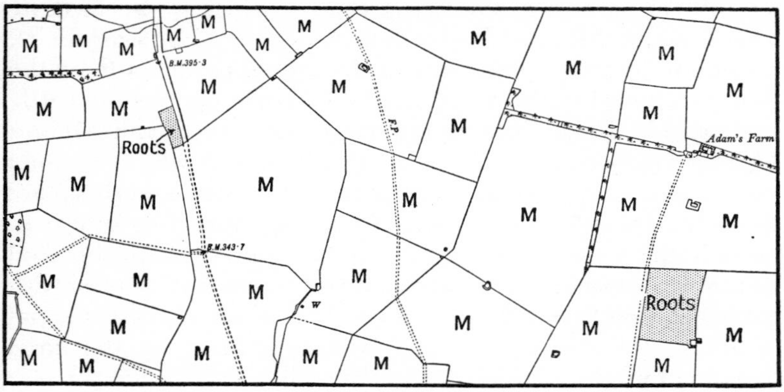

FIG. 105. A section of country in the Midlands of England in 1932

Typical of farming economy in the damp Midland plains or the clay vales. The land is evenly divided into moderate sized fields, which before 1939 were nearly all under permanent grass, with a small field here and there devoted to root crops for winter feed. Scale, 4 inches to 1 mile. (By permission of the Ordnance Survey and of the Land Utilisation Survey of Britain.)

During the plough-up campaign of the Second World War, country of this type showed a greater change than anywhere in Britain and as much as 50 per cent was ploughed.

triangle so delineated includes the southern two-thirds of Staffordshire, practically the whole of the county of Warwick, most of Worcestershire, and extends southwestwards to the Vale of Evesham and the Vale of Gloucester, which lies between the Welsh hills and the scarp of the Cotswolds. To the northeast it includes the whole of Leicestershire and a portion of western

Rutland, as well as the borders of Northamptonshire, the greater part of Nottinghamshire and the western fringe of Lincoln as far east as the scarp of Lincoln Edge. In general terms this is an undulating plain with rather heavy clayey or marly soils derived for the most part from the Keuper Marls and from the clays of the lower part of the Jurassic series (especially the Lias) or, more frequently, from the glacial drifts of local material. Much of the east Midlands is excellent grazing land, and was largely under permanent pasture before 1939. In the Middle Ages it is clear that considerable areas were ploughed and many fields show the well-known ridge and furrow indicative of early attempts to drain heavy soils. During the Second World War there were great changes. Mechanisation made it possible to plough the stiff soils with comparative ease and some very heavy crops, notably of wheat, resulted; but much of this land has since been put back to grass. The heavy soils of the Midland plain are interrupted over considerable areas by tracts of lighter soils. The Keuper Sandstones afford some excellent loams and so do some of the sandy drifts. There are also areas where the Bunter Pebble Beds and Sandstone outcrop and where the soils are light; much of this ground is rather infertile and is still covered with woodland, as, for example, in Sherwood Forest in Nottinghamshire, and in Cannock Chase. There are also hilly or upland areas formed by the outcrop of old rocks, as in Charnwood Forest. In the east, there is a tract of country, occupying roughly the eastern half of Leicestershire, which is intermediate in character between the Midland lowlands and the hills of the scarplands, and in this area there is more arable farming. Lying just to the south on the borders of Northamptonshire is one of the best known centres for cattle fattening in England. These famous fattening pastures of the Melton Mowbray–Market Harborough district are excellent and will fatten one bullock and one sheep on 0.4 hectare (one acre). The cattle and sheep are purchased from March onwards and sold for killing from July onwards. In the southwest in the Vale of Evesham and in parts of Worcestershire soil conditions favour extensive orchards, especially of plums and apples, with which vegetable growing is closely associated. This is one of the principal horticultural areas in Great Britain and is distinguished by the large numbers of small holdings.

Northeast and east Yorkshire

The eastern part of the North Riding and most of the East Riding of Yorkshire fall clearly into four agricultural divisions:

The Cleveland Hills and the North York Moors form a plateau dissected by deep valleys, with rough hill pastures and heather moors occupying the higher parts of the hills; in the valleys there are considerable areas of pasture, but despite a location on the drier eastern side of Great Britain, there is little cultivation largely owing to the prevalence of steep slopes and to the risk of flooding on the low ground. A belt of arable land coincides with the Corallian 'tabular hills'.

The Vale of Pickering was once occupied by a lake, but now consists of well-drained arable land reminiscent of the Fenland. The position of the villages on the margin is worthy of note; from them the central area is farmed.

The Yorkshire Wolds stretch in the form of a broad crescent from the Humber to Flamborough Head. The tops of these hills are almost bare chalk, but the dipslope in the east is covered with varying thicknesses of chalky boulder clay. Thanks to some early and farseeing enclosure initiated by the Sykes family, the Wolds are devoted to arable crops and it says much for the farmers that they can successfully cultivate such thin soil. Farms are large, barley, turnips and swedes and rotation grass are the principal crops, and sheep and beef cattle are fattened. Around Hull, vegetables are grown, the original impetus coming from Dutch immigrants in the 1930s.

Holderness. This lowland, covered with deep boulder clay and patches of sand and gravel, has been drained with some difficulty and is mainly cultivated. Wheat is the chief crop and fat cattle, sheep and pigs are the main livestock products.

Lincolnshire

The Lindsey Division of Lincolnshire repeats the conditions found in the East Riding of Yorkshire. The Trent Vale in the west of the county is part of the Midlands and has the damp cattle pastures already described, although there are considerable areas under cultivation. Lincoln Heath, on the dip slope of the Lincoln Edge scarp, is largely under tillage crops, notably barley, and the lowland which separates the Heath from the Lincolnshire Wolds is an area of mixed farming. The Lincolnshire Wolds repeat many of the features of the Yorkshire Wolds, and the Lincolnshire Marshes are important cattle fattening areas.

The scarplands and clay vales

Stretching across England from the neighbourhood of Lincoln to the Dorset coast, there is a series of discontinuous, westfacing scarps, accompanied by long, gentle dipslopes (cf. pp. 46–50). The uplands are mainly of limestones, calcareous grits or sandstones, and the well drained higher levels are mainly given over to arable land. Barley and rotation grass are the chief crops, although vegetable-growing has extended to the Cotswolds from the Vale of Evesham. This is a land of large farms and mellow stone villages. The dip slopes merge gradually into the great clay vale, which may be said to extend as far as the chalk scarp and from the borders of the Fens on the northeast to the Dorset–Devon coast on the southwest, although south of Bath the valley is ill-defined. In places the main vale is interrupted by low ridges where harder rocks outcrop, but it is mainly a low-lying belt

9

of clay which gives rise to heavy soils. Permanent pasture and cattle-rearing are the keynotes throughout the greater part of the area, although there is now more ploughed land than there was before the Second World War. This description applies to much of the county of Northampton (except the mainly arable ironstone belt with its rich red soils), the northern half of Buckinghamshire, the central tract of Oxfordshire and the northwestern part of Wiltshire. The belt extends into the eastern and southern parts of Somerset and the neighbouring parts of Dorset and Devonshire. It is from these parts of Wiltshire, Somerset, and the borders of Dorset that much of London's milk is obtained, for it is preeminently dairy-farming country. The production of bacon and sausages are important subsidiary industries. In the northeast where the great clay vale abuts on the Fenland, there are large tracts covered with glacial deposits, particularly chalky boulder clay, which afford excellent mixed soils; as a result, large areas in Huntingdonshire and the southern part of Cambridgeshire and Bedfordshire are arable land. Where heavy boulder clay occurs the land is poorer, notably in the western half of Huntingdonshire. Where light loams result from the outcrop of Lower Cretaceous sands or from the occurrence of terrace gravels there are the market gardening areas around Sandy and Biggleswade in south Bedfordshire. This, too, is an area of small holdings, which formerly depended on supplies of London manure to maintain the fertility of its light soils.

The Fenlands

The once watery waste known as the Fens has now been almost completely drained, the great work of reclamation having begun in the seventeenth century with the help of Dutch engineers. Both the dark-coloured mild peat soils of the drained fens and the silts of land reclaimed from the Wash are very fertile, although the peats are gradually disappearing through bacterial action and wastage, and parts of these lands already lie below sea-level. This is undoubtedly the most intensively cultivated arable area in the British Isles and yields of most crops are higher than elsewhere. It comprises the Holland Division of Lincolnshire and the Isle of Ely, together with the neighbouring parts of Lindsey and Kesteven and the fringes of Norfolk. More than three-quarters of the whole area is under the plough and amongst the great variety of crops grown are large quantities of wheat and sugar beet. Special mention must be made of potatoes, since this is the greatest area of potato cultivation in the British Isles. Large acreages on the silts are under vegetables and bulb flowers, the latter especially in the tulip fields near Spalding, and the area around Wisbech produces top fruit and small fruit, especially strawberries. Vegetables are also grown on the peats, notably celery around Littleport. Farms are generally small and few livestock are kept. The limited areas of pasture are found especially on the 'islands' of boulder clay (see Fig. 106) or on the 'washlands' between the main drainage channels.

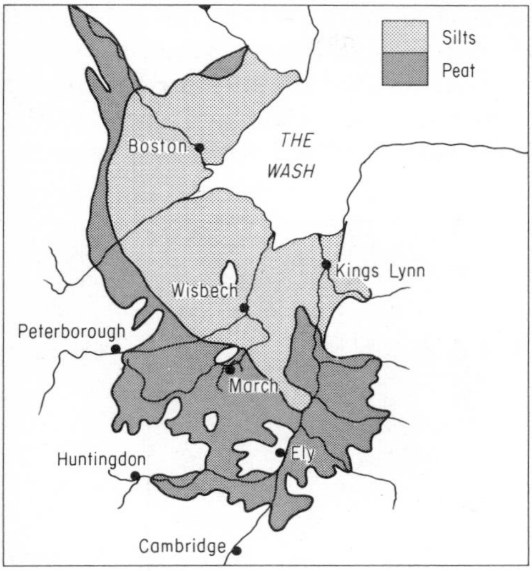

FIG. 106. The Fenlands
Unshaded areas are largely of boulder clay. Notice the boulder clay 'islands'.

The Plain of Somerset

The Plain of Somerset, between the Mendips and the Blackdown Hills, is very different. Lying on the wetter side of England, it has not been so adequately drained and is therefore still occupied by wet pastures; parts are liable to almost annual floods. The Somerset Levels, though also underlain by peat, are largely devoted to dairy cattle. During the winter there is flooding and cattle are kept on surrounding higher land. The Levels are also handicapped by highly fragmented farms. However, there is good arable land in the Vale of Taunton and the little Vale of Porlock, and store cattle and pigs are fattened.

The Chalk lands of the southeast

The Chalk lands comprise the North and South Downs, the open downs of Dorset, Wiltshire and the northern part of Hampshire, and the stretch of Chalk country forming the Chilterns and continuing northwards as the East Anglian Heights. Farther to the northeast the Chalk occurs over wide areas in East Anglia, but it is so masked by glacial deposits that the land is entirely different in character. At least four types of land are found along the Chalk outcrop. The main downland areas, where there are few superficial deposits, are largely under arable cultivation. Farms are large and barley and rotation grass the chief crops, the latter often used for the support of dairy cattle or for the fattening of beef animals. Where the land is not sufficiently good for ploughing or where the elevation is perhaps too great, the Chalk was formerly covered by pastures traditionally used for sheep rearing. In the old days the sheep fed by day on the grass, and at night were folded on the fallow arable land which they enriched with their manure.

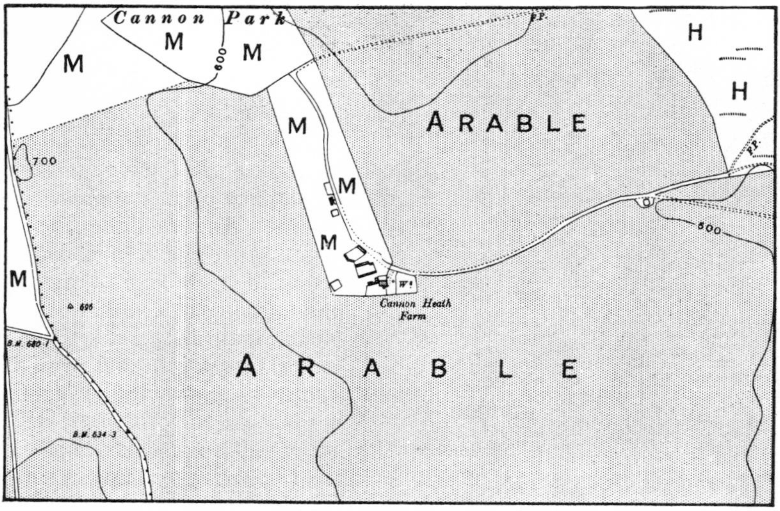

FIG. 107. A section of country on the 'downlands' of southeastern England with huge open stretches of ploughed land, limited areas under pasture (M), and the poorer land left as rough pasture (H) for sheep. Scale, 4 inches to 1 mile

(By permission of the Ordnance Survey and of the Land Utilisation Survey of Britain.)

Later root crops were grown on the fallow for the sheep. Each region of the Chalk lands evolved its own type of sheep, such as the South Downs. High labour costs and artificial fertilisers have made sheep-farming less attractive and less necessary and sheep are no longer characteristic of such areas. Where there is a coating of gravel, the Chalk lands are often not used for agriculture or are under rough pasture, and land of this character has been utilised for the military training grounds of Salisbury Plain. In other areas, like the Chilterns, the surface of the Chalk is covered by a residual deposit known as Clay-with-flints. This tenacious brown clay, from which the lime has been almost entirely leached away, gives rise to stony soils, so that it is difficult to grow crops other than grass and cereals; much of this land is in mixed farming, with dairy cattle as the major enterprise.

East Anglia

East Anglia, comprising the greater parts of the counties of Norfolk and Suffolk, as well as the northern two-thirds of Essex, may be broadly described as a low plateau. Chalk underlies a great deal of the area, but its characteristic feature is the wide mantle of glacial deposits. The surface utilisation and the type of farming largely depend upon the characters of these glacial deposits (see Fig. 108). The central belt is occupied by mixed

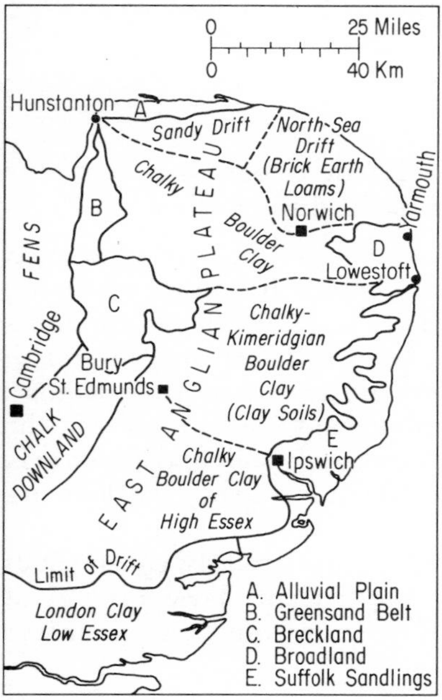

FIG. 108. East Anglia
Agricultural regions (based on those suggested by Professor P. M. Roxby), with the East Anglian plateau subdivided according to the character of the boulder clay (after maps by the late F. W. Harmer).

loamy soils and is excellent arable country. Nearly half the arable land is under cereals; farmers on the lighter soils grow barley, on the heavier wheat, but sugar beet and field crops of vegetables, such as peas for canning and quick freezing, are also important. Blackcurrants are also a distinctive crop, especially in northeast Norfolk, and the acreage under top fruit in East Anglia has been increasing steadily since the Second World War. Formerly sheep were fed on swedes, and big Irish Shorthorn bullocks fattened for Christmas. Now sugar beet tops are used; grass-fed lambs are important, while young bullocks are winter fed on kale and fattened on grass in summer. Broiler production of turkeys is increasingly important. In the west coarse sands occur over the huge tract known as Breckland, which is largely afforested with conifers planted by the Forestry Commission, and a similar tract, the Suffolk Sandlings, occurs near the coast in the east; a post-1945 revolution has been the conversion of these light lands to fertile arable by new techniques. East of Norwich are the Broads, stretches of shallow water now known to occupy old peat workings. On some of the heavier soils dairying became important, but is now declining in favour of more profitable enterprises. The southern limit of the area coincides with the limit of the chalky boulder clay; farther south are heavy lands on London Clay.

The London Basin

Although a comparatively small area, the London Basin is remarkably complex. At least four major types of land must be distinguished:

London Clay gives rise to heavy soils which were formerly under permanent pasture, much of it providing hay for London horses. It is now (where not built over) largely under the plough, especially in Essex where vegetables and soft fruit are distinctive crops. Many areas are still extensively wooded, e.g. Epping Forest which was for many centuries a royal hunting ground.
Sandy areas, more especially the great Bagshot Sand plateau towards the west of the basin, have extremely infertile coarse sandy soils and are largely occupied by heathland and pine woods, although nursery gardens are important in some areas.
Belts of mixed soils, usually excellent loams, are particularly conspicuous along the southern margin of the basin in north Kent. This is the great market gardening and fruit farming belt of Kent, supplying large quantities of fruit and vegetables to the metropolis.
Stretches of brick-earth, terrace gravel, and alluvium occur in the Thames Valley at different levels. The high-level gravels may be overdrained and infertile, but the lower terraces, for example over much of Middlesex, afford excellent soils for market gardening and fruit. Unfortunately, much of this land has been taken for housing or other development and little remains in cultivation.

The Hampshire Basin

In many respects the Hampshire Basin repeats the features seen in the London Basin, although clay lands are less and sandy areas are more important. There are heavy clay areas largely occupied by permanent pasture, a belt of mixed soils, largely under arable crops (and including the specialised strawberry growing around Swanwick), the large tracts of barren sandy soil, occupied in particular by the New Forest, and belts of gravel or alluvium. It should be noticed that both in the Hampshire and London

Basins, as well as in the neighbouring parts of the chalk lands and in the Wealden belt, agricultural use depends very largely on economic conditions and the requirements of the metropolis. Much of this area is thus in semi-agricultural use for part-time or hobby farming.

The Weald

The Weald is the region between the North and South Downs. In the heart is a sandy area occupied largely by Ashdown Forest and tracts of heathland, although the sandstones are very fine grained and fruit growing is important. Towards the margins of the Weald are the sandy ridges of the Lower Greensand which vary greatly in character, from the fruit-growing areas around Maidstone to the extensive heaths and coniferous woodlands between Dorking and Petersfield. Much of the rest of the Weald is occupied by the Weald Clay and other clay beds, which give rise to damp country which was formerly covered with oakwood, but is now cleared and occupied by pasture supporting numerous cattle. Round the fringes of the Weald is a narrow lowland called Holmesdale which coincides with the outcrop of the Gault; on the better drained margins there is a belt of mixed soils very suitable for cultivation. It is on some of the better soils that the hop gardens and orchards for which Kent is well known are found. A small but important region within the Weald is Romney Marsh, now largely drained and carrying the highest densities of sheep in the British Isles. In summer some tracts of this rich pasture land carry and fatten six or eight sheep and lambs per acre, but in winter only the breeding ewes remain. It has now been found that the soils are as suitable for intensive cultivation as those of the Fenland. In contrast are Pevensey Levels which are largely devoted to pasture for cattle.

13
The British fisheries[1]

The post-Second World War period has witnessed a marked upsurge in world landings of fish. This state of affairs, however, has not been evident in the British fishing industry and figures for both employment and landings were in the late 1960s at their lowest levels in modern times. Over the period 1948 to 1967, in which world landings (measured by live weight) increased from 19.6 million metric tons to 60.7 million metric tons, the corresponding figures for the United Kingdom have been 1.2 million metric tons and 1.0 million metric tons.

No western European nation has matched the spectacular postwar growth of fishing that has occurred in Peru, Japan, China and the USSR, but most have had some increase in landings and the Norwegian catch, the largest in Europe, increased from 1.4 million metric tons in 1948 to 3.2 million metric tons in 1967.

In terms of weight of landings, the United Kingdom is thirteenth in the world but, when value is considered, the position is more favourable and the placing is sixth among nations that publish values (i.e. excluding China and the USSR where landings are obviously more significant). British catches contain a good proportion of high value fish whereas some countries concentrate on industrial fishing (i.e. catching fish largely for low value outlets such as meal and oil plants). The prime example of an industrial fishing nation is Peru, where the world's largest catch of over 10 million metric tons (one-sixth of the world total) was landed in 1967. The fish are anchovies which are mainly converted into meal and their value, $117 million, was only two-thirds that of the much smaller United Kingdom catch.

The total value of United Kingdom landings of fish in 1967 was £64 million. Freshwater fisheries, mainly for salmon, contributed just under £3 million to this figure and, although these fisheries may have considerable local significance, particularly on the rivers of the east of Scotland, their overall importance is obviously small and this chapter will concentrate on the sea fishing industry.

Three general categories of fish are normally recognised: demersal fish

1. This chapter has been rewritten by Dr T. D. Kennea, to whom I am much indebted. Dr Kennea also compiled the two maps, Figs 109 and 110.

such as cod, haddock and flat fish, which spend much of their lives on or near the sea bed, pelagic fish such as herrings, mackerel and sprats which are considered as near-surface dwellers, although they usually have demersal phases, and shellfish. It is upon the first of these groups that the British fishing industry is mainly dependent and, in 1967, it comprised 88 per cent by value and 78.6 per cent by weight of the total United Kingdom catch. The corresponding figures for pelagic fish were 5.4 per cent and 16.7 per cent respectively and for shellfish 6.6 per cent and 4.7 per cent respectively.

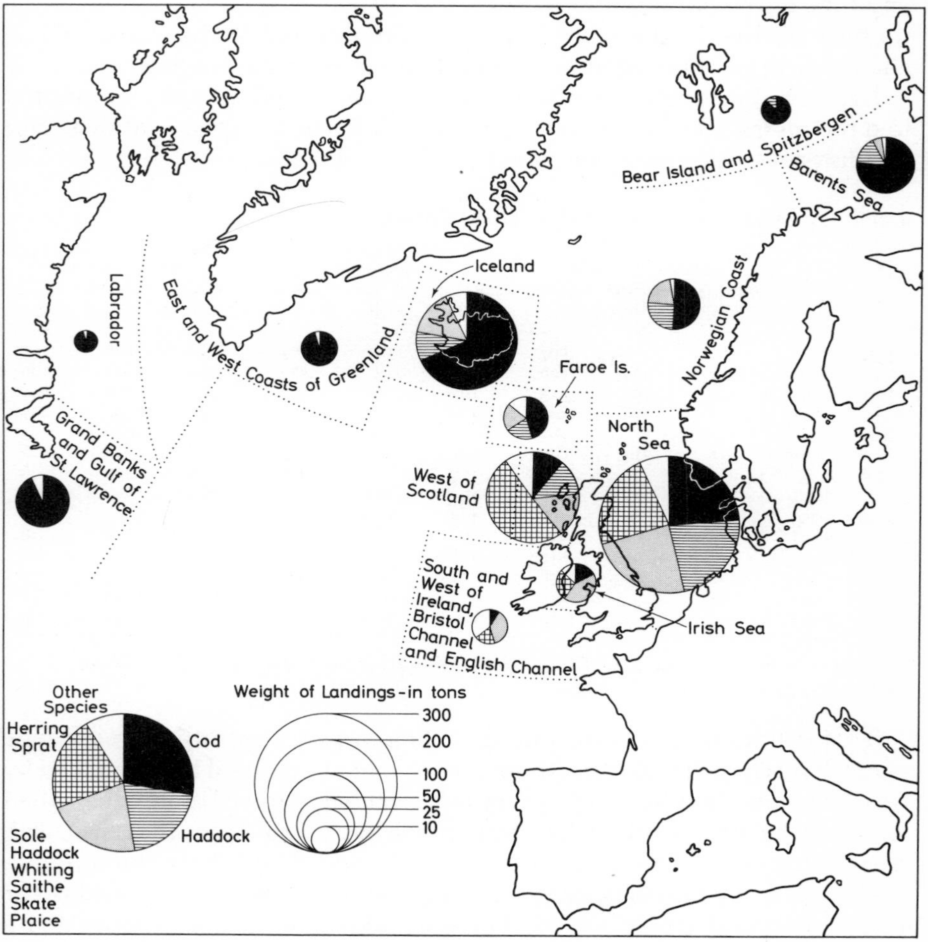

FIG. 109. The main fishing grounds used by British fishermen, and their yields in 1967

It is clear that pelagic fish have a lower value per unit weight than other types. They do not keep as well as most demersal species and many are processed in some form or another. The herring is the most important pelagic fish and its partial disappearance from the North Sea is the principal reason for the considerable drop in pelagic landings (see Table below).

At present, there is rather greater emphasis on pelagic fish in Scotland than in England and Wales and in the heyday of the herring fishery, when biggest catches were in English waters, a high proportion of the landings were made by Scottish drifters which travelled around the coast fishing, in the appropriate seasons, where the shoals were densest.

The Scottish demersal landings have been higher in the 1960s than at any time in the past and this has, to some extent, helped to counteract the postwar decline in the more important English and Welsh catch. These changes will be considered in greater detail later in the chapter.

Landings in Northern Ireland have been small and, in 1967, amounted to 9 100 metric tons (9 000 long tons), which fetched £470 000 at first sale; shellfish accounted for more than half the total value.

Landings ('000 tons) of wet fish in Great Britain

		ENGLAND AND WALES			SCOTLAND			GREAT BRITAIN		
		DEMERSAL FISH	PELAGIC FISH	TOTAL	DEMERSAL FISH	PELAGIC FISH	TOTAL	DEMERSAL FISH	PELAGIC FISH	TOTAL
1913	long	418	389	807	137	227	364	555	616	1171
	metric	425	395	820	139	231	370	564	626	1190
1919	long	319	196	515	107	192	299	426	388	814
	metric	324	199	523	109	195	304	433	394	827
1930	long	573	211	784	135	175	310	708	386	1094
	metric	582	214	802	137	178	315	719	392	1112
1938	long	632	145	777	125	144	269	757	289	1046
	metric	642	147	789	127	146	273	769	294	1063
1949	long	629	80	709	158	135	293	787	215	1002
	metric	639	81	720	160	137	297	800	218	1018
1959	long	516	31	547	185	111	296	701	142	843
	metric	524	31.5	556	188	113	300	712	144	856
1967	long	482	33	515	213	114	327	695	147	842
	metric	490	33.5	523	216	116	332	706	149	855

Sources: *Sea Fisheries Statistical Tables*; *Annual Reports of the Fishery Board for Scotland*; *Scottish Sea Fisheries Statistical Tables*.

To a considerable extent, fishing techniques vary according to the type of catch it is hoped to make. About 80 per cent of demersal fish are taken by trawling, a method by which a very large net bag is towed along the seabed catching the fish in its path. The front of the bag is kept open, in the vertical, by weights on the lower part of the mouth and floats along the top and, horizontally, by the pressure of water against 'otter' boards attached to the towing lines and acting as kites. Trawling takes place to a maximum depth of about 250 fathoms.

Most of the remaining 20 per cent of demersal fish is caught by Danish seining. The method was introduced to the British Isles in 1921 and has been employed principally by Scottish fishermen. It is a system of netting in some ways not unlike trawling, that is particularly suitable for use by medium size vessels fishing on smooth grounds; it accounts for nearly 50 per cent of Scottish demersal landings. Only about 1 per cent of demersal fish are taken by line fishing, which was once a method of some considerable importance.

Trawling is also responsible for the largest share of the catch of pelagic fish (over 50 per cent in 1969). The methods are somewhat different from trawling for demersal species and there are nets that may be operated in midwater, frequently by two vessels, one towing on each side of the instrument; for obvious reasons, this is known as pair trawling. The system was introduced from Scandinavia after the Second World War and is now the principal method by which sprats are taken. About 40 per cent of British landings of herring are also caught by trawling; pair trawls are sometimes used but a modified type of bottom trawl is more important. The fish are

PLATE 7. A modern Grimsby trawler

usually taken in daylight when they are near the seabed. In the evening they move towards the surface and it is then they become enmeshed in drift nets which are, effectively, curtains of netting suspended in the water; each boat may have a fleet of these nets extending for several miles. Drifting, which now accounts for less than 20 per cent of herrings landed, has declined markedly, and even in 1967 was responsible for 40 per cent of the catch; it is a high-cost, comparatively inefficient system, requiring many expensive nets and a large complement of men for each vessel. The remaining 40 per cent of the herring catch is taken by ring nets and purse seines, mainly in the more sheltered of Scottish waters; the fish are trapped by a wall of netting laid around the shoal in a roughly circular form.

Finally, line fishing may be mentioned as the principal method of catching mackerel. The lines are either towed behind a moving boat or lowered into a shoal of fish and immediately pulled up again, often with a fish on each of up to about fifteen hooks. Feathers are most frequently used as bait although other light coloured or shiny material may be employed.

Shellfish are taken in many ways. Lobsters and crabs are caught in baited traps, so also are crawfish though many of these, which are only of any significance to British fishermen in Cornish waters, are captured by skindivers. Oysters and escallops are dredged up, and Norway lobsters, known commercially as scampi, are trawled. Other shellfish fall to methods probably more numerous than the kinds of fish and including suction dredging for cockles and hand gathering and netting of several types.

In terms of total number of vessels, small boats play a large part in the British fishing industry (out of some 6000 fishing vessels, over 4000 are less than 12 metres (40 ft) in length) and although some trawlers regularly fish far afield, the North Sea is still the most important single fishing area, providing about one-third of the total catch (Fig. 109). Nevertheless, the relatively small number of ships in the distant water category (only 182 vessels of over 42.59 metres (140 ft) length), operating over widely separated areas of the northern hemisphere, land about 40 per cent of the demersal fish.

British landings of fresh and frozen demersal fish by main vessel length groups in 1967

VESSEL LENGTH GROUP		QUANTITY '000 TONS	
		METRIC	LONG
Over 42.5 m (140 ft)	England and Wales	311.3	306.4
	Scotland	1.6	1.6
24 m to 42.3 m (80 ft–139.9 ft)	England and Wales	126.0	124.6
	Scotland	86.3	84.9
Under 24 m (80 ft)	England and Wales	50.7	49.9
	Scotland	128.9	126.9
	Northern Ireland	5.5	5.5
All vessels	England and Wales	488.6	480.9
	Scotland	216.8	213.4
	Northern Ireland	5.5	5.5

Source: *Sea Fisheries Statistical Tables.*

The distant grounds are also more productive than those nearer, although the difference is less significant than it appears from the Table on p. 259. The larger craft fishing the remote areas are more powerful, use bigger nets and have a greater catching capacity than smaller boats. Also, as the distant water vessels spend much of each voyage steaming to and from the grounds, they need a higher catch rate as compensation. Nevertheless, the relatively small number of ships in the distant water category (only 161 are vessels over 42.59 metres (140 ft) in length), operating over widely separated areas of the northern hemisphere, land nearly 50 per cent of the demersal fish.

Important though the distant areas are, the reliance of much of the British fishing industry upon less productive near waters cannot be escaped. Parts of this section are doing well, but others continue in operation, with the help of subsidies, on grounds only marginally profitable; as there is no evidence, however, of a spur of strong consumer demand, greater diversion of effort to the deep sea sources is not justified. On the other hand, countries such as the Soviet Union and Japan, with a large market for fish and determined to expand their industry in the postwar period, have built vessels able to fish as far afield as the South Atlantic, and with facilities for freezing and processing the entire catch on board.

Catch of demersal fish per hour fishing time by vessels of 12 metres (40 ft) and over on principal grounds in 1967

	CWT	KG
Barents Sea	12.1	614.7
Norwegian Coast	12.1	614.7
Bear Island and Spitzbergen	13.8	701.0
North Sea	2.0	101.6
Iceland	9.7	492.8
Faroes	7.2	365.8
West of Scotland	4.3	218.4
Irish Sea	1.4	71.1
English Channel	0.7	35.5
Bristol Channel	1.5	76.2
East and West Coast of Greenland	26.3	1335.0
Labrador	32.1	1630.7
Grand Banks	17.8	904.3
Gulf of St Lawrence	20.8	1056.7

Source: Derived from *Sea Fisheries Statistical Tables.*

At the end of 1969, out of a British distant water fleet of 161 craft, there were six such trawlers, another twenty-seven able to freeze their catch and one with facility for part-freezing. On 31 December 1965 there had been twelve of these vessels, and during that year their landings totalled 31 500 metric tons (31 000 long tons). The corresponding figure of 96 500 metric tons (95 000 long tons) for 1969 represented nearly 30 per cent of the distant water catch. Over the same period conventional distant water trawlers decreased in importance (their numbers declined from 184 at the end of 1965 to 127 at the end of 1969) although the vessels going out of service were the least efficient.

Freezer trawlers may stay away from their home ports for six weeks or more (compared with three weeks by conventional distant water trawlers) but, in the main, are smaller than their counterparts from Japan and the Soviet Union. A number are over 61 metres (200 ft) in length but even the largest have a registered length of only about 70 metres (230 ft). Japanese trawlers are up to nearly 91 metres (300 ft) long and the largest Soviet trawler is over 122 metres (400 ft). Both these nations have refrigerated transport vessels which relieve fishing boats of their catches and allow them to remain longer on the grounds. They also use 'mother-ships' which have processing facilities and act as guiding and coordinating centres for fleets of smaller fishing vessels; such a system has not been employed by the British fishing industry, the nearest approach being the provision of a 'guard' ship in Icelandic waters in winter following the sinking of three trawlers in bad weather conditions during the winter 1967–68.

Fishing cannot be regarded as a major employer on a national scale, but the number of persons indirectly dependent upon it for employment is much larger. Probably at least twice as many as those actually fishing are engaged upon such activities as boat building and repairing, net making, fish processing and distribution, providing items of ships chandlery and the general oversight and administration of the industry.

Employment in fishing[1]

	ENGLAND AND WALES		SCOTLAND		NORTHERN IRELAND		UNITED KINGDOM	
	REGULARLY EMPLOYED	PARTIALLY EMPLOYED	REGULARLY EMPLOYED	PARTIALLY EMPLOYED	REGULARLY EMPLOYED	PARTIALLY EMPLOYED	REGULARLY EMPLOYED	PARTIALLY EMPLOYED
1938	26 062	2 949	12 976	4 939	342	556	39 380	8 444
1948	25 946	3 373	12 080	5 148	800	300	38 826	8 821
1967	10 110	3 076	8 057	1 847	508	184	18 675	5 107

1. The figures relate to 31 December in each year.

Employment in fishing has been halved since the war. This is due partly to the generally declining state of the industry, but the powerful counter-attraction of regular, fairly well paid work ashore has also been an important factor. The result has been a manpower shortage at many ports which might have been more acute but for the introduction of efficient modern vessels requiring fewer crew members than older craft with equivalent catching power.

There must be relatively few villages around British coasts which do not have some form of commercial fishing, even if it is only providing mackerel or some shellfish for summer visitors. The most important sections of the industry are highly concentrated, however, and over 62 per cent (by value) of fish landed by British vessels at United Kingdom ports in 1967 was brought ashore at Grimsby (£13.2m), Hull (£12.8m), Aberdeen (£7.9m) and Fleetwood (£4.1m). A further 15 per cent was contributed by vessels landing at Lowestoft, Ullapool, Fraserburgh, North Shields and Leith. A more detailed picture of the distribution is provided in Fig. 110.

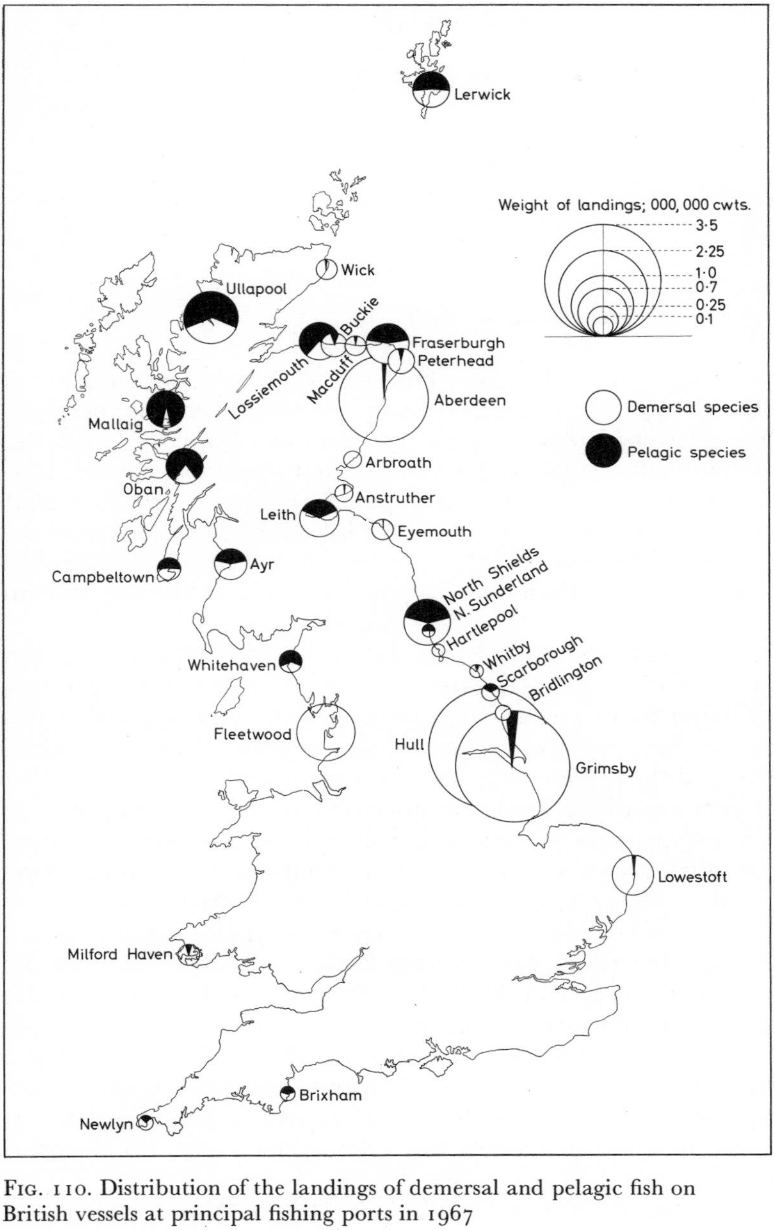

FIG. 110. Distribution of the landings of demersal and pelagic fish on British vessels at principal fishing ports in 1967

Vessels of 24 metres (80 ft) and over registered length at 31 December 1967

LOCATION	24 M–42.5 M (80–139.9 FT)	OVER 42.59 M (OVER 140 FT)	TOTAL
Aberdeen	107	2	109
Fleetwood	50	11	61
Grimsby	79	60	139
Hull		104	104
Leith	20		20
Lowestoft	108	1	109
Milford Haven	20		20
North Shields	5	3	8
Others	9	1	10

Source: Derived from *Sea Fisheries Statistical Tables*.

Most of the distant water fleet is at Hull where there are no vessels less than 42.5 metres (140 ft) in length. Grimsby has more medium and large craft overall but fewer in this category. In terms of landings this has the effect that the Hull catch is rather larger than that made at Grimsby. But, as more of the smaller craft from the latter port fish nearer home, they land fewer distant water cod and more high value fish such as plaice. There are relatively few large trawlers at other centres and these usually exploit grounds no farther afield than the Faroes, Iceland and the Norwegian coast.

Coastal towns or villages normally develop as fishing ports to exploit fish in nearby waters. Early impetus is gained if local grounds are very productive but with major British ports it has been other factors, applied at this stage or later, that have really established their positions. It was in the nineteenth century that the present pattern of port distribution became evident and the railway companies played an important part in the development of the larger centres, not only by providing rail links with major consuming areas and introducing special fish trains, but also by investing in the ports themselves, mainly by providing docking facilities. Probably Grimsby is the best example of a port developed by railway companies. The network reached it in 1848, but there was still little fishing and most vessels on the Humber were concentrated at Hull. During the next five or six years facilities were much improved at Grimsby, while they were still fairly primitive at Hull, where the railhead was over a mile from the landing place. Inducements were offered to owners at Hull and other ports to encourage them to fish from Grimsby. In addition, the railway companies became part owners of a fleet of nine vessels and, by the late 1850s, the port was growing fast.

Aberdeen, Fleetwood, North Shields and Milford Haven were later developing but they all benefited from the help provided by the railway concerns. It must, nevertheless, be remembered that these organisations were only prepared to invest where there was obvious potential. On the east coast this was provided by the discovery and exploitation of good fishing grounds in the North Sea from about the 1830s. The principal west coast ports of Fleetwood and Milford Haven already had railway connections in the late 1880s and early 1890s, when vessels from Grimsby and Hull were based there while fishing, principally for hake, to the west of Scotland, in the Irish Sea and British Channel, and to the south of Ireland. These ventures were successful, the railway companies helped with the provision of facilities on shore and of suitable transport, and the two centres became established in the front rank of British fishing ports.

PLATE 8. The fish market at Aberdeen

From about the middle of the nineteenth century other important changes were also taking place. The increasing use of ice for preservation gave added encouragement for craft to remain longer on the grounds or to fish farther afield. Vessels and equipment were being improved, and with the widespread introduction of the steam trawler from the 1880s onwards, many new areas were opened to British fishermen. By the end of the century fishing had taken place around Iceland, Faroes and in the Bay of Biscay; in

1904–05 it had extended to the Murmansk coast and, during the next thirty years, hardly a fishing ground in the North Atlantic between the latitudes of Spitzbergen and Morocco had not been explored. It was during this latter period that Hull became established as a distant water port.

The pattern that had by now emerged was of many small and medium fishing ports whose vessels were exploiting grounds, usually less than 160 kilometres (100 miles) distant, and of a few major ports whose economy was largely dependent upon the produce of relatively distant seas. For these the nearby grounds, so important less than a century before, were of much diminished significance. The inertia that had been derived from the early provision of railway, marketing, processing, repairing, docking, coaling and other ancillary facilities had been sufficient to keep these places in the forefront.

Subsequently, the industry has declined in overall importance and catches by English and Welsh vessels have been reduced, although the smaller Scottish industry has been in a healthier state.

Some temporary reversals to this general trend of contraction have occurred and the most notable was in the late 1940s following the resting of many fishing grounds during the war. Landings at the principal English and Welsh fishing ports are all below the levels attained in the 1930s, but Aberdeen stands out in marked contrast although the present situation there is not encouraging. Greater landings could almost certainly be made from Grimsby and Hull but vessels are frequently laid up because of an absence of a market for their product. The decline at Lowestoft is due to the repeated failure of the East Anglian herring season. Luckily, the port has a sound basis provided by its long standing demersal fishery conducted in the North Sea but Great Yarmouth, its neighbour, was more heavily dependent upon herring and is now virtually finished as a fishing centre.

Landings of wet fish ('000 tons) at important ports during selected years

YEAR	HULL		GRIMSBY		LOWESTOFT		FLEETWOOD		MILFORD HAVEN		ABERDEEN	
	METRIC TONS	LONG TONS	METRIC TONS	LONG TONS	METRIC TONS	LONG TONS	METRIC TONS	LONG TONS	METRIC TONS	LONG TONS	METRIC TONS	LONG TONS
1919	56.8	56	134	132	63	62	39.5	39	14	14	63.9	63
1930	213	210	196	193	76	75	61	60	36.4	36	84	83
1938	291	287	208	205	52	51	69	68	37.5	37	88	87
1949	251	247	222	219	36.4	36	74	73	29.4	29	102	101
1967	198	195	172	169	23.3	23	46.6	46	6.0	6	107	106

Sources: *Sea Fisheries Statistical Tables*; *Annual Reports of Fishery Board for Scotland*; *Scottish Sea Fisheries Statistical Tables*.

Hake have made up a large part of the landings at Fleetwood and Milford Haven. The stocks of these fish to the west of the British Isles have been severely overfished,[1] not only by British vessels but also by those from Spain, France and other Continental countries. Fleetwood has been the less unfortunate of the two ports, for its economy has not been so dependent on a single species of fish and its vessels have been frequent visitors to more distant grounds around the Faroes and Iceland. Additionally, the large fish-consuming Lancashire market is on its doorstep.

The plight of Milford Haven as a fishing port has not been helped by its location. The common difficulty of obtaining crews has been acute here; many of the trawler companies, hit by declining landings, have been in a poor financial state and unable to replace their old and uneconomic vessels, and a visitor to the fish dock sector of the port is confronted with a most depressing sight. The large fish market is only partly used, the once busy railway sidings are silent and there is a general air of decay. The oil industry, for some years a dominant feature of Milford Haven (cf. p. 355), has had little effect on the fishing industry of this area.

From Scottish ports other than Aberdeen, most fishing is carried out inshore or in near waters, by vessels less than 24 metres (80 ft) in length. Even Aberdeen trawlers rarely fish far afield. That catches have not exhibited the marked decline evident in most other fisheries is probably due to the following main reasons: first, many Scottish grounds have not been severely overfished and, like some other British inshore grounds, may well have been helped, recently, by the restriction of foreign fishing activity round our coasts, following the 1964 Fishery Limits Act; secondly, there has been increasing emphasis on demersal fishing to compensate for the declining herring catch; thirdly, a high proportion of vessels here are family owned and manned and there are strong social incentives for keeping them in operation; fourthly, there are fewer alternative employment opportunities available than in England; fifthly, voyages are fairly short and much fish landed in Scotland has not spent long in the hold of a vessel and there is a good demand for it; finally, Scottish fishermen are rather more mobile than many of their English counterparts—they will take their vessels wherever fish are likely to be rather than fish a nearby ground out of production. Most Scottish vessels fishing west coast grounds are from the east coast; once the craft are there the men will fish during the weekdays out of, perhaps, Ullapool or Lochinver and go home to Lossiemouth or some other North Sea centre by road on Friday, returning to their vessels on Sunday night.

At some smaller centres elsewhere in Britain fishing has been successful, but at others it has ceased altogether, and there are many where it continues only because the fishermen have been able to augment their incomes by catering for tourists or taking additional work ashore.

The importance of cod and haddock to the British fishing industry is clearly shown in the table on p. 266. Neither are inhabitants of warmer

1. Overfishing occurs when, over a period, the weight of fish removed from an area is greater than the difference between the weight added to a fishable stock by natural replacement and growth, and that lost to it due to natural causes.

waters, though the cod exists between a wider range of latitudes and shows a preference for colder regions. The species comprises almost the entire catch from the most northerly waters fished (Fig. 110) and, in some years, is significant in landings as far south as the English Channel. Haddock are in small numbers in these extreme areas and the largest catches are made in the northern North Sea, from where Scottish vessels made almost half the total British landings of the fish during 1967.

Landings of fresh and frozen fish by British vessels at United Kingdom ports in 1967

TYPE OF FISH		QUANTITY ('000 LONG TONS)	VALUE £'000
Demersal fish			
Cod		345	25 235
Haddock		127	10 474
Plaice		44	5 646
Whiting		47	2 818
Saithe		42	1 476
Lemon soles		6	1 165
Skates and rays		11	1 048
Hake		4	976
Halibut		2	802
Soles		2	683
Others		70	3 370
Total	long tons	700	53 693
	metric tons	711	

TYPE OF FISH		QUANTITY ('000 LONG TONS)	VALUE £'000
Pelagic fish			
Herring		101	2 676
Sprats		43	374
Mackerel		4	199
Others		1	29
Total	long tons	149	3 278
	metric tons	151	
Shellfish			
Norway lobsters		9	1 686
Lobsters		1	903
Crabs		4	409
Shrimps		2	228
Cockles		15	218
Others		10	557
Total	long tons	41	4 001
	metric tons	41.6	
Total all fish	long tons	890	60 972
	metric tons	904	

1 long ton = 2240 lb = 1.016 metric ton
Source: Derived from *Sea Fisheries Statistical Tables.*

Four flatfish appear in the above table. Halibut, the largest of them, frequently attain a weight of over 45 kilograms (100 lb); they are caught in deeper waters, particularly around the Faroes, where they form the most important items in the catch of Scottish line fishermen. Good landings are also made by trawlers around Iceland and on the Grand Banks but these fish are generally taken from shallower waters and are somewhat smaller than the line caught fish.

None of the other three flatfish lives in waters as deep as those frequented by the halibut. They are all taken principally from the North Sea. The sole, the least important of the trio, is also least tolerant of low temperatures. It is taken mainly from the shallow waters of the southern North Sea, the English and Bristol Channels and the Irish Sea. Few appear in Scottish catches. Plaice and lemon soles are wide-ranging and important in areas as far apart as the English Channel and Iceland. Further north lemon soles are only taken in small quantities while plaice are significant in the Barents Sea. Generally, lemon soles inhabit deeper waters than those in which plaice normally live; this is shown clearly in the North Sea where the former are taken in largest quantities from the deepest northern parts while plaice, like soles, are caught mainly in the south.

Although caught in quite large quantities, the saithe, or coalfish, a member of the cod family often retailed under the name 'coley', has a low value and cannot be regarded as a popular food fish. It is taken from most of the areas frequented by cod but in only small quantities from the northernmost of these. It is important in catches made around Iceland and Faroes, off the Norwegian coast and the west of Scotland, and in the North Sea.

The whiting is taken in largest numbers by Scottish vessels, principally from the North Sea but also off the west coast. Catches by other British craft in the North Sea, the English and Bristol Channels and the Irish Sea are quite considerable but it is found in only small quantities to the north of the British Isles. The level of exploitation of the whiting stock, particularly by Scottish fishermen, is frequently a reflection of the abundance of the more valuable haddock for, when the latter are scarce, greater emphasis is placed on fishing for whiting.

The remaining fish mentioned in the table are hake and skates and rays.

The general category 'skates and rays' contains a number of different species and some occur in nearly all the regions exploited by British vessels. They are sometimes found in shallow waters, most are taken off the western coasts of Britain but good catches are made from the North Sea, particularly in the north.

Hake are normally inhabitants of deeper waters at the edge of the continental shelf or on the continental slope but some migrate around the north of Scotland into the North Sea during the summer. The greatest landings are made from the west of Scotland, in the Irish Sea and in the northern North Sea. Formerly, large catches were made to the south and west of Ireland and it is important off the coasts of Portugal and Morocco. The severe overexploitation of this fish to the south and west of the British Isles and the decline of Milford Haven have already been mentioned. Cardiff and Swansea, now insignificant as fishing ports, had sizeable fishing fleets, largely dependent upon hake, in the late 1940s and early 1950s. The total British landings of the fish were just over 4064 metric tons (4000 long tons) in 1967, compared with over 25 400 metric tons (25 000 long tons) in 1949 when landings from the south and west of Ireland alone amounted to over 11 180 metric tons (11 000 long tons). In 1967 about 40 metric tons of hake were taken by British vessels from the same area; admittedly, many fewer trawlers are now operating but it is the reduction in catches that has played a major part in making the operations uneconomic. It is interesting to note that, over the postwar period, the decline in the value of hake landings has been almost as great as that accompanying the much publicised fall in the herring catch. In 1948 the hake was fifth in total value of British wet fish landings and fetched £3.5m at first sale; the herring was fourth at £5.4m. The respective figures for 1967 were £1m (ninth) and £2.7m (fifth).

Many of the other demersal species have also been under pressure. Indications may be given by declining catches per 100 hours fishing and a preponderance of small fish in the catch. Alterations in total landings from a particular area can be misleading, for these may only indicate changes in fishing effort. Total national catches are even more suspect in this respect. For example, landings of cod by British vessels in England and Wales were rather lower in 1967 than in 1949 but considerable changes of emphasis are hidden by these figures; during the earlier year nearly two-thirds of the total came from northeast Arctic grounds of the Barents Sea and around Bear Island and Spitzbergen but, because of declining productivity here, the main fishing effort was diverted elsewhere, and by 1967 the largest catches were being made in Icelandic waters and there had been a significant increase in catches from the northwest Atlantic, particularly following the development of freezer trawlers.

Cod landings from principal areas by British vessels at English and Welsh ports in 1949, 1967 and 1969

		LANDINGS ('000 LONG TONS)		
AREA		1949	1967	1969
Barents Sea		139	39	107
Norwegian Coast		19	23	56
Bear Island and Spitzbergen		64	9	26
North Sea		26	40	36
Iceland		62	104	78
Faroes		10	6	6
West Greenland		12	16	*
Grand Banks		*	35	2
Labrador		*	7	2
Others		8	14	10
Total	long tons	340	293	323
	metric tons	345	298	328

* Less than 1000 tons.
1 long ton = 2240 lb = 1.016 metric ton

Source: *Sea Fisheries Statistical Tables.*

The British were not alone in diverting vessels; much of the Soviet fleet operated there following the over exploitation, for which it was largely responsible, of the northeastern Arctic grounds in the period 1960–63.

German, Portuguese and other fleets were also well in evidence. This international reduction in fishing effort in northern European waters allowed stocks to recover, and the figures for 1969 tell the story of the resulting action taken by fishing companies.

If we now turn to an examination of the pelagic species, the dominance of the herring is clear. This fish is far more important to the Scottish fisheries than to the English and the greatest landings are now made off the Scottish west coast, although the east coast used to be more important. It is taken throughout the year from these western areas and, although there are seasonal differences, they are not as marked as in the North Sea. At Ayr the minimum is during the autumn, at Campbeltown it occurs in the winter and, farther north, it is during the summer.

Distribution of the herring catch (in '000 long tons) by ports in 1967

Ullapool		26.2
Mallaig		16.0
Oban		13.6
Fraserburgh		8.3
Lerwick		7.8
Ayr		5.5
Whitehaven		3.8
North Shields		3.5
Campbeltown		3.2
Stornoway		2.2
Lossiemouth		1.5
Aberdeen		1.3
Scarborough		1.2
North Sunderland		1.0
Lowestoft		0.6
Grimsby		0.6
Peterhead		0.5
Yarmouth		0.5
Milford Haven		0.5
Others		3.2
Total	long tons	101
	metric tons	102.6

Ring netting is the most important method used in the sheltered waters of the Clyde and the Minches. It is rarely employed in other Scottish waters where weather conditions are less reliable and more fish are taken in drift or trawl nets. Purse seining, although similar in many ways, has been used more widely and has been responsible for good landings at some Scottish east coast ports, among which Fraserburgh has been notable. Drifting is important on the west coast only from Ullapool, where a number of vessels fish in the more open waters of the North Minch. Trawling accounts for many herrings in the Minches but it is little used in the Clyde.

West coast fisheries other than the Scottish are of small importance. There are two that may be mentioned, both being operated during the summer. One is around the Isle of Man and off northeast Ireland, mainly by drifters and ring-netters; the other, worked mainly by trawlers sometimes landing at Milford Haven, is off southern Ireland between the Smalls lighthouse and the Old Head of Kinsale.

It is well known that in the North Sea large-scale fishing begins each year in the north and moves southwards during the summer and autumn. It must be stressed that although there is clear evidence of some southward movement of mature and maturing fish, it is not the movement of one stock but of several, each appearing progressively farther southwards. After spawning, the fish return northwards to spend the winter in various deeper parts of the North Sea.

Mainly to the north of 55°N the catching of immature herrings and recovering spents (those that have recently spawned) begins in May. By June, feeding is at a much higher rate and good quality maturing and immature fish are taken. Up to this time fish are landed in the Shetlands, along the Scottish east coast, principally at Fraserburgh, but also at Aberdeen, Lossiemouth, Peterhead and other centres and on the English northeast coast, where North Shields is the main centre.

There is a steady improvement during the next two months and shoals spread farther southwards. In August spawning takes place in the northern North Sea and these fish are taken off northeast Scotland; mixed shoals of full and spawning fish occur off the English coast as far south as Scarborough and provide the basis for the main Yorkshire fishery.

These fisheries are mainly prosecuted with drift nets and, by the end of August, there is little activity north of the Yorkshire coast, where fishing usually finishes about a month later.

The annual east coast drift fishery culminates in the southern North Sea and eastern English Channel when, between about the beginning of October and Christmas, shoals of mature fish head southwards to spawn off the northern French and Belgian coasts. This fishery is of small importance to the economy, contributing, in 1967 1 120 metric tons (1 100 long tons) to the British herring landings of 102 600 metric tons (101 000 long tons), but it is notable because of its history.

In the past, large numbers of Scottish and English drifters were based at Yarmouth and Lowestoft during the season but nowadays few Scottish vessels find it worth while to make the trip, particularly as the fisheries in The Minches at the same time are much more profitable. East Anglian landings reached their peak in 1913, a year when English and Welsh herring landings totalled 372 000 metric tons (366 000 long tons) (compared with 12 000 long tons in 1967). Subsequently there has been an almost continuous decline interrupted only by temporary revivals after both world wars.

The British trawl fisheries for herring in the North Sea are of little consequence compared with those carried out by continental fishermen. The Fladen grounds in the northern North Sea between the Scottish and Norwegian coasts were found in 1911, by an Aberdeen skipper, to be productive for herring trawling; the area fished was extended southwards, and vessels from Germany, Denmark, France, Belgium and Sweden were soon operating over a wide area between the Humber and the Orkneys and making very large catches. Since the second war there has been intensive trawling of the spawning stocks off the north French coast, and in 1948 a fishery for immature herrings on the Bløden ground, between the Dogger Bank and the Danish coast, commenced and enormous hauls have been made by continental vessels. Most of these trawled fish are consigned to factories for conversion to meal and oil.

Several factors have almost certainly been responsible for the general decline in herring landings. There was a considerable reduction in demand both at home and on the export market after the First World War. In 1913 the greatest part of the herring catch was exported, in pickled form, mainly to Russia, Germany, France and Belgium. After the war, the trade with Russia and Germany, the principal customers, was seriously curtailed, partly because of their political problems but also because they were developing their own fishing fleets. Subsequently exports have continued to decline and increasing reliance has been placed on the home market, but here, too, consumption has fallen.

It is also true that stocks of herring in the southern North Sea have been seriously depleted. Admittedly, catches might have been expected to fall, if only because of the smaller number of vessels operating, but there is undoubtedly a shortage of fish due, almost certainly, to the extensive trawling by continental boats on the spawning grounds in the southern North Sea and the eastern English Channel and the taking of immature fish on the Bløden grounds.

The British have never developed an interest in large scale exploitation of herring for fish meal although surplus and condemned fish go to this outlet. Nevertheless about 40 per cent of the herring catch goes for processing for human consumption; most are kippered, while good quantities are canned, marinated and pickle cured for export and some are made into bloaters or red herrings. Most of this processing is concentrated at Fraserburgh, Aberdeen and Peterhead and fish are even taken in fair quantities from England to be dealt with there.

Sprats are taken mainly for processing but most of these are consigned to fish meal plants and many go for petfood manufacture. Some are canned at Fraserburgh and brought to the factory from as far away as the south of England. Others are smoked and a few arrive on the fresh market.

The fishery for sprats was transformed during the 1950s following the introduction of the pair trawl, but the main expansion followed the commencement, in the early 1960s, of intensive operations along the Scottish east coast, particularly in the Moray Firth but also in the Firth of Forth and the Buchan area; smaller catches are made around the Shetlands and in the Clyde. The English landings are less and sometimes even minute by comparison, but in most years could be much larger if an outlet were available for them; the prices are so low that it is often not even economical to transport the fish to meal and oil plants. The main catches are, again, made along the east coast; vessels from Grimsby and several other centres fish in the area of the Wash and good landings are made at North Shields.

It was in the Thames Estuary, from Whitstable, that commercial pelagic pair trawling was introduced to this country in 1950, but little is carried on at the port now. Fish were landed in considerable quantities there and at Southend in the early and middle 1950s and again in the early 1960s. At other times fish have not been in the area. The remaining significant fisheries are on the south coast, principally from Poole and the Torbay ports.

The other pelagic fish are mackerel and pilchards; both are landed principally in Cornwall although sizeable catches of the former are made in Scottish waters. Taking mackerel on lines from small boats during the summer and autumn is now the main fishery activity at many ports in Cornwall and, to some extent, has made up for the drastic postwar decline in landings of pilchards and demersal fish in the area. Before, and for a few years after the Second World War, there was an important drift fishery for mackerel by boats from Scotland and the east coast of England, which were based at Newlyn each year after the main herring season was finished farther east. They operated south of Ireland and in the western English and Bristol Channels. Catches were reduced and drifters scrapped as the herring fishery declined, and visits from these vessels finally ceased in the late 1960s.

During this century pilchards have been caught mainly in drift nets but formerly other methods were employed. The fish have been important, but since 1953, when the largest postwar landings of nearly 6100 metric tons (6000 long tons) were made, the picture has been of decline, and less than 1000 long tons were brought ashore in 1967.

Certainly, there have been fewer fish on the traditional inshore grounds, but there has also been an absence of good market demand. Before the war most fish were cured in brine and exported to Italy. The trade collapsed but the curing was replaced by canning, mainly for the home market; unfortunately, this, too, declined considerably as the canners were unable to compete with relatively cheap imports of canned pilchards from South Africa and South-West Africa.

The most marked feature of the shellfishing part of the industry postwar has been the boom in landings of Norway lobsters (scampi) since the late 1950s. Earlier, the market for these had been extremely limited and the creatures were often discarded as valueless but, with the rising standard of living and the acquisition by many people, through foreign holidays, of a taste for similar shellfish, it was not difficult to create a demand.

They are trawled at many places around the Scottish coast, mainly on the western side but also in the east and off the English northeast coast and from Northern Ireland. They are taken by road to processing plants at places such as Aberdeen, Lossiemouth and Buckie where they are deep frozen, packed and dispatched to various parts of the British Isles, perhaps for export.

The other principal crustaceans are lobsters, crabs, shrimps and crawfish. Lobsters prefer rocky areas and this valuable shellfish is taken at many places around the Scottish coasts but nearly one-third of the total catch (by value) in 1967 was made in the Shetlands, and at Wick, Stornoway and Mallaig. The smaller landings in England and Wales are mostly made on the coasts of northeast England, Cornwall and west Wales but they are also significant in other English Channel waters west of Eastbourne. Unfortunately, catches have been declining in the last few years and this may be a sign of overfishing.

Crab landings have been more stable in England although they, too, have declined in Scotland. These crustaceans are more important in England that in Scotland and few are taken in Wales. They may be found in somewhat deeper waters than is normal for lobsters but are also in many of the same areas. The biggest landings are made on the Scottish east coast, in the Shetlands, on the English northeast coast and in the English Channel off Devon and Cornwall, particularly at Dartmouth and Plymouth. In Norfolk, Sheringham and Cromer are famous for crabs.

The remaining larger crustacean, the crawfish, is a warmer water creature and landed in only small quantities outside western Cornish waters. It is a more familiar fish on the continent where high prices are paid and, consequently, most are exported. Shrimps inhabit shallow sandy areas and the main catches are made in Morecambe Bay, the Ribble and Dee Estuaries and the Wash.

About 4 million oysters are now produced annually. This is many fewer than before the war or, indeed, shortly after the conflict. In 1938 there were over 16 million marketed and, for 1949, the number was 8 million. The famous Whitstable beds are now of little importance and are used for fattening small numbers of oysters from other areas. In Essex the beds in the rivers Blackwater, Colne and Crouch still have a good production but it is in Cornwall, on the Helford river and the various inlets leading into the Fal, that the principal beds exist. Even these are dependent, for young oysters, on stock imported from France and other countries and good local spatfalls (layings) are few.

The decline of the east coast beds has been the result of mainly physical disasters. Just as production was being resumed after the war, many oysters were killed in the hard winter of 1946–47. Subsequent misfortunes were the floods of 1953 and the winter of 1962–63. The Cornish stocks escaped the worst of these adversities and the grounds in the west country have also been more free of pests.

Escallops are taken between depths of about 18 and 55 metres (10 and 30 fathoms) from many areas around the British Isles, usually in small quantities. There are grounds near the Isle of Man, in the English Channel off South Devon and southeast Cornwall and off Newhaven in Sussex. In recent years, however, the largest catches have been made in western Scottish waters and brought ashore principally at Campbeltown and also at Mallaig, Oban and Ullapool. Good landings have also been made at Lerwick.

Two other shellfish to be mentioned are cockles and mussels. The former occur in many places but the most significant commercial beds are nearly all at the mouths of large rivers particularly in the outer Thames estuary, the Wash and in the Burry Inlet in South Wales. Mussels are also widespread in occurrence and may be found attached to piers, rocks and jetties but the largest commercial quantities are in estuaries with gravelly or stony beds and most are taken from the Wash, the Conway estuary and the Menai Straits.

Fish marketing has undergone many changes in the postwar period but some aspects are extremely antiquated; it is still not unusual for fish to pass through three markets before reaching a retailer. The effect of the attendant delay and handling inflicted on a perishable product can easily be imagined.

Demersal fish are usually first sold at a port auction market by an agent acting on commission for the vessel owner. The fish may be bought by a firm of freezers or by a major retailing organisation which would possibly send its purchase to a central depot before final distribution. Some might be bought by local retailers or by a wholesaler who would either distribute his fish by rail or road to retail outlets or send it to an inland market where it might be sold, but probably not by auction, to a retailer. The larger markets, as at Billingsgate or Manchester, act not only as gathering points for fishmongers of the region but also distribution points for wider areas. Consequently fish may be bought here by yet another wholesaler who might send some to be sold at a smaller inland market. It is quite likely that at some point along the path, and probably at the port market by the wholesaler, the fish may be filleted.

Many port markets have gone out of existence and the throughput of others has been reduced, partly because of smaller catches but also because more boat owners are dealing directly, or through their agents, with freezing companies and, additionally, because more fish are being frozen at sea and need specialised handling. In 1969 over 20 per cent of the wet fish catch was quick-frozen either at sea or on landing and the amount is increasing every year.

Some fishermen, particularly at small ports without a market, have been sending fish directly to inland markets instead of to the nearest port market.

A number of cooperatives have also been formed, again at smaller centres, and the members have taken over the marketing function at the port, obviously to their benefit.

Inland markets have also been in decline. They are being bypassed as direct trading between retailers and the ports has become more popular and have suffered because of the increase in fish being frozen and then distributed by the processers. This in turn has affected the fishmongers who no longer have a virtual monopoly of fish retail selling now that many types of stores offer frozen foods. There has been a reduction in the number of private fishmongers and this has further reduced the potential market customers. Finally, a greater part of the conventional retail wet fish trade is being undertaken by multiple fish retailers who buy at the ports and do their own distribution.

Pelagic fish may be sold in broadly the same way as demersal fish, but a higher proportion is sent directly to processers, and a particular canner may have a number of vessels fishing for him.

Shellfish are not auctioned and may be disposed of to a wholesaler or by direct sale to a private buyer. Lobsters, crabs, crawfish and Norway lobsters are mainly sold to a port wholesaler, who may process them in some way, prior to dispatch. Lobsters and crawfish, however, are normally sent live.

The postwar period has seen a change of emphasis in fish transport from rail to road. This is partly connected with the decline of the traditional marketing system for, with more direct dealings between the ports and retailers or inland wholesalers outside the largest markets, smaller loads have to be carried to a greater number of places and road transport is obviously more suitable; in addition, the pricing policy of British Rail has not encouraged the use of their transport for small consignments. Many processers and wholesalers now rely largely upon road transport and own fleets of vehicles, often of a specialist type such as those used for carrying frozen foods. Road improvements have encouraged the trend which has been further accelerated by the effects of recurrent labour difficulties and the closure of some railway routes.

More expensive fish, mainly shellfish, are sometimes transported by air, both within Great Britain and to the continent. Frequent consignments of shellfish are exported from Southend, Land's End, Exeter and other airports.

Considerable financial assistance is provided for the industry by the Government, and administered by the White Fish Authority and the Herring Industry Board. Modernisation is encouraged by the payment of substantial grants and loans for the purchase and improvement of vessels and, also, by the provision of loans for processing and ice plants on shore. Aid is given to encourage the formation of cooperatives, and finally there are operating subsidies which, for vessels less than 24 metres (80 ft) in length, are paid at a rate per day at sea or per stone of fish landed, and for larger craft are related to a measure of their operating efficiency.

Even with this assistance, many problems remain and the non-freezer part of the distant water fleet is extremely vulnerable. Its catches are sometimes unsaleable because of poor quality on landing, and it is important that ways are devised of keeping the fish fresher; experiments in transferring it to freezer trawlers on the fishing grounds have been carried out, and if these are extended, they may provide the answer until all the distant water catch is frozen on board the catching vessels.

Inshore fishing is concentrated at rather fewer ports than some years ago and, recently, this section, particularly in Scotland, has been in a much healthier state. It accounts for more than a quarter of the total supplies. Quality of fish is good and catches have been improving, probably at least partly due to the effect of the Fishery Limits Act of 1964.

Nevertheless, catch rates in this sector are low compared with those of vessels fishing more remote waters where the main immediate future must lie. The effects of intensive exploitation on many distant grounds by vessels of several nations have been mentioned and we have witnessed a change of emphasis from the northeast Arctic to the northwest Atlantic. Present international conservation measures are obviously inadequate in such situations and, if fish are to be protected, other action must be taken, but the difficulties of obtaining international cooperation for major revisions are enormous. In the meantime, additional fishing areas need to be explored; experimental voyages have been made in the past few years to the south Atlantic to catch silver hake. Perhaps these and other stranger fish will become regular items on our menu.

Aids to modern fishing are numerous and expensive and the industry now has many extremely complex craft, but in essence its philosophy is the primitive one of badly controlled hunting. One cannot help but wonder if it is not this that really needs revision and if greater money and effort should be channelled into fish cultivation.

14
Fuel and power

In the preceding consideration of agriculture, forestry and fisheries particular emphasis has been laid on the changes that have been wrought, during the period since the First World War in particular, by technological advances and by alterations in the general economic situation of the country. Turning now to the major industries and their bases of resources, fuel and power, we shall find that the changes are even more revolutionary—that we are living in the middle of what may well be described by future historians as the 'Second Industrial Revolution' of the mid-twentieth century. This 'revolution' has been brought about—just as that of 1760–1830 was—by new 'inventions', entailing the use of new materials and new sources of energy, derived perhaps from quite different localities than hitherto and contributing to fundamental changes in the geographical balance and the economic fortunes of the various parts of Britain.

Amongst the most important of these changes are: (*a*) the declining use of coal, with the vast increase in the use of electricity (which, however, is still mostly generated through the agency of coal), an equally massive increase in the use of oil, with all that this entails in the necessity for imports, in the growth of refining industries and petrochemical industries at both old and new ports, and in the almost complete cessation in the use of coal as a fuel in ships (which in turn has resulted in the virtual death of the British coal export trade), and the advent of a completely new source of energy in the shape of North Sea gas; (*b*) the phenomenal growth of the automobile and aircraft industries with their insatiable demand for a thousand-and-one components involving many subsidiary industries; (*c*) the development of manmade fibres, entailing the growth of new chemical industries to make the fibres and with important economic consequences for the older textile trades; (*d*) the growth of a vast array of electrical and electronic industries—domestic and industrial appliances, radio, television and now computers—that have quite different localising factors from those characteristic of nineteenth-century industry.

It is the purpose of the first of these industrial chapters to examine the fuel and energy supplies upon which the British economy is now based.

COAL

Coal has always been Britain's main mineral product, and though (see Chapter 15) gravel and limestone together now represent a greater tonnage, coal remains of overwhelming importance both in terms of the value of the output and in terms of the employment that it offers. In 1967 coal output of 173.7 million metric tons (171 million long tons) compared with gravel 106.7 million metric tons (105 million long tons) and limestone 76.2 million metric tons (75 million long tons); but in the same year the coal industry employed 412 000 people and all other mining and quarrying industries together less than 50 000.

It is obviously true to say that Britain's industrial development has been based on coal. But as a source of energy its dominance has been greatly reduced by the importation of ever-increasing quantities of crude oil (more than 76.2 million metric tons (75 million long tons) in 1968 as compared with 9.1 million metric tons (9 million long tons) in 1950) and more recently by the construction of several nuclear-based power stations mainly in coastal locations. In 1968 North Sea gas was also beginning to make significant inroads into the energy market. The difficulties which beset the coal mining industry immediately after the Second World War have been too loosely interpreted as being related essentially to the exhaustion of workable reserves. This was certainly far from the truth, though it might have been argued that substantial quantities of the more readily accessible coals had already been extracted, particularly in the older coalfields of the country.

Coal has been worked in Britain since very early times. The discovery of coal cinders in the ruins of Roman towns makes it probable that the Romans used coal during their occupation of the country. The *Anglo-Saxon Chronicle* records its use in monasteries in the ninth century. By the thirteenth or fourteenth century there was a well established trade in seaborne coal from Newcastle and Tyneside to London. The early shallow workings were naturally along the outcrops of individual seams, but coal at or near the surface is apt to be badly weathered and unobtainable in lumps suitable for transport and burning. Small adits or drifts following the seams into the hillsides provided better-quality coal, but the opening of these often gave rise to problems of drainage and roof support. Bell pits and small mines with haulage shafts allowed slightly deeper-lying seams to be worked. Generally, however, no systematic form of shallow mining was developed. No records were kept, with the result that at their uppermost levels many seams are still honeycombed with unchartered irregular excavations. In recent years some of this coal lying at no great depth has been extracted by opencast means and, more locally, by small drift mines operated both by the National Coal Board and under licence as private concerns. Where the incidence of old workings is high and a flood risk is known to occur no exploitation of any remaining reserves is now likely to take place.

In general terms the story of development is the same for all the British coalfields. There was first, as described above, the spasmodic local working in open pits or shallow mines; then came larger mines with deep shafts and associated colliery villages or mining towns, with all the attendant network of services and communication—the improvement of roads or construction of tramways, and later the extensive building of canals, rendered obsolete by the advent of railways. The industrial regions took on the high degree of specialisation characteristic of Britain—Lancashire with cottons, the Leeds–Bradford area of Yorkshire with woollens, the Sheffield area with steel and cutlery, the Black Country with iron smelting and so on.

Coal mining, however, is a robber industry and although a state of complete exploitation is not physically possible it should be apparent that in due course the more accessible and better-quality reserves will be largely exhausted. In Britain this has already happened in the old Black Country of southern Staffordshire and neighbouring parts of Worcestershire, and in the Forest of Dean. During the past twenty years many of the older coalfields of Britain have shown a progressive shift of mining activity to the deeper or 'concealed' sections so that capital outlay has been greater and individual units now have an extended geographical range of operations and generally higher outputs.

Nationalisation and recent progress in the industry

The British coal mining industry was nationalised on 1 January 1947 when the National Coal Board and its component Divisional Board were established. The Board was charged with the task of reorganising and re-equipping the industry. Apart from the slight industrial recession in 1951–52, the period from 1947 to the end of 1956 was featured by an expanding economy with an average annual increase in the inland demand for coal of 3.2 million tons. For ten years the industry was therefore, from a production angle, geared to an expansionist programme. The problem of overproduction, which was brought to light in the latter half of 1957, was totally unexpected. To avoid wholesale closures of collieries, some with substantial reserves, and the dismissal of thousands of miners, stocks of coal were allowed to build up and by the end of 1959 these reached a peak level of nearly 36.6 million metric tons (36 million long tons). The main reasons for this decline in demand were the industrial recession in the United Kingdom and the increasing usage of alternative, more convenient and, sometimes, cheaper forms of fuel, particularly oil.

These entirely unforeseen changes within the British coal mining industry, involving as they did the serious problems of mounting stocks and diminishing demand, forced the National Coal Board to draw up its third major plan (1959) within the space of ten years. Forecasts made in this plan for the production and manpower levels in 1965 have subsequently proved to be far too high; nevertheless, much of the future policy then outlined has been implemented in the mining programmes evident up until 1968.

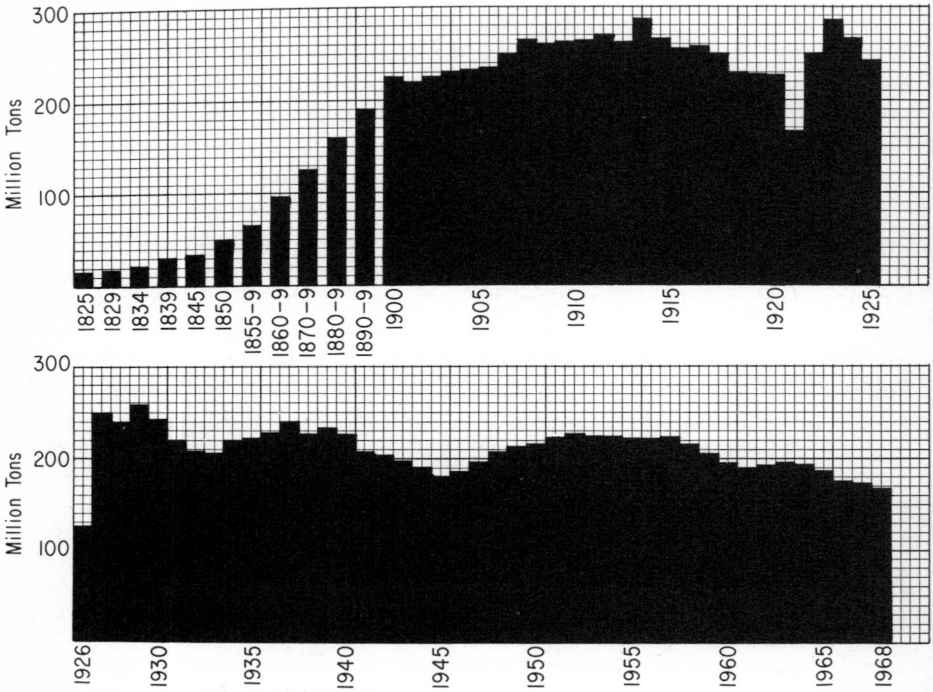

FIG. 111. Graph showing British coal output, 1825–1968

A major effort has been directed at the improvement of all-round efficiency within the industry. In the latter half of 1968 output per manshift (overall) at the Board's collieries had reached the encouraging level of 2.2 metric tons (43 cwt) and it was confidently anticipated that this would exceed 2.5 metric tons (50 cwt) by 1970–71. No other British industry could match this productivity spurt and now it perhaps can rightly be claimed that the British coal mining industry leads the world in technical deep-mining developments. To achieve this end the closure of uneconomic or low-yielding collieries, more especially in the older coalfields of Scotland, Northumberland and Durham, Lancashire and South Wales has been drastic. Between March 1965 and March 1968 no less than 164 collieries, mainly in these categories, were closed or merged. In 1968 more than 90 per cent of the deep-mined output was produced by mechanised methods. Resources are being directed to those collieries with the greatest potential as the less economic collieries are closed. The continuing collieries will be producing from fewer, more productive, faces and at lower costs.

The enforced contraction which the industry has suffered resulted in a certain lack of faith in its future stability. As a consequence the drain of manpower through normal wastage, a reduction in recruiting and transfer into other occupations reached near-flood proportions at times. Thus the average overall colliery manpower has markedly diminished from 693 000 in 1958 to 392 000 for the year ended 30 March 1968. The Board consider it essential to maintain an adequate labour force in the low-cost central coalfields, but this is particularly difficult at a time when because of uncertainty about the long-term future, wastage from the industry will probably increase. It is a corollary of the progressively increasing productivity rates that the rundown of production has not been of such a drastic order. The output of deep-mined coal (National Coal Board and licensed mines) for the year ended 30 March 1968 was 166.6 million metric tons (164 million long tons) as compared with 204.7 million metric tons (201.5 million long tons) in 1958.

PLATE 9. The 'new look' of a modern colliery: Parkside in south Lancashire. The concrete towers house the shaft-heads

The disposition of the coalfields

Unlike her neighbours on the continent of Europe, Britain has practically no production nor resources of lignite or brown coal. The small field containing such coals of Tertiary age at Bovey Tracey in Devonshire is unimportant. Britain's coals are nearly all of Carboniferous age; those of England and Wales occurring in the Coal Measures (Upper Carboniferous), those of

Scotland in both the Lower and Upper Carboniferous. There is an isolated mine at Brora on the coast of Sutherland in northern Scotland, which works coal of Jurassic age. Britain is perhaps unfortunate in that a former wide spread of Coal Measure rocks has been broken up into a number of separate small areas by subsequent earth movements and denudation; and an attempt to reconstruct the geography of the period may assist in the understanding of the disposition of existing fields.

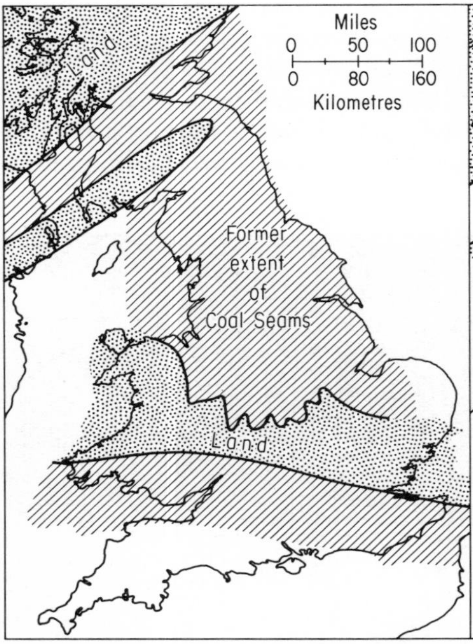

FIG. 112. The geography of the Coal Measure period

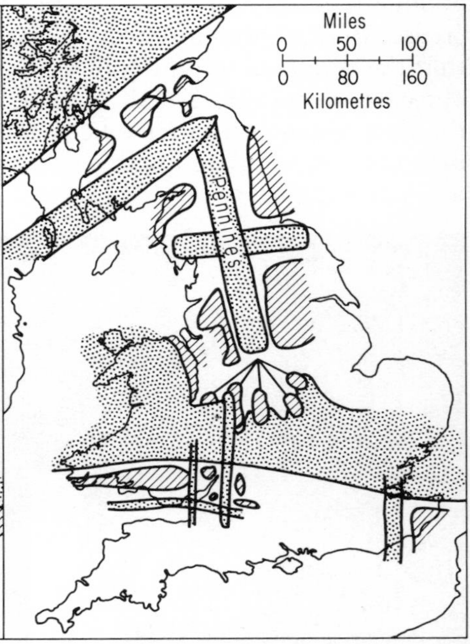

FIG. 113. The effect of subsequent earth movements in separating the British Coal Measures into a number of basins

In Chapter 2 we have already outlined the conditions under which the Coal Measures of Britain were deposited.

In early Carboniferous time the present Highlands of Scotland formed part of a great continental mass. Along its southern fringe were deltaic flats, and on them flourished the extensive swamp forests from which coals of Lower Carboniferous age derive. These older coal seams die out southward except for a few in Northumberland. It was not until Upper Carboniferous time that conditions suitable for the growth of coal forests spread over the larger part of England and Wales. At that time, it is believed, a great deltaic flat stretched from the margin of the Scottish land mass to St George's Land, a low land ridge crossing the Midlands of England. Along the southern fringe of St George's Land conditions were also suitable for the growth of Coal Measure forests, but farther south (in Devon and Cornwall) rocks of the same age are barren. St George's Land remained relatively stable during Coal Measure time, whereas the areas to the north and south underwent successive depressions. It would seem that there were thus originally two enormous coalfields of Upper Carboniferous or Coal Measure age, one reaching from the Highlands of Scotland to the Midlands of England, the other lying south of St George's Land and extending from South Wales across southern England into Kent and on into northern France and Belgium. In the northern area, coal seams traced southward towards the old land bridge are found to get gradually closer together and, in some places, eventually to merge. This is the case with the famous Thick Coal—as much as 11 metres (36 ft) thick—of the South Staffordshire or Black Country coalfield, and this explains why the coals in some of the Midland fields have been virtually worked out.

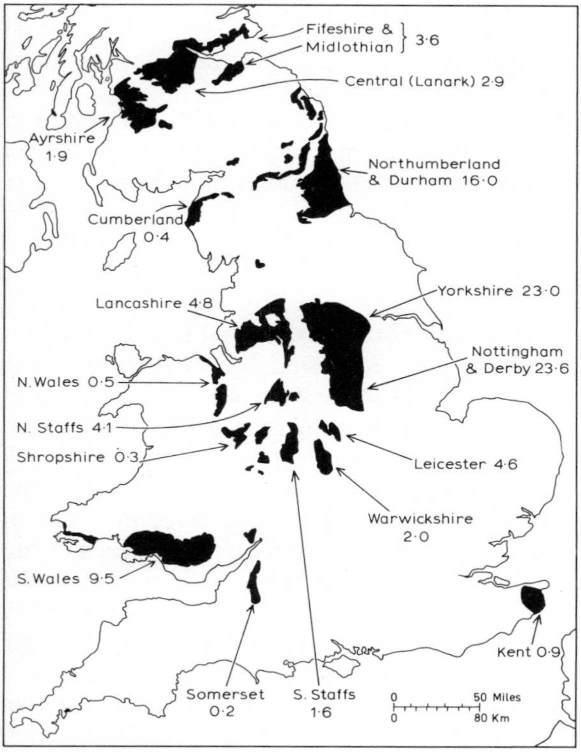

FIG. 114. The coalfields of Great Britain and their production in 1968 expressed as a percentage of the total national output

The Armorican or Hercynian earth movements at the end of the Carboniferous period flexed the British Coal Measures into a series of east–west and north–south folds. Where two downfolds cross, an oval basin may be formed, as in the little Forest of Dean coalfield. Folding and subsequent denudation of the anticlines resulted in the separation of the British coal deposits into a series of basins. Each basin is geologically a distinct unit and may be said to constitute a coalfield. Where the basin is completely surrounded by older rocks the exact extent of the field is known, and total reserves can be closely calculated. The South Wales and Forest of Dean fields are good examples of such basins; the Scottish fields afford other examples. In other places the Coal Measures may plunge down or be faulted down to such depths that the existence of coal can only be assumed; in any case it is beyond workable depth. Thus between the North Wales and Lancashire fields coal probably underlies the whole Cheshire plain, but at depths certainly exceeding 1200 metres (4000 ft). In still other places the Coal Measures plunge beneath younger rocks or the sea, and the precise limits of the field remain unknown. This is the case with the great Yorkshire and Durham fields.

Unfortunately, different parts of a single geological coal field may be given separate names, and in recent nomenclature has been further confused by the adoption of regions with new names.[1]

The extent of the fields as known at present is shown on the official map of Coal and Iron on the scale of 1 : 625 000 prepared by the Maps Research Office of the Ministry of Housing and Local Government and published by the Ordnance Survey.

British coal reserves

No calculations have been made recently of Britain's total coal reserves. A summary made in 1947 from the published Regional Survey Reports of the Ministry of Fuel and Power suggested that the known workable reserves in seams 46 centimetres (18 inches) and more in thickness, to a depth of 1200 metres (4000 ft) and exclusive of reserves considered not economical to work at that time amounted to something like 40 000 million long tons. Despite the extra data now available the National Coal Board has not embarked on the big task of reassessing the reserves quantitatively. For some mining districts precise estimates have been made, but it is considered that the aggregation of all the figures available would be misleading since they would combine estimates varying widely in reliability. Undoubtedly there are extensive reserves of coal available in the country as a whole, but some of the long-worked parts of the fields are becoming, or have been, exhausted of coal which can be worked economically. Full assessments of the concealed extensions to some coalfields have yet to be made and in some instances the details will not be available until mining developments have actually encroached on these virgin areas. As shown by the exceptional structural difficulties encountered in parts of the South Wales and Scottish coalfields

1. Particularly stupid and confusing is the use by the Ministry of Fuel and Power of the term 'North-eastern field' meaning in fact west and south Yorkshire.

a network of boreholes of normal density does not always provide a reliable picture of the actual mining conditions likely to be encountered. The conditions under which mining, even with modern methods, can be carried out economically are relatively narrow. Emphasis must be laid on the fact that much of the best coal, and of the coal which is cheapest to work, has gone. In many areas, therefore, technical advances in mining methods are largely offset by greater physical difficulties of extraction.

In the general estimate of reserves previously quoted the Coal Survey Officers usually disregarded seams lying at depths below 1200 metres (4000 ft) (this was extended to 1350 metres in the case of a few collieries in South Lancashire and North Staffordshire). In some coalfields deep mining could well be extended appreciably below 1200 metres, but in highly disturbed coalfields, like that of South Wales, poor roof and floor conditions over wide areas will not permit mechanised mining even well short of these levels. On a conservative estimate it would appear that Britain has sufficient coal for upwards of 200 years at the present rate of extraction. Whether this will be fully required is open to questioning in the light of developments in the production of other forms of energy. It must be again stressed that the reserves are not shared equally on a unit area basis between the separate coalfields; in some fields economic exhaustion is in sight. Comparison with other European countries will nevertheless show that only Germany (pre-1939 frontiers) is so well endowed with coal resources.

The classification of British coals

British coals include substantial reserves of anthracite in the northwestern quadrant of the South Wales coalfield and minor quantities of this comparatively rare coal in Ayrshire; the remainder are bituminous or humic coals. It has long been the custom to use a rough classification into types based on the suitability of the coals for different purposes. Thus steam coals are hard, burn with little flame and little soot and were therefore much valued for bunker purposes and for ships. Similar types are appreciated for some domestic purposes under the name of 'kitchen nuts' when broken to a small size, and are suitable for consumption in enclosed stoves. By way of contrast, household coals, those which are favoured for burning in open grates, still to be found in English homes, are coals which give a pleasant flame, and are described by the housewife as being 'gassy'. Then the coking property of coals is important. Good coking coals should also, of course, yield a large supply of gas, and if the coke is required for the iron industry, it is essential that it should be a good hard coke, and should not crush when loaded with a considerable weight of iron ore above it. The relative absence of intense folding in the British Isles has resulted in the comparatively small proportion of powdered coals of the types extensively used on the continent of Europe for the manufacture of briquettes. It is indeed only in recent years that coal slack—dust—has been utilised at all in this country, and only a few collieries have briquetting plant for this purpose. The coal dust requires to be mixed with some material, such as pitch, as a binding substance.

In recent years a more exact classification has been brought into use. This scheme was evolved by the Coal Survey officers to assist the Ministry of Fuel and Power in making a census of fuel consumption. The arbitrary 'code numbers' are based on content of volatile matter (on the dry ash-free basis) and coking properties.

I Low-volatile coals (volatile matter 20 per cent or less)
- 100 Anthracite: non-caking, volatile matter less than 10 per cent.
- 200 Low-volatile steam coals (types distinguished as 201, 202, 203, 204, 206).

II Medium-volatile coals (volatile matter 20.1–30.0 per cent).
- 300 Scottish medium-volatile, non-caking or weakly caking.
- 301 Coking coals, strongly caking. (These are the metallurgical coking coals of Durham and South Wales.)

III High-volatile coals (volatile matter over 30.0 per cent). (Each group is divided into 01 and 02, with respectively less and more than 37.0 per cent of volatile matter.)
- 400 Very strongly caking coals
- 500 Strongly caking coals
- 600 Medium caking coals
- 700 Weakly caking coals
- 800 Very weakly caking coals
- 900 Non-caking coals.

All coals have a certain proportion of ash and a high proportion is noticeable in some coal now being mined. It has been authoritatively stated that $2\frac{1}{2}$ per cent should be deducted from post-1950 production to allow for the poorer coals compared with pre-1939 output.

Coal type reserves in the separate fields

Although in need of considerable revision the table opposite (the only one available) gives some indication of the reserves of the various types of coal, as defined in the previous section, within Great Britain as a whole.

In the Northumberland and Durham field the change in the physical and chemical characters of any one seam when it is traced laterally is greater than the difference in seams higher or lower in the succession at a given locality. In Northumberland the predominant type is weakly caking (700), but medium and strongly caking coals (500 and 600) are available in appreciable amounts. The range of coals in the declining western half of the Durham coalfield is rather narrow; about half the production in the past has comprised the special coking coals (301 and 401a). The volatile content increases towards the east where they pass into coking-gas and gas coals (401, 501, 502). Northward they change into medium and weakly caking coals (601, 702) marketed chiefly for power stations, general industrial use and house coal; they are of excellent quality.

Virtually the whole of the limited Cumberland coalfield production is of the high volatile strongly caking class (500).

In the West Yorkshire field types 500 and 600 predominate. More than 70 per cent of the production has come from five seams, but there has been a noticeable move eastward to the deeper part of the field and seams with other types of coal are likely to be worked. In the Sheffield area of South Yorkshire the dominant types are 500, 600 and 700; further south in Nottinghamshire they range on either side of 800 from very weakly caking to non-caking types. The progressive southward change continues into the fields of Leicestershire and South Derbyshire, where the coals are mainly non-caking (900), especially in seams of more than five feet thick. In the other Midland fields very weakly caking and non-caking coals (800–900) again predominate.

Summary of developable coal reserves in Great Britain[1]
(in millions of long tons)

TYPE OF COAL	PLANNED OUTPUT 1942–2042		PROVED ADDITIONAL RESERVES		OUTPUT 1938	
	TONS	%	TONS	%	TONS	%
Anthracite (100)	704.6	3.4	914.3	6.8	6.1	2.7
Steam coals (200, 300; low and medium volatile)	1 861.9	9.1	1 306.6	9.8	20.7	9.1
Coking coals (301, 401; medium volatile)	1 556.2	7.6	1 130.5	8.5	20.7	9.1
Coking-gas and gas coals (400, 500, 600; high volatile)	7 402.3	36.1	3 953.5	29.5	85.0	36.8
Household and industrial coals (700; high volatile, weakly caking)	2 894.4	14.1	1 448.0	10.8	34.2	15.0
Household and general coals (800, 900; high volatile, non-caking)	5 634.1	27.5	4 623.8	34.6	60.7	26.6
Unclassified	446.9	2.2	—	—	1.8	0.7
	20 500.4	100.0	13 376.7[2]	100.0	228.2	100.0

[1] Data from *Rapid Survey of Coal Reserves and Production*, Fuel Research Board, Dept of Scientific and Industrial Research, 1946.

[2] Exclusive of at least 2000 million tons unclassified.

1 long ton = 1.016 metric tons.

Apart from a small output of very strongly caking coal (301 and 400) from the Burnley basin, the coals produced in the Lancashire coalfield range from strongly caking (500) to non-caking, high-volatile types (900). In North Staffordshire the coals show, quite markedly, stronger caking properties with increasing depth. There has been a trend towards the production of larger quantities of very strongly caking coal (400) whilst in the southern concealed area, now being developed, medium-volatile caking coals occur at moderate depths.

South Wales coals range from 100 to 400; anthracite predominating in the northwest, dry steam coals (200) in the heart of the field, and medium or high-volatile coals, including the medium-volatile coking coals (301), towards the southeast. In the entirely concealed Kent field the chief reserves are also of type 200 and anthracites could possibly exist in the deeper seams beyond the eastern coastline.

Scotland has coals of very varied types. Though anthracite is absent, apart from the small quantities in Ayrshire, there are excellent steam coals and a wide range of high-volatile coals.

Opencast working and drift mining

It may seem strange that during the Second World War, after more than a century of essentially deep mining, Britain returned to the open pit or opencast working of coal to such an extent that from 1944 onwards nearly 5 per cent of the production has been obtained in this way. A maximum output of 14.5 million metric tons (14.3 million long tons) was achieved in 1958; the 1968 production totalled 7.1 million metric tons (7 million long tons), the annual output having remained fairly stable around this mark since 1960. In exceptional cases opencast sites are now being worked to depths of more than 150 metres (500 ft). In many of the coalfields, areas of low dip are often defined by slopes of gentle grade at little variance with the underlying structure. Terrain of this type is ideal for opencast working since it often implies that where extractable seams are present the ratio of overburden to coal thickness remains at manageable proportions over extensive sites. Before the advent of opencast mining techniques much of this coal was too deep to quarry and too shallow to mine without giving rise to roof support or subsidence problems.

Large-scale mechanical excavators, dragline scrapers and bulldozers now make it possible to remove greater thickness of overburden and to do it economically. All opencast sites are carefully restored to their former, normally agricultural, usage. In recent years wherever opencast operations can be combined with the reclamation of derelict land the National Coal Board seek to plan and design these activities, in cooperation with local authorities and other bodies, so as to improve the environment of areas of opencast workings and to provide land for recreation or development. When opencast production was at its peak between 1947 and 1959 rather more than 60 per cent of each annual output was obtained from Northumberland, Durham, Yorkshire, Derbyshire and Nottinghamshire, where structural conditions are generally more favourable for opencast workings than in the other coalfields. Stocks of opencast coal remained at a high level during 1968 and the National Coal Board decided that for the time being, at least, production from new sites should be kept at a minimum consistent with supplying market needs and maintaining opencast potential. The Ministry of Power's White Paper on Fuel Policy stated that further authorisations for opencast production would only be given where, because of quality or location the coal produced would not be in competition with deep-mined output. Thus in the western half of the North Crop of the South Wales coalfield the opencast production of anthracite, which reached a peak level of 1 635 000 metric tons (1 610 000 long tons) in 1966, is being maintained at a high rate.

PLATE 10. Opencast coalmine in Northumberland. The huge walking dragline, made by Bucyrus-Erie in Milwaukee, USA, weighs nearly 3000 tons and has a 65 cubic yard capacity bucket (compare the size of the lorry and coach); it can shift 2600 cubic yards of overburden in an hour

Much of the high cost of opencast coal workings in the war years may be attributed to its experimental nature; opencast mining is now a highly profitable operation. Thus in 1967–68 the National Coal Board's deep mines made an operating profit of only 2*s* 9*d* per ton as compared with 18*s* 6*d* per ton for its opencast operations. Initially it was feared that much of the coal might be badly weathered and consequently of poor quality, but now with it being feasible to work to much deeper levels these doubts are to a large degree no longer valid. Past speculations on the likely period of life of future opencast operations have invariably been proved wrong; they seem likely to continue for some years in the Durham and Northumberland, South Wales and Scottish coalfields where there has been an accelerated rundown of conventional mining. Small drift mines, normally employing less than twenty men apiece and operating under licence from the National Coal Board, produced 1.03 million metric tons (1.02 million long tons) of coal in 1967–68, a slight reduction on the 1966–67 output. The success of quite a few of these small units and the difficulties which had beset some of the National Coal Board's new deep mines has resulted in some change of policy with regard to the establishment of new drift mines by the Board. In the past eight years or so several new drift mines, usually employing between 100 and 300 men and directed at the exploitation of relatively shallow-lying reserves not likely to last more than twenty years, have been opened up, more particularly in South Wales, Scotland and the Burnley area of Lancashire. Production-wise many of these have been a great success.

It is perhaps of interest to note the introduction of a modified form of drift mining within a pit near the South Crop of the South Wales coalfield. Horizon mining, widely adopted in some west European coalfields, was introduced into this area in an attempt to work, on a large scale, the strongly dipping seams of high-grade coking coal. As the name implies horizon mining is a system whereby all seams are extracted between horizontal planes which form the main roadways. The incidence of thrust-faulting and disturbed ground was found to be on a much greater scale than originally envisaged whilst there was also some deterioration in seam quality. Horizon mining on a grand scale has therefore been abandoned and replaced by deep-lying drift mining which utilises the facilities provided by vertical shafts and horizontal roadways.

The principal fields

Northumberland and Durham

The Coal Measures in Northumberland and Durham dip away from the Pennine upland and eventually pass under the waters of the North Sea. In eastern Durham they are unconformably overlain by Permian beds, comprising, in upward succession, the Basal Permian Sands, Magnesian Limestone and Upper Permian Marl and reaching a maximum thickness of some 488 metres (1600 ft) in the coastal area near West Hartlepool. The older, shallower workings of the coalfield are thus situated on the flanks of the Pennines in the west whilst the larger and deeper modern collieries are nearly all to the east. In the concealed eastern section of the Durham coalfield much of the production is now being obtained from beneath a considerable thickness of the overlying Permian. The beds of this formation are generally water-bearing and this imposes limitations on the extraction of any coal seams lying immediately below. Percolating water from this source has sometimes exceeded pumping capacity and led to the flooding and abandonment of collieries in the past. Thus mining less than 45.6 metres (150 ft) from water-bearing strata is now prohibited by statute unless it can be shown that the hazard has been overcome.

The relative importance of Britain's coalfields

MINIMUM PROVED RESERVES	FIELD	YEARLY AVERAGE OUTPUT IN MILLION LONG TONS[1] 1909–13	1922–4	1931–5	1950	1960–1	1967–8
1 537	Ayrshire	4.1	4.5	3.9	3.5	3.7	3.2
3 049	Lanarkshire	17.4	19.4	13.6	8.5	6.3	4.8[4]
2 500	Midlothian	6.1	4.4	4.7	3.9	3.4	3.3
3 742	Fifeshire	8.8	8.5	7.8	7.3	4.0	2.7
5 510	Northumberland	14.0	13.7	13.0	12.1	10.9	8.8
870	Durham	40.4	36.6	29.3	26.5	22.5	17.8
1 528	Cumberland	2.2	2.2	1.5	1.1	0.9	0.6
26 000	Yorkshire	39.0	64.7	39.3	32.6	34.4	38.0
	Notts and Derby	31.5	30.2	26.6	36.3	42.6	39.2
4 367	North Staffordshire	13.9	6.3	5.9	11.0[3]	8.9[3]	9.5[3]
1 415	South Staffordshire		1.5	6.2	0.9	1.1	—
1 825	Leicestershire	—[2]	3.1	2.4	3.8	6.7	7.6[5]
1 127	Warwickshire	—[2]	5.1	5.0	5.1	3.9	3.3
4 239	Lancashire	27.3	19.2	13.7	12.5	10.3	7.9
1 736	North Wales		3.2	2.8	2.2	1.8	1.3
26 000	South Wales	51.2	52.3	35.3	23.0	17.9	15.8
259	Forest of Dean	—[2]	1.3	1.2	0.8	—	—
4 198	Bristol and Somerset	2.7	1.3	0.9	0.5	0.5	0.3
2 000	East Kent	—[2]	0.4	1.9	1.7	1.4	1.45
	Shropshire	—	—	—	—	—	0.5

[1] 1 long ton = 1.016 metric tons. [2] Details not available. [3] Includes Cannock.
[4] Including extensions of field into adjoining counties. [5] Including South Derbyshire.

Along the Northumbrian coast many of the coal seams run uninterruptedly out to sea and 6.4 kilometres (four miles) from the coast may be taken as the economic limit for the working of the coalfield. Off the concealed section of the Durham coalfield a programme of undersea deep drilling to ascertain reserves and future mining potential was commenced in 1958. This has established the fact that large areas of thick coal lie ahead of existing coastal workings in several seams. Some seams previously thought to be too thin to exploit have proved to be of workable thickness whilst of equal significance the bore holes have revealed the existence of a thick bed of impervious rock overlying the coal seams and protecting them against possible future inflows of water. New undersea reserves of at least 500 million metric tons have been proved.

The Lower Coal Measures, that is those exposed in the extreme western part of the field, contain a few thin but workable coals. The productive measures of the field begin with the Brockwell or Denton Low Main Coal and contain altogether about twenty-three workable coals. Many of the seams rest on beds of valuable fireclay or seat earth, formerly extensively used for the manufacture of firebricks. Amongst the best known coals are the Hutton and Low Main; the latter is a good gas and house coal in Durham, but north of the Tyne becomes a steam coal. Higher up is the

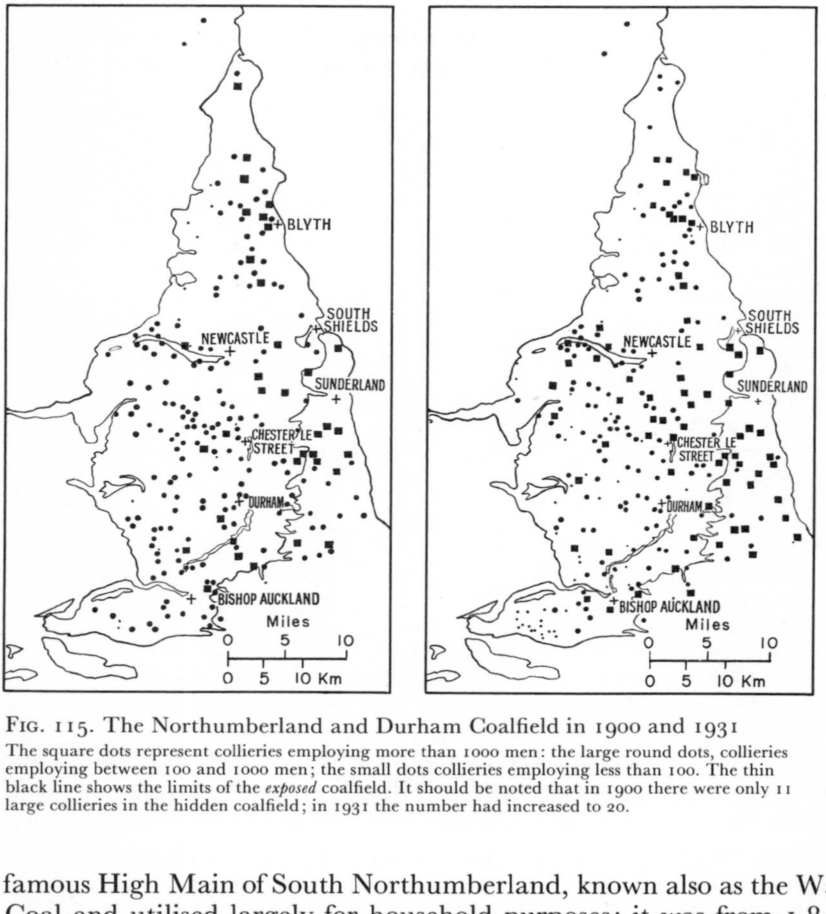

FIG. 115. The Northumberland and Durham Coalfield in 1900 and 1931

The square dots represent collieries employing more than 1000 men: the large round dots, collieries employing between 100 and 1000 men; the small dots collieries employing less than 100. The thin black line shows the limits of the *exposed* coalfield. It should be noted that in 1900 there were only 11 large collieries in the hidden coalfield; in 1931 the number had increased to 20.

famous High Main of South Northumberland, known also as the Wallsend Coal and utilised largely for household purposes; it was from 1.8 to just over 2 metres (six to seven ft) thick, but is now very largely exhausted. Durham coals exhibit a wide range of rank, quality and physical characteristics ranging from soft bright coking coals containing less than 30 per cent of volatile matter to hard, rather dull coals with greater than 36 per cent. These include some of the best coking and gas coals in the kingdom although other seams are much more suitable for household coal. North of the Tyne steam coals become prevalent.

Two sections given here (Figs 116 and 117) show the general disposition of the coal seams and the way in which the Coal Measures are slightly

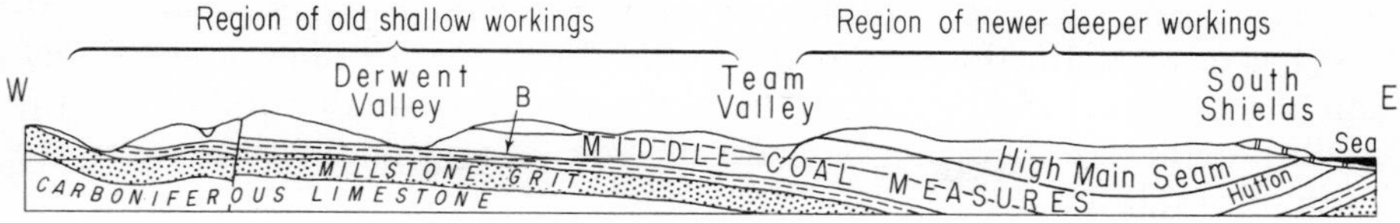

FIG. 116. Section across the northern part of the Durham field (just south of the Tyne), showing the valleys which facilitated the early working of coal. B = Brockwell Seam (after Walcot Gibson)

folded under the cover of the Magnesian Limestone and associated Permian beds. Numerous faults and dykes of igneous rocks cross the field, usually in an east and west direction. The Ludworth Dyke, which pre-dates the Permian rocks, traverses the full width of the concealed coalfield to the east of Durham City. It is encountered in the workings of a number of collieries and has had a severe metamorphic effect on the coal on both its flanks. In places low-volatile, heat-altered coals extend for about three-quarters of a mile on either side of the dyke in all seams being mined. Two of the best known faults are the Butter Knowle in South Durham, with a throw of between 73 and 129 metres (240 and 420 ft), and the famous Ninety Fathoms Fault which in places shifts the Coal Measures no less than 300 metres (1000 ft). The Butter Knowle Fault running eastward for some eight miles from near Ferryhill to the coast just north of Hartlepool separates two areas of contrasted structural aspect within the concealed coalfield of East Durham. To the north folding is gentle, but to the south sharper folds with closures of several hundreds of metres are aligned with their axes parallel to this major fault.

The Carboniferous Limestone Series is exposed to the north and west of the Coal Measures and, as in Scotland, this contains in Northumberland some workable coals. Two collieries to the south of Alnwick and one to the west of Hexham were exploiting seams in this formation in 1968.

The three maps shown in Figs 115 and 118 show the location and size of individual collieries in 1900 compared with those in 1931 and 1968 and demonstrate very clearly how the main weight of mining activity has continued to move eastward during the present century. In the exposed section of the Durham coalfield most of the better-quality seams were worked out from many small shafts and surface adits before or during the nineteenth

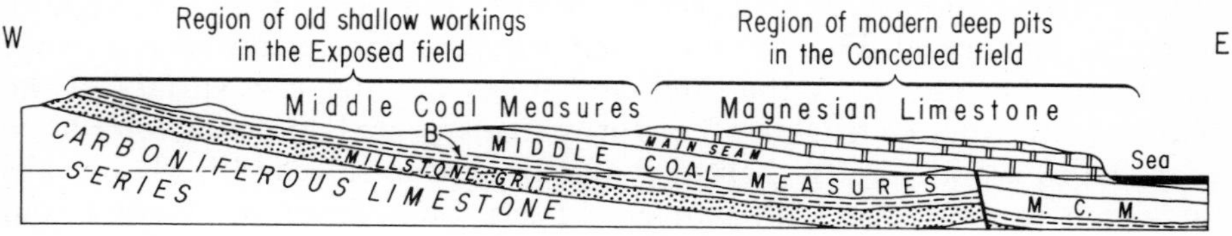

FIG. 117. Section across the southern part of the Durham field, showing the thick mass of Magnesian Limestone covering the concealed coalfield. B = Brockwell Seam (after Walcot Gibson)

century. Mining in the shallower or western sector of the concealed coalfield has now declined appreciably and in the future a still greater proportion of the output will be derived from the relatively small number of large modern collieries operating beneath the coastal and undersea areas to the south of Sunderland.

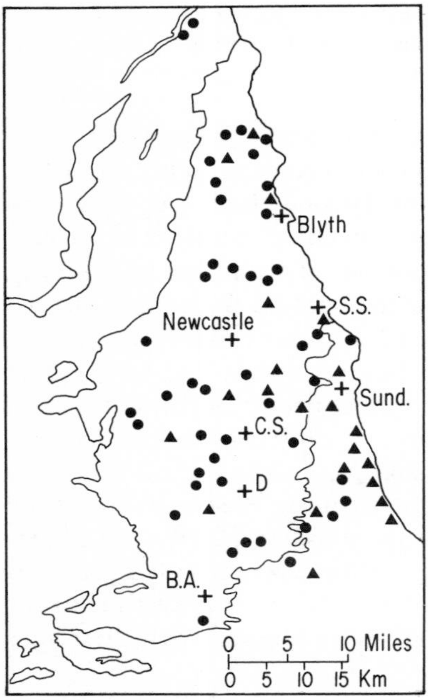

FIG. 118. The Northumberland and Durham coalfield, 1968
Round symbols, mines employing between 100 and 1000 men; triangles, over 1000 men.

Coal mining in the Northumberland and Durham coalfield began at a very early date, and from the fourteenth century 'sea-cole' was shipped from the Tyne and Wear to London. This coal was either picked up on the seashore or obtained from sloping tunnels driven into the sides of the incised valleys of the major rivers, and carried from the mine entrances to navigable water by packhorses. The use of wheeled vehicles on the primitive roadways was rendered difficult by the thick and sticky boulder clay surface of the plateau, and wooden tracks or 'corduroy roads' were laid down, later to be replaced by wooden rails, then by flanged cast iron rails and lastly by rails on which ran vehicles with flanged wheels. Sometimes the loaded coal waggons descended by gravity and pulled up at the same time the empty ones; in other cases the waggons were horsedrawn. The railway had evolved itself; it merely awaited the coming of the steam locomotive. Some of these early waggonways are shown on Fig. 119. The Stockton and Darlington Railway of 1825, with its locomotive haulage, solved the problem of coal transport to the Tees; within a few years it was extended to Middlesbrough and Hartlepool, and numerous coal-carrying railways were constructed, especially in the Durham section of the coalfield and in south Northumberland, leading from the mines to the staithes (wooden piers) from which the waiting seagoing colliers could be loaded.

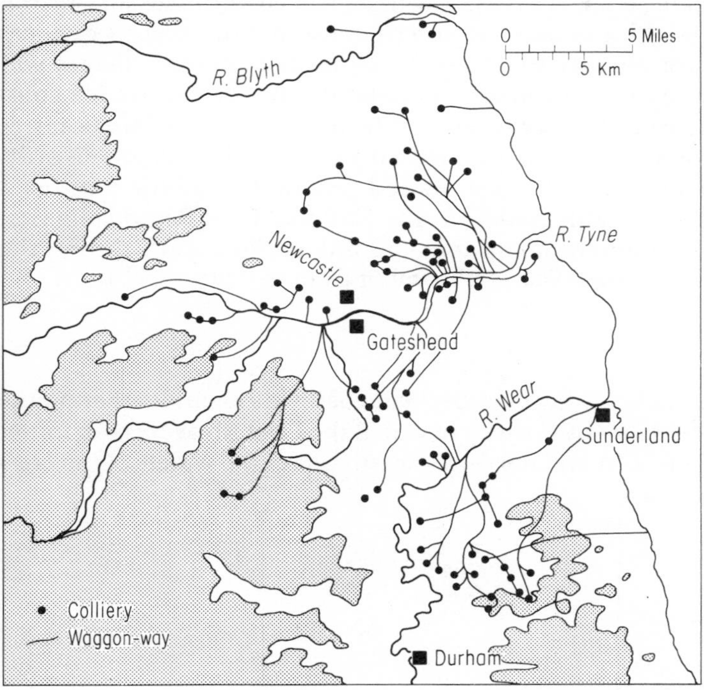

FIG. 119. Old waggonways and collieries. Northumberland and Durham field, 1830, showing the importance of access from navigable water (after Rodwell Jones). Land over 400 ft, stippled

This coalfield is, indeed, more conveniently situated for the export of coal by sea than any other large English field. Hence it is not surprising that in the interwar years 35 per cent of all the coal mined was exported. A substantial proportion of the current production is still carried by coasting vessels to other parts of Britain, and more particularly to Thameside. Because of its former dependence upon the export trade, the Northumberland–Durham coalfield felt the effects of the post-1920 depression more than any other field in the country. In this respect its fortunes compared with those of the South Wales coalfield. Since 1960 the general rundown of the coal mining industry and the concentration of activity at the larger or reconstructed units has given rise to the accelerated closure of dozens of small collieries in the western half of the exposed coalfield. Here a high proportion of the remaining reserves of the thicker seams is situated in the takes of long-abandoned workings or was too far removed from the outlets or shafts of the recently closed units to allow viable extractive operations. Many mining villages to the west and northwest of Newcastle, near Consett and in the vicinity of Bishop Auckland, have been denuded of their active collieries. In the latter town, in particular, a traditional centre for the mining of first-rate coking coal—perhaps the best of all coking coals for the iron smelting industry—this has had serious economic and social consequences for which there are no easy solutions. Some former mining villages will surely die slowly; others will merely become dormitory centres for commuters finding alternative employment in the more accessible large centres of population with a more varied industrial structure. In 1959 the Northumberland and Durham coalfield produced 34.5 million metric tons (34.4 million long tons) of saleable coal from 164 National Coal Board collieries. A production of 27 million metric tons (26 million long tons) during the year ended 30 March 1968 was forthcoming from seventy such units.

Cumberland

Though only a small field, the Cumberland coalfield resembles that on the other side of the Pennines by the way in which the Coal Measures run under the sea, but this time west and northwestwards under the waters of the Irish

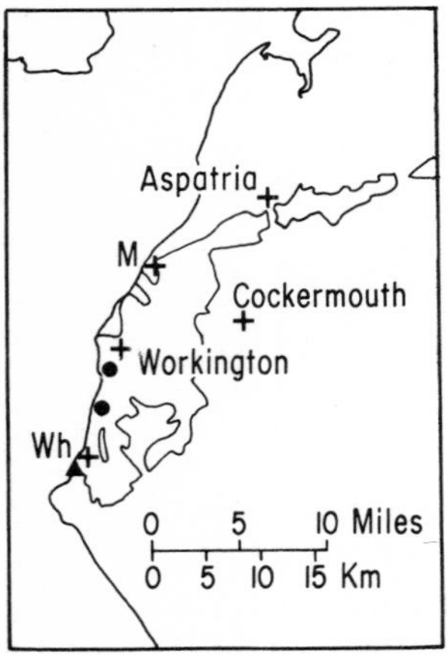

FIG. 120. The Cumberland coalfield, 1968
For symbols see Fig. 118.

Sea and the Solway Firth. In 1968 there were only three productive collieries, all situated on or near the coastline between Workington and St Bees Head. The workings extend for a substantial distance—up to a limit of about 6 kilometres (four miles)—under the sea, the limit being determined approximately by the cost of haulage from the working faces to the shafts, which of necessity, must remain on land. In addition to the exposed area and the area under the sea, there is a small extension of the coalfield under younger rocks towards the south, but a much larger extension to the north of Aspatria, where the Coal Measures are covered by Triassic rocks. It is probable that the Coal Measures extend right underneath the lowlands of the Solway marshes or the Carlisle Basin and reappear as the tiny Canonbie coalfield situated some distance to the north of Carlisle, that is towards the west and northwest. There are numerous faults, with throws of from 91 to 183 metres (300 to 600 ft), running from northwest to southeast across the coalfield, and the northern edge of the worked field in Cumberland is terminated by a complicated belt of fracture. The detailed structure to the north of this belt has not been fully determined, but it now seems unlikely that any coal reserves beneath the Solway lowlands will be exploited. In 1968 the three active collieries within this field had a combined labour force of nearly 3000. Two out of the three collieries had productivity rates of less than half the British average, and it is possible that a complete cessation of coal mining activities is not too far away.

Lancashire and Cheshire

On a geological map the Lancashire coalfield appears as a triangular patch of exposed Coal Measures lying to the west of the Millstone Grit and older rocks of the Pennines. In the heart of the exposed Coal Measures, inliers of considerable extent of Millstone Grit define the general trend of the Rossendale Anticline. The Lower Coal Measures succeeding the Millstone Grit are between 420 and 800 metres (1400 and 2600 ft) thick. They are widely exposed within the coalfield, but are rather poor in coals. Most of the productive and thicker coals occur within the Middle Coal Measures which are of more restricted distribution. The main weight of coal mining activity within the Lancashire coalfield has therefore been concentrated on zones of rather limited area extent. Three such coal mining zones are normally recognised.

(*a*) *The Burnley coalfield.* The Burnley basin of Middle Coal Measures is a broad synclinal tract lying between the Pendle Monocline to the northwest, the Rossendale Anticline to the south and the Pennine Anticline to the east. The continuity of its component coal seams is much disrupted by thrusts, slides and tear faults, mostly with a northwest to southeast or westnorthwest to eastsoutheast trend. Within the northern half of this basin much of the coal has been exhausted and the only important seam remaining unworked at depth over a substantial area is the Lower Mountain (Union). At the beginning of 1968 the southern half of the Burnley basin contained six active mines. Four of these had productivity rates of more than 1.8 metric

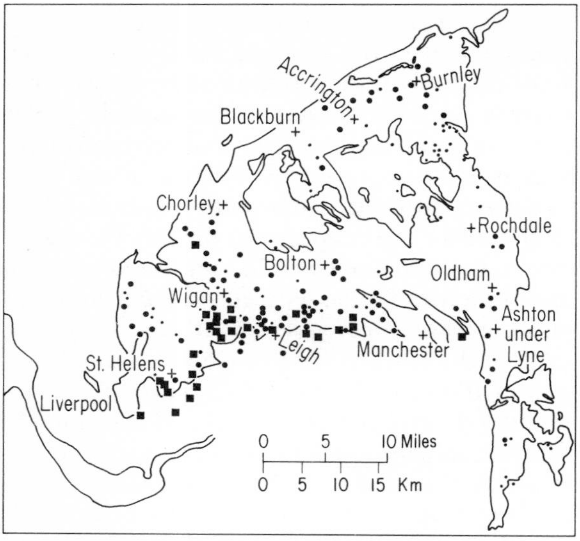

FIG. 121. The Lancashire Coalfield, 1931

tons (36 cwt) per manshift, which was well above the average for the Lancashire coalfield, and this is largely a reflection of the economic viability of drift mining at relatively shallow depths. The Upper Mountain and the Lower Mountain were the main seams being worked, but at a few of these drifts accessible reserves were quickly being exhausted.

(*b*) *The South Lancashire coalfield.* In the south the rocks of the Middle Coal Measures, which succeed those of the Lower Coal Measures and Millstone Grit lying to the north, have a rather steep dip and are quickly concealed by a cover of Triassic rocks. Here is to be found probably the maximum thickness reached by Coal Measure rocks in the British Isles, but unfortunately the southerly dip of the beds increases as they pass under the Triassic cover and thus the concealed coalfield has economically a limited extent towards the south. Even so, the workings of the larger collieries have in places extended to depths of more than 1200 metres (4000 ft) and are the deepest in the British Isles. It is probable that the Coal Measures underlie the whole of the Triassic Plain of Cheshire and are connected directly with the fields of North Wales and North Staffordshire. Oil companies are still interested in the possibilities of discovering new sources of hydrocarbons within any suitable buried structures occurring beneath the Triassic cover rocks, but maybe one should eliminate any thought of future coal mining operations at these depths.

The curiously irregular southern edge of the exposed measures in south Lancashire is due to the numerous and large faults which cut across the Coal Measures in a direction roughly from northwest to southeast. Further east, in the Manchester coalfield the faults assume a more north to south

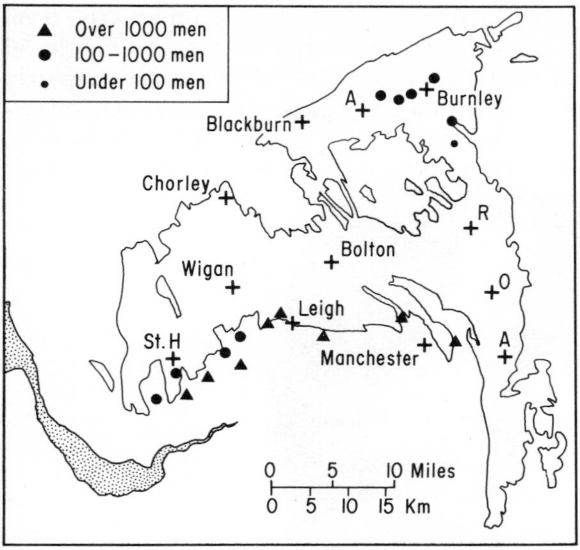

FIG. 122. The Lancashire coalfield, 1968

trend. The Irwell Valley Fault has an estimated throw of 900 metres (3000 ft) in places whilst east of this the Bradford Fault has given rise to a vertical displacement of something like 500 metres (1800 ft) so that one cannot overstress the serious dislocations to the continuity of large-scale mining operations brought about by the presence of such faults. As in so many of our coalfields, the greater part of the faulting took place before the deposition of the succeeding rocks of the Permian period and represents fracturing which was occasioned by the Armorican earth movements (see p. 15). Amongst the famous and important seams of this field, which have been extensively worked, are the Wigan 9-ft, the Arley and Yard coals. In the Wigan district the well-known Wigan cannel coal (a corruption of 'candle' coal because splinters, when lit by a match, will burn with a flame like a candle) overlies the King coal. But this curious coal, which is of rather limited distribution elsewhere in Britain, is now practically exhausted. Its character is believed to be due to a difference in the mother substance of the coal, since it has been found to consist mainly of the spores of the seed-bearing organs of the ancient tree ferns which have gone to make up ordinary coals.

If one includes the two major pits within the built-up area of Manchester, the South Lancashire coalfield contained twelve productive collieries in 1968. The majority of these were large concerns with individual mining complements of more than 1000. They included the new pits of Agecroft, in the northwestern suburbs of Manchester, and Parkside, at Newton-le-Willows. Capital expenditure on these two new pits was more than £10m and £14m, respectively. Agecroft colliery produced 711 000 metric tons

(700 000 long tons) of saleable coal in 1968 with a productivity level approaching 2 metric tons (40 cwt) per manshift. On the other hand Bradford colliery located four miles to the east yielded only 406 000 metric tons (400 000 long tons) despite a £6m major reconstruction scheme, following which its output was expected to rise to 1 million metric tons per annum.

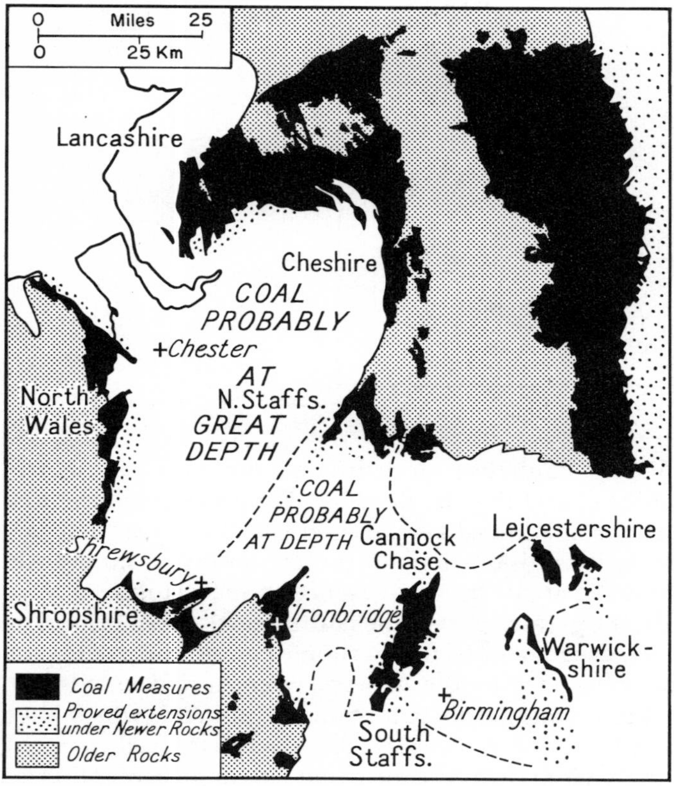

FIG. 123. The exposed and hidden coalfields of the Midlands, and their relationship to one another

(*c*) *The Manchester coalfield.* The southeastern prolongation of the Lancashire coalfield lying east of Manchester and running southward through Ashton under Lyne and Stockport towards Macclesfield is commonly known as the Manchester coalfield. In 1968 it contained no active colliery. Not unexpectedly the Coal Measures in this area can be correlated with those of North Staffordshire to the south, while it is possible to recognise correlatives of some of the seams of the Yorkshire coalfield on the far side of the Pennines, and there is little doubt that the Coal Measures were originally deposited continuously across the area now occupied by the Pennine Uplift. The combined thickness of the Middle and Lower Coal Measures within this coalfield exceeds 1500 metres (5000 ft) and no less than twenty-three seams have been worked in the past. The reserves within this field are by no means exhausted, but in addition to an adverse economic climate the need to pump out large quantities of water from some of the mines hastened their closure. In the concealed segments to the west all the main seams are likely to be present at depth, but despite the presence of several large faults, which throw against the westerly dip and bring the measures nearer to the surface on their western sides, future mining would most likely prove uneconomic.

The North Staffordshire or Potteries coalfield

At its southern end the western margin of the Pennine Uplift is marked by the existence of a number of sharp folds. In the western, and by far the deepest fold, the Coal Measure sequence is preserved intact. In the Cheadle basin very much less remains, whilst farther north only the lowest and least

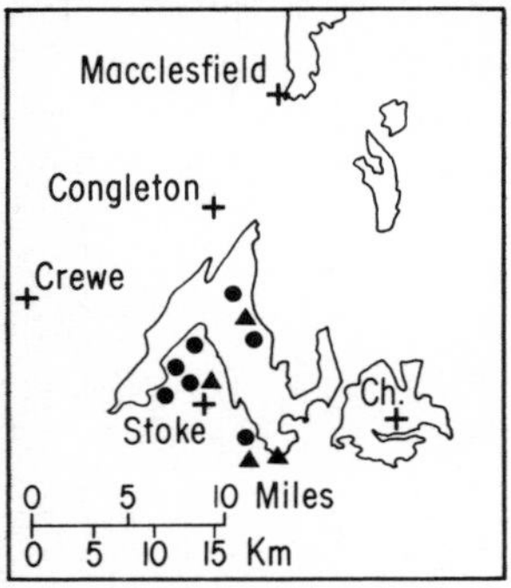

Fig. 124. The North Staffordshire or Potteries coalfield, 1968
For symbols see Fig. 118.

productive parts of the Coal Measures have escaped denudation in the shallow troughs amongst the older Carboniferous rocks. Thus the North Staffordshire coalfield is characterised by extensive folding and faulting of the Coal Measures. The most important coals occur in the Middle Coal Measures. There are some coals in the Lower Coal Measures, but in the Upper Coal Measures, apart from the lower group (Blackband Group), the rocks become reddish and barren, and are held by some to indicate the on-coming of desert conditions towards the close of the Coal Measure period in the British Isles. It is estimated that in 1200 metres (4000 ft) of strata the coalfield contains an aggregate of 42.6 metres (140 ft) of coal in thirty seams of over 60 centimetres (about two ft) in thickness, vertically distributed in such a manner as to permit most of them being worked by one pit at any one place.

The coalfield is especially important because numerous seams of good quality are well adapted to the requirements of the industries which have been established in the field. The potteries, however, no longer use the 'long-flame' coal that was so important to them in the past (cf. p. 602). In the west there are some good gas and coking coals (400 to 800 types). These are now largely worked out, but coking coals are being obtained from deeper seams in the centre of the syncline whilst reserves, only recently tapped, exist in the concealed southern extension of the field. Fireclays are still important in this field, but the formerly valuable ironstones are no longer worked.

In 1958 the North Staffordshire coalfield had twenty productive collieries. By 1968 this number had been reduced to eleven which were all concentrated within, or on the outskirts of, Stoke-on-Trent and Newcastle-under-Lyme. In the late 1950s and early 1960s no less than £27m was spent by the National Coal Board on the reconstruction of three of the larger collieries. It is gratifying to note that in 1968 one of these pits produced more than 1 million metric tons of saleable coal whilst at two of the collieries output per manshift was well above the British average at more than 2.5 metric tons (50 cwt) per manshift (overall).

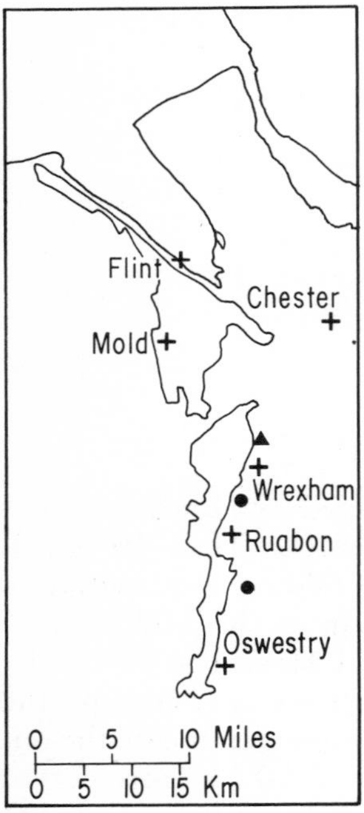

FIG. 125. The North Wales coalfield, 1968
For symbols see Fig. 118.

The North Wales coalfield

This coalfield may be taken next because it represents the western exposed portion of the huge basin which probably underlies Cheshire (Fig. 123).

The Carboniferous rocks rest unconformably on highly folded ancient sediments of the Ordovician and Silurian periods, indicating that the Welsh massif formed a land mass at the time of the deposition of the Coal Measures. So much of the Coal Measures is covered by superficial deposits, in the form of thick glacial sands and gravels and estuarine or river alluvium on Deeside, that the structure is known only as the result of mining. A huge fracture running from westsouthwest to eastnortheast, a continuation of the major Bala Fault, divides the field approximately into a northern, or Flintshire, portion and a southern, or Denbighshire, portion. Some of the most important coals are steam coals (200 types), but in addition there are house and gas coals. Beneath the Triassic cover to the east, the coalfield has been worked in the southern part of the Wirral peninsula; borings show that the concealed segments of the field have a very complicated structure with several major faults, many of which run roughly parallel to the general trend of the exposed field to the west.

None of the collieries within this field have ever shown high productivity rates and in 1968 there were only four active units along its 64 kilometre (40-mile) length.

The Shrewsbury or Central Shropshire coalfield

This little field with its three seams, having a total thickness of two metres (six feet), may be mentioned here because it seems to represent the southernmost extension of the Cheshire basin and the Coal Measures are resting on the ancient rocks of the Welsh massif. Old rocks occupy the whole area southward.

The Yorkshire, Nottinghamshire and Derbyshire coalfield

While it has been common practice to regard as three fields those of West Yorkshire, South Yorkshire and Nottinghamshire and Derbyshire, in reality the three form one huge coalfield with a common geological structure and containing for the most part the same types of coal though changing gradually from 500 types in the north to 900 in the south. The whole area, it is true, is divisible into a western exposed coalfield and an eastern concealed coalfield where the Coal Measures are covered by an easterly-thickening sequence of Permian, Trias and later rocks. There is a certain geographical distinction between the three areas; the West Yorkshire coalfield has been particularly associated with the woollen manufacturing area around centres at Leeds, Bradford and Huddersfield; the South Yorkshire coalfield contains the steel and engineering industries of Sheffield and Rotherham; whilst the Derbyshire and Nottinghamshire coalfield shows more dispersed industrial centres, as at Nottingham, Chesterfield and Mansfield. The precise limits of the concealed coalfield are still not definable despite the continued programme of exploration for natural gas and oil;

but the known area of the whole field, exposed and concealed, is likely to exceed 6475 square kilometres (2500 square miles) or more than twice the size of the South Wales coalfield, and the field as a whole undoubtedly has the greatest reserves of any British field, exceeding in this respect even the

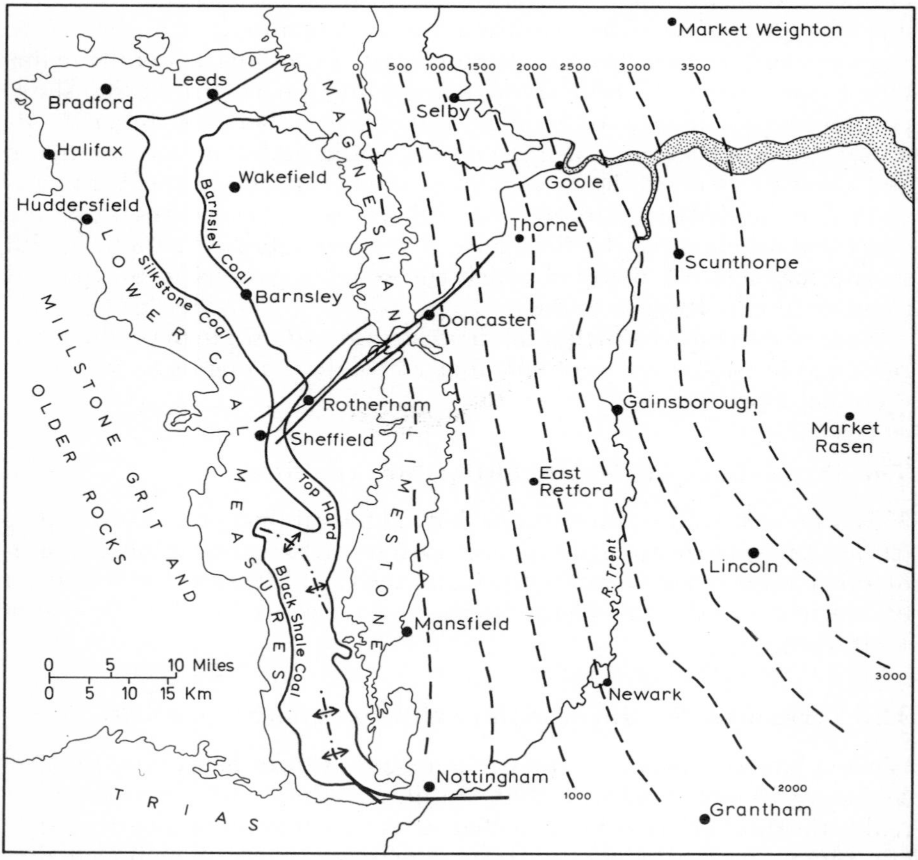

FIG. 126. Map showing the extent and major structural features of the Yorkshire, Nottinghamshire and Derbyshire coalfield

Note in particular the Don 'graben', the anticlines in the exposed Derbyshire section, and the considerable eastward extension beyond the river Trent (depths in feet).

rich South Wales field. The Coal Measures of the fields on the eastern side of the Pennines are less disturbed than those on the western side (Lancashire and North Staffordshire), and this is true of the great coalfield of Yorkshire, Nottingham and Derby. The Coal Measure rocks dip gently away from the Millstone Grit areas of the Pennine Uplift. Consequently there is a long band of Lower Coal Measures exposed in the extreme western part of the field. As usual in the Lower Coal Measures, the coals are on the whole few and poor, but in Yorkshire the Ganister Coal has been extensively mined between Sheffield and Huddersfield, as well as around Halifax, though largely in connection with the underlying ganister and associated fireclays which afford high-class refractory materials of worldwide reputation. Then the Kilburn Coal of the Lower Coal Measures is famous as an almost ash-free house coal. This appears particularly in the southern part of the field and is scarcely recognisable in Yorkshire, where, however, around Bradford, Leeds, and Wakefield, the Better Bed Coal is one of great purity, and formerly much used for iron smelting. Around Leeds the Beeston coal, formed by the union of two coals, is occasionally as much as 2.5 metres (8 ft) thick, and is one of the most valuable seams in West Yorkshire. But on the whole it is the Middle Coal Measures which contain the most seams, and in which the formation of coal reaches its maximum development as regards thickness, quality, and the persistence of the individual seams. The famous Silkstone seam, the chief gas and coking coal, also well known as a house coal, is near the base of the Middle Coal Measures; whilst an almost equally famous seam, the Top Hard Coal of Nottinghamshire (known as the Barnsley coal in the Barnsley area) can be regarded as dividing the Middle Coal Measures into two parts. It is only in the extreme north of the field that the Barnsley coal deteriorates and passes into the Warren House coal. High dips amongst the coal seams are the exception in this great field, and are limited to a few restricted areas. Consequently mining operations are carried on with a greater facility than in any other British coalfield. As shown in the sectional diagram there are local anticlinal folds, especially in the south, and notably the Brimington anticline near Chesterfield and the Erewash anticline between Alfreton and Ilkeston, but on the whole faulting on an extensive scale is much less noticeable in this field than in most British fields. One of the most important groups of faults are those known as the Don faults, passing laterally into a monocline, and along this tectonic zone the Don itself runs.

As one passes eastwards into the concealed coalfield, the cover of Permian and Triassic rocks gradually increases in thickness, so that along the line of the River Trent there is an overlying thickness of more than 600 metres (2000 ft) of strata to be penetrated before the Coal Measures are reached. A boring at Market Weighton passed through 945 metres (3100 ft) of the cover rocks without reaching the Coal Measures. The structure of the explored sections of the concealed coalfield is by no means simple since this is given variation by a few shallow anticlinal folds between which the beds sag in wide troughs. A few of these anticlines are complex with subsidiary folds and may be flanked by substantial normal faults. With the notable exception of the buried northeastward continuation of the Don monocline of the exposed coalfield the trend of all these upfolds approximates more or less closely to the northwesterly strike of the Pre-Cambrian rocks of Charnwood Forest. Mention might be made of the Nocton–Blankey anticline, a large structure running southeastward from near

Lincoln; recent drilling indicates the presence of a further upfold at Stexwould, nine miles to the east. Within this highly important concealed coalfield the major structures discussed above are a deterrent to successful mining operations only in rather restricted zones. In this same context, the seams in the intervening wide troughs are liable to show minor flexures which may locally prove troublesome. It is of interest to note that the concealed Coal Measures lying southeast of a line drawn through Nottingham, Eakring and Lincoln contain bands of igneous rocks, most of which are of intrusive affinities, with olivine dolerites predominating.

The Upper Coal Measures occupy a very restricted area within this great coalfield, but this is of little consequence since the most important seams are

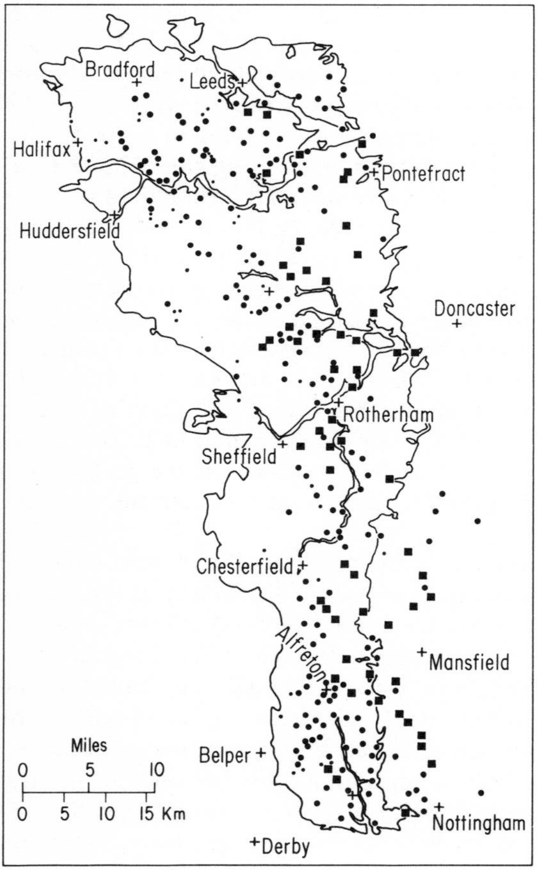

FIG. 127. The Yorkshire, Nottinghamshire and Derbyshire field, 1900

Square dots = collieries employing more than 1000 men. Large round dots = collieries employing 100 to 1000. Small dots = collieries employing less than 100. Note that there are only 11 large collieries in the hidden field.

in the Middle Coal Measures. Even if one includes only the area in which the valuable Barnsley or Top Hard coal has been proved in the concealed coalfield, it is found that this seam alone exists over 1555 square kilometres (600 square miles), and contains at least 2000 million metric tons of high-class coal within a depth of 900 metres (3000 ft) from the surface. The high

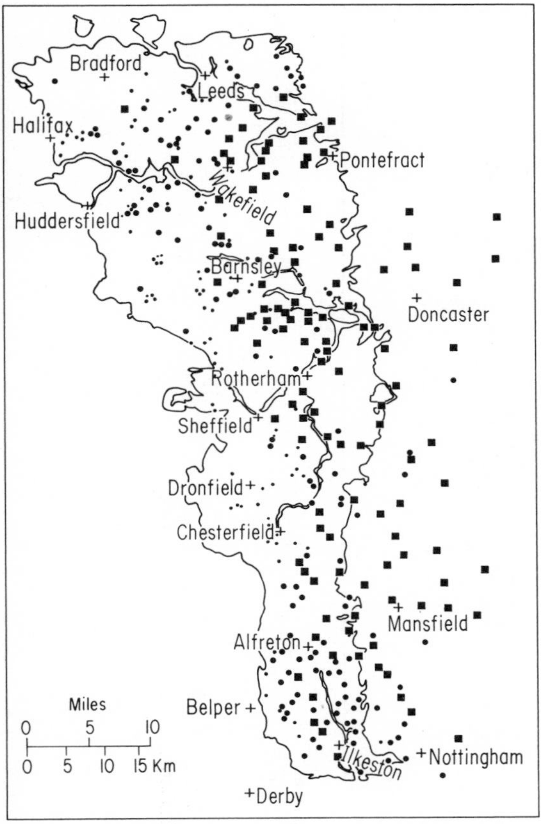

FIG. 128. The Yorkshire, Nottinghamshire and Derbyshire field, 1931

commercial value attached to this particular seam depends largely on the presence of a hard semi-anthracite coal known as 'hards' or 'hard coal', furnishing a really firstclass steam coal whilst other parts of the seam yield a house, manufacturing, and, to a lesser degree, gas coal. In Nottinghamshire this seam varies from a little under 1 metre (3 ft) to just over 1.8 metres (6 ft) in thickness, with an average for the proved area of 1.2 metres (4 ft) of good coal, whilst in Yorkshire an average thickness of 1.8 metres (6 ft) can be reckoned.

If one examines the three maps, Figs 127 to 129, showing the distribution of collieries in the whole coalfield in the years 1900, 1931 and 1968, similar general trends to those noted in the case of the Northumberland and Durham coalfield will be observed. There has been a progressive movement of mining activity eastward, towards and into the concealed coalfield. Many of the older and smaller workings of the exposed coalfield, such as

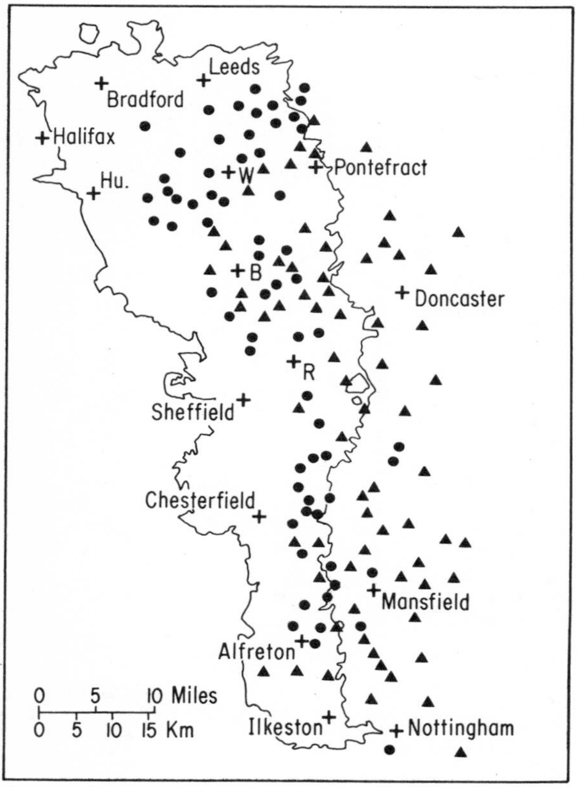

FIG. 129. The Yorkshire, Nottinghamshire and Derbyshire coalfield, 1968
Round symbols, 100 to 1000 men employed; triangles, over 1000 men.

those lying west of Wakefield, Barnsley and Alfreton, respectively, have been closed down because the accessible seams have largely been exhausted and many of the working faces had advanced to locations too remote from the shafts or drift outlets. The concealed coalfield was not touched until 1859. Today it has more than thirty large modern collieries, as a group perhaps second to none in terms of efficiency and the development of modern mining practice. In distribution these collieries range southward in a broad belt between Doncaster, Worksop, Mansfield and Nottingham. Nearly all of these large collieries still have an employment roll of more than 1000 and many of them record productivity levels of more than 3 metric tons (60 cwt) per manshift (overall), which is some 50 per cent above the British average. Three new pits have been sunk by the National Coal Board at individual costs ranging between £12m and £14m. These are Kellingley, lying east of Pontefract, Bevercotes, to the southeast of Worksop, and Cotgrave, located a few kilometres eastsoutheast of the built-up limits of Nottingham. Northeast of Kellingley colliery there are indications that considerable reserves of good-quality coal exist. Coal production began at Bevercotes colliery in February 1967. This is the world's first colliery planned for a complete and integrated system of remote and automatic control. Some initial difficulties were encountered in the operation of this, but when the colliery has been fully developed and its true potential realised, levels of productivity much in excess of the present national average should be attainable. Although a substantial number of working units have been closed or merged in the exposed section of the coalfield since 1960, many of the collieries here are operating at a profit and have large reserves for future working. A few new drift mines are within this category.

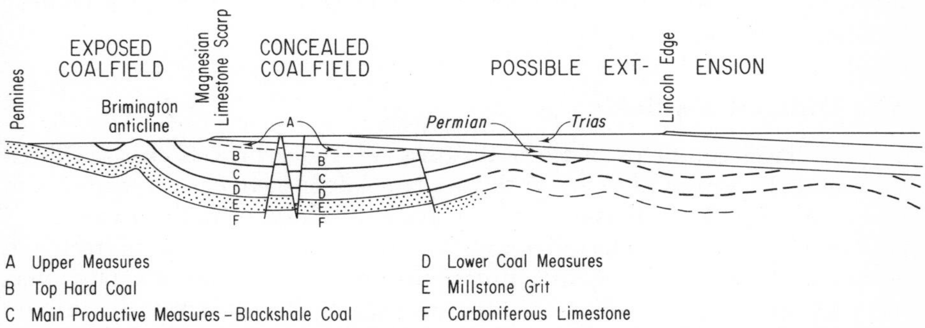

FIG. 130. Diagrammatic section from west to east across the Derbyshire–Nottinghamshire coalfield

This major Yorkshire, Nottinghamshire and Derbyshire coalfield yielded 80.6 million metric tons (79.4 million long tons) of saleable coal in 1959 (from 179 productive colliery units) out of an overall British total of 195.7 metric tons (192.6 million long tons) forthcoming from National Coal Board deep mines (41 per cent of the total). The corresponding figures for the year ending 30 March 1968 were 78.4 million metric tons (77.2 million long tons) in a national total of 165.3 million metric tons (162.7 million long tons) (47 per cent) from 133 producing collieries. One cannot overstress this increasing concentration of the British output of deep-mined coal on this important field, and more particularly on its newer concealed sections. It might be instructive, therefore, to view in rather more detail one of these concealed zones where relatively speaking, at least, coal mining has assumed greater significance. To the east of Mansfield nine large modern collieries produced 8 million metric tons of coal in 1968 at productivity rates up to

4.5 metric tons (90 cwt) per manshift (overall). The greater part of this output was forthcoming from the High Hazles, Top Hard, Deep Soft and Tupton or Low Main seams at depths ranging between 365 and 853 metres (1200 and 2800 ft) below the surface. The uppermost workings (that is in the High Hazles seam) varied between 150 and 300 metres (500 and 1000 ft) below the base of the unconformable cover of Permian and Triassic rocks which succeed the Coal Measures. All these coals are of a bituminous nature with 81 to 85 per cent of carbon and 36 to 47 per cent of volatile matter. They are largely utilised in the nearby coal-fired power stations of the Trent valley. The following factors have contributed to the high yield of this group of collieries: thick seams with good roofs and lying practically flat over wide areas; a rather low incidence of major faults; the moderate depth of mining which is barely sufficient to give rise to great rock heat and unwieldy roofs; the existence of a fairly thick barrier of largely impermeable rocks between the main mining horizons and the heavily water-bearing Bunter Sandstone of the newer cover rocks; an abundant ground water supply for washery purposes; and, finally, a flat or slightly undulating surface configuration allowing for the ready erection of modern colliery buildings and ancillary plant.

The Midland coalfields

The Midland coalfields of Leicestershire, Warwickshire, South Staffordshire and the Forest of Wyre with Coalbrookdale have certain features in common. The Coal Measures were deposited in bays or hollows in the old land mass, previously referred to as St George's Land, which then stretched across south-midland England. Frequently there are no older Carboniferous rocks than the Middle Coal Measures which therefore rest directly on the ancient floor. This ancient floor usually slopes northwards and the Coal Measures nearly always thicken from south to north. In the northern parts of the fields there are often fair numbers of coal seams which, when traced southwards, are found to converge to form one or more very thick seams. After their deposition the structure of the fields was complicated by the formation of a very extensive series of north and south faults and folds with axes of like trend. The combined faulting and folding has resulted in the further separation of the fields into distinct divisions. In addition there are frequently important east–west faults so that the geological structure of the small Midland coalfields is often very complicated.

(*a*) *Leicestershire.* This coalfield lies in a basin that is bounded on the west by the Cambrian rocks of the Nuneaton Ridge and on the east by the Pre-Cambrian rocks of Charnwood Forest. The coalfield includes an area of about 155 square kilometres (60 square miles) in the county of Leicester together with about 39 square kilometres (15 square miles) in South Derbyshire. Within this field the Coal Measures are exposed at the surface over an area of 62 square kilometres (24 square miles) with Ashby-de-la-Zouch as a centre, the most important part of the concealed coalfield lying to the south-east. The Lower Coal Measures are thin and unimportant and only one small seam has been worked. Most of the seams lie therefore in the Middle Coal Measures which occur in the eastern and western areas, these being separated by an anticlinal fold of Lower Coal Measures. The Royster Coal on the east and the Kilburn Coal on the west are usually the lowest workable seams and are regarded as the base of the productive measures. The Main Coal is the standard coal of the district and consists of two seams in the north which unite in the south to form one thick seam of about 4.3 to 4.9 metres (14 to 16 ft). The Main Coal is a steam, house and manufacturing coal. In 1968 the seams most extensively worked were the Woodfield, Main, Eureka and Kilburn in the west and the Middle and Nether Lount in the east. The eastern section had eight productive collieries in 1968 and the western section, which extends into south Derbyshire, had four active units. Productivity levels in this coalfield are amongst the highest in the country, every colliery recording more than 2.3 metric tons (45 cwt) per manshift (overall) in 1968 with a few exceeding 4 metric tons (80 cwt) per manshift.

The Leicestershire coalfield is remarkable in one respect, that it has not given rise to an extensive industrial area and the coal mining centres have remained small towns or more often villages, as for example, Coalville. Ashby-de-la-Zouch is still essentially a country market town barely touched by coalfield development. Swadlincote, however, in south Derbyshire, is an important centre of industries based on the local resources of fireclay.

(*b*) *The East Warwickshire or Nuneaton coalfield.* The total area of this field is about 388 square kilometres (150 square miles), but a large part of it is occupied by the barren Upper Coal Measures to which the productive Measures form a narrow fringe on the east and north. Again the Coal Measure rocks were deposited in an old embayment. Carboniferous Limestone and Millstone Grit are nearly always absent, and the Coal Measures rest directly on the ancient Cambrian rocks. Even the Lower Coal Measures themselves seem to be absent. The Middle Coal Measures, the productive series, are about 300 metres thick in the Tamworth area in the north, but thin southwards. As one goes southwards the coal seams tend to unite so that in the vicinity of the Newdigate collieries, near Nuneaton, the separate seams have coalesced to give a thickness of over 7 metres (23 ft) to the Thick Coal or Hacksbury seam. In the northern part of the field seams with a combined thickness of 10.6 metres (35 ft) occur. In 1968 the coalfield had only six productive collieries, as compared with fifteen in 1950. Mining operations were being directed mainly at the extraction of the Ryder, Nine Feet and Two Yard seams. Productivity levels were not nearly as high as those of the Leicestershire coalfield, but Daw Hill, a new colliery sunk at a cost of over £4m midway between Nuneaton and the eastern suburbs of Birmingham, recorded the highly satisfactory yield of nearly 3 metric tons

(60 cwt) per manshift. The coals are of a bituminous nature and have been utilised for domestic and manufacturing purposes. The remaining collieries are well spaced and there are considerable areas under which the coal has remained untouched. In the southern part of the field there has been some difficulty with water in the overlying beds. The excessive thickness of the Thick Coal has also been an obstacle to successful mining. This deserves to be stressed because it might be thought that a very thick coal would be an extremely valuable one, but the expense of timbering (or, alternatively, of working the coal in horizontal sections) is enormously increased.

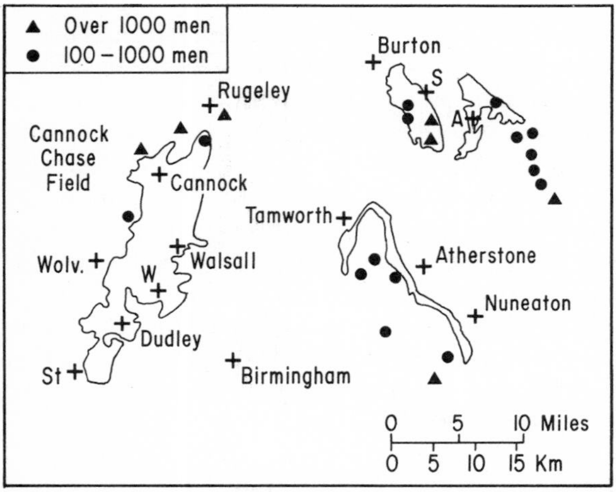

FIG. 131. The Midland coalfields, 1968
Note that mining in the old 'Black Country' is extinct.

(*c*) *The South Staffordshire coalfield.* The total area of this field is about 386 square kilometres (149 square miles). Again, in the southern part, the Coal Measures rest on an irregular floor, usually composed of Silurian rocks. Structurally the field falls into three parts: in the north is the Cannock Chase basin, partly concealed beneath the Trias; this is succeeded, beyond the east–west Bentley Faults, by the northern part of the Black Country field, a shallow basin with its axis lying northwest–southeast from Wolverhampton to West Bromwich; this in turn is separated from the third area by the axial ridge of the Black Country, partly composed of a dolerite mass (the Rowley Hills) and partly of three inliers of Silurian rocks, of which Dudley Castle hill and the Wren's Nest are famous for the highly fossiliferous Wenlock Limestone that was formerly quarried and mined for use in the local blast furnaces. The southern section of the field, south of this ridge, is divided into two basins—the Pensnett and Cradley basins—by the Netherton anticline that trends northnortheast–southsouthwest. Once again the Lower Coal Measures seem to be absent, at any rate in the southern part of the field; and even the Middle Coal Measures are only 76 metres (250 ft) thick in the south although they thicken to nearly 600 metres (2000 ft) in the north (Cannock Chase). The thinner seams in the north progressively coalesce towards the south to form the famous Thick Coal. This has an aggregate thickness of more than 9 metres (30 ft) over a considerable area and occasionally reached nearly 11 metres (36 ft). The coals

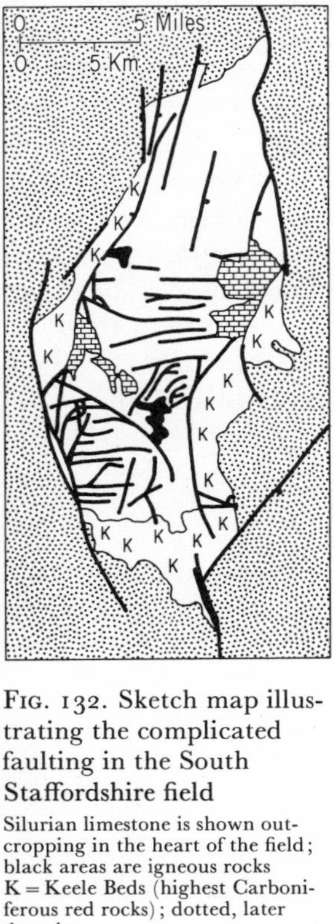

FIG. 132. Sketch map illustrating the complicated faulting in the South Staffordshire field

Silurian limestone is shown outcropping in the heart of the field; black areas are igneous rocks K = Keele Beds (highest Carboniferous red rocks); dotted, later deposits.

of the South Staffordshire field are bituminous in character and suitable for house, manufacturing and local uses. They were formerly much prized for making the type of coke that was used for iron smelting during the Industrial Revolution—though they would not now be regarded as coking coals suitable for treatment in modern byproduct ovens. The seams of Cannock Chase have a specially high reputation as house coal. As in the two previous fields the boundary faults to the east and west are important and it is not fully known to what depths the Coal Measures may be faulted down. Several collieries have worked part of the ground beyond these faults. In 1949 the National Coal Board embarked on an extensive boring programme designed to explore the ground east of the Rugeley Fault at the northern end of the Cannock Chase section of the coalfield. These investigations have revealed a valuable extension of the coalfield beneath the Triassic cover which was proved to have a highly irregular base. The Mealy Grey Coal, the lowest of the workable seams, was found to be succeeded by about 450 metres (1500 ft) of measures containing a dozen, or so, good seams. The Old Park and succeeding Wyrley Bottom Coals are two of the more valuable seams of this concealed coalfield. Lea Hall colliery, near Rugeley, was sunk at a capital cost of £11m to exploit these new resources and, with a 1968 output of 1.27 million metric tons (1.25 million long tons) and a productivity level of 3.5 metric tons (70 cwt) per manshift, is one of the National Coal Board's successes. In this concealed coalfield some of the upper seams incrop and are thus absent over restricted zones because of truncation at the irregular base of the Trias. This irregular plane of junction of the two formations also introduces a drainage or flooding hazard to mining operations because the Bunter Pebble Beds, in particular, are highly water-bearing.

Including Lea Hall, the Cannock Chase or northern section of the field now has only five active collieries. The southern part of the field, in the Black Country proper, is practically worked out and whereas in the mid-nineteenth century there were some 500 shallow pits, in 1968 there were no operative collieries to the south of Wolverhampton.

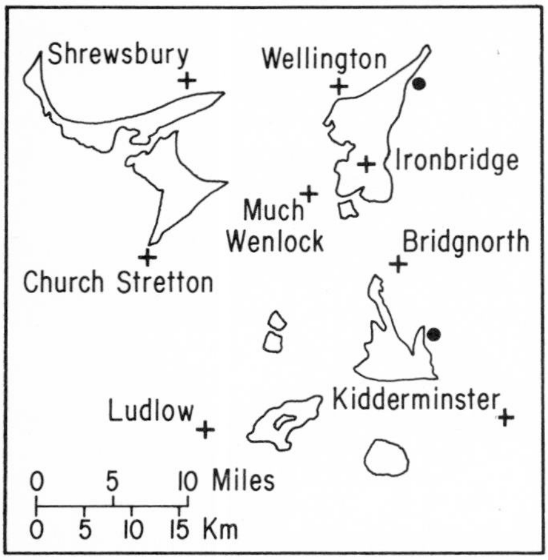

FIG. 133. The Shropshire coalfields, 1968
Only two pits remain, each with under 1000 men employed.

(*d*) *The Forest of Wyre coalfield.* This occupies a hollow in the ancient rocks, and although having an area of 130 square kilometres (50 square miles) it has very small reserves of coal. The Coal Measures here have a maximum thickness approaching 610 metres (2000 ft). The coals of the Upper Measures (Highley Group) were formerly extensively mined in shallow pits and open workings. In the Middle Measures only the Highley–Brooch Coal was worked on a large scale. Only one colliery near Highley was operating in 1968, and that closed down at the end of the year.

(*e*) *The Coalbrookdale field.* This field has small reserves, but formerly held several productive collieries. Only one colliery was functioning in 1968; this had an annual production of rather more than 203 000 metric tons (200 000 long tons). The coalfield is of the greatest interest because of the fame of the district in the history of the iron trade. Here coke-smelted iron was first produced and at Ironbridge the first bridge constructed of iron was erected and is still standing (see Plate 16).

The South Wales coalfield

This is different from the English fields, with the exception of its small neighbour, the Forest of Dean, in that it is a true basin of almost wholly exposed Coal Measures. Indeed, the South Wales field may be likened roughly to a pie dish elongated from east to west and with a rim which is formed of Millstone Grit and Carboniferous Limestone, usually flanked by still older rocks. The southern rim (South Crop) is generally considerably steeper than the northern rim (North Crop). In the centre of the pie dish there is a threefold sequence: the Lower Coal Series, comprised predominantly of shales with many coal seams and subsidiary sandstones; the Pennant Sandstone Series, typified by massive felspathic sandstones or grits; and, finally, the Upper Coal Series, again characterised by shales but with fewer coal seams. The three subdivisions reach their greatest thickness in the western part of the coalfield, thinning fairly consistently to the east and northeast. Although this tripartite division of the Coal Measures is often clearly reflected in the relief of the area, it has long been appreciated that it is geologically unsatisfactory, chiefly because of the markedly diachronous relationship of the Pennant to the underlying and overlying series. In its revised mapping the Institute of Geological Sciences has devised a new classification which is based on palaeontological datum planes equatable with those in other coalfields and providing for a standard form of mapping of the Coal Measures in England and Wales. This new classification is not yet in universal usage because the issue of revised maps for the coalfield is incomplete. To avoid confusion therefore the use of the old nomenclature will be retained in the following account.

One would expect the Lower Coal Series to be at their greatest depth in the centre of the pie dish. But east of Port Talbot there is a line of pronounced upfold, running eastward from west of Maesteg to the vicinity of Pontypridd, which brings many of the valuable seams of the Lower Coal Series comparatively near to the surface even in the centre of the coalfield. The Upper Coal Series are preserved in synclinal or downfaulted outliers which normally provide areas of subdued or lower relief. These include the

Gowerton–Llanelly Syncline, the Llantwit Fardre–Caerphilly and Gelligaer or Blackwood Synclines and the elongated strip of the Duffryn Trough, to the north of Swansea. The whole field has a length from east to west of about 145 kilometres (ninety miles). Its greatest width, 26 to 27 kilometres (sixteen to seventeen miles), is in Glamorgan. An average width of about

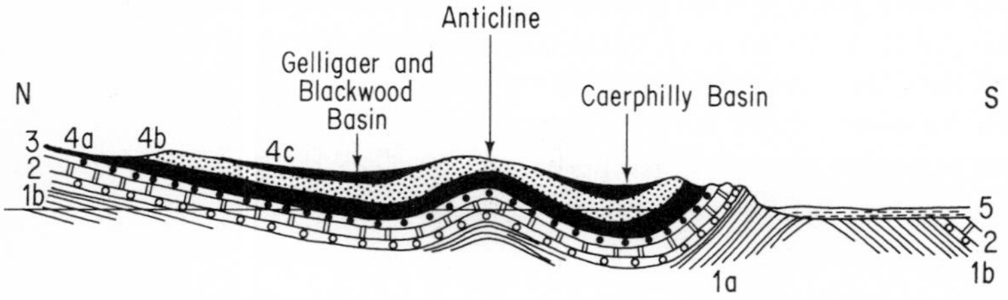

FIG. 134. Diagrammatic section through the east of the South Wales coal basin

1a, Silurian and lower Old Red Sandstone; *1b*, upper Old Red Sandstone (conglomerates, etc.); 2, Carboniferous Limestone; 3, Millstone Grit; *4a*, lower Coal Series; *4b*, Pennant Grit; *4c*, upper Coal Series; 5, Mesozoic and later rocks.

24 kilometres (fifteen miles) is maintained as far as Swansea Bay. Westwards the coalfield narrows and in the western part of Pembrokeshire it is scarcely 5 kilometres. If one includes the portions covered by the sea in Swansea Bay and Carmarthen Bay the area of the coalfield is over 2590 square kilometres (1000 square miles) and it has very extensive reserves. The relief of the greater part of the coalfield is particularly characteristic in that deep transverse valleys have been the main factor determining the location of collieries, villages and towns. In the early days levels were opened up along these steepsided valleys and the first mines thus had natural drainage through their portals. To avoid passing through an unnecessary thickness of the Pennant Sandstone or other barren measures many pits were subsequently sunk on the floors of the valleys. Between the deeper valleys are large tracts of moorland at a considerable elevation above sea level and from the surface of these wide open moorlands it is often impossible to see a colliery and to realise that one is in the heart of a coalfield.

Turning to details of geological structure, apart from the anticlinal fold traversing the central regions of the main coal basin, there are also other smaller anticlines which to some extent bring the lower coals within mineable reach. Then the whole of the main basin is crossed by a pronounced series of faults trending in general from northnorthwest to southsoutheast or northwest to southeast, that is subparallel to the prevailing dips. Some of these are in the nature of trough faults with 'troughs' of Coal Measures let down between them, but on the whole they throw westwards so that it is in the neighbourhood of Swansea that the lower coals are found at their greatest depth. In fact, they are depressed below 1220 metres (about 4000 ft) and cannot under present conditions be mined. Belts of major faulting, completely avoided by mining operations, include the so-called Neath and

Tawe Disturbances of the upper Neath and Tawe valleys and the Moel Gilau Fault of west–central Glamorgan. Equally disturbed zones, perhaps less obvious on the surface, but with repeated low-angled faulting or thrusting have been encountered both on the South Crop and in the western half of the North Crop which forms the anthracite section of the coalfield. Large rivers, notably the Neath and the Tawe, find their way along the faulted belts towards the sea. In Pembrokeshire, folding and faulting have both been very intense; frequently the beds are overfolded and there are great thrust faults and the whole structure is such as to render virtually impossible any serious attempts at renewed mining.

The development of the South Wales coalfield has been influenced to a great degree by the high quality and the variety of the coal. While bituminous coals are present in quantity there are well-known steam coals and anthracites, both of which are characterised by a high percentage of carbon and a low percentage of volatile matter. In addition, in many South Wales coals the ash content is very small. Whilst bituminous coals commonly have an ash content of 5 to 10 per cent, that of the steam coals of South Wales is frequently under 4 per cent, and in the case of the anthracites it is only about one per cent. Anthracite is found in the detached portion of the coalfield, in Pembrokeshire, and also in the northwestern part of the main field from the Gwendraeth Valley approximately as far as the head of the Vale of Neath and the upper Avan Valley. The seams are in the Lower Coal Series. East and south of the limit of the anthracite area, as defined above, the seams change in character, each seam passing first into steam coal and then into a bituminous coal. Thus towards the South Crop of the coalfield, from the Swansea area in the west to the Caerphilly–Bedwas area in the east, the seams in the lower part of the Coal Measures are bituminous whilst between this zone and the anthracite district they are mainly steam coals of various grades. It is particularly around Aberdare and in the Rhondda Valley that the most famous of the steam coals have been mined. The coals of the Upper Series are generally bituminous coals. Broadly speaking, about 50 per cent of the coal available in South Wales is steam coal, about 30 per cent bituminous and about 20 per cent anthracite. Coal was undoubtedly worked in the South Wales field as early as the thirteenth century, while towards the end of the sixteenth century it was being used for the smelting of copper. For some considerable time much of the coal-winning on the North Crop was achieved by what is called 'patching'—digging the low-dipping, or nearly horizontal, seams in open workings. This was succeeded by workings in bell pits, the shallow pits being dug near the outcrop of the seam, and workings being made outward from it in all directions until it was considered unsafe to proceed farther.

In the latter part of the eighteenth century coal began to be used generally in the iron industry and there followed the great expansion in the export trade in iron. In due course this was followed by a similar rise in the export of coal. A detailed map of South Wales will show the way in which the valleys in the southeast of the field join and lead to two main centres—Newport and Cardiff. The coal export trade of Newport developed particularly after the opening of the Monmouthshire Canal and the quantity exported rose from about 10 000 metric tons in 1798 to over 148 000 metric tons in 1809. Cardiff developed rapidly as the main exporting port in the middle years of the nineteenth century. Tramways and canals brought the coal to the ports and the construction of the Taff Vale railway (completed in 1841) to Merthyr and Aberdare helped greatly in accelerating the increase in the export trade. Likewise the opening of the Bute Docks at Cardiff in 1839 was a major contributory factor. In 1913 no less than 70 per cent of

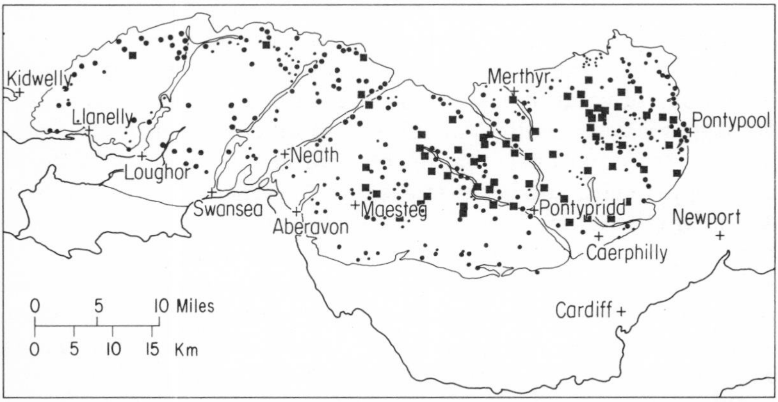

FIG. 135. The South Wales coalfield, 1931. Excluding the western extension

the total output of the coalfield was exported either abroad or to other parts of Britain by water. Cardiff, including Penarth and Barry, shipped nearly two-thirds of this, and next in order of importance were Newport, Swansea and Port Talbot. Thus the former prosperity of the South Wales coal industry depended to a very large degree on the export trade. The field suffered correspondingly in the interwar years from the diminution in that trade. In 1968 the proportion of South Wales coal exported was less than 6 per cent, and this comprised mainly anthracite from Swansea. Coke ovens now consume some 6 million metric tons out of the total of 16 million metric tons of deep-mined coal derived from the South Wales coalfield whilst electricity plants take more than 4 million metric tons.

Subsequent to nationalisation in 1947 the National Coal Board has spent more than £100m on major capital schemes in the South Wales coalfield. These embraced the reorganisation or reconstruction of existing collieries, the sinking of new pits or drifts, the reconstruction and reopening of old collieries formerly disused, and the establishment of ancillary works of a varied nature. Few of the colliery schemes have been unqualified successes.

This can be largely attributed to difficult geological conditions, particularly in the South Crop and anthracite areas, but other factors, such as the persistently high rates of absenteeism, have been partially responsible for this unhappy state of affairs. A few redeeming features are worthy of note. In the anthracite area two major new pits costing more than £10m apiece, have fallen far short of expectation in terms of yield and productivity, but three relatively shallow drift mines are between them producing 406 000 metric tons (400 000 long tons) of anthracite at productivity rates well above the average for the South Wales coalfield. Likewise quite a few of the older collieries in the central steam coal section of the coalfield have now been

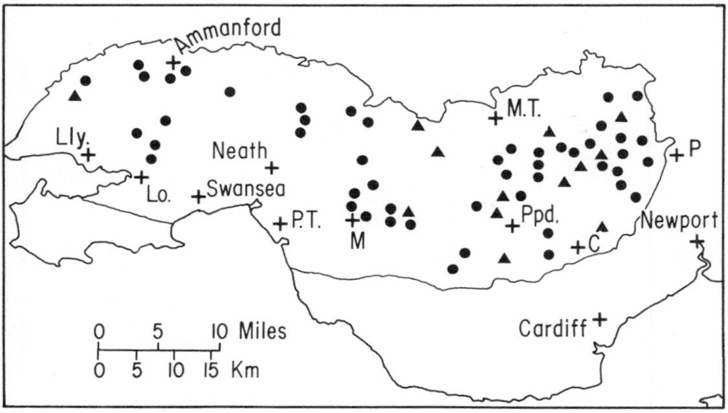

FIG. 136. The South Wales coalfield, 1968
Round symbols, 100 to 1000 men employed; triangles, over 1000 men.

working at a profit for a number of years. In 1950 the National Coal Board operated 163 productive mines in the South Wales coalfield. By March 1968 this number had been reduced to 62. A comparison of Figs 135 and 136 will indicate that the closures have been most in evidence in the eastern half of the anthracite district, along the South Crop and at the northern ends of the Glamorgan and Monmouthshire valleys.

The Forest of Dean coalfield

The small Forest of Dean coalfield comprises a basin of entirely exposed Coal Measures surrounded by a rim of Carboniferous Limestone and separated from the South Wales field by a broad expanse of older rocks. The Coal Measures occupy an area of about 70 square kilometres (44 square miles) and the total thickness of the Measures is about 427 metres (1400 ft). Several coals have been extensively worked, the three main centres being the towns of Coleford, Cinderfoot and Lydney. The last operative National Coal Board colliery ceased production in 1966.

Somerset and Gloucestershire coalfields

In Somerset and Gloucestershire there are six detached areas of Coal Measures completely different from the South Wales field in that each is surrounded by strata newer than the Coal Measures, except where a rim of Carboniferous Limestone exists (for details see Chapter 3), and most of the coal mining has been carried on under the newer formations. The exposed rocks occupy about 130 square kilometres (50 square miles) and the concealed Measures about another 492 square kilometres (190 square miles) so that some four-fifths of the total coalfield areas can actually be described as concealed. In the south there is a total thickness of about 7 metres (23 ft) of coal. Farther north in the Radstock area the seams increase in number and thickness, but the Radstock basin is traversed by several major thrusts, its southern limit being marked by a large thrustfaulted overfold. The Radstock basin had three active collieries in 1968, each showing reasonable productivity levels. In this basin three important coal seams occur in the lowest third of the Pennant Series. There are now no active collieries in the Kingswood field to the north which is poorer in coals.

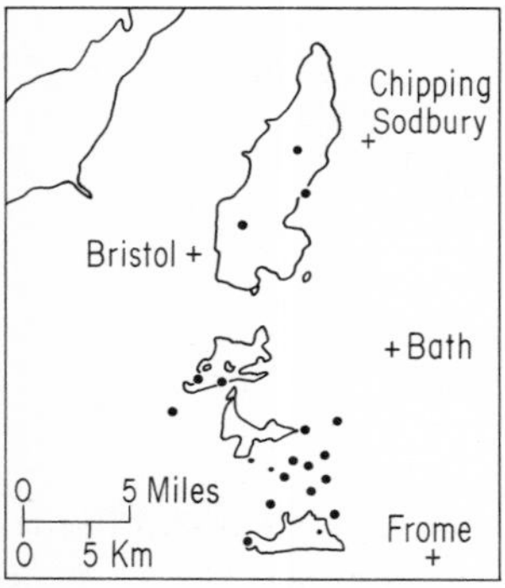

FIG. 137. The Bristol and Somerset fields, 1931

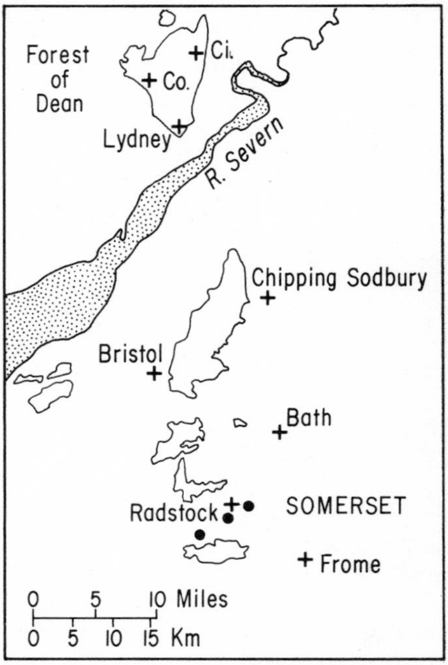

FIG. 138. The Somerset and Gloucestershire coalfields, 1968
Note that the Bristol and Forest of Dean fields are now extinct.

Geologically these coalfields in Somerset and Gloucestershire are interesting in that some of the coals are believed to be of much younger date in the Coal Measures sequence than those in other parts of England.

The East Kent coalfield

Long before the end of last century geologists confidently predicted that a concealed coalfield would be found underneath southeastern England. Prestwich and Godwin Austen, in particular, in the seventies of last century were certain of the matter. The field was first discovered when excavations

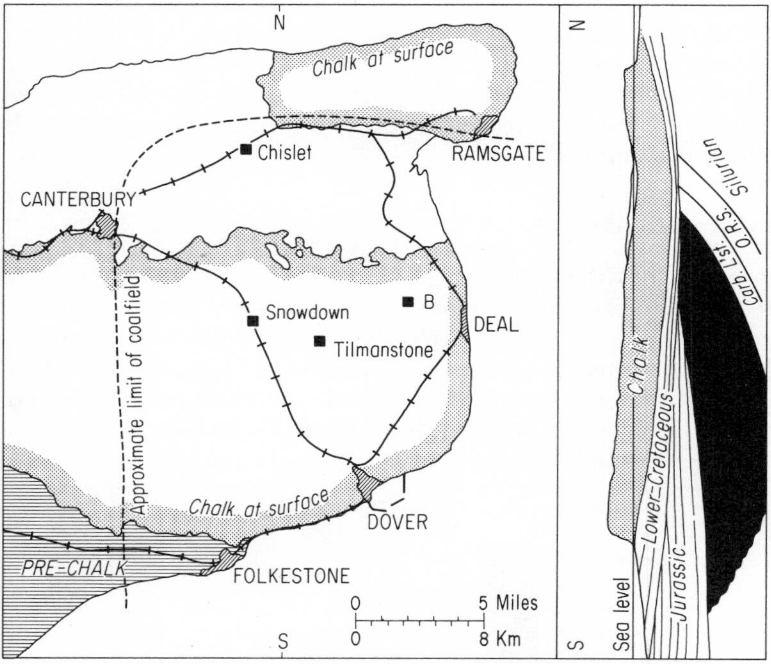

FIG. 139. The East Kent coalfield and a section through it (with the Coal Measures in black)

The area with a stippled margin is where chalk outcrops at the surface. The four collieries are those working in 1961. B = Betteshanger.

for the proposed Channel tunnel near Shakespeare Cliffs, Dover, were temporarily suspended and engineers bored downwards. This occurred in 1890. During the succeeding twenty-five years a number of boreholes were put down and the limits of the coalfield were broadly determined. It forms a basin extending as far north as Sandwich, a little north of Canterbury, and westwards is bounded by a sharp upfold so that there is a rough north–south line limiting the field a short distance west of the longitude of Folkestone. It is now estimated to have an area of 534 square kilometres (206 square miles), of which 145 square kilometres (56 square miles), however, lie at a workable distance from the shore but below the sea. The Coal Measures trough is now thought to be deepest around Waldershore and St Margarets Bay where it reaches to about 1460 metres (3800 ft) below O.D. and the Coal Measures attain a maximum thickness of some 884 metres (2900 ft). On land the top of the Coal Measures lies at depths of 305 to 488 metres (1000 to 1600 ft). Fourteen more or less persistent coal seams have been recognised; some of these are more than 1.5 metres (5 ft) thick, but many are split. Much of the coal has strong caking properties, but in view of its rather friable nature the proportion of fines is rather high.

The four active mines of the coalfield are of comparatively long standing and so have extensive takes, as much as five miles across. A notable proportion of the annual production of 1.5 million metric tons is consumed in the cement, gas and electricity industries. The field is conveniently situated for the port of Dover, and an overhead ropeway was installed to take coal in limited quantities to that port.

The Scottish coalfields

The Scottish coalfields differ very much in character from those of the rest of Britain in that important coal seams occur not only in rocks of Coal Measure age but also in rocks which are contemporaneous with the great mass of the Carboniferous Limestone as developed in England and Wales. Most of the Carboniferous Limestone coals are in the middle subdivision of that series which is known as the Limestone Coal Group. Geologically, of course, the whole Midland Valley of Scotland is a broad syncline of sedi-

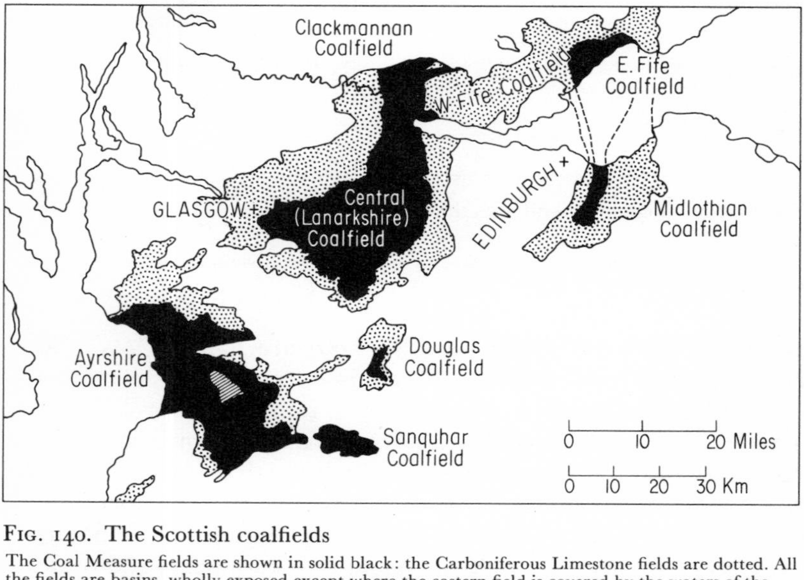

FIG. 140. The Scottish coalfields

The Coal Measure fields are shown in solid black: the Carboniferous Limestone fields are dotted. All the fields are basins, wholly exposed except where the eastern field is covered by the waters of the Firth of Forth and where a patch of Permian occurs in the heart of the Ayrshire field.

mentary rocks let down between the older rocks of the Highlands on the north and of the Southern Uplands on the south. Broadly speaking, the youngest rocks are near the centre of the syncline, the older rocks along its margins. Consequently there is a broad belt of Old Red Sandstone along the northern margin and a narrower, less continuous belt along the south. Carboniferous rocks occupy much of the centre, but it is clear that folding and denudation had gone on before the formation of the Coal Measures and, at least in some cases, the Coal Measures occupy basins filling up old hollows in the pre-existing floor. Most of the ten more or less well defined basins occupied by Coal Measures are, however, folds within Carboniferous rocks which have been formed by subsequent earth movements. The extent of the fields is roughly shown in the accompanying diagram and broadly speaking it can be seen that there are three important areas:

The Ayrshire coalfield.
The Central coalfield, lying largely in Lanarkshire but with extensions northwards into Stirling and Clackmannan.
The Midlothian–Fifeshire coalfield, where actually the Coal Measures as well as the Carboniferous Limestone are continuous under the Firth of Forth which, however, divides this area into two fields, the Fifeshire field to the north and the Midlothian field to the south.

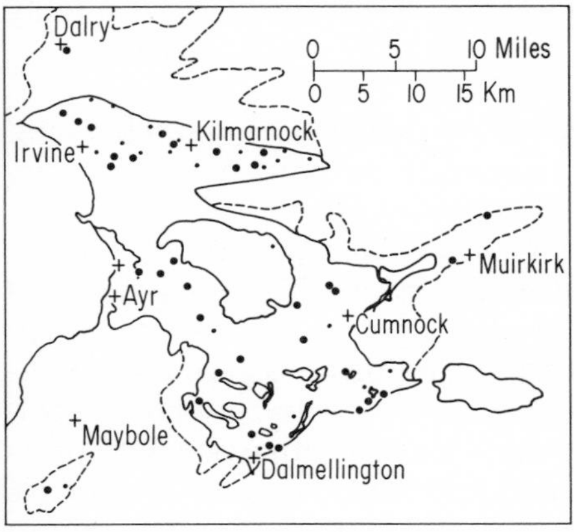

FIG. 141. The Ayrshire fields, 1931, distinguishing the Coal Measure fields from the here unimportant Carboniferous Limestone fields. One important colliery should have been shown in the Sanquhar basin

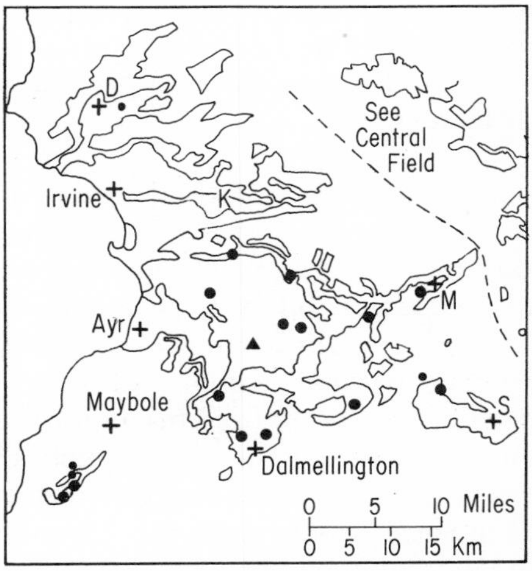

FIG. 142. The Ayrshire coalfields, 1968
Small dots, under 100 men employed; large dots, 100 to 1000; triangles, over 1000.

Few of the Scottish coal seams have a wide lateral extent. This is particularly the case with the Limestone Coal Group. Further, individual seams tend to vary greatly in thickness, often within short distances. Some of the best coals average under three feet in thickness, but locally the seams may swell out to over 6 metres (20 ft). Most of the Scottish coals are bituminous coals, though first-class steam coals are present and there are good bunker coals. There are, in addition, a number of high-quality gas and coking coals.

(*a*) *The Ayrshire coalfield.* Over much of the Ayrshire coalfield the Coal Measures are disposed in a number of synclines with the intervening anticlines often broken by faulting. These structures generally have a northeasterly trend. The Productive Coal Measures have a maximum thickness of about 458 metres (1500 ft), but are succeeded in places by an upper group, the Barren Red Measures. Complex belts of close faulting are locally a feature. The coals are mainly bituminous and are chiefly used for steam raising and domestic purposes. In a few instances seams affected by intrusive sills of teschenite have been rendered anthracitic.

In recent years closures of uneconomic collieries, or those at which the main reserves have been exhausted, bear no comparison with the degree of cessation of mining activity apparent in the Central coalfield. The majority of the Ayrshire collieries still active recorded productivity rates at or above the Scottish average in 1968. The new Killoch colliery, near Ochiltree to the east of Ayr, established with a capital outlay of more than £9m, is now the largest productive unit in the area with an annual output of over one million metric tons, a labour force of 2000 and a productivity rate of more than 2 metric tons (40 cwt) per manshift which in Scottish terms is highly satisfactory.

(*b*) *The Central coalfield.* Coal mining in the Central field of Scotland has long been associated with the iron and steel industry of such centres as Airdrie, Coatbridge, Motherwell and Wishaw. The greater portion of the field lies in Lanarkshire, but to the east and southeast it extends into West Lothian, Stirlingshire, Dunbartonshire and Clackmannanshire. The small outlying Douglas coalfield, which had four active collieries in 1968, lies in south Lanarkshire. Excluding this minor field but including its eastern and northeastern extensions the Central field contained only twelve productive collieries. The scale of colliery closures since 1960 bears comparison with parts of the South Wales coalfield. Disused shafts and drifts are now a feature of the landscape, particularly in the Coatbridge–Hamilton area and again to the east and southeast of Airdrie. Many of the closures can be related to difficult structural conditions or to the exhaustion of the more accessible seams. Quite a few were drifts with limited mining complements. A few new drift mines opened up as major capital projects by the National Coal Board have recorded encouraging yields; on the other hand some reconstruction schemes have proved disappointing mainly because geological conditions have turned out to be more complex and disturbed than was indicated by exploratory boring or surface conditions. A case in point is the Glenochil drift mine near Alloa which was closed in 1961 after expenditure of more than £5m on its development. The ancient ports of Bo'ness and Grangemouth have long served the Stirlingshire and Clackmannanshire extensions to the field by shipping coal and importing pit props. Clackmannan is still largely an agricultural county and the mine workings are not unduly obtrusive.

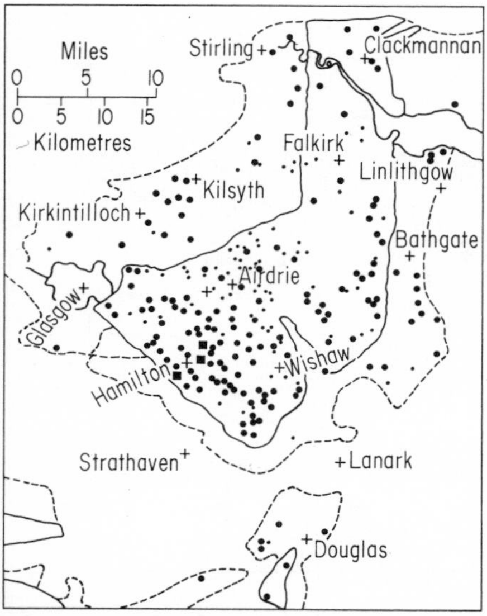

FIG. 143. The central coalfield, 1931

This map shows by a solid line the boundary of the upper (Coal Measure) coal-bearing series and by a pecked line the boundary of the Carboniferous as a whole. FIG. 144 shows more exactly the outcrops of the two coal-bearing series.

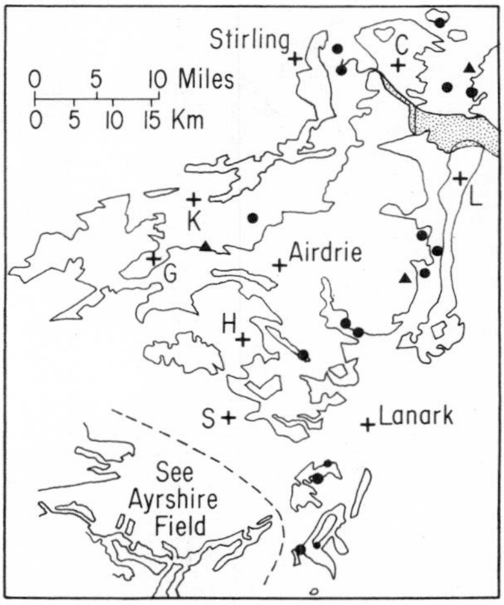

FIG. 144. The central coalfield, 1968

Small dots, under 100 men employed; large dots, 100 to 1000; triangles, over 1000. The reduction in the number of pits since 1931 is remarkable, as is also the small number of large pits.

(*c*) *The Fifeshire coalfield.* This field contains large reserves of coal despite a long history of past mining. These reserves nevertheless are becoming increasingly more difficult and costly to reach. In the eastern half of the field they lie principally in the Productive Coal Measures beneath the waters of the Firth of Forth and at substantial depths in the Limestone Coal Group both on land and in the undersea extension. A deep shaft was sunk by the National Coal Board near Thornton (Rothes colliery), at a capital cost of more than £10m, to tap these reserves in the Limestone Coal Group. This was finally abandoned in 1962 when it was disclosed that exceptional underground conditions had severely affected results. Eight kilometres south on the coastline to the south of Kirkcaldy the new Seafield colliery, costing £15m, has in the past few years started extracting seams of the Limestone Coal Group from beneath the Firth of Forth. Between 1955 and 1957 an offshore boring tower completed six boreholes to an average depth of 915 metres (3000 ft) in the Firth and these verified the former speculation concerning the seaward extension of the coalfield towards the east and south. It is now wellnigh certain that the Coal Measures of East Fifeshire are continuous with those of the Midlothian Basin on the opposite side of the Forth. It seems likely that future undersea workings will be at substantial depths. In the centre of the Firth it has been postulated that there is a deep pre-Glacial channel filled with unconsolidated materials extending to depths reaching beyond 150 metres (500 ft) below O.D.

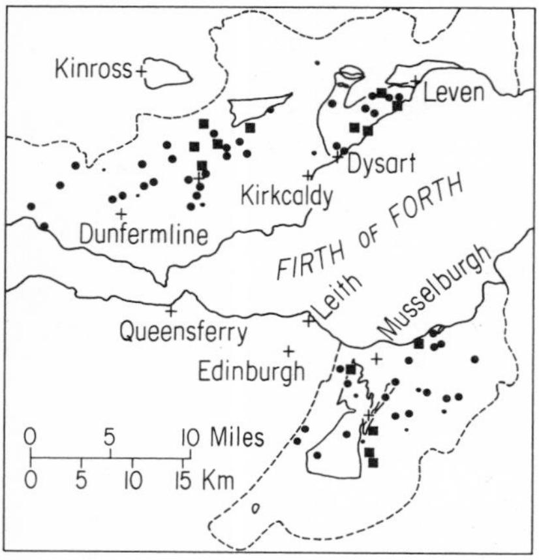

FIG. 145. The eastern coalfields of Scotland, 1931
The importance of the lower group (Carboniferous Limestone group) in Fifeshire is very apparent.

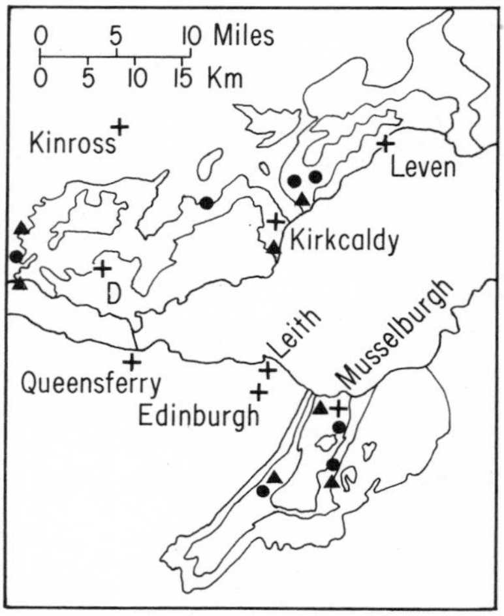

FIG. 146. The eastern coalfields of Scotland, 1968
Symbols as on Fig. 144.

On land the major structure affecting the Coal Measures is the Burntisland Anticline whose axis extends in a northnortheasterly direction from near Burntisland to the vicinity of Markinch. On the eastern flanks of this large upfold the rocks have been flexed into a series of lesser folds trending roughly from north to south and disturbed by a number of east–west faults. The Productive Coal Measures reach their maximum thickness of some 518 metres (1700 ft) between Methil and Kirkcaldy where they contain up to twenty workable seams. West of Kirkcaldy and in the West Fife Coalfield, in general, practically all the workable seams are found in the Limestone Coal Group. This reaches a maximum thickness of 427 metres (1400 ft) in the deepest part of the Lochore syncline where the total thickness of the component seams may reach nearly 30 metres (100 ft). In places the coals have been destroyed or otherwise affected by igneous intrusions. Near Cowdenbeath and Dunfermline there are numerous east–west faults so that the coal-bearing strata are now preserved in a series of small basins bounded to the north and south by dislocations.

The Midlothian and East Lothian coalfields

The Midlothian coalfield is structurally an asymmetrical syncline with a steep western limb, the axis of which runs in a general northeasterly direction to the sea near Musselburgh. The great Pentland fault of similar trend forms its western boundary whilst to the east it is separated from the East Lothian coal basin by the D'Arcy-Cousland anticline. Workable seams are found both in the Limestone Coal Group and in the Middle and Lower subdivisions of the Coal Measures. The Limestone Coal Group averages 244 metres (800 ft) in thickness and contains up to fifteen seams of commercial significance whilst the Productive Coal Measures (i.e. the Middle and Lower subdivisions) are normally about 400 metres (1300 ft) thick and show thirteen workable coals. The Limestone Coal Group thins generally

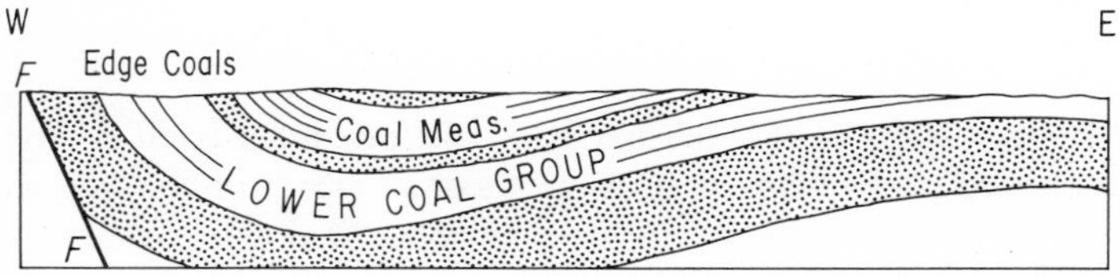

FIG. 147. A section across the Midlothian coalfield

to the south and southeast and as a result is less than 91 metres (300 ft) thick in the extreme south of the basin. From the southern coastline of the Firth of Forth near Musselburgh workings within the Limestone Coal Group have been extended northward for more than 3 kilometres in the undersea extension of the coalfield. Two major new collieries (Monkton Hall and Bilston Glen), whose shafts were sunk near Newcraighall and to the southwest of Dalkeith, respectively, were designed to win coal from the Limestone Coal Group in the deeper, flatter and as yet largely untapped central portions of the basin. In 1968 both were producing coal at the rate of 914 000 metric tons (900 000 long tons) per annum and with highly satisfactory productivity levels. Recent colliery closures have resulted in a cessation of mining in the East Lothian basin and in the southern half of the Midlothian basin. An annual production of over 3 million metric tons is now being achieved from six collieries all lying within 9.5 kilometres (6 miles) of the outer southern or eastern suburbs of the city of Edinburgh. In conclusion one might note the apt name given to the seams of the Limestone Coal Group—Edge Coals—on the steeply upturned western edge of the Midlothian basin.

Northern Ireland

The exposed coalfield of East Tyrone lies to the immediate west of Lough Neagh and is of limited extent. The beds occur within a structural continuation of the Midland Valley of Scotland and workable coals occur in rocks of both Carboniferous Limestone and Coal Measure age. The only other known coalfield lies to the east of Ballycastle. It occupies a hollow in the old highland rocks and coal seams are again present in strata of Carboniferous Limestone age. Small quantities of coal have been produced from both coalfields, but the quality is rather poor.

The Irish Republic

Although a geological map shows several areas of Coal Measures the coal seams in them are unimportant and practically all the coal required by the Irish Republic has to be imported.

PEAT

The Tertiary paleogeography of the British Isles did not lend itself to the formation of great thicknesses of *lignite* such as those of parts of the North European Plain. Only in one tiny area—the Oligocene basin of Bovey Tracey in Devonshire—are seams of lignite known to occur. They were quarried and even mined during the Second World War—though more, it must be admitted, as a source of montan wax than as fuel—and they are unlikely to be worked again.

The peat resources of the country have been estimated at 10 000 million metric tons. This is equivalent to no more than twenty to twenty-five years' consumption of coal at present rates. A considerable volume of peat has been extracted in the past from such lowland bogs as those of Fenland, the Norfolk Broads area and the Somerset Levels, and from isolated bogs at higher levels such as Macclesfield Moss. Little use has ever been made of the upland peat bogs of the Pennines or the Scottish Highlands, though many a Scottish croft has made use of its local resources. Undoubtedly the greatest potentiality lies in central Ireland (see Fig. 75), and here a considerable industry has developed, with milling and briquetting and the use of the fuel in several electric power stations.

Although some 600 000 hectares (1.5 million acres) of peat have probably been cut since 1800, there remain a further 1.2 million hectares (3 million acres), the bulk of which is in the Irish Republic. The modern large-scale utilisation of this resource postdates the Second World War, and an organisation called Bord na Móna has been responsible for much of the development. There are about 40 500 hectares (100 000 acres) of peat bog in patches larger than 400 hectares (1000 acres), and a further 120 000 hectares (300 000 acres) in smaller but still economically workable areas. Mechanical excavators dig the peat, and lorries and light railways carry it to the milling and briquetting plants and to the power stations. Long-distance transport is out of the question since six times the volume of peat is required compared with coal to yield a given quantity of heat energy. Seven power stations now depend on milled and sod peat for their fuel supply (see Fig. 156). The first was at Portarlington, and the largest is at Ferbane, near Athlone. In addition, considerable quantities of processed peat are used as industrial and domestic fuel.

MINERAL OIL AND GAS

The serious search for oilfields in this country began during the First World War under the auspices of the Geological Survey at a time when the German submarine menace made home supplies of all commodities of vital importance. Prior to this, one occurrence of natural gas had long been known. About the middle of the last century a well near the new railway line at Heathfield in Sussex tapped a small gas field and natural gas was used to light the lamps at Heathfield station for some years. Exploration during the war was concentrated on the Carboniferous rocks of the Midlands of England where traces of bitumen had long been known, and in central Scotland in the area where oilshale had long been worked. Some small shows of oil were detected, but the net result was a solitary oil well, at Hardstoft in Derbyshire.

In the period between the wars the Government passed the Petroleum Production Act in 1934, an Act which nationalised the oil resources of the country, at that time unknown except for the Hardstoft occurrence. This first decree of nationalisation by the Government received remarkably little attention, but it permitted the Crown to encourage active exploration for oil, which was undertaken by a subsidiary of the Anglo-Iranian Oil Company.

Many trial borings were made in the south of England and in the Midlands and north, greatly adding to our knowledge of the geological structure,[1] but only in one area has much success followed these efforts. In the East Midlands a number of anticlinal structures in the concealed Carboniferous rocks have yielded oil in commercial quantities since 1939. The first areas to be developed were at Eakring, Kelham and Caunton (near Newark) in Nottinghamshire; their output, which reached a peak in 1943, was sent by rail to Pumpherston in Scotland for refining (see below, p. 330). Later discoveries at Plungar in the Vale of Belvoir, at Egmanton near Tuxford, and in several localities near Gainsborough, brought the East Midlands output to 86 400 metric tons (85 000 long tons) in 1960.

By the end of 1960 the oilfields of Britain had yielded a total approaching a million and a half metric tons of oil. Such figures seem large until they are measured against imports and consumption. In 1960 home production was about 0.3 per cent of consumption.

1. N. L. Falcon and P. E. Kent, *Geological Results of Petroleum Exploration in Britain 1945–1957*. Geol. Soc. Memoir no. 2, 1960.

Oil shale

Oil shale, unlike coal, was worthless until industrial technique had reached a high degree of development. Oil shales were known to occur in the Carboniferous rocks of Scotland and although they had never been worked for any purpose some of them were so rich in oil that they could easily be kindled into flame, and it was in the 1850s that James Young, using a seam near Broxburn, produced oil on a commercial scale. He was so successful that Scotland began to supply almost all the worldwide demand for mineral lubricant and lighting oils, as well as for paraffin wax. It was not until 1859 that petroleum was discovered in commercial quantities in Pennsylvania and American competition appeared. The richer shales of Scotland yielded as much as 364 litres (80 gallons) of oil per ton. When these were exhausted yields from poorer shales dropped to about 91 litres (20 gallons) per ton, but the byproducts proved more valuable than both the oil and wax obtained. In particular large quantities of ammonia were obtained which combined with sulphuric acid made on the spot to form ammonium sulphate, a valuable fertiliser. For the greater part of a century the production of shale oil from Scotland went on, and the countryside of West Lothian is littered with gaunt red spoil heaps of burnt shale. The output of crude oil in the 1930s was about 127 000 metric tons (125 000 long tons) a year. Wartime needs during the Second World War stimulated production, which reached 151 000 metric tons (149 000 long tons) in 1941. The shale was refined at Pumpherston. Production fell to 61 000 metric tons (60 000 long tons) of oil in 1960 and ceased in 1964.

Natural gas[1]

Apart from the isolated occurrence of natural gas at Heathfield, mentioned above, the first discovery of real importance was made in the 1950s in north-east Yorkshire, where a deep boring in Eskdale not only discovered potash salts resembling those of the famous Stassfurt deposits of Germany but also struck methane gas in the Magnesian Limestone. Some of this gas was later piped to Whitby, and in the early 1960s several more successful bores were put down in the same area. These discoveries, together with the development of the great gas fields in the Netherlands, naturally led to the speculation that anticlinal structures beneath the North Sea might yield gas and perhaps oil as well. Towards the end of 1964 intensive undersea drilling began, and during the next four years over one hundred wells were drilled, mostly into the gasbearing horizons in the Permian, or sometimes into the Lower Trias. The first commercial strike was made in September 1965 in the West Sole field, some 65 kilometres east of Holderness (Fig. 148), at a depth of nearly 3000 metres, and a pipeline was subsequently laid beneath

1. T. M. Thomas, 'The North Sea gas bonanza', *Tijds. v Econ. en Soc. Geog.*, 1968, 57–70.

the sea floor to Easington on the Yorkshire coast. The Leman Bank and Hewett fields were proved in 1966, the latter only 25 kilometres from the Norfolk coast, and a number of other successful strikes followed, a pipeline being laid in 1967 to Bacton. Little oil has so far been tapped. The piping of the gas inland to join the existing natural-gas pipeline from the Canvey terminal to Leeds is referred to below (p. 336).

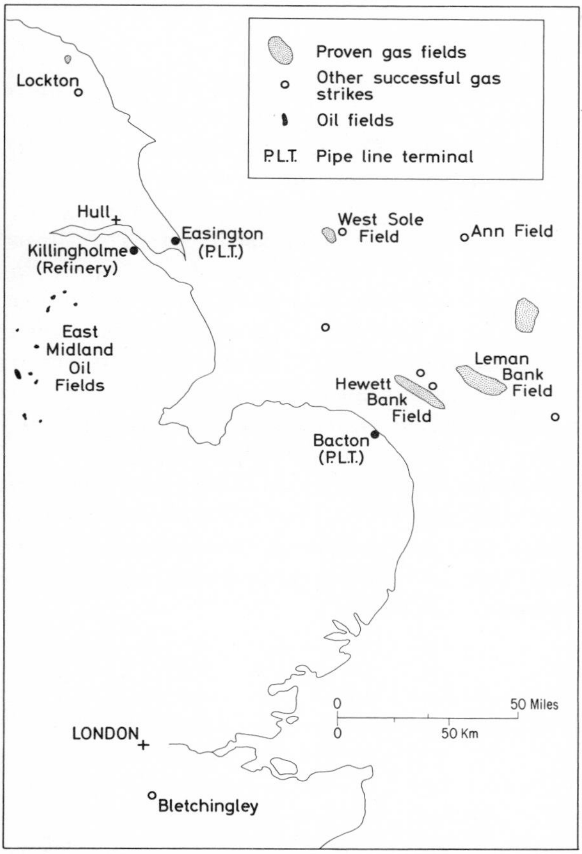

FIG. 148. The oil and natural gas fields of England and the North Sea

FUEL AND ENERGY PRODUCTION AND USE

The total quantity of fuel and energy (including water power) used in the United Kingdom about 1950 was equivalent to 226.5 million metric tons (223 million long tons) of coal. Coal, about 203 million metric tons (200 million long tons), represented about 90 per cent of the whole, and about 10 per cent was derived from imported oil. Water power and all other sources supplied only 0.5 per cent. Since that time coal output has dropped to 162.5 million metric tons (160 million long tons) and oil imports have risen to 76.2 million metric tons (75 million metric tons), whilst electricity derived from nuclear energy has entered the picture, as also has natural gas, and there has been a small but significant increase in the hydroelectricity output in Scotland.

The changing use of coal

In 1913 when British coal production reached its peak of 291.6 million metric tons (287 million long tons) the country was producing more than one-fifth of all the coal mined in the world. During the interwar years, with a world output approximating to 1524 million metric tons (1500 million long tons) a year, the United States was mining roughly one-third, Great Britain one-sixth and Germany rather less than a sixth. In 1913 almost exactly one-third of the total coal mined was sent out of the country as export and bunker coal; an all-time maximum export of 99.2 million metric tons (97.6 million long tons), or over 35 per cent of the output, was reached in the boom year of 1923. During the Second World War the total of export and bunker coal fell to less than 3 per cent of the coal mined, but in the years following the war recovered temporarily to nearly 10 per cent in 1949, only to fall to less than 3 per cent by 1961, and to 1.3 per cent by 1968.

With an increasing population one would expect a fairly steady or slight upward trend in the total home demand for coal. But this came to an end in 1956 in face of competition from cheap imported oil. Considering only the coal retained for home consumption the following table shows, in percentage form, the changes in use to which it was put.

USER	1923	1938	1955	1961	1969
Collieries	9.6	6.9	4.0	2.5	1.2
Railways	7.9	7.5	6.0	4.6	0.1
Coastwise bunkers	0.8	0.7	0.3	0.1	*
Gas works	9.9	10.9	13.2	12.3	4.3
Coke ovens	11.2	10.9	12.7	14.9	15.5
Electricity works	4.1	6.4	20.1	30.6	47.1
Miners coal	3.7	2.6	2.4	2.6	1.8
Domestic } Industrial }	52.8	26.1	15.2	15.8	11.5
		26.0	26.1	16.6	13.3
Miscellaneous	—	—	—	—	5.2

* Included in 'miscellaneous'.

For more recent years the table shows a steady decrease in the coal consumed by gas works and an enormous increase in that used by electricity works. The decline in consumption by the gas industry has accelerated rapidly in recent years with the introduction of North Sea gas; whilst consumption by power stations continues to rise despite the use of oil fuel and atomic energy. The railways ceased to be a significant user of coal after 1966 because of the general replacement of steam engines by diesels or electric traction. The big drop from 1938 to 1955 in domestic consumption was due to rationing. The year 1955 was one of acute shortage and a large import. Many industries were forced to consider the possibilities of utilising other forms of fuel, particularly oil, and thus by 1957–58 there was a complete change around in the fortunes of the coal mining industry—the main problem then became, and this persists to the present day, one of over-production and monthly surpluses. The domestic market has likewise witnessed a steady decline and this is primarily due to wider installation of central heating appliances based on oil, electricity and, in the more recent period, natural gas.

Coke

Domestic coke is a byproduct of the gas industry and as such was produced by almost every coal-burning gas works up and down the country. Metallurgical coke, however, is produced by coke-oven plants for use in iron and steel works, and the industry has an interesting geographical pattern which may be briefly analysed.[1]

Coke for iron smelting was probably first made by Abraham Darby at Coalbrookdale in the early part of the eighteenth century. He used lump coal of relatively low rank (78–79 per cent carbon) and almost free from sulphur, and carbonised it in open heaps. This method, with similar coals, became standard practice in the Black Country and elsewhere during and after the Industrial Revolution. Then, towards the middle of the nineteenth century the 'beehive' oven was developed to use the 'smalls', or 'slack', of strongly-swelling, 'caking' coals of higher rank (carbon 85 per cent or more). Progress in this case was most rapid in the Durham coalfield, particularly rich in such coals and lying in such close proximity to the rapidly growing iron town of Middlesbrough; but the coking coals of Yorkshire and Derbyshire were also coked in beehive ovens. For various reasons the development of the byproduct recovery oven was slow in Britain compared with the continent. There was an abundance, in certain areas, of coking coals of superlative quality, but the relative stagnation of the iron and steel industry during the last quarter of the nineteenth century did not encourage high capital outlay on new coking plant. In 1900, 80 per cent of British coke was still produced from beehive ovens and only 8 per cent from byproduct ovens. But by 1914 the beehive percentage had dropped to 31 and the byproduct figure had risen to 62, and after the First World War the beehive oven rapidly became almost extinct. Byproduct ovens, using

1. S. H. Beaver, 'Coke manufacture in Great Britain: a study in industrial geography', *Trans. Inst. Br. Geogr.*, **17**, 1951, 131–48.

crushed or slack coal of similar quality to that used for beehives, yield considerable quantities of tar, benzole, benzine, naphtha, ammonia and many other products which make coke production a chemical industry of some significance. Nevertheless the main function of the coke oven is still to produce coke for iron smelting.

The modern coke industry is located in two types of situation—at or near the collieries which produce coal of suitable quality and alongside iron and steel works. Only a few of our coalfields and coal seams yield coal of suitable quality—though with the development of scientific blending the range is increasing—and in consequence the coalfield coke industry is located in three main areas only, in south Durham, in south Yorkshire and northeast Derbyshire, and in eastern South Wales. In addition to these pit-head cokeries, however, vast quantities of coke are now made at 'integrated' iron and steelworks (see below, p. 397) both on the coalfields—as at Rotherham, Glasgow and Ebbw Vale—and away from the coalfields—as at Middlesbrough, Scunthorpe, Corby and Newport—for coke is more expensive to transport than coal and the 'waste' gases from the ovens can be used in the works for various power-producing purposes as well as for their by-products. In those areas where coke is made the gas is frequently used to supplement the local gasworks' output for domestic and industrial use. The Sheffield area actually has a 'gas-grid' on the same general principle as the electricity 'grid'.

The total production of oven coke in 1969 was 16.5 million metric tons from 25.0 million metric tons of coal. The South Wales coalfield provided 4.6 million metric tons, the Yorkshire coalfield 4 million metric tons and the Durham coalfield 3.3 million metric tons. Nearly 10.6 million metric tons were disposed of in blast furnaces, the demand from this quarter having diminished by 1 million metric tons, or thereabouts, since 1960. With technological improvements in blast furnaces and iron foundries, less coke is required per ton of metal and the demand for metallurgical coke has been falling on this account. With the installation of smokeless zones in towns there have been local increases in the demand for coke and other manufactured fuels, both in industry and in domestic usage.

Gas

The use of coal to produce gas began in 1805, when Murdock lighted a mill in Manchester with gas; two years later a German, Winzau, who had failed to arouse enthusiasm for his schemes in his own country, raised enough capital in London to carry out the lighting of Pall Mall, the first public thoroughfare in the world to be illuminated by gas. His company received a royal charter in 1812 and later became the Gas, Light and Coke Company. Steady progress in the manufacture and use of gas for town lighting and domestic purposes was made during the nineteenth century. Up to 1890, however, the lighting properties of the gas depended on those vapours it contained which burnt with a luminous flame; later it was discovered that it was better and cheaper to remove from the coal gas these luminous gases and to rely on the heating properties of the gas to raise metallic oxides on gas mantles to so high a temperature that they became incandescent. So the problem became to maintain the heating properties of the gas at a maximum and to recover from the gas the vapours which had previously given luminosity to the flame. Gas is produced by heating bituminous coal in closed vessels called retorts. The volatile gas is removed and the porous coke, which remains, contains as high a proportion of carbon as anthracite and is used for similar purposes, especially for central heating.

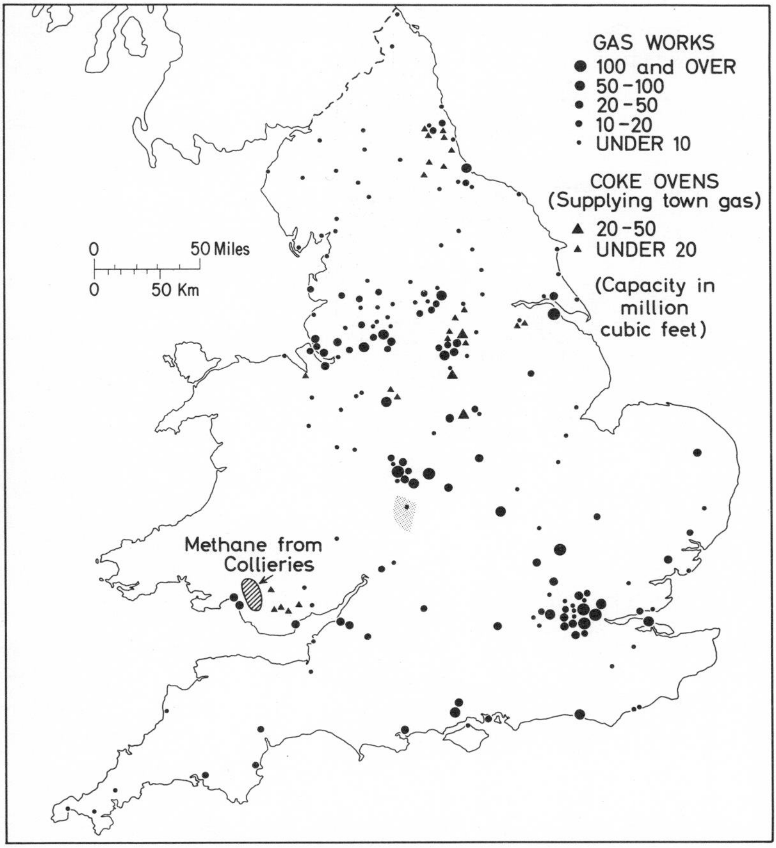

FIG. 149. The gas industry, 1967

On nationalisation in 1949 there were 1050 gasworks in production; the above map shows that in 1967 there were less than 300—but the total capacity had risen by over 25 per cent. In 1971 the total had been reduced to about 100—of which only 3 made gas from coal!

Formerly, gas was produced almost entirely within the main centres of consumption, so that every town had its gasworks, the main siting factors of which were proximity to a railway or navigable waterway, for coal supplies. Before the Second World War a few gas-grids existed in the major conurbations, but they were of limited extent and quite unconnected with each other (see Ordnance Survey 1:625000 map, *Gas and Coke*, 1952—relating to the 1949 position). Since the industry was nationalised in 1949 it has been organised on a regional basis; smaller and less efficient works have been closed, and from being an essentially market-orientated industry it has become concentrated at the larger markets, at the location of its raw materials, and at tidewater sites, whilst an extensive mileage of pipelines has been laid down for regional distribution. To an increasing extent also the regional Gas Boards have purchased bulk supplies of gas from the coke-oven plants of the National Coal Board and the integrated iron and steel works, and in a few localities methane gas pumped from coal mines has contributed to the supply.

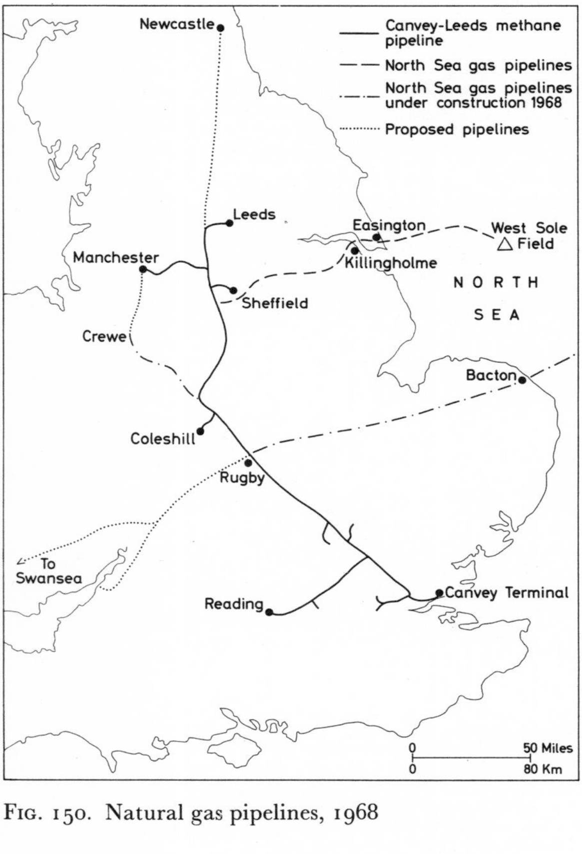

FIG. 150. Natural gas pipelines, 1968

Technological progress has been extremely rapid since 1950, and amongst the most important developments has been the making of gas from oil—either by catalytic gasification at ordinary gasworks or at new, specially built works, or in the normal course of oil refining ('tail gases' which are subsequently modified to the required calorific value). Another development was the gasification of low grade coal by the German 'Lurgi' process; a plant at Westfield in Fifeshire has used opencast coal since 1961, but an even newer works at Coleshill, near Birmingham, has already been closed as out-of-date, so rapid has been the efficient development of oil and of natural gas.

Natural gas, referred to above (p. 330) has been imported in specially constructed tankers from North Africa since 1963, and a pipeline was constructed from the Canvey Island terminal on the Thames estuary to Leeds (Fig. 150). The development of North Sea gas and its piping to the major industrial areas has added an entirely new economic factor in the gas industry, and the precise part to be played in the future by coal-gas, gas-from-oil and natural gas, and the competitive power of the gas industry *vis-à-vis* solid fuel and electric current, have yet to be worked out. To a large extent it is a political as well as an economic matter.

The situation is changing so rapidly that any statistical statements must be out of date before they are printed; and it is also true that an enormous upheaval in the gas industry is inevitable as a result of the changing sources of raw materials. In 1968, just over 20 per cent of the raw materials used in gas works was natural gas, and about two-thirds of this came from the North Sea; another 52 per cent comprised oil, whilst coal, which only a few years previously had been accounting for two-thirds of the gas output, had dropped to only 23 per cent. The repercussions of this on the coal industry must be serious (see note under Fig. 149).

Electricity

The following table shows the phenomenal growth of the electricity supply industry during the last few decades:

YEAR	TOTAL OUTPUT IN MILLION kWh	(HYDRO)	(NUCLEAR)
1929	11 962	165	—
1938	25 708	988	—
1946	42 742	1 139	—
1955	94 076	1 701	—
1966	202 568	4 560	21 009

Thermal generation—coal and oil fuel

Until 1926 the systems of supply of electricity in this country were the result of unplanned growth. Local legislation and piecemeal development had resulted in the existence of numerous isolated area supplies with a great variety of generating plant, frequencies and pressures. Two inevitable consequences followed—a very wide variation in the cost to the consumer of a unit of electricity and a paralysing or stultifying effect on large-scale developments. The Electricity Supply Act of 1926 provided for the setting up of a Central Electricity Board. Within this national scheme electricity was to be generated only at 'selected stations' where generation could be most economically carried out. The network of lines for the transmission of energy at high tension (commonly known as the Grid) rapidly became familiar through the erection of pylons in all parts of the country, and over these lines took place the 'wholesale' transmission of the current to the distributing undertakings. In 1948 the whole passed under the control of the British Electricity Authority. The Electricity Act of 1957 set up a Council, a Generating Board and twelve Area Boards in England and Wales. In Scotland the South of Scotland Electricity Board controls supplies in the Lowlands and Southern Uplands, whilst the North of Scotland Hydro-Electric Board looks after the Highlands.

The main location factors[1] involved in the distribution of power stations are: (1) proximity to the populous areas which the station is designed to serve; this is still important, but with the possibility of large-scale transmission of power at high tension over long distances it is much less so than formerly; (2) the availability of cheap coal, usually of inferior quality, or of fuel oil; water transport facilities, inland or coastwise, are of great importance. In addition to these *location* factors, there are two *site* factors of importance, the availability of cooling water, usually many millions of gallons per hour, and cheap land with room for expansion and for railway sidings and ash disposal. Water front sites will again be important; if adequate river or sea water is not available, large concrete cooling towers will have to be built (Plate 11), so that the water can be used over and over again.

CEGB (England and Wales) power stations and capacity, 1968

TYPE OF INSTALLATION	NO. OF STATIONS	INSTALLED CAPACITY (MW)
Steam (coal or oil)	179	40 000
Gas turbine	8	1 235
Diesel	12	52
Nuclear	7	3 300
Hydro	10	479
Total	216	45 020

1. See E. M. Rawstron, 'The distribution and location of steam-driven power stations in Great Britain', *Geography*, **36**, 1951, 249–62.

Until the Second World War the map of power stations bore some resemblance to a map of major urban concentrations, but postwar technological developments in the utilisation of pulverised coal, in the construction of large power stations with capacities undreamt-of a few decades ago, and in the transmission of high-tension current, have wrought great changes. Of the 179 steam-driven stations, about 40, each rated at over 300 MW (and the largest at 1770 MW), now possess about 67 per cent of the entire generating capacity (Fig. 151). To such an extent is the proximity of a large river now a matter of vital importance that 65 per cent of this 'super-station' capacity is now to be found alongside the lower Thames (5574 MW in ten stations), along the Trent (7638 MW in nine stations), and along the Aire and Calder (4120 MW in seven stations). These 'super-stations' almost all consume pulverised coal—of which the Yorkshire–Nottinghamshire coalfield is the cheapest source in the country—and their thermal efficiency is between 25 and 34 per cent, compared with less than 20 per cent and sometimes even less than 10 per cent for the older stations which are being gradually eliminated or relegated to a stand-by function only, the base load being taken by the big and efficient plants.

The other major development has been the 'super-grid', first of 275 kV and more recently (since 1966) of 400 kV. The total extent of the grid is about 16 000 kilometres (10 000 miles), of which 2575 kilometres (1600 miles) are 275 kV and 2100 kilometres (1300 miles) are 400 kV. The development of the 'super-grid' is a natural consequence of (1) the economies to be reaped by high-voltage transmission (even though this means bigger pylons), and (2) the concentration of the 'super-power' stations in the Trent valley, Yorkshire and Thames-side. Lancashire, still largely served by a multitude of relatively small stations, is increasingly the recipient of current from the Trent valley and West Yorkshire; and the 'super-grid', fed also by the nuclear power stations (see below), now extends to South Wales, southern and southwest England, and the northeast, with both west and east coast links into Scotland.

Thermal generation—atomic energy and nuclear power stations[1]

In conventional steam-driven electric power stations a 'fossil fuel', such as coal, oil, or natural gas, is mixed with air and burned in a boiler furnace. The hot gases of combustion rise and go through tubes in a boiler through which water circulates. The water absorbs the heat and changes to steam, which is then used to drive a turbogenerator, thereby producing electric power. In nuclear power stations, the heat comes from the process of nuclear fission in an atomic reactor and, in British stations, carbon dioxide gas under pressure is pumped over the uranium fuel in the reactor, drawing off the heat to the boilers.

1. This section has been contributed by Dr P. R. Mounfield.

In the early 1950s, it seemed that Britain was faced with a future shortage of coal and oil for electricity generation. Thus, the first programme for the commercial development of nuclear power was introduced, in 1955, and under this programme it was planned to install 5000 MW of nuclear generating capacity by 1969. The power stations constructed under the programme have been based on the 'Magnox' thermal reactor design, first developed at Calder Hall in Cumberland, using natural uranium as a fuel. Nine stations of this type have been built. Three are on the Severn estuary, at Berkeley (276 MW), Hinkley Point (500 MW) and Oldbury (600 MW);

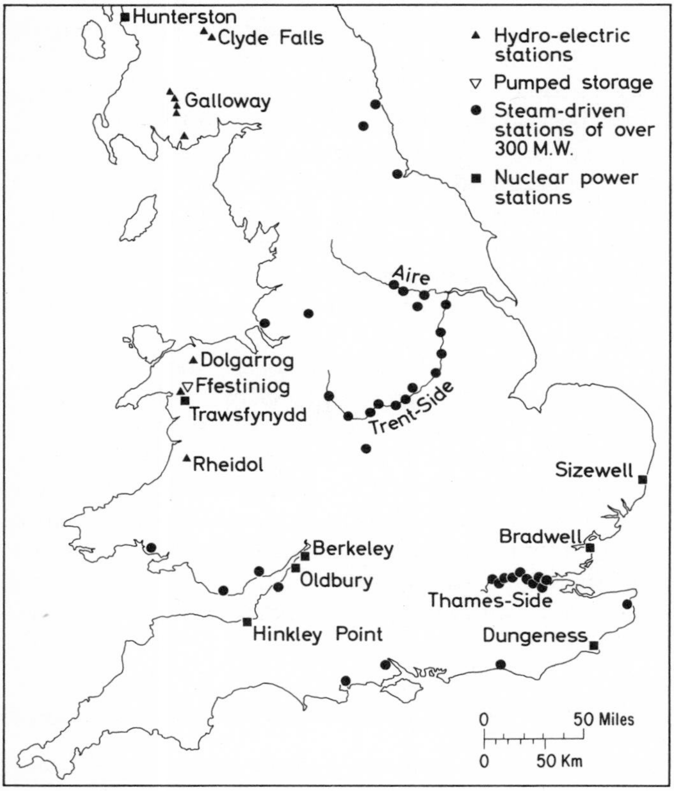

FIG. 151. Power stations, 1968
Of the 216 power stations in existence in England and Wales, 50 are shown on this map, including all the steam stations with over 300 MW capacity. The concentration of the latter on the Trent and the lower Thames is very striking.

two are on the coast of East Anglia, at Bradwell in Essex (300 MW) and Sizewell in Suffolk (580 MW); two are in North Wales, at Trawsfynydd in Merioneth (500 MW) and Wylfa in Anglesey (1180 MW); one is on the south coast, at Dungeness in Kent (550 MW) and one in Scotland, at Hunterston, Ayrshire (300 MW). Because these stations have been costly to build, the electricity that they produce is more expensive than that from coal-fired stations of comparable age and size located on the cheap coal-fields. Thus, they have been located so as to meet the growth of demand for electricity in areas where coal is scarce or expensive, i.e. the southwest, the southeast and the northwest. Within these areas, two other important considerations have influenced the selection of sites. Because of the need for large quantities of water, each of the stations, except for Trawsfynydd, is on the coast. Also, though it is claimed that no danger is involved, to allay public fears on this score, sites far from large concentrations of population

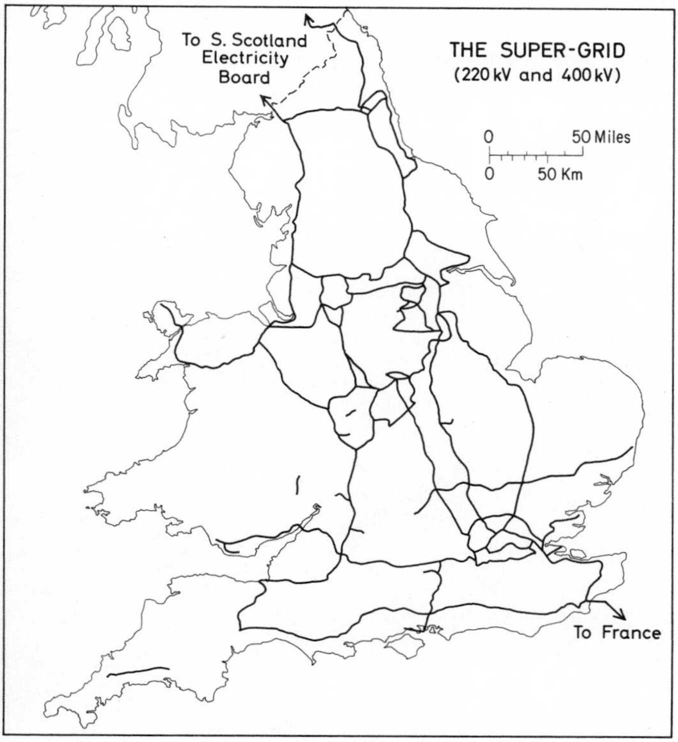

FIG. 152. The super-grid in 1968

Numerous extensions are proposed or in course of construction; the map can be kept up-to-date from the annual statistical yearbook of the Central Electricity Generating Board.

have been selected. On occasion, this policy has led to conflict between the Central Electricity Generating Board and those bodies concerned with preserving the little that remains of rural Britain. It has also meant that rather long and expensive high-voltage transmission lines have had to be built to connect some of these remote stations to the national grid.

In April 1964 the Government announced Britain's second nuclear power programme, for the period 1970 to 1975, allowing for the construction of a further 8000 megawatts of generating capacity. This programme was prefaced by an invitation from the Generating Board for tenders for all types of commercially available nuclear generating systems, including water reactors developed in the USA. Assessment of the tenders in July 1965 showed that the British advanced gas-cooled system (AGR) was the most commercially attractive design and AGR power stations, each of 1320 MW installed capacity, were under construction in 1969, on the same sites as the existing Magnox stations, at Dungeness, Hinkley Point and Hunterston, and at a new site at Seaton, near Hartlepool. A further station is proposed at Heysham on the Lancashire coast, together with a second station at Sizewell and a very large one of 2500 MW near Connah's Quay on the Dee estuary in North Wales.

PLATE 11. West Burton power station, Nottinghamshire (photographed in 1965)
The water consumption of stations such as this is so enormous that cooling towers are necessary in order to re-use the water that is derived from the river Trent. There are now so many power stations on the Trent that if they all simply extracted river water and discharged it at a high temperature after use the river would consist of hot water, with disastrous consequences for the aquatic fauna.

The estimates of the cost of electricity to be produced by the AGR plants have altered the economic conditions under which the locations for nuclear power stations are chosen. By the early 1970s, the AGR plants are expected to generate electricity more cheaply than the best coal or oil-fired power stations available at that time—more cheaply, even, than contemporary coal-fired stations built next to the pit head on the low-cost coalfields. Thus, as nuclear power becomes progressively cheaper compared with power from fossil fuels, it will become increasingly appropriate to choose sites near to large cities and conurbations. This will enable increases in demand for electricity to be met with the minimum long-distance energy movements and with a minimum of new overhead transmission lines, and it will reduce the friction between the Generating Board and amenity preservation bodies. It is fortunate that, through the use of prestressed concrete pressure vessels, and oxide fuel in stainless steel cans, the AGR has excellent safety characteristics. In March 1968 the independent Nuclear Safety Advisory

PLATE 12. Dungeness nuclear power station (photographed in 1964)

Committee advised the Government that, in its opinion, it is safe to use sites near to large urban areas for AGR power stations. The locations that have been chosen to date for several of the AGR units reflect the fact that there is sufficient space at most of the existing nuclear power station sites for a second station, but the new locational parameters have influenced the choice of Heysham and Seaton and doubtless will be reflected in the choice of future sites.

In economic terms, the choice between nuclear and fossil-fuel electricity generation in Britain rests mainly on the advance of nuclear technology on the one hand, and future movements in the cost of conventional fuels on the other. In 1970 three-quarters of the electricity produced in Britain will come from coal-fired power stations, with the remaining quarter divided almost equally between nuclear and oil-fired plants. However, the new generating plant commissioned and provisionally planned to be commissioned by the Generating Board up to 1980 is as follows:

PERIOD	CONVENTIONAL (MW)	NUCLEAR (MW)	GAS TURBINE AND HYDRO-PUMPED-STORAGE (MW)
1961–5	8 638	2 415	1 069
1966–70	21 666	2 670	800
1971–75	8 000–11 000	6 000– 7 000	2 000–3 000
1976–80	6 000–11 000	16 000–20 000	2 000–3 000

These figures underline the fact that nuclear power is now a strongly competitive source of electrical energy. During the 1970s it will be taking an increasing share of the base load generation of electricity and it seems possible that by 1980 a very large proportion of the Generating Board's *new* capacity may be nuclear. There are, however, many imponderables. For example, in January 1968 a 60 MW unit using natural gas from the gas grid was commissioned at Hams Hall power station, near Birmingham, and some further use of North Sea gas in power stations seems inevitable, for it will be cheaper than coal in many areas. Yet again, a substantial reduction of the fuel oil tax would make oil the cheapest fuel for electricity generation in most parts of the country. Since they are twice as expensive to build as conventional stations of the same size, nuclear power stations are particularly vulnerable to rising interest rates, but on base load, the fuel cost of a modern conventional station is about two-thirds of the total generating cost. At a nuclear station it is only about one-fifth. The Seaton AGR power station provides an example of what this can mean in practical terms. Assuming an average load factor of 75 per cent, the estimated overall cost of generation at the Seaton AGR station is 0.52*d* per unit, compared with 0.70*d* per unit for a coal-fired station at the same site burning Durham coal. The National Coal Board's price increases of April 1966, added £30m to the electricity industry's fuel bill, and it could well be that, in the light of rising coal prices, some increase in the nuclear power programme before 1975 would be economically justified. Even if this does not happen, by 1975 nuclear power stations will be providing a quarter of the total electrical power produced in Britain.

If current plans remain unchanged, the total nuclear capacity in Britain in 1975 will be 13 000 megawatts; approximately one-fifth of the total generating capacity then installed. Such a large commercial reactor programme requires the support of extensive nuclear fuel services. Uranium ore has to be mined and the uranium extracted and concentrated. These activities are carried out in Canada, the USA, Australia and other uranium producing countries, but large chemical plants are required for the conversion of the uranium concentrate to metal or to the gaseous compound uranium hexafluoride, which is the feed material for isotope separation plants. The latter are required to enrich uranium and, although the Magnox reactors use natural uranium, the fuel elements for the AGR stations will contain uranium in slightly enriched form. A publicly owned company may well be formed soon to take over the responsibility for nuclear fuel, but at present the production group of the United Kingdom Atomic Energy Authority (AEA) provides all the services except mining and concentration of ore. The AEA developed out of the organisation originally formed to produce Britain's military nuclear deterrent and consequently owns the Springfields factory for the treatment of imported uranium ore concentrate and fabrication of fuel elements, the Capenhurst gaseous diffusion plant and the Windscale fuel reprocessing plant. In addition, it has extensive research and development facilities, particularly at Harwell and Winfreth Heath, and operates the Calder Hall, Chapelcross and Dounreay reactors. The Authority's factories have been largely rebuilt and re-equipped to supply the fuel services for CEGB. The existing Magnox reactors already have been supplied with over 1.7 million fuel elements made at Springfields and when all nine stations are fully operational replacement elements will be supplied at a rate of 150 000 a year. Completely new manufacturing facilities are being provided at Capenhurst for the fabrication of the slightly enriched fuel elements for the AGR stations. A large new reprocessing plant has been built at the Windscale site which has a capacity for treating more than 2000 metric tons a year of irradiated fuel. The Generating Board itself has a comprehensive nuclear power research unit at its Berkeley Nuclear Laboratories, on the river Severn between Bristol and Gloucester. These laboratories provide the electricity supply industry with basic technical and scientific information. The site for the laboratories was chosen for its proximity to one of the Generating Board's early nuclear power stations and because it was close to the University of Bristol.

Hydroelectricity

The Water Power Resources Committee Report of 1921, referred to above, foresaw, on the basis of schemes proposed at that time, the development of no more than 250 MW of hydroelectricity, the bulk of which would come from Scotland. True, all the physical possibilities had not then been investigated, and in fact by 1968 more than 1600 MW of generating capacity was actually in existence—but even so, these figures pale beside the 45 000 MW of thermal-electric capacity installed in England and Wales alone in 1968, and the energy output figures given above (p. 337) show that hydroelectricity represents but one-fiftieth of the total electricity output.

The fact is of course that the physical make-up of Great Britain does not lend itself to large hydroelectric developments. There is plenty of well distributed rainfall in Highland Britain, and there are plenty of swiftly falling rivers, but the available catchments are very small and so the capacity of any plant, even allowing for considerable reservoir construction to augment the supplies, is bound also to be small.

There are really but few possibilities. Clearly the best area is the western side of the Scottish Highlands, where rainfall is heaviest and the relief greatest; but there are also possibilities in the western part of the Southern Uplands. The Lake District is of no use since the catchments are very small and the lakes are at too low an altitude. Snowdonia and the western part of central Wales hold some prospects, and there are minute possibilities in the Dartmoor area. But that is all. In Ireland the existence of the large river Shannon has opened up a possibility of a rather different kind.

Developments in the Scottish Highlands date from 1895. The earliest station was erected at Foyers, on the eastern side of Loch Ness, for the smelting of aluminium. The years 1904–09 witnessed the erection of a 23 MW power station at Kinlochleven, at the head of a marine loch, to which seagoing steamers have access. The water comes from the Moor of Rannoch to the east. Quite a considerable town has grown up around the aluminium works, now belonging to the British Aluminium Company, which were established. The Lochaber Power Company, established in 1921, achieved fame by driving a fifteen-mile tunnel to carry water from Loch Trieg through the flanks of Ben Nevis to near Fort William, there to generate electricity for the British Aluminium Company's smelter built just north of the town in 1929. Lochs Trieg and Laggan were dammed to increase their storage capacity, and the headwaters of the river Spey diverted into Loch Laggan.

The Grampian system, dating from 1930, comprised two power stations utilising the abundant water supply of the great Rannoch upland. The Rannoch installation uses water from Loch Ericht; the Tummel station uses water from Loch Rannoch. Much farther north, in Ross-shire a small station at Loch Luichart used water from the river Conon, and supplied power to Nairn, Dingwall, and Dornoch. The Highlands of Scotland have certain advantages for water development. Temperatures are moderate so that risk of freezing is slight, evaporation is low, and hence the loss of water from reservoirs is small. Moreover, the winter precipitation maximum (even though part of it may be in the form of snow and so not immediately available) ensures that the river flow is greatest just when the demand for electricity is at its highest. There are many sites suitable for dams, and considerable areas are more than 900 metres (3000 ft) above sea-level so that a good fall of water is possible. But it became clear that a fully co-ordinated development was essential.

Under the Hydro-Electric Development (Scotland) Act 1943, a public authority was set up known as the North of Scotland Hydro-Electric Board which was given wide powers for the development of water and the pro-

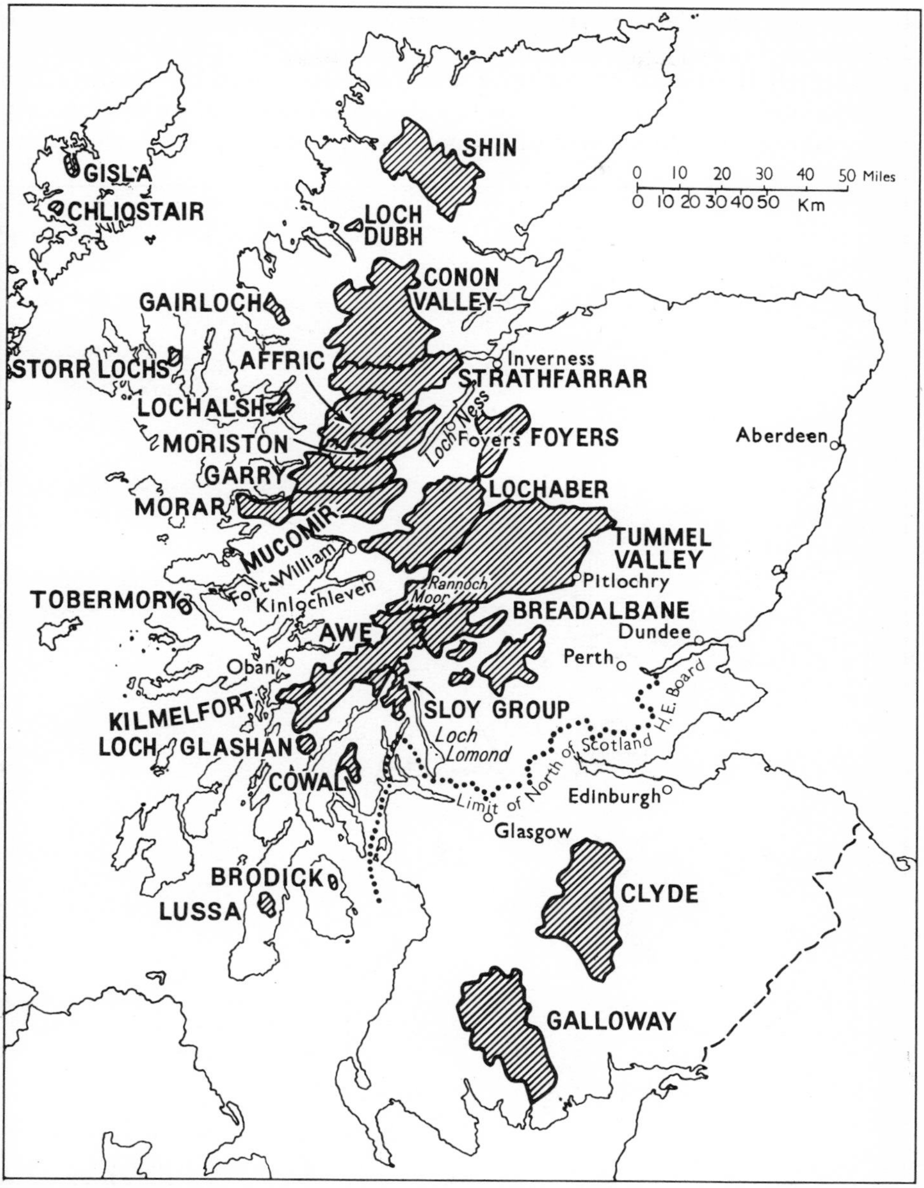

FIG. 153. Map of Scotland showing water-power development—projects and catchment areas

motion of social, industrial, and general rehabilitation within the Scottish Highlands. Its area of operations covers about 57 000 square kilometres (22 000 square miles), approximately three-quarters of Scotland, and is broadly the whole area north of the Central Lowlands (see Fig. 153). The Electricity Act 1947, which nationalised the electricity supply industry in Britain, left the Board out of the pattern for the rest of the country but brought under its control the sixteen existing private and local authority undertakings. The Board is required not only to produce and sell electricity

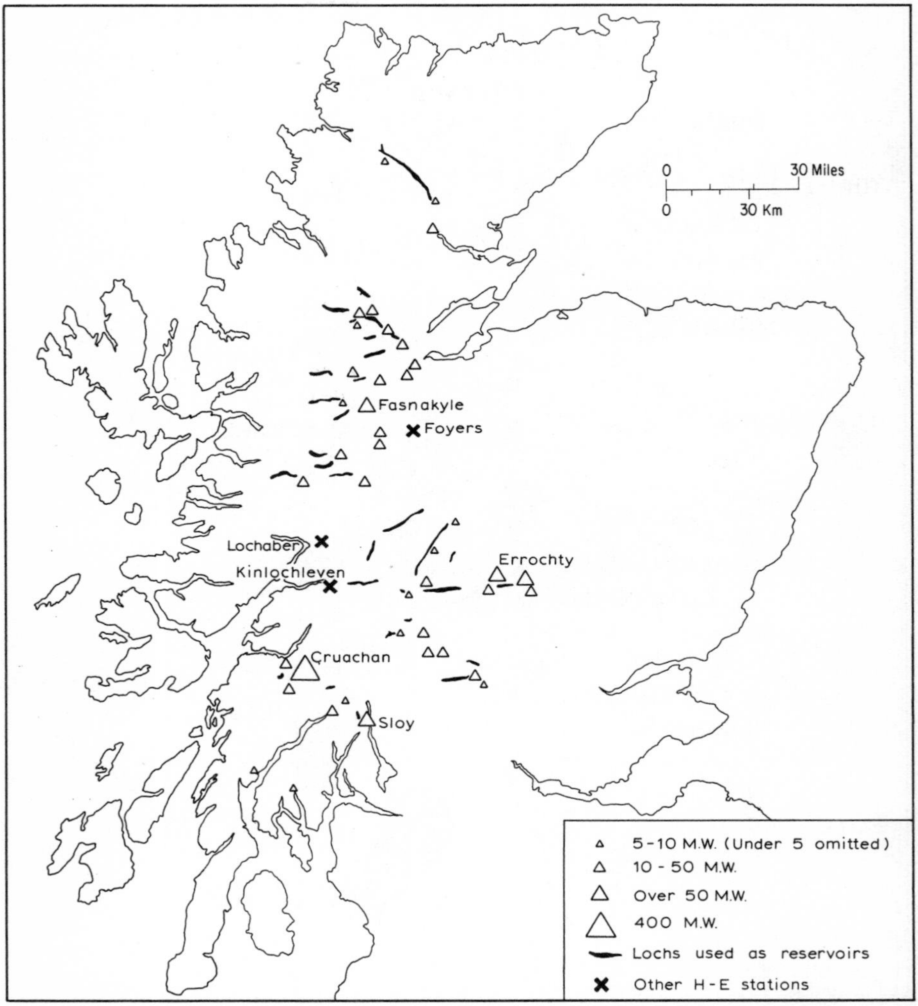

FIG. 154. Water power in the Scottish Highlands
Based on data from the North of Scotland Hydroelectric Board.

but to collaborate in measures for the social and economic development of the whole area.

The first of the new hydroelectric power stations to be completed was a very small one at the Falls of Morar in Inverness-shire in 1948. At that time only one farm in fourteen and one croft in a hundred were connected to the mains. The large Loch Sloy scheme with its power station on Loch Lomond was completed in 1950, and the Glen Affric scheme, with a power station at Fasnakyle in Strathglass, was opened in 1952. By 1948 the Board had fifty-five main hydroelectric power stations in operation, all but two (Rannoch and Tummel) built since the war (Fig. 154). The installed capacity was 1047 MW and the output 3225 million units. The number of consumers was 444 000, or 96 per cent of the potential. The Board had built or rebuilt over 400 miles of roads.

The largest power station is the 400 MW pumped-storage station, part of the Cruachan (Loch Awe) scheme; the station itself is underground. The principle of this scheme is to have high level and low level reservoirs connected by a pipeline. At off-peak periods the water is pumped into the upper reservoir and then electricity is generated by allowing the water to flow from the upper to the lower reservoir through the turbogenerators at times of peak load. Among other large stations may be mentioned Errochty and Clunie in the Tummel valley. The latest big development is based on Foyers; the aluminium works having closed, the Hydro-Electric Board is to establish a 300 MW station by enlarging the catchment and using pumped storage. The project is due for completion in 1974.

Outside the Highlands of Scotland conditions are generally less favourable, potential and actual output is of limited magnitude, so that the British Electricity Authority controls a limited number of relatively small stations. One of the largest is the Galloway Scheme in the Southern Uplands, completed at the end of 1936, with five power stations, a generating capacity of 102 MW and an annual output of about 180 million units. Much earlier, however, the falls on the Clyde were harnessed to supply two power stations, one using the Stonebyres Falls and the other the Bonnington and Corra Linn Falls.

There are small hydroelectric power stations in North Wales at Dolgarrog, Maentwrog, and Cwm Dyli; the first of these provides power for an aluminium rolling mill (see p. 477). In 1963 a large pumped-storage scheme, with a capacity of 360 MW, was completed in North Wales (Ffestiniog) and in 1964 the Rheidol scheme near Aberystwyth, with two power stations and a capacity of 56 MW. There are three tiny stations in the Dartmoor area, two of which are in the Tavy valley north of Plymouth.

What is happening is in fact the coordination in the whole national grid system of what were formerly small isolated schemes, as well as some larger ones and extending or adding to them. Perhaps the most interesting possibility for water power lies in harnessing the energy of the tides. Of the various schemes which have been considered that of the Severn Barrage has attracted most attention and has been the most carefully investigated. Unfortunately the output, estimated at 2300 million units a year from a plant capacity of 800 000 kW, would be rather irregular as the height of the tide varies. Capital cost was estimated at £29m in 1933, at £47m in 1944, and rising costs have since put the whole scheme virtually out of practical consideration.

PLATE 13. Cruachan pumped-storage hydroelectric scheme, Argyll
The fall from the dam to the power station on Loch Awe is 365 metres (1200 ft).

Water power in Ireland

Until the recent developments in the Scottish Highlands, by far the largest and most ambitious scheme in the British Isles was that for harnessing the river Shannon. Ireland is practically devoid of coal, and so was under the necessity of importing her fuel, hence the great incentive to the development of water power from the largest river in the British Isles. The Government entered into an agreement with a German firm—Messrs Siemens Schuckertwerke—in February 1924, the proposals being submitted to Dàil Eireann in 1925, and the Shannon Electricity Act was passed in June of the same year. The river Shannon has a long meandering course over the central drift-covered plain, passing through three large lakes, Loughs Allen, Ree, and Derg, and in 200 kilometres (125 miles) of its length has a

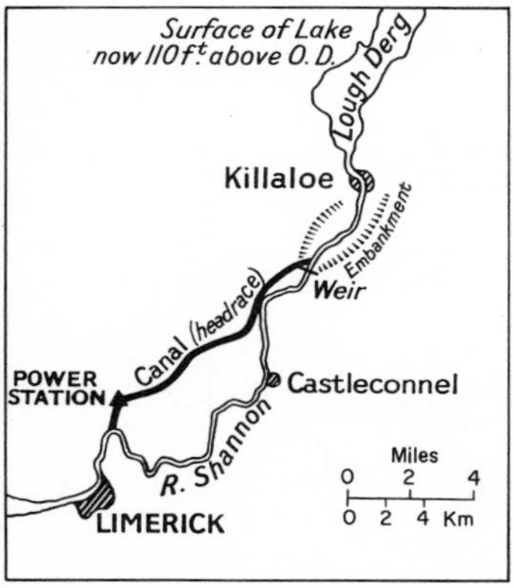

FIG. 155. Details of the Shannon scheme

fall of only 17 metres (55 ft), or less than 15 cm (6 in) per mile. The flow is sluggish, the flooding of adjacent areas common, but from Lough Derg to the sea a remarkable change takes place. The surface of Lough Derg was about 30 metres (100 ft) above mean sea level at Limerick and from Killaloe at the southern end of the lake to Limerick is only a distance of 24 kilometres (15 miles). The river made its way through a series of rapids, cutting almost a gorge through the hard rocks which there cross its bed. The local details of the scheme as carried out are shown in Fig. 155. By means of an embankment below Killaloe the surface of the lake was raised some 3 metres (10 ft) so that it is now 33 metres (110 ft) above O.D. Fortunately, Killaloe is built on rather higher banks of the river, and the little town has not suffered. At the southern end of the embankment a large weir was constructed, and then the bulk of the water taken through a canal or headrace to the power station just above Limerick where the full fall of nearly 30 metres (100 ft) could be utilised, the spare water being allowed to find its way through into the Shannon. The power house is at Ardnacrusha, from whence the race discharges the spent water into the Shannon near Limerick. The water in the tailrace is influenced by the tide, the net fall varying from 26 to 35 metres (86 to 115 ft). Above Killaloe, throughout the Central Plain, the river is navigable and a barge canal was constructed at the side of the power works so as to permit continuous navigation from Limerick. Further

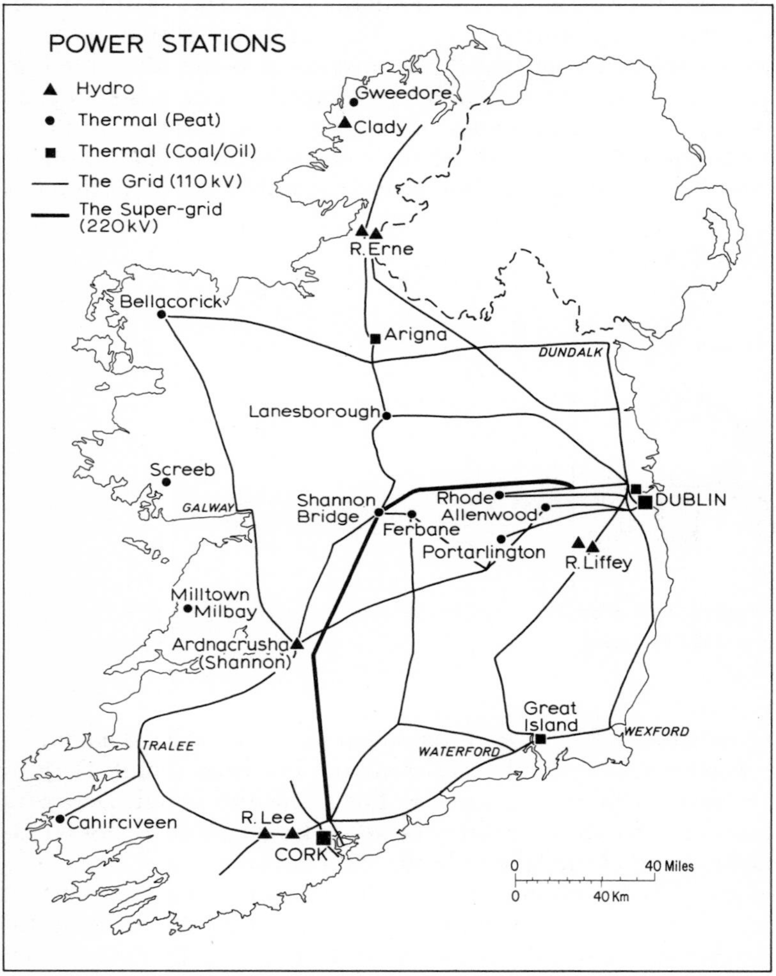

FIG. 156. The Irish electricity grid, 1968

This map can be kept up-to-date from the annual reports of the Electricity Supply Board, Dublin.

a small canal with a series of steps to be utilised by salmon was made (later much improved), since salmon fishing in the Shannon is of very considerable value. Under the Electricity (Supply) Act, 1927, the Electricity Supply

Board took over the task of generating and supplying electricity to the whole Republic. Fig. 156 shows the power stations which in the year ended 31 March 1968 generated 4 246 000 000 units, 19.5 per cent derived from water, 26.7 per cent from peat, 1.8 per cent from native coal and 52 per cent from imported coal and oil.

Petroleum

The consumption of petroleum continues to rise by leaps and bounds, and the industry that supplies it has undergone a major revolution since the Second World War. In 1947 about 2.5 million metric tons of crude oil were refined in Great Britain; in 1968 ten major refineries each had an annual capacity greater than this, and four of them a capacity of over 10 million metric tons, whilst the output of saleable products reached an all-time record of 84.8 million metric tons (83.5 million long tons). The reasons for this vast expansion are partly economic, partly political and partly technological. Crude oil costs much less to import than refined petroleum, and the dollar shortage made it vital to cut American imports and increase the importation of crude oil from the Middle East. Political considerations were also involved: the Arab embargo on the export of Middle East oil to the refinery at the Israel port of Haifa, and the Persian seizure of Abadan, were both factors increasing the desirability of expanding British refining capacity; whilst the Suez crisis of 1956 spurred the development of supertankers that have reduced transport costs but have created port problems. Certain technical factors also played a notable part: the refineries produce many byproducts which can be used in other industries, and the petrochemical industries (cf. Chapter 22) have likewise rapidly expanded; and the variety of petroleum products now used by motor cars, tractors, diesel-engined lorries and locomotives, and aircraft is such that it is obviously more economic to produce them at home refineries from crude oil imported in vast bulk than to import them separately in small tankers that can only carry one product at a time.

Users of oil fuels, 1967

	MILLION METRIC TONS	MILLION LONG TONS		MILLION METRIC TONS	MILLION LONG TONS
Electricity generation	7.9	7.8	Bricks, pottery, glass, cement	2.7	2.7
Central heating	5.7	5.6	Chemical industries	2.4	2.4
Oil refining	4.7	4.7	Paper industry	1.1	1.1
Steel industry	4.5	4.5	Railways	1.0	1.0
Engineering industry	3.1	3.1			
			Total	44.0	43.4

The 1968 output of 84.8 million metric tons (83.5 million long tons) included 44 million metric tons (43.4 million long tons) of gas oil, diesel oil and fuel oil, 13 million metric tons (12.8 million long tons) of motor spirit, 3.1 million metric tons of aviation spirit, and 10 million metric tons of naphtha, used as 'chemical feedstock' in the petrochemical industry and in the manufacture of gas. The table on p. 353 lists the most important users of the heavier fuel oils.

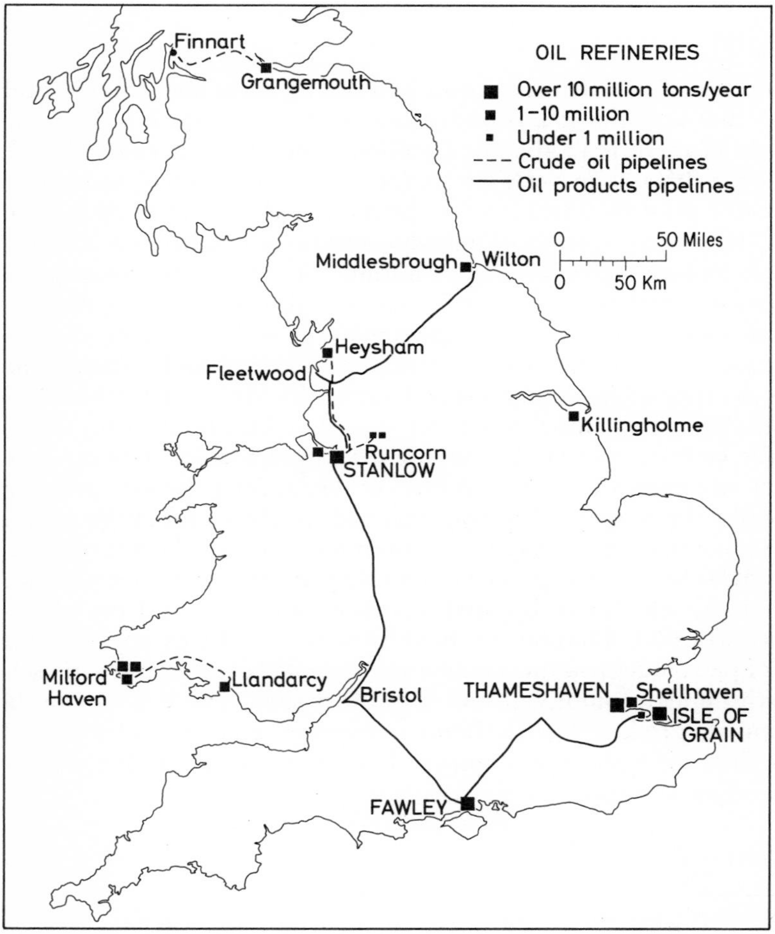

FIG. 157. Oil refineries and major pipelines

Naturally enough, waterfront situations are chosen for oil refineries, since all the crude oil is imported. But because they require very large areas and are somewhat undesirable neighbours, they have been built away from the major ports, and have had to develop their own port or pipeline facilities. Fawley is on Southampton Water, but its Solent approaches had to be dredged to enable fully-laden 70 000 ton tankers to reach it. Stanlow, on the Manchester Ship Canal (which can only take vessels up to 12 000 tons) had to develop a new dock at Eastham to take 30 000 ton tankers, and a jetty (with a 19.3 kilometres (twelve-mile) pipeline) at Tranmere on the Mersey estuary for tankers larger than this. Thames Haven and Shellhaven on the Essex shore of the Thames estuary, and the Kent refinery on the Isle of Grain, can now accommodate very large tankers. Grangemouth, on the Forth estuary, is too shallow for large tankers, so a 92 kilometres (57-mile) pipeline was laid from Finnart on the 'fjord' of Loch Long which has very deep water close to the shore. At Llandarcy, near Swansea, the refinery (which dates from the 1920s) was served by Queens Dock, but as this cannot take vessels of over 20 000 tons a pipeline has been laid to Angle Bay on Milford Haven. Milford Haven has indeed been the scene of very important developments, for in addition to the Angle Bay terminal, three separate oil refineries have now been constructed along this 'ria', which can take 250 000 ton tankers. The search for deep-water facilities has gone on, and the latest refineries are on Tees-side, on the south bank of the outer Humber estuary (where the deep-water channel swings into the shore), and on reclaimed land at the entrance to Belfast harbour. Even more spectacular is the development of a terminal at Bantry Bay, one of the deep rias of southwest Ireland, where tankers of 300 000 tons or more can be accommodated, unloading their liquid cargo into smaller tankers which distribute to British and continental refineries.

The coastal location of the refineries also facilitates an export trade which is growing rapidly. In 1945 the export of fuel oil in ships' bunkers totalled 1.7 million metric tons, and of fuel oil not for bunkers, only 1000 metric tons. By 1951 the figures had risen to almost 3 million metric tons for bunkers and 2.3 million metric tons not for bunkers; whilst in 1968 bunkers totalled 5.5 million metric tons and other exports 13.0 million metric tons.

15
Mining industries other than coal and iron

The tables below show the relative importance, in terms of output and employment, of the various minerals that are mined and quarried in the United Kingdom. As already noted, coal is still by far the greatest, but gravel and limestone are fast catching up. It is significant that this mid-twentieth-century 'age of concrete' demands increasing quantities of aggregate (sand and gravel) and of cement (made from limestone and chalk); significant also that, unlike coal, most of the other minerals are obtained by quarrying, the effect of which on the landscape rivals that of the collieries and their spoilheaps and is geographically more widespread.

Output of minerals

MINERALS	PRODUCTION (MILLION TONS)					
	1938		1955		1967	
	METRIC TONS	LONG TONS	METRIC TONS	LONG TONS	METRIC TONS	LONG TONS
Coal	230.6	227.0	225.1	221.6	173.8	171.5
Iron ore	12.0	11.9	16.4	16.2	12.9	12.7
Chalk	10.5	10.4	16.6	16.5	18.1	17.9
Limestone	19.1	18.9	31.7	31.2	76.3	75.2
Igneous rocks	12.0	11.9	14.1	14.0	29.8	29.4
Slate	0.3	0.3	0.15	0.15	0.1	0.1
Sandstone[1]	5.2	5.2	4.4	4.4	8.9	8.8
Salt	2.6	2.6	4.7	4.7	7.1	7.0
Clay, shale, etc.	27.2	26.8	29.7	29.3	35.2	34.7
China clay	0.6	0.6	1.2	1.2	2.6	2.6
Potters clay	0.2	0.2	0.4	0.4	0.5	0.5
Fireclay	2.6	2.6	2.5	2.5	1.7	1.7
Sand and gravel	22.5	22.2	60.4	59.5	107.0	105.4
Oil shale	1.5	1.5	1.3	1.3	nil	nil
Tin ore (dressed)	0.003	0.003	0.002	0.002	0.002	0.002
Lead and zinc ore (dressed)	0.057	0.057	0.011	0.011	0.005	0.005
Moulding sand	0.8	0.8	0.8	0.8	0.8	0.8
Gypsum (including anhydrite)	1.1	1.1	2.9	2.9	4.5	4.5

[1] Including silica rock and ganister.

Employment in mines and quarries

	1927	1935	1948	1967
Coal mines	1 023 886	769 474	727 565	412 000
Iron ore mines and quarries	11 864	7 981	6 529	3 227
Other metalliferous mines	5 137	3 409		941
Salt works	97 399	84 100	4 824	*
Slate quarries			4 724	1 377
Other non-metalliferous mines and quarries			39 133	42 065

Not including clerical and other non-operative staff.
* Not available.

In general terms we can divide the 'other minerals' into two groups, metallic and non-metallic. Any consideration of metallic minerals in Britain (other than iron ore) must now be largely a matter of historical geography, for, important though Cornish tin, Anglesey copper, Pennine lead, for example, may once have been, present outputs are either nil or very small in quantity. Nevertheless a brief résumé may not be out of place. The industrial significance of the minerals in question will be considered in Chapter 18.

Metallic ores

Although individual deposits may vary widely in details of their mode of occurrence most of the metallic ores found in Britain may be said to occur in one of three major types of geological environment:

(*a*) Associated with the granite masses of Devon and Cornwall.
(*b*) In the Lower Paleozoic rocks of the Highland Zone of Britain, associated with igneous activity of which sometimes there is no evidence at the surface—as in central and north Wales (including Anglesey), the Welsh Border (Shropshire), the Lake District, the Southern Uplands of Scotland, and the Wicklow Mountains of Ireland.
(*c*) In certain regions of the Carboniferous Limestone outcrop, such as the Derbyshire Dome, the northern Pennines of northwest Yorkshire, Durham and Northumberland, the Mendip Hills, and the hills of northeastern Wales (Flintshire).

Devon and Cornwall[1]

One of the later stages of the igneous activity which produced the Armorican granites of Devon and Cornwall was the intrusion of veins and lodes carry-

1. See H. G. Dines, *The Metalliferous Mining Region of South-west England*, Mem. Geol. Surv., HMSO, 1956.

ing metalliferous ores, which are found chiefly in a belt about 9.5 to 16 kilometres (six to ten miles) wide extending from Lands End to Dartmoor (Fig. 158). In general, tin and copper occur nearest to the granites; lead, silver, and zinc farther away. Tin ore (cassiterite) is a very stable mineral and so was to be found not only in the original veins or lodes in the rocks, but also washed out in alluvial gravels, where it was formerly worked as

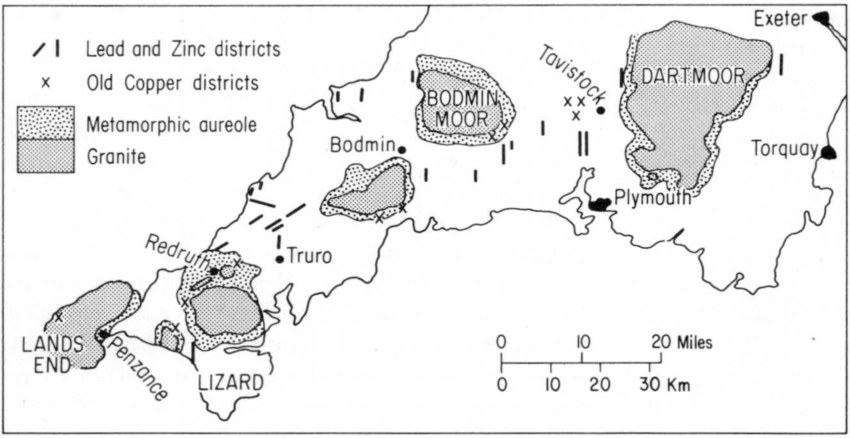

FIG. 158. The metalliferous mineral areas of Cornwall and Devon
The tin-mining tracts corresponded approximately with the copper districts.

'stream tin'. Cornwall was almost the world's only source of tin from very early times until the early nineteenth century. The greatest concentration of mining was around Camborne and Redruth. Copper was also mined from pre-Roman times in several districts of the southwestern peninsula, and Cornish ores contributed in no small measure to the rise of Swansea as the world's greatest copper-smelting centre in the early part of the nineteenth century (cf. p. 465). Mining in Devon and Cornwall is but a shadow of its former self; one or two mines remain productive of tin, wolfram (tungsten ore), and arsenic, but though it is considered by some that much mineral wealth remains to be got, there is unlikely to be any revival without an enormous programme of reorganisation and exploration and the application of vast new capital resources.[1]

Wales, etc.

The Lower Paleozoic rocks of Wales, the Lake District, and the Southern Uplands, have yielded a number of different minerals, but particularly

1. See *Memorandum to the Minister of Reconstruction on the production of non-ferrous metals and minerals other than coal in Great Britain*, published by Institution of Mining and Metallurgy, 1944. In 1968 several firms were prospecting in West Cornwall.

lead, which was worked from Roman times. The most important areas were in central and North Wales, in the Welsh Border district (Shelve in Shropshire), in the Lake District, and in the Leadhills district of the Southern Uplands. Copper was also occasionally important, as in North Wales and Anglesey (Parys Mountain), and in the Lake District (Keswick area). A little gold has been obtained from the Dolgellau area of North Wales and from Carmarthenshire; and the manganese ore found in the Cambrian rocks of North Wales has been worked from time to time, especially during the two World Wars.

Ireland

The Armorican disturbances induced mineralisation in the Paleozoic rocks of southern Ireland, at intervals in a broad belt from the Wicklow Mountains to the mountains of Kerry and in the Paleozoic uplands of Tipperary and Galway. Apart from much past working, there has been a recent resurgence, backed by Canadian and American capital, with new developments in copper in the Wicklow Mountains, in silver-lead-zinc at Tynagh in Co. Galway (now the largest producer in Europe) and in copper-lead-zinc-silver and barytes in the Silvermines Mountains of Tipperary.

Regions of the Carboniferous Limestone outcrop

Fissures and solution hollows in the Carboniferous Limestones are frequently filled with mineral deposits, of which lead and zinc have been most important. Five main lead-fields have been worked, in the Alston–Allendale area of the northernmost Pennines, farther south in northwest Yorkshire, in the Derbyshire Dome, in the Mendips, and in the limestone hills which border the Flint and Denbigh coalfield. In most of these areas the maximum output was reached after the middle of the nineteenth century and a very rapid decline followed; but evidence of the industry, in the shape of old mine shafts, spoil heaps, and tumbledown buildings, is still to be found in places. In 1958 a lead mine near Matlock was the only one working in the country. Zinc ores were associated with the lead veins in some places, particularly in the Mendips and in North Wales. Occasionally, copper ores occurred, as on the western edge of the Derbyshire Dome at Ecton, in Staffordshire. In Ireland, lead and zinc have been worked at many localities on the fringes of the Central Lowland, e.g. in the counties of Sligo, Clare and Monaghan.

Non-metallic minerals

We may divide the non-metallic minerals into two groups, the rarer and more highly localised ones—e.g. salt, gypsum, and anhydrite, fireclay and ganister, fluorspar, china clay—and the commoner and more widespread ones—e.g. limestone, chalk, brick clays, sandstone, igneous rocks (granite, whinstone, etc.) slate, sand, and gravel. Another way of distinguishing the two groups might be to say that of the first group more or less all of the available deposits are likely to be ultimately required, whereas in general, and from a national rather than a local point of view, there is a wider choice of locality for the working of the commoner minerals.[1] One can hardly envisage the extraction and utilisation of the entire chalk outcrop, for example!

Except for the igneous rocks, which are quarried mainly for road metal, all the non-metallic minerals occur in the sedimentary rocks, and every formation from the Cambrian to the Pleistocene yields some mineral or other in some part of its outcrop.

The 'rarer' minerals

The semi-desert conditions under which the later Permian and Triassic rocks were laid down were responsible for the accumulations of salt, gypsum, and anhydrite which are now worked in Cheshire, in South Durham, and elsewhere.

Salt.[2] Rock-salt used to be mined in Cheshire, and still is in one mine at Winsford, but almost all our salt output is now obtained by controlled brine-pumping.[3] There is an enormous reserve underneath the Cheshire Plain—the salt beds are several hundred metres in thickness over an area of some 970 square kilometres (375 square miles)—and the great chemical industries (p. 584) which depend on the salt need have no fear of exhausting the supplies. Other salt deposits occur in the Trias in the vicinity of Stafford, Droitwich (Worcs.), Fleetwood (Lancs.), and Middlesbrough.

Gypsum[4] (calcium sulphate $CaSO_4$, $2H_2O$) is the raw material of plaster of Paris and of the plasterboard which plays such an important part in the building industry. It is quarried or mined in Nottinghamshire (e.g. at Gotham and near Newark), in Staffordshire (near Tutbury), and in the Eden Valley near Appleby; there is also a mine near Battle, in Sussex,

1. This contrast should not be pushed too far; to an increasing extent modern industry requires specialised and standardised products which can often only be obtained from relatively small areas, and the availability of transport and markets exerts a very strong influence over the location of quarries.

2. A. F. Calvert, *Salt in Cheshire*, London, 1915; also *Mem. Geol. Surv., Mineral Resources*, vol. xviii, *Rock-salt and brine*, HMSO, 1921.

3. Pumping of 'wild' brine from the old and flooded salt-mines led to considerable and unpredictable surface subsidence—now represented by 'flashes' or lakes, especially in the Northwich district; controlled pumping does not eliminate subsidence, but reduces it and renders it more or less predictable, by confining it to the vicinity of the bore-hole. About 65 per cent of the brine pumped in Great Britain is obtained from bore-holes on the Holford estate, about 8 kilometres (5 miles) east of Northwich.

4. *Mem. Geol. Surv., Mineral Resources*, vol. iii, *Gypsum and anhydrite*, HMSO, 3rd edn, 1938.

which works gypsum from the Purbeck Beds (Upper Jurassic). The anhydrous form of gypsum is known as *anhydrite*; it is an important raw material for certain branches of the chemical industry, notably the manufacture of ammonium sulphate and sulphuric acid (cf. p. 585). Almost the entire output comes from a large mine at Billingham-on-Tees around which, since the 1930s, the vast works of Imperial Chemical Industries have grown up, and from near Workington in Cumberland.

Potash. Deep borings (to 1220 metres (4000 ft) or more), sunk originally in the search for oil, in the North Yorkshire Moors area, in the vicinity of Whitby, have revealed what is probably the western edge of the great Upper Permian ('Zechstein') potash field that reaches its greatest expression in the Stassfurt area of Germany. The first mine sinking was commenced in 1969 at Boulby, and others are likely to follow.

Fluorspar,[1] used as a flux in the steel industry and in the manufacture of hydrofluoric acid for glass-etching, is obtained from veins in the lead-bearing districts of the Carboniferous Limestone outcrop; the main present source is Derbyshire.

China clay and China stone[2] are derived from the decomposition (probably by superheated gases and steam from below) of certain of the granite masses of Devon and Cornwall. By far the most important field is in the Hensbarrow granite, near St Austell. The clay is got from deep open pits (the deepest is over 91 metres (300 ft)) by hydraulic sluicing, and the impurities (mainly quartz and other minerals) are removed and dumped in the gigantic white conical spoil-heaps which form the major feature of the landscape.[3] The clay is further purified and dried, and is then sent away by rail or exported coastwise and overseas from such small ports as Fowey and Par. While much china clay and china stone still go to North Staffordshire for the pottery industry, and large quantities are exported to Europe and USA (1.75 million long tons in 1965), it is important to realise that pottery manufacture is no longer the major user of china clay. Of the home consumption, 75 per cent is in the manufacture of paper and board; it is also used in textiles, paint, pharmaceuticals, cosmetics, insecticides, as a 'hardener' in the rubber industry, and the list is extending.

Ball-clay[4] is another raw material for the manufacture of pottery, glazed tiles, and sanitary earthenware. The two principal sources are Eocene beds in the vicinity of Poole, in Dorset, and Oligocene lake-bed deposits near

1. *Mem. Geol. Surv., Mineral Resources*, vol. iv, HMSO, 1922.
2. Board of Trade. Working Party Reports. *China Clay*, HMSO, 1948. R. M. Barton, *History of the Cornish China-clay Industry*, Truro, 1966.
3. Between six and eight times as much waste is produced as clay, and the largest spoil-heap contains a million tons of material. Some of this sand and fine aggregate is now used for concrete-making, but little or no impression can be made by this small industry on the size or number of the spoil-heaps, which from a distance look like a gigantic encampment of white tents.
4. *Mem. Geol. Surv., Mineral Resources*, vol. xxxi, HMSO, 1929.

Bovey Tracey, in south Devonshire; in both areas there are quarries and shallow mines.

Fireclay[1] is a special kind of clay with properties of resistance to high temperatures; it is employed in the manufacture of refractory bricks for furnace linings, gas retorts, etc., and also for glazed sanitary pipes (the glazing of

PLATE 14. Goonbarrow china-clay pit, St Austell

which needs temperatures higher than those used for ordinary brick burning). Fireclays generally occur as the seat-earths of coal seams, particularly in the Lower Coal Measures of Durham, Yorkshire, and Lancashire, in the Middle Coal Measures of the south Derbyshire coalfield (Swadlincote area), and of the Black Country, Warwickshire, and North Wales coalfields, and at the base of the Upper Coal Measures in the Potteries coalfield. In all these districts important refractory and glazed-ware industries exist; the greatest concentrations are in the Swadlincote area and in the Black Country near Stourbridge. The fireclays are generally mined, often from coal mines, but they are also sometimes quarried, as in the Swadlincote district.

1. *Mem. Geol. Surv., Mineral Resources*, vol. xiv, HMSO, 1920.

Ganister[1] is a rock consisting almost entirely of silica; like fireclay it occurs underneath coal seams, and is used for the manufacture of refractories. True ganister is mostly obtained in the Lower Coal Measures of the Sheffield district, but somewhat similar material, known generally as *Silica rock*, is obtained from the Millstone Grit and Lower Coal Measures of Derbyshire, Durham, and the fringes of the North and South Wales coalfields, and from the Lanarkshire coalfield.

It is fortunate that the best refractory materials—which are so much in demand by the iron and steel industry—should occur in such close proximity to some of the major centres of that industry, as in Durham, the Sheffield–Derbyshire area, South Wales, the Black Country, and central Lanarkshire.

The commoner minerals[2]

Broadly speaking, every acre of Britain is underlain by minerals (i.e. 'rocks') of which *some* use could be made. But whether or not use *is* made depends partly on the geological circumstances, and is very largely a question of economics. Actual quarries and mines are situated where they are because the operations can be profitably conducted—the quality of the rock is satisfactory for the purpose for which it is intended, the physical setting and available technical aids permit extraction to be undertaken at reasonable cost, and the operations can take place in suitable geographical relationship to the market for the output, and connected thereto by appropriate means of transport. Naturally enough, therefore, in a highly developed country like Britain there will tend to be clay pits and gravel pits widely scattered over the country, serving local needs, but there will also be great concentrations of such pits in those areas where geological and economic circumstances are peculiarly favourable—as with the Oxford Clay brick-making industry of Peterborough, for example, and the gravel industry of west Middlesex; so also with the limestone quarrying of Buxton, and the chalk quarrying for cement on the Thames estuary.

Igneous rocks. Igneous rocks are less widespread in Britain than most of the sedimentary rock types, and the occurrences are almost entirely within the Highland Zone, so that any isolated outcrops in the Lowland Zone—the Leicestershire 'granites' for example—are additionally important. Igneous rocks may be divided into the very coarsely crystalline granites, which are mainly used as ornamental and monumental stones and for heavy con-

1. *Mem. Geol. Surv., Mineral Resources*, vol. xi, HMSO, 1920.
2. S. H. Beaver, 'Minerals and planning', *Geog. Journ.*, **104**, 1944, 166–93; *idem*, 'Surface mineral working in relation to planning', Town Planning Institute, 1949 (*Report of Summer School at St. Andrews*); 'Land Reclamation', *Chartered Surveyor*, **92**, 1960, 669–75 (with bibliography).

structional work, and the finer grained rocks, from fine-grained granites to basalt, which are mainly quarried for road-making materials. The question of accessibility is a major factor in the quarrying of these rocks, and large areas of some of the outcrops (e.g. the Cheviot granite) are quite untouched. Of the ornamental and constructional stones the most noteworthy are certain of the granites of Devon and Cornwall, the Shap granite, and the Aberdeen and Peterhead granites. Of the granitic rocks used for road stone those of Leicestershire (Mount Sorrel, etc.) are most utilised, with others coming from North Wales (the Lleyn), Devon and Cornwall. Of the rocks of basaltic type the chief is the Whin Sill of Northumberland and Durham, and there are other noteworthy occurrences in the Clee Hills of Shropshire, the Rowley Hills of the Black Country, and at Penmaenmawr in North Wales. Metamorphic rocks are quarried for road stone in the Malvern Hills.

Slate. Slaty rocks occupy large areas of the Highland Zone, particularly in the Southern Uplands, the Lake District, Wales, Cornwall, Northern Ireland, and southeastern Eire; but beds with cleavage sufficiently pronounced to render the rock fissile and capable of producing roofing slates are much more narrowly confined. By far the most important area is North Wales, where Cambrian slates are worked in enormous open quarries west of the Snowdon range (the Penrhyn–Dinorwic–Nantlle area) and Ordovician slates are mined underground at Blaenau Ffestiniog. Here there was a vast industry in the nineteenth century, to supply the colossal demand of the growing industrial towns for roofing materials; several narrow-gauge railways were built to cope with the traffic, terminating at Portmadoc, Port Dinorwic, and Port Penrhyn, where coastwise vessels loaded their cargoes. The vast quarries,[1] and even vaster spoil-heaps (for 95 per cent of what is quarried is waste) have considerably altered the natural landscape. There were other slate-quarrying areas in North Wales also, and slates were obtained in the Coniston and Keswick areas of the Lake District and at Delabole in Cornwall. The competition in the twentieth century of clay (and more recently concrete) roofing tiles has all but killed the slate industry, and a considerable legacy of derelict land is left behind.

Limestone and chalk. Chalk is of course a form of limestone, but is generally considered as a separate mineral. There are many sources of limestone in Britain,[2] and many uses for it—building stone, road metal, smelting flux, lime-burning, cement manufacture,[3] chemical industries, and agriculture. The Carboniferous Limestone formation is by far the most important source, and the very pure limestones which occur in parts of the Pennines (particularly the High Peak district near Buxton, the Clitheroe district, and Weardale), in North Wales, in South Wales, in the Mendips, and on the

1. The Dinorwic quarries, near Llanberis, cover 283 hectares (700 acres) of the hillside, and the top level is 548 metres (1800 ft) above the bottom level. They closed in 1970.
2. F. J. North, *Limestones*, London, 1930, especially Chapters 4–12.
3. See P. N. Grimshaw, 'The U.K. Portland cement industry', *Geography*, **53**, 1968, 81–4.

fringes of the Lake District are excavated in very large quarries. The Magnesian Limestone (Permian) yields building stone and *dolomite* at intervals along its outcrop from Sunderland to Nottingham. Dolomite is used for the basic linings of steel furnaces (cf. p. 376); the most important localities for this mineral are Coxhoe (Co. Durham), Conisbrough (Yorks.), and Steetley (near Worksop). At Hopton, Derbyshire, the dolomitised Carboniferous Limestone is quarried for the production of metallic magnesium. In the Jurassic series there are many fine building and facing stones, such as the Ancaster and Weldon stones of Lincolnshire, the Bath stone of the Cotswolds, and the famous Portland stone from the Isle of Portland. Some of the Jurassic limestones are also used for cement making, for example, the Lower Lias in Warwickshire (Rugby, Harbury) and the Lincolnshire Limestone at Ketton in Rutland.

The Chalk has long been used in a small way as a source of agricultural lime, but the twentieth century has witnessed an enormous expansion of chalk quarrying in certain areas to serve the cement industry, and about three-quarters of the country's cement industry is based upon chalk. The chief area comprises the banks of the lower Thames, in Essex and Kent, where huge chalk quarries are accompanied by pits in the London Clay which yield the clay necessary for mixing with the chalk, and by cement works on the river bank, using water transport for incoming coal and exported cement. On the edge of the Chilterns near Tring, Luton, and Cambridge, the Lower Chalk is sufficiently clayey to be used alone for cement making. Other areas include the lower Medway and the Humber above Hull, both with waterfront sites for the cement works.

Brick clays.[1] In 1939 there were more than 1250 brickworks in Great Britain, most of them served by adjacent clay-holes. Nearly one-third of them used clay and shale from the Coal Measures (sometimes obtained as a byproduct of coal mining)—partly because of the suitability of such clays, but also because the coalfields contain so many large urbanised areas where the demand for bricks is great. Nearly another one-third used the most recent clays—glacial, alluvial, brickearth, etc. The remainder mostly used Jurassic and Cretaceous clays. This simple statement, however, conceals a most important fact, namely, that over one-third of the country's brick output came, before the war, from about thirty mass-production works using Oxford Clay in the vicinity of Peterborough, Bedford, and Bletchley, in the 'Great Clay Vale'. The Oxford Clay yields a thick and reasonably homogeneous clay containing about 5 per cent of carbonaceous matter, which makes for very low fuel consumption. The clay is dug by large excavators, and the bricks are mechanically pressed into shape. The works at the new village of Stewartby, near Bedford, is the largest in the world.

1. See *Clay Brickmaking in Great Britain*, National Brick Advisory Council, Paper vi, HMSO, 1950. Also M. B. Gleave, 'Some contrasts in the English brick-making industry', *Tijds. v. Econ. en Soc. Geog.*, 1965, 54–61.

Since the war the concentration has become even more striking; over 600 brickworks have been closed and 54 per cent of the national output of bricks comes from large works in the Oxford Clay.

Roofing tiles are also mostly made from clay. Many small brickworks also make tiles, but a large proportion of the country's output is made from the Etruria Marl formation (Upper Coal Measures) in the North Staffordshire coalfield and in the Black Country. The same formation yields the famous engineering bricks known as 'Staffordshire blues'. Both these Staffordshire products are declining in the face of competition from alternative materials. Concrete tiles are replacing clay tiles, and mass concrete is used instead of blue bricks.

Sandstones and sands. Sandstones, of varying hardness, are used for building and constructional purposes, for road metal, for paving, for grindstones, and sometimes, as already noted, for refractories. As local building material sandstone is often evident in villages and towns, but little is quarried for this purpose now, and to an increasing extent concrete slabs and tarmacadam are replacing the paving flags which used mostly to come from the mid-Pennines of Yorkshire and Lancashire. The Millstone Grit and Coal Measures have been by far the more important sources of sandstone in the past. Red Triassic sandstones are very much in evidence in churches and large buildings all over the Midlands; the Old Red Sandstone has been much used in Scotland.

Sands, from relatively less-consolidated deposits, have many uses, of which the most important are in building (mortar, concrete, etc.), metallurgical work, and glass-making. Foundry sand for metal-casting is mostly obtained from the Trias of the west and east Midlands. Glass-sand, of exceptional purity, comes especially from the Lower Greensand of Leighton Buzzard and King's Lynn, and from a superficial deposit known as the Shirdley Hill Sands in southwest Lancashire. Sand for concrete comes almost entirely from gravel-pits.

Gravel.[1] The three major sources of gravel are (*a*) river-gravels, alluvial, and terrace; (*b*) glacial deposits—sheets of sand and gravel deposited as glacial outwash beyond the limits of the ice-sheets, and occasional morainic accumulations and eskers; (*c*) 'solid' deposits, of which the chief is the Bunter Pebble Beds (Triassic) of the West Midlands (mainly north and south Staffordshire). The river gravels are commonly worked in 'wet' pits, i.e. the gravel is mechanically dug or pumped from beneath the permanent water-level, so that a lake is left behind when the gravel has been extracted. The glacial gravels, more frequently occurring at higher levels, are usually worked in dry pits just like most other minerals. The deposits are very wide-

1. S. W. Wooldridge and S. H. Beaver, 'The working of sand and gravel in Britain: a problem in land use', *Geog. Journ.*, **115**, 1950, 42–57. Reports of the Advisory Committee on Sand and Gravel, HMSO, 1948–53. S. H. Beaver, *The Geology of Sand and Gravel*, Sand and Gravel Association, 1968.

spread and scattered, which is fortunate since the demand for sand and gravel for building, for road-making, etc., is also spread throughout the country. Gravel mostly moves by road to its destination, and relatively little goes beyond an economic margin of about 50 kilometres (thirty miles). There is some tendency to concentrate on the broader and more profitably worked gravel spreads, particularly of river gravels, which are usually cleaner and more homogeneous than the glacial gravels, and about one-third of the country's output comes from the Thames terraces of the London area, where land use problems of considerable magnitude are created owing

PLATE 15. Wet gravel pit in the Soar valley, Leicestershire
The gravel is dug from beneath the water level by a dragline excavator. The islands in the lake are of clay or worthless gravel.

to the high agricultural value of the terrace lands and the many competing uses for land within the Metropolitan region. But at least the 'Great Wen' provides abundant waste materials for filling up the lakes which gravel extraction creates—though the demand is now for the excavations to be left as lagoons for angling, sailing and water sports.

As already noted, the gravel industry has for some time been second only to coal mining in respect of output tonnage. There are about a thousand gravel pits in the country, and their annual land consumption is of the order of 1600 hectares (4000 acres), which is about two-thirds of the total land area consumed annually by quarries of all kinds.

Upwards of 10 million metric tons of sand and gravel are landed annually at various estuarine ports, the result of submarine dredging. The outer Thames estuary (off the Essex coast), the Mersey, the Severn (east of the Holms islands) and the approaches to Southampton are the major sources of this material—which of course creates no land use problems at all.

16
Iron and steel

The origin of the British iron industry is lost in obscurity. The five hundred years before the Christian era, however, are known as the Iron Age, and in all probability the Celtic inhabitants of Britain were fairly expert in the working of the metal: the finding of Celtic pottery in association with iron slags in the Furness[1] district and near Northampton[2] is evidence of at least two localities in which the actual smelting was performed. That the Romans worked the iron ores of our islands is also quite certain. Sites of furnaces and heaps of slag lying near accumulations of Roman coins and pottery have been identified in Furness, in the Forest of Dean, in the Weald, in the Mendips, in Northumberland and Durham, in Northamptonshire, and in South Wales.[3] The earlier furnaces were usually situated in exposed places, where the wind would create a natural blast; later, sites were chosen along streams where a small waterwheel could be used to work the primitive bellows. After the Roman occupation there are few records and, apart from a few scattered notices in the Domesday Survey,[4] where 'ferraria' (ironworks) are occasionally mentioned, we have no positive information until the twelfth century.

The two most important medieval centres of the iron industry were the Forest of Dean and the Weald of Sussex and Kent.

The Forest of Dean. This was for long the chief area in the country for iron smelting.[5] As early as 1282 there were sixty forges in the forest using the local ore, and the industry continued to flourish for many centuries. In the seventeenth century the area was importing richer ore from Lancashire to supplement the local supplies and was sending iron to the Birmingham area for working up into implements and weapons.

The Weald of Sussex and Kent. In the sixteenth and seventeenth centuries this

1. G. M. Tweddell, *Furness Past and Present*, 1876.
2. *Victoria County History*, Northamptonshire, i, 151.
3. Kendall, *Iron Ores of Great Britain and Ireland*, Crosby, Lockwood, 1892, Chapter 2. More detailed references will be found in the volumes of the *Victoria County History*, e.g. *Cumberland*, ii, 385–406; *Durham*, ii, 278–93; *Yorkshire* ii, 341–51; *Lancashire*, ii, 360–4; *Derbyshire*, ii, 356–62; *Gloucestershire*, ii, 216–33; *Worcestershire*, ii, 267–71.
4. For example, Gloucestershire, in the Forest of Dean, and at Pucklechurch; Northamptonshire, at Gretton and Corby; Yorkshire (East Riding), at Hessle.
5. See H. G. Nicholls, *Iron Making in the Olden Times*, 1866.

area was even greater than the Forest of Dean in the importance of its iron industry. The first cast iron guns were made at Buxted in 1543, and a large proportion of the British ordnance was subsequently made in the Weald. In 1574 there were no less than thirty-two smelting furnaces and thirty-eight forges in Sussex, besides numerous others in Kent.[1]

In addition we have definite records of iron making in Northumberland and Durham from the thirteenth century onwards, in Northamptonshire and Lincolnshire in the twelfth and thirteenth centuries, in the West Riding of Yorkshire from the twelfth century, and in Rosedale (North Riding) in the fourteenth century, in Cumberland and in Derbyshire from the twelfth century, in the Furness district from the thirteenth century, and in South Wales from the fourteenth century, together with evidence of the existence and working of iron ore in certain other localities. In fact, during the medieval period, the iron industry in Britain was fairly widespread, owing to the abundance of iron ore near the surface in many parts of the country, and the ample timber supplies which could nearly always be found in the vicinity of the ore deposits. So great was the amount of charcoal necessary, however, that the forests were being rapidly depleted,[2] and in the reign of Queen Elizabeth stringent measures were passed to prevent the reckless destruction of our timber supply at a time when every log was valuable for building ships of war. Only those areas which were especially favoured by extensive forests, like the Weald and the Forest of Dean, were able to maintain their industry on a large scale; for, however rich a deposit might be, overland movement of the ore was impracticable except for short distances when pack horses were the only means of transport available. The Cumberland and Lancashire region, lacking extensive timber resources, but having a seaboard situation, continued to extract ore for export by sea to the Forest of Dean and South Wales and later to Ayrshire and the Clyde.

This distribution of the industry began to suffer a radical change in the eighteenth century owing to the substitution of coal for charcoal in the smelting process. Dud Dudley, a Staffordshire ironmaster, had patented a process of smelting iron with 'pit-cole' and 'sea-cole' as early as 1621, but neither his nor other suggested methods were successful, and owing to the failing timber supply the British iron industry suffered a steady decline for over a century.[3] By 1740, in fact, we were importing mainly from Sweden and Russia nearly twice as much iron as was made at home.

The real beginning of the modern era of iron making came with the

1. See W. Topley, *Geology of the Weald*, HMSO, 1873; also E. Straker, *Wealden Iron*, G. Bell, 1931; and M. Delany, *The Historical Geography of the Wealden Iron Industry*, Benn, 1921.

2. It is probable that 0.4 hectare (an acre) of woodland yielded only sufficient charcoal to make three metric tons of iron, and as a single furnace in the sixteenth century could make 20 metric tons a week it is obvious that the destruction of the forests must have been very rapid.

3. T. S. Ashton, *Iron and Steel in the Industrial Revolution*, 2nd edn, 1951, p. 10. This book is indispensable for a study of the iron industry in the eighteenth century.

introduction, by Abraham Darby of Coalbrookdale in Shropshire, of the use of coke in the blast furnace. Darby had probably smelted iron with coke as early as 1709, but such a revolutionary innovation as this naturally required many years of experimenting for its perfection; since so little was

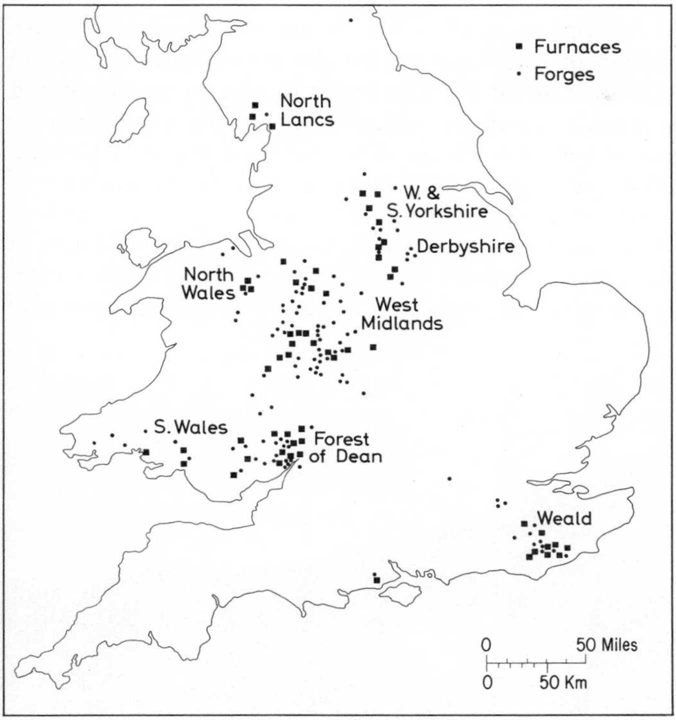

FIG. 159. The iron industry of England and Wales in 1717
(After B. L. C. Johnson, compiled from John Fuller's list.)

Compare Fig. 160 and note that Coal Measure ironstones had already localised part of the industry in and around the coalfield areas where adequate charcoal was available for the furnaces, together with suitable coals for the forges. The subsequent importance of the coalfields of Yorkshire, Derbyshire, Shropshire, North and South Staffordshire, South and North Wales was already foreshadowed half a century before the Industrial Revolution.

known of the properties of the coal and the iron ore or the chemical reactions that went on inside the furnace. Moreover, not all coals were found to be suitable for coking,[1] and the quality of the pig iron could not always be relied upon. It was not until about 1760 then that the erection of new and larger furnaces adapted for using coal and coke inaugurated a period of development and expansion in the iron industry. This development coincided with, and was to a large extent aided by, the perfection of the steam engine, which could be used for pumping water out of flooded coal mines

1. The coal used by Darby was the 'clod', which proved peculiarly suited to the process of carbonisation in large lumps in open heaps—cf. p. 333.

and for creating the more powerful blast which the use of coke in the furnace demanded. Smeaton built the first steam engine for producing blast in 1760, but it was left to James Watt to commence the construction of efficient engines on a commercial scale about 1775, and a few years later to adapt his engines to rotative motion. The consequences were profound. The steam engine needed a large amount of iron in its construction, and an increased iron production in turn necessitated the provision of more and larger engines, not only for blowing the furnaces, but also for pumping and working the winding machinery of the coal mines, which were stimulated by the demand for more coal for smelting. The increased capacity for iron production was also followed by a rapid increase in the number and variety of the uses to which the metal could be put. The first cast iron bridge was built at Ironbridge in 1779, and during the next few decades all kinds of machinery, especially textile machinery, were introduced to replace contrivances formerly made of wood or the less common metals, copper and brass.

PLATE 16. The iron bridge over the Severn at Ironbridge, erected 1779

In 1784 Henry Cort perfected the puddling furnace for making malleable or wrought iron, using coke as fuel. He also introduced the use of rollers in place of hammers in drawing out the iron into bars. These processes provided a further stimulus for the iron industry by enabling much larger outputs to be obtained in very much less time than formerly, and they helped to strengthen a movement which had been going on for twenty years, namely the increasing concentration of the ironworks on the coalfields. Progress was not rapid—in 1788 nearly half the furnaces in Britain were still using charcoal—but slowly and surely the pull of those areas which

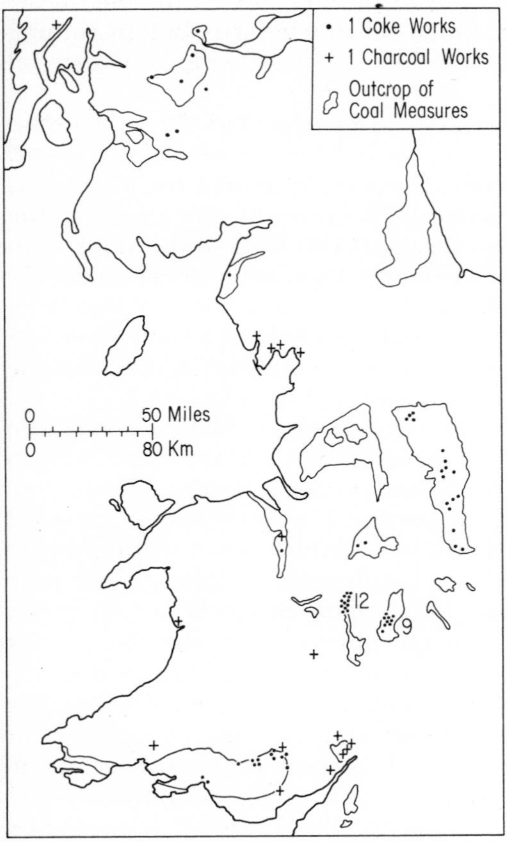

FIG. 160. Blast furnaces in 1796
Exposed coalfields outlined. The last of the Wealden furnaces, at Ashburnham, is not shown on this map. Note the absence of furnaces in south Lancashire and north-eastern England.

were favoured with abundant iron ore in the same measures as the coal seams was beginning to assert itself. By 1806 only eleven charcoal furnaces remained out of the 300 or so that existed 150 years earlier, and the clustering of the ironworks round the coalfields of South Wales, South Staffs., Salop, and Derby was very marked. The coalfields of Northumberland and Durham and South Lancashire, however, being almost devoid of Coal

Measure ironstones (see Fig. 164) and lacking coals which could be coked by the methods then available, or were suitable for using raw in the furnaces, failed to develop extensive iron industries at this time.

The iron industry also received a considerable fillip during this period from the waging of wars, which necessitated large supplies of iron weapons and ammunition. The American War of Independence occupied the years 1776–80, and between 1793 and 1815 wars were almost continuous on the continent. These wars not only stimulated our iron industry but, by ruining the greater part of Europe, placed Britain in a very strong commercial position.[1]

The first half of the nineteenth century was a period of gradual expansion and of improved technique in the iron industry.[2] Two events are important. In 1828, Neilson, a Glasgow gasworks foreman, suggested the use of hot, instead of cold, air in blowing the furnace. This process, which reduced the fuel consumption considerably, gave a remarkable fillip to the industry in Scotland, and was later taken up in England.[3] Then in the 'forties came the 'railway mania', which created an enormous demand for rails and locomotives. The first successful locomotive had been built in 1812 by Blenkinsop, and the Stockton and Darlington Railway was opened in 1825; but the years 1845–47 marked the great boom in railway development.

Throughout the period since the introduction of coke fuel the ores of iron used in Britain had been of the clayband and blackband[4] types occurring in the Carboniferous rocks, together with smaller amounts of haematite from Cumberland and Furness. In 1851 the pig iron production of Britain stood at the level of about 2.5 million metric tons (which was half the world's supply) of which the greater part (*c.* 2.1 million metric tons) came from three areas, Scotland, South Wales, and south Staffordshire. It is not surprising, therefore, to find that the Coal Measure ores, especially in the Midlands, where working had been going on continuously for over a century, were beginning to show signs of a decreasing yield due not so much to actual exhaustion as to the increased cost and difficulty of working the seams of nodules at a considerable depth. At this juncture, however, an entirely new source of ore supply was discovered[5] in the belt of Jurassic scarplands which stretches across England from the Cleveland Hills to the Dorset coast. These ores, first worked in North Yorkshire about 1850, and in Northamptonshire a year or two later, have had far-reaching effects upon

1. L. C. Knowles, *Industrial and Commercial Revolutions of the Nineteenth Century*, 1927, p. 102.
2. 1816, Rogers's improved puddling furnace; 1842, Nasmyth's steam hammer; 1845, first attempt to utilise waste blast-furnace gases for heating blast and raising steam.
3. See, with reference to this and to the matter of the preceding paragraphs, H. Scrivenor, *History of the Iron Trade*, 2nd edn, 1854.
4. Blackband was not discovered till 1801, and not extensively employed until after the introduction of the hot-blast. See D. Mushet, *Papers on Iron and Steel*, 1840.
5. Or rather rediscovered, for, as we have seen, Roman and medieval workings are known to have existed in Northamptonshire, Lincolnshire, and North Yorkshire.

the development of the British iron and steel industry, and their importance is difficult to overestimate. The commencement of iron smelting in Cleveland and Northamptonshire marked the beginning of a decline in that great attraction which had been exercised by the coalfields ever since the introduction of coal as a fuel in the process of smelting. When every ton of pig iron needed eight tons of coal to smelt it the setting up of furnaces away from the coalfields was obviously not an economic proposition. But with coal consumption reduced to two or three tons and the use of the Jurassic ores entailing an ore consumption of about the same amount, it became possible for the costs of coal and ore transport to be reduced almost to level terms, and at once the pull of the coalfields began to decrease in strength. The seaboard situation of Cleveland, together with the nearness of the Durham coalfield, now available as a source of coke through the development of the beehive coke oven, sent this area forging far ahead of the inland Northamptonshire, where coking coal was at least sixty miles away.

The second half of the nineteenth century witnessed remarkable progress in the heavy metallurgical industry of Britain, a progress which was ultimately bound up with the substitution of steel for wrought iron. Huntsman's crucible furnace, invented in 1742, had for over a century been the only efficient means of producing steel, and this was a very costly process. In 1855 only about 50 000 tons of steel were produced in Britain at a cost of £75 per ton. In 1856 Bessemer introduced his 'converter', which, making use of the heat generated by blowing a blast of air through a ladle of molten pig iron, without the employment of the large amount of fuel consumed in the crucible method, could produce much larger quantities of good steel in a much shorter time (about twenty minutes only) at much less expense. Indeed, by 1864 the price of a ton of open-hearth steel rails had been reduced to £17 10*s*.[1] Almost on the heels of Bessemer came William Siemens, who in 1861 patented the open-hearth type of regenerative gas-fired furnace for steel making. As with most revolutionary inventions, however, it took many years for the new steel processes to become firmly set, and nearly thirty years elapsed after Bessemer's invention before steel finally succeeded in supplanting wrought iron. Until the early 'eighties, in fact, the enormous demand for iron rails and iron ships was accompanied by a corresponding rapid increase in the size of the puddling industry and the number of of puddling furnaces rose from 3462 in 1860 to 7575 in 1875.[2] Moreover, except in certain cases, the steel industry was hampered by the necessity, in both the converter and open-hearth process (which employed acid, or silica, furnace linings), for fairly pure, non-phosphoric ores, such as occur in Britain only in Cumberland and North Lancashire. The bulk of British ores, including the Jurassic ironstones, were useless for steel making, and thus we find a new feature introduced into the British iron and steel industry,

1. Lowthian Bell, *The Iron Trade of the United Kingdom*, 1886, p. 20.
2. *Ibid.*

namely, the import of large quantities or rich, non-phosphoric ores from northern Spain into those steel-making areas such as Cleveland and South Wales, which were either on the coast or had easy access thereto. In 1869 scarcely 1 per cent of the ore used in Britain was imported. In 1882 this figure had risen to 18 per cent. The invention in 1879 by Messrs Thomas and Gilchrist of the 'basic process' (i.e. lining the steel furnace with a basic material such as dolomite, in order to get rid of the phosphoric impurities) might have been expected to change this state of affairs, since it permitted the use, for steel working, of the abundant phosphoric ores in the Jurassic rocks of Cleveland and the southeast Midlands. But the basic process, needing special furnace linings and entailing the payment of high royalty charges, was then more costly than the acid process; and so cheap were the rich foreign ores that it was actually less expensive, at Middlesbrough, to convert rich Bilbao ore into steel rails by the acid process than to manufacture iron rails without conversion into steel from the lean phosphoric ore of the Cleveland Hills only a few miles away.[1]

Whether acid or basic, however, the production of steel rapidly increased in the last quarter of the nineteenth century, and steel began to be used for almost every purpose to which puddled iron had previously been applied—of which the most important were for rails, ships, and in constructional engineering.[2] But while British production of iron and steel continued to expand, our position relative to the rest of the world exhibited a slow decline. Between 1850 and 1870 Britain was producing every year about one-half of the world's output of pig iron. The expansion of the industry in the United States, however, and the great development of basic steel in France and Germany, considerably reduced Britain's supremacy, and by the early 'nineties the United States and continental Europe had each exceeded the British output, and the home country produced less than one-third of the world's pig iron. By 1913 we were producing only one-eighth of the world's total (10 million out of 78 million metric tons), and the United States and Germany had both passed our production by a considerable margin.[3] The tale of the steel industry is similar. Before the introduction of the basic process Britain was easily first, but thereafter Germany (using the basic process

1. Lowthian Bell, *op. cit.*, p. 17.

2. *Note on iron and steel.* Pig iron—or cast iron—from the blast furnace is not pure. It contains carbon, and, if made from certain classes of ore, may contain sulphur and phosphorus; all these three elements are injurious and render the iron brittle. The carbon may be eliminated by stirring the molten iron in a puddling furnace; as the carbon disappears the liquid becomes pasty and is removed in lumps to be hammered or rolled. This is wrought iron, very tenacious but not hard enough for many purposes. The acid process of steel making so effectively removes the carbon that a small proportion has to be replaced by the addition of ferromanganese or Spiegeleisen, which contains some carbon. Steel may contain 0.3 to 2.2 per cent of carbon; it becomes exceedingly hard when cooled suddenly, and it is more flexible and elastic than wrought iron, although not so durable when exposed to the weather.

3. Germany, 17.0 million metric tons (16.76 million long tons); United States 31.40 million metric tons (30.97 million long tons).

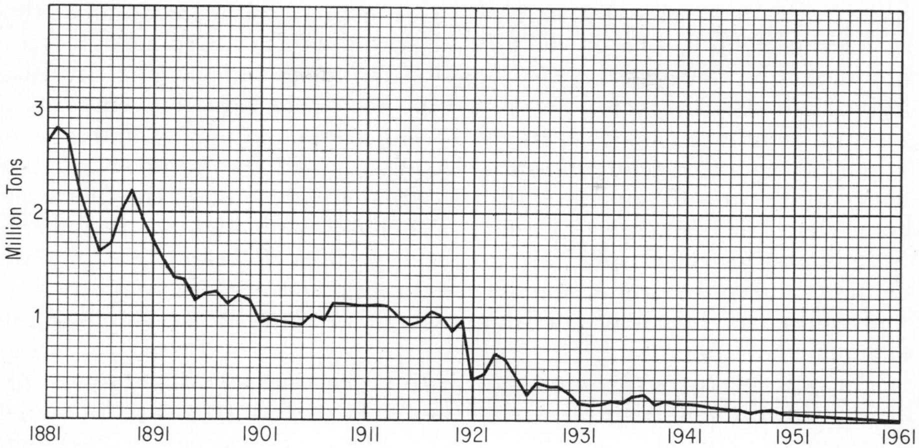

FIG. 161. Production of wrought-iron
In 1961 the total was a mere 14 000 tons.

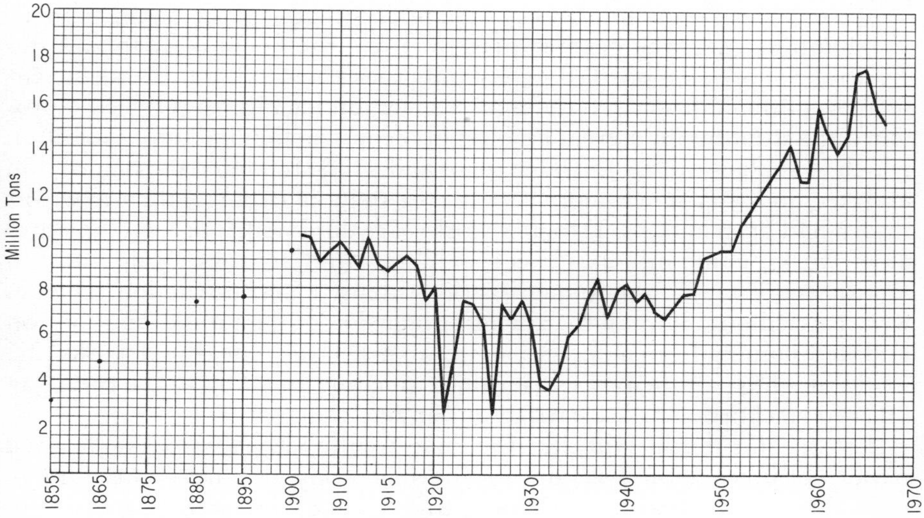

FIG. 162. Production of pig iron, 1855–1967

with Lorraine ores) and the United States (using the acid process with Lake Superior ores) began to develop rapidly, and by 1913 Britain was producing little more than one-tenth of the total world output[1] (7·7 million metric tons out of 75 million metric tons).

The period from the commencement of the supremacy of steel until the

1. See tables on pp. 113–14 of *Survey of Metal Industries*, HMSO, 1928.

First World War is characterised first by the great absolute expansion of the steel industry both at home and abroad, with the relative decline of Britain amongst the other great steel-producing nations;[1] and secondly by vast improvements in the technique of smelting and steel production, entailing a more efficient use of all apparatus and raw materials employed, and especially a considerable reduction in fuel costs. A third feature of note is the concentration on the open-hearth process at the expense of the Bessemer converter. The open-hearth furnace, although taking a longer time (some 6–12 hours) to convert pig iron into steel, permits of greater control of its contents and so the production of more carefully graded and uniform steel and, moreover, it allows the employment of scrap, a very important economic consideration.[2]

The war of 1914–18 found the British steel industry ill-adapted for prompt adjustment to the tasks which had to be performed as a result of the phenomenal demand for steel of all grades. The wartime necessity of relying more on home iron ores and less on imports led to a considerable reorganisation of certain sections of the industry, with a material increase in the output of basic steel.

The recurrent economic crises of the period 1920–33, the boom of 1920, the slump of 1921, the general strike of 1926, the boom of 1929 and the disastrous depression of 1931–33 not only took their toll of the less efficient sections of the industry (cf. the figures given under Fig. 167) but also provided the stimulus for a great amount of reconstruction and reorganisation which took place during the later 1930s and which rendered the British iron and steel industry much more capable, in 1939, of coping with a new war than it had been in 1914. Two new works of major importance, on the site of older works, came into existence—at Corby and at Ebbw Vale—and in almost every major producing district extensive reconstruction schemes were carried out, with an increasing proportion of the total output of iron and steel coming from a decreasing number of large, integrated works (i.e. works in which all the processes from coking and smelting to the rolling of finished steel products are carried out on one site).

The Second World War, like the First, resulted in a somewhat changed pattern of production, with once again increasing emphasis on the use of home-produced Jurassic ironstones, and in addition with a greatly increased proportion of alloy steel (produced especially in Sheffield).[3] The

1. See, on this and other matters, T. H. Burnham and G. O. Hoskins, *Iron and Steel in Britain, 1870–1930*, 1943.

2. On an average some 40 per cent of the raw material of the British open-hearth steel industry consists of scrap, but in individual furnaces the percentage may rise to over 80. Other important considerations are the low melting losses compared with the Bessemer converter (5 per cent, cf. 15–20 per cent), and the fact that gas for firing is often readily available from the coke ovens and blast furnaces of 'integrated' works.

3. The story of British iron and steel during the war is told statistically in the British Iron and Steel Federation's volume covering the years 1939–44. See also *Iron and Coal Trades Review*, 2 Nov., 1945, pp. 667–70, and 29 March 1946, p. 578.

postwar period, however, has not repeated the disastrous history of the 'twenties. The industry has gone from strength to strength; four major new fully integrated plants have been established, all of them involving the construction of hot-strip mills for the production of sheet steel for either tinplate or motor-car bodies. The first, at Shotton on Deeside, added blast furnaces to an existing steelworks; at Margam in South Wales, a huge new plant replaced pre-existing iron- and steelworks, whilst at Ravenscraig, near Motherwell, and at Newport, Monmouthshire, virgin sites have been developed.

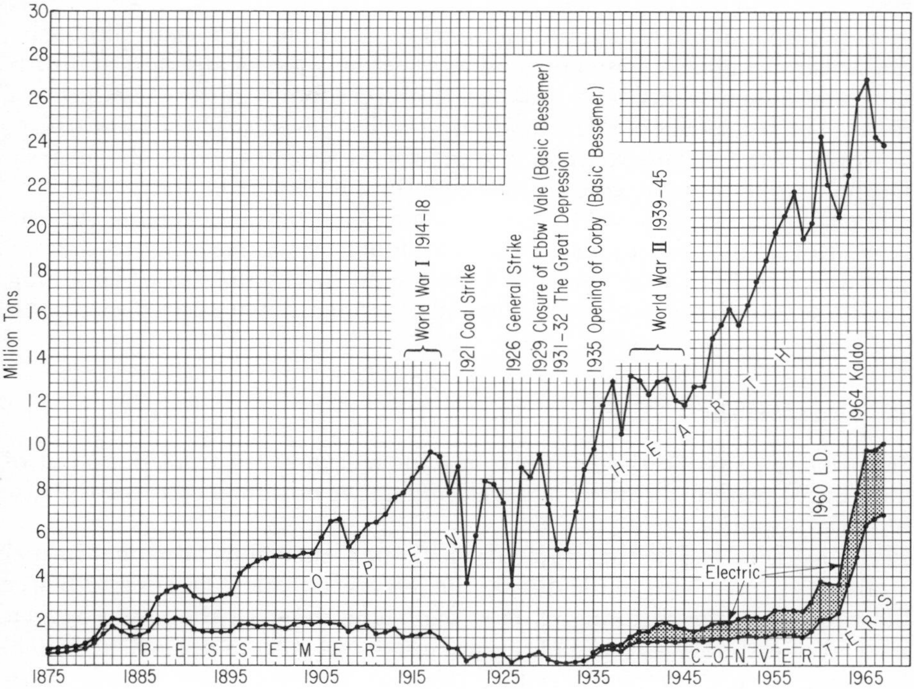

FIG. 163. Output of steel by processes, 1875–1967

Bessemer steel almost ceased in the early 1930s; from 1935 to 1959 the 'converters' section of the graph comprises the outputs of Corby, Ebbw Vale (began 1939) and Workington (acid process); from 1960 the output is greatly swelled by that of the L.D. and later Kaldo converters. Output of electric steel furnaces before 1935 too small to be shown on graph at this scale.

Another important technical development has been the use of oxygen in place of ordinary air, in open-hearth furnaces and in new-type converters (the Kaldo and LD (Linz-Donawitz) processes). In 1961 some 11 thousand million cubic feet of oxygen were used in the iron and steel industry, of which 3.6 thousand million in open-hearths and 2.6 thousand million in converters. By 1969, however, the volume had swelled to 38 thousand million cubic feet of which 17 thousand million in converters, 7 thousand million in open-hearths, and 2 thousand million in blast furnaces. This development, however, will have no effect on the location of the industry, for oxygen-producing plants are being set up alongside the steelworks.

The present conditions of the industry

There are three major factors affecting the localisation of an iron and steel industry—the supply of ore, the supply of fuel, and the market for the produce.[1] One or more of these must be present or easily accessible in order to give rise to such an industry. The earliest British iron industries in the Forest of Dean and the Weald were situated where ores of iron were found in close proximity to an assured charcoal supply from the forests. Similarly, the first iron industry based on coal as a fuel became localised in Staffordshire and Salop, where both coal and iron were found in the same series of rocks. The industries of Cleveland and the Furness district of Lancashire, however, were localised upon ore-producing regions, with the nearby Durham coke and the coastal situation for the export of the produce as other favourable factors. Modern transport facilities may render possible the rise of an industry in an area devoid of both coal and iron ore—as, for example, the Ford iron works at Dagenham, on Thames-side, obtaining foreign ore and Durham coal by sea, and having its own assured market in the adjacent motor works.

Raw materials

In order to examine the British iron and steel industry from the point of view of geographical control of development, we must first consider the raw material supplies.

Fuel. Coal is of course the major item, though enormous advances in fuel technology have been made during the last few decades: bigger and better blast furnaces, the sintering of ores (see below, p. 394), the use of oxygen instead of ordinary air, and of oil fuel instead of coke in open-hearth steel furnaces, have all helped to reduce the coal consumption from 3145 kilogrammes per metric ton (62.9 cwt per long ton) of steel in 1924 to 1860 kilogrammes per metric ton (37.2 cwt per long ton) in 1949 and a mere 680 kilogrammes per metric ton (13.6 cwt per long ton) in 1967. The total coal consumption by the iron and steel industry is of the order of 16.1 to 19.2 million metric tons (16 to 19 million long tons) annually, most of which is coked before use. The distribution of coking coals has already been briefly described (p. 334), and it is apparent that the actual location of coking coal

1. While a supply of limestone is normally essential to the industry (about 5 cwt of limestone flux are used for each ton of pig iron), this raw material is never a localising factor, since limestones are so readily available in most districts where either iron ore or coal are found; for example, Coal Measure ironstones were seldom far from thick Carboniferous or Magnesian Limestone deposits, and the Jurassic ironstones occur in a series, the principal members of which are frequently limestones of greater or less purity.

resources has but slight present influence on the location of iron and steel works. There is certainly no clustering of blast furnaces in south Durham, in south Yorkshire, or in eastern South Wales, and of about thirty smelting works in the country, only about half a dozen lie in close proximity to their sources of coking coal. The transport of coking coal or coke is thus a major item in the cost of production, particularly for the works situated on the Jurassic orefields.

In recent years, at first due to coal shortage, there has been a tendency to employ *oil fuel* instead of producer-gas in the firing of open-hearth steel furnaces. South Wales, with the large Llandarcy refinery in the middle of the steel-making area, has gone furthest in this direction, but Middlesbrough and Scotland have also converted many furnaces to oil firing. In 1964, 1.6 million metric tons of fuel oil were used for this purpose, one-third of it in South Wales; but in view of the increasing importance of oxygen-blown converters this was probably the peak year.

Iron ore. The ores of iron that occur in Britain may be grouped into four broad divisions (see table on p. 390).

1. *Haematite* (Fe_2O_3), including 'kidney ore'. This occurs in Cumberland and northwest Lancashire[1] in various irregular deposits in the Carboniferous Limestone which wraps round the western and southern sides of the Lake District dome. The iron is generally assumed to have been derived by solution from the red Triassic beds which formerly covered the area, and subsequent concentration in cavities in the jointed limestone—the concentration being frequently guided by faults which brought together beds of contrasted texture.

Two separate areas were important for the production of this type of ore, and the mode of occurrence in each of these is rather different. In west Cumberland, in the neighbourhood of Cleator, Egremont, and Beckermet occur numerous irregular masses of ore, sometimes disposed more or less vertically up against faults, sometimes more or less interbedded with the limestone and the sandstone and the shales which accompany it, and in other cases showing no form or structure at all. Farther south, extending on either side of the Duddon estuary from southwest Cumberland into the Furness district are a number of dishlike deposits, practically solid masses of ore occupying great hollows in the limestone. The largest of these, the famous Hodbarrow deposit, near Millom, contained originally over 8 million cubic yards of almost solid ore. In both areas the deposits are within a few hundred feet of the surface, but they are covered by thick deposits of glacial drift, which conceals the 'solid' geology and increases the difficulty of locating and working the ores.

The two areas were formerly of equal importance as ore raisers, but the

1. *Mem. Geol. Survey, Mineral Resources.* vol. viii, *Haematites of West Cumberland, Lancashire, and the Lake District*, 2nd edn, 1924. See also T. H. Bainbridge, 'Iron ore mining in Cumbria', *Geography*, **19**, 1934, 274–87. Also *Geology of the Iron-Ore field of South Cumberland and Furness*, Geol. Surv. Wartime Pamphlet no. 16, 1941.

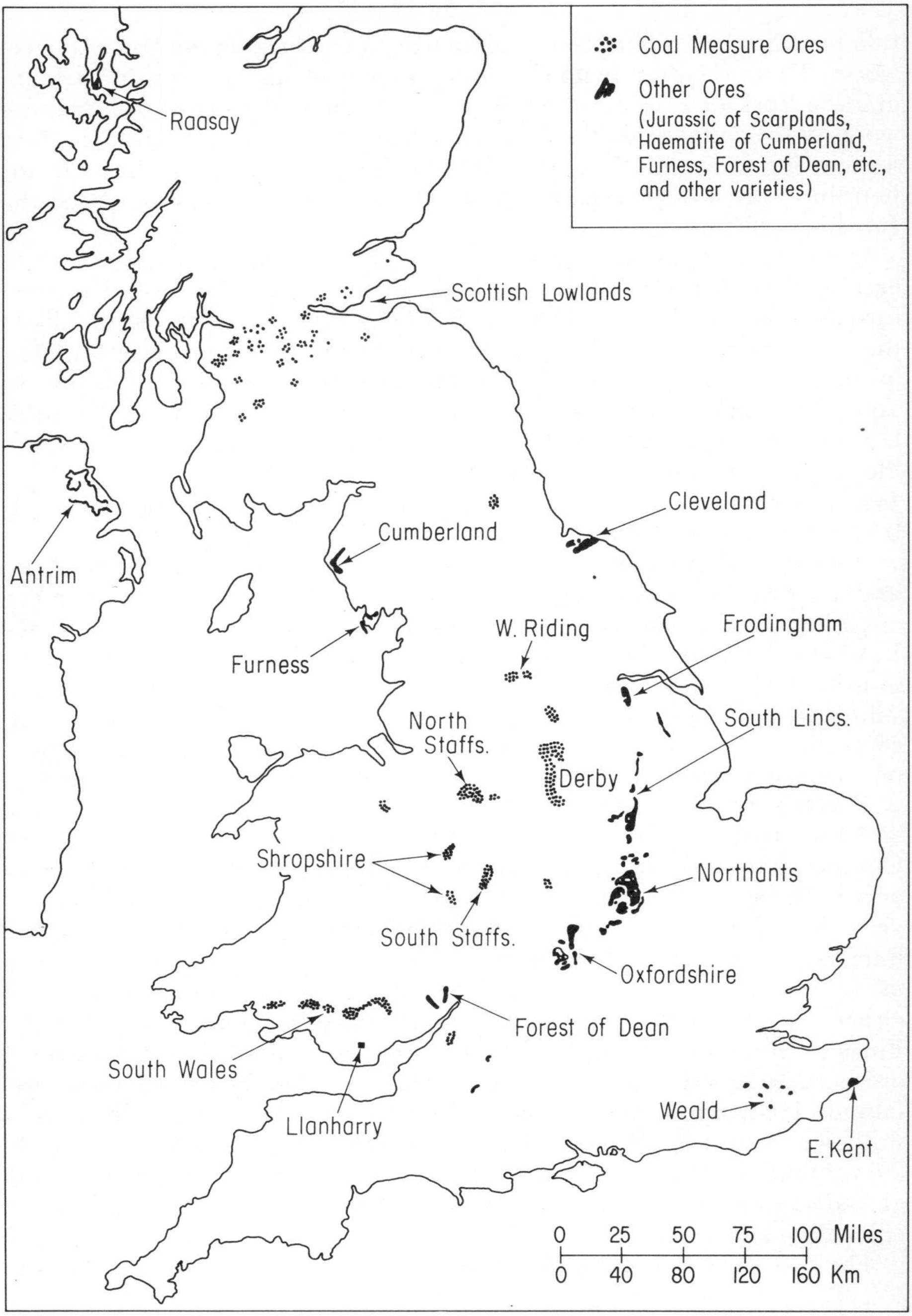

FIG. 164. The iron ores of Britain

The only ones of present importance are the Jurassic ores of Cleveland, Frodingham, South Lincs and Northants, with the Haematites of Cumberland and Llanharry.

greater ease of working the Furness deposits has led to their extinction more rapidly than is the case with the irregular veins and masses of western Cumberland, and whereas in the early 'eighties (the period of greatest production) each area was producing about 1.5 million tons per annum, the Furness area has now ceased to produce, whilst Cumberland has an output of only 0.15 million metric tons (see table on p. 390). Only two mines remain, near Egremont. This haematite is the richest ore produced in Britain, having an iron content of nearly 50 per cent. It is also important as being non-phosphoric.

The modern development of these ores dates from about 1825, and a great fillip was given to their extraction and export by the completion of the Furness Railway in 1846, and of the Whitehaven, Cleator and Egremont line in 1857;[1] whilst the completion of the Stainmore Pass line across the Pennines in 1861 opened up a new route to the Durham coalfield and Middlesbrough.

2. *The bedded ores occurring in the Coal Measures.*[2] These ores are of great historical interest since they were the foundation upon which British supremacy in the iron industry was built up during the hundred years 1750 to 1850. At the end of this period they still accounted for nine-tenths of the entire British output of ore, and production continued to increase in certain areas until the 'seventies. Since then the output has rapidly declined both relatively and absolutely, and none at all has been raised since the Second World War. There were two distinct varieties of ore found in the Coal Measures, 'clayband' and 'blackband'. Clayband ironstone consists of carbonate of iron mechanically mingled with earthy matter. It usually takes the form of thin seams, either continuous or nodular, varying from a few centimetres to several metres in thickness, interbedded with shales or less frequently with sandstones. It is noteworthy that the clayband ores are not evenly distributed throughout the Coal Measures, either stratigraphically or in area. The areas over which they were formerly of greatest importance are South Staffordshire, Shropshire, South Wales, Derbyshire, the West Riding of Yorkshire, and the Scottish Lowlands.[3] The blackband ores are carbonaceous ironstones, i.e. they contain coaly matter sufficient for calcining the ore without the addition of coal. They occur in even closer association with coal than the claybands. They are usually found on the top of coal seams and in Scotland some blackbands are actually found to pass laterally into coal. On the other hand, they usually occur in thinner seams than the claybands. Their value as ores of iron was not realised until 1801,

1. In the late 1850s close on 304 000 metric tons (300 000 long tons) of ore were being exported annually—mostly to South Wales.

2. *Mem. Geol. Survey, Mineral Resources*, vol. xiii, *Pre-Carboniferous and Carboniferous bedded ores of England and Wales*, 1920; also vol. xi, *Iron Ores of Scotland*, 1920.

3. It should be noted that iron ores, as well as coal, occur in the Carboniferous Limestone and Millstone Grit formations of Scotland, in addition to their development in the true Coal Measures.

and it was some time before they were extensively used in the iron industry. The only two coalfield areas in which they were discovered to be developed in quantity were North Staffordshire and Scotland. In Scotland they were especially valuable since they showed such an adaptability to the use of the hot blast, a far greater reduction in fuel consumption being obtained when using blackband ores and the Scottish 'splint' coal than with any other combination of ore and fuel. In contrast with the haematite, the clayband and blackband ores are lean, containing only about 30 per cent of metallic iron.

The decline in the output of Coal Measure ironstone was due to two main causes. In the first place there is the actual exhaustion of many of the best seams, especially in those areas like Shropshire and south Staffordshire, which were earliest worked. But the ores are by no means wholly exhausted. According to an estimate made in 1922 there were 'actual' reserves of over 1000 million metric tons, and a further 'probable' reserve of 1200 million metric tons. The second reason is thus the increasing difficulty and cost of working such thin seams of lean ore at depth (for an enormous amount of 'waste' material has to be removed and brought to the surface before the bands and nodules of ore can be extracted). This cost was rendered prohibitive by the cheapness with which equally good Jurassic ores, quarried or mined in thick bands at small depth, could be obtained.[1] This huge reserve will never be mined under present or foreseeable economic conditions, and in consequence the Coal Measure ores can no longer be said to exert any influence whatsoever over the distribution of the iron and steel industry.

3. *The bedded ores of the Jurassic rocks.*[2] Although certain of these ores, as in Northamptonshire and Lincolnshire, were worked in Roman and medieval times, their value as ores of iron seems to have been completely forgotten for several centuries,[3] and they were hailed as new discoveries about 1850. Since that date they have steadily increased in importance, until at the present time their output represents over 98 per cent of the total ore raised in the British Isles. The ores occur at several different horizons in the Jurassic sequence. Several characteristics are common to them all and serve to distinguish them in a very marked way from the ores which we have previously considered. They are all lean ores, varying in their iron content from 20 to about 33 per cent; they all occur in thick beds, generally about 3 metres (10 ft) thick, but ranging from a metre or two to over 9 metres (30 ft), and in common with the whole Jurassic series they are tilted gently to the east or southeast without being greatly disturbed by folding or fault-

1. The average selling price of Coal Measure ironstone between 1925 and 1931 was just over 13*s* per ton; the figure for the equally rich Northamptonshire stone was little more than 3*s*.
2. *Mem. Geol. Survey, The Northampton Sand Ironstone: stratigraphy, structure and reserves*, HMSO, 1951; *The Liassic Ironstones*, HMSO, 1952.
3. One John Morton, writing in 1712, actually denies the existence of iron ore in Northamptonshire (*Natural History of Northamptonshire*, p. 549).

ing. Furthermore, they are all either quite close to the surface so that they can be quarried, or are easily accessible by shallow mining. In all of them the iron is in the chemical form of chamosite (a silicate of iron) or siderite (carbonate of iron), and is an original constituent of the rock, though in most cases subsequent enrichment and oxidation have occurred through the action of atmospheric waters. It is worthy of note that the 'minette' ores of Lorraine are of precisely the same character and occur on almost the same stratigraphical horizon as the Northampton Sands ores. Four important deposits may be distinguished.

(*a*) In north Lincolnshire, in the neighbourhood of Frodingham and Scunthorpe, certain beds in the Lower Lias formation are ferruginous. This is the thickest of the Jurassic ironstones, between 6 and 9 metres (20 and 30 ft) being worked, and almost all the work is opencast, for, although the thickness of overburden may amount to over 15 metres (50 ft), it consists of soft clays and shales which can be removed mechanically. The ore is, however, very lean, averaging only 20–22 per cent of iron; moreover, it contains up to 25 per cent of lime and an appreciable quantity of manganese—both qualities which influence the technique of its utilisation. The Frodingham ore was first worked in 1859; the field now produces just over one third of the total British output.

(*b*) The 'Marlstone' bed of the Middle Lias yields iron in two quite distinct areas, the Cleveland Hills of Yorkshire and the scarplands from Lincolnshire to Oxfordshire. The marlstone is not always an iron ore. Between north Yorkshire and south Lincolnshire it is barren; a gap separates the south Lincolnshire field from the Leicestershire field, and this again is separated by a barren area from the Banbury ore-bearing district. In north Yorkshire the marlstone crops out on the northern flanks of the Cleveland Hills, dipping gently southeastwards. Owing to the resistant nature of the overlying beds which form the Hills the ore bed quickly disappears underground. It was first quarried in the outliers of Eston and Upleatham only a few miles from the Tees estuary. Almost at once adit mining (i.e. tunnels driven into the hillside) became necessary, and subsequently vertical shafts were sunk to depths of as much as 213 metres (700 ft). The ore bed deteriorates southeastwards and becomes divided by shale partings which quickly reduce its thickness from the 3 metres (10 ft) which was worked on the northwestern edge of the field. The total amount of ore which has been removed from this field is about 355 million metric tons (350 million long tons). Production declined from 6 million metric tons in 1913 to under 2 million metric tons in the years 1931–36, and about 1 million metric tons in 1949–1952; and the last mine closed in 1964.

The other marlstone areas are all worked opencast. The iron in these ores is the result of concentration due to the atmospheric weathering of lean ferruginous mudstones, and consequently, as soon as the bed disappears beneath the cover of newer deposits, where it has been protected from such weathering, the iron content diminishes so rapidly as to render the rock useless as an ore.[1] Consequently mining will probably never be necessary. The three separate fields are: (1) the Caythorpe district of south Lincolnshire (the smallest); (2) the Melton Mowbray ironstone ridge, around Holwell and Eaton in Leicestershire;[2] (3) the Banbury district on the borders of Oxfordshire and Northamptonshire (formerly the most important, but extinct since 1967). In each of these areas the ore bed varies from about 1.8 to 3.6 metres (6 to 12 ft) in thickness, but often much has been lost through denudation.

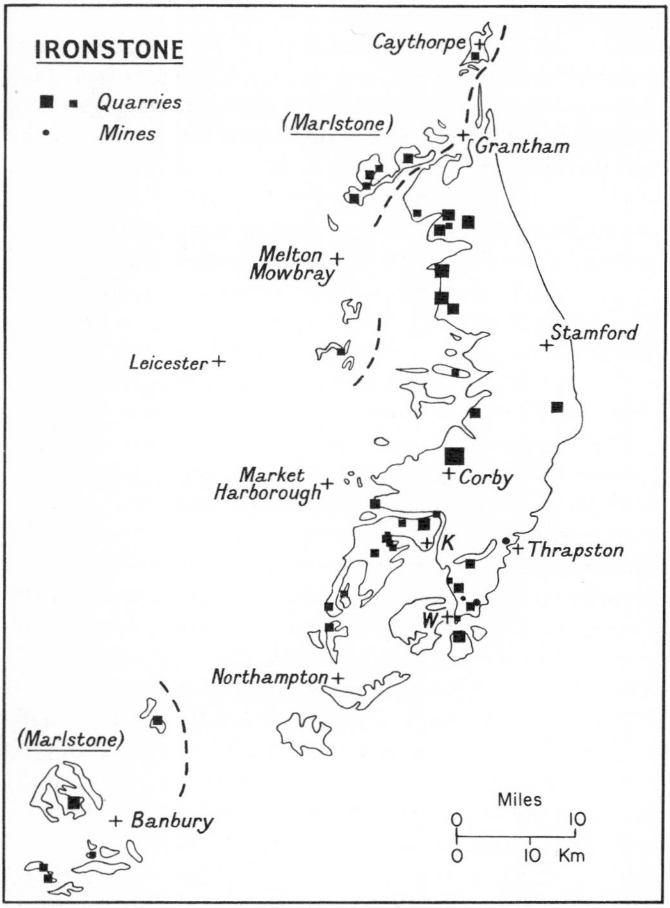

FIG. 165. The Jurassic ironstone fields of the East Midlands

This map represents the situation in the 1950s; since then, the number of individual quarries in central Northamptonshire has been much reduced, without however any reduction in output; the marlstone of Leicestershire has much declined, whilst the Banbury district is completely extinct.

1. *The Liassic Ironstones*, pp. 95, 144.
2. P. T. Wheeler, 'Ironstone working between Melton Mowbray and Grantham'. *East Midland Geog.*, **4**, 1967, 239–50.

All the marlstone districts produce lean ores. The Cleveland ore contains on the average about 28 per cent of iron, and the quarried ores of the scarplands about 25 per cent.

(*c*) That portion of the Inferior Oolite formation in Northamptonshire, Rutland, and south Lincolnshire, known as the 'Northampton Sands', is, and will continue to be, one of the vital factors in the British iron and steel industry.[1] It contains a bed of iron ore, generally between 1.8 to 3.6 metres (6 and 12 ft) in thickness, which is not only the richest of the Jurassic ores (iron content 30–33 per cent) but also offers the most extensive reserve of ore of any of these fields. At the 1949–51 rate of production, about 7 million metric tons a year, the ore was estimated to last for at least 175 years.[2] The field stretches, with slight interruptions due to deterioration and denudation, from Lincoln to Towcester and, unlike the marlstone of the neighbouring areas, the ore does not deteriorate eastwards under cover. The ore is obtained by opencast methods, at depths of up to 24 to 30 metres (80 to 100 ft). It is siliceous, which makes it very suitable for foundry iron, and it is also higher in phosphorus than the other Jurassic ores, which makes the pig iron produced from it suitable for the basic Bessemer process.[3]

In all the Jurassic ore fields, except Cleveland, the railway facilities have had a great bearing upon the working of the ore, and as the vales at the foot of the Marlstone and Inferior Oolite scarps provided excellent railway routes very little additional mineral line construction has been necessary.[4] In Cleveland the more dissected nature of the country led to the building of several special mineral lines and connections with the existing tortuous branches of the North Eastern Railway (see Fig. 182).

Again, except for Middlesbrough, Scunthorpe, and more recently Corby, the working of the Jurassic ore fields has not given rise to any marked change in the distribution of population. The reason is to be found in (*a*) the scattered nature of the quarries, and (*b*) the geological conditions which permit the use of mechanical appliances and consequently a small man-power. The use of mechanical excavators, however, mainly since the First World War, greatly exaggerated the effect of ironstone quarrying on the landscape, for whereas in the days of hand working all the overburden and top soil were replaced and the land restored to agriculture, the mechanical

1. S. H. Beaver, 'The iron industry of Northamptonshire, Rutland and south Lincolnshire', *Geography*, **18**, 1933, 102–17.
2. *Mem. Geol. Surv.*, *The Northampton Sand Ironstone*, p. 7.
3. Iron containing at least 1.8 per cent of phosphorus is necessary for the basic Bessemer process. Most iron ores at present available in Britain contain too much phosphorus for the acid process and too little for basic Bessemer—one reason for the popularity of basic open-hearth. The Corby works, however, having revived the basic Bessemer process in 1935, ceased to use it in 1965, greater economies being obtainable by the use of the L-D oxygen-converter (cf. p. 379).
4. The most important mineral line is the Stainby and High Dyke branch, south of Grantham, which carries Northampton Sands ore from south Lincolnshire, on its way to Scunthorpe and Derbyshire.

PLATE 17. Opencast iron ore mining at Scunthorpe

Large walking dragline removing overburden, which is being re-distributed by a smaller dragline and then flattened by bulldozers. A face-shovel digs ironstone on the extreme right. Steelworks in distance (with gasholders to store surplus gas from blast furnaces and coke ovens).

shovel and dragline create large dumps of overburden in 'hill and dale' formation, and the problems of afforestation and agricultural reinstatement are considerable.[1] Nevertheless, as in the case of opencast coal mining, all worked areas are now regularly restored to farming or else planted with trees.

4. *Miscellaneous ore deposits.* Although of very small importance at the present time (since they provide less than 1 per cent of the total output), certain other occurrences of iron ore have been important at various periods in the past and deserve passing notice.

In the Carboniferous Limestone of the Forest of Dean limonite (oxidised haematite $Fe_2O_3 + 3H_2O$), occurring in the same irregular fashion as the Cumberland haematites, was mined from Roman times, and it gave rise to

1. See, for example, W. D. Evans, 'The open-cast mining of ironstone and coal', *Geogrl J.* **104**, 1944, 102–19; also S. H. Beaver, *The Land of Britain, Part 58, Northamptonshire*, pp. 372–4. On restoration problems see S. H. Beaver, 'Land reclamation after surface mineral working'. *J. Tn Planning Inst.*, **41**, 1955, 146–54.

PLATE 18. Opencast iron ore mine at Cottesmore, Rutland
Dragline removes overburden, dumps it without forming 'hill and dale', and subsequently replaces the soil; agricultural restoration is complete.

an extensive iron industry during the charcoal smelting period. Production declined rapidly after 1880. A similar deposit in the same formation at Llanharry (Glamorgan) is the only one of the 'other occurrences' which is still worked to any extent;[1] it supplements the imports of foreign ore at Cardiff and Port Talbot. The ore in the Upper Lias of Raasay, Scotland, was worked for a time, especially during the First World War, but its remoteness and low iron content (25 per cent) rendered the cost prohibitive. The deposit of magnetic ore occurring in the Inferior Oolite of Rosedale, Yorks, has long since been worked out. The Corallian beds of Westbury (Wilts.) contain an iron ore which formerly fed the furnace there. The concealed Corallian rocks of the East Kent coalfield have also been found to contain similar ore. Certain bodies of bedded ore occurring in the Cretaceous rocks have also been of importance in the past. Most noticeable, of course, are the ironstones in the Wealden rocks of Sussex and Kent, which were for so long the chief sources of British iron. Deposits in the Lower Cretaceous near Claxby (Lincs.) are mined by a Scunthorpe firm, and at Seend (Wilts.) is a similar small deposit which for a short time fed a small ironworks.

1. *Mem. Geol. Surv., Iron Ores*, vol. x, *The Haematites of the Forest of Dean and South Wales*, 1919.

Iron ore production (thousand long tons)

FORMATION	1913	1931	1937	1942[2]	1950	1956	1960	1964	1969	AVERAGE IRON CONTENT PER CENT
HAEMATITE:										
Cumberland	1 361	613	737	594	342	323	315	274	143	48
Lancashire	406	96	120	21	—	—	—	—	—	(54)
Total	1 767	709	857	615	342	323	315	274	143	
JURASSIC:										
Lower Lias	*	1 423	3 047	3 672	3 155	4 485	5 411	5 441	4 408	20
Middle Lias, Cleveland	5 941	1 497	2 037	1 884	1 019	581	463	—	—	28
Middle Lias, other areas	*	1 056	2 001	2 702	1 538	2 879	2 121	1 590	232	24
Inferior Oolite	*	2 851	5 834	10 635	6 804	7 847	8 657	8 868	7 185	31
Total	12 572	6 827	12 919	18 894	12 517	15 793	16 652	15 899	11 825	
COAL MEASURES:										
N. and S. Staffs.	*	50	149	150	—	—	—	—	—	—
Scotland	591	8	22	36	—	—	—	—	—	—
Other areas	*	5	7	1	—	—	—	—	—	—
Total	1 542	73	178	187	—	—	—	—	—	(32)
Other occurrences	116[1]	17	260	209	103	129	120	153	136	50[3]
Total	15 997[1]	7 626	14 215	19 906	12 963	16 245	17 087	16 326	12 103	
Total (metric tons)	16 254	7 748	14 443	20 225	13 171	16 506	17 361	16 588	12 298	

* Not available, as figures given by counties only, not by formations.

1 Includes 60 000 tons from Antrim, Ireland.

Import and internal movement of iron ore

Despite the extensive reorganisation of the British iron and steel industry which was conducted during 1914–18, when our capacity for producing basic steel from the home Jurassic ores was considerably enhanced, and despite the great expansion of the Jurassic ore output, our imports of rich foreign ores have not proportionately diminished. Indeed, they have materially increased. But the reasons for importing ore are now rather different from those which influenced the first importation in the 'seventies. It was then that the demand for steel made by the acid processes became so great that Cumberland and Furness, even though their output rose to over 3 million metric tons yearly, could not supply sufficient non-phosphoric ore to feed the furnaces. By 1900 the amount imported had risen to 30 per cent of the total quantity used. Our earliest imports came almost entirely from Spain, which possessed, in the province of Vizcaya, huge reserves of rich haematite ore, non-phosphoric and yielding 50–60 per cent of iron. During the 1880s, in fact, the greater part of the shipment from Bilbao, amounting to between 3 and 4 million metric tons per annum, was destined for British ports. Swedish ores, though very rich in iron (mostly 60–70 per cent) are mostly phosphoric, and this fact, combined with the lack of transport facilities, prevented any considerable import thereof before the discovery of the basic process. The first Swedish ores to arrive in this country came from central Sweden (the Grängesberg and Dannemora areas). The colossal magnetic deposits of northern Sweden at Gällivare and Kirunavare were not available until railways were built to the coasts. Lulea began to ship ore in 1887, and the Norwegian port of Narvik began exporting Swedish ore in 1903. After 1900, too, considerable quantities of rich low-phosphorus ore were received from French and Spanish territories in North Africa, where there are extensive deposits of ore yielding over 50 per cent of iron.

In recent years between 16 and 18 million metric tons of ore have been imported into Britain annually, and there have been radical changes in the sources of supply. Since the Second World War Sweden has more than regained the dominant position that it held before the war, but North African imports have declined considerably within the last decade, while Spain has fallen—largely owing to the exhaustion of its best deposits—to a minor place. For a time Newfoundland came into the picture again with its oolitic haematites from Wabana, but these mines closed in 1966 and the large quantities of Canadian ore now imported come from the pre-Cambrian deposits on the Quebec–Labrador border that were opened up in the mid-1950s. The greatest changes, however, have been concerned with the opening up of new orefields in the pre-Cambrian rocks of West Africa and South America, and with alterations in the nature of the shipping that carries the ores. Of the West African sources Sierra Leone was first in the field; a Scottish steel company was largely responsible for this development in 1933. Lateritic ore from Conakry, in Guinea, began to arrive in 1953, but both these sources have been far surpassed by the magnetite of the Bomi Hills in Liberia and still more recently (since 1963) the haematite from Mauritania. South American ores come from the Itabira region of Brazil, and from Venezuela. Another source, since 1965, is the USSR; and imports have even been received from as far afield as India and northwestern Australia.

Iron ore imports (thousand long tons)

COUNTRY	1913	1931	1937	1943[4]	1950	1960	1965	1969	AVERAGE IRON CONTENT PER CENT
Canada[1]	100	27	258	3	123	3 307	3 018	2 895	54
Sierra Leone	—	—	337	502	733	738	547	372	61
France	327	77	408	—	373	537	109	26	41
North Africa[2]	1 038	582	2 350	848	2 666	3 662	1 533	437	51
Spain	4 525	888	930	265	750	743	581	571	50
Sweden[3]	854	446	2 387	—	3 443	5 101	6 777	3 509	61
Venezuela	—	—	—	—	—	1 620	1 706	1 529	60
Brazil	—	—	38	262		626	613	1 021	68
Liberia	—	—	—	—	—	533	1 531	1 503	65
Guinea	—	—	—	—	—	381	190	—	47
Other Countries	386	88	242	14		735	2 252	6 314[5]	—
Total (long tons)	7 230	2 108	6 950	1 894	8 402	17 969	18 857	18 177	57
Total (metric tons)	7 346	2 142	7 061	1 924	8 537	18 257	19 160	18 468	

[1] Newfoundland only before 1956; includes Labrador thereafter; Newfoundland ceased 1966.
[2] Morocco, Algeria and Tunisia.
[3] Includes some from Norway, e.g. 652 th. long tons in 1937, 715 th. long tons in 1965.
[4] Lowest war year—French and Scandinavian sources enemy-controlled.
[5] Includes Norway 2065, Mauritania 1957, USSR 1357 (each averaging 62–63 per cent iron).

The reasons for such large imports, and from such distant sources, are (*a*) the fact that the imported ores are in general about twice as rich as the home-produced Jurassic ores, and may be even richer if they have been concentrated or pelletised before shipment;[1] (*b*) the lower fuel consumption per ton of pig iron which the smelting of richer ores entails;[2] and (*c*) the relative cheapness of transporting iron ore in large bulk carriers of up to

1. Of the 15.1 million metric tons (15 million long tons) imported in 1967, 6.5 million metric tons were in the form of concentrates or pellets.
2. In 1967 Jurassic ores needed about 750 kilograms of coke per metric ton (15 cwt of coke per long ton) of pig iron, imported ores only 650 kilograms per metric ton (13 cwt per long ton).

60 000 tons or more, instead of in tramp ships of 10 000 tons or less. The repercussions of this last factor are considerable, for our normal ore-importing ports were incapable of accommodating such large vessels. Thus Middlesbrough has had to develop a new deepwater ore terminal; at Port Talbot the entire port has been reconstructed to take ore-carriers of up to 100 000 dwt.[1] and an entirely new ore terminal to serve the Scottish industry is proposed at Hunterston on the Ayrshire coast. Clearly the coastal or near-coastal location of much of the British iron-smelting industry—a feature which was essentially the product of the importation of foreign ore—is likely to be even more strongly emphasised in the future.

The iron ore imports are by no means evenly distributed amongst the various iron-smelting districts, for clearly the Jurassic orefield smelters (Corby, Scunthorpe) are dependent upon their local ores whilst the remaining Midland plants (Staffordshire, Derbyshire) also use home ores. South Wales (Port Talbot, Cardiff and Newport) is by far the largest importer, taking some 40 per cent of the total; it is followed by the north-eastern ports (especially Middlesbrough), east coast ports (including London and Grimsby), the Clyde, the Mersey and Workington.

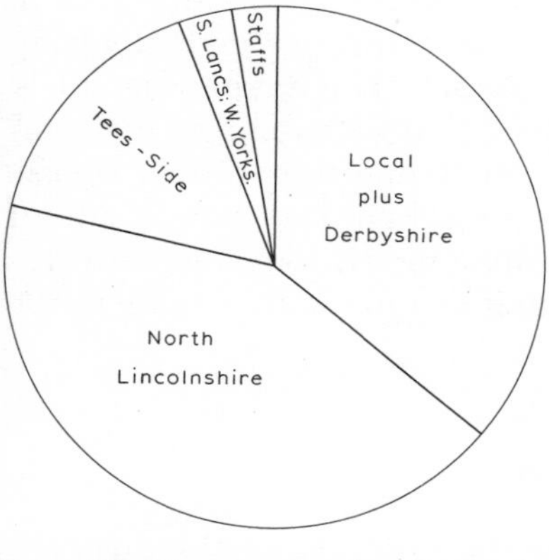

FIG. 166. Diagram showing destination of Northampton Sands iron ore in 1967

An extensive system of internal ore transport also exists in Britain, and it has an interesting geographical background. We have already seen that the presence of iron ores and coal in the same measures gave rise to iron industries in Staffordshire, Yorkshire (West Riding), Derbyshire, and South Wales. The cessation of the supply of Coal Measure ores, however, left these

1. When Australian ore first arrived at Port Talbot it was transhipped at Rotterdam from bulk carriers into smaller vessels capable of entering the port. The Russian ore could be imported at Port Talbot because it came in vessels of 10·000 tons which were the largest that Murmansk, the port of origin, could accommodate.

areas without their local raw material, which must in consequence be drawn from farther afield. The Jurassic scarplands, on the other hand, have huge ore supplies and no coal. Consequently, although furnaces exist in Northamptonshire and at Scunthorpe, a large proportion of the Jurassic ore is 'exported' to these old-established regions. Most of the Frodingham ore is used in the local furnaces, but a considerable proportion of the Marlstone and Northampton Sands ores goes into the furnaces of the Midlands. An interesting transference of ore also takes place as a result of the calcareous nature of the Frodingham ore, which is so limy that it cannot be used alone in the furnace, but requires a siliceous complement—which is supplied by the ore from the Northampton Sands of Lincolnshire and Northamptonshire.[1] The cessation of the Cleveland production is further reflected in the large amount of Northamptonshire and Rutland ore which is sent to the Tees-side furnaces. As a comment upon the facts enunciated above, Fig. 166 shows the destination of the Northampton Sands ore.

Sinter

To an increasing extent the home output of Jurassic ores, and also some of the imported ores, are being subjected to a sintering or agglomerating process before being charged into the blast furnace. This enables the finely fragmented ores to be more effectively smelted, and with reduced fuel consumption. The crushed ores are mixed with small quantities of coke breeze and passed through a furnace, coming out in hard clinkery lumps. About 11 million metric tons of home ores and 11 million metric tons of foreign ores are now treated annually in this way, resulting in a marked increase in the efficiency of the blast furnaces.

Other raw materials

Other raw materials of vital importance to the iron and steel industry—apart from air and water[2]—include limestone, dolomite, refractories, manganese ore, alloying metals, and of course scrap. The first three of these have been briefly dealt with in Chapter 15; suffice it to say that Britain is well supplied with high-quality deposits, which are often most fortunately placed with respect to the iron and steel industries. *Manganese ore* is employed, to the extent of nearly 50 kilograms per metric ton (1 cwt per long ton) of pig iron, mainly to neutralise the harmful effects of sulphur, and so is especially used in blast furnaces producing pig iron for basic steel manu-

1. Cf. the interchange, in Lorraine, of the limy ores of the Briey plateau and the siliceous ores of the Longwy and Nancy regions.
2. Air is paradoxically the heaviest raw material of all, for anything from 3 to 7 metric *tons* of air may be used in a blast furnace to produce a ton of pig-iron, and a large furnace may use a ton of air per minute! Fortunately air is free and ubiquitous.

facture.[1] In the form of ferromanganese (which is produced in blast furnaces just like pig iron) it is used in steel melting as a de-oxidiser, especially in the Bessemer process, and it is also a constituent of high-manganese steel, which has exceptional qualities of toughness and resistance to wear. Of the alloying metals, *nickel*, used in stainless steel and for engineering purposes, *cobalt*, used in magnets and heat-resisting steels, *tungsten*, for high-speed tool steel, *molybdenum*, for high-speed and corrosion-resisting steels, and *chromium*, for tools, magnets, ball-bearings, and stainless steels, are the most important. All have to be imported.[2] Over 1.5 million metric tons of alloy steels are produced every year—nearly 60 per cent of it in Sheffield (see p. 414) and much of the rest in Scotland, in south Lancashire, in South Wales and in the Midlands.

Scrap

In recent years some 17 to 20 million metric tons of scrap have been used annually in iron and steel manufacture. The basic open-hearth furnaces are by far the largest consumers (12 to 14 million metric tons), but the electric furnaces, though with a much smaller output, work on little else but scrap, whilst another 4 million tons is used in iron foundries. Nearly one-half of the scrap supply normally arises from the iron- and steelworks themselves, during the processes of manufacture, and the remainder is purchased from home sources (particularly re-rolling works and other works engaged in processing iron and steel, and also engineering works, ship-breaking yards, and other works having obsolete plant to dispose of) or imported from abroad.

The smelting and steel-making districts

Location factors[3]

The British iron and steel industry affords numerous examples of 'geographical inertia' or 'industrial momentum'—the continuance of a human activity in a region, after some or all of the causes which gave rise to that activity have ceased to operate. By reason of the size and cost of its plant the manufacture of iron and steel tends to be one of the most inert of industries, and, rather than abandon their works and move to a better site, manu-

1. Manganese ore imports 1969: South Africa 129 thousand tons, Congo 64, USSR 31, Ghana 19, India 17, Brazil 77, total 431 thousand tons (metric).

2. Consumption of ferro-alloy materials, 1969 (thousand metric tons): nickel 13.9, molybdenum 3.7, tungsten 0.8, vanadium 0.8, cobalt 0.4; ferrochrome 52.9, ferrosilicon 94.0, ferromanganese 215.1.

3. A concise summary of the main locational characteristics of the British iron and steel industry will be found in an article entitled 'The location of the British steel industry', in the *Monthly Statistical Bulletin of the British Iron and Steel Federation*, **25**, no. 11, Nov. 1950.

facturers will go to great lengths to improve their efficiency, or their transport, or will specialise in certain types of produce. Slowly but surely, however, economic factors in the shape of competition from better situated producers will operate. If the industry originally set up has resulted in the accumulation of a large population in its neighbourhood, it is highly probable that production of some kind will continue by reason of the skilled

Pig iron production (by districts)
(thousand long tons)

DISTRICT	1913	1931	1937	1940[2]	1950	1960	1965	1966	1969
Derby, Leics., Notts, Northants, Essex[1]	1 166	979	1 938	1 787	2 309	2 633	1 971	1 634	1 611
Lancs and Yorks	503	205	476	401	437	1 408	1 685	1 693	1 526
Lincolnshire	450	412	1 043	1 308	1 239	2 290	2 697	2 521	2 945
NE Coast	3 869	1 137	2 429	1 934	2 402	3 412	3 434	2 784	3 109
Scotland	1 369	154	497	659	739	1 299	1 675	1 313	1 908
Staffs, Salop, Worcs, Warwick	851	202	470	447	551	553	585	595	685
South Wales and Monmouth	889	280	814	962	1 232	3 141	4 718	4 611	4 034
NW Coast	1 163	404	825	705	824	1 028	695	559	571
Total (long tons)	10 260	3 773	8 493	8 205	9 633	15 763	17 460	15 710	16 390
Total (metric tons)	10 425	3 833	8 629	8 336	9 787	16 016	17 740	15 962	16 652

[1] Essex only since 1934. [2] War peak year—see footnote to next table.
1 long ton (2240 lb) = 1.016 metric ton.

labour there present; if the original industry was but small it must inevitably die out. Since much of our industry was built upon Coal Measure ores, which are now not worked at all, it follows that one of the main advantages formerly possessed by the iron industries of the coalfields has been lost. We must examine the producing areas individually in order to see how this change in location of the ore supplies has affected them.

It is important to realise that iron smelting and steel making can be and often are two quite separate industries, with different location factors. In the case of iron smelting, between 3 and 3.75 metric tons of raw materials and fuel are consumed per metric ton of pig iron, and the iron ore, which is the largest single item, naturally exerts the greatest influence on the location of the industry. Thus two major types of location are found: (*a*) on the orefields, particularly the low-grade Jurassic fields (e.g. Scunthorpe and Corby); (*b*) at ports, where foreign ores arrive (e.g. Middlesbrough, Workington, Cardiff, Dagenham—the first two having also the original advantage of nearby ore supplies, the third of a nearby source of coking coal). But the 'momentum' referred to above is also responsible for a third type of location: (*c*) on coalfields, where the original works were based on

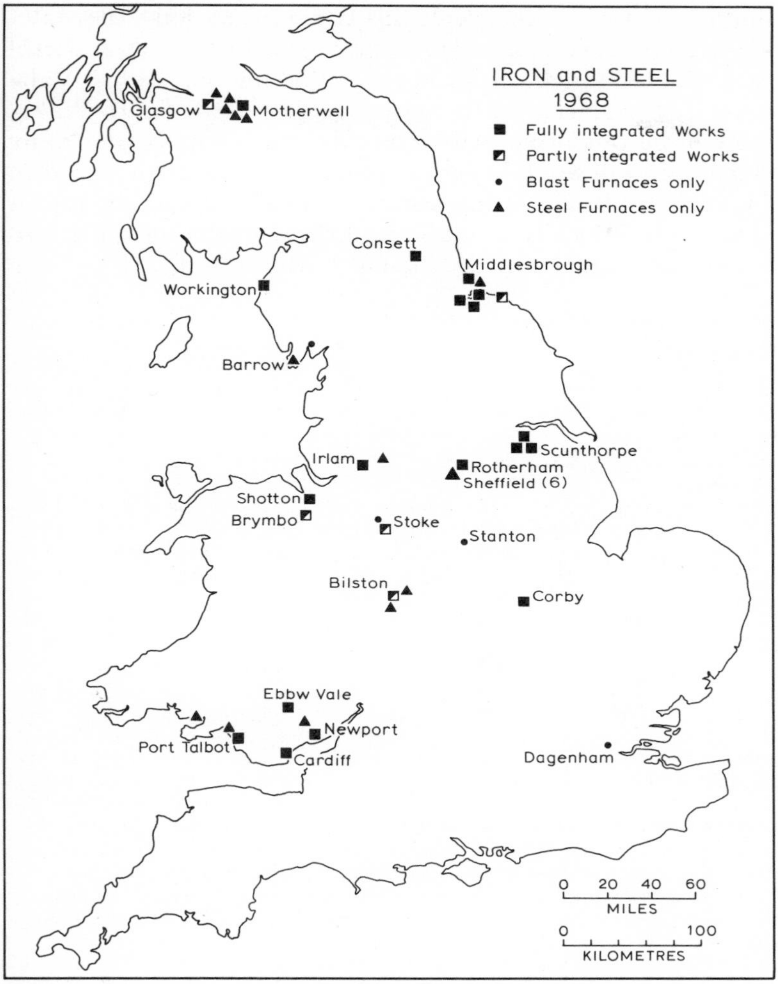

FIG. 167. The iron and steel industry in 1968

The special symbol for Sheffield represents six steelworks.

The number of blast furnaces in existence was 486 in 1921, 285 in 1937, 119 in 1952 and only 71 in 1969 (cf. Fig. 162). Open-hearth steel furnaces numbered 391 in 1952 and 181 in 1969. Electric furnaces numbered 321 in 1962 and 434 in 1969. There were 42 converters of various kinds in 1969. In addition to the works shown on this map, 106 other works, in various parts of the country, had small 'tropenas' converters or electric steel furnaces. Such furnaces belong to the engineering industry rather than to the primary production of steel; in 1969 they operated 15 converters and 348 electric furnaces.

local Coal Measure ironstones as well as suitable fuel (e.g. Consett, Ilkeston, Coatbridge, Bilston, Stoke-on-Trent).

The steel making industry has as its main raw materials iron, either molten or in pig form, and scrap. It may be located (*a*) adjacent to a smelting works, where molten iron from the blast furnaces can be converted directly, without loss of heat, into steel; this type of situation—the 'integrated' works—is coming increasingly to dominate the British iron and steel industry (e.g. Middlesbrough, Scunthorpe, Workington, Ebbw Vale, Corby, Margam); (*b*) adjacent to its market (e.g. western South Wales, where almost all the output formerly went into the tinplate mills; and many scattered and mainly small works in various parts of the country which form part of steel foundries and engineering works); (*c*) in an engineering district where abundant scrap is locally available and the engineering works also form a market for the output (e.g. Wednesbury, Motherwell).

Steel production (*ingots and castings*) (*by districts*)
(thousand long tons)

DISTRICT	1913	1931	1937	1943[1]	1950	1960	1965	1966	1969
Derby, Northants, Notts, Lancs, Yorks (excluding Sheffield), North Wales	512	363	1 511	1 683	2 048	3 589	3 927	3 653	3 822
Lincolnshire	241	392	1 299	1 243	1 562	2 579	3 086	2 770	3 233
NE Coast	2 031	1 142	2 825	2 525	3 353	4 813	4 790	3 857	4 373
Scotland	1 421	676	1 895	2 031	2 426	2 701	3 053	2 678	3 296
Staffs, Salop, Warwick, Worcs	365	419	702	727	856	1 554	1 757	1 769	1 982
South Wales and Monmouth	1 807	1 274	2 629	2 609	3 407	5 666	6 778	6 393	5 828
Sheffield	879	776	1 739	1 960	2 218	3 064	3 272	2 946	3 451
NW Coast	398	161	385	253	423	339	343	250	348
Total (long tons)	7 664	5 203	12 984	13 031	16 293	24 305	27 006	24 315	26 422
Total (metric tons)	7 787	5 286	13 192	13 240	16 554	24 695	27 439	24 704	26 845

[1] War peak year. The wartime peak of steel production was reached later than that of pig iron, for several sources of foreign ore were cut off and scrap was substituted. Thus the 1940 steel output consumed 6839 thousand metric tons (6731 thousand long tons) of pig iron and 7296 thousand metric tons (7181 thousand long tons) of scrap; the 1943 steel output consumed 6222 thousand metric tons (6124 thousand long tons) of pig iron and 8093 thousand metric tons (7965 thousand long tons) of scrap.

Naturally enough, in a country in which the industries are as old-established as they are in Britain (only four new localities of major importance have been added to the iron and steel map during the present century), and in which distances between coal, ore and ports are in no case great, many works fall into more than one category.

1. *Scotland.*[1] Of several dozen iron smelting works, all established between 1760 and 1860, only one remains (in a modernised form, of course); and nearly a century elapsed before the construction of a new plant at Ravenscraig, near Motherwell, in 1957. The first one, apart from a few charcoal

1. See H. Hamilton, *The Industrial Revolution in Scotland*, Chapters 7 and 8, for an excellent account of the development of the Scottish iron industry. Also K. Warren, 'Locational problems of the Scottish iron and steel industry since 1760', *Scott. geogr. Mag.*, **81**, 1965, 18–37.

furnaces erected on the west coast to use local timber and Furness haematite, was established by a Sheffield ironmaster in 1760, at Carron, near Falkirk, on a site within a few miles of the coast, where a good water supply was available, and close to clayband ore and coal reserves. The works quickly became one of the largest and most famous in Europe. Progress generally

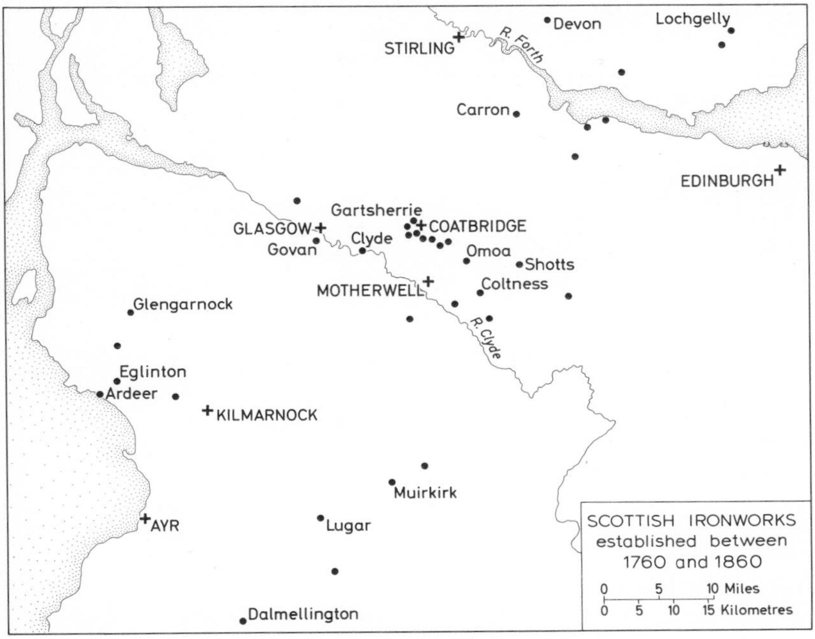

FIG. 168. Scottish ironworks established between 1760 and 1860

was particularly marked, however, after Neilson in 1828 rendered the blackband ores more efficiently usable by means of the hot blast. The output, only 9000 metric tons in 1806, rose to 213 000 metric tons in 1840, and in the 'fifties, with over 150 furnaces available, Scotland was producing a quarter of the entire British output of pig iron. After 1880 the production of blackband ores began rapidly to decline, and the ironworks, finding their ore supplies partly cut off, were obliged to import extensively from abroad. By distribution the smelting works fell into three main groups. The central group, clustered on the Lanarkshire coalfield, had its chief centres at Coatbridge, Airdrie, Motherwell, Wishaw, and Glasgow. Here the Monkland Canal and the Clyde, and later the railways, provided suitable means of transport for the bulky iron products, whilst the local 'splint' coals[1] and the

1. The 'splint' coal, one of the most constant of the Lanarkshire seams, is of a hard splinty character specially valuable for furnace purposes. 'It comes from the pit in big hard blocks which do not readily break up in the furnace under the weight of the overlying material, and the draught is thus kept open'. (*Mem. Geol. Surv., Economic Geology of the Central Coalfield of Scotland, Area V*, 1926, 73.)

blackband ores were the basis of this industry (cf. Fig. 143 and Fig. 164). The North Ayrshire group was centred on Irvine and Kilbirnie, with outlying plants at Lugar and Muirkirk; it had the same basis of ore and fuel. The third group, mostly post-1840 apart from Carron, straddled the upper Firth of Forth, using the coals and blackbands of the eastern part of the central coalfield in the Bo'ness area and of the Fifeshire coalfield around Lochgelly.

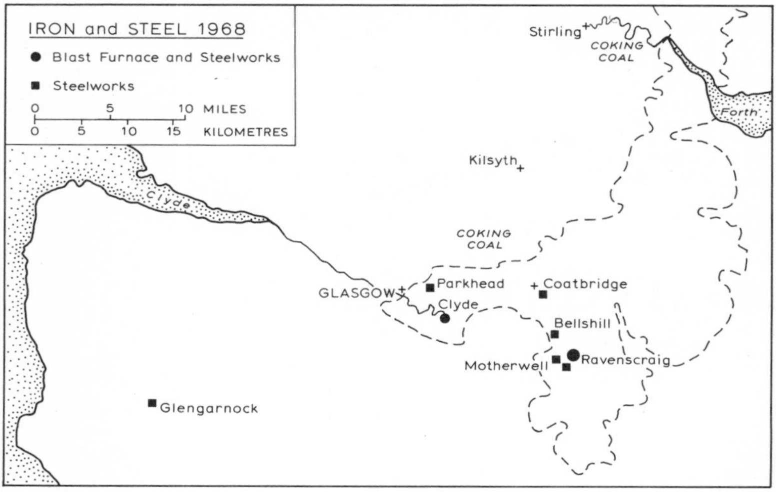

Fig. 169. The Scottish iron and steel industry in 1968
The dotted line is the boundary of the Coal Measures; the coking coal seams are in the Lower Carboniferous.

The prosperity of the Scottish ironworks was seriously undermined by the falling off in the local ore supply, and the situation was aggravated by the approaching exhaustion of the 'splint' coals, which were used raw in the furnaces. These circumstances, together with the periods of depression which characterised the inter-war years, were largely responsible for completely changing the character of the Scottish iron smelting industry, by weeding out those works whose equipment or situation rendered them uneconomic. Pig iron production is now concentrated at two plants only—one near Glasgow and the new one near Motherwell. From more than 100 furnaces which existed in 1913 the number has fallen to only 6; many complete works have been demolished. Yet the pig iron output has since 1960 risen to a higher level than that of 1913. This concentration on a few large plants has been accompanied and aided by the production of coke from certain seams, such as the Kilsyth coking coal, which occur in the Lower Limestone Group (of Carboniferous Limestone age) in north Lanarkshire and Stirlingshire. New large furnaces, comparable with those in other parts of Britain, have been erected to use foreign ore and Scottish coke, and the two works are fully integrated and possess their own coke ovens. Thus the small furnace producing foundry iron from local raw materials has vanished from the Scottish iron industry.

The steel industry is located for the most part in the neighbourhood of Coatbridge, Motherwell, Wishaw, and Glasgow. It grew up apart from the blast furnaces, depending originally on imported haematite pig iron and scrap from the local shipbuilding, ship-breaking, and engineering industries. During and after 1914–18 much of the plant was adapted for the production of basic steel, and in the 1950s about 90 per cent of the output was of the basic open-hearth variety. Scotland, however, has taken its full

PLATE 19. Integrated steelworks at Ravenscraig, Motherwell

share of the recent technological advances, and only two-thirds of the steel is now made in open-hearth furnaces, the remainder coming from LD converters and electric furnaces. Much of the output, together with large quantities of imported semifinished steel, goes into the local shipbuilding and engineering industries, whilst the hot-strip mill at Ravenscraig, opened in 1963, provides sheet steel for the motor vehicle industry (Plate 19).

2. *Tees-side.*[1] The advantages of Tees-side for the setting up of iron and steel

1. See House and Fullerton, *Tees-side at Mid-century*, Macmillan, 1960; K. Warren, 'The shaping of the Tees-side industrial region', *Advmt Sci.*, **25**, 1968, 185–99.

industries were unique. An abundant supply of ore in the Cleveland Hills, less than 8 kilometres (five miles) away from tide water at first, and later well within 32 kilometres (twenty miles) of Middlesbrough; ample supplies of the finest coking coal in the kingdom from southwest Durham, only 40 kilometres (twenty-five miles) away and available by existing railways; limestone in abundance from the Carboniferous Limestone in Weardale and dolomite from the Permian of East Durham: and a seaboard situation favourable, with the improvement of the estuary, for the export of the bulky products. It is little wonder that within twenty-five years of the commencement of the industry Tees-side was producing 1.75 million metric tons of

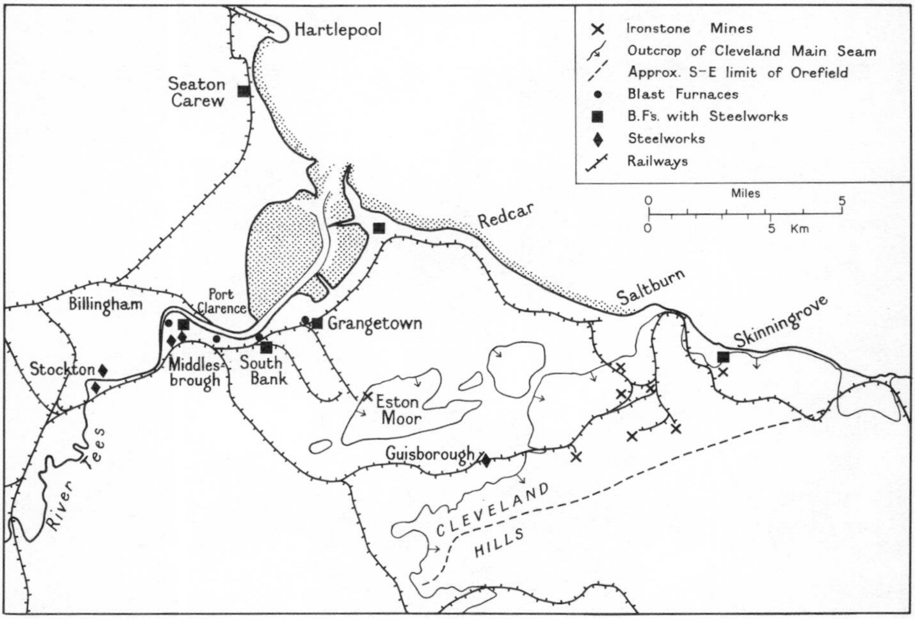

FIG. 170. The Tees-side iron and steel industry in the early 1950s

Apart from a reduction in the number of blast furnaces, the most important change has been the closure of all the iron ore mines. The Lackenby steelworks (1953) and beam mill (1958) lie just north-east of Grangetown.

pig iron, or close on 30 per cent of the total British output. Moreover, after the introduction of the acid steel processes the coastal situation favoured the import of rich Spanish ores, which were rendered cheaper by the availability of a return cargo of coal from the adjacent coalfield, whilst the abundance of flat land alongside the estuary allowed ample room for the expansion of the works. All these advantages enabled Tees-side to build up the greatest iron and steel industry in the whole of Britain. The serious depletion of the local ores, however, combined with the stimulus which was given to the industry during 1914–18, brought about changes in the nature of the industry. The pig iron output has never again approached the 1913 total (see table on p. 396), and none of it is now made from Cleveland ore. Sweden, Africa and the Americas supply rich ores from abroad; Northamptonshire and South Lincolnshire send a million tons per annum of lean ores. The bulk of the pig iron is converted into basic steel, and the once famous foundry iron production has virtually ceased. Both pig iron and steel are exported to Scotland and other coastal centres of the industry. Much of the haematite pig iron and steel made is sent to Sheffield for working up into the finer types of steel products. A large proportion of the steel production is absorbed by the local engineering and shipbuilding industries. The expansion of the steel industry during the First World War resulted in a vast improvement of the existing Tees-side steelworks plant and the erection of a new works at Redcar. Subsequently foreign competition resulted in renewed efforts to modernise the plant and to reduce working costs. As a result huge combines were formed, bringing under a single control the coke and ore supplies, the furnaces, and the steelworks, and even including the engineering industry and the marketing of the produce. An excellent example is furnished by Dorman Long, which united Dorman, Long & Co., Bell Bros., North-Eastern Steel Co., Bolckow, Vaughan & Co., and other smaller establishments. The industry was 'rationalised' and inefficient plant eliminated. For example, Port Clarence works (opposite Middlesbrough), with eleven blast furnaces, closed down in 1930 and was later demolished.

Steel-making capacity was increased in the 1950s by the construction of a new steel plant and beam mill at Lackenby; and a new ore terminal has been built to accommodate vessels of up to 100 000 tons.

The chief works in the northeast coast area away from the Tees are at Seaton Carew just north of the estuary, at Skinningrove, to the east, and at Consett.[1] These outlying centres are supported almost entirely by foreign ore.

3. *The West Coast.* The geographical basis of the iron and steel industry in West Cumberland and Furness was simple. Large supplies of rich haematite ore occurred within a few miles of the coast; the ore was obtained from the Carboniferous Limestone, which could be used as a flux; and the Durham coke lay not far away (by rail) across the Pennines (for the local Cumberland coal is not of first-class coking quality). Almost without exception, then, the works were located on, or quite close to, the sea-shore, and consequently, owing to the absence of a large industrial market in the vicinity, it was the export trade in pig iron which was chiefly developed, the exports being to Sheffield, coastwise to Belfast, South Wales, and Scotland, and

1. The location of the Consett works depended on the existence of a limited amount of clayband ironstone in the Coal Measures of the immediate vicinity; but as against its present disadvantageous situation regarding imported ore, it lies almost on top of the coking coal requirements, and not far from excellent limestone and silica rock deposits. It is a fully integrated works.

abroad. The first works (apart from the ancient charcoal furnaces)[1] were erected in 1841, but the greatest development came after the introduction of Bessemer steel, and nine new works made their appearance in as many years, between 1870 and 1879. The area built up a great reputation for high quality haematite iron and acid Bessemer steel, much of which was exported abroad or to other British industrial areas; and the shipbuilding industry at Barrow provided an additional local outlet. The depressions of the 1920s and 1930s decimated the industry (Fig. 171), which has still

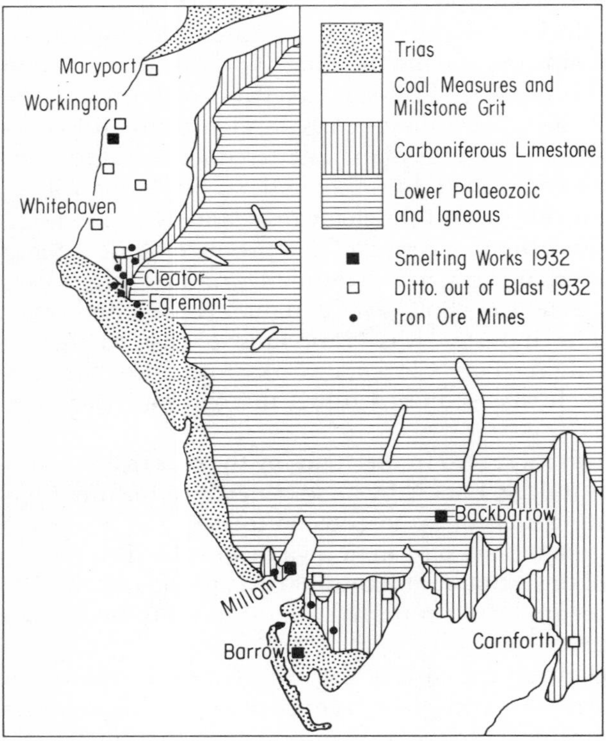

FIG. 171. Map illustrating the west coast iron and steel industry in the 1930s

Almost all the works marked as inactive in 1932 have since been demolished; of those active in 1932 only Workington remained in 1969. Only two mines remained in 1969, near Egremont, and none in the Furness peninsula.

further contracted in recent years; the blast furnaces at Barrow and Millom closed in 1968, and the industry is now represented only by the integrated works at Workington, which has blast furnaces partly fed by imported

1. The ancient Backbarrow works, founded in 1711, continued (in a modernised condition) to make charcoal iron well into the present century; with the virtual extinction of the local charcoal-burning industry it then turned to the use of coke, and it remained until the late 1960s as a rather odd, out-of-the-way relic.

(especially Norwegian) ores, and the only remaining acid Bessemer converters in the country, and by Barrow steelworks (where only the electric furnaces remain).

4. *South Wales*. South Wales illustrates admirably the changes that have been brought about in the location of the iron and steel industry owing to changes in geographical values. The earliest working after the introduction of coke smelting was in the northeastern part of the coalfield, in the uplands at the head of numerous valleys which flow down towards Cardiff and Newport; along a narrow belt, from Aberdare through Merthyr Tydfil, Rhymney, Tredegar, Ebbw Vale, and Blaenavon to Pontypool. Here the clayband ores were richest and the gentle dip of the Coal Measures on this

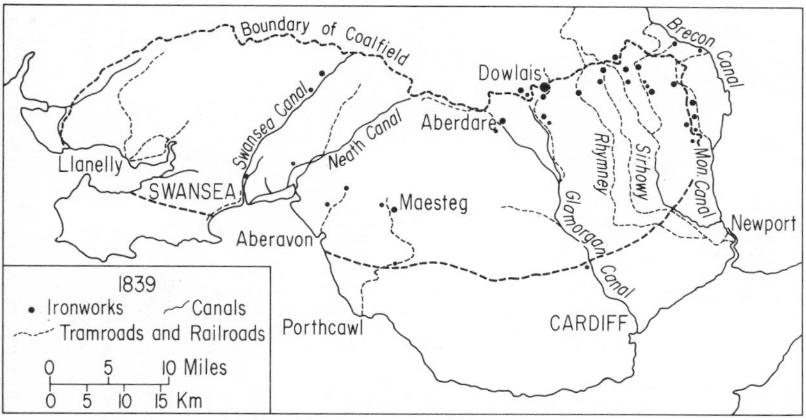

FIG. 172. South Wales iron smelting works, canals and chief tramroads, 1839

northern outcrop of the coalfield permitted the easy extraction of the ores and coal from quarries and adit mines. The setting up of the industry in this inland situation necessitated the growth of improved methods of transport, and the construction of tramroads and canals to the coast further stimulated the iron trade and encouraged the development of docks at Newport and Cardiff for exporting iron and coal (Fig. 172). There were other smelting works at Maesteg and Cwmavon, where the median anticline of the coalfield (cf. p. 315) brought coal and ironstone to the surface. A vast industry developed, reaching its maximum in the 1860s when there were 200 blast furnaces and over 1350 puddling furnaces for wrought iron manufacture.

The introduction of the acid steel industry in the 'sixties, with its accompanying need for non-phosphoric ore, started slowly but surely to undermine the basis upon which the existing iron industry had been built. Interest now centred on the import of rich haematite from Spain. The momentum of the northeastern area sufficed to attract the steel industry to that area, and several large works grew out of the existing smelting and wrought iron works. Dowlais was in fact the largest works in the world at one time.

But this prosperity could not last; all the haematite ore had to be dragged up the valleys from the ports, and the introduction of the basic process gave no relief since by that time the local clayband ores were either exhausted or rapidly becoming uneconomic to work; and competition from better-situated producers in other parts of Britain was intense. So one by one, from the 1880s onwards, the great works—Dowlais, Cyfarthfa, Sirhowy, Blaenavon, and others—closed down, and the last survivor, Ebbw Vale, ceased work in 1929.[1]

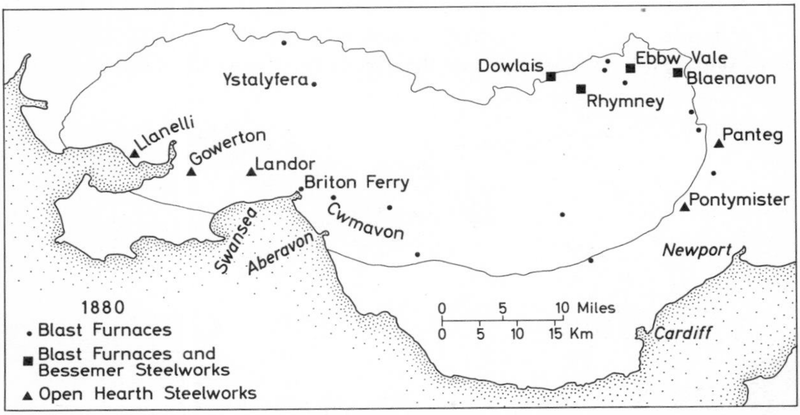

FIG. 173. The South Wales iron and steel industry in 1880

Meanwhile two other trends had developed. First, following the discovery by Siemens in the late 1870s that mild open-hearth steel made an excellent foundation for tinplate, several new steelworks—based on imported pig iron and scrap—were set up in the southwestern part of the coalfield, close to the ports and within the area where the tinplate industry was already largely concentrated—as at Llanelli, Bynea, Gorseinon, Gowerton, Swansea, Briton Ferry, and Port Talbot. A somewhat similar development took place in the east—e.g. at Panteg and Pontymister. Secondly, new 'integrated' iron- and steelworks were set up on the coast—indeed, on the dockside—at Cardiff and at Margam (Port Talbot). Here, obviously, with Spanish, French, and North African ores readily available by sea, was a better situation for the industry than 24 kilometres (fifteen miles) inland and 300 metres (1000 ft) above sea-level.

The extinction of the industry in the northeastern area was the major factor in the severe incidence of the depression, with its attendant unemployment problem, in that part of South Wales, between the wars. The existence of so much 'social capital' in the area, however, prompted the

1. See D. G. Watts, 'Changes in location of the South Wales iron and steel industry, 1860–1930', *Geography*, **53**, 1968, 294–307.

Government in 1936 to encourage the firm of Richard Thomas & Co., which at that time was considering abandoning its interests in South Wales and setting up a new plant at Scunthorpe, to embark on a large scheme for the rehabilitation of Ebbw Vale; and at a cost of over £10m, a vast new integrated works was constructed, with blast furnaces, coke ovens, basic Bessemer and open-hearth furnaces, continuous hot-strip mill and tinplate works. The Bessemer process was first chosen as being less expensive in fuel than the open-hearth, and the need for high-phosphorus iron for basic Bessemer steel entailed the importation by rail of Northampton Sands ironstone from the Wellingborough district (where the Irthlingborough mines had been worked by the previous Ebbw Vale company). Ebbw Vale is now once again one of the greatest single producing units in the country; it has, however, substituted LD converters for basic Bessemer, and has added a continuous galvanising plant.

PLATE 20. Integrated steelworks at Margam, Port Talbot

The success of Ebbw Vale, and particularly the economies to be reaped in tinplate manufacture by the hot-strip process (see below, p. 422) prompted the formation by several South Wales steel firms of the Steel Company of Wales, which in 1947 began a £60m project for the reconstruction of the Margam iron- and steelworks (which is of course dependent on foreign ores) and the installation alongside it of a continuous hot-strip mill (the Abbey works), together with associated cold rolling mills and tinning works at Trostre, near Llanelli and at Velindre near Swansea. These two vast tinplate producing concerns, Ebbw Vale and Margam–Trostre–Velindre, have rendered redundant all the old tinplate mills and most of the smaller steelworks (cf. p. 422); but the hot-strip process also produces other sorts of steel sheet besides that for tinplate, in particular, for motor car bodies.

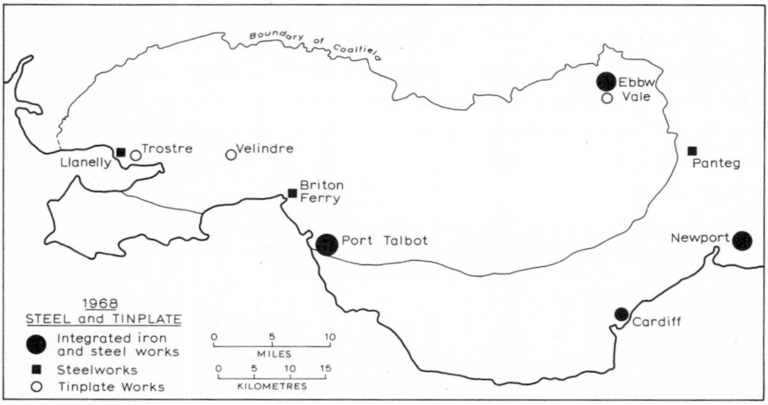

Fig. 174 The South Wales steel and tinplate industry, 1968

Another vast new works—the Spencer works, near Newport, was opened in 1962; with its blast furnaces and LD converters this adds another 1.5 million metric tons to the steel making capacity of South Wales, which is now by far the largest producing district in Great Britain.

So the present picture in South Wales, with a few very large integrated works and a few separate steelworks, is indeed a very different one from that of a hundred years ago—more so, perhaps, than in any other area except Scotland, and the differences are due fundamentally to changes in industrial technique and in the sources of raw materials.

5. *Lincolnshire.*[1] In Lincolnshire, where the first furnace was lighted in 1864, the localisation of the works is due entirely to the existence of the thick, though lean, Lower Lias ore in the neighbourhood of Scunthorpe and Frodingham. The greater thickness of the orebed here and its occurrence over a comparatively small and compact area has permitted a far greater concentration of the smelting industry on this field than was the case, for example, in Northamptonshire. The area is well situated with regard to fuel supplies and export facilities. The nearest mines of the Yorkshire coalfield (which produces good coking coal) are less than 24 kilometres (fifteen miles) to the west, and the port of Grimsby lies only 40 kilometres (twenty-

1. D. C. D. Pollock: 'Iron and steel at Scunthorpe', *East Midland Geogr.*, **3**, 1963, 124–38.

five miles) to the east. The limy nature of the ore, as we have seen, necessitates the import of siliceous Northampton Sands ore from South Lincolnshire, but the presence of appreciable quantities of manganese renders it rather more suitable for basic open-hearth steel making than the Northamptonshire ore. Owing to this fact, and to the compact nature of the industry, this group of works received a marked stimulus during 1914–18, further emphasised during the reconstruction that followed the depression of the 1930s, and the production of steel is now more than ten times what it was in 1913. The plant comprises three huge integrated works, Appleby-Frodingham, Lysaght's and Richard Thomas. The ironstone field is estimated to have a future of at least 200 years before it, and this, together with the relative ease of access to imported ore, provides an assured future for the industry. The momentum of other areas may prevent the rise of any great engineering industry, but Scunthorpe will remain a pillar of strength as a producer of the raw materials of that industry. Pig iron is sent to Yorkshire, Lancashire, Staffordshire, and Scotland, and much of the steel output goes into constructional engineering.

6. *The western Midlands* (*Black Country*, *etc.*). Even in the days of charcoal smelting South Staffordshire, by virtue of its accessible coal supplies,[1] developed an extensive finished iron industry based upon bar iron obtained either from Shropshire and Worcestershire or imported *via* the River Severn from the Forest of Dean and Sweden. Furnaces, forges and slitting mills made use of every available stream for power, and there was especial concentration in the Stour valley.[2] The introduction of coke smelting at once placed the Coalbrookdale area and South Staffordshire in a more favourable position. Rich coal and iron seams, together with fireclays, occurred in the same measures, a supply of flux was locally available in the Wenlock limestone hills of Dudley, and the people were already skilled in metal working. The result was the creation of that vast smelting industry which earned for the South Staffordshire region its unenviable title of 'Black Country'.[3] At the beginning of the nineteenth century the two counties of Staffordshire and Shropshire accounted for 40 per cent of the pig iron production of Great Britain. In North Staffordshire the clayband ores and coking coals of the western part of the coalfield began to be used in the late eighteenth century, and the utilisation of the blackband ores after 1840 brought the smelting industry into the Potteries area.

The Black Country reached its peak in iron production in the late 1850s, with about 180 blast furnaces, but already the local ironstones were showing signs of physical and economic exhaustion and a declining iron output

1. Coal furnaces were used to heat the iron for forging.

2. B. L. C. Johnson, 'The Stour Valley iron industry in the late seventeenth century', *Trans. Worcs. archaeol. Soc.*, 1950, 35–46.

3. See *Birmingham and its Regional Setting*, British Association Handbook, 1950, pp. 161–86, 193–210, and 229–48.

became increasingly dependent on Northamptonshire ores.[1] Wrought iron production, partly assisted by Northamptonshire pig iron, went on increasing until the 'seventies, when there were over 2100 puddling furnaces, but after that appreciable changes took place; iron smelting declined still further, and steel manufacture began to replace that of wrought iron, with an increasing concentration on iron-using industries rather than iron-making. There are now only six furnaces left in Staffordshire, and the last

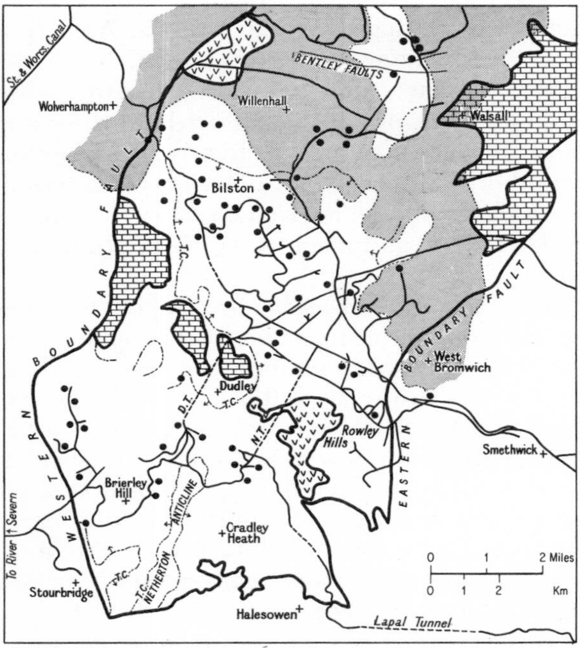

FIG. 175. The Black Country iron industry in the mid-19th century

Within the coalfield are shown (i) Exposed Coal Measures (covered in some areas, however, by Etruria Marl); (ii) Glacial Drift (stippled); (iii) Carboniferous volcanics (V-symbol); (iv) Silurian inliers (brick-work symbol); (v) Outcrop of Thick Coal (T.C.), with arrow indicating dip. Also shown are all the canals and branches, and (black dots) all the ironworks in existence in the 1850s. Note that almost every ironworks lay alongside a canal, and many were served by their own branches and basins. For the ultimate destinations of the canals passing beyond the edge of the map, see Fig. 239.

of the small works left on the Shropshire coalfield, at Oakengates, has been demolished. In North Staffordshire, at Etruria, and in the south, at Bilston, Jurassic ores from Northamptonshire, and some imported ores are used, whilst the small Goldendale works in Stoke-on-Trent uses nothing but

1. The South Staffordshire output of pig iron was 606 500 metric tons (597 000 long tons) in 1858. By 1884 it had declined to 283 500 metric tons (279 000 long tons), 80 per cent of which was made from Northamptonshire ore.

scrap. North Staffordshire, it is true, has coking coal on the spot, but the Shelton works is no longer fully integrated,[1] and Bilston's coke is derived from South Wales. The West Midland iron and steel industry is thus running on 'industrial momentum'. The true Black Country now produces no coal and no iron ore, and, as a result, has come to specialise to an increasing extent in steel making, fostered by the abundance of scrap available from the engineering industries. There are steelworks at Bilston, Round Oak, and Wednesbury. Foundry pig iron is imported from Northamptonshire for working up into cast iron articles, but the last remaining wrought iron works, which produced ships' chains and anchors, closed down in 1961.

7. *The remaining areas* (*except Sheffield*). The remainder of the British iron and steel industry falls into several groups. The former general dominance of pig iron production for foundry work has given way, except in Derbyshire, to a greater concentration on steel. Most of the works are supplied with ore from the marlstone and Northampton Sands fields (cf. Fig. 166). Three principal groups of furnaces may be noted:

(*a*) *Derbyshire and south Yorkshire*, grouped around three centres, in south Derbyshire (Ilkeston), in northeast Derbyshire (Chesterfield), and in south Yorkshire (Rotherham).[2] All these works owed their origin to the clayband ores which were formerly mined in conjunction with the valuable coal seams which occur near the base of the Middle Coal Measures. In a fourth area, around Leeds and Bradford, the Black Bed ironstone and the Better Bed coal were used, and this region was long famous for 'Best Yorkshire' wrought iron. The last surviving works, at Low Moor, was dismantled in 1938, and an alloy steel works has taken its place. In south Yorkshire the Tankersley ironstone and the Silkstone and Park Gate coals provided the basis for the industry which still flourishes in the Rotherham area, where Park Gate is a fully integrated works and Renishaw a small blast-furnace plant producing iron for the steelworks of companies with which it is associated. Farther south, in the Chesterfield area, the Brimington anticline brought the Silkstone coal and several useful ironstone seams nearer to the surface and so localised the furnaces (now dismantled) at Sheepbridge and Staveley, where the speciality is iron pipes for water and gas mains. At Clay Cross an ironworks—also closed—was started in 1847 to provide an outlet for the surplus coke produced by the ovens erected to supply Midland Railway locomotives—perhaps the oddest location factor in the whole of the British iron industry. Farther south still the Erewash valley anticline, bringing the valuable Top Hard (Barnsley) coal to the surface, localised a group of furnaces of which the Stanton works near Ilkeston, world famous for iron

1. Coking coal is mined within a stone's throw of the Shelton works, but when the coking plant needed complete reconstruction in 1968 it was in fact abandoned, and the coal now goes by rail to Shotton on Deeside for coking, returning to Shelton in the same wagons!

2. See K. Warren, 'The Derbyshire Iron Industry since 1780', *E. Midland Geog.*, **16**, 1961, 17–33.

pipes, is the only survivor.[1] All these works now depend entirely on Jurassic ores, and their output (except at Park Gate) is concerned far more with pig iron and foundry products than with steel. At Stanton a recent development is the replacement of the cupolas used for re-melting pig iron and scrap by Kaldo vessels which produce molten iron for the pipe-spinning process.

(*b*) *South Lancashire and North Wales.* The existence of a small quantity of coking coal and the local demand for textile machinery, together with the availability of imported ore supplies *via* Liverpool, gave rise to the iron industry in South Lancashire, and in North Wales the usual association of coal and ironstone in the Flint and Denbigh coalfield led to its development. What remains is either modern or specialised. The smelting works at Wigan and Darwen have long been extinct, and the only works in South Lancashire is the modern plant at Irlam, alongside the Ship Canal; this depends on ore from Northamptonshire and abroad. The huge steelworks at Shotton, to which blast furnaces and coke ovens were added in 1953, are likewise modern; though on Deeside they depend on Birkenhead for imports and exports. The Mostyn ironworks, also on the Dee estuary, which made ferro-alloys, has closed, and the only survivor of the old industrial régime is the Brymbo iron- and steelworks, near Wrexham, which played almost as important a part as Coalbrookdale in the early history of the iron industry.

(*c*) *Northamptonshire and Leicestershire.* In Northamptonshire, as at Scunthorpe, the local ore supplies gave rise to an industry away from the coalfields.[2] The start was slow, for the inland situation and the great momentum possessed by the Midlands as iron producers prevented the rise of an industry comparable with that which developed, based on similar ores, on Tees-side. Moreover, the distance from coal and from the coast prevented the rise of a basic steel industry, and the phosphoric ore produces an easily flowing pig iron which is admirably adapted for making cast iron articles. Until recently therefore the area remained as a producer mainly of foundry and forge pig iron for the vast metallurgical industries of Staffordshire, and the scattered foundry and engineering industries of the southeastern portion of Great Britain. The chief centres of the smelting industry were near Melton Mowbray, in Leicestershire, and at Kettering, Wellingborough and Corby, in Northamptonshire. The last-named village, which saw its first blast furnace in 1910, has since 1933 been transformed into an industrial

1. Both the Silkstone and the Top Hard seams produce hard coal not unlike the Scottish 'splint'; during the nineteenth century many of the Derbyshire ironworks—and there were twenty-six in all—used raw coal rather than coke, and it was only in the first decade of the present century that the introduction of by-product coke ovens altered the balance; the small coal-using furnaces were inefficient, and the collapse of the wrought iron industry in the 1920s removed their market and brought about their demise.
2. S. H. Beaver, 'The development of the Northamptonshire iron industry 1851–1930' (in *London Essays in Geography*, Longmans, 1951, Ch. 3).

town[1] by one of the outstanding developments of the century. Stewarts and Lloyds erected a huge plant, containing coke ovens, blast furnaces, Bessemer and open-hearth steel furnaces, continuous hot-strip rolling mill, and a tube factory, in the heart of the Northamptonshire ironfield. The distance from a coalfield, the requirements of the tube industry, and the phosphoric character of the ores, led to the adoption of the basic Bessemer process, but this has been replaced by the oxygen-using LD process (cf. p. 379).

The declining market for foundry iron, however, has led to the closure of all the remaining blast-furnace works, and Corby thus remains alone, another witness to changing industrial techniques.

Last amongst the 'remaining areas' is Essex. Here, in 1934, at Dagenham on Thames-side, the Ford Motor Co. established coke ovens and a blast furnace, with a motor vehicle assembly plant alongside. Both ore and coal arrive by sea.

8. *Sheffield.*[2] Sheffield must be considered separately, because its industry is so very different from that of the remainder of the region in which it is situated. In common with the neighbouring areas, the Don valley and its tributaries developed, as early as the twelfth century, an iron industry based upon Coal Measure ironstones, local charcoal supplies, and plentiful water power. The Carboniferous sandstones of this region making excellent grindstone material, specialisation commenced in the manufacture of cutlery, and this was encouraged by the settling of skilled Flemish immigrants in the district in the sixteenth century. The impurity of the local ores rendered necessary the import of pure bar-iron from Spain and central Sweden for the finer work. Thus, over 400 years ago, began a branch of the steel industry which, largely owing to the 'deposit' of skilled labour which has accumulated, has remained localised in this region. The only essential changes which have occurred are (*a*) the concentration of the more recently developed heavy steel industries in the Don valley between Sheffield and Rotherham, whilst the manufacture of cutlery and the lighter types of goods is more localised higher up in the Sheaf valley in the centre and south of Sheffield; and (*b*) the specialisation in the finest types of steel goods and in such articles as need a large amount of skilled labour expended upon a small quantity of raw material; this was a result of the inland position and the absence of local ore supplies.

The development of the steam engine and of iron and steel ships gave Sheffield new opportunities for producing fine steel forgings for the crankshafts and axles and, later, huge castings for turbine engines; the constant necessity for improvement in armour-plating and in guns and shells for

1. K. C. Edwards, 'Corby—a New Town in the Midlands', *Tn Planning Rev.*, **22**, 1951, 122–31.

2. For a brief history of the Sheffield steel industry, see Lord Aberconway, *Basic Industries of Great Britain*, Chapter 3; also R. N. Rudmose Brown, 'Sheffield: its rise and growth', *Geography*, **21**, 1936, 175–84; and *Sheffield and its Region* (British Association for the Advancement of Science, Handbook 1956), Chapters 15 and 16.

destroying it opened up further fields;[1] the perfection of high-speed tool steels since 1900 has expanded the steel market still further; whilst the development of chrome-iron alloy, which produces stainless steel,[2] just before the First World War, and the subsequent use of this material not only in the cutlery trade but also for an expanding list of products in the engineering industry, have ensured that, despite its inland position, Sheffield's accumulation of plant and skill will continue to maintain the special branches of the steel industry for which the town is justly famed. The industry underwent a considerable expansion in productive capacity during 1914–18, and a further and even greater stimulus was provided by the Second World War, so that the output in the 1960s was more than three times greater than that of 1913. No pig iron is made in Sheffield, and by far the most important raw material is scrap. Sheffield is almost the only remaining home of the acid open-hearth furnace, and it contains nearly a half of all the electric steel furnaces in the country. In recent years over two-thirds of the local steel output has been derived from electric furnaces, and the city produces 60 per cent of the entire British output of electric steel. In alloy steel the dominance is similar, partly of course since about 80 per cent of all the alloy steel made is produced in electric furnaces. In recent years Sheffield has produced about 60 per cent of the national output of alloy steel.

Ireland. The only steelworks in Ireland is on an island in Cork Harbour; it is based on imported scrap, and the furnaces are oil-fired; in addition there is a small galvanising plant. It serves the Irish market.[3]

The uses of British steel

The following table shows some of the major uses to which the produce of British steelworks is put. An amount of the order of 6 million metric tons a year consists of semifinished steel in the form of blooms, billets, slabs and bars which go to the re-rollers for conversion into finished products. A further 3 million metric tons or so are exported, and almost as much goes into the stockyards of the merchants who supply the multifarious needs of small users. It is worthy of note that the motor vehicle industry is now by far the largest single consumer of steel.

1. Several armour-plate firms, e.g. Brown, Cammell Laird and Vickers, extended their interests and use their Sheffield products in their own shipyards.
2. See Marshal and Newbould, *The History of Firths*, 1924. Stainless steel contains about 18 per cent by weight of chromium and 8 per cent nickel.
3. D. A. Gillmour, 'The Irish Steel Industry', *Irish Geog.*, **6**, 1969, 84–90.

Uses of British steel (thousand long tons)

USER	1965	1967	1969
Stockholding merchants	3 003	2 756	4 382
Motor vehicle industry	1 870	1 568	1 802
Industrial plant and steelwork	1 666	1 330	1 332
Wire manufacturing	1 242	1 045	1 183
Machinery (non-electrical)	1 170	952	1 148
Electrical machinery and goods	553	439	478
Agricultural machinery	131	107	128
Shipbuilding and marine engineering	585	418	574
Railway rolling stock	221	156	134
Coal mining	464	475	398
Construction (civil engineering)	794	589	630
Cans and metal boxes	597	658	691
Hollow-ware	184	146	185
Drop-forgings	762	629	813
Nuts, bolts, screws, etc.	231	220	217
Other users	3 368	3 781	4 185
Exports	3 350	3 712	3 374
Semi-finished steel (blooms, etc.)	7 097	5 875	7 049
Total	27 288	24 856	28 703
Total (metric tons)	27 726	25 255	29 162

The iron and steel trade

The following table gives details of iron and steel imports for certain years.

It will be observed that much of the import is of 'raw' or 'semifinished' materials, destined (pig, blooms, and billets) for remelting and processing, or (sheets, plates, and rods) for further fabrication. The postwar expansion of British output seems to be reducing the quantity of imports, and our nearest continental neighbours are taking an increasing share of the trade. But it is a trade that fluctuates widely from year to year.

[*chapter continues overleaf*]

Iron and steel imports by varieties and countries
(thousand long tons)

	ITEMS	1913	1933	1937	1950	1960	1965	1969
VARIETIES	Blooms and billets	514	230	435	161	220	16	576
	Sheet and tinplate bars	345	85	151	23	19	—	—
	Steel bars, angles, and shapes	134	187	72	8	76	103	268
	Plates and sheets	169	36	49	93	625	250	462
	Iron bars, rods, and angles	200	15	25	—	1	—	—
	Hoops and strips	72	79	72	6	20	36	40
	Girders and beams	109	77	71	13	3	9	35
	Wire rods	95	42	97	66	88	34	57
	Pig iron	185	93	644	195	223	314	169
	Other varieties	408	127	423	192	407[1]	438[2]	1140[3]
	Total	2231	971	2039	757	1682	1200	2747
	Total (metric tons)	2267	987	2072	769	1709	1219	2791

[1] Includes 213 Ferro-alloys. [2] Includes 304 Ferro-alloys.
[3] Includes 325 Ferro-alloys and 80 high-pressure conduits for hydroelectric plants; also 424 steel ingots.

		1913	1933	1937	1950	1960	1965	1969
COUNTRY OF CONSIGNMENT	Belgium	583	468	528	95	115	57	124
	United States	154	2	315	62	331	28	248
	France	37	113	316	301	65	52	79
	Luxembourg	*	57	134	42	17	13	6
	Netherlands	7	11	28	46	191	143	518
	Canada	*	*	164	39	286	72	71
	Germany	1198	55	133	71	127	171	155
	Sweden	209	23	105	14	53	114	211
	Other Countries	43	242	316	87	497	550	1335[1]
	Total	2231	971	2039	757	1682	1200	2747
	Total (metric tons)	2267	987	2072	769	1709	1219	2791

* Not available. 1 long ton (2240 lb) = 1.016 metric ton.
[1] Includes 355 Norway, 127 USSR.

In the next table exports are similarly enumerated.

The 1913 figure has never since been reached, and probably, with world output rising rapidly, it never will be. Naturally enough, it is 'finished' materials rather than 'raw' iron and steel which are exported, and the increasing relative importance of tubes and pipes is a reflection partly of increased British output (notably from Corby) and partly of increased world demand for such products for use in oil transmission (note e.g. exports to Iran) and as tubular scaffolding. The destination of the exports no longer shows the marked Commonwealth bias characteristic of former years; the USA and our European neighbours are now the main customers.

Iron and steel exports by varieties and countries
(thousand long tons)

	ITEMS	1913	1933	1937	1950	1960	1965	1969
VARIETIES	Plates and sheets	204	213	387	471	689	1177	1086
	Pig iron	945	108	153	35	146	88	80
	Tubes and pipes	400	273	376	510	735	386	425
	Railway rails	500	56	148	175	90	267	128
	Steel bars and angles	251	107	231	522	497 }	2205	2393
	Miscellaneous	2669	1165	1314	1468	1468 }		
	Total	4969	1922	2609	3181	3360	4123	4112
	Total (metric tons)	5049	1953	2650	3232	3414	4189	4178

		1913	1933	1937	1950	1960	1965	1969
COUNTRY OF DESTINATION	Australia	567	120	149	462	198	111	52
	South Africa	261	170	304	191	82	195	47
	Iran	4	*	70	101	78	80	128
	India, Pakistan, and Ceylon	896	187	258	253	364	178	144
	New Zealand	154	54	122	179	147	145	90
	Netherlands	146	43	105	78	118	97	110
	British East Africa	19	7	21	96	46	40	44
	British West Africa	46	18	68	95	90	67	79
	Argentina	358	110	192	66	87	109	79
	Finland	*	18	30	78	52	90	106
	Canada	187	123	169	242	200	219	139
	Irish Republic (Eire)	*	33	65	101	63	86	162
	Other countries	2331	1039	1056	1239	1854	2706	3232[1]
	Total	4969	1922	2609	3181	3360	4123	4112
	Total (metric tons)	5049	1953	2650	3232	3414	4189	4178

* Not available. [1] Includes USA 782, Sweden 206, Spain 288, Italy 134.
1 long ton (2240 lb) = 1.016 metric ton.

17
Iron and steel: the secondary industries

The iron and steel industry obviously does not come to an end with the casting of steel ingots and the rolling of plates, bars, and rails. Ingots, plates, and bars, although the finished products of the steel furnaces and mills, are the raw materials of a number of other industries, which thus depend for their existence upon the output of the home steel industry or upon the imported material. Chief amongst these are shipbuilding, tinplates, galvanised sheets, rails, tubes and pipes, constructional steelwork, iron castings (stoves, radiators, cylinder blocks, etc.), wire and wire products (netting, nails, etc.), and the various industries concerned with the manufacture of engines and machinery, and their constituent parts (cf. p. 436). To describe all of these would be impossible within the limits of a single chapter. We may, therefore, concentrate our attention on some which are geographically most interesting. Three groups of industries will be studied:

(*a*) *The tinplate industry* and its allies, concerned with the covering of thin steel sheets with a coating or film of tin, zinc, or a mixture of tin and lead;
(*b*) *The shipbuilding industry*, employing vast quantities of thick steel plates and girders; and
(*c*) The various *engineering industries*, depending for their raw materials upon foundry and forge iron from the blast furnaces and various forms of 'semifinished' steel from the mills. Some branches of engineering industry—the building of steam locomotives for example—have declined: in contrast there is the huge expansion of the automobile and aircraft industries and of the complex electrical machinery industry.

A few simple geographical considerations will reveal certain definite localising factors in each of these groups. In the case of the tinplate industry the bulkiest raw material is the steel plate which is to be coated; moreover, the tin has to be imported and much of the produce is destined for export. It would seem, then, that a situation within one of the great seaboard steel-producing areas is most favourable. With shipbuilding we shall likewise expect to find a concentration mainly on those navigable estuaries or sheltered waters where the heavy iron and steel industry is also developed. The engineering industries, however, being concerned, generally speaking, with more valuable products, do not show the same tendency to be concentrated in close proximity to the parent industry; in fact, since the finished articles are usually more costly to transport than the raw materials of which they are composed, and since also the assembly of many different raw materials may be involved, we shall find that whilst many of the heavy engineering industries are concentrated upon the coalfields, in the case of the lighter types of engineering product the existence of a market for the goods, or the availability of good transport facilities, may exercise as much control over the location of the industry as do the sources of raw materials. Moreover, as with the primary iron and steel producers, there are many examples of engineering industries the location of which is inexplicable in terms of presentday geographical and economic circumstances; we must often delve into the past to discover the location factors involved.

The tinplate and allied industries[1]

Since the tinplate industry has changed out of all recognition since the 1930s most of what follows must now be regarded as historical geography; but a brief outline of the main features of the industry up to 1939 is necessary for the complete understanding of the subsequent developments.

The art of giving a coating of some non-ferrous metal to a thin sheet of iron, in order to preserve it, was first practised in Bohemia about the fourteenth century. The metal used was tin and the sheets thus became known as 'tin-plates'. Subsequently the metals zinc and lead have also been employed for the same purpose, giving rise to the trade names 'galvanised sheets' (coated with zinc) and 'terne plates' (coated with a mixture of tin and lead).[2] Recent developments include the use of chromium and aluminium as coating materials.

The first successful attempt to make tinplate in Britain took place in 1720 at Pontypool, where a small iron industry already existed, and a good water supply was available for working the hammers which produced the flat plates, and for washing the plates before tinning. From this small beginning grew the great industry in South Wales. Its growth was aided by two subsequent events: first the invention in 1728 of a method of rolling plates (a much quicker and more efficient process than hammering), and secondly the substitution of coal for charcoal in the iron smelting industry, permitting a much greater output. By the end of the eighteenth century a dozen works were producing tinplate, and our imports of that commodity had been replaced by a growing export trade. The industry spread rapidly during the first half of the nineteenth century, especially in Monmouth-

1. See J. H. Jones, *The Tin-plate Industry*; Rider and Trueman, *South Wales*, Chapter 10; E. H. Brooke, *Monograph on the Tin-plate Works in Great Britain*, Swansea, 1932.
2. The name 'terne' reflects the fact that such plates are composed of *three* metals—iron, lead, and tin; but it may also be derived from the French *terne* = dull or tarnished, in view of the contrast with the brightness of tinplate.

shire, Glamorgan, Gloucestershire, and Staffordshire (the last two supplied with iron from the Forest of Dean). All the works, however, were subsidiary to pre-existing smelting works or forges which were favoured with abundant water supply.[1] The reasons for this early concentration in South Wales are not clear. Probably the chance selection of Pontypool as the first site for a tinplate works prompted other ironworks in the neighbourhood to adopt this profitable sideline as an outlet for their iron at a time when the iron industry was not very flourishing; the nearness of South Wales to the Cornish tin supplies may also have given that area an advantage. In addition, the momentum derived from an early start sufficed to maintain the supremacy of South Wales in the industry even when the methods of production were radically changed, while the inland position of Staffordshire, and the decline of the iron industry in the Forest of Dean, prevented the rise of those areas in competition with South Wales. In 1850 thirty-five tinplate works existed, twenty-two of which were in South Wales. By 1875 the total had increased to seventy-seven, fifty-seven of which were in South Wales.

The last quarter of the nineteenth century witnessed vast changes in the nature and location of the tinplate industry. By the early 1870s Malayan tin had replaced the failing supplies from Cornwall, but this was of minor importance compared with the substitution of mild steel plates for wrought iron plates. Acid open-hearth steel suitable for rolling into tin plates was first produced at the Landore works (near Swansea) in 1875, and the cheapness of steel compared with puddled iron, together with its greater suitability—steel plates having a smoother surface which absorbed less tin—soon resulted in its adoption in the tinplate works. But acid steel could only be made from imported pig iron, and in consequence steelworks, followed by tinplate mills, began to be set up in the neighbourhood of the ports of Llanelli, Swansea, and Briton Ferry, and the 'centre of gravity' of the tinplate industry in the vales of Swansea and Neath migrated downstream. Eight new steelworks, all associated with tinplate mills, were erected between 1875 and 1900. Many of the older tinplate works persisted for a considerable time; but the momentum possessed by an individual works—usually a small, comparatively inexpensive unit—was not great, and in consequence migration was not difficult. This 'reshuffling' of the industry in the 'eighties, combined with the economic disaster produced by the American tariff of 1890, which almost cut off our chief market for tinplate, naturally resulted in a period of depression, but the first quarter of the present century witnessed a great expansion of the tinplate trade, and a remarkable concentration of the industry upon the Swansea–Llanelli region.

Before considering the reasons for this development, let us further examine the nature and methods of the industry. Tinplates have many uses, and the expansion of the petroleum industry, and of canning industries of all kinds,

1. See H. C. Darby, 'Tin-plate migration in the Vale of Neath', *Geography*, **15**, 1929, 30–5.

has naturally been accompanied by a great increase in the production of the tinplates from which the containers are made. Until the development of plates coated with lacquer, now widely used, tinplate made the only metal container capable of being hermetically sealed; and it is perfectly safe for the canning of vegetables, fruit, fish, meat, and every other kind of perishable article. It is interesting to note the changing markets for tinplate. So long as it was mainly used for containers for fruit, fish, meat, and mineral oil the countries producing those commodities were the chief buyers of tinplate. With the increase in world output of mineral oil, the greater part is bulk handled, but petrol cans still dominate in remoter developing countries. Elsewhere more and more commodities are canned—beer for example—and Britain's great markets now are her European neighbours not producing their own (the Scandinavian countries, Spain and Portugal, Greece) together with South and South-West Africa, Argentina, Hong Kong, and even USA; but the list and the quantities vary widely from year to year (see p. 423).

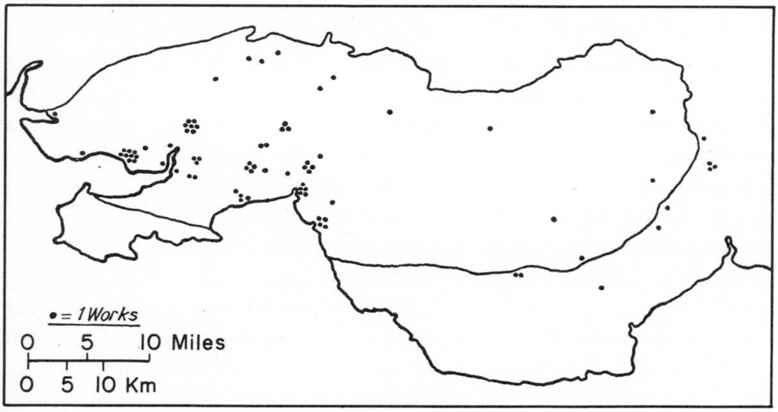

FIG. 176. Tinplate works in South Wales, 1932

Until the introduction at Ebbw Vale, and more recently at Margam, of the continuous hot-strip process, tinplates were produced by rolling out steel bars into thin sheets 0.25 to 0.5 mm (0.01 to 0.02 in) in thickness and cutting to the required sizes. These 'black plates' were then pickled in acid to remove the surface scum of oxide, heated again ('annealed') and re-rolled to produce a smooth, shiny surface, pickled again and then passed through a bath of molten tin. Coal-fired furnaces were used for heating the bars and for the annealing process, and often anthracite was used for maintaining the heat of the tin bath.

The advantages of the South Wales area as a whole for the production of tinplates were fairly obvious from the start. We have further seen how the industry, following the construction of the coastal steel mills, migrated downstream to Swansea and Llanelli. The subsequent dominance of this area, however, was probably due to the coincidence of local fuel, the proximity of the non-ferrous smelting and refining industries which provided a reservoir of skilled labour and a source of sulphuric acid, the good rail communications and the development of the port facilities of Swansea (e.g. Prince of Wales Dock, 1882).

The distribution of tinplate works in South Wales, before the advent of the vast new integrated works, is shown in Fig. 176. With the exception of a few near Newport, the largest and most important works were all located within a few miles of the coast in the Loughor, Tawe, and Neath valleys, or at the ports of Llanelli, Briton Ferry, Swansea, and Port Talbot.

The introduction of the hot-strip process, which uses a succession of rollers to produce a continuous run of steel sheet, which can be coiled and later rerolled and cut as required, has revolutionised the industry. First at Ebbw Vale in 1937, and after the war at Margam, with associated cold-rolling and tinning plants at Velindre, near Swansea, and Trostre, near Llanelli, the new methods have made it possible to produce a greater output of tinplate from two basic plants than from seventy of the old pack mills before the war. As a result, all the old mills have been closed. Seldom can a single technical development have had such a catastrophic effect. Almost the entire national output of tinplate—which in the 1960s stood at a higher level than ever before—now comes from Ebbw Vale and the Margam–Velindre–Trostre complex. A further technological development has been the introduction of electrolytic tinning in place of the old hot-dip method; and almost 90 per cent of the output is now produced in this way.

Isolated centres of the old tinplate industry in Britain were Lydney, Gloucestershire, Stourport, Worcestershire—the last witnesses of the former prosperity of the trade in the Forest of Dean and around the Black Country—and Mold, Flintshire. The last-named centre owed its existence largely to its proximity to the port of Liverpool (which is the chief tin smelting centre in the country), and to the Brymbo steelworks.

Black plates (thin steel sheets without the coating of tin) form the basis of the enamelled hollow-ware industry, which has spread rapidly in South Staffordshire and in other parts of Britain. They are also exported either for this purpose, or for conversion into tinplates by certain countries which, although they can perform the tinning operation, cannot, or do not, produce the required quality of steel.

The manufacture of *galvanised sheets* was formerly associated with that of tinplate. When iron was the raw material South Staffordshire was the chief centre, but with the change-over to steel South Wales became the largest producer. The concentration in the Swansea district was natural enough, bearing in mind that the galvanising process was very similar to tinning, but it was favoured also by the fact that Swansea was the most important centre in the country for the smelting and refining of zinc. Just as the tinplate industry has undergone rationalisation, so has galvanising. In South

The tinplate trade (thousand long tons)

	1913	1921	1929	1931	1950	1956	1961	1969
Production (Tin, Terne, and Black Plates)	822	291	880	717	764	918	1077	1321
Retained in Britain	328	50	269	317	513	615	638	942
Exported	494	241	611	400	251	303	439	379

Exports of tinplate (thousand long tons)

	1913	1921	1929	1931	1950	1956	1962	1969
Australia	29	18	57	37	65	96	12	0
New Zealand					17	14	7	16
India and Pakistan	52	28	23	8	17	19	6	16
Singapore and Malaysia	17	12	27	14	8	17	15	6
Hong Kong						5	12	24
Canada	10	3	28	37	*	*	*	0
British W. Indies						*	5	9
Other Commonwealth						18	20	28
South and SW Africa					19	1	53	18
Argentina	19	4	27	17	33	38	37	33
Brazil	14	2	22	18	3	*	7	6
Japan	28	22	32	22	*	*	*	0
China	15	8	20	16	*	*	*	2
Sweden						12	22	23
Norway	25	5	17	9	*	3	18	5
Denmark					8	3	18	17
Netherlands	43	20	44	37	4	8	17	0
Spain	12	9	28	19	*	16	32	36
Portugal	14	4	18	19	*	3	17	19
Italy						4	29	9
Greece						—	12	9
United States						—	36	42
Total	494	241	611	400	251	303	456	379
Total (metric tons)	502	245	621	406	255	308	463	385

* Under 3000 tons. 1 long ton (2240 lb) = 1.016 metric ton.

Wales the process is now undertaken at the great integrated works at Ebbw Vale and Port Talbot, and also at Gorseinon, which is one of the few remaining independent steelworks (cf. p. 408). One Black Country works survives, at Wolverhampton, whilst the trade in North Wales, formerly favoured by the proximity of the Flintshire zinc mines and carried on at

Mold, is now confined to the great steelworks at Shotton on Deeside. In Scotland two plants in the Motherwell area (one of them the integrated works at Ravenscraig) also produce galvanised sheets.

A coating of zinc protects the steel sheets from corrosion, and galvanised sheets, usually corrugated, are extensively employed for roofing and fencing in tropical countries. Popularly known as 'corrugated iron', they are far more durable than wood, and unaffected by insects. They do, however, rust through quickly under tropical conditions and corrugated asbestos and aluminium are often preferred. Galvanised sheets are also employed to an increasing extent for cisterns and tanks. The production of galvanised sheets is about a quarter that of tinplates. The exports are somewhat more restricted in their distribution than is the case with tinplates, and much of the tonnage is destined for Commonwealth countries.

The galvanising of finished steel products (e.g. tanks, cisterns, dustbins) is associated with the engineering industry rather than with steel making, and the most important area is the Black Country.

Finally, in recent years two new methods of coating thin steel sheets with non-ferrous metals have been developed. At Trostre an alternative for tinplate is now made, using electrolytically deposited chromium and chromium oxide in place of tin; it is a Japanese invention and is known as Hi-Top; it takes a lacquer coating better than tinplate. At Shotton, plant is being erected to use a process of coating steel sheet with aluminium powder; the market for such a product will be the manufacture of motor-vehicle silencers and other articles where corrosion resistance at high temperatures is required.

Shipbuilding

The shipbuilding industry, like the iron industry, has undergone revolutionary changes in its geographical distribution during the last two centuries. The changes have been essentially due to alterations in the nature, and thus the distribution, of the raw materials employed, and to technical progress. The requirements of shipbuilding are two:

1. A navigable sheltered waterway, as near to the sea as possible, in which the vessels can be launched.
2. An easily available supply of the appropriate building materials.

When ships were constructed almost entirely of wood, the presence of fairly good timber supplies in many parts of Britain enabled the industry to be carried on at a large number of small estuaries and harbours all round the coasts, and the ease of import of timber permitted this to survive long after the local supplies were exhausted. The Thames below London and the Tyne were two of the most important centres, and such places as Inverness, Dundee, Whitby, Hull, Bristol, and Newport turned out many of those vessels—merchantment, whalers, and ships of war—which helped to lay the foundations of the British Empire. The substitution, during the second half of the last century, of iron, and later steel, as the basis of the shipbuilding industry was naturally followed by the gradual decline of all those centres which were remote from the iron and steel-producing regions, and the increased importance of those estuaries, such as the Tyne, Tees, and Clyde, which were in close proximity to such regions, and which could accommodate vessels of ever increasing size.

Anything like a detailed history of the shipbuilding industry is impossible here;[1] we can only indicate in broad outline the general trend of events during the past century or so. The principal features may be outlined as follows:

Raw materials

Until about 1850 most ships were built of wood and were of quite small size —in 1815 the average size of the vessels in the British Merchant Fleet was 100 tons, and in 1855 the largest vessel in the world, the Cunard *Persia*, was only 3600 tons. The first iron vessel was launched in 1812, and the first iron vessel to cross the Atlantic (the *Sirius*) did so in 1838, but even in 1850 only 9 per cent of the new tonnage constructed was of iron. By the 1870s, however, iron was fast supplanting wood as the standard material, and in 1880 under 4 per cent of the new tonnage was of wood. From this point, however, steel began to usurp the position which iron had gained and its success by reason of its greater tensile strength per unit of weight was assured. By 1900 the new tonnage built of iron had fallen to nil.

The use of iron and later of steel in shipbuilding proved the salvation of the British industry, for our home timber supplies had been reduced almost to nothing, and the repeal of the Navigation Acts in 1849, by throwing open our commerce to the world's ships, would have put British building at the mercy of other countries, such as the USA, where abundant timber was available near tide water. The advantageous situation of our coal and iron supplies not only prevented any such catastrophe, but gave to the British industry a stimulus which maintained its world supremacy for the century that followed.

Method of propulsion

Steam was first used as a method of propelling a ship in 1788, and the steamer *Sirius* crossed the Atlantic in 1838. By 1850, however, sailing vessels

1. A good short summary will be found in *Survey of Metal Industries*, pp. 363–9. Greater detail is given in D. Pollock, *Shipbuilding Industry*, Methuen, 1905. Some splendid histories of individual shipbuilding firms are available; see for example K. C. Barnaby, *100 years of Specialised Shipbuilding and Engineering* (Thorneycrofts), Hutchinson, 1964; Sir A. Grant, *Steel and Ships: the history of John Brown's*, London, Joseph, 1950; *Two hundred and fifty years of shipbuilding by the Scotts at Greenock*, Glasgow, 1961.

still represented 95 per cent of the total British tonnage, and not until the 1880s did the sail tonnage begin to drop below the tonnage under steam, since when its decline has been very rapid. The earliest steamships were propelled by paddle wheels. After 1850, though many paddle steamers continued to be built, the screw propeller became the more general method. Great advances were made in the efficiency of the steam engines by the employment of the multiple expansion principle; but the greatest revolution came at the end of the century with the introduction in 1897, by Sir Charles Parsons, of Newcastle, of the steam turbine. In recent decades oil has almost completely replaced coal as the fuel for steamships. Oil has, of course, the advantages of being less bulky, more easily stored, cleaner and quicker to load, and requiring less manpower at the boilers. Great strides have been made also, within the last few decades, in the adaptation of the Diesel engine, consuming heavy oil, to marine propulsion, and the tonnage of motor ships launched annually in the United Kingdom is now far greater than that of steam driven vessels (see table opposite). In 1936 of a world total of over 65 million tons of shipping, coal-fired steamers represented 32 million tons, oil-fired steamers 20 million tons, and motor-driven vessels just over 12 million tons. By 1968, the world total had risen to 186 million tons, of which coal-fired steamers represented only 3 million, oil-fired steamers 71 million, and motor-ships 120 million tons. In 1968, only 1.6 per cent of the world's shipping was using coal, as against 45 per cent in 1939 and 97 per cent in 1914. In 1952, for the first time since the introduction of steam, not a single coal-fired ship was launched from British yards. The consequences for the British coal trade and tramp shipping of this wholesale abandonment of coal have been profound.

New types of vessel

The development of the giant passenger liner, of the large mixed-traffic vessel (usually with refrigerated cargo space), and more recently of the 'supertanker', of specialised vessels for the carriage of liquefied natural gas, of bulk carriers for ore and grain traffic, and of the 'container' ship, have added new problems for the shipbuilders to solve, and great advances in the techniques of construction have been made, especially since the Second World War.[1] Ships are now being built of dimensions that would have been thought utterly impossible only twenty-five years ago. Whereas, for example, the standard oil tanker of the 1930s was a vessel of about 10 000 to 12 000 tons, and the Americans built several hundreds of 16 000-ton tankers during the war, tankers of 24 000 tons made their appearance in the late 1940s, only to be superseded a few years later by 'supertankers' of 30–40 000, and then in the 1960s by still larger vessels of over 100 000 tons

1. See S. H. Beaver, 'Ships and shipping: the geographical consequences of technological progress', *Geography*, **62**, 1967, 133–56.

United Kingdom shipbuilding: tonnage launched (excluding warships) (thousand tons)

CLASS	1913	1921	1929	1933	1937	1942[1]	1949	1952	1961	1968
Steamers:										
Coal fired	1911	*	750	78	307	*	23	0	0	0
Oil fired	0	*	306	5	220	*	413	440	572	12
Total Steamers	1911	1430	1056	83	527	814	436	440	572	12
Motor Ships	8	102	464	48	388	448	832	854	682	886
Barges, etc.	13	6	3	2	5	13	0	8	2	0
Total	1932	1538	1523	133	921	1276	1267	1302	1256	898
Tankers	238	251	175	3	144	312	434	370	393	81

[1] War peak year. * Not available.

and indeed up to 350 000 tons. A few such vessels can quickly alter the statistical picture of world's shipping. In the late 1930s oil-tankers represented about 15 per cent of the world's mercantile marine; by 1952 this had risen to 22 per cent, and by 1968 the 4540 tankers then afloat totalled 72.2 million tons, or 39 per cent of the world's fleet. Similarly with the bulk carriers that have largely replaced the old-fashioned tramp ships of a generation ago: ships of between 35 000 and 100 000 tons are now being used for iron ore traffic; they can often be employed for grain or other bulk cargoes as well, and for oil.

The day of the outsized passenger liner is over, largely owing to the competition of air travel (cf. p. 714); the *Canberra* of 1960 was only 45 000 tons; the 80 000 ton *Queens* have gone, and their replacement is a vessel of only 65 000 tons. Even the shape of the big passenger ships has altered. At the other end of the scale the small ferryboat is being replaced by the hovercraft, based on an entirely different principle and capable of two or three times the speed of the conventional ship.

Geographical distribution of shipbuilding

The increase in the size of ships and in the bulk of the machinery and component parts of which they are built has greatly accentuated the localisation of the shipbuilding industry upon the largest estuaries adjacent to the steel-producing regions. Because the shipbuilding industry is essentially an *assembly* industry, however (cf. motor vehicles, p. 444), it is possible for many outlying centres to survive, albeit in most cases by specialising in certain types of craft. Broadly speaking the industry falls into four groups: (1) the major estuaries that build most of the tonnage and all the large vessels—Clyde, Tyne, Wear, Tees, Mersey, Belfast Lough, with Barrow in a non-estuarine situation; (2) the minor estuarine and coastal centres, in general capable of building small general-purpose cargo ships and coasters —such as Dundee, Grangemouth, Aberdeen, Ardrossan and Lowestoft; (3) the 'small-ship' centres, including the fishing-boat builders of the Humber group and the yacht and hovercraft centres on the south coast—Southampton and Portsmouth; (4) the Royal Dockyards, sited for strategic reasons, sometimes very long ago, on certain tidal waters in southern England.

In 1958 the total employment in shipbuilding, ship repairing and marine engineering was 275 000 (including 37 000 in marine engineering), but this figure had fallen to 202 000 at the Census of Production in 1963, including 39 000 in marine engineering. The loss of employment in shipbuilding and repairing is thus of the order of 70 000 in fifteen years.

The relative importance of the various districts is shown in the table below. But an important word of caution is necessary in interpreting the recent figures; sharp fluctuations from year to year have always occurred, for an individual ship takes a long time to build and only appears in the statistics on its launching. A yard may nowadays launch nothing for a whole year and then produce a 100 000-ton tanker—so one must not assume from the table that in 1968 the Wear had unbounded prosperity whilst Barrow was in the depths of depression.

Shipbuilding: tonnage launched[1] (*excluding warships*).
Gross tonnage (thousands)

AREA	1913	1921	1929	1933	1937	1950	1962	1965	1968	1968 No of ships
Clyde	685	505	532	49	337	438	363	316	189	*25*
Tyne	366	355	272	11	102	206	197	159	120	*13*
Wear	300	144	245	12	156	191	214	253	238	*18*
Tees	308	164	92	15	83	141	51	44	171	*7*
Belfast	129	93	144	14	74	131	89	130	98	*2*
Mersey	34	51	55	3	34	67	45	41	25	*2*
Dundee	18	17	17	7	21	19	18	13	4	*1*
Humber	49	31	27	8	16	20	12	14	13	*27*
Barrow	2	64	20	0	48	60	33	62	0	*0*
Leith	19	17	32	7	36	30	32	17	18	*5*
Other Districts	22	97	87	7	14	22	19	24	22	*34*
Total	1932	1538	1523	133	921	1325	1073	1073	898	*134*[2]

[1] Only vessels of 100 tons and over are included in this table and the previous one (*Lloyd's Register of Shipbuilding*—annual summaries).
[2] Of these 134 ships only one, of 12 000 tons, built on the Clyde, was a *steamship*.

The northeast coast

The northeast coast includes the estuaries of the Tyne, Wear and Tees. On the Tyne the major yards are at Walker, Wallsend and Willington Quay on the north bank and Hebburn, Jarrow and South Shields on the south bank. Much of the industry is now in the Swan Hunter group. Ships of all kinds have been launched from these yards, though in the past the emphasis was on tramp steamers, colliers and warships (from Vickers-Armstrong) rather than on passenger liners. The emphasis now is on tankers, bulk carriers and container ships. On the Wear at Sunderland there are five yards, four on the riverside and one, unique in the country, that launches direct into the North Sea. The modern specialities, as on the Tyne, are large tankers, bulk carriers and cargo liners. On the Tees there are two centres, on the estuary itself at Haverton Hill and South Bank, and at West Hartlepool just north of the river mouth. Again, the major output is of freight-carrying vessels of various kinds.

PLATE 21. Shipyards at Clydebank

John Brown's yards (marked by the T-cranes) in which the *Queens* were launched; the building slip is oriented towards the mouth of the river Cart (extreme left) which effectively increases the width of the Clyde at this point.

The Clyde

The Clyde was never as important as the Tyne in the days of sailing ships. Its rise is more recent: it was in 1812 that Bell's *Comet* was launched by John Wood at Port Glasgow, but most of the growth is post-1840. It was not an ideal waterway for shipping—at the end of the eighteenth century no boats drawing more than 1.5 metres could reach Glasgow; only by persistent dredging has it been improved and maintained. Indeed, for 19 kilometres below Glasgow the Clyde has been described as 'artificial as the Suez Canal'. Of the twenty shipbuilding firms formerly located on a 32 kilometre (20-mile) stretch of the river below Glasgow a number have been driven out of business by the economic stresses of the last decade; Upper Clyde Shipbuilders have incorporated most of those at the Glasgow end, with yards at Govan on the south bank and at Scotstoun and Clydebank on the north bank, whilst the Scott Lithgow group controls the yards at Port Glasgow and Greenock; the Denny yard at Dumbarton, that built many cross-channel steamers, closed in 1963. Both naval and merchant vessels up to the largest pre-1940 sizes were constructed—including in the interwar period the battleship *Vanguard* and the two *Queens*. Since the war the fortunes of the Clyde have declined somewhat, though the *Queen Elizabeth II* was launched from the same yard as her predecessors in 1968. The river is not ideal for launching vessels of exceptional size (and the *Queens* berth at John Brown's yard at Clydebank is carefully aligned so as to project the launched vessel into the mouth of the river Cart), and Clyde participation in giant tanker building is likely to be at the Port Glasgow end.

The northeast coast and the Clyde together have been responsible since the First World War for about 75 per cent of the British output of ships, and with the increasing size of bulk carriers and tankers this percentage is likely to rise rather than fall, for it is in these estuaries that there is the greatest capacity for launching large vessels. Indeed in 1968 the percentage was 80. The other areas are much smaller, both in extent and in output.

Belfast

Although not backed by a great iron and steel producing region, the head of the sheltered Belfast Lough, by the estuary of the Lagan, has remained an important shipbuilding centre by reason of the ease of import of the raw and semifinished materials required. Both western Scotland and the English northwest are capable of supplying Belfast with steel, and other materials can be imported via other British ports or directly from abroad. Belfast-built liners, cargo ships and tankers are to be found on most of the world's shipping routes. Harland & Wolff Ltd have extensive shipyards and engineering shops; the largest vessel launched to date is a 250 000-ton tanker for Esso in 1970. In addition to manufacturing all types of propelling machinery Belfast engineers have materially aided the development of the Diesel engine for nautical purposes. Shipbuilding employs nearly 8000 people at Belfast, and marine engineering another 4000.

Birkenhead

At Tranmere, on the southern side of Birkenhead, are the large yards of Cammell Laird, builders of warships, cargo ships, tankers and passenger liners.

Barrow

Shipbuilding was not important here until the local iron ores came to be used in large quantities for steel-making. The first vessel was launched in 1873. The greater part of the industry is under the control of Vickers. Both naval and merchant vessels have been built and Barrow has a distinguished list of liners and tankers to its credit, including the first 100 000-ton tanker launched from a British yard. There has also, for no particular geographical reason, been a specialisation in the building of submarines.

Minor Scottish centres

Aberdeen, at the beginning of the last century, was the chief shipbuilding port in all Scotland, and later on in the 1850s and 60s many famous 'tea clippers' were launched from its yards for service between Britain and China. Subsequently it has come to specialise in vessels for its own particular trade—trawlers, whalers and other fishing craft. Also on the Scottish east coast, Dundee, Grangemouth and Leith build small cargo ships, and there are small yards at Troon and Ardrossan on the Ayrshire coast.

The English east coast

A number of ports on the east coast and its inland waterways have small shipyards, but the vessels constructed are mostly small and of specialised character. The Humber region offers a remarkable example of an industry carried on solely as a result of momentum gathered in past years. Always an important fishing centre, this estuary naturally developed the building of all kinds of fishing boats, and the ease of access, by rail and canal, to the Sheffield district and by sea or by rail to the Tees-side steelworks, together with the old-established import trade in timber, have resulted in a continuation of the industry. Hull itself, Beverley on the river Hull, Selby on the Ouse, together with Knottingley, Goole and Thorne, have yards capable of building trawlers and drifters and other small craft, for which various firms in Hull or elsewhere build the engines. At some of the yards the vessels are launched sideways into the narrow river on which the yard stands. The Humber retains its position in the front rank of fishing craft construction centres (see Fig. 257).

Further south, a somewhat similar specialisation in fishing and small coastal craft is to be found at Lowestoft.

Minor centres

A number of other ports have small shipbuilding industries, but the vessels constructed are mostly small; vessels of under 100 tons are not included, except for certain purposes, in Lloyd's Register, but as an industry the building of small craft is of increasing importance. The motor cruiser or yacht or even a small boat, has now become a 'status symbol'. Southampton, Cowes and Portsmouth specialise in yachts, motor boats and certain types of small naval craft, and more recently in hovercraft. On the North Devon coast a yard at Appledore specialises in tugs, dredgers, trawlers and the like.

The Thames no longer builds ships (though a small yard remains at Faversham on the Medway). But for a long period it was one of the major centres. The Blackwall yard, where the Orient Line had its origin, was founded in 1612, and a number of famous ships, including the *Warrior* (the first ironclad, built at Canning Town 1859) and the *Great Eastern* (built at Millwall in 1855) have been launched from Thames-side yards. During the Victorian period some of the most prosperous firms in the country were located here; but the distance from the major steel-producing areas has driven them all out of business or to other localities, and all that remains is the extensive repair service referred to below. The surprising thing is that the industry managed to overcome the economic difficulties involved for so long a period: the battleship *Thunderer*, the last big vessel to be launched, was only completed in 1911.

In the Irish Republic there is a shipyard, state subsidised like the nearby steel industry, at Cork.

Attention must finally be called to the shipbuilding activities of the Royal Dockyards. Although a considerable proportion of the naval requirements is ordered from public companies, a good deal of warship construction is, or was, carried out at Devonport, Chatham, and Portsmouth. All these places occupy heavily fortified situations where large expanses of tidal water are available for the 'housing' of the British fleet. In many cases only the hulls of the new vessels are erected at the dockyard, the machinery being supplied by public firms of marine engineers.

Ship repairing

In addition to the actual building of new ships, the repairing and overhauling of existing vessels is an industry of considerable importance. In its distribution, however, this industry is much more widespread than shipbuilding. The chief necessity is a dry dock or some other means of raising the ship out of the water so that access to the hull may be obtained (see Fig. 177). It should be remembered, however, that many repairs may be effected without this preliminary procedure and that ordinary building yards may be used for repair work. Since it is obviously most economical to repair a ship on the termination of a voyage, during which the need for repair becomes apparent, the great ports of the country, as well as the shipbuilding areas, will share in the repairing industry; for the amount of material necessary to effect the repairs will not be large and may be of very diverse nature.

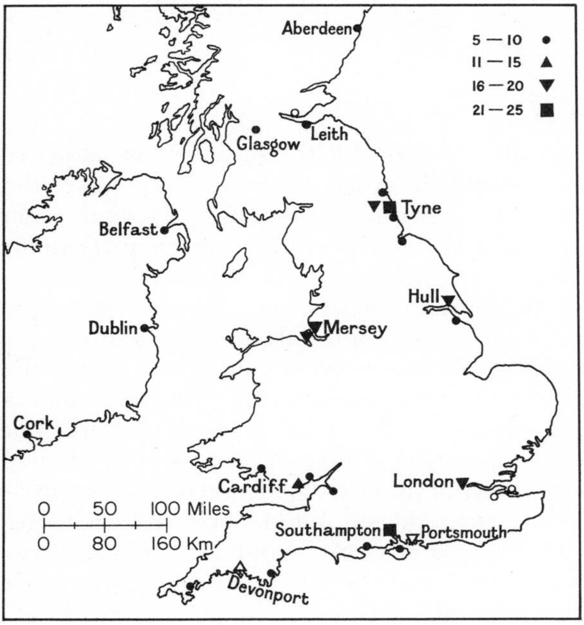

FIG. 177. Facilities for ship-repairing in Britain—number of dry docks and slipways, 1951. Belfast now has twelve

The symbols in outline are naval dockyards. In addition to the ports shown on the map, forty-nine other ports have ship-repairing facilities.

Whilst the Tyne, as judged by the number of dry docks, etc., dominates the industry, dealing with all classes of cargo ships, liners, and tankers, the ports of London, Southampton, Liverpool, and Belfast have extensive facilities, largely controlled by the great shipbuilding firms,[1] for the repair of the large liners and other vessels which visit them. The Clyde is not nearly as important for repairing as for building—although more repairing is done than is suggested by Fig. 177, many building yards, when not engaged in new construction, being used for this type of work.

The advent of the giant tanker and the increasing size of bulk carriers have created problems for the ship repairing industry as they have for the shipbuilders. New dry docks have had to be constructed in order to cope

1. Harland and Wolff, for example, own extensive yards at Liverpool and Southampton and control the repair yards of the Port of London Authority.

with the overhaul of such vessels; such provision has already been made at Birkenhead, London, Newcastle (Hebburn) and Glasgow, whilst the deep water of the Fal estuary has encouraged a firm at Falmouth to offer similar facilities, and in Belfast a new dry dock capable of taking vessels of up to 200 000 tons has been built.

Marine engineering

Although the chief new materials necessary for the shipbuilding industry are steel plates and girders, castings, forgings, tubes and pipes, i.e. the 'heavy' products of the iron- and steelworks, numerous other items enter into the construction of a ship, and there is an increasing tendency to employ aluminium and alloys thereof in the fabrication of the superstructures. A large amount of finished machinery such as winches and pumps is required, and large supplies of furnishing materials, joinery, paint, rope, and nautical instruments are also necessary. Many subsidiary industries are thus involved. Chief of these is marine engineering—the construction of the boilers, turbines, and driving gear for all kinds of vessels. The marine engineering industry, dealing as it does in very bulky, though valuable, pieces of machinery, must of necessity be located in close proximity to the shipyards. In many cases the shipbuilders control their own marine engineering works. The chief centres of the industry are the Clyde (Glasgow, Clydebank and Greenock) and the northeast coast (Newcastle and Sunderland). Employment in the marine engineering industry recorded by the 1948 Census of Production amounted to 54 000, of which over 21 000 were in Scotland and nearly 18 000 on the northeast coast. The 1963 Census of Production recorded 39 000, but this figure is for establishments dealing solely in marine engineering and does not include those employed in the marine engineering sections of shipbuilding firms.

Shipbuilding—Britain and the World

The shipbuilding industry has long been described as a 'trade barometer', as it reflects, perhaps more faithfully than any other trade, the general state of the world's commercial activity. It also reflects in a very remarkable way the incidence of wars, as Fig. 178 shows. At the same time it is the key to the prosperity, or otherwise, of a large number of subsidiary industries. Quite apart from the steel industry, so many other trades are involved that a slackening of the demand for new ships may be followed by a depression, the repercussions of which are felt throughout the country. The shipyards suffer most, however. The iron- and steelworks may have other products, such as boiler plates, girders, and rails, to which they can turn their attention, and the engineering shops may obtain orders for other types of machinery, but a shipyard has difficulty in changing.

The British shipbuilding industry faces many problems. The cream of the world's passenger traffic now goes by air and the days of the great passenger liner are probably over though there is an apparently elastic demand for holiday cruises from which many of the shipping companies derive their main profitable revenue. Whatever the reason may be—high labour costs, restrictive practices, out-of-date methods and equipment, design, tardiness of delivery, unattractive financial terms are all named—Britain has lost the dominating position formerly held in shipbuilding.

The following table lists the output of the world's chief shipbuilding countries in certain selected years, the selection emphasising the booms and depressions. Complete figures for the war peak year, 1943, are not available, but the world total in that year reached the staggering figure of 13 885 000 tons, largely owing to the enormous tonnage launched in the USA. In that same year the British output represented a mere 8 per cent of the world total. In 1958 Britain fell behind both Japan and West Germany in ships launched. Japan continues to lead the world since 1956, and in 1968 British launchings represented only 5 per cent of the world total. Indeed, since 1958 Britain has been a net *importer* of ships, and in 1967 no less than fourteen countries were building ships for British owners!

World's shipbuilding (excluding warships) gross tonnage (thousands)

COUNTRY	1913	1919	1926	1930	1933	1937	1957	1962	1968
United Kingdom	1 932	1 620	639	1 478	133	921	1 414	1 073	916
Germany	465	*	180	245	42	435	1 231	1 010	1 344
France	176	32	121	101	34	26	428	481	502
Netherlands	104	137	94	153	36	183	476	418	293
Italy	40	83	-20	87	17	22	485	348	497
USA	276	4 075	150	247	11	239	359	449	416
Japan	64	612	52	151	74	451	1 511	2 183	8 644
Other countries	265	585	218	427	141	433	2 597	2 413	4 312
Total	3 332	7 144	1 674	2 889	489	2 710	8 501	8 375	16 944
Per cent by UK	58	23	38	51	27	34	17	13	5

* Figures not available.
In 1968 'other countries' include Sweden 996 and Norway 500.

Engineering

If the recent history of shipbuilding makes dismal reading, it is very much otherwise with the engineering industries. The term 'engineering' now covers a vast range of industries. Beginning during the Industrial Revolution with the making of engines and textile machines, it now embraces all kinds of machinery and the machine and hand tools with which to fashion them.

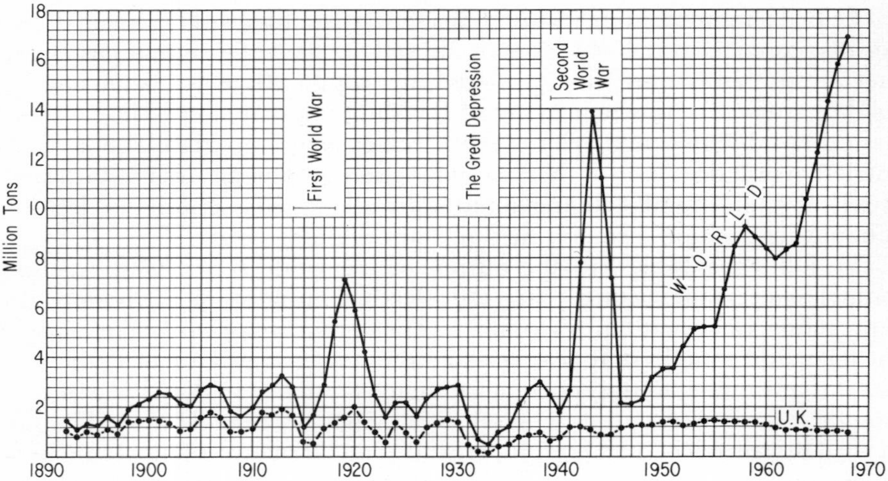

FIG. 178. Shipbuilding in the UK and the World, 1892–1968
In terms of tonnage launched, the UK figure has varied comparatively little in 75 years, but world output since the Second World War has expanded enormously, particularly in Japan.

These fundamental branches have always been in large measure dependent on the iron and steel industry for their raw materials. During the twentieth century, however, other industries have arisen, concerned mainly with electrical apparatus of many kinds, from generators, motors and cables to radios and computers, the raw materials of which include non-ferrous metals, plastics and ceramics as well as iron and steel. In addition, there are the industries that produce self-propelled vehicles—locomotives, automobiles and aircraft; these are categorised separately in official statistics, but we can include them in this chapter since they also depend mainly on metallurgical industries for their raw materials.

The two following tables demonstrate the relative importance of the various branches.

Employment in engineering, 1966 (thousands)

Radio and electronics	306
Electrical machinery	236
Wires and cables	67
Telegraph and telephone apparatus	96
Other electrical goods	215
Scientific and photographic instruments	138
Industrial plant and steelwork	162
Agricultural machinery	38
Textile machinery	59
Machine tools	96
Other machinery	370
Other mechanical engineering	253
Total engineering	2352
Motor vehicles	500
Aircraft	255
Locomotives	36
Railway rolling stock	42
Motor cycles and pedal cycles	26
Total vehicles	865

Value of engineering products (£ million)

	1960	1966
Electrical machinery	312	454
Insulated wires and cables	136	254
Radio, radar and electronic capital equipment	60	329
Domestic electrical appliances	130	157
Other electrical goods (exc. radio)	212	322
Industrial plant and fabricated steelwork	294	527
Contractors' plant and quarrying machinery	93	143
Metal working machine tools	112	167
Mechanical handling equipment	87	133
Engineers' small tools	65	92
Industrial engines	81	138
Pumps and industrial valves	93	144
Textile machinery	84	111
Other machinery (not electrical)	572	775

Note. The overall increase of 60 per cent in the value of the engineering industry's output between 1960 and 1966 is of course in some measure due to inflation, but clearly some branches—the radio and electronic in particular—have expanded at far more than the average rate.

The geographical principles underlying the distribution of the engineering industries have already been touched on (p. 418). It is probably true to say that there are few towns of any size in the country which have not either a foundry or some small factory making use of iron and steel. This being so, a rough classification of the engineering towns is necessary in order that we may better comprehend the distribution of the industry. Engineering towns in Britain may be divided into two distinct types:

(*a*) Those in which the engineering industry is preserved by reason of the local supplies of coal and iron; e.g. the towns of the coalfields. The particular branch of engineering involved will depend primarily on various local factors which we shall examine in detail later;
(*b*) Towns not situated on, or quite close to, the major coalfields and iron-producing centres. These towns may be further subdivided into two classes: (1) Those in which the presence of the engineering industry is due to some definite local demand for certain types of iron products. Under this heading come most of the engineering centres of eastern England, where the manufacture of agricultural implements is of quite early origin. (2) Those in which the engineering industry is of much more recent growth and is due either to the situation of the town with regard to railways—as, for example, former locomotive building towns of Swindon and Ashford (Kent)—or to the presence of large and increasing agglomerations of population which

can be drawn upon as a source of labour supply, e.g. Letchworth (Herts.), Luton, and Slough.

This classification cannot be regarded as comprehensive or exhaustive, but it may serve as a guide in our study of the engineering industry of Britain. The chief engineering provinces are seven in number. They may be briefly summarised as follows:

Manchester and south Lancashire. Textile machinery, constructional engineering, engines and locomotives, and electrical apparatus.
Yorkshire, Nottinghamshire and Derbyshire coalfield. Textile machinery (West Yorkshire), heavy engineering, locomotives; the special trades of Sheffield and the miscellaneous industries of Derbyshire and Nottinghamshire.

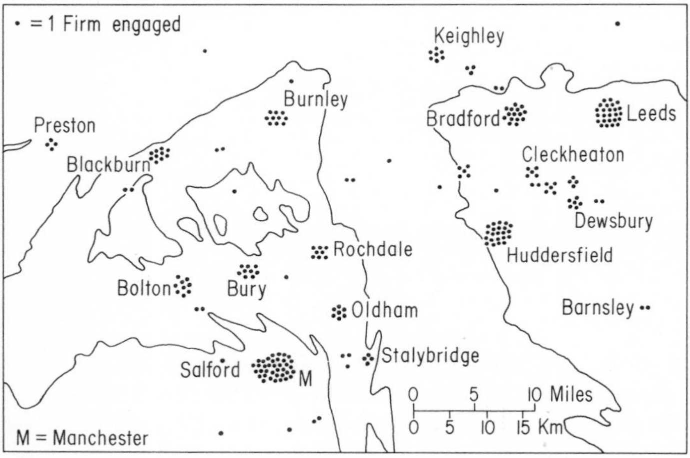

FIG. 179. The textile engineering industry of Lancashire and Yorkshire. Lines show boundaries of exposed Coal Measures. This map refers to the interwar period but the general distribution remains

The northeast coast. Marine engineering (see above), constructional engineering, locomotives.
The Scottish Lowlands. Marine engineering (see above), constructional engineering, heavy machinery, locomotives.
The Black Country and Birmingham. Heavy foundry and forge work, constructional engineering, miscellaneous trades of Birmingham.
The smaller Midland coalfields. Miscellaneous industries of North Staffordshire and Warwickshire.
Southeastern Great Britain. Scattered miscellaneous machinery industries and foundry products, especially agricultural and excavating machinery and locomotives.

Before we consider these provinces in greater detail certain rather specialised industries call for individual comment.

Textile machinery

The manufacture of textile machinery is dominant, as one would expect, in the great textile working regions of southeast Lancashire (nearly two-thirds) and the West Riding (a fifth) (see Fig. 179), the only other centres of any importance lying within the regions of minor specialised textile production. The industry has been located here on both sides of the southern Pennines ever since the first machines for working cotton were invented (i.e. since the end of the eighteenth century), and the growth of the textile industries, together with the presence of coal and the proximity of the iron and steel districts of Yorkshire and the Midlands, have given it such a momentum, that it easily retains the premier position, which it has always held, supplying not only the manufacturers, but also, until comparatively recently, most of the other textile industries of the world. The map shows that nearly every important town in the textile manufacturing area of Lancashire and Yorkshire has one or more factories engaged in producing machinery for working cotton, wool, or the modern manmade fibres. Although the Lancashire towns confined themselves mainly to cotton-manufacturing machinery, and the West Riding towns to woollen and worsted machinery, a few firms in the towns where the two regions approach most closely (e.g. Huddersfield, Keighley, Rochdale, and Oldham) produced machinery for both industries; and firms making machinery for the newer textiles are to be found in both regions. Some of the larger firms turn out practically every machine which is used in the textile industries; others specialise in certain types of machine, or machines for special processes.

Exports of textile machinery (thousand long tons)

COUNTRY	1913	AVERAGE 1921–25	1929	1933	1948	1962	1966
USSR	15.3	0.6	7.0	0.2	—	4.7	1.8
France	12.6	12.2	7.5	0.9	3.5	2.6	2.8
Belgium	10.3	5.8	7.5	1.6	4.0	1.5	1.8
Germany	13.9	2.7	5.1	1.6	—	1.9	3.9
Italy	2.4	4.1	4.3	1.3	0.5	2.7	1.4
China	3.3	9.4	10.6	2.5	2.8	—	1.0
Japan	19.7	15.0	14.4	1.0	—	1.4	0.5
India	50.3	49.1	38.2	24.9	23.0	16.5[2]	23.3[2]
Brazil	11.9	8.2	3.3	1.9	8.7	2.2	1.4
Other countries	38.3	28.3	78.6	20.6	17.5[1]	44.5[3]	46.2[4]
Total	178.1	135.4	126.5	56.5	60.0	78.0	84.1
Total (metric tons)	180.9	137.6	128.5	57.4	60.9	79.2	85.4

[1] Includes Egypt, Argentina, Australia, and Canada. [2] Includes Pakistan.
[3] Includes Australia (3.1), S. Africa (3.0), USA (2.8).
[4] Includes USA (6.2), S. Africa (3.7), Australia (2.5).

Great prosperity was enjoyed in Lancashire while the factories were building machinery for the growing cotton industries of Japan, China, and India, but the excess of productive capacity thus created caused a slump. Foreign firms even bought secondhand machinery from Lancashire's closed mills.

In the textile machinery industry as a whole, employment declined from 70 000 in 1921 to 60 000 in 1924, and 48 000 at the Census of Production in 1930. The revival revealed by the 1948 Census of Production (67 000) was largely due to the manufacture of machinery for working the newer textile fibres (see Chapter 21), but at the 1963 Census of Production the figure was down to 48 000 again.

Of the other localities where textile machinery is made, the chief are Nottingham and Leicester, which between them share the bulk of the trade in hosiery machinery. Nottingham, in addition, is supreme in the manufacture of lace-making machinery. Macclesfield occupies a similar position with regard to silk machinery; and Dundee makes most of the machinery used in the jute and hemp trades. A few other scattered centres in Scotland make various kinds of textile machinery, e.g. Hawick and Galashiels (woollen), Paisley and Glasgow (cotton). Belfast supplies textile machinery for the working of flax, hemp, manmade fibres, and wool to most parts of the world. Much of the produce of the textile machinery industry, as suggested above, is destined for export.

The 1913 export figure has never again been attained. The actual amounts exported to individual countries may fluctuate considerably from year to year—but it is still true that India (now India and Pakistan) is by far our best customer. The Far Eastern market has seriously declined, but our near European neighbours can still be relied upon to take textile machinery, whilst growing textile industries in other parts of the world are buying British machines.

Locomotive building

The locomotive-building industry of Britain, although of long standing (some of the firms are over 100 years old), was distributed in an extraordinary fashion. Two factors contributed to this. First, locomotives can run on wheels under their own power, and so do not have to be built in the locality in which they are to work. This means that while we might expect, by reason of the bulk of the raw materials required, that the industry would be primarily located in those areas where iron and steel were produced, it would not surprise us to find building centres in places remote from such regions where other local factors may have given rise to the industry. Secondly, it was the policy of the principal British railway companies (and in this respect they were almost unique in the world) to build most of their own engines and not to place extensive orders with engineering firms. This resulted in the setting up of a locomotive industry in a number of places where, despite the distance from the raw materials, the railway companies concerned considered that the nodality of the site with regard to their particular system warranted the establishment of the works. Of the sixteen engineering companies which were building locomotives in the thirties, all

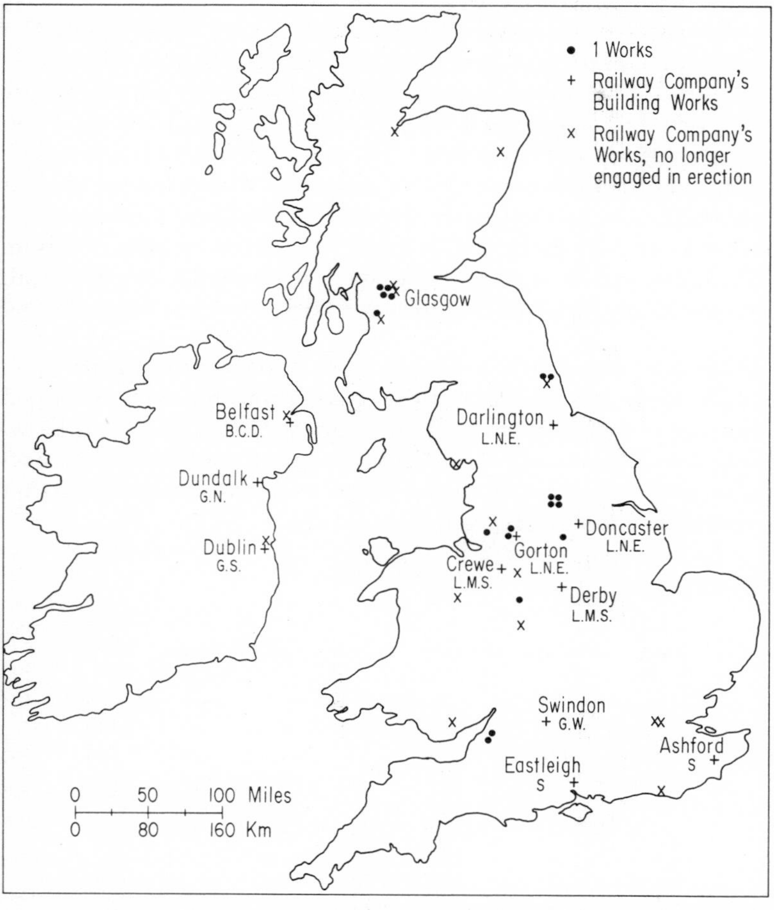

FIG. 180. Map showing locomotive-building centres about 1930. Initials refer to the railway companies which existed before nationalisation in 1948

but five were noticeably grouped about four nodes, each in the heart of one of the engineering provinces, based upon the coalfields, already mentioned (Fig. 180). The Glasgow–Kilmarnock area had four large works, three belonging to the North British Locomotive Co., which was the largest concern of its kind in Europe. Two works were situated on Tyneside and three, the largest that of Beyer, Peacock & Co., in the neighbourhood of Manchester. Another group of four had their headquarters in Leeds. The remaining works were situated at Darlington, Sheffield, Stafford, and two at

Bristol. With the exception of the Bristol works, both of which built locomotives mainly for industrial purposes (works, docks, etc.) and not for ordinary railways, all these locomotive-building establishments were essential components of that great engineering industry of Britain which owes its development to the proximity of iron and coal. Many of the works formerly belonging to the railway companies, on the other hand, were situated at some distance from coal and iron, and the only explanation of their location is that they occupy nodal points on the railway system to which, before nationalisation, they belonged. Such are Crewe, Swindon, Oswestry, Eastleigh, Brighton, Ashford, and Stratford.[1] The works of the railways which served the industrial north, however, were naturally situated near to their sources of raw materials, as Doncaster, Derby, Darlington, Gorton, Horwich, Kilmarnock, and St Rollox (Glasgow). The Irish centres, Dublin, Belfast, and Dundalk, are all ports on the east coast where the raw materials and fuel were most easily obtainable across the Irish Sea from England and Scotland.

After the amalgamation of the principal lines into four groups in 1923, the building of locomotives at many of the smaller and less well equipped works, e.g. Oswestry, Stoke, Barrow, Kilmarnock, Gateshead, and Cowlairs (Glasgow), was abandoned, their activities being confined to the execution of repairs; and subsequently the process of rationalisation still further reduced the number of works engaged in building.

Export of steam locomotives (tons)

DESTINATION	1913	AVERAGE 1921–25	AVERAGE 1926–30	1932	1937	1946	1948	1962
Argentina	11 571	2 686	7 814	91	114	—	3 114	—
Brazil	1 279	158	1 079	—	2 151	748	827	—
Egypt	224	—	2 254	27	1 976	—	835	—
India, Pakistan, and Ceylon	14 810	16 622	14 037	672	1 571	14 142	515	—
Australia	5 287	511	1 552	4	12	964	—	—
South Africa	3 878	2 382	1 868	62	798	9 711	9 039	—
British W. Africa	635	1 533	1 047	501	611	254	2 021	—
British E. Africa	1 094	825	1 338	—	—	474	—	—
Other countries	5 494	8 799	6 917	1 208	2 044	16 810	10 189	—
Total	47 121	33 461	38 495	3 483	9 277	43 103	26 540	64
Number of locomotives	?	662	681	169	147	437	280	2

Note: No *steam* locomotives have been exported since 1965.

1. The railway-created towns, Crewe and Swindon, will be more fully referred to in Chapter 27. See pp. 700–701.

All the preceding account of the locomotive-building industry has been written in the past tense because it refers to the building of steam locomotives, an industry which is virtually dead. The table of exports shows this also but at the same time is an indication of its former importance. No new steam locomotive has been built for British railways for some years; haulage as in most other parts of the world is by diesel or electric locomotives. One of the problems of British Railways (see p. 708) is that many of the building and repair shops shown on Fig. 180 are now redundant. The building and equipping of diesel and electric locomotives is an offshoot of electrical engineering (see p. 448), with major centres at Rugby, Loughborough and Preston, but the railway workshops at Crewe, Swindon and Derby continue to assemble and repair such locomotives for British Rail. Export destinations vary widely from year to year, but are mostly amongst the underdeveloped countries of the world.

Export of locomotives, 1966 (tons)

DESTINATION	DIESEL	ELECTRIC	RAILCARS
Mexico	—	—	1021
Nigeria	890	—	—
Cuba	423	—	—
Mozambique	312	—	—
Canada	—	292	—
India	48	215	—
Malaysia	183	—	—
Total	2414	670	1238

Motor vehicles

The motor industry is of comparatively recent growth. Undoubtedly its early location stemmed from that of the bicycle industry, which expanded greatly after about 1860 in Birmingham, Wolverhampton and Coventry so that by 1914 bicycle manufacture was the third largest employer in the West Midlands, after brassfounding and jewellery. The first Lanchester car was made in Birmingham in 1893, the first Daimler at Coventry in 1896. The Rover factory began in 1896, Standard in 1903 and Austin in 1905. Commercial vehicles began with Daimler at Coventry, followed by Standard in 1912 and Guy at Wolverhampton in 1914. The growth of these car-building plants engendered the development of the components industry—metal castings, stampings and forgings in the Black Country, springs in Redditch and West Bromwich, steel tubes in Birmingham, and so on, and also provided a great stimulus for the rubber industry (Dunlop began in

Birmingham in 1890), and for the machine tools industry that provided the wherewithal to fashion the parts.

By 1907 the motor industry claimed 53 000 employees; by 1931 the total had risen to 190 000, and by 1966 there were half a million.

Production of vehicles, 1956, 1966 and 1969 (thousands)

TYPE OF VEHICLE	1956	1966	1969
Aircraft	1.6	0.4	—
Passenger cars	708	1604	1717
Commercial vehicles	297	439	466
Tractors	109	214	180
Motor cycles	124	105	—
Pedal cycles	2873	1423	—

Between the wars the motor-car industry witnessed a gradual concentration into big firms; the number of manufacturers fell from forty to twenty-five; and after the Second World War, Austin merged with Morris to form the British Motor Corporation, Leyland with Standard-Triumph, and Jaguar absorbed Daimler, Guy and Coventry Climax; and more recently Leyland merged with British Motor Corporation. Jaguar and Rover survive on the basis of high-class products—but both are in other sections of the industry as well, Jaguar with commercial vehicles and Rover with Land Rovers. Only a few of the relatively small firms have survived—like Morgan at Malvern, Jensen at West Bromwich and Reliant at Tamworth.

It cannot be too strongly emphasised that the motor industry is essentially an *assembly* industry; the average motor car has no less than 20 000 components, made from many diverse materials—ferrous and non-ferrous metals, plastics, glass, leather, upholstery, rubber, and so on. Consequently its ramifications extend far beyond the localities—such as Cowley, Dagenham and Longbridge—that catch the public eye. About 24 per cent of the national employment in vehicle manufacture is in the West Midlands (it was 40 per cent in 1931), in which region 11.6 per cent of all the manufacturing employment is provided directly by the motor industry. Such is the importance of component manufacture, however, that no less than 45 per cent of all the manufacturing employment in the region is in firms that have *something* to do with the vehicle industry.

The factors that have influenced the location of the vehicle-building industry are five: (*a*) the fact that it attached itself to localities where the cycle industry already flourished; (*b*) the very wide range of industrial products that enter into a motor vehicle; (*c*) the skilled character of much of the work involved—at least in earlier years and before the development of mass-production on assembly lines—so that an attachment to already existing engineering localities was natural enough; (*d*) the ready transportability both of the component parts and of the assembled vehicles, so that 'raw material' supplies exercise little control over location; and (*e*) Government encouragement or direction towards 'Development Areas' where vehicle assembly can provide much-needed employment and a boost to the local economy.

Outside the West Midlands—where the three major centres, Coventry, Birmingham and Wolverhampton, each have all branches of the industry represented—the main localities are in metropolitan England, and more recently in Lancashire and in Scotland. In the London region the presence of a huge population, the existence of numerous other engineering trades and the great demand for vehicles have contributed towards the rise of the motor industry. The Associated Equipment Co., which builds London's buses, is located in the western suburbs, whilst the Ford works is situated on Thames-side at Dagenham. Luton (Vauxhall) may be regarded as a self-contained 'satellite' of London, as also may Oxford. Here, at Cowley, from small beginnings (actually a bicycle-repair shop) the enormous business of Morris (Viscount Nuffield) was built up.

Outlying older centres are Crewe (the home of Rolls-Royce) and Bristol, together with Manchester and Leyland in south Lancashire, where the existence of many other engineering industries and the presence of a large labour force encouraged the growth. Leyland is the greatest centre for commercial vehicles.

The new areas in the industry owe their existence to Government encouragement of manufacturers to set up in the Development Areas that are in need of economic resuscitation. On Merseyside, since 1960, a vast plant (covering over 140 hectares and employing 11 000 in 1968) has been set up by Ford at Halewood on the Lancashire side, whilst Vauxhall employs nearly 11 000 people at Hooton, near Ellesmere Port on the Wirral side. A third plant, begun in 1966 at Speke, near Liverpool, belongs to Standard-Triumph (now part of the Leyland–BMC group). The total employment in the motor industry on Merseyside in 1968 was over 26 000.[1] In Scotland, the Rootes group have an assembly works at the new industrial town of Linwood, twelve miles southwest of Glasgow, and BMC are located at Bathgate, halfway between Glasgow and Edinburgh.

To an increasing extent the fabrication of motor-car bodies has become separated from the assembly plants. The pressing of sheet steel (much of it from Port Talbot) into body shapes takes place at Llanelli, Swindon, Wolverhampton and other places, and the bodies are transported on double-decked road vehicles or rail cars to the assembly plants. As for components, while it is true that thousands of individual firms contribute in one way or another, there is a remarkable concentration in the west Midlands, and

1. J. Salt, 'The motor industry on Merseyside', *Geography*, **53**, 1968, 320–2.

some firms exercise a most powerful influence. Thus Lucas of Birmingham produce about 90 per cent of all the electrical equipment used by the motor industry (lamps, dynamos, wind-screen wiper motors, etc.), and about 85 per cent of all clutches come from a firm in Leamington Spa. Most of the chromium-plated fittings are produced in the Black Country, as are castings and engine components; wheels are made in Wellington (Salop), Bilston, Darlaston and Coventry; of the major tyre-producing firms Dunlop, Pirelli, Michelin and Goodyear are all located in the west Midlands. All the new assembly plants in other parts of the country have to rely for almost all their component supplies on the west Midlands.

The phenomenal rise of the motor industry as an exporter of major importance is shown in the following tables.

Export of motor vehicles (thousands)

	1913	1931	1935	1950	1960	1964	1969
Motor-cars	8	19	46	274	570	680	772
Tractors				86	155	170	133
Commercial vehicles				70	146	164	179

Export of motor vehicles (cars) (value in £ thousands)

COUNTRIES	1950	1962	1966
Australia	64 858	12 132	12 979
Canada	26 151	17 731	14 291
Sweden	11 451	7 738	6 634
New Zealand	10 192	11 262	13 040
S. Africa	8 883	12 140	17 237
India	6 477	779	22
USA	8 270	40 829	51 704
Brazil	5 158	—	37
Netherlands	5 225	5 512	8 288
Others	43 267	105 811	128 024[1]
Total	189 932	213 934	235 019

[1] Includes Denmark £9.2m, France £9.2m.

Aircraft

Closely allied to the motor industry is the aircraft industry, which in 1966 gave employment to 255 000 people in a large number of factories. It was at first less concentrated, and more widely scattered, than the motor industry, partly, no doubt, for strategic reasons and partly due to its need for airfields. The 'big four' in the industry are Hawker Siddeley, British Aircraft Corporation, Rolls-Royce and Bristol Siddeley, who between them employ 160 000 people. The next largest is Short's of Belfast, and there are many smaller specialised firms. The activities of the 'big four' are more or less evenly divided between four major areas—the northwest (especially Manchester and the Preston area), the Midlands (especially Coventry and Derby), the southwest (Bristol and Cardiff) and the southeast (many centres from Hurn and Hamble to Weybridge and Kingston, Hatfield, Stevenage and Luton), with outlying centres in the Glasgow area and at Brough in East Yorkshire. Engine production is concentrated mainly in Derby, Bristol and Coventry. The industry is also concerned with the production of rockets and other missiles.

Road vehicles and aircraft—exports (£ million)

	CARS	COMMERCIAL VEHICLES	MOTOR CYCLES	CYCLES	AIRCRAFT
1913	2·4				0·05
1931	3·4				1·9
1935	6·3				2·7
1950	190				34
1955	120	37	7	21	40
1960	218	39	5	14	62
1962	214	43	4	11	41
1966	234	136	13	7	130

The totals include also chassis, parts, spares, etc., but not aircraft engines (which in 1966 were valued at £71m).

Electrical engineering

With the development of domestic electricity and more recently of radio and television, the smaller electrical trades have expanded rapidly and have spread over many parts of the country; for the produce comprises for the most part small but valuable consumer goods, manufactured from a great variety of raw materials, and the industry can thus be carried on almost anywhere, the site depending more on the availability of labour and markets than upon railway facilities or the location of raw material supplies. The more prosperous cities and conurbations have attracted a great variety of such industries—radio, batteries, lighting accessories—which together in 1948 employed 235 000 people and 260 000 (115 000 women), in 1962, but which would perhaps be more appropriately treated in the chapter on

Miscellaneous Manufactures since they depend to only an insignificant extent on iron and steel.

The heavy electrical trades, however (i.e. the construction of heavy electrical machinery and power-producing plant), which employ large quantities of iron and steel, often of special qualities, are more definitely localised. They employed in 1962 some 225 000 people (compared with only 149 000 in 1935), of which a third were in the Midland Region, a quarter in the Northwestern Region (mainly south Lancashire) and nearly a quarter in London and the Southeastern Region. In almost every case, the only important exception being Rugby, the industry is located in towns and cities where a flourishing machinery industry of one kind or another already existed; railway facilities have also played a part, for adequate means of transport are essential to an industry which imports much of its raw material (copper, mica, etc., from abroad and heavy steel castings, probably from Sheffield), and produces bulky and valuable goods. The metropolis of the industry is at Manchester, the home of the Metropolitan-Vickers Co., which produces power plant and electric locomotives of all kinds. At Rugby, the forerunners of the English Electric Co. set up their works in 1897, and a huge industry, increased by the advent of the British Thomson-Houston Co. in 1901, has resulted. Heavy machinery and turbo-electric plant are made here. These are the principal centres. Others of less importance are Coventry (radio apparatus and other plant), Preston (electric motors, locomotives, and formerly tramcars), Birmingham (electric motors and other plant), Hebburn-on-Tyne (switchgear), Loughborough (turbo-electric motors and railway equipment), and Stafford (generators and industrial equipment).

Division 72 of the *Export List* is entitled 'Electrical machinery, apparatus and appliances', and includes generating sets, generators, motors, transformers, switch-gear, batteries, bulbs, lamps, radio and TV sets and parts, telegraph and telephone apparatus, cooking and heating and domestic appliances, electric cables and wires, accumulators and a wide variety of minor items. It is obviously meaningless to express exports by weight which was done previously and comparison with the past is difficult. The trade is worldwide: 120 countries are separately listed in the *Annual Statement of the Trade of the United Kingdom*. The value of exports rose from £170m in 1954 to £346m in 1966. In 1966 the chief customers in order were South Africa (£27m), Australia, USA, Netherlands, New Zealand, Canada and West Germany (£14m). Nothing could illustrate more clearly how Britain's prosperity, depending upon exports, depends upon maintaining worldwide trade connections. Sweden, France, Nigeria, Kenya, India, Iran and China are countries selected at random which were all customers to the extent of over £3m.

Cables. The manufacture of cables and wiring for the transmission of electrical energy—an industry which represents probably a half of the total capital invested in electrical concerns in Britain, and which employed some

53 000 people in 1963, mainly in Lancashire and the London area—is deserving of special mention. As an industry it represents a link between heavy electrical machinery and the non-ferrous metal trades (see Chapter 18). A moment's reflection upon the multiplicity of the uses of electric cables—for house wiring, post office and other telephones, railway signalling, power transmission, and submarine telegraphs—is sufficient to establish its importance in modern life.

Like the motor industry the manufacture of cables employs a great variety of raw materials: copper, aluminium,[1] and steel wires, insulating materials in the form of rubber, oiled paper, and cambric, lead and latterly plastics and aluminium for sheathing, jute to form part of the protective covering, and timber for the rollers upon which the finished products are mounted for transport. Many of these items must be imported and a large part of the produce is destined for export, so that we shall expect to find the industry located near the large ports, especially in the vicinity of the non-ferrous metal industry (cf. Chapter 18). The banks of the Thames below London—as at Erith, Barking, and Northfleet—support nearly half the industry, whilst a considerable proportion of the remainder is localised in the important non-ferrous metal district of south Lancashire, at Manchester, Prescot, and Liverpool; Glasgow is the centre of the trade in Scotland, and Newport in South Wales. A recent addition to the list of localities is Wrexham, in the Development Area of northeast Wales.

Engineering provinces

We may now comment briefly upon the various engineering provinces mentioned above, noticing the geographical factors which have helped to influence their development and the present-day trends of their industries. (See table on p. 457).

Manchester and South Lancashire

Manchester is the hub of one of the world's greatest engineering districts. In 1931 some 217 000 people in Lancashire and the adjoining part of Cheshire were employed in the various branches of the engineering industry, about 22 000 being engaged in the textile-machinery industry alone. Yet south Lancashire is not, and never has been, a great iron and steel-producing area. As we have seen (p. 382), the coalfield was almost devoid of Coal Measure ironstones so that no great smelting industry arose; and at the present time there is only one smelting works in the whole of the area—at Irlam, west of

1. The increasing replacement of copper by aluminium as the conductor in cables for electrical distribution is shown by the following figures: use of copper 52 800 metric tons (52 000 long tons) in 1962, 22 300 metric tons (22 000 long tons) in 1968; use of aluminium, 4674 metric tons (4600 long tons) in 1962, 20 300 metric tons (20 000 long tons) in 1968.

Manchester. The momentum acquired by the early textile machinery industry, however, assisted by the availability of coal and the ease of access to supplies of iron and steel from Staffordshire and Yorkshire (by railway) and from Cumberland and Scotland (by sea), has been sufficient to attract a large number of heavy-engineering industries to the area, and the 'deposit' of technical skill, which has been gradually accumulating since the eighteenth century, has found outlets in the designing and building of steam and other engines and all kinds of heavy machinery.

Three of the most important branches have already been noticed—textile machinery, electrical machinery, and locomotives. In addition, many firms are engaged in building stationary steam engines and other power-producing plant (gas and oil engines, boilers, etc.). Since James Nasmyth (of Salford) invented the steam hammer, vast strides have been made in the efficiency of the machines which fashion the parts of the engines and machinery. The heavy machine-tool trade is the greatest in the country, and probably nine-tenths of the machines used in the manufacture of armaments, shafting, and heavy forgings in Sheffield are made in south Lancashire. The list of engineering products is almost unending. Mining, colliery, and saw-mill plant, and machinery for numerous food-preparing trades, wire ropes, cables, and chains, hydraulic machinery, and constructional steelwork are among the most important. After Manchester and its suburbs the chief engineering towns are Blackburn, Bolton, Preston, and Oldham (cf. Fig. 196).

The Yorkshire, Nottingham, and Derby coalfield

(*a*) *The West Yorkshire Conurbation.* The engineering industries of west Yorkshire as a whole employed, in 1931, over 111 000 people. The geographical bases of the industry are similar to those which are found in the case of south Lancashire, namely the early start in the manufacture of textile machinery and the ease of access to coal and iron. In contrast with Lancashire the importance of local iron manufacture—mainly south of Bradford—has been considerable, but the industry, famous for 'Best Yorkshire' wrought iron, is now extinct. Within the area there is a tendency towards the segregation of the textile-machinery industry in the west—at Bradford, Keighley, Bingley, and Halifax—while locomotive manufacture and the heavy iron and steel trades are to be found mainly on the lower ground farther east, at Leeds, Huddersfield, and Wakefield. Apart from the textile machinery and locomotives already dealt with, the following engineering products may be cited: railway rolling stock and the materials therefor (wheels and axles), formerly tramway rails (probably 50 per cent of all the tram rails in Britain were rolled at Leeds),[1] machine tools, drilling and boring machinery, hydraulic apparatus and certain types of con-

1. Aberconway, *op. cit.*, 94.

structional steelwork (e.g. gasholders). All these trades employ iron and steel from Middlesbrough, Scunthorpe, and Sheffield.

(*b*) *South Yorkshire.* The unique industries of Sheffield (cf. Chapter 16, p. 413) are divisible into two groups: (1) cutlery and small articles,[1] e.g. hand tools, clock springs, and pen nibs; (2) the heavy steel trades. The latter include huge castings and forgings for ships and heavy machinery, armour plating, guns, and certain types of railway and electrical apparatus where special hardness, strength or magnetic properties are required. Some of the names in the Sheffield steel industry are world famous: Firth's (stainless steel), Vickers (the Manchester electrical engineers, and Barrow shipbuilders), Cammell Laird (the Birkenhead shipbuilders), John Brown (the Clyde shipbuilders) and Hadfield's (the pioneers of manganese steel) are amongst the best known.

Rotherham takes part in two types of Yorkshire industry, the special steel manufacture of Sheffield, and the wrought and cast iron trade which developed on the coalfield in the early days of iron smelting. Like Sheffield, it makes, at the Park Gate and other works, special steels and their products —heavy castings and forgings for marine engines and other machinery. Side by side with this have developed the railway rolling stock and constructional steelwork trades. Very different, and much older, however, are the wrought-iron industry and the manufacturing of stoves and grates.[2]

(*c*) *Derbyshire and Nottinghamshire.* The industries of this group, while owing their origin to the presence of coal and iron, are more allied by their miscellaneous character to the scattered engineering trades of southeastern Britain. It is probably due to the towns themselves not forming a coherent whole, and to the absence of any vast industrial occupation, such as textiles or shipbuilding, which could generate a machinery industry. Typical of the area (apart from the locomotives and hosiery machinery already referred to) are the chains, castings and refrigerating machinery of Derby, the cycles of Nottingham, the tubes of Chesterfield, and the cast iron pipes produced at the Stanton and Staveley ironworks.

The Northeast coast

The two characteristic engineering industries of this region are the building of marine and locomotive engines, located principally on Tyneside, and the production of ship plates, rails, and constructional steelwork, centred upon Tees-side. Marine engineering is a natural accompaniment of shipbuilding, and locomotive building is a kindred industry which here, as on

1. Employment in cutlery industry, 10 000 in 1960.
2. It is interesting to recall that the plates for the 'Great Eastern' were rolled at Rotherham (cf. p. 432).

the Clyde, assumed large proportions (cf. pp. 434 and 441). The constructional steelwork (girders for bridges and buildings) produced by Dorman Long and other famous bridge builders of Tees-side is a peculiarity the origin of which is less obvious. There are two factors to be borne in mind:

(*a*) The iron industry of Tees-side began much later than those of the coalfields, in an area where there was no previous industrial development and no existing machinery industries.
(*b*) The coastal site favoured the growth of an industry which specialised in bulky, unwieldy products for which a large market existed abroad. Thus the heavy machinery industries never developed, and the principal products, apart from the export of iron and steel to other areas, have been shipbuilding steelworks, rails, and girders. Triumphs of Tees-side include the steelwork of Sydney Harbour Bridge, of the Little Belt Bridge in Denmark and of the Lower Zambezi bridge. Darlington is also famous for its bridge building materials. Stockton is the headquarters of a firm that produces mining equipment and iron- and steelworks plant.

The Scottish lowlands

The western portion of the Scottish lowlands, centring on Glasgow, but extending northeast to Falkirk and southwest to Kilmarnock, is a great engineering province for three reasons:

(*a*) There are excellent facilities for the production of iron and steel from local and imported materials.
(*b*) For a period in the 'thirties and 'forties of last century central Scotland was the most important iron-producing region in Britain, and consequently was a centre of attraction for many engineering industries.
(*c*) The shipbuilding industry naturally gave rise to a marine engineering industry, and the skill acquired in this branch could easily be applied to other branches of engineering.

The region thus partakes of the characteristics of both Manchester and Tyneside. In 1930 about 90 000 people were employed in the engineering trades.[1] The great marine-engineering industry of the Clyde, formerly employing 20 000 people, has already been dealt with, and we have seen that Glasgow was the most important locomotive-building centre in the British Isles. The textile machinery industry is present, though it bears no comparison with that of south Lancashire. One firm at Clydebank, however, employs 10 000 people in the manufacture of sewing machines. As a natural accompaniment to locomotive building, we have boiler making (e.g. Babcock and Wilcox), and the production of stationary steam engines

1. *Industrial Survey of South-west Scotland*, p. 63.

and pumps. These trades, together with marine engineering, have given rise to an extensive manufacture of machine tools, in which branch the Glasgow district seriously rivals the Manchester area. Glasgow leads the world in the production of machine-tools for the building of marine engines; and it is the chief centre in Britain for the production of mining equipment, such as coal-cutting machinery. Constructional engineering is another natural outlet for the steel of a seaboard region; and among the many firms engaged in this branch the most famous is that of Arrol & Co., the builders of the Forth, Tay, and Tower bridges. Other characteristic products of this province are steel tubes, hydraulic engineering machinery, sugar-making machinery (a result of Glasgow's former important trade with the West Indies), and various types of cast iron articles such as stoves, grates and baths, for which the Carron company, for example, is specially noted. The most recent introduction is heavy electrical engineering—a natural result, perhaps, of the development of hydro-electric power schemes in the Highlands.

Northern Ireland

In recent years Northern Ireland has become increasingly important as a centre of engineering, apart from the shipbuilding already noted, aircraft building and textile machinery.

The products of the many engineering firms are numerous and varied, including fans for mine ventilation, machinery for tea and coffee estates, turbines and turbine blades, tabulating machines, electronic computers, telephone exchange equipment, oil well drilling and ancillary equipment, radios, gramophones, tape-recorders, cameras and cutlery, and car tyres.

The Black Country and Birmingham

The Black Country is the oldest of the great engineering provinces, and the origin of its iron and steel industry has already been discussed (Chapter 16, p. 409). Even in the sixteenth century the manufacture of nails, knives, and locks was going on in the area,[1] and the momentum given by this early start, by the fortunate occurrence in juxtaposition of the raw materials of the iron industry, and by the steam-engine trade of Boulton and Watt in the last twenty years of the eighteenth century, enabled a vast engineering industry to be built up. Birmingham, not on the coalfield, quickly began to specialise in small valuable articles, while the heavier industries concentrated in the Black Country. The interior position of the region was originally a disadvantage, but the nodality which resulted from the construction of canals and railways meant that all districts could be equally well served, though shipbuilding and marine engineering could hardly be expected to develop.[2]

1. Leland's *Itinerary*, vol. iv, fol. 186.
2. It is interesting to recall, however, that one of the very earliest iron steamships—the *Aaron Manby* of 1822—was actually built at Tipton and sent in sections by canal to London for assembly and launching!

As a result the dominant note of the engineering industry became *variety*. The decline of iron smelting has been accompanied by an even greater specialisation in all kinds of engineering industries based on local steel produced from non-local ores and scrap. The localisation of many of these industries is not geographically explicable, being often almost accidental and due to the chance decision of a manufacturer of certain goods to set up his factory in a particular spot. Interesting local specialities, the origins of which are buried in history, are to be found at Willenhall (locks), Darlaston (nuts and bolts), Wednesbury (tubes), West Bromwich (coiled springs), Cradley Heath (chains), and Walsall (saddler's ironmongery).[1]

Only the outstanding products can here be indicated. The list is so extensive that any enumeration must omit many important ones. Amongst the principal *groups* of products, however, the smaller usually included under the term 'hardware', the following seem to be characteristic: chains (especially for ships' anchors); locks and keys; nuts, bolts, and screws; steel tubes; iron castings of every description; stoves, grates, and fireirons (and their modern developments, gas and electric fires); constructional steelwork; railway rolling stock; and many kinds of steam and other engines and machinery. The iron hollow-ware (now frequently called in the trade 'holloware') industry has been very largely replaced by the manufacture of similar articles in aluminium (see p. 477)[2]

The trades of Birmingham are of such bewildering variety that it is impossible to give an adequate selection. So many of them, moreover, involve the use of other metals than iron and steel that the discussion may best be deferred (p. 485).

The smaller Midland coalfields, and adjacent areas

(*a*) *North Staffordshire*. Much of the iron smelted in this region is sent away, either as pig iron or as semifinished steel, to other areas, notably south Lancashire and the Black Country. There is a small engineering industry concerned chiefly with foundry products and with machinery for the local pottery industries in Stoke-on-Trent. But Stafford, largely by reason of its excellent rail facilities (for it is off the coalfield), has become an engineering centre of major importance, formerly with locomotive-building, now with heavy electrical engineering, and reinforced concrete engineering. Uttoxeter, long famed as an agricultural market, produces farm machinery.

(*b*) *Warwickshire and Leicestershire*. This group, like Derby and Nottinghamshire, has a number of miscellaneous iron and steel industries. Stoves and

1. See British Association for the Advancement of Science, Handbook, *Birmingham and its Regional Setting*, 1950, pp. 161–248.

2. Employment in 'Hardware and Holloware' industry, 1948 (*Census of Production*):— Great Britain, 175 297, of which 61 723 in Midland Region (i.e. mainly Birmingham and the Black Country).

grates are again prominent, as at Leamington and Warwick (which also has motor-car assembly). Coventry has a vast trade in castings, forgings, and tools for its great motor, cycle, and aeroplane industries. Leicester makes, amongst other things, heating and ventilating plant, machinery for its own hosiery and boot and shoe trades, and stone-crushing apparatus (possibly a result of the proximity of the Charnwood quarries); and Rugby and Loughborough, as mentioned above, are important centres for the manufacture of all kinds of electrical apparatus and machinery.

Southeastern Great Britain

The scattered engineering industries of the region lying southeast of a line from the Humber to the Bristol Channel owe their origin in many cases to the agricultural implement manufacture, which arose at certain nodal points in this the essentially arable part of Britain.[1] In other cases the industries have developed largely because (*a*) good railway facilities permitted easy access to sources of raw material; (*b*) the local population provided at one and the same time a ready market for the articles produced and a source of labour supply. Of the towns where agricultural machinery formed the basis of the engineering industry, the most important are Lincoln, Gainsborough, Grantham, Thetford, Leiston, Ipswich, Colchester, and Rochester.

Reference has been made earlier to the almost complete mechanisation of British agriculture and the huge expansion of the demand for tractors and agricultural machinery of the most varied and increasingly complex types.

The outlook has broadened from the old emphasis on ploughs and reapers. Lincoln is probably the chief centre outside North America for the manufacture of excavating machinery: Ruston-Bucyrus draglines and face-shovels are used the world over. In addition, every type of road locomotive (road rollers, traction engines, etc.) is made, together with a variety of agricultural machines and boilers and engine parts. Gainsborough makes dredges; Ipswich makes cranes, excavators, railway material, and electric road vehicles; Colchester deals in boilers and gas engines; Grantham has a large output of petrol-driven farm machinery and road rollers of all kinds.

Of the second class of towns the locomotive-building centres have already been mentioned. A few others may be cited as examples, but it must be remembered that, as pointed out previously, almost every town has an engineering works of some kind. Northampton makes stoves and grates and boot-making machinery; Bedford such things as pumps, oil engines, and electrical gear; Luton makes motor cars, ball-bearings, refrigerating plant; Guildford makes specialised motor vehicles such as fire engines, refuse

1. This industry began, no doubt, by the keener farmers inventing their own mechanical devices, and became commercialised by the setting up of workshops in the market towns where the farmers congregated. Cf. *Victoria County History, Lincolnshire*, vol. ii, pp. 394–6.

collectors and lawn mowers; Yeovil makes oil engines; and Oxford has already been mentioned in connection with the motor-car industry.

Despite the absence of coalfields, this southeastern region, taken as a whole, is the greatest engineering province of all. True, it is unlike the other regions in being far more widespread and in containing far more numerous and scattered individual centres, but within it the great city of London, as the table opposite shows, is the largest employer of engineering labour in the country. The multifarious engineering trades of London are referred to elsewhere (pp. 485, 673–5), but we might note here the importance of the electrical and motor trades and of the miscellaneous group. To provide raw material for some of these industries London has over 500 foundries (iron and non-ferrous), 10 per cent of all those in the country.

South Wales

Finally, attention may be called to South Wales. In this area neither shipbuilding nor any great engineering industry has developed[1] despite the early importance of the iron industry. The reason is to be found (*a*), in the location of the early smelting works in narrow valleys miles from the coast, and (*b*) in the great development of the tinplate industry (see above) which absorbed much of the steel output. Only the manufacture of rails and sections, an industry lying on the borderline between the *production* of iron and steel and engineering proper, was of any importance. This absence of any great manufacturing industry was largely responsible for the disastrous interwar unemployment in eastern South Wales, which resulted from the decline of the inland centres and the working out of the best coals in that same northeastern region.[2]

The electronics industry

This industry is basically a highly specialised branch of the electrical industry. Half the output is concerned with radio and television reception and transmission but the field includes automation in industry with computers and business machinery, navigational aids and radar, guided weapons and fire control equipment, and sound recording and reproducing apparatus. The basic component in the industry, the thermionic valve, was invented by Ambrose Fleming in 1904, but is now being supplanted by the transistor. The word electronics does not even appear in the 1933 supplement to the *Oxford English Dictionary*; in 1960 the total labour force in the

1. Newport was quite an important shipbuilding centre in the days of wooden ships, but the industry declined when iron came into favour. It was revived in 1953 with the opening of a new shipyard in which prefabricated sections are assembled in dry dock, and the finished hulls floated out into the River Usk and so to Newport Docks for completion.
2. See *Industrial Survey of South Wales*, Chapter 3.

British industry was estimated at 237 000 and, early in 1959, 400 firms were participating. These include subsidiaries or branches of the great electrical firms, set manufacturers concentrating on standard equipment and the makers of specialised components. Most operate in large units of 500 to 5000 workers in modern well-equipped factories. Two-thirds of the labour force are in the Greater London area especially in the outer ring of suburbs —Hayes, Enfield, Ilford, Croydon, and Sidcup—or slightly further out at Chelmsford, Southend, Slough, and Welwyn. A previously little used reservoir of unskilled female labour has been tapped and other factors favouring the choice of Greater London have been industrial linkage between the specialised sections of the industry and the fragile nature of the products making them very suitable for direct delivery in small lots to

Employment in engineering industries in 1966 (thousands)

MINISTRY OF LABOUR REGIONS	ELECTRICAL ENGINEERING	MOTOR VEHICLES	SHIPBUILDING AND MARINE ENGINEERING	AIRCRAFT	MACHINE TOOLS	TOOLS AND CUTLERY	OTHER ENGINEERING INDUSTRIES	TOTAL
1. Scotland	26	30	48	14	7	1	146	272
2. Northern Region	52	12	42	2	4	1	81	194
3. NW Region	142	85	28	35	13	2	202	506
4. Yorks. and Humber	30	35	7	10	28	17	155	283
5. W. Midlands	121	179	1	24	45	6	320	697
6. E. Midlands	37	25	1	27	8	1	114	214
7. Wales	27	153	4	7	2	—	51	245
8. London and SE Region	358	179	32	67	39	11	495	1180
9. London	199	64	8	13	16	6	264	571
Total persons employed in Great Britain	865	579	178	230	153	40	1826	3872
Total areas 1–8[1]	794	560	162	177	147	39	1563	3591
Total employed in GB 1961	726	539	173	267	139	32	1477	3353
Total employed in GB 1950	533	518	278	146	77	52	1786	3390
Total employed in GB 1931	242	348	151	*	*	43	*	1483
Total employed in GB 1921	175	275	410	*	*	56	*	1910

* Comparable figures not available.
[1] Areas omitted from the table are Southwest, South, and East.

retailers in the very large local market. Somewhat similar considerations have favoured development in the West Midlands. Other centres are found in Lancashire, on Tyneside and in central Scotland (especially Fifeshire) where Government direction of industry into Development Areas, and a search for a labour supply for a rapidly expanding industry have been major factors.

18
The non-ferrous metal industries

The term non-ferrous applies to all metals other than iron. Of a somewhat lengthy list, however, we are only concerned with a few which are in everyday use for domestic and industrial purposes. These fall roughly into three groups:

1. Some of the *baser metals*, such as tin, lead, copper, and zinc, have from very early times been wrought extensively in various parts of Britain, and the home-produced ores, though now almost negligible and supplemented by imports of ores, concentrates, and metal, have given rise to smelting and manufacturing industries of major importance.
2. Other of the *baser metals*, such as nickel, chromium, and aluminium, have found an increasing number of industrial uses during the present century. They are mostly imported.
3. Ores of the *precious metals*, gold and silver, have never been worked in any great quantity in Britain,[1] but the demand of a highly civilised and, on the whole, wealthy community for jewellery, plate and ornaments is responsible for the existence of a large industry concerned with the refining and fabrication of the imported metals.

Much metal wealth, especially of tin and lead, probably still remains locked up in British rocks (cf. p. 357), but the once important veins of Cornwall, Derbyshire and elsewhere cannot under present economic conditions hope to compete with the large-scale output from much richer areas abroad; the result being that the mining of non-ferrous ores in Britain is now virtually an extinct industry, and the manufactures to which the home deposits originally gave rise must now be carried on almost entirely with imported foreign ores, concentrates, or crude metal.

There are many areas of the country where non-ferrous ores have been worked, and many thousands of extinct mines (some 4000 disused lead mines in Derbyshire alone). But the life of a metalliferous mine is generally, with some very notable exceptions, comparatively short. Hunt calculated[2] for a thirty-year period in the second half of the last century that of 220 Cornish mines only thirty-five had a life of over twenty years, whilst no less

1. Considerable quantities of silver have from time to time, in the past, been obtained from argentiferous ores of lead, in the Mendips, Derbyshire and elsewhere. See also pp. 359, 461.
2. Quoted in *Mem. Geol. Surv., Min. Res.*, vol. xxvii.

than 114 were productive for less than five years. As every mine must have a dump heap of the useless rock dug out during the mining operations, and an erection of some kind at the head of the shaft, it is obvious that the effect on the landscape of those areas which have been thoroughly worked in the past must be considerable; and many a Cornish and Welsh panorama is marred by the ugly excrescences which betoken an activity which is, alas, rapidly fading into insignificance.

The industries based upon the non-ferrous metals and their extraction fall naturally into two distinct divisions: (*a*) the smelting and refining of the ores, and (*b*) the working up of the metal into manufactured articles. The geographic and economic influences bearing upon the location of the two branches are rather different. In the case of the smelting it must be borne in mind that most non-ferrous ores are very much poorer in their metallic content than ores of iron. A percentage as low as one per cent may prove profitable if the ore is in sufficient quantity and easily accessible. The ore from the world-famous Anglesey mines, once the most productive in the world, only averaged four per cent of metallic copper. It is thus not an economic proposition to smelt the ores far from their place of origin, unless cheap water transport be available, or unless the ore can be conveniently concentrated so that its metallic content is increased, say, to over 50 per cent. With inland ores smelting will most probably take place at the mines; should the ore lie near the coast it may be exported raw or in concentrated form to ports more favourably situated with regard to coal. The Derbyshire lead was always smelted on the spot; the Cornish copper ores were sent across the Bristol Channel to the ports of southwest Wales.

The location of the manufacturing industries is dependent on at least three factors, the existence of a supply of raw material in the form of refined metal, a suitable labour supply, and the presence of a market for the finished goods. Should the market be a scattered one, it can scarcely be expected to influence the siting of the works, for one locality would be as good as another. In these circumstances the factories may either be set up in the vicinity of the smelting and refining plants, or distributed in a haphazard fashion over the country. If, on the other hand, the market is localised in a particular region or regions, the tendency will be for the manufacture to take place as near as possible to those areas. A second consideration concerns the wastage of the raw materials during the process of manufacture. If there is little or no waste the amount of material to be transported is much the same whether the raw materials or the finished goods are sent, and so it matters little where the industry is located on a line drawn from the source of the raw materials to the market. If, however, there is a great wastage of material the market will exert much less attractive power, and the manufacture will tend to be located near the source of supply of the raw material.

With these general principles in mind, we may proceed to examine in some detail the past and present distribution of the non-ferrous metal industries in Britain, paying special attention to the changes in location which have occurred, and to the geographical influences (in this case mainly a combination of geological and economic factors) which have been foremost in producing them.

The development of the non-ferrous metal industries

From the earliest times to the reign of Elizabeth I[1]

The early history of the working of non-ferrous metals, like that of iron, is lost in obscurity. It is probable, however, that the western end of the Cornish peninsula, with its indented rocky coast, and the adjacent Scilly Isles were the Cassiterides to which the Phoenicians came from at least the fifth century B.C. to trade in tin with the natives.[2] By the time of the Roman occupation there is abundant evidence, both literary and *in situ*, of the great use which the Romans (with the help doubtless of their slaves) made of Britain's metal wealth. The historian, Diodorus Siculus, writing of the Cornish tin trade just after Caesar's time, records the collection of the smelted tin on Ictis Isle (probably St Michael's Mount) and its purchase by the merchants for shipment to the coast of Gaul and thence to Marseilles and the Mediterranean, and a block of tin such as he describes has actually been dredged up from Falmouth harbour. But it was lead that the Romans chiefly prized, and the results of their mining and smelting operations are to be found in such widely scattered localities as the Mendips, Derbyshire, Flintshire, western Shropshire, Alston Moor and Leadhills. A very fair technique had been attained, for numerous pigs of lead have been unearthed bearing the inscription 'ex arg' (*ex argento*, freed from silver), and Pliny refers to the large supplies of lead pipes and sheeting which Britain produced. In addition, the Romans are known to have worked the copper ores of Anglesey and Shropshire, while it is not improbable that they obtained a certain amount of gold from mines in North Wales and Carmarthenshire.

All these early efforts were either stream-works or else mere surface scratchings. The natural environment in which the ores occurred was par-

1. Much valuable literature on this subject will be found summarised in the *Victoria County Histories* (vol. ii in each case) of *Cumberland, Derbyshire, Durham, Somerset* and *Yorkshire*.
2. Cassiterides, from Greek *cassiteros* = tin. See W. C. Borlase, *A Historical Sketch of the Tin Trade in Cornwall*, 1874. Herodotus (fifth century B.C.) and Strabo (first century B.C.) each refer to the Cassiterides and their tin, and Polybius (second century B.C.) and Diodorus Siculus (first century A.D.) both mention tin in Cornwall, but no definite pronouncement seems to be made identifying the one with the other. A Phoenician bronze ornament has been found at St Just.

ticularly favourable to their discovery and utilisation. The veins were to be found in upland areas formed by palaeozoic rocks, and the thin soils and scanty vegetation of much of these districts permitted the surface exposure of the minerals; the heavy rainfall of most of the upland regions entailed a great deal of erosion by rushing torrents which would further expose and erode the veins and would sort and re-deposit the ore in their beds; while the peat cover of much of the moorland and the forests of the slopes would provide ample fuel for smelting purposes. The Cornish tin ore was probably all obtained from detrital deposits in which, owing to its high specific gravity (6.8), it accumulated whenever the velocity of the streams was insufficient to carry it further; and the ores of the other regions were obtained either from streams or by shallow diggings at the outcrop of the veins.

There are few records of mining or smelting during the Saxon period, and the only noteworthy reference in the Domesday Survey concerns lead mines at Wirksworth and other places in Derbyshire.[1] The first documentary evidence begins in the twelfth century, and the long series of Pipe Rolls contain frequent references to the mining industry, in which tin and lead are the chief items.

Tin.[2] In the twelfth and thirteenth centuries, the Cornish tin trade was mostly in the hands of Jews who may or may not have been the descendants of Phoenicians who settled in the country. Even to this day certain ruined smelting hearths and slag dumps are known as 'Jews-houses'. The banishment of all Jews from England in 1290 left Cornwall without its merchant smelters, but a revival of industry took place in the early fourteenth century with the passing of the first Stannary Laws (Latin *stannum* = tin). So great a part did tin mining and tin smelting play in the lives of the people of Devon and Cornwall that from this time onwards for over four centuries the 'stannaries' had their own parliaments,[3] and a series of laws governing the mining, coinage and disposal of tin. 'Coinage' was the marking of the tin bars for taxation purposes. It took place generally once a year at certain 'coinage towns', whither the bars were brought from the neighbouring smelting houses. In Cornwall, Lostwithiel, Liskeard, Bodmin, Truro and Helston were appointed as coinage towns, and in Devon, Tavistock, Ashburton, Plympton and Chagford. The chief uses of tin were for the manufacture of pewter, as an alloy in bell-founding and as a soldering material. The pewter trade assumed large proportions in the fifteenth and sixteenth centuries, and a considerable export took place, largely controlled by Venetian merchants.

1. It is difficult to believe that tin mining had died out—but possibly, being considered as royal property, the mines were not recorded in a survey, the main purpose of which was the ascertainment of the value of estates for taxation purposes. (G. R. Lewis, *The Stannaries*, p. 34.)
2. Lewis, *op. cit.*, Chapter ii.
3. The parliament of the Devon 'stannary' met on Crockerntor and later at Tavistock; that of Cornwall met at Lostwithiel and afterwards at Truro.

Lead.[1] The twelfth and thirteenth centuries saw great activity all over the country in the erection of great buildings—especially churches and monasteries—and as a result the demand for lead for roofing and drainage purposes was greatly stimulated. Derbyshire was the chief centre, but the Pennine region of Durham and the Mendip Hills also had many mines and smelting hearths. Smelting of the galena was performed in 'boles' (simple hearths surrounded by a few bricks) using brushwood as a fuel. These boles were nearly always placed on the brow of a west-facing hill, in order to catch the breeze. Many such ancient furnace sites are known in Derbyshire and Durham, and the name 'Bole Hill' is of frequent occurrence in the former county. The fourteenth century probably witnessed the introduction of charcoal as a fuel, and also the development of waterwheels for working bellows which could create the necessary blast—with a consequent descent of the smelting industry into the valleys. At this time lead ranked with wool and leather as one of the chief exports of Britain.

From the reign of Elizabeth I to the present day

The history of the non-ferrous metal industries from about 1550 to the present day may be briefly summed up as follows. A great fillip was given to mining and smelting in the Elizabethan period by the introduction of workmen from the continent who could and did teach the English how best to search for and make use of the metal wealth which the country possessed. The small existing industries were considerably expanded, and a number of new manufactures, such as those dealing with copper and brass, came into being. After a period of comparative quiescence during the troublous times of the middle seventeenth century, a great revival took place. The end of that century and the beginning of the next marked the foundation, in various parts of the country, of many branches of the industry which have survived, though perhaps in a modified form, until the present day. The increasing uses to which the metals were being adapted, together with the new lease of life given to the mining industry by the installation of the steam engine as a means of pumping out water from the ever-deepening mines, brought about a continued expansion of the industry during the eighteenth century. Stimulated by the development of manufacturing which accompanied the Industrial Revolution, and by the increasing employment of non-ferrous metals as well as iron in the fabrication of machinery, the output of British mines reached a maximum during the period 1840–80. About the same time, too, foreign ores, especially of tin and copper, began to be imported, and the smelting trade, notably in the Swansea area, enjoyed a period of great activity. Gradually, however, it became increasingly uneconomic to transport bulky ores for thousands of miles from overseas, and

1. See especially *Victoria County History, Derbyshire*, ii, 323–49; also J. W. Gough, *The Mines of Mendip*, Oxford U.P., 1930, 2nd ed, 1968; and A. Raistrick and B. Jennings, *History of Lead Mining in the Pennines*, Longmans, 1965.

as this trend has coincided with the decline, almost to nothing, of the home ore production, smelting has almost died out, and the structure of the non-ferrous metal industry has been radically changed. Most branches of the industry are carrying on as a result of momentum acquired during the period of prosperity, and are now based upon imported semifinished material in the shape of ingots and bars of refined or partly refined metal.

A more detailed examination of the development and distribution changes during this period will help to explain how the British non-ferrous metal industry and its dependants have been built up, and the part which they play in the economic organisation of the country at the present time.

In the middle of the sixteenth century, although tin and lead were still being worked, England lagged a good deal behind the Continent in industrial development, and early in the reign of Elizabeth it began to be realised that in order to improve conditions at home, to increase foreign trade, and to maintain the defences, metal industries were very necessary, especially those dealing with copper and brass, since those substances were used for the production of ordnance as well as for domestic utensils.[1] Accordingly, invitations were extended to certain German metal workers to take up their abode in this country and pursue their trade with British ores. In 1564 a small group of skilled men from Augsburg, led by one Daniel Höchstetter, landed in England, and in the following year, after rich copper deposits had been located at Keswick, several hundred workmen from the Tyrol were 'imported' and smelting works were set up. Many groups of German miners and metal workers subsequently came to Britain and settled in the mining districts, notably in Cornwall, the Mendips and in Northumberland, or started new metal industries in various parts of the country.[2] Two companies were subsequently formed and granted charters, one the 'Mines Royal Society', whose privilege it was to work for precious metals and copper in certain areas, and the other the 'Society of the Mineral and Battery Works', who were authorised to get calamine (zinc ore), and to make brass and battery goods (i.e. articles, such as pans and kettles, made from copper or brass beaten into thin sheets). In 1583 copper ore began to be worked in western Cornwall, and as there was no fuel there available, a smelting house was set up at Neath, in South Wales, to deal with the ore. A little later copper ore was discovered at Ecton Hill, Staffordshire and Alderley Edge, Cheshire, and smelting works were set up in the vicinity. The chief essentials of the smelting industry were ore supplies and the availability of fuel. At Keswick peat was used; at Neath charcoal and coal. The brass industry, on the other hand, needed calamine and copper as its raw materials, and power for the hammers, and was best placed near to a market. The first brass works were at Tintern (using the calamine

1. See on this subject H. Hamilton, *The English Brass and Copper Industries to 1800*.
2. Many of the early metal-working establishments owe their foundation not to any geographical advantages possessed by the site but to the settling of a group of foreign artisans.

lately discovered in the Mendips, together with fuel from the Forest of Dean), at Nottingham (using Derbyshire calamine and Staffordshire copper), and on small streams near London (at Isleworth and Rotherhithe). One of the principal uses of brass, apart from 'battery goods', was for wire and pin-making—the chief activity of the Mineral and Battery Society was the production of iron and brass wire for wool-cards.

The political instability of the Civil War and Protectorate period, and the monopolistic control exercised by the two companies mentioned, were unfavourable to great progress;[1] but with the removal of the monopolies in 1689, the way was opened for a considerable expansion in the copper and brass trades, and the improvements in mining and smelting technique which naturally followed, further increased the possibilities of development. During the eighteenth century several areas participated in the general growth of the non-ferrous metal industries. Around Swansea and Neath, the chief activity was smelting, using copper ores imported by sea from Cornwall and Ireland (Co. Wicklow), and silver-lead ore from Cardiganshire. Swansea was at this time the chief port in South Wales—and the nearest to Cornwall—and as it possessed a navigable river, easy access to coal supplies and a large area of flat and otherwise useless land behind it, it offered a very favourable site for the growth of the copper trade. All these advantages were largely shared by Neath. In the Bristol district the ease of the import of Cornish copper ore,[2] the proximity of the Mendip calamine deposits, and the water power provided by the Avon and its tributaries, resulted in both smelting and brass manufacturing. The third region comprises north Staffordshire, northeast Cheshire, and south Lancashire. Here the initial impetus was given by the local copper ores and the calamine of Derbyshire, and the ease of import of copper ore from Ireland. Quite early in the eighteenth century, smelting works were established at Warrington,[3] and copper and brass battery and wire works in the Cheadle district, where water power from the River Churnet was utilised. The greatest development here, however, came after the discovery, in 1768, of a whole hill of copper ore in the island of Anglesey.[4] Although some smelting was done at Amlwch, near the mines, much of the ore was exported; St Helens and Liverpool developed smelting works, and the Macclesfield area took up the brass industry. Considerable quantities of Anglesey ore were also exported to Swansea, where many new works were established. Smelting was tried in Cornwall on several occasions, but none of the attempts really succeeded,

1. In 1670 and again later the copper required for a new coinage had to be imported from Sweden.

2. In 1720 no less than forty ships were constantly employed to carry Cornish ore to Bristol and Swansea.

3. Warrington at that time had just, by the dredging of the Mersey, been made available as a tidal port.

4. The Parys mine quickly became the largest in Europe, and at the end of the century was yielding about 3000 metric tons of metallic copper annually.

principally because of the coal difficulty, but also because the greater part of the British copper-smelting industry was under the control of large combines which could effectively crush any competition from less well organised competitors.[1]

The chief outlets for the copper and brass made were the East India Company, which largely controlled the export trade, and the metal trades of Birmingham.[2] These deserve further comment. In the sixteenth century Birmingham was already a centre of the finished iron industry (see above, p. 453). When brass manufacture first began to develop, early in the seventeenth century, Birmingham was thus a natural market; brass is easier to fabricate than iron, and the skill of the ironworkers could be readily adapted to the use of the new metal. The local demand for brass products was stimulated by the gun, saddlery and harness trades, and the output of buckles, ornaments, and toys increased rapidly after the Restoration. Bad road transport and the lack of navigable rivers made Birmingham specialise in small and valuable goods, whilst the heavy iron trades became localised farther west, where coal and water power (e.g. in the Stour valley) were available, with the navigable Severn not far away. The development of the smelting and brass-making industries at Bristol and Cheadle, together with the expansion of the export trade to Africa and the Indies, gave Birmingham an impetus in the manufacture of metal wares that has sufficed to maintain its supremacy in the trades, even to the present time; and the desire to break the power of the combines (see above) led to the setting up of brass manufacturing (as opposed to the fabrication of brass articles) towards the end of the eighteenth century. Besides Birmingham, Wolverhampton and Walsall also began to develop brass and copper industries; in Wolverhampton the industry grew up primarily as an associate of the lock trade; in Walsall of the saddlery and harness trades.

The eighteenth century witnessed the lead industry at the height of its prosperity. Lead had not been affected to such an extent as the copper and brass trades by the disturbing effects of control by large companies, export and import restrictions, and fashion changes, but, favoured by a flourishing export trade, had undergone a steady development. In Derbyshire the lead miners, most of whom were individualists working for their own ends, and selling the ore from their own small digging or mine to merchant smelters, were governed by laws even more numerous and complicated than the Stannary Laws of Devon and Cornwall; and as most of the mines were small and the laws permitted anyone to dig for lead anywhere, and to remove timber for propping and smelting, the effect on the landscape of the lead mining area lying between Wirksworth and the Peak Forest has been considerable.[3] Other lead mining and smelting regions at this time were

1. Hamilton, *op. cit.*, Chapter 6.
2. *Ibid.*, Chapter 5.
3. J. P. Carr, 'The rise and fall of Peak District leadmining', in *Essays in Geography for Austin Miller*, Reading, 1965, pp. 207–223.

Flintshire, the Leadhills region, the Mendips (though the lead here began to be subordinate to zinc—see below), and the Pennines of north Yorkshire and western Durham.[1] Lead was used for sheeting, pipes and bullets.

The tin mining industry of Cornwall was given a considerable impetus after about 1730 by the growth of the tinplate trade in South Wales (cf. Chapter 17). Despite the commencement of the import of tin ore from the East Indian island of Banka in 1760, this trade, combined with the export market provided by the East India Company, sufficed to maintain the Cornish mines in a state of comparative prosperity. A considerable amount of tin smelting was performed in Cornwall—probably owing to the very early start which the industry had, using peat and charcoal as fuel, and to the fact that unlike the copper trades, tin mining was confined to the one area, and so not subject to competition from better situated producers.

The need of the brass industry for calamine has already been mentioned. In the early days of brass manufacture prepared calamine was used to mix with copper. About the middle of the eighteenth century, however, methods of extracting metallic zinc, or spelter, from both calamine ($ZnCO_3$) and blende (ZnS) were discovered, and later spelter was used in brass making. The first zinc smelting works was set up at Bristol in 1743, and thereafter the mining of zinc ores became of still greater importance in the Mendips, where nearly 100 mines were in existence at the end of the eighteenth century.

The outstanding technical developments which influenced metal production in the nineteenth century were concerned with (*a*) more efficient mining methods—i.e. better drainage and ventilation; (*b*) better treatment (washing and crushing) of the ore, so as to get the utmost possible metal out of it; both of these were greatly assisted by the employment of the steam engine; (*c*) improved methods of smelting—the introduction of cupolas and reverberatory furnaces using coal or coke as a fuel; (*d*) the introduction of rolling as opposed to battery in the production of sheet metal. The development of coke smelting and the use of steam power did not, however, as with the iron industry, tend to concentrate the non-ferrous metal industry on the coalfields; for the lean ores were not found in the Coal Measures, and the smelting industry was located either on the ore-fields, as in the case of Derbyshire lead and Cornish tin, or near the coast, where either home or foreign ores could be easily imported, as in the Swansea and Bristol areas and in south Lancashire.

The progress of the non-ferrous metal industries during the nineteenth and early twentieth centuries can be best treated under three headings: ore mining; ore import and smelting; and manufacturing trades.

Mining. Taken as a whole, production of non-ferrous ores reached its maxi-

1. A. E. Smailes, 'The lead dales of the northern Pennines', *Geography*, **21**, 1936, pp. 120–9; *Geology of the Northern Pennine Orefield*, vol. i (*Mem. Geol. Surv.*), 1948; Raistrick and Jennings, *op. cit.*, Chs. 6 and 7; R. T. Clough, *The Lead Smelting Mills of the Yorkshire Dales*, Leeds, 1962.

mum during the middle period of the last century, though different ores and different regions reached their climax at varying dates. In the early years of the century, Cornwall and Devon were producing about half of the world's copper ore, but although the actual amount increased until about 1860, the tremendous outputs of Chile and the United States soon dwarfed this into insignificance. The Anglesey ores were gradually worked out, and although between 1850 and 1870 North Wales and the Lake District were fairly productive, a rapid decline quickly set in. In lead mining, the peak period was 1850–70 when the average output was over 91 400 metric tons (90 000 long tons) of ore annually. Derbyshire no longer dominated the industry, the northern Pennines and North Wales producing large quantities.[1] The Cornish tin mines continued to increase their productivity, reaching a maximum between 1870 and 1890, subsequently declining. Zinc mining attained its greatest output in 1881 and declined gradually.

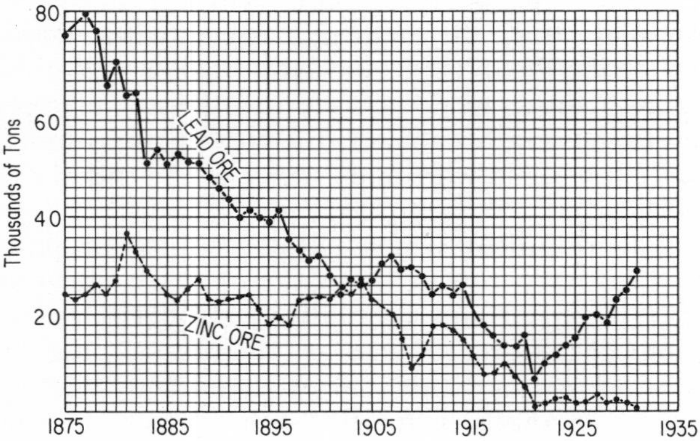

FIG. 181. Lead- and zinc-ore production in Britain, 1875–1931

Since the Second World War, zinc ore has almost ceased to be produced, whilst the output of lead ore has averaged less than 5000 tons a year.

The general rapid decline of ore production in the last quarter of the century may be ascribed to several causes. Mining conditions were becoming more and more unfavourable, and the best ores were worked out; prices during the great depression of the 'seventies dropped to ruinously low levels, rendering the working of many mines quite unremunerative;[2] the rapid growth of steam shipping, and the development of large bodies of ore in foreign countries, made for easy import of ores and concentrates—

1. See G. J. Fuller, 'Lead-mining in Derbyshire in the mid-nineteenth century', *E. Midland Geog.*, **3**, 1965, 373–93.
2. It should be remembered also that unless pumping is carried on a disused mine quickly gets flooded and the outlay involved in putting it again into working order may be prohibitive.

copper from Chile and the United States, lead from Spain (where it was a byproduct of the silver mines), tin from Australia and Malaya.

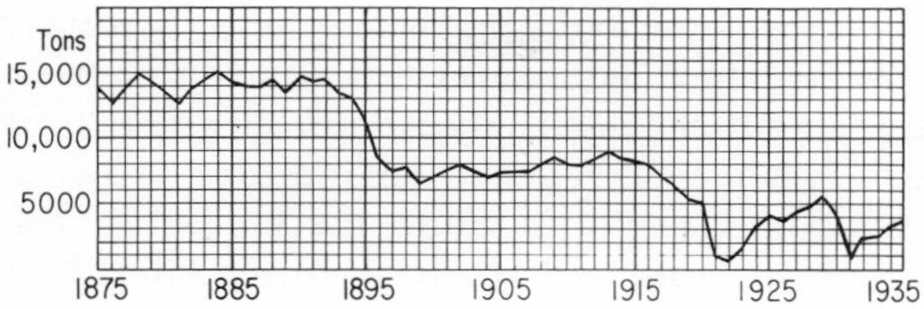

FIG. 182. Tin-ore production in Britain, 1875–1935
Since the Second World War, production has averaged only about 1000 tons a year.

Smelting. The nineteenth-century smelting industry affords some excellent examples of the results of changing geographical values. The rise of Swansea has already been mentioned. The expansion of the Cornish output of copper ore continued to stimulate the erection of new works on the River Tawe; four (also one at Llanelli) were actually built during the first decade of the century. After about 1830, foreign ores from Cuba and Chile began to supplement the Cornish supplies, and the growth of smelting at Swansea was, as it were, cumulative: the very existence of a number of smelting works, and of a labour supply skilled in metal working was sufficient to

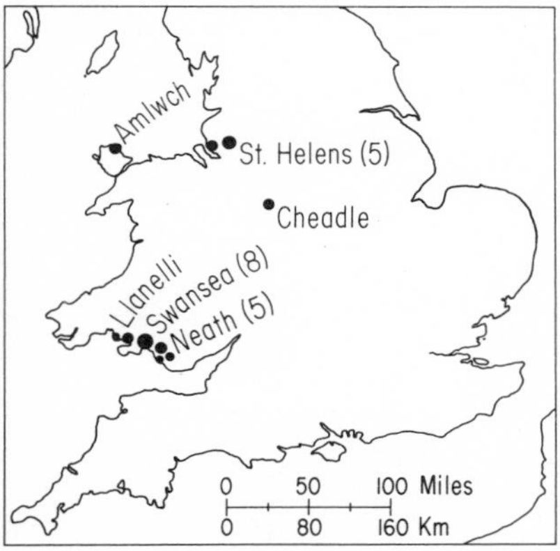

FIG. 183. Copper-smelting works in 1861

attract any new enterprises to the vicinity, and Swansea assumed the position of the world's chief copper smelting centre.[1] In the 1860s, when the trade was at its greatest, Swansea boasted eight copper smelting establishments out of a total of sixteen in South Wales, and twenty-four in the whole

1. See G. Grant-Francis, *History of Copper Smelting in the Swansea District*, and D. T. Williams, *Economic Development of Swansea.*

country. The effect of this vast industry upon the landscape was disastrous. The sulphurous fumes belched forth from hundreds of chimneys during the roasting and smelting operations destroyed the vegetation for miles around, especially on the east side of the Tawe (due to the prevailing westerly winds) and the enormous slag dumps, together with numerous ruined factories, combined to make the entry by rail into Swansea a most depressing journey.[1] The increase of orefield smelting, however, reduced the industry at Swansea to a state when economic competition with Chile, the United States, and Australia was no longer possible and, as a result, from the late 1880s onwards, copper smelting declined until it no longer exists. Instead, smelted copper ('matte' or 'regulus') is imported and refined. The other smelting activities of Swansea (lead and zinc) were formerly of much less importance, but strangely enough they have survived the copper smelting (see below).

The only other copper smelting centre of importance in the nineteenth century (apart from the declining orefield smelters at Amlwch and in North Staffordshire) was St Helens, with the origin of which we have already dealt (Fig. 183).

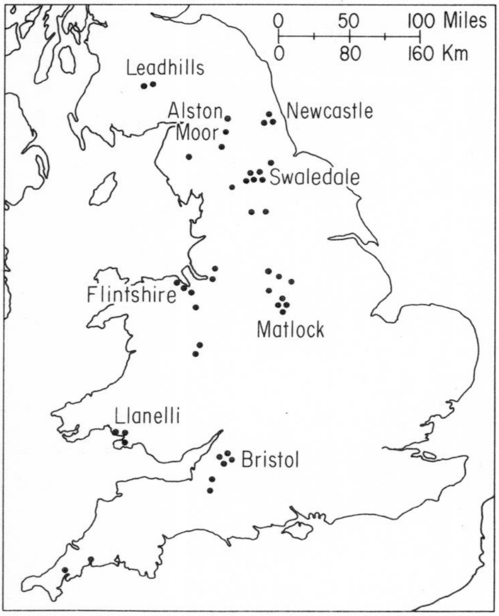

FIG. 184. Lead-smelting works in 1870

The smelting of lead was much more widely distributed, owing chiefly to the fact that rich ores were abundant in many parts of the country, and also to the ease of smelting and the absence of destructive fumes (Fig. 184).

1. The 'Lower Swansea Valley Project' was formed in 1961 to clear up the mess—see K. J. Hilton, ed, *The Lower Swansea Valley Project*, Longmans, 1967.

In Derbyshire (centring on Matlock), in Cornwall, Flintshire, Shropshire, the north Pennines, the Mendips and at Leadhills, the smelting works were located in close proximity to the larger mines. Bristol, also an important centre for other non-ferrous metals, used ore from the Mendips or imported from North Wales. A few works in the Llanelli region used north Welsh ore, and Newcastle upon Tyne smelted ores from Alston Moor, or imported by sea. The rapid decline of mining, however, has considerably reduced the number of works in operation, and the whole of the British lead production is now derived from imported concentrates, which are refined principally at or near the chief seaports.

Although certain of the Cornish tin smelters for a time actually imported East Indian and Australian ore for smelting, the trade has suffered the same fate as the rest of the industry; concentrates are now imported to be smelted at Liverpool or London, and refined tin bars are imported for the tinplate trade.

Manufacturing. If, during the nineteenth century, Swansea merited the title of 'metallurgical capital' of Britain (in non-ferrous metals only, of course), Birmingham to an even greater extent deserved to be regarded as the metropolis of those industries concerned with the working of the non-ferrous metals into articles of commerce.[1] The momentum which that city had acquired in the brass and copper trades during the eighteenth century was sufficient to attract any new developments, and so greatly did the market for copper and brass expand during the first half of the nineteenth century that by 1860 brass manufacture was the leading trade in Birmingham. The development of the steam engine had added a vast new market for brass and copper tubes, steam cocks, pressure gauges, etc., and the invention of a method of making seamless tubes in 1838 gave a further impetus to this branch; the introduction of yellow or Muntz's metal for ship-sheathing early in the century, and the demand for 'naval brassfoundry' to which the expansion of shipping gave rise, created a new market; and the increase in domestic and municipal sanitation generated a large demand for taps, water-cocks, etc., whilst gas lighting opened up a new market for pipes and fittings. In 1830 the crucible method of brass manufacture (using copper and spelter) began to replace the old cementation process, and this, like Bessemer's converter in the steel industry, caused a considerable expansion of output, and a reduction of operating costs. Birmingham was, moreover, particularly well situated, following the cutting of canals, for the assembly of raw materials and coal, and was conveniently near to certain accessories of brass manufacture—fireclay crucibles from the Stourbridge district, and local Triassic deposits which furnished excellent moulding or casting sand. It is little wonder, then, that the number of people employed in the brass industry in the city rose from 1800 in 1831 to 8100 in 1861.

1. See G. C. Allen, *Industrial Development of Birmingham and the Black Country.*

It was natural, too, that a city devoted so largely to the working of the baser metals should turn its attention to silver, gold and the jewellery trade. Birmingham began with silver, but early in the nineteenth century gold was being worked as well, and the increasing demand for jewellery in the early years of Queen Victoria's reign, together with the expansion of the gold trade following the 'rushes' in California and Australia in 1849–51, brought about a rapid growth, and by 1860 the jewellery trade was one of the four largest in Birmingham, employing about 7000 people, mostly small craftsmen working in their own workshop-dwellings. The introduction of electroplating about 1840 opened up a vast new market. The silver-plate trade introduced into Sheffield about 1740 had been shared by Birmingham, and the two cities both profited very largely by the great demand which was set up by the cheapening of plated articles without any loss of utility and attractiveness.

To an even greater extent than the brass and copper industries, the jewellery trade depended on foreign raw materials. As a consequence, when competition from better-situated continental and American producers became keen, concentration upon high-class goods became a feature of the trade.

Both the brass and the jewellery trades survived in Birmingham and even expanded considerably, whilst the iron industry was rapidly declining. The cheapening of copper by reason of the huge foreign supplies available, and the vast increase in the use of steam-driven machinery, together with the fact that Birmingham had always been dependent on distant sources of raw materials, and so did not suffer, as in its iron industry, from the disadvantage of failing local supplies, combined to maintain and increase the prosperity of the brass trade. The jewellery industry, augmented by the introduction of jewel-cutting and by the continual increase of electroplating, flourished likewise.

At the beginning of the present century we thus see the various branches of the non-ferrous metal industry very different in magnitude, and in relative importance, though not radically different in geographical distribution, compared with their condition in 1800. Smelting had declined almost to nothing; instead of ores, ingots of semirefined or pure metal were being imported; and the manufacturing industry, helped by the creation of many new uses for the metals, had grown almost out of all recognition, especially in the Birmingham district.

Before dealing with the present condition of the industry, we must glance briefly at the sources of the raw materials; we can then study the distribution of the various branches of the industry and amplify the explanations hitherto given of the geographical factors involved.

Output of non-ferrous metalliferous ores (long tons)

MINERAL	CHIEF LOCALITIES	AVERAGE PER CENT OF METAL IN DRESSED ORE	1913	AVERAGE 1921–25	AVERAGE 1926–30	1931	1934	1937	1944	1949	1955	1960
Copper precipitate[1]	Cornwall, Anglesey	63	163	149	123	109	23	79	27	Nil	16[3]	16[3]
Lead ore	Derby, Durham, Cumberland, Dumfries	80	24 282	12 048	21 583	29 502	68 122	33 411	3 969	2 465	7 443[3]	1 412[3]
Manganese ore	Merioneth, Caernarvon	30	5 393	1 214	624	—	—	—	17 607[2]	Nil	Nil	Nil
Tin ore	Cornwall	60	8 355	2 195	4 566	919	3 224	3 367	1 289	820	1 037[3]	1 172[3]
Zinc ore	Cumberland, Derby, Flint, Dumfries	46	17 294	1 696	1 913	409	988	13 083	8 663	Nil	1 048[3]	250[3]
No. of persons employed in all non-ferrous mining (including barytes)	—	—	—	3 406	4 603	1 380	3 270	3 711	*	*	*	*

[1] Copper *ore*, 2569 tons, 1913; practically none since 1920. [2] Wartime output only. [3] Metal content. * No comparable figures available.
Apart from 2900 tons of lead ore, no other outputs in 1966 were large enough to be worth recording in the *Statistical Summary of the Mineral Industry 1961–66*, HMSO.

The present condition of the non-ferrous metal industries

Home supplies of ore

Some details of the British metalliferous ores have already been given in Chapter 15. It only remains for us to add the table on p. 473, which demonstrates the demise of a once great industry.

Non-ferrous metal industry: imports of raw material, 1967

I. Ores and concentrates

MATERIAL	THOUSAND METRIC TONS	THOUSAND LONG TONS	CHIEF COUNTRIES OF ORIGIN	CHIEF RECEIVING PORTS[1]
Bauxite	458	451	Ghana, Greece France, India	Burntisland, Newport
Chromium ore	99.5	98	S. Africa, Philippines	Manchester
Manganese ore[2]	411.5	405	S. Africa, USSR, India, Brazil	Middlesbrough, Liverpool Manchester
Pyrites[3]	562	553	Italy, Sweden, Spain	Liverpool[4]
Tin ore and concentrates	63.9	63	Bolivia	Liverpool
Tungsten ores	6	6	Bolivia, China	—
Zinc concentrates	259	255	Australia, Canada	Swansea, Bristol
Lead	32.4	32	Australia, Canada	Newcastle

II. Crude metal

Aluminium	228.5	225	Norway, Canada, USA	Liverpool, London, Manchester Newport
Copper	478.5	471	Zambia, Chile, USA	Liverpool, London, Manchester, Swansea
Lead	182.9	180	Australia, Canada S.W. Africa	London, Liverpool, Manchester, Newcastle
Tin	8.1	8	Nigeria, Malaysia	London
Zinc (Spelter)	162.5	160	Canada, Bulgaria, Australia	London, Liverpool, Swansea

[1] Where no port is given, no port imports in quantities sufficiently large to be recorded separately in Trade Statistics.

[2] Manganese ore is not imported for the production of metallic manganese, but is used in the steel industry; see Chapter 16, p. 394. No further mention will be made of it in this chapter.

[3] Pyrites includes both iron pyrites (FeS_2) and copper pyrites ($CuFeS_2$). Iron pyrites is imported for the sulphur and not for the iron.

[4] Many ports receive iron pyrites since its chief use was in gas-works. Liverpool is the chief recipient of Spanish copper pyrites, used in the Lancashire chemical industry (cf. Chapter 22).

Imports of ores and metals

It is obvious that the small quantities of metal to be obtained from the ores enumerated above could not form the basis of any large manufacturing industry. In order to maintain the vast industries which grew up during the nineteenth century, therefore, recourse must be had to the import of raw materials from abroad. The greater part of the raw material is in the form of crude metal (already smelted and perhaps refined); some ores and concentrates, however (notably zinc from Australia, and bauxite, the ore of aluminium), are still imported by certain ports where the smelting industry, favoured by a coastal situation, is not entirely extinct (e.g. Swansea, Liverpool, Bristol).

Besides continuing their smelting industry, though in a greatly reduced and modified form, these old coastal centres have also turned over to the working up of imported metal into sheets, bars, wire and tubes. But the weight of a given quantity of crude metal will be very little reduced after manufacturing, and in consequence, unlike the ores, this raw material will stand the cost of transport to inland centres. Needing no special accommodation, it can be dealt with to a very large extent by the great ports, London, Liverpool, Manchester, in the course of their ordinary import trade. The large part which these ports play in the import of crude metal is, however, partly accounted for by the existence at all three of important refining and manufacturing industries; but London, especially, imports far greater quantities than its own works can consume, the surplus going to the Midlands or as far afield as South Wales.

Non-ferrous metals in the United Kingdom (tons)

	1950	1960	1968	
	LONG TONS	LONG TONS	METRIC TONS	LONG TONS
Aluminium				
Virgin aluminium production	29 500	28 900	38 200	37 600
Secondary ,, ,,	79 900	109 600	186 000	183 000
Lead (refined) production	73 100	91 100	143 700	141 400
Imported refined lead	163 400	192 100	161 400	158 900
Zinc (slab) production	70 300	74 300	132 800	130 700
Home consumption	330 100	365 800	367 000	361 300
Tin metal production	28 500	27 700	28 100	27 700
Copper home production	190 200	215 400	197 700	194 600
,, home consumption	526 500	722 600	779 600	668 900
Nickel home production	20 900	33 800	41 600	41 000

The non-ferrous metal industries considered separately

Aluminium.[1] This, one of the most abundant metals in the earth's crust, has given rise to the youngest of the great non-ferrous metal industries. Its de-

1. See W. G. Rumbold, *Bauxite and Aluminium*, Imperial Institute Monographs on Mineral Resources.

velopment dates really from about 1900, with the discovery of a reduction process applicable on a commercial scale. Although alumina is present in all clays, bauxite (a mixture of bohmite $Al_2O_3.H_2O$, and gibbsite $Al_2O_3.3H_2O$), the name derived from Baux in southern France, is as yet the chief commercial source of the metal. The production of aluminium is effected in two stages: (1) by a complicated chemical process, nearly pure alumina (aluminium oxide Al_2O_3) is obtained from the bauxite: (2) the alumina is calcined and then reduced in an electric furnace employing a current of great intensity.[1] It is the necessity for electric power on a large scale which has hitherto been the chief obstacle to the spread of aluminium manufacture, and which has caused the concentration of the industry mainly near hydroelectric stations. In Britain, the production of the metal is divided into two quite distinct parts. The extraction of alumina from imported bauxite is effected at Burntisland; the works at Larne which were based on the Antrim bauxites, have been closed, but in 1939 large new works were established at Newport in South Wales. The reduction of the alumina is effected at works using hydroelectricity which have been erected in the Scottish Highlands at Fort William (Inverness) and Kinlochleven (Argyll). Although both Burntisland and Newport, being seaports, are fairly conveniently situated with regard to the import of bauxite it is obvious that a great deal of transport is necessary before the metal aluminium is finally produced; and as the power stations are far removed from the great metal-working centres a further journey is necessary before the metal finally enters the market as a finished article. For this reason it is a great advantage that aluminium is a metal of extreme lightness (Sp. Gr. 2.7).

Something of a revolution in the economic geography of aluminium production was foreshadowed in 1968, however, by Government agreement to the establishment of three large new smelters. The first, at Lynemouth on the Northumberland coast, is to obtain its electricity from a coal-fired power station (part of a conscious effort to boost the coal mining industry); the second, at Invergordon on the Moray Firth, and the third, at Holyhead, will derive their current from the public grid, to which hydro sources from the Highlands will contribute in the case of the former and nuclear power from the Wylfa station in Anglesey in the latter. All three of these new plants are to be located in areas that present special unemployment problems, but the interesting aspect is the breakaway from the apron-strings of hydroelectric stations.

In half a century many uses have been found for aluminium, based mainly on its lightness combined with strength, malleability and ductility, and the ease with which it can be alloyed with other metals. Unalloyed, it is used for electric cable wire (especially the bare overhead lines of the

1. 100 000 ampères at 5 volts, see S. H. Beaver, 'Technology and geography', *Advmt Sci.*, **18**, 1961, 315–27.

Grid and for virtually all low-voltage mains up to 11 kV), in motor-car and aircraft construction, and for hollow-ware (i.e. cooking utensils). Alloyed with copper, zinc, or with two or more other metals, for the purpose of combining lightness with tensile strength, it is used for pistons, cylinders and other parts of aircraft and motor-car engines (as opposed to framework). Two world wars gave a tremendous stimulus to the production of aluminium for aircraft, and the rapid post-1918 expansion of the motor industry provided a new outlet. Aluminium is also employed in the manufacture of the explosive ammonal and the production of metallic paint. The aluminium-manufacturing industry may be divided into three parts: (*a*) Rolling and wire drawing are largely carried on in the metal-working district of southwest Lancashire (Warrington, Prescot, St Helens, etc.); but South Wales, since the last war, has become the major area; at Rogerstone, near Newport, a continuous rolling mill, established in 1950, converts Canadian aluminium ingots into saleable products, while other large plants have been established at Swansea, Resolven (in the Vale of Neath) and Newport. In North Wales, the Dolgarrog hydroelectric plant is concerned with sheet-rolling from imported ingots. An outlying centre, owing its origin largely to cheap land and good rail communications, is Banbury. (*b*) The foundry industry is much more scattered, but its correlation with the motor-car industry is most marked; the most important centres being Coventry, Birmingham (and various Black Country towns), Manchester, the London district and Glasgow. It was natural, considering the importance of the Birmingham-Smethwick-West Bromwich area in the brass and iron-foundry trades, that the first establishment for making aluminium castings should have been set up at Smethwick in 1900. The growth of the industry elsewhere was largely the result of the development of the motor-car and aircraft industries but in later years aluminium has entered into the whole field of general engineering and plays a large part in building (sections and tubing), packaging (aluminium foil), the chemical and food industries (e.g. beer cans) with the consequence that aluminium-using factories are widely scattered. (*c*) The hollow-ware trade, essentially a post-1918 development, is centred at Birmingham, where it is the logical successor of the decayed cast-iron hollow-ware industry.

Production of aluminium products (thousand long tons)

	1956	1968
Sheet and strip	141	189
Castings	79	125
Extrusions	72	135
Forgings	5	4
Total	297	453
Total (metric tons)	301	460

A flourishing export trade in aluminium products has been built up since the Second World War (see table on p. 486).

Lead. With the decline of the home lead mining industry, and the increase of lead smelting at the rich mines of foreign countries, Britain has lost the high position which she formerly occupied in the lead trade. The ores produced in this country now provide less than one per cent of the total lead consumed, the remainder being imported chiefly in the form of pig-lead from abroad (see table on p. 474). To a greater extent than most other metals, lead is used in the production of certain chemical compounds as well as in the metallic state. Of these compounds the most important are white lead, red lead and litharge. They are used in the manufacture of glass, for glazing pottery and earthenware, and for the manufacture of paints and pigments. In the metallic state (when it is soft though tough, flexible and very malleable) lead is made into sheets, pipes, wire and shot; whilst alloyed with other metals it contributes to the production of type metal (lead and antimony), pewter (lead and tin) and certain kinds of brass. Considering this great variety of uses and also the rather scattered nature of the old-time lead industry (cf. Fig. 184), it is not surprising that the manufacture of lead and its products should be much more widely distributed than most of the other non-ferrous metal trades. The last lead-smelting establishments to use locally produced ores were in Derbyshire (near Matlock) and on Deeside in Flintshire (at Bagillt). The establishments on Tyneside which flourished in the days when the Alston Moor mines were at the height of their prosperity have now to rely on imported material; the cessation of Mendip lead mining similarly left the Bristol works without their original basis.

Production of lead and lead products (thousand long tons)

	1956	1968
English refined lead	95	141
Imported refined lead	172	159
Lead scrap used	101	106
Lead used in cables	114	79
Lead used for batteries	28	47
Lead oxides and compounds	72	115
Sheets and pipes	74	65
White lead	10	4
Solder	14	14
Alloys	17	20
Total lead used	358	378
Total lead used (metric tons)	364	384

The most important centres of the lead industry today are to be found at the ports where the pig lead is received. London, Newcastle, Manchester, Bristol and Glasgow are the most important, but as the raw material is imported in a refined condition, and so leaves little or no waste in manufacturing, numerous inland centres also have works devoted to the manufacture of lead sheets and pipes. Nearly 20 per cent of the pig lead consumed goes towards the making of sheets and pipes, nearly 25 per cent is employed in the production of white and red lead and litharge, and 10 per cent in the making of batteries. The remainder finds an outlet in the manufacture of shot, solder and type metal.

Zinc. As with lead, the home production of zinc ores is now almost negligible, and the bulk of the requirements must be imported. In the case of zinc, however, large quantities of ore are imported from Australia, as well as spelter, and smelting is thus still an important side of the industry, with an output of about 100 000 metric tons of metal a year. Consumption was 350 530 metric tons (345 000 long tons) in 1966. The chief uses of zinc are as follows: (*a*) We have already seen its importance in the brass industry, of which, with copper, it forms the raw material—about 32 per cent of the spelter consumed goes towards the making of brass. (*b*) We have examined in Chapter 17 its use in galvanising steel sheets—about 27 per cent of the spelter consumption is employed for this purpose. Wire is similarly given a protective coating; 48 000 kilometres (30 000 miles) of wire so treated were used in the Forth road bridge (1963). (*c*) Lastly, like lead, it has many subsidiary uses—in electric batteries and in the zinco-type printing process, as well as (in the form of various compounds) for the manufacture of lithopone (used in the making of white rubber goods), in the production of pigments and varnishes, in the dyeing and calico-printing industry, and for medicinal purposes. Whilst zinc-using industries are scattered over many parts of the country, therefore, the existence of a large smelting industry, and the necessity for importing spelter as well are bound to have considerable effect upon their distribution.

The smelting of imported ores (i.e. the production of spelter) is carried on in Swansea, where the industry grew up very largely out of the declining copper trade. At first calamine and blende were imported from abroad or from Flintshire, but now the bulk of the supply consists of Australian concentrates. In 1930 smelting both of zinc and copper had practically ceased in Britain. Zinc was produced by only one company—The National (now Imperial) Smelting Company, now a branch of the Rio Tinto Zinc Corporation—which later (1957) developed a new blast furnace system of production at Avonmouth where works had been erected during the First World War. Avonmouth and Swansea are the only smelters. The galvanising industry has two branches: the first, allied to the tinplate trade, deals with corrugated galvanised steel sheets for roofing and fencing purposes (see Chapter 17); the second, with which we are concerned here, is independent of the tinplate industry, and is concerned with the galvanising of steel sheets and their manufacture into articles and wares—cisterns, tanks, dustbins, chimney cowls, hollow-ware, etc. It is true that some of the corrugated-sheet manufacturers of South Wales, Bristol and Flintshire also deal in the second branch of the industry, but in the main this trade is concentrated in the Birmingham area and at certain ports. In Birmingham and the Black Country it is an offshoot of the formerly important tinplate trade in an area which deals largely in zinc for its brass industry. At Liverpool, Manchester, London and Glasgow, the localising factors would seem to be (*a*) the port where, in the course of general trade, spelter ingots are most conveniently imported, and (*b*) the presence in the vicinity of a large market for the type of goods produced.

The general working of zinc, apart from galvanising and brass making, is carried on in a large number of towns, but as with most of the non-ferrous metals, the industry is dominated by Birmingham, where over 40 per cent of the firms engaged in the trade have their headquarters.

Tin. Tin is not used in nearly such large quantities as lead and copper, the reason being that it does not enter into commerce in the form of articles made of tin, but is employed chiefly in the tinplate industry (to the extent of about 50 per cent of the total consumption), in the manufacture of numerous alloys, such as bronze (tin and copper) (see below) and its varieties—bell metal and gun metal, Britannia metal (tin and antimony, largely used in the manufacture of Sheffield plate) and pewter (tin and lead), and in the formation of a number of useful chemical compounds, used especially in the dyeing and calico-printing industries.

Since the Cornish tin mines, like most other non-ferrous metal mines in Britain, now provide only a very small proportion of the total requirements, a large import of concentrates and metal bars is necessary. The tin smelting industry is located chiefly at Liverpool (Bootle), but there is also a works at Northfleet, on the Thames below London. It is doubtful whether the Cornish smelters at Redruth will ever work again. The annual smelter output of metallic tin is of the order of 20 000 metric tons.

Much of the bar tin imported is consumed in the tin-plate industry of South Wales (cf. Chapter 17). The bronze industry is dealt with below.

Copper. Copper was probably the first metal ever adapted by man for his own uses, but its importance in human affairs is now greater than ever before, owing to the part which it plays in the transmission of electrical energy. The valuable properties of copper are its great tensile strength, its ductility, which permits it to be drawn out into the finest of wires, and its capacity for conducting an electric current.

All the copper used in this country now has to be imported, and in consequence the location of the industry is but an interesting reminder of bygone conditions. The early copper industries were founded on such sound geographical bases, however, that the industrial momentum which they have accumulated has sufficed to maintain them, the only alterations being the substitution of refining for ore smelting, and perhaps some change in the nature of the output.

Production of copper and copper products (thousand long tons)

	1956	1968
Refined virgin copper	118	49
Refined secondary copper	103	146
Wire	259	270
Sheet, strip and plate	131	136
Rods, bars and sections	93	113
Tubes	69	86
Castings, etc.	69	59
Total products	633	669
Total products (metric tons)	643	679

The smelting and refining of matte (half smelted copper)[1] is carried on in those two regions which were formerly dominant in the ore-smelting industry—southwest Lancashire and South Wales, Widnes and Port Talbot being the chief centres. Birmingham and Walsall also have smelting works. The refining and working up of imported copper bars and their transformation into rolled sheets and wire is an industry located mainly in South Lancashire (Widnes, St Helens, Prescot,[2] Garston (Liverpool))—note the connection with the electrical machinery and cable industries—but several other places, such as Swansea, Glasgow, Hebburn-on-Tyne, Birmingham, Walsall and Leeds, also share in this branch. About 40 per cent of the total consumption of copper is employed in the production of wire, and another 20 per cent in the manufacture of plates and sheets. The manufacture of copper tubes for boilers employs about 12 per cent of the copper consumption. As far back as the 1860s some 8000–9000 metric tons of tubes were being produced annually, and the growth of railways and steamships increased this quantity materially before the end of the century. The use of the superheater and of higher boiler pressures, however, with the employment of steel tubes reduced the demand. On the other hand copper pipes

1. Copper smelting is a more complicated process than iron smelting. The ore is roasted and once smelted to get rid of most of the sulphur (hence the sulphurous fumes mentioned above) and in this stage it is known as 'blister', 'matte' or 'regulus'; a further roasting follows, and then another smelting, when the copper is ready for a final electrolytic refining.
2. A works was opened at Prescot in 1933 for the working of copper of great purity from the Roan Antelope mine in what was then Northern Rhodesia.

have largely replaced lead pipes in domestic plumbing. The tube industry is concentrated almost entirely on Birmingham, where Boulton and Watt first began to produce steam engines on an economic scale in 1775.

Copper is second only to iron as a metal useful to industry, and of the immense variety of articles that can be stamped, pressed, or otherwise fabricated from copper sheets and bars, the electrical and the machinery industries employ the largest proportion. We may expect the 'coppersmith' trade to be located, therefore, with special reference to these industries (cf. Chapter 17) and it is not surprising that, as judged by the number of establishments, Manchester and Glasgow, the two greatest engineering cities in the country, should head the list. London, Birmingham, Liverpool, Sheffield, the textile engineering towns of the West Riding and southeast Lancashire, and the Tyneside towns are also important—but the industry, like general engineering, is on the whole very scattered.

The Alloys. Alloys are mixtures of two or more metals designed to give physical properties different from those of the metals which compose them. Some of these have already been referred to. The most important groups are the brasses and bronzes.

Brass. Brass is the name given to a whole series of copper-zinc alloys, containing over 50 per cent of copper, the mixing of the metals in different proportions creating new metals of varying properties. Brass, like copper, will take on a brilliant polish, and has a similar high tensile strength, but it is harder than copper. Of the many different varieties in common use, the following may be cited as examples: 'yellow metal' for hot stamping is 58:40 with a little lead; Muntz's metal, a malleable variety, is 60:40; brass for wire 70:30; 'naval' brass 61:38, with a little tin to improve its corrosion-resisting property. It may be as well to remind ourselves of the many ways in which brass enters into commerce and industry. The brass trade falls naturally into two sections: (1) the actual making of the alloy and the production of semi-manufactured material. Of an annual production of something over 300 000 metric tons, about 80 per cent is in the form of rods and sheets (the raw material of the foundry and stamping branches), about 3 per cent is brass wire, and the remainder in the form of tubes (for boilers, curtain rods, and formerly, in the nineteenth century, for brass bedsteads) and castings; (2) the finished goods section, comprising cabinet brassfoundry (locks, hinges, knobs, etc.), lighting (oil lamps, gas and electric-light fittings), plumbers' brassfoundry (taps, etc.), engineers' brassfoundry (steam cocks, whistles, etc.), naval brassfoundry, and a host of general products, such as picture rails and nails.

The brass industry has many times, with changing fashions, been called upon to turn to new activities, and usually the decline of one branch has been accompanied or followed by the rise of another. This has been especially evident during the present century. The declining demand for the elaborate gas fittings, ornamental candlesticks, brass-railed bedsteads and brass hearth furniture of the Victorian era was offset by the rise of the electrical and motor-car industries, both of which were great brass users, and by the great post-1918 development of housing schemes with their accompanying need for 'builders' brassfoundry'. More recently these brass products have been subjected to severe competition from plastics (see p. 594).

The whole of the brass industry is dominated by Birmingham. At the 1931 census, of 40 000 people employed in the making of brass and brassware, over 16 000 were enumerated in that city, whilst several thousands more were not far away in Smethwick and the Black Country towns. As the table on p. 486 shows, the position in 1950 was almost exactly the same. Outside the Birmingham region, the various branches of the brass trade are very widely scattered all over the country, most important towns, and many quite unimportant ones, having some establishment, possibly a huge factory or possibly only a small workshop, dealing with one or another type of product. Much of the heavy brass industry, together with naval brassfoundry, has migrated northwards to the engineering and shipbuilding centres, leaving Birmingham to specialise on the innumerable smaller foundry and stamped products. Thus whilst Birmingham had only 30 per cent of the brassfoundry workers in 1931, it claimed 62 per cent of the workers employed in the manufacture of light brass goods (builders' accessories, etc.). The rapid development of plastics and stainless steel has had a very serious effect on the latter branch. In 1921 it employed 24 000 people; in 1931 only 12 000. The numerous engineering industries of London employ many brassworkers, and Manchester, Glasgow, Wolverhampton, Liverpool, Leeds, Huddersfield, Sheffield, Rotherham, Newcastle and Bristol—to name only a few—are amongst the most important provincial centres of the brass trade.

Bronze. Bronze was the first alloy ever made. Although it is no longer the chief metal for ornaments, utensils and weapons, certain types of bronze still play an important part in industry and art. Bronzes are harder, stronger and more durable than copper or brass, and are particularly resistant to the effects of atmospheric weathering. In industry, bronzes are employed for machinery bearings, pumps, boiler-mountings, valves and cocks, and for parts exposed to damp air or water; and in the arts, bronze is almost unrivalled for beauty of finish and general appearance in the production of statuary and ornaments. In general, bronzes are made up of about 80 per cent copper and 20 per cent tin; gun-metal (so called because it was formerly a favourite material for the making of cannon) has more copper, and more recent varieties which give extra strength and roughness, combined with an even greater resistance to corrosion, are phosphor bronze (containing some lead and a little phosphorus) and manganese bronze (with a little manganese and iron).

The chief centres of the bronze industry are Birmingham and London.

Other towns of importance are Manchester, Coventry and Glasgow (note the correlation with the engineering and motor industries), and Sheffield, where the industry is one of many concerned with non-ferrous metals (especially the rarer ones). The numerous other centres are scattered, and no geographical explanation can be given of them.

Other metals. Antimony, chromium, molybdenum, tungsten, bismuth and other rarer metals are imported into this country in small quantities for special purposes—usually for alloying with other non-ferrous metals or with steel. Antimony is used, largely by reason of its hardness and resistance to corrosion, in Britannia metal and type metal; chromium, molybdenum and tungsten are chiefly employed at Sheffield for the production of special quality steels—chromium for rustless steel[1] and steels of high-tensile strength, molybdenum for high-speed tool steels, tungsten for very hard steels (and also for wire in incandescent electric lamps). These metals are refined either at Sheffield, where their subsequent employment lies, or in south Lancashire (Widnes and St Helens). Bismuth has the important property, which it also imparts to its alloys, of expanding when it solidifies from the molten state. When used as a constituent of type-metal it ensures a good sharp type if cast from moulds. The most important of the other metals, however, is nickel. Nickel matte from Canada is refined at Clydach (Swansea), and the resulting metal is employed in the manufacture of nickel-silver at Sheffield and Birmingham, and in the production of nickel-steel, a high-tensile variety, at Sheffield. An interesting byproduct obtained at Swansea is copper sulphate (the nickel matte contains copper) exported to Mediterranean countries for vine spraying and to Ireland for potato spraying.[2]

The precious metals. Although gold and silver ores have never been worked in any great quantity in Britain, the unceasing demand for plate, ornaments and jewellery has given rise to a flourishing industry based on imported supplies of these precious metals. In 1966, about 28 000 people found employment in the jewellery, precious metal working and plate trades. To a greater extent than in any other major industry except clothing (see p. 612), these trades are characterised by small firms employing less than twenty-five persons. Such firms in fact produce nearly one-quarter of the products, and employ some 6000 people. This section of the non-ferrous metal industry is far more concentrated on a few localities than any of the trades devoted to the baser metals. Birmingham, Sheffield and London are

1. Notice also the amazingly rapid growth of chromium plating replacing the earlier nickel plating.

2. Production of copper sulphate (average, 1928–31), 44 600 metric tons (44 000 long tons). Export of copper sulphate (average, 1928–31), 43 600 metric tons (43 000 long tons). In 1955–60 the export averaged 33 400 metric tons (33 000 long tons) but by 1966 it had fallen to 13 100 metric tons (13 000 long tons), with Greece as the chief recipient.

the only cities in which the precious metals are utilised to any extent. Avoiding details, it may be said that Birmingham largely controls the refining and beating of gold, and the manufacture of gold chains and other jewellery, whilst silver and the electroplating trades are divided between that city and Sheffield. The Sheffield silverplate industry dates from about 1742, when Thomas Bolsover discovered a method of coating a copper ingot with silver in such a manner than it could be subsequently rolled and worked into plate and ornaments. The growth of the silver and electroplating trades in Sheffield (the latter from 1804) is partly the result of this almost accidental beginning, and is partly, no doubt, to be ascribed to the availability of labour already skilled in the working of metals. Finally, London, largely by reason of its immense potential market, shares in all the chief branches of the gold and silver industry.

Regional summary

An attempt may now be made to summarise the non-ferrous metal industries according to the regions of Britain where they are carried on.

In 1950[1] nearly 170 000 people were employed in Great Britain in industries concerned entirely, or almost entirely, with non-ferrous metals. This figure differs little from that recorded in the Census of 1931, at which date about 49 per cent were in Birmingham and the Black Country, 16 per cent in the London district, 13 per cent in the West Riding and 8 per cent in South Lancashire.

Although many branches, as we have seen, are very scattered in their distribution, the non-ferrous metal industry as a whole falls, geographically, into a number of fairly well defined provinces, each characterised by the presence of a different series of trades.

The *Birmingham District*[2] is probably the greatest metal-working area in the whole world. Employing nearly 70 000 people, it engages in almost every possible activity connected with non-ferrous metals, from smelting and refining, through the production of semi-manufactured material to the fabrication of innumerable varieties of finished goods. Its specialities, however, are the making of brass, the rolling of brass and copper, and the manufacture of tubes, the production of all kinds of cast and stamped copper and brassfoundry, the working of gold, and the manufacture of gold, silver and electroplated ware, and the production of aluminium hollow-ware.

The *London district*, including lower Thames-side, also has a great variety of metal trades, owing to the facility for importing raw materials and the

1. Later employment figures are on a different basis and not exactly comparable. In 1962 68 000 men and 15 000 women were engaged in the 'manufacture of copper, brass and other base metals'; and in 1966 the total was 80 000.

2. See *Birmingham and its Regional Setting*, British Association for the Advancement of Science, Handbook, 1950, especially pp. 159–248; also M. J. Wise, 'The evolution of the jewellery and gun quarters in Birmingham'. *Inst. Br. Geogr.*, **15**, 1949, 58–72.

Employment in non-ferrous metal industries, 1950[1] (in thousands)

REGION	SMELTING, REFINING, ROLLING	BRASS INDUSTRY	JEWELLERY AND PRECIOUS METALS	TOTAL
Scotland	6.4	2.2	0.2	8.8
Wales	11.0	0.4	0.5	11.9
Northern	2.5	1.5	0.0	4.0
Northwest	9.2	2.6	0.5	12.3
E. and W. Ridings	5.4	5.5	5.4	16.3
N. Midlands	0.6	0.4	0.0	1.0
Midlands	37.5	21.6	10.8	69.9
Southwest	2.7	0.3	0.0	3.0
South	7.3	0.4	0.2	7.9
East	2.7	0.3	0.1	3.1
London and S.E.	13.9	4.6	10.8	29.3
(*London*)	*13.0*	*4.6*	*10.5*	*28.1*
Total	99.1	40.0	28.6	167.7[2]

[1] Compare table on p. 457, in which the same regional divisions are used.
[2] Compare 1921, 181.6; 1931, 147.5.

Exports of non-ferrous metals and manufactures thereof (thousand long tons)

METAL	1913	AVERAGE 1921–25	AVERAGE 1926–30	1931	1950	1960	1968
Aluminium	—	5.9	9.6	6.8	58.6	53.2	60
Brass	13.4	26.2	21.3	12.1	55.9[1]	55.6[1]	74[1]
Copper	63.4	32.3	33.7	19.4	48.7	113.4	99
Lead	48.4	18.0	12.2	9.3	4.8	—	—
Nickel	—	4.6	7.8	4.8	13.8	26.7	45
Tin	11.5	18.8	29.3	25.0	15.4	7.8	11
Zinc	11.1	6.3	6.5	6.5	5.9	—	—
White Metal	—	6.9	4.0	3.8	3.5	—	—
Total value (million £'s)	12.0	14.4	17.2	6.9	57.5	89.1	168

[1] Includes other copper alloys (other than nickel alloys).
1 long ton (2240 lb) = 1.016 metric ton.

extensive market provided by the eight millions of people in the conurbation. Northfleet has important tin and lead-refining works, and London itself, principally in the East End and also south of the Thames, engages in the jewellery trades, sheet-metal working of all kinds, brass and copper foundry, bronze manufacture, galvanising and the manufacture of lead, and lead products.[1]

The *West Riding* assumes a position of importance, largely by reason of the part played by Sheffield in the manufacture of silver ware and electroplated goods. The baser metals are also worked to a considerable extent, however, notably copper and brass—these industries, located mainly in the towns which make up the West Yorkshire conurbation, as well as in Sheffield, being dependent upon and auxiliary to the great engineering industries of that region. The largest copper works is at Rothwell near Leeds.

South Lancashire has two sides to its industry. In the western part of the region, at Liverpool, Widnes and St Helens, are located the smelting and refining branches, together with rolling and wire drawing, the chief metals dealt with being copper, tin and aluminium. The eastern part of the region, however, is more concerned with copper and brassfoundry as a part of the great engineering industry of Manchester and the other towns that have been mentioned in Chapter 17.

In *South Wales* we find all that remains of the once world-famous smelting industry. In the Swansea–Port Talbot area are the principal zinc and nickel smelters in the country and the last remnant of the Welsh copper smelting trade. It is a good reflection on the geographical environment of South Wales, however, that just as in the iron trade, few or no derived industries should have been set up. The absence of a great engineering industry has rendered impossible the growth of extensive foundry trades, and even rolling and wire drawing are conspicuous by their absence or feeble development. The aluminium fabricating industry, in the Swansea area and behind Newport, dates mainly from the Second World War and after. The smelting and refining industries at Bristol may be considered, having similar geographical bases, as an outlier of the South Wales province.

The *Northeast coast* still retains its interest in the smelting business, lead and zinc being produced from materials which now have to be imported. The brass and copper industries are largely bound up with the engineering and shipbuilding trades, being concerned primarily with the requirements of the shipyards, and the marine and locomotive engineers.

On *Clydeside* the non-ferrous metal industries are mainly dependent on the engineering and shipbuilding trades, but they also owe their development partly, as at other large ports, to the facility for importing raw materials. Copper and brassfoundry, sheet-metal work, jewellery and galvanising are the most important branches.

1. Billiter Street, in London (bellyeter = bell-founder), was a former centre of the bell-founding trade. London has 300 foundries dealing with non-ferrous metals.

19
The textile industries: woollen and worsted

The textile industries: general

The textile industries, which for many centuries were the mainstay of British prosperity, are well supplied with literature, technical and historical, economic and geographical. In this and the following chapters little more can be attempted than a summary of the main features of their development, present distribution, and relative importance.

Not only are the textile industries of major importance in employment and in foreign trade,[1] but they also provide interesting examples of the factors influencing the localisation of industry and the alterations in distribution brought about by changes in geographical values. These changing values are concerned primarily with the development of machinery and sources of power supply, and with the relative part played by the various kinds of raw material.

Although wool was from time immemorial the principal fibre employed in the making of cloth, the cotton industry, only introduced into Britain in the seventeenth century and not really important until the second half of the eighteenth, long since surpassed the woollen in size; and whereas the making of woollen cloth, formerly a very scattered trade based on local raw materials and still carried on in a number of different areas, has suffered radical changes in its geographical distribution, the cotton industry, never very widespread and always using imported fibre, has been localised very largely in the region of its origin—so that its recent serious decline has been all the more noticeable. Of the industries based upon the minor textile fibres, those of long standing, such as linen and hemp, show very definite localisation on home sources of raw material. The newer introductions, rayon and nylon, are essentially chemical industries as far as the production is concerned, but their utilisation has attached itself as a satellite to the older textile trades in regions where a 'deposit' of labour skilled in the working of textiles had accumulated.

The introduction of manmade fibres has had a far-reaching influence on

1. Percentage of total value of U.K. exports, 1950 (1913 figures in brackets): woollen mfs, 6.6 (8.0); cotton mfs, 7.3 (25.6); linen mfs, 1.4 (1.9); silk mfs, 2.3 (0.5). But by 1962 exports had fallen to the following totals: woollens £95m (3.0 per cent of total exports), cottons £88m (2.8), synthetic fibres £33m (1.0), silk, flax, jute and hemp £85m (2.7).

the textile industries as a whole, and it is no longer possible—as it was when this book was first published, in 1933—to identify clearly the various branches of the industry, for manmade fibres are spun and woven in what were formerly simply cotton or worsted mills, and are used to produce mixed fabrics of many kinds. Indeed, 'the whole business of yarn and cloth production and distribution is now so enmeshed that the old distinctions in terms of fibres, processes or location are meaningless. The textile industry is one organism and the health of any one member affects the health of the whole'.[1]

Nevertheless, it is impossible to approach the present-day textile industries except through their historical geography, and so Chapters 19–21 have been allowed to retain their titles.

The following tables show the general trends in employment over the last forty years or so. The fact that it is no longer possible to keep to the old classifications is a further indication of the degree of overlap between the various branches.

Employment in the textile industries, 1924–56 (thousands)

INDUSTRY	1924[1]	1930[1]	1950[2]	1956[6]
Cotton	526	379	326	256
Wool and worsted	273	223	216	210
Fellmongery	2	2	2	—[4]
Hemp and linen	24	16	14	—[4]
Textile finishing[3]	108	98	89	96
Canvas and sacking	9	7	—[4]	—[4]
Silk and artificial silk	40	59	50[5]	97
Lace	17	14	13	10
Hosiery	95	97	123	128
Total	1096	898	1013	1007

[1] Census of Production Reports. [2] Ministry of Labour figures.
[3] Bleaching, dyeing, printing, finishing. [4] Not available.
[5] Includes rayon and nylon *weaving*; rayon and nylon *production* employed 47 300 in 1950 (cf. table on p. 490).
[6] From Annual Abstract of Statistics.

The decline in the numbers employed in almost all branches continues. This is largely (except in the case of cotton) due to technological improvements that give greater output for the expenditure of less labour. But the employment in manmade fibre production is on the increase, as is that in hosiery (which is now largely concerned with manmade fibres) and in car-

1. Sir Frank Rostron, Chairman of the Textile Council, in *The Times*, 25 March 1968.

pets (in which manmade fibres have also created something of a revolution in recent years).

Employment in textile industries, 1961 and 1966 (thousands)

BRANCH OF INDUSTRY	1961	1966
Production of manmade fibres	45	51
Spinning of cotton, flax and manmade fibres	140	110
Weaving of cotton, flax and manmade fibres	130	103
Woollen and worsted	203	177
Jute	18	17
Rope, twine and net	14	13
Hosiery and other knitted goods	130	137
Lace	9	8
Carpets	37	43
Narrow fabrics	22	22
Made-up textiles	45	39
Textile finishing	83	71
Other textile industries	28	27
Total, textile industries	904	818

Regional distribution of textile employment, 1966 (thousands) (Ministry of Labour's New Regions)

North	21	Wales	18
Yorks. and Humber	184	W. Midlands	37
E. Midlands	124	Northwest	222
E. Anglia	4	Scotland	98
Southeast	34	N. Ireland	53
Southwest	16		

The above table shows that despite the decline of the cotton industry, the Northwest (i.e. Lancashire) still remains the most important textile province, with Yorkshire not far behind. The figures reflect the continued importance of the East Midlands in knitwear, of the several kinds of textile industries in Scotland, and of linen and manmade fibres in Northern Ireland. The decline of East Anglia from its one-time supremacy is explained in the following pages.

The historical geography of the woollen and worsted industries[1]

From the twelfth to the nineteenth century the woollen industry was the premier English industry, and as such was largely responsible for the growth of the country's wealth and so for the accumulation of the capital which rendered possible the development of the homeland and the Empire. Thus the existing industry is but the result of many centuries of development in which geographical factors have played a very large part.

From the earliest times to the fourteenth century

It is probable that a primitive domestic woollen industry existed even before the Roman occupation, and it is certain that cloth was made in Britain during that period, for the Romans had an establishment at Winchester for making fine uniform cloths, and evidence of dyeing and fulling operations has been found at various places in southern England. Spinning and weaving are occasionally mentioned in Anglo-Saxon literature, and it is possible that woollen fabrics were being exported to the Continent as early as the eighth century. Not until after the Norman Conquest, however, do we see definite evidences of the growth, helped probably by the skill of artisans amongst William's followers and by numerous refugees from continental wars, of a flourishing industry. This industry in the twelfth and thirteenth centuries was to be found principally in the larger towns of the southern and eastern parts of the country, which, largely owing to their accessibility from the continent and from the Metropolis, were at that time the seat of the chief economic developments. The earliest recorded weavers' guilds, for example, grew up in London, Winchester, Lincoln and Oxford, and other towns which gained a reputation for fine wares were York, Beverley, Colchester and Sudbury. Although the making of cloth was widespread, the industry was probably of no great magnitude, and most of the wool from the English sheep was exported in a raw state to the Continent.

The first economic revolution, fourteenth to sixteenth century

Having reached a peak of production and export in the thirteenth century, the wool trade declined for a long period; the almost incessant political strife was not conducive to its expansion, and many formerly important centres decayed. The seeds of a new period of progress were sown in the fourteenth century, however, when, from 1331 onwards, small bands of

1. Of the mass of historical literature, one of the most valuable items is E. Lipson, *History of the English Woollen and Worsted Industries*, 1921 (especially Chapter 6). The descriptions to be found in Leland's *Itinerary*, Fuller's *Church History*, and Defoe's *Tour through Great Britain* are exceedingly interesting and valuable as giving an account of the distribution and state of the industry at the different periods when they were written.

skilled craftsmen from Flanders were encouraged to settle in various parts of the country. Numerous weavers, dyers and fullers settled in large towns where the woollen industry was already in existence—such as London, York, Winchester and Norwich—or scattered themselves over the countryside. The widespread possibilities for cloth making were largely due to the suitability of such large areas of the countryside for sheep rearing (although from the earliest times the drier limestone and chalk uplands seem to have been the chief regions), and the absence of other localising influences. Water-mills were only just coming into use for working the fulling hammers,[1] and not only was the power required so small that almost any stream would do, but the unfinished cloth could be, and indeed was, sent from scattered weavers' houses to the small streamside establishment of the fuller.[2]

The export trade in wool recovered; it was largely a seasonal trade, for before the introduction of root crops as fodder, large numbers of animals had to be slaughtered in the autumn. Thus in the summer the shorn wool was sent across the Channel, in the autumn and winter the 'fells'—skins with wool still adhering thereto. But manufacturing expanded as well, and gradually the cloth industry began to be more localised and rather more specialised. The need for soft, lime-free water for the washing, scouring, and dyeing processes, combined with the increasing use of water power for the fulling mills, resulted in certain regions offering a more than usually favourable environment for the industry. In Gloucestershire, Somerset and Wiltshire, the importance of the sandstone formations in the Jurassic series, as suppliers of soft water, and the existence of a dissected scarp, providing numerous power sites, together with the extensive sheep pastures on the Cotswolds and in Herefordshire, were favourable factors. In Devonshire a number of centres grew up on the outer edge of the Dartmoor mass, favoured by soft water from the granites or culm measures and a useful power supply. In the Pennine districts of Yorkshire and Lancashire the soft water from the Millstone Grit uplands and the numerous steeply graded streams gave plenty of scope for development. In East Anglia, where many of the Flemish weavers settled, much soft water was available from the boulder clay streams, but little or no power. As a result, this region was not so well fitted for the production of true woollen goods, and came early to specialise in the manufacture of worsteds.[3] The idea of the fulling operation was to felt the cloth by pounding it with hammers in water mixed with soap or fuller's earth, and as worsted fabrics made from longer and finer wools did not require this treatment, power was not necessary. Of these four areas

1. R. A. Pelham, 'Distribution of early fulling mills in England and Wales', *Geography*, **29**, 1944, 52–6.
2. The need of pure water for dyeing was not apparent whilst most of the cloth was exported in a 'grey' state to be finished in Flanders.
3. It is generally agreed that the name 'worsted' is derived from the little village of Worstead, not far from Norwich, one of the earliest centres of the industry.

the two in the west of England were producing, at the end of the fifteenth century, about one-third of the woollen cloth made in England, East Anglia was responsible for about a quarter and Yorkshire for one-eighth (mainly of poor quality), and, in addition, East Anglia produced almost all the worsted material. Finally, it is very noticeable that the sheep-rearing regions of the Jurassic scarplands where limestone is a dominant formation and the stream water consequently hard—e.g. Lincolnshire and Northamptonshire—did not develop the manufacture of woollen fabrics to any great extent.

Thus during this period the whole economic outlook of the country was changed, and from being primarily an exporter of raw wool England became in addition a manufacturer and exporter of cloth. The end of the fifteenth century saw England 'largely a nation of sheep-farmers and cloth-makers'. The wealth derived from the wool trade was spent in church building and road-making, and many a fine church and cathedral and many a now-ruined abbey owes its origin to the sheep. The monks especially were great sheep farmers, as the records of the many old abbeys of Yorkshire bear witness.

Growth and expansion, sixteenth to eighteenth century

The expansion of the woollen and worsted industries brought about an increasing specialisation: (*a*) of different regions in different classes of goods; (*b*) of individual members of a manufacturing community in different processes; and it also contributed to the rise of a new class in society—the 'clothiers' or 'drapers' who purchased raw wool from the farmers, gave it out to the spinners and weavers to be made into cloth, and then sold the finished pieces in local markets or at the London Cloth Fair.[1] Much of the wealth gained by the drapers, and by the companies which they formed, went not into ecclesiastical channels but towards the further expansion of industry and trade. Then political and religious troubles on the continent were continually interfering with the Flemish cloth industry, and from time to time bands of refugees would flee their country and settle in England. In the sixteenth century, for example, after the revocation of the Edict of Nantes, a large body of Huguenots arrived from France and took up their abode in various cloth-making regions, notably in the Stroud area of Gloucestershire. As a result, the English cloth trade began to surpass that of Flanders, and at the end of the seventeenth century woollen manufactures made up two-thirds by value of England's export trade.

We must pause to analyse in a little more detail the geographical background of the principal centres of the industry in the seventeenth and early eighteenth centuries.

1. The markets were known as 'Cloth Halls'—e.g. Blackwell Hall in London.

The West Country.[1] Within the region so designated there were two distinct producing districts, the Cotswold area (extending from Cirencester to Sherborne, and from Devizes to Bristol), and Devonshire. In Gloucestershire, Wiltshire and part of Somerset was concentrated the manufacture of the famous 'broadcloths', while Devonshire and southwestern Somerset specialised in serges. The geographical advantages possessed by the region as a whole may be summed up as follows:

(*a*) The agricultural wealth of the fertile vales and the pastoral wealth of the uplands had long been utilised and had given rise in quite early times to a comparatively dense population.

(*b*) Supplies of raw materials—long-woolled sheep of Dartmoor and the Cotswolds (for the serge industry), short-woolled sheep of the near-by chalk uplands and the rich lands of Herefordshire, of the Forest of Dean and of Exmoor, and fuller's earth from the local 'Fuller's Earth' formation, which is particularly well developed on the dipslope of the Cotswolds—were present in abundance.

(*c*) When the necessity arrived, the geographical situation for the import of foreign wool was distinctly favourable—and Barnstaple and Bristol imported long wools from Ireland and fine merino wool from Spain.

(*d*) The abundance of soft water,[2] which was particularly suitable for dyeing, and of small water-power sites, as mentioned above, rendered the localisation complete.

Broadcloth was, perhaps, the finest variety of woollen fabric ever produced. It was made from the best short wools (i.e. not from the local Cotswold sheep) and was heavily fulled and felted so that when finished the weave was quite invisible. It was used for uniforms, liveries, and the best class of clothing. The wearing of broadcloth was formerly the mark of a gentleman. The importance of a power supply for the fulling is very evident, and it is not surprising that with the growth of the industry the localisation became more definite, and the network of 'clothing towns' and 'clothing villages' which Leland describes became more concentrated. The early town centres, Gloucester, Bristol and Tewkesbury, soon declined, and the less suitable outlying centres as, for example, the villages along the chalk scarp (Devizes, Warminster); those on the Mendip fringe (Frome, Wells); those on the Jurassic scarp of Somerset (Bruton, Castle Cary) and those in the Avon valley (Chippenham, Melksham, Bradford) decreased in importance or became specialised. Wells, for example, took up the hosiery trade; Frome specialised in fine Spanish cloths. It was on the dissected west-

1. See R. H. Kinvig, 'Historical geography of the West Country Woollen Industry', *Geographical Teacher*, **8**, 1916, 243–54; 290–302.

2. Although much of the Cotswold dipslope plateau is composed of shelly limestone (known as 'calcareous grit'), the chief water-bearing bed in the Scarp region is the Cotswold (or Midford) Sand, which yields copious supplies having a very low degree of permanent hardness.

facing scarp of the Cotswolds that the industry became concentrated, and the old centres on the dipslope—Tetbury, Cirencester and Witney—all had to specialise to avoid extinction. Thus Tetbury, devoid of water power (almost, in fact, devoid of water), took up wool-combing and spinning, and Cirencester did likewise—thin yarn from the long-woolled Cotswold sheep being sent to the hosiery and worsted centres. Witney, partly perhaps owing to a peculiarity of the Windrush water which makes it well suited to the bleaching operation and partly to the fact that it had little or no power, specialised in blankets, which are made from short wool and fells and do

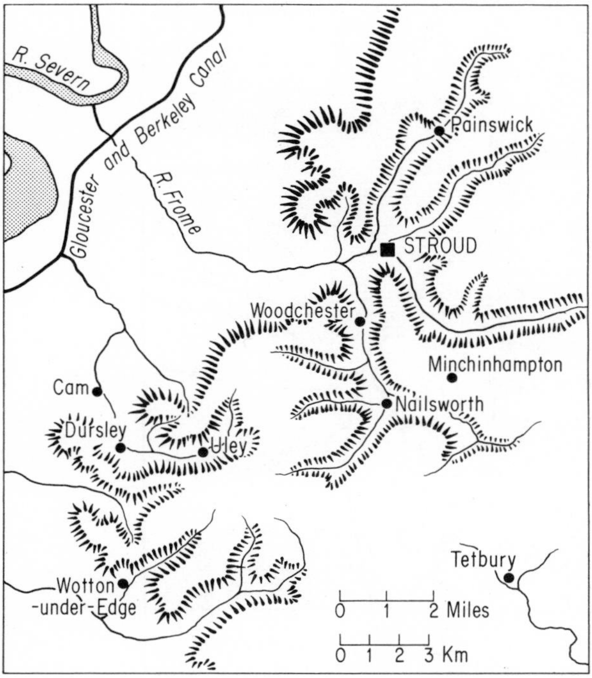

FIG. 185. The Broadcloth region in the dissected scarpland of the Cotswolds

not need heavy milling. On the western slope of the Cotswolds the deeply cut valleys of the Frome and its tributaries contained numerous centres of the industry—Stroud, Painswick, Minchinhampton, Woodchester and Nailsworth, and a little further south the edges of a westerly projection of the scarp provided power sites, for example, at Dursley, Wotton-under-Edge and Uley (Fig. 185). The waters of the scarp were considered to possess some property which rendered them particularly suitable for the production of the fine scarlet dye for which Gloucestershire cloths were famed.

'Serge' was the name given to a fabric made with a warp (longitudinal threads) of long wool, and a weft (crosswise threads) of short wool (or of the short combings derived from the long wool). Both long (Dartmoor) and short (Exmoor) wools were available in Devonshire, and in addition much long Irish wool was imported *via* Barnstaple and other ports, and short wool

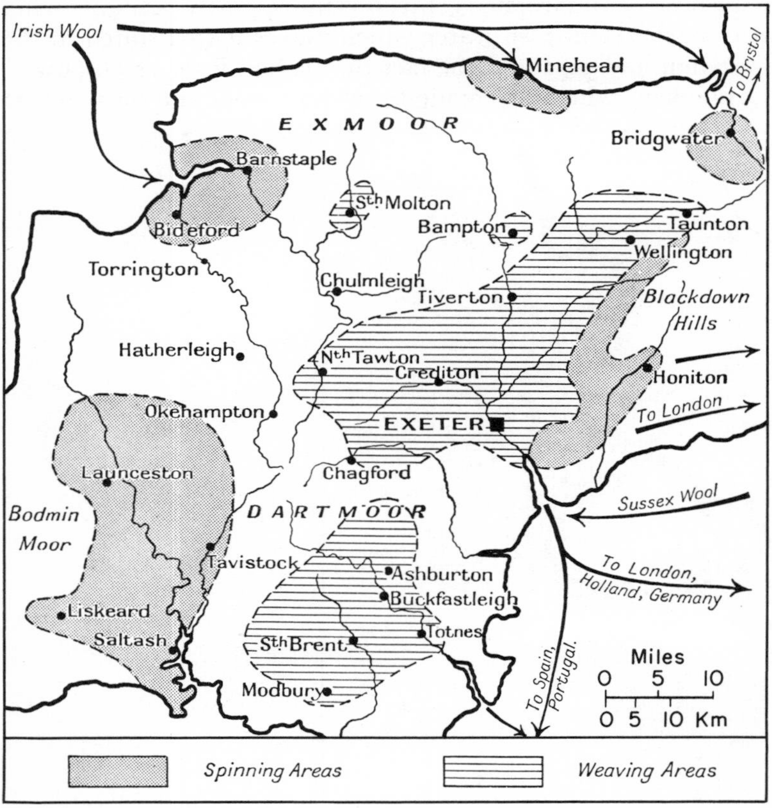

FIG. 186. The West Country woollen industry about 1700 (mainly after Hoskins)

from Kent and Sussex, *via* Exeter. Water power was necessary for milling serges, as for broadcloths, and the numerous small streams radiating from the Dartmoor massif supplied this in plenty. But owing to the comparative isolation of the individual streams many small manufacturing centres grew up, and there was no concentration as at Stroud. Ashburton, Buckfastleigh, Tavistock, Okehampton, North and South Molton, Tiverton and Crediton may be cited as examples, whilst just over the border, in Somerset, Taunton and Wellington were also engaged in the serge trade (Fig. 186). The great market for all this industry was Exeter, which in the eighteenth century rivalled Leeds in this respect.[1]

East Anglia, lacking water power, obviously could not produce broadcloths and serges, and in consequence it was the worsted trade which flourished here. The worldwide fame to which this region attained in the seventeenth and eighteenth centuries was in large measure due to the presence of the Flemish weavers and their descendants—far more artistic skill was necessary for the production of patterned worsteds than for the making and finishing of plain broadcloths. Two separate districts were engaged in the trade. Norwich, once the greatest manufacturing town in all England,[2] was the centre of a whole group of flourishing towns and villages engaged in the production of fine worsteds: for example, Thetford, Diss, Dereham and Attleborough. In Suffolk and Essex a number of towns in or near the Stour valley, the largest of which were Colchester, Sudbury and Halstead, had a twofold interest. Besides making some worsteds, and doing a great deal of combing and spinning for the Norwich weavers, this region, largely owing to the presence of a small amount of water power provided by the Stour and its tributaries, was devoted to the production of coarse cloths made from short wools—baize and kerseys, which were not true woollens, but rough loose fabrics which did not need much milling.

For 400 years East Anglia possessed a virtual monopoly of the worsted trade, and not until the beginning of the eighteenth century did a rival appear in the West Riding of Yorkshire.

Yorkshire and Lancashire. The gradual rise of the north country in the woollen trade is to be associated with the natural suitability of parts of the Pennines for sheep rearing, the abundance of lime-free water, and the existence of innumerable possible sites for waterwheels. The sixteenth-century spread of the industry up the valleys was also due to a countryward movement of the craftsmen away from the guild fettered corporate towns of the lowlands.[3] We must not neglect the fact, also, that a good deal of energy behind the expansion of the industry came from the Nonconformists, whose Puritanism, with its insistence on the duty of work, its teaching that business could be a 'divine calling', and its inculcation of the virtues of prudence, probity, and economy which smoothed the path to riches, was largely responsible for their accumulation of capital and its application to the development of trade. In both Lancashire and Yorkshire the early industry, devoted to the

1. See W. G. Hoskins, *Industry, Trade and People in Exeter, 1688–1800*, Manchester Univ. Press, 1935. Chap. 2 gives an account of the serge industry, which about 1700 was the most important branch of the national woollen manufacture, accounting for over a quarter of the total exports.
2. In 1770 no less than 72 000 people were employed.
3. Of the great West Riding towns, only Wakefield ever harboured the guild system. The serious decline of York at this period is well known.

weaving of coarse woollen cloths called 'kerseys', clung to the upper parts of the valleys, the dwellings where the spinning and weaving were done being situated on the slopes and higher parts (since surface water is very abundant on the Millstone Grit formation and Lower Coal Measures), the fulling mills in the valley bottoms by the larger streams. It was essentially a rural organisation—a combination of domestic industry and agriculture for the home food supply, where each house had its own cultivated patch and urban centres were not developed to any great extent.[1] The industry quickly outgrew the local wool supplies, and the Lancashire region began to import from Ireland and from the Midlands, while the West Riding came to rely more on Lincoln and Leicester wool. About the end of the sixteenth century, the manufacture of baize (using woollen warp and worsted weft) was introduced; but as the use of cotton began to spread soon afterwards in south Lancashire, the woollen trades in that area were pushed further and further eastwards until the Rochdale neighbourhood was the only important district remaining. Then, early in the eighteenth century, the wealthy merchants began to introduce the manufacture of worsted material, and Halifax and Rochdale quickly took to the making of 'shalloons' (light worsted cloth for dresses and linings)—the older baize trade gradually dying or being replaced by the weaving of flannels. By the 1770s the output of worsted cloth from the West Riding equalled that of Norwich, but the Yorkshire worsteds were mostly of much poorer quality.

An important auxiliary industry in the West Riding was the manufacture of wool-cards—stiff wire brushes used for opening out the wool and interlacing the fibres preparatory to spinning.[2] This was located at Brighouse—attracted thither by the old iron forge at Colne Bridge (near the outcrop of the sulphur-free 'Better Bed' coal and near a formerly important seam of ironstone).

In the eighteenth century the main outline of the great conurbation was complete; Leeds, Bradford, Halifax, Huddersfield and Wakefield were flourishing towns, Leeds and Wakefield having large cloth markets. Bradford had, however, not yet assumed special prominence, and neither had the shoddy trade (see p. 514).

Other centres. Mention must finally be made of a few other isolated and rather specialised centres of the woollen industry. Worcester and Kidderminster were really outlying centres of the West Country broadcloth trade. Kendal, in Westmorland, was long famous for 'Kendal cottons' (not made from cotton, but from local wool). In Leicestershire the local long-woolled flocks gave rise to a small woollen industry as early as the thirteenth century; and in the seventeenth century a domestic hosiery industry became established.

1. See the illuminating description in Defoe's *Tour through Great Britain*, which covers the years 1724–27.
2. The name 'card' is derived from Latin *carduus* = a thistle or teazel, since teazel heads were used in the carding process.

In the first half of the eighteenth century we thus see the woollen and worsted industries considerably more specialised and concentrated upon a few areas than they had ever been before. The West Country and East Anglia had almost reached their peak of prosperity, but the West Riding was really only just beginning to be of real importance in the manufacture of any but the poorest cloths. All this was about to be changed, for with the introduction of machinery and the utilisation of steam power and so of coal, the whole basis of the industry was radically transformed.

The Industrial Revolution, 1750–1850

The domestic processes of cloth manufacture had been little changed since the great revival of industry in the fourteenth century, and consequently the inventions which we have now to discuss produced an upheaval of unparalleled magnitude. This upheaval, however, took place earlier and was far more sudden in the case of the Lancashire cotton industry than with the Yorkshire woollen and worsted trades: in the first place because almost all the inventions emanated from Lancashire; secondly, because the woollen fibre did not lend itself so readily to being worked by fast-moving machinery; and thirdly, because an adequate supply of raw wool was not easy to obtain until Australian produce became available after about 1830. The history of these inventions is an oft-told tale, and a very brief summary must here suffice. In 1733 John Kay introduced the flying shuttle, thus rendering the process of weaving rather more rapid. This was perhaps a little unfortunate, for already it took ten spinners to keep one weaver supplied with yarn (a fact which is reflected in the large number of women who were engaged in spinning—and thus in the retention of the term 'spinster' for an unmarried woman); in the 'seventies, however, Hargreaves' spinning jenny and Arkwright's roller-spinning machine remedied this state of affairs, and the application of water power to the latter resulted in such an increased output that a surplus of yarn was produced. The application of mechanical power to weaving was somewhat delayed (see below). All these inventions were applied first to the cotton industry and their adaptation to wool and worsted came later. As a result the 'water power' stage in the West Riding was not of long duration and in some cases did not exist at all—for by the time machinery was introduced on a large scale, the steam engine had been sufficiently perfected as to be the obvious source of power for new mills and new machines. A new control—the existence of productive coal measures—entered the field.

The Lancashire inventions gradually crossed the Pennines and worked their way into the West Riding from the southwest, *via* Huddersfield and Halifax and probably by 1780 the use of the spinning jenny, still worked by hand, and of the scribbling machine (performing part of the carding process), worked by water power, had spread over most of the region. Neither of these could produce much change in the industry apart from a speeding up of certain of its processes—and by the separation of the upland, domestic, spinning and weaving from the valley-bottom scouring, fulling, and carding, much wasteful carriage had to be performed, each piece of wool journeying several times up and downhill before it finally emerged as a finished cloth. From 1785 onwards Watt's steam engine began to be used in the mills of Lancashire and Nottinghamshire, and the first in Yorkshire was set up for driving scribbling and fulling plant at Leeds in 1792[1]—marking the beginning of the end of the short reign of water power. Spinning machinery was introduced into Yorkshire in the 'nineties, and was in fairly general use by about 1810—the quick changeover being due possibly to the large numbers of women and children employed who were unable, like their menfolk, strenuously to resist the introduction of mechanical appliances. It must be noted, however, that it was the worsted branch, in which the longer, silkier fibres were more adaptable to mechanical handling, that progressed most, little headway being made with spinning machinery in the woollen branch until after 1830. Other, more commercial, reasons for the greater mechanisation of the worsted industry, were the greater capitalisation and more efficient organisation (it being a younger industry and essentially the product of Yorkshire's own accumulated wealth) and the large 'outside' demand (from the East Anglian worsted trade and the hosiery trades) for worsted yarn. The introduction of power looms took a much longer time, partly owing to the technical difficulty already alluded to and partly owing to vigorous opposition from the hand loom weavers. Not, in fact, until the early 'thirties was real progress made, but by 1835 Yorkshire possessed over 4000 woollen and worsted power looms out of a total for the country of about 5400 (a further 1100 being only just across the Pennines in Lancashire).[2] Gig mills (rotating drums set with teazels for raising the nap on cloth) and shearing frames (for cropping the nap) were also introduced fairly late, and the famous Luddite Riots of 1812 were largely directed against their use. In the following decade, however, they were erected rapidly in all districts.

Even when, stimulated by the outstanding success of the mechanised cotton industry of Lancashire, the use of machinery was well established, wool continued to lag far behind worsted for reasons given above, and also because there was much less specialisation in the woollen trade, most factories completing all or most of the processes, and a considerable amount of domestic work still taking place. In 1835 the number of looms weaving worsted cloth was four times the number weaving wool, and as late as 1856 only half of all the woollen workers in the West Riding were employed in factories, and handloom weavers remained an important section until the 'seventies, not being finally negligible until about 1900.[3]

1. See *Leeds Woollen Industry, 1780–1820*, ed., W. B. Crump, Thoresby Society, Leeds, 1931.
2. Compare this total with the 114 000 power looms which existed in the cotton industry at the same period.
3. Persons employed in woollen and worsted factories: 1835, 55 461; 1850, 154 180; 1861, 173 046; 1870, 238 503; 1880, 301 556; 1901, 259 909. Cf. cotton, pp. 532–33.

If the introduction of machinery was slow, though comparatively unobstructed, in the West Riding, it was much more retarded and much more bitterly opposed in the West Country, and in East Anglia the industry died before the machine had time to take root. Both in the West Country and in East Anglia the workers in the ancient industries were well organised and the industry was fairly concentrated, and so a much more effective opposition could be raised to the introduction of labour-saving machinery. This opposition proved their undoing. The swamping of the cloth market by cheap machinemade goods from Yorkshire gave a blow to the older industries from which they never recovered. The copying by machinery of all the fancy worsted designs of Norwich effectively killed the trade in that town. By 1830 domestic spinning had ceased to exist, and in 1838, when Yorkshire had 347 steam-driven mills employing over 26 000 people, Norwich had three with only 385 workers. The perfection of Arkwright's combing machinery had allowed short wools as well as long to be used for worsted manufacture, and the rapid spread of new fabrics produced by adding cotton, alpaca, or mohair warps to the worsted weft gave a tremendous stimulus to the Yorkshire worsted industry, which rapidly outpaced the slower growing woollen trade.

The West Country industry did not feel the pressure of Yorkshire competition as soon as East Anglia, owing to the late introduction of machinery and steam power into the woollen branch and to the persistence of the domestic system. After 1840, however, the declining market for the fine broadcloths and the inability of the Cotswold industry to adapt itself rapidly to the new conditions resulted in a period of decline—though the industry was by no means completely extinguished.

The general features of the Industrial Revolution period in the woollen and worsted industries may be summed up as follows:

(*a*) A gradual decline of the domestic system, less rapid in wool than in worsted, and in weaving than in spinning: accompanied by the development of large-scale production in factories.
(*b*) A short period of water power quickly followed by the employment of the steam engine for driving machinery.
(*c*) The rapid expansion of industry in the West Riding, where the localisation was confirmed by the presence of coal which was employed for generating power and for heating and humidifying the mills in accordance with the requirements of the spinning and weaving operations.
(*d*) The rise to supremacy of worsted over woollen in Yorkshire, very largely for technical reasons and owing to the organisation of the worsted industry.
(*e*) The decline and complete extinction of the Norwich worsted trade and the general decline of the West Country industry, where, however, with increasing specialisation the finest woollen cloths continued to be made.
(*f*) The growth of the West Riding, in combination with the rapid ex-

pansion of industry and population in Lancashire (see Chapter 20), brought about a change in the 'centre of gravity' of the English population and an increasing dominance of the north over the south.

Concentration and development, 1850–1950

The essential features of the geography of the woollen and worsted industries remained virtually unchanged for a century following the great transformation wrought by the Industrial Revolution.[1] Despite the great increase in the productivity of the industries there was little expansion after 1850 in the numbers employed, which fluctuated around 260 000 until the 1920s; this of course was due to the increased mechanisation of the processes of manufacture, to the greater concentration in large mills, and to the improvements in speed and efficiency of the machines. After 1900 there was a gradual tendency for steam power to be supplanted by electricity. There were, however, substantial changes in the supplies of raw wool. In the few decades before 1850, about three-quarters of the wool used was home grown, the remainder being fine Saxon and Silesian varieties. Between 1830 and 1860 Australian and Cape wools began to displace all other imports, and with the expansion of the industry the home clip came to assume a less significant position, declining to about one-tenth of the total quantity used (see table on p. 505).

Raw materials

The raw materials of the woollen and worsted industries consist principally of the wool of the domestic sheep, which is the most important of all fibres of animal origin used in the textile industries. There is no wild sheep with a fine fleece, and the sheep—now the most numerous of all domestic animals—was bred by man at an early date in the civilisation of the world. Even before the wool was used in weaving, sheepskins formed a valued protective covering. The fibres of wool differ from those of cotton in being covered with tiny overlapping scales, and the presence of these scales accounts for the 'felting' properties of wool: the fibres can be beaten together into a fabric (felt) without weaving because the scales interlock. It is because the fibres of wool are usually finely curled or crimped that a woollen cloth includes a large proportion of air space. Air is a bad conductor of heat and thus woollen clothes, with their large amount of included air, are very warm.

Without attempting to account for their origin, it may be said that wool-bearing sheep at the present day fall into three main groups:

(*a*) *Original English breeds*. In the Middle Ages wool was not only an im-

1. A useful summary will be found in the Board of Trade's *Survey of the Textile Industries*, HMSO, 1928.

portant product but a leading export of England. The English breeds have become widespread in South Africa, Australia and New Zealand. The animals thrive in cool, comparatively moist climates.

(*b*) *Merino sheep.* These sheep are natives of North Africa, but were introduced into Spain and other grassy areas in Mediterranean lands in the Middle Ages and later into Saxony. They yield but very poor meat and are bred essentially for their wool. They have become very important in South America, South Africa, Australia and New Zealand. The animals thrive in dry climates.

(*c*) *Cross-bred sheep.* These sheep are derived from cross-breeding between merinos and English strains. A large proportion of the Australian and New Zealand flocks are cross-bred. Cross-bred sheep yield both meat and wool.[1]

Shearing by machinery is now usual at most large sheep stations, and as the quality of the wool varies considerably from one part of an animal to another, the fleeces are usually clipped round or 'skirted', the inferior clippings being thrown into a separate bin. According to the age of the animal four grades of wool are distinguished:

Lamb's wool from 7 months old animals—the finest.
Hoggets from 12 to 14 months old sheep.
Wether wool from sheep of all other ages.
Double fleece, representing two years' growth, is poorer in quality than a single-year fleece from the same animal and is cheaper.

Fleeces vary greatly in weight. Australian sheep average between 2.5 and 3.1 kilograms ($5\frac{1}{2}$ and 7 lb); New Zealand sheep 3.4 kilograms ($7\frac{1}{2}$ lb). A prize fleece may be as much as 13.5 or 18 kilograms (30 or 40 lb).

Wool is graded according to the 'count' or number of 512-metre (560-yard) hanks that weigh 0.45 kilogram (1 lb).

Fine counts, from 60 to 90 hanks to 0.45 kilogram (1 lb). These are chiefly merino wools and are short stapled (6.35 to 15.2 centimetres ($2\frac{1}{2}$ to 6 in)).
Medium counts, from 36s to 60s. These wools are usually long stapled (up to 30.4 centimetres (12 in)) and include the wools of English breeds and the cross-bred colonial wools of South America and Australia.
Coarse or low counts, below 36s. These wools are more like hair, and include the wools of southern Russia, Asia and North Africa.

Wool as shorn from the sheep contains a large proportion of grease, called 'yolk', as well as varying proportions of dirt. It is usually exported 'in the grease' and productions are quoted on a 'greasy' basis.[2] The wool may be washed to remove dirt, but if the grease is removed the wool felts or mats together.

1. The introduction of refrigerator ships, by increasing the value of the sheep for meat, and thus concentrating attention on that aspect of sheep farming, led to a change in the character of Australian wool.
2. About four-fifths of the annual import is of 'greasy' wool.

The wool is washed with water containing ammonia or some solvent to remove the grease—a process known as scouring. Greasy wool loses half its weight when scoured. The grease extracted is known as lanoline and is used in the preparation of toilet soaps and cosmetics, and in the pharmaceutical industry. It should be noted that wool taken chemically from pelts is called 'slipes'.

The carding or combing processes result in the separation of 'tops' (the long hairs) and 'noils' (the short hairs), which are combed out.

In general it may be said that the woollen branch uses lower and medium grades of wool, 'noils', mungo (torn rags and tailor's clippings) and shoddy (wool derived from soft woollen rags and knitwear), whilst the worsted branch uses merino and the finer grades of wool.

In addition, other animal fibres are used for certain purposes. Although including some of the finest of textile materials, the rarer animal fibres are usually handled by dealers specialising in 'low wools':

Mohair is obtained from the Angora goat and is an important export from Turkey and South Africa. There the goats flourish on the Karroo, where it is too dry for sheep. Mohair makes strong, lustrous materials.
Cashmere is the fine, downy winter undercoat of the Kashmir (or Cashmere) goat, a native of Kashmir, Tibet and southern China. Each fleece yields only a hectogram (about 3 oz).
Camel's hair is obtained mainly from China and Turkestan. The mane and hump produce strong hair, the remainder of the body downy 'wool'.
Alpaca, llama, vicuna and *guanaco* are all animals native to South America, especially on the high Andes of Peru. The wool of the vicuna, a wild animal, is sometimes said to be the finest of all textile materials, and is certainly the most costly.

Owing to the large sheep population of Britain, to the great amount of cross-breeding which has taken place, and to the fact that sheep named after a particular area are rarely confined to that area, it is difficult to generalise about the home clip of wool. Our flocks may be roughly grouped into two classes, however, long-woolled and short-woolled. In the long-woolled class, the best breeds are the Lincoln, which yields a fleece of 4 to 4.5 kilograms (9 to 10 lb) in weight, and the Leicester; whilst other breeds are the Cotswold, the Romney Marsh, and the numerous varieties to be found in Devon and Cornwall (e.g. the South Devon and Devon Longwool), in many of the Midland counties, and in parts of Yorkshire (e.g. the Wensleydale). Most of the long-woolled sheep yield fairly coarse but lustrous wool which is almost invariably combed and spun by the worsted process. The short-woolled sheep fall into two groups, the mountain sheep yielding fleeces weighing about 1.5 to 1.8 kilograms (3 or 4 lb) and the breeds characteristic of the chalk areas yielding 1.8 to 2.25 kilograms (4 or 5 lb) fleeces. The mountain sheep produce very variable fleeces, according to exact breed and region; the roughest wools are used in the carpet and tweed trades, the fine Cheviot wool for woollens, and the soft short wool of the Welsh and Irish mountain sheep is much in demand for flannels. The Southdown sheep produce the finest type of short wool which, until surpassed by Spanish, later Saxon, and now Australian merino, was the chief source of supply for the fine woollen trade. Now much of the Southdown wool is used either for flannels or is combed for hosiery yarn.

Between one-third and one-half of the home clip is exported—a testimony to its excellent quality—(see table on p. 522) and so extensive imports are necessary to make up the amount required in the wool textile industries.

The following table shows the quantity of wool available for use in the industries in certain years between 1910 and 1960. It should be remembered that the quantity *available* may not be a faithful index of the amount *consumed* in any year, for wool is a non-perishable commodity that can withstand long warehousing.

Raw material of the wool textile industry (million lb)

VARIETY	AVERAGE 1910–14	AVERAGE 1921–25	AVERAGE 1926–30	1931	1935	1950	1960
Home clip[1]	95	52	72	86	65	58	78
Imported sheep and lamb's wool, mohair, alpaca, etc.[1]	506	467	494	601	597	571	355
Wool from imported sheep-skins	35	22	24	27	16	37	*
Mungo and shoddy[2]	206	88	84	*	104	71	68
Total quantity of wool, mohair, and pulled wool available in United Kingdom	843	630	675	804	782	737	769
Total (million kg)	384	286	306	365	356	334	349

[1] Balance retained, after deducting exports (or re-exports).
[2] Estimated quantity.
* Not available.
1 lb = 0.454 kg.

Since the Second World War there has been a great increase in the amount of manmade fibres used in the wool textile industries, and in consequence, as with other branches of the textile industry, the nature of the published statistics has changed. The table on p. 506 shows the raw material position in 1968, from which it is apparent that manmade fibres now contribute one-quarter of the total raw materials used.

Raw material of the wool textile industry, 1968

	MILLION LB	MILLION KG
Raw wool		
Merino	156	70.7
Crossbred	216	98.0
Other wools	20	9.0
Total	392	177.7
Other fibres		
Hair	23	10.4
Broken tops	5	2.3
Wool noils	11	5.0
Wool waste	14	6.3
Mungo and shoddy	50	22.7
Cotton	4	1.8
Synthetic fibres	168	76.2
Total	275	124.7

Finally, the following tables refer to the wool import trade. The greater part of the import of raw wool is of Commonweath origin, Australia and New Zealand being the chief sources. Part of the import from South Africa is mohair.

Gross imports of wool (including re-exports) (million lb)

VARIETY		1913	AVERAGE 1921–25	AVERAGE 1926–30	1931	1935	1955	1962	1968
Sheep and lamb's wool	Merino	801	819	359	364	449	388	304	237
	Crossbred			296	412	332	292	276	252
	Other descriptions			146	73	83	42	43	57
Wool waste and wool noils		3	4	4	4	6	11	11	*
Mohair		28	22	14	11	11	14	20	*
Alpaca, vicuna, llama and camel's hair		13	10	9	8	7	3	4	*
Wool tops		*	4	3	2	1	3	3	*
Woollen, worsted, and hair yarn		33	15	18	19	2	3	7	*
Flocks and shoddy		122	*	51	49	*	*	*	*

* Not available. Re-exports in 1968 amounted to 13.6 million kg (30 million lb).
1 million lb = 453 590 kg.

Imports of wool and mohair by countries (less re-exports) (million lb)

COUNTRY	1913	AVERAGE 1921–25	AVERAGE 1926–30	1931	1935	1949	1955	1966
New Zealand	143	146	117	119	109	162	185	135
Australia	126	123	166	218	278	403	337	138
South Africa	81	60	61	69	65	56	64	33
Argentina	52	46	53	90	69	4	32	58
Other countries	104	92	98	105	94	40	118	156[1]
Total	506	467	494	601	615	665	736	520
Total (million kg)	230	212	224	273	279	302	334	236

[1] Includes Uruguay 37, China 23.

Ports importing raw wool (million lb)

	1913	AVERAGE 1927–30	1931	1935	1948	1960	1966
Goole	6	10	8	9	9	—	19
Grimsby	15	8	6	4	—	—	1
Hull	48	136	123	174	60	160	121
Liverpool	182	143	185	221	282	172	241
London[1]	485	375	391	346	256	162	93
Manchester	0.2	14	25	6	14	10	6
Southampton	61	107	107	97	29	25	22

[1] The former dominance of London in this table was a result of the key position held by that city in the world's wool market.
1 million lb = 453 590 kg.

The chief branches of the woollen and worsted trades

Only the briefest outline of the processes which lie between the raw wool and the finished cloth can be given here, and technical works should be consulted for further details.[1]

1. See, for example, A. F. Barker and others, *Textiles and their Manufacture*, Constable, 1922; or J. A. Hunter, *Wool, from Material to Finished Product*, 4th edn, Pitman, 1930.

The wool is first sorted and classified into grades—long wools (destined for combing and the worsted trade), short wools (for carding, mainly for the woollen trade), and the lowest class for the carpet trade. In this connection it should be remembered that a single fleece is not homogeneous as regards its quality. Different parts of the animal yield wools of varying length and fineness. An allied preliminary process is the sorting of rags and tailors' clippings and their reduction to shreds in tearing machinery. The wool must next be scoured in a soap solution (for which soft water is essential) in order to remove the natural grease which it contains, and machinery must be employed finally to extract all burrs and other foreign bodies which may remain. The dry wool is oiled before passing through the next process in order to render it supple. The short wools are then passed through scribbling and carding machinery, the object of which is to mix up the fibres by taking advantage of their clinging properties and to produce a series of 'rovings' or 'slivers'—thin ropes of roughly parallel fibres—which are subsequently in the spinning process drawn out and given a twist which makes them into thread. During the carding operation any necessary admixtures (i.e. of rag wool, noils, or cotton) may be accomplished. The woollen and worsted branches then follow rather different courses. For worsteds, the finer varieties of carded short wool and also the long wools which have not been carded are put through a combing machine which, by more careful means, so as not to cause damage by breakage and crushing, produces slivers of parallel fibres which are subsequently drawn out into finer and finer threads. The noils (short wools rejected during the combining process) go back into the woollen trade.

Then in both woollen and worsted, the finely drawn-out rovings are spun into a continuous thread. For certain purposes, especially to give strength to the yarn and produce a bi- or multi-coloured yarn, 'doubling' of the thread is performed (i.e. twisting two or more threads into one). All yarns destined to form part of coloured cloths must, of course, have received their dye before being woven. The yarn itself may be dyed, but usually the uncarded wool or the combed tops are dyed before being spun.

Before weaving can begin, the warp and weft threads must be arranged in the required manner. Warping—or building up the warp—is a skilled process, still largely performed by hand; during or after the setting up of the warp, the yarn composing it is treated with size, in order to keep the threads smooth and prevent them from interlocking with one another. The modern high-speed loom is a triumph of automatism, which nothing short of a whole chapter or volume could adequately describe, and the variety of weaves and patterns which can now be mechanically produced is inexhaustible.

The finishing processes are many and varied. The cloth must first be examined for defects and mended where necessary. If woollen, it must be fulled, i.e. shrunk and felted—by being passed through rollers and through soap solutions; the nap must be raised by passing the cloth through drums set with teazel heads and then cropped by a kind of mowing machine. For worsteds, in which it is desired to show up rather than conceal the pattern of the weave, raising and cropping are unnecessary, but steaming and pressing contribute largely to the great variety of finishes which can be produced. If no colour has as yet been given to the wool the cloth may be dyed in the piece before the final finishing processes are completed.

In recent years the wool-textile industry has been diversified—one might almost say enriched—by the advent of manmade fibres, which have been treated as an ally rather than as a competitor. Many varieties of the new fibres have been successfully blended with wool in varying proportions to give better wearing qualities and new textures. Thus a mixture of 80 per cent wool and 20 per cent nylon is used for carpets; 45 per cent wool and 55 per cent polyester fibre for strong lightweight fabrics; bulk is achieved by mixing stretched and unstretched yarns, for sweaters, and so on. The carpet industry, indeed, has been transformed by the introduction of manmade fibres. In 1968 some 90 per cent of all the carpets produced contained some artificial fibre, and wool represented but 40 per cent of the raw materials used in the industry. In the case of the increasingly popular tufted carpets (only introduced in the middle 1950s and now accounting for nearly half the total output), the contribution of wool is a mere 5 per cent, and the bulk of the raw material is rayon, nylon and acrylic fibres (see Chapter 21). For woven carpets, however (e.g. the traditional Axminster and Wilton types), wool still provides 60 per cent of the total fibre usage.

The following tables present in statistical form the recent history of the wool textile industries. The total employment in the woollen and worsted

Employment in woollen and worsted industries, by regions

	WOOLLEN		WORSTED		WOOLLEN AND WORSTED	WOOLLEN AND WORSTED
	1921	1931	1921	1931	1950	1966
Great Britain	139 158	98 525	120 534	103 487	218 700	158 310
West Riding	94 578	65 406	112 376	95 550	168 130	123 680
Lancashire	8 457	6 511	320	575	11 070	7 920
Somerset, Wiltshire, and Gloucestershire	5 726	4 686	31	26	5 080	3 770
Leicestershire	486	504	1 132	2 006	1 630	2 750
Oxfordshire	1 134	1 233	19	15	3 960	2 130
Peebles, Roxburgh, and Selkirk	9 039	8 275	55	58	20 870	19 130

Note. 1950 and 1966 figures are for Ministry of Labour Regions—E and W Ridings, Northwestern, Southwestern, Midlands, Southern and Scotland, and are not strictly comparable with previous Census figures. Included in the total are 7900 in other regions (mostly in the Northern Region).

Employment in woollen and worsted industries, by process, 1953 and 1966 (thousands)

	1953	1966
Combing	13.4	7.9
Worsted spinning	53.5	18.7
Worsted weaving	32.3	18.7
Woollen spinning	22.4	23.4
Woollen weaving	42.1	24.4
Total	163.7	93.1

Source. Wool Industry Bureau of Statistics. The figures relate to 'productive' personnel only, i.e. excluding administrative, clerical, and transport staff.

branches has declined, particularly during the last decade or so; but this has not meant a decline in the prosperity of Yorkshire or indeed of the other major areas, for the manipulation of manmade fibres has occupied the mills and given alternative employment to the workers. The decline is most noticeable in the worsted branch, for worsted is readily mixed with, or replaced by, manmade fibres, while, to quote the advertising slogan, 'there is no substitute for wool', and employment in wool-spinning has actually increased. The carpet industry has also increased quite substantially, for the use of manmade fibres in carpets has greatly increased the range of products available to an increasingly affluent home market.

Employment in carpet industry

	1921	1931	1950	1961	1966
Great Britain	23 625	26 936	28 200	27 830	35 320
Worcestershire	6 945	8 902	9 460[1]	10 800[1]	12 390[1]
West Riding	6 967	5 976	6 480[2]	10 490[2]	12 710[2]
Glasgow	2 917	3 629	9 270[3]	10 000[3]	11 120[3]

[1] Midlands. [2] East and West Ridings. [3] Scotland (Ministry of Labour regions).

Woollen and worsted industries: production, 1907–60 (million lb)

VARIETY OF PRODUCT	1907 (UNITED KINGDOM)	1924 (GREAT BRITAIN)	1930 (GREAT BRITAIN)	1950 (UNITED KINGDOM)	1960 (UNITED KINGDOM)
Tops	243	286	244	316	319
Noils	30	35	28	*	*
Yarns	446	550	373	656	548
Woollen	260	314	191	329	303
Worsted	—	211	158	227	245
Alpaca and mohair	186	15	8	—	*
Other hair or wool	—	10	15	*	*

* Not available.

Woollen and worsted industries: production, 1968

VARIETY OF PRODUCT	MILLION KG	MILLION LB	MILLION SQ. YD	MILLION SQ. M
Tops	96.5	213		
Yarn, woollen	230.0	325		
Yarn, worsted	98.3	217		
Fabrics, woollen			132	121
Fabrics, worsted			162	148
Blankets			33	30

Geographical distribution of the wool-textile industry

The West Riding

The dominance of the West Riding in all branches of the wool textile industry has been a feature of industrial Britain for over a century. Whereas the worsted branch is almost extinct in those areas of East Anglia and the West Country where it once flourished, the woollen section has maintained a somewhat specialised existence in a number of different regions, notably East Lancashire, the Cotswold country and the Tweed Basin. In 1931 no less than 93 per cent of the worsted workers in Great Britain were in the West Riding, but only 67 per cent of the woollen operatives. The carpet industry has persisted at several localities in Scotland and at Kidderminster–Stourport, and only one-third of the people engaged in the industry are in West Yorkshire.

The two features of principal interest within the West Riding are the geographical distribution of the industries and specialities, and the relation between wool textiles and other occupations. Perhaps the outstanding elements in influencing the area covered by the textile-working district, in Yorkshire as in Lancashire, have been the supply of soft, or lime-free water from the Millstone Grit uplands and the outcrop of productive Coal Measures. The central Pennines, between the South Lancashire and West Yorkshire coalfields, are made up entirely of the Millstone Grit, for the most part peat-covered, and so giving an abundant surface run-off. The Grit consists mainly of hard sandstones, with alternations of coarser and more porous grits, which act as efficient filters and render the spring water extremely pure.

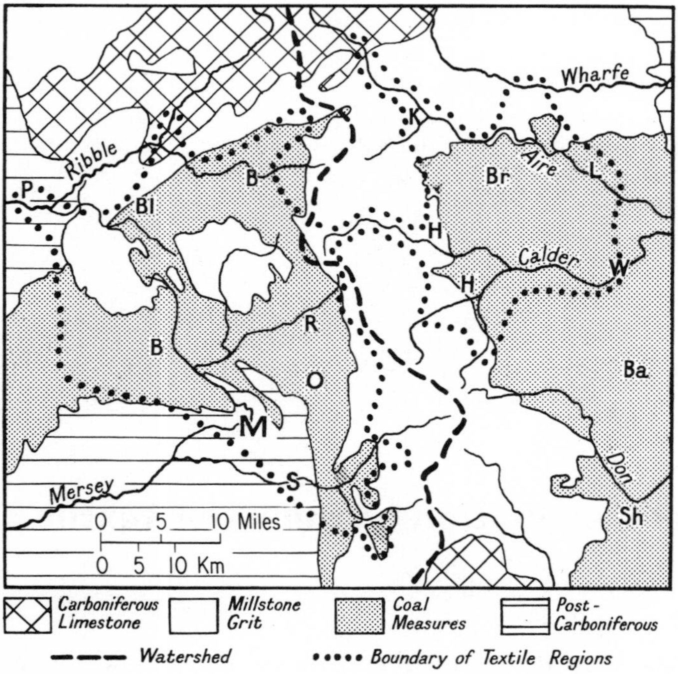

FIG. 187. The textile regions of Lancashire and Yorkshire
Note that the two regions merge across the Roch-Calder watershed.

The West Yorkshire industry is somewhat more localised, however, than the boundaries of the soft-water area would suggest (Fig. 188). Apart from one or two outlying centres on the headwaters of the Dearne and in the Wharfe valley, the industry is confined essentially to the coalfield portions of the Aire and the Colne–Calder valleys, and the area which lies between them, together with the upper portions of those streams on the Grits. Eastwards of Leeds and Wakefield textiles cease to be of any consequence, and coal mining becomes the chief industrial occupation, but westwards of the main region tongues of industry spread up the Colne valley above Huddersfield, up that of the Calder above Halifax to Hebden Bridge and over into Lancashire, and up the Aire to Keighley and Skipton. The northern boundary of the main region is marked by the edge of the coalfield, roughly coincident with the river Aire. It should be noticed that the Aire, unlike the Colne and Calder, rises in a region of Carboniferous Limestone so that its water is not very soft. As a result, no great centres of the textile trade have grown up on it—the chief towns, Keighley, Bingley, Shipley and Guiseley,

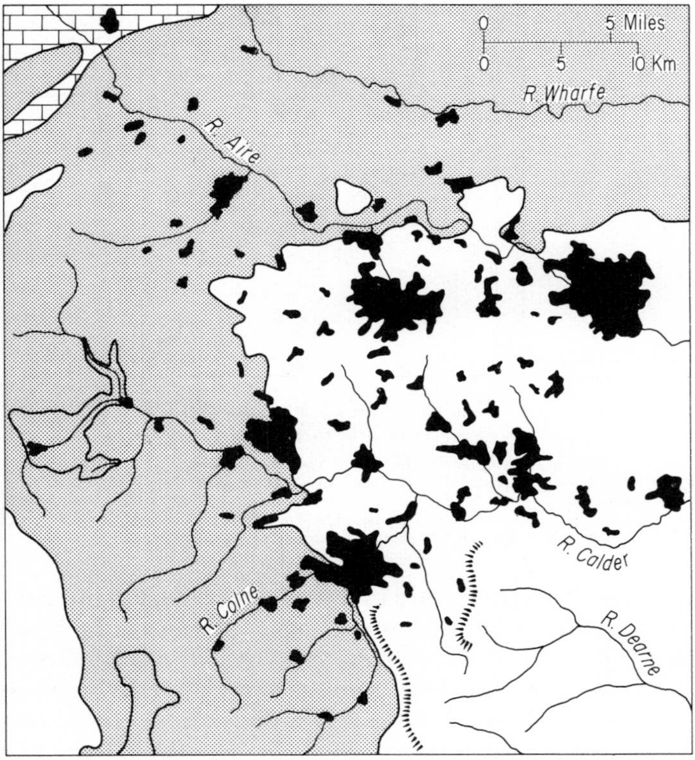

FIG. 188. The woollen towns of Yorkshire in relation to the streams from the Millstone Grit

The Millstone Grit is stippled, Coal Measures left blank. In the southwest are two areas enclosed by lines which are shown on old geological maps as 'Carboniferous Limestone' but are actually of non-calcareous shales now classified with the Millstone Grit. The area in the northwest is of rocks of Carboniferous Limestone age, but is *not* limestone. Notice in the southeast the scarps formed by Sandstones in the Lower and Middle Coal Measures.

being located on small tributary streams rising on the Grits or Coal Measures. The almost sudden cessation of the industry south of the Calder is also remarkable. It is due partly to the paucity of water power in the region of the Dearne headwaters, which rise on the dipslope of the Coal Measure escarpments, but mainly to the long-standing economic differentiation of the Dearne–Don region, where Middle Coal Measure ironstone was formerly smelted and where textile trades (e.g. linen and coarse woollen cloths called 'pennistones') quite early became subordinate to the coal mining and metal trades of the Sheffield region.[1]

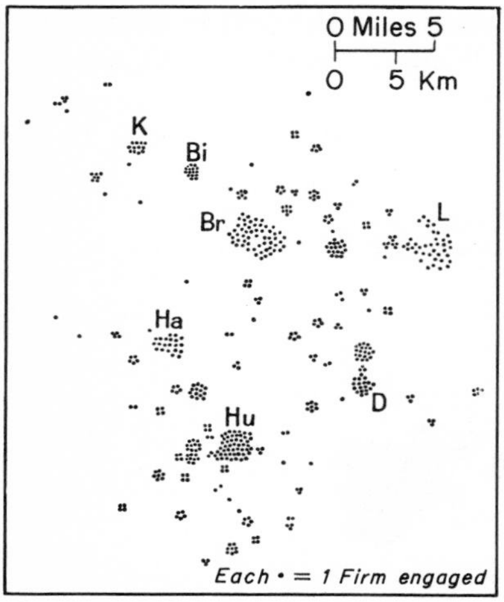

FIG. 189. The woollen industry of West Yorkshire in 1931

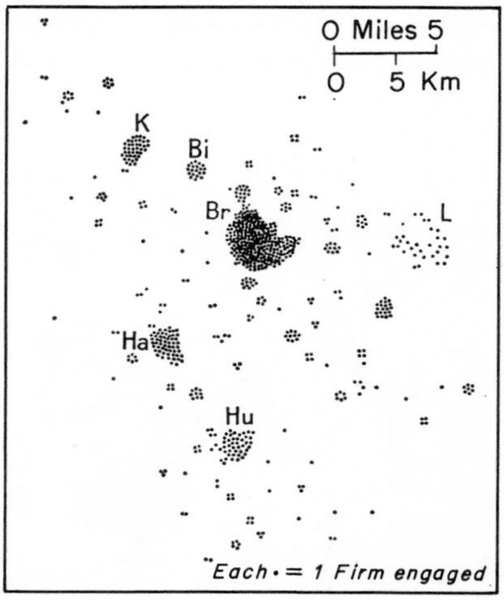

FIG. 190. The worsted industry of West Yorkshire in 1931

Note the general predominance of woollens in the southeast and of worsted in the northwest.
K = Keighley; Bi = Bingley; Br = Bradford; L = Leeds; Ha = Halifax; Hu = Huddersfield; D = Dewsbury.
For a more recent sketch of the regional specialisms see G. L. Hope, 'The wool textile industry of the West Riding of Yorkshire', *South Hampshire Geographer*, **2**, 1969, 30–7 (map on p. 32).

Within this comparatively restricted area there is a good deal of internal differentiation as regards the particular branches or phases of the wool textile trades which are present. Both woollen and worsted manufactures are to be found all over the area, and there is no sharp regional division between them (Figs 189, 190). Worsted, however, is of relatively small importance in the southeastern part of the area—Wakefield and the Dewsbury region—but is dominant in the northwestern part—Bradford, Halifax and Keighley. The region within a radius of about six miles from Dewsbury, comprising the townships of Dewsbury, Batley, Morley, Ossett, Cleckheaton and Heckmondwike, all north of the Calder, is the greatest in the world for the manufacture of mungo and shoddy and their employment in cloth making.[2] In Dewsbury and Batley there is a large number of firms

1. But see also E. Charlesworth, 'A local example of the factors influencing industrial location', *Geogrl J.*, **91**, 1938, 340–51.
2. See S. Jubb, *History of the Shoddy Trade*, London, 1860, for the early development of this industry.

engaged in the sorting of rags which are subsequently torn up and respun and woven into cloth.

Regional specialisation in certain processes—a characteristic feature of the Lancashire cotton industry—is not much in evidence in West Yorkshire, owing to the peculiar organisation of the woollen branch, in which, as we have seen, a large proportion of the firms engage in all or many of the stages between raw wool and finished cloth. Without attempting to overgeneralise, it may be said that in the western portion of the region (Halifax and the upper Calder, Bradford and the upper Aire) spinning and weaving are about equal in the numbers they employ in each centre; in the eastern and southeastern parts, and especially in the small centres south of the Calder, weaving is rather more important than spinning. Dyeing shows a remarkable concentration upon Bradford, attracted thither by the dominance of merchanting and the finishing trades in the city, and is also developed in the middle portion of the Aire valley, between Leeds and Shipley, and in the Calder valley in and around Halifax.[1]

Of individual towns which call for mention, Bradford holds pride of place as the metropolis of worsted and woollen manufacture. This city, apparently in the beginning destined, by reason of its situation on only a tiny stream, to be one of the *less* important centres, has risen since about the 'thirties of last century to a position of prominence unrivalled by its former peers, Leeds and Halifax. In 1800 it had one spinning mill and a population of 13 000. It is probable that the settling within its confines of a number of Jewish merchants, in association with German bankers, soon after 1830, began to increase its importance as a marketing and warehousing centre for worsted goods, and by a process of cumulative growth, and with the aid of the dyeing industry, which was considerably expanded about the same time, it rapidly rose to supremacy. At the present time its activities are concerned principally with combing (i.e. top-making), worsted spinning and weaving and dyeing—but the woollen branch is by no means absent, and Bradford has almost a monopoly in the trades employing alpaca and mohair. Huddersfield concerns itself as much with woollens as with worsteds and is famed for its high-class cloth and its pattern designing. Of the two valleys that converge on Huddersfield, the Holme is devoted mainly to worsted and the Colne to woollens.[2] Halifax, until the rise of Bradford, was the chief worsted centre, and it still deals more in worsted than in woollens.

1. The textile finishing trades employed over 12 000 people in Yorkshire in 1948, about one-half of whom were concerned with wool and worsted and the remainder with cotton, mixed fabrics, knitwear, etc. There has since been a steady increase in the importance of mixed fabrics.

2. An interesting account of modern economic reorganisation, involving a reduction in the number of mills (but not in employment), increased horizontal integration in the woollen branch and vertical integration in the worsted branch, as well as the growth of inter-industry groupings involving both branches, will be found in R. C. Riley, 'Locational and structural change in the Huddersfield wool textile industry'. *Tijd. v. Econ. en Soc. Geog.*, **61**, 1970, 77–84.

It is famed for carpets, although numerically the carpet trade gives employment to only three per cent of the town's insured workers. Dewsbury, Batley and the Spen valley towns, as we have seen, form the headquarters of the shoddy trade. Leeds is actually the third town in the conurbation, in respect of absolute numbers employed in the wool textile industry, ranking after Bradford and Huddersfield. But relatively, wool textile manufacture only employs three per cent of the insured workers, and it is the textile-using trades, especially the clothing industry, which are dominant; employment in the latter represents 14 per cent of the city's total (1961).

PLATE 22. Woollen mills in the Holme valley, near Huddersfield
The environment is typical of the early woollen industry, before so much of it became concentrated in the towns.

As regards the relative importance of wool textiles compared with other industries in the West Riding, some interesting unpublished maps made on the basis of the 1921 Census by Dr H. C. K. Henderson[1] showed how, eastwards of a zone running southwards from Leeds *via* Ardsley and Ossett to the headstreams of the Dearne, textiles became subsidiary to coal mining (Fig. 191, and cf. map of Yorkshire coalfield, p. 308). Few mines remain within the textile region, which has thus to a certain extent lost one of the bases upon which its industry was built.

Fig. 192 shows the relative importance of wool textile industries in the various West Yorkshire centres, thirty years later. In every town the wool

1. Shown to the British Association (Section E) at York, 1932.

textile trades are less important relatively, and frequently absolutely also, than they were in the 1920s. This is partly due to increasing mechanisation and the consequent displacement of many employees, and partly to the great increase in the employment capacity of other industries, e.g. engineering, electrical trades and numerous 'consumer goods' industries, particularly in the larger towns. It is only in a few of the smaller peripheral centres (e.g. Slaithwaite, Haworth, Holmfirth) that wool textiles now employ more than 40 per cent of the insured population.

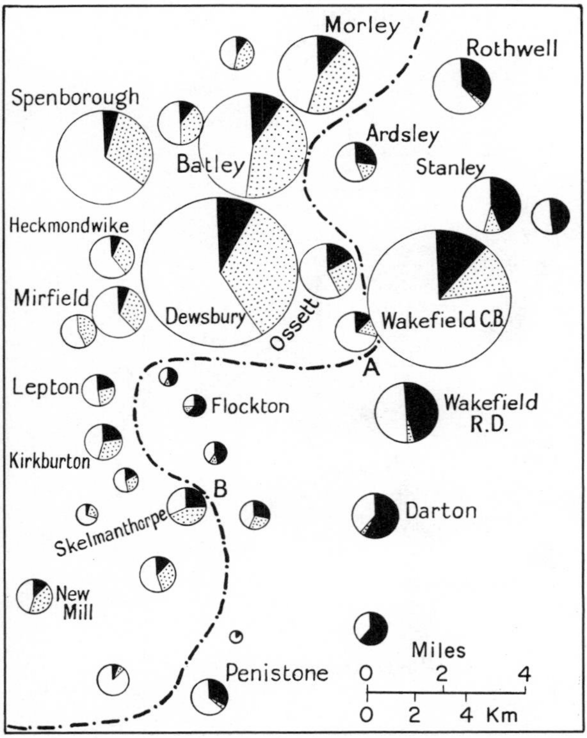

FIG. 191. The transition between textiles and coal mining occupations by census divisions

Circles proportional to the number of people employed in 1921. Black = coal mining; dotted = textiles; blank = all other occupations. West of the broken line, textiles more important than mining: east of the same, mining more important than textiles. This line of division between A and B coincides with the Calder–Dearne water parting (compare Fig. 188). (Map prepared by H. C. K. Henderson.)

It is not yet possible to compile this map afresh on the basis of the 1961 Census. But coal mining is now almost extinct within the wool–textile region.

In the textile zone as a whole, in 1964, 180 000 people found employment in the textile industries—21 per cent of all employment; and there were 47 000 others employed in the clothing trades (including footwear).

Of the major urban centres, Leeds is the most diversified city in the whole conurbation, and several occupations exceed wool textiles in importance, such as tailoring (cf. p. 613), engineering (pp. 438, 450), transport services, distributive trades and professional services. Bradford has a considerable dyeing and finishing industry, together with electrical and general engineering and the making of textile machinery and motor vehicles. Halifax and Huddersfield each make clothing and have textile machinery and other

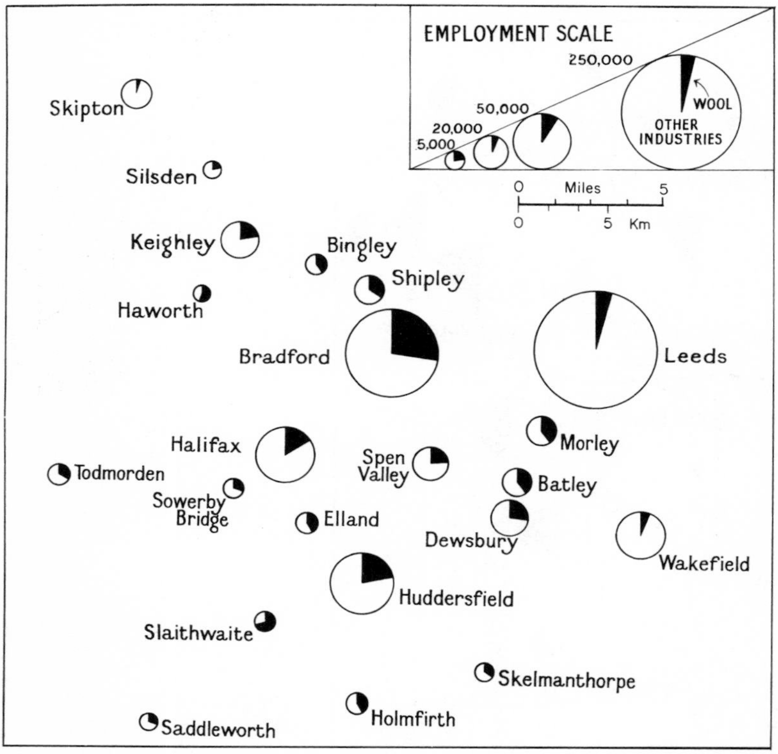

FIG. 192. Map showing the relative importance of the wool-working industries in the industrial economy of the West Yorkshire towns—Census of 1951

engineering industries, whilst Halifax has also the carpet trade and brass and wire industries, and Huddersfield a considerable dyestuffs industry and vehicle building. In Wakefield only 10 per cent of the total employment is in textiles. Dewsbury and the Spen Valley towns still have about one-quarter of their people employed in wool, and there are important textile machinery and other engineering industries. Keighley has textile machinery works (cf. Fig. 179), whilst in the western fringes of the wool-working district we find Skipton using cotton and manmade fibres, Hebden

Bridge with large clothing and cotton manufactures, and Sowerby Bridge with a subsidiary cotton industry.

East Lancashire

The ancient woollen industry of South Lancashire has become very restricted and specialised since the growth of cotton manufacturing. As stated above (p. 498), it has been pushed eastwards up the Pennine valleys, where there are now two areas concerned, one north of Manchester, in the valley of the Roch where Rochdale and Bury are the chief centres, and the other east of Manchester, in the Tame valley about Mossley and Stalybridge. The woollen branch predominates, notably felts (upon which an extensive slipper industry depends), flannels and blankets.

West of England

The decline and increasing specialisation of this region have already been considered (p. 501). The spinning of yarn has practically ceased and the weaving and finishing of special types of cloth is all that remains. Stroud is still the principal centre of the trade in highly finished cloths of the broadcloth type for liveries, uniforms, hunting outfits and billiard tables. Outlying centres continue to flourish in a small way, such as Dursley, making woollens and carpets, Witney,[1] the blanket town, Trowbridge, woollens and some worsted, Frome, Wellington and one or two minor survivals of the Devonshire serge trade, as at Ashburton. The carpet industry continues to flourish at Wilton (Wiltshire) and Axminster (Devon) which, like Kidderminster in the Midlands, have given their names to types of carpet not necessarily manufactured at the centres concerned.

Wales

Many parts of Wales formerly had a considerable domestic woollen industry, using locally produced wool. Much of this industry has been mechanised and factories, most of them small, are to be found scattered in a great many towns and villages in central and west Wales. The greatest concentration is in Carmarthenshire in the valley of the Teifi between Lampeter and Newcastle Emlyn. Flannel and 'Welsh blankets' are the principal products.

Leicestershire

The growth of the woollen and worsted industries is a natural outcome of the expansion of the hosiery trade. As a result, they are of rather a specialised nature, being concerned primarily with the production of worsted and

1. One firm at Witney claims to have been making blankets since 1670. See A. Plummer, *The Witney Blanket Industry*, Routledge, 1934.

some woollen yarn destined for subsequent manufacture, within the same region, into hosiery proper and all allied types of 'knitwear'—underwear, pullovers, bathing costumes, etc. The principal seat of the industry is Leicester, but a number of neighbouring towns share it to a certain extent, as Melton Mowbray, Wigston and Loughborough (cf. Chapter 21).

The Scottish Border

A well established domestic linen and woollen industry existed in the Tweed basin prior to the Industrial Revolution, based upon local flax-growing and wool from the Cheviot and Blackfaced mountain sheep, and aided by copious supplies of soft water from the limestone-free Silurian and Old Red Sandstone formations. The decline of the linen trade due to competition from better situated areas in Fifeshire and Ireland, and the introduction of machinery into woollen manufacture, brought about a changed distribution. Attention became focused on water-power sites on the change of gradient between the narrow tributary valleys and the broader central basin of the Tweed—and towns situated in such places as, for example, Galashiels and Hawick, expanded considerably as a result. Subsequent development was hampered, however, by the absence of coal, the somewhat isolated nature of the region as regards populous markets, and the attendant lack of facilities for easy import of foreign wool. Competition with Yorkshire being out of the question, specialisation has occurred and the region has become world famous for 'tweeds'[1] of high quality, and for hosiery of all kinds, the latter being the speciality of Hawick. In consequence much foreign wool is now imported, and the industry survives today by reason of a foundation laid during a period when local geographical conditions were more favourable. The site conditions, owing to the narrowness of the valleys, are not very favourable for mill and town development, and in the 'seventies of last century the Galashiels industry had to find a new outlet at Selkirk, with the result that the population of the county named after that town increased by 80 per cent between 1871 and 1881.

The depression which followed the First World War, with its accompanying lack of real demand for the costly high-quality products, hit the industry badly. A partial relief was obtained by the introduction, as at Jedburgh, of the artificial silk trade; but the present adverse geographical and economic factors are outweighing even the momentum of several centuries.

The rest of Scotland

Just as in Wales, the natural aptitude of many parts of Scotland for sheep rearing, together with the abundance of soft water, gave rise to a wide-

1. The name was originally 'twill' or 'tweel', which an English clerk's error transformed into tweed—and this misspelling happening to be the name of the river basin, it has stuck to the cloth and the trade.

spread domestic woollen industry, of which, despite the progress of mechanisation and the development of factories, many scattered remnants still remain. Small mills for spinning and weaving tweed and other cloths, blankets and carpets are to be found in nearly every county, and only one or two of the more important regions can here be mentioned. Although completely overshadowed by more modern industries, the old woollen trade survives in Ayrshire, as at Kilmarnock and Ayr, and in the Glasgow–Paisley district, where carpets and blankets are made and where the industry is partly an associate of the cotton industry. Between the Forth and the Tay, on the steep southern slope of the Ochil Hills, where there was abundant water power, the woollen industry still remains centred on Alva, Alloa and Tillicoultry; and numerous small mills are to be found in the valleys running southeastwards and northeastwards from the Grampian massif. Finally, mention must be made of the hand-loom production, in the Hebrides, of the famous 'Harris homespun' tweeds; and of the domestic hosiery industry of the Shetlands. These trades are now much more commercialised than formerly, and machine-spun yarn is used in order to speed up production.[1] The chief spinning centre in the Highlands is Brora, on the small coalfield.

Ireland[2]

Here, as before, we find a scattered domestic woollen industry which has become partly industrialised. A number of towns in Northern Ireland, and some in Eire, notably in the hinterland of Cork, have mills where woollen cloths, tweeds and blankets are produced, but Belfast, Ballymena, Newtownards, Dublin and Cork are the only towns where more than one firm is engaged.

Export trade

The following tables show the fortunes of the export trade in wool and manufactures thereof since 1913. It is interesting to note that the export of British raw wool is still a flourishing business. For the rest, it is clear that semifinished material, in the shape of tops and yarn, is very important—serving the developing woollen and worsted industries of other countries; the export of cloth has declined somewhat from the figures of a few decades

1. The term 'Harris Tweed' is restricted to cloth produced from Scottish wool spun in the Island and woven in the houses of the people. There are several carding and spinning mills, mostly at Stornoway, but there are some 800 members of the Harris Tweed Association; they produce 2.7 to 3.6 million metres (3 to 4 million yards) of cloth a year, all of it of high quality and much of it destined for export. The industry is the mainstay of the economic life of many of the Islanders. See H. A. Moisley, 'Harris Tweed: a growing Highland industry', *Econ. Geog.*, **37**, 1961, 353–70.
2. D. J. Dwyer and L. J. Symons: 'The development and location of the textile industries in the Irish Republic', *Irish Geog.*, **4**, 1963, 415–31.

Exports of wool and woollen goods by variety (in 100 centals = 10 000 lb = 4535·9 kilograms)

VARIETY	1913	AVERAGE 1921–25	AVERAGE 1926–30	1931	1935	1950	1966
Wool (British only)	2 866	5 209	4 118	3 577	*	2 536	4 387
Noils and waste	3 388	3 449	3 166	2 011	3 580	4 938	3 849
Tops	4 363	3 736	3 431	2 799	5 593	7 289	21 301
Yarn, worsted	4 990	3 712	3 786	2 978	3 308	2 396	1 230
Yarn, woollen	481	784	654	515	781	605	1 593
Tissues, worsted (million sq. yd)	62	54	41	30	38	40	24
Tissues, woollen (million sq. yd)	106	129	113	56	71	84	54
Yarn, alpaca, and mohair	1 722	738	761	406	438	220	337
Other yarns of hair and wool	848	307	712	640	*	300	
Flocks, shoddy, and rags	2 326	2 501	3 106	2 269	*	4 350	*
Piece goods (million sq. yd)	187	185	169	95	*	*	*
Carpets (million sq. yd)	11	7	7	3	6	12	15
Blankets (1000 pairs)	1 002	1 235	990	409	417	1 360	*
Flannels (million sq. yd)	—	6	4	3	5	*	*

* Not available.

Exports of wool and woollen goods by countries (£ millions)

COUNTRY	1913	AVERAGE 1921–25	AVERAGE 1926–30	1931	1935	1955	1966
Germany	9.5	7.0	8.7	4.0	2.4	14.0	18.4
Canada	4.4	6.2	6.6	2.6	3.4	17.2	15.9
Australia	2.4	5.3	3.1	0.3	1.1	2.0	4.2
New Zealand	0.5	1.2	1.3	0.6	0.8	5.0	3.4
South Africa	1.5	1.5	1.6	1.2	1.9	7.0	5.0
China	0.6	3.7	3.2	1.8	0.6	5.2	0.3
Japan	1.9	7.3	2.8	1.2	0.7	4.7	10.2
India	1.3	1.0	1.3	0.4	0.7	6.7	—
Other Countries	11.9	27.4	22.4	13.1	18.8	91.6	59.4
Total	34.0	60.6	51.0	25.2	30.4	153.4	117.0

Other countries in 1966 included USA (£20.8m), Denmark (£11.4m) and Hong Kong (£6.8m).
These and similar tables may be kept up to date from the annual *Accounts relating to Trade and Navigation of the United Kingdom*, HMSO.

ago, but it is maintained on the basis of quality—for Yorkshire cloth (like Wedgwood china) still commands a substantial market in North America and the 'white' Commonwealth countries. Liverpool, by reason of its proximity to Yorkshire and its regular worldwide shipping connections, continues to dominate the export trade.

Ports exporting wool and woollen manufactures (millions of £s sterling)

	1913	AVERAGE 1927–30	1931	1935	1948	1960	1967
Goole	2.9	4.9	2.7	3.5	4.7	—	1.1
Grimsby	5.8	3.3	1.4	0.9	0.2	—	0.5
Hull	5.7	11.5	4.4	8.5	9.2	23.0	7.4
Liverpool	11.7	21.1	8.0	10.2	41.7	37.3	14.5
London	6.6	10.2	5.2	7.0	15.3	8.8	9.0
Manchester	0.7	1.8	0.6	1.1	10.5	12.2	4.1
Southampton	1.2	3.0	1.6	2.1	7.8	6.3	2.5
Glasgow	0.5	1.6	0.6	0.9	4.0	1.9	1.9

20
The textile industries: cotton

The cotton industry, unlike that of wool, has no long history stretching back into the Middle Ages; its development and expansion were roughly coincident with the period of the Industrial Revolution. Moreover, it has always been entirely dependent upon imported raw material and during its periods of greatest prosperity was very largely dependent upon foreign outlets for its produce. Since the Second World War, the picture of the cotton industry has been metamorphosed completely, with both yarn and cloth now figuring highly among the imports and the present quantity of exports reflecting only a shadow of the former valuable export trade. That section of the textile industry which is still mainly dependent on cotton now represents only one-sixth of the whole, and indeed it has been asserted with some truth that 'the cotton industry', as we knew it before 1940, no longer exists. Nevertheless, an industry which employed 624 000 people in 1913 is worthy of close consideration, especially since 96 per cent of those employed at that date were to be found in one area, southern Lancashire and the adjacent parts of Cheshire and Derbyshire. Such a remarkable concentration cannot be explained by the simple factors of power supplies and transport facilities alone, the prime necessities of an industry relying on considerable overseas trade. Several other regions of Britain possessed equally good advantages in this respect. Therefore, it will be our business in this chapter to attempt an analysis (*a*) of the factors which contributed to the original localisation of the cotton industry in Lancashire and elsewhere, (*b*) of the physical and economic circumstances which enabled the Lancashire region to adapt itself to new discoveries and new requirements and so to develop the remarkable concentration and specialisation which characterised it during the peak years, and (*c*) of the technological, economic and political influences which have accelerated the decline of the cotton industry since the Second World War.

Historical geography of the cotton industry[1]

1600–1770

It is probable that, from the thirteenth century onwards, small quantities of cotton wool were imported into England for the making of candle wicks, and in the sixteenth century this trade was fairly regular. Definite evidence of the spinning and weaving of cotton in this country is lacking, however, until about 1600. Cotton had been utilised on the Continent for a considerable period (in Spain, Italy, Germany and Belgium, for example) and it is probable that Flemish refugees introduced it into Britain. At Norwich, the home of fine fabrics (cf. p. 497), fustians and bombazines (mixtures of linen and cotton, or silk and cotton) were being made, possibly before 1600 and certainly in 1605, and in south Lancashire, where many foreigners settled, fustians began to be produced about the same time, using cotton imported from Smyrna, the Levant and Cyprus, and linen from Scotland and Ireland. In East Anglia the manufacture was clearly an ally of the worsted industry which we have already discussed (Chapter 19). In south Lancashire it attached itself quite naturally to an existing linen and woollen industry. Manchester was making woollen cloth in the early fourteenth century, and in the sixteenth century the linen trade of Manchester, and the 'Manchester cottons' (made of wool) produced at that town and at Bolton are commented upon by Leland. The use of cotton was slow in developing, however, and as yet the fibre was only used for mixing with others, for it could not be spun into a thread strong enough for employment as warp. By the end of the seventeenth century, aided by the great damage done to the continental industry by the Thirty Years War, and by the increasing demand for fustians, the industry was definitely established and concentrated chiefly in the Manchester region.

Manchester, like Birmingham (cf. Chapter 18, p. 466), was a non-corporate town—'neither walled town, city, or corporation' (Defoe)—free from the strict regulations of the larger populous centres and thus able to accommodate foreigners and new industries without trouble. It lay, too, outside the area dominated by the trading activities of the Merchant Adventurers, and so could develop unhampered by restrictions. Three branches of the textile industry grew up—the woollen 'cottons' referred to above, checks and small-ware (tapes, etc., often made of worsted), and fustians (made from linen warp and cotton weft). At the same time, whilst Manchester was the centre of the new industries, Bolton also made fustians, Rochdale and East Lancashire generally still retained a flourishing woollen trade, and Warrington, developing as a port, was famed for its sail cloths. The prohibition (at the instigation of the silk and woollen manufacturers) of the import of printed and dyed calicoes obtained from India, in 1700, resulted in the setting up of a printing and dyeing industry in London (where the 'grey' cloths were imported) and in Lancashire; and when in

1 (page 525). Of the abundant literature on the history of the cotton industry, the following books are 'classics': E. Baines, *History of the Cotton Manufacture*, 1835; S. J. Chapman, *The Lancashire Cotton Industry*, 1904; G. W. Daniels, *The Early English Cotton Industry*, 1920; Wadsworth and Mann, *The Cotton Trade and Industrial Lancashire, 1600–1780*, 1931. A more popular account will be found in Wood and Wilmore, *The Romance of the Cotton Industry in England*, 1927.

1721 the *use* of printed calicoes was forbidden, Lancashire took up fustian-printing, an industry which was legalised by the famous 'Manchester Act' of 1736.

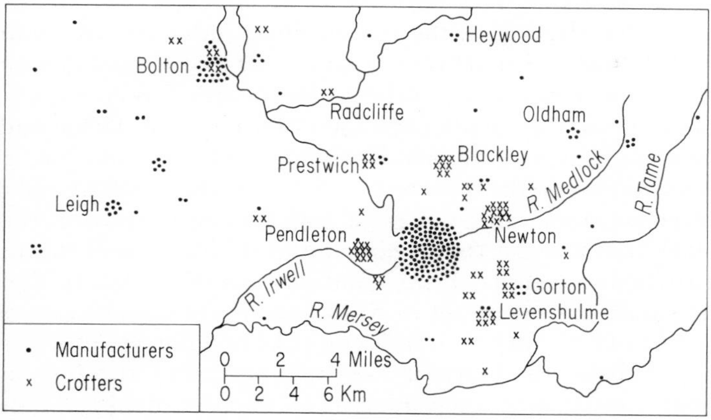

FIG. 193. The distribution of cotton users in south Lancashire at the end of the pre-machinery period

The large cluster of dots represents the manufacturers of Manchester.

The steady, if slow, expansion of the cotton-using industries in Lancashire during the first half of the eighteenth century[1] was accompanied by the rise of Liverpool as a port. With the gradual silting up of the Dee estuary, Chester was declining,[2] and the improvement of Warrington in the 1690s, followed by the construction of the first docks at Liverpool in 1715, and the improvement of the Mersey-Irwell navigation to Manchester, commenced in 1720, are evidence of the need for oceanic inlets and outlets for the growing trade of south Lancashire. Liverpool was not really important as an importer of raw cotton, however, until the main source of supply shifted from the east to the west (i.e. the United States). The one great handicap of the Manchester region (cf. Birmingham) was the lack of good roads. The pack-horse provided the only available means of overland transport and most of the raw cotton was obtained from London by this method. Another feature which prevented much expansion until after the invention

1. In 1701, just under 900 000 kilograms (2 million lb) of raw cotton were imported; in 1751, nearly 1.3 million kilograms (3 million lb).
2. See H. W. Ogden, 'Geographical basis of the Lancashire cotton industry', *J. Textile Inst.*, **18**, Nov., 1957, T573–594 (useful maps).

of machinery was the scattered and rather widespread nature of the domestic spinning and weaving industries, which at this time were largely part-time occupations of families also engaged in farming. Although from quite early times the merchants (the equivalent of the Yorkshire 'clothiers') employed large numbers of people, large-scale output of homogeneous fabrics was obviously impossible before the coming of the factory age.

Fig. 193 shows the distribution of the cotton-using industries in south Lancashire at the end of the pre-machinery period.[1] The concentration on the Manchester district is remarkable, and may be regarded as an expression of the dominance of that town over the Lancashire region. Defoe had described it as 'the greatest mere village in England', with a population, in its parish, of some 50 000; and whilst there was as yet no incentive to move into the comparatively barren hill country in search of water power, the lowland agricultural area around the Medlock and middle Irwell basins proved the more attractive region. Of the 'manufacturers' shown in Fig. 193, the makers of small-ware were all in Manchester; the checkweavers mostly in Manchester and an 'inner circle', comprising what are now the city's suburbs (e.g. Failsworth, Gorton, Levenshulme) and the fustian makers in Manchester, and in an outer semicircle on the edge of the uplands (e.g. Leigh, Bolton, Oldham). The crofters or 'whitsters' who performed the bleaching operations[2] were grouped in the villages around Manchester (Blackley, Newton, Pendleton) and in the Irwell valley (e.g. Prestwich, Radcliffe, Bolton)—a location which, as we shall see, has been preserved even to the present time, though the methods and requirements have changed considerably.

The Industrial Revolution

The factors which contributed to the localisation of the cotton industry in South Lancashire in the seventeenth century—the existence of linen and woollen industries in the soft-water region of the Pennine flanks, and the settling of foreigners in a non-corporate town are not sufficiently exclusive or conclusive to explain the later concentration. Numerous other regions had soft water, Flemish weavers, and an atmosphere humid enough for successful spinning. The secret of the expansion of the industry in Lancashire lies in the fact that as each new development arose, so the natural environment of the region was found capable of being utilised in the desired manner. When machinery was invented, water power was available; when steam power arrived coal could not have been in closer proximity; the development of chemical bleaching was aided by the presence of the Cheshire saltfield, only a few miles away, and by the abundance of soft water; and the need for transport could be satisfied by comparatively easy canal and

1. Data from Daniels, *op. cit.*, pp. 69–70.
2. The method employed was to steep the cloth in sour milk, spread it out on grassy slopes, and allow the sunlight to do the bleaching. It was a process occupying several months.

railway construction, and by the enlargement of the existing ports of Liverpool and Manchester. The Industrial Revolution period witnessed all these factors in operation.

Before the invention of machinery the textile industries were essentially home occupations. The homemade spinning wheel and hand loom were the only essential requirements. The difficulty which weavers experienced in getting adequate supplies of yarn[1] was only aggravated by Kay's flying shuttle (patented in 1733, but not much used until the 1760s), and in consequence the early inventions were all designed to facilitate the spinning process. Hargreaves's 'jenny' (origin of the name is obscure) merely multiplied the number of spindles which could be handled by one operative,[2] and still could not produce a yarn strong enough for warp. Arkwright's invention[3] of roller spinning, however, making use of rollers moving at different speeds for drawing out the rovings into yarn, remedied this deficiency. His machine, although patented at first to be worked by a horse, was quickly adapted for driving by water power, and hence came to be known as the 'water frame'. It may be said to have wrought two great changes in the cotton industry. In the first place, it made possible the weaving of all-cotton cloth (calico)—a manufacture which, owing to the existing prohibitions (see above), had to be legalised in 1774—and thus, by rendering unnecessary the admixture of linen and wool, contributed to the decline of those industries in Lancashire;[4] secondly, it caused the first vital change in the localisation, within Lancashire, of the production of yarn, by making water power an essential. But progress in the use of water power was at first slow. There was a natural reluctance on the part of the people to work in factories; then the lapse of Hargreaves's patent allowed the rapid spread of the jenny, which needed no power, and Arkwright, driven from Lancashire by hostility to his machines,[5] set up his works in Nottingham, the home of flourishing hosiery, lace and silk industries, and later at certain water power sites in the hosiery-making district of Derbyshire (Cromford 1771, Derby 1773, Belper 1776). Another factor contributing to the expansion of the industry was Crompton's mule, constructed in 1779 and so called be-

1. 'It was no uncommon thing for a weaver to walk three or four miles in the morning and call on five or six spinners before he could collect enough weft to serve him for the remainder of the day' (Guest, *Compendious History of the Cotton Manufacture*, p. 12). The situation was aggravated in the summer months by the spinners neglecting their spindles for more urgent agricultural labour.
2. The first jenny, in 1770, had sixteen spindles. Twenty years later machines were being constructed with over 100.
3. Like so many 'inventions', the principle of roller spinning was not the product of the brain of the man whose name is associated with it. It is due to Lewis Paul, whose first machine was made in 1738—thirty years before Arkwright's patent.
4. By 1790 woollen manufacture had disappeared, except in a specialised form in East Lancashire, and the linen industry was almost dead.
5. Arkwright did not at first intend to make calico, but as the Lancashire weavers refused to buy his machinemade yarn he had to use it himself in the manufacture of all-cotton cloth.

cause it combined the principles of the jenny and the roller. This machine spun thread for both warp and weft, and was capable of producing counts of much greater fineness than ever heretofore. As it was never patented, its use quickly spread, and in the 'eighties it began to supersede the jenny. It was not adapted for water power until 1790, after which, during the last decade of the century, it was adopted for producing the finer types of yarn, Arkwright's water frame spinning the coarser counts.

The early machinery age thus falls naturally into two periods. The first, from 1770–90, is characterised by the endeavour to provide an adequate supply of yarn, by the birth of the new cotton industry, by the inauguration of the factory system, consequent upon the use of water-driven machinery, and by an important migration of the industry away from Manchester and into the steeply graded valleys of the western Pennines and the Rossendale upland, where water power was available. The second, from 1790 until 1800, is a period of development and consolidation, in which two pieces of machinery played important parts. The mule enabled the trade in fine fabrics, for so long an Indian monopoly, to be captured by Lancashire and by the Glasgow–Paisley district of Scotland, where the cotton industry began to supersede that of linen (see p. 563). The steam engine, which Watt began to develop for driving machinery about 1782,[1] not only enabled far greater power to be obtained, but also confirmed the existing localisation of the industry on the Lancashire and Lanarkshire coalfields. The increasing use of machinery gave rise to a new industry—the building of machines for the mills which were springing up in many of the coalfield valleys. The import of cotton rose by leaps and bounds, a new and prolific source of supply appearing in the United States.[2]

All this time, however, weaving had lagged seriously behind spinning in technical developments, with the result that the hand-loom weavers, supplied now with a surfeit of machine-spun yarn, were enjoying a period of great prosperity. It is true that Cartwright had invented a power loom in 1785, but although several were erected none was successful until, about 1804, Radcliffe overcame the liability of the cotton yarn to break when subjected to mechanical handling by steeping the warp in boiling size before mounting it in the loom. Thus it was not until about 1806 that the power loom, later improved by Horrocks, became a commercial proposition—to the serious detriment of the hand-loom weavers.

Two trends are to be discerned in the localisation of the weaving industry. At first, there was a temporary migration of many of the cottage looms into weaving sheds attached to the new beckside spinning mills. Then, with the introduction of the power loom, a process of disruption began, due to a

1. The first engine for a cotton mill was erected at Papplewick, Notts., in 1785; Manchester obtained its first in 1789, and Glasgow in 1792. By 1800 Manchester had thirty-two engines.
2. Import of raw cotton in 1781—2.2 million kilograms (5 million lb); 1800—25.4 million kilograms (56 million lb). See also p. 535.

number of causes. The hand-loom weavers were a body of skilled workers who objected to working in 'factories', and who saw in the coming of machinery the grim spectre of unemployment and ruin. Unlike the early spinning machines, the power looms did not need skilled operatives and could be worked or attended by women and children—at, of course, low wage rates. It is little wonder then that many of the early machines and factories were damaged or destroyed in a series of riots during the second and third decades of the nineteenth century.[1] Many weaving masters, potential factory builders, migrated to the northern slopes of the Rossendale upland, where the cotton industry was less highly developed and where the hatred of machinery was less intense. To this migration, and to the increasing separation of spinning and weaving, due to the large number of new fabrics and the impossibility of weaving firms spinning all the varieties of yarn which they required, the beginnings of the modern specialisation in the industry, dating from about 1840, are due.[2] The use of the power loom did not take the industry by storm, however, as the spinning machines had done,[3] and for a long period, just as in the woollen industries, the hand loom continued to be an important factor in cotton manufacture. Even in the 1830s, when the cotton industry in Great Britain possessed about 100 000 power looms, perhaps 250 000 hand-loom weavers remained.[4] Some remained—in Glasgow for example—even after 1880.

It must not be assumed that spinning and weaving were the only two processes in the cotton industry to be mechanically performed. As far back as 1748 Lewis Paul had patented a carding engine, and Arkwright placed a whole series of carding and drawing machines on the market in the late 'seventies. Many other machines were designed to perform the many processes through which the raw cotton goes before it is ready for spinning.

Another very important series of inventions concerned the bleaching and dyeing of yarn and cloth and the printing of calico. The year 1785 witnessed great advances in the methods of both bleaching and printing. Berthollet, a French chemist, discovered the bleaching properties of chlorine and his ideas quickly became known in Lancashire, the centre of the English calico industry. The new process, as improved by Henry and others in Lancashire, reduced the time necessary from many months to a few days. Its essential requirements were chlorine, easily obtained by canal from the salt deposits of Cheshire; lime, sent by canal from the Carboniferous Limestone region

1. We must not assume that the Luddite and other riots were due *entirely* to the fear of machinery. The general resentment of wage levels and food prices during the great depression which followed the Napoleonic wars should also be taken into consideration (Daniels, *op cit.*, pp. 83–91).
2. See J. Jewkes, 'The localisation of the cotton industry', *Econ. Hist.*, **2**, Jan. 1930, 91–106.
3. Domestic spinning was almost extinct in the towns by 1785, although it lingered in the country districts for several decades. In 1813 there were about 100 power looms in the Manchester district, and about 2400 hand looms.
4. This figure, given by Baines (*op. cit.*, p. 396), is generally regarded as being too high.

of Derbyshire,[1] and sulphur, which began to be obtained from pyrites imported from Spain *via* Liverpool. The assembly of these raw materials by canal and sea resulted naturally in the foundation of a chemical industry at the head of the Mersey estuary, whilst the bleaching industry suffered no change in its location. The bleaching works of the pre-machinery period were fortunately (for boiling water of lime-free character is the chief item in the process) situated on the coalfield and well within the soft-water area of the southern flank of the Rossendale upland, and were also near to Manchester, the finishing and marketing centre.

In 1785 also, cylinder printing was invented. Replacing the old woodblock and copper-plate methods, which had been in use in Lancashire for twenty years, this piece of machinery, later assisted by the transfer process of engraving, could perform the work of 100 men, and so greatly speeded up the printing of calico, reduced costs and enabled a vastly greater output to be obtained.

The development of the cotton industry was facilitated during the Industrial Revolution period by the growth of transport facilities, especially in the form of canals (cf. Chapter 26). Although the earliest canals (Sankey Canal, 1760; Bridgewater Canal, 1761) were designed to provide outlets for the coalfield, the rapid development of the cotton industry after 1770 was followed by a period of intensive canal construction. The Leeds and Liverpool Canal provided an outlet for the northern area (Blackburn–Burnley) as well as for the wool textile region of the West Riding; the Rochdale Canal served Rochdale and the southwest of the Yorkshire woollen region; the Manchester, Bolton and Bury Canal served the Irwell valley; and the Huddersfield Canal linked the Ashton–Stalybridge area with Manchester. Many new mills grew up alongside these canals.

The essential features of the Lancashire cotton industry were thus outlined during the Industrial Revolution period, and just as in the wool textile industry the localisation has changed little since that time, although the relative importance of the various centres may have been somewhat modified. Thus in 1838 Manchester still had more people employed in the cotton industry than any other town, and of the towns north of Rossendale only Blackburn had achieved much importance.[2]

1. The Peak Forest Canal, connected by tramway from its terminus at Bugsworth with the limestone quarries of the Doveholes area. Cf. Fig. 203 on p. 584.

2. Cotton operatives in 1838 (Factory Inspectors' Returns, quoted by Chapman *op. cit.*, p. 151)—towns having 10 000 or more ('000 omitted): Manchester 39.4, Stockport 23.8, Oldham 15.0, Bury 13.7, Ashton-under-Lyne 12.1, Rochdale 10.9, Blackburn 10.5, Bolton 9.9. Whalley parish, that included the growing villages of Burnley and Accrington, had about 10 000 cotton workers. See H. B. Rodgers, 'The Lancashire cotton industry in 1840', *Trans. Inst. Br. Geogr.*, **28**, 1960, 135–53; also K. L. Wallwork, 'The calico printing industry of Lancastria in the 1840s', *Trans. Inst. Br. Geogr.*, **45**, 1968, 143–56.

Modern Growth and specialisation

The main trends to be observed in the industry between the Industrial Revolution and the First World War are six in number. (1) An absolute expansion of the British output, accompanied by a decline relative to the world's total (cf. iron and steel, and shipbuilding). The only serious setbacks received until the First World War were the result (*a*) of the cotton famine brought about by the American Civil War; (*b*) of the great depression of 1873–96, during which the general economic depression, the depreciation of silver (affecting the purchasing power of Eastern countries), and the commencement of foreign competition combined to arrest the triumphant progress of the first half of the century. (2) An increased separation of the spinning and weaving branches, with the development of a 'horizontal' system of organisation. (3) An increased specialisation in the finer types of yarn and fabric, and in fabrics for special markets—a consequence of foreign competition in the production of cheap goods and of the comparatively high cost of raw material as a result of distance from its source. (4) Changes in the mode of transport, the railway superseding the canal, and then the road seriously competing with the railway for the carrying of raw cotton and manufactures. (5) The growth of associated industries, notably textile engineering and the manufacture of chemicals. (6) The beginning, in the twentieth century, of a change in the source of power, increasing use being made of electricity.[1] There is one feature which distinguishes the cotton from the woollen industry during the Industrial Revolution period, and that is the earlier mechanisation of cotton manufacture. Cotton was a well-established factory industry in the 1830s when the greater part of the wool industry, with the exception of worsted spinning, was still in the domestic stage.[2]

1. Power employed in cotton industry 1924 and 1930 (Census of Production).

	1924	1930
Prime movers (steam engines and turbines)	328 000 hp	283 000 hp
Electric generators driven by prime movers	20 000 kW	28 000 kW
Electric motors and purchased current	52 000 hp	75 000 hp

At the Census of Production, 1948, the cotton spinning and weaving industries were recorded as having spent £4.9m on coal and £1.8m on electric current.

2. Persons employed in textile factories (*British Commerce and Industry*, ed. J. W. Page, vol. ii, p. 230).

YEAR	COTTON	WOOL
1835	219 286	55 461
1850	330 924	154 180
1861	451 569	173 046
1870	450 087	238 503
1880	528 795	301 556

The state of the cotton industry during its prosperity

Sources of raw material

The cotton industry in Britain was founded on supplies of raw cotton from the Near East, as we have seen. Before the end of the seventeenth century, the West Indies began to rival the Levantine regions as the chief source of supply. London was the principal receiving port, most of the cotton making an overland journey between the capital and Lancashire. Liverpool, although its general trade was growing, was not important as an importer of cotton until the rise of the United States as a cotton-producing region. Towards the end of the eighteenth century Glasgow also began to import West Indian cotton. Little expansion was possible in the supply of raw cotton from these regions, however, while the French were still in a position to intercept cargoes bound for Britain, and it so happened that a fresh source of supply in the Cotton Belt of the newly established United States became available at just about the same time as the Revolution in France temporarily upset the trading and industrial activities of that country. The cotton plant was of some importance in the agricultural economy of Georgia and the Carolinas by about 1790, and the invention of the saw gin, a machine for separating the fibres from the cotton seeds, in 1793, by making the medium-stapled American cottons much more readily usable, gave the signal for a very rapid expansion of cotton cultivation. The Southern States quickly superseded all other sources of supply, and since that time their produce has been the mainstay of the British cotton industry, and every fluctuation in their crop has been reflected in the prosperity or otherwise of the Lancashire mills.[1]

Before the First World War the United States and Egypt provided about 80 per cent of the imports. Since then there has been a great decline in the actual and proportional imports from the United States, accentuated since the Second World War by shortage of dollars; and an increase in the amount received from a variety of other sources, including Turkey, Iran and the USSR. The recovery of Japan and the changed political status of India and Pakistan have reduced British imports from the Indian subcontinent (see table opposite).

Raw cotton varies enormously in quality. The important factors determining quality include length and regularity, fineness, lustre, softness, strength, colour and cleanness. The fibres vary in length from about 12 mm ($\frac{1}{2}$ inch) to 57 mm ($2\frac{1}{4}$ inches). In America, when the fibres are less than 28 mm ($1\frac{1}{8}$ inches) in length, the cotton is referred to as short stapled; long-stapled cottons exceeded 28 mm ($1\frac{1}{8}$ inches). In other countries the terms

1. For example, the American Civil War, 1861–64 or the partial failure of the crop in 1921.

are relative. We may classify the various grades of raw cotton into three principal groups:

Group I or Fine Cottons, including:
True Sea Island, produced only in small quantities in the small islands off Georgia (United States) and in some of the smaller West Indian islands;

Georgia and Florida Sea Island, generally grown on the coast lands of those States near the sea. Of roughly equivalent quality are the finest Egyptian cottons (Sakellaridis);

American 'Long Stapled Uplands', grown mainly in Louisiana and Texas (32 mm to 45 mm: $1\frac{1}{4}$ to $1\frac{3}{4}$ inch staple). Of about the same quality are Peruvian and the best West African cottons.

Group II or American 'Uplands'—the commonest and most abundant quality. Uplands are classified according to the International (US official) standards into eight grades. In Group II are included much of the South American cotton as well as long-stapled Indian[1] and Russian.

Group III or Short Native Indian, Russian and Chinese cottons—short-stapled and harsh.

Retained imports of raw cotton (million lb)

COUNTRY OF ORIGIN	1913	AVERAGE 1921–25	AVERAGE 1926–30	1931	1950	1962	1966
United States	1471	857	838	442	329	152	78
Egypt	288	265	249	238	188	18	12
India	30	78	78	97	36[1]	27[1]	19
Brazil	57	24	20	37	178	52	31
Peru	38	72	83	64	62	36	27
Anglo-Egyptian Sudan	—	12	45	10	97	52	20
Other countries	290	92	370	210	115	331[2]	280[3]
Total	2174	1400	1483	1098	1005	668	467
Total (million kilograms)	986	635	673	498	456	303	212

[1] Includes Pakistan, 28 in 1950, 15 in 1962.
[2] Includes Iran 50, Turkey 49, USSR 30, Nigeria 15.
[3] Includes Turkey 74, USSR 41, Iran 38, Nigeria 13.

In general, it may be said that the longer the staple of the cotton the finer the yarn and fabric that can be produced from it. Yarn is graded in 'counts'. A count is the number of hanks, each 768 metres (840 yards) in length, which go to make 0.45 kilogram (one pound avoirdupois). Thus the finer the yarn the higher the count. Ordinary American cotton of 22 mm

1. The bulk of the cotton imported by Britain from India and Pakistan does not exceed 20 mm ($\frac{3}{4}$ inch).

($\frac{7}{8}$ inch) staple will produce yarn of about 20's counts, but the best Sea Island may give a yarn of almost spider's web fineness, counting 825 hanks to the kilogram (more than 300 hanks to the pound), and counts of up to 200 are produced from the best Egyptian cottons.

Processes in the Cotton Industry[1]

The principles of cotton manufacture resemble those which we have already described for the woollen industry (p. 508). The main processes are as follows:

(*a*) After unbaling the raw cotton is passed through mixing and cleansing machinery (in which spiked rollers and air suction play important parts).
(*b*) Next, the carding machines give a final cleansing, remove the short unusable fibres[2] (see below) and deliver the cotton in slivers—ropes of clean separated fibres, held together by their natural cohesion.
(*c*) In order to remove irregularities of thickness and weight, several slivers are combined in a 'drawing-frame' and drawn out into one, so that the fibres take up a position parallel to each other.
(*d*) The drawn slivers are passed through a succession of machines (fly frames) which gradually reduce their thickness and prepare them for receiving the twist which will make them into yarn.
(*e*) One of two methods may be used in the spinning process. The simplest apparatus is the ring-frame (derived from Arkwright's water-frame), which spins continuously and is used chiefly for warp and coarser yarns. More complicated, needing more attention (for its operation is intermittent), but producing softer and better yarn, is the self-acting mule (derived from Crompton's invention).
(*f*) 'Doubling' (twisting together of spun yarns) may be performed to ensure an even count being produced or to give strength to warp yarn; and all yarn destined for use as sewing thread, or in the lace and hosiery trades, is doubled.
(*g*) Weft yarn needs little or no further preparation, but the 'twist' (warp yarn) must be transferred from the cops or bobbins of the spinner on to a winding frame ready for assembling on the warper's beam.
(*h*) After 'beaming', the yarn on the beams is passed through boiling size and steam dried.
(*i*) The beam is then mounted in the loom, and weaving can commence.
(*j*) The 'grey' woven cloth is then either disposed of as such, or is subjected to several finishing processes. Apart from dyeing, bleaching and printing, the more important of these are calendering and mercerising. The calendering machine gives a smooth and shiny finish to the cloth. Mercerising con-

1. See *The Cotton World*, ed. J. A. Todd, 1927, p. 191.
2. In the production of fine yarns from long-stapled cotton special combing machinery is employed for this purpose between the carding and drawing processes.

sists of steeping cotton yarn or cloth in a bath of caustic soda in such a way that the shrinkage which would ordinarily result from such treatment is prevented. It produces a lustre almost equivalent to that of silk.

The short fibres removed by the carding machines are known as waste. They are worked up (sometimes mixed with short-stapled Indian cotton or even with wool) into coarse yarn (5's to 10's counts) for use in the manufacture of sheetings, blankets, towels, dusters, lamp wicks and a host of other miscellaneous products.

Geographical distribution and its background

(*a*) *Lancashire.* In analysing the factors which have contributed to the remarkable concentration of the cotton industry in Lancashire we must attempt to differentiate between true localising factors, i.e. factors which were responsible for the placing of the industry just where it is, and factors which have merely been assets in confirming that localisation and in hindering any serious migrations into other regions. In the first category we have the historico-geographical influences already dealt with—the physical environment which aided the rise of woollen and linen industries on the western flanks of the Pennines (cf. Chapter 19), and the part played by Manchester, as a non-corporate town, in attracting industry to itself. In the first class, too, are the water power provided by the numerous steeply graded streams and the soft, lime-free character of the water of those same streams. The combination of lime-free water and water power was the most powerful factor in determining the location of the individual producing centres and the boundaries of the cotton-working region. Of the second class, first and foremost is the existence of productive coal measures. Lancashire could scarcely have attained to its present position had it not been for the coalfield; the industry would probably have died a natural death before the middle of last century. Other important auxiliary factors are the naturally high humidity of south Lancashire, which reduced the necessity for expenditure upon humidifying apparatus for spinning mills; the proximity of the Cheshire saltfield, providing essential materials for the bleaching industry; and the facilities for rail, water and road communication offered by the natural routeways of the Pennine and Rossendale streams, and by the flat plain of southwest Lancashire between Manchester and Liverpool.

The physical setting of the industry has already been alluded to; let us now examine it in rather more detail. The core of south Lancashire is the Rossendale anticline, trending in a westsouthwest direction from the monoclinal axis of the Pennines. On the north side of the upland are the towns situated in the valleys of the Darwen and Calder, tributaries of the Ribble; south of the upland are the towns in the middle Irwell and Roch valleys; and in the denuded heart of the upfold lie the towns strung along Rossendale, the upper valley of the Irwell. The fourth group of cotton-working centres lies in the valleys of the Medlock, Tame and upper Mersey, which flow down from the Pennines (Fig. 194). The Pennine region and part of the Rossendale upland are made up of the thick Millstone Grit Series, and the flanks of the latter are composed mainly of Lower Coal Measures. These systems are characterised by similar lithology, consisting mainly of hard sandstones (hence forming uplands) with alternations of shales and porous

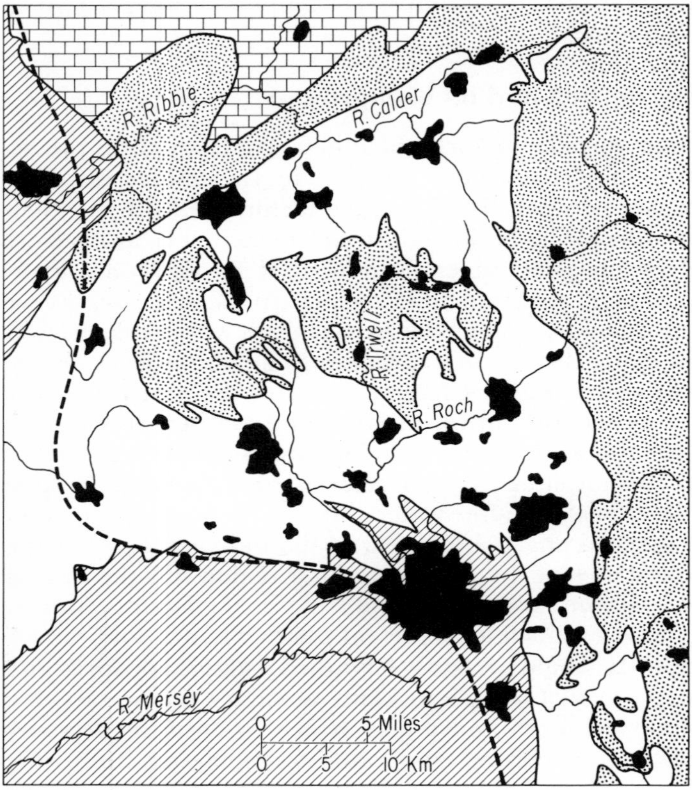

FIG. 194. The cotton-working towns of Lancashire, showing the relation of their position to geological outcrops and soft-water supplies

Carboniferous Limestone outcrop shown on the north; Millstone Grit, dotted: Coal Measures, blank; Trias, lined. The heavy broken line marks the westward limit, according to H. W. Ogden, of public supplies of soft water (hardness under 10); the water used by the mills, however, was often much less pure and of poorer quality.

grit beds (and in the latter formation some coals). They therefore give rise to an abundance of lime-free surface water and although, owing to their low porosity, they are not good water *bearing* formations, the deep narrow valleys which dissect the uplands could easily be dammed in order to ensure copious and constant supplies. The regularity of the stream regime is a result of the comparative evenness of the precipitation through the year (partly, no doubt, due to orographical influence on the rainfall in a west-facing upland area) and of the thick accumulations of spongy, water-holding peat which cover the moors.

The extent to which the need for soft water, at first for washing and cleaning, bleaching and dyeing, and later to an even greater extent for the chemical bleaching process and for the steam-producing boilers, limited the outward expansion of the industry, is seen in Fig. 194. Water having a permanent hardness of more than 10 degrees (i.e. 10 grains of carbonate of lime, or its equivalent in other lime or magnesium salts, per gallon of water) is very difficult to lather, and this makes for much wastage of soap and chemicals; moreover, the excess of lime is deposited as scale in the boilers and pipes of the power-producing plant. Although water-softening apparatus became available, the cost of installation and upkeep was not likely to assist in the construction of new mills outside the soft-water area. We thus find that the cotton industry did not develop on the Triassic, drift-covered area of southwest Lancashire, nor on the flanks of the limestone Pennines; the absence of water power in the former region provided a further check to the westward expansion of the industry. The northern boundary of the cotton-working region is probably the result of the interaction of several factors. The more diversified lithology of the rocks underlying the Ribble basin, together with the fact that the Ribble itself rises in one of the most extensive areas of limestone in northern England, render the softness of the water less reliable. Moreover, two further hindrances to northward expansion were the absence of coal and the distance from the economic centres of the industry—the port of Liverpool and the Manchester market. Thus, north of the coalfield edge, the only two cotton-working centres of any importance are Preston (deriving its soft water from the Millstone Grit of Longridge Fell) and Clitheroe (similarly supplied from Pendle Hill). Finally, it is noteworthy that the cotton industry overstepped the flat watershed between the Roch and the Yorkshire Calder, Todmorden and Hebden Bridge being far more devoted to cotton than to wool.

The importance of soft water must not be overemphasised, except as an original locating factor. As the nineteenth century advanced the water supplies of the individual mills were often polluted and the hardness of the water increased. Further, many of the ordinary spinning and weaving mills had little use for water except for their steam engines, whilst the substitution of electric power still further reduced the water requirements. The industry went on growing through its own momentum, not because of soft water.

Concerning the coalfield as a factor in the growth of the industry, reference has already been made (Chapter 14) to the nature and occurrence of the seams. It is noteworthy here that the major centres of production were never in the vicinity of the principal cotton towns, but lay southwest thereof, in the Lancashire plain. The Bolton–Rochdale group, and the Rossendale group, especially, are removed from large mines. It is obviously, then, the mere existence of the coalfield, rather than the geographical distribution of the mining centres, which was of importance (cf. Chapter 19, p. 516, and Fig. 121). Since the Second World War the almost universal use of electric power from the grid has completely removed any dependence on the coalfield.

PLATE 23. A Lancashire cotton-mill town: Shaw
Typical mill buildings, mingling with nineteenth-century 'bye-law' housing.

The humidity of the atmosphere in Lancashire, although not the vital factor that it was formerly supposed to be, was a valuable asset.[1] For spinning a high relative humidity is required, as otherwise the threads snap under the strain put upon them in the process of drawing and twisting. Dampness causes the fibres to cling together. Even a slight drop in the relative humidity, due perhaps to an east wind, was sufficient to cause considerable inconvenience, and a long dry spell might have proved very costly. From very early times, however—almost in fact from the introduction of the steam engine—artificial steaming or humidifying of the atmosphere was practised.

1. Ogden, *loc. cit.* (above, p. 527).

Finally, a last result of the geological structure is the abundance of building material, so necessary in an area where great factories had to be erected. The sandstones of the Millstone Grit and Coal Measures were employed for domestic and factory architecture, and later the Coal Measure shales were dug in large quantities for brick making. Whilst the older spinning mills, and most of the weaving 'sheds' north of Rossendale, were built of buff-coloured sandstone (now much soot-blackened), most of the modern mills are redbrick buildings,[1] which with their three or four storeys, chimney and tower stand out prominently and give an occasional splash of colour to an otherwise drab landscape (Plate 23).

The development of associated trades is a natural accompaniment of the growth of any large and concentrated industry. It was indeed fortunate for the cotton industry that the principal seat of the heavy chemical industry in Britain should have grown up in the middle Mersey region, backed on the one hand by the saltfield of Cheshire, and on the other by the port of Liverpool, through which were imported the fats for soap making and the pyrites for sulphuric acid. Probably at first the two industries, cotton and chemicals, were interdependent, but the vast expansion of the chemical industry resulted in the textile trades forming only a small part of the market for the produce of Widnes, Runcorn and Northwich (cf. Chapter 22). The growth of the engineering industry, too, especially that part of it devoted to the manufacture of textile machinery, was a natural corollary of the early inventions. Without it Lancashire could never have continued to lead the world in technical efficiency and in the production of the finest types of cotton fabric (cf. Chapter 17, p. 439).

The cotton industry would likewise have been stifled through the inadequacy of its transport system had not the railway come to its aid. The bulk traffic engendered by the cotton trade quickly outgrew the capacity of the canals, and the monopolistic control exercised by the canal owners, the slowness of the transport, and the endless delays due to the locks, and in summer to lack of water and in winter to ice, led a group of merchants in Liverpool and Manchester to embark on the construction of the railway to connect those two industrial foci (cf. Chapter 26, p. 698). In the 1830s the high-water mark of canal transport was reached; then railways began to supersede the stage coach and the barge for passenger and freight traffic, and by 1850 almost all the present railways were in existence. The outstanding features of the railways web of south Lancashire were a reflection of the distribution and organisation of the cotton industry—although, of course, it was not the cotton industry alone which produced them. No less than three main lines connected the market and the port—the direct route across Chat Moss, the southern line *via* Warrington, and the northern line via Bolton. Manchester had a radial web linking it with all the major centres (see Fig. 243, p. 703), and an important link joined Liverpool to the

1. The bricks, which have a smooth, shiny surface, are known as 'Accrington reds'.

weaving centres of East Lancashire. A later expression of the dominating position occupied by Manchester was the Ship Canal, completed in 1894, permitting large ocean freighters to dock thirty-five miles inland from the Mersey Bar.

Mention should finally be made of the expansion of road transport between the ports, the mills and the market. Motor lorries, by reason of their greater flexibility as transporting media, have taken much traffic from the railways. Loading up with raw cotton at the Liverpool or Manchester docks, they can deliver at almost any spinning mill within an hour or two, and are then free perhaps to carry yarn to a weaving mill, and afterwards cloth back to the Manchester warehouse in the same day.[1] Such mobility and speed are impossible for a railway wagon.

Ports importing raw cotton (million lb)

	1913	AVERAGE 1927–30	1931	1935	1948	1961	1967[1]	
							MILLION LB	MILLION KG
Liverpool	1690	1106	744	855	652	380	330	150
Manchester	383	336	338	425	210	120	118	54
London	40	22	13	33	—	5	—	—

[1] Also Glasgow 2.5, Belfast 4.7 million lb.

(*b*) *Scotland.*[2] The growth of a cotton industry in Scotland, although resting on sound geographical foundations, was largely the result of the coincidence, in time, of two events of historical importance. At the beginning of the Industrial Revolution period flourishing linen and silk industries were already in existence, being especially well developed in the Glasgow–Paisley region (cf. Chapter 21). Abundant supplies of soft water from the lime-free rocks of the Central Lowlands, a humid atmosphere favourable to the spinning operation, and a 'deposit' of labour skilled in the manufacture of fine fabrics, thus provided a suitable ground in which the new industry could take root. Then the American War of Independence, by causing the sudden ruin of Glasgow's extensive trade with the Plantations—especially the tobacco trade—left without employment a vast amount of capital and organising ability which had been gained therein; and it so happened that this period, 1775–80, coincided with the period of the great inventions in the cotton industry which we have already discussed. The manufacture of cotton thus provided a very appropriate new outlet for the capital and skill of the Lowlands. Actually, the use of cotton in fustian

1. It has been calculated (W. Smith, 'Trends in Lancashire cotton industry', *Geography*, **26**, 1941, 7–17) that on the average no fewer than six journeys are undertaken from raw cotton to finished piece-goods.
2. See H. Hamilton, *Industrial Revolution in Scotland*, Chapter 6.

making probably began about 1769, and in 1780 muslins began to be made, using Indian spun weft; but it was not until the early 1780s that the use of Crompton's mule enabled all-cotton cloth to be made from homespun yarn, and the real boom in the erection of cotton spinning mills occurred between 1785 and 1795.

The widespread nature of the linen industry and the abundance of soft water and water power in most parts of Scotland resulted in the early cotton mills being scattered in many counties, although the Glasgow region naturally exercised a considerable influence on the location of new enterprises,[1] by reason of its West Indian traffic (most of the cotton came before 1795 from these islands) and its linen and silk trades. With the exception of one or two well placed concerns which managed to survive for a considerable period, however (e.g. Catrine in Ayrshire, Deanston in Perthshire—both of which still exist today), most of the mills outside the Glasgow–Paisley region were comparatively shortlived; distance from the source of raw material (i.e. the port), and later from coal supplies, causing their eventual demise.

Just as in Lancashire, a new factor was introduced into the industry in the 1790s—the steam engine. The expansion of this method of power production was not rapid in Scotland, partly because of the excellent water power facilities which were being utilised, and partly because the engineering industry did not establish itself on the Lanarkshire coalfield as rapidly as in Lancashire, each new mill thus having to make its own machinery. Slowly but surely, however, the steam engine conquered the spinning industry, and the concentration of the mills upon the Lanarkshire coalfield became more marked. By the 1830s nearly all the spinning mills were to be found within 40 kilometres (twenty-five miles) of Glasgow.[2]

In the weaving branch, of course, domestic labour continued to produce the greater part of the output for some time after the spinning industry had been mechanised, and, as in Lancashire, the weavers enjoyed a period of great prosperity whilst yarn was so cheap. In 1831, although there were nearly 15 000 power looms in the Glasgow district, some 50 000 hand looms were still in use in the villages of Lanarkshire, Renfrew and Ayrshire, and hand-loom weavers remained an important section of the community until the 1870s or 80s. The early specialisation of the linen and silk industries in fine fabrics naturally gave an impetus to the production of similar fine wares in cotton. Muslins and ginghams were the ordinary goods produced, but over half the looms, in about 1840, were employed in making the famous Paisley shawls (either all cotton, or cotton and silk), fancy muslins and

1. The first cotton mill in Scotland was erected at Rothesay on the island of Bute in 1779. In 1787 there were nineteen water power spinning mills, distributed as follows: Lanark 4, Renfrew 4, Perth 3, Edinburgh 2, Ayr 1, Galloway 1, Annandale 1, Bute 1, Aberdeen 1, Fifeshire 1.

2. Spinning mills, 1839: Lanarkshire 107, Renfrew 68, rest of Scotland 17. Glasgow alone possessed 98.

decorated cloths. Here lay the greatest difference between the cotton industries of Scotland and Lancashire. Lancashire was thriving on coarse cotton cloths for the Indian market; the fine fabrics from Glasgow went mainly to the continent.

The rapid rise of the cotton industry and its concentration in the Glasgow region were accompanied, as in Lancashire, by the growth of auxiliary trades. Pure water supplies and the facilities for importing raw materials gave rise to a chemical industry which could supply the bleaching and dyeing works which naturally sprang up in the wake of the cotton mills.[1] The ease of production of iron and coal resulted in the establishment of an engineering industry; but although at first this may have been intimately connected with the cotton trade, it soon expanded far beyond the limits set by the mechanical requirements of the factories, and took to the railway and shipbuilding branches (cf. Chapter 17, p. 452). It was the extraordinary geographical basis of the iron industry, in fact (cf. p. 399), which prevented Glasgow from becoming a rival to Manchester, and which was largely responsible for the gradual decline of the Scottish cotton industry in the second half of last century. Iron, and later steel, came so to dominate the economic life of the lowlands, especially of the Lanarkshire coalfield region, that the cotton industry, built from the very beginning on the rather insecure foundation of specialisation in fine and peculiar wares, and so susceptible to changes of fashion,[2] and unable to take advantage of the expanding Indian and Far Eastern markets, was almost swamped.[3] The geographical suitability of the area for cotton manufacture remained unaltered, but the far greater suitability for iron and steel production resulted in the concentration on these trades at the expense of cotton. Such industry as remained was located off the coalfield, as in Glasgow, Paisley and in the Leven valley.

Specialisation

The extraordinary centralisation of the cotton industry in south Lancashire rendered possible a degree of specialisation that is without parallel in any other branch of manufacture. Not only have the various processes of the industry tended to separate, financially and physically, but the relatively unfavourable situation of Lancashire with regard to raw materials and foreign markets produced a further specialisation in the finer varieties of fabrics and in products for particular markets. The focus of this centralisation from the very beginning was Manchester; but from being the principal producer the city changed its role to that of commercial and financial centre. An industry which imported all its raw material from abroad and

1. The dyeing industry was introduced into the Glasgow region by James Watt, who brought Berthollet's invention from France. (Cf. pp. 531, 579.)
2. The manufacture of Paisley shawls, for example, collapsed between 1870 and 1880.
3. See Hamilton, *Industrial Revolution in Scotland*, pp. 147–9.

exported the bulk of its output naturally needed a greater amount of commercial organisation than an industry based upon local supplies and local markets; and Manchester, excellent route centre that it was, assumed the functions of bank and warehouse. The rapid growth which such a position entailed, combined with the city's increasing importance as a port, had the effect of raising land values to such an extent that many of the older mills migrated to the outer suburbs and to the smaller towns. Manchester is still the centre of the industry—no longer the producing centre, but the commercial centre.

Two of the outstanding features of the Lancashire cotton industry were the extreme specialisation of its constituent parts, and the feeble development of integration of any kind. At least six types of firm could be recognised: (*a*) the Liverpool merchants and brokers; (*b*) the spinners; (*c*) the yarn merchants; (*d*) the manufacturers (weavers); (*e*) the dyers and finishers; (*f*) the piece-goods merchants. Many of the producing firms further limited their activities, confining themselves, for example, to fine or coarse yarn, special fabrics, bleaching, sizing, or dyeing; whilst the activities of the Manchester merchants were similarly limited to certain markets.[1]

The distribution of the three main branches of the cotton industry, spinning (including carding), weaving or 'manufacturing' (including winding), and finishing (bleaching, dyeing and calendering) is indicated graphically in Fig. 195.[2] The 'combined' mill, doing both spinning and weaving, was the dominant unit of the industry until well on in the nineteenth century, and it never completely disappeared, but the economic basis of the separation of spinning and weaving, apart from the historical reasons given above, is not difficult to discover. It was due to two main causes. In the first place it was the result of the ever-increasing range of yarns and fabrics which could be produced. Few firms, without being unwieldy and uneconomic, could possibly manufacture all the many varieties of yarn and stuff, and so the business units tended to remain small, specialising in certain types of product only. Secondly, the organising capacity necessary in the spinning industry was very different from that required in weaving.[3] The spinning branch was concerned with a narrower range of products, was more adaptable to large-scale production and horizontal integration, and depended for its market not only on the local weaving industry, but also upon the fairly stable cotton industries of the continent, and to an increasing extent upon the hosiery trades at home and abroad. The weaving trade, on the other hand, dealt in a multitude of different

1. Chapman, *op. cit.*, Chapter 8; G. C. Allen, *British Industries*, 1st edn, pp. 227–50; *Survey of Textile Industries*, pp. 15–30.

2. For an alternative method of demonstrating the distribution of spinning and weaving, by plotting the location of factories, see Fig. 62 of Wilfred Smith's *Economic Geography of Great Britain*, Methuen, 1949.

3. Chapman, *The Lancashire Cotton Industry*, pp. 161–4; cf. Jewkes, *Econ. Hist.*, **2**, 1930, pp. 105–6.

styles of fabric, employing many different types of yarn, and depended largely for its prosperity upon a fluctuating, almost worldwide, market and upon the ability to foresee and cater for changes of fashion, both at

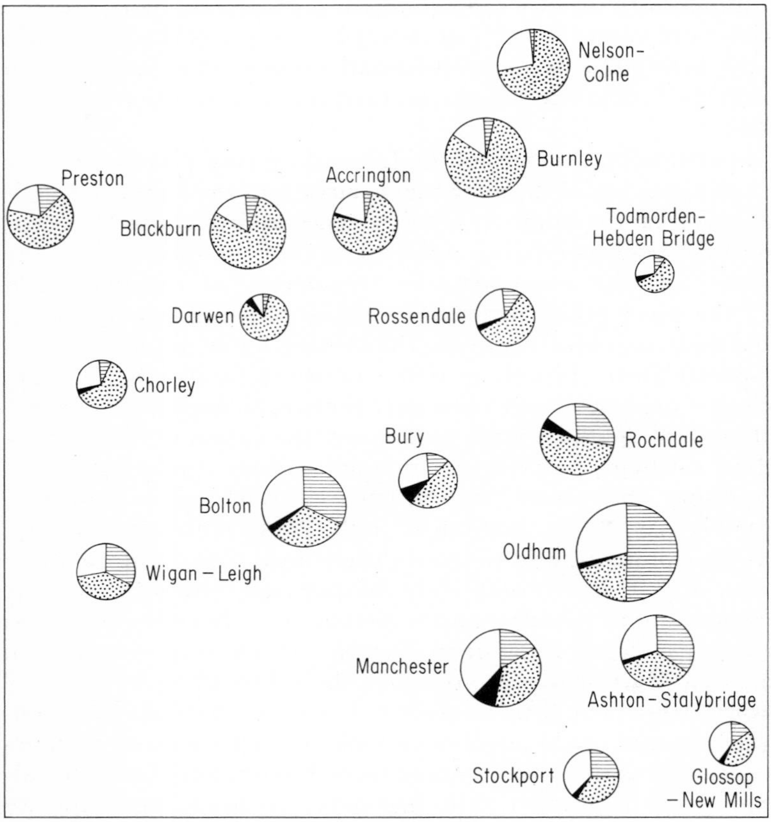

FIG. 195. Distribution of textile occupations in the cotton-working area, 1921

Circles are proportional in area to number of people employed; thus Oldham = 66 000, Darwen = 13 000. The sectors of the circles represent the proportion of the total engaged in the various branches of the industry. Ruled = Carding and Spinning (Census groups 363,365); dotted = Winding and Weaving (groups 367,370); black = Dyeing and Calendering (groups 381,384); blank = all other cotton-working occupations. The people have been grouped around the principal towns; thus Bolton includes Bolton C.B., and the parishes of Farnworth, Kearsley, Little Lever, Turton and Little Hulton; Rossendale includes Bacup, Rawtenstall, Haslingden and Ramsbottom. Notice the feeble development of spinning in the northern area, the prominence of weaving in the so-called 'spinning' area of the south, and the importance of the finishing trades in the Manchester–Bolton–Bury region.

home and abroad. There were still many firms which, whether through sheer momentum, or through the desire to ensure the quality of the yarn which they used, conducted both spinning and weaving operations, but the majority confined themselves to one branch only. The number of separate firms engaged in weaving was much greater than the number in the spinning trade. This was partly due to the greater tendency for amalgamation amongst spinning firms and partly to the extreme specialisation of the weaving trade.[1]

The spinning industry continued to be located principally in the towns of the early cotton-working area—the region of the valleys tributary to the Irwell and the Mersey, i.e. to Manchester. Although the 'horseshoe' of towns stretching from Wigan and Leigh *via* Bolton, Bury, Rochdale, Oldham and Stalybridge to Stockport was primarily devoted to spinning, weaving was by no means absent, and the spinning industry showed much specialisation incapable of geographical explanation. Thus Oldham dealt mainly in medium staple American cotton, producing yarn of 20s to 60s counts. Rochdale's trade was similar. Bolton and Manchester, on the other hand, spun finer yarns from the best American, Egyptian and Peruvian cottons; and in the Stockport district doubling became an important separate branch of the industry. North of the Rossendale upland spinning was of very small importance compared with weaving.

The spinning district—in which about 90 per cent of all the spindles were located—suffered less during the depression of the 1930s than the weaving district, partly because of the additional outlet provided by the hosiery trades and partly since it was within this district that the bulk of the engineering and other industries of south Lancashire were located (cf. pp. 449, 487).

The weaving industry was far more widespread than the spinning, and was less concentrated in the major towns. There were many small weaving sheds outside the urban areas. Besides being dominant north of Rossendale, weaving employed as many or more people than spinning in most of the towns south of the upland, with the exception of Oldham.[2] Here again there were certain towns devoted to certain types of fabric. Within the Manchester province perhaps the chief weaving activity was concerned with the manufacture of goods from 'waste', as at Rochdale and Heywood and in the Stockport–Stalybridge districts, but Oldham still retained something of the old fustian trade, and Bolton produced quilts. The towns in the Rossendale valley specialised in sheeting (made mostly from 'waste'). North of the Fells Preston made fine shirtings, Blackburn and Accrington concentrating mainly on 'dhooties'[3] and other cheap cloths for the Indian and Chinese trade, Burnley on long lengths of narrow cloth destined for printing, Nelson and Colne on 'fancy' fabrics such as sateens, poplins and brocade.

The finishing industry, comprising bleaching, dyeing and calico printing

1. Number of firms engaged in 1924 (*Worrall's Directory*, quoted in *Survey of Textile Industries*, pp. 24–6), spinning only: 620; spinning and weaving: 232; weaving only: over 900.
2. In 1936 some 74 per cent of all the looms were in the main weaving district and 26 per cent were located within the spinning district (W. Smith, *Geography*, **26**, 1941, p. 13).
3. Long, narrow strips of flimsy cloth worn by male Hindus as pantaloons.

and numerous finishing processes, such as mercerising and calendering, remained centred in the Manchester province where it originally grew up.[1] It had been held there by the favourable situation with regard to pure water supplies, and by proximity to the great warehousing centre. The works were to be found alongside the streams which flow down from the Rossendale Fells and the Pennines, the rivers Goyt, Roch, Irwell and Bradshaw Brook being especially important in this respect. The chief centres were Manchester–Salford, Stockport, Bury, Bolton and Rochdale (with Littleborough) and the smaller towns just north of Manchester—Radcliffe, Whitefield and Middleton.

Those centres of cotton manufacture lying just off the edge of the main region in Derbyshire and Yorkshire for the most part resembled, in their industry, the Lancashire region which lay nearest. Thus the Glossop–New Mills group in northwest Derbyshire was devoted, like Stockport, to spinning, to the weaving of cloth from waste, and to the bleaching and dyeing industry. Farther north the Saddleworth–Dobcross area had specialities more akin to those of Oldham. A great tongue of the cotton industry stretched from Rochdale into the Calder valley of the West Riding, and whilst Todmorden and Hebden Bridge were more 'cotton' than 'woollen' towns, numerous woollen centres farther east also engaged to a certain extent in the manufacture of cotton.[2] Huddersfield and Halifax were the chief of these, but Sowerby Bridge, Elland and Brighouse each had more than ten firms engaged in the cotton industry. The main branches were cotton-doubling and weaving. Spinning did not develop to any extent, possibly owing to the lower average of relative humidity on the eastern side of the Pennines. Farther north still, the weaving industry of Nelson and Colne overflowed into the Aire valley. Skipton was the principal centre, but Bradford also had a number of cotton mills, and others were scattered in the small towns which lie in the valley between these two—e.g. Keighley and Bingley. In this region weaving, especially of the Nelson–Colne specialities, was the principal activity.

Rather farther afield we find interesting 'outliers' of the cotton industry in the region around the southern end of the Pennines, where the manufacture survived because of the existence of allied industries. Scattered mills in the Macclesfield district of Cheshire dealt in spinning and doubling and especially in bleaching, dyeing and mercerising, the presence of the silk industry probably having encouraged the last-named activity. In Nottinghamshire, Leicestershire and Derbyshire, the existence of the lace and hosiery trades had much to do with the survival, as at Nottingham, Derby, Mansfield, Long Eaton and a few smaller centres, of cotton doubling and the manufacture of sewing thread.

1. About one-half of the 73 000 workers in the textile finishing trades in 1948 were in the Northwestern Region.

2. Employment in the Yorkshire Region, 1948 (Census of Production): 7542 in cotton spinning and doubling, 7650 in cotton weaving.

The cotton industry in Scotland is but a shadow of its former self. The spinning branch has almost disappeared (except, of course, for the important manufacture of sewing cotton), and yarn is now obtained from Lancashire. Three types of activity remain. The last witness of the former trade in high-quality goods is the manufacture of poplins, muslins, ginghams and fine shirtings, still carried on in Glasgow. Paisley shawls have given place to sewing thread in the making of which some 8000, mostly women, are employed.[1] Lastly, the finishing trades still retain some of their former importance in the Glasgow region,[2] in the Vale of Leven (calico printing), and in north Ayrshire, by reason of the abundance of pure water and the proximity of the chemical industry—although most of their work is now performed upon fabrics which have been woven in Lancashire.

A few mills at Belfast continue to spin cotton, chiefly for admixture with flax in the production of special types of thread and table linen.

In the Irish Republic the cotton industry is mostly of recent origin, post-1930, and has been established partly in connection with the general industrialisation programme to help solve the unemployment problem and partly to reduce dependence on imports. The largest mill is at Athlone, but there are also several in the area between Dublin and the Ulster border (e.g. Slane, Ardee and Drogheda) and several in the far west in Co. Galway.

The present state of the cotton industry

Since 1913, the peak year of the cotton industry, in numbers employed and in production, there has been a marked contraction in all aspects of the industry. It is true that there have been some relatively prosperous years since then, such as 1925, 1937 and 1951, but these have only been temporary halts in the overall gradual decline.

Over the past half century, such is the completeness of the decline that in 1961 the volume of British cloth exports was a mere 5 per cent of the maximum of over 6500 million metres (7000 million linear yards) reached in 1913, and cotton manufactures represented but 1.5 per cent of the total value of UK exports, compared with 25.6 per cent in 1913. Indeed, by 1958–59 the yardage of exports was actually exceeded by cheap imports from Asia, and in 1960 the UK became a net importer of cotton yarn. By 1967 one-third of the home market for cotton goods was being supplied by imports. The main reason for this sad state is primarily the loss of overseas markets, especially in the Far East, where the rapidly growing industries in Japan, Hong Kong, India and Pakistan have entered the world cotton trade as well as supplying their own large home markets. Secondly, the industry

1. Enough thread is made each week in Paisley to encircle the earth 88 times! Employment, 1953: 8436, of whom 5672 were female.
2. Nearly 13 000 people were employed in Scotland in textile finishing trades in 1948. The Vale of Leven industry is much declined, and a new industrial estate has come into being to relieve the unemployment thus created.

has been hampered by the accumulation of redundant and obsolete equipment; the poor trade prospects have discouraged mill owners from modernising their plant and keeping up-to-date with modern techniques. A third factor contributing to the decline has been the shortage of labour. In view of the general contraction of the industry this needs some explanation. During the 1939–45 war many mills were compulsorily closed as the industry was geared to war production. Some of the abandoned premises were used for other purposes, munitions and engineering products, many of the new occupying firms having moved from the more vulnerable Midlands and south of England. Thus many cotton operatives found employment in alternative trades and of course many were drafted into other occupations away from their home region. The dying industry did not attract them back again and thus the United Kingdom was unable to take full advantage of the great demand for goods immediately after the war. The seller's market was lost, and then European and Far East manufacturers quickly recovered to take the trade.

The brief economic slump of 1952 hit the cotton industry severely. A considerable amount of the export trade in quality cottons, the United Kingdom's speciality, was lost to competitors in Western Europe and the United States. The prewar loss of markets for the cheap cotton goods continued and the growth of imports upset the balance of trade still further. Grey cloth has featured among the imports for some time, and much of it was re-exported after finishing in British mills, but in 1958 for example, 65 per cent of this was sold on the home market. The following year, the government attempted to rectify affairs with the Cotton Industry Act 1959. The Act aimed at drastic reorganisation of the industry in two ways; first, the government was to compensate firms who scrapped obsolete equipment and secondly, it would provide grants to help with the cost of installing new machinery. The voluntary application of the Act brought about great changes. In the first year, 40 per cent of the installed looms and 49 per cent of the installed spindles were scrapped. However, much of this equipment had been redundant for a number of years. Of much more significance is the fact that 81 per cent of the looms scrapped were in mills which closed down completely whereas only 56 per cent of the scrapped spindles were in closed mills. Thus, it could be expected that less re-equipment would result in the weaving mills, the branch of the industry on which the country depended for its specialised products to overcome overseas competition. Fine spinning and fine weaving, the manufacturing of good quality cotton goods had also suffered a setback from the rapid development of the manmade fibre industry. Rayon at first, followed by nylon, Terylene, Dacron, etc., have all helped to replace some of the traditional cotton manufactures. Many mills have turned to yarn mixtures, and the reservoir of facilities and skill in the cotton manufacturing areas has meant that factories producing artificial fibres alone have been established in Lancastria. But they are by no means dependent on the facilities and advantages of the region, for nylon and

Courtelle factories are found in many parts of the country, encouraged by more favourable amenities to go to the new light industrial estates in the other Development Areas. Thus it is the fine-spinning town of Bolton for example and the fine-weaving centre Nelson that have suffered from the contraction. On the contrary, the towns of Bury and Rochdale and the small centres in the Rossendale valleys specialising in coarse products have escaped such serious losses; a complete reversal of the effects of the decline in the 1930s.

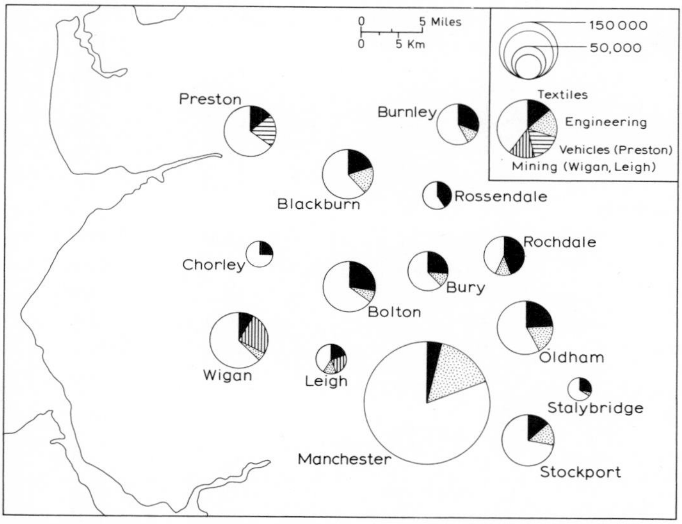

FIG. 196. Employment in textiles and other industries in south Lancashire, 1961

The symbols represent the towns named and their smaller neighbours.

The result of the recent changes has been a more marked redistribution of weaving than spinning. The traditional weaving belt of the Darwen-Calder valley has now less than half of the looms in the industry, the spinning area of southeast Lancashire has gained nearly a quarter of the looms, but has maintained its lead in spinning with 75 per cent of the spindles. The old subdivision of the cotton manufacturing area into weaving predominant in the north and spinning in the south is more realistically altered to give a fourfold division suggested by H. B. Rodgers (1962): (*a*) The Darwen–Calder valley zone, still highly specialised in weaving, but comparatively less important; (*b*) southeast Lancashire, still dominant in spinning but, with the greater loss in spindles, spinning and weaving are more balanced; this is still the most important 'finishing' area; (*c*) Rossendale, where spinning and weaving are roughly equivalent and the area has experienced much less contraction in the industry than others; (*d*) West Central Lancashire, where there is no marked specialisation and contraction has been small.

The cotton industry 1956 and 1966

		1956 (IN MILLIONS)	1966
Raw cotton imports	tons	335	209
	metric tons	340	212
Cotton yarn production	lb	597·5	368.2
	kg	271	167
Cotton waste yarn	lb	104.9	87.7
	kg	47·5	39·7
Spun manmade fibre yarn	lb	99	89.8
	kg	44·9	40.7
Yarn consumed in weaving			
cotton yarn	lb	443.6	248.2
	kg	201.2	122.6
cotton waste yarn	lb	78	59·3
	kg	35·4	27
manmade fibre yarn	lb	227.2	221.6
	kg	103	100.5
Cotton production			
cotton	linear yds	1612	9·5
	m	1474	8.7
manmade fibres	linear yds	605	545
	m	553	498
cotton/manmade mixtures	linear yds	97	71
	m	88.7	64.9
Imports of woven cotton fabrics	sq. yds	375	583
	sq. m	313	487
Exports of woven cotton fabrics	sq. yds	385	152
	sq. m	322	127

In 1939 there were about 1600 cotton mills of various sorts in Lancastria. The actual total in 1951 was 1562; but by 1962 it was down to 868, and by 1968 only 635 were left. Over 900 mills had been closed, but nearly four-fifths of them were converted to new uses so that no great unemployment problem resulted, and industrial diversification was greatly assisted. By 1967, no less than 140 000 people were working in old cotton mills, and the process continues.

The Lancashire textile industry can no longer be thought of merely in terms of cotton. Between one-third and one-half of the cloth output is now made wholly or partly of manmade fibres. Moreover, the economic structure of the industry has changed fundamentally in the 1960s. True, there are still (1968) about 400 independent companies with spinning, doubling and/or weaving operations, together with about 120 finishing firms and over 800 independent converters (merchants and wholesalers). Yet about 20 per cent of these firms control some 60 per cent of the spindles and 40 per cent of the looms and employ 50 per cent of the finishing labour force, and half a dozen very big firms (Courtaulds, Coats Patons, Viyella, English Sewing Cotton, Calico Printers, Carrington & Dewhurst) dominate the industry. Vertical integration is replacing the characteristic horizontal integration of the past, and some of the big firms are far more concerned with manmade fibres than with cotton, so that the textile industry is fast becoming almost an adjunct of the chemical industry that provides the fibres (see Chapter 21)—and indeed the chemical industry's capital is being used to further development.

So, with employment in textiles down to 100 000, representing but 8 per cent of the total employed population of Lancastria, and with only 5 per cent of the school leavers in 1967 entering the industry, the whole economic geography of the region has changed almost out of recognition in a few decades. It is now dominated by engineering, chemicals and manmade fibres. Cotton is no longer king.

21
The textile industries: other textiles

As remarked on p. 489, it is no longer possible to make the same clear distinction as formerly between the industries dependent on cotton, wool and manmade fibres. But silk has an interesting historical geography that is still worth examining, the knitwear industry was always dependent on several raw materials and so has not been affected in its location by the advent of manmade fibres, while the linen, jute and lace industries are still recognisable entities with highly localised distributions. It is with these, together with the production of manmade fibres (that might almost equally well fall into the chapter on Chemical Industries) that we are here concerned.

Employment figures, in so far as it is still possible to separate them by fibres and processes, have been given above, p. 490.

An examination of the geographical distribution of the various branches will show that several different types of factors have been involved in their localisation.

(*a*) In the case of linen, proximity to flax-growing areas led originally to the rise of Ireland and the Scottish Lowlands as manufacturing regions. In the Lowlands the growth of other textile occupations and of heavy industries in the west resulted in the confinement of the linen trade to the eastern region—a situation confirmed by the ease of importing flax and hemp from the Baltic countries. In Ireland the events of the Industrial Revolution conspired to localise the industry on Ulster.
(*b*) The jute industry attached itself, quite naturally, to the allied linen and hemp trades of the Dundee province. It was a Dundee manufacturer who, during a temporary shortage of hemp supplies, experimented with jute as a substitute. It has attained but small dimensions elsewhere.
(*c*) The localisation of much of the silk industry in southeast Cheshire and northwest Staffordshire is not easily explicable on a purely physical basis. Its expansion was due to the pre-existence of a textile smallware and button-making trade, combined with facilities for water power development.
(*d*) The concentration of the knitwear industry in Derbyshire, Leicestershire, and Nottinghamshire is to some extent the result of fortuitous circumstances associated with the invention of the 'stocking frame' near Nottingham, though economic factors also played a part, while the lace industry of

the Nottingham district began as an offshoot of the local hosiery industry. Although the woollen and worsted industry may have had some influence on the early growth of the knitwear industry, the development of silk and cotton spinning in Derbyshire and Nottinghamshire did not take place until the knitwear industry was well established. The growth of the silk and cotton industries in this area was partly a result of demand created by a pre-existing knitwear industry, though the local supply of cotton and silk yarn in its turn stimulated further expansion of knitwear manufacturing.

(*e*) The manufacture of 'artificial' or 'manmade' fibres, such as rayon, nylon and numerous later ones such as Terylene and Courtelle is really a chemical industry, depending in the case of rayon on imported wood pulp and cotton linters, and a very large water supply, and in the case of the synthetic fibres, on chemicals derived from coal or petroleum. But their products, 'artificial' fibres, are the raw materials of textile industries which in general have attached themselves to pre-existing textile centres, where suitable skilled labour could most easily be obtained—as in south Lancashire, west Yorkshire, the Nottingham–Leicester province, the Macclesfield–Leek district, and Northern Ireland.

(*f*) Finally, there are numerous isolated centres of the minor textile industries to be found, as in East Anglia, in the West Country, and in south-west Scotland, where certain specialities are all that remain of once flourishing trades in wool and worsted, silk, or cotton.

With the exception of the artificial fibres, which are products of the twentieth century, all the minor textile industries have long histories. Many features of their early distribution are inexplicable except by the chance settlement of Flemish or other foreign craftsmen; and the geographical and historical factors which contributed to their development in most cases have long since ceased to operate. Without going into an immense amount of historical detail, then—a task which is here impossible—it is difficult to give more than a sketchy account of their origin and growth; and many of the curious features of their distribution must be passed over merely as examples of industrial momentum.

Knitwear

The present-day hosiery industry deals with such a variety of products that hosiery proper now forms only a relatively small part of it, knitted underwear and outer garments (such as pullovers, dresses, and costumes) providing a constantly expanding market. It seems advisable, therefore, in order to avoid confusion of terms, to designate this industry 'knitwear'. For the first 300 or so years of its existence, however, the industry was primarily devoted to the production of hose.[1] With a labour force of 126 500 in Great

1. *Victoria County History, Nottinghamshire*. ii, 352–8; W. Felkin, *History of Machine-Wrought Hosiery and Lace Manufacturers*, 1867; F. A. Wells, *The British Hosiery Trade*, 1935 (see especially chapters 1 to 3).

Britain in 1961 and a further 3000 or so in Northern Ireland, the knitwear industry is by no means insignificant in the national economy, even when compared with the cotton and woollen and worsted industries, and the knitwear province of the east Midlands, with almost 76 000 people employed in the industry in 1961, must be regarded as a major region of industrial specialisation on the same level as the cotton manufacturing region of Lancashire and the woollen and worsted region of the West Riding.

The manufacture of hosiery from worsted and silk by machinery dates from the invention of the stocking frame by William Lee, a clergyman of Calverton, near Nottingham, in 1589. It seems to have been entirely a matter of chance that the machine was invented in Nottinghamshire at this time, for unlike other major technical developments in textile machinery, it was not a response to strong economic incentives. The hosiery industry gradually began to spread in Nottinghamshire and the adjoining counties of Derbyshire and Leicestershire, possibly aided by the local production of worsted yarns from the long-woolled Leicester sheep, but it was in London that the earliest major concentration of the industry took place. Here proximity to the main centre of the silk industry and the main market for luxury goods and fashionable items of clothing was responsible for the early success of machine hosiery manufacturing. The London industry began to decline during the first quarter of the eighteenth century, and most of the machines were subsequently moved to the Nottingham and Leicester districts. The main reason for this migration appears to have been that labour costs were lower in the east Midlands than in London, so although the beginning of hosiery manufacturing in the Nottingham district was largely a matter of chance, the eventual concentration of the industry in the counties of Derbyshire, Leicestershire, and Nottinghamshire was a response to positive economic advantages.[1]

Strutt's invention of a machine for producing ribbed hose, in 1758, gave an impetus to the trade, and the development of factory cotton-spinning in the Derwent valley soon afterwards stimulated further expansion. By the middle of the nineteenth century the hosiery trade, which was still entirely a domestic industry, provided work for 100 000 people, almost all in the east Midlands. The three principal counties had become concerned with different types of hosiery. Nottingham was the first to make cotton stockings from Indian spun yarn, in 1730, and its later connection with Arkwright, Hargreaves, and the early cotton-spinning industry (cf. Chapter 20, p. 529) made it the chief cotton hosiery town, although silk was also employed to a large extent. Derby, the home of the first English silk mill (see p. 571), developed the manufacture of silk hose; and Leicester, always more concerned with long wools than with cotton or silks, specialised in worsted hosiery.

The gradual replacement of the domestic system in the hosiery industry

1. D. M. Smith: 'The British hosiery industry at the middle of the nineteenth century: an historical study in economic geography', *Trans. Inst. Br. Geogr.*, **32**, 1963, 125–42.

by factory production during the second half of the nineteenth century led to further expansion of knitwear manufacturing, as the increasing use of cotton, wool, silk, and later artificial silk, for knitted underwear, and of wool especially for outer garments, greatly extended the market for knitwear. The present-day manufacture of knitwear forms an interesting link with the cotton, woollen, silk and manmade fibre industries, for the finished or semi-finished products of those trades form its raw materials. The introduction of knee-breeches almost killed the silk hose business, but the cheapening of the manufacture of silks, and more particularly the use of artificial silk in the production of ladies' hosiery, led to a revival of this branch of the trade.

The progress of the knitwear industry in Great Britain during the past sixty years is illustrated in the following table:

Employment in knitwear manufacturing

	1911[1]	1961[2]	1966[3]
The east Midlands	49 500	75 600	77 340
Rest of England and Wales	6 900	29 400	31 770
Scotland	11 400	21 600	20 930
Total	67 800	126 600	130 040

[1] Census Report. [2] Ministry of Labour. [3] 'Hosiery and other knitted goods'.

This shows that the general expansion has been accompanied by a reduction in the concentration in the east Midlands, though this area still remains the major knitwear manufacturing region in the country.

The 'knitwear province' of the east Midlands is shown in Fig. 197. Dominated by Leicester and Nottingham the industry is seen to be grouped about four nodes. In Leicestershire there is a concentration in and around Hinckley in the south, and another centred on Leicester and extending down the Soar valley to Loughborough and Shepshed. To the north Nottingham is the focus of the trade centred on the Erewash and Leen valleys, and another concentration exists in the Mansfield and Sutton-in-Ashfield district. At Derby the decline in the silk industry after about 1860 was accompanied by considerable expansion of knitwear manufacturing, but this tended to subside as the town's engineering activities grew; an important local specialisation in Derby is the manufacture of elastic webbing and bandages. The traditional distinction between the Nottingham district specialising in cotton goods, Derby (silk), and Leicester (woollen) is now largely obscured by the widespread use of artificial fibres. Local specialisation still exists, however: the Hinckley area and a number of towns on the Derbyshire and Nottinghamshire coalfields tend to concentrate on ladies' stockings, Nottingham and Leicester have a larger proportion of garment manufacturers, while the dyeing and finishing section of the trade remains largely concentrated in Nottingham in the Leen valley.

Outside the main knitwear province several other centres of the industry are to be found, mainly in association with other textile trades. Several towns in Lancashire and the West Riding, such as Manchester and Keigh-

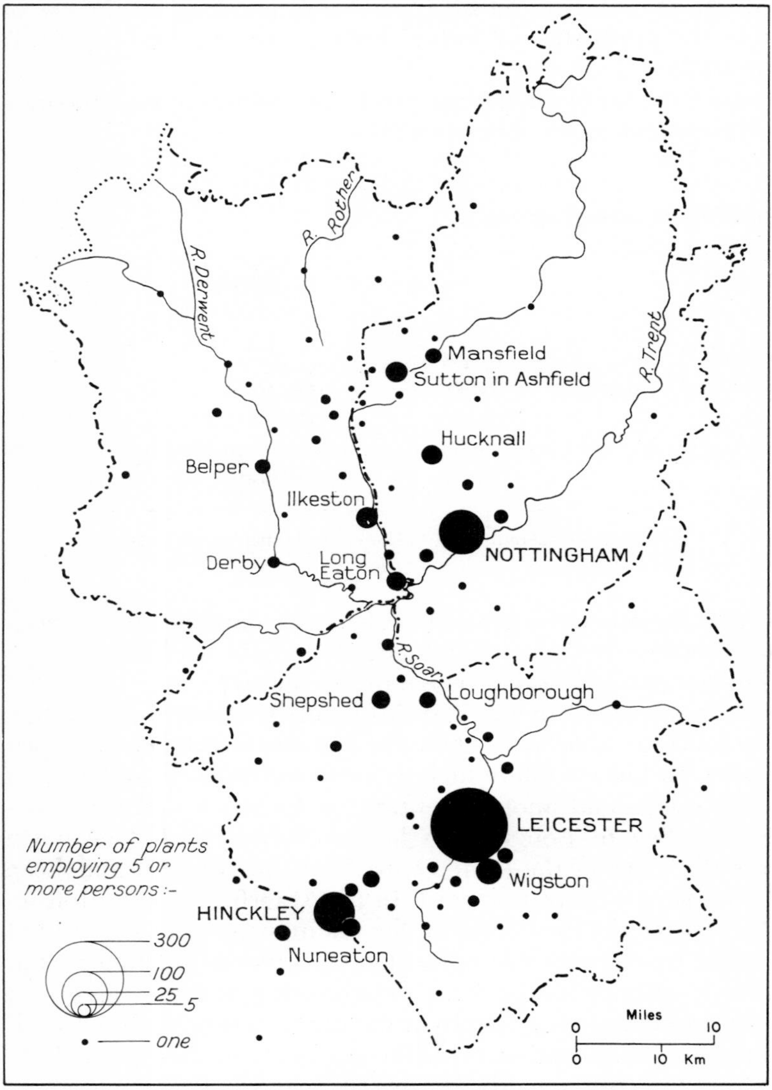

FIG. 197. The knitwear province of the east Midlands, 1957

ley, have knitting mills, as have also the silk-manufacturing centres of Cheshire and Staffordshire—Macclesfield, Congleton, and Leek. In Scotland, Glasgow, Kilmarnock, and Stewarton, together with a number of other Ayrshire towns carry on a trade which has developed out of the decayed cotton industry of the area; and at Hawick woollen knitwear, which began as a sideline to the manufacture of tweed cloth, is now the main interest, employing over 5000 people in the border area as a whole. Numerous other towns in England and Scotland have small knitwear factories, for bulky raw material is not required, and the widespread use of electric power has relaxed the restriction on location previously imposed by the need for access to local supplies of coal. An interesting development during the post-war period has been the setting up of large knitwear factories in areas of relatively high unemployment, such as South Wales, northeastern England, and Northern Ireland, as a result of the relative scarcity of labour in the east Midlands. This represents a continuation of the dispersal of the industry on a national level which has been evident since knitwear manufacturing became a factory industry.

A recent development of considerable significance has been that of warp-knitting, using synthetic filament yarns (see below, p. 575). In addition to catering for new markets such as stretch tights for women, warp-knitted cloth has made great inroads into the traditional markets for Lancashire woven cloth. About one-third of the entire industry is in the hands of Courtaulds, and by 1968 some 80 per cent of women's lingerie and night-wear was produced by warp-knitting, and nearly one-half of the shirt-making material, with a substantial share of the output of sheeting and garment linings.

Lace[1]

The making of lace was probably introduced into this country by refugees from Flanders, and during the seventeenth century it became an important female domestic occupation in many parts of southern and Midland England. The manufacture of lace by machinery began in an area relatively unfamiliar with hand lace making, however, for although lace was being made in Nottingham in the sixteenth century, this part of the Midlands was never one of the more important areas of hand lace making. The machine lace industry originated as an offshoot of the hosiery industry.[2] During the last three decades of the eighteenth century numerous attempts were made to adapt the stocking frame to the production of new meshes, with the result that by 1810 some 15 000 people were employed in machine lace manu-

1. See *Victoria County History, Nottinghamshire*, ii, 358–63. Also Felkin, *op. cit.*, and E. M. Rawstron, 'Some aspects of the location of hosiery and lace manufacturing in Great Britain', *East Midland Geogr.*, **9**, June, 1958, 16–28.
2. For further details, see D. M. Smith, 'The Nottingham lace industry', *Northern Universities Geogr. J.*, **1**, February 1960, 5–15.

facturing. The invention of the bobbin-net machine by Heathcote in 1809 gave further impetus to the industry, and during the next twenty years the population of Nottingham and its surrounding villages rose from 47 000 (1811) to 79 000 (1831). Then in 1834, Leavers adapted the Jacquard principle to the lace-frame, thus enabling patterns to be produced mechanically instead of being sewn in by hand. During this period much of the work was of a domestic nature, and large numbers of women and children were employed in various finishing processes and in preparing yarn for the machines. Most of the cotton yarn used came from Manchester, but the doubling was

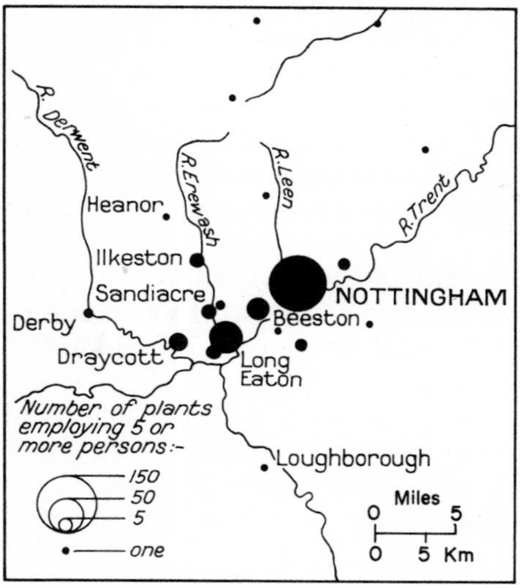

FIG. 198. The lace-making province of the Nottingham area, 1957

done in Nottingham. The lace industry, unlike the hosiery industry, was by no means entirely a domestic industry during the first half of the nineteenth century, for large factories were erected in Nottingham and Derby, and also in the West Country following Heathcote's move to Tiverton in Devon in 1814. For a brief period the West Country threatened to replace Nottingham as the main centre of the machine lace industry, but Nottingham soon reasserted its supremacy. Although the large power-driven factories were relatively rare until the second half of the nineteenth century,[1] there were many small workshops of hand-operated machines, and this, together with the (now defunct) system of hiring out machines to small manufacturers, resulted in the existence, within the industry, of a great number of small firms. This situation has persisted up to the present time, and it is common

1. In 1862, of 120 000 people employed in the lace industry, only 4000 came under the notice of the Factory Acts.

to find several small firms renting their floor space and power, within the same mill.

During the last quarter of the nineteenth century, and up to the First World War, the lace industry of the Nottingham district enjoyed a period of enormous expansion and prosperity. Since this time a marked decline has taken place as the following table shows:

Employment in lace manufacturing

	1911[1]	1962[2]	1966
Nottingham and district	35 600	5 400	6 110
Rest of England and Wales	5 400	1 000	7 200
Scotland	5 100	1 700	1 240
Total	46 100	8 100	14 550

[1] Census Report. [2] Ministry of Labour.

The trade has always been subject to great fluctuation in accordance with changes in fashion, but with the passing of the Victorian era and the adoption of greater simplicity in dress and furnishings the market for lace suffered a serious contraction. The lace industry has retained the remarkable concentration in the Nottingham district which has been its outstanding feature almost from its inception, an excellent example of the cumulative growth of an industry. After the city, Long Eaton is the next most important centre, but Beeston, Sandiacre, Derby and a few other places also participate (Fig. 198). With the exception of isolated mills in the West Country at Tiverton, Barnstaple, Honiton, and Chard the only other noteworthy region is Ayrshire, where lace making, principally of curtain nets, developed after about 1875 at Newmilns, Darvel, and Galston—water power sites on the Irvine river—following the decline of the local weaving industry.

Linen

Flax-growing and the manufacture of linen have been carried on in England, Scotland, and Ireland, and since the industries in each of these countries have had little relation to one another it will be convenient to treat them separately. In each country, however, we shall find that little is known of the origin of the industry, that a considerable advancement was brought about by the influx of the foreign refugees, and that parliamentary action, in the form of duties, and historical events, such as the American Civil War, have also contributed to the development of the industry.

England

Flax was certainly being grown in England in the twelfth century, and late in the fourteenth century a colony of linen weavers, brought by Edward III from the Netherlands, was settled in London; in the fifteenth century Norwich was the centre of the linen trade. Little expansion was possible, however, whilst the woollen industry was receiving such careful attention from the Government; no encouragement was given to linen lest it should interfere with the wool trade, and it was not until the rise of the cotton manufacture with its accompanying demand for linen warp yarn, that any great advance was made. Flax-growing and linen manufacture were domestic industries, scattered over many parts of the country, notably in south Lancashire, but the quality of the product was poor, largely owing to inadequate knowledge of, and lack of care in, the preparation of flax, and in consequence a great deal of fine linen was imported from France. The introduction of spinning machinery in 1787[1] and the development of steam power after about 1820, resulted in the concentration of the industry in the West Riding, where it reached its maximum in the 1850s. Leeds alone possessed nearly half of the 441 000 spindles in England and Wales in 1856. The increasing dominance of the wool textile industry, and the much greater development of linen and its allied fibres in Ireland and Scotland led to the decline of the Yorkshire industry; and at the present time the manufacture of linen in England is practically extinct.

Scotland[2]

Linen was the principal export of Scotland in the sixteenth century, and its manufacture was a widespread domestic occupation. After languishing for a period, it experienced a considerable revival in the eighteenth century after the union with England, largely as the result of State encouragement. A board of trustees was set up in 1727, with funds and power to help flax growing and the linen trade—and this remained in existence for nearly a century. A little colony of French weavers from St Quentin was established at Edinburgh in 1729, and later, Irishmen and Dutchmen were brought to Scotland to teach improved methods of production and manipulation of flax and linen. At first the product was of coarse quality, and most of the export went to the American Plantations, but from the 1740s onwards finer varieties of linen cloth began to be copied from our German competitors. The domestic manufacture of the period was widespread, but with the growth and capitalisation of the industry certain divisions began to be apparent, much of the spinning being done in the northern counties (e.g. Banff, Aberdeen) whilst the weavers, although very scattered, tended to congregate in the commercial and finishing centres of the Lowlands, where,

1. First machine erected in 1787 at Darlington.
2. See Hamilton, *Industrial Revolution in Scotland*, Chapters 4–5.

as at Perth, Glasgow, Edinburgh, Dumbarton, and several places in Fifeshire, large bleaching fields were laid out. To an increasing extent, too, the eastern part of the Lowlands—Forfarshire (Angus)[1]—began to specialise in coarser types of cloth, whilst Lanarkshire and Renfrew developed the manufacture of French lawns and cambrics,[2] using imported yarn.

The phenomenal growth of the cotton industry in the western portion of the Lowlands during the last twenty years of the eighteenth century had a profound effect upon the linen trade. The manufacturers of fine French and Italian varieties of cloth in the Glasgow–Paisley region were the first to take up the new fibre, and the result was an almost complete extinction of the linen industry in that area. Just at this period, however, flax-spinning machinery was introduced, and the linen industry in the eastern counties, aided by the presence of water-power, and, after the application of steam power, of coal, entered upon a period of rapid growth, in the 1820s and 1830s. The county of Angus, with Dundee as its chief town, soon became the most important, with the adjoining county of Fife not greatly inferior. In 1836 Scotland possessed 170 flax-spinning mills (80 per cent of them in these two counties) employing over 13 000 people. The decline of domestic spinning was not paralleled by a similar contraction of the home weaving industry. Flax fibres are inelastic and were not easily worked by mechanical power, so that, although attempts were made to introduce power looms in the 1820s, their adoption was not general until after 1850, when Dundee, Coupar Angus, Brechin, Kirkcaldy, Montrose and Aberdeen became important weaving centres. The American Civil War by almost strangling the cotton trade, gave a distinct fillip to the manufacture of linen, but the prosperity was short-lived, and a steady decline set in. Possibly aided, however, by the allied jute and hemp industries, and by the facility for importing Baltic and Belgian flax (for flax cultivation in Scotland has practically ceased), the linen industry has maintained itself to a far greater extent than in England.

Ireland[3]

Of very early origin, the manufacture of linen in Ireland was for a long period given no encouragement as being prejudicial to the wool trade. It is thus of little moment until the seventeenth century, towards the end of which legislation laid for it a permanent foundation by prohibiting the export of wool from Ireland except to Britain (lest the cheap Irish labour should undercut England's wool trade in foreign markets), and by admitting Irish flax and linen into England free of duty. Its growth was materially

1. For example, Dunfermline (Fife), long renowned for table linen.
2. As late as 1767, forty skilled craftsmen were brought from France to teach the spinning of fine yarns, and settled at Anderston.
3. See H. W. Ogden, 'The geographical basis of the Irish linen industry', *J. Manchester geog. Soc.*, **45**, 1934–35, 41–56.

aided, too, by the influx in 1685 of Huguenot refugees, who settled mainly in Protestant Ulster and in Dublin (those in Dublin being chiefly silk and poplin weavers); while the encouragement of flax-growing by Charles II and the improvement of the methods of cultivation and bleaching by the Huguenots were other contributory factors. As in Scotland, a Board of Trustees was established to assist the growing of flax and to preserve the quality of the produce by grading and marking all cloth; like the Scottish board, this continued in action for more than a century. The vast expansion of the trade during the eighteenth century[1] was achieved entirely without mechanical power, and until about 1830 the linen manufacture was a cottage industry; only in 1828 was the first flax-spinning machine erected in Belfast, and although power looms began to appear from 1850 onwards, hand-loom weavers remained an important section of the linen operatives until the First World War. Power machinery rendered certain the dominance of the Ulster region, by reason of its nearness to imported coal supplies and to the port of Belfast. Over the rest of Ireland production, except perhaps for home use, has practically ceased.

Processes in the linen industry

Flax is by no means so simple a fibre to deal with as cotton, and it is very liable to be injured by careless treatment during the preparatory processes. The pulled flax must first be retted in water in order to remove soft tissues and gummy matter and to facilitate the separation of core and fibre. It is in this process that ignorance or carelessness on the part of the farmer may lead to much damage. The retted stalks are then scutched (beaten) to remove the woody core; the waste fibre produced thereby is called 'tow' and is used for making twine and canvas. After scutching, about 5 per cent by weight of the original flax plant remains. Before spinning, the fibre must be submitted to roughing and hackling processes—i.e. combing out short fibres (producing more tow), untangling and parallelising the fibres, and then cutting out the middle (best) part of each length. The 'line' (as distinct from tow) is combined by machinery into slivers, which are further drawn out in a drawing frame and wound on bobbins for spinning. In Scotland dry spinning is mostly practised—giving strong yarn for towelling and for weft in mixed goods. In Ireland, for finer and more even yarn, the rovings are passed through hot water before spinning. The spun yarn is doubled for use in the lace, tailoring, carpet, and fishing-net trades; and yarn for fine linen goods is bleached and boiled before being woven. The weaving process needs no comment. To a greater extent than any other textile, linen derives benefit from bleaching. Grass bleaching is still done in Ireland, away from the smoky towns, but most of the linen is bleached and finished by chemical and mechanical methods.

1. Annual export 1700: about 180–275 thousand metres (200–300 thousand yards). 1800: about 27–37 million metres (30–40 million yards).

The products of the linen industry are four in number: *Yarn*; *brown cloth* (unbleached)—canvas, duck and drills; *fully bleached*—for shirtings and sheets, damasks and cambrics; *articles* made from fully bleached cloth—sheets, handkerchiefs, table-cloths, and so on, in immense variety, plain and embroidered.

Raw materials

Flax is no longer grown in commercial quantities in Northern Ireland, and the English and Scottish crops being negligible, supplies of raw flax, tow and yarn are imported.

Imports of flax and linen yarn (thousand cwt)

VARIETY OF PRODUCT	1913	AVERAGE 1921–25	AVERAGE 1926–30	1931	1935	AVERAGE 1951–55	AVERAGE 1956–60	1966 METRIC TONS	1966 '000 CWT
Raw flax	1 686	564	708	579	679	572	638	21 900	432
Tow or codilla	364	140	132	286	444	191	238	14 225	280
Flax yarn	248	89	143	138	20	31	23	2 300	46

Ports importing flax and linen yarn (thousand cwt)

TOWN	1913	AVERAGE 1927–30	1931	1935	1948	1955	AVERAGE 1956–60	1966 METRIC TONS	1966 '000 CWT
Belfast	1 363	492	696	681	312	435	520	17 000	338
Dundee	451	182	113	288	100	240	}	10 700	211
Leith	266	149	102	80	—	—	}		—
Aberdeen	106	45	12	1	—	69	} 440		—
Glasgow	33	28	15	16	20	—	}	7 400	146
London	70	16	38	8	—	—	}		—

Flax production of Northern Ireland (thousand cwt)

1913	AVERAGE 1926–30	1931	1939	1948	AVERAGE 1951–55	AVERAGE 1956–60	1962
253	116	28	90	80	61	10	Nil

Imports of flax, tow and linen yarn by countries (thousand cwt)

COUNTRY	1913	AVERAGE 1921–25	AVERAGE 1926–30	1931	1935	AVERAGE 1951–55	AVERAGE 1956–60	1962[2] METRIC TONS	1962[2] '000 CWT
USSR[1]	1 583	74	34	120	458	21 (USSR, Estonia, Latvia, Lithuania)	292 (USSR, Estonia, Latvia, Lithuania)	8 100 (USSR, Estonia, Latvia, Lithuania)	160 (USSR, Estonia, Latvia, Lithuania)
Estonia	—	79	67	6	66				
Latvia	—	168	319	442	168				
Lithuania	—	12	22	2	19				
Netherlands	33	40	46	17	64	94	79	1 400	28
Belgium	517	259	378	340	343	551	415	16 200	319
France	42	17	38	36	5	32	16	2 400	48

[1] Russia prior to 1921. [2] Includes Poland 38.

Before 1914 Russia supplied the bulk of the requirements, but between the Revolution and 1932 only a very small proportion came from the USSR. This proportion notably increased during the 1930s, declined to nothing during the Second World War, but has since partly recovered. The chief flax-growing area of old Russia lay in the northwest, and in the erstwhile republics of Latvia, Estonia, and Lithuania. The main source now is Belgium, and the adjacent parts of France and Holland. From Belgium also most of the imported yarn is derived.

The linen industry today

The United Kingdom possesses about one-third of the world's flax spindles, and Ulster is the greatest linen manufacturing region of all. Belfast is the hub of that industrial area, and three-quarters of the mills are within thirty miles of the city. Belfast dominates the linen industry to an even greater extent than Manchester does the cotton industry, for it is the chief manufacturing centre as well as being the commercial focus and port. Other important centres are Lurgan, Banbridge, Portadown, Ballymena and Lisburn, but many of the small towns are associated in one way or another with the industry (Fig. 199). Research is carried on at Lambeg. There is some separation of spinning and weaving, many firms confining themselves to one branch only, but the division is not so marked, either economically or geographically, as was the case of the Lancashire cotton industry. Nearly all the cloth woven in Northern Ireland is finished there and a considerable section of the industry is engaged in making up and embroidering sheets, pillow-cases, handkerchiefs, etc. The Irish linen industry suffered considerably from the competition of more cheaply produced yet artistically finished cotton goods, and from the decline in the demand for linen blouses and embroidered work; but much was done after 1918[1] to improve the

1. The Linen Industry Research Association was formed just after the First World War. It had Government backing and included all the principal firms in its membership.

quality of the Ulster flax by scientific approach to the problems of cultivation and retting. Many firms, moreover, are now concerned with the spinning and weaving of manmade fibres (see p. 576) as well as flax.[1]

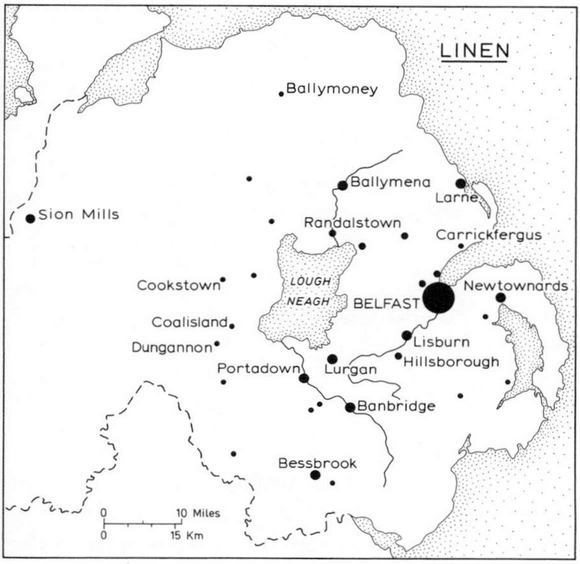

FIG. 199. The linen industry of Northern Ireland
Symbols roughly proportional to the importance of the various centres as measured by numbers employed in the 1950s.

Whereas Ireland has always been famous for its fine quality linen, eastern Scotland has for a long period been associated with the coarser types of product. This is partly, no doubt, due to the remarkable development of the manufacture of the coarser fibres, jute and hemp, in that region. Of a number of towns in the counties of Angus, Perth, and Fife, devoted to the linen industry, the chief are Kirkcaldy, Dunfermline (famous for its damasks), Dundee, Forfar, and Brechin (Fig. 200). Most of the linen yarn is obtained from Belfast.

The linen industry depends primarily upon the export market. Formerly only about 20–30 per cent of its produce was retained in the United Kingdom; about a third of the output is still exported. Unlike cotton its chief market is North America, and it is thus an important dollar earner. The United States has for many years taken one-third of the total exports, and Commonwealth countries are high on the list. West Germany and Italy are the chief customers for yarn.

1. See *Belfast in its Regional Setting* (British Association for the Advancement of Science, Handbook, 1952, p. 151).

Export of linen yarn and manufactures by countries (thousands of £s)

COUNTRY	1913	AVERAGE 1921–25	1931	1935	1950	1960	1966
China	38	85	293	343	7	—	333
USA	3 962	5 906	2 496	2 142	6 559	5 353	4 457
Brazil	212	295	97	208	1 171	—	—
Argentina	334	340	91	134	162	—	—
South Africa	145	224	136	349	588	—	268
India	254	320	163	147	76	—	—
Canada	690	911	565	617	1 070	1 019	498
Other countries	3 829	4 359	2 084	3 252	10 110	10 181	5 760
Total	9 464	12 438	5 925	7 192	19 741	16 553	11 316

In 1960 other countries included Australia (1355), West Germany (883), and Italy (567); in 1966 they included Sweden (588), Italy (513), Hong Kong (476), Australia (421), West Germany (418).

Hemp and Jute

The term hemp is applied very loosely to a number of fibres. Soft, or European, hemp is obtained from the stalk of the hemp plant, like flax, but large quantities of hard fibres, also known as hemp, are obtained from the leaves of subtropical or tropical plants—as manila hemp from the Philippines, phormium from New Zealand, sunn hemp from India, and sisal from West and East Africa and Mexico. The hemp fibres can be used for the coarser varieties of 'linen', and in addition are much in demand for the manufacture of rope and twine, canvas, and sacking. All the hemp used in Britain has to be imported. The hemp-using industries are widespread, but

Import of raw jute (thousand cwt)

	1913	AVERAGE 1921–25	AVERAGE 1926–30	1931	1935	1950	1966 METRIC TONS	1966 '000 CWT
Total import	7016	3095	3749	2955	3635	2253	89 100	1755
From India	6951	3054	3628	2894	3634	86		—
From Pakistan						2166	87 400	1720

Ports importing raw jute (thousand cwt)

TOWN	1913	1931	1935	1948	1960	1967 METRIC TONS	1967 '000 CWT
London	2564	488	668	300	—	—	—
Dundee	4350	2424	2742	1520	2430	113 300	2230

tend to be concentrated (*a*) in the linen-manufacturing areas of north-eastern Ireland and eastern Scotland; (*b*) in the textile districts of south Lancashire and the West Riding, and (*c*) at the principal ports where there is a constant demand for rope and sacking. Belfast has one of the largest rope works in the world.

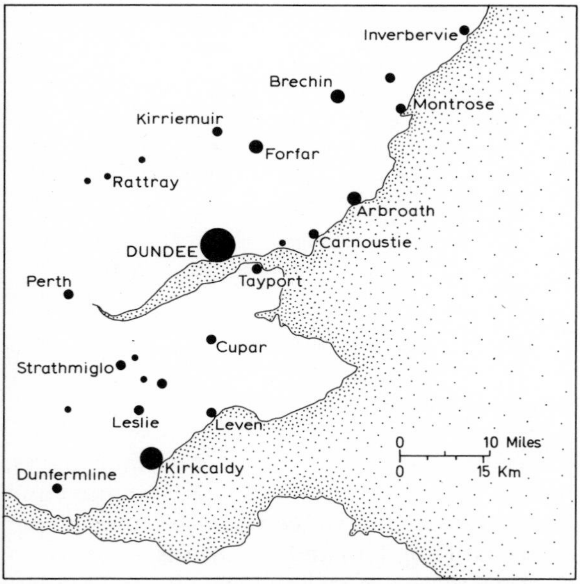

FIG. 200. The east Scottish jute–hemp–linen province
Symbols roughly proportional to the importance of the various centres as measured by numbers employed in the 1950s.

Jute is a coarse fibre which will not bleach but dyes well, and although strong, perishes on exposure. It owes its lead among the minor textile fibres to its cheapness, which is due partly to the great production per acre and partly to the ease with which it can be prepared, spun, and woven by modern methods. The jute industry in Britain grew out of the flax and hemp manufacture of the Dundee region, whither Indian jute began to make its way in the 1830s.[1] Its progress at first was slow, owing to the difficulty of manipulating the fibre and of adapting the flax machinery to its use, but in the 1850s the industry became so profitable that most of the Dundee spinners and weavers changed over from flax to jute and the new fibre became the principal material for sackcloth and hessian, and was used with hemp to produce coarse sheeting. Another important use found for it was in the

1. W. H. K. Turner, 'The evolution of the pattern of the textile industry within Dundee', *Trans. Inst. Br. Geogr.*, **18**, 1952, 107–19; also *Dundee and District*, British Association for the Advancement of Science, Handbook, 1968, 162–72.

manufacture of carpets and linoleum; the town of Kirkcaldy has become the chief centre in Britain for floorcloth manufacture. A very large proportion of the jute industry is still centred at Dundee, very few other places, except one or two nearby towns (e.g. Tayport, Forfar and Kirriemuir) and a few of the principal ports, having adopted it. Indeed, in 1968 'over 90 per cent of the jute spindles in the United Kingdom and two-thirds of the weaving machinery were located within the boundaries of the city of Dundee, and the remainder were to be found in towns within a radius of twenty miles of Dundee; the total number employed in jute was about 16 500'.[1] The tables above illustrate the jute trade.

Export of jute manufactures by countries (including yarn but excluding cordage, etc.) (thousands of £s)

COUNTRY	1913	AVERAGE 1921–25	AVERAGE 1926–30	1931	1950	1960	1966
Netherlands	148	154	289	123	*	230	23
Belgium	104	72	174	44	*	*	*
USA	1653	1891	1525	499	508	930	209
Brazil	299	322	388	214	*	*	*
Argentina	673	549	371	73	*	*	*
South Africa	85	147	146	74	132	152	*
Canada	487	412	464	150	*	459	185
Other countries	1890	1964	2001	1059	*	*	1251[1]
Total	5339	5511	5358	2040	4314	4174	1668

* Not available. [1] Includes Denmark 378, Australia 236.

Silk

Judged by the length and fascination of its history,[2] the silk industry deserves a chapter to itself. The late eighteenth and early nineteenth centuries were the most prosperous days of the industry, and although there have been occasional increases in demand for silk in the twentieth century, developments in artificial fibres since 1945 have largely extinguished the market for the more expensive yarn. Silk, like wool, has been worked by domestic labour in many parts of Britain, and many of the early centres of the industry were influenced by the pre-existing wool-working towns. In subsequent periods other textile industries have exercised an attraction,

1. *Dundee and District*, British Association for the Advancement of Science, Handbook, 1968, p. 342.
2. See Sir F. Warner, *Silk Industry of the United Kingdom*, London, 1921—a very detailed treatment.

such as hosiery, flax, worsted, and cotton, by providing a market for yarn or by using closely allied machinery. Except in Yorkshire, the major centre in the nineteenth century for fabrics using a mixture of different yarns, the mechanised silk industry has tended to occupy sites peripheral to the major textile regions, for example in southeast Cheshire and, along with flax, between the Cotswold and Devonshire wool producing districts.

Although earlier records exist, the real beginning of the silk industry dates from the sixteenth and seventeenth centuries, when skilled Flemish and French craftsmen were seeking refuge in Britain from persecution on the continent. In the sixteenth century Flemish weavers were making bombazines in Norwich and Colchester (early centres of the worsted industry). The influx of Huguenots, in and after 1685, brought further skill to Britain, and refugees were found in many towns, particularly in the southeast where they landed and in the West Country. A colony of considerable size was established in Spitalfields,[1] in the east end of London, which soon became the dominant centre of the industry. By 1700 the silk industry was one of Britain's most flourishing trades and manufacturing was commenced in many likely and unlikely towns all over the country, sometimes by refugees but often by enterprising natives. Protection of the industry by heavy duties, and later the prohibition of imports helped the industry to expand in various parts of the country in the eighteenth century, raw silk being chiefly obtained from Italy, China, and India.[2]

The introduction of mechanical silk throwing to this country from Italy by John Lombe in 1717 paved the way for the establishment of large mills, although it was nearly a century before powered weaving of this delicate fibre was possible. In Derby where Lombe established his mill, silk throwing developed to supply the growing hosiery industry, and by 1830 silk ribbon manufacture had been added to the throwing and silk hosiery industries as the staple trades of the town. Macclesfield, which had made silk buttons in the sixteenth century and had supplied Spitalfields with yarn even before mechanisation, developed into the major mill town for silk in the early nineteenth century. Norwich reached the height of its prosperity between 1740 and 1760, while in Suffolk and Essex, silk weaving providentially replaced the declining worsted industry, particularly in Sudbury. Coventry grew as the major ribbon producer from 1700 and many West Country towns took up the trade. Dublin had a flourishing silk industry mainly producing poplins, in the late eighteenth century, developed by French immigrants, and at Paisley, where silk gauzes began to be made around 1760, no less than 10 000 people were employed in the 1780s, before the coming of cotton almost ruined the trade.

1. Spitalfields already had a wool-weaving industry, carried on mainly by Nonconformists —two very good reasons for the settling of the dissenters there. About 15 000 foreigners settled in London and its eastern suburbs in 1685–86.

2. 1713–65, heavy duties on imported silk manufactures; 1765–1826, total prohibition of import; 1826–60, tariff of 15 per cent *ad valorem*; 1860, abolition of all duty.

Water power had an important locational effect in an industry which until then had had few physical restraints on its distribution. Derby was developed in preference to Nottingham; Leek, although in Macclesfield's sphere as a domestic producer, had no power resources until steam was introduced, and hand-weaving centres such as Spitalfields and Coventry established water powered throwing mills in the Chilterns and north Cotswolds.

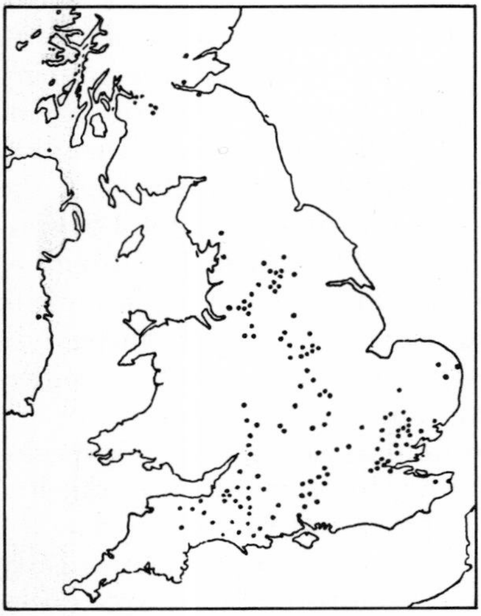

FIG. 201. Map showing all localities where the silk industry has been carried on in Britain

Notice the concentration in (1) London and the Eastern Counties; (2) the West Country; (3) the Midlands, including the West Pennines; (4) the Lancashire–Yorkshire textile regions and (5) the Scottish Lowlands.

The greatest period of the silk industry was the first half of the nineteenth century. Macclesfield was at the heart of the major silk producing area though many towns in East Anglia and the West Country possessed silk mills, and hand-weaving occupied large numbers in Spitalfields, Coventry, and Manchester. In Spitalfields, however, there was a rapid decline after the widespread application of power in the provinces, owing mainly to the higher wage costs. And in Lancashire, hand-loom weaving—introduced when mechanised cotton weaving displaced many workers—also declined, while the large powered branch of the silk industry in Lancashire shrank before further advances by cotton.

The introduction of machinery for spinning 'waste' silk (short fibres) in the 1830s brought the industry to the West Riding, where the Leeds flax industry provided closely allied machinery and where spun silk was widely used for admixture with alpaca and fine worsteds. Fine silk dyeing developed at Macclesfield and Leek, based on the pure water supply of the Pennine streams, though at Congleton, the other major silk town of the southwest Pennines, dyeing never developed as the town supply of water on which the dyers would have to depend was too hard.[1]

After the abolition of the duties in 1860, the English industry shrank before competition and 'dumping' of cheap French silks, although some products, particularly spun silks, survived the onslaught. By contrast, the Coventry ribbon trade was ruined literally overnight. By the beginning of the twentieth century, the West Riding and Macclesfield areas accounted for over half of the total employment in the industry, with a further 12 per cent in East Anglia, while in centres like Derby, Spitalfields, and the West Country towns, the industry had practically ceased to exist. The 130 000 employees of 1851 were reduced to 39 000 by 1901, though part of this decline can be explained by greater productivity following large-scale factory production.

In the twentieth century, silk was the first textile to give way to artificial fibres, both because of its expense and because of the greater suitability of its machinery to handling continuous filament yarns. The Courtaulds, an immigrant family of silk manufacturers, were the first to develop artificial fibres in England and have remained in the forefront ever since. In those towns of the southwest Pennines and Yorkshire most closely associated with silk, manmade fibres have gradually replaced silk in both throwing and weaving processes, although a little pure silk is occasionally manufactured, while East Anglia can only boast of a few hand-loom silk weavers. Since the war, hosiery and knitwear concerns have become important in the Macclesfield area and the manufacturers, though proud of their past,[2] are becoming absorbed into an amorphous clothing industry made up of large-scale concerns.

The following tables illustrate the silk trade.

Imports of raw and semi-manufactured silk (thousand lb)

VARIETY	1913	AVERAGE 1921–25	AVERAGE 1926–30	1931	1935	1950	1967
Raw silk	970	717	1290	1875	4288	1780	424
Knubs and waste	6272	3024	2789[1]	1537	2544	260	283
Noils	1120	183				—	5
Thrown silk	479	45	798[2]	952	162	11	—
Spun silk yarn	575	682				36	59

[1] 1926–1935. 'Cocoons and waste of all kinds'. [2] 1926–1935. 'Silk yarn'.

1. For a detailed examination of the geographical factors, see C. L. Mellowes, 'The geographical basis of the West Pennine silk industry', *J. Textile Inst.*, 1934, 376–88. A more recent work is P. D. Wilde, 'Growth, decline and locational change in the English silk industry of the nineteenth century', Ph.D. thesis, University of Keele, 1970.
2. In the current (1969) official guide to Macclesfield fifty-eight firms are listed as 'silk and associated industries', and of these fifteen are throwsters or (silk) manufacturers.

Import of raw silk by countries (thousand lb)

COUNTRY	1913	AVERAGE 1921–25	AVERAGE 1926–30	1931	1935	1950	1967[1]
China	508	312	369	320	285	41	379
Japan	102	104	526	1208	3549	1414	—
Italy	58	177	206	205	161	381	—
France	194	13	60	40	60	—	—

[1] The total of 424 includes Switzerland 25 and other countries 20 th. lb.
1000 lb = 453.6 kilogram.

Export of silk and manufactures thereof by countries, 1913–66 (thousands of £s)

COUNTRY	1913	AVERAGE 1921–25	AVERAGE 1926–30	1931	1935	1966
USA	413	223	247	59	91	473
Argentina	86	102	59	32	104	—
India	89	67	72	43	82	—
Australia	147	335	348	202	120	53
New Zealand	29	83	60	41	31	—
Canada	204	174	120	42	44	25
France	322	244	170	106	117	21
Germany	241	18	131	56	92	69
Other countries	627	883	895	456	441	155
Total	2158	2129	2102	1037	1142	796

Manmade fibres

The use of 'artificial' fibres in the textile industry is a relatively recent development, for although much of the experimental work was accomplished between 1850 and 1900, and although the first British artificial silk was made by Courtauld's (the Braintree silk firm) at their Coventry factory in 1905, it is really only since the First World War that 'rayon' has become a textile material of serious importance, whilst the rise of the 'nylon' industry can be dated from the Second World War, and the development of polyester and acrylic fibres is even more recent. Fundamentally, manmade fibres production is a chemical industry: rayon may be described as 'regenerated' fibre, derived from organic substances such as wood pulp and cotton linters, whilst nylon and the others are 'synthetic', their raw materials being chemicals derived from coal or petroleum.

The chemical side of the industry will be dealt with in Chapter 22; suffice it here to mention that there are two varieties of rayon or regenerated fibre, viscose and acetate, the former being much the more important. A very large proportion of the cellulosic fibre production and use is in the hands of Courtauld's, whose brand names such as Vincel and Tricel are well known. The synthetics fall into three groups: (*a*) the nylons, including Bri-nylon (made by ICI), Celon (Courtauld's) and Enkalon (made by British Enkalon); (*b*) the polyesters, including ICI's Terylene and British Enkalon's Terlenka; (*c*) the acrylics, including Courtauld's Courtelle and Monsanto's Acrilan.

The products of the chemical side of the industry may take one of two main forms: (*a*) continuous filament produced by extrusion, which can then be converted into yarn by twisting together anything from twenty to one hundred filaments; (*b*) staple fibre, consisting of similar filaments cut into short lengths corresponding to long-staple cotton or short-staple wool. Both continuous yarn and staple fibre (after spinning) can be woven on ordinary textile machinery just like cotton and wool, and as has already been noted in the chapters on wool and cotton, a great deal of admixture now goes on, to produce fabrics with new appearance, new textures and new wearing properties.

The production of manmade fibres in the United Kingdom has had a meteoric rise since the Second World War, and indeed output expanded ten times between 1956 and 1968, to nearly 545 million kilograms (1200 million lb). Since no real silk is produced in Britain these figures may be compared with an import of under quarter a million kilograms (half a million lb) of real silk.

The 1968 output included 160 million kilograms (353m lb) of viscose staple, 47 million kilograms (126m lb) of continuous filament viscose (largely for use in motor tyres), 40 million kilograms (88m lb) of continuous filament acetate and triacetate (largely for knitting and for the production of women's dress fabrics), 13 million kilograms (29m lb) of acetate staple (largely for making filter tips for cigarettes), 144 million kilograms (318m lb) of continuous filament synthetics (which go into ordinary weaving on both cotton and wool systems, and into both warp knitting and weft knitting), and 124 million kilograms (273m lb) of synthetic staple fibre (comprising roughly 60 million kilograms (130m lb) acrylics, 45 million kilograms (100m lb) polyester and the rest nylon).

Since the manmade fibre industry is part chemical and part textile, and since moreover some of the works that produce the filament also spin yarn, it is difficult to offer much in the way of generalisation as to the geographical influences on location. In a sense each installation is peculiar to itself. The earliest works was at Coventry—a development from one of Courtauld's existing silk factories—and others before the Second World War were at Spondon, near Derby (originally a cellulose factory), at Doncaster, at Wolverhampton, at Flint and Greenfield on the Flintshire coast, at Liverpool (Aintree) and at Preston.[1] Since the Second World War there has been a vast expansion, as noted above, particularly in the manufacture of

1. For an analysis of this early stage in the development of the regenerated fibres industry see H. A. Moisley, 'The rayon industry in Great Britain', *Geography*, **34**, 1949, 78–89.

synthetic fibres, and the most notable developments have been on Tees-side at Wilton (part of the great ICI chemical complex), at Grimsby (part of the general industrialisation of south Humberside), and in Northern Ireland (where government policy has attracted an international array of giant firms with American, British, German and Dutch capital to such places as Carrickfergus and Kilroot on Belfast Lough, Coleraine, Antrim, Armagh, Dungannon and Limavady). Northern Ireland, indeed, now produces one quarter of all the United Kingdom output of synthetic fibres. Outlying centres are at Pontypool and Hirwaun in the 'development area' of South Wales, at Manningtree in Essex and at Tiverton in Devon—the last two with a long history of textiles behind them.

However, the *using* of the fibres is definitely a textile industry, and as such, whether it be connected with fabrics made wholly of manmade fibres or mixed with cotton, wool, worsted or linen, it has attached itself to the pre-existing textile industries, in south Lancashire—where probably half the cloth now produced in the weaving area north of Rossendale is either wholly or in part woven with manmade fibres—in west Yorkshire (especially the worsted district), in the erstwhile silk province of Macclesfield–Leek, in the east Midlands (Nottingham, Leicester and Long Eaton), and in west Scotland (Glasgow–Paisley); some of the few remaining centres of the textile trades in East Anglia now use manmade fibres (e.g. Braintree, Sudbury) and there are several factories in the London area and in Northern Ireland.

As the following table shows, a very lucrative export trade has been built up, particularly with our European neighbours, with the Commonwealth and with the United States.

Export of synthetic fibres and manufactures thereof, 1966 (thousands of £s)

Australia	2 457
New Zealand	3 989
Canada	868
India	218
Pakistan	104
Hong Kong	2 186
Ireland	3 042
France	346
Germany	1 525
Sweden	3 843
Switzerland	3 581
South Africa	4 392
USA	1 306
Other countries	19 457
Total	47 014

In concluding this three-chapter study of the textile industries, it is pertinent to call attention to Fig. 202 which shows the volume of the export trade over a period of ten years. Clearly cotton has slumped, while wool has just about held its own; in the case of manmade fibres the home market is clearly absorbing most of the vast increase in fabric output, and only yarn exports are increasing steadily.

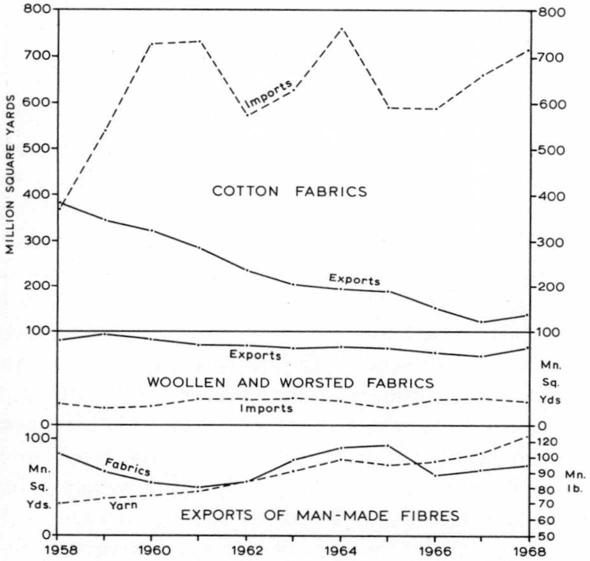

FIG. 202. Exports and imports of textile fabrics, 1958–68

22 The chemical industries[1]

Lord McGowan, former Chairman of Imperial Chemical Industries, Ltd, once described the chemical industry as the most polygamous of all industries. There are few manufacturing industries today which can dispense with the services of the chemist, and the vast field now covered by the chemical industry is the natural result of cooperation between the chemist and his fellow scientists, or between the chemist and the engineer and manufacturer. The chemical industry has become the foundation on which not only British industry as a whole but also modern world industry is erected. Not only has chemistry become the servant of the older industries but in many cases the powerful rival, and in some cases the master. The synthetic products produced by the combined ingenuity of engineer and chemist not only serve to meet demands created by a high standard of living, but come increasingly into competition with substances of natural origin, or even the earlier products of the chemists themselves. Thus, synthetic nitrates are more than adequate competitors for the favours of the agriculturalist requiring nitrates for fertilising. The quantity of artificial silk and chemical fibres used in the world much exceeds the quantity of natural silk. Chromium plating has replaced nickel plating just as nickel plated goods replaced brass and bronze of earlier periods. Similarly, plastics have largely replaced metals—especially brass—and also wood, glass, leather and textiles for many purposes.

The annual turnover of the chemical industry is some £2500m, a figure only exceeded by that of the engineering industries and its growth rate in recent years has been twice that of the national economy.

The development of the heavy chemical industry

The heavy chemical industry is in many respects the chemical industry proper, embracing as it does the manufacture of those commodities which are required in large quantities and have a variety of uses. There are really two branches—the inorganic, founded essentially on two fundamental

1. I am greatly indebted to Professors H. D. Springall and I. T. Millar of Keele University for advice leading to the rewriting of this chapter.

substances, sulphuric acid and sodium carbonate; and the organic, of much more recent large-scale development, based essentially on substances derived originally from the distillation of coal and now, increasingly, on the refining of petroleum.

The birth of the whole chemical industry took place little more than 200 years ago, and indeed at the close of the eighteenth century there was scarcely a chemical industry in this or any other country—apart from the manufacture of gunpowder, a few acids in small quantities, a few drugs, and of course large quantities of soap. The chemical industry that grew slowly during the Industrial Revolution in the late eighteenth and early nineteenth centuries largely revolved around the needs of the textile, glass and metal industries: alkalis were needed for soap and bleaching materials required by the textile trades, and in glass manufacture, and sulphuric acid was used as a sour in textile bleaching and for pickling metals. One of the first chemicals produced in quantity was sulphuric acid, made in England as early as 1720, and for upwards of a century from the 1740s the acid was produced in large reaction chambers made of sheet lead, the source of sulphur being volcanic brimstone imported from Sicily. The discovery of the value of chlorine as a bleaching agent in 1785 opened up a new avenue of alkali manufacture, and towards the close of the eighteenth century the discovery of bleaching powder, or 'chloride of lime', by Charles Tennant, a Scottish linen bleacher, led in 1797 to the foundation of a chemical works at St Rollox in Glasgow. Within a few years the manufacture of bleaching powder by passing chlorine over dried powdered lime had spread to several localities. Then in 1790 the French government awarded a prize to Nicolas Le Blanc for a method of making soda, since France, owing to wars, had found it difficult to obtain a constant supply of this commodity. His method consisted of treating common salt with sulphuric acid, thus making sodium sulphate and liberating hydrogen chloride (hydrochloric acid gas), then roasting the sodium sulphate with limestone and charcoal or coal and obtaining in this way sodium carbonate and calcium sulphide.

The growth of the Le Blanc soda process in this country was slow, largely because there were adequate supplies of sodium carbonate from burnt seaweed or kelp from Scotland and of barilla (a littoral plant of the goosefoot family) from Spain and Portugal, and the first large-scale development was introduced by James Muspratt at Liverpool in 1823 and a few years later at St Helens; these two works quickly drove natural alkali from the Mersey soap factories and laid the foundations of the great chemical industry of that area, in which both alkalis and sulphuric acid were involved. The use of soda in glass-making was perhaps part of the reason for the choice of St Helens (though the local coalfield and the St Helens Canal leading to the Mersey were also contributory factors), and the association with glass certainly favoured Tyneside as an early location (the local soap industry also providing a market), and was responsible for the setting up of works at Oldbury in the Black Country to supply the Smethwick glass factory.

The fact that salt is the primary raw material in the manufacture of soda and alkalis led to the gravitation of the industry to the vicinity of the country's major saltfield in Cheshire, and to the mid-Mersey towns of Widnes and Runcorn, the former the terminus of the St Helens Canal (for coal supplies) and the latter at the point where the River Weaver and the Trent and Mersey Canal, both passing through the saltfields, reached the Mersey.[1] But it was not long before the soda manufactory became larger and more complicated. It made soda, of course, using common salt, sulphuric acid and Buxton lime, and soon added the manufacture of its own sulphuric acid by burning sulphur or pyrites. Large quantities of hydrogen chloride were produced, which at first were allowed to escape into the atmosphere (albeit from very tall chimneys) with terrible results on the areas surrounding the chemical works, and it was not until the invention of the 'Gossage tower' that hydrochloric acid could be recovered for use in making bleaching powder—which was much in demand after 1860 for esparto grass paper-bleaching as well as in the cotton and linen industries.

In the early years of the industry, for every ton of soda made nearly two tons of alkaline waste were produced, an evil-smelling mass containing practically all the sulphur from the sulphuric acid used; and although by a process introduced in 1861 a third of the sulphur was recovered, it was not until 1882 that waste was really eliminated—and some of it still scars the landscape near Widnes and St Helens. The elimination of waste was more or less forced on the chemical manufacturers by the Alkali Act of 1863, which provided for close inspection and for heavy penalties against emitting obnoxious fumes into the atmosphere.

By 1890 the British heavy chemical industry was in the hands of forty or fifty firms whose works were situated principally on the saltfield of Cheshire and the neighbouring parts of the mid-Mersey region of Lancashire, with outlying centres on the Tyne and the Clyde and a few in the west Midlands. As soda manufacturers they were suffering from the severe competition of what is known as the ammonia-soda process for the manufacture of soda. The chemistry of the process involved in the mixing of salt, ammonia, carbon dioxide and water to form bicarbonate of soda and ammonium chloride is very simple, but it was not until the 1860s that the Solvay brothers of Belgium were successful in producing soda in quantity by this process. It was they who, in 1873, granted a licence to Brunner, Mond & Co., a combination of Brunner the administrator and Mond the energetic young chemist, to manufacture in Great Britain—at Winnington, by the river Weaver, on the edge of the Cheshire saltfield. In 1890 the British heavy chemical firms were forced into combination and formed the United Alkali Co. of Liverpool. Although the object of the combination was to facilitate, by lowering costs, the continuance of the manufacture of soda

1. The Trent and Mersey canal actually ends at Preston Brook, and the last four miles to Runcorn form the western end of the Bridgewater canal.

by the Le Blanc process, they were obliged in turn to take up the ammonia-soda process. Some idea of the progress may be gauged from the production figures: in 1863 the world's production of soda was 300 000 long tons, the price about £13 per ton; in 1903 out of an annual production of 1.8 million long tons, 1 676 000 metric tons (1 650 000 long tons) were made by the Solvay process, and the selling price was only about £4 per long ton; shortly afterwards the Le Blanc process was completely abandoned.

Meanwhile, the sulphuric acid industry was also undergoing changes, largely in the sources of its raw materials. In the late 1820s pyrites from North Wales and Ireland began to be used in Liverpool, to be later superseded by richer pyrites from Spain; whilst in the 1850s the sulphur dioxide derived from copper smelting (which, previously discharged into the atmosphere, had such disastrous effects on the landscape of the Swansea area—cf. p. 470) was first used for the recovery of sulphur. Then in 1870, the iron oxide process of removing sulphur from coal gas began to yield sulphur from the spent oxide, at gas works up and down the country. The key position of sulphuric acid in chemical technology became firmly established during the nineteenth century, and by 1900 Britain was producing one million long tons a year, one-quarter of the world's output.

The ramifications of the chemical industry became increasingly apparent in the latter half of the nineteenth century, and only a few of the highlights can be noted here. The production of *cyanides* for making textile dyes such as Prussian Blue began early in the century, and there was some use of potassium cyanide in the early electroplating industry; but the revolutionary discovery in the 1880s by MacArthur that a weak solution of potassium or sodium cyanide would extract gold from low-grade ores led to a great upsurge in demand and the setting up of works at Runcorn and Oldbury to manufacture these products. The production of *phosphorus* began in 1844, for making matches; the process involved the treatment of bone-ash with sulphuric acid and then mixing the phosphoric acid with charcoal and heating in a coal-fired retort. A works was set up at Oldbury which for long remained in a monopolistic position. The use of imported phosphate rock, and the invention of the safety match in 1855, opened up larger possibilities. Also using phosphatic material was the *fertiliser* industry. In the early nineteenth century many thousands of tons of bones were annually imported for agricultural use, and it was the German chemist Liebig who first suggested treating the bones with sulphuric acid—a suggestion that was taken up by J. B. Lawes (who had inherited the Rothamsted estate in Hertfordshire that subsequently became the famous agricultural research station). Lawes set up a works at Deptford in London in the early 1840s to make superphosphate from bones, but he soon turned to mineral phosphates, using coprolites from the Severn valley and later Norwegian apatite. New sources of phosphate rock were tapped in Belgium, the United States and North Africa, and by the 1870s there were eighty works, many of them at ports where the imported rock arrived, and many of them, remote from the major heavy chemical industries, developing their own sulphuric acid plants.

The outbreak of war in 1914 found the chemical manufacturers of this country quite unprepared. There were government factories well equipped for the manufacture of explosives, but they were only on a small scale. Firms such as Nobel had up-to-date works (established as long ago as 1871 on the remote sand dunes of the Ayrshire coast at Ardeer), but again on a scale incommensurate with wartime needs. The two main requirements were explosives and chlorine. The latter, in the form of bleaching powder, was used in large quantities as a disinfectant on the war fronts, and later as liquid chlorine for the production of chlorine as a war gas. It was the upsurge in demand that encouraged the development of the electrolytic process of chlorine manufacture that was first introduced just before the war at Runcorn, St Helens and Winnington, and is now standard practice. As for explosives, at the beginning of the war most of our shells were filled with picric acid (trinitrophenol) as a high explosive, for TNT or trinitrotoluene had only just been adopted. The first government factories for its manufacture were set up in 1915—the toluene produced from petroleum distillation at Portishead near Bristol and nitrating plants at Oldbury and at Queens Ferry on the river Dee; and later the scarce toluene resources were conserved by mixing TNT with ammonium nitrate to produce amatol explosives.

Of necessity the explosive firms in particular and the chemical firms in general had during the war period to work together and to pool their knowledge. The way was thus paved for the formation in 1918 of Explosive Trades Ltd, afterwards known as Nobel Industries Ltd. There thus came to be four firms concerned with the chemical industries of this country: Brunner, Mond & Co., Nobel Industries, the United Alkali Co., and British Dyestuffs Corporation. The amalgamation of these came naturally in 1926 with the formation of Imperial Chemical Industries Ltd.

The main developments in the heavy chemical industry since the First World War have been, on the inorganic side, the considerable expansion of sulphuric acid production, which is now running at about 3 million tons a year, with the manufacture of superphosphates, ammonium sulphate and rayon as major consumers, and on the organic side, the development of a new dyestuffs industry, the production of new materials, such as plastics and manmade fibres, and the synthesis of pharmaceuticals and of non-soap detergents. Sulphuric acid production is widespread and is in the hands of more than fifty firms—as a result of its growth in connection with the fertiliser industry, as mentioned above. During the Second World War, with Spanish pyrites unavailable, emphasis was on the import of sulphur from Texas, and this continues. But to an increasing extent home deposits of anhydrite, on Tees-side and in west Cumberland, have been brought into use, with important plants at Billingham, near Whitehaven, and at Widnes (which uses Cumberland mineral), and about one-sixth of the total output of sulphuric acid is now derived from anhydrite. Further changes are possible using North Sea gas.

Expansion in organic chemicals has been especially rapid since the Second World War, and has accompanied the growth of an enormous oil-refining industry (cf. p. 354). Between the wars, the heavy organic chemicals industry (commonly abbreviated to HOC) was based on fermentation alcohol, coal (as coke or calcium carbide) and coal-tar derivatives. True, in the 1930s ICI had already begun producing fuel petrol by hydrogenation of coal and of creosote oil (a coal distillation product) at Billingham on Tees-side, but this was largely in connection with their use of hydrogen on a vast scale for ammonia manufacture, and it was the shortages created by the war that prompted the further development of the process. But the relative costs of coal and oil changed in the early 1950s, and the Billingham plant was abandoned and replaced by petrochemical plant. In 1949 petroleum feedstocks provided only 6 per cent of the raw material for organic chemical manufacture, but by the mid-1960s this percentage had risen to nearly 70. The first real petrochemical works in England was set up at Spondon, near Derby, by British Celanese in 1942, to provide chemicals for rayon production (cf. p. 575); but most of the subsequent works are adjacent to oil refineries—at Stanlow and Carrington, on the Mersey, at Fawley on Southampton Water, and at Grangemouth, and more recently at Baglan Bay, near Swansea. The vast 800-hectare (2000-acre) site at Wilton on Tees-side began to be developed in 1949; here there was no refinery, but the feedstocks (mainly petroleum naphtha) were brought in by tanker. Another recent development, served in this instance by pipeline (cf. p. 354), is on Severnside, north of Bristol. By 1962 capital investment in petrochemicals had reached £200m. Indeed the chemical industry as a whole is one of the most heavily capitalised of all modern industries. The current (1969) capital of ICI is £1487m, which represents £10 700 for every one of their 139 000 employees. On Severnside ICI has invested £25m, or £30 000 per employee. And yet when the group was formed in 1926 the total capital of the four constituent companies was just under £40m. While it is right to emphasise the capital-intensive character of the heavy chemical industry, and the relatively small number of giant firms engaged in it, we should not forget that there is a vast range of other chemical industries; the Board of Trade's Census of Production in 1963 included nearly 3000 companies engaged in some form of chemical manufacture—but nearly two-thirds of them employed under one hundred workers, most in the pharmaceutical branch and the great majority in the Greater London area.

Geographical distribution of the heavy chemical industry

Geographical factors in the distribution of the various branches of the heavy chemical industry are fairly obvious, and many of the early locational influences—including sources of salt and coal, and inland water transport—continue to be important. But developments since the Second World War have added at least one completely new factor, namely the location of oil refineries (already studied in Chapter 14).

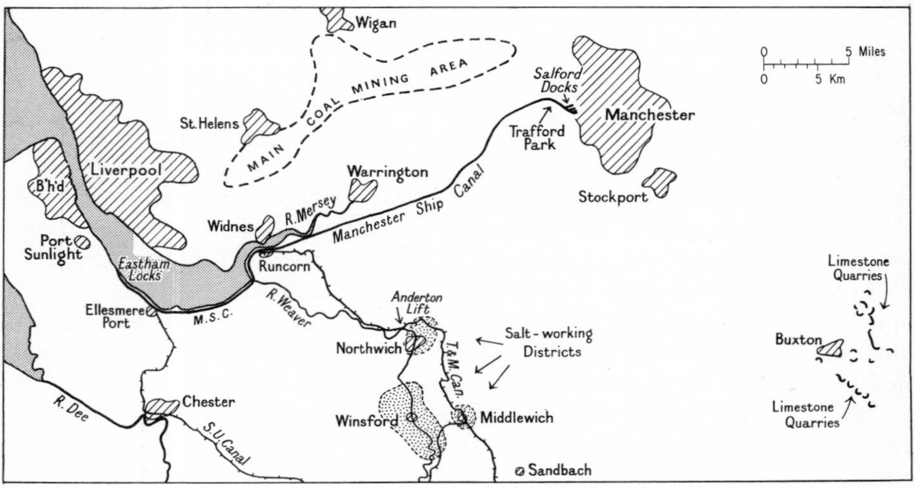

FIG. 203. The mid-Mersey chemical towns, in relation to sources of salt, coal and limestone

The Stanlow oil refinery lies just east of Ellesmere Port. Compare Fig. 255.

Of the older centres, by far the most important are the mid-Mersey region and the Cheshire saltfield (Fig. 203).[1] On the saltfield is the great chemical complex at Northwich, the headquarters of the Alkali Division of ICI. The Cheshire salt industry owed much to the transport facilities provided by the Weaver Navigation and the Trent and Mersey Canal (which are linked by the Anderton lift near Northwich), and the river is still much used. The production of refined salt from pumped brine takes place mainly at Middlewich and Sandbach (the former coarse salt production at Northwich and Winsford having seriously declined), but alkali manufacture is concentrated at three large works in the vicinity of Northwich, and at Runcorn (headquarters of ICI's Mond Division) and Widnes. About half the insured population of the Northwich area is employed in the chemical industry, and about 40 per cent in Runcorn and Widnes. St Helens, despite its early start, is now scarcely a chemical town at all, being much more occupied with glass manufacture (see below, p. 590), and Warrington's connection is mainly through the soap industry. Fig. 203 expresses the space relationship of the main geographical factors involved—the location of the

1. See *A Scientific Survey of Merseyside*, British Association for the Advancement of Science, 1953, pp. 251–64.

mid-Mersey towns halfway between the sources of salt and coal (Runcorn is served with brine by pipeline from the Northwich area), with Buxton lime readily accessible by railway, and imported vegetable oils, pyrites, sulphur and other raw materials available through the port of Liverpool. The importance of Merseyside as a chemical centre has been greatly accentuated by two further developments, the piping of ethylene from the ICI's Wilton plant on Tees-side, across the Pennines to a new plant at Runcorn for the production of vinyl chloride monomer (see below, p. 594), and the advent of the great Shell oil refinery at Stanlow, near the western end of the Manchester Ship Canal, with associated petrochemical works there and at Carrington, on the Ship Canal nearer to Manchester.

PLATE 24. The ICI works at Billingham-on-Tees
The plant covers 280 hectares (700 acres) with tidewater access.

The second most important area is more closely confined, around Tees-side. A Triassic saltfield had provided the basis for the Cerebos salt industry, but the great expansion in the 1920s was due to two quite different factors. The first was the establishment of a government-sponsored nitrate factory at Billingham, in 1918 (which never in fact worked, but which provided a convenient site for Brunner, Mond & Co. to establish their subsidiary Synthetic Ammonia and Nitrates Ltd in 1920), and the second was the fortunate discovery, right underneath the works, of valuable seams of anhydrite (calcium sulphate). There could hardly have been a more appropriate occurrence, for the anhydrite was used to make sulphur dioxide (for acid manufacture), with clinker suitable for making cement as a byproduct. In the 1930s the making of oil from coal was added but the most spectacular developments have occurred since the Second World War, with the addition of petrochemicals and the building of a whole series of new plants at Wilton concerned with heavy organic chemicals for plastics and manmade fibres (see below, p. 592). Wilton and Billingham are connected by pipeline under the river Tees. The more recent addition of oil refining on Teesside adds still further to the importance of the area as a chemical centre of world significance.[1]

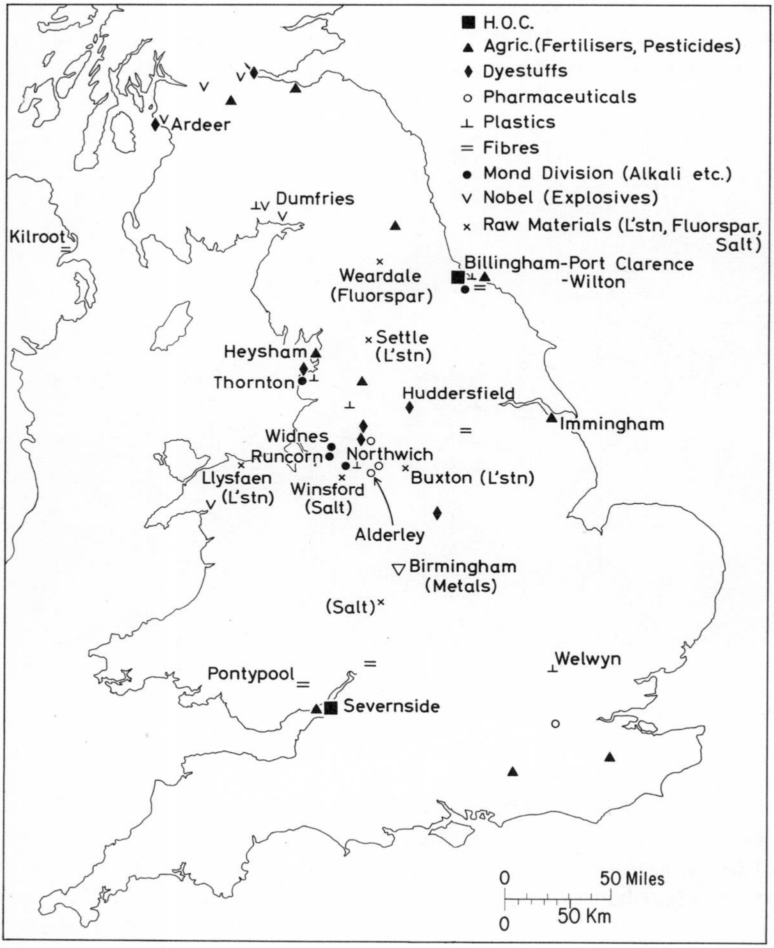

FIG. 204. The ICI 'empire'

The chemical industry is so vast and varied that it is impossible to represent it all on one map; so the principal establishments of ICI have been mapped to give some idea of the wide industrial and geographical range.

1. See P. W. B. Semmens, 'The chemical industry of Teesside and south Durham', in *Durham County and City with Teesside*. British Association for the Advancement of Science, 1970, 330–40.

In west Lancashire, the Fleetwood complex of chemical works had local brine-pumping and port facilities at the mouth of the river Wyre as its basis. In addition to alkali manufacture there are now plants for making dyestuffs and plastics—the latter fed with ethylene by a branch of the trans-Pennine pipeline from Tees-side.

On the Tyne, salt-panning was an ancient practice, and so were the making of glass and soap. Hedley's soap works was founded in 1837, and it remains a major producer of soaps and detergents. In the 1860s Tyneside was producing half the total Le Blanc alkali made in the country, but the industry declined with the introduction of the Solvay process. Sulphuric acid is made at Blaydon, and at Prudhoe-on-Tyne a wartime ammonia plant remains an important producer of sulphate of ammonia.

The association of the west Midlands with the chemical industries arises largely from the metallurgical trades and glass manufacture (see below, p. 590) and Oldbury is a good example of the tendency in the chemical industry to add new processes to existing works.

In Scotland the chemical industries grew up essentially as the servants of other industries, beginning with bleaching materials for textiles and continuing with dyestuffs, paints and fertilisers—in the vicinity of Glasgow, Grangemouth and Edinburgh. The explosives works at Ardeer now makes many other chemical products as well, whilst a great petrochemical industry has grown up at Grangemouth.

A recent addition to the heavy chemical map is Severnside, fed with raw materials through the port of Avonmouth and by pipeline from Fawley. ICI established themselves here on a 400-hectare (1000-acre) site in 1957, to make heavy organic chemicals and fertilisers; other chemical industries in the same area include the fertiliser works of Fisons, a carbon-black factory and of course the numerous chemical byproducts of the Avonmouth zinc smelting plant.

As a commentary on the above, Fig. 204 shows the location of the major chemical plants operated by ICI. Of course this does not represent the entire chemical industry, and some of the great petrochemical localities—such as Fawley, Stanlow and Swansea—are missing, as are some of the manmade fibres and fertiliser plants. But on the whole it gives a reasonably good representation of the widespread distribution, and of the concentration, of the chemical industries.

There is one characteristic of the chemical industry that differentiates it from all others; only the iron and steel industries show anything comparable. It is the extent to which the various branches are interdependent; the finished products of one branch are the raw materials of another. Thus the ICI's Mond Division in Cheshire and Merseyside supplies alkalis and other chemicals to the plastics, dyestuffs, metal and pharmaceutical divisions, the HOC Division on Tees-side and Severnside supplies a multitude of different products for fertilisers, insecticides, plastics, paints, dyestuffs, synthetic fibres, pharmaceuticals, explosives, and so on. In fact, 40 per cent of HOC's output is sold to other sections of ICI. The importance of mass-transport media for these products—pipelines, liner-trains and fleets of road tankers—is considerable.

It remains to add the following tables showing employment in the chemical industry at different dates, and to deal in more detail with some particular branches of the industry.

Employment in chemical industries, 1948, 1961 (thousands)

INDUSTRY	EMPLOYMENT 1948	EMPLOYMENT 1961	CHIEF REGIONS[1] APPROXIMATE PERCENTAGE OF TOTAL
General Chemicals	100	200	NW 31; N. 21; London and SE 15.
Explosives and fireworks	25	33	Scot. 36; Wales 16; NW 16.
Soap, candles, and glycerine	21	45	NW 50; London and SE 15.
Dyes and dyestuffs	17	20	Yorks. 45
Drugs and pharmaceuticals	47	73 (Drugs and pharmaceuticals with Toilet preps. and perfumery)	London and SE 39; N. Mid. 15; NW 15.
Toilet preps. and perfumery	9		London and SE 80.
Fertilisers and insecticides	15		Scot. 20; London and SE 14; Yorks. 13; N. 13.
Paint and varnish	33	49	London and SE 35; NW 15; Yorks. 9.
Plastics materials	—	33	

[1] Ministry of Labour Regions.

Employment in chemical industries, 1966

REGION[1]	THOUSANDS	REGION	THOUSANDS
North	55	Wales	26
Yorks and Humberside	46	W. Midlands	32
E. Midlands	20	Northwest	120
E. Anglia	10	Scotland	34
Southeast	170	N. Ireland	3
Southwest	12		
		Total	527

[1] Ministry of Labour's new regions. The former N. Midlands is now called East Midlands; Yorks (W. and E. Ridings) is now called Yorkshire and Humberside. London is included in Southeast.

The metallurgical industry

There is a close association between non-ferrous metal smelting and refining and the chemical industries, for chemicals are used in metal processing and numerous chemical byproducts are obtained. Thus it was Mond, of Brunner, Mond & Company, who discovered with a collaborator a process for the extraction of pure nickel and floated the Mond Nickel Co. whose large works are at Clydach, near Swansea (cf. p. 484). The chemical by-products of aluminium, lead and zinc smelting have already been referred to (pp. 477, 478–9). Since the Second World War the development of the use of the rarer metals in the electrical industries, in alloy steel making and for lightweight and special-purpose alloys has widened the range of contact between chemical and metallurgical industries, and new developments are frequent. In fact the processing of these metals is for the most part done by the chemical industry and not by firms whose main interest is in metals. Magnesium, molybdenum, tantalum, titanium, tungsten and zirconium are examples. The extraction of magnesia from sea-water at Hartlepool is mainly for refractory products rather than metal. Metallic tantalum, however, has found a use in the rayon industry: it is used for the spinnerettes in the viscose process (see p. 591). Titanium, being highly resistant to corrosion, whilst of high strength and low density, is being developed for use in ships and aircraft, and especially for long-range rockets and spacecraft; it is also used as a white pigment. The industry is based on imported ilmenite, and is a major consumer of sulphuric acid; it is located within the great chemical complexes of Tees-side and south Humberside, and at Swansea. The oxides of some of these rare metals—many of the group referred to by chemists as the 'transition metals'—are used in catalytic reactions, e.g. in the production of synthetic ammonia and in petroleum cracking.

The chemical–metallurgical industries are fairly widespread, but there is a notable grouping in the Birmingham area.

Glass

The manufacture of glass is essentially a chemical process. All types of glass are made by heating in a furnace, silica (which is usually obtained in the form of sand) with soda and lime and the oxides of other metals such as magnesium, aluminium, boron or lead, according to the type of glass required—e.g. a large proportion of borax is used for Pyrex heat-resisting (i.e. low-expansion) glass. The mixtures are very complex; ordinary bottle glass contains no less than twelve chemical elements. Plate glass is rolled in continuous sheets while soft; glass tubing is drawn out; glass bottles are cast in moulds or are blown. The modern float process for plate glass uses a bed of molten tin. The main requirements of the glass industry are thus a suitable supply of fuel, sand, and chemicals, chiefly soda, lime, magnesia, and borax from the heavy chemical industry. For the finer types of glass, including colourless glass bottles, the purest white sand, free from coloured impurities, must be used. Such sand comes from the superficial Shirdley Hill Sands of southwest Lancashire and from occasional pockets in the Lower Greensand formation—as at King's Lynn, Leighton Buzzard, and Redhill—or is imported from Belgium or elsewhere. A new source of high quality sand was discovered during the Second World War at Lochaline in western Scotland.

For coloured bottles, less pure raw material is needed, and several other geological formations, as well as those named above, contribute supplies.

The glass industry in 1963 gave employment to over 72 000 people, of whom more than a third were concerned with bottle-making. The London area, by reason of its huge market for milk and beer bottles, and easy access to Lower Greensand and imported sand supplies, has a very large bottle-making industry, and other centres are Doncaster and St Helens. The latter town is also the chief in the country for glass-making other than bottles. The geographical influences here look deceptively simple—Shirdley Hill Sands and coal almost on the spot and the great mid-Mersey chemical industry only a few miles away. But, in fact, the industry was located here before the Shirdley Hill Sand was 'discovered'; this local sand supply simply confirmed the location and strengthened it. Interesting, if less obvious, locations are Stourbridge, on the edge of the Black Country (where the glass industry was started by foreign refugees several hundred years ago and was based on local fireclay, from which the crucibles, used in large numbers, were made), Smethwick, chief British centre for the making of lighthouse lanterns, and Sunderland, home of heat-resisting glass.

Dyestuffs

The rise of the textile industries in the early nineteenth century did not generate a corresponding development in the making of synthetic dyestuffs, for the organic chemistry of the natural dyestuffs—alizarin from madder, indigo from woad and *indigofera* spp., and certain traditional dyewoods—was not understood. It was in 1856 that W. H. Perkin discovered that mauve could be produced from materials derived from coal tar, and other synthetic dyestuffs based on tar products followed rapidly. But the industry that he founded in England did not flourish, and it was left to Germany—with the help of imported British raw materials—to develop commercial dyestuff production on a large scale after the 1870s. The outbreak of war in 1914 found the British textile industries—despite the existence of two German dyestuffs firms that had set themselves up on Merseyside—quite unable to dye the uniforms that they were called upon to produce! After the war development was rapid; a works was set up at Grangemouth in 1919, and the British Dyestuffs Corporation amalgamated a number of interests in 1924, only itself to be absorbed into ICI in 1926. Thus the dyestuffs industry became inseparably bound up with the heavy organic chemicals industry, and by the outbreak of the Second World War in 1939 nearly 95 per cent of British requirements were home produced.

The dyestuffs industry was presented with a whole series of new problems by the advent of manmade fibres, which do not absorb dyes as cotton and wool do. The result has been the development of many new products and techniques, such as the impregnation of nylon and acrylic fibres with anthraquinone dyes at elevated temperatures.

The chief raw materials of the dyestuffs industry are a small group of aromatic hydrocarbons, including benzene, toluene, naphthalene and anthracene, all derived from coaltar distillation, or in some cases from petroleum refining. Naturally enough, the bulk of the output comes from the north of England, where the combination of coalfields and textile industries on both sides of the Pennines, with chemical industries and more recently oil refineries on both coasts, provides an obvious geographical control. Apart from the Tees-side chemical complex, the major centres are at Ellesmere Port, Manchester and Huddersfield, whilst in central Scotland, with a similar geographical basis, there are dyestuffs works at Grangemouth and Ardeer.

Manmade fibres

There is an unexpectedly close connection between explosives and certain types of what used to be known as 'artificial silk', but are now generally referred to as regenerated 'manmade fibres'; for both involve the use of cellulose, which is the main constituent of dry vegetable matter, and thus forms the bulk of wood, cotton, linen and many other vegetable products. Thus, if cotton rags are treated with caustic soda, washed, bleached and dried the contaminants are removed and cellulose is the result. If the cellulose is treated with a mixture of sulphuric and nitric acid, nitrocelluloses are formed, which are in general highly inflammable or explosive substances. Gun-cotton is a nitrocellulose, and cordite and other explosives are closely associated. The principle of making artificial silk is to treat wood pulp or some other material containing cellulose with caustic soda and then with carbon bisulphide; a yellow viscous liquid is obtained which when extruded into a suitable precipitating bath of acid yields tough fibres, from which the sulphur is removed in a further process, the end product being a thread of almost as great a fineness as that spun naturally by the silkworm. This is the substance now known under the formerly patent name of *viscose* (cellulose xanthate, 1892); it was originally used for lamp filaments, but in 1905 the silk firm of Courtaulds began making it for use as a silk substitute fibre at their Coventry works. An alternative material is *cellulose acetate*, first developed in France about 1910 for photographic film (to replace the highly inflammable nitrocellulose) and made in Britain during the First World War for coating aeroplane wings and making plastic windows. The cellulose is treated with acetic acid (itself made from a byproduct of petroleum refining). A factory was set up at Spondon, near Derby, in 1916, and when the demand for its products came to an end with the cessation of hostilities it used the materials to produce the fibre known as 'Celanese'. The subsequent development of rayon, as these two cellulose-based forms of manmade fibre came to be known, has been dealt with in Chapter 21. Suffice it here to say that the location of the chemical side of the industry is in part more or less fortuitous, though access to vast quantities of water and suitable means of effluent disposal were important siting factors—as at Greenfield on the Flintshire coast, for example.[1]

The other manmade fibres—the 'synthetics'—are of more recent development, and like the plastics, are products of polymer chemistry, a branch that represents what is probably a greater technological revolution than anything since the development of textile machinery and the steam engine in the eighteenth century. Like the plastics, too, their raw materials are largely derived from coal, or more recently from petroleum refining. Indeed, many of the new products, such as nylon and polypropylene, can be used both as plastics and as fibre. It is perhaps not surprising that many of the early developments in macromolecular chemistry took place in the USA, which had a huge oil-refining industry, and in Germany, which with its drive for self-sufficiency was developing artificial rubber and other synthetic materials. Many of the later developments, however, are British, and have become possible by reason of the great postwar expansion of oil-refining and the petrochemical industries (cf. Chapter 14).

Nylon was the first, a purely American development (1937), for which ICI acquired manufacturing rights in 1940. Nylon is a 'condensation polymer' (produced by the condensation of hexamethylene diamine and adipic acid). It was much used during the Second World War for parachutes, glider tow-ropes, and aeroplane tyre cord—produced by British Nylon Spinners Ltd, a firm set up jointly by ICI and the textile firm of Courtaulds; it was also used as a plastic in the wartime engineering industry. After the war, in 1949, production of fibre for the ordinary textile industry began at Wilton on Tees-side, from which it was sent to Pontypool for spinning. Later developments, in the 1960s, have been the establishment of plants at Antrim in Northern Ireland by British Enkalon (an Anglo-Dutch firm) and at Cumnock in Ayrshire by the American Monsanto Company's subsidiary Chemstrand (now Monsanto Textiles Ltd). Some nylon is employed as a plastic rather than as a textile fibre—for brush bristles and fishing lines.

Terylene (polyethylene terephthalate, commonly known as polyester) developed out of British research done during the war (actually in the laboratories of the Calico Printers' Association). The raw materials are xylenes derived from petroleum refining. ICI acquired the British rights, and Du Pont for the United States, and full-scale production of Dacron began in USA in 1953, and of Terylene at the vast new ICI plant at Wilton in 1955; a further ICI development took place at Kilroot near Belfast in 1963. British Enkalon at Antrim produces a similar fibre known as Terlenka, whilst the German firm of Hoechst at Limavady produces Trevira.

Acrylic fibres. Vinyl cyanide (otherwise known as acrylonitrile) began to be produced in 1959, at the ICI Billingham plant, for use in the manufacture

1. See H. A. Moisley, 'The Rayon Industry in Great Britain', *Geography*, **34**, 1949, 78–89.

of synthetic rubber. Somewhat earlier it had been used in the United States as a fibre, and in 1963 the Monsanto subsidiary Chemstrand began making Acrilan at Coleraine in Northern Ireland. Other acrylic fibres (polyacrylonitrile), known under various trade names such as Courtelle, are produced in Courtauld factories at Coventry and Grimsby.

Polypropylene (methyl ethylene) was developed in America and first made in Britain in 1959 by the ICI complex at Wilton, marketed as Propathene. It is based on the products of naphtha cracking at oil refineries. In 1963 ICI started production at its Kilroot plant, where the material is marketed as Ulstron. It can be used as fibre, film or as mouldings.

The geography of the manmade fibres industry clearly shows a number of different influences at work, but the most obvious are attachment to a pre-existing textile industry (e.g. Coventry), or to a great HOC complex (e.g. Wilton), and government encouragement in the Development Areas (e.g. Pontypool and the various centres in Northern Ireland). Manmade fibres are indeed a major prop to the economy of the last-named area (cf. p. 576).

Plastics

The development of the plastics industry, like that of synthetic fibres, is essentially a part of the industrial revolution of the mid-twentieth century. And yet Alexander Parkes produced his Parkesine from cellulose nitrate (nitrocellulose) with castor oil as early as 1861 and in a paper read to the Royal Society of Arts in 1865 he anticipated many of the modern uses of plastics. The American J. W. Hyatt using cellulose nitrate and camphor produced Celluloid in 1869, and Daniel Spill (Parkes's assistant) introduced Xylonite—still made—about the same time. Scientific progress was made but slowly, however. The effective foundation of the industry may be dated from about 1907, when L. H. Baekeland in America discovered a process for producing technically useful resins by reaction of phenol with formaldehyde; this material—subsequently known as Bakelite—was first made in England in 1916, and large-scale operations began at Tyseley, near Birmingham, in 1931.

The plastics industry is thus mainly a product of the last three or four decades. Of small importance before the late 1920s, it was greatly stimulated by the rapid growth of the electrical and radio industries, and great advances were made during the Second World War. The output increased more than fourfold during the decade 1938–48, and has continued to rise steeply. Production in 1961 reached 619 700 metric tons (610 000 long tons), doubling again to 1 239 400 metric tons (1 200 000 long tons) in 1968, in which year the value of the goods produced was about £700m. Over one quarter of the output is exported directly, and a good deal more as components of, for example, cars and refrigerators.

At present roughly a fifth of the total production enters the packaging industry (everything from film wrapping to egg boxes, meat trays and all kinds of bottles and bags); another fifth is taken by the building industry, for guttering, pipes and taps, tiles, chipboard, etc. Two other industries—domestic appliances and household goods and the automotive industry—take another 15 per cent each. Something like 32 kilograms (70 lb) of plastics go into the average car—and the Concorde aircraft contains no less than 2000 plastic components. New plastics are constantly being evolved that will add flameproof, heat-resistant and long-life characteristics to existing electrical and chemical resistance properties, and new materials, such as plastics reinforced with carbon fibres, may have qualities that compare with steel. 'The potential for plastics consumption extends into virtually every industrial sector and plastics are increasingly substituting for materials ranging from glass through pottery, leather and lubricating oils to textiles and metals.'[1]

The plastics industry, like that of manmade fibres, consists of two parts, the actual production of the synthetic resins and moulding powders, which is a chemical industry, and the manipulation of the materials to produce a multitude of industrial components and consumer goods. In 1966 39 000 people found employment in the production of plastics, and a further 95 000 were engaged in plastics moulding and fabricating. As with synthetic fibres, the basic chemicals, which are derived essentially from byproducts of petroleum refining and coal-tar distillation, are married together, by the process known as polymerisation, into plastic materials. There are two major types: (1) thermosetting plastics, which harden by chemical action brought about by heating and cannot subsequently be softened again; they are moulded by compression; (2) thermoplastics, which are moulded by injection or are produced in flexible sheets, rods or tubes, in a wide range of colours. The thermosetting plastics are based on phenol (derived from coal-tar), formaldehyde (from carbon monoxide and hydrogen) and urea (from ammonia and carbon dioxide); they are used for such things as door knobs, laminated sheet, plastic crockery, electrical insulators, tabletops, etc., in paint manufacture and as a bonding material in plywood and furniture. The thermoplastics are of two kinds, those derived from cellulose, the manufacture of which depends on imported cotton linters, and the synthetic materials, derived mainly from coal and petroleum and using also salt and limestone. The synthetic plastics are of fairly recent development, mainly during and since the Second World War; like the synthetic fibres, they are polymerisation products. They include: polythene (based on ethylene derived from oil cracking), used mainly in film form as a wrapping material; Perspex or glass-substitute (derived from acetone); polyvinyl chloride (PVC—based on carbide and chlorine), much in use for raincoats, curtains, table-covers, handbags, wall, floor and seat

1. Supplement to *The Times*, 17 June 1969.

coverings, gramophone records, etc.; polystyrene (from benzene and ethylene), used for toys, table-ware, toilet articles, radio parts, etc.; and polyurethane, used mainly in foamed form for packaging and insulating.

The main sources of the fundamental chemicals used in the industry are of course the great chemical works of ICI—Billingham and Wilton, Northwich, Runcorn, Fleetwood—and the petrochemical works associated with coastal oil refineries (e.g. Stanlow, Fawley, Grangemouth). But the wide variety of raw materials employed, both home produced (coal derivatives, salt, limestone) and imported (petroleum, carbide, cotton linters, wood pulp, resins, etc.) and the equally wide variety of products and markets, result in a widespread distribution both of the making and the utilisation of plastics. Moreover the industry has been taken up by many firms previously engaged in other or allied trades, and so it is not easy to generalise about location factors. But since there is little wastage of raw materials during manufacture, labour supply and markets rather than raw materials tend to be of most significance—hence the importance of the Greater London and Birmingham areas, for example; whilst the light and largely footloose character of the manipulation side of the industry has made it a suitable one for setting up in the New Towns and in Development Areas. The list of localities contains more unexpected and not readily explicable places than is the case with any other manufacturing industry.

There is one last plastic industry that differs from all others in that it is based on inorganic materials. Silicone polymers, used as water-repellent agents and for purposes where a chemically resistant plastic is needed, have a silicon (i.e. sand) base. Production takes place at the ICI works at Ardeer in Ayrshire, at Oldbury near Birmingham and at Barry in South Wales (localised by the availability of a wartime magnesium-from-sea-water factory). Silicones can be produced in the form of liquids, semi-solids and solids; they are used as impregnants, thermally-resistant coatings, waterproofing agents, polishes and lubricants.

Soap and detergents

The early history of the soap industry, and its relationship to alkali manufacture, have already been referred to. In the early days almost any fat or oil was used, and the soap-boiling works were widely scattered. Large-scale production based on imported vegetable oils led inevitably to a concentration on major ports, and the business of Lever Brothers is a good example. W. H. Lever selected a site on the Wirral side of the Mersey estuary, because 'it was a rural area where ample acreage could be secured adjacent to both rail and water transport with reasonable facilities for obtaining the necessary supply of labour'; and the result was Port Sunlight works and 'garden city'. It was also conveniently near to the alkali industry of Merseyside. The Lever interests gradually absorbed many other soap-making companies; and there was close connection also with those who were using vegetable oils for other purposes, such as the British Oil and Cake Mills, Ltd, and finally in 1920, came the merging of interests with the Margarine Union, which had been using similar materials for the manufacture of margarine. The whole great combine is known as Unilever, and its manufacturing business extends into fifty countries and employs more than a quarter of a million people.

Although Port Sunlight dominates the industry, there are other centres in Lancashire, notably Warrington. Outside Merseyside, the London port area, Tyneside, and several centres in Scotland such as Renfrew, Paisley and Grangemouth are concerned with soap manufacture.

The soap industry has turned in part to new products—synthetic detergents or 'syndets', which are now flooding the market under numerous proprietary names. These detergents—which started as soap substitutes and have turned out to be in fact very much better than soap for many purposes, particularly with hard water—are made for the most part from oil refinery products, and both the soap firms and the petrochemical interests are involved. The industry began in the early 1930s with soapless shampoos produced by Hedley's and Unilever, and with Shell's Teepol, but since 1957 the main product has been a detergent alkylate, made on Tees-side and elsewhere. The use of these detergents created considerable problems of indestructible foam that affected sewage effluents, streams and rivers, and which are still not completely solved.

Other chemical industries

There are many other chemical industries that deserve more than a passing mention, and the geographical influences on their location are diverse. It is clear, however, that the labour supplies and markets provided by the great conurbations play an important part, for the raw materials are often of diverse origins and of relatively small bulk. Thus whilst the London area has scarcely been mentioned so far in this chapter, a glance at the table on p. 588 will show that it is in fact the most important region of all in terms of employment in chemical manufacture, particularly in the fields of toilet preparations and perfumery, drugs and pharmaceuticals, i.e. what are usually known as 'fine chemicals', produced for specialised application rather than for a range of uses.

The range of *biologically active chemicals* has increased enormously during the last half-century, mainly as a result of the synthesis of these substances, which modify the behaviour of living organisms by participating in their biochemistry. In the presynthetic age pharmaceuticals were mainly derived from the roots and leaves of plants and from a few chemicals such as Glauber's salt; there was little or no scientific or theoretical basis to their preparation until the middle of the nineteenth century, and there was no manufacture of synthetic pharmaceuticals in Britain before the First World War. Probably three-quarters of all the drugs and medicines in use today were unknown forty years ago; insulin, adrenaline and the preparation of vitamins go back to the 1920s, but products of such far-reaching significance as penicillin, cortisone, the anaesthetic 'fluothane', and the birth control pill, have all been developed since 1940. There is an interesting connection with the synthetic dyestuffs industry in that much of the fundamental research in organic chemistry is of a similar nature. ICI entered the pharmaceutical field in 1936 by forming a medical section within its dyestuffs research division, and though Pharmaceuticals is now a division in its own right, some products are still made at factories within the Dyestuffs division. There are also connections with the foodstuffs industries—a special Unilever subsidiary concerned with the production of vitamins for adding to margarine and animal feeding stuffs was formed in 1946—and with distilling.

The pharmaceutical industry is in the hands of some 500 firms, mostly small and specialised, with a few giant combines such as ICI, Beecham and Boots. The Greater London area—including some of its newer industrial centres such as Welwyn Garden City and Dagenham—is by far the most important, with Manchester, Liverpool and Edinburgh. The case of Nottingham is an interesting example, comparable with Oxford and its motor car works, of a great industry arising from very small beginnings. The parents of Jesse Boot happened to have a small herbalist business in the city, which in 1888 became a retail chemist's shop with its own manufacturing side.

Another side of the biologically active chemicals industry is concerned with *pesticides* and *weed-killers*, in which some 150 different chemicals are now involved. Vine-spraying with lime and sulphur began in France in 1851, but the British industry is largely post-First World War. Considerable developments took place between the wars, in the use of copper salts, derris, pyrethum, tar oil, and so on, and both ICI and Boots entered the field in the 1930s. The link with the fertilisers industry is an obvious one. ICI and agricultural interests formed Plant Protection Ltd in 1937 and the fertiliser firm of Fisons formed Pest Control Ltd in 1954, with a large factory at Harston near Cambridge. Developments since the Second World War have been rapid, especially of insecticides (e.g. DDT), selective weed-killers (e.g. 2,4-D) and the newer general herbicide 'paraquat'.

The main *fertiliser* industry is of much longer standing, as noted above (p. 581). Dependent partly on imported raw materials (phosphates) and partly on home-produced chemicals (e.g. sulphate of ammonia), and having a widespread agricultural market, it is fairly well scattered, with an emphasis on port locations and on centres (e.g. Ely) within the main agricultural areas.

Paint and varnish manufacture, depending on pigments, solvents, oils and resins, is a large employer of labour in several of the major industrial districts, particularly Greater London, south Lancashire and the West Midlands; in

Glasgow and on Tyneside it is clearly linked with the shipbuilding industry. To an increasing extent it is drawing on the products of the heavy organic chemicals industry, replacing its older natural materials with synthetic products.

Exports of chemicals

The following tables demonstrate the importance of the considerable export trade in chemicals, the value of which rose from an average of £29m a year in 1935–38 to £178m in 1953, £295m in 1959 and £493m in 1967.

Exports of chemical products, by value (£ millions)

PRODUCT GROUP	1959	1963	1967
Chemical elements and compounds	70	93	118
Dyeing, tanning and colouring materials	40	48	58
Medicines and pharmaceutical products	46	54	78
Essential oils and perfume materials	30	34	43
Fertilisers, manufactured	3	5	8
Explosives &c.	10	7	9
Plastics	45	64	94
Others	51	63	84
	295	368	493

Exports of chemical products, by weight (thousand tons)

PRODUCT	1938		1948		1959		1967	
	METRIC TONS	LONG TONS	METRIC TONS	LONG TONS	METRIC TONS	LONG TONS	METRIC TONS	LONG TONS
Ammonium sulphate &c*	318	313	224	221	218	215	373	367
Copper sulphate	31.4	31	25.3	25	31.4	31	12.1	12
Disinfectants and insecticides	19.2	19	34.4	34	28.4	28	43.6	43
Sodium compounds	362	356	419	413	615	605	603	593
Dyes and dyestuffs	15.1	15	18.2	18	12.1	12	21.3	21
Soaps	37.5	37	28.4	28	50.8	50	25.3	25
Detergents		†		†	46.6	46	58.9	58

* Including other nitrogenous fertilisers in 1959 and 1967.
† Not available (but virtually non-existent).

About 60 per cent of the exports, by value, leave from the ports of London and Liverpool—the latter because of the wide range of heavy chemical industries in its immediate hinterland, the former because of the high-value products that are made in its many 'fine chemicals' factories. Middlesbrough and Hull—each with chemical industries of its own—are a very long way behind, followed by Manchester and a long list of ports that export in small quantities.

23
Miscellaneous industries

In the preceding chapters we have dealt in turn with the major industries of Britain. It is true that we still have some miscellaneous manufacturing industries to consider but, even allowing for these, there remains the remarkable fact that well over half the population of these islands has still to be accounted for. It is worth while to study with some care the tables which follow in that they illustrate the relative importance of the occupations not yet considered.

The service industries

One of the characteristics of the employment structure of 'developed' countries is the increasing proportion provided by what is known as the 'tertiary' sector—that is, the service industries as opposed to extractive industries and agriculture (primary) and manufacturing (secondary). Britain is no exception to this generalisation, and indeed if 1959 figures are regarded as 100, the figures for 1964 were primary 80.3, secondary 105.0 and tertiary 109.9 (the total employment having risen to 106). In the same year (1964) the actual figures of employment were primary 1 181 000, secondary 8 700 000 and tertiary 12 950 000, the tertiary representing 55 per cent of the total.

In the table on p. 600 the service industries are listed at the bottom, from 'construction' to 'public administration'.

Distribution of total manpower, Great Britain (thousands)

	1938	1961	1966
Total population	46 208	51 350	54 744
Males	22 197	24 833	26 602
Females	24 011	26 517	28 142
Total working population	19 473	24 650	26 236
Males	14 476	16 325	17 045
Females	4 997	8 325	9 191

	1938	%	1961	%	1966	%
HM Forces and Women's Services	385	(2)	474	(2)	417	
Males	385		459		402	
Females	—		15		15	
Agriculture, forestry, fishing	949	(5)	604	(2)	478	
Mining and quarrying	849	(4)	731	(3)	580	(2)
Manufacturing industries: total	6 363	(33)	8 928	(36)	9 055	(34)
Food, drink and tobacco	640	(3)	832	(3)	841	(3)
Chemicals and allied industries	276	(1)	532	(2)	528	(2)
Metal manufacture }			631	(2)	619	(2)
Engineering and electrical goods }			2 147	(9)	2 337	(9)
Shipbuilding }	2 590	(14)	241	(1)	214	
Vehicles }			898	(4)	861	(3)
Other metal goods }			567	(2)	596	(2)
Textiles	861	(5)	842	(4)	810	(3)
Clothing and footwear	717	(4)	585	(2)	552	(2)
Bricks, pottery, glass, cement, etc.	271	(1)	346	(1)	352	
Leather, leather goods and fur }			67		60	
Timber, furniture, etc. }	844	(4)	308	(1)	296	
Paper, printing and publishing }			621	(2)	648	(2)
Other manufacturing	164	(1)	309	(1)	342	
Construction	1 264	(6)	1 617	(7)	1 725	(7)
Gas, electricity and water supply	240	(1)	379	(2)	431	
Transport and communication	1 225	(6)	1 683	(7)	1 629	(6)
Distributive trades	2 882	(15)	3 312	(13)	3 035	(11)
Insurance, banking and finance	414	(2)	573	(2) }	3 222	(12)
Professional and scientific services }	1 806	(9)	2 217	(9) }		
Miscellaneous services }			2 270	(9)	2 246	(9)
Public administration }						
National government service }	1 386	(7)	511	(2)	579	(2)
Local government service }			756	(3)	804	(3)
Unemployed total	1 710	(9)	261	(1)	281	

In 1938 the working population was 42 per cent of the total population (65 per cent of males, 21 per cent of females); in 1961 it was 48 per cent of the total (66 per cent of males, 31 per cent of females); in 1966 it was still 48 per cent, but males had dropped to 64 and females rose to 33. Percentages given above are of the working population.

Perhaps the most striking fact emerging from the table on page 601 is the important, often dominant position occupied by the London area in almost all these miscellaneous industries. The reason is to be found partly in London's premier position as a port for the import of all manner of raw materials, but mainly in the existence within the conurbation of some ten millions of people, providing both a source of labour and an immense market for all the necessities and luxuries of civilised life. London's industrial structure will be referred to in some detail in Chapter 26.

We may begin our examination of these miscellaneous industries with the only one in which London plays little or no part—the pottery industry.

Miscellaneous manufacturing industries employment, 1948 and 1960

INDUSTRY	NUMBER EMPLOYED (THOUSANDS) 1948	1960	CHIEF REGIONS[1] APPROXIMATE PERCENTAGE OF TOTAL
China and earthenware	67	68	Midland (85).
Glass and glassware	62	77	NW (30), London and SE (23), Yorkshire (16).
Leather and leather goods	49	55	NW (20), London and SE (12), Yorkshire (10).
Boots and shoes	114	117	N. Midland (51), NW (11), London and SE (8).
Tailoring and dressmaking	384	399	London and SE (25), NW (18), Yorkshire (15), N. Midland (8).
Furniture and upholstery	93	109	London and SE (33).
Paper and board	66	94	London and SE (22), Scotland (22), NW (20), SW (9).
Printing and publishing, etc.	190	378	London and SE (34), Scotland (9), NW (9), E. (7), Yorkshire (7).
Rubber	89	124	NW (30), Midland (22), London and SE (18), Scotland (11).
Building and contracting	1505	1505	Greater London (16), Scotland (7), SE (7), Lancashire and Cheshire (7).
Tobacco	45	49	*

[1] Ministry of Labour Regions.
* Not available, as regions lumped together.

The ceramic industries

According to the Census of Production, 1948, no less than 85 per cent of all the pottery workers in Great Britain were in the Midlands Region. In fact the concentration is narrower than this and within the Region almost the entire industry is located in the city of Stoke-on-Trent—one of the most remarkable industrial concentrations in the world. The 'Five Towns' of Arnold Bennett's novels (there are actually six, but he omitted Fenton) have become so identified with the pottery industry, that they are known all over the world as 'The Potteries'. The North Staffordshire coalfield (see p. 301) lies in the southwest corner of the Pennine Uplands, drained by several small streams—of which the most important is the Fowlea Brook—which unite to form the upper Trent, and separated by a low and broken ridge from the Cheshire Plain. In early times it was distinctly isolated, and from about the fourteenth century it seems that the local wood and clays, and later the local coals, were used to make coarse earthenware as a sideline to subsistence farming. By the early eighteenth century the village of Burslem had become quite a noted centre, making, amongst other things, butter-pots for sending Uttoxeter butter to London. Old maps show clearly the crofts with their pottery kilns adjacent to the dwelling or to the barn, and the small clay-holes from which the raw material was obtained. Lead and salt for glazing were accessible from the Derbyshire limestone area and from Cheshire, respectively. The clays came from the Blackband Group at the base of the Upper Coal Measures—which outcropped in Burslem and Hanley—and the long-flame coals from the adjacent upper part of the Middle Coal Measures. Devon and Dorset ball clays, and south coast flints, were imported by pack-horse for making finer ware, and the construction

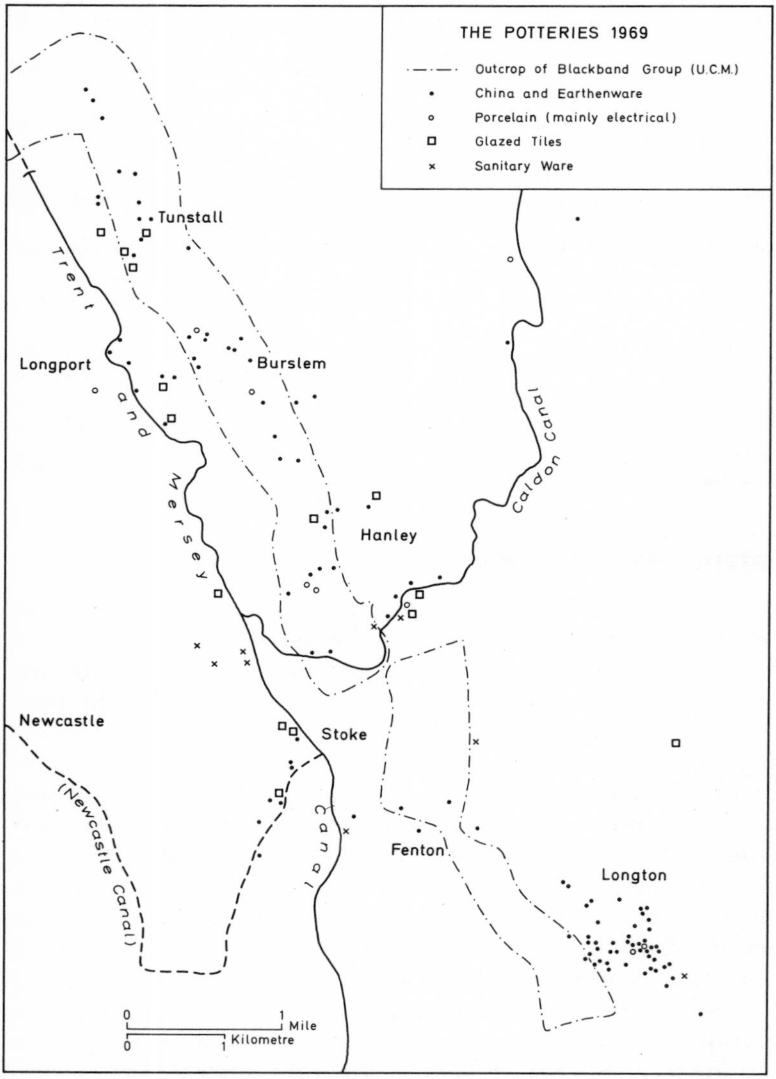

FIG. 205. The Potteries, 1969

of turnpike roads led to the growth of the industry in Longton, at the point where the Derby–Newcastle road crossed the main coal and clay outcrops.

Amongst the skilled families of potters in the mid-eighteenth century were the Wedgwoods. Josiah Wedgwood (1730–95) was a farsighted business man as well as an expert craftsman. It was he who introduced Cornish china clay into the potteries in the 1760s; he, too, who was a leading spirit behind the construction of the Trent and Mersey Canal, opened in 1777, alongside which he placed his Etruria Works. The canal, linking the Trent near Derby with the Mersey at Runcorn, and passing through the western ridge of the coalfield in the famous Harecastle tunnel, gave direct water connection between Cornwall and North Staffordshire. But, curiously enough, the potteries did not migrate to its banks; they remained where they were, in the rapidly growing small towns, for between five and twelve tons of coal were needed for every ton of clay, and the collieries were located close to the towns, whilst the canal ran down the Fowlea Brook valley, which follows the Etruria Marl (barren red Upper Coal Measures) outcrop. The early nineteenth-century location of the industry has thus remained unchanged to the present day. The vast majority of the potteries are still in the built-up areas of Tunstall, Burslem, Hanley, Fenton, Longton, and Stoke; the only canal-side potteries are at Longport (where the old turnpike road from Burslem to Newcastle crossed the canal), at Stoke, and at Hanley (where the Caldon Canal crossed the Blackband outcrop). The china section of the industry (as opposed to earthenware) is located almost entirely in Longton, actually the farthest of all the towns from the canal. Only one firm so far—Wedgwoods—has attempted to leave the congested urban area; in 1939 the old Etruria works were abandoned and a completely new factory, with electric firing and rail transport, was established at Barlaston, a few miles south of Stoke. Two other large works outside the urban area are specialists in the production of electrical porcelain; each lay alongside a canal—one at Stone by the Trent and Mersey Canal, the other at Milton, by the Caldon Canal.

But several 'potters' millers' are located on the canal banks, where many of the raw materials (china clay, china stone, ball clay, flint, chert, felspar, calcined bones, etc.), used to arrive by water and are prepared for the potters. Accompanying the pottery industry are subsidiary industries concerned with the supply of colours and glazes; and Stoke is the headquarters of the British Ceramic Research Association.

The economic geography of the pottery industry has changed fundamentally since the last war. No coal is now used for firing—gas, electricity and oil fuel have been substituted (thus incidentally removing the greater part of the smoke problem in Stoke)—and the china clay arrives from Cornwall by 'clay-liner' railway trains. Only the location remains unchanged, and many of the potteries have been rebuilt on their existing sites. The limited amount of mechanisation that is possible in this industry has reduced the labour requirements, and the employment roll dropped from 53 000 in 1958 to 43 000 (of whom 24 000 female) in 1968.

China and earthenware are not the only clay industries in the Potteries. The Coal Measures' fireclays were the basis of the manufacture of saggars (the containers in which the china and earthenware are placed for firing in the kilns), and of glazed tiles, sanitary ware and sewage pipes, and of refractory products. The purple mudstones of the Etruria Marl supply not only a flourishing brick industry, but also over one-half of all the clay roofing tile industry in the country. The tile industry, unlike the pottery trades, spreads beyond Stoke-on-Trent into the neighbouring borough and ancient market town of Newcastle-under-Lyme.

The ceramic industries outside the Potteries are located almost entirely on their source of clay supplies. Thus the Dorset and Devonshire potteries are located on the ball-clays of Poole and Bovey Tracey respectively. Some of the famous china industries of the past—at Worcester, Coalport, and Derby, for example—are now either extinct or of relatively little importance. The sanitary ware industry, based upon Coal Measures' fireclays, is to be found in such places as Swadlincote (south Derbyshire), Halifax, and Barrhead (near Glasgow).

Fur, and the leather-producing industries[1]

In its distribution the fur industry of Britain is almost entirely distinct from the ordinary leather industry. The dressing and preparation of furs is very largely restricted to London where, in the East End, it employs a large number of people. Three-quarters of the 11 000 workers in the industry are in London and they produce nearly three-quarters of the total output by value. With regard to the *leather* industry, the distribution of tanning and leather dressing in Britain is of considerable geographical interest. Tanning is an old industry and whilst production techniques have changed in detail, the general sequence of operations by which raw hides and skins are transformed into leather has remained broadly the same since very early times. The main stages in the process of production are as follows:

(*a*) *Washing and soaking*. When the hides arrive at a tannery they are often dirty and very stiff. Washing and soaking in water removes some of the dirt and makes them pliable.

(*b*) *Dehairing*. To remove hair from the hides and skins they are immersed in a solution of lime. This causes the skins to swell and the hairs to fall out and partially dissolve.

(*c*) *Fleshing*. After dehairing the hides may still retain shreds of animal

1. This and the next section (pp. 608–612) have been rewritten by Dr P. R. Mounfield, to whom I am much indebted.

flesh. At this stage these are removed by machine scraping or, occasionally, by hand.
(*d*) *Drenching and deliming*. The lime used in dehairing is still on the skin. It is removed during this process by soaking in water.
(*e*) *Tanning*. Tanning is designed to preserve the hides, make them waterproof and to improve their flexibility and wearing qualities. The tanning liquor can be either a solution of vegetable extracts or mineral salts. The latter is nowadays more common for the soft leathers required for shoe uppers, gloves and other leather clothing.
(*f*) *Finishing or dressing*. In this process the leather is oiled, stretched and polished. Some of the leather may have designs stamped upon it whilst other hides may be treated to give a high gloss.

In large tanning firms, all these processes may be carried out in the same premises but it is not uncommon for the final stage of finishing or dressing to be carried out by separate firms. About half the leather-producing firms in Britain start with the raw hides and skins and either finish them right through or sell them 'in the crust' (or rough-tanned state). Others buy the 'crust' leather, from either British or foreign suppliers, and dress it to produce the finished material. It is important to note this distinction between tanning and leather dressing, because they exhibit rather different locational characteristics. The two sections of the industry together employ approximately 35 000 workers.

The nature of the production processes indicates the main requirements of the *tanning* industry to be (*a*) a reliable supply of hides and skins, (*b*) mineral or vegetable tanning agents, (*c*) copious supplies of clean and preferably soft water, (*d*) lime for dehairing. In medieval times tanneries were very small and widely scattered throughout the country; practically every village of any size had its own tan pits. Hides and skins were obtained locally and oak bark, for a considerable period the main source of tanning liquor, was obtained from local woodlands. The individual tanneries served strictly local markets and the smaller ones were frequently ancillary to a farmer's business and worked by farm labour as part of the farm. With the passage of time, however, tanning became a more specialised and separate craft. The complete tanning process was a long one; in medieval tanyards a hide might take twelve months to prepare, and even as late as 1925 the usual period for sole leather was five to six months. This meant that, as it progressed as a separate activity, the industry became one that required increasingly large amounts of capital. Furthermore, as the demand for leather increased, and as individual tanneries became larger, the question of oak bark supplies became progressively more important. The oak bark itself was fragile, bulky and produced only 10 to 20 per cent tannin liquor. This in turn led to an increased concentration of tanning on or near to the large oak forests which grew both on the damp lowlands of central England and on the drier sandstone ridges such as those of the Bunter sandstone. Furthermore, the 'New Husbandry' of the seventeenth and early eighteenth centuries meant that a large proportion of the heavy claylands in the Midland shires was put down to grass. These grass pastures became famous fattening areas for the herds of cattle that were driven to the London meat markets from as far afield as Wales, Shropshire and Cornwall. A constant and reliable supply of hides was thereby assured, and some of the old-established Midland towns, such as Northampton, became important centres for the organisation of the tanning industry. Another centre of early importance was the natural focus of the great agricultural region of East Anglia, that is, Norwich.

However, the nineteenth century witnessed a general decline in the number and relative importance of inland tanneries in Britain. This was mainly due to the increasing dependence of the industry on imported hides and imported vegetable tanning concentrates—a dependence which placed a premium on coastal locations and led to the growth of tanneries at the large ports such as Liverpool, Bristol and London.

In the 1890s, just when it seemed that what remained of the tanning industry in inland centres was doomed to final extinction, a new and revolutionary process was introduced in the industry. This was mineral tanning. Hitherto, tanning agents had been obtained exclusively from vegetable sources such as oak bark and hemlock. Now, it was discovered that chrome salts could be used. By using chrome salts, tanners were able to give a finer and more uniform finish to their products and mineral tanning quickly superseded vegetable tanning, particularly in the tanning of softer leathers, such as those used for shoe uppers. The tanners using vegetable tanning solutions began to specialise in the production of tough, durable leather of the type used for machine belting and the soles of shoes. A large proportion of their hides were imported, from the Argentine, the Union of South Africa, India, Eire and other cattle rearing countries. Thus, the heavy-leather tanneries remained at the ports. Mineral tannage, on the other hand, served to revive the industry in some of the old inland centres as in Northamptonshire, for example, where the footwear industry had grown rapidly at a number of places during the second half of the nineteenth century and provided an important local market for the tanners' products.

Tanners treat raw hides and skins, but not all of their output is fully finished. Moreover, a substantial proportion of the imported hides and skins now enter Britain in a semitanned state and may not go to the tanner. These hides have been rough-tanned in the exporting countries in order to decrease their weight before shipment. Imported leather is subject to lower tariffs if it is semitanned rather than in a finished condition. In addition, for many purposes leather has to be finally worked up near its market because its finished form is dependent upon the dictates of fashion. Thus, it might reasonably be expected that the *leather dressing* industry as a separate trade would be in the same areas of the country as those industries which use leather as their main raw material. This is certainly the situation in

Northamptonshire, where the centres of leather dressing are also shoe manufacturing towns. Indeed, it is leather dressing rather than tanning that has gained from the presence of footwear production in the southeastern Midlands.

The history of leather dressing as a separate occupation is relatively short. Until a century ago, all imported hides entered the country in a raw and virtually untreated state: they went directly to the tanneries, which undertook all the processes of leather manufacture. The first fundamental division between tanning and leather dressing appeared when rough-tanned leather began to be imported in quantity, from about the middle of the nineteenth century. In Northamptonshire the footwear industry was expanding at this time, but the local tanning industry was declining; the leather dressing industry largely took its place. Sometimes old tanneries were converted into leather dressing works but more frequently new buildings were erected, for the old tanneries included a considerable amount of space for tanning pits which was not needed for leather dressing. Nowadays the chief product of the Northamptonshire dressers is a high-grade upper leather, together with lining and slipper leathers. The leather dressing works are generally smaller than the tanneries, each tends to have its own speciality, and no individual works employs more than fifty workers. However, leather dressing in Northamptonshire employs a much larger *total* labour force than tanning.

Thus, there are three types of area where tanning and leather dressing are important at the present day:

(*a*) The old centres in the heart of the country districts, particularly in Northamptonshire, associated with the manufacture of boots and shoes, as well as in Somerset and other southern counties, where it was and often still is linked with local supplies of sheepskins and with the glove industry (p. 613);
(*b*) in the vicinity of the great ports, particularly Merseyside (Liverpool, Warrington and Runcorn), Bristol and London, where the emphasis (mainly the result of hide imports) has been on heavy leathers for the soles of boots and shoes;
(*c*) in the great inland industrial conurbations (West Yorkshire, South Lancashire, and the West Midlands), where the market provided by various types of demand, particularly the use of leather belting for driving machinery in the textile and engineering industries, has been an influential factor.

It must be noted, however, that the heavy leather tanneries have suffered considerably in recent years through the decline in demand for machine belting, through the decreasing use of leather as a sole material in the footwear industry (see table on p. 609) and through competition from a variety of synthetic products.

Leather-using industries : especially footwear manufacture

The small-scale making of leather goods was formerly very widespread throughout the rural counties of England and Wales. These leather workers were, in the main, either saddlers, whose occupation has almost disappeared with the increasing mechanisation of agriculture, and bespoke shoemakers, who similarly have been put out of business through the growth of factory-made footwear. The manufacture of both footwear and leather goods is now concentrated in particular parts of the country. The production of leather bags, trunks, saddlery, and similar articles tends to be concentrated in the Greater London area (which has 40 per cent of the 25 000 people employed), and also in the west Midlands (21 per cent), principally at Walsall. It has already been mentioned that, before modern methods of transportation and food preservation were developed, most of London's meat supply was provided by herds of cattle driven long distances to the London meat markets from the rural rearing and fattening districts. The hides of these animals were processed by London tanners and provided the basic material for local leather workers. In the Middle Ages Birmingham was a smaller and less important place than Worcester, Coventry, Warwick and Stafford, but it became a natural centre, albeit on a somewhat infertile plateau, for the surrounding rich fertile lowlands, and, like the iron hardware industry (cf. pp. 409, 453), the leather industry may be regarded as having grown out of an early response to local farming requirements and local supplies of raw material.

The footwear industry, which employed over 100 000 workers in 1961, has become concentrated in a remarkable way in a few areas (see table opposite).

In the Middle Ages, and even later in remoter parts of the country, individual households commonly made their own shoes. The everyday shoes of the working classes during the Middle Ages were extremely simple leather 'envelopes' worn over tight stockings. The workmanship was of a comparatively crude but sturdy nature, requiring little skill. It was not until horse-riding became more common that the heel was introduced, enabling the foot to be held more securely in the stirrup. After this technical innovation, shoemaking became more of a separate craft. Even so, virtually every village and town in the country had its own shoemakers, producing a local supply of shoes and using local materials (in those parts of the country where leather was in short supply, wood was sometimes substituted for leather soles). At this stage, there was little sign of any concentration of the industry in particular parts of the country. Since each pair of boots had to be made to measure, the shoemaking craft was distributed in accordance with the pattern of population.

It was not until the military spirit of the seventeenth century made itself felt that the need for large quantities of strong and serviceable footwear,

Statistics for the major footwear manufacturing districts of Britain, 1955 and 1965

AREA	NUMBER OF FIRMS		OUTPUT (THOUSAND PAIRS)		LABOUR FORCE		PERCENTAGE OF OUTPUT WITH NON-LEATHER SOLES	
	1955	1965	1955	1965	1955	1965	1955	1965
London, Chesham and East Tilbury	55	36	10 053	15 754	6 092	4 781	51	91
Bristol, Kingswood and Street	26	8	7 204	20 892	6 748	10 988	58	97
Kendal and Scotland	6	4	2 757	5 305	3 852	4 875	12	69
Leeds	12	8	3 182	2 372	2 060	1 052	44	90
Norwich	27	22	7 065	8 556	9 008	7 628	30	76
Desborough, Rothwell and district (Northants)	11	8	2 065	2 399	1 637	1 502	24	65
Kettering and district (Northants)	25	16	5 610	5 444	5 645	4 588	23	56
Rushden and district (Northants)	77	69	12 980	14 273	11 763	10 295	25	67
Northampton	38	24	7 144	7 764	10 543	7 241	15	67
Leicester	76	55	13 430	14 369	11 703	8 792	34	97
Leicester county (excluding Leicester)	66	57	18 523	22 459	11 616	10 830	55	99
Stafford and Stone	9	4	1 738	2 570	2 141	2 361	22	93
Lancashire (especially Rossendale)	54	38	28 280	30 705	12 056	10 117	74	99
Total	482	349	120 031	152 862	94 864	85 060	36	82

Note. Data provided by the Footwear Manufacturers Federation and the Lancashire Footwear Manufacturers Association. Although most of the footwear manufacturing firms in Britain belong to one or the other of these two organisations, there are a few which do not. Thus, the figures in this table may be slightly lower than if all firms were included. The employment statistics in the table refer to all employees, including administrative, technical and clerical staff.

It should be noted that a *firm* may operate more than one *factory*.

made to a standard pattern, for troops, became apparent. The first recorded order for a large quantity of footwear was placed with a group of Northampton shoemakers in 1642. This was an order for 4000 pairs of shoes and 6000 pairs of boots to supply the Royalist armies in Ireland. It probably marks the beginning of wholesale footwear production in Northampton, and perhaps in Britain. Subsequently, similar orders were placed in the town, particularly to supply Cromwell's New Model Army, the first large standing army ever to exist in Britain. Under the transport conditions of seventeenth-century England, Northampton was in a good position to establish and maintain contact with the London market. Given the initial start provided by military contracts, the master shoemakers in the town strengthened their trade links and the fact that the army clothiers needed a fairly standardised product meant that a sensible division of labour could be introduced and the scale of production increased. In Northampton itself, a number of artisans had been left unemployed by the decline of the town's formerly prosperous woollen industry and there was a surplus of agricultural labour caused by enclosures in surrounding parishes. These things, combined with supplies of good quality leather, initially from local sources, and later also from London, provided a favourable economic climate for the steady growth of wholesale footwear production in Northampton.

Stafford (1760) and Norwich (1792) are two other places where the production of footwear on a wholesale basis began fairly early. Stafford, like Northampton, had a flourishing local leather industry but perhaps just as important, at least in the early stages, was the personal friendship between William Horton, the first wholesale footwear manufacturer in the town, and R. B. Sheridan, playwright, influential at Court, and Member of Parliament for Stafford from 1780 to 1806. Through his influence in London, Sheridan obtained sizeable orders for his friend. Norwich, too, had local tanneries but the decline of the woollen industry in the city during the eighteenth century made available a large labour force skilled in manual operations, and when wholesale shoemaking was introduced by James Winter in 1792, it was quickly taken up as an alternative source of employment.

Thus, by 1800, there were three concentrations of wholesale footwear production in England, the one at Northampton being of greater importance than the others. Nevertheless, they were small. Even in 1841, Northamptonshire contained only 7000 shoemakers, barely 4 per cent of the total number in England and Wales, and the local bespoke maker still provided for the largest part of the country's population. The main reason for this was that, before the introduction of machinery, wholesale manufacture was superior to traditional bespoke methods only for the fulfilment of large military orders. However, important changes came in the nineteenth century. Particularly significant was the great increase in the population of Britain under the influence of the Industrial Revolution. This created the opportunity to market a cheap, mass-produced article suitable for the growing number of wage earners manning the factories and mines of the new industrial areas. Footwear machinery began to be introduced from 1840 onwards. It reduced the degree of skill required for all but the better qualities of footwear and reduced the advantage of the experience in the industry that had been accumulated over the years in Northampton, Stafford and Norwich. In these circumstances it was only a question of time before other areas began to develop a factory-based industry. In Northamptonshire itself, the industry rapidly spread out to several other places in the county, notably Rushden, Higham Ferrers, Kettering, Raunds, Rothwell and Wellingborough, in the search for extra labour. Perhaps even more important, however, was the entry into the industry of places elsewhere in Britain which had previously shown no signs of specialisation in wholesale footwear manufacture, notably Street in Somerset (1833); Kendal in Westmorland (1842); Bristol and Kingswood (1843); Leeds (1850); Leicester (1851); the Rossendale area of Lancashire (1876) and, in Scotland, Kilmarnock. At Street, footwear manufacture grew out of currying and the making of sheepskin rugs. Early entrepreneurs at Bristol and Kingswood were able to make use of part-time workers from the local coal mines and could draw upon a well-developed local tanning industry for their leather supplies. In Rossendale, the footwear industry grew from the habit of workers in local felt warehouses of making up ends of felt into slippers, to avoid damaging the material over which they had to walk for the purpose of matching patterns. Leicester, with some smaller nearby towns such as Barwell and Earl Shilton, quickly became the most important of the 'new' centres of footwear manufacture. Leicester gained its start in the industry through the enterprise of Thomas Crick who, in 1853, patented a method of riveting soles and uppers together. Until this time, Leicester lacked a

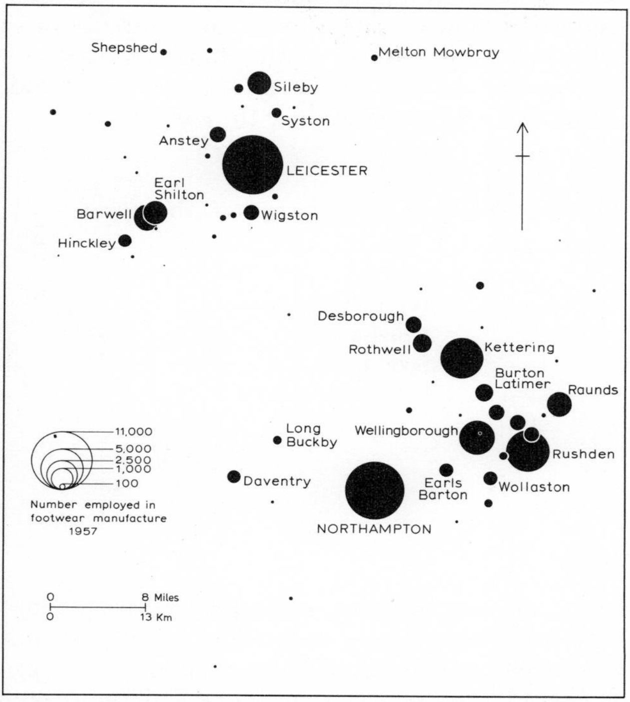

FIG. 206. The footwear industry of the East Midlands (after P. R. Mounfield)

handsewn footwear industry of any size, and this meant that machinery could be introduced more easily than in places such as Northampton, which did have a strong tradition of handsewn work. The decline of the local domestic hosiery industry in Leicestershire provided a source of suitable labour.

Thus it was in the period from approximately 1850 to 1914 that many of the existing centres of footwear manufacture in England and Wales achieved their present importance. The reasons for the location of the industry at each place tend to be slightly different, but it is notable that footwear manufacture has often provided a replacement for other formerly important local industries.

The longest period of continuous prosperity for the industry was from 1890 to 1914, when footwear exports boomed and many modest fortunes were made. However, several important overseas markets were lost during the First World War and after, when foreign countries which had formerly imported shoes from Britain began to develop their own footwear industries. The total number of boot and shoe *factories* in England and Wales fell by half between 1914 and 1955, from 1021 to 550. As for more recent years, it is clear from the table on p. 609 that, whilst production per worker and total output of footwear have increased in nearly all of the major centres of production, both the labour force and the number of *firms* have decreased in nearly every case. A striking feature has been the substitution of rubber and synthetic materials for leather as a sole material since the early 1950s.

Employment in clothing and footwear industries, 1966 by regions (thousands)

North	33	Wales	16
Yorks. and Humber	59	West Midlands	22
East Midlands	78	Northwest	94
East Anglia	14	Scotland	32
Southeast	150	Northern Ireland	27
Southwest	26	Total	551

The clothing trade

Everyone must wear clothes and the industry, excluding footwear, employed 425 000 in 1968. The little dressmakers' and tailors' establishments which were so important in the past still persist in towns of almost every size up and down the country; indeed, in 1948 over 40 per cent of all the 12 000 firms in the industry employed less than ten persons each,[1] but the large-scale manufacture of articles of clothing has become concentrated in a number of distinct centres, and it is perhaps because the requirements of clothing are broadly proportional to the population that these centres are the great conurbations. It would seem that the proximity of the market is more important than local supplies of raw material, though that too is seen to exercise an important influence in a number of areas. A leading place amongst the list of centres must be given to Leeds, not only because it con-

1. There are no comparable later figures; but the Census of Production 1963 records that in the manufacture of women's and girls' tailored outerwear 678 out of a total of 1135 firms employed under 25 people; and in the manufacture of men's and boys' tailored outerwear 584 out of 1238 firms had an employment roll of under 25. There has undoubtedly been a very great reduction in the number of firms, for the 1958 Census showed a total of 1383 firms in the women's branch and 1767 in the men's branch.

tains the largest number of clothing operatives and because the variety of clothing trades carried on within its boundaries is very great, but because it is really the only large town of which clothing may be said to constitute the staple industry. The influence of the Yorkshire woollen industry is seen in the character of the clothing industry of Leeds, which specialises in outer garments of which wool is the chief material. In Lancashire, where Manchester is the principal clothing centre, dresses of light material, shirts, and underclothes are more important, obviously again indicating the importance of the local supplies of cotton and other fabrics. The Manchester industry spreads to Stockport and to Wigan, whilst that of Leeds spreads to Halifax and Huddersfield. A third centre is afforded by Birmingham, Walsall, and neighbouring towns of the Midlands. A perhaps greater geographical interest attaches to the group of clothing manufacturing towns in the west of England of which Bristol is the centre; it also includes Gloucester and the Stroud valley, Taunton and elsewhere. Doubtless the clothing firms here are a legacy of the once important cloth industry now largely disappeared. It is natural that the hosiery centres of Nottingham, Leicester, and Kettering should not cease with the manufacture of knitwear, but should include also the manufacture of underclothing of different types. In the southern and eastern counties there are many towns, such as Colchester, Norwich, Portsmouth, Basingstoke, and Reading which have individually quite important clothing industries, but it is in Greater London that the industry is really important (see Chapter 26). To a considerable extent the clothing industries are 'footloose' and can be located wherever suitable labour can be recruited and a local market exists. Portsmouth with its corset factories employing mainly women is an interesting example of a deliberate attempt to use available labour: here the dockyard employs almost exclusively male labour. Luton, in Bedfordshire, was the chief centre in Britain for the manufacture of hat shapes, an interesting later development of the former domestic industry in straw plaiting and weaving which in turn was the result of a situation in the midst of a rich cereal-growing country.[1] In Scotland there is really only one important clothing centre—Glasgow.

Glove manufacture is a specialised branch of the clothing industry, linked, however, not with the main clothing industry but rather with the present or former production of fine leather and with the West Country textile industry. Small towns in Worcestershire, Wiltshire, Dorset, and Oxfordshire contain much of the industry (nearly 40 per cent of the 10 700 employees in 1948 were in the South-West Region), which in part arose out of the declining woollen trades (cf. p. 501), and was accompanied, as noted above (p. 607), by the development of small-scale tanneries for the local sheepskins which are still largely used.

1. See C. M. Law and D. J. M. Hooson, 'The straw-plait and straw-hat industries of the South Midlands', *E. Midland Geog.*, **4**, 1968, 329–50.

Food industries

Naturally, if one includes bakers, workers in the preparation of foodstuffs are very widespread throughout the country. A map of the distribution of bakers and flour confectioners would show the same pattern as a population map, and some of the other food industries are also located mainly in the major urban centres, with the London area dominant almost throughout, but in some cases other geographical or economic factors may be involved.

Employment in food, drink and tobacco industries, 1966 (thousands)

Bread and flour confectionery	159	Cocoa and chocolate	95
Grain milling	43	Sugar refining	16
Biscuits	51	Brewing and malting	96
Bacon, meat and fish products	88	Other drinks	69
Fruit and vegetable products	73	Tobacco	50
Milk products	41	Total	850

Employment in food, drink and tobacco industries, 1966, by regions (thousands)

North	34	Wales	22
Yorks. and Humber	81	West Midlands	72
East Midlands	46	Northwest	126
East Anglia	39	Scotland	99
Southeast	229	Northern Ireland	30
Southwest	63	Total	841

Bread and flour confectionery occupies 20 per cent of the total employed and is the most widely distributed, but London has a quarter of the total. Even there the universal tendency towards larger units is seen. The same is true of *brewing and malting* (11 per cent of employees) and the *soft-drink* industry (5 per cent). *Milk products* (5 per cent) are made in the country districts still (only a seventh of the employees in London and the southeast). More localised are *biscuit making* (6 per cent), *cocoa and chocolate* (11 per cent), *sausages and preserved meats*.

We may perhaps distinguish three types of location: (*a*) The larger towns, where industries may exist, based originally on local agricultural produce and often still in part dependent thereon—e.g. mustard at Norwich. In some cases perhaps a local traditional occupation has affected the establishment of allied factory industries, and Reading's biscuit manufacture may be an example of this. Certainly the fruit and vegetable preserving industries of such places as Peterborough, Wisbech, and Dundee come into this category. Rather different in character is the milk products industry which, though sometimes located in the market towns, is more commonly completely rural in location, depending upon good rail and road transport. The importance of the Northwestern Region (which includes the Cheshire Plain), and of Southwest England in this industry is clear from what has been said (pp. 197–9). (*b*) Certain types of food processing are naturally concentrated on the great ports where the imports (e.g. grain and sugar) arrive. Large-scale grain milling in particular tends to be concentrated at ports, notably Liverpool, London, Bristol, Hull, Southampton, and Manchester (though there are, of course, many inland flour mills, mainly served by rail or inland waterway). So does sugar refining, in which London and Liverpool again lead; and the manufacture of margarine (from imported fats) is another example. (*c*) Food industries, like many other partly 'footloose' industries, often exist in localities which have been chosen for essentially non-geographical reasons—e.g. the chocolate industries of Bournville (near Birmingham), and York. And food processing being often a 'light industry', there are numerous examples of twentieth-century factories on the periphery of the great conurbations, or in trading estates, or more recently in the Development Areas. Thus half the country's output of baked beans is produced at Wigan, in what is in fact the largest food-processing plant in the Commonwealth.

Paper

The manufacture of paper and cardboard is a widely distributed industry, and has been so ever since it began in the late fifteenth century. Formerly rags and abundant clear water were the main necessities; at the end of the eighteenth century there were over 500 small paper mills in the British Isles, all manually operated. Then water power and bleaching chemicals became of importance and by about 1860, straw, mechanically formed wood pulp, chemical pulp and esparto grass had entered the field, largely to supplant the use of rags. Mills increased in size and decreased in number; by 1900 there were only 280, and the process of eliminating the smaller rural mills and concentrating on larger establishments has continued, so that the total in 1948 was about 228 mills distributed as shown on p. 616. Water supply is still a major factor, since very large quantities (amounting to millions of gallons a day) are required by the mills; but facilities for the disposal of the effluent are almost of equal importance (compare the artificial silk industry, p. 591). Soft water is desirable in general (and is always an asset where steam-driven plant is employed) but purity and freedom from colouring matter (particularly iron) are more important; hard water is not objectionable in the newsprint branch of the industry, since chalk is in any case often used as a filler for the paper.

The regional distribution of the paper industry (cf. employment table on p. 601) is as follows:

AREA	NO. OF MILLS
Lancashire (and adjacent parts of Cheshire and Derbyshire)	38
Kent	32
SW England (Gloucester, Somerset, Devon)	22
Yorkshire	16
Chilterns (Bucks, Herts)	12
East Scotland (Fife, Stirling, Clackmannan)	14
Midlothian	13
West Scotland (Lanark, Renfrew)	10
Aberdeen	6
Other areas	65
Total	228

The annual output of paper and board in recent years has been steadily rising. Average for 1956–60: Newsprint, 666 000 tons; Other paper and board, 2 911 300 tons; Total, 3 577 300 metric tons. As production has risen, so the tendency has been for a concentration in larger units.

Two of the most important regions in the industry are the fringes of the Mid-Pennines and North Kent. In Lancashire and Yorkshire, pure water from the Millstone Grit, early water power possibilities, later the ready availability of coal and chemicals and an abundant supply of cotton rags from the local textile industry, and then the proximity of the Mersey, Ribble, and Humber ports for the import of wood pulp and exports contributed to the rise and persistence of paper manufacture, while the large local population provides not only a market for the output but also a source of waste paper and rags as further raw materials.[1] In the case of North Kent (Dartford–Gravesend and the Maidstone–Medway area) where a large proportion of the newsprint industry is concentrated, large water supplies from the Chalk, and river frontages for the disposal of effluent and the import of fuel and raw materials, together with the proximity of the enormous London market, have been the major factors involved.

There are many inland centres of paper-making, many of them of long standing and often highly specialised—e.g. banknote paper on the flanks of the Mendips, near Wells, fine writing paper and blotting paper at various mills in the Chilterns (e.g. Apsley, Loudwater); fine transfer paper for the pottery industry at Cheddleton, near Leek; and highly specialised packaging paper for the food industry, at Watchet, in Somerset.

In Scotland, paper-making also has a long history and a wide distribution. The Edinburgh district produces upwards of three-quarters of all the

1. In Radcliffe, for example, 2000 out of a total working population of 16 000 are employed in the paper industry (which is more important than textiles), and in Bury, paper employs 3500 out of a total working population of 30 000.

esparto paper in the country, and has long been famed for the variety and high quality of its products—which are much used locally in the stationery and printing trades, as well as having worldwide markets. Glasgow is the main newsprint centre, Aberdeen has several mills, and there are numerous other centres, mostly on the eastern side of the Central Lowlands, and mostly specialising in particular varieties of paper products.

An allied industry is the conversion of paper and board into products for the use of other industries. There are actually more paper-converting mills than paper-making mills; many of them are in the same areas as the paper mills, but there are also very many in the Midlands where are located so many manufacturing industries needing boxes, wrappings, cardboard tubes, and so on for the marketing of their products.

Printing and bookbinding

Of the workers enumerated in Great Britain, approximately one-third are located in the London area. Further, many printing firms have, for reasons of economy, migrated to towns which, although accessible from the metropolis, are outside it. Thus, this book is printed at Beccles, in Suffolk. Other well-known firms have chosen locations such as Colchester, Guildford, Maidstone, and Rochester. There is also still an interesting association between the printing, bookbinding, and publishing trades and the great centres of learning. One may cite particularly Edinburgh in the case of Scotland, and Oxford in the case of England.

The furniture industry[1]

Although furniture-making is widespread there are significant concentrations of the industry. Measured by the percentage of total value of manufacturers' turnover, the chief producing areas of Britain in 1957 were London and southeastern (45.3), southern (15.1, of which High Wycombe accounted for 12.0), and northwestern (11.4). In 1956 London led in cabinet and upholstered furniture (respectively 52.6 and 34.4 per cent of Britain), south in chairs (41.4, though the making of chair parts in the Chiltern beechwoods ceased in 1960).

In Greater London the Shoreditch and Bethnal Green district remains the home of small manufacturers and of manufacturers' suppliers, but most furniture is now made in a belt along the River Lea, from Bow through Lea Bridge (Leyton), Walthamstow, Tottenham, Edmonton and Enfield. Large quantities of timber are brought by lorry and barge from the Port of London to Lea-side merchants' and manufacturers' premises. New centres are developing with easy access to main roads, as at Barnet, Watford, and

1. See J. L. Oliver, *Development and Structure of the Furniture Industry*, Pergamon Press, 1966.

Letchworth, all near the A1 or M1 roads, and as at Romford, Brentwood, and Southend on the Southend Road or within short distances from it.

In the concentration of the furniture industry on the capital London follows the pattern of Copenhagen, Oslo, Stockholm, Vienna, and Paris. In very few towns in the world does furniture-making dominate local economic activity. High Wycombe, Buckinghamshire, is almost unique in this respect.

The rubber industry

Although Hancock set up a factory in London in 1819 to process raw rubber and later collaborated with Mackintosh, the inventor of waterproof garments, the rubber industry may be quoted as an example of an industry of comparatively recent origin—Dunlop invented the pneumatic tyre in 1888—which illustrates the varying strength of factors determining location. The raw material is, of course, of equatorial or tropical origin, and must be imported. One would therefore expect the industry to be concentrated near the great ports. On the other hand the question of market arises. A large proportion of the rubber is required for tyres for the motor industry, and in connection with the electrical industries which have become established—particularly in south Lancashire and the west Midlands, where rather over half the workers in the rubber industry are located. Avon tyres at Melksham, Michelin at Stoke, Goodyear at Wolverhampton each suggest interesting studies in industrial location.

Tourism

This somewhat inappropriate term is coming to be widely used for what, some claim, is now the world's most important industry. Alternatively we may refer to the 'holiday industry'. In the past holidays with pay were enjoyed by only a minority of the population and holiday for the majority consisted of short trips arranged actually on statutory bank holidays, especially the first Monday in August. It is now true to say that the majority of jobs in Britain include two or three weeks' holiday per year during which normal rates of wages or salary are paid. In 1962 over 4 million Britons out of a total population of some 50 million left the country to holiday on the continent. Figures for tourists or holiday-makers thus going abroad are known with considerable accuracy but it is much more difficult to assess the importance of tourism at home. Sample surveys suggest that 80 per cent—let us say 40 million—leave their homes for a holiday of some sort during the year. But there are 10 816 000 private cars and 1 324 440 motor cycles registered in Britain (1968) costing to run 7*d* out of every £1 earned (1962). The huge mileage of non-business journeys, with the cost of meals taken en route, in reality is all part of the great business of tourism, the full extent of which it is impossible to measure.

The attraction of visitors and catering for their varied needs have become the major preoccupation of many local authorities. One method of assessing the importance of the traffic is by accommodation available. We may use the number of beds available but since many hotels are open for the summer season only a better measure is bed-nights, and this is the best available measure of the use made of accommodation. Caravan and dormobile users escape this census however. The average cost of a bed-night gives some measure of money which changes hands either for accommodation alone or on a bed and breakfast basis. Since, however, most families set aside a more or less definite amount for holidays we have another measure. At £10 per head £400 million would change hands in this country, at £25 the total rises to £1000m. In the mid-fifties (traffic has been increasing since) it was shown that summer visitors brought into and spent more money in the county of Devon than was represented by the total output of agriculture in that large and rich farming county. The £15m per annum spent by visitors to the Channel Isles is the major source of revenue.

It follows that a high economic importance attaches to the possession of what tourists want or the amenities to be provided for them. It has been calculated that over 40 per cent of all recreation is 'water based', on the sea or inland waters, and that, as in America, a boat on some lake (probably a reservoir) or sheltered estuary has become a 'status symbol', probably taking precedence of a second car. A country or seaside cottage is now within reach of many and the demand for such solves one problem but creates another. As agriculture becomes more efficient and more fully mechanised, a smaller labour force is needed to maintain or even increase production from the land. There is rural depopulation and cottages formerly occupied by agricultural workers become redundant, as do a proportion of farmhouses. Provided the area is scenically attractive and the cottages are fundamentally sound in construction, they become occupied by townsfolk, first for weekends or summer use and later for retirement. This 'adventitious' rural population (p. 659) brings both manpower needed to sustain the social structure of the village or countryside and a certain amount of money earned outside. A problem is however created when demand for cottages exceeds supply and the adventitious townsman outbids the rural worker, or when the demand is such that extensive building upsets the balance and agricultural land is threatened.

An allied problem is provided by the caravan. It was estimated in 1968 that about 5.5 million people, or one-seventh of all British holiday-makers, now take their holidays in a caravan, usually rented for a short period at one of the 5000 licensed sites that are now to be found round our coasts and at inland localities where scenery or the presence of water (lakes or rivers) provide the attraction. Nearly sixty of these sites have places for over 500 caravans, and the three largest—at Porthcawl in South Wales, at Selsey near Portsmouth and at Canvey Island on the Thames estuary—each have space for over 1500 caravans.[1] Many a delectable piece of coastal scenery has been marred by caravan sites—but clearly this is a form of holiday that is much appreciated by large numbers of people; and of course the rent from the sites provides a useful source of income for farmers and landowners.

The establishment of National Parks and Nature Reserves has already been discussed (pp. 132–3). In Scotland chair-lifts have been constructed in the Cairngorms to encourage winter sports: they are equally popular with summer tourists.

The development of resort towns is far older. The Romans were quick to appreciate the curative value of hot mineral springs—as seen in Bath (and inland watering places where the sick sought to drink the waters), which enjoyed a fluctuating fortune for many centuries. In the eighteenth century they began to share with the new type of watering places—those by the sea—a prosperity associated with Royal and noble patronage. In particular the Prince Regent, afterwards George IV (1820–30), made Brighton, where he built the fabulous oriental-style Brighton Pavilion (now carefully preserved by the Corporation) in 1784. Other members of the royal family are associated with the rise of Weymouth (Duke of Clarence), and as the development of railways facilitated access 'watering places' grew up in many places round the coast, inland spas—either new or resuscitated—grew up at places like Buxton, Matlock, Harrogate, Leamington, Cheltenham, Tunbridge Wells, and even as far afield as Strathpeffer beyond Inverness. The pattern of Victorian and Edwardian life for the wealthier included some weeks *en famille* by the sea, often at old fishing ports which assumed new functions and gained new features—such as Whitby, Scarborough, Cromer, Sheringham, Felixstowe, Margate, Ramsgate, Hastings, Eastbourne, Torquay, Brixham, Penzance, Newquay, Ifracombe, Aberystwyth, and many others. These are apart from other seaside resorts, exemplified by Blackpool and Southport, which grew up as such (p. 702).

Another aspect of tourism is the attraction to Britain of foreign visitors, who in 1968 numbered over 4 million (compared with 1.8 million in 1961). These tourists spent some £274m in Britain, and their fares paid to British shipping, airlines and railways brought the total income to £375m—which compares with the estimate of £272m spent on foreign travel (including business visits as well as holidays) by United Kingdom residents. Tourism thus has an important part to play in helping to solve the nation's balance of payments problems.

One of the greatest attractions for foreign visitors is undoubtedly London, with its wealth of historic buildings and its array of cultural facilities. But for many, including the Americans who come in large numbers and who have ancestral roots in Britain and claim our cultural heritage as their own, the interest is primarily in the historic towns and cities—the cathedral

1. *Caravan Sites 1969*, published by *Modern Caravan*.

cities of Canterbury and York, the castles of Edinburgh and Caernarvon, the colleges of Oxford and Cambridge, and of course Stratford-on-Avon. The 'stately homes' in the countryside, especially those with gardens, and many now owned by the National Trust, are another attraction. Overseas visitors also look for the best of British scenery—the Highlands, the Lakes, Devon and Cornwall—but boating and bathing they can probably enjoy better at home.

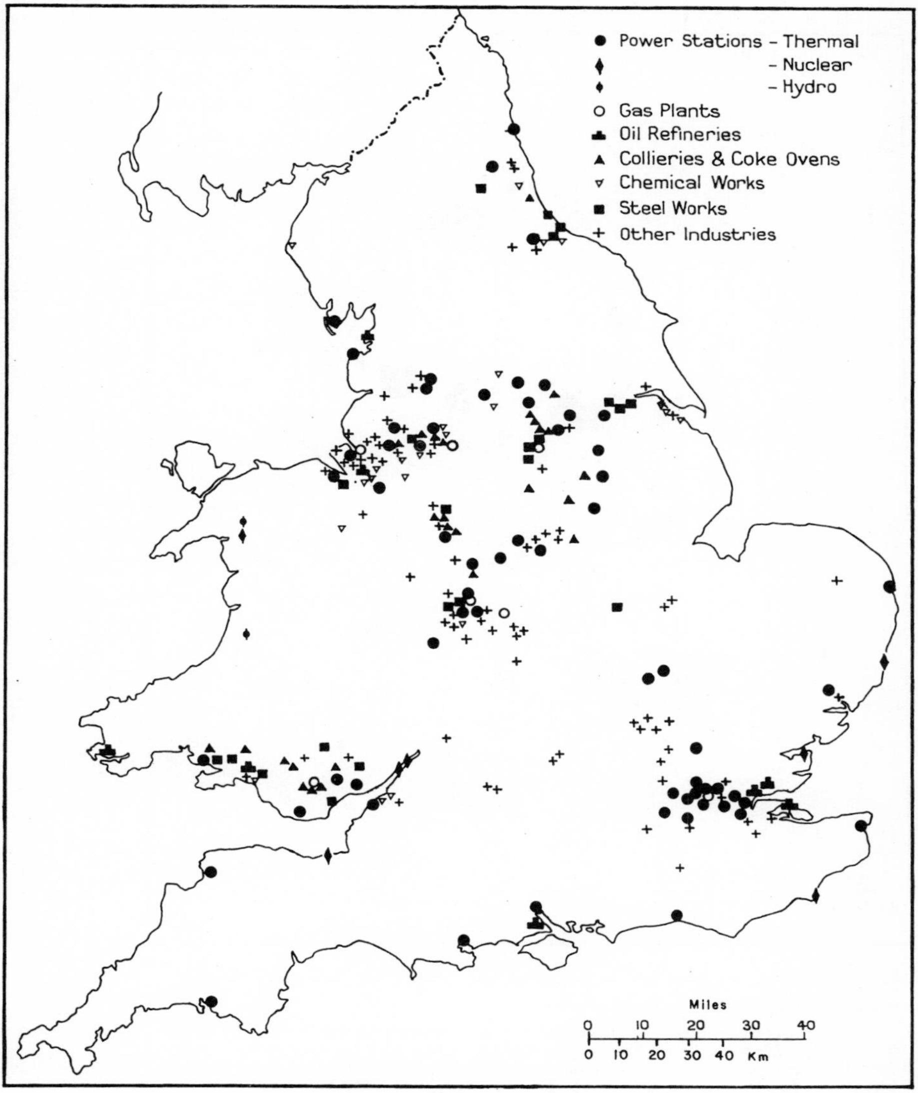

FIG. 207. The location of new factories and power plants, 1945–61

The increase in tourism of all kinds has brought new pressures on the countryside and has enhanced the importance of intelligent conservation. The desire to see and enjoy the amenities of the natural scene encourages the provision of the very facilities—motor roads, caravan camps, hotel and motel accommodation—that are capable, without the most careful planning, of destroying those same amenities.

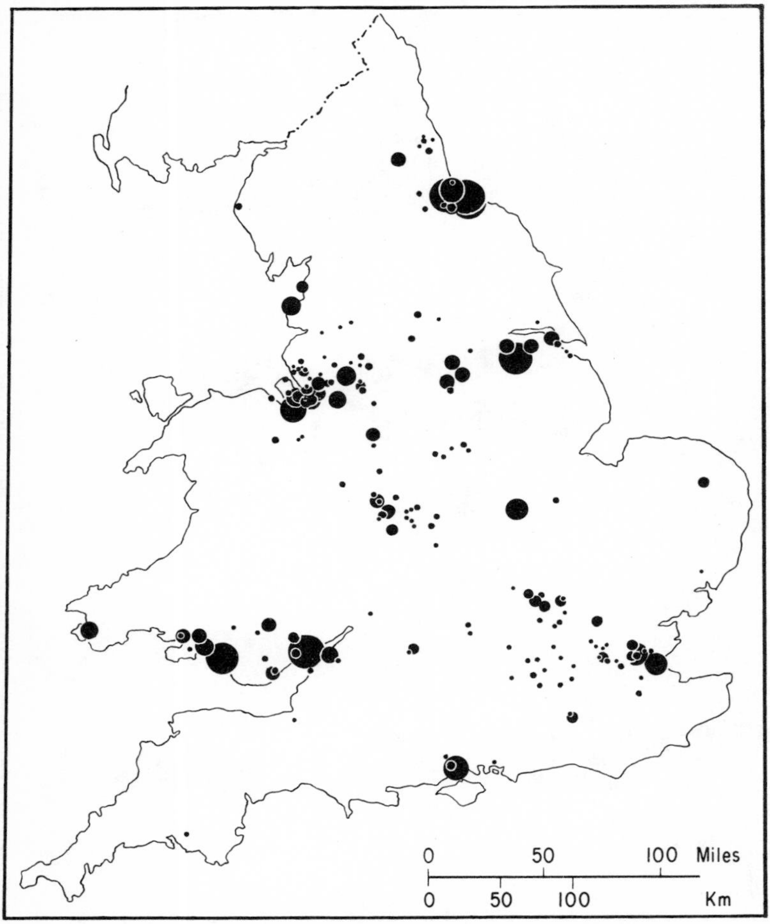

FIG. 208. Major postwar industrial projects (to 1961) shown individually and graded according to capital cost

Certain major features are readily recognisable: (*a*) steelworks projects (e.g. Scunthorpe, Middlesbrough, Newport, Port Talbot, Corby, Consett, Shotton); (*b*) chemical projects (e.g. Wilton (Tees-side), Severnside); (*c*) oil refineries (e.g. Milford Haven, Fawley). Despite the emphasis on capital-intensive developments in the peripheral 'Development Areas' of South Wales and the northeast, the continued dominance of the 'axial belt' from Thames to Mersey is still evident.

Postwar industrial development in general

The interwar years were marked by the contrast between the decline, with accompanying unemployment, of the old outer industrial areas—mid-Scotland, Tyneside, West Cumberland, and South Wales in particular—

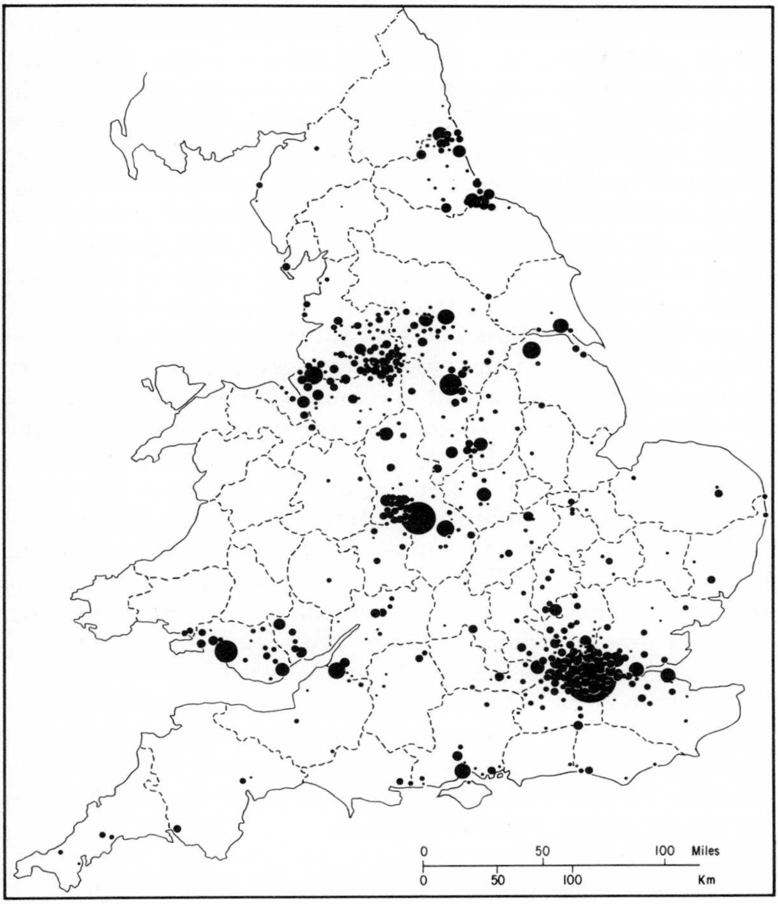

Fig. 209. The rateable value of industry, 1961, showing concentration on Greater London, Birmingham and Lancashire–Yorkshire

on the one hand and the expansion and prosperity of the two great industrial regions of Greater London and the West Midlands on the other. The decline in the old cotton area of Lancashire was balanced by the growth of new industries in the Liverpool–Ship Canal–Manchester area. Worried by this growing unbalance the government of the day set up the Royal Commission on the Geographical Location of the Industrial Population under the chairmanship of Sir Montague Barlow and the resulting Barlow Report, issued shortly after the outbreak of the Second World War, advocated a planned dispersal of industry.

A rapid dispersal of industry quickly took place on the outbreak of war for other reasons—to avoid the concentration of war-material factories in vulnerable easily bombed concentrated sites.

The government realised that the dispersal of industry, whether deliberately planned or necessitated by wartime conditions, would profoundly affect life in what had previously been purely rural areas and set up the Committee on Land Utilisation in Rural Areas under Lord Justice Scott. The Scott Report took a broad view and in implementing its recommendations the government in due course introduced the Agriculture Act, 1947 which stabilised farming by giving farmers a guaranteed market and guaranteed prices, and the Town Planning Act, 1947 which made the preparations of plans for future development, on a county and county borough basis, compulsory over the whole country. There followed also the National Parks Act, 1949 which set up a National Parks authority and also the Nature Conservancy (see pp. 132–3 and Fig. 77). In the postwar period it has been the policy of successive governments (*a*) to encourage new industrial development in the older industrial areas, (*b*) to secure some dispersal of population by building new towns (Fig. 77) and (*c*) to discourage—not very successfully—the further growth of London and Birmingham in part by restricting licences for factory building, in part by laying down 'green belts' in which any building or other development would be strictly curtailed. Three maps, prepared by Dr E. C. Willatts, show the results on industrial development of these various government measures.[1] The first, Fig. 207, shows the location of new factories and power plants (1945–61) each costing more than £5m. This map should be read together with that showing new towns (Fig. 77) and the Electricity Grid map (Fig. 152). The same facts are shown differently in Fig. 208 where no distinction is made between the different industries. Finally Fig. 209 shows that the new developments, important though they are, have not changed the supremacy of the great industrial centres of London and Birmingham.

1. E. C. Willatts, 'Post-war development: the location of major projects in England and Wales', *Chartered Surveyor*, 1962, 356–63.

24
The peopling of the British Isles

Two sets of factors may be said to have exercised a dominating influence on the early peopling of the British Isles. The first set of factors is climatic, the second is physiographic. There is no doubt that there were human inhabitants in the British Isles before, or at least in the earliest stages of, the great Ice Age. As glacial conditions spread southwards so man was forced to retreat before the advancing cold, and River Drift or Paleolithic man left the open valley bottoms and took refuge in caves. But it is clearly incorrect to picture a continuous southward spread of glacial conditions and then a continuous northward retreat. Periods of intense glaciation were succeeded by comparatively warm interglacial periods which in turn were terminated by a renewed onset of colder conditions. The extremely difficult, if fascinating, work of correlating the glacial and interglacial deposits of this country and of tracing their connection with the movements of early man is one which has for long periods unceasingly occupied the attention of both geologists and archaeologists. If we consider the period of maximum extension of glaciation we may rightly picture the whole of Ireland and the whole of northern Britain, as far as a line joining the mouth of the Thames and the mouth of the Severn, as being covered by ice sheets of greater or less extent and of varied origin (see Fig. 14). At this period the extreme south of Britain, therefore, would be occupied by land comparable in climatic and probably in vegetational characteristics with the great Tundra lands of the present day. On these Tundras or Arctic grasslands the reindeer, amongst other animals, flourished, and attracted the attention of early man, the hunter. When the ice sheets finally retreated these Tundra grassland conditions moved gradually northwards and probably man, still the hunter, went with them. The place of the Tundra in Britain was then gradually taken by forests. In recent years, especially as the result of the work of Prof. H. Godwin, precision has been given to the determination of climatic fluctuations during and since the Ice Age by the analysis of pollen grains found in the successive layers of peat deposits. Tundra conditions were succeeded by forests in which coniferous trees predominated while milder conditions were marked by an influx of deciduous trees. After several climatic cycles, the establishment of a mild, moist climate resulted in the general spread over the lowlands of the deciduous forests which form the characteristic natural vegetation of these islands at the present day.[1] The spread of forest increased the difficulty of sustaining life from the spoils of the chase, and so encouraged the settlement of man in more open areas on the uplands and along the coast. The coast dwellers apparently obtained shell fish, and their implements are of 'Tardenoisian' type. Later came the introduction of primitive agricultural and domestic animals, probably by invaders who were forerunners of the Megalithic and Beaker peoples. With the development of a more settled life there was no longer the necessity to be continually on the move, and several writers have properly stressed the importance of the change, especially on child life. No longer was it necessary for the children to be carried about continuously on their mothers' backs. Infant mortality lessened, and there was an increase in the population, and with the increase an improvement in moral and physical conditions. It must be remembered that simultaneously the great vegetation belts of the world which we know at the present day must have moved northwards, and this northward movement of environmental conditions with which they were familiar in itself encouraged the northward movement of peoples. This invited naturally a migration into, and a settlement of, Britain from the Continent.

The main physical features of the British Isles profoundly affected the lines of movement both of traders and of settlers. Prehistoric immigrants who entered Britain from the south or from the east spread westwards and northwards, though avoiding the thickly forested clay lowlands and using as their avenues of movement, for the most part, the more open hill belts. Their movements were stopped, or at least hindered, by the hilly barriers afforded by the Pennines, the edge of the Welsh massif, and the hills of Devon and Cornwall. It might be thought that they would penetrate through what is now called the Midland Gate into the plain of Cheshire and Lancashire and thus reached the Irish Sea, but it would seem that that lowland was covered by a very heavy growth of damp forest which prevented access to the western seaboard. Later, it is clear that during the Roman period the settlements of the Romano-British population were in the main limited[2] to the 'lowland zone', and it is still clearer when one comes to the succeeding period and considers the distribution of Anglo-Saxon settlements. On the other hand there was the stream of traders and settlers who approached the British Isles by the seaway from the west and southwest. It is clear that, though they were able to spread over the whole of Ireland, their colonies were largely restricted to the coastlands of Devon, Cornwall, the Scillies, Wales (especially Glamorgan, Pembrokeshire, Caernarvonshire and Anglesey), the Isle of Man, the Western Isles and adjacent coasts of Scotland, Orkney, Shetland, the plain of Caithness and

1. For a short summary see Chapter 14 of L. D. Stamp's *Britain's Structure and Scenery*, Collins, 1946; also above, pp. 86–7, and p. 118.
2. Later work, especially by O. G. S. Crawford, has demonstrated the considerable extension of Roman control and influence into southern Scotland.

the shores of the Moray Firth. Only when they had overcome the intervening mountain barriers—and still more the forest and marsh barriers—were they able to descend on, or mingle with, the people of the lowlands to the east. It was not apparently till a much later stage, that of the Scandinavian invasions, that a movement of people coastwise from the north of Britain became important.

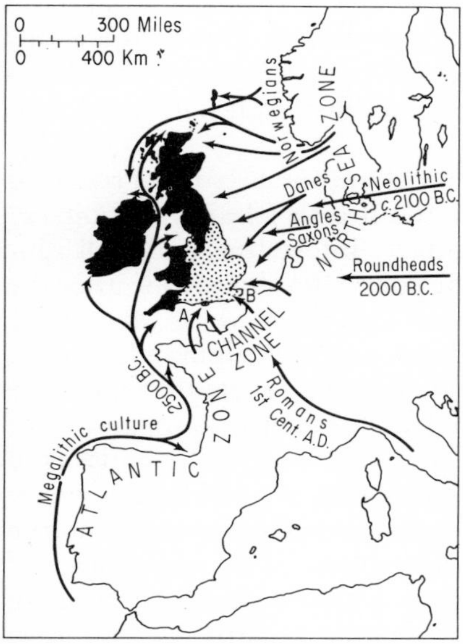

FIG. 210. The routes from Europe into Britain followed by early traders and invaders

The 'highland zone' is shown in black; the 'lowland zone' by dots. A and B = routes followed by invaders and traders of the late Bronze Age; B = routes followed by Romans.

There is, thus, in the peopling of Britain a fundamental distinction to be made between the lowland zone of the south and east and the highland zone of the north and west. Already, before the dawn of written history, a frontier region of peoples and cultures came into existence between the two. The dividing line between the zones corresponds roughly with the outcrop of the youngest Paleozoic rocks—the boundary between Highland Britain and Lowland Britain already discussed in Chapter 3. It would seem that the distinction between the two zones has been preserved for several reasons. Amongst them two stand out. One is that until the extensive clearance of forests in the lowland zone the habitable regions were mainly those raised some distance above sea-level, forming islands of habitable or cultivable land in a sea of forest, and where those more readily cultivable regions reached the coast there grew up the trading centres. By way of contrast the cultivable or habitable regions amongst the hills of Scotland or Wales were the valley regions, which may be described as islands of inhabitable country within a sea of comparatively useless hills. In the second place the lowland zone is that neighbouring to, and easily accessible from, the Continent, and so successive waves of invaders came in and imposed their culture, and often their racial characteristics, on the existing inhabitants. On the other hand, in the highland zone, such of the few invaders as penetrated into the valleys tended to be absorbed by the existing population. This is important, because it helps to explain the persistence of differences between the Highland Scot or the Welshman on the one hand, and the English lowlander on the other.

Professor H. J. Fleure presented a summary of the main results of research before 1920 on the pre-Roman peopling of the British Isles in *The Races of England and Wales* (1923).[1] Later a particularly interesting and well illustrated summary was drawn up by Sir Cyril Fox,[2] who shows how after the final retreat of the ice, but earlier than 2000 B.C., a powerful Megalithic civilisation spread over the whole of Ireland and the highland zone of Britain, including the plateau of Caithness and the lowlands round the Moray Firth. The culture had been brought by sea from the south and west, that is from Spain and Atlantic France. The invaders were the builders of the dolmens and other huge stone monuments which are still found widely distributed in Ireland. In Britain they evidently pressed eastwards, and the stone circles of Stonehenge and Avebury are evidence of the importance of their dominance in the Salisbury Plain region. Forty of the lesser stones of Stonehenge were actually transported from Pembrokeshire. The builders of the great stone monuments seem to have been long-headed people, probably of short stature and dark skin, and the evidence points to them as the oldest large element in our population. They buried their dead in long barrows, and hence they are sometimes known as 'long barrow' people.[3] Simultaneously the east of Britain seems to have been strongly influenced by a Neolithic culture of peoples coming from the east, from the Baltic region, or possibly from farther eastwards from the Kiev region or from Upper Silesia, passing on their way to Britain through Denmark and Holland. In Britain, the remains of these people, often known as the 'Beaker' people as they are associated with rough pottery of curious form known as beaker pots, are left most characteristically along the east coast from Caithness to the Humber, and in the southeast, where they evidently penetrated along the chalk ridges. The earliest arrivals brought no metal, but copper and bronze daggers were a little later commonly buried with the dead. They buried their dead in round barrows. Burials of the succeeding stage

1. In 1951 Professor Fleure summarised his long life's work in this field in *A Natural History of Man in Britain*.

2. *The Personality of Britain* (see Bibliography, p. 829).

3. Some authorities regard the long barrows as a variety of megalith belonging to a zone farther east than the true megalith and of doubtful cultural derivation.

were also in round barrows, but usually in cinerary urns, since by that time the corpses were generally burnt. The Beaker people were short-headed people, thus allied in character to the Alpine race of the Continent of Europe or perhaps a Nordic–Alpine cross, whereas the Megalithic people may be said to be allied to the Mediterranean races of Europe.

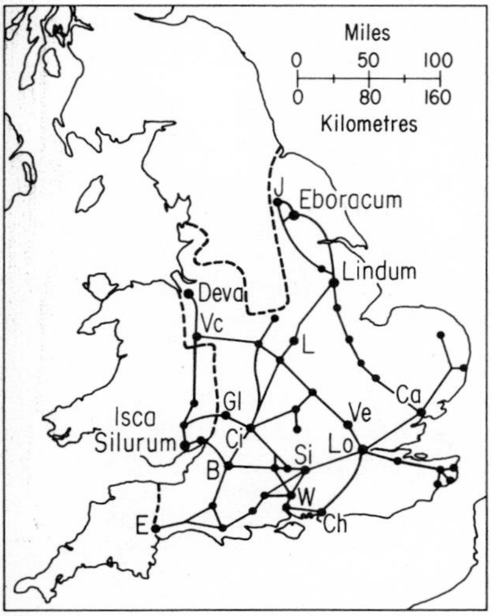

FIG. 211. The civil districts of Roman Britain (after Haverfield and Macdonald)

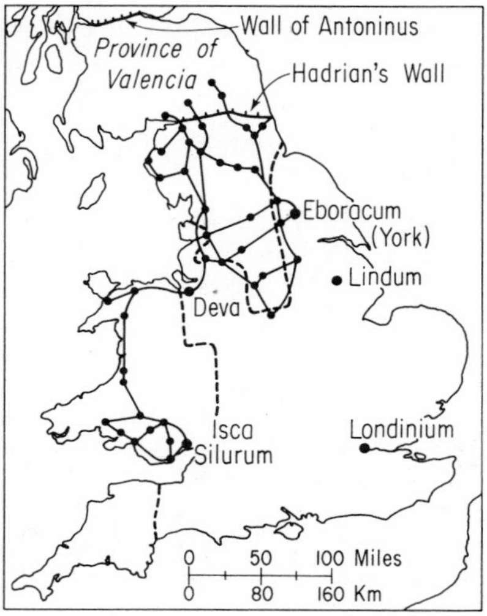

FIG. 212. The military districts of Roman Britain (after Haverfield and Macdonald)

The chief Roman roads connecting (Fig. 211) the civil settlements and (Fig. 212) the military posts.

For the next stage in the peopling of Britain Fox gives the provisional date of about 2000 B.C. The invaders were from the east, the Nordic–Alpine roundheads (predominantly but not exclusively roundheaded) who came and occupied the whole of the lowland zone and penetrated far into the highland zone. They made Salisbury Plain an important centre and assimilated some of the Megalithic traditions and possibly reconstructed Stonehenge. The trade from the southwest also developed at this time and the Hampshire 'Gate' seems to have been used for the importation of bronze tools which were taken *via* Salisbury Plain to the Midlands and possibly through the Bala cleft into Wales. Many of the people of the southeastern lowlands, however, were too poor at the time to acquire these imported tools. Almost contemporary with this, Fox says, a new source of copper and bronze tools was opened up in Ireland, and these Irish products were traded in both highland and lowland Britain. There was at this time an important trade in Irish gold (obtained in the Wicklow Mountains) to the Continent, and this trade seems to have been captured by the lowland people of Britain.

By 1000 B.C. (in the late Bronze Age) there was marked activity in trading. New invaders brought with them a high culture, and developed metallurgy, particularly the art of bronze working, in Britain itself. They entered the country by the east and south coast estuaries and seem to have been most active in the Thames Basin—the middle and lower Thames valley. Here during the last five centuries B.C. the Bronze Age gave place to the Iron Age, and close contact developed between the iron-sword makers of

FIG. 213. Cultural zones of the Angles, Saxons and Jutes in Britain *c.* A.D. 550 (after E. T. Leeds)

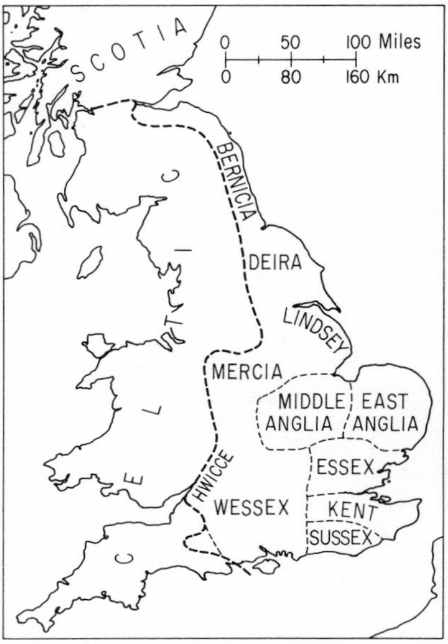

FIG. 214. Anglo-Saxon Britain at the end of the sixth century A.D., showing the kingdoms. Notice the significance of the Forth as a barrier (after E. T. Leeds)

south-eastern England (Iron Age 'A' culture) and the neighbouring parts of the Continent, with the result that the southeast had a cultural pre-eminence, and strong British kingdoms had their capitals at St Albans and Colchester. At the same time there seems to have been an important cultural centre (Iron Age 'B' culture) in the southwest, probably connected with the exploitation of Cornish tin, and the consequent stimulation of the old sea routes to the southwest.[1]

In A.D. 43 the Roman conquest of Britain began by an entry in the southeast and an advance northwestwards towards the Thames. A Roman commercial centre was quickly established at London, and a uniform control

1. Much information is now available on the Ordnance Survey Map of Southern Britain in the Iron Age, with descriptive text, 1962.

was imposed on the lowlands. Two maps are given here to illustrate the Roman occupation of Britain. The first shows the area with civil settlements in Roman Britain, and the remarkable way in which the civil districts correspond to what has been described in this work as the 'lowland zone' will be noticed at once. The Romans established cities and farms (*villae*), and made their long straight roads all over the lowland zone. In the highland zone they established military camps and military districts, but not Romanised civil settlements, though roads were extended from the lowlands into the highlands. This is shown very clearly in the second map. The distribution of Roman villas in the country—almost restricted to the lowland zone—illustrates once again the significance of the division between these two fundamental parts of Britain. After some four centuries of occupation, the breaking up of the Roman Empire resulted in the withdrawal of all Romans from Britain.

In the fifth and sixth centuries A.D. history repeated itself. This was the period of the invasions, conquest and colonisation of the British lowlands by the Angles and Saxons. The maps, Figs 213, 214, show clearly how the political and cultural division of England in the sixth century A.D. illustrate once more the contrast between the Lowland Zone and the Highland Zone; the Lowland Zone predominantly Anglo-Saxon, the Highland Zone remaining Celtic. Thus, since the Anglo-Saxons were pagans at first, the Celtic Christian Church was cut off from the Roman Christian Church of the Continent. Many of the earlier writers on the early history of Britain fell into the error of thinking that all invasions of Britain—cultural and military—had come from the east, and that each invasion in turn had pushed the earlier peoples into the highland fastnesses of Scotland and Wales, and into the outpost of Ireland. We have seen that this is fundamentally wrong; and it can again be proved so during the fourth, fifth and sixth centuries A.D. when there was extensive colonisation from Ireland of the western coasts of Scotland (where the Scots from Ireland drove out the native Picts in Argyllshire), Wales, the southwestern peninsula and Brittany; and it was indeed the coming of these Irish to western Britain that spread alarm in the waning years of Roman rule. The Anglo-Saxon colonisation largely 'fixed' the settlements of at least the lowland zone and the process was later extended.

It was in the ninth and tenth centuries A.D. that a new movement of invasion and colonisation occurred which had a lasting influence on parts of Britain. This was the invasion of Vikings or Norse and Danes which was mainly from the northeast. The Norse colonised the Shetlands and Orkneys, and a broad coastal fringe of northern Scotland, including most of Caithness.[1] The Danes colonised many places, as the distribution of place names

1. The Viking invasions so weakened the Picts of Scotland that they were conquered with ease by the Scots under Kenneth MacAlpine, who thus became the ruler of the united Picts and Scots.

21

shows, in eastern Britain, tending to remain on the whole along the coast, though spreading far inland along the valleys of navigable rivers. The name Danelaw is given to those districts of northeast and eastern England conquered by the Danes in the ninth and tenth centuries and in which Danish customary law prevailed. The stand made by King Alfred prevented the Danes from engulfing Wessex and between 880 and 890 a line running northwest from the River Lea roughly along the line of Watling Street was agreed as the western limit of the Danish domains, but by 920 the Danes

FIG. 215. The Norse settlements of the ninth and tenth centuries

were conquered. Another stream of Norse invaders had passed down the western coast of Scotland, colonising at intervals as they went, and forming a broad area of settlement in what is now the Lake District, the Isle of Man, and Lancashire. They showed themselves adept at recognising the more important ports of entry into Ireland, colonising round Dublin, Waterford, Cork and Limerick. In the meantime, it should be noticed, the Anglo-Saxons had penetrated farther northwards and had colonised the east of the Midland Valley of Scotland as far north as the Forth, where Lothian formed the northern part of the Kingdom of Bernicia.[1] Thus we see the British Isles at the time of the Norman Conquest in 1066 with an Anglo-Saxon or Lowland Zone, a Celtic-speaking Highland Zone, with important Scandinavian infiltrations in the north and west. The Romans had imposed their rule and to some degree their language, but can scarcely be said to have altered the racial characteristics of the inhabitants of these islands. The significance of the Anglo-Saxon and Scandinavian invasions was that they marked a new beginning in the human geography of the British Isles. The Norman invasion was not one of colonisation, but represented a replacement of the aristocratic government of the Anglo-Saxons by a feudal system.

Having learnt now something of the various strains of people that have gone to make up the British nation, we may turn to a consideration of the distribution of population in the islands.

An immense wealth of information concerning England in the latter part of the eleventh century is contained in the Domesday survey. For long, difficulties of interpretation resulted in this material being neglected in its geographical aspects until a team of workers under the general direction of Professor H. C. Darby undertook a systematic study county by county.[2] The study has virtually reached completion, and Professor Darby has kindly provided the distribution map of population density in Domesday England (Fig. 216). Certain problems present themselves in its analysis. The counties of Northumberland and Durham, and most of Cumberland and Westmorland, were not included in the survey, while Lancashire is treated in a far from thorough fashion. Thus in Fig. 216 there is no information of population density in the four northern counties, and Lancashire is estimated as having a density of under 2.5 per square mile. Domesday does not record total population but only heads of households, and to obtain total population a multiplier must be used, based on the believed size of the medieval family household unit. This has not been attempted on this map. A further problem is that serfs may not have been recorded as heads of households but as individuals: Fig. 216 has not been adjusted for this. What remains is the density per square mile of the *recorded* Domesday population. The resulting map has the advantage of revealing relative densities from area to area. A distinction may be made between the recorded counties of northern and west midland England, and the remainder of midland, southern and eastern England. The former was marked by a low density of population, with few areas above 12 per square kilometre (5 per square

1. On the importance of the Firth of Forth as a geographical barrier and the origin of the present Scottish counties, see W. C. Dickinson, 'The Sheriff Court Book of Fife', *Scottish History Society*, 1928.

2. The first of six volumes was published by the Cambridge University Press in 1952. The five regional volumes are now complete, and the sixth concluding volume is awaited (1969). Reference should also be made to Professor Darby's paper on 'The changing English landscape', *Geogrl J.*, **117**, 1951, 377–98.

mile). The latter was more densely populated, the greater part having a density of between 13 and 38 per square kilometre (5 and 15 per square mile), with Norfolk, Suffolk and parts of Lincolnshire and Sussex having even higher densities. The low density of population in the north may be related both to its poor development economically at this time and the devastation wrought by William I in his harrying of the north between

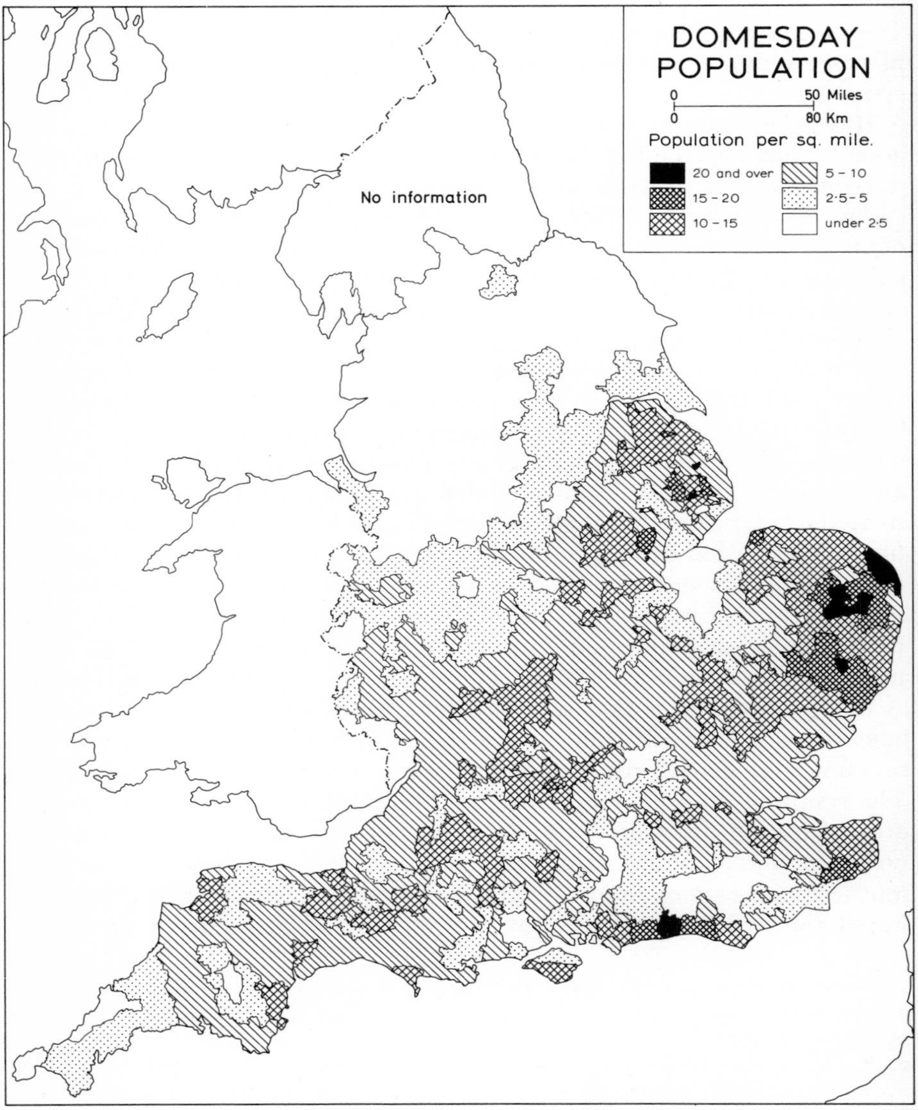

FIG. 216. Population of England at the time of the Domesday survey

1068 and 1070. Southern, eastern and midland England were areas of better agricultural land, which supported a higher density of population. This population contrast reflecting those areas with a better agricultural resource base was maintained until the eighteenth and nineteenth centuries and the revaluation of the north through industry. The influence of areas of difficulty on population density is also readily seen. The uplands of Cornwall, Dartmoor and the Pennines have low population densities, while the Fens and the woodlands of the Weald are marked by restricted settlement.

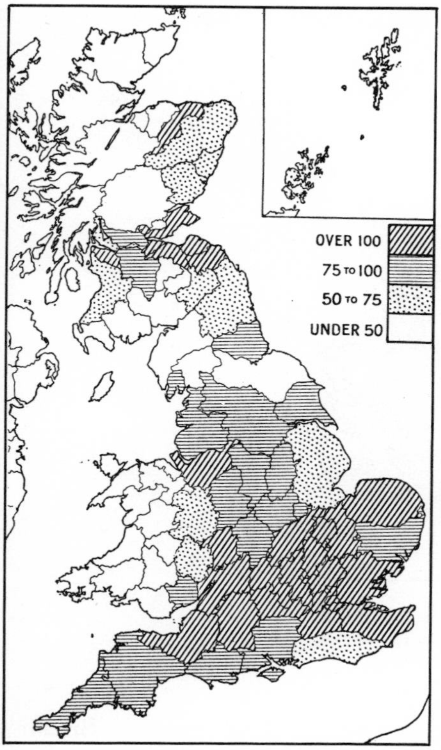

FIG. 217. The population of Britain in 1700 per square mile (Scotland in 1755)

The densest population was in the better agricultural areas: the coalfields had not yet exerted their influence.

The emergence of the English people as a whole really dates from the days of Chaucer (*c.* 1340–1400) who was the first great writer to use the English language as opposed to Anglo-Saxon or Norman French. After the Norman conquest, there was no mass invasion of the country, but there were certain population movements. One of these was the influx of Flemings and Huguenot refugees, which had an important and lasting effect on the development of economic life in this country.[1] Another was the intermittent incursions and peaceful settlement of western Scotland by migrants from Ireland, particularly early in the seventeenth century during the reign of James I of England.

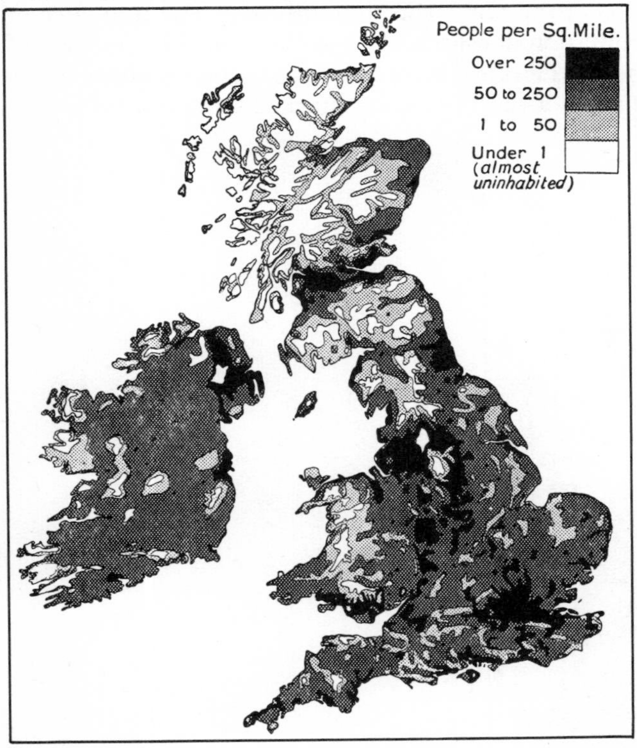

FIG. 218. The population of the British Isles in 1931
The divisions correspond roughly with industrial and intensive agricultural, good agricultural, poor agricultural and remote moorland tracts.
1 per square mile = 2.59 people per square kilometre.

To Scotland falls the honour of having taken the first census in Britain, compiled in 1755 by Dr Alexander Webster, minister of the Tolbooth Church in Edinburgh. Webster used his influential position as Moderator of the General Assembly in 1753 to secure from the parish ministers a return of the number of souls in their parishes, differentiating the two groups of Protestants and Papists. These early records of Scotland are particularly interesting since they show the distribution of population just prior to the period when Scotland changed from an agricultural and fishing country to one characterised by large-scale industrialisation in the Central Valley. Thus in 1755 the most densely populated counties in order were Banff, Berwick, Midlothian, Clackmannan, Fife and West Lothian, all, it will be

1. See pp. 493, 571.

noticed, on the drier eastern side of the country which has already been shown (see Chapter 11) to be the most suitable agriculturally to support a considerable population. It will be seen that the Midland Valley counties had not at this time succeeded in drawing to themselves the large populations which characterised them shortly after. It was largely owing to the influence of Malthus and the not inconsiderable stir that his predictions produced that the first official census of the British Isles was taken in 1801. From that time onwards the census was taken every ten years until 1931, and the table given on p. 640 shows the population of each of the constituent parts of the British Isles at each census and also the decennial rate of change. Throughout, the rapid increase at first and then the diminishing rate of increase is clearly indicated. An attempt has also been made to incorporate the effects of migration. Of course the key note of the last hundred years has been industrialisation—the increase of the industrial and urban population—accompanied by rural depopulation. An actual decrease in population did not set in as a rule until about the middle of last century or later. A study of the movement of population county by county, indicates at first a rise, practically speaking, in all counties, then a general decrease in the rural counties, but continued increase in all those counties which had industries. Quite frequently even the possession of a small industrial tract on the county margins was sufficient to turn the scale as, for example, in Denbighshire and Flintshire in Wales.

In general terms it may be said that there are in Britain two superimposed population patterns. One is the rural-agricultural with its isolated farms and farm-workers' cottages, villages and market towns, the whole strongly influenced by quality of land. The other is the urban-industrial, still expanding and spreading over the older pattern. At the present day rural depopulation is not an indication of decadence but of increasing agricultural efficiency—less labour needed to maintain production.[1]

Because the general movement of population has long been from the country to the towns it must not be presumed that all towns have increased in size. The rise and fall of settlements will be discussed in the next chapter. But whilst continued growth is the rule in the great urban agglomerations, which once they attain a certain size tend to increase of their own momentum, some of the smaller towns, especially those in Scotland, are losing their population at a greater rate than even the purely rural parishes. It is scarcely necessary to emphasise the way in which the coalfields have been the magnet for the attraction both of industries and the population which went with the development of industries. Exceptions were few. Naturally some of the

1. In some areas the 1951 Census revealed a rise in the population of rural districts and hence an apparent rise in the population officially classed as rural. Actually the increase represented an overspill from the towns into the surrounding rural districts. The same phenomenon is seen in Fig. 219 for the 1961 Census which also shows for London and other large cities a decreasing population in the centres where offices and shops are taking the place of homes.

larger ports continued to attract a population as their trade developed, but in reality they were serving for the most part as inlets or outlets for the industrial regions on the coalfields. The one main exception was London, in so far as its relationship to the coalfields is concerned, but after all London is really the port for the greater part of Britain. But post-1918 years brought about a distinctly new tendency. It may be described as the flight of industry *from* the coalfields, in large measure of course due to the more extensive use of electricity which could be generated on the coalfields or from waterborne coal and transmitted where required. To sum up, the tend-

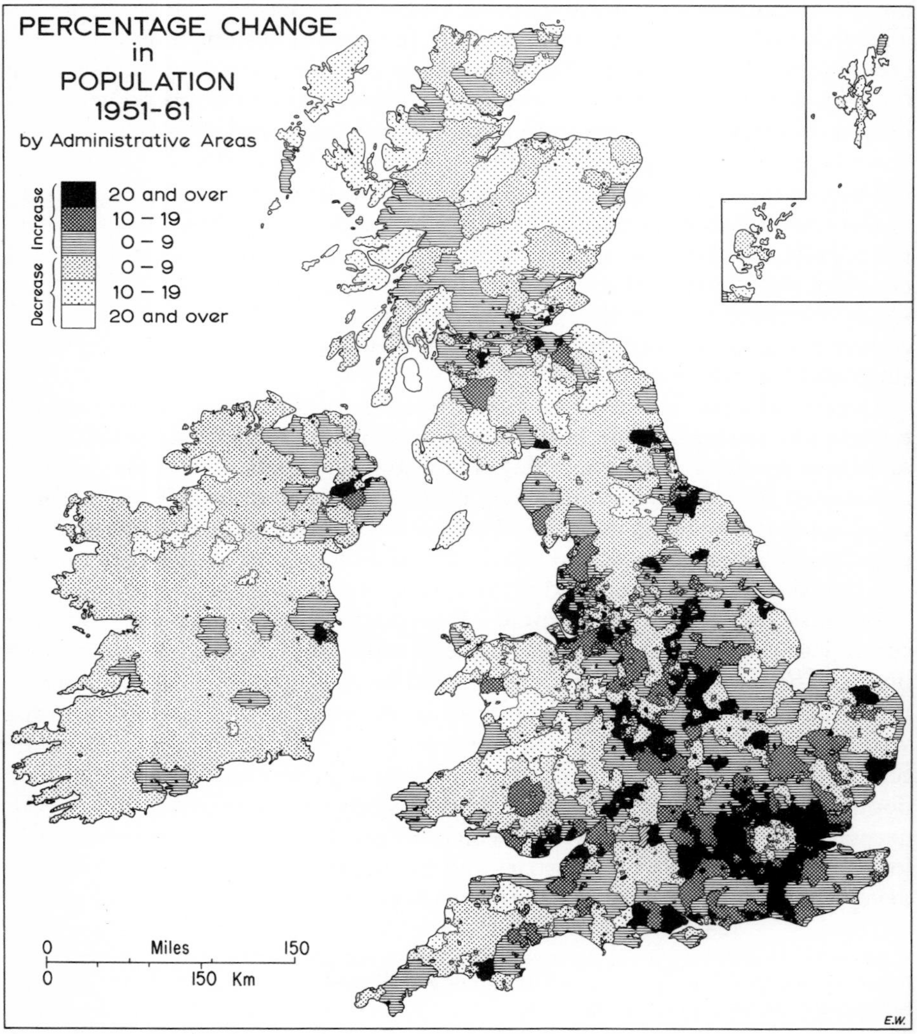

FIG. 219. Population changes in the British Isles 1951–61
Map specially prepared by the Geography Maps Office of the London School of Economics.

encies in the intercensal period of 1921–31 may be described as showing continued rural depopulation, virtual or actual cessation of growth, and in cases even a decrease in the population of industrial regions and towns in the north compensated for by the continued phenomenal growth of London and of the development of the London region as a whole as a manufacturing area.

As a result of these interwar changes many of Britain's older industrial areas, associated notably with parts of the coalfields approaching exhaustion, suffered severely from unemployment. They became and for a time were known as Depressed Areas. When Government decided to take positive action to help them, they were designated and remain 'Development Areas' and are officially demarcated with additions made from time to time. Parts of central Scotland, the northwest and northeast coalfields, parts of Lancashire, North Wales coalfield and South Wales are the chief areas.

The main areas of really marked population increase were Greater London and Greater Birmingham. It was said that industry was moving south—actually what was happening was the establishment of new industries and new factories in the south and Midlands whereas in the older industrial areas obsolescent and abandoned factories were not being replaced. This meant that in the older peripheral areas there was much unemployment and taxes collected from the business of the prosperous centre were being used to relieve distress there. The Report of the Royal Commission on the Geographical Location of the Industrial Population (Barlow Report) recommended that there should be a national plan to secure a wider distribution of industry. This dispersal of industry was in fact secured by the wartime conditions of 1939–45 and is now part of national policy. It is made easy for manufacturers to establish new factories or industries in the 'Development Areas'. Despite official deterrents the results of both the Census of 1951 and that of 1961 showed a continued increase in the 'belt' stretching from Lancashire on the one hand to London on the other.[1]

The population of the Irish Republic decreased from 2 971 992 in 1926 to 2 965 854 in 1936 and to 2 960 593 in 1951, the period 1946–51 showing a slight increase. In the decade 1951–61 there was again a decrease—to 2 814 703 in 1961, rising slightly to 2 884 002 according to the Census of April 1966.

At first it might be thought that Ireland offers a different picture from Britain. But that is not the case. Ireland is essentially rural, and so has suffered depopulation in the same way as all rural parts of the British Isles. But as the diagram (Fig. 220) shows, depopulation was continuous from the decade 1841–51 to 1921 and was initiated by the great famines of the 1840s.

1. There has been much discussion on the reality or otherwise of this 'belt'. See *Geogrl J.* **103**, 1944, 49–72; also A. E. Smailes, in *Geography*, **29**, 1944, 41–51.

One of the remarkable features of recent years, especially from 1954, has been the influx into Britain of large numbers of British West Indians of Negro stock, especially Jamaicans. By 1963 Britain had a black population, many Negro, of some 300 000. As citizens of the British Commonwealth they were free to come and go. Large numbers of Pakistanis and Indians also came to Britain. They have been absorbed into the British economic system, especially as manual workers, in transport undertakings, and into the medical services. Numerous Hungarians fled to Britain in 1956 to escape the Russian military control, their numbers being added to the numerous Poles and other Europeans who had found refuge or political asylum in Britain during and after the Second World War.

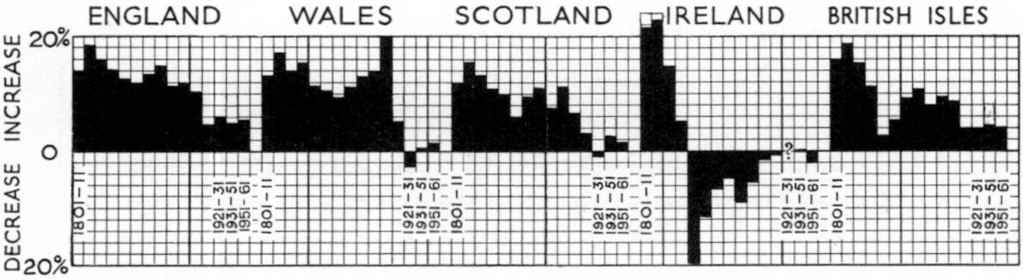

Fig. 220. Population changes in the British Isles, 1801–1961, showing decennial changes

Population

YEAR	BRITISH ISLES	ENGLAND AND WALES	SCOTLAND	IRELAND
1801	—	8 892 536	1 608 420	—
1811	—	10 164 256	1 805 864	—
1821	20 893 584	12 000 236	2 091 521	6 801 827
1831	24 028 584	13 896 797	2 364 386	7 767 401
1841	26 730 929	15 914 148	2 620 184	8 196 597
1851	27 390 629	17 927 609	2 888 742	6 574 278
1861	28 927 485	20 066 224	3 062 294	5 798 967
1871	31 484 661	22 712 266	3 360 018	5 412 377
1881	34 884 848	25 974 439	3 735 573	5 174 836
1891	37 732 922	29 002 525	4 025 647	4 704 750
1901	41 458 721	32 527 843	4 472 103	4 458 775
1911	45 213 347	36 070 492	4 760 904	4 381 951
1921	—	37 886 699	4 882 497	4 228 533[1]
1931	—	39 952 377	4 842 554	
1951	53 327 333	43 744 924	5 095 969	4 329 587
1961	55 487 924	46 071 604	5 178 490	4 237 830
1968 (estimate)	—	48 593 000	5 187 500	—

[1] Census year 1926 for Irish Free State and Northern Ireland.

Decennial population changes (percentages)

YEAR	BRITISH ISLES	ENGLAND AND WALES	SCOTLAND	IRELAND
1801–11	—	14.00	12.3	—
1811–21	—	18.06	15.8	—
1821–31	15.03	15.80	13.0	14.3
1831–41	11.24	14.27	10.8	5.5
1841–51	2.47	12.65	10.2	−19.8
1851–61	5.62	11.90	6.0	−11.8
1861–71	8.55	13.21	9.7	−6.7
1871–81	10.80	14.36	11.2	−4.4
1881–91	8.16	11.65	7.8	−9.1
1891–1901	9.89	12.17	11.1	−5.2
1901–11	9.04	10.89	6.5	−1.7
1911–21	—	4.93	2.6	−3.4[1]
1921–31	—	5.16	−0.8	
1931–51	—	9.5 (4.75)	5.2 (2.6)	2.4[2]
1951–61	4.1	5.3	1.6	−2.1

[1] 1911–1926. [2] 1926–1951.

Owing to the Second World War there was no Census in 1941. The figures in the penultimate row thus refer to twenty years (ten-year period in brackets).

Number of passengers of British nationality leaving and entering the United Kingdom for and from countries outside Europe (thousands)[1]

	1909–13	1926	1930	1933	1938	1946	1950	1960	1967
Emigrants:									
To the Commonwealth	276.3	132.3	59.2	20.8	29.0	110.2	112.9	79.4	203.1
To foreign countries		166.6	32.9	5.5	5.1	56.6	17.3	9.2	59.8
Immigrants:									
From the Commonwealth	104.3	39.1	51.4	44.6	32.6	54.1	56.1	74.3	114.1
From foreign countries		12.0	14.8	14.7	8.0	9.0	10.0	5.9	32.2

[1] From *Statistical Abstract of United Kingdom* and *Annual Abstract of Statistics*, 1926 was a peak year for emigration after the First World War, 1933 a low record.

25
The evolution of the form and functions of British villages and towns

It seems clear that the settlements of Stone Age man were restricted to those areas where the natural vegetation cover was easily cleared (see p. 625). That such areas were available on the comparatively open belts, such as the chalk downlands of southeastern England, is reasonably certain (but see p. 119), though it has been argued also that there were other sites, notably gravel plains in the valleys, which were equally attractive.[1] As our knowledge of postglacial climatic fluctuations increases it becomes clear that in pre-Roman Britain when Neolithic man and his successors occupied the land the climate of these islands was more humid than at present, and that water supply in upland situations did not present the difficulty that it would do today. The Briton at the time of the first Roman raids relied upon the hoe for scratching the surface of the small square fields which he had cleared on the uplands or on the valley gravels, and this field system appears to have continued during the Roman occupation. The network of straight roads linking strategically sited towns developed by the Romans bore no relation to the agricultural land-use pattern of the earlier inhabitants. When the Romans withdrew, the earlier Anglo-Saxon invaders came as warring conquerors, who seem almost to have eliminated the Romano-British inhabitants, although this is debatable. But later they appear as land hungry settlers, penetrating by water routes to almost every part of Lowland Britain. By early Saxon times the normal human settlement had five primary requirements. (*a*) A supply of water; (*b*) an area of good lowland grazing, e.g. meadows on alluvium or by the side of streams; (*c*) Drier undulating land suitable for ploughing; (*d*) an area of common rough hill pasture for grazing. Such comprised a typical valley settlement; (*e*) a woodland area for fuel and building material. In the broader valleys the settlements would be on the banks of the stream, and the land proper to the village would extend from the damp pastures along the banks of the stream to the high ground on one side of the valley. The villages might be at intervals of a mile or more along the banks with a corresponding line along the other side of the stream. In the case of narrower valleys the village itself might

1. E. T. Leeds, *Geography*, **14**, 1928, 527–35. Probably, as suggested on p. 125, the alder woodland of these damp areas was more easily attacked by men armed only with stone tools than oakwood or other types of forest.

bridge the stream and its domain extend from the hills on one side to the hills on the other. In other cases a line of villages might be situated along a line of springs issuing from the hillside, the pasture land occupying the lower ground to the one side, the ploughed land the rough pasture the higher ground to the other, giving what are known today as spring line villages.[1] It is thus clear how the vill or smallest unit of administration came into existence. It was the land proper to a single village or settlement and its boundaries were naturally so arranged that it included areas of the three types of land mentioned.[2] With the reintroduction of Christianity into Britain at the end of the sixth century A.D., it was natural that a church should be added to the existing settlements, and the vill took on a new aspect; it became the parish, the smallest unit of our existing administrative system and originally a purely ecclesiastical area. It was the district served by the parish church and indeed the area from which tithe was payable to a given church, or in the first instance to the priest in charge. It should be noted that as the number of churches increased, so the size of parishes decreased. Examples are numerous in southeastern England of the apparently curious shape of parish boundaries which are due to the old-time necessity of including with the parish sufficient areas of the land of different types required by the rural economy of the period. Excellent examples are afforded in the south of Surrey in the parishes of Wootton, Abinger, etc. With the development of the manorial system sometimes the vill or township coincided not only with the parish but also with the manor. Sometimes, however, the vill had become divided into two or more manors, each of which had a parish church and so each became a distinct parish. Often the component parts in the original vill retained the old name, distinguished, however, by the addition of an adjective—such as the name of the lord of the manor or the saint to which the church was dedicated. Many of the picturesque names in the lowland counties of England are thus derived.[3]

It is clear that the typical arrangement just described would be characteristic of predominantly arable areas, but it must be remembered that large tracts of the wetter lowlands of England remained for long under damp oakwood. Probably the earliest settlements in these were mere clearings in the forest, that is, isolated homesteads. Later much of the damp oakwood became replaced by permanent pasture, and to this day in England the pastoral counties are characterised by disseminated settlements or iso-

1. Both types of village correspond to what some continental authors have called 'wet point villages'. It is only in the wet marshy district, e.g. plain of Somerset, that there is the necessity for the human settlement to occupy a drier point than the surrounding marshy lowlands, giving what may be termed a 'dry point' village. See B. M. Swainson, 'Rural settlement in Somerset', *Geography*, **20**, 1935, 112–24.

2. Vill seems a better term for these units than township, which tends to suggest an urban area.

3. For example, Compton Bassett, Berwick Bassett, Winterbourne Bassett (Wiltshire), Wiggenhall St Germans, Wiggenhall St Peter, Wiggenhall St Mary the Virgin, Wiggenhall St Mary Magdalene (Norfolk).

lated farms, whereas arable areas are characterised by the nucleated village.[1] Even when a number of the pioneer settlers were close together and formed a hamlet the population of the whole area would remain scanty and probably also poor. Not one of these hamlets or small vills would be sufficiently rich to support a church and a priest, and in such areas of Britain

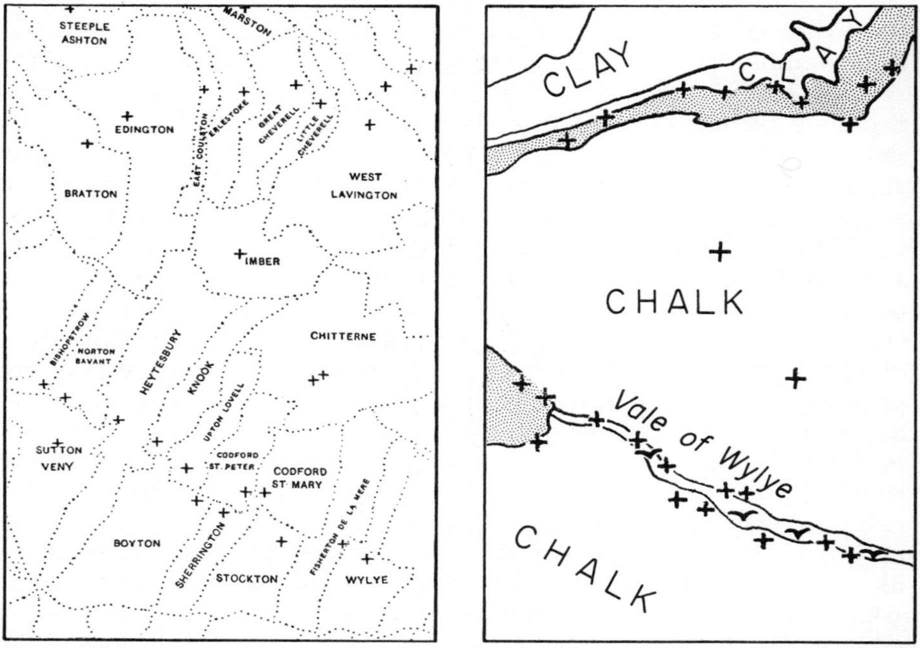

FIG. 221. Wiltshire parishes

Illustrating a line of valley settlements along the Vale of Wylye, with the village (the cross represents the parish church) near the stream in each case. In the north are 'spring line' villages along the outcrop of the water-bearing Upper Greensand on the southern side of the Vale of Pewsey. (Scale 4 miles = 1 inch.)

as Cheshire and Shropshire, and the Marches of Wales, a church had to serve a large area of this sparsely peopled country, and a parish came to consist of as many as ten to twenty of the small vills or townships. Not infrequently these larger churches, collegiate churches as they were afterwards known, had two rectors; probably the duty of one being to tour the large parish.

1. See P. W. Bryan, *Man's Adaptation of Nature*, University of London Press, 1932. But in many cases when it was supposed that the isolated homestead was the original form of settlement, the supposition has been disproved. By way of contrast for different areas see E. G. Bowen, 'A study of rural settlements in south-west Wales', *Geog. Teacher,* **13**, 1926; H. King, 'The geography of settlements in south-west Lancashire', *Geography,* **14**, 1927, 193–200, and *J. Manchester Geog. Soc.,* **39–40**, 137–44; Dorothy Sylvester, 'The hill villages of England and Wales', *Geogrl J.,* **110**, 1948, 76–93. See also H. J. E. Peake, 'Geographical aspects of administrative areas', *Geography,* **15**, 1930, 531–46, and H. Thorpe, 'The green villages of County Durham, *Inst. Br. Geogr.,* **15**, 1949, 155–80.

Such large parishes of the west seem to have been designed to provide the maximum of convenience to their population. Although they are large they are usually roughly circular or oval without awkward prolongations, and the parish church is generally to be found near the centre. On the other hand, there are large, and often irregularly shaped, parishes in the arable eastern counties due to the action of lords of the manor. Where one man held a lordship over two or three adjoining manors he tended, for the sake of economy, to combine these and to be satisfied with one church and one priest for the whole of his estate. Some of the still more irregularly shaped

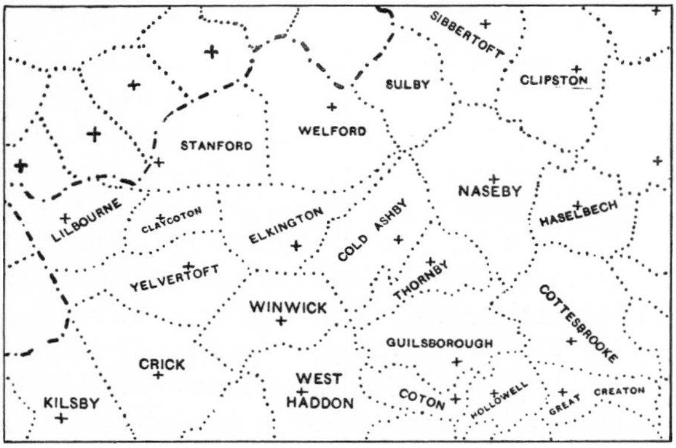

FIG. 222. Regular shaped parishes with the church and village centrally placed

Typical of the pasture lands of the Midlands and clay vales. (Scale 4 miles = 1 inch).

For a classification of these villages by type of site see S. H. Beaver, *The Land of Britain, Part 58, Northamptonshire.* Land Utilisation Survey, 1943, pp. 364–8.

and unwieldy parishes owe their origin to the action of the monasteries, who endeavoured to augment their incomes from tithes by combining parishes irrespective of their boundaries, grouping them around the parish church which belonged to the monastery. This practice seems to have been prohibited in 1123, but already by that time a number of large and awkwardly shaped parishes that contradict all rational geographical principles had been formed. Each had, of course, one parish church, and the churches which had previously been parish churches, and which were still included within the boundaries, became chapels or chapels of ease. Other chapels of ease were often erected in large and populous parishes.

The majority of villages found today had been established by 1086 and were recorded in the Domesday survey. Additions to the village pattern have been relatively few. Of more importance is that since that time many villages have been lost to the landscape. It is estimated that there are more than 1300 deserted villages in England, with two main concentrations appearing—namely the Inner Midlands of Buckinghamshire, Leicestershire, Northamptonshire, Nottinghamshire, Oxfordshire and Warwickshire, and an Eastern Margin of Lincolnshire, Norfolk, Suffolk and Yorkshire. Thus in Northamptonshire and Oxfordshire respectively there are 80 and 100 recorded lost villages. Desertion has occurred at all times and for a variety of reasons. But in midland England the main period was between *c.* 1350 and *c.* 1450. In this area deserted villages were not the direct result of the Black Death, but were related to the economic depression that followed the plague. Cereal prices declined, and there was a movement from arable to sheep-grazing, the result of the high price of wool. Villages which had formerly been arable-orientated were depopulated to provide grassland for flocks.[1]

Most of the parishes of Britain are of very ancient origin, and retained their boundaries until a little over a century ago, when in the early part of the nineteenth century the growth of population, consequent upon the Industrial Revolution, necessitated the frequent carving up of very populous parishes into smaller units. Even this practice was not general until after the passing of an Act in 1856. It should be noticed that until Tudor times the parish had been a purely ecclesiastical unit, and it was not until the decay of the manor following the Black Death and the first agrarian revolution that the parish became a civil unit. When parish councils were created by the Local Government Act of 1894, the civil parishes almost invariably coincided with the ecclesiastical parishes. County councils were given power to subdivide large parishes, and although the power was not very widely exercised,[2] where it was, the new civil parishes were made to follow the ancient boundaries of the vills or townships. This was done, for example, in Cheshire.[3]

Returning now to the old vills or townships—these were grouped into hundreds which normally consisted of ten or twelve townships, at least in southeastern England.[4] In the northeastern counties of England under Danish influence larger units were formed known as wapentakes. Many of the old hundreds are mentioned in the Domesday survey. Some of them are named after spots remote from villages lying in the middle of waste land; and one may look upon such a hundred as consisting of a ring of vills or parishes having a large area of common grazing land in the middle of which was a convenient meeting place. Others take their names from larger villages which had been growing into market towns. A meeting place in the midst of waste land proved to be less convenient than a meeting place in a large village, and undoubtedly many of the old market towns originated in this way. It has been suggested that when the hundreds take their names

1. See M. W. Beresford, *The Lost Villages of England*, 1954; also W. G. Hoskins, *The Making of the English Landscape*, 1955, pp. 93–5.

2. For although alterations were made to some 6000 parishes, the changes were in most cases very small.

3. See the *Historical Atlas of Cheshire*, ed. D. Sylvester, Chester, 1958.

4. Sometimes believed, at least in some cases, to have comprised roughly a hundred families.

from waste land it was a common practice for the men of the townships to meet there and sort out their cattle just as is done at the present day at the spring round-up in the great pastoral countries of the newer lands of the world. Disputes were settled by the hundred court, and hence the association of the hundred court later with market towns. The areas of the hundreds became irregular in just the same way as did the areas of the parishes, and gradually the hundred as a unit became less and less important, and local administration was based on the parish and on the county. After the Napoleonic Wars problems arose which were beyond the powers of parishes to solve, and a new unit came into existence which was the Poor Law Union created by the Act of 1834. The Unions were devised in a haphazard way regardless of geographical conditions, with the result that in less than a hundred years they have entirely disappeared. Their place has now been taken by Rural Districts.

The geographical counties of England are also of very early origin.[1] The majority go back to the time of the Saxons and a large number at any rate were in existence at the time of King Alfred. The counties south of the Thames, broadly speaking, correspond to old kingdoms. Thus in the south-east of England the Anglo-Saxon Kingdom of Kent (Cantii) occupied an area roughly conterminous with Kent. It is to be observed that the areas of these old counties are natural geographical units, and their boundaries are natural geographical features. The frontiers particularly used were the sea, a river, a line of hills—such as the chalk scarp—a tract of dense almost impenetrable woodland or marshland, or an area of barren heath. Thus Kent stretched to the sea and the river on the north, to the sea on the east and to the south as far as the great impenetrable mass of woodland which then occupied the Weald. It must be remembered of these natural barriers that the woodlands have disappeared, even the areas of barren heathland have been largely utilised. Another example is afforded by Sussex, which represents the territory of downland held by the South Saxons (Regni) and which was cut off by the woodland of the Weald from the rest of England. As the woods of the Weald were gradually cleared and settled so that territory was divided between Kent and Sussex. Norfolk and Suffolk form an interesting example of a natural region, occupied in pre-Roman days by the Iceni. It was bounded by the sea on the north and on the east; by the marshland of the Fens on the west; by the thick forests, which must have covered the London Clay lowlands of Essex, on the south. The only landward entry into this region was the narrow belt of chalk downland stretching away to the southwest.[2] When the territory of the Iceni was invaded and settled

1. The fifty-two ancient or geographical counties of England and Wales should not be confused with the sixty-two administrative counties which themselves exclude the eighty-three county boroughs or towns with the status of a county.

2. Along which was the Icknield Way (cf. Ic(k)eni Way, a possible, but unproved derivation) crossed by a succession of dykes or protective earthworks.

by the East Anglians they divided it into the North Folk and the South Folk —hence the modern counties of Norfolk and Suffolk.

Turning to the midland counties of England, dense, damp oak woodland covered their lowlands to a much later date. As we have just seen, this woodland was only gradually cleared and occupied by settlers. It would seem that the Midlands of England were arbitrarily divided into shires or counties in the tenth century in the course of the wars between Wessex and the Danes. The method followed seems to have been that certain leading

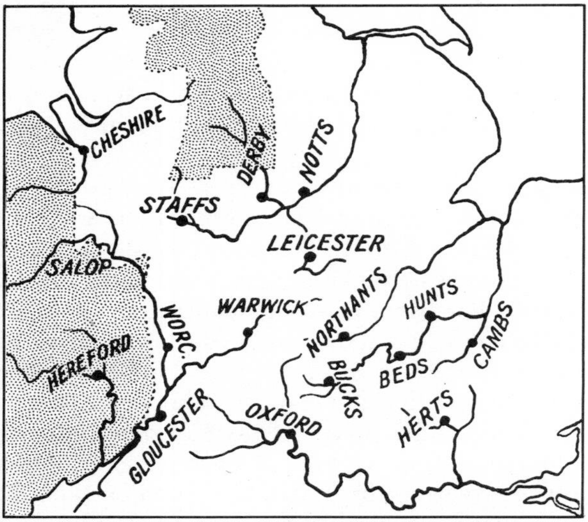

FIG. 223. Map showing the Midland 'shires' or counties of England grouped about the county town, in each case on a navigable river (after C. B. Fawcett)

settlements or military strongholds, such as a Danish borough,[1] were chosen as capitals of the shires, and around these were grouped such areas as at that time could conveniently be administered. Thus the midland shires of England are not the natural geographical units that the southern and eastern counties are. One notices how many of these midland shires are still named after the principal town. The very names of the old southern and eastern county kingdoms do not need the addition of the word shire, and the name of the county town often bears little or no connection with that of the name of the county, whereas in the Midlands of England we have Bedford, Bedfordshire; Northampton, Northamptonshire; Oxford, Oxfordshire, Warwick, Warwickshire; and so on. It is very interesting to notice how many of these artificially arranged midland shires are still awkward

1. The majority on navigable rivers, emphasising the importance of river transport in low land, still largely forested.

administrative units, and present difficulties in administration even to the present day which are not found in those counties based on the natural geographical units of the old kingdoms.[1]

Returning now to the development of settlements, we may take first of all purely rural areas: that is areas which have remained rural to the present day. If one looks upon a village as a convenient point of settlement from

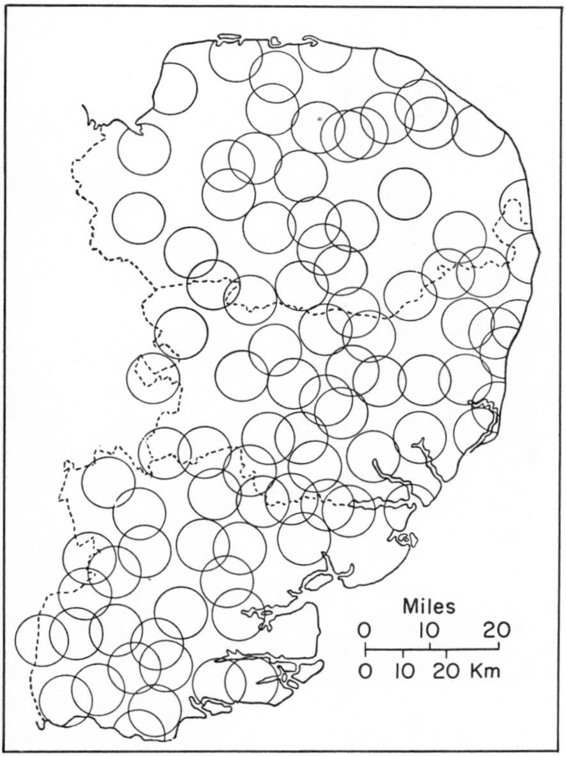

FIG. 224. The medieval market towns of East Anglia

Showing each with an arbitrary limit of 6.4 kilometres (4 miles) radius (after R. E. Dickinson).

which the land of the surrounding vill was cultivated then one gets the idea of the primitive village as an essentially agricultural settlement. The first requirement of the people would obviously be a market centre to serve a small collection of vills, where they could exchange their commodities with one another, could sell the surplus that they had, and buy such of the simple

1. An immense amount of information is to be gained by a study of place names. Many county volumes have been published by the Place Name Society, and a convenient general guide is *The Oxford Dictionary of English Place-Names*, by E. Ekwall, Oxford University Press, 2nd edn, 1940.

necessities from the outside world as the requirements of early days demanded. But there was already an organisation which required the federation of eight or a dozen vills and this was the hundred. So it is often the case that one of the larger villages became the market town or centre of the commercial life of a hundred. It is an obvious step from this to the same town becoming the administrative centre of the hundred, e.g. for purposes of the

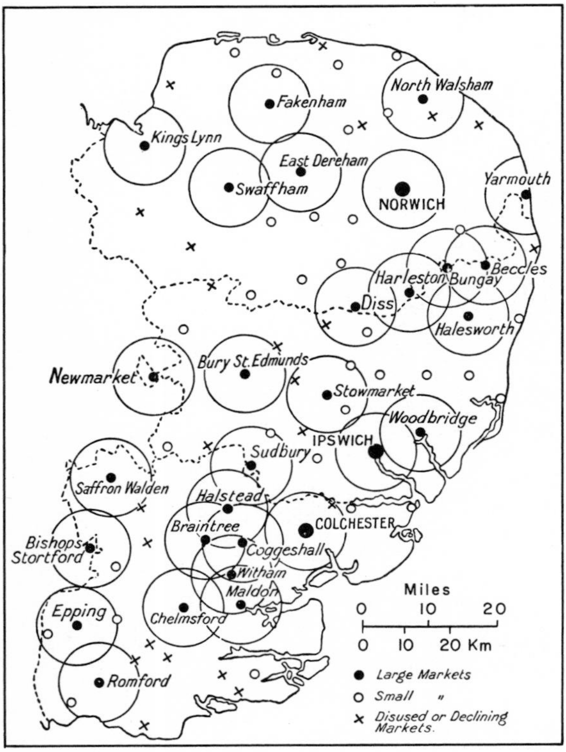

FIG. 225. The market towns of East Anglia, about 1834

Showing each with a limit of 10 kilometres (6 miles) radius (after R. E. Dickinson).

administration of the law. In other cases the administrative function may have preceded the development of a town as a market or commercial centre.

The market towns of medieval England were closely spaced. The visit to the market town had to be made on foot, or if a carriage or other conveyance were available the condition of the tracks or roads of the countryside was so execrable that the radius served by a market town was not very appreciably increased. Although the use of rivers may have been important in appropriate cases it is clear that in the more settled rural parts of England between 11 and 16 kilometres (seven to ten miles) was regarded as the proper distance between marketing centres. Indeed, there is an old law still in existence which makes it illegal to establish a market within 10.7 kilometres ($6\frac{2}{3}$ miles) of an existing legal market. In an interesting study of the distribution and functions of the urban settlements of East Anglia, R. E. Dickinson[1] suggested that the maximum range of influence of the medieval market was about 6.4 kilometres (four miles), and he drew a map to show an arbitrary market area of 6.4 kilometres (four miles) radius to each medieval town in East Anglia (Fig. 224).

Not all towns grew naturally. In the Middle Ages, many 'new towns' were established where previously there had been no settlement.[2] In England and Wales there are 256 recorded 'new towns'. Over 90 per cent of these came into existence between 1066 and 1350, a period of economic growth and colonisation. During these three centuries trade, industry and population were growing sufficiently to permit the siting of 'new towns' between the established market centres. Landlords were aware of the value in terms of increased rent-roll of having merchants and traders centred at one place on their land. In Wales the majority of plantations were fortified, being associated with Edward I's Welsh campaigns, but they developed market functions simultaneously. Many of the 'new towns' prospered, and for example Caernarvon and Newcastle-under-Lyme, founded in 1283 and between 1154 and 1162 respectively, are today thriving centres. But not all 'new towns' were successful: of the 256 recorded plantations, 16 per cent were failures. Thus New Radnor in Radnorshire founded in 1257 is but a village today.

It is remarkable how long this primitive arrangement of marketing and administrative centres remained; and it was not until about the middle of the eighteenth century that changes occurred. The gradual development of road transport after about 1780 in particular resulted in the concentration of marketing in fewer towns due to the increased marketing radius which was possible. In the main, nodality, with ease of communications in different directions, was the factor which determined the survival of the fittest. In the early part of the nineteenth century it was possible to classify the market towns of the rural countryside into three groups, large, small and disused or rapidly declining (Fig. 225). This was the state of affairs in 1834 when the Poor Law Unions were brought into existence, and the market towns were constituted headquarters of the Poor Law Union districts and the seat of the Board of Guardians. But the bad designing of the unions soon became apparent; for there followed the great development of railways and the macadamisation of roads. People could easily go 12 or 15 kilometres (eight or ten miles) to or from their market town far more easily than their forefathers two or three generations ago could travel half that distance.

1. *Geography*, **17**, March 1932, 19–31; see also 'The town plans of East Anglia', *Geography*, **9**, 1934, 37–50.
2. M. W. Beresford, *New Towns of the Middle Ages*, 1967.

Roughly speaking, every alternate market town decayed, and the prosperity of the intervening ones increased. The remaining market towns were given what may be described as a new lease of life when they became the centres of the new rural districts. In the separate county parts of *The Land of Britain*, the Final Report of the Land Utilisation Survey, the distribution and functions of the agricultural markets are considered as they were in the 1930s. Broadly speaking, livestock markets, for example in the southwest, are closely spaced whereas grain and produce markets, as in East Anglia, draw from a much wider area. The reasons are obvious.

The early progress of towns in what are now industrial areas was, of course, similar. Early industrialisation seems to have been fostered by one or two main causes: (*a*) the inhabitants of the town tried to utilise for manufacture raw materials supplied to them by the visitors to the market; the rise of the woollen industry using the wool sold by local farmers is thus characteristic of Norwich and certain towns of East Anglia; (*b*) the inhabitants found that they could supply the needs of some of their neighbouring agriculturalists by goods made in their own centre. It would seem that the early trade in horseshoes and other small iron objects in Birmingham started in this way—with a supply to farmers in the local districts; the iron ore being available near at hand and charcoal for smelting it from the neighbouring forests. The cutlery industry of Sheffield may be cited as a similar instance. Natural advantages and a near-at-hand market for the produce were responsible for the inception of the industry. Thus, leaving on one side altogether the ports, a number of small manufacturing centres sprang up all over England. The Industrial Revolution and the flight of the industries to the coalfields resulted in the disappearance of many of these small industrial centres and in the immense development of others.

Functions of urban settlements

Here we may break off for a moment and consider what are the essential functions of a town or an urban settlement. Grouped into broad categories the functions may be described as follows:

(*a*) Commercial.
(*b*) Administrative.
(*c*) Industrial.
(*d*) Social.
(*e*) Residential.

A study of the urban settlements of the British Isles shows that the relative importance of these functions varies from town to town. Sometimes the one may be so important as to overshadow all the others. There are reasons why the study of the functions of a town are of the utmost importance, particularly at the present day. One of these reasons is that it is perfectly clear that town planning must be varied not only according to the site which is available, but according to the functions of the town concerned. Let us attempt, therefore, to analyse in slightly more detail each function.

(*a*) *Commercial.* The function is concerned primarily with the buying and selling of goods. The larger the town the greater the cleavage or difference between wholesale and retail. In all the larger towns there is usually a definite commercial centre. It may be represented in the large market town of a rural county by the cattle market and its surrounds—the storehouses of the corn chandlers and of the vendors of agricultural implements. In a town of a different type it is represented by the closely spaced streets of large warehouses. But in either case the wholesale commercial centre is divorced from the retail shopping area. The growth of a town as a wholesale commercial centre depends above everything else on its nodality and its transport facilities. Under this heading comes naturally the relationship between the commercial centres of the larger towns and the railway and road systems on the one hand, and the facilities for the import of goods on the other. Thus in the larger ports we find the warehouses, representing the commercial centre, grouped near or around the docks.

(*b*) *Administrative.* For purposes of administration, particularly for administration applying to the whole county, undoubtedly one of the factors of greatest importance is ease of accessibility to all parts of the area concerned from the centre chosen. Quite frequently the county town has ceased to be ideal from this point of view—especially when it is essential to retain vital and immediate contact with some large centre on the borders of the county. Thus the county offices of both Lanarkshire and Dunbartonshire are in Glasgow. For many purposes Kingston-on-Thames and not Guildford is the county town of Surrey. Much of the business of the county of Essex is conducted from its London office.

(*c*) *Industrial.* It is important to realise how many of our larger towns are essentially industrial, whilst they are neither commercial nor administrative in an important sense. The reverse is also true. Manchester and Leeds are primarily the commercial and to some extent administrative centres, as well as in some degree social centres, of a manufacturing area in each case, rather than being primarily industrial. We have considered elsewhere in this book the requirements of industrial centres, and these points need not be reiterated: but just as the commercial and the administrative offices of a large town are frequently collected together in definite areas, so also—even more markedly—are the industrial works. Provided the essential requirements of easy receipt of raw material and easy despatch of finished articles are satisfied then the town planner can do much to direct industrial development round an existing town in those ways which will best serve the whole community.

(*d*) *Social.* The social functions of an urban settlement are not always fully realised or given their proper importance. Women form more than half the population of the British Isles, and it is calculated that over three-quarters of the money passed over counters in retail stores is passed over by women. In other words, women do the shopping. Yet how many women pay a visit to a town with the purely utilitarian motive of shopping and nothing else? This question might have a double question mark after it. For is it not true to say that the choice of the town and the choice of the route are not infrequently determined by the attractive nature of the displays in the shop windows; the possibility of a lunch in a pleasant restaurant with music, and a visit to a cinema where light and life—real and unreal—afford a relaxation from the daily round and common task? In the larger towns or for longer journeys, such as a trip to London, there may be the added attraction of the theatre. The hotel and the club must be near at hand. It is particularly in the evening that the town exercises its social influence over men and women together. This conjunction of the social services is of the utmost importance, because in town planning one cannot divorce the shopping centre from the centres of amusement such as we have described. What is the quintessence of the importance of the West End of London and of other cities which boast a West End? Or of Broadway and Fifth Avenue in New York? In certain towns another factor of importance comes in and that is the influence of the church. No one who has lived in a smaller cathedral city can fail to appreciate the importance of this factor and its influence. In some areas schools and colleges exert a somewhat comparable influence.

It is often forgotten that there are large numbers of towns in the British Isles where the social influence is paramount, and where the fostering of the social influences becomes the main industry of the town. This is, of course, the case with seaside resorts and with inland spas. With all her richness in scenic beauty and historic remains Britain has not realised the full possibilities of what has now come to be called the tourist traffic or 'tourism' (see above, p. 618). For example, how many British seaside resorts have so far developed their attractions in the winter months that one may unhesitatingly go for a weekend being assured of a lively and sustained period of relaxation from daily business? Here the modern generation, not unreasonably, demands things on a large and lavish scale. Nothing could be more miserable than the seaside resort with three-quarters, perhaps all, of its places of amusement closed for the winter; and nothing could be more attractive than a fine pavilion—well lit, with music, food, and a view of the sea—in the winter months. In the preceding chapters of this book, it will be found that a number of quite large towns have scarcely been mentioned. They have little or no concern with industry, they are not ports nor commercial nor administrative centres. They are in fact essentially social-residential cities and towns. A leading member is Bournemouth—the youngest large town in Britain; others include Harrogate, Bath, Buxton (spas); Scarborough, Cromer, Margate, Eastbourne, Torquay, Newquay,

Llandudno, Blackpool and Douglas (I. of Man) (seaside resorts). A pioneer study of their evolution was made by E. W. Gilbert (*Scott. Geogr. Mag.*, **55**, 1939, 16–35), and he has since analysed the development of Brighton in detail (*Geogrl J.*, **114**, 1949, 30–53).

(*e*) *Residential.* There are some towns which are mainly residential. They are either dormitories for the large cities such, for example, as many of the smaller towns in a ring round London, or they may be the residential town for an industrial area, as Newcastle-under-Lyme is for the once smoky Potteries towns of the North Staffordshire coalfield. But a fact, again too often forgotten at the present day, is that there are very few areas which can be purely residential in this sense. They must either have absolutely first-class facilities for communication with the larger centres, or they must develop their own social life. Expensive housing estate schemes and garden city suburb schemes have proved failures for this very reason; and here arises a big question which the Britisher has not yet decided. His choice at present is between the semidetached villa with the little strip of garden where he may amuse himself in the evenings, but from which he has to face daily his half-hour's or his hour's journey to and from his business, and the flat in a large block where he has at hand the social attractions of the city, including the public parks with their beds of flowers, probably so superior to anything that he could have produced in his own little garden had he been a dweller in the suburbs.

This disquisition on the functions of urban settlements has been rather a lengthy one; but it is a subject to which more and more thought is being given in England. For a true interpretation of trends is a necessary prelude to a successful planning for the future.

Town and country planning

It is true that a town or city in the fullest sense of the term has all its functions fully developed. Fifty years ago the late Professor C. B. Fawcett, in a stimulating little book,[1] outlined a scheme for the division of England and Wales into provinces, each province, of course, with a provincial capital. It is clear that he had in mind the necessity of a provincial capital having fully developed all the functions above outlined for towns.

When Fawcett wrote, it seemed unlikely that Britain would ever be divided into provinces and such was the comment made by us in the first

1. *The Provinces of England*, recently edited by W. G. East and reissued, 1960.

edition of this book. The outbreak of the Second World War and the imminent danger of invasion led to the division of the country into Civil Defence Regions each with a Commissioner representing the Central Government and with headquarters in a centrally placed city or regional capital. The regions were quickly adopted by many government departments for their own purposes, with this remarkable difference—that each department, and frequently individual divisions within a department, decided for itself the number, boundaries, and capitals of its regions. When the war came to an end the regions or provinces were firmly established and civil servants allotted by their departments to the regions carried in many cases the title 'provincial'—for example the Provinicial Land Commissioner of the Ministry of Agriculture—or in other cases 'regional' such as the Regional Planning Officer. Most departments recognise about nine or ten provinces for England; Wales forms at least one other, whilst Scotland for many purposes is divided into four. A comparative view of the many different regional divisions adopted up to the time he wrote has been given by E. W. Gilbert (*Geogrl J.*, **94**, 1939, 29–44).

Some of the provinces suggest themselves with their provincial capitals, others are far from satisfactory. For example some parts of the Southwestern Province are more difficult to reach from Bristol, the provincial capital, than from London. Similarly although East Anglia is a natural province, its obvious capital Norwich is less conveniently situated in many respects than Cambridge, which several ministries use for the purpose. Cambridge has the advantage of easier and quicker access from London, yet Norwich has the natural attributes of a provincial capital. Centrally situated on the East Anglian plateau, it is even so a port. Its large cattle, sheep, and pig markets point it out as the natural capital of a predominantly agricultural area; and it is, of course, the administrative centre of the large county of Norfolk. It has developed manufactures of two main types: the food industries utilising the produce of the farmers of the region; and side by side with them the manufacture of agricultural implements and such things as wire netting which are required in quantity by a farming community. In other cases its industries have undergone an interesting process of evolution. When the woollen and worsted industries departed to the coalfields, manufacture of boots and shoes—of recent years fancy shoes for women—was deliberately introduced. The totality of its civic and religious life, the intense local patriotism, the extent and variety of its shopping centres, and its amusement facilities leave no doubt as to the importance of the city as a social centre.

The study of towns and their zones of influence or 'urban hinterlands' has become of great practical importance in connection with physical planning and reconstruction following the Second World War. In a pioneer study of Leeds and Bradford some years ago, Professor R. E. Dickinson showed the complexity of the problem—that there might be tracts of country relying on one centre for certain purposes, on another for other purposes.[1] In the Land Utilisation Survey's Report on Hampshire, F. H. W. Green paid special attention to public road services in determining urban hinterlands or 'umlands', and he developed this idea when he became Maps Officer to the Ministry of Town and Country Planning (a Ministry created in 1943, but merged into Housing and Local Government in 1951). On the basis of bus services, he demarcated the whole of England and Wales into 'urban hinterlands'. The main criticism of the method is that the picture can be quickly and radically changed by simple alteration of the bus services provided.[2]

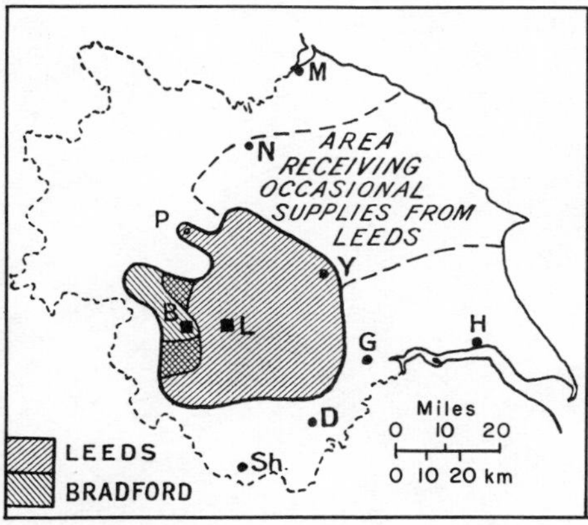

FIG. 226. The zones of influence of Leeds and Bradford as distributing centres

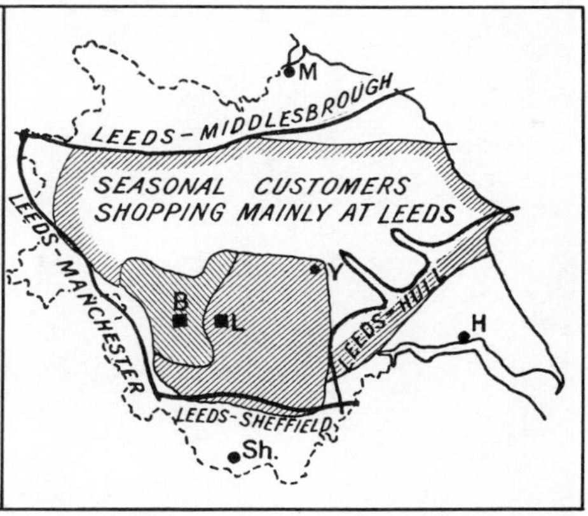

FIG. 227. The zones of influence of Leeds and Bradford as market or shopping centres

The heavy lines mark lines of equal accessibility or time by train of the two towns mentioned in each case.

A practical attempt to overcome the disadvantages of a long journey to work was initiated by the Government after the Second World War in two ways. One was by encouraging industry and consequent development in some of the smaller towns, the other was by the deliberate creation of a dozen New Towns—a ring around London in Crawley, Bracknell, Stevenage, Hemel Hempstead, Welwyn, Hatfield, Harlow and Basildon; at Corby; Aycliffe and Peterlee in Durham, Cwmbran in South Wales, East Kilbride and

1. "The regional functions and zones of influence of Leeds and Bradford', *Geography,* **15**, 1930, 548–57. Here Leeds is the regional capital, Bradford the great manufacturing city. For a modern treatment of this theme see A. J. Brown, 'What is the Leeds Region?', in *Leeds and its Region.* British Association for the Advancement of Science, 1967, pp. 200–14.

2. F. H. W. Green, 'Urban hinterlands in England and Wales', *Geogrl J.*, **114**, 1950, 64–88. See also Ordnance Survey 1/625,000 map of 'Local Accessibility', 1955. A more general treatment is that given by A. E. Smailes, 'The urban mesh of England and Wales', *Trans. Inst. Br. Geogr.*, **11**, 1946, 87–101.

Cumbernauld near Glasgow, and Glenrothes in Fifeshire.[1] These were planned *ab initio* on what are usually called garden city lines with a spacious layout and a low density both of houses and people per square mile. The New Towns thus take part at least of their inspiration from the pioneer garden cities of Letchworth and Welwyn. They differ from garden suburbs (such as Hampstead Garden Suburb and Wythenshawe, Manchester)

PLATE 25. A 'New Town'—Hemel Hempstead, Hertfordshire

This illustrates the grafting of a New Town on to an older settlement. The New Town centre, with its blocks of buildings and its water garden, lies in the Gade valley. In 1969 the total population was 66 000, some 40 000 of whom were in the New Town section.

which are mainly residential. Elsewhere trading estates (i.e. estates where factory buildings are constructed for letting) have been used as nuclei of new or extended urban developments—as at Trafford Park (Manchester), which dates from 1902, Team Valley (Tyneside), and Slough (Greater London), which were developments mainly of the interwar years.

Side by side with such planned urban development has grown the national desire to preserve the best of the past, whether historic buildings

1. Others have since been added, notably Skelmersdale in Lancashire and Dawley, Shropshire (now called Telford). See Fig. 77.

(many now owned by the independent National Trust, or 'scheduled' as such by the Government) or the countryside—hence the activities of such bodies as the Council for the Protection of Rural England (CPRE) and the creation of National Parks under the official National Parks Commission.

Modern developments in town and country planning have also rendered it imperative to study more precisely the problems of rural population—including rural depopulation. Official figures show rather more than 80 per cent of the British population as 'urban', rather less than 20 per cent 'rural'. The rural population as officially defined is that living in Rural Districts which may include quite large towns (e.g. Didcot, the railway town in Berkshire). The truly rural population living in isolated farms or cottages, hamlets, and villages does not exceed about 10 per cent of the total. Here agricultural mechanisation may well lead to a further decrease in the labour force required, increased mobility by bicycle, motor-bicycle and car as well as by buses leads to a concentration of retail supply sources in the towns, the smaller families now usual may result in such small numbers of children in the villages that schools can no longer be kept open. Indeed the whole social structure of country life is threatened. The suggestion made by Stamp some years ago to distinguish in the rural populations three groups is now commonly used.[1] These groups are:

(*a*) The primary rural population of farmers, farm workers, and their families,
(*b*) The secondary rural population of those who exist to provide essential services to the first group,
(*c*) The adventitious rural population living in the country by choice.

It has been found that group (*c*) may be entirely absent in country valuable agriculturally, but less attractive residentially (such as large parts of the Fens), and that in such cases (*a*) and (*b*) are in the proportion of 2:1. In most cases it is found that a vigorous rural life—an active parish council, live social, religious, and educational institutions—often depends largely on the adventitious population, including retired people, hence its importance.

Conurbations

It has long been recognised that the British census figures gave a quite inadequate measure of the relative size and importance of the larger centres of population because the figures refer to the areas defined by local government boundaries. Actually the densely populated areas are contiguous and form continuous urban areas. One of the best known examples of this, of course, is that of Manchester and Salford. Thus the term conurbation—suggested by the late Sir Patrick Geddes—has come to be widely adopted.

1. *The Land of Britain, Its Use and Misuse*, first edition, p. 448.

Professor Fawcett defined a 'conurbation' as 'an area occupied by a continuous series of dwellings, factories, and other buildings, harbours, and docks, urban parks and playing fields, etc., which are not separated from

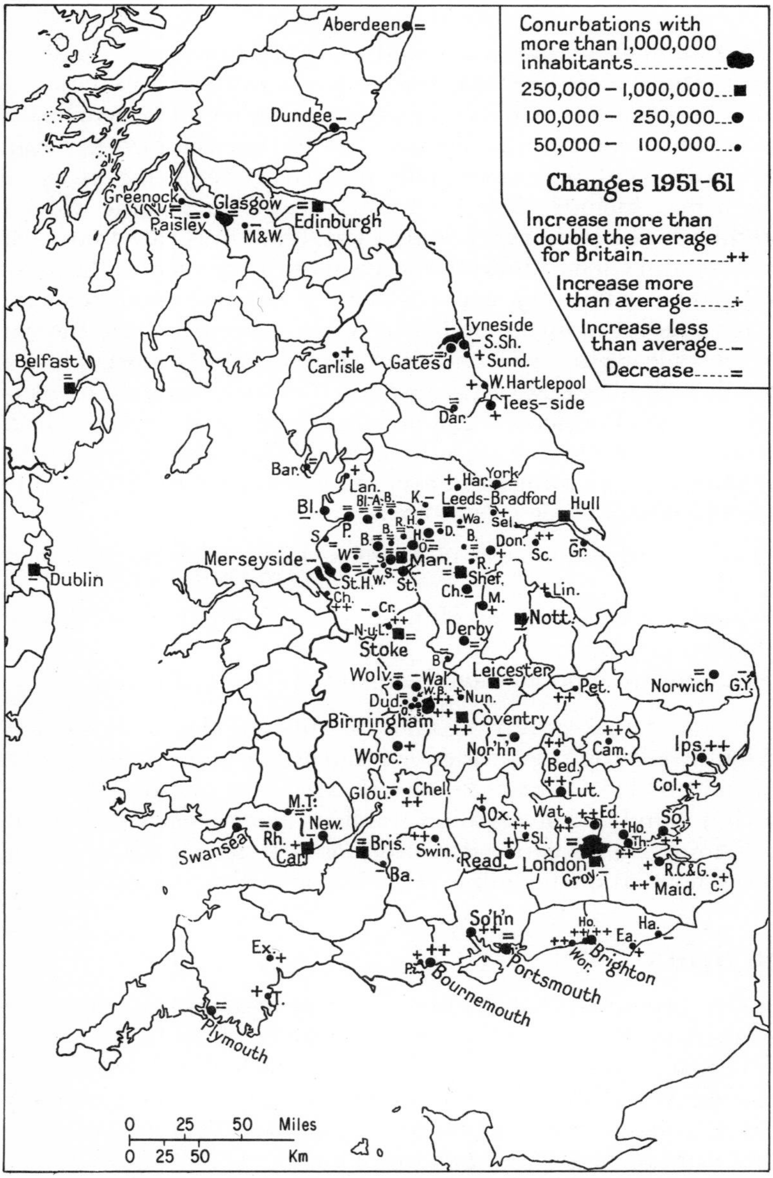

FIG. 228. The larger towns of Britain (all with more than 1 000 000 inhabitants are marked and County Boroughs over 50 000), and their population changes, 1951–61

each other by rural land; though in many cases in this country such an urban area includes enclaves of rural land which is still in agricultural occupation'. On this basis there were at the time of the 1931 Census no less than seven large conurbations in Great Britain, six of which had more than a million people; and there were also thirty other towns with more than 100 000 people.[1] It was found that 40 per cent of the total population of Britain was living in the seven 'million cities' or conurbations—half the total urban population. The Census of 1951 gave official recognition to each of these conurbations which were defined in terms of complete local government areas. The seven conurbations thus officially recognised are as follows:

1. Greater London, with an aggregate population of 8 346 137 in 1951, and covering some 1865 square kilometres (720 square miles). Separate consideration is given below to London (Chapter 26). The same area had 8 171 902 in 1961, and 7 764 000 in 1968.
2. Southeast Lancashire or Greater Manchester—with the continuous urban area of Manchester and Salford in the centre, and a number of smaller urban districts closely joined therewith, thus giving an inner ring with more than 1 million inhabitants. Round this, at a distance of from twelve to eighteen miles from the central point, is what may be called the Manchester ring: the towns of Bolton, Bury, Rochdale, Oldham, Stockport, etc., all being linked to the central core by regular bands of urban character. The total population in 1951 was 2 421 011 over an area of 982 square kilometres (379 square miles). It had increased to 2 427 000 in 1961, and 2 441 000 in 1968.
3. The West Midlands or Greater Birmingham and the Black Country. The city of Birmingham contains about half the total urban population in this total area of 694 square kilometres (268 square miles) and 2 236 723 people in 1951, increased to 2 344 000 in 1961, and to 2 425 000 in 1968.
4. The West Yorkshire conurbation, of which Leeds and Bradford are the two largest members, and which includes most of the woollen towns of the West Yorkshire coalfield, has a total area of 1243 square kilometres (480 square miles); its population of 1 692 190 rose to 1 703 000 in 1961 and to 1 730 000 in 1968.
5. Merseyside—including Liverpool, with two-thirds of the total population, and Birkenhead and Wallasey on the opposite side of the Mersey—covers 383 square kilometres (148 square miles) and had 1 382 244 people in 1951 but only 1 386 000 in 1961, with a further decline to 1 351 000 in 1968.
6. Tyneside, of which the natural centre—Newcastle—contains about a quarter of the total population, covers 233 square kilometres (90 square

1. Where the urban areas are not continuous the term 'town cluster' may be used and is appropriate for the Black Country, or the ring of towns around Manchester mentioned above, or the West Riding woollen towns outside Leeds and Bradford.

miles), and had 835 332 people in 1951, 852 000 in 1961, and 843 000 in 1968.

7. Glasgow. The Central Clydeside conurbation, focusing upon Glasgow, covers 834 square kilometres (326 square miles) and contains just over one-third of the population of Scotland. In 1951 it had 1 758 000 people, in 1961 1 766 000, and in 1968, 1 755 000 (of whom 945 000 were in Glasgow itself).

A comprehensive study of these and other smaller conurbations is contained in T. W. Freeman, *The Conurbations of Great Britain*, Manchester University Press, 1959. From a different point of view C. A. Moser and W. Scott, in *British Towns*, Oliver & Boyd, 1960, have developed a 'typology' of towns.

26
London

What is London? Before attempting any description of London and its activities, it is necessary to attempt to define what the name 'London' connotes. For at least half a dozen different boundaries are in common use, each enclosing a tract which, for specific purposes, is considered as 'London'.[1] Two of these are precisely defined administrative units—the City of London which is the original heart of the whole, 2.6 square kilometres (one square mile) in extent, and the Greater London Council area, created in 1963, covering 1606 square kilometres (620 square miles). The former County of London had been created by the Local Government Act of 1888; it was carved out by taking parts of the counties of Kent, Surrey, Middlesex and Essex, and was divided into forty-one districts, which were re-grouped in 1899 into twenty-eight metropolitan boroughs. Despite its area of 303 square kilometres (117 square miles) the County proved inadequate before many years had passed to contain the population whose life and work were centred in London. The loose designation 'Greater London' came to include the City, the County, and a variable outer ring. Specific definitions of Greater London have been used for different purposes: the London Transport Board area covers about 5180 square kilometres (2000 square miles), the Metropolitan Police area 2020 square kilometres (780 square miles), the Metropolitan Water Board area 1475 square kilometres (570 square miles), and the London postal area 608 square kilometres (235 square miles). The population of 'Greater London' given by the Census figures for 1921 and 1931 refers to the Metropolitan Police area. For the purpose of the 1951 Census Greater London or the London conurbation was precisely defined in terms of administrative units, and this Registrar General's area is more or less the same as the Police area, with minor modifications that reduce its extent to 1865 square kilometres (720 square miles). It should be noted that when Sir Patrick Abercrombie prepared the Greater London Plan, 1944, to cover postwar redevelopment and expansion, a much wider area was taken into consideration.

A Royal Commission on Local Government in Greater London was appointed in 1957 and produced its report in 1960; its recommendations

1. For a map showing all the various boundaries see Jones and Sinclair's *Atlas of London*, 1968, Plate 8.

were radical—a drastic reduction in the number of local authorities and the abolition of the Counties of London and Middlesex, and the creation of an overall planning and traffic authority, the Greater London Council. The result was the London Government Act of 1963, which established the GLC, the Inner London Education Authority (whose area covers the old County) and thirty-two London Boroughs. The population of the area was about 8 million, incorporating 3.25 million from the former County, 2.25 million from Middlesex, about one million from each of Surrey and Essex, half a million from Kent and about 60,000 from Hertfordshire.

The City

The smallest unit which may be designated 'London' is the City of London, commonly called the City, coinciding roughly with Roman London and with medieval walled London, though overlapping both to some extent. The City is only a little over 2.6 square kilometres (678 acres) and, lying wholly to the north of the river, includes the two hills separated by the long since obscured Walbrook. To the west the City extends beyond the medieval Lud Gate and the valley, where once the Hol-bourne flowed into its estuary the 'Fleet', as far as Temple Bar. Here, until 1878, a bar in the form of an archway across Fleet Street actually existed to mark the limit of the City of London, and at this point it is still the custom of the Lord Mayor to present the sword of the City to the ruling sovereign on his entry. The City is still the hub about which the great wheel revolves. London became a world exchange for almost every commodity as well as the greatest centre of banking and insurance, and as such earned the proud title of the commercial capital of the world. The City is still the heart of this commercial London, but it no longer has the monopoly that it had until the First World War. Every important business house in the world has offices or representatives in London. Before the war a deliberate policy of limitation of height of buildings prevented the building of skyscrapers, and commercial London had to expand laterally and so invaded the formerly residential or 'social' areas of Westminster and the West End. Great office buildings of the interwar period, such as Bush House, are outside the City, whilst other office buildings of the same period such as Thames House and Imperial Chemical Building are even farther west than the Houses of Parliament. But the City still has within its bounds the Bank of England (The Old Lady of Threadneedle Street—rebuilt in the interwar years, from within, with the exterior unaltered), the Stock Exchange, and the great commodity exchanges as well as the world-famous insurance corporation of Lloyd's, the ancient Guildhall, and the official residence of the Lord Mayor (the Mansion House). The City suffered severely by bombing during the Second World War, especially the section between St Paul's Cathedral and the Bank and rebuilding in large tall blocks has altered its character. The preservation of St Paul's itself, almost unscathed, was virtually a miracle.

The ever increasing pressure on space required for office accommodation —half a million office workers are employed in the City and a further 600 000 in the West End—has naturally resulted in a steadily decreasing residential population. Compared with 128 129 in 1801, by 1931 only 10 996 persons, largely resident caretakers, were recorded as actually living in the City, but nearly half a million came in daily to work in its offices. By 1961, the total had fallen to 4771. The deserted City on a Sunday morning is a sight not to be forgotten.

Inner London

'Inner London' comprises the City of London and the area formerly known as the County of London. The latter includes twelve of the new London Boroughs (see Fig. 230) which have replaced the City of Westminster and twenty-seven former metropolitan boroughs. The new borough of Tower Hamlets (formerly Bethnal Green, Stepney and Poplar) lying to the east of the City coincides roughly with what is popularly designated the 'East End'. The East End is still essentially industrial, and some of the leading industries will be noted later, whilst the southern parts, Stepney and Poplar, include some of the docks of the Port of London. Several of its outstanding features—its rows of small, too frequently squalid, houses, its innumerable little shops—the East End shares with the majority of industrial towns, but the large alien population is a distinctive feature. Whitechapel, lying within this area, is popularly, and largely correctly, associated with a major part of London's Jewish population; Limehouse with London's 'China Town'. The East End suffered severely from wartime bombing which destroyed or seriously damaged approximately 20 per cent of all houses in Britain, thus creating a very serious housing shortage. This led, in London as elsewhere, to a conflict of policies. Any house which could be rendered habitable was patched up; any vacant space might be used for temporary prefabricated homes erected from sections ('prefabs') leaving but limited space for imaginative rebuilding on modern lines. One of the best examples of the latter is the Lansbury Estate of Poplar. Elsewhere sheer necessity has led to the building of blocks of flats, despite the strongly held belief among many that the Englishman will always prefer an individual home.

To the immediate west of the City of London is the City of Westminster. Less than 200 years ago it was still a pleasant walk through the fields from London to Westminster, but it has long since been impossible to the ordinary Londoner to distinguish where one begins and the other ends. In Westminster are the Houses of Parliament and that street of Government buildings, Whitehall, with its famous, if insignificant, offshoot Downing Street. Westminster merges into and in many respects is part of the 'West End'. Here the fashionable residential area still clings round the parks and squares, whilst London's great shopping centres lie along the main thoroughfares.

But blocks of flats have largely replaced ducal mansions, offices and shops are invading the quiet residential squares, office buildings are replacing hotels. The West End includes also that curious enclave of somewhat squalid streets, famous for its varied foreign population and its restaurants, known as Soho—a local industrial area largely dependent on the main shopping centres near by. The West End is ill-defined and merges outwards on the west and north into the upper-class residential areas. The East End, the City, the southern parts of the new boroughs of Camden and Islington (formerly Holborn and Finsbury), and the West End may be regarded as

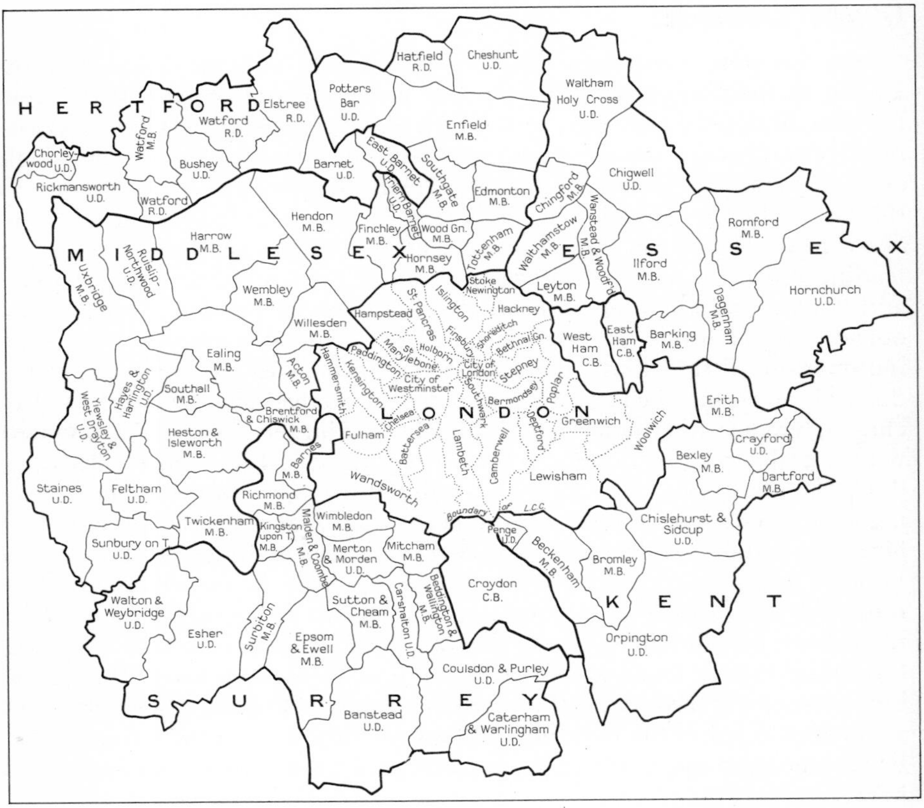

FIG. 229. The administrative divisions of Greater London, 1961
Compare with Fig. 230 which shows the post-1963 position.

constituting central London, but to the north and west, within the county, there lies a large area, partly residential, partly industrial (the former Metropolitan Boroughs of Paddington, Marylebone, Hampstead, St Pancras, Islington, Stoke Newington, Hackney, Chelsea, Fulham, and Hammersmith). That part of London lying south of the Thames is largely industrial and commercial in its inner ring, and residential towards its outer margins. Much of the housing—as well as other building—is obsolete or obsolescent and awaits reconstruction.

Greater London

The area administered by the Greater London Council comprises Inner London, as defined above, plus twenty London boroughs. It is a slightly smaller area than the Greater London of the 1961 Census (compare Figs. 229 and 230). This outer ring of boroughs, largely suburban in character though with numerous local centres and industrial zones, may be described as London's dormitory, for a fair proportion of those who live therein journey daily to some point in Inner London to earn their daily bread. But the ring includes areas of very different character:

(*a*) Some of the boroughs nearest to Inner London are really an integral part of London proper. Thus the largest of London's docks lie in the borough of Newham (formerly East Ham and West Ham), and the industrial district of the East End merges insensibly into Newham and Barking (including the former borough of Dagenham). Similarly on the south side the Woolwich industrial area is continued into Erith (now part of the London Borough of Bexley); and on the northwest Willesden (now part of the borough of Brent), Acton (now part of Ealing) and Brentford (now part of Hounslow) continue the industrial and nineteenth-century residential areas of Paddington and Hammersmith.
(*b*) On the other hand, some boroughs in the outer ring retain an entity of their own as local centres—for example, Croydon, Kingston-upon-Thames and Barnet.
(*c*) In other tracts, notably in the northwest sector and especially along the main lines of the former Great Western and LNW railways, new industrial centres have developed in the heart of the outer ring (see below, p. 681).

Greater London in another sense (as used, for example, by Abercrombie in the Greater London Plan) embraces an even larger area stretching to the crest of the chalk hills on the north and even beyond them on the south, and is thus equivalent to rather more than the central part of the London Basin. An increasingly large number of those whose business takes them daily to London take a pride in living 'outside the suburbs' and this they are enabled to do by the increased transport facilities. By the 1930s the ever-extending electrified services of the Southern Railway ran out as far as the coast at Hastings and Brighton: on the north the Metropolitan Railway extended beyond Aylesbury, whilst to the east the number of season ticket holders to Southend was very large. Since the war, the Liverpool Street suburban lines have been electrified, and the main-line electrification from Euston has brought places like Northampton and Rugby within commuting range of London. The ever-extending sprawl of London has led not only to an apparently insoluble traffic problem of rush-hour traffic, to a journey to work absorbing two or even three hours of each day, but also to a virtual extinction of any rural country within 30 or 40 kilometres (twenty or twenty-five miles) of the centre. This has resulted in conscious planning to limit the growth of London by imposing a green belt, wherein building is prohibited or severely limited, by offering inducements to manufacturers to

FIG. 230. Administrative areas of Greater London, as reorganised in 1963.

expand elsewhere, and by building New Towns to serve as self-contained 'overspills' for London. Most of the towns on this periphery of the London area have their local functions as market towns serving (with the help of local bus services) the immediate countryside, as well as their functions as dormitory towns for Londoners. One solution to part of the London problem is to develop them as self-contained units, rather than as dependants upon London itself.

The influence of the metropolis extends, of course, much farther. A very large part, if not the whole, of the four Home Counties (Hertfordshire, Essex, Kent, and Surrey) as well as Sussex, southern Buckinghamshire, etc., is engaged in supplying dairy produce and vegetables to the London markets. The 'economic tentacles' of the metropolis thus extend out in all these directions. The motor-car has brought the whole of the southeast coast from Bournemouth to Yarmouth within the normal limits of the car-owning Londoner's Saturday or Sunday trip—with a corresponding congestion on most of the direct roads.

Physical factors influencing the growth of London

The site of early London was determined in the main by the presence, near the navigable river, of the hills, safe above flood level, now crowned by St Paul's Cathedral and the Royal Exchange or Cornhill. From the early

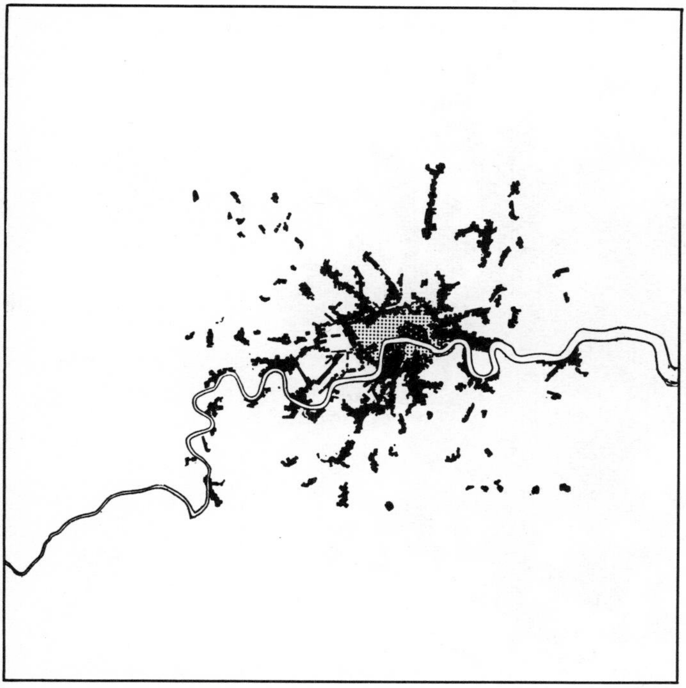

FIG. 231. London in 1820

The solid black shows the built-up area at that date. White on black: The City; dotted: built up 1666 (from Mayne's *The Growth of London*, by permission of Messrs George Harrap & Co. Ltd.).

days the physical features of the whole of the London Basin have not failed to exert their influence on the growing city. Residences spread outwards along the gravel terraces and ridges where a water supply was available, but where drainage prevented a waterlogging of the soil. The lower valleys of some of the streams draining to the Thames and many tracts of clay remain to us to this day as the open spaces of Hyde Park, St James's Park, and others; the Lea Marshes still remain open land. For long the flood plain of the Thames itself must have presented a picture of a waste of marshland, flooded at high tide, but gradually embankment along the southern shore (opposite the City) permitted the formation of 'polders' occupied by cattle pastures. Below London, the great areas of marshland, such as the Isle of Dogs, remained until the great dock building companies began to utilise them in the nineteenth century. With the embanking of the river on both sides the water channel was restricted within narrow limits and little now remains to remind us of the extent of the old flood plain. But as London grew, the better residences sought the well-drained heights capped by gravel and the low-lying London Clay tracts remained undeveloped—occupied by pastureland. The gravel terraces west of London furnished

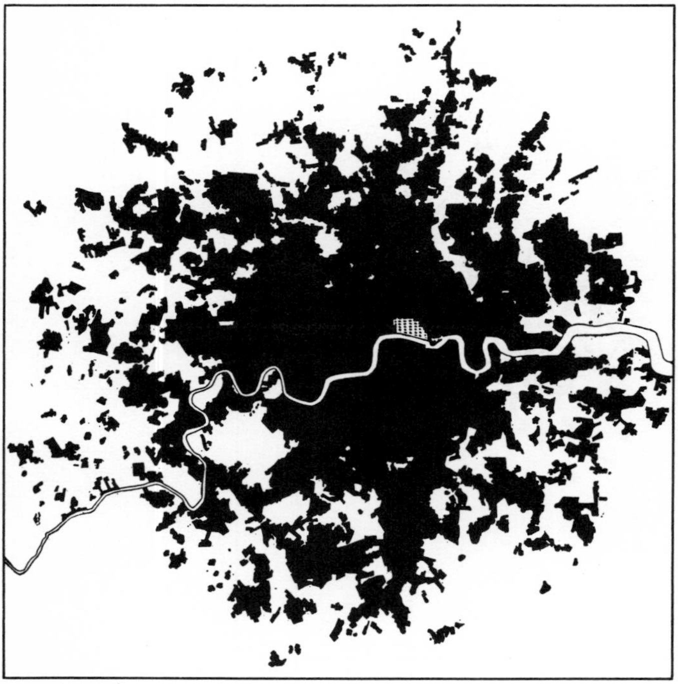

FIG. 232. London in 1945

The solid black shows the built-up area at that date. Figs 231 and 232 are on the same scale (from Mayne's *The Growth of London*, by permission of Messrs George Harrap & Co. Ltd.).

arable land, and the area that was formerly southwest Middlesex still sends much market-garden produce to London, though London's great airport at Heathrow has taken up much of the open land which remained. The roads out of London of necessity made for the gaps through the chalk ring; settlement followed along these roads and give an early example of what has later been called 'ribbon development' (Fig. 232). At a much later stage the railways had to seek the chalk gaps and triangular tracts of farmland were left between them. A few tracts still remain: others were built over in the interwar years. It is found that most which remain are low-lying London Clay tracts. Modern drainage, water supply and improved foundations have played their part in making these clay lands usable, but the better residences sought the chalk slopes or the gravel-capped heights of the Surrey Hills or the Northern Heights.

The population of London

The following table serves to illustrate the changing nature of population distribution in London:

	CITY	REMAINDER OF COUNTY	OUTER RING	TOTAL GREATER LONDON
1801	128 129	831 181	155 334	1 114 644
1841	123 563	1 825 714	286 067	2 235 344
1881	50 569	3 779 728	936 364	4 766 661
1921	13 709	4 484 523	2 995 678	7 480 201
1931	10 996	4 385 825	3 805 997	8 202 818
1951	5 268	3 343 068	4 997 801	8 346 137
1961	4 771	3 190 343	4 976 788	8 171 902

Note. All figures before 1961 are adjusted to the pre-1963 administrative areas. In 1968 (Registrar General's estimate) the population of Greater London had fallen to 7 764 000.

These figures are sufficient to indicate the general trend: the decreasing population of the City and adjoining 'business' divisions of London. Indeed, Inner London as a whole has shown a declining population since 1901. The enormous increase is in the outer ring, whilst if one takes the area *outside* the 'Greater London' of official reports (i.e. the Metropolitan Police area) the percentage increase in the new outermost ring is even greater. This is likely to become even more marked when the ring of new towns (see p. 657) is complete. In the area outside the county considered in the Abercrombie plan the population rose from 4 084 900 in 1919 to 6 117 300 in 1939. Greater London of the Plan had thus over 10 million people, or a quarter of the total for Britain.

There is thus an ever-increasing outward movement of the population, but it must not be forgotten that this is accompanied by an ever-increasing *daily* movement of the people from their homes in the suburbs to their offices, shops, and factories in central London. Thus the resident population of Central London was, according to 1957 estimates, 226 000, whilst the employed day population was 1 352 000. In most London boroughs there is a daily movement outwards of workers going to their occupations elsewhere, and also a daily movement inwards of workers resident elsewhere. For the County of London alone the number of persons so moving daily was over 2.5 million, a stupendous figure representing 11 per cent of the total occupied population of the whole of England and Wales at that time.

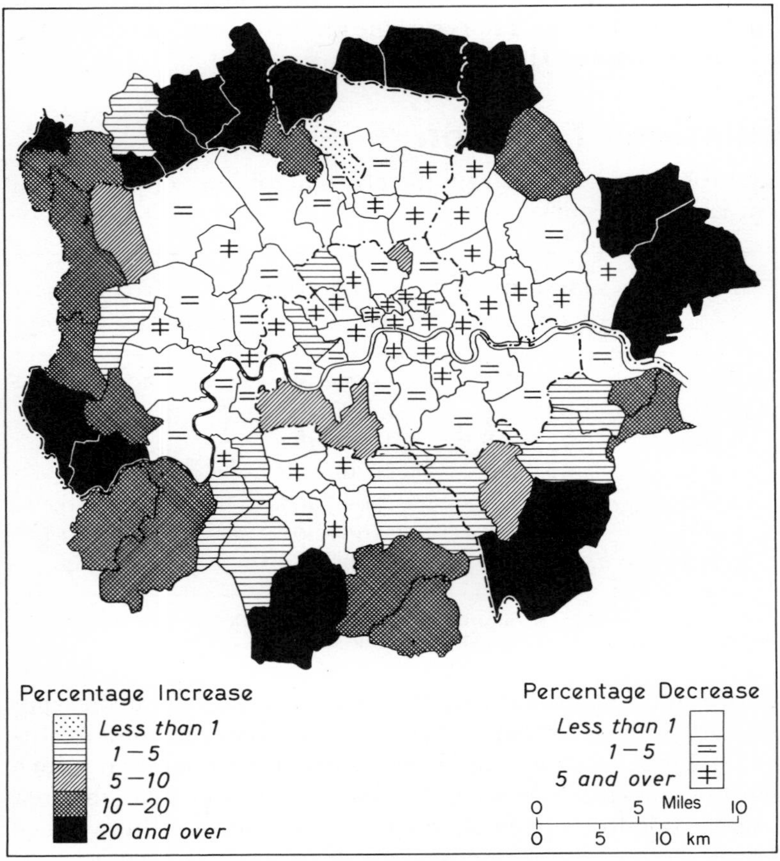

FIG. 233. Population changes in Greater London, 1951–1961

Even as long ago as 1921, the resident population of the City, Westminster, Finsbury, and Holborn was far smaller in each case than the transient population of workers who moved in and out daily. As the resident population of the central boroughs has decreased, so the daily movement has increased. Broadly speaking, it is the shop and office workers who come in from the suburbs to the City and the central boroughs: the industrial workers live near or at least nearer their work though they often move outwards from the very areas which receive a daily influx of black-coated workers.

Employment in Greater London

The tables that follow give figures for the main groups of employment in Greater London in 1921, 1951, 1961 and 1966. This period was one of great increase in employment in the London conurbation which is the largest single employment region in the British Isles.

Employment in Greater London, 1921 and 1951
(arranged in Standard Industrial Classification Groups)

CLASSIFICATION		THOUSANDS 1921	THOUSANDS 1951
I.	Agriculture, forestry, fishing	27.7	17.1
II.	Mining and quarrying	1.3	2.7
III.	Treatment of non-metalliferous mining products	17.6	33.1
IV.	Chemicals	56.2	95.7
V.	Metal manufacture	12.2	24.7
VI.	Engineering	160.1	357.5
VII.	Vehicles	59.3	143.8
VIII.	Other metal goods	38.8	73.8
IX.	Precision instruments, jewellery, etc.	45.4	70.0
X.	Textiles	23.3	26.8
XI.	Leather, leather goods, etc.	27.4	21.3
XII.	Clothing	218.1	185.0
XIII.	Food, drink and tobacco	136.0	146.3
XIV.	Wood and cork manufactures	68.2	89.9
XV.	Paper and printing	139.6	173.3
XVI.	Other manufacturing	50.4	81.4
XVII.	Building	146.9	283.1
XVIII.	Gas, electricity and water	50.4	85.2
XIX.	Transport and communication	346.6	420.3
XX.	Distributive trades	534.9	599.3
XXI.	Insurance, banking and finance	109.9	186.9
XXII.	Public administration and defence	210.3	317.0
XXIII.	Professional services	207.1	365.0
XXIV.	Miscellaneous services	483.4	484.7
	Other occupations	45.0	4.5
	Total	3216.1	4288.3

Source: P. G. Hall, *The Industries of London since 1861*, Hutchinson, 1962.

Employment in Greater London, 1961 and 1966
(arranged in Standard Industrial Classification Groups)

CLASSIFICATION		THOUSANDS 1961	1966
I.	Agriculture, forestry, fishing	11.6	7.3
II.	Mining and quarrying	3.7	3.6
III.	Food, drink and tobacco	128.0	123.0
IV.	Chemicals and allied industries	93.9	80.1
V.	Metal manufacture	26.0	24.5
VI.	Engineering and electrical goods	462.8	407.0
VII.	Shipbuilding and marine engineering	10.8	8.1
VIII.	Vehicles	103.2	77.2
IX.	Metal goods not elsewhere specified	82.2	79.0
X.	Textiles	22.8	21.3
XI.	Leather, leather goods and fur	16.4	15.7
XII.	Clothing and footwear	128.4	109.7
XIII.	Bricks, pottery, glass, cement	36.8	29.6
XIV.	Timber and furniture	80.6	67.5
XV.	Paper, printing and publishing	195.2	173.5
XVI.	Other mfg. industries (rubber linoleum, plastics, toys, etc.)	72.3	64.2
XVII.	Construction	380.9	298.1
XVIII.	Gas, electricity and water	78.1	78.7
XIX.	Transport and communication	373.7	422.6
XX.	Distributive trades	663.6	625.3
XXI.	Insurance, banking and finance	240.0	255.2
XXII.	Professional and scientific services	431.8	462.7
XXIII.	Miscellaneous services	584.3	589.4
XXIV.	Public administration and defence	280.9	280.3
	Other occupations	22.3	22.6
	Total	4530.3	4326.2

If we look more carefully at the list of employment groups, the statistics can be assembled in three main groups.[1] The *Primary* (sometimes called *extractive*) group of occupations (Groups I and II) is unimportant and accounts for less than 0.3 per cent of the employed population. Market gardening and gravel-digging are the major representatives of this group.

1. The Standard Industrial Classification was modified in 1958; the three major groupings remain the same, but there are important differences in the numbering and specification of individual Groups, so that continuity of tabulation is impossible.

The *Secondary* or *manufacturing* industry groups (Groups III–XVI) include about 30 per cent of the total; the most important industries are engineering (including electrical goods), the paper and publishing trades, food-processing industries and the clothing trade. All these, it may be noted, are industries that have been growing nationally in the post-1918 period, and London is conspicuously lacking in the major occupations that have been declining as employers of labour, such as coal-mining, cotton textiles and agriculture.

London has long been a great centre of the *Tertiary* group of occupations or *servicing* industries (Groups XVII–XXIV), and these groups together employ 70 per cent of the employed population of the conurbation. This is not surprising in view of London's position as the capital city, exercising a national role in administration, banking and insurance, wholesale and retail distribution, and as the main centre of specialised medical, legal, educational, cultural and other services. Also, over 400 000, or nearly 10 per cent of the total employed population of Greater London, are engaged in the transport and communication industries. While the role of the port of London and the function of London as a railway centre are remembered, account must also be taken of the recent growth of London as an international focus of air routes. In any case, the task of transporting London's workers from home to work is itself one of great magnitude, for some 1.25 million travel each day from the suburban areas, and from towns outside London, to work in the centre.

The following table shows how the major groups have fluctuated since the First World War:

Employment in Greater London, by industrial sectors (thousands)

	1921		1951		1961		1966	
	TOTAL	%	TOTAL	%	TOTAL	%	TOTAL	%
Primary (Groups I, II)	29.0	0.9	19.8	0.4	15.3	0.3	10.9	0.25
Secondary (Groups III–XVI)	1052.6	33	1522.6	35	1459.4	32	1280.4	30
Tertiary (Groups XVII–XXIV)	2089.5	65	2741.5	64	3033.3	67	3012.3	70

The Primary group has declined steadily, for more and more of London's market-garden land has been swallowed up, and gravel pits have either moved further out or become highly mechanised. The Secondary group rose to a maximum in the years after the Second World War, but since then the Government's policy of clamping down on industrial expansion in London and encouraging firms to move into the Development Areas has begun to take effect. Industrial Development Certificates issued by the Board of Trade have been increasingly hard to get in the London area; in (the years 1956–59 such certificates offered some 6.5 per cent of the country's total new employment, but by 1964–67 this percentage had been reduced to 2. Thus between 1961 and 1966 every major industrial group showed a decline in employment.

The figures for the Tertiary group, however, the servicing industries, tell a different story. The continued growth of employment in central London is a phenomenon that has given rise to serious concern in respect of practical problems of congestion. Estimates suggest that in the late 1950s and early 1960s the number of office jobs in central London was increasing by at least

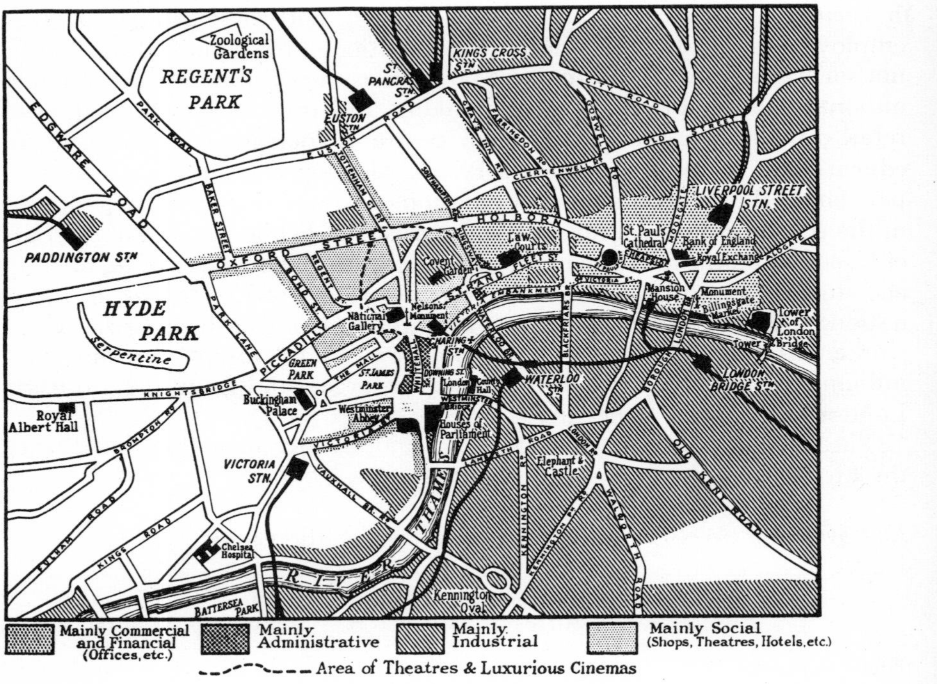

FIG. 234. The 'functions' of London

London is an excellent example of a large city in which definite areas are devoted to the main functions of the city. The blank areas are mainly residential.

15 000 a year. Whilst the growth of manufacturing industry is subject to control by the Board of Trade (and undoubtedly the Secondary group would have increased materially since 1945 had the natural inclination of industrialists been allowed to prevail) it is less easy to control the growth in the number of jobs in the servicing industries—and of course postwar reconstruction and the development of skyscraper office blocks in the City have helped to swell the employment opportunities. It is true that some restrictions have been imposed since 1963 on the rebuilding of office blocks in the centre, and further attempts have been made to decentralise office jobs to suburban centres and to New Towns and other towns situated

beyond the conurbation (see below, p. 687). Nevertheless the percentage of the total employment represented by the 3 million jobs in servicing industries continues to rise; and what is quite clear is that London must continue to develop as a service centre on an international scale.

The industrial districts of London

In the years 1932 to 1938 inclusive out of 3635 new factories opened in Great Britain no less than 1573 were opened in Greater London; out of 2994 closed only 1055 were in Greater London. Taking the net gain in numbers of 641, no less than 518 were in Greater London, or 80 per cent of the whole of Britain. The outstanding feature in London itself was the general movement towards decentralisation. It must be admitted that the development of new factory areas in and near London was, in the main, haphazard. It is obvious that (*a*) labour supply, (*b*) space for expansion, (*c*) transport facilities, (*d*) relation to markets, and (*e*) water, gas, and electricity supplies and costs, and rates were leading factors.

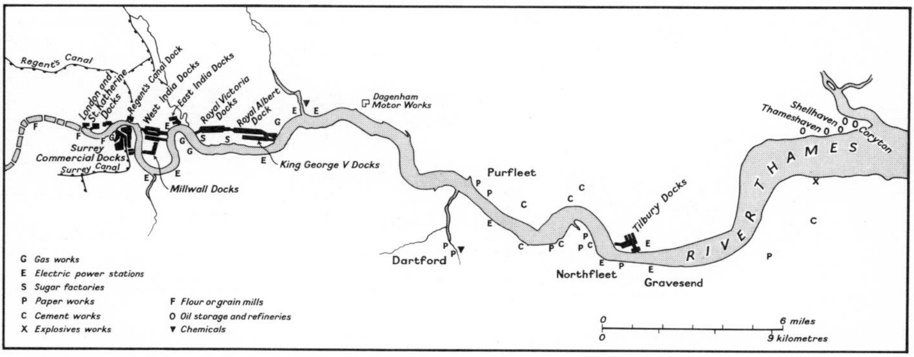

FIG. 235. The docks and riverside industries of the port of London

The small factory must needs be erected near an existing labour supply. But labour is mobile and a large unit, complete with housing scheme, can attract labour to itself. So there was the rise of new industrial centres, such as Letchworth (no less than 56 kilometres (thirty-five miles) from London), Welwyn (34 kilometres (twenty-one miles)) and, nearer in, Slough. There is a difference of opinion among manufacturers whether the factory to be erected near an existing residential tract should be on the outskirts so that the workers go *outwards* to their work, but have the amenities of town life at their doors, or whether the factory should be as central as possible and the workers come *inwards* to their work from homes where circumstances permit of small gardens for each. There is no doubt that want of space for expansion is by far the most important reason for moving an established industry. The modern mechanised factory requires a horizontal layout rather than a vertical one, hence the great demand for space. In choosing the new site, transport facilities play a large part. For heavy and exporting industries (and for industries dependent upon bulky imported raw material) the importance of the nearness of the river or docks is paramount. This is very clear in the case of such industries as:

(*a*) Electric power works and gas works—using water-borne coal and practically all situated near the river. Those on the Regent's Canal now receive coal by rail or road.
(*b*) Cement works, an example of a heavy and exporting industry, using chalk, mud or clay and water-borne coal, all along the Thames below Dartford and the Medway.
(*c*) Paper works, petroleum refineries, grain mills, and sugar factories using bulky imported raw materials.

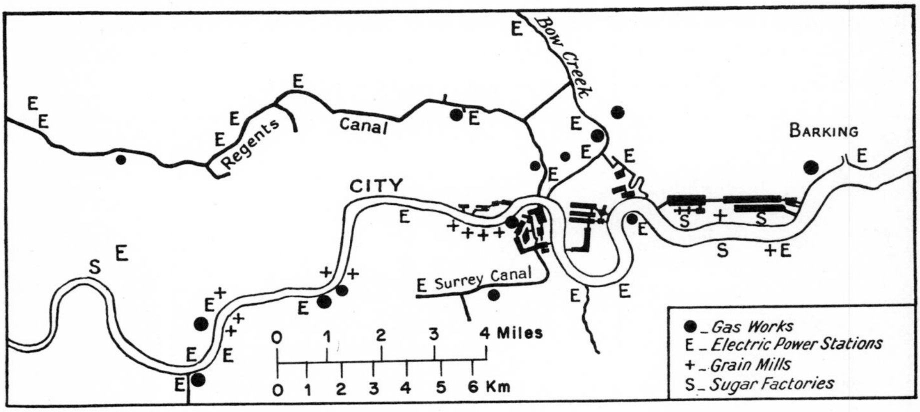

FIG. 236. Water-side industries of London

On the other hand, for lighter industries and those supplying primarily or largely the home market, nearness to the main railway lines or arterial roads is more essential. This is clearly exemplified by the almost continuous succession of factories built between the wars along the old Great Western main line from Ealing through Slough with such examples as the gramophone works (HMV) at Hayes, Middlesex, and the gigantic bakeries of J. Lyons & Co., Ltd, or the Park Royal Breweries of Arthur Guinness & Son, Ltd.

This separation of heavy and light industries fortunately operates to a considerable extent in another way. It coincides to some extent with a separation between 'dirty' or 'noxious' and 'clean' industries—to the advantage of residential areas. There is an element of danger associated with explosives and even with oil refining, with a consequent attempt to isolate them. Shellhaven and the great refineries on the Isle of Grain afford excellent examples.

There is, of course, another great factor at work where essentially skilled labour is required—the factor which may be called inertia. It operates in the clothing industry, which has expanded in the east and northeast of London rather than changed its location.

Mention was made above of the relation to markets. There are several points of view here. Those manufacturers who depend on the London area as their chief market must be near at hand for delivery; those who rely on London as an international mart and are manufacturing for export must be near both for shipment of goods and to permit foreign buyers to inspect their goods. A foreign buyer might well cut off from his list a factory whose warehouse was inconveniently far away for him to visit. The makers of bulky or standardised articles, of course, get over this by a showroom in London, but even then comes the difficulty that the buyer cannot talk personally with the principals of the business.

We list below the present industrial areas of Greater London:

The East End

This traditional industrial area of London lies mainly in the former Metropolitan boroughs of Shoreditch, Bethnal Green, Stepney, and Poplar, together with those parts of West Ham comprising Canning Town and Silvertown. South of the river, Bermondsey may be included. Some medieval crafts long survived. There is still one bell-foundry and until the 1914 war there were silk-weavers at Spitalfields using hand looms as old in design as the industry itself. In the 1880s, when transport was entirely horse drawn or the docks reached by the sulphur-laden 'underground' of the Metropolitan Railway, shipbuilding was important along the river, ship repairing even more so. Shipbuilding is dead, ship repairing almost so, but to some extent modern engineering industries have grown out of the old shipbuilding, and the close connection with the sea is maintained by very large numbers of dockers and lightermen. Away from the river, furniture making, the clothing industry, printing and cardboard-box-making, tobacco industries, and food processing rank high. By number employed and value of output, London ranks first among the urban centres of Britain in many industries. Before the bombing and destruction of 1940–45 about a third of a million workers were employed in the East End. Shoreditch and Bethnal Green thus forms the 'city of the smaller trades and the lesser ingenuities'.

Since the nineteenth century clothing and furniture trades have clustered here. Furniture is still made in several hundred workshops in Bethnal Green and Shoreditch, where the small man often specialises in one process such as turning legs for tables, veneering or upholstery. The area produces a great variety of output but is no longer the metropolis of the trade. Stepney, especially Whitechapel, remains important in clothing manufacture principally the women's outerwear trades. Small workshops exist alongside factories with a few hundred workers, but mechanisation here scarcely extends beyond the electric sewing machine and some sectional division of operations. In recent decades clothing manufacture has spread to the decaying suburbs, notably Hackney and further afield into the Lea Valley and Essex. London does not to any appreciable extent manufacture textiles. The textiles required for the clothing trades are brought in from other regions to the factories or to wholesale merchants. Food, drink and tobacco industries are also important in the East End while printing works are clustered on the fringe of the City. Immediately beyond the Lea, in West Ham, is the principal area of chemical manufacture in London, which at one time 'benefited' here from laxer bye-laws on noxious industries.

While the home of leather tanning and the leather industry is in Bermondsey across the river, the manufacture of leather goods is by no means unimportant in the East End where, however, fur-dressing and furriery is particularly important. But what must again be stressed is the immense variety of miscellaneous industries—old crafts being found side by side with the manufacture of radio and television parts, or a range of plastic 'gadgets' inseparable from modern life.

Soho and the West End

Behind the great shopping streets of the West End is a major concentration of the clothing industry concerned especially with outerwear for women. The factory or work room units are usually small, many concentrate on expensive garments.

The Lea Valley

This is really an offshoot of the congested East End boroughs, from which population, soon followed by industry, began to move from 1880 onwards and the quiet fertile valley from Waltham Abbey southwards to Enfield, Edmonton, Tottenham, and Walthamstow was changed to a broad ribbon of small homes and factories. Up to 1914 the dominant industries were those of the East End—furniture, clothing, and metal working later followed a great diversification. Well served by waterways and rail, the later development came to rely more and more on road transport. In the Lea Valley the intensive production (under glass in heated greenhouses) of tomatoes, cucumbers, and flowers is organised as an industry rather than as a branch of farming, but necessitated the conservation of considerable areas of land for its use. Once it was good local soil, abundant water, and good sunshine average which attracted the industry, now proximity of markets and a large local labour supply are more important in retaining the industry, although it has declined in importance in recent years.

The Lower Thames-side

This is London's heavy industrial area: in contrast with the areas just described it is essentially one of large units which have occupied the erstwhile marshlands. Examples are the great Ford works at Dagenham on the north of the river; cement works at Erith, Dartford, Northfleet to the south with the great oil refineries nearer the mouth of the river.

West and Northwest London

With the exception of a few big pre-1914 firms at Willesden, Hayes and Southall, these areas grew up after the First World War, some parts indeed from munition factories, whilst much of the 1924–25 Wembley Exhibition grounds was given over to light industry. Industries are located in an inner zone or nucleus and in areas in four principal directions from the nucleus. Among the inner districts are Park Royal, Wembley Park, Acton Vale, Willesden and Cricklewood. Those on radial routes include (*a*) New Brentford and Feltham to the southwest along the Great West and Staines roads, (*b*) Hayes and Southall to Slough (actually to Buckinghamshire) along the former GWR line to the West, (*c*) Alperton, Perivale and Greenford along Western Avenue and the former GWR and LMS lines to the northwest, (*d*) along Edgware Road, e.g. Colindale; finally, (*e*) along the North Circular Road.

West London is particularly important in light engineering and vehicle manufacture and in the preparation of many types of proprietary articles, including branded foods and toilet preparations.

Rail freight is very significant for some districts, especially Park Royal and Southall. By contrast factories on Edgware Road depend mainly on road transport and the Wembley Park Estate makes little use of the rail facilities that surround it.

Kingston bypass, *Wandle Valley* and *Cray Valley* are three rather small and isolated areas of development south of the River Thames.

London's wholesale markets

The covered retail markets of London, small and few, are insignificant when compared with the great covered markets of such towns as Liverpool and Birmingham. London's street markets are more comparable with the covered retail markets of the provinces, and play an important part in London life.[1] But London's wholesale markets occupy (or at least did prior to the outbreak of war in 1939) a unique position in that to a large extent they determine or influence prices throughout the country, and are an outward and visible sign of London's pre-eminence as a commercial centre. In a

1. See *New Survey of London Life and Labour*, iii, Chapter 13, p. 290.

very large number of commodities transactions are carried out by sample so that the 'markets' are or were merely certain streets in the City where firms specialising in certain commodities have their offices located. The tea market is or was in Mincing Lane, the jute market, sugar market, etc., near at hand. But in the case of foodstuffs where freshness is essential (meat, fish, and vegetables) the commodities are actually brought to the markets of the metropolis for sale.

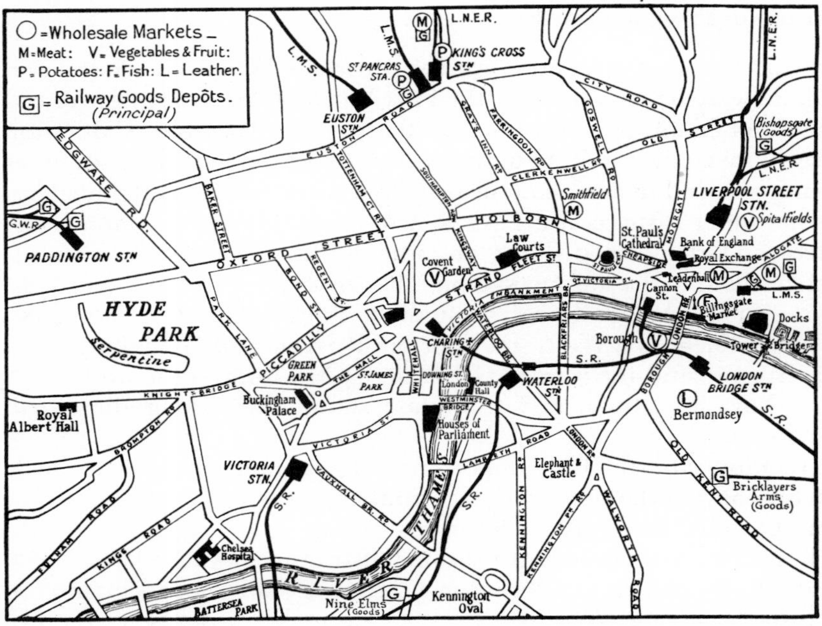

FIG. 237. London's wholesale markets
Shown in relation to the main railway termini and the docks

The City Corporation of London owns four markets: the London Central Meat Market at Smithfield, markets at Spitalfields, Billingsgate, and Leadenhall. Covent Garden is owned by a public company, two railhead markets have fallen to the control of British Rail. It is interesting that no markets were controlled by the London County Council which came really too late on the scene. Some of the markets, such as the LC Meat Market, serve mainly the London area; others, such as Covent Garden, serve practically the whole country, and there has been much discussion as to devising some means to obviate the delay and expense of repeated handlings necessary to bring such commodities as imported fruit to Covent Garden before reconsigning it to distant parts of the country.[1]

1. A South African farmer once told the writer that a case of oranges was handled fifteen times before it was opened in a retailer's shop in England. Five of these were necessitated by the existence of the Covent Garden system.

Covent Garden. Covent Garden is still the principal centre of Great Britain dealing in imported fruit and vegetables, and also handles a seasonal surplus of fruit from southeastern England. The market was founded in 1670 in the reign of Charles II. The market itself covers 2.3 hectares ($5\frac{3}{4}$ acres) including open squares, covered market buildings and a Floral Hall where auctions take place. Most of the premises in the neighbouring streets are occupied by firms in the fruit and vegetable trade. The market is chiefly active between 3 a.m. and 6 a.m., when the homegrown supplies reach the market, and over 5000 vehicles go into the market in one day. It cannot be claimed that the market premises are up to date, and the congestion is notorious. There are active plans to move the market to a site at Nine Elms.

Spitalfields. The market founded originally in 1682 was long associated with the old fine silk industry of the area. It is now the market for fruit and vegetables, mainly from Essex and the eastern Home Counties supplying the populous east and northeast of London.

Stratford. This is a fruit and vegetable market adjoining, and constructed in 1878 by, the old Great Eastern Railway. It derives its supplies from the counties on that line. The railhead depots at King's Cross and Somer's Town had a similar function—handling the potatoes and vegetables of the Fenlands in particular; while the Borough Market serves the south of London. Greenwich has also a small wholesale fruit market.

The London Provision Exchange. Established in 1887, this market normally handles the whole of the bacon and ham imported into London—about half of the total imports of the country. It is concerned also with butter, cheese, lard, and canned goods.

Smithfield. The London Central Market, owned and operated by the Corporation of the City of London under a charter of Edward III, covers now an area of 4 hectares (10 acres) and is the principal meat market, dealing also in eggs, poultry, game, butter, and cheese. From the point of view of ease of approach and facilities for handling the meat, Smithfield is the best of London's markets: 60 000 sides of beef (about 9000 tons) can be displayed at once; there are external loading points for 350 three-ton lorries at one time and thirty-one ample gates to the market itself. There are numerous cold stores adjacent to the market. The incoming lorries deliver their loads and are away between 4 a.m. and 6 a.m. The retail butchers do most of their purchasing between 6 a.m. and 8 a.m.

Leadenhall Market. Handles mainly poultry and, being not far from Billingsgate, is convenient for retailers who sell both fish and poultry; though more poultry is being handled at Smithfield. There is also an important retail market.

Billingsgate. Billingsgate fish market more than rivals Covent Garden in historic interest. It is the oldest of the markets controlled by the City Corporation, and its site—by the riverside around a small haven just below London Bridge—was inevitable when most of the supplies were waterborne. Actually the proportion of waterborne deliveries has now dropped to a small fraction of the total, and the bulk has therefore to be brought from the great railway termini. Although the market serves primarily London and the southeastern counties, not a small proportion is conveyed to distant points in the south—possibly not far from where the fish was originally landed. The market itself, with an area of about 0.5 hectare (an acre), is unable to accommodate the quantity of fish to be sold. Thus much of the selling is by samples, and delivery can be made from the railway companies' vans which line the 'Inner Circle' of streets surrounding the market direct to the waiting buyers' vans which line the 'Outer Circle' of side streets. The market opens at 5 a.m. when deliveries arrive from the special night fish trains. Retailers arrive at 6 o'clock and most of the business is over by 8 a.m. and the streets clear before the great throng of city workers pours through the neighbouring thoroughfares at 9.0 or 9.30.

The other markets are indicated in Fig. 237. The old Hop Exchange was off the Borough.

London during the Second World War

London was so obviously the nerve centre of Britain and the Commonwealth that it was reasonable to presume an immediate massed air attack in the event of war. Consequently, when war broke out in September 1939, prearranged plans for the evacuation and the setting up of autonomous Civil Defence Regions covering the whole country, as well as the dispersal of commerce and industry, were immediately put into effect. The serious attack did not in fact come for nearly a year, but in the winter of 1940–41 nightly raiders caused much damage, especially by incendiary bombs. Dockland, the East End and parts of the City suffered severely. After April and May there was something of a respite until the advent in the later stages of the war of the guided missiles (flying bombs, or V1s), and then the giant projectiles, or V2s, with great destructive power. Although large numbers of evacuees, including children, had drifted back to London, London's normal activities remained greatly reduced. The Port handled but a fraction of its prewar volume of trade, many of the City's commercial and business firms carried on from addresses scattered widely through the country, few industries of national importance continued to function in London. Even so, shops, restaurants, hotels, cinemas, and theatres carried on and because many businesses did not do more than move from the centre to the suburbs the population of Greater London probably never dropped below two-thirds of its 1939 total. That of the County of London reached a low of 2 314 700 in December, 1941, compared with 4 062 800 in mid-1938.

London after the Second World War

The end of the war was marked by an immediate rush to return to London—of individuals, of business and commercial houses, of industry and even of Government departments. Decentralisation, previously advocated as desirable, necessitated by the war, had proved to have many disadvantages. Although careful and imaginative plans had been prepared for the rebuilding of city, county, and suburbs, it was difficult for several reasons to put these into effect. Bombing had resulted in spasmodic rather than systematic clearing of large sites, and the shortage of houses was so acute that any dwelling which could be repaired and made habitable had to be so used, thus postponing demolition of obsolescent buildings indefinitely. Priority of labour and materials had to be given to housing, and work on large office blocks, as well as hotels, cinemas, department stores, and other 'luxury' work, even including factories and warehouses, had to take second place. By 1952 scarcely a start had been made on rebuilding the City. On the other hand, the expansion of the civil service to staff such new ministries as Food and Defence, Housing and Local Government and to take care of nationalised industries—such as coal and transport—involved the spread of Government offices to many parts of London. In some cases, as in the east side of Regent's Park, their use as Government offices saved much of Regency London—houses which private occupiers could no longer afford to maintain. With the destruction of some large shopping areas, the remaining areas had become much congested, and shops and offices have still further invaded the formerly residential areas, notably Mayfair. The westward migration of varied light industries became more marked, partly because of the relatively slight war damage when compared with the East End. Shipping and trade returned to the London docks and the influence of water transport is still strong enough to concentrate the development of power stations and oil refineries on Thames-side and an expansion of the great self-contained vehicle plant of Ford at Dagenham.

The future development of London

Modern London illustrates in a remarkable way the separation, which is characteristic of most of the very large modern centres, of areas serving each of the five great functions of a city: the commercial, the administrative, the industrial, the social, and the residential. As a result of the destruction wrought by bombing in 1940–45, the areas have become less clearly defined and the expansion of central administration in particular has caused Government offices to appear in most unexpected places. Normally the heart of commercial London is the City with its banks, its insurance houses, its business premises, its warehouses, and its markets. On the one side to the east it is very closely linked with the Port of London. Much of the buying and selling is actually done by samples in the City whilst the goods them-

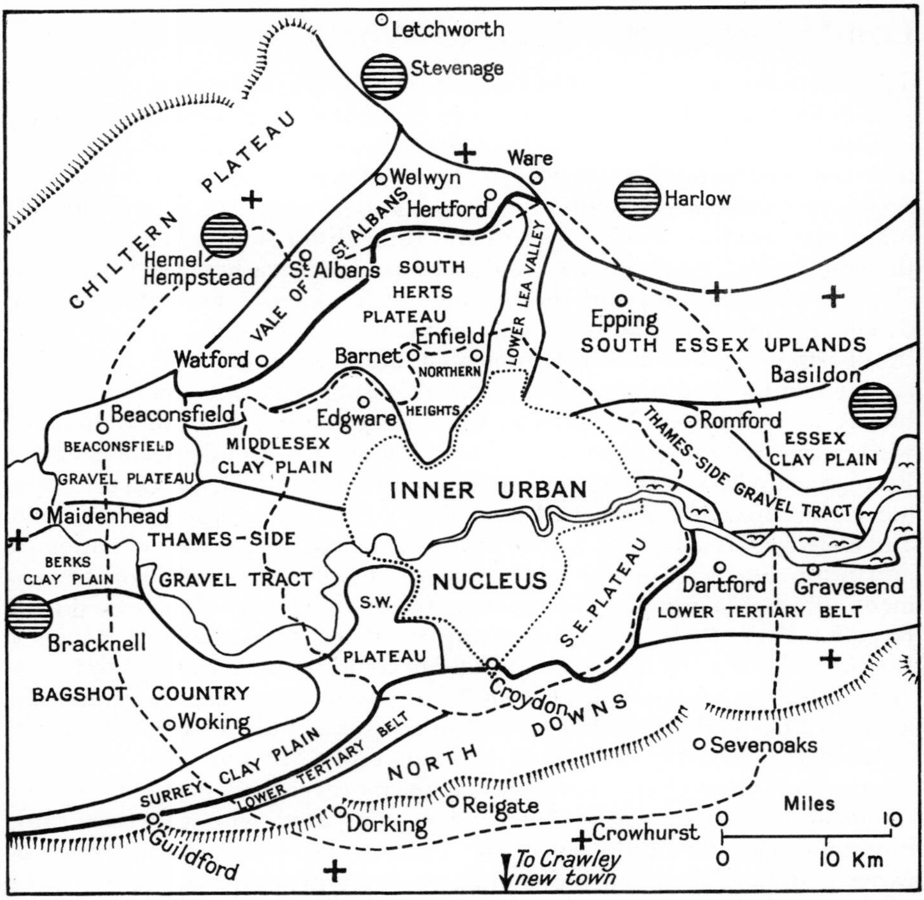

FIG. 238. Greater London in relation to the surrounding physical regions (after S. W. Wooldridge, *Trans. Inst. Brit. Geog.* 1946)

Crosses: sites proposed for new or satellite towns in the Greater London Plan of 1944. Circles: new towns: Hatfield, Welwyn Garden City not shown.

selves remain in the Port. The growth of commercial London was driving out the resident population in many western areas long before the outbreak of war in 1939. Bush House is outside the city limits. The replacement of old buildings on the South Bank by the giant Shell Centre (1962) is another indication of the spread of commercial London. Social London remains in the West End. Here in juxtaposition are the theatres, the cinemas, the large stores, and attractive shops, the clubs, restaurants, and hotels within reasonable access to the principal railway termini; but new building is mainly of office blocks.

A question brought very much to the fore is whether London should be *allowed* to grow. Between the wars more than 10 000 new factories were built. The transport of London's workers from their homes to their work threatens to become an insoluble problem despite the coordination of transport services (especially under the London Transport Executive) and schemes for further railway electrification.

Consequently the London Plans emphasise physical limitation by a green belt and accommodation of 'overspill' population in self-contained New Towns 30 to 80 kilometres (twenty to fifty miles) from the centre. In the meantime the concept of the 'neighbourhood unit'—a town within a town—has grown, though it merely crystallises the old local allegiance denoted by such neighbourhood names (they are not administrative units) as Bloomsbury, Mayfair, Belgravia, and Chelsea. If people *want* to live in London should they, in a free society, be prevented?

In accordance with this policy the building of a ring of New Towns was undertaken. Some are shown in Fig. 238—Crawley in the south, Bracknell in the west, Hemel Hempstead, Welwyn, Stevenage, Hatfield and Harlow to the north, Basildon to the east in Essex.

The original population of the areas designated as New Towns was 98 500; in December 1968 it was 450 000 and it is expected to rise to about 642 000. A main characteristic of the New Towns is the provision of industrial employment as well as residence. By 1968 there were over 100 000 jobs in manufacturing in the eight towns, mainly in the expanding industries such as electrical goods, engineering, vehicles, chemicals, and food and drink industries.

In addition there has been a planned decentralisation to towns that have been expanded under the Town Development Act, 1952. No less than twenty-seven schemes have been agreed between London and such towns as Ashford, Basingstoke, Bletchley, Haverhill, Swindon, Thetford and Wellingborough. By 1967, 29 378 houses had been built under these schemes and 410 firms had moved to 'expanded' towns. Attempts have also been made since 1964 to control the growth of office employment in central London, and to decentralise office employment to the suburbs and to New and 'expanded' towns. Over and above the planned movement of people and jobs from London to other parts of the region there has also been a substantial 'voluntary' outward movement to 'commuter' areas beyond the conurbation. The Metropolitan Area extending outwards from the edge of the conurbation for about 40 kilometres (twenty-five miles) (i.e. to some 64 kilometres (forty miles) from central London) grew by 800 000 between 1951 and 1961 and the tendency has continued. It is expected that the total overspill from the conurbation will be about one million in the period 1966–81.

Estimates of future population growth suggest that, while the population of the Greater London Conurbation may fall slightly by 1981 there may be a growth of 2.14 million people in the South East Region between 1964 and 1981. Differences of view exist on the planning strategy to be adopted. The *South East Study* (1964) advocated a second generation of new and expanded towns of larger size than the first New Towns. Not all its proposals have been accepted although plans for the new town of Milton Keynes, near Bletchley, are well advanced. *A Strategy for the South East* (1967) put forward suggestions for the development of 'sectors' following the main radial routes out of London and including a number of major expansion schemes large enough to serve as foci of counter-attaction to London itself. But new proposals for planning the London region were expected late in 1969 from a study being made by the Ministry of Housing and Local Government.

27
The growth of communications

The history of the development of facilities for communication in the old-established and highly industrialised country of Britain is a subject so vast, and withal so well supplied with literature,[1] that in this chapter, fascinating though excursions into economic history might prove to be, we can scarcely hope to present more than a brief essay in the geography of transport and an analysis of the relative importance of geographical and other factors in influencing the growth of roads, canals, and railways.

Two features of fundamental importance have played a part in modelling our present transport system. In the first place, one may say that Britain is, on the whole, by its physical nature, well favoured for the development of two out of the three major modes of communication—road and rail. There exist very few real barriers to road construction in the shape of high mountain ranges or wide marshes, and the 'negative' areas are of such small extent that both roads and railways can round the obstacles without long detours. The all-important raw materials, both for road making and for the road beds of railways, are widely distributed (cf. p. 363), and railways were, in addition, favoured by the existence of fuel supplies of excellent quality—a fact which had no little influence on British locomotive design and practice. For canals, however, the undulating surface of Britain, with its industrial regions separated for the most part by upstanding areas of harder rock or by alternating scarps and dip-slopes, is not nearly so well adapted as, for example, the flat plains of the Netherlands and North Germany, whilst long navigable rivers free from vexatious sinuosities are non-existent. Although Britain passed through a canal era of great importance in its industrial development, it is not surprising that this form of transport should have seriously declined with the rapid expansion of railways.

Secondly, a characteristic feature of the development in Britain of railways, canals, and the 'turnpike' roads has been the dominance of private enterprise and the virtual absence, from the Roman period until quite

1. See References, p. 831; standard works are Jackman, *Development of Transportation in Modern England* (a solid and well-documented piece of research); and Pratt, *History of Inland Transport and Communication in England* (a more popular and more readable account). Also Appleton, *The Geography of Communications in Great Britain.*

recently, of Government assistance.[1] This strict adherence to laissez-faire principles, with its preservation at all costs of open competition, lest a dreaded 'monopoly' should come into being, has been responsible for many of the difficulties of the present transport system, and for many of the differences which exist between Britain and Continental countries. There was no national plan, as in the case of the railways and 'routes nationales' of France; instead, the systems grew during periods of boom—the canal 'mania' of the 1790s and the railway 'mania' of 1845–47—in haphazard fashion, and sometimes without either sound geographical basis or real economic need. Turnpike trusts were established in large numbers, in many parts of the country, with little reference to the economic needs of the period; canals—long since derelict—were constructed through areas where neither through nor local traffic could reasonably be expected to yield a profit. Some of the early railway lines were similar; others were constructed merely to act as competitors to already existing lines.

With these preliminary considerations in mind, we may attempt very briefly to trace the history of transportation in this country.

Roads

The Roman roads, military in origin and well planned and constructed, were for the most part stone causeways following a straight course from beacon to beacon across the higher and more open ground above the forests and marshes of the lowlands.[2] Even at this early stage the importance of London as a focal point was well marked (cf. Fig. 211). For a long period after the departure of the Romans little attention was paid to communications, and although many improvements were made in the thirteenth and fourteenth centuries conditions of transport subsequently deteriorated considerably. Rivers were undoubtedly more important than roads, and nearly every town of any size was a river port (e.g. York, Lincoln, Gloucester, Chester) (cf. Fig. 223). The accessibility of the university towns of Oxford and Cambridge was certainly improved by the waterways of the Thames and Cam. Towns such as Birmingham and Bradford, not on navigable streams, were non-existent or of no consequence.[3] The medieval roads were mere trackways, the actual route of which was constantly shifting to avoid the more dilapidated patches.[4] There was but a meagre demand for intercommunication between towns and villages when subsistence agriculture

1. Note, however, the military roads of the Scottish Highlands, constructed in the eighteenth century by General Wade and his successors, and the costly but rather useless Caledonian and Crinan Canals built with Government money.

2. See Ordnance Survey Map of Roman Britain.

3. Birmingham remains an example of one of the very few large towns in the world actually on or near a water-parting.

4. This continual departure from a direct course may possibly explain some of the curious sinuosities in the present-day roads.

and domestic industry were the rule, and the upkeep of the roads was regarded as a charitable occupation and so left mainly to the monks. With the breakdown of the manorial system, the decline of the fairs and the cessation of pilgrimages, and, finally, the dissolution of the monasteries, the roads grew worse and worse. An Act passed in 1555 delegated the labour of road mending to the parishes. This measure actually remained in force until 1835, but it really cannot be said to have succeeded in greatly improving the road system, for the statutory parish labour was easily evaded and the methods employed were of the most primitive order. There was still no pressing need for efficient roads until the trade of the country, both internal and external, began to expand in Elizabethan times. The fairly late introduction of industry into Britain, when compared with certain parts of the Continent, is largely due, in fact, to the difficulties of internal transport.

The increase of wheeled traffic played havoc with the layers of mud and stones which passed as roads in the seventeenth century. Long covered wagons had begun to be used in the sixteenth century, and stage coaches made their appearance fairly early in the seventeenth century, and the result was a series of regulations concerning weights to be carried and width of wheels, it being thought that wide rims would cut up the roads less than narrow ones. The legislation, it should be noted, was concerned with adapting the vehicles to the roads, not with improving the roads to accommodate the vehicles. Descriptions of roads and journeys during this century and a half (1600–1760) are numerous and entertaining. The Tours of Defoe[1] and Young have been previously referred to in this book. It was indeed an adventure almost equivalent to a modern crossing of Central Africa to undertake a long journey through Britain, and it is little wonder that those who performed such travels wrote at great length of their experiences. The many clay belts of England were areas of especial difficulty. In the winter the roads across these regions were almost impassable, and the sparse settlements were isolated for months on end. Of particular ill-fame were the roads across the Weald Clays of Sussex, across the London Clay, Gault, and Oxford Clay belts which intervene between London and the Midlands, and across the bogs of South Lancashire. Heavy lumbering carts with their numerous horses cut the roads into deep ruts, and the laying of stones only served to make progress more dangerous and uncomfortable for travellers on horseback or in wheeled vehicles. Of the road to Wigan, Arthur Young says: 'I know not in the whole range of language terms sufficiently expressive to describe this infernal road . . . eighteen miles of execrable memory'. Obviously industrial development was not aided by such conditions, and south Lancashire and the Birmingham region, especially, found themselves hampered by the difficulty of disposing of their goods. Road speeds, too, were extremely slow. In the middle of the eighteenth century, Edinburgh

1. See especially Appendix to vol. ii of Defoe's *Tour thro' the island of Great Britain* (original edition, 1724–26).

was 10 to 12 days' coach journey from London, Exeter 4 days, Birmingham and Dover 2 days, and so on. It was with the object of improving road conditions that the Turnpike Trusts were set up. The first of these was instituted in 1663 on a section of the Great North Road in the clay belt between Hertfordshire and Huntingdon; their object was to obtain money for maintaining the roads in good condition by charging tolls. About 1100 separate trusts were formed, the greatest period being 1760–75; but many of them controlled only a few miles of road, and large numbers were thoroughly inefficient, most of the tolls going towards the payment of trustees' salaries. There is no doubt, however, that the turnpike movement did an enormous amount of good for road transport, especially after the advent of new methods of road making. Until the beginning of the nineteenth century the construction of roads was not regarded as an occupation worthy of the skill of engineers, and, as we have seen, the authorities tried in vain to adapt the traffic to their poor surfaces. Between 1810 and 1820, however, two men, Telford and McAdam, began to apply scientific principles to road building; Telford, who commenced reconstructing the Holyhead road in 1815, concentrating upon the creation of a solid foundation and adequate draining; McAdam, who attained the position of Surveyor-General of Roads in 1827, devoting his attention to the production of the durable, impermeable surface which still bears his name.[1] A great impetus was thus given in the 'twenties and 'thirties to the development of coaching traffic. Just when the Turnpike Trusts were beginning to set the roads of Britain in good order a new form of transport, the railway, entered the field and deprived them of much of their revenue. During the second half of the century they were all wound up, the control of the roads passing into the hands of Parish Councils and Highway Boards, and later into those of the reconstituted Local Government bodies, County, Borough, Urban, and Rural District Councils. Thus road transport for several decades became a matter of local importance, until the evolution of the petrol motor rendered the construction and maintenance of roads of first-class national significance.

Rivers and canals

The age of bad roads, in the seventeenth and eighteenth centuries, is marked by an increased attention to river navigation. The natural waterways had been for so long neglected that their beds had become silted up, and disastrous floods occurred after periods of heavy rainfall. Thus, many medieval ports, such as Lewes, Ely, Bawtry, York, and Doncaster, had been deprived of their position and had lost in trade and importance thereby.

1. The essential point of his work was the discovery that stone broken to a uniform size and of angular shape could be made to bind together. The tarring of the pieces (and the making of tar-macadam) with the consequent elimination of dust, is a twentieth-century development. The reinforced concrete road has gone still further to solve the problems of roadmaking in country with a soft subsoil.

The first Act for improving a river was actually passed in 1424 concerning the River Lee (an important highway for London's wheat supply), but the great age of dredging and artificial cutting (to avoid the frequent meanders) was between 1660 and the beginning of the canal era. Although rivers all over the country were subjected to much improvement, the greatest incentive came from the north of England, where industries were beginning to develop rapidly. Thus the Mersey was improved as far as Warrington in the 1690s, and in 1720 three new projects were sanctioned—the Mersey and Irwell navigation, giving navigable water as far as the growing town of Manchester; the Weaver navigation, opening up the Cheshire salt-field; and the Douglas navigation, providing an outlet for the Wigan coalfield to Preston. The Aire and Calder navigation, commenced in 1699, stimulated the growth of Leeds and Hull, and the improvement of the Don enabled the manufacturers of Sheffield to obtain their Swedish iron more easily.

The various disabilities attaching to river navigation, however, such as time wasted in following the innumerable windings, the difficulty of towing upstream, and the fluctuation in depth of water according to season, together with the fact that several growing industrial areas, such as Birmingham and the Potteries, were not served by navigable rivers, led to the development of artificial waterways or canals. The link between the two is the Sankey Canal, sanctioned in 1755 as a river improvement scheme to provide an outlet for the Wigan coalfield. The improvement of the Sankey Brook being found impracticable, an entirely artificial cut was made. From this small beginning an extensive canal system came into being within the next sixty years. The canals were built by private enterprise, competing with the Turnpikes, and the companies were modelled on the lines of the Trusts, that is, they were toll-takers, and not carriers. As a result, there was great variation in depth and width, size of locks, and gauge of tunnels, etc., and through long-distance traffic was compelled to pass over the property of several different companies.[1] At first, however, the improvement in speed upon road transport, the reduction of freight rates to about a third or a quarter of the amounts charged on the roads, and the ability of the canals to carry bulky raw materials and finished goods in hitherto inconceivable quantities sufficed to enable many of the canals to pay enormous dividends.

Geographical influences in the growth of the principal elements in the canal system—if it can be called a system—are very evident. The increasing use of coal in industry and as a household fuel, together with the industrial development of the Midlands and North, where the roads were particularly bad, were responsible for the greater part of the canal cutting taking place in those areas, whilst the South was left—with one or two exceptions—comparatively untouched. The Black Country, South Lancashire, and the West Riding became the principal foci, London, with its river navigation

1. For example, Birmingham to Liverpool, six canal companies, each canal of different dimensions; Liverpool to Hull, ten companies.

and coasting trade, being distinctly ex-centric in marked contrast to its position as regards the roads and later railway nets. In Lancashire and Yorkshire three needs were being catered for: (*a*) more adequate disposal of coal; (*b*) easier transport between the cotton and woollen centres and the coast; (*c*) coast to coast communication, in order to avoid long coastal voyages. Thus, the Worsley Canal linked the Duke of Bridgewater's collieries with Manchester, the Bridgewater Canal gave the cotton capital a new and better outlet to the Mersey estuary, and the Leeds and Liverpool Canal, and also the Rochdale and the Huddersfield canals, linked the navigable waters on either side of the Pennines. The Leeds and Liverpool Canal, especially, was responsible for much new industrial development in the Aire valley and in the valleys north of Rossendale Forest. The great canals of the Midlands fall into two groups. In the first place there is the complicated system in the Birmingham–Black Country region, which afforded much-needed outlets for coal and the bulky produce of the iron and other metal industries; secondly, there are the canals designed to link up the major navigable rivers. Of these the most important were the Grand Trunk from Trent to Mersey, which had a truly remarkable effect upon the development of the Potteries, where Wedgwood had just recently (1763) begun his improvement of the staple industry (cf. p. 603); the Shropshire Union, linking the Birmingham system with the Mersey; the Staffordshire and Worcestershire, linking the Birmingham system with the Severn; the Grand Junction, giving navigable water from London to Birmingham and the Trent; the Thames–Severn (across the Cotswolds to Stroud) and the Kennet–Avon. These interriverine canals were instrumental in displacing a great amount of coastal sailing; when coasting steamers developed they lost most of their traffic, and the last two, for example, have long been disused. South Wales also developed canals as an aid to its iron and coal export trade—the Monmouthshire and Glamorganshire valleys providing obvious lines of movement to the ports of Newport and Cardiff. It is noteworthy, however, that Northumberland and Durham—the home of wooden and iron tramways (see Chapter 14 and below)—never adopted a canal system. In Scotland the Forth and Clyde Canal from Bowling to Grangemouth had as its primary object the connection of the coasting trades of east and west Scotland;[1] but the Monkland Canal (from Coatbridge to the Forth and Clyde Canal at Glasgow) and the Union Canal (from the same canal at Falkirk to Edinburgh) were both constructed to give outlets for the Lanarkshire coalfield. The state-aided Caledonian and Crinan Canals (the former from Fort William to Inverness and the latter across the head of Kintyre) have never been of any real economic importance.[2]

1. Its western terminus was 16 kilometres (10 miles) below Glasgow, owing to the shallowness of the Clyde. It was finally closed about 1963.

2. Even modern pleasure steamers start from above the famous 'Neptune's staircase' of locks at the southern end of the Caledonian Canal. The British Waterways Board's cruiser carried 12 000 passengers in 1967.

The great boom in canal construction came between 1791 and 1794, during which period eighty-one new canal and navigation Acts were passed. Many of these were for quite useless canals which either soon went out of business or became absorbed in the larger concerns. The coming of the railway after 1830 was the beginning of the end for a large part of the canal system. In that year the British Isles possessed 6872 kilometres (4270 miles) of canals and inland navigations (i.e. improved rivers), over 5150 kilometres (3200 miles) in England and Wales, nearly 322 kilometres (200 miles) in Scotland, and nearly 1368 kilometres (850 miles) in Ireland. By reason of the great industrial expansion of Britain, traffic on many of the canals actually increased until the end of the century, but the total canal traffic was very small beside that carried by the railways.[1] We may profitably summarise the principal reasons why the decline of the canals has taken place and why their resuscitation is impossible.[2]

1. The narrow canals and rivers of Britain are ill adapted for speedy carriage, for fast-moving vessels create a wash which would quickly undermine the banks.

2. Britain is not physically suited to canals. Locks are required in great number and tunnels (the older ones without towing paths) are not infrequent, and the resultant delays add considerably to all journey times. Between London and Avonmouth, for example, in 286 kilometres (178 miles), there are 125 locks (including a remarkable 'staircase' of 29 at Devizes); between Liverpool and Hull, 256 kilometres (159 miles), there are 147 (92 in 51 kilometres (32 miles) over the summit of the Rochdale Canal); between London and Birmingham *via* Blisworth, 159 locks in 217 kilometres (135 miles); and between Birmingham and Sharpness 62 locks in 121 kilometres (75 miles). At Anderton (near Northwich) a hydraulic lift raises barges 15 metres (50 ft) from the River Weaver navigation to the Trent and Mersey Canal.

3. A large part of the canal system is of small dimensions, incapable of taking boats drawing more than 1.2 metres (4 ft) of water, or more than 2.1 metres (7 ft) in width. Narrow canals are especially characteristic of the Birmingham system, on which special narrow boats must be employed.[3] The impossibility of widening these canals is evident when it is realised that over much of their extent in the Black Country the banks of the waterways are completely built over with factories, works, and even dwellings,

1. 1898: Canal traffic 39 million long tons; railway traffic 379 million long tons. These are 'unreal' figures, since traffic passing from one company to another was recorded by each company and so may figure several times in the total. However, the truth of the generalisation made above is apparent.

2. See Royal Commission on Canals and Inland Navigation, Cd. 4979, 1909, also E. A. Pratt, *Canals and Traders*, which sets out clearly the arguments against the revival scheme proposed by the Commission.

3. It is not the open channels of the canals which are narrow, but the locks and bridges, which it would be very difficult and costly to widen.

many of which, though possibly owing their site to the facilities for water transport, now make little or no use of them.

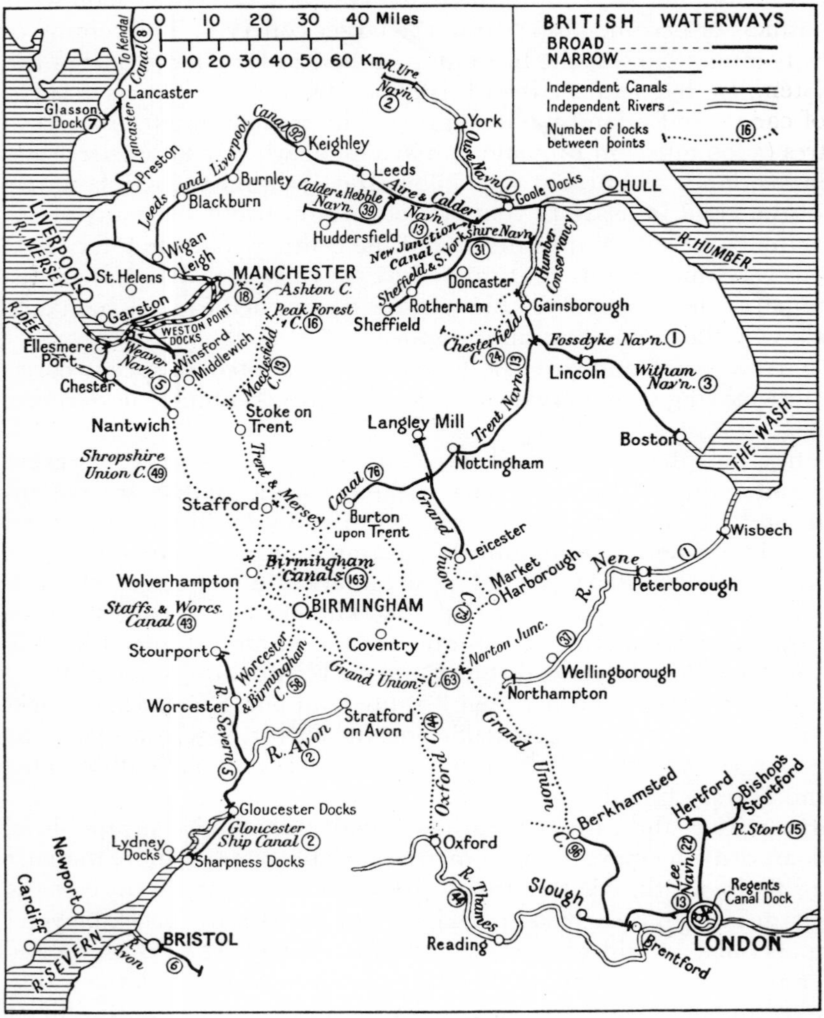

FIG. 239. Navigable waterways of England and Wales, 1959

The new junction canal, in Yorkshire, joins those to north and south.

4. Many canals, designed to facilitate coal transport, pass through coal mining areas in which ground subsidence is of frequent occurrence, and the maintenance of the waterway consequently difficult. Thus, in the Black Country, in Lancashire, and in the Potteries, subsidence has occurred to such an extent that the canals now run in places above the general level of the land, like an embanked river over its floodplain.

5. Canals which cross watersheds are likely to experience difficulty in obtaining adequate water supply. Were such canals to be enlarged, great reservoirs would need to be constructed in order to render navigable the deeper and wider channels.
6. The great disadvantage of the canal is its lack of flexibility and its capacity for serving adequately only those factories, mines, and farms which lie along its banks. Owing to the initial cost and difficulty of construction, a canal is very much less flexible than a railway. Canals, moreover, are not well adapted for carrying small loads to a number of different points, and in any case only short haulages are possible, owing to the small size of the country.

Fig. 239 shows the navigable waterways existing in 1959—with an indication of the number of locks. They may be divided into three classes: first, the 'open' river navigations (such as the Crouch, Hull and Wharfe) totalling 200 kilometres (124 miles); secondly, the independent waterways (most of the navigable rivers, the Manchester Ship Canal, and canals that are in fact mainly used for drainage, as in the Fenland) amounting to about 2736 kilometres (1·700 miles); thirdly, the canals and river navigations under the control of the British Waterways Board, totalling just over 2575 kilometres (1600 miles). British Waterways traffic totalled 12 million long tons in 1953 and 9 million long tons in 1963, and the decline continues, particularly since the National Coal Board ceased to use water transport in 1965; in 1967 the total was just over 7 million long tons. About 20 per cent of the waterway system carries 90 per cent of the traffic, and the principal remaining waterways are the River Trent (below Nottingham), the Aire and Calder, the Sheffield and South Yorkshire, the Calder and Hebble, the Fossdyke, the river Weaver, the Berkeley Canal, the River Lee (below Enfield), and the southern end of the Grand Union Canal (below Uxbridge). The greater part of the canal system now carries little commercial traffic, though it remains of great potential value for amenity purposes—boating, crusing and fishing—and parts of it are valuable for water supplies or drainage.[1]

Railways

Just as the canal system owed its origin to the growing dissatisfaction with the bad roads of the eighteenth century, so a large part of the railway system grew up in the first place to supplement the inadequate services provided by the waterways, and to introduce better transport into those areas where canals had not penetrated. Once again we find that private enterprise was responsible, and the result was a haphazard growth almost completely devoid of plan or any suggestion of a possible national system. Fortunately,

1. In 1967 the British Waterways Board issued over 10 000 licences for pleasure craft; and on a June Sunday a census recorded 27 000 anglers fishing in the canals and reservoirs!

however, with one major exception, the companies all adopted the standard gauge of 1.435 metres (4 ft 8½ in). The exception was the old Great Western which used a broad gauge until the 'nineties. Parliament, moreover, did all it could to promote competition and prevent any line from having a monopoly of traffic. Railways in Britain were regarded as dangerous innovations, to be resisted alike by turnpike trusts, canals, and landowners, and the result was that from their very beginning they were hampered by excessive costs—heavy legal expenses in order to overcome opposition to the passing of their bills, and exorbitant charges for land.[1]

To an even greater extent than that of the canals, the early history of the railways is bound up with the coal trade. Long before the invention of the locomotive, wooden, and later iron, tramways had been utilised in the Northumberland coalfield for transporting coal from the mines to Tyneside (cf. Fig. 119), and similar systems arose in Shropshire and in South Wales. The Tyne had for centuries been an avenue for coal traffic, and the increasing distance of the collieries from the river was not easily bridgeable by canals, owing to the nature of the land surface. In South Wales, too, away from the main valley bottoms, canals were virtually impossible, and thus an extensive system of tramways grew up around Merthyr Tydfil and between that town and Cardiff. Between 1801 and 1825, when the first real 'railway' was opened, no less than twenty-nine 'iron railways' were constructed in various parts of the country, mostly connected with canals, ironworks, or collieries.

The influence of the coal trade upon the early railway system may be gauged from Fig. 240.[2] The Stockton and Darlington line, the first public railway, was intended to provide an outlet for coal from Witton Park to the Tees, and its promoters had no intention of carrying passengers. A network of lines quickly developed in the northeastern area, linking the collieries with the mouth of the Tyne and with the ports of Sunderland, Hartlepool, Stockton, and Port Clarence. In the Scottish lowlands the earliest lines (Monkland and Kirkintilloch; Glasgow and Garnkirk) were built to connect the Lanarkshire coalfield with the Forth and Clyde canal and with the port of Glasgow; in South Wales the Llanelly railway and the Taff Vale lines were likewise developed to facilitate coal movement; and the Leicester and Swannington line was designed to carry coal from the Leicestershire coalfield to the county town at a cheaper rate than that charged by the Soar navigation from Derbyshire. In Lancashire the inability of the existing system of waterways to accommodate the vastly increased traffic between Liverpool and Manchester engendered by the cotton industry was mainly responsible for the step taken by a group of merchants in promoting the Liverpool and Manchester railway, opened in 1830, but several subsequent

1. The London and Birmingham, for example, paid £72 868 in legal costs, and an average of £6300 per mile for land. See Pratt, *History of Inland Transport*, Chapter 20. Also H. G. Lewin, *The Railway Mania and its Aftermath*. London, 1936.

2. See H. G. Lewin, *The British Railway System* (to 1844), 2nd edition, 1925.

lines had as their main object the improvement of the coal trade (e.g. the Wigan Branch railway).

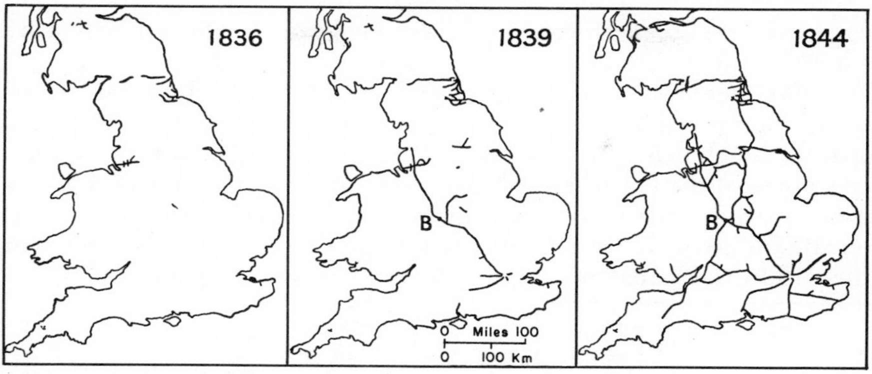

FIG. 240. The growth of the British railway network

B = Birmingham. The two curious outlying lines, Bodmin–Wadebridge (Cornwall) and Canterbury–Whitstable (Kent) are interesting. The former was constructed to carry shelly sand from the Camel estuary to the agricultural lands around Bodmin; the latter to carry coal to Canterbury owing to the silting of the river Stour.

In the 1840s the nucleus of the subsequent Midland railway began to appear. This series of lines (Midland Counties, Rugby–Leicester–Derby; North Midland, Derby–Chesterfield–Leeds; Derby and Birmingham junction) had as its main object the improvement of Derbyshire coal trade —and it is interesting to note in this connection the way in which the subsequent Midland railway, with the same intention, extended long tentacles to all parts of the country, its powers extending as far as Yarmouth, York, Carlisle, Liverpool, Bristol, Bournemouth, Swansea, and Southend.

Many of the early railways, as we have seen, were primarily coal carriers; passenger transport was a subsidiary business. It soon became apparent, however, that except in the colliery districts of Northumberland and Durham, Lanarkshire, South Wales, and South Lancashire—all of which were close to navigable water—the canals still held a great advantage in cheapness of conveyance, and that the railways would derive far greater benefit from the carriage of human freight. The second great object of the railway promoters was thus to link up the existing large centres of population with each other and with London, an object which, as Fig. 240 shows, was in an advanced stage of progress before the mania years. By 1844 through communication was established between London and Folkestone, Brighton, Southampton, Exeter, Bristol, Manchester, Liverpool, Preston, Birmingham, York, Leeds, and Newcastle; and the future importance of Birmingham and Manchester as junctions was foreshadowed. No less than three trans-Pennine connections were complete. The absence of the Great Northern line from these maps is an interesting reflection of the nature of the country through which that line afterwards passed—an extensive agricultural tract where there was little possibility of large local traffic.

The bulk of the mileage, then, until the mania years of 1845–47, was dependent mainly upon passenger traffic for its revenue.[1] By this time the energy of the canal companies in trying to retain their traffic was beginning to wane, and from thenceforward goods traffic began to play an increasing part in the economy of the railways.

The subsequent history of the railway system is largely a story of development in hitherto neglected areas, and of amalgamations to form the great companies which existed before the grouping of 1921. We may profitably observe some of the geographical and economic consequences of that development. In the first place, the railways stimulated the growth of population and industries at their terminals and crossing points. Folkestone was the first railway-created port, but numerous others—e.g. Grimsby, Im-

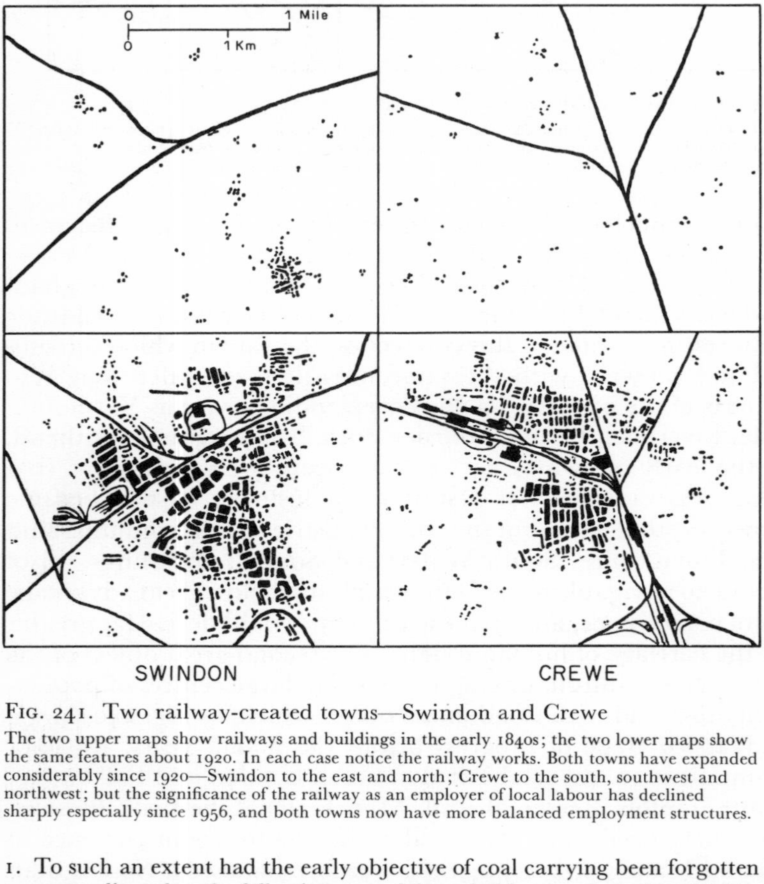

FIG. 241. Two railway-created towns—Swindon and Crewe

The two upper maps show railways and buildings in the early 1840s; the two lower maps show the same features about 1920. In each case notice the railway works. Both towns have expanded considerably since 1920—Swindon to the east and north; Crewe to the south, southwest and northwest; but the significance of the railway as an employer of local labour has declined sharply especially since 1956, and both towns now have more balanced employment structures.

1. To such an extent had the early objective of coal carrying been forgotten by some of the passenger lines that the following remark is probably representative of the more aristocratic attitude towards railways: 'Coal!' a certain Mr B. of the London and Birmingham is reported to have exclaimed when it was first suggested that his railway should carry so humble a commodity—'why, they'll be asking us to carry dung next!' (Acworth, *Railways of England*, p. 153.)

mingham, Middlesbrough, Fleetwood, Southampton, and the South Wales ports—were largely developed, if not actually created, by the forerunners of the railway companies which, before nationalisation, owner-operated them. There are many examples, too, of towns which grew up at railway junctions. The outstanding examples are Crewe and Swindon (see Fig. 241). At Crewe, before the coming of the railway, not even a village existed; and the original Swindon was a small market town on the top of an outlier of Portland stone over a mile south of the railway junction which lay in the clay vale beneath. In both these cases the growth was aided by the development of railway works. Ashford (Kent), Bletchley, and Rugby are other examples. At the crossing of rail and river the railway frequently gave a new lease of life to the decayed river ports—e.g. Lincoln, Gloucester, Chester, and Selby.

The power of the railway to attract commerce and industry was so obvious that towns which had not yet been reached pressed for new lines, lest their development should be arrested. Not only did the railways help to concentrate industry on the coalfields by transporting raw materials to the fuel supply, but, by working in the opposite direction, they allowed the survival and renewed development of old industries in localities far removed from coal—as, for example, the engineering industries of the eastern counties. With the declining dominance of the coalfields as iron-producers the railways have also contributed to the scattering of industry over the countryside. In the development of the great conurbations the railways have been of prime importance. The vast daily movement of passenger and goods traffic in these thickly populated areas would be impossible without the railway. The railway web of a conurbation is well worth examining. It consists essentially of radial lines with belt connections. The most symmetrical example is Paris, but London and Manchester (Figs. 242 and 243) may be taken as equally representative. In the case of London, the radial web is particularly well developed; but it is noteworthy that the belt connections are mainly situated on the north and northwest sides—for the obvious reason that most of the traffic arrives from the Midlands and North. The function of the North London line, from Acton and Willesden to Camden, Broad Street, and the Docks; of the North and South-west Junction line, from Cricklewood (Brent sidings) *via* Neasden and Willesden to the London and South Western line, and of the West London Extension railway, linking Willesden and Old Oak Common with the great Southern Region depôts at Battersea, should be specially noted. The distribution of the goods depôts is also interesting. These are of two kinds—the terminals, where the traffic is transferred to the markets or to road vans for distribution, and the marshalling yards in the suburbs near the belt lines. Fig. 243 shows that the same general plan can be detected in the case of Manchester—although here, as might be expected, the belt lines are mainly on the south and east (i.e. on the side of the great industrial regions of the Midlands and Yorkshire). The suburban railways of London pioneered in electrification—

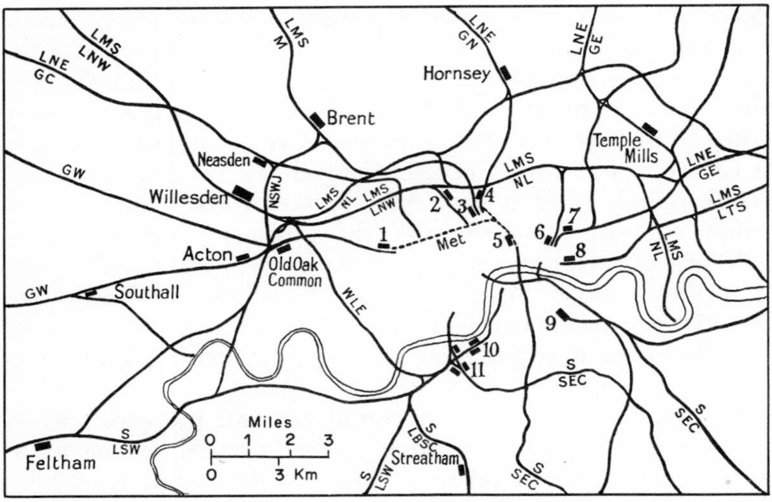

FIG. 242. The radial lines and belt connections of London, as they were before nationalisation

The principal marshalling sidings are named; terminal goods depots are numbered 1 to 11. 1, Paddington; 2, Camden; 3, Somers Town; 4, Kings Cross; 5, Farringdon; 6, Broad Street; 7, Bishopsgate; 8, Fenchurch Street; 9, Bricklayers Arms; 10, Nine Elms; 11, Battersea.

especially the Southern Railway—and by 1939 the Southern Railway had so extended its electrified lines on the third rail system as to have the largest suburban electrified network in the world. London led the world in electric tube railways—unified as the 'Underground' under the London Passenger Transport Board with trams (which became extinct in 1952) and buses.

The part played by the railways in the development of holiday resorts has been of immense value both to the favoured towns and to the people who are thus enabled to visit them. Many a West of England fishing village was given a new lease of life by railborne holiday traffic, and a number of the foremost resorts, for example Bournemouth, Cleethorpes, Blackpool, and Clacton, were almost non-existent before the coming of the railways.

Lastly, the railways have frequently chosen somewhat barren and thinly populated sites for the establishment of huge marshalling yards where the traffic from many areas can be re-sorted and distributed. Such are Toton, on the edge of the formerly flooded Trent lowland between Derby and Nottingham (where most of the coalfield traffic is collected before being passed on to London and the south); March, only completed in 1932, a similar concentration point for the LNER; South Crewe, at the junction of three main lines of traffic on the old LNWR (cf. Fig. 241), and Stoke Gifford, which collects Bristol and South Wales traffic on the GWR.

Two of the outstanding features of the British railway system are the perfection of its permanent way (and consequent reputation for speed) and the small size, when compared with the Continent or the United States, of its rolling-stock. The former is largely due to the way in which the lines

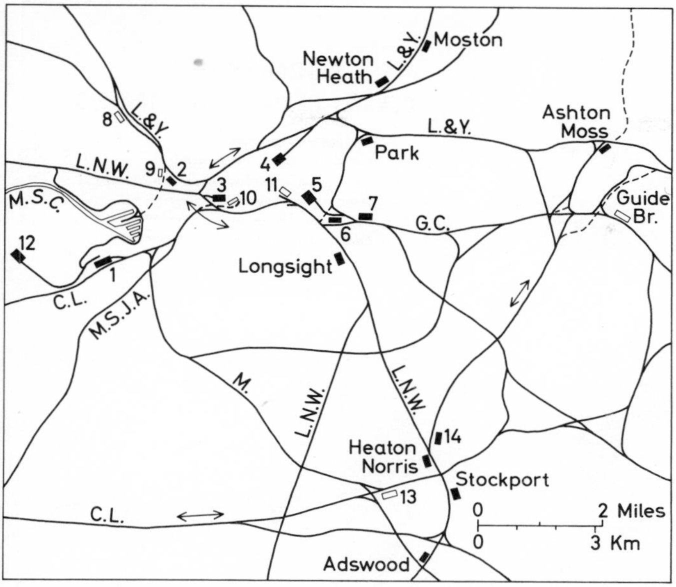

FIG. 243. The radial lines and belt connection of Manchester, 1969

Closed depots are shown in hollow symbols. Key to numbers: 1, Trafford Park; 2, Hope St; 3, Liverpool Road; 4, Oldham Road; 5, Ancoats; 6, Ashburys; 7, Ardwick; 8, Brindle Heath; 9, Windsor Bridge; 10, Deansgate; 11, London Road; 12, M.S.C. 'Containerbase'; 13, Heaton Mersey; 14, Jubilee Sidings.

It is not possible to make quite the same distinction between suburban marshalling yards and terminal goods depots as it was in London. But No. 4 is the main N.C.L. depot, 3 is the 'continental' customs depot, and 1, 12 and Longsight are the freightliner terminals. Double-ended arrows show the main routes used by through traffic.

were originally built. In the first place, solidarity of construction was a policy carried to extreme degrees in order to satisfy those who feared for the safety of the trains; secondly, the early engineers were for the most part haunted by a fear that the locomotive would only run on level or nearly level lines, hence the extraordinary care taken, by the provision of deep cuttings and tunnels and lofty embankments, to ensure the gentleness of gradients.[1] Another legacy from the early days is a small loading gauge (i.e. width and height of carriages and engines allowed)—from our pioneer experience of which continental builders profited by employing a larger one—but full development under such conditions would have been difficult but for our excellent coal supplies of high calorific value.

During the First World War, the railways were taken over temporarily by the State. It may be said that experience thus gained in unified working led to the consolidation of the numerous pre-existing companies into four great groups from 1 January 1923—London, Midland and Scottish;

1. See S. H. Beaver, 'Geography from a railway train', *Geography*, **21**, 1936, 265–83.

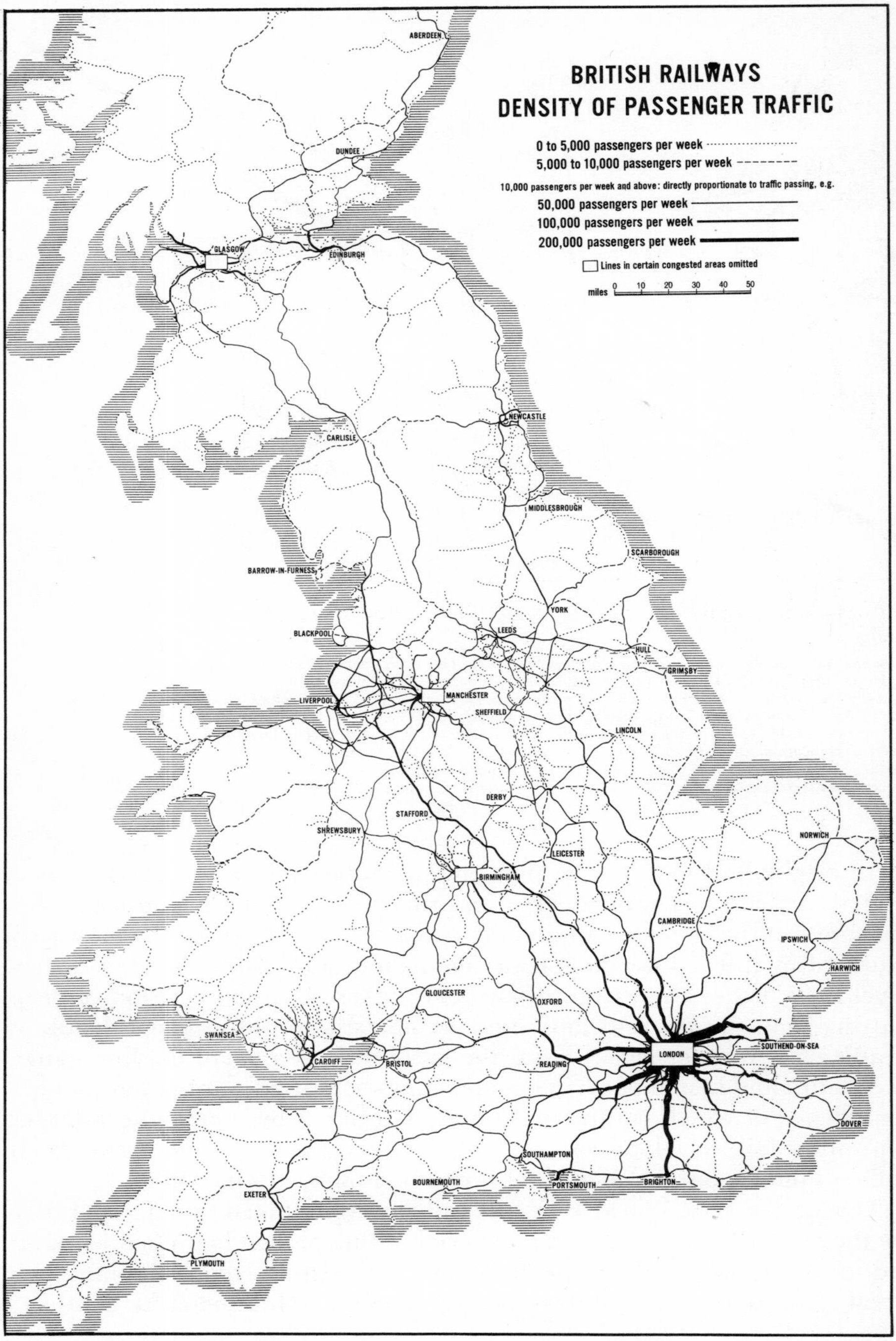

FIG. 244. The volume of passenger traffic on British railways, 1962

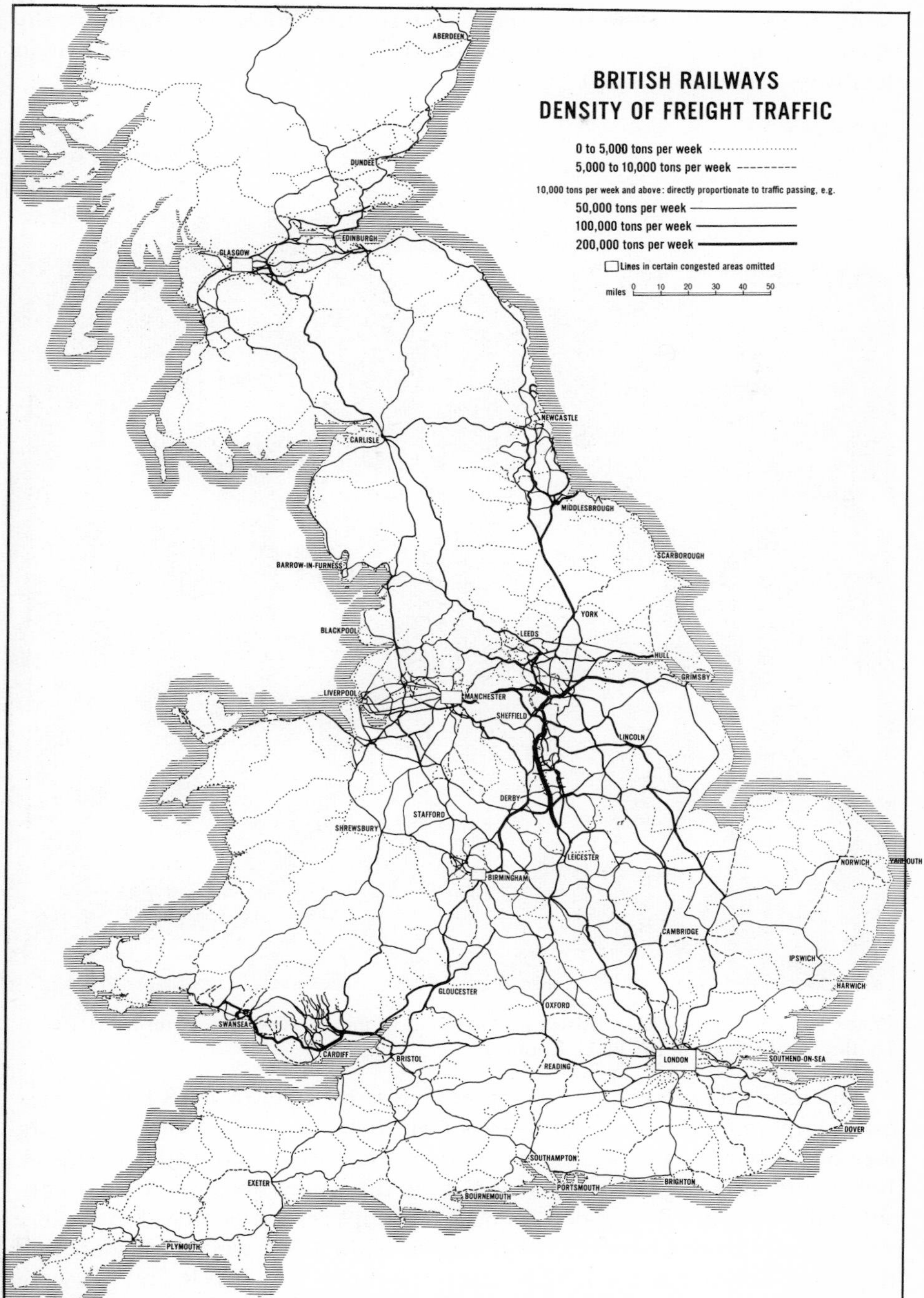

FIG. 245. The volume of freight traffic on British railways, 1962

London and North Eastern; Great Western; and Southern. Again, in the Second World War, the State took control and nationalisation as British Railways followed in 1948.

PLATE 26. The 'new look' in British Rail's freight traffic: the freightliner terminal at Dudley, in the heart of the Black Country

The four railway systems which existed from 1923 to 1948 had carried out a large measure of integration within their areas by absorbing canals, steamer services, road transport services for both goods and passengers, hotels and catering services. At the same time they had preserved a considerable measure of competition. Two groups served Scotland and there was friendly rivalry between the *Royal Scot* of the LMS west coast route and the *Flying Scotsman* of the LNER east coast route. The GWR and SR were rivals in the South-west, both serving Exeter and Plymouth. London to the Midlands traffic brought the GWR and LMS into competition—as to

Birmingham. With nationalisation road services were separated from rail and the hotels-catering was also divorced: there was little element of competition left. Largely as a result of road competition and the decline of freight traffic, the nationalised railway system showed ever-increasing annual losses, despite such radical changes as main line electrification, continued electrification of suburban lines, including all the southeast coast; the substitution of diesel locomotives for steam, and the extensive use

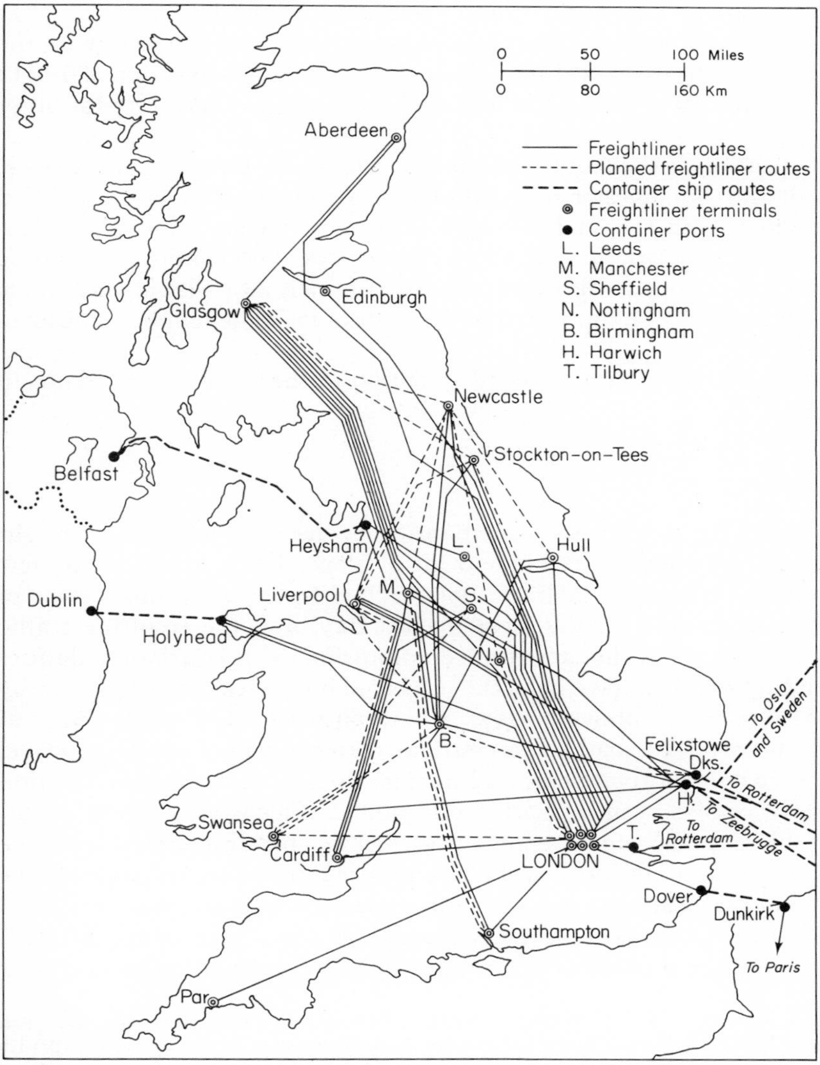

FIG. 246. Freightliner and container ship routes, 1968
(From *Geographical Digest* 1969 by permission of George Philip and Son, Ltd.)

of diesel rail cars. The position in 1962 is shown by the two official maps here reproduced, giving density of passenger and freight traffic respectively.

The desperate financial position led to the report prepared by Dr Beeching and published in April 1963. Its drastic proposals included the closing of about one third of the total railway mileage and some 4000 stations, and although the report's recommendations were not implemented in their entirety, there has been a steady reduction in passenger services. The number of stations has been reduced from 5474 in 1956 to 2888 in 1966, and the route from 30 617 kilometres (19 025 miles) to 21 067 kilometres (13 721 miles) in the same period. Freight services have been reorganised, with the introduction of the express 'Liner Trains', and the rationalisation of freight depots in many large towns has released much railway property for other uses.[1]

Electrification of the trunk lines between London, Birmingham, Crewe, Liverpool and Manchester was completed in 1967 and the last scheduled steam-hauled train ran in June 1968. The most recent railway plan envisages a basic network of some 17 700 kilometres (11 000 miles), including lines which it is hoped will eventually be commercially viable and others which will probably be supported on grounds of social benefit by some form of subsidy.

It remains in this chapter to call attention to the more recent trends in transport.

Roads

Undoubtedly the extraordinary expansion of the road haulage of freight and the use of the private car take pride of place. There are now very few villages in the country which are not reached by a public bus service of some sort, be it only on the local market day, and the resulting traffic patterns, which are at the same time emphasising existing urban nodalities and creating new foci, have been the subject of interesting investigations by F. H. W. Green (see above p. 657). About 60 per cent of all the internal freight now travels by road and an estimated 10 per cent of passenger travel is by bus, coach or private car, and in consequence the economic position of the railways has been seriously undermined. This is of course a worldwide problem by no means confined to Britain, but in contrast with the United States and certain European countries, the reorganisation of the road system necessary to cope with this expansion of traffic has only been initiated in the last decade. A few bypasses and a few 'arterial roads' leading out of the larger cities were built during the 1920s and 1930s and after

1. See J. A. Patmore, 'The changing network of British Railways', *Geography*, **47**, 1962, 401–5; also J. H. Appleton, 'Some geographical aspects of the modernisation of British railways', *Geography*, **52**, 1967, 357–73. A further 1209 kilometres (751 miles) were closed in 1967–68; see J. H. Appleton, *Disused Railways in the Countryside of England and Wales*, a report to the Countryside Commission, HMSO, 1970.

the war, but in general the roads remained until recently much as they were in 1900 and the problems of congestion and accidents were immense.

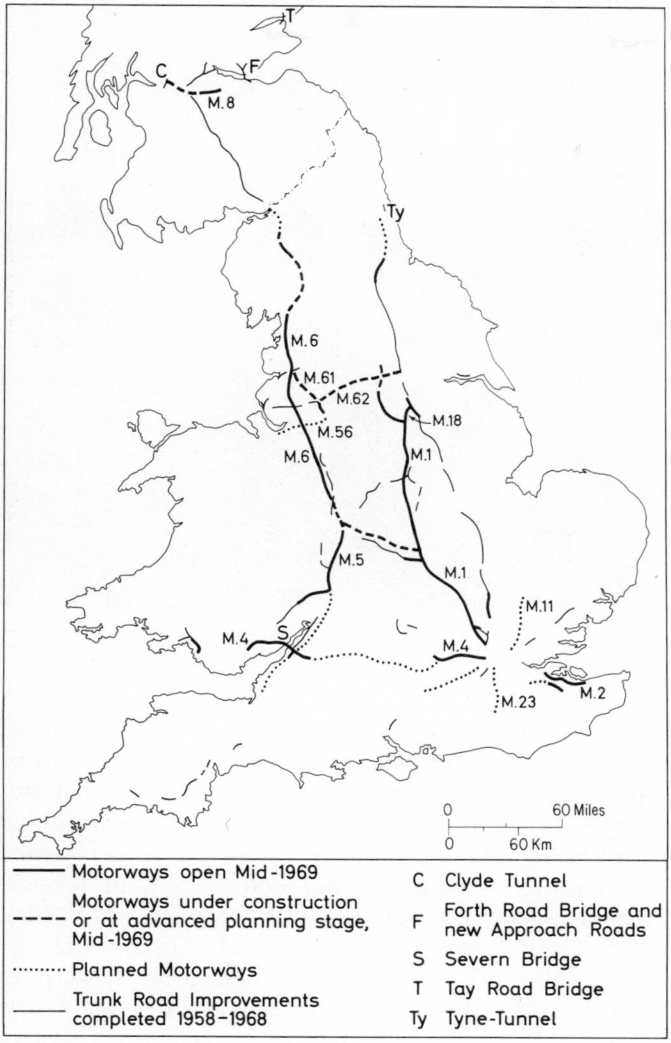

FIG. 247. Motorways in 1969
This map bears an almost uncanny resemblance to the railway map of 1844 (Fig. 240).

After the First World War the public roads of Britain were classified as 'A', which were numbered, 'B' (likewise numbered) and 'C', or unclassified roads. At a later date a small number of the chief A roads were recognised as trunk roads and their upkeep (except where they pass through large towns) became the responsibility of the central government. Other-

PLATE 27. The Severn Bridge
Opened in 1966, this bridge forms a vital link in the road communications between England and South Wales.

wise the county is the highway authority. National road-planning initiated during and after the 1939–45 war culminated in the publication in 1948 by the Ministry of Transport of a proposed new road system of trunk and motor roads. The Special Roads Act of 1949 restricted the use of the proposed motorways to motor traffic only and in 1958 the Preston bypass was opened as the first section of the planned 1600 kilometres (1000 miles) of motorway. This total has now been increased to 2175 kilometres (1350 miles) of which about 1200 kilometres (750 miles) form the basic network of interconnected routes (M1, M4, M5 and M6) with the remaining mileage in the form of isolated sections, such as the M2 Medway Towns bypass in Kent. At the end of 1968 853 kilometres (530 miles) of motorway were open, and a further 240 kilometres (150 miles) were under construction including the important M62 trans-Pennine section linking Manchester and Leeds (Fig. 247).

This national programme for the construction of entirely new motor routes is supplemented by an ambitious plan for the improvement of trunk routes. The A1 has now been rebuilt throughout much of its length, with many bypasses of motorway standard, and the replacement of estuarine ferry links on the trunk road system is eliminating frustrating delays to traffic. The Forth Road Bridge, just west of the railway bridge, was opened in 1964 and followed two years later by the Tay bridge and by that spanning the Severn estuary (Plates 27 and 28). In urban areas additional tunnels are being driven to alleviate congested river crossings: the second Blackwall tunnel in London and the Tyne tunnel were opened in 1967, and a second tunnel under the Mersey is in progress.

PLATE 28. The Forth bridges, rail and road

Improvements in urban transport have been designed to accommodate the ever-increasing numbers of private cars, and most large cities have now produced road plans incorporating sections of urban motorways. Such roads are highly expensive to construct as a result of land prices and the need for frequent viaducts, cuttings and even tunnels, and to date the only such roads completed are the M4 in West London, the Hendon extension of the M1, and the 'Mancunian Way' in Manchester.[1] The authorities in most of Britain's conurbations have now initiated land-use/transportation surveys involving the collecting of data on all aspects of travel and associated industrial, commercial and social activities and with the general aim of integrating transport planning with future city development as a whole.

1. The most recent and most spectacular example was opened in 1970—in the Tame valley between Walsall and West Bromwich. Here the M1, M5 and M6 meet in a series of curved viaducts that quickly became known as 'spaghetti junction'!

Pipelines[1]

As a means of transportation the pipeline is now an integral part of the whole system—quite apart of course from its long-established use for the transference of water and gas from source to consumer. The pipeline has many advantages for the transport of materials in liquid or slurry form—it is laid underground and so is unseen, and interferes but little with surface land use, it reduces considerably the amount of tanker traffic on both road and railway, and it can ensure a constant flow of materials.

Most of the now considerable pipeline network has already been referred to in previous chapters. Crude oil pipelines are shown on Fig. 157; in addition there are petroleum products pipelines linking London Airport (Heathrow) with the oil refineries at Fawley and Isle of Grain, linking Thames-side refineries with those on Merseyside, and linking the Merseyside refineries with the ICI Severnside chemical complex. Natural gas pipelines are shown on Fig. 150; with the advent of North Sea gas this network is likely to be considerably extended. Petrochemical feedstock pipelines are referred to on p. 587; the most important link Fawley oil refinery with Severnside, and the Merseyside refineries with the chemical industries on Tees-side and at Fleetwood. Lastly an interesting pipeline carries chalk slurry from quarries in the Chiltern Hills to a cement works at Rugby, where the original basis of Lower Lias limestone has been worked out (cf. p. 365).

Airways

Distances in Britain are too small for internal air services to displace rail to the extent that they have done in countries of great distances, such as the United States. When the time taken to reach one of the London airports from the centre of London is added to that from the provincial airport to the city centre, the margin of time saved is small over distances of under 300 kilometres (200 miles). Advertisements for the high-speed electric train services between London, the Midlands, Manchester and Liverpool emphasise the advantages of 'city centre to city centre' travel. Nevertheless, the air age has come to stay, and the increase in both passenger and freight traffic during the last two decades has been phenomenal, as the following table shows:

Domestic air traffic

	1952	1961	1967
Passengers (thousands)	669	2841	5314
Passenger-kilometres flown (millions)	186	965	1941
Passenger-miles flown (millions)	116	600	1206
Cargo freight (thousand short tons)	3	19	74

1. See R. T. Foster, 'Pipeline development in the United Kingdom', *Geography,* **54**, 1969, 204–11.

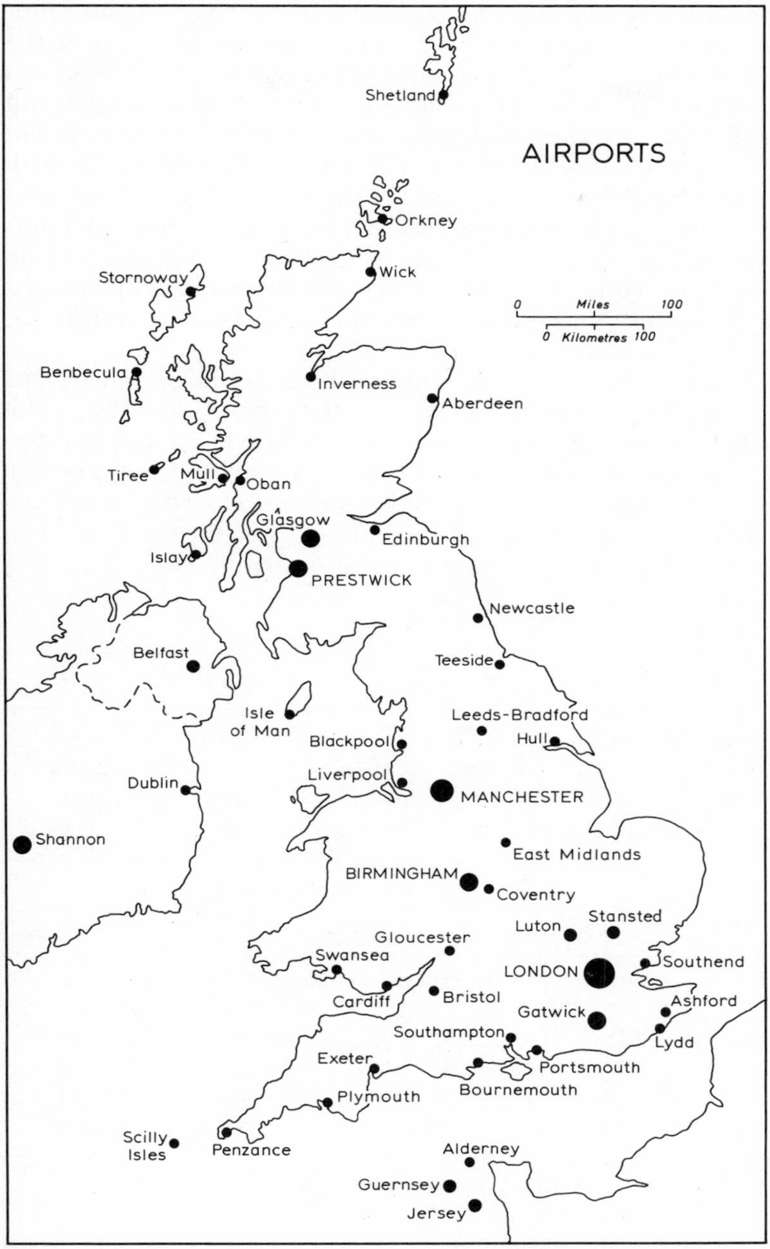
AIRPORTS
Shetland
Orkney
Wick
Stornoway
Benbecula
Inverness
Aberdeen
Tiree
Mull
Oban
Glasgow
Edinburgh
Islay
PRESTWICK
Newcastle
Belfast
Teeside
Isle of Man
Leeds-Bradford
Hull
Blackpool
Dublin
Liverpool
MANCHESTER
Shannon
East Midlands
BIRMINGHAM
Coventry
Stansted
Luton
Gloucester
Swansea
LONDON
Southend
Cardiff
Bristol
Ashford
Gatwick
Southampton
Lydd
Exeter
Portsmouth
Bournemouth
Plymouth
Scilly Isles
Penzance
Alderney
Guernsey
Jersey
0 Miles 100
0 Kilometres 100

FIG. 248. Airports in 1969

Though such services as London–Glasgow and London–Manchester are well used, air transport, especially for passengers, has come into most prominence where a sea crossing is involved—notably for holiday traffic to the Channel Islands and Isle of Man and for regular traffic to Belfast and Dublin, from Penzance to the Scilly Isles and from the Scottish mainland to the Outer Hebrides, Orkney, and Shetland. Car ferries for motorists and their cars across the Channel form a special type of 'foreign' traffic with fourteen different routes from Southend, Lydd or Ferryfield (Kent), and Hurn (Hants)—two going direct as far as Switzerland. Normal international services, especially long distance, tend to be concentrated on London (Heathrow), equipped to take the largest aircraft in existence, but Manchester, Prestwick (for Glasgow) and Shannon (near Limerick) are extensively used as ports of call.

As with domestic air traffic, international air traffic has increased enormously since the Second World War, as the tables below show. Not only has the amount of travel increased, but the share of aircraft in international passenger movement is also increasing steadily at the expense of the ocean liner. In 1960, out of 13 million persons entering or leaving Britain, 5.9 millions (47 per cent) did so by air; in 1968 the total had risen to 25 million travellers, of whom 63 per cent travelled by air.

International air traffic (UK airlines only)

	1952	1961	1967
Passengers (thousands)	1064	4010	7004
Passenger-kilometres flown (millions)	1814	6326	12 126
Passenger-miles flown (millions)	1127	3931	7535
Cargo freight (thousand short tons)	32	233	245

Foreign trade of airports, 1967 (in £m)

AIRPORT	IMPORTS	EXPORTS	RE-EXPORTS	TOTAL
London	475.5	431.2	55.0	961.8
Manchester	34.6	32.6	1.5	68.6
Prestwick	30.5	31.8	1.1	63.4
All others	139.9	79.4	5.6	229.3

Total trade by air, £1323.2m; by sea, £10 956.6m; by land route to Eire, £83.2m.

Naturally enough, the aeroplane cannot compete with the ocean freighter, but the amount, and in particular the value, of air freight, is also rising rapidly, so that in 1967 it represented 10.7 per cent of the total value of foreign trade.

London airport, indeed, in terms of the total value of its trade, is the third 'port' in the United Kingdom after the seaports of London and Liverpool (cf. table on p. 719). Its imports, unlike those of almost all the seaports, include almost nothing in the foodstuffs and raw materials categories, and are mainly made up of valuable machinery (including aircraft parts) and manufactured goods; the same classes of commodity make up the bulk of the export traffic, including again aircraft engines and parts and office machinery; the re-exports include quantities of furskins, and more machinery.

British airports have undergone a rapid evolution, parallel to the aircraft they serve. Before the Second World War London was served by Croydon on a plateau surface on the chalk of the North Downs and by Northolt to the northwest; it was during the war that a search was made for the much larger area which would be needed. The only site seemed to be an extensive area a dozen miles west of the heart of London occupied by market gardeners producing intensively from one of the finest stretches of brick-earth soils in

PLATE 29. London Airport, Heathrow

the country. It was one of the first head-on collisions between urban needs and the newly declared policy of conserving good agricultural land. It would be wrong to say agriculture lost because all land planning is in the national interest, and above all Britain's capital had to have a first-class airport. It is interesting to note that there is no rail access: it is solely by road. Croydon in due course was abandoned, Northolt was discontinued as a civil airport, but congestion at Heathrow led to the opening of Gatwick some thirty miles south on the main electrified line to Brighton in 1958. Blackbushe and Stansted (Essex) act as emergency subsidiaries. The trouble in Britain, as all over the world, is to find the necessary space—with runways two miles and more in length for giant jets—sufficiently near the urban centres they are to serve.

A large proportion of Britain's internal air services are run by BEA (British European Airways) which, as its name implies, links Britain with most European countries. Britain's other state-owned organization is BOAC (British Overseas Airways Corporation) serving extra-European destinations. The bulk of long-distance traffic is handled by London (Heathrow), Manchester (Ringway) and Prestwick, together with Shannon (Irish Republic).

28
The seaports of Great Britain

The following six tables present statistically some aspects of the fortunes of British ports during the last half-century. Tables 1, 3, 4 and 5 are expressed in percentages and so give a measure of the relative importance of the various ports at different periods. In reading Table 2, however, which is expressed in terms of value, the great change in the value of money must be borne in mind; because London's trade is now worth eight times as much as in 1913 this does not mean that the actual traffic has increased eightfold in volume. The figures in Table 6, giving the tonnage of vessels cleared from the ports, have of course been considerably affected by changes in the character of shipping. Southampton's figures for many years were swelled by the 80 000 tons a week represented by the transatlantic sailings of the *Queens*, but quite fundamental changes are now being wrought by the 'supertankers' which have, for example, converted Milford Haven from a small fishing creek into the fourth freight port in the United Kingdom.

Table 1 illustrates two facts of outstanding importance. The first is the concentration of the huge trade of the United Kingdom in a few major ports. Thus the first six on the list handle nearly three-quarters of the total traffic. Even more remarkable are the figures for the first two—London and Liverpool between them handling over one-half of the total foreign seaborne trade of the United Kingdom. The second point of importance is that this concentration of trade on the major ports has been a feature of the growth of British trade for a long time and, what is perhaps still more significant, it is still maintained, despite the temporary eclipse of London during the Second World War. The table also reveals, however, the decline of the coal exporting ports of Cardiff and the Tyne, and also of the Clyde and of Liverpool; and the footnote indicates that, despite the decline of many of the minor ports round the coasts, certain ports have increased in importance, notably the East Anglian ports of Harwich and Felixstowe, with their mainly short-sea-route European trade, whilst new ports concerned with the oil trade, such as Milford Haven, have come into the picture.

Table 2 tells something of the same story in a different way, using figures of the value of trade. Whereas the total United Kingdom trade has increased in value by just over 8 times between 1913 and 1967, and that of London in almost exactly the same proportion, the value of Liverpool's trade has increased by only 5 times, that of the Tyne by only $4\frac{1}{2}$ times, that of Glasgow by $5\frac{1}{2}$ times, and that of Cardiff by only $2\frac{1}{2}$ times; whilst that of Harwich has increased by $9\frac{1}{2}$ times, and that of the 'other ports' by no less than fourteen times.

Tables 3 and 4, based on the value of trade, show the fluctuations in the relative importance of the ports in terms of exports and imports. London has clearly maintained its overall position with an increasing share of exports balancing a declining share of imports, while Liverpool has declined on both counts. The improvement in the relative positions of Harwich, Felixstowe and Dover reflects our increasing trade with the near Continent; whilst Cardiff's virtual fade-out from the exports list results from the extinction of its coal trade, and Milford Haven, Swansea and Grangemouth have all risen in the import list as a result of petroleum imports.

The entrepôt or re-export trade is shown in Table 5. In terms of the value of such trade, three facts stand out clearly: first the continuing dominance of London, secondly the decline of Liverpool and thirdly the importance of re-exports via the short sea routes to the Continent. If one takes re-export *tonnage* figures, a rather different picture emerges, for considerable recent changes have been brought about by the oil industry, which imports oil in large tankers and re-exports it in smaller tankers to refineries in other countries. Thus, in terms of tonnage, Milford Haven is now second to London as a re-exporter, with 27 per cent of the total as against London's 46 per cent. Liverpool is third with 7 per cent (partly made up of oil) and Swansea (another oil port) fourth with 3.5 per cent. Excluding oil, however, London is now more dominant than ever before in the entrepôt trade, with about two-thirds of the total tonnage.

Table 6, which deserves careful study and comparison with the previous tables, brings out a number of interesting points: (*a*) the importance of coastwise traffic, spread over a wide range of ports; (*b*) the 'passenger' ports—transatlantic like Southampton and short-sea-route like Dover and Holyhead (where the numerous daily services of cross-channel ships cause a large tonnage total to mount up), together with the inter-island ferry ports such as the Isle of Wight, Portsmouth and Belfast; (*c*) the rise of the 'other ports' in foreign traffic—including the purely oil ports such as Milford Haven and the recently expanded 'container' port of Felixstowe; (*d*) the general large increases in ocean-going tonnage since 1952 at several ports, such as London and Southampton, which now have substantial oil refineries and are visited at frequent intervals by giant tankers.

1. Trade of the leading ports expressed as a percentage of value of the total trade

PORT	1913	1926–30	1935	1948	1960	1967
London	29.3	34.5	37.7	31.8	33.9	33.3
Liverpool	26.4	23.3	22.0	27.3	21.4	18.0
Hull	6.3	5.3	6.0	5.3	5.4	6.7
Manchester	4.0	4.7	4.3	5.6	5.0	4.5
Southampton	3.8	4.5	4.4	3.0	3.9	4.2
Glasgow	3.9	4.0	3.8	4.4	3.6	3.3
Harwich	2.4	2.5	2.0	0.7	1.8	3.2
Tyne ports	1.7	1.9	1.9	1.5	1.4	1.1
Dover and Folkestone	2.5	1.8	1.2	1.1	1.7	2.3
Bristol	1.5	1.8	2.0	2.9	2.6	2.6
Grimsby	2.7	1.7	1.4	1.0	1.0	1.1
Goole	1.3	1.3	1.1	0.8	0.9	1.0
Leith	1.6	1.3	1.1	0.8	0.7	0.9
Cardiff	1.7	1.1	1.1	0.8	0.6	0.6
Newhaven	1.5	0.7	0.6	0.4	0.4	—
Other ports, Gt. Britain	8.0	8.3	8.3	11.3	14.8	16.2
Northern Ireland	1.4	1.3	1.3	1.3	0.9	1.0

The first six (London, Liverpool, Hull, Manchester, Southampton, and Glasgow) 73.7 per cent of the total in 1913; 76.3 per cent in 1926–30; 77.4 per cent in 1931; 80.2 per cent in 1935; 77.4 per cent in 1948; 73.2 per cent in 1960; 69.7 per cent in 1967. In 1967 among 'other ports' Felixstowe (2.4) and Milford Haven (1.3) have risen considerably in importance.

2. The leading British ports arranged according to the value of their trade (in £m)

PORT	1913	1926–30 AVERAGE	1935	1948	1960	1967
London	411.8	681.9	466.7	1 179.9	2 793.1	3 406.5
Imports	*253.9*	*470.4*	*321.4*	*673.2*	*1 523.4*	*1 773.8*
Exports	*99.1*	*148.1*	*112.2*	*483.2*	*1 212.4*	*1 580.4*
Re-exports	*58.8*	*67.5*	*33.1*	*23.5*	*57.3*	*52.2*
Liverpool	370.8	460.6	271.8	1 091.6	1 759.4	1 817.4
Imports	*175.5*	*220.4*	*139.8*	*545.8*	*809.9*	*893.3*
Exports	*170.1*	*222.8*	*125.5*	*533.4*	*923.6*	*910.2*
Re-exports	*25.2*	*17.4*	*6.5*	*12.4*	*25.9*	*13.9*
Hull	84.6	104.1	74.4	198.7	444.4	677.3
Imports	*49.8*	*71.4*	*48.5*	*127.0*	*259.0*	*353.6*
Exports	*29.2*	*31.2*	*24.8*	*64.6*	*182.3*	*319.4*
Re-exports	*5.6*	*1.5*	*1.1*	*5.1*	*3.1*	*4.3*
Manchester	56.3	93.1	52.9	208.7	414.0	449.9
Imports	*35.3*	*63.0*	*39.8*	*138.6*	*285.2*	*301.1*
Exports	*20.6*	*29.4*	*12.8*	*69.4*	*127.9*	*147.7*
Re-exports	*0.4*	*0.7*	*0.4*	*0.7*	*0.9*	*1.1*

PORT	1913	1926–30 AVERAGE	1935	1948	1960	1967
Southampton	53.6	88.9	54.9	113.3	320.3	429.6
Imports	*25.5*	*40.6*	*26.1*	*53.5*	*191.8*	*246.5*
Exports	*20.7*	*37.2*	*23.5*	*57.4*	*123.5*	*177.7*
Re-exports	*7.4*	*11.1*	*5.3*	*2.4*	*5.0*	*5.3*
Glasgow	54.8	79.5	46.7	162.5	293.8	312.1
Imports	*18.5*	*29.9*	*20.1*	*73.0*	*137.0*	*152.3*
Exports	*35.9*	*48.6*	*26.1*	*89.2*	*154.9*	*158.7*
Re-exports	*0.4*	*1.0*	*0.5*	*0.3*	*1.9*	*1.1*
Harwich	34.3	48.4	25.0	25.8	147.2	323.1
Imports	*25.6*	*41.8*	*20.1*	*14.3*	*84.1*	*175.3*
Exports	*6.0*	*4.9*	*3.7*	*10.2*	*60.2*	*141.4*
Re-exports	*2.7*	*1.7*	*1.3*	*1.3*	*2.9*	*6.5*
Tyne ports	24.6	36.9	23.1	55.6	111.8	110.3
Imports	*11.4*	*20.9*	*11.6*	*29.2*	*63.9*	*63.6*
Exports	*13.2*	*15.8*	*11.3*	*26.1*	*47.6*	*45.7*
Re-exports	*0.0*	*0.2*	*0.1*	*0.3*	*0.3*	*1.0*
Dover and Folkestone	35.2	35.3	15.6	41.2	140.4	241.0
Imports	*24.4*	*22.7*	*8.7*	*23.2*	*66.2*	*120.8*
Exports	*6.7*	*6.9*	*4.4*	*14.4*	*67.7*	*169.2*
Re-exports	*4.1*	*5.7*	*2.5*	*3.6*	*6.5*	*11.0*
Bristol	22.1	35.0	24.6	108.4	212.9	259.0
Imports	*18.0*	*30.9*	*23.4*	*100.1*	*179.8*	*216.8*
Exports	*4.0*	*3.7*	*0.9*	*7.8*	*32.1*	*47.0*
Re-exports	*0.1*	*0.4*	*0.3*	*0.5*	*1.0*	*1.1*
Grimsby	37.9	34.0	17.4	33.6	85.9	111.6
Imports	*15.9*	*21.6*	*12.3*	*20.5*	*69.7*	*83.5*
Exports	*21.9*	*12.0*	*5.1*	*11.3*	*16.0*	*27.4*
Re-exports	*0.1*	*0.4*	*0.05*	*1.8*	*0.2*	*0.7*
Goole	18.8	25.8	13.1	28.1	73.5	106.2
Imports	*8.4*	*12.2*	*5.0*	*10.0*	*36.2*	*55.5*
Exports	*10.3*	*13.5*	*8.0*	*17.6*	*36.7*	*49.8*
Re-exports	*0.1*	*0.1*	*0.1*	*1.5*	*0.6*	*0.8*
Leith	23.0	24.6	13.3	28.6	61.3	87.8
Imports	*15.8*	*19.0*	*10.1*	*22.4*	*44.7*	*55.2*
Exports	*6.9*	*5.4*	*3.1*	*6.2*	*16.5*	*32.1*
Re-exports	*0.3*	*0.2*	*0.1*	—	*0.1*	*0.5*
Cardiff	23.9	22.5	13.1	29.0	48.7	61.1
Imports	*6.7*	*9.6*	*4.8*	*17.9*	*37.5*	*43.8*
Exports	*17.2*	*12.9*	*8.3*	*10.2*	*10.5*	*17.2*
Re-exports	*0.0*	*0.0*	*0.0*	*0.9*	*0.7*	*0.1*

PORT	1913	1926–30 AVERAGE	1935	1948	1960	1967
Newhaven	21.0	13.5	7.0	14.0	36.7	34.5
Imports	*13.5*	*8.8*	*3.2*	*10.2*	*20.2*	*18.0*
Exports	*5.0*	*3.5*	*2.2*	*3.3*	*15.7*	*15.6*
Re-exports	*2.5*	*1.2*	*1.6*	*0.5*	*0.8*	*1.0*
Other ports Great Britain	111.6	164.0	101.0	357.1	1 218.7	1 532.5
Imports	*53.3*	*86.2*	*49.3*	*181.4*	*668.5*	*984.9*
Exports	*57.8*	*74.8*	*49.9*	*166.1*	*517.2*	*547.6*
Re-exports	*0.5*	*3.0*	*1.7*	*9.6*	*33.0*	*83.7*
Ports of Northern Ireland	19.5	26.4	16.6	48.4	74.5	109.3
Imports	*17.3*	*18.7*	*11.8*	*36.7*	*63.6*	*91.4*
Exports	*0.7*	*6.6*	*4.1*	*11.4*	*10.0*	*17.9*
Re-exports	*1.4*	*1.1*	*0.7*	*0.3*	*0.9*	*0.5*
United Kingdom Total	1 403.6	1 974.2	1 237.2	3 724.5	8 236.6	11 462.9
Imports	*768.7*	*1 184.0*	*756.0*	*2 078.0*	*4 540.7*	*6 434.1*
Exports	*525.3*	*677.2*	*425.8*	*1 581.8*	*3 554.8*	*5 028.8*
Re-exports	*109.6*	*113.1*	*55.3*	*64.7*	*141.2*	*119.6*

In 1967 among 'other ports' Felixstowe reached a total trade of £239m, Milford Haven £135m, and Swansea £108m.

3. *Export trade of the leading ports expressed as a percentage of the total seaborne export trade*

PORT	1913	1926–30	1935	1948	1960	1967
London	18.9	21.9	26.2	30.4	34.1	36.2
Liverpool	32.4	32.9	29.4	33.6	26.0	20.9
Hull	5.6	4.6	5.8	4.1	5.1	7.3
Manchester	4.0	4.3	3.0	4.4	3.6	3.4
Southampton	4.0	5.5	5.5	3.6	3.5	4.0
Glasgow	6.9	7.2	6.1	5.6	4.4	3.6
Harwich	1.1	0.7	0.9	0.6	1.7	3.2
Tyne ports	2.5	2.5	2.6	1.6	1.3	0.8
Dover and Folkestone	1.3	1.0	1.1	0.9	1.9	2.5
Bristol	0.8	0.5	0.2	0.5	0.9	1.1
Grimsby	4.2	1.8	1.2	0.7	0.5	0.6
Goole	2.0	2.0	1.9	1.1	1.0	1.1
Leith	1.3	0.8	0.8	0.4	0.5	0.7
Cardiff	3.3	1.9	2.0	0.6	0.3	0.4
Newhaven	1.0	0.5	0.5	0.2	0.4	0.3
Other ports. Great Britain	—	—	—	—	14.6	12.6
Northern Ireland	—	—	—	—	0.3	0.3

In 1967 the 'other ports' included Felixstowe (2.4), Grangemouth (2.0), Tees and Hartlepool (1.6) and Swansea (1.1).

4. Import trade of the leading ports expressed as a percentage of the total seaborne import trade

PORT	1913	1926–30	1935	1948	1960	1967
London	33.3	39.7	42.5	32.5	33.5	31.1
Liverpool	22.8	18.6	18.5	26.4	17.8	15.4
Hull	6.5	6.0	6.4	5.1	5.7	6.2
Manchester	4.6	5.3	5.3	5.2	6.3	5.3
Southampton	3.3	3.4	3.5	2.6	4.2	4.3
Glasgow	2.4	2.5	2.7	3.5	3.0	2.9
Harwich	3.3	3.5	2.6	0.5	1.9	3.0
Tyne ports	1.4	1.8	1.5	1.4	1.4	1.3
Dover and Folkestone	3.2	1.1	1.2	1.1	1.5	2.1
Bristol	2.3	2.6	3.1	4.8	4.0	3.7
Grimsby	2.1	1.8	1.6	1.0	1.5	1.5
Goole	1.1	1.0	0.6	0.4	0.8	1.0
Leith	2.1	1.6	1.3	1.1	1.0	1.0
Cardiff	0.9	0.8	0.7	0.9	0.8	0.8
Newhaven	—	—	—	0.4	0.4	0.3
Other ports. Great Britain	—	—	—	—	14.8	17.3
Northern Ireland	—	—	—	—	1.4	1.6

In 1967 'other ports' included Felixstowe (2.4), Milford Haven (2.1), Tees and Hartlepool (1.3), Swansea (1.0) and Grangemouth (0.9).

5. Entrepôt or re-export trade of the leading ports expressed as a percentage of the total seaborne entrepôt trade (by value)

PORT	1913	1926–30	1935	1948	1960	1967
London	53.7	59.7	59.9	36.3	40.6	43.7
Liverpool	23.0	15.4	11.8	19.1	18.3	11.7
Hull	5.1	1.3	2.0	8.0	2.2	3.7
Manchester	0.4	0.6	0.7	1.0	0.6	1.0
Southampton	6.7	9.8	9.6	3.7	3.5	4.5
Glasgow	0.4	0.9	0.9	0.5	1.3	1.0
Harwich	2.5	1.5	2.3	2.0	2.1	5.4
Tyne ports	0.0	0.2	0.2	0.5	0.2	1.0
Dover and Folkestone	3.7	5.0	4.5	5.8	4.6	0.2
Bristol	0.1	0.4	0.5	0.8	0.7	1.0
Grimsby	0.1	0.4	0.1	2.7	0.1	0.6
Goole	0.1	0.1	0.1	2.3	0.4	0.7
Leith	0.3	0.2	0.2	—	0.1	0.5
Cardiff	0.0	0.0	0.0	1.4	0.5	0.1
Newhaven	2.3	1.1	2.8	0.8	0.6	1.0
Other ports. Great Britain	—	—	—	—	23.3	14.4
Northern Ireland	—	—	—	—	0.6	0.5

In 1967, *seaborne* entrepôt trade represented 65 per cent of the total; 34 per cent was carried by air and 1 per cent across the Irish land boundary (cf. p. 718).

6. The leading British ports, showing net tonnage of vessels cleared (millions of tons)

PORT	1913		1926–30		1952		1967	
	FOREIGN	COASTAL	FOREIGN	COASTAL	FOREIGN	COASTAL	FOREIGN	COASTAL
London	11.4	8.6	19.4	7.9	18.5	11.1	34.0	9.4
Liverpool	11.2	4.2	13.0	3.5	12.7	3.8	16.2	4.2
Hull	4.4	1.4	4.4	1.3	4.3	1.6	5.6	1.6
Manchester	1.5	1.2	3.0	1.0	3.4	—	5.5	1.7
Southampton	6.6	1.6	10.4	1.5	13.8	4.1	20.7	6.3
Glasgow	4.3	2.0	4.8	1.5	4.9	1.8	6.0	1.6
Harwich	0.9	0.3	2.3	0.1	3.2	—	6.7	—
Tyne ports	8.5	3.4	7.4	2.2	3.7	4.4	3.9	3.0
Dover and Folkestone	3.2	0.3	2.8	0.2	4.5	—	12.2	—
Bristol	1.1	1.6	2.0	1.3	2.3	2.1	3.6	2.0
Grimsby	2.8	0.3	2.0	0.3	1.5	—	4.0	1.6
Goole	0.8	0.7	0.7	0.4	—	—	—	—
Leith	1.5	0.8	1.5	0.7	0.6	0.4	0.8	—
Cardiff	10.4	2.2	7.0	1.2	2.2	1.8	1.7	1.0
Newhaven	0.5	0.2	0.6	0.1	0.5	—	0.9	—
Swansea	2.8	0.6	3.2	0.6	4.3	1.5	2.3	1.5
Blyth	2.2	0.3	1.3	0.9	0.5	2.1	—	1.2
Plymouth	3.8	0.9	6.3	0.5	1.7	—	0.5	—
Middlesbrough	2.1	1.3	2.4	0.8	2.9	0.7	4.6	1.0
Holyhead (and Beaumaris)	0.0	1.5	1.4	0.7	1.4	—	2.0	—
Cowes and Isle of Wight	0.0	1.9	2.0	2.1	—	4.2	—	4.6
Portsmouth	0.1	1.6	0.2	2.0	—	2.8	—	3.2
Sunderland	2.0	1.5	1.4	1.5	—	2.0	—	1.4
Belfast	0.3	3.1	2.5	2.9	0.7	5.2	2.1	7.1
Newport (Mon.)	—	—	—	—	1.7	0.5	2.0	0.4
Lancaster	—	—	—	—	0.7	1.2	0.3	1.4
Falmouth	—	—	—	—	1.7	—	1.5	0.5
Milford Haven	—	—	—	—	—	—	8.5	3.8
Other ports	—	—	—	—	7.9	24.5	24.6	22.7

The study of the development of British ports affords many interesting examples of the interrelation of geographic and economic factors. In the first place it is true to say that the site of every British port was determined originally by local geographical conditions. The first requirement was the provision of a safe harbourage. In the second place the situation of that safe harbourage or anchorage relative to important parts of the country and the ease of communication therewith played a leading part. Perhaps the first great test of the suitability of an existing port in relation to changing conditions came with the development of inland transport and the Industrial Revolution—the canal era and the concentration of industry on the coalfields—and then again later with the developments of the railway age. Where the port was so situated that it could utilise to the full these new means of communication it survived and expanded. But a still greater test was to come. Could the port adapt itself to the increasing size of the steamship? A harbourage of limited size, a rock-girt basin, a river channel liable to silting or difficult and expensive to dredge: these are factors which have resulted in the downfall of once significant ports. Whatever their original advantages, all the great modern ports have had to adapt themselves to changing conditions. Two factors are absolutely essential to this development. The first is the suitability of the site to adaptation, the second the existence of sufficiently wealthy or powerful interests to carry out the actual work of organisation and construction. The one, it should be noticed, is useless without the other. It is significant how often the geographical factor which originally rendered the site of value or of importance as a port, as for example the existence of a small safe anchorage or pool at Liverpool and Hull, has become, with the changing requirements of shipping, of very little importance, and has passed both out of existence and out of knowledge.

The years since 1950 have witnessed the influence of a new technological

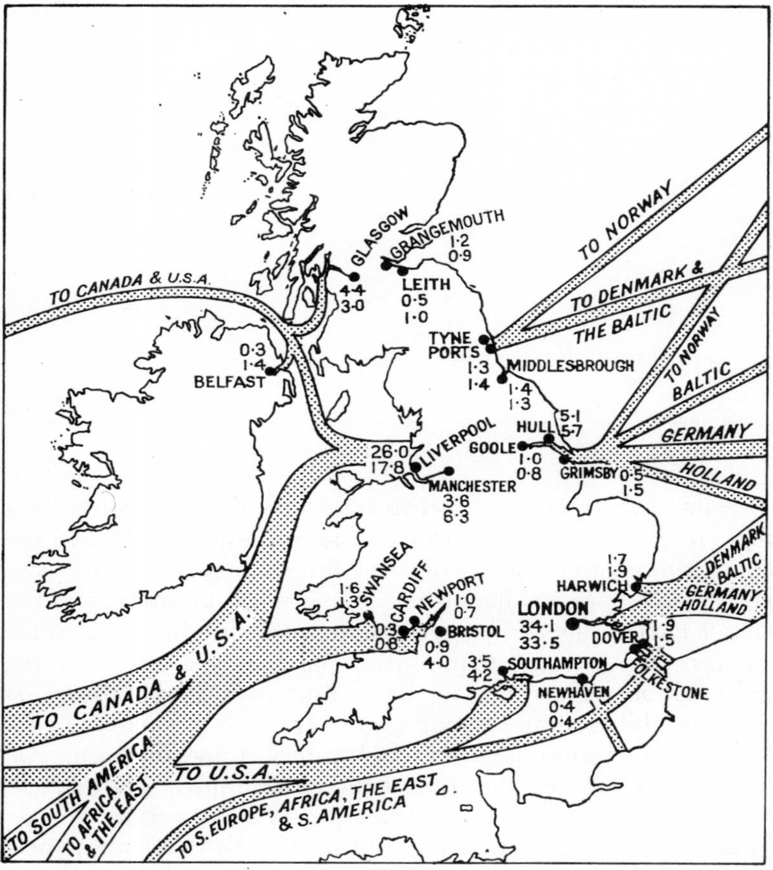

FIG. 249. General map of the Ports of the United Kingdom showing the proportions of the total export trade (upper figures) and import trade (lower figures) handled by each in 1960. Compare the 1967 figures given on pp. 721–2.

Some attempt is made to show the countries *principally* served by each port. It should be noted that most of the passenger and cargo liner services with South America are now from London with Southampton of lesser importance.

factor in the phenomenal increase in the size of oil tankers and other bulk carriers. The enormous size and deep draught of these vessels has led to considerable new port developments such as the creation of oil terminals in Milford Haven, the dredging of the approaches to Fawley on Southampton Water, the construction of a new oil terminal at Tranmere on the Mersey, the creation of deep-water ports at the mouth of the Tees and on the southern shores of the Humber estuary, and the construction of an entirely new port at Port Talbot to take large iron-ore carriers.

In the sections that follow the history of each port is briefly traced in order to show how the adaptation to changing economic and technological circumstances has been effected.

London

There is little doubt that London was a port as soon as it was a settlement. Below the site of London the banks of the River Thames were low and marshy and unsuitable for building, and we have seen how the settlement grew up where firm ground approached sufficiently near to the river and where there was also a possible fording place. Those who know London at the present day find it hard to believe that the Thames was ever fordable in the neighbourhood, but one must remember that man in the last 2000 years has consistently been training the river into a narrow channel, whereas in early times, especially over what is now the Surrey side around Southwark, the waters must have wandered over a very wide area, and have been correspondingly shallow. From the early settlement trackways radiated to different parts of the country both to north and to south of the river, and there can be little doubt indeed that the early inhabitants of London had their primitive boats on the River Thames and that London was, therefore, a meeting place of land and water routes and a port. We may go so far as to say that the history of the port of London falls into four stages:

(*a*) the early period (to the Norman Conquest)
(*b*) the medieval period to the eighteenth century
(*c*) the nineteenth century—the great dock building era
(*d*) the modern period dating from the establishment of the Port of London Authority in 1908.

The early period

The estuary of the Fleet as well as the well-known Pool of London below London Bridge must have afforded excellent anchorage for ships, and there is certainly no lack of evidence that Londinium was an important commercial centre much frequented by merchants and trading vessels at the time of the Romans. These facts are recorded by Tacitus in A.D. 61. It was natural, therefore, that London should later become the chief town of the East Saxons, and that in the eighth century the Venerable Bede should describe it as a market of many nations whose traders came to it both by sea and by land. Later, London fell into the hands of the invading Danes from whom it was rescued by King Alfred the Great who, by encouraging the building of ships, helped materially the commerce of the port.

The medieval period to the eighteenth century

There seems little doubt that London benefited on the whole from the Norman Conquest, for it was brought into closer relationship with the then more advanced countries of Europe. Merchants from France and from Flanders, as well as from more distant countries, came and settled in London and developed the city's foreign trade. The construction of the Tower of London by William the Conqueror illustrates the importance that was attached by the Normans to the stronghold. Even before the Norman invasion bands of German merchants had settled in what is now the area of Billingsgate, and it was from the descendants of these German settlers that the Hanseatic League developed. The centuries succeeding the Norman Conquest are marked especially by the development of the Hanseatic League (which had its headquarters where Cannon Street station now stands) and by the stranglehold which it gradually obtained over the commerce and shipping of the port of London. With the discovery of America by Columbus in 1492 the great age of exploration began. As early as 1505 the Merchant Adventurers was incorporated, and this association of Englishmen rapidly became a great band of merchant shipowners as well as trading adventurers. The English merchants rapidly became so strong that in 1598 the Hanseatic League was expelled from the country by Queen Elizabeth. The sixteenth and seventeenth centuries witnessed a great development of English foreign trade and with it the development of the trade of the port of London. The Russian Company, the Turkey Company, the East India Company, the Hudson's Bay Company and other concerns came into existence during this period, particularly under the stimulus of promises of monopolies to those companies which first opened up communication and trade with new or undeveloped countries. There is no doubt, too, that London benefited by the sack of Antwerp in 1585, since Antwerp was at that time the centre of European trade, and one is justified in saying that from that event onwards London became the commercial and financial centre of the world.

During this time London was a great river port. The small ships were beached or anchored by the side of the stream and their cargoes off-loaded in that position. Later it became desirable or necessary to construct small wooden piers or wharves of stone and wood at which the vessels could lie to be discharged or loaded. Alternatively, rectangular areas of the river bed were excavated, and the sides shored to prevent them slipping inwards. Such was the origin of Queenhithe and Billingsgate. Queenhithe—on the north bank above Southwark Bridge and so, like the Fleet anchorage, some

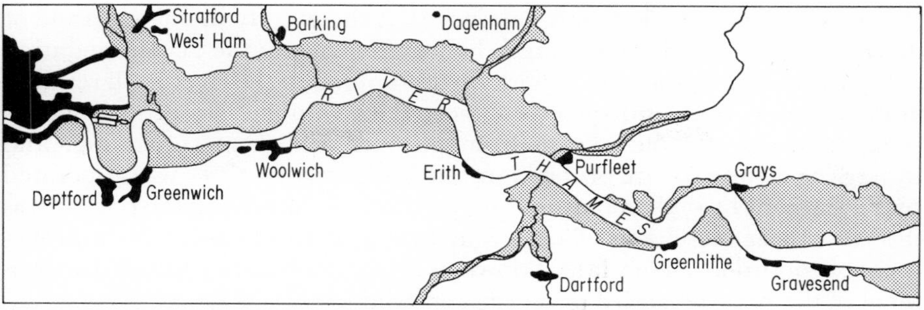

FIG. 250. Riverside settlements on the Thames below London in 1802

The stippled area is the alluvial flood plain—practically without any habitations at this date. All the riverside settlements were on bluffs where firmer rocks reached the river side.

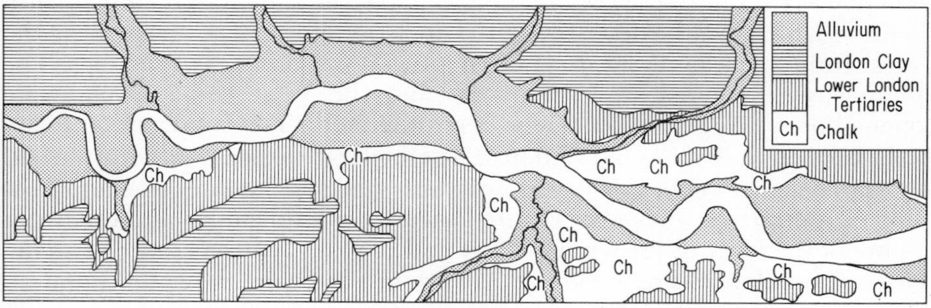

FIG. 251. The geology of the Thames Valley below London

Comparing this map with Fig. 250 it will be seen that the majority of the early riverside settlements are where the chalk affords firm ground.

distance above London Bridge, was probably the first. Old London Bridge, with its double lines of shops and houses and its numerous narrow arches, played an important part in limiting the activities of the port. The rush of water through the narrow arches, both with the flow and ebb of the tide, was so severe that navigation was virtually limited to small boats and then to short periods of the day when the water was comparatively slack. Thus the port developed below London Bridge, and it is significant that all the great docks of the Port of London today are in the area below London Bridge. London Bridge is, indeed, the head of ocean navigation (except for colliers and craft of comparable size up to about 2800 gross tonnage able to pass under the arches of the bridge) on the Thames today just as it was 500 years ago. The Great Fire of London in 1666 destroyed most of the wharf and warehouse accommodation existing up to that time, and the reconstruction was on improved lines. The quays built were of two types: the legal quays where loading and discharging were permitted only in daylight under conditions enforced by the Commissioners of Customs and the sufferance wharves established by occasional licence to relieve congestion at the legal quays.

It was during the eighteenth century that the greatly increased trade of the Port of London demonstrated the insufficiency of the accommodation then available. Continuous congestion of shipping in the river itself resulted in great delay, loss, and inconvenience. It was difficult to protect vessels lying at anchor in the stream from plunder and from smuggling, and smuggling assumed huge proportions. Although a committee was appointed by Parliament in 1796 to inquire into methods of improving the port, it was the West India merchants who drew up practical proposals for the improvement of conditions. They laid it down as an axiom that any future development of the port depended upon the construction of wet docks.

The nineteenth century

There was thus initiated the great period of development in the nineteenth century which may be described as the dock building era. The scheme of the West India merchants was to construct two docks on the Isle of Dogs. The plan was sanctioned by Parliament, and the West India Docks were opened on 27 August 1802. They were the first docks as understood today to be opened in the Port of London. The Howland Dock at Rotherhithe had been opened in 1696, but it was only intended for the safer anchorage of ships and, indeed, trees were planted as far as possible all round it in order to break the force of the winds. What had previously been regarded as the curse of London was now to be its salvation. For below the site of London, stretching practically to the sea and to a large extent along both banks, were enormous stretches of useless marshland, unsuitable alike for settlement and building, and for reclamation by the agriculturalists; this land for the most part had been lying entirely waste. Thus there were huge tracts where enormous docks could be constructed. Further, the land was a soft alluvium easily excavated, and below that gravel and London Clay[1] which also presented little difficulty. The land to start with was at river level. The London Clay did not present difficulties in the construction of docks which a very pervious substratum might have done; but at the same time the solid

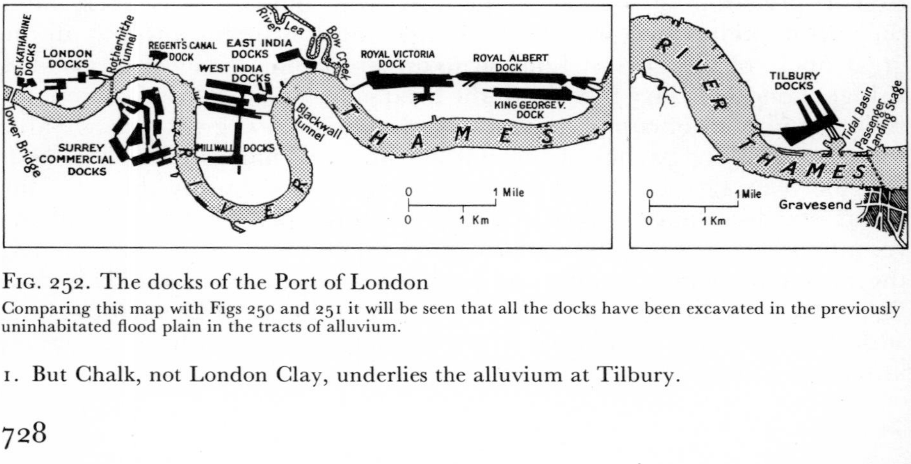

FIG. 252. The docks of the Port of London

Comparing this map with Figs 250 and 251 it will be seen that all the docks have been excavated in the previously uninhabitated flood plain in the tracts of alluvium.

1. But Chalk, not London Clay, underlies the alluvium at Tilbury.

clay was sufficiently firm for the foundation of quays and warehouses and, later, for great buildings such as flour mills. The London Dock was opened in 1805, the East India Dock in 1806, the St Katharine Docks in 1828, the Royal Victoria Dock in 1855, the Millwall Dock in 1868, and the Royal Albert Dock in 1880. That curious collection of docks, now known as the Surrey Commercial Docks, came into existence piecemeal between 1807 and 1876. At a later stage came construction of what is really the outport of London, Tilbury Docks, which were opened in 1886. In addition to the docks there were numerous riverside wharves and warehouses. The docks, warehouses, and wharves were built and owned by different companies. There was little coordination; instead destructive competition was the usual rule. Companies found themselves with insufficient resources to carry out the improvements and reconstruction which the growing size of steamers demanded. Towards the close of the nineteenth century there was a very real danger than London might pass into the position of only a second-class port.

The modern period

But the danger passed, when, it is true, after a considerable delay, Parliament passed the Port of London Act in 1908. This Act created a new authority, a public trust—the Port of London Authority—which was to take over and administer all the docks and the whole of the tidal portion of the river Thames between Teddington and a line about 113 kilometres (seventy miles) to the east across the estuary. The PLA, as it is usually called, has thus jurisdiction over the docks and their associated warehouses and storage yards, but on the main river itself the limit of the Authority's jurisdiction on both banks of the river is the high-water mark. Thus there are numerous quays and wharves lining the river which are privately owned, the best known of which is perhaps Hay's wharf. In the river itself the duties of the Port Authority include all matters relating to navigation, regulation of traffic, and the maintenance of adequate river channels; and undoubtedly one of its most important works has been the improvement of the river channels. In 1909, just after the Port of London Authority took charge, the deepest draughted vessel that had used the Port of London up to that time drew 8.2 metres (27 ft) of water. Now vessels which draw up to 11.2 metres (37 ft), the normal draught of the largest vessels in the world (other than supertankers), can use the Port of London. Fairly large seagoing steamers can ascend right to the Pool of London, to London Bridge.

Outstanding features

We can now proceed to examine some of the outstanding features of the Port of London. One of the most remarkable features is undoubtedly the extensive use of lighters or barges. Despite the enormous area of wharfage accommodation, something like four-fifths of all the cargo reaching the

Port of London is off-loaded into lighters or barges, of which there are about 7000 on the waters of the Thames. The owners of these lighters or barges still have the rights which were given to their predecessors when the first docks were sanctioned by Parliament. They can enter or leave any of the docks belonging to the Port of London Authority and remain free of dues for seventy-two hours, if engaged on bona fide business. They are continually plying between the docks and wharves and the factories which line the 225 kilometres (140 miles) of banks of the River Thames. Most barges are towed by motor and steam tugs. Only a few of the old sailing barges remain, whilst a comparatively small number are self-propelled. Although coal can be delivered by colliers of moderate size which are able to pass under London Bridge to such points as the Battersea power station, many riverside works above London Bridge depend upon the continued use of the barges. In the second place London illustrates remarkably well that the successful modern port must not only be well equipped for handling all types of general cargo, but must have the special equipment necessitated by special types of cargo. It is one of the features of the London docks that there is marked specialisation in the cargoes handled by the principal docks. Then there is no doubt at all that the Port of London derives an enormous benefit from its huge storage accommodation, for it enables the Port of London Authority to act as warehouseman, more especially of goods which are subject to heavy customs dues. Merchants and wholesalers can rent storage space in the Port of London Authority's warehouses, or can pay so much for the storage of goods, and thus defer the payment of customs duty until the goods are actually required and can be cleared. Thus enormous quantities of tobacco are normally stored. Further, there are facilities for the cold storage of meat and other commodities requiring very specialised storage conditions unrivalled by any individual firm. For these reasons London had formerly a virtual monopoly of several types of imports into the country, such as tea and rubber. The destruction of warehouse accommodation, however, altered this position, which has never been quite regained—though the proportion of the country's re-exports handled by London remains high (see also p. 718). The table opposite shows the percentage of different imports into the United Kingdom which were handled by the port in 1929 and 1967.

The Surrey Commercial Docks deal with the greater part of the still largely seasonal timber trade. Storage accommodation is provided for nearly half a million long tons, and there are specially constructed sheds where timber can be seasoned, and, in addition, ponds for floating. The London and St Katharine Docks were those situated just below Tower Bridge—that is, nearest to London Bridge. As they were small, without direct rail connections, they could not be extended and used by large vessels, and were concerned mainly with coastwise and continental including Mediterranean trade, and St Katharine Docks closed in 1969. The storage arrangements here have been specially made for the more valuable

Percentage of UK import trade in various commodities handled by London, 1929 and 1967

COMMODITY	1929	1967	
Meat	48	43	(Meat and meat preparations)
Grain and flour	24	21	(Cereals and cereal preparations)
Wool	45	9	(Textile fibres)
Butter	44	33	(Dairy products and eggs)
Wood	31	24	
Crude mineral oil	50	16[1]	
Vegetable oils	35	25	(Animal and vegetable oils)
Tea	93	72	
Non-ferrous metals	38	23	
Iron and steel	22	31	
Hides and skins	43	24	(Hides, skins and furs)
Paper	50	26	(Paper and pulp)
Tobacco	30	30	
Rubber	80	29	

[1] The drop in the proportion of imported crude oil is merely relative because only small amounts of oil were refined in this country before the war. The Port of London embraces the great Thameshaven-Shellhaven and Isle of Grain groups of refineries, with almost a third of the UK refining capacity. This has resulted in a phenomenal postwar rise in the imports of crude oil into the port as is illustrated by the following figures (in million gallons): 1938, 82; 1947, 71; 1954, 2088, and 1966, 5696.

types of merchandise such as wine, spirits, spices, sugar, ivory, gums, and essences. Here it is interesting to note other functions carried out by the Port of London Authority. Samples of commodities are taken by their experts, and the sales in the City are based on these samples which are in a way guaranteed by the independent and unbiased Port of London Authority. Farther downstream there is the great loop of the River Thames which almost cuts off the once pastoral marshy area known as the Isle of Dogs. It was only in 1929 that the two separate series of docks, the West India and the Millwall, which occupy this area, were united. The West India Docks, the oldest docks of the Port of London, were constructed specially for handling cargo from the West Indies; and it is remarkable that more than a century and a half later the most important commodities dealt with at the West India Docks still come from the West Indies. Hardwood is another of the commodities handled by the West India Docks. The Millwall Dock specialises in the handling of grain, and it is here that the grain is sucked from the holds of vessels by pneumatic elevators and passed into the central granary, which with a capacity of 24 300 metric tons (24 000 long tons) holds sufficient grain for London's needs for at least a week. Farther downstream the East India Dock formerly handled large quantities of goods from the East, particularly tea and silk; but now deals only with small coastwise and near continental traffic. At Royal Albert Dock special arrangements have been made for the banana traffic of London. Here, too, there is a disease-proof quarantine station established for pedigree stock for export to various parts of the world. The Royal Victoria, Albert, and King George V Docks are in reality one huge dock divided into three sections. They form the largest sheet of enclosed dock water in the world, with a total

PLATE 30. London river and the Royal group of docks
Note the sheaves of lighters moored in the river; and compare Fig. 250.

area of 445 hectares (1 100 acres), of which 95 hectares (235 acres) are water, and with 16 kilometres (10 miles) of quay. In these docks the water is kept at a height of 0.76 metre ($2\frac{1}{2}$ ft) above high-water mark. To the north of the Royal Victoria Dock are the storage warehouses, whilst to the south are four large flour mills. The Royal Albert Dock handles most of the meat imported by London, much of the meat being taken into huge cold stores which have been erected to the north side of the dock, and which are capable of accommodating well over half a million carcasses of mutton. The King George V Dock was opened in 1921, and, with a depth of 11.6 metres (38 ft), it can accommodate vessels up to 35 000 tons gross (such as the *Mauretania*), despite the fact that it is comparatively near to the heart of London. Large vessels, such as the P. & O. liners of 40 000 tons, can be accommodated in the Tilbury Docks, where an entrance 305 metres (1000 ft) long and 33.5 metres (110 ft) wide was opened in September 1929, and where a magnificent dry dock was later completed. Tilbury handles most of the passenger traffic using the port of London, and there is a floating landing stage which can be used at all stages of the tide. It is served directly by rail and is within 45 minutes of the heart of London in addition to having easy communication with all parts of the country. Although built by the combined East and West India Docks Company, Tilbury might have developed into a separate 'outport' and rival of London itself, but the unification of control has prevented this. The latest development at Tilbury is the construction of a large container terminal.

Naturally the docks of London were a priority target for enemy bombing from 1940 to 1945; destruction, especially of warehouse accommodation, was great and the port was virtually unused. But the main structures remained and the docks have been restored. The damaged Poplar Dock was converted to a specialised oil-terminal in 1958.

We have indicated elsewhere how the once significant shipbuilding industry of the Thames has disappeared, and London illustrates rather well the separation of shipbuilding from ship repairing. The Port of London is

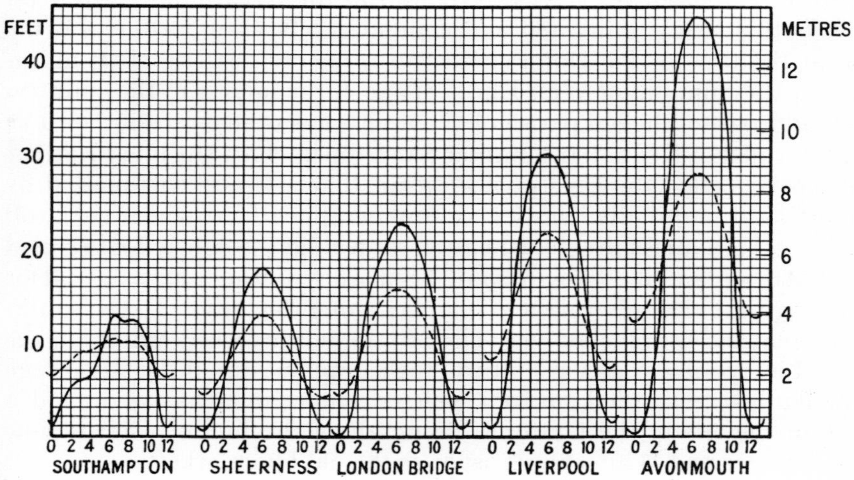

FIG. 253. Tidal graphs of some characteristic British ports

The two graphs in each case are for a typical spring tide and a typical neap tide. Figures below show the time in hours. Notice the effect of the double tide at Southampton and the small range; the increasing tidal range in the Thames as one goes from Tilbury to London Bridge; and the enormous range at Avonmouth.

very well equipped for ship repairing. It has no less than nine dry docks, including one at Tilbury which is 228 metres (750 ft) long and 30 metres (100 ft) wide and can, when the increasing size of vessels demands it, be extended to over 305 metres (1000 ft) in length. In these docks every facility for the repair and overhaul of vessels is provided. One very important factor in the maintenance of London's pre-eminence as a port is the close cooperation between the port and the commercial centres of London. This is possible despite, in fact one might say because of, the separation of London into zones of functional utilisation. Thus going westwards from dockland one comes immediately to the commercial and business centre of London—first to the network of narrow streets where are situated so many of the wholesale firms. This juxtaposition is responsible for the retention in London of a great woollen market—for so long and to some extent even now a world market—despite the fact that practically none of the wool is used for manufacture in the neighbourhood of London itself. Then there is very close connection between the Port of London and industrial London. On p. 678 we have given a map showing the situation of so many of London's industries along the banks of the Thames and the still important canal systems.

Liverpool and Merseyside

If London has been a great port for 2000 years the same can scarcely be said of Liverpool, for the real rise to importance of Liverpool is within the last two hundred years. A thousand years ago, when London was already an important centre, Liverpool was just one of a group of small vills comprised within the ecclesiastical parish of Woolton in the Greathundred of West Derby. Both sparsely inhabited and comparatively unimportant was the region at the time of the Domesday survey, hence (because of its unimportance) the hundred of West Derby is one of the largest in the country. The greater part of the old parish of Woolton was situated on an islandlike upland, formed of Keuper and Bunter Sandstone, which the late Professor P. M. Roxby called the Liverpool Plateau. It was almost surrounded by low-lying land, originally 'mosses' or low-lying peatland which cut it off from the rest of Lancashire. Northeastwards a ridge of slightly higher land connected this islandlike site with south Lancashire through Prescot, and for a very long time the only carriage road lay along this ridge. To the southwest the plateau approached very close to the bottlenecked estuary of the Mersey. Liverpool was an agricultural township, but it had the advantage of a small tidal creek called the Pool, which extended inland for about half a mile from the site of the Customs House along the line of what is now Paradise Street and Whitechapel as far as the old Haymarket.

King John seems first to have visualised the possibilities of Liverpool as a port for Ireland—a military port in that case—and so made it into a borough in 1207. And it was from the quiet waters of the Pool that fishing and coastal traffic was built up, including a not inconsiderable trade with

Ireland. In these early days Liverpool was overshadowed by the importance of Chester—indeed, it was claimed as being merely a creek within the port of Chester. But, owing to the silting up of the Dee estuary which was specially marked from the fourteenth century onwards, Chester became unimportant as a port even before the rise of the trans-Atlantic trade which was destined to be of such significance to Liverpool. The great age of exploration initiated by the discovery of America in 1492 first gave Liverpool its real opportunity, but for long Bristol dominated in the western trade. There seems little doubt that the greater security of a route to the north of Ireland compared with the route to the south of Ireland was by no means unimportant in view of the long series of wars with Holland and France in the seventeenth and eighteenth centuries. Although the immediate situation of Liverpool rendered communication with its hinterland in Lancashire difficult, the importance of the Midland Gate which facilitated communication between the merchants of London and Liverpool soon came to be recognised. From the latter part of the seventeenth century the growth of the port was rapid. First came the recognition of Liverpool as the chief port for the Irish trade as far as the north of England was concerned, as well as for increasing coastal traffic with western Scotland. Then there was the rapid development of trade with the West Indies, infamously associated from about 1730 with what has come to be known as the great Trade Triangle and which dominated Liverpool shipping in the latter half of the eighteenth century. Ships from Liverpool sailed to West Africa with cheap manufactured goods such as beads, indifferent muskets, gunpowder, and raw spirits which they traded with the African slave-traders or so called 'kings', who organised slave raids into the interior. These same ships then took on board full cargoes of Negroes and made the famous middle passage with the help of the trade winds, disposing of the slaves in the West Indies, returning thence to Liverpool with a cargo of molasses, tobacco, and cotton. The abolition of the slave trade in 1807 did not, as many Liverpool merchants had anticipated, check the growth of the port. By that time the Industrial Revolution was in full swing, and there was a huge demand for raw cotton from the southern United States, and Liverpool became what it has since remained—the chief importing port for raw cotton. Then came the development of trade in cotton goods, particularly after the cessation of the monopoly of the East India Co., as well as the development of more varied trade with the North American continent and an emigrant traffic.

Just as in the case of London, it was found that Liverpool was so situated that she was able to adapt herself to changing requirements. The mouth of the old pool was converted into a wet dock—one of the first in the world—and the remainder of the pool filled in. There was a marshy fringe running along the side of the Mersey and bordering the sandstone plateau on which the settlement was situated, and this afforded possibilities for the excavation of docks just as the marshy land of the lower Thames had done. The docks were extended all along the waterfront southwards until the natural limit was reached where there is an outcrop of sandstone on the river bank at Dingle Point. Here is the residential district of Aigburth. Beyond this are more marshes, and here has been developed the group of docks forming the port of Garston owned, before the nationalisation of the railways, by the London, Midland and Scottish Railway. To the north of Liverpool the limit has not yet been reached, and here it was claimed that the Gladstone group of docks when opened was amongst the largest and best equipped in the world. Further extensions were in progress in 1969. The development of docks along the whole waterfront has had two main results. The old shipbuilding yards have disappeared, and not only have the warehouses and mills been forced inland, but still more has industrial development. Few of the factories of Liverpool can be supplied direct from lighters as in the case of London or Hull, and so lighters play but a small part in the life of the port. Whilst the excellent arrangement in the port itself renders loading and offloading possible in very short time, the old overhead railway running the length of the docks enabled workers to get quickly to their work, but hindered the development of industries with direct access to the docks.

As in London the early dock construction was carried out by separate companies; but the need for a unifying authority was appreciated much earlier, and the Mersey Docks and Harbour Board came into existence in 1858. It now controls the whole dock estate on both sides of the river, except for the nationalised Garston docks which are under the Docks and Inland Waterways Executive. The rapid development of the whole waterfront of Liverpool rendered the utilisation of the Cheshire side inevitable, which happened in the middle of the nineteenth century—about the initial nucleus of Wallasey Pool, an inlet corresponding roughly in character with the old Liver Pool. There are now over 186 hectares (460 acres) of docks on the Liverpool side with a quay frontage of 43 kilometres (27 miles), and on the Cheshire side a water area of 73 hectares (181 acres) and 14.5 kilometres (9 miles) of quay. There is not as yet a continuous line of docks on the Cheshire side as there is on the Liverpool side, and so a considerable number of industrial concerns there have their own water frontage. There one finds also the shipbuilding yards, and the Tranmere oil jetty. Thus, on the Cheshire side, there has grown up the great industrial and commercial town of Birkenhead, and more recently the residential area known as Wallasey, which may fitly be described as a dormitory for both Birkenhead and Liverpool. Indeed the greater part of the Wirral Peninsula is rapidly becoming a residential area for Merseyside. Immense numbers of workers cross over morning and evening by ferry and by the Mersey railway from the Cheshire to the Lancashire side, and the need for the construction of the Mersey road tunnel (opened 1934) became apparent.

It has been pointed out that the Liverpool plateau is separated from the main part of Lancashire by a belt of low-lying 'moss', a large proportion of which is now extremely fertile agricultural land. This emphasises the isolation of the Liverpool region from the manufacturing and industrial regions of south Lancashire, an isolation which is borne out by the character of the industries of Merseyside. For the major industries are based essentially on imported materials—milling, soap, and candle manufacturers, cattle-food industries, and so on. Liverpool shows to some extent the zoned character of London. In the rear of the docks there is the business part of the

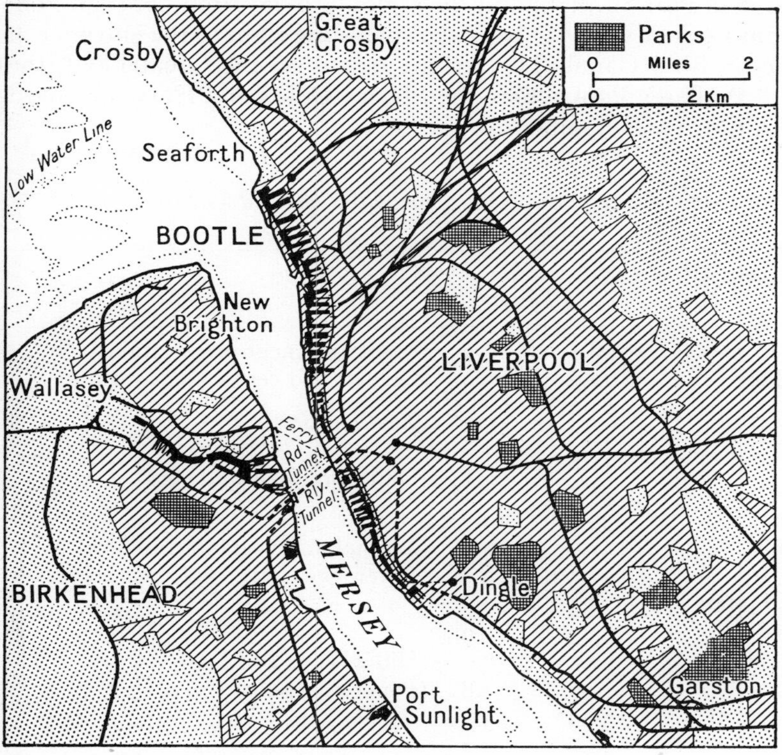

FIG. 254. The port of Liverpool

A unique feature of Liverpool's transport system was the electric overhead railway, supported on wrought iron columns about 6 metres (20 ft) from the ground which ran for 10.5 kilometres ($6\frac{1}{2}$ miles) alongside the docks, from Seaforth to Dingle, thus affording facilities for travelling from one part of the long dock estate to another. It was however closed on 31 December 1956 and has been dismantled. The famous road tunnel cost over £7 000 000 and was opened in 1934.

city, concentrated especially round the Town Hall and coinciding very closely with the centre of the old township. Near at hand is what may be described as the social centre with fine public buildings such as the Picton Library, St George's Hall, the Walker Art Gallery, and many of the finest shops. Then, forming an irregular ring, is the residential area, some of it still consisting of extremely congested slums—a legacy of the early days of the Industrial Revolution which Liverpool has done her utmost to remove. On the high ground of the sandstone plateau stand the University and two cathedrals. The industrial development tends to be concentrated near a labour supply, and as far as possible near the supplies of raw materials from the docks. In some cases the industrialisation is considerably removed from the centre of the city, as in the Aintree district, in the new estates of Kirkby, and at Speke and Halewood. On the Cheshire side lie two main areas of industrialisation. One is to the south of Birkenhead on low ground where the industrial area of Port Sunlight and the region around Bromborough Pool (converted into a dock in 1931) has been spreading right to the entrance of the Manchester Ship Canal. The second area is on the Great Float, the lower part of Wallasey Pool, where the Mersey Docks and Harbour Board hold land for future development.

Percentage of UK import trade in various commodities handled by Liverpool

COMMODITY	1948	1967	
	PER CENT		
Meat	26.1	10.7	(Meat and meat preparations)
Grain and flour	22.9	15.9	(Cereals and cereal preparations)
Cotton	84.0	45.9	(Textile fibres)
Wool	40.3		
Butter	11.6	12.1	(Dairy products and eggs)
Eggs	21.5		
Wood	37.0	10.7	
Vegetable oils	41.0	53.0	(Animal and vegetable oils)
Tea	25.3	19.9	(Beverages)
Non-ferrous metals	8.3	23.7	
Iron and steel	5.3	11.9	
Hides and skins	61.5	8.2	(Hides, skins and furs)
Paper	3.7	1.8	(Paper and pulp)
Tobacco	35.9	23.4	
Rubber	48.0	42.7	

It is quite clear from the above table—and indeed from the table on p. 722—that Liverpool's share of freight traffic has declined, in some cases quite seriously, during the last two decades. This is partly due to the increased emphasis in the nation's trade pattern on trade with European countries, for which east coast ports can cater more expeditiously, and to the declining relative importance of trade with the Commonwealth (see Fig. 290). Thus whilst the overall value of London's trade has trebled since 1948, that of Liverpool has not even doubled (see table on p. 719). The largest major category of imports is foodstuffs, including grains, sugar, meat (especially lamb, the beef trade having gone to London) and fruit; many types of raw materials come in, including cotton, wool, ores and crude metal of various kinds, especially tin and copper, and of course petroleum. The exports are really an epitome of British exports as a whole, with machinery and transport equipment (especially motor vehicles of all kinds) as the major category, followed by manufactured goods including textiles, iron and steel, non-ferrous metals, and chemicals. Amongst the re-exports is Guinness beer imported from Dublin in coasters and sent out in oceangoing ships all over the world.

Manchester

As an ocean port, Manchester only dates from 11 January 1894, when the Manchester Ship Canal, constructed between 1887 and 1893, was opened for traffic. The Manchester Ship Canal extends from Eastham on the south side of the Mersey to the heart of Manchester,[1] and has a total length of 57 kilometres ($35\frac{1}{2}$ miles) and a minimum depth of 8.5 metres (28 ft). Docks at Eastham have been reconstructed to take tankers up to 30 000 tons and the new Tranmere jetty still larger ones. Vessels of up to 10 000 tons can go the whole length of the canal. The bottom width of the canal at the full depth is, with a very few exceptions, 36.5 metres (120 ft). This is sufficient to allow large ships to pass one another, and at the bend at Runcorn the bottom width has been increased to 47 metres (155 ft). In Manchester itself, the Trafford Park industrial estate has developed adjoining the docks. In 1894, the first year that the port of Manchester was opened, the value of the trade was £6.9 million sterling, of which about 40 per cent represented imports. The trade had grown tenfold in value by 1929. The capital expenditure on the canal by the end of 1914 was nearly £17m, and it was not until 1915 that the first dividend was paid on the preference stock. The canal extends between two of the busiest industrial regions of Britain, and several important industrial sites are now located along its banks, including Trafford Park at the Manchester end, Irlam iron and steel works, several at Runcorn, and of course the great Stanlow oil refining and petrochemical complex near the western end (Fig. 255).

The port of Manchester (which for statistical purposes includes the whole of the Ship Canal) is now the fourth port of the United Kingdom in terms of the value of its trade—though its imports greatly outweigh its exports. The most important individual items in recent years have been imports of petroleum and of refined copper (for the Lancashire engineering and cable-making trades), but there are considerable imports of foodstuffs (especially maize), tobacco, pulp and paper. The exports, naturally, are of manufactured goods and machinery, including textiles (with woollens much more important than cottons), textile machinery, electrical machinery and vehicles, and petroleum products.

Hull

Hull is an example of a port whose commerce has been continuously active, and whose position in relation to other English ports has changed very little

1. Most of the docks are actually in Salford.

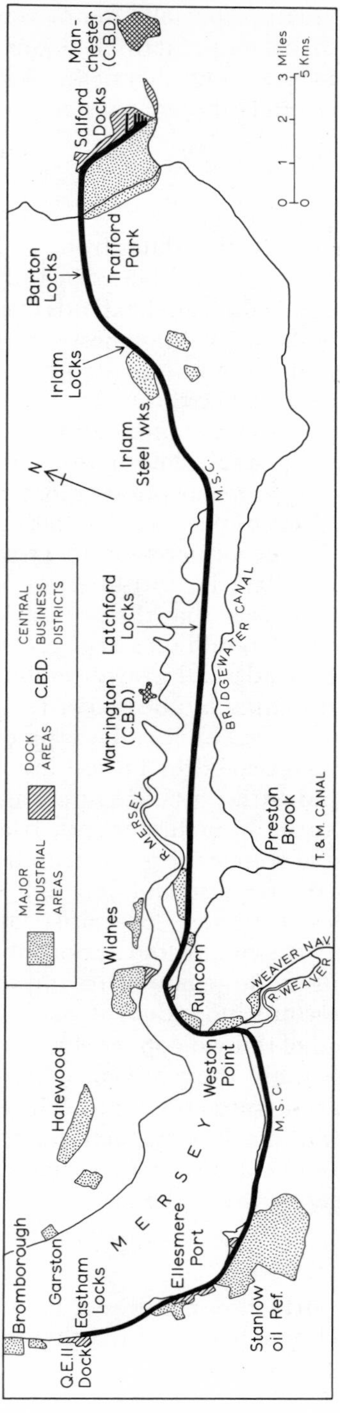

FIG. 255. The Manchester Ship Canal

since the Middle Ages. In this respect Hull can be compared with London. Again, we have an example of a port where geographical surroundings permitted its adaptation to modern conditions—as in the cases of London and Liverpool. By way of contrast other ports of the vicinity were not so fortunate. In the thirteenth and fourteenth centuries the commerce of Boston, which was the outport of Lincoln, exceeded that of Hull, but is now entirely insignificant. The possibility of development was precluded for one reason by the silting up of the approaches to Boston. The port of Hedon flourished in the twelfth and thirteenth centuries and stood, like Kingston-upon-Hull, on a tidal creek of the Humber to the east of Hull. But it was too far inland for the approach of modern vessels and suffered, again, from the choking of its channels. Finally, Ravenserodd, formerly situated on a small sandbank behind Spurn Point, entirely disappeared in the middle of the fourteenth century—a victim of the tidal scour which somewhat earlier had created the very land on which it was built.

The little River Hull enters the Humber from the north just where the line of the Humber curves northwards in such a way that the river current and the tidal current hug the shore and guarantee permanent deep water. The river Hull is navigable for some distance to the north, and, as is so frequently the case, near the head of navigation a small port and town sprang up—the town of Beverley—situated some distance away from the marshy banks of the river itself with which it is connected by an artificial channel. The first stage in the history of the rise of the port of Hull was when the little creek offered shelter or anchorage for boats on their way to its older neighbour Beverley. A little marsh-surrounded settlement grew up to the immediate west of the mouth of the creek, and it was Edward I who, in passing through this little settlement, caused it to be known as King's Town upon Hull (Kingston-upon-Hull is still the full name of the city of Hull), and granted the town its first charter. A plan of Hull dating from the fourteenth century shows a small settlement with quays on the east at which sailing boats are being unloaded with the help of hand cranes, and the settlement guarded on the north, west, and the south by a wall outside of which is a moat connecting the waters of the Hull with the waters of the Humber to the west of the settlement. A glance at a physical map will show that Hull is situated on the Humber a few miles to the east of the point where the river cuts through the chalk escarpment. To the west, the northwest, and the southwest lies the Trent and Ouse Basin: in all covering an area of about one-sixth of the whole of England. Most of the rivers of the basin were navigable for considerable distances. Doncaster was about 5 kilometres (three miles) above the old limit of navigation of the Don and York lies near that of the Ouse. Thus, in early days, a place of shelter near the mouth of the Humber could not compete with the ports which were situated well inland along these navigable rivers (cf. Fig. 258).

The second stage in the development of the port came with the increasing size of oceangoing vessels. Hull became the point of transhipment for river craft trading with towns on the navigable parts of the Ouse and Trent system. It clearly had the advantage of position, and could fulfil this function in a way in which Beverley could never do. So Beverley gradually became what it is today—a small town constructing trawlers for the fishing industry of Hull. The appalling condition of roads in England gave Hull a very considerable importance as an outlet from all central England, even for goods from such areas as Cheshire and Lancashire destined for London.

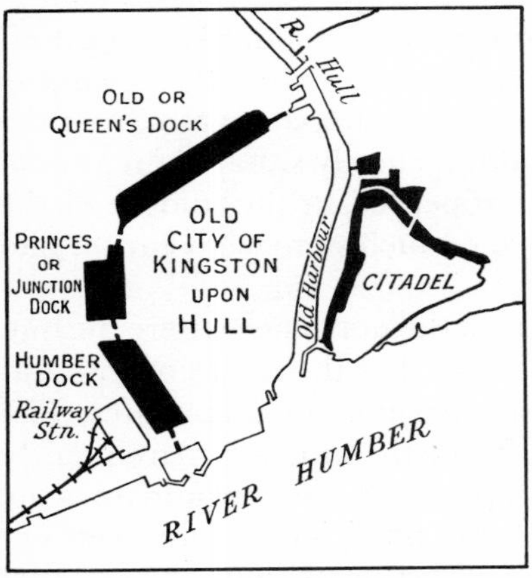

FIG. 256. The port and docks of Hull in 1840

The third stage in the development of the port came with the canal era, when the natural waterways were improved by a network of canals, of which the Aire and Calder was, and remains, the most important, which brought the growing industrial centres, particularly of West Riding, into easy communication with Hull. Thus the outstanding features of the port of Hull today—especially the immense amount of transhipment into lighters for distribution—developed at an early date. Further, Hull is still unique amongst the ports of the British Isles in the extent and significance of inland water navigation from its docks.

The fourth stage in the development of the port came with the construction of docks. As Rodwell Jones has said, 'the increase in size of vessels together with the increasing volume of trade made it necessary to supply means whereby ships could be in harbour for considerable periods without grounding, and cargoes could be dealt with at quaysides without change of level, since the tidal range at Hull is about 19 feet'. The old wall and moat became the site of the earliest docks. The Queen's Dock or Old Dock was opened in 1778, Humber Dock in 1809, Princes or Junction in 1829. The coming of the railway is emphasised by the name Railway Dock—a small offshoot from the Humber Dock opened in 1846. The earlier line of approach to Hull by railway (from Selby, opened in 1840) followed along the Humber where there was sufficient space between the chalk scarp and the river to obviate the necessity of constructing a tunnel. A later line which approached the town from the northwest had to cross the chalk scarp; the gradients were considerable, and there was also a tunnel. Marshy, unoccupied land to the southeast of the town has provided further opportunity for the construction of docks, and there followed here the Victoria Docks (1850). Subsequent dock construction resembled that at Liverpool in that it extended along the extensive water fronts, but it differs somewhat in the methods adopted. For farther to the southwest the work was carried out by constructing a great embankment along the line of the estuary and thus producing behind it the St Andrew's Dock (1883), the Albert Dock, and William Wright Dock (1869), these three being to the west of the town. Of necessity, later development had to be farther downstream, where there is the giant Alexandra Dock opened in 1886, and the King George V Dock opened in 1914 and enlarged in 1959–62. At first it is to be noticed that railway construction merely emphasised the existing lines of communication, and amongst the early disconnected portions of railway construction, that from Hull to Selby, and the industrial West Riding, was both noteworthy and early.[1] Subsequently railway construction extensively widened the hinterland served by the port. It is interesting in this connection to notice that with the regrouping of British railways in 1923, Hull became preeminently the port of the London and North Eastern Railway.

The value of the export trade has never afforded a very good index of Hull's importance because of the great bulk of coastwise traffic and the large fish trade. Since the fish is landed from British-based ships it does not figure as an import. The port resembles London in the very general nature of cargoes handled, and in that it is primarily an importing port, particularly of foodstuffs. Hull is the leading British port for the import of oilseeds. The seed is sent by lighters from the deep water docks to the crushing mills along the Hull itself and also to Selby. Similarly with wheat, of which there is a huge import; one finds flour mills (with the seed-crushing mills) lining the banks of Hull for something like two miles. The concentration of flour milling at the great ports of the British Isles is a very marked feature and has been responsible for the decay of milling in many smaller towns. For example, some of the wheat imported at Hull was formerly sent for milling at York, but later the York mills were closed. There is a large import trade in butter and bacon—obviously connected with Hull's suitability for distributing these commodities to the large industrial population of the north of England, and also obviously connected with the situation of Hull with regard to the continental ports, including those of Denmark, from which these commodities are exported. Similarly with the huge imports of timber—partly the result of the connection of the port with the great coalfields, and partly because of its position in relation to the European

1. See Fig. 240.

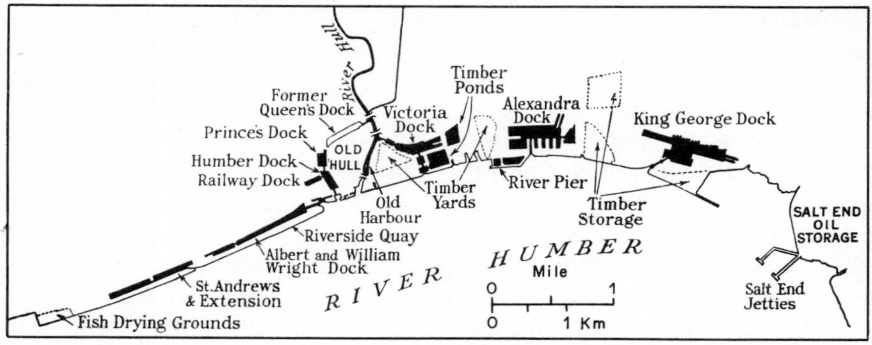

FIG. 257. The port and docks of Hull. Queen's Dock had outlived its usefulness and was filled in to form an open space in 1934

countries from which much of the timber is derived. As a wool importer Hull is second to Liverpool, for the latter has better regular shipping connections with Australia, New Zealand and other wool-producing countries than does Hull. Petroleum products are imported at the Salt End jetties, especially for the adjacent chemical works.

As an exporting port Hull is largely concerned with the products of its hinterland, whilst the nature of the commodities is also influenced by the continental destination of much of the exports. Vehicles, textile machinery, manufactured goods including textiles, non-ferrous metals and iron and steel products, chemicals, and also wool, wool tops and yarn, figure largely in the total.

Something has already been said of the immense importance of Hull as a fishing port (pp. 261–2). The majority of Hull trawlers are big vessels, often absent for several weeks at a time, and therefore requiring large stocks of fuel and ice, and really excellent facilities for handling the catch when they reach port. The St Andrew's Docks are entirely given over to this traffic.

Hull had more than its share of bombing and the heart of the city was virtually eliminated. In plans for reconstruction land transport presented a major problem. The main docks are and must remain to the east of the city, the hinterland lies to the west. Railways crossed roads by a very large number of level crossings. Tunnelling is difficult because of a high water level in the alluvium: a succession of viaducts would be extremely expensive. The Humber cuts Hull off from direct communication with the south and a road–rail bridge has long been proposed.

Grimsby, Immingham and Goole

It has been pointed out that the development of Hull as a port is closely bound up with its extensive hinterland and the waterways therein. It is clear that, provided deep-water facilities for oceangoing vessels are available, there must be other sites on or near the mouth of the Humber which could also handle the traffic of the same hinterland. There are now three ports which share with Hull the Humber trade—Grimsby, Immingham, and Goole. Grimsby lies to the south of the estuary of the Humber in the county of Lincolnshire, 27 kilometres (seventeen miles) southeast of Hull.

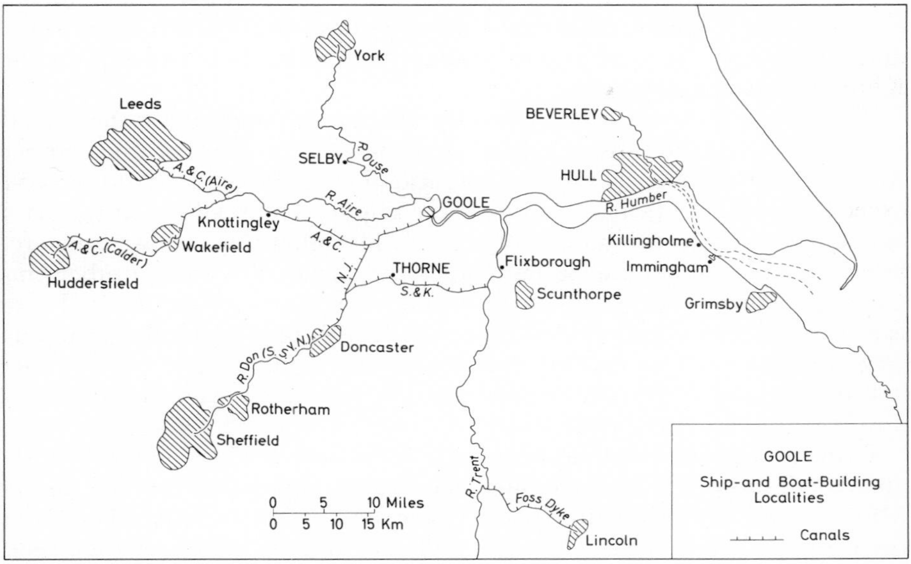

FIG. 258. The Humber ports and their inland waterway connections
The ship- and boat-building localities have been specially distinguished (cf. p. 431).

The potentialities of the site had long been apparent, but the development was left to the railways in the 1850s when the initiative of the Manchester, Sheffield, and Lincolnshire railway, later part of the London and North Eastern system, began the transformation of a fishing village into a town of over 100 000 inhabitants. Grimsby is, of course, pre-eminently a fishing port, handling a quantity of fish which in interwar years reached nearly a quarter of a million tons (cf. p. 264). There was a steady development of the fish traffic in the latter part of last century, but it was not until 1900 and the opening of No. 2 Fish Dock that an enormous extension of the fish trade took place, and in the early decades of the present century the fish expresses to all parts of Great Britain were a characteristic feature of the port. A third fish dock was added in 1934.

The entrance to Grimsby Docks is through a tidal basin into the Royal Dock and its Alexandra extension, and through locks into the Fish Docks. Moreover, the main channel of the Humber does not swing along the coast here and there is a large stretch of mud at low tide. Eight kilometres west of Grimsby, however, there is a position where the main deep-water channel approaches the shore. Here, in 1912, Immingham Dock was created by the former Great Central Railway. For various reasons, mainly the economic disturbance resulting from the First World War and the depressions of the 1920s and 1930s, Immingham, despite a large coal export and iron ore and timber import, never lived up to the expectations of its promoters, and it is only in the last decade or so that with the increasing industrialisation of south Humberside, it has come into its own, to serve in particular the oil, chemical and fertiliser industries. New oil jetties were constructed in 1963, and nearly half the total import tonnage is now crude petroleum for the Killingholme refinery.[1]

The foreign trade of Grimsby and Immingham is combined in the official statistics, but in fact Immingham deals mostly in mineral and timber traffic. The trade of the combined port is somewhat unbalanced, imports far exceeding exports in value. Amongst the imports foodstuffs, mainly bacon and butter from continental sources, are of high value, whilst iron ore, other minerals (including sulphur for local chemical works), timber (including pit props) and of course crude oil, represent a greater bulk. There is also an import of fish landed from non-British (e.g. Icelandic and Norwegian) vessels. Of the exports, coal is still of some significance both in bulk and in value, while petroleum products, chemicals, iron and steel products and machinery figure prominently.

Grimsby and Immingham were both, from 1923 to 1948, on the London and North Eastern Railway system; the corresponding port on the London Midland and Scottish Railway was Goole, 80 kilometres (fifty miles) from the open sea on the river Ouse but still accessible to vessels of 1000 tons. Goole is directly connected to Leeds by the Aire and Calder Canal system which, with its trains of compartment boats, is one of the most important inland waterways in the country. Its trade is largely with continental ports, and includes imports of timber, foodstuffs, fertilisers and some wool and other textile fibres, with exports of manufactured goods including wool tops, textile fabrics, metal goods, chemicals and coal.

Southampton

Southampton is the chief commercial port on the south coast. Although the Docks are of comparatively modern origin, dating from 1842, the port itself has played a long and notable part in the history of Britain. In A.D. 43 the Romans established a station on the east bank of the River Itchen; the Norman Conquest established it as the port for the royal city of Winchester, then capital of England, and by 1450 Southampton ranked as the third port of Britain.

Good geographical position and natural advantages have contributed to making Southampton a foremost port. Situated in the centre of the south coast, within easy reach of London and the continental ports of Havre and Cherbourg, the Docks stand at the head of Southampton Water, a well

1. See R. V. Leafe, 'The port of Immingham', *E. Midland Geog.*, **4**, 1967, 127–42.

sheltered estuary leading from the English Channel, with the Isle of Wight forming a natural breakwater at the entrance. The approaches to the Docks enjoy a great natural depth of water, in fact it was not until 1882 that dredging had to be resorted to for deepening, but with the advent of the big ocean liners, drawing up to 11.9 metres (39 ft) of water, dredging has, of course, been necessary, and today the main channel of Southampton Water is 244 metres (800 ft) wide with a minimum depth of 10.7 metres (35 ft) at low water. The advent of the giant oil tanker made further dredging of the approaches to Southampton Water necessary, to a minimum depth of 13.7 metres (45 ft), in order that vessels of 80 000 tons, drawing 14.3 metres (47 ft) when fully laden, might reach the Fawley refinery.

PLATE 31. The port of Southampton
Compare Fig. 260.

Another natural advantage is the relatively small tidal range of only 3.9 metres (13 ft), making closed docks unnecessary, but undoubtedly the greatest natural advantage which has aided Southampton is the phenomenon of a double high tide whereby the period of high water is maintained for two hours twice during the twenty-four hours. In addition, there is the 'young flood' stand, which is an interruption of normal tidal rise causing a slack-water period occurring from $1\frac{1}{2}$ to 3 hours after low water; thus during the twenty-four hours of each day there are seven hours slack water at a level navigable by all types of ships. Various theories[1] have been advanced as to the cause of the double tides and the unusual feature of such a short ebb but no one theory completely accounts for all the features experienced in the port.

The modern system of docks at Southampton was not started till 1838, when a small group of business men, realising the potentialities of Southampton as a port, founded the Southampton Dock Company, and the first dock was opened for trade in 1842. Well-equipped quays were laid out in such a way that passengers and cargo could be brought from and sent to London and other inland destinations with the maximum of speed. In 1892 the Docks were transferred from the Southampton Dock Company to the London and South Western Railway (later the Southern Railway) and in 1948 passed to the British Transport Commission, being subsequently placed under the control of the Docks and Inland Waterways Executive (now the British Transport Docks Board).

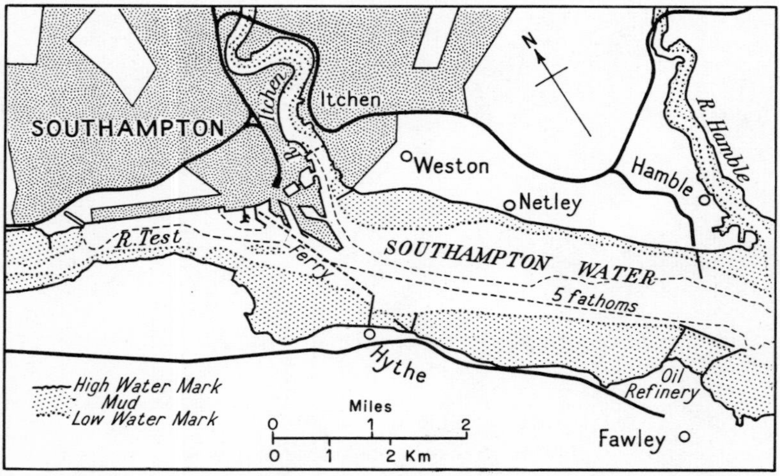

FIG. 259. The port of Southampton

Some measure of the prosperity the Docks have brought to Southampton is shown in the growth of population of the town, from 65 621 in 1892 to 180 000 in 1953 and 204 707 in 1961.

The Old Docks, covering some 80 hectares (200 acres), form a triangle with the apex at the confluence of the rivers Itchen and Test. In addition to the river quays there are three large tidal basins, the Ocean Dock, Empress Dock, and Outer Dock. The Ocean Dock is the main base of the

1. F. H. W. Green, 'Tidal phenomena, with special reference to Southampton and Poole', *Dock and Harbour Authority*, Sept., 1951. See also J. H. Bird, *The Major Seaports of the United Kingdom*, pp. 164–8.

North Atlantic express passenger services, and the Ocean Terminal, a double-storey passenger and cargo reception station on the eastern side of this dock, completed in 1950, after severe wartime bombing and destruction of older installations, is acknowledged to be one of the best of its kind in the world.

To the northwest of the Old Docks, facing the River Test, are the New Docks, begun in 1926, completed in 1934. A bay of 160 hectares (400 acres) of tidal mudland was reclaimed to give a straight line of 2½ kilometres (1½ miles) of deep water quay, with adjacent passenger and cargo sheds, railway sidings and appliances for the rapid handling of passengers and freight. At the western end of the New Docks is the King George V dry dock, which at the time of its construction in 1933 could accommodate vessels larger than any yet built, and which was regularly used by the *Queens* of 80 000 tons in later years. Immediately behind the New Docks quays are 52.5 hectares (130 acres) of reclaimed land which is gradually being developed as an industrial estate.

Southampton is Britain's premier passenger port, dealing with about

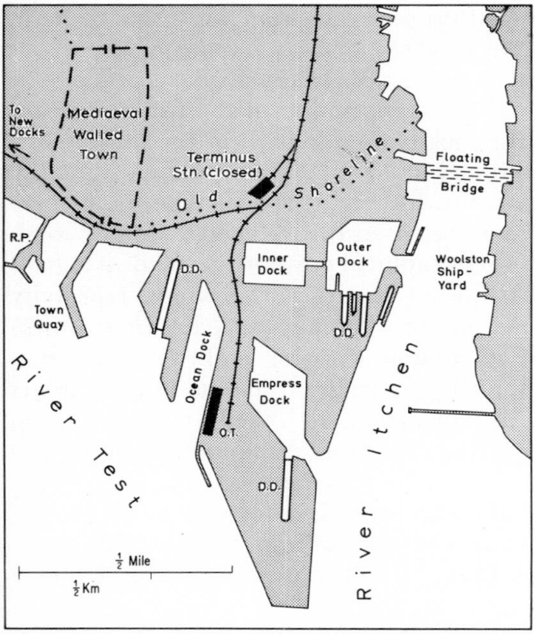

FIG. 260. The older docks of Southampton

Note the relation to the medieval town and the old shoreline, at the confluence of the rivers Test and Itchen. R.P. Royal Pier; D.D. Dry Dock; O.T. Ocean Terminal. Owing to the small tidal range and sheltered position there is only one small non-tidal dock (the Inner Dock).

half of all the oceangoing passengers to and from the United Kingdom, especially to and from the United States and South Africa. Thirty of the world's principal shipping companies used to maintain regular passenger services from Southampton to all parts of the world, and from the inception of the Docks in 1842 Southampton has always dealt with the world's largest liners. In this connection it is interesting to note the situation of Southampton relative to the position of Britain described in Chapter 1. It will be seen that steamship services from the northern coasts of Europe, for example, Germany and Holland, proceeding to the Americas or elsewhere are not taken out of their way to any appreciable degree in order to call at Southampton. Hence it is or was the regular calling place of the German liners of the Hamburg-Amerika and Norddeutscher Lloyd, and of the Dutch Holland-America line.

Southampton also ranks fifth in the list of Britain's cargo ports. Practically the whole of the South African deciduous fruit shipped to Britain is received at the Docks as well as about three-quarters of the citrus fruit. There is a large cold store for meat from Australia and New Zealand. Wool, hides, skins, wines, canned fruit, and jams are also received from South Africa. Other imports at Southampton are bananas from the West Indies and West Africa, fresh fruit and vegetables from the Channel Islands and France, timber from the Baltic and Central Europe, grain from Australia, Canada and South America, as well as from English ports, and also coastal cargoes from Scotland and Ireland. The construction of the Esso oil refinery at Fawley in 1952 materially altered the composition of the freight traffic; crude petroleum is now by far the most valuable item in the import list, whilst petroleum products—including bunker oil for foreign ships using the port—are prominent in the export list. Other exports include motor cars and practically every variety of manufactured British goods, shipped to all parts of the world. Southampton's geographical position has made it a good centre for the reception and distribution of cargo of all kinds, especially perishable and express goods. Within 160 kilometres (a hundred miles) radius there is a population of 16 million, an area embracing London (which is reached in under two hours by passenger train and in three hours by freight train), the industrial Midlands, etc., all linked to Southampton by regular rail and road services giving rapid and economic transport and distribution.

Although the bulk of the general cargo traffic is dealt with at the Docks, about one million tons of cargo—much of it to and from the Isle of Wight—is handled annually at the Town Quay, which is owned by the Harbour Board.

For the dry docking and repair of ships there are seven dry docks, ranging in length from 85 to 365 metres (281 to 1200 ft). Overhauls of the largest liners in the world are carried out at the Docks. Thornycroft's shipbuilding yard at Woolston, on the eastern bank of the River Itchen, is noted for the building of naval and commercial vessels.

Harwich, Dover, Folkestone and Newhaven

It is from these ports that the passenger ferry services to the Continent leave Britain, and to which the now obsolescent term 'packet station' was formerly applied. Harwich serves Holland (the Hook and Flushing) and Denmark (Esbjerg); Dover serves France (Calais and Dunkerque) and Belgium (Ostend); Folkestone serves France (Boulogne), and Newhaven, France (Dieppe); apart from passengers they all have a trade somewhat similar in character and function broadly comparable in each case, though Harwich and Dover far exceed the other two in freight traffic, and also have car ferry services. They all have an import trade made up of perishable foodstuffs such as butter, eggs, fresh meat, poultry, fish, and fruit, as well as manufactured goods in great variety and usually of relatively high value in proportion to their bulk. Exports are mainly of manufactured goods including machinery and motor cars—again valuable goods of relatively small bulk.

Bristol

Bristol is an excellent example of a port which had initial geographical advantages of which it made full use, but whose advantages were not of the character that could be so readily adapted to supply modern requirements as was the case, for example, with London and Liverpool. Thus Bristol, though remaining a port of no mean significance, has failed to remain in the first rank. There is no evidence of a Roman settlement at Bristol, but the low sandstone hill naturally protected by the marshes of the River Frome on the north and the marshes of the River Avon on the south, the two rivers joining farther to the southwest, supplied an excellent defensible position in the troublous times of Saxon England. Below Bristol the River Avon passes through its famous limestone gorge and empties into the lower part of the estuary of the Severn. The shallow and tortuous course of the upper part of the estuary of the Severn gave Bristol an advantage in competing as an outlet not only for the region to the east of it, but also for the Severn valley.[1] The route eastwards from Bristol was well known because of the Roman spa at Bath which was popular at an early date. Connections with Ireland date from an early period and almost equally fundamental relations with France and Spain are indicated by the early development of the wine trade, wine being an important item in the imports of Bristol then as it is today. Soap making, tanning and wool weaving developed in the thirteenth century, and in 1353 Bristol was made one of the staple towns for the export of wool. The growing importance of the centre was recognised in 1373 when Edward III granted a charter whereby the town and suburbs of Bristol were

1. Despite the construction of the Berkeley Canal, allowing the passage of vessels of 3·3 metres (11 ft) draught, Gloucester fell behind in the competitive race.

made into a separate county. In the meantime the settlement had spread to other sandstone hills in the neighbourhood, and the low ground was utilised for the construction of quays.

The rediscovery of America[1] opened a new field for Bristol; but at first there was severe competition between the port and London. The Merchant Adventurers Society of Bristol received its charter in 1552, but London shot ahead and monopolised much of the new trade. However, the foundation of colonies in Virginia in 1606, and Newfoundland in 1610, saw many men from the west country taking part. The famous Hakluyt himself was Dean of the Cathedral from 1586 onwards. So in the early part of the seventeenth century came the development of the American trade. Though a decree of 1631 had enacted that tobacco should only be imported into London, there was so much smuggling into Bristol that its importation was legalised in 1649. Then came the development of the great Trade Triangle from Bristol just as from Liverpool; Bristol vessels going to West Africa, taking a cargo of slaves to the West Indies and returning to Bristol.

As early as 1612 there were evidently sugar houses in Bristol because there was a protest demanding the removal of one such owing to the danger of fire. The first mention of the establishment of the chocolate industry is in the granting of a patent in 1731 to Walter Churchman of Bristol, whilst in 1753 Joseph Fry was admitted as a freeman of Bristol after five years' residence. But the tortuous course of the Avon practically prohibited the ascent of vessels exceeding 150 tons, and the Merchant Adventurers were compelled in the early part of the eighteenth century to spend considerable sums on additional moorings and the removal of rocks. There was much discussion about the construction of new docks, but nothing definite was done. Bristol largely lost the sugar trade which it has never quite recovered. By the time the docks were constructed in the early part of the nineteenth century, it was too late and prohibitive dues annulled the advantages of the new docks.

With the coming of the railway era Bristol was unfortunate in its close relationship with the network of 2.1-metre (7-ft) gauge lines of the old Great Western Railway. These held back the trade of the city especially in connection with the trade of the Midlands; the change of gauge rendered necessary the handling of goods at Gloucester, putting up transport costs and resulting in the diversion of the traffic to Liverpool. It might be thought that the situation of Bristol so close to the Bristol coalfield would have been a tremendous advantage; but there was never any measure of agreement between the coal-owners and workers and the city authorities in Bristol. Indeed, in 1727, a bill was passed which permitted the setting up of toll gates and taxation on every ton of coal entering Bristol for consumption.

But Bristol occupies an essentially valuable position in the west of England, and the obvious though bold move was the construction of

1. It was John Cabot, a naturalised Venetian of Genoese birth, who had settled in Bristol as a merchant, who really rediscovered the North American continent by landing on Cape Breton Island in 1496.

modern deep-water docks at the mouth of the Avon. This was undertaken both to the north of the Avon at Avonmouth in 1877 and to the south at Portishead in 1879, but whilst Avonmouth went ahead, Portishead became

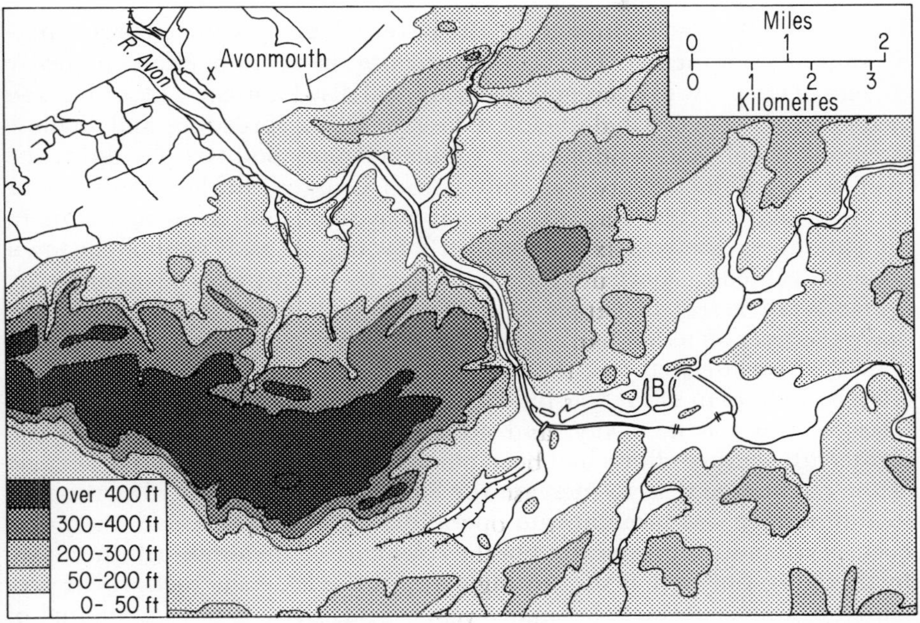

FIG. 261. The physical setting of the city and port of Bristol (B)

Note the ridge of high ground through which the River Avon cuts in the famous Avon gorge *between* Bristol and the sea. This has effectually prevented Bristol from becoming a modern deep-water port, hence the growth of the outport Avonmouth.

almost disused, except for coal and fuel oil to supply the power stations, and phosphates for a dockside fertiliser factory. One disadvantage of Avonmouth is the enormous rise and fall of the tide, so that vessels have to wait for high tide before they can leave the docks. But facilities have been provided particularly for petroleum storage, the cold storage of butter and meat, the handling, storage, and milling of grain, and the warehousing of tobacco, and a special feature of Avonmouth is the docking there of the West Indian banana vessels. Other imports serve the metallurgical and chemical industries of Severnside—zinc concentrates, aluminium and chemicals. Thus the import trade of the port of Bristol has again shown a marked tendency to increase; but the exports are small, and include paper, chemicals, metals and machinery. The manufactures of the city itself remain those connected with its old West Indian trade—tobacco, chocolate and soap in particular, but the great new industrial complex that is growing up on Severnside is giving a new aspect to the Bristol region. The imaginative proposal for a completely new port—to be called Portbury[1]—has not met with Government approval.

Glasgow

The city of Glasgow is situated on the River Clyde 35 kilometres (twenty-two miles) from the sea. The port is in reality the result of efforts made by citizens of Glasgow to overcome geographical disadvantages. Less than 200 years ago the River Clyde below Glasgow was a spreading and shallow stream of shoals and sandbanks, fordable at many points as far down the river as 19 kilometres (twelve miles) from Glasgow Bridge. Only about 100 years ago the river was only navigable by small craft drawing not more than about two metres (six or seven feet) of water. As early as 1668 the town council decided to construct their own port by buying a piece of land 5.25 hectares (13 acres) in extent at a point 29 kilometres (eighteen miles) down the river on its left bank. The construction of the town and harbour at New Port was undertaken, the name being changed subsequently to Port Glasgow. Here, in 1812, was built the first dry dock in Scotland. But Port Glasgow was too far away, and already towards the latter part of the eighteenth century efforts had been made to confine the water to the centre of the channel and so to increase the effect of scouring. In 1824 the first steam dredger was brought into operation, and since that date there has been a systematic improvement of the river carried on almost continuously by dredging—as well as the cutting away of the Elderslie rock which presented a serious obstacle for many years. Thus there is now a channel of about 8 metres (26 ft) in depth at low water which, added to a tidal rise of 3.3 to 3.6 metres (11 to 12 ft), makes the port accessible for steamers of the largest trading class. Docks have been constructed and the port is now well equipped.

The expenditure on the improvement of the River Clyde below Glasgow was warranted by the development of the hinterland. The occurrence of coal and iron close together in the immediate vicinity of Glasgow converted it into the centre of a great manufacturing region. The fact that the bed of the river below Glasgow was filled by easily dredged material and mostly soft rocks rendered possible also that extension in width which has enabled the great shipbuilding yards along the Clyde to continue in operation as the size of vessels built there has increased. Then there is, further, the fact that Glasgow shares with Liverpool the advantage of facing the New World. It is true that the North American and West Indian trade began as a smuggling trade before the union of the English and Scottish Parliaments, but after the Act of Union it so flourished that Glasgow led all its English rivals in the import of tobacco.

Glasgow, unlike most of the ports of Britain, has developed an exporting

1. See F. Walker: 'Economic growth on Avonside', *Trans. Inst. Brit. Geog.*, **37**, 1965, 1–13.

trade that is slightly greater in value than its importing trade. The imports include foodstuffs (large quantities of maize, wheat and butter), tobacco, together with petroleum (which is actually discharged at Finnart on Loch Long and sent by pipeline to the Grangemouth refinery—cf. p. 354) and iron ore (at a special quay on the south side of the river in Glasgow itself, with direct rail connection to the Ravenscraig iron and steel works—cf. p. 401). The most valuable export is one of small bulk—whisky; others are the machinery, transport equipment and manufactured goods produced in Central Scotland.

At the mouth of the Clyde, just below Port Glasgow, is Greenock. As a port it has a peculiar trade pattern, for there is really only one import—sugar, for the local refinery; and one export—ships, launched for foreign owners from its shipyards.

Ports of Eastern Scotland

With the exception of Leith, the ports on the east coast of Scotland are all more or less specialised, and serve very limited hinterlands. Leith has an import trade similar in many respects to that of Hull, and serves as an inlet for cereals (wheat and maize) and for bacon, butter, cheese, eggs and other continental produce required not only for the Edinburgh district but for the more populous areas that lie further west. Its exports include whisky and manufactured goods, including some of the machinery and textile goods produced in central Scotland that are destined mainly for continental markets.

Grangemouth has an oil refinery and a petrochemical industry, and in consequence crude petroleum dominates its import trade—with timber, fertilisers and wood pulp as other imports. Petroleum products and chemicals are the most important exports, together with iron and steel goods and whisky. It is peculiar amongst oil ports in having an export trade greater in value than its imports, but that is because much of its oil, as noted above, is recorded in Glasgow's import trade.

The little port of Burntisland exists almost solely to import bauxite for its alumina works (cf. p. 476); whilst Methil is moribund, with but a very small inwards traffic in wood pulp and timber and a small export of coal.

On the Tay, Dundee's trade is mainly inwards, and is virtually confined to the import of jute, jute fabrics and flax; while farther north, Aberdeen, apart from its important fishing interests (cf. p. 261) is largely concerned with the import of wood pulp, paper and board for its local paper industries.

Ports of northeast England

The River Tyne from Newcastle and Gateshead to the North Sea, a distance of 16 kilometres (10 miles), forms what is really one large sheltered port. The river valley is entrenched in the low plateau of the coalfield, but the rocky floor of the valley lies well below sea-level and has been partly infilled with glacial drift. This drift can be excavated with relative ease and this has permitted a dredging and deepening of the river channel to keep pace with the increasing size of vessels launched from Tyneside shipyards. As a port Tyneside has been proverbially (coals and Newcastle) associated with the export of coal for at least six centuries (see above, Chapter 14); but most of the coal now shipped is for coastwise destinations, particularly Thames-side. The several bridges connecting Newcastle and Gateshead are the lowest on the river; colliers and grain ships ascend higher, passing under the high-level bridges and by the help of swing spans through the low level. The river mouth with Tynemouth to the north and South Shields to the south is sheltered from North Sea storms by extensive stone piers or breakwaters.

The improvement of facilities on the Tyne, however, dates only from the middle of the last century, when Northumberland Dock (1857) on the north bank and Tyne Dock at South Shields on the south bank (1859) were constructed to provide space and staithes for coal shipment; the Albert Edward Dock was added at North Shields in 1884. Between the bridges and the docks the river became lined for seven miles with coal staithes, shipyards and other industrial establishments.

In the modern trade of the Tyne coal plays but a very subsidiary role, though there is some coke export to the Continent. The main imports are foodstuffs (bacon, butter, wheat) and raw materials including iron and non-ferrous ores and timber; but machinery, in the form of ships' engines made abroad, is also important, and petroleum products are unloaded at a terminal on the site of the filled-in Northumberland Dock. Iron ore is unloaded at a riverside quay built in 1953, adjacent to Tyne Dock, and goes in special trains to Consett; the non-ferrous ores include lead concentrates for riverside works that once depended on Pennine ores. Exports partly reflect the nature of the hinterland and partly the importance of the Scandinavian trade. Machinery and ships launched for foreign owners play a large part, and many varieties of manufactured goods including textiles from Lancashire, Yorkshire and the recently developed textile industries in the north-east. Clearly the function that the Tyne is best able to perform is that of a link with Scandinavia; the passenger and freight services to Bergen and Oslo (including roll-on, roll-off car ferries) are concentrated at the Tyne Commission Quay adjacent to Albert Edward Dock.

North of the mouth of the Tyne, the former coal port of Blyth stands at the mouth of the river of the same name. Its staithes are idle and there is little traffic of any kind except some import of pit props.

South of the Tyne is the mouth of the Wear, with the port of Sunderland. Here the physical conditions were different; there is no long glacially deepened channel but a rocky bed of Magnesian Limestone, so that the port and its shipyards are much more closely confined to the shore and the immediate vicinity of the river mouth. Petroleum products are brought in by coastwise tankers, and some pitwood is still imported, but there are few exports other than ships launched for foreign owners.

On the Tees estuary stands Middlesbrough, created from nothing in the nineteenth century, first in the 1830s as a small coal shipment point at the terminus of the Stockton and Darlington and Port Clarence railways and later (after 1875) as a great importer of iron ore and exporter of iron and steel. The wide open estuary and its often shallow stream have been altered fundamentally by training walls built of iron slag and by land reclamation, with recent facilities for oil and iron ore imports in the huge vessels that now characterise these traffics. The increasing variety of large-scale industry on Tees-side, including the great chemical and manmade fibres plants and now oil refineries, have greatly altered the character of the trade, and in terms of value petroleum and products and chemicals take precedence over iron and manganese ore, whilst chemical exports are more valuable than iron and steel. The availability of these valuable and bulky cargoes attracts regular shipping services from all over the world.

The South Wales ports

South Wales has the distinction of having seven ports in 112 kilometres (seventy miles) of coastline, and in the heyday of the coal trade at the beginning of the present century all were extremely active. For long the prosperity of South Wales depended in large measure on the export of coal, especially the hard steam coals used for bunkering steamers and for the maintenance of supplies in overseas coaling stations. From the narrow mining valleys to the coast is downhill, so that gravity aided the movement of coal by rail, whilst the convergence of valleys into the Taff and Usk led naturally to the development respectively of Cardiff and Newport at their mouths. Towards the western end of the coalfield the valleys were more separated, so that Aberavon (later Port Talbot) grew at the mouth of the Avon, Briton Ferry at the mouth of the Neath, Swansea at the mouth of the Tawe and Llanelli on the estuary of the Loughor. During the nineteenth century one port after another expanded its dock facilities, as more and more competitive railway lines were built to tap the coal-mining valleys. Cardiff developed an outport, at Penarth, and in the 1890s Barry and its railway came into existence in response to the enormous demand for Rhondda coal. All the ports were equipped with coal hoists for loading coal from railway trucks into ships; and in addition of course the steel, tinplate and non-ferrous metal industries, contributed to both import (ores, etc.) and export traffic.

But the coal export trade (cf. p. 318) has collapsed, apart from some anthracite sent out from Swansea. Cardiff and Newport are but shadows of their former selves, though both still have important iron ore imports, Cardiff for its dockside works and Newport for Ebbw Vale and for the great new steelworks at Llanwern; both import pitwood for the mines, Newport takes aluminium for the Risca smelter and Cardiff has some coastwise oil traffic; both export iron and steel products. Penarth is closed, and Barry, apart from a little coal export (a mere 406 000 metric tons (400 000 long tons) in 1967 compared with 11.1 million metric tons (11 million long tons) in 1913), is largely concerned with the import of bananas and with coastwise oil traffic. Swansea has an advantage for general trade in that it is nearer the open sea than its two rivals; and it still imports crude petroleum in tankers of up to 20 000 tons for the Llandarcy refinery, and nickel matte and zinc concentrates for its remaining non-ferrous metal works; in addition to anthracite it exports tinplate. Port Talbot is simply a specialised iron ore port, that has recently (1969) extended its facilities to accommodate ore carriers of up to 100 000 tons.

PLATE 32 A 'VLCC' (very large crude carrier) in Milford Haven

The *British Explorer*, 215 000 tons. Looking upstream, the BP terminal at Angle Bay is just above the ship's superstructure; the Esso refinery is above the ship's bow.

The outstanding development of recent years in South Wales has been the revival of Milford Haven, with the construction of oil refineries and terminals that can take tankers of 200 000 tons or more. Oil imports in vessels of this size can have a very potent effect on trade statistics. As mentioned above (p. 717), Milford Haven is now the fourth port in the United Kingdom in terms of tonnage of vessels entered and cleared; the value of its trade far exceeds that of any other South Wales port, and its coastwise traffic in petroleum products renders it the third most important port after London and Liverpool for coastwise traffic (if one disregards the 'packet' ports such as Southampton, Isle of Wight and Belfast).

Minor ports

There remain for consideration numerous small but interesting ports that still play a significant part in the life of the British Isles. The numerous fishing ports of present and past have been considered in Chapter 13 and many of the old fishing ports have a new function in that they cater for pleasure boating and sailing for summer visitors. Then quite a considerable number of ports are significant today for coasting trade, especially for heavy and bulky commodities of which coal is the outstanding example. There is a coastwise despatch of coal from such ports as Ayr, Methil, or Whitehaven, and quite large quantities are received at such centres as Ipswich and Shoreham.

Some ports exist to handle the shipment of a local product—one thinks of Fowey, Par and Charlestown despatching the china clay of Cornwall, whence it goes to Holland and even to America. Building stones such as the granite of Peterhead or road metal are advantageously handled by direct water transport. Many manufacturing centres have their own port facilities—such as the cement ports of the Thames and Medway, where the wharves are normally owned by the industrial concerns and do not handle commodities other than their own. The Medway ports are expanding, and Rochester has a large import of wood pulp for the paper industry.

Dockyards and naval ports such as Rosyth, Chatham, Portsmouth and Devonport (Plymouth) form another group. Still another class are those ports serving Ireland or outlying parts of the British Isles: Stranraer, Larne, Heysham, Preston, Holyhead, Fishguard, Penzance, Weymouth, Wick, Thurso, Stornoway and Oban are a few examples which spring to mind.

A number of minor ports in southeastern England have expanded considerably during the last two decades, taking advantage of their proximity to the Continent with which an increasing proportion of our trade is done (cf. p. 811). Shoreham has specialised since 1951 in the bulk import of French wines and brandies, though its export trade is but small. Felixstowe, reconstructed after the east coast floods of 1953, and profiting by the shelter and deep water of the approach to its neighbour Harwich, has developed a tanker terminal, a roll-on, roll-off terminal and a container base—i.e. all the elements of modern progressive shipping—and has built up a considerable short-sea trade with continental ports such as Antwerp and Rotterdam, with the Mediterranean and with America, offering quick turn-round facilities and freedom from the labour troubles that have plagued London and other large ports. Ipswich, Lowestoft, Yarmouth (transformed from a fishing port into a service station for North Sea gas exploration), King's Lynn and Boston are also far from moribund, and they have an appreciable coastwise traffic as well as foreign connections.

All in all, then, and despite the decadence and demise of some ports, the general impression is one of the extreme richness of the British Isles in natural inlets and harbours that continue to function as gateways for the coastwise and foreign trade of the country.

PLATE 33. The container terminal at the port of Felixstowe

The hinterlands of the ports of Britain

It is not possible to delimit with accuracy the hinterlands of the ports of Britain. Several points may be emphasised. The first is the great extent to which the hinterlands overlap. Thus London serves an ever-increasing area, including not only the greater part of the Midlands of England, but much of the industrial north. Obviously Liverpool embraces within its hinterland the whole of the Lancashire and the Yorkshire industrial regions as well as the industrial regions of the Midlands of England. Hull, whose hinterland was in general coextensive with the Ouse–Trent Basin, now for some purposes extends its tentacles farther, e.g. to east Lancashire. But a factor which it is essential to remember is the specialisation of the modern port for the handling of certain classes of goods. Just to take one small example, Avonmouth has been specially equipped to handle the bananas which are imported in huge quantities into this country. It is true that in this traffic it has rivals in Barry and London, but notwithstanding that bananas are delivered by rail to all parts of Britain from Avonmouth. In this sense, therefore, the whole of Britain may be regarded as lying in the hinterland of Avonmouth. It is only, therefore, in the broadest possible sense that one can attempt any sort of delimitation of British hinterlands.[1]

1. See, however, the very interesting study by J. H. Bird, 'Traffic flows to and from British seaports', *Geography*, **54**, 1969, 284–302.

29
The Irish Republic[1]

In the earlier chapters of this book the British Isles have been considered as a whole. It is impossible in any general study of the geology, geographical evolution or climate of the British region to ignore either the whole or part of the island of Ireland. When, however, one comes to consider the various aspects of economic geography which have been taken up in turn the emphasis has been on the main island of Great Britain or on the political unit of the United Kingdom of Great Britain and Northern Ireland.

The present chapter on the Irish Republic has been included for the sake of completeness, but it should not be regarded as more than the merest introduction to the geography of a very interesting country.

Historical note

The Irish Republic is a sovereign independent state and its jurisdiction covers twenty-six of the thirty-two counties of Ireland, including the whole of the three historic provinces of Leinster, Munster and Connaught (Connacht), together with three of the counties (Cavan, Monaghan and Donegal), of the former province of Ulster.

After what has become known as the Easter Rebellion of 1916 a Republic was proclaimed and in due course the British parliament recognised its independence. On 6 December 1921 the Treaty was signed and a boundary was demarcated between the Irish Republic and Northern Ireland. From 1921 to 1937 the official name used for the Republic was Saorstat Éireann, or the Irish Free State. Later the name Eire (literally Ireland, since the State does not officially recognise the existence of Northern Ireland) came to be used, to be changed in 1949 to the present official title, the Irish Republic, or Poblacht na h Éireann.

Apart from the fact that there are close commercial ties between the Irish Republic and the United Kingdom in that the large population of Britain forms a natural market for Irish agricultural produce, the Republic is independent in every way of the United Kingdom Government and ceased to be a member of the Commonwealth in 1949. The head of the Irish Republic is the President, and government is by the Dail and Senate.

1. We are deeply grateful to Mr T. W. Freeman for most valuable comments on this chapter and the next.

FIG. 262. Political map of Ireland

Population

The population of the island of Ireland expanded rapidly from about 1770 to the 1840s. This expansion was made possible by the great development in the cultivation of potatoes, which became the staple article of diet of the Irish farmer and farm worker. The failure of successive potato harvests led to the terrible famines of the years 1845–47, in the course of which very large numbers died of starvation, and which gave rise to the great streams of migrants, especially to the United States. Ireland has in fact never recovered from the effects of those famines of over 100 years ago, and in the past century the total population has been reduced by half.

The first actual census of the whole island was taken in 1821 and recorded a population of 6 802 000. This total by 1841 had reached 8 175 000 and by 1845, when the famine struck, was probably approaching 8½ million despite the considerable emigration which had already taken place. This may be contrasted with the population of the Irish Republic and Northern Ireland in 1961 of 4 240 000. It will be noted that the population of Northern Ireland is now steadily increasing due mainly to the vigorous policy of industrialisation in Belfast and neighbourhood. In the Irish Republic, on the other hand, the population continued to decline slowly, though there was a slight increase from 1946–51, to 2 960 593. This was followed by ten years of decline to 1961, with 2 814 703 but an increase to 2 884 002 by 1966.

In contrast to the present population in the Irish Republic of less than three million the number of emigrants has been truly remarkable. There was no count of the immigrants at the ports of entry before 1851, but it was calculated that there were already nearly one million in the United States, three-quarters of a million in Britain, and one-quarter of a million in Canada. In the year 1847 alone more than a quarter of a million Irish refugees landed at Liverpool, the majority of whom settled in the growing factory towns of the north of England, where their descendants remain to this day.

In the ten years 1851–61 another 1¼ million emigrants left the ports of the British Isles, mostly destined for the United States and Canada. So migration went on and although it steadily slowed down, especially after 1891, over two million have left the island in the past fifty years. Since 1930 the main migration from Ireland has been to Great Britain. It is of course difficult to give anything approaching exact figures, but it has been estimated that people of Irish descent living in America and elsewhere total something like 16 million or more than five times the total number remaining in the Irish Republic.

Considerable parts of Ireland are actually uninhabited—the mountains and the lowland bogs—so that if one excludes these uninhabited areas the population density over the settled parts presents a very different appearance from population density calculated over the whole. At the census of 1961 average rural density in the whole Republic was about 23 per square kilometre (60 per square mile), but excluding the uninhabited areas over half the country had an average density of between 20 and 39 per square kilometre (50 and 100 per square mile), much of the remaining half between 39 and 77 per square kilometre (100 and 200 per square mile) whilst the inhabited fringes of the remote west, the so-called congested districts, supported between 77 and 115 per square kilometre (200 and 300 persons per square mile), in some cases actually over 155 per square kilometre (400 per square mile) of cultivated land.

Over the greater part of the Irish Republic the rural population exceeds 75 per cent of the whole. The settlement is scattered, villages are rare. Although the word 'town' is used to cover nucleated settlements, many of the so-called towns boast less than 200 people and indeed many places with between 800 and 1500 people are, in social and economic functions, towns. The needs of farmers are served especially, however, by those market towns which have between 1500 and 5000 people. There are nearly seventy of this size in the Irish Republic, and a much smaller number of larger ones. In the Irish Republic Dublin with its port, Dun Laoghaire, boasts over 700 000 people, and stands in a class by itself. The expansion has been particularly marked since 1946. If one includes the surrounding residential areas Cork exceeds 130 000, Limerick has now nearly 60 000 and Waterford has almost

30 000. These four towns, however, have exhibited the phenomenon of urbanisation which is almost universal. Over the period 1891–1961 the four together had increased by 43 per cent, and at the 1961 census contained more than one-quarter of the total population. By way of contrast the purely rural areas, including settlements of less than 1500, had decreased by 29 per cent over the same period, and from embracing three-quarters of the total now have only a little over 60 per cent.

It will be clear that apart from the four towns specially mentioned the Republic remains essentially rural and agricultural.

Agricultural regions

The agricultural regions of Ireland show a close coincidence with those determined on a basis of geological structure and relief, although the old familiar statement that Ireland consists of a central plain—more strictly a low plateau so plastered with glacial deposits as to have everywhere impeded and irregular drainage—with an interrupted rim of mountains and hills remains broadly true.

One must remember, however, that the rim is very irregular in character and consists really of a number of isolated hill masses, while the central plain itself is interrupted especially towards the southwestern margins by numerous ranges or isolated hill masses. The central plain further reaches the coast in a number of points.

The physical regions which may also be discussed as agricultural regions are shown on Fig. 263.[1] This may be compared with the next figure, showing the types of farming in Ireland.

The regions may now be taken in order.

(*a*) The mountains and uplands of the southeast (Wicklow and Wexford).
(*b*) The parallel ranges and valleys of the southwest.
(*c*) The mountain masses of the northwest (Connemara, Mayo and Donegal).
(*d*) The uplands of the northeast which are a continuation of the uplands of Northern Ireland.
(*e*) The central lowland and its fringing areas.

The mountains and uplands of the southeast or the Leinster Chain

This well-marked area was doubtless once continuous with north and central Wales, with which the southeastern part in particular is structurally similar; the northern part (actually forming the Wicklow Mountains) consists in the main of the largest granitic intrusion in the British Isles. There is thus geographically a twofold division of the whole area:

1. For a more recent interpretation see D. A. Gillmor: 'The agricultural regions of the Republic of Ireland', *Irish Geography*, 5, 1967, 245–61.

(*a*) The *Wicklow Mountains*, which narrow southwards on the other side of the gorge of the River Slaney to Mt Leinster and the Blackstairs Mountains.
(*b*) The *low plateau* or *uplands of County Wexford*, which extend northwards, narrowing to form the coastal belt of the eastern part of Wicklow.

The whole region is remarkable in the first instance because of the completeness of the barrier which it offers between the southeastern coast of Ireland and the central lowlands. The whole region may, alternatively, be called the Leinster Chain, and to this day no railway crosses this barrier. Further, the main mass of the Wicklow Mountains is uncrossed even now by a motor road.

The Wicklow Mountains

The Wicklow Mountains, reaching northwards almost to the outskirts of Dublin, are remarkable not only for the barrier which they offer, but also

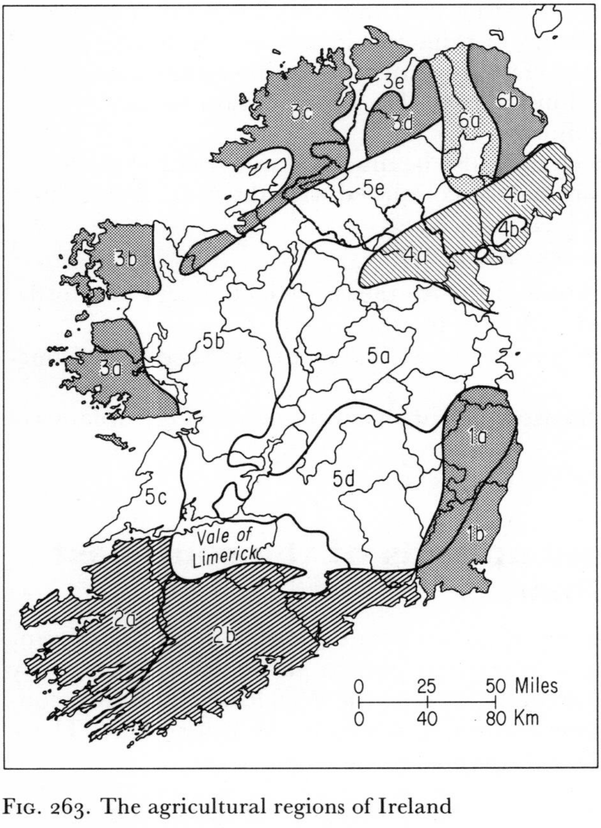

FIG. 263. The agricultural regions of Ireland
For explanation, see text.

for the contrast between the wide open moorlands of the higher parts, and the deep secluded valleys of the east. The moorlands reach elevations of over 925 metres (about 3030 ft) in Lugnaquillia, the highest summit in eastern Ireland, while a very large number of the rounded summits of the moorlands reach over 610 metres (2000 ft). The breadth of the Wicklow Mountains varies between 16 and 25 kilometres (ten and fifteen miles). The streams which rise in the moors flow in comparatively broad shallow valleys until they reach the areas of slope which flank the chain itself. Here the descent is continued in deep gorge-like valleys which are frequently richly wooded, and these glens have long been famous for their scenic beauties, well-known examples being the Glendalough valley and the Avoca Vale.

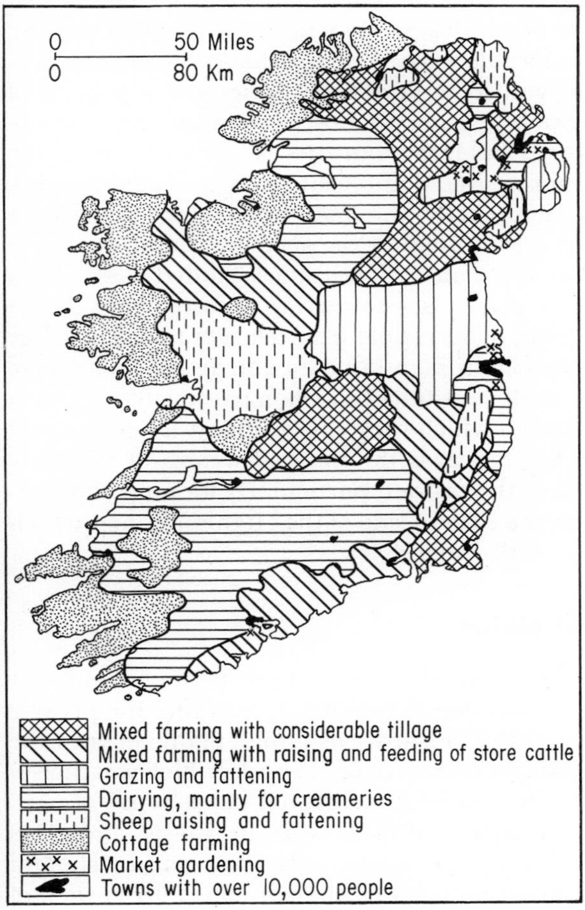

FIG. 264. Types of farming in Ireland

Simplified from T. W. Freeman, Ireland, by permission of the author and Messrs. Methuen & Co. Ltd.

It is towards the south that the granite ridge is breached by the River Slaney which passes through a deep gorge guarded by the village or small town of Clonegall. To the southwest of the Slaney gorge the Mt Leinster–Blackstairs range has two nuclei each over 730 metres (2400 ft) in height separated by the Scullogue Gap, a defile which has been used in the past by bold chieftains desiring to travel from Enniscorthy, the tidal head of navigation on the River Slaney, to Kilkenny, the next important centre towards the heart of the country. Because of their elevation the Wicklow Mountains experience a heavy annual rainfall, in spite of their situation on the eastern or drier side of Ireland. But in the secluded glens of the east the rainfall is less, and these glens benefit from the high summer temperatures, the July mean being over 15.5°C (60°F), although it is of course lower than in the corresponding regions in eastern England. These eastern glens, being sheltered from the rainy westerly or southwesterly winds, form one of the few areas in Ireland where considerable extents of woodland have been preserved. Wicklow timber was valued in very early times and a process of systematic deforestation began when the Anglo-Normans of the Pale exported the oak and other woods in large quantities. The suitability of the area for afforestation has been recognised in recent years, and considerable areas have been planted. Agriculturally, the main importance of the area is for the sheep pastures which are afforded by the open moorland, but there are restricted though good areas of cultivation in the secluded vales. Thus the sheep farming of the centre gives place to rearing of store cattle on the margin, or to dairy farming where accessible from Dublin and Bray. For long the tribes of the Leinster Chain maintained a sturdy independence. They had their strongholds at the entrances to the narrow valleys which led to the high moorlands, and to which they could retreat if need should arise. Yet from the Bronze Age onwards the mineral wealth of Wicklow caused traders to be attracted to the district, particularly for gold and copper, ores of which occurred on the eastern side of the Highlands, and which became known to the people of all Ireland.

The Wexford uplands and plains

To the south and east of the Wicklow Mountains there lies an area almost completely cut off from the remainder of Ireland. It occupies the greater part of Wexford and narrows northwards to form a small plain between the Wicklow Mountains and the sea. It is an area of old rocks which weather to form a moderately good soil. Over large areas glacial deposits are absent. Where they occur they consist mainly of shallow sands, marls, and clays which help to produce soil of excellent quality. As elsewhere in Ireland mixed farming is the rule: here more crops than usual. This corner of Ireland has relatively dry warm summers, and the climatic conditions combined with the soil have produced here what is *par excellence* the barley–wheat–oats region of the country, in which potatoes and pigs are also important. The country is undulating, and generally well drained so that bogs are almost non-existent. Although naturally not nearly so predominantly arable as the eastern parts of England, nearly a third of Wexford is recorded in the returns as arable. Despite this agriculturally favourable aspect of the country its isolation by nature is apparent from the numerous simple little

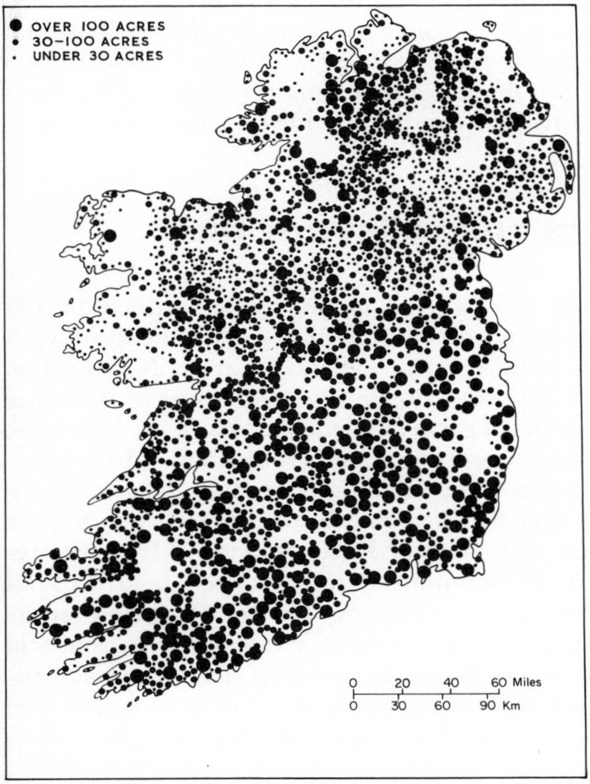

FIG. 265. The distribution of farms of different sizes in Ireland

(From T. W. Freeman, Ireland, by permission of the author and Messrs. Methuen & Co. Ltd.)

whitewashed cabins which are so reminiscent of the remote west. Northwards, where the plain narrows to the strip between the Wicklow Mountains and the Wicklow coast, is an interesting area sometimes referred to as the 'Garden of Ireland'. It is pleasant, comparatively well-wooded 'close' country of very English aspect, free from bogs, and supporting numbers of dairy cattle as well as sheep. It is from this area that the valleys penetrate into the mountains. It might be thought that this pleasant coastland would have been subject to invasions from the east, that is, from the other side of the Irish Sea, but actually, throughout historic time it was dominated by the tribesmen of the Wicklow Hills. The presence of such a stronghold of hill people near Dublin was for very long a source of danger and difficulty to those who sought to establish authority over the whole of Ireland from its natural centre at Dublin. Thus as late as 1800 it was necessary to construct a military road to traverse the high moorlands from Dublin to the Aughrim Valley. Even today the one main road and railway which connects Dublin with the southeast of Ireland runs along the narrow coastland through the picturesque watering place of Bray; whilst the famous Round Tower of Glendalough remains there as a permanent reminder of the long-held strongholds of early Christianity in the secluded valleys of the mountains.

The parallel ranges and valleys of the southwest

Southwestern Ireland is built up of a series of long, comparatively barren ridges of Old Red Sandstone trending roughly from eastnortheast to west-southwest, separated by damp, fairly fertile valleys of Carboniferous Limestone covered by superficial deposits. The country thus owes its structure and relief to the Armorican series of earth movements. Whilst the hill ridges with their rough sheep pastures and the valleys with their damp cattle pastures and famous dairy herds form one natural twofold division of this part of Ireland, there is another which should be considered. There is the west, corresponding roughly with County Kerry, so cut off from the remainder of Ireland by ridges of mountains that it has been described, not ineptly, as a region under the title of the Munster Barrier. It is here that the wild mountains of Old Red Sandstone reach their greatest elevation, and where the intervening valleys pass seawards into long narrow arms of the sea known as rias,[1] in contradistinction to fiords of different character and origin. To the east the mountains are less rugged and less wild, the valleys broader and of greater importance to the country as a whole. Here is part of the greatest dairying region in Ireland, with such important centres as Cork and Waterford, as well as an area devoted rather to feeding of cattle. Actually, dairying and feeding are commonly found on the same farm.

The mountains of County Kerry and West Cork

This region really stretches from the wide estuary of the Shannon on the north to Bantry Bay on the south. The high mountain rampart which separates it from the remainder of southern Ireland on the east and southeast is lofty, bare or bog-encumbered country, intervening between the long valleys opening westwards to the Atlantic and the wide basins of the Lee and

1. A ria becomes progressively deeper seawards; there is not the submerged lip so commonly found in the case of fiords and due to a morainic ridge. It is not without significance that Bantry Bay, like Milford Haven in South Wales, which is also a ria, should have been selected as the site of a great modern oil terminal to take vessels of 300 000 tons.

Blackwater, rivers draining eastwards and then south to the sea. Amongst the mountains of Kerry are the famous Macgillycuddy's Reeks, with the highest mountain in Ireland. In these peninsulas of the west the mountains occupy most of the country and support on their rough pastures numerous sheep, whilst the farms include many of 12 to 20 hectares (30–50 acres) but

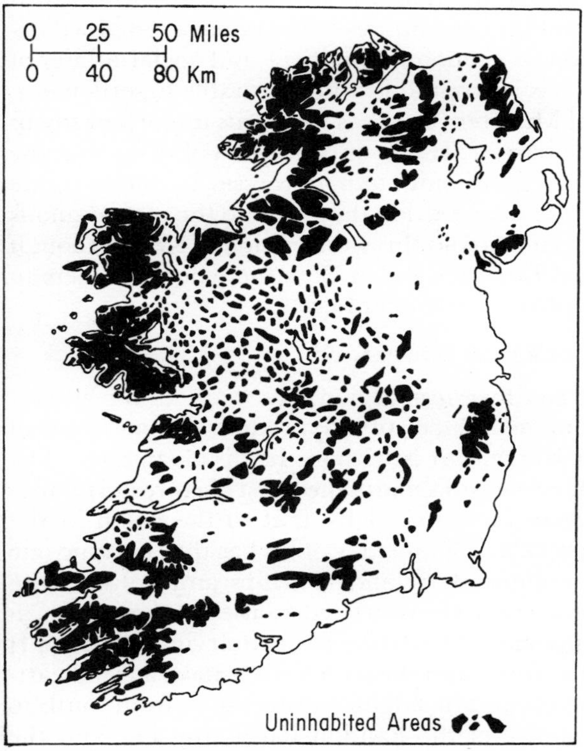

FIG. 266. The uninhabited areas of Ireland
(From T. W. Freeman, Ireland, by permission of the author and Messrs. Methuen & Co. Ltd.)

also numerous small holdings—cottage farming comparable with the crofting of Scotland. The whole region is essentially a pastoral one, for cultivation is rare in Kerry, and even the fertile tracts are generally used for cattle rearing owing mainly to conditions of climate. Western Kerry has the heaviest annual rainfall for the whole of Ireland, the total in places actually exceeding 2500 millimetres (100 in) per annum. At the same time the climate is remarkably mild, especially in the winter months, when an average of over 6.6°C (44°F) is maintained, and a mean January temperature of 7.7°C (46°F) is recorded in parts of western Kerry, being the highest figure for any area in the British Isles. The heavy moisture and excessive mildness of the climate is reflected in certain local features of the vegetation, rich in ferns and mosses, and even including plants native to the western Mediterranean. Although to the west the force of winds from the Atlantic may prohibit tree growth, over restricted areas in the more sheltered valleys are the famous woods of Kerry, including in particular the strawberry tree (*Arbutus unedo*). Modern roads no longer leave this an isolated tract, and the wild country is much loved by visitors to Killarney. Previously the district was one of great isolation; the farming communities of Kerry have remained detached from the main stream of economic, political and social affairs of Ireland. But much of the area is inhospitable and unsuitable to settlement, and the traditional capital of Munster (Cork) as well as its important towns are situated to the east of the barrier. It was only in times of stress that the people naturally withdrew to their mountain fastnesses in the extreme southwest. Even the Viking invaders, used as they were to the mountainous conditions of Norway, preferred to avoid this western side of Kerry; though they established settlements at Limerick and at Cork there does not seem to be evidence that they attempted a settlement here.

The parallel valleys of Cork and Waterford

This, the eastern half of the southwestern region, has many of the advantages (such as mildness of climate and moisture to produce fine pastures) of the mountainous regions of Kerry, but is without its disadvantages. The drift-covered limestone lowlands afford some of the finest pasture in Ireland. The country to the south may be matched by that to the north in the famous Golden Vale of Limerick and Tipperary. This has thus become one of the main dairy farming regions of Ireland. Turnips and potatoes are grown in the lowlands, oats are mainly restricted to the southern part in County Cork. Pigs are an important byproduct of the dairying industry. It will be seen that in general the rivers and the river valleys have a trend eastwards, parallel to that of the mountain ridges. In succession from south to north one may notice the course of the Bandon River, the Lee and the Blackwater, but the region is not as isolated from the central lowland of Ireland as might be expected, because of the transverse valleys which interrupt the east–west mountains. An excellent example is that followed by the railway from Mallow to Cork, affording an easy line of movement between Cork and Limerick. In earlier days these routes were not as easy nor as practical as they are today; thus, although Limerick and Cork were settled by allied bands of Northmen, contact was closer between Cork and Waterford than between Cork and Limerick although the settlers in the two latter areas were originally more closely allied. Intercommunication between the farms in the valleys and the main centres has been an essential factor in the development of the cooperative dairy farming. In many parts 90 per cent of the milk produced on the farms, notably in the county of Limerick, is dealt with in cooperative dairies, an indication of the high pitch of efficiency to which the industry has there been taken. In the east the important and fertile valley of the Suir, Nore and Barrow focus on Waterford.

The mountains of the northwest

These mountains are built up of the same ancient metamorphic rocks as those which make up the Highlands of Scotland. The mountain rampart is exposed to the full force of the relentless waves of the Atlantic Ocean. There are innumerable rocky headlands and deep inlets overshadowed by barren rocky heights. In two places structural weaknesses have allowed the sea to penetrate the mountain rampart as far as the fringes of the central lowlands. These two inlets are Clew Bay and the wider Donegal–Sligo Bay, and they have the effect of separating the mountain rampart into three parts: the mountains of Connemara in the south, the mountains of Mayo in the centre, and the mountains of Donegal or Tirconnail in the north. The first two are often linked together as the Connacht Highlands, whilst the latter is the northwestern Highland properly speaking. The whole of this part of Ireland is exposed to the full force of the rain-bearing winds from the Atlantic Ocean. Large areas are so bleak as to be uninhabitable and tree growth is impossible. Extensive areas of the higher land were swept bare of soil during the great Ice Age, whilst between the barren mountains there are huge glaciated surfaces, waterlogged and occupied by vast boggy moorlands which are again practically uninhabited. The population exists crowded together in the valleys and especially along the coast, and like the crofters of Scotland, the people live by carrying on subsistence farming. Sheep live on the better-drained slopes and furnish the wool for the famous Irish and Donegal tweeds. Potatoes are often almost the only crop possible, and there is frequently clear evidence of conscious and unconscious attempt of man and animal alike to seek shelter on the lee side of hills away from the full force of the Atlantic winds. In such situations are the little homesteads; here alone will trees grow.

The mountains of Connemara

The region corresponds with the western third of Galway and the southwestern corner of County Mayo. Running northwards from the town of Galway is the Limestone belt which is described below as part of the fringe of the Central Lowlands. Westwards the junction between the often bare limestone surfaces and the ancient rocks of the highlands is usually quite sharp—so sharp that the line can often easily be drawn on a map. Actually along the junction there are frequently prosperous farms in wooded sheltered hollows; but away from this margin stretch great expanses of almost uninhabited moorland. Shallow treacherous lakes occupy every hollow, and are in turn fringed by bogs; whilst between the lakes are extensive stretches of bare glaciated rock surface. Rounded mountain masses often practically bare of soil rise in lonely grandeur from the lake-studded lowlands. Their more fertile slopes may be covered by a moorland in which bracken and heather are important. Some of the scenic effects, such as the view of the Twelve Bens or Pins of Connemara seen from the south, are both majestic and awe-inspiring. Where the glaciated mountains reach the coast, the scenery again is often very fine, as in the fiord known as Killary Harbour. 'Much of the sparse settlement in this region is along the coast,

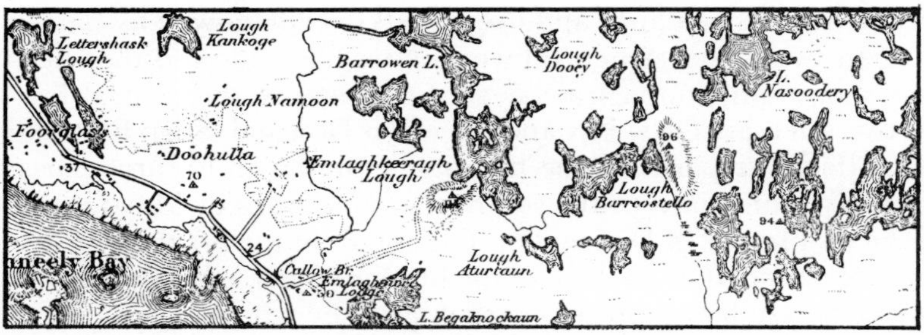

FIG. 267. Part of the lake-studded lowland of Connemara

Note the restriction of settlements to the coast. Scale, 1 inch to 1 mile. Reproduced from the Ordnance Survey map by permission.

where fishing may be combined with subsistence farming, and where seaward drainage helps to improve the natural conditions. Little whitewashed single-storied thatched cabins lie scattered along the coast wherever a few fields sufficiently free from boulders may be secured. Frequently the little farm is situated on a slope with rough sheep pastures above and where hay, oats and potatoes may be grown on a narrow strip of land between the farm and the sea. A few small black cattle, an occasional pig and a few poultry form the rest of the livestock. Such is the character of the country around Clifden.'[1] It should be noticed that in this far west even good pasture is scarce.

The mountains of Mayo

These are broadly similar to the mountains of Connemara and Joyce's Country to the south of Clew Bay. The width of the mountains of Mayo from north to south—that is from Clew Bay to the north—is roughly 50 kilometres (thirty miles), but only one road forces its way across them in this distance. The 147 square kilometres (fifty-seven square miles) which make up Achill Island, the largest island off the Irish coast, consist almost entirely of wild moorland with only very occasional patches of cultivation. No districts in Ireland are more isolated from the main currents of national life than are these desolate tracts of western Galway and western Mayo. It is there, not unnaturally, that we find today the descendants of the earliest inhabitants of the island. Through the ages the sturdy hillsmen remained in defiance of foreign overlords coming there from across the plains to the east. To this day dark-skinned descendants of Neolithic man

1. L. D. Stamp, *An Agricultural Atlas of Ireland*, p. 60.

are to be found in the hill country of Galway and Mayo. This is, indeed, one of the remotest fringes of Europe.[1] Railways reach Ballina, in north Mayo, Westport or Clew Bay, and the City of Galway. From all these places bus services run to places in the extreme west and Coras Iompair Eireann, which organises all public transport, also provides lorry and van services.

Donegal or Tirconnail[2]

In the windswept land of Conall the barrenness and rugged character of the Irish highlands reach their maximum, but though the coast is usually very broken and rockbound the main mountain masses terminate abruptly before reaching the sea, there being usually a low, though narrow, coastal plain which makes possible the existence of a larger population in Donegal than in the bleaker, but less majestic, mountain country of Mayo and Galway. This is readily apparent in the maps showing the distribution of potatoes in the Irish Republic (Fig. 270), there being obviously more land under cultivation on the fringe of the Donegal mountains than in either of the preceding areas. This is true, for example, of the coastal fringe of the peninsula of Inishowen.[3] The climate is, of course, characterised by the prevalence of strong westerly and southwesterly winds, bringing a heavy annual rainfall, and by a mildness of temperature at all seasons. This is important. The absence of frost is marked particularly, and it is thus possible for the small cattle breeder of Donegal to allow his animals to remain in the fields even during the winter, at least in most years. The cattle thrive on the verdant pastures which are possible in many of the valleys, whilst on the hillsides are numerous sheep. Woodland is naturally absent in Donegal except on the sheltered, usually the eastern, sides of the hill slopes. On the east the mountainous massif of Donegal abuts against the broad, comparatively fertile, corridor which is formed in the main by the valley of the Foyle River and, by analogy with Scotland, may be called the Foyle Strath. Along it there now runs the boundary between the Irish Republic and Northern Ireland. The rugged mountain scenery of the northwestern massif appears again to the east of the Foyle Strath in the Sperrin Mountains of Northern Ireland. The lowland basin of the Foyle has long been the focus of human activities. Strabane in Northern Ireland is one of the most important road centres of the area, and here the chief tributary of the River Foyle, the River Finn, joins the main stream. The east side of Donegal is far more fertile than the west, and a light railway formerly ran to the towns of Donegal and Killybegs (closed in 1959). The natural centre for the Foyle basin is Londonderry, in Northern Ireland, but the customs frontier is close to the town.

1. E. Estyn Evans, 'The Atlantic ends of Europe', *Advmt Sci.*, **15**, 1–58, 54–64.
2. Tir Chonaill = the Land of Conall.
3. Inishowen = island of Owen.

The uplands of the northeast

Lying in the counties of Cavan, Monaghan and Louth is the continuation of the rolling country more fully described under Northern Ireland. Though the old rocks are largely masked by glacial deposits—this is part of the great drumlin belt—the drainage here is much better than in the plains of central Ireland to the south; bogs become infrequent or have been drained, but as in the neighbouring parts of Northern Ireland, there are rich pastures, more accessible than those amongst the bogs and so giving rise to a country where dairy cattle are important, and where there is an extensive cultivation of potatoes, as well as of oats, and in the drier east some barley and wheat. Pigs are numerous as a byproduct of the dairy farming industry; sheep are numerous on the drier pastures.

The central lowlands

Now that the fringing highland masses of the Irish Republic have been described, there remains a great central region which is on the whole a lowland. It seems best to consider it as made up of four parts:

(*a*) The central lowland which is mainly 60–120 metres (200–400 ft) above sea level with only low hills.
(*b*) The western fringe, where well-drained areas of glacial deposits and bare limestone tracts make a varied landscape.
(*c*) The limestone uplands of County Clare.
(*d*) The southern area, where great tongues of lowland are separated by hill masses, and where the fertile river valleys merge insensibly into the similar valleys of southwestern Ireland.

The central lowland

On the ordinary solid geological map this tract appears as a broad sweep of Carboniferous Limestone, which extends also to the western fringe and far to the south. Over much of the central lowland, however, the limestone is rarely seen. It is masked by a spread of glacial and later deposits. There are wide areas of waterlogged boulder clay interrupted by infertile glacial sands and occasionally by loam. On a low-lying area of such a character, drainage is naturally bad. It is rendered worse by the presence of the limestone below, for water tends to pass through fissures in the limestone rather than across the surface by regular watercourses. The curse of the central lowland is bad drainage and consequent formation of huge bogs. Away from the bogs it is a land of wet pastures where little cultivation is possible. The whole may indeed well be described as the beef- and bog-land of Ireland. Some of the larger bogs may be 8 or even 16 kilometres (five or ten miles) across; and it is not infrequently a journey of some distance from a main road to an isolated farm. With such difficulties of communication it is obvious that dairy farming is practically impossible. The regular collection of the milk for a central creamery would be out of the question. If dairy cattle are kept, as they are in small numbers, butter is made at the individual farms. On the other hand the damp pastures are, of course, excellent for cattle. Hence, as a map showing the distribution of beef cattle would indicate, there is an

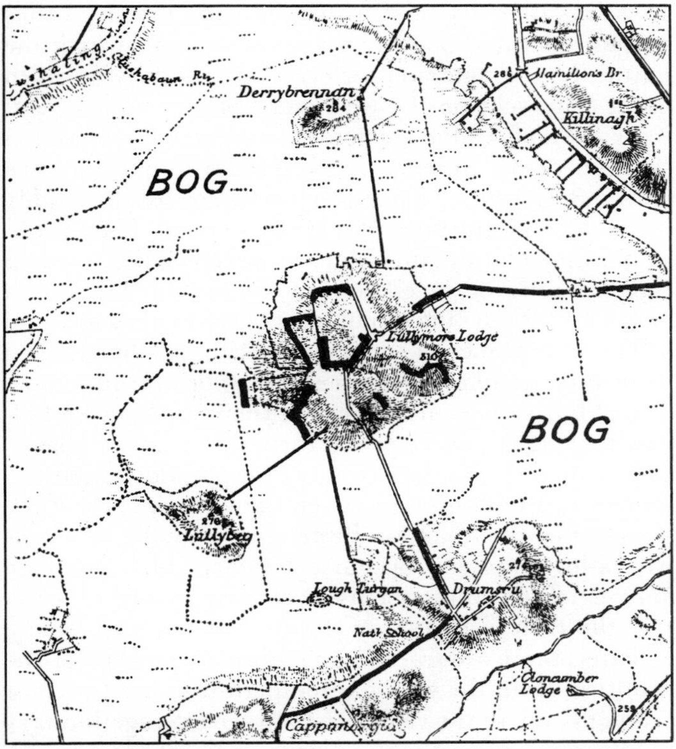

FIG. 268. Part of the central lowland of Ireland, in the region of the great bogs, showing 'islands' of well-drained sands, very difficult of access, in waterlogged bogland. It is not surprising that Lullymore on this map has been abandoned as a farm
Scale, 1 inch to 1 mile. Reproduced from the Ordnance Survey map by permission.

immense concentration of the stock-rearing industry on the central lowland. Especially in the immediate hinterland of Dublin are there large numbers ready for export to Britain. There is little cultivation of land, but the importance of potatoes relative to oats indicates the greater adaptability of potatoes as a food crop. In the south turnips become important—obviously grown as a cattle food.

The central lowland reaches the Irish Sea in the lowland stretch between the Wicklow Mountains on the south and the low hills of County Louth on the north. Here is the obvious gateway to the heart of Ireland, and the natural position for the capital. Notwithstanding this fact, communication across the central lowland is not easy. It has been facilitated, however, by the presence of ridges of glacial origin and the old roadways carefully avoided the peat bogs by traversing the well-drained glacial deposits including, in some places, sandy ridges called eskers, some of which run conveniently from east to west. Even when the land of the great bogs has been traversed, there is the difficulty of crossing the wide marshy valley of the Shannon or the considerable bog-fringed lakes through which the river passes. Thus, naturally, the Shannon formed the boundary between the ancient kingdoms of Connacht on the west and Leinster on the east; whilst the position of the town of Athlone, where a crossing of the Shannon is rendered possible, is doubly emphasised by its presentday importance as a railway junction and as a road centre. The esker ridges consist of roughly stratified sands and gravels, and are normally grass-covered. They probably mark the courses of subglacial streams which were developed towards the close of the Ice Age. On some of the eskers and comparable mounds of glacial origin in the north and south of the main part of the central lowland sheep are numerous. The importance of these glacial ridges is heightened during the heavy rains of autumn and winter when the subterranean waters, such a common feature of limestone country, rise in the neighbouring hollows, locally known as 'turloughs', and convert them into shallow lakes.

To the southwest of Dublin is the Kildare country—especially famous for its breeding of race-horses and Irish hunters. Even the wettest parts of the central lowland—for example, the Shannon Basin—are actually at a considerable height above sea-level, and it is, of course, this fact which has made possible the development of the Shannon hydroelectric power scheme. Consequently, towards the eastern section of the central lowland, where drainage to the sea is better, there are tracts much more favourable for the development of agriculture. Here the seasonal temperatures are the most extreme for Ireland, though even so the variation between average January and July mean temperatures is only about 11 degrees C (20 degrees F). The effect of prevailing westerly or southwesterly winds on vegetation is much less marked, and tree growth tends to be more abundant. On the other hand cold easterly and northeasterly winds in winter are able to penetrate a considerable distance into the central lowlands. Along the coastal fringe, the cultivation of barley, wheat and potatoes is seen to assume a greater importance. It is a matter of the greatest significance that this better-drained land should be on the eastern side.

The central lowland has been in each epoch of invasion the home of the foreigner who has entered from the Irish Sea. The Vikings established their settlement in Dublin, and the port became the stronghold of the stranger just as it has been at many succeeding dates. The Anglo-Normans established in Dublin their outpost from England and their headquarters for the conquest of the wide central lowland. Not unreasonably the holder of the port of Dublin would feel confident ultimately of establishing authority throughout the island, and at the same time ensuring protection to commerce in the Irish Sea by preventing raiders leaving *from* the natural gateway of the country. Although clansmen might remain virtually independent in the distant hills, the lord of the central lowland was virtually the King of Ireland. This is, when one considers it, obvious, although at first sight remarkable in view of the by no means favourable conditions of the whole of the central lowland.

The western fringe

This seems a convenient designation for a belt of country lying between the central lowland as here described and the old mountains of the northwest. Actually it consists of two contrasted types of country. There are areas where the Carboniferous Limestone reaches the surface and gives rise to dry limestone country covered with sparse sheep pastures, and other areas where the surface soils are of glacial origin but comprise comparatively well-drained mounds or drumlins and eskers. These mounds of sandy glacial material contain few boulders, so that stone is not available for the construction of

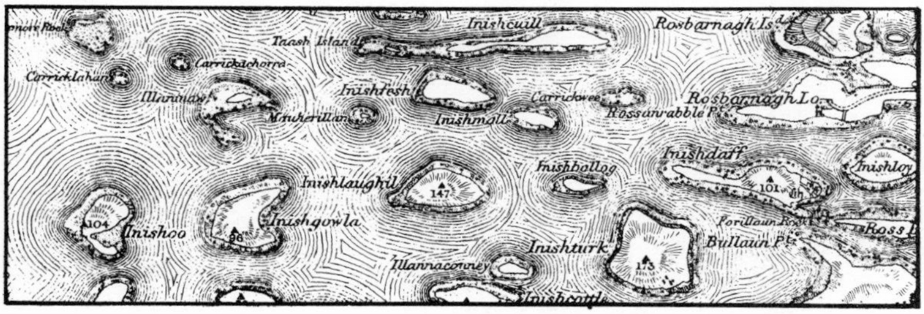

FIG. 269. Clew Bay—an example of 'drowned' country of drumlins
Scale, 1 inch to 1 mile. Reproduced from the Ordnance Survey map by permission.

stone walls. Instead the fields are divided by hedges. On the other hand the western position of the area and the dampness of the climate favour the growth of grass for hay, and the region is to be described therefore as a land of hay and hedges with oats, potatoes and dairy cattle. In addition, especially in the north, there are outlying masses of the ancient metamorphic rocks of the highlands which stand up as hill ranges, particularly out of the limestone country. To consider the two types of land in somewhat greater detail, over considerable tracts the limestone may be almost bare, its grey-white surface seamed with solution channels, and supporting but little vegetation of any sort. This may be the case even on low ground, as to the north of Galway on the shores of Lough Corrib. Frequently the limestone is covered by patches of drift, and fades thus into the drumlin or esker type of country. The lower parts of the valleys near watercourses are often ill-drained and occupied by large bogs. The slopes are cultivated. The limestone blocks are used for the construction of walls, which become grassed over and divide the fields. Oats and other crops are largely grown; both cattle and sheep are numerous, though sheep are specially important. The farmhouses have an air of comparative prosperity, and this belt of mixed soils is obviously an important one. It is thus clearly incorrect that the

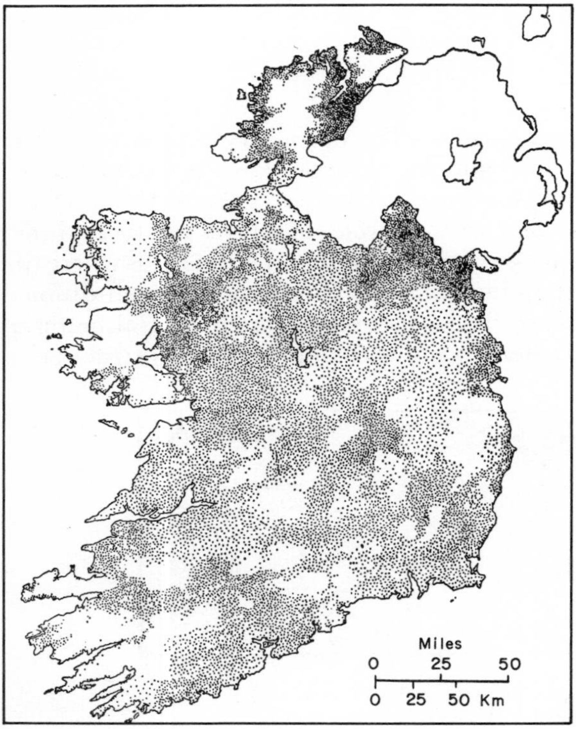

FIG. 270. Distribution of potato cultivation in the Irish Republic in the 1930s
Each dot represents 10 hectares (25 acres).

country though hilly should be linked with the barren desolate tracts of the mountains of Connemara and Mayo by which it is bordered on the west. The glacial country, on the other hand, is built up in the main of a series of drumlins or mounds of glacial material. It would require a map contoured at ten-foot intervals to show adequately its character. But where such country has been drowned, as in Clew Bay, the innumerable low islets give a clue to its general appearance. Near the sea the hollows are drowned, but elsewhere they are occupied by small scattered peat bogs, whilst reedy pastures occur on the more level stretches, the gentle slopes of the mounds being occupied either by cropped land or hay; whilst the driest slopes are given over to sheep. This type of country is well seen in the plains of Mayo or in the country round Clew Bay, or from Westport to Castlebar and Swineford. It stands out on the agricultural maps as the belt where the cultivation of oats and potatoes is important, and where large numbers of cattle, sheep and pigs are reared. Where masses of the older rocks appear through

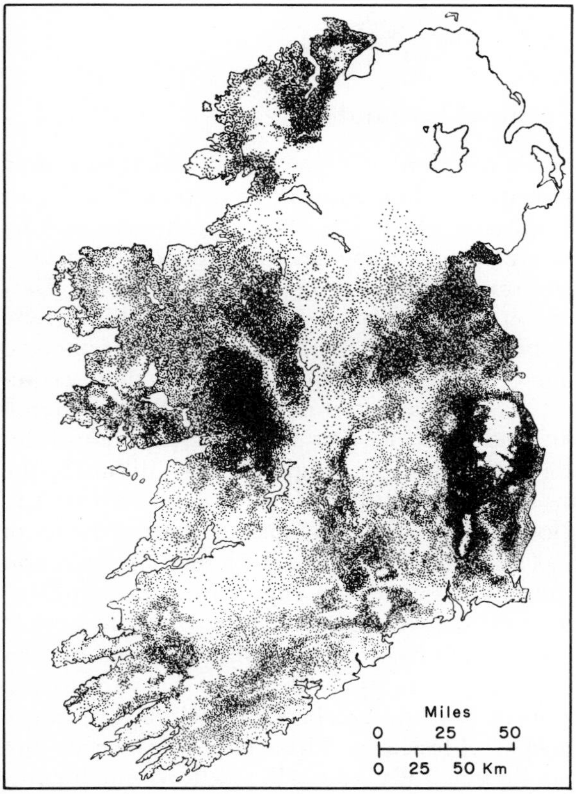

FIG. 271. Distribution of sheep in the Irish Republic in the 1930s
Each dot represents 100 sheep.

the limestone or the cover of glacial deposits they give rise to mountains (of which the Ox Mountains may be quoted as an excellent example) forming a sort of outer rampart or bulwark of the Connaught (Connacht) Highlands against the central lowlands.

The limestone uplands of County Clare

Here in the west is a typical limestone area, but one which has few glacial deposits. There are wide stretches of open grassy moorland comparatively free from peat, whilst flat-topped hills with abrupt edges, built up of almost horizontal limestone beds, break the monotony of the scenery. These limestone tracts are sparsely inhabited, and support mainly a limited number of sheep. Isolated tracts of a similar character occur fringing Sligo Bay near Sligo itself. In the southern part of County Clare are drift deposits which support pastures and share in the dairy farming industry of County Limerick.

The southern area of the central lowlands

This, perhaps, is the most difficult part of Ireland for which one may attempt to give a general description. The country of farmland and vast bogs passes southwards into an area where the plains are interrupted by numerous hills. Some of these are anticlinal masses where the older rocks—the Old Red Sandstone—are found outcropping from beneath the Carboniferous Limestone. Others, on the other hand, are synclinal areas where patches of Millstone Grit have been preserved in basins in the Carboniferous Limestone, but owing to their greater resistance to subaerial denudation stand up as hill masses. In the heart of the anticlinal hills of Old Red Sandstone still older rocks appear, and thus one gets barren rocky mountains with poor pasture, such as are found in Slieve Aughty, Slieve Bernagh, the Arra Mountains, Slievefelim, and Slieve Bloom. It will be noticed that in the neighbourhood of Killaloe on the Shannon, just to the northeast of Limerick, two of these masses of ancient rock approach close to the Shannon itself. It is here that the Shannon passes over the rapids from Lough Derg (35 metres: 116 ft above sea-level) before reaching the town of Limerick, and it is the succession of rapids which has made possible the construction of the hydroelectric power works (see p. 351). Between the various hill masses there are broad tongues of lowland or corridors, which can be regarded as off-shoots from the central lowland. These fade southwards into important river valleys. Speaking generally, the valleys afford much cultivated land, especially on the slopes. Oats, potatoes and turnips are grown. In the drier and more sheltered valleys farther to the southeast, barley becomes important. There are also very extensive cattle pastures, and the drier hill slopes above support numbers of sheep, whilst in the centre of the valleys themselves there are often extensive bogs. The easternmost of the larger valleys is that of the Barrow in which sugar beet and mangolds are cultivated. The western part of the whole tract comes within the main dairying belt of southwestern Ireland, and it is here that perhaps the most fertile part of Ireland—the Golden Vale of Limerick—lies between the region now under consideration and that which has been described under southwestern Ireland. On the other hand the northeastern portion of this varied tract is more closely allied with the central lowland and, like the central lowland, is famous for its beef cattle.

The industries and towns of Ireland

Many of the manufacturers of the Irish Republic are concerned primarily with the processing of home agricultural products. Of outstanding importance is the manufacture of butter and the dairying industry is organised essentially around the cooperatives which collect the milk and make the butter. With a relatively small home urban market there is not the demand for liquid milk which characterises the dairying industry of England, Wales and Scotland, and consequently the emphasis is on butter.

There is an associated cheese industry, though much less important. Mitchelstown, Co. Cork, is the main centre. Butter is made at a large number of rural creameries, and collected in cold stores at Cork and Dublin, whilst the condensed milk trade is centred at Limerick.

An old established industry is that of bacon curing. There are bacon factories at the four chief towns—Dublin, Cork, Limerick and Waterford—as well as in a number of provincial centres. Efforts have been made to spread bacon factories throughout the country in order to provide a convenient market for the pigs produced by the smaller farmers. Some of the factories also provide sausages and other pork products.

Centres of meat canning have also been established, notably at Dublin, Waterford and Roscrea. The home production of sugar from sugar beet has been carefully fostered since 1925 and the output is about enough to supply home needs. There are four factories in the heart of the country at Carlow, Thurles, Mallow and Tuam. Along with the growth of home production of sugar has been the development in the manufacture of jams and confectionery.

Although production of barley is not large, Irish barley has a high reputation as malting barley and goes largely to the breweries found in Dublin, Cork and other towns, especially in the east. The most famous and the largest of the breweries is of course that of Guinness beside the River Liffey in Dublin. Irish whiskey is equally famous and distilleries are situated in Dublin, Cork and Tullamore. Irish whiskey is quite distinct in character from Scotch and there is a considerable export market. There has long been a widespread appreciation of the dangers of alcoholism, especially from illegally home-produced spirits and the wide distribution of plants manufacturing soft drinks is an indication of the effects of the abstinence campaign.

Amongst other industries using agricultural products one finds naturally spinning, weaving and dyeing of woollens, with a number of woollen mills as well as a large production of homespun cloths made by individual workers in the west.[1] There are some famous mills near Cork, especially Blarney and Dripsey. Hosiery and knitwear are also to be noted, and the industry has

1. See D. J. Dwyer and L. J. Symons, 'The development and location of the textile industries in the Irish Republic', *Irish Geography*, **4**, 1963, 415–31.

spread to the making of clothes and a range of woollen rugs, blankets and tweeds for export. A widespread leather industry and the manufacture of footwear reflects another use of home-produced raw material.

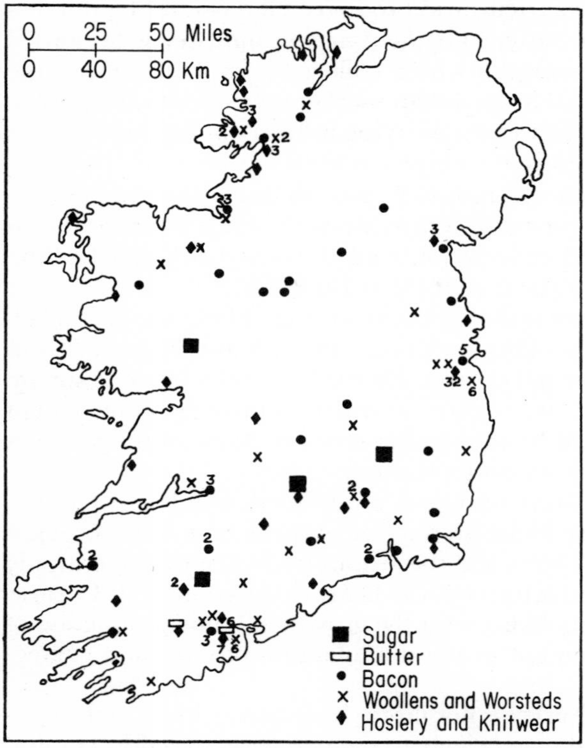

FIG. 272. The industries of the Irish Republic
(*Modified from T. W. Freeman, Ireland, by permission of the author and Messrs. Methuen & Co. Ltd.*)
More than one plant is indicated by a number.

A group of industries is concerned to supply the needs of the farmers, notably with tools and agricultural implements and fertilisers. The milling industry is an interesting one. Few of the old mills still grind the wheat, oats and barley supplied by farmers and return the flour to them after grinding. The mills grinding imported wheat and maize have become important in the bigger towns. Limerick is now a milling centre.

Those industries making goods intended for the home market employ an increasing number of people but they tend to be concentrated particularly in and around Dublin, despite the Government's aim to spread industry widely. Paper and printing affords a good example, whilst one of Dublin's largest factories makes biscuits and chocolate for distribution throughout the country. Other firms are concerned in Dublin, Dundalk and Drogheda with tobacco manufacture. Engineering and metal works have also increased in importance, but it was not until 1938 that steel making was established in Ireland on an island in Cork harbour, a former British naval base with deep-water berths. Ireland's first oil refinery was opened at Whitegate, Cork, in 1959.

A description has already been given in an earlier chapter of the great Shannon hydroelectric power scheme from which electricity is distributed over most of the country, though now providing only a fraction of national consumption. In view of the absence of coal, oil and timber this water power development has been of the greatest importance. The old staple Irish fuel was peat, never a very satisfactory one, although obtainable in many areas just for the labour of cutting and drying. Many isolated habitations and towns have gone direct from a peat age to an electric age. In some cases, oddly enough, the electricity may be generated using peat as a fuel in the power stations (see above, pp. 328, 352).[1]

The ports of the Irish Republic

The great bulk of shipping which serves the Irish Republic uses the port of Dublin, including its outport at Dún Laoghaire, formerly Kingstown, used by the regular service of mail steamers to Holyhead in Anglesey. Apart from passenger services to Britain, all the port trade is of cargoes as the rapid air services through Shannon Airport in County Clare cater for transatlantic passengers. The numerous small ports have a limited and generally declining coastal traffic.

Dublin

As regards its navigation, harbour facilities, and internal communications, Dublin is the obvious rival of Belfast, and is far and away the most important port of the Irish Republic. It handles the export trade with Scotland, the Midlands and south of England. There are regular cargo or cargo-passenger services to Glasgow, Liverpool, Manchester, and by the relatively short sea route to Holyhead, with express connections therefrom on the other side. The Liffey on which Dublin stands is but a small river with a small catchment basin, but owing to the lack of gradient the channel in the estuary was formerly shallow and the deposition of sand continuous. Improvements have continually been made to provide deep-water berthage of at least 10.6 metres (35 ft) accommodating the large ocean freighters normally using the port. Larger vessels must wait for high tide to cross the bar over which there is 6 metres (20 ft) of water at low tides, thus enabling the port to be used by cross-channel steamers at all times. Constant and extensive dredging, however, will always be necessary. Above the loopline railway bridge steam lighters come up to the breweries of Messrs Guinness at St James's.

1. Chapter 8, 'Peat', in *A View of Ireland*, British Association, Dublin, 1957.

The port is equipped for the bulk handling of oil and of various other commodities but side by side with modern methods of loading and off-loading may be seen numerous horse-carts and the handling of goods by hand-cranes. There is no direct passenger railway service in connection with the quays and this has diverted traffic to Dún Laoghaire, which has direct rail connections. The port of Dublin itself, however, is so near to the heart of the city that the absence of rail facilities is no great disadvantage and there are several regular, but not daily, passenger sailings to ports in Great Britain, other than the daily service to Liverpool. The once-important Royal Canal is disused and the Grand Canal system which once linked Dublin with a large part of the heart of the island has become merely a pleasure route, as barges ceased to run in 1959. Nevertheless rail, road and water place practically the whole of the Irish Republic in the hinterland of the port of Dublin.

In view of the absence of home production of coal there is everywhere throughout Ireland a demand for imported coal in large quantities, though the railways now run on diesel oil. Naturally Dublin is still the chief importing port and it is to Dublin that are sent most of the manufactured goods

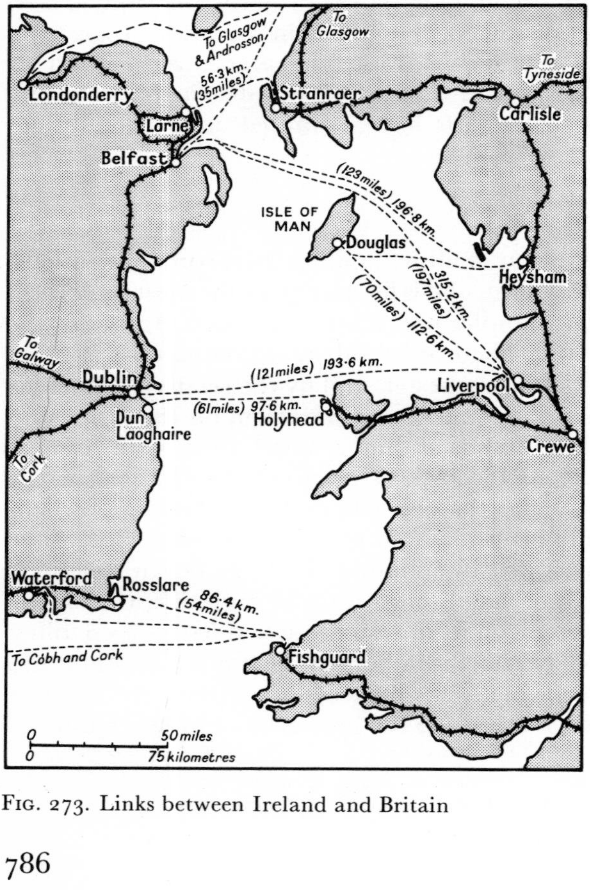

FIG. 273. Links between Ireland and Britain

for distribution throughout the Republic. As a collecting centre for commodities for export Dublin is also pre-eminent. More than a third of the exports of the Republic are live animals, cattle in particular, but also sheep and pigs. There is in addition the movement in both directions of racehorses and bloodstock and even greyhounds, which travel by air. Live animals demand quick and efficient transport, hence the advantage in the situation of Dublin, only 98 kilometres (61 miles) from Holyhead and 162.5 kilometres (121 miles) from Birkenhead. Fat stock rapidly lose condition and the time taken in crossing is very important, hence they are commonly sent to Holyhead and Birkenhead. Store cattle destined either for fattening or addition to the dairy herds of Britain are not so affected by a longer voyage and may go to other ports.

Though there is still a large export in stout and porter manufactured in Dublin the establishment by Messrs Guinness of breweries elsewhere, notably at Park Royal in the west of London, has considerably altered the position in recent years.

Most of the other exports from Ireland will be found passing through Dublin, which also handles a large part of the import traffic, less important than formerly, of feeding stuffs for animals. By contrast the coastwise traffic from Dublin is less important than from many of the smaller ports.

Although the harbour of Dún Laoghaire, or Kingstown, was built as long ago as 1817 as a refuge for vessels during south-easterly gales, it was developed as a result of interest of the railway companies into the premier passenger port of the Irish Republic, favoured by the short distance from Holyhead in Anglesey, terminus of the 'Irish Mail' rail route to London. Its old rival was Rosslare, in the southeast with a service from Fishguard on the former Great Western Railway.

Other ports

North of Dublin is the small port of *Dundalk*, importing coal, but more important is *Drogheda*, which has a considerable import of coal. The port, however, is poorly equipped and though small ocean vessels use the port cargo has to be unloaded by gangways and there are no direct rail facilities to the quayside.

Southwards from Dublin is the small port of *Wicklow*, importing a little coal, but more significant is *Arklow*, which was developed as the Republic's largest fishing port. Like the other ports of the east coast, however, its significance has faded as Dublin's has been improved, but it imports china clay for a local pottery.

The small port of *Wexford* lies at the mouth of the Slaney and is served direct by railway, but more significant is *Rosslare* harbour, almost an eastern continuation of Wexford, where passenger and goods trains run alongside the vessels moored to the quay. Goods can be distributed with considerable facility to the south and southwest of Ireland. As a passenger port it has therefore long rivalled Dublin, to which it also occupies second place as a cargo port. Though the sea passage is about the same as Holyhead–Dublin, the overall time of the journey from Cork to London *via* Rosslare is between two and three hours shorter than from Cork to London *via* Dún Laoghaire and Holyhead.

Along the south coast of Ireland the port of *Waterford* lies in a sheltered estuary where the combined Nore and Barrow are joined by the Suir. It is, however, open to small ocean-going vessels only at certain states of the tide, and the city and port of Waterford on the south side of the river are cut off from the railway on the other side. Formerly river traffic by barges inland was significant and at that time the port took a large share in the export of live animals.

Cork is the second port of the Irish Republic and the very large sheltered harbour includes the lower harbour of Cork itself as well as Cóbh or Queenstown situated on the south side of Great Island and with a quay adjacent to the railway station for reception of mails and passengers. The new oil refinery at Whitegate is on Cork Harbour. Other very small ports along the south coast include Kinsale, Baltimore and Youghal.

Bantry Bay, one of the west-facing rias on the southwest coast, has recently become an oil terminal. With an almost unlimited water depth, it will become the major Atlantic terminal for tankers of up to 300000 tons employed by the Gulf Oil Company. The oil will be transhipped into smaller tankers for distribution to British and continental European ports which are unable to accommodate such huge vessels. In terms of shipping tonnage Bantry Bay will quickly become the largest port in Ireland.

Turning to the west coast of the Irish Republic exposure to westerly gales is a serious deterrent to the use of those ports which exist, which is unfortunate in view of the fact that Limerick at the head of the Shannon estuary, a tidal port for all vessels, includes the whole of the Shannon basin in its natural physical hinterland. Fifty-eight kilometres (36 miles) from the open sea, on the south side of the estuary, is Foynes, which achieved a greater importance as a trans-Atlantic airport, formerly used both as a regular stopping place as well as for emergency landings when the airports of Britain were fogbound. It has been replaced by Shannon on the north side of the river.

Midway along the west coast, protected by the Aran Islands, is Galway Bay, a deep indentation reaching the plain of central Ireland. Unfortunately, however, the approach to *Galway harbour* is not favourable to shipping because of the natural shelving which takes place and the existence of a ridge of hard rock crossing the channel, which can only be blasted away, not dredged. There have been many proposals to develop Galway as a trans-Atlantic port, and for some years from about 1926, trans-Atlantic liners anchored in the roadstead a mile or so off the port and transferred their passengers by tender. But all one is likely to see in Galway harbour now is a few fishing vessels, probably from Scotland, and occasional coasting ships bringing coal, raw materials for the various industries of Galway, including fertilisers, and bags of cement as building materials. And most of the other small ports are similar, such as Westport and Ballina (on Donegal Bay), Sligo (on Sligo Bay), and Ballyshannon on the northwest side of Donegal Bay.

The foreign trade of the Irish Republic

The diagrams illustrating the foreign trade of the Republic (Figs 274, 275) show at once the overwhelming importance of the exports of agricultural origin, but there has been a significant change since the Second World War, as now the export of meat in various forms—mainly beef, some bacon—exceeds that of cattle. In effect this indicates both the industrial growth in the Republic and the humanitarian objections to the export of live animals. Eggs and poultry exports have now practically ceased as a result of the intensification of British poultry farming, but butter exports have increased with the use of cold storage plants giving supplies throughout the year. Still, however, some live animals are exported, including cattle for immediate slaughter as well as stores for fattening. There is also an export of sheep and lambs, and an important bloodstock trade. Beer and whiskey also form important exports. The imports into Ireland bring out the dependence of the

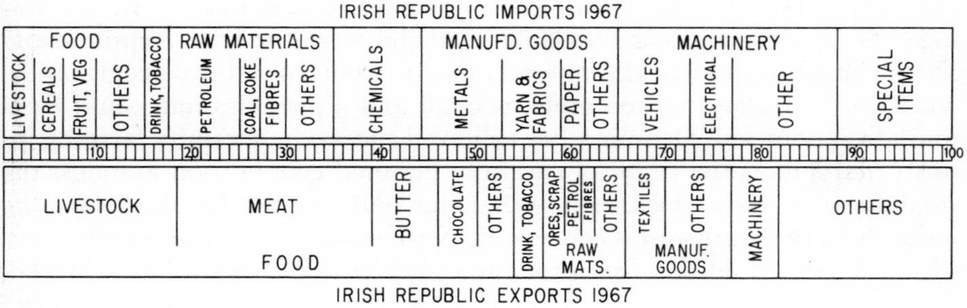

FIG. 274. Trade of the Irish Republic, 1967

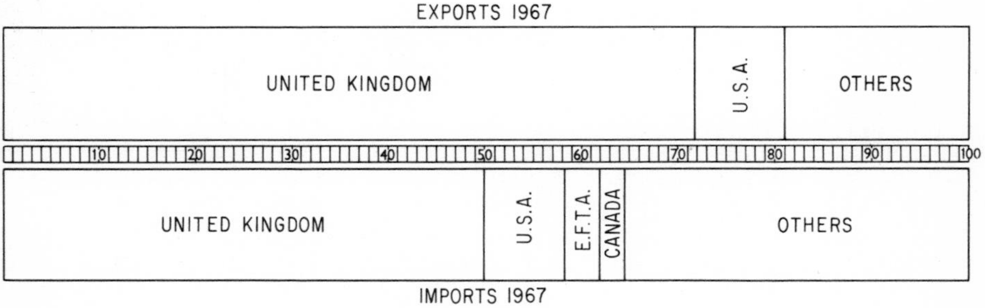

FIG. 275. Trade of the Irish Republic by countries, 1967

country on foreign supplies of coal, petroleum and many manufactured goods as well as its dependence—as is true also of the United Kingdom—on foreign supplies of the essential foodstuffs. As we have shown elsewhere in this book, wheat used to be grown over large areas in Ireland, but one must admit that the geographical conditions of the country are quite unsuited to the production of this crop, and it cannot be grown economically in competition with other countries of the world where the geographical conditions are more suitable, as in Canada or Australia, though production is encouraged by Government.

There are, then, three special aspects of the foreign trade of the Irish Republic worthy of notice. In the first place, Ireland sells various commodities, particularly foodstuffs which are not produced in sufficient quantity in Britain, to that country; whilst Great Britain supplies manufactured articles that cannot be made in Ireland. It is not surprising, therefore, to see that the Republic in 1967 sold 60 per cent of all its exports to Great Britain and a further 12 per cent to Northern Ireland and purchased over 50 per cent of all its requirements from the same sources. A feature of recent years has been the large import from the United States.

The second point is that in the supply of agricultural products to Britain, and indeed to any other country which may serve as a market for these goods, the Irish Republic has a great rival in Denmark. But in the third place the contrast with Denmark is interesting. Ireland's leading exports are live cattle and meat, Denmark relies on butter and bacon. An interesting geographical comparison can be made between the Irish Republic and Denmark, both countries hampered to some extent by natural geographical conditions—Ireland by too much rainfall and a poor drainage, and Denmark by a poor soil. Denmark has achieved success in her dairy farming industry largely as the result of carefully planned cooperation amongst the small farmers. Ireland is treading the same path as far as her dairy farming industry in the southwest is concerned. No geographical reasons really exist why Ireland should not attain the same success as Denmark has achieved.

30
Northern Ireland

Under the Government of Ireland Act, 1920, as subsequently amended in certain details, a separate parliament and executive government were established for Northern Ireland, comprising the parliamentary counties of Antrim, Armagh, Down, Fermanagh, Londonderry and Tyrone, together with the Boroughs of Belfast and Londonderry. Although the name Ulster is often used as if synonymous with Northern Ireland, in fact Northern Ireland embraces only six of the nine counties of the historic province of Ulster; Donegal, Cavan and Monaghan are included in the Irish Republic.

In broad general terms Northern Ireland is that part of the island where, largely for historical reasons, Protestants form either an absolute majority or a substantial minority of the population. Over the whole, Protestants form about two-thirds of the total. By contrast in the Irish Republic, Roman Catholics practically everywhere form a majority and over about half the country the population is almost exclusively Catholic.

Northern Ireland forms an integral part of the United Kingdom of Great Britain and Northern Ireland which, since 1921, has replaced the United Kingdom of Great Britain and Ireland. It returns twelve members to the House of Commons sitting in London but its own Parliament has power to act in a wide range of matters. The importance of separating statistics which refer to the United Kingdom from those which refer only to Great Britain (England, Wales and Scotland), or to England and Wales alone has already been emphasised.

Northern Ireland contains 13 577 square kilometres (5242 square miles) or 1 358 838 hectares (3 355 156 statute acres) of land (excluding water), with a population which has been slowly increasing since the beginning of the century and reached 1 484 800 in 1966. In marked contrast to England 40 per cent of these people are classed as rural and 30 per cent actually live in the open countryside—contrasted with about 10 per cent in England—where the isolated family farm averaging 16 hectares (40 acres) is the characteristic unit of settlement. Although thirty-six places have the official status of 'towns' only four, Belfast (400 000), Londonderry (56 000), Newtown Abbey (47 000) and Bangor (27 000) had more than 25 000 persons in 1966, and only ten of the others had more than 10 000. The greater part of Northern Ireland is, in many ways, the Belfast Region.

The close connection in geological structure and relief between Northern Ireland and Scotland is paralleled by human associations between the two countries through the ages, especially from the time when the Scots from northeastern Ireland overcame the Picts in Argyll and gave their name to Scotland. To this day such western Scottish clan names as Macrae are found in Irish form (Rae or Rea and O'Rea) in Ireland. Following the long delayed conquest of Ulster by the English in the early seventeenth century was the organised plantation of English and Scottish settlers, followed by a steady settlement of Scottish Presbyterians and English Episcopalians. Thus the contrasts between Northern Ireland and the Irish Republic are deep rooted: further, the rise of industrialism in Belfast was on the English model. Also, the markets for Northern Ireland's main products, ships and textiles, lie either in Britain or beyond.

Regions of Northern Ireland

Since in Northern Ireland are to be found continuations of the great structural units of Scotland from which the country is separated only by the North Channel with an average width of a little over 32 kilometres (twenty miles), it might be expected that Northern Ireland would fall into three primary divisions:

(*a*) The northern mountains akin to the Highlands of Scotland lying north of the great boundary faults.
(*b*) The continuation of the Midland Valley of Scotland occupied by the Carboniferous Limestone and other Carboniferous rocks.
(*c*) The continuation of the Southern Uplands of Scotland comprising the country to the south of the boundary fault.

Actually, however, the structure is complicated by the fact that the Chalk Sea spread over the greater part of Northern Ireland and wore down the ancient rocks and deposited over them, as well as over the rocks of the Midland Valley, thin layers of chalk. At a later date, that is in the Tertiary Period, these beds of chalk were covered by enormous stretches of basaltic lavas poured out from great fissures. Hence there is a huge lava plateau over a large part of the country. But this lava plateau has subsided towards the west-centre, where it is occupied by the shallow water of the largest lake in the British Isles, Lough Neagh, and the Bann valley. There is thus at the present day a rather remarkable contrast between the higher parts of the lava plateau around its rim and the subsided central portion. The regions which result, which are both natural or physical regions and agricultural regions, have been shown in Fig. 263. It must also be remembered that Northern Ireland was severely glaciated during the great Ice Age, so that soil and loose rocks were removed from the higher levels of the old rock masses whilst the lower levels were covered with a thick though irregular mantle of glacial deposits. Great numbers of drumlins cover much of the country.

The uplands of County Down and County Armagh

This unit is convenient because the region is a natural continuation of the uplands of southern Scotland. There are to be found the same Ordovician and Silurian sediments, but they are in Ireland masked to a greater extent by glacial deposits. There is a further contrast with Scotland in that the whole tract is of lower elevation. Only limited areas rise to over 150 metres (500 ft), and so instead of wide tracts of moorland are miles of pleasant farming country. To the east, indeed, the uplands pass into fertile lowlands which are in turn covered by the shallow waters of the sea in Strangford Lough. Broadly speaking, in the higher parts the soils are stony and poor,

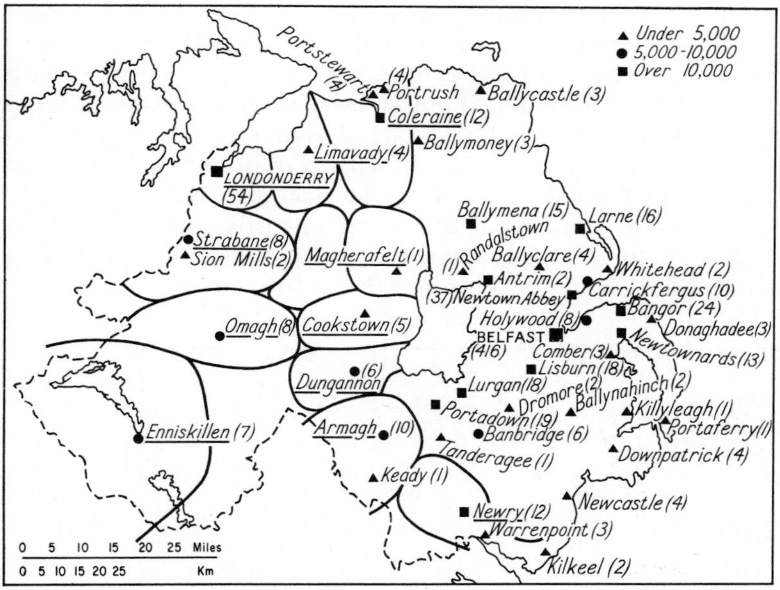

FIG. 276. The market towns of Northern Ireland

The population of each town in 1961 is indicated to the nearest thousand. In the west the large area served by the market town (underlined in each case) is shown by the heavy lines.

the farms small, the farmhouses unpretentious, and sheep pastures an important feature of the surrounding land. The lower undulating country, on the other hand, is a land of relatively prosperous farms, and over all this lower ground cattle, dairy as well as beef, are widely distributed; barley, oats and potatoes are leading crops. Taking the region as a whole, sheep are very numerous; their concentration in the higher areas is very marked. The region is generally well populated; market towns are numerous. To the north lie the industrial towns of the Lagan Valley; the rather deserted port of Newry, once a rival to Belfast, lies in an important fertile valley to the southwest, while the prosperous seaside resorts of Bangor and Newcastle are both within this area. The proximity of these considerable areas of settlement, but more especially the proximity of Belfast with its population approaching half a million, has a marked influence on the agricultural occupations of the population.

That part of the region lying in County Armagh differs somewhat from County Down. It is a county of small-holdings, focusing economically on Portadown, where jam factories are found. In the south of the County Down upland belt is a distinct region, small but remarkably well defined—the Mourne Mountains, formed by a great intrusive mass of granite of comparatively recent age, probably Tertiary. The mountains are rounded in outline, but they rise in Slieve Donard to 852 metres (2796 ft) above sea-level. Cultivation is absent from the central mass, but very large numbers of sheep are reared on the rough pastures of the slopes and there are some recent conifer plantations. The mountains themselves reach the coast in Carlingford Lough, which may be described as a fiord, and also to the south of Newcastle; but between these two points there is an interesting tract of lowland centring on Kilkeel, which is a tract of small farms and sheep pastures, but where oats and potatoes can be grown in quantity, and where many cattle are kept. Seed potatoes from this area are widely exported.

Since other hill masses, coinciding with other intrusive igneous rocks, lie to the west of Carlingford Lough, Estyn Evans uses the name Carlingford Lough Mountains to cover both these and the Mourne Mountains.

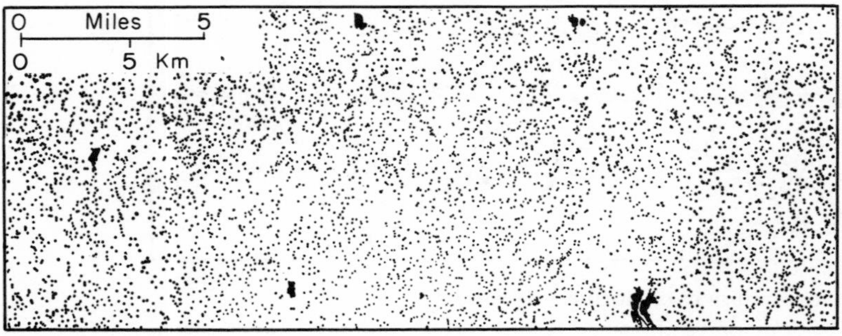

FIG. 277. Map indicating the scattered nature of rural settlements in Ireland

Each dot represents a single inhabited house, but there are only five villages in the whole area. That marked in the southeast is Newry.

The plateau and glens of Eastern Antrim

This region comprises the higher eastern portions (the land over 150 metres (500 ft)) and the edge of the basalt plateau, together with the coastal strips which sometimes lie between the edge of the plateau and the sea, and also the deep glens which gash the edge of the plateau itself. Agriculturally, these three parts are to a considerable extent distinct:

(*a*) The surface of the plateau is wide open moorland, useful as pasturage for a limited number of sheep and cattle.
(*b*) The coastal strips vary greatly. Sometimes there is a low plateau with a rolling surface formed by the basalt itself, as in Island Magee southeast of Larne. Such country is fertile, and dairy-farming may be important. In the northeast of Antrim there is a considerable tract of ancient rock—a continuation of the Highlands of Scotland—cropping out from beneath the chalk and the basalt. These rocks give rise to boulderstrewn moorland sheep pastures, whilst on sheltered valley slopes many small mixed farms may be found. In a few places tracts of chalk are exposed, and there is a sudden change to short springy grass which is indistinguishable, except to the botanist, from that to be found on the chalk down of southern England; and the white chalky farm lanes and the numerous sheep make the comparison complete.
(*c*) The deep glens are particularly interesting. They are, of course, famous for their scenery. The summer visitor might be surprised if he observed the conditions of these glens in the winter. They are narrow and bordered by high, often vertical, basalt cliffs, so that the southern side of the valley may not be in sunlight in the winter until as late as 2 p.m. and suffers accordingly. Agricultural conditions and the health of the people improve as one goes to the other side of the valley. In general, the centre of the valley is occupied by ill-drained cattle pastures, and on either side of the road or lane, along the valley side, is a succession of small farms where the farmer carries on a varied mixed farming. In the broader glens and on part of the coastal strip, particularly on the northern shores of Belfast Lough—Belfast to White Head—Keuper Marls appear and afford excellent soil capable of intensive cultivation. No one needs to be reminded that where the basalt reaches the northern coast is to be found the most famous of all localities in the whole of Ireland—the Giant's Causeway—the stones of the causeway being naturally formed hexagonal columns of basalt. Larne serves as an outpost for Belfast on the short sea route to Stranraer in Scotland, but the other little ports at the mouths of the glens—Glenarm, Cushendun, Cushendall and Ballycastle—occupy themselves with summer visitors.

The Lagan Corridor

The Lagan Corridor, only a few kilometres wide, lies between the basalt edge on the north and the uplands of County Down. It is the trough in which Belfast lies and which opens out in Belfast Lough.

The Lough Neagh Basin and the Lower Bann Valley

Except for the west, the greater part of Northern Ireland may be described as the Ulster Basin, in that a great tract of it drains towards Lough Neagh;

agriculturally and otherwise, however, it seems better to separate the lower central part of the great basalt region which lies almost entirely below 150 metres (500 ft). The underlying basalt is often hidden by the glacial deposits, and there is a gently rolling surface rather than a level plain. If the basalt itself is exposed, there is often a rich, red-brown, fertile soil, but in many places the gentle slope towards the central lake has waterlogged glacial soils, though the lighter glacial deposits may be well drained. Thus there are some true fens and large areas of damp pastures characterised by clumps of rushes. However, considerable drainage work has substantially increased the numbers of cattle such land can support. Where drainage and soil conditions are better, arable land is found. This is particularly the case on the superficial clays and alluvium lying to the southwest and west of the lake. Here oats are grown in quantity, and in the heyday of the flax industry this region was the great area of flax cultivation which was particularly important in the valley of the Main. A basalt ridge separates the Main and lower Bann valleys, and rises to over 150 metres (500 ft). This is sufficient to render cultivation unimportant and to bring in sheep pastures. Otherwise sheep are unimportant in the basin itself. In the broad lower Bann valley, centring on the small port of Coleraine, mixed farming is typical.

The mountains of Londonderry and Tyrone

Geologically this area is part of the ancient massif of Donegal from which it is separated by the broad, fertile valley of the Foyle. The highest parts form the Sperrin Mountains, rising to 683 metres (2240 ft), whilst near at hand is to be found the high western edge of the basalt plateau. The higher areas of both the basalt and the ancient rocks are unoccupied save for a few sheep, though recent afforestation has changed the appearance of peaty slopes. Towns and large villages are absent over the greater part of the area, the inhabitants being found in small isolated farms in the valleys. Here the valley farmers have a few cattle and a few pigs, and succeed in growing crops of potatoes—perhaps some oats; but other crops are unimportant. The valleys open out westwards into the Foyle Valley.

The Foyle Valley and the shores of Lough Foyle

The significance of this corridor connecting the lowlands of central Ireland with the port of Londonderry has already been stressed. It is sheltered from the rain-bearing westerly winds; there is much arable land devoted especially to oats and to a much smaller extent to potatoes and turnips. As a result of this cultivation, the area of cultivated land in County Derry almost balances the area under permanent grass. The Foyle Valley has already been likened to a Scottish strath. In its continuation northeastwards along the southern shores of Lough Foyle there is a wide stretch of marine alluvium largely given over to cattle pastures, and further inland a belt of lowland floored by red Keuper Marls which give good arable land, and which may therefore be said to correspond roughly to a Scottish carse.

The Rift Valley lowlands

To the southwest of Lough Neagh there is a corridor of lowland which connects the Lough Neagh basin with the central lowland in the Irish Republic. It lies between the ancient metamorphic rocks of the Sperrin Mountains on the north and the Ordovician-Silurian sediments on the south. Structurally it is, of course, a continuation of the rift valley, or midland valley, of Scotland. As in the midland valley of Scotland, there are large tracts of Old Red Sandstone which give rise to an extensive hilly region northeast of Lower Lough Erne, in the basin of the upper Foyle around Omagh. As in Scotland, too, there are Carboniferous sandstones and shales giving rise to an area of hills to the northeast of Upper Lough Erne. The remaining area consists largely of Carboniferous Limestone worn to a lower level and masked by glacial deposits, as in the ill-drained tracts of the central lowland. This forms hummocky lowlands with the hollows frequently occupied by shallow, tortuous-sided lakes. The region includes the greater part of Fermanagh, the southern portion of Tyrone, and Derry, the main centre of the area being Enniskillen between Upper and Lower Lough Erne. Where this corridor links with the corridor of the Foyle valley is the town of Omagh, whilst Armagh is on the southern fringe of the area. It is on the whole a region of small, scattered farmsteads, whilst here and there only are there tiny market towns such as Aughnacloy. Dairy and store cattle are numerous, pig production is fairly widespread. Oats are grown only in more favoured tracts.

Industries and industrial regions

One-third of the population of Northern Ireland lives in *Belfast*, which has become a great manufacturing centre with a population approaching half a million. In Northern Ireland as a whole nearly 200,000 persons are employed in manufacturing, and 55 per cent of these in 1962 were at work in Belfast itself, though many travelled daily from their homes in towns and villages over a wide area. The development of industrial Belfast is remarkable because Northern Ireland is practically devoid of native resources of power or minerals and, with only a small home market, is separated by the Irish Sea from its principal domestic markets.

Shipbuilding is virtually synonymous with the one firm of Harland and Wolff, whose modernised shipyards, employing 9000 people, can undertake the construction of the largest tankers, liners, cargo ships and special purpose vessels including warships. Their huge engineering works can supply the necessary propelling machinery (see Chap. 16). In combination with Short Brothers, formerly of Rochester, Kent, an aircraft industry has been developed by the shipbuilding interests—at first flying-boats, then heavy bombers, and later jet aircraft. Active Government encouragement has been given to the expansion of light engineering works such as those producing precision instruments, radios, vacuum cleaners and machine tools (see p. 453). This is in addition to the older range of textile, agricultural and other machinery. The textile machinery is a natural corollary

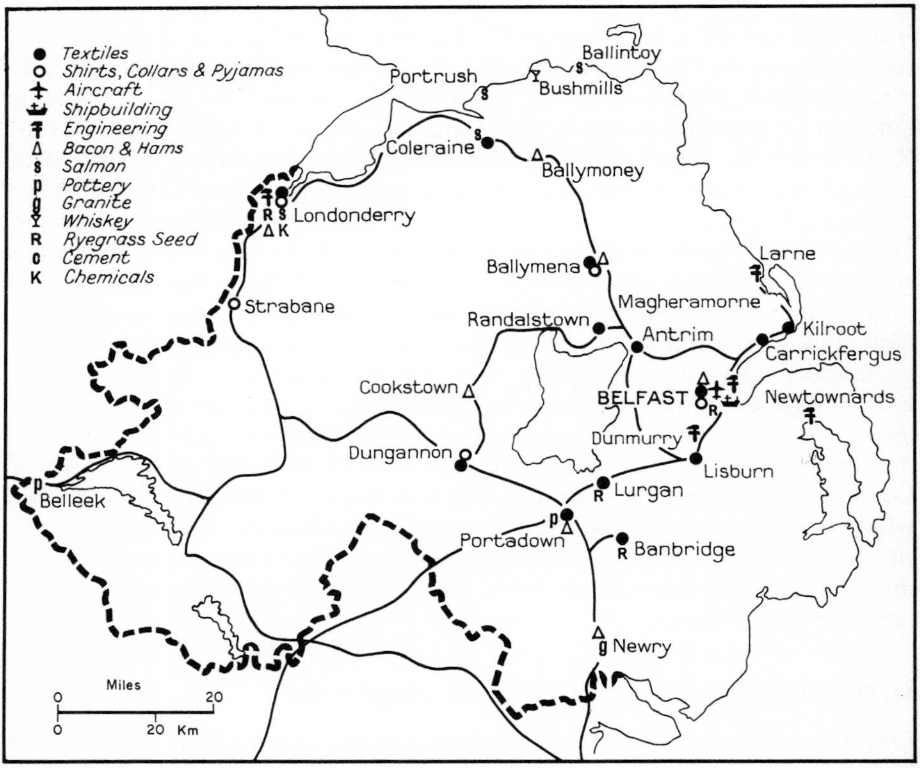

FIG. 278. The towns and industries of Northern Ireland
See also Fig. 199 (p. 567).

to the other great industry, that of textiles, which employs nearly half the total of industrial employees—70 per cent of them women. The textile industry has undergone great changes since the Second World War, with the declining importance of linen and much increased emphasis on manmade fibres, into the manufacture of which an enormous amount of new British, American and continental capital has been poured, with great new plants at Carrickfergus, Kilroot, Limavady, Antrim, Coleraine and elsewhere (see p. 576). Northern Ireland, indeed, produces almost one-quarter of all the synthetic fibre output of the United Kingdom. Cotton and wool textiles are still made, as well as a large output of ropes and cordage, whilst 10 per cent of the textile workers are engaged in making up materials into sheets, cloths, handkerchiefs, etc., apart from the actual textile industry. There is an expanding carpet industry.

Two other groups of industries in the Belfast area call for notice. One is the processing of home agricultural products—bacon-curing, canning of milk and vegetables, grain milling, baking, brewing and distilling. The other is associated with the imports of a great port, and includes the tobacco industry and a new oil refinery.

Londonderry has an industrial life of its own with an emphasis on clothing such as shirts and collars.

The ports of Northern Ireland

The port of *Belfast* dominates Northern Ireland. The sheltered, easterly facing Lough made it worth-while to dredge and maintain a navigable channel for the largest liners afloat. This was facilitated by the nature of the materials filling the old trough (cf. Glasgow and Newcastle). The natural hinterland of Belfast—the Lagan valley—soon grew to include the whole region readily accessible through a succession of lowland corridors in due course served by rail and road. Formerly canal transport was possible from Belfast *via* the lowland corridors to distant parts of Ireland. With its superior facilities for dealing expeditiously with passenger traffic (overnight or by day direct to Heysham or Liverpool), with live cattle, perishable products such as eggs and poultry, as well as the bulk handling of coal and grain, and more recently of oil, Belfast has almost eliminated its older rivals. It handles 60 per cent of the seaborne trade of Northern Ireland (or 90 per cent of the total trade including the land boundary and Belfast airport). Wharves and other facilities are being extended, and the channel further dredged. The most valuable items in the export list are textiles and textile machinery.

Londonderry, the second port, is at the head of Lough Foyle, twenty-five miles from the open sea on a very stormy coast. As a port it was greatly improved during the Second World War. Above Londonderry the Foyle is navigable for barges till the canal though Strabane is entered. The natural hinterland of the port is the basin of the Foyle: it has been extended further by railways. The export traffic is characteristic of all Irish ports other than Belfast. Agricultural products dominate but are small in total value, and include an increasing number of cattle, sheep, bacon and hams, and eggs (the Londonderry area specialises in the last three). Small quantities of pigs, oats, meal, hides, grain, offal, potatoes and grass seed are exported—the same type of traffic as is exported through the port of Belfast from the Lough Neagh basin. The manufactured products consist chiefly of textiles.

There remain to be considered three other small ports in Northern Ireland. The most important of these is *Larne*, at the mouth of the entrance to Larne Lough, twenty miles northeast of Belfast and, therefore, nearer to the Scottish mainland. To this factor the importance of the daily passenger service to Stranraer was due.

Coleraine is a very small port on the River Bann four and a half miles from the sea.

Although the Newry river was canalised to connect the Carlingford Lough with the Lough Neagh and Lagan basins, the port of *Newry* is only just within Northern Ireland and much of its former hinterland lay across the present frontier. Further, its way to the open sea is obstructed by a bar.

Trade

The trade of Northern Ireland in a recent year is shown in Fig. 279. On the import side, equipment for the country's industries, and motor vehicles, loom largely, whilst the raw material for the textile industries occupies but a very minor place. Of the exports, however, textiles are the largest individual item; livestock and food products are important, whilst the item 'machinery &c' includes the ships launched at Belfast.

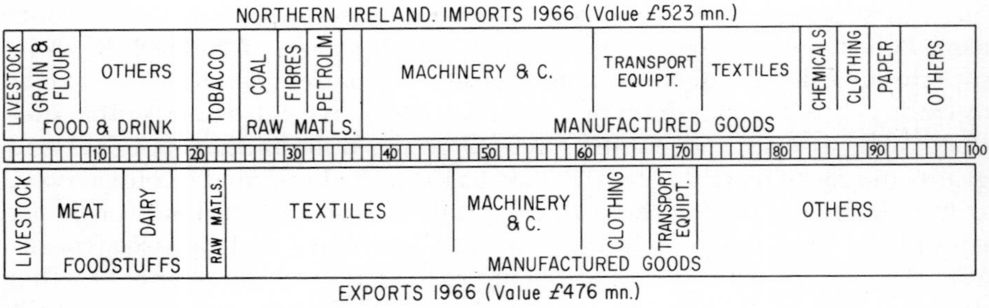

FIG. 279. The trade of Northern Ireland

31
The foreign trade of the United Kingdom

In early times and during the Middle Ages the great feature of English trade was the export of raw materials and the import of manufactured articles. For long the most important of the exported raw materials was wool, but it was only one of several, the export duties levied on which furnished a large part of the revenue of the Crown. In order to collect this revenue, trade was regulated at an early date from the reign of Edward III, and particularly by the Ordinance of Edward III in 1353. This decreed that all the more important commodities (which were named and formed thus the staple commodities) should be exported exclusively through certain English, Welsh and Irish ports where the duties would be collected. The staple commodities enumerated are wool, sheepskins with the wool on, leather or hides, and tin; but on other occasions lead, cheese, butter, alum, tallow and worsted are also mentioned; the last, however, infrequently. The ports specified include most of those of any significance on the east coast of England except Berwick-on-Tweed, together with Southampton and Exeter on the south coast and Bristol on the west. Carmarthen was the sole staple port for Wales. In Ireland there were four: Dublin, Cork, Waterford and Drogheda.

The trade in the staple commodities was mainly in the hands of a privileged body known as the staplers who were, for the most part, foreigners. This was largely, it may be said, because Englishmen were liable to smaller dues than foreigners, and thereby the revenue of the king suffered. Amongst the foreigners engaged in the staple trade of England were many Italians, but members of the Hanseatic League were particularly important (see p. 726). English merchants therefore specialised in the trade in non-staple commodities. Their attempts at trading were adventurous, and hence they became known as Merchant Adventurers and as such constituted themselves into organised companies. As English manufactures grew these became the most valuable commodities outside the staples. Woollen goods were the chief commodities whose sale abroad was pushed by the Adventurers. The Merchant Adventurers had a charter granted to them as early as 1404, and shortly afterwards the company established its headquarters at Antwerp. Other companies followed, such as the Eastland, the Levant or Turkey, the East India, the Africa or Guinea, as well as the Hudson's Bay Company. The East India Company obtained its first charter on 31 December 1600, and retained a monopoly for trade with India until 1813, and with China until 1833, by which time the company had become a great territorial power. But in the fifteenth, sixteenth and seventeenth centuries English manufactures gradually became the principal exports. Throughout the eighteenth century woollens were the most important, and every effort was made to check the rise of rivals. In the course of the eighteenth century cotton goods came to acquire a very considerable importance, and were sent in quantities from Bristol and Liverpool to West Africa to be exchanged for the slaves to be sold in the West Indies. The Industrial Revolution resulted in the placing of cotton manufactures first amongst our exports, a position which they continued to hold until the nineteen-thirties. To give an example of the position in the last century, in the years 1871–75 (average), cotton manufactures represented no less than 31.3 per cent of the total exports, followed by iron and steel 12.9, and woollen manufactures about the same quantity. At that time coal and coke were only about 4.3 per cent. Half a century later the position was still substantially the same, though with the broadening of the country's industrial base the dominance of the major items was slightly less. In 1911–13 cotton represented 25.6 per

United Kingdom, exports of native produce and manufactures

PRINCIPAL ARTICLES	PERCENTAGE OF TOTAL VALUE											
	1881–85	1886–90	1891–95	1896–1900	1901–05	1906–10	1911–13	1926–30	1931–35	1950	1962	1967
Cotton manufactures[1]	31.9[1]	30.2	29.2	26.9	27.2	26.0	25.6	19.2	15.3	7.3	1.2	0.5
Iron and steel	11.4	11.1	9.4	10.4	10.0	10.8[2]	10.4	8.3	6.9	7.2	5.3	4.6
Coal, coke, etc.	4.3	5.5	7.3	9.0	9.5	9.8	9.3	6.4	8.7	2.8	0.8	0.3
Woollen manufactures	—	—	10.7	9.7	8.5	8.4	8.0	7.2	6.9	6.6	2.1	1.5
Machinery and engines	5.1	5.6	6.4	7.3	6.9	7.6	7.0	7.4	8.3	14.6	22.2	20.6
Chemicals, drugs, dyes	4.2	4.2	5.1	4.9	4.5	4.3	4.3	3.5	4.7	8.1	9.0	9.8
Linen yarn and manufactures	2.7	2.7	2.6	2.3	2.2	2.1	1.9	1.4	1.5	1.4	0.1	0.1
Apparel and haberdashery	3.1	2.8	2.7	2.6	2.4	1.8	2.1	3.7	3.0	1.6	1.0	1.2
Leather manufactures including boots	1.7	1.7	1.7	1.5	1.6	1.6	1.8	1.2	0.9	*	1.0	0.6
Hardware, implements, etc.	2.1	1.9	1.6	1.6	1.6	1.3	1.4	—	—	2.4	4.1	3.1
Fish	0.8	0.7	0.8	1.0	1.2	1.2	1.4	1.1	1.1	—	—	0.2
Earthenware and glass	—	—	1.2	1.2	1.1	1.0	1.0	1.9	2.0	2.5	1.0	0.6
Copper and yellow metal	1.4	1.4	1.4	1.2	1.2	0.9	0.7	—	—	3.5	1.5	1.5
Jute, yarn and manufactures	1.1	1.1	1.2	1.0	0.9	0.8	0.7	—	—	*	—	*
Spirits[3]	0.3	0.5	0.6	0.8	0.9	0.8	0.8	1.3	1.6	1.3	2.1	2.6
Electrical goods, excluding machinery	—	—	—	—	0.9	0.7	0.9	1.8	1.9	3.9	6.5	6.9
Books	0.5	0.5	0.6	0.6	0.6	0.5	0.6	—	—	*	—	0.6
Silk yarn and manufactures	1.3	1.2	0.8	0.7	0.6	0.5	0.5	1.5	1.3	2.3	—	*
Beer and ale[3]	0.7	0.7	0.7	0.7	0.6	0.5	0.4	—	—	*	—	*
Ships	—	—	—	—	—	—	—	1.8	1.1	1.9	1.0	1.4
Automobiles	—	—	—	—	—	—	—	2.4	3.3	8.1	11.1	4.2

[1] Large quantities of piece goods of mixed materials in which wool predominated were erroneously entered as cotton prior to 1884, annual value about £500 000.

[2] In 1906–10 'iron and steel' includes 'tyres, wheels, axles' to the value of £1.08m, also small amounts of old rails and telegraph wire.

[3] Ex-ship stores. * Less than 1 per cent.

cent, iron and steel 10.4 per cent, coal and coke rather more, at 9.3 per cent, woollen manufactures 8 per cent, and machinery 7 per cent (see table on p. 802). After another two decades that included the First World War and the great depression, the period 1931–35 saw cotton manufactures reduced to 15.3 per cent, iron and steel to 6.9 per cent, and woollen to 6.9 per cent; coal and coke remained high, at 8.7 per cent, for the full impact of oil had not yet been felt, whilst machinery had risen to 8.3 per cent, and electrical goods and automobiles had begun to figure significantly in the list.

The percentages referred to in the last paragraph relate to *values*. If tonnage is taken into consideration the significance of coal is at once apparent since it formed for long more than half the total exports of the country. The huge export of coal reaching a maximum of 76.2 million metric tons (75 million long tons) in 1913 (see above, Chapter 14) not only encouraged the

United Kingdom, general imports, excluding diamonds and bullion and specie

PRINCIPAL ARTICLES	PERCENTAGE OF TOTAL VALUE											
	1881–85	1886–90	1891–95	1896–1900	1901–05	1906–10	1911–13	1926–30	1931–35	1950	1962	1967
Grain and flour	15.7	13.6	13.8	12.9	12.5	12.0	11.4	7.9	8.7	6.1	5.5	3.5
Wheat	*7.0*	*5.5*	*5.6*	*4.9*	*5.5*	*6.3*	*5.9*	*6.9*	*4.1*	*3.6*	*2.3*	*1.6*
Maize	*2.2*	*2.1*	*2.0*	*2.3*	*2.1*	*1.9*	*1.7*	*1.9*	*1.5*	—	*2.0*	*1.3*
Wheat meal and flour	*2.6*	*2.3*	*2.3*	*2.1*	*1.6*	*1.0*	*0.8*	*0.6*	*0.5*	*1.0*	*0.3*	*
Raw cotton	10.8	10.6	8.5	7.2	8.7	10.0	10.1	6.0	4.6	6.2	1.3	0.6
Meat	6.3	6.6	7.5	8.7	9.1	7.9	7.1	9.2	12.2	7.8	7.9	5.8
Fresh beef and mutton	*0.8*	*1.2*	*1.9*	*2.4*	*2.9*	*3.0*	*3.2*	—	*5.5*	*1.0*	*2.8*	*1.1*
Bacon and hams	*2.3*	*2.3*	*2.6*	*2.9*	*3.1*	*2.8*	*2.5*	*3.8*	*4.5*	*2.4*	*2.1*	*1.9*
Animals	*2.4*	*2.2*	*2.1*	*2.2*	*1.8*	*1.1*	*0.2*	*1.4*	*1.2*	—	—	*0.8*
Wool, sheep, alpaca, etc.	6.2	6.6	6.3	5.1	4.0	4.9	4.6	6.1	4.9	7.3	3.0	1.5
Butter and margarine	2.9	3.2	3.9	4.0	4.3	4.1	3.8	4.2	5.2	3.5	3.0	2.3
Wood, total	4.1	4.0	4.0	5.0	4.6	4.1	4.0	3.7	4.4	3.5	4.3	3.0
Sugar	5.6	4.6	4.7	3.7	3.2	3.3	3.4	2.0	2.0	3.1	1.4	1.6
Rubber	0.6	0.7	0.8	1.2	1.3	2.2	2.8	2.0	0.9	2.3	1.4	0.7
Silk yarn and manufactures	2.8	2.9	3.1	3.5	2.5	2.1	1.9	1.2	0.6	*	—	0.2
Oil, seeds and nuts	2.1	1.9	1.7	1.4	1.6	1.9	2.0	1.6	1.5	8.2	1.2	0.6
Hides, skins and furs, raw	1.7	1.6	1.6	1.5	1.4	1.8	1.8	2.2	2.1	1.9	1.0	0.8
Tea	2.7	2.6	2.4	2.2	1.7	1.7	1.8	3.1	3.6	2.2	2.6	1.6
Chemicals	2.9	3.0	2.1	1.8	1.7	1.7	1.7	1.3	1.0	1.4	3.8	5.1
Fresh fruit and nuts	1.1	1.2	1.4	1.5	1.7	1.7	1.5	2.8	4.0	3.6	2.5	5.0
Woollen yarn and manufactures	2.1	2.8	2.9	2.6	2.4	—	—	0.9	0.6	*	0.1	0.2
Cotton yarn and manufactures	—	—	1.0	1.2	1.4	1.6	1.6	0.9	0.5	1.1	1.3	0.6
Leather	1.3	1.5	1.7	1.7	1.5	1.5	1.5	1.3	1.1	*	0.6	0.4
Iron and steel manufactures	—	1.1	1.0	1.2	1.5	1.3	1.8	2.3	1.5	1.0	2.0	1.9
Machinery				0.6	0.8	0.8	0.9	1.5	1.6	1.7	5.6	8.0
Eggs	0.7	0.8	0.9	1.0	1.2	1.1	1.2	1.5	1.2	1.0	1.0	0.7
Flax and hemp, raw and tow	1.4	1.4	1.2	1.1	1.3	1.1	1.1	—	—	*	—	—
Cheese	1.2	1.1	1.2	1.2	1.2	1.1	1.0	1.2	1.1	1.0	0.7	0.7
Tin	0.6	0.7	0.6	0.9	0.9	1.1	1.2	0.8		*	0.5	0.4
Copper	0.6	0.7	0.5	0.8	0.9	1.1	0.9	—	1.8	1.8	2.8	—
Iron ores	0.6	0.7	0.7	1.0	0.9	0.9	0.9	0.4		1.5	1.4	1.0
Petroleum	—	—	—	—	—	—	—	3.2	4.2	5.9	11.9	11.1

* Less than 1 per cent.

shipbuilding industry, but made it possible to offer very low rates for suitable return freights, e.g. iron ore.[1]

We see, then, that after the Industrial Revolution, the import trade assumed the general features that continued to characterise it for a century, showing an overwhelming importance of the imports of raw materials and foodstuffs, with raw cotton rivalling grain and flour for first place by value; and an export trade that apart from coal was primarily in the products of the textile and metallurgical industries. It would indeed have been very difficult for a citizen of Victorian England to imagine that by the late 1960s the two most important items on the import list would be petroleum and machinery, with cotton manufactures and coal reduced to complete insignificance amongst the exports. We may briefly examine the world setting in which these fundamental changes have taken place.

The changing pattern of British trade

As British trade expanded during the nineteenth century it became a characteristic feature that, year by year, the value of imports greatly exceeded that of exports. The difference was made up by what are known as 'invisible exports'. Under this heading the principal receipts were interest on overseas investments, profits from banking and insurance business overseas, payments for services rendered by British technicians and other exports abroad and receipts from shipping and the carriage of goods. All over the world, especially in the so-called 'new' countries, Britain had built and owned railways and ports together with such public utilities as gas, electricity and water supply companies; mining and other companies working natural resources such as timber; in every city in the world British banks and insurance offices were to be found and innumerable commercial companies. Half the world's shipping, carrying at least half the world's passenger and freight traffic, was British whilst British technical experts were to be found in every country in the world. The receipts from all these varied sources came to the home country not as money but as goods—especially foodstuffs, and raw materials—which thus flowed automatically into the country. Indeed at times the flow threatened to become a flood and both raw materials and manufactures were dumped at prices undercutting the home producer. Overseas countries anxious to buy British manufactures sold their foodstuffs to us at under cost. Such manufactured goods as Japanese silks sold at less in the shops here than in Japan.

Whilst it was clear that such a trade pattern could not last indefinitely it was the Second World War which completely changed the whole position.

Already and at an increasing pace as the newer countries of the world grew and developed they sought to control their own affairs—either for the state to take over such essential services as railways or for companies con-

1. On some aspects of this subject, see A. J. Sargent, *Seaways of the Empire*, 2nd edn, 1930.

trolled by their own nationals to replace the foreigners. While the foreigners —the British in so many cases—were usually compensated, the source of their income disappeared. Further, all countries in the world were tending towards industrialisation—the home production of manufactured goods—often in factories equipped with British machinery and staffed by those trained in Britain or by British technicians. When the Second World War cut off supplies from Britain there was added a final incentive to the development of the home countries' resources.

Thus Britain emerged from the Second World War with many, one may say most, of her overseas investments sold, a large part of her banking and insurance business passed into other hands, a large proportion of her merchant shipping at the bottom of the sea, a large number of her old customers either supplying themselves or buying from other sources—especially the United States. Broadly speaking Britain was faced with the task of paying her way, selling exports of manufactured goods in sufficient quantities to pay for the import of raw materials and the 45 to 50 per cent of food which is not, and can scarcely be, home-produced. In all the markets of the world British manufactured goods have to compete both with the home-produced article and with those from other exporting countries such as the United States and the older countries of Europe including (since her recovery from the war) her old rival Germany. When she has succeeded in selling her exports, which can only be by superior quality and lower prices than rival products, Britain has to buy her raw materials in the world's markets in competition with other buyers, often for surpluses far less abundant and more costly than in the past. Some countries, to protect their own industries, put up barriers in the form of import duties and other restrictions including currency restrictions. Britain in her turn must restrict imports for which she cannot pay—in particular from dollar countries.

The world has thus become divided into a number of trade regions—or alternatively the countries of the world may be said to have become linked into a small number of groups. These are:

(*a*) The Soviet bloc, or the USSR and the Comecon countries, including Poland, Eastern Germany, Hungary, Romania, Bulgaria and Czechoslovakia. China may perhaps be included with this group.
(*b*) The Sterling Area (now officially called the Scheduled Territories) comprising the Commonwealth, except Canada, together with those countries which have linked their currency with the pound sterling.
(*c*) The Dollar Area, primarily the United States and those countries which are linked financially to the United States dollar.
(*d*) The European Economic Community, often called the Common Market, brought into being on 1 January 1958 by a treaty signed in Rome the previous year, and consisting of France, West Germany, Italy, Netherlands, Belgium and Luxembourg.
(*e*) The European Free Trade Association (EFTA or 'the Seven') came

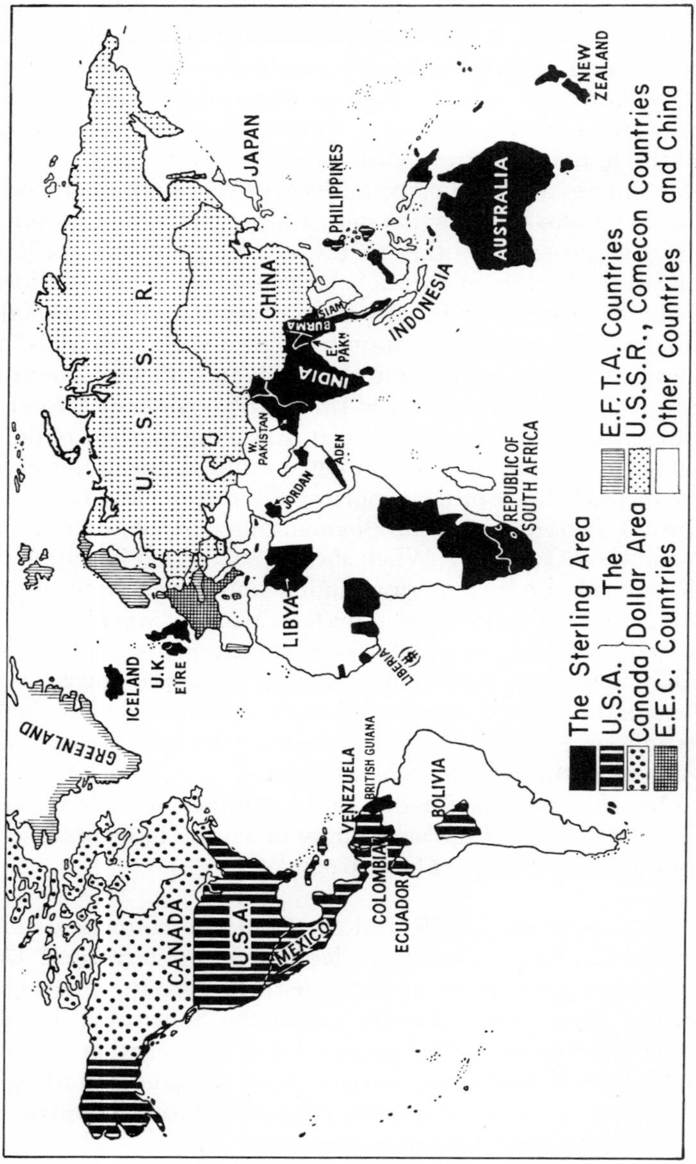

Fig. 280. Map of the world showing the Soviet Bloc behind the Iron Curtain, the Sterling area, the Dollar countries, the European Economic Community or Common Market and the European Free Trade Area (EFTA comprising the United Kingdom, Austria, Denmark, Norway, Sweden, Portugal and Switzerland; Finland is an Associate Member)

into being in 1960 and consists of the United Kingdom, Austria, Switzerland, Portugal, Denmark, Norway and Sweden with Finland joining in 1961.

The relative importance of the 'blocs' in British trade is shown in Figs 289 and 290. For fourteen years, 1947–61, most of the countries of Western and Central Europe were linked as the OEEC countries (Organization for European Economic Cooperation), the members of which received American aid in their postwar rehabilitation.

There is relatively little foreign trade between the Soviet countries and the outside world so that this bloc is almost self-contained. The countries of the sterling area trade with one another with relative freedom and funds

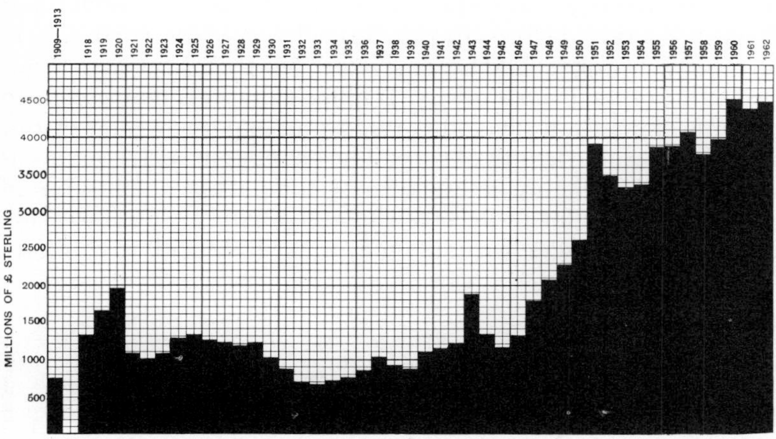

FIG. 281. The fluctuations in the declared value of imports into the United Kingdom

This diagram ignores the change in the value of money, and should be compared with the table showing the changing volume of trade.

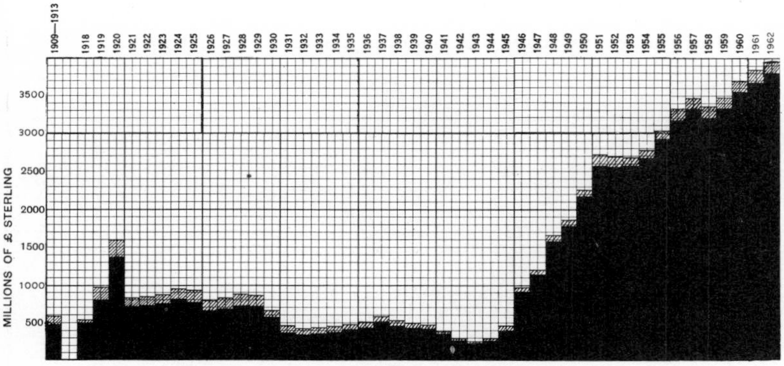

FIG. 282. The fluctuations in the declared value of exports from the United Kingdom. Exports of home origin shown in black; re-exports lined

can be sent from one country to another, but the group as a whole tries to limit purchases from dollar countries and to conserve its gold and dollar reserves.

In the early part of the present century, invisible exports accounted for over 30 per cent of the whole of British exports. This figure dropped to 20 per cent in the interwar period and became almost negligible during the Second World War. In the 1949–51 period it recovered to about 3 per cent, exceeded 10 per cent in 1953–54 but, as a net figure, has since dropped.

When pound notes were first introduced to take the place of gold coins, they were freely exchangeable for the actual gold coins by those who wished to do so. This has long since ceased to be the case and in 1952 a gold sovereign had become worth nearly £3 in notes. The value of the old pound had thus become reduced to about 6*s* 8*d*. Other currencies in other countries had suffered still more severely: before 1914 the French franc was worth nearly 10*d* in British money; in 1953 it had become worth less than $\frac{1}{4}d$ even in terms of the lowered value of the British penny. It follows that it is now useless to compare the value of British trade, either imports or exports, with previous years over any considerable length of time. The changes in such commodities as coal or iron and steel may best be seen by comparing weights, but of course this cannot be done for trade as a whole involving as it does a wide range of commodities. Changes in quality may make it difficult to compare

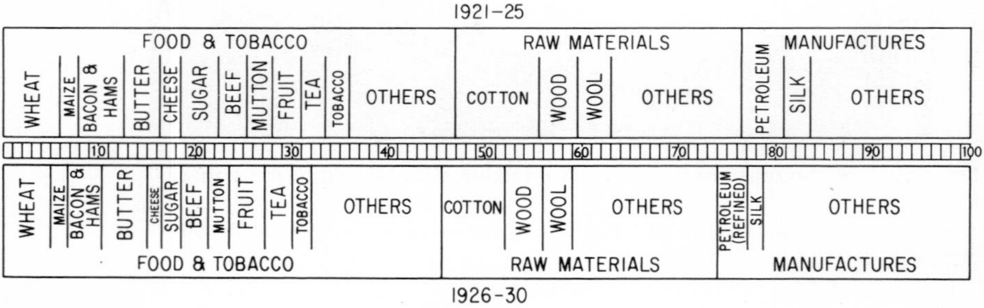

FIG. 283. The interwar trade of the United Kingdom—imports

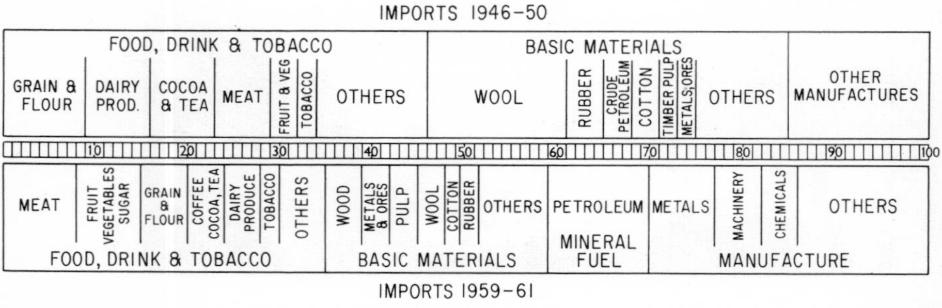

FIG. 284. The postwar trade of the United Kingdom—imports

quantities directly in many cases. In order to make comparisons possible various systems and series of index numbers may be used. One year may be taken as a standard or starting point and later years expressed as percentages of that standard, taking into account changes in the value of money. The Board of Trade, taking first 1938 as the standard (= 100), showed that in 1947 imports had dropped to 78 but exports of British origin had risen to 109. Re-exports, after dropping to 5 in 1942 had recovered to 45. The Board of Trade then took 1947 as a standard year and showed a rise from 100 to 144 for imports in 1957 and of exports from 100 to 184. The year 1954

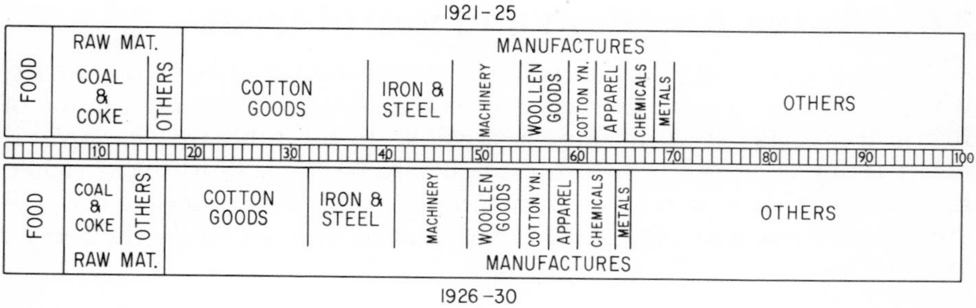

FIG. 285. The interwar trade of the United Kingdom—exports

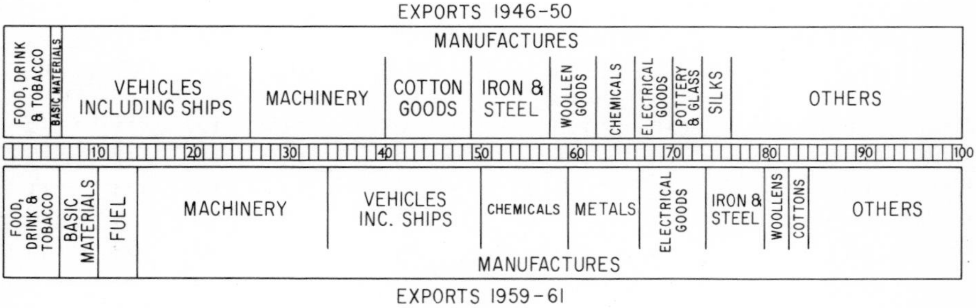

FIG. 286. The postwar trade of the United Kingdom—exports

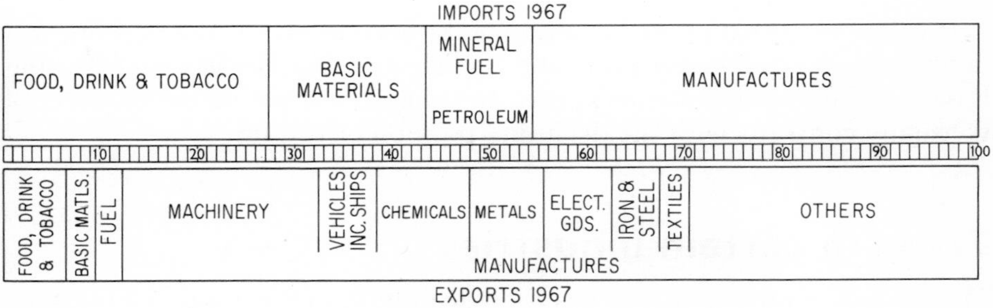

FIG. 287. Imports and exports, 1967

was the next standard used (=100). By 1961 imports had climbed to 135, exports to 125. Then, using 1961 as a standard, imports had climbed by 1967 to 109, and exports to 114.

The diagrams illustrating this chapter express the main categories of imports and exports as percentages of the whole and so enable changes in the relative importance of any individual commodity or group of commodities to be compared. Similarly the direction of foreign trade can be compared with past years.

The United Kingdom and world trade

Although it is difficult to get figures on a comparable basis from all countries, it is possible to measure at least approximately the value and volume of British trade against world trade as a whole. In this table the year 1913 is taken as one of a peak in British trade before the First World War (when British coal exports were at their maximum); 1931 is representative of the great depression, and 1950 of the period immediately following the Second World War.

World trade 1913–67

COUNTRY	RETAINED IMPORTS				DOMESTIC EXPORTS			
	1913	1931	1950	1967	1913	1931	1950	1967
United Kingdom	16	22	12	9	14	12	11	7
United States	9	12	16	13	13	15	18	16
Germany	14	9	5	9	12	15	4	11
France	8	9	5	6	7	8	5	6
Other countries	53	48	62	63	54	50	62	59
	100	100	100	100	100	100	100	100

It will be seen that up to the period of the Second World War Britain was taking a larger and larger proportion of imports, but already contributing less to the sum total of world exports. In the post-war period the recovery of Germany contrasts with the declining position of Britain.

Trade in certain industries

The trade in many industries has been dealt with in the appropriate chapters. Some general points of interest may be recalled here.

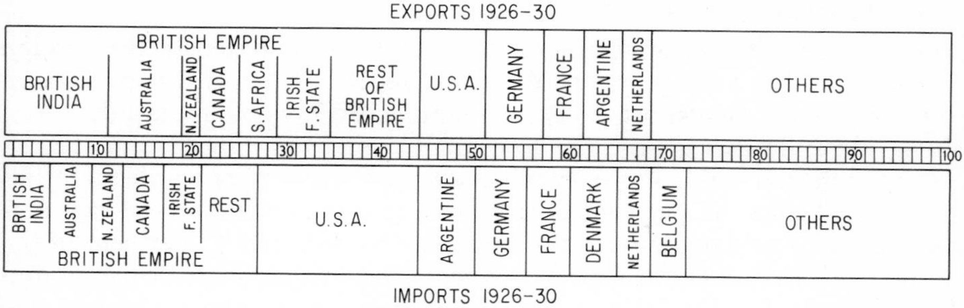

FIG. 288. The direction of foreign trade, 1926–30

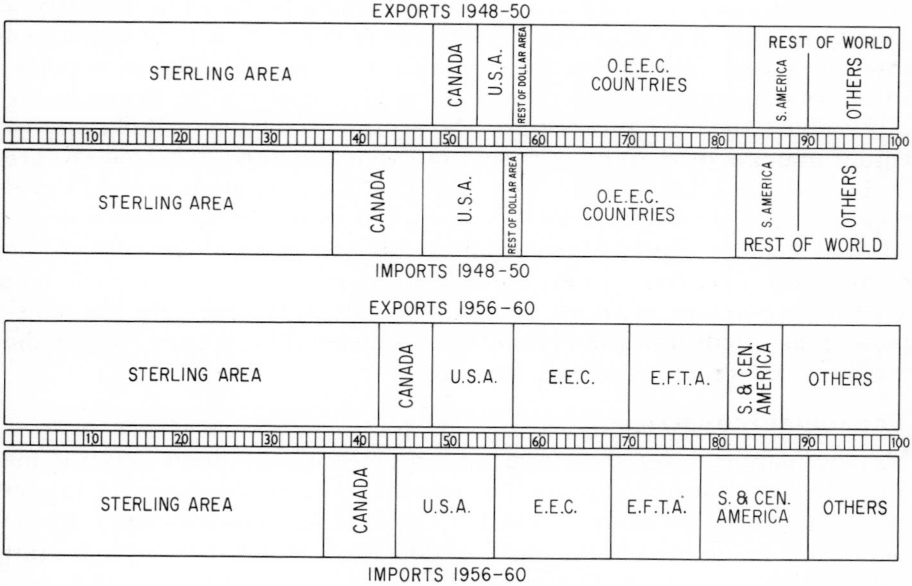

FIG. 289. The direction of foreign trade, 1948–50 and 1956–60

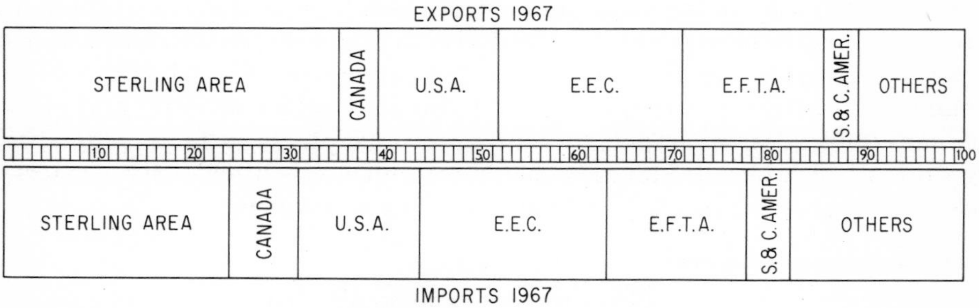

FIG. 290. Direction of trade, 1967

The textile industries

During much of the nineteenth century textiles dominated British foreign trade—on the one hand import of cotton, wool and other raw materials, on the other hand the export of cotton manufactures, woollen manufactures, linen, silk and other goods. The long-maintained supremacy from 1881 to 1913 is well seen in the summary tables above. Even in 1924 textile materials constituted some 52 per cent of the value of retained imports of raw materials, and goods made from the materials contributed 37 per cent of the value of all British exports or 48 per cent of the value of all British manufactures exported. Or again in 1931 the figures were 39 per cent of the value of imports of raw materials and 25 per cent of all exports. By 1952 the corresponding figures had fallen to 13 per cent of imports and 15 per cent of exports. In 1913 *cotton* yarns and manufactures alone formed nearly a quarter of the value of *all* exports. By way of contrast in 1952 imports of raw cotton had fallen to less than 4 per cent of the total value of imports; cotton manufactures to less than 6 per cent of exports. As shown in the tables above the fall has continued; raw cotton to 0.6 per cent of imports, cotton manufactures to 0.5 per cent of exports in 1967. The reasons are many and cumulative; there is no hope that the cotton industry will ever regain its old position (see Chapter 20). The other textiles have also declined—woollen manufactures from 10 per cent around the turn of the century to 1.5 per cent in 1967, linen from 2.5 per cent to 0.1 per cent, and silk from 0.7 to 0.03 per cent. To a limited extent, however, the rise of exports of manmade fibres and manufactures thereof has compensated for the decline in the other textiles (cf. Fig. 202).

The metal industries

Metals, manufactures therefrom and engineering products account for about half of all British exports. The emphasis is naturally upon the export of manufactured goods upon which much skill has been expended. By far the largest single item in the entire export list is motor-cars, with aircraft and aircraft engines very high in the list and commercial vehicles and tractors making an important contribution. Indeed, if 'engines' are transferred from the 'machinery' category in which they are shown on Fig. 287, the total contribution of the motor and aircraft industries to the export trade in 1967 was nearly 13 per cent. Finished steel in many shapes and forms occupies a high place, as do various non-ferrous metals. Electrical goods of many kinds, from power plant, switchgear and cables to radio and electronic equipment, are important, and prominent places in the 'machinery' group are occupied by textile machinery, office machinery (typewriters, calculating machines, etc.) and earth-moving machinery.

Other manufactures

On the export side, the sales overseas of chemicals, drugs, dyes and colours account for nearly 10 per cent of total exports—more than ten times that of pottery, glassware, and china. An interesting recent change is the jump in export of refined petroleum products. The list of miscellaneous manufactures exported is very long—ranging from heavy bulky commodities like cement from home produced raw materials, and asbestos, from entirely imported, to plastic goods, floor coverings, jewellery, toys, paper, books and curios.

On the import side manufactured and semimanufactured goods have been increasing rapidly in recent years, and whereas in the early 1950s they represented between 20 and 25 per cent of the total value of imports, by 1967 this figure had risen to 45 per cent (Fig. 287). Semimanufactures comprise non-ferrous metals, chemicals, plastics, etc., whilst in the fully-manufactured category machinery, including electrical apparatus and transport equipment, bulks largely, with clothing and wood manufactures as other important items.

Food, drink and tobacco

The trade here is largely on the import side, and includes wheat, maize, meat, butter, cheese, eggs, fresh fruit and vegetables, sugar, molasses, preserved, dried and tinned fruit, tea, coffee, cocoa and tobacco. The increasing affluence of the British people has resulted in a number of recent changes, including a substantial increase in the relative importance of fruit imports (see table on p. 803) and the doubling of the wine imports in less than a decade. But there is also an export, reaching between 6 and 7 per cent of total exports. The largest single item is Scotch whisky (13 million gallons valued at £36m in 1952, rising to 30 million gallons valued at £80m in 1961 and 48 million gallons valued at £132m in 1967), which goes mainly to North America; others include refined sugar, chocolates, cigarettes, and in some years a substantial quantity of barley.

Raw materials

The virtual disappearance of the coal export trade has already been emphasised. The replacement of the former very large import of refined petroleum products by a huge increase in crude petroleum marks an important new industrial development (cf. p. 353). China clay is now the only important raw material export ('Basic Materials' on Fig. 287). Most of the varied raw materials imported go directly to feed British factories—the textile materials, timber and pulp, rubber, hides, skins, furs, vegetable oils and oil seeds, and whale oil. The great expansion of British iron and steel is dependent not only on the imports of iron ore, but also on tungsten, manganese, and nickel for the manufacturing alloys. The home production of metalliferous non-ferrous ores now being negligible, the great non-ferrous metal industries depend upon imported zinc, aluminium, copper, lead and tin as well as several minor metals.

The entrepôt trade

The entrepôt trade suffered severely from the partial destruction of the Port of London during the Second World War. It has recovered, and continues to be dominated by London's seaport and airport (cf. pp. 715 and 719); its monetary value has continued to increase, but its value relative to the export trade has declined, from 5 per cent in 1952 to 4.1 per cent in 1961 and 3.6 per cent in 1967. Outstanding items are rubber, wool and raw furskins, with tea, coffee, spices, tobacco and non-ferrous metals. More than half the re-exports are destined for western Europe.

References and further reading

Additional references are given in footnotes to the text

Chapter 2 The physiographic evolution of the British Isles

BEAVER, S. H. *The Geology of Sand and Gravel*, Sand and Gravel Assocn, 1968.
CHARLESWORTH, J. K. *The Historical Geology of Ireland*, Oliver & Boyd, 1963.
CRAIG, G. Y., ed. *The Geology of Scotland*, Oliver & Boyd, 1965.
LEWIS, C. A., ed. *The Glaciations of Wales and adjoining regions*, Longmans, 1970.
STAMP, L. D. *Introduction to Stratigraphy*, 4th edn, Thomas Murby, 1958 (1st edn, 1923).
—— *Britain's Structure and Scenery*, Collins (New Naturalist), 1946; new edn, Fontana, 1960.
WEST, R. G. *Pleistocene Geology and Biology*, Longmans, 1968, ch. 12.
WILLS, L. J. *Physiographic Evolution of Britain*, E. Arnold, 1939.
—— *Palaeogeographical Atlas*, Blackie, 1951.

Chapter 3 The physiography of the British Isles

The detailed study of the physiography and geomorphology of the British Isles has not yet been fully undertaken on a uniform plan. There are, of course, innumerable accounts of the physical features of the islands on general lines, and incidental accounts of local details will be found especially in the *Memoirs* of the Geological Survey and the geological papers in the Quarterly Journal of the Geological Society and the Proceedings of the Geologists' Association. Amongst other contributions of importance, with details of physiography, apart from those cited in the text, are the following:

BALCHIN, W. V. G. 'Erosion surfaces of Exmoor and adjacent areas', *Geogrl J.* **118**, 1952, 453–76.
BRITISH ASSOCIATION FOR THE ADVANCEMENT OF SCIENCE. The local handbooks issued for the annual meetings of the BA often have excellent physiographic sections. See especially those on *Oxford* (1954), *Sheffield* (1956), *Glasgow* (1958), *Aberdeen* (1963), *Southampton* (1964), *Nottingham* (1966), *Leeds* (1967), *Exeter* (1969) and *Durham* (1970).
British Regional Geology. Series of memoirs by various authors. HMSO.
BROWN, E. H. 'The physique of Wales', *Geogrl J.* **123**, 1957, 208–30.
—— *The Relief and Drainage of Wales*, University of Wales Press, 1960.

EDWARDS, K. C. *The Peak District*, Collins (New Naturalist), 1962.
GEORGE, T. N. 'British Tertiary landscape evolution', *Science Progress* **43**, 1955, 291–307.
LINTON, D. L. 'The origin of the Wessex rivers', *Scott. geogr. Mag.* **48**, 1932, 149–65.
—— 'The origin of the Tweed drainage system', *Scott. geogr. Mag.* **49**, 1933, 162–75.
—— 'Problems of Scottish scenery', *Scott. geogr. Mag.* **57**, 1951, 65–85.
—— 'The landforms of Lincolnshire', *Geography* **39**, 1954, 67–78.
—— and MOISLEY, H. A. 'The origin of Loch Lomond', *Scott. geogr. Mag.* **76**, 1960, 26–37.
MILLER, A. A. 'The entrenched meanders of the Herefordshire Wye', *Geogrl J.* **85**, 1935, 160–78.
PEEL, R. F. and PALMER, J. 'The physiography of the Vale of York', *Geography* **40**, 1955, 215–36.
SHOTTON, F. W. 'The physical background of Britain in the Pleistocene', *Advmt Sci.* **19**, 1962, 193–206.
STAMP, L. D. *Britain's Structure and Scenery*, Collins (New Naturalist), 1946; new edn, Fontana, 1960.
STEERS, J. A. *The Sea Coast*, Collins (New Naturalist), 1953.
SWINNERTON, H. H. 'The physiographic subdivisions of the East Midlands', *Geography* **15**, 1929, 215–26.
WHITTOW, J. B., DAVIES, G. L. and STEPHENS, N. 'Physiographic evolution in Ireland', *Advmt Sci.* **56**, 1958, 381–91.
WOOLDRIDGE, S. W. 'The upland plains of Britain', *Advmt Sci.* **7**, 1951, 162–75.
—— 'The changing physical landscape of Britain', *Geogrl J.* **118**, 1952, 297–308.
—— and GOSSLING, F. *The Weald*, Collins (New Naturalist), 1953.
—— and LINTON, D. L. *Structure, Surface and Drainage in South-east England*, Inst. Br. Geogr., Publication no. 10, 1939; reissued G. Philip, 1955.

Chapter 4 British weather and climate

BEAVER, S. H. and SHAW, E. M. *The Climate of Keele* University of Keele, 1970.
BILHAM, E. G. *The Climate of the British Isles*, Macmillan, 1938. This is the standard work of reference and summarises the wide range of material collected by the Meteorological Office.
BROOKS, C. E. P. *Climate through the Ages*, 2nd edn, Benn, 1949.
—— *Climate in Everyday Life*, Benn, 1950.
BRUNT, SIR DAVID. *Weather Study*, Nelson, 1941.
CHANDLER, T. J. *The Climate of London*, Hutchinson, 1964.
FORSDYKE, A. G. *Admiralty Weather Manual; Meteorological Glossary; The Weather Map*; all HMSO.
Climatological Atlas, HMSO, 1952.

KIMBLE, G. H. T. *The Weather*, Penguin (Pelican), 1951.
MANLEY, G. *Climate and the British Scene*, Collins (New Naturalist), 1952.
STAMP, L. D. *The Land of Britain: its use and misuse*, 3rd edn, Longmans, 1962. Includes a summary of the influence of climate on land use.
TAYLOR, J. A. and YATES, R. A. *British Weather in Maps*, 2nd edn, Macmillan, 1967.

Classification of rainfall:

SHAW, E. M. 'An analysis of the origins of precipitation in Northern England, 1956–1960', *Q. Jl R. met. Soc.* **88**, 1962, 539–47.
—— 'A decade of precipitation at Keele, 1952–61', *N. Staffs. Jl Field Studies* **2**, 1962, 132–40.

The Meteorological Office issues a *Daily Weather Report* (with charts both of the Northern Hemisphere and of the British Isles in detail), which forms the basis of maps published daily in *The Times* and other papers. The Meteorological Office also publishes a *Monthly Weather Report.*

Founded in 1860 the British Rainfall Organisation was a voluntary organisation until the retirement of Dr Hugh Robert Mill in 1919; the carefully compiled annual volumes of *British Rainfall* are a mine of information. For modern advances in knowledge constant reference should be made to the *Quarterly Journal of the Royal Meteorological Society* and to the popular monthly, *Weather*, also published by the Society.

Sections on the climate of each county of Britain are published in the separate parts of *The Land of Britain* (London 1936–46).

Chapter 5 The inland waters of the British Isles

British Waterworks Yearbook and Directory.
METROPOLITAN WATER BOARD. Annual Reports.
Annual Reports of the various River Authorities.
The Surface Water Yearbook of Great Britain, 1937–1945. HMSO, 1952. Also later years.
THAMES CONSERVANCY. Monthly Reports.

BALCHIN, W. G. V. 'A water use survey', *Geogrl J.* **124**, 1958, 476–93.
EDMUNDS, F. H. 'Outlines of underground water supply in England and Wales', *Trans. Inst. Water Eng.*, 1941.
GEOLOGICAL SURVEY. The *Water Supply* Memoirs, HMSO.
GREGORY, S. 'The contribution of the uplands to the public water supplies of England and Wales', *Trans. Inst. Br. Geogr.*, **25**, 1958, 153–65
MILL, H. R. 'The English Lakes, with bathymetrical maps and illustrations', *Geogrl J.* **6**, 1895, 135–66.
MURRAY, SIR JOHN. 'Bathymetrical survey of the freshwater lochs of Scotland', *Geogrl J.* **4**, **9**, **15–18**, **22–27**, **30**, **31**, **36**.

ROSEVEARE, J. C. A. 'Land drainage in England and Wales', *Water and Water Engineering* **34**, 1932, 637–65.
SYMPOSIUM, 'Water and planning', *Town and Country Planning*, June 1966.
WALTERS, R. C. S. *The Nation's Water Supply*, Nicholson & Watson, 1936.

Chapter 6 The soils of Britain

BRADE-BIRKS, S. G. *Good Soil*, English Universities Press, 1944.
BUNTING, B. T. *The Geography of Soil*, Hutchinson, 1967.
BURNHAM, C. P. 'The soils of Herefordshire', *Woolhope Trans.* **38**, 1964, 27–35.
—— and MACKNEY, D. 'Soils of Shropshire', *Field Studies* **2**, 1964, 83–113.
CROWTHER, E. M. and others. 'The soils of Britain and their classification', *Geography* **21**, 1936, 106–19.
HALL, A. D. and RUSSELL, E. J. *Agriculture and the Soils of Kent, Surrey, and Sussex*, HMSO, 1911.
HARMER, F. W. 'The Pleistocene Period in the Eastern Counties of England', in *Geology in the Field.* Geologists' Association Jubilee Volume, 1910, 103–23.
JACKS, G. V. *Soil*, Nelson, 1954.
LAND UTILISATION SURVEY OF GREAT BRITAIN. Report, *The Land of Britain*, ed. L. D. Stamp, in 92 parts (one for each county), or 9 vols, Geographical Publications, 1937–46.
ROBINSON, G. W. *Soils: their origin, constitution, and classification,* Thomas Murby, 1932.
RUSSELL, E. J. *Soil Conditions and Plant Growth*, 6th edn, Longmans, 1932.
—— *The World of the Soil*, Collins (New Naturalist), 1957.
SOIL SURVEY OF GREAT BRITAIN. *Annual Reports*, HMSO, 1948 onwards. The Survey also issues memoirs on individual map sheets.
STAMP, L. D. *The Land of Britain: its use and misuse*, 3rd edn, Longmans, 1962; chapter on Soils.
THIRD INTERNATIONAL CONGRESS OF SOIL SCIENCE. *Guidebook for the Excursion round Britain*, Oxford, 1935. The best guide to British soils yet available.

Chapter 7 The natural vegetation of Britain

GODWIN, H. *The History of the British Flora*, Cambridge University Press, 1956.
ORME, A. R. 'Ireland's vegetation: an essay in biogeographic change', *Geogrl Viewpoint* **1**, 1968, 241–50.
NATURE CONSERVANCY, THE. *The First Ten Years*, HMSO, 1960. The NC also issues *Annual Reports*.
PEARSALL, W. H. *Mountains and Moorlands*, Collins (New Naturalist), 1950; new edn, rev. by W. Pennington, Fontana, 1968.
PENNINGTON, W. *The History of British Vegetation*, English Universities Press, 1969. A simpler treatment than that provided by H. Godwin.

TANSLEY, SIR A. G. *The British Islands and their Vegetation*, 2nd edn, 2 vols, Cambridge University Press, 1949. The standard work.

Sir George Stapledon initiated several surveys of grassland (see above, p. 125), adopting a broad classification which is both ecological and agricultural. See:

DAVIES, W. in *A Survey of the Agricultural and Waste Lands of Wales*, ed. R. G. Stapledon, Faber, 1936.

STAPLEDON, R. G. *The Hill Lands of Britain, Development or Decay?* Faber, 1937.

The Ordnance Survey has published two vegetation maps on the scale of 1:625 000: Sheet 1, *Reconnaissance Survey of Scotland*, by A. Geddes and L. D. Stamp (1953) with explanatory text by A. Geddes (1958); Sheet 2, *Grasslands of England and Wales* (1940), by R. G. Stapledon and W. Davies (published 1945, with explanatory text, 1952).

Chapter 8 Forestry and afforestation

ACKERS, C. P. *Practical British Forestry*, Oxford University Press, 1938.

COLLINS, PETER. 'The Work of the Forestry Commission', *Geogrl Mag.* **34**, 1961, 125–34.

EDLIN, H. L. *Trees, Woods and Man*, Collins (New Naturalist), 1956.

FORESTRY COMMISSION. *Annual Reports*.

—— *Timber! Your Growing Investment*, F.C. Booklet no. 23, HMSO, 1969.

TAYLOR, W. L. *Forests and Forestry in Great Britain*, Crosby, Lockwood, 1946.

Census of Woodlands and . . . Home-grown Timber 1924, HMSO, 1928.

Census of Woodlands, 1947–49, HMSO, 1952.

Census of Woodlands, 1965–67, HMSO, 1970.

Chapter 9 Land use in the British Isles

ARVILL, R. *Man and Environment*, Penguin Books, 1967, chapters 3 and 4.

BEST, R. H. 'Recent changes and future prospects in land use in England and Wales', *Geogrl J.* **131**, 1965, 1–12.

—— and COPPOCK, J. T. *The Changing Use of Land in Britain*, Faber, 1962.

LAND UTILISATION SURVEY, Report, *The Land of Britain* (see chapter 6).

Report of the Committee on Land Utilisation in Rural Areas, Cmd 6378, HMSO, 1942.

STAMP, L. D. *The Land of Britain: its use and misuse* (1948), 3rd edn, Longmans, 1962.

—— 'Planning and agriculture', *J. Town Planning Inst.* **36**, 1950, 141–52.

—— *Our Undeveloped World*, Faber, 1953.

—— *Man and the Land*, Collins (New Naturalist), 1954.

In 1955 the Government appointed a Royal Commission on Common Land which issued its Report in 1958 (Cmd 462, HMSO). A lengthy appendix gave details of existing common lands, county by county, covering a total area of 1 054 661 acres in England in 4515 units, and 450 341 acres in Wales in 631 units. The whole subject is considered from the geographical angle in:

HOSKINS, W. G. and STAMP, L. D. *The Common Lands of England and Wales*, Collins (New Naturalist), 1963.

The memorial volume to Sir Dudley Stamp entitled *Land Use and Resources: studies in applied Geography* (Inst. Br. Geogr. special publication no. 1, 1968) contains, in Part 2 (pp. 85–142) several essays on the theme 'The land of Britain'.

Land Utilisation maps, 1 inch scale. London, Edward Stanford.

Land utilisation, land classification, 1:625 000 (2 sheets), Ordnance Survey, 1944, 1945.

Second Land Utilisation Survey, 1:25 000 scale maps; available from Edward Stanford.

Chapter 10 Agriculture

STAMP, L. D. *The Land of Britain: its use and misuse*, 3rd edn, Longmans, 1962.
SYMONS, L., ed. *Land-use in Northern Ireland*, University of London Press, 1963.

These two works study at length the subjects considered in this chapter.

Official statistics are published annually by HMSO, with separate volumes for England and Wales, for Scotland and for Northern Ireland. These give statistics for individual counties. Figures for the constituent countries of the United Kingdom are published in separate volumes of UK statistics, and a centenary volume was published in 1968.

Agricultural statistics for all Irish counties appear in:

Statistical Abstract of Ireland. Central Statistical Office, Dublin. Annual.

Many other official publications relating to agriculture include:

CENTRAL OFFICE OF INFORMATION, Pamphlet 43, HMSO, outlines government measures.

There is a vast literature dealing with the agriculture of the British Isles. A summary of books and papers with a marked geographical content relating to Great Britain and published between 1945 and 1964 is given in:

COPPOCK, J. T. 'Postwar studies in the geography of British agriculture', *Geogrl Rev.* **54**, 1964, 409–26.

Others are listed in:

HUNT, K. E. and CLARK, K. R. *The State of British Agriculture 1965–1966*, Oxford, Agricultural Economics Research Institute, 1966.

Agricultural atlases:

ORDNANCE SURVEY. *England and Wales*, 2nd edn, 1932.
COPPOCK, J. T. *An Agricultural Atlas of England and Wales*, Faber, 1964.
STAMP, L. D. *An Agricultural Atlas of Ireland*, Gill, 1931.
WOOD, H. J. *An Agricultural Atlas of Scotland*, Gill, 1931.

Other maps appear in:

Types of Farming in Scotland, HMSO, 1952.
The Atlas of Britain and Northern Ireland, Oxford University Press, 1963.

Chapter 11 The agricultural regions of Scotland

The Land of Britain (see Chapter 6). Parts 1–30 deal with Scottish counties.
STAMP, L. D. *The Land of Britain: its use and misuse*, 3rd edn, Longmans, 1962; esp. Chapter 15.
SYMON, J. A. *Scottish Farming Past and Present*, Oliver & Boyd, 1959.
Types of Farming in Scotland, HMSO, 1952.
WOOD, H. J. *An Agricultural Atlas of Scotland*, Gill, 1931.

For details of certain parts of Scotland, including accounts of agriculture, see *inter alia*:

CAIRD, J. B. *Park: a geographical study of a Lewis crofting district*, Geog. Field Group, Universities of Nottingham and Glasgow, 1958.
GRANT, J. F. 'The Highland openfield system', *Geogr. Teacher* **13**, 1926, 480.
KAY, G. 'Agricultural patterns and soil types in north east Scotland', *Scott. geogr. Mag.* **77**, 1961, 131–47; also *ibid.* **78**, 1962, 100–11.
LEPPARD, H. M. 'Scottish carse agriculture: the carse of Gowrie', *Econ. Geog.* **10**, 1934, 217–38.
MCQUEEN, J. D. 'Milk surpluses in Scotland', *Scott. geogr. Mag.* **77**, 1961, 93–105.
MAXTON, J. P., ed. *Regional Types of British Agriculture*, by fifteen authors. Allen & Unwin, 1936.
MOISLEY, H. A. *Uig: a Hebridean parish*, Geog. Field Group, Universities of Nottingham and Glasgow, 1962.
Natural Resources in Scotland, Symposium, Scottish Council, 1961.
SNODGRASS, C. P. 'Stock farming in Scotland and its relation to environment', *Scott. geogr. Mag.* **49**, 1933, 24–34.
—— 'The influence of physical environment on the principal cultivated crops of Scotland', *Scott. geogr. Mag.* **48**, 1932, 329–47.

The county volumes of the new (Third) *Statistical Account* of Scotland are a mine of information. There are also many articles about postwar agriculture in Scotland in:

Scottish Agricultural Economics

Scottish Agriculture
Transactions of the Royal Highland and Agricultural Society.

The relevant British Association Handbooks contain sections on agriculture: South-Eastern Scotland (1951), Glasgow (1958), The North-East of Scotland (1963) and Dundee (1968).

Chapter 12 The agricultural regions of England and Wales

COPPOCK, J. T. *An Agricultural Atlas of England and Wales*, Faber, 1964.
LAND UTILISATION SURVEY, Report, *The Land of Britain* (see Chapter 6), Parts 31–90 contain full accounts of each county in England and Wales under prewar conditions.
MAXTON, J. P., ed. *Regional Types of British Agriculture*, Allen & Unwin, 1936.
STAMP, L. D. *The Land of Britain* . . . , 1962. The third edition of 1962 has a long chapter discussing changes from 1947 to 1960.

The annual Handbooks of the British Association for the Advancement of Science usually contain sections on agriculture; see especially Norwich (1961), Southampton (1964), Cambridge (1965), Nottingham (1966) and Exeter (1969).

Chapter 13 The British fisheries

DAY, E. E. D. 'The British sea fishing industry', *Geography* **54**, 1969, 165–80.
GRAHAM, MICHAEL, *The Fish Gate*, Faber, 1943.
——, ed. *Sea Fisheries*, Arnold, 1956.
HARDY, A. C. *Fish and Fisheries*, Collins (New Naturalist), 1959.
HICKLING, C. F. *The Hake and Hake Fishery*, Arnold, 1935.
HODGSON, W. C. *The Herring and its Fishery*, Routledge, 1957.
——, ed. *Herring Atlas*, published by International Council for the Exploration of the Sea, 1951.
RUSSELL, E. S. *The Overfishing Problem*, Cambridge University Press, 1942.
TAYLOR, R. A. *The Economics of White Fish Distribution in Great Britain*, Duckworth, 1960.

Official publications:

Annual Fish Stock Records.
Annual Reports of the White Fish Authority.
Fisheries in War-time, HMSO, 1946.
Report of the Committee of Inquiry into the Fishing Industry, Cmnd 1266, HMSO, 1961.
Scottish Sea Fisheries Statistical Tables, HMSO, annual.
Sea Fisheries Statistical Tables, HMSO, annual.
Laboratory leaflets published by the Ministry of Agriculture, Fisheries and Food include, e.g. *North Sea Plaice Stocks*, 1966, *The Cornish Pilchard and its Fishery*, 1965.

Useful articles appear in the following periodicals:
World Fishing, John Trundell Ltd.
Fishing News, Arthur Heighway Pubns.
Fishing News International, Arthur Heighway Pubns.

Chapter 14 Fuel and power

COAL

Official publications:

FUEL AND POWER, MINISTRY OF. *Coal Mining: Report of the Technical Advisory Committee* (The Reid Report), Cmd 6610, HMSO, 1945.

FUEL AND POWER, MINISTRY OF. *Regional Survey Reports*, HMSO:

Northumberland and Cumberland Coalfields (Northern A Region), 1945.

Durham Coalfield (Northern B Region), 1945.

North Eastern Coalfield (the official designation of the Yorkshire fields), 1945.

North Western Coalfields (Lancashire and North Wales), 1945.

North Midland Coalfield (Nottinghamshire, North Derbyshire, South Derbyshire and Leicestershire), 1945.

The Coalfields of the Midland Region (North and South Staffordshire, Shropshire and Warwickshire), 1945.

Kent Coalfield, 1945.

South Wales Coalfield (including Pembrokeshire), 1946.

Bristol and Somerset Coalfield, 1946.

FUEL RESEARCH BOARD (Dept. of Scientific and Industrial Research), *Rapid Survey of Coal Reserves and Production: a first appraisal of results*, FR Survey Paper no. 58, 1946. This is the first official estimate of coal reserves. Attention is restricted to those in 'the opinion of colliery owners and of independent mining engineers and surveyors . . . likely to sustain the country's coal output during the next hundred years'. Other publications of the Board are concerned with detailed technical studies, including those of individual seams.

FUEL RESEARCH BOARD, *Methods of Analysis of Coal and Coke*, FR Survey Paper no. 44, HMSO, 1941. This gives the basis for the classification of coal outlined above.

ROYAL COMMISSION ON THE COAL INDUSTRY, 1925, *Report*, vol. i, Cd 2600, HMSO, 1926. An historic document.

SCOTTISH HOME DEPARTMENT, *Scottish Coalfields*, HMSO, 1944.

ORDNANCE SURVEY, 1:625 000 maps, *Coal and Iron* (two sheets), 1945; mines plotted as at 1940; sections across coalfields.

General:

BIRCH, T. W. 'The development and decline of the Coalbrookdale coalfield', *Geography* **19**, 1934, 114–26.

BROOKFIELD, H. C. 'A study in the economic geography of the pre-war coastal coal trade', *Trans. Inst. Br. Geogr.* **19**, 1953, 81–94.

CROWE, P. R. 'The Scottish coalfields', *Scott. geogr. Mag.* **45**, 1929.

DRON, R. W. *The Coalfields of Scotland*, Blackie, 1902.

GRAY, G. D. B. 'The South-Yorkshire coalfield', *Geography* **32**, 1947, 113–31. An important study in the shift in the focus of the mining industry, with maps showing collieries in the seventeenth century and in 1855, 1895 and 1934.

HUMPHRYS, G. 'The Coal Industry', chapter 3 of *South Wales in the Sixties*, ed. G. Manners, Pergamon Press, 1964.

JEVONS, H. STANLEY. *The British Coal Trade*, Kegan Paul, 1915.

LEBON, J. H. G. 'The development of the Ayrshire Coalfield', *Scott. geogr. Mag.* **49**, 1933, 138–54.

LERRY, G. G. *The Collieries of Denbighshire*, Wrexham, 1946.

MITCHESON, J. C. 'The East Warwickshire Coalfield', in *Birmingham and its Regional Setting*, British Association for the Advancement of Science, Handbook 1951, pp. 289–302.

NEF, J. U. *The Rise of the British Coal Industry*, 2 vols, Routledge, 1932 (historical: pre-1800).

NORTH, F. J. *Coal and the Coalfields of Wales*, 2nd edn, National Museum of Wales, 1931.

RITCHIE, A. E. *The Kent Coalfield: its evolution and development*, London, 1919.

SIMPSON, E. S. *Coal and the Power Industries in Post-war Britain*, Longmans, 1966.

SMAILES, A. E. 'The development of the Northumberland and Durham Coalfield', *Scott. geogr. Mag.* **51**, 1935, 201–14.

THOMAS, T. M. 'Coal mining in Britain: a declining industry', *Tijds. v. Econ. en Soc. Geog.* 1961, 267–76.

TRUEMAN, A. E. *The Coalfields of Great Britain*, Edward Arnold, 1954. Contains an excellent summary of the character and resources of the British coalfields.

WILLIAMS, D. T. 'The economic geography of the western half of the South Wales Coalfield (excluding Pembroke)', *Scott. geogr. Mag.* **49**, 1933, 274–89.

WILLS, L. J. *Concealed Coalfields*, Blackie, 1956.

WISE, M. J. 'The Cannock Chase Region', in *Birmingham and its Regional Setting*, British Association for the Advancement of Science, Handbook, 1951, pp. 296–88.

OIL

LUCKAS, M. R. 'Recent developments in the United Kingdom oil industry', *Geography* **50**, 1965, 152–60.

PETROLEUM INFORMATION BUREAU. *U.K. Petroleum industry statistics*. Annual.

GAS

J. A. DEMONT, 'The introduction of North Sea Gas into the East Midlands', *East Midl. Geogr.* **4**, 1969, 379–86.

MANNERS, G. 'Recent changes in the British Gas Industry', *Trans. Inst. Br. Geogr.* **26**, 1959, 153–68.

ELECTRICITY

CENTRAL ELECTRICITY GENERATING BOARD. *Statistical Yearbook.*

ELECTRICITY SUPPLY BOARD (IRELAND). *Annual Report.*

NORTH OF SCOTLAND HYDRO-ELECTRIC BOARD. *Power from the Glens*, 1964.

RAWSTRON, E. M. 'The distribution and location of steam-driven power stations in Great Britain', *Geography* **36**, 1951, 249–62.

—— 'The salient geographical features of electricity production in Great Britain', *Advmt Sci.* **12**, 1955, 73–82.

—— 'Power stations and the river Trent', *East Midl. Geogr.* **14**, 1960, 27–32.

Chapter 15 Mining industries other than coal and iron

GEOLOGICAL SURVEY. *Special Reports on the Mineral Resources of Great Britain*, 35 volumes, HMSO, published at intervals since 1916. These *Reports* cover all the metallic ores and most of the rarer non-metallic minerals. There is no comparable treatment of the commoner minerals. For a general survey see:

BEAVER, S. H. 'Minerals and planning', *Geogrl J.* **104**, 1944, 166–93.

—— 'Land reclamation', *Chartered Surveyor*, 1960, 669–75.

—— *The geology of sand and gravel.* Sand and Gravel Association, 1968.

Reports of the Advisory Committee on Sand and Gravel, Parts 1–18, HMSO, 1948–1953.

The following maps in the 'National Atlas' 1:625 000 series have been published by the Ordnance Survey: Limestone (including Chalk), sheets 1 and 2, 1955, Gravel, sheet 2 only, 1965.

Chapter 16 Iron and steel

ASHTON, T. S. *Iron and Steel in the Industrial Revolution*, 2nd edn, Manchester University Press, 1951.

BRITISH STEEL CORPORATION. *Annual statistics*; also quarterly review, *British Steel.*

BURNHAM, T. H. and HOSKINS, G. O. *Iron and Steel in Britain, 1870–1930*, Allen & Unwin, 1943.

CARR, J. C. and TAPLIN, W. *History of the British Steel Industry*, Blackwell, 1962.

DEARDEN, J. *Iron and Steel To-day*, Oxford University Press, 1939; 2nd edn, 1956.

GEOLOGICAL SURVEY. *Memoirs on Mineral Resources*—see footnotes to text.

SCHUBERT, H. R. *History of the British Iron and Steel Industry, 450* BC *to* AD *1775*, Routledge, 1957.
WARREN, K. *The British Iron and Steel Sheet Industry since 1840*. Bell, 1970.

Chapter 17 Iron and steel: the secondary industries

ABERCONWAY, LORD. *Basic Industries of Great Britain*, Benn, 1927.
ALLEN, G. C. *British Industries and Their Organisation*, Longmans, 1933 (4th edn, 1959), Chapter 4–7.
COMMITTEE ON INDUSTRY AND TRADE. *Survey of Metal Industries*, HMSO, 1928.
JONES, J. H. *The Tinplate Industry*, P. S. King, 1914, for early history.
POLLOCK, D. *The Shipbuilding Industry*, Methuen, 1905, *also* for early history.
TURTON, B. J. 'The British Railway Engineering Industry', *Tijds. v. Econ. en Soc. Geog.* 1967, 193–202.

Chapter 18 The non-ferrous metal industries

ALLEN, G. C. *Industrial Development of Birmingham and the Black Country*, Allen & Unwin, 1929.
GEOLOGICAL SURVEY. *Special Reports on Mineral Resources* (see Chapter 15).
GRANT-FRANCIS, G. *History of Copper Smelting in the Swansea District*, 1881.
HAMILTON, H. *The English Brass and Copper Industries to 1800*, Longmans, 1926.
HOPKINS, T. G. L. 'Developments in the British aluminium industry', *Geography* **44**, 1959, 266–7.
PERCY, J. *Metallurgy:* Vol. i, *Copper;* vol. ii, *Lead*, Murray, 1875.
WILLIAMS, D. T. *The Economic Development of Swansea*, University of Wales Press, 1942.

Chapter 19 The textile industries: woollen and worsted

CLAPHAM, J. H. *Woollen and Worsted Industries*, Methuen, 1907.
COMMITTEE ON INDUSTRY AND TRADE. *Survey of Textile Industries*, HMSO, 1928.
CRUMP, W. B. and GHORBAL, G. *History of the Huddersfield Woollen Industry*, Tolson Museum Handbook, no. 9, 1935.
KINVIG, R. H. 'Historical geography of the West Country woollen industry', *Geogrl Teacher* **8**, 1916, 243–54, 290–302.
LIPSON, E. *History of the English Woollen and Worsted Industries*, A. and C. Black, 1921.
MORRIS, G. W. and WOOD, L. S. *The Golden Fleece*, Oxford University Press, 1931.
TRADE, BOARD OF, Working Party Report, *Wool*, HMSO, 1948.
WOOL INDUSTRY BUREAU OF STATISTICS. *Monthly Bulletin.*

Chapter 20 The textile industries: cotton

BAINES, E. *History of Cotton Manufacture*, London, 1835.
CHAPMAN, S. J. *The Lancashire Cotton Industry*, Manchester University Press, 1904.
COMMITTEE ON INDUSTRY AND TRADE. *Survey of Textile Industries*, HMSO, 1928.
DANIELS, G. W. *The Early English Cotton Industry*, Manchester University Press, 1920.
DWYER, D. J. and SYMONS, L. J. 'The development and location of the textile industries in the Irish Republic', *Irish Geogr.* **4**, 1963, 415–31.
HAMILTON, H. *Industrial Revolution in Scotland*, Oxford University Press, 1932, Chapter 6.
OGDEN, H. W. 'Geographical basis of Lancashire cotton industry', *J. Manchester geogrl Soc.* **43**, 1927, 8–30.
ROBSON, R. *The Cotton Industry in Britain*, Macmillan, 1957.
RODGERS, H. B. 'The Lancashire cotton industry in 1840', *Trans. Inst. Br. Geogr.* **28**, 1960, 135–53.
—— 'The changing geography of the Lancashire cotton industry', *Econ. Geog.* **38**, 1962, 299–314.
SMITH, W. 'Trends in the geographical distribution of the Lancashire cotton industry', *Geography* **26**, 1941, 7–17.
TRADE, BOARD OF. Working Party Report, *Cotton*, HMSO, 1948.
WALLWORK, K. L. 'The Cotton industry in north west England: 1941–1961', *Geography* **47**, 1962, 241–55.
—— The calico printing industry of Lancastria in the 1840's, *Trans. Inst. Br. Geogr.* **45**, 1968, 143–56.
WOOD, L. S. and WILMORE, A. *The Romance of the Cotton Industry in England*, Oxford University Press, 1927.

Chapter 21 The textile industries: other textiles

BRADBURY, F. *Flax Culture and Preparation*, Pitman, 1920.
FELKIN, W. *History of Machine-wrought Hosiery and Lace Industries*, Longmans, 1867. Reprinted David & Charles, 1967.
HAMILTON, H. *Industrial Revolution in Scotland*, Oxford University Press, 1932, Chapters 4 and 5, Linen.
MOISLEY, H. A. 'The rayon industry in Great Britain', *Geography* **34**, 1949, 78–89.
MOORE, A. S. *Linen*, Constable, 1922.
RAWSTRON, A. M. 'Some aspects of the location of hosiery and lace manufacturing in Great Britain', *E. Midland Geogr.* **9**, 1958, 16–28.
ROBSON, R. *The Man-made Fibres Industry*, Macmillan, 1958.
SMITH, D. M. 'The Nottingham lace industry', *Northern Universities Geogr. J.* **1**, 1960, 5–15.

SMITH, D. M. 'The British hosiery industry at the middle of the nineteenth century', *Trans. Inst. Br. Geogr.* **32**, 1963, 125–42.
—— 'The location of elastic-web manufacturing in England and Wales', *E. Midland Geogr.* **22**, 1964, 326–36.
—— 'The location of the British hosiery industry since the middle of the nineteenth century', *E. Midland Geogr.* **5**, 1970, 71–9.
TURNER, W. H. K. 'The textile industries of Dunfermline and Kirkcaldy, 1700–1900', *Scott. geogr. Mag.* **73**, 1957, 129–45.
—— 'The textile industry of Perth and district', *Trans. Inst. Br. Geogr.* **23**, 1956, 123–40.
WARNER, F. *The Silk Industry of the United Kingdom*, Drane's, 1921.
WELLS, F. A. *The British Hosiery Trade: its history and Organisation*, Allen & Unwin, 1935.

Chapter 22 The chemical industries

BRITISH ASSOCIATION FOR THE ADVANCEMENT OF SCIENCE. *A Scientific Survey of Merseyside*, 1953, pp. 251–64.
—— *Durham County and City with Teesside*, 1970, pp. 330–40.
CLOW, A. and CLOW, N. L. *The Chemical Revolution*, Batchworth Press, 1952.
GITTINS, L. The development and location of the soap manufacturing industry in Great Britain, 1700–1850', unpublished Ph.D thesis, University of London, 1962.
HARDIE, D. W. F. *A History of the Chemical Industry in Widnes*, ICI, 1950.
—— and PRATT, J. D. *A History of the Modern British Chemical Industry*, Pergamon, 1966.
MIALL, STEPHEN. *A History of the British Chemical Industry*, Benn, 1931. Written for the Society of Chemical Industries on the occasion of the fiftieth anniversary of its foundation.
WALLWORK, K. L. 'The mid-Cheshire salt industry', *Geography* **44**, 1959, 171–86.
WOODER, L. G. 'The paint and varnish industry of Great Britain', unpublished M.Sc thesis, University of London, 1962.

Chapter 23 Miscellaneous industries

BEAVER, S. H. 'The Potteries', *Trans. Inst. Br. Geogr.* **34**, 1964, 1–31.
BURTON, T. L. and WIBBERLEY, G. P. *Outdoor Recreation in the British Countryside*, Wye College, 1965.
DOBBS, S. P. *The Clothing Workers of Great Britain*, Routledge, 1928.
MOISLEY, H. A. 'The industrial and urban development of the North Staffordshire conurbation' [The Pottery industry], *Trans. Inst. Br. Geogr.* **17**, 1951, 151–65.
MOUNFIELD, P. R. 'The footwear industry of the east Midlands', *East Midland Geogr.* **3**, 1964–5, 293–306, 394–413, 434–54; **4**, 1966–7, 8–23, 154–75.

RODGERS, H. B. *Pilot National Recreation Survey Reports Nos. 1 and 2.* British Travel Association, 1967, 1969.

The paper industry:

BRITISH PAPER AND BOARD MAKERS' ASSOCIATION. *Paper Making*, 1950.
COLEMAN, D. C. *The British Paper Industry, 1495–1860*, Oxford University Press, 1958.
JERVIS, W. W. and JONES, S. J. 'Paper making in Somerset', *Geography* **15**, 1930, 625–30.
SHORTER, A. H. *Paper Mills and Paper Makers in England, 1495–1800*, Hilversum, 1957.

Chapter 24 The peopling of the British Isles

CHILDE, V. G. *Prehistoric Communities of the British Isles*, 2nd edn, Chambers, 1947.
DARBY, H. C., ed. *A Historical Geography of England before A.D. 1800*, Cambridge University Press, 1936; reprinted 1951.
FITZGERALD, W. *The Historical Geography of Early Ireland*, George Philip, 1925.
FLEURE, H. J. *The Races of England and Wales*, Benn, 1923.
—— *The Natural History of Man in Britain*, Collins (New Naturalist), 1951.
FOX, C. *The Personality of Britain—its influence on inhabitant and invader in prehistoric and early historic times*, National Museum of Wales, Cardiff, 1932; 4th edn, 1950.
HAVERFIELD, F. and MACDONALD, G. *The Roman Occupation of Britain*, Oxford University Press, 1924.
HUNT, A. J., ed. *Trans. Inst. Br. Geogr.* **43**, 1968. Special number on population maps of the British Isles, 1961.
KEITH, A. 'The ethnology of Scotland', *Nature* **100**, 1917, 85–8.
KENDRICK, T. D. and HAWKES, C. F. *Archaeology in England and Wales, 1914–1931*, Methuen, 1932.
LAWTON, R. 'Population changes in England and Wales in the later nineteenth century', *Trans. Inst. Br. Geogr.* **44**, 1968, 55–74.
LEEDS, E. T. *The Archaeology of the Anglo-Saxon Settlements*, Oxford University Press, 1913.

MAPS:

Roman Britain 1:1 000 000. Ordnance Survey, 3rd edn, 1956.
Ancient Britain (two sheets) 1:625 000. Ordnance Survey, 2nd edn, 1964.
Monastic Britain (two sheets) 1:625 000. Ordnance Survey, 2nd edn, 1954.

Chapter 25 The evolution of the form and functions of British villages and towns

CHISHOLM, G. G. 'On the distribution of towns and villages in England', *Geogrl. J.* **9**, 1897; 76–87; **10**, 1897, 511–30.

COSSAR, J. 'The Distribution of towns and villages in Scotland', *Scott. geogr. Mag.* **26**, 1910, 183–91, 298–318.

CROWE, P. R. 'The population of the Scottish lowlands', *Scott. Geogr. Mag.* **43**, 1927, 147–67.

DICKINSON, R. E. 'Some new features of the growth and distribution of population in England and Wales', *Geogrl Rev.* **22**, 1932, 279–85.

FAWCETT, C. B. 'The distribution of the urban population in Great Britain, 1931', *Geogrl J.* **79**, 1932, 100–16.

FREEMAN, T. W. *The Conurbations of Great Britain*, Manchester University Press, 1959.

LAWTON, R. 'Recent trends in population and housing in England and Wales', *Sociol. Rev.* **11**, 1963, 303–21.

MEIKLEJOHN, G. *Settlements and Roads of Scotland*, Edinburgh, 1927.

MOSER, C. A. and SCOTT, W. *British Towns*, Oliver & Boyd, 1960.

O'DELL, A. C., The population of Scotland, 1755–1931', *Scott. geogr. Mag.* **48**, 1932, 282–90.

—— 'The urbanisation of the Shetland Islands', *Geogrl J.* **81**, 1933, 501–14.

SMAILES, A. E. 'Population changes in the colliery districts of Northumberland and Durham' *Geogrl J.* **91**, 1938, 220–32.

—— *The Geography of Towns*, Hutchinson, 1953.

TRUEMAN, A. E. 'Population changes in the eastern part of the South Wales coalfield', *Geogrl J.* **53**, 1919, 410–19. An example of population immigration to a coalfield.

VINCE, S. W. E. 'Reflections on the structure and distribution of rural population in England and Wales, 1921–31', *Trans. Inst. Br. Geogr.* **18**, 1952, 53–76.

Chapter 26 London

ABERCROMBIE, L. PATRICK. *The Greater London Plan, 1944*, HMSO, 1945.

BIRD, J. H. *The Geography of the Port of London*, Hutchinson, 1957.

BROMEHEAD, C. E. N. 'The influence of its geography on the growth of London', *Geogrl J.* **60**, 1922, 125–35.

CENTRE FOR URBAN STUDIES. *London, Aspects for Change*, MacGibbon & Kee, 1964.

CLAYTON, K. M., ed. *Guide to London Excursions*, 20th Internat. Geog. Congress, London, 1964.

CLAYTON, R., ed. *The Geography of Greater London*, George Philip, 1964.

COPPOCK, J. T. and PRINCE, H. *Greater London*, Faber, 1964.

DEPARTMENT OF ECONOMIC AFFAIRS. *Strategy for the South East*, HMSO, 1967.

FORSHAW, J. H. and ABERCROMBIE, L. P. *County of London Plan*, Macmillan, 1943.
HALL, P. G. *The Industries of London since 1861*, Hutchinson, 1962.
—— *London 2000*, Faber, 1963.
HOUSING AND LOCAL GOVERNMENT, MINISTRY OF. *The South-East Study*, HMSO, 1964.
JONES, E. and SINCLAIR, D. J. *Atlas of London and the London Region*, Pergamon Press, 1968 (in progress).
JONES, LL. RODWELL. *The Geography of London River*, Methuen, 1932.
KEEBLE, D. E. 'Industrial decentralization and the metropolis: the North West London case', *Trans. Inst. Br. Geogr.* **44**, 1968, 1–54.
MARTIN, J. E. *Greater London: an industrial geography*, Bell, 1966.
MAYNE, DEREK. *The Growth of London*, Harrap, 1952. A simple account which grew out of researches undertaken for the making of a film.
New Survey of London Life and Labour, The, vols i–vi. P. S. King, 1931–35. The standard work covering London of 1930.
ORMSBY, H. R. *London on the Thames*, Sifton Praed, 1924.
REES, G. and WISEMAN, J. 'London's commodity markets', *Lloyds Bank Review* **91**, 1969, 22–45.
REES, HENRY. 'A growth map for North-east London during the Railway Age', *Geogrl Rev.* **35**, 1945, 458–65.
ROYAL COMMISSION ON LOCAL GOVERNMENT IN GREATER LONDON, *Report*, HMSO, 1960.
SMITH, D. H. *The Industries of Greater London*, P. S. King, 1933.
SPATE, O. H. K. 'London 1600–1800', in H. C. Darby, ed., *Historical Geography of England before 1800*, Cambridge University Press, 1936.
THOMAS, R. *London's New Towns*, PEP, 1969.
WILLATTS, E. C. *Middlesex and the London Region*, part 79 of *The Land of Britain*, Land Utilisation Survey, 1937.
WOOLDRIDGE, S. W. 'Some geographical aspects of the Greater London Regional Plan', *Trans. Inst. Br. Geogr.* **11**, 1946, 1–20.

Chapter 27 The growth of communications

General:

APPLETON, J. H. *The Geography of Communications in Great Britain*, Oxford University Press, 1962.
JACKMAN, W. T. *Development of Transportation in Modern England*, 2 vols, Cambridge University Press, 1916.
PRATT, E. A. *History of Inland Transport and Communication in England*, Kegan Paul, 1912. Reprinted, David & Charles, 1970.

Air transport:

SEALY, K. R. *The Geography of Air Transport*, Hutchinson, 1957, esp. pp. 125–39, 183–95; rev. edn, 1966.

SEALY, K. R. and HERDSON, P. C. L. *Air Freight and Anglo-European Trade*, ATS Co. Ltd for Armstrong Whitworth Aircraft Ltd, 1961.

Inland Waterways:

CADBURY, G. and DOBBS, S. P. *Canals and Inland Waterways*, Pitman, 1929.

BRITISH TRANSPORT COMMISSION. *Canals and Inland Waterways: Report of the Board of Survey*, HMSO, 1955.

DOCKS AND INLAND WATERWAYS EXECUTIVE. British Waterways, also official map, 7 miles to 1 inch.

EDWARDS, L. A. *Inland Waterways of Great Britain and Northern Ireland*, Imray, Laurie, Norie and Wilson, 1950.

HADFIELD, C. *British Canals: an illustrated history* [to 1844], Phoenix House, 1950. 4th edition, David & Charles, 1969.

—— *The Canals of the West Midlands*, David & Charles, 1966.

—— *The Canals of the East Midlands*, David & Charles, 1966.

—— *The Canals of South Wales and the Border*, David & Charles, 1960.

PRATT, E. A. *Canals and Traders*, P. S. King, 1910.

—— *Scottish Canals and Waterways*, Selwyn & Blount, 1922.

ROYAL COMMISSION ON CANALS AND INLAND NAVIGATION, Command 4979, HMSO, 1909.

SALIS, H. R. DE. *Bradshaw's Canals and Navigable Rivers of England and Wales*, 1928. The 1904 edition reprinted by David & Charles, 1969.

Railways:

ACWORTH, W. M. *The Railways of England*, 5th edn, Murray, 1900.

—— *The Railways of Scotland*, Murray, 1890.

APPLETON, J. H. 'Some geographical aspects of the modernisation of British Railways', *Geography* **52**, 1967, 357–73.

ELLIS, C. HAMILTON. *British Railway History*, vol. i, *1830–1876*; vol. ii, *1877–1947*, Allen & Unwin, 1954, 1959.

LEWIN, H. G. *The British Railway System* [to 1844], 2nd edn, Bell, 1925.

—— *The Railway Mania and its Aftermath*, Railway Gazette, 1936.

MARSHALL, H. DENDY. *A History of British Railways* [to 1830], Oxford University Press, 1938.

O'DELL, A. C. 'A geographical examination of the development of Scottish railways', *Scott. geogr. Mag.* **55**, 1939, 129–48.

PATMORE, J. A. 'The changing network of British railways', *Geography* **47**, 1962, 401–5.

Road transport:

GREEN, F. H. W. 'Urban hinterlands in England and Wales: an analysis of bus services', *Geogr. J.* **116**, 1950, 64–88.

—— 'Bus services in the British Isles', *Geogrl Rev.* **41**, 1951, 645–55.

GREGORY, J. W. *The Story of the Road*, Maclehose, 1931, 2nd edn, revised by C. J. Gregory, 1938.
TURTON, B. J. 'The changing transport geography of the East Midlands', *E. Midland Geogr.* **4**, 1969, 387–99.

Chapter 28 The seaports of Great Britain

ABERCROMBIE, L. PATRICK. *County of London Plan*, Macmillan, 1943.
ALLISON, J. E. *The Mersey Estuary*, Liverpool University Press, 1949.
BIRD, J. *The Geography of the Port of London*, Hutchinson, 1957.
—— *The Major Seaports of the United Kingdom*, Hutchinson, 1963.
BRITISH TRANSPORT DOCKS BOARD. *Report and Accounts*, HMSO, Annual.
COMMISSIONERS OF HM CUSTOMS AND EXCISE. *Annual Statement of the Trade of the United Kingdom*, HMSO, vol 5, gives statistics of imports, exports and re-exports for each port.
EAST, W. G. 'The port of Kingston-upon-Hull during the Industrial Revolution', *Economica* **42**, 1931, 190–212.
—— 'The historical geography of the transport and roads of Whitby', *Geogrl J.* **80**, 1932, 484–97.
JONES, LL. RODWELL. *The Geography of London River*, Methuen, 1931.
JONES, S. J. 'The growth of Bristol', *Trans. Inst. Br. Geogr.* **11**, 1946, 57–83.
NATIONAL PORTS COUNCIL. *Digest of Port Statistics*. Annual.
NICHOLAS, R. *City of Manchester Plan*, Manchester, 1945.
RAILWAY COMPANIES. *The Ports of the London and North Eastern Railway* (LNER), *Great Western Ports* (GWR), *The Ports of the London, Midland and Scottish Railway* (LMS). Published annually until 1939.
REES, H. *British Ports and Shipping*, Harrap, 1958.
Teesside Survey and Plan, vol. 1, HMSO, 1969.
THOMPSON, L. F. *Merseyside Plan*, HMSO, 1945.
THORNTON, R. H. *British Shipping*, Cambridge University Press, 1939.
WALKER, F. 'Economic growth on Severnside', *Trans. Inst. Br. Geogr.* **37**, 1965, 1–13.

BRITISH ASSOCIATION FOR THE ADVANCEMENT OF SCIENCE. Many of the *Handbooks* produced for the annual meetings of the British Association have excellent sections on ports, notably Belfast, 1952; Merseyside, 1953; Bristol, 1955; Glasgow, 1958; Southampton, 1964; Dundee, 1968; Durham, 1970 (Wear and Tees).

Chapter 29 The Irish Republic

BRITISH ASSOCIATION FOR THE ADVANCEMENT OF SCIENCE. *A View of Ireland*, 1957.
FREEMAN, T. W. *Ireland: a general and regional geography*, 4th edn, Methuen, 1969.

Recent work on Ireland may be followed in the journal *Irish Geography*, published by the Geographical Society of Ireland, Dublin.

Chapter 30 Northern Ireland

BRITISH ASSOCIATION FOR THE ADVANCEMENT OF SCIENCE. *Belfast in its Regional Setting*, 1952.

EVANS, E. ESTYN. *Mourne Country*, Dundalk, 1952.

FREEMAN, T. W. *Ireland: a general and regional geography*, 4th edn, Methuen, 1969.

GREEN, F. H. W. 'Town and country in Northern Ireland from a study of motor-bus services', *Geography* **34**, 1949, 8k–96.

SYMONS, L., ed. *Land Use in Northern Ireland*, University of London Press, 1963. This is the general report of the Land Utilisation Survey of Northern Ireland, organised by Mr D. A. Hill. All the one inch sheets have been published. The classification of land was modified in detail from that used in Britain to meet local needs.

Ulster Year Book. HMSO, Belfast.

Chapter 31 The foreign trade of the United Kingdom

Accounts relating to the Trade and Navigation of the United Kingdom, HMSO; contains elaborate details; the December issue summarises the year.

Annual Abstract of Statistics, HMSO; gives ten-year summaries.

Board of Trade Journal, HMSO; published a few weeks after 31 December, giving details of British trade for the preceding year.

COMMISSIONERS OF HM CUSTOMS AND EXCISE. *Annual Statement of the Trade of the United Kingdom*, HMSO, vol. 1, abstract tables of imports and exports; vol. 2, details of trade with individual countries; vol. 3, details of exports; vol. 4, details of imports; vol. 5, port statistics.

Addenda

Whilst this book was in the press, an important series of essays on Ireland was published, *Irish Geographical Studies in honour of E. Estyn Evans*, edited by N. Stephens and R. E. Glasscock (Belfast, 1970). Of particular relevance are:

(Chapter 3, p. 816)

SYNGE, F. M. 'The Irish Quaternary: current views 1969'. Ch. 3, pp. 34–48.

STEPHENS, N. 'The coastline of Ireland. Ch.8, pp. 125–45.

(Chapter 9, p. 820)

SYMONS, L. 'Rural land utilisation in Ireland'. Ch. 16, pp. 259–73.

Index

The more important references are in heavy type

A

Abberley Hills, 35, 41, 42
Aberavon, 318, 405, 406
Abercrombie, Sir Patrick, 663
Aberdare, 317, 318, 405
Aberdeen, 85, 232, 261, 262, 264, 265, 269, 433, 563, 565, 616, 617
  granite, 364
  (as seaport), 755
Aberdeenshire
  forests, 137
  linen industry, 562
Aberystwyth, 74
Accrington, 546, 547
Achill Island, 774
acid process, 376, 377, 379, 405
acrylic fibres, 592–3
adit mining, 385
administrative function, towns, 653
Adur Gap, 54
Ae, Forest, 143, 144
afforestation, **141**, 232, 234, 252 (*see also* forestry)
  need for more, 136
  Scotland, 142, 143, 144
  Wales, 143, 144, 240
Africa (Guinea) Company, 801
Agricultural Atlas of Scotland, 229
agricultural holdings, **209–13**
  definition, 209
  numbers, 209 *et seq.*
  size, 209 *et seq.*
  tenure, 211, 212
agricultural land, good, map, 157
agricultural output, UK, **218–19**
agricultural regions
  England and Wales, **236–53**; Highland, 239–43; Lowland, 244–53; Transitional, 243–4
  Scotland, 229–35
Agricultural Research Council, 105
Agricultural Returns, 4 June, 148
agricultural revolution
  first, 165
  second, 161, **173**
agricultural statistics, 148 *et seq.*, **151**
agriculture, **160–228**
  changes, current, 174–5
  changing land use in 1871–1952, 172
  cheap food policy, 160
  climatic control of, 176
  Corn Laws repeal, effect, 160
  crops and livestock distribution, 175–209
  employment in, 160–1
  enclosures, 164, 165
  First World War, 226
  historical economic influences on, 160–1, 162
  Industrial Revolution and, 160
  interwar years, 167
  labour force decline, 160, 174
  land devoted to, 161
  lowland England, 162–4
  marketing, 174; Acts, 168; Boards, 168
  mechanisation of, 167, 169, 173, 210, 246; effect on industry, 455; rural communities, 659
  pre-enclosure, 162–5
  pre-First World War, 162–7
  production, postwar, 172 *et seq.*
  Second World War and after, 168–75
  State support, postwar, 169 *et seq.*
  subsidies, interwar, 168
  today, 161 *et seq.*
  Victorian, 165–6
  wartime policy, 169
Agriculture Act, 1947, 171, 624
  1957, 172
Agriculture and Internal Improvement, Board of, 104
Agriculture, Ministry of, 92, 95, 125, 148

Agriculture and Soils of Kent, Surrey and Sussex, 104
Agrostis setacea, 130
aircraft industry, **446–7**, 453, 797–8
centres, 447
exports, 447, 812
firms involved in, 447
Airdrie, 324, 325
Aire, R., 44
Aire and Calder navigation, 693, 696
airlines, 716
air masses, British Isles, 68, 70
airports, **713–16**
1969 map, 713
car ferry, 714
evolution 715–16
foreign trade, 714
airways, 5, **712–16** (*see also* airports)
car ferry routes, 714
domestic traffic, 712, 714
internal traffic, 714
'Albion', 1
alder (*Alnus rotundifolia*), 119; and willow (*Salix*) vegetation, **125**
Alderley, 586
Alderley Edge, copper smelter, 464
Alfred, King, 632, 647, 726
alkalis, 579 *et seq.*, 584, 587, 595; Act, 580
Allerston forest, 144
Alloa, 325, 521
allotments, 154, 155
alloys, 482–4
Allscott, 220
alpaca, 504
alpine orogenesis, 20
aluminium, 459, 474, **475–8**
location of smelters, 476
production and uses, **476–7**
smelting, 346
aluminium foundry industry, 477
Alva, 521
amatol, 582
Amlwch, 469
ammonal, 477
ammonia, 583
ammonium sulphate, 582, 587
Amwell, 97
Anglesey, 35, 359
agriculture, 240
copper ore, 465, 468, 473
copper smelting, 469
Anglo-Saxon
agriculture, 162
cultural zones map, 630
invasions, 631
kingdoms, 630
settlements, 626
Anglo-Saxon Chronicle, 278
Angus, 233, 563, 567
anhydrite (calcium sulphate), 356, 359, **360**, 582, **585**
animal husbandry, 174
Annan, wood processing, 146
Anstey, 611
antimony, 484
Antrim, 21, 791, 798
Plateau, 57–8
apatite, 581
apparel and haberdashery, exports, 802
Appledore shipyard, 432
apples, 193, 194, 195, 246
Appleton, J. H., 708
Apsley, 616
arable farming, 233
England and Wales maps, 237
arable land, 149, **151** *et seq.*, **175** *et seq.*
1937 map, 170
1944 map, 171
Highland Zone, 239 *et seq.*
Lowland Zone, 244 *et seq.*
Transitional Zone, 243
Arbutus unedo, 772
Arctic-Alpine grassland, 130
Ardeer, 582, 586, 587, 590, 595
Ard forest, Loch, 144
Ardrossan, 431
area, British Isles, Great Britain, United Kingdom, 7, 8
Areas of Outstanding Natural Beauty, 133
Arklow, 787
Arkwright, 529 *et seq.*, 787
Armagh, 791, 793–4, 797
Armorica, 15
Arra nuts, 782
arsenic, 358
artificial silk, 591
Arundel, 54
Arun Gap, 54
Ashburton, 496, 519
Ashby-de-la-Zouch, 311
Ashdown Forest Ridges, 52
Ashdown Sands, 53
Ashton, T. S., 370
ash trees (*Fraxinus excèlsior*), 121, 122, 123, **125**, 142
Athlone, 549, 778
Atlantic period, 119
atmospheric pollution, 84–5

Atomic Energy Authority, 345
atomic power (*see* nuclear power)
Attleborough, 497
Aughnacloy, 797
Aughrim Valley, 770
automobiles, exports, 802
Avebury, 628
Avoca Vale, 767
Avon, R., 41, 751
Avonmouth, 587, 753
  zinc smelting, 479
Awe, Loch, 349, 350
Axholme, Isle of, 45
Axminster, 519
Aycliffe, 657
Aylesbury, Vale of, 50, 164
Ayr, 269, 521
Ayrshire, 186
  coalfield, 283, 287, 322, 323, **324**
  lace, 561
Azores high pressure system, 62, 63, 64, 66, 70

B

Backbarrow, 404
bacon, 224, 225, **227**, 783, 798, 799
  imports, 743, 755
Bagillt, 478
Baglan Bay, 583
Bagshot Beds, 126
Bagshot Sand, 124, 252
Bainbridge, T. H., 381
baize, 497, 498
Bakelite, 593
Balchin, W. G. V., 88
ball-clay, **361**, 602, 604
Ballina, 775
Ballintoy, 798
Ballycastle, 328, 795
Ballymena, 566, 567, 798
Ballymoney, 567, 798
Balmoral, 74
Banbridge, N. Ireland, 566, 567, 798
Banbury, 386, 477
Bandon, R., 772
Banffshire
  forests, 137
  linen industry, 562
Bangor, N. Ireland, 791, 794
Bann valley, 792, 796
Bantry Bay, 355
  oil terminal, 770, **788**
Bardney, 220
Barking, 449, 678
Barlaston, 603
Barley, 174, **181–2**
  distribution map, 1931, 180
  Highland Zone, 239 *et seq.*
  Ireland, N., 793
  Ireland, Republic of, 768, 776, 778, 782, 783
  for livestock feed, 182
  Lowland Zone, 245 *et seq.*
  for malting, 182
  Northumbria, 243
  Scotland, 232, 233, 235
  statistics 1938 and 1966, 177
Barlow, Sir Montague, 624
Barnet, 617
Barnstaple, 494, 496, 561
Barrhead, 604
Barrow, 431
  steelworks, 397, 404, 405
Barrow valley, 782
Barry, 318, 595, 758
Barwell, 611
barytes, 359
basalt, for roads, 364
basic process, 376
Basildon, 132, 657, 686, 687
Basingstoke, 613
Bath, 654
Bathgate, 445
Bath stone, 18, 365
Batley, 514
Battle, 360
bauxite, 476
  imports, 474, 476, 755
beaches, raised, 25
Beaker people, 628
beans and peas
  for fodder, 184
  for freezing, 192–3
Beaver, S. H., 47, 333, 363, 366, 645, 703
Beccles, 617
Bedford, 50, 455
  bricks, 365
Bedfordshire, market gardening, 167
beech (*Fagus sylvatica*) hangers, 124
beech trees, 119, 122, 123, **124**, 140, 142
beer, brewing and consumption, 223
  exports, 802
Beeston, 560, 561
Belfast, 718, 723, **791**, 794, 795, **797** *et seq.*
  distilling, 799
  linen industry, 565, **566–7**
  rainfall, 77

Belfast—*contd.*
  as seaport, 565, 799
  shipyards, 430, 433, 434
Belleek, 798
Bell metal, 480
Bellshill, 400
Belper, 558
Ben Nevis, 28, 73, 346
Beresford, M. W., 163, 646, 651
Berkeley, 340, 345
Berkeley, Vale of, 44, 45
Berkshire, 51
Bernicia, Kingdom of, 633
Berwick, Merse of, 234
Bessemer process, 375, 379, 405, 406, 413
Best, R. H., 155
Beverley, 431, 741, 742, 745
Biggleswade, 248
bilberry (*Vaccinium myrtillus*), 123, 124, **126**
  128
Bilham, E. G., 74
Billingham-on-Tees, 361, 402, 582, 583, 585, **586**, 592, 595
Billingsgate, origin, 726
Billingsgate fish market, 274, 682, **684**
Bilston, 397, 446
Bingley, 450, 513, 514, 548
birch trees (*Betula verrucosa*), 119, 121, **123**, 126, 128, 140, 142
Bird, J. H., 748, 761
Birkenhead, 431, 434, 584, 736
Birmingham, 41, 74, 586
  aluminium, 477
  bicycles, 443
  brass manufactures, **466**, 483
  bronze, 483
  clothing, 613
  copper, 481
  engineering province, 438, 453–4
  jewellery, 484–5
  motor vehicles, 443, 445, 446
  non-ferrous metal industry, **485**
  non-ferrous metal manufactures, 19th century, **471–2**
  other manufactures, 454
  plastics, 595
  rateable value, industry, 623
  water supply, 98
  zinc, 480
Birmingham, Greater, population increase, [639
Birr Castle, 77
biscuits, 614, 615
bismuth, 484
Blackburn, 450, 532, 546, 547
Blackbushe airport, 716
'Black Country', 43, **409–11**, 424
  clays, 366
  engineering, 453–4
  fireclay, 362
  motor vehicle components, 446
blackcurrants, 193, 251
Black Death, 163
Blackdown Hills, 50, 51
black earth, 111
Black Isle forest, 144
Blackmore, Vale of, 50
Blackpool, 655
Blackstairs mts, 766, 768
Blackwall tunnel, 711
Blackwater, R. (Ireland), 771, 772
Blaenau Ffestiniog slate, 364
blanket making, 495, **519**
Blarney, 783
Blaydon, 587
bleaching powder, 580, 582
Bledisloe, Lord, 92
Bletchley, bricks, 365
Blyth, 723, 756
Bodmin Moor, 242, 358
bogs, 126, 770, 773, 776 *et seq.*, 782
boiler making, 452
Bolton, 450, 547
books, exports, 802
Bord na Móna, 328
Boreal period, 119
Boston, 759
Boulby, 361
Boulder Clay, 49, 113–14
Bournemouth, 654
Bournville, 615
Bovey Tracey, 281, 328, 362, 604
Bowland Forest, 44
bracken, 122, 123, 124, 130
Bracknell, 132, 657, 686, 687
Bradford (Avon valley), 494
Bradford (Yorks), 450, 498, 514, **515**, 657
  cotton, 548
Bradwell, 340
Braintree, 576
brass, 471–2, **482–3**
  crucible manufacturing method, 471
brass works, 464–5, 483
bread and flour confectionery, 614
Brechin, 563, 567
Breckland, 143, 251
  afforestation, 252
Brecon Beacons, 36
  National Park, 132

Brentwood, 617
Brewing and malting, 223, 614, 783, 799
brick clays, 360, **365–6**
brick-earth, 25, 115
bridge building, 452
Bridgewater canal, 532, 694
Brigg, 220
Brighouse, 498, 548
Brighton, 54, 655
Bristol, 354
  aircraft industry, 447
  brass making, 466, 483
  clothing, 613
  food, 615
  footwear, 609, 610
  lead smelting, 471; imports, 479
  leather industry, 607
  motor vehicles, 445
  wood processing, 146
  woollens, 494
Bristol (as seaport), **719** *et seq.*; with Avonmouth, **751–4**, 802
  deep-water docks, 753
  development, 751
  commodities handled, 753
  physical setting maps, 753
  as staple port, 801
  wool imports, 16th–18th century, 494
Bristol–Mendip region physiography, 45
Britain (Great Britain)
  area, 7, 8
  definition, 7
  population, 8, 640
  position, 1–7
Britain and the British seas, 1
Britannia metal, 480
British Electricity Authority, 338
British Islands and their Vegetation, The, 120
British Isles, political units area and population, 7–8
British Medical Association, 85
British Sugar Beet Society, 219
British Sugar (Subsidy) Act, 167, 220
Briton Ferry, 406, 408, 420, 757
broadcloth, 494, **495**
Broads, The, 251, 252
  origin, 57
bronze, **483–4**
Bronze Age, 119, 629–30
Brora, 282
Brough, 447
brown earth, 113
brown forest soils, 103, 106, 114
Brunner, Mond & Co., 580, 585, 588
Bruton, 494
Brymbo iron and steelworks, 397
Buchan Plateau, 30, 232, 233
Buckfastleigh, 496
building stones, 365
bulbs, 248
Bunter pebble beds, 246, 366
Bunter sandstones, 16
  in Lancastria, 44
  in Midlands, 42, 43
  in NE lowlands, 44, 45
Burnham, T. H., 378
Burnley, 532, 546
  coalfield, 297–8
Burntisland, 476
  as seaport, 755
Burslem, 601, 602, 603
Burton, 41, 77, 584, 586, 654
Burton Latimer, 611
Burton-on-Trent, 223
Bury, 519, 546, 547
Bury St Edmunds, 220, 251
Bushmills, 798
bus services and urban hinterlands, 657
butter (*see* dairy produce, milk)
  imports, 227, 738, 743, 755, 803
Buxton, 654
Bynea, 406

C

cabbages, 192
cables, manufacture, 449–50
Cabot, John, 752
Cader Idris, 12, 35
Caernarvon, 651
  manganese ore, 473
Caerphilly, 318
Cairngorms and tourism, 620
Caithness, 232
  forests, 137
calamine, 465, 466, 479
calcium sulphide, 579
Calder, R., 45
Calder Hall reactor, 345
Caldon Canal, 603
Caledonian canal, 694
  folding, 12
  system (trend) 12
Calvert, A. F., 360
Camborne, 358
Cambrian period, 10
Cambrian slates, 364

Cambridge, 84, 365
Cambridgeshire, 193
camel's hair, 504
Campbeltown, 269, 274
canals, 100, 102, 279, 532, 584, 603, 689, 690, **693–7**
  decline, 695–7
canning industry, **221–2**
Cannock Chase, 41, 42, 43, 245
  woodland, 142
Canonbie coalfield, 297
Canterbury, 54
Cantii, 647
Cantley sugar beet factory, 219–20
Canvey Island
  caravans, 620
  gas terminal, 337
Capenhurst gaseous diffusion plant, 345
Caravans, 619–20
Carboniferous Limestone, 13, 322
  in Bristol–Mendips, 46
  in Ireland, 58
  in Lake District, 34
  as mineral resource, 364–5
  minerals associated with, 357, 359
  in NE lowlands, 44
  in Pennines, 39, 40, 98
  vegetation, 127
  in Wales, 35
Carboniferous Limestone period, 10, 13
  geography map, 12
Carboniferous period, 10, 13–15, 282
Carbo-Permian period, 10, 15–16, 17
  mountains, 17
Cardiff, 267, 318, 405
  aircraft industry, 447
  as seaport, 118 *et seq.*, **757–8**
  ship repairing, 433
  steelworks, 396, 397, 408
Carlingford L., 794
Carlow, 221, 783
Carmarthen (as staple port), 801
Carmarthenshire, 198
Carnforth, 404
car ownership, 618
carpet making, 505, 511, **516**, **519**, 570, 799
carr, marsh and swamp, 125
Carrickfergus, 798
Carrington, 583
carrots, 245
Cartwright's power loom, 536
cashmere, 504
Cassiterides, 461
Castlebar, 781
Castle Cary, 494
catchment areas, 97, 98
Catmoss, Vale of, 48
cattle, 164, 168, **197–203** (*see also* dairy farming, dairy produce, Ireland, N., and Republic)
  breeds, **165**, 201, 235
  dairy, **197–201**, 214, 216
  beef, **201–3**, 214, 216, 233, 240 *et seq.*, 243
  fattening, 214, **215**, 245, **246**, **247**, 251
Caunton, 329
Cavan, 762, 776
Caythorpe, 47, 386
celery, 248
cellulose
  acetate, 591
  in explosives, 591
  in plastics, 593
  in rayon, 591
Celts, 1, 631
cement, 356, **365**, 585, 759
  works, location, 365
Cenozoic era, 9, 10
census, 636, 637, 639
Central Electricity Generating Bd., 338, 341, 343, 344
  nuclear research, 345
Central (Lanark) coalfield, 283, 322–3, **324–5**
Central Lowlands (Midland Valley) of Scotland, 32–3
  agric. region, **233–4**
  coalfields map, 283, 322 *et seq.*
  iron and steel, 397, **398–401**
  paper, 617
ceramic industry, **601–4**
  employment, 604
  exports, 813
  location, 601, 603, 604
  power in, 603
  products, 604
  raw materials, 602, 603
Ceramic Research Association, British, 603
Chadwell, 97
chain manufacture, 450, 451
chalk, 360
  downland vegetation, 130
  in East Anglia, 57
  escarpment, 50
  formation, 19–20
  in Hampshire Basin, 56
  in London Basin, 54, 55
  as mineral resource, **365**
  soil, 116

chalk—*contd.*
in Weald, 52, 53
in Yorks, S., 47
Chalklands, The
agric. region, 249–50
physiography, 50–2
Chalk Sea, 19
Chandler, T. J., 85
Channel Islands, 195
area, 8
cattle, 201
legal situation, 7
population, 7
tourism, 619
Channel Tunnel, 4
Chapelcross reactor, 345
charcoal, 53, 121, 463
Chard, 561
Charlestown, 759
'Charnian' Folds, 11
Charnwood Forest, 17, 43, 246
Chatham, 432, 759
Cheadle, 465, 466, 469
Cheddleton, 616
cheese (*see* dairy produce, milk)
imports, 227, 755, 803
Chelmsford, 457
chemical industries, **578–98** (*see also* petrochemicals)
capital investment, 583
development, 578–83
employment, 584; statistics, **588**
exports, 598, 802
geographical distribution, 583
heavy organic chemicals (HOC), **578–88**, map 586, 598
inorganic, 578–9, 582
interdependence in, 587
locational factors, 584
locations, 578 *et seq.*, maps, **584**, **586–7**
mass transport in, 588
in metallurgical industry, 587
organic, 579, 582–3
products, 578 *et seq.*
raw materials used, 578 *et seq.*; 1920 to date, **583**, 585
chemicals, biologically active, 596
chemicals, exports, 802, 812
imports, 803, 813
chernozem, 103
cherries, 193, 194
Cheshire, 198
chemical industry, 580, **584**
saltfield, 580, 584
Cheshire Plain, salt of, 360
Chester, 223, 584
Chesterfield, 451
chestnut, Spanish, 122, 138
Cheviot Hills, 39
granite, 364
Chiltern Hills, 51, 73
agriculture, 164
beechwoods, 124
cement, 365
paper, 616
woodland, 142
china clay, 356, 359, **361**, 362, 759
exports, 813
Chippenham, 494
chlorine, 582
chocolate, 752, 784
Chorley, 546
chromium, 395, 424, 459, 474, 484
churches, 493, 643–5, 654
cider, 194, 242
Circle routes, Great, 3–4
Cirencester, 494, 495
Civil Defence Regions, 656
Clackmannan coalfield, 322
Clacton, 74
Claerwen reservoir, 98
Clare, Co., 781–2
Clashindarrock forest, 143, 144
Claxby, Lincs, 389
Claxton, J., 144
clay, 10, 11, 18, 46, 111, 113, 114, 116, 360, 361
output, **356**
clay with flints, 115
Clay Vales, 47–50
Clayton, K. M., 104
Clean Air Act, 84
Cleator, 381, 404
Cleckheaton, 514
Clee Hills, 364
Clent Hills, 43
Cleveland Hills, 47, 48
Cleveland, iron industry, 375
iron ores, 374, 381, 385
Clew Bay, 773, 774, 779, 780
climate, **59–87**
climate, British Isles, 68 *et seq.*
and health, 85–6
local, 73–6; aspect and, 73
and Neolithic man, 642
urban, and respiratory diseases, 85–6
variations, 86–7
Climate and the British Scene, 86

climate, NW Europe, **62–8**
summer, 64–8
winter, 62–4
Clitheroe, 365
Clonegall, 768
clothiers and drapers, 493
clothing industry, **612–13**
employment, 600, 601, 612
gloves, 613
location, 612–13, 679, 799
cloud formation, 67
clover, 165, **189**
wild white (*Trifolium repens*), 129
Clun Forest, 241
Clydach, 589
Clydebank, 429, 430, 434
Clydeside
non-ferrous metals, 487
shipyards, 429, 430, 433
steelworks, 400
Clyde Falls, 340
Clyde Valley, 234
coal, **278–328**
adit mines (*see* drift mining), 278
anthracite, 317, 318, 319
bell pits, 278
Board, National, 278, 279, 318, 324, 325, 336
cannel, 299
changing use, 332–3
in chemical industry, 583
classification, 285–6
in Coal Measure period, 282
coking (*see* coke)
competitors to, 278
disposition of, 281–4
drift mines, 278, **288** *et seq.*, 324
(and coke) exports, 802, 809
fields, 42, 281–4, **290–327**; production map, 283; statistics, relative importance, 291
forests, 282
Ganister, 305
gas, 285
hydrogenation of, 583
and Iron Map, 1:625,000, 284
lignite, 281, 328
opencast mining, 278, 288–90
output (graph), 280, 281, **291**
pulverised, 339
reserves, 284–5; distribution, 286–8, 291; exhaustion, 279
'splint', 399
in steelmaking, 380–1
users, 332
working, history, 278–9
Coalbrookdale, 371
coalfield, 315, 409
Coal Measure period, 14, 15
rocks, 282
Coal Measures, map 37; 39, 40; maps 41, 42; 43–5, 58, 290 *et seq.*
in brickmaking, 365
in Ireland, 58
iron ore maps, 382, 383–4
in Pennines, 98
in NE lowlands, 44
in Wales, 35–6, map 37
coal mining industry, 279–81, **286–328** (*see also* coal)
contraction, 279–80
nationalisation, 279, 318
coasts, vegetation, 131–2
Coatbridge steelworks, 324, 397, 400, 401
cobalt, 395
Cóbh, 786, 788
cockles, 266
and mussels, 274
cocoa and chocolate, 614, 615, 752, 784
cod, 262, 265–6, **268**
landings, main areas, 268
Coed Morgannwg, 143, 144
'coinage towns', 462
coke, 285, 292, 302, 305, 313, 318, **333–4**, 380, 802
for iron smelting, 333, 371, 372, 375, 380, 394, 400, 405
Colchester, 455, 491, 497, 613, 617
Coleford, wood processing, 145
Coleman, Alice, 158
Coleraine, 796, 798, 799
Columbus, Christopher, 2, 3
Colwick, 220
Comecon, 805, 807
commercial junction, towns, 653
common land, 162, 164
cultivation, 162
grazing, 163, 164–5, 240
Pennines, 239
common rights, 163
communications, **689–716**
physical factors, 689
concrete, 356, 366
Congleton, 559
conifers, 123 (*see also* forestry and afforestation and timber)
Conisbrough, 365
Coniston slate, 364

Connacht Highlands, 773
Connah's Quay, 342
Connaught (Connacht), 762, 778
Connemara mts, 765, **773–4**
  lowland, 774
Conon, R., 346
conservation, buildings and countryside, 659
Consett, 397, 403
consequent streams, 52
Continental shelf, 6, 60
conurbations, **659–62**, map 660
  Glasgow, 662
  Greater London, 661
  Merseyside, 661
  Southeast Lancashire or Greater Manchester, 661
  Tyneside, 661–2
  West Midlands or Greater Birmingham, 639, 661
  water supply, 97
Conway estuary, 274
Cookstown, 798
copper, 358, 359, 459, 461, 463, 464, **465**, 474, **480–2**
  alloys, 482
  (and yellow metal) exports, 802
  imports, 803
  smelting, 464, 465, **469**, **481–2**
  sulphate, 484
copper industry
  location factors, 480
  production, 481
  smelting, **481–2**
  tubes, 482
coppice, **121–2**, 123, 138, 139
Coppock, J. T., 155, 160
coprolites, 581
Corallian rocks, 47, 49, 50
Corby, 132, 386, 396, 657
  iron and steel, 378, 379, 387, 393, 396, 397, **413**
cordite, 591
Cork, 85, 414, 770, 772, 783, 788
  as staple port, 801
corn, mixed, 184, 242
'Cornish Riviera', 83
Corn Laws, repeal of, 160
cornstones, 36
Cornwall
  agricultural region, 242
  china clay, 361
  copper mining, 464, 473
  early potatoes, 186
  flowers, 195
  granite, 364
  igneous rocks, quarrying, 364
  lead, smelting, 471
  market gardening, 167
  metallic ores, **357–8**
  rotation grass, 189
  small fruit, 193
  tin mining, 462, 473; smelting, 471
Corpach, wood processing, 146
Corrib, L., 779
corrie (cwm) lakes, 90
corrugated asbestos, aluminium, iron, 424
Cort, Henry, 372
Cotswolds, 45, 48, 49, 247
  beechwoods, 124
  grassland, 130
  woodland, 142
  woollen textiles, 492, 494–5, 511
cotton grass (*Eriophorum vaginatum*) moors, 128
cotton, raw, imports, 803
  yarn and manufactures, imports, 803
Cotton Industry Act, 1959, 550
cotton textile industry, **525–53**
  associated trades, 541, 544
  canals, 532
  Derbyshire, 548
  employment, 1835–1880, 533
  exports, 802, 812
  fibre qualities, 534–5
  geographical distribution, 537–44
  historical geography, 526–34
  importing ports, 542
  Industrial Revolution, **528–33**, 542
  Lancashire, 537–42, 551
  localising factors, 537, 539, 540
  modern growth and specialisation, 533
  occupations map, 1921, 546
  power consumption 1924 and 1930, 533; today, 540
  present state, 549–53; statistics, 552
  processes, 536–7
  prosperous, 534–49
  railways, 541
  raw material, sources, **534–6**
  Scotland, 542–4
  specialisation, 544–9, 551
  Yorkshire, W. Riding, 548
counties, **647–9**
  origin, 647
county towns of midland shires, 648
County War Agricultural Executive Committees, 170

Coupar Angus, 563
Courtelle, 593
Covent Garden market, 682, **683**
Coventry, 41, 591
  aircraft industry, 447, 455
  aluminium, 477
  bicycle industry, 443, 455
  bronze, 484
  manmade fibres, 575
  motor vehicles, 443, 445, 446, 455
  other manufactures, 455
  silk, 571, 573
Cowdenbeath, 326
Cowes, 723
  shipbuilding, 432
Cowley, 444, 445
Coxhoe, 365
crabs, 258, 266, 273
crawfish, 273
Crawley, 132, 657, 687
Crediton, 496
Cretaceous clays, 50
  period, 10, 18, 19
  seas, 19
  soils of, 116
Crewe, 41, 443, 445, **700**, 701
Crinan canal, 694
Crofters Commission, 212
crofts, 231
Cromer, 77, 273, 654
Crompton's mule, 529–30
crop
  distribution, 175–96
  farming, **217**
  rotation, triennial, 162; 4-course, 165; 6-course, 232, 233
  statistics, 1938 and 1966, 177
  yields, 163, 165, 177, 181, 194
Croydon, 457
  airport, 715
Cruachan HEP, 350
Cuckmere Gap, 54
cuestas, 10
Cumberland
  anhydrite, 582
  coalfield, 283, 287, **296–7**
  lead ore, 473
  zinc ore, 473
Cumberland, West, steelworks, 403
Cumbernauld, 132, 658
Cumbria, *see* Lake District
Cumnock, 592
Cupar, 188, 220, 233
Cupressus macrocarpa, 76
currency, changing value, 808
Cushendall, 795
Cushendun, 795
cutlery, 451, 453
Cwmavon, 405, 406
Cwmbran, 132, 657
Cwm Dyli, 349
cyanides, 581
cyclones (depressions) and Polar Front hypothesis, 61
Cyfarthfa, 406

D

Dagenham, 444, 445, 597
  steelworks, 380, 396
dairy farming, 214, **215** (*see also* cattle)
  England and Wales map, 237
  Highland Zone, 239 *et seq.*
  Irish Republic, 783
  Lowland Zone, 244 *et seq.*
  Northumbria, 243
  Scotland, 234, 235
  water requirements, 91
dairy produce, **166**, 167, 168 *et seq.*
  Cheshire and N. Salop, 244
  Highland Zone, 239 *et seq.*
  Lowland Zone, 244 *et seq.*
Danelaw, 632
Danes, 726
Darby, Abraham, 371
Darby, H. C., 420, 633
Darent Gap, 54
Darlaston, 446
Darlington, 452
Dartford, 616
Dartmoor, 73, 242, 358
  HEP, 349
Dartmoor National Park, 132
Dartmouth, 273
Darwen, 546
Daventry, 611
Davies, William, 125
Davis, W. M., 52
Dawley (Telford), 658
Deal, 54
Dee estuary, 273
deer forests, 150, 231
Delabole slate, 364
Delamere Forest, 44
Delany, M., 370
depopulation
  industrial areas, 638, 639
  rural, 232, 637, 639
  urban, 167, 637

Depressed Areas, 639
depressions
  influences of, 61 *et seq.*
  secondary, 65
  typical formation and path, 60–2, 63–4, **67–8**, **69**
Derby, 41, 548, 572, 575, 604
  aircraft industry, 447
  hosiery, 556, 557, 558
  knitwear, 556
  lace, 560, 561
  railway workshops, 443
  water supply, 99
Derbyshire
  cotton, 548
  Dome, 357
  engineering, 451
  iron and steel, 411–12
  lead mining, 459, 463, 466, 468, 473
  lead smelting, 471, 478
  zinc ore, 473
Dereham, 497
Derg, Lough, 782
Derwent, R., 97
Derwent valley water resources, 99
Desborough, 611
detergents, 582, 596
Development Areas, 445, 593, 595, 615, 639
Devizes, 494, 695
Devon, 130, 193, 194
  agricultural region, 242
  china and ball-clays, 361–2
  copper mining, 468
  igneous rocks, quarrying, 364
  metallic ores, **357–8**
  paper, 616
  potteries, 604
  tin mining, 462
  woollen textiles, 492, 494
Devon and Cornwall
  climatic influence, 38
  geological map, 39
  granite, 364
  physiography, 36–8
  soil, 38
Devonian period, 12
  series, 13
Devonport, 432, 759
dew, 77
Dewsbury, 514, 518
Didcot, 659
Dines, H. G., 357
Diss, 497
disseminated settlement, 643
distilling, **223–4**, 783, 799
docks (*see* seaports)
Dogs, Isle of, 670, 728
Dokuchaiev, V. V., 104
Dolgarrog, 340, 349, 477
Dolgellau, 359
dollar area, 805, 806
dolmens, 628
dolomite, 365
Domesday survey, 633, 645, 646
  population map, 634
Don, R., valley, 45, 92
Donaghadee, 85
Doncaster, 575, 590, 741
Donegal, 762, 765, **773**, **775**
Donegal–Sligo Bay, 773
Dorking, 54
dormitory towns (London), 655, 667
Dorset, 51
  Basin, 48, 50
  gloves, 613
  potteries, 604
Douglas, Isle of Man, 655
Douglas coalfield, 322, 324
Douglas fir, 143
Douglas navigation, 693
Dounreay reactor, 345
Dover, 54, 85
  as seaport, 718 *et seq.*, 751
  Strait of, 52
Dovey forest, 144
Dowlais, 405, 406
Down, 791, 793–4
Downs
  Hampshire, 51, 54
  North, 51 *et seq.*, 115, 249; beechwoods, 124; gap and gap towns, 54
  South, 51 *et seq.*, 249; beechwoods, 124; gap and gap towns, 54; Way, map, 132
Draycott, 560
drift nets (fish), 269–70, 272
drift deposits, 107
drift maps, 24, 108
drift mining (coal), 288–90
Dripsey, 783
Drogheda, 784, 787
  as staple port, 801
Droitwich, 360
drought, 80
drugs, export, 802, 812
drumlins, 115, 793
dry point villages, 643
Dryas, Lower and Upper, 86

Dublin, 147, 571, 770, **778**, 783, 784
as seaport, **785–7**; commodities handled, 787; hinterland, 785
ship repairing, 433
as staple port, 801
Dudley, 41, 409
Dumbarton, 430, 563
Dumfries, 586
Dumfriesshire
lead ore, 473
zinc ore, 473
Dunbartonshire, 324
Dundalk, 784, 787
Dundee, 431, 563, 567, **569**
as seaport, 565, 755
Dundry Hill, 45
Dunfermline, 326, 563, 567
Dungannon, 798
Dungeness, 85, 340, 342
Dún Laoghaire, 786, **787**
Dunlop rubber, 443
Dunmurry, 798
Durham, Co., 180, 186
agriculture, 243
lead ore, 473
Durham coalfield (*see* Northumberland and Durham coalfield)
Dursley, 495, 519
Dwyer, D. J., and Symons, L. J., 521
dyes, exports, 802, 812
dyestuffs, 582, map 586, 587, **590–1**
Dysart, 326

E

Eakring, 329
Earl Shilton, 611
Earls Barton, 611
earthenware and glass exports, 802
earth movements, 10, 12
Alpine, 10, 20, 21, 28, 51, 52
Armorican, 10, 16, 36, 58, 283, 770
Caledonian, 10, 12, 15, 28, 30, 32, 33, 35
Carbo-Permian, 15, 16, 17, 26, 36
Charnian, 10, 11
effect on Coal Measures, 282
Hercynian, 15, 283
Pre-Cambrian, 10, 26, 35
Silurian, 10, 31
Siluro-Devonian, 10, 28, 30
earthworms, 113
East, W. G., 655
East Anglia, 21, 249, **251–2**
grassland, 129
market towns, 1834, 650, 652
markets, medieval map, 649
moorland, 127
peat, 328
physiography, 57
sugar beet, 188
wheat, 178
woodland, 125
woollen textiles, 493, 497, 499, 500, 501
worsteds, 492–3
East Anglian Heights, 51, 57
Eastbourne, 54, 654
East India Company, 466, 467, 726, 735, **801–2**
East Kent coalfield (*see* Kent coalfield)
East Kilbride, 132, 657
Eastland Company, 801
Ebbw Vale, 757
iron and steel, 378, 379, 397, 406
tinplate, 422 *et seq.*
economic groups, 226, 805–7
Ecton Hill, Staffs, 464
Eden Valley, 239, 360
Edinburgh, 77, 233, 326
chemicals, 587
linen, 562, 563
paper, printing, bookbinding, 616–17
pharmaceuticals, 597
Edwards, K. C., 413
eggs, 169, 209; imports, 755, 803
Egremont, 381, 404
Eire (*see* Ireland, Republic of)
Elan reservoir, 98
electrical engineering, 447–8, 453, 454, 455, [456
port location, 449
electrical goods, 802
exports, 812
Electricity, **337–53**
Act, 1957, 338
Boards, 338, 341
grids, 338, 341, 352
hydro-, 337, **345–53**
nuclear, 337, **339–45**
power stations and capacity, 338, 344; maps, **340**, 342
thermal (excluding nuclear), **337–45**; location factors, 338
electronics industry, 456–8
definition, 456
location, 457–8
Elland, 548
Ellesmere Port, 584, 591
wood processing, 146
elm trees (*Ulmus*), 119, 142

Ely, 220, 597
Ely, Isle of, 180, 186, 193, 248
emigration (*see* peopling)
Empire Marketing Board, 226
enclosure of land, 163–4
Enfield, 457
engineering industry, **435–58**, 798
  aircraft, 446–7
  distribution, 438
  electrical, 447–8
  electronics, 456–8
  employment, 436, 440, 457
  light, 798
  localising factors, 418–19, 437, 444, 445, 447, 449, 451, 452, 453, 454, 455, 456, 457
  locomotive building map, 441, 440–3
  marine, 434, 438, 451, 452
  motor vehicles, 443
  products, 450; value, 437
  textile machinery, map 438, 439–40, 450
  town types, 437
engineering provinces, 438, 449–56
  Black Country and Birmingham, 438, 453–4
  Ireland, N., 453
  Manchester and S. Lancs, 438, 449–50
  Midlands coalfields, smaller, 438, 454–5
  Northeast Coast, 438, 451–2
  Scottish Lowlands, 438, 452–3
  Southeastern Gt Britain, 438, 455–6
  South Wales, 456
  Yorks, Notts and Derbyshire coalfield, 438, 450–1
England, area and population, 8
English Channel, 6
English Pale, 147
Enniskillen, 797
entrepôt trade, 814 (*see also* London *and* London as port)
Eocene period, 10, 20
  sea, extent of, 20
Epping Forest, 252
equinoxes, and climate, 70
Ericht, L., 346
Erith, 449
Erne, L., 797
eskers, 115, 778
Essex, 57, 193, 194
  oysters, 273
ethylene pipeline, 585, 587
Etruria Marl, 366, 603, 604
European Economic Community (Common Market), 6, 805, 806
European Free Trade Association (EFTA), 805, 806, 807
Evans, E. Estyn, 775
evaporation, 80
evapotranspiration, 80
Evesham, Vale of, 42, 44, 245, 247
Exe, R., 26
Exeter, 497; as staple port, 801
Exmoor, 38
Exmoor National Park, 132
explosives manufacture, 582, 591
exports, 801, 802 *et seq.* (*see also* individual industries)
  invisible, 804

F

factories (*see* industry)
Fal, R., 273
Falkirk, 325
Falmouth, 74, 77, 85, 723
  ship repairing, 434
FAO (Food and Agriculture Organisations), 107
farmhouses, 164
farming, types of, **213–18**, 230, 237
Farming in the Eastern Counties, 215
Farming in Scotland, Types of, 215, map, 230
Farming Map, Types of, Assoc. Agric., 215
Farming Map, Types of, MAF, 213
farm land, use of, 1937 map, 170; 1944 map, 171
Farm Survey, National, 210–11
Farningham, 54
Fasnakyle, 349
Fawcett, C. B., 655, 660
Fawley, 583, 587, 595
  oil refinery, 354, 747, 750
Felixstowe, port, 717 *et seq.*, **759**, **760**
Felstead, 220
fenland, 48, 57, 90, 111–13
  agric. region, 248–9
  market gardening, 167
  rotation grass, 189
  sugar beet, 188
Fenton, 602, 603
Fenton, E. Wyllie, 120
Ferbane, 329
Fermanagh, 791, 797
Ferryfield airport, 714
fertilisers, 165, 169, 174
  chemical, 581, 587, 597
fescue grass on downland, 130

feudal system, 163
Ffestiniog, 340, 349
Fifeshire, 233, 567
Fifeshire and Midlothian coalfield, 283, 322, 323, **325–7**
Finnart oil terminal, 354, 355, 755
fireclay, 15, 305, 311, 356, 359, **362**
fish, **254–76**
  categories (demersal, pelagic, shell fish), present catch, 255 *et seq.*, **259**, map 261
  cultivation, 276
  demersal, definition, 254–5
  exports, 802
  landings statistics, 266, 268
  marketing and markets, 274–5
  pelagic, definition, 255
  post-1948 catch, 254
  processing, 271, 273, 274
  shell fish, 255, 258, 266, 272–4
  trains, 262
  transport, 275
fisheries, **254–76**
  development and decline, 263–5, 272, 274–5
  conservation, 265, 269, 276
  distant grounds, 258–9, 276
  grounds, map 255, **258–9**, 263, 265, 266–268
  inland, 101–2
  inshore and local, 262, 265, 276
  overfishing, 265, 267–9, 271
Fishery Limits Act, 1964, 276
Fishguard, 759
fishing
  employment in, 260
  industry, 263 *et seq.*; influence of rlys. on, 262–3
  line, 257
  ports map, 261, 262, 264
  seasons, 270
  techniques, 256–8, 263, 269–72
fishing vessels, 258, **259–60**, 262, 276
  cooperatives, 275
  drifters, 269–70
  improvement, 263
  ownership, 265
  trawlers, 265 *et seq.*, 270
fishmongers, 275
'Five Towns', 601
fjord coast, 28
flannel, 519
flax, 189–90
  hemp and tow, imports, 803
  N. Ireland, 796
Fleetwood, 261, 262, 263, 264–5, 354, 587, 595
  salt, 360
Flemish craftsmen, 492, 526, 555, 564, 571, 635
Fleure, H. J., 628
Flint, 575
flints, 115, 602
Flintshire
  lead smelting, 471, 478
  zinc ore, 473
floods, 92–4
flowers, **195**, 243; under glass, 196
fluorspar, 360, **361**
fodder crops, miscellaneous, 169, 188–9
fog, 68, 84–5
Folkestone, 54; as seaport, 719 *et seq.*, 751
food
  foreign trade, 801, 802, 803, 804 *et seq.*
  processed, exports, 813
  processing, N. Ireland, 799
  supply, UK, 219, **224–8**; statistics, **225**
food industry, **614–15**
  employment, 600, 614
  location, 614–15, 678
foreign trade, **801–14** (*see also* agriculture, *and individual industries*)
  proportions handled by airports, 714; by UK ports, map, **724**
Forest of Dean, 45, 141, 143, 144
  coalfield, 36, 284, 315, **319**
  iron industry, **369–70**, 380, 388
Forest Marble, 49
forest and woodland, natural, **121–5**
  postglacial to present day, 119–20
Forest of Wyre coalfield, 43, 314–15
forestry and afforestation, **134–47**, 148, 149 (*see also* timber)
  distribution statistics, 136–8
  map 1947 census, 139
  Northern Ireland, **147**
  primeval remnants, 141
  state, 143–4
Forestry Commission, 136 *et seq.*, 252
  plantations map, 144
Forfar, 567
Forth Bridges, 709, 711
Forth, Firth of, and coal, 326
Forth and Clyde canal, 694
Fort William, 476
fossils, 13, 18, 20
Foster, R. T., 712
Fowey, 361, 759
Fowlea Brook valley, 603

Fox, Sir Cyril, 628
Foyers, 346, 349
Foyle, L., 796–7, 799
Foyle, R., 775
valley, **796–7**
Foynes airport, 788
Fraserburgh, 261, 269, 270, 272
Freeman, T. W., 662, 762, 766 *et seq.*
freezing of foodstuffs, 222
freightliner and container ship routes, 1968
map, 707
Frome, 494, 519
Frome, R., 497
fronts
cold, 66, 67, 68
occluded, 66, 67
Polar, 61–3, 64, 66
warm, 66, 67, 68
frost
hoar, 77
incidence, 74–5
pockets, 73, 76, 242
fruit
fresh, and nuts, imports, 803
small, **193**, 233, 251
fruit farming
East Anglia, 251
England and Wales map, 237
Fenland, 248
frost and, 75, 76
Lowland Zone, 246 *et seq.*
Worcestershire, Vale of Evesham, 246
fuel and power, **277–355**
production and use, **331–55**
(*see also* coal, coke, gas, electricity, petroleum)
Fuller, G. J., 468
fuller's earth, 494
fur industry, 604
Furness
early iron industry, 369, 370
iron ore, 381–3
steelworks, 403, 404
furniture, **617–18**
employment, 600, 601
Fylde, 244

G

Gainsborough, 329, 455
Galashiels, 520
Galloway, 31, 340; Rhinns of, 235
galvanising, 422–4, 479
Galway, 359, 773, 788–9; City of, 775
Ganister, 15, 360, 363
garden cities, 658
suburbs, 658
Garry, R., 78
Gas, Light and Coke Co., 334
gas, natural, 330–1, 583
fields, 331
methane, 336
pipelines, 336, 337
gas from oil, 336–7
gas, producer, 381
gas, town, **334–7**
industry, 335
Gateshead, 755, 756
Gatwick airport, 713, 714, 716
Gault Clay, 19, 53
Geddes, Arthur, 126
Geddes, Sir Patrick, 659
'geographical inertia', 395
geological maps, 31, 33, 37, 39, 41, 55
Geological Survey, 91, 104
geology
eastern England map, 109
eras, 9–10
periods, 9–10 *et seq.*
Giant's Causeway, 795
Giekie, Sir A., 108
Gifford, J., 93
Gilbert, E. W., 656
Gillmor, D. A., 766
Girvan, 234
glacial deposits, 23–5, 57
lakes, 25
Glacial period (Ice Age), 21–5, 89
chronology, 24
climate and vegetation, 86
climatic fluctuations, 625
effects of, 24–5, 625
Gipping, 22, 23
Lowestoft, 22, 23
man in, 24
Weichsel, 22, 23
Glamorgan, Vale of, 37
agriculture, 241
Glasgow, 74, 85, 132, 400, 401, 453, 563, 565
aircraft industry, 447
aluminium, 477
brass, 483
bronze, 484
cables, 447
chemicals, 587
copper, 481, 482
cotton industry, 530, 531, 543, 544, 549

Glasgow—*contd.*
electrical engineering, 449
knitwear, 559
lead, 479
locomotives, 441
manmade fibres, 576
paint and varnish, 598
paper, 617
shipbuilding, 430, 433, 434
steelworks, 397
woollen industry, 521, 524
Glasgow (as seaport), 565, 719 *et seq.*, **754–5**
commodities handled, 755
oil refinery, 755
glasshouse crops, 195–6
Scottish Lowlands, 234
glassmaking, 579, 587, **589–99**
glassware, exports, 802, 813
glassworts (*Salicornia*), 131
Gleave, M. B., 365
Glen Affric HEP scheme, 349
Glenarm, 795
Glendalough valley, 767
Glengarnock, 400
Glen Morey, 28
Glenochil drift mine, 324–5
Glenquoich, rainfall, 77
Glenrothes, 132, 658
Glen Trool forest, 143, 144
gley (glei) soils, 106
Glossop, 546, 548
Gloucester, 494, 613, 696
Gloucester, Vale of, 45, 245
Gloucestershire, 49
basin of deposition, 49
coalfield, 320–1
woollen textiles, 492, 493
glove industry, **613**
Godwin, H., 87, 118, 625
gold, 459, 461, **484–5**; value 808
Golden Vale (Limerick and Tipperary), 772, 782
golf courses, 131
Goole, 431, 524; as seaport, 719 *et seq.*, **746**
Goring Gap, 51
gorse, 126, 130
Gorseinon, 406
Gotham, 360
Gowerton, 406
Gowrie, Carse of, 193, 233
grain and flour imports, 803
Grain, Isle of, 354, 355
Grampian HEP stations, 346
Grampians, 28
Grand Junction (Union) Canal, 694 *et seq.*
Grand Trunk canal, 694
Grand Union Canal, 696
Grangemouth, 354, 355, 431, 583, 587, 591, 595, 596
as seaport, 718, 755
oil refinery, 755
Grangetown steelworks, 402
granite, 10, 360
in Ireland, 58
intrusions, 21
minerals associated, **357–8**
quarrying, 364
in southwest peninsula, 36, 38
Grantham, 386, 455
grass for hay, 163
area and yield statistics, 1938 and 1966, 177
Ireland, 779
meadow, 189
seeds, 189
grass moorland, **128**
grass, rotation, **189**, 250
Highland Zone, 231, 232, 239 *et seq.*
Lowland Zone, 247 *et seq.*
grassland map, 125
grassland, natural, 130
grassland (pasture), permanent, 149, 151 *et seq.*, **168** *et seq.*, 175 *et seq.*, 199
1937 map, 170
1944 map, 171
fattening cattle, 203, 204, 237
Highland Zone, 239 *et seq.*
improvement, 207
Lowland Zone, 244 *et seq.*
Scotland, 233, 234
Transitional Zone, 243
grassland, seminatural, 119, **129–30**
acidic, 129
Agrostis festuca (bent-fescue), 207
Arctic-Alpine and mountain, 130
corresponding with forest types, 119
fescue, 119
limestone or basic, 130
Molinia (flying-bent), 207
Nardus (mat grass), 207
Nardus and *Molinia* moors, 130
neutral, 129
siliceous, 129
types, 119–20, 128, **129–30**
gravel, 356, **366–8**, 675
Gravesend, 616
Great Britain
area, 7, 8

Great Britain—*contd.*
definition, 7
population, 8
Great Clay Vale, 50, 365
Great Yarmouth, 264, 269, 270
Green, F. H. W., 657, 708, 748
green belt, 624, 668
Greenfield, 575
Greenock, 430, 755
Greensand, 19
in chalklands, 51
in Weald, 52, 53, 54
Greensand, Lower, 116, 124
Greenwich, 85
Gregory, J. W., 29
Grimsby, 261, **262**, 263, **264**, 269, 272, 524, 576
Grimsby as seaport, 719, **744–6**
commodities handled, 746
fish trade, 745
grouse moors, 232
guanaco wool, 504
guano, Peruvian, 165
Guernsey, 74
cattle, 201
Guildford, 54, 455, 617
Guiseley, 513
Gulf Stream, 6
gun-cotton, 591
gun-metal, 480, 483
gypsum, 17, 356, 359, **360**

H

haddock, 265–6
hake, 264, 266, 267–8
Hakluyt, 752
Halewood, 445
halibut, 266
Halifax, 450, 604
clothing, 613
cotton, 546
woollen textiles, 498, 499, 514, 515, 518
Hall, A. Daniel, 104
Hall, P. G., 673
halophytes, 131
Halstead, 497
Hamble, 447
Hambleton Hills, 47
Hambleton forest, 143
'hammer ponds', 101
Hampshire, 193
woodland, 137, 138
Hampshire Basin, 20, 252–3
physiography, 56–7
vegetation, 127
Hampshire 'Gate', 629
Hanley, 602, 603
Hanseatic League, 726, 801
hardpan, 106, 126
Hardstoft, 329
hardware, 454
implements, etc., exports, 802
Hargreaves's 'jenny', 529
Harland and Wolff shipyards, 433, 797
Harlow, 132, 657, 686, 687
Harrogate, 654
Harston, 597
Hartlepool, 589
Harwell, 345
Harwich, port, 717 *et seq.*, 751, **759**
Hastings, 54
Hastings Sand, 18, 53
Hatfield, 447, 657, 687
Haverton Hill, 429
Haweswater, 98, 99
Hawick, 520, 559
hay
meadow, 189
pre-enclosure, 163
seeds, 189
statistics, 1938 and 1966, 177
Hayes, 457
hazel, 119, 121, 122, 138
Heanor, 560
heather (*Calluna vulgaris*), 124, **126**
Heathfield, 329, 330
heathland, 252
and moorland, **125–30**
Heathrow (*see* London airport)
Hebburn, 429, 434, 481
Hebden Bridge, 519, 546, 548
Hebrides, 521; Outer, 72
Heckmondwike, 514
hedges, 164
Helford, R., 273
Helvellyn, 98
Hemel Hempstead, 132, 657, 686, 687
hemp and jute industry, **568–70**
hemp fibres, varieties and place of origin, 568
jute imports, 568
location factors, 554
locations, 568–9
manufactures, exports, 570, 802
raw and tow, imports, 803
Henderson, H. C. K., 516
Hereford, Plain of, 35, 36, 241–2

Herefordshire, 190, 193
Herne Bay, 54
Herring Industry Board, 275
herrings, 256, 264, 265, 266, 269, **270–71**
Hexham, wood processing, 146
Heysham, 343, 586, 759; oil refinery, 354
hides, skins and furs, raw, imports, 803
Highland boundary fault, 30
Highland Zone, 11, **28–40**, 88
  agricultural regions, 239–43
  agriculture, 162
  farming, 238
  limit, 26
  minerals, 357, 363, 364
  peopling, 626, 627–8, 629, 631
  soils, 115
  temperatures, 72–4
Highlands, Scottish, 11, 205
  agric. region, **231–2**
  hydroelectricity, **346** *et seq.*
  vegetation, 128, 130
High Wycombe, 617, 618
hill sheep farming, 214, **215**
Hinckley, 557–8, 611
Hinkley Point, 340, 342
historic buildings, preservation, 658–9
History of the British Flora, The, 87
Hi-Top steel coating process, 424
Hog's Back, 50, 53, 54
holloware, 454, 477
holly (*Ilex aquifolium*), 123
Holmesdale, 53, 54, 253
Holyhead, 476; as seaport, 718, 723, 759
Home Grown Cereal Authority, 174
Honiton, 561
Hooton, 445
Hop Marketing Board, 190
hop poles, 138
hops, 190, 242, 253
Hopton, 365
horses, 174, **196**, 197, 778
horticulture, **214**, 217
hosiery (*see* knitwear)
Hoskins, G. O., 378
Hoskins, W. G., 497
hovercraft, 427
Howe, G. Melvyn, 85
Hucknall, 558
Huddersfield, 450
  brass, 483
  chemicals, 586, 590
  clothing, 613
  cotton textiles, 548
  woollen textiles, 498, 499, 514, 515, 518
Huddersfield Canal, 532, 694
Hudson's Bay Company, 726, 801
Huguenots, 493, 571, 635
Hull, 51, 85, 196, 261, **262**, 263, **264**, 431, 433, 524, 598
  food, 615
Hull (as seaport), 719 *et seq.*, **739–44**
  commodities handled, 743–4
  communications, water and rail, 742, 743, 744; difficulties, 744
  development, 741–3
  docks maps, 742, 744
  fish trade, 743, 744
Hull, R., 741
Humber, R., 51, 742
  cement, 365
  ports map, 745
  shipyards, 431
humus, 112, 113
hundred court, 647
hundreds, 646–7
Hunstanton, 51
Hunterston, 340, 342
Huntingdonshire, 180
Hurn airport, 714; aircraft industry, 447
hydraulic machinery, 450, 453
hydrochloric acid, 580
hydroelectric power, 89, 101, 337, **345–53**, maps 347, 348, 352
  potential, 346, 349
hydrogen chloride, 580

I

Ice Age, Pleistocene, **21–25**, map 22
Iceland, low pressure system, 62, 63, 66
Iceni, 647
ice sheets, 21, 22 *et seq.*
Icknield Way, 647
igneous rocks, 10, 21, 356, **363**
Ilford, 457
Ilkeston, 397, 558, 560
ilmenite, 589
immigration (*see* peopling)
Immingham, 586
  as seaport, **745–6**
Imperial Chemical Industries (ICI), 361, 578, 583, 587, 592, 595
  chemical plant map, **586**
  formation, 582
  pharmaceuticals development, 597
imports, 801, 802 *et seq.*
industrial function, towns, 653
'industrial momentum', 395

Industrial Population, Royal Commission on the Geographical Location of, 623–4, 639
Industrial Revolution, 499–502, 528–32, 610
  and foreign trade, 802
  and parish boundaries, 646
  Second, 277
industy (*see also individual industries*)
  assembly, 444
  dispersal, 624, 639, 657, 675, 687
  factories and power plant, new, 1945–61 map, 621
  postwar development, 623–4
  primary, secondary, tertiary, 599–600
  projects, major postwar to 1961, map 622
  rateable value, 623
infield/outfield arable farming, 164
Inishowen, 775
Inland Water Survey Committee, 91
inland waters, 88–102
interglacial periods, 23
Invergordon, 476
Inverness, 232
  wood processing, 146
invisible exports, 804
Ipswich, 220, 251, 455, 759
Ireland (*see also* Ireland, Northern and Ireland, Republic of)
  agricultural regions map, 766
  agriculture, 160–1
  barley in, 181
  Bronze Age, 629
  cattle, dairy, 198
  Central Plain, 58
  distilling, 223–4
  Easter Rebellion, 762
  emigration, 764
  famine, 763
  farm holdings and tenure, 210, 212
  farm mechanisation, 197
  farm size and distribution map, 769
  farming types map, 767
  flax, 190
  geological structure, 765
  gold, 629
  HEP, 351–3
  land use, 176
  linen industry, 563–4
  Megalithic culture in, 628
  metallic minerals, 359
  moorland, 130
  oats, 182, 183
  peat-bogs, 112
  peopling of, 631 *et seq.*, **639–41**
  physical regions map, 29
  physiography, 57–8
  political division, 7
  ports serving, British, 759
  potatoes, 185
  rural depopulation, 167
  sheep, 204, 207
  steelworks, 414
  sugar beet, 188
  uninhabited areas, 771
  vegetables for freezing and canning, 193
  Vikings in, 778
  wheat in, 177–8
  woollen industry, 521
Ireland, Northern
  afforestation, 794, 796
  agricultural and physical regions, **792–7**
  agriculture, employment in, 161
  aircraft industry, 797–8
  area, 8, 791
  bacon, 798, 799
  barley, 793
  boroughs and counties, 791
  carpet industry, 799
  cattle, beef, 793, 795, **796**, 797
  cattle, dairy, 793, 795, 797
  cement, 798
  chemicals, 798
  clothing, 798, 799
  coalfield, 327–8
  cotton, 549
  crops, 793, 794, **796**
  drumlins, 793
  engineering, 453, 798
  farm holdings, 211
  farming, types of, 215
  flax production, 565
  food processing, 794, 799
  Foyle valley and Lough Foyle, **796–7**
  geological structure, 792
  glaciation, 792
  granite, 798
  industries and industrial regions, **797–9**, map 798
  knitwear, 556
  linen industry, 565, **566–7**
  Londonderry and Tyrone, mts, **796**
  manmade fibres, 576, 586, 592, 798
  mixed farming, 796
  Neagh, Lough, basin and lower Bann valley, **795–6**
  oats, 793, 794, **796**, 797
  pigs, 796

Ireland, Northern—*contd.*
plateaus and glens, E. Antrim, **794–5**
political, 791
population, 8, 791
ports, 799–800
potatoes, 793, 794, 796
pottery, 798
religion, 791
Rift Valley lowlands, **797**
rural settlement map, 794
rye grass seed, 798
salmon, 798
and Scotland, 792
seaports, 719 *et seq.*
settlers, English and Scottish, 792
sheep, 793, 794, 795, 796
shipbuilding, 430, 433, 797, 798
textile machinery, 798
textiles map, 798
towns, 791; industrial, 793, map 798; market, map 793, 797
tourism, 795
turnips, 796
trade, 800
uplands, counties Down and Armagh, **793–4**
whiskey, 798, 799
Ireland, Republic of (*see also* Ireland), **762–90**
afforestation, 768
agricultural holdings, 210, 212
agricultural output, 219
agricultural products, 783, map 784
agricultural regions, **765–82**
agriculture, employment in, 160–1
airports, 788
Anglo-Normans in, 778
area, 8
bacon, 783
barley, 768, 776, 778, 782, 783
bogs, 770, 773, 776 *et seq.*, **782**
breweries, 783
butter, 783
canning and freezing, 222
cattle, beef, 768, 770, 771, 774, **776**, **781**, **782**
cattle, dairy, 198, 768, 769, **770**, 772, 776, 779, **782**
Central Lowlands, 90, 112, 765, 773, **776–82**; western fringe, 779–81
cheese, 783
chocolate, 784
climatic conditions, 768, 771, 772, 773, 775, 778
communication obstacles, 776–8
cooperative dairying, 772, **783**, 790
cotton, 549
counties and provinces, 762
distilleries, 783
electricity, 352
emigration, 764
eskers, 778
farming, mixed, 768
farming types map, 767
farms, small, 771
food supply and consumption, 228
food processing, 783–4
foreign trade, 789–90
frontier, 775
'Garden of', 769
granite, 58
history, 762
horses, 197, **778**
industries and towns, **783–5**
invasions, foreign, 778
meat canning, 783
northeast uplands, 765, 776
northwest mountains, 765, **773–5**
oats, 768, 772, 774, 776, 777, 779 *et seq.*
oil refinery, 785
peat, 785
physical regions, **766–82**
political, 762, 763
population, 8, 639, 763–5, 774; density, 764
ports, **785–9**
potatoes, 768, 772, 773 *et seq.*, map 780
railways, 772, 775
religion, 791
roads, 770
sea routes to Britain map, 786
sheep, 768, 769, **771**, 774, 775, **780–1**, 1930 map, 781, 782
shipyard, 432, 433
silk, 571
southeast, mountains and uplands of (Leinster Chain), **765–70**
southwest ranges and valleys, 765, **770–3**
steel making, 414, 785
sugar beet, 221, 782
tobacco, 784
trade with Great Britain, 790
transport, 775
turnips, 772, 782
tweed, 773, 784
urban development, 764–5
water power, 351–3
whiskey, 783

Ireland, Republic of—*contd.*
  woodland, 768, 769, 772, 775
  woollen mills, 783–4
Irlam, 397, 739
iron
  production, 369–374, **377**; districts, 396–8, 409
  smelting, early, 121, 369
  wrought, 372, 410, 451
Iron Age, 119, 630
Ironbridge, 315, 372
Ironbridge coalfield, 41, 42, 43, 315
iron industry, 369–417 *passim*
  blackband and clayband ores in, 374, 399, 405, 409, 411
  blast furnaces 1796 map, 373
  charcoal in, 53, 370, 373
  coal in, 370
  coalfield concentration, 373–4; decline, 375
  Coal Measure ores in, 374, map 382, 383–4
  coke in, 333–4, 371, 380
  Derbyshire and S. Yorks, 411
  Iron Age to 1855, **369–375**; 1717 map, 371
  Jurassic ores in, 374–5, 376, 378, 381, map 382, 384–8
  Lincolnshire, 408
  location factors, 395–8
  Northants and Leics, 412–13
  railways and, 387
  Scotland, 1760–1860, 399
  Sheffield, 413–14
  South Wales, 1839, 405
  steam engine influence, 371–2
  in Weald, 53, 369, 371
  West Midlands (Black Country), 409–11
iron ore
  blackband and clayband, 374, 399, 405
  Coal Measures, **383–4**, 403
  haematite, 381, **382–3**
  imports, 375, **391–3**, 405, 406, 407, 803
  internal transport, 393–4
  Jurassic, **384–8**, map 386, 393
  limonite, 388–9
  magnetic, 389
  opencast working, 387
  ports of import, 393
  production statistics, 390
  and railways, 383, 387
  sintering of, 394
  smelters, 393
  Tees-side maps, 402
  West Cumberland and Furness, 1930s map, 404
iron and steel, **369–417** (*see also* iron, iron ore, steel)
  alloying metals, 394–5
  alloy steel, 414
  centres, 371, 373, 374, 376, 378, 379
  Derbyshire and S. Yorks, 411–12
  districts, **396–414**
  exports, varieties and destination, 416–417, 802, 809, 812
  historical background, 369–80
  hot-strip process, 407, 408
  imports, varieties, and source, 416
  integrated works, 378, 379, map 397, 404, 408, 409
  Lincolnshire, 408–9
  locational factors, 380, **395–414**
  manufactures, exports, 416–17, 802, 809; imports, 416, 803
  and motor vehicle industry, 414
  Northants and Leics, 412–13
  postwar, 379–417
  raw materials, 380–90, 394–5
  scrap, 395, 414
  in Scotland, 1968 map, 400
  secondary industries, **418–58**
  sources of iron ore, 381–90
  South Lancs and North Wales, 412
  South Wales, 405–8
  Tees-side, 401–3
  trade, 415–17
  West Coast, 403–5
  West Midlands (Black Country), 409–11
  works map, 397
irrigation, 80, 192
Irvine, 132
  wood processing, 146
isotope separation plants, 345

J

jam-making, 193
Jarrow, 429
Jedburgh, 520
jewellery, 472, 486
Johnson, B. L. C., 371
juniper, 141
Jurassic clays, 245, 365
Jurassic period, 10, 18
Jurassic rocks
  Bristol–Mendips, 45
  in chalklands, 50–2
  in scarplands, 46–50

Jurassic scarplands, SE England
  map and sections, 48–9
  physiography, 46–50
jute, yarn and manufactures, exports, 802
  (*see also* hemp and jute)

K

Kainozoic era, 9, 10
Kaldo process, 379
kale, 188, 251
Kay's flying shuttle, 529
Keele, 78
Keighley, 450, 513, 514, 518, 548, 558
Kelham, 220, 329
Kemsley, wood processing, 146
Kendal, 610
  woollens, 498
Kennea, T. D., 254
Kennet–Avon canal, 694
Kent, 186, 190, 647
  orchards and small fruit, 193–5
  paper, 616
  woodland, 137, 138
Kent coalfield, 283, 287, **321–2**
Kerry, Co., **770** *et seq.*
Kersey, 497, 498
Keswick, 359, 364
Kettering
  clothing, 613
  footwear, 609, 610
  iron industry, 412
Keuper marls, 16, 17, 223, 245
  in Midlands, 42, 43
  in NE lowlands, 44, 45
  in Somerset, 46
  water, 100
Keuper sandstones, 17
  in Lancastria, 44
  in Midlands, 42, 43
Keuper (Triassic) times, 10, 17
Kew, 84
Kidderminster, 41, 220, 498, 519
Kidson, C., 93
Kielder Forest, 143, 144
Kildare, 778
Kilkeel, 794
Kilkenny, 768
Killaloe, 782
Killary Harbour, 774
Killingholme, 354, 746
Kilmarnock, 521, 559, 610
Kilroot, 586, 592, 593, 798
Kilsyth, 325, 400
Kimmeridge Clay, 50
Kincardine forests, 137
King's Lynn, 220, 759; sand, 366
Kingston-upon-Hull, 741
Kingswood coal basin, 46, 320
Kinlochleven, 346, 476
Kinvig, R. H. 494
Kirkcaldy, 325, 326, 563, 567, 569–70
knitwear industry, **555–9**
  employment, 557
  fibres used, 557
  hosiery, 556
  location factors, 554–5
  postwar dispersal, 559
Knottingley, 431, 745
krilium, 110

L

lace industry, **559–61**
  centres, 560–1
  employment, 561
Lackenby, 403
Ladybower Reservoir, 99
Lagan valley, 793, 795, 799
Lake District, 359
  copper, 468
  denudation, 34
  drainage, map 34
  physiography, 33–5
  sheep, 203
  water resources, 97
Lake District National Park, 132, 239
Lambeg, 566
Lambourn Downs, 51
Lanarkshire, 324, 563
Lanarkshire (Central) Coalfield, 33, **324–5**
Lancashire, 196
  clothing, 613
  cotton textiles, 526 *et seq.*
  employment 1961 map, 551
  footwear, 609
  iron and steel, 412
  leather industry, 607
  manmade fibres, 555, 576
  paint and varnish, 597
  paper, 616
  rateable value, industry, 623
  rubber industry, 618
  silk, 572
  south, non-ferrous metals, 487
  textile machinery, 438, 439
  woollen textiles, 498, 500, 502, **519**
Lancashire coalfield, 283, 284, 287, **297–301**

Lancaster, 723
Lancastria, Plain of, 186
agric. region, 244
physiography, 44
Land of Britain, The, 104, 156
land classification, **156–8**
land drainage, **92–5**
Act, 94
and flooding, 92
mole, 92
Land Drainage in England and Wales, Cmd 916, HMSO, 92
Land's End, 242, 358
land use, British Isles, **148–59**
statistics, 148–9, 151
land use territories, 158–9
Land Utilisation in Rural Areas, Committee on (Scott Committee), 624
Land Utilisation, Survey of Britain, First, 104, 121, 125, 129, **152–8**, 175, 229, 238
Second, 158–9
lanoline, 504
larch, 123, 143, 145
European (*Larix europaea*) and Japanese (*L. kaempferi*), 143
Larne, 567, 759, 795, 798, **799**
lava, 10, 11, 12
lava plateaus, 21, 29
Lawes, J. B., 581
Laxton, Notts., 163
Lea, R., 97, 99
as London supply route, 693
Valley, 195
leaching, 250
lead, 359, 459, 461, **463**, 465, **466–8**, 474, 602
imports, production, uses, **478–9**
smelting, **470–1**, 478
and zinc ore, 356, 358, 359
Leadenhall market, 682, **683**
Leadhills, 359, 471
Leamington, 446, 455
Leatherhead, 54
leather, imports, 803
leather industry, **604–7**
dressing, 606–7
employment, 600, 601, 605
location, 605, 606, **607**
processes, 604–5, 606
leather manufactures, exports, 802
leather using industries, **608–12**
footwear, 600, 601, **608–12**; employment, 612
location, 608
Leatherhead, 54
Le Blanc soda process, 579, 581
Lee, R. (Ireland), 771, 772
Leeds, 450, 515, **518**, 657
brass, 483
clothing, 613
cloth market, 498
copper, 481, 487
footwear, 609
woollen textiles, 498
Leeds and Liverpool Canal, 532, 694
Leek, 559, 572
Leicester, 41, 386, 455, 520
clothing, 613
footwear, 609, 611
hosiery, 556
knitwear, 557, 558
manmade fibres, 576
water supply, 99
Leicestershire, 245
engineering, 454–5
footwear, 609
hosiery and knitwear, 498, 520, 548
iron and steel, 412–13
Leicestershire Coalfield, 43, 283, 287, **310–11**
Leicestershire granite, 364
Leigh, 299, 547
Leighton Buzzard, 366
Leinster, 762, 778
Leinster Chain, 766, 768
Leinster, Mt., 766, 768
Leiston, 455
Leith, 85, 261, 326, 431, 433, 719 *et seq.*; as seaport, 565, 755
Lerwick, 77, 269, 274
lettuces, 196, 617, 658, 677
Leven, 326
Leven valley, 544, 549
Lewes, 54
Lewis, G. R., 462
ley farming, 176, 213, 235
Leyland, 445
lias, 10, 18, 44, 47, 49, 50
clays, 47, 48, 116
deposits, Bristol–Mendips, 46
limestones, 47, 49, 365
marlstone, 48, 49, 385–7
Lickey Hills, 17, 41, 42, 43
Liffey, R., 783, 785
Limavady, 798
lime trees, 119
Limerick, 772, 783, 784
Limerick, Co., 782

limestone, 18, 356, 359, **364–5**
(and chalk) quarrying, 356, 359, **364–5**
Lincoln, 47, 455
Lincoln Cliff (Edge), 47, 48, 245, 247
Lincoln Vale, 50
Lincolnshire, 186, 245, 247, 248
Holland, 193, 195
iron and steel, 408–9
limestone, 47, 48
scarplands, 47
Lincolnshire Wolds, 51
linen industry, **561–8**
England, 562
centres, 566, N. Ireland map, 567
exports, destination, 567
flax processing, 564
importing ports, 565
Ireland, 563–5; Northern, **566–7**
location factors, 554
present state, 566–8
products, 565
raw materials, imports and sources, 565–566
Scotland, 562–3
linen yarn and manufactures, exports, 567, 568, 802, 812
ling, 126 (*see also* heather)
Linlithgow, 325
linoleum, 570
Linton, D. L., 89
Linwood, 445
Linz-Donawitz process, 379, 413
Lisburn, 566, 567, 798
lithosols, 106
Littleport, 248
Liverpool, 74, 85, 132, 223, 524, 575
brass, 483
cables, 449
chemicals, 581, 584, 585, 586–7; exports, [598
copper, 481
cotton industry, 527 *et seq.*, 534, 542, 545
electrical engineering, 449
food, 615
leather, 607
pharmaceuticals, 597
ship repairing, 433
smelting works, 465, 480
water supply, 97, 99
Liverpool (as seaport) and Merseyside, **717** *et seq.*, **734–9**, 802
commodities imported, 738
communications, 736, 737
development, 734–6
docks and quays, 736
dormitory areas, 736
exports, 738–9
freight traffic decline, 738
industries, 737–8
Irish trade, 735
oil terminal, 736
port map, 737
trans-Atlantic trade, 735
livestock
distribution, **196–209**
farming, 166, 168, 231–2, 251; localisation of, 196
rearing, 214, **215**; England and Wales map, 237;
Highland Zone, 239 *et seq.*
Livestock and Meat Commission, 174
Livingston, 132
Lizard, 242, 358
llama hair, 504
Llandarcy oil refinery, 354, 355, 758
Llandudno, 655
Llanelli, 405, 406, 420, 757
copper smelting, 469
lead smelting, 471
motor industry, 445
Llanharry, Glam., 389
Llanwern (Spencer) steelworks, 408, 757
Lleyn granite, 364
lobsters, 258, 266, 273
Lochinver, 265
lochs, origin, 90
Scottish, hydroelectricity, 346 *et seq.*
locomotive building, 440–3, 450, 451, 452, 454, 455
exports, 442;
destination, 443
map, 441
engines, 451
loess, 25
London, ii, 74
as administrative centre, 665, 675, 685
administrative divisions 1961 map, 666; 1963 map, 668
aluminium, 477
area and definition, 663
boroughs, 664
brass, 483; brassworks, 464
built-up area, 1820 map, 669; 1945 map, 670
City of, 663, **664–5**, 1820 map, 669; markets in, 682
cultural centre, 675, 685, 686
commuting, 667–8, 671–2, 687
copper, 482

London—*contd.*
cotton imports, 534, 542
Country, 663
East End, 665, 679–80
Education Authority, Inner, 664
employment in, 671–2, **673–7**, primary, 674, secondary, 675, tertiary, 675–7
expanded towns, 687, 688
financial centre, 664, 675
flax, linen yarn imports, 565
functions map, 676
fog, 84
food supplies, 668, 670
future development, 685–8
Government Act, 1963, 664
Great Fire, 727
green belt, 668, 687
growth, influence of physical factors, 669–61, map 686
hotels, 666, 685, 686
housing, 665–6, 667, 668, 669, 671, 685
industrial, 665, 666, 667, 675, **677–81**; location factors, 678–9
influence of, 668–9
Inner, 665–7, 671
lead, 479
markets, wholesale, 681–4, 734
Metropolitan Police area, 663, 671
Metropolitan Water Board, 663
neighbourhood units, 687
New Towns, 657, 668, **687**
non-ferrous metal industry, 485–7
offices, 666, 676, 685, 686
overspill, 668
population, 671, changes map, 672, growth, 687
Provision Exchange, 683
rainfall, 77
during Second World War, 684
post-Second World War, 685
suburbs, 667
tin, 480
Tower of, 726
transport centre, 675, 687
water supply, 97, 99
West End, 665–6, 680, 686
woollen textiles, 491, 492, 524
(*See also* London, Greater; London, as port)
London, Greater, 663, 667–9, 671, map **686**
Council, 663, 664
employment, 600
Local Govt. in Roy. Commission on, 663
Plan, 663, 667, 671
London, Greater, industrial areas and industry, 679–81, 687
cement, 678, 681
chemicals, 596, 680
clothing, 613, 679–80
electronics industry, 457
East End, 679–80
electronics, 680
food, 615, 678, 679–80
footwear, **609**
fur industry, 604, 680
furniture, 617, 679
leather industry, 607, 680
leather using industry, 608, 680
Lea Valley, 680
light engineering, 681, 685
motorworks, 681, 685
oil refining, 678, 681, 685
paint and varnish, 597
pharmaceuticals, 583, 597
plastics, 595
power installations, 678
printing and boxmaking, 679–80
rateable value, industry, 623
ship repairing, 734
soap, 596
Soho and West End, 680
Thames-side, Lower, 681
West and Northwest, 681
tobacco, 679–80
transport serving, 677, 678, 679, 680, 681
London, as port, 565, 598, 665, 717 *et seq.*, **725–34**
Authority, Port of, **729** *et seq.*
commodities handled, trade, 731–3
docks, 728 *et seq.*; building, 670; and industries, 677
medieval to 18th century, 726–8
19th century, 728–9
to Norman Conquest, 725–6
oil refineries, 678
oil-terminal, 733
Port of, 727 *et seq.*
Second World War, 733
ship repairing, 734
Tilbury, 84, 733, 734
trade, **717–23**
warehouses and storage, 730–1
London airport (Heathrow), 670, 713, **714–716**
London Basin, 20, 21, 52, 56
agric. region, 252
geology, 55
physiographic regions, 55

London Basin—*contd.*
physiography, 54–6
soil, 116
vegetation, 124, 126
London Bridge, 100, 727
London Clay, 252; in cement, 365
London Transport Board, 663
Londonderry, 775, 786
borough, 791, 799
Company, 791, 796
as seaport, 796, **798**, 799
'long barrow' people, 628
Longbridge, 444
Long Buckby, 611
Long Eaton, 548, 558, 560, 576
Longport, 602
Longton, 602, 603
Lossiemouth, 261, 269
Lothian, West, 324
Lothian, agric. region, 233
Loughborough, 443, 455, 557, 560
Louth, 776, 777
Lowestoft, 261, 264, 269, 270, 431, 759
Lowland Zone, **41–57**
agriculture, 162–4
farming, 238
limit, 26
peopling, 626, 627–8, 629, 631
soils, 116
temperatures, 72–4
Luddite riots, 531
Ludworth Dyke, 293
Lugnaquillia, 767
Luichart, L., 346
Lundy Island, 21
Lurgan, 566, 567
Luton, 365, 445, 447, 455, 613
airport, 713, 714
Lydd airport, 713, 714
Lynemouth, Northumberland, 476
Lynmouth, 93

M

McAdam, 692
Macclesfield, 75, 465, 559
cotton, 548
silk, 572, 573
manmade fibres, 576
Macgillycuddy's Reeks, 771
Machinery, imports, 803
and engines, exports, 802
machinery manufacture 450–55 *passim* (*see also* textile machinery)
machine tools, 450, 453
mackerel, 258, 260, 266, 272
Mackinder, Sir Halford, 1
Maentwrog, 349
Maesteg, 318, 405
Magheramorne, 798
Magnesian Limestone, 16, 293
as mineral resource, 365
in NE lowlands, 44, 45
Sea, 16
magnesium, 589
Maidstone, 616, 617
Main, R., valley, 796
maize, for feed, 226–7
Malin Head, 85
Mallaig, 269, 274
Mallow, 221, 783
Malthus, 637
Malvern, 444
Malvern Hills, 16, 35, 36, 130, 364
Malvernian folds, 46
Man, Isle of, area and population, 8
Manchester, 132, 223, 274, 524, 598
aircraft industry, 447
aluminium, 477
brass, 483
bronze, 484
cables, 449
chemicals, 584, 591
clothing, 613
copper, 482
cotton industry, **526** *et seq.*, 542, **544** *et seq.*
electrical engineering, 449
food, 615
knitwear, 558
lead, 479
motor vehicle industry, 445
pharmaceuticals, 597
as seaport, 719 *et seq.*, **739**
water supply, 98, 99
Manchester airport (Ringway), 713, 714, 716
Manchester, Bolton and Bury Canal, 532
Manchester coalfield, 300–1
Manchester Ship Canal, 355, 542, 584, 585, 738, **739**, map 740
industrial area, 739–40
Manchester and S. Lancashire engineering, 449–50
manganese ore, 359, 394, 474
mangolds, **187–8**
Irish Republic, 782
Lowland Zone, 245 *et seq.*
statistics, 1938 and 1966, 177

Manley, G., 86
manmade fibres, 505, 557, 559, 573, **591–3**, 798
  cellulose and, 591–2
  centres, 575–6, 592
  exports, 812
  location factors, 555, 575, 591, 593
  trade statistics, 576–7
  synthetics, 592–3
  types, 574–5
  use in textiles, **576**
Manningtree, 576
Mansfield, 548, 557, 558
manufacturing industries, miscellaneous, **600–18**
Margam steelworks, 379, 406, 407
  tinplate, 422
Margate, 54, 85, 654
marine platforms, 38
market gardening, 167
  England and Wales map, 237
  Lowland Zone, 248 *et seq.*
  Scotland, 233
market gardening and fruit farming map, 191
market towns, 646
Market Weighton, 47
  Uplift, 48
marl, definition, 111
Marlborough Downs, 51
marram (star) grass (*Ammophila arundinacea*), 131
marshland vegetation, **130–2**
Maryport, 404
match making, 581
Matlock, 359
Mayo, Co., 765, 773, 781
Mayo mts, 767, 773, **774–5**
meat and live animals, imports, 803
meat (*see also* Livestock), 169
Meath, plains of, 216
Medway Gap, 54
Medway, lower, cement, 365
Medway ports, 759
Megalithic culture, 628
Melksham, 494, 618
Melton Mowbray, 246, 386, 611
Menai Straits, 274
Mendip Hills, 17, 46, 47, 48
  lead mining, 463; smelting, 471
  metallic ores, 359
  Uplift, 48, 49–50
Merchant Adventurers, 726, 752, **801**
Merioneth, 473
Mersey, R., 693
  estuary, 595
  mid-, chemical towns, 584–5
  sand and gravel, 368
  tunnels, 711, 737
Mersey Docks and Harbour Board, 736, 738
Merseyside (*see* Conurbations)
  employment in, 445
  motor vehicles, 445
Merstham Dry Gap, 54
Merthyr, 318, 319, 405
Mesozoic era, 9, 10, 19–20
Mesozoic rocks, soils of, 116
metal industries, non-ferrous, **459–87**
  consumption and production, of metals, 475
  decline in mining, 463–4, 468–9, 471
  development to end 19th century, 461–73
  location factors, 460
  manufacturing, 19th century, 471–2; locational factors, 460
  metals and ores, imports, 803; origin, receiving ports, 474
  port locations, 475
  present position, **474–87**
  refineries at ports, 475
  regional summary, 2, 485–7
  smelting, 469–71, 475, 486; locational factors, 460, 464
metallic ores, **357–9**
  in Carboniferous Limestone, 359
  in Devon and Cornwall, 357–8
  in Ireland, 359
  in Wales, 358–9
  occurrence, 357
metalliferous ores, non-ferrous
  alloys, **482–4**, 486
  aluminium, **475–6**, 486
  copper, **480–2**, 486
  employment, export statistics, 486
  home produced, statistics, 473
  lead, **478**, 486
  and metals, imports, 474
  nickel, 484, 486
  to end 19th century, 459–473
  precious metals, 484–5
  tin, **480**
  zinc, **479**
metallurgical industry and chemicals, 588–589
metals
  base, 459
  precious, 459, 486
Meteorological Office, 60, 69, 79, 91
methane gas, 335, 336

Middlesbrough, 598, 723
iron and steel, 376, 387, 397, 402
salt, 360
as seaport, 723, **757**; deep water ore terminal, 393, 396
Middlewich, 584
Midland counties and county towns, 648
Midland Gate, 42, 689
Midlands of England, 27
agric. region, 245–6
coalfields, 310–15; engineering province of smaller, 438, 454–5
definition, 41–2
'islands' in, 41, 43
physiography, 41–4
soil, 42
Triassic plain, 41
Midlands, East
footwear map, 611
knitwear, 557; map 558
Midlands, West
chemicals, 587
footwear, **609**
industry, 444
iron and steel, 409–11
leather industry, 607
leather using industry, 608
motor vehicle components, 446
paint and varnish, 597
rubber industry, 446, 618
Midlothian coalfield, 283, 322, 323; and East Lothian coalfield, **327**
Midlothian–Fifeshire coalfield, 33, 283, 323, 325–6
Milford Haven, 262, 263, 264, **265**, 269, 270, **717** *et seq.*, **758**
oil port, 265
oil refineries, 354, **355**
milk, **166–9** *et seq.*
Cheshire, N. Salop, 244
Highland Zone, 239 *et seq.*
Lowland Zone, 244 *et seq.*
production and distribution, 199
products, 614, 615
Milk Marketing Board, 168, 242
Millar, I. T., 578
Millom ironworks, 404
Millstone Grit, 10, 13–14, 304, 498
in Lancastria, 44
in NE lowlands, 44
Pennines, 39, 40, 98
Millstone Grit streams and
cotton towns map, 538
woollen towns map, 513
Milton, 603
Milton Keynes, 132, 688
Minchinhampton, 495
Mineral and Battery Works, Society of, 464
minerals, production, 356
feasibility of exploitation, 363, 364
Mines Royal Society, 464
mining
coal, 278–9, 290–327 *passim*
employment in, 357
opencast, 288–90
other minerals, **356–68**
Miocene period, 10, 20
Mitchelstown, 783
mixed farming, **217**, 241, 250
England and Wales map, 237
mohair, 504
Moisley, H. A., 521, 575, 592
molinia (*Molinia caerulea*) moors, 130
Molybdenum, 395, 484, 589
Molton, North and South, 496
Mole Gap, 54
Monaghan, 762, 776
Mond Nickel Co., 589
Monkland canal, 694
Montgomery, 241
Montrose, 563
moorland (*see also* heathland), 127–8, 130, 230
moorpan, 126
'mor' (soil), 113
Moray Firth
lowlands, 232, 233
woodland, 142
Morayshire forests, 137, 143
Morecambe Bay, 273
Morley, 514
morphological map, 27
Mossley, 519
Motherwell, 400, 401
steelworks, 324, 397
motor vehicles industry, 443–6
aluminium, 477
amalgamation of companies, 444
bodies and components, 445–6
centres, 445, 455, 456
exports, 446, 447, 802, 809, 812
production, 444
motorcars, exports, 446, 812
Mounfield, P. R., 339, 604, 611
Mourne, mts, 21, 58, 794
Munster, 762
Munster Barrier, 770
Musselburgh, 326

mustard, 614
myxomatosis, 130

N

Nailsworth, 495
Nairn, forests, 137
Nantes, Edict of, 493
naphtha, 354, 583
Nardus (*Nardus stricta*) moors, 130
Nasmyth, James, 450
National Atlas of Disease Mortality, 85
National Farm Survey, England and Wales, 210, 211
National Parks, 132, 133
National Parks Act, 1949, 624
National Parks Commission, 133, 659
National Trust, 659
National Water Policy, Cmd. 6515, HMSO, 91
Nation's Water Supply, The, 95
natural gas, 330–1, **336–7**
  fields, 331
  pipelines, map 336
Nature Conservancy, 133, 624
Nature Reserves, 133
Neagh, Lough, 58, 792
Neath, 318
  copper smelting, 464, 465, 469
Neath, Vale of, aluminium industry, 477
Nelson-Colne, 546, 548
Neolithic man, 119, 628
Ness, Loch, 346
Newcastle, N. Ireland, 794
Newcastle-under-Lyme, 651
Newcastle (Staffs) Canal, 602
Newcastle-on-Tyne, 132, 756
  brass, 483
  lead, 479
Newcraighall, 327
New Forest, 57, 143, 144, 252
  tree species, 142
Newhaven, port, 719 *et seq.*, 751
Newmarket, 51
Newport, S. Wales, 318, 405, 449, 723
  aluminium, 476, 477
  as seaport, **757**, 758
  steelworks, 379, 397, 408, 757
Newquay, 654
New Radnor, 651
New River Scheme, 1606–13, 97
Newry, 794, 798, 799
Newton Aycliffe, 132
Newtown Abbey, 791
Newtownards, 567, 798
New Towns map, 132, **657–8**
  industry, 595
nickel, 395, 459, **484**
Nidd, R., 44
nitrate of soda, 165
Nobel Industries Ltd., 582
non-ferrous metalliferous ores (*see* metalliferous ores, non-ferrous)
non-metallic minerals, **359–68**
  common, 360, 363–8
  'rare', 360–3
Norfolk, 193, 194, 248, 647
  crop rotation, 165
  vegetation, 126
Normans, 633
Northampton, 386, 455
  footwear, **609**, 610, 611
Northampton Sands, 387, 393, 409, 411
Northamptonshire, 48, 49, 245
  footwear, **609**
  iron industry, 375
  iron and steel, 412–13
  leather industry, 606 *et seq.*
North Atlantic Drift, 6, 59–60, 63
Northeast coast engineering province, 438, 451–2
Northeastern lowlands, physiography, 44–5
Northfleet, 449
Northolt airport, 715
North Sea, 7, 21, 266, 270
North Shields, 261, 262, 269
North Staffordshire Coalfield, 41, 42, 44, 283, 287, **301–2**, 601
North Staffordshire
  engineering, 438, 454
North Sunderland, 269
Northumberland, 180
  coalmining, opencast, 289
  forestry, 143
Northumberland and Durham coalfield, 283, 284, 286, **290–6**
Northumberland National Park, 132
Northumbria agric. region, 243
North Wales Coalfield, 35, 283, 284, **302–3**
Northwich, 584, 586, 595
Norway spruce (*Picea abies*), 142
Norwich, 57, 571, 656
  clothing, 613
  cotton and other textiles, 526
  footwear, 609, 610
  woollen textiles, 492, **497**, 498, 501
Nottingham, 41, 451, 464, 548
  clothing, 613

Nottingham—*contd.*
cotton industry, 529
knitwear, 556, 557–8
lace, 559–61
manmade fibres, 576
pharmaceuticals, 597
water supply, 99
Nottinghamshire, 245
and Derbyshire, engineering, 451
lace, 548
woollen textiles, 500
nuclear power, 337, **339–45**
reactors (AGR), 342–3, (Magnox) 340–2
stations, 340–3
Nuclear Safety Advisory Committee, 343
Nuneaton, 558
Nuneaton coalfield, 43
Nuneaton Ridge, 42, 43
nurseries, 153, 154
nylon, **592**

O

oak (*Quercus*) trees, 119, **121–5**, 126, 129, 141
oasthouses, 190
oats, **182–3**
Highland Zone, 239 *et seq.*
Ireland, N., 793, 794, **796**, 797
Ireland, Republic of, 768, 772, 774, 776, 777, 779 *et seq.*
Northumbria, 243
Scotland, 232, 233, 234, 235
statistics, 177
Oban, 269, 274, 759
obsequent streams, 52
Ochil Hills, 521
Offa's Dyke Path, 132
oil, mineral (*see also* petroleum)
imports, 803, 804, 808, **813**
(and gas), **329–31**
oil pipelines, maps 354, 712
oil refineries, map **354**, 746, 747, 750, 755, 757, 758, 785
oil refining, 583, 584, 592
oil, seeds and nuts, imports, 743, 803
oil shale, 330, 356
fertiliser from, 330
Okehampton, 496
Oldbury, 340, 581, 582, 587, 595
Oldham, 450, 546, 547
Old Red Marls, 10, 42
Old Red Sandstone, 10, **13**, 28, 232, 323
in Bristol–Mendips, 46
in Central Lowlands, 33
in Ireland, 58, 782
in Scottish Highlands, 13, 29, 30
in Wales, 13, 36
Oligocene period, 10, 20
deposits, 361
Oliver, J. L., 617
Omagh, 797
oolites, 10, 47, 48, 49, 50
Oolitic Limestone, 18, 49, 116
open field system, 162–4
orchards, **193–5**, 234, 246
siting and local climate, 73
Ordovician period, 10, 31, 32, 33
volcanic activity, 11
Ordovician slate, 364
Orkney Islands, 30, 232
osier (*Salix viminalis*), 125
Ossett, 514
Otford, 54
Ouse Gap, 54
Ouse, R. (Bedford), 50
Ouse, R. (Yorks), 97, 745
Oxford, 456
rainfall, 77
Vale of, 50
Oxford Clay, 50, 365
Oxfordshire, 49
gloves, 613
Oxfordshire Uplift, 48, 49
Ox mts, 781
Oysters, 258, 273–4

P

Painswick, 495
paint and varnish, 587, **597–8**
Paisley, 521, 530, 543, 544, 549, 563
manmade fibres, 576
silk, 571
soap, 596
Paleolithic man, 24, 625
Paleozoic
deposits, 11
era, 9, 10
platform, 28
rocks, soils of, 116
Panteg, 406
paper industry, **615–17**
centres, 616–17
distribution, regional, 616
employment, 601, 616
raw materials, 715, 616
wood pulp for, 142

Par, 361, 759
paraquat, 597
parishes, 643–6
  monasteries and, 645
  names, 643
  origin, 643
  shape, 238, 644–5
Parkhead steelworks, 400
pasture (*see* grassland)
paths, long distance, maps, 132
Patmore, J. A., 708
Peak District National Park, 132
pears, 193
peas, 251 (*see also* beans and peas)
peat, **328–9**; bogs, 112, 780
pedalfers, 103
pedocals, 103
pedology, 104
Pelham, R. A., 492
Pembroke, 85
Pembrokeshire Coast National Park, 132
Penarth, 718, 757
Penmaenmawr basalt, 364
Pennine Uplift, 304
Pennine Way, 132
Pennines, 16, 23, 149
  agric. region, 239–40
  geological sections, 40
  lead mining, 463
  limestone, 364
  metallic ores, 359
  physiographic regions, 40
  physiography, 38–41
  vegetation, 128, 129
  water resources, 97, 98
Pentland fault, 327
Penzance, port, 759
peopling of the British Isles, **625–41** (*see also* depopulation *and* population)
  Anglo-Saxons, 626, 631, 642
  Bronze Age, 629
  cultural zones *c.* A.D. 550, 630
  Danes, 631–2
  emigration and immigration statistics, 641
  Ice Age, 625
  immigrants, Commonwealth, 640
  immigrants, German miners and metal-workers, 464
  immigrants, prehistoric, 626, map 627, 628–9
  immigrants, refugee, 635, 640
  immigrants, statistics, 641
  Iron Age, 630
  Norman times, 633, map 634
  Norse settlements map, 632
  population density, 633 *et seq.*, Domesday Survey map, 634; 1700 map, 635; 1931 map, 636
  Roman times, 626, **629**, 642
  Vikings, 631
permanent pasture (*see* grassland)
Permian period, 10, 17
  limestones, 365
perspex, 594
Perth, 563, 567
Pest Control Ltd., 597
pesticides and weed killers, **597**
Peterborough, 220; bricks, 365
Peterhead, 232, 269, 759; granite, 364
Peterlee, 132, 657
petrochemical industry, **583**, 584, 585–6
  centres, 583, 585, 586, 587
  detergents, 596
  feedstocks, transport, 583
  manmade fibres, 592, 595
petroleum, **353–5** (*see also* oil)
  crude, imports, 278
  exports, refined, 355, 813
  imports, 803
  in iron and steel industry, 381
  in petrochemical industry, 353
  ports, 354–5
  Production Act, 329
  refineries and pipelines map, 354
  refineries, locational factors, 354
  users, 353
Pevensey Levels, 253
Pevensey Marsh, 53, 54
Pewsey, Vale of, 51
pewter, 462, 480
pharmaceutical industry, 582, 583, map 586, **596**; exports, 812
Phoenicians, 461, 462
phosphorus, 581
physical regions, British Isles, 29 *et seq.*
Physiographic Evolution of Britain, The, 90
physiographic evolution, British Isles, 9–25
physiography, British Isles, 26–58
Pickering, Vale of, 50, 247
Picts, 631
pigs, 169, **208**, 214, **217**
  Cornwall, 242
  Ireland, N., 796, 797
  Ireland, Republic of, 768, 772, **781**
  Somerset, 249
  Transitional Zone, 243
pilchards, 272
Pimlott, J., 147

pine trees, 119, **123–4**, 126, 142–3, 145
Corsican (*Pinus laricio*), 143
lodgepole (*P. contorta*), 143
Scots (*P. sylvestris*), 123–4, 128, 141, 145
pipelines, **712**, 755
gas, natural, map, 336
oil, map, 354
Pitlochry, 101
pitprops, 142, 143
plaice, 262, 266, 267
plant indicators, 131–2
Plant Protection Ltd., 597
plant recolonisation, postglacial, 118
plastics, **593–5**
in electronic and electrical industries, 593
employment in, 594
inorganic materials in, 595
location factors, 595
map, 586
production, 593
raw materials in, 594, 595
types and characteristics, 594
uses in industry, 594–5
Pleistocene Ice Age, 21, **22**
effects of, *et seq.*, **24–5**
Pliocene Sea, 21
plums, 193, 194, 195, 246
plungar, 329
Plymouth, 85, 273, 358, 723
Poblacht na h Éireann, 762 (*see* Ireland, Republic of, 762)
podzols, 103, 106, 114
Polar Front, 61–63, 64, 66
Polar Front hypothesis, 59, 61–3
Polden Hills, 46
pollen analysis, 118
Pollock, D., 425
pollution
air, 84–5, 239, 580
water, 95, 96, 596
polypropylene, 592, 593
polythene, 594
polyurethane, 595
polyvinylchloride (PVC), 594
Pontymister, 406
Pontypool, 318, 419, 586, 592
Poole, 361, 604
Poor Law Union, 647; districts, 651
Poppleton, 220
population
density, 634, 635, 636
distribution, changes, 1951–61, map 638, **639**, graph 640, map 660
rural, adventitious, 619
rural, classified, 659
rural-agricultural, 637
statistics, 8, 599, 640, 641
urban, 637; in Rural Districts, 659
working, 599–600, 601
Portadown, 566, 798
Portarlington, 329
Porthcawl, 405, 619
Portishead, 582, 753
Portland, Isle of, 365
Portland stone, 18, 365
Portrush, 798
Ports, 6, 7 (*see also* airports, seaports)
medieval, 692
staple, 801
Portsdown Hill, 56
Portsmouth, 85, 613, 718, 723, 759
shipyards, 432, 433
Port Sunlight, 584, **595**, 738
Port Talbot, 318, 406, 408, 725, 757, 758
copper, 481
iron and steelworks, 397, 406, 407
ore terminal, 393
potatoes, 169, **184–7**, 224, 225
Cornwall, 243
crisps, 224
cultivation, 1966, map, 185
Highland Zone, 243 *et seq.*
Ireland, N., 793, 794, 796
Ireland, Republic of, 768, 772, 773, 774, 776, 777, 778, 779, 1930 map, 780, 781, 782
Lowland Zone, 245 *et seq.*
Northumbria, 243
Pembrokeshire, 241
Scotland, 233, 234
seed, 186
statistics, 1938 and 1966, 177
potash, **361**
Potteries, The, 41, **601** *et seq.*, 694
potter's clay, 356, 602
poultry, 169, **208–9**, 214, 217
broiler, 224
transitional agric. zone, 243
power producing plant, 450
Powis, Vale of, 241
Pre-Cambrian era, 9–11
precipitation, 76–82
Prescot, 449, 477, 481
pressure (*see also* fronts)
high, 60, 62, 63 *et seq.*
low, 60, 62
Preston, 443, 447, 450, 546, 575; as port, 759

Prestwick airport, 4, 714, 716
printing and bookbinding, **617**
  employment, 600, 601
Protection of Rural England, Council for the (CPRE), 659
provinces, 656
Prudhoe-on-Tyne, 587
Pumpherston, 329, 330
Purbeck, Isle of, 20, 51, 56
purse seining, 269
pyrites, 474, 580, 581

Q

Quantock Hills, 38, 46, 242
quartzites, 11
Quaternary era, 9, 10
Queenhithe, 726
Queens Ferry, 582
Queensferry, 326

R

rabbits, 130
Radnor Forest, 241
railways, 294, 689, 690, **697–708**
  amalgamation of companies, 703–4
  coal and, 698
  contraction of network, 708
  effect on industry, 701
  1845–47, 374
  freight traffic, 1962 map, 704
  goods depot location, 701
  growth 1836–44 maps, 699
  and iron working, 387
  marshalling yards, 702
  nationalisation, 707
  passenger traffic 1962 map, 704
  radial webs, 701–2, 703
  rolling stock, 450, 451
  towns created by, 700–1
  and town development, 700–1, 702
rainfall, **77–81**
  and agriculture, 78 *et seq.*
  annual, British Isles, 77, 78
  causal factors, **78**, 81
  limitations imposed by, 78–80
Ramsgate, 54
ranching, 232
Randalstown, 798
Rannoch upland, HEP, 346
raspberries, 193, 233
Raunds, 610, 611
Ravenscraig, 755; steelworks, 379, map 400, 401, 424
raw materials, imports, 803–4 *et seq.*
Rawstron, E. M., 338
rayon, 582, 583, 591–2
Reading, 613, 614
recreation, 101, 132, 239 (*see also* tourism)
Redditch, 132, 443
Redesdale forest, 143
Redhill, 54
Redruth, 358, 480
reed moors (*Scirpus*), 128
references and further reading, **815–34**
refrigerated vessels, effect on agric., 166
  and markets, 227
Reigate, 54
rendzina, 114
Renfrew, 563, 596
residential function, towns, 655
resorts, seaside, 654–5
Resolven, 477
retail function, towns, 653, 654
Rhaetic limestones, 47
Rhaetic period, 10, 18, 44
  seas, 17–18
Rhayader, 98
Rheidol, 340
Rhondda Valley, 317
rhubarb, 192, 244
rias, 355, 770
Ribble estuary, 273
ribbon development, 671
ring netting (fish), 269
River Authorities, 94, 95
River Boards, 95
River Drift man, 625
river system, evolution, 52, 88–90
river transport, 690, 692 *et seq.*
  improvements, 693
rivers
  British Isles map, 89
  England and Wales map, 94
  evolution, 88–90
  pollution, 101
  water resource, 97
road metal, 43, 360, 364, 759
roads, 651, **690–2**, **708–11**
  classification, 709
  freight carried, 708
  macadam, 692
  medieval to 1830s, 692
  modernisation, 710–11
  motorways 1969 map, 709, 710
  Roman, 690

roads—*contd.*
tunnels, 711
turnpike, 603, 689, 690, 692
wool trade, 15th century, 493
Robinson, G. W., 105
Rochdale, 519, 546, 547
woollen textiles, 498
Rochdale Canal, 532
Rochester, 54, 455, 617, 759
rockets and missiles, 447
rocks, 9, **10**
crystalline, 9–11, 35
igneous, 10, 11, 35
metamorphic, 9–11
sedimentary, 10, 11
Rodgers, H. B., 532, 551
Rogerstone, 477
Roman Britain, 626, 630, 633
civil and military districts map, 629, 631
Romans, 369, 461, 491, 620, 690, 725, 746
Romford, 617
Romney Marsh, 53, 54, 253
Romney Marsh sheep, 204, 207
roofing slates, 364
tiles, 366
Roscrea, 783
Rossendale, 546, 551
footwear, 609, 610
Rossendale Forest, 44
Rosslare, 786, 787
Ross-shire forest, 144
Rosyth, 759
rotation of crops, 162
Norfolk four-course, 165
six-course, 232, 233
triennial, 162
Rothamsted Experimental Station, 165, 581
Rotherham, 451
brass, 483
steelworks, 397, 411
Rothwell
(Northants), 610, 611
(W. Yorks), 487
rough grazing, 149, **151** *et seq.*
common, 162
Scotland, 231
Rowley Hills, 364, 410
Royal Geographical Society, 154
Royal Dublin Society, 147
rubber industry, 443, 618
imports, 738, 803
Rugby, 443, **448**, 455
Runcorn, 132, 354, 455, 580, 582, **584**, 585, 586, 595, 607, 739
Rural Districts, 659
rural population, classified, 659
rurban fringe, 159
Rushden, 609, 610, 611
Russell, E. J., 104
Russian Company, 726
Rutland, 48, 245
rye, **183–4**
pre-enclosure, 162–5
whiskey, 184
rye grass (*Lolium perenne*), 129

S

St Austell, 361, 362
St George's Land, 14, 35, 282, 283, 310
St Helens, 465, 469, 470, 477, 481, 579, 582, 584, **590**
saithe, 266, 267
Salisbury, Sir E. J., 123
Salisbury Plain, 50, 51, 56, 173, 250, 628
salmon, 101, 352
salt, 356, 359, **360**, 602
in chemical industry, 580
industry, 585
refined, **584**
salt marsh, 131
sand, 10, 18, 20
in building materials, 366
glassmaking, 366
moulding, 356, 366
sources and use of, 366
sand (and gravel), 356, 360, **366–8**
Sandbach, 584
sand-dunes, 131
Sandiacre, 560, 561
Sandlings, Suffolk, 251, 252
sandstone, 356, 360
for construction, 366
sandstones, 11, 18
Sandy, 248
Sankey Canal, 532, 693
Sanquhar coalfield, 322
sausages, 248; and preserved meats, 614
scallops, 258, 274
scampi (Norway lobsters), 258, 266, 272
Scarborough, 85, 269, 654
scarplands, 27, 46–50
Scarplands and clay vales agric. region, 247–8
Scheduled Territories, 805, 806
Scilly Isles, 84, 195
Scotland
agricultural regions, **229–35**

Scotland—*contd.*
agriculture, 161, 164, 210
aircraft industry, 447
area, 8
barley in, 182, 232, 233
cables, 447
canals, 694
carpet making, 511
catchment areas map, 347
cattle, 198, **202**, 234
chemical industry, 586, **587**, 591
clothing, 613
coalfields, **322–6**
cotton industry, 530, **542–4**, **549**
crofting, 210
dairying, 234, 235
distilling, 223
Electricity Boards, 338
engineering industries, 452–3, 458
explosives, 582, 586
farm holdings, 210
farming, types of, 215, 230 *et seq.*
fisheries, **254–76**
footwear, 609, 610
forests, 137, 144, 233
grassland, 234
HEP map, 347
jute map, 569
knitwear, 557, 558
lace, 561
land use, 149, 175
linen industry, 543, **562–3**
manmade fibres, 592
motor vehicles industry, 445
moorland, 150
oats, 182, 233, 234
orchards, 234
paper, 616–17
peopling, 626 *et seq.*, **636–7**
plastics, 595
population, 8, 640
ports, 754–5
potatoes, 185–7, 233, **234**
rotation grass, 189
sheep, 203, 205, 206, 234
small fruit, 193, 233
soap, 596
sugar beet, 188, 220, 233
tourism, 231
towns, new, 657–8
wheat, 177, 179, 233
woollen industry, 511, **520–1**
Scottish Highlands, 14, 28–30
Central, 28, 29
divisions, 28
in glacial period, 28
granite outcrops, 28
Northwest, 28, 29
soil, 30
Scottish Lowlands
engineering, 452–3, 458
Scots, 631
Scots pine, **123–4**, 128, 141, 142, 145
Scott Report, 95, 624
scrubland, 119, 122, 123
scrub woodland, 137
Sculloghe Gap, 768
Scunthorpe, 385, 393, 396, **408–9**
sea couch grass (*Agropyrum junceum*), 131
sea mists, 84
seaports, Great Britain, **717–61**
for coasting trade, 759
container, 718, **759–60**
deepwater, 725
entrepôt trade, 718, **722**
export trade, direction, and proportion of total, map, 724
ferries, roll-on, roll-off, 756, 759
flour milling, 743
giant vessels and, 725
hinterlands, 761
locational factors, 723–4
major, **717–59**
minor, 759
naval, and dockyards, 759
oil, 718, 725, 736
passenger, 718, 751, 756
staple, 801
tidal graphs, 733
trade, **717–23**
seaside resorts, 654–5
Seathwaite, 77
Seaton, 342, 343
Seaton AGR power station, 344
Seaton Carew, 403
Seend, Wilts, 389
seining, 256–7
purse, 269
Selby, 431, 745
Selkirk, 520
Semmens, P. W. B., 586
serge, 494, 495–6, 497, 519
service industries, **599–601**
Settle, 586
settlements
conurbations, 659–62, map 660
evolution, **642–62**
industrial, 652

settlements—*contd.*
rural, 649
townships, 646–7, 649
urban, functions, **652–53**
valley, 644
villages, 642 *et seq.*, 649
Severn, R., 41, 45, 97, 495, 751
gorge, 43
Severn, sand and gravel, 368
Severn Barrage, 349
Severnside petrochemicals, 583, 586, **587**
Shannon airport, 4, 716, 788
Shannon R., 770, 778
HEP scheme, 351–2, 778, **782**, 785
Shap granite, 364
Shaw, E. M., 78
sheep, **164**, 168, **203–8**, 214, 246, 247
breeds, 165, 206
chalklands of South East, **250**
East Anglia, 251
England and Wales map, 237
Highland Zone, 239 *et seq.*
hill, 215, map 230, 231, 235
Hill Sheep Subsidy, 231
Ireland, N., 793, 794, 795, 796
Ireland, Republic of, 768, 769, **771**, 774, 775, **780–1**; 1930 map, 781, 782
Lowland Zone, **250** *et seq.*
Northumbria, 243
Romney Marsh, **253**
Scotland, 203, 205, 206, map 230, 234
Scottish lowland, 234
Wales, 203, 240–1
wool, 503–4
Sheffield
brass, 483
copper, 482
electroplating, 485
industry, 451
iron and steel, 397, 403, **413–14**
silverplate, 472
water supply, 99
shellfish, 258, 260, 266, 274
Shellhaven, 354, 355
Sheppey, 54
Shepshed, 557, 558, 611
Sherborne, 494
Sheringham, 273
Sherwood Forest, 44, 143, 245
Shetland Islands, 273, 521
shipbuilding industry, **424–35**
Barrow, 431
Belfast, 430–1, 797
Birkenhead, 431
Clyde, 430
employment in, 428
England, east coast, 431; minor centres, 432, 750
geographical distribution, 427–32
historical background, 424–7
locational factors, 424
marine engineering, 434
new types of vessel, 426–7
NE coast, 429
output, leading nations, 1913–68, 435
propulsion methods, 425–6
raw materials, 425
Scotland, minor yards, 431
tonnage launched 1913–68, by class 427, by area 428
as 'trade barometer', 434–5
UK and world graph 1890–1969, 436
ship repairing, 432–4
Shipley, 513
ships, exports, 802
Shirdley Hill Sands, 366, 590
shoddy, **514**
Shoeburyness, 85
Shoreham, 759
Shotover Hill, 50
Shotton steelworks, 379, 397, 424
Shrewsbury, 41
Shrewsbury (Central Shropshire) coalfield, 303
shrimps, 266, 273
Shropshire, 190
coalfields, 283, **314**
lead smelting, 471
Shropshire Union canal, 694, 696
Sidcup, 457
Siemens open-hearth process, 375, 376, 395
silage, 189
silica rock, 363
silicone polymers, 595
silk industry, **556**, **570–4**
centres, 559, 571, map 572
in East Anglia, 571
location factors, 554, 570–1, 572
manmade fibres and, 573
trade statistics, 573–4
silk, yarn and manufactures, exports 802; imports 803
silver, 359, 459, 465, **484–5**
Silvermines mts, Tipperary, 359
silverplate, 472, 485
Sites of Special Scientific Interest, 133
Sitka spruce (*Picea sitchensis*), 142
Sizewell, 340, 342

skates and rays, 266, 267
Skelmersdale, 132, 658
Skinningrove, 402, 403
Skipton, 518, 548
Skye, 29
Slaney, R., 766, 768
slate, 11, 356, 360, **364**
slave trade, 735, 752, 802
Slieve Aughty, Bernagh, Bloom and Slievefelim, 782
Slieve Donard, 794
Sligo Bay, 782
Slough, 457
Slough, trading estate, 658, 677
Sloy, Loch, 349
Smailes, A. E., 467, 639, 657
Small Farmers' Scheme, 173
small fruit (*see* fruit)
smallholdings, statutory, 212
Smethwick
  aluminium, 477
  brass, 483
  glass, 579, 590
Smithfield meat market, 682, **683**
smog, 84
smokeless zones, 85
Snowdon, 12, 78
Snowdonia in Ice Age, 23
Snowdonia National Park, 132
snowfall, Br. Is., map, 79
soap and detergents, 579, 584, **595–6**
social function, towns, 654–5
soda, 579 *et seq.*
sodium carbonate, 579
sodium sulphate, 579
soil, 10, 17, **103–17**
  acid, 113, 114, 128
  aclimatic, 104
  alluvial, 114
  azonal, 106
  boulder clay, map, 109, 113, 128; chalky, 114–15
  brick-earth, 115
  calcareous, 111
  classification, 110–13
  clay, 108, 111, 113–14, 115
  and climate, 103, 109
  creep, 105
  Fenland, 111–13, 128
  fertile, 112
  fertilisers, 110
  and former vegetation, 109
  in geological time, 10
  glacial sands, 115
  gley (glei), 106
  gravelly, 115, 126
  groups, 103, 106
  horizons, 105–6
  humus in, 106, 112
  intrazonal, 104
  iron in, 106
  leaching of, 105–6, 111, 116, 126, **127**
  on limestone, chalk, 106, 127
  loamy, 111
  loamy glacial drift, 115
  maps, 104, 105
  mild humic, 113
  mineral, 110–11; from drift deposits, 113–15; from solid rocks, 115–16
  organic, 111–13, 114
  particles, 110
  peaty and moorland, 113, 116, 127–8
  profile, 105–6
  sandy, 111, 116, 126, 127
  scientists, 104, 105
  series, 107–10
  structure, 110
  texture, 110
  types distribution, 113–16, map 114
Soil Map of Europe, International, 116–17
Soil Survey of Great Britain, 105, 116
soles, 266, 267
Solvay process, 580, 581
Solway Firth, 235
Solway Plain, 239
Somerset, 193, 194, 198
  coalfield, 283, **320–1**
  leather industry, 607, 610
  lowlands, 50
  paper, 616
  woollen textiles, 492, 494
Somerset, Plain of
  agric. region, 249
  physiography, 46
Southampton (as seaport), 717 *et seq.*, **746–750**
  commodities handled, 524, 750
  development, 746–9
  docks, 748–9, 750
  food industries, 615
  freight traffic, 750
  hinterland, 750
  oil refinery, 747
  passenger traffic, 749–50
  port, 747, map, 748
  shipbuilding, 750
  shipyards, 432, 433
Southampton (as staple port), 801

Southeastern Britain
  engineering, 438, 455–6
South East Study (1964), 687
Southend, 457, 617
  airport, 713, 714
Southern Uplands (Scotland), 128, 149
  agric. region, 234–5
  dales, 32
  granite intrusions, 31
  HEP, 349
  physiography, 30–2
  section, 32
South Lancashire coalfield, 298–300
South Shields, 429, 756
Sowerby Bridge, 519, 548
spa towns, 654
Spalding, 220, 248
Spartina townsendii, 131
Speeton Clay, 18
Speke, 445
spelter, 467, 474, 480
Spencer (Llanwern) steelworks, 408, 757
Sperrin mts, 775, 797
Speymouth forest, 143
Sphagnum moss, 92, 128
spirits, exports, 802
Spitalfields, 571, 572, 679, 682, **683**
Spondon, 583, 591
sprats, 266, 272
Springfields (AEA) factory, 345
spruce, 142–3, 145
Stafford, 41, 454
  footwear, 609, 610
Staffordshire, 186, 245
  bricks, 366
  coalfield, South, 42, 43, 283, **312–14**
Staffordshire and Worcestershire canal, 694
Stalybridge, 519, 546, 547
Stamp, L. D., 626, 659, 774 (*see also* Land Utilisation Survey of Britain, First)
Stanlow, 583, 584, **585**, 587, 595
  oil refineries, 354, 739
Stannary Laws, 462, 466
Stansted airport, 716
Stanton, 397, 412
staple commodities, definition, 801
  ports, 801
Stapledon, Sir George, 125, **207**, 232
staplers, 801
steel
  constructional, 450, 451, 452
  uses, **414**
Steel Company of Wales, 407
steelmaking
  electricity in, 401, 405, 414
  history, **375–80**
  location factors, 395–8
  oxygen in, 379, 381
  processes, 375, 376, 378, **379**
  production by districts, 398–414
  products, users, 414, **415**
  scrap in, 378, 395
  works map, 397
steel products
  heavy, 451
  special, 451
Steetley, 365
steppe, semi-steppeland survival in Britain, 129
sterling area, 805, map 806, 807–8, 811
Stevenage, 132, 447, 657, 686, 687
Stewartby brickworks, 365
Stewarton, 559
Steyning, 54
Stirling, Carse of, 234
Stirlingshire, 324
Stockport, 546, 547, 584
  clothing, 613
Stockton, 452
  steelworks, 402
Stoke-on-Trent, 397, 454, 601–4, 618
Stone (Staffs), 603, 609
Stonehaven, 30
Stonehenge, 628
Stornoway, 84, 85, 269, 759
Stourbridge, 362, 590
Stour Gap (Kent), 54
Stour, R. (E. Anglia), 495
Stour valley (W. Midlands), 409
Strabane, 775, 798
Straker, W., 370
Strangford L., 793
Stranraer, 759
Strategy for the South East (1967), 688
Stratford market, 683
Strathmore, 233
strawberries, 193, 248, 252
streams, consequent, obsequent, subsequent, 52
Street, 610
Stroud, 495, 519; valley, 613
subsequent streams, 52
Sudbury, 491, 497, 571, 576
Suez Canal, 3
Suffolk, 57, 194, 647
  vegetation, 126
Suffolk Sandlings, 252

sugar, imports, 803
sugar beet, 169, **188**, 218, **219–21**
in East Anglia, 251
factories, 220–1
Highland Zone, 242
Ireland, Republic of, 188, 221, 782
Scotland, 233
sugar refining, 188, **219–21**, 614, 615
sulphur, 579 *et seq.*
dioxide, 581, 585
sulphuric acid, 579 *et seq.*, 587, 589
Sunderland, 429, 434, 590; as seaport, 723, **756**
sunshine and cloud, 82–3
superphosphates, 165, 581, 582
Surrey, 186, 193, 195
coppice, 138
farming, 210
Sussex, 193, 647
Vale of, 54
woodland, 137, 138, 140
Sutton-in-Ashfield, 557, 558
Swadlincote, 311, 362, 604
Swale, R., 44
Swansea, 267, 358, 406, 420 *et seq.*, 587
aluminium, 477
copper, 481; smelting, 465, 469
as 'metallurgical capital', 471
nickel smelting, 484
zinc smelting, 479
Swansea, as seaport, 318, 718, 757, 758
Swanwick, 252
Swindon, 443, 445, 700, 701
Swineford, 781
Swinnerton, H. H., 96
sycamore trees (*Acer pseudoplatanus*), 142

T

Tadcaster, 223
Tamworth, 444
tankers, oil, **426–7**, 431, 433, 717, 718, 747, 758
tanneries (*see* leather industry)
Tansley, A. G., 120, 122, 126
tantalum, 589
Taunton, 496
Taunton Deane, Vale of, 46, 249
Tavistock, 358, 496
tea, imports, 803
Team Valley, trading estate, 658
Teddington, 729
Teddington Weir, 93, 97
Tees, R., 26, 97
Tees-side
anhydrite, 582
cement, 585
chemicals, **585–6**, 587, 588, 592
engineering, 451
manmade fibres, 576
oil refineries, 757
petrochemicals, 583, 586
shipyards, 429
steelworks, 401–3, map 402
Teifi valley woollens, 519
temperature, British Isles, 71–6
quadrants, 72
range, 74–6
summer, 71, 79
winter, 71
temperature, factors influencing, 72–3, 74
temperature, NW Europe
summer, 64–5
winter, 63–4
tenant farmers, England and Wales, map, 211
Tertiary era, 9, 10, 20
Tertiary rocks
in East Anglia, 57
in Hampshire Basin, 56–7
in London Basin, 54
soils of, 116
terylene, 592
Tetbury, 495
Tewkesbury, 494
textile industries, **488–577**, 798
and chemical industry, 553, 555
cotton (*q.v.*), 525–53
employment statistics, 489, 490
exports, 521–4, 552, 574, 576–7, 809, 812
in foreign trade, 801 *et seq.*, **812**
locational factors (*see* cotton, manmade fibres, hemp, etc., woollen)
miscellaneous fibres, 554–77 (*see* hemp and jute, knitwear, lace, linen, manmade fibres, silk)
provinces, 490
trade, fabrics compared, 1958–68, 577
woollen and worsted (*q.v.*), 491–524
textile machinery, 439–40, 450, 452, 453, 798
exports, 439, 812
Ireland, N., 798
map, Lancs and Yorks, 438
Yorkshire, 450
Thames, R., 50, 51, 55, 90, 93, 97, **99**, **725** *et seq.* (*see also* London, London (Greater) industrial areas, London as port)
embanking in London, 670

Thames, R.—*contd.*
geology, below London, map 727
lower, industry, 365, 681
proto-, 89
settlements, below London, map, 727
shipyards, 432, 433, 434
water supply, function, 90, 93, 97, 99
Thames Basin, 55
Thames estuary, sand and gravel, 368
Thames Haven oil refinery, 354, 355
Thames–Severn canal, 694
Thames-side power stations, 340
Thanet, 51, 54
Thetford, 455, 497
wood processing, 146
Thetford Chase, 142, 143, 144
Thirlmere, 98, 99
Thorne, 431, 745
Thornton, 586
Thurles, 221, 783
Thurso, 232, 759
tidal scour, 6, 100
Tilbury, 84, 729, 733, 734
Tillicoultry, 521
timber
imports, 743
preindustrial use, 134–5
present use, 135, 145–7
processing factories map, 146
resources, UK, 135–45
timothy meadows, 189
tin, 459
'coinage towns', 462
Devon and Cornwall, 461, 462, 467, 468, 469, 471, 473
Elizabeth I to present, 463, 468
imports, 463, 480, 803, 813
industrial uses, 462, 480
manufactures, 462, 480
metal production, UK, 475
mines, location, 461–2
Phoenician traders, 461
Roman times, 461
smelting, 460, 462, **467**, 469, 471
Stannary Laws, 462
12th and 13th centuries, **462**
tin ore, 356, 358, 459 (*see also* tin)
production 1875–1935, 469; 1913–1960, 473; 1967, 474
tinplate, 406, **407**, map **408**, 480
uses, 421
tinplate industry, 418, **419–24**, 467, **480**
localising factors, 418
processes, 421
Tintern, 464
Tipperary, 359, 772
Tirconnail (Donegal), 773, **775**
titanium, 589
tithes, 643, 645
Tiverton, 496, 561, 576
tobacco imports, 738, 752, 753, 755
Todmorden, 546, 548
tomatoes, 73, 195
Topley, W., 370
Torquay, 83, 358, 654
Tortworth Ridge, 46
tourism, 231, 618–22
foreign visitors, 620–1
town and country planning, 655–9
Town and Country Planning, Ministry of, 657
Town Planning Act, 1947, 624
towns
expanded, 687
functions, **652–5**
large, map, 660
market, 650–2, 657
medieval, 650
'new', Middle Ages, 651
New, postwar, 657, 668; population, 687
zones of influence, 657
Trade, Board of, 101, 583, 809
Trade Triangle, 735, 752, 802
trading estates, 658
Trafford Park, trading estate, 658
Tranmere oil terminal, 725, 736
Trans-Atlantic air services, 4–5
'transition metals', 589
transport (*see* airways, communications, railways, roads, waterways)
trawling, 256 *et seq.*, 270, 273
Trawsfynydd, 340, 341
Trent and Mersey Canal, 584, 603, 696
Trent, R., 97, 697
Trent-side power stations, 340
Trias, marls of, 116
Triassic deposits, 16–17, 42
Bristol–Mendips, 45, 46
divisions, 16
period, 10
Triassic (Keuper) period, 10, 17, 42
Triassic Sea, 17
trinitrophenol (TNT), 582
Troon, 431
Trostre tinplate works, 408, 422, 424
trout, 101
Trowbridge, 519
Truro, 358

Tuam, 221, 783
tulips, 248
Tullamore, 783
Tunbridge Wells Sands, 53
tundra, in Ice Age, 625
tungsten, 395, 484, 589; ores, 474
Tunstall, 602, 603
Turkey Company, 726, 801
turkeys, 251
'turloughs', 778
turnips
  Ireland, 772, 782, 796
  Scotland, 232, 233, 234
turnips and swedes, 165, **187**
  Highland Zone, 239 *et seq.*
  Lowland Zone, 245 *et seq.*
  Northumbria, 243
  statistics, 177
Tutbury, 360
tweed (cloth), 520
  Harris, 521
Tweed, R., 511, 520
Tweed Basin, 234
Tynagh, Co. Galway, 359
Tyne, R., 755 *et seq.*
Tynemouth, 77, 85
Tyne tunnel, 709, 711
Tyneside industries
  chemicals, 587
  electronic industry, 458
  engineering, 451
  paint and varnish, 598
  shipyards, 429, 433
  soap, 596
Tyneside ports, 719 *et seq.*, **755–6**
  commodities handled, 756
  docks, 756
Tyrone, 791, 796

U

Uley, 495
Ullapool, 261, 265, 269, 274
Ullswater, 99
Ulster, 762, 791, 792
Unilever, 596, 597
Union canal, 694
United Kingdom, definition, 7
  population, 8
United Kingdom, foreign trade, **801–14**
  with British Empire, 1926–30, 811
  in certain industries, 810–13
  changing pattern, **802–9**
  changing value, 808–10
  coal, 802 *et seq.*, 813
  cotton goods, **802** *et seq.*, 812
  with EEC, 811
  with EFTA, 811
  entrepôt, 814
  exports (value) 1881–1967, 802; inter-war and postwar, 809; 1967, 809; fluctuations, 807, 812
  exports, direction, 811
  exports, invisible, 804, 808
  food, drink, tobacco, 813
  history, 801–4
  imports (value) 1881–1967, 802; interwar and postwar, 808, 809; 1967, 809, 813; fluctuations, 807
  imports, direction, 811
  Industrial Revolution, 802
  iron and steel, 802 *et seq.*, 813
  leather, hides, 801
  manufactures, 812
  metal industries, 812
  with OEEC countries, 811
  post-Second World War, 805 *et seq.*
  raw materials, 813
  sheepskins, 801
  with South (and Central) America, 811
  staple trade, 801
  with Sterling Area, 811
  textiles in, 812
  and trade 'blocs', 805–7, 811
  wool, 801
  woollens, 801, 802, 812
  and world trade, 1913–67, 810
United Kingdom and overseas trading partners, some selected commodities and manufactures
  Argentina, butter, 227; iron and steel, 417; jute manufactures, 570; linen, 568; maize, 227; meat, 227; silk, 574; tinplate, 423; wheat and wheat flour, 226. Proportion of total UK overseas trade, 811
  Australia, butter, 227; elec. mach., etc., 448; iron ore, 392; iron and steel, 417; linen, 568; meat, 227; motor vehicles, 446; poultry, 227; silk, 574; synthetic fibres, 576; tin, 469; tinplate, 423; wheat and wheat flour, 226; wool and woollen goods, 523; zinc and lead concentrates, zinc (spelter) and lead metal, 474. *See also* UK foreign trade, British Empire.
  Belgium, eggs, 227; flax, etc., 566; iron and steel, 416; jute manufactures, 570;

UK and overseas trading—*contd.*
Belgium—*contd.*
textile machinery, 439. Proportion of total UK overseas trade, 811
Bolivia, tin ore and concentrates, 474; tungsten ores, 474
Brazil, cotton, raw, 535; iron ore, 392; jute manufactures, 570; linen, 568; manganese ore, 474; motor vehicles, 446; textile machinery, 439; tinplate, 423
Bulgaria, zinc (spelter), 474
Canada, aluminium, 474; cheese, 227; electrical machinery, 448; iron ore, 391–2; iron and steel, 416, 417; jute manufactures, 570; linen, 568; locomotives, 443; meat, 227; motor vehicles, 446; nickel, 484; silk, 474; synthetic fibres, 576; tinplate, 423; wheat and wheat flour, 226; wool and woollen goods, 523; zinc and lead concentrates, zinc (spelter) and lead metal, 474. Proportion of total UK overseas trade, 811
Ceylon, iron and steel, 417
Chile, copper, 469, 474
China, electrical machinery, 448; linen, 568; silk, raw, 574; textile machinery, 439; tinplate, 423; tungsten ores, 474; wool and woollen goods, 523
Cuba, locomotives, 443
Denmark, bacon and meat, 227; butter, 227; eggs, 227; motor vehicles, 446; poultry, 227. Proportion of total UK overseas trade, 811
East Africa, Commonwealth, iron and steel, 417
Egypt, cotton, raw, 535
Finland, iron and steel, 417
France, bauxite, 474; electrical machinery, 448; flax, etc., 566; iron ore, 391, 392; iron and steel, 416; motor vehicles, 446; silk and raw silk, 574; synthetic fibres, 576; textile machinery, 439. Proportion of total UK overseas trade, 811
Germany, iron and steel, 416; silk, 574; synthetic fibres, 576; textile machinery, 439; wool and woollen goods, 523. Proportion of total UK overseas trade, 811
Germany, West, electrical machinery, 448; linen, 568
Ghana, bauxite, 474
Greece, bauxite, 474; tinplate, 423
Guinea, iron ore, 391, 392
Hong Kong, linen, 568; synthetic fibres, 576; tinplate, 423
India, bauxite, 474; cotton, 535; electrical machinery, 448; iron ore, 392; iron and steel, 417; jute, 568 linen, 568; locomotives, 443; manganese ore, 474; motor vehicles, 446; silk, 574; synthetic fibres, 576; textile machinery, 439; tinplate, 423; wool and woollen goods, 523
Iran, cotton, raw, 535; electrical machinery, 448; iron and steel, 417
Ireland, Republic of, butter, 227; eggs, 227; iron and steel, 417; poultry, 227. *See also* UK foreign trade, British Empire
Italy, cheese, 227; copper and iron pyrites, 474; linen, 568; silk, raw, 574; textile machinery, 439; tinplate, 423
Japan, silk, raw, 574; textile machinery, 439; tinplate, 423; wool and woollen goods, 523
Kenya, electrical machinery, 448
Liberia, iron ore, 392
Luxembourg, iron and steel, 416
Malaysia, locomotives, 443; tin, metal, 474; tinplate, 423
Mauritania, iron ore, 392
Mexico, locomotives, 443
Middle East, crude oil, 353
Mozambique, locomotives, 443
Netherlands, cheese, 227; eggs, 227; electrical machinery, 448; flax, etc., 566; iron and steel, 416, 417; jute manufactures, 570; meat, 227; motor vehicles, 446; tinplate, 423. Proportion of total UK overseas trade, 811 *See also* UK foreign trade, British Empire
New Zealand, butter, 227; electrical machinery, 448; iron and steel, 417; meat, 227; motor vehicles, 446; silk, 574; synthetic fibres, 576; tinplate, 423; wool and woollens, 523
Nigeria, cotton, raw, 535; electrical machinery, 448; locomotives, 443; tin metal, 474
Norway, aluminium, 474; tinplate, 423
North Africa, iron ore, 391, 392
Pakistan, cotton, raw, 535; iron and steel, 417; jute, 568; synthetic fibres, 576; tinplate, 423

UK and overseas trading—*contd.*
Peru, cotton, raw, 535
Philippines, chromium ore, 474
Poland, bacon, 227; eggs, 227
Portugal, tinplate, 423
Romania, maize, 227
Sierra Leone, iron ore, 391, 392
Singapore, tinplate, 423
South Africa, electrical machinery, 448; chromium ore, 474; iron and steel, 417; jute manufactures, 570; linen, 568; maize, 227; manganese ore, 474; motor vehicles, 446; poultry, 227; synthetic fibres, 576; tinplate, 423. Proportion of total UK overseas trade, 811
Southwest Africa, lead metal, 474; tinplate, 423
South America, iron ore, 391
Spain, copper and iron pyrites, 474; iron ore, 391, 392; lead, 469; tinplate, 423
Sudan, cotton, raw, 535
Sweden, copper and iron pyrites, 474; electrical machinery, 448; iron ore, 391, 392; iron and steel, 416; linen, 568; motor vehicles, 446; synthetic fibres, 576; tinplate, 423
Switzerland, silk, raw, 574; synthetic fibres, 576
Turkey, cotton, raw, 535
Uruguay, meat, 227
USA, aluminium, 474; copper, 469; copper metal, 474; cotton, 534, 535, 550; electrical machinery, 448; iron and steel, 416; jute manufactures, 570; linen, 568; maize, 227; meat, 227; motor vehicles, 446; silk, 574; synthetic fibres, 576; tinplate, 423; wheat and wheat flour, 226. Proportion of total UK trade, 811
USSR, cotton, raw, 535; flax, 566; iron ore, 392; manganese ore, 474; textile machinery, 439
Venezuela, iron ore, 392
West Africa, Commonwealth, iron and steel, 417
West Indies, Commonwealth, tinplate, [423
Zambia, copper, 474
Upper Greensand, 50
uranium, 344–5
urban climates, 85–6
hinterlands, 656–7
population, 659
settlements, functions, 652–5
Ure, R., 44
Uttoxeter, 454, 601

V

Valentia, 77, 85
vanadium, 395
vegetables, **191–3**, 243, 247, 248, 251
as field crops, 191–2
freezing of, 192, 251
Lowland Zone, **248** *et seq.*
relation to markets, 192
Scotland, 233
specialised, favourable locations, 192
vegetation, natural (Britain), **118–33**
Atlantic period, 119
Boreal, 119
forest and woodland, 121–5
grassland, 129–30
heather and moorland, 125–8
Iron Age, 119
marshland, 130–3
moorland, 113
postglacial recolonisation, 118–19
preglacial, 25
present day, 120–32
sea coast and sand dune, 131
types, **120–32**
Velindre tinplate works, 408, 422
vicuna wool, 504
Viking invasions, 631
villages, 642 *et seq.*
deserted, 645–6
dry point, 643
nucleated, 162
spring line, 644
wet point, 643
vinyl chloride monomer, 585
viscose yarn, 591
volcanic activity, 11, 12
Vyrnwy, L., 97

W

Wadsworth, J., 80
Wakefield, 450, 514, 518
cloth market, 498
Wales
afforestation, 142, 143, 144
agricultural holdings, 210
agricultural regions, 240–42
agriculture in wartime, 169
aluminium industry, 477
area, 8

Wales—*contd.*
canals, 694
coal, 279 *et seq.*
coalfields: North, 35, 283, 284, 302–3; South, 283 *et seq.*, **319–19**
collieries, closure, 280
copper smelting, 481
farming, types, 237
galvanising, 423, 479
geology, map, 37
glaciation, 23
HEP, 349
iron and steel, 405–8
limestone, 364
manmade fibres, 576, 592
metallic ores, 358–9
peopling, 626 *et seq.*
petrochemicals, 583
physical map, 37
physical regions, 29
physiographic regions, map, 37
plastics, 595
population, 8
rough grazing, 210
sheep, 203, 240–1
slate, 364
tinplate industry, 419–24, 480
town development, 651, 657
water resources, 97
woodlands, distribution, 137, 139, 142
woollen industry, 519
Wales, South
coal basin, 15, 279 *et seq.*
coalfield, map 283, *et seq.*, **315–19**
drift mines, 290
engineering, 456, 477
iron smelters, canals, tramroads 1839 map, 405
iron and steel 1880 map, 406
non-ferrous metals, 487
ports, 757–8
Walker, 429
Wallasey Pool, 736
Wallsend, 429
wood processing, 146
Wallwork, K. L., 532
Walsall, 41, 608, 613
brass and copper industries, 466, 481
Walters, R. C. S., 95
wapentakes, 646
Wark forest, 143, 144
War of Independence, American, 374, 542
Warminster, 494
Warrington, 223, 465, 477, 584, 596, 607
Warwick, 455
Warwickshire, 49, 245
coalfield, 41, 42, 283, 310, **311–12**
(and Leicestershire) engineering, 454–5
Wash, The, 51, 273, 274
reclaimed land, 248
Washington, 132
Watchet, 616
water
'burtonisation', 100
consumption, 91
fluoridation, 100
pollution, 95, 96
power, 100–1, 409, 413, 492, 494, 495–500 *passim*, 529–30
quality, 99, 100
reservoirs, major, 97–99
soft, **492**, 498, **512**, 520, **538–9**, 616
urban supplies map, 99
wheels, 101
Water Power Resources Committee, 101, 345
water resource utilisation, 90–2
areas map, 94
Water Resources Act, 94
water supply, 95–100
artesian, 95, 96
bearing beds, 96
in Second World War, 91
'soft', 98, 99
sources, 95
Waterford, 770, 772, 783, 786, 788
(as staple port), 801
watermills, 492 (*see also* water power)
watershed, definition, 95
waterways
navigable inland 1959 map, 696
for recreation, 101–2
for transport, 100
Watford, 617
Watling Street, 632
Watt, James, 372
Watts, D. G., 406
Weald, 56
agric. region, 253
Clay, 18, 53, 253
Forest Ridges, 53
gaps and gap towns, 54
Greensand Ridge, 53, 54
iron industry, 121, 135, **369–70**, 380
physiographic regions map, 54
physiography, 52–4
sands, 52
vegetation, 127

wealden dome, 20, 52
lake, 18
Wear, R., shipyards, 429
Weardale, 365, 586
weather, 59–87
air masses, 68, 70
British, factors influencing, 59–61, 65, 68
equinoxes, 70
NW Europe, 62–8
Weaver, R., 693
Weaver Navigation, 584
Wedgwood, Josiah, 603, 694
Welland Valley, 48
Wellingborough, Northants, 412, 610
Wellington (Som.), 496, 519
Wellington (Salop), 446
wells, 95, 96
Wells (Som.), 494, 616
Welsh massif
physiography, 35–6
Welshpool, 241
Welwyn, 457, 586, 657, 677, 686, 687
Welwyn Garden City, 132, 597, 658
Wensum, R., 93
Westbury, Wilts, corallian beds, 389
West Bromwich, 443, 444
West Hartlepool, 429
West Lothian, 324
Westport, 775, 781
wet point villages, 643
Wexford (port), 787
Wexford uplands and plains, 58, 765, 766, **768–70**
Weybridge, 93, 447
Wey Gap, 54
Weymouth (port), 759
Wharfe, R., 44
wheat, **177–81**
distribution map, 1931, 178
imports, 743, 803
Irish Republic, 768, 776, 778
limits to cultivation, 179
Lowland Zone, 245 *et seq.*
maximum acreages, 179
New World, 166
Northumbria, 243
pre-enclosure, 162–5
Scotland, 233, **234**, 235
S. W. Lancs, 244
statistics, 1938 and 1966, 177–8
strains, 180–1
wartime production, 169
yield, 165
Wheeler, P. T., 386
Whin Sill basalt, 364
Whinstone, 360
whiskey and whisky, **223–4**, 755, 783, 798, 799
Whitby, 361
White Fish Authority, 275
Whitehaven, 269, 404
White Horse, Vale of, 49, 50
whiting, 266, 267
Whitstable, 272, 273
Wick, 77, 84, 85, 232, 759
Wicklow (port), 787
Wicklow mts, 58, 765, **766–8**, 777
minerals, 359, 629, 768
vegetation, 128
Widnes, 580, 582, 584, 586
copper, 481
Wigan, 299, 546, 547, 584
clothing, 613
food, 615
Wight, Isle of, 20, 51, 56, 57, 718, 723
Wigston, 558, 611
Wigtownshire, 235
Wilde, P. D., 573
Willatts, E. G., 624
Willington Quay, 429
willow (*Salix*), 125
Wills, L. J., 90
Wilton, Tees-side, 583, 585, 586, 592, 595; oil refinery, 354
Wilton, Wilts, 519
Wiltshire, 51
gloves, 613
parishes, 644
woollen textiles, 492, 494
Winchester, woollens, 492
Windrush, R., 495
winds, 60, 84–5
planetary, 59
westerly, 62, 64
Windscale, 345
wine, imports, 813
Winfred Heath, 345
Winnington, 580, 582
Winsford, 360, 584, 586
Wirral, 595
Wisbech, 193, 248
Wishaw steelworks, 324, 401
Wissington, 220
Witham Gap, 47
Witney, 495, 519
wolfram (tungsten ore), 358
Wolverhampton, 41, 575
bicycles, 443

Wolverhampton—*contd.*
brass and copper, 466, 483
motor vehicles, 443, 445
rubber, 618
Women's Land Army, 169
Wood, H. J., 229
wood
imports, 803
processing, 145, 146
pulp, 142, 574
woodland, *see* forestry
Woodchester, 495
wool, **502–4**
imports, 803
merino, 503–4
processing, 503–4
Tudor times, 163
qualities, 503
wool-cards, 498
Wooldridge, S.W., 55, 56, 89, 366
woollen and worsted textile industries, **491–524**
animal fibres in, 504
branches of trade, 507–11
and coalmining, 1921 map, 51
East Anglia, 492–3, 497, 499, 500, 501
employment, 509, 510
export trade, 521–4, 812
geographical distribution, 511–21
historical geography, 491–502
Industrial Revolution, **499–502**
Ireland, 521
Irish Republic, 783
Lancashire, East, 519
Leicestershire, 519–20
localising factors, 492, 493, 494, 495, 496
manmade fibres in, 505
manufacturing techniques, 508–10
mungo, 504
noils, 504
production, 511
raw materials, **502–7**
Scottish Border and Scotland, 520–1
shoddy, 498
specialisation, 16th–18th centuries, 493
Wales, 519
worsteds, original areas, 492–3
Yorkshire and Lancashire, 497–8, 499, 500, 501, 502, **512**
Yorkshire, W. Riding, 499, 500, **501**, **511–19**
West Country, 494, map 496, 499, 501, 511, **519**
woollen manufactures, exports, 802
woollen yarn and manufactures, imports, 803
Woolston, 750
Worcester, 498, 604
Worcestershire, 190, 193, 195, 245
gloves, 613
Workington, 361
steelworks, 379, 396, 397, 404
'worsted', derivation, 492
Worsley canal, 694
Worthing, 54, 73–4, 196
Wotton-under-Edge, 495
Wrekin, the, 17, 35, 41, 42, 43
Wrexham, 449
Wylfa, 340, 476
Wyre, R., 97
Wyre, Forest of, coalfield, 43, 314–15

X

xylonite, 593

Y

Yarmouth, Great, 85, 759
yellow (Muntz's) metal, 471
Yeovil, 456
yew trees, 124, 141
York, 615
woollen textiles, 492
York, Vale of, 45, 90, 245
York Moors, North, National Park, 132
Yorkshire
cotton towns and employment, 548
dales, 44, 243
paper, 616
rateable value, industry, 623
textile machinery, 438, 439
woollen textiles, 493
Yorkshire, NE and E, agric. regions, 246–7
Yorkshire, North Riding
vegetation, 127
Yorkshire, south
engineering, 451
iron and steel, 411–12
Yorkshire, W. Riding, 186
conurbation, 450–1
cotton textiles, 548
engineering, 450–1
footwear, 609
knitwear, 558
leather, 607
manmade fibres, 576; textiles, 555

Yorkshire, W. Riding—*contd.*
non-ferrous metals, 487
silk, 572, 573
woollen textiles, 498, 499, **501**, **511–19**
Yorkshire Dales, 44, 243; National Park, 132
Yorkshire, Nottinghamshire and Derbyshire coalfield, 283, 284, 287, **303–10**; engineering province, 450, 451
Yorkshire Wolds, 51, 247
Ystalyfera, 406

Z

zinc, 359, 459, 467–8, 474, 486
alloys, 482
consumption and uses, **479–80**
zirconium, 589

THE FUTURE OF EARLY CHRISTIANITY

Helmut Koester

ESSAYS IN HONOR OF HELMUT KOESTER

The Future of Early Christianity

Edited by
Birger A. Pearson

In collaboration with
A. Thomas Kraabel
George W. E. Nickelsburg
Norman R. Petersen

FORTRESS PRESS   MINNEAPOLIS

THE FUTURE OF EARLY CHRISTIANITY
Essays in Honor of Helmut Koester

Cover design by Pollock Design Group
Typesetting and book design by The HK Scriptorium, Inc.

Library of Congress Cataloging-in-Publication Data

The Future of early Christianity : essays in honor of Helmut Koester /
edited by Birger A. Pearson in collaboration with A. Thomas Kraabel,
George W. E. Nickelsburg, and Norman R. Petersen.
p. cm.
Includes bibliographical references and indexes.
ISBN 0-8006-2521-8 (alk. paper)
1. Bible. N.T.—Criticism, interpretation, etc. 2. Church history—Primitive and early church, ca. 30–600. 3. Bible. N.T.—Antiquities. 4. Judaism—History—Post-exilic period, 586 B.C.–210 A.D. 5. Christian literature, Early—History and criticism. 6. Gnosticism. I. Koester, Helmut, 1926– . II. Pearson, Birger Albert. III. Kraabel, A. Thomas. IV. Nickelsburg, George W. E., 1934– . V. Petersen, Norman R., 1933– .
BS2395.F87 1991
270.1—dc20 91-31975
CIP

The paper used in this publication meets the minimum requirements of American National Standard for Information Sciences—Permanence of Paper for Printed Library Materials, ANSI Z329.48–1984.

Manufactured in the U.S.A. AF 1-2521

94 93 92 91 1 2 3 4 5 6 7 8 9 10

Contents

Preface xi

Curriculum Vitae of Helmut Koester xi

Contributors xiii

Abbreviations xvi

Introduction
Birger A. Pearson 1

Part One
The Environment of Early Christianity

1. Early Christianity as a Religious-Historical Phenomenon
   Kurt Rudolph 9

2. Reflections of a New Testament Scholar on Plutarch's Tractates *De Alexandri Magni Fortuna aut Virtute*
   Dieter Georgi 20

3. New Testament Papyrus Manuscripts and Letter Carrying in Greco-Roman Times
   Eldon Jay Epp 35

4. The Godlessness of Germans Living by the Sea according to Philo of Alexandria
   Dieter Lührmann 57

5. The Messianic Banquet Reconsidered
   Dennis E. Smith 64

Part Two
Archaeology and Early Christianity

6. The Bethsaida Excavations: Historical and Archaeological Approaches
Heinz-Wolfgang Kuhn and Rami Arav 77

7. Archaeology and Eschatology at Thessalonica
Holland Lee Hendrix 107

Part Three
Ancient Judaism

8. Moses Servant of God and the Servants: Text and Tradition in the Prayer of Nehemiah (Neh 1:5–11)
Klaus Baltzer 121

9. Philo and the Sabbath Crisis: Alexandrian Jewish Politics and the Dating of Philo's Works
Robert A. Kraft 131

10. The Tests of the Twelve Patriarchs: Forensic Rhetoric in Josephus's *Antiquities of the Jews* 2.7–200
Wilfred F. Bunge 142

11. Iael Προστάτης in the Jewish Donative Inscription from Aphrodisias
Bernadette J. Brooten 149

12. Adolf Harnack's "The Mission and Expansion of Judaism": Christianity Succeeds Where Judaism Fails
Shaye J. D. Cohen 163

Part Four
New Testament

13. The Q Trajectory: Between John and Matthew via Jesus
James M. Robinson 173

14. *Logoi Prophētōn?* Reflections on the Genre of Q
Richard Horsley 195

15. The Divinization of Disorder: The Trajectory of Matt 8:20//Luke 9:58//*Gos. Thom.* 86
Robert Doran 210

16. The Apocalyptic Son of Man Sayings
Adela Yarbro Collins 220

17. The Antithetic Saying in Mark 16:16: Formal and Redactional Features
Paul Allan Mirecki 229

18. *Secret Mark* and the History of Canonical Mark
Philip Sellew 242

19. The Sermon on the Mount in Matthew's Interpretation
Hans Dieter Betz 258

20. The God-fearers Meet the Beloved Disciple
A. Thomas Kraabel 276

21. Salvation Is *for* the Jews: Secret Christian Jews in the Gospel of John
Sarah J. Tanzer 285

22. Contending with God: The Death of Jesus and the Trial of Israel in Luke-Acts
David L. Tiede 301

23. Community of Goods in Acts: Idealization or Social Reality?
S. Scott Bartchy 309

24. Four Problems in the Life of Paul Reconsidered
Hans-Martin Schenke 319

25. The Man from Heaven in Paul's Letter to the Philippians
Wayne A. Meeks 329

26. On the Ending(s) to Paul's Letter to Rome
Norman R. Petersen 337

27. The Incarnation: Paul's Solution to the Universal Human Predicament
George W. E. Nickelsburg 348

28. The Revelation of John and Pauline Theology
Eduard Lohse 358

29. A Genre for 1 John
Julian V. Hills 367

Part Five
Early Christian Literature

30. The *Gospel of Thomas* and Christian Origins
Ron Cameron 381

31. The Suspension of Time in Chapter 18 of *Protevangelium Jacobi*
François Bovon 393

32. "Masculine Fellowship" in the *Acts of Thomas*
Harold W. Attridge 406

33. "Seneca" on Paul as Letter Writer
Abraham J. Malherbe 414

34. God Language in Ignatius of Antioch
Bishop Demetrios Trakatellis 422

Part Six
Gnosticism

35. New Testament Christologies in Gnostic Transformation
Pheme Perkins 433

36. The "Mystery of Marriage" in the *Gospel of Philip* Revisited
Elaine H. Pagels 442

37. Pre-Valentinian Gnosticism in Alexandria
Birger A. Pearson 455

Epilogue: Current Issues in New Testament Scholarship
Helmut Koester 467

Bibliography of Helmut Koester
David M. Scholer 477

Index of Ancient Sources 488

Index of Modern Authors 505

Preface

THIS BOOK HAD its inception during the course of the Annual Meeting of the Society of Biblical Literature and the American Academy of Religion held in Atlanta, Georgia, in late November 1986. An informal discussion among old friends from graduate student days at Harvard University turned to the subject of Helmut Koester, and the appropriateness of someone arranging for a Festschrift in his honor to celebrate his sixty-fifth birthday some five years thence. A meeting was arranged with Harold W. Rast, then Director of Fortress Press, in the Fortress Press hotel suite, with A. Thomas Kraabel, George Nickelsburg, Norman Petersen, and myself participating. Dr. Rast, on behalf of Fortress Press, offered to publish such a Festschrift. During this and other planning sessions it was proposed that I be the editor of the Festschrift, with the promise of the collaboration of Kraabel, Nickelsburg, and Petersen. We began to put together a list of scholars who might be invited to contribute, and also discussed the possible shape of the book. A tentative title was also agreed upon: "The Future of Early Christianity." We set as our goal to present the Festschrift to Prof. Koester sometime during the course of the 1991 Annual Meeting of the Society of Biblical Literature. Of course, we could not know at the time that Helmut Koester would be the President of the Society of Biblical Literature at that 1991 meeting!

In my letter inviting contributions, sent out early in 1987, I included the following paragraph:

> The volume that we propose to publish will be broad-ranging in its scope, as befits the range of Helmut Koester's contributions to scholarship in the field of New Testament and early Christianity. As you know, these contributions have illuminated such diverse areas as gospels and gospel traditions, the Pauline epistles, the problem of theological diversity in early Christianity, and archeological evidences for early Christian history. We hope that the volume to be published in his honor will serve as a statement of the current state of scholarship on key areas of early Christianity, and also serve as a pointer toward the future of scholarship in the field. Following a suggestion made by Norman Petersen, we propose to entitle the Koester Festschrift "The Future of Early Christianity."

The readers of this book will have to judge for themselves how well this project has succeeded.

It is my pleasant duty here to acknowledge with thanks those who have assisted me in bringing this project to fruition. First of all, I wish to thank all of the contributors, without whose articles there would have been no book at all. My collaborators, A. Thomas Kraabel, George W. E. Nickelsburg, and Norman R. Petersen, have been of enormous help to me. Each has read and commented on a portion of the articles submitted and has been otherwise involved in the work of planning and executing this book. To my old Harvard schoolmates, I tender my sincere thanks.

I also want to acknowledge here the assistance I have received from some of my students at UCSB. Robert Petty produced the English translation of H.-W. Kuhn's contribution on Bethsaida, submitted in German. Kristen Wilson assisted me in some of the early stages of the editing process. Bradley Hawkins created both the table of abbreviations and the indexes for the book. To all of them I offer my hearty thanks. Nor should I omit to mention here the support for this project that I have received from my university: research grants from the UCSB Academic Senate, and secretarial assistance, postage, and other administrative assistance from the Department of Religious Studies. (Additional acknowledgments from individual contributors are found in notes to some of the articles in this book.)

Finally, I wish to acknowledge the various people associated with Fortress Press, the publishers of this book. I have already mentioned Harold Rast, former Director of Fortress Press, whose initial encouragement got the project started. His successors at Fortress Press, the late John A. Hollar, and the current Director, Marshall D. Johnson, have continued to support and encourage the work. J. Michael West, Senior Editor at Fortress Press, has been the person in the press's administration most closely involved with the process of publishing the book. Maurya P. Horgan and Paul J. Kobelski of The HK Scriptorium, Inc., have done the copyediting and typesetting for the book. To all of them, and to the Fortress Press staff, I offer my heartiest thanks and congratulations for a publication of very high quality.

As the book was in production an epilogue was added to it at the suggestion of Michael West: an address given by Helmut Koester to a group of Lutheran professors at the 1990 Annual Meeting of the Society of Biblical Literature in New Orleans on the topic "Current Issues in New Testament Scholarship." Thus, appropriately enough though unbeknownst to him until the publication of this book, our jubilarian has the final word in his own Festschrift.

To our friend Helmut Koester: εἰς ἔτη πολλά, φίλε.

Birger A. Pearson
The University of California, Santa Barbara

Curriculum Vitae of Helmut Koester

HELMUT KOESTER was born December 18, 1926, in Hamburg, Germany, the son of Karl Köster (architect) and Marie-Luise née Eitz. He has one brother, Reinhard, a sociologist and pastor in Essen, Germany. He attended primary and secondary schools in Hamburg (1933–36) and Berlin (1936–43). He served in the German armed forces from 1943 to 1945, when he was taken prisoner by the American forces shortly before the end of World War II. He married Gisela G. Harrassowitz in 1953. They have four children: Reinhild (b. 1956), Almut (1958), Ulrich (1962), and Heiko (1966).

Koester studied theology under Rudolf Bultmann in the University of Marburg (1945–50) and took his first theological examination at Marburg in 1950. He served as Vicar (intern pastor) in the Lutheran Church of Hannover (1951–54). He took his second theological examination in the Lutheran Church of Hannover in 1954 and was ordained to the Lutheran ministry in 1956.

He received his Doctor of Theology degree at the University of Marburg in 1954, with a dissertation on synoptic traditions in the Apostolic Fathers (published in 1957; see bibliography). He served as research and teaching assistant to Professor Günther Bornkamm at the University of Heidelberg (1954–56) and submitted his Habilitation dissertation in 1956. He was Privatdozent (assistant professor) in the University of Heidelberg from 1956 to 1959, interrupted by a year of teaching as a visiting assistant professor at Harvard University Divinity School, Cambridge, Massachusetts (1958–59). He returned to Harvard in 1959 as an associate professor, and he has been at Harvard ever since. Named John H. Morison Professor of New Testament Studies in 1963 and Winn Professor of Ecclesiastical History in 1968, he continues to hold both chairs. In 1963 he went back to Heidelberg as a visiting professor. He has also been a visiting professor at Drew University and the University of Minnesota (1990).

Fellowships and awards include a Guggenheim fellowship (1964–65); American Council of Learned Societies fellowships (1971–72 and 1978–79);

and a research fellowship in the American School of Classical Studies in Athens (1978–79). In 1981 he gave the Schaeffer Lectures at Yale University, and in 1986 he gave the Sigmund Mowinckel Lectures at the University of Oslo, Norway. He was awarded the honorary degree of Doctor of Theology at the University of Geneva, Switzerland, in 1989.

Koester is a Fellow of the American Academy of Sciences, and a member of the Societas Novi Testamenti Studiorum, the American Schools of Oriental Research, the Society of Biblical Literature (President 1990–91), and the Institute for Antiquity and Christianity of the Claremont Graduate School (Claremont, Calif.).

Since 1975 he has served as editor of *Harvard Theological Review.* He is also chairman of the New Testament section of the editorial board of the Hermeneia commentary series (Fortress Press), editor (with Holland Hendrix) of *Archaeological Resources for New Testament Studies,* director of the Research Team on Religion and Culture of the New Testament Lands (ASOR/Harvard Divinity School), and coeditor of the *Encyclopedia of Archaeology in the Biblical World* (Oxford University Press).

Professor Koester's fields of teaching and research at Harvard include New Testament exegesis and theology, history of ancient Christianity, Hellenistic religions, Greek, and archaeology. His interest in archaeology was stimulated by his sojourn in Athens as a research fellow at the American School (1978–79). Since his arrival at Harvard University he has directed a great number of doctoral dissertations. His numerous publications are listed in the bibliography prepared for this volume by David M. Scholer.

His avocations, which he shares with his wife, Gisela, are chamber music (violin), gardening (mostly vegetables), hiking, and camping.

Contributors

Rami Arav
Research Associate of Zinman Institute of Archaeology
University of Haifa
Haifa, Israel

Harold W. Attridge
Professor of New Testament
Department of Theology, University of Notre Dame
Notre Dame, Indiana

Klaus Baltzer
Professor of Old Testament Theology
Evangelisch-Theologische Fakultät, Universität München
Munich, Germany

S. Scott Bartchy
Adjunct Associate Professor of History
University of California
Los Angeles, California

Hans Dieter Betz
Shailer Mathews Professor of New Testament Studies
The Divinity School and The Division of the Humanities
The University of Chicago
Chicago, Illinois

François Bovon
Professor of New Testament
Faculté Autonome de Théologie Protestante
Université de Genève
Geneva, Switzerland

Bernadette J. Brooten
Associate Professor of Scripture and Interpretation
Harvard University Divinity School
Cambridge, Massachusetts

Wilfred F. Bunge
Professor of Religion and Classics
Luther College
Decorah, Iowa

Ron Cameron
Associate Professor of Religion
Wesleyan University
Middletown, Connecticut

Shaye J. D. Cohen
Ungerleider Professor of Judaic Studies
Brown University
Providence, Rhode Island

Adela Yarbro Collins
Professor of New Testament
The Divinity School, The University of Chicago
Chicago, Illinois

Robert Doran
Professor of Religion
Amherst College
Amherst, Massachusetts

Eldon Jay Epp
Harkness Professor of Biblical Literature
Case Western Reserve University
Cleveland, Ohio

Dieter Georgi
Professor of New Testament Theology and Dean
Fachbereich Evangelische Theologie
Johann Wolfgang Goethe-Universität Frankfurt am Main
Frankfurt, Germany

Holland Lee Hendrix
President
Union Theological Seminary
New York, New York

Julian V. Hills
Assistant Professor of Theology
Marquette University
Milwaukee, Wisconsin

Richard Horsley
Professor of Religion
Study of Religion Program, University of Massachusetts
Boston, Massachusetts

A. Thomas Kraabel
Qualley Professor of Classics and Dean of the College
Luther College
Decorah, Iowa

Robert A. Kraft
Professor of Religious Studies
University of Pennsylvania
Philadelphia, Pennsylvania

Heinz-Wolfgang Kuhn
Professor of New Testament Theology
Evangelisch-Theologische Fakultät, Universität München
Munich, Germany

Eduard Lohse
Professor of New Testament Theology, Emeritus
Bishop of the Evangelical Church of Hannover, ret.
Göttingen, Germany

Dieter Lührmann
Professor of New Testament Theology
Fachbereich Evangelische Theologie
Philipps-Universität Marburg
Marburg, Germany

Abraham J. Malherbe
Buckingham Professor of New Testament
The Divinity School, Yale University
New Haven, Connecticut

Wayne A. Meeks
Woolsey Professor of Biblical Studies
Department of Religious Studies
Yale University
New Haven, Connecticut

Paul Allan Mirecki
Assistant Professor of Religious Studies
University of Kansas
Lawrence, Kansas

George W. E. Nickelsburg
Professor of Religion
School of Religion, University of Iowa
Iowa City, Iowa

Elaine H. Pagels
Harrington Spear Paine Professor of Religion
Princeton University
Princeton, New Jersey

Birger A. Pearson
Professor of Religious Studies
University of California
Santa Barbara, California

Pheme Perkins
Professor of New Testament Theology
Boston College
Chestnut Hill, Massachusetts

Norman R. Petersen
Washington Gladden Professor of Religion
Williams College
Williamstown, Massachusetts

James M. Robinson
Arthur Letts Jr. Professor of Religion and Dept. Chairman
Director, Institute for Antiquity and Christianity
The Claremont Graduate School
Claremont, California

Kurt Rudolph
Professor of the History of Religions
Philipps Universität Marburg
Marburg, Germany

Hans-Martin Schenke
Professor of New Testament Theology
Humboldt Universität Berlin
Berlin, Germany

David M. Scholer
Distinguished Professor of New Testament and Early Church History
North Park College and Theological Seminary
Chicago, Illinois

Philip Sellew
Associate Professor of Classical and Near Eastern Studies
University of Minnesota
Minneapolis, Minnesota

Dennis E. Smith
Associate Professor of New Testament
Phillips Graduate Seminary
Enid, Oklahoma

Sarah J. Tanzer
Associate Professor of Judaism and Christian Origins
McCormick Theological Seminary
Chicago, Illinois

David L. Tiede
Professor of New Testament and President
Luther Northwestern Theological Seminary
Saint Paul, Minnesota

Demetrios Trakatellis
Bishop of Vresthena
Distinguished Professor of Biblical Studies and Christian Origins
Holy Cross School of Theology
Brookline, Massachusetts

Abbreviations

AASOR	*Annual of the American Schools of Oriental Research*
AB	Anchor Bible
ACW	Ancient Christian Writers
AJA	*American Journal of Archaeology*
AnBib	Analecta Biblica
ANET	*Ancient Near Eastern Texts,* ed. J. B. Pritchard (Princeton: Princeton University Press, 1950)
ANRW	*Aufstieg und Niedergang der römischen Welt,* ed. H. Temporini and W. Haase (Berlin and New York: de Gruyter)
APOT	*Apocrypha and Pseudepigrapha of the Old Testament,* ed. R. H. Charles, 2 vols. (Oxford: Clarendon Press, 1913)
ASORDS	American Schools of Oriental Research Dissertation Series
ATD	Das Alte Testament Deutsch
BA	*Biblical Archaeologist*
BAC	Biblioteca de autores cristianos
BAG	W. Bauer, W. F. Arndt, and F. W. Gingrich, *Greek-English Lexicon of the New Testament and Other Early Christian Literature* (Chicago: University of Chicago Press, 1952)
BAR	*Biblical Archaeologist Reader*
BBB	Bonner biblische Beiträge
BCH	*Bulletin de Correspondance Hellénique*
BCNH	Bibliothèque copte de Nag Hammadi
BDF	F. Blass, A. Debrunner, and R. W. Funk, *A Greek Grammar of the New Testament and Other Early Christian Literature* (Chicago: University of Chicago Press, 1961)
BETL	Bibliotheca ephemeridum theologicarum lovaniensium
BG	(Codex) Berolinensis Gnosticus
BGU	*Ägyptische Urkunden aus den Kgl. Museen zu Berlin*
BHT	Beiträge zur historischen Theologie
Bib	*Biblica*
BJRL	*Bulletin of the John Rylands University Library of Manchester*
BJS	Brown Judaic Studies
BMCI	*The Collection of Ancient Greek Inscriptions in the British Museum*

BMCRE	*The Coins of the Roman Empire in the British Museum*
BZ	*Biblische Zeitschrift*
BZAW	Beihefte zur ZAW
CBQ	*Catholic Biblical Quarterly*
CG	(Codex) Cairensis Gnosticus (=NHC)
CIG	*Corpus inscriptionum graecarum*
CII	J.-B. Frey, *Corpus inscriptionum iudaicarum,* 2 vols. (Vatican City: Institute of Christian Archaeology, 1936, 1952)
CPJ	*Corpus Papyrorum Judaicarum,* ed. V. A. Tcherikover and A. Fuks, 3 vols. (Cambridge, Mass.: Harvard University Press, 1957–64)
CRAI	*Comptes Rendus de l'Académie des Inscriptions et Belles-Lettres*
CRINT	Compendia Rerum Iudaicarum ad Novum Testamentum
CSCO	Corpus scriptorum christianorum orientalium
Ebib	Etudes bibliques
EJ	*Encyclopaedia Judaica* (Jerusalem: Encyclopaedia Judaica; New York: Macmillan, 1971)
EKKNT	Evangelisch-katholischer Kommentar zum Neuen Testament
ER	*Encyclopedia of Religion*
ETL	*Ephemerides theologicae lovanienses*
EvT	*Evangelische Theologie*
FBBS	Facet Books, Biblical Series
FRLANT	Forschungen zur Religion und Literatur des Alten und Neuen Testaments
GAASG	Vetus Testamentum Graecum, Auctoritate Academiae Scientiarum Gottingensis editum
GCS	Griechische christliche Schriftsteller
GNS	Good News Studies
GOTR	*Greek Orthodox Theological Review*
GPM	*Göttinger Predigmeditationen*
GRBS	*Greek, Roman, and Byzantine Studies*
GTA	*Göttinger theologische Arbeiten*
HAT	*Handbuch zum Alten Testament*
HDB	*Harvard Divinity Bulletin*
HDR	Harvard Dissertations in Religion
HNT	Handbuch zum Neuen Testament
HNTC	Harper's NT Commentaries
HR	*History of Religions*
HTCNT	Herder's Theological Commentary on the New Testament
HTKNT	Herders theologischer Kommentar zum Neuen Testament
HTR	*Harvard Theological Review*
HTS	Harvard Theological Studies
HUCA	*Hebrew Union College Annual*
HUT	Hermeneutische Untersuchungen zur Theologie
ICC	International Critical Commentary

IEJ	*Israel Exploration Journal*
Int	*Interpretation*
JBL	*Journal of Biblical Literature*
JEH	*Journal of Ecclesiastical History*
JETS	*Journal of the Evangelical Theological Society*
JJS	*Journal of Jewish Studies*
JPOS	*Journal of the Palestine Oriental Society*
JRS	*Journal of Roman Studies*
JSNT	*Journal for the Study of the New Testament*
JSNTSup	Journal for the Study of the New Testament—Supplement Series
JTC	*Journal for Theology and the Church*
JTS	*Journal of Theological Studies*
KAT	Kommentar zum Alten Testament
KEK	Kritisch-exegetischer Kommentar über das Neue Testament (Meyer)
Koester, *Introduction*	Helmut Koester, *Introduction to the New Testament.* Vol. 1: *History, Culture and Religion of the Hellenistic Age.* Vol. 2: *History and Literature of Early Christianity* (Berlin and New York: de Gruyter, 1982)
LCL	Loeb Classical Library
LPGL	*A Patristic Greek Lexicon,* ed. G. W. H. Lampe (Oxford: Clarendon, 1961)
LSJ	Liddell-Scott-Jones, *A Greek-English Lexicon* (Oxford: Clarendon, 1925–40)
MAMA	*Monumenta Asiae Minoris Antiqua*
MGWJ	*Monatsschrift für Geschichte und Wissenschaft des Judentums*
MT	Masoretic Text
NCB	New Century Bible
NHC	Nag Hammadi Codex (= CG)
NHS	Nag Hammadi Studies
NovT	*Novum Testamentum*
NovTSup	*Novum Testamentum,* Supplements
NPNF	Nicene and Post-Nicene Fathers
NRSV	New Revised Standard Version
NTApoc	*New Testament Apocrypha,* ed. E. Hennecke and W. Schneemelcher, trans. R. M. Wilson, 2 vols. (Philadelphia: Westminster, 1964)
NTD	Das Neue Testament Deutsch
NTS	*New Testament Studies*
OLP	*Orientalia lovaniensia periodica*
OLZ	*Orientalische Literaturzeitung*
OTP	*The Old Testament Pseudepigrapha,* ed. J. H. Charlesworth, 2 vols. (Garden City, N.Y.: Doubleday, 1983, 1985)
PEFQS	*Palestine Exploration Fund, Quarterly Statement*

PG	*Patrologiae cursus completus. Series graeca,* ed. J. P. Migne, 161 vols. (Paris, 1857–66)
PL	*Patrologiae cursus completus. Series latina,* ed. J. P. Migne, 221 vols. (Paris, 1844–64)
PO	Patrologia orientalis
PTS	Patristische Texte und Studien
PW	Pauly-Wissowa, *Real-Encyclopädie der classischen Altertumswissenschaft* (Stuttgart: Metzler, 1893)
PWSup	Supplement to PW
RAC	*Reallexikon für Antike und Christentum*
REG	*Revue des études grecques*
RGG	*Die Religion in Geschichte und Gegenwart,* ed. K. Galling, 3rd ed., 7 vols. (Tübingen: Mohr-Siebeck, 1957–65)
RHPR	*Revue d'histoire et de philosophie religieuses*
Robinson-Koester, *Trajectories*	James M. Robinson and Helmut Koester, *Trajectories through Early Christianity* (Philadelphia: Fortress Press, 1971)
RSR	*Recherches de science religieuse*
RSRev	*Religious Studies Review*
RSV	Revised Standard Version
RTP	*Revue de théologie et de philosophie*
SAC	Studies in Antiquity and Christianity
SBB	Stuttgarter biblische Beiträge
SBLDS	Society of Biblical Literature Dissertation Series
SBLMS	SBL Monograph Series
SBLSBS	SBL Sources for Biblical Study
SBLSP	SBL Seminar Papers
SBT	Studies in Biblical Theology
SC	Sources chrétiennes
SCHNT	Studia ad Corpus Hellenisticum Novi Testamenti
SD	Studies and Documents
SEG	*Supplementum Epigraphicum Graecum*
SHR	Studies in the History of Religions (Supplements to *Numen*)
SJLA	Studies in Judaism in Late Antiquity
SNTSMS	Society for New Testament Studies Monograph Series
ST	*Studia theologica*
Str-B	H. L. Strack and P. Billerbeck, *Kommentar zum Neuen Testament aus Talmud und Midrasch,* 6 vols. (Munich: Beck, 1922–61)
SUNT	Studien zur Umwelt des Neuen Testaments
TAPA	*Transactions of the American Philological Association*
TBü	*Theologische Bücherei*
TDNT	*Theological Dictionary of the New Testament,* ed. G. Kittel, G. Friedrich, and G. Bromiley. 10 vols. (Grand Rapids: Eerdmans, 1964–76)

THAT	*Theologisches Handwörterbuch zum Alten Testament,* ed. E. Jenni and C. Westermann, 2 vols. (Munich: Kaiser, 1971, 1976)
TKHNT	Theologischer Handkommentar zum Neuen Testament
TLZ	*Theologische Literaturzeitung*
TQ	*Theologische Quartalschrift*
TRE	*Theologische Realenzyklopädie*
TRu	*Theologische Rundschau*
TU	Texte und Untersuchungen
TWAT	*Theologisches Wörterbuch zum Alten Testament,* ed. G. J. Botterweck and H. Ringgren (Stuttgart: Kohlhammer, 1970–)
TWNT	*Theologisches Wörterbuch zum Neuen Testament,* ed. G. Kittel, 10 vols. (Stuttgart: Kohlhammer, 1933–)
UNT	Untersuchungen zum Neuen Testament
UPZ	*Urkunden der Ptolemäerzeit,* ed. U. Wilckens, 2 vols. (Berlin and Leipzig: de Gruyter, 1927–57)
USQR	*Union Seminary Quarterly Review*
VC	*Vigiliae christianae*
VF	*Verkündigung und Forschung*
VTSup	*Vetus Testamentum,* Supplements
WMANT	Wissenschaftliche Monographien zum Alten und Neuen Testament
WUNT	Wissenschaftliche Untersuchungen zum Neuen Testament
ZAW	*Zeitschrift für die alttestamentliche Wissenschaft*
ZDPV	*Zeitschrift der deutschen Palästina-Vereins*
ZKG	*Zeitschrift für Kirchengeschichte*
ZKT	*Zeitschrift für katholische Theologie*
ZNW	*Zeitschrift für die neutestamentliche Wissenschaft*
ZST	*Zeitschrift für systematische Theologie*
ZTK	*Zeitschrift für Theologie und Kirche*

Introduction

BIRGER A. PEARSON

THE TITLE CHOSEN for this volume honoring Helmut Koester,[1] a title that could admittedly be read as an oxymoron, is meant to be both allusive and evocative. It is allusive in two respects: First, it alludes to the title of the English version of a Festschrift published several years ago in honor of Koester's *Doktorvater*, Rudolf Bultmann, *The Future of Our Religious Past.*[2] Second, and more importantly, it alludes to the nature of Helmut Koester's own work in the study of ancient Christianity and its sources: always on the cutting edge of scholarship, always open to future developments in the field, and always challenging others to new thinking about old subjects.[3] Indeed, the essays in this book provide ample evidence of the impact of Koester's work on scholars of this generation, an impact that arguably outweighs that of any other of Bultmann's students.

The book's title is also meant to be evocative in two respects: Initially, it was meant to evoke from some of Koester's colleagues, many of whom are also former students of his, essays for the book that would in one way or another follow his example in opening new vistas in the study of early Christianity. And, of course, the essays here presented, together with Koester's own massive oeuvre, are meant to challenge the book's readers to enter into "the future of early Christianity" with new thinking and, as well, to make new contributions to the ongoing work of elucidating anew the origins and early history of the Christian religion.

[1] The title was suggested by Norman Petersen at an early stage in the planning for the volume.

[2] *The Future of Our Religious Past: Essays in Honour of Rudolf Bultmann,* ed. J. M. Robinson, trans. C. E. Carlston and R. P. Scharlemann (New York: Harper & Row, 1971). The original German version was published in 1964 to commemorate Bultmann's eightieth birthday (*Zeit und Geschichte: Dankesgabe an Rudolf Bultmann zum 80. Geburtstag,* ed. E. Dinkler [Tübingen: Mohr-Siebeck]).

[3] The evidence is found in the bibliography of Helmut Koester published in this volume (pp. 477–87) and now also in this volume's epilogue (pp. 467–76).

The essays submitted for this book organized themselves into six categories of scholarly research, each of which has also been the object of our esteemed jubilarian's attention. Thus, the book is divided into six parts.

Part One is somewhat loosely entitled "The Environment of Early Christianity." The lead essay actually speaks more to issues of methodology, while the others take up aspects of the historical environment of emergent Christianity. Thus, Kurt Rudolph expands on the work of the *religionsgeschichtliche Schule* in Germany by challenging this generation of scholars of early Christianity to treat it for what it is, namely, a religious phenomenon in the real world of history.[4] Helmut Koester's own work, of course, is paradigmatic of such scholarly treatment.[5] Dieter Georgi probes some key tractates of Plutarch's famed *Moralia* for insights into the New Testament, especially for the thought world of the apostle Paul. Eldon Epp examines the massive evidence of the papyri preserved in Egypt's dry sands for information on how letters were sent and delivered in the ancient world, thus shedding light on the circumstances of the sending and delivery of letters preserved and alluded to in the New Testament. Dieter Lührmann, in a subtle allusion to Koester's North German origins, discusses a piece of Hellenistic ethnographic lore, passed on by Philo of Alexandria, pertaining to certain Germanic tribes living by the North Sea in antiquity. (Needless to say, Helmut Koester embodies in himself, as does Dieter Lührmann, the remarkable advances made by the erstwhile barbarians over two millennia of history.) Finally, Dennis Smith examines some ancient examples of sacred banquets, Jewish and non-Jewish, and mythical traditions pertaining to ritual feasting, to shed some light on the concept of the messianic banquet.

Part Two contains essays on an area of scholarship that attracted Helmut Koester's attention at an advanced stage in his career, that is, the use of archaeology for the elucidation of early Christian history.[6] In a two-part study, the site of ancient Bethsaida in the Golan area of Palestine is treated, with a study by H.-W. Kuhn of ancient literary and documentary sources relating to Bethsaida and a report by Rami Arav on recent excavations there. Thus important new light is shed on a key geographical locus for the activities of Jesus of Nazareth and his disciples in the first century. Holland Hendrix utilizes archaeological data to good advantage in the interpretation of aspects of the eschatology of Paul's first letter to the Thessalonians.

[4] See B. A. Pearson, "On Treating Christianity as a Religion," *Soundings* 71:2–3 (Summer/Fall 1988) 355–63.

[5] See esp. Koester, *Introduction*.

[6] Koester is primarily interested in the archaeology of Greece and the Aegean area; see esp. *Archaeological Resources for New Testament Studies,* vol. 1, ed. H. Koester and H. L. Hendrix (Philadelphia: Fortress Press, 1987), a valuable resource including both text and slides. See A. T. Kraabel's comments at the beginning of his essay (chapter 20 below).

Part Three is devoted to the study of ancient Judaism, the matrix of early Christianity. Klaus Baltzer, alluding to a short but important article that he coauthored with Helmut Koester many years ago,[7] analyzes the "Servant of God" motif in the Prayer of Nehemiah (Neh 1:5–11). Robert Kraft offers some innovative suggestions on the use of Philo Judaeus's exegetical treatment of the biblical patriarch Joseph for clues to the dating of portions of Philo's extensive corpus. Wilfred Bunge analyzes the rhetorical strategy of Josephus in his treatment of the Joseph story in *Antiquities of the Jews*, book 2. Bernadette Brooten treats one of the persons named in a now-famous Jewish inscription from Aphrodisias in Caria, "Iael," and argues persuasively that the person in question was a prominent woman and a leader in the Jewish community of Roman Aphrodisias.[8] Shaye Cohen examines the Protestant theological bias inherent in Adolf Harnack's treatment of Judaism in his famous work on the expansion of Christianity in the first three centuries of the Common Era.[9]

As might be expected, the bulk of this Festschrift, Part Four, consists of essays bearing directly on the New Testament. Nine of them deal with gospels and/or gospel traditions. Two of these essays address the issue of the genre of the sayings source "Q." James M. Robinson argues, largely on the basis of Helmut Koester's work on the *Gospel of Thomas* and Q,[10] that the redactors of Q turned a presumably nonapocalyptic, wisdom-oriented Jesus into the apocalyptic Son of Man. Robinson's understanding of the compositional history of Q is heavily influenced by John S. Kloppenborg's recent work.[11] Richard Horsley mounts a vigorous critique of Kloppenborg's and others' findings and argues for the "prophetic" rather than "apocalyptic" or "wisdom" orientation of the sayings in Q.[12]

[7] Klaus Baltzer and Helmut Koester, "Die Bezeichnung des Jakobus als 'ΩΒΛΙΑΣ," *ZNW* 46 (1955) 141–42. The enigmatic epithet ὠβλίας in Hegesippus's account of James the Just (in Eusebius *Historia ecclesiastica* 2.23.7) is plausibly treated as a textual corruption of 'Ωβδίας = "Servant of God" (cf. James 1:1).

[8] The Aphrodisias inscription, with its reference to people called *theosebeis* ("God-fearers"), is an important piece of evidence in the ongoing controversy over the existence in antiquity of a special category of Gentile sympathizers of Judaism, distinct from "proselytes," that is, converts who accepted circumcision and the ritual laws. See A. T. Kraabel's essay (chapter 20 below) and the studies cited in his notes.

[9] A. Harnack, *Die Mission und Ausbreitung des Christentums in den ersten drei Jahrhunderten* (Berlin: de Gruyter, 1902). Other editions are referred to in Cohen's article.

[10] The key essay is the one reprinted in the volume jointly published by the two longtime friends, "One Jesus and Four Primitive Gospels," in Robinson-Koester, *Trajectories*, 158–204. It is, of course, cited often in this Festschrift.

[11] John S. Kloppenborg, *The Formation of Q: Trajectories in Ancient Wisdom Collections* (SAC 2; Philadelphia: Fortress Press, 1987).

[12] The "prophetic" (and political) orientation of the historical Jesus is elaborated by Horsley in his recent book *Jesus and the Spiral of Violence: Popular Jewish Resistance in Roman Palestine* (San Francisco: Harper & Row, 1987).

Robert Doran analyzes a Son of Man saying in Q and *Gos. Thom.* 86 (the only Son of Man saying in *Gos. Thom.*) and discusses the various ways in which the saying could be understood in the history of its transmission. Adela Yarbro Collins takes up the problem of the apocalyptic Son of Man sayings in the Synoptic Gospels. She discusses the various ways in which Daniel 7:13 was interpreted in pre-Christian Judaism and then argues, against much current scholarship,[13] that it is illegitimate to exclude from the material attributable to the historical Jesus such apocalyptic sayings as reflect the use of Daniel 7:13 (e.g., Mark 13:26).

Paul Mirecki discusses the formal and redactional features of a dominical saying in the secondary ending of Mark. Philip Sellew, utilizing Helmut Koester's work on the *Secret Gospel of Mark*,[14] advances a new theory concerning the compositional history of the canonical Gospel of Mark. Hans Dieter Betz develops his previous work on the Sermon on the Mount,[15] arguing for its pre-Matthean Jewish Christian origin and showing how the author of Matthew interpreted this source in the composition of the Gospel.

The Gospel of John is treated in two essays. A. Thomas Kraabel suggests that the figure of the Beloved Disciple in John can be interpreted symbolically, in a manner comparable to the God-fearers in the book of Acts.[16] Sarah Tanzer probes the passages dealing with various kinds of Jews in the Fourth Gospel, such as Nicodemus, and suggests ways in which the author of the Gospel utilizes these figures in his narrative to refer to that author's actual social situation and intended audiences in the late first century.

Four essays deal in some way with the book of Acts. Kraabel's essay has already been mentioned. David Tiede analyzes the theology of Luke-Acts in relation to the question of the role of the people of Israel in the author's understanding of the divine plan of judgment and salvation. S. Scott Bartchy argues in favor of the historicity of the communal nature of the earliest Jerusalem church, as presented by the author of Acts. Hans-Martin Schenke takes up four problems relating to the life and career of the apostle Paul, utilizing both Acts and Paul's own letters in his discussion. The most surprising part of this essay is the doubt that is cast on the tradition, found only in Acts, concerning Paul's Tarsian origins.

[13] Besides the influential work of Norman Perrin, with which Yarbro Collins expresses her basic disagreement, see also the articles in this book by Robinson (chapter 13) and Doran (chapter 15).

[14] See esp. Koester's article "History and Development of Mark's Gospel (From Mark to *Secret Mark* and 'Canonical' Mark)," in *Colloquy on New Testament Studies: A Time for Reappraisal and Fresh Approaches*, ed. B. C. Corley (Macon, Ga.: Mercer University Press, 1983) 35–57.

[15] See esp. his *Essays on the Sermon on the Mount* (Philadelphia: Fortress Press, 1985).

[16] Kraabel treates the God-fearers in Acts as more of a Lukan theological construct than an actual historical category referring to Gentiles interested in Judaism; see his n. 8.

Letters of the apostle Paul are the focus of three exegetical studies. Wayne Meeks employs the same method that he used in his well-known study of the Gospel of John[17] in an interpretation of the Christ hymn in Philippians 2. Norman Petersen challenges some recent rhetorical and epistolographic studies that argue in favor of the integrity of Romans, including chapter 16, and in a careful analysis argues the contrary, that is, that chapter 16 did not originally belong with chapters 1–15.[18] George Nickelsburg utilizes the Two Ways/Two Spirits traditions found in early Jewish literature (especially 1QS iii–iv) to interpret some passages in Galatians (5:16–6:10) and Romans (chaps. 5–8).

Eduard Lohse takes up the problem of the relationship between the (presumably Ephesian) author of the book of Revelation and the Pauline tradition previously established in Ephesus and elsewhere in Asia Minor. Lohse argues for a hint of Pauline influence in Revelation and also suggests a rationale for the lack of more explicit Pauline influence in that apocalypse. Finally, Julian Hills explores the problem of the literary genre of 1 John and relates this epistle generically to the community rule or church order.

Part Five of the book is devoted to noncanonical early Christian literature. Building on the work of Helmut Koester on the *Gospel of Thomas,* Ron Cameron probes the importance of that gospel for the elucidation both of the historical Jesus and of the origins of Christianity. François Bovon takes up for extended discussion the vision of Joseph presented in chapter 18 of the *Protevangelium of James,* with special attention to the motif of the "suspension of time" found in that passage. Harold Attridge focuses on the notion of "masculine fellowship" found in the *Acts of Thomas,* and he interprets this concept with reference to gnostic sources. Abraham Malherbe takes up the problem of Paul's rhetorical effectiveness in his letters, with reference to the third/fourth-century apocryphal correspondence between "Paul" and the philosopher "Seneca." Malherbe finds that "Seneca" has a greater appreciation for Paul's letter-writing skills than Paul's own historical contemporaries did. Finally, Demetrios Traketellis explores the various ways in which Ignatius of Antioch speaks about God and the Christian's relationship to God and Christ.

The sixth and last part of the book is devoted to three studies of Gnosticism. Pheme Perkins, building on some of Helmut Koester's studies, discusses the various christologies reflected in Christian gnostic sources. Elaine Pagels explores the various contradictory theories regarding the nature of the Valentinian sacrament of the "Bridal Chamber," particularly as treated in the *Gospel of Philip,* and argues that the gnostic author of that text

[17] W. Meeks, "The Man from Heaven in Johannine Sectarianism," *JBL* 91 (1972) 44–72.

[18] This is the view also espoused by Helmut Koester (*Introduction* 2:138–39), who suggests that chapter 16 is part of a letter sent to Ephesus.

was not interested in the question of whether there should be a sexual component to the "mystery of marriage." Finally, the editor of this book explores the nature of that "Gnosticism" that presumably existed in Alexandria before the time of Valentinus. A "revisionist" stance is also taken vis-à-vis the arguments of Walter Bauer regarding the nature of early Christianity in Alexandria.[19]

The essays in this book reflect, of course, various interpretations and approaches, some of them conflicting one with another. But that is the nature of a vibrant scholarly tradition (and of the humanistic and social sciences in general). The editor and his collaborators express herewith the hope that this book, devoted to their beloved teacher and friend on the occasion of his sixty-fifth birthday, will live up to the intentionality of its title in opening up for its readers the challenge of exploring anew the perennial and ever-fascinating issues involved in the study of the origins and early history of Christianity.

[19] W. Bauer, *Orthodoxy and Heresy in Earliest Christianity,* trans. and ed. R. Kraft and G. Krodel (Philadelphia: Fortress Press, 1971) esp. 44–60.

PART 1

The Environment of Early Christianity

1

Early Christianity as a Religious-Historical Phenomenon

KURT RUDOLPH

THE INCONTESTABLE MERIT of having comprehended early Christianity as a phenomenon in the history of religions belongs to the history-of-religions school (*religionsgeschichtliche Schule*) of Protestant theology in Germany, which evolved at the close of the last century.[1] Stimulated and influenced by the pioneering works of the time on the history of the Near East, Hellenism, and late antiquity, this school understood nascent and developing Christianity as a part of its environment and thereby liberated it from the ivory tower to which it had been banned by dogmatics and theological church historiography. Even if today a number of theses and claims propagated by some of the leading figures, such as W. Bousset, H. Gressmann, H. Gunkel, W. Heitmueller, J. Weiss, W. Wrede, and R. Reitzenstein, may no longer be blindly adopted, one should nevertheless rigorously maintain its basic position. Recently it has often become a matter of course to subject certain views of the history-of-religions school to exaggerated criticism (or even to treat them as a scapegoat) and, on the basis of this, to place the entire effort in disrepute. But it cannot be denied that everyone who is involved in this field of study is somehow indebted to the school, even those who formerly opposed it (e.g., A. von Harnack and K. Holl) and those who believe that they still must do so. There is nothing to say against the justifiable criticism of such untenable and exaggerated theories as the notion

[1] A more extensive version of this article has been published previously: "Das frühe Christentum als religionsgeschichtliches Phänomen," in *Das Korpus der Griechischen Christlichen Schriftsteller: Historie, Gegenwart, Zukunft,* ed. J. Irmscher and K. Treu (TU 120; Berlin: Akademie-Verlag, 1977) 29–42. It was translated for publication here by F. Stanley Jones and edited by Birger Pearson.

On the history-of-religions school, see my article, "Religionsgeschichtliche Schule," in *ER* 10:230–39.

of the (gnostic) "redeemed redeemer."[2] These often arose amid exuberant joy over new discoveries and were propounded in sharp opposition to the narrow theological view. One should not forget, however, the pioneering thoughts of the school and the impetus it provided for further work. One may recall that H. Gunkel wrote in 1903 that Christianity is a "syncretistic religion" and that the last great representative of the school, R. Bultmann, expressly adopted this stance and employed it as the guiding principle for his excellent presentation of primitive Christianity.[3] Since that time, this perception has again been applied in productive ways.[4]

These brief remarks on the history of investigation are intended to serve only as a sort of recollection and to point out the underlying basis for that which has become for us more or less a matter of course, namely, an understanding of Christianity as a phenomenon in the history of religions. These introductory remarks indicate also the point of view I employ in dealing with this topic. The following treatment can be only a sketch, for the subject easily leads to endless discussions and a comprehensive presentation is yet to be accomplished. When I speak of an approach in terms of the history of religions, I mean in this context the historically developed form of Christianity seen as *conditioned* by the contemporary and older religious traditions, that is, by the history of religions in its surrounding world (Hellenism and late antiquity). Also involved is the task of a closer phenomenological description and definition on the basis of a comparison of religions—that is, the application of phenomenological categories for religion to the developmental history of Christianity and to its individuality as such. This, however, is a side issue in the present discussion.

If one takes a general view of Christianity as it is documented in its earlier writings and in the form of numerous churches and orientations, one notices above all two components that have been decisive for Christianity even up to the present: the Jewish heritage and the Hellenistic heritage. The former always stood at the center of interest for investigation and plays a role even in the older theological historiography—this for obvious reasons: the "Old Testament" constituted the scripture of the early church; the Greek-Hellenistic material came only slowly into view, first through study of the language and then through study of terminology and imagery. Indeed,

[2] C. Colpe, *Die religionsgeschichtliche Schule: Darstellung und Kritik ihres Bildes vom gnostischen Erlösermythos* (Göttingen: Vandenhoeck & Ruprecht, 1961); see my review in *TLZ* 88 (1963) 28–33.

[3] H. Gunkel, *Zum religionsgeschichtlichen Verständnis des Neuen Testaments* (Göttingen: Vandenhoeck & Ruprecht, 1903) 95; R. Bultmann, *Primitive Christianity in Its Contemporary Setting* (New York: Meridian, 1956) 175–79.

[4] E.g., Koester-Robinson, *Trajectories,* esp. 1–19 (Robinson) and 114–19 (Koester); Koester, *Introduction;* see his prefaces (1:xxi–xxiii; 2:xxxiii–xxxiv).

classical philology has rendered important service, ever since the age of humanism, to the elucidation of this side of Christianity; it has worked to recover the textual basis of Christian tradition and to explicate this tradition by using the extant writings of ancient authors. The real religious historical investigation begins, however, in the second half of the nineteenth century. Hand in hand with the development of the so-called ethnological school of philologists represented by E. Rhode, A. Dieterich, R. Wuensch, and F. Boll, there was carried out a corresponding interpretation of the New Testament and early Christian literature, which also featured a close working relationship with the history-of-religions school (R. Reitzenstein is the most prominent example of this). This sphere of studies has grown ever since and has led, especially in recent times, to entirely new insights.

The Jewish heritage too has become so differentiated that one can no longer speak of Judaism as a clearly defined and unitary entity at the time of the New Testament and the early church; one can only point out various definite phenomena that influenced Christianity. The discoveries at the Dead Sea (Qumran and others) have not only disclosed previously unknown sides of the Judaism of New Testament times (and other first stages of Jewish esoteric thought) but have also supplied new material for the analysis of primitive Christian literature—even if through a stronger emphasis on the contrasts.[5] Since a detailed presentation of these relationships would be too involved, we shall venture here a short list of the "components" that probably were of decisive importance for early Christianity and its subsequent development:

1. The Israelite-Jewish idea of God, the most fundamental presupposition of nascent Christianity.

2. Old Testament prophecy, that which became the immediate model for Jesus of Nazareth through one of its last representatives, John the Baptist, and would often form in the history of the church the starting point for revolutionary, antiauthoritarian movements.

3. Apocalyptic, with its eschatological-messianic view of history and prophetic "futurology" and its dualistic cosmology and anthropology. It should be noted here that, contrary to popular opinion, apocalyptic is not a purely intra-Jewish phenomenon but is rather involved in various ways with Hellenistic-oriental syncretism and cannot be viewed in an isolated manner.[6]

4. The "intensification of the Torah" in contemporary Jewish radicalism,

[5] See, e.g., H. Braun, *Qumran und das Neue Testament* (Tübingen: Mohr-Siebeck, 1966); G. Vermes, *Jesus and the World of Judaism* (Philadelphia: Fortress Press, 1973) 100–139.

[6] See esp. D. Hellholm, ed., *Apocalypticism in the Mediterranean World and the Near East: Proceedings of the International Colloquium on Apocalypticism, Uppsala, August 12–17, 1979* (Tübingen: Mohr-Siebeck, 1983; 2nd ed. 1989).

as is seen in the Qumran writings, which was of decisive importance for Jesus' ethic and finally for Christian ethics.[7]

5. Dualistic wisdom, an area that recently is increasingly moving to the focal point of research both regarding primitive and early Christianity (collections of sayings)[8] and regarding gnosis or Gnosticism.[9] Here too one should not neglect the close relations to Hellenistic thought (e.g., Philo).[10]

6. Jewish esoteric thought and gnosis, which, though not of central importance for the Christianity that finally became authoritative, were of importance for the birth and development of Christian Gnosticism and left behind undisguisable traces, as is shown by the Johannine and Pauline traditions or "schools" and also by the major heresiological antipodes of the second and third centuries, Irenaeus, Clement of Alexandria, and Origen.[11] The aftermath of this gnostic infiltration of the early church (next to physical persecution its greatest crisis) may be clearly observed both in the formation of the canon and in the fiction of apostolic tradition, as well as in the orientation of theological doctrines and the development of dogmatic terminology (e.g., ὁμοούσιος).

As a whole, it is clear from these components that it was *Hellenistic* Judaism, in its various traditions and forms, that was decisive for nascent Christianity, as exemplified by its theistic theology, the doctrine of angels, the dualism of body and soul, ethics, and eschatology, as well as, in the cultic sphere, the so-called Service of the Word, Baptism, and the Lord's Supper. Christianity began as a Jewish-Hellenistic sect and first spread in this form. The separation of Judaism and Hellenism primarily arose from matters regarding mission and the stance to be taken on the Jewish ceremonial law, not from the problem of "Judaism" or "Hellenism." Whereas Jewish Christianity maintained for a time the forms of the oldest community in

[7] See the groundbreaking study of H. Braun, *Spätjüdisch-häretischer und frühchristlicher Radikalismus* (2nd ed.; Tübingen: Mohr-Siebeck, 1969).

[8] Koester-Robinson, *Trajectories,* chaps. 3 (Robinson), 4 (Koester, esp. 135ff.), 6 (Koester, esp. 219ff.).

[9] G. W. MacRae, "The Jewish Background of the Gnostic Sophia Myth," in MacRae, *Studies in the New Testament and Gnosticism,* ed. D. J. Harrington and S. B. Marrow (GNS 26; Wilmington, Del.: Michael Glazier, 1987) 184–202; K. Rudolph, "Sophia und Gnosis: Bemerkungen zum Problem 'Gnosis und Frühjudentum,'" in *Altes Testament-Frühjudentum-Gnosis: Neue Studien zu "Gnosis und Bibel,"* ed. K.-W. Tröger (Berlin: Evangelische Verlagsanstalt, 1980) 221–37.

[10] B. Mack, *Logos und Sophia: Untersuchungen zur Weisheitstheologie im hellenistischen Judentum* (Göttingen: Vandenhoeck & Ruprecht, 1973).

[11] See, e.g., K. Rudolph, *Gnosis: The Nature and History of Gnosticism,* trans. R. McL. Wilson et al.; Edinburgh: T. & T. Clark; San Francisco: Harper & Row, 1983) esp. 209–309; J. M. Robinson, "Gnosticism and the New Testament," in *GNOSIS: Festschrift für Hans Jonas,* ed. B. Aland (Göttingen: Vandenhoeck & Ruprecht, 1978) 125–43; G. W. MacRae, "Nag Hammadi and the New Testament," in *Studies in the New Testament,* 165–83.

Jerusalem,[12] the so-called Hellenistic Christianity went beyond the Hellenistic material that was already inherent in Jewish Christianity and became receptive to other contemporary religious ideas of the Greek and Roman spheres of expansion, simultaneously abandoning older material connected with the Christian faith. Here Paul stands in a key position.[13] To a certain extent there is a break between the primitive community in Jerusalem and the Hellenistic "church," not in terms of organization but in terms of the history of religions. Through its leap into the non-Palestinian Roman world, Christianity evolves increasingly as an independent religion alongside Judaism. While developing indigenous forms, it constantly takes up and assimilates more and more Hellenistic material from late antiquity (especially from the second to the fourth century).[14]

The Greek-Hellenistic culture supplied to the *oikoumenē* of the time, stretching from central Asia to Spain, the ubiquitously visible ferment of its unity (which may be viewed even today in the architectural and artistic remains of the period). Through its various expressions it also affected Christianity in a more or less deep and irrevocable manner. The following traditions and ideas deserve special mention here:

1. The Platonic, especially the Middle Platonic, school, which through its terminology for dialectics and cosmology assisted in the foundation of Christian theology (in Alexandria).[15] This process formed an important moment in Christian self-assertion over against paganism and led to the birth of the Greek-Christian tradition of education and finally to the connection of Christianity and humanism.[16]

2. The Cynic-Stoic popular philosophy, which was a model already for Paul in its literary mode of expression (the diatribe) and had its effect on early Christianity especially in the moral-ethical sphere.[17] At various times reference has been made to the importance of its negative attitude toward the world for the emergence of Christian asceticism.[18]

[12] Koester, *Introduction* 2:198–201.

[13] Ibid., 97–145.

[14] On the origin of the different "churches" and their ideologies, see C. Andresen, *Die Kirchen der alten Christenheit* (Die Religionen der Menschheit 29:112; Stuttgart: Kohlhammer, 1971).

[15] See esp. H. J. Krämer, *Der Ursprung der Geistmetaphysik: Untersuchungen zur Geschichte des Platonismus zwischen Platon und Plotin* (2nd ed.; Amsterdam: Gruner, 1967); J. Dillon, *The Middle Platonists 80 B.C. to A.D. 220* (Ithaca: Cornell University Press, 1977).

[16] See esp. W. Jaeger, *Early Christianity and Greek Philosophy* (Cambridge, Mass.: Harvard University Press, 1961).

[17] R. Bultmann, *Der Stil der paulinischen Predigt und die kynisch-stoische Diatribe* (Göttingen: Vandenhoeck & Ruprecht, 1910).

[18] H. Strathmann, *Geschichte der frühchristlichen Askese bis zur Entstehung des Mönchtums im religionsgeschichtlichen Zusammenhang*, vol. 1, *Die Askese in der Umgebung des werdenden Christentums* (Leipzig: Dörffling, 1914); J. Leipoldt, *Philosophie und frühchristliche Askese*

3. The characteristically Roman relationship to God, which noticeably corresponded to the Old Testament conception and was put to use for the doctrine of God in Roman-Latin Christianity, as Tertullian and Lactantius clearly demonstrate.[19]

4. The mystery religions, which through language and action transformed the originally simple Christian-Jewish cult to such an extent that the Christian church itself became a mystery religion, something that was repeatedly noticed by the opponents of the church.[20] "The mysteries create the outer form in which Christianity conquered a good deal of the world."[21]

5. Gnosis, in the form of the Christian Gnosticism of the second and third centuries, designated by Adolf von Harnack as "the acute secularising of Christianity."[22] Harnack's formulation is today valid only in a modified way, because the origin of Gnosticism must be sought independently of Christianity and because Christian Gnosticism makes up only a part of this movement. In this form, however, it is a particular expression of hellenized Christianity and was probably the most dangerous foreign infiltration of Christianity.[23] The importance and vitality of the gnostic heritage are demonstrated by its further effects, for example, Manichaeism and its influence on Augustine[24] or the sectarian movements of the late Middle Ages.

6. Finally, mention should be made of the various popular beliefs (or superstitions) that were appropriated by Christianity from its environment and were propagated in its mission (e.g., in the Germanic countries). Even in this respect Christianity assumed the heritage of late antiquity as its own.[25]

This list of traditions and ideas from the early and later imperial periods that have exercised in various ways an influence on the ideological and

---

(Sitzungsbericht der Sächs. Akademie der Wissenschaften zu Leipzig, Philol.-hist. Kl. 106:4; Berlin: Akademie-Verlag, 1961).

[19] A. Wlosok, "Römischer Religions- und Gottesbegriff in heidnischer und christlicher Zeit," *Antike und Abendland* 4 (1970) 39–53.

[20] See esp. G. Anrich, *Das antike Mysterienwesen in seinem Einfluss auf das Christentum* (Göttingen: Vandenhoeck & Ruprecht, 1894); J. Leipoldt, *Von den Mysterien zur Kirche: Gesammelte Aufsätze* (Leipzig: Koehler & Amelang, 1961).

[21] Leipoldt, *Von den Mysterien,* 49.

[22] A. von Harnack, *History of Dogma,* trans. N. Buchanan (New York: Dover, 1961) 1:223–66, esp. 227: "The Gnostic systems represent the acute secularising or hellenising of Christianity. . . ."

[23] See Rudolph, *Gnosis,* passim.

[24] A. Böhlig, "Zu gnostischen Grundlagen der Civitas-Dei-Vorstellung bei Augustinus," in Böhlig, *Gnosis und Synkretismus: Gesammelte Aufsätze zur spätantiken Religionsgeschichte* (Tübingen: Mohr-Siebeck, 1989) 1:127–34.

[25] See, e.g., P. Wendland, *Die hellenistisch-römische Kultur in ihren Beziehungen zu Judentum und Christentum* (2nd ed.; Tübingen: Mohr, 1912) 215f.; R. L. Fox, *Pagans and Christians* (New York: Alfred A. Knopf, 1987) esp. 325–35.

practical-cultic level of Christianity could, of course, be differentiated and expanded. We were concerned only with the more important ones, which, just as was the case with the Jewish heritage, achieved an enduring effect on central expressions of the Christian life and faith, lasting even up to the present. It has been noticed that Christianity "apparently at no time seriously questioned the structure of the ancient school, its teaching program, and its methods of instruction."[26] Thus, Christianity was able to become the heir of ancient education. "Why do you nibble on the Greek sciences if the reading of your holy scriptures is sufficient?" Emperor Julian asked the Christians.[27] Concerning this issue, there is the temptation to exaggeration and false evaluation because of the great importance of the Greek-Hellenistic tradition in culture and education; this has already vitiated several presentations.[28] One may often show that there is a Jewish-oriental thought deriving from the biblical tradition hidden behind a Greek formulation; on the other hand, Greek style and material are sometimes employed to polemicize indirectly against the conventional meanings.[29]

A neglected point of view in this context has received more attention and more precise formulation first of all by my teachers J. Leipoldt and S. Morenz: the notion of "book religion." What is meant here is a type of religion that, in contrast to traditional "cultic" or "popular" religion, is based on a written source of revelation.[30] This special type constitutes a specifically Jewish legacy and became so strong a factor that one must on that account differentiate Christianity from the religious cults of its environment, regardless of the interrelationships.[31] This involves simultaneously the dominance of history in Christianity over against the mythic character of Greek cultic religion. Morenz has also made reference to another hardly investigated share of the orient in the formation of Christian theology. It has to do with the effect, albeit "unconscious," of ancient Egyptian theology on the problem of the Trinity and the Incarnation. This involves "traditional modes of thought" deriving from Egyptian speculation on trinities and identities of the gods (not simply groups of gods), which noticeably affected Christian thinkers, particularly in Alexandria.[32] Surely there are many other

[26] O. Gigon, *Die antike Kultur und das Christentum* (Gütersloh: Mohn, 1966).

[27] Quoted in Gigon, *Die antike Kultur*, 123.

[28] See C. Schneider, *Geistesgeschichte des antiken Christentums* (2 vols.; Munich: Beck, 1954). For criticisms, see, e.g., S. Morenz, "Um Herkunft und Frühgeschichte des Christentums," *TLZ* 80 (1955) 525–32.

[29] See the classic study by E. Norden, *Agnostos Theos: Untersuchungen zur Formengeschichte religiöser Rede* (Berlin/Leipzig: Teubner, 1913); cf. A. Momigliano, *Alien Wisdom: The Limits of Hellenization* (Cambridge: Cambridge University Press, 1974).

[30] J. Leipoldt and S. Morenz, *Heilige Schriften: Betrachtungen Religionsgeschichte der antiken Mittelmeerwelt* (Leipzig: Harrassowitz, 1953).

[31] Morenz, "Um Herkunft," 529.

[32] Ibid., 529–30.

oriental contributions to developing Christianity that could be listed or that still remain to be discovered. Much of this, however (e.g., Iranian material), was mediated through Judaism and Hellenism and should be evaluated as an indirect contribution. With the passing of time, the individual Christian churches adopted and assimilated themselves to other religious traditions from the areas in which they had spread. This is a broad area for research that has not even been staked out, much less investigated.[33]

This, however, is not all there is to say about Christianity. Its *habitus*, or quality—that which even allows us to talk about what is typically *Christian*—is its hard-to-define core. Alongside a number of statements of faith which increasingly led to the creation of "symbols" or set confessions and which still today determine the dogmatic framework of Christian theology (doctrines of God and the Trinity, Christology, soteriology, and eschatology), there are a few characteristic traits of the outer form of Christianity, regardless of its dissolution into the various denominations (ecclesiology, priesthood and laity, charitable and social establishments, and the basic ethical and moral attitudes). These were not just incidental factors in the final victory of Christianity.[34] The political and social processes that led to this victory have always remained obscure. The key figure in this process, Emperor Constantine, and the motives that led him to decide for the Christian church are controversial.[35]

Of no little importance here was the well-established organization of the church throughout the empire, a characteristic missing from all other competing oriental religions, with the exception of Judaism and Manichaeism. But it was detachment from a nationally exclusive Judaism, with its observance of the Jewish law, that first rendered Christianity ripe as a world religion.[36] Several additional factors aided Christianity to achieve recognition, such as its liberated, universal-monotheistic, and ethical conception of God, together with its insight into the unity and equality of all humans and its impetus for a relationship to one's neighbor (above all to the socially disadvantaged), which was not based on traditional prejudices. The Christian attitude, for example, left the Stoic ideal regarding humanity far behind it and was made accessible to all believers in the exemplary actions of the founder, Jesus. He promised help and comfort and even access to the future

33 See Leipoldt, *Von den Mysterien*, 98ff., 165ff. On the problem of Buddhist–Christian relationships, see, e.g., H. Haas, *Bibliographie zur Frage nach Wechselbeziehungen zwischen Buddhismus und Christentum* (Leipzig: Hinrichs, 1922).

34 See, e.g., Gigon, *Die antike Kultur*, 142–81.

35 See, e.g., T. D. Barnes, *Constantine and Eusebius* (Cambridge, Mass.: Harvard University Press, 1981); R. MacMullen, *Christianizing the Roman Empire (A.D. 100–400)* (New Haven: Yale University Press, 1984).

36 J. Leipoldt, "Die Ablösung des frühen Christentums vom Judentums," in *Von den Mysterien*, 211–30; cf. 170–73.

world to "sinners" and broken humans, those who had been rejected by official religion. Also to be considered here are its critical and distanced stance vis-à-vis the world and the state (the imperial cult), which was born out of an eschatological consciousness, and, finally, its missionary aspect and concern for conversion.[37] Thus, it was not just assimilation to contemporary culture, to its "tenor" and to the needs or the tendencies of the individual classes in the population, but also that which exceeded the contemporary culture, the overpowering content of the Christian faith, which allowed Christianity to rise to dominance. It was also this "kernel" that apparently enabled Christianity to avoid a total foreign infiltration that could have resulted in its dissolution.

This process, so interesting in its various expressions, begins to appear already in the Pauline letters (Corinth) and continues increasingly until it reaches its first major climax in its opposition to Gnosticism, a battle that proved to be of decisive importance in the evolution of the "great" church.[38] Throughout its later course, the church repeatedly attempted to steer its way between the Scylla of total assimilation and the Charybdis of isolation. One clear example of this is Augustine's anti-Manichaean struggle and his intense confrontation with the culture of late antiquity.[39] Many sects and heresies were not only expressions of social and intra-Christian tensions but also attempts to shroud Christian doctrine totally in the dress of the surrounding world. One may thus say that Christianity, like every other major religion, preserved its form through a long process of reception and rejection, which is continuing even today. This process simultaneously tests Christianity's strength of life and self-preservation.

These remarks seek to observe the proper balance between form and content. They provide no support for the notion that there was a "pure and unadulterated" Christianity in a historical sense even in its beginnings.[40] This indeed could not have been the case, since the canonical writings of the New Testament, including the Gospels, and even Jesus himself did not propagate a message that was "pure" and isolated from the surrounding world. For the history of religions, there has never been a "pure religion"; this would be an ahistorical construct. Indeed, every religion is a syncretistic

[37] MacMullen, *Christianizing the Roman Empire,* 74–101.

[38] W. Kamlah, *Christentum und Geschichtlichkeit: Untersuchung zur Entstehung des Christentums und zu Augustins "Bürgerschaft Gottes"* (2nd ed.; Stuttgart: Kohlhammer, 1951) esp. 101ff. The term "great church" is used by the famous second-century opponent of Christianity Celsus (Origen *Against Celsus* 5.59).

[39] Kamlah, *Christentum und Geschichtlichkeit,* 133–340; see also P. Brown, *Augustine of Hippo: A Biography* (Berkeley: University of California Press, 1967).

[40] It makes no historical sense to speak of an "essence" of Christianity, except to say that the "essence" of Christianity is its history. See my methodological observations in *Historical Fundamentals and the Study of Religions* (New York: Macmillan, 1985) esp. 47–58.

phenomenon. This is the insight toward which the study of religions is progressing: it no longer understands the designation "syncretism" as a derogatory category.[41] This observation should not be neglected in the study of early Christian sources; it is an axiom arising from scientific insight and integrity that this knowledge should be employed in future work. Only from this perspective does the early history of the church become understandable and *historically* determinable. In the light of the new sources now available, such as the texts from Nag Hammadi, this remains a burning issue. Thus, the statement once made by Harnack concerning the study of religions (*Religionswissenschaft*), that a historian of religions faces a large task when concerned with the early church, has proved to be true in an unsuspected way.[42] The history of religions, however, always maintains simultaneously that one may not divert one's perspective from the wide field of religions whenever one investigates a single epoch in the history of religions.[43]

If one views the rise and development of early Christianity from the perspective of a comparison of religions, one may make the following observation: Christianity arose out of a messianic sect of a monotheistic popular religion; the one who initiated it, a prophetic, messianic preacher of repentance and reform, became a founding figure first at a later time when, after his death, the movement that he kindled finally abandoned contemporary Judaism and became an independent religion. One may designate this process as the transformation of a (Jewish) "heresy" into a "world religion."[44] A decisive role here was played by the former Pharisee Paul (Saul) of Tarsus. He has often been called the founder of Christianity, and this cannot be rejected out of hand. At the very least, he took measures, through his determined adoption of already existing tendencies in the Hellenistic congregation, that prevented Christianity from remaining a Jewish sect. This involved the promotion of a critical position vis-à-vis law and cult which was already implicit in the message of Jesus, with the result that Christianity became an independent movement. From him derives the theologically reasoned openness of primitive Christianity to the Hellenistic world, and the further development (which may be traced even in the New Testament writings) is basically a consequence of the direction that he took. This is what led to the

[41] K. Rudolph, "Synkretismus: Vom theologischen Scheltwort zum religionswissenschaftlichen Begriff," in *Humanitas Religiosa: Festschrift für Harald Biezais zu seinem 70. Geburtstag* (Stockholm: Almqvist & Wiksell, 1979) 194–212.

[42] A. (von) Harnack, *Reden und Aufsätze* (Giessen: Töpelmann, 1904) 2:170–71, 184–85.

[43] See Rudolph, *Historical Fundamentals*, 43–58.

[44] On "heresy" as a category in the history of religions, see my article "Heresy: An Overview" in *ER* 12:293–96, and literature cited there. On "heresy" in early Christianity, see the groundbreaking study by W. Bauer, *Orthodoxy and Heresy in Earliest Christianity*, trans. R. Kraft and G. Krodel (Philadelphia: Fortress Press, 1971).

establishment of historical "Christianity," a *religio christiana* that understood itself as a *genus tertium* alongside Judaism and Hellenism (paganism).[45]

Thus, the problem of Christianity in the history of religions involves equally both "outer" and "inner" questions and cannot even be grasped, much less solved, without consideration of both.

[45] See Kamlah, *Christentum und Geschichtlichkeit,* esp. 99–115.

2

Reflections of a New Testament Scholar on Plutarch's Tractates *De Alexandri Magni Fortuna aut Virtute*

DIETER GEORGI

PLUTARCH'S TRACTATES on the fortune or the virtue of Alexander, like the other theological and ethical works of the scholar from Chaeronea, are interesting for the New Testament scholar because they show important perspectives on the linguistic world of New Testament times.[1] In the following inquiry I shall start with some general remarks on both tractates and then concentrate on the first one, which yields more for the direct comparison with the New Testament.[2]

Both tractates of Plutarch on the fortune or virtue of Alexander belong, like Plutarch's two other studies on τύχη (*De fortuna* and *De fortuna Romanorum*), to the author's rhetorical exercises, trial runs in the category of the γένος ἐπιδεικτικόν. I share the opinion of most scholars that these tractates are authentic works of the man from Chaeronea. There is reason to suspect that the impression of incompleteness conveyed by these studies is not simply a rhetorical trick played by the author but that these works indeed were never finished. Their fragmentary nature shows most of all at the ends

[1] This study had its origin in a project at the Institute for Antiquity and Christianity (Claremont, Calif.) engaged in the study of parallels between Plutarch and the New Testament. I want to thank John Huddlestun of the University of Michigan for reading, correcting, and thus vastly improving my translation of the original German version.

On Plutarch, see Hans Dieter Betz, ed., *Plutarch's Theological Writings and Early Christian Literature* (SCHNT 3; Leiden: Brill, 1975); idem, *Plutarch's Ethical Writings and Early Christian Literature* (SCHNT 4; Leiden: Brill, 1978).

[2] A good introduction to Plutarch's work is given by Konrat Ziegler in *Der kleine Pauly: Lexikon der Antike von Pauly's Realencyclopädie der classischen Altertumswissenschaft* (5 vols.; Stuttgart: A. Druckenmüller, 1964–1975) vol. 4, cols. 945–53.

of both speeches of Alexander. On the other hand, the beginnings of these speeches also appear incomplete. This may result from the fact that both tractates were never really worked out for publication but were merely drafted as rhetorical sketches. Perhaps they were composed by the young Plutarch, like the two other studies on fortune, but never delivered as real orations or brought on the book market by Plutarch himself. Perhaps they were found among Plutarch's papers after his death and published posthumously. Whatever the details, the lack of originality, often decried, reflects a school milieu and represents the average tendencies of the time.

A critical comparison between ethical concepts and topics like τύχη and ἀρετή was commonplace since the first sophists, adopted by the rhetoricians long before Plutarch. The later ones needed historical personalities and events for the presentation and discussion of average contemporary issues. Those exercises had to have a lofty as well as an authentic flavor. They were used for philosophical and rhetorical training long before the first century. These historical phenomena and their actions and reflections were simulated in a schematized fashion, thus presenting them as types for the purpose of a paradigmatic discussion of such problems.

As regards the thematic concept of τύχη, it is not consistently treated by Plutarch. For a philosophically trained mind τύχη evoked some embarrassment; therefore, in the more Hellenic tracts Plutarch yields more to the philosophical suspicion and criticism of the chancy and immoral nature of fortune. In the tract on the Roman fortune, however, he accommodates the fact that the Roman intelligentsia as much as Roman culture had a higher opinion of the goddess Fortuna—her character, actions, and gifts—than Greek philosophers usually could muster. The Romans viewed Fortuna in two ways, in the context of individual welfare and that of the state.[3] In *De fortuna* and *De fortuna Alexandri Magni* Plutarch instead has to anticipate the apprehension Greek intellectuals had toward τύχη as being unpredictable and immoral—indeed, blind and moody—chance. Therefore, τύχη in these tracts appears in a more ambivalent light. But one side of this ambivalence, the positive one, could not be neglected in a Greek environment either. Readers of Plutarch would recognize already from many of their common coins that theirs and other city goddesses all resembled the goddess τύχη. This was, in fact, parallel to Roman understanding and practice. The common experience would relate Fortuna and commonweal.

Read against this background, most strongly coming out in the treatise on the Roman fortune, the Pauline invocation of grace and peace at the end of the prefaces of his letters would be associated by his readers with the claims made out of reverence for local city goddesses resembling

[3] See n. 18 below.

τύχη, namely, that the safety and welfare of the community depended entirely on the goddess invoked. All the more so, since Paul in each case emphasizes the name of the respective *polis* and views the *ekklēsia* there as being in competition with the local assemblies of free citizens of the city congregating in the local theater. Thus, there is a clear social and political dimension to these prayers in Pauline prefaces addressing the community's urban spirit, or *daimōn,* as Plutarch would call it in *De fortuna Romanorum.* This is the power that creatively governs and supports the place and its people. It reminds one of the peaceful consequences the presence of that spirit and prayer to it entail.

This Hellenistic phenomenon and its Roman counterpart create a status or expectation similar to the Hebrew *šālôm* or the English concept of salvation, if not misunderstood in an individualized and internalized fashion. In the case of Paul's praying for grace and peace, the source and maintainer of these powers and gifts are, of course, the God of Israel and his reflection, the Christ, but in direct competition with the divine power allegedly supporting and protecting the *polis.* Thus political, not only religious, competition is also indicated in this case.

The discussion about the dependability of τύχη, particularly in a Greek philosophical context, casts unexpected light on the Pauline problem of justification.[4] None would doubt Paul's acquaintance with the Hellenistic Jewish diaspora, but whenever Jewish sources are used for the purpose of clarifying his understanding of justification, Palestinian Jewish references tend to be given primary place and thus usually dominate in contemporary Pauline scholarship. But does it help, for instance, to explain Paul's concentrated discussion of τὰ ἔργα τοῦ νόμου? Does this not appear as an obsession and indeed a caricature, when compared with Palestinian Jewish concerns as we know them from rabbinic writings—most of all Pharisaic rabbinic ones? When viewed, however, in the light of the diaspora synagogue and its missionary theology, Paul's efforts make sense because there the missionary concern dwells on ethical considerations and actions as the essence not only of the law alone but of Judaism as a whole.[5]

Hellenistic Jewish missionary wisdom was passionately concerned with elucidating the moral dimensions of the law, enhancing the scribal interest of charismatic wisdom like that of Jesus ben Sirach and systematizing this

[4] For Paul's understanding of justification, see Dieter Georgi, "Gott auf den Kopf stellen: Überlegungen zu Tendenz und Kontext des Theokratiegedankens in paulinischer Praxis und Theologie," in *Theocracy in Paul's Praxis and Theology,* ed. J. Taubes (Minneapolis: Fortress Press, 1991).

[5] In my book *The Opponents of Paul in Second Corinthians* (Philadelphia: Fortress Press, 1986), I have presented a detailed picture of this Jewish missionary theology, its context, its activity, and its relationship to the early church.

ethical concern. There was a mutual interpretation of ethics and law, and the latter was portrayed as the constitution of the world, not only the human world but also the world as divine creation. This was adopted from earlier Jewish wisdom and further developed. This interplay between law, ethics, social and world order, and general stability was at the heart of that missionary theology and constituted the rather attractive and successful effort of this branch of the biblical Jewish wisdom movement, unjustly called Jewish apologetics. But there is no doubt that it took into consideration Hellenistic pagan criticism and responded to it. The argument of universal meaning, power, and dependability of the Pentateuch would also address pagan questions about the biblical concepts of grace and election, because it was evident that such ideas for a Hellenistic reader came close to chance, luck, and fate. The stress of Jewish missionary theology on the credibility and the universally stabilizing nature of Jewish ethics helped to refute this pagan criticism. The adoption of the term πίστις within the homiletics and theology of the diaspora synagogue belongs within this context, not in support of a theology of grace but in opposition to it, for in that use it supported the idea of stability. Election and grace were deemphasized, whereas the credibility and stabilizing nature of Jewish ethics were stressed instead.

Paul's presentation of the issue of God's grace enters into debate with this missionary theology of the diaspora synagogue. Whereas in Galatians and in 2 Corinthians two different Jesus-oriented versions of that theology are in view, the Letter to the Romans speaks to the missionary activity and thought of the diaspora synagogue directly. This explains why the Pauline discussion of a Jewish theology of works is found most of all in Romans and the term πίστις occurs there so often. This letter also makes Paul's own mission a predominant topic. In critical response to Jewish missionary theology, Paul's attempt to pursue a theology and practice of mission is based on election and grace, despite Hellenistic criticism of the immorality of the concept of chance and associated terms. But this critical response is not invented by Paul or the church at large. Jewish wisdom since the Wisdom of Solomon—and thus a major element of Paul's own tradition—tended in that very direction. Josephus's work proves also that the correspondence of divine providence and chance could be seen in a positive light as well. There is also the understanding of task and mission well known to the readers of the New Testament, particularly in Paul but not limited to him.

Plutarch's tractates on Alexander show us a divinely inspired determination of the hero, reminiscent of the understanding of delegation, motivation, and responsibility in texts like Mark 6:7–13 and even more in 1 Corinthians 4 and 9, 2 Cor 2:14–7:4; 10–13; and Romans 1; 9–11; and 15. Our first Alexander tractate of Plutarch poses as a correction of another work of his on Fortuna. Plutarch mentions that writing in his first sentence, namely, that

Alexander the Great had been only the ἔργον of τύχη.[6] Lamprias, who lists our tract as the one "On the luck of Alexander" (no. 176) and the second one as "On the virtue of Alexander" (no. 186), knows of no tractate whose first line would correspond to this. Therefore, the mention of a speech on Fortuna just held could be a rhetorical means for increasing the actuality and liveliness of the theme to be discussed in what follows. It would use a common philosophical and rhetorical understanding of Alexander as a creation of Fortuna.

The New Testament presupposes the ideal of human beings as divine creations, a concept not only familiar in the Bible and in oriental circles but also in the Mediterranean world at large. Romans 9 shows that Paul is very much aware of the association of God-willed sovereign creation and arbitrariness, but he avoids any camouflaging of that controversial issue, contrary to Jewish missionary theology and later Christian apologetics. He underlines instead that element of arbitrariness rather strongly.

In 1 Cor 3:6–15 Paul goes even further, coming close to the concept discussed by Plutarch and others, namely, of the origin and use of various human beings as products of chance. In v. 10, Paul introduces the term χάρις, which his Jewish and pagan contemporaries in such a context certainly would have understood as synonymous with τύχη. Paul uses here the circumlocution of "natural" relation and processes parabolically for a model discussion of the differences between various missionary situations and functions. But the missionaries are seen as instruments in the development of a divine work and construction enterprise—first of mission itself, but then even more clearly of the building of the divine temple with Christ as the foundation and the Holy Spirit as dweller therein. It is not unimportant that Paul here plays with the ambivalence of temple as a symbol for the single person as well as for the community of believers. He has both perspectives in mind, a personal and a social one. This brings him close to the Hellenistic and Roman understanding of the function and blessings of Fortuna, who is the foundation of individual and societal excellence, personal and public achievement.

Plutarch's intended corrective to the discussion of this issue at first seems to put philosophy in antithesis to τύχη, but that contradiction is later evened out. More obvious and important for the entire tractate is the fact that Alexander here can stand for philosophy itself. Alexander is represented as the true philosopher. Plutarch presents the achievements of Alexander's life as manifestations of authentic philosophy itself.

The contrasting of Fortuna's work and Alexander's personal activity is essential not only for the following reflections on Plutarch but also for the

[6] On the relationship of Alexander and ἔργον and the relevance of the latter for the New Testament, see below.

exegesis of the New Testament. It should be mentioned that the personal achievement of the young Macedonian king is here described as having come about through the "price of much blood and wounds." The theme of hurtful and personally taxing exercises is maintained throughout the entire tractate and is characteristic of the concept of the περιστάσεις.[7] Therefore, many catalogues of circumstances (περιστάσεις) can be found. These catalogues are well known from the letters of Paul, particularly 2 Corinthians, and must be presumed for Paul's opponents as well, although in a more heroic light than Paul wants to give them.[8]

At the end of the catalogue of circumstances in §1, Plutarch presents a catalogue of virtues. This form is known from the literature of the early church as well, especially from Paul, but usually they are not connected with catalogues of circumstances. 2 Cor 6:4–10 is an exception; here we find a catalogue of virtues worked over and integrated into a catalogue of circumstances.

At the beginning of §2, Plutarch describes τύχη not as a force behind the origin of Alexander's deeds (as was done in §1) but as a partner of Alexander in his successes. He is peer to the goddess. Ignatius in *Romans* 2:1 uses the term ἐπιγράφειν for the description of a partnership with the achievements of another person. Plutarch lets Alexander start with a speech that disclaims any title of τύχη on his successes. The conclusion of this speech is found at the end of §2 because there the first person singular ends, but §3 certainly is meant as a supplement.

Alexander's fictitious sermon begins with self-acclaim by means of depreciating others—a practice for which Paul usually denounces his opponents,

[7] The interest of Jewish missionary theology/apologetics in suffering is evident most prominently in 4 Maccabees but is not limited to this document. A martyr theology was developed that anticipated its later Christian counterparts—martyrdom understood as heroic achievement and by that token not merely of religious but also of propagandistic, social, and indeed political benefit. 4 Maccabees shows that the basic link to general Hellenistic ideals was the concept of *agōn*, easily connected with ἀρετή in its double meaning of virtue and divine active power. As much as there were pagan missionaries and apologetics, there were also pagan martyrs and exemplary accounts of their triumphs and communal-societal benefits through suffering, the most prominent pagan martyr being Socrates. Philostratus also presents Apollonius as a martyr in his *Life of Apollonius.*

[8] The endurance of adversity and duress as a major element of mission is already present in the Heracles myth, of great importance for Greek colonialism and even more for Alexander's and Hellenism's understanding of cultural mission. In Euripides' missionary tragedy *Bacchae,* Dionysus illustrates the connection between suffering and mission as well. The descriptions of the mission of the authentic Cynic philosopher by Epictetus in *Dissertationes* 1.24 and 3.22, and of Peregrinus Proteus by Lucian, prove (as two of many examples) the conscious integration of harsh circumstances into the kerygmatic efforts of the delegates of God in pagan missionary propaganda. In the case of Peregrinus Proteus, self-immolation is part of the execution of that mission, with a clear communicative intention of the dying person as well as of his epigones and messengers.

particularly in 2 Corinthians, although his opponents and his churches on occasion seemed to have viewed him as not being free from that habit himself.[9] The direct self-recommendation that follows is also known from the New Testament, not only from the epistles but also from Acts and the Gospels—here especially as Jesus' self-recommendation, predominantly in self-revelatory pronouncements. The irony at the end of 326F applied to Fortuna is found in the depiction of the demonic in the Revelation of John. For the main part of Alexander's self-recommendation Plutarch again uses the form of the catalogue of circumstances (327A and B), now like Paul (2 Cor 11:22–33) in the form of an immediately autobiographical summary. In both cases emphasis is placed on the adverse circumstances. Both instances belong to the complex genre of the *res gestae.*[10] Apparently, Plutarch uses historical information for this report—although from sources unknown to us—but he is not interested in a correct historical sequence for the events reported.

Although Alexander's speech had ended with §2, the enumeration of circumstances is continued, yet now in an even more summary fashion and less chronologically organized than the preceding section. But Plutarch keeps the biographical flavor alive. A change of style within the account like that in §§2 and 3 is not rare in Pauline examples of the form of the catalogue of circumstances, as evidenced by the examples in 2 Corinthians. Concerning the contrast between the youthful age of the hero on the one side and expectation and achievement on the other as described in 321D, one is reminded here of Luke's story of the young Jesus in the temple (Luke 2:41–52) and the Lukan reference to the beginning of Jesus' public career in Luke 3:23. It is important for our comparison that Luke does this while emphasizing the universal dimensions of Jesus' mission. The rule that those whom the gods love they let die early is known rather early in Greek tradition, and it affected the Alexander tradition as well as the Jesus tradition. An older version of that maxim occurs in Wisdom 3–5, here as description of the end of the just one(s), especially in 4:7–14, thus demonstrating the incorporation of this idea by the diaspora synagogue prior to the first century C.E.

At the beginning of §4 is a rhetorical question about the reasonability of Alexander with respect to the beginning of his undertakings. This kind of question and the expected negative answer are known from the style of the diatribe, used there for the purpose of emphasis. The literature of the early church adopted this rhetorical device, as Paul already proves. The use of ἀφορμή in the beginning of §4 for the description of a moral advantage of a certain character in the context of general praise finds an important parallel in the two passages in 2 Cor 5:12 and 11:12 where Paul speaks of his own

[9] See Georgi, *Opponents,* index under "recommendation" and "self-recommendation."
[10] Ibid., 294 n. 122, 406–9.

respectable self-recommendation and denounces the self-recommendations of others as immoral. It should be noted that, according to 327E, these ἀφορμαί could be taught. The catalogue of virtues that follows has at least formal parallels in the literature of the early church. It consists of an enumeration of the gifts one may receive through studying philosophy. An interesting substantial parallel is the listing of the fruits of the spirit in Gal 5:22–23, remarkable because of the central orientation of these gifts and in this sense resembling the Plutarch reference in question.

The personification of philosophy as found here in Plutarch is not rare in Hellenism, although the idea of philosophy as an inspiring and empowering force is not as common. The opponents in Col 2:8 would be an example of the latter idea.

At the beginning of 328, one might discover interesting analogies within documents of the early church if the meaning of ὑπομνηματισμοί and their relation to λόγος could be clarified. The use of scriptures in the early church has to be seen in a much wider frame of reference than the church or even Judaism at large.[11] Principles of establishing and using authoritative holy writings, including the idea of "canon," have many parallels in Greek and Hellenistic culture and more direct ones in contemporary Roman culture since Augustus.[12] Hellenistic culture, and its education in particular, depended on knowing and using writings by and written traditions about Homer, the Seven Sages, Socrates, Plato, the founders of the other Socratic schools including Aristotle, the classical tragedians, comedians, lyricists, rhetors, historians—later also the Roman greats, poets, historians, laws and lawyers, and the *Aeneid* of Virgil.

The tendency to canonize authoritative writings was first and most of all a Hellenistic-Roman principle. Judaism and the early church simply adopted this practice; they did not invent it. This was part of a communicative strategy, without which the victory of the Pentateuch would not have been possible. That this was already the case in the time of Ezra cannot be demonstrated, but from the Hellenistic period of Judaism on—that is, since the times of Alexander—this communicative strategy existed in Hellenistic culture.

In our text Plutarch goes so far as to consider λόγος and Alexander's ὑπομνηματισμοί (of the various virtues) superior to most authoritative writings, even to the bible of Hellenistic culture—the *Iliad* and the *Odyssey* of Homer. The intention of Plutarch is to demonstrate that Alexander represents a philosophy of action superior to theoretical philosophy. The distinction between ἔργον (as important) and λόγος (as less important) is known

[11] Ibid., 84–90, 110–16, 122–48, 160–64, 246–71, 394–409, 422–34.

[12] Ibid., 427–34.

from many writings of the early church, for instance 2 Cor 10:11, where Paul uses this argument to denigrate his opponents.

The essential philosophical achievement of Alexander, according to Plutarch, is the spread of civilization, that is, the universal expansion of law and peace. It might be natural to presume here the influence of the image of Augustus, but this would be a short-circuiting of the problem. It overlooks the fact that Augustus very consciously modeled his activity and propaganda after the paradigm of Alexander. For example, Augustus sealed his correspondence with the image of Alexander, and his most important court theologian, Virgil, paralleled Augustus in book 6 of the *Aeneid* with the great Macedonian.

The fact that Alexander—like Socrates, the biblical patriarchs, or Jesus—did not leave any writings behind is not considered a disadvantage, but an advantage intimating an authority superior to the written one, the ἀγράμματα regarded as of a higher quality than the γράμματα. This motif played an important role in the traditions of the Jesus movement and their redactional processes, most of all in Paul and Christian Gnosticism. Alexander, according to Plutarch, is superior to all philosophers who wrote philosophical tractates. He is a universally successful philosopher of action. His praxis is philosophical reality, more all-embracing and comprehensive, more penetrating and decisive than all theory.

The question must be asked whether Paul's missionary activity and that of other Jesus missionaries (including that of Jewish predecessors and contemporaries) stand consciously or subconsciously in the long line of individuals and institutions exercising an *imitatio Alexandri.* Alexander's example had been of tremendous influence among the learned and the uneducated alike, a true mass phenomenon in the Mediterranean world for a long period of time, later even bridging the borders between the Christian and Islamic worlds. The history of tradition of the Alexander romance is itself proof of this influence. A further question results from this, namely, whether or not imitation of Alexander did not also, as a matter of course, include the idea of urbanization and worldwide civilization among the many missionaries of the various missionary religions—Judaism and its newly emergent version of the Jesus movement included. For Hellenistic Jewish missionary theology, this was an essential motivation. Read against this background, the discussion of mission in Paul's Letter to the Romans (particularly chaps. 2, 11, and 15) gains a new perspective and certainly also a new critical dimension.

As the two following sections of Plutarch's tractate discussed demonstrate, philosophical activity for this writer is synonymous with worldwide education—education most of all understood as ethical formation. This concept, be it understood positively or as a critical counterimage, is of great importance for Jewish missionaries and those of the early church. The high point of philosophical and missionary activity is the change of human nature, which Alexander, more than anyone else, brought about. Because of this ability to change humanity from within, Alexander (for Plutarch) is the most authentic and essential philosopher.

The relationship of mission to internal change is also a common concept in the early church. It appears to me that the above idea of Alexander's mission, not invented but adopted by Plutarch, should be included in any discussion of conversion in the early church, especially within the Hellenistic Jewish mission—mission here, as in the case of Alexander, being understood as demand and expansion of world civilization.[13]

Gal 3:23–4:7 shows that Paul critically discusses the idea and praxis of worldwide education leading toward reason and order under the guidance of the law. It is commonly assumed that he here addresses individual rather than social issues, but the interplay of law and education is being brought by him into a universal, cosmic perspective. This dimension emerges more clearly when held against the Plutarch text in question. The common claim that in Paul the political dimension would be replaced by what modern exegetes and theologians call the eschatological understanding, identical with a privatizing and individualizing intention, is premature; in fact, contrary to the point, Paul engages in concrete critical dialogue with his whole culture, not merely the Jewish one.

In Plutarch's eyes, the empire of Alexander had realized one way of life, one common law, and one people—all ideals of Zenon's state. Plutarch describes this in almost hymnic fashion. Alexander's empire is a well-ordered philosophical community. This reminds one of the concept of unity and reconciliation in the letters to the Ephesians, the Colossians, and already in Paul. The difference between Zenon's state as dream or as εἴδολον and the transformation of this dream into an ἔργον by Alexander (329B) makes one think of the antithesis between shadow and reality in the Letter to the Hebrews.

Plutarch stresses that Alexander's policy of universal reconciliation and unity consciously contradicted the counsel of Aristotle, who insisted on the lasting separation of Greeks and barbarians. It appears to be an element of royal panegyrics to present Alexander as sent from heaven, as κοινὸς ἁρμοστὴς καὶ διαλλακτὴς τῶν ὅλων. This is similar to the image of Jesus Christ in Ephesians, and even more so in Colossians and Ignatius. Alexander's policy of integration is presented as a mixture in a κρατὴρ φιλοτήσιος, an idea similar to the concept of ἀγάπη in Paul, John, and Ignatius. The idea that moral differences on the international level were intended to replace ethnic differences and polarization—that even the terms "Greek" and "barbarian" should become subtitles for ethical values, instead of ethical values becoming

[13] Ibid., 148–51, 366–77, 390–409.

subtitles to the terms "Greek" and "barbarian," as was the custom heretofore—goes beyond any statement of the New Testament.

In the seventh section, the famous wedding scene is portrayed as a welding of Asia and Europe. This is described as love presenting the common bond (although understood more in the sense of marital and parental love) and presents a clear parallel to the ecclesiological concepts of Pauline, Johannine, and Ignatian writings. The discussion of Alexander's policy of accommodation with respect to clothing and customs is also similar to Jewish missionary theology and practice, reflected in Paul's rule of being a Jew to the Jews, to those under the law as one under the law, and to those without the law as one without the law (1 Cor 9:19–23).

The scholarly discussion of the ἁρπαγμός passage in Phil 2:6 has on the whole overlooked the soteriological dimensions of the Plutarch parallel in 330D. The contrast to Plutarch is not between οὐδ' ὥσπερ ἅρπαγμα and δικαίως (or something similar) but between an attitude resembling robbers, and universal leadership/reconciliation: ἀλλ' ἑνὸς ὑπήκοα λόγου τὰ ἐπὶ γῆς καὶ μιᾶς πολιτείας ἕνα δήμων ἀνθρώπους ἅπαντας ἀποφῆναι βουλόμενος. Alexander is someone who brings ὁμονοία, εἰρήνη, and κοινωνία to all humans (330B). This corresponds to Plutarch's previous statement about Alexander's being a god-sent ἁρμοστὴς καὶ διαλλακτής (329C).

In the passage that follows (330D), Alexander is presented again as one sent from god. That passage develops, as noted above, Alexander's policy of accommodation. He subjects himself to the subjugated ones. Plutarch does not say anything about exaltation. He had not spoken before about a real *kenōsis* either, but the text has in mind a sudden recall of Alexander by the deity who sent him. The pattern chosen is sufficiently close to the hymn in Philippians 2 and similar texts of the early church to commend itself to exegetes as a possible counterfoil.

There is a lamenting remark that is interesting. It states that the whole of humanity could have been unified under one law and under one just person as leader had the life of Alexander not been so brief. This is portrayed in revelatory terms, as participation or nonparticipation in a common light, and as owning or not owning the sun. Alexander is the revealing personality. The closeness to the soteriological ideas of Romans 5; 15; and Ephesians is obvious: universal unity established by a heavenly delegate in human form. The difference is clear also: Plutarch emphasizes that Alexander's undertaking was but fragmentary. No heavenly postexistence is reported, no efficacious afterlife, and the major unifying element in the case of Alexander is the law.

Following the presentation of the heroic conduct of Alexander and his political intentions, the tractate continues with a treatment of his sayings (logia). What we have here is a collection of (biographical) apophthegms (the term the older form critics would have used), as defined in 331A. Plutarch provides brief anecdotes or chriae, each around a logion of Alexander. Naturally these apophthegms/chriae/anecdotes and their collection are of great interest to Gospel criticism. It appears to me that we learn from these also something about the self-understanding of Papias and about the character and criteria of his work.

The introductory line of this portion of Plutarch's tractate intimates that this recording of collected sayings and/or apophthegms/chriae/anecdotes of kings and political leaders (partly quoted in the following introduction of the collection) corresponds to the conception and assessment of kings usual in Hellenism and elsewhere.[14] This points to the possible existence of similar collections—although of persons who did not have the flair of Alexander, and especially not the interests of Plutarch. Therefore, these other collections did not receive similar attention from later generations and eventually were lost.

In the section preceding his collection of anecdotes, Plutarch has made statements that betray his dependence on Hellenistic discussions of true kingship as they were conducted by philosophers but also reflected in school exercises. This underlines the closeness of Plutarch to Hellenistic traditions. In those discussions and exercises on kingship, Alexander was presented as a model of kingship, although he was not always seen as a positive example but more frequently a negative one.

Plutarch's presentation of the collection of apophthegms manifests itself as a secondary elaboration. It presupposes a previous collection and reflects on it as the author/redactor presents it. Plutarch adds comments, both preceding and inserted into the collection, some of which are of considerable length. From the standpoint of form criticism this collection of anecdotes is more fully developed than the collections in the Synoptic Gospels, but less advanced than the Semeia source in John's Gospel. There is yet no serious interest in a systematic arrangement; for the biographic appearances, only the youth of Alexander is correctly placed with these stories at the beginning.

In contrast to the tendency of the redactors of the Jesus tradition, Plutarch's comments are distinctly set apart from the mass of the traditional material collected, on occasion even distancing themselves by a nonemotional, reflective style. These secondary, sometimes even tertiary, comments are not integrated into the narrative, as could have been done by presenting them as (fictitious) remarks of contemporaries of Alexander. The one exception occurs at the end of 331E, where Plutarch himself inserts a piece of historical information, as well as the clearly inauthentic deliberations in §12.

Further, the technique of weaving redactional comments into longer speeches of the main figure, as one finds, for example, in John's Gospel and

[14] Ibid., 51, 404–6.

Acts, is attested only once in the tractates discussed—in the invented speech of Diogenes in 332. It is interesting that this speech is presented in a brief redactional remark as an extensive interpretation of a logion of Alexander: εἰ μὴ 'Αλεξανδρὸς ἤμην, Διογένης ἤμην. Therefore, the comparability with Johannine method and style is limited. The apophthegms Plutarch found already collected contained in some cases secondary additions from the hands of earlier collectors/redactors. Such a secondary addition, for instance, is found in 331E, where everything following 'Αχιλλέως κέκτημαι (at least from a form-critical perspective) is unnecessary and secondary. This apophthegm could have easily ended earlier after the line οὐδὲν τῆς ἐκείνου δέομαι.

This collection of Alexander anecdotes continues up to §10. Whereas the preceding stories had been collected in order to portray the wit and alertness of Alexander, the chriae in §11 were collated to support and illustrate the theme of the truly royal attitude of Philip's son. Plutarch transforms this tendency into the overall subject of the true philosopher, not a very radical change for Hellenistic taste.

It is questionable whether §12 contains any material from the previous collection of Alexander anecdotes. In the first place, there is only one narrative, and if it is taken as an anecdote, then it is one of a completely different kind from the others in the preceding collection—a correspondence story, as it were. The stringency of the other stories is absent. There is no grouping of individual units under one theme. The narrative is integrated more strongly into Plutarch's intentions, namely, to debate and depict morality extensively. Thus, the last redactor, Plutarch, seems to have added this episode from another source. This method is known to us from the gospel tradition, where in similar fashion the late or last editor remained under the influence of form and genre as he completed his collection.

There are also fascinating parallels to the documents of the early church in Plutarch's redactional remarks in §§9–12. The motif in 331C is important for the Hellenistic understanding of victorious and salvific suffering and as such provides a significant parallel to certain narrations and interpretations of the death of Jesus, and also the lives and martyrdoms of apostles, bishops, prophets, and others in the early church: τοῖς ἰδίοις ἀγάλλεσθαι τραύμασι, καθ' ἕκαστον μέρος ἔθνους μνημονεύοντα καὶ νίκης καὶ πόλεων ἁλισκομένων καὶ βασιλέων παραδιδόντων . . . (τὰς οὐλάς) . . . ὥσπερ εἰκόνας ἐγκεχαραγμένας ἀρετῆς καὶ ἀνδραγαθίας περιφέροντα.

Plutarch uses the story in §11 in order to treat the true philosopher-king, who supersedes the earlier models for the θεῖος ἀνήρ. This motif is well known from Hellenistic Jewish missionary theology and has influenced greatly the self-understanding of the early church.[15] It gave propagandistic

[15] Ibid., 148–51, 366–77, 390–409.

models and structures to missionaries and their enterprises and was copied by many Jesus missionaries, who formed the traditions about Jesus and the so-called apostles and then shaped their own work accordingly. They followed themselves the θεῖος ἀνήρ model and connected this with the biblical tradition, comparing and competing with other religious and philosophical traditions and their actual representatives and followers. This was a peculiar way of exchange, a communication with the surrounding culture that made one's own message understandable to the environment—much to the chagrin of Paul, who firmly resisted this kind of communication.[16]

In 332AB this motif is taken up again, this time including heroes and deities, for example, Heracles, Perseus, Dionysus, all of whom are seen as models. In 331E Plutarch further reveals the existence of a pagan wisdom tradition. Here sapiential sentences form a string of sayings demonstrating the presence and force of wisdom in various ways.

Plutarch's new interpretation of Alexander's strategic intentions, found in 332A, calls to mind, even more than the previous version, Paul's reflections concerning his missionary strategy in Rom 15:19–25. Paul's use of Jesus as a model in Rom 15:3, and especially in v. 8, corresponds to the practice of Jewish missionaries, who, like Alexander, followed the examples of earlier heroic and even divine individuals who through their own energetic action, interfering in human affairs, had brought peoples and other cultures under their own religious and cultural reign.

The example of the gymnosophists presents an interesting version of a problem common to all forms of Hellenistic propaganda (cultural, philosophical, religious, pagan, Jewish, and early church), namely, that the missionary message had to be new but also had to presuppose consciously the work of others as preparatory to one's own message and action. Missionary success needed to relate to those for whom the propaganda was intended, integrating essential elements that had been known before and elsewhere. This was necessary for the establishment of one's own authenticity.[17]

Given the interest within literature of the early church in metaphors such as seal, image, type, reflection, coining, etc., a simile found at the end of §10 should be of importance: δεῖ κἀμὲ νόμισμα παρκόψαι καὶ παραχαράξαι τὸ βαρβαρικὸν Ἑλληνικῇ πολιτεία.

Only a few observations remain to be made on the last sections of the first tractate on the fortune of Alexander. Section 11 begins with a catalogue of virtues and vices. The dialectic pairs in 332D are also important from a form-critical standpoint. This is preceded by a discussion of the Stoic concept of correct individual actions, as the incorporation and comprehension of all virtues united in one. This and the view that an individual may be αὐτονόμος

[16] Ibid., indexes under "divine man" and "θεῖος ἀνήρ."

[17] Ibid., index under "tradition."

(332B) are similar to Paul's preference for the singular in the case of ἔργον, or where he speaks of work or action in a positive sense, particularly in the case of Gal 6:4 and Rom 2:14–15—the latter passage even with respect to the action of Gentiles. The statements of Paul and John on the ἔργον of God, the Lord, and Christ, belong here (cf. John 4:34; 6:28; 10:32–33; 17:4; Rom 14:20; 1 Cor 15:58; 16:10; Phil 1:6; 2:30; note also the end of 333B).

A last surprising parallel is found in 333B. Here Plutarch says that owning philosophy had made Alexander free to share all he had with others, a statement similar to Paul's description of sovereignty in Phil 4:10–13.[18]

[18] The tractate *De Fortuna Romanorum* is not unrelated to the Alexander tradition, as its conclusion already shows. This tractate portrays a contest between Fortuna and Virtus, which is resolved by making them both powers, that is, deities, who correspond and cooperate, actually in the end dissolving Virtus into Fortuna. This presupposes the ambivalence of the meaning of ἀρετή as being virtue as well as miraculous power and action. Fortuna, as based on Roman virtue, brought about stability and security, a world order (κόσμος in its double meaning of order and world [317B]).

The conclusion of this tractate reads like a continuation of the tractates on the fortune of Alexander (326A and B). Once more the issue of Alexander's early death is picked up. It is said that it was the will and action of Fortuna that Alexander died prematurely before he could move toward the west and thus become a threat to the Romans. Here Plutarch also praises the prowess and success of Alexander and describes his intention as surpassing even Dionysus and Heracles (ὑπερβαλέσθαι τὰ Διονύσου καὶ Ἡρακλέους πέρατα τῆς στρατηλασίας). This relates to the tendency of the *Vita* of Alexander as portrayed by Plutarch in the *Parallel Lives*.

3

New Testament Papyrus Manuscripts and Letter Carrying in Greco-Roman Times

ELDON JAY EPP

Issues, Purpose, and Limitations

IT IS WELL KNOWN that the earliest extant manuscripts of the New Testament were written on papyrus and were all found in Egypt.[1] The first was published in 1868 (P11), but B. P. Grenfell and A. S. Hunt's discoveries at Oxyrhynchus in 1897 occasioned the first genuine excitement over such finds, and eventually twenty-seven New Testament papyrus fragments were recovered from that site alone. More significant discoveries, in terms of extensive manuscripts of early date, were to come in the 1930s and 1950s, and currently some eighty-six different New Testament papyrus manuscripts are in hand. These manuscripts reflect a variety of textual complexions, which has given rise to the intractable questions as to whether or not the papyri represent an array of early "text-types" and—even more basic—whether there were or could have been "text-types" in Egypt in the period of the earliest group of New Testament papyri—those dating prior to ca. 300 C.E. There also are subsidiary questions, whose answers could help resolve the larger issues; these include the following: Though all New Testament papyri were found in Egypt, did they all actually originate in Egypt? If not, how easily and quickly could they or their ancestors have been transferred to Egypt from other parts of the Greco-Roman world? And

[1] To Helmut Koester, a demanding but always supportive mentor and a career-long colleague in *Hermeneia,* I owe far more than can be conveyed in a brief statement that he inspired his students to seek out important issues in early Christianity, to pursue them armed with a thorough grasp of the Greco-Roman world, and to persist in their resolution despite obstacles or opposition.

how readily did written documents in general—but especially letters and literature—move from place to place in that period?

In a recent article, the present writer undertook in a preliminary way (though not using the term) a "social-world" approach to this whole matter, and the simple intention of the present exploratory essay is to attempt a further step in that investigation.[2]

The New Testament Papyri in Their Setting

The papyrus manuscripts of the New Testament did not exist in a vacuum but were part of an active, vibrant world of agriculture, commerce, travel, education, literary activity, medicine, religion, law, and everyday life in the society of the day. All of this—and more—is abundantly attested by the papyrus documents and letters that have come down to us from ancient Egypt. Among the activities of business, legal, and public life that have been documented by the papyri are edicts, codes, reports, declarations, and announcements of government officers; applications, nominations, and appointments to official positions; petitions, summonses, depositions, minutes, and judgments in legal proceedings; and business orders, contracts, statements, receipts, accounts, and audits. Education, literature, and philosophy are attested by copies of works by Homer, Hesiod, Sappho, Pindar, Bacchylides, Sophocles, Euripides, Menander, and Callimachus, to mention only the most prominent poets and playwrights; by portions of the historical writings of Herodotus and Thucydides, of orations by Aeschines, Demosthenes, and Hyperides, of philosophers such as Plato, Theophrastus, and various Sophists, Cynics, and Stoics; as well as by school exercises, folk poetry, and an array of miscellaneous literary texts. Among the myriad events and social interactions of everyday life that are reflected in this material are marriage and divorce; birth, adoption, civil rights, death, wills, bequests, and even the exposure of children; sons in military service and children away at school; concern about health, safety, and welfare; invitations to visit and the sending of gifts; crime, fraud, and vandalism; and prayers, charms, and horoscopes. In addition, this real-life, flesh-and-blood world that the papyri reveal to us is replete with the wide array of human perceptions and emotions, including feelings of accomplishment and disappointment, anger and approval, estrangement and reconciliation, loneliness and comfort, anxiety and relief, depression and elation, and joy and

[2] Eldon Jay Epp, "The Significance of the Papyri for Determining the Nature of the New Testament Text in the Second Century: A Dynamic View of Textual Transmission," in *Gospel Traditions in the Second Century: Origins, Recensions, Text, and Transmission*, ed. William L. Petersen (Christianity and Judaism in Antiquity 3; Notre Dame, Ind./London: University of Notre Dame Press, 1989) 76–84, esp. 81–84 and 89–90.

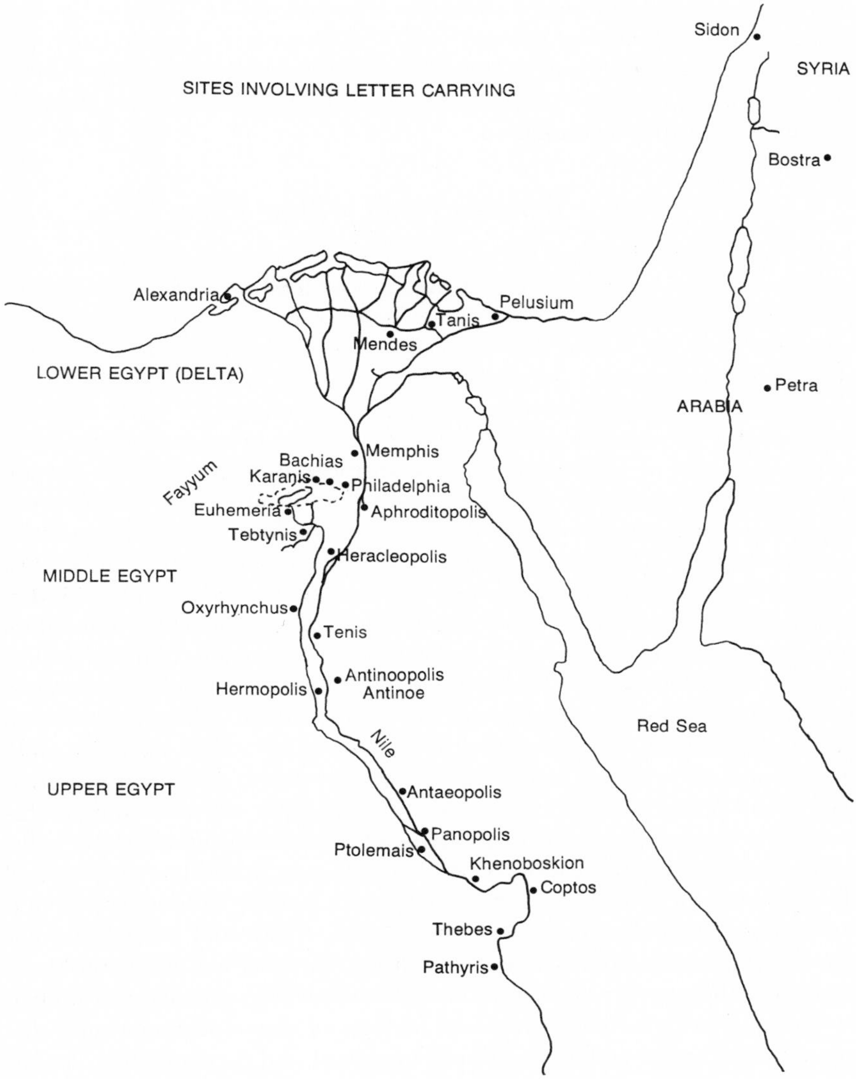
SITES INVOLVING LETTER CARRYING
Sidon
SYRIA
Bostra
Alexandria
Pelusium
Tanis
Mendes
LOWER EGYPT (DELTA)
Petra
ARABIA
Memphis
Bachias
Fayyum
Karanis
Philadelphia
Euhemeria
Aphroditopolis
Tebtynis
Heracleopolis
MIDDLE EGYPT
Oxyrhynchus
Tenis
Antinoopolis
Antinoe
Hermopolis
Red Sea
Nile
UPPER EGYPT
Antaeopolis
Panopolis
Ptolemais
Khenoboskion
Coptos
Thebes
Pathyris

sorrow. The papyri were sent, received, and employed in a down-to-earth, everyday social environment, and it was within this same world that the New Testament papyrus texts were transmitted and used.

The quantity of this variegated material is immense.[3] In the New Testament field, this material has been used since its discovery to explore the nature of the vocabulary, diction, and syntax of New Testament Greek and to locate parallels to the content of the New Testament. Yet this social world of the New Testament papyrus manuscripts has seldom been related directly to those New Testament papyri themselves in an effort to discover how such texts were transmitted; from where, to where, and by whom they were carried; and how and how fast they traveled. To be sure, this analysis may not in any specific fashion illumine the New Testament papyri text-critically or even assist in locating them precisely and individually in their own immediate settings, but it can help us to see them for what they are: artifacts of a real-life setting that was in no way isolated from the daily flow of people and events. Above all, we are permitted—indeed, compelled—to see that the New Testament papyri neither originated nor functioned in a vacuum, nor did they move in and through the Greco-Roman world via a kind of sacred superhighway, as if unrelated or insensitive to the surrounding world.

That the New Testament papyrus manuscripts were part of and participants in this vibrant social environment is perhaps in no way so poignantly confirmed as by the fact that the vast majority of the New Testament papyri appear to have been discovered in the rubbish heaps of Egypt—one of the great levelers in society short of death itself. Contrary to what a pious Christian might believe or wish to believe, these priceless portions of "sacred scripture" suffered the same ignominious fate that befell thousands of legal, official, and business documents, personal letters, and school exercises, and also copies of the works of great secular writers, historians, and philosophers of antiquity that have been mentioned earlier. Whether the biblical papyri were worn out by use and discarded or were abandoned because of neglect and nonuse, they rested unceremoniously for hundreds upon hundreds of years along with other remnants and cast-offs of an active social milieu. As a matter of interest, some of our more extensive New Testament papyri—the Chester Beatty—were rumored to have been found in a pitcher in a ruined

[3] For a convenient summary, see E. J. Epp, "The New Testament Papyrus Manuscripts in Historical Perspective," in *To Touch the Text: Biblical and Related Studies in Honor of Joseph A. Fitzmyer, S.J.*, ed. M. P. Horgan and P. J. Kobelski (New York: Crossroad, 1989) 264–65 and the references cited there. Some of the relevant material can be found conveniently in A. S. Hunt and C. C. Edgar, *Select Papyri: I. Non-Literary Papyri, Private Affairs* and *II. Public Documents*, and Denys L. Page, *Select Papyri: Literary Papyri: Poetry* (LCL 266, 282, 360; Cambridge, Mass.: Harvard University Press, 1932–42) [cited as LCL 1, etc.], and in John L. White, *Light from Ancient Letters* (Foundations and Facets; Philadelphia: Fortress Press, 1986) [abbreviations of papyri follow White].

church or monastery near Aphroditopolis in the Fayyum, which might suggest that they, too, had outlived their usefulness and were given a customary form of "burial" for unwanted manuscripts.[4] Overall, rubbish heaps, collapsed and rubbish-filled buildings, ruined structures filled with windblown sand, and an occasional jar have been the common resting places for New Testament papyri and for the tens of thousands of other literary and nonliterary manuscripts from Egypt. Others, no more nobly treated, were reused in the bindings of later books or by being turned into cartonnage or "paper-mache" for wrapping mummies.[5]

This, then, constitutes the general setting and the larger context for the treasured fragments of papyrus that carry texts of the New Testament writings.

Scholarly Attitudes toward Nonliterary Papyri

It has long been customary for New Testament textual critics to pick up (so to speak) the New Testament papyrus documents as precious, independently existing artifacts, dust them off, and then utilize them for text-critical purposes largely in isolation both from the immediate environment out of which they were "rescued" (a common expression which itself makes the point!) and from the social setting in which they originated and functioned. This attitude is perhaps understandable when one recalls that early archaeologists discarded untold numbers of papyri in favor of finding instrinsically valuable artifacts or those of museum quality[6] and that classical scholars in the first half of the nineteenth century were dismayed that Greek papyrus discoveries throughout that period were predominantly documentary rather than literary. Overall, until the twentieth century little attention was paid to those nonliterary documents that reflected the socioeconomic history of the Hellenistic and Roman periods, for "papyri were rated according to literary content, and these were regarded as pretty mediocre."[7]

This preference for literary papyri over the nonliterary continued into the twentieth century, so that Adolf Deissmann in 1922 could say "it is regettable, therefore, to see the merest scrap of an ancient book treated as if it were something sacred—immediately published with notes and facsimile, even it be a fragment of some forgotten scribbler who deserved his fate—

[4] Colin H. Roberts, *Manuscript, Society and Belief in Early Christian Egypt* (Schweich Lectures, 1977; London: Oxford University Press, 1979) 7.

[5] To complete the picture, it should be added that tombs also yielded a few Greek papyrus manuscripts that had been buried with the dead.

[6] Leo Deuel, *Testaments of Time: The Search for Lost Manuscripts and Records* (Baltimore: Penguin Books, 1970; original, New York: Alfred A. Knopf, 1965) 92, cf. 88.

[7] Ibid., 92–93.

while on the other hand the non-literary items are often not even printed in full."[8] Papyrologists, when publishing papyri, routinely make the same distinction between literary papyri and documentary or nonliterary papyri, further subdividing the latter into private documents (including letters) and public documents (as is done, e.g., in LCL 1 and 2, respectively). Further, when publishing literary papyri, papyrologists often assign biblical fragments to a category different from that given to texts of classical authors. All of these procedures and attitudes tended not only to separate the documentary papyri from the literary but at times even to separate biblical from classical texts.

Naturally, these characterizations are not meant to suggest any reform in how the papyri are classified or published. The point is a much simpler one, though not thereby any less important: the attitude that separated documentary from literary papyri, or personal letters from literary works, or biblical papyri from secular manuscripts has impoverished the study of the New Testament papyri by abstracting them from their "bedfellows" in the rubbish heaps and thereby isolating and insulating them from their proper social environment or life setting. Rather, the New Testament papyri need to be studied in their proper social context.

Purpose and Limitations of the Present Study

The proper procedure—restoring the New Testament papyri to their life setting—not only can enlighten us about their immediate social context but also can help in answering the questions posed earlier—how far, how easily, and how quickly New Testament manuscripts might have moved around the Greco-Roman world of earliest Christianity, and by what means of transfer. Answers to these puzzles are directly relevant to the other questions raised earlier about New Testament textual criticism: (1) Were there distinctive and identifiable text-types in the earliest period of New Testament textual transmission? (2) If so, to what extent are the Egyptian papyri representative of that spectrum of texts? (3) And did they originate only in Egypt?

This present effort is only a beginning, and space restrictions further require that the investigation be limited to a single facet of the New Testament papyri's social world: *letter carrying.* The purpose of these limited pages, then, will be to show how Greco-Roman letters and their movement reveal aspects of the social-world environment of the time that are relevant to answering the basic but intractable questions just posed about the New Testament papyri.

[8] See Adolf Deissmann, *Light from the Ancient East* (New York: Harper, 1927; German original, 4th ed. 1922) 39.

The illustrative material will be restricted to private letters (though with occasional reference to public documents), and it will range over papyri originating in the broad Greco-Roman period (generally, from Alexander to Constantine). Obviously, the random nature of the data—tens of thousands of manuscripts found but hundreds of thousands lost, with the survivors offering mainly a selection of documents discarded in antiquity—leaves us in a far less than desirable situation, though we remain immensely grateful for what we do possess. We quickly discover, however, how important letters were. For example, a slave writes to her master in the second century CE, "I beg you, my lord, if it seems good to you, to send us a letter also, since we die if we do not see you daily. Would that we could fly to you and greet you. . . ." (*PGeiss* 17; LCL 1:115).[9] Or a marine writes from Misenum, a port near Naples, to Philadelphia in the Fayyum (second century CE), begging his father to write even "a little letter, telling me first of your welfare, secondly of my brother's and sister's, and enabling me thirdly to make obeisance before your hand[writing]" (*BGU* 423; LCL 1:112). The son, newly settled at his naval assignment, thinks of his family, and even a "little letter" written in his father's own hand would bring to him all the warmth of home and hearth. "And do not hesitate to write letters," a man writes to his brother in Karanis (in the Fayyum) on 23 August 133, "since I rejoiced exceedingly, as if you had come. From the day that you sent me the letter I have been saved (*PMich.* VIII 482), and it goes on, incidentally, to report that "Peteeus, who is writing this letter for me, salutes you repeatedly as well as your wife and your daughter and Bassus your horse" (!).

In addition, the extant papyri provide evidence covering the full range of human endeavor and of human emotion. Human feelings emerge with special force and poignancy, of course, in papyri of a private nature, and it is impossible to avoid the impression that most social interactions of everyday life in the Egypt of the period surrounding the earliest Christian era bear close resemblance to aspects of modern life. A few examples must suffice. Disease and calamity occur: "I beg you, brother, to write to me about your being all well, as I heard at Antinoopolis that there has been a plague in your neighborhood. So do not neglect to write, that I may feel more cheerful about you," writes Pausanias to Heraclides in Oxyrhynchus in the third century (*POxy.* 1666; LCL 1:149). Another letter, from 95 BCE says, "We heard that mice have eaten up the crop. Pray come to us and buy wheat here . . ." (*PGrenf.* II 36; LCL 1:103). Bills were sometimes hard to collect: "Let me tell you that you owe me seven years' rents and revenues, so unless you send remittances you know the risk you run" (late third century; *PTebt.* 424; LCL 1:154). Caution is needed during travel: "When you come, bring

[9] For this translation, see John Garrett Winter, *Life and Letters in the Papyri* (Jerome Lectures; Ann Arbor: University of Michigan Press, 1933) 130.

your gold ornaments, but do not wear them on the boat," writes Paniskos to his wife in 296 CE (*PMich.* III 214). Propriety triumphs over feelings in this postscript to a second-century letter from mother to son: "At your wedding the wife of my brother Discas brought me 100 drachmae; and now that her son Nilus is about to marry, it is right that we should make a return gift, even if we have grievances against them still pending" (*PFlor.* 332; LCL 1:114). Above all, family conflicts occur, as in the second-century CE letter from one brother to another:

> Sempronius to Maximus his brother, very many greetings. . . . I learned that you are treating our revered mother harshly as if she were a slave. Please, dearest brother, do not distress her in anything. If any one of the brothers talks back to her, you ought to box their ears. . . . For we ought to reverence her who bore us as a god, especially when she is so good. This I have written to you, brother, since I know the sweetness of dear parents. Please write me about your health. Farewell, brother. (LCL 1:121; trans. Winter, 48–49)

A daughter, Plutogenia, writes from Alexandria to her mother in Philadelphia (ca. 296 CE) in severe language: "It is already eight months since I came to Alexandria, and not even one letter have you written to me. Again then you do not regard me as your daughter but as your enemy" (*PMich.* III 221), and the phraseology indicates that the problem is not mere delinquency in letter writing. Then, too, a mother (who happens to be a Christian) writes to her son (fourth/fifth century), referring to herself:

> . . . Your mother Cophaena is ill, look you, thirteen months, and you had not the good grace even to write me a letter, since you yourself know that I have dealt more kindly with you than my other children [?], and you had not the grace, on hearing that I am ill, you had not the grace to send me at once anything at all. . . . I pray for your welfare for many years. (*BGU* 948; trans. Winter, 154–55)

A son can chastise a father just as effectively, as in this tantrum letter, though by the time one reaches the last line it seems to be good natured and written out of serious concern (January, second or third century CE):

> Theon to Theon his father, greeting. You did a fine thing; you didn't take me with you to the city. If you do not wish to take me with you to Alexandria, I'll not write you a letter or talk to you or wish you good health. What's more, if you go to Alexandria, I won't take a hand from you or greet you again. So if you do not wish to take me with you, that's that! . . . But you did a fine thing; you sent me presents, big ones, locust beans! . . . But send for me, I beg you. If you do not send, I won't eat, won't drink! There! I pray for your good health. (*POxy.* 119; trans. Winter, 60)

A son away at school reassures his father (third century CE): "Now do not be uneasy, father, about my studies; I am working hard and taking relaxation;

I shall do well" (*POxy.* 1296; LCL 1:137). Finally, the famous second-century letter from a penitent son, Antonius Longus, to Nilous, his mother, deserves quotation, at least in part: "I was ashamed to come to Karanis, because I go about in filth. I wrote to you that I am naked. I beg you, mother, be reconciled to me. Well, I know what I have brought on myself. I have received a fitting lesson. I know that I have sinned" (*BGU* 846; LCL 1:120).

These glimpses into real life—which are abundant in the papyri—serve to highlight the enmeshment of the New Testament papyri in that same day-by-day, week-by-week routine, and as we explore the evidence on sending and receiving letters in the Greco-Roman world, this view of the social world for its own sake will in itself be an attendant benefit, even though available space often will prevent us from quoting the full text of the letters cited.

Letter Carrying as Disclosed in the Papyri

It is common knowledge that letters in late antiquity were carried by family members, friends, acquaintances, employees, slaves, and soldiers; by businessmen or passing travelers headed for places of the letters' destinations; by soldiers given a letter-carrying commission; and by government postal services. Sometimes, too, letters were sent to an intermediary place or person, whence they would be forwarded to the addressee.

Official and Private Transfer of Letters

Apart from government postal service, letter carrying was personal and unstructured. Expressions such as "many people have sailed down" or "if I find someone going to you . . ." are common, and the occasions for sending letters were obviously frequent, for we often hear complaints that "I have sent you three letters this month" or "I have sent you so many letters and you have written none in return." As for letter carriers:

> Engaged in their own concerns, they passed up and down the land in never-ceasing motion, executing minor commissions and stolidly bearing, after the manner of modern postmen, the business of a great people, as well as a people's cares and joys. They carried the letters entrusted to them, but they were unlike our postmen in that they had no official status except in the case of the imperial post.[10]

The Roman imperial postal service, as E. G. Turner notes, "must have been well organized; but so was that of the Ptolemaic kings," and he documents both points from papyri evidence.[11] First, regarding the Ptolemaic

[10] Ibid., 82.

[11] E. G. Turner, *Greek Papyri: An Introduction* (Oxford: Clarendon, 1968) 139–40.

post, there is extant a fragment (of sixty-three lines) from a postal register dating about 255 BCE, which comes from a daybook listing postal items that have passed through an intermediate station on the government's postal service. It shows items checked in by day and hour, the names of the carrier, the receiver, and the subsequent carrier, as well as the sender and designated recipient. Seven times King Ptolemy is recorded as the sender and twice as the recipient of papyrus rolls in this particular list (LCL 2:397). Second, concerning the later Roman imperial post, a file of papyrus copies of letters sent from the strategus of the Panopolite nome in September of 298 CE reveals that this official had six clerks writing his letters and that as many as seventeen letters were sent in a single day (*PBeatty Panopolis* 1). In addition, a file of letters that came to the same stategus from the procurator, covering January-February of 300 CE, lists the dates when the letters were sent and received. Many of these were meant to be forwarded to other destinations, but the interesting point is that some letters arrived in Panopolis the same day they were sent—120 miles away—(*PBeatty Panopolis* 2), if one assumes that the procurator was stationed at Hermopolis.[12]

Government postal service—Hellenistic and Roman—was patterned after the highly successful Persian relay service. The Ptolemies, for example, set up two major routes in Egypt, one following the Nile, using mounted couriers operating in relay, the other across country using foot messengers. Boats on the Nile and camels across land carried parcels. In the Roman Empire, the *cursus publicus* functioned by messengers changing horses at fixed posts or stations and later by using chariots on the highway network. These Greek and Roman systems were efficient, but almost exclusively for state and military purposes.[13]

But private correspondence lacked this organization and support, to say nothing of the efficiency of the government post. Yet private communication, which would be the usual mode of travel for New Testament papyri, was a widespread and everyday practice:

> It was an easy matter to take a sheet of papyrus (the back of a business document would do), write on it, roll or fold it, pull out a fibre to act as a wrapping string, and close it with a lump of clay impressed with one's seal ring; it was more difficult to find a friend or messenger to carry it to its destination, and no doubt letters often went astray.[14]

Yet the degree of difficulty encountered in sending and receiving letters remains a relative matter and it should be assessed from the papyri themselves.

[12] Ibid., 139.

[13] White, *Light from Ancient Letters,* 214–15; *The Oxford Classical Dictionary,* ed. N. G. L. Hammond and H. H. Scullard (2nd ed.; Oxford: Clarendon, 1970) 869.

[14] Turner, *Greek Papyri,* 130.

Ease and Difficulty of Private Correspondence

That the writer of private letters had to find his or her own letter carrier is abundantly illustrated from the papyrus letters themselves. Often the carrier is nameless and, apparently, merely a chance or casual acquaintance. For example, a late third century letter begins, "Having chanced on someone going up to you, I have been moved to write and tell you of my plight, how I was afflicted with illness for a long time so that I could not even stir." This papyrus, however, contains a fragmentary postscript along its margin, which refers to the receipt (and perhaps forwarding) of an earlier letter, "a letter sent from the praefect," and it mentions "our friend Morus the letter-carrier" (*PSI* 299; LCL 1:158). If the latter is a reference to a professional carrier, this single letter would attest both the chance private letter carrier and the imperial post professional. Almost identical is a third/fourth century explanation for a father writing his son: "Having had the luck to find someone going up to you I felt obliged to address you. I am much surprised, my son, that to date I have received from you no news of your welfare. . . . Reply to me promptly, for I am quite distressed at having no letter from you" (*POxy.* 123; LCL 1:159).

A happier report goes from a son to his father in Hermopolis about 117 CE: "Heliodoros to his father Sarapion, greeting. I have just received your letter, and I rejoiced that you are well. . . . I am always glad to send you greetings by anyone I find sailing up-river, even when there is no news to tell you" (*PBad.* 36; *CPJ* 2:440). The same Heliodorus, however, encounters some difficulty in communicating with his brothers, as shown in two other letters of the same general date (*PBad.* 39; *CPJ* 2:441): "For there has still been no one sailing up to bring you letters except [. . .]" and "I am very glad that you get the letters I send. I greet you at least in writing. That is why I watched wearily for anyone who is sailing up." Possibly these communication difficulties were due to the Jewish revolt in Egypt and elsewhere during 115–117 CE.[15]

A third-century letter, found at Oxyrhynchus and sent from Serenus to Diogenes his brother, reports that "I had been intending to come up myself . . . , since Sarapion's people said that he was ill; wherefore I am writing to you to write me news of him from time to time by anyone you can send" (*POxy.* 935; LCL 1:136). A later Oxyrhynchus papyrus of the fifth century (*POxy.* 2156) refers—in similar fashion—to the writing of a letter because of "a favorable opportunity by a man who is going to you."

[15] This view is based largely on the words "harm" and "danger" at the end of the second letter: "May the gods preserve you from harm and make you prosper among every danger." Cf. *PBrem.* 11; *CPJ* 2:249–51, col. II. 24–26, though the text lacks most of a line: "We took much trouble to write to one another [. . .], however, because of the Jewish disturbances."

Frequently the letter carrier is named, as in this papyrus of 41 CE, which reports sending letters to Alexandria by two individuals and receiving another: "Sarapion to our Heraclides, greeting. I sent you two other letters, one by Nedymus and one by Cronius the sword-bearer [or: police officer]. For the rest, I received the letter from the Arab, read it, and was grieved" (*BGU* 1079; LCL 1:107). Naming the letter carrier, of course, does not mean that we are thereby any better informed about the relationship of letter writer to letter carrier, but the examples are numerous. In 168 BCE, a wife expresses relief at learning that her husband is safe in a retreat at the Serapeum at Memphis, but then complains bitterly that he has not returned home to rescue her and his son from virtual bankruptcy and starvation, concluding "now that Horus who brought the letter has told us about your having been released from your retreat, I am utterly distressed" (*PLond.* 42).[16] A fourth-century letter concerns a woman reported seriously ill in earlier correspondence who has now improved: "But as she seems to have taken a turn for the better, I have made haste to have another letter brought to you by Euphrosynus, in order to cheer you" (*POxy.* 939; LCL 1:163). A wife (who happens to be a Christian) writes to her husband in the same century: "I send you through Apon [= Apion?] your fellow-soldier a letter and a cloak" (*PGrenf.* I.53).[17] Other letters naming the carrier include *PBour.* 12 (88 BCE); and *PFay.* 123 (110–111 CE): "your man Mardon."

In at least one case, however, a letter carrier—though not named—is recommended to the addressee as qualified to expand on the situation treated in the letter: a woman seeks Zenon's help against a third party, who allegedly is mistreating her son, and her letter concludes, "The rest please learn from the man who brings you this letter. He is no stranger to us" (*PCol.* III 6).

Other letters show that various named and unnamed messengers were used: a second-century letter: "I sent you many letters both through the slave of Sarapion and by means of the son of the crown scribe" (*PAmh.* II 131); or a third-century letter, written by Herculanus to Aplonarion: "I rejoiced greatly on receiving your letter which was given to me by the cutler, though I have not yet received the one which you say you have sent me by Platon the dancer's son" (*POxy.* 1676; LCL 1:151), or a Tebtynis papyrus from late in that century, in which Sarapammon, the writer, says to Piperas, "I sent you a letter by the baker" (*PTebt.* 424; LCL 1:154).

Occasionally we discover an effort to increase letter-carrying efficiency, as in a letter of 256 CE from a landowner to his steward, reporting that "the agent at Euhemeria has sent another carrier with a few things, though both

[16] George Milligan, *Selections from the Greek Papyri* (Cambridge: Cambridge University Press, 1910) 8–11.

[17] See Winter, *Life and Letters in the Papyri*, 157–58.

of you could send by the same man after notifying each other" (*PFlor.* 176; LCL 1:141). The reference here seems to be to carrying goods rather than merely letters, but the same principle applies. Alternatively, the writer could specify a carrier for the reply: "Send me a letter quickly by means of Polydeukes. . . ." (*UPZ* I 68).

The availability of letter carriers, then, presents a mixed picture. Yet even in the Roman frontier province of Arabia, a soldier stationed at Bostra finds frequent letter carriers to Karanis, though that does not prevent him from registering a complaint—that his father still does not write back (19/20 February, 107 CE):

> But this has troubled me, that I have very often written to you through Saturninus the standard-bearer, likewise through Julianus the son of Longinus [and through Dius], and not yet have you answered me concerning your health. But nevertheless, now that you have been asked, do give your attention necessarily before all else to writing to me concerning your health. A number of times I asked Longinus, who brings you the letter, to take something for you, and he refused, saying he was unable. . . . If, then, you love me, you will straightway take pains to write to me concerning your health. . . . (*PMich.* VIII 466)

At the same time, the arrival of numerous travelers from a location can be used more directly to chide the nonwriter of letters, as in this second-century letter from a centurion of the Alexandrian (?) legion to his brother in Karanis:

> Julius Clemens to Arrianus his brother, greeting. This is now the third letter I am writing to you, and you have sent no reply, although you know that I am worried if you do not write me frequently about your affairs, and in spite of the fact that many persons come here from your vicinity. I therefore ask you, brother, . . . to write to me about your well-being, which is my prayer to all the gods. I pray for your good health. (*PMich.* VIII 484)

From the same century, though more succinct, is the complaint of a son to his mother: "How many letters have I sent you and not one have you written me in reply, though so many people have sailed down!" (LCL 1:121), and a pregnant woman, in two letters to her family around 200 CE, speaks of several people going to or from them; yet she complains bitterly: "You have not even thought fit to write me one letter" (*PMich.* VIII 508).

On the other hand, the lack of a readily available letter carrier can be an excuse for not writing, as in this otherwise touching letter with deep personal affection, probably from father to son (second century CE):

> . . . I received Antinus' letter and yours, in which I seemed to see you. Wherefore I beseech you to do the same [i.e., to write] continually, for so

> our love will be increased. . . . When I am slow in writing to you, this is easily accounted for by the fact that I can find no one who is going to you. (*PMich.* Inv No. 241)[18]

At least one letter writer complains of negligent letter carriers who excuse themselves by accusing the letter writers of negligence (second century CE, found at Karanis): "I have written to you often, and the negligence of those who carry [the letters] has slandered us as negligent" (*PMich.* VIII 499).

There are, however, other ways to reprimand a lax correspondent (second century, Karanis):

> Apol[. . .] to Apollinarius, his brother, greeting. Having learned that you are in Bacchias I salute you, brother, and I urge you to write to us immediately concerning your health. For I have already used up a papyrus roll in writing to you, and I received barely one letter from you. . . . (*PMich.* VIII 496)

The writer adds, at the end, that Bacchias is only two hours away (!) from Karanis, indicating that letter writing was not only used for bridging long distances. And a son away at school sends a scolding but plaintive letter to his father (early third century)

> To my lord and father Arion from Thonis greeting. . . . Look you, this is my fifth letter to you, and you have not written to me except only once, not even a word about your welfare, nor come to see me; though you promised me saying, "I am coming," you have not come to find out whether the teacher is looking after me or not. . . . If you had come up with me, I should have been taught long ago. And when you come, remember what I have often written you about. [postscript] Remember our pigeons. (LCL 1:133)

A businessman anxious to conclude a deal tries to get his associate to act by referring to menacing letters from his father (first century CE, Alexandria [?] to Philadelphia):

> . . . Please do not neglect to write me, through anyone you may find, what you decide about the thirty items. Since, from when I sailed downriver, this is the fifth letter my father will be writing me about them, and he is growing angry, and I am going to buy them, and will you make up your mind? Tell me through anyone you can . . . , and please be sure to write me. . . . (*PCol.* Inv 316)[19]

If recipients do not respond, one remedy is to send them papyrus, as did the writer of an early second century letter from Alexandria (?) to Karanis: "I sent

[18] Ibid., 60, 82.

[19] Jacqueline Long, "Confidential Business: P. Col. Inv. 316," *Bulletin of the American Society of Papyrologists* 24 (1987) 9–12.

you papyrus so that you might be able to write me concerning your health" (*PMich.* VIII 481). A third-century CE letter has the same theme:

> Aurelius Theoninus to the most honorable Didymus, greeting. . . . For though I have often written to you and sent you papyrus for letter-writing, to enable you to write to me, you have never deigned to remember me in any way; but evidently your pride in your wealth and the great abundance of your possessions make you look down on your friends. Now do not behave in this sort towards your brother Theoninus, but write to me more frequently that by means of your letters your friend may be fully informed about your affairs. (*PFlor.* 367; LCL 1:147)

Yet there were more ingenious ways than these to solicit replies. For example, a fifth-century letter carrier apparently has been instructed to "bribe" the recipient for a response: "Please ask the letter carrier for six melons. Do not fail to send me a reply" (*PMich.* Inv No. 497),[20] but perhaps the most unusual pressure placed upon the noncommunicating addressee is found in this Karanis letter from the second century CE, from a soldier seeking to be reconciled to his brother: "I ask you to write to me, and the gods ask the same thing of you" (*PMich.* VIII 502).

What steps could be taken to ensure delivery? Normally a letter was addressed by writing the name of the addressee on the outside of the folded letter. This might be simply "To Ptolemaeus" or "To Ptolemaeus and Apollonius" (LCL 1:98, 99); or with a title, "To Apollonius the strategus" (LCL 1:115); or with the location, "To Zenon. To Philadelphia" (LCL 1:93) or "Deliver at Pathyris to my father" (LCL 1:101); or with a return address, "Deliver at Karanis to Taesis, from her son Apollinarius of Misenum" (LCL 1:111) or "Deliver the letter to Horina sister of Apollonius, of Coptos, from Tare daughter of her sister, of Apamea" (LCL 1:165) or, more elaborately, "To Apion, gymnasiarch and ex-strategus of the Antaeopolite nome, from Philosarapis, holding office as sacrificial magistrate of Antaeopolis" (LCL 1:148); or "To Dionysios, who is also called Amois, son of Ptolemy and brother of Apollonios the village secretary of Tholthis, who is staying near Theon, the son of Ischyrion" (*POxy.* VII 1061, 22 BCE); or with special instructions, "Deliver in Alexandria in the Imperial Market . . . to Heraclides from Sarapion" (LCL 1:107); or "At the gymnasium. To Theon the son of Nikoboulos, the olive supplier" (*POxy.* II 300, late first century CE). (See also *POxy.* VII 1061, 22 BCE; *PMert.* II 63, 57 CE.) In general, however, the simpler forms of address predominate.

The papyri, though, do furnish an interesting additional example of care in assuring delivery. A church official in the early third century began to draft some instructions for a letter carrier, then revised them in the second part of the surviving papyrus. Although the instructions remain problematic,

[20] See Winter, *Life and Letters in the Papyri,* 82.

we here catch a glimpse of someone struggling to provide full directions for transmitting an obviously important letter to the famous bishop, Theodotus (though the letter itself did not survive):

> I wish to send a letter to Antioch. . . . Deliver [it] so that it comes into the hands of him whom I wish, to this end, that it be delivered to the bishop of Laodicea, which is two stations before Antioch. . . . [Revision:] Go to the bishop of Antioch and place this letter in his own hands . . . in order that he may deliver it into the hands of Theodotus, the bishop of Laodicea. For such is in fact the address. But since there are two Laodiceas, one in Phrygia and one in Syria, he will dispatch it to Laodicea of Coelesyria, two stations before Antioch. Theodotus is the bishop there. Deliver it now to . . . incomparable brother. (*PSI* 311)[21]

These various forms of address may tell us something about letter carriers: the presence of the addressee's name only, especially on a family letter, may suggest that the letter carrier was well known to the writer or addressee, while a more complete address may imply a stranger or a chance carrier. However, a more detailed or formal address, complete with titles, may indicate the status or measure of respect afforded the addressee and should not be understood to mean that the person was more difficult to find—the opposite would be the case. Overall, therefore, the relative simplicity of addresses suggests and supports the view that letters moved with general ease throughout the Greco-Roman world.

In the event that a direct letter carrier is not readily available, a letter might be sent to an intermediary for forwarding, as was done by a second-century Egyptian marine stationed at Misenum (near Naples) when trying to reach his father. The letter's additional address directed that it be sent (presumably by military post) to the camp of the cohort in Egypt (doubtless at Alexandria) and then forwarded to the father in Philadelphia (*BGU* 423; LCL 1:112). Another writer, perhaps in the third century, reports that "the letter which you forwarded to me to deliver to Bolphius I have delivered" (*PSI* 1080; LCL 1:132), and a sailor writing to his mother in Karanis from Ostia in Italy (second century) suggests to her that she send her letter to an intermediary for forwarding:

> Apollinaris to Taesion, his mother, many greetings. . . . From Cyrene, where I found a man who was journeying to you, I deemed it necessary to write to you about my welfare. . . . And now I am writing to you from Portus [two miles north of Ostia], for I have not yet gone up to Rome and been assigned [to a fleet]. . . . Do not delay to write about your health and that of my brothers. If you do not find anybody coming to me, write to Socrates and he forwards it to me. (*PMich.* VIII 490)[22]

[21] Ibid., 170–71; see the discussion there of the textual problems.

[22] See ibid., 40–41.

Interestingly, this letter was found excellently preserved in a house, presumably the mother's, along with a second written by the same son a short time later from Rome, in which he reports his safe arrival there and his assignment to the fleet at Misenum. "Please write to me about your welfare and that of my brothers and all your kinfolk," he says. "And for my part, if I find someone [to carry the letters], I will write to you; I will not delay to write to you" (*PMich.* VIII 491; LCL 1:111).

Another military son writes to his mother in the same city of Karanis (early second century) and hopes to visit her under a military commission to carry letters, though he has some fears of losing the opportunity:

> Saturnalus to Aphrodous his mother, very many greetings. . . . I wish you to know that I sent you three letters this month. . . . If I find an opportunity of putting my plan into effect, I am coming to you with letters [i.e., he has a commmission for carrying letters]. . . . I was afraid to come just now because they say: "The prefect is on the route," lest he take the letters from me and send me back to the frontier, and I incur the expense in vain. . . . You wish to see me a little; I wish it greatly and I pray daily to the gods how I may find a good chance to come. . . . (Preisigke-Bilabel 7356)[23]

The "expense" to which Saturnalus refers is undoubtedly the bribe he would have paid for the letter-carrying assignment, for "in the army everything depends on the right opportunity."[24]

Finally, on occasion a copy was made of a letter and both were sent, presumably by different carriers, as seems to be indicated in this sentence of a second-century CE Karanis papyrus: "I sent you a copy so that it might not go astray" (*PMich.* VIII 500).

All of these examples suggest that, in spite of occasional difficulties, letters moved with frequency and ease throughout the Hellenistic and Roman worlds. If papyrus was needed, it could be sent; if forwarding was required, that could be arranged; if detailed delivery instructions were essential, they could be provided; if a reply was urgent, a return letter carrier might be designated. Apparently addressees were easily enough located, both by the letter writer and by the carrier; certainly letters were lost, but important communications could be sent in copies via different carriers; and it appears that human failure far more commonly was that of the letter writer—the failure to write—and not of the letter carrier.

[23] Ibid., 50–51; F. Preisigke, F. Bilabel, et al., *Berichtigungliste der griechischen Papyrusurkunden aus Ägypten* (5 vols.; Leiden: 1913–).

[24] For this interpretation, see M. P. Speidel, "Furlough in the Roman Army," *Papyrology*, ed. Naphtali Lewis (Yale Classical Studies 28; Cambridge/New York: Cambridge University Press, 1985) 292–93.

The Speed of Transferring Letters

How fast did letters like these travel? We reported earlier that governmental mail could move letters more than a hundred miles the same day. What about private letters? A third-century letter from Isis to Thermouthion, her mother, says, "I wish you to know that I have arrived in Alexandria safe and sound in four days" (*BGU* 1680). This letter was found at Philadelphia in the Fayyum, some 150 miles from Alexandria, presumably the daughter's home. Even to and from out-of-the-way places, there was daily traffic available for mail transfer. A letter (mentioned earlier) written by a soldier stationed on the frontier at Bostra ("eight days' journey from Petra," the letter itself tells us) to his father in Karanis on 27 March 107 CE, complains that his father has not answered his numerous letters sent through various named individuals, and then he says, "If, then, you love me, you will straightway take pains to write me concerning your health and, if you are anxious about me, to send me linen garments through Sempronius, *for merchants come to us from Pelusium every day* (*PMich.* VIII 466 [italics added]).

The possibility of replying the same day as the receipt of a letter appears to be documented in the impassioned communication between a husband and his wife in the second century CE; the wife seems to have run off with a man named or nicknamed "Bobtail" (*Kolobos*), and strong emotion is conveyed in striking ways, though we possess only the husband's (uneducated and therefore at points obscure) response:

> Serenus to Isidora, his sister and wife, very many greetings. . . . I want you to know that ever since you left me I have been in mourning, weeping at night and lamenting by day. After I bathed with you on Phaophi [= month] 12th I had neither bath nor oil-rub till Hathyr 12th [the next month], when I received from you a letter that can shatter a rock, so much did your words upset me. I wrote you back on the instant, and sent it on the 12th with your letter enclosed. . . . But look, I keep writing you and writing you. Are you coming [back] or not coming? Tell me that. (*POxy.* 528; LCL 1:125).[25]

Not only has he responded on the very day of receipt, but he has returned her letter as well—perhaps so that his wife can reread the letter that has so disturbed him and be brought to her senses.

In addition, there are invitations to dinners and weddings, asking the invitee to come "today" or "tomorrow" (see *POxy.* 1485, 1487; LCL 1:172, 174), though undoubtedly these would be invitations to local events. There also are letters ordering items for specific dates, such as birthdays or festivals. For example, on the 18th of the month Choiak in 100 CE,

[25] For this translation, see Naphtali Lewis, *Life in Egypt under Roman Rule* (Oxford: Clarendon, 1983) 56.

Gemellus, a landowner in the Fayyum, writes an order: "And send the fish on the 24th or 25th for Gemella's birthday feast" (*PFay.* 114; LCL 1:109), presumably six or seven days after the letter was written; of course, we do not know where in the Fayyum this letter originated or was sent, but the interval between order and delivery is relatively short.

The best and most detailed evidence on the transfer of private letters, however, comes from the famous Zenon archives, consisting of the papers of a certain Zenon, manager of the 6,800-acre Philadelphia estate of Apollonius, the finance minister under Ptolemy II. It is the largest single papyrus archive ever found, consisting of nearly two thousand items very well preserved and covering the years 260–240 BCE. It is of interest that these papers include not only lists, inventories, accounts, records of deposits, petitions, and letters from court officials and of a business nature but also more personal letters and some ten works of literature; in addition, they place us in contact with Zenon's hometown of Caunus (or Kaunos) on the coast of Caria in Asia Minor.[26] Zenon, we learn, even employed a commercial traveler, Promethion, who—among other duties—bought papyrus rolls for Zenon.[27] Zenon himself traveled widely, and in 256 BCE, when he settled permanently in Philadelphia, he brought with him the documents he had carefully collected over the preceding four years.[28] This is significant, of course, because it preserves for us far more than might normally have been expected, but also because it shows how a group of documents might have been collected and circulated in antiquity.

What interests us most, however, is that Zenon frequently dockets his incoming letters, noting (on the outside) the contents and/or the date of receipt. If a letter carries its date of sending (as is the usual practice), a comparison with the docket's date of receipt will indicate the time required for delivery, and if places of origin and destination are stated or known, additional information of value is gained.

A first example is an order for logs for the Isis festival in 256 BCE (*PCairoZen.* 59154; LCL 1:90): "Apollonius to Zenon greeting. From the dry wood put on board a boat as many of the thickest logs as possible and send them immediately to Alexandria that we may be able to use them for the festival of Isis. Goodbye." The letter is dated Phaophi 23 (=17 December 256 BCE), and it was received on Hathur 18 (11 January 255 BCE), or

[26] Turner, *Greek Papyri,* 35, 48, 77–78; Naphtali Lewis, *Greeks in Ptolemaic Egypt: Case Studies in the Social History of the Hellenistic World* (Oxford: Clarendon, 1986) 42–43, 52–55; for a full description, see Campbell Cowan Edgar, *Zenon Papyri in the University of Michigan Collection* (Ann Arbor: University of Michigan Press, 1931) 1–50; P. W. Pestman, *A Guide to the Zenon Archive: A. Lists and Surveys* and *Indexes and Maps* (Papyrologia Lugduno-Batava, 24A–B; Leiden: Brill, 1981).

[27] Lewis, *Greeks in Ptolemaic Egypt,* 54–55.

[28] Edgar, *Zenon Papyri,* 25–26.

twenty-five days later; unfortunately, however, something went awry with the letter delivery, and it arrived too late, for the festival ran from Hathur 17–20. Perhaps it was sent at the last minute, for the address (on the outside) says "To Zenon. At once," indicating that the letter should be immediately dispatched.

More information can be garnered from a letter in the Zenon archive written a year earlier, in 257 BCE, which tells of a trip by two travelers, Ariston and his sister (presumably the Doris mentioned in the letter's docket), from Alexandria to southern Asia Minor, who experienced delays in their ship passage and spent two months before reaching their destination (cf. *PCairoZen.* 59029). Their host in Cilicia, a certain Sosipatros, reports their arrival to a certain Antimenes, who (presumably) lives in Alexandria, and this letter, dated Apellaios 26 (= 31 January 257 BCE), reaches Antimenes about two months later, having traveled perhaps some eight hundred miles. At that time, on Peritios 28 (= 1 April 257 BCE), Antimenes sends to Zenon a copy of Sosipatros's letter, with a covering note (*PMich.* I 10; cf. *PCairoZen.* 59052). Zenon receives this double letter nineteen days later in the city of Mendes (in the Delta), that is, on Dystros 17 (= 20 April 257 BCE), which we learn from Zenon's docketing of its receipt. Since Mendes is about eighty miles from Alexandria, we obtain some definite information on the time required to move letters not only from Asia Minor to Alexandria, but also from Alexandria to Mendes.[29]

A letter to Zenon in Philadelphia from Artemidorus, a physician writing from Sidon in Syria, was written on Peritios embolimos [intercalary] 6 (= 14 April 252 BCE) and was docketed by Zenon in Philadelphia on Phamenoth 6 (= 28 April 252 BCE), after traveling some four hundred miles, more or less, in fourteen days (*PCairoZen.* 59251).[30] Two letters of Toubias to Apollonios, sent from Transjordan (*CPJ* 1:125–29) to Alexandria (perhaps 350 miles) reached Zenon in thirty-six days (*CPJ* 4 and 5 = *PCairoZen.* 59075 and 76), for they were sent on Xandikos 10 (= 13 May 257 BCE) and docketed in Alexandria on Artemisios 16 (= 17 June 257 BCE). In addition, we know that *PSI* V 514 moved the 150 miles from Alexandria to Philadelphia in four days. It was written on Peritios 28 (= 25 April 251 BCE) and docketed on Phamenoth 7 (= 29 April 251 BCE).[31] *PSI* V 502 traveled between the same two points in seven days, and *PMich.* I 48 also may have been sent from Alexandria to Philadelphia; if so, it traveled there in six days (double-dated Panemos 28 and Epeiph 30 [= 20 September 251 BCE] to

[29] Ibid., 69–71; Pestman, *Guide,* 266. It is not clear why Lewis (*Greeks in Ptolemaic Egypt,* 12) states that the letter came to Zenon in Philadelphia rather than Mendes—the latter is clear enough in the docket.

[30] See Pestman, *Guide,* 234–35.

[31] Edgar says "within seven days" (*Zenon Papyri,* 119); see Pestman, *Guide,* 236.

Mesore 7 [= 26 September 251 BCE]).[32] Lastly, a brief letter about two rams' fleeces is sent from Memphis by Nikon to Zenon in Alexandria on Pharmouthi 25 (= 17 June 257 BCE), and its receipt was docketed on Daisios 11 (= 11 July 257 BCE), indicating a delivery time of about three weeks for the 125-mile distance (*PMich.* I 16).[33]

Actually, more than 150 of the Zenon papyri have been docketed as to their date (and often place) of receipt; these cover the years 258–247 BCE. Many, however, did not or no longer contain their dates of composition, and often the places of origin and/or of destination cannot be determined. We do have examples, however, of letters received within a day or two, such as a letter from Sosos in Aphroditopolis, which is dated Mecheir 5 [Egyptian year] (= 29 March 256 BCE) and was docketed by Zenon near or in Philadelphia on Peritios embolimos 6 (= 29 March 256 BCE)—the same day—after covering a distance of something like fifteen miles (*PMich.* I 28).[34] Other letters that were sent and received on the same day include *PMich.* I 32, circulating somewhere in the Fayyum; *PLond.* VII 1951, in the Delta; *PMich.* I 35; *PHib.* I 43; and *PCol.* IV 121. At least the following letters moved within the Delta region in two days: *PHib.* I 44 = *PYale 33; PRyl.* IV 560; *PCol.* III 16; and *PMich.* I 18. Finally, *PCol.* III 10 was received in Memphis five days after it was written (probably) in the Fayyum.

Conclusion

The evidence sampled here—and there is much more—documents both the vibrant, everyday quality and the prompt transfer of letters throughout the Greco-Roman world. This lively activity occurred not only within Egypt (i.e., between the Delta, the Fayyum, and upper Egypt) but between Egypt and places as far removed as Ostia in Italy, Cilicia in Asia Minor, Sidon in Syria, and Arabia—to mention only a few specific examples cited above. This data can be combined with other evidence of brisk "intellectual commerce"[35] and dynamic interchanges of people, literature, books, and letters between Egypt and the vast Mediterranean region during the broad New Testament period to permit at least two claims about the early New Testament manuscripts: (1) the various textual complexions (usually called "text-types") represented by the earliest New Testament papyri—all of which were found in Egypt—did not have to originate there, but could easily, in a matter of a few weeks, have moved anywhere in the Mediterranean area. Moreover, if

[32] See Pestman, *Guide,* 238–39.

[33] We know Nikon's location from *PMich.* I 14. For dates, see Pestman, *Guide,* 267.

[34] See Pestman, *Guide,* 226–27, 268.

[35] See Epp, "Significance of the Papyri," 81–84, 89–91.

some of these textual complexions did originate in Egypt, the dynamic situation meant that they would not—could not—have been confined to Egypt. Therefore, (2) it is not only theoretically possible, but quite probable, that the present array of text-types represented in the Egyptian New Testament papyri do, in fact, represent text-types from the *entire* Mediterranean region, and, furthermore, that they could very likely represent *all* of the existent text-types in that large region in the early period of New Testament textual transmission.

4

The Godlessness of Germans Living by the Sea according to Philo of Alexandria

DIETER LÜHRMANN

PHILO WAS AN EDUCATED man with encyclopedic knowledge who even knew something about the Germans.[1] As examples of peoples who were so "full of folly that they feel a violent irritation if the world does not follow their wishes" (*De somniis* 2.117), he first mentions the Persian king Xerxes and then goes on:

> A very populous portion of the Germans, the story goes, force back with haste the oncoming waters—the sea has tides in their land—stretching out their bare swords and running in array to encounter the sea when it rises in waves. It is right to hate them, for because out of godlessness they dare take opposing weapons against the unenslaved part of nature. And it is right to jeer at them, because they attempt impossible things as though possible, thinking that like a living being water too could be pricked, injured, killed, and, in addition, feel pain, be anxious, flee in fear of attackers, and admit what are the soul's passions corresponding to pleasure and pain. (120–21).[2]

German readers will immediately think of the East Frisians, the people living at the estuary of the river Ems, which runs into the North Sea; they are frequently subjected to the same kind of jokes the Dutch tell about the Belgians, or the Americans about hillbillies. Philo, however, says not only

[1] I am grateful to Hendrikus Boers for his revision of my English text.

[2] The Greek text is that of the Loeb Classical Library, ed. F. H. Colson and G. H. Whitaker (12 vols.; London: Heinemann, 1929–62; reprint, Cambridge, Mass.: Harvard University Press, 1968–85), My translation here is an attempt to present the Greek text as literally as possible.

that one should jeer at the Germans; one should hate them because of their godlessness (ἀθεότης).[3]

How could Philo be so sure about such ridiculous behavior of these Germans? To begin with, he must have been abreast of his time to have had knowledge about Germans at all. Neither Herodotus not the geographer Erasthotenes, perhaps not even Posidonius, had such knowledge. Pytheas on his famous journey of about 325 BCE may have gone as far as the Kattegat, the link between the North and the Baltic seas, but at that time it was assumed that the western part of the world, north of the Mediterranean, was inhabited by the Celts, as was the east by the Scythians.

It was probably only after Caesar's ethnographic excursus on the differences between the Celts and the Germans that the Mediterranean world became aware of the latter (*De bello Gallico* 6.11–24).[4] The Roman attempts to expand their empire to the east and to make the river Elbe instead of the Rhine their new border brought more information about the Germans. For centuries there had already been contacts with Germanic tribes, especially to get amber from them. At the end of the second century BCE the Cimbri and their allies had raided the Roman Empire, finally to be beaten back by Marius. On the other hand, Scandinavian museums show many Greek and Roman statues and coins, which reached these parts through trade from the Mediterranean world.

Since the time of Caesar all the tribes east of the Rhine were seen as related to each other but different from the Celts; they were called *Germani*, a name probably of only one tribe, the *Germani cisrhenani*, who lived on "this side" of the Rhine, the Roman left side, somewhere in the area of the present-day Netherlands (Tacitus *Germania* 2.5).[5] So "German" was not a self-designation but a technical term of ancient ethnography. An Alexandrian of Philo's time could have found descriptions of the Germans, supplementing Caesar's, in Strabo's *Geographica* (7.1.2) and in the elder Pliny's lost books on the German wars and in his *Historia naturalis* (4.99–101).[6] Later readers could consult Pomponius Mela's *Chorographia* (3.25–32) and

[3] The standard German translation of Philo omits this passage: *Die Werke Philos von Alexandria, sechster Teil*, ed. I. Heinemann and M. Adler (Breslau: Jüdischer Buchverlag Stefan Münz, 1938) 245–46. The reason for the omission is not a problem with the transmission of the text; it can only be the historical circumstances of the edition. Obviously the editors of the time tried to avoid a Jewish offense against the Germans.

[4] Ed. H. J. Edwards (LCL; Cambridge, Mass.: Harvard University Press, 1979).

[5] Ed. M. Hutton (LCL; Cambridge, Mass.: Harvard University Press, 1980). Strabo traces this designation back to the Latin *germanus*, indicating that the Romans thought the Germans were the "genuine" Celts (*Geographica* 7.1.2, ed. H. L. Jones [LCL; Cambridge, Mass.: Harvard University Press, 1967–83).

[6] Ed. H. Rackham (LCL).

Tacitus's *Germania.*[7] The picture more or less dominant in all these books is that of a sinister country and of people who had always been dangerous to the Roman Empire, which never succeeded in conquering the areas east of the Rhine, north of today's Frankfurt or Wiesbaden. In southern Germany, on the east side of the Rhine, the Romans had very early erected the *limes.*[8] With this wall the Romans marked their border beyond the Rhine, as they did later in Britain with Hadrian's Wall and similarly with a wall in Arabia. In northern Germany the Romans lost a few legions when Varus was defeated by the Cherusci in 9 CE (Tacitus *Annales* 1.55);[9] after that they more or less acknowledged the Rhine as their border.

The miserable conditions of living in Germany "where the sea has tides" are described by the elder Pliny, who expresses only contempt for the pride of the inhabitants:

> There, twice in each period of a day and a night the ocean with its vast tides sweeps in a flood over the measureless expanse, covering Nature's age-old controversy and dispute as to whether the region belongs to the land or to the sea. There this miserable race occupies elevated patches of ground or platforms, built up by hand above the level of the highest tide they experienced, living in huts erected on the sites so chosen, and resembling sailors in ships when the water covers the surrounding land, but shipwrecked people when the tide has retired; and round their huts

[7] Pomponius Mela, *Chorographia,* ed. K. Frick (Leipzig: Teubner, 1880); Tacitus, ed. M. Hutton (LCL).

[8] This *limes* can be followed through major parts of southern Germany, thanks to a program of excavations at the end of the last century. One of the centers is the Saalburg Museum in the Taunus mountains near Frankfurt, a reconstructed Roman fortress. Visitors can get an impression how the German Prussian empire, established in 1871, tried to legitimate itself as the successor of the Roman Empire by reanimating the concept of a "Holy Roman Empire of the German nation" of the Middle Ages: at the entrance are a Roman-style Latin inscription by *Kaiser* Wilhelm II and a statue of the Roman Caesar Antoninus Pius, the original builder of the fortress, dedicated to him by its reconstructor, Wilhelm. On the other hand, the very existence of the Limes Program under the auspices of leading German historians of that era can be considered a result of archaeologists' success in getting funds for their excavations by making extensive use of the same myth of legitimation.

[9] Ed. J. Jackson (LCL). One of the many monstrous monuments erected at the end of the last century in Germany is the *Hermannsdenkmal* near the city of Detmold commemorating the victory of the Cherusci. Their leader had been a certain Arminius, a former Roman soldier whose name became the German "Hermann." The program for this monument does not contradict the one mentioned in the previous footnote; it only shows the eclecticism of such myths. In this case the ideology is the Rhine border, which even the Romans did not master. The French emperor Napoleon, however, did succeed in doing so, but eventually, in 1815, the Prussians took large parts west of the Rhine. Thus the famous Hermann stood raising his sword toward the west in the name of the German Prussian empire against the Romanic French, west of the Rhine. See also the *Germania* monument with its marvelous view of the Rhine near Koblenz.

> they catch the fish escaping with the receding tide. It does not fall to them to keep herds and live on milk like the neighboring tribes, nor even to have to fight with wild animals, as all woodland growth is banished far away. They twine ropes of sedge and rushes from the marshes for the purpose of setting nets to catch the fish, and they scoop up mud in their hands and dry it in the wind more than by sunshine, and with earth as fuel they warm their food and also their own bodies, frozen by the north wind. Their only drink is supplied by storing rain-water in tanks in the forecourts of their homes. And these are the races that, when they are now vanquished by the Roman nation, say they are reduced to slavery! That is indeed the case: Fortune oft spares men as punishment. (*Hist. nat.* 16.1.3–4)[10]

Contrary to Pliny, Tacitus, generations after him, in his *Germania,* would praise the Germans for their style of living in contrast to that of the Romans and for their desire for independence and for not being "reduced to slavery."

Philo shares the Roman perspective, according to which the Rhine and the Euphrates formed the boundaries not only of the Roman Empire but of what according to him properly bears the name οἰκουμένη, the inhabited world of civilization and culture (*Legatio ad Gaium* 10). On the other side of the Rhine lived the Germans and other more "brutish" nations; and on the other side of the Euphrates the Parthians, Sarmatians, and Scythians, no less "wild" than the Germans. This he wrote in his encomium on the first weeks of the reign of Caligula, who had succeeded Tiberius as *princeps* after the latter's death. Philo praises the harmony of the Roman Empire, where all former oppositions are annulled: Greeks and barbarians are of one mind, and soldiers as well as civilians enjoy the *pax Romana* (*Legatio* 8; cf. 13). Thus, if barbarians gained respect as human beings inside the empire, those outside, on the other side of the two rivers, could no longer be called "barbarians"; they must count as "beasts."

Therefore the Jews offered sacrifices not only at Caligula's accession to the throne and when he had escaped a severe illness but also in the hope of victory in Germany, according to Philo's report of what the Jewish delegates had told Caligula (*Legatio* 356).[11] The desired victory over the Germans refers to Caligula's campaign of the years 39 and 40. That, however, according to Suetonius had by no means been a military expedition, but staged

[10] This passage refers to the Chauci, a Germanic tribe settled between the rivers Ems and Weser (Latin *Amisia* and *Visurgis*). Dikes were erected against the oncoming floods only centuries later, in the Middle Ages. Traveling there today one can still see the centers of the villages built on artificial mounds (*Wurt* or *Warft* in German), crowned by a church as a defense against the oncoming tides.

[11] The German translation of the *Legatio* came out in 1964: *Philo von Alexandria: Die Werke in deutscher Übersetzung,* ed. L. Cohn et al. (Berlin: de Gruyter, 1964). In this case the passages on the Germans could be given in detail (cf. n. 3, above).

skirmishes—camouflaged Roman soldiers playing the role of the German enemy, who were then easily beaten by the Caesar (*Caligula* 43–48).[12] This campaign is one of the reasons for Tacitus's ironic statement that in recent times the Romans had too often celebrated triumphal processions even though victories over the Germans had been rare (*Germania* 37).[13] At the end of his campaign Caligula brought his armies down to the Rhine estuary, let his soldiers march on the beach with all their military equipment, and then ordered them to collect seashells as war booty from his victory over the ocean. A lighthouse was erected in memory of that "achievement." Is that not "godlessness," to use Philo's expression?

What Philo blamed some Germans for did indeed happen at the North Sea, but under Caligula, and we are brought back to our starting point. Thus far we have seen that Philo's detestation of the Germans was due to the Roman point of view, which he shared. But what about that special detail about running against the oncoming waves? Many strange stories may have been told about the Germans, either by the shipwrecked soldiers during Germanicus's naval campaign in the North Sea[14] or by soldiers blustering into Alexandria. Today we can, on the basis of the preserved written sources, only identify a typical *Wandermotiv* that had been taken as fact by Philo.[15]

Aristotle in his *Ethica Eudemia* (3.1.1229b28–29) mentions as an example of anger (θυμός) that the Celts take their weapons to meet the oncoming waves, what is for him the opposite to true bravery.[16] Aristotle does not name sources for his statement, but it shows that such opinions must have been common in his time. His authority was so great that about five hundred years later the Roman author Claudius Aelianus repeated this as something he had heard (*Varia historia* 2.23).[17] In fact, he may have gotten it from his reading of Aristotle.

Aelianus could have known better, and Philo, too, had they read Strabo's *Geographica.* Discussing the Germans, Strabo tries to correct false opinions

[12] Ed. J. C. Rolfe (LCL; Cambridge, Mass.: Harvard University Press, 1979).

[13] See his no less ironic statement (also in 37) that the Roman conquest of Germany has been going on for centuries.

[14] Tacitus *Annales* 2.24; the last sentences of Tacitus *Germania;* or Caesar *De bello Gallico* 6.25–28 (probably a later addition).

[15] For many details of this article I am indebted to the monograph by the famous philologian Eduard Norden, *Die germanische Urgeschichte in Tacitus Germania* (Leipzig: Teubner, 1920). Norden calls himself "a son of the East Frisian coast" (296) and recounts his own observations. As far as I can see, he did not recognize the special item I am discussing in my article, though he did identify many other such "Wandermotive." Norden (born 1886) got into serious trouble in the University of Berlin after 1933 because of his Jewish descent. In 1938 he had to emigrate to Switzerland, where he died in 1941.

[16] I. Becker, ed., *Aristotelis Opera* 2 (2nd ed.; ed. O. Gigon; Berlin: de Gruyter, 1960).

[17] Ed. R. Hercher (Leipzig: Teubner, 1887).

about the Cimbri, who had interested the Mediterranean world ever since their incursions into the Roman Empire:

> As for the Cimbri, some things that are told about them are incorrect and others extremely improbable. . . . And the man who said that the Cimbri took up arms against the flood-tides was not right either; neither is the statement that the Celts as training in the virtue of fearlessness meekly abide the destruction of their homes by the tides, and then rebuild them, and that they suffer greater loss of life as a result of water than of war, as Ephorus says. (7.2.1)

Strabo's source for this passage seems to be no less than the famous Posidonius, to whom he refers explicitly in the beginning of the next paragraph.[18] There may be some doubt whether Posidonius already knew about the Germans or whether in fact Caesar had been the first to describe them as different from the Celts. However, Strabo's text argues against someone who transferred to the Cimbri what Aristotle had said about the Celts. Strabo places it in the wider framework of his ethnography, which was better informed and could therefore identify the Cimbri as belonging to the Germans.

Obviously it had been a matter of dispute why the Cimbri had left their land in the Jutland peninsula. Strabo, following Posidonius, denied that the reason could have been a great flood, which must therefore have been argued by some. Others adduced their emigration to overpopulation, because not all of the Cimbri had left: even in Tacitus's time some still stayed there (*Germania* 37). Whatever may have been the reason, Strabo's text shows that the motif of fighting against the oncoming waves had not only been linked to the Celts, but to the Cimbri as well. Therefore Philo's verdict of a "very populous part of the Germans" may refer to the Cimbri, and not the East Frisians.

Posidonius had investigated the tides of the ocean. For that purpose he had gone to Gades in Spain. He had confirmed the dependence of ebb and flood on the planets, especially the moon, which had already been observed by Pytheas (see Strabo *Geographica* 3.5.7–9). That had become common knowledge in the ancient world. Even Philo took the matter up in his interpretation of Genesis 1:14–19, the creation of the planets (*De opificio mundi* 113). For Posidonius such knowledge justified rejecting false stories about the Celts and the Cimbri:

> Indeed, the regularity of the flood-tides, and the fact that the part of the country that was subject to inundations was well known, should have precluded such absurdities; since this phenomenon occurs twice every day, it is of course improbable that the Cimbri did not so much as perceive

[18] The passage is taken to be from Posidonius by F. Jacoby, *Fragmente der griechischen Historiker* 2a (Berlin: Weidmann, 1926) 240–42 (FGH 87 F 31).

> that the reflux was natural and harmless, and that it occurred, not in their country alone, but in every country that lay on the ocean. (Strabo *Geographica* 7.2.1)

Not so Philo. Neither his ethnographic and geographic knowledge nor what he had learned about the connection between the tides and the planets hindered him from passing on the rumors. His judgment of "godlessness" seems to be derived less from religious than from political concerns. His other example of "godlessness" referred to above, ἀσέβεια in this case (*De somniis* 2.119), the Persian Xerxes, also comes from the political realm. The Persians had been the enemies of the Greeks, in the same way as their successors, the Parthians, were the enemies of the Romans. Persians and Parthians lived across the Euphrates, as the Germans lived across the Rhine and therefore outside the Roman Empire, which was for Philo the οἰκουμένη. Thus, what Philo calls their "godlessness" may simply have been that they did not accept the Roman order of peace.

5

The Messianic Banquet Reconsidered

DENNIS E. SMITH

THE CONCEPT OF the messianic banquet is a pervasive one in Jewish and early Christian literature, but one that has received little systematic analysis. As a result, it is often referred to in a facile way, as if we all know what it is. In fact, it is a complex phenomenon that deserves more attention than it has received.[1] The phenomenon is exhibited in varied forms: in references to meals of the Israelites portrayed on a heroic scale, in allusions to the banquet of the end-time, in a description of the community meal at Qumran, as a motif in the parables of Jesus, and even as a motif in defining the actual historical meals of Jesus. What is involved in these various references is an interplay of mythological and literary motifs with allusions to ritualized versions of actual meals. The problem is distinguishing what we are dealing with in any particular instance, whether we have a reference to a mythological or imaginary story or whether we are dealing with an actual "messianic" banquet being celebrated at a particular time and place. In this essay I propose to reassess the data and previous scholarly analysis and to offer a more satisfactory definition of the term "messianic banquet."

The term "messianic banquet," strictly speaking, should refer to that form of an "apocalyptic banquet" at which the Messiah is expected to be present. In practice, however, it is used without such a distinction—and rightfully so because of the complexity of the data. It is therefore appropriate, first of all, to broaden the concept to refer to the general phenomenon in which a meal is used symbolically to represent a mythological event or realities on the

[1] Standard resources for the motif of the messianic banquet include *APOT* and *OTP* (see indexes); G. F. Moore, *Judaism in the First Centuries of the Christian Era: The Age of the Tannaim* (3 vols.; Cambridge, Mass.: Harvard University Press, 1927–30) 2:364–65; Str-B 4:1156–65; Joachim Jeremias, *Jesus' Promise to the Nations* (London: SCM, 1958) 59–65; Frank Moore Cross, Jr., *The Ancient Library of Qumran and Modern Biblical Studies* (Garden City, N.Y.: Doubleday, Anchor Books, 1961) 85–91, 234–36.

mythological level. It is primarily connected with the thought world of apocalyptic, but aspects of the symbolism are widespread in the ancient world. Like other apocalyptic motifs, it has its origins in a complex mythological heritage from the ancient Near East and is especially developed during the Hellenistic and Roman periods; in this period it is supplemented with parallel motifs from the Hellenistic world. In order to understand better the complexity of the phenomenon, we shall look at examples of a variety of types of meals located in the mythological realm, whether or not they have clear reference to future eschatology.

A Summary of the Data

The messianic banquet in Jewish and early Christian literature is almost entirely a mythological/literary motif. There are two ways in which the data can be broken down. On the one hand, there is the motif of sacred food that imparts divine blessing, usually some form of immortality. One of the early foundation myths for this concept is that of the tree of life whose fruits impart life (Gen 2:9).[2] A parallel tradition is found in Greek mythology, where the "food of the gods" that imparts life is nectar and ambrosia (e.g., Homer *Odyssey* 5.93; *Iliad* 5.335–42; 19.38–39). This concept is taken up in apocalyptic literature to represent the blessing of eternal life at the end time.[3] On the other hand, there is the motif of a sacred banquet in which the emphasis is placed on the banquet proper. A foundation myth for this motif is that of the victory banquet held after a great battle of the gods.[4] It then becomes a part of the repertoire of apocalyptic literature whereby the end-time is described in terms of combat and victory motifs.[5] The festive banquet was also utilized as a symbol for the joyous afterlife among the Greeks and Romans, but never in as prominent a form as in the ancient Near Eastern tradition.[6]

[2] For other examples of this motif in ancient Near Eastern myth, see T. H. Gaster, *Thespis: Ritual, Myth, and Drama in the Ancient Near East* (Garden City, N.Y.: Doubleday, 1961) 29–34, 336–38.

[3] *1 Enoch* 24:4–25; *Testament of Levi* 18:11; 4 Ezra 8:52; Rev 2:7; 22:2, 14, 19. On the connection of this motif to the symbolism of the menorah in the biblical cult, see Carol L. Meyers, *The Tabernacle Menorah: A Synthetic Study of a Symbol from the Biblical Cult* (ASORDS 2; Missoula, Mont.: Scholars Press, 1976) 95–202.

[4] See, e.g., *Enūma eliš* VI:69–94 [*ANET* 69]; Isa 34:5–7; Zech 9:15. See further Gaster, *Thespis*, 93–94; Paul D. Hanson, "Zechariah 9 and the Recapitulation of an Ancient Ritual Pattern," *JBL* 92 (1973) 46 n. 25, 53–55.

[5] On the combat and victory motif in apocalyptic literature, see Paul D. Hanson, *The Dawn of Apocalyptic* (Philadelphia: Fortress Press, 1975) 300–322; Adela Yarbro Collins, *The Combat Myth in the Book of Revelation* (HDR 9; Missoula, Mont.: Scholars Press, 1976) 207–9, 224–30.

[6] See, e.g., Plato *Republic* 2.363.c–d; Richmond Lattimore, *Themes in Greek and Latin Epitaphs* (Urbana: University of Illinois Press, 1962) 52. The common motif on Greek funerary

The motif of sacred food comes to be applied to various specific foods, usually basic foods such as water, fish, bread, and wine.[7] Water, for example, is referred to as the "living water of eternity" that snatches the soul from death (*Odes of Solomon* 6:8–18), as "a spring of water gushing up to eternal life" (John 4:10–14), and as the "water of life," which along with the "tree of life" imparts eternal life (Rev 22:1–2, 17–19). The symbolism of fish is often connected with the sea monster Leviathan, a mythological symbol of chaos, whose destruction represents God's power over chaos and on whom the righteous will feast in the new age.[8]

Bread as a numinous food is referred to as "bread of the angels" (Ps 78:25; Wis 16:20; 4 Ezra 1:19) and "bread of life" (*Joseph and Aseneth* 16:8, 14–16; John 6:25–59). Here there is special reference to a midrashic tradition in which the miraculous "bread from heaven" or manna is connected with divine food or food that confers eternal life on those who eat it (Exod 16:1–17:7; Num 11:7–9; 20:2–13).[9]

Wine as a form of numinous food is especially prominent in the Greek tradition, where it is associated with the god Dionysus and his blessings on humanity. These blessings range from pleasure to literary inspiration to

reliefs whereby the deceased is pictured reclining at a banquet has been interpreted as a reference to an eschatological banquet (F. Cumont, *Recherches sur le symbolisme funéraire des Romains* [Haut-Commissariat de l'Etat français en syrie et au liban, Service des antiquités, Bibliothèque archéologique et historique 35; Paris: Geuthner, 1942] 417–22), but that interpretation is not widely accepted; for objections, see A. D. Nock, "Sarcophagi and Symbolism," *AJA* 50 (1946) 145 [reprinted in *Essays on Religion and the Ancient World*, ed. Z. Stewart (2 vols.; Cambridge, Mass.: Harvard University Press, 1972) 2:613]; and J.-M. Dentzer, *Le motif du banquet couché dans le proche-orient et le monde grec du VIIe au IVe siècle avant J.-C.* (Bibliothèque des écoles françaises d'Athènes et de Rome 246; Rome: Ecole française de Rome, 1982) 530–32.

[7] E. R. Goodenough has collected useful data on the symbolic use of these foodstuffs in Jewish art in *Jewish Symbols in the Greco-Roman Period* (13 vols.; New York: Pantheon, 1953–68) vols. 5 and 6, 12:94–131. See also Joachim Jeremias, *The Eucharistic Words of Jesus* (3rd ed.; London: SCM, 1966) 233–34.

[8] On God's destruction of Leviathan, see Ps 104:26; Job 40–44; Rev 12:3–9; 21:1. On the provision of Leviathan as divine food for the righteous in the new age, see Ps 74:13–14; *2 Baruch* 29:1–4; *1 Enoch* 60:7–10, 24; 4 Ezra 6:49–52. References to this motif in rabbinic literature and Jewish legend are collected and discussed in L. Ginzburg, *The Legends of the Jews* (7 vols.; Philadelphia: Jewish Publication Society of America, 1909–38) 1:27–28; 5:41–46; and Str-B 4:1156–65. On fish symbolism in Jewish art, see Goodenough, *Jewish Symbols*, 5:3–61; 6:3–61; for Christian art, see Graydon F. Snyder, *Ante Pacem: Archaeological Evidence of Church Life Before Constantine* (Macon, Ga.: Mercer University Press, 1985) 24–26, 64–65. "Fish stories" in the NT with possible symbolic overtones include Matt 14:13–21//Mark 6:32–44//Luke 9:10–17//John 6:1–15; Matt 15:32–39//8:1–10; Luke 24:42–43; John 21:9–14.

[9] Both Philo (*Legum allegoriae* 2.86; 3.166–70) and Paul (1 Cor 10:1–13) interpret manna and the miraculous water from the rock symbolically. Philo connects them with the word and wisdom of God, which nourish the soul. Paul's interpretation connects them with "spiritual food" and "spiritual drink," which are taken to be symbolic of the food and drink at the Christian Lord's Supper.

intimations of immortality.[10] Although it is not as prominent in the Jewish tradition, the wine motif is still present and as a numinous food is consistent with other versions of the sacred food tradition.[11] What is different about the wine motif, however, is its reference to the actual imbibing of a physical beverage. Here we have a clear crossover from literary and mythological motif to actual food and drink. However, ritual drinking of wine in the cult of Dionysus, although a significant form of religious activity, is not clearly related to myth. Henrichs notes, for example, that it was "a 'social' rather than a 'sacramental' experience."[12] The problem that arises is whether we can extrapolate evidence for ritualized consumption of food and drink from mythological texts or otherwise connect ritual eating and drinking with myth. This problem will be dealt with further below.

The sacred banquet motif is especially exemplified in Isa 25:6–8 (NRSV):

> On this mountain the LORD of hosts will make for all peoples a feast of rich food, a feast of well-aged wines, of rich foods filled with marrow, of well-aged wines strained clear. And he will destroy on this mountain the shroud that is cast over all peoples, the sheet that is spread over all nations; he will swallow up death for ever. Then the Lord GOD will wipe away the tears from all faces, and the disgrace of his people he will take away from all the earth, for the LORD has spoken.

This text combines the primary themes connected with the banquet motif: victory over the primordial enemies, eternal joyous celebration, abundance of food, the presence of the messiah (assumed), judgment, and the pilgrimage of the nations.

These themes are operative in such texts as *1 Enoch* 62:12–14, where "the righteous and elect ones . . . shall eat and rest and rise with that Son of Man forever and ever." This will happen "in that day" when the Lord shall triumph over the kings and other rulers of the earth. This is a banquet at which there will be lavish provisions of food and wine, as is appropriate to a festive meal.[13] It further emphasizes judgment in the form of divine reversal. The idea is that those who suffer now will rejoice "in that day," and

[10] See esp. Albert Henrichs, "Changing Dionysiac Identities," in *Jewish and Christian Self-Definition*, vol. 3, *Self Definition in the Greco-Roman World*, ed. Ben F. Meyer and E. P. Sanders (Philadelphia: Fortress Press, 1982) 140–43, 159–60.

[11] See esp. Morton Smith, "On the Wine God in Palestine (Gen. 18, Jn. 2, and Achilles Tatius)," *Salo Wittmayer Baron Jubilee Volume*, ed. S. Lieberman (American Academy for Jewish Research; Jerusalem: Central Press, 1975) 815–29.

[12] Henrichs, "Changing Dionysiac Identities," 141. Note that, although Henrichs implies here that "social" may be less than "religious," he goes on to point out that "organized worshippers of Dionysus [in Dionysiac cult associations] elevated social wine drinking to a ritualized form of religious group expression, thus making it a hallmark of their Dionysiac identity."

[13] On the motif of lavish feasting, see also Joel 2:24–26; 3:18; Isa 25:6–8 (quoted above); compare the "unfailing table" of 4 Ezra 9:19.

those who hunger now will feast in the future. Here the enemy that is vanquished is historicized. In other texts the enemy is defined in mythological terms, as in *2 Bar.* 29:1–4, where the flesh of the primordial monsters Behemoth and Leviathan will be eaten when the "messiah is revealed."[14]

In the New Testament, the messianic banquet theme is especially prominent in the gospel tradition. The parables make lavish use of the theme to represent the joys of the end-time, as seen especially in the parable of the Great Banquet (Matt 22:1–10//Luke 14:16–24//*Gospel of Thomas* 64). This theme is echoed in other sayings and stories about Jesus, such as his feeding miracles, the beatitude "Blessed are you who are hungry now, for you will be filled," and the tradition whereby Jesus is criticized for being "a glutton and a drunkard" and "a friend of tax collectors and sinners."[15] Here we can identify a combination of such themes as the joyous banquet, the presence of the messiah, judgment, and the pilgrimage of the nations. The gospel writers, especially Luke, expand upon these ideas with numerous references to the motif of table fellowship with Jesus.[16] Especially important for the emerging Gentile church is the idea of the pilgrimage of the nations, which, when combined with the theme of divine reversal, is interpreted to mean that they will take the place of Israel at the table: "I tell you, many will come from east and west and will eat with Abraham and Isaac and Jacob in the kingdom of heaven, while the heirs of the kingdom will be thrown into the outer darkness, where there will be weeping and gnashing of teeth" (Matt 8:11–12 [//Luke 13:28–29 NRSV]).[17]

Another variation of the messianic banquet theme is the wedding banquet. This idea seems to derive from mythological traditions connected on the one hand with a celebration of the victory and kingship of the god and on the other hand with the idea of a sacred marriage.[18] It is utilized as a symbol for the relationship of God with God's people in both the Old Testament (Hos 2:1–23; Isa 54:4–8; Ezek 16:7–8) and the New Testament (John 3:39; 2 Cor 11:2; Eph 5:23–32). It is specifically connected with the apocalyptic banquet tradition in such texts as Isa 54:5–55:5 and, in the New Testament, in the parables and in the Apocalypse of John.[19]

[14] Compare the reference to death being swallowed in Isa 25:8 (quoted above).

[15] See respectively Matt 14:13–21//Mark 6:32–44//Luke 9:10–17//John 6:1–15; Matt 15:32–39//Mark 8:1–10; John 2:1–11; Luke 6:21 [= Matt 5:6 = *Gos. Thom.*]; Matt 11:19//Luke 7:34.

[16] On this theme, see esp. Dennis E. Smith, "Table Fellowship as a Literary Motif in the Gospel of Luke," *JBL* 106 (1987) 613–38.

[17] Compare Luke 16:19–31; 14:16–24 [//Matt 22:1–10]; 22:28–30; *Didache* 9.4. See also Jeremias, *Jesus' Promise to the Nations,* 59–63.

[18] On the connection of the wedding banquet with the mythological motif of the victory banquet, see Yarbro Collins, *Combat Myth,* 223–24. On the theme of "sacred marriage" in ancient Near Eastern myth and ritual, see esp. Marvin Pope, *Song of Songs* (AB 7C; Garden City, N.Y.: Doubleday, 1977) 374–75, 504–10.

[19] Matt 9:15//Mark 2:19–20//Luke 5:34–35; Matt 22:1–14; 25:1–13; Luke 14:7–11; John

These themes as traced thus far are primarily motifs operating on the literary level. What is being portrayed is a banquet of a mythological nature. It is a potent symbol for the joys of the afterlife or of the mythological world, since it carries with it the basic cultural imagery of the life-giving nature of food and the celebrative nature of the banquet. The question to which we must now turn is the extent to which actual meals may have utilized this imagery.

Defining Historical Banquets

Dealing with the interaction between the mythological world and the real world is especially difficult because of the nature of our data. What we have in the data is not direct historical description but rather, nearly always, literary idealization. What people represent in the literature is not what we would like to find, that is, history "as it really happened," but rather they represent themselves and their world as they would like it to be. What we find in literary documents can be referred to as a "narrative world."[20] On the one hand, it is a valid representation of one aspect of reality in that it represents the values of their social world. On the other hand, it cannot be considered an exact equivalent to the "real" world, in the historical sense of that term, without some qualifications.

This point can be illustrated from the literary side with an example from Plutarch. In his *Table Talk,* Plutarch recounts conversations held at several meals he supposedly attended. In actuality, Plutarch is self-consciously writing from the perspective of the literary tradition of the symposium, as he himself tells us:

> To consign to utter oblivion all that occurs at a drinking-party . . . has the most famous of the philosophers to bear witness against it,—Plato, Xenophon, Aristotle, Speusippus, Epicurus, Prytanis, Hieronymous, and Dio of the Academy, who all considered the recording of conversations held at table a task worth some effort. (612D–E)[21]

Certainly many of these meals may have actually taken place, but Plutarch's descriptions must be taken for what they are, exercises in the art of literature.

1:1–11; 3:29; *Gos. Thom.* 104; Rev 19:7–9; 21:2, 9; 22:17; see also Yarbro Collins, *Combat Myth,* 223–31.

[20] This category has especially been brought to the attention of biblical scholars by Norman R. Petersen in *Rediscovering Paul: Philemon and the Sociology of Paul's Narrative World* (Philadelphia: Fortress Press, 1985).

[21] Plutarch, *Moralia,* ed. F. C. Babbitt (LCL; Cambridge, Mass.: Harvard University Press, 1967–84). On the literary form of the symposium, see Josef Martin, *Symposion: Die Geschichte einer literarischen Form* (Paderborn: F. Schöningh, 1931). On its relation to the NT, see Klaus Berger, "Hellenistische Gattungen im Neuen Testament," *ANRW* 2.25.2, esp. 1310–15.

That he is skilled in this literary form is shown by his use of it in describing an imaginary meal of the legendary seven sages but doing so in the form of a first-person account, a form that was common to the symposium tradition.[22] A similar skill is shown by the author of the Gospel of Luke, who makes rich use of symposium literary motifs as well as the messianic banquet theme in his creative retelling of the Jesus story.[23]

Similar problems arise in analyzing mythological stories. Albert Henrichs, for example, has pointed out the problems involved with interpreting various mythological stories connected with Dionysus as if they represent actual ritual practices.[24] He especially refers to the traditional interpretation of the maenadic ritual eating of raw flesh and drinking of undiluted wine. This has been interpreted as a meal with sacramental overtones, in which eating raw flesh is interpreted as eating the god himself. Rather, Henrichs points out that the primary source for this idea is myth, notably the version found in Euripides' *Bacchae,* in which maenads are said to tear a wild animal apart with their bare hands and eat the flesh raw. Henrichs argues for a greater gap between myth and ritual. Maenadic ritual, insofar as we can reconstruct it, at best involved the handling (not eating) of raw meat taken from regular sacrificial victims. He refers to this as "hardly more than a token tribute to the ritualistic savagery of maenadic myth."[25]

The same distinctions should be drawn in dealing with such texts as the references in *Joseph and Asenath* to the "cup of immortality," "bread of life," and "ointment of immortality," which are said to impart eternal life to those who partake of them. There have been many attempts to interpret these as ritual texts, but a more correct interpretation would be one that recognizes their inherent literary nature.[26]

A similar text is found in John 6:53–54 (NRSV): "Very truly, I tell you, unless you eat the flesh of the Son of Man and drink his blood, you have no life in you. Those who eat my flesh and drink my blood have eternal life, and I will raise them up on the last day." This text has been widely interpreted to be reflective of eucharistic theology in the Johannine community.[27] Bultmann reminds us, however, of its nature as a mythological text. He then

[22] See Plutarch's *Dinner of the Seven Wise Men* (*Septem sapientium convivium*). A useful analysis of this treatise by David E. Aune is found in *Plutarch's Ethical Writings and Early Christian Literature,* ed. H. D. Betz (Leiden: Brill, 1978) 51–105.

[23] See esp. D. E. Smith, "Table Fellowship as a Literary Motif."

[24] Henrichs, "Changing Dionysiac Identities," 143–47, 159–60.

[25] Ibid., 144.

[26] On this point, see esp. John J. Collins, *Between Athens and Jerusalem: Jewish Identity in the Hellenistic Diaspora* (New York: Crossroad, 1983) 213–18.

[27] See, e.g., Raymond E. Brown, *The Gospel According to John I–XII* (AB 29; Garden City, N.Y.: Doubleday, 1966) 284–91.

connects that symbolic meaning with the eating of a "sacramental meal."[28] The problem is that the text itself does not indicate how such a connection with ritual is to be made. Although we may conclude that it represents an attempt to mythologize the community's ritual meal, we do not have sufficient data to determine how mythology and ritual would have been related in this case. The problem is that a distinction must be made between myth and the reconstruction of ritual. The actions of mythological figures may be incorporated into ritual, but how this is done must be carefully and cautiously reconstructed.

The "Messianic Banquet" at Qumran

The most famous example of a communal meal being celebrated as a "messianic banquet" is that at Qumran, as indicated in 1QSa ii.11–22.[29] Here, in a context where ritualized communal banquets were a regular part of community life, we have a text describing what appears to be a normative ritual for those banquets. In the text, the messiah is said to be present and presiding at the meal:

> This is the order of the session of the "Men of the Name who are invited to the Feast" for the communal council when God sends the Messiah to be with them: The Priest shall enter at the head of all the congregation of Israel and all the fathers of the Aaronids . . . and they shall sit before him each according to his rank. Next the Messiah of Israel shall enter, and the heads of the thousands of Israel shall sit before him each according to his rank. . . . When they solemnly meet together at a table of communion or to drink the wine . . . the Messiah of Israel shall stretch out his hand to the bread. Next all the congregation of the community shall give thanks and partake, each according to his rank. (1QSa ii.11–18, 20)[30]

The motif here is clearly that of the messianic banquet. The question is the extent to which this text describes the actual "liturgy" utilized at the Qumran meals. What it does do is provide a literary idealization of those meals in which not only the normal membership is deemed to be present but the messiah as well. In the literary account, therefore, their meals are raised to a mythological level, but how this idea was actually realized when they gathered for their meals is the question that the text leaves unanswered.[31]

[28] Rudolf Bultmann, *The Gospel of John: A Commentary* (Philadelphia: Westminster, 1971) 222–24.

[29] The classic argument for this text as representing a messianic banquet is that of Cross, *Ancient Library*, 85–91.

[30] Trans. Cross, *Ancient Library*, 87–89.

[31] According to K. G. Kuhn, "At the actual meals of the Essenes there was, to be sure, no one who could represent the Messiah of Israel" ("The Lord's Supper and the Communal Meal

The Messianic Banquet and the Historical Jesus

One of the favorite themes in studies of the historical Jesus is the idea that Jesus offered a messianic banquet to those with whom he dined.[32] This is certainly the way the gospel tradition represents the meals of Jesus, but the tradition is clearly idealizing the figure of Jesus as the Messiah. The question is the extent to which the historical Jesus could be envisioned as hosting a meal that would be perceived by the participants as a messianic banquet.

When we consider that the messianic banquet is in essence a mythological meal, we have to raise the question whether there can be a messianic banquet with Jesus at any point before Jesus has become a mythological figure. Furthermore, if we use the Qumran banquet as a model for what a messianic banquet might have looked like, we also must take into account that it requires a highly developed community self-consciousness, particularly a self-identity as an apocalytic community. It is possible to attribute such a social identity to certain early Christian groups, but it is highly unlikely that such social development existed in a "Jesus movement" in Jesus' own lifetime.

---

at Qumran," in *The Scrolls and the New Testament,* ed. K. Stendahl [New York: Harper & Row, 1957] 71). Cross, on the other hand, states: "No doubt in the assemblies of the Essenes the lay head and the priestly head of the community (the types of the Messiahs to come) stood in the stead of the Messiahs of Aaron and Israel" (*Ancient Library,* 88 n. 6). Thus, for Cross the Qumran common meal is "a liturgical anticipation of the Messianic banquet" (ibid., 90). A helpful description of the Qumran perspective on the relationship between this world and the mythological world is provided by B. E. Thiering, who notes "the extent to which heaven was conceived structurally and spatially in Qumran thought. The heavenly temple and the earthly community are understood as two different structures, both existing at present in two different places, far away from one another. . . . In the present time, the community members belong to the heavenly community of angels, but they are parted from them by the distance between heaven and earth" (*Redating the Teacher of Righteousness* [Australian and New Zealand Studies in Theology and Religion 1; Sydney: Theological Explorations, 1979] 62, 70). Thiering relies especially on John Strugnell's study of the angelic liturgy at Qumran, "in which the presence of the angels is in a sense invoked" (Strugnell, "The Angelic Liturgy at Qumran—4Q Serek Šîrôt 'Ôlat Haššabbāt," in *Congress Volume: Oxford 1959* [VTSup 7; Leiden: Brill, 1960] 320).

[32] Examples abound. The most influential argument for this position is that of Norman Perrin, *Rediscovering the Teaching of Jesus* (New York: Harper & Row, 1967) 102–8. Recent proponents of this view include E. P. Sanders (*Jesus and Judaism* [Philadelphia: Fortress Press, 1985] 174–211, 271–73); Richard Horsley (*Jesus and the Spiral of Violence: Popular Jewish Resistance in Roman Palestine* [San Francisco: Harper & Row, 1987] 178–80), and Marcus Borg (*Jesus: A New Vision* [New York: Harper & Row, 1987] 101–2, 131–33). I have addressed the question of the table fellowship texts in the Jesus tradition in my article "The Historical Jesus at Table," in *Society of Biblical Literature 1989 Seminar Papers,* ed. D. J. Lull (Atlanta: Scholars Press, 1989) 466–86.

The Messianic Banquet and Early Christian Meals

It is clear that the messianic banquet theme is prominent in the representation of early Christian meals in early Christian literature.[33] What is not clear is how we are to evaluate this material. On the one hand, this theme is clearly a mythological idea, a way to represent in the narrative world the presence and accessibility of the divine. On the other hand, we have seen in our analysis of various types of data how difficult it is to define the form a messianic banquet might take as an actual meal. Furthermore, it is unclear how mythological texts are to be related to ritual. They cannot simply be read as liturgy. This mistake is made, for example, when John 6:53–54 is read as if it were a ritual text. The same point may be made in regard to all of the texts of the "eucharistic words" of Jesus. In all of these cases an etiological legend is being presented.[34] How it relates to liturgy is not at all clear, however. The lack of clarity is indicated in the tradition by the fact that the Pauline tradition speaks of repeating the rite ("Do this in remembrance of me" [1 Cor 11:24, 25]), but without clarity as to how this textual tradition functioned when that was done. In Mark, however, the tradition is placed within a narrative as one of many other stories about Jesus.[35] Here there is even less clarity as to how it would have functioned as a liturgical text.

The problems are complex. At the least, I suggest that the term "messianic banquet" (and its cognate terms) is not at all helpful in describing a historical banquet. Rather, it is best to reserve this term for the depiction of a mythological meal in the "narrative world." Actual meals may aspire to the experience of the numinous as expressed in the myth, but the description of how that happens needs to be nuanced much more carefully than has been done in the past.[36]

[33] See Cross, *Ancient Library*, 234–36; Jeremias, *Eucharistic Words*, 59–61, 205–7, 233–37; Eduard Schweizer, *The Lord's Supper according to the New Testament* (FBBS 18; Philadelphia: Fortress Press, 1967) 18–22.

[34] This point is made by Burton Mack in *A Myth of Innocence: Mark and Christian Origins* (Philadelphia: Fortress Press, 1988) 120.

[35] Ibid., 299.

[36] This essay is an adaptation and expansion of my article "Messianic Banquet," forthcoming in *The Anchor Bible Dictionary* (Garden City, N.Y.: Doubleday).

PART 2

Archaeology and Early Christianity

6

The Bethsaida Excavations: Historical and Archaeological Approaches

HEINZ-WOLFGANG KUHN AND RAMI ARAV

I. Bethsaida and the Ancient Sources

Bethsaida in the Canonical Gospels

OF ALL THE PLACES that link Jesus with Galilee and the Gaulanitis, only three can make the claim with a high degree of historical probability that Jesus worked there, namely, Capernaum, Bethsaida, and Chorazin.[1] Nazareth, on the other hand, can be viewed only as the

[1] The author of the first part of this article is Professor Heinz-Wolfgang Kuhn from the Evangelical-Theological Faculty of the University of Munich. Along with twenty-seven other individuals, almost exclusively theology students from the University of Munich, he took part in the excavation at Bethsaida from 2 April through 16 April 1989. He visited the site once again 21–23 July 1989 with the classical archaeologist Doris Hefner from Munich, who was the supervisor of Area B in April.

The author of the second part, Dr. Rami Arav, chief curator at the Eretz Israel Museum in Tel Aviv, has led the systematic excavation at Bethsaida and el-Araj since 1987. The preliminary excavations were carried out in March and April 1987 at et-Tell and in el-Araj. In January, May, June, and July of 1988 further excavations at et-Tell took place; the excavation of April 1989 was continued in June and July of that year.

The excavation in April 1989 was made possible by generous grants made, above all, by the Ludwig-Maximilians-Universität München, the Evangelisch-Lutherische Kirche in Bayern and the Gesellschaft von Freunden und Förderern der Universität München. Prof. Kuhn received assistance in the collection and evaluation of materials for Part I from Doris Hefner, Monika Bernett, Wolfgang Fenske, and Ruth Fränzel. The translation of Part I was done by Robert Petty, a student of Prof. Pearson.

In the meantime further excavations took place in 1990, which will be continued in the following years. In 1990 Prof. Kuhn and his collaborator Monika Bernett visited the site 27–31 July.

place in which Jesus grew up (in the oldest gospel tradition only the expression of origin Ναζαρηνός is established).[2] Capernaum is well attested as a primary site for the activity of Jesus both in the Gospel of Mark and in Q,[3] but Chorazin is encountered only once in a saying of Jesus in Q. Alongside the emphasis on Capernaum as a site of Jesus' activity, Chorazin and Bethsaida are mentioned in Luke 10:13–15 par. Matt 11:21–23. The saying is presumably authentic, but at least it reflects the activity of the historical Jesus and would therefore have been formulated not long after his death. This is supported by the following points (the first suggests authenticity): (1) The reversal of the Old Testament folk oracle uttered against the enemies of Israel, Tyre and Sidon (Isaiah 23 and Ezekiel 26–28), in a saying directed against certain minor Jewish settlements—which proves a great originality of the author—is most likely to be attributed to Jesus himself. (2) The later preaching of the community cannot be equated here with the preaching of Jesus, since it is a matter of Jesus' "mighty works" (see, e.g., the authentic saying of Jesus in Luke 11:20 par. Matt 12:28). (3) The curious grouping of three locations has geographical significance (they form a tight triangle at the north end of the Sea of Galilee) and can, with respect to Capernaum (including its emphasis here) and Bethsaida, be brought into accord with other historical considerations concerning the locations of Jesus.

The Gospel of Mark also mentions Bethsaida twice. In 6:45 the original goal of the journey by boat in the direction of Bethsaida (in the Gaulanitis) could be traditional, since in 6:52 the evangelist puts in the boat not around Bethsaida but rather at the site or in the area of Gennesaret in Galilee (could the reason be that it was fitting that Jesus meet the Pharisees from Jerusalem which appear in 7:1 in Galilee rather than the more pagan Gaulanitis on the other side of the Jordan?). Not adhering to Markan tradition, Luke somewhat awkwardly transfers the feeding of the five thousand in 9:10 to Bethsaida (according to v. 12 the place of the feeding is termed "a lonely place").[4] On

[2] Besides Capernaum, Bethsaida, Chorazin, and Nazareth, the only place-names associated with the activity of Jesus in this region according to the canonical Gospels are Nain (Luke 7:11), Cana (John 2:1, 11; 4:46), and Gennesaret, provided that this is not merely a general designation for the area (Mark 6:53 par. Matt 14:34). Apparently Dalmanutha (Mark 8:10) par. Magadan (Matt 15:39) belong(s) to the west shore of the Sea of Galilee, and the country of the Gergesenes (as only some manuscripts read in Mark 5:1 par. Matt 8:28 and Luke 8:26, 37) to the east shore. In the very north of the territory of Philip the area of his capital, Caesarea Philippi, is said to be a place of Jesus' stay (Mark 8:27 par. Matt 16:13).

The expression Ναζαρηνός appears especially in the oldest Gospel in traditional settings: Mark 1:24; 10:47; 14:67; 16:6; cf. also 1:9; 6:1. In Q there is no reference to Nazareth.

[3] Capernaum appears as a type of "center" for the activity of Jesus both in Mark 1:21–2:12, in fact in 1:16–4:34 (one notices the "house" motif in the Gospel, which no doubt refers mostly to Capernaum; and Jesus, according to Mark 9:33, stayed in Capernaum once more before his final departure from Galilee) and in Luke 10:15 par. Matt 11:23 (concerning which see immediately below). Cf. also Matt 4:13; 9:1.

[4] Luke here uses the place-name Bethsaida, which Mark mentions in 6:45 and 8:22, at the beginning and at the end of the Mark-section which was omitted by Luke (which incidentally

the other hand, that the healing of the blind man in Mark 8:22–26 takes place in Bethsaida (is 8:22a traditional?) before the journey of Jesus to the area of Caesarea Philippi (8:27) and that the evangelist previously has Jesus travel across from the western shore of the Sea of Galilee (8:13), as it seems, say much for his geographical knowledge (which despite the usual statements to the contrary is really not so poor!); the healing of the blind man directly before the entrance into Jerusalem correspondingly takes place in Jericho. As the narrative itself already had done (v. 23), Mark too in the redactional command to secrecy mentions the place as κώμη in v. 26b.[5]

Both occurrences of Bethsaida in the Gospel of John, which do not speak expressly of Jesus' activity there, are clearly traditional and could go back to old sources. In 1:44 it is related that the newly called disciple Philip comes from Bethsaida, and that it is also the hometown of the brothers Andrew and Peter; here, in contrast to Mark 8:23, 26, Bethsaida is characterized as a πόλις. Had Peter—if one may connect John 1:44 with Mark 1:29–31—married in Capernaum, which was situated nearby, where his mother-in-law now attended Jesus and his followers?[6] In 12:21 Philip is once again newly introduced as "Philip from Bethsaida," this time also with the addition "in Galilee," which could indicate tradition.[7] Here "Greeks" turn to Philip, who in turn speaks with Andrew. It is fitting in this regard that only for both of these disciples from Bethsaida are Greek names alone transmitted; as Dr. Arav communicated to me, at the end of July 1989 an earthenware sherd with an inscription of a few Greek letters, obviously from the Hellenistic-Roman period, was discovered at et-Tell.

In summary, besides Capernaum and (according to Luke 10:13 par.) Chorazin, only Bethsaida is relatively well established in the older gospel tradition as a location for the activity of Jesus.

Bethsaida and Julias in Other Ancient Texts and in Scholarly Discussion

The search for the location of Bethsaida must begin with Josephus, who in *Antiquities of the Jews* (18.2.1 §28) identifies Bethsaida with Julias:

> Φίλιππος δὲ Πανεάδα τὴν πρὸς ταῖς πηγαῖς τοῦ Ἰορδάνου κατασκευάσας ὀνομάζει Καισάρειαν, κώμην δὲ Βηθσαϊδὰ πρὸς λίμνῃ τῇ Γεννησαρίτιδι πόλεως

---

proves that Luke was aware of the section Mark 6:45–8:26!); but Luke differs here with Mark 8:23, 26 in his use of πόλις.

[5] For Bethsaida as πόλις or κώμη, see p. 87 below.

[6] Andrew, James, and John in Mark 1:29 could be a Markan addition; or did Matthew and Luke not read these three names in Mark (see Matt 8:14 par. Luke 4:38)?

[7] For the much-debated statement "in Galilee," see pp. 86f. below.

> παρασχὼν ἀξίωμα πλήθει τε οἰκητόρων καὶ τῇ ἄλλῃ δυνάμει Ἰουλίᾳ θυγατρὶ τῇ Καίσαρος ὁμώνυμον ἐκάλεσεν.[8]
>
> Philip for his part made improvements at Paneas, which is situated at the headwaters of the Jordan, and called it Caesarea; he further granted to the village Bethsaida on the Sea of Galilee both by means of a large number of settlers, and through further expansion of strength, the rank of a city and named it after Julia, the daughter of Caesar [Augustus].

Difficulties arise in the translation of the text regarding the transition from Bethsaida to Julias. Depending on how one translates the passage, Bethsaida, for Josephus, either was a significant location before the change of name to Julias with respect to the number of inhabitants and further expansion of strength, or the Tetrarch Philip first made it such (the latter is probably the correct translation).

οἰκήτωρ as a rule means only "inhabitant," but it can with Josephus have the special meaning of "settler" (see especially *Jewish War* 1.21.2 §403). This translation conforms to the fact that it is grammatically less probable—in contrast to the archaeological results up to now, which show no enlargement of the site with the change of name from Bethsaida to Julias—to render both the datives πλήθει and δυνάμει with "because of." As an examination of Josephus's usage regarding (τῷ) πλήθει as an instrumental dative indicates, one finds with verbs of action in an active usage—that is, in the case of verbs with an active sense that describe a *change of condition* (here παρέχειν)—usually the dative of instrument or means (e.g., *Ant.* 1.2.2 §61; 9.4.4 §60; for the instrumental also as comitative, see, e.g., 18.4.1 §86), while with descriptions of a *condition* (e.g., "superiority") the instrumental has a causal meaning (e.g., *Ant.* 1.11.1 §194; *J.W.* 4.7.5 §432). If Josephus had here wished to say "because of," διά with the accusative would be expected instead (cf. *Ant.* 11.8.3 §315).[9] In addition, the emphatic grammatical opposition of κώμη and πόλις in our text rather speaks for the fact that Josephus's meaning is that Bethsaida did not previously possess a sizable population or means of power. The new settlement of citizens is common in Josephus; thus in Samaria by Herod the Great, when he refounded the city and called it Sebaste (*J.W.* 1.21.2 §403). One can also compare the settling of Tiberias by Herod Antipas in *Ant.* 18.2.3 §§36–38.[10] Did Josephus perhaps err in the case of Bethsaida-Julias?

[8] The text of Josephus is cited according to the *editio maior* of B. Niese (7 vols.; Berlin: Weidmann, 1885–95; reprint, 1955) compared with the edition of H. St. J. Thackeray et al. in the Loeb Classical Library (9 vols.; London: Heinemann; Cambridge, Mass.: Harvard University Press, 1926–65 [reprints]). For this citation there is no deviation.

[9] For the instrumental dative, see the following grammars: E. Schwyzer/A. Debrunner, *Griechische Grammatik* (4 vols.; Munich: Beck, 1939–71) 2:159–68; R. Kühner/B. Gerth, *Ausführliche Grammatik der griechischen Sprache* (4 vols.; 3rd ed.; Hannover/Leipzig: Hahn, 1890–1904) 2/1 §425.6, 7, 11.

[10] The sense of the passage as here set forth appears also in the translations of H. Clementz (*Des Flavius Josephus Jüdische Altertümer* [2 vols.; Berlin and Vienna: Harz, 1923] 2:509) and

On the basis of other statements in Josephus—above all, the authentic report in *Life* 398–406—and in connection with the excavations at et-Tell begun in 1987, Julias can today be clearly identified with that mound. Et-Tell covers 80,000 square meters in all and rises 25 meters above the surrounding area.[11] The hill is somewhat more than 2 kilometers air-line distance from the mouth of the Jordan at the Sea of Galilee and a good 500 meters from an eastern branch of the Jordan. The altitude is 165 meters below sea level, and the large plain between et-Tell and the sea lies 206 meters below sea level.[12] In *J.W.* 3.10.7 §515 Josephus says accurately that the Jordan flows "after passing the city of Julias" (μετὰ πόλιν 'Ιουλιάδα) into the Sea of Galilee (thus it is not "at" the city!). This sentence already excludes the possibility that Julias can be identified with el-Araj or el-Mesadiyeh, which lie east of the mouth of the Jordan. In *Life* 398–406 Josephus gives an account that contains geographical information of his battle with the force of Agrippa II, ally of the Romans. He himself encamped with his soldiers "near the Jordan" (πλησίον τοῦ 'Ιορδάνου ποταμοῦ), only one stade (approximately 200 meters) away from Julias. All of these statements fit neatly only with et-Tell, especially the sentence which relates that the soldiers of Josephus, upon the resumption of combat following his accident, advanced from their camp "as far as the plain" (μέχρι τοῦ πεδίου) and then were ambushed by opposing troops (this statement obviously presupposes the plain between et-Tell and the sea, so that the sea at the time of Josephus did not by any means reach as far as et-Tell).

Is this Julias to be identified with the Bethsaida of the New Testament? First of all, it must be emphasized that the identification of Julias with Bethsaida, which Josephus makes in *Ant.* 18.2.1 §28, is the only reference to it in the whole of ancient literature. Although the canonical Gospels speak exclusively of Bethsaida (otherwise the place-name Bethsaida or Julias does not appear in the oldest Christian literature consulted by Bauer/Aland[13]) and thus constitute the oldest evidence of any kind for a place named Bethsaida or Julias on the Sea of Galilee, there appears in Josephus, apart from the passage in *Antiquities* 18 cited above, only Julias.[14]

L. H. Feldman (*Josephus* [LCL, 1965] 9:25). In contrast, it has recently been translated as a causal ("à cause du grand nombre de ces habitants . . .") by J. F. Baudoz (*Bethsaide-Julias au premier siècle* [Mémoire, Ecole Biblique et Archéologique Française de Jerusalem, June 1981] 63); "Bethsaïde," *Le Monde de la Bible* No. 38 [March–April 1985] 28).

[11] R. Arav, "Et-Tell, 1988," *IEJ* 39 (1989) 100a; see also section II, p. 94.

[12] According to a map from המדידות ישראל ("Survey of Israel") Scale 1 : 50,000 from 1986; see also section II, p. 94.

[13] W. Bauer, *Griechisch-deutsches Wörterbuch zu den Schriften des Neuen Testaments und der frühchristlichen Literatur*, ed. K. Aland and B. Aland (6th ed.; Berlin/New York: de Gruyter, 1988) s.v.

[14] Julias at the north end of the Sea of Galilee is intended in *J.W.* 2.9.1 §168 (at the first reference); 3.3.5 §57; 3.10.7 §515; 4.8.2 §454; *Ant.* 18.2.1 §28; 18.4.6 §108; *Life* 398; 399; 406.

In the ancient Jewish literature Bethsaida or Julias appears as a location on the Sea of Galilee in the Jerusalem Talmud in tractate *Šeqalim* 6.50a and very likely too in the *Midraš Qohelet Rabbah* at 2.8 as ציידן (*varia lectio* probably falsely צידון).[15] The one text that appears as a Baraita in the Jerusalem Talmud and whose alleged author belongs to the second century CE makes it quite sure on the basis of its connection with an interpretation of Ezek 47:8–10 that the location is to be sought not far from the issue of the Jordan into the Sea of Galilee. The present textual connection concerns the effect of the Jordan on the Sea, which—here according to Ezek 47:9—obviously at its mouth, thus near "Saidan," was considered to be especially rich in fish.[16] At most, the occurrence of Saidan in the scene in *Midraš Qohelet Rabbah,* which takes place in the first half of the second century CE, can be interpreted as a Jewish town in or near Galilee on the basis of the other place-names in the context (see another scene in "Saidan" for that time in the Babylonian Talmud in tractate *Niddah* 52b). Did Bethsaida-Julias still exist at all at that time or later? (See also for the fourth century "Rabbi Josi of Saidan," who appears several times in the Jerusalem Talmud, e.g., *Berakot* 4.8a.)

In the ancient pagan literature Bethsaida or Julias appears, as far as I know, only twice, once in the first century CE as Julias in Pliny the Elder (*Hist. nat.* 5.15.71), and in the second century CE as Ἰουλιάς in Ptolemy Claudius (*Geographia* 5.16.4). Since the identification of Julias with et-Tell on the basis of Josephus and the more recent excavations can no longer be disputed, these two references do not provide further help. Pliny the Elder mentions four "lovely cities" on the Sea of Galilee in his work, which appeared in the second half of the first century CE, among them "in the east" Julias and Hippos.[17] Ptolemy (ca. 90–168 CE) lists four cities in Galilee(!): along with Sepphoris, Capernaum, and Tiberias, also "Julias" (the problem of Ptolemy's statements concerning latitude and longitude cannot be addressed here).[18]

[15] The Geniza Fragment of the Jerusalem Talmud also reads ציידן with our passage; see L. Ginsberg, *Yerushalmi Fragments from the Genizah* 1 (Texts and Studies of the Jewish Theological Seminary of America 3; New York: Jewish Theological Seminary of America, 1909) 135. Other rabbinical texts, which speak of ציידן, צידן, ציידנייה, and the like, are still less clear; see the references in J. Levy, *Wörterbuch über die Talmudim und Midraschim* (4 vols.; 2nd ed.; Berlin and Vienna: Harz, 1924) 4:183b; G. Reeg, *Die Ortsnamen Israels nach der rabbinischen Literatur* (Beihefte zum Tübinger Atlas des Vorderen Orients B. 51; Wiesbaden: Reichert, 1989) 534. This holds further for the citation that is not mentioned by Levy and Reeg: *'Abod. Zar.* 3.7 (reading צידן or צידון). ציידן or the like as interpretation of בית ציידה presents few difficulties; in the Gospel of Mark the indeclinable noun Βηθσαϊδά is encountered as Βηθσαϊδάν. For the lack of בית, see S. Klein, "Hebräische Ortsnamen bei Josephus," *MGWJ* 59 (1915) 168.

[16] So also Klein, "Ortsnamen," 168 with n. 2; Baudoz, "Bethsaïda," 31 n. 7.

[17] For the limited value of the reference, see D. Urman, *The Golan: A Profile of a Region during the Roman and Byzantine Periods* (BAR International Series 269; Oxford: B.A.R., 1985) 136 n. 81.

[18] Concerning this text, see P. Thomsen, "Untersuchungen zur älteren Palästinaliteratur. 1.

Nor do the two oldest texts of the early church that make relevant geographical statements have anything to contribute to the question of the identification of Julias with Bethsaida or the location of Bethsaida. In both cases we are dealing with texts of Eusebius, who in one writing speaks of Julias and in the other of Bethsaida. In the *Chronicorum libri duo,* vol. 2, which was published around 303 CE, with its characteristic chronological inaccuracy (whether of Eusebius himself or some copyist) the (re)founding of Caesarea Philippi and also of Julias is connected with the tetrarch Philip in the year 25 CE. In the *Onomastikon* Eusebius merely combines a statement corresponding to John 1:44 concerning Bethsaida as the city of Andrew, Peter, and Philip, with the above cited remark of Josephus (*Ant.* 18.2.1 §28), that Bethsaida-Julias is situated on the Sea of Galilee.[19]

Of worth is the oldest pilgrim itinerary that mentions Bethsaida: a conglomeration of reports written in the first half of the sixth century concerning Palestine, which in some manuscripts is attributed to a certain archdeacon Theodosius.[20] In chapter 2 there appears a geographically plausible route (Tiberias, Magdala, Seven Springs [Tabgha], Capernaum; from here 9 kilometers [as by modern roads] to Bethsaida [et-Tell] and in the far distance Paneas), which conforms to an identification of Julias with Bethsaida, even though the statements about distances are inexact.[21]

In any case, since the twelfth century a Galilean Bethsaida (John 12:21!) has been assumed, above all in the area of el-Minyeh on the northwest shore of the Sea of Galilee.[22] The renowned theologian and archaeologist from New York, Edward

Ptolemaeus," *ZDPV* 29 (1906) 106f.; C. McCown, "The Problem of the Site of Bethsaida," *JPOS* 10 (1930) 35. On Ptolemy as geographer in general, see E. Polaschek, "zum Art. Klaudios Ptolemaios: Das geographische Werk," *PWSup* 10, cols. 680–833.

19 A translation of the Armenian text of the chronicle, which is complete only in this version, is found in J. Karst, *Eusebius Werke* 5 (GCS 20; Leipzig: Hinrichs, 1911); see p. 212. An edition of the Latin version of this writing by Jerome has been produced by R. Helm, *Eusebius Werke* 7 (GCS 47; 2nd ed.; Berlin: Akademie-Verlag, 1956); see pp. 172f. (for the reconstruction of the original Greek text, the Greek fragment on p. 397 should be compared); see here also a general discussion of the dates given in the chronicle (pp. XXXVIII–XLVI). E. Klostermann has provided an edition of the *Onomastikon* together with the Latin version of Jerome in *Eusebius Werke 3/1* (GCS 11/1; Leipzig: Hinrichs, 1904; reprint, Hildesheim: Olms, 1966); see pp. 58f.

20 See H. Donner, *Pilgerfahrt ins Heilige Land: Die ältesten Berichte christlicher Palästinapilger (4. - 7. Jahrhundert)* (Stuttgart: Katholisches Bibelwerk, 1979) 190–225.

21 El-Araj, however, lies much nearer to Capernaum than et-Tell (the square brackets in the text are the author's). The main approach to et-Tell has always been from the north (see section II, p. 94).

22 The area of el-Minyeh lies southwest from Tell el-ʻOreimeh/Chinnereth; see the map in C. Kopp, *Die Heiligen Stätten der Evangelien* (2nd ed.; Regensburg: Pustet, 1964) 213. A map from around 1300 shows "*Betsaida civitas*" in exactly that location; see Z. Vilnay, *The Holy Land in Old Prints and Maps* (2nd ed.; Jerusalem: Mass, 1965) 251 (cf. Kopp, *Stätten,* 241). For the medieval locating of Bethsaida on the western shore, see Kopp, *Stätten,* 239; McCown, "Site of Bethsaida," 39, 57. For a good description of the area of el-Minyeh (including Khan Minyeh), see E. Robinson in the next note.

Robinson, although he himself in his diary from 1838 identified et-Tell as Julias-Bethsaida in the Gaulanitis—as the Anglican bishop Richard Pococke, who visited Palestine exactly one hundred years before him had done—still firmly maintained a second Galilean Bethsaida, which he identified with Tabgha.[23]

El-Araj and el-Mesadiyeh, east of the mouth of the Jordan in the Sea of Galilee, were first clearly considered as possibilities for Bethsaida, as far as I know, from the nineteenth century on, for example, in detailed fashion by the vicar from Zurich, K. Furrer, who in 1879 emphatically denied that et-Tell was Bethsaida.[24] The prevailing opinion has for some time given up the Galilean Bethsaida, which had nothing to do with the Bethsaida of the Gaulanitis, and has gladly distinguished between Bethsaida-Julias at et-Tell and a fishing village Bethsaida at el-Araj which belonged to the former. For Gustav Dalman, et-Tell was still above all the "Acropolis of Julias" established by Philip, while the new city also had an important quarter here on the shore of el-Araj.[25] Albrecht Alt (despite a reference to Dalman) identified only el-Araj with Bethsaida-Julias.[26] The three most important voices of the eighties that set out a precise knowledge of location and made themselves heard before the preliminary excavations of 1987 were Jean-François Baudoz, who obtained his doctorate at the Ecole Biblique et Archéologique in Jerusalem in 1981 with a work concerning Bethsaida, the Israeli archaeologist Dan Urman with concise remarks in his study of the Golan in the Roman and Byzantine period (1985), and the Benedictine priest and archaeologist Bargil Pixner, working in Tabgha and Jerusalem, whose activities are partly responsible for the realization of the recent excavations.[27] With regard to the Bethsaida-Julias of the New Testament era all three posit—with differences in certainty and nuance—a city at et-Tell and a related settlement in el-Araj (Urman also in el-Mesadiyeh).

[23] E. Robinson, *Biblical Researches in Palestine and Adjacent Regions: A Journal of Travels in the Years 1838 & 1852* (2nd ed.; 3 vols.; London: Murray, 1856) (for et-Tell, see 2:412–14; for Tabgha as Bethsaida, see 2:404–6; 3:358f.; for el-Minyeh as Capernaum, see 2:403f.; 3:344f.); R. Pococke, *Beschreibung des Morgenlandes und einiger anderer Länder* (2 vols.; Erlangen: Verlag des Stiftshauses, 1754) 2:100, 106f. (the English original edition, *Description of the East and Some Other Countries* [2 vols.; London, 1743–45] was not accessible to me).

[24] K. Furrer, "Die Ortschaften am See Genezareth," *ZDPV* 2 (1879) 66f. Furrer refers illegitimately to many old witnesses (p. 67); however, he correctly realized that there was only *one* Bethsaida on the Sea of Galilee and this was Bethsaida Julias (p. 67).

[25] G. Dalman, *Orte und Wege Jesu* (Schriften des Deutschen Palästina-Instituts 1; 3rd ed.; Gütersloh: Bertelsmann, 1924) 172–98, esp. 173.

[26] A. Alt, "Galiläische Probleme" (1937–40), in *Kleine Schriften zur Geschichte des Volkes Israel* (3 vols.; Munich: Beck, 1953–59) 2:393; idem, "Die Stätten des Wirkens Jesu in Galiläa territorialgeschichtlich betrachtet" (1949), in *Kleine Schriften,* 2:447. So still the just edited supplement volume of the *Tübinger Atlas des Vorderen Orients* (Reeg, *Ortsnamen,* 533).

[27] Baudoz, *Bethsaide-Julias;* idem, "Bethsaïda," 28–31; Urman, *Golan,* 120f.; B. Pixner, see esp. "Searching for the New Testament Site of Bethsaida," *BA* 48 (1985) 207–16. Also worthy of mention is R. Riesner, whose recent publications presuppose the probe excavations at et-Tell and in el-Araj in 1987; see esp. "Ausgrabungen in Bethsaida," *Das Heilige Land* 120 (1988) 12–14.

In summary, the identification of Julias (surely et-Tell) with Bethsaida made by Josephus requires critical scrutiny, since in view of the ancient texts—apart from the references in the Jerusalem Talmud and Theodosius, which are admittedly not to be overestimated—its accuracy can be supported only by the single citation in Josephus. The hypothesis of a fishing village directly on the sea in the time of Jesus is in any case in view of the ancient tradition a mere conjecture.[28] The assumption of a possible second Galilean Bethsaida on the west shore of the Sea of Galilee has been justly abandoned.

Julias = Bethsaida?

Three arguments that speak against the identification in Josephus do not withstand a critical examination.

1. The fishing village Bethsaida cannot have been so far (today a good 2 kilometers air-line distance) *away from the sea.* But nowhere is it mentioned in the ancient literature that Bethsaida lay directly on the water. This could at the most be deduced from the place-name. But this is not unambiguous: בית צי(י)דא can signify in Aramaic "House of the Hunt" as well as "House of Fishing"; the above-mentioned rabbinical text in *Midraš Qohelet Rabbah* speaks of "pheasants from Saidan," and the sentence quoted from the Jerusalem Talmud attests to a great plentitude of fish in "Saidan."[29] From the wording of Josephus that Julias lies "on the Sea of Gennesaret" (*Ant.* 18.2.1 §28: πρὸς λίμνῃ τῇ Γεννησαρίτιδι), or that one can "travel to Julias by boat" (*Life* 73 §406: καταπλεῖν εἰς Ἰουλιάδα), only a larger or smaller mooring place can be inferred, precisely because Josephus clearly equated Julias with et-Tell. This also holds true for the journey by boat "in the direction" of Bethsaida (πρὸς Βηθσαϊδάν) in Mark 6:45, which was mentioned earlier. In fact, fishing utensils have been discovered at et-Tell during the latest excavations. According to Rami Arav, lead weights for nets, fishing hooks, and a large needle for mending nets and sails from the Hellenistic-Roman period have come to light.[30] Conversely, no archaeological site for the time of Jesus directly on the present-day shore at el-Araj or el-Mesadiyeh—a partially swampy area around a larger lagoon—where existing remains could perhaps point to a larger settlement,[31] has actually been proved. The probe excavations by Rami Arav in the spring of 1987 discovered no evidence for

[28] See p. 84 above.

[29] For the clarification of the place-name, see H. P. Rüger, "Aramäisch II," *TRE* 3 (1978) 604. Cf. German place-names, for example, "Fischhausen" (on the Schliersee). E. Nestle would connect Bethsaida with the Hebrew צידה ("travel expense") and the feeding of the five thousand (צידה = ἐπισιτισμός [Luke 9:12!]) ("Chorazin, Bethsaida," *ZNW* 7 [1906] 184–86).

[30] See p. 91 below and section II, esp. p. 104.

[31] So Urman, *Golan*, 121.

Hellenistic or Roman occupation at el-Araj.[32] In May 1989 Prof. J. F. Strange from the University of South Florida informed me by letter about his excavations at el-Mesadiyeh (more precisely map square 209 254) in 1982 to the effect that he at this point cannot say "whether there were any clear Hellenistic or early Roman wares."[33] On the other hand, Dan Urman believed that during an investigation of el-Araj and el-Mesadiyeh in 1974—together with Mendel Nun—he had found sherds that indicated inhabitation "from the early Roman period" on.[34] Until systematic excavations are carried out at those sites, the assumption of an additional Bethsaida directly on the sea will be viewed only as a hypothesis. The excavations at et-Tell show that at any rate a rather large settlement at et-Tell existed prior to Philip. That the sea in the New Testament era perhaps reached considerably nearer to et-Tell is—apart from the description in Josephus—not very probable, since Rami Arav has also ascertained a history of settlement on the present-day shore at el-Araj from the fourth to the sixth centuries CE.[35]

2. The argument from John 12:21, according to which *Bethsaida* was situated *in Galilee,* is weakened inasmuch as at the time in which the Gospel of John was composed (toward the end of the first century), Bethsaida could well have been considered a part of Galilee.[36] Indeed, for Josephus, Galilee is bounded by the Gaulanitis, but he does not indicate the Jordan as a boundary, and instead of the Sea of Galilee he places Hippos and Gadara at its boundary (*J.W.* 3.3.1 §37). Since there is still no clear conclusion to be drawn from this, it is all the more significant that from Nero to the end of the century, a part of Galilee, the Gaulanitis, and other territories were politically connected under Agrippa II (after the death of Agrippa this area apparently became part of the province of Syria).[37] Of still greater significance is the fact that the geographer Ptolemy Claudius in the text mentioned earlier considers our Julias to be a part of Galilee. Eusebius does this also in his *Onomastikon* in the text quoted before, but he knows the Gospel of John! The Talmud also considers Gamala on the east shore of the sea, and even Caesarea Philippi itself to be part of Galilee (*b. ʿArak.* 32a; *b. Sukk.* 27a).[38] The admittedly very hypothetical conjecture of Bargil Pixner

[32] R. Arav, "Et-Tell and el-Araj," *IEJ* 38 (1988) 188b; see also section II, pp. 94, 104.

[33] Letter from 31 May 1989. My inquiry referred to J. F. Strange, "Survey of Lower Galilee, 1982," *IEJ* 32 (1982) 255b.

[34] Urman, *Golan,* 121.

[35] Arav, "Et-Tell and el-Araj," 188b; see also section II, pp. 94, 104.

[36] So already—without all arguments being cogent—Furrer, "Ortschaften," 69f., and Urman, *Golan,* 23.

[37] See E. Schürer, *The History of the Jewish People in the Age of Jesus Christ (175 B.C.–135 A.D.),* rev. and ed. M. Black et al. (3 vols.; Edinburgh: Clark, 1973–87) 1:472f., 483.

[38] A. Neubauer, *La géographie du Talmud* (1868; reprint, Amsterdam: Meridian, 1965) 240, 237f.

should also be recalled (made with reference to the geomorphologist Moshe Inbar), according to which the Jordan, before its influx into the sea, could have taken a straight course so that the fishing village Bethsaida would have been situated west of the present-day lagoon and therefore still in Galilee.[39]

3. In general, it is assumed on the basis of Josephus (*Ant.* 18.2.1 §28) that Philip, at the beginning of his rule, still before the banishment of Augustus's daughter Julia (2 BCE)—thus between 4 and 2 BCE—changed the name of Bethsaida to Julias.[40] Why then does *the old name Bethsaida* always appear *in the New Testament?* The new name could, of course, have been only partially successful,[41] as the rabbinical literature obviously shows, which still speaks of "Saidan." But also the explanation of the name Julias by Josephus in *Ant.* 18.2.1 §28 and the chronological dating of the name change that is deduced from it are false. It will be shown in the next section that this change of the name more likely took place between 29 and 31 CE and referred to the wife of Caesar Augustus and mother of Tiberius Caesar, Livia, later called Julia. In this case the name change would first take place around the time of Jesus' death, for the dating of which the year 30 CE or a year close to it has a large claim.[42] Corresponding to the characterization of Bethsaida as κώμη and of Julias as πόλις by Josephus (*Ant.* 18.2.1 §28), the New Testament speaks of Bethsaida both as κώμη (as at the time of Jesus) and as Bethsaida the πόλις (as at the time of the composition of the Gospels). The narrative of the healing of the blind man (Mark 8:22–26), which was taken over by the Gospel writer and need not have taken place in Bethsaida, and a Markan addition at that point call Bethsaida a κώμη (vv. 23, 26). On the other hand, the later Gospels, while retaining the old name, speak of Bethsaida as a πόλις, corresponding to their period (Luke 9:10; John 1:44; so Pliny the Elder also calls Julias "oppidum").

Who Was Julia?

The first doubt concerning the usual equation of the name of the city with that of the daughter of Caesar Augustus, which Josephus expressly made in *Ant.* 18.2.1 §28, I owe to Dr. Arav, who on the basis of the coinage of Philip bearing the inscription ΕΠΙ ΦΙΛΙΠΠΟΥ ΤΕΤΡΑΡΧΟΥ ΚΤΙΣ[ΤΗΣ] and the date given, year 34 (=30/31 CE [or already 29/30?])[43] considered the

[39] Pixner, "Searching," 213f.; see also Riesner, "Ausgrabungen," 14a. Both refer for a similar conjecture to C. W. Wilson, "The Sites of Taricheae and Bethsaida," *PEFQS* 4 (1877) 10–13.

[40] Schürer, *History,* 2:172.

[41] See the detailed treatment of name changes of cities in the Hellenistic-Roman period in O. Keel/M. Küchler/C. Uehlinger, *Orte und Landschaften der Bibel* (presently 2 vols.; Zurich et al.: Benziger; Göttingen: Vandenhoeck & Ruprecht, vol. 1, 1984; vol. 2, 1982) 1:305–16.

[42] See H.-W. Kuhn, "Kreuz I: Urchristentum," *TRE* 18 (1990) 716.

[43] See the reproduction and description of the coinage in Y. Meshorer, *Ancient Jewish*

possibility of a later reestablishment of Julias and therefore also another Julia. An examination by my collaborators and myself of all Juliae from the Julian-Claudian house (for which see immediately below) in connection with the numerous variations in the coinage of Philip revealed that only Livia, the wife of Caesar Augustus and mother of Tiberius Caesar, was a possibility. On the basis of Augustus's will she was accepted into the Julian family in 14 CE and then officially took on the name Julia Augusta, and often was also simply called Julia; she appears now on numerous coins, above all in the east, as Julia Sebaste.[44] This result was confirmed for me later, when I saw that the distinguished Israeli archaeologist Michael Avi-Yonah in 1972 and the Israeli numismatist Jacob Maltiel-Gerstenfeld in 1982 had both already thought of this Livia-Julia, but without referring to the opposing scholarly opinion or the contradiction in Josephus.[45]

The identification proposed here is, on the basis of Philip's coinage, quite clear: Philip not only described himself in 30/31 as a founder of cities but also minted in the same year in a series of at least three coins of various weights[46] a coin with the inscription ΙΟΥΛΙΑ ΣΕΒΑΣΤΗ and the portrait of Livia-Julia.[47] This Julia doubtless of about 30/31 CE cannot be the emperor's daughter who was banished in 2 BCE and who died in 14 CE,[48] but rather only the wife of Augustus and mother of Tiberius, for whom Philip also obviously displayed a special admiration. He also portrayed Augustus together with his wife Livia-Julia (the earlier wife of Augustus, Scribonia, who had already been put aside in 39 BCE, is therefore not a candidate) as

Coinage (2 vols.; New York: Amphora Books, 1982) 2:42, 47–49, 246 (no. 11), plate 8; J. Maltiel-Gerstenfeld, *260 Years of Ancient Jewish Coins: A Catalogue* (Tel Aviv: Kol Printing Service, 1982) 143, 148 (no. 119), 270f.

44 See L. Ollendorff, "Livius (Livia) 37," PW 13/1, cols. 900–924, esp. 900.63ff., 906.61f., 916.26ff., 917.41ff. See also R. Hanslik, "Livia 2," *Der Kleine Pauly: Lexikon der Antike* (Stuttgart: Druckenmüller, 1964–75) vol. 3, cols. 687f. See also n. 47.

45 M. Avi-Yonah, "Bethsaida," *Encyclopaedia Judaica* (Jerusalem: Encyclopaedia Judaica, 1972) vol. 4, col. 748; Maltiel-Gerstenfeld, *260 Years*, 143; here in paragraph 3, line 8 it should read more precisely: "the emperor's [Tiberius's] mother [instead of wife] Livia or Julia. . . ."

46 For this, see Maltiel-Gerstenfeld, *260 Years*, 143; see also Meshorer, *Coinage* 2:49.

47 Meshorer, *Coinage* 2:278 (Suppl. III/1), plate 29 above (no. 1); Maltiel-Gerstenfeld, *260 Years*, 148 (no. 120). As far as I can judge, there is no other Julia in the Julian-Claudian house that had ever been called Julia Augusta or, in Greek, Julia Sebastē. Research by my collaborator Doris Hefner showed that Livia-Julia is very often named in this way on coins from the time of her being accepted into the Julian family in 14 CE after the death of Augustus (*Livia in familiam Iuliam nomenque Augustum adsumebatur*, "Livia was adopted into the Julian family and the Augustan name" [Tacitus *Annals* 1.8]) until her consecration by Claudius in 42 CE, from which time she was often called *Diva Augusta* or Θεὰ Σεβαστή; cf. W. H. Gross, *Iulia Augusta: Untersuchungen zur Grundlegung einer Livia-Ikonographie* (Abhandlungen der Akademie der Wissenschaften in Göttingen, Phil.-Hist. Klasse, 3. Folge, 52; Göttingen: Vandenhoeck & Ruprecht, 1962) 34.

48 See K. Fitzler, "Julius (Julia) 550," PW 10/1, cols. 896–906; R. Hanslik, "Julius (Julia) A 95," *Der Kleine Pauly*, vol. 2, cols. 1539f.

ΣΕΒΑΣΤΩΝ on yet another coin.[49] Since the Julia coin was found in the same series as the κτίστης coin and therefore the Julia who was exiled in 2 BCE can no longer be intended, the possibility may doubtless be ruled out that the founding of a city must refer to the thirtieth anniversary of the reestablishment of Paneas as Caesarea Philippi. Note also that Caesarea Philippi had already been established in 3 or 2 BCE, thus not exactly thirty years before.[50] Clearly, the name change of Bethsaida took place in remembrance of the honored mother and quasi coregent[51] of Tiberius; Livia-Julia died in 29 CE,[52] not long before the issue of the above-mentioned coin, which is up to now the oldest coin of Philip that expressly carries her name (in 33/34 CE [or 32/33?] Philip once again—on the fifth anniversary of her death?—had a coin minted with her name ΙΟΥΛΙΑ ΣΕΒΑΣΤΗ[53]). From a literary standpoint connections are verified especially between Livia-Julia and Herod the Great and his sister Salome;[54] the coins of Philip now show also a strong connection between Livia-Julia and Philip.

The erroneous statement in Josephus is further compromised by the fact that in *J.W.* 2.9.1 §§167f. he obviously means that the two cities Julias in the Gaulanitis and Julias in Perea are named after the Julia who was mentioned twice immediately before, that is, "Julia, the wife of Augustus" (§167) or the Julia whose son was Tiberius (§168). This section in §168 is oriented toward the period following the death of Augustus (14 CE), that is, toward Tiberius, and it appears that Josephus transferred the founding of Caesarea Philippi falsely to the period *after* 14 CE (but in return correctly connected Julias in the Gaulanitis with the mother of Tiberius). On the other hand, the section in *Ant.* 18.2.1 §§27f. is dealing with the reign of Augustus and names four cities in this connection which are to be associated with him: Sepphoris, which Antipas dedicated to Augustus; Julias in Perea, which had been named by him in honor of the wife of Augustus; Caesarea Philippi, which Philip named after Augustus; and Julias on the Sea of Galilee, which he named after the daughter of the emperor. Josephus thus clearly in *Ant.* 18.2.1 §§27f. became a victim to the organization of his account in favor of Caesar Augustus that made the mistake possible.[55]

On the basis of the coins of Philip, Livia-Julia appears to be the only possible candidate, not Julia the daughter of Augustus and temporary wife of

[49] See the reproduction and description of the coin (without date) in Meshorer, *Coinage* 2:245 (no. 6 and 6a), plate 7; Maltiel-Gerstenfeld, *260 Years,* 148 (no. 118).

[50] Schürer, *History* 2:170; contra Meshorer, *Coinage* 2:49. The arguments above disprove A. Kasher, who believes that Julias/Bethsaida "became a *polis* only under Agrippa II" (*Jews and Hellenistic Cities in Eretz-Israel* [Texte und Studien zum Antiken Judentum 21; Tübingen: Mohr, 1990] 220f.); like Schürer (*History* 2:172), he confuses Julias in Peraea with Julias in the Gaulanitis (e.g., Josephus, *Ant.* 20.8.4 §159 par. *J.W.* 2.13.2 §252).

[51] Ollendorff, "Livia 37," cols. 916–23 passim.

[52] Ibid., col. 922.27ff.; Hanslik, "Livia 2," col. 688.42ff.

[53] Description and reproduction in Maltiel-Gerstenfeld, *260 Years,* 89 (no. 123), 149.

[54] See Ollendorff, "Livia 37," cols. 905.35ff., 906.25ff., 914.39ff.

[55] My attention was drawn to the different orientations of the two accounts in Josephus by my collaborator Wolfgang Fenske.

Tiberius, who was erroneously named by Josephus in *Ant.* 18.2.1 §28 and who, as far as I know, had no connection with the Herod family.

Still less of a possibility among the other Juliae of the Julian-Claudian house is the granddaughter of the Livia-Julia suggested above (often called Livilla), who in her second marriage was wed to Drusus, the son of Tiberius, until she took part in his murder and died in disgrace in 31 CE.[56] The case is even worse with the granddaughter of Augustus, who was exiled in 8 CE,[57] and with Livilla, usually called Julia, the daughter of Germanicus, who was born in 18 CE (her father was a grandson of the Livia-Julia here under discussion).[58]

Concerning the Excavations

The focal point of the excavations in 1988 and 1989 lay in Hellenistic-Early Roman times; on the basis of the excavation results up to now, it is the opinion of the archaeologist Dr. Arav that we are dealing in regard of that period with the centuries up to the first Jewish revolt.[59] This period is also the focus of the following excavation report. The excavation is therefore of particular interest for the New Testament scholar, not only because it concerns the New Testament period but especially because for the first time the settlement of Bethsaida—in which Jesus, on the basis of a critical analysis of the canonical Gospels, apparently worked—can be quite clearly (as Julias = Bethsaida) identified with et-Tell. It must be assumed on the basis of the excavations that already before the tetrarch Philip (4 BCE–34 CE) and Jesus (+ca. 30 CE) Bethsaida was relatively important and that no traces of an enlargement by Philip (elevation of the settlement to the status of city probably 30/31 CE or shortly before) are to be discerned up to now. A coin, almost certainly of Philip, shows, as it seems, on the obverse side the head of Tiberius and on the reverse side a temple (presumably the Augusteum in Caesarea Philippi).[60] The find corresponds to the typical coins of Philip, esp. to the large group with the head of Tiberius.[61] On the other hand, an oil lamp with winged Erotes, which can be clearly determined chronologically,

[56] See L. Ollendorff, "Livius (Livia) 38," PW 13/1, cols. 924–27; R. Hanslik, "Livia 3," *Der Kleine Pauly*, vol. 3, cols. 688f.

[57] See K. Fitzler, "Julius (Julia) 551," PW 10/1, cols. 906–8; R. Hanslik, "Julius (Julia) A 96," *Der Kleine Pauly*, vol. 2, col. 1540.

[58] See K. Fitzler, "Julius (Livilla) 575," PW 10/1, cols. 938f.; R. Hanslik, "Julius (Julia) A 105," *Der Kleine Pauly*, vol. 2, col. 1542.

[59] See section II, p. 104.

[60] See section II, p. 97, and illustration 1.

[61] The closest parallels are those coins of this group whose roof of the temple shows two parallel lines on both sides. See the description and reproduction of these coins in Meshorer, *Coinage* 2:245f. (no. 8,11,14; no. 11 is the above-mentioned κτίστης-coin), plate 8; see also Maltiel-Gerstenfeld, *260 Years,* 143ff. Earlier I believed that the coin shows Philip himself, corresponding to a coin in Meshorer, *Coinage* 2:44, 46, 244 (no. 2), plate 7: H.-W. Kuhn, "Bethsaida: Ausgrabung einer Stadt Jesu," *Gesellschaft von Freunden und Förderern der Universität*

belongs to the period of the second and the beginning of the first centuries BCE.[62] To this early period belong also two silver Seleucid coins of Demetrius II from the second half of the second century BCE.[63] Dr. Arav mentions in the following report further coins and an abundance of other finds, especially ceramic, from the Hellenistic-Early Roman period.

While in Area A it is rather clear that we are dealing with a large and obviously public building, which originated—as we learned in 1990—in the Iron Age and was reused in the Hellenistic-Early Roman period, in Area B a considerable, obviously Jewish, courtyard house (without any elements of Hellenistic architecture) has been excavated, which belonged to a fishing family who lived there even during the time of Jesus (see for Area B the "Conclusions" of section II). Several fishing implements (net weights, a needle, probably for repairing nets and sails, and possibly also fishing hooks) are described in the excavation report.[64]

It is hoped that the first detailed report on the excavations since 1987 at et-Tell, which is given below in Part II, will contribute to the removal of some of the uncertainty in New Testament research that has existed up until now, especially concerning the location of Bethsaida. With respect to that I would point out once again that a recently published volume of the *Tübinger Atlas des Vorderen Orients* shifts Bethsaida only toward el-Araj.[65] The double location of Bethsaida above at et-Tell and below on the sea is also presently without archaeological justification.[66]

II. Bethsaida Excavations

References to Bethsaida in antiquity place this town on the north side of the Sea of Galilee, just east of the Jordan River.[67] A rectangular plain, located

München 68: 1989 (1990) 29. But now I agree with Dr. Arav that the coin shows probably Tiberius Caesar (Arav refers to Meshorer type no. 10 as best parallel; see above, n. 60).

[62] See section II, p. 97 and plate 1:4; illustration 2; see also Y. Israeli/U. Avida, *Oil-Lamps from Eretz Israel: The Louis and Carmen Warschaw Collection at the Israel Museum, Jerusalem* (Jerusalem: Israel Museum, 1988) 17.

[63] See section II, pp. 97, 103. Seeing the original coins in 1990, my collaborator Monika Bernett recognized that on one of the two coins the year HΞP = 168 of the Seleucid era (145/144 BCE) is rather surely recognizable (both coins read Demetrios and show an eagle, that is, as far as we know, used on Demetrios coins only for Demetrios II [ca. 145–139 and 129–125 BCE]). From our photographs we do not believe that the third letter (from r. to l.) could be read as ς = 6.

[64] See section II, pp. 102, 104 ("Conclusions") and plate 1:11–13; illustrations 5, 6.

[65] See above, n. 26.

[66] See pp. 85f. above; see also section II, p. 94.

[67] The author wishes to acknowledge the editorial assistance of Dr. Frederick Strickert in the preparation of this part of the article.

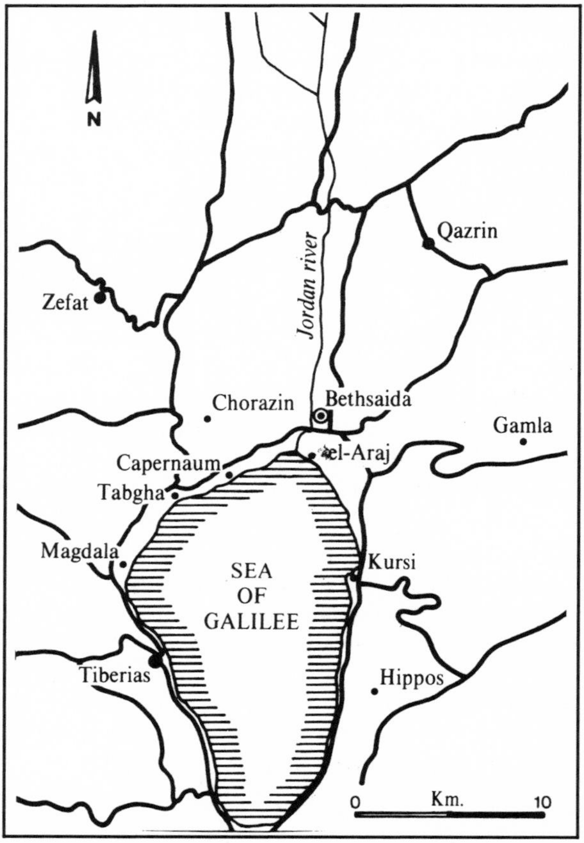

Figure 1

at about 200 meters below sea level, extends over six square miles and is bordered by the Jordan River on the west, the Sea of Galilee in the south, and the Golan Heights in the east and north. The plain of Bethsaida is known also by the Arabic name *Bateḥa,* perhaps derived from the Aramaic *Betaḥ,* which according to M. Jastrow means "a hollow column-like receptacle of rain water near the house."[68] The name indicates that this is an area of swamps and marshes; that, in fact, is the case during the rainy winter months. Presumably, in ancient times the delta was covered with water most of the year (figure 1). Several sites within the plain have been suggested as

[68] M. Jastrow, *A Dictionary of the Targumim, the Talmud Babli and Yerushalmi, and the Midrashic Literature* (Philadelphia: Traditional Press, 1903).

candidates for the town of Bethsaida. In the mid-nineteenth century, E. Robinson identified Bethsaida with et-Tell, a large mound situated in the northwestern corner of the plain.[69] In the 1880s, G. Schumacher proposed el-Araj, a site closer to the shore, since it seemed unlikely that a fishing village should be located one and a half miles away from the lake.[70] Other surveys briefly examined two sites.[71] On the basis of these surveys, Pixner argued for two Bethsaidas: one at et-Tell and another at el-Araj.[72]

The Excavations

In 1987, The Golan Research Institute on behalf of the University of Haifa launched a regional study program on the plain of Bethsaida with a series of test excavations at el-Araj and et-Tell.[73] On the basis of initial findings, more extensive excavations have been undertaken at et-Tell; the first season lasted for five weeks in 1988, and the second season lasted for eight weeks in 1989.[74]

El-Araj

At el-Araj, a low mound extending over ten dunams near the mouth of the Jordan River, remains of a public building are visible on the ground and were possibly incorporated in a building erected early in the twentieth century.

69 Robinson, *Biblical Researches* 2:413–14.

70 G. Schumacher, *The Jaulân* (London: R. Bentley, 1888) 246.

71 M. Kochavi, S. Gutman, and C. Epstein, *Judea, Samaria, and the Golan: Archaeological Survey, 1967–1968* [Hebrew] (Jerusalem: Israel Exploration Society, 1972).

72 Pixner, "Searching," 207–16.

73 The test excavations in 1987 were sponsored by the Golan Research Institute. The participants were a group of students from the University of Waterloo, Waterloo, Ontario. A preliminary report was published in *IEJ* 38 (1988) 188.

74 The first season, in 1988, was sponsored by the Ministry of Science. Area supervisors for the 1988 season were Rachel Pollak and Ruth Negri. The participants were students from St. John's College, Collegeville, Minnesota; students from Wartburg College, Waverly, Iowa, headed by Dr. Frederick Strickert; students from Michigan State University, East Lansing, Michigan, headed by Dr. John T. Greene; and other students and volunteers from throughout Europe and North America.

The main sponsors for the 1989 season were the Jewish Agency and the Golan Regional Council, with additional sponsorship provided by the participants. Preliminary reports were published in *IEJ* 39 (1989) 99–100 and *Hadshot Archaeologiot* [Hebrew] 93 (1989) 15. Area supervisors for the 1989 season were Doris Hefner, George Spanos, Katherine Dempsey, Dr. Frederick Strickert, and Dr. John T. Greene. Surveying was done by Franz Pfeifer, architect; drawing by Dawn Tipka; and photography by Dirk Stoller and Thomas Goeke. Participants in the 1989 season were students from the University of Munich, headed by Prof. Dr. H.-W. Kuhn; students from Wartburg College, headed by Dr. Frederick Strickert; students from Michigan State University, headed by Dr. John T. Greene; and volunteers from Europe and North America. We would like to thank the Israel Defense Forces for providing tarpaulins.

Visitors in the 1920s reported seeing a mosaic floor there.[75] The area selected for the probe was 50 meters east of these remains. A random square of 4 by 4 meters was excavated, yielding a floor and two walls forming a corner.

The pottery from this square dates from the Byzantine period. A few representative samples are (1) a bowl of pseudo terra sigillata with a pattern of circular grooves near the base (plate 2:7, 9), dating from the Byzantine period, similar to those found in many sites, including Capernaum;[76] (2) a large cooking pot (plate 2:6), which corresponds to Khirbet Shemaʿ level V, dating from Byzantine 2 or 419–640 CE;[77] (3) the base of a glass cup (?) dating from the fourth to the early fifth century CE (plate 2:8).[78].

There was no evidence found for Roman or Hellenistic occupation of the site. Rather, a sterile level was found underneath this Byzantine structure. El-Araj was not to be identified with Bethsaida, the site mentioned by both Josephus and the Gospels. There were no remains consistent with expectations for a site designated as a πόλις, nor was the site even in use in New Testament times. Rather, it would seem that el-Araj had been settled several centuries later, perhaps after the destruction of Bethsaida itself.

Et-Tell

Topography

Et-Tell, the largest mound on the plain, rests on the basalt extension that forms the Golan Heights. It measures 400 meters in length, 200 meters in width, and rises 25 meters above its immediate surroundings. The elevation for the peak of the mound is 165.96 meters below sea level. The summit, formed by two peaks with a shallow saddle between them, lies on the eastern part of the mound with a steep slope down to the plain. The southern and western sections slope more gradually; however, the main approach to the town was from the north where the mound protrudes from the basalt extension.

As mentioned earlier, this area has an abundance of water. In addition to the Jordan River, which lies 500 meters west of the mound, there exist

[75] R. De Haas, *"Galilee": A historical and geographical description of Lake Galilee and surroundings* (Jerusalem: n.p., 1933).

[76] This type corresponds to those discussed in S. Loffreda, O.F.M., *Cafarnao II* (Jerusalem: Franciscan Printing Press, 1974) 65–88.

[77] E. Meyers et al., *Ancient Synagogue Excavations at Khirbet Shemaʿ, Upper Galilee, Israel, 1970–1972* (AASOR 42; Durham, N.C.: Duke University Press, 1976) pl. 7:16, 25.

[78] Similar glass was found in Khirbet Shemaʿ; see Meyers, *Ancient Synagogue Excavations*, pl. 8.7:18–21.

two springs of high-quality water in the eastern and western foothills of the mound.

Procedures

An initial test excavation, near the highest point of the mound, revealed a 4-meter accumulation of layers dating from the Iron Age to the early Roman period. In order to carry out a more systematic excavation, the mound was then divided into a network of 5-by-5-meter squares and a topographical plan was prepared. Two areas were selected for excavation (figure 2). Area A, located near the initial square at the summit, would provide a cross section of the mound running from east to west. Area B, located 50 meters to the north, would provide a wide-area excavation.

Area A: Excavations

The lowest level excavated in Area A contained an Iron Age II house (tenth to eighth century BCE). Two walls with six courses of stone remaining were found at a depth of 0.50 meters below the surface. They measure 3.80 and 5.50 meters in length, but their width has not yet been determined. A plaster floor was discovered at an elevation of 168.15 meters below sea level. Many vessels were unearthed on the floor, among which was an Aramaic ostracon bearing the letters *'kb'*, which may indicate the proper name Akiba. This building was presumably destroyed in the eighth century BCE.[79]

The next level provides evidence for an extensive construction, including a large public building. The construction was established in the Iron Age (and reused in the Hellenistic-Roman period). The terrain was leveled, with bricks and stones brought in to fill the depressions. A new floor was established at -167.10 meters, one meter above the earlier level. Large boulders were installed to create a solid foundation for a building with walls 18 and 11 meters in length. Because of destruction, the plan of this building is not yet clear. The importance of this building is attested by the presence of a few dressed stones, some of which were decorated. Among these are the following: (1) a basalt lintel decorated with meander and floral motifs (plate 2:5), similar to a lintel discovered at Capernaum that was carved in limestone and without the floral motif;[80] (2) a basalt architectural fragment with a

[79] During the eighth century BCE, a few other sites on the northeastern shores of the Sea of Galilee were destroyed with no later Iron Age resettlement. These were En Gev ("En Gev Stratum I"; see B. Mazar, A. Biran, and I. Dunayevski, "En Gev Excavations in 1961," *IEJ* 14 [1964] 1–49) and the recently discovered Tel Soreg and Tel Hadar I (see M. Kochavi, "The Land of Geshur Project: Regional Archaeology of the Southern Golan [1987–1988 Seasons]," *IEJ* 39 [1989] 1–17).

[80] G. Orfali, O.F.M., *Capharnaüm et ses ruines* (Paris: August Picard, 1922) figs. 103, 104.

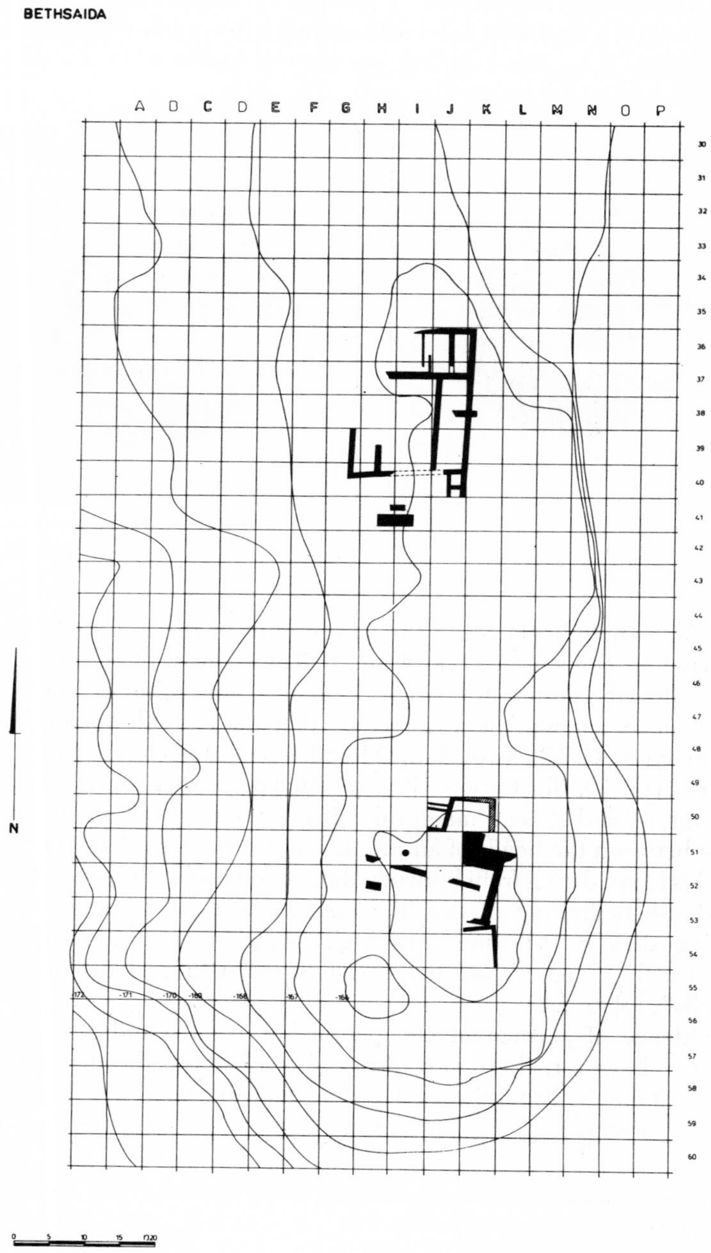
BETHSAIDA
A B C D E F G H I J K L M N O P
30
31
32
33
34
35
36
37
38
39
40
41
42
43
44
45
46
47
48
49
50
51
52
53
54
55
56
57
58
59
60
-172
-171
-170
-169
-168
-167
-166
N
0
5
10
15

Figure 2

flower surrounded by leaf scrollwork (plate 2:4), which has parallels found at Chorazin;[81] (3) a section of lintel with acanthus decoration with the center mutilated (plate 2:3). The building was largely destroyed in the mid-first century CE.

Illustration 1
Obverse

Illustration 1
Reverse

Other finds include (1) coins; the scarce numismatic finds at et-Tell include forty-four coins from Areas A and B. They consist of one silver stater from Tyre (fourth century BCE), eight Ptolemaic coins, four Seleucid coins, six Hasmonean (among them are coins that date to Alexander Janneus [Meshorer types C, E]), two Philip Herod (one dates clearly to 29/30 CE [Meshorer type 10, illustration 1][82]), six Roman second-century CE coins, one Byzantine, and sixteen medieval coins; (2) a lamp ornamented with a palmette between the heads of antithetic winged Erotes (plate 1:4; illustration 2) (this lamp, dating from between the second half of the second century BCE and the beginning of the first century BCE, is common to many Hellenistic sites in Palestine,[83] its high quality suggesting that it is an import); (3) the female head of a clay figurine with curled hair and veil (Livia/Julia?) (plate 2:2).

No evidence of permanent occupation has been found after the first century CE; however, there is evidence for visitors to the mound during subsequent periods. From the medieval period, coins and sherds of pottery were discovered, which suggests that much stone looting took place during

[81] Z. Yeivin, "Chorazin Excavations, 1962–1964," *Eretz Israel* 13 (1973) 144–57; and in limestone (see Orfali, *Capharnaüm*, figs. 49, 50).

[82] Meshorer, *Coinage* 1:49, pls. 5–12; 2:245, pl. 8.

[83] This is no. 25 in the Schloessinger collection; see R. Rosenthal and R. Sivan, *Ancient Lamps in the Schloesinger Collection* (Qedem 10; Jerusalem: Hebrew University, 1978) no. 25.

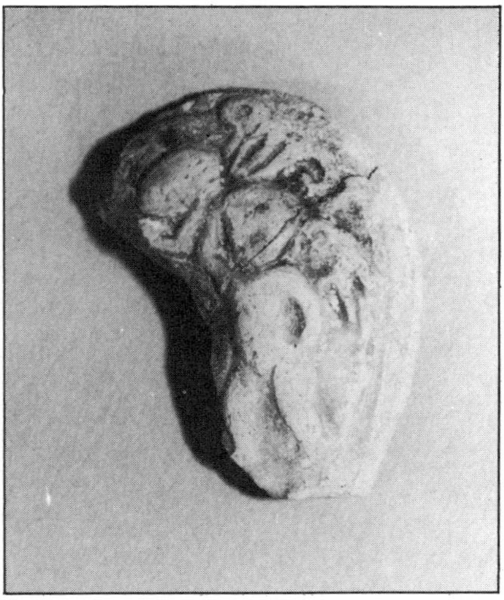

Illustration 2

Illustration 3

this time. During the nineteenth and early twentieth centuries CE, the bedouin buried their dead on the mound. Thus far sixty-two tombs have been excavated in Area A. In addition, between 1948 and 1967 the Syrian army turned the site into a military fortification. Trenches crisscrossed the site, particularly at the summit and at the edges of the mound.

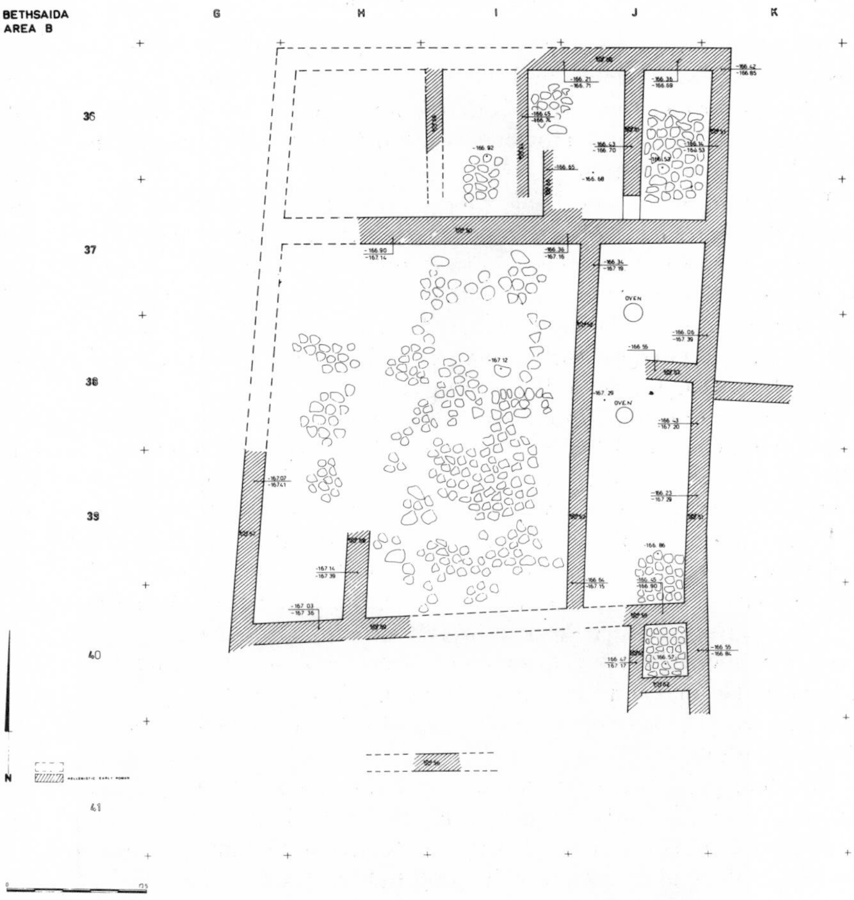

Figure 3

Area B: Excavations

An initial 3-by-3.5-meter test square provided evidence for two levels of occupation: Early Bronze and late Hellenistic-early Roman. The evidence for the earlier level corresponds to the presence of a thick Bronze Age wall surrounding the mound. However, work in Area B has concentrated on the later level of occupation.

Excavation of the late Hellenistic-early Roman level of Area B has uncovered the remains of a private residence (illustration 3). This can be deduced from the floor plan and from the size of the blocks that form the structure. All stones were small field stones, smaller than the stones and boulders of Area A. The materials used in Area B are of a size handled easily by one or two persons. Unlike the public building in Area A, this building was not constructed on a filling of brick material.

The state of preservation in Area B is much better than in Area A. There were neither bedouin tombs nor Syrian military remains; however, there is clear evidence of stone looting. Piles of stones from the residence were found in a depression excavated in the northwest section of the structure. Whereas the eastern walls (W 51) were preserved to about 1.3 meters in height, the western section (W 57) was almost completely looted. The floor of the courtyard was found only a few centimeters below the surface.

The house is quite large and typical of Hellenistic Palestine courtyard houses (figure 3).[84] It covers an area of 430 square meters, similar in size to a house in Gezer,[85] and larger than houses in Philoteria (280 square meters)[86] and Samaria (130 square meters),[87] all dating from late Hellenistic and early Roman periods.

The floor plan resembles that of a courtyard house, that is, a house built around a central courtyard that is also the main feature of the house. The courtyard in Area B is located at the center of the building. It measures 7.1 by 13.5 meters and is paved with basalt fieldstones of about 20 to 40 centimeters in diameter. The entrance to the house has not yet been determined but was perhaps in the west. A cluster of rooms surround the courtyard. The interior eastern wall is 60 centimeters wide and built with one row of stones. The outer eastern wall is 70 centimeters wide and built with two faces.

The rooms in the east include a kitchen with two ovens. The ovens were stone-faced with clay, about 1 centimeter thick; they are preserved to a height of about 30 centimeters. Kitchenware was found scattered in the area

[84] R. Arav, *Hellenistic Palestine: Settlement Patterns and City Planning, 331–37 B.C.E.* (BAR International Series 485; London: B.A.R., 1989) 166.

[85] Ibid., fig. 34.

[86] Ibid., fig. 71.

[87] G. A. Reisner, C. S. Fisher, and D. G. Lyon, *Harvard Excavations at Samaria (1908–1910)* (Cambridge, Mass.: Harvard University Press, 1924) 141.

of the ovens, beneath the debris from the walls. To the south, there was a large rectangular room. Here the floor was made of beaten earth, with only a small section of an elevated area paved with fieldstones. The outer wall (W 51) was found inclined toward the rooms; this inclination is also marked on the floor plan. Whether this inclination was the result of an earthquake or another cause is still unknown.

To the south of this room, there was a rather small room, measuring 1.5 by 2 meters. The interior western wall (W 63) measures 45 centimeters in width and the southern wall (W 62) measures 55 centimeters. However, the northern wall (W 59) is thicker, 70 centimeters, and perhaps served as the southern wall of the courtyard. It seems that W 63 extends southward to include another room. This area has not yet been excavated. W 59 and W 56 mark the row of rooms in the south. The floors of these rooms were made of beaten earth. Because of the poor state of preservation in the west, very little was left of these rooms. W 58 disappears on reaching the courtyard. W 57 was not completely excavated. The depression in the northwest corner eliminates any remains from the corner of W 57 and W 60.

A row of four rooms was preserved in the north. The northeastern room measures 5.5 by 2.4 meters. This room was paved with fieldstones. The elevation of the floor measured at -166.53 meters corresponds to the elevation of the small room in the south.

A threshold at the corner of W 61 and W 50 leads to a room that measures 3.5 by 5.5 meters. The room was perhaps smaller at one time and closed by W 65. Later this room was enlarged, and W 64 was built farther west. The entrance to this room was near the corner of W 64 and W 50. The adjoining room to the west was bordered by W 66. Little of this wall was preserved, and in this section it was completely looted. The room to the west of W 66 has not yet been excavated.

Area B: Pottery

With the exception of one globular cooking pot, all vessels were found smashed under the debris of the walls. The pottery is divided into two main groups: (1) local ware, and (2) eastern terra sigillata.

Cooking pots. One intact cooking pot was found near the north oven next to W 50 (plate 1:2). It is a globular pot: the walls are thin and have fine ribbing, and it has a vertical, slightly concave neck, similar to Lapp type 71.[88] A fairly large number of similar cooking pots were found broken.

[88] P. W. Lapp, *Palestinian Ceramic Chronology* (New Haven: American Schools of Oriental Research, 1961) 184; for other parallels, see E. Netzer, *Greater Herodium* (Qedem 13; Jerusalem: Hebrew University, 1981) 60.

Jugs. A complete jug was found next to the intact cooking pot (plate 1:1). This jug has a wide neck, a thick rim, and a sack-shaped body, similar to Lapp type 21. Parallels include Beth Zur II (175–165 BCE), Shechem BI (200–150 BCE), and Beth Zur 279 (175–100 BCE).[89]

Flasks. A single sample of a flask is made of fine ware, with an everted rim and red slip (plate 1:3), similar to Lapp type 29.[90]

Oil lamps. Few oil lamps were discovered in Area B, yet they represent the life span of the house. The oldest pieces are of brown clay with black glaze, similar to Schloessinger collection no. 10,[91] dated to the second quarter of the fourth century BCE to the first quarter of the third century BCE. Another type is an oil lamp with a ray motif and black glaze (plate 1:5), similar to Lapp type 83.2,C, dated to 75–25 BCE.[92] The latest type is the so-called Herodian lamp with a bow spout, similar to Lapp type 82.1, common to sites dating from the first century BCE to the first Jewish revolt.[93]

Eastern terra sigillata. Area B is particularly rich in eastern terra sigillata. Almost every sherd basket contained a few items. Among the noteworthy examples are deep small bowls with black glaze (plate 1:7), large shallow bowls with decorations of palmettes, and "fish plates" with black glaze (plate 1:8), similar to Lapp type 153.1,A[94] dated to 200–150 BCE. A few molded "Megarian" bowls bearing floral motifs (plate 1:9; illustration 4; see also for Area A plate 1:10), similar to Lapp type 158,[95] are dated to 150 BCE to 20 CE.

Other Finds from Areas A and B

Among the other finds from both areas are the following: (1) Fishing implements. Found in the courtyard of the residence were lead weights for fishing nets. These weights, measuring 2 to 5 centimeters are simple flat plaques of lead that were folded on both sides (plate 1:12; illustration 5). (2) An iron hook, 6.5 centimeters in length (plate 1:13). (3) A bronze needle, 15 centimeters long with an eye at one end, found in the eastern rectangular room (plate 1:11; illustration 6). (4) A clay seal, measuring 25 millimeters in height and 20 millimeters at the base. The seal depicts, through deep incisions, a scene that can be interpreted as a boat with an elevated prow in the shape of an animal head (horse?). Two persons seem to be standing in the boat. In

[89] Lapp, *Chronology,* 157.

[90] Ibid., 161.

[91] Rosenthal and Sivan, *Lamps,* 10.

[92] Lapp, *Chronology,* 194.

[93] Ibid., 193; Rosenthal and Sivan, *Lamps,* 80–81.

[94] Lapp, *Chronology,* 206.

[95] Ibid., 209; see also J. Gunneweg, I. Perlman, and J. Yellin, *The Provenience, Typology and Chronology of Eastern Terra Sigillata* (Qedem 17; Jerusalem: Hebrew University, 1983) pl. 22:2.

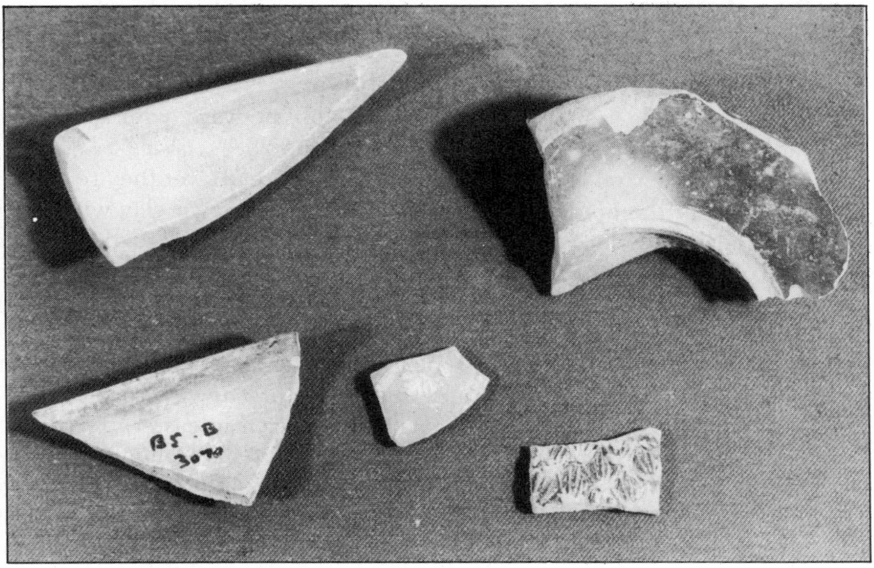

Illustration 4

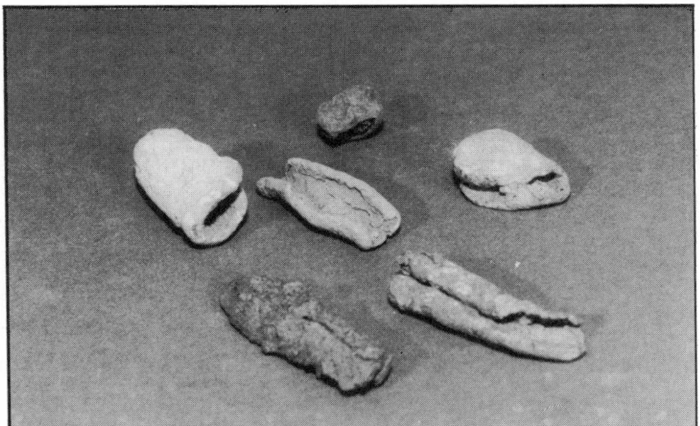

Illustration 5

front of the boat is a stylized reed. Fish can be discerned below the boat (plate 2:1). (5) Among a few Hellenistic coins were two silver tetradrachmas assigned to Demetrius II (145–138 BCE) that were found in the eastern large rectangular room. (6) A single Rhodian stamped handle of a wine jar was found near the ovens (plate 1:6).

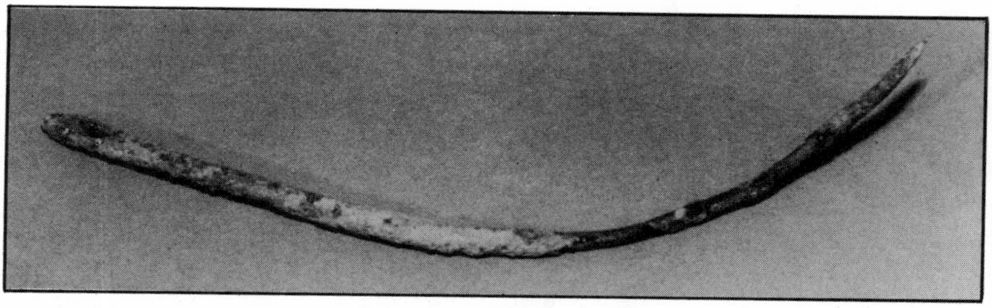

Illustration 6

Conclusions

El-Araj provided no evidence for occupation prior to the Byzantine period. On the other hand, three main occupation levels were discerned at et-Tell: the earliest dating from the Early Bronze Age II, the second dating from Iron Age, and the last dating from the second century BCE until 65/66 CE. There is thus sufficient evidence to identify et-Tell as ancient Bethsaida.

A spacious courtyard house from the last period of occupation was excavated in Area B. The house existed through some modifications until the onset of the Jewish–Roman war, when it was destroyed and never resettled. The settlement of Bethsaida moved perhaps to a nearby location. The finds in the house, such as fishing net weights, hooks, and a needle for repairing nets and sails, indicate that fishermen owned the house. The architectural elements of this house do not reveal any Hellenistic influence; neither columns nor capitals nor typical Hellenistic architectural designs were unearthed in Area B. Some such elements were found in Area A and are apparently associated with the public building. Absence of Hellenistic architectural elements is typical of Jewish settlements during the Hellenistic and Roman periods. In addition to this, the find of Jewish coins supports the idea that the inhabitants of Bethsaida were Jewish.

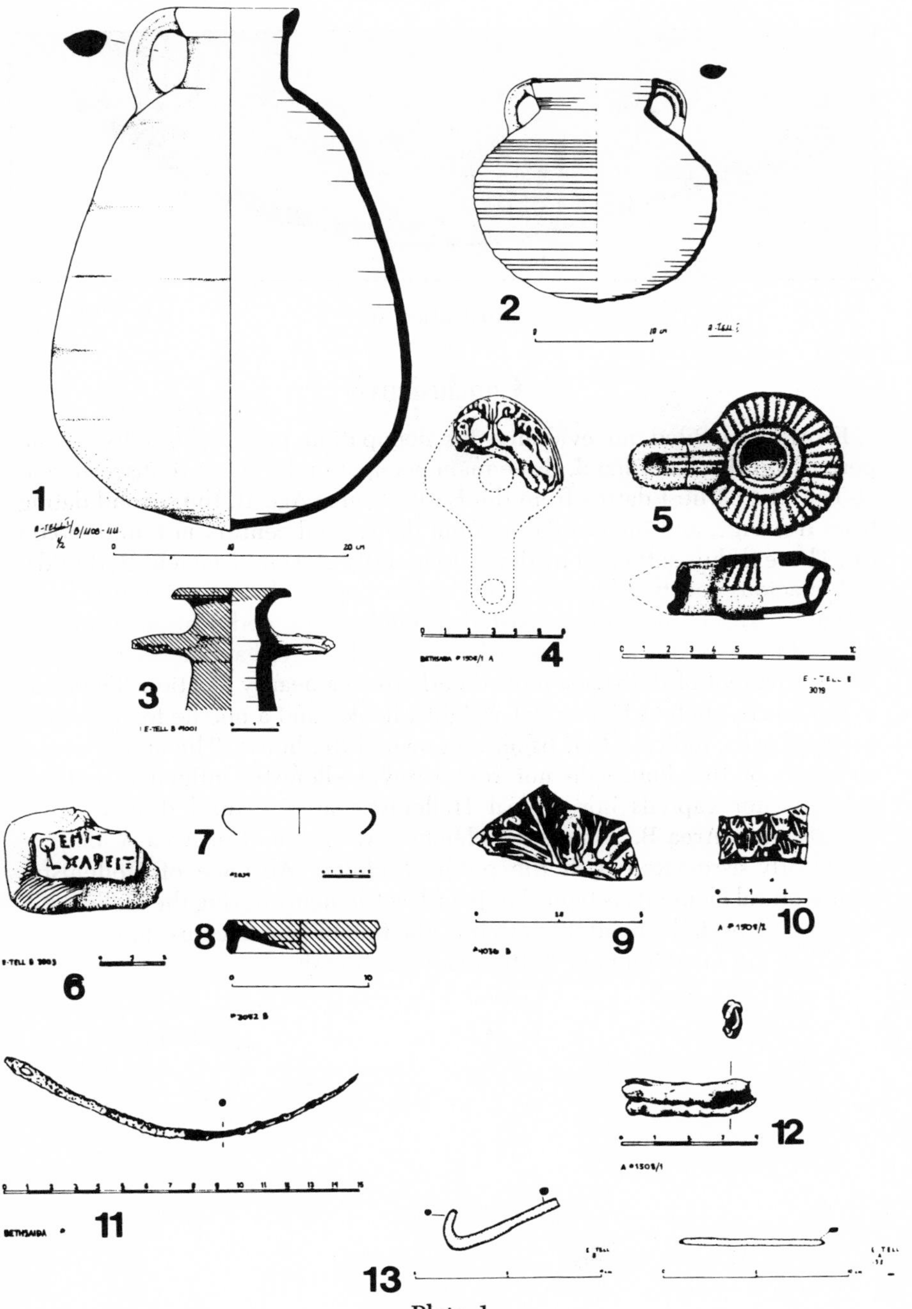

Plate 1

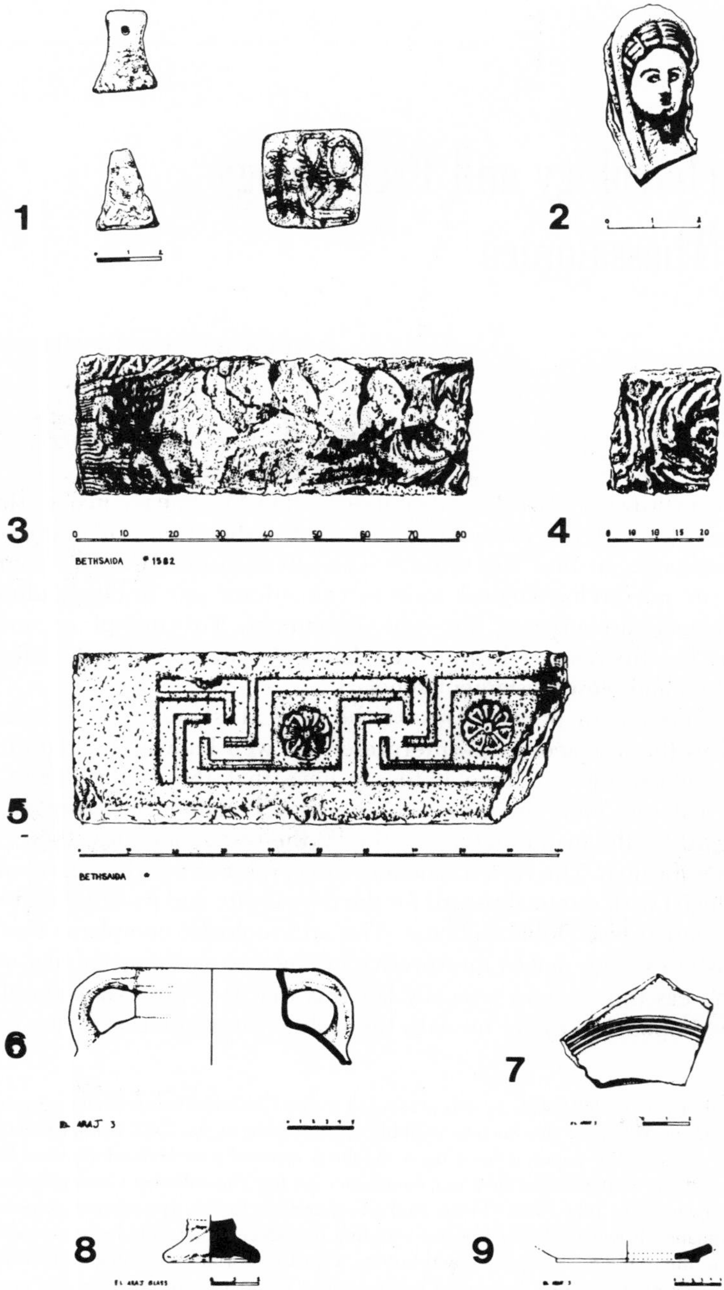

Plate 2

7

Archaeology and Eschatology at Thessalonica

HOLLAND LEE HENDRIX

"ARCHAEOLOGY" AND "ESCHATOLOGY" stand in uneasy juxtaposition: the study of the material evidence of earlier times as opposed to discourse on the "last times."[1] The question posed in this study is whether or not archaeological sources can inform our understanding of eschatological discourse in the New Testament. To attempt an answer requires a healthy respect for the often divergent interests of archaeological interpreters and New Testament scholars.

The difference in perspectives of the New Testament interpreter as opposed to the archaeological interpreter are well known and require no extensive elaboration. Suffice it to say here that the archaeologist and regional historian mine the sources of the New Testament interpreter with little regard for the overall interpretation of the texts, much less their theological significance. The New Testament interpreter mines the quarry of the archaeologist with minimal regard for the overall site and its situation in any regional, much less global, scheme. The archaeologist complains that the enthusiastic exegete makes interpretive mountains out of artifactual molehills, whereas the exegete typically laments that it is professionally, if not humanly, impossible to get on with the task of interpretation if one has to

[1] An earlier version of this paper was presented to the Consultation on Archaeology of the New Testament World of the Society of Biblical Literature at its 1987 annual meeting in Boston. In revising the paper, I have been indebted especially to Helmut Koester for the manuscript of a presentation he gave to a conference on the Thessalonian Correspondence at Leuven University in July 1988, "From Paul's Eschatology to the Apocalyptic Schemata of 2 Thessalonians." It was Professor Koester who first introduced me to the broad Macedonian plain and to the richness of its people and history. That I can bring something of its history to bear on interpreting the New Testament is the highest honor I could hope to offer one who has done so much in illuminating both Macedonian and New Testament studies.

master every territory's molehills. What is of principal import to one is extraneous to the other.

The possibility of a constructive dialogue between the archaeological interpreter and the exegete exists only if their respective and divergent interests can be encouraged to intersect. This requires some mutual education. For the archaeologist, such education entails cultivating a more sophisticated interest in religious phenomena and a more *critical* regard for religious documents in general and New Testament materials in particular.[2] For the New Testament interpreter, more education is required in the painful process of being weaned from secondary compendia and analyses of material evidence and being directed to the primary sources of archaeological data. One searches in vain most bibliographies of recent New Testament studies for references to the most rudimentary collections of archaeological data—even in works whose authors purport to take material evidence seriously. To guard against making mountains out of molehills, New Testament interpreters must begin to gain archaeological field experience if they are to appreciate the precision as well as the methodological limitations of archaeological enterprises.[3]

In addition to developing some familiarity with field archaeology and the appropriate sources for the full range of archaeological corpora (inscriptions, coins, architecture, statuary, artifacts, various categories of organic remains, etc.), the New Testament interpreter should attempt to formulate questions or hypotheses that may fruitfully be applied to the archaeological evidence.

[2] For over a decade there has been increasing interest in religion on the part of some "new" or "scientific" archaeologists. See, e.g., Robert Hall, "Ghosts, Water Barriers, Corn and Sacred Enclosures in the Eastern Woodlands," *American Antiquity* 41 (1976) 360–64; Kent Flannery and Joyce Marcus, "Formative Oaxaca and the Zapotec Cosmos," *American Scientist* 64 (1976) 374–83; Ian Hodder, *Symbolic and Structural Archaeology* (Cambridge: Cambridge University Press, 1982); Mark Leone, "Some Opinions About Recovering Mind," *American Antiquity* 47 (1982) 742–60. This movement has yet to have a significant impact on "classical" archaeologists recovering and studying Greco-Roman materials. For the most part, classical archaeologists confine their interest in religion to overtly religious phenomena, and even these seldom are studied from a religious-historical (as opposed to an art-historical or a political-historical) perspective. There is also a tendency among classical archaeologists to treat NT sources with insufficient critical regard. Note, e.g., John Camp's presumption of the historical accuracy of Acts 17 in *The Athenian Agora* (New York: Thames & Hudson, 1986) 211. For the limitations of Syro-Palestinian archaeology in NT studies, see Eric Meyers and James Strange, *Archaeology, the Rabbis and Early Christianity* (Nashville: Abingdon, 1981) 22–30.

[3] A criticism sometimes leveled by NT scholars against the use of archaeological materials in NT interpretation is the "accidental" nature of archaeological remains. Such criticism is misguided and counterproductive. As Lewis Binford has observed, "the practical limitations on our knowledge of the past are not inherent in the nature of the archeological record; the limitations lie in our methodological naivete . . ." (*New Perspectives in Archeology,* ed. S. Binford and L. Binford [Chicago: Aldine, 1968] 23). On the nature of error in data collection, see P. J. Watson, S. A. LeBlanc, and C. L. Redman, eds., *Archeological Explanation* (New York: Columbia University Press, 1989) 169–75.

This might ensure some economy in the task of marshaling data and could ease the interpreter's burden in approaching admittedly vast corpora of evidence.

As a case study in the use of archaeological material in New Testament interpretation, we turn now to the issue of archaeology and eschatology at Thessalonica. There are a number of interpretive puzzles in the apocalyptic core of 1 Thess 4:13–5:11. In 4:13 to 5:1, Paul provides new information about those who have "fallen asleep." His intention is to grant some comfort to those who are still alive by revealing that their being caught up into the clouds with the Lord will be preceded by the raising up of those asleep.[4] After encouraging his readers to comfort one another with this disclosure, he turns in 5:1 to a consideration of the "times and seasons" of the coming day of the Lord, presuming as he does that the Thessalonians already are aware of instructions on the subject.

In what follows, we encounter a pastiche of traditional apocalyptic imagery. The day of the Lord comes like a thief in the night; those of light, likened to the sober, are contrasted to those in gloom and drunkenness; the suddenness of the destruction is illustrated by a woman in travail. Much of this imagery we find in other letters of Paul, and substantial work has been done in locating it in apocalyptic traditions known from other sources in the Hebrew scriptures, the New Testament, and extracanonical literature.[5]

One of the distinctive features of this Pauline formulation of the end-times is the saying he introduces in 5:3: "When people say, 'there is peace and security,' then sudden destruction will come upon them" (RSV). The resonance of this passage with Hebrew prophetic denunciation of delusions of peace on the eve of destruction has long been noted by commentators on the passage.[6] The clearest parallels are, of course, Jeremiah 6 (and 8) and Ezekiel 13. There are, however, significant differences between the Hebrew

[4] The most detailed analysis is that of B. Rigaux, *Saint Paul: Les Epîtres aux Thessaloniciens* (Ebib; Paris: Gabalda, 1956) 24–74. For a more recent discussion of the passage with pertinent bibliography to 1980, see Raymond F. Collins, *Studies on the First Letter to the Thessalonians* (BETL 66; Leuven: Leuven University Press, 1984) 154–72.

[5] Gerhard Friedrich has questioned the authenticity of 1 Thess 5:1–11 on a number of occasions; see esp. "1. Thessalonicher 5,1–11, der apologetische Einschub eines Späteren," *ZTK* 70 (1973) 288–315. Arguing in favor of the passage's authenticity and in response to Friedrich are Raymond F. Collins ("A propos the Integrity of 1 Thes," *ETL* 65 [1979] 67–106) and Joseph Plevnik ("1 Thess 5,1–11: Its Authenticity, Intention and Message," *Bib* 60 [1979] 71–90). On traditional apocalyptic elements in 1 Thess 5:1–11, see B. Rigaux, "Tradition et rédaction dans 1 Th. V. 1–10," *NTS* 21 (1974–75) 318–40; Collins, *Studies*, 163–71; Plevnik, "1 Thess 5,1–11," 80–87; Koester, "Eschatology," 6–17; Wolfgang Harnisch, *Eschatologische Existenz: Ein exegetischer Beitrag zum Sachanliegen von 1. Thessalonicher 4.15–5,11* (FRLANT 110; Göttingen, Vandenhoeck & Ruprecht, 1973).

[6] See Rigaux, *Thessaloniciens*, 557–58 and references there. Also useful is the summary discussion of Traugott Holtz, *Der erste Brief an die Thessalonicher* (EKKNT 13; Neukirchen-Vluyn: Neukirchener Verlag, 1986) 215–16.

prophetic tradition and the passage in Paul's letter to the Thessalonians. Paul quotes the declaration as "peace and security" (εἰρήνη καὶ ἀσφάλεια). "Security," or any functional equivalent thereof, is not to be found in any of the Hebrew scriptural allusions.[7] Ἀσφάλεια occurs only here in the Pauline corpus.[8] Also distinctive to Paul's formulation is the implication that the pronouncement of "peace and security" is a condition of the last times and that sure destruction is the sudden fate of those who proclaim such a message.[9]

What does this "peace and security" represent? Some interpreters have suggested that Paul was attempting to guard against an eschatological lassitude among Thessalonian Christians.[10] Other scholars would go further in identifying as the object of the polemic a gnostic or gnosticizing group in the congregation which promoted a noneschatological "peace and security."[11] The principal difficulty with such interpretations is that, in the context of Paul's admonition, those to whom he attributes the saying "peace and security" seem to stand outside the congregation addressed by the apostle.[12]

[7] A common interpretation has been to assume that Paul replaces the second "peace" of Jeremiah's formulation with "security." See, e.g., Rigaux, *Thessaloniciens,* 558; Holtz, *Erste Thessalonicher,* 79–80. Koester challenges this assumption in "Eschatology," 10–11.

[8] Koester points out that ἀσφάλεια occurs in the NT only here and in Luke 1:4 and Acts 5:24 ("Eschatology," 31 n. 44). Paul uses an adjective from the same root in Phil 3:1.

[9] If Paul has in mind Hebrew prophetic denunciation of false purveyors of peace, he takes the retribution one important step beyond what we find in Jer 6:14 (8:11) and Ezek 13:10, 16. In these passages, false prophesying of peace is condemned, but it is not made a condition for divine destruction. For Paul, the pronouncement of "peace and security" seems to serve as a temporal qualifier for the "sudden" imposition of God's wrath. Note also the clearly sequential force of Paul's use of ὅταν . . . τότε in 1 Cor 15:28 and 54.

[10] So Franz Laub, *Eschatologische Verkündigung und Lebensgestaltung nach Paulus: Eine Untersuchung zum Wirken des Apostels beim Aufbau der Gemeinde in Thessalonike* (Regensburg: Pustet, 1973) 133; Plevnik, "1 Thess 5,1–11," 88. This interpretation is explicit or implicit in a number of other studies: Lieselotte Mattern, *Das Verständnis des Gerichts bei Paulus* (Zurich and Stuttgart: Zwingli, 1966) 77–82; David A. Black, "The Weak in Thessalonica: A Study in Pauline Lexicography," *JETS* 25 (1982) 307–21, esp. 318; Stephen Smalley, "The Delay of the Parousia," *JBL* 83 (1964) 49–52; Collins, *Studies,* 169. A highly nuanced variation of the interpretation is that of Robert Jewett, *The Thessalonian Correspondence: Pauline Rhetoric and Millenarian Piety* (Philadelphia: Fortress Press, 1986) 171: "The church had evidently interpreted Paul's message about being saved from the wrath to come as the beginning of permanently altered conditions of immortality and bliss." For criticism of the assumption that the "delay of the parousia" was at issue in Paul's letter, see Koester, "Eschatology," 16–17.

[11] Major proponents of this view are Walter Schmithals (*Paul and the Gnostics,* trans. J. E. Steely [Nashville: Abingdon, 1972] 128–318) and Harnisch (*Eschatologische Existenz,* 52–158). In response to the antignostic hypothesis, see Gerhard Friedrich, "Der erste Brief an die Thessalonicher" in J. Becker, H. Conzelmann, G. Friedrich, *Die Briefe an die Galater, Epheser, Philipper, Kolosser, Thessalonicher und Philemon* (NTD 8; Göttingen: Vandenhoeck & Ruprecht, 1976) 206–8.

[12] Plevnik is sensitive to the issue but wants to have it both ways. He concludes that "Paul's motive in 5,2–3 is to put an end to any false security anchored in the emerging realization that

If those responsible for the saying were within the congregation (and even if they were gnostic opponents), one would expect the type of formulation we find in 1 Cor 15:12: "Now if Christ is preached as raised from the dead, how can some of *you* say that there is no resurrection of the dead?" (RSV, emphasis mine). Throughout 1 Thess 5:1–11, the overwhelming emphasis is on "you," "we," and "us," as opposed to "others," "they," and "them." With the exception of 5:11, the contrast between "us/you" and "them" is explicit in every verse of the passage. The climactic contrast of the passage occurs in 5:9: "For God has not destined *us* for wrath, but to obtain salvation through our Lord Jesus Christ" (RSV, emphasis mine). Those responsible for the saying "peace and security" are "destined for wrath" in that promotion of their message coincides with their "sudden destruction" from which "there will be no escape" (5:3). As opposed to the Christians of Thessalonica, promoters of the saying are arrayed on the side of gloom, drunkenness, and slumber.

If the victims of Paul's apocalyptic condemnation are outside the Thessalonian congregation, at whom exactly is he pointing the finger in isolating proponents of "peace and security"? Perhaps the apostle offers a general and traditional prophetic condemnation of all those not committed to his particular view of divine retribution, preferring instead an attitude supportive of a peaceful status quo. For two reasons, this appears unlikely. First, the addition of "and security" and the omission of "when there is no peace" do not follow the Hebrew prophetic condemnation of a false view of peace. This suggests that the saying specifies something other than a traditional prophetic construal of a false sense of peace. If Paul's citation of the saying reflects prophetic tradition, it is something other than what we find in Jeremiah and Ezekiel. Second, the temporal specificity of the destruction of those proclaiming "peace and security" is striking. To be sure, Paul employs traditional prophetic language in describing their destruction—"as travail comes upon a woman with child" (Isa 13:8; Jer 6:24; Hos 13:13). But in the prophetic tradition destruction is not linked temporally (or causally) with an inappropriate proclamation of peace. Paul's employment of the formula "when . . . then" (ὅταν . . . τότε) underscores the temporal and causal connection between the proclamation of "peace and security" and the destruction of those promoting it. Such specificity seems to engender more precision than a prediction of judgment directed generally against all non-Christians on prophetic analogy with "the nations" (Isa 13:8) or a recalcitrant Israel (Jer 6:24; Hos 13:13). It is almost as if Paul is singling out for particular mention

the day of the Lord will not come as soon as it was first expected." He goes on to observe, "This judgment is, indirectly, a real possibility also for the faithful—if they ever abandon their readiness and vigilance. . . ." But then he adds: "However, the threat of condemnation is really not directed against those are 'in Christ,' but rather against the outsiders" ("1 Thess 5,1–11," 88).

a subset of those "of the gloom" with whom he contrasts the Thessalonian Christians and himself, a subset of those "of the day." A further element of specificity is the encouragement which the *Thessalonian* congregation is to derive from the knowledge that they, as opposed to those proclaiming "peace and security," are not destined for the sudden devastation wrought by divine wrath (5:9–11).

What is the source of the saying "peace and security"? One possibility that has been largely ignored or rejected is that the phrase refers to Roman imperial sloganeering.[13] Helmut Koester and Karl Donfried have revived this interpretation in recent studies of the Thessalonian correspondence.[14] A major impediment to presuming a connection between Paul's allusion to the phrase and propaganda about Roman rule is the lack of a comprehensive impetus or warrant for the apostle's critique.[15] Why should Paul seize this particular opportunity to lash out against promoters of Roman "peace and security"?

[13] Ernst Bammel proposed this in "Ein Beitrag zur paulinischen Staatsanschauung," *TLZ* 85 (1960) 837–40, esp. 837: "*Pax et securitas* . . . ist das Programm der frühprinzipalen Zeit, in der Form, wie es ausserhalb von Rom seit den Tagen des Pompeius . . . verkündet wurde. Dabei ist zu berücksichtigen, dass *securitas* das Korrelat zu *aeternitas* ist, dass beide einem religiösen Anspruch, den der politischen Heilsverwirklichung beihalten." Holtz dismisses the suggestion without discussion (*Erste Thessalonicher,* 215). See Koester, "Eschatology," 32 n. 48.

Norman DeWitt assumes that the phrase "peace and security" reflects an Epicurean outlook that is condemned by Paul (*Epicurus and His Philosophy* [Minneapolis: University of Minnesota Press, 1954] 85, 189, 338). Abraham Malherbe has drawn attention to this connection without explicitly endorsing it: "With people in mind who, like the Epicureans, sought security in this life (5:3), he urges his readers to live in the light of the Day (5:1–10) . . ." (*Paul and the Thessalonians* [Philadelphia: Fortress Press, 1987] 81). Neither DeWitt nor Malherbe has provided a thoroughgoing justification of this identification, but the suggestion clearly calls for further research.

[14] Emphasizing the political provenance of "security," Koester attributes the phrase to imperial Roman propaganda. He concludes that Paul's condemnation "is entirely in keeping with older Jewish and later Christian apocalyptic protest against imperial establishments" ("Eschatology," 11). Donfried considers 5:3 a "frontal attack on the *Pax et Securitas* programme of the early Principate" ("The Cults of Thessalonica and the Thessalonian Correspondence," *NTS* 31 [1984–85] 336–56, 344, 355 n. 55); he cites W. H. C. Frend, *Martyrdom and Persecution in the Early Church* (Oxford: Blackwell, 1965) 96, 124 n. 69.

[15] Donfried calls attention to an "emphasis on royal theology in Thessalonica at the time of Paul's visit . . ." ("Cults," 347). Jewett has gone even further in associating the "enthusiasm" with which Thessalonians "entered into honorific cult of Rome" with political messianism (*Thessalonian Correspondence,* 126). Both authors assume that a particularly "high" royal theology involving the emperor had developed at Thessalonica. This presumption is not warranted by the evidence. Relative to other quarters of the Roman Empire, Macedonia manifests a rather low imperial theology and a comparatively restrained religious response to Roman benefactors, magistrates, and emperors. On this, see further my "Beyond 'Imperial Cult' and 'Cults of Magistrates,'" in *Society of Biblical Literature 1986 Seminar Papers,* ed. K. H. Richards (Atlanta: Scholars Press, 1986) 301–8. However, what the Thessalonians may have lacked in theologically qualitative regard for the emperor, they more than compensated for in quantitative attention to the imperial establishment.

The "Roman Peace" was promoted emphatically in Augustan and Julio-Claudian propaganda. It was a characteristic feature of imperial media—be they coins, monuments, or official proclamations.[16] Even before Augustus, Greeks had acclaimed the "peace and security" provided by Romans.

> Decree of the people of Pergamum. "In the presidency of Cratippus, on the first of the month Daisios, a decree of the magistrates. As the Romans in pursuance of the practices of their ancestors have accepted dangerous risks for the common safety (ἀσφάλεια) of all humankind and strive emulously to place their allies and friends in a state of happiness and lasting peace (εἰρήνη), the Jewish nation and their high priest Hyrcanus have sent as envoys to them. . . . (Josephus *Antiquities of the Jews* 14.10.22 §§247–48)[17]

In Augustan, Julio-Claudian, and Flavian propaganda "security" (*securitas/* ἀσφάλεια) figured prominently.[18] Perhaps the most cogent example of how

[16] For coin issues projecting *Pax* under Octavian/Augustus, see, e.g., *BMCRE* 605, 612, and esp. 691; "universal peace" was celebrated on issues of Nero (e.g., *BMCRE* 321); "pax Augusti" as a characteristic feature of numismatic propaganda soon after Nero's reign (Galba, *BMCRE* 261; Vespasian, *BMCRE* 558). C. H. V. Sutherland discusses the issues in *Roman Coins* (New York: Putnam, 1974) 119, 125, 168, 180. Among the more dramatic examples of Augustan monuments to peace is the altar of *pax Augusta* dedicated in Rome in 9 BCE. Of particular import to our study is Claudius's mention in his letter to the Alexandrians of two gold statues, one representing the "Claudian Augustan Peace" to be erected in Rome, and the other to be carried in processions by the Alexandrians (British Museum Papyrus no. 1912; Eng. trans. in K. Chisholm and J. Ferguson, *Rome, The Augustan Age* [New York: Oxford University Press, 1981] 539–41). Perhaps the best known and most widely distributed proclamation of Augustus as promoter of peace (and security) is the *Res Gestae Divi Augusti.* For Augustus as superior champion of Roman peace, see tablet 2, lines 42–45 of the *Monumentum Ancyranum* (= *MA*); as restorer and extender of peace, *MA* tablet 5, lines 9–23; as promoter of public security and safety of the republic, *MA* tablet 1, lines 6–9. For the altar of *pax Augusta,* see *MA* tablet 2, lines 37–41. F. Danker provides an English translation and commentary in *Benefactor* (St. Louis: Clayton, 1982) 256–80. On the "universal" extent of the *pax Augusta,* see Velleius Paterculus 2.126.3.

[17] Trans. Ralph Marcus (LCL; Cambridge, Mass.: Harvard University Press, 1933) 7.581. On the phenomenon of Romans "as common benefactors of all," see L. Robert, "Théophane de Mytilène a Constantinople," *CRAI* (1969) 42–64. The evidence for this phenomenon is widespread (Athens, Chalcis, Isthmia, Mylasa, Magnesia on the Meander, Cyrene, Lesbos, Antioch on the Meander, and elsewhere). Robert traces the formula of common beneficence of Romans to the establishment of the *Nikephoria* at Pergamum in 182 BCE. Robert does not treat, however, the traditional Greek attribution of "common" peace (εἰρήνη) and security (ἀσφάλεια) to "Hermes Koinos" (see, e.g., Diodorus Siculus 5.75.1–2).

[18] On the *securitas Augusti,* see *BMCI* 1, 241 no. 212, and for the *securitas* of the Roman people, *BMCI* 1, 361 no. 266, and 3, 313 no. 570. For ἀσφαλής as characteristic of Augustus's treatment of foreign peoples, consult the *Res Gestae Divi Augusti* (*MA* tablet 1, line 15). There is a suggestive coordination of εἰρήνη and ἀσφάλεια in Dio's description of Gaius's assumption of legionary command in 1 BCE (55.17). Seneca epitomizes the universal *securitas* of the Roman peace in *Epistulae* 91.2. On coinage of Gaius ("Caligula"), the emperor's sister, Agrippina, was represented as *Securitas* (C. H. V. Sutherland, *Roman History and Coinage 44 BC — 69 AD* [Oxford: Clarendon, 1987] 73). For *Securitas* in the coinage of Vitelleius, see Sutherland,

peace and a secure order could be related to imperial beneficence is in the Asian League's widely publicized announcement of celebrations for Augustus's birthday.

> Whereas Providence that orders all our lives has in her display of concern and generosity in our behalf adorned our lives with the highest good: Augustus, whom she has filled with ἀρετή for the benefit of humanity, and has in her beneficence granted us and those who will come after us [a Savior] who has made war to cease and who shall put everything [in peaceful] order. . . .[19]

If Paul's citation of "peace and security" is a direct allusion to Roman propaganda or to Greek propagandistic responses to Roman beneficence, why does the issue arise in an epistle to the Thessalonians?[20] Put more pointedly, is it fortuitous that *only* in 1 Thessalonians does Paul engage in an apocalyptic critique of a stock element of propaganda about Romans? From this we might frame an inquiry directed to Thessalonica's archaeological record. Is there any evidence to suggest a distinctive sensitivity to propaganda about Roman rule in the Julio-Claudian period on the part of Thessalonians?

From the Thessalonian epigraphic record, a significant political and civic religious shift is apparent in the evidence from the first centuries BCE and CE. In this period, the city's assembly began to issue many of its decrees no longer on its own but in association with an official Roman group (συμπραγματευόμενοι ῥωμαῖοι).[21] "Roma and Roman Benefactors" were added to the cultic patrons of the gymnasium, the city cult of "the gods."[22] In the pecking order of civic religious institutions, the priesthood of "the gods" descended gradually until it disappeared entirely in the second century CE.[23] Ascending in the pecking order was a new civic religious office established

---

Roman History and Coinage, 119–20. Vitelleius's commitment to *securitas* is reflected in Tacitus's account of his campaigns (*Histories* 3.53; note the coordination with *pax*).

[19] The decree is dated conventionally to 9 CE, but the precise date is unknown. For presentation and thorough discussion of the texts, important fragments of which have been recovered at Priene, Apameia, Dorylaion, and Eumeneia, see Umberto Laffi, "Le iscrizione relative all' introduzione nel 9 a.C. del nuovo calendario della Provincia d'Asia," *Studi Classici e Orientali* 16 (1967) 5–98. The English translation followed here is from Danker, *Benefactor,* 215–22.

[20] Donfried's assertion that Paul is attacking the "*Pax et Securitas* programme of the early Principate" may be overstated. The peculiar correlation of εἰρήνη and ἀσφάλεια as applied to Romans originally may have been a Greek convention as the Pergamene declaration cited above suggests. Although the correlation may have been commonplace in Greek responses to Roman beneficence, it may not have been internalized systematically in imperial propaganda. The complex relationship of the two sets of terms warrants a separate study.

[21] *Inscriptiones graecae Epiri, Macedoniae, Thraciae, Scythiae, Pars II Inscriptiones Macedoniae, Fasciculus I Inscriptiones Thessalonicae et viciniae,* ed. C. Edson (Berlin: de Gruyter, 1972) (= *IT*) nos. 32 and 33.

[22] Ibid., no. 4 (95 BCE).

[23] Ibid., nos. 4, 31, 32, 132, 133, 226.

at the city in the last quarter of the first century BCE, a "priest and agonothete of the Imperator Caesar Augustus son of god."[24] The office quickly assumed premier status in the hierarchy of civic offices at Thessalonica and superseded ultimately the priesthood of "the gods," which formerly had been at the apex of civic religious offices.[25]

There is also evidence from the epigraphic record of a temple (ναός) of Caesar dating probably to the same period as the institution of the priest and agonothete of the emperor.[26] I should emphasize that no remains of the ναός have been recovered at the city.[27] We have only a rather poorly executed inscription attesting its existence. Although the epigraphic record does not provide clear evidence of a *distinctive* sensitivity to propaganda about Romans (except perhaps in the case of the acknowledgment of Augustus as "son of god"), the record does establish that Thessalonica's interests increasingly were influenced by Romans and by regard for the Roman emperor.

In surveying the numismatic evidence, one encounters a significant number of issues of a coin type that was novel in Thessalonica's minting history. It features the laureate head of Julius on the obverse with the legend θεός and a bare-headed Octavian on the reverse with the legend "of the Thessalonicans."[28] Some of the issues in the series bear the additional inscription *Sebastos,* suggesting that part of the series was issued prior to Octavian's assumption of the title *Augustus* in 27 BCE and part issued after that event.[29] It is clear from the issue that the Thessalonians corporately were acclaiming both the divine status of Julius and Octavian's official association with Julius. What is of interest to our inquiry is the particular way in which the Thessalonians expressed themselves.

The issues are a rather unoriginal imitation of an *as* issued by Octavian in

[24] Ibid., nos. 31, 32, 132, 133. For 133, I follow L. Robert's identification of Rhoimetalces as Prince (later King) Gaius Julius Rhoimetalces, son of the Thracian king Rhescuporis, which demands an early first century date for the inscription (after 18–19 CE) ("Les Inscriptions de Thessalonique," *Revue de Philologie* [1974] 180–246, 212–15). At *IT* 133, Edson dates the work at least a century later.

[25] The last known inscription from Thessalonica that records a priest of "the gods" is *IT* 226, dated by Edson without absolute certainty to the second century CE. Civic inscriptions from the later second and third centuries do not attest the priesthood.

[26] *IT* no. 31; Edson dates the inscription to between 27 BCE and 14 CE.

[27] Jewett speaks of "impressive archaeological remains of the large temple of Roma" at Thessalonica (*Thessalonian Correspondence,* 126). Perhaps he has mistaken the extensive remains of the much later palace of Galerius for an imperial cult temple. The only evidence for a temple is *IT* no. 31, which mentions a ναός of Caesar (and not of Roma).

[28] B. V. Head, *A Catalogue of the Greek Coins in the British Museum,* Volume 5, *Macedonia, etc.* (London: Longman's, 1879) (= *BMC*) 115 nos. 58–59, 61; H. Gaebler, *Die antiken Münzen von Makedonia und Paionia: Die antiken Münzen Nord-Griechenlands,* Band III, erste Abteilung, ed. F. Imhoof-Blumer (Berlin: G. Reimer, 1906) (= *AMMP*) II, 125 no. 43.

[29] Head, *BMC,* 115 no. 61.

38 BCE in honor of Julius's deification.[30] It is a direct imitation of Augustan propaganda, and in the context of Greek coinage during the period, it is unusual in being so mechanical an imitation.[31] The only substantial differences between the Octavian issue and the Thessalonian are (1) the date of the issues (38 BCE for Octavian and just prior to and after 27 BCE for the Thessalonians); (2) the Octavian issue bears Octavian on the obverse and Julius on the reverse, whereas the Thessalonian has Julius obverse, Octavian reverse; (3) the Octavian obverse bears the legend *divi filius* and the reverse has *divus,* whereas the Thessalonian obverse legend does not translate *divi filius* (a noteworthy omission) but simply bears the citizens' appellation.[32] These differences may not be insignificant in ascertaining the nature of Thessalonian religious regard for Augustus and his successors.[33] For our immediate purposes, however, what is significant is the unusual extent of imitation of a medium of Augustan propaganda in the Thessalonian issue.

An investigation of architectural, sculptural, and other artifactual evidence from the city yields one other phenomenon that may be of import to our inquiry. Fragments of a statue of Augustus were found north/northeast of the Serapeion in Thessalonica.[34] The head of the statue discovered in Thessalonica seems to be related intimately to that of the famous representation of Augustus found at Prima Porta.[35] However, the Thessalonian statue's date seems to be somewhat later than the Prima Porta exemplar. Extant portrayals of the emperor in the particular "hip-cloaked" subgenre found at Thessalonica are largely western, executed primarily in the mid-to-late

[30] E. A. Sydenham, *Coinage of the Roman Republic,* rev. G. C. Haines; ed. L. Forrer and C. A. Hersh (London: Spink & Son, 1952) 208 no. 1335. The issue also is reproduced in S. Weinstock, *Divus Julius* (Oxford: Clarendon, 1971) pl. 30 no. 3.

[31] Compare the evidence collected by Weinstock, *Divus Julius,* esp. pl. 30.

[32] On the date of the Thessalonian issues, see C. Edson, "Macedonia, II. State Cults in Thessalonica," *Harvard Studies in Classical Philology* 51 (1940) 127–36, 132. Weinstock's description of the Thessalonian issue (*Divus Julius,* pl. 30 nos. 1 and 2) is incorrect: the obverse is Julius *Theos,* not Octavian, who is portrayed on the reverse.

[33] On this, see Hendrix, "Beyond 'Imperial Cult,'" 307–8.

[34] N. Kotsias reported the discovery to O. Walter, who published the fragments in "Archäologische Funde in Griechenland vom Frühjahr 1939 bis Frühjahr 1940," *Archäologischer Anzeiger* (1940) 265–66, 261–62 Abb. 71–73. The restored statue is now on display in Thessalonica's Archaeological Museum (no. 1065). For analysis of fragments of a Thessalonican statue identified as divine Claudius, see G. Bakalakas, "Vorlage und Interpretation von römischen Kunstdenkmälern in Thessaloniki," *Archäologischer Anzeiger* 88 (1973) 671–84, esp. 677–78. If the identification is correct, the statue provides further evidence of Thessalonica's attention to early Roman imperial religious propaganda.

[35] See, e.g., H. G. Niemeyer, *Studien zur statuarischen Darstellung der römischen Kaiser* (Monumenta artis Romanae 7; Berlin: Mann, 1968) 102–3. For a discussion of the controversial issues involved in the utility of "Prima Porta" typology and citation of the extensive literature on the subject, see U. Hausmann, "Zur Typologie und Ideologie des Augustusporträts," *ANRW* 12.2, 513–98.

Tiberian period and during the reign of Claudius.[36] A number of analysts have concluded that the schematic idealization of the type recovered at Thessalonica is indicative of portrayals of Augustus executed during Claudius's reign.[37] If this dating is accurate, then the statue is only one of a very few archaeological phenomena dating to the immediate period of Paul's missionary activity.

It is assumed generally that the Augustus statue recovered at Thessalonica was a native production.[38] This is quite uncertain. Adaptation of the Greek "hip-cloaked" portrayal to imperial portraiture appears to have been accomplished in the west. The statue at Thessalonica is the earliest known instance of such a depiction in the east.[39] Although the model may have been introduced to the city by any number of means, it is also possible that the statue itself was imported. The composition's extensive disassembly might support such a conclusion. If the statue came from a workshop in Thessalonica, one must wonder why at least five cuts would have been essential for movement over a presumably short distance.[40] It may be more reasonable to assume that the work was produced elsewhere by artists familiar with Roman models and disassembled for extended transport, as was known to have been the case for portraiture in the Claudian period.[41]

Whether the work is a local product or not, what is clear is that the most complete and imposing statue of an imperial figure recovered at Thessalonica represents a Claudian adaptation of an Augustan prototype. Moreover, such an imitation was unusual in the east.[42] As in their numismatic expression of attention to the imperial establishment, so also in their statuary the Thessalonians chose to imitate, if not import, imperial media.

Returning to the question derived from the exegetical query, we may now answer in the affirmative that there is significant archaeological evidence of a distinctive sensitivity to propaganda about Roman rule on the part of Thessalonians. This enhances on circumstantial grounds established through archaeological evidence the plausibility of the following conclusion: Paul's

[36] See Niemeyer, *Studien,* 101–3 and Tafel 24.1–4. For discussion of the rendering of the head, consult Hausmann, "Augustusporträts," 579 and Abb. 36, 47–48, 52, 57, and 61.

[37] Niemeyer, *Studien,* 103; Hausmann, "Augustusporträts," 587 and other sources cited there.

[38] In the discussions of which I am aware, only Walter's analysis might imply a non-Thessalonian origin.

[39] Niemeyer, *Studien,* 103.

[40] Following the report of Kotsias, Walter observed, "Die Statue war offenbar zwecks leichteren Transportes langs des Mantelkonturs und der Hufte gestuckt, desgleichen der Kopf und der rechte Arm, sowie der linke Unterarm angesetzt" ("Funde," 266). Examination of the statue reveals an additional cut in the left forearm beneath the gathering of the cloak.

[41] M. Stuart, "How Were Imperial Portraits Distributed Throughout the Roman Empire?" *AJA* 43 (1939) 601–21.

[42] Niemeyer, *Studien,* 103.

exceptional citation of a slogan associated with Roman beneficence in his apocalyptic message to the Thessalonians might have been made in specific reference to the Thessalonian environment and to the experience of the city's inhabitants.

The implications of this reading of the passage are more or less far-reaching depending on how one interprets other aspects of the letter (e.g., the nature of the "affliction" and/or "pressure" [θλίψις] to which Paul declares the Thessalonians subject).[43] The most we can conclude from this study is that if the citation of "peace and security" was intended to resonate with a feature of the Thessalonian political environment, those at the city broadcasting such propaganda were aligned by Paul on the side of gloom, sleep, drunkenness, and wrath. Indeed, Paul would have been proposing that they should be the first to fall victim to the sudden wrath of God, perhaps in comforting counterposition to the precedence afforded those who had "fallen asleep."

I leave to another occasion the further analysis of Paul's apocalyptic message in 1 Thessalonians and its implications for appreciating the apostle's attitudes toward Roman imperial ideology. Here I hope to have fulfilled a more straightforward objective: the bearing archaeological materials may have on hearing more clearly Paul's eschatological message. Without a thorough knowledge of the material evidence for circumstances addressed by Paul, we would miss what might be a critical and provocative dimension of his indictment of the times.

[43] Donfried, for example, supports an interpretation that links the deaths of Thessalonian Christians (4:13–18) with the "pressure" to which Paul observes they are subject (1:6; 2:14; 3:3–4) ("Cults," 342–47); this follows F. F. Bruce, *The Acts of the Apostles* (Grand Rapids: Eerdmans, 1951) 327; compare J. E. Frame, *The Epistles of St. Paul to the Thessalonians* (ICC; Edinburgh: T. & T. Clark, 1912) 82–83. If such "pressure" had been the result of political opposition involving Roman or Roman-related interests, Paul's apocalyptic critique of Roman "peace and security" might seem more comprehensible. Malherbe criticizes such a construal of θλίψις (*Paul,* 46–48 and 65–66).

PART 3

Ancient Judaism

8

Moses Servant of God and the Servants: Text and Tradition in the Prayer of Nehemiah (Neh 1:5–11)

KLAUS BALTZER

THE PRAYER OF NEHEMIAH in Nehemiah 1 has not received a particularly warm reception among exegetes.[1] Its authenticity has been the main issue in the discussion. Depending on whether it is regarded as "genuine," that is, authored by Nehemiah, different literary-critical procedures follow. It has already been well established that verses in the prayer are reminiscent of Deuteronomy, even to the extent of "loose quotation."[2] The

[1] To my friend Helmut Koester, in recollection of our first collaborative publication: "Die Bezeichnung des Jakobus als 'ΩΒΛΙΑΣ," *ZNW* 46 (1955) 141–42. I wish to thank Christopher R. Seitz for providing this English translation.

For the text of the prayer, see the commentaries, esp. Loring W. Batten, *The Books of Ezra and Nehemiah* (ICC; Edinburgh: T. & T. Clark, 1913; reprint, 1961); Wilhelm Rudolph, *Esra und Nehemia* (HAT 20; Tübingen: J. C. B. Mohr, 1949); Kurt Galling, *Die Bücher der Chronik, Ezra, Nehemia* (ATD 12; Göttingen: Vandenhoeck & Ruprecht, 1954); J. de Fraine, *Esdras en Nehemias* (De Boeken van het Oude Testament 5; Roermond: J. J. Romen, 1961); Jacob Myers, *Nehemiah* (AB; Garden City, N.Y.: Doubleday, 1965); U. Kellermann, *Nehemia: Quellen, Geschichte und Überlieferung* (BZAW 102; Berlin: Töpelmann, 1967); F. Charles Fensham, *The Books of Ezra and Nehemiah* (Grand Rapids: Eerdmans, 1982); Antonius H. J. Gunneweg, *Nehemia* (KAT 19.2; Gütersloh: Mohn, 1987).

For an example of the opinion of exegetes, see Batten, *Ezra and Nehemiah,* 188: "But it is difficult to believe that we have in vv. 5–10 the words he [Nehemiah] used. There are favourite words of the Chr[onicler] like מעל, v. 8, and the whole prayer is made up of passages and phrases from Dt. It is true that in Christian praying there is an unhappy tendency to use stock and hackneyed expressions, and so the resemblance of this prayer to others in the OT may not justify suspicion. But Neh. was a common man, and would be unlikely to use such phrases."

[2] Rudolph, *Nehemiah,* 105: "freiem Zitat."

language is classified as "deuteronomistic."[3] Others assume a "chronistische Redaktion"[4] or believe that the passage represents the "stereotypical language of prayer."[5]

But what prevents prayers from being quite precise in their choice of words? We shall attempt to establish in what follows that the reference to existing texts is not necessarily coincidental and that the text of the prayer is more closely related to the larger context of the book of Nehemiah than is generally acknowledged. On the basis of our findings, conclusions will be drawn concerning the position of Nehemiah himself as he is portrayed in the text.

The Text of the Prayer

The prayer stands at the beginning of the book of Nehemiah. With respect to genre the book should be classified as "biography," in the sense of an "Ideal-Biography" from antiquity.[6] The superscription ("The words of Nehemiah the son of Hacaliah" [1:1]) conforms to the genre. In comparing the various *Gattungen,* the original Ideal-Biography in Egypt was a tomb inscription. In such a manner, the dead would "speak" to the living, to posterity. Following the superscription, there is a description of the dire circumstances leading up to Nehemiah's prayer (cf. Judges 6). The prayer itself takes up the position occupied by the inauguration account in the Ideal-Biography, including as it does Nehemiah's account of his life and conduct before God and humanity. The sort of graphic detail that is usually found in an inauguration account is lacking here. Nehemiah is not a prophet. Nevertheless, even in a foreign country there can be a direct encounter with God.[7] Nehemiah experiences God's sovereignty in the course of his daily business transactions: "the good hand of my God was upon me" (2:8). In this context the appeal to God is tied up with his commissioning by the Persian king (2:1–10).

At the beginning of the prayer the divine name is invoked, "O Yahweh . . ." (אנא יהוה). There could not be a more prominent location for the divine

[3] Gunneweg, *Nehemiah,* 47–48.

[4] Galling, *Nehemia,* 218–19; M. Noth, *Überlieferungsgeschichtliche Studien* (1943; reprint, Darmstadt: Wissenschaftliche Buchgesellschaft, 1957) 148. Noth's formulation is peculiar, because of his starting point: "Auf ihn (den Chronisten) wird man zurückführen müssen das im Stile von Dtr formulierte Gebet Nehemias in 1,5–11a" (p. 127).

[5] Gunneweg, *Nehemia,* 48: "stereotyper Gebetssprache."

[6] See Gerhard von Rad, "Die Nehemia-Denkschrift," *ZAW* 76 (1964) 176–87: "der antiken Ideal-Biographie"; Sigmund Mowinckel, *Studien zu dem Buche Ezra-Nehemia* (Oslo: Universitäts-forlaget, 1964) esp. 122–24; Klaus Baltzer, *Die Biographie der Propheten* (Neukirchen-Vluyn: Neukirchener Verlag, 1975) esp. 180ff.

[7] For this theme, compare Ezek 1:1ff.; Daniel 7; 8:2; Acts 9.

name—and this is the only time it is specifically mentioned in the entire book.[8] With the title "God of heaven" (אלהי השמים), one could make oneself understood with the Persian authorities (cf. Ezra 5:11; 6:9, 10; 7:12), but the divine name Yahweh is used only in relation to Israel (cf. v. 6). Perhaps one should say here that it is the divine name that was revealed to Moses, the servant of Yahweh, when he was commissioned at the burning bush (Exod 3:13–15). Last but not least, when at this juncture Nehemiah utters the divine name, his "orthodoxy" as an Israelite is also made clear.

At the end of the prayer the interjection "O" is repeated again (v. 11), in connection with "O *Lord* . . ." (אנא אדני). On the basis of the correlation of "Lord" with "servant" a special sociomorpheme is used in this text. This is made clear by the fact that the term "servant" (עֶבֶד) is used eight times in a relatively brief context.

As one considers other expressions that appear in the prayer, one gets the impression that traditional religious language has been used. It is striking, however, that the commentaries, in putting forward passages for comparison, repeatedly point to Deuteronomy. In my view, the connection with Deuteronomy must be taken even more seriously if one is to understand the text as it stands. Deuteronomy consists of "these words, which Moses spoke to all Israel beyond the Jordan" (Deut 1:1). The present text gives a clear signal: Nehemiah is speaking the language of Deuteronomy. He speaks with the words of Moses from Deuteronomy—not from, say, Leviticus or Numbers.

Relation to Deuteronomy

From this general observation one can proceed further to ask whether specific texts from Deuteronomy have not played a role in the formulation of the text of Nehemiah as we have it. Such a hypothesis requires a measure of caution; still, I would like to point out several peculiarities. In making comparisons it is critical (1) that something more substantial than isolated words appear; (2) that a combination of verses from a single context forms the basis for discussion, if at all possible, when it appears that a text from Deuteronomy has been utilized; and (3) that the appropriate context be respected when pointing out the relationship to the present text and to the rest of the book of Nehemiah and its larger thematic perspective.

A prior classifying of the texts for discussion often occurs in the commentaries, which after all represent a substantial history of exegesis. So Rudolph writes of Nehemiah's prayer: "Nehemiah, like Ezra (Ezra 9:6ff.), moves in the same circles as Deuteronomy with respect to its turns of expression

[8] According to 5:13 a "Halleluia" (ויהללו את יהוה) is struck up as the people give assent to their liberation from slavery.

(5 = Deut 7:9.21 [Dan 9:4]; 10 = Deut 9:29; 8f. is a loose quote from Deut 30:1–4). . . ."[9]

Deuteronomy 7:21 and 9

Neh 1:5 gives evidence of composition on the basis of Deut 7:21 and 9. In the context in which Deut 7:21 speaks of "a great and terrible God," what is announced is that Israel is not to stand in dread of the other nations (v. 21). The larger unit begins thus: "If you say in your heart: These nations far outnumber me . . . you shall not fear them" (7:17–18). What is emphasized is that Yahweh will act as he did during the exodus from Egypt, only now "little by little" (מעט מעט [v. 22]).

In the book of Nehemiah the theme of "dread before the nations" appears in concrete form in connection with the building of the walls (3:33–4:17).

> Now when Sanballat and Tobiah and the Arabs and the Ammonites and the Ashdodites heard that the repairing of the walls was going forward . . . they were very angry. . . . (4:1 Heb.)
>
> But Judah said: "Strength is failing . . . we are not able to work on the wall." (4:4 Heb.)

In this situation Nehemiah preaches:

> "Do not be afraid of them. Remember the Lord (אֲדֹנָי) who is great and terrible!" (4:8 Heb.)

This is the same divine titulature as in Neh 1:5 and Deut 7:21.

The second correspondence between the wording of Deuteronomy 7 and the same verse of Nehemiah's prayer occurs in Deut 7:9. There we read: "who keeps covenant and steadfast love with those who love him and keep his commandments." In the same immediate context "redemption from the house of bondage" is referred to (v. 8; cf. Deut 9:26; 13:6; 21:8). With the same verb פדה ("redeem, ransom, release"), the fundamental saving act of Yahweh is affirmed in v. 10 of Nehemiah's prayer. "Redemption" is a concrete problem for the book of Nehemiah.[10] According to the penitential prayer in Neh 9:36, the Israelites are "servants, slaves" (עבדים) under foreign domination. With only minor modification, the beginning of the unit at v. 32 ("and now . . .") takes up the formulation of Deut 7:21 and 9, and with it Neh 1:5 as well.[11] By recalling the exodus, the appeal to God is applied to the present predicament—this is the common thread.

[9] Rudolph, *Nehemia,* 105.

[10] See Klaus Baltzer, "Liberation from Debt Slavery after the Exile in Second Isaiah and Nehemiah," in *Ancient Israelite Religion: Essays in Honor of Frank Moore Cross,* ed. P. D. Miller, Jr., et al. (Philadelphia: Fortress Press, 1987) 477–84.

[11] In the penitential prayer of Daniel in Dan 9:4, Deut 7:9 and 21 are likewise combined, and in the same sequence (v. 21 and v. 9) as in Neh 1:5. The question therefore arises whether Daniel 9 already presupposes the Nehemiah text.

The theme of the larger context of Deuteronomy 7, however, is the election of Israel as the people of Yahweh and their relationship to the peoples of the land (7:1–8). It reads like a program for Nehemiah's measures to live up to, in terms of their rigorous standards. Politically speaking, Nehemiah has to do with Judah's constitution as a distinct *ethnos* within the Persian empire. The reference to Deuteronomy 7 also indicates that this is a theological program.

Deuteronomy 30

A second text in Deuteronomy that gives evidence of more than general literary proximity to Nehemiah 1 is Deuteronomy 30. Neh 1:9 ("If you return to me . . . though your dispersed be under the farthest skies, I will gather them thence and bring them . . .") corresponds almost word for word to Deut 30:4. In this instance too, the context must be taken into consideration. Deuteronomy 30 is the closing speech of Moses before he installs his successor (chap. 31). "Life and death, blessing and curse" are set before Moses (vv. 15, 19), but, most important, the first section (Deut 30:1–10) speaks of the promise that follows upon repentance. It is a good omen from the mouth of Moses (cf. v. 9) that Nehemiah makes his own.

It is the modifications that become all the more conspicuous as further comparisons are made. Deut 30:5 continues: "and Yahweh your God will bring you into the *land* (הארץ) which your fathers possessed. . . ." In place of this Neh 1:9 reads: "and I will bring them to the *place* (המקום) which I have chosen, to make my name dwell there." The question of possession is thereby bracketed out. With the chosen "place" another *topos* from Deuteronomy is recognized (Deut 12:5; 14:23, 25). This terminology has become critical for Jerusalem's legitimation. It remains an open question whether the chosen place refers to the temple complex itself or the entire city.[12] The precise way in which the temple and the city are to be related is a major problem of the postexilic period. Nehemiah's task, an account of which is supplied in the following section, concerns Jerusalem's new constitution as a city. As such, this is further evidence that Nehemiah's prayer is closely related to its larger context.

1 Kings 8: Prayer for the Dedication of the Temple

The mention of "the place which I have chosen to make my name dwell" (v. 9) quite possibly points to another key text: the prayer of Solomon for the

[12] See Helmut Koester, "τοπος," *TDNT* 8:187–208, esp. 195–99; J. Gamberoni, "מָקוֹם, *māqom*," *TWAT* 4:1113–24.

dedication of the temple. For several reasons it is likely that the Deuteronomic presentation of 1 Kings 8 is presupposed here, and not that of the Chronicler (2 Chronicles 6).[13] Significantly, according to Neh 1:8 the message is mediated through "[God's] servant Moses."

This corresponds to 1 Kgs 8:53. At a similar juncture, 2 Chron 6:42 speaks of "thy steadfast love for thy servant David." Nehemiah does that which was made possible by the prayer of consecration itself: he prays in "the land of their enemies, who carried them captive" (1 Kgs 8:48). He is in a "land far off" (v. 46) in Susa (Neh 1:1). Nehemiah confesses the sins of the people (cf. 1 Kgs 8:47f.). He lays claim to the promise for which, according to the text, Solomon had prayed, that is, that God would hear just such a prayer as Nehemiah's. The connection to the people's prayer of repentance in Nehemiah 9 is clear, even when they are now in "a near land" (1 Kgs 8:46).

There are further indications of a connection with 1 Kings 8. To the divine titulature at the beginning of the prayer before the altar in the presence of all the assembly of Israel (vv. 22–53) belongs "who keeps covenant and steadfast love" (v. 23). This corresponds to the same formula at the beginning of the prayer of Nehemiah in v. 5. Then Nehemiah prays (v. 6): "let thy ear be attentive, and thy eyes open, to hear. . . ." Difficulties are created in v. 6 in the relationship between "ear," "eye," and "hear." Furthermore, it is not clear how "now, today" is to work with "day and night."[14]

Placed next to the text of 1 Kgs 8:28–29, however, this becomes clear: the open eyes function there in relationship to "this house" with some further expansion, and only then follows "that thou mayest hearken to the prayer." "Now, today" belongs to the prayer, "night and day" (in this order) to the open eyes. In this instance the literary dependence of Nehemiah 1 on 1 Kgs 8:28, 29 is patent; more precisely, one should speak here of conscious alteration, especially in the deletion of any reference to "this house"—that is, the temple! The key phrase in 1 Kgs 8:29 is picked up again in the same chapter in v. 52. The two verses comprise a sort of frame around this section of Solomon's prayer.[15] It is curious that v. 52 stands closer to the formulation of Neh 1:6. There is no filling out of the phrase "and let thy eyes be open . . . to hear" with reference to "ear" as in Neh 1:6.

The two preceding verses in 1 Kgs 8:50b–51 are lacking in the Chronicler's exposition. This unit might help explain a problem at the end of Nehemiah's prayer. The final sentence reads: "and grant him [thy servant]

[13] See Gamberoni, "*māqom*," 1122.

[14] See Rudolph, *Nehemia*, 105ff.: "Kleinlich ist der Einwand v. 4 rede von tagelangem Weinen und Beten, v. 11a dagegen spreche nur von 'heute' . . . dass man aber 'heute' nicht pressen darf, zeigt 'heute Tag and Nacht' v. 6. . . ." See also Mowinckel, *Studien*, 17: "Dass hayyom hier »wie so oft 'jetzt, nunmehr' bedeute« (Rudolph) ist eine kümmerliche Ausflucht. . . ."

[15] See Ernst Würthwein, *Das erste Buch der Könige* (ATD 11.1; Göttingen: Vandenhoeck & Ruprecht, 1977) 95.

mercy in the sight of this man" (v. 11). 1 Kgs 8:50b has "and grant them mercy in the sight of those who carried them captive, that they may have compassion on them." Nehemiah can hardly say of his master, the Persian king Artaxerxes, that he is one who carries away and holds captive, so he simply says "this man." But anyone sensitive to the connection with 1 Kgs 8:46–50 and aware of the familiar wordplay שבה ("deport") and שוב ("repent, turn around") knows what is being said. It requires a miracle to turn the situation around (compare chap. 2). To such a situation the prayer of petition in Neh 9:32–37 speaks in no uncertain terms.[16] But does Nehemiah feel particularly at ease in his role under "this man" האיש הזה)?[17]

In view of all the similarities between 1 Kings 8 and Nehemiah 1, the differences should also be elaborated, involving the use of the terms "servant" and "servants."[18] Solomon speaks repeatedly in his prayer of "thy servant my father David" (vv. 24, 25, 26). He characterizes himself in relation to God as "thy servant" (v. 28). He makes reference to the dynasty as a legitimizing institution in v. 25.

To be sure, Nehemiah can no longer pray in this way. But it is worth considering whether he does not refer to the Davidic dynasty in his prayer after all. He includes himself in the confession of sin in behalf of the people of Israel (v. 6) and then explicitly adds, "Yea, I and my father's house have sinned." That makes sense if Nehemiah is capable of inclusion within the Davidic dynastic line. In favor of such a possibility is the existence of a family burial vault within the walls of Jerusalem (2:3–5)."[19] A plan enabling Nehemiah to become king (6:7) would fit within this same context. Yet this is expressly refused by Nehemiah; his theological and civil-administrative charge has a grounding other than that of the Davidic dynasty. A confession of sin on the part of the dynasty must have been an annoyance to monarchists in view of the messianic expectation associated with the Davidic covenant. In the Prayer of Nehemiah this points to an acknowledgment of the law of

[16] It is possible that the text of Nehemiah 9 makes a connection between action and consequence: "they cast the law behind their back" (אחרי גום [v. 26]); therefore, "they have power over our bodies" (על גויתינו [v. 37]).

[17] "This man" sounds rather sharp if one assumes that Nehemiah, as a high Persian official, was made a eunuch. Already the Septuagint has in v. 11 εὐνοῦχος for οἰνοχόος (see the commentaries and, more recently, Edwin M. Yamauchi, "Was Nehemiah the Cupbearer a Eunuch?" *ZAW* 92 [1980] 132–42; compare also Isa 53:3–5 over against Deut 23:1. The "power over our bodies . . . at their pleasure (ועל גויתינו משלים . . . כרצונם)" would be intelligible with respect to Nehemiah's own person.

[18] See Claus Westermann, "עֶבֶד ʿebed Knecht," *THAT* 2:182–200; H. Ringgren, U. Rüterswörden, and H. Simian-Yofre, "עָבַד," *TWAT* 5:982–1012; C. Lindhagen, *The Servant Motif in the Old Testament* (Uppsala: Lundequist, 1950); I. Riesener, *Der Stamm* עבד im Alten Testament (Berlin: Töpelmann, 1979).

[19] See Gunneweg, *Nehemia*, 180; cf. Kellermann, *Nehemia*, 154–59 on "Nehemias Amt und Abstammung."

God as also binding on rulers.[20] A comparison of the texts clearly reveals the nature of the modification. The prayer of Solomon concludes in the Deuteronomic formulation (1 Kgs 8:52): "Let thy eyes be open to the supplication of thy servant, and to the supplication of thy people Israel, giving ear to them. . . ." This becomes in the Prayer of Nehemiah (Neh 1:6): "Let thy ear be attentive, and thy eyes open, to hear the prayer of thy servant which I now pray before thee day and night for the people of Israel thy servants. . . ." That Nehemiah prays for the Israelites (על בני ישׂראל) is explicable from the context. An essential difference, minor as it seems, is that Nehemiah refers not only to himself as "thy servant" but also to the Israelites as "thy servants" (עבדיך).

In the Deuteronomic formulation of 1 Kings 8, the use of language is consistent in rendering "thy servant and thy people Israel" (vv. 30, 36). Those instances where plural forms of servant are found are not entirely unambiguous, text-critically. In v. 23 the Septuagint reads the singular "thy servant" (τῷ δούλῳ σου), and in v. 32 instead of "thy servants" we find "thy people Israel" (τὸν λαόν σου 'Ισραηλ). The basic conception remains: the kings are the servants of "Yahweh, the God of Israel" (v. 25); the "people" are a collective entity.

The Israelites in the Nehemiah text occupy a role as (God's) "servants," and three levels of "servant of God" can be distinguished in the text:

1. Moses, Servant of God (vv. 7 and 8). First, Moses is the law-giver. Through him God transmitted "commandments, statutes, ordinances" (v. 7). This corresponds to his function in Neh 9:14; 10:30. As such, it is striking that when the prayer of petition in Nehemiah 9 looks back on the wonders that accompanied the exodus, they are attributed to God alone. Moses is here no wonder-worker! Second, Moses is a "prophet." By his word Israel's destiny, in blessing and in curse, is brought to pass. Just as the curse of dispersion has come about, so too there is hope for the future (cf. Deuteronomy 28–30).
2. Nehemiah, Servant of God (vv. 6 and 11 [twice]). Nehemiah assumes the authority of Moses. He speaks for the Israelites (בני ישׂראל [v. 6]) on behalf of the people of God (עמך [v. 10]) in prayer before God (cf. 3:36). He acts in God's name (2:20). He proclaims that "God will fight for us" (4:14), and he admonishes them to walk in the "fear of God" (5:9; cf. 13:27). In particular he sees to it that the law given through Moses is again put into effect (Nehemiah 10), and he secures its recognition at a practical level (Nehemiah 5: the redemption of slaves; 13: cleansing of the temple, organization of the cult, honoring of the sabbath).

[20] See Klaus Baltzer, "Das Ende des Staates Juda und die Messias-Frage," in *Studien zur Theologie der alttestamentlichen Überlieferungen*, ed. R. Rendtorff and K. Koch (Neukirchen-Vluyn: Neukirchener Verlag, 1961) 33–43.

3. The Israelites, Servants of God (vv. 6, 10, 11). Both individually and collectively (v. 10) the Israelites are "servants" (of God). As such, in this text they are classified with the same term as the individual Nehemiah. They are "servants" of God not by dint of birth or position but on account of and insofar as they "delight to fear thy name" (v. 11). In this sense, they are "servants" of "Yahweh, God of heaven" (v. 5), who is Lord (v. 11). The alternative is whether to "serve" him or another lord (cf. Neh 9:32–37, esp. 35–37).

The important role played by the sociomorpheme Lord–Servant in Nehemiah also reveals a link to Deutero-Isaiah. The connection between "servant" (sg.) and "servants" (pl.) in the Prayer of Nehemiah corresponds to the theological stance of Deutero-Isaiah. With the aid of the familiar sociomorpheme Lord–Servant, the community is able to articulate its self-understanding in a fresh way and to achieve a better conception of the relationship to God and neighbor.[21]

Other terms are used in the book of Nehemiah for external reference. In the service of the Persian empire, Nehemiah is termed "governor" (פחה [5:14, 18; 12:26]) over the "land of Judah" (ארץ יהודה [5:14]) or "the province" (מדינה [1:3; 7:6; 11:3]), whose capital is Jerusalem. Ethnically, the inhabitants are "Jews" (יהודים [1:2; 2:16; 3:33f.; 4:6; 5:1, 8, 17; 6:6; 13:23]). The relationship between these two language usages, both in internal and external terms, demands further study.[22]

Conclusions

Conclusions and further questions for interdisciplinary research can be summarized as follows: (1) To a greater degree than is normally acknowledged, the book of Nehemiah is a literary unity, including the prayers found in chapters 1 and 9. One is entitled to speak of a conceptual unity as well.[23] (2) The prayer of Nehemiah 1 exhibits a programmatic character. It uses formulaic language—which is not to say that such language has been used indiscriminately. Here is old tradition, developed on the basis of Deuteronomy, whose legitimacy derives from "Moses, the servant of God." (3) The text of the prayer reflects a complex exposition of text and tradition. This

[21] See Baltzer, "Debt Slavery," 478–80.

[22] See the commentaries, esp. Gunneweg, *Nehemia*, 42–45, 92; Hans G. Kippenberg, *Religion und Klassenbildung im antiken Judäa* (Göttingen; Vandenhoeck & Ruprecht, 1978); Sara Japhet, "People and Land in the Restoration Period," in *Das Land in biblischer Zeit: Jerusalem-Symposium 1981 der Hebräischen Universität und der Georg-August-Universität*, ed. G. Strecker (Göttinger Theologische Arbeiten 25; Göttingen: Vandenhoeck & Ruprecht, 1983) 103–25.

[23] This would not exclude from consideration the addition of individual units, e.g., the material associated with Ezra in Nehemiah 8.

exposition serves to communicate present experience as well as a program for the future.[24] (4) In historical terms, the project linked to the name of Nehemiah involves a new constitution for Jerusalem and Judah.[25] It is an attempt to overcome the trauma of the collapse of kingship and the exile by political and theological means. Implicitly the formula "the servant and the servants" points to equality before God—and before the law of "Moses, servant of God." This is a step whose significance reaches well beyond the Old Testament itself.[26]

[24] There is much to be done in the future to firm up our appreciation of the process involved. For literature, see Michael Fishbane, *Biblical Tradition in Ancient Israel* (Oxford: Clarendon, 1985); D. A. Carson and H. G. M. Williamson, eds., *It is Written: Scripture Citing Scripture: Essays in honour of Barnabas Lindars* (Cambridge: Cambridge University Press, 1988); Helmut Utzschneider, *Künder oder Schreiber? Eine These zum Problem der "Schriftprophetie" auf Grund von Maleachi 1,6—2,9* (Frankfurt am Main: Lang, 1989); Klaus Baltzer, "Schriftauslegung bei Deuterojesaja—Jes 43,22–28 als Beispiel," in *Die Väter Israels: Festschrift J. Scharbert*, ed. M. Görg (Stuttgart: Katholisches Bibelwerk, 1989) 11–16. The problem can also be seen with reference to developments outside the OT; see, e.g., H. Tadmor, M. Weinfeld, eds., *History, Historiography and Interpretation: Studies in Biblical and Cuneiform Literatures* (Jerusalem/Leiden: Brill, 1986); Richard Garner, *From Homer to Tragedy: The Art of Allusion in Greek Poetry* (London: Routledge, 1990). The significance of the Moses tradition for the book of Jeremiah has been the subject of recent analysis by Christopher R. Seitz ("The Prophet Moses and the Canonical Shape of Jeremiah," *ZAW* 101 [1989] 3–27; "Mose als Prophet: Redaktionsthemen und Gesamtstruktur des Jeremiabuches" *BZ* 34/2 (1990) 234–45.

[25] The date can be established with a degree of probability on the basis of the note at 2:1, "the twentieth year of King Artaxerxes." If Artaxerxes I (465–424) is meant, then the year of Nehemiah's commissioning would be 445 BCE. De Fraine correctly points out in his commentary that in Athens this is the time of Pericles (ca. 495–429). It would be important to compare the transition from a system where all are equal before the law (isonomy) to democracy in Athens. Certainly one would like to know more about the political situation in the cities of Asia Minor and the Levant (including Egypt) in the Persian period.

[26] See Baltzer and Koester, "Jakobus als 'ΩΒΛΙΑΣ."

9

Philo and the Sabbath Crisis: Alexandrian Jewish Politics and the Dating of Philo's Works

ROBERT A. KRAFT

YEARS OF STUDYING with Helmut Koester and reaping the benefits of his work have helped to underline and bring into clearer focus that cornerstone of critical research: "Things are not always what they seem" or, better, ". . . what others have made them to seem." Illustrations can be drawn from every corner. In what follows, I wish to explore and reopen some aspects of that still largely unmined treasure trove, the works of Philo the Jewish Alexandrian, with particular reference to some hints in Philo's writings that seem to me to refer to a hitherto unexplored aspect of Jewish involvement in the Alexandrian political scene.[1]

[1] This essay is a report on "work in progress," with many open leads and loose ends left to explore. A related aspect is examined in my article "Tiberius Julius Alexander and the Crisis in Alexandria according to Josephus," (in *Of Scribes and Scrolls: Studies on the Hebrew Bible, Intertestamental Judaism, and Christian Origins Presented to John Strugnell on the Occasion of his Sixtieth Birthday*, ed. Harold W. Attridge et al. [College Theological Society Resources in Religion 5. Lanham, MD/New York/London: University Press of America, 1991]).

Some use has been made of the convenient electronic texts prepared and distributed by the Thesaurus Linguae Graecae project directed by Theodore Brunner at the University of California, Irvine, and of the IBYCUS Scholarly Computer system for searching and manipulating this material. Of conventional scholarly publications, special use has been made of the Loeb Classical Library volumes on Philo, edited and translated by G. H. Whitaker and F. H. Colson (vols. 1–5, 1929–1934) and by Colson alone (vols. 6–10, 1935–1962), with indexes by J. W. Earp (in vol. 10) and two supplementary volumes by Ralph Marcus (1953) (Cambridge, Mass.: Harvard University Press). The older English translation by C. D. Yonge (London: H. G. Bohn, 1854) has also been consulted at points. Frequent reference has also been made to the works of E. R. Goodenough, especially his *Introduction to Philo Judaeus* (2nd ed.; Oxford: Blackwell, 1962) and his *Politics of Philo Judaeus* (New Haven: Yale University Press, 1938). For matters

My main conclusions and their immediate ramifications are as follows; (1) Philo's *negative* treatments of Joseph as a symbol of the political person often reflect a specific set of political events experienced by Philo (in Egypt) involving problematic actions of a Jewish political figure. (2) Philo's *positive* treatment of Joseph as a symbol of the (Jewish?) political person was almost certainly written prior to the crisis reflected in the negative treatments. (3) The most obvious candidate for sparking the negative treatment would seem to be Philo's own nephew Tiberius Julius Alexander, who first appears in preserved sources as a major political figure around 42 CE and disappears from the sources shortly after 70.[2] (4) If Philo is reacting to political activities of Tiberius Alexander, the date of the publication of Philo's allegorical treatises may be considerably later than usually has been assumed.

The larger context of these observations is an interest on the part of myself and my students in examining more closely the chronological clues present in Philo's writings.[3] We have convinced ourselves that some significant, perhaps even startling, things remain to be said about the course of Philo's life and the sequence of his literary activities. Goodenough, for all of his foundational and magisterial work on Philo, has probably done us a disservice by encouraging us to abandon the search for evidences of chronological progression within the Philonic corpus. That Philo envisioned different audiences for different writings or series of writings seems highly probable, but it by no means follows that chronological distinctions between various works might not also be possible.

The Crisis over Jewish Public Attitudes to Rulers

The one certain date in Philo's career that every commentator recognizes is the crisis that led to the Jewish embassy to Rome around the year 40 of

dealing with the *Embassy to Gaius* and associated issues, E. M. Smallwood's *Philonis Alexandrini Legatio ad Gaium* (Leiden: Brill, 1961) has been very useful.

[Indeed, after the initial draft was submitted to the editors, the following directly relevant article was brought to my attention: "Philonic Anonyms of the Roman and Nazi Periods: Two Suggestions," by Daniel R. Schwartz, in *The Studia Philonica Annual* 1 (1989) 63–73. The "suggestion" by Schwartz anticipates and neatly complements the present study! See below, n. 7.]

2 My main source of detailed information on Tiberius Julius Alexander and related subjects is E. G. Turner, "Tiberius Iulius Alexander," *JRS* 44 (1954) 54–64.

3 Our route to Philo was via an examination of translation techniques in antiquity, which led us to Philo's etymologies, and thence to such tantalizing phenomena as Philo's (early?) use of "Chaldean" to designate the language that he consistently calls "Hebrew" in the (later?) "allegorical" treatises (C. K. Wong has prepared a preliminary study of this usage). This has led us to look (1) for other possible systematic changes in the Philonic corpus as clues to the internal sequence of writing and also (2) for Philo's own cross-references and autobiographical allusions within the corpus. My thanks are offered to the various students and other associated colleagues in my advanced seminars who have shared in this work—especially William Adler, Kass Evans, Noel Hubler, Alan Humm, Allen Kerkeslager, Ross Kraemer, Lynn LiDonnici, David Rech, Jay Treat, C. K. Wong, and Benjamin Wright.

the Common Era. Philo presents himself as a leader and an elder statesman in that group of (five) Jewish envoys (*Embassy to Gaius* [*Legatio ad Gaium*] 182), but the names of his companions are not recorded. It has been suggested that Philo's brother Alexander might have been with the group since he somehow found himself in prison (in Rome?) when Claudius became emperor in 41 CE and released him.[4] I do not know if anyone has suggested that Philo's nephew, Tiberius Julius Alexander, might also have been present, since he emerges at the outset of Claudius's reign with a civil position in Egypt (ca. 42–44) and soon thereafter becomes prefect of Judea (46–48). There is a strong possibility that the Jewish envoys (and their supporters?) were still in Rome when Gaius Caligula was succeeded by Claudius (so Turner).

The background and course of events leading to the embassy are described in some detail by Philo in his essays known as *On Flaccus* and *Embassy to Gaius*. Josephus also mentions these events rather briefly (*Antiquities of the Jews* 18.8.1 §§257–60). The main public issue of contention that is reported by these sources is the failure of Jews to erect honorific statues to the Roman rulers, which became a catalyst for rioting against the Jewish meeting places and populace and a reevaluation of traditional Jewish privileges. The disastrous results led to the sending of embassies, from the Jews and from their accusers, to the emperor Gaius, who died before the issues could be resolved. Claudius inherited the problem and finally brought it under control by means of official letters and edicts.

The Crisis over Sabbath Keeping

This is not the only public political crisis concerning Jewish practice and privilege that Philo describes in his writings, although it receives by far the most detailed attention. In the treatise entitled *On Dreams* (*De somniis*), of which two of the original three (or more?) "books" have survived, Philo becomes uncharacteristically autobiographical and confrontationally indignant about a series of recent events that challenged the traditional Jewish sabbath observance in Egypt. The context is a discussion of the two dreams of the young man Joseph in Genesis 37:5–11. Philo's picture of Joseph here is quite negative: Joseph represents human vanity that seeks "addition" of sense-related luxuries to the ideally simple life. His brethren rightly criticize him, reflecting the attitude of right reason toward vainglory. In the end, Joseph will change his stance and be remembered (see *Dreams* 2.105–9), but the main focus in *Dreams* 2.5–109 and 2.110–154 is on Joseph as a symbol of failings due to conceit.

[4] Turner ("Tiberius," 58) discusses the details, including the close family ties with Agrippa and his family. See Josephus *Ant.* 19.5.1 §§276–77.

Joseph's first dream, where sheaves of wheat bow down, introduces the problem of earth-generated vanity and luxury. The second, where the heavenly bodies bow down, draws attention to the folly of humans exalting themselves over nature itself (2.115–17). Thus the Persian king Xerxes tried to change nature and even attacked the sun (2.117–20), and the Germans are reported to use their weapons to try to repel floodwaters (2.121–22)! At this point we find a third example, based on Philo's own experience, the main features of which are as follows (in an intentionally mechanical rendering):

> (123) But not a day or two ago I knew a certain one of the rulers who, since he had charge of the leadership and protection of Egypt, determined to upset our traditions, and especially to abrogate the most holy and most awesome law that concerns the sabbath, . . . and to do other things that ignore established custom, thinking that it would be the beginning of a change of habit concerning the other things and of transgression of all things, if he were able to destroy the sabbath tradition.
>
> (124) And when he saw that those he was pressuring neither were submitting to the commands nor did they subdue the remaining multitude but they took the matter gravely and heavily, and since they were mournful and downcast as at enslavement and sacking and destruction of a native land, he decided with a word to instruct them to transgress, saying:
>
> (125–126) [Speech describes possible calamaties and asks] (127) "Will you sit in your synagogues assembling the usual group and safely reading the holy books and if anything is not clear explaining it and extensively spending time and studying the native philosophy? (128) No, but discarding all these you will strip down to help yourselves and parents and children and the other relations and loved ones, and if truth be told, also possessions and money, to prevent their destruction." (129) "Indeed, I my very self am," he said, "all the preceding—whirlwind, war, cataclysm, thunderbolt, a plague of famine and disease, the earthquake shaking and overthrowing what firmly stood; not just a name for fate's necessity but a power, visible, standing near!"
>
> (130) What then shall we say that the one who proclaims such or merely thinks it is? Is he not from somewhere else? Beyond the ocean, then, or metacosmic, some new evil, since indeed he dared to compare his all-unfortunate self to the all-blessed? (131–132) [Further rhetorical examples of his conceit] . . . insofar as he a man thinks himself superior to the other creatures.

There can be little doubt that Philo intends to speak of a real person of authority in Egypt (parallel to Xerxes and the Germans), or that the events to which he refers happened recently and derive from his personal knowledge. The Greek phraseology is not detached and formalistic. On the contrary, Philo's flow of words is lively and impassioned. The issues are extremely serious to him, involving not simply the unnamed ruler's expression of blasphemous vanity but also the situation that produced such insolence: an attack on the Jewish sabbath tradition and, through it, on Jewish law and practices in general.

But who is this dastardly villain, and when did such events happen? F. H. Colson is content to note (in agreement with Edersheim and Ewald) that Flaccus does not seem to fit the bill (despite Mangey's claim), and that perhaps one of his immediate predecessors, Iberus or Vitrasius Pollio, is in view.[5] Goodenough devotes an entire chapter of his *Politics* to this and similar passages to argue that here Philo is expressing "politics in code" to attack Roman oppression in general in a manner that "would seem quite innocuous if, as was unlikely, it fell into Roman hands."[6] Goodenough declines to identify the specific ruler or crises described by Philo. It "may have been Flaccus, but I doubt it. . . . [Philo's] reference . . . seems to indicate the prefect immediately preceding the incumbent at the time of writing."[7] Goodenough does not think there was enough time left in Philo's life for him to write this and associated works after the reign of Gaius (and Flaccus).

It seems to me that in such discussions, the commentators miss some crucial features of Philo's invective throughout *Dreams* 2 and similar passages, especially passages about Joseph. Goodenough is mostly correct that the specific reference to a specific ruler in 2.123, which seems to depart from "the general allegorical mazes" of the surrounding discussions, "is no break at all since Philo has been talking about the Romans all along."[8] My only quarrel with Goodenough here would be the precise definition of "Roman." Goodenough clearly means "hated Roman outsider." But I think Philo is concerned in these passages primarily with the (suspect) Roman insider—that is, with political authority exercised by persons of Jewish origin within the Roman system. Joseph is an obvious model: one of the brethren who becomes second in command in ancient Egypt (note *Dreams* 2.43–47).

The specific problems described in *Dreams* 2.123–32 all deal with basically internal Jewish customs and concerns. The key issue highlighted is sabbath observance, which admittedly could easily be a point of contention for non-Jewish authorities since it impacts on such key economic issues as work schedules. The privilege of retaining customary observances—including sabbath—among Jews in the Roman world was, according to Philo and other sources from that period, consistently reaffirmed by Augustus and his

[5] Philo (LCL) 5:609.

[6] Goodenough, *Politics,* 21.

[7] Ibid., 29–30. Schwartz takes issue with these conjectures and takes a step toward what seems to be a more reasonable solution by identifying the culprit as Tiberius Julius Alexander around the year 42 ("Suggestions").

[8] Ibid., 30.

successor (see *Embassy* 155–61; sabbath observance is mentioned specifically only in passing in 158). It is true also that in discussing the Gaius Caligula crisis, Philo can view Jewish customs as a connected unit, so that a challenge to one element constitutes a threat to all (*Embassy* 117–18). Nevertheless, there is no evidence to suggest that any non-Jewish Roman ruler tried to use sabbath observance as the wedge to overthrow Jewish customs in general or that the motivation of Flaccus and/or Gaius was to overturn all Jewish customary observances.

The villain of *Dreams* 2.123, however, is described as wanting to attack sabbath observance as a step toward overthrowing Jewish customs in general. The various hints that surround the central passage suggest that he is an insider, who should know better (see, e.g., 2.135–38, on the pseudo-dream nature of the justification presented by the "not well cleansed" oppressor; or 2.144, which suggests that a traitor from the inside is responsible for the crisis; or the images of fountain and herd in 2.150–54, which seem to reinforce that picture). Similarly, the Joseph introduced in the general statements of 2.10–16 seems to represent inside pressures caused by vanity and conceit, which threaten to overthrow the existing equilibrium. With regard to Joseph's first "dream," Philo makes no attempt at explaining away the obvious indications in the biblical story that Joseph is functioning among his parents and brethren (e.g., 2.33; 2.41–47). Similarly, it seems to be the insider who is described as in danger of failing in such passages as 2.68–70 or 2.78–84, and the praise of the brethren who oppose this tyrant (e.g., 2.93–104) best fits the picture of inner-Jewish tensions. Philo even looks to the time of reconciliation for this vain and misguided antagonist (2.105–9).

Philo's Uses of the Joseph Figure/Story

As is well known, Philo's treatments of Joseph vary greatly throughout the Philonic corpus, from the largely sympathetic presentation in *On Joseph* (one of the "expositional" treatises) to the ambivalent or critical passages scattered throughout the "allegorical" series of writings.[9] The evidence in Goodenough's brief footnote on this matter is filled out very helpfully by Colson's comments in the general introduction to the appropriate volume of Philo, and in even greater detail by the extremely useful annotated index of names

[9] The general distinction between Philo's "expositional" writings (*On Creation, On Abraham, On Joseph;* perhaps also *Life of Moses*), which tend to deal with the biblical text in a fairly straightforward manner, and his "allegorical" treatises (LCL vols. 1–5, except *On Creation*) is widely accepted and rests on strong internal and external evidence. See L. Cohn, "Einteilung und Chronologie der Schriften Philos," *Philologus Supplementband* 7 (1899) 385–436.

by J. W. Earp.[10] Colson follows Goodenough in explaining the differing depictions as due to Philo's "chronic vacillation of character" (or, in Colson's rephrasing, "chronic tendency to see both sides of a question alternately or even simultaneously"). Goodenough, of course, also notes that the different series of writings were aimed at different audiences. I find these explanations less than satisfactory.

The Joseph of Philo's exposition *On Joseph* is the representation of the political person, a life-style that stands over against the life of learning/instruction (Abraham), of "nature" (Isaac), and of practical application (Jacob). This image of Joseph is highly favorable. It is his brothers, filled with envy, who are villains in the story concerning Joseph's two dreams—in contrast to what has been summarized above from the treatment of Joseph in *Dreams*. Philo spins off no allegories at this point in *Joseph*, nor does he draw any pointed lessons. There is no hint of the negative Joseph imagery found in *Dreams* 2 and elsewhere in the allegorical series of writings. Outside these allegorical treatises of Philo and *Joseph*, references and allusions to Joseph are rare and seem quite positive (e.g., *On Rewards and Punishments* [*De praemiis et poenis*] 65, on Jacob's twelve ideal sons/tribes), and where Philo has occasion to speak of apostasy within Israel in this material (as in *Special Laws* [*De specialibus legibus*] 1.54–58) the Joseph imagery seems to play no role.

Several of the allegorical treatises, on the other hand, make explicit mention of Joseph and often represent him as symbolic of negative features, in general accord with the picture in *Dreams*. The following passages seem closely related to the treatment in *Dreams* and to each other in some of their emphases: *Worse Attacks Better* (*Quod deterius potiori insidiari solet*) 5–31; *God's Immutability* (*Quod Deus immutabilis sit*) 111–21; *Agriculture* (*De agricultura*) 55–56; *Sobriety* (*De sobrietate*) 10–15; *Flight* (*De fuga et inventione*) 126–31. Notable features include the contrast between Joseph and his various types of (half) brothers, the "youthfulness" of Joseph, the stages of Joseph's quest to find his brothers and his need for worthy instructors. The passage in *Flight* seems much less specific, much less personally involved than the others, and may have been written significantly earlier or later than the crisis mentioned in *Dreams* 2.

Another group of passages from allegorical treatises presupposes the negative imagery of Joseph but holds out explicit hope for his rehabilitation: *Change of Names* (*De mutatione nominum*) 89–96, 171–74, 214–15; *Migration of Abraham* (*De migratione Abrahami*) 16–24, 158–63, 203–7. Similarly, *Allegorical Laws* (*Legum allegoriae*) 3 both chides Joseph the statesman (3.26, 179) and praises Joseph as a model for withstanding temptation (3.237–42). A few other, only mildly critical references to Joseph occur in the allegorical

[10] Goodenough, *Politics*, 33 n. 50; Colson, vol. 6 of LCL, pp. xii–xiv; Earp, vol. 10 of LCL.

treatises: *Cherubim* (*De cherubim*) 128 (Joseph was imprecise in assigning the cause of true interpretation of dreams), *Cain's Posterity* (*De posteritate Caini*) 78–82 (even Joseph is deemed "successful" in things God gives him), *Confusion of Tongues* (*De confusione linguarum*) 71–72 (Joseph symbolizes the least mature of the "good" tendencies, slightly better than the "bodily" Egyptians), *Who Is Heir* (*Quis rerum divinarum heres*) 251 and 256a (Jacob is amazed that Joseph "still lives to virtue and rules the body").

Identifying Philo's Historical Joseph

In several of these negative portrayals of Joseph, the details sometimes seem to be more precise than might be expected from some sort of general allegory, based on what we know of the biblical narratives and of Philo's usual procedures. Philo appears to have a specific person and situation in mind, perhaps supplementing the picture found in *Dreams* 2. Thus, "Joseph" is depicted as engaging in philosophical debate—see especially *Worse* 6–12 (17, 28b) on how "Joseph" is motivated by the "political" rather than by "truth" in his position that the one perfect "good" involves the combination of the traditional three types of "goods"; compare *Agriculture* 55–66, which spells out more clearly the biblical textual base of this symbolism in the contrast between "cattle tending" (political controlling) and "shepherding" (rational leadership). Philo's "Joseph" is able to achieve his political goals, to a point, but then significant opposition occurs from the "brethren" (e.g., *Agriculture* 59). It is not clear to me whether the tirade against superficial religious ritual in *Worse* 20–21 is aimed at Philo's "Joseph" (the analogous attack on illegitimate acts of "self-control" in *Worse* 19 seems not to be), although certainly political activity in Philo's world would involve a leader in such issues and activities.

The emphasis on "Joseph's" wealth (e.g., *Change* 91) and his connection with a wealthy family (e.g., *Worse* 13–14) find sufficient explanation in the biblical narrative. That he is really an older person, although described as "young," may border on historical allusion (see *Immutability* 120 and *Agriculture* 56—does Philo have someone specific in mind?), but *Sobriety* 10–15 also provides a biblical textual basis for the observation. Indeed, the idea that "Joseph" needs to return to the "older" viewpoints (*Sobriety* 15), to have a change of perspective (*Dreams* 2.105–9), is propounded by Philo on the basis of his biblical texts with such firm conviction that one wonders whether this also reflects a perceived historical turnabout by "Joseph"—or even whether the historical "Joseph" villain is dead by the time *Migration* 16–24 is penned.

This much seems to me to be clear: the real crisis described in *Dreams* 2.123–32, which is sparked by the Joseph story but is not directly linked to explicit "Joseph" imagery at that point, has to do with a Jewish political leader and Jewish community issues. This crisis has spilled over to the surrounding "Joseph" symbolism throughout *Dreams* 1 and 2 (e.g., 1.219–25; 2.78–84; 2.101–4). It probably leaves its mark also in some of the other "Joseph" lessons in other tractates in the allegorical series and may in fact have helped Philo to create some characteristics of his generalized allegorical "Joseph." I suspect that a careful study of the Joseph material from this perspective may help to determine the order in which Philo wrote the relevant passages, some of which are rife with emotional involvement, others of which are quite calm and detached. It seems to me virtually impossible that Philo could have written *On Joseph* after these developments!

But who is this Jewish political figure? Our knowledge of political details in Philo's world is very spotty, but we do have examples from Philo's own family of very involved Jewish leaders. At some point, Philo's brother Alexander bore the title *alabarch* (or perhaps *arabarch*), the exact implications of which are not known. It is usually presumed to relate directly to matters of money on the general (not simply the Jewish) Alexandrian political scene. One of Alexander's sons, Marcus Julius Alexander, died relatively young (around the year 44, probably in his twenties) but seems to have had some significant exposure to the Egyptian (Alexandrian?) fiscal and civic scene. Another son, Tiberius Julius Alexander, was clearly active in eastern Mediterranean political life from the forties through the sixties (the reigns of Claudius and Nero) in various connections: he was *epistratēgos* in the Thebaid area of Egypt around the year 42, when his brother Marcus was also active in commerce in that area; he became procurator of Judea from about 46 to 48; sometime in the reign of Nero (54–68) he was procurator of Syria;[11] around the year 63 he was a military officer in the Armenian area; in 66 he was appointed prefect of Egypt, and we lose sight of him after his involvement as a staff officer with Titus in the siege of Jerusalem in 70, although he may reappear as a prefect of the Praetorian Guard in Rome.[12]

On the face of things, Tiberius Julius Alexander makes an excellent candidate for Philo's "Joseph" of the *Dreams* tractates. He is politically active in Egypt (if not in Alexandria) at a relatively early date, is described by Josephus (*Ant.* 20.5.2 §100) as one who abandoned the ancestral customs, and is thought by many commentators to be the "Alexander" of Philo's philosophically argumentative treatises *On Providence* (*De providentia*) and

[11] See J. P. Reys-Coquais, "Syrie Romaine, de Pompée à Dioclétien," *JRS* 68 (1978) 71 n. 369 (see also *L'Année épigraphique* for 1978, #819). I am indebted to Kass Evans for this information.

[12] For details, see Turner, "Tiberius," esp. 58–61. An updated study of the lengthy edict of Tiberius Alexander to the Alexandrians in 68 CE in the context of the present essay might be instructive. For bibliography on the edict, see Turner, "Tiberius," 60 n. 32, to which should be added G. Chalon, *L'Edite de Tiberius Julius Alexander: Étude historique et exégétique* (Bibliotheca Helvetica Romana 5; Olten: Graf, 1964).

Alexander: That Irrational Animals Possess Reason (*De animalibus*)[13]—a conjecture that may be relevant to the discussion of the "Joseph" description in *Worse* 6–12. The possibility that Philo's "Joseph" is his own brother Alexander cannot be dismissed out of hand, although there is no evidence that Alexander ever challenged Jewish custom in the way *Dreams* 2.123–32 suggests. Nor do we know enough about Alexander to determine whether he might have had the political power suggested by Philo's tirade. We know less about Marcus and about other Jewish political figures in Egypt at that time.

But is it possible that Philo could have written a large portion of his "allegorical" treatises after Tiberius Julius Alexander had gained the sort of power indicated in *Dreams* 2?[14] The most obvious situation would be in the late sixties, when Tiberius Julius Alexander was prefect of Egypt. Josephus describes in some detail, as a precipitating factor in the development of hostilities in Palestine between Jews and the Roman rulers, problems encountered by Tiberius Alexander at the beginning of his governance of Alexandria and Egypt (*J.W.* 2.18.7–8 §§487–97). Although Tiberius Alexander at first tries to talk the Jewish rebels out of their precarious position, Josephus says nothing to suggest that the "ancestral customs" are at issue. If Philo's "Joseph" of *Dreams* 2 is Josephus's Tiberius Alexander of the year 66, we will need to read a great deal between the lines. But it may well be worth the try.

How old would Philo have been when Tiberius Julius Alexander was governor of Egypt? Probably no younger than in his seventies, assuming that his "appropriate age" among the representatives to Gaius around the year 40 (*Embassy* 182) means that he was born no later than 5 BCE, and probably a few years prior to that.[15] He might even have been in his eighties by the

[13] E.g., Turner, "Tiberius," 56; Goodspeed, *Introduction,* 50 (ambiguously); Colson, Philo (LCL) 9:447.

[14] A further consideration to be noted is the apparent intention voiced by Philo in *Dreams* 1.168 of writing a treatise on Abraham's being guided by instruction. For various reasons I would resist the conclusion that this is a reference to the existing work *On Abraham,* although the description in *Dreams* 1.168 invites that possibility.

[15] The commentators differ widely on the questions of Philo's birth and floruit and thus on how long after the *Embassy* crisis Philo might have been literarily active. The key passage is *Embassy* 182, which, combined with *Embassy* 1, has been taken to suggest that Philo is somewhere around fifty years old—and possibly older—in 40 CE (Philo's numerological periodization of life's stages in *Creation* [*De opificio mundi*] 103–5 suggests that "elderly" and "old" apply after forty-nine years of age; the partial parallel in *Allegorical Laws* 1.9–10 does not deal with the older periods). It should be noted that elsewhere in Philo the word used in *Embassy* 182 ("age") frequently, if not normally, occurs in references to youth and vitality, not old age (e.g., *Abraham* 195), and thus Philo might be comparing his prime-of-life status to the more advanced ages of his fellow ambassadors. *Embassy* 1 does use a more normal word for "aged," presumably referring to the time when Philo writes the essay (not the time of the embassy visit itself), but

year 66 CE. There is no question that some authors in their seventies and eighties have produced cogent and extensive writings. Whether Philo was one of them remains to be explored in greater detail. If that is deemed improbable, other possibilities for the "Sabbath Crisis" situation at an earlier date (perhaps under a younger Tiberius Julius Alexander; see Schwartz) deserve consideration.

---

it is not necessarily to be taken at face value. Other pertinent issues include the possible age of Philo's brother Alexander—and thus of Alexander's children Marcus and Tiberius. A. D. Nock argues that for Tiberius Alexander to be *epistratēgos* of Thebais in 42 CE, he must have been born around 10 CE (he thinks Goodenough's estimate of around 20 CE "is too late"). See Nock, "Philo and Hellenistic Philosophy," *Classical Review* 57 (1943) 78 and n. 13 (reprinted in Nock's *Essays on Religion and the Ancient World,* ed. Z. Stewart [Cambridge, Mass.: Harvard University Press, 1972] 2:561). If Philo's periodization of the fifth hebdomad of life, from twenty-nine to thirty-five, as childbearing age is accepted as a convenient measure (*Creation* 103–5), Philo's brother might have been born around 20 BCE, with perhaps a ten-year window on either side. Was Marcus older than Tiberius? Was Alexander older than Philo? I am assuming that Philo would have been about twenty years older than Tiberius Alexander, which is certainly neither impossible nor improbable, given the data currently at our disposal.

10

The Tests of the Twelve Patriarchs: Forensic Rhetoric in Josephus's *Antiquities of the Jews* 2.7–200

WILFRED F. BUNGE

A NUMBER OF analyses of the whole or parts of Josephus's *Antiquities* have appeared in recent years. H. W. Attridge's study of Josephus's interpretation of biblical history approaches the work comprehensively; T. W. Franxman presents a detailed comparison of the Genesis narrative materials in Josephus and the Bible; and L. H. Feldman has published several articles on Josephus's presentation of individual biblical figures.[1] What is common to all of these studies is the attempt to define how Josephus has reconceived the biblical story, to identify his intentionality or distinctive motifs in retelling the story.

Josephus clearly does not confine himself to re-presenting the biblical story in a narrowly precise way, despite the ostensible meaning of his promise in *Ant.* 1 Proem 3 §17, that he will give the exact details of scripture without adding or omitting anything. Whereas he claims in *Against Apion* 1.10 §53 that the duty of the historian is to present an accurate account either on the basis of experience or as learned from other witnesses—in general a Thucydidean approach to history—the *Antiquities* is actually closer in style to Herodotus. Josephus is very inclusive, whether he has his

[1] H. W. Attridge, *The Interpretation of Biblical History in the "Antiquitates Judaicae" of Flavius Josephus* (HDR 7; Missoula, Mont.: Scholars Press, 1976); T. W. Franxman, *Genesis and the "Jewish Antiquities" of Flavius Josephus* (Biblica et Orientalia 35; Rome: Biblical Institute Press, 1979); L. H. Feldman, "Abraham the Greek Philosopher in Josephus," *TAPA* 99 (1968) 143–66; idem, "Josephus' Portrait of Saul," *HUCA* 53 (1982) 45–99; idem, "Josephus as an Apologist to the Greco-Roman World: His Portrait of Solomon," in *Aspects of Religious Propaganda in Judaism and Early Christianity*, ed. E. Schüssler-Fiorenza (Notre Dame: Notre Dame University Press, 1976) 69–97.

additions from other sources or from his own imaginative expansion, though he also omits details and episodes from the biblical narrative in deference to his own purposes in re-presenting the material.

Josephus's chief aim was to present the rich and ancient traditions of his people as worthy of the attention of the wider Hellenistic/Roman world (*Ant.* 1 Proem 2 §§5–9; *Ag. Ap.* 1.13 §§69–72). Secondarily, he argues that these traditions offered outstanding examples of character—wisdom, skill, and virtue—an argument underscored by the key role of Moses (*Ant.* 1 Proem 2 §6 passim) and the dedication to Epaphroditus (*Ant.* 1 Proem 2 §8), a man of deep intellectual curiosity whose own virtue matched the central concerns of Jewish history and made him an apt audience for it.

Josephus presents a moral history, with frequent editorial moralizing, lest the reader miss the point. The chief lesson of history (*Ant.* 1 Proem 3 §14) is that those who follow the will of God prosper and those who disregard the law suffer.[2] This accounts for the central position of Moses as lawgiver in Josephus's understanding of Jewish history. Moses presents God as possessing pure virtue; the corollary responsibility for human beings is to embody this virtue (*Ant.* 1 Proem 4 §23).

This essay will focus on the story of Joseph and his brothers as presented in *Ant.* 2.2.1–2.8.2 §§7–200. Josephus conceives the story as occupying a key position in Jewish history, marking the transition from the accounts of the earliest ancestors to the settling of the promised land. Joseph and his brothers adumbrate the structure of the nation of Israel. It is important that they exhibit those virtues, those solid character traits which Josephus regards as central to his people. These patriarchs are also the means of the departure from Egypt and the settling of the promised land (*Ant.* 2.2.1 §8). Egypt becomes for Josephus the staging ground for the settlement of Canaan (*Ant.* 2.7.2–3 §§170–75), in contrast to Genesis, which speaks simply of going to Egypt and returning (Gen 46:4).

The basic emphasis of the Joseph stories in Genesis is on the ongoing history of salvation. Joseph's characterization of his role in Egypt as assuring the survival of the Jewish community (Gen 45:7) provides an important indicator of narrative intention. The test of character is there, surely, both for Joseph and for his brothers. But the primary concern is for the continuity of the people, manifested in part through the recurrent theme of the true heir.[3] Notably, Josephus omits Genesis 49, in which Jacob's blessing singles out Judah as the true heir, a clue that the continuity of Israel, so important to Genesis, is not a central concern for Josephus.

For Josephus, Joseph and his brothers are the community of Israel. What he intends to demonstrate is their tested and proven character. They

[2] See Moses' testamentary speech in *Ant.* 4.8.1–2 §§175–193.

[3] See L. H. Silberman, "Listening to the Text," *JBL* 102 (1983) 18–24.

constitute the exemplars of all Israel. When Josephus establishes the case for their character, he has successfully commended the entire Jewish community as worthy of the attention and respect of his Hellenistic/Roman audience.

The speeches of Reuben (Gen 37:21–22; *Ant.* 2.3.1–2 §§20–31) and Judah (Gen 44:18–34; *Ant.* 2.6.8 §§140–58) are among the most striking examples of editorial expansion by Josephus, one near the beginning of the narrative and the other near the end. The speeches together form a rhetorical frame for Josephus's conception of the story. These are speeches of defense, Reuben summing up the defense of Joseph before the court of his brothers, and Judah presenting a defense summation for Benjamin before Joseph as judge—forensic rhetoric, an appeal for and to character, for the merits of the defendant and to the mercy of the judges.[4] The framing of the narrative with these highly developed defense speeches suggests that Josephus intends the entire narrative of Joseph and his brothers as an extended piece of forensic rhetoric, in which a case is made for the exemplary character of the Jewish community as a whole.

As in Genesis, Joseph's story—the premier content and continuity of the narratives both of Genesis and of Josephus—is a kind of *Bildungsroman,* an account of character development from youth to maturity. All through this development Joseph encounters tests of character—betrayal by his brothers, the temptation and false charge of Potiphar's wife—and he comes through with remarkable steadfastness and great honor. But the speech of Judah challenges even Joseph to be true to his character. He has passed difficult tests of character and enjoys almost unlimited power—a noteworthy shifting of the burden back onto the plaintiff.

Josephus presents the brothers of Joseph as examples of successful character reform. Though Benjamin was an innocent bystander and only Reuben and Judah appear in any profile, the narrative views the brothers as a group in their plot against Joseph and in their positive change. The tests of character become the center of the narrative; the outcome demonstrates the achievement of integrity of character in the brothers. Despite their earlier enmity toward Joseph, the brothers appear at the end of the narrative as exemplary, decent men, worthy of the extravagant description with which Josephus introduces them at the beginning (*Ant.* 2.1.1 §1). Internally, the narrative argues for the character transformation of the brothers; externally, it presents a case to Josephus's Hellenistic/Roman audience for the noble character of the Jewish people as represented by these brothers. The omission of counterevidence—Reuben's consorting with his father's concubine

[4] The chiastic relationship between the two speeches—first a defense of Joseph before his brothers, and then a defense of the brothers, in particular Benjamin, before Joseph—provides the basic architecture of the narrative.

(Gen 35:22) and Judah's sexual union with his daughter-in-law, Tamar (Genesis 38)—provides further evidence that Josephus is making a case for character. One should not expect him to include details that would put such a severe strain on his case for character. Genesis can tell all, since there the central point is the continuity of God's promise. Character is a secondary issue.

So much for general observations. We turn now to more detailed observations on selected passages.

Genesis 37 introduces the account of the family of Jacob by turning immediately to Joseph. Joseph appears as an ingenuous younger brother who tattles on his older brothers (Gen 37:2) and is hated by them because of his father's favoritism toward him (Gen 37:4). He annoys even his father, Jacob, by wild dreams of his family's future deference to him.

In contrast to the spare economy of the Genesis narrative, Josephus begins with a general summary of the situation of Jacob and his family and an announcement that by divine providence the story of misfortune he is about to tell will come to a good end (*Ant.* 2.2.1 §§7–8). Jacob enjoys almost unparalleled prosperity and has outstanding children, hardworking and intelligent. The tone Josephus sets in this introduction suggests the key position of this story in the larger history of his people. They have reached a level of prosperity and quality as a people that poises them on the brink of successful settlement of the promised land (*Ant.* 2.2.1 §8). Their imminent sojourn in Egypt overshadows the fact that they are already in the promised land and flourishing there. The important barrier to permanent settlement is the stay in Egypt, and that obstacle Joseph and his brothers overcome.

After the extravagant introduction of the brothers, their subsequent behavior toward Joseph is quite jarring. Josephus takes considerable rhetorical risk in juxtaposing such an introduction with the sordid events that immediately follow. No such abrupt shift occurs in the Genesis narrative. Josephus can take the risk because he applies a heavy editorial hand throughout the narrative and consequently never leaves the reader in suspense about the final outcome.

In Genesis the brothers are eventually humbled by experience, but nowhere do we find the idealized generalization about their character that we find in *Ant.* 2.2.1 §7. They display, from their murderous envy at the beginning of the story to their varied assortment of vices and virtues in Jacob's blessing in Genesis 49, a credible range of character. Jacob's blessing foresees a continuation of this complex range of character into the future of the community in the promised land.

Josephus, on the other hand, sanitizes the narrative and thus removes a large measure of the ambiguity of character, not so much as to destroy the credibility of the narrative but a fairly radical revision nonetheless. He omits entirely the content of Genesis 49 and thus removes even those minimal profiles of the brothers. However, at the beginning of the narrative he retains the jealousy and murderous intent of the brothers, while at the same time, as noted above, introducing them as exemplary young men, pointing to the future distinction of the community in the land of promise. The false note of their treachery to Joseph is overcome by the thoroughness of their eventual reformation.

Josephus alters Jacob's response to Joseph's dream. Whereas in Gen 37:10 Jacob scolds Joseph for the pretentiousness of his dream, in *Ant.* 2.2.3 §§15–16 he understands immediately the meaning of the dream for the wonderful destiny of Joseph and accepts that destiny as beneficial for them all. There remains, therefore, no hint of disapproval of Joseph by Jacob.

There is considerable awkwardness in the Genesis interruption of the story of Joseph with the account of Judah's relationship with his daughter-in-law, Tamar (Genesis 38). Nonetheless, it fits in as a link in that chain of events through which God assures the continuity of the history of salvation, as part of the genealogy of Judah, a central figure in the history. Josephus's primary concern, however, is character, not the history of salvation. Therefore, he omits the episode as an embarrassing stain on the character of one of the most prominent of the brothers. He ignores as well a similarly difficult episode—Reuben's consorting with his father's concubine (Gen 35:22)—involving the other brother prominent in the narrative.

Josephus's chief addition to the introduction to the Joseph story, prior to his experience in Egypt, is a running moralizing commentary on the conflict between Joseph and his brothers. Josephus editorializes both on the brothers' perverse failure to recognize that they would share in Joseph's good fortune (*Ant.* 2.2.4 §17) and on the heinous character of their treachery (*Ant.* 2.3.1–3 §§20–33). The latter comes in an elaborate expansion of Reuben's simple exhortation in Genesis not to kill Joseph. Josephus has Reuben deliver an extended defense plea, with emotional appeals to the feelings of their parents, the youth and good character of Joseph, the will of God, their conscience, and their own self-interest (*Ant.* 2.3.1 §§21–28). He urges them to exercise self-control (*Ant.* 2.3.1 §23), a fundamental virtue for Josephus's audience. In sum, the speech presents an elaborate argument for good character. This stands in stark contrast to the spare economy of the Genesis narrative at this point (Gen 37:21–22).

The speech of Judah appears in Gen 44:18–34 as a brief summary of events that have led to the crisis of the charge of theft against Benjamin. Judah acts as spokesman for his brothers, offering his life in ransom for Benjamin, for the sake of their aged father. Josephus expands this speech of Judah into a major forensic rhetorical appeal. Judah is the defense attorney; he offers a case that turns the test back on Joseph (*Ant.* 2.6.8 §§140–58). Joseph, he argues, must show mercy; to do otherwise would violate his basic character.

Judah begins his case with an appeal to Joseph's character, his kindness

(*Ant.* 2.6.8 §140). Rather than focusing on the wrongdoing, Joseph should consider his own nature: don't fall victim to wrath, but be noble in the face of it (*Ant.* 2.6.8 §141). Judah draws a parallel between Joseph's rescue of them from starvation and withholding punishments (*Ant.* 2.6.8 §143). In fact, he argues to Joseph, God very likely brought them to this disaster to provide him with an opportunity to display virtue by forgiveness of wrongs against him (*Ant.* 2.6.8 §145). Joseph can in fact share the character of God himself by avoiding wrath against those whose wrongs he has every right to punish (*Ant.* 2.6.8 §146). Judah then heightens the poignancy of his father's situation, should Benjamin not return with them, and pleads with Joseph to let mercy for him supersede the wrong (*Ant.* 2.6.8 §§147–52).

The effect of Judah's argument is to put Joseph on trial, a test of his character. His action in this case will reveal whether he imitates the character of God himself or, contrary to his prior behavior in generously alleviating human suffering, acts on the basis of anger. In making his case, Judah follows the principle that the best defense is a good offense. Reuben had followed a similar path in dealing with his brothers' charge against Joseph. He put them on trial instead, though without success. There is deep irony in Judah's plea to Joseph for restraint of vengeance, since he and his brothers had earlier wrought severe vengeance on Joseph. The plea is not mere self-serving, however. Rather, the irony underscores the genuineness of the brothers' reform. Judah's argument is successful—Joseph reveals himself and confesses that he has been testing their brotherly love (*Ant.* 2.6.9 §§160–61), a motif not explicit in Genesis. The brothers have passed the test and should now move to Egypt.

The chief impression at the conclusion of the narrative is that here is a community of proven virtue, a community that has come through difficult tests with nobility. When we seek specific content for this virtue, however, we must look to the example of Joseph, particularly in the episode with Potiphar's wife. Josephus ends the entire narrative with Joseph, as does Genesis, and makes the general observation that Joseph was a person of remarkable virtue who managed everything with reason (*Ant.* 2.8.2 §198).[5] His wisdom and skill in administration were present in all that he did, but the primary test of character was the temptation of Potiphar's wife. There we learn in some detail what Josephus wants his audience to know about the character of the Jewish people.

Joseph introduces the episode with Potiphar's wife with a generalization about the outcome (*Ant.* 2.4.1 §40): Joseph did not abandon virtue, in spite of his opportunity to take advantage of his favorable situation. We have in the narrative (*Ant.* 2.4.1–5 §§39–59) a prime example of the sharp contrast

[5] See 4 Macc 2:2–3, which credits Joseph's mastery over sexual passion to his reason.

between what I have called the spare economy of the Genesis narrative and Josephus's expansion, in this case particularly in erotic details.[6]

That this is a test of character becomes clear early on (*Ant.* 2.4.2 §42) in the editorial observation that Potiphar's wife was viewing Joseph as a slave—there to do her bidding—rather than observing his character. Joseph urges her to get control of her passion (*Ant.* 2.4.2 §43) and turn it toward reason (*Ant.* 2.4.5 §53). He resists the promise of special favors, should he submit, and stands firmly on his responsibility to his master. He appeals to conscience and the superiority of living well over wrongdoing (*Ant.* 2.4.4 §52). Finally he endures the humiliation of false charges for the sake of maintaining his virtue and self-control (*Ant.* 2.5.2 §69), trusting in the providence of God (*Ant.* 2.5.1 §60).

Judging the quality of life by character rather than social status, controlling passions with reason, exercising self-control, trusting the providence of God—these constituents of the virtuous character of Joseph and finally of his brothers as well, which Josephus accents in his revision of the Genesis narrative, were commonplaces in the moral world of his Hellenistic/Roman audience, whether one labels them Stoic in the narrower sense or not. Josephus makes the case that the Jewish people exhibit the highest ideals of character in that world, all the way back to their very ancient beginnings. They are a people worth attending to.

[6] See M. Braun, *Griechischer Roman und Hellenistischer Geschichtsschreibung* (Frankfurt am Main: Klostermann, 1935); idem, *History and Romance in Graeco-Oriental Literature* (Oxford: Blackwell, 1938); H. Sprödowski, *Die Hellenisierung der Geschichte von Joseph bei Flavius Josephus* (Greifswalder Beiträge zur Literatur und Stilistik 18; Greifswald: Hans Adler, 1937).

11

Iael προστάτης in the Jewish Donative Inscription from Aphrodisias

BERNADETTE J. BROOTEN

THE GOAL OF this article is to ascertain the possible range of meanings of the title προστάτης applied to Iael in line 9 of the principal Jewish inscription from Roman Aphrodisias in Caria.[1] I suggest that several meanings of "president" and "patron" are historically plausible. I further demonstrate that Iael was not the only female religious leader involved in philanthropic activity within Judaism or within the larger Aphrodisian community. Other women in the Roman period served as Jewish leaders and as donors, and other Aphrodisian women are memorialized in inscriptions for their official religious roles and their public benefactions. Thus, Aphrodisian Jews shared with the larger Aphrodisian culture the practice of honoring female religious officials and benefactors by an inscription. This inscription is therefore one further piece in the emerging mosaic of diaspora Judaism in the context of the Roman world.

I shall first present face *a* of the inscription, then summarize the arguments that Iael is a feminine name, then outline several readings of προστάτης, and finally give some selected examples of female religious functionaries and benefactors in Roman Aphrodisias.

[1] Thanks are due to those who have assisted me in various ways with this project: Denise Buell, Ruth Clements, Sara Hazel, Melanie Johnson-DeBaufre, John Lanci, Janet McDaniel, and Laurel Schneider. Deepest thanks and honor are due to Helmut Koester, my teacher, colleague, and friend, for teaching us all that the Graeco-Roman world is not just the backdrop to early Christianity and ancient Judaism, but a vibrant world of competing philosophies and religions, political machinations, great building projects, and penetrating images, all of which deeply affected people's religious lives. May this piece communicate some of the excitement I have found seeking out the new sources that he has always encouraged us to pursue.

The Jewish Inscription from Aphrodisias

The principal Jewish inscription from ancient Aphrodisias in Caria is inscribed on a marble block on two faces; faces *a* and *b* are from different hands. Joyce Reynolds and Robert Tannenbaum, who have provided the scholarly world with an exemplary edition of and commentary on the inscription date both faces to the third century.[2] They transcribe face *a* of the inscription as follows:

Col. (i) Θεὸς βοηθός, πατέλλα̣ ? δο̣[.1 *or* 2.]
Οἱ ὑποτεταγμέ-
νοι τῆς δεκαν(ίας)
τῶν φιλομαθῶ̣[ν]
τῶν κὲ παντευλογ̣(--ων)
εἰς ἀπενθησίαν
τῷ πλήθι ἔκτισα[ν]
ἐξ ἰδίων μνῆμα
Σα- 'Ιαηλ προστάτης
μου *v.* σὺν υἱῷ 'Ιωσούα̣ ἄρχ(οντι?)
ηλ Θεόδοτος Παλατῖν(ος?) σὺν
πρεσ *v.* υἱῷ 'Ιλαριανῷ *vac.*
βευ- Σαμουηλ ἀρχιδ(έκανος?) προσήλ(υτος)
τῆς 'Ιωσῆς. 'Ιεσσέου *vacat*
Περ- Βενιαμιν ψαλμο(λόγος?)
γε- 'Ιούδας εὔχολος *vacat*
ούς 'Ιωσῆς προσήλυ(τος)
Σαββάτιος 'Αμαχίου
'Εμμόνιος θεοσεβ(ής) *v.v.*
'Αντωνῖνος θεοσεβ(ής)
Σαμουηλ Πολιτιανοῦ
Εἰωσηφ Εὐσεβίου προσή(λυτος)
κα[ὶ] Εἰούδας Θεοδώρ(ο̣υ)
καὶ 'Αντιπέος 'Ερμή(ου?)

[2] Joyce Reynolds and Robert Tannenbaum, *Jews and God-Fearers at Aphrodisias: Greek Inscriptions with Commentary* (Cambridge Philological Society, Supp. 12; Cambridge: The Cambridge Philological Society, 1987). The dimensions of the marble block are as follows: faces *a* and *c*, 45–43 cm. [w] x 280 cm. [h]; face *b*, 46–42.5 cm. [w]. Faces *a* and *b* are from different hands; the editors date face *a* only slightly later than face *b* and both to the third century (pp. 3–5, 20–22).

καὶ Σαβάθιος νεκτάρις
[?κα]ὶ Σαμο[υ]ηλ πρεσ-
βευτὴς ἱερεύς[3]

Reynolds and Tannenbaum give a tentative translation of lines 1–8:

> God our help. {Givers to/Give to/Gift to/Building for} the soup kitchen.[4] Below (are) listed the (members) of the decany of the {students/disciples/sages} of the law, also known as those who {fervently/continually} praise God, (who) erected, for the relief of suffering in the community,[5] at their personal expense, (this) memorial (building).[6]

Following the commentary of Reynolds and Tannenbaum, I offer the following tentative translation of lines 9–27:

(Margin:)
Samouel,
envoy(?),
from
Perge

Iael, {president/patron};
with (her) son Iosouas, archon (?);
Theodotos, former court employee (?), with
(his) son Hilarianos;
Samouel, head of the decany (?), proselyte;
Ioses, son of Iesseos;
Beniamin, psalm-singer (?);
good-tempered Ioudas;
Ioses, proselyte;
Sabbatios, son of Amachios,
{pious Emmonios/Emmonios, God-Fearer};
{pious Antoninos/Antoninos, God-Fearer};
Samouel, son of Politianos;
Eioseph, proselyte, son of Eusebios;
and Eioudas, son of Theodoros;
and Antipeos, son of {Hermes/Hermeas};
and sweet Sabathios;
and (?) Samouel, en-
voy (?), priest

[3] Reynolds and Tannenbaum, *Jews*, 5. For face *b*, which contains another list of names, see pp. 6–7.

[4] Reynolds and Tannenbaum suggest an alternative for line 1: "God help the {givers to/gift to/building for} the soup kitchen" (*Jews*, 41).

[5] Reynolds and Tannenbaum give an alternative for lines 6–8: "for the alleviation of grief in the community . . . (this public) tomb" (*Jews*, 41). Reynolds and Tannenbaum deserve congratulations for their care in presenting and explaining several alternative translations.

[6] Reynolds and Tannenbaum, *Jews*, 41.

Iael appears first in this list (line 9). The sons of only two persons are mentioned, Iosouas, archon (?) and son of Iael (lines 9f.), and Hilarianos, son of Theodotos (lines 11f.). The titles of Jewish leadership (president or patron, archon [?], head of the decany [?], and envoy [?]) are clustered together at the beginning.[7] These two facts—namely, the listing of only two persons' sons (and these at the beginning) and the clustering of Jewish leadership titles at the beginning—make it probable that the head of the list was a place of special honor. Notice that although Iael has a son, a spouse is not mentioned. Perhaps the spouse had died or was not as active as Iael in the leadership of the Jewish community.

Reynolds and Tannenbaum first state that the name Iael could be feminine and that the title is not an obstacle in this case, since other Jewish women of the diaspora bore "titles of high synagogue or community office," but they then suggest that the name is more probably a masculine name.[8] I have argued elsewhere that they have adduced no convincing evidence to read Iael as a masculine name.[9] Their only stated argument is that "the lists here are otherwise demonstrably and consistently masculine."[10] This argument does not hold, since women in leadership positions are by definition in the minority in male-dominated religions and societies.[11] As evidence that a masculine form of the name Ιαηλ existed, Reynolds and Tannenbaum refer to several Septuagintal manuscripts that have Ιαηλ as a masculine name in 1 Esdr 10:26, 43.[12] Against this interpretation, I argue that the Septuagintal manuscript variants inform us about practices of scribal transliteration but not about actual Jewish naming practices. The transliteration of Hebrew names in the Septuagint is extremely varied and often outright chaotic. Further, obscure manuscript variants of 1 Esdras were not as influential in the Jewish community, since they did not enjoy the same distribution as the book of Judges, in which a feminine Jael is mentioned six times.[13] The feminine Jael of Judges is referred to in postbiblical Greek, Hebrew, and Aramaic Jewish literature, including Josephus, Pseudo-Philo, rabbinic

[7] On the placement of Samouel's name in the top left margin, see Reynolds and Tannenbaum, *Jews*, 10, 30, 41f.

[8] Ibid., 41; see also 101.

[9] Bernadette J. Brooten, "The Gender of Ιαηλ in the Jewish Inscription from Aphrodisias," in *Of Scribes and Scrolls: Essays in Honor of John Strugnell*, ed. H. W. Attridge et al. (Lanham, Md.: University Press of America, 1990) 163–73.

[10] Reynolds and Tannenbaum, *Jews*, 101.

[11] See Brooten, "Gender of Ιαηλ," n. 22, for the examples of British Prime Minister Margaret Thatcher, who, with one exception, presided over all-male cabinets, and the third-century BCE Nikippe, [προ]ερανίστρια of a cultic club of Serapis worshipers, named first in a list of men.

[12] Reynolds and Tannenbaum, *Jews*, 101.

[13] Ιαηλ is the best-attested form of the name in the Septuagint in Judg 4:17, 18, 21, 22; 5:6, 24, but variants do occur. My argument is not primarily a text-critical one, but rather that the Jael of Judges is far better known than anyone in the lists in 1 Esdr 10:18–44 (= Ezra 10:18–44).

sources, and a synagogal prayer preserved in the Christian *Apostolic Constitutions;* moreover, this portion of Judges may have been read aloud in the synagogue as part of the cycle of scriptural readings. I have demonstrated that Jael was known in this period primarily as a female figure of the book of Judges and that the masculine names in the inscription include a number of well-known (not obscure) masculine biblical names.[14] Thus, it is far more plausible to assume that the Ιαηλ of this inscription was a woman than a man.

Reynolds and Tannenbaum do not state that Ιαηλ's prominent position in the inscription hinders us from taking it as feminine. Nevertheless, it is at the minimum surprising to find a Jewish woman called προστάτης at the head of a long list of Jewish men. The task of the interpreter is to face head on the surprises presented by new sources. What does προστάτης mean? Would a prominent female title-bearer have been anomalous in Roman Aphrodisias?

The Meaning of προστάτης

Several readings of προστάτης[15] make sense. The term has three general meanings: (1) leader, chief, president, presiding officer; (2) guardian, champion, patron; (3) one who stands before a deity to entreat him or her, a suppliant.[16] Jewish sources are quite in line with normal Greek usage, as a few examples can demonstrate. Josephus describes Solomon as προστάτης over the construction of the temple and over the kingdom (*Antiquities of the Jews* 7.14.10 §376). Philo says that Joseph had taken over the "guardianship and superintendence" (ἐπιμέλεια καὶ προστασία) of Egypt (*On Joseph* 157; see also 248). He speaks of the true statesman as having "superintendence and guardianship" (προστασία καὶ ἐπιμέλεια) (*On Joseph* 67). Philo says that some governors at the time of Tiberius and his father Caesar perverted their office of "guardianship and superintendence" (ἐπιμέλεια καὶ προστασία) into domination and tyranny (*Flaccus* 105). A Jewish inscription from the Via Appia in Rome refers to a holy προστάτης,[17] and another inscription from the Via Portuensis in Rome speaks of a προστάτης

[14] For references and discussion, see Brooten, "Gender of Ιαηλ," n. 29.

[15] The -ης form is not a hindrance to taking Ιαηλ as feminine. Grammatically masculine forms of titles can occur for women, e.g., Rufina, a Jew, ἀρχισυνάγωγος (*CII* 741 = *Inscriptiones graecae ad res romanas pertinentes* IV 1452); Phoebe, διάκονος (Rom 16:1). See n. 43 below.

[16] LSJ, s.v. προστάτης. In Christian usage the term can refer to ecclesiastical rulers, such as bishops; see *LPGL*, s.v. προστάτης. See the very useful survey of recent epigraphical and papyrological evidence for the term by G. H. R. Horsley, *New Documents Illustrating Early Christianity* (5 vols.; North Ryde, N.S.W.: Macquarie University, 1981–90) 4:241–44.

[17] *CII* 100: "Here lies Gais (= Gaius?), holy president/patron, who lived 72 years. In peace your sleep!" Ἐνθάδε κειτε/ Γαις προστάτης/ ὅσιος ἔζησεν/ ἔτη οβ'. Ἐν εἰρή[νῃ ἡ]/ κοίμησίς σου. Menorah at right side.

of the Agrippensians.[18] Another Jewish inscription, probably from Alexandria, employs what may be an abbreviation for προστάτης.[19] These Jewish examples confirm the plausibility of Reynolds and Tannenbaum's suggestion that προστάτης could mean either "president" of a community or "patron," as in the patrons and patronesses of Hellenistic religious societies.[20]

The editors make the intriguing proposal that the πάτελλα of line 1 (loanword from Latin *patella*, "dish," "plate," or "pan") here refers to a soup kitchen. They note that the Mishnaic Hebrew word for "dish," תַּמְחוּי, can carry the extended sense of "charitable institution."[21] The inscription could be the donative inscription set at the entrance to this soup kitchen. This can be a help in interpreting προστάτης. Iael could have been the president or patron of the soup kitchen or its governing board. If Iael was the president of the board (the decany?) that administered the soup kitchen, her duties could have included raising funds, arranging for food to be donated, seeing to its preparation, overseeing the volunteer or paid staff, identifying the persons in need, and carrying out the daily work and organization of the soup kitchen. Alternatively, she could have presided over the board (again, possibly the decany) that donated the building (if the μνῆμα of line 8 denotes a building), in which case her work could have consisted of fund-raising, negotiations concerning the plot of land (her own land?), and arrangements with the builders. If Iael was a patron, she could have donated a significant amount of money, building materials, or labor (if we are speaking of a building), or could have agreed to contribute agricultural goods or labor for the daily running of the πάτελλα.[22] If the inscription were to refer to a tomb (the more common meaning of μνῆμα), rather than to a soup kitchen, Iael's presidency or patronage would imply slightly different functions.

[18] *CII* 365: "Here lies Kailis (= Caelius?), president/patron of the Agrippensians. May (Kailis) rest in peace." 'Ενθάδε κειτε/ Καιλις προστάτης 'Αγριππη/σίων. 'Εν εἰρή/νῃ κοιμάσθω.

[19] *CII* 1447; B. Lifshitz, *Donateurs et fondateurs dans les synagogues juives* (Cahiers de la Revue Biblique 7; Paris: Gabalda, 1967) no. 98: "Artemon, (son of) Nikon, president/patron, the eleventh year, to the synagogue. . . ." 'Αρτέμων/ Νίκωνος πρ(οστατής)/ τὸ ια' (ἔτος) τῇ/ συναγωγῇ/ . . ντηχηι. (*CII* 1447 has πρ[οστατήσας].) G. H. R. Horsley gives three further examples of Jewish inscriptions with the terms προστασία or προστάτης: *I. Berenike* 17 (24 Oct., 24/5)—honoring a Roman's patronage; *SEG* 537 (Larisa)—a Jew who was an "advocate and patron"; *SEG* 969—epitaph for a Jewish man from the area of Naples, who, Horsley suggests, was either a patron or the equivalent of a gerousiarch (*New Documents* 4:242).

[20] Reynolds and Tannenbaum, *Jews,* 41. For examples of associations, see Lellia Cracco Ruggini, "Stato e associazioni professionali nell'età imperiale romana," in *Akten des VI. Internationalen Kongresses für Griechische und Lateinische Epigraphik, München 1972* (Vestigia 17; Munich: Beck, 1973) 271–311; Guido Clemente, "Il patronato nei collegia dell'impero romano," *Studi Classici e Orientali* 21 (1972) 142–229 (both articles include some references to religious associations).

[21] Reynolds and Tannenbaum, *Jews,* 26f.; on תַּמְחוּי, see, e.g., *m. Pesaḥ.* 10:1; *m. Pe'a* 8:7.

[22] These meanings of προστάτης would still hold, *mutatis mutandis,* if πάτελλα did not mean soup kitchen.

Perhaps one might object that the inscription lists Ιαηλ as a member of "the decany of the {students/disciples/sages} of the law, also known as those who {fervently/continually} praise God,"[23] and that a woman could not be called φιλομαθής within Judaism. Reynolds and Tannenbaum propose four possible meanings for οἱ φιλομαθεῖς οἱ καὶ παντευλογ(?) (lines 4f.): (1) the pious name of the synagogue, in which case the decany could be the governing body; (2) those attending weekly public lectures at the *Beth Midrash* or who study in the evenings there, the decany being the governing body or association; (3) a yeshiva; (4) a private study group, with the decany as the private association itself.[24] At this point, the commentary of Reynolds and Tannenbaum so strongly presupposes the norm of rabbinic Judaism as to preclude historical interpretations that are plausible for diaspora Judaism. Although the variety of possible meanings of the two Greek terms is well laid out and documented (including from nonrabbinic sources), rabbinic institutions of higher learning are presented as if they were normative for the diaspora. Although the language of their commentary at times seems to include women,[25] it focuses primarily on rabbinic institutions of learning for men.[26] An example of a nonrabbinic Jewish institution for the study of the Torah is the community of the Therapeutrides and Therapeutai described by Philo of Alexandria. This group of ascetic women and men, a group which, according to Philo, existed not only in Egypt but in many other places as well, devoted itself to the contemplative life and the allegorical interpretation of the law (*On the Contemplative Life* 21). Philo describes the Therapeutrides as having a "zeal and yearning for wisdom" (ζῆλος καὶ πόθος σοφίας), as spurning the pleasures of the body and desiring no mortal offspring in order to behold the doctrines of wisdom, and as having the same zeal and sense of purpose as the men (*On the Contemplative Life* 68, 32).[27] I do not mean to suggest that the Jews listed in the Aphrodisias inscription were members of this group, but only to point to it as a nonrabbinic group promoting female love of study. Since the Greek-language Jewish literature from Asia Minor, Greece, and Italy is far less extant than the rabbinic literature of Palestine and Babylonia, it may seem reasonable to interpret an

[23] Face *a*, lines 6–7; Reynolds and Tannenbaum, *Jews*, 41.

[24] Ibid., 30–34.

[25] E.g., "the clear requirement, laid down in Mishnaic times, that *every* Jew become, as far as he was able, a scholar of the Law" (Reynolds and Tannenbaum, *Jews*, 31; emphasis theirs). Do they mean that this requirement refers to *every* Jew, or only to every male Jew?

[26] Dispute concerning women's Torah study existed among the rabbis, of course; see, e.g., *m. Soṭa* 3:4 (dispute between ben Azzai and R. Eliezer on whether a man has a duty to teach his daughter the Torah).

[27] For an excellent and comprehensive study of this group, see Ross S. Kraemer, "Monastic Jewish Women in Greco-Roman Egypt: Philo Judaeus on the Therapeutrides," *Signs* 14 (1989) 342–70.

inscription from Asia Minor by drawing heavily upon rabbinic literature. But there is no reason to assume that rabbinic teachings were normative for the diaspora. Further, since rabbinic literature does not describe Jewish institutions in which a woman can be a προστάτης and one of the φιλομαθεῖς, I suggest that we draw upon rabbinic sources with extreme caution. Otherwise we miss the challenge and the surprise of this inscription.

This inscription is actually not that unusual if we see it in the contexts of (1) female leaders within Judaism, (2) ancient female donative activity within the Jewish community, and (3) female religious leadership and philanthropy in Roman Aphrodisias. If Iael was president of a Jewish religious association, she would not have been an anomaly within Judaism, since other Greek and Latin inscriptions from around the ancient Mediterranean confirm that women were heads of synagogues, elders, mothers of synagogues, leaders, and priests.[28] If Iael was primarily a patron and had donated goods or money to the Jewish institution alluded to in the inscription, she would have been in the company of other women who donated entire synagogues or parts of synagogues in this period.[29] Iael was also not an anomaly among Aphrodisian women, as the following material demonstrates.

Women's Civic and Religious Leadership in the Surrounding Culture

The inhabitants of Asia Minor were accustomed to seeing women in positions of religious and civic leadership. Inscriptions from Aphrodisias contain ample evidence that Aphrodisian women functioned as leaders in the Roman period. Attalis, daughter of Menekrates, is a good example. Inscriptions attest to the seventh, ninth, eleventh, thirteenth, and sixteenth years of her functioning as στεφανηφόρος of Aphrodisias.[30] She probably flourished at

[28] See Bernadette J. Brooten, *Women Leaders in the Ancient Synagogue: Inscriptional Evidence and Background Issues* (Brown Judaic Studies 36; Chico, Calif.: Scholars Press, 1982); Ross S. Kraemer, "A New Inscription from Malta and the Question of Women Elders in the Diaspora Jewish Communities," *HTR* 78 (1985) 431–38.

[29] See Brooten, *Women Leaders,* 157–65, for a collection of these donative inscriptions (discussion, pp. 141–44).

[30] *Monumenta Asiae Minoris antiqua* (= *MAMA*), ed. Sir William M. Calder and J. M. R. Cormack (Manchester: Manchester University Press, 1962). On the seventh year, see *MAMA* VIII, 413 (pl. 22); Théodore Reinach, *REG* 19 (1906) nos. 138–41, pp. 231–43. Two inscriptions attest to the ninth year: *MAMA* VIII, 556a (pl. 27); Reinach, *REG* 19 (1906) no. 168, pp. 272–74; and Philippe Le Bas and W. H. Waddington, *Voyage archéologique en Grèce et en Asie Mineure* (pts. 1–4 in 7 vols.; Paris: Didot, 1870) 3 (1870) (= Le Bas) no. 1634. On the eleventh year, see *MAMA* VIII, 553 (pl. 33). On the thirteenth year, see *MAMA* VIII, 554 (pl. 30); *CIG* 2829 and p. 1115; Le Bas 1630. On the sixteenth year, see *MAMA* VIII, 555 (pl. 19); Reinach, *REG* 19 (1906) no. 169, pp. 274–76; cf. Louis Robert, *BCH* 52 (1928) 411; see also *MAMA* VIII, 556b (pl. 27); Reinach, *REG* 19 (1906) no. 175, pp. 280–81. In the latter inscription the number of the term of office as στεφανηφόρος is missing.

the turn of the second to the third century and was thus a contemporary of Iael.[31] The office of στεφανηφόρος (literally, "bearer of a crown") included religious and political functions.[32] *Eponymia,* or having the year named after oneself, was associated with the office. In the case of Attalis, official inscriptions were dated by the year of her functioning as στεφανηφόρος. Typical inscriptions in which this occurs are grave markers in which the owners identify themselves and prohibit anyone else from burying someone in their grave. A typical closing to such an inscription is the following:

> A copy of this inscription has been deposited in the office in which the registry of public debtors is kept, in the eleventh term of office of Attalis, daughter of Menekrates, as στεφανηφόρος, in the fifth month.[33]

Thus, the official act was dated according to the term of the officiating στεφανηφόρος, in this case a woman, Attalis.

Tata, a leading woman of Aphrodisias involved in philanthropic activity and the support of religious and cultural events, presents a particularly interesting case. Following is an inscription honoring her:

> The council and the people and the senate have granted first honors to Tata, daughter of Diodoros, son of Diodoros (by adoption), son of Leon by birth; holy priestess of Hera for life; mother of the city; who became and remained wife of Attalos, son of Pytheas, στεφανηφόρος; (who is) also herself of foremost and illustrious stock; who served as priestess of the emperors for the second time; who twice supplied oil most abundantly for small vessels running from the bathing tubs even for the greater part of the night; who functioned as στεφανηφόρος; who sacrificed during the course of entire years for the health of the emperors; who sponsored feasts for the people which were both frequent and involved reclining dinners for the whole populace; who primarily on her own maintained the top performances in Asia in both musical and theatrical competitions and who offered to (her) native city for the neighboring towns to assemble together for the display of the performances and to celebrate (the festival) together; who spared expenses on no one's wife; loving glory; adorned with virtue (and) prudence.[34]

[31] See Otto Braunstein, *Die politische Wirksamkeit der griechischen Frau: Eine Nachwirkung vorgriechischen Mutterrechtes* (Leipzig: August Hoffmann, 1911) 53 n. 1.

[32] Ibid., 52–56. Erich Ziebarth says that the term may mean "mayor" ("etwa Bürgermeisterin") (*Kulturbilder aus griechischen Städten* [Leipzig: Teubner, 1907] 53).

[33] *MAMA* VIII, 553 (pl. 33). In a field below Eymir. Marble sarcophagus. Lines 12b–18: ταύτης/ τῆς ἐπιγραφῆς ἀντίγρα/φον ἀπετέθη εἰς τὸ/ χρεοφυλάκιον ἐπὶ στε/φανηφόρου τὸ ια' 'Ατταλίδος/ τῆς Μενεκράτους μηνὸς/(scroll) πέμπτου (leaf). The other Attalis inscriptions of this type are *MAMA* VIII, 554, 555, 556a, 556b; Le Bas 1634.

[34] Inscription *b: MAMA* VIII, 492 (pl. 35); Le Bas 1602; *CIG* 2820a. Geyre, Stadium north wall. Marble block (138 x 112 cm.) with one complete inscription (*b*) and two fragmentary inscriptions (*a* and *c*). Additional marble fragment (32 x 17 cm.) contains the ends of the first

Through Tata's financial support of religious and other civic activities, she gained power and prestige. As was the case with men, Tata's family ties and wealth gave her access to power, but she functioned as a civic leader in her own right, not simply as a daughter or a wife. The very constellation of the three inscriptions attests to this. The only stated connection between Tata's husband, Attalos (probably inscription *a*), and Tata's father, Diodoros (inscription *c*), is Tata herself. Tata's father, Diodoros, was probably (the lacunae are rather large) a member of the council, a high priest for life in the emperor cult, a gymnasiarch, and a chief magistrate; he is honored for a public largesse similar to that of Tata. Tata is thus in the tradition of the philanthropic wealth and power of her father. The inscription emphasizes that she does not merely receive her honor from her husband but is "also herself of foremost and illustrious stock." Women and men living in the city of Aphrodisias would have seen and experienced these public displays of benefaction and power. Jews would have had sufficient opportunity to know of Tata as a religious official ("holy priestess of Hera for life"; "who served as priestess of the emperors for the second time"; "who sacrificed . . . for the health of the emperors") and as a civic official (στεφανηφόρος). They may have

---

seven lines of *c*. The fragmentary inscription to the left (*a*) seems to honor Tata's husband, Attalos, while the fragmentary inscription to the right seems to honor her father, Diodoros. The inscription is probably to be dated to the late second or possibly the early third century. Inscription *b*: ἡ βουλὴ καὶ ὁ δῆμος καὶ ἡ γερο[υσία]/ ἐτείμησαν ταῖς πρώταις τειμα[ῖς]/ Τάταν Διοδώρου τοῦ Διοδώρου το[ῦ φύ]/σει Λέοντος, ἁγνὴν ἱέρειαν Ἥρας διὰ βίου,/ μητέρα πόλεως, γυναῖκα γενομένην/ καὶ μείνασαν Ἀττάλου τοῦ Πυθέου/ στεφανηφόρου, καὶ αὐτὴν γένους πρώ/του καὶ λαμπροῦ, ἱερατεύσασαν τῶν/ Σεβαστῶν ἐκ δευτέρου ἀλείψασαν/ δὶς δρακτοῖς ἐκ λουτήρων ἐπιρύτοις/ δαψιλέστατα τὸ πλεῖστον μέρος καὶ τῆς/ νυκτός, στεφανηφορήσασαν, θύσασαν/ παρ' ὅλους τοὺς ἐνιαυτοὺς ὑπὲρ τῆς ὑγή/ας τῶν Σεβαστῶν, ἑστιάσασαν τὸν δῆμον/ πλεονάκις καὶ πανδήμοις κατακλίσεσιν,/ ἔν τε τοῖς θυμελικοῖς καὶ σκηνικοῖς ἀγῶ/σιν τὰ πρωτεύοντα ἐν τῇ Ἀσίᾳ ἀκροά/ματα αὐτὴν πρώτως ἀγαγοῦσαν καὶ δεί/ξασαν τῇ πατρίδι, ὡς ἐπὶ τὴν δεῖξιν τῶν/ ἀκροαμάτων συνελθεῖν καὶ συνεορτά/σαι τὰς ἀστυγειτνιώσας πόλεις, γυναῖκα/ μηδένος ἀναλώματος φεισαμένην, φι/λόδοξον, ἀρετῇ σωφροσύνῃ κεκοσμημένην. For further bibliography on this inscription, see H. W. Pleket, *Epigraphica* (2 vols.; Leiden: Brill, 1969) vol. 2, *Texts on the Social History of the Greek World,* no. 18, pp. 31f. Pleket's collection contains thirty-two inscriptions relating to women in the Graeco-Roman world (pp. 10–41). See also R. A. Kearsley, "Asiarchs, *Archiereis,* and the *Archiereiai* of Asia," *GRBS* 27 (1986) 184.

For a fuller discussion of the Roman imperial cult, see S. R. F. Price, *Rituals and Power: The Roman imperial cult in Asia Minor* (Cambridge: Cambridge University Press, 1984). He mentions this inscription on p. 211. Price argues against seeing Roman politics, diplomacy, the military, and economics as "real," and the imperial cult as merely an ideological overlay, which was not real worship and which was not at the center of the real power of the empire. Price rather argues for a complex interweaving between religion and politics: "The imperial cult, like the cults of the traditional gods, created a relationship of power between subject and ruler. It also enhanced the dominance of local élites over the populace, of cities over other cities, and of Greek over indigenous cultures. That is, the cult was a major part of the web of power that formed the fabric of society" (p. 248). Although Price does not spell out the implications for female cultic officials, his thesis implies that the high priestesses of the imperial cult had not only a religious but also a political function.

attended the musical and theatrical events sponsored by her, and they may even have participated in the feasts, such as by partaking only of the vegetarian parts of the meal. In any case, this one example of Tata makes it implausible that Aphrodisian Jews would not have known that women could be leaders in the community.

Nor does Tata stand alone in this respect. In addition to the Aphrodisian women who bear the title στεφανηφόρος, a number bear the title "high priestess" (ἀρχιέρεια): Apphia, high priestess for life of the *divi Augusti* and priestess of Artemis; Phlabia (i.e., Flavia) Apphia, high priestess of Asia; the wife (name broken off) of Neikomachos, high priestess (presumably in the emperor cult); Ioulia Paula, high priestess; Aristoneike, high priestess and στεφανηφόρος; and Ailia Laibilla (i.e., Aelia Laevilla), high priestess of Asia.[35]

Scholars have disagreed on whether or not high priestesses of the emperor cult gained their titles as the wives of high priests[36] and, if so, whether they actually had public functions.[37] R. A. Kearsley has convincingly demonstrated

[35] Apphia: *MAMA* VIII, 478 (pl. 34); Reinach, *REG* 19 (1906) no. 38, pp. 116f. Phlabia Apphia: *MAMA* VIII, 517 (pl. 25); *CIG* 2782. Wife of Neikomachos: *MAMA* VIII, 546 (pl. 24). Ioulia Paula: *MAMA* VIII, 564 (pls. 28, 33); *CIG* 2845. Aristoneike: Le Bas 1592. Ailia Laibilla: *CIG* 2823.

[36] See, e.g., Jürgen Deininger, who argues that the high priest (ἀρχιερεύς; 'Ασιάρχης, etc.; *sacerdos;* or *flamen,* depending on the region) presided over the provincial councils (κοινά, *concilia*) during the imperial period, posits that the ἀρχιέρειαι were the wives of these politically powerful high priests. He does not produce positive evidence to support this hypothesis, but rather argues from the negative evidence: "Aus den Inschriften läßt sich grundsätzlich keine Sicherheit darüber gewinnen, ob diese Priesterinnin jeweils die Frauen von Oberpriestern waren oder nicht. Festgehalten zu werden verdient jedoch, daß es sich wohl bei keiner Provinzialpriesterin ausschließen läßt, daß sie jeweils die Frau eines Landtagsvorsitzenden war" (*Die Provinziallandtage der römischen Kaiserzeit* [Vestigia 6; Munich: Beck, 1965] 154). He refers to the *lex Narbonensis,* which contains the regulations of the *concilium* in Narbonne, Gaul, and which refers to the [*uxor fla*]*minis* (*flamen* being the Gallic Latin equivalent of the Eastern ἀρχιερεύς), and suggests that the ἀρχιέρεια was responsible for the cult of the female members of the imperial family (*Provinziallandtage* 154; see also 41, 75f.). See also David Magie, *Roman Rule in Asia Minor* (2 vols.; Princeton: Princeton University Press, 1950) 1:649 (who holds that "[t]heir duties were presumably purely honorary," but does not really argue his case); 2:1518f. n. 50 (in apparent contradiction to the above: "In most cases the woman seems actually to have been an official. In others she seems to have had the title merely because it was borne by her husband . . ."); 2:1603f. (list of high priestesses in Asia); 2:1611 (list of high priestesses in Lycia-Pamphylia); 2:1614 (reference to a priestess of Roma and Julia Augusta). See further E. Beurlier, *Essai sur le culte rendu aux empereurs romains* (Paris: Thorin, 1890) 152: "Les *Flaminicae* [the equivalent of the ἀρχιέρειαι of the Eastern provinces] sont ainsi appelées parce qu'elles sont associées au sacerdoce de leur mari."

[37] The scholars arguing that women actually carried out priestly functions respond to the arguments of their opponents, while those arguing that they were simply wives of priests do not answer their opponents. See, e.g., Robert Étienne, who suggests that there were two kinds of *flaminicae:* (1) those who were the wives of provincial priests and had a temporary function, and (2) those who were appointed by the provincial council for life. In support of his position, Étienne refers to the inscriptional evidence for the *flaminica perpetua.* He also lists those

(1) that the ἀρχιέρειαι of Asia had religious functions, as was the usual Greek practice for priestesses (including priestesses of male deities), and (2) that the term "asiarch" was not coterminous with "high priest" (as assumed by those who argue that a high priestess's asiarch husband was actually a high priest, whence she derived her title).[38] Steven J. Friesen, on the basis of a comprehensive survey of the extant epigraphic and numismatic evidence for high priestesses, also concludes that the title was functional.[39]

Women and men who attained religious and civic office were usually members of elite families who married into other elite families and who displayed their wealth through public benefactions. We cannot separate their official duties from these elite family ties and public benefactions. The Tata of the inscription above would probably have been incredulous, not to say irritated, at the question of what functions she actually had, since a number of them are expressly mentioned. The inscription emphasizes that both her family of origin and her husband were illustrious, and in this Tata is probably typical of female title-bearers. Rather than manifesting modern Western concepts of individual merit or individual duties, the Tata inscription

---

priestesses whose husbands were priests, those whose husbands were not priests, and those whose husbands' sacral status is unknown (*Le culte impérial dans la péninsule ibérique d'Auguste à Dioclétien* [Bibliothèque des Ècoles Françaises d'Athènes et de Rome 191; Paris: De Boccard, 1958] 166–75). See also J. Toutain, who points out that the [*uxor fla*]*minis* of the *lex Narbonensis* has certain obligations and privileges. Toutain notes that the documents do not imply that the wife of a provincial priest was forced to be a provincial priestess, but that she sometimes was one. He suggests that provincial priestesses were probably appointed by the provincial councils (*Les cultes païens dans l'empire romain* [1 pt. in 3 vols.; Bibliothèque de l'École des Hautes Études, Sciences Religieuses 20; Paris: Leroux, 1907–20] 1:144–48).

The question of sacerdotal functions is not laid to rest even in those cases in which a high priestess is the wife of a high priest. Ramsay MacMullen addresses himself to the problem of female religious functions: "Pierre Paris spends many pages discussing whether women in public positions actually *did* very much. If that is a real question, it is not easily answered for male magistrates and liturgists, either" ("Women in Public in the Roman Empire," *Historia: Zeitschrift für Alte Geschichte* 29 [1980] 215). MacMullen is referring to the extensive study by Pierre Paris, *Quatenus feminae res publicas in Asia Minore, Romanis imperantibus, attigerint* (Paris: Thorin, 1891). See also Anthony J. Marshall, "Roman Women and the Provinces," *Ancient Society* 6 (1975) 109–27, esp. 123–27 (epigraphical evidence cited on p. 123); and Otto Braunstein, *Die politische Wirksamkeit der griechischen Frau.*

[38] R. A. Kearsley, "Asiarchs," 183–92. Kearsley points to instances in which the wife bears a title while the husband bears no title or a different title, and to cases in which the husband bears a title while the wife does not. Kearsley gives the Aphrodisian example of *CIG* 2782 (see also *CIG* 2783; *MAMA* VIII, 517 [pl. 25]), in which Flavia Apphia is ἀρχιέρεια, while her husband is not an ἀρχιερεύς, even though the inscription has been unconvincingly restored to make him one. She also notes *CIG* 2823, in which an Aphrodisian woman is ἀρχιέρεια and her husband is only a municipal ἀρχιερεύς ("Asiarchs," 188f.).

[39] Steven J. Friesen, "Ephesus, Twice Neokoros" (Ph.D. diss., Harvard University, 1990) 106–18; see also 119–24. Friesen's original contribution to the study of high priestesses of the imperial cult is his thesis that women were admitted to the high priesthood around the second quarter of the first century CE.

and others like it bear witness to elite women and men who gained honor and prestige through skillfully using their complex webs of family wealth and connections. Riet Van Bremen suggests that the important public roles played by elite women in Greek urban society from around the second century BCE through the third century CE are to be seen "as a result of the social and ideological components of the system of euergetism."[40] Families gained and held power through their public benefactions.

Iael's office is not comparable in every respect to those of the non-Jewish Aphrodisian women described above. Nevertheless, the connection between philanthropic activity and public office may be common to both. To be sure, Tata's sponsorship of musical events and large public meals involved great sums of money and/or agricultural products, while Iael's presidency or patronage of a Jewish soup kitchen (or a burial institution) was probably relatively modest. Further, Tata's religious offices, especially her priesthood in the emperor cult, were tied into the official public life of the city, while Iael's activities would have been restricted to the Jewish community (although the beneficiaries of a soup kitchen surely included non-Jews). Nevertheless, despite the different scale, philanthropic activity and religious recognition are common to both. But would not the Jewish community have done everything possible to avoid any commonalities with a pagan priestess of Hera and of the divinized emperors? And how is a Jewish soup kitchen, harking back to such ancient Israelite traditions as helping the orphan and the widow, in any way like the self-aggrandizing efforts of an Aphrodisian elite seeking the recognition of the Roman rulers? Perhaps the philanthropy of elite Aphrodisian women and men was not only self-aggrandizement. And perhaps the Jewish community sought to be part of and to gain the recognition of Aphrodisian society, including its more prosperous parts. The presence of nine city councillors among the θεοσεβῖς listed on face *b*[41] attests to good relations between leading people of the city and the Jewish community or to Jewish representation in the city's leadership.[42]

[40] Riet Van Bremen, "Women and Wealth," in *Images of Women in Antiquity,* ed. Averil Cameron and Amélie Kuhrt (Detroit: Wayne State University Press, 1983) 237.

[41] Lines 34–38; the names are clustered together first in the list. The meaning of θεοσεβ(ε)ῖς is one of the most disputed questions about this inscription. See esp. Robert S. MacLennan and A. Thomas Kraabel, "The God-Fearers—A Literary and Theological Invention," *Biblical Archaeology Review* 12:5 (1986) 46–53, 64; Robert F. Tannenbaum, "Jews and God-Fearers in the Holy City of Aphrodite," *Biblical Archaeology Review* 12:5 (1986) 54–57; Louis H. Feldman, "The Omnipresence of the God-Fearers," *Biblical Archaeology Review* 12:5 (1986) 58–64, 66–69.

[42] Face *b* is of a different hand, but, according to Reynolds and Tannenbaum, only slightly earlier than face *a*. Therefore, I am including it in this discussion.

Conclusions

Several plausible historical reconstructions of Iael's role in the Jewish community of the Aphrodisian inscription have emerged. (1) She served as president of the governing board that built a soup kitchen (or possibly a tomb) and/or of the board that administered it; (2) she served as patron to the governing board that built a soup kitchen (or tomb) and/or of the board that administered it; her patronage included economic support. Iael was not an anomaly as a female religious leader involved in philanthropic activity; a number of leading Aphrodisian women were cultically and philanthropically prominent in this period. Nor was Iael anomalous in the Jewish community at large, since Jewish women elsewhere both held office and made donations to the synagogue.[43]

[43] A separate study is required to elucidate the implications of the use of προστάτης for Rom 16:2, in which Paul calls Phoebe προστάτις. See n. 15 above.

12

Adolph Harnack's "The Mission and Expansion of Judaism": Christianity Succeeds Where Judaism Fails

SHAYE J. D. COHEN

IN 1902, ADOLF HARNACK[1] (1851–1930) published his *Die Mission und Ausbreitung des Christentums in den ersten drei Jahrhunderten* (in English: *The Mission and Expansion of Christianity in the First Three Centuries*). The book added to the already immense prestige of the author and went through four editions, the last of them published in Leipzig by J. C. Hinrichs in 1924. English translations of the first and second editions were published in England and the United States in 1904–5 and 1908.[2] In many respects the book still dominates the field; it was the first modern detailed study of its subject and has not yet been replaced.[3] The opening chapter of the book, a study of the expansion of Judaism in the diaspora, deserves attention because it well illustrates how Christian theology can sometimes govern the interpretation of Jewish history.[4]

[1] Or, after his ennoblement in 1914, Adolf von Harnack. For a biography, see Agnes von Zahn-Harnack, *Adolf von Harnack* (2nd ed.; Berlin: de Gruyter, 1951). For discussions of Harnack in English, see G. Wayne Glick, *The Reality of Christianity: A Study of Adolf von Harnack as Historian and Theologian* (New York: Harper & Row, 1967); and *Adolf von Harnack: Liberal Theology at its Height*, ed. H. Martin Rumschiedt (London: Collins, 1989).

[2] Adolf Harnack, *The Mission and Expansion of Christianity in the First Three Centuries*, trans. James D. Moffatt (New York: Putnam; London: Williams & Norgate).

[3] In 1984 the fourth German edition was reprinted by VMA-Verlag in Wiesbaden.

[4] On the anti-Jewish animus of classic German scholarship on Judaism, see George F. Moore, "Christian Writers on Judaism," *HTR* 14 (1921) 197–254; E. P. Sanders, *Paul and Palestinian Judaism* (Philadelphia: Fortress Press, 1977) 33–59; Charlotte Klein, *Anti-Judaism in Christian Theology* (London: SPCK, 1978) with the thorough review by George W. E. Nickelsburg, *RSRev* 4 (1978) 161–68; Shaye J. D. Cohen, "The Political and Social History of the Jews in

The thesis of the chapter is that the expansion of the Jewish diaspora prepared the way for the growth of Christianity. Harnack argues that there were Jews in most provinces of the Roman Empire (p. 5);[5] that they were especially numerous in Syria, Egypt, Rome, and Asia Minor (pp. 6–9); and that their numbers, although difficult to estimate precisely, amounted to some four or four and a half million, out of a total population of some fifty-four to sixty million in the Roman Empire (pp. 9–13). Such enormous growth in Jewish numbers implies that Judaism must have engaged in missionary activity and that it did so successfully (p. 13). Harnack then gives a brief account of Jewish missionary theology (pp. 13–14) and argues that proselytes were attracted by Judaism's morality and philosophic character (pp. 15–17). The Christian mission owed its success in large measure to what it inherited from the Jewish mission (pp. 17–20). Jewish syncretism and "concentration on great principles" also helped prepare the way (pp. 20–21). The chapter concludes with an appendix on the ambiguous attitude of Palestinian Judaism toward the mission and toward the universal impulses of Judaism (pp. 21–23).

All of this may seem rather innocuous, the dry stuff of German scholarship. Indeed, in the preface to the fourth edition Harnack writes that the book "contains virtually no hypotheses but [merely] assembles facts."[6] Whether Harnack's tongue was in his cheek when he wrote those words, I do not know, but *The Mission and Expansion of Christianity,* no less than all his other works, contains its share of assumptions, prejudices, and hypotheses. In all his writings Harnack was a theological historian (or a historical theologian), and his description of diaspora Judaism is a decidedly Christian (liberal Lutheran) description.

According to Harnack the Greek-speaking Judaism of the diaspora was a *praeparatio evangelica* in two senses: first, through an inner transformation Judaism was becoming more universal and less national, more philosophical and less ritualistic; second, through its propaganda and mission Judaism was spreading the knowledge of God and the Bible among the Gentiles, thereby predisposing them to an acceptance of Christianity. For Harnack these processes are interrelated and virtually synonymous. The Jewish mission to

Greco-Roman Antiquity," in *Early Judaism and Its Modern Interpreters,* ed. R. A. Kraft and G. W. E. Nickelsburg (The Bible and Its Modern Interpreters 2; Atlanta: Scholars Press, 1986) 33–56, esp. 34–37. Cf. A. T. Kraabel, "Greeks, Jews, and Lutherans in the Middle Half of Acts," *HTR* 79 (1986) 147–57; and John J. Collins, "Judaism as *Praeparatio Evangelica* in the Work of Martin Hengel," *RSRev* 15 (1989) 226–28.

[5] The page numbers refer to the fourth German edition. When citing Harnack in English, I base my translation on Moffatt's and tacitly adjust it to match the German.

[6] "Nachrühmen darf ich dem Werk, daß es so gut wie keine Hypothesen enthält, sondern Tatsachen zusammenstellt."

the Gentiles was a vital component of Judaism's increased universalism, and the main goal of the universal spirit was to bring the knowledge of God to all humanity. The term that Harnack uses repeatedly to describe these twin processes is *Entschränkung*, a word for which there is no precise English equivalent but which perhaps is best rendered "unfettering" or "release from constraints."[7] The first chapter of the book is entitled "Das Judentum, seine Verbreitung und Entschränkung," "Judaism, Its Expansion and Its Release from Its Constraints."[8] The application of this term to Judaism seems to have been Harnack's coinage.[9] By its deemphasis of ritual, its concentration on moral and philosophic truths, and its outreach to the Gentiles, Judaism was undergoing *Entschränkung* and thereby preparing both itself and the world for Christianity.

Harnack's account of Jewish missionary theology shows how Judaism's "inner transformation" was a preparation for the church (p. 14; the emphasis is Harnack's):

> [Judaism's missionary success is] proof that *Judaism, as a religion, was already releasing itself from its constraints*[10] *through external influences and an inner transformation*, with the result that it had become a cross between a national religion and a world-religion[11] (confession and church). The Jew felt proud that he had something to say and was compelled to bring to the world which concerned all humanity—*the one spiritual God, creator of heaven and earth, and his holy moral law*—and it was from this consciousness (Rom. ii. 19f.) that he felt missions to be a duty. *The Jewish propaganda in the empire was primarily the proclamation of the one God, of his moral law, and of his judgment;* to this everything else became secondary.

"The proclamation of the one God and his moral law" would become even more central for Christianity than for Judaism, especially the ethical and cultural Christianity of the sort that is given expression in Harnack's own *Das Wesen des Christentums* published in 1900, only two years before *Mission and Expansion*.

I do not dispute Harnack's right to believe that Christianity is superior to Judaism and all other religions,[12] or to construct a Christian theology to his

[7] "Emancipation" might have served except that it is a technical term with other meanings. "Unfettering" is a wonderful translation suggested to me by my friend Robert Schine, but it is somewhat awkward as a noun.

[8] Moffatt fails completely with his rendering "Judaism: Its Diffusion and Limits."

[9] Emil Schürer believes that "Entschränkung des Judentums" is a coinage of Harnack (*Geschichte des jüdischen Volkes im Zeitalter Jesu Christi* [3 vols.; 3rd ed.; Leipzig: Hinrichs, 1909] 3:163 n. 44).

[10] "Entschränkt," translated by Moffatt "blossoming out."

[11] "Volksreligion" . . . "Weltreligion."

[12] Harnack had no doubt that Christianity is the only real religion; for this tendency in

liking, but I do dispute his right to inflict Christian theology on Jewish history.[13] Many scholars, both before and after Harnack, have argued that diaspora Judaism was dominated by a missionary impulse and a universalist tendency,[14] but the view's popularity cannot change the fact that it is based on remarkably little evidence. The argument from the numerical expansion of Judaism (7 percent of the population, Harnack says) is as weak as all other arguments from ancient population statistics, which are notoriously unreliable.[15] The entire calculation rests on Philo's statement that the Jewish population of Egypt amounted to one million, but the context of that statement shows that it may well have been a gross exaggeration.[16] Judaism certainly experienced geographical expansion during the Hellenistic and Roman periods, but the degree of its numerical expansion is unknown and unknowable.

As for the rest of Harnack's construct, a new consensus is beginning to emerge according to which the Greek Jewish literature of antiquity was not propaganda directed to outsiders, diaspora Judaism was not a missionary religion, and Jews were not seeking to find the "essence" of their religion in

---

German Protestant thought, see Claude Welch, *Protestant Thought in the Nineteenth Century* (2 vols.; New Haven: Yale University Press, 1972, 1985) 2:125–26. Note especially Adolf Harnack, *Reden und Aufsätze* (2 vols.; 2nd ed.; Giessen: Töpelmann, 1906) 2:110, a lecture entitled "Grundsätze der Evangelisch-Protestantischen Mission" and delivered on 26 September 1900 to the general assembly of the German Evangelical Protestant Missionary Society, "die unerschütterliche Überzeugung unserer Missionspflicht fließt aus der Erkenntnis, daß das Christentum nicht eine Religion neben anderen, sondern daß es die Religion selbst ist, daß daher erst in ihr und durch sie jedes Volk und die Menschenheit das wird, was sie sein sollen."

[13] My colleague Prof. David Lotz of Union Theological Seminary, to whom I am much indebted for a careful reading and critique of this essay, objects to this formulation, suggesting that Harnack was not so much "inflicting Christian theology on Jewish history" as interpreting Jewish history in the framework of nineteenth-century German historicism. Perhaps such a formulation would be fairer to Harnack, but his Christian perspective—which Harnack himself would clearly acknowledge and defend as *true*—remains all the same.

[14] The fullest recent statement is Dieter Georgi, *The Opponents of Paul in Second Corinthians* (Philadelphia: Fortress Press, 1986) 83–151, who is much indebted to Harnack.

[15] In the foreword (p. v) Harnack comments that the value of ancient population statistics is "useless." Why are the Jewish numbers better than the others?

[16] Philo, *Against Flaccus* 6.43. P. M. Fraser calls Philo's statement "very imprecise, but there is no better figure" (*Ptolemaic Alexandria* [3 vols.; Oxford: Clarendon, 1972] 2:164 n. 315). Harold Hegermann says that "the figure given by Philo is clearly meant as a rough total with a certain inherent tendency towards exaggeration" (*Cambridge History of Judaism II: The Hellenistic Age*, ed. W. D. Davies and L. Finkelstein [Cambridge: Cambridge University Press, 1989] 149). Emil Schürer calls the figure "rhetorical exaggeration" (*The History of the Jewish People in the Age of Jesus Christ 175 B.C.–35 A.D.*, rev. and ed. Geza Vermes, Fergus Millar, Martin Goodman et al. [3 vols. in 4; Edinburgh: T. & T. Clark, 1973–1986] 3:44). The original Schürer (3:37–38) believed Philo but ignored Harnack's other calculations. In fact, neither the old Schürer nor the new attempts to calculate the number of Jews in antiquity. Presumably they both recognized that such an attempt would be futile. Contrast the certainty of Georgi, *Opponents*, 83–84.

universal ethics. The shift in scholarly consensus is evident in the contrast between the old Schürer and the new. Harnack's colleague Emil Schürer (1844–1910),[17] in his famous *The History of the Jewish People in the Age of Jesus Christ,* believed that diaspora Judaism was missionary in character and universalist in tendency and that Greek Jewish literature was propaganda for the Jewish cause, but almost all the passages of his book that express this view have been excised or muted in the revision of 1986.[18] This change in scholarly perspective is the result not of new discoveries but of a new sensitivity in the study of ancient Judaism. Elsewhere I have attempted to demonstrate that there simply is insufficient evidence to prove that Judaism in antiquity was a missionary religion, at least a missionary religion as understood by Harnack.[19] Matt 23:15 is the only ancient text that explicitly ascribes a missionary policy to a Jewish group, but that passage, whether exaggerated or not, does not help Harnack much because it is speaking of the Pharisees of Palestine. According to Harnack (and Schürer[20]), diaspora Jews were the missionaries, while Palestinian Jews, especially the "strict" Pharisees, were opposed to conversion—or at least not comfortable with it. But this view slights the evidence that exists in favor of evidence that does not. The depiction of diaspora Jews as proto-Christian missionaries and of Pharisaic Jews as narrow-minded ritualists, derives, of course, from a Christian reading of Jewish history.

Harnack's theological prejudice goes much further. Diaspora Judaism's mission to the Gentiles and anticipation of some of the central teachings of Christianity not only prepare the world for salvation through grace and faith but also demonstrate Judaism's inadequacy and failure. *Entschränktes Judentum* might have succeeded in conquering the world had it been able to resolve its tension between being a national religion and a world religion (pp. 17–18):

> [There is] one vital omission in the Jewish missionary preaching: viz., that no Gentile, in the first generation at least, can become a real son of Abraham. His rank before God remains inferior. Thus it also remains very

[17] Schürer and Harnack were collegial friends; Harnack's obituary of Schürer appeared in the 1910 volume of the *Theologische Literaturzeitung,* a journal they coedited for many years.

[18] Schürer, *Geschichte* 3:3, 162–63, 420–23, 545, 553–54, 595, 610–11, 618; contrast the new Schürer, *History* 3:4, 159–60, 470–73, 609, 617, 656, 679, 690. The shift is apparent also in German scholarship; contrast, e.g., Peter Dalbert, *Die Theologie der hellenistisch-jüdischen Missionsliteratur* (Hamburg: H. Reich, 1954) with Karl-Wilhelm Niebuhr, *Gesetz und Paränese: Katechismusartige Weisungsreihen in der frühjüdischen Literatur* (WUNT 28; Tübingen: Mohr, 1987).

[19] Shaye J. D. Cohen, "Was Judaism in Antiquity a Missionary Religion?" in *Assimilation, Acculturation, and Accommodation,* ed. Menahem Mor.

[20] Schürer, *Geschichte* 3:162, a view that should have been deleted from the new Schürer (3:159).

> doubtful in what measure the proselyte—to say nothing of the "God-Fearer"—will have a share in the glorious promises of the future. The religion which will repair this omission will drive the Jewish mission from the field. When it fully proclaims that the last will be first, and when it explains that freedom from the Law is the normal and higher life, and that the observance of the ceremonial Law is at best a thing to be tolerated and no more, it will win thousands where the previous missionary preaching won but hundreds.

Judaism is Christianity *manqué*. It tried to conquer the world, but, hobbled by its ethnocentrism and (later) by its ritualism, was doomed to failure. The fact that Harnack could not quote a single piece of evidence to prove either that the Greek-speaking Jews of the diaspora sought in the pre-eschatological present to conquer the hearts and minds of the world or that, having decided to do so, they were hampered by their own inability to treat proselytes as equals[21]—this failure did not stop Harnack. His theological history was (at least here) more theology than history, and a theologian does not need footnotes. The following paragraph is certainly not history (pp. 76–77):

> By its rejection of Jesus, the Jewish people disowned its calling and brought on itself its own death-blow; its place was taken by the new People, the Christians; it appropriated the whole tradition of Judaism; whatever was useless in it was reinterpreted or allowed to drop. . . . Gentile Christianity brought a process to completion which had in fact commenced long since in a part of Judaism—the release of Judaism from its constraints and its transformation to a world religion.[22]

[21] The statement "No Gentile, in the first generation at least, can become a real son of Abraham. His rank before God remains inferior" seems to derive from Schürer, *Geschichte* 3:163 (= new Schürer 3:160), "Wenn die Heiden durch ihre Bekehrung zum Judentum auch nicht Vollbürger in Israel wurden. . . ." On p. 187 (corresponding to new Schürer, 176) Schürer explains further, ". . . im weßentlichen die Proselyten in bezug auf Pflichten und Rechte doch als den geborenen Israeliten gleichstehend betrachtet werden. Die Kluft freilich, die zwischen einem geborenen Kinde Abrahams und einem Nichtabrahamiden durch die Geburt begründet war, konnte doch niemals überbrückt werden." Schürer then demonstrates that in (some strands of) rabbinic law the proselyte never achieved equality with the native born. (In the new Schürer [p. 176] the first of the two sentences just quoted is modified and the second is omitted, thus producing a contradiction between pp. 160 and 176.) Harnack would have read the 1898 edition of Schürer pp. 114 and 134, but the only evidence that Schürer quotes for the inequality of the proselyte is rabbinic, which does not help Harnack's thesis at all. Philo *Life of Moses* 1.27 §147 might support Harnack's case.

[22] "Das jüdische Volk hat durch die Verwerfung Jesu seinen Beruf verleugnet und sich selbst den Todesstoß versetzt; an seine Stelle rückt das neue Volk der Christen; es übernimmt die gesamte Überlieferung des Judentums; was unbrauchbar in derselben ist, wird umgedeutet oder fallen gelassen . . . das Heidenchristentum führt doch nur einen Prozeß zu Ende der in einem Teile des Judentums bereits längst begonnen hatte—die Entschränkung der jüdischen Religion und ihre Transformation zur Weltreligion." See too the introduction to the fourth

The *Das Wesen des Christentums* has a similar passage,[23] and so does the fourth edition (1909) of the *Dogmengeschichte:*[24]

> [The Church] is the final development of the Synagogue itself, insofar as the Synagogue had extended itself throughout the world and by stripping away its outer shell had established itself as a world religion. . . . [The Synagogue] demonstrated that her strength was insufficient, and that she had undertaken propaganda with a not entirely good conscience, because she was always compelled to make concessions which she really could not make. Thus in the end she turned back from the attempts to be a world religion in order to be a national religion of the strictest sort.

This is *Dogma,* not *Geschichte.* The theory that diaspora Judaism was characterized by missionary activity and universalist trends is an integral part of a larger and decidedly Christian conception of ancient Judaism, in which Judaism is viewed not only as a preparation for the church but also as Christianity *manqué.* Such a conception may have a place in Christian theology but not in Jewish history.[25] The diverse attitudes of the Judaisms of antiquity toward Gentiles, converts, and conversion, and the history of Jewish expansion, require renewed investigation.[26]

German edition (p. 2): "Die Christliche Religion . . . erscheint als die entschränkte und dadurch vollendete jüdische Religion."

[23] See *Das Wesen des Christentums* (Leipzig: Hinrichs, 1900; reprint, Stuttgart: Klotz, 1950) 104 = *What Is Christianity?* (New York: Harper Torchbooks, 1957) 174. Note again the use of the phrase "Entschränkung der jüdischen Religion."

[24] Adolf Harnack, *Lehrbuch der Dogmengeschichte* (3 vols.; Tübingen: Mohr, 1931; reprint of the fourth edition of 1909) 3:132.

[25] See A. T. Kraabel, "The Roman Diaspora: Six Questionable Assumptions," *JJS* 33 (1982) 445–64 = *Essays in Honour of Yigael Yadin.* Harnack's portrait of Roman paganism is to some extent as artificial as his portrait of Judaism; see Ramsay MacMullen, *Paganism in the Roman Empire* (New Haven: Yale University Press, 1981) 206 n.16. Many Jewish writers in both the first part of this century (notably Moritz Friedländer and G. Klein) and later endorsed the idea that Judaism was once a missionary religion with a universalist impulse. The idea was so well suited to their own apologetic and/or reform tendencies that its Christian origins were ignored. This subject deserves a separate study. See now Scot McKnight, *A Light among the Gentiles* (Minneapolis: Fortress Press, 1991).

[26] Lest I be misunderstood I would like to state that nothing I have read leads me to think that Harnack was an "anti-Semite." An "anti-Semite" could not have written what Harnack wrote in *Mission* (p. 76): "Eine solche Ungerechtigkeit wie die der Heidenkirche gegenüber dem Judentum ist in der Geschichte fast unerhört." Harnack, like Schürer, Wellhausen, Bousset, and virtually every other German liberal Protestant academic of his era, had no doubt that Judaism was much inferior to Christianity. Theodor Mommsen thought that the *Judenfrage* should be solved by the conversion of the Jews to Christianity, and I suspect that Harnack would have agreed. This is not anti-Semitism; this is Christianity.

PART 4

New Testament

13

The Q Trajectory: Between John and Matthew via Jesus

JAMES M. ROBINSON

. . . the problem of the *continuity* between Jesus and the community, i.e. the basic problem of New Testament theology as a whole . . .[1]

HELMUT KOESTER IS CLEARLY the most creative of the younger generation of pupils of Rudolf Bultmann, those who completed their doctorates under him in Marburg after World War II, in distinction from the older generation between the wars. Koester began his academic career in Heidelberg, as Dozent under the patronage of one of the older Bultmannians, Günther Bornkamm, who with his numerous students formed what one might call the central strand of the Bultmannian school. But Koester soon moved from Heidelberg to Harvard University and subsequently resisted the temptation to return to Heidelberg as Bornkamm's successor. Koester has thus combined the German *Gründlichkeit* of the Marburg and Heidelberg contexts in which he was formed with the openness and creativeness of the Harvard and American context in which he has flourished.

The Bultmannian impetus, though it has largely died out in Germany, has continued in America—and, of course, first of all in the steady stream of highly gifted and thoroughly trained Harvard graduates who by now dominate the American scene in New Testament studies. Yet the impact of Koester's work has extended far beyond the circle of his actual students. For one of the growing edges of American New Testament scholarship, most visible in the Jesus Seminar of the Westar Institute and the Q Seminar of the Society of Biblical Literature, has built on creative insights he developed on the basis of his Bultmannian heritage.

[1] Hans Conzelmann, "Gegenwart und Zukunft in der synoptischen Tradition," *ZTK* 54 (1957) 279.

Such a sweeping panorama, painted with too broad a brush, needs of course to be nuanced and made specific, in order to clarify precisely where it is and is not fully valid. The present essay is intended to trace only a single strand, which is nonetheless central and of major importance.

Albert Schweitzer's Apocalyptic Paradigm

Albert Schweitzer championed apocalyptic as a new paradigm in terms of which Jesus and primitive Christianity became more intelligible than they were on the previous model of ethical idealism implemented as the social gospel. The power of Schweitzer's position lay largely in his posture as the inevitable outcome of the preceding century of critical scholarship ("from Reimarus to Wrede"). Actually, it was only after publishing his own solution to the problem of the historical Jesus that Schweitzer turned to studying the history of the problem, which then, not by coincidence but of necessity, vindicated his solution. That this thesis was foisted upon the evidence has gone largely unnoticed, since no one has controlled the literature to the extent Schweitzer did.

Schweitzer's schematization of the quest of the historical Jesus was in terms of three decisive either-or decisions reached in the 1830s, 1860s, and 1890s:

> [David Friedrich] Strauss posed the first: Either purely historical or purely supernatural. The Tübingen School and [Heinrich Julius] Holtzmann worked out the second: Either Synoptic or Johannine. Now we have the third: Either eschatological [Johannes Weiss and Albert Schweitzer] or uneschatological.[2]

Schweitzer's tendentiousness is evident already in the way he posed the first either-or alternative. Actually Strauss had transcended a standoff between the "historical" interpretation of the rationalists and the "supernatural" interpretation of the conservatives, by advocating the "mythical" interpretation. On occasion Schweitzer did formulate Strauss's alternative correctly: "Myth or history."[3] But, since neither alternative fitted Schweitzer's own, he actually modulated out of this either-or dilemma to the

[2] Albert Schweitzer, *Geschichte der Leben-Jesu-Forschung* (Tübingen: Mohr, 1913), second revised edition of *Von Reimarus zu Wrede: Eine Geschichte der Leben-Jesu-Forschung* (Tübingen: Mohr, 1906). The sixth edition of 1951 is cited here (p. 232). A seventh, two-volume paperback edition appeared in 1966. Eng. trans. of the first German edition: *The Quest of the Historical Jesus: A Critical Study of Its Progress from Reimarus to Wrede* (London: Macmillan, 1910), first Macmillan Paperback Edition (New York: Macmillan, 1961; fifth printing 1968) cited here (p. 238).

[3] *Geschichte*, 115; *Quest*, 113.

Hegelian both-and model, with Strauss becoming the "synthesis" of the supernatural and the historical.[4]

Strauss's position can be described as the "synthesis" only as a combination of supernaturalism's insistence that the point of the text is to affirm the supernatural and rationalism's insistence that this supernatural point is nonhistorical, from which Strauss's mythical position results. But Schweitzer's own solution was a converse synthesis, a combination of supernaturalism's insistence on abnormal conduct being historical, and rationalism's insistence that the historical is not miraculous, from which Schweitzer's apocalyptic history resulted. Schweitzer derived Jesus' abnormal conduct not from any miraculous powers but from Jesus' apocalyptic ideology. Thus he was able to rescue the narrative's historicity without recourse to some modern, often-ridiculous rationalization, as did the rationalists, but rather by making the events intelligible as the conscious planning of a somewhat ridiculous apocalypticist.

Schweitzer conceded that he made of Strauss's position "something different from what it was for his contemporaries," in that Strauss was "the prophet of a scholarship to come" that would discover "a Jewish Messianic pretender who lived in a purely eschatological world of thought."[5] It is this "something different" that leads directly to Schweitzer's position, since it is simply his position projected back onto Strauss.

By turning Strauss on his head Schweitzer could claim him as his own: "Thus the terrain was prepared on which research today operates."[6] Actually, Strauss's mythical interpretation points not to Schweitzer's apocalyptic historical Jesus but rather to Rudolf Bultmann's abandoning of the quest of the historical Jesus in favor of the demythologization of the kerygmatic text, whose existential meaning, rather than the historical Jesus, was to become the essence of Christianity.

Strauss's mythical interpretation laid the groundwork for twentieth-century form criticism's skepticism about the historicity of most Jesus traditions, a skepticism Schweitzer himself recognized in his own day as unfavorable to his own apocalyptic solution. Schweitzer is in fact the last stage in the reaction against Strauss, an effort to rescue the historicity of the narrative to an almost gullible extent.

The second either-or decision, "either Synoptic or Johannine," had been decided in favor of the Synoptics, in view of the theory that the Synoptics are historically more reliable because they rest upon two early sources, Mark and Q.

Schweitzer could only endorse this decision, since the Gospel of John is

[4] *Geschichte,* 82; *Quest,* 80.
[5] *Geschichte,* 97; *Quest,* 95.
[6] *Geschichte,* 85; *Quest,* 84.

the least apocalyptic of the canonical Gospels. But he could not accept the justification for this decision, namely, that Matthew and Luke are secondary conflations of Mark and Q. For neither Mark nor Q provides an adequate basis for his solution, which depends primarily on the Gospel of Matthew, seen not as a secondary conflation but as a primary and historically reliable source in its own right.

Schweitzer's own innovation had been to move beyond Johannes Weiss's apocalyptic interpretation of Jesus' sayings, in order to show how the apocalyptic sayings explain the narrative in which they are imbedded: Jesus' action was motivated by the same apocalypticism that came to expression in his sayings. But Q, like Weiss, was limited to the sayings, and Mark had too little by way of sayings to justify the apocalyptic interpretation of the action (especially since Schweitzer recognized that the Markan apocalypse did not go back to Jesus). Protestant liberalism had hence succeeded in reading a modern psychology rather than a Jewish apocalypticism into the Markan narratives.[7]

The most important instance of the intertwining of Jesus' sayings and actions is put together by Schweitzer as follows: Jesus' identification of himself as the apocalyptic Son of man is "for us the great fact of His self-consciousness."[8] The most important saying is Matt 10:23, ". . . you will not have gone through all the towns of Israel before the Son of man comes."[9] But this is not in Mark, and perhaps not even in Q (since it is not in Luke). Yet it is Schweitzer's key to the mission discourse, with its message: "The kingdom of God has drawn near" (Matt 10:7, derived from Q 10:9). After sending the disciples out, Jesus actually never expected to see them again until after the parousia.[10] The return of the disciples (Mark 6:30) was the first time Jesus was forced out of his dogmatic obsession and made to face up to reality. Thus Schweitzer pulled together a mosaic from various Synoptic sources and elevated this secondary mosaic to a primary causal connection that should explain historically Jesus' odd behavior.

Yet Schweitzer could not argue the historicity of this causal nexus in terms of its disparate pre-Synoptic sources, but had to maintain the historicity of Matthew's own mosaic: "Without Matt. 10 and 11 everything remains enigmatic."[11] But even Matthew left out Mark's return of the disciples that triggered the encounter with reality and hence the march on Jerusalem. "The Life of Jesus cannot be arrived at by following the arrangement of a single Gospel, but only on the basis of the tradition which is preserved more

[7] *Geschichte,* 407; *Quest,* 360.
[8] *Geschichte,* replaced after the first edition (p. 363) by an expanded text; *Quest,* 367.
[9] *Geschichte,* 407; *Quest,* 359–60.
[10] *Geschichte,* 431; *Quest,* 386.
[11] *Geschichte,* 407; *Quest,* 360.

or less faithfully in the earliest pair of Synoptic Gospels."[12] That is to say, Schweitzer built his apocalyptic life of Jesus on Matthew and Mark, but only by disregarding the classical solution to the Synoptic problem that gave to the Synoptics their priority as historical sources. Thus he had no moral claim to the advance marked by the second either-or decision, even though he was a pupil of Heinrich Julius Holtzmann in Strassburg.

The third either-or decision was this: "either eschatological or uneschatological." But alongside of this either-or alternative Schweitzer put another:

> One must either be quite sceptical, as was Bruno Bauer, and contest equally all reported facts and connections in Mark; or, if one proposes to build a historical Life of Jesus on Mark, one must recognize the Gospel as a whole as historical, in view of its connections running through the whole material.[13]

Schweitzer considered the renewed skepticism of his day to be merely a desperate effort to avoid the inescapable eschatological conclusion: "But what survives as historical in the Gospels for the main stream of theology, if it considers itself obliged to sacrifice hand and foot and eye because of the offense of pure eschatology?"[14] Thus Schweitzer merged the two decisions into one:

> There is either the eschatological solution, which then at one stroke elevates the unsoftened, disconnected and contradictory Marcan presentation as such to the status of history; or there is the literary solution, which regards the dogmatic and foreign element as the earliest evangelist's interpolation into the tradition about Jesus and thus eliminates from the historical life of Jesus his Messianic claim as well. *Tertium non datur.*[15]

Rather than being scared off by such a heretical-sounding outcome as the denial that Jesus claimed to be the Messiah, critical scholarship of the twentieth century has in fact built upon the three either-or decisions reached by the nineteenth century: The canonical Gospels are in their primary intent mythical (we have become accustomed to saying "kerygmatic") rather than historical. What can be known about the historical Jesus lies behind the Synoptics, in Mark and Q, more than behind John. But one must be skeptical as to the historicity even of the Synoptic Gospels, since, as form criticism insisted, they are primarily witnesses to the life of the primitive church and only secondarily witnesses to the life of Jesus.

Yet with regard to the other either-or decision that Schweitzer merged

[12] *Geschichte,* 441; *Quest,* 394.
[13] *Geschichte,* 338; *Quest,* 307–8.
[14] *Geschichte,* 256 (cf. 597); *Quest,* 265.
[15] *Geschichte,* 375; *Quest,* 337.

with the decision concerning historical versus skeptical—namely, eschatological versus uneschatological—the twentieth century has in fact followed a sort of *tertium,* even though Schweitzer had warned: *non datur:* Although a messianic self-consciousness is often no longer ascribed to Jesus, his emphatic reference to an apocalyptic Son of Man other than himself, and hence his basically apocalyptic orientation, has been maintained throughout the first half of the century. Schweitzer's thesis that the more skeptical the less apocalyptic has been ignored.

But then when Jesus' expectation of an apocalyptic Son of Man other than himself also came to be questioned in the last half of the century, Matt 10:23 and all, the apocalyptic organizing principle for understanding Jesus was decisively undermined. A new paradigm is needed.

Philipp Vielhauer's Elimination of the Son of Man

Rudolf Bultmann followed the dominant liberal Protestant view of his day in maintaining that Jesus spoke of a future apocalyptic Son of Man, though not identifying himself with that figure. Yet, by the end of Bultmann's career, a shift away from this apocalypticism, the temporal nearness of the kingdom, was well under way, even within his own school. Werner Georg Kümmel noted this anomaly as follows:

> Rudolf Bultmann introduces the description of Jesus' proclamation at the beginning of his *Theology of the New Testament* with the following statements: "The dominant concept of Jesus' message is the *Reign of God* (βασιλεία τοῦ θεοῦ). Jesus proclaims its immediately impending irruption, now already making itself felt. Reign of God is an eschatological concept. It means the regime of God which will destroy the present course of the world. . . ." This basically futuristic-eschatological understanding of Jesus' message, for which J. Weiss and A. Schweitzer had laid the groundwork, seems to Bultmann so self-evident that he adduces no proof of it and mentions no contrary opinions. And yet this view, according to which Jesus proclaimed the temporal nearness of the coming of the Reign of God, has always met with serious opposition and in the last few years has again been energetically disputed.[16]

[16] W. G. Kümmel, "Die Naherwartung in der Verkündigung Jesu," in *Zeit und Geschichte: Dankesgabe an Rudolf Bultmann zum 80. Geburtstag,* ed. E. Dinkler (Tübingen: Mohr-Siebeck, 1964) 31–46; reprinted in *Heilsgeschehen und Geschichte* (Marburger Theologische Studien 3; Marburg: Elwert, 1965) 351–63; Eng. trans., "Eschatological Expectation in the Proclamation of Jesus," in *The Future of Our Religious Past: Essays in Honour of Rudolf Bultmann,* ed. J. M. Robinson (London: SCM; New York/Evanston/San Francisco/London: Harper & Row, 1971) 29–48 (here 29).

Kümmel himself could hardly understand this departure from standard procedure and proceeded to refute it by presenting proof for the authenticity of sayings containing the imminent expectation: Q 10:9 (in the wording of Matt 10:7; Mark 1:15 is at least partially edited by the church); Mark 9:1; 13:28–29, 30; Luke 18:2–8a; Matt 10:23b.

The fact that this departure from the established critical view took place even within the Bultmannian movement may nonetheless be due to Bultmann himself. His existentialistic interpretation assumed a futuristic eschatological meaning of Jesus' preaching only on the surface level of the mythological language, for the demythologized existential meaning applies to the present. Even eschatological existence refers to the present, though this present is called eschatological because it is lived out of the future. Yet this future out of which the present is lived is not a duration of time that will fill a segment of time sometime in the future, but rather refers to the futures or options that one may actualize right now through an act of existential decision. Thus Bultmann recognized that though Jesus talked about the future and in this sense was eschatological or even an apocalypticist, the meaning of that futuristic talk had to do with the openness of every present moment to free decision, to choose a future to constitute one's being in the present. This focusing of the meaning of Jesus' message on the present, though at the hermeneutical level rather than on the usual exegetical level, may nonetheless have made possible the exegetical advances that did take place in the left wing of his school.

Philipp Vielhauer had taken the first major step within the Bultmannian movement toward reducing the centrality of eschatology, in that he argued that traditions in Judaism and early Christianity concerning the Son of Man represent a separate strand of eschatology from that represented by the kingdom of God. Since the kingdom of God is central in the authentic sayings of Jesus, all eschatological Son of Man sayings are to be excluded from those ascribed to Jesus and are to be ascribed first to the primitive church.[17]

Vielhauer's position was not simply based on the distinction of two separate strands of tradition, but also substantively on the incompatibility of

[17] Philipp Vielhauer, "Gottesreich und Menschensohn in der Verkündigung Jesu," in *Festschrift für Günther Dehn* (Neukirchen Krs. Moers: Buchhandlung des Erziehungsvereins, 1957) 51–79; "Jesus und der Menschensohn: Zur Diskussion mit Heinz Eduard Tödt und Eduard Schweizer," *ZTK* 60 (1963) 133–77; "Ein Weg zur neutestamentlichen Christologie? Prüfung der Thesen Ferdinand Hahns," *EvT* 25 (1965) 24–72. All three are reprinted in Philipp Vielhauer, *Aufsätze zum Neuen Testament* (TBü 31; Munich: Kaiser, 1965) 55–91, 92–140, 141–98 respectively, to which reference is here made. Vielhauer pointed out (pp. 82–83) that the use of Son of Man in Daniel 7 was not yet titular, but referred generically to a human. Hence, though Daniel 7 also refers to kingdoms (though without literal use of the expression "kingdom of God"), Daniel for him did not present an exception to the generalization: "Where the Son of Man is an individual figure and plays an active role, there is no mention of the kingdom of God. The Son of Man is not an integral part of the hope in the eschatological kingdom of God" (p. 86).

Jesus' "strict orientation to God being king," an "object of lively hope," with any apocalyptic expectation:

> In such an eschatology the figures of the Son of Man and the Messiah have as little place as do speculations about the date of the end or fantasies about the future world. On the basis of the strict concept of God's reign it is impossible that Jesus awaited the coming Son of Man or even more that he identified himself with him.[18]

Hans Conzelmann presented on 22 October 1957 at the annual Bultmannian meeting of "Old Marburgers" a first endorsement of Vielhauer's position:

> The question is whether Jesus' expectation of the kingdom of God is accurately interpreted when it is presented as combined *in any way* with the expectation of a personal eschatological Fulfiller, i.e., whether the *structure* of his thought tolerates a synthesis of kingdom of God and Son of Man. What one finds in the texts seems to me to lead to denying this question. . . . Jesus' person is taken up into the procedure in a way that no room remains for a further intervening person.[19]

Conzelmann focused attention on the way in which the removal of the futuristic Son of Man from the teaching of Jesus fits with collapsing the time between Jesus' present and the imminently expected kingdom of God, a mythologoumenon that in effect should not be taken literally and in that sense not seriously. The eschatology of the kingdom functioned only existentially, not temporally and hence not futuristically.[20] This nontemporal eschatology is what Koester would come to call "Jesus' radicalized eschatology."

Vielhauer was soon able to appeal to most of the important representatives of the Bultmannian school in his support: Ernst Haenchen, Ernst Käsemann, Hans Conzelmann, and even Eduard Schweizer, though more a Barthian than a Bultmannian.[21]

[18] Vielhauer, "Gottesreich und Menschensohn in der Verkündigung Jesu," 88.

[19] Conzelmann, "Gegenwart und Zukunft," 281.

[20] Ibid., 286–88.

[21] Vielhauer ("Ein Weg," 146) cited Haenchen, "Die Komposition von Mk viii,27–ix,1 und Par.," *NovT* 6 (1963) 81–109. Haenchen ascribed Mark 8:38 // Q 12:8–9 to the community, which at first distinguished terminologically between the past Jesus on earth and the future Jesus coming as the Son of Man on the clouds (pp. 93–96).

Vielhauer ("Jesus und der Menschensohn," 93 n. 4) cited Käsemann, *VF* 1958–59 [1960–62] 99–102, esp. 101. Käsemann's emphasis on apocalyptic as the matrix of Christian theology presupposes that apocalypticism was ignited by the Easter experience and that Jesus himself was not an apocalypticist. See the following works by Käsemann: "Die Anfänge christlicher Theologie," *ZTK* 57 (1960) 161–85, esp. 179; reprinted in *Exegetische Versuche und Besinnungen* (Göttingen: Vandenhoeck & Ruprecht, 1960–64) 2:82–104, esp. 99; Eng. trans., "The Beginnings of Christian Theology," *JTC* 6: *Apocalypticism* (New York: Herder & Herder, 1969) 17–46, esp. 39; and in Käsemann, *New Testament Questions of Today* (London: SCM;

Günther Bornkamm was already committed in print to Bultmann's view of the Son of Man, to the effect that Jesus expected an apocalyptic Son of Man other than himself.[22] Bornkamm became in effect the leader of that strand of the Bultmannian movement that retained this classical position.[23]

Philadelphia: Fortress Press, 1969) 82–107, esp. 101–2. "Zum Thema der urchristlichen Apokalyptik," *ZTK* 59 (1962) 257–84; reprinted in *Exegetische Versuche und Besinnungen* 2:105–31; Eng. trans., "On the Topic of Primitive Christian Apocalyptic," *JTC* 6: *Apocalypticism,* 99–133, esp. 104; "On the Subject of Primitive Christian Apocalyptic," in Käsemann, *New Testament Questions of Today,* 108–37.

Vielhauer ("Ein Weg," 146) cited Conzelmann without specific reference. See Conzelmann, "Jesus Christus," *RGG*³ 3 (1959) 631; Eng. trans., Conzelmann, *Jesus* (Philadelphia: Fortress Press, 1973) 44–45: "The firming up of the language there [Dan 7:13] of 'a' figure like a human to 'the' Son of Man" is "not thinkable apart from the Christian (community) exegesis of Dan 7 and its application to the person of Jesus."

Eduard Schweizer ("Der Menschensohn [Zur eschatologischen Erwartung Jesu]," *ZNW* 50 [1959] 185–209, esp. 192) agrees with Vielhauer "that Jesus apparently did *not* await the coming of the Son of Man," and that Q sayings referring to the Jesus of the public ministry as Son of Man are held to be authentic (Q 7:34; 9:58; 11:30) (pp. 199–200), and that the term is not a generic designation ("human") but presupposes a latent Christology ("this circumlocution at once veiling and suggesting the mystery of his person," p. 198). It is this titular though nonapocalyptic use of Son of Man as a self-designation that is opposed by Vielhauer ("Jesus und der Menschensohn," 114–37). See also Schweizer's English summary and adaptation, "The Son of Man," *JBL* 79 (1960) 119–29.

[22] G. Bornkamm, *Jesus von Nazareth* (Stuttgart: Kohlhammer, 1956) Exkurs 3, "Zur Frage der messianischen Hoheitsnamen in den Selbstaussagen Jesu" (pp. 206–10); Eng. trans., *Jesus of Nazareth,* trans. I. and F. McLuskey with J. M. Robinson (London: Hodder & Stoughton; New York: Harper, 1960) Appendix 3, "The Messianic Titles in Jesus' References to Himself" (pp. 226–31). This is in substance the same, with but minor variations, as the presentation by Rudolf Bultmann, *Theologie des Neuen Testaments* (Tübingen: Mohr-Siebeck, first fascicle 1948) 29–31; Eng. trans., *Theology of the New Testament,* trans. K. Grobel (2 vols.; New York: Scribner, 1951, 1955) 1:28–31.

[23] Bornkamm's position was carried out by his pupils in their dissertations: Heinz Eduard Tödt, "Hoheits- und Niedrigkeitsvorstellungen in den synoptischen Menschensohnsprüchen" (1956), published as *Der Menschensohn in der synoptischen Überlieferung* (Gütersloh: Mohn, 1959); Eng. trans., *The Son of Man in the Synoptic Tradition* (London: SCM; Philadelphia: Westminster, 1965). Tödt argued for the authenticity of most of the futuristic Son of Man sayings in Q: 11:30; 12:8, 9, 40; 17:24, 26, 30 (not 17:28–29) (*Son of Man,* 60). The cohesiveness of the Heidelberg school on the Son of Man is evident from the fourth and fifth editions of Bornkamm's *Jesus von Nazareth* (1960 [not in the Eng. trans.) 195–96 n. 6a), where he rejected Vielhauer's original essay by appeal to Tödt, and where Tödt's book is praised as "the best investigation of the Son of Man sayings" (p. 209). See Vielhauer, "Jesus und der Menschensohn," in *Aufsätze zum Neuen Testament,* 92–140. Another dissertation under Bornkamm by Ferdinand Hahn, entitled "Anfänge christologischer Traditionen" (1961), was published as *Christologische Hoheitstitel: Ihre Geschichte im frühen Christentum* (FRLANT 83; Göttingen: Vandenhoeck & Ruprecht, 1963); Eng. trans., *The Titles of Jesus in Christology: Their History in Early Christianity* (London: Lutterworth; New York/Cleveland: World, 1969). See Vielhauer, "Ein Weg," in *Aufsätze zum Neuen Testament,* 141–98. Vielhauer had already added a refutation of Hahn in a "Nachtrag" to "Jesus und der Menschensohn" (pp. 138–40), beginning with a recognition of the togetherness of Tödt and Hahn's positions: "Hahn takes over Tödt's overall concept of

Günther Bornkamm's Revival of Q Studies

The revival of Q studies over the past generation took place in large part within the strand of the Bultmannian movement led by Günther Bornkamm. It is documented in the work of his pupils Heinz Eduard Tödt, Odil Hannes Steck, and Dieter Lührmann.

Tödt located the dominant trend in Q as the identification of Jesus with the apocalyptic Son of Man about whom Jesus himself had spoken, but only in the third person. Given the presence of the resurrected Jesus, the Q community experienced already the acquittal awaited at the judgment from the Son of Man, and thus came to identify Jesus with that figure and ascribe to him proleptically that title and authority.[24] Thus the basic orientation of Q itself is to Jesus as future Son of Man:

> The sayings source, more strongly than any other collection of material within the Synoptic tradition, preserved the eschatological character of the proclamation of Jesus. . . . Thus the eschatological sayings are now brought together in a substantive thematic group [Q 17:23–30]. In this group all sayings of the coming Son of Man appear, except for Luke 12:8–9 par. and Luke 11:30 par. . . . An important position in the structure of the whole is accorded to the Son of Man sayings.[25]

This eschatological christological definition of Q is basically different from the traditional view of Q as a parenetic supplement to the kerygma of cross and resurrection. Q now has a kerygma in its own right, thus suggesting that Q comes from an independent strand of primitive Christian tradition: ". . . the continued transmission of Jesus' teaching, in view of the divine authorization of the teacher, does not appear from the same source and with the same meaning as the passion kerygma, but has a source and a meaning by itself."[26]

---

the problem of the Synoptic Son of Man with unimportant modifications in detail (13–53 [Eng. trans., 15–53]). In the already-mentioned debate he defends the togetherness of 'kingdom of God' and 'Son of Man' in the proclamation of Jesus (27–32 [Eng. trans., 24–28])." The unpublished Heidelberg dissertation of 1953 by G. Iber, "Überlieferungsgeschichtliche Untersuchungen zum Begriff des Menschensohnes im Neuen Testament," was nonetheless appealed to by Vielhauer ("Jesus und der Menschensohn," 106 n. 22 [133–35 as Vielhauer's own view]): The distinction of Jesus from the Son of Man in Q 12:8–9 need not be taken as supporting the authenticity of sayings where this distinction is made (on the grounds that Jesus, but not the church, would have distinguished Jesus from the Son of Man), for it merely defines them as an early layer of the church's thinking when it had not yet come to describe the earthly status of Jesus in the language of his future apocalyptic status.

[24] Tödt, *Der Menschensohn*, 248–49 (Eng. trans., 273).

[25] Ibid., 246–47 (Eng. trans., 270).

[26] Ibid., 267 (Eng. trans., 296). This view is summarized by Bornkamm ("Evangelien, synoptische," *RGG*³ 2 [1958] 753–66, "Spruchquelle" cols. 758–60, esp. col. 759). Bornkamm's *Jesus von Nazareth* (pp. 198–99 [Eng. trans., 217]) makes no such claim for Q. It may be that *Jesus von Nazareth*, which appeared in the same year as the submission (in May 1956) of Tödt's

This is the origin of the current idea of a distinctive Q community or movement.

Odil Hannes Steck traced the history of the deuteronomistic view of history, to the effect that both exiles had been due to the disobedience of Israel producing "the violent fate of the prophets." His point of departure, however, is a detailed reconstruction of three Q texts, 6:22–23; 11:47–51; and 13:34–35 (though he doubts that the last belongs to Q), each of which presupposes that deuteronomistic tradition. Indeed he considers the deuteronomistic view of history as "the presupposed comprehensive conceptual framework" of Q.[27]

Dieter Lührmann's study had its focus in the redaction of Q. He defined redaction narrowly as "a conscious formation under theological points of view, to be distinguished from 'collecting' according to catchword or topical arrangement."[28] He located Q's redactional focus in the apocalyptic judgment pronounced on Israel ("this generation") for having irrevocably rejected the Q movement. While arguing against Tödt that the identification of Jesus with the Son of Man had taken place in the Q community prior to the redaction and hence was not itself first introduced by the redaction,[29] Lührmann does see in the apocalyptic judgment by the Son of Man a decisive redactional trait of Q:

> Even if this [apocalyptic] expectation of judgment goes back to Jesus himself, it is at least onesidedly emphasized in Q and has become in the redaction the decisive interpretive tool for Jesus' proclamation of the βασιλεία. One can hence even speak of a "re-apocalypticizing" of the proclamation of Jesus in Q.[30]

---

dissertation, was completed prior to that submission and that Tödt perhaps more than Bornkamm is responsible for the emphasis on the independence of the Q tradition, which Bornkamm then took up into his article that appeared two years later.

[27] Odil Hannes Steck, *Israel und das gewaltsame Geschick der Propheten: Untersuchungen zur Überlieferung des deuteronomistischen Geschichtsbildes im Alten Testament, Spätjudentum und Urchristentum* (WMANT 23; Neukirchen-Vluyn: Neukirchener Verlag, 1967) 288. (His doubt about ascribing 13:34–35 to Q [p. 283 n. 1] is not shared by D. Lührmann [*Die Redaktion der Logienquelle* (WMANT 33; Neukirchen-Vluyn: Neukirchener Verlag, 1969) 44 n. 5].) According to the preface, this is a dissertation of 1965 under Bornkamm (p. 13). Ferdinand Hahn listed Steck as an assistant who helped him with proofreading and indexing (*Christologische Hoheitstitel,* preface 6).

[28] D. Lührmann, *Die Redaktion der Logienquelle,* 84; see also 8, 16. The book was dedicated to Bornkamm. The preface reported that it was a 1968 *Habilitationsschrift* in Heidelberg, where Lührmann was assistant from 1965 to 1968 (p. 7).

[29] Lührmann, *Die Redaktion der Logienquelle,* 41 n. 6; see also 85.

[30] Ibid., 94. Here (n. 4) Lührmann referred to Kümmel's essay "Eschatological Expectation in the Proclamation of Jesus" for the "status of the discussion" about the Son of Man, thereby implicitly reaffirming the position of Bultmann and Bornkamm over against Vielhauer. However, Lührmann seemed (*Die Redaktion der Logienquelle,* 41 n. 6) to be moving toward Vielhauer's position: Lührmann considered Q 12:8–9 decisive as to whether Jesus referred to

Similarly with regard to Steck's thesis Lührmann argued that the deuteronomistic view of history is one ingredient, but only one ingredient, in the redactional focus of Q.[31] It is especially the Sophia orientation of Q 11:49–51; 13:34–35, which are two of Steck's three primary texts (along with 6:23c), as well as other Sophia texts in Q (7:35; 10:21–22; 11:31–32) and the sapiential genre of Q in general,[32] that led Lührmann to bring wisdom motifs into new focus for defining the redaction of Q: "That means first of all that, in terms of the history of religions, the taking up of Jesus' proclamation of the βασιλεία into the apocalyptic announcement of judgment is rooted in motifs derived from wisdom."[33] The redaction of Q would thus seem to be a history-of-religions hodgepodge without profile or directionality.

Helmut Koester's Early Sapiential Layer in Q

It is at this juncture that Lührmann quoted in an extended footnote a just-published essay ("now") by Helmut Koester as "an interesting thesis" where "new paths are indicated for the further work on the *Gospel of Thomas*":

> The basis of the *Gospel of Thomas* is a Sayings collection which is more primitive than the canonical Gospels, even though its basic principle is not related to the creed of the passion and resurrection.
>
> It must have been a version of Q in which the apocalyptic expectation of the Son of Man was missing and in which Jesus' radicalized eschatology of the Kingdom and his revelation of divine wisdom in his own words were the dominant motives.[34]

---

a future Son of Man, and he was inclined to think that the language of confessing and denying with its courtroom overtones was more likely to be a creation of the community. Similarly (p. 75) Q 17:24, 26–27 are considered inauthentic, though (in the comments appended when reading proofs, p. 8) he conceded that R. A. Edwards ("The Eschatological Correlative as a Gattung in the New Testament," *ZNW* 60 [1969] 9–20) "contests more strongly than do I that these comparisons are original sayings of Jesus."

[31] Lührmann, *Die Redaktion der Logienquelle*, 88.

[32] Ibid., 91, 102; Lührmann appropriated my genre definition, λόγοι σοφῶν.

[33] Lührmann, *Die Redaktion der Logienquelle*, 100; see also 97–98: "As the latest, and hence temporally (even if not necessarily tradition-historically) nearest layer to the redaction of Q there has emerged a series of logia that are clearly shaped by late Jewish wisdom. At first glance this may not seem surprising, for the influence of just this stream already on Jesus' proclamation is after all recognizable on all sides in the Synoptic tradition. Yet the frequency and special shape of these sayings, and the formation of the logia source as a whole in terms of a genre coming from wisdom literature, speak for the view that precisely this influence had significant weight in the transmission of the logia source."

[34] Ibid., 92–93 n. 4. He quoted Koester, "One Jesus and Four Primitive Gospels," *HTR* 61 (1968) 229–30; now reprinted in Robinson-Koester, *Trajectories*, 186. Lührmann's rejection of attempts to "distinguish in terms of *literary criticism* younger and older sources in Q" (*Die Redaktion der Logienquelle*, 89 n. 2) was directed against older, unrelated views.

It is clear that Lührmann himself did not follow up this "interesting thesis" in his own work on Q. It required that one be prepared to build upon Vielhauer's thesis of the secondary role of the futuristic sayings about the Son of Man to an extent that Lührmann, given his Heidelberg context, was not yet fully prepared to do. It also presupposed that the *Gospel of Thomas* is not built primarily upon the Synoptic Gospels—as was assumed by most European scholars at the time, following Wolfgang Schrage's *Habilitationsschrift* at Kiel[35]—but rather on oral tradition, as most American scholarship has tended to assume, following the prompt refutation of Schrage in the unpublished Claremont dissertation of John Sieber.[36] Thus Lührmann, though obviously attracted to Koester's thesis, did not in fact introduce it in a meaningful way into Q research.

If thus the Heidelberg branch of the Bultmannian movement did not investigate further a preapocalyptic, sapiential collection of sayings behind Q, such a possibility was envisaged in Dieter Zeller's 1976 *Habilitationsschrift* at nearby Freiburg im Breisgau, though rather isolated from the developments within the Bultmannian movement but at home in the somewhat different context of emergent Roman Catholic Q scholarship. "One can in any case also go about disengaging complexes of logia that precede Q, which possibly had their own 'Sitz im Leben.' Among them are six rather large groups of sayings that may have grown up around a kernel of admonitions."[37] The six complexes of sayings that Zeller listed are as follows:

1. Conduct toward enemies: Q 6:(20–23), 27–33, 35b–37a, 38b, 41–42, (43–49)
2. Conduct of the messengers: Q 10:2–8a, 9–11a, 12(+16?)
3. Prayer: Q (11:2–4?), 9–13
4. Conduct under persecution: Q [11:33–36?]; 12:(2–3), 4–9, (10)
5. Attitude toward material things: Q 12:22–31, 33–34
6. Watchfulness: Q 12:(35–37?), 39–40, 42b–46

Zeller's complexes 1–5 are, with but minor variations, the first five sapiential speeches ascribed by John S. Kloppenborg, in his comprehensive analysis of the literary layering of Q, to the first edition of Q.[38]

[35] W. Schrage, *Das Verhältnis des Thomas-Evangeliums zur synoptischen Tradition und zu den koptischen Evangelienübersetzungen: Zugleich ein Beitrag zur gnostischen Synoptikerdeutung* (BZNW 29; Berlin: Töpelmann, 1964).

[36] J. Sieber, "A Redactional Analysis of the Synoptic Gospels with Regard to the Question of the Sources of the Gospel of Thomas" (Ph.D. diss., Claremont Graduate School, 1964). Sieber is currently preparing for publication a new book based on his dissertation.

[37] D. Zeller, *Die weisheitlichen Mahnsprüche bei den Synoptikern* (Forschung zur Bibel 17; Würzburg: Echter Verlag, 1977) 191. Zeller adds with somewhat less assurance that one might consider as a seventh complex the Q apocalypse, 17:23–24, 26–27, 30, 34–35, 37b.

[38] J. S. Kloppenborg, *The Formation of Q: Trajectories in Ancient Wisdom Collections* (SAC; Philadelphia: Fortress Press, 1987). Kloppenborg ascribed apocalypticism, and hence Zeller's

Only somewhat less striking is the list of six pre-Q collections of aphoristic sayings, each displaying a similar structure, presented by Ronald A. Piper:[39] Q 6:27–36 (in Matthew's order); 6:37–42; 6:43–45; 11:9–13; 12:2–9; 12:22–31. The first three of Piper's six collections are parts of the first cluster on Zeller and Kloppenborg's list, while the other three in Piper's list comprise major parts of items 3 through 5 of Zeller and Kloppenborg's list.

Whereas Kloppenborg, at the conclusion of his analysis of the sapiential speeches, does refer in passing in a note to Zeller's list, Piper, though making use in general of Zeller's work, nowhere refers to this listing of sapiential complexes; Kloppenborg's book appeared too late for Piper to include it.[40] Thus his conclusions are relatively independent.

Another striking aspect of these converging lists of sapiential collections is their focus on the Sermon on the Mount: The first collection listed by Zeller and Kloppenborg is the Sermon in Q, from which three of the six Q collections of Piper also come. The enlargement of Q's Sermon into the Sermon on the Mount (Matthew 5–7) adds collections 3 and 5 from the list of Zeller and Kloppenborg, and two of the remaining three collections of Piper. Thus the disengaging of sapiential collections behind Q arrives at a position somewhat analogous to, though quite independent of, Hans Dieter Betz's claim that the Sermon on the Mount goes back behind Matthew to about 50 CE, that is, prior to Q.[41] Thus Betz in his way supports those seeing a sapiential layer behind Q.

To be sure, the independent existence of the Q Sermon prior to Q is hardly provable,[42] much less that of the Sermon on the Mount. But, just as

---

sixth and seventh complexes (and 12:8–9), to the second edition of Q, while himself disengaging a sixth sapiential speech in the first edition of Q scattered through Luke 13–17. Kloppenborg, in an unpublished paper prepared for the Q Seminar of SBL in 1988, "Redactional Strata and Social History in the Sayings Gospel Q," 5, n. 1, presented a slightly revised list of materials assigned to the two editions of Q: "To the instructional layer I assign: (1a) Q 6:20b–23b, 27–35, 36–45, 46–49; (1b) 9:57–62; 10:2–11, 16; (1c) 11:2–4, 9–13; (1d) 12:2–7, 11–12; (1e) 12:22b–31, 33–34; (1f) 13:24; 14:26–27; 17:33; 14:34–35 and probably also 15:4–7, (8–10?); 16:13; 17:1–2, 3b–4, 5–6 [probably 5 is not meant to be included, see Kloppenborg, *Q Parallels: Synopsis, Critical Notes and Concordance* (Sonoma, CA: Polebridge, 1988), 186–187]. The second layer consists of five large blocks of sayings, (2a) Q 3:7–9, 16–17; (2b) 7:1–10, 18–28, 31–35; 16:16 [presumably meant to precede 31–35, see *Q Parallels* 56–57]; (2c) 11:14–26, (27–28?), 29–32, 33–36, 39b–42b, 43–44, 46–52; (2d) 12:39–40, 42–46, 49, 51–59; (2e) 17:23–24, 26–30, 34–35; 19:12–27; 22:28–30, and various interpolations: 6:23c; 10:12, 13–15; 12:8–9, 10; 13:25–27, 28–30, 34–35; 14:16–24. At a third level, Q 4:1–13; 11:42c and 16:17 were added."

[39] R. A. Piper, *Wisdom in the Q-tradition: The Aphoristic Teaching of Jesus* (SNTSMS 61; Cambridge/New York/New Rochelle/Melbourne/Sydney: Cambridge University Press, 1989).

[40] Ibid., 209 n. 61.

[41] H. D. Betz, *Essays on the Sermon on the Mount*, trans. L. L. Welborn (Philadelphia: Fortress Press, 1985); see also his contribution to the present volume.

[42] Leif E. Vaage, "Composite Texts and Oral Myths: The Case of the 'Sermon' (6:20b-49)," in *Society of Biblical Literature 1989 Seminar Papers*, ed. D. J. Lull (Atlanta: Scholars Press, 1989) 424–39.

the existence of Zeller's collections 1, 3, and 5 is not dependent on their initial collection into the Sermon on the Mount, so the existence of three of Piper's six collections is not dependent on their initial collection in a Q Sermon prior to the composition of Q. The important thing is the detection of some clustering activity at the early, formative stage of Q. Rather than having to do merely with a number of sapiential sayings, one has to do with a structuring of such sayings into clusters, a process reflecting some intentional activity on the part of some person or persons largely restricted to the Q community.[43]

When one turns from the question of literary layering to that of the history of traditions, the distinction drawn by Siegfried Schulz between two stages in the tradition, "the kerygma of the Jewish-Christian Q community" and "the kerygma of the younger Q community of Syria," presented as the first layer a surprisingly high degree of overlap with the sapiential collections, which is all the more surprising given Schulz's orientation to an apocalyptic point of departure for the Q community.[44] He listed as the older layer Q 6:20b–21, 27–38, 41–42; 11:1–4, 9–13, 39, 42–44, 46–48, 52; 12:4–9, 22–31, 33–34; 16:17–18. Again it is striking how much of this is in the Q Sermon (6:20b–21, 27–38, 41–42) or in additions included in the Sermon on the Mount (Q 11:1–4, 9–13; 16:17–18; 12:22–31, 33–34). Actually in Schulz's oldest layer of tradition only a very few passages (Q 11:39, 42–44, 46–48, 52; 12:4–9) are not in the Sermon on the Mount. And only a few passages (11:39, 42–44, 46–48, 52; 16:17–18) are not in the sapiential collections of Zeller and Kloppenborg (who also left out 12:8–9).

Of the three monographs by Zeller, Kloppenborg, and Piper oriented to sapiential collections imbedded in Q, only that of Kloppenborg built consciously on the initiative of Koester, carrying through its implications in terms of redaction criticism.

> Koester observes that the forms most typical of the wisdom gospel or *logoi sophon* are wisdom sayings, legal pronouncements, prophetic sayings ("I"-words, blessings and woes) and parables. Least typical of this genre are apocalyptic sayings, especially apocalyptic Son of Man sayings. Therefore, as far as *Gattungsgeschichte* is concerned, the *Gos. Thom.* reflects a stage antecedent to the final form of Q. By including Son of Man sayings, Q produced a secondary version of a "wisdom-gospel." Koester conjectures that the introduction of apocalyptic eschatology was a means to attenuate the radicalized eschatology and gnosticizing tendencies at work in earlier forms of Q. . . .

[43] Piper, *Wisdom,* 161: "The distinctiveness of structure and argument which has been found to characterize several aphoristic sayings-collections of the double tradition leads one to infer the existence of a unique circle of people who formulated these collections. . . ." This relatively restricted source-critical range within which the collections are found strengthens the theory of a unique sapiential circle behind the collections.

[44] S. Schulz, *Q: Die Spruchquelle der Evangelisten* (Zurich: Evangelischer Verlag, 1972).

> His conclusions regarding the formative elements of Q are based on two assumptions: that Q belongs to the genre of "wisdom gospel" and that only certain kinds of sayings and theological tendencies are typical of the genre. According to Koester, apocalyptic Son of Man sayings and sayings which evince a strongly future-oriented eschatology run counter to the tendencies of the genre, and for that reason are to be judged secondary. In practice, Koester's method is comparative and the *Gos. Thom.* serves as a criterion for deciding what was formative in Q. *Gos. Thom.* lacks an apocalyptic thrust and has only one (non-apocalyptic) Son of Man saying (saying 86).[45]

Kloppenborg himself saw it as his task to carry through the redactional analysis that shows the Son of Man apocalyptic layer to be later than the sapiential instructional layer:

> It must be shown on redactional grounds that certain elements (e.g., apocalyptic Son of Man sayings) belong to a secondary compositional level and that compositionally and literarily the wisdom sayings, and the wisdom-gospel format, are foundational and formative for the document. Such a conclusion can be obtained in the first place only from an analysis of Q itself, not by comparative analysis.[46]

Thus Kloppenborg implemented Koester's working hypothesis of an early sapiential layer in Q in a way that Lührmann has not. For Lührmann, the sapiential layer responsible for the genre λόγοι σοφῶν was the latest layer, for here Sophia Christology is presupposed (Q 7:35; 10:21–22; 11:31–32, 49–51; 13:34–35). The result is that for Lührmann it would be at the redactional stage that sapiential influences would have been introduced, even though he recognized that sapiential sayings going back to Jesus himself should lead one to expect a sapiential orientation even earlier.[47]

Yet the emergence of Sophia Christology not at the oldest layer of Q but only at the redactional level should not in itself be surprising, once one notes that Christology as such really only emerges at this secondary level. In the first edition of Q "sons ‹of God› " are all those who are godlike in loving their

[45] Kloppenborg, *Formation of Q,* 32–33, 38.

[46] Ibid., 38–39.

[47] Lührmann, *Die Redaktion der Logienquelle,* 97–98, 100. The situation is similar in this regard with the 1984/85 Bern dissertation of Migaku Sato, *Q und Prophetie* (WUNT 2.29; Tübingen: Mohr, 1988) 161: "A few 'functional elements' of personified Wisdom have flowed into the sayings of the Exalted. . . . This tendency of Q sayings is then picked up in a certain way by one of the Q redactions—no doubt C [the latest]." The dissertation is designed to replace the definition of the genre of Q in terms of sapiential literature with a genre definition in terms of OT prophecy. To this end a number of Q sayings are reconstructed and their genre defined as prophetic. Since Kloppenborg's thesis was not available to Sato, the fact that these "prophetic" sayings are practically all from what Kloppenborg has classified as the apocalyptic second edition of Q, in distinction from the sapiential first edition, is not taken into consideration. Rather the genre of the sapiential sayings is passed over in silence, as of necessity is that of the first edition of Q itself, where the designation λόγοι σοφῶν would be most appropriate.

enemies (Q 6:35), and it is only in the second edition of Q that sonship becomes an exclusive christological title of Jesus (Q 10:22; 4:3 and 9 may be even later). In the first edition of Q, the term Son of Man in Q 9:58 apparently goes back to a generic meaning "human" (*Gos. Thom.* 86), though it has become a reference to Jesus here and in 6:22 (lacking in Matt 5:11); however, in the second edition of Q it becomes, in addition to a reference to the earthly Jesus (7:34; 12:10; and perhaps 11:30), the christological title for Jesus as an apocalyptic figure who functions at the last judgment as character witness (12:8) or even as judge (12:40; 17:24, 26, 30). In the first edition of Q κύριος can refer to God (10:2; 16:13, both metaphorically), whereas for Jesus it is a form of address just meaning "Sir" (9:59). It develops into a title for Jesus in the first edition of Q only as teacher (6:46) and here is used only by persons who are criticized for their lack of conformity to the teaching. Only in Matt 7:22, does κύριος develop beyond Q into a title for the character witness at the last judgment, building there upon the metaphorical use of the secular meaning "Sir" (Q 13:25; Matt 25:11). Thus the relative absence of Christology from the first edition of Q and the relative prominence of Christology in the second edition of Q is striking. It is hence not surprising that the first edition of Q, though its genre and sayings are largely sapiential, does not present a Sophia Christology, but that this christological development can be sensed first among the christological developments of the second edition of Q. Thus in spite of the Sophia Christology emerging first in the second edition of Q, it is the first edition that is primarily a sapiential collection of λόγοι σοφῶν; in the second edition the literary genre moves in a narrative, chreia-like direction.

A New Trajectory

The recognition of a preapocalyptic layer lying behind Q, which Koester first identified and which has subsequently come to expression in such a variety of ways, poses a new alternative for tracing the movement from Jesus to the church.

In modern scholarship Jesus had usually been placed historically between John the Baptist, into whose movement he was baptized, and Paul, whose letters are the first documentation of the religion venerating Jesus. Since both John and Paul were apocalypticists, the easiest working hypothesis has been to bridge the gulf of two decades between them with a straight-line development: Jesus too was an apocalypticist.

The idea of Jesus as apocalypticist had originally commended itself in the same way as did the Copernican revolution: As an organizing principle, the theory that the earth rotates around the sun left less by way of unresolved problems than did the previous geocentric model. Apocalypticism won on the aesthetic criterion of providing a cleaner, less-cluttered model. And so it became the working hypothesis for the quest of the historical Jesus in the twentieth century.

Now, almost a century later, though Schweitzer's apocalyptic derivation of Jesus has become the establishment view, it no longer plays that liberating role. As the old model, it is now frayed, blemished by broken parts, no longer a heuristic tool drawing attention to new insights on all sides, but rather a Procrustean bed in which the discipline squirms, ill at ease. Today's growing edges are no longer edges of that given model, but rather dangle off in space on their own, in a largely disintegrated discipline.

Emergent layering in Q may well provide the possibility to replace the apocalyptic model from John to Paul with a Q trajectory between John and Matthew, on which a major sapiential deviation and a re-apocalypticizing may be plotted. There may be no other name significant enough to associate with such a sapiential deviation than Jesus (especially since Q names by name only John and Jesus), though academic rigor may make us prefer "John Doe."

Such a rethinking should not, in an excess of exuberance, seek to deny the apocalyptic nature of the two poles, John and Paul. John in Q 3:7–9, 16–17 is presented in a way that can be characterized as apocalyptic—that is, forewarning of judgment imagined like natural disasters such as hurricane and lighting, what in modern legal parlance are still called "acts of God." There is a "coming wrath" (3:7); "already" an ax is poised to "cut down and throw into the fire" trees not bearing good fruit (3:9); "the Coming One . . .mightier than I"—some divine agent—will baptize with "[wind and] fire" (3:16); "the winnowing fork" is poised to separate the "wheat" into the "granary" from the "chaff" to be cast into the "unquenchable fire" (3:17). These heavy metaphors tend to point to some superhuman final resolution to the human dilemma, such as the term apocalypticism tends to evoke. Rather than appealing behind this apocalyptic portrayal of John to the standard Cynic critique of the "soft" life reflected in Q 7:25 as distinguishing the historical John as having been a Cynic,[48] we need to cope with the probability that Jesus underwent John's baptism and thus entered an apocalyptic movement[49] and hence must have

[48] Leif Vaage documented quite fully the pejorative use of μαλακός ("soft") as Cynic ("Q: The Ethos and Ethics of an Itinerant Intelligence" [Ph.D. diss., Claremont Graduate School, 1987] Appendix 3, "Matt 11:8 / Luke 7:25—Clarifying a Characterization," [pp. 485–502]). Vaage has prepared a revised version of the appendix in article form, "Q and the Historical Jesus: Q 7:25—Characterizing a Characterization" (forthcoming).

[49] Kloppenborg has summarized the discussion, concluding that Jesus' baptism was not in Q (*Formation of Q*, 84–85; and *Q Parallels: Synopsis, Critical Notes and Concordance* [Sonoma, Calif.: Polebridge, 1988] 16). Yet it is not fully satisfactory to assume that "the title 'Son of God' in Q 4 does not require an explanatory narrative any more than does the title 'Son of man,' which is by far the more common title for Q" (*Q Parallels*, 16). For the temptation narrative would be the first place in Q where Jesus is presented as saying or doing anything, if his baptism were not mentioned. Yet the title Son of God occurs in the temptation not as a familiar and

begun by believing its apocalyptic message with considerable fervor.

Jesus, though initially such a fervent convert of John, would seem not to have continued in a straight-line way the program or life-style of John. He seems not to have continued John's symbolic act of baptism. Though both ate and dressed very simply, John seems not to have depended on civilization, but to have had an uncooked diet and an unwoven garb (Mark 1:6) typical of the bedouin,[50] and to have frequented uninhabited places like an anchorite—the people had to come out and hunt him up (Q 7:24; in Mark 1:4 the wilderness may be derived from Isa 40:3 quoted in Mark 1:3). Jesus, on the other hand, seems to have depended on civilization, to have lived in Capernaum (Q 7:1 // John 2:12 and 4:46; Q 10:15; Mark 1:21; 2:1), though at times to have been a mendicant itinerant (Q 9:58; 10:2–11). Jesus' (lack of) gear is not that of John, but apparently clothes of the day of human-made cloth (though on the other hand not the garb of the Cynic, but even more rigorous [Q 10:4], though perhaps with a similar symbolic meaning). Thus John's and Jesus' life-styles could only be contrasted, even when caricatured (Q 7:34). We might use the contrast between the raw and the cooked. Given these divergences, which are all the more remarkable in view of Jesus' beginning with John's baptism, there is no strong reason to assume that Jesus continued John's ideology. The apocalypticism of the second edition of Q may in fact be a re-apocalypticizing of the Jesus tradition.

The early efforts by Karl Barth to argue that Paul, though occasionally borrowing categories from Jewish apocalypticism, was himself not an apocalypticist, were shown to be tendentious by Rudolf Bultmann: In such a text as 1 Cor 15:22–28 Paul did reason apocalyptically.[51] This is not just an

---

unchallenged title, as is usual with christological titles (e.g., Son of Man, or Son ‹of God› in Q 10:22), but rather is challenged and made the issue. This seems to presuppose some provocative identification of Jesus with that title, which the devil then contests. Thus to assume the inclusion of the baptism of Jesus in Q seems relatively prudent.

[50] Philipp Vielhauer concluded: "As surely as John awaited no political Messiah 'in the desert,' just as certainly his eschatological message connected up with the old desert typology. From this the unusualness of his clothing and nourishment is to be explained in a better and more unified way than on the basis of asceticism or hostility to culture. His clothing and nourishment have their meaning as eschatological demonstration" ("Tracht und Speise Johannes des Täufers," in *Aufsätze zum Neuen Testament*, 54).

[51] Karl Barth distinguished between "Schlussgeschichte," apocalypticism's series of final events in time and space, and "Endgeschichte," the ultimate substantive reality behind such language, that is, ultimately God (*Die Auferstehung der Toten: Eine akademische Vorlesung über 1. Kor. 15* [Munich: Kaiser, 1924] esp. 56–62, 94–99). So as to limit Paul to the latter, Barth twisted illegitimately the exegesis of 1 Cor 15:22–28 so as to eliminate from the text a series of final events. (The Eng. trans., *The Resurrection of the Dead* [London, 1933] is so inadequate that it might best be ignored.) Rudolf Bultmann had full appreciation for Barth's identification of the Pauline point behind the language, but insisted that Paul's language was sometimes inadequate to that point—e.g., when Paul himself became distracted into laying out a series of final things, as in 1 Cor 15:22–28 ("Karl Barth, Die Auferstehung der Toten," *Theologische*

unintelligible lapse on the part of Paul, but is a built-in proclivity of finite human experience seeking to express ineffable ultimacy in its finite language that again and again gets the upper hand.[52]

Paul's theology is not derived in a significant way from that of Jesus, and therefore Paul's apocalypticism might not weigh heavily in defining Jesus' ideology. Only if that were all one had from the first generation might one by default be obliged to follow the apocalyptic interpretation of Jesus. But there is in fact Q, whose layers span the first generation, the only other surviving "apostolic" text (in a chronological sense—the noun "apostle" is hardly in Q's vocabulary [Q 11:49?], though the verb "send" is present [Q 10:3, 16; 11:49; 14:17; the substantivized aorist passive participle 13:34]). Q is the extant text that reflects most nearly, though not exclusively, Jesus' own thought. The question of Jesus' apocalypticism is basically a question of the interpretation of Q.

If the earlier layer of Q would seem to be oriented heavily to sapiential traditions (though not without apocalyptic flickers or interpolations), there are in the later layer strong indications of apocalyptic indulgences and indeed of a re-apocalypticizing of the tradition. Those responsible for the eschatological[53] or prophetic[54] correlatives were closely related to the Q movement, in that four correlatives are in the second edition of Q (Q 11:30; 17:24, 26–27, 30), and only one elsewhere in the Synoptic Gospels (Matt 13:40–41). These correlatives are closely related to the introduction of the future Son of Man into Q, in that at least half the instances occur in correlatives: Q 17:24, 26–27, 30 (whether Q 11:30 refers to the Son of Man as future is unclear), whereas only two occur elsewhere in Q (12:8, 40). The apocalyptic

Blätter 5 [1926] 1–14; reprinted in *Glauben und Verstehen* [1] [Tübingen: Mohr, 1933]; Eng. trans., "Karl Barth, The Resurrection of the Dead," *Faith and Understanding* [London: SCM; New York: Harper & Row, 1969; reprint, Philadelphia: Fortress Press, 1987) 66–94, esp. 84–86).

[52] Hans Jonas, *Augustin und das paulinische Freiheitsproblem: Eine philosophische Studie zum pelagianischen Streit* (FRLANT, ed. Rudolf Bultmann, 44; Göttingen: Vandenhoeck & Ruprecht, 1930; 2nd ed., 1965) 82: "All this derives from an unavoidable fundamental structure of the spirit as such. That it interprets itself in objective formulae and symbols, that it is "symbolistic," is the innermost nature of the spirit—and at the same time most dangerous! In order to come to itself, it necessarily takes this detour via the symbol, in whose enticing jungle of problems it tends to lose itself, far from the origin preserved symbolically in it, taking the substitute as ultimate. Only in a long procedure of working back, after an exhausting completion of that detour, is a demythologized consciousness able terminologically to approach directly the original phenomena hidden in this camouflage (cf. the long path of the dogma of original sin up to Kierkegaard!)."

[53] Edwards, "Eschatological Correlative," 9–20, esp. 11. This essay recurs with minor alterations in his dissertation, *The Sign of Jonah in the Theology of the Evangelists and Q* (SBT 2.18; London: SCM, 1971).

[54] Daryl Schmidt, "The LXX *Gattung* 'Prophetic Correlative,'" *JBL* 96 (1977) 517–22, esp. 521–22.

title John used to refer to the future judge, "the Coming One," which the Q movement identified with Jesus, is also limited to the second edition of Q: 3:16; 7:19; 13:35 (though Ps 118:26 is quoted at the triumphal entry in all four Gospels). The broadly attested polemic against those who cry out "Here!" or "There!" is indicative of such trends: Luke (Q?) 17:20–21, 23; Mark 13:21; *Gos. Thom.* 3 (// Matt 24:26) and 103; *Gospel of Mary* (*PBerol.* 8502, 8, 15–19).[55]

Kloppenborg has argued that even after the second edition of Q there was a final redaction that introduced Q 4:1–13; 11:42c; 16:17, with an emphasis on Jesus as advocate of strict Torah observance, perhaps as a last desperate effort to gain acceptance in Jewish circles. From here it is not far to the emphatically particularistic sayings in Matt 10:5–6, 23 (cf. Rom 15:6), which hardly reflect that evangelist's own view (Matt 28:18–20), but either some otherwise unknown strand of tradition, further attestation for the final redaction of Q which Luke might readily have omitted, or an addition to Q by the Matthean community after the Lukan copy of Q had been made.

If thus a clear distinction between a third edition of Q, a QMt and even a kind of Ur-Matthew cannot be drawn, since all these entities are themselves obscure, it would seem clear that the Q movement—at least a significant part of it—merged into the Matthean community, bringing into Matthew and the Gentile church, and thus into the canon and the modern world, the traditions of Jesus that Q had transmitted:

> Therefore we support the thesis that the Gospel of Matthew comes from a community which was founded by the wandering messengers and prophets of the Son of man of the Sayings Source and remains in close contact with them. The traditions of Q thus reflect, for the community, experiences from its own history. They are "its own" traditions.[56]

Thus the model of an unbroken apocalypticism from John to Paul is to be replaced by a trajectory of the Q movement between John's apocalypticism and that of Matthew, but with a more nuanced, since better documented, course from one to the other. Here the early sapiential layer, which may well

[55] James M. Robinson, "The Study of the Historical Jesus after Nag Hammadi," *Semeia* 44: *The Historical Jesus and the Rejected Gospels* (1988) 45–55, esp. 50–53; James G. Williams, "Neither Here Nor There: Between Wisdom and Apocalyptic in Jesus' Kingdom Sayings," *Forum* 5.2: *The Jesus of Q* (1989) 7–30; Risto Uro, *Neither Here nor There: Lk 17:20–2 and Related Sayings in Thomas, Mark and Q* (Occasional Papers 20; Claremont, Calif.: Institute for Antiquity and Christianity, 1990).

[56] Ulrich Luz, *Das Evangelium nach Matthäus (Mt 1–7)* (EKKNT 1.1; Zurich/Einsiedeln/Cologne: Benziger; Neukirchen-Vluyn: Neukirchener Verlag, 1985) 66; Eng. trans., *Matthew 1–7: A Commentary* (Minneapolis: Augsburg, 1989) 50.

involve a "paradigm shift" in our understanding of Jesus,[57] is the most important discovery of the current phase of Q research, for which we are primarily indebted to Helmut Koester.

[57] Hans Küng has popularized for theology this concept presented by Thomas S. Kuhn, *The Structure of Scientific Revolutions* (International Encyclopedia of Unified Science 2.2; Chicago: University of Chicago Press, 1962; 2nd ed. enlarged, 1970). F. Gerald Downing calls for "a 'paradigm shift'" with reference particularly to his emphasis on Cynic parallels to Jesus (*Jesus and the Threat of Freedom* [London: SCM, 1987] 149); see n. 48.

14

Logoi Prophētōn? Reflections on the Genre of Q

RICHARD HORSLEY

HELMUT KOESTER'S SEMINAL ARTICLES written during the 1960s have proved to be a major stimulus to multifaceted analysis of early Christian literature. In "GNOMAI DIAPHOROI," he demonstrated how, from the very beginning, Christianity was characterized by diversity that varied according to geographical area and type of literary production. In "One Jesus, Four Primitive Gospels" he further demonstrated the correlation between literary types and theological/christological viewpoint. In "The Structure and Criteria of Early Christian Beliefs," finally, he demonstrated how particular creedal formulations or Christologies were correlated with particular cultural environments and particular social characteristics of nascent communities.[1] In those programmatic pieces Koester laid groundwork and offered paradigms for further study according to geographical area, literary type, and christological viewpoint. He also insisted that some of the old theologically determined categories were distorting historical analysis, and his delineation of the extreme diversity of early Christianity has provoked even further questioning of the received conceptual apparatus of our field.

One of the areas in which Koester's groundbreaking scholarship has stimulated highly productive investigations has been in analysis of the Synoptic sayings source. Koester argued that the *Gospel of Thomas* is a development from an early stage of a "wisdom gospel"—in the genre of *logoi sophōn*

[1] H. Koester, "GNOMAI DIAPHOROI: The Origin and Nature of Diversification in the History of Early Christianity," *HTR* 58 (1965) 279–318 [Robinson-Koester, *Trajectories*, 114–57]; "One Jesus and Four Primitive Gospels," *HTR* 61 (1968) 203–47 [*Trajectories*, 158–204]; "The Structure and Criteria of Early Christian Beliefs," in Robinson-Koester, *Trajectories*, 205–31.

expounded by his friend James M. Robinson[2]—the gnostic proclivities of which were blocked by the inclusion of the apocalyptic Son of Man sayings in Q, which can thus be seen as a secondary redaction of an older collection of wisdom sayings. This suggestion of Koester has been the key step leading to the distinction of a formative, sapiential stratum from a redactional, apocalyptic layer in Q by John S. Kloppenborg and others.[3] The way in which that distinction between sapiential and apocalyptic strata of Q has been described may be problematic precisely because advances in our understanding of the diversity of concrete expressions of early Christianity force further criticism and dismantling of our inherited conceptual apparatus. But once certain key conceptual adjustments are made, it seems clear that what Koester discerned twenty-five years ago as the crucial difference between Q and the *Gospel of Thomas,* that is, the "apocalyptic son of man sayings," may still be a key to understanding the distinctive concerns of Q.[4]

The Question of Apocalyptic and Sapiential Strata in Q

Kloppenborg's imaginative reconstruction of the formation of Q, although apparently definitive with regard to the composition of the various clusters of sayings in Q, seems questionable in its hypothesis of a formative "sapiential" layer and a secondary "apocalyptic" or judgmental layer.[5] The discernment of these two strata may be rooted more in the conceptual apparatus of modern New Testament scholarship than in the text of Q.[6] Ironically, it

[2] J. M. Robinson, "LOGOI SOPHŌN: On the Gattung of Q," in Robinson-Koester, *Trajectories,* 71–113.

[3] J. S. Kloppenborg, *The Formation of Q: Trajectories in Ancient Wisdom Collections* (SAC 2; Philadelphia: Fortress Press, 1987) 32–33.

[4] James M. Robinson presented his programmatic article on the genre of the Synoptic sayings source as a tribute to Rudolf Bultmann ("LOGOI SOPHON: Zur Gattung der Spruchquelle Q," in *Zeit und Geschichte: Dankesgabe an Rudolf Bultmann zum 80. Geburtstag,* ed. E. Dinkler [Tübingen: Mohr-Siebeck, 1964]). In the same tradition, but with a far more limited scope, range, and focus, it may be appropriate to offer this minor adaptation of Robinson's, Koester's and others' groundbreaking work on Q in tribute to the last great Schuler of Bultmann, Helmut Koester.

[5] Kloppenborg, *Formation of Q.* The following analysis is heavily dependent on the work of Kloppenborg. He has been a generous and patient mentor in my attempt to enter the complex world of Q scholarship. It seems only fair that, if I am to question his hypothesis regarding the stratigraphy of Q, I should suggest some alternative hypothesis regarding the development, composition, and function of the document.

[6] Many of the points made briefly in the next few paragraphs were stated in R. A. Horsley, "Questions about Redactional Strata and the Social Relations Reflected in Q," in *Society of Biblical Literature 1989 Seminar Papers,* ed. D. J. Lull (Atlanta: Scholars Press, 1989) 186–203; see the response by Kloppenborg, "*The Formation of Q* Revisited: A Response to Richard Horsley," in the same volume, pp. 204–15.

is precisely sophisticated analyses of texts like those by Koester and Kloppenborg that make it possible and necessary to call into question the very conceptual apparatus with which we have been working.

Kloppenborg assigns five complexes of sayings in Q (3:7–9, 16–17; 7:1–10, 18–35; 11:14–52; 12:39–59; 17:23–37) to a secondary redaction on the basis of three common features discerned in those complexes—projected audience, form, and motifs. But those common features are not consistently present in the five complexes of sayings. First, only one of the five clusters of sayings, Luke 11:14–26, 29–32, 39–52, appears to be clearly directed at the "outgroup" of "this γενέα," or impenitent opponents, as the ostensive or implied audience. All or most of the sets of sayings in the other four complexes are addressed directly to the Q people themselves. Moreover, there is no reason internal to the sayings in these complexes to think that "this γενέα" refers to "Israel" as opposed to "Gentiles," no indication of a mission to Gentiles, and no indication outside of Luke 7:1–9 of Gentile faith—hence, little evidence that "Gentile faith" is a significant theme, let alone that it functions as an *Unheilszeichen* for Israel.[7] Second, although many of the sayings in these complexes are clearly prophetic, it is difficult to find many that are arguably "apocalyptic words." Third, it is difficult to find in these five complexes motifs that could be identified as apocalyptic. Kloppenborg and Burton Mack have both pointed out that Q is much less apocalyptic than previously imagined.[8] But we can press that critical realization far more sharply: there are virtually no apocalyptic motifs in the supposedly apocalyptic stratum of Q. For example, Luke 12:54–56 does not suggest "signs of the end" or "the impending catastrophe" but refers to a present crisis, and the division of families in 12:51–53 is a prophetic, not an apocalyptic, motif (see Mic 7:6). It is difficult to find "the catastrophic destruction of the world" by fire or flood in Luke 3:9, 17; 12:49; 17:27, 29. Luke 12:40, 42–46 and 17:23–37 indicate the suddenness of judgment, but hardly an apocalyptic *Naherwartung*.[9]

Indeed, by strict analysis, only two sets of sayings, both in the same

[7] It will be necessary to develop fuller explanations of these points in another context. For now it might be noted, e.g., with regard to (τ)αυτη γενέα, on which so much weight is placed by Kloppenborg and others, that "this generation" may not even be an appropriate translation. Immediate literary context is surely the key. Thus, in reference to the scribes/lawyers and Pharisees, "this kind/type/group" is the appropriate translation in Luke 11:49–51 (and probably in 11:29–31 in the same complex of sayings), as can be seen from the comparison with, e.g., Mark 9:19, where γενέα refers to the disciples, or Mark 8:12, where it refers to the Pharisees, in contrast to Mark 8:38 and 13:30, where the reference is something broader, like "this generation" or "era."

[8] J. S. Kloppenborg, "Symbolic Eschatology and the Apocalypticism of Q," *HTR* 80 (1987) 292; B. Mack, "The Kingdom That Didn't Come: A Social History of the Q Tradents," in *Society of Biblical Literature 1988 Seminar Papers*, ed. D. J. Lull (Atlanta: Scholars Press, 1988) e.g., 614.

[9] *Pace* Kloppenborg, *Formation of Q*, e.g., 151–52; "Symbolic Eschatology, 296, 299–300, 306.

complex (11:29–32 and 11:49–51), actually contain the three common features used as criteria for differentiating the supposedly secondary "apocalyptic" or "judgmental" layer, and even then not quite in the distinctive ways Kloppenborg has characterized them: that is, they are prophetic (but not apocalyptic) sayings in form; they contain the motif of rejection of Jesus' preaching as a basis for condemnation (but no apocalyptic traits); and they also focus on "this generation" (but not "Israel") as the projected audience (in fact six of the seven occurrences of "this generation" occur in these two brief passages!). This would not appear to be a sufficient basis for assigning five whole clusters of sayings to a particular redactional stratum.

There are similar difficulties with the purported common features of the supposedly formative "sapiential" stratum.[10] First, this stratum cannot be differentiated from the judgmental stratum on the basis of "implied audience" since (a) (as just noted) most of the latter is also addressed directly to the members of the community and (b) at least two clusters in the "formative" stratum include material ostensibly directed at outsiders, which must then be dismissed as later redactional insertions (e.g., Luke 10:13–15; 13:28–30, 34–35; 14:16–24). But that same argument could be made for materials in the supposedly secondary clusters (e.g., that Luke 7:31–35, ostensibly directed at outsiders, is a redactional addition to 7:18–28, which is addressed directly to the community). Second, the argument from characteristic forms is particularly weak. In order to purify the stratum it must be purged of prophetic sayings, which are dismissed as later insertions. But even the material left is *not* particularly *sapiential* "with respect to traditional forms of conventional wisdom," and appears "sapiential" only by comparison with materials in the "apocalyptic" secondary stratum.[11] Since the supposedly secondary layer is not particularly apocalyptic, this ostensible distinction between the strata would appear to collapse. And since the supposedly formative layer contains "some rather specialized instructions which go beyond what is usually understood as sapiential admonitions," such as sayings regarding mission, discipleship, and the Holy Spirit,[12] there appears even less basis for its characterization as distinctively and consistently "sapiential." Third, the motifs claimed as characteristic for the supposedly formative stratum do not run across the component clusters, and it is questionable whether the texts cited actually illustrate the motifs listed. Fourth, the references provided as evidence for characteristic structural features throughout this stratum are not convincing, in some cases (12:13–14; 12:33a) not even clearly part of Q.

[10] The following observations respond to Kloppenborg's summary in *Formation of Q*, 238–43.

[11] Mack, "Kingdom That Didn't Come," 613.

[12] Kloppenborg, *Formation of Q*, 239–40.

Thus it appears, upon closer examination, that the criteria used to differentiate the supposedly secondary, apocalyptic stratum from the supposedly formative, sapiential stratum in Q—that is, the different sets of common features in each stratum—are either difficult to find in the actual Q clusters or are not distinctive to one stratum or the other.

These problems of characterizing and distinguishing strata are compounded by generic considerations. Kloppenborg claims that "the formative stratum has the strongest generic contacts with the genre of 'instruction.'"[13] Yet the "two notable departures from the typical form of instruction" would appear to be decisive. In contrast to the instructional genre, the "sapiential" speeches in Q do not take the form of parental instruction. Even more important, "in contrast to the generally conservative comportment of the instruction, Q presents an ethic of radical discipleship which reverses many of the conventions which allow a society to operate. . . ."[14] The explanation? "Q has moved towards the form of gnomologium." And "although Q infuses the form with new content, and although it shifts from a presupposition of this-worldly order to eschatological order, the basic hermeneutic of the instruction is preserved."[15] Yet Kloppenborg himself, besides drawing attention explicitly to how different Q's hermeneutic is from that of "instructional" literature, has set up our discernment that Q's hermeneutic matches none of the three hermeneutical modes of gnomological literature.[16] That of "penetration and research" surely fits the *Gospel of Thomas,* but not Q. "Fittingness" fits Q even less. Kloppenborg seems to be suggesting that the supposedly formative sapiential speeches of Q presuppose the gnomological hermeneutic of "obedience and assimilation." But whereas such gnomologia require study, reflection, and interpretation toward the attainment of a perfect and untroubled condition of the soul (again *Gos. Thom.* might fit!), Q requires obedience in the sense of response to a new social order of troubled social interaction and conflict ("love your enemies"; being sent out "as sheep in the midst of wolves"; "Do not fear those who (only) kill the body") in an ethos concerned about the basic human necessities of food and shelter (see Luke 6:20–21; 6:27–36; 10:5–8; Q/Matt 6:11–12; Luke 12:22–31). The new wine of the kingdom would appear to have burst the old wineskins of instruction and gnomologia. The hermeneutic of the formative layer of Q, some of which is not sapiential instruction anyhow, is simply not that of an assimilation of a wisdom ethos (not in 6:20–49, concerned with community interaction; nor in 10:1–16, concerned with mission; nor in

[13] Ibid., 317.
[14] Ibid., 318–19
[15] Ibid., 319, 321.
[16] Ibid., 301–6.

11:2–4, 9–13, concerned with prayer; nor in 12:2–12, concerned with struggle; nor in 12:22–31, concerned with anxiety).

If, therefore, the "apocalyptic" stratum of Q is not particularly apocalyptic in form or motif, and the "sapiential" layer is not particularly sapiential in substance or hermeneutic, perhaps another look at the formation and genre of Q would be in order.

Characteristics of Q Complexes

Kloppenborg and others have relied on Koester's analysis of the *Gospel of Thomas* as the basis for the claim that "as far as *Gattungsgeschichte* is concerned, the *Gos. Thomas* reflects a stage antecedent to the final form of Q."[17] With that claim as an operative assumption, the first step would appear to be a critical review of the characteristics of the *Gospel of Thomas* and the tradition behind it.[18]

Although he accepted Robinson's view that both *Gos. Thom.* and Q belong to the genre of *logoi sophōn*,[19] Koester also drew attention to the prominence of prophetic and apocalyptic sayings in *Gos. Thom.*[20] Indeed, the prophetic and apocalyptic materials in *Gos. Thom.*, including the "kingdom" sayings and parables and the other, largely prophetic parables taken together constitute nearly half (50 +) of the 114 logia. They are far more prominent in *Gos. Thom.* than proverbs and other wisdom sayings (roughly 15–20 in various judgments), which have roughly the same frequency as the I-sayings and what were apparently "community rules" in the pre-Thomas traditions and which are less prominent than the apparently "gnostic" material. Of the prophetic and apocalyptic materials that dominate the collection, there are several that are apocalyptic in motif or could be classified as "apocalyptic" sayings, even if we are careful to follow Bultmann's more restrictive usage of that category (as opposed to the rather loose and synthetic concept that often still obscures our scholarly discourse).[21] This includes even a few that are reminiscent of motifs otherwise distinctive of "apocalyptic" literature proper, concerning the heavens passing away or being rolled up (11, 111), speculation about the end or fate of the dead and the new world (e.g., 18, 51; cf. 19 and 85), and elements known through Paul (17; cf. 1 Cor 2:8–9). Far more prominent and typical of *Gos. Thom.* are prophetic sayings,

[17] Ibid., 33.

[18] On *Gos. Thom.* and Koester's important contribution to its interpretation, see now Ron Cameron, "Thomas, Gospel of," in *The Anchor Bible Dictionary*, ed. D. N. Freedman (Garden City: Doubleday, forthcoming); idem, "The *Gospel of Thomas* and Christian Origins," in this volume (chapter 30).

[19] Robinson, "LOGOI SOPHŌN."

[20] Koester, "One Jesus," 166–85.

[21] R. Bultmann, *The History of the Synoptic Tradition* (Oxford: Blackwell, 1963) 120–25.

particularly those that have parallels in Q, and a remarkable number of parables, particularly parables of the kingdom and/or with parallels in Mark. The hermeneutic of *Gos. Thom.*, however, can be discerned more clearly in the "gnostic" materials located in a score of logia scattered throughout the collection, materials that have few parallels in the Synoptic Gospels.

The implications of this review of Koester's analysis of materials in *Gos. Thom.* for assessment of Q appear to lead in a direction different from that taken in recent discussions of stratigraphy in Q. First, although the absence of apocalyptic Son of Man sayings in *Gos. Thom.* is striking in comparison with Q, there are far more apocalyptic (and much more vividly apocalyptic) materials in *Gos. Thom.* than in Q. Thus the difference between (the tradition of sayings leading to and/or reflected in) *Gos. Thom.* and (the final version of) Q cannot depend on the absence or presence of apocalyptic sayings or motifs generally. But that appears to eliminate the basis on which Kloppenborg and others posited a stage of a sayings genre antecedent to the final form of Q that was basically sapiential and distinguishable from a redactional apocalyptic layer in the final form of Q.[22]

Second, although there are indeed many wisdom sayings in *Gos. Thom.* (along with several apocalyptic sayings), the most striking impression received from Koester's (form-critical) analysis of logia in *Gos. Thom.* is the dominance of prophetic sayings and kingdom parables.[23] But rather than contradict or call into question the seminal research of Robinson adopted by Koester (and now virtually assumed in the field) that *Gos. Thom.* (and supposed proto-Thomas collections) belonged to the broad general genre of *logoi,* this merely moves toward greater specificity and precision. Robinson made it quite clear that the literary label or self-designation *logoi* was used far more broadly than for collections of wisdom sayings. In fact, particularly when he focused on Christian literature, *logos/logoi* referred to prophetic (even apocalyptic) "words/sayings of the Lord," often understood prophetically and sometimes understood explicitly as transmitted through the Lord's

[22] That *Gos. Thom.* as we have it may (re-)interpret apocalyptic sayings does not change the situation, because what are properly categorized as apocalyptic sayings and motifs were thus still contained in the tradition (and in the genre?) of sayings that leads to or is reflected in *Gos. Thom.* It may be indicative of the hermeneutic of *Gos. Thom.* that what appears to be a typical apocalyptic motif of the end being the same as the beginning (#18) and a statement of seemingly "realized eschatology" (#51) and a saying that rejects apocalyptic-style calculations (#113//Luke 17:20–21) can stand, as it were, side by side.

[23] A related impression is that there are fewer changes in the wisdom sayings in *Gos. Thom.* compared with their parallels in the Synoptic tradition, while many of the prophetic sayings have been adapted with specific changes, twists, and additions. As Koester notes, "we can see in it a distinctive reinterpretation of originally eschatological sayings and their terminology" ("GNOMAI DIAPHOROI," 137). This suggests that the wisdom sayings were more susceptible of understanding according to the special hermeneutic presupposed in Thomas, whereas the prophetic sayings required explicit adaptation and interpretation.

prophets, as is clear in literature from Paul to Justin.[24] The designation *logoi* is very general and fluid. If we are to take our cue from the type of sayings dominant in *Gos. Thom.* (or in the cultivation and transmission of Jesus sayings behind it), *logoi prophētōn* would appear to be a more appropriate specification than *logoi sophōn.*

Rather than focus the argument on the most suitable label for the apparent genre, however, it may be more fruitful to compare *Gos. Thom.* and Q for ways in which *Gos. Thom.* may reflect a stage antecedent to the final form of Q in terms of generic development. If we think in compositional terms rather than types of sayings, a major difference between *Gos. Thom.* and Q is immediately evident. Whereas in Q the sayings are clearly formed into coherent larger clusters or complexes, in *Gos. Thom.* most of the material stands in much smaller units, usually as single, double, or triple sayings. Certain units (e.g., logia 14, 21, or 47) show development toward the fuller clusters found in Q. A useful comparison can be focused on Luke 12:49 (50), 51–53, 54–56 (which is apparently part of a still larger complex in Q): *Gos. Thom.* 16 joins the same two sayings as Luke/Q 12:51–53, but the parallel to Luke 12:49 is isolated in *Gos. Thom.* 10 and that to Luke 12:56 is the answer to a question of Jesus' identity in *Gos. Thom.* 91. Clusters of sayings, such as those in logia 14, 16, or 47, are rare in *Gos. Thom.;* however, they dominate Q and indeed give it an internal structure lacking in *Gos. Thom.* This suggests an approach to understanding the character and composition (perhaps even the genre) of Q as a whole document quite different from (and no longer dependent on) the attempt to characterize Q as a whole on the basis of the forms and motifs of individual sayings and sets of sayings. In this connection much of Kloppenborg's compositional analysis and reconstruction can be accepted as definitive quite apart from the stratigraphical hypothesis and the sets of questionable common features on which it is based.[25] That is, if Q is composed almost entirely of larger or smaller complexes of sayings, then the composition, character, and function of those complexes may be the key to understanding Q as a whole. Outlines and divisions of Q have been proposed with increasing specificity, from T. W. Manson to W. Schenk.[26] But they have been basically topical or thematic

[24] Robinson, "LOGOI SOPHŌN," 95–103.

[25] Although much critical analysis remains to be done on the development of clusters, building on such investigations as the chapter "Aphoristic Cluster" in J. D. Crossan, *In Fragments: The Aphorisms of Jesus* (San Francisco: Harper & Row, 1983); and P. H. Sellew, "Early Collections of Jesus' Words: The Development of Dominical Discourses" (Th.D. diss., Harvard University, 1985).

[26] T. W. Manson, *The Sayings of Jesus* (London: SCM, 1949; orig. 1937); W. Schenk, *Synopse zur Redenquelle der Evangelien: Synopse und Rekonstruktion in deutscher Übersetzung mit kurzen Erläuterungen* (Düsseldorf: Patmos, 1981).

labels or sequential indicators. We may get further by looking for the functions, the possible purposes and/or likely effects of the various complexes.

In a few cases the functions appear immediately evident. Luke 10:2–16 (one of those sapiential speeches that goes beyond what is usually understood as sapiential admonitions, as Kloppenborg noted) is instruction regarding mission. Luke 11:2–4, 9–13 is instruction specifically on prayer. The Q material underlying Luke 17:23–37, the contents of which are exhortation on preparedness in the face of the suddenness of judgment, appears to have functioned as the sanction on the whole of Q (somewhat analogously to the way in which Luke 6:46–49 is the sanction on the exhortations in 6:27–45).

The functions of other complexes may not be far to seek. Luke 6:20–49 is, to be sure, Jesus "inaugural sermon." In addition, it is a set of opening admonitions that corresponds to the set of sanctions that closes the document in Luke 17:23–37. But, more precisely, as can be discerned from the contents of such admonition as 6:27–38, it appears intended as instruction on social-economic relations within the community, and not merely religious teaching to individuals. More than that, the complex has a fairly clear structure or sequence: the initial blessings set the stage for the exhortations regarding local social-economic interaction, which are followed by sanctional sayings that reinforce motivation to observe the preceding injunctions. Luke 7:18–35 deals not simply with Jesus, John, and "this generation" but with the significance of what is happening with John and Jesus, that is, the fulfillment of expectations and prophecies of salvation. Luke 11:39–52 and possibly the whole of 11:14–52 condemns the principal opponents of the Q community and/or of the people with whom the Q people identify. The Q material in Luke 13:28–30, 34–35; 14:16–24, similarly, appears to be another cluster of sayings directed against opponents, in this case the rulers in Jerusalem. The fragments of Q utilized in Luke 14:26–27, 34–35; 15:4–7; 16:13, 17, 18; and 17:1–6 apparently formed a cluster of stringent demands on discipleship and community discipline with the appropriate encouragement (although this material could also be viewed as two shorter clusters divided on either side of 16:13). Also not too far to seek, the sayings by John in 3:7–9, 16–17 on the crisis of impending judgment and salvation and that by Jesus in 22:28–30 on the restoration or liberation of Israel function respectively as the opening and closing sayings of the whole collection.

Less evident but nevertheless intelligible are the division, coherence, and functions of the remaining materials, largely in Luke 12. Luke 12:2–12, apparently following immediately after the complex that condemned the community's principal opponents, exhorts Jesus' followers to be confident and bold in their witness, with the specter of heavenly judgment as sanction. Luke 12:22–31(33–34) addresses the (Q) people's anxieties about necessities of life, which will take care of themselves if they are single-minded in pursuit of the kingdom. Luke 12:39–40, 42–46 could be sanctions on the previous exhortation or part of a larger complex of sanctions addressed to the Q community. Luke 12:49–56(57–59) proclaims the disruptive, conflictual effect of Jesus' practice or movement, with a challenge to those who do not respond to the crisis. Luke 13:18–21 are simply two parables indicating the amazing expansion of the kingdom (of the Q/Jesus movement?). With or without the exhortation to bold confession in Luke 12:2–12, those four or five smaller clusters could be taken together as one larger complex, offering positive encouragement followed by two sets of sanctions and rounded out by two encouraging parables of the kingdom's growth. The resulting complex could then be seen as parallel (and roughly comparable in length) to 6:20–49: the Q material behind Luke 12:22 through 13:21 addresses particular understandable anxieties of Q people with appropriately sharp sanctions, while 6:20–49 addresses intracommunity affairs with less ominous sanctions.

The dominant, unifying theme of the whole document is clearly the kingdom of God. Featured prominently at crucial points in most of the complexes (6:20; 7:28; 10:9, 11; 11:2; 11:20; 12:31; 13:18–21; 13:28–29; 16:16?; 22:28–30), the kingdom of God is virtually assumed or "taken for granted" as the focus of Q discourse as well as the comprehensive agenda of preaching, practice, and purpose in Q. The kingdom of God, moreover, is double-edged, having positive, salvific benefits for those who respond to its presence, but negative, judgmental implications for those who do not (see esp. 10:9 and 11; 11:20; 13:28–29).

In fact, by focusing on the kingdom theme, we can discern how the various complexes cohere as a whole document. Luke 3:9–11, 16–17 and 22:28–30 provide, respectively, a threatening as well as promising opening and a highly positive, anticipatory ending, in which the kingdom clearly means the renewal of Israel. The opening discourse in 6:20–49, after announcing the kingdom for the poor, etc., presents fundamental commandments for interaction in the kingdom community(ies) and is followed by a discourse that affirms the fulfillment of longings now happening with Jesus and the kingdom. The closing two discourses correspondingly articulate, respectively, the stringent demands of discipleship and community discipline and admonition about preparedness in the face of judgment that provides sanction for Q as a whole. Depending on how Luke 16:16 is placed, that these complexes, particularly 17:23–37, lack the kingdom theme makes sense insofar as the kingdom does not have negative implications for those who respond—that is, the community itself. In between the opening programmatic complexes and the closing disciplinary and sanctioning clusters are successive instructions (respectively) on the mission of spreading the kingdom, on petitioning God boldly for the kingdom, on confidence in confession and no anxiety in pursuit of the kingdom, followed by sanctions on those encouraging teachings and then sayings on the crisis constituted by Jesus' ministry, which is in turn followed by two encouraging parables of growth of the kingdom. Between the exhortation on boldly petitioning God and the other encouraging exhortations directed to the community and just following the latter are two clusters of sayings in which Jesus stands in conflict with or condemns the Pharisees (= "this γενέα"?) and the ruling house/families in Jerusalem, for both of whom, in their presumption of their own salvation, the kingdom means condemnation.

Throughout the sequence of complexes, the types of sayings and motifs correspond to the function of the complex. The clusters addressed to community relations and discipline (i.e., 6:27–49; 12:22–31; and the pieces behind Luke 14, 15, 16, 17) are strongly sapiential—as we might expect, given the traditional function of popular wisdom (in contrast to the more individually addressed parental instruction of professional sages). The mission discourse and prayer do not correspond to conventional forms of wisdom. Prophetic forms come to the fore in the complexes directed to the community as sanctions (sections of Luke 12 and 17:23–37) as well as in the clusters of sayings against the Pharisees and Jerusalem rulers—again not surprising considering the traditional function of prophetic woes, laments, etc. Not surprisingly, the motif of the killing of the prophets occurs in the two prophetic clusters ostensibly addressed to the opponents (11:47–51; 13:34–35), and the (at one point overlapping) polemic against "this γενέα" is almost exclusively concentrated in one of those clusters, that directed against the Pharisees/lawyers (11:29–32, 49–51).

There are kingdom sayings or parables also scattered throughout *Gos. Thom.* But they do not play the same role in providing the unifying theme because *Gos. Thom.* is a collection of various sayings without any (as yet clear) internal structure and sequencing corresponding to that provided by the clusters that constitute Q. The clusters with their distinctive functions would appear to be the key to understanding Q, to what makes Q different from that earlier stage in the vague genre of sayings collection behind *Gos. Thom.*

It is in this connection that the presence of the "apocalyptic" son of man sayings may be a key to Q in comparison with *Gos. Thom.* We must be careful not to continue to project the modern synthetic concept of "the Son of Man" onto Q texts in this regard. It seems clear that when "son of man" is a self-reference by Jesus in Q it does not refer to judgment, and when "(the day of) the son of man" refers to judgment, it does not refer to Jesus. Thus, "son of man" is not a christological title and apparently does not even refer to an individual agent of redemption in Q/Luke 12:8–9; 12:40; 17:24, 26, 30. Rather, "son of man" in 12:8–9 is an advocate figure in the divine court of judgment and "(the day of) the son of man" in 17:24, 26, 30 may simply be an image of the divine judgment (i.e., so standardized that no reference to the text of Daniel 7 is involved), with greater or lesser emphasis on an individual heavenly figure. Moreover, it is not clear at all that these "(day of) the son of man" sayings in Q evoke a particularly apocalyptic scenario of "the last judgment" with attendant signs and cosmic disturbances. In fact, the references to "the day(s) of the son of man" in Q/Luke 17:23–30 are almost antiapocalyptic in their explicit rejection of watching for signs and emphasis on the suddenness of judgment.[27] In every case, of course, these "son of man" sayings function as sanctions on the community's or members' discipline and courage, positively in 12:8–9 and negatively as a threat in 12:40 and 17:23–30. Thus these sayings do not lend Q an apocalyptic orientation, but they do provide a sanction of the suddenness of judgment for a community caught in the midst of a struggle.

It would seem an obvious next step, following up Koester's observation about the absence of these "apocalyptic" son of man sayings in *Gos. Thom.*, to look for other materials that function importantly in Q but are absent in *Gos. Thom.* Significantly, the latter has no parallels to the series of woes against the Pharisees (a parallel only to Luke 12:52 in logion 39; cf. 102) or to the prophetic sayings directed against the rulers in Luke 13:28–29 and 34–35 (contrast the guarding against the "world" in logion 21). Nor does *Gos. Thom.* have parallels to the sayings that involve or suggest a community in struggle, such as Luke 7:31–35; 11:14–20; and 12:3–9 (only the general saying 12:2 is paralleled, in logia 5–6). It is also significant that many of the prophetic sayings in *Gos. Thom.* have been explicitly adapted or interpreted in an individualizing and/or gnosticizing direction, as can be seen by comparison with some counterparts in Q, which still have a social thrust. The effect becomes clear, however, particularly when we consider the cluster composition in Q in contrast to relatively isolated sayings in *Gos. Thom.* The clusters provide a social context in which the sayings have significance in Q, whereas in *Gos. Thom.* we are left without much of any context for interpretation of individual sayings. For example, in logion 73 the saying about sending out workers into the harvest has no particular connotations of mission, whereas in Q/Luke 10 it functions as the keynote to the mission of spreading the kingdom, which evokes sharp social conflict. In *Gos. Thom.* 35 the saying about binding the strong man and plundering his house has no connotations of the struggle against Satan's rule that not only has been engaged but is being won, as suggested by the complex of sayings in Luke 11:14–23. "Cleansing the outside of the cup" and the Pharisees' hiding the key to knowledge in *Gos. Thom.* 89 and 39, respectively, have no religious-political context at all because they are not part of a series of woes against the Pharisees, as in Q. What is hidden becoming revealed in *Gos. Thom.* 5

[27] Similarly Kloppenborg ("Symbolic Eschatology," 301–3)—although terms such as "the parousia" and "events prior to the end" and "universal destruction" appear to be derived from Christian theology and/or from synthetic modern scholarly concepts of apocalypticism rather than from the Q text.

and 6 gives no sense of encouragement or vindication in the face of acute social conflict that it has in Q because it is part of 12:2–9.

The clusters and their functions thus also appear to be the key to the hermeneutic implicit in Q, in contrast to that in *Gos. Thom.* The latter is a matter of "penetration and research" basically of particular sayings toward the goal of individual enlightenment, with no concern for a social group and no social conflict in view. Q, by contrast, is concerned not so much with a "radical mode of existence" for individuals but with a new or renewed social order, which entails social conflict as well, and is structured into a series of clusters of sayings focused on particular aspects of that social renewal and social conflict.

Q and Community Instruction

Once we recognize that Q has been composed by/into clusters of sayings, we should be comparing Q not only with the *Gos. Thom.* but with other sayings collections that are composed in clusters as well. The most obvious case might be the *Didache*. Indeed, there are some striking similarities between Q and *Didache* in the function or focus (and the sequence) of certain clusters.

The *Didache* opens with a traditional two-way teaching in chapters 1–5 (closely related to that in *Barnabas* 18–20).[28] The first major section then happens to be a cluster of sayings with close affinities to Q/Luke 6:27–35/ Matt 5:38–48, and continues with exhortations in the form "Do not . . . ," and in the form of "parental instruction." More to the point here, however, the overall complex is covenantal in substance (decalogue and related prohibitions and "fences around" the decalogue prohibitions) and is concerned with social-economic interaction within a community. (*Did.* 1.3b–6 in context, like the more explicit covenantal structuring of Q material in Matthew 5, further confirms that Q/Luke 6:20–49 is a cluster of *logoi* concerned with social relations in a community and not simply with individual ethic admonition.) Thus in function the opening complex corresponds to "Jesus' inaugural sermon" in Q, both in itself and in its place at the opening of the document.

The *Didache* ends with what has been termed "eschatological admonition." Substantively it has more affinities with Mark 13 and Matthew 24 than with Q (e.g., Luke 12:35, 40), is replete with apocalyptic motifs (such as "the world-deceiver," "signs spread out in heaven," etc., and climaxes with "the Lord coming on the clouds of heaven") that are utterly lacking in Q. But the function of *Did.* 16 is parallel to that of the terminal complex of sayings in

[28] See Robert A. Kraft, *The Apostolic Fathers*, vol. 3, *The Didache and Barnabas* (New York: Nelson, 1965).

Q/Luke 17:23–37 regarding the suddenness of judgment, that is, a sanction on the exhortation in the whole document.

In between these opening and closing complexes of *logoi* (*Did.* 1.3a) are several clusters of instructions on various topics. Q has no parallels, of course, to the brief sections concerning food, baptism, and fasts or to the longer section on the Eucharist. But it does have a parallel instruction on the Lord's Prayer (*Did.* 8.2–3; Luke 11:2–4) and a parallel to the brief section on community discipline placed immediately before the closing "eschatological"/judgmental sanction (*Did.* 15.3–4; Luke 17:1–4). Considering the later stage in the development of the early Christian movement represented by the *Didache*—and assuming that Q is dated much earlier in the "mission" of Jesus' followers—the lengthy discussion concerning the support and treatment of itinerant apostles and prophets (*Did.* 11–13) is a complex of teachings that corresponds to the mission discourse in Q (Luke 10:1–16). Thus we have parallels to five of the Q complexes in the *Didache* which exhibit the same or similar function and the same sequence.

These parallels do not suggest, however, that Q is merely a proto-Didache, an early form of "manual of discipline" for the nascent Christian movement in Palestine. That is clearly an important aspect of its composition and apparent function, but it has the form of *logoi* of *Jesus*. And the bulk of the *logoi* organized in respective complexes are exhortations of promise and encouragement as well as of crisis and warning directed to the community(ies) of his followers: 7:18–28, 31–35 about the fulfillment at hand, 12:2–9 about fearless confession, 12:22–31 on not being anxious, 12:49–59 on the crisis at hand, and 11:14–52 plus 13:28–30, 34–35; + 14:16–24 condemning the rulers and their retainers (in Q for the benefit of the hearers/readers). The keynotes with which the whole (hypothetical) document apparently begins and ends, moreover, are prophetic threat and promise: the "stronger one who is coming" will baptize "with holy spirit" as well as fire and "gather the grain" as well as burn the chaff (Q/Luke 3:16–17, and (once we translate terms more appropriately) the twelve are to be "liberating/making justice for" (not negatively "judging") the twelve tribes of Israel (Q/Luke 22:28–30). Finally, Jesus, whose *logoi* constitute the contents of the clusters, is clearly understood as a prophet—indeed (along with John) as the culminating prophet in a long line of prophets (3:16–17; 7:18–28; 11:49–50; 13:34).

Although comparison with similarly functioning complexes of sayings in the *Didache* enables us to discern that Q is a document concerned with community life, it is also clearly a perpetuation of the prophetic preaching of Jesus (and John), announcing the presence of the kingdom, which means fulfillment of longings and renewal of community life in Israel for those who respond, but condemnation for "Pharisees" (were any others included in "this γενέα"?) and Jerusalem rulers who oppose. But if Q is more than a

Didache-like manual for community order, it is much more than "instruction" addressed to individual disciples in the tradition of wisdom teaching evident in literature such as Sirach. The sayings tradition that culminates in the *Gospel of Thomas* does indeed focus individual penetration and interpretation on particular sayings of Jesus—and in pursuit of its hermeneutic must adapt and alter the dominant prophetic components of that tradition. Q, on the other hand, is concerned less with instruction of individuals than with the social life and conflicts of a movement. Besides shaping sapiential materials (of which it has much more than does *Gos. Thom.*) into clusters concerned with community relations, prayer, and discipline, it utilizes sets and whole complexes of prophetic materials as sanctions on community discipline and as polemic against the authority figures who oppose the movement. Most distinctive and important among the prophetic materials directed to the community, as Koester noted, are the threatening "(day of) the son of man" sayings, which are utterly lacking in *Gos. Thom.*, but which constitute the final sanctioning cluster in Q.

It is conceivable that determination of the precise literary genre of Q is not of crucial importance for understanding its composition and function. Robinson's survey of literature designated as *logoi* turned up a great variety, some of it sections of larger wholes, most of it "sapiential" in character, but some of it "prophetic." It is difficult to understand how, when we find hermeneutics as widely variant as those of Q and *Gos. Thom.*, the classification of both under *logoi sophōn* helps to elucidate either. Assuming that some term of reference to genre may be appropriate in dealing with literature, however, we should focus on the composition of Q in a series of complexes with particular functions for the community to which it was addressed and not so much on the types of sayings included in those complexes. Moreover, if the authority (and founder?) of the Q community(ies) is understood as a prophet in a series of prophets including John, then an appropriate specification of the document of the clusters of his and John's sayings would appear to be *logoi prophētōn*.

15

The Divinization of Disorder: The Trajectory of Matt 8:20// Luke 9:58//*Gos. Thom.* 86

ROBERT DORAN

THE CHALLENGE OF form criticism has been to understand an individual unit of a tradition without regard to the later literary contexts in which that unit is found. Only after one has attempted that difficult task of imagination can one begin to discuss a trajectory of the unit. As so stated, the form-critical approach has a built-in diachronic stance: an early saying, for example, is said to develop during transmission into a scene in which a question is asked and the saying provides the answer, or a maxim may become a saying when so-and-so is said to have expressed it. One might debate whether such a chronological development is essential to the process of imagination involved in the form-critical exercise, or whether one should speak simply of different levels of reading a unit from the more abstract to the more particular. Whatever the case, one must investigate what individual units of the tradition may have meant.

One particular case is the saying about homelessness found in Matt 8:20// Luke 9:58//*Gos. Thom.* 86.[1]

Matt 8:19–20	*Luke 9:57–62*
19 καὶ προσελθὼν εἷς γραμματεὺς εἶπεν αὐτῷ· διδάσκαλε, ἀκολου-	57 Καὶ πορευομένων αὐτῶν ἐν τῇ ὁδῷ εἶπέν τις πρὸς αὐτόν· ἀκο-

[1] I have maintained the literal translation "Son of Man." For a sensitive discussion of the problem of balancing traditional translation of this phrase with more inclusive translations such as "human" or "child of humanity," see Adela Yarbro Collins, "The Origin of the Designation of Jesus as 'Son of Man,'" *HTR* 80 (1987) 391–407, esp. 391–92.

θήσω σοι ὅπου ἐὰν ἀπέρχῃ.
20 καὶ λέγει αὐτῷ ὁ Ἰησοῦς· αἱ
ἀλώπεκες φωλεοὺς ἔχουσιν καὶ
τὰ πετεινὰ τοῦ οὐρανοῦ κατασκηνώσεις, ὁ δὲ υἱὸς τοῦ ἀνθρώπου οὐκ ἔχει ποῦ τὴν κεφαλὴν
κλίνῃ.

λουθήσω σοι ὅπου ἐὰν ἀπέρχῃ.
58 καὶ εἶπεν αὐτῷ ὁ Ἰησοῦς· αἱ
ἀλώπεκες φωλεοὺς ἔχουσιν καὶ
τὰ πετεινὰ τοῦ οὐρανοῦ κατασκηνώσεις, ὁ δὲ υἱὸς τοῦ ἀνθρώπου οὐκ ἔχει ποῦ τὴν κεφαλὴν
κλίνῃ.

ⲡⲉϫⲉ ⲓ̅ⲥ̅ ϫⲉ [ⲛⲃⲁϣⲟⲣ ⲟⲩⲛ̅ⲧⲁ]ⲩ ⲛ[ⲉⲩⲃⲏⲃ]
ⲁⲩⲱ ⲛ̅ϩⲁⲗⲁⲧⲉ ⲟⲩⲛ̅ⲧⲁⲩ ⲙⲙⲁⲩ ⲙ̅[ⲡⲉ]ⲩⲙⲁϩ
ⲡϣⲏⲣⲉ ⲇⲉ ⲙ̅ⲡⲣⲱⲙⲉ ⲙⲛ̅ⲧⲁϥ ⲛⲛ[ⲟⲩ]ⲙⲁ
ⲉⲣⲓⲕⲉ ⲛ̅ⲧⲉϥⲁⲡⲉ ⲛϥⲙ̅ⲧⲟⲛ ⲙ̅[ⲙⲟ]ϥ.

And a scribe approached and said to him, "Teacher, I will follow you wherever you go." And Jesus says to him, "The foxes have dens and the birds of heaven quarters, but the Son of Man has nowhere to lay his head."

And as they were going along the road someone said to him, "I will follow you wherever you go." And Jesus said to him, "The foxes have dens and the birds of heaven quarters, but the Son of Man has nowhere to lay his head."

Jesus said, "[The foxes have] their dens and the birds have their nests, but the Son of Man has nowhere to lay his head and rest.

In the *Gospel of Thomas*, the saying is found without the disciple–leader interaction present in Matthew and Luke, and Helmut Koester suggested that the witness of *Gos. Thom.* seemed to confirm that the logion did not apply to Jesus.[2] Since then, John S. Kloppenborg has well argued for the independent development of the saying in *Gos. Thom.*, as the setting in the canonical Gospels is artificial.[3]

The saying shows evidences of careful craftsmanship. Bultmann had already noted its antithetic parallelism, with the first part containing synonymous parallelism.[4] The use of an indirect deliberative question as the object

[2] Robinson-Koester, *Trajectories*, 170 n. 34.

[3] John S. Kloppenborg, *The Formation of Q: Trajectories in Ancient Wisdom Collections* (SAC 2; Philadelphia: Fortress Press, 1987) 191 n. 83; see also Rollin Kearns, *Das Traditionsgefüge um den Menschensohn* (Tübingen: Mohr-Siebeck, 1986) 26 n. 83.

[4] Rudolf Bultmann, *The History of the Synoptic Tradition* (New York: Harper & Row, 1963) 81. John Dominic Crossan also comments sensitively on the parallelism (*In Fragments: The Aphorisms of Jesus* [San Francisco: Harper & Row, 1983] 77–78).

of the second stich contrasts emphatically with the substantives of the first stich. The word choice in the saying is also well made with assonance at ἀλώπεκες φωλεούς and κεφαλὴν κλίνῃ. There is no figure of speech in the second half of the first stich (πετεινὰ τοῦ οὐρανοῦ κατασκηνώσεις), but the choice of κατασκηνώσις instead of the more usual word for bird's nest (νοσσιά; Att. νεοττιά) is revealing. A rare word, κατασκήνωσις is found with the meaning of bird's nest only here and reflects the Septuagint usage, where birds lodge (κατασκηνοῦν) under trees in Ps 103:12 LXX (τὰ πετεινὰ τοῦ οὐρανοῦ κατασκηνώσει) and Dan 4:21 (see also Dan 4:12). In these contexts, as in its other appearances in the Septuagint, κατασκηνοῦν has the resonances of settled living.[5] Such a word choice is particularly apt, for the first stich contrasts the social habits of animals with homeless human behavior.[6] This sense of community versus the individual is further suggested by the contrast of the plurals "foxes" and "birds" with the singular human. The Septuagint Son of Man (see Sir 17:30; Jer 2:6) has a double article, and the article is generic, corresponding to the generic article governing "foxes" and "birds," as the class of humans is contrasted with the classes of animals.[7] The specific animals chosen have interest too. On a Lévi-Straussian grid, foxes live under the ground, birds live above the ground in the air, and humans live on the ground. Foxes are seen as inimical to human culture, invading vineyards (Song 2:15) and prowling, almost repossessing, ruined cities (Lam 5:18 LXX; Ps 63:10). The sarcasm of Tobiah's remark in Neh 4:3 relies on the constant pressure of foxes against cultivation. Birds too are the freest of animals. Aristophanes' *Birds* plays on the incongruity of birds building a *polis*.[8] The saying has been well polished.

The classic form-critical view of the saying was stated by R. Bultmann:

> The dominical saying could have circulated without any framework. That must indeed have been the case if *ho huios tou anthrōpou* has been incorrectly substituted for "man." And "man" must have been in fact the original meaning, man, homeless in this world, is contrasted with the wild beasts. This is presumably an old proverb which tradition has turned into a saying of Jesus.[9]

[5] Wilhelm Michaelis, "σκηνή," *TDNT* 7:368.

[6] Arland D. Jacobson finds κατασκήνωσας here "impossibly stilted" and suggests a reflection in this saying of Septuagint usage, where the word refers to the dwelling place of God (Ezek 37:27; Tob 1:4; Wis 9:8; 2 Macc 14:35) ("Wisdom Christology in Q" [Ph.D. diss., Claremont Graduate School, 1978] 132). He does not discuss the Septuagint usage mentioned above.

[7] There is thus no reason to posit that the titular Son of Man was substituted for a first-person singular (see C. Colpe, *TDNT* 8:435). The reconstruction of the saying in Aramaic by M. Casey is sound, although the Septuagintal flavor of the Greek, as well as its niceness, argues against the necessity of retroversion into Aramaic. Casey also notes that the Greek article could be read as generic; see "The Jackals and the Son of Man (Matt. 8.20//Luke 9.58)," *JSNT* 23 (1985) 3–22.

[8] The same incongruity is found in the fable of Aesop about apes who wanted to dwell in a *polis*. The fable is found in Hermogenes *Progymnasmata* 1.14–15 (ed. H. Rabe; Leipzig: Teubner, 1913). The ascription to Hermogenes is doubted by Rabe.

[9] Bultmann, *History*, 28.

It is a secular *mashal*, "a saying which is completely full of the pessimism of folklore."[10] Kloppenborg basically concurs with this judgment.[11] Adela Yarbro Collins also holds that "the aphorism is probably an adaptation of a widely known proverb," but further suggests that the pessimistic contrast between humans and animals "could easily be adapted to a philosophically dualistic, apocalyptic or gnostic perspective."[12]

Bultmann's analysis of the saying has not always been accepted. Barnabas Lindars states that, as a description of humanity in general, this saying is "manifestly untrue of people in general, who usually do have houses and beds."[13] Lindars claims that Jesus used *bar nāšā'* in this saying as an oblique self-reference that could also include anyone who shared in the conditions of Jesus' own missionary vocation.[14] Richard Bauckham also claims that the generic meaning "human" makes the saying incredible.[15] Maurice Casey counters the claim that as a general statement about humans the saying is manifestly untrue by appealing to a situational context of the idiom "son of man" "where the speaker used a general statement containing the term בר אנש to refer to himself. At this level, the saying asserts the divine provision of ample places for animals and birds to go, and contrasts the lack of such provision for men."[16] The situational context, Casey contends, is Jesus' migratory preaching,[17] and the meaning of "son of man" would be restricted to the social group constituted by such wandering preachers.[18] The text that Casey adduces to support his agreement that "son of man" can be used only of a restricted group—a saying of R. Hiyya bar Adda at *y. Ber.* 2.8.5b—contains the expression "the disciple of a son of man," a reference to a circumscribed group, that is, one where disciples are found.[19] No such restriction is found within the saying under discussion. Furthermore, there is no mention at all in the saying about a *divine* provision of resting-places

[10] Ibid., 98, 102.

[11] Kloppenborg, *Formation of Q*, 192.

[12] Yarbro Collins, "Origin," 400–401.

[13] Barnabas Lindars, *Jesus Son of Man* (Grand Rapids: Eerdmans, 1984) 30; see also Barnabas Lindars, "Response to Richard Bauckham: The Idiomatic Use of Bar Nasha," *JSNT* 23 (1985) 35–41.

[14] Lindars, *Jesus Son of Man*, 30–31.

[15] Richard Bauckham, "The Son of Man: 'A Man in My Position' or 'Someone'?" *JSNT* 23 (1985) 28.

[16] Casey, "Jackals," 15.

[17] Ibid., 9–10, 15.

[18] Rollin Kearns is influenced by Casey's arguments about a situational context for the idiom, but confounds it with his theory that "Son of Man" reflects an earlier title *br nš*, which at the turn of the eras in Palestine had come to mean "wandering charismatic teacher"; see *Die Entchristologisierung des Menschensohnes* (Tübingen: Mohr-Siebeck, 1988) 185–88.

[19] Casey, "Jackals," 11–12. In a later article, he shows himself aware of the distinction of this saying from others: "General, Generic and Indefinite: The Use of the Term 'Son of Man' in Aramaic Sources and in the Teaching of Jesus," *JSNT* 29 (1987) 25.

for the animals, so that Casey has placed the saying within a certain interpretative reading. One might also note that itinerant charismatics often had friends in towns and villages they could visit. Neither Lindars nor Bauckham considers seriously Bultmann's claim that the saying is proverbial, and Casey notes that no such proverb has ever been found.[20]

In support of that proverbial claim, Bultmann made reference to one similar contrast found in Plutarch.[21] In the life of Tiberius Gracchus, Gracchus makes a speech in defense of his proposed agrarian legislation and begins thus:

> The wild beasts that roam over Italy have everyone of them a cave or lair to lurk in; but the men who fight and die for Italy enjoy the common air and light, indeed, but nothing else; houseless and homeless they wander about with their wives and children. And it is with lying lips that their imperators exhort the soldiers in their battles to defend sepulchres and shrines from the enemy; for not a man of them has an hereditary altar, not one of all these many Romans an ancestral tomb, but they fight and die to support others in wealth and luxury, and though they are styled masters of the world, they have not a single clod of earth that is their own. (*Tib. Gracc.* 9.4–5.828c)[22]

Bultmann was referring to the first sentence. Joseph A. Fitzmyer is right to reject this as not being proverbial in form,[23] but the context and content deserve attention. Plutarch is concerned to show in his life of Tiberius Gracchus that the initial cause of Gracchus was just but that he was led astray by an immoderate desire for glory (*Agis* 2.4; *Tib. Gracc.* 9.4). This first speech by Gracchus, then, is in an honorable and just cause as he pleads for the poor. The primary thrust of his speech is not to contrast animals and humans but to highlight the wretched conditions of the poor commoners with the wealth and luxury of the rapacious rich landowners. The point of Gracchus's speech was that all Romans should have a home, that the situation in the Italy of his day was unjust and improper. What is correct is that wild beasts live in caves, humans in houses, in towns—that is, in society. Aristotle summed up an attitude that would remain a constant in the antique Mediterranean world: humans are political animals; other animals do not live in cities (*Politica* 1.1.11.1253a). Such an attitude finds expression in the proverb in Sir 36:33, as well as in the incident during the fifth century CE when towns barred their gates against roaming bands of unkempt monks.[24] A

[20] Casey, "Jackals," 13 and n. 29.

[21] Bultmann, *History*, 98; Casey, "Jackals," 13 and n. 29.

[22] Trans. B. Perrin (LCL; Cambridge, Mass.: Harvard University Press, 1969–82).

[23] J. A. Fitzmyer, *The Gospel According to Luke I–IX* (AB 28; Garden City, N.Y.: Doubleday, 1981) 835. Johannes Geffcken found a parallel to the saying of Tiberius Gracchus in *Sibylline Oracles* 8.17–36, but this parallel deals solely with the rapaciousness of the rich ("Ein Wort des Tiberius Gracchus," *Klio* 23 [1930] 453–56).

[24] *Vie d'Alexandre l'Acèmète*, ed. J. de Stoop, PO 6:684–86.

human who does not live in society, in a *polis,* must be either a beast or a god (Aristotle *Politica* 1.1.9.1253a). Tiberius is thus using that rhetorical commonplace as the basis for his attack on the economic conditions of his day. The wisdom behind Tiberius Gracchus's speech, therefore, is not "pessimistic folklore" as, for example, in the adage "the rich get richer and the poor get poorer"; it is more fundamental, as it is based on the very premise of human social living—that is, living in a *polis*—as opposed to animal existence.

The saying ascribed to Jesus in Matt 3:20//Luke 9:58//*Gos. Thom.* 86 is much more radical. Tiberius Gracchus seeks to right the present injustice, to return to the proper status quo where the veterans will live like the rest of humanity. Assuming that "son of man" means "humanity" in general, the saying ascribed to Jesus states not that just some members of society do not have homes who should but that all humans, not just a specific group, are contrasted with the animal world. The saying reverses proverbial wisdom; it upends the status quo. Whereas human living in towns was seen as the top end of the scale and animals were pictured as wandering, now animals are said to have a settled existence and humans wander. Animals are cultured, humans stateless. Such reversal is part of that "widespread ancient Near Eastern topos that can be formulated negatively to depict a chaotic world upside down (WUD) or positively to depict a messianic or utopian situation where the present chaotic world will be overturned."[25] Daniel 7 portrays the course of human history as a succession of beasts; *1 Enoch* 1–5 contrasts the lawfulness of the stars and seasons with the asocial behavior of humans.[26] The saying in Matt 8:20//Luke 9:58//*Gos. Thom.* 86 thus portrays a chaotic world, a world upside-down, and constitutes an apocalyptic condemnation of contemporary human society. Both Lindars and Bauckham have misunderstood how the saying functions as applied to humans. The audience addressed by such a saying may not be similar to the economically exploited addressees of Tiberius Gracchus, but it is certainly a group that feels itself marginalized.[27]

When the article governing "son of man" is read not as generic but as contrasting this figure with other humans in the same class, the thrust of the

[25] Raymond C. Van Leeuwen, "Proverbs 30:21–23 and the Biblical World Upside Down," *JBL* 105 (1986) 602. The *topos* in this saying does not attain the full development found elsewhere in antiquity and discussed in detail by Hedwig Kenner (*Das Phänomen der verkehrten Welt in der griechisch-römischen Antike* [Klagenfurt: Rudolf Habelt, 1970]) and Giuseppe Cocchiara (*Il mondo alla rovescia* [Turin: Boringhieri, 1963]), where animals are depicted in human garb and roles.

[26] The theme of the flight of the gods from humanity's evil is found in Hesiod *Works and Days* 195–210 in his description of the fifth race of men.

[27] Margaretha Lelyveld suggests a situation of persecution, and the saying would be "un Dit apocalyptique annonçant la condition des disciples avant la fin" (*Les Logia de la Vie dans l'Evangile selon Thomas* [Leiden: Brill, 1981] 54). Her interpretation does not take cognizance of the universality of the logion.

saying changes. The titular usage of Son of Man in early Christianity made for a different reading of the saying.[28] It would then reflect that the Son of Man, who should live with humans, has not been received or given hospitality, the great asocial sin as in Judges 19 and throughout the *Odyssey*.[29] The Son of Man has been locked out, as was Wisdom in *1 Enoch* 42:1–2.[30] Kloppenborg has argued against this interpretation of the saying: "Q9:57–58 says nothing of rejection and it does not state that the Son of Man *could not* find a place of rest or that he subsequently found one among the angels (as in *1 Enoch* 42). Instead, the saying describes the vagrant existence of the Son of Man."[31] Given the proverbial context sketched above—that to be human is to live in a *polis*, in society—such a reading of the saying misses the plaintive tone of the contrast between the home life of animals and the human, even the Human *par excellence* excluded from such happiness. The tone is similar to that in the haunting poem of Sappho, who contrasts mythic Selene sinking into the seas to join Endymion with the human woman who must sleep alone.

> The Moon and Pleiades have set,
> Midnight is nigh,
> The time is passing, passing, yet
> Alone I lie.[32]

[28] Over ten years ago Joseph Fitzmyer declared the literature on the Son of Man problem to be so vast as to be almost uncoverable ("The New Testament Title 'Son of Man' Philologically Considered," in *A Wandering Aramean: Collected Aramaic Essays* [SBLMS; Missoula, Mont.: Scholars Press, 1979] 145–60), and that the link between the indefinite or generic Aramaic usage and the titular usage was still missing (p. 150). Recently Adela Yarbro Collins has suggested that Jesus himself alluded to the generic phrase in Dan 7:13, and "in order to refer to that figure, Jesus probably used a definite form as a way of referring to the figure known on the basis of that text" (Yarbro Collins, "Origin," 404).

[29] See, e.g., Susan Niditch, "The 'Sodomite' Theme in Judges 19–20: Family, Community, and Social Disintegration," *CBQ* 44 (1982) 365–78.

[30] One thinks of the theme of the rejection of prophets, as in the proverb in Mark 6:4 ("A prophet is not without honor except in his own country") and the woe in Luke 13:34 ("O Jerusalem, Jerusalem, killing the prophets and stoning those who are sent to you"). The choice of the general expression "the son of man" deals with this specific theme on a broader plane, an expansion at work also in Jer 1:10–11.

[31] Kloppenborg, *Formation of Q*, 192.

[32] Diskin Clay has argued convincingly for Sappho as the author ("Fragmentum Adespotum 976," *TAPA* 101 [1970] 119–29). I thank my colleague, Professor Rebecca Hague, for this reference.

The text is in D. Page, *Poetae Melici Graeci* (Oxford: Clarendon, 1962) fragmentum adespotum 976. The translation is that of C. R. Haines, *Sappho, The Poems and Fragments* (London: Routledge, 1926).

The sad tone of rejection runs throughout the saying of Matt 8:20//Luke 9:58//*Gos. Thom.* 86. The addition "to rest" in *Gos. Thom.* 86 continues this tone, as it explicates the phrase "to lay his head," and this doublet in some sense balances the doublet found in the first stich.[33] The verb "to rest" in *Gos. Thom.* 86 (*emton emmof*) is the same as that found in *Gos. Thom.* 61 where it has no gnostic overtones of heavenly repose: "Two will repose (*eemton emmau*) on a couch: one will die, one will live."[34] The preferred term for heavenly repose in *Gos. Thom.* is ἀνάπαυσις (*Gos. Thom.* 50, 51, 60, 90), and its connotations should not be read into *Gos. Thom.* 86. Whether the context in *Gos. Thom.* supports a gnostic reading of the saying is a different question, which will be discussed below.

There are two trajectories of interpretation of this saying: discipleship and dichotomy. Both Jacobson and Kloppenborg agree that the saying in its present Q form is about discipleship.[35] Connecting it with the second logion makes this clear. The difference between them is one of emphasis: Jacobson stresses that the Son of Man is rejected as Wisdom was; Kloppenborg stresses the disciple–master relationship.

This sense of discipleship has been taken over in both Matthew and Luke, but differently. Luke situates the saying just after the beginning of the travel account to Jerusalem, "as the days of his assumption drew near." The allusion to Elijah (2 Kgs 2:11; 1 Macc 2:58; Sir 48:9) finds a counterpart in the saying in Luke 9:61–62, referring to the call of Elisha in 1 Kgs 19:19–21. These Old Testament allusions underscore the call to discipleship, to follow Jesus along the way.

Matthew, however, has used the saying differently. It comes after the healings of three marginal persons (a leper, a Gentile, a woman), and the double apophthegm points forward to the crossing of the lake (Matt 8:23–27). Such boundary crossings in Matthew's narrative world are times of danger, times to be wary.[36] The inhabitants on the other side of the lake clearly perceive Jesus' crossing as a danger as they beg him to leave their neighborhood (Matt 8:34). Before Jesus crosses the lake boundary, he warns would-be disciples that dangers abound if they choose to follow him.[37]

[33] See A. Strobel, "Textgeschichtliches zum Thomas-Logion 86 [Mt 8, 20/Lk 9,58]," *VC* 17 (1963) 222–23.

[34] As suggested by Jan Helderman, *Die Anapausis im Evangelium Veritatis* (Leiden: Brill, 1984) 75 n. 48; see also Crossan, *In Fragments*, 242. The extent to which "rest" is gnostic in *Gos. Thom.* has been challenged by Steven L. Davies, *The Gospel of Thomas and Christian Wisdom* (New York: Seabury, 1983) 33–34, 39.

[35] Kloppenborg, *Formation of Q*, 192; Jacobson, "Wisdom Christology" 143.

[36] The notion of space in Mark has been well examined by Elizabeth Struthers Malbon, who notes the crossing of the sea of Galilee as crossing traditional limits (*Narrative Space and Mythic Meaning in Mark* [San Francisco: Harper & Row, 1986] 76–79).

[37] Jack Dean Kingsbury argues that the scribe has arrogated to himself the authority to

Once the saying was christologically oriented, alienation from society was seen as divinely sanctioned: the human who lived alone, away from society, from towns, was not beastlike but imitating Christ. The logic of this interpretation can be seen when, in 337 CE, Aphrahat alludes to the saying in his exhortation to monks to lead the angelic life away from society,[38] and one can see played out in the history of Syrian monasticism how literally some monks would shun society as they lived, sometimes naked, in the open air eating grass for food like wild animals.[39]

The saying of Matt 8:20//Luke 9:58//*Gos. Thom.* 86 also found another line of interpretation, one that stressed the dichotomy inherent in the contrast between the animal world and the world of Jesus. Clement of Alexandria interpreted the saying this way:

> That utterance of the Savior "The foxes have holes, but the Son of Man has no place to lay his head" hints at this in some way. For I think the head of what exists, the good and gentle Word, rests upon the believer alone, who is distinguished completely from those others called by the scripture beasts. (*Stromateis* 1.3.24.2)[40]

Clement interpreted the saying to distinguish between those who have true knowledge and those who do not, between those who use philosophy well and the sophists, who do not.

This same interpretive strategy is applied also to the saying in *Gos. Thom.* As mentioned above, the saying in itself has no hint of dualism. However, the context of the saying seems to stress levels of existence. Saying 83 speaks of visible images and images of the father's light; saying 84, with reference to Gen 1:27, distinguishes between one's visible appearance and one's preexistent image; saying 85 states that Adam is not on the same level as Jesus' disciples.[41] *Gos. Thom.* 87 argues against having one's priorities misplaced: one should not depend on the body. Within this cluster of sayings, then, is found the notion of levels of existence, and saying 86, situated within this cluster, is to be interpreted as distinguishing between this world, which is

---

become Jesus' disciple and that Jesus turns him away in alluding to the repudiation Jesus must endure ("On Following Jesus: The 'Eager' Scribe and the 'Reluctant' Disciple [Matthew 8.18–22]," *NTS* 34 [1988] 45–59). Kingsbury sensitively notices the differences between the two logia, but perhaps pushes the distinction too far.

[38] In the Sixth Demonstration, edited (with Latin translation) in Patrologia Syriaca 1, cols. 239–312; an Eng. trans. is found in *NPNF* 13:362–75.

[39] See Arthur Vööbus, *History of Asceticism in the Syrian Orient: A Contribution to the History of Culture in the Near East,* vol. 2, *Early Monasticism in Mesopotamia and Syria* (CSCO 17; Louvain: Secrétariat du Corpus SCO, 1960) 25–27.

[40] Clement of Alexandria, *Clemens Alexandrinus,* Band 2, *Stromata Buch I–VI* (GCS 15; Leipzig: Hinrichs, 1906). My translation.

[41] Lelyveld links logion 86 to 85 through this notion of the community of disciples (*Les logia,* 53–54).

a body (cf. *Gos. Thom.* 56, 80), and the gnostic, who does not belong to this visible world of visible images—who is a passerby (*Gos. Thom.* 42).

Throughout early Christianity, then, this saying maintained the sense of alienation from society. What had been an apocalyptic description of a chaotic world, a world turned upside-down, with an implicit expectation that a better world would come, became interpreted, on the one hand, as an ethical exhortation to lead a vagrant life and, on the other, as a metaphor for setting a boundary between the group and outsiders.

16

The Apocalyptic Son of Man Sayings

ADELA YARBRO COLLINS

MANY SCHOLARS NOW hold that none of the apocalyptic Son of Man sayings goes back to the historical Jesus. Norman Perrin, for example, argued that all the apocalyptic Son of Man sayings originated in early Christian interpretation of scripture in light of the experience of Jesus as risen. A very important preliminary argument in his overall case is that there was no defined concept of the apocalyptic Son of Man in ancient Judaism. Since the apocalyptic Son of Man sayings in the Synoptic tradition presuppose a well-defined concept of the Son of Man and his eschatological role, that concept must have developed during the time between the resurrection of Jesus and the writing of the oldest texts we possess. Using especially the work of Barnabas Lindars and H. E. Tödt as models, Perrin attempted to reconstruct the development of a very early Christology, that is, the understanding of the risen Jesus as the apocalyptic Son of Man.[1]

I agree that the rediscovery of the importance of the interpretation of scripture among the earliest Christians is an advance. Likewise, it is crucial to keep in mind the diversity of eschatological ideas in Judaism at the turn of the era. I have no desire to return to an approach that assumes fixed and widely accepted concepts, such as *the* apocalyptic Son of Man and *the* Messiah, in the sense of a definite set of qualities and functions regularly connected with a specific title. There is, however, a weak link in Perrin's impressive chain of argument. It is the failure to consider seriously that there

[1] Norman Perrin, *Rediscovering the Teaching of Jesus* (New York: Harper & Row, 1967) 197–98; idem, *A Modern Pilgrimage in New Testament Christology* (Philadelphia: Fortress Press, 1974) 23–40; Barnabas Lindars, *New Testament Apologetic: The Doctrinal Significance of the Old Testament Quotations* (London: SCM, 1961); H. E. Tödt, *The Son of Man in the Synoptic Tradition* (Philadelphia: Westminster, 1965).

may have been certain features in the understanding of Daniel 7 common to many Jews around the turn of the era.

Jewish Interpretation

It is important to begin with the meaning for the author of Daniel of "one ancient of days" and "one like a son of man" (Dan 7:9–10, 13–14). The meaning of "one ancient of days" is clear: this is the Most High (see vv. 18, 22, 25, 27), that is, God. The meaning of the "one like a son of man" continues to be disputed.

According to Perrin, the one like a son of man

> represents "the people of the saints of the Most High," almost certainly the Maccabean martyrs, and his coming to dominion, glory and greatness is their coming to their reward for the sufferings they have endured. In other words, the use of Son of man in Daniel is a cryptic way of assuring the (Maccabean) readers of the book that their suffering will not go unrewarded.[2]

An interpretation that fits the evidence better by far is that the one like a son of man is an angelic being. It has been argued that the angelic interpretation does not fit the context of Daniel 7. The vision is a symbolic vision containing images that are not to be taken literally. The four beasts represent kings and kingdoms but are not to be taken as actually existent heavenly beings. Since they are allegories or symbols of earthly political realities, the manlike figure should, by analogy, be taken as a collective symbol for the Jewish people. Several responses may be made to this argument. In a Jewish apocalyptic allegory composed at roughly the same time as Daniel, animals represent human beings and human figures represent angels (the Dream Visions of Enoch). Further, there was an ancient narrative pattern in which a superhuman, but humanlike, hero did battle with a monster.[3] In the Hebrew Bible, this mythic pattern was historicized so that the monster or beast signified a political power hostile to Israel. It was usually Yahweh himself who took the hero's role as the divine warrior. In Daniel 7, this role is delegated to an angelic being, as in the *War Scroll*. Thus one could conclude that the vision of Daniel 7 is a mixed type, combining allegorical symbols with heavenly entities. It would be more appropriate to say that this is not a symbolic vision in the sense of fortuitously chosen images. Rather, this is a mythic vision in which the beasts represent in a traditional, narrative way the hidden reality of the political kingdoms to which allusion is made and the manlike figure represents divine power.

[2] Perrin, *Rediscovering the Teaching of Jesus*, 166–67.

[3] The most recent extensive study of this narrative pattern is Neil Forsyth, *The Old Enemy: Satan and the Combat Myth* (Princeton: Princeton University Press, 1987).

The angelic interpretation is the most likely meaning for the one like a son of man from the point of view of the author of the book of Daniel as a whole. There is, however, an aspect of the text that may hint at a more complex original meaning or at least may have provided the occasion for the development of a new meaning. This aspect of the text is the particular phrase used to describe the manlike figure in Dan 7:13. He is described as כְּבַר אֱנָשׁ ("[one] like a son of man" or "a son of man, as it were"). This particular phrase does not appear in any of the other passages in Daniel referring to angelic beings in human form. In part, of course, this is because Daniel 7 is in Aramaic, whereas chapters 8–12 are in Hebrew. The Hebrew equivalent of בַּר אֱנָשׁ would be בֶּן אָדָם. This precise phrase occurs only once in Daniel 8–12, and there it is used not to describe an angelic being but as an address of Daniel by Gabriel (Dan 8:16).[4] This use of the term simply means "O man" or "O human one" and draws a contrast between humanity and heavenly beings. This usage appears frequently in the book of Ezekiel.

The use in Dan 7:13 of the Aramaic equivalent of the Hebrew בֶּן אָדָם is interesting because there is some evidence that הָאָדָם ("the man") of Gen 1:27 and בֶּן אָדָם (the "son of man," apparently a poetic equivalent of "man") in Psalm 8 were understood especially with reference to the Davidic king, that is, as royal terms.[5] A royal term could easily have been understood messianically after the demise of the monarchy. Ps 8:4 (MT 8:5) is especially interesting because בֶּן אָדָם ("son of man") appears in parallelism with אֱנוֹשׁ ("man"). The latter is a Hebrew word that has the same root as the Aramaic word used for "man" in Dan 7:13.

In Gen 1:27, a Mesopotamian royal designation (צֶלֶם אֱלֹהִים, "image of God") was used by the Priestly writer to counter a common notion of Mesopotamian anthropology: humankind as the servants of the gods. Instead, the Priestly writer portrays all humanity as sharing in the king's role of executing the divine rule over creation.[6] Psalm 8 is generally seen as a hymn of praise, extolling God as creator and expressing wondering gratitude at the godlike role the Creator has given to humanity: dominion over the rest of creation.[7] If the psalm is early, it may have been sung at the enthronement festival, postulated by Sigmund Mowinckel, at which the kingship of God and his representative, the Davidic king, was celebrated.[8] In such a context, the king would be the paradigmatic or representative man. Even if the psalm was

[4] In Dan 10:18 the word אָדָם alone is used of an angel in the phrase כְּמַרְאֵה אָדָם (one having the appearance of a man); in 10:16 the phrase בֶּן אָדָם is used of an angel, but in most manuscripts it is in the plural (כִּדְמוּת בְּנֵי אָדָם, one in the likeness of the sons of men).

[5] Phyllis A. Bird, "'Male and Female He Created Them': Gen 1:27b in the Context of the Priestly Account of Creation," *HTR* 74 (1981) 140–44.

[6] Ibid., 144.

[7] Claus Westermann, *The Praise of God in the Psalms* (Richmond: John Knox, 1965) 139.

[8] S. Mowinckel, *The Psalms in Israel's Worship* (Nashville: Abingdon, 1967) 1:167.

composed later—for example, in the Persian period[9] —it clearly draws upon royal tradition and images. God's crowning the man (v. 5 [MT v. 6]) with glory and honor would call to mind the diadem of the king (cf., e.g., 2 Sam 12:30; Ezek 21:26 [MT v. 31]). Giving him dominion and putting all things under his feet are also notions that would recall kingly power. It is likely that, in the postexilic period, this psalm and others like it were understood messianically, that is, with reference to a future king of a restored Israel.[10] The targums interpret the "son of man" in Pss 8:3; 80:17 (MT v. 18) and 144:3 as the messiah.[11] The fact that these verses are read messianically, in spite of the fact that the Christians understood them analogously of Jesus, suggests that the Jewish messianic interpretation is early.

Thus, the choice of words in Dan 7:13 may be a deliberate allusion to the wording of Psalm 8 and related psalms, in which the phrase בֶּן אָדָם ("son of man") was understood messianically at the time Daniel was composed. Even if the author did not intend an allusion to those psalms, the messianic significance of the phrase "son of man" in them was probably connected to the similar phrase in Dan 7:13, by messianically-minded audiences, soon after the book of Daniel was published.

Perrin was quite correct in pointing out the considerable differences between the use of Daniel 7 in the Similitudes of Enoch and in 4 Ezra 13, but he was wrong in saying that the only thing the two have in common, apart from the attribution of a kind of preexistence to the two redeemer-figures, is the dependence on Dan 7:13.[12] Perrin overlooked the fact that there is a further similarity between the two: both texts assume that the manlike figure of Dan 7:13 is the messiah.[13] The term "messiah" is not used in 4 Ezra 13. Apart from the epithet "man," derived from Daniel 7, the figure is designated "my son" (4 Ezra 13:32, 37, 52).[14] Behind the Latin "son" (*filius*) may have been the Greek word παῖς, which could mean either "child" or "servant." Some scholars believe that the Greek παῖς was a translation of the

[9] Charles A. Briggs, *A Critical and Exegetical Commentary on the Book of Psalms* (ICC: New York: Scribner, 1906) 1:61–62.

[10] Brevard S. Childs, *Introduction to the Old Testament as Scripture* (Philadelphia: Fortress Press, 1979) 516–18.

[11] S. Mowinckel, *He That Cometh: The Messiah Concept in the Old Testament and Later Judaism* (Nashville: Abingdon, 1956) 357.

[12] Perrin, *Rediscovering the Teaching of Jesus,* 167–72; idem, *Modern Pilgrimage,* 24–26, 28–32.

[13] Perrin recognized the messianic character of the man from the sea in 4 Ezra 13, but not that of the Son of Man in the Similitudes (*Rediscovering the Teaching of Jesus,* 167–70; *Modern Pilgrimage,* 25–26, 31–32).

[14] See Jacob M. Myers, *I & II Esdras* (AB 42; Garden City, N.Y.: Doubleday, 1974) 305–7, 310; B. M. Metzger, "The Fourth Book of Ezra," in *OTP* 1:522–53.

Hebrew עֶבֶד ("servant").[15] In the context of 4 Ezra as a whole, this "son" or "servant" is the messiah (cf. 7:28–29). In the Similitudes of Enoch, the redeemer-figure is referred to sometimes as "the Chosen One," sometimes as the messiah, and sometimes as "that Son of Man." The parallelism between that Son of Man and the messiah in chapters 48 and 52 suggests that the two are identical (cf. *1 Enoch* 48:2–7 with 48:10 and 52:1–4 with 52:5–9). The Chosen One is characterized in chapter 49 in terms of the messianic prophecy of Isaiah 11 (v. 3). It is clear from many passages that the Chosen One and that Son of Man are the same figure (cf. *1 Enoch* 45 and 55 with 69:24–29).

Since the Similtudes of Enoch and 4 Ezra are literarily independent of one another, it appears that a tradition had developed prior to the composition of both works that the "one like a son of man" in Daniel 7 should be understood as the messiah. This is especially interesting for the life and teaching of Jesus in light of the early date of the Similitudes. In spite of J. T. Milik's argument that the Similitudes is a Christian composition of the third century, most specialists date the work between the reign of Herod the Great and the destruction of the temple in 70 CE.[16] Since the latest historical allusions relate to the Parthian invasion of Palestine in 40 BCE and Herod's treatment in the warm springs of Callirrhoe, the usual methods of dating lead to a date around the turn of the era.[17] The significance of this date is that it makes this document evidence for the messianic interpretation of Dan 7:13 before the public life of Jesus.[18]

The New Testament

Perrin's influential argument that the use of Dan 7:13 in the New Testament presupposes the resurrection of Jesus is based primarily on passages

[15] Michael Stone presupposed this hypothesis in his article "The Concept of the Messiah in IV Ezra," in *Religions in Antiquity: Essays in Memory of Erwin Ramsdell Goodenough,* ed. J. Neusner (SHR 14; Leiden: Brill, 1968) 295, 307.

[16] J. T. Milik, *The Books of Enoch* (Oxford: Clarendon, 1976) 89–98; Adela Yarbro Collins, "The Origin of the Designation of Jesus as 'Son of Man,'" *HTR* 80 (1987) 404–5. See also the literature cited by John Donahue, "Recent Studies on the Origin of 'Son of Man' in the Gospels," in *A Wise and Discerning Heart: Studies Presented to Joseph A. Fitzmyer, S.J. in Celebration of His Sixty-Fifth Birthday, CBQ* 48 (1986) 486 n. 8.

[17] John J. Collins, "The Jewish Apocalypses," in *Apocalypse: The Morphology of a Genre, Semeia* 14 (1979) 39; idem, *The Apocalyptic Imagination* (New York: Crossroad, 1984) 143.

[18] It has been pointed out by a number of scholars, including Perrin (*Rediscovering the Teaching of Jesus,* 171–72), that the manlike figure of Dan 7:13 is interpreted as the messiah in rabbinic literature. Once again this Jewish interpretation is probably early, because it is unlikely that Jews would have adopted this interpretation after Christians had used it with reference to their claim that Jesus was the Messiah.

in Acts and Mark.[19] His working hypothesis was that the original understanding of the resurrection of Jesus was in terms of Ps 110:1—"The Lord says to my lord, 'Sit at my right hand, till I make your enemies your footstool.'" He finds support for this thesis in Peter's speech in Acts 2 on the occasion of Pentecost, in particular in Acts 2:34, where Ps 110:1 is cited. Like others, Perrin concluded that Luke did not invent this interpretation of the resurrection but made use here of very early tradition. The earliest use of Dan 7:13 came in the next step, that is, the interpretation of Jesus' resurrection as his ascension to heaven as Son of Man, an interpretation that involved linking Ps 110:1 with Dan 7:13.[20] Perrin found evidence for this second stage in Mark 14:62a and in Acts 7:56.

Now the argument that the Christian combination of Psalm 110 and Daniel 7 is older than Mark is quite weak. Let us look at the first passage adduced as evidence, Mark 14:62. The context is the trial of Jesus before the sanhedrin. It gives Jesus' reply to the question of the high priest, "Are you the Christ, the Son of the Blessed?": "I am; and you will see the Son of Man seated at the right hand of Power, and coming with the clouds of heaven." Perrin argued that Jesus' reply is "the end-product of a Christian pesher tradition" and that it is based on two originally separate exegetical traditions.[21] One of these traditions portrays the exaltation of Jesus to the right hand of God as a fulfillment of both Psalm 110 and Daniel 7. In this tradition the Son of Man goes from *earth* to *heaven*. It has nothing to do with the parousia, that is, with the return of the Son of Man from *heaven* to *earth*. The other tradition is the more familiar one, the interpretation of Dan 7:13 as a prophecy of the parousia: the Son of Man will come with the clouds in the last days, presumably from heaven to earth. Perrin's argument is that the words "the Son of Man seated at the right hand of Power," in the first part of v. 62 of Mark 14, represent the first tradition, the exaltation tradition. The words "coming with the clouds of heaven," in the second part of the verse, represent the second tradition, the parousia tradition.

[19] Perrin, *Modern Pilgrimage,* 10–18; *Rediscovering the Teaching of Jesus,* 176–81.

[20] Perrin, *Rediscovering the Teaching of Jesus,* 179–80. William O. Walker, Jr., accepted Perrin's overall thesis, but proposed to strengthen it by explaining why Ps 110:1 and Dan 7:13 were brought together. The reason was exegetical plays on words, and the missing link is Psalm 8. It was the similarity between the phrase ὑποπόδιον τῶν ποδῶν σου in Psalm 110:1 (LXX 109:1) and the phrase ὑποκάτω τῶν ποδῶν αὐτοῦ in Ps 8:6 (LXX 8:7) that led to the connection. The link between Psalm 8 and Dan 7:13 was made because of the occurrence of υἱὸς ἀνθρώπου in Ps 8:4 (LXX 8:5). Walker believed that these connections could only have been made in Greek ("The Origin of the Son of Man Concept as Applied to Jesus," *JBL* 91 [1972] 487–90). Perrin accepted this suggestion of Walker as strengthening his case (*Modern Pilgrimage,* 19, 21–22).

[21] See the title of his article originally published as "Mark 14:62: The End Product of a Christian Pesher Tradition?" *NTS* 12 (1965–66) 150–55; reprinted with a postscript in *Modern Pilgrimage,* 10–22.

It appears of course quite gratuitous to divide a single verse and claim that the parts represent two separate exegetical traditions. The only external support that Perrin can muster for this procedure is a dubious analysis of Acts 7:55–56. These verses report Stephen's vision of the exalted Son of Man: "But he, full of the Holy Spirit, gazed into heaven and saw the glory of God, and Jesus standing at the right hand of God; and he said, 'Behold, I see the heavens opened, and the Son of Man standing at the right hand of God.'" Perrin begins with the sound observation that Stephen's vision contains no reference to the parousia. Rather than attributing this lack to Lukan redaction, he concludes that Stephen's statement (v. 56) was taken by the author of Luke-Acts from a source and that it reflects the hypothetical tradition in which Dan 7:13 is interpreted as the exaltation of Jesus.[22] In his recent commentary on Acts, however, Hans Conzelmann concludes that the evidence is insufficient to distinguish between source and redaction in these verses.[23] If the use of a source in Acts 7:56 is dubious, Perrin's whole theory of a pre-Markan tradition that combined Psalm 110 with Daniel 7 disintegrates. The demise of this theory raises the question whether the author of Mark was the first to combine these two texts in Christian interpretation of Jesus.[24] I hope to address this question on another occasion.

The refutation of Perrin's theory about an exaltation tradition using Daniel 7 has significant implications for the origin of the apocalyptic Son of Man sayings. If such an exaltation tradition did not exist, the apocalyptic Son of Man sayings may have originated in the life of Jesus. One of these sayings is Mark 13:26: "And then they will see the Son of Man coming in clouds with great power and glory." This is the climax of the apocalyptic discourse of Jesus in Mark 13.

In Perrin's discussion of this saying, he entertained only two possibilities. *Either* there was a clearly defined conception of the Son of Man "coming with the clouds" among Jews of Jesus' time and Jesus alluded to it *or* this saying is a Christian production.[25] He failed to consider the possibility that Jesus

[22] Even though Perrin accepts C. K. Barrett's theory that the motif of the Son of Man *standing* rather than *sitting* is redactional, he nevertheless concludes, following Tödt, that the rest of v. 56 comes from a source. The only hard evidence he cites is the use of the singular "heaven" in the narrative introduction to the vision (v. 55) and the plural "heavens" in the report itself (v. 56). See Perrin, *Rediscovering the Teaching of Jesus*, 177–79.

[23] H. Conzelmann, *Acts of the Apostles* (Hermeneia; Philadelphia: Fortress Press, 1987) 59–61.

[24] Acts 7:56 may lack a reference to the parousia because it is modeled on Luke 22:69. Luke may have omitted the reference to the parousia in Mark 14:62, at least in part, because of the awkwardness of portraying Jesus *both* as seated at the right hand of God *and* coming with the clouds. This awkwardness may be a sign that Mark is doing something new.

[25] Perrin rejected the hypothesis that Mark 13:26 comes from a Jewish source because it has certain linguistic features that do not appear in any known Jewish allusion to Dan 7:13, but do appear in other Christian sayings. He did accept the hypothesis that Jewish material was used

interpreted Dan 7:13 in an innovative way in his teaching.

Perrin did not argue that the historical Jesus could not have alluded to scripture in his teaching. His argument was that the use of Dan 7:13 in the New Testament presupposes the resurrection of Jesus. Such an argument is difficult to refute given that all the early Christian writings that survive presuppose the resurrection, exaltation, or at least vindication of Jesus. The present use and context of most, if not all, of the sayings are colored by this presupposition. Second, it is becoming more and more difficult to make a case for attributing a particular saying, even in its earliest recoverable form, to the historical Jesus. This difficulty is due mainly to the acceptance of the criterion of dissimilarity and to the attitude that, if a saying has a plausible social setting in an early Christian community, it probably originated there. In other words, the burden of proof is now generally thought to rest on the shoulders of one who would attribute a saying to Jesus, and that burden is getting heavier. Since many, if not all, of the sayings of Jesus are ambiguous if read without a context, and since the contexts they have in the tradition presuppose the resurrection, I agree with E. P. Sanders that it is methodologically more sound to begin with the known events of Jesus' life rather than with the teachings.[26]

The events of Jesus' life that are generally accepted as historical, or for which one could make a sound case for historicity, imply that Jesus understood himself and was understood in an apocalyptic or restoration-eschatological context. He accepted the apocalyptic message of John the Baptist by going to him to be baptized. He chose twelve disciples to have a special role, apparently in relation to the notion of the renewal of the twelve tribes of Israel. He performed a prophetic symbolic action in the temple that alluded to its destruction and possibly to its replacement by the eschatological temple. He was executed by the Romans as a threat to public order, possibly for claiming to be or allowing himself to be treated as the king of the Jews (the Messiah of Israel). Shortly after Jesus was crucified, his death and subsequent vindication were interpreted by a significant and influential number of his disciples in an apocalyptic context. The origin of Jesus' activity in the apocalyptic movement of John the Baptist, the known events of his life, and the apocalyptic movement initiated by his followers after his death suggest that Jesus understood himself and his mission in apocalyptic terms.

If Jesus understood himself in an apocalyptic or restoration-eschatological context, it is illegitimate to exclude, a priori, all the apocalyptic sayings from the material attributed to the historical Jesus. Perrin, or anyone else for that

---

in Mark 13 (*Rediscovering the Teaching of Jesus,* 173–75). Another theory is more persuasive, i.e., that the source used in Mark 13 was Jewish Christian (Egon Brandenburger, *Markus 13 und die Apokalyptik* [Göttingen: Vandenhoeck & Ruprecht, 1984] 65–73).

[26] E. P. Sanders, *Jesus and Judaism* (Philadelphia: Fortress Press, 1985) 3–13.

matter, has not made a case against Mark 13:26 as a saying of Jesus. It does not presuppose the resurrection of Jesus if the Son of Man in that saying was not originally identified with Jesus but was understood as a heavenly being who was to have an eschatological role in the future.[27] It may not be possible to reconstruct the form of the saying as spoken by Jesus. It is noteworthy, though, that the discourse of Mark 13 is introduced with a pronouncement story in which the telling saying is a prediction of the destruction of the temple. This prediction is pre-Markan tradition.[28] Although it is impossible to reconstruct a specific saying, it is likely that Jesus did prophesy the destruction of the temple.[29] Thus, the notions of the destruction of the temple and the revelation or epiphany of the Son of Man in Mark 13 may both be elements in the teaching of Jesus upon which the apocalyptic discourse is based.[30] In other words, Jesus may be seen as the first to understand Dan 7:13 as the "coming" of the manlike figure to earth in an epiphany as an eschatological event. Perrin made a case for the dissimilarity of Jesus' teaching about the kingdom of God in his speaking of it as "coming." In Daniel 7, God is portrayed as ruling through the manlike figure, the saints of the Most High, and the people of the saints of the Most High, as agents of the divine power. In Dan 7:14 it is explicitly stated that the manlike figure is given kingdom or kingly rule. Most scholars agree that Jesus' teaching about the kingdom of God had both a present and a future dimension. It is a credible hypothesis, and one worth serious attention, that Jesus used language about the rule of God to express the present dimension and, at least at times, language about "the" son of man of Daniel 7 to express the future dimension.

[27] Rudolf Bultmann concluded that Jesus spoke of a heavenly Son of Man with whom he did not identify himself (*The History of the Synoptic Tradition* [rev. ed.; New York: Harper & Row, 1968] 112, 122, 128, 151–52).

[28] John Donahue, *Are You the Christ?* (SBLDS 10; Missoula, Mont.: Scholars Press, 1973) 107–8.

[29] Sanders, *Jesus and Judaism,* 71–76.

[30] The epiphanic character of the coming of the Son of Man is due to the use of the preposition ἐν ("in"); in the theophanies of the OT, the phrase "in the clouds" is typical (Perrin, *Rediscovering the Teaching of Jesus,* 174). The preposition ἐν is not found in any Greek version of Dan 7:13 known to us; ἐπί ("on") and μετά ("with") are the prepositions used. The change from one of these to "in" may have been a deliberate change to emphasize the already epiphanic character of Dan 7:13 and its context; on the latter, see Stone, "Concept of the Messiah," 308.

17

The Antithetic Saying in Mark 16:16: Formal and Redactional Features

PAUL ALLAN MIRECKI

Formal and Redactional Features of Mark 16:16

Mark 16:16 ὁ πιστεύσας καὶ βαπτισθεὶς σωθήσεται
ὁ δὲ ἀπιστήσας κατακριθήσεται

MARK 16:16 IS AN independent saying structured in antithetic parallelism and centered on the cause-and-effect relationship between belief and salvation and their logical antitheses, disbelief and condemnation.[1] The use of antithetic sayings in the redactional composition of discourses is a well-known feature of the Johannine redaction and has recently been identified in the primary redactional stratum of the *Apocryphon of James*.[2]

[1] The following study is a revision of a section of my dissertation directed by Prof. Koester: "Mark 16:9–20: Composition, Tradition, and Redaction" (Th.D. diss., Harvard University, 1986).

The most thorough discussions of prophecies of judgment and salvation are Donald N. Swanson, "Basic Forms of Christian Prophetic Speech" (Th.D. diss., Harvard University, 1981) esp. 1–170; and Klaus Koch, *The Growth of the Biblical Tradition: Form-Critical Method* (New York: Scribner, 1969); see also John Hug, *La Finale L'Evangile de Marc (Marc 16,9–20)* (Paris: Gabalda, 1978) 101, 170–71; Rudolf Pesch, *Das Markusevangelium* (2 vols.; HTKNT 2; Freiburg: Herder, 1977) 2:553, B. J. Hubbard, *The Matthean Redaction of a Primitive Apostolic Commissioning: An Exegesis of Matthew 28:16–20* (Missoula, Mont.: Scholars Press, 1974) 144–45.

[2] Rudolf Bultmann, *The Gospel of John: A Commentary* (Philadelphia: Westminster, 1971) 140 n. 2, 155–56; Heinz Becker, *Die Reden des Johannesevangeliums und der Stil der gnostischen Offenbarungsrede* (FRLANT 50; Göttingen: Vandenhoeck & Ruprecht, 1956) 24, 65. See John 3:18, 31, 36; 4:13–14; 5:43; 8:23; 9:39; 11:9–10; 15:2. Ron Cameron, *Sayings Traditions in the Apocryphon of James* (HTS 34; Philadelphia: Fortress Press, 1984) 44–46.

The secondary use of an antithetic prophetic saying as a saying of Jesus is a redactional feature of Mark 16:16.[3] The text appears to be a form-critically discrete unit that is capable of existing independently of its present narrative context. The two major indicators of the traditional nature of Mark 16:16 are: (1) the use of a structural and terminological formulation found in other antithetic prophetic sayings (e.g., belief and salvation in antithetic parallelism with disbelief and condemnation),[4] and (2) the conceptual and syntactic independence of the saying from the surrounding text.

Donald Swanson and Klaus Koch note that the basic structure of a *prophecy of salvation* contains four elements: (1) identification formula, (2) identification of situation, (3) a prediction of salvation or promise, and (4) a concluding characterization which reaffirms divine authorization of the prophecy.[5] The structure of the *prophecy of judgment* is similar: (1) an introductory address to the accused, (2) an accusation, (3) identification formula of the divine judge, (4) the announcement of the judgment, and (5) a conclusion which often summarizes the accusation and the divine authority of the accuser.[6] The antithetic prophetic saying in 16:16 appears to have conceptual similarities with both of these forms. The announcements of salvation and judgment are brought together into a concise antithetical statement.

The parallelism of this saying is clear.[7] The subject of each line is in participial form, and the main verb of each line is a future passive. The antithetic nature of the parallelism is observed between the two subjects (ὁ πιστεύσας and its antithesis ὁ δὲ ἀπιστήσας) and the two verbs (σωθήσεται and its antithesis κατακριθήσεται).[8]

[3] Cameron identifies Mark 16:16 as a creed (*Sayings Traditions,* 82–85). Although this text shares some structural and terminological similarites with various creedal traditions (as will be demonstrated in the following discussion) it finds its closest generic and conceptual parallels in prophecies of salvation. On the diverse use of creedal traditions, see Helmut Koester, "One Jesus and Four Primitive Gospels," in Robinson-Koester, *Trajectories,* 198–204; idem, "The Structure and Criteria of Early Christian Beliefs," *Trajectories,* 208.

[4] Cf. John 3:18. Joachim Jeremias notes that "antithetic parallelism in the sayings of Jesus cannot be attributed to the process of redaction" (*New Testament Theology* [New York: Scribner, 1971] 18), but I would add that antithetic traditions can enter a text through that process.

[5] Swanson, "Christian Prophetic Speech," 124–26; Koch, *Form-Critical Method,* 207–10, 213–15.

[6] Swanson, "Christian Prophetic Speech," 13–124, esp. 31–79; Claus Westermann, *Basic Forms of Prophetic Speech* (Philadelphia: Westminster, 1967) 131.

[7] On antithetic parallelism in general, see Stanislav Segert, "Semitic Poetic Structures in the New Testament," *ANRW* 2.25.2, 1433–62 and the literature cited there; Otto Eissfeldt, *The Old Testament: An Introduction* (New York: Harper & Row, 1965) 57–64; Koch, *Form-Critical Method,* 103–4; Jeremias, *NT Theology,* 14–20.

[8] Segert ("Semitic Poetic Structures," 1438) notes that "the term and concept of antithetic parallelism is clearly defined by opposition of half-verses, based on semantic oppositions of their parts . . . syntactic similarity and parallelity stresses this opposition . . . thetic and antithetic parallelism is in most instances developed within one verse consisting of two half verses."

	subject	*middle element*	*verb*
line 1	ὁ πιστεύσας	καὶ βαπτισθεὶς	σωθήσεται
line 2	ὁ δὲ ἀπιστήσας		κατακριθήσεται

The parallelism is broken in the first line by the almost intrusive reference to baptism. This variable middle element is a regular feature of other antithetic prophecies and need not be considered a secondary textual interpolation.

The saying lacks its own redactional introduction[9] yet shares the connective that introduced the preceding saying (καὶ εἶπεν αὐτοῖς [16:15]). The main redactional device is a *Stichwort* linkage employing the πιστ- stem (16:10b, 13b, 14, *16*, 17a), which has securely attached the formulation in 16:16 to the surrounding text. A more subtle compositional device is the placement of this antithetic parallel saying immediately after the synthetically parallel commissioning saying in 16:15, which results in the (apparently tolerable) redundant repetition of similar forms.[10]

Comparative Texts: Similar Antithetic Sayings

The formulation in 16:16 is independently attested,[11] yet comparative analysis demonstrates that it belongs to a group of traditionally formulated texts that share strikingly similar stylistic, structural, and terminological features. Compare and contrast the following texts.

Mark 16:16	ὁ πιστεύσας	καὶ βαπτισθεὶς	σωθήσεται
	ὁ δὲ ἀπιστήσας		κατακριθήσεται
John 3:18	ὁ πιστεύων	εἰς αὐτὸν	οὐ κρίνεται
	ὁ δὲ μὴ πιστεύων		ἤδη κέκριται

Kerygma Petrou (Clement *Stromateis* 6.6.48)

οἱ ἀκούσαντες	καὶ πιστεύσαντες	σωθῶσιν
οἱ δὲ μὴ πιστεύσαντες	ἀκούσαντες	μαρτυρήσωσιν . . .

[9] The prophecies both of salvation and of judgment employ an introductory identification formula, as noted.

[10] On the redactional use of the *Stichwort* technique and the association of traditions by formal relationship, see Rudolf Bultmann, *The History of the Synoptic Tradition* (2nd ed.; New York: Harper & Row, 1963) 325.

[11] Hug notes that 16:16 is "une formulation particulière independante" (*Finale,* 170). Hubbard discusses the relationship between Mark 16:16; Matt 28:19b; and John 20:23 (*Matthean Redaction,* 145). He suggests that 16:16 may have been redacted from those texts, but he goes on to note that 16:16 is "substantially different from either the verse in Matthew or that in John . . . in composing v. 16, [the author] may have had access to an independent tradition, just as he did in composing v. 15."

Ascension of Isaiah 3:18 (Amherst Papyri 1, frag. 2.4–4.4)

οἱ πιστεύσαντες	τῷ σταυρῷ αὐτοῦ	σωθήσονται

Isa 28:16 LXX (= Rom 10:11)

ὁ πιστεύων	ἐπ' αὐτῷ	οὐ καταισχυνθήσεται

Rom 10:9

ἐὰν ὁμολογήσῃς	ἐν τῷ στόματί σου . . .	[σωθήσῃ]
καὶ πιστεύσῃς	ἐν τῇ καρδίᾳ σου . . .	σωθήσῃ

Mark 13:13b

ὁ δὲ ὑπομείνας	εἰς τέλος	οὗτος σωθήσεται

Didache 16.5

οἱ δὲ ὑπομείναντες	ἐν τῇ πίστει αὐτῶν	σωθήσονται

An analysis of these texts will enable us to define a sphere of reference in which to interpret the form and content of the saying in Mark 16:16. It will also clarify the manner in which such antithetic prophetic sayings were appropriated at the textual level for various purposes of compositional redaction.

John 3:18

	subject (participial)	*middle element*	*verb*
line 1	ὁ πιστεύων	εἰς αὐτὸν	οὐ κρίνεται
line 2	ὁ δὲ μὴ πιστεύων		ἤδη κέκριται

This text clearly reflects the realized eschatology of the Johannine gospel.[12] C. H. Dodd and R. E. Brown consider John 3:18 and Mark 16:16 to be variants of the same saying.[13] These texts, however, exhibit particular differences which prohibit any theory of derivation from a common traditional

[12] Raymond E. Brown, *The Gospel According to John* (2 vols.; AB 29, 29A; Garden City, N.Y.: Doubleday, 1982) 1:CXVI–CXXI, 345; Bultmann, *John,* 155 n. 1; Rudolf Schnackenburg, *The Gospel According to St. John* (HTCNT; London: Burns & Oates; New York: Herder & Herder, 1968) 1:380–81, 401–3; Hug, *Finale,* 98.

[13] C. H. Dodd, *Historical Tradition in the Fourth Gospel* (Cambridge: Cambridge University Press, 1963) 357–58; Brown, *John* 1:148. But Dodd also notes that "both writers are following a current tradition" (p. 357). See 1 John 5:10 and the relevant comments on redaction by R. Bultmann (*The Johannine Epistles* [Hermeneia; Philadelphia: Fortress Press, 1973] 81–82).

saying. At the same time, however, they exhibit structural and conceptual similarities which suggest that they are independent formulations of a particular type.

Note that the two texts are structurally identical.[14] Each is constructed of two lines in antithetic parallelism.[15] In both texts the subject derives from the πιστ- stem. In Mark 16:16 the antithetic subject employs the alpha-privative (ἀπιστεύω), and in John 3:18 it employs the negative μή. The Markan text places σωθήσεται and κατακριθήσεται in antithesis, while John 3:18 employs οὐ κρίνεται in antithesis with ἤδη κέκριται.[16]

Both texts also employ an extra element in the first line that has no complementary element in the second. This middle element functions to apply the saying to a particular issue, whether christological (εἰς αὐτόν [John 3:18]) or sacramental (καὶ βαπτισθείς [Mark 16:16]) and so is suggestive of its *Sitz im Leben*. The two texts are neither terminologically nor thematically identical.

Such similarities and differences demonstrate that these two texts are not variants of the same saying but are rather two independent expressions or formulations of a clearly defined traditional type. The basic structure of the type has set belief and salvation into a causal relationship and then set this first couplet into antithesis with the second couplet representing disbelief and condemnation (also in a causal relationship). The *Sitz im Leben* of any particular formulation is most clearly seen in the middle element, which applies the saying to a particular issue.

Kerygma Petrou (Clement *Stromateis* 6.6.48)

subject (participial)	*middle element*	*verb*
οἱ ἀκούσαντες	καὶ πιστεύσαντες	σωθῶσιν
οἱ δὲ μὴ πιστεύσαντες	ἀκούσαντες	μαρτυρήσωσιν . . .

[14] Dodd notes that the texts are "virtually identical, and they are molded in the same form" (*Historical Tradition*, 357). Their similarity, however, is mostly structural, while terminological similarity is confined to the πιστ- stem. John 3:18 is followed by an interpretive comment (ὅτι . . .), which Bultmann describes as "certainly the work of the evangelist" (*John*, 155 n. 1).

[15] The poetic features of the Johannine sources and redaction have received detailed attention by both Segert ("Semitic Poetic Structures," 1454–55) and Brown (*John* 1:CXXXII–CXXXV). Compare D. Moody Smith, who isolates the materials that Bultmann had attributed to the revelation discourse source and demonstrates their poetic nature (*The Composition and Order of the Fourth Gospel* [New Haven: Yale University Press, 1965] 23–34).

[16] On the Johannine use of κρίσις, see C. H. Dodd, *The Interpretation of the Fourth Gospel* (Cambridge: Cambridge University Press, 1953) 208–12; see also Friedrich Büchsel, "κρίνω," *TDNT* 3:933–35, 938–39; Brown, *John* 1:345.

This text in the *Kerygma Petrou* (= *KP*) exhibits the formal features of an antithetic prophetic saying.[17] It comprises two lines in antithetic parallelism and is unique among the comparative texts because of its use of a middle element in the second line (ἀκούσαντες). The structure and syntax of the traditional formulation have been coordinated to the syntactic demands of the surrounding narrative. This can be seen by the use of the subjunctive leader ὅπως[18] and by the continuation of the formulation's second line into the following narrative: μαρτυρήσωσιν οὐκ ἔχοντες ἀπολογίαν εἰπεν· οὐκ ἠκούσαμεν.

The two-part schema of belief–salvation in Mark 16:16 and John 3:18 is not employed in *KP*, which favors a three-part schema of hearing–belief–salvation. It appears that a traditional antithetic prophetic saying that spoke of belief-and-salvation (and the antithetic disbelief-and-condemnation) has been expanded by the addition of elements referring to the hearing (ἀκούω) of the message (ὅτι εἷς θεός ἐστιν).[19]

Neither the Johannine christological element (εἰς αὐτόν [John 3:18]) nor the Markan sacramental element (καὶ βαπτισθείς [Mark 16:16]) is considered in this peculiar formulation. In the first line the participle built on the πιστ-stem, which occupies first position in the other texts, has been relegated to second position. The peculiar οἱ ἀκούσαντες occupies first position with the implication that the hearing of the message is temporally prior to belief.[20]

The author places the redundant ἀκούσαντες rather awkwardly in the middle section of the second line, thereby further obscuring the paral-

[17] The *KP* is extant only in patristic quotations. Clement of Alexandria preserves the largest number (*Strom.* 1.29.82; 2.15.68; 6.5.39–41; 6.6.48; 6.15.128). G. Quispel and R. M. Grant point out that *KP* is also quoted by Theophilus, without, however, being identified as part of *KP* ("Note on the Petrine Apocrypha," *VC* 6 [1952] 31–32). The *KP* fragments have been collected and discussed by Ernst von Dobschütz, *Das Kerygma Petri. Kritisch Untersucht* (TU 11.1; Leipzig: Hinrichs, 1893) esp. 22–24. See also the discussions by W. Schneemelcher, "The Kerygma Petrou," *NTApoc* 2:94–102, esp. 101; P. Nautin, "Les citations de la Predication de Pierre dans Clement d'Alexandrie, Strom VI.V.39–41," *JTS* 25 (1974) 98–105; and Terence V. Smith, *Petrine Controversies in Early Christianity* (WUNT 15; Tübingen: Mohr-Siebeck, 1985) 38–40. Schneelmelcher suggests Egypt as the place of origin (*NT Apoc* 2:95) and agrees with Dobschütz's dating of 80–140 CE (*Kerygma Petri*, 67). More recently, however, H. Paulsen has dated the composition of the *KP* text more precisely: 100–120 CE ("Das Kerygma Petri und die urchristliche Apologetik," *ZKG* 88 [1977] 1–37).

[18] See BDF §369.

[19] On the pre-Christian use of this confession in Hellenistic Judaism, see Vernon H. Neufeld, *The Earliest Christian Confessions* (Leiden: Brill, 1963) 36–41; Klaus Wengst, *Christologische Formeln und Lieder des Urchristentums* (Gütersloh: Mohn, 1972) 136–43.

[20] A similar theological issue was addressed by Paul in Rom 10:14–21; see Ernst Käsemann, *Commentary on Romans* (Grand Rapids: Eerdmans, 1980) 292–98; Ulrich Wilkens, *Der Brief an die Römer* (3 vols.; EKKNT 6; Zurich: Benziger; Neukirchen-Vluyn: Neukirchener Verlag, 1960) 2:227–28.

lelism.[21] By its emphasis on the hearing of the message, the text functions as a warning to those who have heard and yet excuse themselves, saying **οὐχ ἠκούσαμεν**; it attempts to give one solution to the theological problem of the fate of those who have heard and yet do not believe.

Single Member (Nonantithetic) Formulations

Ascension of Isaiah 3:18 (Amherst Papyri, frag. 2.4–4.4)

οἱ πιστεύσαντες τῷ σταυρῷ αὐτοῦ σωθήσονται

Isa 28:16 LXX (= Rom 10:11)

ὁ πιστεύων ἐπ' αὐτῷ οὐ καταισχυνθήσεται

Rom 10:9

ἐὰν ὁμολογήσῃς ἐν τῷ στόματί σου . . . [σωθήσῃ]
καὶ πιστεύσῃς ἐν τῇ καρδίᾳ σου . . . σωθήσῃ

Mark 13:13b

ὁ δὲ ὑπομείνας εἰς τέλος οὗτος σωθήσεται

Didache 16.5

οἱ δὲ ὑπομείναντες ἐν τῇ πίστει αὐτῶν σωθήσονται

Each of these texts exhibits the formal features of the first line of an antithetic prophecy and so each can be considered a prophecy of salvation. The logical redundancy inherent in the antithetic second line of the two-line formulations was probably the reason for the elision of the antithesis. The antithetic members, which most likely never existed in these particular texts, can easily be supplied by generation out of the extant line, which further demonstrates the formal relationship between the full antithetic formulations and the one-line versions. For example:

Ascension of Isaiah 3:18

οἱ πιστεύσαντες τῷ σταυρῷ αὐτοῦ σωθήσονται
(οἱ δὲ μὴ πιστεύσαντες κατακριθήσεται)

Isa 28:16 LXX (= Rom 10:11)

ὁ πιστεύων ἐπ' αὐτῷ οὐ καταισχυνθήσεται
(ὁ δὲ μὴ πιστεύων καταισχυνθήσεται)

[21] Segert notes the phenomenon of the dissolution of parallel structures through the process of redaction ("Semitic Poetic Structures," 1451–52).

These reconstructed antithetic formulations are structurally and terminologically similar to the antithetic sayings in Mark 16:16 and John 3:18.[22] Except for Mark 13:13b, the one-line versions are incorporated into narratives without any indication that they are understood as sayings of Jesus, which further demonstrates the diverse use of antithetic prophetic sayings.

Greek papyrus fragments of the *Ascension of Isaiah,* discovered by B. P. Grenfell and A. S. Hunt and published in 1900, contain a prophecy of salvation which, like others, lacks a second line.[23] Again, one finds a conformity to a traditional type. The participle built on the πιστ- stem occupies first position and maintains the subject. The middle section defines the object of belief as τῷ σταυρῷ αὐτοῦ. Unlike the christological and baptismal concerns in John 3:18 and Mark 16:16, the middle section of this formulation focuses on a theological speculation concerning the cross in which an unspecified belief in the cross is understood as efficacious for salvation.[24] This prophecy of salvation does not occur as a saying of Jesus, but is instead part of a retrospective description by the narrator in a story containing a postresurrection commissioning (*Asc. Isa.* 3:17–21) demonstrating the transformation of an antithetic prophetic saying into a narrative.

Note also the two formulations in Rom 10:9 and 11:

Isa 28:16 LXX (=Rom 10:11)

ὁ πιστεύων	ἐπ' αὐτῷ	οὐ καταισχυνθήσεται

Rom 10:9

ἐὰν ὁμολογήσῃς	ἐν τῷ στόματί σου . . .	[σωθήσῃ]
καὶ πιστεύσῃς	ἐν τῇ καρδίᾳ σου . . .	σωθήσῃ

[22] Conversely, the two-line formulations can function effectively without their antithetic members, as the following "deconstructions" demonstrate:

Mark 16:16a:	ὁ πιστεύσας	καὶ βαπτισθεὶς	σωθήσεται; and
John 3:18a:	ὁ πιστεύων	εἰς αὐτὸν	οὐ κρίνεται,

further exhibiting the formal and functional similarities between the one-line and two-line versions.

[23] B. P. Grenfell and A. S. Hunt, *The Amherst Papyri* (2 vols.; London: Oxford University Press, 1900) 1:1–22, pls. III–IX, esp. pp. 11, 21; see J. Flemming and H. Duensing, "The Ascension of Isaiah," in *NTApoc* 2:642–63 and the literature cited there, esp. 648. On the Old Slavonic, Coptic, and complete Ethiopic versions, see *NTApoc* 2:643. Hug notes that "ici, seulement, le 1er membre de l'alternative" (*Finale,* 99–100).

[24] See Johannes Schneider, "σταυρός," *TDNT* 7:572–80. The cross as an object of belief is also found in one of the dialogues in the *Apocryphon of James* (I,2) from Nag Hammadi, esp. 5:31–6:11. See the discussion by Cameron (*Sayings Traditions,* 82–90). The word "cross" is possibly used here as a euphemism for the word "death" or the phrase "death on the cross" (see Phil 2:8c), suggesting belief in the soteriological implications of that death. The cross, however, follows the risen Jesus from his preaching tour of the underworld and even speaks in *Gospel of Peter* 10:39–42 (cf. 4:11; *Barnabas* 9:8). On the cross in the apocryphal acts, see Schneider, "σταυρός," 580 n. 70. Other texts that suggest a salvific power within the cross are Col 1:20; 2:14 (see Schneider, "σταυρός," 577 n. 39); and Eph 2:16. On the theological significance of the cross in Ignatius, *1 Clement, Barnabas,* and Polycarp *Philippians,* see Schneider, "σταυρός," 579–80, 583.

Both the Isaianic text and the more developed formulation in Rom 10:9 also exhibit structural and terminological conformity to a traditional type.[25] In Rom 10:11 a participle built on the πιστ- stem occupies the usual first position and also maintains the subject. The variable middle section defines the object of belief with a christological focus (ἐπ' αὐτῷ).[26] The structural and terminological similarities with the formulation in John 3:18 suggest that the two texts are independent expressions of a traditional type rather than two versions of a common traditional saying. Compare the following:

Rom 10:11	ὁ πιστεύων	ἐπ' αὐτῷ	οὐ καταισχυνθήσεται[27]
John 3:18	ὁ πιστεύων	εἰς αὐτὸν	οὐ κρίνεται

The Johannine reading οὐ κρίνεται is not attested as a variant for οὐ καταισχυνθῇ in Isa 28:16 LXX.[28] Paul introduces the Isaianic quote with the editorial connective λέγει γὰρ ἡ γραφή and emphasizes the universality of salvation by the interpretive addition of πᾶς to the beginning of the quote.[29] Both texts employ the variable middle section for christological purposes (Rom 10:11: ἐπ' αὐτῷ; John 3:18: εἰς αὐτόν).

Of special interest is the unique and complex formulation of the traditional type that is found in Rom 10:9:

[25] Isa 28:16 LXX is quoted also in Rom 9:33 and 1 Pet 2:6. On the Septuagintal and early Christian interpretations of Isa 28:16, see C. E. B. Cranfield, *A Critical and Exegetical Commentary on the Epistle to the Romans* (2 vols.; ICC; Edinburgh: T. & T. Clark, 1975, 1979) 2:511–12. The antithetic nature of much of the Pauline "homologia" has been discussed by Neufeld, who notes that primitive confessional traditions were often "bipartite, appearing as contrasts, though at times the adversative aspects have been softened by qualifying phrases so as to make them complementary rather than antithetical" (*Confessions,* 45–49, 66–67).

[26] Hans-Jürgen van der Minde notes that "das ἐπ' αὐτῷ bezieht sich nun nicht mehr auf Gott, wie im ursprünglichen Kontext, sondern auf den in V.9 genannten Kyrios Jesus" (*Schrift und Tradition bei Paulus* [PTS 3; Munich: Schöningh, 1976] 116); see Cranfield, *Romans* 2:531.

[27] Cranfield notes that "Paul understands οὐ καταισχυνθήσεται as equivalent to δικαιωθήσεται/σωθήσεται" (and not the Johannine οὐ κρίνεται) (*Romans* 2:531). Compare the discussions on the general relationship between Paul and John in Anton Fridrichsen, *The Root of the Vine* (New York: Philosophical Library, 1953) 37–62; and Pierre Benoit, "Paulinisme et Johannisme," *NTS* 9 (1962–63) 193–207.

[28] *Septuaginta: Isaias,* ed. Joseph Ziegler (GAASG; Göttingen: Vandenhoeck & Ruprecht, 1983) 218.

[29] The editorial introductory formula λέγει γὰρ ἡ γραφή, with slight variations, is the second most common Pauline introductory formula (5 occurrences: Rom 4:3; 9:17; 10:11; 11:13; Gal 4:30; also 1 Tim 5:18). The most common formula is γέγραπται (29 occurrences); see E. Earle Ellis, *Paul's Use of the Old Testament* (London: Oliver & Boyd, 1957) 22–37, esp. 22–25. Still useful is the comprehensive study of NT quotation formulas by David McCalman Turpie, *The New Testament View of the Old* (London: Hodder & Stoughton, 1872) esp. 101–76. On the universality of salvation, see Käsemann, *Romans,* 291–92; Cranfield, *Romans* 2:531; van der Minde, *Schrift und Tradition,* 117. On πᾶς in the universal sense of "anyone," see BDF §275(3), (6).

verbal subject	*variable middle element*	*creedal element*	*final element*
ὅτι ἐὰν			
ὁμολογήσῃς	ἐν τῷ στόματί μου	κύριον Ἰησοῦν	———
καὶ			
πιστεύσῃς	ἐν τῇ καρδίᾳ σου	ὅτι ὁ θεὸς αὐτὸν ἤγειρεν ἐκ νεκρῶν	
			σωθήσῃ

The text appears to be the result of a conflation of two single-line creedal formulations into a synthetic parallelism. Note that each line is structured in four sections. The first line (introduced by ὅτι ἐὰν) contains the usual verbal subject in first position, but it is based on ὁμολογέω rather than the expected πιστεύω.[30] The variable middle element of each line defines the instrument or location of either action by a prepositional phrase, whether related to ὁμολογέω (ἐν τῷ στόματί σου) or πιστεύω (ἐν τῇ καρδίᾳ σου). The final element, σωθήσῃ, occurs only once, and at the end of the entire formulation so as to avoid a redundancy.

Unique to this formulation is the presence of creedal statements in both lines which have been identified by Käsemann and others as pre-Pauline traditional materials:[31] (1) κύριος Ἰησοῦς, and (2) (ὅτι[32]) ὁ θεὸς αὐτὸν ἤγειρεν ἐκ νεκρῶν.[33]

Finally, the structural and terminological similarities that indicate a traditional type behind the preceding comparative texts are also evident in two apocalyptic texts.

Mark 13:13b	ὁ δὲ ὑπομείνας	εἰς τέλος	οὗτος σωθήσεται[34]
Didache 16.5	οἱ δὲ ὑπομείναντες	ἐν τῇ πίστει αὐτῶν	σωθήσονται

[30] On ὁμολογία, its cognates and antonyms, and the peculiarities of the Pauline homologia, see Neufeld, *Confessions,* 13–33, 42–68; and Otto Michel, "ὁμολογέω," *TDNT* 5:199–220, esp. 209.

[31] Käsemann notes that "in this case a pre-Pauline formula is adopted . . . into which the apostle imports the allusions to Deut 30:14" (*Romans,* 291), and van der Minde speaks of "eine vorpaulinische Formel" (*Schrift und Tradition,* 113–14).

[32] On ὅτι-recitativum, see BDF §§397 (5), 470 (1). The variant reading ὅτι κύριος Ἰησοῦς (introduction of ὅτι and alteration into the nominative case) in the Alexandrian witnesses (B cop^{sa} Clem, joined by 81 syr^{pal} cop^{bo} et al.) reflects a scribal attempt to make more explicit the reference to the independent and oral nature of the creedal acclamation. This evidences a tendency to restore the oral nature of the creed that Paul has textualized in the accusative case without the ὅτι-recitativum.

[33] On the traditional nature of these two confessional statements, see Paul-Emile Langevin, "Sur la Christologie de Romains 10,1–13," *Laval Théologique et Philosophique* 35 (1979) 35–54, esp. 41–44; Cranfield, *Romans* 2:526–30; Neufeld, *Confessions,* 43; Wengst, *Formeln und Lieder,* 131–35.

[34] The Markan text is twice copied verbatim, in Matt 10:22 and 24:13.

Each of these texts expresses a traditional formulation without a complementary antithetical second line.[35] The virtue, however, is not the usual believing (πιστεύω) but rather enduring (ὑπομένω)[36] and suggests a persecution and/or parousia context. The variable middle section of each text refers to either an eschatological event (εἰς τέλος [Mark 13:13b])[37] or the locus of remaining (ἐν τῇ πίστει αὐτῶν [*Did.* 16.5]).[38]

The occurrence of the single-line formulation in Mark 13:13b demonstrates another instance in which a prophetic statement is used as a saying of Jesus in the construction of a discourse—and in this case an apocalyptic discourse. Each text employs the postpositive δέ, which, as an editorial device, links the formulation to the surrounding text.[39] The saying in *Didache* 16:5 is also attached to its text by the use of an antonymous *Stichwort* device: σκανδαλίζω/ὑπομένω. It is not, however, considered a saying of Jesus in its present narrative. Both texts are employed in a persecution/parousia narrative context (especially suggested by the use of ὑπομένω),[40] attesting to another special application of traditional prophetic formulas.

Observations on Formal and Redactional Features of Mark 16:16

The preceding analysis of the structural and terminological similarities among comparable texts suggests that each of the texts is an independent expression of a traditional type. Mark 16:16 is one textual formulation among many which represent that traditional type. Differences between the texts are due to performancial variations in both the oral and textual (redactional) spheres.

The one-line and two-line antithetic formulations appear to share structural and terminological similarities with another traditional type commonly

[35] *Did.* 16.5 continues with ὑπ' αὐτοῦ τοῦ καταθέματος (omitted in *Apostolic Constitutions*). See the text and discussion in *Didache (Apostellehre), Barnabasbrief, Zweiter Klemensbrief, Schrift Diognet* (Schriften des Urchristentums; ed. Klaus Wengst; Darmstadt: Wissenschaftliche Buchgesellschaft, 1984) 3–100, esp. 90–91.

[36] Compare the use of ὑπομονή in Luke 21:19: ἐν τῇ ὑπομονῇ ὑμῶν κτήσασθε τὰς ψυχὰς ὑμῶν. On the technical use of ὑπομένω/ὑπομονή as a virtue in Greek ethics and early Christian literature, see Hauck, "ὑπομένω, ὑπομονή," *TDNT* 4:581–88. See also Klaus Berger, "Hellenistische Gattungen im Neuen Testament," *ANRW* 2.25.2, 1031–1432, 1831–35, and the discussion entitled "Tugend- und Lasterkataloge," pp. 1088–92 and the literature cited there.

[37] See Werner H. Kelber, *The Kingdom in Mark* (Philadelphia: Fortess Press, 1974) 118–19.

[38] On the relationships between Matthew 24, Mark 13, and *Didache* 16, see Bultmann, *History,* 122, 125–27; and Helmut Koester, *Synoptische Überlieferung bei den apostolischen Vätern* (TU 10; Berlin: Akademie-Verlag, 1957) 180, 183–84.

[39] *Did.* 16.5: τότε . . . καὶ . . . δέ. Mark 13:13: καὶ . . . δέ.

[40] Hauck, "ὑπομένω, ὑπομονή," 586–88.

called creed or homologia.[41] The variety of modern terminology that has been employed to describe these traditional materials is clearly seen, for example, in descriptions of the formulation in Rom 10:9. This text has been described as creed, creedal formula, acclamation, acclamation-homologia, homologia-confession, baptismal confession, and liturgical confession.[42]

The concise nature of the traditional formulations suggests that they were understandable within their original contexts, but once removed from those contexts and redacted into secondary literary contexts they lost their earlier frame of reference and inadvertently acquired a more obscure nature, which further resulted in an increase in the saying's polyvalence.[43]

The particular formulations do not constitute the textual record of one traditional saying's evolution. They are instead independent expressions of a traditional type. It is the type that generates the particular formulations. The structural and terminological features of the particular formulations suggest poetic and mnemonic traits, further suggesting usage within the oral sphere.[44]

Some of the texts exhibit oral features with little or no influence from textuality (Mark 16:16; John 3:18), and others evidence influence of a scribal hand (Rom 10:9 [B cop$^{bo, sa}$ syp^{pal} 81 Clem]), a redactional hand (*KP;* Rom 10:9 [in its use of earlier traditional materials]), or dependence on a textual and exegetical tradition (Rom 10:11 = Isa 28:16 LXX).

The structural and terminological diversity that is evident among the particular formulations makes especially problematic any attempt to describe a single *Sitz im Leben* for the type and instead indicates the type's applicability in various contexts. It has already been noted that the variable middle element is the least stable terminological element in the formulation. This element is perhaps the best indicator of the *Sitz im Leben* of any of the

[41] Neufeld, *Confessions,* 13–33.

[42] Creed: C. K. Barrett, *A Commentary on the Epistle to the Romans* (New York: Harper, 1957) 200; creedal formula: H. Sasse, "Jesus Christ, the Lord," in *Mysterium Christi,* ed. G. K. A. Bell and A. Deissmann (New York: Longmans, Green, 1932) 93; acclamation: O. Michel, *Der Brief an die Römer* (Göttingen: Vandenhoeck & Ruprecht, 1955) 227; acclamation-homologia: van der Minde, *Schrift und Tradition,* 113–14; homologia-confession: Käsemann, *Romans,* 290–91, and Neufeld, *Confessions,* 43; baptismal confession: C. H. Dodd, *The Epistle of Paul to the Romans* (London: Hodder & Stoughton, 1949) 166; liturgical confession: Hans Lietzmann, *An die Römer* (Tübingen: Mohr, 1928) 97.

[43] Hug, for example, does not speak of the prophetic, confessional, or creedal aspects of 16:16 (*Finale,* 94–102). He interprets it as "l'alternative" in the light of the acceptance or rejection of τὸ εὐαγγέλιον in 16:15.

[44] Ernst Lohmeyer appears to be unique among researchers by his insightful identification of "eine bestimmte Form der mündlichen Überlieferung" (*Das Evangelium des Markus* [KEK; 14th ed.; Göttingen: Vandenhoeck & Ruprecht, 1957] 362). The oral nature and *Sitz im Leben* of both the prophecy of judgment and that of salvation are discussed by Swanson, "Christian Prophetic Speech," 168, esp. n.3.

formulations. The middle element, in virtue of its variable nature, appears to be the point at which any particular formulation makes direct contact with its own *Sitz im Leben*. The middle element in Mark 16:16 (καὶ βαπτισθείς) has led to the suggestion that this particular formulation is a prophetic acclamation that was recited in a baptismal catechism or baptismal ritual.[45]

Mark 16:16 also emphasizes belief (ὁ πιστεύσας). The object of belief, however, remains obscure because it does not have a referrent within the syntactical confines of the saying. We cannot suppose that the original object of belief can be found elsewhere in the formulation's present narrative context (e.g., ὅτι ζῇ καὶ ἐθεάθη).[46] Whether the act of believing in 16:16 originally referred to a belief in resurrection, as it does in its present narrative, or to the popular confession κύριος Ἰησοῦς, or to some other confessional tradition cannot be demonstrated.

Mark 16:16 is an antithetic prophecy of salvation and condemnation that entered the Markan text from the oral sphere in a process of compositional redaction. It is one particular formulation of a traditonal type. This text not only demonstrates the secondary use of antithetic prophetic sayings as sayings of Jesus; it also demonstrates the use of such sayings in the redactional composition of discourses.

[45] Researchers have not generally attempted descriptions of the *Sitz im Leben* of Mark 16:16. Note, however, that V. Taylor refers to a "confession made at baptism" (*The Gospel According to St. Mark* [2nd ed.; New York: Macmillan, 1966] 612). John Alsup speaks of a "confessional statement" (*The Post-Resurrection Appearance Stories of the Gospel-Tradition* [Stuttgart: Calwer, 1975] 123), and Walter Grundmann describes the text as an "Akklamation" related to baptism (*Das Evangelium nach Markus* [THKNT 2; 3rd ed.; Berlin: Evangelische Verlagsanstalt, 1965] 328).

[46] A form-critical and redaction-critical study which suggests that an earlier narrative composition (16:9–15, 20a) was later expanded by the editorial addition of traditional materials (represented by the following units: v. 16; vv. 17–18, 20b; and v. 19) from elsewhere, can be found in my dissertation.

18

Secret Mark and the History of Canonical Mark

PHILIP SELLEW

ONE OF THE MOST important contributions Helmut Koester has made to our understanding of early Christian history and literature has been his insistence on paying full attention not only to the writings that were eventually made part of the New Testament canon but also to other, often equally ancient writings that were ultimately left to the side. Apocryphal or noncanonical writings, he argues, must be examined and given their full weight in considering the history of early Christian literary forms as well as the origins and development of the Jesus sayings tradition.[1] It is fully consonant with this approach that the *Secret Gospel of Mark* quoted in a purported letter of Clement of Alexandria, published by Morton Smith in 1973, has impressed Professor Koester as an important key to understanding the history of the Gospel of Mark.[2] In a significant but unfortunately neglected article, Professor Koester has outlined a provocative hypothesis that places *Secret Mark* on a line of development subsequent to the original writing but prior to the canonical Gospel, which he views as the product of a secondary, ecclesiastical redaction.[3] Although these suggestions have

[1] See esp. H. Koester, *Synoptische Überlieferung bei den Apostolischen Vätern* (TU 65; Berlin: Akademie-Verlag, 1957), and numerous other works listed in the Koester bibliography published in this volume.

[2] Morton Smith, *Clement of Alexandria and a Secret Gospel of Mark* (Cambridge, Mass.: Harvard University Press, 1973); see Koester's review in the *American Historical Review* 80 (1975) 620–22.

[3] H. Koester, "History and Development of Mark's Gospel (From Mark to *Secret Mark* and 'Canonical' Mark)," in *Colloquy on New Testament Studies: A Time for Reappraisal and Fresh Approaches,* ed. B. C. Corley (Macon, Ga.: Mercer University Press, 1983) 35–57; reprinted in Koester, *Gospel Traditions in Early Christian Literature: Collected Essays,* ed. P. Sellew (London/Philadelphia: Trinity Press International, 1992). Koester's paper was originally presented at a colloquy on New Testament studies convened at Fort Worth, Texas, in November 1980.

attracted some notice,[4] for the most part New Testament scholarship has not yet fully come to terms with Koester's proposal.[5] Because of his essay's origin as a contribution to a conference, Koester's argument is often rather abbreviated, and some implications of his observations and suggestions are only hinted at and not always made clear. My purpose in this brief contribution in his honor is to scrutinize Koester's hypothesis more thoroughly than has yet been done and then to suggest how his proposal, which I believe to be correct in its basic insights, will necessarily affect our understanding of the composition and history of the canonical Gospel of Mark.[6] It gives me great pleasure as Helmut Koester's student to draw the attention of colleagues more fully to this very intriguing part of his work.

Summary of Koester's Proposal

I shall begin with a summary of Koester's hypothesis, which will require some detail. There is no need or space to review here the circumstances and

---

Koester has now published a brief updated version of his hypothesis, with some new suggestions about chaps. 8–10 in Mark, in his book *Ancient Christian Gospels: Their History and Development* (Philadelphia: Trinity Press International, 1990) 273–303, esp. 293ff.

[4] Most notably Hans-Martin Schenke, "The Mystery of the Gospel of Mark," *Second Century* 4 (1984) 65–82; John Dominic Crossan, in *Four Other Gospels: Shadows on the Contours of Canon* (Minneapolis: Winston/Seabury, 1986) 91–121; and Marvin W. Meyer, "The Youth in the *Secret Gospel of Mark*," in *The Apocryphal Jesus and Christian Origins, Semeia* 49, ed. Ron Cameron (Atlanta: Scholars Press, 1990) 129–53; idem, "The Youth in Secret Mark and the Beloved Disciple in John," in *Gospel Origins & Christian Beginnings: In Honor of James M. Robinson*, ed. James E. Goehring, Charles W. Hedrick, et al. (Sonoma, Calif.: Polebridge, 1990) 94–105. My thanks are due to Professor Meyer for his generous permission to use his articles in prepublication form. See also Burton L. Mack, *A Myth of Innocence: Mark and Christian Origins* (Philadelphia: Fortress Press, 1988) 157 n. 16.

[5] The scholars mentioned in the previous note (with the partial exception of Schenke) build on Koester's proposal without fully evaluating it in any detail. The first response to Koester's proposal, by David Peabody (printed in the volume of proceedings of the Fort Worth conference [*Colloquy*, ed. Corley, 87–132]), addresses almost nothing but the issue of Synoptic Gospel relationships, instead of engaging Koester's ideas about *Canonical Mark* arising as a revision of *Secret Mark*. A recent survey article on *Secret Mark* fails even to mention Koester's proposals (Saul Levin, "The Early History of Christianity, in Light of the 'Secret Gospel' of Mark," *ANRW* 2.25.6, 4270–92). However, Levin's bibliography and the publication history of the *Ausfstieg und Niedergang* suggest that his essay was written about ten years before its publication in 1988, and thus also before Koester's proposal was published.

[6] For clarity's sake I shall employ here some terms that refer to specific proposed stages in Mark's history: *Original Mark* = the presumptive source of Luke; *Augmented Mark* = the presumptive source of Matthew; *Secret Mark* = the revision of *Original Mark* quoted by Clement; and *Canonical Mark* = the NT Gospel of Mark. A mention of "Mark" or "Mark's Gospel" in roman type refers to the Gospel at any or all stages, or to the Gospel document undifferentiated as to edition(s). Though these are not Koester's labels, they do reflect his views. His own term for what I am calling *Original Mark* is "Proto-Mark," which, however, has an unfortunate association with the term "Ur-Markus," which he wants to avoid.

basic character of Clement's letter,[7] though it will be helpful to mention the two fragments of *Secret Mark* that Clement quotes: an episode found after Mark 10:32 where Jesus raises a youth from the dead and subsequently teaches him about the mystery of the kingdom, and a briefer remark found at Mark 10:46 about Jesus not receiving the youth's sister and Salome at Jericho (Clement of Alexandria *Ad Theodorem* 1^{v} 22–2^{r} 11 and 2^{r} 14–16).[8]

1. Koester accepts the reliability of Clement's report about several versions or editions of the Gospel of Mark being known and used in Alexandria at the close of the second century: a "public" gospel, apparently more or less equivalent to the canonical text (= *Canonical Mark*); a "mystical" or "secret" gospel, also the property of the Alexandrian church but reserved for those specially enlightened (baptized?) (= *Secret Mark*); and a Carpocratian gospel that Clement considered an unacceptable version of the "secret" gospel.

2. Koester disagrees with Clement that the "secret" or "more spiritual" gospel was a secondary version of the "public" gospel, arguing instead for the reverse sequence.[9] Koester's suggestion of multiple stages—or, better, unfolding history—in the development of *Original Mark* to *Canonical Mark* is part of his larger interest in drawing attention to the diversity and multiplicity of gospel traditions and texts in the first two centuries. He suggests that John's Gospel provides the most useful analogue for what he proposes must also have occurred in the case of *Canonical Mark:* a complexity of stages in writing, rewriting, and redacting a document, a process that was probably never entirely completed.[10] I can best explain Koester's specific proposals for the sequence of editions of the Markan gospel with the aid of a diagram (see fig. 1): *Original Mark* was composed on the basis of pre-Markan traditions and was more or less equivalent to sections 1:1–6:44 + 8:27–16:8 of our received gospel. This text was used as a source by the author of Luke,

[7] See Smith, *Clement and a Secret Gospel.* For a survey of responses to this publication see Morton Smith, "Clement of Alexandria and Secret Mark: The Score at the End of the First Decade," *HTR* 75 (1982) 449–61.

[8] These and subsequent references from *Secret Mark* are taken from the text and photographs of Clement's letter as published in Smith, *Clement and a Secret Gospel,* 448–53. The text is also available in the second edition of Otto Stählin, ed., *Clemens Alexandrinus* 4/1 (GCS; ed. U. Treu; Berlin: Akademie-Verlag, 1980) xvii–xviii.

[9] On this basic point of the chronological priority of *Secret Mark* to *Canonical Mark,* Koester is in agreement with Smith, though otherwise the two often disagree in their opinions about likely Markan sources and editions, as well as the implications of Clement's report for our understanding of first- and second-century Christianity.

[10] Koester, "History and Development," in *Colloquy,* ed. Corley, 36–37. For the case of John's Gospel, Koester refers to Raymond E. Brown, *The Community of the Beloved Disciple* (New York: Paulist, 1979) and Ernst Haenchen's commentary; I would add Mack, *Myth of Innocence,* 221 n. 12.

Figure 1
Chart Illustrating Helmut Koester's Proposal

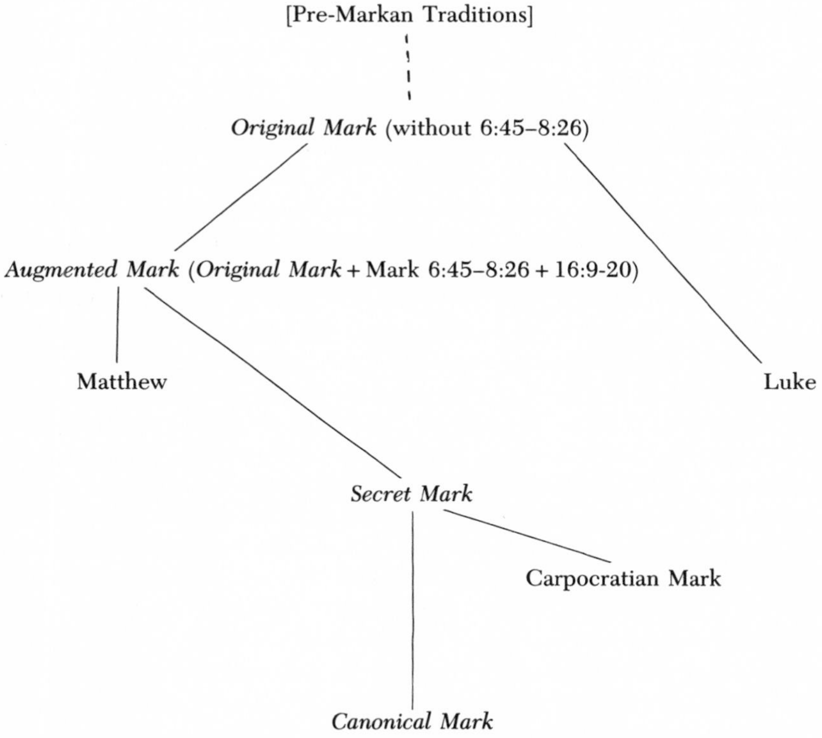

whereas Matthew employed a version of *Original Mark* that had been enlarged by the section now labeled 6:45–8:26. This lengthier version (= *Augmented Mark*), most likely now also including the "Longer Ending" of 16:9–20, was further expanded to produce *Secret Mark*. At some point in the second century, *Secret Mark* was slightly abridged to produce the currently known *Canonical Mark*.

3. *Canonical Mark* contains frequent disruptions in its narrative flow, some apparently secondary glosses and some unusual phrases that have puzzled many readers. Koester argues that many of these difficulties can be explained as due in large part to a not entirely successful expurgation of *Secret Mark* for public use by ordinary believers. Some of the more famous of these puzzles include the abrupt arrival and departure of Jesus and his retinue at Jericho in 10:46 (καὶ ἔρχονται εἰς ’Ιεριχώ, καὶ ἐκπορευομένου αὐτοῦ ἀπὸ ’Ιεριχώ . . .); the unprepared and unexplained appearance of a young man

clothed in a linen cloth (shroud?) in 14:51–52; and a pattern of language and episodes connected with mysterious or magical practices (e.g., the stop-and-start miracle of 8:22–26) that were not read, unless they were independently omitted, by *Original Mark*'s first known revisers, the authors of Matthew and Luke.

4. In his search for terms, themes, and narrative features of Mark's material that accord with the language of the excerpts from *Secret Mark* as quoted by Clement, Koester found several that are normally included among the so-called minor agreements of the later Synopticists against *Canonical Mark,* such as the plural τὰ μυστήρια and the "addition" of γνῶναι in their parallels to Mark 4:11, where *Canonical Mark* has instead simply ὑμῖν τὸ μυστήριον δέδοται τῆς βασιλείας τοῦ θεοῦ (cf. Matt 13:11 and Luke 8:10), or the "suppression" of Aramaic spells or formulas found in Mark 5:41 (ταλιθὰ κοῦμ; cf. Matt 9:25 and Luke 8:54) and 7:34 (ἐφφαθά, no complete parallel). The exorcist's command quoted in Mark 9:25 is not repeated in Matt 17:18 or Luke 9:42. Mark's threefold reference to "baptism" in 10:38, repeated virtually verbatim in 10:39, is lacking in Matthew's parallel (the episode is not found in Luke). Koester suggests that these and similar materials were added to create *Secret Mark* at some point after *Original Mark* and *Augmented Mark* had formed the basis for Luke and Matthew. Koester has also found it striking, though ultimately less decisive, that the material passed over at Luke 9:17 (the famous "Great Omission" of the material in Mark 6:45–8:26) contains doublets or repetitions of several stories, including, as it happens, most of these "magical" pericopes.[11]

5. In addition to clearly magical elements, Koester identifies the Markan emphasis on "teaching" (διδαχή/διδάσκειν) and the unqualified references to "the message" (ὁ λόγος) as likely related to the *Secret Mark* redaction. Frequently Mark's references to Jesus' teaching, found even when introducing or closing miracle stories, are not paralleled by either Matthew or Luke.[12] Matthew repeats only one of Mark's absolute references to "the gospel," often writing instead τὸ εὐαγγέλιον <u>τῆς βασιλείας (τοῦ θεοῦ)</u>.[13] Koester

[11] Koester qualified his reliance on this "Lucan omission" as evidence of the extent and contents of *Original Mark* in his discussion of Peabody's response to his 1980 paper (see "Seminar Dialogue with Helmut Koester," in *Colloquy,* ed. Corley, 75), though the view that Luke used a version of Mark without 6:45–8:26 reappears in *Ancient Christian Gospels,* 284–86. For my comments see below.

[12] Koester ("History and Development," in *Colloquy,* ed. Corley, 44–46) lists Mark 1:27// Luke 4:36; Mark 2:13, cf. Matt 9:9//Luke 5:27; Mark 4:1–2//Matt 13:1–3//Luke 8:4; Mark 6:30//Luke 9:10; Mark 6:34//Matt 14:14//Luke 9:11; Mark 8:31//Matt 16:21//Luke 9:22; Mark 9:31//Matt 17:22//Luke 9:43–44; Mark 10:1//Matt 19:2; Mark 11:17//Matt 21:13//Luke 19:46; Mark 12:35//Matt 22:41–42//Luke 20:41; Mark 12:37–38//Matt 23:1//Luke 20:45.

[13] See, e.g., Mark 1:39//Matt 4:23; Mark 6:6//Matt 9:35; Mark 13:10//Matt 24:14; Mark 14:9// Matt 26:13.

notes that in four other cases Matthew neglects to repeat a Markan mention of "the gospel" for no apparent reason.[14] Luke "omits" all of them.[15]

6. Koester also identifies the special interest in words related to noetic "understanding" (e.g., συνιέναι in Mark 4:12; 6:52; 7:14; 8:17, 21; νοεῖν Mark 7:18; 8:17; 13:14) as typical of the material that he would connect with the *Secret Mark* redaction. He points for possible help in explaining these data to the similar language of the pseudo-Pauline epistles Colossians and especially Ephesians, where an analogous absolute use of the term "the gospel" is linked with statements about disclosing a "mystery."[16]

Evaluation of Koester's Proposal

The insight on which Koester bases his proposal is fundamental. The discovery of Clement's letter about the ancient existence of more than one version of the Gospel of Mark provides us with an important clue to realize that the Gospel of Mark that we have in our received New Testament collection is not a single, unchanged document that resulted from a single act of written composition. Even without appealing to the evidence of *Secret Mark,* the New Testament *Canonical Mark* has long appeared to many to be a secondarily redacted document.[17] Three or four examples must suffice. The Markan version of the sending out of messengers in 6:7–14 has struck many interpreters as an abbreviated version of the story as told in the Q parallel (Q 10:2–16). Koester argues that Mark 2:27 ("The sabbath was made for Human Being, not Human Being for the sabbath") is a secondary intrusion into 2:22–28; it is not found in either the Matthean or Lukan parallels.[18] Mark 10:29 is the famous case of Jesus adding "for the sake of the gospel" to his statement that his followers must renounce hearth and home for *his*

[14] Mark 1:15a//Matt 4:17a; Mark 1:15b//Matt 4:17b; Mark 8:35//Matt 16:25; Mark 10:29//Matt 19:29 (Koester, "History and Development," in *Colloquy,* ed. Corley, 43).

[15] As Koester notes, Luke's Gospel (in distinction from the Acts) never uses the noun εὐαγγέλιον! (*Ancient Christian Gospels,* 9–14).

[16] Koester mentions Eph 3:1–7 and esp. 6:19: ἐν παρρησίᾳ γνωρίσαι τὸ μυστήριον τοῦ εὐαγγελίου ("History and Development," in *Colloquy,* ed. Corley, 48).

[17] Most frequently, Mark has been seen as a secondary redaction of other known gospel documents, namely, Matthew (and/or Luke) or Q. Among the copious literature, see, e.g., Emil Wendling, *Ur-Marcus: Versuch einer Wiederherstellung der ältesten Mitteilungen über das Leben Jesu* (Tübingen: Mohr-Siebeck, 1905); John Pairman Brown, "An Early Revision of the Gospel of Mark," *JBL* 78 (1959) 215–27; idem, "Mark as Witness to an Edited Form of Q," *JBL* 80 (1961) 29–44; O. R. Linton, "Evidences of a Second-Century Revised Edition of St. Mark's Gospel," *NTS* 14 (1967/68) 321–55; David L. Dungan, "Reactionary Trends in the Gospel Producing Activity of the Early Church: Marcion, Tatian, Mark," in *L'Évangile selon Marc: Tradition et rédaction* (BETL 34; ed. M. Sabbe; Leuven: Leuven University Press, 1974) 179–202; C. M. Tuckett, *The Revival of the Griesbach Hypothesis* (SNTSMS 44; Cambridge: Cambridge University Press, 1983).

[18] Koester, "History and Development," in *Colloquy,* ed. Corley, 39–40.

sake (Matt 19:29 has "for my name's sake"; Luke 18:29 has "for the sake of the kingdom of God").[19] Koester follows G. Bornkamm in considering Mark 12:32–34 to be a secondary appendix to the story about the scribe's question about the great commandment.[20]

Not all will agree about which of these and similar features should ultimately be judged to be secondary additions, but their awkwardness would call for some explanation even in the absence of the other Synoptic Gospels. The lack of many of these apparently secondary notes in Matthew and Luke provides an important comparative check for our tracing of the history of Mark's text. If for other reasons we are convinced that Matthew and Luke used Mark (in whatever form) as a narrative source, then the apparently intrusive editorial features present in *Canonical Mark* that are missing in both later Synoptics need to be explained.

The orthodox approach of the two-source hypothesis to the problem of the "minor agreements" is typified by B. H. Streeter's appeal to harmonization in the scribal tradition,[21] and this is no doubt correct in some or even many instances. But that sort of solution was directed almost entirely to the particular literary source difficulties of the classical Synoptic problem. Koester's hypothesis of second-century edition(s) of the Markan Gospel has the great virtue of trying to explain the data in a way that transcends the narrowly construed questions of the older source criticism, by specifically addressing the development of the Markan tradition itself.[22] This focus on Mark's own history, apart from the narrow issues of the Synoptic problem, is one reason why Koester appropriately resists associating his hypothesis of Markan editions with older "Ur-Markus" hypotheses.[23]

Separation of Mark's sources, redaction, and new composition is notoriously difficult, because of a lack of comparative material and the continuity of language and style in the various possible stages. Koester himself has made this point: "It is not surprising to find in this section [Mark 6:45–8:26] redactional features which are typically 'Markan.' . . . Also the additions of *Secret Mark* to Mark are typical for Markan redaction."[24] Koester's argument about

[19] Ibid., 43–44.

[20] Ibid., 40–41.

[21] B. H. Streeter, *The Four Gospels: A Study of Origins* (London: Macmillan, 1924) esp. 295–331.

[22] See Koester's own remark: "To be sure, ad hoc explanations for the several agreements of Matthew and Luke against Mark can be proposed. But such a procedure does not offer an explanation for the problem of Mark as a whole . . ." ("History and Development," in *Colloquy*, ed. Corley, 36).

[23] Ibid.

[24] Ibid., 39 n. 15. I have discussed this problem of the continuity of language in Mark's tradition and composition in greater detail in two recent articles: "Composition of Didactic Scenes in Mark's Gospel," *JBL* 108 (1989) 613–34; and "Oral and Written Sources in Mark 4.1–34," *NTS* 36 (1990) 234–67.

the instability of Mark's text is important, as is his observation about the paucity of evidence for knowledge and especially use of Mark's Gospel until the third century.[25] This all suggests, however, that we must be very cautious about drawing overly sweeping conclusions about the history of particular sections in Mark from comparison with Matthew and Luke alone. When Koester argues that the so-called Great Omission of Luke (of Mark 6:45–8:26) was added to *Original Mark* as an initial step in the direction of *Secret Mark*,[26] for example, we must consider a wider range of evidence.

David Peabody's critique of Koester's original conference presentation included a detailed treatment of typically Markan vocabulary, phrases, and syntactic structures found within the presumed addition of 6:45–8:26. He also tried to show connections, mostly linguistic "reminiscences," of particular pericopes in this section with pericopes elsewhere in Mark.[27] Many of Peabody's data do in fact show a linguistic connection between Mark 6:45–8:26 and the bulk of the gospel, but, as hinted above, this is only to be expected within the perspective of Koester's hypothesis of an organic development of the gospel document.[28] In other words, we would not expect to find linguistic and stylistic dissimilarity in this section unless it were a secondary intrusion from outside Mark's trajectory, such as we see in the Longer Ending of 16:9–20.

It is more customary to cite other grounds for doubting that Luke used a version of Mark lacking this section. Luke typically avoids repetition and the duplication of similar stories, and this section of Mark contains many doublets with other stories told just previously in chapters 4–6 (the boat trip, the feeding miracle, the healing of a blind man).[29] This clear tendency in Luke's use of his sources, when combined with the linguistic data assembled by Peabody, tends to lessen the probability of Luke having used a substantially different version of Mark from that used by Matthew.

More decisive for me than those sorts of arguments, which are after all at times rather difficult to adjudicate, is the question of how the section

[25] Koester, "History and Development," in *Colloquy*, ed. Corley, 37–38; see also Koester, *Ancient Christian Gospels*, 273–75.

[26] Koester, "History and Development," in *Colloquy*, ed. Corley, 38–39. Cf. also n. 11 above.

[27] Peabody, "The Late Secondary Redaction of Mark's Gospel and the Griesbach Hypothesis: A Response to Helmut Koester," in *Colloquy*, ed. Corley, 88–132 (esp. 102–13).

[28] See Koester's comments in the discussion of his paper as reported in *Colloquy*, ed. Corley, 75–76.

[29] On Luke's avoidance of repetition in a stylistic sense, see Henry J. Cadbury, *The Style and Literary Method of Luke* (HTS 6; Cambridge, Mass.: Harvard University Press, 1920). On Luke's avoidance of duplicating similar material, see esp. Heinz Schürmann, "Die Dublettenvermeidungen im Lukasevangelium," in *Traditionsgeschichtliche Untersuchungen zu den synoptischen Evangelien* (Düsseldorf: Patmos, 1968) 279–89.

6:45–8:26 fits within Mark's plotted story. This approach requires a recognition that Mark's plot and structure involve much more than simply a lengthy introduction to the passion account (though assuredly the themes of fated suffering and betrayal are important throughout).[30] I believe that any analysis of the Gospel that focuses on its narrative development will reveal that several significant elements of Mark's plot are located precisely here.

The only aspect of the story that I have space to discuss is the dramatic portrayal of the increasing incomprehension of the disciples, along with a correspondingly progressively stern response on the part of Jesus. The section that Koester believes may have been missing from *Original Mark* is crucial in the portrayal of this central narrative theme. The disciples are mystified by Jesus' ability to walk on water in 6:45–52, and the narrator informs us in 6:52b that their hearts had been "hardened" (a typical motif of biblical narrative suggestive of dangerously careless attitudes or behavior). When Jesus is confronted by the Pharisees and scribes in 7:1–13, he accuses them with Isaiah's picture of unclean lips and wayward hearts; then when the disciples ask for a private explanation of his meaning in 7:14–23, Jesus accuses them of sharing the Pharisee's ignorance: "So you also are stupid (ἀσύνετοι)?" (7:18). Just before the end of this section, Mark constructs a wholly new scene of Jesus and the disciples in the boat, 8:14–21, an occasion where the master addresses his pupils with the same prophetic abuse he had earlier directed at the ill-fated outsiders in 4:11–12 and the Pharisees in 7:6–13.[31] While thematic motifs and favorite phrases could quite conceivably be shared by more than one writer or editor working with one basic story within a particular socioreligious situation (as we see in the case of John), or perhaps by the same writer working at different times (as we see in Paul's letter to the Philippians), basic elements of the narrative plot of a writing like Mark were much more likely to be included from the start.[32]

Koester's suggestion that many of Mark's references to Jesus' "teaching" (διδαχή and διδάσκειν) derive from the *Secret Mark* redaction also requires some scrutiny. It is difficult to determine in several individual instances whether Koester is right that Matthew or Luke did not read the words

[30] Contrast Koester's statement in the Fort Worth discussion of his paper: "Mark wants to order his material as a preface to the passion narrative; I think that still stands, no matter what kind of sources Mark used" (*Colloquy*, ed. Corley, 74; see now also *Ancient Christian Gospels*, 291–92). When we look beyond the issues of tradition and redaction to those of composition and authorial choice, however, other narrative themes, some just as prominent, emerge more clearly from Mark's story.

[31] The connections between Mark 4:1–20; 7:1–23; and 8:14–21 are discussed further in Sellew, "Composition of Didactic Scenes in Mark's Gospel."

[32] There is an important and profitable discussion of this section of Mark's plot from a different perspective in Norman R. Petersen, "The Composition of Mark 4:1–8:26," *HTR* 73 (1980) 185–217.

relating to teaching in their copies of Mark, or whether they instead independently removed that characterization of Jesus' miracle stories when they considered it inappropriate. To take only the first of Koester's examples, the famous case of the crowd's exclamation about "new teaching" in Mark 1:27 upon Jesus' first miracle (exorcism), it is true that Luke 4:36 rewrites Mark's language and substitutes ὁ λόγος οὗτος for Mark's διδαχὴ καινή.[33] But surely it is also significant that both Luke 4:31–32 and Matt 7:28–29 (though there deployed in a different context) nonetheless repeat Mark's statements ἐξεπλήσσοντο ἐπὶ τῇ διδαχῇ and ἦν διδάσκων αὐτούς! Luke may depart from Mark's use of this teaching language at the close of the exorcism account, but he and Matthew certainly give evidence of having read it in their source.

Finally, the question of the enigmatic figure of the youth taught and loved by Jesus in the two fragments of *Secret Mark* quoted by Clement also requires some discussion. Koester proposes that at the literary stage of the production of *Secret Mark*, the story quoted by Clement of the initiation of the young man (νεανίσκος) was inserted at 10:32–34. The scene in 14:51–52 of the youth running away without his linen cloth is thus an additional episode added at the same time, or else the remnant of such an addition. Koester's main interest in the initiation episode is its associations with baptismal and mystery concepts. Others, however, have made more of the role of the youth.[34] I cannot summarize their arguments here, except to say that they consider 14:51–52 in *Canonical Mark* to be a remnant of an earlier stage. This is not necessarily incorrect, but I would point to a feature of Mark's narrative style as employed in 14:51 that would then require some explanation.

These scholars seem not to have noticed that Mark begins this little note with the phrase "And *a certain* youth was following . . . (καὶ νεανίσκος τις συνηκολούθει . . .)." Mark and the other Gospel writers consistently employ the normal Greek narrative practice of using either this construction with τις or, more commonly, an anarthrous noun or proper name, when introducing a *previously unmentioned character*. Study of the introduction of even very well known characters in Mark's opening pages illustrates this stylistic feature.[35] The further example of the unprepared appearance of Simon of

[33] Koester discusses this and other examples in "History and Development," in *Colloquy*, ed. Corley, 44–47.

[34] See Robin Scroggs and Kent I. Groff, "Baptism in Mark: Dying and Rising with Christ," *JBL* 92 (1973) 531–48; also the works cited in n. 4 above, esp. the articles by Meyer.

[35] John first appears on the stage as simply Ἰωάννης βαπτίζων ("[a] John was baptizing") but is subsequently mentioned anaphorically as ὁ Ἰωάννης in 1:6, 14 ("John, the one mentioned"). So too with Ἰησοῦς ἀπὸ Ναζαρέτ in 1:9 as contrasted with ὁ Ἰησοῦς in 1:14, 17; the anarthrous first appearance of Simon, Andrew, and the brothers Jacob and John in 1:16, 19; contrast ἄνθρωπος ἐν πνεύματι ἀκαθάρτῳ in 1:23 with τὸ πνεῦμα τὸ ἀκάθαρτον in 1:26. Mark does not always use this device in the somewhat different circumstance of names used in the genitive case, esp. when the genitive has an adjectival function: e.g., ἐβαπτίσθη . . . ὑπὸ Ἰωάννου (1:9);

Cyrene in 15:21 is instructive: ἀγγαρεύουσιν παράγοντά τινα Σίμωνα Κυρηναῖον. Luke uses this device to great effect, especially at the beginning of parables.[36] Mark's parables tend to start not with τις but instead with the equivalent construction with anarthrous nouns (ἄνθρωπος βάλῃ [4:26]; ὡς κόκκῳ σινάπεως [4:31]; ἀμπελῶνα ἄνθρωπος ἐφύτευσεν [12:1]).[37]

This suggests very strongly that the use of the word τις within *Canonical Mark,* at least, is a conscious editorial or authorial step taken to signal that the νεανίσκος of 14:51–52 had not yet been mentioned in the story. If *Canonical Mark*'s predecessor(s) had earlier featured this character in the initiation scene in chapter 10, then earlier versions of 14:51 *could not have read* καὶ νεανίσκος τις. Proof of this is found in the second fragment from *Secret Mark* quoted by Clement, which refers back to the earlier story of the youth's initiation: καὶ ἦσαν ἐκεῖ ἡ ἀδελφὴ τοῦ νεανίσκου ὃν ἠγάπα αὐτὸν ὁ Ἰησοῦς (2r 14–15). It is not irrelevant, by the way, that the textual basis for the introductory note in 14:51 is quite insecure: among other variants is the very appealing καὶ εἷς τις νεανίσκος, read in A W Θ f1.13 al. This reading may be "original" in *Canonical Mark.* The odd-seeming use of the numeral "one" with or in place of the indefinite pronoun is a common feature of unliterary Koine. It is employed just before this in Mark 14:47 (εἷς δέ τις τῶν παρεστηκόντων; see also 12:42 ἐλθοῦσα μία χώρα; John 11:49: εἷς δέ τις ἐξ αὐτῶν Καϊαφᾶς). In fact the first fragment of *Secret Mark* quoted by Clement uses the same construction: καὶ ἦν ἐκεῖ μία γυνή . . . (1v 23).

We can account for this introductory note with (εἷς) τις in our text of 14:51 in *Canonical Mark* in one of three ways. (1) Perhaps this νεανίσκος is not meant to be identified with the youth of the *Secret Mark* fragment (or the youth in the tomb at 16:5). This is possible but unsatisfying, since we would then have three unconnected references to unrelated νεανίσκοι. (2) Perhaps the enigmatic and unexplained references to unnamed νεανίσκοι were present in *Original Mark* and prompted *Secret Mark*'s additions of the two fragments quoted by Clement. This option has the difficulties that neither Matthew nor Luke shows any knowledge of the νεανίσκος of 14:51 and, more troubling, that the person(s) who inserted the additional episodes was

---

ἦλθον εἰς τὴν οἰκίαν Σίμωνος (1:29). Current NT editors do not pay much attention to this narrative feature, e.g., at 1:36, where on the important internal criterion of author's style we should read ὁ Σίμων with A C 090 al.

[36] E.g., in Luke, ἄνθρωπός τις in 10:30; 15:11; 16:1, 20; 19:12; also Σαμαρείτης δέ τις in 10:33; γυνὴ δέ τις ὀνόματι Μάρθα (10:38); πτωχὸς δέ τις ὀνόματι Λάζαρος (16:20); κριτής τις (18:2); τυφλός τις (18:35); in Acts, καί τις ἀνὴρ χωλός in 3:2; ἀνὴρ δέ τις Ἀνανίας ὀνόματι (5:1); ἀναστὰς δέ τις ἐν τῷ συνεδρίῳ Φαρισαῖος (5:34); ἀνὴρ δέ τις ὀνόματι Σίμων (8:9); ἦν δέ τις μαθητής (9:10); εὗρεν δὲ ἐκεῖ ἄνθρωπόν τινα ὀνόματι Αἰνέαν (9:33); etc. John also uses this device: καὶ ἦν τις βασιλικός in 4:46; ἦν δέ τις ἄνθρωπος ἐκεῖ (5:5); ἦν δέ τις ἀσθενῶν Λάζαρος (11:1); ἦσαν δὲ Ἕλληνές τινες (12:20).

[37] The opening of "the" Sower in 4:3 (ὁ σπείρων . . .) is an exception that likely derives from its pre-Markan attachment to the allegorical interpretation given in 4:14–20.

prompted by the reference in 14:51–52, but neglected to alter the latter to refer to those additions. (3) A more promising possibility is that when *Secret Mark* was edited to produce the public *Canonical Mark*, the editor(s) took care to disguise the previous reference. This last option is preferable within the basic hypothesis Koester has outlined. But it means that we should no longer view the editing of *Secret Mark* to produce *Canonical Mark* as the mere excision of one or two offending passages. The process must have been more thoroughgoing. In that case it would not be surprising that someone who took the trouble to excise the story at 10:32 would also alter the wording of 14:51.[38]

Some Implications for Our Understanding of Mark's History

One important question to consider is whether the themes or motifs isolated by Koester as specific to the stratum of the *Secret Mark* redaction should (or even could) be separated successfully from the document's history as a whole. It may be better to understand most of these themes as fully integral to the interests and tendencies of the document at all its stages, even if some of them received additional emphasis in one or another stratum. What this implies is that we should not view the various stages of writing, rewriting, and redacting Mark's gospel as discontinuous or disruptive of the basic interests and themes of the story viewed overall. Some of the more sensational suggestions about the *Secret Mark* text and its interpretation when first published have apparently clouded many scholars' perspectives on this point. The *Secret Gospel of Mark* no doubt differs somewhat from *Canonical Mark* in its specific wording at places, as well as by including more episodes; though the two stages probably differ to a greater extent than is admitted by Koester and Crossan,[39] *Secret Mark* should not be seen as unrepresentative of the originary impulses and interests that operated within the Markan

[38] In any event, this analysis also has critical implications for those who would connect the youths of 14:51 and 16:5, e.g., Scroggs and Groff ("Baptism in Mark"). They and others do not take account of the fact that even in our received text of Mark 16:5 the women encounter an apparently previously unmentioned youth (εἶδον νεανίσκον καθήμενον; Aland mentions no variants). Marvin Meyer's theory about *Secret Mark*'s "sub-plot involving the [*sic*] νεανίσκος, . . . [which] communicates *Secret Mark*'s vision of the life and challenges of discipleship . . ." encounters the same difficulty ("The Youth in the *Secret Gospel of Mark*," 139). His suggestions about the exemplary value of (the) youth are nonetheless important.

[39] Koester ("History and Development," in *Colloquy*, ed. Corley, 56) mentions the episode of the raising and initiation of the youth as perhaps the only major excision from *Secret Mark* to produce *Canonical Mark*, followed by Crossan (*Four Other Gospels*, 103–4). In *Ancient Christian Gospels*, however, Koester now says more cautiously: "On the basis of the information that is provided by Clement, it is not possible to say whether there were any other differences between these two gospels as Clement knew them" (p. 295).

tradition from the start. We must think in terms of lines of development ("trajectories") rather than disruptive external redaction or tampering.

The emphasis on Jesus' teaching and the need for "understanding" that Koester has connected with the *Secret Mark* redaction may in fact be one of the most pervasive themes of the gospel throughout its various editions. Mark's use of the terms διδαχή and διδάσκειν in editorial contexts is not the whole story. The characterization of Jesus' miraculous powers as "teaching" is deeply embedded in Mark's plotted narrative. I have already mentioned the narrator's repeated descriptions of Jesus' followers as not "understanding" Jesus' identity and authority. They remain uncomprehending despite his mastery of nature as demonstrated in the boat stories (4:35–41 and 6:45–52) and especially in the feeding miracles (6:30–44 and 8:1–10). When Jesus walks to them on the water, the disciples are greatly astonished, "because they didn't understand (οὐ γὰρ συνῆκαν) about the loaves" (6:52). The disciples are still at a loss in the boat trip that immediately follows the second feeding story and are sternly rebuked for their confusion by Jesus' rhetorical questions, ending with his exasperated retort, "You still don't understand!?" (οὔπω συνίετε 8:21).

Perhaps this special Markan theme of teaching and understanding can already be recognized in the gospel's characterization of Jesus' followers as "learners" (μαθηταί). Here I feel the need to tread cautiously, since it is part of our unexamined common "knowledge" about Christian origins that those who surrounded Jesus, more specifically his followers, were (in historical fact) his "disciples." What does it mean that the narrator of the earliest surviving story about Jesus specifically chose to call those attached to him "disciples"? Was this term inevitable? Is it not true that this portrait of master and learners is itself a crucial part of the gospel writer's narrative aims? Everyone agrees that the evangelist has a great interest in picturing the fate of Jesus and its implications for those called "to be with" him.[40] As part of this theme the narrator quite deliberately uses the device of Jesus instructing his followers, as well as the fascinated "crowds" and various religious authority figures, nearly always with poor results.

It may go beyond the state of our evidence to claim that the term μαθηταί was first applied to the followers of Jesus in the circles that produced Mark's gospel in its various editions, but the idea is intriguing.[41] It is worth

[40] The modern theological interest in "the cost of discipleship," of course, ultimately derives largely from this poignant story in the Gospel of Mark.

[41] There is a provocative and very interesting discussion of this idea in Mack, *Myth of Innocence*, 78–97, esp. 79 n.1: ". . . Thus the disciples in Mark betray thematic interests. Their prominent place in Mark's story of Jesus cannot be used to argue for 'discipleship' as a common concept among Jesus movements before Mark's time. It is not unthinkable that Mark was active in turning lore about the 'pillars' Cephas, James and John (Gal 2:9) into stories about 'disciples' of Jesus. . . .'"

observing that we have no attestation of the term for this group prior to Mark's story. The term μαθητής is not used by Paul or indeed anywhere in New Testament literature outside the Gospels and Luke's Acts. The sayings gospel Q never clearly calls those around Jesus his μαθηταί, though it does use this word for the "disciples of John (the Baptist)."[42] Instead we find Matthew or Luke inserting the term μαθηταί to identify Jesus' audience more closely when introducing sayings material based on Q material.[43]

A full consideration of this question would take us far beyond the scope of this essay, but even if we were to grant that the term μαθηταί was readily available in Mark's tradition or environment to describe Jesus' retinue,[44] the importance of the concept in the Markan narrative suggests that it was precisely there that the term took on its deeper significance. We know that other aspects of Mark's story were enormously influential on subsequent Gospel writers: Matthew, Luke, and John all take over Mark's basic plot. Since they clearly borrow Mark's basic structural pattern, it may also be that other, less prominent narrative features were just as appealing to the later Gospel writers, including the strong impulse to label Jesus' associates or followers his "disciples." In any case, I would emphasize that not only the theme of "teaching" but also that of "learning" is integral to Mark's gospel, from its start in *Original Mark* through its later forms known to us as *Secret Mark* and the New Testament *Canonical Mark*. A similar case could be made that the concepts of "understanding" and "mysteriousness" were important within the Gospel of Mark at every stage, even if they were further emphasized in the *Secret Mark* redaction as Koester has suggested.

It is important to stress that neither the tendency nor the implications of Koester's basic proposal need be taken as contradicting the results of other Markan scholars who are currently working from the very different perspectives of composition criticism, narrative analysis, or reader-response theory. If Koester is correct that the version of Mark that we read in our New

[42] Q 7:18; see also Mark 2:18//Matt 9:14//Luke 5:33; Mark 6:29//Matt 14:12; Matt 9:14. Matt 22:26 also mentions the disciples of the Pharisees and Herodians.

[43] Q (Luke) 9:59 mentions simply "another (person)"; Matt 8:21 says ἕτερος <u>τῶν μαθητῶν</u>. Q 10:2 reads ἔλεγεν δὲ πρὸς αὐτούς; Matt 9:37 says τότε λέγει τοῖς μαθηταῖς αὐτοῦ. Luke seems to have added the phrases <u>πρὸς τοὺς μαθητάς</u> at Q 12:22 and εἶπέν <u>τις τῶν μαθητῶν αὐτοῦ</u> at Q 11:1 (contrast Matt 6:9, 25). The only possible exception is at Q 14:26–27 (virtually a "Markan thunderbolt" in the Q material!), where Jesus is shown challenging someone (who?) who would be his μαθητής to reject family ties and "pick up his cross." The proverbial image contrasting the honor of teacher and pupil is found in the saying at Q 6:40 (οὐχ ἔστιν μαθητὴς ὑπὲρ τὸν διδάσκαλον; see Matt 10:25).

[44] Note that the *Gospel of Thomas* also uses the term ⲘⲀⲐⲎⲦⲎⲤ in editorial contexts, and of course the Gospel of John incorporates the image of (John's and) Jesus' disciples quite thoroughly within its own narrative. Mack deals with this difficulty by suggesting (perhaps a bit desperately) that "early Q traditions that were taken up into the Gospel of Thomas may have passed through the Markan milieu or sphere of influence . . ." (*Myth of Innocence,* 79 n. 1).

Testament is the result of an editorial process one or two generations after Matthew and Luke composed their works largely on the basis of *Original Mark,* then in fact a more free-standing literary analysis of the version of Mark's text that we have in the canon is all the more necessary. I would only insist that we not attempt to distinguish too finely the word choice, style, key motifs, and narrative plot of the various proposed stages in Mark's history. Matthew, Luke (and John) already show that *Original Mark* was itself quite similar in all those respects to what we see in *Canonical Mark.*

A final and very intriguing consideration has to do with how we should try to understand the origin of the *Secret Mark* stage in the gospel's history of writing and rewriting. Here Koester's observations about the gospel's use of language appropriate to the disclosure of mysteries when referring to Jesus' miracles and teaching are of help. In the longer fragment of *Secret Mark* quoted by Clement, Jesus "teaches" the youth the "mystery" (singular) of the kingdom of God. Clement explains that access to this version of Mark's Gospel is limited to those (being?) initiated into the church (πνευματικώτερον εὐαγγέλιον εἰς τὴν τῶν τελειουμένων χρῆσιν [1^{r} 21–22]). Because of the fragment's baptismal elements, it seems quite plausible that this and related *Secret Mark* materials were introduced into the Markan story deliberately by the Alexandrian church early in the second century for use by catechumens or baptized believers.[45] If this were the case, then the copy of *Original Mark* used in Alexandria for this revision would likely be lost or at least go out of use. Koester has gathered convincing evidence that Mark was little known and less used until the mid-third century.[46] (What this means, of course, is "Mark" in the sense of any possible edition: *Original Mark, Secret Mark,* or the *Public* [*Canonical*] *Mark* known to Clement.) *Original Mark* was replaced by those who wrote new gospel documents inspired by its basic format and plot structure: Matthew, Luke, John, and *Secret Mark. Canonical Mark* was created from *Secret Mark* because *Original Mark* was no longer available to the people involved or because it was no longer so attractive as a point of departure.

If *Secret Mark* did originate in some such setting of second-century Alexandria, then we must recognize further that those involved chose to work on the basis of *Original Mark,* instead of some other gospel document, because

[45] This indeed has been the interpretation given by Scroggs and Groff ("Baptism in Mark"), Schenke ("The Mystery of Mark"), and esp. Meyer ("The Youth in the *Secret Gospel of Mark*"). Thomas J. Talley has argued that the baptismal practice of the ancient Egyptian church made use of a liturgical calendar that would quite likely have meant that this section of the Gospel of Mark was read on the sixth day of the sixth week (the day of baptism for new believers) ("Liturgical Time in the Ancient Church: The State of Research," *Studia liturgica* 14 [1982] 34–51, esp. 44ff.). Thus the *Secret Mark* passage would be a very appropriate reading at just the right spot.

[46] Koester, "Apocryphal and Canonical Gospels"; *Ancient Christian Gospels,* 273–75.

they found the tone and substance of Mark's portrait of Jesus with his deeds, words, and associates most congenial for their purposes. This leads to my conclusion. *Secret Mark* is in no sense a deviation from the general character and themes of the Markan gospel in any of its stages of development. From the start, the traditions incorporated and elaborated by Mark pictured Jesus as a miracle worker along (naïvely?) magical lines; from the start, there was an interest in portraying the mysterious nature of Jesus' speech, his "mysteries of the kingdom" (Mark 4:11 in *Original Mark* with the plural μυστήρια). In the later stage of the Markan development represented by *Secret Mark*, there is less interest in focusing on the mysterious words than on the central mysterious act of the baptismal sacrament as now explained ("taught") by Jesus as hierophant. Initiation into the Christian mystery of salvation is portrayed in the prototypical example of the youth, using the characters of Jesus the "teacher" and his faltering "learners." Though Jesus loved him and baptized him, the youth fled at his master's arrest. These themes of mysterious teaching, frail disciples, and betrayal are elaborations of motifs central to Mark's story at every point of its development, not foreign intrusions into the text. *Secret Mark* is an organic development from *Original Mark* and fits as well as could be expected into what we know from Clement and others about the mysterious and murky life of second-century Christian Alexandria.[47]

[47] On this thorny topic see most recently the collection of essays in *The Roots of Egyptian Christianity*, ed. Birger A. Pearson and James E. Goehring (SAC; Philadelphia: Fortress Press, 1986), esp. Pearson's own contribution, "Earliest Christianity in Egypt: Some Observations" (pp. 132–59), with further references there.

19

The Sermon on the Mount in Matthew's Interpretation

HANS DIETER BETZ

GIVEN THE PRESENT controversies regarding the Gospels and their sources, it is worth noting that there is considerable agreement among New Testament scholars about two related issues.[1] These issues can be summed up by saying that the Sermon on the Mount (Matt 5:3–7:27 [henceforth abbreviated SM]) is a decisive passage for determining the theology of Matthew, whose name stands for the final redactor and author of that Gospel, whatever one may think about the meaning of the SM itself. Both of these issues are related as two sides of the same coin. Whatever view one holds about the one determines one's view about the other. This situation requires that careful consideration be given to the presuppositions on which answers to these issues are based, before turning to our main topic itself.

Presuppositions

1. The first presupposition concerns the origin of the SM. Present New Testament scholarship offers several options: (a) The SM was composed by the evangelist, who used smaller textual components from the Q tradition and other pre-Synoptic traditions (*Sondergut*).[2] (b) The SM was composed by the evangelist, who used pre-Synoptic redactional units of greater length and

[1] This article originated as a contribution to the seminar entitled "The Gospel of Matthew"; it was presented at the general meeting of the Society for New Testament Studies in Dublin, Ireland, July 1989. It is published here in recognition of Helmut Koester's lifelong work on the Gospels and many years of friendship.

[2] This is the conventional view held by most scholars today.

complexity and arranged these units, not without adding his own contributions.[3] (c) The SM existed prior to Matthew as a complete unit, redactional in nature; it was taken over into the Gospel and inserted at its present place with little or no change.[4]

These options must be seen also in relation to the question of Q because of the parallel Sermon on the Plain (Luke 6:20b–49 [henceforth abbreviated SP]). Before the question of Matthean authorship can be treated, the prior questions must be answered: Which version, the SM or the SP, was part of Q? Is it to be assumed that either of the two versions was part of Q? Or were only those parts common to both the SM and the SP part of Q? Again, there are a number of options. If the SP was "identical or almost identical"[5] to the hypothetical Q Sermon, then the SM is a further elaboration and expansion of this Q Sermon, produced either by Matthew or a pre-Matthean author. If, on the other hand, the SM was identical to the Q Sermon, then the SP is a reduced version of it. Since most scholars subscribing to the Q hypothesis prefer the former option, it follows that they regard the SM as a product of Matthew's redaction. Yet the relationship between the two sermons is more complicated.

As I have pointed out elsewhere, the redactional character of *both* sermons must be recognized.[6] If that is so, the question is whether the Gospel authors Matthew and Luke were responsible for these two secondary elaborations, whether they have taken over already existing sources, or whether in each case we have a combination of both.

The answer to this question requires careful Synoptic comparison, involving not only the wording of the Greek texts but also their compositional makeup, structure, genre, and function. Difficult as these comparisons are, they reveal that the SM and the SP are related to each other by as many similarities as differences. Contrary to what has often been said, not everything that is in the SP is also in the SM. Indeed, when examined in detail, the composition of the two sermons is very different, although they share a great deal of the material, internal order, literary genre, and function. Both

[3] For this view, which at least approximates mine, see the commentaries by Georg Strecker, *The Sermon on the Mount: An Exegetical Commentary,* trans. O. C. Dean, Jr. (Nashville: Abingdon, 1988); and Ulrich Luz, *Das Evangelium nach Matthäus (Mt 1–7)* (EKKNT 1.1; Zurich/Einsiedeln/Cologne: Benziger; Neukirchen-Vluyn: Neukirchener Verlag, 1985).

[4] This option was first stated as a hypothesis in my *Essays on the Sermon on the Mount,* trans. L. L. Welborn (Philadelphia: Fortress Press, 1985).

[5] This ambiguous phrase, telling as it should be, has been in use almost since the beginning of the Q hypothesis. See Heinrich Julius Holtzmann, *Die synoptischen Evangelien: Ihr Ursprung und geschichtlicher Charakter* (Leipzig: Engelmann, 1883) 174–75.

[6] H. D. Betz, "The Sermon on the Mount and Q: Some Aspects of the Problem," in *Gospel Origins and Christian Beginnings, in Honor of James M. Robinson,* ed. J. E. Goehring et al. (Sonoma, Calif.: Polebridge, 1990) 19–34.

are *epitomai* of the teachings of Jesus, composed for the purpose of instructing disciples—the SM for disciples coming from a Jewish background, and the SP for those coming from a Gentile background. Theologically, the sermons operate at levels that are pre-Matthean and pre-Lukan but compatible with Matthew's and Luke's overall purposes and intentions.

The conclusion I draw from this situation is that the SM is not an elaboration of the SP (or Q Sermon) but that both sermons are parallel and independent elaborations of essentially the same sayings material. They represent instructional material intentionally focusing on two different categories of disciples, one from a Jewish and the other from a Gentile background.[7]

Moreover, I take it that there were two versions of Q: Q^{Matt} and Q^{Luke}. When they were included in the Gospels of Matthew and Luke, they were at an advanced stage of development and contained one of the sermons, the SM in Q^{Matt} and the SP in Q^{Luke}. It is interesting that the two sermons maintain their function as teaching material even within the contexts of Q^{Matt} and Q^{Luke}.

If this conclusion implies a decision against the Gospel writers as having composed their respective sermons, it does not of course *per se* preclude any possibility of their redactional interference. Whether or not the Gospel authors interferred internally in the texts of the SM and the SP must be demonstrated by the analysis of the composition, language, and content of these texts. Leaving aside the SP now and turning to the SM, I do not see any place within the SM where I would be able to recognize sufficient reasons for assuming the interferring hand of the Gospel writer Matthew. The fact that terms such as "kingdom of the heavens," "law," and "righteousness" occur in the Gospel elsewhere is not sufficient reason for postulating that Matthew introduced these terms in the SM; surely, he did not invent these terms but took them over from the tradition, just as the SM did. Moreover, once it is admitted that all of the SM is redactional, the identity of specifically Matthean traits must be distinguished from pre-Matthean redaction. In this regard it can be said that, although there is plenty of Matthean redaction in the framework surrounding the SM (Matt 4:23–5:2; 7:28–29), there is nothing within the SM that has the specific character of Matthew's redaction. In addition, the theological language and thought world of the SM are Jewish, not Christian. Scholars, including prominent Jewish scholars, have long recognized that the theological language and ideas in the SM can without exception be accounted for in terms of first-century Judaism.[8] This

[7] For detailed evidence and arguments, I refer to my unpublished full commentary on the Sermon on the Mount and the Sermon on the Plain.

[8] See already Johann Gottfried Herder, *Erläuterungen zum Neuen Testament aus einer neueröfneten Morgenländischen Quelle* (Riga: Hartknoch, 1775) 106–9; idem, "Regel der Zusammenstimmung unserer Evangelien aus ihrer Entstehung und Ordnung," in *Sämmtliche Werke:*

assessment pertains in particular to terms such as βασιλεία τῶν οὐρανῶν, νόμος, and δικαιοσύνη. It is a peculiar fact that for reasons further to be examined the evangelist Matthew did not remove or "christianize" this Jewish language. He let the text stand, and he could do so because his Christian interpretation of the SM is located in the framework around the SM and in the Gospel as a whole. It can be shown also that there are characteristic differences between the way some terminology is used within the SM and its use elsewhere in the Gospel. These differences point to older source material adapted by the evangelist, who, not unlike the other Gospel writers, abstains from bringing all his sources systematically into conformity with his own theological language.

This view will, of course, be unacceptable to those who understand the evangelist Matthew to be the author of the SM. These scholars then have the choice between finding "Christian" elements in the SM and making Matthew as "Jewish" a theologian as possible. The former choice is typically made in the commentary on Matthew by Walter Grundmann.[9] Grundmann presents Jesus as a Jewish teacher analogous to the Qumran Teacher of Righteousness,[10] yet he has Jesus at crucial points "transcend" Judaism.[11] Therefore, in spite of the heavy emphasis on Jesus' Jewishness, in the final analysis Jesus turns out to be a Christian in Jewish disguise. Not surprisingly, then, the Matthean SM can be presented as an early Christian catechism based on Christian Christology.[12] Grundmann inherited this peculiar, and to us

---

Zur Religion und Theologie (Tübingen: Cotta, 1810) 12:3–56, esp. 32–33. Jewish scholars include Joseph Klausner, *Jesus of Nazareth: His Life, Times, and Teaching,* trans. H. Danby (New York: Macmillan, 1929) 361–97, esp. 363–68. The opposite view was stated most clearly by Gerhard Kittel, "Die Bergpredigt und die Ethik des Judentums," *ZST* 2 (1925) 555–94; idem, *Die Probleme des palästinischen Spätjudentums und das Urchristentum* (BWANT 3.1; Stuttgart: Kohlhammer, 1926) 88–140.

[9] W. Grundmann, *Das Evangelium des Matthäus* (THKNT 1; 2nd ed.; Berlin: Evangelische Verlagsanstalt, 1971) 111: "Mit der Bergpredigt gibt Matthäus die erste seiner fünf grossen Redekompositionen; sie ist von ihm aus einer Reihe von Einzelsentenzen und Lehraussagen, von denen einige die Form von Lehrgedichten haben, zusammengestellt. Der Stoff entstammt zum Teil der Spruchquelle, deren älteste für uns erkennbare Gestaltung der Bergpredigt aus Luk. 6, 20–49 zu erschliessen ist. Ihr sind durch Matthäus andere Stücke aus der Spruchquelle zugefügt, ferner hat er Material aus seiner Sonderüberlieferung übernommen. Aus diesen verschiedenen Elementen gestaltet er die Bergpredigt."

[10] Ibid., 115: "Dass Matthäus Jesus in der Bergpredigt als den Lehrer der Gerechtigkeit darstellt, fällt auf, nachdem die Funde von Qumran die Gestalt des Lehrers der Gerechtigkeit als eine entscheidende Erscheinung für die Qumrangemeinde haben sichtbar werden lassen."

[11] Ibid., 154, with reference to the ἐγὼ δὲ λέγω ὑμῖν ("But I say to you"): "Wohl benutzt Jesus damit eine Formel, die in rabbinischer Diskussion als Einleitung einer 'dem allgemeinen Urteil widersprechenden Meinung' Verwendung gefunden hat, jedoch setzt sie in unserem Zusammenhang eine autoritative Aussage, deren Grund nur in der Person des Redenden liegt."

[12] See Grundmann's excursus "Das theologische Problem der Bergpredigt" (ibid., 181–90) and also p. 206: "Ist die Bergpredigt ein Katechismus der Urchristenheit, gebildet aus Worten

contradictory, concept from Gerhard Kittel, to whom he refers, with reference also to Karl Barth's christological interpretation.[13]

The view of making Matthew as "Jewish" a theologian as possible has been advocated by many distinguished scholars. Among the more recent ones is Ulrich Luz, in his commentary on Matthew. For Luz, Matthew is the author of the SM, but he uses a Jewish-Christian source, Q^{Matt}. Luz allows for the pre-Matthean origin of some compositional elements, but he refuses to consider the possibility that Q^{Matt} could have contained the whole of the SM.

According to Luz, the evangelist Matthew himself was an exponent of Jewish Christianity and faithful to the Torah.[14] How this same author could at the same time have broken with the synagogue and approved the mission to the Gentiles, apparently without circumcision, and how he could have subscribed to a highly developed Christology and Christian eschatology, Luz will still have to explain. As I have pointed out elsewhere, Matthew at no point interjects his own Christology into the SM.[15] Indeed, the very peculiar fact that the SM contains no Christology at all calls for a special explanation. This has been recognized also by earlier scholars, in particular Adolf Schlatter, who keenly observed the fact and who made several attempts to solve the problem.[16] We cannot, of course, enter into a full discussion here of all those passages that could be interpreted christologically. Rather than forcing a Christology into the texts where there is none to be found, we ought to let the phenomenon stand and try to explain it. To be sure, it is astonishing that Matthew passes up the opportunity to insert his Christology into the SM, even at those places where we might expect it.[17] A similar conclusion can be reached with regard to eschatology. The eschatology of the SM is conventionally Jewish, devoid of apocalyptic characteristics and quite different from the Christian apocalyptic worldview of Matthew, as expressed especially in Matthew 24–28.[18]

Jesu, sowohl des vorösterlichen wie des erhöhten, so bekommt er seine innere Ordnung als Auslegung des Herrengebetes, das sich darin bewährt als breviarium totius evangelii, wie es Tertullian genannt hat."

[13] See above, n. 8; see also Grundmann, *Matthäus*, 190: the basis of SM is "die christologische Vollmacht Jesu."

[14] See Luz, *Matthäus* 1:62–73.

[15] H. D. Betz, "The Problem of Christology in the Sermon on the Mount," in *Text and Logos: The Humanistic Interpretation of the New Testament*, Festschrift for Hendrikus W. Boers, ed. T. W. Jennings, Jr. (Atlanta: Scholars Press, 1990) 191–209.

[16] Schlatter took varying positions in several of his works on the subject; see esp. his imaginative article "Das Bild Jesu nach der Bergpredigt," in *Der Einzige und wir anderen* (Velbert: Freizeiten-Verlag, 1929) 149–62. On Schlatter's ideas, see Betz, "Problem of Christology."

[17] In my article "Problem of Christology" I have attempted to answer pertinent critical questions raised by scholars critical of my own position as stated in *Essays*.

[18] See H. D. Betz, "Eschatology in the Sermon on the Mount and the Sermon on the Plain,"

Finally, the composition of the SM can be shown to be internally intact. Its structure is elaborate, pointing to an advanced stage of redactional development and reflecting a coherent theological thought world that is Jewish in character.

In terms of its composition, however, the SM is not unique. Besides the parallel composition of the SP, there is the *Didache* (esp. chaps. 1–6), and the Greek *Vorlage* of the Latin *Doctrina apostolorum;* from Hellenistic Judaism there are the texts recently investigated by Karl-Wilhelm Niebuhr;[19] and from the Greek world we possess many comparable *epitomai,*[20] the most striking parallels being Epicurus's *Kyriai Doxai* and Epictetus's *Encheiridion.*[21] Matthew, by contrast, never presents another such composition in his Gospel. The instruction to the missionary apostles in chapter 10 has some similarity with the SM, but closer examination reveals that it is quite different. Finally, when in the concluding speech the risen Jesus orders the eleven to teach the Christian converts "to keep all that I have commanded you" (28:20), this commandment is different from the SM (cf. 7:24–27) in that "all" includes the whole Gospel, not only the SM.

2. The second presupposition pertains to the goals of the evangelist Matthew. If, as it has been suggested, this evangelist composed the SM, what could have motivated him to create a text that is thoroughly Jewish in theology and thus different from his own theology? It is then only consistent that those who attribute the SM to Matthew's authorship also regard the evangelist as a Jew, a converted rabbi or scribe, or perhaps even the repentant and converted tax collector of Matt 9:9; 10:3.[22] These scholars must minimize the fact that Matthew was a Christian theologian, writing at the end of the first century, whose theology was not based on the Jewish Torah but on the salvific death and resurrection of Jesus Christ. It is inconceivable, however, that an author for whom the separation between Judaism

---

in *Society of Biblical Literature 1985 Seminar Papers,* ed. K. H. Richards (Atlanta: Scholars Press, 1985) 343–50.

19 K.-W. Niebuhr, *Gesetz und Paränese: Katechismusartige Weisungsreihen in der frühjüdischen Literatur* (WUNT 2:28; Tübingen: Mohr-Siebeck, 1987). These materials should be seen in comparison with Egyptian texts, for which see the collection by Hellmuth Brunner, *Altägyptische Weisheit: Lehren für das Leben* (Zurich/Munich: Artemis, 1988).

20 The basic studies are by Henricus Bott, *De epitomis antiquis* (Marburg: Hamel, 1920); Ilona Opelt, "Epitome," *RAC* 5:944–73. Already Erasmus had pointed out that the SM is a compendium of the *dogmata Christi;* see Friedhelm Krüger, *Humanistische Evangelienauslegung: Desiderius Erasmus als Ausleger der Evangelien in seinen Paraphrasen* (BHT 28; Tübingen: Mohr-Siebeck, 1986) 177–204.

21 See Betz, *Essays,* 7–15.

22 On this point, see Luz, *Matthäus,* 1:62–73; the latest study is Martin Hengel, "Zur matthäischen Bergpredigt und ihrem jüdischen Hintergrund," *TRu* 52 (1987) 327–400, esp. 341–48: "Der erste Evangelist als Judenchrist und Schriftgelehrter."

and Christianity was a historical fact and who advocated the inclusion of Gentiles in the church by baptism without ever mentioning circumcision, would compose a text that is pre-Christian in language and theology.

The hermeneutical consequences are clear: Those who consider a Jewish author of the Gospel to have composed the SM will tend to interpret that Gospel as a whole in terms closest to Judaism, but this interpretation will not be capable of accommodating Matthew's Christology, soteriology, ecclesiology, and eschatology. Thus, there emerge two entirely different Matthews, depending on whether one views his theology as based on the Jewish SM or on the Christian gospel as contained in the entirety of Matthew's work. Our view is that, in order to be adequate, the interpretation of the Gospel must be able to accommodate all the complexities of the pre-Matthean sources, their traditions and tendencies, as well as Matthew's overall composition and theology. The final test must be the Matthean text itself, and not a postulated "historical background" supplanting it.[23]

3. What were the purpose and aim of Matthew's Gospel? In my view, the author attempted to accomplish two major purposes at the same time.[24] His primary goal was the critical revision of the life of Jesus as he encountered it in the Gospel of Mark. His second goal was to take into account the historical developments from the time of Jesus to the situation of his church at his own time. It is because of the literary and theological ingenuity of this author that he was able to achieve these goals in one book—instead of in two, as the author of Luke-Acts did. Matthew is at this point similar to the Fourth Gospel. He must, therefore, be appreciated not only as a compiler and redactor of sources, but also as an author in his own right, who tried to explain to his readers how the momentous changes in the course of the history of the church came about and how these changes can be accounted for as historically and theologically legitimate. Matthew was no doubt also motivated by his disappointment at the inadequacy of the Gospel of Mark's account of Jesus' life and teaching.

Although Mark's overall narrative framework, when drastically revised, could serve Matthew's aims and purposes, he saw the need to use Q*Matt* so

[23] Hengel's way of approaching the subject is almost entirely that of exploring the "background." The danger of this approach is to get lost in speculations which then prove hard to reconcile with the complexities of the text.

[24] The disadvantage of the literary-critical approach as practiced by Jack Dean Kingsbury is that he does not pay enough attention to non-narrative dimensions of the text, such as the thoroughgoing historical and theological arguments. These concerns should be made part of the literary-critical analysis or should complement it. See Kingsbury, *Matthew as Story* (2nd ed.; Philadelphia: Fortress Press, 1989); idem, "The Place, Structure, and Meaning of the Sermon on the Mount within Matthew," *Int* 41 (1987) 131–43.

as to take Jesus' teachings more fully into account, and part of that happened to be the SM.

The Delimitation of the Sermon on the Mount

As has been shown by scholars previously, and especially recently by David Hellholm, the textual unit called the SM is clearly set apart by Matthew's redactional framework and should be viewed in relation to other such delimitations of the major speeches in that Gospel, all of them the result of Matthew's redaction.[25] The fact that the SP also contains a short narrative frame in Luke 6:20a and 7:1 may indicate that Q^{Matt} and Q^{Luke} already had narratives introducing and concluding the body of parenetic material of which these units are composed. Subsequently, Matthew added a second introduction to whatever he found in Q^{Matt} and thus brought things in line with his own narrative.

Matt 5:1–2 points out three objectives. The beginning phrase ἰδὼν δὲ τοὺς ὄχλους ("seeing the crowds") connects the passage with the preceding summary (4:24–25), in which the ὄχλοι are mentioned as following Jesus. The continuation by ἀνέβη εἰς τὸ ὄρος ("he went up on the mountain") seems to have come from the source. Notably, in the parallels in Mark 3:13 and Luke 6:12 similar language occurs in connection with the calling of the twelve apostles. Yet Matthew more than anyone else uses the motif of Jesus going up to a mountain for making revelatory statements.[26] Most important is Matthew's little vignette portraying Jesus as a typical teacher: He sits down, his disciples draw near and presumably stand or sit around him; his speech is then introduced by the somewhat solemn words καὶ ἀνοίξας τὸ στόμα αὐτοῦ ἐδίδασκεν αὐτοὺς . . . ("he opened his mouth and taught them"), clearly attributing extraordinary significance to the occasion and the speech to follow.

There is little doubt that the concluding statement in 7:28–29 is also the result of Matthew's redaction. The phrase καὶ ἐγένετο ὅτε ἐτέλεσεν ὁ Ἰησοῦς τοὺς λόγους τούτους ("and when Jesus finished these sayings") refers back to

[25] David Hellholm, "Probleme und Bedeutung substitutioneller Gliederungsmerkmale für die Komposition des Matthäusevangeliums," forthcoming in the Festschrift for Birger Gerhardsson. See also Terence J. Keegan, "Introductory Formulae for Matthean Discourses," *CBQ* 44 (1982) 415–30; Gerhard Lohfink, "Wem gilt die Bergpredigt? Eine redaktionsgeschichtliche Untersuchung von Mt. 4,23–5,2 und 7,28f," *TQ* 163 (1983) 264–84; Luz, *Matthäus* 1:178–81, 197–98.

[26] See Matt 4:8; 5:1; 8:1; 14:23 (//Mark 6:46); 15:29; 17:1, 9 (//Mark 9:2, 9//Luke 9:28, 37); 21:1(//Mark 11:1//Luke 19:29); 24:3 (//Mark 13:3); 26:30 (//Mark 14:26//Luke 22:39); 28:16. See also the study by Terence L. Donaldson, *Jesus on the Mountain: A Study in Matthean Theology* (JSNTSup 8; Sheffield: JSOT Press, 1986).

the SM. The recurrence of similar conclusions to other speeches in the Gospel (see also 11:1; 13:53; 19:1; 26:1) has often been pointed out by scholars. The term λόγοι ("sayings") takes up the literary category of the components of the SM from the text itself (7:24–27). Matthew's evaluation of the speech endorses the reaction by the ὄχλοι to this "striking" teaching, and then explains it as being endowed with authoritative power: ὡς ἐξουσίαν ἔχων καὶ οὐχ ὡς γραμματεῖς αὐτῶν ("as one who had authority, and not as their scribes"). This explanation is certainly derived from Mark 1:22 and made to fit the Matthean context. There is also to be noted a small but significant inconsistency. If Matthew wanted to contrast Jesus' teaching (διδαχή) with that of other Jewish teachers inimical to Jesus, he should have referred to them as οἱ γραμματεῖς καὶ οἱ Φαρισαῖοι ("the scribes and the Pharisees") as in 5:20, and not simply as οἱ γραμματεῖς (7:29); the inconsistency was noticed and "corrected" by some manuscripts (C* W 33 1241 *pc* lat sy).

These observations permit us to determine the nature of the framework in 5:1–2 and 7:28–29 as metatextual substitutions, to use Hellholm's text-linguistic term. They indicate essentially five things: (1) They delimit the SM (5:3–7:27) by pointing forward and leading into it (5:1–2), and by reflecting back on it (7:28–29). (2) They thereby place the SM at a prior textual level. (3) They determine the character of the narrative framework as being of a different sort compared with the parenetic material bracketed by it. (4) They classify the SM formally as "sayings" (λόγοι) and materially as "teaching" (διδαχή), categories derived from the SM itself (see 5:19; 7:24–27). (5) They identify Jesus as speaker and author of the SM. It should be noted also that no similar second-level or metatextual statements occur in the SM itself. The conclusion, therefore, is that the evangelist Matthew regarded the SM as one textual unit and treated it almost as a long quotation. After 7:29, the Gospel never explicitly refers to the SM again, a fact that requires further explanation.

The Place of the Sermon on the Mount in Matthew's Life of Jesus

Matthew's account of the life of Jesus is intended to correct what he perceived to be inadequacies and improbabilities in Mark's Gospel, which I assume was one of his sources. He wanted to present more credibly how things developed in Jesus' life as well as in the early church.

To begin with Jesus' baptism by John the Baptist: this event requires, in Matthew's view, special explanation. Clearly, Jesus could not have been one of the sinners in need of repentance who came to John to obtain forgiveness (Matt 3:1–2, 6). In the eyes of Matthew, Jesus was a righteous man (see 3:15; 10:41; 27:4, 19, 24), so that, if he was baptized by John, the reason for this baptism must have been a special one. Therefore, Matthew rewrites the story so that it now serves to demonstrate both men's righteousness. For this reason Matthew has Jesus say to John, who has questioned the need for his baptism: ἄφες ἄρτι, οὕτως γὰρ πρέπον ἐστὶν ἡμῖν πληρῶσαι πᾶσαν τὴν δικαιοσύνην ("Let is be so now; for thus it is fitting for us to fulfill all righteousness" [3:15]). Therefore, the ritual was not an occasion for Jesus to confess his sins and repent, but God used the moment to proclaim Jesus as his beloved son (3:17). Being God's son was for Matthew synonymous with being righteous.

Jesus' righteousness is then tested, no doubt at God's behest, by the devil in the temptation story (4:1–11). If Matthew preferred the version of the story Q*Matt*, he did so because again Mark's version (Mark 1:12–13) leaves things unclear. The only reason for tempting Jesus could have been, according to Matthew, that his righteousness was to be tested. Nobody's righteousness can be trusted unless it has been tested. After having passed his test successfully, Jesus is entitled and equipped to start his own ministry in Galilee. This move was also necessitated by John the Baptist's arrest, as told by Mark (1:14a), and also because of the prediction by the prophet Isaiah (Matt 4:12–16). In Matthew's view, Jesus' message at that time was the same as that of John: μετανοεῖτε· ἤγγικεν γὰρ ἡ βασιλεία τῶν οὐρανῶν ("Repent, for the kingdom of the heavens is at hand" [4:17; cf. 3:2]).

Comparison with Mark 1:14b–15 shows an important point of disagreement. Obviously, Matthew had difficulties with Mark's use of the term εὐαγγέλιον τοῦ θεοῦ ("gospel of God"). It is at this point that Matthew's historical judgment comes to the fore. As a Jew and a follower of John the Baptist, Jesus could not have suddenly begun to proclaim what Matthew knew was the Christian gospel. Mark in fact fails to give any explanation at this point, so Matthew felt he should set the record straight. Accordingly, when Jesus "*began* to preach" (ἤρξατο . . . κηρύσσειν) he called for repentance and justified it by the nearness of "the kingdom of the heavens" just as John had done (4:17; cf. 3:2). What then was the difference between Jesus and John? Further, did the church's εὐαγγέλιον have no connection with the message of its founder? Matthew's solution is contained in his peculiar term τὸ εὐαγγέλιον τῆς βασιλείας ("the gospel of the kingdom"), which is clearly a Mattheanism (4:23; 9:35; 24:14; cf. 26:13).

What does this term mean?[27] (1) Matthew found it unacceptable when Mark attributed the term εὐαγγέλιον to Jesus' message before his death and

[27] On this Matthean concept, see Georg Strecker, *Der Weg der Gerechtigkeit: Untersuchung zur Theologie des Matthäus* (FRLANT 82; 3rd ed.; Göttingen: Vandenhoeck & Ruprecht, 1971) 128–30; Luz, *Matthäus,* 1:37, 73, 173, 181–83; Wolfgang Schenk, *Die Sprache des Matthäus: Die Textkonstituenten in ihren makro- und mikrostrukturellen Relationen* (Göttingen: Vandenhoeck & Ruprecht, 1987) 265–68; Hubert Frankemölle, *Evangelium: Begriff und Gattung: Ein Forschungsbericht* (SBB 15; Stuttgart: Katholisches Bibelwerk, 1988) esp. 149–55.

resurrection.[28] Matthew seems to know that Mark's term implied a Greek interpretation of Jesus' message—an anachronism in Matthew's view. As a Jew, Jesus must have preached a Jewish message not different from that of John the Baptist. Historically Jesus was not a Gentile Christian, as Mark seems to imply. Hence, the post-Easter *kerygma* of the church must have been different from the pre-Easter *kerygma* of Jesus. (2) Strictly speaking, therefore, the expression "the gospel of the kingdom" is a compromise.[29] It is intended to state that, if Jesus preached a "gospel," it was that of the nearness of "the kingdom of the heavens."[30] (3) Matthew has reservations about using the term "gospel" for the pre-Easter message of Jesus. He omits the term whenever Mark has it, except for the story of the anointment at Bethany, where the Markan τὸ εὐαγγέλιον (Mark 14:9) is allowed to stand.[31] Probably the term τὸ εὐαγγέλιον τοῦτο ("this gospel") refers to the story as a whole (Matt 26:13). A similar historical judgment is responsible for Luke's complete avoidance of the term in his Gospel, although he uses it to designate the Christian message in Acts (15:7; 20:24).[32] (4) When Matthew characterizes Jesus' activities in the summaries in 4:23 and 9:35, the evangelist is again critical of the description of Mark in 1:39. Mark's claim that Jesus preached (κηρύσσειν) in the Galilean synagogues apparently looked anachronistic to Matthew, and he, therefore, reformulated it by letting Jesus do three things: He *taught* (διδάσκειν) in the synagogues, but he *preached* (κηρύσσειν) "the gospel of the kingdom" outside where also the *healings* took place (4:23).

In other words, Matthew could not imagine Jesus preaching the Christian gospel in Jewish synagogues, but he could imagine using the term εὐαγγέλιον in connection with healings because for this he found confirmation in Isa 61:1 LXX, where the verb εὐαγγελίζεσθαι occurs in combination with miracles: "(the) blind receive their sight and (the) lame walk, (the) lepers are cleansed and (the) deaf hear, and (the) dead are raised up, and (the) poor have the gospel preached to them" (Matt 11:5).[33] Yet the gospel is more than

[28] Mark 1:1, 14, 15; 8:35; 10:29; 13:10; 14:9; cf. 16:15.

[29] See Luz's excursus, "Verkündigen, Lehren und Evangelium bei Matthäus," in *Matthäus* 1:181–83; he interprets the concept differently. In my view, he underestimates Matthew's critical difficulties concerning Mark's use of the term εὐαγγέλιον. See also Helmut Koester, "From the Kerygma-Gospel to the Written Gospels," *NTS* 35 (1989) 361–81, esp. 367; idem, *Ancient Christian Gospels: Their History and Development* (Philadelphia: Trinity Press International, 1990) chap. 1: "The Term 'Gospel.'"

[30] The *kerygma* is the same for John the Baptist (3:2), Jesus (4:17), and the Jewish-Christian missionary apostles (10:7), but not for Matthew's church.

[31] For the passages, see n. 28 above.

[32] So, rightly, Frankemölle, *Evangelium,* 155–59.

[33] Frankemölle has shown that Isa 61:1 LXX was of interest to Matthew because the Septuagint version uses εὐαγγελίζεσθαι, a term associated with miracles. This association is secondary as far as Matthew is concerned; it presupposes the existence of the Christian concept

the message announcing the occurrence of miracles. As the important statement in Matt 24:14 reveals, the expression "the gospel of the kingdom" also involves the entire apocalyptic scenario of the parousia, and it is this message that the church is to proclaim "in the whole world as a witness to all the nations." The message is, therefore, identical not only to the Great Commission to the Matthean church in 28:18–20 but also to the content of the Gospel of Matthew as a whole.[34]

Matthew's distinction between Jesus' preaching (κηρύσσειν) and teaching (διδάσκειν) applies also to his audiences.[35] Whereas his preaching addresses all the people, his teaching is directed toward special groups of disciples, first a small and then a larger group. After having called into discipleship Simon Peter, his brother Andrew, and the two sons of Zebedee (4:18–22), he gives this group the SM as their first major piece of instruction. This instruction is not to be confused with what is being taught in the synagogues, be it by Jesus or other Jewish teachers. Its programmatic purpose is to set the standards for discipleship specifically for Jesus' disciples. Therefore, we see Jesus turn away from the crowds and go up the mountain, where he is alone with the four just called (5:1–2). This setting is indeed appropriate if one considers the content of the SM as special instructional material for Jesus' disciples.

Matthew's retrospective evaluation in 7:28–29, however, makes clear that the SM did not remain hidden from the crowds. Somehow the SM made it into the open, so that the crowds became excited about its content—as excited as the readers of the Gospel are supposed to become. From these crowds, of course, all future disciples were recruited, so that their loyal response to the call becomes plausible.

Implementing the programmatic summary in 4:23, Matthew then inserts chapters 8 and 9, featuring miracle stories. These miracles, it is said, occur in the presence of the crowds, an assumption confirmed also by the summary in 9:35, which repeats the words of 4:23.

The new section in 9:36–38 turns again to teaching, addressing now the crowds. The reason, as Jesus sees, is that the crowds need more than to witness miracles, but the teaching of the crowds is delegated to the disciples. Because of the greater needs of the people, Jesus calls the twelve disciples

---

of "gospel," rather than generating it. See Frankemölle, "Jesus als deuterojesajanischer Freudenbote? Zur Rezeption von Jes 52,7 und 61,1 im Neuen Testament, durch Jesus und in den Targumim," in *Vom Urchristentum zu Jesus: Festschrift für Joachim Gnilka*, ed. H. Frankemölle and K. Kertelge (Freiburg/Basel/Vienna: Herder, 1988) 34–67.

[34] So also Luz, *Matthäus* 1:182.

[35] For κηρύσσειν, see Matt 3:1; 4:17, 23; 9:35; 10:7, 27; 11:1; 24:14; 26:13; cf. 12:41. For διδάσκειν, see 4:23; 5:2, 19; 7:29; 9:35; 11:1; 13:54; 15:9; 21:23; 22:16; 26:55; 28:15, 20; 26:18. The διδάσκαλος is always associated with the μαθητής (8:19; 9:11; 10:24, 25; 12:38; 17:24; 19:16; 22:16, 24, 36; 23:8, 26:18).

(10:1), who are then installed as missionary apostles (10:2–5). Once this group is assembled, further instruction for them is needed for their new work; it is provided in the missionary instruction. The missionary instruction of chapter 10, therefore, adds another piece of foundational teaching. It is different from the SM in content, genre, and function but adds to what is already in circulation through the SM. Jesus' teaching, therefore, occurs cumulatively, seeking out one group after another and delivering to them the kind of instruction they need to hear. Thus in the course of his life Jesus progressively reveals all his teaching, so that by the end of the Gospel the readers have learned what the author thinks they must know.

For Matthew as well as for his church, the life of Jesus on earth is considered a matter of the past, and so are his preaching, teaching, and working of miracles. What is the lasting importance of this past? In Matthew's view Jesus' life and teaching serve as a *speculum* of the faith of the Christian readers of the Gospel, who of course live in different times and under different circumstances from those described in the Gospel. What are the readers to do with Jesus' teaching? When Jesus orders his disciples in his post-Easter commission (28:18–20) to "keep everything that I have commanded you," this command should not be taken to imply total obedience to a rigid code of rules and regulations. The term τηρεῖν[36] should rather be interpreted as "preserve" a legacy, and this is what the Gospel of Matthew is attempting to provide. Thus, the life and teaching of Jesus during his earthly existence constitute the fundamental framework and standard for the church of later times, a foundation that no doubt requires interpretation of the kind Matthew himself is providing.

This framework also serves to interpret—and thus to preserve—the sources, among them the SM. In Matthew's Gospel the SM, which internally pays no attention to Jesus' life, has become part of that life. Thereby the SM has been relegated to the past and thus historicized. Matthew presumes, of course, that Jesus' life was in full conformity with the prescripts and principles of the SM, so that he becomes the prototypical example of how it should be lived out. In this way the SM has become part of the whole legacy of Jesus on which the "gospel of the kingdom" is based. Together with all the sources included in the Gospel, the SM has also been supplemented and superseded by having become a part of a larger whole. This process has come to a conclusion with the Gospel of Matthew. This Gospel will certainly be in need of further interpretation, but that interpretation will have to be of a different genre, namely, the genre of the commentary on the Gospel of Matthew as an authoritative text.

[36] See also the uses of the term in 19:17; 23:3; 27:36, 54; 28:4.

The Place of the Sermon on the Mount in Matthew's History of the Church

As we had indicated before, one of Matthew's aims was to explain his church's place in history. This involves the past, the present, and the future, seen from the vantage point of Matthew's present perspective. His own time schedule is constituted by the charter Christ has given to the church in his postresurrection commission (28:18–20). Since then, of course, time has progressed. At present the church lives in expectation of the parousia of the Lord, but there are uncertainties about "when these things will be, and what (will be) the sign of your coming and (of the) consummation of the eon" (24:3). These uncertainties were not in any way unique to Matthew; other New Testament texts as well point to a general crisis of confidence in post-70 Christianity.[37]

Without entering into a full discussion of the complexities of Matthew's eschatology, it is fair to say that he not only admits but actually argues in favor of a delay of the parousia. "But concerning that day and hour no one knows, not even the angels of the heaven, nor the Son, but the Father only" (24:36). At the present time there exists great danger for the church to be misled by false prophets who announce the end to have arrived with them (24:5). Although according to Matthew it is true (24:6) that the messianic signs of "wars and rumors of wars" must happen, he issues stern warnings, such as: "See that someone does not mislead you!" (24:4) or "See that you do not get confused! For they must happen, but this is not yet the end" (24:6). "Nation will rise against nation, and kingdom against kingdom, and there will be famines and earthquakes in various places" (24:7), but this hardly announces novelty and surprise. It does, however, indicate the point in the time schedule at which Matthew believes to be living: "All these things are (the) beginning of (the) birthpangs" (24:8) of the great cosmic "rebirth" (παλιγγενεσία [19:28]). In Matthew's estimation, therefore, he and his church are presently experiencing the phase entitled ἀρχὴ ὠδίνων, the beginning but no more.

What is still to come is the "great tribulation" (ἡ μεγάλη θλῖψις)[38] with its persecution and apostasy, during which also the proclamation of "the gospel of the kingdom" will be completed throughout the world and to all the nations (24:9–14), "and (only) then the end will come" (24:14). This "great tribulation" will be introduced by the infamous βδέλυγμα ἐρημώσεως

[37] See Glenn S. Holland, *The Tradition that You Received from Us: 2 Thessalonians in the Pauline Tradition* (HUT 24; Tübingen: Mohr-Siebeck, 1988) esp. 134–42.

[38] Matthew distinguishes between general θλῖψις καὶ διωγμός predicted earlier by Jesus (5:10, 11, 12, 44; 10:23; 13:21; 23:34) and the θλῖψις μεγάλη immediately preceding the parousia (24:9, 21–29).

("desolating sacrilege" [24:15 RSV]) predicted by the prophet Daniel,[39] and by the subsequent flight to the mountains (24:16–20). While the Matthean church may have witnessed these things already, the worst of the great tribulation is still to come (24:21–29). Only when that tribulation has come to an end, the "sign of the Son of Man" will appear "in the sky" (ἐν οὐρανῷ) and usher in the parousia (24:30–31). Given this vantage point, Matthew sees the greatest danger for the church in the false prophets and false messiahs that have appeared and threaten to lead the faithful astray (24:4–5, 11, 23–28). For this reason the great eschatological discourse of chapters 24 and 25 abounds with warnings: "See that someone does not mislead you!" (24:4; cf. 24:5, 11, 24); "Wake up!" (24:42; 25:13); and "Be prepared!" (24:44; cf. 25:10).

If the great danger of misjudging the eschatological time schedule is to be avoided, the legacy of Jesus as laid down in Matthew's Gospel must carry its full weight. Jesus' seemingly incidental remark in 24:25 ἰδοὺ προείρηκα ὑμῖν ("Lo, I have told you beforehand") betrays Matthew's understanding of the significance not only of this but also of all of Jesus' speeches. Whatever the readers need to know about the present and the future has been foretold by Christ in the past and is contained in Matthew's record. This past, however, has its own problems. Matthew was aware that the incompleteness and inadequacy of the sources posed a serious problem. Paradoxically, therefore, what he perceived to be a firm foundation had first to be reconstructed by a critical revision of the sources of Mark and Q^{Matt}.

Regarding the past, to be sure, Matthew's work amounted to far more than the best sources still available, so as to arrange them in as plausible a sequence as possible. Matthew's aim in this certainly was apologetic. He knew that the available sources raised grave doubts and had led to serious misunderstandings.

One of Matthew's main concerns was to explain how the church could have developed legitimately out of its Jewish beginnings, which were so different from the conditions of his own church. Matthew's church, to be sure, was a Christian community that was no longer part of the Jewish religion. This church was "ecumenical" in scope and included former Jews and Gentiles. The members of this church did not obey the Jewish Torah, nor did they subject new converts to circumcision. Their main rituals were baptism (28:19) and the Eucharist (26:17–30). How did the changes occur, and why were they legitimate?

Matthew confirms that the church originated in Judaism, and that Jesus was a Jew. In other words, Matthew does not claim that Jesus was the first Christian. Yet, Jesus' genealogy and the infancy narratives show that his

[39] The notion comes from Mark 13:14, and ultimately from Daniel (9:27; 11:31; 12:11; cf. 1 Macc 1:54).

origins were a particular strand of Judaism: He was the "son of David" and hence the "son of Abraham" (1:1). This Abrahamic genealogical line runs straight through to Joseph and Mary, Jesus' parents (1:2–17). The fact that Jesus' ancestry was Abrahamic determined his line of Judaism and led consistently to the inclusion of the Gentiles into the kingdom of God.

When Jesus came to John the Baptist for his baptism, he came to a prophet who opposed the claims to Abrahamic descent by the Pharisees and the Sadducees (3:1–12). When John announced Jesus as "the stronger one" (3:11–12), he did so in line with the Abrahamic tradition, and this is also the reason why Jesus' Jewish teaching of the SM was so different from that of the Pharisees and scribes (5:20; 7:29). In the chapters following the SM, the differences between Jesus and the Jewish leadership become more and more apparent, but this does not mean that Jesus becomes less Jewish. On the contrary, as the opposition becomes increasingly threatening, Jesus' Abrahamic Judaism comes more and more to the fore.

The missionary instruction (10:5b–42) assumes further developments. Jesus realizes the needs of the Jewish crowds, whom he likens to "a flock without a shepherd" (9:36–38). The twelve disciples are then charged with the mission among the Jews only: "On the way of the Gentiles do not go, and do not enter into (a) town of the Samaritans, but go rather to the lost sheep of the house of Israel" (10:5b–6). Matthew was certainly aware that there was a mission to the Gentiles and to the Samaritans, but that mission had to wait until after the resurrection of Jesus, when the then-reconstituted body of the eleven was charged with carrying out that mission too (28:16–20).[40] Matthew, therefore, knew that at first the Christian mission was to the Jews, preaching the same message as John the Baptist and Jesus (10:7; cf. 3:2; 4:17).[41] This division of the mission also corresponds to Paul's account about the separation of the mission in Gal 2:1–10.[42] It may be that already the source of Q*Matt* reflected this division, so that here also the evangelist was able to draw on an earlier source to make it fit his scheme.[43]

[40] See Matt 10:17–18, where the apostles are warned: "Beware of the people! For they will hand you over to the law-courts, and in their synagogues they will flog you. And you will be dragged before governors and kings because of me as a testimony to them and the Gentiles." This prediction, contrary to Mark 13:9–10 but in agreement with Luke 21:12–13, does *not* refer to the mission and proclamation of the gospel to the Gentiles, but to the apostles' testimony of their persecution; καὶ τοῖς ἔθνεσιν explains that these governors and kings were Gentiles who, therefore, became early witnesses even before the mission to the Gentiles began. For a different view, see Kingsbury, *Matthew*, 38–39.

[41] See also 15:24, where Jesus says about himself to the Syrophoenician woman, a Gentile: "I was sent only to the lost sheep of the house of Israel." See also 7:15; 9:36; 18:10–14; 12:11–12; 25:32–33; 26:31.

[42] See on this passage H. D. Betz, *Galatians: A Commentary on Paul's Letter to the Churches in Galatia* (Hermeneia; Philadelphia: Fortress Press, 1979) 81–103.

[43] So, rightly, Heinz Schürmann, "Mt 10,5b–6 und die Vorgeschichte des synoptischen

The following chapters of the Gospel describe how Jesus gradually separated from John the Baptist (11:1–19), how he withdrew from "this generation" (11:16; 12:39–45; etc.),[44] and how his criticism of the Jewish leadership resulted in his being rejected by them.[45] This growing mutual rejection is completed at the end of the great debates in the temple, when Jesus leaves the temple after having silenced both the Pharisees and the Sadducees (22:46; 24:1). The reason for Jesus' alienation was no coincidence: His message and teaching are "Abrahamic" and thus diametrically opposed to the Pharisees and the Sadducees. As a result of their rejection Jesus then gradually and somewhat hesitatingly turns to the Gentiles. This process begins with the healing of the son of the centurion at Capernaum (8:5–12). When Jesus sees the great faith of that Roman officer, he invokes the prophetic promise: "I tell you, many will come from east and west and recline with Abraham, Isaac and Jacob in the kingdom of the heavens, but the sons of the kingdom will be thrown out in the outer darkness" (8:11–12; cf. 22:32).[46] Indications of the transition to the Gentiles steadily increase when Jesus addresses the great crowds (9:36; 13:1–2; 14:14; 15:32; cf. 18:27; 20:34) by telling them parables (13:3, 10, 13, 34–36). The parables of the kingdom proclaim in an oblique way the true dimensions of the kingdom of God.[47] While the crowds at first do not understand these implications (13:2–3, 10–13), Jesus explains them to his disciples separately (13:11,

---

Aussendungsberichtes," in *Traditionsgeschichtliche Untersuchungen zu den synoptischen Evangelien* (Düsseldorf: Patmos, 1968) 137–49; differently, Joachim Gnilka, *Das Matthäusevangelium* (Freiburg/Basel/Vienna: Herder, 1986) 1:361. Paul Hoffmann shows that a decision depends on one's presuppositions with regard to the Q hypothesis ("Lk 10,5–11 in der Instruktionsrede der Logienquelle," *EKK-Vorarbeiten*, Heft 3 [Zurich/Einsiedeln/Basel: Benziger; Neukirchen-Vluyn: Neukirchener Verlag, 1971] 37–53). See also John S. Kloppenborg, *The Formation of Q: Trajectories in Ancient Wisdom Collections* (SAC; Philadelphia: Fortress Press, 1987) 12 n. 50; 78; 195 n. 105; idem, *Q-Parallels: Synopsis, Critical Notes and Concordance* (Sonoma, Calif.: Polebridge, 1988) 72.

[44] See 11:16; 12:29, 41, 42, 45; 16:4; 17:17; 23:36; 24:34. The expression ἡ γενεὰ αὕτη refers to the Jewish contemporaries of John the Baptist and Jesus. See Strecker, *Der Weg*, 43, 102–3, 111, 113, 168, 233 n. 7.

[45] See on this Kingsbury, *Matthew*, 59–76; "The Ministry of Jesus to Israel and Israel's Repudiation of Jesus (4:17–16:20)"; idem, "The Developing Conflict between Jesus and the Jewish Leaders in Matthew's Gospel: A Literary-Critical Study," *CBQ* 49 (1987) 57–73.

[46] For the background and the present state of research of Matt 8:11–12//Luke 13:28–29, see Gnilka, *Matthäus* 1:303–6; Kloppenborg, *Q-Parallels*, 156.

[47] See Jack Dean Kingsbury, *The Parables of Jesus in Matthew 13* (London: SPCK; St. Louis: Clayton, 1977); idem, *Matthew*, 73–74; Gnilka, *Matthäus* 1:473–512. The seven parables in chapter 13 are addressed to the crowds who, however, do not understand them; the right interpretation is given to the disciples, who think they understand them (13:51–53) but they really do not. Differently, the three parables of 21:28–32, 33–46; 22:1–14 are addressed to the chief priests and elders of the Jews, who pretend they do not understand although in truth they do (21:23–27, 43–46).

16–17, 36, 51): "He who sows the good seed is the Son of Man; the field is the world, and the good seed means the sons of the kingdom" (13:37–38a). The following chapters disclose more and more who these true "sons of the kingdom" are.[48] Again, these revelations occur in the form of parables, interspersed with cryptic sayings, such as "Many that are first will be last, and the last first" (19:30; 20:16), and "Many are called, but few are chosen" (22:14; cf. 20:16 *v.l.*). The matter comes to a climax in the three great parables of chapters 21 and 22, the parable of the Two Sons (21:28–32), the parable of the Wicked Tenants (21:33–41), and the parable of the Great Supper (22:1–14).[49] The prediction of 21:43 discloses to the chief priests and the Pharisees the meaning of these parables: "Therefore, I tell you, the kingdom of God will be taken away from you and given to a nation producing the fruits of it." Then they know that the kingdom of God will be given to the Gentiles (21:45).

In conclusion, Matthew is able to show the way in which the church gradually developed out of Judaism and became the worldwide Christian community of which he and his readers are members. In view of this development, the SM constitutes the point of departure. The words of 5:13 and 5:14–16, defining the disciples as "salt of the earth" and "light of the world" provide first inklings[50] of which the vast changes occurring later in the Gospel are nothing but legitimate consequences. Thus, Matthew's worldwide church of Jews and Gentiles has its roots in Jesus' first programmatic pronouncement of the Sermon on the Mount.

[48] Whereas the SM speaks of the disciples as "sons of God" (5:9) and "sons of your Father in the heavens" (5:45), the special designation "sons of the kingdom" (υἱοὶ τῆς βασιλείας), like "gospel of the kingdom," is a Mattheanism (see 8:12; 13:36–43; cf. 9:15; 17:25–26). See also Strecker, *Weg*, 100–101, 106 n. 2; Schenk, *Sprache*, 120.

[49] The three parables interpret the historical phases of the repudiation of John the Baptist (21:28–46), Jesus (21:33–46), and the missionary apostles (22:1–14). See also Kingsbury, *Matthew*, 82–83; idem, "The Parable of the Wicked Husbandmen and the Secret of Jesus' Divine Sonship in Matthew: Some Literary-Critical Observations," *JBL* 105 (1986) 643–55.

[50] The SM passage of 5:13–16 has, as scholars have noted long ago, "universalist" implications. At the pre-Synoptic level, these implications can be accounted for in terms of Jewish self-definition; at the level of Matthew's theology they belong to the roots of Christ's cosmic rulership (28:19).

20

The God-fearers Meet the Beloved Disciple

A. THOMAS KRAABEL

I

FESTSCHRIFTEN ARE NOT for everyone. A scholar must first be so productive as to have students enough and theories or findings enough to create the pool of contributors and to give them subjects to which to direct their attention in constructive criticism and in commendation. And there must be an occasion, some milestone for the *Jubilar*, for the rest of us to join in celebrating.

But in addition to seniority and productivity, is there not a third qualification? I mean the willingness to learn from one's students, to take instruction from them in such things as the pages of a Festschrift—and even earlier, during the time one is responsible for their graduate education.

One remarkable aspect of Helmut Koester's scholarly career has been his enthusiastic embrace of archaeology and the realia of the Aegean world, both as objects of study and thought in their own right and as illustrative of the social world of the early church. What is striking is that he took up this new and extensive subject only long after becoming a senior faculty member at Harvard. As he worked his way into the new area, a number of students and junior colleagues accompanied him, often as members of Harvard's Research Team for Religion and Culture of New Testament Lands. On occasion they had advanced farther in one subject or another than he had, and so they became not only associates but tutors as well. Some of them are represented in this volume. It is this openness to other scholars and to new and demanding areas of research that I particularly want to recognize with this essay.

Deans teach seldom, and so we usually have few pupils. Nevertheless, the impetus for the present study did come from the ideas of undergraduate students, members of my New Testament classes at Luther College.

Additionally, one half of my topic, the issue of the God-fearers, has involved the interaction of archaeology and the New Testament, a central concern of the Harvard Research Team. For both these reasons it seems an appropriate offering on this occasion.

II

In discussing the Beloved Disciple in the Fourth Gospel and the God-fearers in the Acts of the Apostles, my intent is not to recount fully either debate or to go much beyond the evidence within the New Testament; rather, it is to point to parallels between the two issues and, finally, to one way in which they have very different implications.[1]

Of the canonical Gospels, the Fourth is generally recognized to have the least concern with things historical or, rather, the greatest interest in what is behind and before history, and beyond it. As one of Helmut Koester's students once wrote for her pupils: "What we know of Jesus' preaching comes from the three synoptic gospels. The fourth gospel reflects on the tradition from the perspective of the resurrected and exalted Jesus and rarely provides any historical information."[2]

Increasingly the third gospel, Luke's, is being recognized too as "theological history" or even "theology in historical guise," to employ a phrase used by Jacob Neusner in discussing a related issue.[3] Luke's willingness to rearrange and revise details in the early Christian story is known well enough. A simple example is the displacement of the lament over Jerusalem (13:34–35) to lower its apocalyptic "temperature"; in Luke this story is located ahead of the events of Palm Sunday rather than after the entry into Jerusalem, as Matt 23:37–39 has it. Another is the account of the baptism of Jesus. If we had only the Gospel of Luke we would not know who it was who baptized Jesus; we would have to say, however, that it could not have been John the Baptist, because he was in prison (Luke 3:19–22). Another is what Michael Cook calls Luke's "Myth of the Myriads," the picture in Acts of great numbers of Jews joining the Christian movement in the very earliest stages of Christian missionary activity.[4]

[1] The standard commentaries on John and Acts are thus assumed as background for what follows.

[2] P. Perkins, *Reading the New Testament: An Introduction* (New York/Ramsey, N.J.: Paulist, 1978) 85.

[3] R. Maddox, *The Purpose of Luke-Acts* (Edinburgh: T. & T. Clark, 1982) 15–18 (for "theological history"); J. Neusner, *Ancient Judaism: Debates and Disputes* (BJS 64; Chico, Calif.: Scholars Press, 1984) 251–55.

[4] M. Cook, "The Mission to the Jews in Acts: Unraveling Luke's 'Myth of the "Myriads,"'" in *Luke-Acts and the Jewish People: Eight Critical Perspectives*, ed. J. Tyson (Minneapolis: Augsburg, 1988) 102–23. See also Koester, *Introduction* 2:315–23.

However, although the creativity and the symbolism brought to the story of Jesus by the author of the Fourth Gospel are generally well accepted, many students of the New Testament have been hesitant to recognize the occurrence of something quite similar in the work of Luke. One reason for their reluctance has been the "historical" importance attributed to that other composition of Luke, the Acts of the Apostles. Erwin Goodenough was fond of repeating a story to this point:

> Kirsopp Lake said to a graduate class years ago that if Acts is not an historically reliable account of the beginnings of Christianity, we know nothing of that beginning, and so he and Foakes Jackson compiled their great work called The Beginnings of Christianity, which was almost exclusively a study of Acts.[5]

But Goodenough quoted Lake only to call Lake's view into question. It was particularly the Paul represented in Acts that Goodenough could not accept. The conclusion to one of his last publications is characteristically pointed:

> One wonders if it was someone thinking like the author of Acts whom Paul had in mind when he wrote to the Galatians: "Even if we, or an angel from heaven, should preach to you a gospel contrary to that to which we preached to you, let him be accursed" (Gal. 1:8). For no one in the Galatian or Corinthian churches would have recognized in the pages of Acts the Paul they had heard preach or had read in his letters.[6]

III

In the New Testament the God-fearers are mentioned only in the middle half of Acts.[7] The first one, Cornelius, appears in chapter 10, set in Caesarea

[5] E. R. Goodenough, "Paul and the Hellenization of Christianity," in *Religions in Antiquity: Essays in Memory of Erwin Ramsdell Goodenough,* ed. J. Neusner (SHR 14; Leiden: Brill, 1968) 24; see also his "The Perspective of Acts," in *Studies in Luke-Acts: Essays Presented in Honor of Paul Schubert,* ed. L. Keck and J. Martyn (Nashville: Abingdon, 1966) 51. Both essays are reprinted in *Goodenough on the Beginnings of Christianity,* ed. A. T. Kraabel (BJS 212; Atlanta: Scholars Press, 1990). His reference is to F. J. Foakes Jackson and K. Lake, *The Beginnings of Christianity. Part I: The Acts of the Apostles* (5 vols.; London: Macmillan, 1922–33; reprint, Grand Rapids: Baker, 1979); see "Paul and the Hellenization of Christianity," 24 n. 3.

[6] Goodenough, "Perspective," 58.

[7] The bibliography on this issue grows steadily. See A. T. Kraabel, "The 'Disappearance' of the God-fearers," *Numen* 48 (1981) 113–26; two contributions to *Christians Among Jews and Gentiles: Essays in Honor of Krister Stendahl on his Sixty-Fifth Birthday,* ed. G. W. E. Nickelsburg (Philadelphia: Fortress Press, 1986 [= *HTR* 79/1–3]): J. Gager, "Jews, Gentiles, and Synagogues in the Book of Acts" (pp. 91–99), and A. T. Kraabel, "Greeks, Jews, and Lutherans in the Middle Half of Acts" (pp. 147–57); three articles in *Biblical Archaeology Review* 12.5 (1986): R. MacLennan and A. T. Kraabel, "The God-fearers—A Literary and Theological Invention?" (pp. 46–53), R. Tannenbaum, "Jews and God-fearers in the Holy City of Aphrodite" (pp. 54–57),

Maritima, for Luke the most "Gentile" of all the cities of Israel. Here Cornelius encounters the apostle Peter.[8] All other instances are set in the Mediterranean diaspora: Pisidian Antioch (13:16, 26, 43, 50), Philippi (16:14), Thessalonica (17:4), Athens (17:17), and Corinth (18:7). In each case the God-fearers are involved with Paul. The letters of Paul, however, make no reference to these particular individuals or to "God-fearers" as groups within Mediterranean society.

In the traditional reconstruction of the historical situation, the characteristics of the God-fearer are as follows: (1) They are Gentiles interested in Judaism, but not converts (=proselytes); the men are not circumcised. (2) They are found in some numbers attached to the synagogues of the diaspora, from Asia Minor to Rome. (3) The God-fearer as traditionally understood is particularly significant for students of the New Testament and early Christianity; it was from the ranks of the God-fearers that Christianity supposedly had recruited a great number of its first members.

Finally, and all too often, their image was given an anti-Jewish coloration, a direction already pointed out by Luke himself: (4) The existence of the God-fearers could be seen as an indication that Jews in the Roman period, and particularly diaspora Jews, were prepared to compromise traditional standards and beliefs to attract Gentiles and win allegiance and support to their faltering creed. In this scenario the God-fearer became an element of the "fullness of time" (Gal 4:4); part of what set the stage for the advent of Christianity was the supposed bankruptcy of the faith of the erstwhile "chosen people." Thus Christianity must supersede Judaism.[9]

---

and L. Feldman "The Omnipresence of the God-Fearers" (pp. 58–63). See also *Luke-Acts and the Jewish People,* ed. Tyson; J. T. Sanders, *The Jews in Luke-Acts* (Philadelphia: Fortress Press, 1987); P. Esler, *Community and Gospel in Luke-Acts* (SNTSMS 57; Cambridge: Cambridge University Press, 1987) with my review of Sanders and Esler in *JBL* 108 (1989) 160–63. New impetus to the discussion comes from an inscription discovered in Aphrodisias in Caria (southwest Turkey) and published by J. Reynolds and R. Tannenbaum, *Jews and God-Fearers at Aphrodisias: Greek Inscriptions with Commentary* (Cambridge Philological Society, Supp. 12; Cambridge: Cambridge Philological Society, 1987); see also Kraabel, "Disappearance," 121 n. 26; Tannenbaum, "Jews and God-fearers"; P. van der Horst, "Jews and Christians in Aphrodisias," *Nederlands Theologisch Tijdschrift* 43 (1989) 106–21.

[8] Some later developments of this story are instructive for the issues argued here; see P. Stuehrenberg, "Cornelius and the Jews: A Study in the Interpretation of Acts Before the Reformation" (Diss., University of Minnesota, 1988).

[9] Kraabel, "Greeks"; idem, "*Synagoga Caeca:* Systematic Distortion in Gentile Interpretations of Evidence for Judaism in the Early Christian Period," in *"To See Ourselves as Others See Us": Christians, Jews, "Others" in Late Antiquity,* ed. J. Neusner and E. Frerichs (Chico, Calif: Scholars Press, 1985) 219–46. A statement by M. Hengel illustrates this view: "The large number of [God-fearers] standing between Judaism and paganism in the New Testament . . . shows the insoluble dilemma of the Jewish religion in ancient times. As it could not break free from its nationalist roots among the people, it had to stoop to constant and ultimately unattainable compromises" (*Judaism and Hellenism* [2 vols.; London: SCM, 1974] 1:313. See

I have argued instead that in Acts the God-fearers serve as a symbol to help Luke argue that Christianity had become a Gentile religion *legitimately*, without losing its Old Testament roots. The Jewish outreach to Gentiles recalled in the God-fearers would provide ample precedent for the far more extensive mission to Gentiles which Christianity had in fact undertaken with good success. Once Luke had made that point, provided that precedent, he could let the God-fearers disappear from his story.[10] The movement of the Jewish sect of the Christians into Gentile society was God's will, as Luke demonstrated—for example, in the Cornelius story. But there is also justification in Jewish history itself, says Luke: witness the God-fearers.

In a recent article Shaye Cohen identifies seven degrees of involvement between Jews and Gentiles from the Gentile side, from "admiring some aspect of Judaism" all the way to full conversion to Judaism. Two important questions, however, are not taken up: "the relative numbers of 'god-fearers' . . . [and] the role of 'god-fearers' in the book of Acts."[11] But these are just the issues most intriguing to the student of the New Testament: the *numbers* of such persons, and the *value* of the evidence in Acts. There is some historical basis for these characters in Luke's story, but how important were they in the earliest expansion of Christianity? Were they as frequent in Greco-Roman society as (some scholars have concluded) Luke suggested? If their absolute numbers were low and their occurrences scattered, as I suspect, then as evidence they are not sufficient to bear the weight of Luke's argument, and the few details that Luke provides about them should not be accepted uncritically as historical data. Their importance has been greatly inflated by Luke to serve the purposes of his narrative.

Luke gives us names for only three of the God-fearers in Acts: Cornelius, the first one; Titius Justus, the last one (18:7); and one woman, Lydia (16:14). For the Beloved Disciple the text provides no name at all. Nevertheless, most students of the Gospel of John have always had a name in mind. For some he was the disciple John the son of Zebedee; for others John the Presbyter, or John Mark, or Lazarus. The text itself (21:24) tells us that the Beloved Disciple was the source of all that it narrates. In some sense he is responsible for the gospel, the one with the greatest claim to be called its

also two studies of Hengel's work in *RSRev* 15.3 (1989): J. J. Collins, "Judaism as *Praeparatio Evangelica* in the Work of Martin Hengel" (pp. 226–28), and W. Long, "Martin Hengel on Early Christianity" (pp. 230–34). "Judaism" in this context might well appear in quotation marks, so nonhistorical and theologized has it become. See also J. Neusner, "From Moore to Urbach and Sanders: Fifty Years of 'Judaism': The End of the Line for a Depleted Category," *Religious Studies and Theology* 6 (1986) 7–26.

[10] Hence the title of my 1981 article "The 'Disappearance' of the God-fearers."

[11] S. J. D. Cohen, "Crossing the Boundary and Becoming a Jew," *HTR* 82 (1989) 13–33; the quotation is from p. 33 n. 70.

"author"—no wonder the Beloved Disciple is usually called "John."[12]

He is also of great importance as a character within the story—that is, after he enters the narrative, two-thirds of the way through the account. He makes his first appearance at the Last Supper, itself one of the most embellished and augmented elements of the Fourth Gospel (chaps. 13–17). (A story that takes an average of fifteen verses to tell in each of the Synoptics requires ten times that number in John.) There he is "one of his disciples, reclining on Jesus' bosom" (13:23); of all in attendance he is the closest to Jesus. At the crucifixion, standing with Mary beneath the cross, he is entrusted by Jesus with her care (19:25–27). On Easter morning he and Peter make for Jesus' tomb; he outruns Peter and finds the tomb empty (20:2–10). In Galilee shortly afterward Peter does not recognize a figure standing at the lakeshore until the Beloved Disciple identifies him as the risen Lord (21:7).

Despite the Beloved Disciple's obvious significance in the Fourth Gospel, there are only one or two possible points of contact in the Synoptic Gospels with any of John's stories about him. These are the weakly attested Luke 24:12, which may rather derive from the account in the Fourth Gospel, and Luke 24:24; both these texts would parallel elements in the story of the footrace to the tomb in the Fourth Gospel. But if they are all the evidence available, then the Synoptics really have nothing at all to tell us about the Beloved Disciple.

Who was the Beloved Disciple? The disciple John the son of Zebedee has traditionally been the favored candidate among named individuals in the New Testament. But the "sons of Zebedee" are mentioned in the Fourth Gospel only at 21:2, and John is never referred to by name. Nor does this Gospel present any of the stories about the "sons of Zebedee" that are found in the Synoptics.

The foremost American student of the Gospel of John, Raymond E. Brown, concluded in his Anchor Bible commentary that John the son of Zebedee was the likeliest of all possible candidates to have been the Beloved Disciple.[13] A decade later, after much more research, he had decided that *none* of the known historical figures fits; the Beloved Disciple was some unknown person.[14]

If the Beloved Disciple was an actual disciple of Jesus, that is, a contemporary, his role still has been vastly expanded in the Fourth Gospel—even more so if he was a generation later. Not all of what John intended with this

[12] See the commentaries, especially R. E. Brown, *The Gospel According to John* (AB 29, 29A; Garden City, N.Y.: Doubleday, 1966, 1970); idem, *The Community of the Beloved Disciple* (New York/Ramsey/Toronto: Paulist, 1979).

[13] Brown, *John* 1:xcviii.

[14] Brown, *The Churches the Apostles Left Behind* (New York/Ramsey: Paulist, 1984) 84 n. 120.

expansion is clear to us, but the main conclusion at least is evident. Although there probably was someone, some actual person, whom the author of the Fourth Gospel had in mind as he wrote about the Beloved Disciple, in the text the Beloved Disciple plays a very different role from what he did in the career of Jesus, because that suited the community's concerns and the author's theology and the movement of his narrative. Something like this expansion occurs in Acts with the God-fearers, I would argue, and for similar reasons. Someone who now objects to such a "distortion of the record" on the part of "John" or Luke may well have a different understanding of their purposes than did these authors themselves.

IV

Teachers of literature or history often use particular and limited examples from their texts to illustrate larger themes. In many of my classes I have cited the God-fearers to make a point about how Luke operated as an author. In recent years I have also employed the figure of the Beloved Disciple to the same purpose for the Fourth Gospel. Several years ago one student pointed out to me the similarity between the two examples, both as regards the authors' purposes and as to the historical and other problems their technique raises. Since then a number of others have independently made the same connection. It is this stylistic parallel between the two authors that I would stress in this brief paper. Exploring the example from one writer can help to understand also what the other intended. It may also make it simpler to distinguish historical bedrock from the more important theological point John or Luke wished to make.

There surely were some Gentiles interested in their Jewish neighbors and their piety.[15] And, I believe, there is some historical figure somewhere behind the Beloved Disciple. But in each case Luke and the author of the Fourth Gospel took over a kernel of fact and magnified and transformed it, shaping it to their own purposes. In both cases traditional views of the historicity of the New Testament drove commentators to search for a historical identity for these literary characters and symbolic agents.

Finally, in each case and all too often, to fix on the question of historicity was to miss the symbolism and the more important theological point the author wished to make. When theology is mistaken for history, historians and theologians both suffer a loss.

But there is one *difference* between these two examples that is more important than any of their similarities. If interpreters of the New Testament insist on identifying the Beloved Disciple with one or another of the major

[15] But for what reasons? See Cohen, "Crossing the Boundary"; and Kraabel, "The Roman Diaspora: Six Questionable Assumptions," *JJS* 33 (1982) 445–64.

players during the career of Jesus, the result will be to confuse that story, but nothing except Christianity is much distorted. But the accounts in Acts are made to touch repeatedly on *Jewish* history. One example is what Acts reflects of Palestinian Judaism, and especially of Paul's supposed connection to it. Samuel Sandmel once put it succinctly: "If Acts had never been written, or if Acts had been lost and not made its way into the New Testament and we had the Epistles [of Paul] alone, I doubt that any scholars would have supposed that there was some close relationship between Paul and Palestinian Judaism."[16] As it is, of course, studying Palestinian Judaism or the later rabbis in order to "explain" Paul is a common methodology of our field.

Another example is the present concern, the God-fearers. They figure prominently in reconstructions of Jewish diaspora history in the Greco-Roman period. After all, the God-fearers would be pagans attracted originally to *Judaism;* it would be bad method not to include them if the data are reliable. And that is the central question.

I have argued that Luke employed the God-fearers to provide a precedent for the movement of Christianity, originally a Palestinian Jewish sect, into the Gentile world. But his larger theological agenda in Acts was to show how Judaism was superseded in that process. For Luke there was no legitimate place for Judaism in the diaspora now that the newer message of the Christian missionaries was available; what they preached was ideally a kind of "Judaism for Gentiles," replacing its mother religion in the process.

Thus, not only is it true that Luke had no need to tell, and perhaps no interest in telling, an accurate story about first-century Jews. Given his theology and the way it set up the relationships between Judaism and the new Christian movement, he had both motivation and justification to rewrite that story, to inflate or to minimize, as it suited his agenda. As it happened, that agenda combined with the theological concerns of later students of the New Testament, particularly Protestant interpreters, to produce the degrading and one-sided image of the Jewish diaspora already mentioned, a picture perhaps forever distorted, and so persuasive that even Jewish scholars and Jewish reference works were taken in.[17]

If Acts had been written by Mark, Matthew, or John—or Paul—the story would not have had the same results. That is because the theology carried by the narrative would have been quite different.

The purposes behind the presence of the Beloved Disciple in the Fourth Gospel are becoming clear to students of that text. They are aided by the existence of the Synoptics, which allow detailed comparisons to be made among the Gospels. More along that same line needs to be done now for

[16] S. Sandmel, *RSRev* 4 (1978) 159, in a review of E. P. Sanders, *Paul and Palestinian Judaism* (Philadelphia: Fortress Press, 1977).

[17] Kraabel, "Roman Diaspora."

Acts, even though the "parallels" here are more remote from the New Testament text: the history, literature, and archaeological evidence of the Greco-Roman world including diaspora Judaism.

Luke has in many respects a wonderful and winning theology of the early Christian movement. It is time to get beyond his distortions of Jewish history to the larger view of Christianity in the world of the diaspora—our world—which he wished to present to us. A fresh look at the Beloved Disciple provides some unexpected assistance at the beginning of that task.

21

Salvation Is *for* the Jews: Secret Christian Jews in the Gospel of John

SARAH J. TANZER

OVER THE PAST three decades a significant focus of Johannine scholarship has been the setting, purpose, and audience of the Fourth Gospel. This study reexamines the last two of these, inquiring into *one* purpose and *one* potential audience of the Gospel of John. A presupposition of this study is that John[1] may well have more than one purpose and more than one intended audience.[2] Along the way, three previously well defined positions will be cursorily reviewed. The first sees this Gospel as

[1] Whenever "John" is used, it refers to the canonical Gospel, and not to the author(s) or to other literature which bears that name.

[2] I have preferred the term "audience" over "reader" in recognition of the fact that at the time in which the Gospel of John began circulating, most readings were public readings, done from manuscripts or memory, such that audience or hearers seem more appropriate to a discussion about the end of the first century C.E. Stephen D. Moore has succinctly described the danger of failing to recognize that the aural appropriation of a text by "hearers" is different from the visual appropriation by the private, silent "reader": "After all, to dub the evangelist's intended listening audience 'the reader,' and then produce minute analyses of a 'reading' that in all probability never occurred—at least not in the modern, private, silent sense—would seem the ultimate waste of time" ("Stories of Reading: Doing Gospel Criticism As/With a 'Reader,'" in *Society of Biblical Literature 1988 Seminar Papers*, ed. D. J. Lull [Atlanta: Scholars Press, 1988] 146).

By *intended* audience I mean to indicate an audience for whom the author (or authors) intended this Gospel to be heard in the first century, that is, to the extent that one can reconstruct an intended audience based on the Gospel text itself. In this way, I distinguish between an intended first-century audience, any actual first-century audiences, or, for that matter, other audiences or readers throughout the centuries. I have deliberately stayed away from most of the vast and often confusing terminology of reader-response criticism.

intended to serve as a missionary document for diaspora Jews.[3] This article does not take up exactly this position, but it explores whether or not there is a missionary purpose to John, which is directed toward Christian Jews.[4] The second position is one that views John as written in a setting of sharp dialogue with the synagogue.[5] Though this article does not take up the possible historical reasons for the sharp dialogue, it does inquire about the purpose behind the portrayal of this polemic in John and what it may tell us about an intended audience of the Gospel. The third position views the intended audience of John as "insiders," those squarely within the Johannine Christian community, because the "closed metaphorical system" of the Gospel could hardly be understood by an outsider.[6] According to this position, one "of the primary functions of the book, therefore, must have been to provide a reinforcement for the community's social identity."[7] This view, which has gained wide currency among contemporary scholars, is clearly at odds with the "missionary purpose" position.[8] This leads one to consider whether John might indeed have more than one purpose and one intended audience—written on the one hand for the edification of "insiders," and yet also written to deliver a hortatory message for those on the fringe of the Johannine community, caught between Johannine Christianity and Judaism. It is this latter possibility that this study explores.

In order to discern these issues, one needs also to inquire into the role of "the Jews" in the Gospel of John and what that role can or cannot tell us about the intended audiences of the Gospel.[9] Finally, since the named (and

[3] See esp. K. Bornhäuser, *Das Johannesevangelium: Eine Missionsschrift für Israel* (Gütersloh: Bertelsmann, 1928); T. C. Smith, *Jesus in the Gospel of John* (Nashville: Broadman, 1959); W. C. van Unnik, "The Purpose of St. John's Gospel," *Studia Evangelica* 1 (1959) 382–411; J. A. T. Robinson, "The Destination and Purpose of St. John's Gospel," *NTS* 6 (1959–60) 117–31.

[4] "Christian Jews" in this study refers to those people whose public mode of religious expression was found in the synagogue and whose primary identity was as Jews, yet who privately or secretly maintained some form of belief in Jesus (however inadequate by Johannine community standards).

[5] This position was put forward by K. L. Carroll ("The Fourth Gospel and the Exclusion of Christians from the Synagogue," *BJRL* 40 [1957] 19–32) and further developed by Erich Grässer ("Die antijüdische Polemik im Johannesevangelium," *NTS* 11 [1964–65] 74–90). But the most thoroughly developed argument of this position is the seminal study of J. Louis Martyn, *History and Theology in the Fourth Gospel* (New York: Harper & Row, 1968).

[6] Wayne A. Meeks, "The Man from Heaven in Johannine Sectarianism," *JBL* 91 (1972) 44–72.

[7] Ibid., 70.

[8] As Meeks writes, "It could hardly be regarded as a missionary tract (ibid.).

[9] This is another area that has received increased attention in recent years. The most compelling contemporary work has been done by Urban C. von Wahlde ("The Terms for Religious Authorities in the Fourth Gospel: A Key to Literary Strata?" *JBL* 98 [1979] 231–53; "The Johannine 'Jews': A Critical Survey," *NTS* 28 [1982] 33–60; *The Earliest Version of John's Gospel* [Wilmington, Del.: Michael Glazier, 1989] 31–36).

sometimes unnamed) characters of the Gospel tell us something about the intended audience and purpose of John, the admittedly ambiguous role of Nicodemus deserves a reevaluation. Too often, while noting that he represents secret Christian Jews, scholars have too quickly dismissed him with the evaluation that the Gospel judges him as no better than the Jewish authorities or superficial signs believers. Neither a positive nor a negative view of Nicodemus tells us whether or not he represents an intended audience of John or what the message is to that audience.[10]

There are many indicators of purpose and intended audience(s) in John. The stated purpose of the Gospel of John in 20:30–31 is "these (signs) are written (in order) that you may believe that Jesus is the Christ, the Son of God, and that believing you may have life in his name."[11] The purpose, then, is to bring people to belief, and not to a bare belief at that, but a deep faith, one which holds "that Jesus is the Christ, the Son of God." This tells us something about the intended audiences for this Gospel. But this does not tell us at what stage of belief the intended hearers were located. For example, were they completely outside the Johannine community—open to missionary activity, but beginning with no belief? Or were they closer to the Johannine community, perhaps straddling the fence between Judaism and Christianity—with the seeds of belief already implanted (perhaps they viewed Jesus as a Prophet)? Or were they perhaps well inside the Johannine community with a solid faith, but one that needed to be nurtured to a deeper level?

Another indicator of intended audience is the structure of John, much of it made up of vignettes, little scenes involving individuals (the Samaritan woman; Mary, Martha, and Lazarus; Mary Magdalene; Thomas; etc.) whom Jesus encounters, rather than simply crowds. These varied vignettes involving different characters in the Gospel, all of whom are at different stages on the way to faith or to a deeper comprehension of who Jesus is and what that means, represent the variety of people for whom this Gospel was intended. It is important to recognize that the characters span a wide spectrum of belief. Among the named and unnamed individuals whom Jesus encounters there is a kind of continuum that extends from Nicodemus, and others whose faith is unarticulated or incipient at best, to the Beloved Disciple, who is the disciple *par excellence,* at the other end of the continuum. In this way, these vignettes tell us that the audience for whom John was intended was very diverse, like the individuals along this continuum.[12]

[10] My purpose is not to argue that Nicodemus has been treated unfairly, but rather to explore what this character tells us about the purpose of the Gospel and about its intended audiences.

[11] Translations of the Gospel of John are from the RSV, though any clarifications or additions in parentheses are my own.

[12] Those characters who do not represent any intended audience include those *groups* of

The plot of the Gospel is correspondingly directed to an audience who could identify with these characters. As R. Alan Culpepper pointed out, it is largely "a matter of how Jesus' identity comes to be recognized and how it fails to be recognized. . . . This literary dynamic pushes the reader to embrace the ideological point of view of the author, that is, the confession that Jesus is 'the Christ, the Son of God' (20:30)."[13] Thus, the plot that incorporates these diverse vignettes can be said to utilize "a strategy for wooing readers to accept its interpretation of Jesus."[14] And it is a strategy that is aimed at a diverse audience, similar to the wide spectrum represented by its characters.

One of the perplexities of John is that to some scholars it seems like the most Jewish of the four canonical Gospels, whereas to others it represents a Christianity the most removed from Judaism. It is not difficult to comprehend the basis for such divergent views. On the one hand, John, with its use of Jewish festivals, its comparisons with major Jewish heroic figures, its occasional use of midrashic techniques of scripture interpretation,[15] and its references throughout the Gospel to "the Jews," appears indeed to be the most Jewish of the Gospels. On the other hand, its unambivalently negative portrayal of "the Jews" and their unbelief, the great distance it puts between Jesus and "the Jews,"[16] and the well-developed Christology all point to a Christianity seemingly removed from its Jewish roots. These seeming contradictions are not only reconciled but can be well understood if one considers the plausibility of a Johannine Christian community in competition with its Jewish counterpart for closet Christian Jews.

A subtlety that is significant but often overlooked is the nuanced distinction between different groups of Jews or Jewish characters in John. Once again, this is easy to understand because of the overwhelmingly negative use of "the Jews" (οἱ Ἰουδαῖοι) to represent the hostile rejection of Jesus' revelation. As Culpepper has noted, "Through the Jews, John explores the heart

---

people (it is interesting that they are mostly not individuals) who reject Jesus with hostility and whom Jesus consequently rejects unambiguously (the Jews, the Pharisees, certain Jews who believe because of signs but cannot respond further to the Word, etc.). Thus, not all of the characters in the Gospel represent intended audiences. The Gospel does not seem interested in addressing those represented by characters whom it judges in an insultingly negative way.

[13] R. A. Culpepper, *Anatomy of the Fourth Gospel* (Philadelphia: Fortress Press, 1983) 88–89.

[14] Ibid., 98.

[15] On the midrashic character of John, see esp. Peder Borgen, "Observations on the Midrashic Character of John 6," *ZNW* 54 (1963) 232–40; idem, *Bread from Heaven: An Exegetical Study of the Concept of Manna in the Gospel of John and the Writings of Philo* (NovTSup 10; Leiden: Brill, 1965).

[16] If it were not for the Samaritan woman's view of Jesus as a Jew (4:9) and a few other references, one might forget that Jesus was a Jew in this Gospel, because of this great distance between him and "the Jews."

and soul of unbelief."[17] Urban C. von Wahlde has shown that this use of "the Jews" in John usually refers to religious authorities.[18]

This usage of "the Jews" in a hostile sense is generally agreed to be characteristically Johannine, though there are numerous other uses of "the Jews" in this Gospel that are neutral in tone.[19] In addition, there are other references to Jews (negative, neutral, and positive) in this Gospel: (1) Following encounters with Jesus, we are sometimes told that there are Jews who believe because of signs (2:23; 12:11); less often the implication is that they believe because of what they have heard (8:30). But in these cases Jesus denounces this group of Jews, because their belief is shown to be superficial. (2) There is also the recurring theme of division (7:43; 9:16; 10:19–21) among the Jews (usually also following a sign, e.g., 11:45), which leads some Jews to believe (or at least to stand up for Jesus in the ensuing debate), while others do not believe, call him unattractive names, or report him to the authorities. In these instances the text merely reports that there are Jews who believe or stand up for Jesus, and their belief is not denounced. (3) There are various groups of Jews which seem to overlap: those Jews of whom it is written that for "fear of the Jews" they will not speak explicitly of Jesus or of their belief (7:13; the blind man's parents in 9:22; Joseph of Arimathea, identified as a secret disciple of Jesus in 19:38; the secret belief of many of the authorities who fear the Pharisees in 12:42; but this "fear of the Jews" theme extends to the disciples in 20:19). Apart from the stinging reprimand in 12:43, the Gospel seems unresolved and ambiguous in its response to these Jews. (4) Not unrelated to these Jews is the individual Nicodemus (ruler of the Jews/teacher of Israel), who in three ambiguous scenes (3:1–21; 7:50–52; 19:38–42) appears to be a slowly emerging believer. All too often, Nicodemus (and those Jews whose belief in Jesus is not explicit because of fear of the Jews) is evaluated negatively and ultimately as belonging with "the Jews"—those who represent total hostility to Jesus and also those Jews who believe only because of signs and who are denounced for their superficiality.[20] (5) There are several other individual Jews (e.g., Nathanael in

[17] Culpepper, *Anatomy,* 129.

[18] Von Wahlde, "The Johannine 'Jews,'" 41–42. Further, he has shown that two literary strata are marked off in John by different linguistic terms for designating religious authorities: the Jews, on the one hand; Pharisees, chief priests and rulers, on the other ("Terms for Religious Authorities," 231–53, esp. 238–39).

[19] Von Wahlde provides the best survey of these neutral uses, including references to Jewish religious/national customs, to the land of Judea, to individuals as Jews in a context that separates them from non-Jews, to people who are termed "Jews" but who clearly do not share the hostility of the characteristically Johannine Jews, to the phrase "King of the Jews" ("Johannine 'Jews,'" 33–60, esp. 46).

[20] It strikes me that this is much too sweeping a judgment, based on only two verses in the Gospel, 12:42–43. These verses will be discussed further below. Martyn typifies this point of view. But *ex hypothesi* this means only that, from the point of the separated Johannine

1:45–51[21] and the blind man in chapter 9 who are judged favorably by the Gospel, because their belief in Jesus becomes overt and exemplary rather than covert, like the belief of Nicodemus.

What could these diverse references to Jews in John mean in terms of a possible audience and purpose? At one extreme there are "the Jews" (and Pharisees, chief priests, and rulers) who are constantly hostile to Jesus, while at the other extreme there are certain individual Jews (most notably, the blind man) who respond to Jesus without fear of the consequences. Then there are those Jews who seem to believe in Jesus, but have that belief unmasked for what it is, a very superficial belief. Opposite them are those who see and come to truly believe. Located in between these opposite groupings are those Jews who are afraid to be explicit about what they believe about Jesus (e.g., the blind man's parents, Joseph of Arimathea, and Nicodemus).

Now, many would judge that the great distancing implied in phrases such as "the Passover of the Jews" (2:13) and the hostile sense of "the Jews" shows not only that the narrator is placing some distance between himself and Judaism but also that the reader is not a Jew.[22] Just the opposite may be true concerning the "reader." Although it is indeed unusual, it is not by accident that the Gospel uses "the Jews" in the way that it does throughout.[23] The distancing from "the Jews" and from Jewish festivals and the negative portrayal of the Jews would have a great hortatory effect on secret Christian Jews, exhorting them not to be like the hostile Jews and not to be afraid to distance themselves from their Jewish customs. As Raymond Brown suggested,

> There are rather clear indications that the Fourth Gospel makes an appeal to these Jews who believed in Jesus and who were torn between their faith

---

community, the attempt on the part of these secret believers, these so-called Christian Jews, to straddle the fence is wholly unsuccessful; their attempt constitutes, in fact, what Wayne Meeks has correctly characterized as a diabolic lie. Because they do not take their stand absolutely in the word of Jesus, they only prove that his word does not have any place at all among them and that in the final analysis they are not "the Jews who had believed in him," but merely "the Jews" ("Glimpses into the History of the Johannine Community," in *The Gospel of John in Christian History* [New York/Ramsey/Toronto: Paulist, 1978] 113–14).

[21] Culpepper has pointed out that when a positive sense is intended for the Jews, "the evangelist normally uses the term 'Israel' (1:31, 47, 49; 3:10; 12:13)" (*Anatomy,* 127). This would include Nicodemus in that positive sense (3:10). But there seems to be a contrast intended between "the true Israelite," Nathanael, and the ironic reference to Nicodemus as "the teacher of Israel" in 3:10.

[22] Culpepper, *Anatomy,* 220.

[23] This is true whether one agrees with von Wahlde ("Terms for Religious Authorities," 238) that this negative usage is unique in its reference to religious authorities or whether one finds in John that the term often implies the common people as well.

> and a natural desire not to desert Judaism. The generally hostile attack on "the Jews" would not apply to them. . . . The heavy emphasis on Jesus as the Messiah (especially xx 31) would be designed to strengthen their faith in this crucial confession which had become the testing stone of continued admission to the synagogues. The theme of Jesus' replacement of Jewish institutions and feasts would be an encouragement to them, for they would have to leave such practices behind if they withdrew from the synagogues.[24]

They should be fearless of the consequences, like the man born blind. It is precisely those texts in which fear of the Jews or expulsion from the synagogue is mentioned (7:11–13; 9:18–23; 12:10–11, 42–43; 16:1–4) that implicitly exhort one not to be afraid, not to worry about being put out of the synagogue, rather to leave Judaism behind and confess Jesus openly.

Similarly, Nicodemus, as both a ruler of the Jews and yet someone with a beginning belief in Jesus (albeit *only* a beginning belief), is used to exhort an intended audience of this Gospel. It is interesting that we do not find Nicodemus in one long scene (as, e.g., the Samaritan woman); instead he makes three appearances—toward the beginning of the Gospel (chap. 3), toward the middle of the Gospel (chap. 7), and toward the end of the Gospel (chap. 19). In the first scene (3:1–21) he comes out of the darkness of night to speak with Jesus; by the third (19:38–42), he comes more publicly (and in daylight?) to bury Jesus. In between he defends Jesus' right to fair treatment before his fellow Jewish leaders. These three scenes could be characterized as a three-part "coming out of the closet": Nicodemus becomes gradually more public in his support of Jesus. On the other hand, all three scenes are ambiguous, both in their evaluation of Nicodemus and in their meaning. This ambiguity is puzzling to commentators, precisely because most of the other characters in John are not fraught with such ambiguity. As Culpepper has noted, the characters represent responses to Jesus and choices which the audience is being challenged to make: "The characters are, therefore, particular sorts of choosers. Given the pervasive dualism of the Fourth Gospel, the choice is either/or. All situations are reduced to two clear-cut alternatives, and all the characters eventually make their choice. So must the reader."[25] Such a reading of the Gospel does not allow for the ambiguity introduced by a character like Nicodemus.[26] Many commentators are also unable to allow for this ambiguity and, as a result, tend to conclude

[24] R. E. Brown, *The Gospel according to John I–XII* (AB 29; Garden City, N.Y.: Doubleday, 1966) LXXV. Although Brown writes this in the introduction, at several points in the commentary he does not appear persuaded that there was an intentional appeal being made to these Christian Jews or that exhortation to these Christian Jews was a purpose of this Gospel.

[25] Culpepper, *Anatomy,* 104.

[26] I agree with Culpepper that *most* of the situations and characters are presented as either/or alternatives, but not all.

that in the end Nicodemus's place is with the hostile Jews[27] or superficial signs believers,[28] that he should be judged negatively,[29] and that he is without representative value for any intended audience of this Gospel.[30]

There are a number of interesting features in the account of Nicodemus's first encounter with Jesus in 3:1–21. Nicodemus is identified as "a man of the Pharisees" and "a ruler of the Jews" (v. 1). In 3:2 he makes a beginning confession of faith: "Rabbi, we know that you are a teacher come from God; for no one can do these signs that you do, unless God is with him."[31] We are told in this verse also that Nicodemus came to Jesus by night. In the ensuing dialogue Nicodemus plays a role that many characters in this Gospel also play: the hearer who misunderstands Jesus. Nicodemus misses out on what Jesus means about being born from above.[32] In 3:10 Jesus reprimands Nicodemus for his lack of understanding, and in vv. 19–21 Jesus speaks of the judgment of those who so love the darkness (σκότος) that they do not come to the light lest their deeds be exposed. But Nicodemus himself does not speak again after v. 9. Much of what is said by Jesus in the intervening verses is implicitly hortatory (e.g., 3:16–18 with its strong appeal to believe in God's son). Another intriguing aspect of this dialogue-turned-discourse is the use of "we" by Nicodemus and "you" (plural) by Jesus. To whom does this refer? One possibility is that it refers generally to the Jews or the Pharisees (based on 3:1). Another possibility, put forward by David Rensberger, is that Nicodemus represents secret believers and that it is these secret believers who are being exhorted in vv. 3 and 7 to be born again:

> Our first observation must be that this demand is made not of unbelievers in the strict sense, but of people with at least some faith in Jesus. To be sure, it is implied that such half-belief is in fact little better than unbelief.

[27] Culpepper writes, "He remains, therefore, 'one of them,' not one of the children of God" (*Anatomy,* 136).

[28] See M. de Jonge, "Nicodemus and Jesus: Some Observations on Misunderstanding and Understanding in the Fourth Gospel," *BJRL* 53 (1971) 355; Meeks, "Man from Heaven," 55; David Rensberger, *Johannine Faith and Liberating Community* (Philadelphia: Westminster, 1988) 38.

[29] For an example of an especially negative reading of Nicodemus's character, see Rensberger, *Johannine Faith,* 37–41, esp. 40.

[30] See de Jonge, "Nicodemus and Jesus," 349.

[31] However, the reference in this verse to "signs" has led many to assume that Nicodemus belongs with the men whom Jesus does not trust, who believe only because they saw signs (2:23–25).

[32] Meeks has pointed out that this genre was widespread in the Greco-Roman world: "Nicodemus plays a well-known role: that of the rather stupid disciple whose maladroit questions provide the occasion (a) for the reader to feel superior and (b) for the sage who is questioned to deliver a discourse" ("Man from Heaven," 53). Misunderstanding in John is typical of both those who are hostile to Jesus and those who are ultimately brought to faith (e.g., the Samaritan woman in chap. 4).

> But it remains true that this call is issued in what could be termed a "missionary" or "evangelistic" context only with very careful qualification.[33]

In the case of Nicodemus, the scene is ambiguous, beginning on a hopeful note and ending with his misunderstanding. But Jesus' response, one of ironic reprimand, is hardly the same harsh repudiation one finds in scenes with Jewish authorities or in encounters with unnamed Jews who believe only because of signs. The message about Nicodemus is that he has misunderstood, even as a teacher of Israel. The message to those hearers whom he represents is to do better than Nicodemus.

But Wayne Meeks has argued from this dialogue that someone such as Nicodemus was not intended to be able to read and respond to the Gospel:

> The form of the dialogue itself is such that the reader without special prior information would be as puzzled as Nicodemus. Only a reader who is thoroughly familiar with the whole Fourth Gospel or else acquainted by some non-literary means with its symbolism and developing themes (perhaps because he belongs to a community in which such language is constantly used) can possibly understand its double entendre and its abrupt transitions. For the outsider—even for an interested inquirer (like Nicodemus)—the dialogue is opaque.[34]

Such an analysis does not take into account that the message *about* a particular character in the Gospel (such as Nicodemus) is not necessarily the same as the message *to* the audience whom that character represents (namely, secret Christian Jews). If a Gospel is truly to *affect* its audience, to move and sway them,[35] then it seems quite plausible that it may have a negative and even a "tough" message about that audience, which is intended to challenge them to move in the direction in which the Gospel writer wants them to go.

In 7:50–52, there is a cameo appearance of Nicodemus. It occurs in the midst of a scene portraying an encounter between Jesus and the chief priests and Pharisees. In this scene, the authorities are annoyed that Jesus has not been arrested, and they claim that those who believe in Jesus are ignorant of the law and therefore accursed. Nicodemus is introduced as one "who had gone to him (Jesus) before, and who was one of them (the authorities)." Nicodemus defends Jesus, saying, "Does our law judge a man without first giving him a hearing and learning what he does?" (v. 51). He is then rebuked by his cohorts. Again, if we try to apply labels such as positive or negative, we are left only with ambiguity. The scene reflects positively on Nicodemus insofar as he steps in to defend Jesus. It seems to evaluate him negatively insofar as Nicodemus is identified as "one of them." Commentators have

[33] Rensberger, *Johannine Faith,* 55.

[34] Meeks, "Man from Heaven," 57.

[35] Moore, "Stories of Reading," 152.

pointed out also that Nicodemus still falls short of making a public confession of faith:

> I do not think that the Gospel wants to suggest that Nicodemus in fact has come to believe in Jesus and is, as such, an exception to the general rule laid down by his fellow-Pharisees in verse 48. After all it refers the reader to chapter iii and there is no indication of a development in Nicodemus' attitude since this rather unsatisfactory discussion with Jesus.[36]

But the passage does not bring up his lack of public confession, so once again there is ambiguity—though this presents a more flattering portrait of Nicodemus than chapter 3. After all, Nicodemus is not creeping stealthily out of the night here; rather, he is publicly defending Jesus before his Pharisaic cohorts.

In Nicodemus's final scene (19:38–42), we are told that he came with Joseph of Arimathea, "who was a disciple of Jesus, but secretly, for fear of the Jews," to bury Jesus. We are reminded (19:39) that Nicodemus had first come to Jesus "by night." In addition to a brief description of the burial, Nicodemus is described as having brought a very heavy weight of spices for the burial. Compared to chapter 3, this is a very positive portrayal of Nicodemus. After all, he is paired with a "disciple" of Jesus; he has come to bury Jesus with a great deal of honor (not to mention spices); and he comes not by night but publicly. Yet his partner, Joseph of Arimathea, was a disciple of Jesus only secretly, "for fear of the Jews." There is no confession of faith (as we find with other characters in the Gospel who are favorably portrayed), and Jesus is now dead. So the interpretation of this scene is not without some ambiguity. Still, the persistent appearance of Nicodemus in this Gospel cannot be insignificant, and the pairing of Nicodemus with Joseph of Arimathea, a secret disciple, tells us that he is representative of such secret disciples. Culpepper notes that the affective power of the plot, making use of the representative responses of the characters, pushes the audience toward a response to Jesus.[37] This final scene with Nicodemus indeed challenges its intended audience. As the concluding scene to a gradual coming to faith on the part of Nicodemus, 19:38–42 subtlely exhorts an intended audience (those closet believers of the author's own time) to do as Nicodemus does and yet better than Nicodemus—to publicly confess Jesus and not to fear the Jews or expulsion from the synagogue.[38]

[36] De Jonge, "Nicodemus and Jesus," 345; see also Rensberger, *Johannine Faith,* 39; C. K. Barrett, *The Gospel According to St. John* (2nd ed.; Philadelphia: Westminster, 1978) 332. A more positive evaluation of Nicodemus in these verses is found in Brown, *John I–XII,* 1:330; Ernst Haenchen, *John 2,* trans. R. W. Funk, ed. R. W. Funk and U. Busse (Hermeneia; Philadelphia: Fortress Press, 1984) 18.

[37] Culpepper, *Anatomy,* 148.

[38] Most commentators seem to view this pericope as a positive portrayal of Nicodemus. Brown is an especially good example of this (*John* 2:959–60). He sees crypto-believers in the

There is a wrinkle introduced in 12:42–43 into this theory that the Gospel is intended to address secret Christian Jews such as Nicodemus: "Nevertheless many even of the authorities (ἀρχόντων) believed in him, but for fear of the Pharisees they did not confess it, lest they should be put out of the synagogue: for they loved the praise of men more than the praise of God." This damning statement is certainly unambiguous enough. The writer's judgment is emphatic with regard to these believers and their inability to confess their faith. Although it is intriguing that Nicodemus is not named in these verses, it is difficult not to think of him as included in this judgment. The description seems to fit him, and in his two scenes prior to these verses he has been linked with the Pharisees (3:1; 7:45–52) and described as an ἄρχων (an authority, a ruler [3:1]). If the Gospel ended here and there were not yet one more scene with Nicodemus (19:38–42), one would be tempted to conclude with most commentators that John places Nicodemus with "the Jews" and the Pharisees and, consequently, neither holds out any hope for these characters nor intends to address an audience whom they represent. But the scenes with Nicodemus *are* ambiguous and *are* increasingly positive in their portrayal of him as the Gospel moves on. For that reason, in passages such as 12:42–43, the fearful believing rulers (such as Nicodemus) present a negative paradigm to the intended audience. Once again, the message *about* the secret believers among the Jews is not the same as the message *to* that intended audience. The audience is admonished *not* to do as they do, *not* to love the praise of men more than the praise of God. Instead it is implied that they should reveal themselves and their faith openly and, if that means being put out of the synagogue, that they should not fear such consequences. Nicodemus might also be said to present a positive paradigm to an intended audience of secret believers insofar as the three scenes in which he is named depict a gradual coming out of the closet. However, insofar as these scenes remain ambiguous, it seems as though the audience is being challenged to go further than Nicodemus does.

In addition to the scenes with Nicodemus, there are several other features which suggest that a purpose of this Gospel is to reach secret Christian Jews

synagogue exhorted to follow the positive paradigms of Nicodemus and Joseph of Arimathea, who finally have the courage of their convictions. He also views the large outlay of spices as symbolic of the appropriately kingly burial of Jesus. However, a negative interpretation is given by Rensberger, who builds upon the earlier interpretation of Alfred Loisy (*Le quatrième évangile* [Paris: Picard, 1903] 895–96): "Alfred Loisy pointed out long ago that Nicodemus and Joseph confess nothing and have nothing to do with Jesus except with his corpse. Nicodemus shows himself capable only of burying Jesus, ponderously and with a kind of absurd finality, so loading him down with burial as to make it clear that Nicodemus does not expect a resurrection any more than he expects a second birth. Throughout the gospel, then, Nicodemus appears as a man of inadequate faith and inadequate courage, and as such he represents a *group* that the author wishes to characterize in this way" (*Johannine Faith,* 40). See also Meeks, "The Man from Heaven," 55.

and to convince them to cross over from the synagogue to the Johannine community. First, there are a variety of more general indications in the Gospel. The Jewishness of John has been noted by many scholars and, in particular, the diversity of Judaism revealed in this Gospel. As has already been noted, one of the most Jewish and yet anti-Jewish aspects of the Gospel is the hostile use and distancing from "the Jews" throughout. Even when "the Jews" are not explicitly named (e.g., in 1:11), the message is clear that this is not the desirable group to belong to. A message such as this would have been much more meaningful directed toward those caught between the Johannine community and its Jewish counterpart than toward those already firmly within the bounds of a Christian Johannine community and clearly separated from Judaism. This argument also applies not so much to the quotation of Jewish scriptures in John as to the use of midrashic techniques for interpreting them. Chapter 6 remains the most fully explored example of this.[39] The midrashic content of vv. 31–33 (as well as vv. 49–51, 58) is directed to an audience whose primary identity is Jewish. These verses are intent on shifting that audience from Moses and the manna in the wilderness to Jesus—the true bread from heaven (and the better consequences of that true bread): "Your fathers ate the manna in the wilderness and they died. This is the bread which comes down from heaven, that a man may eat of it and not die. I am the living bread" (vv. 49–51).[40] To secret Christian Jews the message would be clear: the Johannine Jesus offers them something better than they will find in the Jewish tradition.

Another way in which John seems to appeal to those people who are straddling the fence between Judaism and the Christian Johannine community is in its comparison and contrast of Jesus with major Jewish heroes. In the first nine chapters of the Gospel one finds Jesus at various points contrasted with Jacob, Abraham, and Moses. Jesus' encounter with the Samaritan woman takes place by Jacob's well (4:4–6), and in the misunderstanding over living water the Samaritan woman asks Jesus (v. 12): "Are you greater

[39] It focuses especially on vv. 31–33, where Jesus alters the biblical view from "Moses gave (bread from heaven)," to "God gives (the true bread from heaven)." The midrash is carried out on a saying of Jesus (v. 31) and includes an interpretation of the subject to whom the pronoun "he" refers and a repointing of the Hebrew verb to put it in the past tense (from the present participle *nōtēn* to *nātan*). For a much more detailed study of the midrashic character of chapter 6, see Borgen, *Bread from Heaven;* see also Martyn, *History and Theology,* 125–28.

[40] I am aware of arguments for literary stages in the compositon of John—in particular, arguments that at an earlier stage or even in a pre-gospel phase of the Johannine community the message of this community was directed to Jews and that consequently one sees evidence of that in the Gospel. The midrash in chapter 6 may well reflect such a stage. However, material that seems to make a hortatory appeal to secret Christian Jews cannot all be relegated to earlier stages, and it is entirely plausible that material which was originally directed to a Jewish audience was included in the later redaction of the Gospel precisely because it could be poignantly directed to an intended audience of Christian Jews.

than our father Jacob, who gave us the well?" This is of course an ironic question,[41] and Jesus tells her (vv. 13–14): "Every one who drinks of this water (from the well of Jacob) will thirst again, but whoever drinks of the water that I shall give him will never thirst." The figures of Abraham and especially Moses serve purposes other than simply contrast with Jesus in this Gospel. Nevertheless, Jesus' superiority is made quite evident. In a discussion with the Jews in chapter 8, another ironic question emerges (vv. 52–53): "Abraham died, as did the prophets; and you say, 'If any one keeps my word, he will never taste death.' Are you greater than our father Abraham, who died?"[42] Of the three biblical heroes, Moses has the most complex role in John.[43] But he is also contrasted with Jesus, as one can see from the midrash in chapter 6. The manna linked with Moses in the wilderness does not offer what Jesus offers as the living bread from heaven (vv. 49–51): "Your fathers ate the manna in the wilderness, and they died. . . . I am the living bread. . . if any one eats of this bread, he will live for ever. . . ." Each of these biblical heroes is connected with death or only temporary sustenance, whereas Jesus is connected with life and eternal sustenance. The meaning of such contrasts between Jesus and the biblical heroes of Judaism is evident also in 1:17: "For the law was given through Moses; grace and truth came through Jesus Christ." The Johannine Jesus (and, consequently, Johannine Christianity) has something better to offer than what Judaism can offer. To closet Christian Jews, such contrasts would point out the limitations of their Judaism next to what Christianity offers and encourage them to leave their Judaism behind.

Finally, a very significant passage that points to an intended audience of those straddling the fence between Judaism and the Johannine Christian community is chapter 9, the healing of the blind man. Chapter 9 can be divided into seven distinct scenes.[44] Verses 1–7 establish the setting, the miracle, and its demonstration and include disciples, "a man blind from his birth," and Jesus. Verses 8–12 portray the neighbors questioning the man born blind about the miracle. There is division (confusion really) among the neighbors about the identity of the man born blind. In this scene the man

[41] Culpepper points out, "The most common device employed by the evangelist [for irony], however, is the unanswered question, often based on a false assumption, in which the character suggests or prophesies the truth without knowing it" (*Anatomy,* 176).

[42] Jesus' superiority is further played out in the ensuing verses and when Jesus finally says to them (v. 58): "Truly, truly, I say to you, before Abraham was, I am."

[43] See T. Francis Glasson, *Moses in the Fourth Gospel* (Naperville, Ill.: Allenson, 1963); W. A. Meeks, *The Prophet-King* (Leiden: Brill, 1967).

[44] The most thorough study of these scenes and their possible historical context is presented by Martyn (*History and Theology,* 24–62). A recent and very intriguing analysis of the significance of chapter 9 and the issue of sin is presented by Rensberger (*Johannine Faith,* chap. 2: "Nicodemus and the Blind Man: Choices of Faith and Community," 37–51).

born blind refers to Jesus as "the man called Jesus" (v. 11). Verses 13–17 describe the questioning of the man born blind by the Pharisees. There is division among the Pharisees regarding Jesus (and the miracle), the implication being that some find Jesus to be a "sinner" while others find him to be a man from God. When asked, the man born blind identifies Jesus as "a prophet" (v. 17).

The fourth scene, in vv. 18–23, portrays a questioning of the man's parents by "the Jews."[45] The characters include the Jews (not the Pharisees!), the parents, and, by inference, the man born blind (though he does not speak). The Jews ask the parents whether or not this is their son, whether their son was really born blind, and how he now sees. The parents acknowledge that this is indeed their son, that he was really born blind, but they refuse to touch the third issue, deferring to the son (vv. 20–21). In v. 22 we are given the reason why they will not address the issue of how their son now sees: "His parents said this because they feared the Jews, for the Jews had already agreed that if any one should confess him to be Christ, he was to be put out of the synagogue." It would seem that the parents are closet Christian Jews who fear being put out of the synagogue if they identify Jesus as "Christ."

Verses 24–34 describe a second questioning of the man born blind by unnamed Jewish authorities. This scene seems to refer back to the first interrogation by the Pharisees (vv. 13–17). It echoes the themes of sin and man from God; it continues the discussion of who Jesus is (from vv. 13–17) and involves only the Pharisees(?) and the man born blind. Finally, in a resolution of the division among the Pharisees over whether Jesus is a man from God or a sinner, the man born blind makes it clear that he knows Jesus is a man from God (v. 33).[46] At that moment the Pharisees "cast him out," as one "born in utter sin."

In vv. 35–38, Jesus reenters the drama upon hearing that the man born blind has been cast out. In this scene, unlike the previous scenes, it is Jesus who does the questioning of the man born blind. Jesus reveals himself as

[45] It is interesting that this scene involves "the Jews," whereas the previous scene involved the Pharisees (as does the final scene); the next scene refers back to "they" (only this is seemingly not the Jews but the Pharisees). Von Wahlde makes a compelling case for the different terminology in 9:13–41 as representative of different literary strata ("Terms for Religious Authorities," 248–51). This suggests that if this scene represents a later stratum, integrated into already developed scenes involving the Pharisees, this scene involving the man born blind's parents is very significant at this later stage of the Gospel. One surmises that the parents represent secret and fearful Christian Jews and that this scene directs a potent message to this intended audience.

[46] Some of the same themes—e.g., man (teacher) from God (3:2), confrontation with the Pharisees (7:48–52), a faith that gets its start from signs and the interpretation of what these signs mean about Jesus (3:2)—are present, though used differently in the scenes involving Nicodemus. Haenchen looks at some of the similarities between the Nicodemus encounter in chapter 3 and chapter 9 (*John 2,* 35–42).

"Son of Man," and the man responds, "Lord, I believe" (v. 38). Verses 39–41 follow, with a description of the Pharisees questioning Jesus, the ironic question of the Pharisees ("Are we also blind?" [v. 40]) and Jesus' deeper and more provocative response (v. 41).

An important feature of this seven-scene drama is that Jesus is present only in three of the scenes (vv. 1–7, 35–38, and 39–41).[47] How is it that the man born blind comes to a progressively stronger faith (from "the man called Jesus" in v. 7 to "Lord" in v. 38)? "What is especially significant about the blind man's progressive christological enlightenment is the circumstances under which it develops. He reaches deeper understanding, not in a reflective encounter with Jesus, as Thomas and the Samaritan woman do, but in the process of *confrontation* with the Pharisees."[48] Two things should be said about this confrontation. The issue on which the confrontation centers is the interpretation of Jesus' performance of the miracle (sign) and what this means about who he is. The man born blind is a positive example of one whose faith grows genuinely out of a sign.[49] Second, the confrontation creates a polarity between the Pharisees, who cast the man born blind out, and the man born blind, whose faith develops fully in the course of the drama. He is aligned with Jesus and therefore epitomizes the proper response to the synagogue and to the threat of being cast out. The point of the story seems to be that good things come to those who are cast out of the synagogue. Or, put in the position of the man born blind, one should choose as he did, to confess his faith publicly and not to fear being cast out. For Jesus does not abandon those who are cast out of the synagogue, and the faith of the man born blind develops even further after he is cast out.

Although such a drama would prove reassuring for those already squarely in the Johannine Christian community, it would carry a much more potent message to those caught between the synagogue (the Pharisees and the Jews) and the Johannine community (the man born blind and Jesus). The parents of the man born blind (and perhaps even those secret believers among the Pharisees [v. 16]) are being exhorted here to follow the example of their fellow Jew and not to fear the consequences of publicly confessing their faith. If, as seems likely, vv. 18–23 have been added into the drama involving the Pharisees, the man born blind, and Jesus, at a later stage, then the intrusive force of such a centrally located scene is not such that it would be lost upon an intended audience for the Gospel of John. The negative portrayal of the parents, caught between the Jewish authorities and their own son, and yet who will not confront the Jews for fear of being put out of the

[47] Rensberger, *Johannine Faith,* 42.

[48] Ibid., 46.

[49] This reminds us of the carefully maintained tension in the Gospel of John between signs as an incipient basis for genuine faith and signs as leading to at best a superficial faith, not to be trusted. There are Jews who fit both of these categories in the Gospel.

synagogue, delivers a most powerful message to those whom the parents represent: closet Christian Jews. Their own stance is shown to be shamefully inadequate, and the example of the man born blind is held up for them to follow.

I began this inquiry into one purpose and one intended audience of the Gospel of John by noting the seemingly contradictory evaluations of scholars, some of whom find a missionary purpose, others of whom find that the Gospel is directed to an audience of insiders. Although one intended audience of the Gospel was most likely made up of insiders, those well within the bounds of the Johannine Christian community, another intended audience is represented by characters such as Nicodemus, Joseph of Arimathea, and the parents of the man born blind. These are all characters about whom there is some ambiguity in the Gospel. In fact, often the message to those whom they represent is not to do as they do. Rather, they are exhorted to come out of the closet, even if this means leaving their Judaism behind, because the Christianity of the Johannine community can offer them something more. Should one think of this intended audience as insiders? Surely not, when compared with those firmly within the Johannine community, those whose primary identity was clearly Christian. On the other hand, these closet Christian Jews had a foot in the door—they must have had some connections with the Johannine community—even though they were admittedly on the fringe. To the extent that they were incipient Christians and that the Gospel holds out hope that they could be brought along to a deeper faith, they were insiders. Perhaps, however, as John seems to have an edifying message for insiders, and as these are characters who are pictured most ambiguously, we would be better off thinking in terms of a missionary intent toward these closet Christian Jews. After all, their primary identity was as Jews. Although the insider versus missionary debate is difficult to resolve when one is confronted with an intended audience of fence straddlers, it is clear that John makes a powerful hortatory appeal to these closet Christian Jews. One only wishes that history had preserved the appeal made by the other side.

22

Contending with God: The Death of Jesus and the Trial of Israel in Luke-Acts

DAVID L. TIEDE

LUKE'S NARRATIVE OF the death of Jesus is a theodicy, a justification of God's ways in the history of Jesus, Israel, and the early church. The same may be said generally of all Christian accounts of the crucifixion, but the term is more specific when applied to Luke-Acts because of its similarity in mode and genre to various histories of its day. These authors interpreted what had happened in terms of human and divine necessity, justice, virtue, mercy, and freedom. Luke joined a class of writers who drew on sacred traditions and eyewitness accounts to legitimate and interpret the significance of "the things which have been accomplished among us" (1:1–4). Luke's theodicy may be compared first with those narratives that testified to the benediction of the gods on the victories of the Greeks and Romans. Hellenistic historiography had its own understandings of "salvation history."

Luke's theodicy also belongs within "the old Jewish literary tradition."[1] This narrative imitates the prose of the scriptural histories and displays close dependence on the deuteronomistic understanding of history as the arena of repentance and restoration.[2] Israel's scriptures are distinctive in their convictions about how God works in history, not least because the Law,

[1] See Henry J. Cadbury, "The Greek and Jewish Traditions of Writing History," in *The Beginnings of Christianity*, ed. F. J. Foakes Jackson and Kirsopp Lake (5 vols.; London: Macmillan, 1920–33) 2:7–29; 2:121.

[2] See David P. Moessner, "Luke's Preview of the Journey of the Prophet Like Moses of Deuteronomy," *JBL* 102 (1983) 575–605; idem, "Paul in the Acts: Preacher of Eschatological Repentance to Israel," in *The Glory of Christ in the New Testament: Studies in Christology in Memory of George Bradford Caird*, ed. L. D. Hurst and N. T. Wright (Oxford: Clarendon, 1986).

Prophets, and Writings were largely composed and collected in the era of the exile, when the triumph of the adversaries was evident. Among the Hellenistic histories, Luke's narrative imitates and draws on literary and theological traditions that are particular to Israel's past.[3]

To describe Luke's project as a theodicy requires further analysis of the literary conventions, theological traditions, and social setting of the narrative. The force of any theodicy is immediately tied to the values, convictions, and interpreted experience of particular communities. Thus, Luke's place among the Hellenistic historians must be discerned with great care lest the content of his theodicy be misappropriated and misinterpreted. The dangers of perverting the social implications of Luke's narrative are real, especially if "Luke-Acts is a Jewish Christian story that fell into gentile hands.[4]

An assessment of Luke's distinctive theodicy provides a critical perspective on a cluster of issues that have been heavily debated in Lukan interpretation: the saving significance of Jesus' death in Luke's account, Jesus' death and the fate of Jerusalem, and Jesus' reign and the promise to Israel.

The Saving Significance of Jesus' Death

Luke's theology of the death of Jesus is distinct from that of the other Gospels. Interpreters have taken particular notice of Luke's neglect of traditional Christian emphases on the expiatory value of the crucifixion.[5] Those who use the standard of Mark or Paul to judge Luke's presentation of Jesus' death regularly find it to be deficient for proclaiming the forgiveness of sins. Reginald H. Fuller grasped Luke's soteriology more adequately by emphasizing the theodicy of Jesus' execution: "the remission of sins is the consequence of passion and resurrection. . . . Luke invariably interprets the resurrection as vindication."[6]

Luke's narrative no longer leaves Jesus' death shrouded in the Markan mysteries of its efficacy and Jesus' identity. Even Mark's messianic secret has

[3] See Thomas Louis Brodie, "Greco-Roman Imitation of Texts as a Partial Guide to Luke's Use of Sources," in *Luke-Acts: New Perspectives from the Society of Biblical Literature Seminar,* ed. Charles H. Talbert (New York: Crossroad, 1984) 26–34; William S. Kurz, "Hellenistic Rhetoric in the Christological Proof of Luke-Acts," *CBQ* 42 (1980) 171–95; Eckhard Plümacher, *Lukas als hellenistischer Schriftsteller* (SUNT 9; Göttingen: Vandenhoeck & Ruprecht, 1972).

[4] David L. Tiede, "'Glory to Thy People, Israel': Luke-Acts and the Jews," in *The Social World of Formative Christianity and Judaism: Essays in Tribute to Howard Clark Kee,* ed. J. Neusner et al. (Philadelphia: Fortress Press, 1988) 327.

[5] Hans Conzelmann states: "Nor is there any direct soteriological significance drawn from Jesus' suffering and death" (*The Theology of St. Luke* [New York: Harper & Row, 1960] 201).

[6] R. H. Fuller, "Luke and the Theologia Crucis," in *Sin, Salvation, and the Spirit,* ed. D. Durken (Collegeville: Liturgical Press, 1979) 216–17.

been transformed. In Luke, Jesus' identity and mission are clear, and he dies knowingly obedient to God's will. The only secret is why the Messiah must die at all. Many have argued that Jesus' death has been reduced either to a martyrdom or to a sadly unavoidable prelude to exaltation. In either case, Luke's emphasis on the resurrection appears to some to be more of a theodicy of glory, vindicating the Christian triumph, than a confrontation with the depth of human sin or the powers of evil.[7]

But Luke is not merely a revision of Mark, and more is at stake than a displacement of Mark's theology of the cross. Richard Glöckner has explored Luke's emphasis on God's mission of exalting the lowly, demonstrating that God's determined will is a force with which the self-righteous contend in this narrative. This conflict between divine and human wills reaches its climax in the death of Jesus.[8] Jerome Kodell shows further that Jesus' death is not a mere martyrdom. It "has meaning in itself as the confrontation of human sinfulness by lowliness, which in God's plan is the state of openness to divine salvation."[9]

Confrontation, contention, and rejection persist from the beginning to the end of Luke-Acts. Norman Petersen insists that "the rejection of God's agents by God's people in connection with God's sanctuaries (synagogues and temple) is the plot device by which the movement of the narrative as a whole is motivated."[10] In fact, the protagonists (God, the angels, Jesus, the apostles) uncover and prompt both rejection and reception.

The angelic visitations to Zechariah and Mary are divine initiatives, provoking differing responses of disbelief and faith (Luke 1). Simeon's oracles both reveal God's determined will to save and glorify Israel (2:29–32) and disclose the rejection that awaits the infant Messiah (2:33–35). Jesus' declaration of his mission in Nazareth immediately prompts rejection and hostility (Luke 4:14–30). The mild reproof of Jesus by "certain Pharisees" at his arrival in Jerusalem evokes a harsh oracle of judgment for not knowing the "time of your visitation" (19:38–44), and the disagreement among Paul's fellow Jews in Rome causes him to invoke a severe prophetic judgment (Acts 28:23–29).

The speeches in Acts explicate this plot with a strong emphasis on God's initiative. The wise Gamaliel perceives the danger of harassing the apostles and cautions the sanhedrin, "If it is of God, you will not be able to overthrow

[7] Jerome Kodell provides an excellent summary of this discussion, which has persisted since the work of Martin Dibelius, Hans Conzelmann, and Ernst Käsemann in "Luke's Theology of the Death of Jesus," in *Sin, Salvation, and the Spirit,* ed. Durken, 221–30.

[8] R. Glöckner, *Die Verkündigung des Heils beim Evangelisten Lukas* (Walberger Studien, Theologische Reihe 9; Mainz: Grünewald, 1976) 155–95.

[9] Kodell, "Luke's Theology," 229.

[10] N. R. Petersen, *Literary Criticism for New Testament Critics* (Guides to Biblical Scholarship; Philadelphia: Fortress Press, 1978) 83.

them. You might even be found opposing God" (5:39). So also Peter must accede to God's will in the conversion of Cornelius because, "who was I that I could withstand God" (11:17), and Paul recalls his confrontation with the exalted Lord as a consequence of his "opposing the name of Jesus of Nazareth" (26:9–20).

The problem of history for Luke is anchored in the conviction that God's determined will encounters rejection and faith in the arena of human history. This theodicy is not original with Luke. Abraham Heschel says of Israel's prophets, "History is where God is defied, where His judgment is enacted, and where His kingship is to be established."[11] So also in 2 Maccabees, divine vengeance is an inescapable consequence for those who have tried God's justice by killing the righteous because God's righteous reign is an active force. The sixth son who is martyred does not claim to be guiltless, but he warns his executioners, "Do not think that you will go unpunished for having tried to fight against God" (7:19).

In Luke's story, God's determined will and plan is never an abstract determinism, nor is it merely a moral appeal to a quality such as lowliness. Robert J. Karris has written a perceptive study of the centurion's verdict on Jesus death in which he argues that "*dikaios* does not mean innocent, but means righteous."[12] Of course Jesus was a model of lowliness and innocence, but more critically he was the agent of God's righteous rule.

Those who attack the righteous are also testing God. The logic is explicit in Wis 2:17–24, where the ungodly test the righteous who is God's son with insult, torture, and shameful death only to discover that they have been ignorant of God's secret purposes and now are contending with God. As Richard J. Dillon says, "the centurion's *dikaios* is, in fact, the *messianic victor* about to be vindicated by God in spite of human onslaught against him (Acts 3:14–15)."[13]

The saving significance of Jesus' death in Luke is not invested in its expiation for sin. This death is rather portrayed within God's strategy for Israel, revealing both God's judgment and saving rule. The crucifixion is a predicted consequence of God's anointing "Jesus of Nazareth with the Holy Spirit and with power" (Acts 10:38). This salvation of this "Savior" is directly linked to God's initiative, which surpasses the reign of the Roman emperor or any other benefactors of humanity who claim divine authorization for their mighty acts in history (see Luke 2:11; Acts 5:31; 13:23).[14]

[11] A. Heschel, *The Prophets* (New York: Harper & Row, 1962) 190–91.

[12] R. J. Karris, "Luke 23:47 and the Lucan View of Jesus' Death," *JBL* 105 (1986) 65–74.

[13] R. J. Dillon, *From Eye-Witnesses to Ministers of the Word: Tradition and Composition in Luke 24* (AnBib 82; Rome: Biblical Institute Press, 1978) 101.

[14] Joseph A. Fitzmyer, *The Gospel According to Luke I–IX* (AB 28; Garden City, N.Y.: Doubleday, 1981) 222–23; see also Frederick W. Danker, *Benefactor: Epigraphic Study of a Graeco-Roman and New Testament Semantic Field* (St. Louis: Clayton, 1982). Jerome Neyrey

God's initiative in the reign of this Savior is not immediately salvific in the crucifixion. Jesus' death is a confrontation, in which God's will is tried. Those who resist the king's reign (see 19:11–27) or kill the royal heir (20:9–19) place themselves in grave peril, testing God's forbearance. Even Peter's announcement that in the resurrection "God has made him both Lord and Christ, this Jesus whom you crucified" is heard first as threat (Acts 2:36–37). Luke's theodicy insists that God's righteous rule was profoundly challenged in the death of the "Messiah of God, his Chosen One . . . the King of the Jews" who was truly "the righteous one" (Luke 23:35–38, 47).

Jesus' Death and the Fate of Jerusalem

Only Luke relates Jesus' dire oracles as he wept for the fate of Jerusalem on his arrival and rejection (19:41–44; see also 13:34–35) and to the "daughters of Jerusalem," who bewailed and lamented him on his way to be executed (23:27–31). The literary significance of these oracles is to alert the reader that Jesus is not tragically blind to or ignorant of what lies ahead, but those around him are, especially his own disciples and the people.[15] The Messiah explicitly identifies the focus of greatest anguish to be not on him alone as he dies but on the peril of his death for all those who surround him. Jesus will die in the assurance of committing his spirit to the Father (23:46), but his prayer will be for those who crucify him, because they do not know what they do (23:34).[16]

One of the most poignant lines in the narrative distinguishes "the people" who "stood by watching" from "the rulers" who "scoffed at him saying, 'He saved others, let him save himself, if (or sarcastically "since") he is the Messiah of God, his Chosen One'" (23:35). The rulers are strictly adversaries, filled with blind rage, but ironically identifying Jesus correctly. In Luke's view, they have misunderstood the consequences of his identity and therefore have not understood the "utterances of the prophets" and have "fulfilled these by condemning him" (Acts 13:27).

---

offers helpful comments on Jesus' obedience and faith as a "saved Savior" in his death (*The Passion According to Luke* [New York: Paulist, 1985] 129–55). Neyrey, however, sees only the exemplary character of Jesus' death to the neglect of Luke's testimony to God's righteous reign and rule being established in this "Savior" who is obedient to God's determined will.

[15] See David L. Tiede, *Prophecy and History in Luke-Acts* (Philadelphia: Fortress Press, 1980) 65–125.

[16] The textual authenticity of v. 34 remains a difficulty, but Luke's repeated comments on the "ignorance" of Israel broaden the base of this interpretation (see Acts 3:17; 13:27; 17:30; and 7:60). The argument for the inclusion of v. 34 will rest on internal grounds, but it is worth noting that its omission fits well with the anti-Judaic bias of the Western text. See E. J. Epp, *The Theological Tendency of Codex Bezae Cantabrigiensis in Acts* (SNTSMS 3; Cambridge: Cambridge University Press, 1966).

The opposition of the rulers is not simple ignorance. They gather Israel in opposition "against the Lord and against his Anointed" (see Acts 4:26–27; Ps 2:1–2). The tragedy, therefore, grows deeper because these rulers have also implicated "the people" or "those who live in Jerusalem" (Acts 4:27; 13:27). The complicity of the "people" is culpable in Luke, but much more passive, just as Judas's active betrayal (see 22:4, 22) may be distinguished from Peter's denial (22:31–34, 54–62)—but both are guilty. So the failure of the people to continue to defend Jesus before Pilate's court is not the same as the plots on his life by the temple leadership.

As the people stand by "watching" at the cross, they have not yet truly "seen" what is happening, but neither are they crying out against Jesus, as they did three times when their will to protect him (see Luke 19:48, 20:6, 26; 22:2, 6) was tried in Pilate's court (see 23:14–25). Like Peter, who was warned by Jesus yet denied him three times and went out and wept bitterly (chap. 22), the people bewail and lament him as he goes to his execution (23:27), watch the specter in silence (23:35), and return home at his death "beating their breasts" (23:48).

When Jesus dies, the reader shares the privileged position of the narrator and God, observing all the human actors in various levels of ignorance and insight. Only the centurion and Jesus' followers who stood at a distance have truly "seen" (23:47, 49: ἰδών, ὁρῶσαι), but the multitudes who had assembled to "see the sight" (23:35, 48: θεωρεῖν) have now at least observed enough to return home beating their breasts. The risen Messiah will be required to open the scriptures before even his followers will fully understand (24:13–35), but at his death the multitudes do not gloat. Whatever they have "seen," they already know that it requires their repentance (23:27, 28, 35, 48).

Within the narrative, Luke's theodicy is an exposition of the "visitation" of God's reign in Israel. The purpose of this divine initiative was prophetically discerned as God's salvation and the forgiveness of Israel's sins (1:67–79). But the tragedy that evokes the tears of the Messiah is that Jerusalem (Israel) "did not know the time of your visitation" (19:44). The first consequence of the initiation of God's reign in the Messiah's mission, therefore, was lamentable for Jerusalem and Israel.

Within the real world of Luke's era, this message could never be merely a tale well told. It was a diagnosis of why Jerusalem had been destroyed. This theodicy was a social commentary, justifying God's ways in the horrendous "days of vengeance" in which Jerusalem was "trodden down by the Gentiles" (21:22, 24). Luke's presentation of Jesus as the Savior, Messiah of God, God's Chosen One, and King of the Jews had to explicate the twin mysteries of why the Messiah had been crucified and why Jerusalem had been destroyed. Both were brutal facts. Neither could be understood without reference to Israel's scriptural understanding of history as the arena of repentance and restoration.

Jesus' Reign and the Promise to Israel

Israel's understanding of history was imbued with repentance, but even the prophetic and deuteronomistic interpretations of the Babylonian exile debated its exact content. Various Jewish groups in the era of Roman occupation offered differing definitions of faithfulness, from proper observance of temple ritual to courageous revolt against the oppressor, fidelity to the Torah, and fidelity to the reign of the Messiah from Nazareth. Once Jerusalem had been destroyed by Rome, all who read Israel's scriptures could agree that restoration could only follow repentance.[17] But of what must Israel repent? And does this theodicy of deserved divine judgment hold any hope of restoration even with repentance?

In Josephus's account of Titus's speech to besieged Jerusalem, the Roman general indicts the Jews for sins against Roman generosity (*Jewish War* 6.333). Titus insists that Vespasian graciously gave them time for repentance for such offenses against virtue (6.339), but now their fate was governed only by the laws of war and reprisal. Josephus affirmed Titus's severe theodicy, observing the convergence of "the power of God over unholy men and the fortune of the Romans" (6.399; see also §433).

2 Baruch also was written after the Roman destruction, projected back on the scriptural stories of the Babylonian triumph. *2 Baruch*, however, was confident God took no pleasure that "the idols in the cities of the nations are happy and the flavor of the smoke of the incense of the righteousness of the Law has been extinguished everywhere in the region of Zion" (67:6). The hope was that "after a short time, Zion will be rebuilt again, and the offerings will be restored, and the priests will again return to their ministry. And the nations will again come to honor it" (68:5–6); but first there must be repentance. The content of this repentance is not respect for Roman virtue, as Titus insisted, but return to the observance of the law of Moses, relying upon the mercy of the Mighty One (84:10). This is the way to full restoration (85:4), but even the time of repentance will have its end (85:12).

The content of repentance for Luke was faith in the Messiah, "this Jesus whom you crucified . . . whom God raised from the dead" (Luke 24:46; Acts 2:36–38; 3:12–15, 19–24; 4:10–12; 5:30–31; 10:39–43; 13:28–39). The resurrection of Jesus was God's gift of repentance unto faith, providing the means of forgiveness of sins (Luke 24:47; Acts 2:38; 3:19; 5:31; 10:43; 13:38–39; 26:18). The end of this divinely initiated process of repentance unto faith and forgiveness was "the gift of the Holy Spirit" (Luke 24:49; Acts 1:4–8), the fulfillment of God's promises to Israel, and finally the "restoration of all" (Acts 3:21; see also 2:38–39; 10:44; 11:18).

[17] David L. Tiede, *Jesus and the Future* (Cambridge/New York: Cambridge University Press, 1990).

Luke's conviction that Israel was contending with God in its history was thoroughly unremarkable in Jewish sources. Even understanding the destruction of Jerusalem as a divine verdict on sinful Israel was commonplace before and after the Roman conquest. But the identification of Israel's sin and the definition of Israel's required repentance varied sharply. Luke's judgment that the trial and death of Jesus were Israel's tragically defiant rejection of God's will and reign illumines the dying Messiah's oracles about the dire fate of Jerusalem. Most remarkable, however, is Luke's confidence that in this trial of Israel, God's will is indeflectably determined to accomplish Israel's salvation and restoration of her mission.

Luke's theodicy is not simply wrought at Israel's expense, as Titus's speech in Josephus. It goes beyond *2 Baruch*'s reliance on God's mercy by stressing God's action in raising Jesus as direct proffering of repentance unto forgiveness. In contrast to Mark, Luke declined to invest Jesus' death with expiatory efficacy. Like both *2 Baruch* and Mark, Luke saw the destruction of Jerusalem as an event of apocalyptic significance in the divine scheme of history, but Luke interpreted the death and resurrection of Jesus as God's means to fulfill the scriptural promises in the face of human opposition.

For Luke, the destruction of Jerusalem was a sign of divine vengeance (see also Luke 21:22) for Israel's rejection of the reign of God's Messiah, requiring repentance. Because "those who live in Jerusalem" had tragically failed to "know the time of your visitation" (Acts 4:27; Luke 19:44), God was justified in judgment. But the present time was an era of renewed promise, restoring Israel's glory and vocation of preaching "repentance and forgiveness of sins . . . in his name to all nations, beginning in Jerusalem" (Luke 24:47).

Luke's theodicy did not merely vindicate the Roman triumph or portend the wrath to come. This testimony to God's determined will was confident of God's promises to Israel, even when messianic Israel often received a better hearing from Gentiles than from Jews (Acts 28) and even after Jerusalem had been "trodden down by the Gentiles . . . until the times of the Gentiles" were fulfilled (Luke 21:24). The problem of history for Luke was not merely to justify God's vengeance but to understand God's determined will to bless. In Jesus' death, Israel had indeed been "found opposing God," for which repentance was required. In raising Jesus from the dead, however, God was contending for Israel's restoration.

23

Community of Goods in Acts: Idealization or Social Reality?

S. SCOTT BARTCHY

I

IN HIS COMMENTARY on the Acts of the Apostles, Hans Conzelmann claims that Luke's depiction of the sharing of goods by the first generation of Christians in Jerusalem is "idealized" and fictional.[1] Thus Luke's portrayal of these Christians "should not be taken as historical," "despite the existence of communistic groups in the vicinity of Jerusalem" (by which he is referring at least to the Essene settlement at Qumran). If such sharing had actually been the norm for those Christians, Conzelmann insists that "some sort of organized means of support would have been necessary, as in those groups."[2]

Apparently, Conzelmann is convinced that apart from sharing in the means of production of crops and goods, as seems to have been the case at Qumran, there could have been no Christian "community of goods" worthy of that description. In any case, from this claim that there is no historical

[1] An earlier version of this article was read at the annual meeting of the Pacific Coast Region of the Society of Biblical Literature, March 1989. During my research and revising, I gratefully received important suggestions from K. C. Hanson and financial assistance from the Westwood Christian Foundation.

H. Conzelmann, *Acts of the Apostles* (Hermeneia; Philadelphia: Fortress Press, 1987) 24. For a useful history of the interpretation of the relevant passages in Acts 2 and 4, see B. H. Mönning, "Die Darstellung des Urchristlichen Kommunismus nach der Apostelgeschichte des Lukas" (Diss., Göttingen, 1978).

[2] Conzelmann, *Acts,* 24. In his *History of Primitive Christianity* (New York: Abingdon, 1973) 36, Conzelmann notes the absence in Acts of "the one necessary mark of any communistic community: such can exist only if not only consumption is communally regulated but, above all, production is organized."

basis for Luke's description, Conzelmann concludes: "Thus we cannot speak of a 'failure of the experiment,' nor can we draw conclusions for a primitive Christian communistic ideal."[3] Conzelmann urges us not to speak of a "failure" precisely because there was no such "experiment"!

In addition, Conzelmann asserts that "Luke does not present this way of life as a norm for the organization of the church in his own time. It is meant as an illustration of the uniqueness of the ideal earliest days of the movement."[4]

Each of these assertions is quite vulnerable to challenge. For example, in light of the strong emphasis in Luke's Gospel on sharing goods and property, it seems highly unlikely that Luke had no interest in presenting "this way of life as a norm" for the church in his own time or that he was motivated to compose the two summaries regarding a sharing of goods only to illustrate the unique, ideal beginnings of the Christian movement.

II

If not on the basis of historical reports, on what kind of sources, if any, did Luke base his summary statements in Acts 2 and 4? According to Conzelmann, Luke worked from reports of such rare generosity as that of Joseph Barnabas (4:36–37) and (negatively) of Ananias and Sapphira (5:1–11), which he then generalized as if such sharing had been characteristic behavior for all the Christians in Jerusalem. For his summary descriptions Luke then drew on his knowledge of so-called communistic groups, "whether real (Essenes and the Qumran community) or ideal"—for example, the original community of Pythagoreans, about whom Iamblichus later (ca. 300 C.E.) commented: "For all things were common and the same to all, and no one possessed anything privately" (*De vita Pythagorica* 30.167).[5]

Luke's motive for presenting the earliest Christians in such idealized terms, according to Conzelmann, was to make clear to his readers that in their earliest days these Christians were no less admirable than the citizens of primeval Athens (as described and esteemed by Plato) or than the original Pythagoreans. For, notes Conzelmann, "idealized communal portraits are associated with utopian dreams or accounts of primeval times."[6]

Yet where can confirming evidence be found elsewhere in Acts to support Conzelmann's claim that Luke intended to present the early days of the Jewish Christians in Jerusalem as a "primeval time" or a "golden age" of the

[3] Conzelmann, *Acts*, 24.

[4] Ibid.

[5] In the next section (30.168) he emphasized again that "they held their property in common."

[6] Conzelmann, *Acts*, 24.

Christian movement?[7] To be sure, there is much evidence in chapters 2 and 4 that it was indeed important to Luke to describe the life of these Christians in glowing terms that would call forth the high respect of any person acquainted with Greek ideals. Yet these texts present no basis for reading them with reference to a "golden age" associated with the Pythagoreans rather than in the context of the everyday ideals for friendship advocated by Aristotle.

III

The Greek proverb κοίνα τὰ φιλῶν ("the belongings of friends are held in common") is reported with approval by Plato, Aristotle, Cicero, and Philo.[8] Aristotle claims that "all the proverbs agree with this: 'Friends have one soul between them' and 'Friends' goods are common property'" (*Nicomachean Ethics* 9.8.1168b 6ff.) The fact that Luke uses language that evoked memories of such ideals in many of his readers does not, however, in itself imply that there was no historical basis for Luke's report. Conzelmann himself observes that Josephus (*Antiquities of the Jews* 15.10.4 §371) compares the Essenes to the Pythagoreans, without in any way suggesting that the Essenes never really shared their goods.[9]

Furthermore, Conzelmann carefully notes, apparently ignoring Acts 27:3, that two of the ancient catchwords characteristic of such idealization cannot be found in Luke as a designation for the community, namely, ἰσότης ("equality") and φίλοι ("friends"). Yet even if Luke had thus employed these terms, it would be difficult to argue that they had no positive relationship to everyday social behavior in the early Christian movement. For the term ἰσότης does appear in Paul's language in one of his letters to the Corinthian Christians, by which he exhorts them to share their goods with the Christians in Jerusalem: "as a matter of equality (ἰσότητος) your abundance at the present time should supply their want, so that their abundance may supply your want, that there may be equality (ἰσότης). As it is written [Exod 16:18], 'He who gathered much had nothing over, and he who gathered little had no lack'" (2 Cor 8:14–15 RSV). This passage has frequently been overlooked in relation to Acts 2 and 4, especially by scholars who have sought to stress

[7] Without citing any further evidence, R. I. Pervo (*Profit with Delight: The Literary Genre of the Acts of the Apostles* [Philadelphia: Fortress Press, 1987] 69–70) echoes Conzelmann while stressing the "utopian coloration" of the "idealistic fiction" in Luke's first two summaries. For a recent alternative approach to this material, see G. Lüdemann, *Early Christianity according to the Traditions in Acts* (Minneapolis: Fortress Press, 1989) 60–63.

[8] Plato *Republic* 5.46 2c; Cicero *De officiis* 1.16.51 (referring to a Greek proverb: "Amicorum esse communia omnia"); Philo *Quod omnis probus liber sit* 75–86.

[9] Conzelmann, *Acts,* 24; idem, *History,* 36.

the experimental and temporary character of the sharing among the Christians in Jerusalem.

What, then, are the characteristic terms for the community and for the sharing of goods that Luke uses? ἡ κοινωνία (2:42); ἦσαν ἐπὶ τὸ αὐτὸ καὶ εἶχον ἅπαντα κοινά (2:44); ἅπαντα κοινά and ἦν καρδία καὶ ψυχὴ μία (4:32) (yet this is also a common Hebrew idiom).[10] With the following evidence and arguments I seek to show that Luke employs Greek utopian language as part of his description, not of what he wished had happened or of what he fantasized in order to edify his readers but of what he believed actually had taken place among the Jewish Christians in Jerusalem. He had a substantial cultural context for such a conviction.

IV

Since Josephus uses similar utopian language to describe the praxis of the Essenes (presumably at the Qumran settlement), it seems significant to note that no scholar known to me has suggested that a community of goods in some form was never practiced at Qumran. Josephus comments that the Essenes despise wealth and have everything in common, appointing special stewards to handle their affairs (*Jewish War* 2.8.3 §§122–23; see 1QS v.1–2, 12).

Conzelmann points to the "organized means of support" (through sharing in the means of production of crops and goods) that has been claimed to characterize the life of the Essenes at Qumran. Yet when comparing the evidence from the Dead Sea Scrolls and from Acts for "having things in common," it is essential to observe that the Essene documents tell us nothing about *how* this group supported itself. As G. Vermes astutely remarks, only from the remains discovered at Qumran can we conclude that they "farmed, made pots, cured hides, and reproduced manuscripts."[11] If we did not have such archaeological support, in the absence of textual evidence for how these Essenes actually supported themselves, would many scholars, including Conzelmann, argue that the group at Qumran never really shared their goods and that their writing about it was utopian fantasy?

V

In the absence of archaeological evidence for the means by which the Jewish Christians in Jerusalem supported themselves and shared their goods, as Luke claims, I suggest that we will most profitably seek the content

[10] See Deut 6:5; 10:12; 11:13, 18; 13:4.

[11] G. Vermes, *The Dead Sea Scrolls: Qumran in Perspective* (rev. ed.; Philadelphia: Fortress Press, 1977) 89.

of the phrase "having all things in common" in an analysis of first-century Mediterranean kin groups and of the relations between patrons in such groups and their clients, whereby I propose that the Jewish Christians in Jerusalem regarded themselves (and certainly were regarded by Luke) as a so-called fictive kin group, that is, a group practicing general reciprocity not based on blood ties.[12] Some of the characteristics of such a group are loyalty and trust, truth telling, homes open to all in the group, obligation to be certain that the needs of everyone in the group are met (generalized reciprocity),[13] and a sense of shared destiny.

Loyalty and trust. In the first century there was no such thing as a sense of the "kinship of all human beings," that is, a universal social commitment or loyalty to all people. Loyalty was to blood and kin.

> [Beyond this group] all people were presumed dishonorable, guilty unless proved otherwise, a presumption based on the agonistic quality of competition for the scarce commodity, honor. . . . No one outside the family of blood can be trusted until and unless that trust can be validated and verified. So men of the same village or town who are not blood relatives relate to each other with an implied deep distrust which in practice prevents any effective form of cooperation.[14]

Truth telling. Since loyalty and truth telling were owed only to kin, no obligation existed to tell the truth to outsiders. "The right to the truth only exists where respect is due, that is to the family and superiors. . . . It is honorable to lie in order to deceive an 'outsider' who has no right to the truth."[15]

Open homes to all in the fictive kin group. In his pathbreaking book *The New Testament World: Insights from Cultural Anthropology*, Bruce Malina describes the ideal man in first-century Mediterranean cultures:

> [He] maintains a culturally predictable, transparent, socially open existence. What this means is that he lives in a way that allows others to know what he is up to. . . . One way of showing this openness, to reveal that he is no threat to others, is to allow children to roam freely in and out of his house, workplace, or any other situation that might harbor a secret threat to others. . . . Another form of signaling such openness—giving others the

[12] See J. Pitt-Rivers, "Pseudo-Kinship," *International Encyclopedia of the Social Sciences*, ed. D. L. Sills (New York: Macmillan, 1968) 8:408–13. The community at Qumran, of course, was also a fictive kin group; this group practiced particularly stringent social boundaries.

[13] B. J. Malina, *Christian Origins and Cultural Anthropology* (Atlanta: John Knox, 1986) 101–6; see also M. Sahlins, *Stone Age Economics* (Chicago: Aldine-Atherton, 1972).

[14] B. J. Malina and J. H. Neyrey, "Honor and Shame in Luke-Acts: Pivotal Values of the Mediterranean World," in *The Social World of Luke-Acts: Models for Interpretation*, ed. J. Neyrey (Peabody, Mass.: Hendrickson, 1991) 32.

[15] Ibid., 37.

> opportunity to check up on one—is to keep the door to one's courtyard and/or house open when the village or neighborhood is up and about.[16]

Thus Malina concludes that "regular meeting in people's houses points to fictive kinship groups."[17] This brings to mind Luke's report of John Mark's mother opening her substantial home (with a gate) for meetings of the Christians (Acts 12:12). Evidently she and these Christians together had become a kin group.[18]

Obligation to be sure the needs of everyone in the group are met. Each member of a (fictive) kin group was obligated to provide assistance "without specification of some return obligation in terms of time, quantity, or quality. However, the expectation is always implied but left indefinite and open-ended."[19] Members with substantial resources were expected to function as patrons of the kin group.

In his stimulating study of patrons and clients in the Roman Empire, Luis Roniger describes the role of a patron as that of securing for his or her clients in both private and public affairs "all the tranquility of which they particularly stood in need . . . doing everything for them as fathers do for their sons with respect to money and to contracts that related to money."[20] This relationship between patrons and clients is well described by Halvor Moxnes: "a patron has instrumental, economic, and political resources and can therefore give support and protection. A client, in return, can give promises and expressions of solidarity and loyalty." Moxnes calls attention to the "strong element of solidarity in these relations, linked to personal honor and obligations. There may be a spiritual attachment, however ambivalent, between patrons and clients."[21]

Within the kin group, the honored patron functioned as a river of blessing for his people, his clients. His honor depended on his initiative in sharing his wealth rather than in hoarding it, in being a giver and not just a receiver of life's limited goods.[22]

[16] B. J. Malina, *The New Testament World: Insights from Cultural Anthropology* (Atlanta: John Knox, 1981) 77–78.

[17] B. J. Malina, "'Religion' in the World of Paul," *Biblical Theology Bulletin* 16 (1986) 99.

[18] See J. H. Elliott, *A Home for the Homeless: A Sociological Exegesis of 1 Peter* (Philadelphia: Fortress Press, 1981) 188–200.

[19] Malina, *Christian Origins*, 102.

[20] L. Roniger, "Modern patron–client relations and historical clientelism: some clues from ancient Republican Rome," *Archives européennes de sociologie* 24 (1983) 69.

[21] H. Moxnes, *The Economy of the Kingdom: Social Conflict and Economic Relations in Luke's Gospel* (Philadelphia: Fortress Press, 1988) 42.

[22] See Sahlins, *Stone Age Economics;* also S. N. Eisenstadt and L. Roniger, *Patrons, Clients, and Friends* (Cambridge: Cambridge University Press, 1984).

A sense of shared destiny. That such a sense prevailed in most extended families seems clear. This was true also for a fictive kin group in which patron–client relations were usually regarded as binding and long-range. Yet since they were entered into voluntarily by both patron and clients, such relations could also be abandoned (with the pain of shame) by either party.

VI

When this fictive-kinship understanding of interpersonal relationships is brought to the exegesis of Acts 2, 4, and 5, the texts describe recognizable social realities. In ignorance of this cultural context, exegetes commonly state that Luke presents the tradition about Joseph Barnabas's generosity for one of two reasons. Either his gift was one of the few specific acts known to Luke of a Jerusalem Christian's selling property for the benefit of the congregation there (and thus the only positive historical basis of his summaries regarding sharing of goods), or Luke regarded this information as a fitting way to introduce Joseph Barnabas to his readers, a man who in the narrative will soon play an important role as a coleader with Paul of Tarsus both in Antioch and in the mission to the west.

But if Joseph Barnabas is regarded first of all as one of the significant patrons in the Jewish Christian community in Jerusalem, Luke's focus on his generous behavior makes even more sense. It seems relatively certain that most of those belonging to this new fictive kin group did not own houses or lands that they could sell; rather they lived from day to day at the subsistence level—that is, although they owned relatively little, they usually were not "in need." Those disciples of Jesus who had come to Jerusalem from Galilee would most likely have had to resort to working as day laborers to earn their own living.

Although most of the disciples in Jerusalem would have had few resources that they could share with others, what they could share, of course, was their open homes, their loyalty and trust, truthfulness, a sense of shared destiny—that is, all the rich personal benefits of living as sisters and brothers in a kin group. Indeed, this easily presents itself as the social reality to which Luke refers with the phrases "being of one heart and soul" and "having everything in common."

Patrons such as Barnabas would have been relatively rare among the Jerusalem Christians; he was an owner of a field outside of Jerusalem (perhaps on Cyprus?), whose relative wealth and status as a Levite made him a natural patron in the Christian community. He sold that property in order to help those specifically in need among his clients, who as Christians were also his fictive brothers and sisters. By that act of sharing rather than hoarding, he functioned as a river of life for his people, and he maintained and augmented his honor as a patron.

Thus in contrast to the person in Jesus' parable of the Great Banquet (Luke 14:18) who could not come to the feast because of the field he had bought, Barnabas sold his field in order to contribute to the feast. And in contrast to the rich and pious ruler whose apparent need to control his wealth made it impossible for him to accept Jesus' invitation to cast his lot with Jesus' group of followers (Luke 18:18–25), Barnabas demonstrated that he had indeed cast his lot with Jesus' disciples by selling a field and making the proceeds available to his new kin group. By bringing all the proceeds to the apostles, Barnabas both demonstrated to his clients his truthfulness, openness, and solidarity and publicly honored the apostles (who in Jewish culture were probably his social and economic inferiors) as the superior patrons (and brokers) in the fictive kin group.[23]

On the other hand, Ananias and Sapphira, whose wealth also qualified them to function as patrons for the Jerusalem Christians, secretly hoarded part of the money they received from the sale of their property. Luke's narrative strongly suggests that not only Ananias but also Sapphira then claimed to have given the entire selling price to the apostles in order to meet pressing needs among those in the congregation. By making such a claim they openly were seeking the honor appropriate to a truthful and faithful patron, honor appropriate to one who functioned as a flowing river of life for his or her clients.

Yet by lying in order to achieve an honor they had not earned, Ananias and Sapphira not only dishonored and shamed themselves as patrons but also revealed themselves to be outsiders, non-kin. By not telling the truth, especially about a matter so central to their relationship with their fictive kin group, Sapphira and Ananias seriously violated the honor of the group.[24] In light of Luke's presentation of the creation of this fictive kin group as an act of God's Holy Spirit (see Acts 2:38–42), it makes sense for this couple's lying about their relation to the group, denying solidarity, and rejecting a shared destiny to be designated as lying to the Holy Spirit, as lying not to human beings but to God (5:3–4).

Luke's narrative stresses Sapphira's and Ananias's freedom to dispose of the property as they saw fit. They had freely entered the Jewish Christian community in Jerusalem; and although they would have brought shame on themselves if they had abandoned it, they could indeed have done so. When specific needs arose among the brothers and sisters of the congregation, no doubt those who were regarded as patrons, such as Barnabas, Ananias, and Sapphira, became especially aware of their expected role as benefactors. Yet

[23] For patrons acting as brokers, see B. J. Malina, "Patron and Client: The Analogy Behind Synoptic Theology," *Forum* 4 (1988) 2–32, esp. 11–13.

[24] See Juliet du Boulay, "Lies, mockery and family integrity," in *Mediterranean Family Structures*, ed. J. G. Peristiany (New York: Cambridge University Press, 1976) 389–405.

how they would respond remained in their control. That is why honor—or shame, or even death—could result from their actions.

As a faithful patron, Barnabas did not claim that his property was his alone; rather, he sought to protect the honor of his new fictive kin group precisely by functioning as a generous and honorable patron. Other Christians of lesser means would have protected the kin group's honor by opening their modest homes to each other, by loyalty and truth telling, and by sharing what they had so that no one among them was "in need."

That they did indeed bring such honor, even divine honor, to the Jewish Christians in Jerusalem is claimed by Luke in Acts 4:33: "And great grace was upon them all." One proof of God's blessing was the fact that (in the words of Deut 15:4) "there were no poor among them," or (in the words of Luke 4:34) "there was not a needy person among them." In his next summary statement Luke tells his readers that the people held the Jerusalem Christians "in high honor." "And more than ever believers were added to the Lord, multitudes both of men and women" (Acts 5:13 RSV).

Luke clearly intends to stimulate admiration among both Jews and Greeks for the Jewish Christians in Jerusalem by showing that they related to each other quite effectively as a fictive kin group. The sharing of their lives, including their property, was a social reality.[25]

To be sure, the fact that a group of Jews in Jerusalem, not related by blood, decided to share their lives as a fictive kin group is surely noteworthy but not in itself astonishing. What is especially remarkable, however, is the radical inclusiveness that characterized this kin group. Luke presents the climax of Peter's sermon on the day of Pentecost following the crucifixion of Jesus as an invitation addressed to those whom Peter held responsible for that crucifixion. He invited them to change their minds and the directions of their lives, to accept forgiveness from God and from the 120 persons in the core kin group, and to become family members of this new kin group. According to Acts 2:42, those former enemies who responded favorably were then quickly invited to share in the breaking of bread in the various homes and in the economic κοινωνία.

Soon thereafter, this push toward inclusiveness brought some hellenized Jews into the new kin group. Luke's interest in presenting this extraordinarily open kin group in a very positive and admirable manner does not

[25] Luke's interest in emphasizing this fact may well be the reason for his omission of the tradition (Deut 15:11) found in a saying of Jesus in Mark 14:7, "For you will always have the poor with you, and whenever you will, you can do good to them." See R. Pesch, *Die Apostelgeschichte* (EKKNT 5.1–2; Neukirchen-Vluyn: Neukirchener Verlag, 1986) 184. Pesch also stresses "wie sehr Lukas am verpflichtenden Vorbild der Urgemeinde interessiert bleibt, deren Sozialverfassung er als Erfüllung nicht nur der biblischen Verheissung, sondern auch der Sehnsucht der Menschheit interpretiert, indem er auf einen Topos griechischer Tradition zurückgreift."

prevent him, however, from noting carefully a major weakness in their functioning as a kin group: namely, the dissension caused by a lack of proper attention (for whatever reasons) to the needs of the Hellenistic Jewish Christian widows (Acts 6; see Jas 1:27). No doubt there were many other problems in living as a new kin group, which Luke does not mention. The problem caused by the initial neglect of these widows, however, became particularly noteworthy for Luke in the context of his awareness of the fact that the honor of any kin group was dependent in large measure on its willingness to care for *all* its members, especially persons in the older generation. In Acts 6, therefore, Luke seeks to document the integration of the weakest members of the most recently integrated group: the Hellenistic Jewish Christians. His motives for describing the episode in Acts 6 would include presenting the method of problem solving as exemplary and introducing to his readers some esteemed leaders among the Hellenistic Jewish Christians.[26]

VII

Thus I conclude that in Acts 2:42–47 and 4:32–5:11, Luke uses language that echoes Greek utopian hopes to describe the actual meeting of individual needs among the Jewish Christians in the Jerusalem house-churches by means of their pervasive acts of sharing, which Luke believed had indeed happened. Such sharing would have been expected in any well-functioning kin group; for Luke these Christians constituted such an exemplary, fictive kin group. To support his goal of moving the members of Christian house congregations in his own time toward increased sharing of their goods (and awareness of themselves as a kin group), Luke relies not only on his pointed presentation of Jesus' teaching regarding the use of property to benefit others (in his first book), but also on the earned reputation and honor of the first Christians in Jerusalem as a powerful motivation for a change in their attitude and praxis regarding possessions, that is, for acting in faith, especially by potential Christian patrons.

[26] L. T. Johnson, *Decision Making in the Church: A Biblical Model* (Philadelphia: Fortress Press, 1983) 64–65.

24

Four Problems in the Life of Paul Reconsidered

HANS-MARTIN SCHENKE

The Origin of Paul

PAUL CAME FROM the Cilician city of Tarsus.[1] This passes, or passed, as absolutely certain in the view of New Testament scholars. It never entered my mind that one could doubt this and at the same time doubt the tradition concerning Paul's Roman citizenship inherited from his father (Acts 22:25–29). Rather, this doubt, together with the different view to which it ultimately leads, comes from Helmut Koester.[2] As a matter of fact, only Acts says that Paul came from Tarsus (9:11; 21:39; 22:3), whereas in his own letters nothing is reported about this. Incidentally, Koester refers to the Tarsian origin of Paul, before calling it into question, as "quite conceivable."[3]

If one wants to go beyond Koester's "conceivableness" to more serious doubt, one has to explain how this view of Paul's origin could have occurred to the author of Acts or where he may have gotten it from. It is totally improbable that he produced it himself, for it obviously contradicts his tendency to make Paul as much as possible a Jerusalemite. He ought to have gotten it from one of his sources or materials. If one looks at those passages in Acts where Ταρσεύς or Ταρσός occurs (9:11; 21:39; or 9:30; 11:25; 22:3), it is immediately obvious that only 9:11 can be taken into account as a possible source. In other words, Luke would have derived his conviction that Paul

[1] This paper is an abridged form of a lecture entitled "Chapters in a Life of Paul," which was originally prepared for and read at Union Theological Seminary (25 April 1985) and in New Haven (Harvard–Yale Day, 26 April 1985).

[2] Koester, *Introduction* 2:97f. Regarding the problem of Paul's Roman citizenship, see esp. W. Stegemann, "War der Apostel Paulus ein römischer Bürger?" *ZNW* 78 (1987) 200–229.

[3] Koester, *Introduction* 2:97.

came from Tarsus from the legend of Paul's conversion near or in Damascus, which was originally independent before Luke included it in his work. Luke has considerably revised this "source," especially in order to make it fit his overall perspective. Critical research on Acts has been able to give us an idea of the original shape of the legend, but this analysis cannot be provided here. What matters in this context is that the tradition on which Luke depends tells only that Paul (or Saul) was known in Damascus as a man from Tarsus.[4] One should not blame Luke for taking and using this information in the most natural way, namely, as meaning that Paul is a citizen of the city of Tarsus (21:39) and that he was even born in Tarsus (22:3).

But there is still another way of understanding the tradition that Paul is (sur)named "the man from Tarsus." Paul could have been called "the man from Tarsus" in the same way that Barnabas was known as "the man from Cyprus" (Acts 4:36) and Simon the father of Alexander and Rufus as "the man of Cyrene" (Mark 15:21). Accordingly, Ταρσεύς would be something like a patronym and would have been used to distinguish this Saul from all the other Jews bearing the same name. In such a case, the actual relationship to Tarsus presupposed by this surname need not indicate more than the fact that the family of Paul had originally come from Tarsus.

In the conversion legend Paul is called "the man from Tarsus" when he has just arrived at Damascus. It might seem less logical to apply such a name to a traveler like Paul than to a resident of the city, raising the question of whether, behind this unmotivated detail, there might not lie an earlier historical fact that Paul was known to the Jews as well as to the Christians of Damascus as "the man from Tarsus."

At this point our problem intersects with another very difficult question, namely, how it could be that Paul, the historical persecutor of Christians, would come to Damascus in order to carry out his purpose. His supposed "coming to" Damascus is presupposed not only by the larger context of Acts, which is historically impossible (Paul is sent by the high priests from Jerusalem, etc.) but already by the self-contained conversion legend, though here it is unclear where he comes *from*. Critical research on Paul is unable to answer this question in a plausible way. Perhaps the reason is not that critical research has gone astray but that the question itself is wrong—all the more since Paul himself, when he speaks of this event in Gal 1:17, does not at all presuppose his "coming to" or "having come to Damascus," but merely his "being" or "having been" in Damascus: "nor did I go up to Jerusalem to

[4] Strictly speaking, the phrase of Acts 9:11 ζήτησον . . . Σαῦλον ὀνόματι Ταρσέα does not mean "inquire . . . for a man of Tarsus named Saul" (RSV) but "inquire . . . for a Saul named the man of Tarsus," i.e., ὀνόματι belongs to Ταρσέα. See M.-É. Boismard and A. Lamouille, *Le Texte occidental des Actes des Apôtres: Reconstitution et réhabilitation* (2 vols.; "Synthèse" 17; Paris: Editions Recherche sur les Civilisations, 1984) 2:64.

those who were apostles before me, but I went away into Arabia; and again I returned to Damascus" (RSV). This would mean, in fact, that Paul did not *come* to Damascus at all, but he *was* in Damascus and had been for some time. Whatever he may have done, good or evil, before his conversion—especially all the evil he did as a persecutor against the Christian community—he did in Damascus as a member of one of the synagogues there.[5] So it would actually have been as an inhabitant of Damascus that Paul was called "the man from Tarsus."

Paul in Arabia

The next problem in Paul's life lies hidden in the same verse that was important in the first section of this paper, Gal 1:17: "I went away into Arabia; and again I returned" (RSV). In Acts there is no corresponding narrative. The problems posed by these words are well known, and it is not for their sake that I touch this point. Rather, there is a new element to which I want to direct attention, though this is only a kind of "reification" of an exegetical alternative. Since Paul gives only hints of what actually happened in this passage, his words contain many enigmas for scholarship. Systematically, they can be seen as posing four riddles: (1) Where did Paul go? That is, what is meant here by Arabia? (2) Why did Paul go there? (3) How much time did Paul spend in Arabia? That is, how much of the three years between his conversion and his first visit to Jerusalem was occupied by a sojourn in Arabia? Since the words εὐθέως of v. 16 and ἀλλά of v. 17 suggest that Paul's departure for Arabia took place *very soon* after his conversion, how much of the three years remained *after* his return to Damascus and *before* his departure for Jerusalem? (4) Does Damascus belong to Arabia, or is it to be reckoned among τὰ κλίματα τῆς Συρίας ("the regions of Syria" [v. 21])?

In the past scholars were inclined to take "Arabia" as a geographical expression (which in terms of lexicography is alsolutely possible), to understand it as the Syrian-Arabian desert, and to interpret Paul's sojourn in this wilderness—in analogy to the tradition of the forty days that Jesus spent in the desert (Matt 4:1f.//Luke 4:1f.)—as a time necessary for consideration and contemplation before he felt able to depart and fulfill his mission. Today this interpretation is mentioned mainly in order to dismiss it, as, for example, by G. Bornkamm: "It is wrong to imagine the 2½ to 3 years of Paul's sojourn there as a time of monastic seclusion while he would have prepared by meditation for his later work."[6]

[5] The idea that Paul may have been a Damascene comes from Helmut Koester as well (*Introduction* 2:97f., 100). Once more my own share is the attempt to display it a little more and to transpose it into my "coordinate system."

[6] G. Bornkamm, *Paulus* (Urban Bücher 119; Stuttgart: Kohlhammer, 1969) 48f., my translation.

On this hypothesis, Paul's stay in Arabia must not have been very long. Yet the assumption that he stayed only briefly in Arabia is not necessarily bound to this hypothesis. So F. Mussner says: "Presumably the stay in Arabia was only short-lived since a date is missing (unlike 1:18 and 2:1)."[7] But as for how "Arabia" is to be understood and what Paul intended to do there, Mussner shares the usual contemporary interpretation.

This modern interpretation takes the word "Arabia" politically, as meaning the Nabatean-Arabic kingdom (east of Palestine), which was ruled at that time by Aretas IV. Paul would have gone there to begin immediately his mission to the Gentiles, which he felt to be his obligation. In Damascus itself there was already a Christian community, and the Christians there may also have preached to the Gentiles sporadically. It is quite conceivable that Paul thought there was nothing more for him to do and simply looked to the nearest virgin land for his mission. But how near was Arabia to Damascus? Was Damascus itself situated in the territory of Arabia, though at its extremity, so that Paul only moved from the border to the interior? Such must be the supposition of Koester when he writes that "Paul first went as a missionary to 'Arabia,' i.e., Damascus, its environs, and the areas to the south."[8] Did the way from Damascus to Arabia include a frontier crossing from the Roman province of Syria to the kingdom of Aretas?

It is, of course, easier to ask such questions than to answer them. At all events, Damascus was located within the borderland of Syria and Arabia, and therefore the political situation must have been very complicated. It is also certain that this city in the period concerned was normally under Roman rule; nevertheless, the suzerainty seems to have changed once again for a short period. The dating of the three years is of great importance in this connection. The space of time in which Damascus may have been Nabatean comprises only the period from 37 to 65 CE, but the call of Paul and the beginning of the three years cannot be that late.

"Arabia" is large. Where, then, in this large area have we to imagine Paul's first missionary attempts? In the cities, of course, which existed even in this large and mostly infertile country. There is a certain tendency in present-day scholarship not to have Paul go away too far from Damascus. It is said, for example, that Paul would have gone "into the area south-east of Damascus, which includes the northern parts of the Nabatean kingdom."[9] I do not consider this limitation, common as it is, to be very cogent. If it could

[7] F. Mussner, *Der Galaterbrief* (HTKNT 9; reprint, Leipzig: St. Benno, 1974) 93, my translation.

[8] Koester, *Introduction* 2:101.

[9] H. Schlier, *Der Brief an die Galater* (MeyerK 7; 13th ed.; Göttingen: Vandenhoeck & Ruprecht, 1965) 58, my translation. In principle the same view is held by Mussner, *Galaterbrief,* 91f.; Bornkamm, *Paulus,* 48; for Koester's view, see above.

be presumed that Paul already at that time proceeded in the way we know from his later period, namely, to build up his headquarters in the capital of the country to be missionized, then we would have to imagine that above all he felt drawn to the royal residence, that is, to the city of Petra, which was located far in the south of the country. I prefer to imagine that in this period of about two years, Paul missionized Petra above all.

In addition, this would better explain the search for him later in Damascus by an official of the king (2 Cor 11:32f.). That this search was actually connected with Paul's mission in Arabia and was a belated reaction to it has justly been taken for granted by many scholars. It seems that by this mission Paul had incurred the suspicion and wrath of the king himself.

As for the results of Paul's mission during these two obscure years, I join the widespread suspicion of scholars that they must have been limited at best. Perhaps his early return to Damascus must be seen in connection with this suspected fact that Paul's first missionary attempt remained without any results worth mentioning.

The Flight from Damascus

I have already mentioned the danger that Paul encountered in Damascus. The pertinent text is 2 Cor 11:32f.

> At Damascus, the governor under King Aretas guarded the city of Damascus in order to seize me, but I was let down in a basket through a window in a wall, and escaped his hands (RSV).

We are concerned here with two problems, first, the political status of Damascus that is presupposed in this passage. More specifically, does this passage necessarily imply that the city of Damascus belonged to the sphere ruled by the Nabatean king Aretas IV in this period? Second, we have to deal with the time of Paul's flight from Damascus within the chronological frame of his life.

Regarding the first of these problems we are faced with a choice between general political probability (the Romans, once they have a place, will never give it up) and the wording of the text. In fact, the wording of the Greek is not exactly that of the RSV translation. The Greek word for "governor" here is ἐθνάρχης, and this problematic term is decisive in the discussion. The matter is difficult, for, as A. Negev has put it, "The existence of a Nabatean ruler at Damascus at this time has never been satisfactorily explained."[10]

The difficulty lies in the connection of three elements: (1) ὁ ἐθνάρχης, whose technical meaning is in dispute; (2) Ἀρέτα τοῦ βασιλέως, where the sense of the genitive is in doubt; and (3) ἐφρούρει, where the question is the

[10] A. Negev, "The Nabateans and the Provincia Arabia," *ANRW* 2.8, 569.

kind of guarding that is meant. The term ἐθνάρχης usually has three meanings: (a) the ruler of a larger territory to whom his suzerain does not want to grant the title of a king; (b) the chief of a tribe; and (c) the leader of a national minority in a *polis*. On the other hand, there is no evidence that the word could also mean "governor." Rather, Nabatean governors bore the title of στρατηγός.[11] But a genitive such as follows here, "*of* King Aretas," does not make sense with any of these three meanings. Finally, for the verb ἐφρούρει, we must choose between the alternatives "to safeguard from inside" or "to besiege from outside."

Regarding the overall interpretation of this difficult phrase by scholars, there appears to be a clear polarization. Roughly speaking, the opinion of the exegetes is opposed to that of the historians. Within the realm of present-day exegesis one is used to starting from the axiom that at the time of Aretas IV, as well as before and after, Damascus as a part of the province of Syria was under Roman rule. Accordingly, one has to assume that the ἐθνάρχης was a bedouin chief in the charge of the Nabatean king who by order of King Aretas lay in wait for Paul outside the gates of Damascus. This theory leaves room for many special nuances in detail.

A review of this interpretation, including a convincing disclosure of its weak points, is found in Robert Jewett's *chronology*.[12] Jewett also gives new arguments in support of the opposite position (taken by the historians) that infers another Nabatean rule over Damascus, but he dismisses the relevance of the numismatic arguments.[13] In this he is not in agreement with the opinion of the present-day specialists. What is essentially at issue is the gap of the (pseudo-)autonomous (that is, performed under Roman rule) minting of Damascus under Caligula (37–41 CE) and Claudius (41–54 CE). This gap also extends deep into the reign of Nero; the minting of Damascus is resumed only in the year 65 CE. In the eyes of Y. Meshorer and T. Fischer this numismatic evidence is a clear hint that at that time, say from 37 to 65, Damascus temporarily did not belong to the Roman province of Syria, but to the kingdom of the Nabateans.[14] The explanation of the political status of Damascus to the effect that this city between 37 and 65 CE generally, and especially at the time of the event recorded in 2 Cor 11:32f., was Nabatean means for the chronology of Paul that his flight from Damascus must have

[11] See E. A. Knauf, "Zum Ethnarchen des Aretas 2 Kor 11,32," *ZNW* 74 (1983) 145f.

[12] R. Jewett, *Paulus—Chronologie: Ein Versuch* (Munich: Kaiser, 1982) 58–63.

[13] Ibid., 61f.

[14] See Y. Meshorer, *Nabataean Coins* (Qedem: Monographs of the Institute of Archaeology, The Hebrew University of Jerusalem, 3; Jerusalem: Institute of Archaeology, Hebrew University, 1975) 63f., 67; T. Fischer, review of Meshorer, *Nabataean Coins, OLZ* 74 (1979) 242, 244 (plus letter from Fischer of 24 October 1979).

taken place between 37 (the presumed recommencement of Nabatean rule over Damascus) and 40 CE (the death of Aretas IV).

As is well known, 2 Cor 11:32f. has a parallel in Acts 9:23–25. It is well known also that the relationship between these two passages is problematic, especially since in Acts it is the Jews who search for Paul. But, as the matter of the basket shows, there can be no doubt that both passages refer to the same event. In Acts, however, Paul after escaping goes directly to Jerusalem to pay his first visit to the Christian community there (9:26). It is quite natural, though Acts suppresses the three years including Paul's stay in Arabia, that scholars generally see 2 Cor 11:32f. and Gal 1:18 as the same event. In other words, they take 2 Cor 11:32f. as the description of the way in which the ἀνῆλθον εἰς Ἱεροσόλυμα ἱστορῆσαι Κηφᾶν ("I went up to Jerusalem to visit Cephas" [Gal 1:18]) took place. This indeed is really feasible only for those who either date the conversion of Paul fairly late (in the years 34 or 35 CE) or, like Jewett, are prepared to subject their dating of Paul's conversion to the chronological deduction from 2 Cor 11:32f. under discussion here. On the other hand, many exegetes who advocate a more or less early date for the conversion of Paul seem by this chronological deduction to face a dilemma. The identification of 2 Cor 11:32f. and Gal 1:18 is not at all beyond doubt. As a matter of fact, the words of Gal 1:18 taken by themselves do not at all give the impression that the departure from Damascus was forced and precipitate. On the other hand, in 2 Cor 11:32f. Paul does not say a single word about the point in his life when the flight from Damascus took place.

That means, if one dates the conversion, say, about 30/31 CE—as is my opinion—Paul's departure from Damascus and first visit to Jerusalem would have taken place in the year 33 CE. Afterward, four to seven years later, between the first visit to Jerusalem and the Apostolic Council there, when he was in τὰ κλίματα τῆς Συρίας καὶ τῆς Κιλικίας ("the regions of Syria and Cilicia" [Gal 1:21]), Paul would have been once more in Damascus. And it would have been only then that the humiliating flight happened. On the other hand, from such a perspective—apart from the dates of the years mentioned only as an example—three further conclusions follow: (1) One must no longer take for granted that after leaving Jerusalem Paul marched along more or less directly to Antioch and that he left this city and its environs again only in order to travel to the Apostolic Council. (2) According to Paul, Damascus—seen in geographical perspective—is a part of the κλίματα τῆς Συρίας, whether politically it belonged to the Roman province of Syria (as at the time of Gal 1:17) or was under the rule of the Arabic Nabateans (as at the time of 2 Cor 11:32f.). (3) Paul's close connection with Damascus in the period before his conversion would also have continued after his conversion and after his contact with Jerusalem, possibly even during the Antiochian period.

The Secrecy of the First Visit to Jerusalem

From Paul's being imperiled in Damascus we look back once again to his first visit to Jerusalem, which, according to our considerations, would have taken place some years before. There seems to be a mystery about this visit, a mystery that becomes clearer as one looks more closely at the wording of Paul's text (Gal 1:18f., 22–24). Paul's visits to Jerusalem may always have been problematic, even the very first one.

> Then after three years I went up to Jerusalem to visit Cephas, and remained with him fifteen days. But I saw none of the other apostles except James the Lord's brother. (Gal 1:18–19)
>
> And I was still not known by sight to the churches of Christ in Judea; they only heard it said, "He who once persecuted us is now preaching the faith he once tried to destroy." And they glorified God because of me. (Gal 1:22–24)

One wonders just how it happened that of all the Christians in Jerusalem Paul contacted only Peter and James. According to the wording of Gal 1:18f. one has to assume that Paul stayed the fourteen days in the home of Peter and that he saw James only by chance when the latter happened to pay Peter a visit. Before asking for reasons we want to describe the phenomenon somewhat more clearly in terms of method. We are not concerned with all the problems contained in the text. Furthermore, we are interested only in a special perspective. Why Paul *says* here what he says is by and large clear. In the context of his *apologia* to the Galatian Christians he wants to prove his independence from the human authorities in Jerusalem. But our question is why things were such as Paul affirms on oath they were. Paul states that the purpose of this journey was to become acquainted with Peter. This is certainly true in the sense that Peter was at that time the most important figure in Jerusalem that he could meet. But at the same time, one may also consider whether Paul did not simply state what he *obtained* as what he wanted, what he *achieved* as the purpose, namely, his contact with Peter. The same statement by Paul can be interrogated from a second perspective: Paul wanted to contact Peter, but whether Peter wanted to see Paul is not said. On the other hand, regarding the shortness of the stay in Jerusalem, it is not explicitly said that this short stay was in accordance with Paul's plans. Was this nevertheless Paul's intention, or would the reasons for his short stay have been outside his desires and intentions? Had Paul actually come from Damascus to Jerusalem alone? That he says "I" does not necessarily mean that no one else was with him. Such attendants from Damascus could be hidden in the word ἡμεῖς of v. 23, who seem to be more enigmatic than is dreamt of in our usual exegetical procedures; it could be they that *say* what the Christian communities of Judea (including) Jerusalem) *hear.*[15] At the same time, in this verse there is the only (though indirect) hint at what Paul and Peter might have negotiated during those fifteen days. The topic should essentially have been whether Paul was to be recognized as a legitimate preacher of the Christian faith, even though so recently he was such a passionate persecutor of the church.

Regarding the question why this stay of Paul in Jerusalem may have been so secret, the first set of possibilities that might come to mind would be either that it was dangerous for Paul to show up in Jerusalem or that the Christian community did not want to see him. Although the concrete statements in the parallel of Acts 9:26–30 contradict the assertions of Galatians and are incompatible with them, their general purport and the wider context virtually seem to suggest sort of a commentary on our passage from Galatians. In fact, A. Oepke interprets the situation along these lines. He says concerning Gal 1:19:

> He did not even get sight of the other apostles, much less of the other members of the community. The danger required the strictest incognito. As much as the Jews pursued him, as little the Christians trusted him. The report of Acts (9:26ff.) sets off *this* difficulty correctly, but is otherwise incompatible with the statement of Paul.[16]

H. Lietzmann thinks similarly but mentions only one of the two aspects: "When Paul did not see another apostle except Peter and James, the reason for this would hardly have been that all the apostles were on journeys, but that Paul had to keep himself hidden from the Jews: this may also glimmer through in Acts 9:29."[17] In my opinion, the actual acceptance of such a possibility (which, incidentally, Hans Dieter Betz also takes into consideration[18]) depends on the question whether such problems for Paul in Jerusalem are conceivable if Paul's persecution of the Christians had not at all taken place in Jerusalem and had not been nearly as cruel as Luke imagines, but had only made use of the usual means of synagogue punishment, as critical scholarship supposes.[19] In spite of this consideration, I take this situation to be quite imaginable. Actually, between Paul's changing sides in Damascus and his visit to Jerusalem there were about three years; during a

[15] Regarding this problem, however, see the short but interesting remarks of G. Lüdemann, who takes v. 23 to be a personal tradition connected with the missionary work of Paul in the regions of Syria and Cilicia (*Paulus, der Heidenapostel*, vol. 1, *Studien zur Chronologie* [FRLANT 123; Göttingen: Vandenhoeck & Ruprecht, 1980] 44, 72 n. 40, 80 n. 44).

[16] A. Oepke, *Der Brief des Paulus an die Galater* (THKNT 9; 2nd ed.; Berlin: Evangelische Verlagsanstalt, 1957) 35, my translation.

[17] H. Lietzmann, *An die Galater* (HNT 10; 3rd ed.; Tübingen: Mohr, 1932) 9, my translation.

[18] H. D. Betz, *Galatians: A Commentary on Paul's Letter to the Churches in Galatia* (Hermeneia; Philadelphia: Fortress Press, 1979) 78 n. 202.

[19] See, e.g., Koester, *Introduction* 2:99f.

time of that length news could bridge far greater distances. Moreover, one may assume that there were sufficient contacts and common interests between the Jews of Damascus and Jerusalem as well as between Christians of the two places. No doubt, this "turn" of Paul was sensational enough to tell.

Nevertheless, I do not think it proper to restrict oneself to considering only this possibility. It may be just as well to keep this question open. In this perspective, I do not even want, as is usually done, to exclude the suggestion of W. M. Ramsay and F. Sieffert that perhaps Paul could not meet the other apostles simply because they were out of town at the time.[20] After all, Paul's problems during his visit to Jerusalem and the secrecy and shortness of his stay there might be explained as resulting from an unfortunate timing of the visit: the churches of Judea altogether (Gal 1:22) could just then have been in a phase of oppression by their unbelieving compatriots, such as is presupposed by 1 Thess 2:14.

[20] W. M. Ramsay, *A Historical Commentary on St. Paul's Epistle to the Galatians* (2nd ed.; London: Hodder & Stoughton, 1900) 283; F. Sieffert, *Der Brief an die Galater* (MeyerK 7; 9th ed.; Göttingen: Vandenhoeck & Ruprecht, 1899) 70.

25

The Man from Heaven in Paul's Letter to the Philippians

WAYNE A. MEEKS

IN HELMUT KOESTER'S enormous contribution to the history of early Christianity, one of the things of which he has never tired of reminding us is the exuberance of Jesus' followers that created, in the first decades of the movement's existence, the wildest diversity of mythic portraits of him.[1] Students of the New Testament had often been blinded to this diversity by confusing the church's canon with the canon of the historian. However, we do not have to look beyond the canonical documents to see one of these developments that is among the most astonishing of all: the subject of this diverse myth making was a Jewish man from Galilee who died early and in public shame. In both the Fourth Gospel and in Paul's letter to the Philippians, this Jewish man is said to have been a divine being, "a god" and "with God" or "equal to God," who descended to earth in human form, obeying the Father's command to the point of suffering human death, for which he was rewarded by exaltation, enthroned above with even greater honor than before.

Debate over the "meaning" of such mythic texts has become mired in two questionable assumptions. The first is that meaning is determined by antecedents: if we can discover whence the Christians borrowed their myth of the descending/ascending redeemer, we will then know what it means. If that assumption were valid, we would still be far from an answer to our question, for we still have no consensus about the origins of the myth, despite the most diligent research and imaginative reconstructions. Even the categories

[1] Of Koester's many articles that could be mentioned in this connection, two have become classics: "GNOMAI DIAPHOROI: The Origin and Nature of Diversification in the History of Early Christianity," and "One Jesus and Four Primitive Gospels," both reprinted in Robinson-Koester, *Trajectories*, 114–204.

by which we identify the antecedents (Jewish or Hellenistic? gnostic or pre-gnostic?) have proved to be leaky vessels. Second, we assume that the meaning of a myth is a constant "content" carried on by the myth from one context to another and translatable either into nonmythic concepts to which the myth merely refers in an obscure fashion or into existential dispositions that the myth expresses symbolically. Both assumptions run counter to most present theory about language and culture, which emphasizes rather the way language (including the language of myth) works within a particular social setting and practice. Meaning—although perhaps not simply identical with use, as Wittgensteinians have sometimes incautiously said—is at least inextricably connected with use.

Despite the necessary "dismantling" of scholarly categories,[2] enough remains of earlier form-critical analysis to enable us to say something about the *Sitz-im-Leben* of the depiction of Jesus as a descended-and-ascended divine being. It was in the liturgical poetry—hymns and psalms—produced in the early Christian gatherings that members of the new cult used this pattern, whatever its precise antecedents may have been.[3] Poetry can have divers uses, however, and its meaning may change with use. In the Fourth Gospel and in Philippians we have two quite different uses of the hymnic tradition.

The Johannine portrayal of Jesus as the Son of Man come from heaven is exceedingly complicated because it is part of an intricate and relatively long literary composition that patently incorporates complex preliterary traditions and probably several stages of redaction. Several years ago I tried to untangle some of the main features of the resulting social and linguistic web in an article that has stimulated considerable discussion and fairly wide agreement.[4] I argued that, in the final form of the Gospel, the descending/ascending motif is used to depict Jesus' essential strangeness to "the world"—a world that, "though it came into existence through him," was incapable of knowing him. The evangelist accomplished this effect by interweaving this motif in the discourses of Jesus with statements in a riddling and ironic style

[2] James M. Robinson, "The Dismantling and Reassembling of the Categories of New Testament Scholarship," in Robinson-Koester, *Trajectories,* 1–19.

[3] Martin Hengel, "Hymns and Christology," *Between Jesus and Paul* (Philadelphia: Fortress Press, 1983) 78–96, nn. 188–90. In order to keep this essay within the strict limits of space in this volume—limitations necessitated by the enthusiastic response of Helmut Koester's friends and students to this opportunity to express our affection and admiration for him—I have kept references to scholarly literature to an absolute minimum. For an overview of the massive literature on Phil 2:5–11, see R. P. Martin, *Carmen Christi: Philippians ii.5–11 in Recent Interpretation and in the Setting of Early Christian Worship* (SNTSMS 4; Cambridge: Cambridge University Press, 1967) 17–95; and Reinhard Deichgräber, *Gotteshymnus und Christushymnus: Untersuchungen zur Form, Sprache und Stil der frühchristlichen Hymnen* (SUNT 5; Göttingen: Vandenhoeck & Ruprecht, 1967) 11–21.

[4] W. A. Meeks, "The Man from Heaven in Johannine Sectarianism," *JBL* 91 (1972) 44–72.

and by connecting the discourses with narratives that portray Jesus in conflict with Jewish leaders. Thus John's Gospel gave to its intended audience, through the narrative and the self-presentation of Jesus in it, a template for interpreting their own experience. The conflict they had endured over their assertions about Jesus' identity, their resultant separation from the dominant Jewish communities, and thus their alienation from their world all are predicted, caused, and foreshadowed in this Gospel's depiction of Jesus' own mission and fate.

Paul's earlier use of the Christ hymn in Phil 2:6–11 is obviously quite different from the later Johannine use, both in style and in function. What the two have in common, besides the basic pattern, is that both use the christological motif to interpret the experience of the community and thus to shape and reinforce certain attitudes and patterns of behavior in that community. This usage accords with what Martin Hengel finds to be characteristic of the hymnic tradition: early Christian singing not only created Christology; it simultaneously "created community."[5] In the letter, Paul's community-forming use is much more direct and overt than in the Gospel; the letter as a whole is a letter of friendship with a range of parenetic aims,[6] and Paul quotes the poem to support a central part of his exhortation.

By calling the letter and Paul's use of the hymn "parenetic," I will seem to be taking sides in the debate that has raged over Phil 2:6–11 since Ernst Käsemann, in a seminal essay published in 1950, insisted that the dramatic and mythical form of the hymn portrayed an objective *Heilsakt* and therefore requires the interpreter to abandon altogether the parenetic interpretation.[7] Käsemann was reacting to the moralizing typical of traditional Protestant reading. He rightly insisted that Christ is not presented in the hymn as merely a moral *Vorbild,* the exemplar of a virtue or an attitude to be emulated. Käsemann's position won a wide following. Those who disagreed

[5] Hengel, "Hymns" 96.

[6] I was formerly convinced that our received Philippians is a composite of two or three letter fragments, for reasons that Koester ably summarized in his "The Purpose of the Polemic of a Pauline Fragment (Philippians III)," *NTS* 8 (1961–62) 317–32. However, as study of ancient epistolography has advanced rapidly in recent years, the scholarly consensus appears to have shifted, and for good reason. I now take the letter to be single and complete. On the friendly letter and the parenetic letter and their social functions, see Stanley K. Stowers, *Letter Writing in Greco-Roman Antiquity* (Library of Early Christianity 5; Philadelphia: Westminster, 1986) 58–70, 94–106. An important discussion of Paul's use of the conventions of friendship and enmity is to be found in Peter Marshall, *Enmity in Corinth: Social Conventions in Paul's Relations with the Corinthians* (WUNT 2.23; Tübingen: Mohr-Siebeck, 1987) 130–64. Kenneth Berry is presently writing a dissertation at Yale (under the direction of A. J. Malherbe) on the use of the friendship *topos* in Philippians.

[7] Ernst Käsemann, "Kritische Analyse von Phil. 2, 5–11," *ZTK* 47 (1950) 313–60; reprinted in his *Exegetische Versuche und Besinnungen* 1 (2nd ed.; Göttingen: Vandenhoeck & Ruprecht, 1960) 51–95.

sought either (with considerable success) to undermine his starting point, the identification of the myth "behind" the hymn with the "gnostic primaeval man-redeemer myth,"[8] or simply to show that Käsemann's denial of the obvious hortatory function of the hymn in its context was a valiant attempt to make water run uphill.[9] However, both Käsemann's supporters and his opponents construe parenesis very narrowly. We would do better to let ourselves be guided by Paul's own language.

The elliptical clause that introduces the hymn has perplexed not a few interpreters: Τοῦτο φρονεῖτε ἐν ὑμῖν ὃ καὶ ἐν Χριστῷ Ἰησοῦ. I would translate this, for reasons that will appear later, "Base your practical reasoning on what you see in Christ Jesus." The verb φρονεῖν occurs ten times in this short letter. Only in the latter chapters of Romans does Paul use it nearly as frequently (including the compound ὑπερφρονεῖν [12:3], nine times, and the noun φρόνημα 4 times); otherwise it occurs only in 1 Cor 13:11; 2 Cor 13:11; Gal 5:10. Of the other occurrences in Philippians, the closest to 2:5 is in the curious admonition 3:15, ὅσοι οὖν τέλιοι, τοῦτο φρονῶμεν ("We who are mature should keep to this way of thinking" [REB]). Paul has just offered a remarkable self-presentation, a nutshell theological autobiography (vv. 4b–14), explicitly as a model (τύπος) to be imitated (συμμιμηταί μου γίνεσθε [v. 17]). Even though this self-description is bracketed by warnings against "dogs, evildoers, the mutilation," "the enemies of Christ's cross" (vv. 2, 18–19), reminding us of 2 Corinthians 10–13 and perhaps based on Paul's recollection of that recent controversy, the section as a whole is not polemical but hortatory.[10] It is about the way believers ought to behave (περιπατεῖν) and, logically prior to that, how they ought to think. For both there are good models (Paul and Christ) and bad (the enemies of Christ's cross, who are among other things οἱ τὰ ἐπίγεια φρονοῦντες ["their minds are set on earthly things" (NRSV; REB) v. 19]). Yet Paul as τύπος is not a simple *Vorbild* in the sense Käsemann abhors; there is not some heroic virtue or set of cognitions that the Philippians ought to copy—perhaps it is precisely to avoid that misconstrual that Paul adds the puzzling second clause in v. 15, καὶ εἴ τι ἑτέρως φρονεῖτε, καὶ τοῦτο ὁ θεὸς ὑμῖν ἀποκαλύψει ("and if you think differently about anything, this too God will reveal to you" [NRSV]). Rather, just as the way one ought to reason ὡς ἐν Χριστῷ ("as in Christ") is defined not abstractly but by a "drama" (Käsemann), so Paul defines his own example by telling

[8] Among the throng, see, e.g., Dieter Georgi, "Der vorpaulinische Hymnus in Phil 2, 6–11," in *Zeit und Geschichte: Dankesgabe an Rudolf Bultmann zum 80. Geburtstag*, ed. E. Dinkler (Tübingen: Mohr-Siebeck, 1964) 266–75.

[9] Most recently, Ulrich B. Müller, who goes farther in trying to show that the hymn itself, not just the epistolary use of it, was parenetic from the outset ("Der Christushymnus Phil 2, 6–11," *ZNW* 79 [1988] 17–44).

[10] *Pace* Koester, "Purpose." All translations in the present essay are my own unless otherwise indicated.

his own story—in terms almost as telegraphic and paradoxical as the hymn.

What the myth of Christ's descent and ascent and Paul's story of his conversion and subsequent striving have in common is not that the two subjects have done the same thing or thought the same thoughts but that the dramatic structure of the two "plots" is analogous, though not the same. That is the sense in which "to know him and the power of his resurrection and the partnership of his sufferings" is to be "conformed to his death, in order (somehow, miraculously: εἴ πως) to attain to the resurrection from the dead" (vv. 10–11). That is the sense too of the inclusive description of Paul and the letter's recipients in 3:20–21, in language that, as most commentators now acknowledge, echoes the hymn: they are people whose moral reasoning is not determined by the ἐπίγεια, because they are resident aliens, not merely in Philippi but on earth. Their πολίτευμα ("civic community") is in heaven, where Christ has been enthroned and whence they will receive him, when, as he once transformed his own divine μορφή ("form") to take on human σχῆμα ("shape," "form"), now he will transform (μετασχηματίζειν, σύμμορφος) the faithful to share his δόξα ("glory") as they have shared his ταπείνωσις ("humiliation").

Φρόνησις, often translated "practical reasoning" or "practical wisdom" to distinguish it from the more theoretical or contemplative wisdom,[11] was, of course, an important concept in Greco-Roman moral philosophy. Although Paul does not use the noun, we may say with some cogency that this letter's most comprehensive purpose is the shaping of a Christian *phrōnesis*, a practical moral reasoning that is "conformed to [Christ's] death" in hope of his resurrection. This practical reasoning ought to issue in a civic life (πολιτεύεσθαι) "worthy of the gospel of Christ" (1:27) and therefore not the civic life of the ordinary πόλις, the arena of classical Greco-Roman ethics, but that of citizens of the heavenly πολίτευμα. The opening thanksgiving, as often in Paul's genuine letters, signals some of the principal concerns of the letter. Verses 9–11 confirm that one of the letter's aims is parenetic. What is wanted is the maturity of the believers' moral knowledge so that they can discern τὰ διαφέροντα and thus lead such a life that they will be found "pure and blameless for the day of Christ" (1:10 RSV).

There are two specific areas of concern on which this letter wants to focus the moral reasoning of the recipients: unity and harmony within the Christian community and confidence in the face of opposition and suffering. For both, Paul sets up, as models to think from, specific descriptions of his own experience and the myth of Christ. For the former, Paul's friendship with the

[11] The distinction is nicely summed up by Synesius, the third-fourth century rhetorician-turned-bishop, *Epistle* 103: δύο γὰρ αὗται μερίδες φιλοσοφίας, θεωρία καὶ πρᾶξις· καὶ δῆτα δύο δυνάμεις ἑκατέρα παρ' ἑκατέραν μερίδα, σοφία καὶ φρόνησις, κτλ. (*PG* 66:1476D; cited in *LPGL* 1491a).

Philippians, including their "contractual" exchange for the sake of the gospel (1:5, 7; 4:15–16), is both model and context. Their harmony (τὸ αὐτὸ φρονεῖν) will thus make Paul rejoice (2:2). "Joy" is a repeated motif in this letter, always associated with friendly relations—not only with Paul (1:4, 18; 2:2, 17; 3:1; 4:1, 4, 10) but also with Epaphroditus (2:25–30). "To think the same" is a commonplace in Greco-Roman descriptions of friendship, and in 2:2–4 the phrase is connected with a plethora of other common expressions of friendship. In 4:2, however, the phrase recurs in a specific admonition addressed to Paul's "fellow athletes" for the gospel, Euodia and Syntyche. Perhaps, considering the weight placed on it here, their dispute is one of the major reasons for Paul's writing this letter as he does. "Fellow workers" can be mediators of unity and harmony as well as causes of discord; thus Paul also heaps up friendship language in describing both Timothy (2:19–23) and Epaphroditus (2:25–29). They are, moreover, models of "not seeking one's own" but the good for others, "the things of Jesus Christ" (2:21; cf. v. 30). And, of course, so is Paul: in one of the boldest of his assertions of his own friendship with the Philippians, he says that he will survive his present imprisonment and coming trial, contrary to his own desire to "depart and be with Christ," for their sakes—for their moral progress (προκοπή) and faith's joy (1:21–26).

At the same time, Paul's careful assertion of indifference to life or death provides a model for Christian *phronēsis* in the face of the other major concern of the letter, dealing with hostility from without. Hence, he follows this description of his own situation with the first exhortation of the letter, which introduces and weaves together both themes ("live your life in a manner worthy of the gospel of Christ, so that . . . I will know that you are standing firm in one spirit, striving side by side with one mind for the faith of the gospel, and are in no way intimidated by your opponents" [1:27–28, NRSV]), and includes them both in the recipients' relationship with Christ (ἐχαρίσθη . . . τὸ ὑπὲρ αὐτοῦ πάσχειν ["It was granted you . . . to suffer for him," v. 29]) and with Paul (τὸν αὐτὸν ἀγῶνα ἔχοντες, οἷον εἴδετε ἐν ἐμοί κτλ. ["having the same struggle that you saw I had . . ." v. 30]). Paul's assertions of his studied equanimity toward those who preach from motives hostile to himself—not quite what a reader of 2 Corinthians 10–13 would expect!—serve the same end (1:14–18). While Paul's παρρησία ("boldness") in the face of life or death (1:20), like his αὐτάρκεια ("self-sufficiency") in abundance or want (4:11), is a virtue especially prized by Cynics and widely adopted by others as well in the popular philosophy of his day, Paul's confidence that he will not be "put to shame" has another source, as the context makes clear. The competitive values of Greek rhetoric are tacitly reversed both here and in the inverted boasting of 3:4–16. As Nicholas Walter has acutely observed, Paul's connecting the essentially active ἀγών with the essentially passive πάσχειν in 1:29–30 would confound the ordinary understanding of both.[12] In neither place does Paul quite make explicit what is the basis for this reversal of values, except that it is "for Christ's sake" (ὑπὲρ Χριστοῦ, διὰ τὸν Χριστόν). It is fairly obvious, however, that it is Christ's own obedience to the point of death and subsequent exaltation, in short the Christ drama encapsulated in the hymn (2:6–11), that is the basis and model. The analogy is reinforced in Paul's description of Epaphroditus's experience, for Epaphroditus is mediator between Paul and the Philippians not only in his practical service but also here in Paul's rhetoric. His obedience to Christ's task (τὸ ἔργον Χριστοῦ) led him μέχρι θανάτου ("to the point of death," 2:30)—like Christ's own obedience (2:8).

Thus we see that the hymn's story of Christ is the master model that underlies Paul's characterization of his career and of the mediating Epaphroditus. This model sets the terms of the thinking and acting expected of the Philippians in the face of conflict inside and hostility from outside the community. It is within this larger context, the controlling structure of the whole letter, that we should understand the specific verbal connections between the hymn and the immediate parenetic context. The ταπεινοφροσύνη ("humility") that ought to characterize Christian behavior (2:3) is exemplified by the one who ἐταπείνωσεν ἑαυτόν (v. 8); as Christ did not regard (ἡγεῖσθαι) equality with God a windfall to be exploited (v. 6), so Christians ought to regard (ἡγεῖσθαι) each other as superior to themselves (v. 3); Christ's becoming obedient to the point of death (ὑπήκοος μέχρι θανάτου [v. 8]) sets the parameters of the obedience Paul expects of the readers (ὑπηκούσατε [v. 12], with the implied imperative in the following phrase).

The fourth evangelist wrote a Gospel beginning with a poem about a Stranger from Heaven. The Gospel draws the insider-reader into the story of Jesus, replicating and interpreting the community's experience in the Stranger's enigmatic statements about himself and in his confrontations with "the Jews." In John "the Jews" represent a world that is essentially "from below," that loves darkness rather than light; it is a world hostile to the mediator of its own creation and his "friends." His victory over it is visible

[12] Nicholas Walter, "Die Philipper und das Leiden: Aus den Anfängen einer heidenchristlichen Gemeinde," in *Die Kirche des Anfangs: Festschrift für Heinz Schürmann zum 65. Geburtstag,* ed. R. Schnackenburg et al. (Leipzig: St. Benno, 1977) 431. I see nothing in the text, however, to support Walter's conjecture that the letter (only "letter B" in his reading, since he accepts Bornkamm's division) was occasioned by a report that the Philippians were upset and bewildered by having to suffer. The notion that the ἀγών of the wise person entailed patient endurance of hardships is in itself not at all foreign to Hellenistic philosophy, especially in the Cynic and Stoic traditions. What is novel in Paul's view of suffering is that it is not his own inner strength that is exhibited but an external power that is revealed precisely in his own weakness. See John Fitzgerald, *"Cracks in an Earthen Vessel": An Examination of the Catalogues of Hardships in the Corinthian Correspondence* (SBLDS 99; Atlanta: Scholars Press, 1988).

only through the deeply ironic narrative of his trial and "elevation" on a cross. Paul wrote to the Christians in Philippi a letter of gratitude, friendship, and exhortation, the fabric of which is interwoven with motifs from a poem he quotes, very like the poem that begins the Fourth Gospel. In the letter, too, these motifs suggest a duality between outsiders and insiders, between citizens of this world and citizens of heaven. Paul's world, nevertheless, seems a somewhat brighter and more open world than that of John. Irony, so characteristic of the Johannine narrative and, in a different way, of Paul's more polemical writing, is virtually absent from Philippians. This letter encourages a practical moral reasoning that incorporates language and concerns of Greco-Roman philosophy and rhetoric, even though it transforms those common cultural categories, sometimes radically, by the generative image of the one who did not exploit his superior status but humbled himself, accepting the shape of a slave, and was obedient to the point of death, only by that means and for that reason being exalted and enthroned by God and acknowledged by the invisible powers of the universe. Paul's supple and allusive use of the mythic pattern in his moral advice to the Philippian Christians binds the Christian *phronēsis* to that pattern, but opens wide ranges for the unfolding of a moral reasoning based on it.

26

On the Ending(s) to Paul's Letter to Rome

NORMAN R. PETERSEN

ALTHOUGH MANY CRITICS have for some time questioned the originality of Romans 16 to Paul's letter to Rome, in recent decades some new arguments have been presented in defense of it.[1] In this essay in honor of my former teacher, Helmut Koester, himself a disbeliever in its originality,[2] I wish to align myself with the disbelievers while at the same time attempting to advance the ongoing discussion of the composition of Paul's letters. In this instance, the composition of the letters is as much at issue as the chapter in question, because composition provides the criteria for judging its originality. Epistolographers, who read Paul's letters as letters, and recent rhetorical critics, who read them as speeches, do not agree about much, but among the recent studies in support of a sixteen-chapter letter to Rome are some substantial essays from both camps. A critique of their positions will therefore also shed some light on the increasingly significant question of the relationship between the epistolographic and the rhetorical in the composition of Paul's letters.

Three studies are focal. From the epistolographic side, Harry Gamble has argued that there is no text-historical or epistolographic basis for separating Romans 15 from Romans 16.[3] Text-historically, Romans 15 is never found without 16:1–23, and 15:14–16:23/24 is consistent both with Paul's epistolary style and with ancient epistolary practice. Also from the epistolographic

[1] On the history of the problem, see C. E. B. Cranfield, *A Critical and Exegetical Commentary on the Epistle to the Romans* (2 vols.; ICC; Edinburgh: T. & T. Clark, 1975, 1979) 1:5–11; and Harry Gamble, Jr., *The Textual History of the Letter to the Romans: A Study in Textual and Literary Criticism* (SD 42; Grand Rapids: Eerdmans, 1977).

[2] H. Koester, *Introduction* 2:138–39.

[3] Gamble's *Textual History* is the most significant study of both text-historical and literary issues, although it is cited almost solely for text-historical matters.

side, Wolf-Henning Ollrog maintains that Romans 1–16 is consistent with Paul's practice if 16:17–20a and 16:25–27 are excised as interpolations.[4] From the rhetorical side, on the other hand, Wilhelm Wuellner argues that Romans 16 belongs, together with 15:14–33, to the concluding epilogue or peroration of an epideictic rhetorical argument that begins in Romans 1.[5] Gamble and Ollrog focus on the relationship between the ending of Romans and the endings of other Pauline letters, and Wuellner raises issues concerning the relationship not only between epistolography and rhetoric but also between the beginnings and the endings of Paul's letters. We begin with the endings.

Romans 15–16 and the Endings of Paul's Letters

The most thorough epistolographic study of the endings of Paul's letters is contained in a section of Gamble's *Textual History*.[6] While recognizing that we have too few of Paul's letters for conclusions to have any statistical significance, and that there is considerable diversity among the letters that we do have, Gamble nevertheless finds the following pattern to their major components.[7]

(1) hortatory remarks
(2) wish of peace
(3) greetings
([3a] greetings with a holy kiss)
(4) grace benediction.

Gamble concludes that, regardless of the presence of other elements in the epistolary endings, "no matter what else occurs in the conclusions or which of these formulaic elements is omitted, the sequence as such is never violated."[8] Applying the results of his survey to Romans, he claims that

[4] W.-H. Ollrog, "Die Abfassungsverhältnisse von Rom 16," in *Kirche: Festschrift für G. Bornkamm zum 75. Geburtstag*, ed. D. Lührmann and G. Strecker (Tübingen: Mohr-Siebeck, 1980) 221–44.

[5] W. Wuellner, "Paul's Rhetoric of Argumentation in Romans: An Alternative to the Donfried–Karris Debate," in *The Romans Debate*, ed. K. P. Donfried (Minneapolis: Augsburg, 1977) 152–74 (= *CBQ* 38 [1976] 330–51). Wuellner's case for Romans 16 being a part of Romans' rhetorical peroration is based only on a quotation from W. J. Brandt in which Brandt says that "a peroration will sometimes be found to contain a kind of double conclusion" (Wuellner, "Paul's Rhetoric," 163). This is an inadequate basis for the conclusion that 15:14–16:24 were originally part of a single composition. In what follows, therefore, I shall concentrate on other aspects of Wuellner's argument.

[6] Gamble, *Textual History*, chap. 3, "The Problem of Integrity: The Pauline Epistolary Conclusions," 56–95.

[7] Ibid., 83.

[8] Ibid.

15:30–32 is ". . . the conclusion of the body of the letter, but not [the] conclusion of the letter as a whole." That begins with the peace wish in 15:33, which is the "first formulaic item of the conclusion."[9] After the nonformulaic recommendation in 16:1–2, in 16:3–15 we have the greetings, which end with the reference in v. 16 to greeting one another with a holy kiss. "The sequence is then 'interrupted' by the hortatory remarks of 16:17–20, and these are followed by the grace-benediction of 16:20b."[10] Although it is a departure from the practice in other letters, greetings are resumed in 16:21–23, following which there is in some manuscripts a second grace benediction (16:24), one that Gamble argues is original to the letter.[11] With most other critics, he views 16:25–27 as a later addition.

Now within the composition of 15:33–16:24—and assuming their unity—Gamble observes two anomalies: the doubling of the grace-benediction in 16:20b and 24 and the repetition of the peace wish in 15:33 and 16:20a. However, he finds that the former anomaly, although "unique in Paul, is not unusual in the ancient letter"[12] and that the latter anomaly has a "structural" though not verbal parallel in Phil 4:9 and 19.[13] Gamble does not pay much attention to the apparently unusual hortatory "interruption" of the greetings by 16:17–20 or to the formally related exhortation in 15:30–32. However, these, together with the anomalies, require that we reconsider his conclusions.

Gamble's emphasis on the rigidity of the sequence of elements in his proposed pattern suggests a different reading of the repetitions that occur in 15:33–16:24. He misses one, underestimates another, and thereby renders a third more problematical. The one he misses is the repetition of exhortations in 15:30–32 and 16:17–19; the one he underestimates is the peace wish in 15:33 and 16:20a; and the one rendered more problematical is the double grace benediction in 16:20b and 24. Most interesting in these anomalous repetitions is that in two cases the first appearance is in Romans 15 and the second in Romans 16. This means that all that is lacking of a bona fide ending in Romans 15 is the mandatory grace benediction. But the force of this point was lost when Gamble overlooked the hortatory character of 15:30–32. This is all the more surprising because, following C. J. Bjerkelund, he observes that concluding παρακαλῶ sentences differ from others of a more structurally transitional sort by lacking the latter's usual prepositional phrase, διά plus the genitive.[14] In fact, in both 15:30 and 16:17 the formula παρακαλῶ δὲ

[9] Ibid., 90 n. 154, cf. p. 87.

[10] Ibid., 88.

[11] Ibid., 88, 129–32.

[12] Ibid., 88.

[13] Ibid. Gamble is not in favor of seeing Philippians as a composite letter (pp. 45–46). I disagree.

[14] Ibid., 80.

ὑμᾶς, ἀδελφοί is followed by an infinitive, as also in the concluding exhortations in 1 Thess 5:12 and Phil 4:2. Thus, on his own grounds, 15:30–32 is a terminal epistolary exhortation which, he rightly claims, is usually followed by a peace wish, as it is in 15:33. Strangely, however, Gamble identifies 15:30–32 as a request for prayer, even though the parallels he cites for this all lack the hortatory introduction of 15:30.[15] In this light, we can return to Gamble's pattern in order to see where the repetitions appear in the composition of 15:30–16:24. The numbers in parentheses on the left correspond to the numbers of the elements in the pattern.

(1) hortatory remarks	15:30–32
(2) wish of peace	15:33
(recommendation)	16:1–2
(3 + 3a) greetings, including the kiss	16:3–16
(1) hortatory remarks	16:17–19
(2) wish of peace	16:20a
(4) grace benediction	16:20b
(3) greetings	16:21
(scribe's greetings)	16:22–23
(4) grace benediction	16:24

Given Gamble's pattern and criteria, which I accept, the anomalies represented in this outline are sufficient to warrant suspicion concerning the originality of Romans 16 to the letter to Rome. On the one hand, the anomalies begin only in 16:1–2 and then continue throughout Romans 16. On the other hand, if we read Romans 15 as the end of the letter, it lacks just one mandatory item, a grace benediction, whereas the exhortation in 16:17–19, the peace wish in 16:20a, the greetings in 16:21–23, and the grace benediction in 16:24 look like end matter from another letter. Only the textually problematic 16:20b is anomalous. In this light, it would then appear that it is not the resumption of greetings after the exhortation that anomalous, but the appearance of greetings before it in 16:3–16! The greetings after 16:17–20a are strange only on the assumption that 16:1ff. are continuous with 15:33. But if they are not, 16:1–16 constitutes one problem, and the grace benediction in 16:20b another, for without it 16:17–24 fit the pattern perfectly. Given the text-historical problem of both 16:20b and 24, neither of these is as significant an anomaly as 16:1–16.

However, there is another solution to the problems posed by my outline; if 16:17–20a is an interpolation, and if 16:24 is textually secondary, 15:33–16:23 is much more typical of the endings to Paul's letters, assuming the originality of 16:1–23, which is the position taken by Ollrog.

[15] Ibid., 81.

The strength of Ollrog's argument, that the exhortation in 16:17–20a is an interpolation, is that the exhortation interrupts a scheme of greetings in which 16:3–16a is oriented to the *recipients* of greetings while 16:16b and 21–23 are oriented to the *senders* of greetings.[16] Less persuasive are arguments having to do with matters of form and content in 16:17–20a. Materially, Ollrog finds suspicious seven *hapax legomena*, an allegedly un-Pauline use of the word διδαχή, and an un-Pauline style of argument against what he thinks is a problem of doctrinal deviance. However, the *hapax legomena* are not decisive; the teachings referred to are probably more comprehensive than doctrinal (cf. 6:17; 1 Cor 4:6, 26), and the problem addressed appears to be more potential than actual, which would explain the stylistic character of the exhortation. But Ollrog's formal arguments are considerably weaker and tend to turn the table on his case for an interpolation. Of the dozen post-Pauline parallels he cites as evidence that the hortatory formula in 16:17 could well be late (the nineties), only one, Heb 13:22, is a strict parallel. Conversely, and as Bjerkelund (not cited by Ollrog) has shown, the hortatory formula in 16:17 is typically Pauline (cf. Rom 15:30; 1 Thess 5:12; 1 Cor 16:15; Phil 4:2; see also 2 Cor 13:1 and the discussion above of 15:30–32). Equally immaterial is the argument that the expression "the God of peace" (16:20) is typically Jewish and therefore could have come from others than Paul. It could, to be sure, but its form and function in Romans 16 are also typically Pauline (see Rom 15:33; 2 Cor 13:11; Phil 4:9b [cf. 4:7]; 1 Thess 5:23; Gal 6:16).[17] Accordingly, I see no reason to consider 16:17–20a un-Pauline. However, the question still remains whether or not it is an interpolatlon.

Ollrog begins his argument by observing that the exhortation interrupts a homogeneous greetings section that begins in 16:16b and is concluded in 16:21–23. But as we saw in our review of Gamble's study, what is peculiar to Romans 16 is that greetings also *precede* Paul's exhortation, rather than only appear after it, as in 16:21–23; 1 Cor 16:19–20; 2 Cor 13:12–13; 1 Thess 5:26; and perhaps Philemon 23–24. In this light, we must redirect our attention to Rom 16:16, the second part of which Ollrog sees as leading to 16:21–23. If, with Gamble,[18] we grant that 16:16a ("greet one another with a holy kiss") appears where it does because it formulaically concludes the greetings in 16:3–15, then we must also acknowledge that 16:16b ("all the churches of Christ greet you") appears where it does because when both of these expressions appear in a letter they always appear together, as in 16:16; 2 Cor 13:12–13; Phil 4:21–22; and, in inverted order, in 1 Cor 16:20 (1 Thess 5:26 has only "Greet all the brethren with a holy kiss"). Thus the two

[16] Ollrog, "Die Abfassungsverhältnisse," 226–29.

[17] Gamble, *Textual History*, 67–73.

[18] Ibid., 75–76.

expressions in 16:16a and b constitute a bipartite formula. So Rom 16:16b appears where it does because of its relationship to 16:16a, which appears where it does because of its relationship to 16:3–15, whose location before the exhortation is anomalous. The exhortation itself is not anomalous; indeed, the pattern of Paul's usual closings begins with it. Only the textually problematical grace benediction in 16:20b is anomalous in 16:17–24.

I conclude from these epistolographic considerations: (1) that Rom 16:17–20a is not an interpolation; (2) that 16:1–24 is the ending of a letter other than Romans 1–15, one in which the recommendation and greetings in 16:1–16 anomalously appear before the concluding exhortation and end matter; (3) that 15:30–33 is the ending of the letter to Rome, lacking only a grace benediction; and (4) that, of the textually problematical grace benedictions, 16:20b is of dubious origins while 16:24 appears in its proper position. Let us turn to other evidence and issues that support the conclusion that Romans 16 is not original to the letter to Rome.

Chiasm and the Relationship between Epistolary Beginnings and Endings

It is often noted that certain items introduced in Rom 1:1 or 8–15 are repeated in 15:14–33. Supporters of the originality of Romans 16 note this too, but all insist that 15:14–32/33 marks the end of the body of the letter but not of the whole letter. A classic formulation of this position is Otto Michel's assertion that "the point for point" correspondences between 1:8–15 and 15:14–33 render these sections as the bracketlike opening and close of the body of the letter.[19] Apparently aware that this conclusion could be used to argue against the originality of Romans 16, Michel, like Gamble, then claims that the greetings which dominate Romans 16 are both common in the conclusions of ancient letters and not without parallel in other Pauline letters, specifically in 1 Corinthians and Philemon.[20] Gordon Wiles follows Michel's lead but goes a step further by speaking more specifically of a sequential parallelism between items in 1:8–15 and 15:14–33.[21] But this picture of a point-for-point or sequential parallelism is sharply altered by Wuellner's rhetorical assessment of the evidence. He acknowledges the repetitions but extends the beginning to include 1:1–7, and then he identifies a chiastic structure in 1:1–15, which he sees as the letter's rhetorical

[19] Otto Michel, *Der Brief an die Römer* (KEK; 3rd ed.; Göttingen: Vandenhoeck & Ruprecht, 1966) 362.

[20] Ibid., 375–76.

[21] Gordon P. Wiles, *Paul's Intercessory Prayers: The Significance of the Intercessory Prayer Passages in the Letters of Paul* (SNTSMS 24; Cambridge: Cambridge University Press, 1974) 186–88; cf. 72–73.

exordium or opening. Wuellner's argument raises two issues, one concerning the relationship between the epistolographic and the rhetorical composition of 1:1–15, the other concerning the implications of the chiasm in 1:1–15 for the sequence of repetitions in 15:14–33. Consideration of these issues will be facilitated by a diagram showing the relationship between Wuellner's text-rhetorical chiasm and the epistolographic structure of 1:1–15.[22]

address, 1:1–7a	A Paul's interpretation of the gospel and faith	1:1–5
	B his apostolic relation to churches in Rome	1:6
salutation, 1:7b	B^1 his relation to churches in Rome	1:7–12
thanksgiving, 1:8–15	A^1 interpretation of his gospel ministry (including reference to the frustration of his plans, 1:13)	1:13–15

Comparison of the epistolographic and the rhetorically chiastic segmentations of 1:1–15 immediately discloses that Wuellner gains his rhetorical point at the cost of the total erasure of the obvious epistolary structure of address, salutation, and thanksgiving. His case is undercut, however, by other instances in Paul's letters in which chiasms operate on the epistolary level and serve to relate epistolary sections to one another. But in addition to disconfirming his conclusions, these instances also require us to reopen the question of chiasm, which he has introduced to the discussion of the composition of Romans. Let us first look at some chiastic aspects of letter openings and then turn to chiastic relations between the beginnings and the endings of some of Paul's letters, for the latter has a distinct bearing on the question of the original ending of Romans. For reasons of space, my examples will be few and brief.

Galatians offers two excellent examples of the use of chiasm to integrate epistolary segments at the beginning of a letter.[23] As often noted, the address (1:1–2), salutation (1:3–5), and "thanksgiving" (1:6–9/10) sections of Galatians are distinctive because both the address and the salutation contain more context-specific material than most other letters, and because the "thanksgiving" is transformed by Paul's response to the Galatians' lack of anything for him to be thankful for. But it is also apparent that the unusual material in the address and salutation is related to the two main points in the

[22] The differences between this outline and that in the published version of Wuellner's essay are based on the manuscript version of a revision of it.

[23] My comments on Galatians are based on another study (in progress) concerned with chiasm and composition in Galatians. Further support could be drawn from 1 Cor 1:1–9 for my argument that chiasms relate addresses, salutations, and thanksgivings in some of Paul's letters but not, as far as I have been able to determine, in all of them.

"thanksgiving."[24] In 1:1 Paul adds to his identification of himself as an apostle, "not from men nor through man, but through Jesus Christ and God the Father who raised him from the dead." The focus here is Paul's denial that his apostleship has come to him from other people, that he is the emissary (apostle) of human beings. In the salutation, on the other hand, he adds to his customary reference to the Lord Jesus Christ, "who gave himself for our sins to deliver us from the present evil age, according to the will of our God and Father; to whom be the glory for ever and ever. Amen" (1:4–5). "Christ" is here elaborated upon, as "apostle" was in the address. When we turn to 1:6–10, we find that the significance of Christ and the nature of Paul's apostleship are again taken up, but now in chiastic or inverted order. In 1:6–9 Paul is concerned with the perversion of the gospel of Christ, and in 1:10 with the question of whether he is pleasing humans or is a slave of Christ. Thus the chiasm:

A	Paul's apostleship not from humans but through Jesus Christ	1:1
	B Christ gave himself for our sins (= gospel)	1:4–5
	B^1 some are perverting the gospel of Christ	1:6–9
A^1	I am not pleasing humans but am a slave of Christ	1:10

Like Wuellner's, this chiasm governs the composition of the address, salutation, and thanksgiving, but unlike his, it bridges rather than erases the boundaries of epistolary segments. But there is a further chiasm that serves the same function. For 1:6–10 participates in a second chiasm that governs the first part of the body of the letter, that is, up to the beginning of the hortatory section in 5:1. In 1:11–2:21 Paul elaborates on 1:10 and his repudiation of the charge that he is a person pleaser and apostle of humans. In 3:1–4:31 he is elaborating on 1:6–9, now concentrating on the gospel from which the Galatians have deviated. The epistolary chiastic structure of Gal 1:1–4:31 may be outlined as follows:

address	A		1:1–2	
salutation		B	1:3–5	
thanksgiving		B^1	1:6–9	A
	A^1		1:10	B
			1:11–2:21	B^1
			3:1–4:31	A^1

We shall be looking at some other chiasms that function in the same way, but for the moment these are sufficient to show that at the beginnings of Paul's letters chiasms function on the epistolary rather than the rhetorical

[24] In the above-mentioned study on Galatians, I shall show why I differ with Joachim Jeremias's identification of chiasms in that letter; see his "Chiasmus in den Paulusbriefen," *ZNW* 49 (1958) 145–56.

level and that they serve to relate epistolary sections. These conclusions, together with Wuellner's unexplained inclusion of the epistolary prescript in Romans' alleged rhetorical *exordium,* allow us to return to those other critics who see 1:8–15 as the source of items repeated in 15:14–33.

The procedure for identifying repeated elements conforms to the reader's experience of the text, for one only perceives repetitions when one finds that something has been repeated. This means that 15:14–33 is the source of items for which we seek counterparts in 1:8–15. We need not rehearse here Michel's point-for-point list, although we should note that he overlooks the item concerning the frustration of Paul's desire to visit Rome (1:13; 15:22). More important, we need to see that a search for repeated items reveals that they are repeated not on some vague point-for-point basis (Michel), and not "sequentially"(Wiles), but chiastically. Five items from 1:8–15 are repeated in inverse order in 15:14–33, as the following outline shows:

A 1:8 Paul thanks God for the Romans' faith
  B 1:9 Paul prays for the Romans
    C 1:10–12 Paul desires to visit Rome
      D 1:13 but has thus far been prevented from doing so
        E 1:14–15 Paul's mission to the Gentiles
        E¹ 15:14–16 Paul's mission to the Gentiles
      D¹ 15:17–22 why Paul was hindered from going to Rome
    C¹ 15:23–29 now, after a journey, he will go to Rome
  B¹ 15:30–32 Paul exhorts the Romans to pray for him
A¹ 15:33 Paul invokes God's peace upon the Romans

It is evident from this outline that the material involved in the chiasm includes all of the thanksgiving section that begins the body of the letter, and the ending of the letter's body, including the peace wish. This indicates that in Romans the peace wish in 15:33 is bound up with the ending of the letter's body, even though it is a separate sentence, as also in Gal 6:16; 1 Thess 5:23; and Phil 4:7 (the latter being from one of the letters in a now-composite letter). Indeed, that the peace wish belongs to the body ending is further supported by Rom 16:20a; 2 Cor 13:11; and Phil 4:9, where the peace wish is grammatically integrated into the preceding body-ending matter. Thus, contrary to Gamble's argument, the peace wish appears to conclude the body of the letter rather than to begin its postscript.[25] Be this as it may, the more significant conclusion to draw from the chiasm and what it includes is that this evidence supports the view that 15:30–33 is the incomplete (because of the lack of a grace benediction) ending of the body of one letter and that 16:17–20a is the ending of the body of another letter. No other

[25] Gamble, *Textual History,* 90 n. 154; cf. p. 87.

Pauline letter has the double ending Romans would have if chapter 16 were original to it.

The chiastic relationship between the beginning and the ending of Romans now raises the question whether or not other of Paul's letters are similarly composed. I conclude my case with 1 Corinthians, which happens to be one of the letters Michel cited in defense of the originality of Romans 16 to the letter to Rome.

Although a number of chiasms have been identified in 1 Corinthians,[26] I am not aware that the one involving 1:10–4:21 and 16:1–18 has been observed. Despite some differences, it is very much like the one we found in Romans and serves to support our conclusions about the present double ending to that letter. The difference is that while in Romans the bracketing chiasm was between the beginning of the letter body's thanksgiving section and the end of its hortatory section, in 1 Corinthians the bracketing chiasm is between the beginning and the ending of the hortatory section of the letter, 1:10–16:18. Suffice it to say for the present argument that I do not think these differences are significant. The significant points are the similarities to Romans 1–15 and what they tell us about the endings of Paul's letters.

Remembering the procedure by which repetitions are identified by what in the end is repeated from the beginning, we find a chiasm based on the inverted sequence of four items linked to four names:

A 1:16 the household of Stephanas
  B 3:4–9 Apollos (like Paul, absent)
    C 4:17 Timothy has been sent
      D 4:19–21 Paul is coming to Corinth
      D¹ 16:1–9 Paul is coming to Corinth
    C¹ 16:10–11 Timothy has been sent
  B¹ 16:12 Apollos is absent
A¹ 16:15–18 the household of Stephanas

Following the terminal unit in this chiastic sequence (16:15–18), which is also in the form of a concluding exhortation like its relatives in Rom 15:30–32 and 16:17–20a, we lack a peace wish while finding the more or less usual postscript material in 16:19–24. The less than usual material is of no immediate interest, however. What is of interest is that the particular exhortation in 16:15–18 is contained within the chiastic bracket, just as in Rom 15:30–32. The ending of 1 Corinthians, therefore, reinforces both what we

[26] In addition to Jeremias ("Chiasmus"), see Robert W. Funk, "The Letter: Form and Style," in *Language, Hermeneutic, and Word of God,* ed. R. W. Funk (New York: Harper & Row, 1969) 250–74.

saw in Romans and the conclusion that Romans 15 is the original ending of that letter.[27]

[27] Although following a different stylistic principle, the ending of 1 Thessalonians is closely comparable to those of Romans and 1 Corinthians. In 1 Thess 5:12–22, a concluding exhortation is integrated into the hortatory section of that letter's body by the catchwords παρακαλῶ and ἐρωτάω, which are introduced at the beginning of the hortatory section in 4:1 and repeated throughout 4:1–5:22 (4:10, 18; 5:11, 12, 14). Indeed, the two verbs introduced in 4:1 are repeated sequentially at the beginning of the section's close in 5:12 and 14. Like Rom 15:33 and 16:17–20, the concluding exhortations of 1 Thessalonians are followed by a peace wish in 1 Thess 5:23.

27

The Incarnation: Paul's Solution to the Universal Human Predicament

GEORGE W. E. NICKELSBURG

IT CAN BE PLAUSIBLY argued that if the last word has not been said on Romans 7, it should have been—many moons and reams ago. Moreover, in view of the sophisticated and provocative discussions by such giants as Kümmel, Bultmann, Bornkamm, Käsemann, and others,[1] it might seem unlikely that anything new could be added to the subject. But occasionally a new lens brings out previously unseen details in an old object of scrutiny. In this case, the viewing device will be the Jewish and early Christian scheme of the two ways and the two spirits, and I offer the essay as a piece of unfinished business from the appendix of a dissertation that was much indebted to the tutelage and critique of Helmut Koester.[2]

My thesis is as follows. In Romans 7–8 Paul's categories of Sin and Spirit correspond to the two spirits, especially as expounded in the Qumran *Community Rule* (1QS iii–iv). In the case of the Jew, Sin's domination over Flesh (all humanity *qua* humanity) prevents obedience to the Torah and results in condemnation. This domination is overcome when God's Son

[1] See, e.g., Werner Georg Kümmel, *Römer 7 und die Bekehrung des Paulus* (UNT 7; Leipzig: Hinrichs, 1929); Rudolf Bultmann, *Theology of the New Testament,* trans. K. Grobel (2 vols.; New York: Scribner, 1951) 2:227–53; Günther Bornkamm, "Sin, Law, and Death (Romans 7)," in *Early Christian Experience,* trans. P. L. Hammer (New York: Harper & Row, 1969) 87–104; Ernst Käsemann, *Commentary on Romans,* trans. and ed. G. W. Bromiley (Grand Rapids: Eerdmans, 1980) 191–229.

[2] The form of the dissertation presented for examination ("Resurrection, Immortality, and Eternal Life in Intertestamental Judaism" [Harvard, 1967]) included an appendix of one hundred pages that surveyed some of the dissertation's possible implications for NT texts. Pages 452–56 treat Romans 6. In the published form of the dissertation (*Resurrection, Immortality, and Eternal Life in Intertestamental Judaism* [HTS 26; Cambridge, Mass.: Harvard University Press; London: Oxford University Press, 1972), the material on the two ways and two spirits is treated on pp. 156–65.

becomes Flesh-without-Sin, obeys the Torah's requirement, and through his death and resurrection makes available the Spirit that facilitates the obedience that was required by the Torah. Specifically to the point of this essay, Paul's view of Sin-dominated Flesh has as its counterpart a notion of the Incarnation that is crucial to his theology, though it has been greatly underemphasized by critical scholarship, in spite of the correct intuition of the second-century exegete Irenaeus. I present my argument here largely without documentation, because the critical literature is well known and detailed citation of it would double the length of the essay.

The Teaching of the Two Ways and the Two Spirits

Numerous Jewish and early Christian texts organize their ethical teaching according to the scheme of the two ways. In addition to the book of Proverbs, these texts include 1QS iii.13–iv.26; *1 Enoch* 91–105; the Wisdom of Solomon 1–6; *Didache* 1–6; *Barnabas* 18–20; *Doctrina Apostolorum* 1–5; the *Mandates* of the *Shepherd of Hermas,* and the *Testaments of the Twelve Patriarchs.* Human deeds are spelled out in terms of one's "walking" along the right or the wrong path and as leading to or participating in "life" or "death." Some of these texts also envision two angels or two spirits as the guides along the respective paths. Although not all the texts evidence a single literary form, certain elements do recur with some frequency: lists of good and evil deeds, which are sometimes construed as the deeds of the respective spirits; a conflict between the two angels; reference to or descriptions of the "end" of the paths in life and death and the respective rewards and punishments for human deeds. Some texts express a notion of continuity that is compatible with the image of the ways: to walk on the path of life or death is already to participate in the life or death that lies at its end.

For the present topic, the two-ways section of the Qumran *Community Rule* is of special interest (1QS iii.13–iv.26). The cosmic principles of good and evil are present in the Spirit of Truth and the Angel of Darkness, which reside, in various portions, in every human heart (iii.18–iv.1), where they war against each other until the time of the end, when God will deal definitively with evil (iv.15–26). Cosmic dualism is anthropologized; and although the respective spirits are described as angels ("the prince of light, the angel of darkness, the angel of truth" [iii.20, 21, 24]), this particular version of the two-spirits scheme is close to the later, rabbinic notion of the two *yēṣers.* This anthropological slant is given another nuance in 1QS xi.9–22. The human predicament, which columns iii–iv describe as the spirits' warring within the human heart, is here described as God's righteousness bringing salvation to impotent "flesh" (xi.9, 12), the clay that is humanity "born of woman" (xi.20–22). The motif and first-person form of description recur in the *Thanksgiving Hymn* (e.g., 1QH i.21–27; iv.29–33; xii.24–35; xiii.13–21).

The notion that one or the other or both spirits dwell in human beings occurs in other two-ways texts. The *Mandates* of Hermas repeatedly use the verbs κατοικεῖν and κατοικίζειν to describe how the holy spirit (or the Lord, ὁ κύριος) and the evil spirit dwell in "flesh" (σάρξ) or how God causes the good spirit to dwell in humans (3.1 [28:1]; 5.1.2–6.2.2 [33:2–36:2]; 10.1–2 [40:6; 41:5]). Because of the presence of the holy spirit, the righteous "live to God" (ζῆν τῷ θεῷ). Similar usage of the verb κατοικεῖν appears in the *Testaments of the Twelve Patriarchs* (*T. Reub.* 6:4; *T. Dan* 5:1; *T. Jos.* 10:2–3; *T. Benj.* 6:4). In the Wisdom of Solomon, "Wisdom" is identified as God's spirit, who enters the human heart and brings about the righteousness that makes people "friends of God" (1:1–7; 7:22–30). The presence of Wisdom brings with it the immortality (2:23–3:4) that is opposed to death, which was brought by the devil (1:12–14; 2:24; 5:13) and characterizes wicked humanity.[3]

The Pauline Appropriation of the Two-Ways, Two-Spirits Scheme

The Epistle to the Galatians

Paul's use of the scheme of the two ways and two spirits is evident already in Gal 5:16–6:10. The metaphor of the ways is presumed in the verb "walk" (περιπατεῖν [5:16]) and in the notion that the Spirit "leads" (ἀγεῖν [5:18]) the Christian. The two alternatives are identified as "the Spirit" and "the Flesh." Different from Romans, as we shall see, Paul does not refer here explicitly to the power of "Sin" dwelling in the Flesh, but only to Flesh. As in other two-ways documents, the two principles are "opposed" to each other (5:17; cf. 1QS iv.16–17, 23–25; *Herm. Man.* 5.1–2 [33:1–34:8]; 12.6.4 [49:4]; *T. Jud.* 20), and this antagonism prevents people from doing what they wish (5:17; cf. Rom 7:15–19). Paul lays out a catalogue of vices and virtues, which are identified as the "deeds of the Flesh" and the "fruits of the Spirit" (5:19–21, 22–23). The form parallels 1QS iv.2–6, 9–11, where the catalogues of vices and virtues are ascribed to the two spirits. Similarly, *Herm. Man.* 6.2.3–4 (36:3–4) describes human deeds as the deeds (ἔργα) of the two angels. Also typically, Paul anticipates the rewards and punishments that follow from the deeds of the two ways: "corruption" and "eternal life" (6:8).

The unique contours of Paul's reuse of the tradition of the two ways and two spirits lies in his attitude toward the Torah and his identification of the

[3] Ibid., 162–64.

Spirit. For the Qumranites, the right way consisted in obeying the Torah as it was revealed to the community (1QS v.8–9). For Paul the Torah was problematic. Jews were unable to obey it in such a way as to obtain the covenantal promise of "life" (chap. 3; esp. vv. 10–12); instead they faced its curse. Paul indicates the reason for this in 4:3; the Jews were slaves to the elemental spirits of the universe. Strikingly, Paul goes on to use the same term to designate the spirit powers associated with the Galatians' idolatry (4:8–10). Thus, the Jew under the Torah and the idolatrous Gentile have a common predicament; both are subject to demonic powers that stand in opposition to God. Although Paul does not explicitly locate the evil spirit within human beings, he does find all flesh to be alienated from God (cf. 2:16).

This situation notwithstanding, Paul finds a single solution for the common human predicament. Eternal life awaits all whose deeds are the fruits of the Spirit (5:8). Moreover, he identifies this Spirit as the Spirit of the incarnate Son of God, the risen Christ; and therein lies the heart of Paul's appropriation of the scheme of the two ways and two spirits. The key passage is Gal 4:4–7. Different from Qumran, the good Spirit is not resident, in some portion, in all humans. Rather, at the eschaton ("the consummation of the time"), God sends his Son to take on human flesh ("born of a woman"; cf. 1QS xi.21; 1QH xiii.14), to live under the Torah that could not be obeyed because it was associated with evil spirits. Thus the Son of God-become-human has redeemed the Jews, who were under the Torah, and has made them into what tradition said they were by birth (cf. Exod 4:22; Hos 11:1); they have become "sons" of God by virtue of their possession of the Spirit of the Son. Moreover, that status as children of God is available not only to Jews but to Greeks as well—by virtue of their baptism into Christ (3:26–28). Thus, in the idiom of the two spirits, with its christological twist, it is no longer the "I," the human, who lives, but Christ who lives in me (2:20).

Romans 5–8

The soteriological scheme that Paul sketches in Galatians is developed and explicated in Romans 5–8. As is well known, from the beginning of chapter 5 to the end of chapter 9, Paul abandons references to "faith" and "believing" and, to a large extent, the use of the δικαι- group, although he continues to speak in soteriological language. What is striking for our purposes is his use of vocabulary that is at home in the tradition of the two ways and two spirits: "death, life, the end, to walk, to dwell, the Spirit." A review of these chapters, read in the light of this tradition, will clarify this point and reveal important parallels to the interpretation of Galatians sketched above.

Although in chapter 5 Paul abandons much of the vocabulary of chapters 1–4, he returns to his original problem: the universal predicament of Jews and Gentiles. He reworks the theme by tracing the whole human race back to its common origin in Adam and by attributing its common problem of "death" to the first father's sin, which is repeated in every instance. He then indicates his solution to the problem by identifying Jesus as the new, one man, whose obedience will result in "life." Chapter 6 identifies the means of one's transferral from death to life as baptism, in which one is incorporated into Jesus' death and resurrection. Paul's use of the singular "sin" here as the subject of verbs normally applied to rulers and slave masters suggests a personification that is consonant with Sin's function as an evil power and is reminiscent of the Qumranic notion of the ruling of the two spirits (cf. 1QS iii.20–22). Similarly, Paul vacillates in his use of "life" and "to live." As in the two-ways tradition, the right life participates in eternal life. One can reckon oneself as having passed from the dominion of death to the realm of life.[4] For Paul, one is transferred from the realm of the death that pertains to the children of Adam to the new life brought by the death and resurrection of the second Adam. This structure of thought, which I have identified with the tradition of the two ways, is explicated in chapters 7 and 8 with a set of conceptions related to the imagery of the two spirits.

Like chapter 5, chapter 7 is remarkable in the structure of Romans for its return to a subject treated earlier in the epistle. In chapters 1–3 Paul not only stressed the predicament of the whole human race; he explicitly focused on the Jews' solidarity with humanity in this respect, on their inability to achieve righteousness (2:17–3:20). In chapter 7 he treats this issue within the scheme of the two ways and two spirits. His language is both specific to the Jews and common to all humanity. The basic anthropological category is "Flesh," in which Jews as well as Gentiles participate. Humanity's predicament is that "Sin" "dwells" (οἰκεῖν [7:17, 18, 20; cf. v. 23, ὄντι]) in Flesh. The use of this verb with reference to the Spirit of God and Christ in 8:9, 11 indicates that in chapter 7 Sin is playing the role of the evil spirit. This role is further evident in the fact that Sin catalyzes the disobedience that leads to death (7:9–13), just as the evil spirit does in texts of the two-ways and two-spirits tradition. The Adamic overtones often seen in the language in 7:8–12 are not surprising; Paul has already spoken of human's descent from Adam and their participation in the death that started with him (chap. 5). Here, death is a function of Sin's deceit (ἐξαπατᾶν [v. 11]), just as Adam's original disobedience, which led to his death, was caused by the serpent's deception of Eve, according to 2 Cor 11:3 (ἐξαπατᾶν). In a text that describes the common experience of "Flesh," Paul alludes to the experience of humanity's common forebear.

However, we must not lose our focus on the problem of the *Jew* as a human being. According to Jewish covenantal theology, the Torah not only required

[4] Ibid., 164–67.

but also facilitated the obedience that led to the life it promised (see Lev 18:5; Deut 30:15–16). Crucial is the notion that heavenly Wisdom, which is personified as a divine power, resides in the Torah and enables one to obey the commandments and thus obtain life (Bar 3:9–4:4; Sirach 24). Similarly, the Wisdom of Solomon identifies personified Wisdom with God's Spirit, which "enters" human souls (1:4–7; 7:27). Thus the righteous can obey the Torah and obtain "life"—indeed, eternal life and immortality, according to the Wisdom of Solomon. The Qumran *Community Rule* expresses a similar view; the machinations of the Prince of Darkness notwithstanding, in the children of light the Spirit of Truth catalyzes the obedience that leads to life (iv.6–8).

In Romans 7 Paul plays out a fascinating variation on this theme and related elements in two-ways, two-spirits texts, notably the struggle between the two spirits. Most basic, all Jews, by virtue of their humanity (Flesh), have Sin dwelling within them. Although the Torah is the repository of the Spirit (πνευματικός [7:14]), which is the equivalent of ben Sira's Wisdom, the Jew, being human (σαρκινός), is under the power of Sin. This evil power has captured the Torah, neutralized its spiritual element, and used the commandment to trigger disobedience. Thus, there is no effective counterpart to oppose Sin. Following the model of the two-spirits texts, Paul describes an inner struggle (vv. 15–23) between the "I," (the law of) my mind, and (the law of) Sin that dwells in me. I wish to do good (the problem here is not a bondage of the *will*), but Sin prevents me from executing the desire to do good (cf. Gal 5:17 and its very similar wording). The Jew, like the rest of humanity, is under Sin's domination and is bound for Death. Except for the anticipatory v. 25ab, chapter 7 ends with the Jew at a dead end. Torah and covenant notwithstanding, the people of God—like the rest of humanity—are bereft of life because they are incapable of obedience. The situation is much more radical than in 1QS iii–iv, where the children of light are able, in part, to struggle effectively with the evil spirit—even if the resolution of the struggle lies in the eschatological future.

If humanity, and specifically the Jew, has reached an impasse according to chapter 7, Paul explicates a definitive solution in chapter 8. Sin in the Flesh is overcome by the good Spirit, which is identified as the Spirit of the Risen Christ. Paul solves the anthropological problem by reshaping the scheme of the two spirits in eschatological and christological terms, as he did in Galatians.

Paul reiterates the dilemma: the Torah is weakened by the Flesh that is inhabited by Sin (v. 3). But he describes how God deals with this by sending his Son in the likeness of sinful flesh. As in Galatians, the Incarnation is pivotal. Because Flesh *qua* Flesh is incapable of obedience—and therefore even the Jew is under the dominion of the evil power—God must break the universal human impasse by sending his Son in "the likeness" of Flesh which is under Sin's bondage. The notion of likeness suggests not that the Son is quasi-human but that his humanity is not possessed by the virus of Sin, even if it is like sinful flesh.

This sin-free human being now makes possible what was previously impossible, namely, the obedience that leads to life, the fulfillment of God's righteous demand previously expressed in the Torah. To begin with, the Son-become-human fulfills the law's demands, presumably by obedience in his life and by his submission to death. Through this death "for sin" and the resurrection effected by God, the good Spirit—which was unavailable to Jews and Gentiles, that is, which was not present in Flesh—is now offered to all who are in Christ. Because the Son of God became human, all human beings who are "in Christ" have their Flesh transformed by the power of the Spirit of the Risen Christ, which is the Spirit of God's Son. Thereby, they are children of God, having become such through baptism, which effects participation in Christ's death and resurrection (chap. 6).

Furthermore, in the imagery of the two-spirits scheme, the Spirit of God—or Christ, God's Son—dwells in the Christian (8:9–11), as Sin dwells in Flesh, and "leads" the children of God, as the good angel of the two-spirits tradition leads the righteous. Through this Spirit's direction, those in Christ, though they continue to struggle in their body (8:10), can live according to the Spirit and thus await the "life" which is theirs as heirs of God and joint heirs with the Son of God. The struggle that was ineffectual in the flesh—the "spiritual" character of the Torah notwithstanding (chapter 7)—is now effective through the power of the Spirit made available through the resurrection of Christ.

Thus, the scheme of chapters 7 and 8 as a whole repeats the scheme of Romans 5: Flesh, the descendants of Adam, at the prodding of "Sin," disobey and are bound for death. The new human being, free of sin and obedient to God, makes possible a new humanity whose obedience promises life.

In conclusion, Paul's soteriology in Romans 5–8 is informed by the categories of the Jewish ethical tradition of the two ways and two spirits. As in Qumran, Paul sees the problem as anthropological, but in a much more universal sense. All humans—not just the children of darkness—by virtue of their humanity are under the domination of the evil power and cut off from salvation (cf. 3:9, 19, 23). Because the problem is universal, it must be solved by the creation of a new human being in whom is the potentiality for the renewal of the human race. This happens when God's preexistent Son is born as a human being, lives in obedience to God, dies as only a human being can and must, and rises to be present as Spirit. Because that Son has become human, other humans who are incorporated into him can become children of God whose lives the Spirit leads along the way that culminates in the full receipt of the inheritance and glory that belong to God's children.

Philippians 2:5–11

The incarnation plays a role in yet another Pauline text. In drawing the parallels, I leave open the question of its authorship. This "Christ hymn" traces the path of a divine being from heaven to earth and back again. Although the figure is never named, the description of God as "Father" (2:11) suggests that this central character is the Son. He is not said to be "sent," but his arrival on earth in human form is underscored by threefold repetition and the use of terminology reminiscent of both Gal 4:4 (γενόμενος) and Rom 8:3 (ἐν ὁμοιώματι ἀνθρώπων). Also essential to the Son's career is his obedience (Phil 2:8; cf. Rom 5:19), which leads to the death that Romans sees as the common fate of humanity. An explicit contrast with Adam has sometimes been perceived in this first section of Phil 2:5–11. In Philippians 2, the Son's return to heaven (v. 11) diverges strikingly from the scheme of Galatians and Romans, which stress, at least in these contexts, the presence of the Spirit (of the Son). This emphasis on the heavenly enthronement of the Son is consonant with both Phil 1:23 and 3:20–21. Nonetheless, a counterpart of the presence of the Spirit does appear in the introduction to the hymn, where the Christian is to be "minded" as Christ was, or as one is "in Christ" (cf. Rom 8:6, 7, 27).

The hymn in Philippians 2 stands out as quite different from the two-ways material discussed above, but its emphasis on the Incarnation, obedience, and death of the Son is strikingly similar to the pivotal role played by these events in the scheme of salvation in Galatians and Romans.

Some Implications

If the major points of this brief essay prove to be valid, they have significant implications for a broad range of topics relating to Pauline studies. They can only be suggested, in even more sketchy form.

1. Although Paul claims to have been a Pharisee and his language in Romans 7 seems close to the rabbinic notion of the *yēṣer*s, taken as a whole, his appraisal of the human condition and his expression of it are strikingly close to the formulation of the Qumran *Community Rule.* Such a parallel has often been noted with reference to his use of justification language. The parallels to the two-spirits tradition strengthen the connection. It also suggests some caution in setting up a simple Pharisee/Essene distinction in early Judaism.

2. The centrality of the Incarnation in a section of Romans that does not use the language of "faith," but parallels sections that do, may well support the interpretation of πίστις χριστοῦ as the faith that Jesus possessed as a human being. Such faith may have comprised Jesus' obedience to God, both with respect to the Torah and the decision to die. According to this

interpretation, those in Christ are then justified by identifying with or emulating the faith of Jesus the human being.

3. The centrality of the Incarnation as the mechanism that facilitates salvation when humans become children of God like God's Son also seems to favor the view of scholars who place the center of Paul's theology in his participation language. It is possible to be "in Christ" because the Son became human.

4. If this observation is correct, then Irenaeus was much closer to the mind of the apostle than has often been thought. His citation of Gal 4:4–5 and Rom 8:3 to support his incarnational theology is based on an exegesis of those texts remarkably closer to their theological function than much of the interpretive tradition that has derived from Augustine.[5]

5. The scheme that has been laid out here helps to clarify some of the difficulties that arise when one compares Paul's language about justification by faith with his undeniable allusions to a judgment on the basis of works. The scheme of the two ways always presumes that one is rewarded or punished for one's deeds. On the one hand, Paul affirms that human beings as such are incapable of righteousness and, specifically, that Jews as such cannot obtain the covenantal promise of life. Nonetheless, Paul's theology requires obedience and a right life as much as any Jewish document requires it. Paul resolves the problem by positing that such obedience and righteousness are possible in spite of one's humanity through participation in Christ and the consequent prodding and leading of the Spirit. When humanity is at a dead end, God takes the initiative.

6. Within this context it may be worth reconsidering the Pauline notion of δικαιοσύνη θεοῦ. If the life in Christ is a function of the Spirit of the Son of God, then this Greek term could mean, in some of its occurrences, the righteousness, or life of righteous deeds, that are, properly speaking, a righteousness alien to humanity and belonging to God, who is its author. Similarly, if one considers the soteriological scheme from start to finish, the verb δικαιοῦν can also designate the whole process and mean, as is semantically quite possible, "to make righteous."

7. Theoretically, the Pauline soteriological scheme could permit the salvation of both Christians and Jews. God changes the whole human situation. Nonetheless, Romans 7 appears to require a reading of Romans 9–11 that in turn requires that the Jews must believe in order to be saved. If Romans 8 is the answer to the problem in Romans 7, and if the two together—along

[5] For Gal 4:4–5, see *Adversus haereses* 3.16.3, 7; 21.1; 5.21.1; for Rom 8:3, see 3.20.2. For a classic exposition of the contrast between Paul and Irenaeus, see Wilhelm Bousset, *Kyrios Christos*, trans. J. E. Steely (Nashville: Abingdon, 1970) 446–53. Whatever the validity of some of Bousset's observations, Irenaeus helps us to recover a major element in Paul's thought that has been overlooked in the scholarship dominated by Augustinian tradition.

with chapters 5–6 parallel Romans 1–4, then the justification of the Jews, who are condemned by God along with the rest of humanity, depends on their transforming faith in Christ, which appears to be exactly what Rom 11:23 states. As twentieth-century Christians wrestle with this theological problem, they need to affirm Paul's view of the universal grace of God while recognizing that time has belied the exclusivism of his formulation.[6]

[6] The basic line of argument in this essay was developed in a seminar on the interpretation of Paul in Irenaeus and Augustine, which my colleague James F. McCue and I conducted at the University of Iowa in 1988. Various points of the essay were clarified and sharpened in conversation with Professor Jouette Bassler, who led a seminar on the Law and Faith in Paul at the University of Iowa in the spring of 1990, at the time when I was writing the first draft. I am indebted to both colleagues for comments and suggestions, but assume full responsibility for the final product.

28

The Revelation of John and Pauline Theology

EDUARD LOHSE

THE AUTHOR OF the book of Revelation sends to seven churches in Asia Minor, from Ephesus to Laodicea, the message that he had received from the risen and exalted Lord. In speaking to them, he testifies at the same time to the whole of Christianity the proclamation that only one is the Lord of Lords and King of Kings. Therefore, Christians who have understood the meaning of their confession cannot worship other deities or authorities.

This clear statement has to be considered in view of the difficult situation into which it could lead the congregations in Asia Minor at the end of the first century CE. The emperor Domitian demanded that all in his vast empire should address him as Lord and God and prove their loyalty by participating in the cultic veneration of the Caesar. For the pagan population in Asia Minor this demand did not create particular problems, because they were familiar with the widespread Hellenistic idea that the deity was present in the person of the ruler or other outstanding personalities. So they could do what they were asked without much hesitation. For members of the Christian congregations, however, it was absolutely impossible to adore a human being as divine. So they had to be prepared to suffer the consequences of this demand and to follow their Lord in becoming martyrs in the true sense of the word: to give witness to the sincerity of their faith and to be prepared to be hit by persecution and death.[1]

John the prophet wishes to prepare the believers so that they might stand this test of faith and testimony. In order to explain what this situation means he describes a series of colorful pictures and visions that unfold "what must soon take place" (1:1). Christians are not allowed to have any illusions about

[1] Koester, *Introduction* 2:150–51.

the hard realities of history. Yet whatever might happen cannot hinder the coming of the kingdom of God. The most decisive event already took place: the almighty God demonstrated to whom the kingdom belongs, in Christ's suffering, death, and resurrection. Whoever, therefore, remains true and faithful in the final period of tribulation and temptation will participate in the coming glory, which shall be revealed soon. The assurance that God's Anointed One will come after a very short while may give strength and hope to the Christian congregations and help them to survive until the last judgment. Then all those who have remained faithful will inherit the kingdom of Christ and share his final triumph over the powers of evil.

In the seven letters addressed to the churches, the prophet describes the concrete conditions under which Christians lived during this period. The situation is in no way presented in an idealized fashion. On the contrary, a realistic description is given about life in the congregations, what is being done by their members, and what was left undone in their daily life. There is light, but there is also much shadow and darkness. Appreciation for the endurance and steadiness of quite a number of Christians is expressed, but it is not overlooked that other groups are weak in their faith and have abandoned the love they had at first. Some of them are inclined to listen to false teachers who try to explain that Christian freedom includes the permission to do whatever one likes. Following them they do not hesitate to "eat food sacrified to idols and practice immorality" (2:14). Thus they fully participate in the social-religious life of the Hellenistic world and are convinced that even this is allowed for them.

The prophet John preaches to the seven congregations in Christ's name testifying that he knows their deeds and their failures. The Lord is well informed about patient endurance, tribulation, and suffering among them, but he knows as well what false teachers have said. Their activities are criticized and the congregations are being invited to come back to a clear and convincing confession practiced in a way of life obedient to God's commands. They must repent; otherwise they will miss the future salvation and be left out when the Lord comes to lead them to everlasting glory.

The first of these letters is sent to the church in Ephesus, the capital of the province and residence of the Roman governor. The congregation of Ephesus had been the center of the apostle Paul's activity during his stay in Asia Minor nearly half a century earlier. In view of the preaching of Paul as explained in his letters, it is surprising to find no hints of an ongoing influence of Pauline theology in the congregations reflected in the book of Revelation. Not a single verse mentions what Paul had said about justification by faith and the freedom of Christians who are no longer servants of the law but have become slaves of righteousness. Once they had been slaves of sin, law, and death, but now they have become obedient from the heart to the standard of teaching to which they were committed (Rom 6:17). Why is the sermon of repentance and renewal that is given by John the prophet to Christians in the former area of Pauline mission not combined with a reference to the gospel as it had been interpreted by the apostle?

Paul on his part had not hesitated to use apocalyptic terms and images to underline what Christian faith and hope really mean, although he did not develop a picture of world history as it is set forth in the book of Revelation. However, this difference cannot explain the failure to mention a single syllable of Pauline thought. This fact is all the more astonishing in view of the fact that at the end of the first century CE there were some influential persons in Ephesus who were informed about Pauline theology and doctrine. We read in the Pastoral letters a clear testimony that Paul's work and theology were not entirely forgotten in this period. They were still being spoken of and discussed in order to find answers to new problems. Reading the book of Revelation, on the other hand, gives the impression that its author had never heard about Paul the apostle and his theology.

John the prophet speaks of the twelve apostles in 18:20 and 21:14 without even mentioning that Paul too had been called to be an apostle. John points to the Twelve as to a circle that was closed. The names of the twelve apostles are written on the twelve foundations of the heavenly city of God, but the name of Paul the apostle is not mentioned. Was he forgotten? Or why is there not anywhere in the book of Revelation an allusion that would point either to the person or to the theology of Paul?

When attempting to find an answer to this question a more thorough investigation may help us to go beyond a first impression.

1. John the prophet gives two introductions to his book. In the first three verses we read a foreword that mentions in solemn words the origin of his prophecy, its content, and those who should listen to his preaching. At the end a beatitude is pronounced to those who read aloud the words of the prophecy and to those who keep what is written therein, "for the time is near" (1:3).

Then John begins a second time, saying "John to the seven churches in Asia" (1:4). Now he starts to formulate the preamble of a letter as we know it from early Christian documents in the New Testament. The author does not use the short formula of letters conventional in the Hellenistic world, in which usually only the sender and the addressee were named and a very short salutation was expressed: χαίρειν ("greeting"). In the New Testament writings this form is found in very few passages (Acts 15:23; 23:26; Jas 1:1). The normal introduction of a Christian letter followed the tradition common in the oriental world. Here the introduction of a letter had two parts. The first stated the names of sender and addressee, and the second contained a new sentence expressing the greeting: "Peace be with you." This sentence could be expanded by adding other wishes for the welfare of those who receive and read the letter.

It was Paul who formulated this greeting, which describes the Christian message in a very concise form. Right at the beginning of his letters he wrote to the congregations: "Grace to you and peace" (1 Thess 1:1) or, in a more expanded form: "Grace to you and peace from God the Father and our Lord Jesus Christ" (Gal 1:3) . Further words might be added to explain that grace and peace are the gift of Christ who offered himself for our sins. At the end a doxology could be added: To him "the glory for ever and ever" (Gal 1:5). In this formula phrases shaped by Christian liturgy were used to pronounce the blessings sent to the addressees. The liturgical structure of the formula at the beginning of a letter gives evidence that the letter was to be read aloud when the members of the church came together for worship.

The last verses of Pauline letters underline this "setting in life": those who are not full members of the church must leave. The Christians kiss one another to demonstrate by this sign the reality of peace in which they belong together. And they pray *maranatha,* that is, "Our Lord, come" (1 Cor 16:22). The final blessing, "The grace of the Lord Jesus be with you" (1 Cor 16:23), repeats the blessing that was expressed at the beginning and leads to the eucharistic liturgy that was celebrated when the sermon or the reading of the epistle had finished.

In the book of Revelation we find the same elements of introduction and conclusion as in the epistles of Paul. In the latest exegetical discussion this correlation has rightly been underscored.[2] The introduction in the form of a letter was quite unusual in Jewish apocalyptic writings of that time. Yet this form was quite common in early Christianity, as can be seen from the Pauline letters. The epistolary form not only is an outward framework, but reveals the specific Christian character of the following message. This message is sent to the addressees who call on the name of the Lord. They are to listen to the greeting and blessing: "Grace to you and peace" (1:4).

Because John the prophet makes use of this formula at the beginning of his book, the possibility of a connection with the common Christian practice as shaped by Paul the apostle cannot be overlooked.

2. In discussing whether the author of the book of Revelation should be considered a member of a so-called Johannine school, one must recall that the Johannine epistles do not include a single reference to or parallel with the Pauline formula. The first and third letters of John begin in totally

[2] See M. Karrer, *Die Johannesoffenbarung als Brief: Studien zum literarischen, historischen und theologischen Ort des Werkes* (Göttingen: Vandenhoeck & Ruprecht, 1986); J. Roloff, *Die Offenbarung des Johannes* (Zürcher Bibelkommentare; Zurich: Theologischer Verlag, 1984) 15f.; E. Lohse, "Wie christlich ist die Offenbarung des Johannes?" *NTS* 34 (1988) 321–38, esp. 325–28.

different fashion; only the second letter might suggest a certain allusion to the introductory greeting as it is used in the Pastorals: "Grace, mercy, and peace" (2 John 1:3). In view of the differences between the opening passage of the book of Revelation and the epistolary formula in the Johannine letters, one must be skeptical about the theory of a so-called Johannine school to which John the prophet might have belonged.[3] The formula with which the epistle directed to the seven churches in Asia Minor is begun shows far more similarities with the post-Pauline tradition that was developed in different ways in the deutero-Pauline documents. Despite the indisputable fact that there are nearly no theological references to Pauline thinking in the book of Revelation, these connections found in the opening formula of the epistle should not be overlooked.

The author of the book of Revelation makes use of the formula as it had been passed on in early Christian tradition, but he forms the content of the opening verses with a view to the message of his book. The origin of grace and peace is not identified as God the Father and the Lord Jesus Christ, but a threefold expression is formulated that already intones the melody of the whole book: "from him who is and who was and who is to come—and from the seven spirits who are before his throne—and from Jesus Christ the faithful witness, the firstborn of the dead, and the ruler of kings on earth" (1:4f.). The title by which God's sovereignty is named does not speak of an unchangeable eternal being but points out that God, who was and is, will come. The seven spirits demonstrate in an apocalyptic expression the fullness of spirit that is given to each one of the seven congregations. The majesty of Jesus Christ is described in view of the testimony he had given until his death on the cross, his resurrection from the dead, and his enthronement as King of Kings and Lord of Lords. In these phrases apocalyptic traditions and the Christian confession are connected to illustrate the universality of the good news of the gospel.

3. It is thus consistent that the author continues by connecting the introductory greeting with a doxology that also is expressed by phrases of the common Christian creed: "To him who loves us and made us a kingdom, priests to his God and Father, to him be glory and dominion for ever and ever. Amen" (1:5b–6). This doxology might be compared to the words of praise by which Paul concludes the introductory passage in the Letter to the Galatians (1:5). By means of the key concepts of redemption and the calling to kingdom and priesthood, the christological confession is combined with ecclesiology. The church of God belongs to the exalted ruler and is

[3] The hypothesis of a so-called Johannine school is critically discussed by E. Schüssler Fiorenza, "The Quest for the Johannine School: The Fourth Gospel and the Apocalypse," *NTS* 23 (1977) 402–27; reprinted in *The Book of Revelation: Justice and Judgment* (Philadelphia: Fortress Press, 1985) 85–113.

appointed to participate in his kingdom, being obliged to serve him in priestly holiness and praise him as is his due.[4]

Although the apocalyptic terminology may appear a strange tool to interpret the meaning of the Christian faith, it is quite evident from the introduction of the book of Revelation that its author is a Christian prophet who wishes to proclaim the gospel of Christ.

4. The final passage of the book corresponds to the opening. Here also the author follows the pattern as developed by Paul. In these verses the wish that God's grace might remain with the addressees is articulated: "The grace of the Lord Jesus be with all the saints" (22:21). A sharp division between those who believe in Christ and those who are standing outside is made, and the eschatological hope is expressed in the words "Amen, come, Lord Jesus" (22:20). This suggests that the Eucharist was to be celebrated after the reading of the letter. Thus the framework of the book of Revelation fits perfectly into the pattern shaped by Paul in 1 Corinthians.

This pattern had in the meantime become quite common in early Christianity. It was used whenever someone wished to send a Christian message in written form to potential readers or hearers in the church. We find the influence of such a pattern not only in the deutero-Pauline literature but also in some of the so-called Catholic letters, and John the prophet also brings his message to the seven churches into the framework of such a Christian letter.

5. Not only the formal connection but also the content that is put into this pattern reminds us of the intention that Paul had in mind: to preach the gospel and to interpret its meaning in view of the actual situation of the Christian church. We find a quotation of the common Christian creed (1:5f.) not only in the opening passages of the book of Revelation but also within the corpus of apocalyptic visions and images: Again and again christological titles and traditional phrases of Christian confession are used. As in other early Christian writings, Christ is here named Messiah, Son of David, Lord, Son of God, and, very often, the Lamb (of God). These titles are used in different passages, one emphasized more than another, but none of them is missing.[5]

In this context it is striking that only in 2:18 is Christ named Son of God. In the letter to the church in Thyatira a comprehensive quotation from Psalm 2 (vv. 8–9) is given, and although v. 7 is not quoted here, it may be alluded to in the use of the title Son of God: "You are my son, today I have begotten you." But apart from this passage of scripture, the Messiah was not

[4] See P. van der Osten-Sacken, "Christologie, Taufe, Homologie—Ein Beitrag zu Apc Joh 1.5f.," *ZNW* 58 (1967) 255–66.

[5] See T. Holtz, *Die Christologie der Apokalypse des Johannes* (2nd ed.; Berlin: Akademie-Verlag, 1971).

called "son of God" in contemporary Judaism. In the syncretistic world of the Hellenistic period this title could be misunderstood to imply a physical descent from God. To avoid this misunderstanding the Jews were extremely careful about applying a title to the Messiah that could possibly lead to a false interpretation of the eschatological hope. John the prophet shares this careful use of the second psalm and the title Son of God. Since he is closely enough related to Jewish presuppositions to understand the messianic hope, he tries to interpret the christological confession in such a way as to enable people brought up under Judaism to grasp its meaning.

The author of the book of Revelation shares with early Christians in general the common creed expressed by the titles to describe Christ's majesty. John the prophet uses these titles always in view of their Old Testament background and their interpretation in the Jewish tradition. By quoting these titles in this context he wishes to stress the continuity from prophecy to fulfillment. What was promised in the Holy Scripture is fulfilled in Christ. That means that everyone who believes in Christ receives salvation and freedom from him.

6. The experience of redemption can in no way be won by human activity or effort; it is given by God's overwhelming mercy. Therefore, John the prophet explains the meaning of the good news he has to proclaim in words that come quite close to terms we find also in Pauline theology: That Christ has freed us from our sins by his blood, confessed in traditional phrases (1:5; cf. Rom 3:25), means that those who trust in him "have washed their robes and made them white in the blood of the Lamb" (7:14; cf. 22:14). Gratuitously they have received the total renewal of their life. They are called to accept the invitation: "To the thirsty I will give from the fountain of the water of life without payment" (21:6). This invitation is repeated at the end of the book: "And let him who is thirsty come, let him who desires take the water without price" (22:17). Christ who suffered for our sake gives freedom to those who trust in him and are willing to follow him no matter what might happen. In these verses we read applications of the common early Christian message by which the prophet wishes to comfort and strengthen the congregations in their tribulation, difficult times in which they might be tempted to give up their faith.

7. It is not only the danger coming from outside but also the uncertainty within the Christian church that might weaken faithfulness and perseverance. In the seven letters that are sent to the congregations in Asia Minor this threat is often described.[6] There are false teachers who are labeled "Nicolaitans" (2:6, 16). They claim to be true in interpreting the scriptures, but they lay claim to an unrestricted liberty that allows them free sexual behavior and unhindered participation in the way of life of the non-Christian

[6] See Robinson-Koester, *Trajectories*, 148.

surrounding society. They pretend to have the right knowledge, that is, insight into "the deep things of Satan" (2:24), so that they feel free to come in contact with heathen practices.

It is not impossible that these tendencies represent certain consequences of early gnostic teaching and ethics already developed in some congregations founded by Paul. Some of those inclined to adhere to these tendencies tried to argue that they had understood what Christian freedom, about which Paul had preached, really means. Paul is very sharp in his criticism of this movement, as we learn especially from his correspondence with the congregation in Corinth. But he could not prevent gnostic teachers, both during his lifetime and later on, from declaring themselves to be true followers of the apostle. Probably certain influences from such circles were active in the church of Asis Minor at the end of the century.

Some of these false teachers claimed to be apostles (2:2), possibly using slogans that could have been derived from Pauline sentences interpreted in a way that would justify gnostic teaching and behavior. One can only speculate about loose connections of that sort. In the book of Revelation it is stated only that these teachers are heretics and therefore really not apostles at all (2:2). But no polemic is found against slogans of misinterpreted Pauline sentences such as the polemical arguments put forward by the author of the epistle of James, fighting against positions that are falsely derived from Pauline theology. John the prophet stresses that deeds are required as witness of the totality of Christian life, but he seems never to have heard of the problem of the relation of faith to works. He is eager to defend Christian orthodoxy by his prophetic message, which he preaches in the language of apocalyptic to explain that Christ alone is Lord and king.[7]

To sum up these observations: It still remains surprising that no explicit traces of Pauline theology are found in the book of Revelation. A historical reflection might help to explain this lack of specific Pauline influence in the book of Revelation. The Jewish war and the capture and destruction of Jerusalem in 70 CE made quite a number of Palestinian Christians leave their country and come to Asia Minor. Their arrival changed the character of the congregations in that region. It is to be supposed that the prophetic traditions that stand behind the author of the book of Revelation are of Palestinian origin and became influential when the time of the Pauline mission had passed. In these traditions the name and theology of Paul were nearly unknown. They were entirely related to the inheritance of the twelve apostles.

[7] See W. Bauer, *Orthodoxy and Heresy in Earliest Christianity,* trans. and ed. R. A. Kraft and G. Krodel (Philadelphia: Fortress Press, 1971) 179.

Although there are some similarities in the interpretation of the common creed between the Pauline letters and the book of Revelation, John the prophet writes his message without taking notice of the work of Paul the apostle. Only by the fact that his book is written in the formal shape of a Christian letter does he give a weak indication that he intends to continue proclaiming the same gospel that had been preached by Paul in Asia Minor. Despite the different character of the letters sent by Paul and John the prophet to the churches in Asia Minor the two agree in underlining what is most important for the church in every period: to trust in the good news that grace and peace are given by God the Father and the Lord Jesus Christ.

29

A Genre for 1 John

JULIAN V. HILLS

HELMUT KOESTER, one of the last of Rudolf Bultmann's dissertation advisees and in the United States his best-known student, has advanced what in modern idiom might be termed his teacher's "agenda," especially in the insistence that the New Testament be interpreted in light of and along with the wider Hellenistic world. Such faithfulness to a basic scholarly vision has been exemplified by numerous substantial exegetical judgments, inspired in part by the broader fund of primary materials accessible to Koester than to Bultmann. One such judgment, whose implications have not yet been fully explored, is that the final paragraph of 1 John is not, *contra* Bultmann, the work of a redactor. This judgment is the present essay's starting point.

Bultmann held that the epistles of John, like the Gospel before them, underwent a revision at the hands of an "ecclesiastical redactor."[1] Bultmann maintained that 1 John 5:13 is a postscript with which the original writing ended and, hence, that 5:14–21 was added by the redactor as an "appendix."[2] To this position Koester has responded with the observation that, although "the final section of 1 John . . . gives the impression of an appendix which was secondarily added," this impression is subject to a major qualification, for "its language and content would still argue for the same author."[3] Near the end of his review of the contents of the epistle Koester offers the following summary:

[1] Stated most succinctly in Bultmann, *The Johannine Epistles* (Hermeneia; Philadelphia: Fortress Press, 1973) 2: "the text of 1 John was reworked to bring it into conformity with ecclesiastical tradition." For the Gospel, see Bultmann, *The Gospel of John: A Commentary* (Philadelphia: Westminster, 1971) 11; here he speaks of the redaction's tendency to "heighten ecclesiastical interests."

[2] Bultmann, *Epistles,* 83.

[3] Koester, *Introduction* 2:194; see also Wolfgang Nauck, *Die Tradition und der Charakter des ersten Johannesbriefes* (WUNT 3; Tübingen: Mohr-Siebeck, 1957) 136–38. For a detailed discussion of the relation between the beginning and ending of 1 John, see Julian Hills, "'Little children, keep yourselves from idols': 1 John 5:21 Reconsidered," *CBQ* 51 (1989) 285–310.

> 1 John not only emphasizes the necessity to forgive sins repeatedly (1:8–10), but also gives instructions in a church order for this forgiveness (5:16–17) and warns of the seduction of the world (2:15–17). It is clear from these interests that the author is a later church politician from the Johannine circle, who argues in this writing for the practical aspects of the continuation of the Johannine inheritance.[4]

These clues to the purpose of the writing will be taken up here in a new suggestion concerning the genre of 1 John as a whole: that it be considered an early Christian example of the "community rule" or "church order," indeed, to the extent that our evidence allows, *the* Johannine church order.

The Genre of 1 John: The State of the Question

No reader of Raymond E. Brown's monumental commentary on the Johannine epistles can fail to be struck by a paradox.[5] On the one hand, as far as possible Brown interprets the whole of 1 John in terms of the communal situation commonly held to have inspired it, namely, the departure of secessionist brethren from the Johannine fold and hence the perceived need for a defense of the Johannine gospel. On the other hand, having reviewed and judged as inconclusive the history of research on the question of genre, Brown himself abstains from classifying 1 John according to any of the suggested categories: tract, tractate, manifesto, circular epistle, homily, diatribe, pastoral encyclical, and the like.[6] Brown writes: "I shall offer no new name for the literary genre represented by I John but simply attempt to describe what the work basically does."[7]

Brown's caution is understandable, and he is not without an explanation for the difficulty: "the peculiar format of I John may have been influenced by the author's attempt to refute the secessionists by commenting on GJohn [= the Gospel of John] to which they also appealed as a justification for their

[4] Koester, *Introduction* 2:195.

[5] R. E. Brown, *The Epistles of John* (AB 30; Garden City, N.Y.: Doubleday, 1982).

[6] Brown, *Epistles,* 86–90; see also Werner Georg Kümmel, *Introduction to the New Testament* (rev. ed.; Nashville: Abingdon, 1975) 437.

[7] Brown, *Epistles,* 90. Philipp Vielhauer (*Geschichte der urchristlichen Literatur* [Berlin/New York: de Gruyter, 1975] 463) quotes Bultmann: "the form of 1 John is 'without analogy.'" It is worth noting that the influential survey of Greco-Roman epistolography presented by Stanley K. Stowers (*Letter Writing in Greco-Roman Antiquity* [Library of Early Christianity 5; Philadelphia: Westminster, 1986]) tacitly accepts 1 John among NT epistles: "Exhortation plays a major role in all the letters of Paul. . . . This is also the case for Hebrews, James, 1 Peter, 1 and 2 John" (p. 96); but see David E. Aune, *The New Testament in Its Literary Environment* (Library of Early Christianity 8; Philadelphia: Westminster, 1987): "First John is a deliberative homily rather than a letter" (p. 218).

views."[8] This does not mean that, for Brown, 1 John is a commentary in the usual sense, but rather that because of its purpose this so-called epistle almost necessarily imitates the Gospel of John in form and style, especially in its opening and closing.

To be sure, Brown's decision to refrain from a literary judgment has this in its favor, that it addresses the issue of form without recourse to an elaborate source theory, such as those of J. C. O'Neill or a host of predecessors.[9] But in evading a literary judgment Brown places almost the entire burden of exegesis on his reconstruction of the "situation" behind the writing, and it must therefore be asked whether sufficient weight is given to any interpretive clues inherent in the epistle's genre—assuming that it is possible to define it.

One further attempt to define 1 John deserves mention, not only because it moves solidly in the direction of the option to be explored more fully below but also because it takes into account both the probable situation of communal division and those parts of the epistle which are not inherently polemical. Kenneth Grayston has recently described 1 John as "neither epistle nor treatise but an enchiridion, an instruction booklet for applying the tradition in disturbing circumstances."[10]

Church Order(s) in the Early Church

There is, of course, a difference between church order as a general description of materials relevant to a community and church order as a distinct literary genre,[11] and for the genre there is as yet no fully articulated definition. If one is to be forthcoming, its foundation will presumably be a morphology of constitutive elements. Three preliminary points of method must be mentioned. First, as is the case with other endeavors of this kind,[12]

[8] Brown, *Epistles,* 90.

[9] J. C. O'Neill, *The Puzzle of 1 John* (London: SPCK, 1966). The various source theories are reviewed in Brown, *Epistles,* 36–46.

[10] K. Grayston, *The Johannine Epistles* (NCB; Grand Rapids: Eerdmans; London: Marshall, Morgan & Scott, 1984) 4. The best known *encheiridion* from antiquity is that of Epictetus, whose maxims were epitomized in manual form by Arrian.

[11] Thus although Pheme Perkins can describe 1 John as "an instructional tract" (*The Johannine Epistles* [New Testament Message 21; Wilmington, Del.: Michael Glazier, 1979] xvi), and "a treatise for the instruction of Christians in the community" (p. 3), she perhaps reaches for greater generic precision in suggesting that "1 Jn seems intended to be a 'rule' for the community life of those who follow the teaching of 'the elder'" (pp. 4–5). In this connection she departs from traditional interpretation in stating that "ethics, not christology, is the author's concern throughout" (ibid.). But these insights are not developed in terms of generic definition or comparable literature.

[12] E.g., in recent definition of the genre "apocalypse"; see esp. John J. Collins, ed., *Apocalypse: The Morphology of a Genre, Semeia* 14 (1979), esp. idem, "Introduction: Towards the

a morphology will comprise a list of features the majority of which are usually present. Second, allowance will have to made for the fact that a number of writings may also include features that fall outside the regular morphological range. Third, it is best to see this, like other generic types, as the result of an evolution.[13] In the case of the community rule or church order, it seems that we are dealing with the substantial coalescence of smaller forms or genres[14] whose social origin cannot always be determined.

What, then, are the constitutive elements? This question may be asked at two levels: the genre as a whole and the individual units within it. Before these latter are set out in a tentative list, it will be helpful to make some preliminary remarks about the genre as a whole. Recently Klaus Berger has presented evidence which allows the possibility that the pedigree of the church order may be traced in terms of the development of Hellenistic tractate literature, from collections of gnomic sayings promoting an "old social ethic," through Hellenistic Jewish instructions on mutual responsibility (e.g., Ps.-Phocylides; Philo *Hypothetica*), compilations of examples of communal responsibilities (including the New Testament *Haustafeln*), the emergence of an ecclesial self-consciousness in the New Testament, to the Syriac *Didascalia.*[15] One other, principally Jewish, element must also be mentioned: the "testament" genre, which has been suggested as a literary analogy both to deutero-Pauline and to deutero-Petrine letters in the New Testament, especially 2 Timothy and 2 Peter respectively.

The following writings will serve as the pool of resources from which the morphology will be drawn. In each case there is substantial scholarly agreement on the appropriateness of the church order label for all or part of the

---

Morphology of a Genre" (pp. 1–19). Collins states that "a genre is identified by the recognizable similarity among a number of texts"; hence "the only firm basis which can be found [for generic classification] is the identification of recurring elements which are explicitly present in the text" (pp. 1–2). George A. Kennedy states that "it may be a mistake to try to classify individual [NT] epistles within a traditional scheme of classical letter forms," and "in general, identification of genre is not a crucial factor in understanding how rhetoric actually works in units of the New Testament" (*New Testament Introduction through Rhetorical Criticism* [Studies in Religion; Chapel Hill, N.C./London: University of North Carolina Press, 1984] 32–33), but these observations do not diminish the heuristic value of generic classification, the measure of whose usefulness will be convincing exegesis.

[13] See Alastair Fowler, *Kinds of Literature: An Introduction to the Theory of Genres and Modes* (Cambridge, Mass.: Harvard University Press, 1982) 24: "Genres are . . . in a continual state of transmutation."

[14] Fowler speaks of "generic mixtures" (*Kinds of Literature,* 107).

[15] K. Berger, *Formgeschichte des Neuen Testaments* (Heidelberg: Quelle & Meyer, 1984) 135–41 (see esp. the diagrammatic summary on p. 141); idem, "Hellenistische Gattungen im Neuen Testament," *ANRW* 2.25.2, 1078–88. Berger finds a parallel development in Stoic teaching on responsibility, in parts of the Gattung *oikonomikos* ("the duties of domestic life"), and in Pythagorean *Letters to Wives.*

writing. The texts are these:[16] the Pastoral epistles, especially 1 Timothy;[17] the *Didache;*[18] Hippolytus *Apostolic Tradition;* the third-century Syriac *Didascalia;*[19] and the fourth- or fifth-century *Testamentum Domini.*[20] To these I have added the Qumran *Manual of Discipline*[21] and the *Damascus Document.*[22] From these documents the following list of characteristic features may be assembled.[23]

1. *Declaration of authority or credentials, apostolic or pseudonymous, with emphasis on tradition (e.g., scriptural authority).* 1QS i; 1 Tim 1:3–5; 2 Tim 1:13–14; 2:1–2; 3:14–15; Titus 1:1–3; *Didache* 1–2 and passim; *Apost. Trad.* 1; *Didasc.* 2, 24; *Test. Dom.* 1.1, 18; 1 John 1:1–3 and passim.

2. *Affectionate address ("child," "my children," etc.).* CD ii; 1 Tim 1:2, 18; 2 Tim 1:2; 2 Tim 2:1; Titus 1:4; *Didache* 3.1 and passim; *Didasc.* 1; 6; 7 and passim; 1 John 2:1 and passim.

3. *Communal discipline.* 1QS v.25–vi.1; CD ix.1–3; Matt 18:15–17; 1 Tim 5:19–21; Titus 3:10–11; Jas 5:13–20; *Didache* 15.3; *Didasc.* 6; 10; *Test. Dom.* passim; 1 John 5:16–17.

4. *Warning against heresy and/or insistence on orthodoxy.* 1 Tim 1:6–7; 4:1–3; *Didache* 16; *Apost. Trad.* 43.3; *Test. Dom.* 8; 1 John 2:18–27.

5. *Ethical exhortation in gnomic form.* 1QS passim; 1 Timothy passim; 2 Timothy passim; *Didache* 3–4; *Didasc.* 3 and passim; 1 John 1:6–10 and passim.

6. *Teaching about eschatology.* 1 Tim 4:1–3; 6:14–16; 2 Tim 3:1–17; 4:3–4; *Didache* 16; *Didasc.* 20; *Test. Dom.* 3–11; 1 John 2:28.

16 See also Matthew 5–7 and 18–19 (see Koester, *Introduction* 2:176); Jas 5:13–20 (ibid. 2:157); and the *Epistula apostolorum* 46–50 (ibid. 2:238).

17 Koester, *Introduction* 2:301: "The basic structure of 1 Timothy was provided by the genre of the church order."

18 Ibid. 2:158: "The oldest Christian church order."

19 R. Hugh Connolly, *Didascalia Apostolorum: The Syriac Version Translated and Accompanied by the Verona Latin Fragments* (Oxford: Clarendon, 1929).

20 Syriac text and Latin translation in Ignatius Ephraem II Rahmani, ed., *Testamentum Domini nostri Jesu Christi* (Mainz: Kirchheim, 1899); Eng. trans. in James Cooper and Arthur John MacLean, *The Testament of Our Lord* (Edinburgh: T. & T. Clark, 1902).

21 Hebrew text and German translation in Eduard Lohse, ed., *Die Texte aus Qumran* (2nd ed.: Munich: Kösel, 1981) 4–51.

22 Ibid., 66–107.

23 This list is to be considered provisional only; clearly what is needed is some degree of scholarly consensus. It is recognized that there is some overlap between several of the features; thus, e.g., items 1 to 3 might have been subsumed under one heading, but the distinctive character of some of the works cited would thereby be lost. Similarly, it is understood that the *function* of the various features is not necessarily identical in every text.

7. *Lists of responsibilities directed to specific groups within the community.* 1 Tim 5:3, 17; 6:1, 17; 2 Tim 2:2–10; *Apost. Trad.* passim; *Didasc.* passim; *Test. Dom.* passim; 1 John 2:12–14.

8. *Qualifications for or tests of vocation/ministry.* 1QS passim; 1 Timothy 3; Titus 1:7–9; *Didache* 11–13; *Apost. Trad.* passim; *Didasc.* passim; *Test. Dom.* passim; 1 John 4:1–6.

9. *Instructions concerning liturgy/sacraments.* 1QS passim; *Didache* 7–10; *Apost. Trad.* passim; *Didasc.* passim; *Test. Dom.* passim; 1 John 5:6–8.

10. *Other testamentary features (e.g., farewell).* 2 Timothy passim; *Test. Dom.* passim; 1 John 1:4.

A glance at this list reveals what closer inspection confirms, that as Christian church orders came more and more to have independent existence and use, their content became streamlined; this development presumably coincided with the establishment and dissemination of an authoritative canon of New Testament scriptures. Thus in the *Didascalia* and the *Testamentum Domini* personal elements completely recede as ecclesiastical matters become dominant.

1 John and the Church Order Genre

It will be seen that for each element I have offered a reference to 1 John. Some, of course, are stronger than others, and some at first sight have little to be said for them. The gnomic character of much of 1 John, the cornerstone of several source hypotheses, is frequently acknowledged; on the other hand, there is no pretending that 1 John presents a full discussion of sacraments. These differences may be explained on the basis of differences not so much in genre as in community structure; the lack of an established hierarchy among Johannine Christians, for example, and the resulting problem of succession are already recognized.[24] Limitations of space preclude full commentary on these texts, but several items call for special emphasis:

1. *Declaration of authority or credentials, apostolic or pseudonymous, with emphasis on tradition (e.g., scriptural authority).* The opening verses of 1 John are a notorious crux. I have argued elsewhere that the choice of vocabulary in 1:1–3 is directly or indirectly indebted to Old Testament texts that speak of witness to God's mighty deeds, and further, with the majority of modern commentators, that the problematical neuter relative ὅ ("that which") refers to Jesus Christ, revealed in time and place.[25] The question

[24] See esp. D. Bruce Woll, *Johannine Christianity in Conflict: Authority, Rank, and Succession in the First Farewell Discourse* (SBLDS 60; Chico, Calif.: Scholars Press, 1981).

[25] Hills, "'Little children,'" 302–7.

remains: Who are the "we," who write or speak as if from nowhere? The assertion that the "we," whether in fact one or many, are spokespersons for the Johannine tradition hardly settles the issue.[26] Rather, it is only the first step in seeking to explain the role of 1 John 1:1–3. Nor do these verses themselves imply or require a polemical context, for only in light of the later invective against the "they" who have apparently seceded does this we" acquire any polemical coloring.

It is often noticed that there are several places in the Gospel of John where precisely this kind of language is already used, for example, in 3:11, 32; 8:26, 38; 15:15;[27] less often that a stress upon seeing, hearing, knowing, and bearing witness is also characteristically Lukan;[28] less often still that from the last decades of the first century there is increasing interest in the use of such testimony formulas as instruments of legitimation. What apparently sets 1 John apart is that the appeal to authoritative witness is not made explicitly apostolic; there is, in fact, no pseudonymous pretense at all. To this phenomenon the closest literary analogy is to be found in a recognized church order, in which the author(s) address(es) his/their readers from a similar anonymity. The opening of Hippolytus *Apostolic Tradition* is of interest also for its use of the phrase "from the beginning":

> *We* have set down those things which are worthy of note about the gifts which God has bestowed on man *from the beginning* according to his own will, presenting to himself that image which had gone astray. And now, led on by love for all the saints, we have proceeded to the summit of the tradition which befits the churches, in order that those who have been well taught by our exposition may guard that tradition which has remained up to now, and by recognizing it may remain firm. . . .[29]

Thus the "we" are those who have the incontestable right to remind the local community of that which was from the beginning and of that teaching which can confirm the κοινωνία or fellowship (even "community") of the author(s) with the readers—and, in 1 John, of both with God (1:3).

[26] Brown, *Epistles*, 160; see also J. L. Houlden, *The Johannine Epistles* (HNTC; San Francisco: Harper & Row, 1973) 53: "[The writer] consciously takes the mantle of orthodoxy."

[27] See Rudolf Schnackenburg, *Die Johannesbriefe* (HTKNT 13/3; 7th ed.; Freiburg/Basel/Vienna: Herder, 1984) 54.

[28] See, e.g., Luke 2:17, 20; 7:22; Acts 3:16; 4:20; 19:26.

[29] *Hippolytus: A Text for Students*, ed. Geoffrey J. Cuming (Grove Liturgical Studies 8; 2nd ed.; Bramcote, Notts.: Grove, 1987) 8; it is unclear whether the "we" is the authorial "we" of Hippolytus or the voice of an implied apostolic college. The work, which is usually dated ca. 215 CE, is generally held to have been conservative in character. Gregory Dix suggests that "it was already on the way to becoming obsolete as a manual of Christian practice the day it was first published" (*The Treatise on the Apostolic Tradition of St Hippolytus of Rome* [London: SPCK, 1937] xi).

2. *Affectionate address.* Five times in 1 John the readers or hearers are addressed as τέκνα ("children"), seven times as τεκνία ("little children"). It is commonly and rightly held that τεκνίον "has a caritative or endearing force, setting up an affectionate relationship between the speaker and his audience";[30] and it is true that τέκνον persists in 2 John 1, 4, 13, and in 3 John 4 (τεκνίον does not reappear in 2 or 3 John). Yet neither 2 John nor 3 John is capable of classification as other than a letter, whether actual or fictive. But if, as seems probable, both 2 and 3 John are dependent on 1 John,[31] this carryover of terminology is easily explained, and the word remains a viable indicator of genre in 1 John.[32]

3. *Communal discipline.* 1 John 5:16–17 reads:

> If any one sees his brother committing what is not a mortal sin, he will ask, and God will give him life for those whose sin is not mortal. There is sin which is mortal; I do not say that one is to pray for that. All wrongdoing is sin, but there is sin which is not mortal. (RSV)

This passage, of perennial interest because of the theological question of the "sin unto death," is of special importance in the present quest, because its perspective is undeniably communal, even legal, and because it has numerous form-critical parallels in Hellenistic Jewish and early Christian writings, most notably in Matt 18:15–17; Gal 6:1–2; Titus 3:10; Jas 5:19–20; 1QS v.25–26; and CD ix.1–3.[33] Of course, 5:16–17 bears marks of Johannine theology, possibly indicating redaction of an earlier written source, but in any case these verses are form-critically discrete and as a unit point to a distinct life setting.

Surprisingly, the secondary literature on 1 John, while frequently citing one or more of the analogous texts, makes little use of them in assessing the overall character of 1 John. In reality, however, 5:16–17 is of the utmost importance. Not only do these verses have nothing intrinsically to do with the issue of the secessionists' exit; they also fit one of the best externally attested literary forms in the whole writing, that of instruction for communal discipline.[34] Doubtless these verses are viewed by the epistle's author as

30 Brown, *Epistles,* 214.

31 The relation between 2 and 3 John is a matter of debate. Grayston remarks that "the writer [of 2 John] was trying to convey the main thrust of I Jn in his own more limited way" and adds that "the two Epistles were probably more or less contemporary responses to the same disturbance" (*Epistles,* 7). Houlden conjectures that 2 John preceded 1 John, which is "the full statement of the position which 2J sketched out" (*Epistles,* 140–41).

32 See also under (10) below.

33 For additional references, see, e.g., Sophie Laws, *The Epistle of James* (HNTC; San Francisco: Harper & Row, 1980) 238–39.

34 So, correctly, Perkins, *Epistles,* 63: "The section (5:14–21) is the most direct reflection of community rules that we find in the Johannine writings even though [?] much of the early language of 1 Jn had parallels in essene rules and in Didache."

conceptually linked with the teaching in 3:15, that "anyone who hates his brother is a murderer," and such hate may further be linked with secession. But the "if" form, the impersonal verbs, and the explicitly casuistic distinction between different kinds of sinners, or sins, or punishments[35] stand outside of a specific application to secession and, as in the similar texts, point to inner-community regulation.

4. *Warnings against heresy and/or insistence on orthodoxy.* This is probably the litmus test of the argument, in that the now-standard context for the interpretation of 1 John takes as its charter only one paragraph, namely, 2:18–27.[36] Yet comparison with other church order materials shows that such polemic is the norm. Therefore the possibility remains open that the topical inventory of the emerging genre encouraged this strong warning and condemnation; or, to reverse the formulation, precisely the situation of 1 John—a congregation in which, *among other things,* there is dissention and secession or the threat thereof—may be that in which the earlier church orders were composed. The fact that in the case of 1 John the danger appears to have been real and immediate cannot prejudice the literary judgment, especially in light of recent work on the Pastorals and their critiques of actual opponents.[37]

7. *Lists of responsibilities directed to specific groups within the community.* The directions addressed to children, fathers, and young men in 2:12–14 have long proved baffling. They are, on inspection, hardly instructions at all, since they serve mainly to encourage only in the most general way. But as with the previous item, their presence in a genre in which such appeal is becoming a commonplace considerably lessens the burden of detecting a distinct and unique Johannine purpose. These groups, whatever their identity, are addressed because the genre "community rule" recommends that such distinctions be made; or, again to reverse the formulation, the emerging genre seems to have taken up the Hellenistic *captatio.*[38]

10. *Other testamentary features.* This is admittedly a slippery category and hence one to be employed with caution, since a number of the elements

[35] For the variety of approaches to this question, see Brown, *Epistles,* 612–19.

[36] It is an interesting and not entirely fatuous question, whether 1 John, if preserved *without* 2:18–27 (or, indeed, without only the one verse, 2:19), would have supplied the evidence for anything approaching the precision of scholarly reconstructions of its communal situation presently offered.

[37] E.g., Robert J. Karris, "The Background and Significance of the Polemic of the Pastoral Epistles," *JBL* 92 (1973) 549–64.

[38] See Berger, "Hellenistische Gattungen," 1350; and Duane F. Watson, "1 John 2.12–14 as *distributio, conduplicatio,* and *expolitio,*" *JSNT* 35 (1989) 97–110, for a rhetorical analysis of the passage. Watson's conclusions are not incompatible with my generic analysis.

collected above might well have been subsumed under the broader genre heading "testament."[39] With reference to Jewish testaments, R. P. Spittler has gone so far as to suggest that "the mere phrase 'My son(s),' found already in short units of wisdom literature (e.g. Prov 5:1, 7), implies the essence of the testament (*diathēkē*): A wise aged (and usually dying) father imparts final words of ethical counsel to his attentive offspring."[40]

Rather than press 1 John's "my little children" further, the present discussion will briefly focus on 1 John 1:4: "We are writing this that our joy may be complete."[41] In the Johannine writings χαρά ("joy") is an eschatological term; on this there is general agreement among the commentators. Occurring nine times in the Gospel of John (seven of these in the farewell discourses: 15:11 [twice]; 16:20, 21, 22, 24; 17:13), and once in each of the epistles of John, χαρά is found in combination with the passive of πληροῦν ("to fulfill") six times: John 3:29; 15:11; 16:24; 17:13; 1 John 1:4; 2 John 12. The suggestion is prompted that in 1 John 1:4, under the guise of the "we" who testify, the author implies a testamentary farewell. This claim, although not essential to the generic definition of 1 John as a church order, can perhaps find support in the following observations.

First, in John 3:29–30 the Baptist declares: "He who has the bride is the bridegroom; the friend of the bridegroom, who stands and hears him, rejoices greatly at the bridegroom's voice; therefore this joy of mine is now full. He must increase, but I must decrease." Even if from the perspective of the Gospel narrative the Baptist's ministry continues (but this is not certain; cf. 4:1), he has completed his mission of testimony: the time for his "decrease" has come, and the privilege of witness passes to others.[42] Second, in the farewell discourses the joy of Jesus and of his disciples is "fulfilled" precisely in light of Jesus' departure—and, of course, his future return.[43] A third observation concerns 2 Timothy. Koester asserts that "the genre of the testament was consciously chosen for 2 Timothy and was applied consistently in its composition."[44] It is therefore of special interest to find that the Pauline author, writing as if in prison and "on the point of being sacrificed" (2 Tim 4:6), begins his exhortation to Timothy with an assurance of his prayers; for "as I remember your tears I long night and day to see you, *that*

[39] See Berger, *Formgeschichte,* 75–80 and literature cited; for a review of Jewish testaments, R. P. Spittler, "The Testament of Job," *OTP* 1:831–32.

[40] Spittler, "Testament of Job," 832. He includes the *Testamentum Domini* in his brief discussion of "subsequent Christian testaments" (p. 832).

[41] For the text-critical problem, whether "*our* joy" or "*your* joy" is to be read, see Brown, *Epistles,* 173.

[42] Cf. perhaps the words of Simeon in Luke 2:29–32.

[43] See Rudolf Schnackenburg, *The Gospel According to St John* (3 vols.; New York: Crossroad, 1987) 3:160–61.

[44] Koester, *Introduction* 2:300.

I may be filled with joy" (2 Tim 1:4)—or, to venture a paraphrase, "that I may die in the assurance that my witness has not been in vain." So too, it may be claimed, in the literary fiction of 1 John: the source of Johannine authority bequeaths a "rule of life"—a series of "Tests of Life," as they have been called[45]—to a community in crisis.

Conclusion

One of the lasting achievements of the past century of research on 1 John has been the liberation of this passionate little text from the muting confines of classification among so-called Catholic epistles into the cut and thrust of a specific and vociferous communal exchange. The time has now come for 1 John to speak to us not only from the depth of its convictions but also from the contours of its genre—the community rule or church order. Only through these shall we hear again what those first readers heard, not only in theological, polemical word and speech but also in generic, literary deed and truth (see 1 John 3:18).

[45] Robert Law, *The Tests of Life: A Study of the First Epistle of St. John* (3rd ed.; Edinburgh: T. & T. Clark, 1914).

PART 5

Early Christian Literature

30

The *Gospel of Thomas* and Christian Origins

RON CAMERON

WHEN WALTER BAUER advanced his thesis that the beginnings of Christianity were exceptionally diverse, varied dramatically from region to region, and were dominated by individuals and groups whose practice and theology would be denounced as "heretical," he launched a new era in the study of Christian origins.[1] Bauer's monograph truly was a milestone. It set an imaginative agenda and offered a breathtaking reconstruction of Christianity in Edessa, Egypt, Antioch, Asia Minor, Macedonia, Achaia, and Rome.[2] Moreover, Bauer's fresh perspective was controlled by a close reading of nearly all the ancient sources that were known in 1934. Thirty-one years later, following the publication of the second edition of this landmark work, Helmut Koester would hail its documentation, design, and sheer clairvoyance as "ingenious," "convincingly" demonstrated, and "essentially right."[3] Therefore, Koester argued:

[1] W. Bauer, *Orthodoxy and Heresy in Earliest Christianity*, ed. G. Strecker, R. A. Kraft, and G. Krodel (Philadelphia: Fortress Press, 1971; German original, Tübingen: Mohr-Siebeck, 1934; 2nd ed. 1964).

[2] Since a full-scale treatment of the reception of Bauer's book would take us far afield, let me simply note that bibliographical references to and summaries of the scholarly discussions of his work can be readily found in G. Strecker and R. A. Kraft, "Appendix 2: The Reception of the Book," in *Orthodoxy and Heresy*, 286–316; D. J. Harrington, "The Reception of Walter Bauer's *Orthodoxy and Heresy in Earliest Christianity* During the Last Decade," in *The Light of All Nations: Essays on the Church in New Testament Research* (GNS 3; Wilmington, Del.: Michael Glazier, 1982) 162–73; T. A. Robinson, *The Bauer Thesis Examined: The Geography of Heresy in the Early Christian Church* (Studies in the Bible and Early Christianity 11; Lewiston, N.Y./Queenston, Ont.: Mellen, 1988) 1–33.

[3] H. Koester, "ΓΝΩΜΑΙ ΔΙΑΦΟΡΟΙ: The Origin and Nature of Diversification in the History of Early Christianity," *HTR* 58 (1965) 279–318 (the citations are from p. 279); reprinted in Robinson-Koester, *Trajectories*, 114–57 (the citations are from p. 114). All subsequent references to this article will be cited from the latter edition. Note that, when published (with a

> a thorough and extensive reevaluation of early Christian history is called for. The task is not limited to a fresh reading of the known sources and a close scrutiny of the new texts in order to redefine their appropriate place within the conventional picture of early Christian history. Rather, it is the conventional picture itself that is called into question.[4]

Here, in a few deft strokes, Koester announced the implications of the way he conceived of the reorientation of biblical studies as a discipline. The conventional picture of Christianity must be dismantled, new categories developed, a different framework constructed, and established criteria for exegesis reviewed. Obsolete distinctions between canonical and noncanonical, orthodox and heretical were to be renounced in favor of a sustained assessment of γνῶμαι διάφοροι, the views of distinct movements within the spectrum of the early church. Koester would eventually describe this procedure theoretically as "the construction of trajectories." Ultimately, the intention is to provide a systematic "reconstruction of the historical development of early Christianity," whose "primary concern is to present" a critical "history of the early Christian churches." A commitment was deliberately made to situate the investigation methodologically within "the context of the history of religions" of late antiquity, without restricting the analysis artificially to those writings which came to be included in the New Testament.[5]

The impulse for the plan of Koester's *Introduction to the New Testament* may thus be regarded as having emerged as foundational in 1965, when its features were first proposed in his essay "ΓΝΩΜΑΙ ΔΙΑΦΟΡΟΙ." But to say that this undertaking simply reflects Koester's own inevitable scholarly trajectory would surely be inadequate. True, that developing position might seem latent in his initial treatments of the theological aspects of early Christian heresy;[6] was adumbrated, to some degree, in his insistence that apocryphal literature be taken seriously and considered of equal historical value to the canon in any discussion of early Christianity;[7] and, possibly, had been

transliterated title) in its revised version, the term "ingenious" was altered to "brilliant."

[4] "GNOMAI DIAPHOROI," 114–15.

[5] H. Koester, *Introduction* 1:xxi–xxiii, 2:xxi–xxiii. See also idem, "Conclusion: The Intention and Scope of Trajectories," *Trajectories,* 269–79; idem, "New Testament Introduction: A Critique of a Discipline," in *Christianity, Judaism and Other Greco-Roman Cults: Studies for Morton Smith at Sixty,* ed. J. Neusner (4 vols.; SJLA 12; Leiden: Brill, 1975) 1:1–20.

[6] H. Koester, "Häretiker im Urchristentum," *RGG* (3rd ed. 1959) 3:17–21; idem, "Häretiker im Urchristentum als theologisches Problem," in *Zeit und Geschichte: Dankesgabe an Rudolf Bultmann zum 80. Geburtstag,* ed. E. Dinkler (Tübingen: Mohr-Siebeck, 1964) 61–76; Eng. trans. "The Theological Aspects of Primitive Christian Heresy," in *The Future of Our Religious Past: Essays in Honour of Rudolf Bultmann,* ed. J. M. Robinson (New York: Harper & Row, 1971) 65–83.

[7] H. Koester, "Die ausserkanonischen Herrenworte als Produkte der christlichen Gemeinde," *ZNW* 48 (1957) 220–37; Eng. trans. "The Extracanonical Sayings of the Lord as Products of the Christian Community," *Semeia* 44 (1988) 57–77.

germinating ever since Koester demonstrated that, even with the composition and circulation of the Synoptic Gospels, the oral tradition persisted throughout the period of the apostolic fathers, concurrent with but not limited to the Synoptics.[8] Nevertheless, the intimations of Koester's earlier work now became an agenda for scholarship, which he explored programmatically in a number of his subsequent research and publication projects. To single out this one essay for special review, therefore, recognizes that its import far exceeds any reiteration of, or extra nuance given to, previously entertained points of view. In fact, to grasp the distinctive contribution that "ΓΝΩΜΑΙ ΔΙΑΦΟΡΟΙ" makes to the quest for Christian origins, one must come to grips with its fundamental challenge and promise. The set of questions that are asked issues a challenge to the privileged assumptions of biblical scholarship. The basic aims that have motivated the energies of that enterprise, moreover, are repositioned by Koester's selection of noncanonical texts for consideration, a marshaling of other data of great importance that promises to transform what constitutes the basis for argumentation. Together with his call for a paradigm shift, the choice of examples to treat as test cases and the critical acumen with which they are assessed have marked this article for repeated reference.

It is significant that Koester discussed the *Gospel of Thomas* for the first time here, for that gospel would absorb much of Koester's own imaginative labor as he went on to explicate the characteristics and contours of his understanding of Christian origins. Starting, then, with this initial sketch of the profile of the earliest churches that emerged in eastern and western Syria, Asia Minor, and Greece, Koester designed "a blueprint for further work in the history of early Christian theology." In pursuit of that initiative, he highlighted the particular importance of *Gos. Thom.*, arguing that the proper placement of this gospel in a reconfiguration of the beginnings of Christianity "will doubtless have far-reaching consequences for the study of early Christianity as a whole."[9] The ramifications of this insight would be traced through a series of wide-ranging publications dealing with *Gos. Thom.* explicitly, including Koester's classifications of the forms and genres of the gospel tradition,[10] calls for a reappraisal of the significance of the apocryphal gospels for the development of the Jesus tradition,[11] analyses of the use of

[8] H. Koester, *Synoptische Überlieferung bei den apostolischen Vätern* (TU 65; Berlin: Akademie-Verlag, 1957).

[9] Koester, "GNOMAI DIAPHOROI," 119.

[10] H. Koester, "One Jesus and Four Primitive Gospels," *Trajectories,* 158–204; idem, "Formgeschichte/Formenkritik II: Neues Testament," *TRE* 11/2–3:286–99; idem, "Überlieferung und Geschichte der frühchristlichen Evangelienliteratur," *ANRW* 2.25.2, 1463–1542.

[11] H. Koester, "Dialog und Spruchüberlieferung in den gnostischen Texten von Nag Hammadi," *EvT* 39 (1979) 532–56; idem, "Apocryphal and Canonical Gospels," *HTR* 73 (1980) 105–30; idem, "Gnostic Writings as Witnesses for the Development of the Sayings Tradition,"

sayings to compose discourses and dialogues in the Gospel of John,[12] identifications of the sources and literary character of the *Dialogue of the Savior,*[13] reflections on early Christian responses to the historical Jesus,[14] accounts of the origins of Gnosticism,[15] and descriptive introductions to and critical interpretations of *Gos. Thom.* itself.[16]

Because *Gos. Thom.* is given such prominence in Koester's rich scholarly corpus, let me present in the form of theses what I consider to be some of his major findings. This will enable us to define several key issues for further discussion.

1. *Gos. Thom.* is a representative of the genre "sayings collection," directly continuing "the most original gattung of the Jesus tradition" (the λόγοι σοφῶν).[17] Showing "the characteristic features of wisdom books," *Gos. Thom.* is composed according to the pattern of those antique anthologies, of identifiable types, that served as the catalyst for the literary production of the Jesus tradition in the form of sayings gospels.[18]

---

in *The Rediscovery of Gnosticism: Proceedings of the International Conference on Gnosticism at Yale, New Haven, Connecticut, March 28–31, 1978,* ed. B. Layton (2 vols.; Supplements to *Numen* 41; Leiden: Brill, 1980), vol. 1, *The School of Valentinus,* 238–61; idem, "Q and Its Relatives," in *Gospel Origins and Christian Beginnings: In Honor of James M. Robinson,* ed. J. E. Goehring et al. (Forum Fascicles; Sonoma, Calif.: Polebridge, 1990) 49–63.

[12] H. Koester, "Gnostic Sayings and Controversy Traditions in John 8:12–59," in *Nag Hammadi, Gnosticism, and Early Christianity,* ed. C. W. Hedrick and R. Hodgson, Jr. (Peabody, Mass.: Hendrickson, 1986) 97–110.

[13] H. Koester and E. H. Pagels, "The Dialogue of the Savior (III, 5): Introduction," in *The Nag Hammadi Library in English,* ed. J. M. Robinson (San Francisco: Harper & Row, 1977) 229; 3rd ed. (1988) 244–46; idem and Pagels, "Report on the *Dialogue of the Savior* (CG III, 5)," in *Nag Hammadi and Gnosis: Papers read at the First International Congress of Coptology (Cairo, December 1976),* ed. R. McL. Wilson (NHS 14; Leiden: Brill, 1978) 66–74; idem and Pagels, "Introduction," in *Nag Hammadi Codex III,5: The Dialogue of the Savior,* ed. S. Emmel (NHS 26; Leiden: Brill, 1984) 1–17.

[14] H. Koester, "The Structure and Criteria of Early Christian Beliefs," *Trajectories,* 205–31; idem, "The Historical Jesus: Some Comments and Thoughts on Norman Perrin's *Rediscovering the Teaching of Jesus,*" in *Christology and a Modern Pilgrimage: A Discussion with Norman Perrin,* ed. H. D. Betz (2nd ed.; Missoula, Mont.: Scholars Press, 1974) 81–89.

[15] H. Koester, "The History-of-Religions School, Gnosis, and the Gospel of John," *ST* 40 (1986) 115–36; idem, "La tradition apostolique et les origines du Gnosticisme," *RTP* 119 (1987) 1–16.

[16] H. Koester, "The Gospel of Thomas (II, 2): Introduction," in *The Nag Hammadi Library in English,* 117; 3rd ed., 124–26; idem, "Three Thomas Parables," in *The New Testament and Gnosis: Essays in Honour of Robert McL. Wilson,* ed. A. H. B. Logan and A. J. M. Wedderburn (Edinburgh: T. & T. Clark, 1983) 195–203; idem, "The Gospel According to Thomas: Introduction," in *Nag Hammadi Codex II,2–7 together with XIII,2*, Brit. Lib. Or. 4926(1), and P. Oxy. 1, 654, 655,* ed. B. Layton (2 vols.; NHS 20–21; Leiden: Brill, 1989) 1:38–49; idem, *Ancient Christian Gospels: Their History and Development* (London: SCM; Philadelphia: Trinity Press International, 1990) 75–128.

[17] Koester, "GNOMAI DIAPHOROI," 135; cf. 139.

[18] Koester, "The Gospel According to Thomas," 41; cf. 44–45.

2. The basis of *Gos. Thom.* "is a sayings collection which is more primitive than the canonical gospels."[19] Accordingly, this gospel belongs not only "to an early stage of the transmission of Jesus' sayings,"[20] but to a stage "that is comparable to the sources which were used by the gospels of the NT."[21]

3. *Gos. Thom.* displays no vestige of the narratives of the canonical Gospels, nor any sign of their kerygma of the cross and resurrection, nor any trace of redactional dependence on one or more Synoptic versions of its sayings.[22] "The entire (or almost entire) tradition contained" in this gospel thus derives "from an independent early stage of the sayings tradition."[23]

4. Most of the sayings in *Gos. Thom.* are preserved in forms "more original" than their parallels in the New Testament or are "developed from forms which are more original."[24] A comparative analysis of the parables makes this conclusion especially evident, demonstrating that the author of *Gos. Thom.* "is a collector rather than a (Gnostic) interpreter."[25]

5. The parallels to *Gos. Thom.* that are found in the New Testament appear most frequently in older collections of sayings embedded in the biblical texts (e.g., Mark 4:1–34; Matt 13:1–52; Q 6:20–49; 12:22–34, 39–59), as well as in special Lukan materials that are closely related to defined contexts in the Synoptic Sayings Gospel Q (e.g., Luke 12:13–14, 16–21, 35, 49).[26] It is particularly striking that the prophetic sayings in *Gos. Thom.* have their parallels in Q, not in the "detailed apocalyptic predictions" contained in the Synoptic apocalypse (Mark 13 par.).[27]

6. The majority of the sayings in *Gos. Thom.* are wisdom sayings (including parables) and prophetic sayings. Most of the former "have exact parallels in the synoptic gospels."[28] Since many of the sayings formulated apocalyptically in the Synoptics have been preserved as proverbial forms of speech in *Gos. Thom.*, moreover, what "now emerges as peculiar to Jesus' teaching" is his "wisdom teaching."[29]

7. In *Gos. Thom.* "Jesus appears as a teacher of wisdom" or as one who "speaks with the authority of the heavenly figure of Wisdom."[30] Such a

[19] Koester, "One Jesus," 186.

[20] Koester, "Gnostic Writings," 238.

[21] Koester, "Apocryphal and Canonical Gospels," 112.

[22] Koester, "GNOMAI DIAPHOROI," 138; "Apocryphal and Canonical Gospels," 113; "Überlieferung und Geschichte," 1494–95.

[23] Koester, "GNOMAI DIAPHOROI," 132.

[24] Koester, "The Gospel According to Thomas," 42.

[25] Koester, "Three Thomas Parables," 198; see also R. Cameron, "Parable and Interpretation in the Gospel of Thomas," *Forum* 2/2 (1986) 3–39.

[26] Koester, "GNOMAI DIAPHOROI," 132; "One Jesus," 170, 182; "Q and Its Relatives," 53–61.

[27] Koester, "GNOMAI DIAPHOROI," 138.

[28] Koester, "One Jesus," 179.

[29] Koester, "The Historical Jesus," 84.

[30] Koester, *Introduction* 2:150.

characterization substantiates the hard evidence, accumulated from Q and the pre-Markan collections of chreiai and parables, that "the interpretation of Jesus' sayings in terms of revealed wisdom" is "a tradition which apparently goes back to the earliest period of Christianity."[31]

8. Conversely, in *Gos. Thom.* Jesus is neither presented as an apocalyptic preacher nor characterized as the coming "Son of man" (saying 86 preserves a generic, nontitular usage of this term).[32] Instead, this gospel advances "an interpretation of the sayings of Jesus which has no futuristic eschatological component."[33]

9. *Gos. Thom.* does not presuppose "the particular apocalyptic expectation," so characteristic of late stages of Q, that "is epitomized in the sayings about the coming of the Son of man."[34] Rather, it attests to "a stage and form of the tradition of eschatological sayings which did not yet contain [such] an apocalyptic expectation."[35] Consequently, *Gos. Thom.* is comparable to an early version of Q, though one "in which the apocalyptic expectation of the Son of man was missing. . . . Such a version of Q is, however, not secondary, but very primitive."[36]

10. Therefore:

> if the genre of the wisdom book was the catalyst for the composition of sayings of Jesus into a "gospel," and if the christological concept of Jesus as the teacher of wisdom and as the presence of heavenly Wisdom dominated its creation, the apocalyptic orientation of the *Synoptic Sayings Source* [Q] with its christology of the coming Son of man is due to a secondary redaction of an older wisdom book.

Gos. Thom. is an example of "such a wisdom book."[37]

11. *Gos. Thom.* bears witness to "the 'gnosticizing proclivity' of the gattung" λόγοι σοφῶν.[38] As a result, it was "to check the gnosticizing tendencies of this [type of] sayings gospel" that "the apocalyptic expectation of the Son of man had been introduced" into Q in the first place. "Stemming from a more primitive stage of such a 'gospel,'" *Gos. Thom.* "attests its further growth into a gnostic theology."[39]

12. Although *Gos. Thom.* does not presuppose a theology of the cross, it is not therefore "theologically mute."[40] On the contrary, it "proclaims the

[31] Ibid. 2:152.

[32] Koester, "One Jesus," 170–71, 177, 186–87.

[33] Koester, *Introduction* 2:153.

[34] Koester, "One Jesus," 170.

[35] Ibid., 171.

[36] Ibid., 186.

[37] Koester, "Apocryphal and Canonical Gospels," 113.

[38] Koester, "GNOMAI DIAPHOROI," 137; citing J. M. Robinson, "The Problem of History in Mark, Reconsidered," *USQR* 20 (1964–65) 135.

[39] Koester, "One Jesus," 187.

[40] Ibid., 164.

presence of divine wisdom as the true destiny of human existence."[41] "The criterion controlling" its sayings is "the authority of the word of wisdom as such, which rests in the assumption that the teacher is present in the word which he has spoken."[42]

13. The fundamental theological tendency of *Gos. Thom.* is "the view that the Jesus who spoke these words was and is the Living One, and thus gives life through his words."[43] By providing "a distinctive reinterpretation of originally eschatological sayings,"[44] this gospel presents an "elaboration of Jesus' most original proclamation."[45]

14. *Gos. Thom.* is neither "a random collection of sayings" nor a pastiche pieced together by harmonizing the various Gospels of the New Testament. Rather, it "is a writing claiming formal authorship and manifesting theological tendencies which govern the selection and interpretation of traditional materials. Developments in the ecclesiastical structure, theology, and cultural experience of Christianity must be expected to have left traces in such a writing."[46]

15. Attribution of authorship to Didymus Judas Thomas situates *Gos. Thom.* at a time in which appeals of authority were made to individual disciples or apostles by name, in order to secure the identity and guarantee the reliability of the tradition of those communities which looked to such individuals as their patron. Thus, sayings 12 and 13 "are intended to confirm Thomas's authority in contrast to" the competitive "claims made in behalf of ecclesiastical traditions under the authority of James, Peter, and Matthew."[47]

16. Ascribing *Gos. Thom.* and other "wisdom books to the authority of an apostle is certainly an early form of pseudepigraphical literary production in the history of Christianity." Indeed, as early as the writing of 1 Corinthians there is evidence that certain (groups of) persons claimed to possess special wisdom in the name of individual followers of Jesus. "This establishes an early date for the claiming of apostolic authority for secret wisdom."[48]

17. "The wisdom orientation" of *Gos. Thom.* is closely aligned with other developments from the beginnings of "the early Christian wisdom traditions." The similarities in theological themes, technical terms, and patterns of speech which are shared by *Gos. Thom.*, the formative stage of Q, and "the Corinthian wisdom movement" suggest that the gospel of all these groups

[41] Koester, *Introduction* 2:153.

[42] Koester, "GNOMAI DIAPHOROI," 138–39.

[43] Ibid., 139.

[44] Ibid., 137.

[45] Koester, "One Jesus," 172; cf. 173, 203.

[46] Koester, "The Gospel According to Thomas," 40.

[47] Ibid., 41.

[48] Ibid., 45.

was marked by a common religious perspective.[49]

18. *Gos. Thom.* was composed, in its original form, in the first century CE in Edessa.[50] As such, this gospel must be considered the prime documentary witness to the Jesus movements in eastern Syria, for it confirms "that the Thomas tradition was the oldest form" of indigenous "Christianity in Edessa, antedating the beginning of both Marcionite and orthodox Christianity in that area."[51]

The insights that provide the raw material for Koester's conclusions in these theses can also be used as the basis for a redescription of *Gos. Thom.* and the beginnings of Christianity. A sayings gospel with its own compositional integrity, generic identity, and transmissional history has been identified, situated at a particular juncture in early Christian history, and seen to be conceptually governed by a sapiential way of viewing the world. What are we to make of such a gospel, which offers its own account of the significance of Jesus and the Jesus movements that is neither authorized by an apocalyptic vision nor sustained as a kerygmatic cult? For the student of religion, the importance of *Gos. Thom.* is not limited to what can be learned by an exposition of the text or an assessment of its position among the expanding body of primary sources that help clarify the developments of the Jesus tradition. In fact, I would argue that the challenge of this gospel ultimately lies elsewhere, in the larger issues it raises for determining the questions we ask, evidence we need, arguments we make, and theories we employ to reconceive the history of early Christianity. It is difficult to avoid the suspicion that *Gos. Thom.* has been treated in isolation, if not actually ignored, by most biblical scholars because its account of Christian origins does not square with the conventional picture gathered from the writings of the New Testament. Nevertheless, one cannot give *Gos. Thom.* its due simply by placing it on an independent, parallel track alongside such strong texts as the letters of Paul, the Gospel of Mark, or the Synoptic Sayings Gospel Q. By recognizing differences in rhetorical composition and historical context, a comparative analysis precludes either an easy equation or familiar conflation of Q or *Gos. Thom.*'s cultivation of Jesus' sayings with Paul's theology of the cross and Mark's narratives of the passion. However, the comparative method also requires that those writings be positioned at the intersection of complex textual and social histories.[52] Such an approach

[49] Koester, "Apocryphal and Canonical Gospels," 116; see also "One Jesus," 186; "Gnostic Writings," 249; "Überlieferung und Geschichte," 1513–14; "La tradition apostolique," 4–7; "Q and Its Relatives," 50–53.

[50] Koester, "Dialog und Spruchüberlieferung," 554; "Apocryphal and Canonical Gospels," 119; *Introduction* 2:152–53; "Überlieferung und Geschichte," 1518; "La tradition apostolique," 7.

[51] Koester, "GNOMAI DIAPHOROI," 129; cf. 133, 141, 142.

[52] See J. Z. Smith, *Drudgery Divine: On the Comparison of Early Christianities and the*

can then enable one to determine how ancient authors entertained the various encounters with groups and repeated engagements with texts that constituted the cultural tapestry of the times. To take *Gos. Thom.* seriously, therefore, is to situate it intertextually within the spectrum of early Christian history, and that means we must revise our understanding of Christian origins.

Perhaps the most pressing problem in need of a sane and sober review is the assumption of the apocalyptic origins of the Jesus movements. Since the publication of the still influential studies about Jesus by Johannes Weiss and Albert Schweitzer in 1892 and 1906, respectively, it has become axiomatic to regard apocalyptic eschatology as the all-pervasive matrix of earliest Christianity.[53] Recent scholarship on the first Christian gospels, however, has given us reason to call this consensus into question. John S. Kloppenborg has demonstrated that the composition of the Synoptic Sayings Gospel Q may be understood in two main phases, whose formative stratum comprised a collection of six similarly structured instructional units, which underwent a secondary literary expansion through the addition of several blocks of prophetic and polemical sayings.[54] With the shift in discourse and ideology that took place between Q's first and second literary layers, an apocalyptic

---

Religions of Late Antiquity (Jordan Lectures in Comparative Religion 14; London: School of Oriental and African Studies, University of London, 1990).

[53] J. Weiss, *Jesus' Proclamation of the Kingdom of God* (Lives of Jesus Series; Philadelphia: Fortress Press, 1971; German original, Göttingen: Vandenhoeck & Ruprecht, 1892); A. Schweitzer, *The Quest of the Historical Jesus: A Critical Study of Its Progress from Reimarus to Wrede* (New York: Macmillan, 1968; German original, Tübingen: Mohr-Siebeck, 1906). Prominent recent works that advance an apocalyptic hypothesis to explain the origins of Christianity include E. P. Sanders, *Jesus and Judaism* (Philadelphia: Fortress Press, 1985); and P. Fredriksen, *From Jesus to Christ: The Origins of the New Testament Images of Jesus* (New Haven/London: Yale University Press, 1988).

[54] J. S. Kloppenborg, *The Formation of Q: Trajectories in Ancient Wisdom Collections* (SAC; Philadelphia: Fortress Press, 1987). Attempts to discuss the composition, genre, theology, or social history of Q must attend to the literary stratigraphy of this gospel (against J. G. Williams, "Parable and Chreia: From Q to Narrative Gospel," *Semeia* 43 [1988] 85, 103–10; A. Yarbro Collins, "Narrative, History, and Gospel," *Semeia* 43 [1988] 152; H. C. Kee, "Synoptic Studies," in *The New Testament and Its Modern Interpreters*, ed. E. J. Epp and G. W. MacRae [The Bible and Its Modern Interpreters 3; Atlanta: Scholars Press, 1989] 255; R. A. Horsley, "Questions about Redactional Strata and the Social Relations Reflected in Q," in *Society of Biblical Literature 1989 Seminar Papers*, ed. D. J. Lull [Atlanta: Scholars Press, 1989] 186–203). To argue that Q is a unitary document with an unqualified apocalyptic eschatology, composed on the model of other texts in which wisdom and apocalyptic discourse appear together in the same context (e.g., *1 Enoch* 91–104), fails to take seriously the order of the sayings in Q; to discern their compositional effect, redactional contexts, unifying structures, and distinctive rhetoric; to grasp what the framers of Q did when they arranged and construed their tradition; and to determine how Q functioned programmatically as a written gospel text, central to the intellectual life and social concerns of an identifiable Christian community (see J. S. Kloppenborg, "*The Formation of Q* Revisited: A Response to Richard Horsley," in *SBL 1989 Seminar Papers*, 204–15).

idiom was entertained in the text to make sense of a perceived social crisis. Yet not even at that later stage of social history was Jesus remembered as an apocalyptic preacher, nor did apocalyptic assumptions ever become constitutive even for the community of Q. Instead, the fundamental concerns of Q are rather like those of *Gos. Thom.*, indicative of reflective activity pertaining to and characteristic of the phenomenon of wisdom.[55]

The apocalyptic eschatology broached in late strata of Q permeates the entire narrative of Mark's Gospel. Burton L. Mack has established that Mark himself is responsible for reinterpreting the sayings and stories that he received to produce the apocalyptic script that has come to dominate the quest for Christian origins.[56] Mark's activity is not merely a peculiar redactional exercise, however; it is also representative of "a scribal response to a social history" thought to have gone awry, and "functions where strong social identities are already in place, though threatened." Accordingly, apocalypticism should neither be understood as a popular sentiment or pervasive mentality characteristic of the culture at large, nor regarded as "a sufficient rationale" to generate "novel social formations" such as the Jesus movements.[57] The apocalyptic imagination is best described as a learned mode of mythmaking by literate elites who sought to reinforce community solidarity, in accordance with traditional precedents, by devising ways to redress the disparity between the archaic ideal and the actual order, as well as to rationalize the failed expectations of groups that originated, in Christian circles, after the time of Jesus.[58]

If apocalyptic language and imagery are second-order, corrective elaborations of wisdom patterns of discourse in Q and Mark, how are we to understand the apparent conjunction of wisdom and apocalyptic in 1 Corinthians? To say that both arose simultaneously—or that the diversity of early Christian interpretations can be reconciled by imagining that Jesus himself proclaimed a paradoxical message in the form of generative "words and deeds that could have been, plausibly and persuasively, sincerely and honestly, interpreted in both directions by different followers at the same time"—simply will not work and is an inadequate substitute for spirited social

[55] See J. S. Kloppenborg, "Symbolic Eschatology and the Apocalypticism of Q," *HTR* 80 (1987) 287–306; B. L. Mack, "The Kingdom That Didn't Come: A Social History of the Q Tradents," in *Society of Biblical Literature 1988 Seminar Papers*, ed. D. J. Lull (Atlanta: Scholars Press, 1988) 608–35; R. Cameron, "'What Have You Come Out To See?' Characterizations of John and Jesus in the Gospels," *Semeia* 49 (1990) 35–69.

[56] B. L. Mack, "The Kingdom Sayings in Mark," *Forum* 3/1 (1987) 3–47; idem, *A Myth of Innocence: Mark and Christian Origins* (Philadelphia: Fortress Press, 1988).

[57] Mack, *Myth of Innocence*, 40 n. 10.

[58] See J. Z. Smith, "Wisdom and Apocalyptic," in *Map Is Not Territory: Studies in the History of Religions* (SJLA 23; Leiden: Brill, 1978) 67–87; idem, "A Pearl of Great Price and a Cargo of Yams," in *Imagining Religion: From Babylon to Jonestown* (Chicago Studies in the History of Judaism; Chicago/London: University of Chicago Press, 1982) 90–101, 156–62.

settings as the occasions for religious reflection at the beginning of things.[59] Early Christian texts and traditions are contested constructs, the products of intellectual labor by persons engaged in forging self-definition and social identity, authority and legitimacy, forms of leadership and profiles of roles, group stability and flexibility, shared norms and values, codes of etiquette and maintenance of boundaries, the acquisition of a history and a cultural legacy. Authored in concrete circumstances to address specific situations, texts were written to render critical judgments on the patterns of practice of the times and served to differentiate a particular group from the variety of other configurations of Jewish and Christian movements in and around the Levant. Therefore, if wisdom and apocalyptic cannot be identified as partial perceptions or theological persuasions of a single originary impulse, then they may be distinguished in 1 Corinthians by observing that their correlation there is the creation of Paul himself. In objecting to the wisdom speculation of certain members of the Corinthian church, Paul criticizes their beliefs and behavior by appealing to his theology of the cross, and he buttresses his argument by presenting an apocalyptic interpretation of the kerygma's implications in order to use the threat of judgment for ethical admonition.[60] In the Pauline corpus, the kerygma functions as a rationale for sustaining the fabric of a stable society; the introduction of an apocalyptic persuasion, moreover, requires a prior investment in social formation based on other commitments and concerns.[61]

Gos. Thom. is also acquainted with the apocalyptic responses of other, threatened groups, but it rejects them by redirecting the disciples' queries about the future (e.g., sayings 18, 51, 113) with answers which employ the aphoristic imagination that was cultivated from the outset of the Jesus movements. Moreover, *Gos. Thom.* does not interpret Jesus' death by means of a theology of the cross, but advances a Christology in which such a proclamation was not necessary. When the disciples are aware that Jesus will pass away, they reflect on the implications of his departure in terms of group leadership (sayings 12, 13). Accordingly, there is no need to appeal to the cross and resurrection in order to imagine the origins of Christianity, for *Gos. Thom.* documents an alternative rationale sufficient to account for its

[59] Against J. D. Crossan, "Divine Immediacy and Human Immediacy: Towards a New First Principle in Historical Jesus Research," *Semeia* 44 (1988) 125; idem, "Materials and Methods in Historical Jesus Research," *Forum* 4/4 (1988) 11.

[60] Koester has also seen that Paul both advances an apocalyptic interpretation and introduces a theology of the cross when discussing the significance of Jesus and wisdom in 1 Corinthians (review of U. Wilckens, *Weisheit und Torheit: Eine exegetisch-religionsgeschichtliche Untersuchung zu 1. Kor. 1 und 2, Gnomon* 33 [1961] 590–95; "Primitive Christian Heresy," 78; "Structure and Criteria," 220 n. 28; "Gnostic Writings," 240). Note, however, that Koester has not drawn the conclusion that I am arguing is most pressing here.

[61] See Mack, *Myth of Innocence*, 98–123.

beginnings and presents a wisdom paradigm as a mythic precedent to reflect upon its subsequent history. Jesus' death is conceptually linked to the lives of his disciples, who bear their own crosses in imitation of Jesus' stance of endurance (sayings 55, 101; cf. Q 14:26–27; Mark 8:34–35).[62]

The challenge of *Gos. Thom.* is nothing less than a call to see early Christianity in a fresh light, not as something given but as itself an unsettled issue to be investigated by all students of the New Testament as historians of religion in antiquity. As the guiding religious statement of autonomous scribal origins, *Gos. Thom.* took Jesus seriously as a teacher who spoke with authority. It celebrated his memory by preserving sayings in his name that sanctioned the formation of a distinctive community. The gospel locates its group's position within the Christian tradition as an independent Jesus movement, which persisted over the course of several decades of social history without becoming an apocalyptic or kerygmatic sect. *Gos. Thom.* defines the role of its community in constructing the fabric of its society as a process of sapiential insight and research. Jesus was characterized as the very embodiment of wisdom, whose appearance made a difference in the way the social order would be established, sought, and found. By charting the course of salvation as a study in interpretation, this gospel locates the realm of imaginative discourse as the social space for cultivating a sane and circumspect society made possible by the wisdom remembered in Jesus' name.

[62] See also D. Seeley, "Was Jesus Like a Philosopher? The Evidence of Martyrological and Wisdom Motifs in Q, Pre-Pauline Traditions, and Mark," in *SBL 1989 Seminar Papers,* 540–49; J. S. Kloppenborg, "'Easter Faith' and the Sayings Gospel Q," *Semeia* 49 (1990) 71–99.

31

The Suspension of Time in Chapter 18 of *Protevangelium Jacobi*

FRANÇOIS BOVON

I

THE VISION OF JOSEPH in chapter 18 is situated within the context of the birth of Jesus. In the preceding chapters, the author of the *Protevangelium Jacobi* has told the story of Joachim and Anna, the parents of Mary, of the birth and youth of the Virgin, and of her bond with Joseph (chaps. 1–10). Then, concurring with Luke, he tells of the annunciation (chap. 11), the visitation (chap. 12), her pregnancy (chaps. 13–14), an ordeal (chaps. 15–16), and of the edict of Caesar Augustus and the consequent trip from Galilee to Judah. As they approach Bethlehem, Mary, both sad and joyful, feels that her hour is near. Joseph gets her settled in a cave along with his sons and then goes to find a midwife (chaps. 17–18.1). At this point there occurs an evocation of a vision seen by Joseph (18.2–3), marked by a sudden change in the narration from the third to the first person. Joseph continues speaking in the first person until he has found the midwife and spoken to her.

When the midwife arrives, a cloud that was previously overshadowing the cave dissipates, she sees a bright light and the infant appears to her (chap. 19). She comes out of the cave and meets a certain Salome, whose disbelief is first punished and then pardoned as she is forced to admit the postpartum virginity of Mary (chap. 20). The narrative goes on to tell of the visit of the three wise men (chap. 21), the sheltering of Jesus during the massacre of the innocents, the miracle of the split boulder that protected Elizabeth and her son, John (chap. 22), and the martyrdom of Zacharias, the father of John (chaps. 23–24). In the last chapter (25), the author declares himself to be James, explains certain circumstances of his life and indicates the title of his work.

Joseph's vision occupies a precise place in the book: Mary, in her cave, is about to give birth to her only son and Joseph has left to fetch a midwife who will not even be needed. He is separated from the event, just as it was necessary that he should be separated from Mary at the time of her conception (9.3). But separation does not necessarily mean indifference; Joseph is going to have a vision that must coincide, even if the text does not expressly say so, with the birth of Jesus. What he sees gives meaning to what is happening: the cessation of nature and of the activities of beasts and of humans, underscoring the importance of the event. The midwife arrives at the cave too late to assist Mary, but early enough to be a witness. The cloud that overshadowed the cave is symmetrical to Joseph's vision; in the same instant, the last prophet and the first witness meet—both are contemporary to the saving event. Joseph is a prophet—not as a foreteller of events but as an interpreter of the event because he has been given a vision. He is the witness not only of what happens, but of Truth itself.

II

The following is the Greek text of 18:2–3, according to the edition of E. de Strycker, and my translation of it.

> 2. Ἐγὼ δὲ Ἰωσὴφ περιεπάτουν καὶ οὐ περιεπάτουν. Καὶ ἀνέβλεψα εἰς τὸν πόλον τοῦ οὐρανοῦ καὶ εἶδον αὐτὸν ἑστῶτα, καὶ εἰς τὸν ἀέρα καὶ εἶδον αὐτὸν ἔκθαμβον καὶ τὰ πετεινὰ τοῦ οὐρανοῦ ἠρεμοῦντα. Καὶ ἐπέβλεψα ἐπὶ τὴν γῆν καὶ εἶδον σκάφην κειμένην καὶ ἐργάτας ἀνακειμένους, καὶ ἦσαν αἱ χεῖρες αὐτῶν ἐν τῇ σκάφῃ. Καὶ οἱ μασώμενοι οὐκ ἐμασῶντο καὶ οἱ αἴροντες οὐκ ἀνέφερον καὶ οἱ προσφέροντες τῷ στόματι αὐτῶν οὐ προσέφερον, ἀλλὰ πάντων ἦν τὰ πρόσωπα ἄνω βλέποντα. 3. Καὶ εἶδον ἐλαυνόμενα πρόβατα, καὶ τὰ πρόβατα ἑστήκει· καὶ ἐπῆρεν ὁ ποιμὴν τὴν χεῖρα αὐτοῦ τοῦ πατάξαι αὐτά, καὶ ἡ χεὶρ αὐτοῦ ἔστη ἄνω. Καὶ ἐπέβλεψα ἐπὶ τὸν χείμαρρον τοῦ ποταμοῦ καὶ εἶδον ἐρίφους καὶ τὰ στόματα αὐτῶν ἐπικείμενα τῷ ὕδατι καὶ μὴ πίνοντα. Καὶ πάντα θήξει ὑπὸ τοῦ δρόμου αὐτῶν ἀπηλαύνετο.
>
> 2. But I, Joseph, was walking and yet I was not walking. I lifted my gaze toward the vault of heaven[1] and saw it standing still; then at the air and I saw it seized with dread; and the birds of heaven, motionless. Then I looked upon the earth and saw a cooking-pot placed there and workmen reclining with their hands in the pot. Those who were chewing[2] did not chew; those who were in the midst of serving themselves[3] did not take;[4] and those who were raising food toward their mouths did not raise it. But the faces of all were turned upwards. 3. Then I saw sheep being driven

[1] On πόλος, see below.

[2] Μασάομαι ("to chew") must not be confused with μάσσω ("to knead"), an error found in the first two Armenian versions.

[3] Literally, "to lift up."

[4] Literally, "to carry."

> and the sheep were stopped. The shepherd raised his hand to smite them,[5] but his raised hand was immobilized. Then I looked upon the flow of the river[6] and I saw kidgoats with their mouths posed over the water, but they did not drink. Then all things, in one instant, were being driven on[7] again by their own impetus.[8]

Though brief, this fragment presents several textual problems. Three manuscripts omit the vision—the *Vaticanus graecus* 455,[9] the *Vaticanus graecus* 654,[10] and, most important, the *Papyrus Bodmer* V (third century).[11] However, the evidence provided by the versions and by other Greek manuscripts, especially the *Turin Papyrus* (fourth century),[12] convinces us that the vision did belong to the original text.

The second problem is that the evidence of the manuscripts and the versions vacillates between the first and third person: should the text be read with "I"[13] or "he"?[14] If external criticism hesitates, internal criticism imposes the first person; it comes so much as a surprise, that the reader naturally senses why the text has been modified. The sudden changeover to "I," shocking as it may seem, is not an aberration in an ancient text which seeks to substantiate the truth of its message.[15]

5 In πατάσσω ("to beat," "to knock") the sound of the blow is heard; cf. Mark 14:27 (a quote from Zech 13:7).

6 Ὁ χείμαρρος has the meaning of "torrent"; the author clearly wants to emphasize the movement of the river.

7 Note the imperfect tense ἀπηλαύνετο.

8 Ὁ δρόμος, meaning "course," "race."

9 F^b in the edition by E. de Strycker (*La forme la plus ancienne du Protévangile de Jacques* [Subsidia Hagiographica 33; Brussels: Société des Bollandistes, 1961] 31). Particularly useful for the manuscript tradition is E. de Strycker, "Die griechischen Handschriften des Protevangeliums Jacobi (Originalbeitrag 1971/1975)," in *Griechische Kodikologie und Textüberlieferung*, ed. D. Harlfinger (Darmstadt: Wissenschaftliche Buchgesellschaft, 1980) 577–612.

10 G in the edition of de Strycker (*La forme*, 31).

11 Z in the edition of de Strycker (*La forme*, 34). This manuscript was edited by M. Testuz, *Papyrus Bodmer V: Nativité de Marie* (Cologny/Geneva: Bibliotheca Bodmeriana, 1958).

12 Y in the edition of de Strycker (*La forme*, 34). This manuscript was edited by E. Pistelli, *Papiri greci e latini* I (Pubblicazioni della Società italiana per la ricerca dei Papiri greci e latini in Egitto; Florence: E. Ariani, 1912) 9–15.

13 The following Greek manuscripts have "I": Y, A, C, D, E, H, and R; and the versions Syr^a, Syr^b, Arm^a, Arm^b, and Georg, as well as the edition of J. A. Fabricius, *Codex apocryphus Novi Testamenti* I (Hamburg: B. Schiller, 1703) and that of C. de Tischendorf, *Evangelia Apocrypha* (2nd ed.; Leipzig: H. Mendelssohn, 1876; reprint, Hildesheim: G. Olms, 1987) 34. I follow the abbreviations of de Strycker (*La forme*, 30–49).

14 The following Greek manuscript have "he": S, B, I, L, M, and N; the versions or adaptions: Aeth, Lat^a, Lat^b; the *Armenian Gospel of the Infancy* (Tay) and the Latin text of G. Postel published by T. Bibliander, *Protevangelion s. de natalibus Jesu Christi et ipsius matris virg. Mariae, sermo historicus divi Jacobi minoris, etc.* (Basel: J. Oporinus, 1552) 43.

15 See. H. R. Smid, *Protevangelium Jacobi, A Commentary* (Apocrypha Novi Testamenti; Assen: Van Gorcum, 1965) 176–78 (Appendix 3, Transition from the third to the first person); de Strycker, *La forme*, 149.

In the first sentence, I retain, with the best manuscripts, the words "and yet I was not walking."[16] Joseph himself participates in the suspension of movement and of time that is characteristic of his vision.

In the second sentence of the Greek, I follow de Strycker's reconstruction of the text, based on the very old *Turin Papyrus* (even though the papyrus is fragmentary at this point).

In the last sentence of par. 2, should one read ἄνω βλέποντα ("turned upwards") or κάτω νεύοντα ("bending down one's head")?[17] The latter reading, rarely attested, does not accord with the movement of the text, which orients the gaze of everyone toward the heavens. With de Strycker, therefore, I read the words ἄνω βλέποντα.

The last problem is to decide which form, which construction, and which meaning to give to the little word θῆξις. Under the influence of the Syriac and Georgian versions, de Strycker conjectures the dative case without a preposition. All the Greek manuscripts, however, use the preposition ὑπό before θῆξις, rendered with the dative, the genitive, or the accusative. Although it is impossible to reconstruct the text with any certitude, the meaning at least seems sure: "in an instant." One Greek lexicographer defines the rare word θῆξις as "impulse," "prick," "point," or "speed."[18]

III

Although the *Protev. Jacobi* has been known in the West since the voyage of G. Postel to the orient in the sixteenth century and his subsequent edition of a Latin translation of his discovery in 1552,[19] scientific study of the

[16] The following Greek manuscripts omit these words: B, D, H, I, L, R, and the Syriac, the Armenian, and the Georgian versions, as well as the Latin edition by G. Postel and the Greek edition of J. A. Fabricius.

[17] Κάτω νεύοντα is attested by the Greek manuscript A and apparently by one Armenian version (Arm[a]).

[18] See Hesychius of Alexandria (probably fifth century CE), Συναγωγὴ πασῶν λέξεων κατὰ στοιχεῖον ("Alphabetical Collection of all the words" [="Lexicon," "Dictionary"]), ed. M. Schmidt (2nd ed.; Jena: H. Dufft, 1867) 730. Θῆξις is often confused with θίξις. Several Latin glossators quote θίξις and translate it with *tactus* (θίξει, "touching," with *tactu*); see references in the index of G. Goetz, *Thesaurus Glossarum emendatarum* (Corpus Glossariorum Latinorum 7; Leipzig: Teubner, 1901) 329.

[19] See n. 14. It has been known now for several years that several Latin versions and adaptations of the *Protev. Jacobi* did exist and were circulated in ancient times and certainly in the Middle Ages. See de Strycker, *La forme,* 39–41 and 363–71; J. A. de Aldama, "Fragmentos de una versión latina del Protoevangelio de Santiago y una nueva adaptación de sus primeros capítulos," *Bib* 43 (1962) 57–74; E. de Strycker, "Une ancienne version latine du Protévangile de Jacques, avec des extraits de la Vulgate de Matthieu 1–2 et Luc 1–2," *Analecta Bollandiana* 83 (1965) 365–402; and an appendix by J. Gribomont, 402–10; E. de Strycker, "Une métaphrase inédite du Protévangile de Jacques," *Miscellanea in hon. I. Vergote, OLP* 6/7 (1975/76) 174–84; J. Gijsel, "Het Protevangelium Jacobi in het Latijn," *L'Antiquité classique* 50 (1981) 351–66;

document, particularly of our passage, dates back only to the nineteenth century. In 1832, J. C. Thilo presented a good critical edition and a commentary, which are still worthwhile consulting.[20] In 1850, A. Hilgenfeld argued that the text as it had thus far been edited could not be the original;[21] our fragment, with its change of grammatical subject, was proof in his view that the document contains interpolations. The introduction by C. Tischendorf to his *Evangelia apocrypha* remains today an important source of information.[22] In 1880, R. A. Lipsius believed he recognized gnostic characteristics in the chapter under discussion.[23] A. Harnack does not hesitate to identify three sources behind the *Protev. Jacobi:* a biography of Mary up until the age when the canonical Gospels take charge of her (chaps. 1–17), an *Apocryphum Josephi* (chaps. 18–20), and a legend about Zachariah (chaps. 22–24).[24] He holds the change of subject in 18:2 as a decisive criterion for his hypothesis of an *Apocryphum Josephi.* The reworking of these sources must date from the end of the second or third century.

In 1904, A. Meyer made some important philological observations.[25] He understands πόλος not as the fixed pole, but as the celestial vault (grounding his idea on an expression of a certain Alexis: τὸ τοῦ πόλου τοῦ παντὸς ἡμισφαίριον ("the hemisphere of the whole celestial vault").[26] That same year, G. A. van den Bergh van Eysinga was the first to remark that a suspension of time similar to that in *Protev. Jacobi* accompanied the birth of the Buddha.[27] He concluded that the vision of Joseph had its origins in India and that we are thus plunged into the marvelous world of oriental tales. In 1909, W. Bauer summarized well the function of the incident: "Die Natur nimmt Anteil an dem weltgeschichtlichen Ereignis, das sich vorbereitet."[28] He

H. Fros, *Bibliotheca Hagiographica Latina Antiquae et Mediae Aetatis, Novum Supplementum* (Subsidia Hagiographica 70; Brussels: Société des Bollandistes, 1986) 137–38.

[20] J. C. Thilo, *Codex apocryphus Novi Testamenti* (Leipzig: F. C. G. Vogel, 1832).

[21] A. Hilgenfeld, *Kritische Untersuchungen über die Evangelien Justins, der clementischen Homilien und Marcion's: Ein Beitrag zur Geschichte der ältesten Evangelien-Literatur* (Halle: Schwetschke, 1850) 153–54.

[22] Tischendorf, *Evangelia Apocrypha.*

[23] R. A. Lipsius, *Die apokryphen Apostelgeschichten und Apostellegenden* . . ., I–II und Ergänzungsband (Braunschweig: C. A. Schwetschke, 1883–1890; reprint, Amsterdam: Philo Press, 1976).

[24] A. Harnack, *Geschichte der altchristlichen Literatur,* Teil II, *Die Chronologie bis Eusebius* (Leipzig: Hinrichs, 1897) 1:600–601.

[25] A. Meyer, "Protevangelium des Jakobus," in *Handbuch zu den Neutestamentlichen Apokryphen,* ed. E. Hennecke (Tübingen: Mohr, 1904) 125–27.

[26] Quoted by Athenaeus, *The Deipnosophists* (Δειπνοσοφιστῶν), 2.60A; cf. 2.61B; Euripides, *Orestes* 1685.

[27] G. A. van den Bergh van Eysinga, *Indische Einflüsse auf evangelische Erzählungen* (FRLANT 4; Göttingen: Vandenhoeck & Ruprecht, 1904) 65–67.

[28] W. Bauer, *Das Leben Jesu im Zeitalter der neutestamentlichen Apokryphen* (Tübingen: Mohr, 1909; reprint, Darmstadt: Wissenschaftliche Buchgesellschaft, 1967) 67.

indicates a parallel in the *Sibylline Oracles* 8.474–75 (upon the birth of the infant, the earth stretches out joyfully, the throne of heaven laughs, and the world rejoices).

A year later, E. Amann added two other parallels to the list (Ignatius of Antioch *Ephesians* 19.1; Wis 18:14–15) and made the suggestion that if Joseph was able to observe the celestial vault in an arrested state, the cessation of its movement must have happened at sunset.[29] A later Christian tradition connects the midnight prayer with the suspension of time. Nor should one forget that Christians situated the birth of Christ and the Christmas celebration near the time of the winter solstice. Along with polemical factors, they must have had a doctrinal reason for doing so: it is from this day forward that the sun, therefore light and life, waxes in strength. The etymological meaning of "solstice" is that the sun is made to stand still. There is an instant when the pendulum of time, before swinging in the opposite direction, seems to stop. E. Amman examines in detail the patristic notices and the reception of the *Protev. Jacobi* in the east and west.

A quarter of a century later, A. Klawek denied the Buddhist origin of the motif of the suspension of time, rooting it rather in the biblical and extrabiblical Jewish tradition of miraculous signs that usually accompany a theophany.[30] In 1958, M. Testuz published the Greek text of the *Protev. Jacobi* in its abbreviated form (without our chapter) according to the *Papyrus Bodmer* V and picked up again, with some modifications, the literary hypothesis of A. Harnack.[31] The commentary by H. R. Smid has a good presentation of the textual evidence and a list of religious-historical parallels that are useful for our particular study.[32] Smid also makes the following two assertions: (1) What Joseph sees in his ecstasy is not just a dream: in the eyes of the narrator it corresponds to reality. (2) The account in Luke 2:8–14 is not at all used by the narrator, nor does it constitute the literary background of the scene (a point of view I do not share). In an appendix, Smid expounds the literary phenomenon common in antiquity of the sudden use of the first person in a text written in the third person (so the sudden switch-over does not necessarily indicate a new source).[33] More recently, A. M. di Nola has

[29] E. Amann, *Le Protévangile de Jacques et ses remaniements latins: Introduction, textes, traduction et commentaire* (Les Apocryphes du Nouveau Testament; Paris: Letouzey et Ané, 1910) 248–49. At the same time, two scholars published two important volumes of annotated translations: C. Michel and P. Peeters, *Evangiles apocryphes* I–II (Textes et Documents pour l'étude historique du christianisme 18; Paris: Picard, 1914).

[30] A. Klawek, "Motyw bezruchu w Protevangelium Jacobi," *Collectanea Theologica*, Lwów, 17 (1936) 327–38. I express my thanks to Mrs. Irena Backus who helped me understand the content of this Polish contribution.

[31] Testuz, *Nativité*, 16–18.

[32] Smid, *Commentary*, 127–30.

[33] Ibid.

interpreted the vision of Joseph in the light of the biblical notion of the silence of creatures whenever God speaks and manifests himself.[34] The vision is "un esempio di reazione cosmico-creaturale alla teofania-epifania."[35] Di Nola provides the most complete assessment of Jewish, Greek, and Buddhist parallels.

IV

The theme of the suspension of time is extremely common.[36] One can find it in the fairy tale of Sleeping Beauty as well as in a recent novel by M. Kundera.[37] It emerges often in ancient texts that tell of the intervention of a god or of the birth or death of a hero. It has not been forgotten in the Latin Christmas liturgy where Wis 18:14–15 is quoted in the Introit of the Mass of the Dawn. Although such far-flung parallels cannot explain the origin of our text, they can throw light on similarities and particularities as well as underline the coherence of the theme (cf. *Lalita Vistara,* 1; Limenios, *Delphic Paean to Apollos;* Homer, *The Odyssey* 6,42–46; *Homeric Hymn to Athena* (no. 28); Euripides, *Bacchae* 1084–87; Sophocles, *Oedipus Coloneus* 1620–30; Plato, *Politicus* 273E–274A; Plutarch, *De defectu oraculorum* 17, quoted by Eusebius, *Praeparatio Evangelica* 5, 17, 6–9; *Corpus Hermeticum* 13, 16; Pseudo-Callisthenes, *Historia Alexandri Magni* 1,12; 1 Kgs 19:11–13; Hab 2:20; Zeph 1:7; Zech 2:13; Wis 18:14–15; Pss 65:8; 107:29; Job 4:12, 16; *Sifre* Deut 32:1 piska 306; 4 Ezra 7:39–43; *Sib. Or.* 3:199–201; *Testament of Adam* [Syriac and Greek]; Josh 10:12–14; Sir 46:4; *Midrash Rabbah* Exod 29:9; *Targum Ps.-Jonathan* Deut 28).

Although the *Protev. Jacobi* is one of the few to indicate the suspension of time, other ancient Christian texts do mention miracles of nature in connection with the birth or the crucifixion of Jesus. The Synoptic Gospels

[34] A. M. di Nola, "Sospensione della vita cosmica," in A. M. di Nola, *Antropologia religiosa: Introduzione al problema e campioni di ricerca* (Florence: Vallecchi, 1974) 173–99. Cf. A. M. di Nola, *Vangeli apocrifi. Natività e infanzia* (Biblioteca della Fenice, Milan: Guanda, 1977) 26–28.

[35] Di Nola, "Sospensione," 173.

[36] A modern example: a journalist, L. Greilsamer, writes that upon the death of Salvador Dali, ". . . lundi matin, à 10h. 13, les aiguilles de toutes les 'montres molles' du monde se sont arrêtées" (*Le Monde,* 25 January 1989) 10. A Greek friend recently explained to me that at sunset there are a few minutes of silence when the passing of time is interrupted: cicadas have become quiet and the chirring of crickets is not yet heard.

[37] M. Kundera, *La plaisanterie* (Folio, Paris: Gallimard, 1985) 86–87 and 113. See also M. Tournier, *Gaspard, Melchior & Balthazar* (Folio, Paris: Gallimard, 1987) 166: "Le temps s'était effacé dans une éternité sacrée"; G. G. Marquez, *Des feuilles dans la bourrasque* (*La Hojarasca*) (Paris: Grasset, 1983) 106; R. M. Rilke, Acht Sonette aus dem Umkreis der Sonette an Orpheus, 6 ("Welche Stille um einen Gott!" Muzot, 16.–17. Februar 1922), in R. M. Rilke, *Werke* II,1 (3rd ed.; Frankfurt am Main: Insel, 1984) 250; and, of course, the poem by A. de Lamartine, *Le Lac,* and his famous line "O temps, suspends ton vol. . . ."

indicate three hours of darkness and the tearing of the temple curtain at the time of the crucifixion.[38] One can understand how the church fathers exploited as much as they could the text by Phlegon concerning a certain eclipse of the sun.[39] Although for Matthew the standing of the star over the place where Jesus was born had an informative function (Matt 2:9), the same theme is given other meanings in the *Syriac History of the Virgin;* miracles were to accompany the miraculous birth and to symbolize the bonds God was renewing with the earth.[40] The *Protev. Jacobi,* the *Gospel of Pseudo-Matthew,* as well as other apocryphal infancy gospels, make mention of the supernatural light which filled the cave where Mary had taken refuge to give birth to Jesus.[41] Origen also seems to suppose that miracles accompanied the birth of Jesus (*Against Celsus* 1.34 and 38). Later, one would even tell how miracles occurred in Rome;[42] and the *Golden Legend*[43] would contain attempts to list those supernatural events.[44]

V

In my opinion, the search for the origins of the motif has stood in the way of progress toward an exact defining of its contours. Scholars have preferred to study the origin and growth of the text rather than the coherent meaning of its structural content. The latter is what we now take up here.

The emphatic "I," with which our fragment begins, fulfills a double function: it makes the vision personal in the manner of apocalyptic writing (see

[38] Matt 27:45–51//Mark 15:33–38//Luke 23:44–45. Luke adds the eclipse of the sun.

[39] P. de Labriolle, *La Réaction païenne: Etude sur la polémique antichrétienne du Ier au VIe siècle* (Paris: L'artisan du livre, 1948) 204–20.

[40] Suspended over the cave, the star became a column of light or of fire which reached from the earth to heaven; see P. Peeters, *Evangiles apocryphes* 2:2–6.

[41] *Protev. Jacobi* 19:2; *Pseudo-Matt.* 13:2; *Arabian Infancy Gospel* 3.

[42] See C. Druthmar, *Expositio in Matthaeum* 3 (*PL* 106:1287). See Amann, *Protévangile,* 150.

[43] *Legenda aurea* 6, ed. T. Graesse, *Jacobi a Voragine Legenda Aurea* . . . (3rd ed.; Dresden/Leipzig, 1890; reprint, Osnabrück: Zeller, 1969) 39–47: concomitant miracles to the nativity: the fall of the temple of peace, the springing up of a fountain of oil which runs into the Tiber, three suns, the appearing of a heavenly altar to the Sibyl who was consulted by the emperor Augustus, and so on. Concerning this work, see A. Boureau, *La Légende dorée: Le système narratif de Jacques de Voragine (†1298)* (Cerf-Histoire; Paris: Cerf, 1984).

[44] A very important text that contains the motif of the suspension of time linked to the hour and the prayer of midnight is to be found in some versions of the *Apostolic Tradition* 41: "For the elders who handed down the tradition taught us that at this hour all creation rests a moment to praise the Lord: the stars, the trees, the water stop an instant and all the host of angels that serve him praise God at this hour with the souls of the righteous . . ."; see Hippolyte de Rome, *La tradition apostolique d'après les anciennes versions: Introduction, traduction et notes,* ed. B. Botte (2nd ed.; SC 11bis; Paris: Cerf, 1968) 130–31; H. Chadwick, "Prayer at Midnight," in *Epektasis: Mélanges Patristiques offerts au Cardinal J. Daniélou,* ed. J. Fontaine and C. Kannengieser (Paris: Beauchesne, 1972) 47–49. The motif reappears in numerous medieval and Byzantine texts.

sources of water. The more agile kidgoats are there already and the sheep are approaching.

Before saying what the author desires to communicate by this, let us suggest one hypothesis: if we surmise that the workers are agricultural laborers and that a tie binds them to the shepherds, we could have here a narrative based on a verse in Luke's Gospel. Luke begins his story with the angels' appearing to the shepherds who were spending the night out in the open air, watching over their flocks (Luke 2:8). Does not the description of the laborers at table evoke ἀγραυλοῦντες ("dwelling in the field"), and the episode with the shepherd, φυλάσσοντες ("keeping watch") in Luke's story? If this is the case, the author of the *Protev. Jacobi* takes his inspiration from a brief piece of information from the Gospel, which he then illustrates and develops.

The mysterious vision given to Joseph corresponds to the appearance of the angels to the shepherds in the Gospel of Luke. What then is the function of this vision, which adds to the canonical narrative the temporary suspension of movement and of time? The religious significance of ἔκθαμβος ("seized with dread") gives us a hint: it is the awe felt before the presence of the divine. The created world is immobilized because God is about to act. When God intervenes, one feels it on earth; the author, who must be more Greek than Jewish, is trying to express in his own fashion the eschatological character of the birth of Jesus: he knows that in the end times, there will be no more day or night (see 4 Ezra 7:39–43). This means, within his cultural horizons, that there will be no more movement or time. The birth of Jesus is part of this end of time, but it is only the first phase; that is why the cosmic horizon is limited, just as the divinity of the Son is reduced to incarnation. It is just as important that the eschatological immobility be only temporary, for salvation history is not yet at its completion, several stages must still be crossed before the end. The author of the vision of Joseph, by evoking the universe and nature in Greek fashion, points to a decisive moment in the Jewish history of salvation: the birth of Jesus as the beginning of a new age, the last times.

VI

A history of the reception of the *Protev. Jacobi* has not yet been written.[51] The eastern church seems not to have condemned it, skillfully according it an honorary, though not canonical, status. The Byzantines just call it a "story" after one of its titles.[52] The word ἱστορία ("written account," "narrative," "history") could denote a narrative or a historical document. In any case, the

[51] See, however, chap. 3 ("Histoire du livre") of Amann, *Protévangile,* 61–169.

[52] E.g., Pseudo-Eustathius *Commentary on the Hexaemeron* (*PG* 18:772); see Amann, *Protévangile,* 116–17.

Byzantines generally accorded it their confidence and used it as source material for historical, homiletic, or liturgical works. The western church was more reserved. Jerome condemned it, as did Pope Innocent I and the *Decree* of Pseudo-Gelasius.[53] What is less known, is that it was not only adapted but also translated into Latin several times, as recent discoveries have shown.[54] Its destiny in the West was therefore maybe not so grim as has been thought.

The time will come when, with the help of that still-unwritten story of its reception, one will be able to follow the theme of the suspension of time, our chapter 18, down through the centuries of the Christian church. What I am able to indicate at present is the translations and recastings of the work that use this theme. Several western adaptions are ignorant of it, such as the *Gospel of Pseudo-Matthew*, the *De nativitate Mariae*, and the *Golden Legend*.[55] The *Story of Joseph the Carpenter* tells of the birth of Jesus but does not mention our vision of Joseph. Nor is it used, apparently, by Roswitha of Gandersheim.[56] However, the survival of the theme was assured in the East: first, by the *Turin Papyrus* and by the Byzantine manuscripts from the tenth to the seventeenth century, which reproduce the vision of Joseph; then by the oriental versions—two in Syriac, two in Armenian, the Georgian translation, the Ethiopic (which contracts our chapter 18 into a thin summary), a fragment of a Slavic-Glagolithic translation; and, finally, by the Armenian *Gospel of the Infancy*.[57]

When G. Postel published his work in 1552, he believed he was presenting something new to scholars and to devotees.[58] This was not incorrect, since the work had been lost to the West. However, in spite of its absence from the most notable texts, the theme of the suspension of time had not entirely disappeared; the *Liber de infantia salvatoris*, neither forgot it nor omitted it,[59] and Irish monks possessed this work—and

[53] Jerome, *De perpetua virginitate beatae Mariae adversus Helvidium* 8 (*PL* 23:192); Innocent I, *Letter* 6, to Exuperius of Toulouse 7:13 (*PL* 20:501); *Decree* of Pseudo-Gelasius, No. 8: Evangelia nomine Jacobi minoris (see Amann, *Protévangile*, 143 and 104).

[54] See the works cited in n. 19.

[55] *Pseudo-Matthew* 13:2 is content to use the miracle of the illuminated cave. Obviously polemical, *De nativitate Mariae* 10.2 asserts that Mary had childbirth "as the Evangelists taught us," understood "not as the Apocryphal texts tell"!

[56] *Story of Joseph the Carpenter* 7; and Roswitha of Gandersheim, *Historia nativitatis laudabilisque conversationis intactae dei genitricis* . . . (*PL* 137:1065–80).

[57] See de Strycker, *La forme*.

[58] G. Postel, *Protevangelion*, 43–44.

[59] See *Latin Infancy Gospels*, ed. M. R. James (Cambridge: Cambridge University Press, 1927) manuscripts of Arundel *404* and Hereford *0.3.9*. The text has been reedited and translated into Spanish by A. de Santos Otero, *Los Evangelios Apócrifos* (BAC 148; Madrid: La Editorial Catolica, 1963) 266. New manuscripts have been found: see J. Gijsel, "Les 'Evangiles latins de l'enfance' de M. R. James," *Analecta Bollandiana* 94 (1976) 289–302.

thus the vision of Joseph—as attested by the book called *Leabhar Breac.*[60]

[60] The *Leabhar Breac* was edited and translated into English by E. Hogan, *The Irish Nennius from L. Na Huidre and Homilies and Legends from L. Brecc* (Todd Lecture Series 6; Dublin: Academy House, 1895) 38–73. The translation has been reproduced by M. R. James (*Latin Infancy Gospels,* 111–19). On our motif in this text, see M. McNamara, *The Apocrypha in the Irish Church* (Dublin: Dublin Institute for Advanced Studies, 1975) 43.

I express my deep gratitude to my friend Carlo Ossola who put me on the trail of this fascinating theme. I would like also to thank warmly Mrs. Jane Haapiseva-Hunter, lic. theol, who made this translation with interest and competence.

32

"Masculine Fellowship" in the *Acts of Thomas*

HAROLD W. ATTRIDGE

HELMUT KOESTER HAS long advocated the importance of studying the New Testament in as broad a framework as possible. He has been particularly concerned with Christian apocryphal literature, and one of the "trajectories" he has attempted to trace involves the Thomas tradition of early Syriac Christianity.[1] This essay deals with a problem in that tradition that can be illuminated by data from sources on a distinct but related "trajectory." Exploring such interconnections of various "trajectories" is one way in which Koester's work can be usefully continued.

In the *Acts of Thomas* there are numerous liturgical passages, descriptions of rituals, invocations, and epicleses, with intriguing elements.[2] A particularly knotty problem is posed by the phrase "masculine fellowship," which occurs in two invocations. In chap. 27 Thomas initiates King Gundafar[3] and

[1] See, e.g., his "GNOMAI DIAPHOROI: The Origin and Nature of Diversification in the History of Early Christianity," *HTR* 58 (1965) 279–318; reprinted in Robinson-Koester, *Trajectories,* 114–57.

[2] For special studies of eastern liturgical traditions, see G. G. Willis, "What Was the Earliest Syrian Baptismal Liturgy?" *Studia Evangelica* 6 (1973) 651–54; A. J. F. Klijn, "Baptism in the Acts of Thomas," in *Studies on Syrian Baptismal Rites,* ed. J. Vellian Kottayam (Syrian Churches Series 6; Kottayam, 1975) 57–62; Gabriele Winkler, "The Original Meaning of the Prebaptismal Anointing and Its Implications," *Worship* 52 (1978) 24–45; Sebastian Brock, "The Syrian Baptismal Ordines (with special reference to the anointings)," *Studia Liturgica* 12 (1977) 177–83; Ruth A. Meyers, "The Structure of the Syrian Baptismal Rite," in *Essays on Early Eastern Initiation,* ed. P. Bradshaw (GROW Joint Liturgical Series 8; Bramcote: Grove, 1988) 31–43.

[3] The transcription of the name varies. The Greek regularly reads Gundaphoros. The Syriac manuscripts vary between Gudnafar and Gundafar. The combination of Greek and Syriac witnesses and the external attestation of the name favors Gundafar.

his brother Gad in a ritual called "sealing with the seal."[4] Before the anointing the apostle invokes the Spirit with a series of epithets: "holy Name of Christ," "the Power of the Most High," "highest Charism," "merciful Mother," "masculine Fellowship (ἡ κοινωνία τοῦ ἄρρενος),"[5] "Lady who reveals the hidden mysteries," "Mother of the seven houses." In chap. 50, the apostle baptizes and then celebrates the Eucharist for a woman who had been possessed of a demon. Before breaking the bread he offers a prayer similar to his earlier baptismal epiclesis and invokes the Spirit as "perfect Compassion," "masculine Fellowship (ἡ κοινωνία τοῦ ἄρρενος)," "Lady, you who understand the mysteries of the chosen one," "Lady, you who share in all the contests of the noble athlete," "Respite, you who reveal the magnitudes of every greatness," "Lady, you who make manifest what is secret and render visible what is hidden," "sacred Dove who gives birth to twin nestlings," "hidden Mother."[6]

The translations are of the Greek text;[7] the Syriac[8] replaces "masculine fellowship" with unobjectionably pious phrases,[9] in conformity with its tendency to sanitize the text. Although the work was probably composed in Syriac,[10] the Greek, as often, preserves a more original form.

What does it mean to invoke the Mother-Spirit as "Masculine Fellowship"? One explanation has appealed to the presumed Syriac source. According to Burkitt, the "male" in the phrase is the Syriac equivalent of the Son of Man and the invocation appeals to the spirit associated with Christ.[11] A problem with this interpretation is the equation of "male" and "son of man." Even though the term "Son of Man" is rendered in early Syriac texts by "Son of

[4] This term appears only in the Greek: ἐπισφράγισμα τῆς σφραγῖδος; the Syriac makes a simple reference to baptism.

[5] Literally, "fellowship of the male." The genitive is best understood as descriptive or of "quality"; see BDF §165.

[6] The invocations of the "dove" and "mother" are lacking in the Syriac.

[7] R. A. Lipsius and M. Bonnet, *Acta Apostolorum Apocrypha* (Leipzig: Teubner, 1903; reprint, Hildesheim/New York: Olms, 1972) 2.2.99–291. The text is reprinted in Matthias Lipinski, *Konkordanz zu den Thomasakten* (BBB 67; Frankfurt am Main: Athenäum, 1988).

[8] The edition of the principal manuscript is W. Wright, *Apocryphal Acts of the Apostles* (London/Edinburgh, 1871). A fragmentary fifth-century palimpsest was edited by A. Smith Lewis, *Acta Mythologica Apostolorum* in *Horae Semiticae* 3 (London: Clay, 1904). The readings of another major witness are to be found in P. Bedjan, *Acta Martyrum et Sanctorum* (3 vols.; Paris/Leipzig: Harrassowitz, 1892; reprint, Hildesheim: Olms, 1968) 3:1–175. In general, see A. J. F. Klijn, *The Acts of Thomas: Introduction-Text-Commentary* (NovTSup 5; Leiden: Brill, 1962) 4–13.

[9] In chap. 27 the Syriac reads "fellowship of blessing" (*šawtâpûṭâ' debûrkeṭâ'*); in chap. 50 the invocation is a radically different invocation of the Spirit.

[10] See Klijn, *Acts of Thomas*, 5–7, with references to other literature. There remain doubters, e.g., J. Ysebaert, *Greek Baptismal Terminology: Its Origins and Early Development* (Nijmegen: Dekker & Van de Vegt, 1962) 4; and Michael Lafargue, *Language and Gnosis* (HDS 18; Philadelphia: Fortress Press, 1985) 9.

[11] See F. C. Burkitt, "The Original Language of the Acts of Judas Thomas," *JTS* 1 (1900) 280–90.

the male" (*b^e^rêh d^e^gabrâ'*),[12] we do not have here "*son of*" anyone. Moreover, "Son of Man" does not appear anywhere in the *Acts of Thomas,* either in the narrative or in embedded liturgical elements, as a designation of Christ.[13] Nor is the phrase "fellowship of (or participation in) the Son of Man" attested elsewhere in early Christian literature.[14] Even if Burkitt's unlikely view could be sustained, it would not be clear what such κοινωνία was thought to involve.

An attractive alternative is to see the problematic phrase as part of an archaic baptismal formula that used sexual imagery to describe initiatory transformation. By the agency of the Spirit invoked in the two sacramental acts, the Christian is enabled to join and continue in a true spiritual fellowship.

The notion that the phrase is to be explained by appeal to unusual or "heterodox" traditions is not entirely new.[15] It can now be confirmed and given more precision. The confirmation comes from the widespread attestation of the motif of sacramental transformation found in patristic sources and now reinforced with material from the Nag Hammadi library. Several important pieces of evidence merit citation.

Valentinian sources provide clear references to relevant baptismal theology. In the *Excerpta ex Theodoto* the unbaptized are "children of the female only, . . . incomplete, childish, without understanding, weak, and without form, brought forth like abortions, in short, . . . children of the woman." The formation given by the Savior makes initiates "children of the man (husband) and of the bride chamber" (*Exc. Theod.* 68).[16] Some Valentinian sources insist that the formation as "sons of the bridal chamber" takes place through the instruction that accompanies baptism:

[12] Burkitt cites Mark 8:38 in Syr^s^; Luke 7:34 in Syr^sc^; Luke 9:26 in Syr^c^; Luke 22:48 in Syr^c^; John 13:31 in Syr^s^; and "the Palestinian Syriac texts *passim*" ("Original Language," 289).

[13] The phrase does appear once, in chap. 66 (Lipsius and Bonnet, *Acta,* 183,11), on the lips of Thomas, who declares that he is a "human being" like his listeners. "Son of God," however, is common as a christological title.

[14] Klijn (*Acts of Thomas,* 215), accepting Burkitt's suggestion, cites examples of the Spirit united with Christ: *Hermas, Similitudes* 5.6.5; *Epistula apostolorum* 13; Irenaeus *Adversus haereses* 1.21.3; *Sophia Jesu Christi* 102,15, but these are not cases of "participation in the Son of Man."

[15] Richard Lipsius associated the phrase with gnostic sources and translated it as "Companion of the Male Aeon" (*Genossin des Männlichen*) (*Die apocryphen Apostelgeschichten und Apostellegenden* [Braunschweig: Schwetschke, 1883] 314). Burkitt rightly objected to taking κοινωνία as "companion," but he does not entertain any reference to "gnostic" speculation ("Original Language," 289 n. 4).

[16] The translation is that of Werner Foerster, *Gnosis: A Selection of Gnostic Texts,* Eng. trans. R. McL. Wilson (2 vols.; Oxford: Clarendon, 1972) 1:230.

> It is not the bath (washing) alone that makes us free, but also the knowledge. . . . So long as the seed is still unformed, they say, it is a child of the female. But when it is formed, it is changed into a man and becomes a son of the bridegroom. No longer is it weak and subjected to the cosmic (powers), visible and invisible, but having become a man, it becomes a male fruit. (*Exc. Theod.* 78–79)[17]

Irenaeus cites a similar Valentinian formula (*Adv. haer.* 1.21.5).[18] The text contains instructions for anointing the dying with oil and water. They then receive formulas to recite on their postmortem ascent through the heavenly spheres. The deceased will tell the archons that they are sons of the preexistent Father, while they express disdain for the lower Sophia, Achamoth, "who is female and who has made these (bodily) things for herself." To the Demiurge the ascendant soul says:

> I am a precious vessel, more precious than the female which made you. If your mother does not know her origin, I know myself and am aware whence I am, and I invoke the Incorruptible, who is in the Father, mother of your mother, who has no father nor any male consort. A female sprung from a female made you, and she did not know her mother, but believed that she existed all alone. But I call upon her mother.

Like the *Excerpta,* this passage envisions the combination of ritual action and catechesis about the initiand's true identity. The obscure language alludes to cosmogonic myth, in which the nonspiritual universe is created by a fallen Sophia (Achamoth), the inferior "mother." Ultimately, the gnostic hopes to return to the Father, and be a son of the Father, through the intervention of the true spiritual mother whose knowledge is conveyed or reinforced by the rite. That is, through the feminine maternal spirit, the initiand escapes the works of the inferior female and attains to a rightful filial status.[19] Although the cosmogonic myth is lacking in *Acts Thom.* 27, the soteriological structure is similar.

Valentinian sacramental practice was apparently based on earlier and widespread traditions. One such, exemplified in the Book of Baruch by Justin, on which Hippolytus reports (*Refutatio* 5.23–27),[20] postulated that attaining spiritual perfection meant escape from "femininity."[21] Similarly,

[17] See Michael A. Williams, "Variety in Gnostic Perspectives on Gender," in *Images of the Feminine in Gnosticism,* ed. K. L. King (SAC 4; Philadelphia: Fortress Press, 1988) 14.

[18] The translation is from Foerster, *Gnosis* 1:220.

[19] There may be an allusion to the same notion of transformation of a "female" initiand into a male in Heracleon, Frag. 5, in Origen, *In John* 6.20f. "I do not know how, without any explanation, he asserts that 'the voice which is akin to Logos becomes Logos, just as woman is transformed into man.'"

[20] See Williams, "Variety," 13; and Luise Abramowski, "Female Figures in the Gnostic *Sondergut* in Hippolytus's *Refutatio,*" in *Images,* ed. King, 36–52, esp. 143–48.

[21] A useful survey of several of the most important texts is provided by Frederik Wisse, "Flee

the Sethian tractate *Zostrianos* (NHC VIII,*1*:130,20) urges, "Flee from the madness and the bondage of femininity, and choose for yourselves the salvation of masculinity. You have come not [to suffer], but to escape your bondage."

Femininity in these texts may be symbolic of bodily or material existence in general. Elsewhere the term has a more obvious practical referent. The *Dialogue of the Savior* portrays Matthew interpreting the words of Jesus, saying, "'Pray in the place where there is [no woman],' he tells us, meaning, 'Destroy the works of womanhood,' not because there is any other [manner of birth], but because they will cease [giving birth]" (NHC III,*5*:144,15).[22] That the destruction of or escape from the "works of femininity" frequently meant sexual asceticism[23] is clear from numerous sources both in patristic literature bearing on the phenomenon of encratism[24] and in the Nag Hammadi corpus.[25]

The destruction of or escape from "femininity" and the achievement of "masculinity" could be understood as the return to the primordial state of the androgynous protoplast. This widespread myth[26] apparently played an important part in early baptismal traditions.[27] Paradoxical, perhaps, yet illuminating for our text, is that the primordial androgynous state, or the spiritual entity which is its source and goal, could be labeled a *male*.[28]

Femininity: Antifemininity in Gnostic Texts and the Question of Social Milieu," in *Images*, ed. King, 297–307.

[22] For the translation, see Stephen Emmel, *Nag Hammadi Codex II.5*: *The Dialogue of the Savior* (Leiden: Brill, 1984) 89; see also Wisse, "Flee Femininity," 301.

[23] See Antoinette Clark Wire, "The Social Functions of Women's Asceticism in the Roman East," in *Images*, ed. King, 308–24.

[24] On the sayings from the *Gospel of the Egyptians*, cited in Clement of Alexandria *Stromateis* 3.9.63, and 66, see Dennis R. MacDonald, *There Is No Male and Female* (HDR 20; Philadelphia: Fortress Press, 1987) 30. On Julius Cassianus in Clem. Alex. *Strom.* 3.13.92–93, see MacDonald, *There Is No Male*, 36–37.

[25] See, e.g., *Thomas the Contender* II,7:144,8 and *Testimony of Truth* (NHC IX,3) 30,18; see the discussion of both in Wisse, "Flee Femininity," 302.

[26] See the seminal article by Wayne A. Meeks, "The Image of the Androgyne: Some Uses of a Symbol in Earliest Christianity," *HR* 13 (1974) 165–208.

[27] See most recently MacDonald, *There Is No Male*. For a brief statement of the hypothesis see his "Corinthian Veils and Gnostic Androgynes," in *Images*, ed. King, 276–92.

[28] MacDonald highlights the importance of this type of speculation on the androgyne (*There Is No Male*, 98–102, relying on Wendy O'Flaherty, *Women, Androgynes and Other Mythological Beasts* [Chicago: University of Chicago Press, 1980]). Some texts operate with a less complex set of symbols in which the soul qua feminine is simply united with a male spiritual counterpart. Such a scheme is presupposed in the bridal chamber imagery of the *Gospel of Philip* (NHC II,3) 65,1–26 and 70,9–21, and it is most clearly expressed in the *Exegesis on the Soul*, where the primordially androgynous virgin soul (127,22–24), after falling into matter, is sent her heavenly bridegroom (132,1–15), with whom she unites in a heavenly marriage (132,24–133,11). On this text, see MacDonald, *There Is No Male*, 54–55; Williams, "Variety," in *Images*, ed. King, 2–22;

The Nag Hammadi texts provide examples of the virginal spirit understood as male, including the classical description of Barbelo-Pronoia in the *Apocryphon of John:*

> the image of the invisible, virginal Spirit who is perfect. [The first power], the glory, Barbelo, the perfect glory in the aeons, the glory of the revelation, she glorified the virginal Spirit and praised him, because thanks to him she had come forth. This is the first thought, his image; she became the womb of everything for she is prior to them all, the Mother-Father, the first Man, the holy Spirit, the thrice-male, the thrice powerful, the thrice named androgynous one, and the eternal aeon among the invisible ones, and the first to come forth. (NHC II,*2:*4,34–5,11)[29]

Similar descriptions of the Spirit are found in other Nag Hammadi texts.[30]

The best-known text involving a transformation of a female to a male may reflect this understanding of the virginal male spirit. Much has been written on the *Gospel of Thomas,* saying 114:[31]

> Simon Peter said to them, "Let Mary leave us, for women are not worthy of Life." Jesus said, "I myself shall lead her in order to make her male, so that she too may become a living spirit resembling you males. For every woman who will make herself male will enter the kingdom of heaven."

We need not resolve the problems besetting this text in order to affirm that the realm of the spirit attained in baptism is associated with the "male."

Thus far we have illustrated a complex of interrelated motifs in various texts, primarily from the Nag Hammadi collection. The world of the spiritual is not characterized by sexual differentiation. It may, however, be envisioned as "male" even when it is represented by a "maternal" spirit. Baptism is an initiation into that world in which the self is liberated from "femininity," understood either as a general symbol of matter, change, and decay or as the specific social conditions in which men and women play their sexually defined roles. At least one text uses language for the resultant social unit that approaches the specific designation used for the Spirit in the problematic passage of the *Acts of Thomas.* The *Apocalypse of Peter* (NHC VIII,3)

---

and Madeleine Scopello, "Jewish and Greek Heroines in the Nag Hammadi Library," in *Images,* ed. King, 71–90.

[29] See also BG 27,17–28,4.

[30] See, e.g., the hymn to the "male virginal" Barbelo in *Three Steles of Seth* (NHC VII,*5:*121,21–124,14), and see the discussion in Pheme Perkins, "Sophia as Goddess in the Nag Hammadi Codices," in *Images,* ed. King, 96–112, esp. 107. In that text (120,29) it is the Father who is "thrice male."

[31] Among recent treatments are Jorunn Jacobsen Buckley, "An Interpretation of Logion 114 in the *Gospel of Thomas,*" *NovT* 27 (1985) 245–72; Marvin W. Meyer, "Making Mary Male: The Categories of 'Male' and "Female' in the Gospel of Thomas," *NTS* 31 (1985) 554–70; Williams, "Variety," in *Images,* ed. King, 19; MacDonald, *There Is No Male,* 100.

78,31–79,20 contains a polemical passage contrasting the true spiritual fellowship of the gnostics with that of their ecclesiastical competitors:

> And still others of them who suffer think that they will perfect the wisdom of the brotherhood which really exists, which is the spiritual fellowship with those united in communion, through which the wedding of incorruptibility shall be revealed. The kindred race of the sisterhood will appear as an imitation. These are the ones who oppress their brothers.

It would probably not be unfair to describe the spiritual "brotherhood" as a "masculine fellowship" in contrast to the inferior "sisterhood." In each case sexual language is used to describe religious associations symbolically. Unfortunately, this text does not make clear how it is that one enters such a communion.

The baptismal symbolism of sexual transformation may now be applied to the problematic passages. That the *Acts of Thomas,* like many of the apocryphal acts, is interested in promoting radical sexual asceticism hardly needs demonstration.[32] Most of the theories that have been advanced to explain the theological and social significance of the baptismal transformation could be illustrated from its pages. The daughter of King Gundafar embraces a life of celibacy in expectation of union with her true heavenly "bridegroom" (see *Acts Thom.* 13–14). The heroine Mygdonia, like her literary cousin Thecla in the *Acts of Paul and Thecla,* displays "manly" courage in the face of familial and social adversity as she renounces the roles assigned to her sex and pursues a life of holy chastity.

It is the basic contention of this paper that the background for the peculiar designation of the Spirit in the baptismal and eucharistic epicleses of the *Acts of Thomas* is to be found in the conceptual world we have been exploring. This world survives primarily in documents that are more or less gnostic, that is, that operate with the protological myth found in paradigmatic cases of the phenomenon such as the *Apocryphon of John.* That myth and the gnostic label that strictly goes with it are not found explicitly in literature of the "Thomas tradition," a fact that has led to the lengthy debates over whether the *Gospel* and *Acts of Thomas* are aptly labeled "gnostic." The problem posed by both of these texts is part of a much larger issue which Helmut Koester's work has raised and which remains a problem for future research. The relationship between the earliest strata of Syriac Christian

[32] See Yves Tissot, "Encratisme et Actes apocryphes," in F. Bovon et al., *Les Actes apocryphes des apôtres: Christianisme et monde païen* (Geneva: Labor et Fides, 1981) 109–19; and Giulia Sfameni Gasparro, "Gli Atti apocrifi degli Apostoli e la tradizione dell' enkrateia (Discussione di una recente formula interpretativa)," *Augustinianum* 23 (1983) 287–307. In general, see Peter Brown, *The Body and Society: Men, Women, and Sexual Renunciation in Early Christianity* (New York: Columbia University Press, 1988).

sources and the various forms of Christianity represented by the Nag Hammadi collection requires much further study. The baptismal traditions that we have been exploring constitute an interesting example of the connections between the Syrian traditions and the Sethian[33] and Valentinian gnostics. The extent and character of other connections await exploration.

[33] For baptismal traditions in Sethian sources in general, see most recently Jean-Marie Sevrin, *Le dossier baptismal Séthien: Etudes sur la sacramentaire gnostique* (BCNH, Etudes 2; Quebec: L'Université Laval, 1988).

33

"Seneca" on Paul as Letter Writer

ABRAHAM J. MALHERBE

FORCED BY CIRCUMSTANCES to do so, Paul in his correspondence with the Corinthians denied that he spoke with rhetorical finesse but claimed to be a layman in speech (2 Cor 11:6; 1 Cor 2:1–5). Measuring him by their own classicistic canons, most of the church fathers agreed with him. It is true that Augustine, although he thought that Paul was not trained in rhetoric, nevertheless discovered in him an eloquence issuing from inspiration that at times corresponded to classical rules.[1] On the other hand, some writers such as Tatian evidently sought to improve Paul's style by paraphrasing his letters.[2] For the most part, however, those writers who commented on Paul's style were content to describe the rudeness of his speech as earthen vessels (2 Cor 4:7) in which divine knowledge and wisdom were kept and to discover two purposes for it: (1) that it be evident that the power of the Christian message resided in God and not human eloquence,[3] and (2) that rudeness of style was appropriate to and effective with the humble social ranks where the gospel was hospitably received.[4]

In recent years, New Testament scholars have returned with some vigor

[1] Esp. in his *De doctrina christiana.* See E. A. Judge, "Paul's Boasting in Relation to Contemporary Professional Practice," *Australian Biblical Review* 16 (1968) 38–40.

[2] According to Eusebius *Historia ecclesiastica* 4.29.6, despite the criticism by Tatian himself (*Or.* 26) of pagan linguistic fastidiousness. As further representatives of this tendency one should also include those Atticizing copyists who were obviously unsatisfied with Paul's language.

[3] See, e.g., Origen *Commentarii in Ioannem* 4.2; *Contra Celsum* 6.2; *De princ.* 4 (*ap. Philocalia* 7). For references to patristic discussion of the subject in general, see *Arnobius of Sicca: The Case Against the Pagans,* trans. and ed. G. E. McCracken (ACW 7; Westminster, Md.: Newman Press, 1949) 295 n. 280, on *Adv. nat.* 1.58–59; and esp. *The Octavius of Marcus Minucius Felix,* trans. and ed. G. W. Clarke (ACW 39; New York: Newman Press, 1974) 18–22.

[4] See, e.g., Origen *C. Cels.* 6.58–61; cf. 6.1–2; Lactantius *Div. inst.* 5.1.15–21; Jerome *Ep.* 53.10.1.

to the examination of Paul's rhetorical strategy in his letters.[5] Interest has also of late been shown in a particular aspect of rhetoric, namely, epistolary theory, and the ways in which it may illuminate Paul's letters for us.[6] The present article represents this latter interest. Writers of rhetorical bent frequently commented on different types of letters and the styles appropriate to them; handbooks containing some theory and sample letters were composed; and instruction in letter writing on this level began at the beginning of tertiary education and perhaps as early as the latter stages of the secondary curriculum.[7] The subject was thus not arcane. This material makes us aware of a different dimension of Paul's letters, as I wish to illustrate by drawing attention to 2 Cor 10:10 and, especially, the apocryphal correspondence between Paul and the Roman philosopher Seneca.

I

Paul's correspondence with the Corinthians contains a striking number of references to and comments on his letter writing. Already in 1 Corinthians, it is evident that Paul had not been successful in communicating by letter (1 Cor 5:9–11), and he is at pains to state explicitly what his intention in writing is (4:14; 9:15).[8] Perhaps Paul protests too much when he later insists that he only writes what his readers can understand (2 Cor 1:13–14), but his insistence does underline the self-consciousness with which he wrote letters to the Corinthians. He stresses that he would rather see his readers in person (1 Cor 16:5–7; 2 Cor 1:15–16),[9] yet he is ambivalent about visiting them (1 Cor 4:18–21; 2 Cor 1:23). In any event, circumstances, sometimes of his own making, forced him to communicate with them by letter.

One such letter, which Paul claims to have written out of his own grief

[5] The leader in this effort has been H. D. Betz. See his survey, "The Problem of Rhetoric and Theology according to the Apostle Paul," in *L'Apôtre Paul: Personalité, style et conception du ministère*, ed. A. Vanhoye (BETL 73; Louvain: Louvain University Press, 1986) 16–48.

[6] E.g., H. D. Betz, *Galatians: A Commentary on Paul's Letter to the Churches in Galatia* (Hermeneia; Philadelphia: Fortress Press, 1979) 14–15, 223, 232–33; idem, *2 Corinthians 8 and 9* (Hermeneia; Philadelphia: Fortress Press, 1985) 129–40; M. Bünker, *Briefformular und rhetorische Disposition im 1. Korintherbrief* (GTA 28; Göttingen: Vandenhoeck & Ruprecht, 1984); F. W. Hughes, *Early Christian Rhetoric and 2 Thessalonians* (JSNTSup 30; Sheffield: JSOT Press, 1989); A. J. Malherbe, *Paul and the Thessalonians* (Philadelphia: Fortress Press, 1987) 68–78; idem, *Paul and the Popular Philosophers* (Minneapolis: Fortress Press, 1989) 6, 51, 52 n. 20, 56 n. 38, 64 n. 74, 74.

[7] The material is collected and discussed in *Ancient Epistolary Theorists*, ed. A. J. Malherbe (SBLSBS 19; Atlanta: Scholars Press, 1988).

[8] For a similar reticence about writing, see Demosthenes *Ep.* 1.3; Isocrates *Ep.* 1.2; *To Philip* 25–26, and Hughes, *Early Christian Rhetoric*, 19.

[9] Cf. 1 Thess 2:17–18; 3:10. Given Paul's anxiety for his churches (see 2 Cor 11:28), this epistolary cliché nevertheless can be taken to express Paul's genuine feeling.

(2 Cor 2:4), was successful because it made his readers grieve to the point of repenting (2 Cor 7:8–11). This letter was evidently written in the style of the letter of grief described in the epistolary handbooks, in which a writer expressed his sorrow but did so in a manner to show clearly how vexed he was. A sample letter of grief is supplied by Pseudo-Libanius:

> You caused me extremely much grief when you did this thing. For this reason I am very much vexed with you, and bear a grief that is very difficult to assuage. For the grief people cause their friends is exceedingly difficult to heal, and holds in greater insults than those they receive from their enemies. (*Epistolimaioi characteres* 90) [10]

Letters such as this must have been in the minds of Paul's opponents when they expressed the criticism recorded in 2 Cor 10:10.

The rhetorical background of this verse has received considerable attention,[11] although some notice of the chiastic structure of the criticism would sharpen further discussion. I wish here only to draw attention to one dictum of epistolary theory implicit in the opponents' criticism of Paul that has, so far as I can determine, gone unnoticed. I agree with Peter Marshall that the opponents thought that Paul's painful letter was rhetorically effective but considered his performance in person an abject failure.[12] But this inconsistency in Paul's performance was, according to writers on epistolary theory, a grave stylistic as well as moral shortcoming.

Epistolary theory held that, as one part of a dialogue,[13] or a sort of talk,[14] a letter should bring "real traces, real evidences of an absent friend."[15] One should see the writer's soul in his letters.[16] As to a letter's style, Seneca wrote to Lucilius, ". . . my letters should be just what my conversation would be if you and I were sitting in one another's company or taking walks together. . . ."[17] Such consistency was proof of one's integrity and invited confidence in what was said in a letter, which was but a surrogate for one's personal presence.[18]

[10] Cf. 43 (p. 80, 29–31 Malherbe).

[11] Particularly P. Marshall, *Enmity in Corinth: Social Conventions in Paul's Relations with the Corinthians* (WUNT 2.23; Tübingen: Mohr-Siebeck, 1987) 323, 375, 390–93.

[12] Ibid., 390–93.

[13] Demetrius *De elocutione* 223 (p. 16 Malherbe); Cicero *Ad familiares* 12.30.1 (p. 26 Malherbe).

[14] Cicero *Ad Atticum* 9.10.1; Ps.-Libanius *Epistolimaioi characteres* 2; 58 (pp. 66, 74 Malherbe); Basil *Epistulae* 163. See K. Thraede, *Grundzüge griechisch-römische Brieftopik* (Zetemata 48; Munich: Beck, 1970) 27–38, 47–52, 152–54.

[15] Seneca *Epistulae* 40.1; cf. Cicero *Ad fam.* 16.16.2 (p. 24 Malherbe); Demetrius *De eloc.* 227 (p. 18 Malherbe).

[16] Basil *Ep.* 163; see Thraede, *Grundzüge,* 157–61.

[17] Seneca *Ep.* 75.1–2 (p. 28 Malherbe); see Thraede, *Grungzüge,* 39–47.

[18] Cicero *Ad fam.* 12.30.1; Synesius *Ep.* 138 (p. 724 Hercher); see Thraede, *Grundzüge,* 146–49, 164 n. 306.

Seen in this light, the opponents' criticism of Paul does not merely express a negative assessment of his ability as a speaker, although that was important in their list of particulars against him. They could take advantage of Paul's absence (1 Cor 4:18), accuse him of vacillation when his plans changed (2 Cor 1:15–23), and charge him with changing his demeanor when he was not with them (2 Cor 10:1–2). Paul took great care to answer them. What was at issue between them in this battle was not just a suspicion that Paul was a chameleon, but a profound difference in their views of what an apostle should be.[19]

As one part of their strategy, Paul's opponents zeroed in on his letters. His letters were more in line with what they expected of an apostle's style of communication, and, taken by itself, their rhetorical description of his letters could be taken as a compliment. But, implicitly basing their criticism of his oral style on epistolary theory, they charged him with being different when he spoke. Paul understood that at *this* point in the argument their criticism was not, in the first place, of his oral speech as such, but of his inconsistency in expression, for that inconsistency is what he responds to in 10:11 (cf. 13:10).

So, the earliest stylistic comment on Paul's letters judged them favorably as to their rhetorical style; yet, tacitly appealing to one of the rules of epistolary theory, the same persons who showed such generosity toward his letters drew attention to his totally different demeanor in person. Implicit in this accusation of inconsistency was thus a challenge to the integrity of the writer and to confidence in his letters.

II

The situation is completely different in the *Epistolae Senecae et Pauli.*[20] These fourteen letters, composed in the third or fourth century,[21] probably

[19] See Malherbe, *Paul and the Popular Philosophers,* 91–119.

[20] The critical text is published in *Epistolae Senecae ad Paulum et Pauli ad Senecam quae vocantur,* ed. C. W. Barlow (Papers and Monographs of the American Academy in Rome 10; Rome: American Academy in Rome, 1938); reprint, in *PL* Sup. 1:673–78. English translations are available in M. R. James, *The Apocryphal New Testament* (reprint, Oxford: Clarendon, 1955) 480–84; *New Testament Apocrypha,* ed. E. Hennecke and W. Schneemelcher, trans. R. M. Wilson (Philadelphia: Westminster, 1965) 2:133–41; the best translation is that of C. W. Barlow (pp. 139–49).

[21] See the discussion by A. Kurfess in Hennecke-Schneemelcher, *New Testament Apocrypha* 2:133–34; and L. Bocciolini Palagi, *Il carteggio apocrifo di Seneca e San Paolo* (Accademia toscana di scienze e lettere La Colombaria 46; Florence: Olschi, 1978) 7–11. Bocciolini Palagi's later book, *Epistolario apocrifo di Seneca e San Paolo* (Biblioteca patristica 5; Florence: Nardini, 1985), is an abridged version of the earlier edition. See the review by A. Moda, "Seneca e il Cristianesimo," *Henoch* 5 (1983) 93–109.

to exalt Paul despite his epistolary style,[22] purport to be a correspondence between Paul and his philosophic contemporary. It is ironic that this Seneca should be represented as a critic of style, for his own style was considered commonplace and devoid of elegance, though not without a certain severity and dignity.[23] Despite these shortcomings, he was not loathe to criticize others.[24] It is not impossible that the author of the letters collapsed into one person Seneca the Elder, the writer on rhetoric, and his philosophic son.[25] Be that as it may, the letters have been held in very low esteem for their "meaningless insignificance and insipid, exaggerated flattery."[26] As for our immediate interest, the letters are sometimes adduced with other, patristic citations that claim Paul's rhetoric to have been different from that of the world.[27]

We are interested in epistolary theory rather than rhetoric in general, and it is noteworthy how shot through the letters are with epistolary conventions, which suggests a knowledge of epistolary theory. Seneca, for example, is made to express his longing for Paul's presence (*tui praesentiam optavimus*), a very common convention,[28] and he bemoans Paul's continuing absence (*nimio tuo secessu angimur*), which was equally common.[29] In addition, he sprinkles his letters with epistolary clichés like "I would like you to know this (*hoc scias volo*)."[30]

For his part, Paul also is portrayed as accomplished in the art of letter writing. He gives evidence of his epistolary sophistication by properly expressing his joy upon receiving a letter from Seneca,[31] apologizing for his

22 So M. Dibelius, "Seneca," *RGG*² (1931) 5:431.

23 Aulus Gellius *Noctes Atticae* 12.2.1; Fronto *Ad Marcum Antoninum* (p. 155 Naber; 2.102 Haines).

24 Quintilian *Inst. or.* 10.1.125–31. See further M. Schanz and C. Hosius, *Geschichte der römischen Literatur* (Handbuch der Altertumswissenschaft 8.2; Munich: Beck, 1935) 2:715–16; W. Trillitzsch, *Seneca im literarischen Urteil der Antike* (Amsterdam: A. M. Hakkert, 1971) 2:333–38.

25 So Bocciolini Palagi, *Il carteggio apocrifo,* 100–101.

26 J. N. Sevenster, *Paul and Seneca* (NovTSup 4; Leiden: Brill, 1961) 13.

27 E. Norden, *Die antike Kunstprosa* (reprint, Darmstadt: Wissenschaftliche Buchgesellschaft, 1958) 2:501–2; Judge, "Paul's Boasting," 41–42.

28 *Ep.* 1; cf. *Ep.* 4. See H. Koskenniemi, *Studien zur Idee und Phraseologie des griechischen Briefes bis 400 n. Chr.* (Annales Academiae Scientarum Fennicae, Series B, 102.2; Helsinki: Suomalainen Tiedeakatemia, 1956) 38–42, 174–75; R. Andrzejewski, "Nova et vetera in epistulis latinis IV p. Chr. saeculo apparent," *Eos* 57 (1967/68) 245–50; Thraede, *Grundzüge,* index, s.v. *pothos.*

29 *Ep.* 5. See Thraede, *Grundzüge,* 53–55; Bocciolini Palagi, *Il carteggio apocrifo,* 113–14.

30 *Ep.* 1; cf. Phil 1:12; Col 2:1. See Koskenniemi, *Idee,* 77–79. For such clichés, see H. A. Steen, "Les clichés épistolaires dans les lettres sur papyrus grecques," *Classica et Mediaevalia* 1 (1938) 119–76.

31 See Koskenniemi, *Idee,* 75–77.

delay in replying because he did not have a suitable messenger available,[32] and assuring Seneca that he was not negligent in his choice of the right person to send (*Ep.* 2).[33] And when he says, "As often as I hear your letters, I think that you are present and I imagine nothing else than that you are continually with us" (*Ep.* 4), he is not referring to the practice of reading aloud, but rather reflects the view of the epistolary theorists that letters are a conversation between separated friends whose presence is mediated by a letter.[34] Clearly, the correspondents' comments on Paul's style are made by writers accomplished in letter writing. After Paul in *Ep.* 6 makes some puzzling remarks about the clarity of his letters and the ability of his readers to understand them, Seneca in *Ep.* 7 addresses the issue of Paul's epistolary style and ends up being ambivalent about it. On the one hand, Seneca had explained to Nero that Paul's thoughts were not dependent on the usual education but that their power derived from the gods who speak through the mouths of the guiltless. When Seneca further mentioned a Roman precedent for this, Nero was satisfied. Seneca believes that the Holy Spirit is in Paul and with elevated speech brings to expression his high and revered speech. Seneca would thus seem to agree with the patristic tradition that distinguished between the divine efficacy of the Christian message and its human means of communication. But then he goes on to express the wish that when Paul expresses such thoughts, a beautiful form of discourse (*cultus sermonis*) not be lacking. In *Ep.* 9 he says that he is sending Paul a book on facility in the use of words (*de verborum copia*), evidently to help remedy what he saw as a problem.[35]

In *Ep.* 13 Seneca returns to his criticism with a specificity that betrays his concern with epistolary theory. He tries to convince Paul that eloquence does not have to obscure the sense of what he has to say. Indeed, Paul writes

[32] Cf. Cicero *Ad Att.* 6.72; 8.14.2; Pliny *Epistulae* 2.12.6; Symmachus *Epistulae* 1.87; 3.4; 3.28; and see Koskenniemi, *Idee,* 81–87; Bocciolini Palagi, *Il carteggio apocrifo,* 94–95.

[33] Cf. Cicero *Ad fam.* 2.1.1; Symmachus *Ep.* 3.16.

[34] Hearing and speaking: Pliny *Ep.* 3.20.10; see Thraede, *Grundzüge,* 27–38, 71–72; cf. Cicero *Ad Att.* 8.14.1; 9.10.1; 12.53 (pp. 22, 24 Malherbe); *Ad Quintum fratrem* 1.1.45; Seneca *Ep.* 75.1–2 (p. 28 Malherbe); see Koskenniemi, *Idee,* 42–47. Presence: Seneca *Ep.* 41 (p. 28 Malherbe); cf. Cicero *Ad fam.* 16.16.1 (p. 24 Malherbe); see Koskenniemi, *Idee,* 38–42; Thraede, *Grundzüge,* 39–47. "With us": Ps.-Libanius *Epistol. charact.* 2 (p. 67 Malherbe): "A letter, then, is a kind of written conversation with someone from whom one is separated, and it fulfills a definite need. One will speak in it as though one were in the company of the absent person."

[35] For *verborum copia,* see Cicero *De orat.* 3.124.7; 125.1–2; *Tusculanae disputationes* 2.29.12; 30.1; *Brutus* 216; Quintilian *Inst. or.* 12.10.11; Fortunatus *Ars rhetorica* 3.4. It serves to adorn or amplify speech (Cicero *Orator* 97). For *De verborum copia* as a title of a book and attempts to identify it with other books of the same title, see Bocciolini Palagi, *Il carteggio apocrifo,* 151–54.

allegorically and enigmatically,[36] and Seneca urges him to adorn what he has been granted not with mere ornamentation of words but with a certain refinement. This, Seneca insists, would not debase the thought or weaken the power of the subject matter. Paul should at least have regard for Latinity and the outward form for beautiful words.[37]

We have here to do with concerns that exercised epistolary theorists. They commented on allegory and enigmas, and the handbooks included an allegorical type among the letters they discussed, which was to be intelligible only to the persons to whom it was addressed, and an enigmatic letter in which some things were left unsaid.[38] Generally, however, clarity in expression was desired,[39] even though enigmas were thought to help sweeten speech when used in moderation.[40]

Such comments belonged to the larger discussion of the degree of ornamentation allowed to adorn a letter. A writer should be careful not to adopt an excessive loftiness of speech nor to aim too low; the main thing was to write clearly.[41] One should aim at striking a happy balance between a complete lack of embellishment, which avoided enigmas, among other devices, and a self-conscious effort to write beautifully.[42] A particular feature of style that concerned Greek writers was the proper degree to which Atticism might be used in a letter, the decision being that proper epistolary style should be "more Attic than everyday speech, but more ordinary than Atticism."[43] It is such considerations that are brought to bear, *mutatis mutandis,* on Paul's letters.

Paul also is made to refer to current epistolary theory and practice. In the salutations of all (*Ep.* 2, 4, 6, 8, 10) except the last (*Ep.* 14) of his letters to Seneca, Paul changes the usual order of names, so that his name follows that of Seneca (*Senecae Paulus salutem*). Seneca, on the other hand, follows traditional usage (*Seneca Paulo salutem*). In *Ep.* 10, Paul draws attention to his practice and acknowledges that, in view of his status in the church, it is a mistake for his name to appear last; nevertheless, his practice is justified by his desire to be all things to all people (1 Cor 9:22) and his respect for the

[36] For lack of clarity in the scriptures, see Clement of Alexandria *Stromateis* 6.15.126,1; Origen *De principiis* 4 (*ap. Philocalia* 10), and on Paul, see Origen *Epistula ad Romanos* praef; 9 (*ap. Philocalia* 9).

[37] Ps.-Demetrius *Typoi epistolikoi* 15 (p. 39 Malherbe).

[38] Ps.-Libanius *Epistol. charact.* 41 (p. 70 Malherbe); *Ep.* 6 may have such letters in mind.

[39] See Philostratus of Lemnos *De epistulis* (p. 42, 20–24 Malherbe); Julius Victor *Ars rhetorica* 27 (p. 62, 15–25 Malherbe); Ps.-Libanius *Epistol. charact.* 49 (p. 72, 9–29 Malherbe).

[40] Gregory Naz. *Ep.* 51 (p. 60, 4 Malherbe).

[41] Ps.-Libanius *Epistol. charact.* 47 (p. 72 Malherbe).

[42] Gregory Naz. *Ep.* 51.5–7 (p. 60, 1–15 Malherbe); cf. Demetrius *De eloc.* 232 (p. 18 Malherbe).

[43] Ps.-Libanius *Epistol. charact.* 46–47 (p. 72, 7–15 Malherbe), quoting Philostratus of Lemnos *De epistulis* (p. 42, 9–13 Malherbe), who had gone ahead to warn against covert allusions.

Roman Senate. In *Ep.* 12, a letter paralleled in unctiousness only by Paul's concluding letter (*Ep.* 14), Seneca insists that in view of Paul's exalted status, Paul fully deserves to be named first in his letters. A particular convention in letter writing has thus provided the author of the correspondence with an occasion to intone the Roman philosopher's respect for Paul, an insistence so effective that Paul relents and mentions himself first in the last letter!

A glance at epistolary theory and practice casts a little more light on the author's procedure. In Christian letters from the second century on, the name of the writer appeared quite frequently in the second position, which was viewed as an index to the writer's Christian faith.[44] Thus, Paul reflects his Christian humility. More than Christian practice, however, appears to have been involved in the correspondence between Paul and Seneca. Epistolary theorists differed on whether the traditional usage should be tampered with. Thus, Julius Victor permitted the beginnings and endings of letters to reflect contemporary practice which conformed to the degree of one's friendship with one's correspondent, or with his rank.[45] Ps.-Libanius, on the other hand, insisted on the traditional practice.[46] The correspondence between Paul and Seneca is made to reflect this debate on status, with Paul first showing the view represented by Julius Victor, only to be convinced that the traditional usage was, in his case at least, more appropriate. In the process, Paul accepts the higher status accorded him by the Roman philosopher. Epistolary theory and practice have been put to service in the apologetic effort to secure Christianity its proper status in society.

These texts show that Paul's letters were evaluated quite differently by Christian writers familiar with epistolary theory. Paul's opponents in Corinth thought highly of Paul's epistolary style, only to use it to his detriment in their polemic against him. The author of the *Epistolae Senecae et Pauli*, engaged in an apology designed to place Paul in a more elevated position, made a less straightforward approach. While portraying Paul as an accomplished letter writer, he nevertheless acknowledged that Paul did not measure up to Seneca's standards, but invoked the traditional, theological, patristic argument to blunt the criticism. But by manipulating the epistolary salutation in light of epistolary theory, in the end he attained what he set out to do.

44 See F. Ziemann, "De epistularum graecarum formulis solemnibus quaestiones selectae," *Dissertationes Philologicae Halensis* 18 (Halle: Niemeyer, 1911) 268–76. See also M. Naldini, *Il Cristianesimo in Egitto: Lettere private nei papiri dei secoli II–IV* (Florence: Le Monnier, 1968) 21–22; J. L. White, *Light from Ancient Letters* (Foundations and Facets; Philadelphia: Fortress Press, 1986) 195, 198, 200. F. X. J. Exler modifies Ziemann (*The Form of the Ancient Greek Letter: A Study in Greek Epistolography* [Washington: Catholic University of America, 1923] 65–67). Ziemann (p. 269) draws attention to Mark 9:35; cf. 10:31, 43; Matt 19:30; 20:26; 23:12.

45 Julius Victor *Ars rhetorica* 27 (p. 64, 8–9 Malherbe).

46 Ps.-Libanius *Epistol. charact.* 51 (p. 74 Malherbe).

34

God Language in Ignatius of Antioch

BISHOP DEMETRIOS TRAKATELLIS

IGNATIUS OF ANTIOCH has been an engaging author among the early Christian writers. One of the reasons for his attractiveness is his language, with all its singular, suggestive, and enigmatic characteristics. The present article dedicated to Helmut Koester, a creative contributor to Ignatian scholarship,[1] deals with a particular phenomenon within the Ignatian language. It examines the striking way in which the word God (θεός) has been used in the letters of the Antiochian bishop.[2] For convenience we call this usage the God language in Ignatius.

What are the precise data that define this phenomenon? What is the explanation for its occurrence? What can we say about its possible origin and signification?

[1] Helmut Koester, *Synoptische Überlieferung bei den Apostolischen Vätern* (TU 65; Berlin: Akademie-Verlag, 1957); idem, "History and Cult in the Gospel of John and in Ignatius of Antioch," *JTC* 1 (1965) 111–23; idem, *Introduction* 2:279–87.

[2] This paper presupposes the authenticity of the seven letters of Ignatius preserved in the so-called middle recension (*Ephesians, Magnesians, Trallians, Romans, Philadelphians, Smyrnaeans, Polycarp*). The recent challenges to the scholarly consensus by A. Weijenborg (*Les Lettres d'Ignace d'Antioch* [Leiden: Brill, 1969]), J. Rius-Camps (*The Four Authentic Letters of Ignatius the Martyr* [Rome: Pontificium Institutum Orientalium Studiorum, 1979]), and R. Joly, (*Le Dossier d'Ignace d'Antioche* [Brussels: Université de Bruxelles, 1979]), are interesting but not convincing. See William A. Schoedel, *Ignatius of Antioch: A Commentary on the Letters of Ignatius of Antioch* (Hermeneia; Philadelphia: Fortress Press, 1985) 4–7; C. P. H. Bammel, "Ignatian Problems," *JTS* n.s. 33 (1982) 62–97; Christine Trevett, "Anomaly and Consistency: J. Rius-Camps on Ignatius and Matthew," *VC* 38 (1984) 165–71; cf. J. Speigl, "Ignatius in Philadelphia: Ereignisse und Anliegen in den Ignatiusbriefen," *VC* 41 (1987) 360.

God Language in Ignatius: The Data

The Ignatian letters provide us with a considerable number of items related to our topic, which can be listed under six subdivisions or categories:[3]

1. The term θεός ("God") occurs about 180 times in the seven letters of Ignatius.[4] In the Bihlmeyer-Schneemelcher edition of the apostolic fathers the entire text of Ignatius's letters covers 820 lines, which means that the word "God" is to be found once in every 4.5 lines. A comparison will be helpful in determining the significance of this ratio. Three texts taken at random from the same edition of the apostolic fathers show the following figures: In the *Didache* "God" appears once in every 17.5 lines, in *Barnabas* once in every 12.7 lines, and in *1 Clement* once in every 9.2 lines. The difference from the ratio in Ignatius is noticeable. If we add to the comparison a Pauline epistle that Ignatius knew, namely, 1 Corinthians, the difference will remain (once in every 7.2 lines). The unusual frequency of the word θεός in the letters of the bishop of Antioch cannot be accidental.

2. Ignatius favors compound words in which one of the components is the word θεός. Thus we come across the words θεοφόρος ("God-bearer")[5] (found in the inscriptions of all of the seven letters and also in *Eph.* 9.2), θεοδρόμος ("God's runner"; *Phld.* 2.2; *Pol.* 7.2), θεομακάριστος ("blessed of God"; *Smyrn.* 1.2; *Pol.* 7.2) or θεομακαρίτης (*Smyrn.* 1.2 as an alternative reading), θεοπρεπής ("befitting God"; *Magn.* 1.2; *Smyrn.* inscr.; 11.1; 12.2; *Pol.* 7.2), θεοπρεσβευτής or θεοπρεσβύτης ("ambassador of God"; *Smyrn.* 11.1), and ἀξιόθεος ("worthy of God"; *Magn.* 2.1; *Trall.* inscr.; *Rom.* inscr.; 1.1; *Smyrn.* 12.2).

Compound words with θεός are encountered in the Septuagint, the New Testament, and in some of the early Christian texts.[6] They are also found in several of the authors of the classical or Hellenistic periods.[7] What is remarkable in Ignatius, however, and what sets him apart, is the accumulation of so many such words in a limited body of literature and, all the more, the fact that some of them, e.g., θεοδρόμος, θεομακάριστος (or θεομακαρίτης), and θεοπρεσβευτής (or θεοπρεσβύτης) are *hapax legomena* in Greek literature.[8]

3. Ignatius uses a number of short phrases in which the word θεός appears

[3] The data presented here come from the text of the middle recension of Ignatius's letters published in K. Bihlmeyer, *Die Apostolischen Vätern* (2nd ed.; ed. W. Schneemelcher; Tübingen: Mohr-Siebeck, 1956).

[4] Milton P. Brown speaks of 178 instances, omitting the double occurrences (*The Authentic Writings of Ignatius* [Durham, N.C.: Duke University Press, 1963] 22).

[5] For an interesting discussion see Schoedel, *Ignatius of Antioch,* 36–37.

[6] See BAG, 356.

[7] See LSJ, 789–92.

[8] See Brown, *Authentic Writings,* 16.

in the genitive together with an abstract or concrete substantive: ἐν αἵματι θεοῦ ("in the blood of God"; *Eph.* 1.1), πληρώματι θεοῦ ("in the fullness of God"; *Eph.* inscr.), χρῶμα θεοῦ λαβόντες ("having received God's variation or key"; *Eph.* 4.2), ἐν ὁμονοίᾳ θεοῦ ("in God's concord"; *Magn.* 6.1; 15:1; *Phld.* inscr.), ὁμοήθειαν θεοῦ λαβόντες ("having received God's unity of spirit"; *Magn.* 6.2; *Pol.* 1.3), τὸ πάθος τοῦ θεοῦ ("the passion of God"; *Rom.* 6.3), πόμα θεοῦ ("the drink of God"; *Rom.* 7.3), ἐλάλουν θεοῦ φωνῇ ("I spoke with the voice of God"; *Phld.* 7.1), εἰς ἑνότητα θεοῦ ("to the unity of God"; *Phld.* 8.1), τῇ γνώμῃ τοῦ θεοῦ ("with God's purpose"; *Eph.* 3.2 etc.), ἄρτον τοῦ θεοῦ ("the bread of God"; *Eph.* 5.2), ἐν ἡσυχίᾳ θεοῦ ("in the quietness of God"; *Eph.* 19.1), ἐν ἑνότητι θεοῦ ("in the unity of God"; *Eph.* 14.1, etc.), χαρακτῆρα θεοῦ ("the character of God"; *Magn.* 5.2), μιμηταὶ θεοῦ ("imitators of God"; *Trall.* 1.2), ἐγὼ λόγος θεοῦ ("I, word of God"; *Rom.* 2.1), σῖτος θεοῦ ("the wheat of God"; *Rom.* 4.1), ἐν ἀγάπῃ θεοῦ ("in the love of God"; *Phld.* 1.1), τὴν χαρὰν τοῦ θεοῦ ("the joy of God"; *Phld.* 10.1), ἀμεριμνία θεοῦ ("godly freedom from care"; *Pol.* 7.1).

Noteworthy in this instance is the variety of nouns connected with God and the rather bold usage of that word in reference to human conditions or material entities. Ignatius did not say θεῖον χρῶμα or θεία φωνή, but χρῶμα θεοῦ, φωνὴ θεοῦ, which means that he shows a preference for the noun θεός over the adjective θεῖος ("divine"). Of course, he knows the adjective θεῖος, but he uses it only once, in a reference to the prophets (*Magn.* 8.2). This signifies that in the phrases listed above, where the word θεός is employed in a qualifying genitive, something more than an adjectival understanding is implied.

4. Ignatius uses a number of expressions in which the word "God," in the genitive again, is the object of a verb indicating intimate and/or strong relationship with the believers. Five such expressions are encountered in the letters of Ignatius: γέμειν θεοῦ ("being full of God"; *Magn.* 14.1), μετέχειν θεοῦ ("to participate in God"; *Eph.* 4.2), εἶναι θεοῦ ("to be of God"; *Eph.* 8.1; *Phld.* 3.2), λείπεσθαι θεοῦ ("to lack God"; *Trall.* 5.2), and ἐπιτυγχάνειν θεοῦ ("to attain God"; *Magn.* 14.1; *Trall.* 12.2; *Rom.* 4.1; *Smyrn.* 11.1, etc.).

In this category Ignatius is once more unique among the early Christian authors. Phrases like the above are not easily found, much less accumulated, in the other writers. But even outside of early Christian literature, it is difficult to find examples similar to the Ignatian ones.[9] The biblical texts do not offer direct pertinent data, and, with the exception of the μετέχειν ("to partake," "to participate," "to have a share in") terminology known from the Platonic and the Aristotelian traditions, ancient Greek literature does not

[9] Schoedel cites a few examples (e.g., θεοῦ μεστός, πλήρης θεοῦ, ψυχὴ πληρωθεῖσα θεοῦ) related to the Ignatian γέμειν θεοῦ (*Ignatius of Antioch,* 131, interpreting *Magn.* 14.1). But none of them uses the verb γέμειν, and πλήρης θεοῦ does not have the force of γέμειν θεοῦ.

seem to be of decisive assistance either. The Ignatian terminology clearly presupposes the possibility of an intense and intimate relationship between the believers and God. Viewed from another angle, the same terminology reveals a tacit assumption referring to the transcendence of God, a transcendence that obviously is not absolute and inaccessible.

5. Ignatius favors the prepositional phrase ἐν θεῷ. It appears within differing contexts and in a variety of references: ἀποδεξάμενος ἐν θεῷ ("having received in God"; *Eph.* 1.1), ἡ ἐν θεῷ εὐταξία ("orderliness in God"; *Eph.* 6.2), εὔχομαι ἐν θεῷ ("I pray in God"; *Magn.* inscr.), ὡς φρόνιμοι ἐν θεῷ ("as wise in God"; *Magn.* 3.1), φρονεῖν ἐν θεῷ ("to think in God"; *Trall.* 4.1), τὸ ἐν θεῷ πλῆθος ("God's crowd"; *Trall.* 8.2), ὀναίμην ἐν θεῷ ("may I have joy in God"; *Pol.* 1.1), μέρος ἔχειν ἐν θεῷ ("having a lot in God"; *Pol.* 6.1), etc.

It has been appropriately pointed out that "this broad and somewhat flexible use of ἐν θεῷ constitutes one of the most remarkable features of Ignatius's practice with regard to prepositions."[10] The sentences in which ἐν θεῷ occurs may be read as implicit statements of belief in a deep and direct involvement of God in the life of the believers and of the church communities. Hence, they could also be read as statements reinforcing the idea of a transcendence that is not absolute and disconnected from all human reality.

6. The final category consists of some impressive examples in which Ignatius applies the term θεός to Jesus Christ. R. M. Grant lists eleven passages that he considers "definitive examples of this usage."[11] Of these only the first six are direct and explicit in their application of the word θεός to Christ:

Eph. inscr. Ἰησοῦ Χριστοῦ τοῦ θεοῦ ἡμῶν . . . ("of Jesus Christ our God")
Eph. 18.2 ὁ γὰρ θεὸς ἡμῶν Ἰησοῦς Χριστός . . . ("for our God Jesus Christ")
Rom. inscr. Ἰησοῦ Χριστοῦ τοῦ θεοῦ ἡμῶν . . . ("of Jesus Christ our God")
Rom. 3.3 ὁ γὰρ θεὸς ἡμῶν Ἰησοῦς Χριστός . . . ("for our God Jesus Christ")
Smyrn. 1.1 Ἰησοῦν Χριστὸν τὸν θεὸν ἡμῶν . . . ("Jesus Christ our God")
Pol. 8.9 ἐν θεῷ ἡμῶν Ἰησοῦ Χριστῷ ("in our God Jesus Christ")
Eph. 1.1 ἐν αἵματι θεοῦ . . . ("in the blood of God")
Eph. 7.2 ἐν σαρκὶ γενόμενος θεός ("God who became incarnate")
Eph. 15.3 αὐτὸς ἐν ἡμῖν θεὸς ἡμῶν ("he in us our God")
Eph. 19.3 θεοῦ ἀνθρωπίνως φανερουμένου . . . ("God being manifested as human")

10 Brown, *Authentic Writings*, 70. On the other hand, Schoedel, while seeing the significance of the phrase ἐν θεῷ, thinks that it has a rather "stereotyped quality" (*Ignatius of Antioch*, 19).

11 Robert M. Grant, *Ignatius of Antioch* (The Apostolic Fathers 4; Camden, N.J.: Nelson, 1966) 7. Brown lists only six as directly related and explicit (*Authentic Writings*, 22). C. C. Richardson, on the other hand, refers to about thirteen cases (*The Christianity of Ignatius of Antioch* [New York: Columbia University Press, 1935] 40). See also Virginia Corwin, *St. Ignatius and Christianity in Antioch* (New Haven: Yale University Press, 1960) 116–18.

Rom. 6.3 τὸ πάθος τοῦ θεοῦ μου . . . ("the passion of my God")

M. P. Brown suggests that in the above passages "Ignatius does not make a theological issue of this usage; the epithet (i.e., God) is applied casually, for the most part, and apparently without fear of being misunderstood. . . . Thus, it is difficult to avoid the conclusion that the peculiar assignment of ὁ θεός to Jesus Christ is unselfconscious."[12]

Such an assertion seems problematic. How can "a peculiar assignment of ὁ θεός to Jesus Christ," which is consistent, appears in five out of the seven Ignatian letters, surfaces in diversified contexts, and occurs several times, be unself-conscious? Is the application of ὁ θεός to Christ casual or matter of fact? Although Ignatius "does not make an issue of this usage," he does make a clear statement.[13]

The God Language in Ignatius: Evaluation of the Data

The data assembled thus far support the assumption that Ignatius uses the word θεός in a noticeably singular way. The high frequency of occurrence of "God," and its use in forming atypical compound words, short uncommon phrases, sentences with strong relational verbs, prepositional theocentric phrases, and, finally, christological formulas stating the divinity of Christ constitute a special phenomenon, the Ignatian God language. How can we explain such a phenomenon? What can we say about its possible origin and significance?

1. There have been suggestions in the past linking certain features of the Ignatian language and Christology to gnostic influences or sources. H. Schlier, for instance, and H. W. Bartsch have made valuable contributions to this discussion, showing the possibilities and the degrees of the gnostic connections in Ignatius but also revealing the limitations and the uncertainties of such connections.[14] When one focuses on the God language in Ignatius in its concrete forms and expressions, one has serious difficulties in explaining such a language on the basis of gnostic sources.

"Asianism" is another suggestion that has been advanced as a description of the language and the style of Ignatius.[15] Such a suggestion certainly

[12] Brown, *Authentic Writings,* 22–23.

[13] For Richardson, there is no doubt that Ignatius's application of the word "God" to Christ is deliberate (*Christianity of Ignatius,* 40–41).

[14] Heinrich Schlier, *Religionsgeschichtliche Untersuchungen zu den Ignatiusbriefen* (Giessen: Töpelmann, 1929); Hans Werner Bartsch, *Gnostisches Gut und Gemeindetradition bei Ignatius von Antiochien* (Gütersloh: Bertelsmann, 1940); see Arthur D. Nock's critical review of Schlier's book in *JTS* 31 (1930) 308–13; cf. Schoedel, *Ignatius of Antioch,* 16.

[15] See H. Riesenfeld, "Reflections on the Style and the Theology of St. Ignatius of Antioch," *Studia Patristica,* vol. 4 (TU 79; Berlin: Akademie-Verlag, 1961) 312–22. See also O. Perler,

applies to a number of rhetorical and linguistic features found in the letters of the Antiochian bishop. It constitutes, however, a rather general, and primarily stylistic, frame of reference, which does not seem to provide the means and criteria needed for a satisfactory explanation of the specific phenomenon of the Ignatian God language. Beyond style and rhetoric, God language involves concrete theological concepts, ideas and tenets for the understanding of which Asianism is only partially helpful.

A third way of explaining the God language in Ignatius is based on the idiosyncratic, personal, and passionate character of the Ignatian letters. In this view, it is the extreme pathos of the author that accounts for the uncommon constructions, the unusual vocabulary, and the unexpected imagery in Ignatius's letters.[16] There is no doubt about the general validity of such an observation concerning pathos, peculiarity, and exaggeration. The specific theological content of a God language, however, is another matter. Thus, the idiosyncratic and passionate element in Ignatius, although fundamental, cannot adequately explain his God language in its essence, content, and theological intent.

2. The fundamental factor that appears to explain the particularity, the complexity, and the magnitude of Ignatius's God language is, I submit, the Christology of Ignatius in conjunction with his ecclesiology. It is a Christology and an ecclesiology with specific emphases and clearly discernible focuses.

For Ignatius Jesus Christ is God.[17] The expression ὁ θεὸς ἡμῶν Ἰησοῦς Χριστός repeatedly used in a number of variations (see above) constitutes a definitive and unambiguous christological statement. Christ is preexistent (*Magn.* 6.1); he came from the Father and returned to the Father (*Magn.* 7.2), with whom he is inseparably united (*Magn.* 7.1; *Smyrn.* 3.3; *Eph.* 5.1). Ignatius makes no effort to prove that Jesus Christ is God or to develop apologetic strategies in that direction. He simply issues his high christological statement as a matter of fact, as a truth taken for granted and fully shared by the recipients of his letters.

Christ is God, but he is God who came in flesh (ἐν σαρκὶ γενόμενος θεός [*Eph.* 7.2]), God who was revealed as human (θεὸς ἀνθρωπίνως φανερούμενος [*Eph.* 19.3]), God who became perfect human being (τέλειος ἄνθρωπος γενόμενος [*Smyrn.* 4.2]). Ignatius places a strong emphasis on Christ's real, full, and perfect humanity. Hence, he uses impressive christological statements

"Das vierte Makkabäerbuch, Ignatius von Antiochien und die ältesten Martyrberichte," *Rivista di Archeologia Christiana* 25 (1949) 47–72; and Bammel, "Ignatian Problems," 72–73.

16 E. Norden speaks about the Ignatian letters as characterized by the "highest pathos" and by "personal word formations and constructions which are of unprecedented boldness" (*Die antike Kunstprosa* [2 vols.; 2nd ed.; Leipzig: Teubner, 1909] 2:511).

17 Grant, *Ignatius of Antioch*, 8.

to this end: Christ ἀληθῶς ἐγεννήθη, ἔφαγέν τε καὶ ἔπιεν . . . ἀληθῶς ἐσταυρώθη καὶ ἀπέθανεν ("Christ was truly born, both ate and drank . . . was truly crucified and died"; *Trall.* 9.1), ἀληθῶς ἔπαθεν ("he truly suffered"; *Smyrn.* 2.1; see also *Smyrn.* 1.2).[18] Writing to the Magnesians Ignatius voices his eagerness to have them fully convinced ἐν τῇ γεννήσει καὶ τῷ πάθει καὶ τῇ ἀναστάσει . . . πραχθέντα ἀληθῶς καὶ βεβαίως ὑπὸ Ἰησοῦ Χριστοῦ ("of the birth and passion and resurrection . . . for these things were truly and certainly done by Jesus Christ"; *Magn.* 11.1).

Ignatius has serious reasons to insist on the humanity of Christ. They are related to the docetists, those dangerous opponents who denied that Jesus was fully and truly human.[19] Against them he develops a Christology that forcefully projects a θεὸς ἐν σαρκί, a "God in the flesh."[20] Within this kind of christological argumentation Ignatius overtly accuses of blasphemy anyone who does not confess Jesus Christ as σαρκοφόρον ("bearer of flesh"; *Smyrn.* 6.2). He further boldly declares ἐγὼ γὰρ καὶ μετὰ τὴν ἀνάστασιν ἐν σαρκὶ αὐτὸν οἶδα καὶ πιστεύω ὄντα ("for I know and believe that he was in the flesh even after the resurrection"; *Smyrn.* 3.1), and unhesitantly characterizes as ἀθέους ("atheists, godless") those who do not believe that Christ really and truly suffered (*Trall.* 10.1). Within the same christological frame one should interpret the σάρξ–σαρκικός vocabulary in Ignatius.[21]

Ignatius, because of his antidocetic priorities, emphasizes Christ's humanity, which is basically expressed in his birth, passion, and death. Yet he never loses sight of the other basic attribute. Statements like ἐν σαρκὶ γενόμενος θεός ("God who became incarnate"; *Eph.* 7.2) underline the human side of the Incarnation without abandoning the God terminology. Two relevant passages should be mentioned here as having particular importance. The first is *Eph.* 7.2, in which six antithetical pairs are encountered referring to Jesus: fleshly–spiritual, begotten–unbegotten, in flesh (human)–God, death–true life, of Mary–of God, passible–impassible. What we observe here is an advanced and extended mixture of a θεός terminology with an ἄνθρωπος

[18] For the antidocetic force of the term ἀληθῶς, see W. F. Bunge, "The Christology of Ignatius of Antioch" (Th.D. diss., Harvard University, 1966) 14–16.

[19] Docetic opponents are explicitly mentioned in *Trall.* and *Smyrn.*, but as E. Molland ("The Heretics combatted by Ignatius of Antioch," *JEH* 5 [1954] 1–6) and Bunge ("The Christology of Ignatius," 121–37) have plausibly argued, even the judaizers of *Magn.* and *Phld.* were treated by Ignatius as having a docetic Christology. See Richardson, *Christianity of Ignatius,* 53.

[20] See Koester, "History and Cult," 114–15, for a discussion of the pertinent terminology in Ignatius and in the Gospel of John; see also Bunge, "Christology of Ignatius," 26–28; Corwin, *St. Ignatius,* 91–115. The term "sarkocentric," flesh-centered, has been used as indicative of the Ignatian Christology and soteriology; see J. Romanides, "The Ecclesiology of St. Ignatius of Antioch," *GOTR* 7 (1961–62) 62.

[21] For a recent detailed study of the σάρξ terminology in Ignatius, see H. E. Lona, "Der Sprachgebrauch von Σάρξ-σαρκικός bei Ignatius von Antiochien," *ZKT* 108 (1986) 383–408.

terminology occasioned by a christological declaration.[22] The second passage, *Eph.* 18.2, despite its brevity, is equally revealing: ὁ γὰρ θεὸς ἡμῶν Ἰησοῦς Χριστὸς ἐκυοφορήθη[23] ὑπὸ Μαρίας κατ' οἰκονομίαν θεοῦ ("for our God Jesus Christ was carried in the womb by Mary according to the plan of God").

These two and similar passages reveal traces of the genesis, formation, and intent of the God language in Ignatius: immediate christological concerns cause the formulation of christological statements within which the term θεός is directly linked to Christ. As a consequence, the word θεός takes up new conceptual elements and connotations defined by a Christology concerned with the true and full humanity of Christ and with the reality and facticity of his passion.[24] In all probability, it is such a christologically defined concept of God that is to be detected behind the God language in Ignatius. The basic conceptual focus is not the transcendent absolute God but the θεὸς ἐν σαρκί, the incarnate God.[25] In that case we may have a significant interpretive key for the phenomenon of the God language in Ignatius, and we may perhaps be in a better position to explain the data presented in the first part of this paper. The phrase ἐν θεῷ, for instance, could be viewed as a quasi synonym of the phrase ἐν Χριστῷ, and expressions like ὁμοήθεια θεοῦ and γέμειν θεοῦ might be interpreted as signifying ὁμοήθεια Χριστοῦ and γέμειν Χριστοῦ.

Ignatius's strong projection of a Christology in which Jesus is declared ἀληθῶς ἐν σαρκὶ γενόμενος θεός ("God who truly became incarnate") is directly linked to his ecclesiological concerns. For him the central ecclesiological issue is the unity of the church and unity in the church.[26] He constantly speaks about it using an amazing variety of words. His ecclesiological concept of unity, however, depends on and is determined by his Christology, in two ways. First, the church's unity is viewed as founded on and authentically reflecting the unity between Christ and the Father (*Eph.* 3.2; 5.1; *Magn.* 7.1–2; *Smyrn.* 3.3; 8.1; *Phld.* 7.2, etc.). Second, ecclesial unity is actualized in the eucharistic gathering of the community, over which the bishop presides,[27] and in the sacramental partaking of the flesh and the blood of

[22] The same observation holds true for *Pol.* 3.2.

[23] Correctly translated "carried in the womb," in Schoedel, *Ignatius of Antioch,* 84–85.

[24] See Richardson, *Christianity of Ignatius,* 40.

[25] T. Preiss discerns in Ignatius a lack of respect for the notion of transcendence ("La mystique de l'imitation du Christ et de l'unité chez Ignace d'Antioche," *RHPR* 18 [1938] 227). It is not so much that, as it is an emphasis on incarnation that is operative here.

[26] Schoedel, *Ignatius of Antioch,* 21: "The theme of unity may well represent the central concern of the letters of Ignatius." See K. D. Nouskas, Ἡ ἐν τῇ Ἐκκλησίᾳ ζωή κατὰ τὸν θεοφόρον Ἰγνάτιον (The Life in the Church according to Ignatius the Theoforos) (Thessalonike, 1971) 19–25.

[27] See John Zizioulas, Ἡ ἑνότης τῆς Ἐκκλησίας ἐν τῇ θείᾳ Εὐχαριστίᾳ καὶ τῷ Ἐπισκόπῳ κατὰ τοὺς τρεῖς πρώτους αἰῶνας (The Unity of the Church in the Eucharist and the Bishop during the First Three Centuries) (Athens, 1965) 63–64, 87–102.

Christ (*Eph.* 20..2; *Magn.* 7.2; *Trall.* 7.1–2; *Phld.* 4; *Smyrn.* 7.1; 8.1–2; 12.2).[28] Here the ecclesiological concern for unity has brought together, via Christology, the concepts of God or Father, Jesus Christ, the church, the believers, and the Eucharist. As a result, the word "God" seems to have acquired ecclesiological connotations focused on the eucharistically interpreted unity of the church.[29] Thus, it can plausibly be argued that the God language in Ignatius is also strongly related to his special ecclesiological concerns, which, nonetheless, are christologically oriented, since they contemplate the unity of the church from the angles of the Eucharist and of the unity between Christ and the Father.

Ignatius, the bishop of Antioch, evidently did not invent his Christology. His two fundamental tenets, namely, that Jesus Christ is ἐν σαρκὶ γενόμενος θεός ("God who became incarnate"; *Eph.* 7.2) and that he ἀληθῶς ἐσταυρώθη καὶ ἀπέθανεν . . . καὶ ἀληθῶς ἠγέρθη ἀπὸ νεκρῶν ("he was truly crucified and died . . . who also was truly raised from the dead"; *Trall.* 9.1–2) can very well be seen as echoes of John 1 and 1 Corinthians 15. What Ignatius did was to interpret the Johannine and the Pauline christological traditions or formulas in a way that could serve the immediate and pressing needs of the church and, by extension, his own needs in view of his pending martyrdom. One of the results of his interpretation is his fascinating God language.

[28] Koester, "History and Cult," 122–23; idem, *Introduction* 2:284; Schoedel, *Ignatius of Antioch,* 21; Bunge, "Christology of Ignatius," 118; F. Bergamelli, "Nel Sangue di Christo: La vita nuova del Christiano secondo il martyre S. Ignazio di Antiochia," *Ephemerides Liturgicae* 100 (1986) 157–70; Lona, "Der Sprachgebrauch von Σάρξ," 390–95; Richardson, *Christianity of Ignatius,* 56–57.

[29] Bunge, "Christology of Ignatius," 111–20.

PART 6

Gnosticism

35

New Testament Christologies in Gnostic Transformation

PHEME PERKINS

Christology, Form Criticism, and Genre

IN HIS GROUNDBREAKING article "One Jesus and Four Primitive Gospels," Helmut Koester posed a challenge for research into the Christology of the ancient church.[1] Form-critical analysis of the Gospels showed that there were theological principles behind the development of Jesus traditions that did not issue in a narrative dominated by the passion/resurrection creed, the canonical Gospel genre. These "gospels," the sayings of Jesus the wise One, the miracles of Jesus the divine man, and the revelations of Jesus the revealer from heaven, must be studied in noncanonical materials. In the canonical Gospels such traditions are dominated by the narrative of how Jesus came to suffer on the cross. Hints of realized eschatology, mythological speculation, inner awakening through wisdom and the like are domesticated by the historicizing requirements of the gospel understood as a demonstration of the passion/resurrection creed.[2]

Koester's original article demonstrated the importance of the methodological issue by analyzing the sayings material in the *Gospel of Thomas.* Though the distribution of types of sayings is close to what one finds in Q, there are notable differences that cannot simply be the result of the second-century gnosticizing of the collection, but must tell us about the tradition history of the sayings material before it became part of the canonical tradition. The radicalized understanding of the kingdom of God as part of the individual's quest for self-realization is central to the eschatological perception

[1] H. Koester, "One Jesus and Four Primitive Gospels," *HTR* 61 (1968) 203–47; reprinted in Robinson-Koester, *Trajectories,* 158–204.

[2] Ibid., 198–204.

of these sayings. However, the Son of Man imagery with its overtones of apocalyptic parousia is completely missing.[3] Reconstructions of the historical Jesus that fail to take this radical wisdom eschatology into account, but presume that they can begin with the apocalyptic orientation of Q, are on weak historical ground.

This challenge has led scholars to begin examining the sayings traditions in other gnostic writings as well as *Gos. Thom.*[4] Efforts to use such analyses to rewrite the history of the Synoptic sayings tradition continue to be plagued by the difficulty of dating different traditions relative to one another. James Robinson has pointed out that neither the "text" of *Gos. Thom.* nor that of Q was ever stable, so that all comparisons involve reconstructed histories of the tradition.[5] Reconstructions need not be limited to material that formally resembles a collection of sayings or proverbs. Koester's work on the *Dialogue of the Savior* and the discourse material in John traces a line of development in which sayings become part of the dialogue and discourse in the "revelation dialogue."[6]

Koester acknowledges the need for a new understanding of how sayings materials develop. Analyses which presume that one simply compares fixed texts, as was typical in Synoptic criticism, will fail to discover how sayings become discourses.[7] Interpretations are not simply additions to the tradition such as one finds in the Synoptics. Instead, the gnostic discourse radically transforms traditional materials. Even the form of a saying will not be

[3] Ibid., 166–86.

[4] See H. Koester, "Gnostic Writings as Witnesses for the Development of the Sayings Tradition," in *The Rediscovery of Gnosticism: Proceedings of the International Conference on Gnosticism at Yale, New Haven, Connecticut, March 28–31, 1978*, ed. B. Layton (2 vols.; SHR 41; Leiden: Brill, 1980), vol. 1, *The School of Valentinus*, 238–56; R. Cameron, *Sayings Traditions in the Apocryphon of James* (HTS 34; Philadelphia: Fortress Press, 1984); C. Hedrick, "Kingdom Sayings and Parables of Jesus in the *Apocryphon of James:* Tradition and Redaction," *NTS* 29 (1983) 1–24; P. Perkins, "The Rejected Jesus and the Kingdom Sayings," *Semeia* 44 (1988) 74–94.

[5] J. M. Robinson, "On Bridging the Gulf from Q to the Gospel of Thomas (Or Vice Versa)," in *Nag Hammadi, Gnosticism, and Early Christianity*, ed. C. Hedrick and R. Hodgson (Peabody, Mass.: Hendrickson, 1986) 152–62.

[6] H. Koester, "Gnostic Sayings and Controversy Traditions in John 8:12–59," in *Nag Hammadi*, ed. Hedrick and Hodgson, 97–110; idem, "Dialog und Spruchüberlieferung in den gnostischen Texten von Nag Hammadi," *EvT* 39 (1979) 532–56.

[7] Koester, "Gnostic Sayings," 109. C. Tuckett attempts to use verbal correlations and identification of citations to show that gnostic writers are generally dependent on the canonical Gospels, but he fails to realize that such a result is predetermined by the method of analysis (*Nag Hammadi and the Gospel Tradition: Synoptic Tradition in the Nag Hammadi Library* [Edinburgh: T. & T. Clark, 1986]). Similarly, J. A. Williams proceeds on the assumption that Valentinus is interpreting a "fixed text" (*Biblical Interpretation in the Gnostic Gospel of Truth from Nag Hammadi* [SBLDS 79; Atlanta: Scholars Press, 1988]). She notes Koester's earlier work on oral tradition in the second century and his "One Jesus" article but is unaware of the methodological complexity introduced in his more recent work on the gnostic sayings material.

immune to modification. The discourse context also attracts other material that does not fit the genre of sayings, such as creeds, wisdom lists, and fragments of exegesis. Koester's observations suggest that while the narrative realism of the Synoptic tradition could fix a saying by setting it in the narrative context of the apophthegm,[8] gnostic discourses dissolve the sayings themselves.[9]

This transformation may be associated with the shift in Christology from Jesus as teacher of wisdom confronting the hostile authorities to Jesus as revealer of heavenly wisdom similar to that which Koester has discerned in the "I am" sayings of the Fourth Gospel and *Gos. Thom. Gos. Thom.* uses the "I am" formulation to identify Jesus, whereas John uses "I am" sayings as recognition formulas in a narrative plot that ends with the glorification of Jesus on the cross.[10] The timeless universality of the wisdom saying or proverb points to interpretation through application to the myriad circumstances of human life in a world whose structures are those of everyday experience. The revelation of the gnostic redeemer severs all such connections. Not surprisingly, the move from sayings tradition toward aphoristic dialogue is most pronounced in the Fourth Gospel, where Jesus consistently affirms that he is not of this world.[11]

Traditionally, exegetes look for links between New Testament Christology and gnostic speculation in the hymnic materials such as Phil 2:6–11 and Col 1:15–20.[12] Koester's analysis suggests that we need to go beyond the usual discussions of christological hymns and titles to the treatment of sayings material in discourse and dialogue. Christians are so habituated to the narrative realism of the canonical Gospels that they fail to recognize how peculiar the Christian identification of heavenly wisdom with narrative about a human historical figure would have appeared in antiquity.[13]

Jesus as Heavenly Revealer

The revelation discourse is characteristic of gnostic writings. Both the form and content of many of these revelations are only marginally related to

[8] So R. Bultmann, *The History of the Synoptic Tradition*, trans. J. Marsh (2nd ed.; New York: Harper & Row, 1968) 61–64.

[9] See P. Perkins, "Pronouncement Stories in the Gospel of Thomas," *Semeia* 20 (1981) 121–32.

[10] Koester, "One Jesus," 177–79.

[11] See Perkins, "Rejected Jesus," 83.

[12] For an argument supporting the claim that the NT hymns depend on the mythic structure of gnostic thought about the heavenly redeemer, see H.-M. Schenke, "Die neutestamentliche Christologie und der gnostiche Erlöser," in *Gnosis und Neues Testament*, ed. K.-W. Tröger (Berlin: Evangelische Verlagsanstalt, 1973) 205–29.

[13] See the observations of J. Ashton, "The Transformation of Wisdom: A Study of the Prologue of John's Gospel," *NTS* 32 (1986) 161–96.

Christian traditions. However, scholarly analysis continues to show that the gnostic myths of the origins of the cosmos and the heavenly redeemer have appropriated heterodox Jewish traditions.[14] Use of a revelation dialogue to present the risen Jesus as gnostic revealer in works that appear to have been christianized by the addition of a frame story, dialogue, and some scriptural allusions to a non-Christian story (e.g., *Sophia of Jesus Christ, Apocryphon of John*) suggests that the dialogue genre did not evolve within Christian gnostic circles but was already a familiar genre.[15]

Three examples of gnostic revelation in which the revealers and the recipients of revelation are heavenly or ancestral figures, *Hypostasis of the Archons, Zostrianos,* and *Apocalypse of Adam,* suggest that the revelation dialogue emerges from the exchanges between the seer and revealing angel in apocalyptic writings.[16] Studies of the content of gnostic mythology show particular affinities to Enoch traditions.[17] M. Scopello links the heavenly journey of the seer in *Zost.* with *2 Enoch.* The secrets revealed to Zostrianos/Enoch make him like one of the glorious ones around the divine throne. These mysteries are not even known to the angels (*Zost.* 5,15–17; 128,15–18; *2 Enoch* 22:10 [B]; 24:3 [A]).[18] *Hyp. Arch.* contains a tradition that the son of the demonic creator, Sabaoth, repented upon hearing the voice of heavenly Wisdom and was taken up by angels to be enthroned above the angelic powers of the lower world (95,13–96,3). The enthronement of Sabaoth is associated with defeat for the evil creator, who is cast into Tartaros (95,11–13; cf. *1 Enoch* 88:1, the leader of the fallen angels is cast into the Abyss). However, in the gnostic cosmos, such a heavenly throne with its angels cannot represent the divine light world. Sabaoth, a creature of the lower cosmos, cannot enter that realm but must be instructed about it by Wisdom's daughter, Life (95,31–34).[19] The gnostic, seed of the enlightened Norea who receives this revelation from the light angel, does not belong to the lower world but to the imperishable light (96,18–28).

Hyp. Arch. concludes with the eschatological revelation of the True Man, whose coming anoints the Sethians with the Spirit, destroys death and the

[14] See the extensive discussion of B. Pearson, "Jewish Sources in Gnostic Literature," in *Jewish Writings of the Second Temple Period,* ed. M. Stone (CRINT 2:2; Philadelphia: Fortress Press, 1984) 443–81.

[15] See M. Krause, "The Christianization of Gnostic Texts," in *The New Testament and Gnosis: Essays in Honour of Robert McL. Wilson,* ed. A. H. B. Logan and A. J. M. Wedderburn (Edinburgh: T. & T. Clark, 1983) 190–92.

[16] See P. Perkins, *The Gnostic Dialogue* (New York: Paulist, 1980) 79–91.

[17] So Pearson, "Jewish Sources," 451–70.

[18] M. Scopello, "The Apocalypse of Zostrianos (Nag Hammadi VIII, 1) and the Book of the Secrets of Enoch," *VC* 34 (1980) 377–79.

[19] See the detailed study of this motif by F. Fallon, *The Enthronement of Sabaoth: Jewish Elements in Gnostic Creation Myths* (NHS 10; Leiden: Brill, 1978) 25–78.

powers of the lower world and brings the children of light to their true home. The concluding doxology invoking the Spirit, Father, and Son probably belongs to the Christian gnostics who preserved the version of the work that we possess. *Hyp. Arch.* uses apocalyptic motifs of heavenly journey and enthronement to provide a limited validity for the traditions connected with the Jewish God while finally denying their applicability to the gnostic elect. When the more developed variant of this same tradition in *On the Origin of the World* puts Jesus Christ among the divine beings at the right hand of Sabaoth along with the angelic church, a similar demotion is clearly intended (105,23–29). Christian traditions that speak of the exaltation of Jesus to the right hand of God in fact refer to enthronement over the lower world, not entry into the divine Pleroma.[20]

Another example of the gnostic challenge to orthodox christological claims in a work dependent on Jewish gnostic traditions can be found in the Hymn of the Divine Child from *Apoc. Adam* (77,27–82,19).[21] This passage contains a series of false accounts of the origins of the Illuminator. The first twelve appear to be abbreviated myths of an unusual birth, rescue, and/or nourishment of the divine child apart from civilization and then the coming of the savior to glory, power, and "the water." Angels, the muses, or other divine beings are responsible for nourishing the child. The thirteenth explanation, also false, departs from the others by attributing the birth of the Savior to the Word. Pointing to other gnostic writings in which Jesus is either Word (*Trimorphic Protennoia* 47,13–15) or a "Logos-begotten" body prepared by the great Seth (*Gospel of the Egyptians* CG III 63,9–13), Stroumsa suggests that the thirteenth explanation is that offered by a group of Christian gnostics.[22] *Orig. World* also identifies its Savior with the Logos and invokes Matt 10:26 as evidence that the Logos had come to reveal the unknown Father (125, 14–19).[23] The true explanation in *Apoc. Adam* rejects all forms of "begetting," whether mythic stories of divine birth or the Logos-begotten Savior. The Illuminator has come forth from a "foreign air." As in *Hyp. Arch.*, the appearance of the redeemer marks the eschatological conclusion of the work. The gnostic race is revealed while the rest of humanity laments its subjection to the powers and coming death (83,4–85,18).

The eschatological condemnation of the wicked at the end of *Apoc. Adam* includes charges of persecuting the elect and defiling the waters of baptism by subjecting it to the "powers." Ritual as well as theology divides the author

20 Fallon points to Valentinian texts in which the psychic Christ is seated at the right hand of the Demiurge (e.g., *Excerpta ex Theodoto* 38.3) (*Enthronement*, 106–9).

21 See the discussion of this section in G. Stroumsa, *Another Seed: Studies in Gnostic Mythology* (NHS 24; Leiden: Brill, 1984) 88–101.

22 Ibid., 100–103.

23 See P. Perkins, "Logos Christologies in the Nag Hammadi Codices," *VC* 35 (1981) 380–82.

of *Apoc. Adam* from this group, which apparently claimed to attain gnosis through baptism in the name of the Logos-begotten Savior. The Logos account itself is opposed to mythic stories of divine begetting, secret upbringing, and manifestation to the world, a pattern that emerges in Revelation 12 as well as in the historicized infancy narratives of Matthew and Luke. *Apoc. Adam* apparently seeks to isolate the gnostic elect from any form of syncretistic accommodation with outsiders.[24] The protest against identifying the Illuminator with the Logos-born shows that the "gospel" of an eschatological manifestation of the true gnostics brought about by the appearance of the heavenly revealer did not develop out of the christological traditions of orthodox Christianity. In some instances, the Christian Savior may be assimilated into that pattern either by identification with the revealer or with some emanation of the revealer, or treated as a lower "image" of the Savior as in *Orig. World.* On the other hand, *Apoc. Adam.* marshals its revelation against syncretistic assimilation.

The Heavenly Revealer as Jesus

When Jesus is simply equated with the heavenly revealer(s) of gnostic speculation, one finds patterns of discourse and speculation about the origin and mission of the revealer that are quite independent of the christological models found in the canonical narratives. Similarly, the christological titles that play a role in structuring narrative and formulaic confessions in the canon are either missing, secondary, or developed on the basis of pre-Christian speculation.[25] Viewed from this perspective, gnostic syncretism appears to have little concern to make its Savior recognizable as the Jesus of the canonical writings.[26] Heresiologists, who accused gnostic teachers of destroying the gospel picture of Jesus (e.g., Irenaeus *Adv. haer.* 3.praef.) would certainly concur. However, the polemic against christianizing syncretism in *Apoc. Adam* suggests that the question may be put the other way

[24] Koester has emphasized the importance of cultic structures and communal identity in the emergence of diverse patterns of gnostic mythologizing ("The History of Religions School, Gnosis and the Gospel of John," *Studia Theologica* 40 [1986] 115–36).

[25] Gnostic use of "Son of Man," for example, belongs to a tradition of speculation about the heavenly "Man" (so F. H. Borsch, *Christian and Gnostic Son of Man* [SBT 2.14; London: SCM, 1971]; on rare occasions a gnostic text may be dependent in its usage on a canonical text as in *Treatise on Resurrection* 46,14–20, which apparently depends on John 9:35 [Borsch, 87f.]). Though gnostic texts speculate on relationships of filiation between the divine Father and Son(s), use of "Son of God" appears limited to christianizing contexts (cf. *Trim. Prot.* 38,24–25), where it is part of the hymnic praise of the "Perfect Son."

[26] The question very aptly put by C. Tuckett, who observes that the close relationships between *Gos. Thom.* and the Synoptic traditions are not typical of the rest of the corpus; nor do works that claim to be discourses of Jesus feel constrained to echo the canon (*Nag Hammadi and the Gospel Tradition,* 4f., 154–56).

around: What happens when the heavenly revealer assimilates to the figure of Jesus?

Koester's work on sayings traditions already points to two instances in which the content of the revelation dialogue, not merely an external frame story, fits the Jesus tradition: *Dial. Sav.* and *Apocryphon of James.* Both writings also maintain a formal connection with the passion/resurrection creed as normative for authentic Christian revelation. *Ap. Jas.* emphasizes the significance of the passion of Jesus (5,9–6,7).[27] *Dial. Sav.* maintains a tension between the present life of the baptized disciple "in the flesh" and the future entry into glory.[28] The redactor of *Dial. Sav.* has used a traditional piece on the sayings of Jesus to prevent a completely spiritualized understanding of the life of the disciples (139,6–7; 145,23–34) and may even presume that this revelation occurs before rather than after Jesus' resurrection.[29]

Ap. Jas. combines beatitudes and woes, parables and their interpretation, kingdom sayings and allusions to discourse material from John.[30] Woe sayings condemn those "pretenders to truth" who are asleep when they should have been awake in order to enter the kingdom (9,24–35). The polemic exhortation alternates between encouragement to seek the kingdom and condemnation. Its expressions of affirmation include sayings that point to the certainty of salvation (e.g., 10,1–6; 14,14–18).[31] Peculiarly gnostic mythologoumena are not found in *Ap. Jas.* Its language of salvation can be given a conventional Christian rendering as well as a gnostic one, though the concluding description of future believers for whose sake the revelation has been made (15,35–16,30), a *topos* reminiscent of the apocalyptic genre, does presume a division within the Christian community.[32] D. Rouleau finds the polemic in *Ap. Jas.* "irenic." Though Peter and the other apostles are inferior to James, they are not subject to overt attack such as one finds in polemical writings like *Apocalypse of Peter.* He suggests that *Ap. Jas.* stems from a community that is still within the "great church," though critical of its ecclesiology.[33] Faced with similar ambiguities in *Gospel of Truth,* H. Attridge proposed that *Gos. Truth* is an exoteric text seeking to win a sympathetic

[27] Y. Janssens, "Traits de la passion dans l'Epistula Iacobi Apocrypha," *Muséon* 88 (1975) 97–101; D. Rouleau, *L'Épître Apocryphe de Jacques (NH I,2)* (BCNH 18; Quebec: Université Laval, 1987) 107–9.

[28] See H. Koester and E. Pagels in *Nag Hammadi Codex III,5: The Dialogue of the Savior,* ed. S. Emmel (NHS 26; Leiden: Brill, 1984) 11–15.

[29] Ibid., 14f.

[30] For discussion of the Synoptic-like Jesus tradition in *Ap. Jas.,* see Cameron, *Sayings Traditions;* Hedrick, "Kingdom Sayings"; for the Johannine parallels, see P. Perkins, "Johannine Traditions in *Ap. Jas.* (NHC I,2)," *JBL* 101 (1982) 403–14.

[31] The "sons of light" in 10,1–6 are apparently baptized Christians rather than members of a gnostic sect within the community (so Rouleau, *L'Épître,* 121).

[32] Rouleau, *L'Épître,* 136f.

[33] Ibid., 18–28.

hearing from those who are not part of the sect.[34] They may discover that they too are "beloved children" of the Father.[35]

The text of *Dial. Sav.* is too fragmentary for analyses of the literary structure of the work. Koester has identified several divergent traditions patched together to make up the whole: (a) dialogue between the Lord and the disciples, whose most extensive part consists in short units with sayings that have parallels in *Gos. Thom.* as well as various apocryphal and canonical Gospels (124,23–144,17); (b) fragments of a creation myth (127,19–128,23; 129,16–131,18); (c) a cosmological wisdom list (133,23–134,24), and (d) an apocalyptic vision, which perhaps included the installation of a heavenly figure before God[36] as well as the fate of souls in the abyss (134,24–137,3).[37] The primary soteriological emphasis of *Dial. Sav.* lies in its eschatology. The Savior is about to depart from this cosmos to the eternal divine, "standing at rest" (120,3–8).[38] He has opened the way for the ascent of the gnostic soul, which has shed its earthly garments through ascetic praxis and death.[39]

This aspiration to divinization through contemplation of the divine appears in both philosophic and religious traditions of the period. The opening cosmological vision in *Dial. Sav.* (129,20–131,16) apparently referred to the activity of the Word in stabilizing the heavenly realm. Judas's praises are the expected response to such a revelation (131,17–18).[40] Typically, the vision of the divine world is not possible in this life, though it may be

[34] H. Attridge, "The Gospel of Truth as an Exoteric Text," in *Nag Hammadi, Gnosticism, and Early Christianity*, ed. Hedrick and Hodgson, 239–55.

[35] A further indication that, despite its esoteric framework, *Ap. Jas.* is intended to be an exoteric document may be the concluding ascent of Jesus and James/Peter (15,5–27). They see the warring factions of the lowest aeons and the angelic praises of intermediate aeons, nothing more. These heavens correspond to those over which Sabaoth or the Demiurge with Jesus sits in other traditions as we have seen. Therefore, this treatise appears to be for those of the lower world. Its revelation is limited to understanding the earthly or psychic Jesus. (Cf. *Concept of Our Great Power* [41,13–42,11], which attributes the crucifixion to the psychic aeon.)

[36] Since the angelic interpreter shifts from the Savior who has accompanied the disciples to the mountain to the "Son of Man," the vision tradition may be another example of gnostic appropriation of Enoch material. The Similitudes of Enoch combine visions of the Son of Man and judgment of the fallen angels with cosmological speculation and the fragment of a book about Noah and the flood (*1 Enoch* 58–69; see J. Collins, *The Apocalyptic Imagination* [New York: Crossroad, 1984] 142–53). The creation myth, cosmological wisdom list, and the apocalyptic vision may well belong to a single tradition.

[37] Koester-Pagels, in *Dialogue of the Savior*, ed. Emmel, 2–9.

[38] M. Williams has traced the development of this theme in ancient literature as well as in the gnostic writings from Nag Hammadi (*The Immovable Race: A Gnostic Designation and the Theme of Stability in Late Antiquity* [NHS 29; Leiden: Brill, 1985] 8–157). Standing before God in glorious garments typifies the seer who has been transformed into an angelic existence and may even have been ritually enacted (pp. 82–85).

[39] See Perkins, *Gnostic Dialogue*, 107–11.

[40] The issue of cosmic stability and motion is continued in Judas's question about what shakes the earth (132,19–133,24).

anticipated in self-knowledge (132,9–18; 137,9–138,2). As in the ascetic doctrine of *Zost.*, attaining the divine vision requires dissolving the works of femaleness (144,12–145,7). The eschatology of *Dial. Sav.* may also have dictated its appropriation of sayings similar to those in *Gos. Thom.* along with the designation "solitary and elect," (120,26; 121,18).[41] Mary's formulation of a saying, the "mystery of truth," that the disciples will also "stand" in the eternal world (143,6–10), demonstrates that the eschatological dialogue has achieved its purpose of enlightening the disciples. Their questions belong to the genre as "instruction," not as ironic demonstrations of ignorance. Allusions to the tradition of Jesus' sayings and lists of parables ("mustard seed" [144,6–8]; "wickedness of each day," "laborer is worthy of his food," and "the disciple and the teacher" [139,8–13]), connect the teaching in *Dial. Sav.* with words that the reader knows were spoken by Jesus.

Conclusion

The program of research suggested by Helmut Koester's article some twenty years ago continues to provide fruitful insights into the significance of noncanonical material for the study of Christian origins. Such investigation poses serious questions to the theological community, which has seen a flourishing of Christologies "from below" based often on assumptions about the historical Jesus, the Jewish background of particular christological titles, or the eschatology of "Q" that Koester's work renders problematic. Assimilation of the gnostic materials from Nag Hammadi raises questions about the adequacy of our models of religious syncretism in early Christianity.

The significance of particular themes such as "exaltation to the divine throne" can be radically altered by the cultic or literary context in which the motif is used. The canonical option for realistic narrative dominated by the passion/resurrection kerygma may have served to establish the crucifixion as an identifying mark of the Savior, Jesus, but the other options—apocalyptic revelation and sayings collections—provided richer fare for gnostic speculations. Incorporation of kingdom sayings and lists of parables in *Ap. Jas.* and *Dial. Sav.* identify the revealer as the "Jesus" of the larger Christian community. The most radical question this research poses is not about the plurality of primitive "gospels" but the sense in which Christian orthodoxy affirms that there is "one Jesus."

41 See the treatment of the ascetic doctrine in *Zost.* by Williams (*Immovable Race*, 86–100). *Gos. Thom.* uses "standing" for the "single ones" (Log. 16), the "elect" (Log. 23) and those who do not experience death (Log. 18) (p. 89f. n. 37). The question of mortality and immortality also emerges in *Dial. Sav.* (140,1–14).

36

The "Mystery of Marriage" in the *Gospel of Philip* Revisited

ELAINE H. PAGELS

SINCE HANS-MARTIN SCHENKE published the first modern edition and translation of the *Gospel of Philip* in 1959, the theme of the "mystery of marriage" has figured centrally in scholarly discussion of this text.[1] Interpreting the bridal imagery that dominates this text (and occurs often in parallel sources of Valentinian theology) seems to offer an essential key not only for understanding the *Gospel of Philip* but also for reconstructing, so far as our fragmentary sources allow, the Valentinian movement in the history of second-century Christianity.

In his introduction to that first edition, Schenke himself interprets the "mystery of marriage" and the "bridechamber" as ritual acts symbolically enacted through "a holy kiss that the *mystes* receives from the mystagogue."[2] Such ritual acts, Schenke's account implies, had nothing to do with actual marriage or with ordinary sexual practice, and Schenke refrains from speculating about Valentinian attitudes toward either.

Gilles Quispel has challenged Schenke's interpretation. On the basis of his reading of such texts as the *Gospel of Philip* together with Irenaeus's account of Valentinian practice in *Adversus haereses* 1.6.4, Quispel contends instead that Valentinian theology concerning spiritual marriage presupposed—

[1] For their comments on and criticism of an earlier draft of this article, I wish to thank the members of the seminar on late antiquity at Princeton University, and especially to its chairman, Professor Peter Brown. I owe special thanks to Professor Glen Bowersock and the members of the Historical School of the Institute for Advanced Study, where this article was written.

Following the pseudonymous title of *Gos. Phil.*, I refer to its author as "he," without any presumption as to the actual gender of the text's author.

[2] H.-M. Schenke, "Das Evangelium nach Philippus," *TLZ* 84 (1959) 5.

perhaps even required—actual marriage, at least between fellow gnostic Christians.

Such opposite interpretations of readings have set the terms for scholarly debate. Did Valentinian theology concerning the "mystery of marriage" *include* or *exclude* actual marriage? Did Valentinian Christians understand their "bridechamber" ritual as antithetical to marriage, or did they regard marriage itself as a religious symbol? Are we to understand their sacramental theology as more analogous to the symbolic "marriages" later practiced by celibate Catholic religious or to medieval kabbalistic interpretations of marriage as a symbol of Israel's union with God, a symbol embodied in the marital union of the devout—or neither of the above?

For the past thirty years since Schenke's edition appeared, scholars have sharply divided over such questions. Eric Segelberg, writing in 1960, agreed with Schenke that the bridechamber sacrament was purely symbolic and inferred that the Valentinians endorsed only encratistic practices.[3] Yvonne Janssens, writing in 1968, agreed, as have D. H. Tripp, writing in 1982, and Michael Williams in articles published in 1971 and 1986.[4]

On the other hand, Quispel's side of the argument was joined by Jacques Ménard, in his 1964 French edition and translation, and in a qualified way by Robert M. Grant, A. H. C. van Eijk, and Jorunn Jakobsen-Buckley.[5]

Having previously adopted the latter point of view, especially in the form presented most fully by Ménard,[6] I have more recently been challenged, especially by the work of Janssens and Williams, to rethink the interpretation of the bridal imagery. Furthermore, during the past ten years, like many of my colleagues, I have been concerned to place Valentinian gnosticism into the context of the social history of second-century Christianity. Consequently, for me, as for Williams and Buckley, the question of interpreting the bridechamber ritual relates to the larger question that perplexed and divided

[3] E. Segelberg, "The Coptic-Gnostic Gospel according to Philip and its Sacramental System," *Numen* 7 (1960) 189–200.

[4] Y. Janssens, "L'Évangile selon Philippe," *Muséon* 81 (1981) 79–133; D. H. Tripp, "The 'Sacramental System' of the Gospel of Philip," *SP* 17, ed. E. A. Livingstone (Oxford: Pergamon, 1982) 1:251–60; M. A. Williams, "Realized Eschatology in The Gospel of Philip," *Restoration Quarterly* 14 (1971) 1–17; idem, "Uses of Gender Imagery in Ancient Gnostic Texts," in *Gender and Religion: On the Complexity of Symbols*, ed. C. W. Bynum et al. (Boston: Beacon, 1986) 196–227.

[5] J. E. Ménard, *L'Évangile selon Philippe* (Theologica Montis Regii 35; Montreal: Université de Montréal, 1964; R. M. Grant, "The Mystery of Marriage in The Gospel of Philip," *VC* 15 (1962) 129–40; A. H. C. van Eijk, "The Gospel of Philip and Clement of Alexandria: Gnostic and Ecclesiastical Theology on the Resurrection and the Eucharist," *VC* 25 (1971) 94–120; J. Jacobsen-Buckley, "A Cult-Mystery in the Gospel of Philip," *JBL* 99 (1980) 569–81.

[6] See, e.g., E. H. Pagels, "Adam, Eve, Christ, and the Church: A Survey of Second Century Controversies concerning Marriage," in *The New Testament and Gnosis: Essays in Honour of Robert McL. Wilson*, ed. A. H. B. Logan and A. J. M. Wedderburn (Edinburgh: T. & T. Clark, 1983) 146–75.

many second-century Christians—whether Christians may marry or whether, instead, they should practice celibacy.[7] Such recent investigation has convinced me that, in the case of *Gos. Phil.* scholars on both sides of the argument are equally right—or equally wrong. I have come to conclude that the traditional way of formulating this argument (i.e., whether *Gos. Phil.* advocates celibacy or marriage) misleads us into missing the author's main point about what *gnōsis* is and what kinds of acts and attitudes characterize one who has received it. As I now read the text, its author intends to reject entirely the question concerning sexual practice, the same question that contemporary scholars have been trying to use the text to answer.

Once we begin to analyze this thirty-year debate, we can see that it turns, first of all, on interpretation of key passages from *Gos. Phil.* and, second, on interpretation of key passages from Irenaeus and Clement. Examining the disputed passages, we note, first, how scholars on opposite sides of the argument, by selecting different sections of the same passage and translating them differently, actually read the same passage as "proving" opposite conclusions. Let us take, for example, various interpretations of the passage that contrasts the "marriage of defilement" with the "undefiled marriage" that is "pure . . . not fleshly, but holy; not of desire, but will" (*Gos. Phil.* 82, 2–8). Yvonne Janssens, agreeing with Schenke and Segelberg in an encratistic reading, takes this passage as evidence that, for the Valentinians,

> Le lit nuptial (παστός) des élus n'est pas l'union sexuelle—impure—des animaux, des esclaves et . . . des femmes! (en tant quelles se livrent à l'homme, sans doute, puisque l'auteur leur oppose les vierges—παρθένος). Il s'agit d'une union spirituelle, réservée aux hommes libres et aux vierges (qui restent donc vierges dans cette union).[8]

Taking up the same line of argument, Tripp takes the terms παστός and νυμφών to refer to the Eucharist as a kind of symbolic marriage feast. Tripp infers that the use of these terms in *Gos. Phil.* has nothing to do with ordinary marital or sexual union, much less endorsement of either. Williams, interpreting this same passage, simply inserts his own interpretation as a gloss on the text, as if to indicate that the "marriage of pollution" is, by (Williams's) definition, "ordinary marriage, in which there is intercourse." From this he concludes that the "undefiled marriage" must refer to "spiritual marriage, in which Christians lived together without sexual intercourse."[9] Williams goes on to insist that the Valentinian Christians regarded ordinary marriage as antithetical to "spiritual marriage" and that they endorsed, in practice, only the latter.

[7] See P. R. L. Brown, *The Body and Society: Men, Women, and Sexual Renunciation in Early Christianity* (New York: Columbia University Press, 1988).
[8] Janssens, "L'Évangile selon Philippe," 107.
[9] Williams, "Uses of Gender Imagery," 206.

Yet other scholars have read the same passage quite differently. Grant found in it no clear evidence to decide whether or not the author intends to describe marriage in exclusively symbolic terms:

> In its eschatological actuality this heavenly/earthly marriage is a mystery or secret, just as it is in Eph. 5:32. . . . *It is impossible to tell whether these gnostics were describing a human or spiritual marriage, or whether in their minds there is a significant difference between the two*. . . . What the Gospel of Philip reveals to us is a highly significant picture of salvation as equivalent to marriage and of marriage as an archetype of salvation.[10]

When Ménard published his edition and translation of *Gos. Phil.* in 1964, he referred approvingly to Grant's assessment, while omitting Grant's perceptive and cautious qualifications. Challenging those who were interpreting *Gos. Phil.* ascetically, Ménard declared, on the contrary:

> Le ἱερος γάμος est enfin le grand sacrement de L'Évangile selon Philippe. . . . Le mariage terreste est bel et bien un sacrement, un symbole de plénitude, et il semble qu'il ne se concluait pas uniquement dans un baiser mais dans l'union sexuelle des corps (cf. 82:3–8).[11]

Both van Eijk and Buckley, who develop similar lines of argument allude, as Ménard did, to the same phrases from Grant's article, and, like Ménard, omit Grant's qualifications. Van Eijk assumes without argument that, according to the Valentinians, spiritual union is "effectuated . . . by the sacrament of marriage."[12] Buckley goes much further, insisting that earthly marriage "forms the condition necessary for eligibility for the bridal chamber marriage."[13] When Buckley comments on a passage that describes the interaction of male and female forms of unclean spirit (65,1–26), she concludes from the sections she selects that "only by acquiring male or female power, respectively, may the female or male human being delude the earthly powers. 'Spiritual' power asserts itself exclusively in earthly marriage."[14]

Williams, whose selection and translation of the same passage differs considerably from Buckley's, draws the opposite conclusion: "[this] passage in particular reveals much about this text's rationale for the importance of cohabitation, even though the 'defilement' of sexual intercourse is to have no part in this 'undefiled marriage.'"[15]

Those patristic passages in which Irenaeus and Clement comment on Valentinian practice have evoked similarly divided interpretations from

[10] Grant, "Mystery of Marriage," 136–37; emphasis added.

[11] Ménard, *L'Évangile*, 50.

[12] Van Eijk, "Gospel of Philip," 104.

[13] J. J. Buckley, "The Holy Spirit is a Double Name," in J. J. Buckley, *Female Fault and Fulfillment in Gnosticism* (Chapel Hill: University of North Carolina Press, 1988) 121.

[14] Buckley, "Cult-Mystery," 571.

[15] Williams, "Uses of Gender Imagery," 206.

modern commentators. Variations in the Greek and Latin texts of *Adv. haer.* 1.6.4 allow Grant (who assumes, with Quispel, that "the Valentinians were not devoted to asceticism"[16]) to find evidence in Irenaeus's account that Valentinian Christians regarded marriage as essential for the spiritual development of gnostic Christians. Williams, who translates the key phrase ὥστε αὐτὴν κρατηθῆναι in an entirely different sense, takes the same passage as evidence for Valentinian practice of *encratite* marriage.[17]

What this thirty-year debate shows most clearly is that scholars all agree on only one thing: that there is *no unambiguous evidence,* either in *Gos. Phil.* or in the church fathers, to show how this author intended to use sexual imagery. There is, furthermore, *no unambiguous evidence* to prove that Valentinian Christians in general or the author of *Gos. Phil.* in particular exclusively advocated either celibacy or marriage. If those on either side of the argument were right—that is, had the Valentinians insisted either on actual marriage, sacramentally interpreted, or upon celibacy (including celibate marriage) and if this fact (whichever you prefer) were central to their religious understanding, why is it that *not a single one of the extant texts states this clearly?* After all, the Nag Hammadi discovery has yielded a harvest of major Valentinian texts, including the *Tripartite Tractate,* the *Interpretation of Knowledge,* the *Gospel of Truth, A Valentinian Exposition,* and the *Epistle to Rheginos*—besides the *Gospel of Philip.* Are we to assume that every one of these Valentinian authors has failed to communicate the central theme of their theology? Shall we assume, in addition, that such perceptive and critical observers as Tertullian, Irenaeus, Clement, and Origen completely failed to clarify the Valentinians' sexual practices? Finally—and perhaps most puzzling of all—how have the texts managed to be *so* unclear as to have generated two totally contradictory interpretations?

What I suggest is this: The author of *Gos. Phil.* was well aware of the controversies raging between various teachers and groups on matters of marriage versus celibacy. As Peter Brown has shown in his learned and perceptive book *The Body and Society,* these questions exercised and divided Christians throughout the Mediterranean world.[18] Yet the author of *Gos. Phil.* expresses, precisely through his ambiguity on this topic, a deliberate refusal to take sides on this issue. Note, by contrast, how completely *unambiguous* are the positions taken by his Christian contemporaries! Although the apostle Paul strongly urged celibacy upon his converts, but added that marriage is, nevertheless, "not sin" and is certainly preferable to

[16] Grant, "Mystery of Marriage," 133.

[17] M. Williams, "'Gnosis' and 'Askesis,'" *ANRW* 2.22 (forthcoming). Because translation so obviously involves interpretation, I have used my own translation throughout, attempting to adhere as closely as possible to the Coptic text.

[18] See n. 7 above.

promiscuity (1 Cor 7:1–10), few Christians in the following generations could tolerate such ambivalence. Such deutero-Pauline letters as Ephesians, Colossians, and the Pastoral epistles advocated marriage, while modifying traditional Jewish marital patterns in the direction of greater strictness.[19] Many other first- and second-century sources, from the *Acts of Paul* to the *Gospel of Thomas*, rejected marriage and advocated celibacy. Other teachers, including Justin Martyr and Clement of Alexandria, like Paul, took more moderate positions, preferring celibacy yet allowing marriage. Every one of these, whatever his position, obviously regarded this question as an important one and took care to make his position entirely clear. Shall we take it as an accident or an oversight, then, that Valentinian Christians, who went so far as to place marital imagery at the center of their theology, *never said anything definitive about practice* in any of their writings known to us?

I suggest, on the contrary, that the author of the *Gos. Phil.* has deliberately refused, on the basis of his understanding of the ambiguity of language and his consequent rejection of dualistic patterns of thought, to answer a question posed in terms of such a putative opposition (celibacy versus marriage). This Valentinian author apparently shares with certain Neoplatonist philosophers and allegorists a sense of the ambiguous relationship between language and reality—divine reality.[20] Yet unlike pagan Neoplatonists, this author expresses such ambiguity mythologically in the form of gnostic midrash on the creation account of Genesis 2.[21] He describes conflict between the divine truth above, which, he says, "loves humanity" and intends its enlightenment, and the hostile rulers of this world (those whom Paul calls the ἄρχοντες τοῦ κόσμοῦ τούτου [1 Cor 2:6]). According to *Gos. Phil.* 54,14, at the first stage of this drama, "Truth brought names into the world for our sakes, for it was not possible to teach it without names. There is one truth . . . and for our sakes it shows this one thing in love by means of many (names)." Language, then, is essential to convey truth:

> Truth did not come into the world naked, but clothed in types and images; it cannot be perceived in any other way [67,10–13]. . . . But the archons wanted to deceive humanity, since they saw that it had a kinship (συγγενεία) with the truly good. . . . They took the names of those things that are good, and gave them to those that are not good, in order to deceive

[19] See E. Pagels, *Adam, Eve, and the Serpent* (New York: Random House, 1988); see also Dennis R. MacDonald, *The Legend and the Apostle: The Battle for Paul in Story and Canon* (Philadelphia: Westminster, 1983).

[20] See Robert Lamberton, *Homer the Theologian* (Berkeley: University of California Press, 1986) 83–197.

[21] For discussion of similar gnostic exegetical midrashim, see E. Pagels, "Exegesis and Exposition of the Genesis Creation Accounts in Selected Texts from Nag Hammadi," in *Nag Hammadi, Gnosticism, and Early Christianity*, ed. C. Hedrick and R. Hodgson, Jr. (Peabody, Mass.: Hendrickson, 1986) 257–79.

> humanity by means of the names and to bind them to those that are not good. (54,18–23)

Consequently, the author continues, "names given to things in this world have a great deception. For they separate the heart from the things that are established [or: real] and give them to those which are not established" (53,23–29).

In order to effect this ruse, the archons induced Adam to partake of the fruit of the tree of knowledge—not the fruit of the tree of *true* knowledge, but of a poisonous and destructive kind of knowledge. According to this author, eating of that fruit "killed Adam," since that tree was "the law," which "has power to convey the knowledge of good and evil, but never removed Adam from evil, nor placed him in the good. For when he [the archon] said, 'Eat this, do not eat that,' the law became the beginning of death."

In such passages, the author of this gospel seems to reject the kind of modified dualism that dominates so many second-century Christian sources, for a wide range of diverse texts seem to urge their readers to reject the phenomenal world in favor of divine and eternal reality. But in *Gos. Phil.*, as Klaus Koschorke has observed, we do not find the kind of antithesis in which certain terms automatically bear negative connotations (such as "flesh," "body," "darkness") and others bear consistently positive ones (such as "spirit," "wisdom," or even "gnosis").[22] Instead, what any word connotes in this text depends on whether it is understood "in the aeon" (with reference to transcendent reality) or "in the world" (without such reference): "Light and darkness, life and death, right and left, are brothers to one another; they are inseparable. Therefore the good are not good; and the evil are not evil; and life is not life, nor is death death" (53,15–20).

Because of the deceptive potential involved in language, the use of any word whatsoever involves ambiguity. Koschorke points out several examples, including the following: γνῶσις makes one free, as *Gos. Phil.* often declares (see 44; 65; 67; 93; 124; and 127); yet the author also knows of a γνῶσις that brings death (74,5–10); σάρξ ordinarily indicates the sphere that is to be overcome (see 82,28), but the "true" flesh conveys the heavenly inheritance (68,35ff.; 56,34–57,8).[23]

The same principle applies not only to words but also to the physical elements of experience, including those understood as religious symbols—for example, baptismal water. According to *Gos. Phil.*, some people "go down into the (baptismal) water" and only get wet; others descend into it and undergo spiritual rebirth (59,23ff.). Whether the same act remains an empty form or becomes the vehicle of transformation depends, apparently, on the

[22] K. Koschorke, "Die 'Namen' in Philippusevangelium: Beobachtungen zur Auseinandersetzung zwischen gnostischem und Kirchliche Christentum," *ZNW* 64 (1973) 307–22.

[23] Ibid., 310.

participant's level of *gnōsis* and on the absence or presence of the spirit in the process. As Koschorke says, "Wo die leiblich Existenz des Menschen undualistisch gesehen ist, steht deutlich die Sakramentstheologie im Hintergrund."[24]

Perceiving the relationship between sign and reality to be essentially ambiguous, the author of *Gos. Phil.* refuses to engage in the various controversies, both theological and practical, that commonly exercised his contemporaries. For example, in one central theological debate, second-century Christians argued about the nature of the resurrection: Does resurrection mean resurrection "in this flesh"? Or does resurrection involve only the spirit, or soul, and not the flesh? This author refuses to engage the question, declaring "I find deficiency in both" positions (57,11–12)—apparently the deficiency inherent in language. From this point of view, apparently, those who engage in such controversy over resurrection, whether they side with Tertullian, Marcion, or Basilides, nevertheless share a common understanding of *flesh* and *spirit* as opposites—not as "brothers" (53,17), that is, interdependent terms that mutually imply each other.

Similarly, I suggest, the author refuses to engage in argument about whether Christians should marry or remain celibate. Posed as opposites, these alternatives, too, present a false dichotomy. Instead, this author advises: "Do not fear the flesh, nor love it. If you fear it, it will gain mastery over you. If you love it, it will devour and paralyze you" (66,5–7).

While rejecting false dichotomies, this author does not neglect matters of ethical practice, much less imply that they are not important. Instead, he transposes questions of ethical practice into a new key. Now the question becomes not whether to marry or remain celibate but rather how to reconcile the freedom *gnōsis* conveys with the Christian's responsibility to love. The central moral teaching of *Gos. Phil.*, contained in 77,16–84,12, focuses on this theme. This passage both begins and ends by referring to John 8:32 ("You shall know the truth, and the truth shall make you free"), and explicates the apparent contradiction between the Johannine saying and Paul's qualified comment in 1 Cor 8:1 ("All of us have *gnōsis* . . . *Gnōsis* puffs up, but love builds up"). For in that same passage, Paul goes on to say that he regards himself, because of his own *gnōsis*, as being ethically free—free to eat and drink whatever he wishes, free to travel with a Christian sister as a wife, and free to live as an evangelist at community expense (1 Cor 8:1–9). He explains that he has chosen to relinquish his freedom for the sake of love, in order not to offend potential converts or even immature Christians. The author of *Gos. Phil.* seems to follow Paul's lead as he engages this central practical question: How is the Christian to avoid sin? Or, put in positive

[24] Ibid., 313.

terms, how is one to act in harmony with *gnōsis,* on the one hand, and with love (*agapē*), on the other?[25]

Gospel of Philip 77,14 *begins,* as we noted, paraphrasing John 8:32: "Whoever has *gnōsis* of the truth is free," but goes on to add that "the free person does not commit sin," for "whoever commits sin is a slave of sin" (John 8:34). How can this be reconciled with the ambivalence toward *gnōsis* that Paul expresses in 1 Cor 8:1–2? The author of *Gos. Phil.* suggests that truth and *gnōsis* must be joined in union to produce the mature Christian: "The mother is truth, and the father is *gnōsis.*" Apparently intending to give a positive interpretation to 1 Cor 8:1b (usually translated to say that knowledge "puffs up") this author explains instead that since those who no longer sin are called "free," one could say (conflating John 8:32 and 1 Cor 8:1) that *gnōsis* "makes them free," that is, "lifts up" or "exalts" (**ϪⲒⲤⲈ**) them above the world.[26] Yet the author goes on immediately to qualify this by quoting the rest of Paul's sentence: "but love builds up." Throughout 1 Corinthians 8 and 9, as we noted above, Paul claims: "although I am free from all, yet I have made myself a slave unto all" (1 Cor 9:19). Following his lead, the author of *Gos. Phil.* declares that "whoever is made free through *gnōsis* is a slave for the sake of love to those who have not yet attained the freedom of *gnōsis*" (77,27).

Describing the potential harmony of *gnōsis* with *agapē,* the author praises spiritual love, which does not claim what belongs to it as its own prerogative but offers what it has to others (77,31–35). So, the passage continues, spiritual love, like a fragrance, even graces those who do not themselves possess it (77,66ff.). Thus the true *gnostic,* like the Good Samaritan, extends himself to help heal the wounds of those still suffering from the effects of sin, for "love covers a multitude of sins" (78,11–12; note that in this single sentence the author both alludes to Luke 10:3–37 and quotes 1 Pet 4:8).

Amplifying the theme of the effects of spiritual love, the author goes on to invoke an image from ancient eugenic lore[27] to exhort those who "live with the Son of God"—that is, those who are members of the "bride of Christ," the church, to love the Lord and not the world, so that they may bear spiritual offspring who resemble the Lord and not the world (78,12–25). The next passage (78,26–79,12) shows the transforming power of love, for "what you become depends upon what you love" (and vice versa):

> If you become human, the human will love you; if you become spirit, the spirit will be joined to you; if you become logos, the logos will be joined with you; if you become light, the light will become your companion

[25] Note that in the following discussion I have retranslated the text, intending to adopt the simplest possible translation.

[26] See the perceptive comments of Ménard on translation of **ϪⲒⲤⲈ** (*L'Évangile,* 227).

[27] See Brown, *Body and Society,* 20, 439.

> (ⲔⲞⲒⲚⲰⲚⲈⲒ). If you become one of those who belong above, those who belong above will find rest in you. (78,32–79,5)

The next passage describes the process of spiritual growth, which begins rooted in faith, is nourished through hope and love, and ripens to maturity through *gnōsis* (79,20ff.) Then the author returns to the theme of spiritual love: "Blessed is the one who has not caused grief to anyone" (79,34). Jesus Christ is the paradigm of the one who, far from grieving or offending anyone, refreshes and blesses everyone he encounters, whether "great or small, believer or unbeliever" (80,9–10). The text goes on to relate the parable of the owner of a great estate that includes children, slaves, dogs, pigs, and cattle. The owner feeds each kind the diet appropriate to its condition—an image of the disciple of God, who perceives the condition of each person's soul, and speaks to each one accordingly, recognizing that since each one is at a different level of spiritual maturity, each has different needs:

> There are many animals in the world in human form. If he recognizes that they are pigs, he will feed them acorns; if cattle, then barley chaff, and fodder; if dogs, he will give them bones; if slaves, he will give them only the first course; if children, a complete meal. (81,8–14)

The author goes on to elaborate the image of the "mystery of marriage":

> No one will be able to know when a man joins with his wife except the two of them alone. For marriage in the world, indeed, is a mystery. . . . Indeed, if the marriage of pollution is hidden, how much more is the unpolluted marriage a true mystery! It is not counted as fleshly but holy; it does not belong to desire, but to will. It is not in darkness and night, but in the day and the light. A marriage that is exposed has become fornication. . . . Even if [the bride] leaves the bedchamber and is seen. . . . Bridegrooms and brides belong to the bridalchamber. No one shall be able to see the bridegroom with the bride unless he becomes such (as they are). (81,35–82,26)

Those who read this passage either as advocating celibacy (Janssens, Williams) or as sacramental practice of sexual union (Ménard, Buckley) are, I believe, pressing the text to answer questions its author does not address. I take this passage instead as a warning to initiated Christians to keep secret the "mystery of marriage"—that is, not to reveal to outsiders that one has *gnōsis:* to do so betrays the "true marriage" properly shared only among gnostic Christians. Read this way, the message of the passage becomes obvious: Just as ordinary men and women keep their intimacies private, so one who "lives with the son of God" (78,21) is not to display the intimacies of that relationship in public. Yet despite the gnostic Christian's practice of spiritual discretion, those who stand outside the "bridechamber" may, nevertheless, be graced by the spiritual fragrance of love which the gnostic Christian exudes and may thereby receive spiritual nourishment (82,19–23).

The following saying describes Abraham's circumcision, as showing that "it is fitting to destroy the flesh" (82,26–29). Read in context, this saying suggests to me that although those on a lower level may appropriately eat a coarser diet, just as cattle eat fodder or chaff, this author considers it "fitting" that those on a higher level should practice ascetic discipline. Yet, while regarding it as "fitting," this author does not characterize such discipline as essential. What *is* essential is described on pages 82 and 83 (of the manuscript): What is hidden within one, the author says, has great power until it is exposed. When one's inward parts are exposed, one is destroyed, as in the case of a human being whose intestines are exposed or a tree whose roots are exposed. In the same way, the "root of evil" is hidden within every person, and, "so long as the root of evil is hidden, it is powerful; but when it is recognized, it is destroyed." So, this author continues:

> As for us, let each of us dig down to the root of evil within us, and pull out the root from the heart. It will be plucked out if we recognize it. But if we do not recognize it, it takes root in our hearts and produces its fruits in our hearts. It masters us, and makes us its slaves. It takes us captive, so that we do what we do not want, and what we do not want to do, we do. It grows powerful because we have not recognized it (м̄пн̄соуωнс̄). (83,18–29)

One essential element of *gnōsis*, then, is to know one's own potential for evil. To remain unaware of the potential for evil within us is ignorance, which leads to sin and death. ("Ignorance is the mother of all evil. Ignorance brings about death" [83,30–32].) Yet recognizing evil within is necessarily an individual process: "each one" must strive to recognize his or her own truth and to identify impulses and acts that come from the "root of evil" (which consists, apparently, in such sources as anger, lust, envy, pride, and greed). The author assumes that when one recognizes that a certain impulse derives from such sources, one can no longer sustain the action; doing evil seems to require the illusion that one's action is justified or that one is acting for right reasons.

Although contemporary scholars all too often presume that gnostic Christians were dualists, this passage suggests an opposite position. Here, as throughout the entire text, the author of *Gos. Phil.* abandons the modified dualism that characterizes most Jewish and Christian teaching of the second century.[28] Instead of envisioning the power of evil as an alien force that threatens or invades humanity from without, the author of *Gos. Phil.* urges the Christian to recognize the evil within himself or herself and consciously to suppress it.

[28] See, e.g., J. B. Russell, *The Devil: Perceptions of Evil from Antiquity to Primitive Christianity* (Ithaca: Cornell University Press, 1977) 227. But Russell assumes throughout his work that gnostic forms of Christianity tend even more toward dualism than their orthodox counterparts.

Having finished discussing how to overcome the "root of evil" within oneself, the author returns to the opening theme, quoting John 8:32:

> Truth, like ignorance, when hidden, indeed, remains in itself; but when it is revealed or recognized, it is praised, in that it is more powerful than ignorance or deception, it makes us free. Thus says the Logos, "You shall know the truth, and the truth shall make you free." Ignorance is slavery; *gnōsis* is freedom. (84,2–11)

Explicated through the entire passage (77,14–84,11) and repeated at its conclusion, this saying now implies that those who "know the truth" avoid sin because they recognize—have *gnōsis* of—the potential for evil within themselves and are continually watchful to uproot it. The author expresses the optimistic conviction that "truth is more powerful than ignorance or error." Yet "knowing the truth" involves much more than mental or spiritual illumination; it involves also transformation of one's being, transformation of one's way of living. For, the author continues, "if we know the truth, we shall find fruits within us, if we join ourselves with it, we shall receive our fulfillment" (84,12–15).

What about specific practical questions? The attitude of this author reminds me of that expressed in Logion 6 of *Gos. Thom.*, where Jesus' disciples ask him for specific directions: "Do you want us to fast? How shall we pray? Shall we give alms? What diet would we observe?" According to the Synoptics, Jesus *does* offer specific instructions in answer to such questions. But according to *Gos. Thom.*, he says only "Do not tell lies, and do not do what you hate"—giving, in effect, an ironic answer, for it turns one back to one's own resources; for only the disciple alone can discern what is a lie and what he or she hates. In *Gos. Phil.*, too, beyond the expressed preference for asceticism (no doubt intended to mirror the preference Paul expressed in 1 Cor 7:1ff.) the author refrains from offering specific instructions and, in particular, refrains from exclusively advocating either celibacy or marriage. What matters, apparently, is not so much which practice one chooses but the quality of one's intention and the level of one's *gnōsis*. Hence *Gos. Phil.* remains nonprescriptive, but with two important provisos. These act, in effect, as two interdependent moral imperatives. First, the gnostic Christian must temper the freedom *gnōsis* conveys through love; second, the believer must remain continually aware of the potential for evil within, since such awareness can free the Christian—even the gnostic Christian—from involuntary enslavement to sin.

Finally, a word about social setting: The ethical attitudes expressed in *Gos. Phil.* clash completely with those of the majority of second-century Christians—or, at least, those represented by extant texts, from the Pastoral epistles, the apostolic fathers, and the apocryphal Acts of the Apostles to many of the Nag Hammadi texts as well. For the majority of Christians of that era, leading a Christian life meant above all learning to differentiate between those acts which are prohibited to Christians and those that are prescribed. Many Christian writings—both those later canonized as "apostolic" and those later denounced as gnostic—consist of little more than lists of virtues and vices. The author of this gospel no doubt intends to criticize such moral attitudes on the part of his fellow Christians—not only the Jews—when he characterizes the destructiveness of "the law" in words such as these: "The law was the tree (of knowledge). . . . When it said, 'Eat this,' or 'Do not eat that,' it became the beginning of death" (74,5–13). But the author goes on to contrast the law with "that Paradise [apparently the paradise in which gnostic Christians dwell] . . . where they will say to me, 'Eat this, or do not eat that, just as you wish.' This is the place where I may eat anything, since the tree of *gnōsis* is there" (73,33–35). For, indeed, the other tree (the law) "destroyed Adam, but the tree of *gnōsis* brought humanity to life" (74,4–5).

What, then, if anything, can we infer about gnostic practice? Our most explicit contemporary observer, Irenaeus, tells us that Valentinian Christians followed no consistent practice: some of them ate meat offered to idols; some attended pagan festivals and were sexually active (which Irenaeus took to mean promiscuous); others claimed to live as ascetics, either in celibate marriages or in solitude (*Adv. haer.* 1.6.3). Michael Williams, arguing that all Valentinians were encratites, suggests that we entirely discredit Irenaeus's account as mere rhetorical polemics.[29] I suggest that we accept that account insofar as it is descriptive, while discounting its polemical insinuations. What Irenaeus actually *says* is that some Valentinian Christians were married, others engaged in celibate marriages, and still others were solitary celibates (*Adv. haer.* 1.6.3)—in short, that groups of Valentinian Christians demonstrated the same range of practice that we find among other second-century Christians. Clement of Alexandria tells us that the Valentinians "approve of marriage" (*Stromateis* 3.1), without specifying whether they endorse *ordinary* marriages or *celibate* ones. Everything in the extant sources, primary and secondary, suggests to me that both were practiced among Valentinian Christians, as they were among their "catholic" contemporaries.

[29] Williams, "'Gnosis' and 'Askesis.'"

37

Pre-Valentinian Gnosticism in Alexandria

BIRGER A. PEARSON

"ALREADY WALTER BAUER . . ."—so begins one of Helmut Koester's most important and seminal essays, "GNŌMAI DIAPHOROI: The Origin and Nature of Diversification in the History of Early Christianity."[1] What had Bauer done? As is by now well known, he "had demonstrated convincingly that such Christian groups which were labelled 'heretical' actually dominated in the first two or three centuries, both geographically and theologically."[2] Fortunately, Koester did not content himself simply with reporting Bauer's results. Instead, he pointed out the necessity of "a thorough and extensive re-evaluation of early Christian history," and proceeded to embark upon such a re-evaluation in his own essay. Koester concentrated his attention on Palestine and Syria, and on the Aegean lands. In my view, his most important results are those relating to the early history of Edessa and the Osrhoene and the role of the Thomas traditions in that history. It should be noted that his reconstruction involves major corrections of the results earlier obtained by Bauer.[3] Thus, Koester has taught us that Bauer has not, after all, pronounced the final word on the subject of early Christian diversity.

Bauer's views have, of course, been criticized by others, particularly with

[1] H. Koester, "GNOMAI DIAPHOROI: The Origin and Nature of Diversification in the History of Early Christianity," *HTR* 58 (1965) 279–318; reprinted with slight revision in Robinson-Koester, *Trajectories*, 114–57. See Walter Bauer, *Rechtgläubigkeit und Ketzerei im ältesten Christentum* (BHT 10; Tübingen: Mohr-Siebeck, 1934; Eng. trans. *Orthodoxy and Heresy in Earliest Christianity*, trans. and ed. R. A. Kraft and G. Krodel (Philadelphia: Fortress Press, 1971).

[2] Koester, "*GNŌMAI DIAPHOROI*," 279.

[3] See esp. "*GNŌMAI DIAPHOROI*," 290–306; cf. Bauer, *Orthodoxy and Heresy*, 1–43.

respect to certain geographical areas.[4] It is fair to say, however, that Bauer's theory has gained the most acceptance in the case of Egypt.[5] Nevertheless, inspired by my beloved teacher, I propose to subject Bauer's reconstruction of early Egyptian Christianity to critical scrutiny, believing as I do that Bauer's views regarding Egypt require as much revision as his views on Syria and other geographical areas of early Christian expansion. Out of consideration of space limitations I restrict my discussion here to Bauer's argument that earliest Christianity in Egypt was essentially "gnostic" in character.[6]

The starting point for Bauer's reconstruction of early Egyptian Christianity is the paucity of solid evidence for the early history of the Egyptian church. Discounting altogether the legend of the founding of the Alexandrian church by the evangelist Mark, and the list of early Alexandrian bishops used by Eusebius in his *Ecclesiastical History* (2.16,24; 3.14,21; 4.1,4, 5, 11, 19; 5.9), Bauer notes that the only representatives of early Alexandrian Christianity of which we have any solid knowledge are all gnostic heretics: Basilides and his son Isidore, Carpocrates, and Valentinus. The earliest real glimpse that we get of "ecclesiastical" Christianity in Alexandria, according to Bauer, is with Demetrius, under whose episcopal rule (189–232) an "orthodox" form of Christianity first developed under the influence of the Roman church. Bauer is thus driven to conclude that the earliest form of Christianity in Egypt was not "orthodox" but "heretical," specifically "gnostic." In coming to that conclusion Bauer is implicitly extrapolating backward from the great heresiarchs Valentinus, Basilides, and Carpocrates, all of whom were active in Egypt in the time of Emperor Hadrian (117–138).

[4] See, e.g., Thomas A. Robinson, *The Bauer Thesis Examined: The Geography of Heresy in the Early Christian Church* (Studies in the Bible and Early Christianity 11; Lewiston, N.Y./ Queenston, Ont.: Mellen, 1988) and literature cited there; Robinson concentrates mainly on Asia Minor. See also James McCue, "Orthodoxy and Heresy: Walter Bauer and the Valentinians," *VC* 33 (1979) 118–30; McCue's article is more relevant to the Egyptian situation, discussed below.

[5] See, e.g., Hans Lietzmann, *A History of the Early Church,* trans. B. L. Woolf (Cleveland/ New York: Meridian, 1961) 2:275; Robert M. Grant, *From Augustus to Constantine* (New York: Harper & Row, 1970) 198; Koester, *Introduction* 2:220. Koester's discussion of Christian origins in Egypt (pp. 219–39) is, however, more careful in that he speaks of the probability of "several competing Christian groups" in the earliest period (p. 219). He also looks at a wider range of sources.

[6] Bauer, *Orthodoxy and Heresy,* 47–53. Bauer's discussion of Egypt is concentrated in chapter 2 (pp. 44–60), but he makes comments relevant to the Egyptian case elsewhere as well. For my own view of Christian origins in Egypt, see Pearson, "Earliest Christianity in Egypt: Some Observations," in *The Roots of Egyptian Christianity,* ed. B. A. Pearson and J. E. Goehring (SAC 1; Philadelphia: Fortress Press, 1986) 132–59; idem, "Christians and Jews in First-Century Alexandria," *HTR* 79 (1986) 206–16; idem, "Egyptian Christianity," *Anchor Bible Dictionary* (forthcoming). An expanded version of my discussion here occurs as chapter 13 ("Gnosticism in Early Egyptian Christianity") in my book, *Gnosticism, Judaism, and Egyptian Christianity* (SAC 5; Minneapolis: Fortress Press, 1990).

The fact is, we know as little about pre-Valentinian Gnosticism in Egypt as we do about pre-Valentinian non-gnostic Christianity there. Of course, in accordance with his theory, Bauer necessarily regards as essentially "gnostic" the early Alexandrian gospels of which we have some fragments preserved: the *Gospel According to the Hebrews* and the *Gospel According to the Egyptians*. (Bauer did not know the *Secret Gospel of Mark*.)[7] Even the *Epistle of Barnabas* is "gnostic," according to Bauer.[8]

Leaving aside a discussion of the aforementioned Alexandrian writings (which can hardly be regarded as "gnostic" in any meaningful sense), I propose to do something that Bauer did not do: probe the traditions relating to the three heresiarchs Valentinus, Basilides, and Carpocrates, to see if we can determine something about the sources they used. In that way we can arrive at a picture of pre-Valentinian, pre-Basilidian, pre-Carpocratian Gnosticism. In the process we can also gain some insights that might provide a partial answer to the larger question of the nature of pre-Valentinian Christianity in general in ancient Alexandria and thus test the viability of Bauer's famous thesis.

Valentinus

According to information preserved by Epiphanius of Salamis (*Panarion* 31.2.3), Valentinus was born in a village on the Egyptian seacoast, presumably sometime around the turn of the second century;[9] he was educated in Alexandria. Irenaeus (*Adversus haereses* 3.4.3) reports that Valentinus moved to Rome in the time of Hyginus (bishop of Rome 138–141). It was in Alexandria that Valentinus acquired his substantial learning in Greek rhetoric and philosophy. It was there that he encountered Gnosticism. It was probably there too that he became a Christian and eventually a Christian teacher. The relationship between Christianity and Gnosticism in Valentinus's teaching, and the relationship between Valentinus's own elaboration of *gnōsis* and his source material, was apparently well known to Bishop Irenaeus of Lyon. His summary assessment of Valentinus's teaching is expressed in the following sentence: "Valentinus adapted the fundamental principles of the so-called 'Gnostic' school of thought to his own kind of system" (*Adv. haer.* 1.11.1).[10]

[7] See now Morton Smith, *Clement of Alexandria and a Secret Gospel of Mark* (Cambridge, Mass.: Harvard University Press, 1973).

[8] Bauer, *Orthodoxy and Heresy*, 47.

[9] Bentley Layton's dates for Valentinus (ca. 100–ca. 175 CE) seem reasonable; see his valuable discussion in *The Gnostic Scriptures* (Garden City, N.Y.: Doubleday, 1987) 217–24.

[10] As translated by Layton (*Gnostic Scriptures*, 225); see also Tertullian *Adversus Valentinianos* 4. For a valuable discussion of the relationship between Valentinus and the mythological system of *Apocryphon of John*, see G. Quispel, "Valentinian Gnosis and the Apocryphon

What Irenaeus refers to here as "the so-called 'Gnostic' school of thought" is treated at length by him in book 1, chapter 29 of his *Adversus haereses.* There Irenaeus presents an account, obviously based on a written source, of the mythological system of a group of sectarians he refers to as "Gnostics" (*gnōstikoi*). The designation "Gnostic" is to be understood as a self-designation chosen by a specific group of people claiming to be in possession of a special, esoteric *gnōsis.*[11] As is well known, the system described by Irenaeus is essentially reproduced in a well-defined section of the *Apocryphon of John* (BG *2;* NHC II,*1;* III,*1;* IV,*1*).[12] The kind of Gnosticism represented by this and other related texts is often referred to in modern scholarship as "Sethian" Gnosticism, on the basis of a prominence in the texts of the figure of Seth and the use of such terms as "seed of Seth" and "children of Seth" as a sectarian self-designation.[13] (Curiously, the term "gnostic" does not occur in the Nag Hammadi texts.) Bentley Layton refers to the writings of this group as "classic gnostic scripture" and rightly sees in Valentinus both a Christian teacher bent on a "revision" of the gnostic tradition and an innovative "mythmaker" in his own right.[14]

The essential relationship between the myth of the *Apocryphon of John* and the Valentinian myth as elaborated by Valentinus's pupil Ptolemy (Irenaeus *Adv. haer.* 1.1.1–8.5) is evident when the two are compared. The problem here, though, is that Ptolemy's version was itself a revision of Valentinus's original system, which, in turn, was a revision of the Sethian gnostic myth.[15] Unfortunately, we are imperfectly informed about Valentinus's own version, though Irenaeus presents a somewhat sketchy account (1.11.1), from which it can be inferred that Valentinus was, indeed, using a myth like that of *Ap. John.*

The extant fragments of Valentinus consist mainly of quotations from letters and homilies; therefore, on the grounds of their literary genres, they cannot be expected to provide any systematic information on Valentinus's

---

of John," in *The Rediscovery of Gnosticism: Proceedings of the International Conference on Gnosticism at Yale, New Haven, Connecticut, March 28–31, 1978,* ed. B. Layton (SHR 41; Leiden: Brill, 1980, 1981) 1:118–32.

[11] For a valuable discussion of the term *gnōstikos,* see Morton Smith, "The History of the Term Gnostikos," in *Rediscovery,* ed. Layton, 2:796–807.

[12] See n. 10; see also the section on "Barbelognosis" in W. Foerster, *Gnosis: A Selection of Gnostic Texts,* trans. R. McL. Wilson (2 vols.; Oxford: Clarendon, 1972, 1974) 1:100–120; this contains a translation of Irenaeus *Adv. haer.* 1.29.1–4 and the BG version (short recension) of *Ap. John,* with introduction. See also Layton, *Gnostic Scriptures,* 163–69 (Irenaeus's account) and 23–51 (*Ap. John,* long recension [NHC II,*1*]).

[13] See esp. H.-M. Schenke, "The Phenomenon and Significance of Gnostic Sethianism," in *Rediscovery,* ed. Layton, 2:588–616.

[14] Layton, *Gnostic Scriptures,* 220f.

[15] Ibid., 276–79. Layton's discussion is followed by a translation of Ptolemy's version of the myth (pp. 281–302).

mythological system. Even so, allusions to the myth do occur. For example, fragment C[16] deals with the awe of the creator angels in the presence of Adam; here we can easily see the use of the anthropogonic portion of a gnostic myth like that of *Ap. John.* Allusions to the myth occur also in the *Gospel of Truth* (NHC I,3), a contemplative homily on the Christian message of salvation ("the gospel of truth") likely written by the great heresiarch himself.[17]

That Valentinus knew and used the basic myth of the *Ap. John* is therefore clear. But did he know and use the apocryphon itself? That seems to me to be improbable. Indeed, it is doubtful that Irenaeus himself, in quoting part of the myth, was using *Ap. John* as his source.[18] That tractate, in the form(s) that we now know it, is probably later than Valentinus. It is clearly a composite document with a complicated literary history. Indeed, those elements in it that are clearly "Christian" seem to belong to the later stages of its redaction.[19]

So it is an open question whether the form of the gnostic myth used by Valentinus in Alexandria already had some Christian elements in it and, therefore, was at home among *Christian* gnostics in Alexandria. The other possibility is that Valentinus took it over from a non-Christian group of *Jewish* gnostics in Alexandria and added Christian elements of his own.

Where did the myth originate? Alexandria? Or Syria? Syria is often regarded as the birthplace of Gnosticism, and some scholars, Helmut Koester among them, locate some of the most important Nag Hammadi texts there, including *Ap. John* itself.[20] It should be noted that the system of Saturninus (Satornil) summarized by Irenaeus (*Adv. haer.* 1.24.1–2) presupposes the same basic myth as that of *Ap. John.* Saturninus, a Christian gnostic, was active in Syrian Antioch. It is therefore possible that the myth used by Valentinus had been brought to Egypt from Syria by gnostic Christians early in the second century or perhaps even before the end of the first century. It is also possible that Saturninus in Antioch independently christianized an earlier version of the myth, one that was available both in Antioch and in Alexandria. In that case the place of origin of the myth remains an open question.

[16] The fragments of Valentinus are usually cited by the numbers assigned to them in W. Völker, *Quellen zur Geschichte der christlichen Gnosis* (Tübingen: Mohr-Siebeck, 1932) pp. 57–60; followed by Foerster, *Gnosis* 1:239–43. Layton has recently devised a different system, arranging the fragments in a different order and identifying them with letters of the alphabet (*Gnostic Scriptures,* 229–49). I use Layton's system here.

[17] Layton, *Gnostic Scriptures,* 250–64.

[18] Foerster, *Gnosis* 1:100–103; cf. B. A. Pearson, "The Problem of 'Jewish Gnostic' Literature," in *Nag Hammadi, Gnosticism, and Early Christianity,* ed. C. W. Hedrick and R. Hodgson, Jr. (Peabody, Mass.: Hendrickson, 1986) 15–35, esp. 19–25.

[19] Pearson, "'Jewish Gnostic' Literature," 19–25.

[20] Koester, *Introduction* 2:212f.

In discussing the gnostic sources used by Valentinus, we must not overlook another important text from the Nag Hammadi corpus: *Eugnostos the Blessed* (II,*3;* V,*3*). This tractate, which shows no obvious Christian elements, is a learned philosophical-theological treatise devoted to an exposition of the true nature of God and the divine world. It was probably written in Alexandria by a Jewish gnostic with considerable knowledge of Greek philosophy, especially Platonism. Its essential content is preserved also in a christianized version, the *Sophia of Jesus Christ* (III,*4;* BG 3). In the latter tractate the material in *Eugnostos* has been "christianized" by expanding the text into a post-resurrection revelation discourse given by Christ to his disciples. The *Soph. Jes. Chr.* was probably edited in Alexandria by Christian gnostics sometime in the second century, probably after the time of Valentinus.[21]

The importance of *Eugnostos* for our purposes is that its speculations on Anthropos and Sophia seem to have been utilized by Valentinus in developing his doctrine of the divine Pleroma. This has recently been shown by Rouel van den Broek, who accounts for the entities in Valentinus's primary Ogdoad (Irenaeus *Adv. haer.* 1.11.1; cf. 1.1.1) with reference to the speculations in *Eugnostos.*[22] Van den Broek also shows that the gnostic speculations involved grew out of a Jewish milieu that was strongly influenced by Platonism. For example, the entities *Nous* and *Aletheia,* the second set of aeons in Valentinus's primary Ogdoad, ultimately derive from the sixth book of Plato's *Republic* (*Resp.* 490b), though Valentinus probably got them from a Jewish Gnostic myth such as is found in *Eugnostos.*[23]

In considering the background and intellectual milieu of Valentinus, we cannot overlook the strong possibility that Valentinus was personally acquainted with Basilides. Indeed, Layton has recently suggested that Basilides "may somehow have exerted a major influence upon the development of Valentinus' system."[24] We shall return to Basilides in the next section of this essay.

Before we leave Valentinus, however, it is essential that we take into account the non-gnostic background of his thought. We have already alluded to his heavy indebtedness to Greek philosophy. We can go further and assert that Valentinus, like Philo Judaeus, whose writings he probably knew,[25] belongs to the general history of Middle Platonism.[26] But more important for

[21] See Martin Krause's discussion and translation in Foerster, *Gnosis* 2:24–39.

[22] R. van den Broek, "Jewish and Platonic Speculations in Early Alexandrian Theology: Eugnostos, Philo, Valentinus, and Origen," in *Roots of Egyptian Christianity,* ed. Pearson and Goehring, 190–203.

[23] Ibid., 198f.

[24] Layton, *Gnostic Scriptures,* 417.

[25] Ibid., 217.

[26] See John Dillon, *The Middle Platonists 80 B.C. to A.D. 220* (Ithaca: Cornell University Press, 1977) 384–89. G. C. Stead's study of Valentinus's thought lays great importance on his Platonism; see "In Search of Valentinus," in *Rediscovery,* ed Layton, 1:75–95.

our purposes is Valentinus's use of nongnostic Christian sources. The best place to look for the evidence is Valentinus's fragments, all of them presumably dating from his Alexandrian period. These fragments reflect the use by Valentinus of (at least) the canonical Gospel of Matthew (frg. H) and the Pauline epistles (Romans in frgs. D and G), and probably also the Gospel of John (frg. E). Indeed, Valentinus refers in one of his homilies to the writings of "God's church" (frg. G), which implies something like a collection of normative scripture. One need not add to this the numerous canonical scriptures alluded to in the *Gospel of Truth*[27]—which is probably a work of the master himself but, perhaps, not from his Alexandrian period—in order to see that many of the Christian writings that were destined to become canonical scriptures of the "orthodox" church were circulating in Alexandria in the early second century. It was precisely such writings that gave Valentinian *gnōsis* its special "Christian" character.

Basilides

We know nothing of Basilides' background. According to Clement of Alexandria (*Stromateis* 7.106) he was active in Alexandria during the reigns of the emperors Hadrian (117–138) and Antoninus Pius (138–161), but where he spent his early years is not at all clear. Eusebius, in his *Chronicle* (according to Jerome's Latin version), lists as one of the items for the sixteenth year of Hadrian's reign (132) the following notation: "Basilides the heresiarch was living in Alexandria. From him derive the Gnostics."[28] The implications of this terse comment seem to be that Basilides came to Alexandria from somewhere else. If that is the case, the most likely place for Basilides' point of departure is Antioch in Syria. Irenaeus (*Adv. haer.* 1.24.1–2) puts Basilides in close association with Saturninus of Antioch and claims that both of them were pupils of Menander, who had come to Antioch from Samaria (Justin *1 Apology* 26.4).

Eusebius traces the origin of the "Gnostic" sect to Basilides. This cannot be correct, if by "Gnostic" Eusebius means the sect so named by Irenaeus. It is nevertheless the case that Basilides' mythological system, like that of Saturninus, stands in close relationship to the basic myth identified by Irenaeus as that of the "Gnostics" (*Adv. haer.* 1.29; cf. *Ap. John*).[29] Thus

[27] On the use of canonical scripture in *Gos. Truth* see now Jacqueline A. Williams, *Biblical Interpretation in the Gnostic Gospel of Truth from Nag Hammadi* (SBLDS 79; Atlanta: Scholars Press, 1988).

[28] "Basilides haeresiarches in Alexandria commoratur," in R. Helm, ed., *Die Chronik des Hieronymus* (in *Eusebius Werke* 7:7 [GCS 47; rev. ed.; Berlin: Akademie-Verlag, 1956]). Cf. the Armenian version (ed. A. Schoene, *Eusebi Chronicorum canonum quae supersunt* [Dublin/Zurich: Weidmann, 1967] 2:168): "Basilides haeresiarcha his temporibus apparuit" (Basilides the heresiarch appeared at this time).

[29] I accept the view of Layton (*Gnostic Scriptures,* 417–19) that Irenaeus's version of

Basilides would appear to be one of the links in the nexus between Antioch and Alexandria involved in the spread of the Gnostic religion.

Basilides was reputedly a very prolific author; but, unfortunately, very little remains of his literary production. Bentley Layton has recently made a significant advance in scholarship on Basilides by isolating eight fragments that contain quotations from or references to Basilides' own works, as distinct from testimonia that refer to "Basilidians" in general. Seven of these fragments are found preserved in the works of Clement of Alexandria; the other one is preserved by Origen of Alexandria.[30]

Like that of Valentinus, Basilides' teaching was heavily imbued with Greek philosophy, but in his case, as has been shown by Layton, the greatest influence was from the Stoic school.[31] Also like Valentinus, Basilides was an exegete of scripture and commented on some of the apostolic writings that would later become canonical in the catholic church.

The fragments of Basilides, all presumably from works produced after he came to Alexandria, show knowledge and use of the Pauline epistles (frg. F) and the Gospel of Matthew (frg. G). The last-named fragment, the most extensive one preserved, is from book 23 of Basilides' lost *Exegetica*[32] and may constitute part of a commentary on 1 Peter 4.[33] If Irenaeus's discussion of Basilides' version of the crucifixion narrative is authentic, according to which Simon of Cyrene was crucified in Jesus' place (*Adv. haer* 1.24.4),[34] we have possible evidence of Basilides' use of the Gospel of Mark, for the wording of the narrative about Simon's bearing Jesus' cross is closer to that of Mark 15:20–21 than to its parallels in Matt 27:32 and Luke 23:26.[35]

Thus, we find reflected in Basilides' writings, as we did in the case of Valentinus, the presence in Alexandria of scriptures destined to become canonical in the catholic church. We can also make the same assertion about Basilides' Christian Gnosticism that we did about Valentinus's: it was his use of such non-gnostic Christian writings that gave Basilides' *gnōsis* its special Christian character.

Basilides' system is the one closest to that of the heresiarch himself, rather than the version preserved by Hippolytus (*Refutatio* 7.20.1–27.13).

[30] Layton, *Gnostic Scriptures,* 429–44 (fragments A–H).

[31] Ibid., 418.

[32] According to Clement of Alexandria, who quotes it (*Strom.* 4.81.1–83.1). See Agrippa Castor's report (in Eusebius *Hist. eccl.* 4.7.7) that Basilides composed "twenty-four books on the gospel," probably a reference to Basilides' *Exegetica* (commentaries).

[33] So Layton, *Gnostic Scriptures,* 440.

[34] Irenaeus may have misunderstood an account of the crucifixion such as that preserved in the *Second Treatise of the Great Seth* (NHC VII,2) 55,30–56,19; cf. the *Apocalypse of Peter* (NHC VII,3) 82,17–83,15.

[35] Basilides is said to have produced, or edited, his own gospel (Origen *Hom. in Luc.* 1), but of this nothing remains.

Carpocrates

With Carpocrates we run into some special problems of definition. There is no question, of course, that Carpocrates was a "heretic," according to the canons of later orthodoxy. But was he a "gnostic"? Layton, for example, says that "the doctrine of the Carpocratians bears no noticeable resemblance to gnostic myth, and so there are no grounds to conclude that the Carpocratians were gnostics in the classic sense of the word, although they may have borrowed the name 'gnostic,' perhaps as a form of self-praise."[36] Morton Smith associates the core doctrines of the Carpocratians with early Palestinian Jewish Christianity, and plays down any connection with Gnosticism.[37]

In the case of Carpocrates, we are at a serious disadvantage, too, in that we have no writings at all of his. The evidence on the Carpocratians supplied by Irenaeus, which Smith describes as "the only account of Carpocratian theology which can pretend to reliability,"[38] is decidedly ambiguous, particularly as to any connection with Gnosticism. Reference to world-creating archons (*Adv. haer.* 1.25.1) would seem to imply some connection with gnostic myth, but may not be enough to classify the Carpocratians as "gnostics," even if Irenaeus does claim that the Carpocratians in Rome led by Marcellina "call themselves gnostics" (*Adv. haer.* 1.25.6). In any case, it is the emphasis on libertine practice that sets Carpocrates apart from his Alexandrian contemporaries (or near-contemporaries)[39] Valentinus and Basilides. Nor is there any evidence at all of any contact between Carpocrates and either of the other two heresiarchs, though they were active in the same city.

What is of primary importance for the present discussion is the written sources used by Carpocrates, to the extent that we can ascertain them from the account presented by Irenaeus. These sources turn out to be, chiefly, New Testament books. The dominical saying about agreeing with one's adversary (Matt 5:25–26; Luke 12:58–59) is used to bolster the doctrine that all sins must be completed in this life in order to escape reincarnation (*Adv. haer.* 1.25.4). A saying in the Gospel of Mark (4:10–11) is used to bolster the Carpocratian claim to be in possession of Jesus' esoteric teaching (*Adv. haer.* 1.25.5). And there is an allusion to the (deutero-)Pauline doctrine of salvation by faith (Eph 2:8), cited as a basis for Carpocratian ethics (*Adv. haer.* 1.25.5).

Unfortunately, the nature of our chief source, Irenaeus, prevents us from ascertaining more precisely what gospels were used by Carpocrates, in

[36] Layton, *Gnostic Scriptures*, 199.

[37] Smith, *Clement of Alexandria*, 267–78.

[38] Ibid., 270. In Appendix B of his book (pp. 295–350) Smith provides all of the references to Carpocrates found in patristic literature.

[39] Carpocrates flourished before 125, according to Smith (*Clement of Alexandria*, 267).

addition to an epistle or epistles in the Pauline corpus. The Gospel of Matthew, at least, seems to have been used, as well as a version of the Gospel of Mark. Clement's letter to Theodore, published by Morton Smith, raises the possibility that the version of Mark used by Carpocrates was really the longer version now known as *The Secret Gospel of Mark.*[40]

Be that as it may, we can certainly conclude from such little evidence that we have that Carpocrates had access in Alexandria to several of the writings that would later become part of the canonical New Testament of the church. There is little or no evidence that he used any written gnostic sources. His doctrine of reincarnation reflects popular Platonism more than anything specifically "gnostic." Where he got his "libertinism" is uncertain, though again we may have to look eastward, to Syria. We recall in that connection that another expression of early Christian libertinism, the Nicolaitan sect (Rev 2:6, 15), seems to have derived from Nicolaus of Antioch, one of the seven leaders of the "Hellenist" wing of the Jerusalem church in its earliest history (Acts 6:5).[41]

Results

In our brief look at the three arch-heretics which, for Bauer, represent the core of Alexandrian Christianity in its earliest stages, we have certainly noted the presence of a pre-Valentinian, pre-Basilidian Gnosticism in Alexandria. But what we have also noted is the heavy reliance on the part of our heresiarchs upon non-gnostic writings of the (later) canonical New Testament. This itself is a strong indication that Alexandrian Christianity included in its mix groups of non-gnostic Christians, people whom Bauer would have to put into the camp of the "orthodox" or (to use a better term) "proto-orthodox." It is, in any case, hardly likely that the people who brought the aforementioned apostolic writings to Alexandria were all gnostics.

We should recall here the existence in early second-century Alexandria of noncanonical literature of a non-gnostic stamp. To be sure, all of those writings are pseudonymous.[42] The fact remains, therefore, that the earliest

[40] See n. 7 above. Clement's letter claims that Carpocrates obtained a copy of the *Secret Gospel of Mark* from an Alexandrian Christian presbyter and then produced a revised version of it (Smith, *Clement of Alexandria,* p. 446 [Eng. trans.], 450 [text]).

[41] The chief sources for the Nicolaitans are Irenaeus (*Adv. haer.* 1.26.3), who affirms a connection with Nicolaus of Antioch, and Clement of Alexandria (*Strom.* 3.4.25–26), who tries to absolve Nicolaus himself of the charges tradition had brought against him and his sect. Epiphanius brings the libertine "gnostics" he encountered in Egypt into association with Nicolaus and the Nicolaitans (*Haer.* 25–26). On these "gnostics," see Layton, *Gnostic Scriptures,* 199–214.

[42] *Hebrews, Egyptians, Secret Mark, Barnabas,* mentioned above. To these might be added the *Kerygma of Peter,* on which see Schneemelcher's discussion in E. Hennecke and W.

Egyptian Christians about whom we have solid historical evidence are the heresiarchs treated above. What this probably indicates is that, during the first half of the second century, the intellectual life among Alexandrian Christians was dominated by the "heretics." But, as has already been shown, the writings utilized by these teachers included not only gnostic ones but non-gnostic ("proto-orthodox") ones as well.

Nor does the intellectual prominence of the aforementioned heretics indicate anything at all about the numerical ratio of gnostics to non-gnostic Christians. We can certainly not simply assume, with Bauer, that the gnostics were in the majority. Does that mean, then, that there is no evidence one way or the other?

No. Quite apart from the theoretical extrapolations that might be ventured by a sociologist of religion regarding the relationship between esoteric, elitist groups and their "mainline" cousins in antiquity, and the statistical conclusions that could be drawn from modern social theory,[43] we have the testimony of the heretics themselves. The Valentinians provide us with the best evidence, and this has to do with the very structure of their ecclesiology. Simply put, the "pneumatic" gnostics were the elite few, over against the mass of ordinary "psychic" Christians, those who lacked the *gnōsis* prerequisite for entering the eschatological pleromatic "bridechamber."[44] Scriptural proofs were even offered for this state of affairs: The pneumatic elite were referred to as the *eklektoi,* the "chosen," whereas the ordinary "psychic" Christians were the *klētoi,* the "called," recalling the words of the Savior: "Many are 'called' but few are 'chosen'" (Matt 22:14).[45] Indeed, one Valentinian text is very explicit on the relative strengths of non-Christians, non-gnostic Christians, and gnostics: "Therefore many are material (ὑλικοί), but not many are psychic (ψυχικοί), and few are spiritual (πνευματικοί) (*Exc. Theod.* 56.2).[46]

Schneemelcher, *New Testament Apocrypha,* trans. R. McL. Wilson (2 vols.; Philadelphia: Westminster, 1963, 1965) 2:94–102.

[43] For a discussion of such little work as has been done on "sociology and Gnosticism," see Henry A. Green, *The Economic and Social Origins of Gnosticism* (SBLDS 77; Atlanta: Scholars Press, 1985) 1–19. Green's own work reflects a Marxist approach. For an interesting theoretical discussion of how religious groups form and develop, see the seminal study by Rodney Stark and William Sims Bainbridge, *A Theory of Religion* (Toronto Studies in Religion 2; New York/Bern/Frankfurt/Paris: Peter Lang, 1987).

[44] James F. McCue makes a major point of this in his study "Orthodoxy and Heresy."

[45] This terminology is found in Clement of Alexandria's *Excerpta ex Theodoto* 58.1, part of a passage that is derived from an early Valentinian source also used by Irenaeus (*Exc. Theod.* 43.2–65//*Adv. haer.* 1.4.5–7.1). See, e.g., Otto Dibelius, "Studien zur Geschichte der Valentinianer, I: Die Excerpta ex Theodoto und Irenäus," *ZNW* 9 (1908) 230–47; Völker, *Quellen,* 104–18; McCue, "Orthodoxy and Heresy," 125.

[46] As translated by Casey (*The Excerpta ex Theodoto of Clement of Alexandria* [SD 1; London: Christophers, 1934] 77); cf. McCue, "Orthodoxy and Heresy," 127.

To be sure, the gnostics were eager to convert to their groups individuals from the masses of "ordinary" Christians. We have already seen how they could utilize the non-gnostic apostolic writings for their purposes, even devising commentaries that provided the "true" interpretation of these writings. (The Alexandrian gnostics produced the first commentaries on the New Testament.) The later Basilidians and Valentinians even provided arguments based on "apostolic succession": Basilides was said to have drawn his teachings from the apostle Peter through the mediation of one Glaukias; Valentinus drew his from the apostle Paul through one Theudas (Clement of Alexandria *Stromateis* 7.106). But, in assessing the cases of "Glaukias" and "Theudas," are we not entitled to borrow Bauer's phraseology (his reference to the Alexandrian episcopal succession list): "a mere echo and a puff of smoke"?[47]

To conclude: In our effort to scrutinize the traditions relating to the great gnostic heretics of early second-century Alexandria to find evidence of pre-Valentinian Gnosticism, we did indeed find some. We found evidence of a Jewish Gnosticism in Alexandria that the heresiarchs "christianized" with liberal use of "proto-orthodox," potentially canonical, traditions that were *also* existing in Alexandria. Bauer's theory of Christian origins in Alexandria and his views regarding the numerical ratio of "heretics" to "orthodox" there have been found to be seriously defective. I would like to think that my esteemed teacher, had he studied the Egyptian evidence as he did the Syrian, would have arrived at the same conclusions.

[47] Bauer, *Orthodoxy and Heresy*, 45.

Epilogue: Current Issues in New Testament Scholarship

HELMUT KOESTER

Where I Began

LOOKING BACK CAN sometimes be helpful. It was forty-four years ago; I was a student at the end of my second semester of theological studies at the University of Marburg in Germany—very young still, and fresh from two years of service in the German army and half a year as a prisoner of war, less than a year from my release from an American POW camp. My teacher Ernst Fuchs had told me that I should apply for admission to the New Testament seminar of Rudolf Bultmann. I was instructed that I had to make a pilgrimage to the house of the master at Calvinstraße 14 in Marburg. He would ask me questions about any one of a dozen classic publications in the field of New Testament studies. I got the list of these classics and spent the entire summer of 1946 reading.

It is these classics that I want to talk about first. The list was dominated by works of scholars from the history-of-religions school and their successors. There were William Wrede's *Messianic Secret*, Wilhelm Bousset's *Kyrios Christos* and his *Religion of Judaism in the Late-Hellenistic Age*, Eduard Norden's *Agnostos Theos*, Paul Wendland's *Hellenistic-Roman Culture* and his *Early-Christian Literary Genres*, and Richard Reitzenstein's *Hellenistic Mystery Religions*, as well as Albert Schweitzer's *Quest of the Historical Jesus* and his *Mysticism of Paul the Apostle*, and, last but not least, Hans Jonas's *Gnosis und spätantiker Geist* and Walter Bauer's *Orthodoxy and Heresy in Earliest Christianity*.[1] I was lucky that Rudolf Bultmann asked me some

[1] W. Wrede, *Das Messiasgeheimnis in den Evangelien: Zugleich ein Beitrag zum Verständnis des Markusevangeliums* (Göttingen: Vandenhoeck & Ruprecht, 1901), Eng. trans. *The Messianic Secret*, trans. J. C. G. Greig (Cambridge: J. Clarke, 1971); W. Bousset, *Kyrios Christos:*

questions about William Wrede's *Messianic Secret,* a book that I had studied in detail—and I was admitted to his seminar.

I did not know anything at that time about Carl Kraeling's and Erwin Goodenough's work on the spectacular finds of the synagogue and the Christian house-church at Dura Europos, or about George Foot Moore's pioneering study of Judaïsm, or of J. Foakes Jackson and Kirsopp Lake's monumental study, *The Beginnings of Christianity.*[2] However, I was to learn soon that the works of these leading English-speaking scholars enlarged the horizon of New Testament studies in a way that was congenial to the original impact of the message that had come from the history-of-religions school a generation earlier.

What made a lasting impression on me as a student at the University of Marburg after World War II was the opening of the New Testament canon. I learned that there were not only the twenty-seven books of the New Testament but also writings called Apostolic Fathers. The Nag Hammadi documents had not yet become widely known, but there was the second edition of the *New Testament Apocrypha* by Edgar Hennecke.[3] There also were materials from the Greco-Roman world that we were asked to study: the gospel inscriptions of Augustus, magical papyri, the so-called Mithras Liturgy that Albrecht Dieterich had discussed,[4] and many other documents.

Geschichte des Christusglaubens von den Anfängen des Christentums bis Irenaeus (Göttingen: Vandenhoeck & Ruprecht, 1913), Eng. trans. *Kyrios Christos: A History of the Belief in Christ from the Beginning of Christianity to Irenaeus,* trans. J. E. Steely (Nashville: Abingdon, 1970); idem, *Die Religion des Judentums im späthellenistischen Zeitalter* (3rd ed. edited by H. Gressmann; Tübingen: Mohr, 1926); E. Norden, *Agnostos Theos: Untersuchungen zur Formengeschichte religiöser Rede* (Leipzig and Berlin: Teubner, 1913); P. Wendland, *Die hellenistisch-römische Kultur in ihren Beziehungen zur Judentum und Christentum* and *Die Urchristlichen Literaturformen* (HNT 1.2, 3; Tübingen: Mohr, 1912); R. Reitzenstein, *Die hellenistischen Mysterienreligionen, nach ihre Grundgedanken und Wirkungen* (3rd ed.; Leipzig and Berlin: Teubner, 1927), Eng. trans. *Hellenistic Mystery-Religions: Their Basic Ideas and Significance,* trans. J. E. Steely (Pittsburgh: Pickwick, 1978); A. Schweitzer, *Von Reimarus zu Wrede: Eine Geschichte der Leben-Jesu Forschung* (Tübingen: Mohr, 1906), Eng. trans. *The Quest of the Historical Jesus: A Critical Study of its Progress from Reimarus to Wrede,* trans. W. Montgomery (London: A. & C. Black, 1910); idem, *Die Mystik des Apostel Paulus* (Tübingen: Mohr, 1930), Eng. trans. *The Mysticism of Paul the Apostle,* trans. W. Montgomery (London: A. & C. Black, 1931); H. Jonas, *Gnosis und spätantiker Geist,* 1: *Die mythologische Gnosis* (Göttingen: Vandenhoeck & Ruprecht, 1934), 2.1: *Von der Mythologie zur mystischen Philosophie* (Göttingen: Vandenhoeck & Ruprecht, 1954); W. Bauer, *Rechtgläubigkeit und Ketzerei im ältesten Christentum* (BHT 10; Tübingen: Mohr-Siebeck, 1934), Eng. trans. *Orthodoxy and Heresy in Earliest Christianity,* trans. R. A. Kraft and G. Krodel (Philadelphia: Fortress Press, 1971).

[2] F. J. Foakes Jackson and K. Lake, *The Beginnings of Christianity, Part I: The Acts of the Apostles* (5 vols.; London: Macmillan, 1920–33).

[3] E. Hennecke, *Neutestamentliche Apokryphen* (2 vols.; 2nd ed.; Tübingen: Mohr-Siebeck, 1924; 3rd ed. edited by W. Schneemelcher; Tübingen: Mohr-Siebeck, 1959, 1964), Eng. trans. *New Testament Apocrypha,* trans. R. McL. Wilson (2 vols.; London: Lutterworth; Philadelphia: Westminster, 1963, 1965).

[4] A. Dieterich, *Eine Mithrasliturgie* (3rd ed.; Leipzig and Berlin: Teubner, 1923).

I learned that in order to understand the New Testament it was necessary to explore all of the extant early Christian literature, study the Hellenistic world, and explore the religious movements of the Greco-Roman period. Moreover, the history-of-religions school challenged the understanding of the New Testament as a text that could be easily translated into modern theological categories. It wanted to achieve a fresh understanding of religion and piety rather than indulge in theological reflections. What was real for these scholars was cult, ritual, and celebration of common people who could neither write nor read. Texts like the New Testament and the Apostolic Fathers were seen as only secondary expressions of the religious experience and theological abstractions of cultic and ritual celebration.

A Theological Interlude

But on the continent, and especially in Germany, the catastrophe of the First World War caused a change in focus. The rise of "dialectical theology," resulting from the need to establish authorities for a reorientation, implied a return once more to the writings of the New Testament canon and their theological interpretation. It came as a surprise when Rudolf Bultmann—evidently one of the foremost young scholars educated in the history-of-religions school—endorsed Karl Barth's commentary on the Epistle to the Romans. But it was a signal. The return to New Testament theology was reinforced by the need to defend traditional Christian values against Nazi ideology, and it received new impulses through the rebuilding of traditional institutions after World War II, both in church and state—albeit without emperor and state church.

Rudolf Bultmann's famous and controversial program of demythologizing the New Testament message was not produced in the interests of the history of religions or for a better understanding of the relationship of myth to cult and ritual. Rather, it was meant to rescue traditional Christian values embedded in the canonical texts of the Bible. It was no less apologetic than the more recent conservative defense of the New Testament canon by such scholars as Martin Hengel and Peter Stuhlmacher. However, not only the new Tübingen evangelicals but also scholars from the second generation of Bultmann's students in Germany, who have dominated in German universities during the last decades, have concentrated their work on the canonical biblical writings and their theological interpretation. Erudition devoted to the work with other materials, more often than not, has had an apologetic component. It is usually taken for granted that noncanonical, apocryphal texts are secondary, derivative, and theologically inferior. It is no surprise that the contributions of (West) German New Testament scholars to the study of such new discoveries as the Coptic Gnostic Library from Nag Hammadi have been minimal.

New Beginnings on This Continent

American New Testament scholarship has developed in an entirely different direction during the last few decades. The New Testament apocrypha, the Nag Hammadi Library of Gnostic texts, the Dead Sea Scrolls, the social world of the New Testament, archaeology of the lands of the New Testament all have been made part of its agenda. In this respect American New Testament scholarship has had less in common with scholarship in West Germany than with the orientation of research in Switzerland, Holland, Scandinavia, and even East Germany. To be sure, anyone who comes to the annual meeting of the Society of Biblical Literature has noticed that about anything is available in this huge cafeteria of biblical scholarship. But such bewildering variety should not distract from some of the outstanding features that characterize research, publications, and teaching in American universities, theological schools, and religion departments. Let me characterize briefly some of the new departures that have given fresh impulses to scholarship in this country.

Orthodoxy and Heresy

Walter Bauer's book *Orthodoxy and Heresy in Earliest Christianity,* one of the most brilliant monographs in the field of New Testament studies in this century, went almost unnoticed when it was first published in Germany in 1934. Interest in Bauer's thesis began thirty years later on this side of the ocean. Inquiries concerning a possible English translation of the book prompted a renewed interest on the part of the German publisher, resulting in a second edition of the work in 1964, prepared by Georg Strecker, which was subsequently translated into English and published by Fortress Press.[5] It was around that time, in the early 1970s, that Fortress Press also began to emerge as the leading American theological publishing house, which had an enormous impact on biblical scholarship in this country.

The English translation of Walter Bauer's book came at an opportune moment. The American public was discovering the fact of religious pluralism in our society. Walter Bauer demonstrated that earliest Christianity was a pluralistic movement and that the claim of the later "orthodox" fathers that they alone had been there first was historically not verifiable. This was apparently a finding more welcome to Americans than to Europeans. In Europe, everybody belongs to some kind of orthodox establishment, either Protestant or Catholic, at least in theory. Few people want to disturb the delicate equilibrium of church-and-state concordats. In our "Christian" country, however, everyone is a heretic in the eyes of everybody else.

[5] See n. 1.

The discovery of pluralism justified a renewed investigation of noncanonical, so-called apocryphal, early Christian materials. But New Testament scholarship has even gone beyond that stage. Other religions of the Greco-Roman period, including early Judaism, have been investigated and interpreted in their own right, and not just as a "background" for the New Testament. America had a head start with respect to the investigation of early Judaism anyway. The Hitler period in Germany, the concomitant prejudice against anything "Jewish," and the complete disruption of any connection with Jewish scholarship, had a debilitating effect even on those scholars in Germany who emphasized the Jewish character of the New Testament writings.

Openness to hear also the other side of a religious controversy in early Christianity came at a time when spectacular discoveries of ancient texts presented new challenges.

Qumran and Nag Hammadi

When an international team was established thirty-five years ago and charged with editing the Dead Sea Scrolls, the majority of the team members were American scholars. As a result, criticism of the failures of this team to publish these texts expeditiously also occupied especially the American scholarly, and not so scholarly, debate. Nevertheless, the contributions of American scholars to the publication and interpretation of these texts has been remarkable, and it was certainly aided by the close American cooperation with Jewish and Israeli scholars.

The contribution of American scholars to the publication and interpretation of the documents from the Nag Hammadi Library is even more evident. The library was discovered in 1945. In the following two decades, the slow progress of publication by West-European scholars, the illegal export from Egypt of one of the codices, and the exploitation of these texts before their actual publication left little hope that those who had access to these new texts would ever make them appropriately and speedily available to the world of scholarship. It was James M. Robinson of The Claremont Graduate School who had the vision and energy to mobilize and organize American resources for this task. The project which he has directed did exactly what should have been done with the Dead Sea Scrolls, namely (1) publication of a facsimile edition of all texts, (2) a preliminary English translation of the entire Nag Hammadi Library, (3) critical scholarly editions of the individual texts. The first of these two tasks was accomplished speedily during the seventies; and there is considerable progress also in the publication of critical editions—again mostly accomplished by the cooperation of American scholars.

It was no accident that American New Testament scholars could become involved so deeply in the work on the Nag Hammadi Library. They had participated in the discussion of these texts from the beginning, encouraged younger scholars to learn Coptic, and brought a good deal of common sense to the interpretation of the new documents. If these texts are heretical, so be it; let's try anyway to understand what they have to say! The only comparable European effort was made with much more limited resources in what was then the German Democratic Republic by Hans-Martin Schenke and his colleagues and students, while the efforts of French-speaking scholars have found their new center in the Nag Hammadi project of Laval University in Canada.

The sheer quantity of the newly discovered materials and their potential for contributing substantially to our knowledge of earliest Christianity are overwhelming. Substantial efforts of many scholars are still needed in the future. At the same time, other early Christian texts that had been known for a century but had not received much attention are demanding to be drawn into the process of reconstructing the entire history of ancient Christianity. In most instances, scholarship is still in the process of constructing and debating exploratory hypotheses for the understanding of the new materials. The critical discussion of such hypotheses and the development of alternatives of interpretation are urgent needs of New Testament scholarship today and should remain primary items on its agenda for the future.

The Destruction of Borders

There are three borders which had been erected traditionally in order to protect the integrity of New Testament studies: (1) the border between New Testament and the history of ancient Christianity; (2) the treatment of the New Testament as if it were not a part of early Judaism; (3) the investigation of the New Testament and early Christian literature as a phenomenon distinct from Greco-Roman culture and religion of its period. All three borders are artificial. If they are maintained, parochialism will be the result. American New Testament scholarship has the potential to bring these borders down, but there are excuses and defenses. Let me discuss some of these excuses.

(1) "The New Testament canon designates these twenty-seven writings as part of a special book that is different from other early Christian writings." However, this distinction has been introduced several centuries after the fact. The canon was the result of a deliberate attempt to exclude certain voices from the early period of Christianity: heretics, Marcionites, Gnosticism, Jewish Christians, perhaps also women. It is the responsibility of the New Testament scholar to help these voices to be heard again.

(2) "Pharisaic and rabbinic Judaism is a different religion with its own traditions and characterized by the rejection of the belief in Jesus as the Christ." But it should be said that it is a tragic turn of history that Christianity and Judaism later became different religions and that the New Testament writings and the Mishnah were canonized in order to underscore the distinction. Paul and other Christian missionaries did not know anything about such a division. For them, the new converts were the true Israel of the last age to which God would eventually join also those whom Paul called "Israel according to the flesh" (1 Cor 10:18).

(3) "Christians were a people altogether different in their piety and morality from the immoral and polytheistic pagan world." However, Christians lived in the same cities, belonged to the same classes of society, spoke the same language, engaged in the same trades, and organized themselves according to the same structures of religious associations that were also used by their non-Christian fellow citizens. Thus, early Christianity is just one of several Hellenistic propaganda religions, competing with others who seriously believed in their god and who also imposed moral demands on their followers.

Demands for New Testament Scholarship

To achieve a better understanding of the New Testament and of early Christian history efforts have to be made to educate ourselves better in order to achieve the necessary scholarly tools for the investigation of the religions of the late Hellenistic and Roman periods and of early Christianity and Judaism as part of that history of religion and culture. Not everyone can do everything. But we need to give more young scholars the opportunity to equip themselves with the scholarly tools for this task. This implies education of students in more Greek than just New Testament Greek, in more Hebrew than just biblical Hebrew. Students have to learn to read Greek inscriptions or rabbinic texts. Many of the important texts are preserved only in translations into other languages—Latin, Coptic, Syriac, Armenian, and Ethiopic. Students have to be encouraged to acquire expertise in one or several of these languages.

History can no longer be treated as battles and conquests and dates of imperial reigns. To understand the history of religions, it is necessary to study all materials relating to the life of a society, including nonliterary data—not as the "background" of early Christianity but as the world of the early Christians. This world includes also those who did not leave written records but whose lives can be studied and understood by investigating city architecture, temples and synagogues, private and religious associations, honorary inscriptions and records of slave manumissions, coin issues of the imperial and local mints, courts and legislation, trade routes and business records.

It is evident that this implies new demands for the education of future scholars, and that these demands can be met only in the major university settings in which other disciplines are represented so that students can find opportunities to learn languages and to become acquainted with the various methods and tools for the study of history, literature, archaeology, and religion in general. Theological schools whose curriculum is not integrated with that of a major research university and which are not located in academic institutions that are free from sectarian control do not have the resources to provide such education.

New Methods

What about new methods and approaches, from literary criticism to feminist interpretation and social history? This is not the place to discuss any of these methods and approaches as such. There is no question that every new approach can function hermeneutically as a tool for new discoveries. I am not advocating a value-free, objective agenda for the work of highly trained technicians who have no questions. It is too easily forgotten that the historical-critical method was by no means such an agenda. Rather, it was designed as a hermeneutical tool for the liberation from conservative prejudice and from the power of ecclesiastical and political institutions. Those who fear that the historical-critical method threatens their control over the religious orientation and theological judgment of their constituencies are absolutely correct.

There are two tests that should be used in order to determine the validity of any new approach: (1) Does such an approach go beyond the treatment of already established and well-known texts, and does it open up a fresh understanding of materials that have hitherto not been considered? If literary criticism simply rehearses the same old New Testament text without considering analogies in newly discovered literatures, such as the Nag Hammadi Library, it fails this test. That would also be true if a feminist critique of the letters of Paul simply argues that Paul was a villain rather than a saint, without drawing into the debate fresh materials that help to provide a better understanding of the moral values of Paul's world. Or if the description of the social setting of Paul's letters works exclusively with just these letters, without considering archaeological and epigraphical materials from the ancient world. Or if rhetorical criticism is informed exclusively by some modern rhetorical theory and fails to draw into the discussion ancient sources about the art of rhetoric.

(2) The second test could be called "political." Some more recent efforts of a literary-critical interpretation of New Testament writings seem to be

ingenious, but may be nothing else but a self-serving exercise. It can be worse. Literary criticism often disregards the results of text, source, and form criticism—for example, considering John 21 as a part of the writing "as it has come to us," although most scholars agree that this chapter is a secondary appendix. Such method not only displays a disregard for historical development; it is also more palatable to certain ecclesiastical circles because it does not challenge the integrity of the New Testament canon.

Interpretation of the Bible is justified only if it is a source for political and religious renewal, or it is not worth the effort. Martin Luther's discovery of the word of the gracious God in scripture provided not only the justification for liberation from ecclesiastical control; it also encouraged the voices of those who called for social justice—regardless of how successful the magisterial reformation was in this respect. Biblical interpretation must be capable of translating the message of freedom and justification into the issues of liberation and justice in our own time. Those who support and defend the existing structures of power and injustice in our own time do not need any kind of scholarship. From Rome to the centers of power in this country, those who are in power can find a biblical excuse for their suppressive policies perfectly well without ever consulting a biblical scholar. If the Bible has anything to do with justice and freedom, biblical scholarship must be able to question those very structures of power and expose their injustice and destructive potential.

There is a great need for Afro-American New Testament scholars. Because there are so few, the political agenda of black Americans has little effect as a hermeneutical tool. Feminist critique as a hermeneutical tool can serve as a better example because it has already successfully challenged established assumptions, which have been imposed on our reading of biblical texts as well as on our views of the role of women in our society and our churches. Of course, the view that Phoebe of Romans 16 was the presiding officer of the church in Cenchreae and that Junia was a female apostle must be argued on the basis of established philological methods. It is also necessary that newly discovered materials be drawn into the discussion, as in Elaine Pagels's controversial work *The Gnostic Gospels*[6] and in her more recent and more mature book *Adam, Eve, and the Serpent,*[7] which draws traditional patristic texts into the debate with Gnostic materials. Another example is Bernadette Brooten's spectacular work *Women Leaders in the Ancient Synagogue,* which demonstrated on the basis of archaeological and epigraphical data that women were in positions of leadership in early Judaism.[8] To be

[6] Elaine Pagels, *The Gnostic Gospels* (New York: Random House, 1979).

[7] E. Pagels, *Adam, Eve, and the Serpent* (New York: Random House, 1988).

[8] Bernadette Brooten, *Women Leaders in the Ancient Synagogue: Inscriptional Evidence and Background Issues* (BJS 36; Chico, Calif.: Scholars Press, 1982). Cf. chap. 11 in this volume.

sure, the political agenda is evident, but it is exactly this political agenda that has led to new scholarly discoveries.

If new methods are explored, they should thus be capable of transcending the artificial borders drawn around the field of New Testament studies and lead to a comprehensive understanding of the entire political, social, and religious world of early Christianity. But such understanding is possible only if it is inspired by the search for equality, freedom, and justice in our own world. In this respect, the current issues of New Testament scholarship are a renewal of the agenda of the history-of-religions school in a more comprehensive political perspective.

Bibliography of Helmut Koester

DAVID M. SCHOLER

ALTHOUGH HELMUT KOESTER has published a considerable amount, it is not the quantity that is significant. Rather, it is the combination of the quality of his scholarship and its profound influence on his colleagues and the disciplines involved that is significant.

One suspects that Helmut Koester's most enduring work is his already famous *Einführung/Introduction* (nos. 110, 114-115, 137). This work enshrines, among much else, two of his seemingly deepest and most passionate concerns: gospel traditions and early Christian literature "beyond" the New Testament.

Helmut Koester's interest in gospel traditions certainly spans his publication record. From his 1956 Habilitationsschrift (3) to his recent (1990) *Ancient Christian Gospels: Their History and Development,* Helmut Koester's studies of the gospel traditions, often concerned with Q and the *Gospel of Thomas,* are many and profound and have stimulated countless discussions among his colleagues.

True to his intellectual heritage, Helmut Koester has demonstrated his commitment to the study of early Christian literature without a limiting commitment to the so-called canonical boundary of the New Testament. This is reflected, among other places, in his significant collaboration with James M. Robinson (72, 78) and in his repeated attention to literature from the Nag Hammadi collection.

Of course, these two areas hardly exhaust Helmut Koester's interests. "For time would fail me to tell of" the Thessalonian correspondence, archaeology, Hellenistic religions, and more.

The following bibliography is an attempt to present a complete and accurate record of Helmut Koester's publications. As an experienced bibliographer, I am certain that neither goal is probably achieved to perfection. The items are arranged by years. Within each year the order is books, articles, reviews, and edited materials.

This small contribution on my part is but one way for me to honor and thank a wonderful Doktorvater and friend.

1953

1. "Glaube und Verkündigung in der evangelischen Unterweisung." *Evangelische Unterweisung* 8 (1953) 20–23.

1955

2. (with Klaus Baltzer) "Die Bezeichnung des Jakobus als 'ΩΒΛΙΑΣ." *ZNW* 46 (1955) 141–42.

1956

3. "Septuaginta und synoptischer Erzählungsstoff im Schriftbeweis Justins des Märtyrers." Habilitationsschrift. Heidelberg, 1956.

1957

4. *Synoptische Überlieferung bei den apostolischen Vätern.* TU 65. Berlin: Akademie-Verlag, 1957.
5. "Die ausserkanonischen Herrenworte als Produkte der christlichen Gemeinde." *ZNW* 48 (1957) 220–37. [English translation in 141.]
6. "Geschichte und Kulte im Johannesevangelium und bei Ignatius von Antiochien." *ZTK* 54 (1957) 56–69. [English translation in 57.]
7. (with Klaus Baltzer and Friedemann Merkel) "Revelation 3:1–6." *GPM* 12:1 (1957/58) 8–11.
8. Review of Johannes Becker, *Die Reden des Johannesevangeliums und der Stil der gnostischen Offenbarungsrede,* in *Zeitschrift für Pastoraltheologie* (1957) 447.
9. Review of Martin Dibelius and Hans Conzelmann, *Die Pastoralbriefe* (3. Aufl.), in *VF* (1957) 156–57.
10. Review of Lukas Fischer, *Die Auslegungsgeschichte von I. Korinther 6,1–11,* in *VF* (1957) 155–56.

1958

11. (with Klaus Baltzer and Friedemann Merkel) "Apostelgeschichte 2:42-47." *GPM* 12:8 (1957/58) 249–52.
12. (with Klaus Baltzer and Friedemann Merkel) "Apostelgeschichte 9:1-20." *GPM* 12:5 (1957/58) 183–85.
13. (with Klaus Baltzer and Friedemann Merkel) "Hebräer 5:1–10." *GPM* 12:2 (1957/58) 81–84.

1959

14. "Häretiker im Urchristentum." *RGG*³ 3:17–21.
15. (with Klaus Baltzer and Friedemann Merkel) "Jesaiah 62:1–12." *GPM* 13:11 (1959) 18–20.

16. (with Klaus Baltzer and Friedemann Merkel) "Matthäus 25:14–30." *GPM* 13:8 (1959) 280–82.
17. Review of Frank W. Beare, *The First Epistle of Peter* (2d ed.), in *HDB* 24:1 (1959) 26–27.
18. Review of Rudolf Bultmann, *Jesus Christ and Mythology,* in *The Christian Advocate* 3 (1959) 90–92.
19. Review of Frederic Kenyon, *Our Bible and the Ancient Manuscripts* (rev. by A. W. Adams), in *HDB* 24:1 (1959) 24–25.
20. Review of Joachim Jeremias, *Die Gleichnisse Jesu* (4. Aufl.), in *VF* (1959) 173–78.
21. Review of Willi Marxsen, *Der Evangelist Markus,* in *VF* (1959) 178–81.
22. Review of C. F. D. Moule, *The Epistles of Paul to the Colossians and to Philemon,* in *HDB* 24:1 (1959) 27.
23. Review of James M. Robinson, *Das Geschichtsverständnis des Markus-evangelium,* in *VF* (1959) 181–84.
24. Review of Erik Lane Titus, *Essentials of New Testament Study,* in *HDB* 24:1 (1959) 26.

1960

25. Review of J. A. Allen, *The Epistle to the Ephesians,* in *HDB* 24:2 (1960) 36–37.
26. Review of Alan Richardson, *The Gospel According to St. John,* in *HDB* 24:2 (1960) 35–36.

1961

27. "Die Auslegung der Abrahamverheissung in Hebräer 6." In *Studien zur Theologie der alttestamentlichen Überlieferungen: Gerhard von Rad zum 60. Geburtstag,* ed. Rolf Rendtorff and Klaus Koch, 95–109. Neukirchen: Neukirchener Verlag, 1961.
28. (with Klaus Baltzer and Friedemann Merkel) "1 Korinther 13:1–13." *GPM* 16 (1961/62) 115–20.
29. "John xiv.1–20: A Meditation." *Expository Times* 73:3 (1961) 88.
30. "Philippus, Apostel." *RGG*³ 5:337–38.
31. "Segen und Fluch im Neuen Testamentum." *RGG*³ 5:1651–52.
32. Review of Günther Bornkamm, *Jesus of Nazareth,* in *Religion and Life* 30 (1961) 296–97.
33. Review of Ulrich Wilckens, *Weisheit und Torheit,* in *Gnomon* 33 (1961) 590–95.

1962

34. "Luke, Gospel According to Saint." *Encyclopaedia Britannica* (1962) 14:476–78.
35. "Mark, Gospel According to Saint." *Encyclopaedia Britannica* (1962) 14:910–12.
36. "Mark, Saint." *Encyclopaedia Britannica* (1962) 14:909–10.

37. "Matthew, Gospel According to Saint." *Encyclopaedia Britannica* 15 (1962) 96–98.
38. "Outside the Camp: Hebrews 13:9–14." *HTR* 55 (1962) 299–315.
39. "The Purpose of the Polemic of a Pauline Fragment (Philippians III)." *NTS* 8 (1961/62) 317–32.
40. "σπλάγχνον, σπλαγχνίζομαι, εὔσπλαγχνος, πολύσπλαγχνος, ἄσπλαγχνος." *TWNT* 7:548–59. [English translation in 84.]
41. "Stephanus, Märtyrer." *RGG*³ 6:358.
42. "Thaddäus." *RGG*³ 6:725.
43. "Verdammnis im Neuen Testament." *RGG*³ 6:1260.
44. Review of J. Lawson, *Historical and Theological Introduction to the Apostolic Fathers,* in *JBL* 86 (1962) 416–19.

1963

45. "Barnabas, Saint." *Encyclopaedia Britannica* (1963) 3:171.
46. "Gospels." *Encyclopaedia Britannica* (1963) 10:536–38.
47. "Ignatius, Saint." *Encyclopaedia Britannica* (1963) 13:1070.
48. "Pastoral Epistles." *Encyclopaedia Britannica* (1963) 17:444–46.
49. "Polycarp, Saint." *Encyclopaedia Britannica* (1963) 18:190–91.

1964

50. "Häretiker im Urchristentum als theologisches Problem." In *Zeit und Geschichte: Dankesgabe an Rudolf Bultmann zum 80. Geburtstag,* ed. Erich Dinkler, 61–76. Tübingen: Mohr-Siebeck, 1964. [English translation in 87.]
51. "συνέχω, συνοχή." *TWNT* 7:875–85. [English translation in 86.]

1965

52. "Bardesanes." *Lexikon der alten Welt* (Zurich: Artemis, 1965) 436.
53. "Basilides." *Lexikon der alten Welt,* 438.
54. "GNOMAI DIAPHOROI: The Origin and Nature of Diversification in the History of Early Christianity." *HTR* 58 (1965) 279–318. [Reprinted in 80; German translation in 67; reprinted in 73.]
55. "Gnosis." *Lexikon der alten Welt,* 1100–1102. [Reprinted in 81.]
56. "Herakleon." *Lexikon der alten Welt,* 1257–58.
57. "History and Cult in the Gospel of John and in Ignatius of Antioch." *Journal for Theology and the Church* 1 (1965) 111–23. [English translation of 6.]
58. "Karpocrates." *Lexikon der alten Welt,* 1491.
59. "Markion." *Lexikon der alten Welt,* 1854–55.
60. "Paul and Hellenism." In *The Bible in Modern Scholarship,* ed. J. Philip Hyatt, 78–95. Nashville: Abingdon, 1965.
61. "Ptolemaios." *Lexikon der alten Welt,* 2479.
62. "Simon Magus." *Lexikon der alten Welt,* 2800–2801.
63. "τέμνω, ἀποτομία, ἀπότομος, ἀποτόμως, κατατομή, ὀρθοτομέω." *TWNT* 8:106–13. [English translation in 89.]

64. "Valentinus." *Lexikon der alten Welt,* 3176–77.

1966

65. "τόπος." *TWNT* 8:106–13. [English translation in 90.]

1967

66. Review of Robert M. Funk, *Journal for Theology and the Church,* Volumes 1–3, in *HDB* (1967) 16.

1968

67. "GNOMAI DIAPHOROI: Ursprung und Wesen der Mannigfaltigkeit in der Geschichte des frühen Christentums." *ZTK* 65 (1968) 160–203. [German translation of 54; reprinted in 73.]
68. "NOMOS PHYSEOS: The Concept of Natural Law in Greek Thought." In *Religions in Antiquity: Essays in Memory of Erwin Goodenough,* ed. Jacob Neusner, 521–41. Leiden: Brill, 1968.
69. "One Jesus and Four Primitive Gospels." *HTR* 61 (1968) 203–47. [Reprinted in 83; German translation in 75.]
70. "The Role of Myth in the New Testament." *Andover Newton Quarterly* 8:3 (1968) 180–95.

1969

71. "ὑπόστασις." *TWNT* 8:571–88. [English translation in 91.]

1970

72. (with James M. Robinson) *Entwicklungslinien durch die Welt des frühen Christentums.* Tübingen: Mohr-Siebeck, 1970. [German translation of 78; see 73, 74, 75 and 77; Japanese translation in 96.]
73. "GNOMAI DIAPHOROI: Ursprung und Wesen der Mannigfaltigkeit in der Geschichte des frühen Christentums." Kapitel 4 in 72 (1970) 107–46. [Reprint of 67; English translation in 54 and in 80.]
74. "Grundtypen und Kriterien frühchristlicher Glaubensbekenntnisse." Kapitel 6 in 72 (1970) 191–215. [English translation in 85.]
75. "Ein Jesus und vier ursprüngliche Evangeliengattungen." Kapitel 5 in 72 (1970) 147–90. [English translation in 69 and in 83.]
76. "φύσις." *TWNT* 9:246–71. [English translation in 95.]
77. "Schluss: Das Ziel und die reichweite von 'Entwicklungslinien.'" Kapitel 8 in 72 (1970) 251–61. [English translation in 79.]

1971

78. (with James M. Robinson) *Trajectories through Early Christianity.* Philadelphia: Fortress Press, 1971. [English translation of 72; see 79, 80, 83 and 85; Japanese translation in 96.]

79. "Conclusion: The Intention and Scope of Trajectories." In 78 (1971) 269–79. [English translation of 77.]
80. "GNOMAI DIAPHOROI: The Origin and Nature of Diversification in the History of Early Christianity." In 78 (1971) 114–57. [Reprint of 54; German translation in 67 and in 73.]
81. "Gnosis." *Taschenlexikon Religion und Theologie,* 1:362–65. Göttingen: Vandenhoeck & Ruprecht, 1971. [Reprint of 55.]
82. "The Historical Jesus: Some Comments and Thoughts on Norman Perrin's *Rediscovering the Teachings of Jesus.*" In *Christology and a Modern Pilgrimage: A Discussion with Norman Perrin,* ed. Hans Dieter Betz, 123–36. Claremont, 1971.
83. "One Jesus and Four Primitive Gospels." In 78 (1971) 158–204. [Reprint of 69; German translation in 75.]
84. "σπλάγχνον, σπλαγχνίζομαι, εὔσπλαγχνος, πολύσπλαγχνος, ἄσπλαγχνος." *TDNT* 7:548–59. [English translation of 40.]
85. "The Structure and Criteria of Early Christian Beliefs." In 78 (1971) 205–31. [German translation in 74.]
86. "συνέχω, συνοχή." *TDNT* 7:877–87. [English translation of 51.]
87. "The Theological Aspects of Primitive Christian Heresy." In *The Future of Our Religious Past: Essays in Honor of Rudolf Bultmann,* ed. James M. Robinson, 65–83. New York: Harper & Row, 1971. [English translation of 50.]
88. Eduard Lohse. *Colossians and Philemon: A Commentary on the Epistles to the Colossians and to Philemon,* ed. Helmut Koester. Hermeneia. Philadelphia: Fortress Press, 1971.

1972

89. "τέμνω, ἀποτομία, ἀπότομος, ἀποτόμως, κατατομή, ὀρθοτομέω." *TDNT* 8:106–12. [English translation of 63.]
90. "τόπος." *TDNT* 8:187–208. [English translation of 65.]
91. "ὑπόστασις." *TDNT* 8:572–89. [English translation of 71.]
92. Martin Dibelius and Hans Conzelmann. *The Pastoral Epistles: A Commentary on the Pastoral Epistles,* ed. Helmut Koester. Hermeneia. Philadelphia: Fortress, 1972.

1974

93. (with Charles W. F. Smith) *Lent.* Proclamation, Series A. Philadelphia: Fortress Press, 1974.
94. "Lefkopetra: Inscriptions from the Sanctuary of the Mother of the Gods." *Numina Aegaea* 1 (1974) [3 pages].
95. "φύσις." *TDNT* 9:251–77. [English translation of 76.]

1975

96. (with James M. Robinson) [A Japanese translation of 72/78.] Tokyo: Shinkyo Suppansha, 1975. [This contains Japanese translations of 73/80; 74/85; 75/83; 77/79.]

97. "New Testament Introduction: A Critique of a Discipline." In *Christianity, Judaism, and Other Greco-Roman Cults: Studies for Morton Smith at Sixty,* Volume 1, *New Testament,* ed. Jacob Neusner, 1–20. Studies in Judaism in Late Antiquity 12. Leiden: Brill, 1975.

98. Review of Morton Smith, *Clement of Alexandria and a Secret Gospel of Mark,* and *The Secret Gospel: The Discovery and Interpretation of the Secret Gospel According to Mark,* in *American Historical Review* 80 (1975) 620–22.

1976

99. "Literature, Early Christian." *Interpreter's Dictionary of the Bible: Supplementary Volume,* 551–56. Nashville: Abingdon, 1976.

100. "Philippians, Letter to the." *Interpreter's Dictionary of the Bible: Supplementary Volume,* 665–66.

101. Response to R. H. Fuller, *Longer Mark: Forgery, Interpolation, or Old Tradition?* Protocol of the Colloquy of the Center for Hermeneutical Studies in Hellenistic and Modern Culture 18. Berkeley: The Center for Hermeneutical Studies in Hellenistic and Modern Culture, 1976, 29–32.

102. Martin Dibelius and Hans Greeven. *James: A Commentary on the Epistle of James,* ed. Helmut Koester. Hermeneia. Philadelphia: Fortress Press, 1976.

1977

103. (with Elaine Pagels) "The Dialogue of the Savior (III, 5): Introduction." In *Nag Hammadi Library in English: Translated by Members of the Coptic Gnostic Library Project of the Institute for Antiquity and Christianity,* ed. James M. Robinson, 229. San Francisco: Harper & Row; Leiden: Brill, 1977. [See 140.]

104. "The Gospel of Thomas (II,2): Introduction." In *The Nag Hammadi Library in English: Translated by Members of the Coptic Gnostic Library Project of the Institute for Antiquity and Christianity,* ed. James M. Robinson, 117. San Francisco: Harper & Row; Leiden: Brill, 1977). [See 142.]

1978

105. "Mark 9:43 and Quintilian 8.3.75." *HTR* 71 (1978) 151–53. [Reprinted as 114.]

106. (with Elaine Pagels) "Report on the *Dialogue of the Savior* (CG III, 5)." In *Nag Hammadi and Gnosis: Papers read at the First International Congress of Coptology (Cairo, December 1976),* ed. R. McL. Wilson, 66–74. Nag Hammadi Studies 14. Leiden: Brill, 1978.

1979

107. "Dialog und Spruchüberlieferung in den gnostischen Texten von Nag Hammadi." *Evangelische Theologie* 39 (1979) 532–56.

108. "I Thessalonians—Experiment in Christian Writing." In *Continuity and Discontinuity: Essays Presented to George H. Williams,* ed. F. Forrester Church and Timothy George, 33–44. Leiden: Brill, 1979.
109. Hans Dieter Betz, *Galatians: A Commentary on Paul's Letter to the Churches in Galatia,* ed. Helmut Koester. Hermeneia. Philadelphia: Fortress Press, 1979.

1980

110. *Einführung in das Neue Testament im Rahmen der Religionsgeschichte und Kulturgeschichte der hellenistischen und römischen Zeit.* De Gruyter Lehrbuch. Berlin/New York: de Gruyter, 1980. [English translation in 115 and 116; Spanish translation in 138.]
111. "Apocryphal and Canonical Gospels." *HTR* 73 (1980) 105–30.
112. "Apostel und Gemeinde in den Briefen an die Thessalonicher." In *Kirche: Festschrift für Günther Bornkamm zum 75. Geburtstag,* ed. Dieter Lührmann and Georg Strecker, 287–98. Tübingen: Mohr-Siebeck, 1980.
113. "Gnostic Writings as Witnesses for the Development of the Sayings Tradition." In *The Rediscovery of Gnosticism,* Volume 1, *The School of Valentinus,* ed. Bentley Layton, 238–61. Supplements to Numen 41. Leiden: Brill, 1980.
114. "Using Quintilian to Interpret Mark." *Biblical Archaeology Review* 6:3 (May/June 1980) 44–45. [Reprint of 105.]

1982

115. *History, Culture and Religion of the Hellenistic Age.* Introduction to the New Testament 1. New York/Berlin: de Gruyter, 1982. [English translation of part 1 of 110; corrected paperback edition, 1987.]
116. *History and Literature of Early Christianity.* Introduction to the New Testament 2. New York and Berlin: de Gruyter, 1982. [English translation of part 2 of 110; corrected paperback edition, 1987.]
117. "Foreword." Pp. 9–10 in Ron Cameron, *The Other Gospels: Non-Canonical Gospel Texts.* Philadelphia: Fortress Press, 1982.

1983

118. "Formgeschichte/Formenkritik II: Neues Testament." *Theologische Realenzyklopädie* (1983) 11:286–99.
119. "History and Development of Mark's Gospel (From Mark to *Secret Mark* and 'Canonical' Mark)." In *Colloquy on New Testament Studies: A Time for Reappraisal and Fresh Approaches,* ed. Bruce Corley, 35–57. Macon: Mercer University Press, 1983. ("Seminar Dialogue with Helmut Koester," 59–85).
120. "The Imperial Cult in Greece on the Basis of Archaeological Finds." *Deltion Biblikon Meleton* 12 (1983) 5–14 [in Greek].
121. "Three Thomas Parables." In *The New Testament and Gnosis: Essays in Honor of Robert McL. Wilson,* ed. A. H. B. Logan and A. J. M. Wedderburn, 195–203. Edinburgh: T. & T. Clark, 1983.

1984

122. (with Elaine Pagels) "Introduction." In *Nag Hammadi Codex III,5: The Dialogue of the Savior,* ed. Stephen Emmel, 1–17. Nag Hammadi Studies 26. The Coptic Gnostic Library edited with English Translation, Introduction and Notes published under the auspices of The Institute for Antiquity and Christianity. Leiden: Brill, 1984.
123. "The Synoptic Sayings Source and Wisdom Sayings of Jesus." In *AAR/SBL Abstracts 1984,* ed. K. H. Richards and J. B. Wiggins, 225. Chico, CA: Scholars Press, 1984.
124. "Überlieferung und Geschichte der frühchristlichen Evangelienliteratur." *ANRW* 2.25.2, 1463–1542.

1985

125. "The Churches of Macedonia." *Biblical Illustrator* 11 (1985) 40–49.
126. "The Divine Human Being." *HTR* 78 (1985) 243–52.
127. "Early Christianity from the Perspective of the History of Religions: Rudolf Bultmann's Contribution." In *Bultmann: Retrospect and Prospect,* ed. Edward C. Hobbs, 59–74. Harvard Theological Studies 35. Philadelphia: Fortress Press, 1985.
128. "Harvard (Universität)." *Theologische Realenzyklopädie* (1985) 14:469–72.
129. "In Memoriam George W. MacRae." *HTR* 78 (1985) 233–35.
130. "The Text of 1 Thessalonians." In *The Living Text: Essays in Honor of Ernest W. Saunders,* ed. Dennis E. Groh and Robert Jewett, 219–27. Lanham, MD: University Press of America, 1985.
131. William Schoedel, *Ignatius of Antioch: A Commentary on the Epistles of Ignatius,* ed. Helmut Koester. Hermeneia. Philadelphia: Fortress Press, 1985.

1986

132. "Dedication." In *Christians among Jews and Gentiles: Essays in Honor of Krister Stendahl,* ed. George W. E. Nickelsburg, vii–ix. Philadelphia: Fortress Press, 1986. [= *HTR* 79:1–3 (1986) vii–ix].
133. "The History-of-Religions School, Gnosis, and the Gospel of John." *Studia Theologica* 40 (1986) 115–36.
134. "Gnostic Sayings and Controversy Traditions in John 8:12–59." In *Nag Hammadi, Gnosticism & Early Christianity,* ed. Charles W. Hedrick and Robert Hodgson, Jr., 97–110. Peabody, Mass.: Hendrickson, 1986.

1987

135. (with Holland L. Hendrix) Editor, *Archaeological Resources for New Testament Studies.* Volume 1. Philadelphia: Fortress Press, 1987. [300 pages of text and 282 35mm slides on Athens, Corinth, Olympia, and Thessalonica.]

136. "Athens A." In *Archaeological Resources for New Testament Studies*. Volume 1. Philadelphia: Fortress Press, 1987.
137. "La tradition apostolique et les origines du gnosticisme." *Revue de Théologie et de Philosophie* 119 (1987) 1–16.
[See also 115 and 116.]

1988

138. *Introducción al Nuevo Testamento: Historia, cultura y religión de la época helenística e historia y literatura del cristianismo primitivo*. Biblioteca de Estudios Bíblicos 59. Salamanca: Ediciones Sígueme, 1988. [Spanish translation of 110.]
139. (with Vasiliki Limberis) "Christianity." In *Civilizations of the Ancient Mediterranean: Greece and Rome*, ed. Michael Grant and Rachel Kitzinger, 2:1047–73. 3 vols. New York: Charles Scribner's Sons, 1988.
140. (with Elaine Pagels) "The Dialogue of the Savior (III,5): Introduced." In *The Nag Hammadi Library in English: Translated and Introduced by Members of the Coptic Gnostic Library Project of the Institute for Antiquity and Christianity, Claremont, California*, ed. James M. Robinson, 244–46. 3d ed. San Francisco: Harper & Row, 1988. [See 103.]
141. "The Extra-Canonical Sayings of Jesus as Products of the Christian Community." *Semeia* 44 (1988) 57–77. [An English translation of 5.]
142. "The Gospel of Thomas (II,2): Introduced." In *The Nag Hammadi Library in English: Translated and Introduced by Members of the Coptic Gnostic Library Project of the Institute for Antiquity and Christianity, Claremont, California*, ed. James M. Robinson, 124–26. 3d ed. San Francisco: Harper & Row, 1988. [See 104.]

1989

143. "From the Kerygma-Gospel to Written Gospels." *NTS* 35 (1989) 361–81.
144. "Introduction" to "Tractate 2: The Gospel According to Thomas." In *Nag Hammadi Codex II,2–7 together with XIII,2*, Brit. Lib. Or. 4926 (1), and P. Oxy. 1, 654, 655;* Volume One: *Gospel According to Thomas, Gospel According to Philip, Hypostasis of the Archons, and Indexes*, ed. Bentley Layton, 38–49. The Coptic Gnostic Library edited with English Translation, Introduction and Notes published under the auspices of The Institute for Antiquity and Christianity. Nag Hammadi Studies 20. Leiden: Brill, 1989).
145. "The Text of the Synoptic Gospels in the Second Century." In *Gospel Traditions in the Second Century: Origins, Recensions, Text, and Transmission*, ed. William L. Peterson, 19–37. Christianity and Judaism in Antiquity 3. Notre Dame and London: University of Notre Dame Press, 1989.
146. "Theology and Wisdom in the Earliest Collections of Sayings." *Abstracts: American Academy of Religion/Society of Biblical Literature 1989*, ed. James B. Wiggins and David J. Lull, 99. Atlanta: Scholars Press, 1989.

147. "Three Tributes to James M. Robinson." *Forum* 5/2 (June 1989) 5 [the others are by John S. Kloppenborg (p. 4) and Robert W. Funk (p. 60)].

148. Harold W. Attridge. *The Epistle to the Hebrews: A Commentary on the Epistle to the Hebrews,* ed. Helmut Koester. Hermeneia. Philadelphia: Fortress Press, 1989.

1990

149. *Ancient Christian Gospels: Their History and Development.* London: SCM; Philadelphia: Trinity Press International, 1990.

150. "From Paul's Eschatology to the Apocalyptic Schemata of 2 Thessalonians." *The Thessalonian Correspondence,* ed. Raymond F. Collins, 441–58. Bibliotheca Ephemeridum Theologicarum Lovaniensium 87. Leuven: University Press; Leuven: Peeters, 1990.

151. (with Stephen J. Patterson) "The Gospel of Thomas: Does It Contain Authentic Sayings of Jesus?" *Bible Review* 6:2 (April 1990) 28–39.

152. "Melikertes at Isthmia: A Roman Mystery Cult." *Greeks, Romans, and Christians: Essays in Honor of Abraham J. Malherbe,* ed. David L. Balch, Everett Ferguson, Wayne A. Meeks, 355–66. Minneapolis: Fortress Press, 1990.

153. "Q and Its Relatives." In *Gospel Origins & Christian Beginnings: In Honor of James M. Robinson,* ed. James E. Goehring, Charles W. Hedrick, Jack T. Sanders, with Hans Dieter Betz, 49–63. Forum Fascicles 1. Sonoma, Calif.: Polebridge Press, 1990.

Index of Ancient Sources

Old Testament/ Hebrew Scriptures

Genesis
1:27 218, 222
2:9 65
35:22 145, 146
37:10 146
37:2 145
37:21–22 144, 146
37:4 145
37:5–11 133
44:18–34 144
45:7 143
46:4 143
49 143, 145

Exodus
3:13–15 123
4:22 351
16:18 311
16:1–17:7 66

Leviticus
18:5 353

Numbers
11:7–9 66
20:2–13 66

Deuteronomy
1:1 123
6:5 312n
7:1–8 125
7:17–18 124
7:21 124
7:22 124
7:9 124
9:26 124
9:29 124
10:12 312n
11:13 312n
11:18 312n
12:5 125
13:4 312n
13:6 124
14:23 125
15:11 317n
15:4 317
21:8 124
23:1 127n
25 125
28-30 128
30 125
30:1–10 125
30:1–4 124
30:15 125
30:15–16 353
30:19 125
30:4 125
31 125

Judges
4:17 152n
4:18 152n
4:21 152n
4:22 152n
5:24 152n
5:6 152n
6 122
19 216
19-20 216n

2 Samuel
12:30 223

1 Kings
8 126, 127
8:22–53 126
8:23 126, 128
8:24 127
8:25 127, 128
8:26 127
8:28 127
8:28–29 126
8:30 128
8:32 128
8:36 128
8:46 126
8:46–50 127
8:47f. 126
8:48 126
8:50b–51 126
8:52 128
8:53 126
19:11–13 399
19:19–21 217

2 Kings
2:11 217

Isaiah
11:3 224
13:8 111
23 78
25:6–8 67
26:16 240
28:16 235, 236, 237
34:5–7 65n
40:3 191
53:3–5 127n
54:4–8 68
54:5–55:5 68
61:1 268n

Jeremiah
1:10–11 216n
2:6 212
6 109
6:14 110n
6:24 111
8 109
8:11 110n

Ezekiel
1:1ff 122n
13 109
13:10 110n
13:16 110n
21:26 223
26–28 78
37:27 212
47:8–10 82

Hosea
11:1 351
13:13 111
2:1–23 68

Joel
2:24–26 67n
3:18 67n

Micah
7:6 197

Habakkuk
2:20 399

Zephaniah
1:7 399

Zechariah
13:7 395n
2:13 399
9:15 65n

Psalms
2:1–2 306
2:8–9 363
8 222
8:3 223
8:4 222, 225n
8:5 223
8:6 225n
63:10 212
65:8 399
74:13–14 66n
78:25 66
80:17 223
103:122 212
104:26 66n
107:20 399
110 226
110:1 225
144:3 223

Job
4:12 399
4:16 399
40–44 66n

Proverbs
5:1 376
5:7 376
30:21–23 215n

Song of Solomon
2:15 212

Lamentations
5:18 212

Daniel
4:12 212
4:21 212
7 79, 122n, 205, 215, 221
7:13 4, 216n, 222, 223, 224, 225, 226, 227, 228
7:13–14 221
7:18 221
7:22 221
7:25 221
7:27 221
7:8–12 222
7:9–10 221
8:16 222
8:2 122n
9:27 272n
9:4 124
10:16 222n
10:18 222n
11:31 272n
12:11 272n

Ezra
5:11 123
6:9 123
7:12 123
9:6ff. 123
10 123
10:18–44 152n

Nehemiah
1 125, 127
1:1 122, 126
1:2 129
1:3 129
1:5 124, 126, 129
1:5–11 3
1:6 123, 126, 127, 128, 129
1:7 128
1:8 126, 128
1:9 125
1:10 124, 128, 129
1:11 123, 128, 127, 129
2:1–10 122
2:8 122, 124
2:16 129
2:20 128
2:3–5 127
3:33–4:17 124, 129
3:36 128
4:1 124
4:3 212
4:4 124
4:6 129
4:14 128
5 128
5:1 129
5:8 129
5:9 128
5:14 129
5:17 129
5:18 129
6:6 129
6:7 127
7:6 129
9 126, 128
9:14 128
9:26 127n
9:32–37 127, 129
9:37 127n
10 128
10:30 128
11:3 129
12:26 129
13 128
13:23 129
13:27 128

2 Chronicles
6 126
6:42 126

New Testament/ Christian Scriptures

Q (cited from Luke)
3:16 192
3:16–17 190, 97
3:7–9 190, 197
4:1–13 193
4:3 188
6:20–23 185
6:20–49 199, 385
6:20b–21 187
6:22 188
6:22–23 183
6:23c 184
6:27–33 185
6:27–36 186
6:27–38 187
6:35 188
6:35b–37a 185
6:37–42 186
6:38b 185
6:39 187
6:40 255n
6:41–42 185, 187
6:42–44 187
6:43–45 186
6:43–49 185
6:46–48 187
6:52 187
7:1 191
7:1–10 197
7:18 255n
7:18–28 208
7:18–35 197
7:19 192
7:24 191
7:25 190
7:31–35 208
7:34 181, 188, 191
7:35 188
9 188
9:57–58 216
9:58 181, 188, 191
9:59 189, 255n
10:1–16 199
10:2 189
10:2 255n
10:2–11 191

Q (cont.)
10:2–16 247
10:2–8a 185
10:3 192
10:4 191
10:9 176, 179
10:9–11a 185
10:12 185
10:15 191
10:16 185
10:16 192
11:2–4 185, 200
11:9–13 186, 187, 200
11:14–52 197, 208
11:30 181, 188, 192
11:31–32 188
11:42c 193
11:47–51 183
11:49 192
11:49–51 184, 188
12:2–12 200
12:2–3 185
12:2–9 186, 208
12:8 189, 192
12:8–9 108n, 182n, 183n, 186n
12:10 185, 188
12:22 255n
12:22–31 185, 186, 187, 208
12:22–34 385
12:33–34 185, 187
12:35–37 185
12:39–40 185
12:39–59 197, 385
12:4–9 187
12:40 189, 192
12:49–59 208
13:25 189
13:28–30 208
13:34 192
13:34–35 183, 184, 188, 208
13:35 192
14:16–24 208
14:17 192
14:26–27 255n, 392
16:13 189
16:17 193
16:17–18 187
17:23–30 182
17:23–37 197
17:24 184n, 189, 192
17:26 189
17:26–27 184n, 192
17:30 189, 192

Matthew
1:1 273
1:2–17 273
2:9 400
3:1 269n
3:1–2 266
3:1–12 273
3:2 267, 268n, 273
3:6 266
3:11–12 273
3:15 266, 267
3:17 267
3:20 215
4:1–11 267
4:12–16 267
4:13 78n
4:17 267
4:17 268n, 269n, 273
4:17a 247n
4:17b 247n
4:18–22 269
4:23 246n
4:23 267, 268, 269, 269n
4:23–5:2 260
4:24–25 265
4:8 265n
5 207
5–7 186, 371n
5:1–2 265, 266, 269
5:2 269n
5:3–7:27 258n, 266
5:6 68n
5:9 275n
5:10 271n
5:11 188, 271n
5:12 271n
5:13 275
5:13–16 275n
5:14–14 275
5:19 266, 269n
5:20 266, 273
5:25–26 463
5:38–48 207
5:44 271n
5:45 275n
6:9 255n
6:11–12 199
6:25 255n
7:15 273n
7:22 189
7:24–27 263, 266
7:28–29 251, 260, 266, 269
7:29 266, 269n, 273
8:1 265n
8:1–10 66n
8:5–12 274
8:11–12 68, 274n
8:12 275n
8:14 79n
8:18–22 218n
8:19 269n
8:19–20 210, 211
8:20 210, 215, 217, 218
8:21 255n
8:23–27 217
8:34 217
9:1 78n
9:9 246n, 263
9:11 269n
9:14 255n
9:15 68n, 275n
9:25 246
9:35 246n, 267, 268, 269n
9:36 273n, 274
9:36–38 273
9:37 255n
10 176
10:1 270
10:2–5 270
10:3 263
10:5–6 193
10:5b–42 273
10:5b–6 273
10:7 176, 179, 268n, 269n, 273
10:17–18 273n
10:22 238n, 269n
10:23 176, 178, 193, 271n
10:24 269n
10:25 255n
10:26 437
10:41 266
11 176
11:1 266, 269n
11:1–19 274
11:5 268
11:8 190n
11:16 274
11:16 274n
11:19 68n
11:21–33 78
11:23 78n
12:11–12 273n
12:28 78
12:29 274n
12:38 269n
12:39–45 274
12:41 269n, 274n
12:42 274n
12:45 274n
13:1–2 274
13:1–3 246n
13:1–52 385
13:2–3 274
13:3 274
13:10 274
13:10–13 274
13:11 246, 274
13:13 274
13:16–17 275
13:21 271n
13:34–36 274
13:36 275
13:36–43 275n
13:37–38a 275
13:40–41 192
13:51 275
13:51–53 274n
13:53 266
13:54 269n
14:12 255n
14:13–21 66n, 68n
14:14 246n, 274
14:23 265n
14:34 78n
15:9 269n
15:24 273n

Matthew (*cont.*)
15:32 274
15:32–39 66n, 68n
15:39 78n
16:4 274n
16:13 78n
16:21 246n
16:25 247n
17:17 274n
17:18 246
17:22 246n
17:24 269n
17:25–26 275n
18–19 371n
18:10–14 273n
18:15 374
18:15–17 371
18:27 274
19 266
19:1 266
19:2 246n
19:17 270
19:28 271
19:29 247n, 248
19:30 275, 421n
20:16 275
20:26 421n
20:34 274
21:13 246n
21:23 269n
21:23–27 274n
21:28–32 274n, 275
21:28–46 275n
21:33–41 275
21:33–46 274n, 275n
21:43 275
21:43–46 274n
21:45 275
22:1–14 274n, 275
22:1–10 68
22:1–14 68n
22:14 275, 465
22:16 269n
22:24 269n
22:26 255n
22:28–30 68n
22:32 274
22:36 269n
22:41–42 246n
22:46 274
23:1 246n
23:3 270
23:8 269n
23:12 421n
23:15 167
23:34 271n
23:36 274n
23:37–39 277
24 207, 239n, 266, 272
24–25 262
24:1 274
24:3 271
24:4–5 272
24:11 272
24:13 238n
24:14 246n, 267, 269
24:15 272
24:16–20 272
24:21–29 271n, 272
24:23–28 272
24:24 272
24:25 272
24:26 193
24:30–31 272
24:34 274n
24:36 271
24:4 271, 272
24:42 272
24:44 272
24:5 271, 272
24:6 271
24:7 271
24:8 271
24:9 271n
24:9–14 271
25 272
25:1–13 68n
25:10 272
25:11 189
25:13 272
25:32–33 273n
26:1 266
26:13 246n, 267, 268, 269n
26:17–30 272
26:18 269n
26:31 273n
26:55 269n
27:4 266
27:25 193
27:32 462
27:36 270
27:45–51 400n
27:54 270
28:4 270
28:15 269n
28:16–20 273
28:18–20 193, 269, 270, 271
28:19 272, 275n
28:19b 231n
28:20 263, 269n

Mark
1:1 268n
1:1–6:44 244
1:3 191
1:4 191
1:6 191, 251n
1:9 78n, 251n
1:12–13 267
1:14 251n, 268n
1:14a 267
1:14b–15 267
1:15 179, 268n
1:15a 247n
1:15b 247n
1:16 251n
1:16–4:34 78n
1:17 251n
1:19 251n
1:21 191
1:21–2:12 78n
1:22 266
1:23 251n
1:24 78n
1:26 251n
1:27 246n, 251
1:29 252n
1:29–31 79
1:36 252n
1:39 246n, 268
2:1 191
2:13 246n
2:18 255n
2:19–20 68n
2:22–28 247
2:27 247
3:13 265
4–6 249
4:1–2 246n
4:1–20 250n
4:1–34 248n, 385
4:3 252n
4:10–11 463
4:11 246
4:11–12 250, 257
4:12 247
4:14–20 252n
4:26 252
4:31 252
4:35–41 254
5:1 78n
5:41 246
6:1 78n
6:4 216n
6:6 246n
6:7–13 23
6:7–14 247
6:29 255n
6:30 176
6:30 246n
6:30–44 254
6:32–44 66n, 68n
6:34 246n
6:45 78, 85
6:45–52 250, 254
6:45–8:26 79n, 245, 246, 248, 249, 250
6:46 265n
6:52 247
6:52b 250
6:53 78n
7:1 78
7:1–13 250
7:1–23 250n
7:6–13 250
7:14 247
7:14–23 250
7:18 247, 250
8:1–10 68n, 254
8:10 78n
8:13 79

Mark (cont.)
8:14–21 250
8:17 247
8:21 247
8:21 254
8:22 78n
8:22–26 79, 87, 246
8:22a 79
8:23 79
8:26b 79
8:27–16:8 244
8:31 246n
8:34–35 392
8:35 247n, 268n
8:38 180n, 197n, 408n
9:1 179
9:2 265n
9:9 265n
9:19 197n
9:25 246
9:31 246n
9:33 78n
9:35 421n
10 252
10:1 246n
10:29 247, 268n
10:31 421n
10:32 244, 253
10:32–34 251
10:39 246
10:45 421n
10:46 245
10:47 78n
11:1 265n
11:17 246n
12:1 252
12:32–34 248
12:35 246n
12:37–38 246n
13 207, 227n, 385
13:3 265n
13:9–10 273n
13:10 246n, 268n
13:13b 232, 235, 238, 239
13:14 247, 272n
13:21 193
13:26 3, 226, 228
13:28–29 179
13:30 179, 197n
14:7 317n
14:9 246n, 268
14:26 265n
14:27 395n
14:47 252
14:51–52 246, 251, 252, 253
14:62 226n
14:62a 225
15:20 462
15:21 252, 320
15:29 265n
15:33–38 400n
16:5 253n
16:6 78n
16:9–15 241n
16:9–20 245, 249
16:10b 231
16:13b 231, 236
16:14 231
16:15 231, 268n
16:16 229, 230, 231, 232, 233, 234, 236, 240, 241
16:17–18 241n
16:17a 231
16:19 241n
16:20a 241n
16:20b 241n
17:1 265n
17:9 265n

Luke
1 303
1:1–4 301
1:67–79 306
2:8 403
2:8–14 398
2:11 304
2:17 373n
2:20 373n
2:29–32 303, 376n
2:33–35 303
2:41–52 26
2:42 312
3:2 252n
3:7–9 203
3:9 197
3:9–11 204
3:16–17 203, 204
3:17 197
3:19–22 277
3:23 26
4:1f 321
4:14–30 303
4:31–32 251
4:34 317
4:36 246n
4:38 79n
5:1 252n
5:27 246n
5:33 255n
5:34 252n
5:34–35 68n
6:12 265
6:20–21 199
6:20–49 203, 204, 207
6:20a 265
6:20b–49 259
6:21 68n
6:27–49 205
6:27–35 207
6:27–36 199
6:27–38 203
6:27–45 203
6:46–49 203
7:1 78n, 265
7:1–9 197
7:18–28 198
7:18–35 203
7:22 373n
7:25 190n
7:31–35 198, 206
7:34 68n, 246, 408n
8:4 246n
8:9 252n
8:10 246
8:54 246
9:10 78, 87, 246n, 252n
9:10–17 66n, 68n
9:11 246n
9:17 246
9:22 246n
9:24 246
9:26 408n
9:28 265n
9:33 252n
9:37 265n
9:43–44 246n
9:57–62 210, 211
9:58 210, 215, 217, 218
10:1–16 208
10:2–19 203
10:3–37 450
10:5–8 199
10:9 204
10:11 204
10:13 79
10:13–15 78, 198
10:15 78n
10:30 252n
10:33 252n
10:38 252n
11:1 252n
11:2–4 203, 208
11:9–13 203
11:14–20 206
11:14–23 206
11:14–26 197
11:14–52 203
11:20 78, 204
11:29–31 197n
11:29–32 197
11:29–32 198, 205
11:30 182
11:39–52 197, 203
11:47–51 205
11:49–51 197n, 198, 205
12 78, 205
12:2 206
12:2–12 203, 204
12:3–9 206
12:8–9 205, 206, 182
12:13–14 198, 385
12:16–21 385
12:20 252n
12:22–31 199, 203, 205
12:22–13:21 204
12:33–34 203
12:33a 198
12:35 207, 385
12:39–40 203
12:40 197, 205, 206, 207

Luke (*cont.*)
12:42–46 197, 203
12:49 197, 202, 385
12:49–56 204
12:51–53 197, 202
12:52 206
12:54–56 197, 202
12:57–59 204
12:58 463
13–17 186n
13:18–21 204
13:28–29 68, 204, 206, 274n
13:28–30 198, 203
13:34 216n
13:34–35 198, 203, 205, 206, 277, 305
14 205
14:7–11 68n
14:16–24 68, 68n, 198, 203
14:18 316
14:26–27 203
14:34–35 203
15 205
15:4–7 203
15:11 252n
16 205
16:1 252n
16:13 203
16:16 204
16:17 203
16:18 203
16:19–31 68n
16:20 252n
17 205
17:1–4 208
17:1–6 203
17:20–21 192, 201n
17:23 192
17:23–30 206, 197
17:23–37 203, 204, 205, 208
17:24 205
17:26 205
17:27 197
17:29 197
17:30 205
18:2 252n
18:2–8a 179
18:18–25 316
18:29 248
18:35 252n
19:11–27 305
19:12 252n
19:29 265n
19:38–44 303
19:41–44 305
19:44 306, 308
19:46 246n
19:48 306
20:6 306
20:9–19 305
20:26 306
20:41 246n
20:45 246n
21:1 265n
21:19 239n
21:22 308
21:24 308
22 306
22:2 306
22:4 306
22:6 306
22:22 306
22:24 306
22:28–30 203, 204, 208
22:31–34 306
22:39 265n
22:48 408n
22:54–62 306
22:69 226n
23:14–25 306
23:26 462
23:27 305, 306
23:28 306
23:34 305
23:35 305, 306
23:35–38 305
23:44–45 400n
23:46 305
23:47 305
23:47 306
23:48 306
23:49 306
24:3 265n
24:12 281
24:13–35 306
24:24 281
24:42–43 66n
24:46 307
24:47 307, 308
24:49 307
28:16 265n

John
1:1–11 69n
1:11 296
1:31 290n
1:44 79
1:44 83, 87
1:45–51 290
1:47 290n
1:49 290n
2:1 78n
2:1–11 68n
2:12 191
2:13 290
2:23 289
3:1 292, 295
3:1–21 289, 291, 292
3:2 292, 298n
3:3 292
3:10 290n, 292
3:11 373
3:16–18 292
3:18 229n, 230n, 231, 232, 233, 234, 236, 237, 240
3:19–21 292
3:23 373
3:29 69n
3:29–30 376
3:31 229n
3:36 229n
3:39 68
3:7 292
3:9 292
4:1 376
4:4–6 296
4:9 288n
4:10–14 66
4:12 296
4:13–14 229n, 297
4:34 34
4:46 78n, 191
5:43 229n
6:1–15 66n, 68n
6:25–59 66
6:28 34
6:31–33 296
6:49–51 296
6:53–54 70, 73
6:58 296
7:11–13 291
7:13 289
7:38 299
7:39–41 299
7:43 289
7:45–52 295
7:48 294
7:48–52 298n
7:50–52 289, 293
7:51 293
8:26 373
8:30 289
8:32 449, 450
8:34 450
8:38 373
8:49–51 297
8:52–53 297
9 290
9:1–7 297, 299
9:8–12 297
9:11 298
9:13–17 298
9:16 289, 299
9:17 298
9:18–23 291, 298, 299
9:20–21 298
9:22 289, 298
9:24–34 298
9:33 298
9:35 438n
9:35–37 299
9:35–38 298
9:39 229n
9:39–41 299
10:19–21 289
10:32–33 34
11 78n
11:9–10 229n
11:45 289

John (cont.)
12:10–11 291
12:11 289
12:13 290n
12:21 79
12:21 83, 86
12:42 289
12:42–43 289n, 291, 295
12:43 289
13–17 281
13:23 281
15:2 229n
15:11 376
15:15 373
16:1–4 291
16:20 376
16:21 376
16:22 376
16:24 376
17:13 376
17:4 34
19:25–27 281
19:38 289
19:38–42 289, 291, 294, 295
19:39 294
20:2–10 281
20:19 289
20:23 231n
20:30 288
20:30–31 287
21:2 281
21:7 281
21:9–14 66n

Acts
1:4–8 307
2 310, 311, 315
2:34 225
2:36–37 305
2:36–38 307
2:38 307
2:38–39 307
2:38–42 316
2:42 317
2:42–47 318
3:12–15 307
3:14–15 304
3:16 373n
3:17 305n
3:19 307
3:19–24 307
3:21 307
4 311, 315
4:10–12 307
4:20 373n
4:26–27 306
4:27 306, 308
4:32–5:11 318
4:33 317
4:36 320
4:36–37 310
5 315
5:1–11 310
5:3–4 316
5:13 317
5:30–31 307
5:31 304, 307
5:39 304
6 318
6:5 464
7:55–56 226, 401
7:56 225
7:60 305n
9 122n
9:11 319, 320n
9:23–25 325
9:26 325
9:26–30 327
9:29 327
9:30 319
10 278
10:38 304
10:39–43 307
10:43 307
10:44 307
11:17 304
11:18 307
11:25 319
12:12 314
13:16 279
13:23 304
13:26 279
13:27 305, 306
13:28–39 307
13:38–39 307
13:43 279
13:50 279
15:7 268
15:23 360
16:14 279, 280
17:4 279
17:17 279
17:30 305n
18:7 279, 280
19:26 373n
20:24 268
21:24 280
21:39 319, 320
22:3 319, 320
22:25–29 319
23:26 360
26:9–20 304
26:18 307
28 308
28:23–29 303

Romans
1 23
1–3 352
1–4 351, 357
1–16 338
1:1 342, 344
1:1–15 342, 343
1:1–2 343
1:1–7 342
1:3–5 343
1:4–5 344
1:6–10 343, 344
1:8–15 342, 345
1:11–2:21 344
1:13 345
2 28
2:14–15 34
2:17–3:20 352
2:19f. 165
3:1–4:31 344
3:9 354
3:19 354
3:23 354
3:25 364
4:3 237n
5 30, 352
5–6 357
5–8 5, 354
5–9 351
5:1 344
5:11 352
5:19 355
6 352, 354
6:17 360
7 352
7–8 348
7:3 353
7:8–12 352
7:9–13 352
7:14 353
7:15–19 350
7:15–23 353
7:17 352
7:18 352
7:20 352
7:23 352
7:25 353
8 352, 356
8:3 355, 356
8:6 355
8:7 355
8:7–27 355
8:9 352
8:9–11 354
8:10 354
8:11 352
9–11 23, 356
9:17 237n
9:33 237n
10:9 232, 235, 236, 237, 240
10:11 232, 235, 236, 237, 240
10:14–21 234n
11 28
11:13 237n
11:23 357
12:3 332
15 23, 28, 30, 337
15:3 33
15:3–16:24 339
15:6 193
15:8 33
15:14–33 338, 342, 343, 345

Romans (cont.)
15:14–16:24 337
15:19–25 33
15:22 345
15:30 341
15:30–32 339, 340, 341, 346
15:30–33 342, 345
15:30–16:32 340
15:33 339, 340, 341, 347n
15:33–16:24 339
16 337, 340, 342
16:1 153n
16:1–2 339
16:1–16 342
16:1–23 337, 340
16:1–24 342
16:16 339
16:16a 342
16:16b 341, 342
16:17–19 340
16:17–20 339, 347n
16:17–20a 338, 341, 342, 345, 346
16:17–24 340, 342
16:2 162 n
16:3–15 339, 341
16:3–16 340
16:3–16a 341
16:20 341
16:20a 340, 345
16:20b 339, 340
16:21–23 339, 340, 341
16:24 339, 340
16:25–27 338, 339

1 Corinthians
1:1–19 343n
1:10–4:21 346
2:1–5 414
2:6 447
2:8–9 200
3:6–15 24
4 23
4:6 341
4:14 415
4:18 417
4:18–21 415
4:26 341
5:9–11 415
7:1–10 447
7:1ff. 453
8:1 449
8:1–9 449
8:1b 450
9 23
9:15 415
9:19 450
9:19–23 30
9:22 420
10 24
10:1–13 66n
10:18 473
11:24–25 73
13:11 332
15:12 111
15:22–28 191
16:1–18 346
16:5–7 415
16:10 34
16:15 341
16:15–18 346
16:19–20 341
16:19–24 346
16:20 341
16:22 361
16:23 361

2 Corinthians
1:13–14 415
1:15–16 415
1:15–23 417
1:23 415
2:4 416
2:14–7:4 23
4:7 414
5:12 26
6:4–10 25
7:8–11 416
8:14–15 311
10–13 23, 332, 334
10:1–2 417
10:10 415, 416
10:11 28, 417
11:2 68
11:3 352
11:6 414
11:12 26
11:22–33 26
11:28 415n
11:32f 323, 324, 325
13 332
13:1 341
13:10 417
13:11 341, 345
13:12 341
13:12–13 341

Galatians
1:3 361
1:5 361
1:8 278
1:16 321
1:17 320, 321, 325
1:18 322, 325
1:18–19 326
1:18f. 326
1:19 327
1:21 321, 325
1:22 328
1:22–24 326
1:23 326
2:1 322
2:1–10 273
2:9 254n
2:16 351
2:20 351
3:10–12 351
3:23–4:7 29
3:26–28 351
4:3 351
4:4 279, 355
4:4–5 356
4:4–7 351
4:8–10 351
4:30 237n
5:8 351
5:10 332
5:16 350
5:16–6:10 5, 350
5:17 350, 353
5:18 350
5:19–21 350
5:22–23 27, 350
6:1–2 374
6:4 34
6:8 350
6:16 341, 345

Ephesians
2:8 463
2:16 236n
3:1–7 247n
5:23–32 68
5:32 445
6:19 247n

Philippians
1:4 334
1:5 334
1:6 34
1:7 334
1:9–11 333
1:10 333
1:12 418n
1:14–18 334
1:18 334
1:20 334
1:21–26 334
1:23 355
1:27 333
1:27–28 334
1:29 334
1:29–30 334
1:30 334
2 5, 30, 355
2:2 334
2:2–4 334
2:11 355
2:12 335
2:19–23 334
2:21 334
2:25–30 334
2:3 335
2:5 332
2:5–11 330n, 355
2:6 30, 335
2:6–11 331, 335, 435
2:6c 236n
2:8 335, 355
2:30 34

Philippians (*cont.*)
2:30 334, 335
3:1 334
3:2 332
3:4–16 334
3:4b–14 332
3:10–11 333
3:15 332
3:17 332
3:18–19 332
3:20–21 333, 355
3:25–39 334
4:1 334
4:2 334, 340, 341
4:4 334
4:7 341, 345
4:9 339, 345
4:9b 341
4:10 334
4:10–13 34
4:11 334
4:15–16 334
4:19 339
4:21–22 341

Colossians
1:15–20 435
1:20 236n
2:1 418n
2:8 27
2:14 236n

1 Thessalonians
1:1 361
1:6 118n
2:14 118n, 328
2:17–18 415n
3:3–4 118n
3:10 415n
4:1–5:22 347n
4:13–18 118n
4:13–5:11 109
5:1–11 109n, 111, 112
5:12 340, 341
5:12–22 347n
5:23 341, 345, 347n
5:26 341

1 Timothy
1:2 371
1:3–5 371
1:6–7 371
1:18 371
3 372
4:1–3 371
4:18 237n
5:17 372
5:19–21 371
5:3 372
6:1 372
6:14–16 371

2 Timothy
1:2 371
1:4 376
1:13–14 371
2:1 371
2:1–2 371
2:2–10 372
3:1–17 371
3:14–15 371
4:3–4 371
4:6 376

Titus
1:1–3 371
1:4 371
1:7–9 372
3:10 374
3:10–11 371

Hebrews
13:22 341

James
1:1 3n, 360
1:27 318
5:13–20 371, 374

1 Peter
2:6 237n
4 462
4:8 450

1 John
1:1–3 371, 372, 373
1:3 373
1:4 372, 376
1:6–10 371
1:8–10 368
2:1 371
2:12–14 372, 375
2:15–17 368
2:18–27 375
2:28 371
3:15 375
3:18 377
4:1–6 372
5:6–8 372
5:13 367
5:14–21 367, 374n
5:16–17 368, 371, 374

2 John
1 374
3 362
4 374
12 376
13 374

3 John
4 374

Revelation
1:1 358
1:3 360
1:4 360, 361
1:4f. 362
1:5 362, 364
1:5b–6 362
1:5f 363
1:9 401
2:2 365
2:6 364, 464
2:7 65n
2:14 359
2:15 464
2:16 364
2:18 363
2:24 365
7:14 364
9 69n
12 438
12:3–9 66
14 65n
18:20 360
19 65n
19:7–9 69n
21:1 66
21:2 69n
21:6 364
21:14 360
22:1–2 66
22:2 65n
22:14 364
22:17 69n, 364
22:17–19 66
22:20 363
22:21 363

Apocrypha and Pseudepigrapha

Ascension of Isaiah
3:17–21 236
3:18 235

Baruch
3:9–4:4 353

2 Baruch
29:1–4 66n, 68
67:6 307
68:5–6 307
84:10 307
85:4 307

1 Enoch
1–5 215
2:1–2 216
24–25 65n
42 216
45 224
48:2–7 224
55 224
58–69 440
60:24 66n
60:7–10 66n
62:12–14 67
88:1 346
91–105 349

2 Enoch
22:10B 346
24:3A 346

1 Esdras
10:18–44 152n
10:26 152
10:43 152

4 Ezra
1:19 66
6:49–52 66n
7:28–29 224
7:39–43 399, 403
8:52 65n
9:19 67n
13 223
13:32 223
13:37 223
13:52 223
48 224
48:10 224
52 224
52:1–4 224
52:5–9 224
69:24–29 224

Joseph and Asenath
16:14–16 66
16:8 66
passim 70

1 Maccabees
1:54 272n
2:58 217

2 Maccabees
14:35 212n
7:19 304

4 Maccabees
passim 25n

Odes of Solomon
6:8–18 66

Sirach
17:30 212
24 353
36:33 214
46:4 399
48:9 217

Sibylline Oracles
3.199–201 399
8.474–75 398

Testament of Benjamin
6:4 350

Testament of Dan
5:1 350

Testament of Joseph
10:2–3 350

Testament of Levi
18:11 65n

Testament of Reuben
6:4 350

Tobit
1:4 212n

Wisdom of Solomon
1–6 349
1:1–7 350
1:4–7 353
1:12 350
2:17–24 304
2:24 350
2:33–3:4 350
3–5 26
4:7–14 26
5:13 350
7:22–30 350
7:27 353
9:8 212n
16:20 66
18:14–15 398, 399

New Testament Apocrypha

Acts of Thomas
13–14 412
27 406, 407n, 409
50 407n
66 408n
passim 5

Apocalypse of James
passim 229

Apocryphum Josephi
18–20 397

Arabian Infancy Gospel
3 400n

De nativitate Mariae
10:2 404n

Epistolae Senecae et Pauli
1 418n
2 420
4 418n, 419, 420
5 418n
6 419, 420
7 419
8 420
9 419
10 420
12 421
14 420, 421
passim 417

Epistula apostolorum
13 408n

Gospel of Peter
10:39–42 236n

Protevangelium of James
1–10 393
9:3 393
11 393
12 393
13–14 393
15–16 393
17–18.1 393
18:2–3 393
19 393
19:2 400n
20 393
21 393
22 393
23–24 393
25 393

Pseudo-Matthew
13:2 400n, 404n

Secret Gospel of Mark
passim 242
In Clement of Alexandria, *Ad Theodorum*
1v 23 252
1v22–2r11 244
2r 14–15 252
2r14–16 244

Story of Joseph the Carpenter
7 404n

Qumran Scrolls

1QH
i.21–27 350
iv.29–33 350
xii.24–35 350
xiii.13–21 350
xiii.14 351

1QS
i 371
iii.20–22 352
iii.13–iv.26 349
iii.18–iv.1 349
iii.20 349
iii.21 349
iii.24 49
iii–iv 348, 353
iv.2–6 350
iv.15–26 349
iv.16–17 350
iv.23–25 350
iv.6–8 53
iv.9–11 350
v.1–2 312
v.8–9 351
v.12 312
v.25–26 37
v.25–vi.1 371
xi.9 349

1QS (*cont.*)
xi.9–22 349
xi.20–22 350
xi.21 351

1 QSa
ii.11–20 71
ii.11–22 71

Nag Hammadi & Gnostic Writings

Apocryphon of James (NHC I, *2*)
5, 9–6, 7 439
9, 24–35 439
10, 1–6 439
14, 14–18 439
15, 35–16, 30 439
15, 5–27 440n

Apocalypse of Adam (NHC V, *5*)
77, 27–82, 19 437

Apocalypse of Peter (NHC VII, *3*)
78, 31–79, 20 411
82, 17–83, 15 462n

Apocryphon of John (NHC II, *1*)
4, 34–5, 11 411
passim 458

Dialogue of the Savior (NHC III, *5*)
120, 3–8 440
120, 26 441
124, 23–144, 17 440
127, 19–128, 23 440
129, 16–131, 18 440
129, 20–131, 16 440
131, 17–18 440
132, 9–18 441
132, 19–133, 24 440n
133, 23–134, 24 440
134, 24–137, 3 440
137, 9–138, 2 441
139, 6–7 439
139, 8–13 441
140, 1–14 441n
143, 6–10 441
144, 6–8 441
144, 12–145, 7 441
144, 15 410
145, 23–34 439

Eugnostos the Blessed (NHC II, *3;* V, *1*)
passim 460

Exegesis on the Soul (NHC II, *6*)
127, 22–24 410n
127, 24 133, 11 410n
132, 1–15 410n

Gospel of Mary (BG *1*)
8 193
8, 15–19 193

Gospel of Philip (NHC II, *3*)
44 448
53, 15–20 448
53, 17 449
53, 23–29 448
54, 14 447
54, 18–23 448
56, 34–57, 8 448
57, 11–12 449
59, 23ff 448
65 448
65, 1–26 410n
66, 5–7 449
67 448
68, 35ff. 448
70, 9–21 410n
73, 33–35 454
74, 4–5 454
74, 5–10 448
74, 5–13 454
77, 14 450
77, 14–84, 11 453
77, 16–84, 12 449
77, 27 450
77, 31–35 450
77, 66ff. 450
78, 11–12 450
78, 12–25 450
78, 21 451
78, 26–79, 12 450
78, 32–79, 5 451
79, 20ff. 451
79, 34 451
80, 9–10 451
81, 35–82, 26 451
81, 8–14 451
82, 19–23 451
82, 2–8 444
82, 26–29 452
82, 28 448
82:3–8 444
83, 18–29 452
83, 30–32 452
84, 12–15 453
84, 2–11 453
93 448
124 448
127 448
passim 5

Gospel of Thomas (NHC II, *2*)
3 193
5 206
5–6 206
6 207, 453
10 202
11 200
12 387, 391
13 387, 391
14 202
16 202, 441n
17 200
18 200, 201n, 391, 441n
19 200
21 202
23 441n
35 206
39 206
42 219
47 202
50 217
51 200, 201n, 217, 391
55 391
56 219
60 217
61 217
64 68
73 206
80 219
83 218
84 218
85 200, 218
86 4, 210, 215, 217, 218
87 218
89 206
90 217
91 202
101 391
104 69n
111 200
113 201n, 391
144 411
passim 3, 5, 184n, 185, 187, 188, 195, 200, 201, 205, 209, 255n, 383, 384, 386, 388

Gospel of Truth (NHC I, *3*)
passim 459

Hypostasis of the Archons (NHC II, *5*)
83, 4–85, 18 437
95, 11–13 436
95, 13–96, 3 436
95, 31–34 436
96, 18–28 436
105, 23–29 437

On the Origin of the World (NHC II, *5*)
125, 14–19 437

Second Treatise of the Great Seth (NHC VII, *2*)
55,30–56,19 462n

Sophia of Jesus Christ (NHC III, *4;* BG *3*)
102 408n
115 408n
passim 460

Testimony of Truth (NHC IX, *3*)
30, 18 410n

Thomas the Contender (NHC II, *7*)
144, 8 410n

Three Steles of Seth (NHC VII, *5*)
121, 21–124, 14 411n

Trimorphic Protennoia (NHC XIII, *1*)
38, 24–25 438n
47, 13–15 437

Zostrianos (NHC VIII, *1*)
5,15–17 436
128, 15–18 436
130, 20 410

Basilides, *Exegetica*
23 462

Excerpta ex Theodoto
38.3 437
43.2–65 465n
56.2 465
58.1 465n
68 408
78–79 409

Hellenistic Jewish Writers

Josephus
Against Apion
1.10 §53 142
1.13 §§69–72 143

Antiquities of the Jews
1 Proem 2 §§5–9 143
1 Proem 2 §6 143
1 Proem 2 §8 143
1 Proem 3 §8 -143
1 Proem 4 §17 142
1 Proem 4 23 143
1.2.2 §61 80
1.11.1 §194 80
2.1.1 §1 144
2.2.1 §7 144
2.2.1 §§7–8 144
2.2.1 §8 144
2.2.1–2.8.2 §§7–200 143
2.2.3 §§15–16 146
2.2.4 §17 146
2.3.1 §§21–28 146
2.3.1 §23 146
2.3.1–2 §§20–31 144
2.3.1–3 §§20–33 146
2.4.1 §40 147
2.4.1–5 §§39–59 147
2.4.2 §42 148
2.4.2 §43 148
2.4.4 §52 148
2.4.5 §53 148
2.5.1 §60 148
2.5.2 §69 148
2.6.8 §140 147
2.6.8 §§140–58 144, 146
2.6.8 §141 147
2.6.8 §143 147
2.6.8 §145 147
2.6.8 §146 147
2.6.8 §§147–52 147
2.6.9 §§160–61 147
2.7.2–3 §§170–75 143
2.8.2 §198 147
7.14.10 §376 153
9.4.4 §60 80
8.4.6 §108 81n
11.8.3 §315 80
14.10.22 §§247–48 113
15.10.4 §371 311
18.2.1 §§27f. 89
18.2.1 §28 79, 81, 83, 85, 87, 90
18.2.3 §§36–38 80
18.4.1 §86 80
18.8.1 §§257–60 133
19.5.1 133n
20.5.2 §100 139
passim 3

Jewish War
1.21.2 §403 80
2.8.3 §§122–23 312
2.9.1 §§167f. 89
2.9.1 §168 81n, 89
2.18.7–8 §§487–97 140
3.3.1 §37 86
3.3.5 §57 81n
3.10.7 §515 81
4.7.5 §432 80
4.8.2 §454 81n
6 §333 307
6 §339 307
6 §399 307

Life
398 81n
398–406 81
399 81n
406 81n, 85

Philo
De Abrahamo
195 140n
passim 136n

De agricultura
55–56 137
55–66 138
56 138
59 138

De animalibus
passim 140

De Cherubim
128 138

De confusione linguarum
71–72 138

De fuga et inventione
126–31 137

De Iosepho
157 153
67 153
passim 136, 137, 139

De legatione ad Gaium
8 60
10 60
13 60
117–18 136
155–61 136
182 133, 140
356 60

De migratione Abrahami
16–24 137, 138
158–63 137
203–7 137

De mutatione nominum
171–74 137
214–15 137
89–96 137

De opificio mundi
103–5 140n
113 62

De posteritate Caini
78–82 138

De praemiis et poenis
65 137

De providentia
passim 139

De sobrietate
1.54–58 137
10–15 137, 138

De somniis
1.168 140n
1.219–25 139
2 135, 137, 138
2.5–109 133
2.10–16 136
2.33 136
2.41–47 136
2.43–47 135
2.68–70 136
2.78–84 136, 139
2.93–104 136
2.101–4 139
2.105–9 133, 136, 138

De somniis (cont.)
2.110–154 133
2.115–17 134
2.117 57
2.117–20 134
2.119 63n
2.120–121 57
2.121–22 134
2.123 134, 135, 136
2.123–32 135, 138, 140
2.124 134
2.125–126 134
2.130 134
2.135–38 136
2.144 136
2.150–54 136

De vita contemplativa
21 155
32 155
68 155

De vita Mosis
1.27 §147 168n
passim 136n

In Flaccum
6.43 166n
105 153
passim 133

Legum allegoriae
1.9–10 140n
2.86 66n
3.166–70 66n
3.237–42 137
3.26 137

Quis rerum divinarum heres
251 138
256a 138

Quod deterius potiori insidiari solet
5–31 137
6–12 138, 140
13–14 138
19 138
20–21 13

Quod deus immutabilis sit
111–21 137
120 138

Quod omnis probus liber sit
75–86 311n

Rabbinic Literature

Midrashim
Qohelet Rabbah
2.8 82
passim 85

Exodus Rabbah
29.9 399

Targums
Pseudo-Jonathan
Deut 28 399

Mishnah and Talmud
b. ʿArakin
32a 86

b. Niddah
52b 82

b. Sukkah
27a 86

m. Peʿa
8:7 154n

m. Pesaḥ
10:1 154n

m. Soṭa
3:4 155n

y. Berakoth
2.8.5b 213
4.8a 82

y. Seqalim
6.50a 82

Patristic Writers

1 Clement
passim 236n

Barnabas
18–20 207, 349
9:8 236n

Didache
1–2 371
1–5 207
1–6 263, 349
1.3b–6 207
3–4 371
3.1 371
7–10 371
8.2–3 208
9:4 68n
11–13 208, 371
15.3–4 208
16 207, 371
16.5 235, 238, 239
passim 209

Didascalion
2 371
3 371
6 371
10 371
20 371
24 371

Doctrina apostolorum
1–5 349

Hermas, Mandates
3:1 350
5.1.2–6.2.2 350
6.2.3–4 350
10.1–2 350
12.6.4 350
28:1 350
33:2–36:2 350
36:3–4 350
40.6 350
41:5 350
49:4 350

Hermas, Similitudes
5.6.5 408n

Aphrahat
Demonstratio 6
13:362–75 218

Augustine
De doctrina christiana
passim 414

Basil
Epistulae
163 416n

Clement of Alexandria
Ad Theodorum
see *Secret Gospel of Mark*

Stromateis
1.29.82 234n
1.3.24.2 218
2.15.68 234n
3.1 454
3.4.25–26 464n
3.9.63 410n
3.9.66 410n
4.81.1–83.1 462n
6.15.126 420n
6.15.128 234n
6.5.39–41 234n
6.6.48 231, 233, 234n
7.106 461, 466

Epiphanius of Salamis
Panarion
25–26 464n
31.2.3 457

Eusebius
Historia Ecclesiastica
2.16.24 456
2.23.7 3n
3.14.21 456
4.1.9–11 456

Historia Ecclesiastica (*cont.*)
4.1.11 456
4.1.4 456
4.1.5 456
4.7.7 462n
4.29.6 414n
5.9 456

Onomasticon
passim 83, 86

Praeparatio Evangelica
5 399
6–9 399
17 399

Gregory Nazianzus
Epistulae
51 420n
51.5–7 420n

Hippolytus
Apostolic Tradition
1 371
41 400n
43.3 371

Refutatio
5.23–27 409
7.20.1–27.13 462n

Ignatius of Antioch
Ephesians
1.1 424, 425
14.1 424
15.3 425
18.2 425, 429
19.3 425, 427
20.2 430
3.2 424, 429
4.2 424
5.1 427, 429
5.2 424
6.2 425
7.2 425, 427, 428, 430
8.1 424
9.2 423
19:1 398

Magnesians
1.2 423
11.1 428
14.1 424
15:1 424
2.1 423
3.1 425
5.2 424
6.1 424, 427
6.2 424
7.1 427
7.1–2 429
7.2 427, 430
8.2 424

Philadelphians
1.1 424
2.2 423
3.2 424
4 430
7.1 424
7.2 429
8.1 424
10.1 424

Polycarp
1.1 425
1.3 424
6.1 425
7.2 423
8.9 425

Romans
2:1 25, 424
3.3 425
4.1 424
6.3 424, 426
7.3 424

Smyrnaeans
1.1 425
1.2 423
3.1 428
3.3 427, 429
4.3 427
7.1 430
8.1 429
8.1–2 430
11.1 423, 424
12.2 423, 430

Trallians
3.1 425
7.1–2 430
8.2 425
9.1 428
10.1 428
12.2 424

Irenaeus
Adversus haereses
1.1.1 460
1.1.1–8.5 458
1.4.5–7.1 465
1.6.3 454
1.6.4 442, 446
1.11.1 457, 460
1.21.3 408n
1.21.5 409
1.24.1–2 459, 461
1.24.4 462
1.25.1 463
1.25.4 463
1.25.5 463
1.25.6 463
1.26.3 464
1.29 461
1.29.1–4 458n
3. praef. 438
3.4.3 457
3.16.3 356n
3.16.7 356n
3.20.2 356n
3.21.1 356n
5.21.1 356n

Jerome
De perpetua virginitate
8 404n

Epistulae
53.10.1 414n

Justin
1 Apology
26.4 461

Lactantius
Divinae institutiones
5.1.15–21 414n

Origen
Contra Celsum
1.34 400
1.38 400
6.1–2 414n
6.2 414n
6.58–61 414n

Commentarii in Ioannem
4.2 414n

De principiis
4 414n, 420n

Epistula ad Romanos
9 420n

Hom. in Luc.
1 462n

Polycarp
Philippians
passim 236n

Pseudo-Eustathius
Commentary on the Hexaemeron
passim 403n

Synesius
Epistulae
103 333n
138 416n

Tatian
Oratio
26 414

Tertullian
Adversus Valentinianos
4 457n

Other Greek & Roman Writers

Aristophanes
Birds
passim 212

Aristotle
Ethica Eudemia
3.1.1229b28–29 61

Nicomachean Ethics
9.8.1168b 6ff. 311

Politica
1.2.12531 214
1.2.1253a 215

Aulus Gellius
Noctes Atticae
12.2.1 418n

Caesar
De bello gallico
6.11–24 58
6.25–28 61n

Cicero
Ad Atticum
6.72 419n
8.14.1 419n
8.14.2 419n
9.10.1 416n
12.53 419n

Ad familiares
2.1.1 419n
12.30.1 416n
16.16.1 419n
16.16.2 416n

Ad Quintum fratem
1.1.45 419n

Brutus
216 419n

De officiis
1.16.51 311

De oratore
3.124.7 419n
125.1–2 419n

Orator
97 419n

Tusculanae disputationes
2.29.12 419n
30.1 419n

Claudius Aelianus
Varia historia
2.23 61

Demetrius
De elocutione
223 416n
227 416n
232 420n

Demosthenes
Epistulae
1.3 415n

Epictetus
Dissertationes
1:24 25n
3:22 25n

Encheiridion
passim 263

Epicurus
Kyriai Doxai
passim 263

Euripides
Bacchae
1084–87 399
passim 25n, 70

Fortunatus
Ars rhetorica
3.4 419n

Fronto
Ad Marcum Antonium
passim 418n

Hermogenes
Progymnasmata
passim 212n

Hesiod
Works and Days
195–210 215

Homer
Iliad
5.335–42 65
19.38–39 65
passim 27

Odyssey
5.93 65
6 399
42–46 399
passim 27, 216

Homeric Hymns
To Athena
passim 399

Iamblichus
De vita Pythagorica
30.167 310

Isocrates
Epistulae
1.2 415n

Julius Victor
Ars rhetorica
27 420n

Limenios
Delphic Paean to Apollos
passim 399

Livy
Ab urbe condita
2:32 402n

Lucian
Peregrinus
passim 25n

Philostratus
Life of Apollonius
passim 25n

Philostratus of Lemnos
De epistulis
passim 420n

Plato
Laws
10.893C 401n

Parmenides
165D 401n

Phaedrus
252E 401n

Politicus
273E–274A 399

Republic
2.363. c–d 65n
4.436c 401n
4.90b 460
5.46 2c 311

Sophist
252A 401n

Symposium
175B 401n

Theaetetus
181E 401n

Pliny
Epistulae
2.12.6 419n
3.20.10 419n

Pliny the Elder
Historia naturalis
4.99–101 58

Historia naturalis (*cont.*)
5.15.71 82
16.1.3–4 59–60

Plutarch
Moralia
passim 2

De defectu oraculorum
17 399

De fortuna
passim 20, 21

De fortuna Alexandri Magni
§ 1 25
§ 2 25, 26
§ 3 25, 26
§ 4 26
§ 9 32
§ 10 32, 33
§ 11 32, 33
§ 12 31, 32
317B 34n
321D 26
326A 34n
326B 34n
326F 26
327A 26
327B 26
327E 27
328 27
329B 29
329C 30
330B 30
330D 30
331A 30
331C 32
331E 31, 32, 33
332 32
332A 33
332AB 33
332B 34
332D 33
passim 21

De fortuna Romanorum
passim 20

Septem sapientium convivium
passim 70n

Quaestionum convivalium
612D–E 69

Parallel Lives
Agis.
2.4 214

Tib. Gracc.
9.4–5.828c 214
passim 34n

Pomponius Mela
Chorographia
3.25–32 58

Pseudo-Demetrius
Typoi epistolikoi
15 420n

Pseudo-Libanius
Epistolimaioi characteres
2 416n
2 419n
41 420n
46–47 420n
47 420n
49 420n
51 421n
58 16n
90 416

Pseudo-Callisthenes
Historia Alexandri Magni
1 399
2 399

Ptolemy Claudius
Geographia
5.16.4 82

Quintilian
Inst. or.
10.1.125–31 418n
12.10.11 419n

Sappho
Fragmentum Adespotum
976 216n

Seneca
Epistulae
40.1 416n
41 419n
75.1–2 416n, 419n

Sophocles
Oedipus Coloneus
1620–30 399

Strabo
Geographica
3.5.7–9 62
7.1–2 58
7.2.1 62

Suetonius
Caligula
43–48 61

Symmachus
Epistulae
1.87 419n
3.4 419n
3.16 419n
3.28 419n

Tacitus
Annales
1.8 88n
1.55 59
2.24 61n

Germania
2.5 58
37 61, 62
passim 59,61n

Historiae
3.53 114n

Vellius Paterculus
Historiae Romanae
2.126.3 113n

Virgil
Aeneid
passim 27

Inscriptions

Aphrodisias Jewish
passim 3
1–8 150
9 149, 152
9–27 150

CIG
2782 160n
2782–2783 159n
2783 160n
2820a 157n
2823 159n
2829 156n
2837b 156n
2845 159n

CII
100 153n
1447 154n
1447; B 154n
365 154n
741 153n

Le Bas
1592 159n
1602 157n
1630 156n
1634 157n

MAMA
413 156n
478 159n
492 157n
517 159n, 160n
546 159n
553 156n, 157n
554 156n, 157n
555 157n, 156n
556a 156n, 157n
556b 156n, 157n
564 159n

REG
19 (1906) no. 168 156n
19 (1906) nos. 138–41 156n
19 (1909) no. 169 156n
19 (1909) no. 175 156n
19 (1909) no. 38 159n

SEG
537 154n
969 154n

Papyri

BGU
1079 46
1680 52
423 41, 50
846 43
948 42

CPJ
1:125–29 54

LCL
1:93 49
1:98 49
1:99 49
1:101 49
1:107 49
1:111 49
1:115 49
1:121 42, 47
1:133 48
1:148 49
1:165 49
2:397 44

PAmh. II
131 46

PBad
36 45
39 45

PBeatty Panopolis
1 44
2 44

PBerol. 8502 (= BG) 193

PBrem.
11 45n

PCairo Zen.
59029 54
59154 53
59052 54
59075 54
59076 54
59251 54

PCol.
6 46
10 55
16 55
121 55
316 48

PFay.
114 53
123 46

PFlor.
176 47
332 42
367 49

PGeiss
17 41

PGrenf.
I.53 46
II 36 41

PHib.
43 55
44 55

PLond.
42 46
1951 55

PMert.
63 49

PMich.
10 54
14 55n
16 55
18 55
28 55
32 55
35 55
48 54
214 42
221 42
241 48
466 47
466 52
481 49
482 41
484 47
490 50
491 51
496 48
497 49
500 51
502 49
508 47

POxy.
119 42
123 45
300 49
528 52
935 45
939 46
1061 49
1296 43
1485 52
1666 41
1676 46
2156 45

Preisigke-Bilabel
7356 51

PRyl.
560 55

PSI
1080 50
299 45
311 50

PTebt.
424 41, 46

UPZ I
68 47

Index of Modern Authors

Abramowski, L., 409n
Adler, M., 58n
Aland, B, 12n
Alsup, J., 241n
Alt, A., 84
Amman, E., 398, 400, 403n
Andresen, C., 13n
Andrzejewski, R., 418n
Anrich, G., 14n
Arav, R., 81n, 86n, 100n
Ashton, J., 435n
Attridge, H., 5, 131n, 142, 406-413, 439
Aune, D. E., 70n, 368n
Avi-Yonah, M., 88n
Avida, U., 91n

Babbitt, F. C., 69n
Bainbridge, W. S., 465n
Bakalakas, G., 116n
Baltzer, K., 3, 121-130
Bammel, C. P. H., 422n, 427n
Bammel, E., 112n
Barlow, C. W., 417n
Barnes, T. D., 16n
Barrett, C. K., 226n, 240n, 294n
Bartchy, S. S., 4, 309-318
Barth, K., 191, 292, 469
Bartsch, H. W., 426
Batten, L. W., 121n
Bauckman, R., 213, 214, 215
Baudoz, J. F., 81n, 84
Bauer, W., 6, 18n, 81n, 365n, 381, 397, 455, 456, 457, 464, 466, 467, 470
Becker, H., 229n
Becker, I., 61n
Becker, J., 110n
Bedjan, P., 407n
Bell, G. K. A., 240n
Benoit, F., 237n
Bergamelli, F., 430n
Berger, K., 69, 370, 375n, 376n
Berry, K., 331n
Bertram, G., 401n
Betz, H. D., 4, 20n, 70n, 186, 258-275, 327, 415n
Beurlier, E., 159n
Bihlmeyer, K., 423n
Bilabel, F., 51n
Binford, S, 108n
Biran, A., 95n
Bird, P. A., 222n
Bjerkelund, C. J., 339n, 341
Black, D. A., 110n
Black, M., 86n
Boers, H. W., 262n
Böhlig, A., 14n
Boismard, M.-É, 320n
Boll, F., 11
Bonnet, M., 407n
Borg, M., 72n
Borgen, P., 288n, 296n
Bornhäuser, K., 286n
Bornkamm, G, 173, 181, 182, 248, 321n, 322n, 348
Borsch, F. H., 438n
Bott, H., 263n
Boureau, A., 400
Bousset, W., 9, 356n, 467
Bovon, F., 5, 393-405, 412n
Bradshaw, P., 406n
Brandenburger, E., 227n
Brandt, W. J., 338n
Braun, H., 11, 12n
Braun, M., 148n
Braunstein, O., 157n, 160n
Briggs, C. A., 223n
Brock, S., 406n
Brodie, T. L., 302n
Bromiley, G. W., 348n
Brooten, B. J., 3, 149-162, 475
Brown, J. P., 247n
Brown, M. P., 423n, 425n, 426n
Brown, P. R. L., 17n, 412n, 444, 446, 450n
Brown, R. E., 70n, 232, 233n, 244n, 281n, 291n, 294n, 368, 369, 374, 373
Bruce, F. F., 118n
Brunner, H., 263n
Büchsel, F., 233n
Buckley, J. J., 411n, 443, 445
Bultmann, R., 1, 10, 13n, 71n, 173, 178, 181, 190, 192n, 200, 211n, 213, 214, 228n, 229n, 231n, 232n, 233n, 239n, 348, 367n, 368n, 435n, 467, 469
Bunge, W. F., 3, 142-148, 428n, 430n
Bünker, M., 415n
Burkitt, F. C., 407n, 408n
Busse, U., 294n

Cadbury, H. J., 248n, 301n
Calder, W. M, 156n
Cameron, A., 161n
Cameron, R., 5, 200, 229n, 230n, 243n, 381-392, 434, 439n
Camp, J., 108n
Carroll, K. L., 286n
Carson, D. A., 130n
Casey, M., 212n, 213, 214
Chadwick, H., 400
Chalon, G., 139n
Childs, B. S., 223n
Chisholm, K., 113n
Clarke, G. W., 414n
Clay, D., 216n
Clemente, G., 154n
Clementz, H., 80n
Cohen, S. J. D., 3, 163-169, 280, 282n
Cohn, L., 60n, 136n
Collins, J. J., 70n, 164n, 224n, 280n, 369, 440n
Collins, R. F., 109n, 110n
Colpe, C., 10n
Colson, F. H., 57n, 131n, 135, 136, 137, 140n
Connolly, R. H., 371n
Conzelmann, H., 110n, 173n, 180, 302n, 303n, 309, 310, 312

Cook, M., 277
Cooper, J., 371n
Corley, B. C., 4
Cormack, J. M. R, 156n
Corwin, V., 425n
Cranfield, C. E. B., 237n, 238n, 337n
Cross, F. M., 64n, 71n, 72n, 73n
Crossan, J. D, 202n, 211n, 217n, 243n, 253, 390n
Culpepper, R. A., 288, 289n, 290n, 291, 292n, 297n
Cuming, G. J., 373n
Cumont, F., 66n

Dalbert, P., 167n
Dalman, G., 84
Danby, H., 261n
Danker, F., 113n
Davies, S. L., 217n
Davies, W. D., 166n
de Aldama, J. A., 396n
de Fraine, J., 121n, 130n
De Hass, R., 94n
de Jong, M, 292n, 294n
de Labriolle, P., 400
de Lamartine, A., 399n
de Stoop, J., 214n
de Strycker, E., 394, 395n, 396, 404n
Dean, O. C. Jr., 259n
Debrunner, A., 80n
Deininger, J., 159n
Deissmann, A., 39-40, 240n
Denker, F. W., 304n
Dentzer, J.-M., 66n
Deuel, L., 39n
DeWitt, N., 112n
di Nola, A. M., 398, 401n
Dibelius, M., 303n, 418n
Dibelius, O., 465n
Dieterich, A., 11, 468
Dillon, J., 13n, 460n
Dillon, R. J., 304n
Dinkler, E, 1n, 178n, 382n
Dix, G., 373n
Dodd, C. H., 232, 233n, 240n
Donahue, J., 224n, 228n
Donaldson, T. L., 265n
Donfried, K. P., 114n, 118n, 338n
Donner, H., 83n
Doran, R., 4, 210-219
Downing, F. G., 194n
Druthmar, C., 400
du Boulay, J., 316n
Dunayevski, I., 95n
Dungan, D. L., 247n

Earp, J. W., 137
Edgar, C. C., 38n, 53n, 54n
Edson, C., 114n, 116n
Edwards, H. J., 58n
Edwards, R. A., 184n, 192

Eisenstadt, S. N., 314n
Eissfeldt, O., 230n
Elliot, J. H., 314n
Ellis, E. E., 237n
Emmel, S., 410n
Epp, E. J., 2, 35-56, 305n, 389n
Epstein, C., 93n
Esler, P., 279n
Étienne, R., 159n
Exler, F. X. J., 421n

Fabricius, J. A., 395n, 396n
Fallon, F., 436n, 437n
Feldman, L. H., 81n, 142, 161n, 279n
Fenshaw, F. C., 121n
Ferguson, J., 113n
Finkelstein, L., 166n
Fischer, T., 324
Fishbane, M., 130n
Fisher, C. S., 100n
Fitzgerald, J., 335n
Fitzler, K., 88n, 90n
Fitzmyer, J. A., 214, 216n, 304n
Flannery, K., 108n
Foakes-Jackson, F. J., 278, 301n, 468
Foerster, W., 458n, 459n
Fontaine, J., 400
Forrer, L., 116n
Forsyth, N,, 221n
Fowler, A., 370n
Fox, R. L., 14n
Frame, J. E., 118n
Frankemölle, H., 267n, 268n, 269n
Franxman, T. W., 142
Fraser, P. M., 166n
Fredricksen, P, 389n
Frend, W. H. C., 112n
Frerichs, E., 279n
Frick, K., 59n
Fridrichsen, A., 237n
Friedrich, G., 109n, 110n
Friesen, S. J., 160
Fuller, R. H., 302
Funk, R. W., 294n, 346n
Furrer, K., 84, 86n

Gager, J., 278n
Galling, K., 121n, 122n
Gamberoni, J., 126n
Gamble, H., 337, 338n, 339, 340, 341, 345
Garner, R., 130n
Gasparro, G. S., 412n
Gaster, T. H., 65n
Geffcken, J., 214n
Georgi, D., 2, 20-34, 166n, 332n
Gerth, B., 80n
Gigon, O., 15n
Gijsel, J., 404n
Ginzburg, L., 66n, 82n
Glasson, T. F., 297n

Glick, G. W., 163n
Glöckner, R., 303n
Gnilka, J., 274n
Goehring, J. E., 243n, 257n, 259n, 384n, 456n, 460n
Goetz, G., 396n
Goodenough, E. R., 66n, 131n, 135, 136, 137, 278, 468
Goodman, M., 166n
Görg, M., 130n
Graesse, T., 400n
Grant, R. M., 234n, 425n, 427n, 443, 445, 446
Grässer, E., 286n
Grayson, K., 369, 374n
Green, H. A., 465n
Greilsamer, L, 399n
Gressmann, H., 9
Gribomont, J., 396n
Groff, K. I., 251n, 253n, 256n
Gross, W. H., 88n
Grundmann, W., 241n, 261, 262n
Gunkel, H., 9, 10
Gunneweg, A. H. J., 121n, 122n, 127n, 129n
Gunneweg, J., 102n
Gutman, S., 93n

Haas, H., 16n
Haenchen, E., 180, 244n, 294n
Haines, C. R., 216n
Haines, G. C., 116n
Hall, R., 108n
Hammer, P. L., 348n
Hammond, N. G. L., 44n
Hanslik, R., 88n, 90n
Hanson, K. C., 309n
Hanson, P. D., 65n
Harlfinger, D., 395n
Harnack, A. von, 3, 9, 14, 18n, 163-169 passim, 397, 398
Harnisch, W., 109n, 110n
Harrington, D. J., 12n, 381n
Hausmann, U., 116n
Head, B. V., 115n
Hedrick, C. W., 243n, 384n, 434, 439n, 440n, 447n
Hefner, D., 88n
Hegermann, H., 166n
Heinemann, I., 58n
Heitmueller, W., 9
Helderman, J., 217n
Hellholm, D., 11, 265n
Helm, R., 83n, 461n
Hendrix, H. L., 2, 107-118
Hengel, M, 263n, 264n, 279n, 280n, 330n, 331, 469
Hennecke, E., 417n, 464n, 468
Henrichs, A., 67n
Hercher, R., 61n
Herder, J. G., 260n
Hersh, C. A., 116n
Heschel, A., 304n

Hilgenfeld, A., 397
Hill, J. V., 367-377
Hinrichs, J. C., 163
Hodder, I., 108n
Hodgson, R., Jr, 384n, 434, 447n
Hoffmann, P., 274n
Hogan, E,, 405n
Holl, K., 9
Holland, G. S, 271n
Holtz, T., 109n, 110n, 363n
Holtzmann, H. J., 174, 259n
Horgan, M. P., 38n
Horsely, G. H. R., 153n
Horsley, R. A., 3, 72n, 195-209, 389n
Hosius, C., 418n
Houlden, J. L., 373n, 374n
Hubbard, B. J., 229n, 231n
Hug, J., 229n, 231n, 232n, 240n
Hughes, F. W., 415n
Hunt, A. S., 38n
Hurst, L. D., 301n
Hutton, M., 58n,59n

Imhoof-Blumer, F., 115n
Irmscher, J., 9n
Israeli, Y., 91

Jackson, J., 59n
Jacoby, F., 62n
Jaeger, W., 13n
James, M. R., 404n, 405n, 417n
Janssens, Y., 439n, 443, 444
Japhet, S., 129n
Jastrow, M, 92
Jennings, T. W. jr., 262n
Jeremias, J., 64n, 66n, 73n, 230n, 344n, 346n
Jewett, R., 110n, 115n, 324
Johnson, L. T., 318n
Joly, R., 422n
Jonas, H., 192n, 467
Jones, H. L., 58n
Judge, E. A., 414n

Kamlah, W., 17n, 19n
Kannengieser, C., 400
Karrer, M., 361n
Karris, R. J., 304n, 375n
Karst, J., 83n
Käsemann, E., 180, 234n, 237n, 238, 240n, 303n, 331, 348
Kearns, R., 211n, 213
Kearsley, R. A., 158n, 159
Keck, L., 278
Kee, H. C., 389n
Keegan, T. J., 265n
Keel, O.. 87n
Kelber, W. H., 239n
Kellermann, U., 121n, 127n
Kennedy, G. A., 370n
Kenner, H., 215n
Kertelge, K., 269n
Kiersley, R. A., 160n
King, K. L., 409n
Kingsbury, J. D., 217n, 264n, 274n, 275n
Kippenberg, H. G., 129n
Kittel, G., 261n, 262
Klausner, J., 261n
Klawek, A., 398, 401n
Klein, C., 163n
Klein, S., 82n
Klijn, A. J. F., 406n, 407n, 408n
Kloppenborg, J., 3, 185, 186, 187, 188, 190n, 193,196, 197, 198, 199, 200, 201, 206n, 211n, 213, 216, 217n, 274n, 389, 390n, 392n
Klostermann, E., 83n
Knauf, E. A., 324n
Kobelski, P. J., 38n
Koch, K., 229n, 230
Kochavi, M., 93n, 95n
Kock, K., 128n
Kodell, J., 303
Koester, H., 1-6 passim, 10n, 12n, 13n, 109n, 110n, 112n, 125n, 173, 184n, 187, 188, 189, 194, 195, 196, 197, 200, 201, 209, 211, 230n, 239n, 242, 243, 244, 245, 247, 248, 249, 253, 254, 255, 256, 276, 319, 322n, 327n, 329, 331n, 337, 348, 358, 364n, 368n, 371n, 377n, 381, 382, 383, 384, 385n, 386n, 387n, 388n, 391n, 406, 422n, 428n, 430n, 433, 434, 435, 438n, 439, 440, 441, 455
Kopp, C., 83n
Koschorke, K, 448, 449
Koskenniemi, H., 418n, 419n
Kotsias, N., 116n
Kottayam, J. V., 406n
Kraabel, A. T., 2, 3, 4, 161n, 164n, 169n, 276-284
Kraeling, C., 468
Kraemer, R. S., 155n, 156n
Kraft, R. A. , 3, 6, 18n, 131-141, 164n, 207, 455n
Krämer, H. J., 13n
Krause, M., 436n, 460n
Krodel, G., 6, 18n, 455n, 468n
Küchler, M., 87n
Kuhn, H.-W., 2, 87n, 90n
Kuhn, K. G., 71n
Kuhn, T. J., 194n
Kühner, R., 80n
Kuhrt, A., 161n
Kümmel, W. G., 178, 183n, 348, 368n
Kundera, M., 399
Küng, H., 194n
Kurfess, A., 417n
Kurz, W. S., 302n
Lafargue, M., 407n
Laffi, U., 114n
Lake, K., 278, 301n, 468
Lamberton, R., 447n
Lamouille, A., 320n
Langevin, P.-E, 238n
Lapp, P. W., 101n, 102n
Lattimor, R., 65n
Laub, F., 110n
Law, R., 377n
Laws, S., 374n
Layton, B., 384n, 434, 457n, 458n, 459n, 461n, 462, 463n, 464n
Le Bas, P., 156n
LeBlanc, S. A., 108n
Leipoldt, J., 14n, 15, 16n
Lelyveld, M., 215n, 218n
Leone, M., 108n
Levin, S., 243n
Levy, J., 82n
Lewis, N., 52n, 53n, 54n
Lietzman, H., 240n, 327, 456n
Lindars, B., 213, 214, 215, 220
Lindhagen, C, 127n
Linton, O. R., 247n
Lipsius, R. A., 397, 407n, 408n
Loffreda, S., 94n
Logan, A. H. B., 384n, 436n
Lohmeyer, E., 240n
Lohse, E., 5, 358-366
Loisy, A., 295n
Lona, H. E., 428n, 430n
Long, J,, 48n
Long, W., 280n
Lüdemann, G., 327n
Lührmann, D., 2, 57-63, 182, 183, 184, 185
Lull, D. J., 196, 197n, 389n, 390n
Luz, U., 193n, 259n, 262, 265n, 269n
Lyon, D. G., 100n

MacDonald, D. R., 410n, 411n, 447n
Mack, B. L., 12n,73n, 198, 244n, 254, 390n
MacLean, A. J., 371n
MacLennan, R. S., 161n, 278n
MacMullen, R., 16n, 17n, 160n, 169n
MacRae, G. W., 12n, 389n
Maddox, R., 277n
Magie, D., 159n
Malbon, E. S., 217n
Malherbe, A. J., 5, 112n, 118n, 331n, 414-421
Malina, B. J., 313n, 314n, 315n
Maltiel-Gerstenfeld, J., 88n, 89n, 90n
Manson, T. W., 202n
Marcus, J., 108n
Marcus, R., 131n

Marquez, G. G., 399n
Marshall, A. J., 160n
Marshall, P., 331n, 416
Martin, J., 69n
Martin, R. P., 330n
Martyn, J. L., 278, 286n, 296n, 297n
Mazar, B., 95n
McCown, C., 83n
McCracken, G. E., 414n
McCue, J. F., 456n, 465n
McKnight, S., 169n
McNamara, M., 405n
Meeks, W. A., 5, 286n, 292n, 293n, 295n, 329-336, 410n
Ménard, J., 443, 445, 450
Meshorer, Y., 87n, 89n, 324
Metzger, B. M., 223n
Meyer, A., 397
Meyer, B. F., 67n
Meyer, M. W., 243n, 253n, 411n
Meyers, C. L., 65n
Meyers, E., 94n, 108n
Meyers, R. A., 406n
Michaelis, W., 212n
Michel, O., 238n, 240n, 342
Milik, J. T., 224
Millar, F., 166n
Miller, P. D, 124n
Milligan, G., 46n
Mirecki, P., 4, 229-241
Moda, A., 417n
Moessner, D. P., 301n
Molland, E., 428n
Momigliano, A., 15n
Mommsen, T., 169n
Mönning, B. H., 309n
Moore, G. F., 64n, 163n, 468
Moore, S. D., 285n, 293n
Morenz, S., 15
Mowinckel, S., 122n, 126n, 223n
Moxnes, H., 314
Müller, U. B., 332n
Mussner, F., 322
Myers, J. M., 121n, 223n

Naldini, M., 422n
Nauck, W., 367n
Nautin, P., 234n
Negev, A., 323
Nestle, E., 85n
Netzer, E., 101n
Neubauer, A., 86n
Neufeld, V. H., 234n, 238n, 240n
Neusner, J., 277, 279n, 280n, 302n, 382n
Neyrey, J. H., 304n, 305n, 313n
Nickelsburg, G., 5, 163n, 164n, 278n, 348-357
Niditch, S., 216n
Niebuhr, K.-W., 263
Niemeyer, H. G., 116n, 117n
Niese, B., 80n
Nock, A. D., 66n, 141n, 426n
Norden, E., 15n, 61n, 418n, 427n, 467
Noth, M., 122n
Nouskas, K. D., 429n

O'Flaherty, W., 410n
O'Neill, J. C., 369
Ollendorff, L., 88n, 89n, 90n
Ollrog, W.-H., 338, 340, 341
Opelt, I, 263n
Orfali, P. G., 95n

Page, D., 216n
Page, D. L., 38n
Pagels, E. H., 5, 384n, 4 39n, 440n, 442-454, 475
Palagi, L. B., 417n, 418n, 419n
Paris, P., 160n
Paulsen, H., 234n
Peabody, D., 243n, 248
Pearson, B. A., 1-6, 257n, 436n, 455-466
Peristiany, J. G., 316n
Perkins, P., 5, 277n, 369, 374n, 411n, 433-441
Perler, O., 426n
Perlman, I., 102n
Perrin, B., 214n
Perrin, N., 4, 71n, 220, 221, 224, 225, 226, 227, 228, 384n
Pesch, R., 229n, 317n
Pestman, P. W., 53n, 54n, 55n
Petersen, N. R., 1, 5, 69n, 250, 303, 337-347
Petersen, W. L., 36n
Pistelli, E., 395n
Pitt-Rivers, J., 313n
Pixner, B., 84, 87n, 93
Pleket, H. W., 158n
Plevnik, J., 109n, 110n
Pococke, R., 84n
Polaschek, E., 83n
Pope, M., 68n
Postel, G., 396n, 404
Preisigke, F., 51n
Preiss, T., 429n
Price, S. R. F., 158n

Quispel, G., 234n, 442, 446, 443, 457n

Rabe, H., 212n
Rackham, H., 58n
Ramsey, W. M., 328n
Redman, C. L., 108n
Reeg, G., 82n
Reinach, T,, 156n
Reisner, G. A., 100n
Reitzenstein, R., 9, 11, 467
Rendtorff, R., 128n
Rensberger, D., 292n, 293n, 294n, 297n, 299n
Reynolds, J., 150n, 151, 152, 154n, 155, 279n
Reys-Coquais, J. P., 139n
Rhode, E., 11
Richards, K. H., 112n, 263n
Richardson, C. C., 425n, 426n, 428n, 429n, 430n
Riesener, I, 127n
Riesenfeld, H., 426n
Rigaux, B., 109n, 110n
Rilke, R. M., 399n
Ringgren, H., 127n
Rius-Camps, J., 422n
Robert, L., 113n, 115n, 156n
Roberts, C. H., 39n
Robinson, E., 84n, 93
Robinson, J. A. T., 286n
Robinson, J. M., 1, 3, 4, 10n, 12n, 173-194, 196, 200, 202n, 211, 330n, 364n, 382n, 384n, 386n, 434
Robinson, T. A., 381n, 456n
Rolfe, J. C., 61n
Roloff, J., 361n
Romanides, J., 428n
Roniger, L., 314
Rosenthal, R., 97n, 102n
Rouleau, D., 439
Rudolph, K., 2, 9-19 passim
Rudolph, W., 121n
Rüger, H. P., 85n
Ruggini, L. C., 154n
Rumschiedt, H. M., 163n
Russell, J. B., 452n
Rüterswörden, U., 127n

Sabbe, M., 247n
Sahlins, M., 313n, 314n
Sanders, E. P., 67n, 72n, 163n, 227, 228n, 389n
Sanders, J. T., 279n
Sandmel, S, 283n
Sasse, H., 240n
Sato, M., 188n
Schanz, M., 418n
Schenk, W., 202n, 267n, 275n
Schenke, H.-M., 4, 243n, 256n, 319-328, 435n, 442, 444, 458n
Schlatter, A., 262
Schlier, H., 322n, 426
Schmidt, D., 192n
Schmidt, M., 396n
Schmithals, W., 110n
Schnackenburg, R., 232n, 335n, 376n
Schneemelcher, W., 234n, 417, 464n, 465n, 468n
Schneider, C., 15n
Schoedel, W. A., 422n, 423n, 425n, 429n
Schoene, A., 461n

Schrage, W., 185
Schulz, S., 187
Schumacher, G, 93
Schürer, E., 86n, 89n, 165n, 166n, 167
Schürmann, H., 248n
Schüssler Fiorenza, E., 142n, 362n
Schwartz, D. R., 132n, 135n
Schweitzer, A., 174, 175, 176, 177, 178, 189, 389, 467
Schweizer, E., 73n, 80n 180, 181n
Scopello, M., 411n, 436n
Scroggs, R., 251n, 253n, 256n
Scullard, H. H., 44n
Seeley, D., 392n
Segelberg, E., 443, 444
Segert, S., 230n, 233n
Seitz, C. R., 130n
Sellew, P. H., 202n, 242- 257
Sevenster, J. N., 418n
Sevrin, J.-M., 413
Sieffert, F., 328n
Silber, J., 185
Silberman, L. H., 143n
Sills, D. L., 313n
Simian-Yofre, H., 127n
Sivan, R., 97n, 102n
Smalley, S., 110n
Smallwood, E. M., 132n
Smid, H. R., 395n, 398
Smith, D., 2, 64-73
Smith, D. M., 233n
Smith, J. Z., 388n, 390n
Smith, M., 67n, 242, 244n, 457n, 458n, 463n, 464
Smith, T. C., 286n
Smith, T. V., 234n
Smith Lewis, A., 407n
Snyder, G. F., 66n
Speidel, M. P., 51n
Speigl, J., 422n
Spittler, R. P., 376
Sprödowski, H., 148n
Stählin, O., 244n
Stark, R., 465n
Stead, G. C., 460n
Steck, O. H., 182, 183, 184
Steen, H. A., 418n
Stegemann, W., 319n
Stendahl, K., 72n
Stewart, Z., 66n, 141n
Stone, M., 224n, 436n
Stowers, S. K., 331n, 368n
Strange, J. F., 86n, 108n
Strathmann, H., 13n
Strauss, D. F., 174, 175
Strecker, G., 129n, 259n, 267n, 275n
Streeter, B. H., 248
Strobel, A., 217n
Stroumsa, G., 437n
Strugnell, J., 72n
Stuart, M., 117n
Stuehrenberg, P., 279n
Stuhlmacher, P., 469
Sutherland, C. H. V., 113n
Swanson, D. N., 229n, 230
Sydenham, E. A., 116n

Tadmor, H., 130n
Talbert, C. H., 302n
Talley, T. J., 256n
Tannenbaum, R. F., 150n, 151, 152, 154n, 155, 161n, 278n, 279n
Tanzer, S., 4, 285-300
Taubes, J, 22n
Taylor, V., 241n
Testuz, M., 395n, 398
Thackery, H. St. J., 80n
Thiering, B. E., 72n
Thilo, J. C., 397
Thomsen, P., 82n
Thraede, K., 416n
Tiede, D., 4, 301-308
Tischendorf, C., 395n, 397
Tissot, Y., 412n
Tödt, H. E., 181n, 182, 220, 226n
Tournier, M., 399n
Toutain, J., 160n
Trakatellis, D., 5, 422-430
Treu, K., 9n
Trevett, C., 422n
Tripp, D. H., 443, 444
Tröger, K.-W., 12n
Tuckett, C. M., 247n, 434, 438n
Turner, E. G., 43n, 44n, 53n, 132n, 133n, 139n, 140n
Turpie, D. McC., 237n
Tyson, J., 277n

Uehlinger, C, 87n
Urman, D., 82n, 84, 85n, 86
Uro, R., 193n
Utzschneider, H., 130n

Vaage, L. E., 186, 190n
Van Bremen, R., 161n
van den Bergh van Eysinga, G., 397
van den Broek, R., 460n
van der Horst, P., 279n
van der Minde, H.-J., 237n, 238n, 240n
van der Osten-Sacken, P., 363n
van Eijk, A. H. C., 443, 445
Van Leeuwen, R. C., 215n
van Unnik, W. C., 286n
Vanhoye, A., 415n
Vermes, G., 166n, 312
Vielhauser, P., 179, 180, 181n, 182n, 183n, 185, 191n, 368n
Völker, W., 459
von Dobschütz, E. , 234n
von Rad, G., 122n
von Wahlde, U. C., 286n, 289, 290n, 298n
Vööbus, A., 218n

Waddington, W. H., 156n
Walker, W. O. jr., 225
Walter, N., 334, 335n
Walter, O., 116n
Watson, D. F., 375n
Watson, P. J., 108n
Wedderburn, A. J. M., 384n, 436n
Weijenborg, A., 422n
Weinfeld, M. , 130n
Weiss, J., 9, 174, 176, 178, 389
Welborn, L. L., 259n
Welch, C., 166n
Wendland, P., 14n, 467
Wendling, E., 247n
Wengst, K., 239n, 234n
Westermann, C., 127n, 222n
Whitaker, G. H., 57n, 131n
White, J. L., 38n, 421n
Wiles, G., 342
Wilkens, U., 234n
Williams, H. G. M., 130n
Williams, J. A., 434, 461n
Williams, J. G., 193n, 389n
Williams, M. A., 409n, 411n, 440n, 441n, 443, 444, 446, 454
Willis, G. G., 406n
Wilson, R. McL., 384n, 408n
Wilson, W., 87n
Winkler, G., 406n
Winter, J. G., 41n, 44n, 46n, 49n
Wire, A. C., 410n
Wisse, F., 409n, 410n
Wlosok, A., 14n
Woll, D. B., 372n
Wrede, W., 9, 467, 468
Wright, N. T., 301n
Wright, W., 407n
Wuellner, W., 338, 342, 343, 344
Wuensch, R., 11
Würthwein, E., 126n

Yamauchi, E. M., 127n
Yarbro Collins, A., 4, 65n, 68n, 69n, 210n, 213, 216n, 220-228, 389n
Yeivin, Z., 97n
Yellin, J., 102n
Ysebaert, J., 407n

Zeller, D., 185, 186, 187
Ziebarth, E,, 157n
Ziegler, J., 237n
Ziemann, F, 421n
Zizioulas, J., 429n